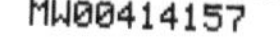

UNIVERSITY CASEBOOK SERIES

READINGS, NOTES, AND QUESTIONS

HEALTH CARE LAW AND POLICY

SECOND EDITION

by

CLARK C. HAVIGHURST
William Neal Reynolds Professor of Law, Duke University

JAMES F. BLUMSTEIN
Professor of Law, Vanderbilt Law School, and Director,
Health Policy Center, Vanderbilt Institute for Public Policy Studies

TROYEN A. BRENNAN
Professor, School of Medicine and School of Public Health
Harvard University

NEW YORK, NEW YORK
FOUNDATION PRESS
1998

11 Penn Plaza, Tenth Floor
New York, NY 10001
Phone (212) 760–8700
Fax (212) 760–8705

Printed in the United States of America

Library of Congress Cataloging-in-Publication Data

Havighurst, Clark C.

Health care law and policy : readings, notes, and questions / by Clark C. Havighurst, James F. Blumstein, Troyen A. Brennan. — 2nd ed.

p. cm. — (University casebook series)

Includes index.

ISBN 1–56662–617–X

1. Medical care—Law and legislation—United States—Cases. 2. Medical laws and legislation—United States—Cases. 3. Medical policy—United States—Case studies. I. Blumstein, James F., 1945– II. Brennan, Troyen A. III. Title. IV. Series.

KF3821.A7H38 1998

344.73'0321—dc21 98–8152

EDITORS' NOTE

No single volume can contain all that an instructor would like to convey to law students concerning personal health care and the legal environment in which it is financed and provided to patients. As a teaching tool, this book seeks, first, to impart basic factual information concerning the health care industry in the United States and the legal doctrines and statutes by which it is governed and, second, to provide analytical and policy insights useful in applying law to this challenging field of human endeavor. While still organized along the same functional, policy-oriented, and history-tracing lines as were followed in the 1988 edition, the book reflects the ongoing revolution in health care financing and delivery by expanding the coverage of certain topics or issues and by altering the emphasis given to others. The addition of two co-editors has made it possible to provide both a reasonably current snapshot of the fast-moving field and the requisite depth of insight in all the many areas that the book must cover. Although the entire book could probably not be studied in less than a four-hour course, attention has been paid to organizing the material to facilitate selective coverage in a course of any length.

Readings herein are drawn from a vast body of literature and, as before, are often chosen because they are especially informative, interesting, or provocative rather than because they are representative of mainstream thinking or necessarily right in their reasoning. The cases reproduced are not always leading ones or sound in their legal and factual analysis. The various selections should therefore be viewed, like the editorial opinions possibly detectable in the extensive textual material, as appropriate objects of criticism, and students should be encouraged to read them critically, not merely to absorb the material presented. Citations of authorities, while numerous, are not always representative and are often provided principally to give students a sense of the currency and dimensions of a particular topic or issue.

In order to avoid as much clutter as possible, cases, readings, and quotations have been edited without indicating where footnotes and citations of authorities are omitted. Omissions of text (of varying lengths) have been shown simply by asterisks (* * *'s), leaving ellipses (. . .'s) to show omissions in the original source. Bracketed material replacing anything in the original text may also represent a lengthy omission.

Professor Havighurst desires to credit almost a generation of research assistants at the Duke University School of Law whose efforts are reflected in this volume, and he especially dedicates his share of the finished work, for many reasons, to Karen Havighurst. Professor Blumstein would like to acknowledge the research assistance of the following students at the Vanderbilt Law School: Keith Koegler, Scott Elder, Melissa Herring, and Holly Larkin (Class of 1997); Lisa Phelps ('98); Julie Dombrosky, Mary Beth Fortugno, Alison Fowler, Paul Gontarek, and Amanda Vaughn ('99). He also gratefully acknowledges the ongoing support of his wife, Andree, who has nurtured not only this project but his entire career. Professor Brennan thanks his wife, Wendy Warring.

CLARK C. HAVIGHURST
JAMES F. BLUMSTEIN
TROYEN A. BRENNAN

June 1998

ACKNOWLEDGMENTS

Berenson, Robert, Beyond Competition, Health Affs., March-April 1997, p. 171, 172, 174-75. Reprinted with permission of Health Affairs.

Berlant, Jeffrey, Profession and Monopoly, A Study of Medicine in the United States and Great Britain 82, 87-88, 91-94 (University of California Press 1978). Reprinted with permission of Jeffrey Berlant.

Bovbjerg, Randall, New Directions for Health Planning, in Cost, Quality and Access in Health Care: New Roles for Health Planning in a Competitive Environment 206, 214-16 (F.Sloan, J. Blumstein & J. Perrin eds. 1988). Reprinted with permission of Jossey-Bass Publishers.

Blumstein, James, Health Care Reform and Competing Visions of Medical Care: Antitrust and State Provider Cooperation Legislation, 79 Cornell L.Rev. 1459, 1464-69 (1994). Reprinted with permission of the Cornell Law Review.

Brennan, T. & D. Berwick, New Rules: Regulations, Markets, and the Quality of American Health Care, 152-54 (1995). Reprinted with permission of Jossey-Bass Publishers.

Brown, Lawrence, Some Structural Issues in the Health Planning Program, in 2 Health Planning in the United States: Selected Policy Issues 20-25 (1981). Reprinted with permission of the Institute of Medicine, National Academy of Science.

Charrow, Robert P., David C. Main & Joseph N. Onek, Retooling Medicine Through PSOs and Medicare+Choice Plans: Can Providers Catch the Brass Ring?, AHLA Health Law Digest, Oct. 1997, p.3. Reprinted with permission of the American Health Lawyers Association. Copyright © 1997, American Health Lawyers Association.

Danzon, Patricia, Medical Malpractice: Theory, Evidence, and Public Policy 9-15 (Cambridge, Mass., Harvard University Press): Copyright © 1985 by the President and Fellows of Harvard College. Reprinted by permission of the publisher.

Elhauge, Does Interest Group Theory Justify More Intrusive Judicial Review?, 101 Yale L. J. 31, 35-44 (1991). Reprinted with permission of the Yale Law School.

Enthoven, Alain, What Medical Is and Isn't, in A. Enthoven, Health Plan: The Only Practical Solution to the Soaring Costs of Health Care 1-12

(1980). Reprinted with permission of the Addison-Wesley Publishing Co.

Enthoven, Alain, Why Financial Incentives Make a Difference, in A. Enthoven, Health Plan: The Only Practical Solution to the Soaring Costs of Health Care 9-11 (1980). Reprinted with permission of the Addison-Wesley Publishing Co.

Etheredge, Lynn, Reengineering Medicare: From Bill-Paying Insurer to Accountable Purchaser, Health Insurance Reform Project, George Washington University (June 1995). Reprinted with permission of Lynn Etheredge.

Etheredge, Jones & Lewin, What is Driving Health System Change?, Health Affs., Winter 1996, p.93, 94-95, 95-96. Reprinted with permission of Health Affairs.

Goode, William, Community Within a Community: The Professions, 22 Am. Soc. Rev. 194 (1957). Reprinted with permission of the American Sociological Association.

Gaumer, Gary, Regulating Health Professionals: A review of the Empirical Literature, 62 Milbank Mem. Fund Q. 380, 406-08 (1984). Reprinted with permission of the Milbank Quarterly.

Goldberg, Lawrence & Warren Greenberg, The Effect of Physician-Controlled Health Insurance: U.S. v. Oregon State Medical Society, 2 J. Health Pol., Pol'y & L. 48, 69-73 (1977). Reprinted with permission of the Duke University Press. Copyright © 1977, Duke University Press.

Gray, Bradford, The New Health Care for Profit, National Research Council News Report, July-Aug., 1983 at 16-17, 21. Reprinted with permission of the National Academy of Sciences.

Hansmann, Henry B., Reforming Nonprofit Corporation Law, 129 U. Pa. L.Rev. 497 (1981). Reprinted with permission of the University of Pennsylvania Law Review.

Harris, Jeffrey, Regulation and Internal Controls in Hospitals, 55 Bull. N.Y. Acad. of Med. 88 (1979). Reprinted with permission of the New York Academy of Medicine.

Havighurst, Clark C. & N. King, Correspondence, 10 Am.J.L. & Med. 459-61 (vol. 10, no. 4 1983). Reprinted with permission of the American Journal of Law, Medicine & Ethics and Boston University School of Law.

Havighurst Clark C. & N. King, Private Credentialing of Health Care Personnel: An Antitrust Perspective (Pt. 1), 9 Am.J.L. & Med., 138-151. Reprinted with permission of the American Journal of Law, Medicine & Ethics and Boston University School of Law.

Havighurst Clark C. & N. King, Private Credentialing of Health Care Personnel: An Antitrust Perspective (Pt. 2), 9 Am. J. L. & Med., 263, 278-80 (1983). Reprinted with permission of the American Journal of Law, Medicine & Ethics and Boston University School of Law.

Havighurst, Clark C. & Laurence Tancredi, "Medical Adversity Insurance"—A No-Fault Approach to Medical Malpractice and Quality Assurance, Milbank Mem. Fund Q. 125 (1975). Reprinted with permission of the Milbank Quarterly.

Havighurst, Clark C., Developing Noninstitutional Health Services: The Role of Certificate-of-Need Regulation, in Cost, Quality, and Access in Health Care: New Roles for Health Planning in a Competitive Environment 71, 78-81, 87-89 (F.Sloan, J. Blumstein & J. Perrin eds. 1988). Reprinted with permission of Foundation Press.

Havighurst, Clark C., Doctors and Hospitals: An Antitrust Perspective on Traditional Relationships, 1984 Duke L.J. 1071, 1122-26, 1149-51. Reprinted with permission of Duke University School of Law.

Havighurst, Clark C., Foreward: The Place of Private Accrediting Among the Instruments of Government, Law & Contemp. Probs., Autumn 1994, at 1, 7-10. Reprinted with permission of the Duke University School of Law.

Havighurst, Clark C., Health Care Choices: Private Contracts as Instruments of Health Reform 14-19, 22, 75-80, 90-109 (1995). Reprinted with permission of AEI Press. Copyright © 1995, the American Enterprise Institute.

Havighurst, Clark C., Practice Guidelines as Legal Standards Governing Physician Liability, Law & Contemp. Probs., Spring 1991, passim. Reprinted with permission of Duke University School of Law.

Havighurst, Clark C., Professional Peer Review and the Antitrust Laws, 36 Case W. Res. L. Rev. 1118, 1164-65 (1986). Reprinted with permission of the Case Western Reserve Law Review.

Havighurst, Clark C., The Changing Locus of Decision-Making in the Health Care Sector, 11 Health Pol., Pol'y & L. 697, 708-10 (1986). Reprinted with permission of the Duke University Press. Copyright © 1986, Duke University Press.

Institute of Medicine, Assessing Medical Technologies 41, 47-48, 50-51 (1985). Reprinted with permission of the Institute of Medicine, National Academy of Sciences.

Institute of Medicine, Improving the Medicare Market, 13-15, 22-23 (1996). Reprinted with permission of the Institute of Medicine, National Academy of Sciences.

Jost, Timothy, Medicare and the Joint Commission on Accreditation of Healthcare Organizations, Law & Contemp. Probs., Autumn 1994, at 15, 16-17. Reprinted with permission of the Duke University School of Law.

Kuttner, Robert, Columbia/HCA and the Resurgence of the For-Profit Hospital Business, 335 New Eng. J. Med. 362-67, 446-51 (1996). Reprinted with permission of the New England Journal of Medicine. Copyright © 1996, Massachusetts Medical Society.

Leape, Error in Medicine, 272 J.A.M.A. 1851, passim (1994). Copyright © 1994, American Medical Association. Reprinted with permission of the American Medical Association.

Light, Donald, Is Competition Bad?, 309 New Eng. J. Med. 1315 (1983). Reprinted with permission of the New England Journal of Medicine. Copyright © 1980, Massachusetts Medical Society.

McCoid, Allan, The Care Required of Medical Practitioners, 12 Vand. l. Rev. 549, 558-560, 605-09 (1959). Reprinted with permission of the Vanderbilt University School of Law.

Metzloff, Thomas B., Arbitrating Malpractice Disputes: Insights from the Real World, Duke Law Magazine, Spring 1996, 7. Reprinted with permission of Duke University School of Law.

Okuno, Takashi, The Cunningham Case and Blood Usage, 220 J.A.M.A. 1015 (1972). Copyright © 1972, American Medical Association and Doctor Takashi Okuno.

Rakich, J. & K. Darr, Hospital Organization and Management: Text and Readings 25-29 (3d ed. 1983). Reprinted with permission of the Spectrum Publications Co.

Relman, Arnold, The New Medical-Industrial Complex, 303 New Eng. J. Med. 963, 966-67 (1980). Reprinted with permission of the New England Journal of Medicine. Copyright © 1980, Massachusetts Medical Society.

Safriet, Impediments to Progress in Health Care Workforce Policy: License and Practice Laws, 31 Inquiry 310, 314-15 (1994). Reprinted with permission of Blue Cross and Blue Shield Association.

Sloan, F., R. Bovbjerg & P. Githens, Insuring Medical Malpractice 4-7, 10 (1991). Reprinted with permission of Oxford University Press.

Starr, Paul, New Critics of Medical Care: The Politics of Therapeutic Nihilism (1976), Hastings Center Rep. Oct. 1976, at 24. Reprinted with permission of the Hastings Center.

Starr, Paul, A National Health Program: Organizing Diversity (1975) Hastings Center Rep. Feb. 1975, at 11. Reprinted with permission of the Hastings Center.

Starr, Paul, The Social Transformation of American Medicine 226-27 (1982). Copyright © 1982 by Paul Starr. Reprinted with permission of Basic Books, Inc., Publishers.

Weiler, Paul, Howard H. Hiatt, J.P. Newhouse, W.G. Johnson, T.A. Brennan, and L.L. Leape, A Measure of Malpractice: Medical Injury, Malpractice Litigation, and Patient Compensation, passim (Cambridge, Mass., Harvard University Press): Copyright © 1993 by the President and Fellows of Harvard College. Reprinted by permission of the publisher.

Weiler, Paul, The Impact of Malpractice Legislation, in Medical Malpractice on Trial, 33, 35-37 (Cambridge, Mass., Harvard University Press): Copyright © 1991 by the President and Fellows of Harvard College. Reprinted by permission of the publisher.

Wennberg et al., An Assessment of Prostatectomy for Benign Urinary Tract Obstruction: Geographic Variations and the Evaluation of Medical Care Outcomes, 29 J.A.M.A. 3027-28, 3030 (1988). Copyright © 1988, American Medical Association. Reprinted with permission of the American Medical Association.

*

FOREWORD

HEALTH CARE AS A LABORATORY FOR THE STUDY OF LAW AND POLICY

Unlike most law school subjects, health care law cannot be learned or taught simply as a discrete body of legal doctrine. Instead, the student or teacher of health care law finds numerous points at which some larger body of public law (e.g., tax or antitrust) or private law (e.g., torts or insurance) impinges on health care providers or patients, creating special problems that warrant separate study. There are also, of course, numerous statutes, regulations, and legal rules that do apply exclusively to the provision or financing of health care. However, these legal requirements affect so many different matters, emanate from such diverse sources, and are so uncoordinated, inconsistent, and incomplete that they fail to constitute a coherent legal regime that can be studied as an integrated whole. In short, it quickly appears that the common denominator that best unifies the study of health care law is the health care industry itself.

In developing these materials, we have attempted to organize the subject around the industry's special functions and institutions and the public policy concerns and issues to which they give rise. This foreword attempts to show some of the substantive scope of this book and why we regard a course in this area as potentially more than just a curricular frill and preparation for practice in a relatively new legal specialty. Precisely because the legal framework within which the health care industry operates in the current era has been so amorphous and unsettled, health care law provides a uniquely valuable vantage point from which to view generally the operation of legal institutions and the interplay of law and policy. It is a fortuitous additional benefit that the course also includes lessons in ethics, professionalism, and professional regulation that carry over to the law student's own profession.

Law in Action

Making a single complex industry the focal point of a law school course is something of a pedagogical innovation. To be sure, there have been courses in transportation, communications, and banking law, but those courses have mostly focused on particular, relatively coherent regulatory regimes. Perhaps occasional courses in sports law, education law, entertainment law, or agricultural law have addressed a range of legal problems besetting a single field of activity, but those fields of human endeavor lack the magnitude, complexity, and universality of health care. Although the study of law in such specific industry contexts does have the virtue of capturing some of the reality of law practice—with problems popping up in all directions rather than in accordance with some internal logic of the law itself—, health care law offers superior opportunities for conveying information about, and insights into, the legal system itself. In our more idealistic moments, we visualize the course as an elective that students should value not so much as a bread-and-butter subject but as an exercise in applied jurisprudence, showing how law evolves and how it influences, for better or for worse, the overall performance of a single, intrinsically fascinating industry. Students are invited to take a "systems" approach to the study of health care law, attempting to isolate contributions that various legal rules make toward achieving coherent and consistent policy results.

There are several specific reasons why the health care sector of the economy offers a unique opportunity for the study of law in action. First, it has undergone extraordinary changes in the last quarter-century as professional dominance has given way to other influences. The rapidity of the industry's transformation and the absence of any single watershed event or impelling cause create numerous opportunities for observing the legal system's performance in promoting, retarding, and adapting to developments. Although the legal system originally bolstered the old medical regime and embodied most of its tenets, changes in legal rules and doctrine eventually contributed to the old system's demise and its replacement by a more chaotic, partly market-driven system. Legislation's contribution to the industry's evolution has been mixed, reflecting old ways of thinking as often as new ones. At the same time, many of the most crucial developments in health care law, especially in the all-important antitrust sphere, have been the result of judicial decisions. Again and again, the student may be asked whether a particular statute, regulatory action, legal doctrine, or judicial decision comports with new developments or with any clear-cut public policy toward the health care field.

A related feature of health care law is that many significant issues affecting the industry and its legal environment remain unsettled. Indeed, the numerous questions yet to be resolved include not only legal fine points but many fundamental policy issues of a kind that are rarely open for more than academic discussion. In addition to a continuing regulation-versus-competition debate, there has been an even more fundamental tension between, on the one hand, centralization of decision making in professional or governmental hands and, on the other hand, devolution of authority to consumers and their voluntarily selected agents. There are many useful lessons to be learned from witnessing the legal system's efforts to accommodate the aspirations of professionals, the interests of consumers, the rights of patients, the imperatives of the political system, and the democratic appeal of a system based on consumer sovereignty and restored cost-consciousness.

Another reason why the health care industry provides a valuable laboratory for the study of the legal system itself is the diversity of the sources of law governing health care. Both Congress and state legislatures have major roles. In addition to presenting issues of statutory policy and interpretation, the course offers numerous illustrations of federalism in action (e.g., the Medicaid program and numerous delegation and preemption issues, including several under antitrust law's state-action doctrine, the McCarran–Ferguson Act, and ERISA). The administrative process is also heavily involved in health care, with the Health Care Financing Administration, the Federal Trade Commission, and state licensing, certificate-of-need, and other regulatory agencies as major players. Local government is involved in the provision and financing of services and in health planning.

Defining the proper law-making role of the judiciary presents especially challenging issues in the study of health care law. There are several important areas that are governed by courts acting primarily in a common-law mode (e.g., in redressing medical malpractice and in defining hospital/physician relations and the powers of voluntary associations). Federal and state courts are also involved in evaluating health care legislation under constitutional norms, in interpreting statutes and their underlying (and sometimes conflicting) policies, and in supervising administrative action. Perhaps most tellingly, there are numerous enlightening opportunities for questioning the need for any legal intervention at all. The question of the appropriate scope of judicial activism arises vividly in the health care field in the interpretation and enforcement of private contracts, in the supervision of private actions (e.g., hospital staffing decisions), in the oversight of voluntary organizations (e.g., accrediting and credentialing bodies), in judicial review of questionable statutes and administrative actions, and in the administration of antitrust law.

Finally, cutting across everything else that the student must consider are social policy issues of the first magnitude. In addition to engaging the student's political interest as an advocate for or opponent of extensive in-kind redistribution, the health care sector offers a good opportunity to address such issues pragmatically, seeing both the legal and practical details of entitlement programs and the disadvantages as well as the benefits of different ways of addressing the needs of the poor. Without losing sight of the important patient interests at stake, issues relating to costs, including the hidden cross-subsidies implicit in expedient legislative or judicial policies, may be brought tellingly into view. Because American society falls well short of honoring its frequently professed commitment to providing health care to those who cannot finance it for themselves, law students have an excellent opportunity to encounter these volatile public issues in the context of the real-world governmental institutions and private actors that must be employed in any redistributive effort.

Policy and Economic Issues

In addition to shedding important light on the workings of the legal system, the study of health care law can illuminate a number of basic problems of public policy that a student may not encounter so explicitly or so forcefully elsewhere in law school. The problem of controlling health care costs, which absorbs so much public and private energy, is best understood as a challenge to achieve efficiency in the allocation of societal resources. Emerging evidence about wasteful spending in the system, about the limits of medicine, and about the extent of scientific uncertainty dramatizes the allocational challenge. Similarly, many of the claims made on behalf of the quality of care also raise (or should be seen to raise) questions of the how-much-is-enough variety. Although allocative efficiency is a central theoretical concern of economics, attempts to achieve it in health care by either market or nonmarket means encounter major political and practical difficulties emanating from the prevalent belief that health (and, by implication, health care) has, or should have, no price. Law students would seem well served by an introduction to such societal dilemmas and to the practical problems they present to advocates and to both public and private decision makers.

Other persistent themes in the rigorous study of health care law include those twin market imperfections that bedevil all risk shifting and insurance: "moral hazard" and "adverse selection." At stake here is the viability of private health care financing and the currently dominant policy of relying upon competition between financing plans to achieve efficiency. On another level, these phenomena complicating health care financing explain many of the public and private actions that accompany attempts to control costs without sacrificing essential quality. A course in health care law can serve as an excellent introduction to the complexities of both social and private insurance.

Other large policy themes to which a student may be introduced through the study of health care law include the tension in the American polity between centralized and decentralized decision making—that is, between an orderly, regulated system featuring homogeneity, paternalism, and orthodoxy, on the one hand, and a disorderly, pluralistic marketplace featuring producer independence, consumer sovereignty, and competitive diversity, on the other. Although it is customary to speak of a health care *system,* developments in recent years appear to have moved the nation away from earlier visions of a social enterprise operated under fairly strict professional or governmental control. Related to this theme is the question of the relative utility of government regulation versus more market-oriented alternatives as a solution to the severe dysfunctions of the health care economy.

Breaking down the foregoing general themes further should lead the student to contemplate numerous other issues that may not surface explicitly or with the same force elsewhere in legal training. The student is confronted at numerous points by questions concerning the performance of the legislative branch of government. Indeed, health manpower regulation and statutory prohibitions on commercial practices in health care provide some stark illustrations of interest groups' ability to use state legislative processes to secure their own advantage. In this connection, some awareness of "public choice" theory may impart some desirable sophistication and prepare the student for the legislative struggles that are a constant feature of health care law at both the state and federal levels.

The study of health care law also invites attention to the role and utility of economic incentives and self-interest in motivating market participants, both lay and professional. Questions concerning the deterrent function of tort law are vividly (to say the least) dramatized in the law of medical malpractice. In addition, a great deal of health care law revolves around the appropriateness of various economic incentives for cost containment and the legitimacy of private corporate agents, both nonprofit and for-profit, as intermediaries between professional and patient. Few law students are otherwise introduced to issues of this kind, to the not-for-profit corporation, or to federal, state, and local tax exemptions. Here these introductions can be particularly memorable because of the policy context.

Health care law also deals at numerous points with information, the quantity and quality of which are vital to optimal industry performance and to social control through either governmental action or market forces. The supply and quality of scientific information and the alternative ways of putting such information to use are vital issues. The student will be interested to witness the parallel use of first amendment (commercial speech) principles and antitrust law to lift artificial restraints on professional advertising. Although industry-sponsored accrediting of health care institutions and credentialing of personnel help to offset the market's chronic underproduction of information, the book asks whether consumers may lack a sufficient diversity of sources and views on matters of sometimes intense interest. There are opportunities here for law students to ponder the function of information and the legal system's power to influence its production and dissemination under various auspices. In many respects, the health care sector is appropriately viewed as a malfunctioning marketplace of competing ideas and not merely as a market for technical services. In this same connection, these materials raise some surprising questions concerning the education system, which must simultaneously impart valid technical information and be open to alternative ways of thinking and doing.

This Course and "Bioethics"

The table of contents shows the coverage of the course as we visualize it. The introductory Part I presents the most basic policy issues, introducing the student at the same time to the institutional and policy frameworks within which health care is financed and delivered. Part II develops the legal and policy tensions between altruism and professionalism, on the one hand, and commercialism reinforced by antitrust policy, on the other. It provides many insights into legal and other relationships between physicians and corporate actors in the health care field. Part III covers the quality side of "the quality/cost trade-off," reviewing public and private initiatives and the role of tort law in disciplining providers. Part IV turns to modern developments integrating financing and delivery and addresses the large issues of accountability that are presented as the industry moves into unfamiliar territory, where law is not yet formulated.

Because a course covering the ground surveyed here easily fills the time available in a typical law school elective, something must be left out. Unfortunately, efficiency seems to dictate that, as fascinating as they are, most issues that go under the heading of "bioethics" should be left in the background for another course or seminar. This book does, however, at a number of points raise cross-cutting issues requiring a synthesis of cost, quality, and access concerns, areas where ethical values are at stake. In particular, the student can expect to encounter some dilemmas related to medical technology and the rationing of health services. The largest questions involving such hard choices and many others in the bioethical sphere seem to us to be best addressed, however, in context, after one has a firm sense of the health care industry, its financing and cost problems, its mix of public and private decision making, and the various mechanisms by which resources are or might be allocated to health care uses. In an ideal curriculum, bioethics would be taught in a last-semester seminar.

We hope that other teachers and students will conclude, as we have, that the health care industry provides a useful vehicle—a laboratory, as it were—in which to gain perspective on legal institutions and public policy. They should also find here a solid foundation for further sober reflection, both philosophical and practical, on society's means of addressing "tragic choices" and some other essential features of the human condition.

SUMMARY OF CONTENTS

TABLE OF CONTENTS

*

TABLE OF CASES

Principal cases are in bold type. Non-principal cases are in roman type. References are to Pages.

GLOSSARY OF ACRONYMS

AAHP	American Association of Health Plans
AAPCC	Adjusted average per capita cost
ABMS	American Board of Medical Specialties
ACGME	Accreditation Council for Graduate Medical Education
ACP	American College of Physicians
ACPE	American Council on Pharmaceutical Education
ACS	American College of Surgeons
ADA	Americans with Disabilities Act, or American Dental Association
ADR	Alternative dispute resolution
AHA	American Hospital Association
AHCPR	Agency for Health Care Policy and Research
AIDS	Acquired immunodeficiency syndrome
AMA	American Medical Association
AMAP	American Medical Accreditation Program
AMCRA	American Managed Care and Review Association
APN	Advanced practice nurse
ASO	Administrative services only
AWP	"Any willing provider" (laws)
BBA	Balanced Budget Act of 1997
BCBSA	Blue Cross and Blue Shield Association
CAHEA	Committee on Allied Health Education and Accreditation (AMA)
CME	Council on Medical Education (AMA)
CON	Certificate of need
COPA	Council on Postsecondary Accreditation
CORPA	Commission on Recognition of Postsecondary Accreditation
CPR	Customary, prevailing, and reasonable (fees)
CQI	Continuous quality improvement
CRNA	Certified registered nurse anesthetist
DCE	Designated compensable event

DHEW	Department of Health, Education and Welfare
DHHS	Department of Health and Human Services
DME	Durable medical equipment
DRG	Diagnosis-related group
DSH	Disproportionate-share hospital
DSA	Disproportionate-share adjustment
ECFMG	Educational Council for Foreign Medical Graduates
ED	Emergency department
EEOC	Equal Employment Opportunity Commission
EMTALA	Emergency Medical Treatment and Active Labor Act
ER	Emergency room
ERISA	Employee Retirement Income Security Act
FASF	Freestanding ambulatory surgical facility
FCA	False Claims Act
FDA	Food and Drug Administration
FEHBP	Federal Employee Health Benefits Plan
FMG	Foreign medical graduate
FTC	Federal Trade Commission
GAO	General Accounting Office
GDP	Gross domestic product
HCFA	Health Care Financing Administration (DHHS)
HCQIA	Health Care Quality Improvement Act
HEDIS	Health plan employer data and information set
HHA	Home health agency
HHI	Herfindahl-Hirschman index
HI	Hospital Insurance (Medicare)
HIAA	Health Insurance Association of America
HIO	Health-insuring organization
HIPAA	Health Insurance Portability and Accountability Act of 1996 (Kassebaum-Kennedy)
HIV	Human immunodeficiency virus
HMO	Health maintenance organization
HSA	Health systems agency (health planning)
IDS	Integrated delivery system
IOM	Institute of Medicine (National Academy of Sciences)
IPA	Individual practice association
IRS	Internal Revenue Service
JCAH	Joint Commission on Accreditation of Hospitals

JCAHO	Joint Commission on Accreditation of Healthcare Organizations
LCME	Liaison Committee on Medical Education
LPN	Licensed practical nurse
MAI	Medical adversity insurance
MCO	Managed care organization
MCP	Medicare+Choice Program
MedPAC	Medicare Payment Advisory Commission
MFN	Most favored nation
MSA	Medical savings account
NAIC	National Association of Insurance Commissioners
NCHCA	National Commission for Health Certifying Agencies
NCQA	National Committee for Quality Assurance
NHPRDA	National Health Planning and Resource Development Act (Public Law 93-641)
NLN	National League for Nursing
OBRA	Omnibus Budget Reconciliation Act (various years)
OIG	Office of Inspector General (DHHS)
OR	Operating room
OTA	Office of Technology Assessment
PA	Physician assistant
PBM	Pharmacy benefit manager
PCP	Primary care provider
PE	Physician extender
PHO	Physician-hospital organization
PHP	Prepaid health plan
POS	Point of service
PPA	Preferred-provider arrangement
PPO	Preferred-provider organization
PPRC	Physician Payment Review Commission
PPS	Prospective Payment System
PRO	Peer review organization
ProPAC	Prospective Payment Assessment Commission
PSO	Provider-sponsored organization
PSRO	Professional standards review organization
RAP	Radiologists, anesthesiologists, and pathologists (hospital-based physicians)
RBRVS	Resource-based relative value scale
RCP	Royal College of Physicians

RN	Registered nurse
RNP	Registered nurse practitioner
RVS	Relative value scale
SCHIP	State Children's Health Insurance Program
SHCC	State health coordinating council (health planning)
SHPDA	State health planning and development agency
SMI	Supplementary Medical Insurance (Medicare)
SNF	Skilled nursing facility
SSI	Supplemental Security Income
TPA	Third-party administrator
TQM	Total quality management
UCR	Usual, customary, and reasonable (fees)
USFMG	United States foreign medical graduate
VA	Veterans Administration
VPS	Volume performance standard rate of increase (Medicare)

READINGS, NOTES, AND QUESTIONS

HEALTH CARE LAW AND POLICY

*

PART I

INTRODUCTION TO THE DILEMMAS OF AMERICAN HEALTH POLICY

CHAPTER 1

ACCESS TO HEALTH CARE: OF OBLIGATIONS AND ENTITLEMENTS

SECTION A: A CASE STUDY IN TRAGIC CHOICES

Muse v. Charter Hospital of Winston–Salem, Inc.

Court of Appeals of North Carolina, 1995.
117 N.C.App. 468, 452 S.E.2d 589, *affirmed per curiam*, 464 S.E.2d 44 (1995), *rehearing denied*, 467 S.E.2d 718 (1996).

■ LEWIS, JUDGE.

This appeal arises from a judgment in favor of plaintiffs in an action for the wrongful death of [Joe Muse, the plaintiffs' son]. * * * The jury found that defendant Charter Hospital of Winston–Salem, Inc. (hereinafter "Charter Hospital" or "the hospital") was negligent in that, inter alia, it had a policy or practice which required physicians to discharge patients when their insurance expired and that this policy interfered with the exercise of the medical judgment of Joe's treating physician, Dr. L. Jarrett Barnhill, Jr. The jury awarded plaintiffs compensatory damages of approximately $1,000,000. The jury found that Mr. and Mrs. Muse were contributorily negligent, but that Charter Hospital's conduct was willful or wanton,[1] and awarded punitive damages [totaling $6,000,000].

The facts on which this case arose may be summarized as follows. On 12 June 1986, Joe, who was sixteen years old at the time, was admitted to Charter Hospital for treatment related to his depression and suicidal thoughts. Joe's treatment team consisted of Dr. Barnhill, as treating physician, Fernando Garzon, as nursing therapist, and Betsey Willard, as social worker. During his hospitalization, Joe experienced auditory hallucinations, suicidal and homicidal thoughts, and major depression. Joe's insurance coverage was set to expire on 12 July 1986. As that date neared, Dr. Barnhill decided that a blood test was needed to determine the proper dosage of a drug he was administering to Joe. The blood test was scheduled for 13 July, the day after Joe's insurance was to expire. Dr. Barnhill requested that the hospital administrator allow Joe to stay at Charter Hospital two more days, until 14 July, with Mr. and Mrs. Muse signing a promissory note to pay for the two extra days. The test results did not come back from the lab until 15 July. Nevertheless, Joe was discharged on 14

1. Ed.: The court stated later in its opinion that "contributory negligence does not bar recovery in a wrongful death action where, as here, the defendants' conduct was found to be wanton or willful."

July and was referred by Dr. Barnhill to the Guilford County Area Mental Health, Mental Retardation and Substance Abuse Authority (hereinafter "Mental Health Authority") for outpatient treatment. Plaintiffs' evidence tended to show that Joe's condition upon discharge was worse than when he entered the hospital. Defendants' evidence, however, tended to show that while his prognosis remained guarded, Joe's condition at discharge was improved. Upon his discharge, Joe went on a one-week family vacation. On 22 July he began outpatient treatment at the Mental Health Authority, where he was seen by Dr. David Slonaker, a clinical psychologist. Two days later, Joe again met with Dr. Slonaker. Joe failed to show up at his 30 July appointment, and the next day he took a fatal overdose of Desipramine, one of his prescribed drugs.

On appeal, defendants present numerous assignments of error. We find merit in one of defendants' arguments [namely, that the jury should not have been permitted to make separate awards of punitive damages against both Charter Hospital ($2,000,000) and its parent corporation ($4,000,-000).]

II.

Defendants [also] argue that the trial court submitted the case to the jury on an erroneous theory of hospital liability that does not exist under the law of North Carolina. As to the theory in question, the trial court instructed: "[A] hospital is under a duty not to have policies or practices which operate in a way that interferes with the ability of a physician to exercise his medical judgment. A violation of this duty would be negligence." The jury found that there existed "a policy or practice which required physicians to discharge patients when their insurance benefits expire and which interfered with the exercise of Dr. Barnhill's medical judgment." Defendants contend that this theory of liability does not fall within any theories previously accepted by our courts.

* * *

Our Supreme Court has recognized that hospitals in this state owe a duty of care to their patients. In Burns v. Forsyth County Hospital Authority, Inc., 344 S.E.2d 839, 845 (1986), this Court held that a hospital has a duty to the patient to obey the instructions of a doctor, absent the instructions being obviously negligent or dangerous. Another recognized duty is the duty to make a reasonable effort to monitor and oversee the treatment prescribed and administered by doctors practicing at the hospital. In light of these holdings, it seems axiomatic that the hospital has the duty not to institute policies or practices which interfere with the doctor's medical judgment. We hold that pursuant to the reasonable person standard, Charter Hospital had a duty not to institute a policy or practice which required that patients be discharged when their insurance expired and which interfered with the medical judgment of Dr. Barnhill.

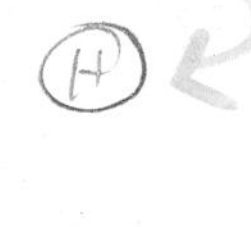

III.

Defendants next argue that even if the theory of negligence submitted to the jury was proper, the jury's finding that Charter Hospital had such a practice was not supported by sufficient evidence. * * *

Plaintiffs' evidence included the testimony of Charter Hospital employees and outside experts. Fernando Garzon, Joe's nursing therapist at Charter Hospital, testified that the hospital had a policy of discharging patients when their insurance expired. Specifically, when the issue of insurance came up in treatment team meetings, plans were made to discharge the patient. When Dr. Barnhill and the other psychiatrists and therapists spoke of insurance, they seemed to lack autonomy. For example, Garzon testified, they would state, "So and so is to be discharged. We must do this." Finally, Garzon testified that when he returned from a vacation, and Joe was no longer at the hospital, he asked several employees why Joe had been discharged and they all responded that he was discharged because his insurance had expired. Jane Sims, a former staff member at the hospital, testified that several employees expressed alarm about Joe's impending discharge, and that a therapist explained that Joe could no longer stay at the hospital because his insurance had expired. Sims also testified that Dr. Barnhill had misgivings about discharging Joe, and that Dr. Barnhill's frustration was apparent to everyone. One of plaintiffs' experts testified that based on a study regarding the length of patient stays at Charter Hospital, it was his opinion that patients were discharged based on insurance, regardless of their medical condition. Other experts testified that based on Joe's serious condition on the date of discharge, the expiration of insurance coverage must have caused Dr. Barnhill to discharge Joe. The experts further testified as to the relevant standard of care, and concluded that Charter Hospital's practices were below the standard of care and caused Joe's death. We hold that this evidence was sufficient to go to the jury.

Defendants further argue that the evidence was insufficient to support the jury's finding that Charter Hospital engaged in conduct that was willful or wanton. An act is willful when it is done purposely and deliberately in violation of the law, or when it is done knowingly and of set purpose, or when the mere will has free play, without yielding to reason. It is wanton when it is done of wicked purpose, or when it is done needlessly, with reckless indifference to the rights of others. We conclude that the jury could have reasonably found from the above-stated evidence that Charter Hospital acted knowingly and of set purpose, and with reckless indifference to the rights of others. Therefore, we hold that the finding of willful or wanton conduct on the part of Charter Hospital was supported by sufficient evidence.

IV.

Defendants' next argument is that * * * the superseding negligence of the Muses [who allegedly allowed Joe access to his medication, contrary to instructions] and Dr. Barnhill [who allegedly failed to urge the Muses, either sufficiently or at all, to hospitalize Joe at an available public psychiatric hospital] insulated the negligence of Charter Hospital as a matter of law, and that, therefore, the hospital's negligence was not a proximate cause of the suicide.

The doctrine of superseding, or intervening, negligence is well established in our law. In order for an intervening cause to relieve the original wrongdoer of liability, the intervening cause must be a new cause, which intervenes between the original negligent act and the injury ultimately suffered, and which breaks the chain of causation set in motion by the original wrongdoer and becomes itself solely responsible for the injury. * * *

The evidence, when viewed in the light most favorable to plaintiffs, with all reasonable inferences being afforded to plaintiffs, tended to show that the hospital had a policy of requiring the discharge of patients when their insurance expired and that this policy interfered with Dr. Barnhill's medical judgment regarding Joe's discharge. Dr. Barnhill was thereby put in a position such that he could not disclose the severity of Joe's condition to the Muses. He then discharged Joe, transferring him to outpatient treatment at the public facility. Any negligence of Dr. Barnhill in discharging Joe and in not warning the Muses, or of the Muses, in not properly supervising Joe after discharge, did not turn aside the natural sequence of events set in motion by the hospital's misconduct. Rather, the alleged intervening acts, in the natural and ordinary course of things, could have been anticipated by defendants as not entirely improbable. Thus, the hospital's negligence was not superseded, and thereby insulated, as a matter of law. Accordingly, the trial court properly denied defendants' motion for judgment notwithstanding the verdict.

Defendants also contend that the trial court erred in directing a verdict for plaintiffs on the issue of whether Dr. Slonaker's alleged negligence was a superseding cause of Joe's death. * * * [T]he evidence tended to show that Joe saw Dr. Slonaker at the Mental Health Authority on two occasions after his discharge from Charter Hospital, that Dr. Slonaker had reviewed Joe's discharge summary, and that Joe reported to Dr. Slonaker that he was still having hallucinations. Further, one of plaintiffs' experts testified that Dr. Slonaker's treatment was "[s]o totally inadequate that he could possibly not have had [the documents in Joe's Charter Hospital file] to review, or if he did review them, he paid no damned attention to them." However, defendants have pointed to no evidence in the record which tends to show that Dr. Slonaker's treatment of Joe was a cause of Joe's suicide. Thus, there was not sufficient evidence to submit to the jury the issue of whether Dr. Slonaker's alleged negligence was a superseding cause of Joe's death, and the trial court did not err in directing a verdict for plaintiffs on this issue.

* * *

For the reasons stated, we find no error in the judgment of the trial court, except for that part of the judgment awarding punitive damages, which is reversed and remanded for proceedings consistent with this opinion.

* * *

■ ORR, JUDGE, dissenting.

After a careful review of the record and applicable law, I must respectfully dissent from the majority on the submission of the issue on wilful or wanton conduct. * * *

[T]here is * * * evidence that defendant hospital had a policy or practice of discharging patients when their insurance ran out. This practice was obviously done for a business purpose; however, the evidence reveals that the policy was subject to being overridden on occasion by request of the treating physician or other financial consideration. Although there also was some evidence that this policy may have affected Dr. Barnhill's decision to discharge the plaintiffs' son, such evidence, while perhaps supporting a negligence theory, does not go beyond that.

Dr. Barnhill testified that the policy did not influence his decision, and more importantly, that a range of treatment options including a state psychiatric hospital were available for the patient. No evidence was presented that could lead a jury to conclude that the policy in question involved a deliberate purpose not to discharge some duty necessary to the safety of the person in question. While it can be said that the policy to discharge was deliberate, there is no evidence that the hospital expected, anticipated or intended for the patient to be released in circumstances that put the person's safety in jeopardy. In fact, [Joe] was discharged into the custody and care of another physician and a community based mental health facility as well as the care of his parents with specific instructions for his care.

* * *

While the jury found that defendant was negligent, I find insufficient evidence to raise the defendant's conduct to the level required to submit the issue of willful and wanton conduct to the jury. A policy to terminate a patient's hospitalization based upon insurance benefits ending in and of itself is not wilful or wanton conduct. To sustain plaintiff's contention there must be, according to our law, a deliberate purpose not to discharge a duty necessary for a person's safety. If the hospital had simply discharged the patient with no referral to another physician or medical facility, then a cognizable claim for wilful or wanton conduct would have been established. Such was not the case here, as I read the record, and although Dr. Barnhill's care in discharging the patient may well have been negligent, there is nothing to suggest that the hospital's policy or its implementation by Dr. Barnhill was done with reckless or deliberate disregard for the patient's safety. Therefore, I conclude that the trial court erred in submitting the issue of wilful and wanton conduct to the jury and would accordingly vote to reverse.

NOTES AND QUESTIONS ON THE ROLES OF THE VARIOUS ACTORS IN THE MUSE TRAGEDY

1. *"Tragic Choices."* Health care necessarily involves hard choices. Indeed, many decisions affecting the treatment of individual patients are so-called "tragic choices," reflecting the regrettable but inevitable tension between society's desire to see unlimited care provided for each afflicted individual and the limits of the available resources. Cf. G. Calabresi & P. Bobbitt, Tragic Choices (1978) (examining "the conflicts society confronts in the allocation of tragically scarce resources," not only in health care but in other potentially tragic situations as well). As in the *Muse* case, tragic consequences sometimes flow from decisions made under difficult circumstances by various actors in the complex system by which health care is financed and delivered in the United States. Sometimes such tragedies are caused by a failure of a particular actor to fulfill appropriate legal responsibilities. Many hardships, however, may be attributable in the last analysis only to the inability or unwillingness of individuals or the government to commit the resources needed to avert the potential harm. Calabresi & Bobbitt, supra, document the immense difficulty that modern society has in acknowledging that, if resources are to be wisely used, tragic outcomes must be tolerated in some specific cases.

In the *Muse* case, the jury found that the hospital had grossly failed to discharge its legal duties to the patient and his family. Yet the most pivotal fact—antecedent to the hospital's involvement—was the contractual 30–day limit on inpatient mental-health benefits in the health plan in which Joe was enrolled. Since the hospital was not responsible for the limits of the Muse family's insurance coverage, one might ask whether it was made a scapegoat for the faults of those who selected or designed that coverage or for the circumstance that resources, societal as well as individual, are "tragically scarce." It is helpful at the outset of our study of the legal environment of the health care industry to consider the various collective and individual actions that contributed to Joe Muse's death. Although the *Muse* case is not a perfect microcosm of all the issues that the law confronts in the health care field, it brings to light a surprisingly large number of the issues, both general and specific, that we will be encountering in the material ahead. To be sure, the court's ruling is of only limited importance as legal precedent. Nevertheless, the circumstances that the court encountered highlight many of the dilemmas with which policymakers, courts, and private parties (employers, payers, hospitals, physicians, and others) must grapple in making "macro" and "micro" decisions that are truly "tragic choices."

2. *The Role of Government.* One might suppose that the Muse tragedy would have been averted if the United States in some way guaranteed health insurance to all its citizens. Even public programs have coverage limits, however, and the administrative controls or financial incentives adopted to contain program costs inevitably operate to deny some patients beneficial care. See the materials on the "prudent purchasing" of health care in chapter 2(§§ C & D) and the *Wickline* case reproduced in chapter 8(§B). Nevertheless, one of the most ambitious reforms proposed by the Clinton administration in its ill-fated Health Security Act in 1993 would have guaranteed all Americans very generous coverage for mental-health care. Pear, White House Plans Would Cover Costs of Mental Illness, N.Y. Times, March 16, 1993, p.1. Although enactment of the Clinton bill would have ensured that patients would not have to be discharged in a condition as precarious as Joe Muse's, the high cost of such generous benefits, together with other factors, prevented that proposal from becoming law. Most Americans must therefore still depend, for better or for worse, on their private coverage.

Perhaps Joe Muse's death was simply one of the costs of not giving everyone (as the Clinton bill would have done) a legal entitlement to all health care care deemed "medically necessary or appropriate." Would you be prepared to argue that the political decision not to provide such a universal entitlement implies that society and individuals must accept the consequences of "tragic choices" made conscientiously and non-negligently by private actors? If not, why not? If so, would you be surprised if a judge or jury was not impressed by your argument?

In fact, government does routinely make some provision for persons in Joe Muse's condition. Joe's family had the option, after all, of having him hospitalized in a state mental hospital, the provider of last resort for those who cannot pay for care in a better institution. Charter Hospital strongly argued that the availability of a public hospital to which Joe might have been transferred relieved it of the duty to provide uncompensated care. Is there any virtue in this argument?

3. *The Role of the Legal System*. In the absence of universal health coverage, should the legal system fill inevitable gaps by creating legal duties on the part of private hospitals to finance vital care for any patient whose privately procured coverage is inadequate? The next section of this chapter examines the scope of hospitals' common-law and statutory duties to treat patients who cannot pay. After studying those materials, you should consider whether the *Muse* court imposed unprecedented obligations on Charter Hospital.

The outcome in the *Muse* case, while tragic, resulted from a combination of factors, including the limits of the Muses' private insurance coverage, the hospital policy of requiring payment for services rendered, and choices made by the family with medical advice. In personal-injury litigation occasioned by a tragic outcome, the legal system must determine whether the injury resulted from some legitimate constraint, legitimately imposed and enforced, or from a failure by one or more defendants to fulfill some legal duty reasonably assigned in the larger system. Regrettably, constraints on the provision of costly services are commonly encountered in health care and, indeed, are an essential feature of an efficient health care system. Thus, courts must attempt to think in terms of the entire complex system through which difficult choices about health care are made. Cumulatively, such choices, both "micro" and "macro," determine how society's resources are allocated between providing health services and other uses. As we will see, excessive spending on health care in the United States may result in part because the legal system, failing to take a systemic view or to weigh benefits against costs, has been unrealistically demanding in defining the substantive obligations of both payers and health care providers.

In this connection, consider the standard of care to which the court held Charter Hospital: "We hold that pursuant to the reasonable person standard, Charter Hospital had a duty not to institute a policy or practice which required that patients be discharged when their insurance expired and which interfered with the medical judgment of Dr. Barnhill." What do you think of the court's invocation of the "reasonable person" standard? To what other source might the court have looked for a standard to apply? How can a court, as a practical matter, take the systemic view that cases like *Muse* seem to require?

4. *The Role of the Patient and His Family.* In the absence of universal government financing of health care, most consumers in the United States are, like the Muses, responsible for providing their own (and their dependents') financial protection against future medical needs. Only in limited circumstances (to be examined in § B of this chapter) does a patient lacking the ability to pay for desirable care have a legal right to receive it from a private provider. Thus, without either insurance coverage or the ability to pay out of pocket, a patient may be unable to obtain care that, rationally or irrationally, he might desire to have and that might have been provided to him without question under more comprehensive private or social insurance.

Would you be prepared to argue that the Muse family's choice of health coverage with a 30–day limit on inpatient mental-health care was the essential cause of the tragedy and that the hospital had no duty to make up for the deficiencies of that coverage? Would you want to know more about how that coverage was obtained and how much choice the family exercised in fact?

What was the legal significance of the family's decision not to hospitalize Joe in the state hospital? Does it depend on how much information the family was given by the treating physician?

5. *The Role of the Employer Providing the Family's Insurance Coverage.* Most Americans obtain financial protection against health care costs through the employer of a family member. See generally M. Pauly, Health Benefits at Work: An Economic and Political Analysis of Employment-based Health Insurance (1998). For complex reasons to be explained later, most employers of significant size, rather than simply buying conventional health insurance, are self-insured. Thus, they pay directly, on some basis (fee-for-service or otherwise), for services provided through provider networks, with which they contract either directly or through an agent—often an insurance company acting not as an insurer but as a "third-party administrator" (TPA). Although a TPA may offer benefit design as one of its services, the extent of coverage is ultimately determined by the self-insured employer itself or negotiated with an employee union.

Other employers, mostly smaller ones, simply assist their employees in purchasing group coverage provided by insurance companies or by organized health plans, such as health maintenance organizations (HMOs). In these cases, coverage limits may be established by the individual insurer or plan rather than by the employer. In some cases, employees are offered a choice of plans, with benefits either prescribed by the employer or specified by the individual plans.

Would you argue that in all of these contexts, because the employer designs the coverage or selects the plan or plans in which employees can enroll, consumer choice does not operate well enough to legitimize the occasional tragic consequences of coverage limits? Or would you argue that the employer is an effective agent of its employees in making choices in the larger market and that its contractual bargains can therefore be enforced or otherwise accepted as legitimizing tragic outcomes? Although it is easy to view the interests of employers and employees as antagonistic, all employers have some incentive, due to pressures of the labor market, to offer attractive benefits and to help employees get good value for their compensation dollars.

To be sure, the 30–day limit on inpatient care was not itself an issue in the *Muse* case, and it may be hard to see how an employer could be legally faulted for procuring coverage with such a limit. In one case, an employer was permitted to reduce prospectively the lifetime benefit limit under its health plan from $1 million to $5000—for AIDS care only. McGann v. H & H Music Co., 946 F.2d 401 (5th Cir.1991) (federal Employee Retirement Income Security Act, known as ERISA, held not to prescribe coverage or plan design or to prohibit contractually permissible amendments). However, the subsequent enactment of the Americans With Disabilities Act, 42 U.S.C. §§ 12101–213 (1994), probably means that employers who reduce benefits now must do so across the board and not in a way that discriminates against those with a particular disability; indeed, benefit design generally must avoid discrimination against particular afflictions—such as mental illness. Although mostly symbolic due to its limited scope and numerous loopholes, the federal Mental Health Parity Act of 1996, Pub. L. No. 104–204, codified at 42 U.S.C. § 300gg–5 (Supp. 1997), requires group health plans maintained by large employers, if they cover mental illness at all, not to discriminate between mental and physical conditions in setting annual or lifetime dollar limits on coverage. By one estimate, eliminating a $25,000 lifetime cap on mental health benefits (a common limitation) would increase premiums by only about $1 per enrollee per year, assuming utilization management. Sturm, How Expensive Is Unlimited Mental Health Care Coverage under Managed Care?, 278 J.A.M.A. 1533 (1997).

It is often proposed that government prescribe the terms of the coverage that all employers must provide to their employees. What effect might such an "employer mandate" have on employees' wages? on employment opportunities generally? What advantages or disadvantages do you see in allowing employers substantial freedom to select their workers' health benefits?

6. *The Role of the Health Insurer.* The designers of health coverage obviously play a potentially pivotal role in making and implementing the hard choices that medical care often requires. Private health coverage in the United States is obtained through a wide variety of entities. At one time, most coverage was provided by local Blue Cross (hospital) and Blue Shield (medical) plans. These nonprofit entities tended to be allied with provider interests and were thus inclined to write coverage with few limits on the services providers could render at plan expense. Although commercial insurers shared the market with the "Blues," they tended to be quite passive in their dealings with providers until competitive pressures in the 1980s forced them to assume more active roles in controlling costs. Other financing vehicles, such as HMOs, were quite rare until the 1970s, but have since spearheaded the movement to offer more cost-effective medical care.

All private financing entities have contracts with their subscribers that place some limits on the care they provide or underwrite. Although exclusions and benefit limitations in health care contracts can create some apparent hardships, they also serve crucial purposes in controlling costs, illustrating once again the tensions that concern us here. Many state legislatures, however, have mandated certain benefits or prescribed certain coverage terms of health insurance contracts. There are also regular proposals to have the federal government prescribe coverage rather than leaving its generosity and its details to state regulators and the marketplace. For example, the Clinton proposals of 1993–94 went quite far in prescribing—although they would not have preempted entirely—the terms of private contracts. See C. Havighurst, Health Care Choices: Private Contracts as Instruments of Health Reform 43–55 (1995). What effects would you expect mandated-benefits regulation to have on the cost of coverage, on employee wages, on the number of citizens lacking private coverage, and on the overall efficiency of the health care system?

Limits on the amount of inpatient mental-health care for which an insurer will pay are common in health insurance policies. The arbitrariness of the 30–day limit in the *Muse* case is notable, however, because it leaves no room for exceptions based on a patient's exigent need. Yet any alternative to such an objective limit on coverage would require heavy reliance on subjective judgment. As we will see, many health care plans have sought to curb inappropriate spending by employing various forms of "managed care" or "utilization management"—administrative techniques aimed at tailoring coverage in specific cases closely to each individual patient's need. See generally Hall & Anderson, Health Insurers' Assessment of Medical Necessity, 140 U.Pa.L.Rev. 1637 (1992). In many cases, these limitations are applied prospectively—before care is provided—through a process known as "predetermination of benefits" or "prior authorization." Use of these techniques has been especially controversial and difficult in the field of mental health and substance-abuse (behavioral health) care. You should begin to recognize the relative advantages and disadvantages of different ways of defining and administering health benefits in the modern era. Materials in chapter 8 will address the vexing legal issues presented in administering various kinds of health coverage.

The literature on cost-containment measures in the behavioral health field is extensive. See generally Institute of Medicine, Managing Managed Care: Quality Improvement in Behavioral Health (1997); P. Boyle & D. Callahan, eds., What Price Mental Health? The Ethics and Politics of Setting Priorities (1995); Iglehart, Managed Care and Mental Health, 334 New Eng.J.Med. 131 (1996); Shore & Beigel, The Challenges Posed by

Managed Behavioral Health Care, 334 New Eng.J.Med. 116 (1996) ("In containing costs, the clinical aim of managed behavioral health care is to limit treatment to whatever will return patients to a reasonable level of functioning as soon as possible, * * * a marked departure from traditional behavioral health care, in which treatment of the underlying clinical illness is primary, and functional improvement a secondary goal"); Symposium, Mental Health in the Age of Managed Care, Health Affs., Fall 1995; Morreim, The New Economics of Medicine: Special Challenges for Psychiatry, 15 J. Med. & Philos. 97 (1990). Cf. Weithorn, Mental Hospitalization of Troublesome Youth: An Analysis of Skyrocketing Admission Rates, 40 Stan. L. Rev. 778, 826 (1988) ("A combination of factors, including laissez-faire judicial policies, insurance coverage favoring inpatient treatment, the rise of corporate medicine, a mental health establishment willing to assume control over troublesome youth, and the symbolic appeal of a medical perspective on deviance appear to have converged to promote the inappropriate use of inpatient mental health services for the management of difficult children and adolescents.").

Despite their arbitrariness, purely objective coverage limits of the kind encountered in the *Muse* case have certain attractions for health plans. Not only do they save administrative costs, but they also reduce certain legal risks by avoiding ambiguity (which invites courts to apply the interpretive principle under which contractual ambiguities are resolved against the party drafting the contract). Plans with unambiguous coverage limits are also less vulnerable to suits for "bad faith" in the administration of coverage and to suits for personal injuries allegedly resulting from debatable utilization management. It is possible that insurers use arbitrary coverage limits principally because they do not trust courts to make allowances for the difficulty of drafting and administering other kinds of limits in health care contracts.

Health insurance policies of the kind found in the *Muse* case—essentially, a contract to indemnify the insured for certain incurred expenses (with indemnification rights assignable by the patient to the provider of covered services)—are increasingly disfavored in today's health care marketplace. Such three-cornered "indemnity" arrangements are rapidly being replaced by health plans that feature substantial integration of financing and delivery. Integration may be achieved either organizationally—by having a single prepaid entity actually provide the covered services, as in some HMOs—or through a wide variety of contractual relationships between the financing entity and providers. Note how the Muses might have benefitted if, instead of merely indemnifying them for certain costs incurred in patronizing a provider of their (unlimited) choice, their insurer had contracted with Charter Hospital (or some other provider) in a way that allowed it to negotiate the price and prevent utilization abuses while also meeting the demonstrable needs of individual patients.

Are you beginning to see the possible (though still debatable) benefits of competition in a health care marketplace featuring a variety of financing arrangements and including payers that play active rather than merely passive roles in procuring services for their enrollees?

7. *The Role of the Hospital.* The *Muse* case raises specific questions about the respective responsibilities of a private hospital and a treating physician under circumstances created by consumer and insurer choices that, without being unreasonable, were pregnant with potential hardship. One possible interpretation of the hospital's role is that it was simply implementing economizing choices made by others. Again, it is helpful to ask whether the various actors performed their respective functions in a manner consistent with the smooth operation of the total process by which society makes necessary, but potentially tragic, choices concerning the care of individual patients.

a. *Profits vs. Charity.* The case against Charter Hospital was strongly colored by its status as a profit-making rather than a charitable enterprise, with obligations to shareholders as well as to patients. As we shall see in chapter 3(§§ B & C), there has been controversy over the role of for-profit institutions in the health care field. At the time the *Muse* case was tried, there had been much publicity, including a TV exposé, concerning another proprietary chain of psychiatric hospitals that seemed to keep troubled adolescents hospitalized as long as, but no longer than, their insurance coverage held out.

In *Muse*, it was argued on behalf of the hospital that the role of private hospitals in the health care system is such that they should have a legal duty to provide free care only in extraordinary circumstances. Private charity and the provision of uncompensated care are of course common in the health care system and perform a valuable role, often serving as a critical buffer against harms that might otherwise result from inevitable gaps and shortfalls in private or public financing. Many private hospitals are explicitly organized as tax-exempt, charitable corporations and provide, in varying degrees, uncompensated care as a service to their communities. The role of these community hospitals is often supplemented by public hospitals (such as the state psychiatric hospital in *Muse*), which are supported by public funds for the express purpose of caring for those who lack the ability to pay for their own care. Investor-owned, tax-paying hospitals, on the other hand, argue that they play a different role in the larger system and should not be expected, or required, to perform redistributive or charitable functions—particularly since they pay local, state, and federal taxes that are used in part to support care for those unable to pay.

In the next section of this chapter, we will see some statutes that require private hospitals to provide needed emergency care without regard to ability to pay. Such statutes all stop well short, however, of creating an unlimited duty to serve all comers without compensation. In light of the legislation on this subject, would it seem anomalous—and possibly inappropriate under the separation of powers—for a court to define a new set of circumstances under which hospitals must provide free care? Would it be an unconstitutional "taking" for a legislature (or a court) to impose, without compensation, an unconditional duty of this kind on a private actor?

b. *A Duty to Continue Treatment Once Begun?* Presumably, a state's police power can be invoked to justify compelling a private hospital to continue rendering care, regardless of the prospects for payment, to a patient who faces an imminent hazard if care is discontinued. As we will shortly see, such a requirement has long been embodied in a common-law duty not to "abandon" a patient under treatment. Under this doctrine, which is incorporated in provider ethics as well as law, it is an incident of all provider/patient relationships that the provider will not walk away from a patient in emergent need. Providers, on notice of this implied term in their contract with patients, can predict the probable extent of their obligations under this doctrine and price their services accordingly. In general, the rule against abandonment reflects the special nature of health care and represents a reasonable effort to define the responsibilities of providers to patients facing significant danger.

On the *Muse* defendants' appeal to the North Carolina Supreme Court (addressed only to the issue raised in the dissenting opinion and decided without opinion), the plaintiffs argued that the hospital was guilty of willful and wanton conduct in abandoning Joe when he badly needed continued hospitalization. To be sure, the decision to discharge Joe was in the hands of Dr. Barnhill. But, according to the plaintiffs' brief, the evidence showed that the hospital "(1) required [Joe's] discharge solely because the patient's health insurance benefits expired, (2) compromised the medical judgment of the patient's treating physician and the physician's ability to place the patient into appropriate treatment, and then (3) deceived the patient's parents concerning the extent of the danger." In support of its claim that the hospital had essentially abandoned Joe, the plaintiffs cited the awareness of several hospital employees of the seriousness of his condition. Although the lower court had not invoked abandonment as its principal theory, the plaintiffs effectively recast the issues in these terms on appeal, making the case seem less of a departure from precedent than it had previously seemed.

On the other hand, the abandonment principle permits a provider to withdraw from a case if satisfactory alternative arrangements are made for the patient's care. In this case, the hospital could maintain that Dr. Barnhill was charged with making such arrangements and, for all it knew, had done so in consultation with the family. Would you be impressed by the argument that, in Joe's case, neither outpatient care nor the state mental hospital was a satisfactory alternative to continued hospitalization at Charter? Would you worry that accepting such an argument would make superior providers unwilling to accept the sickest patients or would discourage providers from striving for superiority?

The hospital might claim that it did nothing more than advise the patient's physician of the exhaustion of insurance benefits and of the consequent need to consider alternative sources of treatment. Would you agree that the hospital's role in this tragedy was simply that of the bearer to Joe's physician of the bad news that his insurance coverage was exhausted and that hospitalization at Charter would not be available as a treatment option much longer? Note that the trial court's instruction to the jury appeared to treat the expiration of the patient's insurance coverage as an event having little effect on his right to receive additional services. Do you agree that a discharge for financial reasons might violate the hospital's duty even if the patient's condition was such that his discharge would not constitute abandonment?

The hospital, it appears, maintained a policy of providing adequate care "regardless of [the] source of financial support." This policy, contained in a statement of "Rights of Patients" that was given to the Muses on Joe's admission, was apparently required by a hospital accrediting body. Did this document constitute, as plaintiffs claimed, a commitment to provide services for which no payment was likely to be forthcoming? Should an accreditor's standard be treated as a standard to which all accredited institutions have a duty to adhere?

c. *May Hospitals Influence the Behavior of Physicians?* Plaintiffs' main theory was that Charter, for financial reasons, corrupted Dr. Barnhill's medical judgment. Do you agree that a hospital should never attempt to influence a doctor in making decisions for his patient? In fact, hospitals have and legitimately exercise many methods to ensure that physicians do not overuse hospital resources in providing unremunerative care. See generally Hall, Institutional Control of Physician Behavior: Legal Barriers to Health Care Cost Containment, 137 U. Pa. L. Rev. 431 (1988). Indeed, Congress anticipated when it enacted the so-called Prospective Payment System for Medicare in the early 1980s (under which hospitals are paid a fixed amount per patient depending on the diagnosis) that hospitals would enlist physicians in the effort to control costs; physician cooperation was necessary to enable a hospital to stretch its Medicare allowances, and it was accepted that hospitals might earn a profit in treating some individual patients. For evidence of how increased financial pressures on hospitals in recent years have changed relationships between hospitals and physicians, see S. Shortell, Effective Hospital–Physician Relationships (1991); Blum, Evaluation of Medical Staff Using Fiscal Factors: Economic Credentialing, 26 J. Health & Hosp.L. 65 (1993); Burns, Anderson & Shortell, Trends in Hospital/Physician Relationships, 12 Health Affs. 213 (1993); Burns et al., The Effect of Hospital Control Strategies on Physician Satisfaction and Physician–Hospital Conflict, 25 Health Services Res. 527 (1990); Hall, supra.

Although the instruction to the jury in the *Muse* case implied that hospitals' economic interests should have no place in medical decisions, that idea reflects old and cherished, but ultimately unsustainable, beliefs concerning the nature of medical care and its distribution and the locus of decision-making responsibilities. If entities such as for-profit hospitals cannot impose cost constraints of any kind on physicians, the entire managed-care movement may be legally unsupportable. Managed care depends heavily, after all, on inducing physicians to observe resource constraints in their medical judgments.

To be sure, one should not be sanguine about a health care system in which tragic choices are made by actors having clear conflicts of interests and only limited legal or other accountability for their actions. Nevertheless, a judicial ruling that doctors cannot be told (or consider) the limits of a patient's insurance or encouraged to take financial considerations into account in clinical decisions would set back efforts to rationalize spending on the treatment of individual patients. Is the *Muse* decision such a ruling? Do you now see the immense difficulty of maintaining in law and public discourse the fiction that economic incentives do not and should not influence medical decision making? It is in the nature of "tragic choices" that society and its agents, observing a kind of "political correctness," systematically avoid acknowledging that some economizing choices must be made and implemented and that society must tolerate the regrettable consequences of such choices.

Plaintiffs' most telling argument in the *Muse* case may have been that the hospital compromised Dr. Barnhill's ability to advise the Muses to hospitalize Joe in the state hospital by creating a need to preserve the appearance that he was being discharged for reasons other than financial ones. According to the court of appeals, "Dr. Barnhill was thereby put in a position such that he could not disclose the severity of Joe's condition to the Muses." And the plaintiffs' brief in the state supreme court conceded as follows:

> If the record in this case showed merely that Charter Hospital had proposed to terminate Joe Muse's hospital stay for lack of insurance, while so advising Joe's parents and leaving Dr. Barnhill free to make the medical decision whether and under what circumstances a discharge was appropriate, then there would be no basis for a finding of willful or wanton conduct. Indeed, the present lawsuit would never have been filed.

Do you see the irony in making a hospital liable for not being more forthright about its commercial motives?

8. *The Role of the Treating Physician.* Was Dr. Barnhill in a position, legally or practically, to commandeer the hospital's facilities—without payment—for continued treatment of his patient? Did the instruction to the jury convey the impression that a physician's unconstrained medical judgment alone determines a patient's entitlement to continued hospitalization?

A possible role for the physician in modern, cost-conscious medical care is to serve as the principal advocate for patients in contexts featuring substantial constraints. There is some case law suggesting that a physician must not passively accede to constraints imposed by a payer if he or she perceives a real danger to the patient and an appeal is possible. See, e.g., dicta in the *Wickline* case in chapter 8(§B). Dr. Barnhill was able, it will be noted, to persuade the hospital to extend the patient's stay for two days beyond his coverage. Conceivably, Dr. Barnhill might have had a duty to seek further hospitalization at Charter if there was no adequate treatment alternative—that is, if discharge would have constituted abandonment. The duty to advocate the patient's cause within the established decision-making framework would seem vital to ensure that patients are not abandoned by hospitals and that utilization managers have all the information they need to administer coverage limitations of any but the most arbitrary kind.

In some managed-care settings, however, the financing intermediary, rather than merely limiting its contractual obligation to pay for certain services, imposes constraints directly on physicians. The financial incentives they employ create for the physician at least a minor conflict of interests. And in all managed-care systems physicians practice under an awareness that their continued participation in the plan is contingent on their overall performance, including their cooperation in controlling costs. Likewise, hospitals under payer-imposed constraints may attempt to influence physicians to economize in their use of hospital resources by threatening to withdraw certain perquisites or privileges. In all such situations, physicians are placed in the position of making choices with their own welfare as well as the welfare of the individual patient in mind, thus creating a risk of an unwarranted tragic outcome. Yet public policy today clearly contemplates that medical decisions will regularly be influenced, though not compromised, by financial considerations. Great faith is placed, it would seem, in physician ethics as a protection against abuses. In these circumstances, the need for some legal recourse for aggrieved patients seems clear. Our study will in due course consider the adequacy of the legal regime under which health plans and providers currently operate and are held more or less accountable for the choices they make.

The duty of a physician in circumstances such as those encountered in the *Muse* case may be framed in another way—namely as a duty to assist the patient in solving his health problem with the resources at the patient's disposal. In this case, the exhaustion of insurance benefits clearly created a new and more difficult problem for the patient (perhaps explaining why one witness thought Dr. Barnhill appeared "frustrated"). There was a conflict in the evidence, however, over how fully the doctor advised the family of the new situation and over how strongly he urged them to pursue the option of transfer to the state mental hospital before he arranged for outpatient care by a community provider. Do you agree that the key question was whether Dr. Barnhill adequately informed the Muses concerning their newly limited options? Joe's mother testified that "If I'd just known that [Joe] wasn't well and was leaving because of money matters, then we could have * * * done things differently, but nobody told me that." The claim against Dr. Barnhill was settled before the trial of the case against Charter.

For his part, Dr. Barnhill testified that he did not order Joe's discharge because his insurance had run out. Whether or not that statement was credible, was he right to take the position that financial considerations did not enter in? Does it appear that, as the plaintiffs suggested, the doctor was trying to conceal the hospital's profit motive and, in so doing, failed in his duty to the family? Once again, we encounter the irony that liability might have been avoided if the hospital and the physician had been candid about the financial dimension of the relationship instead of trying to maintain the fiction that, when it comes to medical care, the patient's welfare is the only thing that counts. Would you counsel Dr. Barnhill (and the hospital) in the future to be more forthright with patients in making decisions in which insurance limits are a factor?

9. *Another Case.* Consider the elements contributing to a similar tragedy in Tabor v. Doctors Memorial Hosp., 563 So.2d 233 (La.1990). In *Tabor*, the physician on duty in the emergency room of a community hospital elected not to admit a youth to the hospital's psychiatric ward. The court discussed the evidence as follows (id. at 238):

> The record supports a finding [by the trial court, contrary to the jury's verdict,] that Dr. Dunn's conduct was below the appropriate standard of care. He knew that Andy was depressed and had taken an overdose of sleeping pills. He knew that this combination was dangerous and created a suicide risk. He knew that alcohol increased the effects of quaaludes. Dr. Dunn first decided to admit Andy, but changed his treatment when the admission was blocked by [a hospital policy requiring a $400 deposit when insurance coverage could not be immediately verified]. He was advised * * * by all three nursing personnel [(it was the doctor's first night working in this particular hospital) that the hospital's policy allowed him to waive the $400 deposit in a "true emergency"], and at least one nurse told Dr. Dunn that he felt that Andy's condition presented [such] an emergency.

Although the doctor recognized the risk associated with the combination of depression and drugs, he testified (id. at 237) that he

> did not feel that Andy presented an emergency or that Andy was suicidal. Dr. Dunn stated that he initiated discussion of in-patient treatment, not because he felt that Andy would hurt himself, but because he wanted to help the Tabor family who obviously cared about their son. When the admission was blocked, Dr. Dunn did not change his diagnosis but did change the treatment, recommending that Andy's family watch him and that Andy see his private physician.

A "medical review panel" investigating the incident stated that "Dr. Dunn's change in recommended treatment from hospitalization to outpatient care lowered the level of care from optimal to satisfactory." Id. at 236 n.3. Was it unreasonable, in your view, for the physician to change his prescription when he learned that the family might not have insurance coverage? If he was willing to impose the cost on an insurer, why was he not willing to impose the cost on the hospital (by waiving the deposit)? Or was he still concerned that the family might end up paying the cost out of pocket?

Dr. Dunn was employed, not by the hospital, but by an independent organization which supplied ER physicians under contract to area hospitals (and which was held vicariously liable for the negligence found in this case). The hospital itself escaped liability, having met its statutory duty "in no event [to deny] emergency treatment to anyone on account of inability to pay." As to the $400 requirement, the court stated as follows (id. at 239–40):

> Hospital policy also provides that: " * * * In the event that a patient does not meet the financial standards of the hospital and cannot produce the necessary deposit, the patient is to be denied admission UNLESS the patient is a true emergency admission AND the physician signs the 'Emergency Admission Confirmation' form...." Testimony established that Doctors Memorial Hospital is a privately operated, for profit facility. Dr. Baker [an expert] testified that he was familiar with emergency room procedures and policies across the nation and that they were analogous to those at Doctors Memorial Hospital. Dr. Cenac [another expert] stated that the policies at the hospital constituted "perfectly normal hospital operation." Dr. Dunn testified that he worked as a consultant at numerous emergency rooms across the nation all having rules and policies similar to those at Doctors Memorial Hospital. Further, Drs. Baker and Dunn reported that the Joint Commission on Accreditation of Hospitals outlines the policies which hospitals must follow to uphold their accreditation. Under these policies, the physician decides whether a patient is appropriate for waiver of the $400.00 admission deposit. This is a reasonable delegation of authority for determination of which patients present a true emergency. Based on the record, we do not find the hospital negligent as a result of the policies it had in operation.

On the basis of the insights gained from your consideration of the *Muse* case, be prepared to discuss the systemic issues presented in *Tabor*.

PROBLEM

Your client is a North Carolina hospital that provides obstetrical services to enrollees of CarePlus, a managed-care plan. It expects obstetricians on its medical staff to discharge CarePlus patients after no more than one full overnight stay following a birth because that is normally all CarePlus will pay for. Like other hospitals in the modern era, the hospital routinely monitors the costs incurred by the patients of individual practitioners and considers such data in deciding whether to renew a physician's staff privileges. What is the hospital's exposure to liability under the *Muse* case if a newborn should suffer a complication that might have been managed more effectively if the hospital stay had been extended another 24 hours? How would you advise the hospital to reduce its risks? How would you advise the OB staff concerning their responsibilities in treating CarePlus patients? Consider the issues in the problem in systemic terms, as suggested in the discussion of *Muse*. Can you visualize a combination of contracts among the various actors that would rationalize the situation eliminate the need for legislative intervention?

Should the apparent problem be solved by legislation? In fact, media coverage of the issue generated a startling amount of legislative attention to it in 1995 and 1996, including regulatory legislation passed by 29 state legislatures and by Congress. Newborns' and Mothers' Health Protection Act of 1996, Pub. L. No. 104–102, tit. VI (Sept. 26, 1996), codified at 42

U.S.C. § 300gg–4 (Supp. 1997) (prohibiting insurers from limiting coverage for less than 48 hours after normal vaginal delivery). See generally Declercq & Simmes, The Politics of "Drive–Through Deliveries": Putting Early Postpartum Discharge on the Legislative Agenda, 75 Milbank Q. 175 (1997) ("early discharge laws can be seen as relatively insignificant legislation," but "legislators will no doubt seek further instances where low cost (financially and politically) actions can be taken against unpopular institutions (i.e., insurers, tobacco companies) to reassure constituents symbolically that they are concerned about their interests").

SECTION B: UNCOMPENSATED CARE

NOTES ON PROVIDERS' COMMON–LAW DUTY TO RENDER CARE

1. *Physicians.* The AMA's Principles of Medical Ethics § VI (1980) provide that a physician is "free to choose whom to serve"—"except in emergencies." Legally, physicians have only rarely been held to have a duty to render emergency care in the absence of a pre-existing professional relationship with the patient. E.g., Noble v. Sartori, 799 S.W.2d 8 (Ky.1990) (liability found where physician, though not on duty in the emergency room, was "the only physician available at the hospital * * * who could have treated a heart attack victim"). For a case imposing liability on a physician who had accepted "on call" status in a hospital emergency room, see Hiser v. Randolph, 617 P.2d 774 (Ariz.App.1980). This case was discussed in a later Arizona decision holding a hospital liable for failing to stabilize an indigent patient prior to transfer:

> The duty of care owed by a physician to a patient is different from the hospital's duty. No statute requires the physician to provide services separate and apart from those which the hospital is required to provide. Thus, the duty of care owed by a physician is determined by common law principles which require reference to that which is usually done by members of the profession [citing AMA Principles of Ethics, supra]. It is distinct from the hospital duty. * * *
>
> * * *
>
> The trial court directed a verdict in favor of the vascular surgeon, Dr. Hillegas [who had been consulted by telephone]. The court of appeals found no error. We agree. Plaintiff argues, however, that the vascular surgeon breached his duty in failing to come to the hospital to attend Jessee, and is liable under the principles set forth in *Hiser v. Randolph, supra*. We disagree. In *Hiser* the hospital did not have a physician on duty in the emergency room. Several local physicians were "on call" to come to the emergency room to render emergency care. By assenting to the hospital bylaws, rules and regulations these physicians "personally became bound" to come to the emergency room when called. The doctor in *Hiser* was called to the emergency room to treat a patient in a diabetic coma and flatly refused to fulfill his obligation.

> In the case at bench, physicians were on duty and present at Boswell [Hospital] to care for emergency patients; specialists were "on call," prepared to come to the hospital and treat patients who needed specialized attention. Dr. Hillegas was one of the latter. Unlike the hospital in *Hiser*, Boswell did not request this physician to come. To the contrary, Boswell's refusal to admit Jessee would have made Dr. Hillegas' arrival at the hospital an empty gesture.

Thompson v. Sun City Community Hosp., Inc., 688 P.2d 605, 612–13 (Ariz.1984) (en banc).

2. *Abandonment.* Once a physician has undertaken to treat a patient, there is a legal duty not to "abandon" him. The physician may, however, withdraw from the relationship upon giving reasonable notice (to allow the patient to obtain another physician) or by finding a suitable replacement. See, e.g., Cox v. Jones, 470 N.W.2d 23, 26 (Iowa 1991) ("Even if a jury could determine that defendants refused to treat Cox because her bill was past due, expert evidence would be required to establish that Cox was at a critical stage of medical care when defendants allegedly withdrew medical treatment."); Surgical Consultants, P.C. v. Ball, 447 N.W.2d 676, 682 (Iowa App.1989) (doctor's office advised plaintiff that she was no longer a patient because of unpaid bill; however, valid abandonment claim also required "evidence that the physician has terminated the relationship at a critical stage of the patient's treatment, that the termination was done without reason or sufficient notice to enable the patient to procure another physician, and that the patient is injured as a result thereof"); Ricks v. Budge, 64 P.2d 208 (Utah 1937) (physician withdrawal from case at critical juncture held improper despite unpaid bills for earlier treatment). See generally Hall, A Theory of Economic Informed Consent, 31 Ga. L. Rev. 511, 527–33 (1997) (discussing "the law of economic abandonment").

Hospitals have a similar common-law duty not to abandon a patient once a contractual relationship has been established. See, e.g., Payton v. Weaver, 131 Cal.App.3d 38, 182 Cal.Rptr. 225 (1982) (hospital allowed, under circumstances, to sever relationship with trouble-making patient); LeJuene Road Hosp., Inc. v. Watson, 171 So.2d 202 (Fla.App.1965) (refusal to complete treatment when patient's parent could not provide payment held wrongful); Meiselman v. Crown Heights Hosp., 285 N.Y. 389, 34 N.E.2d 367 (1941) (discharge of patient because of inability to pay treated as abandonment). As the following materials show, hospitals are now subject to a variety of legal requirements to provide emergency care to patients requiring it. Having provided the required emergency care, what continuing duty should the hospital have to the patient? Should the principle of abandonment apply when the original relationship was entered into by the hospital under legal compulsion rather than voluntarily? Consider how, in cases like *Muse* and *Tabor*, the abandonment principle dovetails with other obligations of providers and with the normal obligation of patients to pay for services.

What may a private hospital do about a hospitalized patient who has exhausted his Medicaid benefits? Cf. Virginia Hosp. Ass'n v. Kenley, 427 F.Supp. 781 (E.D.Va.1977) (upholding under federal law a state's 14–day and 21–day limits on Medicaid coverage for hospitalization). In the cited case, it was shown that 92% of Medicaid patients were discharged within 21 days, raising the question why federal law should not be construed to require states to cover needed care for the remaining 8%. Is it legitimate for a state to legislate on the assumption that most hospitals would be willing (or feel legally compelled) to continue to provide needed services without payment? What is, in fact, the legal obligation of the first hospital if no other institution will accept the (nonpaying) patient?

3. *Hospitals.* For a review of the early case law on hospitals' duty to provide care to patients unable to pay, see Mercy Med. Center v. Winnebago County, 206 N.W.2d 198, 200–01 (Wis.1973) (dictum stating that hospital has a duty to treat, on ground that to hold otherwise "would shock the public conscience," but holding that county government had duty to reimburse hospital for such care).

The question whether a hospital has a responsibility to provide at least emergency care was sharply focused in the 1980s by the practice followed by some hospitals (mostly, but not exclusively, private ones) of turning away patients who failed the so-called "wallet biopsy"—that is, those who could not demonstrate an ability to pay for needed services. Hospitals that maintain emergency rooms may of course attract many patients requiring immediate and costly attention. The usual policy with respect to such patients is not to refuse treatment altogether but to accept the patient only for emergency treatment; once the patient is "stabilized," he is transferred to another, usually public, institution. This "patient dumping," although not inconsistent with the law on abandonment, has occasional adverse consequences and has often been decried in the media.

Lawyers interested in improving access to care for the poor have actively explored legal doctrines that may limit hospital discretion in refusing to treat patients on grounds of inability to pay. In addition to the following case on the common-law obligations of hospitals and the authorities cited therein, see Hunt v. Palm Springs Gen. Hosp., Inc., 352 So.2d 582, 584–85 (Fla.App.1977) (hospital liable for failure to admit debtor patient if his condition was "critical"); Guerrero v. Copper Queen Hosp., 112 Ariz. 104, 537 P.2d 1329 (1975) (hospital operated solely for employees of a single company held liable for not providing emergency care to illegal alien; discussed in the *Thompson* case, infra).

4. *References.* See generally Furrow, Forcing Rescue: The Landscape of Health Care Provider Obligations to Treat Patients, 3 Health Matrix 31 (1993); Rothenberg, Who Cares? The Evolution of the Legal Duty to Provide Emergency Care, 26 Houston L. Rev. 21 (1989).

Hospitals' Duties Toward Nonpaying Patients

Stanturf v. Sipes

Supreme Court of Missouri, 1969.
447 S.W.2d 558.

■ STOCKARD, COMMISSIONER.

By his fourth amended petition plaintiff sought compensatory and punitive damages in an amount exceeding $400,000. The trial court entered summary judgment for defendants and plaintiff has appealed.

* * * After visiting with his children in Trenton, Missouri, on February 26, 1962, plaintiff started to drive back to Mercer, Missouri, a distance of approximately thirty miles. The temperature was in the neighborhood of zero degrees. When plaintiff had traveled about two miles he developed a "terrible headache" and "started blacking out." He stated in his deposition that he had been taking some medicine and that this may have been the cause of his condition. He stopped his automobile, but apparently left the lights on. During the night he regained consciousness but could not start his automobile because the battery had run down. He remained in the automobile until the next morning when he obtained transportation on a school bus to Trenton, and he went to the home of his eldest daughter. She called Dr. Oliver Duffy who determined that plaintiff's feet had been frozen. He administered some treatment and told plaintiff that he would "have to have medical treatment," and that he would try to get him admitted to the Wright Memorial Hospital located at Trenton. The next morning Dr. Duffy returned and told plaintiff that he could not get him admitted to the hospital unless plaintiff paid in advance a $25 admittance fee which plaintiff did not have.

In the depositions there is some indefiniteness as to what was thereafter said and what subsequently occurred. However, plaintiff stated in his deposition that his son-in-law went to see Mr. Donald Sipes, the administrator of the hospital, and offered to pay the $25 but that admission to the hospital was still refused. * * * Mr. Sipes * * * stated that Mr. A.L. Palmer, a local minister, called on him in behalf of plaintiff, and that Mr. Palmer stated "that the church had an emergency fund from which it was possible they could take $25," but according to Mr. Sipes, it was "not in the form of an offer." However, Mr. Sipes admitted that he understood that Mr. Palmer would pay the $25 if that would "help the situation." Mr. Sipes also testified that when Dr. Duffy called him he asked if plaintiff would be eligible as a charity patient, and he stated to Mr. Sipes "that it would be an amputation." It also appears that an appeal to Mr. Sipes on behalf of plaintiff was made by some unidentified lady and by the mayor of Trenton. During cross-examination Mr. Sipes testified, in effect, that when a patient paid the $25 admission fee he was accepted without question and it would be assumed he "would be a paying patient," and he would later be billed, but that the hospital did experience some "bad debts."

Mr. Sipes further testified on deposition that he "took the request [of Dr. Duffy for the admission of plaintiff to the hospital] to the Board of Trustees" of the hospital, and they told him that plaintiff was "not eligible," but it appears that he contacted only one member of that board, Mr. W.W. Alexander, Sr., the chairman. This determination of ineligibility apparently was based on the terms of a charitable trust, referred to subsequently, and as stated by Mr. Sipes, "If the person does not live in the county [Grundy], they [sic] are not eligible for charity." It is not clear if the position of Mr. Sipes and Mr. Alexander was that the hospital was prohibited from accepting charity patients from outside of Grundy County, or if the hospital refused to do so as a matter of policy. We note, however, that plaintiff alleges that he was a resident of Grundy County. * * *

Plaintiff was not admitted to the Wright Memorial Hospital. In the meantime, apparently through the efforts of Dr. Duffy, other arrangements for medical care were being sought. Applications to the University of Iowa Hospital and to another hospital referred to in the deposition as "Broadlawns" were not successful. One or both of these hospitals apparently declined to accept plaintiff on the basis that he was not a resident of Iowa. A request for admission to the University of Missouri Hospital was unsuccessful, and Dr. Duffy reported to plaintiff that the reason was that the hospital could not "handle" him. Through the efforts of Mr. Palmer, and possibly others, on March 4, admission of plaintiff was obtained to the University of Kansas Medical Center, although there apparently was no contention that plaintiff was a resident of Kansas. After therapy treatments at the medical center proved to be unsuccessful, both of plaintiff's feet were amputated.

Wright Memorial Hospital is the only hospital in the immediate area. It is operated by the Trenton Trust Company pursuant to an "Irrevocable Trust Agreement" executed in 1932 by Dr. J.B. Wright. By that trust agreement Dr. Wright conveyed the title of property known as the Wright Hospital to the Trenton Trust Company as trustee, and it was therein provided that the property should constitute a trust "to be applied to the maintenance of a hospital and training school for nurses to be used for the gratuitous treatment of medical and surgical diseases of the sick poor, as herein provided, or for such other charitable purposes as herein set forth." In the provision pertaining to the appointment of a general staff for the management of the hospital, it was provided that "the expenses incident to the operation of the hospital shall be minimized as far as possible without impairing the efficiency and effectiveness of the said Hospital to the end that as many free patients as possible may be served and as much good as possible be accomplished by said Hospital." The General Staff was to have full and complete charge of the affairs of the hospital, but the "purpose of this Trust" was declared to be "to give free hospital, surgical, and medical care to as many poor sick of the City of Trenton, Missouri, or of Grundy County, Missouri, as possible." The Trenton Trust Company receives fees as trustee "in the neighborhood of $500 a month." At the time plaintiff sought admission to the hospital, Mr. W.W. Alexander, Sr., was chairman of the General Staff of the hospital and also chairman of the board of directors of the Trenton Trust Company.

Prior to the incident giving rise to plaintiff's claim, Wright Memorial Hospital applied for federal funds under what is known as the Hill–Burton Act. Federal funds in the amount of $70,000 were eventually paid, but it is not certain from the record that they were paid prior to February 26, 1962. Subsequently, additional federal funds were made available to the hospital under the Hill–Burton Act. The applications for these funds were processed through a state agency, and in connection with the applications the state agency certified that Wright Memorial Hospital was a voluntary non-profit institution, and that it had "given assurance that a reasonable volume of free patient care will be provided in the proposed facility." Its service area was stated to be Grundy and Mercer Counties. * * *

Defendants contend that (1) Wright Memorial Hospital is a private hospital and as such it owes no duty to admit anyone it does not want and may refuse admission without assigning a reason therefor; (2) the receipt of public funds under the Hill–Burton Act did not alter its status as a private hospital or create a duty to admit plaintiff; (3) plaintiff has no cause of action against defendants for a breach by the Wright Memorial Hospital of a contract between it and the federal government; * * *.

* * * [S]ummary judgment may not be entered for defendants if there be any theory within the scope of the pleadings, or within the broad scope of probable evidence (authorizing an amendment to the pleadings to conform to the proof) as revealed by the "depositions, and admissions on file, together with the affidavits, if any," (Civil Rule 74.04(c)) which if believed by a jury or the trier of facts would authorize a recovery by plaintiff.

For the purpose of ruling on the issue before us, we shall accept as a fact, but we do *not* rule, that Wright Memorial Hospital is a private hospital, and that subject to the circumstances hereafter noted, it owes no duty to admit anyone it does not want and may refuse admission without assigning a reason therefor, and that neither the acceptance of Hill–Burton funds nor the terms of the Trust agreement imposed a duty on the hospital to admit plaintiff under the attending circumstances, even if plaintiff was in fact a resident of Grundy County, as he alleged. However, the deposition of Mr. Sipes clearly would authorize a finding that Wright Memorial Hospital maintained an emergency hospital service, and the depositions of plaintiff and of Mr. Sipes clearly would authorize a finding that plaintiff's condition created an emergency, and that that condition was known to Mr. Sipes by reason of the communication to him from Dr. Duffy. In addition, the depositions clearly would authorize findings that it was the established policy, regularly carried out, to admit any person seeking admission upon the payment of the $25 admission fee, even if there was reason to believe that the patient could not thereafter meet the cost of hospitalization, and that the admission fee of $25 was tendered in this case. Whether the evidence at trial would authorize findings of these facts is not a matter with which we are now concerned.

Restatement of the Law of Torts 2d, § 323, announces a principle of tort liability as follows:

> "One who undertakes, gratuitously or for consideration, to render services to another which he should recognize as necessary for the protection of the other's person or things, is subject to liability to the other for physical harm resulting from his failure to exercise reasonable care to perform his undertaking, if
>
> (a) his failure to exercise such care increases the risk of such harm, or

(b) the harm is suffered because of the other's reliance upon the undertaking."

In Wilmington General Hospital v. Manlove, 54 Del. 15, 174 A.2d 135, this principle was applied in a factual situation which in some respects was remarkably similar to this case. There a "private hospital" which had received public funds maintained an emergency ward although it admittedly was under no legal obligation to the public to do so. The parents of an infant took their child to the reception room of the emergency ward where treatment was refused. The child was taken home by its parents and it died shortly thereafter. The hospital defended a suit by the parents on the ground that a private hospital owes the public no duty to accept any patient not desired by it, and it is not necessary to assign any reason for its refusal to accept a patient for hospital service. The Delaware Court recognized that this was the general rule. The court then stated:

"But the maintenance of such a ward to render first-aid to injured persons has become a well-established adjunct to the main business of a hospital. If a person, seriously hurt, applies for such aid at an emergency ward, relying on the established custom to render it, is it still the right of the hospital to turn him away without reason? In such a case, it seems to us, such a refusal might well result in worsening the condition of the injured person, because of the time lost in a useless attempt to obtain medical aid.

"Such a set of circumstances is analogous to the case of the negligent termination of gratuitous services, which creates a tort liability. Restatement, Law of Torts, 'Negligence,' § 323."

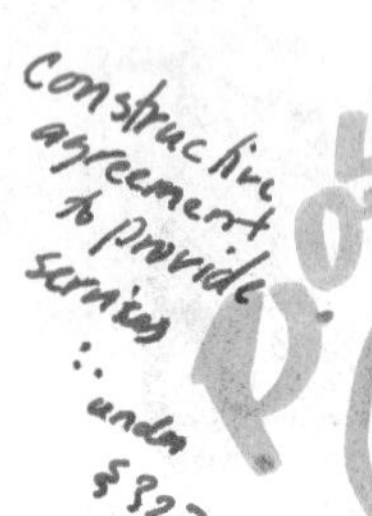

In this case the pleadings, depositions, and admissions would authorize findings that Wright Memorial Hospital was the only hospital in the immediate area, it maintained an emergency service, and through his agent and representative, Dr. Duffy, plaintiff applied for emergency treatment and was refused. In addition, it could also be found that it was the long established rule of the hospital to accept all persons for treatment upon the payment of a $25 admittance fee, that the fee was offered, but admission was refused. We consider that the practice of admission upon the payment of a $25 fee (even in those cases where it is known that $25 will not cover the entire cost) is comparable to the admission for emergency treatment on a gratuity basis. In either case, the members of the public, and particularly plaintiff's agent, Dr. Duffy, had reason to rely on the practice, and in this case it could be found that plaintiff's condition was caused to be worsened by the delay resulting from the futile efforts of Dr. Duffy, to obtain treatment from the Wright Memorial Hospital.

We are not holding by this opinion that the factual situation of this case brings it within the rule announced in Wilmington General Hospital v. Manlove, supra. What we are holding, but only this, is that whether the rule should be held to be applicable cannot be determined on the meager record before us, and that the record does not now demonstrate "by unassailable proof" that plaintiff is not entitled to recover "as a matter of law." Such issues can, and should, be determined only after a development of all the evidence and facts in a trial.

* * *

The judgment is reversed and the cause remanded.

QUESTIONS

The *Stanturf* case simply holds that the hospital must comply with its own policy of accepting emergency patients who can pay $25 up front. Why is the plaintiff entitled to enforce that policy, a promise for which no consideration was given? (It should be noted that, as shown in chapter 3(§B), the law has other ways of forcing charities to be charitable.) Did the hospital make an offer for a unilateral contract or create a promissory estoppel? Was there detrimental reliance—as there arguably was in *Manlove*, because the child in that case might have been taken to another hospital if the parents had known of the first hospital's policy? (Note the anomaly that results if a monopoly hospital can claim that the plaintiff was not induced to forgo any alternative.) Does the *Restatement* clause quoted really apply, or does the court's formulation beg the question whether the hospital actually "under[took] * * * to render services to another"? Indeed, wasn't the *Restatement* provision meant simply to cover abandonment of a patient with whom a relationship had definitely been established? What if a hospital—e.g., the Bad Samaritan—had made it clear that it wanted only paying patients?

NOTES AND QUESTIONS ON HOSPITAL OBLIGATIONS UNDER THE HILL–BURTON ACT

1. In 1946, Congress passed the Hospital Survey and Construction Act, Act of Aug. 13, 1946, ch. 958, 60 Stat. 1040 (codified as amended in scattered sections of 42 U.S.C.) Commonly known as the Hill–Burton Act, this statute was invoked unsuccessfully by the plaintiff in *Stanturf* to support his claimed entitlement to care at the defendant hospital. The act's stated purpose was "to assist the several States in the carrying out of their programs for the construction and modernization of such public or other non-profit community hospitals and other medical facilities as may be necessary, in conjunction with existing facilities, to furnish adequate hospital, clinic, or similar services to all their people." States desiring federal financial assistance were required to submit a "state plan" meeting certain requirements spelled out in regulations. The statute provided that these regulations "may * * * require that [applicants for assistance will give] assurance * * * that (1) the facility or portion thereof to be constructed or modernized will be made available to all persons residing in the territorial area of the applicant; and (2) there will be made available in the facility [etc.] a reasonable volume of services to persons unable to pay therefor * * *." The numbered assurances came to be known, respectively, as the "community service assurance" and the "reasonable volume" or "uncompensated care assurance."

From 1947 to 1972, as over $6 billion in grants, loans, and loan guarantees were dispensed, the agency's regulations essentially tracked the quoted statutory language. Hospitals receiving aid were often slow to provide charitable care, however, and courts refused to find that they had any legal duty, under the general assurances given, to do so in specific cases. E.g., Stanturf v. Sipes, 224 F.Supp. 883, 890 (W.D.Mo.1963) (rejecting claim that Hill–Burton grant created third-party beneficiary contract in favor of plaintiff). Nevertheless, litigation by public interest groups, e.g., Euresti v. Stenner, 458 F.2d 1115 (10th Cir.1972) (finding potential standing to enforce free-care obligation), eventually caused the agency (then DHEW) to issue regulations setting quantitative standards for compliance with the assurances—e.g., what would be deemed a "reasonable volume of services" to "persons unable to pay." Challenges by hospitals to these regulations generally failed. E.g., American Hosp. Ass'n v. Schweiker, 721 F.2d 170 (7th Cir.1983) (holding regulations justified by statutory language quoted above). The result was that hospitals that had received Hill–Burton funds found themselves saddled with burdensome obligations they had not anticipated in accepting federal assistance. Congress eventually revamped the program overall, clarifying the Secretary's duty to issue the regulations in question. 42 U.S.C. § 300q et seq. (1994).

2. A question naturally arose whether the regulations created an entitlement for any individual or only an obligation on the part of hospitals to comply with the regulations. This issue, which might also arise in a suit for damages for denial of care, arose in a case involving the constitutional right of an individual to procedural due process (notice, hearing, etc.) before a denial of eligibility for free care. Newsom v. Vanderbilt Univ., 653 F.2d 1100 (6th Cir.1981) (holding that "neither the statute nor the regulations provided any certain right to free services to any particular individual"). Do you favor a health care system based on individual rights? Or do you agree with the *Newsom* court that the Hill–Burton objective should be achieved by government enforcement to ensure that hospitals receiving federal subsidies for capital construction apply sums roughly equivalent to the interest and depreciation allowances on that free capital to the meeting of societal obligations?

For discussions generally sympathetic to the course that events surrounding the Hill–Burton program took, see Rosenblatt, Health Care Reform and Administrative Law: A Structural Approach, 88 Yale L.J. 243 (1978); Rose, Federal Regulation of Services to the Poor Under the Hill–Burton Act: Realities and Pitfalls, 70 Nw.U.L.Rev. 168 (1975).

3. *Blumstein's Critique.* The effort of public interest lawyers in the 1970s to exploit the language of the original Hill–Burton Act was obviously successful in getting government to adopt regulatory free-care requirements. The strategy of putting litigation pressure on hospitals and political pressure on the government worked effectively to overcome bureaucratic inertia. It is possible, however, that that inertia accurately reflected Congress's original intent. In an appraisal of the dynamics of this law reform effort, Blumstein has suggested, largely in accord with the *Newsom* court's reading, that the language of the original act was merely a symbolic statement of legislative aspiration. Such precatory language, he observes, is frequently found in modern health care legislation but may not be accompanied by the regulatory or other enforcement tools that are needed to realize the stated goal. Blumstein, Court Action, Agency Reaction: The Hill–Burton Act as a Case Study, 69 Iowa L.Rev. 1227, 1233–35 (1984). Blumstein thus disputes (id. at 1255–56) the court's statement in the *AHA* case, supra at 177, that "one may infer from the provision's mere presence in the statute that the free care obligation was intended to have some effect." It is possible, as Blumstein observes, to view the provision for assurances in the Hill–Burton Act as "a sop to access egalitarians" that was easy to enact precisely because it lacked teeth. Blumstein suggests that the 25–year agency neglect to enforce the free-care obligation reflected, if not the only, at least a reasonable interpretation of the statute. (Under the widely cited doctrine of Chevron U.S.A. v. NRDC, 467 U.S. 837 (1984), courts are expected to accept an agency's interpretation of a statute it administers, if that interpretation is not unreasonable.)

Blumstein notes that the ability of the astute lawyers representing indigents to obtain early recognition of their clients' standing to sue grantee hospitals for withholding free care had the effect of forcing DHEW to put the issue back on its political agenda. Once there, he suggests, the symbolic importance of the issue (in the era just following the enactment of Medicaid and in the midst of the campaign for a "right to health care" and national health insurance)—coupled with the fact that the hospitals rather than the government would bear the cost of the gesture being sought—practically ensured a favorable political response. Blumstein also observes that DHEW and later the Department of Health and Human Services (DHHS) failed to contest vigorously or effectively the plaintiffs' claims in the courts by advancing a coherent view of the original statute, suggesting that the bureaucracy shared or was ultimately converted to the plaintiffs' policy views. Blumstein's discussion (id. at 1240–43) of Corum v. Beth Israel Medical Center, 373 F.Supp. 550 (S.D.N.Y.1974), is particularly interesting in this regard; by virtually conceding a seemingly minor point of interpretation (whether DHEW had to require a hospital to identify a patient as eligible for free care prior to treatment), the government essentially confirmed the plaintiffs' view of the Hill–Burton program as a redistributive scheme creating affirmative patient rights—a view that was substantially at odds with the agency's earlier practice and arguably with Congress's original intent.

Blumstein also observes how regulations issued by DHHS in 1979 were a direct and immediate response to the district court decision in *Newsom* and that that decision was subsequently reversed on appeal in an opinion largely reinstating the agency's original understanding of the statute. He duly notes the irony in the deference given to agency discretion by the court in *AHA v. Schweiker* despite the facts that (1) that "discretion was exercised only in response to repeated scoldings by federal district judges"

(69 Iowa L.Rev. at 1259) and (2) the agency interpretation of the statute was not its own but that of a particular (mistaken) district court. Finally, Blumstein concludes (id. at 1255) that "HEW and HHS discretion was more narrowly circumscribed by the courts when the agency was perceived as 'pro-hospital' and insufficiently attentive to the interests of indigent patients than when it aggressively promoted Hill–Burton as a program of medical entitlements to indigent patients."

4. Although the history of the Hill–Burton free-care obligation is interesting and instructive, the practical importance of this obligation is greatly reduced by the 20-year limit on its duration imposed by the regulations. 42 C.F.R. § 124.501(b)(i) (1996). Because the Hill–Burton program flourished in the 1950s and 1960s and stopped granting subsidies for hospital construction in 1974, hospitals have generally discharged their free-care obligations or will do so in the near future.

5. *The "Community-Service" Obligation.* Seemingly more important than the free-care obligation of hospitals receiving Hill–Burton aid is the so-called and apparently perpetual "community-service" obligation provided for in 42 U.S.C. § 300s–1(b)(1)(k) (1994). The current regulations embodying this obligation require that a grantee facility "shall make the services provided in the facility * * * available to all persons residing * * * in the facility's service area without discrimination on the ground of race, color, national origin, creed, or any other ground unrelated to an individual's need for the service or the availability of the needed service in the facility." 42 C.F.R. § 124.603(a)(1) (1996). This provision creates hospital obligations to all patients, not just those eligible for free care under the free-care requirement. As the obligation is interpreted in DHHS regulations (id. at §§ 124.603(a)-(d)), hospitals must provide emergency services regardless of a patient's ability to pay and may not require pre-admission deposits that result in the denial of admission to certain persons, may not discriminate against patients covered by Medicare or Medicaid, and may not deny admission to a patient because he or she lacks a personal physician on the hospital's medical staff.

Although the "community-service" obligation imposed upon Hill–Burton hospitals seems to compel them to provide services to historically underserved persons, it has apparently not been very successful in fulfilling this mission. See generally Dowell, Hill–Burton: The Unfulfilled Promise, 15 J. Health Pol., Pol'y & L. 153 (1987); Conard, Granny Dumping: The Hospital's Duty of Care to Patients Who Have Nowhere to Go, 10 Yale L. & Pol'y Rev. 463, 470 (1992) ("so many faults remain that [Hill–Burton] cannot be viewed as a successful health-care access program"). The act contains no sanctions for noncompliance with its requirements, and DHHS has not enforced the statute with any vigor. Moreover, individuals have not been allowed to bring actions to compel it to effect compliance. E.g., Gillis v. U.S. Dep't of Health and Human Servs., 759 F.2d 565 (6th Cir.1985). Finally, the act has not been construed to require hospitals to spend money to ensure that its goals are met. Indeed, one court of appeals noted, "[The act] imposes upon Hill–Burton hospitals a duty not to discriminate, not a financial obligation." Metropolitan Med. Ctr. v. Harris, 693 F.2d 775, 788 (8th Cir.1982). Notably, in this connection, DHHS administrative decisions on pre-admission deposits have not greatly limited the ability of hospitals to insist upon prior assurance of payment. See Dowell, supra, at 166.

6. *Hill–Burton Costs Under Medicare.* Should a hospital incurring free-care costs under a Hill–Burton obligation have been allowed to treat those costs as reimbursable indirect costs (i.e., overhead) for Medicare cost-reimbursement purposes? Regulations, eventually reinforced by definitive legislation in 1982, 42 U.S.C. § 1395x(v)(1)(M) (Supp. 1997), excluded such costs. Hospitals challenged these regulations, arguing in effect that the obligation they incurred should be viewed as a cost of capital, equivalent to interest on borrowed funds. Most of the many courts that addressed this question rejected the hospitals' arguments and upheld the Secretary. E.g., Catholic Med. Center v. New Hampshire–Vermont Hospitalization Serv., Inc., 707 F.2d 7 (1st Cir.1983) (concluding that "it strains the bounds of logical reasoning to believe that Congress would require hospitals to provide a certain amount of free health care to indigents in reciprocation for receiving federal funds from one program and then allow reimbursement with federal funds from another program").

NOTES ON STATE STATUTES MANDATING INDIGENT CARE

1. *State and Local Governments.* Some state statutes expressly mandate that local governments provide indigent medical care. California, for example, provides,

> Every county * * * shall relieve and support all incompetent, poor, indigent persons, and those incapacitated by age, disease, or accident, lawfully resident therein, when such persons are not supported and relieved by their relatives or friends, or by their own means, or by state hospitals or state or private institutions.

Cal. Welf. & Inst. Code § 17000 (1991). This provision is supplemented by section 17001, which requires counties to set "standards of aid and care." A public interest group obtained a degree of judicial review of a county's standards in Poverty Resistance Center v. Hart, 213 Cal.App.3d 295 (1989).

Other states merely authorize state or local governments to provide care for the indigent. Arizona's statute, for example, states, "The board of [county] supervisors, under such limitations and restrictions as are prescribed by law, may [p]rovide for the care and maintenance of the indigent sick of the county." Ariz. Rev. Stat. Ann. § 11–251(5) (1990). Despite this permissive language, the Arizona Supreme Court has held that the provision of indigent medical care is mandatory. Arnold v. Arizona Dep't of Health Services, 775 P.2d 521 (Ariz.1989) (holding county has a duty to provide medical care, including mental health services, to indigents). But see Zuravsky v. Asta, 569 P.2d 1371 (Ariz.App.1977) (holding county has discretion not to pay expenses incident to elective abortions).

Still other states, although making no express reference to medical care, require local governments to provide "relief," "support," or "maintenance" for the poor. Such statutes have often been construed to include medical care, or at least those services necessary for survival. See generally Dowell, State and Local Government Legal Responsibilities To Provide Medical Care For The Poor, 3 J. Law & Health 1 (1988–89).

2. *Private Hospitals.* A number of states have enacted statutes creating an explicit duty on the part of private hospitals to provide essential care. E.g., Cal. Health & Safety Code § 1317 (West 1990); Fla. Stat. § 395.1041 (1993); S.C. Code Ann. § 44–7–260(E) (Supp. 1996). See generally Dowell, Indigent Access to Emergency Room Services, 18 Clearinghouse Rev. 483 (1984). An Arizona decision has discussed the application of such a statute as follows:

> In this state, the duty which a hospital owes a patient in need of emergency care is determined by the statutes and regulations interpreted by this court in Guerrero v. Copper Queen Hospital, 112 Ariz. 104, 537 P.2d 1329 (1975). Construing the statutory and regulatory scheme governing health care and the licensing of hospitals as of 1972, we held that it was the "public policy of this state" that a general "hospital may not deny emergency care to any patient without cause."
>
> In *Guerrero,* we referred primarily to former A.R.S. § 36–405(A) in construing the statutes governing the licensing of hospitals. We then referred to specific regulations promulgated under the authority of that statute. Subsequently, as a part of a general rewriting of title 36 in 1973, the Director of Health Services was required to adopt regulations for the licensure of health care facilities.
>
> As guidelines for minimum requirements, the director was mandated to use the standards of the Joint Commission for Accreditation of Hospitals (JCAH). * * * The emergency services section of the JCAH states that:
>
>> no patient should arbitrarily be transferred if the hospital where he was initially seen has means for adequate care of his problem.
>
> JCAH, Accreditation Manual for Hospitals 69 (1976). The "Patient's Rights" section of the JCAH manual makes it clear that the financial resources of a patient are among the "arbitrary" considerations within the contemplation of the above language:
>
>> no person should be denied impartial access to treatment or accommodations that are available and *medically indicated,* on the basis of such considerations as . . . the nature of the source of payment for his care.
>
> Id. at 23 (emphasis supplied).
>
> Principles governing the functioning of hospitals were not left in the abstract. Specific regulations were adopted and in 1976, A.C.R.R. R9–10–248, concerning "emergency departments," provided that "general hospitals shall provide facilities for emergency care." In addition, such hospitals were required "to have on call one or more physicians licensed to practice medicine and surgery in Arizona or resident physician or intern physician." Our holding in *Guerrero* is reinforced by A.R.S. § 41–1837(A). This

statute is of particular relevance in understanding the entire legislative scheme bearing on the issue of emergency care. It reads as follows:

> A. When an indigent emergency medical patient is received by an emergency receiving facility from a [licensed] ambulance ..., the county shall be liable pursuant to § 11–297.01, to the ambulance service for the cost of transporting the patient and to the facility for the reasonable costs of all medical services rendered to such indigent by the facility until such patient is transferred by the county to the county hospital, or some other facility designated by the county.

> The quoted statute was in effect in 1975 when we decided *Guerrero* and is still in effect. It provides the answer to a serious problem. Charging hospitals with a legal duty to render emergency care to indigent patients does not ignore the distinctions between private and public hospitals. Imposition of a duty to render emergency care to indigents simply charges private hospitals with the same duty as public hospitals under a statutory plan which permits reimbursement from public funds for the emergency care charges incurred at the private hospital.

> This legislative and regulatory history provides no reason to retreat from or modify *Guerrero*. We therefore affirm its holding that, as a matter of public policy, licensed hospitals in this state are required to accept and render emergency care to all patients who present themselves in need of such care. The patient may not be transferred until all medically indicated emergency care has been completed. This standard of care has, in effect, been set by statute and regulation embodying a public policy which requires private hospitals to provide emergency care that is "medically indicated" without consideration of the economic circumstances of the patient in need of such care. Thus, the word "cause" used in the quoted portion of *Guerrero* refers to something other than economic considerations. Interpreting the standard of care in accordance with the public policy defined in *Guerrero,* we hold that reasonable "cause" for transfer before completion of emergency care refers to medical considerations relevant to the welfare of the patient and not economic considerations relevant to the welfare of the hospital. A transfer based on the forbidden criterion of economic considerations may be for the convenience of the hospital but it is hardly "medically indicated." Given the duty imposed in Arizona—that a general hospital may not deny emergency care to any person without valid cause—there are three possible defenses a hospital may raise in an appropriate fact situation: (1) that the hospital is not obligated (or capable) under its state license to provide the necessary emergency care, (2) there is a valid medical cause to refuse emergency care, (3) there is no true emergency requiring care and thus no emergency care which is medically indicated.

Thompson v. Sun City Community Hosp., Inc., 688 P.2d 605, 609–11 (Ariz.1984) (en banc).

Since the passage in 1986 of the federal legislation reproduced immediately below, state statutes declaring the duties of private hospitals are of diminished practical importance. The New York statute, however, states, "No general hospital shall transfer any patient to another hospital or health care facility on the grounds that the patient is unable to pay or guarantee payment for services rendered." N.Y. Pub. Health Law § 2805–b(1) (McKinney 1993). This provision not only carries criminal sanctions but seemingly goes well beyond the federal statute in prohibiting the financially-motivated transfer of "any" patient, not just a patient with an emergency condition.

3. *Nursing Homes.* Most states maintain regulatory controls over the number of nursing home beds as a way of controlling Medicaid costs for nursing-home care. (See chapter 5(§D).) The resulting shortage, together with the homes' preference for more profitable private-pay patients, has created a problem of "discrimination" against Medicaid patients in filling vacancies. Some states have sought to prohibit discriminatory practices. See, e.g., New Jersey Ass'n of Health Care Facilities v. Finley, 83 N.J. 67, 415 A.2d 1147 (1980) (upholding regulation requiring homes to accept a reasonable number of indigent persons, including Medicaid eligibles, as a condition of licensure but allowing hearing on whether burden prevented reasonable overall return on investment); N.J.Stat.Ann. § 10:5–12.2 (West 1993) (later statute prohibiting discrimination by homes with low Medicaid occupancy). See generally Edelman, Discrimination by Nursing Homes Against Medicaid Recipients: Improving Access to Institutional Long-term Care for Poor People, 20 Clearinghouse Rev. 339 (1986).

On 1987 federal legislation barring nursing homes from requiring guarantors as a condition of admission, see Carlson, Illegal Guarantees in Nursing Homes: A Nursing Facility Cannot Force a Resident's Family and Friends to Become Financially Responsible for Nursing Facility Expenses, 30 Clearinghouse Rev. 33 (1996).

Federal Legislation Mandating Emergency Care

Emergency Medical Treatment and Active Labor Act of 1986, as Amended

42 U.S.C.A. § 1395dd (1995)

§ 1395dd. Examination and treatment for emergency medical conditions and women in labor

(a) Medical screening requirement

In the case of a hospital that has a hospital emergency department, if any individual (whether or not eligible for [Medicare]) comes to the emergency department and a request is made on the individual's behalf for examination or treatment for a medical condition, the hospital must provide for an appropriate medical screening examination within the capability of the hospital's emergency department, including ancillary services routinely available to the emergency department, to determine whether or not an emergency medical condition (within the meaning of subsection (e)(1)) exists.

(b) Necessary stabilizing treatment for emergency medical conditions and labor

(1) In general

If any individual * * * comes to a hospital and the hospital determines that the individual has an emergency medical condition, the hospital must provide either—

(A) within the staff and facilities available at the hospital, for such further medical examination and such treatment as may be required to stabilize the medical condition, or

(B) for transfer of the individual to another medical facility in accordance with subsection (c)[, which permits transfers of an unstable patient if appropriate informed consent is obtained, if a physician certifies in detail that the medical benefits of transfer "outweigh the increased risks * * * from effecting the transfer," and if certain other requirements are met].

[Subsections (2) and (3) absolve the hospital of the foregoing obligation if the individual or his representative, after being informed of the "risks and benefits * * * of such examination and treatment [or] such transfer," refuses to consent thereto. The hospital must "take all reasonable steps to secure the individual's (or person's) written informed consent" to forgo further care.]

* * *

(d) Enforcement

(1) Civil monetary penalties

(A) A participating hospital that negligently violates a requirement of this section is subject to a civil money penalty of not more than $50,000 (or not more than $25,000 in the case of a hospital with less than 100 beds) for each such violation. * * *

(B) Subject to subparagraph (C), any physician who is responsible for the examination, treatment, or transfer of an individual in a participating hospital, including a physician on-call for the care of such an individual, and who negligently violates a requirement of this section, including a physician who—

(i) signs a certification under subsection (c)(1)(A) that the medical benefits reasonably to be expected from a transfer to another facility outweigh the risks associated with the transfer, if the physician knew or should have known that the benefits did not outweigh the risks, or

(ii) misrepresents an individual's condition or other information, including a hospital's obligations under this section,

is subject to a civil money penalty of not more than $50,000 for each such violation and, if the violation is gross and flagrant or is repeated, to exclusion from participation in this title and State health care programs.

* * *

[Paragraph (C) frees the physician from liability if he determines that an individual needs the services of an on-call physician, notifies that person, and the on-call physician fails or refuses to appear.]

(2) Civil enforcement

(A) Personal harm

Any individual who suffers personal harm as a direct result of a participating hospital's violation of a requirement of this section may, in a civil action against the participating hospital, obtain those damages available for personal injury under the law of the State in which the hospital is located, and such equitable relief as is appropriate.

(B) Financial loss to other medical facility

Any medical facility that suffers a financial loss as a direct result of a participating hospital's violation of a requirement of this section may, in a civil action against the participating hospital, obtain those damages available for financial loss, under the law of the State in which the hospital is located, and such equitable relief as is appropriate.

(C) [Two-year statute of] **Limitations on actions**

* * *

(e) Definitions

[Defined terms include "emergency medical condition" (quoted in the *Baber* case, reproduced below), "participating hospital" (i.e., any hospital participating in the Medicare program), "stabilized," "transfer," and "hospital." " 'To stabilize' means * * * to provide such medical treatment of the condition as may be necessary to assure, within reasonable medical probability, that no material deterioration of the condition is likely to result from or occur during the transfer * * *."]

(f) Preemption

The provisions of this section do not preempt any State or local law requirement, except to the extent that the requirement directly conflicts with a requirement of this section.

(g) Nondiscrimination

A participating hospital that has specialized capabilities or facilities (such as burn units, shock-trauma units, neonatal intensive care units, or (with respect to rural areas) regional referral centers as identified by the Secretary in regulation) shall not refuse to accept an appropriate transfer of an individual who requires such specialized capabilities or facilities if the hospital has the capacity to treat the individual.

(h) No delay in examination or treatment

A participating hospital may not delay provision of an appropriate medical screening examination required under subsection (a) or further medical examination and treatment required under subsection (b) in order to inquire about the individual's method of payment or insurance status.

(i) Whistleblower protections

A participating hospital may not penalize or take adverse action against a qualified medical person described in subsection (c)(1)(A)(iii) or a physician because the person or physician refuses to authorize the transfer of an individual with an emergency medical condition that has not been stabilized or against any hospital employee because the employee reports a violation of a requirement of this section.

NOTES AND QUESTIONS ON THE SCOPE OF HOSPITALS' OBLIGATIONS

1. Note the extent to which hospitals' obligations are limited to the provision of emergency care. A large fraction (estimated between 40% and 55%) of visits to hospital emergency departments (EDs) are for nonurgent conditions. The excess cost of treating these patients in EDs rather than in conventional settings was estimated at $5–7 billion in 1993. Baker & Baker, Excess Costs of Emergency Department Visits for Nonurgent Care, Health Affs., Winter 1994, p. 162. (It is unclear how much of these costs, if any, are attributable to the need to comply with EMTALA.) As to patients with real traumatic injuries, prompt treatment (within the so-called "golden" first hour) is crucial in effecting a good outcome, yet EDs are often overcrowded and overworked. Although many hospitals opened highly sophisticated "Level I trauma centers" in the 1980s, many of these were soon scaled back to provide only more conventional ED service—principally as a result of excessive cost burdens prompted by influxes of uninsured victims of violence and drug abuse.

2. What should be a hospital's legal duty to a patient once the legally mandated treatment is completed? In addition to reviewing the earlier note on abandonment, see Harper v. Baptist Medical Center–Princeton, 341 So.2d 133 (Ala.1976) (hospital treating emergency held not to have accepted patient for further treatment). In this case, the hospital was held to have met its responsibilities to the patient by arranging for his transfer to a charitable institution. But what if the first hospital is somewhat better equipped to treat the patient's condition? What is the legal obligation of the first hospital if no other institution will accept the (nonpaying) patient? In answering these questions, what effect should be given to the accreditation standards quoted in the excerpt from the *Thompson* case, supra (and essentially unchanged since)?

One court of appeals has stated that, although treatment "does not always stop when a patient is wheeled from the Emergency Room into the main hospital," EMTALA was passed to require hospitals to provide emergency treatment only; it is "not a measure to force hospitals to provide long-term care for uninsured patients." Thornton v. Southwest Detroit Hosp., 895 F.2d 1131, 1135 (6th Cir.1990). See also Green v. Touro Infirmary, 992 F.2d 537, 539 (5th Cir.1993) ("EMTALA requires only that a hospital stabilize an individual; it does not require a hospital to cure the condition").

3. What is the responsibility of a public or charitable institution to accept the transfer of a patient from another hospital? See Hospital Development and Service Corp. v. North Broward Hosp. Dist., 619 F.Supp. 535, 538–41 (S.D.Fla.1985) (rejecting claim that a public hospital was constitutionally obligated to accept indigent patients transferred for financial reasons from private hospitals and holding that the hospital's "transfer policy is rational as a matter of fiscal responsibility, medical practice, and medical ethics"); Dade County v. American Hosp., 502 So.2d 1230 (Fla.1987) (finding no statutory duty on part of county hospitals in Florida either to accept post-emergency transfers or to compensate private hospitals for post-emergency care). In chapter 3(§B), you will have a chance to consider whether federal or state tax exemptions for private hospitals entail any general or specific responsibilities to accept nonpaying patients.

4. In the absence of a legal duty to render uncompensated care, what other factors might cause a hospital to render it?

Baber v. Hospital Corporation of America

United States Court of Appeals, Fourth Circuit, 1992.
977 F.2d 872.

■ WILLIAMS, CIRCUIT JUDGE:

* * *

Mr. Baber's complaint charged the various defendants with violating EMTALA in several ways. Specifically, Mr. Baber contends that Dr. Kline, RGH [Raleigh General Hospital], and its parent corporation violated EMTALA by: (a) failing to provide his sister with an "appropriate medical screening examination;" (b) failing to stabilize his sister's "emergency medical condition;" and (c) transferring his sister to BARH [another hospital] without first providing stabilizing treatment. * * *

II.

* * * Brenda Baber, accompanied by her brother, Barry, sought treatment at RGH's emergency department at 10:40 p.m. on August 5, 1987. When she entered the hospital, Ms. Baber was nauseated, agitated, and thought she might be pregnant. She was also tremulous and did not appear to have orderly thought patterns. She had stopped taking her anti-psychosis medications * * * and had been drinking heavily. Dr. Kline, the attending physician, described her behavior and condition [as unrestrained. Around midnight, while wandering in the ED, she convulsed and fell, lacerating her scalp. She regained consciousness quickly, and Dr. Kline

examined her and sutured the wound. In his examination, he found no signs that might indicate a serious injury, other than some anxiety, disorientation, restlessness, and some speech problems, all of which he attributed to her pre-existing psychiatric problems (psychosis with paranoia) and alcohol withdrawal. He also observed her for approximately an hour from across the room, looking for focal neurological signs and finding her stable, easily arousable, and not struggling at random.]

Because Dr. Kline did not conclude Ms. Baber had a serious head injury, he believed that she could be transferred safely to BARH where [a] CT report revealed a fractured skull and a right subdural hematoma. BARH personnel immediately transferred Ms. Baber back to RGH because * * * BARH did not have the facility or staff to treat serious neurological problems. When RGH received Ms. Baber for treatment around 7 a.m., she was comatose. She died later that day, apparently as a result of an intracerebrovascular rupture.

III.

The district court granted summary judgment for Dr. Kline * * * because it found that EMTALA does not give patients a private cause of action against their doctors. * * *

Although the statute clearly allows a patient to bring a civil suit for damages for an EMTALA violation against a participating hospital, no section permits an individual to bring a similar action against a treating physician. Instead, the enforcement sections of EMTALA allow an action against a physician only by the Department of Health and Human Services to bar his participation in Medicare programs and/or to seek administrative sanctions in the form of civil monetary penalties. Thus, nothing in the language of the statute permits a private individual to recover personal injury damages from a physician for an EMTALA violation.

* * *

IV.

Mr. Baber also alleges that RGH, acting through its agent, Dr. Kline, violated several provisions of EMTALA. * * *

Mr. Baber first claims that RGH failed to provide his sister with an "appropriate medical screening". He makes two arguments. First, he contends that a medical screening is only "appropriate" if it satisfies a national standard of care. In other words, Mr. Baber urges that we construe EMTALA as a national medical malpractice statute, albeit limited to whether the medical screening was appropriate to identify an emergency medical condition. We conclude instead that EMTALA only requires hospitals to apply their standard screening procedure for identification of an emergency medical condition uniformly to all patients and that Mr. Baber has failed to proffer sufficient evidence showing that RGH did not do so. Second, Mr. Baber contends that EMTALA requires hospitals to provide some medical screening. We agree, but conclude that he has failed to show no screening was provided to his sister.

The requirement that hospitals provide "an appropriate medical screening" is found in § 1395dd(a) * * *. While this section requires a hospital's emergency department to provide an "appropriate medical screening examination," it does not define that term other than to state its purpose is to identify an "emergency medical condition." See Cleland v. Bronson Health Care Group, 917 F.2d 266, 271 (6th Cir.1990) (referring to "appropriate" as "one of the most wonderful weasel words in the dictionary[, and a great aid to the resolution of disputed issues in drafting legislation]").

EMTALA specifically defines "an emergency medical condition" as:

> a medical condition manifesting itself by acute symptoms of sufficient severity (including severe pain) such that the absence of immediate medical attention could reasonably be expected to result in—(i) placing the health of the individual . . . in serious jeopardy; (ii) serious impairment to bodily functions; or (iii) serious dysfunction of any bodily organ or part.

42 U.S.C.A. § 1395dd(e)(1)(A). Thus, the goal of "an appropriate medical screening examination" is to determine whether a patient with acute or severe symptoms has a life threatening or serious medical condition. The plain language of the statute requires a hospital to develop a screening procedure[6] designed to identify such critical conditions that exist in symptomatic patients and to apply that screening procedure uniformly to all patients with similar complaints.

We recognize that application of the procedure necessarily requires the exercise of medical training and judgment. Hospital personnel must assess a patient's signs and symptoms and use their informed judgment to determine whether a critical condition exists. Thus, while EMTALA requires a hospital emergency department to apply its standard screening examination uniformly, it does not guarantee that the emergency personnel will correctly diagnose a patient's condition as a result of this screening.[7]

6. While a hospital emergency room may develop one general procedure for screening all patients, it may also tailor its screening procedure to the patient's complaints or exhibited symptoms. For example, it may have one screening procedure for patients suffering a heart attack and another for women in labor. Under our interpretation of EMTALA, such varying screening procedures would not pose liability under EMTALA as long as all patients complaining of the same problem or exhibiting the same symptoms receive identical screening procedures. We also recognize that the hospital's screening procedure is not limited to personal observation and assessment but may include available ancillary services through departments such as radiology and laboratory.

7. Some commentators have criticized defining "appropriate" in terms of the hospital's medical screening standard because hospitals could theoretically avoid liability by providing very cursory and substandard screenings to all patients, which might enable the doctor to ignore an emergency medical condition. See, e.g., Karen I. Treiger, Note, Preventing Patient Dumping: Sharpening the COBRA's Fangs, 61 N.Y.U.L.Rev. 1186 (1986). Even though we do not believe it is likely that a hospital would endanger all of its patients by establishing such a cursory standard, theoretically it is possible. Our holding, however, does not foreclose the possibility that a future court faced with such a situation may decide that the hospital's standard was so low that it amounted to no "appropriate medical screening." We do not

The statutory language clearly indicates that EMTALA does not impose on hospitals a national standard of care in screening patients. The screening requirement only requires a hospital to provide a screening examination that is "appropriate" and "within the capability of the hospital's emergency department," including "routinely available" ancillary services. 42 U.S.C.A. § 1395dd(a). This section establishes a standard which will of necessity be individualized for each hospital, since hospital emergency departments have varying capabilities. Had Congress intended to require hospitals to provide a screening examination which comported with generally accepted medical standards, it could have clearly specified a national standard. Nor do we believe Congress intended to create a negligence standard based on each hospital's capability. EMTALA is no substitute for state law medical malpractice actions. See 42 U.S.C.A. § 1395dd(f) (EMTALA does not preempt state law, except to the extent state law directly conflicts with this statute).

Congress enacted EMTALA to address its concern with preventing patient dumping. The avowed purpose of EMTALA was not to guarantee that all patients are properly diagnosed, or even to ensure that they receive adequate care, but instead to provide an "adequate first response to a medical crisis" for all patients and "send a clear signal to the hospital community . . . that all Americans, regardless of wealth or status, should know that a hospital will provide what services it can when they are truly in physical distress." 131 Cong.Rec. S13904 (Oct. 23, 1985) (statement of Sen. Durenberger).

We note that other jurisdictions faced with this issue have reached the same conclusion and have rejected a medical malpractice standard in favor of an individualized standard. In Gatewood v. Washington Healthcare Corp., 933 F.2d 1037, 1041 (D.C.Cir.1991), the D.C. Circuit held that a hospital provides an appropriate medical screening if it "conforms in its treatment of a particular patient to its standard screening procedures." The court in *Gatewood* also concluded a hospital would be liable for any deviation from its standard screening, regardless of its motivation.

The Sixth Circuit has also held that an appropriate medical screening means "a screening that the hospital would have offered to any paying patient" or at least "not known by the provider to be insufficient or below their own standards." Cleland, 917 F.2d at 268, 271.[8]

* * *

decide that question in this case because Ms. Baber's screening was not so substandard as to amount to no screening at all.

8. The one distinction between the tests used by the Sixth and D.C. Circuits is that the D.C. Circuit would impose liability for any disparate treatment, regardless of the hospital's motive, Gatewood, 933 F.2d at 1041, while the Sixth Circuit will only impose liability if the hospital had a bad motive in providing the disparate treatment, Cleland, 917 F.2d at 272. For the Sixth Circuit, such bad motives for the disparate treatment might include the patient's indigence, drunkenness, political affiliations, or medical condition, such as AIDS. In this case, we are not required to decide which view is correct since Mr. Baber did not make any allegation of disparate treatment.

Dr. Kline testified that he performed a medical screening on Ms. Baber in accordance with standard procedures for examining patients with head injuries. He explained that generally, a patient is not scheduled for advanced tests such as a CT scan or x-rays unless the patient's signs and symptoms so warrant. While Ms. Baber did exhibit some of the signs and symptoms of patients who have severe head injuries, in Dr. Kline's medical judgment these signs were the result of her pre-existing psychiatric condition, not the result of her fall. * * * Although Dr. Kline's assessment and judgment may have been erroneous and not within acceptable standards of medical care in West Virginia, he did perform a screening examination that was not so substandard as to amount to no examination. No testimony indicated that his procedure deviated from that which RGH would have provided to any other patient in Ms. Baber's condition.

* * *

Mr. Baber also asserts that RGH inappropriately transferred his sister to BARH. * * * EMTALA's transfer requirements do not apply unless the hospital actually determines that the patient suffers from an emergency medical condition. Cleland, 917 F.2d at 271. Accordingly, to recover for violations of EMTALA's transfer provisions, the plaintiff must present evidence that (1) the patient had an emergency medical condition; (2) the hospital actually knew of that condition; (3) the patient was not stabilized before being transferred; and (4) prior to transfer of an unstable patient, the transferring hospital did not obtain the proper consent or follow the appropriate certification and transfer procedures.

* * *

Although Ms. Baber's tragic death indicates that her condition at some point in time was an emergency medical condition as defined in the statute, the record is not clear when. Analysis by hindsight is not sufficient to impose liability under EMTALA. Mr. Baber failed to demonstrate that RGH knew Ms. Baber had an emergency medical condition at the time she was transferred to BARH.

* * * Section 1395dd(b)(1) states the stabilization requirement exists if "any individual ... comes to a hospital and the hospital determines that the individual has an emergency medical condition." Thus, the plain language of the statute dictates a standard requiring actual knowledge of the emergency medical condition by the hospital staff.* * *

AFFIRMED

NOTES AND QUESTIONS ON EMTALA

1. *Origins of EMTALA.* The original version of EMTALA was adopted by Congress in 1986, not as a separate bill, but as part of an immense budget reconciliation act ("COBRA") affecting almost every major area of government spending. Was it in fact a budget measure? What do you think of the legislative process that produced this legislation? No public hearings were held prior to the initial enactment.

To be sure, one legislative hearing on EMTALA was held in 1988. House Comm. on Gov't Operations, Equal Access to Health Care: Patient Dumping, H.R. Rep. No. 531, 100th Cong., 2d Sess. (1988). But one critic alleges that that hearing, and indeed the whole campaign for anti-dumping legislation, relied too much upon untruthful anecdotes rather than upon reliable information about actual hospital practices in transferring patients to public or community hospitals. Hyman, Patient Dumping and EMTALA: Past Imperfect/Future Shock, 8 Health Matrix 29 (1998). Hyman observes, among other things, that the story most widely told by advocates of anti-dumping legislation was largely disproved in a subsequent hearing in Tennessee, that other horror stories also fall apart under scrutiny, and that empirical studies purporting to document dumping fall short of showing that patients were actually worse off because of transfers (or obtained improved care at transferee hospitals) or that private hospitals were systematically neglecting their legal and moral responsibilities.

Note that the EMTALA requirements apply to hospitals that elect to participate in the Medicare program. Does a hospital have a choice, realistically, about whether to participate in Medicare (which finances care for virtually the entire elderly population)? On the other hand, EMTALA applies only to hospitals that operate EDs. Would you expect some hospitals to close their EDs to avoid the act's burdens? Patients admitted through EDs tend to be costlier to treat than comparable patients admitted by staff physicians and thus to be money losers for hospitals under some forms of payment (even assuming that the patient has some means of payment). See Stern et al., The Emergency Department as a Pathway to Admission for Poor and High–Cost Patients, 266 J.A.M.A. 2238 (1991).

Is the subject of patient dumping an appropriate one for federal action? for treatment in the Medicare legislation? Should the law be subject to constitutional challenge? See Jones v. Wake County Hosp. System, Inc., 786 F.Supp. 538, 546–47 (E.D.N.C.1991) (EMTALA prohibition against patient dumping by hospitals receiving Medicare funds is not unconstitutionally vague, is a legitimate exercise of Congress's spending power, and satisfies the constitutional requirement of due process).

2. *Basic Principles*. Other courts have generally agreed with the conclusions reached in *Baber* on the principal legal issues. E.g., Summers v. Baptist Med. Ctr. Arkadelphia, 69 F.3d 902, 904 (8th Cir.1995) ("EMTALA is not a federal malpractice statute and it does not set a national emergency health care standard; claims of misdiagnosis or inadequate treatment are left to [state law]"); Eberhardt v. City of Los Angeles, 62 F.3d 1253 (9th Cir. 1995) (holding that EMTALA provides no private right of action against physicians, creates no national standard of emergency medical care, and requires stabilization of the patient only after an "emergency medical condition" is discovered). See generally 42 C.F.R. § 489.24 (1996) (HCFA regulations on "special responsibilities of Medicare hospitals in emergency cases"); Annot., Construction and Application of Emergency Medical Treatment and Active Labor Act, 104 A.L.R. Fed. 166 (1991); Singer, Look What

They've Done to My Law, Ma: COBRA's [i.e., EMTALA's] Implosion, 33 Houston L.Rev. 113 (1996); Furrow, An Overview and Analysis of the Impact of the Emergency Medical Treatment and Active Labor Act, 16 J. Legal Med. 325 (1995).

Note that EMTALA is apparently satisfied once an "appropriate" screening has been provided and no "emergency medical condition" has been identified. On the question whether the individual received any screening at all, see Correa v. Hospital San Francisco, 69 F.3d 1184 (1st Cir.1995) (hospital that gave a number to patient in ED with chest pains and failed to attend to her for two hours held to have engaged in "constructive dumping" and to be liable under EMTALA even though "disparate treatment" was neither alleged nor proved).

3. *A Later Case in the Fourth Circuit.* The facts in Vickers v. Nash General Hosp., Inc., 78 F.3d 139 (4th Cir.1996), were strikingly similar to those in *Baber*, also involving an undiagnosed and ultimately fatal hematoma. The court held (2–1), however, that the plaintiff had not stated an EMTALA claim even though he had alleged that the decedent "received less screening, both in quantity and quality, than * * * other patients presenting in this same medical condition received." The majority took the view that EMTALA's screening requirement applied only to the initial evaluation, in which the doctor concluded that further diagnostic tests for intracranial injury were not needed. In its view, the accuracy of that evaluation and the appropriateness of the steps taken or not taken after that initial judgment were reviewable only under state law applicable to misdiagnosis and malpractice. Recall that the same court had previously recognized (in *Baber*, footnote 7) that EMTALA, as there construed, might cause hospitals to employ only cursory initial screenings for ED patients.

The dissenting judge in *Vickers* would have distinguished *Baber* on the ground that it involved a grant of summary judgment for failure to offer proof of "disparate treatment," whereas *Vickers* involved only a challenge to the sufficiency of the complaint, which the judge viewed as providing adequate notice of an EMTALA claim.

4. *An "Appropriate" Screening Exam?* Consider a plaintiff's problems in proving that a hospital failed to provide "an appropriate medical screening examination within the capability of the hospital's emergency department." May a hospital defend an arguably inadequate screening exam by claiming that the ED was overburdened on that particular Saturday night? Cf. *Correa*, supra (seeming to require at least triage—that is, a screening to assign treatment priorities to patients according to the degree of urgency). Can EMTALA be invoked to challenge the unavailability of functioning or up-to-date diagnostic equipment in the ED? Does your answer to this question suggest one reason why the court in Gatewood v. Washington Healthcare Corp., 933 F.2d 1037, 1041 (D.C.Cir.1991), said that EMTALA "does not create a broad federal cause of action for emergency room negligence or malpractice"?

Although the *Baber* court opined that Dr. Kline's examination of Ms. Baber was "not so substandard as to amount to no examination" at all, does that fact alone make the examination "appropriate"? Do you agree with the implication in the court's first quotation from the *Cleland* case (as amplified) that Congress used the term *appropriate* to resolve a disputed issue in drafting the legislation? What issue? For what other reason might the term have been chosen? To what sources do courts usually turn for standards of medical or hospital practice in the absence of precise statutory or contractual provisions or in applying common-law requirements of due care, etc.? Should the court have given some weight to Congress's use of the term *appropriate* instead of requiring only that each hospital adhere to its own standards?

If (as the *Baber, Gatewood,* and *Cleland* cases hold) the test is whether the patient received "disparate treatment," how would you proceed? Presumably there had never been another case identical to Ms. Baber's at RGH, making it hard to know whether the hospital departed from its usual, "individualized standard" in examining her. Many other emergency situations may be similarly unprecedented.

To what sources might one look for evidence of the hospital's standard with respect to emergency care? Would the treating doctor, hospital administrators, or other staff physicians be reliable witnesses on whether that standard was adhered to? Where might you look for written standards? Would you expect to find a protocol or guideline for handling the particular conditions or merely general statements to the effect that the policy is to provide care meeting general professional standards? What about asking hospital officials whether the hospital had a general policy of adhering to prevailing standards for ED care? Presumably state law requires such adherence. Would an affirmative answer to the question posed lay a sufficient foundation for calling experts who could testify to such standards? In light of your answers to the foregoing questions, do you still agree that EMTALA "does not create a broad federal cause of action for emergency room negligence or malpractice"?

5. *Effect of State Restrictions on Personal Injury Actions.* Are private actions under EMTALA subject to state laws restricting the procedural or substantive rights of injured patients suing hospitals for malpractice or other torts? See, e.g., Power v. Arlington Hosp., 42 F.3d 851 (4th Cir.1994) (Virginia's special procedural requirements for "malpractice" cases held preempted by EMTALA § 1395dd(f), but state cap on amount of damages and state statute limiting tort liability of insured charitable hospitals held to apply to EMTALA actions in view of § 1395dd(d)(2)(a)); Brooks v. Maryland General Hosp., 996 F.2d 708 (4th Cir.1993) (Maryland law requiring arbitration of malpractice claims held inapplicable by its terms to EMTALA action). In addition to providing a way around at least some state-imposed restrictions on suits against hospitals and physicians, EMTALA allows many plaintiffs to bring their cases in federal rather than state courts.

6. *Motive; Indigent Status of Patient.* In Burditt v. DHHS, 934 F.2d 1362 (5th Cir.1991), the court upheld a $20,000 fine in the first federal anti-dumping case brought by DHHS against an individual physician. Evidence indicated that the doctor had transferred a woman in active labor with dangerously high blood pressure not because she could not pay for care but because he feared that the likely complications would result in a malpractice suit. Although the woman gave birth in the ambulance, neither she nor her baby suffered actual harm. Nevertheless, the court upheld the civil monetary penalty, concluding that EMTALA is not restricted to cases in which the transfer was economically motivated. Do you agree that the statute should apply even though the doctor's motive was to avoid a malpractice risk by practicing "defensive medicine"?

Several courts have concluded that even though Congress's purpose in enacting EMTALA was to prevent hospitals from refusing to provide emergency care on the basis of patients' inability to pay, the statute's plain language extends the law's protections to all patients—that is to "any individual." E.g., Collins v. DePaul Hosp., 963 F.2d 303, 308 (10th Cir. 1992) ("fact that Congress viewed [EMTALA] as a so-called 'anti-dumping' bill does not subtract from its use of the broad term 'any individual' "). See also Roberts v. Galen of Virginia, 111 F.3d 405, 409 (6th Cir.1997) (besides indigency or lack of insurance, other improper motives for denying emergency care "include race, sex, politics, occupation, education, personal prejudice, drunkenness, or spite"); Cleland v. Bronson Health Care Group, 917 F.2d 266, 272 (6th Cir.1990) (plaintiff must show that the hospital provided disparate treatment for any improper reason). Might a plaintiff nevertheless derive some benefit from showing that the hospital was aware of his indigent status?

7. By its terms, EMTALA's screening requirement would seem to be triggered only when an individual physically "comes to" a hospital's ED. See, e.g., Fingers v. Jackson–Madison County Gen. Hosp. Dist., 1996 WL 678233 (6th Cir.) (unreported) (ED without surgeon on duty sought to transfer gunshot victim to other hospitals, all of which declined to receive him; court found latter hospitals had no EMTALA duty to screen patient who was not physically presented or to accept transfer under § 1395dd(g) where hospital was not alleged to have "specialized capabilities or facilities"); Miller v. Medical Center of Southwest Louisiana, 22 F.3d 626 (5th Cir.1994) (no EMTALA claim stated when hospital administrator, upon learning patient being referred for emergency care lacked insurance, instructed referring doctor to send him elsewhere); Johnson v. University of Chicago Hosp., 982 F.2d 230, 233 (hospital-operated telemetry system directed ambulance to "fly by"—i.e., take patient to another hospital because ED was overburdened; hospital held not liable under EMTALA because the patient never "came to the [hospital] or to its emergency department").

A few courts, however, have found, under subsection (c) of the act (which seems to apply when a patient is merely "at a hospital"), that a duty to stabilize the patient and to obey the rules concerning transfer can arise anywhere in the institution, not just in the ED. See, e.g., Reynolds v. Mercy Hosp., 861 F.Supp. 214 (W.D.N.Y.1994) (patient admitted for prearranged surgery permitted to invoke EMTALA when complications created emergency); McIntyre v. Schick, 795 F.Supp. 777, 781 (E.D.Va.1992) ("the anti-dumping statute is not based upon the door of the hospital through which a patient enters, but rather upon the notion of proper medical care for those persons suffering medical emergencies, whenever such emergencies occur at a participating hospital"); Smith v. Richmond Mem. Hosp., 416 S.E.2d 689 (Va. 1992) (patient discharged without stabilizing emergency condition held entitled to recover under EMTALA despite resemblance of claim to ordinary malpractice suit). But see James v. Sunrise Hosp., 86 F.3d 885 (9th Cir.1996) (holding that, although "the question is close," the restrictions on transfer in § 1395dd(c) "apply only to patients who go to the emergency room" and do not apply "unless there has been a determination [of an emergency medical condition] under subsection (b)").

8. Would members of Congress be surprised to learn that EMTALA creates statutory entitlements unconnected either to the patient's indigent status or to the hospital's emergency room? The next case reproduced below may seem even more surprising.

9. *Enforcement*. A consumer advocacy group reported in 1996 that, since 1986, only 32 hospitals had been fined (and none had been excluded from the Medicare program) under EMTALA even though some 500 violations had been found. Public Citizen, Patient Dumping in Hospital Emergency Rooms (1996). Does lax enforcement suggest that the federal government does not really believe that EMTALA is wise public policy?

10. *Policy Questions*. For a provocative critique of EMTALA, see R. Epstein, Mortal Peril: Our Inalienable Right to Health Care? 91–105 (1997). Professor Epstein aggressively questions the policy underlying EMTALA on the basis of its hidden costs and unanticipated effects. He first argues, citing reports of the financial problems and closing of trauma centers, that the supply of emergency services is likely to suffer as the burden of uncompensated care rises and hospitals cannot compensate, short of closing their emergency rooms, by cutting back on treatment to nonpaying patients. More controversially, he notes the frequency of emergencies caused by irresponsible personal behavior (drug use, etc.) by the persons injured and argues that providing free emergency care lowers the cost of such behavior, thus encouraging it: "Absent the political will to cut [chronic offenders] off, we get what we pay for: more self-destructive conduct. EMTALA is part of the problem, not its cure." Id. at 104. See also id. at 103 ("To the question, 'you cannot let them die, can you?' we have to avoid the reflexive answer, no. To restore long-term stability to the system of emergency care, the answer has to be, 'yes, we can sometimes.' ").

Another critic comments as follows:

> EMTALA effectively pegs the level of emergency care above the amount people are voluntarily willing to pay for—and imposes it to a first approximation on the hospitals which are least capable of spreading the cost. This "solution" is a recipe for disaster. Only two things have kept the system from a complete meltdown: the increasingly strained efforts of the courts to maintain a distinction between EMTALA and state malpractice law and HCFA's *sub silentio* acknowledgment that EMTALA is a symbolic law.

> * * * [E]ven symbolic laws are subject to the laws of economics. EMTALA will be repealed—although whether the repeal will be *de jure* or *de facto* remains to be seen.

Hyman, supra, at 55–56.

PROBLEM

Consider a patient with good health coverage who is nevertheless limited as to the services for which her health plan will pay or as to the providers eligible to render covered services—except under conditions that the plan regards as a true emergency. If a hospital, aware of the existence of these limitations but not of how they apply to the case in question, makes inquiry before providing a screening examination or provides a more limited exam than it would normally provide (omitting an MRI scan for a head injury, for example), has it violated EMTALA? What if, having identified what it regards as an emergency medical condition, the hospital is asked by the managed care plan to transfer the patient to a participating provider or to take only minimal steps to stabilize the condition? If the hospital has a contract with the health plan in question, what should it provide with respect to care in the ED?

On what grounds might an HMO resist paying a hospital for a screening exam or for certain types of emergency care rendered to its enrollee? See Pear, H.M.O.'s Refusing Emergency Claims, Hospitals Assert, N.Y.Times, July 9, 1995, p. 1; Loder & Clark, Hospitals in Code–Blue Catch–22, Nat'l L.J., Sept. 18, 1995, p. B9. Federal legislation to require payment by HMOs for services rendered pursuant to EMTALA's mandate has been proposed from time to time. Should such legislation, or something similar, be adopted? What arguments can be made for and against letting payers, rather than Congress or a state legislature, finally define the entitlements of insured patients seeking emergency care? Chapter 8(§C) will further consider the possibility of regulatory solutions to this problem.

Does Federal Legislation Override Professional Standards?

In the Matter of Baby "K"

United States Court of Appeals, Fourth Circuit, 1994.
16 F.3d 590, cert. denied, 513 U.S. 825, 115 S.Ct. 91, 130 L.Ed.2d 42 (1994).

■ WILKINS, CIRCUIT JUDGE:

The Hospital instituted this action against Ms. H, Mr. K, and Baby K [all parties are referred to by anonyms], seeking a declaratory judgment that it is not required under [EMTALA][2] to provide treatment other than

2. The Hospital also sought declaratory relief under § 504 of the Rehabilitation Act of 1973 (Rehabilitation Act), 29 U.S.C.A.§ 794 (West Supp.1993); the Americans with Disabilities Act of 1990 (ADA), 42 U.S.C.A.§§ 12101 et seq. (West 1993); the Child Abuse Prevention and Treatment Act (Child Abuse Act), 42 U.S.C.A. §§ 5101–5106h (West Supp.1993); and the statutes and common law of Virginia. In addressing

warmth, nutrition, and hydration to Baby K, an anencephalic infant. Because we agree with the district court that EMTALA gives rise to a duty on the part of the Hospital to provide respiratory support to Baby K when she is presented at the Hospital in respiratory distress and treatment is requested for her, we affirm.

I.

Baby K was born at the Hospital in October of 1992 with anencephaly, a congenital malformation in which a major portion of the brain, skull, and scalp are missing. While the presence of a brain stem does support her autonomic functions and reflex actions, because Baby K lacks a cerebrum, she is permanently unconscious. Thus, she has no cognitive abilities or awareness. She cannot see, hear, or otherwise interact with her environment.

When Baby K had difficulty breathing on her own at birth, Hospital physicians placed her on a mechanical ventilator. This respiratory support allowed the doctors to confirm the diagnosis and gave Ms. H, the mother, an opportunity to fully understand the diagnosis and prognosis of Baby K's condition. The physicians explained to Ms. H that most anencephalic infants die within a few days of birth due to breathing difficulties and other complications. Because aggressive treatment would serve no therapeutic or palliative purpose, they recommended that Baby K only be provided with supportive care in the form of nutrition, hydration, and warmth. Physicians at the Hospital also discussed with Ms. H the possibility of a "Do Not Resuscitate Order" that would provide for the withholding of lifesaving measures in the future.

The treating physicians and Ms. H failed to reach an agreement as to the appropriate care. Ms. H insisted that Baby K be provided with mechanical breathing assistance whenever the infant developed difficulty breathing on her own, while the physicians maintained that such care was inappropriate. As a result of this impasse, the Hospital sought to transfer Baby K to another hospital. This attempt failed when all of the hospitals in the area with pediatric intensive care units declined to accept the infant. In November of 1992, when Baby K no longer needed the services of an acute-care hospital, she was transferred to a nearby nursing home.

Since being transferred to the nursing home, Baby K has been readmitted to the Hospital three times due to breathing difficulties. Each time she has been provided with breathing assistance and, after stabilization, has been discharged to the nursing home. Following Baby K's second admission, the Hospital filed this action to resolve the issue of whether it is

these provisions, the district court [in an opinion partially reproduced below] concluded that a failure to provide respiratory support to Baby K because of her condition of anencephaly would constitute discrimination in violation of the ADA and the Rehabilitation Act but declined to rule on the application of the Child Abuse Act or Virginia law. Because we conclude that the Hospital has a duty to render stabilizing treatment under EMTALA, we need not address its obligations under the remaining federal statutes or the laws of Virginia.

obligated to provide emergency medical treatment to Baby K that it deems medically and ethically inappropriate. Baby K's guardian ad litem and her father, Mr. K, joined in the Hospital's request for a declaration that the Hospital is not required to provide respiratory support or other aggressive treatments. Ms. H contested the Hospital's request for declaratory relief. After the district court issued its findings of fact and conclusions of law denying the requested relief, the Hospital, Mr. K, and Baby K's guardian ad litem (collectively referred to as the "Hospital") noticed this appeal.

II.

Congress enacted EMTALA in response to its "concern that hospitals were 'dumping' patients [who were] unable to pay, by either refusing to provide emergency medical treatment or transferring patients before their emergency conditions were stabilized." Brooks v. Maryland Gen. Hosp. Inc., 996 F.2d 708, 710 (4th Cir.1993). Through EMTALA, Congress sought "to provide an 'adequate first response to a medical crisis' for all patients," Baber v. Hospital Corp. of America, 977 F.2d 872, 880 (4th Cir.1992), by imposing two duties on hospitals that have entered into Medicare provider agreements.

First, those hospitals with an emergency medical department must provide an appropriate medical screening to determine whether an emergency medical condition exists for any individual who comes to the emergency medical department requesting treatment. A hospital fulfills this duty if it utilizes identical screening procedures for all patients complaining of the same condition or exhibiting the same symptoms.

An additional duty arises if an emergency medical condition is discovered during the screening process. [Citing EMTALA § 1395dd(b)(1) and the definitions of "emergency medical condition" and "to stabilize," the court observed that] once an individual has been diagnosed as presenting an emergency medical condition, the hospital must provide that treatment necessary to prevent the material deterioration of the individual's condition or provide for an appropriate transfer to another facility.

In the application of these provisions to Baby K, the Hospital concedes that when Baby K is presented in respiratory distress a failure to provide "immediate medical attention" would reasonably be expected to cause serious impairment of her bodily functions. Thus, her breathing difficulty qualifies as an emergency medical condition, and the diagnosis of this emergency medical condition triggers the duty of the hospital to provide Baby K with stabilizing treatment or to transfer her in accordance with the provisions of EMTALA. Since transfer is not an option available to the Hospital at this juncture,[5] the Hospital must stabilize Baby K's condition.

5. * * * Since Ms. H objects to the transfer of Baby K, since the Hospital has not obtained a certification that the benefits of a transfer would outweigh the medical risks involved, and since no qualified medical facility has agreed to accept Baby K, the requirements for transfer prior to stabilization have not been met. * * *

The Hospital acknowledged in its complaint that aggressive treatment, including mechanical ventilation, is necessary to "assure within a reasonable medical probability, that no material deterioration of Baby K's condition is likely to occur." Thus, stabilization of her condition requires the Hospital to provide respiratory support through the use of a respirator or other means necessary to ensure adequate ventilation. In sum, a straightforward application of the statute obligates the Hospital to provide respiratory support to Baby K when she arrives at the emergency department of the Hospital in respiratory distress and treatment is requested on her behalf.

III.

In an effort to avoid the result that follows from the plain language of EMTALA, the Hospital * * * claims: (1) that this court has previously interpreted EMTALA as only requiring uniform treatment of all patients exhibiting the same condition; (2) that in prohibiting disparate emergency medical treatment Congress did not intend to require physicians to provide treatment outside the prevailing standard of medical care; [and] (3) that an interpretation of EMTALA that requires a hospital or physician to provide respiratory support to an anencephalic infant fails to recognize a physician's ability, under Virginia law, to refuse to provide medical treatment that the physician considers medically or ethically inappropriate * * *. We find these arguments unavailing.

A.

Relying on the decisions of this court in [*Baber* and *Brooks*], the Hospital contends that it is only required to provide Baby K with the same treatment that it would provide other anencephalic infants—supportive care in the form of warmth, nutrition, and hydration. * * *

* * * [W]e conclude that the duty of the Hospital to provide stabilizing treatment for an emergency medical condition is not coextensive with the duty of the Hospital to provide an "appropriate medical screening." Congress has statutorily defined the duty of a hospital to provide stabilizing treatment as requiring that treatment necessary to prevent the material deterioration of a patient's condition. If, as the Hospital suggests, it were only required to provide uniform treatment, it could provide any level of treatment to Baby K, including a level of treatment that would allow her condition to materially deteriorate, so long as the care she was provided was consistent with the care provided to other individuals. The definition of stabilizing treatment advocated by the Hospital directly conflicts with the plain language of EMTALA.

* * * In the case of Baby K, the treatment necessary to prevent the material deterioration of her condition when she is in respiratory distress includes respiratory support.

Even if this court were to interpret EMTALA as requiring hospitals to provide uniform treatment for emergency medical conditions, we could not find that the Hospital is only required to provide Baby K with warmth, nutrition, and hydration. As the Hospital acknowledged during oral argument, Baby K resides at the nursing home for months at a time without requiring emergency medical attention. Only when she has experienced episodes of bradypnea or apnea has Baby K required respiratory support to prevent serious impairment of her bodily functions. It is bradypnea or apnea, not anencephaly, that is the emergency medical condition that brings Baby K to the Hospital for treatment. Uniform treatment of emergency medical conditions would require the Hospital to provide Baby K with the same treatment that the Hospital provides all other patients experiencing bradypnea or apnea. The Hospital does not allege that it would refuse to provide respiratory support to infants experiencing bradypnea or apnea who do not have anencephaly. Indeed, a refusal to provide such treatment would likely be considered as providing no emergency medical treatment.

B.

The second argument of the Hospital is that, in redressing the problem of disparate emergency medical treatment, Congress did not intend to require physicians to provide medical treatment outside the prevailing standard of medical care. The Hospital asserts that, because of their extremely limited life expectancy and because any treatment of their condition is futile, the prevailing standard of medical care for infants with anencephaly is to provide only warmth, nutrition, and hydration. Thus, it maintains that a requirement to provide respiratory assistance would exceed the prevailing standard of medical care. However, the plain language of EMTALA requires stabilizing treatment for any individual who comes to a participating hospital, is diagnosed as having an emergency medical condition, and cannot be transferred. * * * The Hospital has been unable to identify, nor has our research revealed, any statutory language or legislative history evincing a Congressional intent to create an exception to the duty to provide stabilizing treatment when the required treatment would exceed the prevailing standard of medical care. We recognize the dilemma facing physicians who are requested to provide treatment they consider morally and ethically inappropriate, but * * * [t]he appropriate branch to redress the policy concerns of the Hospital is Congress.

C.

The Hospital further argues that EMTALA cannot be construed to require it to provide respiratory support to anencephalics when its physicians deem such care inappropriate, because Virginia law permits physicians to refuse to provide such care. Section 54.1–2990 of the Health Care Decisions Act (HCDA) of Virginia provides that "[n]othing in this article shall be construed to require a physician to prescribe or render medical treatment to a patient that the physician determines to be medically or ethically inappropriate." Va.Code Ann. s 54.1–2990 (Michie Supp.1993). The Hospital maintains that EMTALA only obligates a hospital to provide stabilizing treatment "within the staff and facilities available at the hospital." It reasons that because its physicians object to providing respiratory support to anencephalics, it has no physicians available to provide respiratory treatment for Baby K and, therefore, is not required by EMTALA to provide such treatment. We disagree.

The duty to provide stabilizing treatment set forth in EMTALA applies not only to participating hospitals but also to treating physicians in participating hospitals. EMTALA does not provide an exception for stabilizing treatment physicians may deem medically or ethically inappropriate. Consequently, to the extent § 54.1–2990 exempts physicians from providing care they consider medically or ethically inappropriate, it directly conflicts with the provisions of EMTALA that require stabilizing treatment to be provided.

* * * EMTALA provides that state and local laws that directly conflict with the requirements of EMTALA are preempted. The Hospital does not allege that EMTALA is an invalid act of Congress. Therefore, to the extent that § 54.1–2990 applies to medical treatment decisions on behalf of infants[10] and to the extent that § 54.1–2990 exempts treating physicians in participating hospitals from providing care they consider medically or ethically inappropriate, it is preempted—it does not allow the physicians treating Baby K to refuse to provide her with respiratory support.

IV.

It is beyond the limits of our judicial function to address the moral or ethical propriety of providing emergency stabilizing medical treatment to anencephalic infants. We are bound to interpret federal statutes in accordance with their plain language and any expressed congressional intent. Congress rejected a case-by-case approach to determining what emergency medical treatment hospitals and physicians must provide and to whom they must provide it; instead, it required hospitals and physicians to provide stabilizing care to any individual presenting an emergency medical condition. EMTALA does not carve out an exception for anencephalic infants in respiratory distress any more than it carves out an exception for comatose patients, those with lung cancer, or those with muscular dystrophy—all of whom may repeatedly seek emergency stabilizing treatment for respiratory distress and also possess an underlying medical condition that severely affects their quality of life and ultimately may result in their death. Because EMTALA does not provide for such an exception, the judgment of the district court is affirmed.

AFFIRMED.

■ SPROUSE, SENIOR CIRCUIT JUDGE, dissenting:

I respectfully dissent.

10. By its terms the application of § 54.1–2990 is limited to the HCDA. The HCDA governs advance medical directives by adults and surrogate medical treatment decisions on behalf of adults. No part of the HCDA sets forth provisions for dealing with medical treatment decisions on behalf of infants. Therefore, the Virginia legislature presumably did not intend § 54.1–2990 to apply to medical treatment decisions on behalf of infants.

I have no quarrel with the majority's conclusion that the duty imposed on hospitals by EMTALA to provide stabilizing treatment for an emergency condition is different from its duty to provide "appropriate medical screening." There is no question that once a medical condition is characterized as an "emergency medical condition" contemplated by EMTALA, the patient must be stabilized to prevent material deterioration of the condition.

I simply do not believe, however, that Congress, in enacting EMTALA, meant for the judiciary to superintend the sensitive decision-making process between family and physicians at the bedside of a helpless and terminally ill patient under the circumstances of this case. Tragic end-of-life hospital dramas such as this one do not represent phenomena susceptible of uniform legal control. In my view, Congress, even in its weakest moments, would not have attempted to impose federal control in this sensitive, private area. Rather, the statute was designed narrowly to correct a specific abuse: hospital "dumping" of indigent or uninsured emergency patients. There is no indication in the legislative history of EMTALA that Congress meant to extend the statute's reach to hospital-patient relationships that do not involve "dumping." Clearly, there is no suggestion of patient "dumping" in this case. To the contrary, Baby K's introduction to the hospital was not for emergency treatment—she was born there. She was twice readmitted and after her subsidiary medical condition was stabilized, transferred back to a nursing home. In light of the purposes of the statute and this child's unique circumstances, I would find this case to be outside the scope of EMTALA's anti-dumping provisions.

I also submit that EMTALA's language concerning the type and extent of emergency treatment to be extended to all patients was not intended to cover the continued emergencies that typically attend patients like Baby K. The law was crafted to effect the purpose of preventing disparate treatment between emergency patients. In my view, Baby K is not that kind of emergency patient contemplated by the statute, although by the very nature of her terminal illness, she will suffer repeated medical emergencies during her day-to-day maintenance care. The hospital argues that anencephaly, not the subsidiary respiratory failure, is the condition that should be reviewed in order to judge the applicability vel non of EMTALA. I agree. I would consider anencephaly as the relevant condition and the respiratory difficulty as one of many subsidiary conditions found in a patient with the disease. EMTALA was not designed to reach such circumstances.

The tragic phenomenon Baby K represents exemplifies the need to take a case-by-case approach to determine if an emergency episode is governed by EMTALA. Baby K's condition presents her parents and doctors with decision-making choices that are different even from the difficult choices presented by other terminal diseases. Specifically, as an anencephalic infant, Baby K is permanently unconscious. She cannot hear, cannot see, and has no cognitive abilities. She has no awareness of and cannot interact with her environment in any way. Since there is no medical treatment that can improve her condition, she will be in this state for as long as she lives. Given this unique medical condition, whatever treatment appropriate for her unspeakably tragic illness should be regarded as a continuum, not as a series of discrete emergency medical conditions to be considered in isolation. Humanitarian concerns dictate appropriate care. However, if resort must be had to our courts to test the appropriateness of the care, the legal vehicle should be state malpractice law.

In my view, considering the discrete factual circumstances of Baby K's condition and previous treatment, if she is transferred again from the nursing home to the hospital in respiratory distress, that condition should be considered integral to the anencephalic condition, and I would hold that there has been no violation of EMTALA. I emphasize that this view contemplates a case-by-case determination. Individual cases involving victims of trauma, cancer, heart attack, or other catastrophic illness, who are denied potentially life-saving treatments, may well require different analyses.

FURTHER NOTES AND QUESTIONS ON EMTALA

1. Note the absence of any reference in *Baby "K"* to the hospital's economic interests. In fact, Baby K's care was being paid for through a combination of private insurance and Medicaid. By the end or 1994, the total cost of that care approached half a million dollars. Tousignant & Miller, Baby K's Mother Gives Her the Prayer that Many Deny She Has, Wash. Post, Oct. 7, 1994, at A1. If the hospital was being fully compensated for its services, why it did object to treating Baby K?

2. Are you surprised to learn that a state would spend large amounts of its citizens' tax dollars on so-called "futile" care? Would it have been relevant if, in *Baby "K,"* the state Medicaid program had refused to pay for the treatment in question? To a significant extent, federal law currently prescribes what specific services states must cover in their Medicaid programs in order to qualify for federal funds. How should the federal Medicaid law be construed in light of other federal legislation, such as EMTALA? For example, should a state Medicaid program be permitted to deny eligible persons coverage for care that EMTALA mandates? Conversely, should EMTALA be construed to require a hospital to provide futile care that states are not federally required to cover under their Medicaid programs? The opinion next reproduced below indicates the potential relevance of the other federal legislation on such sensitive issues.

3. Could EMTALA have been read to reach a different result? Or is the matter, as the court said, simply "a straightforward application of the statute"?

4. Commentators have suggested that Congress should revise EMTALA to refer not to "any individual" but only to indigent patients. E.g., Smith, The Critical Condition of [EMTALA]: A Proposed Amendment to the Act After *In the Matter of Baby K*, 48 Vand.L.Rev. 1491 (1995). What would be the rationale for such an amendment? Would such an amendment resolve the problem evident in *Baby "K"*? Do you think it likely that courts would construe the amended statute to require stabilization of an indigent patient under circumstances where, because care was deemed to be futile and therefore not "medically necessary," there would be no similar duty, either legal or contractual, toward a paying patient?

5. Consider how EMTALA would apply to the facts of the *Tabor* case (the last case noted in the previous section of this chapter). Could a jury find, on the evidence in *Tabor*, that an emergency medical condition existed? Assuming it could, would the fact of disparate treatment occasioned by the absence of (verifiable) insurance coverage be determinative of EMTALA liability? See Helton v. Phelps County Regional Med. Center, 817 F.Supp. 789 (E.D.Mo.1993) (EMTALA action on facts similar to *Tabor*; summary judgment for county hospital denied where its policy called for discharge or transfer of "patients with inadequate financial coverage"). Is it unthinkable that persons with no coverage might receive more aggressive treatment than those with good protection? Does EMTALA mandate equal treatment in a *Tabor*-like situation?

Note that the physician but not the hospital was held liable in *Tabor* and that only the hospital is subject to private suit under EMTALA. Would the hospital have been liable in an EMTALA action? Consider in this connection the relationship of the physician and the hospital. What terms would you, as a lawyer for a hospital concerned about EMTALA liability, want to see included in the contract between the hospital and the corporation operating the ER?

6. Numerous commentators have protested the extension of EMTALA's reach in the *Baby "K"* case. The main criticisms, echoing concerns in Judge Sprouse's dissenting opinion, have to do with the interference with ethical decisions by doctors and terminally ill patients. E.g, Morreim, Futilitarianism, Exoticare, and Coerced Altruism: The ADA Meets Its Limits, 25 Seton Hall L.Rev. 883, 897 (1995); Nealy, Medical Decision–Making for Children: A Struggle for Autonomy, 49 SMU L.Rev. 133, 135 (1995); Dzielak, Physicians Lose the Tug of War to Pull the Plug: The Debate about Continued Futile Medical Care, 28 J.Marshall L.Rev. 733, 748 (1995). Without EMTALA, could a hospital and its doctors safely terminate treatment in a case like *Baby "K"*? Where would their legal warrant come from? How would you amend EMTALA to restore some autonomy to doctors and hospitals in such matters? Note in the opinion reproduced below how other federal statutes likewise interfere with medical decision making in difficult cases.

7. *A Later Decision*. The Fourth Circuit court of appeals had a subsequent opportunity to address an issue similar to that in *Baby K* and reached a strikingly different result. In Bryan v. Rectors and Board of Visitors of the University of Virginia, 95 F.3d 349 (4th Cir.1996), an elderly patient was transferred to a university medical center for treatment of severe respiratory distress. This condition was stabilized and treated by means of a respirator for twelve days, at the end of which the hospital, perceiving further care to be futile, issued a "Do Not Resuscitate" order over the objection of the patient's family, which instructed the hospital "to take all measures to keep her alive and trust in God's wisdom." Pursuant to this order, care was withheld when a new emergency ensued eight days later, and the patient died. The court affirmed the dismissal of an EMTALA claim, distinguishing *Baby K* on the ground that it dealt only with the duty immediately to treat emergency cases even when the doctors considered the treatment inappropriate. EMTALA, the court reasoned, was designed only to create and enforce a duty to stabilize an emergency medical condition and to prevent patient-dumping and did not purport to address the quality of long-term care, which the court viewed as a matter of state law.

In the Matter of Baby K

United States District Court, Eastern District Virginia, 1993.
832 F.Supp. 1022.

■ HILTON, DISTRICT JUDGE.

[The district court's conclusions on the applicability of two other federal statutes referred to in footnote 2 of the court of appeals opinion are presented here.]

II. Rehabilitation Act

Section 504 of the Rehabilitation Act Prohibits Discrimination Against an "otherwise qualified" handicapped individual, solely by reason of his or her handicap, under any program or activity receiving federal financial assistance. Hospitals such as plaintiff that accept Medicare and Medicaid funding are subject to the act. Baby K is a "handicapped" and "disabled" person within the meaning of the Rehabilitation Act of 1973. A "handicapped individual" under the Rehabilitation Act "includes an infant who is born with a congenital defect." Bowen v. American Hospital Ass'n, 476 U.S. 610, 624 (1986).

Section 504's plain text spells out the necessary scope of inquiry: Is Baby K otherwise qualified to receive ventilator treatment and is ventilator treatment being threatened with being denied because of an unjustified consideration of her anencephalic handicap? The Hospital has admitted that the sole reason it wishes to withhold ventilator treatment for Baby K over her mother's objections, is because of Baby K's anencephaly—her handicap and disability.

To evade this textual mandate, the Hospital relies on two cases which held that a hospital's decision not to override the desire of the parents of babies with congenital defects to withhold treatment did not violate section 504. Johnson v. Thompson, 971 F.2d 1487, 1493 (10th Cir.1992), cert. denied, 113 S.Ct. 1255 (1993); United States v. University Hospital, State U. of New York, 729 F.2d 144, 156–57 (2d Cir.1984). Because the parents in *Johnson* and *University Hospital* consented to the withholding of treatment, the two cases are factually distinguishable from this case.

When the Rehabilitation Act was passed in 1973, Congress intended that discrimination on the basis of a handicap be treated in the same manner that Title VI of the Civil Rights Act treats racial discrimination. *University Hospital*, 729 F.2d at 161–163 (Winter, J., dissenting). This analogy to race dispels any ambiguity about the extent to which Baby K has statutory rights not to be discriminated against on the basis of her handicap. It also shatters the Hospital's contention that ventilator treatment should be withheld because Baby K's recurring breathing troubles are intrinsically related to her handicap. No such distinction would be permissible within the context of racial discrimination. In addition, the Hospital was able to perform a tracheotomy on Baby K. This surgery was far more complicated than linking her to a ventilator to allow her to breathe. Cf. *Bowen*, 476 U.S. at 655 ("if an otherwise normal child would be given the identical treatment, so should the handicapped child") (White, J., dictum in dissent). Just as an AIDS patient seeking ear surgery is "otherwise qualified" to receive treatment despite poor long term prospects of living, Baby K is "otherwise qualified" to receive ventilator treatment despite similarly dismal health prospects. Cf. Glanz v. Vernick, 750 F.Supp. 39, 45–46 (D.Mass.1990). Thus, the Hospital's desire to withhold ventilator treatment from Baby K over her mother's objections would violate the Rehabilitation Act.

III. Americans with Disabilities Act

Section 302 of the Americans with Disabilities Act ("ADA") prohibits discrimination against disabled individuals by "public accommodations." A "disability" is "a physical or mental impairment that substantially limits one or more of the major life activities" of an individual. This includes any physiological disorder or condition affecting the neurological system, musculoskeletal system, or sense organs, among others. Anencephaly is a disability, because it affects the baby's neurological functioning, ability to walk, and ability to see or talk. "Public accommodation" is defined to include a "professional office of a health care provider, hospital, or other service establishment." The Hospital is a public accommodation under the ADA.

Section 302(a) of the ADA states a general rule of nondiscrimination against the disabled: "General rule. No individual shall be discriminated against on the basis of disability in the full and equal enjoyment of the goods, services, facilities, privileges, advantages, or accommodation of any place of public accommodations by any person who owns, leases (or leases to), or operates a place of public accommodation." In contrast to the Rehabilitation Act, the ADA does not require that a handicapped individual be "otherwise qualified" to receive the benefits of participation. Further, section 302(b)(1)(a) of the ADA states that "[i]t shall be discriminatory to subject an individual or class of individuals on the basis of a disability ... to a denial of the opportunity of the individual or class to participate in or benefit from the goods, services, facilities, privileges, advantages, or accommodations of an entity."

The Hospital asks this court for authorization to deny the benefits of ventilator services to Baby K by reason of her anencephaly. The Hospital's claim is that it is "futile" to keep alive an anencephalic baby, even though the mother has requested such treatment. But the plain language of the

ADA does not permit the denial of ventilator services that would keep alive an anencephalic baby when those life-saving services would otherwise be provided to a baby without disabilities at the parent's request. The Hospital's reasoning would lead to the denial of medical services to anencephalic babies as a class of disabled individuals. Such discrimination against a vulnerable population class is exactly what the American with Disabilities Act was enacted to prohibit. The Hospital would therefore violate the ADA if it were to withhold ventilator treatment from Baby K.

NOTES AND QUESTIONS ON THE REHABILITATION ACT, THE ADA, AND THE CHILD ABUSE AMENDMENTS

1. The *Baby K* case obviously dramatizes the troubling and divisive issues that can arise in the health care field between, on the one hand, rationalist-economizers and, on the other hand, vitalists, who believe that law should honor biological human life in all its forms instead of inviting distinctions that put the matter on the proverbial "slippery slope." It also demonstrates the extraordinary potential reach of legislation aimed at protecting persons with disabilities. The effect of such laws on public and private health insurance coverage will be considered at one point in § C of this chapter and again in chapter 2(§C).

2. *The ADA and Baby K.* Consider the court's reading of the ADA in *Baby K.* A crucial goal of Congress in passing the ADA was to "assure equality of opportunity, full participation, independent living, and economic self-sufficiency for [disabled] individuals"; its preamble also expressed congressional concern that "individuals with disabilities * * * have been * * * relegated to a position of powerlessness in our society * * * resulting from stereotypic assumptions not truly indicative of the individual ability of such individuals to participate in, and contribute, to society." 42 U.S.C. §§ 12101(a)(7), (8) (1994). Noting the tragic irrelevance of these concerns to the case of Baby K, ethicist Haavi Morreim has summarized as follows her legal arguments against applying the ADA in such situations:

> *First*, the purposes of the ADA, as expressed in its preamble, arguably do not apply to extreme situations such as that of Baby K. If disability law is to help citizens participate more fully in their community, it obviously does not encompass individuals who are utterly incapable of "participation" in human social life.
>
> *Second*, the law's protections apply only to "eligible" or "qualified" individuals. In health care, the criteria for "eligibility" for a medical service are equivalent to "medical indications" for treatment. These are ordinarily established by the medical community and acknowledged by the judiciary as medicine's professional standards of care. Important questions arise concerning whether or when some nonmedical authority may permissibly intervene in medical standards.
>
> *Third*, although the ADA requires those who provide services or programs to make "reasonable accommodations" to include a disabled person, it does not expect them to go beyond reasonableness into undue

burdens or hardships. In the context of health care, the cumulative costs of meeting the needs, not just of one individual with costly demands, but of everyone else similarly situated, can exact an undue toll on other citizens by inordinately raising the cost of care. These costs can be found excessive on two grounds.

Foremost, the ADA is based not just on values of a collective societal obligation to help the less fortunate among us, but on a coerced private altruism that requires private citizens to use their own money to make up for others' misfortunes that they in no way caused. If the public generosity extracted through taxes should be limited, such coerced private altruism should be even more restrained.

Additionally, once we recognize that concessions to Baby K cases logically commit us also to support a wide array of costly marginal treatments for patients with comparably dismal prognoses, the financial costs can quickly become prohibitive. And so can the opportunity costs as it forecloses other projects people value.

Fourth, the ADA does not require programs to "fundamentally change" their essential character in order to accommodate a disabled individual. When health plans must divert vast portions of their limited resources to cover "exoticare" for disabled patients, they may no longer be able to provide basic care for the main group of their subscribers. If providing basic care was the initial and legitimate purpose of the health plan, then such a change would be fundamental.

This change, in turn may trigger a *fifth* ADA-based caveat. Providers of a program or service are not required to endanger the health or safety of others in order to accommodate the disabled. If large numbers of people no longer receive basic care in order to provide exoticare to a minority, it is virtually certain that some of them will suffer adverse effects, as some diseases may not be diagnosed as quickly or treated as effectively.

Sixth, decisions under these circumstances to limit some of the care available to disabled people cannot be said to be based "solely" on their disabilities.

Morreim, Futilitarianism, Exoticare, and Coerced Altruism: The ADA Meets Its Limits, 25 Seton Hall L.Rev. 883, 889–90 (1995).

The district court in *Baby K* is the only court that has faced the question whether denial of truly futile care, like that desired on behalf of Baby K, would violate the ADA. Several courts have decided, however, that denial or termination of such care would not violate the Rehabilitation Act. To state a claim under the Rehabilitation Act, a "plaintiff must prove (1) that he is a 'handicapped individual' under the act, (2) that he is 'otherwise qualified' for the [benefit] sought, (3) that he was [discriminated against] solely by reason of his handicap and (4) that the program or activity in question receives federal financial assistance." Johnson by Johnson v. Thompson, 971 F.2d 1487, 1492 (10th Cir.1992), quoting Strathie v. Department of Transp., 716 F.2d 227, 230 (3d Cir.1983). It has been held that the "otherwise qualified" element of this test is satisfied only when the individual's disability is unrelated to the medical services being withheld (e.g., where a deaf individual is denied treatment for burns solely because she is deaf). United States v. University Hosp., State Univ. of New York, 729 F.2d 144, 156 (2d Cir.1984); *Johnson*, supra, at 1493–94. Under this analysis, Baby K would not be "otherwise qualified" because the treatment sought on her behalf was intended to treat the handicap itself. But, of course, the ADA does not include this requirement.

3. *The Child Abuse Amendments*. The Child Abuse Prevention and Treatment Act Amendments of 1984 (CAA), 42 U.S.C.A. §§ 5101–5106i (West Supp. 1997), make unlawful "the withholding of medically indicated treatment from disabled infants with life-threatening conditions." 42 U.S.C.A. § 5106a(b)(2)(B) (West Supp. 1997). See generally Crossley, Of Diagnosis and Discrimination: Discriminatory Non–Treatment of Infants with HIV Infection, 93 Colum. L. Rev. 1581, 1612–17 (1993). The phrase "withholding of medically indicated treatment" is defined to mean "the failure to respond to the infant's life-threatening conditions by providing treatment (including appropriate nutrition, hydration and medication) which, in the treating physician's or physicians' reasonable medical judgment will be most likely to be effective in ameliorating or correcting all such conditions * * *." 42 U.S.C.A. § 5106g(6) (West Supp. 1997). Standing alone, these provisions would appear to prohibit a hospital from terminating care like that sought on behalf of Baby K. Nevertheless, the CAA created an exception for treatment that would "(i) merely prolong dying, (ii) not be effective in ameliorating or correcting all of the infant's life threatening conditions, or (iii) otherwise be futile in terms of the survival of the infant." DHHS has indicated that these exceptions should be construed narrowly. See, e.g., 45 C.F.R. § 1340 app. at 300–01 (1997) (stating that clause (i) does not apply "where the prognosis is not for death in the near future, but rather the more distant future"). Nevertheless, at least one court has held that the removal of a ventilator used to treat an infant born with severe permanent mental and physical abnormalities who would be forever unable to breathe unassisted would not violate the CAA because the ventilator was merely prolonging death. In Re Baby Girl Muller, described in Bopp & Nimz, A Legal Analysis of the Child Abuse Amendments of 1984 in Compelled Compassion: Government Intervention in the Treatment of Critically Ill Newborns 73, 91–92 (A. Caplan et al. eds. 1992). Might these exceptions be expanded to provide a legislative basis for limiting the level of care adult patients or their surrogates could demand under the ADA or the Rehabilitation Act? For an argument to that effect, see Morreim, supra, at 925.

4. *References*. For further treatment of the challenging legal issues raised by the application of the Rehabilitation Act and ADA in the "heroic" care context, see Mehlman et al., When Do Health Care Decisions Discriminate against Persons with Disabilities?, 22 J. Health Pol., Pol'y & L. 1385 (1997); Crossley, As We Lay Dying: Medical Futility and Disability Discrimination, 81 Iowa L. Rev. 179 (1995); Orentlicher, Rationing and the Americans with Disabilities Act, 271 J.A.M.A. 308 (1994); Peters, Health Care Rationing and Disability Rights, 70 Ind. L.J. 491 (1995); Hadorn, The

Problem of Discrimination in Health Care Priority Setting, 268 J.A.M.A. 454 (1992).

Financing Uncompensated Care

NOTES AND QUESTIONS ON UNCOMPENSATED CARE AND INTERNAL CROSS–SUBSIDIZATION

1. Remembering that (as economists constantly remind us) "there is no such thing as a free lunch," consider how the costs of complying with the various legal mandates reviewed in this chapter are borne. Specifically, how are private hospitals supposed to finance fulfillment of their obligations under the ADA, the Rehabilitation Act, EMTALA, the Hill–Burton Act, state statutes, and the common law (as applied, for example, in *Stanturf* and *Muse*)? Do you sense a pervasive policy of (in Morreim's words) "coerced private altruism that requires private citizens to make up for others' misfortunes that they in no way caused"? Might it be possible to raise constitutional objections to at least some of the mandates identified? If not, why not? How, if at all, does the case differ from, say, the obligation imposed on some public utilities to provide so-called "lifeline" rates to low-income or elderly customers? What is your opinion, as a policy matter, of this method of financing health care for the poor?

2. The EMTALA requirement that emergency services be given to indigent patients makes no provision for payment. Is the requirement therefore unconstitutional? Should the cost of providing such services at least have been reimbursable as an overhead expense under Medicare (as long as Medicare payments to hospitals were based on their actual costs)? Formulate the arguments both ways. Cf. Baptist Hosp. v. Secretary of Health and Human Services, 802 F.2d 860, 866–70 (6th Cir.1986) (pre-EMTALA case rejecting claim that Medicare should bear a fair share of charity allowances and bad debts; emphasis placed on hospitals' voluntary acceptance of burdens of Medicare participation and tax exemptions).

Professor Hyman predicts that new squeezes on hospital revenues will cause many institutions to rethink their commitments to emergency care. He observes not only that patients having coverage that enables them to pay their own way will no longer pay as generously as they have in the past but also that payers are increasingly likely to refuse to cover care sought in emergency rooms of nonparticipating hospitals. Hyman, Patient Dumping and EMTALA: Past Imperfect/Future Shock, 8 Health Matrix 29 (1998). See also R. Epstein, Mortal Peril: Our Inalienable Right to Health Care? 95–101 (1997) (challenging policy underlying EMTALA on basis of its unanticipated effects on supply of emergency services).

3. Do states have a constitutional obligation to provide payment to private hospitals for uncompensated care that is mandated under state law? Regulations under Illinois legislation provided that the state would pay a per diem rate to the hospital for mandated treatment in cases where the patient could not afford to pay. Although the allowance was lower than the hospital's normal charge, the Illinois Supreme Court refused to find a "taking" in violation of the Due Process Clause. Methodist Med. Center v. Ingram, 82 Ill.2d 511, 522–24, 45 Ill.Dec. 924, 929–30, 413 N.E.2d 402, 407–08 (1980) (state's police power to protect the public health was "sufficient to justify, in proper circumstances, uncompensated deprivation of * * * property").

Consider the disputes that would arise under a statute like the one in Illinois over whether the state was obligated to reimburse the hospital for care given to patients whose accounts were subsequently found to be uncollectible. How should a hospital establish its entitlement to reimbursement under such a state program? How should the state protect its funds?

4. *Cross–Subsidization as a Means of Financing Indigent Care.* If, as hospitals and nursing homes often allege, Medicaid allowances are inadequate to allow them to provide quality care, how are deficits to be covered? Can society reasonably expect hospitals to continue treating the uninsured either voluntarily or involuntarily without adequate (or any) compensation? Is it appropriate, and constitutional, for a state to finance indigent care by restricting competition (through entry regulation) in the private-pay market and then compelling institutional providers to apply some of their resulting excess profits to taking care of the poor?

"Uncompensated care" became a burning issue in policy debates as the number of persons with inadequate financial protection grew and as hospitals' ability to finance services for indigent patients was eroded by competition and other pressures. See, e.g., F. Sloan et al., eds., Uncompensated Hospital Care: Rights and Responsibilities (1986); S. Rogers et al., Hospitals and the Uninsured Poor: Measuring and Paying for Uncompensated Care (1985). An important theme linking health care economics, recent industry developments, and the problem of access is that of internal subsidies or cross-subsidization, which is described and placed in policy perspective in the following excerpt:

> The current financial problems of hospitals are in large measure a consequence of their historical practice of relying on liberal payments from all third-party payers, including governments, to support services that the market cannot support. As long as payers were unable or unwilling to resist paying more than the marginal cost—that is, a competitive price—for covered services, nonprofit hospitals were able to cross-subsidize such generally desirable activities as manpower training, research, and the care of patients who could not afford to pay for the care they received and did not qualify for support under any public program. As the government has become less free with its reimbursements, many hospitals, particularly nonprofit ones, are not willing, or do not consider themselves free, to discontinue these activities. Therefore, wherever possible, they have sought to finance continuation of these good works by charging even higher prices to those patients who, usually because they have indemnity insurance, can afford to pay and do not question their bills.
>
> The term "cost shifting" has been coined to characterize the federal government's alleged policy of paying less than the full cost of caring for its beneficiaries. The government is said to have shifted some of its costs to

the hospitals, which in turn—to whatever extent they have been able to get away with it—have shifted their unrecovered costs to private payers. Although this may be an accurate description of what has occurred, the central issue is not whether the government is in fact getting services for its beneficiaries at prices below average or marginal costs. The more important fact is that the government's new aggressiveness as a buyer is threatening to upset the delicate system of cross-subsidies that has developed over the years to meet important needs. Moreover, the government is not the sole culprit in creating these troubles, for many private purchasers are also having good success in obtaining hospital discounts in competitive markets. Indeed, however liberal or illiberal government payment policies may be, it seems only a matter of time before increasing competitive and cost-pressures on private insurers and health care providers will eliminate most of the system's historical capacity for cross-subsidization.

Although "cost shifting" may not be the right name for it, a problem certainly exists. Increasing aggressiveness on the demand side of increasingly competitive markets for both health insurance protection and insured services is indeed having disruptive effects on the supply side of those markets. Private insurers that have heretofore borne the cost of the hospitals' internal subsidies without much complaint now find themselves being exploited more than ever before. Many hospitals are running out of such payers of last resort, however, and, as a consequence, many former beneficiaries of internal subsidies, particularly the poor, are feeling real hardships.

Deregulation and the Destruction of Cross–Subsidies

The troubles being experienced in the health care industry are essentially indistinguishable from dislocations that occur in industries newly subjected to deregulation. Although the health care industry has never been subject to comprehensive regulation by a single agency similar to the Civil Aeronautics Board or the Interstate Commerce Commission, it has long been a regulated industry in the sense that its members have been systematically protected against the operation of normal economic forces. The de facto exemption from the antitrust laws that the industry enjoyed until the late 1970s permitted many private arrangements that effectively foreclosed price competition. Over a long period, the medical profession, claiming special expertise and high ethical principles, succeeded in establishing its cultural authority and its political influence and in preempting decision-making authority over a wide variety of economically important matters. In addition, organized providers, by directly controlling or otherwise influencing the nature and behavior of health insurers, were able to insulate themselves from cost pressures that would normally be transmitted from the demand side of the market. Providers succeeded in establishing in law, in the operation of public and private financing plans, and in the public mind their preferred view of the health care sector as a monolithic self-regulating system, not a competitive industry.

A common feature of most industries subject to comprehensive economic regulation is cross-subsidization of some services out of monopoly returns earned by the regulated firms on other business. To ensure that regulated firms can generate the excess revenues needed for such internal subsidies, regulation must protect them against competition by maintaining entry controls and prohibitions against price cutting. The quid pro quo for these protections is the regulated firms' willingness to plow at least some of their profits back into serving other customers at prices below the cost of service. Some, though certainly not all, of the services supported by such cross-subsidies would be deemed vital by society and would be discontinued or not adequately provided if the subsidy were removed.

The cross-subsidies that regulation fosters are financed by what is in effect a hidden tax paid by one group of consumers and earmarked for the benefit of others. This method of redistributing income and financing public services has been called taxation by regulation, and it is in such widespread use that it is hard to argue that it is anything but a legitimate exercise of governmental power.[9] Nevertheless, it is worth observing that the incidence of the "tax" may be quite inequitable and that the redistribution of income is not necessarily always in the direction of the less well off. Moreover, the usual constitutional steps for levying a tax are bypassed, and neither the need for the particular subsidy nor its amount is established through the normal process of legislative authorization and appropriation. Public officials may also have little occasion to monitor expenditures or the performance of the subsidized tasks. Although worse forms of financing public services can be imagined, taxation by regulation cannot be regarded as an optimal means of defining and meeting public objectives.

Cross-subsidies in the health care industry are a clear instance of taxation by regulation. Indeed, they may constitute the most entrenched, most extravagant, and least closely supervised government-tolerated use of private monopoly to generate resources for public purposes anywhere in the U.S. economy. By the same token, the destruction of this system of internal subsidies by increased cost-consciousness and competition may threaten dislocations and hardships more serious than any that have been associated with deregulation in other industries. The issues that must be addressed in deciding whether to let market forces continue to take hold in the hospital industry are thus very similar to those that have arisen in other deregulation debates and must be taken at least as seriously.

To be precise, of course, the specific policy question is not whether to deregulate the health care industry but whether to "reregulate" it. Just as beneficiaries of internal subsidies in other regulated industries have routinely made common cause with the providers of subsidized services in opposing deregulation, a coalition of health care interests now supports explicit regulation of hospitals as a way of replacing old bulwarks against competition that are rapidly crumbling.

Havighurst, The Debate over Health Care Cost–Containment Regulation: The Issues and the Interests, in J. Meyer ed., Incentives vs. Controls in Health Policy: Broadening the Debate 9, 15–18 (American Enterprise Institute for Public Policy Research, 1985). For a study of the economic

9. Richard A. Posner, "Taxation by Regulation," *Bell Journal of Economics and Management Science*, vol.2 (1971), p. 22.

theory and empirical evidence of differential pricing in health care, see M. Morrissey, Cost Shifting in Health Care: Separating Evidence from Rhetoric (1994).

5. In the remainder of this section, the student will suddenly confront the complexity of modern health care law as well as the complexity of the modern system for financing health care. In studying the difficult *Travelers* case, the next case reproduced below, consider how it relates to the subject of this chapter.

INTRODUCTORY NOTE ON ERISA

The *Travelers* case involves the federal Employee Retirement Income Security Act of 1974 (ERISA), as amended, 29 U.S.C. § 1001 et seq. (1994), and, in particular, section 514(a) thereof, 29 U.S.C. § 1144(a) (1994). Section 514(a) states that ERISA "shall supersede any and all State laws insofar as they may now or hereafter relate to any employee benefit plan * * *." Because this preemptive legislation has important consequences in other contexts to be encountered later in these materials, the student should begin to understand how it may affect state law governing various aspects of the health care industry. Although the *Travelers* case interprets ERISA to leave the states more regulatory freedom with respect to health care than they were previously thought to have, ERISA remains a serious impediment to many state reforms addressing the problem of uncompensated care and the uninsured. The student will see at later points how ERISA also bars other state regulatory initiatives and many lawsuits that aggrieved private parties might wish to bring against employers or organized health plans under state law.

ERISA was enacted in 1974 in response to rapid growth in the number and size of employee benefit plans and to some highly publicized instances of fraud and mismanagement of pension funds. Its effect was to extend preemptive federal regulation to "employee benefit plans"—specifically, to "employee pension benefit plans" (which provide retirement income) and "employee welfare benefit plans" (which provide benefits for incidents of illness, accident, disability, death, or unemployment). The stated purpose of ERISA's preemptive provisions was to assure large employers having workers in several states that they would face uniform federal requirements rather than a myriad of differing regulatory rules and other requirements. See Shaw v. Delta Air Lines, 463 U.S. 85, 105 n. 25 (1983) ("ERISA's comprehensive preemption of state law was meant to minimize [state] interference with the administration of employee benefit plans").

A striking feature of ERISA for present purposes is that it was not enacted as a health care measure at all. In the 1970s, nearly all private health coverage took the form of private health insurance purchased by employers from nonprofit Blue Cross and Blue Shield plans or from commercial health insurers. ERISA was specifically designed not to interfere with the business of insurance or with state regulation thereof. Thus, § 514(b) makes an exception (the so-called "saving clause") from the preemption provision of § 514(a) for state laws that regulate insurance. As summarized by the Supreme Court in a 1987 case, the "pure mechanics" of ERISA's preemption provisions are as follows: "If a state law 'relate[s] to ... employee benefit plan[s],' it is preempted. The saving clause excepts from the pre-emption clause laws that 'regulat[e] insurance.' The deemer clause makes clear that a state law that 'purport[s] to regulate insurance' cannot deem an employee benefit plan to be an insurance company." Pilot Life Ins. Co. v. Dedeaux, 481 U.S. 41, 45 (1987). Under this statutory scheme, ERISA had virtually no effect on employer-purchased health insurance in the 1970s.

Reflecting its assumption that health coverage would continue to be governed by state insurance law, Congress did not conceive ERISA's regulatory scheme with health benefits particularly in mind. Instead, it designed ERISA principally to govern the establishment and administration of pension and welfare funds, setting uniform standards for participation, funding, vesting, disclosure, and reporting and for the conduct of fiduciaries. Thus, ERISA did not even purport to provide a federal substitute for state laws and regulations specifically aimed at the health care industry.

ERISA eventually proved, however, to have important unintended consequences in the health care field. One of its main effects was, in time, to induce nearly all employers large enough to do so to self-insure their employees' health benefits, most often with the help of a so-called "third-party administrator" (TPA) or an insurance company providing "administrative services only" (ASO). The inducement to self-insure was inherent in ERISA's preemptive provisions, which permit self-insured plans alone to escape both the burdens of state insurance regulation and the impact of other state laws applicable to health insurers. See, e.g., *Pilot Life*, supra (state's common-law tort remedy for bad-faith breaches of contract held preempted because it was not so specifically directed at insurers as to be a state law that "regulates insurance," which would be preserved from preemption by ERISA's saving clause); Metropolitan Life Ins. Co. v. Massachusetts, 471 U.S. 724 (1985) (state's mandate that insurers cover mental health needs held insurance regulation not preempted by ERISA; note that such mandates directed at employers *are* preempted); Insurance Board Under Social Ins. Plan of Bethlehem Steel Corp. v. Muir, 819 F.2d 408 (3d Cir.1987) (state held barred from regulating the practices of insurers serving self-insured employers on an ASO basis). The opportunity to escape not only the regulatory burdens of state law but also state premium taxes applicable to health insurers proved an irresistible incentive for employers to switch to self-insurance. As a result, approximately 70% of the roughly 160 million Americans covered by employer-sponsored health plans are in self-insured plans enjoying the benefits of ERISA (including relief from some $3 billion per year in premium taxes).

Although employers have clearly benefited from escaping state taxes and legal constraints, some would argue that the resulting legal regime applicable to the design and administration of employee health benefits is incomplete and inadequate to deal with many issues and with many grievances requiring legal redress. To be sure, ERISA was originally not expected to replace state regulation of health plans and benefits, and Congress has so far not seen fit either to remove ERISA as an impediment to state action or to fill the resulting vacuum by establishing a comprehensive regulatory regime of its own. One might therefore conclude that a vital part of American health care is underregulated or inadequately policed. Nevertheless, the absence of comprehensive state or federal regulation may have been, in some respects at least, a blessing in disguise. Indeed, the revolution that has occurred in American health care since the late 1970s might not have been possible if ERISA-protected health plans had not been free from regulatory restraints and thus able to adopt innovative approaches to the design and administration of health benefits. Later materials will allow the student to draw conclusions on ERISA's overall impact and on whether there is any need to strengthen legal oversight of employer-sponsored health plans.

Although ERISA preemption has undoubtedly enabled many employers to lower the cost of providing health coverage for their workers, the need for an employer to self-insure health benefits in order to qualify for ERISA preemption has limited the value of ERISA to small employers. Employers that are too small to self-insure must obtain coverage for their employees, if at all, from a health insurer or HMO that is subject to state regulatory requirements that may make the cost of coverage prohibitive for some of them. In fact, many small employers do not offer health coverage of any kind, leaving their workers among the large (and increasing) number of uninsured Americans.

The following case, in addition to presenting a particular state's strategy in providing otherwise uncompensated care for its uninsured citizens, illustrates how ERISA, although not intended by Congress to have much effect on health care as such, has become a major factor in many state efforts to reform health care at the local level.

New York State Conference of Blue Cross & Blue Shield Plans v. Travelers Insurance Co.

Supreme Court of the United States, 1995.
514 U.S. 645, 115 S.Ct. 1671, 131 L.Ed.2d 695.

■ JUSTICE SOUTER delivered the opinion of the Court.

A New York statute requires hospitals to collect surcharges from patients covered by a commercial insurer but not from patients insured by a Blue Cross/Blue Shield plan, and it subjects certain health maintenance organizations (HMOs) to surcharges that vary with the number of Medicaid recipients each enrolls. N.Y.Pub.Health Law § 2807–c (McKinney 1993). This case calls for us to decide whether [ERISA] pre-empts the state provisions for surcharges on bills of patients whose commercial insurance coverage is purchased by employee health-care plans governed by ERISA, and for surcharges on HMOs insofar as their membership fees are paid by an ERISA plan. We hold that the provisions for surcharges do not "relate to" employee benefit plans within the meaning of ERISA's pre-emption provision and accordingly suffer no pre-emption.

I

A

New York's Prospective Hospital Reimbursement Methodology (NYPHRM) regulates hospital rates for all in-patient care, except for services provided to Medicare beneficiaries. The scheme calls for patients to be charged not for the cost of their individual treatment, but for the average cost of treating the patient's medical problem, as classified under one or another of 794 Diagnostic Related Groups (DRGs). [The student will encounter another variety of "DRGs"—diagnosis-related groups—in connection with the Medicare program.—Eds.] The charges allowable in accordance with DRG classifications are adjusted for a specific hospital to reflect its particular operating costs, capital investments, bad debts, costs of charity care and the like.

Patients with Blue Cross/Blue Shield coverage, Medicaid patients, and HMO participants are billed at a hospital's DRG rate. Others, however, are not. Patients served by commercial insurers providing in-patient hospital coverage on an expense-incurred basis, by self-insured funds directly reimbursing hospitals, and by certain workers' compensation, volunteer firefighters' benefit, ambulance workers' benefit, and no-fault motor vehicle insurance funds, must be billed at the DRG rate plus a 13% surcharge to be retained by the hospital. For the year ending March 31, 1993, moreover, hospitals were required to bill commercially insured patients for a further 11% surcharge to be turned over to the State, with the result that these patients were charged 24% more than the DRG rate.

New York law also imposes a surcharge on HMOs, which varies depending on the number of eligible Medicaid recipients an HMO has enrolled, but which may run as high as 9% of the aggregate monthly charges paid by an HMO for its members' in-patient hospital care. This assessment is not an increase in the rates to be paid by an HMO to hospitals, but a direct payment by the HMO to the State's general fund.

B

ERISA's comprehensive regulation of employee welfare and pension benefit plans extends to those that provide "medical, surgical, or hospital care or benefits" for plan participants or their beneficiaries "through the purchase of insurance or otherwise." The federal statute does not go about protecting plan participants and their beneficiaries by requiring employers to provide any given set of minimum benefits, but instead controls the administration of benefit plans, as by imposing reporting and disclosure mandates, participation and vesting requirements, funding standards, and fiduciary responsibilities for plan administrators. It envisions administrative oversight, imposes criminal sanctions, and establishes a comprehensive civil enforcement scheme. It also pre-empts some state law.

Section 514(a) provides that ERISA "shall supersede any and all State laws insofar as they . . . relate to any employee benefit plan" covered by the statute, although pre-emption stops short of "any law of any State which regulates insurance." (This exception for insurance regulation is itself limited, however, by the provision that an employee welfare benefit plan may not "be deemed to be an insurance company or other insurer . . . or to be engaged in the business of insurance. . . .") Finally, ERISA saves from pre-emption "any generally applicable criminal law of a State."

C

On the claimed authority of ERISA's general preemption provision, several commercial insurers, acting as fiduciaries of ERISA plans they administer, joined with their trade associations to bring actions against state officials in United States District Court seeking to invalidate the 13%, 11%, and 9% surcharge statutes. * * * The District Court consolidated the actions and granted summary judgment to the plaintiffs. The court found that although the surcharges "do not directly increase a plan's costs or [a]ffect the level of benefits to be offered" there could be "little doubt that the [s]urcharges at issue will have a significant effect on the commercial insurers and HMOs which do or could provide coverage for ERISA plans and thus lead, at least indirectly, to an increase in plan costs." It found that the "entire justification for the [s]urcharges is premised on that exact result—that the [s]urcharges will increase the cost of obtaining medical insurance through any source other than the Blues to a sufficient extent that customers will switch their coverage to and ensure the economic viability of the Blues." The District Court concluded that this effect on choices by ERISA plans was enough to trigger pre-emption under § 514(a) and that the surcharges were not saved by § 514(b) as regulating insurance. The District Court accordingly enjoined enforcement of "those surcharges against any commercial insurers or HMOs in connection with their coverage of . . . ERISA plans."

The Court of Appeals for the Second Circuit affirmed, relying on our decisions in Shaw v. Delta Air Lines, Inc., 463 U.S. 85 (1983), and District of Columbia v. Greater Washington Board of Trade, 506 U.S. 125 (1992), holding that ERISA's pre-emption clause must be read broadly to reach any state law having a connection with, or reference to, covered employee benefit plans. * * *

The Court of Appeals agreed with the trial court that the surcharges were meant to increase the costs of certain insurance and health care by HMOs, and held that this "purposeful interference with the choices that ERISA plans make for health care coverage . . . is sufficient to constitute [a] 'connection with' ERISA plans" triggering preemption. The court's conclusion, in sum, was that "the three surcharges 'relate to' ERISA because they impose a significant economic burden on commercial insurers and HMOs" and therefore "have an impermissible impact on ERISA plan structure and administration." In the light of its conclusion that the surcharge statutes were not otherwise saved by any applicable exception, the court held them pre-empted. It recognized the apparent conflict between its conclusion and the decision of the Third Circuit in United Wire, Metal and Machine Health and Welfare Fund v. Morristown Memorial Hosp., 995 F.2d 1179 (1993), which held that New Jersey's similar rate setting statute "does not relate to the plans in a way that triggers ERISA's preemption clause." We granted certiorari to resolve this conflict, and now reverse and remand.

II

Our past cases have recognized that the Supremacy Clause, U.S. Const., Art. VI, may entail pre-emption of state law either by express provision, by implication, or by a conflict between federal and state law. And yet, despite the variety of these opportunities for federal preeminence, we have never assumed lightly that Congress has derogated state regulation, but instead have addressed claims of pre-emption with the starting presumption that Congress does not intend to supplant state law. Indeed, in cases like this one, where federal law is said to bar state action in fields of traditional state regulation, we have worked on the "assumption that the historic police powers of the States were not to be superseded by the Federal Act unless that was the clear and manifest purpose of Congress."

Since pre-emption claims turn on Congress's intent, we begin as we do in any exercise of statutory construction with the text of the provision in question, and move on, as need be, to the structure and purpose of the Act in which it occurs. The governing text of ERISA is clearly expansive. Section 514(a) marks for pre-emption "all state laws insofar as they ... relate to any employee benefit plan" covered by ERISA, and one might be excused for wondering, at first blush, whether the words of limitation ("insofar as they ... relate") do much limiting. If "relate to" were taken to extend to the furthest stretch of its indeterminacy, then for all practical purposes pre-emption would never run its course, for "[r]eally, universally, relations stop nowhere," H. James, Roderick Hudson xli (New York ed., World's Classics 1980). But that, of course, would be to read Congress's words of limitation as mere sham, and to read the presumption against pre-emption out of the law whenever Congress speaks to the matter with generality. That said, we have to recognize that our prior attempt to construe the phrase "relate to" does not give us much help drawing the line here.

In *Shaw*, we explained that "[a] law 'relates to' an employee benefit plan, in the normal sense of the phrase, if it has a connection with or reference to such a plan." The latter alternative, at least, can be ruled out. The surcharges are imposed upon patients and HMOs, regardless of whether the commercial coverage or membership, respectively, is ultimately secured by an ERISA plan, private purchase, or otherwise, with the consequence that the surcharge statutes cannot be said to make "reference to" ERISA plans in any manner. But this still leaves us to question whether the surcharge laws have a "connection with" the ERISA plans, and here an uncritical literalism is no more help than in trying to construe "relate to." For the same reasons that infinite relations cannot be the measure of pre-emption, neither can infinite connections. We simply must go beyond the unhelpful text and the frustrating difficulty of defining its key term, and look instead to the objectives of the ERISA statute as a guide to the scope of the state law that Congress understood would survive.

A

As we have said before, § 514 indicates Congress's intent to establish the regulation of employee welfare benefit plans "as exclusively a federal concern." We have found that in passing § 514(a), Congress intended "to ensure that plans and plan sponsors would be subject to a uniform body of benefits law; the goal was to minimize the administrative and financial burden of complying with conflicting directives among States or between States and the Federal Government ..., [and to prevent] the potential for conflict in substantive law ... requiring the tailoring of plans and employer conduct to the peculiarities of the law of each jurisdiction." Ingersoll–Rand Co. v. McClendon, 498 U.S. 133, 142 (1990). * * * The basic thrust of the pre-emption clause, then, was to avoid a multiplicity of regulation in order to permit the nationally uniform administration of employee benefit plans.

Accordingly in *Shaw*, for example, we had no trouble finding that New York's "Human Rights Law, which prohibit[ed] employers from structuring their employee benefit plans in a manner that discriminate[d] on the basis of pregnancy, and [New York's] Disability Benefits Law, which require[d] employers to pay employees specific benefits, clearly 'relate[d] to' benefit plans." These mandates affecting coverage could have been honored only by varying the subjects of a plan's benefits whenever New York law might have applied, or by requiring every plan to provide all beneficiaries with a benefit demanded by New York law if New York law could have been said to require it for any one beneficiary. Similarly, Pennsylvania's law that prohibited "plans from ... requiring reimbursement [from the beneficiary] in the event of recovery from a third party" related to employee benefit plans within the meaning of § 514(a). The law "prohibited plans from being structured in a manner requiring reimbursement in the event of recovery from a third party" and "required plan providers to calculate benefit levels in Pennsylvania based on expected liability conditions that differ from those in States that have not enacted similar antisubrogation legislation," thereby "frustrating plan administrators' continuing obligation to calculate uniform benefit levels nationwide." Pennsylvania employees who recovered in negligence actions against tortfeasors would, by virtue of the state law, in effect have been entitled to benefits in excess of what plan administrators intended to provide, and in excess of what the plan provided to employees in other States. Along the same lines, New Jersey could not prohibit plans from setting workers' compensation payments off against employees' retirement benefits or pensions, because doing so would prevent plans from using a method of calculating benefits permitted by federal law. In each of these cases, ERISA pre-empted state laws that mandated employee benefit structures or their administration. Elsewhere, we have held that state laws providing alternate enforcement mechanisms also relate to ERISA plans, triggering pre-emption.

B

Both the purpose and the effects of the New York surcharge statutes distinguish them from the examples just given. The charge differentials have been justified on the ground that the Blues pay the hospitals promptly and efficiently and, more importantly, provide coverage for many subscribers whom the commercial insurers would reject as unacceptable risks. The Blues' practice, called open enrollment, has consistently been cited as the principal reason for charge differentials, whether the differentials resulted from voluntary negotiation between hospitals and payers as was the case prior to the NYPHRM system, or were created by the surcharges as is the case now. See, e.g., * * * Thorpe, Does All–Payer Rate Setting Work? The Case of the New York Prospective Hospital Reimbursement Methodology, 12 J. Health Politics, Policy, & Law 391, 402 (1987).[5] Since the surcharges are presumably passed on at least in part to those who purchase commercial insurance or HMO membership, their effects follow from their purpose. Although there is no evidence that the surcharges will drive every health insurance consumer to the Blues, they do make the Blues more attractive (or less unattractive) as insurance alternatives and thus have an indirect economic effect on choices made by insurance buyers, including ERISA plans.

An indirect economic influence, however, does not bind plan administrators to any particular choice and thus function as a regulation of an ERISA plan itself; commercial insurers and HMOs may still offer more attractive packages than the Blues. Nor does the indirect influence of the surcharges preclude uniform administrative practice or the provision of a uniform interstate benefit package if a plan wishes to provide one. It simply bears on the costs of benefits and the relative costs of competing insurance to provide them. It is an influence that can affect a plan's shopping decisions, but it does not affect the fact that any plan will shop for the best deal it can get, surcharges or no surcharges.

There is, indeed, nothing remarkable about surcharges on hospital bills, or their effects on overall cost to the plans and the relative attractiveness of certain insurers. Rate variations among hospital providers are

5. Although respondents argue that the surcharges have become superfluous now that all insurers have become subject to certain open enrollment requirements, it is not our responsibility to review the continuing substantive rationale for the surcharges. Even so, the surcharges may well find support in an effort to compensate the Blues for the current makeup of their insurance pool, which presumably continues to reflect their longer history of open enrollment policies. See J. Corcoran, Superintendent of Insurance, Position Paper of New York State Insurance Department on Inpatient Reimbursement Rate Differential Provided Non–Profit Insurers 8 (1984) ("If there is any possibility of an abrupt abandonment of the current hospital discount, consideration should be given to the past history of health insurance enrollment in New York which has left the Blue Cross/Blue Shield Plans with a core of uninsurables obtained over the years and the ongoing liability resulting from that enrollment").

accepted examples of cost variation, since hospitals have traditionally "attempted to compensate for their financial shortfalls by adjusting their price . . . schedules for patients with commercial health insurance." Thorpe, supra, at 394. Charge differentials for commercial insurers, even prior to state regulation, "varied dramatically across regions, ranging from 13 to 36 percent," presumably reflecting the geographically disparate burdens of providing for the uninsured. Id., at 400; see id., at 398–399.

If the common character of rate differentials even in the absence of state action renders it unlikely that ERISA pre-emption was meant to bar such indirect economic influences under state law, the existence of other common state action with indirect economic effects on a plan's costs leaves the intent to pre-empt even less likely. Quality standards, for example, set by the State in one subject area of hospital services but not another would affect the relative cost of providing those services over others and, so, of providing different packages of health insurance benefits. Even basic regulation of employment conditions will invariably affect the cost and price of services.

Quality control and workplace regulation, to be sure, are presumably less likely to affect premium differentials among competing insurers, but that does not change the fact that such state regulation will indirectly affect what an ERISA or other plan can afford or get for its money. Thus, in the absence of a more exact guide to intended pre-emption than § 514, it is fair to conclude that mandates for rate differentials would not be pre-empted unless other regulation with indirect effects on plan costs would be superseded as well. The bigger the package of regulation with indirect effects that would fall on the respondent's reading of § 514, the less likely it is that federal regulation of benefit plans was intended to eliminate state regulation of health care costs.

Indeed, to read the pre-emption provision as displacing all state laws affecting costs and charges on the theory that they indirectly relate to ERISA plans that purchase insurance policies or HMO memberships that would cover such services, would effectively read the limiting language in § 514(a) out of the statute * * *. While Congress's extension of pre-emption to all "state laws relating to benefit plans" was meant to sweep more broadly than "state laws dealing with the subject matters covered by ERISA[,] reporting, disclosure, fiduciary responsibility, and the like," *Shaw*, 463 U.S., at 98, and n. 19, nothing in the language of the Act or the context of its passage indicates that Congress chose to displace general health care regulation, which historically has been a matter of local concern.

In sum, cost-uniformity was almost certainly not an object of pre-emption, just as laws with only an indirect economic effect on the relative costs of various health insurance packages in a given State are a far cry from those "conflicting directives" from which Congress meant to insulate ERISA plans. See *Ingersoll-Rand*, 498 U.S., at 142. Such state laws leave plan administrators right where they would be in any case, with the responsibility to choose the best overall coverage for the money. We therefore conclude that such state laws do not bear the requisite "connection with" ERISA plans to trigger pre-emption.

* * *

D

It remains only to speak further on a point already raised, that any conclusion other than the one we draw would bar any state regulation of hospital costs. The basic DRG system (even without any surcharge), like any other interference with the hospital services market, would fall on a theory that all laws with indirect economic effects on ERISA plans are pre-empted under § 514(a). This would be an unsettling result and all the more startling because several States, including New York, regulated hospital charges to one degree or another at the time ERISA was passed. And yet there is not so much as a hint in ERISA's legislative history or anywhere else that Congress intended to squelch these state efforts.

Kind of a slippery slope thing –

Even more revealing is the National Health Planning and Resources Development Act of 1974 (NHPRDA) [repealed in 1986], which was adopted by the same Congress that passed ERISA, and only months later. The NHPRDA sought to encourage and help fund state responses to growing health care costs and the widely diverging availability of health services. * * * The scheme called for designating state health planning and development agencies in qualifying States, [which agencies] would be eligible for federal funding, including grants "[f]or the purpose of demonstrating the effectiveness of State Agencies regulating rates for the provision of health care . . . within the State."

* * * To interpret ERISA's pre-emption provision as broadly as respondent suggests, would have rendered the entire NHPRDA utterly nugatory, since it would have left States without the authority to do just what Congress was expressly trying to induce them to do by enacting the NHPRDA. Given that the NHPRDA was enacted after ERISA and by the same Congress, it just makes good sense to reject such an interpretation.

III

That said, we do not hold today that ERISA pre-empts only direct regulation of ERISA plans, nor could we do that with fidelity to the views expressed in our prior opinions on the matter. We acknowledge that a state law might produce such acute, albeit indirect, economic effects, by intent or otherwise, as to force an ERISA plan to adopt a certain scheme of substantive coverage or effectively restrict its choice of insurers, and that such a state law might indeed be pre-empted under § 514. But as we have shown, New York's surcharges do not fall into either category; they affect only indirectly the relative prices of insurance policies, a result no different from myriad state laws in areas traditionally subject to local regulation, which Congress could not possibly have intended to eliminate.

The judgment of the Court of Appeals is therefore reversed and the case remanded for further proceedings consistent with this opinion.

NOTES AND QUESTIONS

1. Be prepared to describe the New York regulatory scheme in detail. Can you discern its rationale and how the state's policy relates to the material already covered in this chapter?

2. In a decision following the *Travelers* case, the Supreme Court held that New York, seeking "additional revenue to reduce the [Medicaid] program deficit," could impose a gross receipts tax on hospitals, including hospitals owned and operated by an ERISA plan. De Buono v. NYSA–ILA Medical and Clinical Services Fund, 117 S.Ct. 1747, 1749, 1753 (1997) ("Any state tax, or other law, that increases the cost of providing benefits to covered employees will have some effect on the administration of ERISA plans, but that simply cannot mean that every state law with such an effect [even a direct effect, as in the case at bar] is preempted * * *.").

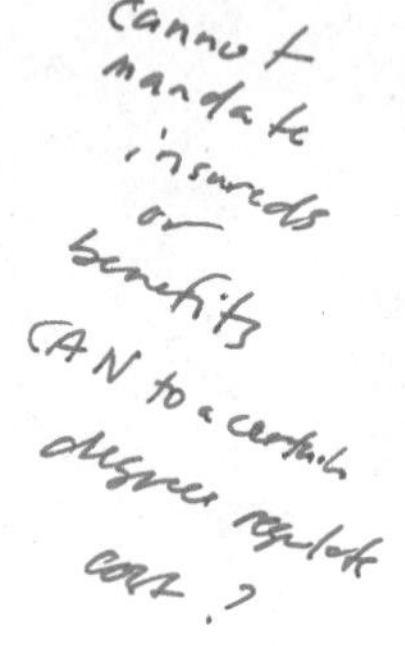

3. After *Travelers* and *De Buono*, could a state require a self-insured employer to participate along with other health insurers in an insurance pool extending coverage to uninsurables? See General Split Corp. v. Mitchell, 523 F.Supp. 427 (E.D.Wis.1981) (preemption found). It seems clear that states cannot, under ERISA, mandate employer provision of health coverage. See Standard Oil Co. of California v. Agsalud, 633 F.2d 760 (9th Cir.1980), affirmed mem. 454 U.S. 801 (1981) (invalidating Hawaii Prepaid Health Care Act, for which Congress subsequently enacted a special exception).

NOTES AND QUESTIONS ON STATE REGULATION OF HOSPITAL RATES

1. *History of Hospital Rate Regulation.* As the opinion in *Travelers* observes, a number of states have experimented with some form of mandatory revenue controls or rate setting for hospitals. A study published in 1981 reported as follows:

> By the end of 1980 eight states had active mandatory hospital rate regulation programs administered by a state agency. Colorado had such a program, but it was terminated in 1980. Several states have established rate review agencies, whose powers are largely advisory. * * * [T]he institutional structure and methods used to regulate hospital rates vary enormously from state to state, and both the coverage and sophistication of these programs have increased over time. These formal state programs are supplemented by "voluntary" private rate review programs, generally implemented by Blue Cross plans, in 12 states. * * *
>
> * * * [H]ospital associations have been * * * cautious in their attitudes toward formal state regulation of hospital payments. They correctly view such legislation as having the potential to impose severe financial constraints on hospital behavior. * * * The hospital association in New York has expressed extreme dissatisfaction with the New York regulatory program because it has placed severe financial burdens on the hospitals. Of course, this is exactly what a program that imposes severe budgetary constraints should be expected to do.

The state programs differ considerably in terms of organizational structure, methods of controlling reimbursement rates, types of payers covered, resources devoted to regulatory efforts, and the extent of interaction and cooperation with providers and insurers.

P. Joskow, Controlling Hospital Costs: The Role of Government Regulation 113–16 (1981).

The high-water mark of the movement to regulate hospital rates was a proposal by the Carter administration under which the federal government would have undertaken to regulate revenue growth in all hospitals. H.R. 6575, 95th Cong., 1st Sess. (1977). That proposal was viewed by its proponents as preferable, for egalitarian reasons, to government measures to control only the costs of public programs of health care financing (e.g., Medicare and Medicaid). It was also envisioned as an essential part of the infrastructure that had to be in place before a system of national health insurance (expanding Medicare to the entire population, for example) could be enacted. The Carter bill was defeated in the House of Representatives in 1979, however. That action, more than any other single event, crystalized Congress's resistance to domination of the health care system by the federal government. Defeat of the Carter initiative was followed in the 95th Congress by a spate of proposals designed to strengthen market forces in the health care sector. It is historically significant that the watershed events heralding a more market-oriented policy toward health care in the United States occurred before, not after, the advent of the conservative Reagan administration.

2. *Medicare and State Rate Setting.* Since 1982, federal law has provided that, under certain circumstances, the Medicare program would pay hospitals according to state-established rates rather than under its regular rules for determining hospital payments. 42 U.S.C. § 1395ww(c)(1) (1994). By obtaining a so-called "Medicare waiver," a state could engage in what was referred to as "all-payer" rate regulation. Specifically, a state could set payment rates for all third-party payers, including Medicare and Medicaid, as long as it "provided satisfactory assurances as to the equitable treatment under the system of all entities (including Federal and State programs) that pay hospitals for inpatient hospital services, of hospital employees, and of hospital patients." In a significant departure from a purely regulatory strategy, however, the federal statute also required that a state regulatory system "not preclude an [HMO or competitive medical plan, as defined] from negotiating directly with hospitals with respect to the organization's rate of payment for inpatient services." The statute also made it clear that the Secretary was *required* to grant a waiver to any state all-payer prospective payment system that met the statutory requirements. This mandate was introduced by Congress because the Reagan administration did not appear anxious to encourage state regulation by granting waivers.

A final condition for obtaining a Medicare waiver was that "the amount of payments made under this subchapter under such [state] system will not exceed the amount of payments which would otherwise have been made under this subchapter not using such system." This final condition caused such high-cost states with waivers as New York and Massachusetts to allow them to lapse. In such states, regulation that squeezed hospitals enough to protect Medicare against higher costs than it would incur under the new prospective payment system would have seriously jeopardized the hospitals' financial health. At the same time, a low-cost state (e.g., Maine) would have found that getting Medicare to pay the same cost-based, state-set rates as other payers might mean forgoing income that would otherwise have been available to the state and its hospitals. Of the few states that retained rate-setting regulation through the 1980s, only Maryland retained its Medicare waiver.

3. *Current Status.* Nearly all the state programs for regulating hospital rates or revenue growth were repealed by the early 1990s. One of the two remaining ones was New York's, which was itself repealed in 1996. The new legislation in New York eliminated the $4 billion in annual surcharges on hospital bills that were contested in the *Travelers* case but added two new taxes: a tax on health insurance policies to finance graduate medical education (that is, residency programs, on which many New York hospitals depend heavily in providing indigent care) and a tax on hospital services to finance care for the poor and uninsured. Under the new plan, "private insurance companies would be able to negotiate their fees with hospitals, a right that only managed care companies currently have." Levy, New Era in Albany Hospital–Rate Plan, N.Y.Times, July 2, 1996, at A1, col. 6 (predicting "a seismic shift in health care, affecting $16 billion in hospital services" and reporting policymakers' belief "that lifting price controls would set market forces loose in the industry, driving costs down for insurers and, eventually, for patients as well").

The repeal of the New York legislation left Maryland as the only state with a program for regulating hospital charges. For arguments in favor of reintroducing rate regulation in the mid–1990s, see Wallack et al., Redefining Rate Regulation in a Competitive Environment, 21 J. Health Pol., Pol'y & L. 489 (1996).

4. *Changing Rationales; Cost Shifting.* It is possible to see the primary concern supporting hospital rate and revenue regulation in the 1980s (and today, to the extent it is still advocated) as being not that price competition is unworkable in the hospital industry, as was alleged in the 1970s, but that it works altogether too well. Some payers, including the federal government and aggressive private purchasers, have succeeded in forcing providers to cut their prices in return for the privilege of treating their beneficiaries—with the result either that other payers must pay higher prices or that hospitals must cease cross-subsidizing desirable services to the same extent as in the past. All-payer regulation can thus be supported as a way of maintaining the health care system's ability to finance its unremunerative good works and sparing government from the necessity to impose explicit taxes to accomplish the same objectives. How promising and desirable is the strategy of financing indigent care by "re-regulating" health care and attempting to curb fast-moving competitive developments?

Is it possible that private purchasers will find ways to steer patients to institutions that, because of their location, clientele, and policies, do not impose a hidden tax on their customers?

How seriously should one take complaints about cost shifting? Is it possible to see cost shifting by hospitals as a desirable development, because it revealed how some payers—mostly commercial health insurers—previously lacked the means or the willingness to steer patients to low-cost institutions and to resist providers' overcharges? By always being available to pick up any cost that a hospital could not recover elsewhere, such payers of last resort long represented an important leak in the public's defenses against runaway health care costs. At one time it was possible to view complaints about cost shifting as an effort by producers of an inefficient product to obtain governmental protection against competition. Now that all payers have finally discovered ways of negotiating effectively with hospitals, it is the hospitals themselves that may prefer regulation as a way of preserving their ability to cross subsidize uncompensated care, medical education, and other unremunerative activities they regard as desirable.

5. *Is Rate Regulation Effective?* A number of older studies produced evidence that rate and revenue control programs can reduce the rate of increase of hospital expenditures. E.g., Coelen & Sullivan, An Analysis of the Effects of Prospective Reimbursement Programs on Hospital Expenditures, Health Care Fin. Rev., Winter, 1981, at 1; Biles, Schramm & Atkinson, Hospital Cost Inflation Under State Rate–Setting Programs, 303 New Eng. J. Med. 664 (1980); Sloan & Steinwald, Effects of Regulation on Hospital Costs and Input Use, 23 J. Law & Econ. 81 (1980). Questions persisted, however, as to the effects of particular programs, calling attention to issues of methodology and political support for aggressive cost containment. See, e.g., Morrisey, Sloan & Mitchell, State Rate Setting: An Analysis of Some Unresolved Issues, Health Affs., Summer 1983, at 36, 45 ("there have been only two clear direct hits at a moving cost-containment target—New Jersey and New York").

A more recent study compared cost trends from 1980 to 1991 in California, which had pursued a competition-based managed-care strategy since the early 1980s (when legislation first expressly authorized both private insurers and the state Medicaid program to contract selectively with providers), with trends in the four states employing the most stringent regulatory strategies for health care cost containment: Md., N.Y., Mass., and N.J. (The latter two states discontinued regulation in 1988 and 1992, respectively.) Melnick & Zwanziger, State Health Care Expenditures under Competition and Regulation, 1980 through 1991, 85 Am.J.Pub. Health 1391 (1995). The study focused on cost increases in three categories (hospital services, physician services, and retail drugs), which together account for approximately 70% of all health care expenditures. California, with its procompetitive health care policy, experienced the lowest growth in total per-capita expenditures across all three categories—39%, versus 59% in Md., 85.4% in N.Y., 70.2% in Mass., and 86.4% in N.J. The study also found

> no evidence that health expenditures were shifted from the hospital sector to other sectors in California as a result of competition. Rather, it appears that states with hospital regulatory programs are the ones to show evidence of the so-called "ballooning or unbundling" effect, in which expenditures in the unregulated sectors grew by much more than the national average for many of the regulatory states.

Of the four states employing regulation, only Maryland had a lower percentage growth rate than the national average. Maryland officials claim that hospital costs there are 6% below the national average, having been 25% above that average in 1976.

A commentary on the foregoing study provides some useful perspective:

> California's reduced flow of dollars into hospital, physician, and drug services might mean better efficiency (value for money) without compromises in quality and access, or it might reflect trade-offs on these counts. [Eds.—Note for future reference the authors' premise that "efficiency" involves no "compromises" or "trade-offs."] The growth of competition in California hospital markets has not only forced hospitals to reduce their margins but has also changed the nature of care. Length of stay in California hospitals has dropped so much that California's average hospital stay today is more than 4 days shorter than that of New York, and the number of hospital beds has declined much more sharply in California than in the regulated states or in the nation as a whole. Similarly, a study comparing Minneapolis (a highly competitive market) found major differences in staffing patterns, outpatient use, length of stay, and more. Evidently, competition not only squeezes "excess" revenues from the system faster than do regulators, but it also changes—perhaps "fundamentally"—the behavior of providers in ways whose impact on quality of care is little understood.
>
> Moreover, as Melnick and Zwanziger remark, competition-induced changes in the behavior of providers raise special concerns about access to care for the uninsured and other vulnerable groups. Policymakers exclusively preoccupied with costs may be willing to let more citizens go without coverage, tolerate obstacles to timely care for the uninsured and public clients, refuse fair compensation to hospitals serving the poor, or shift tasks and fiscal burdens to county governments that are ill-prepared to shoulder them. The uninsured proportion of California's population runs about 60% higher than the population-weighted average among the regulated states. Although many uninsured get care in hospital emergency rooms, California hospitals provide relatively little uncompensated care, committing 5.5% of expenses to this purpose in 1991, below the national average of 5.9% and well below the regulated states' population-weighted average of 6.4%. Regulation in the rate-setting states aims at policy objectives that competition may choose to ignore, for example, subsidizing care for high-risk insured people (as in New York), covering care for the uninsured (by means of uncompensated care pools), and leveling the fiscal playing field among better off and worse off hospitals. These may or may not be worthy objectives, and regulation may or may not pursue them

efficiently, but policymakers should weigh them explicitly when pondering the relative merits of competition and regulation.

Glied, Sparer & Brown, Comment: Containing State Health Care Expenditures—The Competition vs. Regulation Debate, 85 Am.J.Pub. Health 1347, 1347–48 (1995). Observing that California was particularly proactive on behalf of competition, the authors observe that "it is misleading to equate 'competition' with 'weak role of government' " (id. at 1348) and question how easy it would be to replicate the California experience in more sparsely populated states or areas or in states with different political or health care institutions. They warn, "Data-based portraits of the health system too often are followed by prescriptive leaps of faith (make markets, not rates) without the benefit of a crucial intervening level of analysis, one that ponders whether and how [political] institutions may explain outcomes and thus shape generalization and replication." Id.

6. *Maryland's Experience with Rate Setting and Uncompensated Care.* Maryland's Health Services Cost Review Commission (HSCRC) has long built into each hospital's allowed charges the anticipated cost to the hospital of providing uncompensated care. In 1992, the HSCRC was authorized to

> adopt regulations establishing alternative methods for financing the reasonable total costs of hospital uncompensated care provided that the alternative methods:
>
> (1) Are in the public interest;
>
> (2) Will equitably distribute the reasonable costs of uncompensated care;
>
> (3) Will fairly determine the cost of reasonable uncompensated care included in hospital rates;
>
> (4) Will continue incentives for hospitals to adopt efficient and effective credit and collection policies; and
>
> (5) Will not result in significantly increasing costs to Medicare or the loss of Maryland's Medicare Waiver * * *.

Md. Ann. Code § 19–207.3 (1990 & Supp. 1995). Although no action was taken under this authority for several years (you should be able to see why), in late 1995 some members of the Maryland Hospital Association proposed that the HSCRC create an Uncompensated Care Pool through an assessment of 1% of gross revenues against all hospitals and an additional assessment against "low uncompensated care [UC] hospitals." The pool would be distributed to high UC hospitals and otherwise applied to meet the needs of the uninsured in Maryland. The MHA Executive Council approved the pool proposal in 1996, observing "that expanding tax revenues [to take care of the uninsured] would be impossible in the current political environment."

Do you see any potential legal objections to the method of financing proposed? What specific forces and interests do you suppose prompted the 1992 legislation in Maryland and the 1995 renewal of pressure to act on it? What significance do you see in the fact that, even though Maryland purports to maintain an all-payer system, it allows any payer to negotiate a lower price with a regulated hospital? How do you suppose the various members of the MHA reacted to this proposal?

NOTES AND QUESTIONS ON THE UNINSURED

1. *Rising Numbers.* The accessibility of costly health services depends heavily on having health insurance or other financial protection. The number of Americans lacking any health coverage, public or private, at any single time was estimated to be as high as 39.7 million in 1993. That number had begun to increase steadily around 1978 and has continued to rise among low-and middle-income groups in the 1990s. Hellander et al., The Growing Epidemic of Uninsurance: New Data on the Health Insurance Coverage of Americans, 25 Intl.J. Health Services 377 (1995). Moreover, the Census Bureau reported in 1996 that, during a 28–month period beginning in early 1992, about 27% of Americans, or 66.6 million people, lacked health insurance for at least one month; approximately 11.9 million people went uninsured during the entire period. Although 87% of full-time workers were insured throughout the period, the percentage dropped to 74% for part-time workers and 58% for persons experiencing one or more job interruptions. Census Bureau, U.S. Dep't of Commerce, Dynamics of Economic Well–Being: Health Insurance 1992–1993 (1996). See also U.S. General Accounting Office, Private Health Insurance: Continued Erosion of Coverage Linked to Cost Pressures (GAO/HEHS–97–122, 1997). Very few individuals have public or private coverage (other than the catastrophic protection provided by the Medicaid program) for one of the costliest health care needs—long-term care.

2. *Who? Why?* Some people may lack health insurance because it is not provided by their employers. Others may become uninsured by aging out of coverage under a parent's policy, by losing or changing employment, by having their coverage cancelled by an insurer, and by the operation of a "pre-existing conditions" clause when assuming new coverage. A hard core of individuals have conditions that render them uninsurable or make the cost of insurance prohibitive. The Prospective Payment Assessment Commission (ProPAC), a legislative-branch agency assisting Congress in monitoring the Medicare program, hospital payment issues, and the general state of American health care, has discussed the prevalence of health insurance as follows:

> [The uninsured are] not necessarily restricted to the unemployed or the poor. In 1989, for example, of 24 million uninsured adults, 18.5 million were employed. Of the 9.2 million uninsured children, only 14% were in households headed by an unemployed person. In addition, about 30 percent of the uninsured had incomes below the poverty line in 1989, but 12 percent had incomes greater than four times the poverty line. Explanations for this lack of coverage are varied and complex. The cost of coverage for small employers and individual employees with certain medical conditions is in many cases prohibitive. Moreover, in some industries, such as agriculture and construction, both the nature of the work and employment

> patterns have meant higher than average proportions of uninsured workers. Further, new accounting requirements [for listing unfunded retirement benefits as a liability on employer balance sheets] will increase the financial pressures on employer-funded post-retirement health benefits (PRHBs). If employers drop PRHBs because of these requirements, the number of uninsured retirees not yet eligible for Medicare benefits may rise.

ProPAC, Medicare and the American Health Care System (Report to Congress, June 1991), reprinted in Medicare & Medicaid Guide, Extra Edition (CCH) No. 658, June 24, 1991, p. 3. On the subject of "PRHBs," ERISA, though enacted for the benefit of employees, does not prevent an employer from terminating retiree health benefits if it has expressly reserved the right to do so. Sprague v. General Motors Corp., 133 F.3d 388 (6th Cir. 1998) (en banc). Retiree coverage has in fact declined in recent years. U.S. General Accounting Office, Retiree Health Insurance: Erosion in Employer-based Health Benefits for Early Retirees (GAO/HEHS-97-150, 1997).

One discussion of firms that do not offer health insurance coverage found that they "tend to be small, are disproportionately represented in retail trade, are more frequently in the South than in other regions, have fewer full-time employees, offer lower-than-average wages, have higher-than-average turnover, and are often unincorporated." Lippert & Wicks, Critical Distinctions: How Firms That Offer Health Benefits Differ From Those That Do Not (Health Insurance Association of America, 1991). The high cost of coverage for individuals and small employment groups reflects in part the problem "adverse selection," which occurs because individuals seeking coverage tend to present greater than average risks and because insurers lack effective, low-cost ways of screening them and accurately pricing their coverage.

Precisely why has the percentage of uninsured Americans increased in the 1980s and 1990s (rather than continuing to decline as national wealth increased)? As noted, the problem is mostly evident in the working population. One possible explanation is that the cost of health insurance rose faster than wages, pricing many persons out of the market. See Kronick, Health Insurance, 1979–89: The Frayed Connection Between Employment and Insurance, 28 Inquiry 318 (1991) (concluding tentatively that "the major reason for the decline in coverage is the increase in medical care prices" and in the price, relative to wages, of health insurance); Hall, Reforming the Health Insurance Market for Small Business, 326 New Eng. J. Med. 565, 568–69 (1992) (noting the "extreme price sensitivity of purchasers in the small-group market").

A relevant question, rarely asked, is why self-employed individuals and low-income workers (through their employers), instead of "going bare," do not buy less extensive, less expensive coverage—truly "bare-bones" insurance. One possible answer is that they find it cheaper (and tolerable) to free-ride on local providers' willingness (or legal obligation) to provide uncompensated care for serious conditions. Another possible explanation is that—for reasons that the student should ponder throughout this course—very low-cost options may simply not be available in the marketplace. Indeed, a possible clue to some of the dilemmas of American health policy may be found in the observation that low-cost options (limiting the quality or availability of desirable care) might not be well received by the American legal system and may therefore not be feasible. In any event, it is a striking fact that the ostensibly "free" market has for some reason failed to offer products to meet the vital needs of some 40 million American consumers, not all of them poor.

3. *Caring for the Uninsured.* No systematic provision has been made for this population, which generally experiences poorer outcomes from such health care as they receive. E.g., Franks, Health Insurance and Mortality: Evidence from a National Cohort, 270 J.A.M.A. 373 (1993); Ayanian, The Relation Between Health Insurance Coverage and Clinical Outcomes among Women with Breast Cancer, 329 New Eng.J.Med. 326 (1993). As earlier materials demonstrate, however, services are frequently available, more or less, to the uninsured through a combination of legal requirements imposed on providers, special state and local programs, and private charity (which government often facilitates by protecting or enhancing the revenue of hospitals providing uncompensated care). The haphazardness and unevenness of the system under which indigent care is currently provided are certainly troublesome features. It is possible, however, that many communities have pieced together a mixed public/private network of protections that comes close to satisfying reasonable expectations. Nevertheless, evaluation is difficult, and it is clear that many communities fall far short of meeting this standard. Also, new financial pressures on hospitals are eroding their capacity to fill gaps that some of them previously filled fairly well. It is reasonable to believe that there is a great deal of unfinished public business here. See generally Smith, Trends in Health Care Coverage and Financing and Their Implications for Policy, 337 New Eng. J. Med. 1000 (1997) (summarizing decline of private insurance and system's ability to finance uncompensated care).

4. *Legislative Approaches.* Both the federal government and the states have adopted or considered numerous incremental measures designed to reduce the number of the underinsured by making private coverage easier to purchase. For example, because many individuals become uninsured as a result of unemployment, divorce from or death of an employed spouse, or exclusion from a parent's policy upon attaining a certain age, 1986 federal legislation (called "COBRA") amended the Internal Revenue Code and ERISA to require firms offering group health coverage to 20 or more employees to ensure that continuation coverage is available to such persons without evidence of insurability and at rates favorable in comparison to individual coverage. (Similar state laws had been preempted by ERISA.) Such incremental measures are distinguishable from truly fundamental reform since they address only the availability of coverage and do nothing to ensure that people will purchase it.

For the most part, the states took the lead on these matters. Although ERISA has blocked measures impacting too directly on self-insured health benefits plans, states have been free to regulate the business of insurance and HMOs in ways that make coverage more available to small employers. Thus, many states have rules requiring health plans to accept all applicants for coverage ("guaranteed issue"), limiting exclusions of pre-existing conditions, and preventing cancellation of policies because of bad experience. States have also addressed the affordability of health coverage by regulating health plan premiums in ways that cause good risks (e.g., low-risk employment groups) to pay premiums higher than anticipated costs and thereby lower the price for poorer risks; the most extreme such regulation, adopted in New York in 1992, requires "open enrollment" of all comers and "community" rating (based on aggregate experience in the area) rather than "experience" rating (based on the actuarially anticipated costs of covering an individual or group). In general, the strategies mentioned here are aimed at breaking down, or at least weakening, the distinction between pure *private* insurance (schemes by which individuals pool risks with others facing similar risks) and *social* insurance (schemes by which poor risks are subsidized by lumping them, under compulsion, with good ones). Note that regulation of this kind, although it increases both the availability and the security of coverage, also raises cost of coverage to those who might have obtained it otherwise. Is this a legitimate method of financing public objectives?

Some states have attempted to make coverage more affordable by lifting, for some purchasers, certain regulatory requirements that allegedly raise the cost of coverage unduly. Responses to coverage offered pursuant to these measures were reportedly disappointing, however. See Families USA, No Sale: The Failure of Barebones Insurance (1993). Other state initiatives have included provision for cooperative purchasing of health coverage by small employers and self-employed individuals; many of these initiatives may be seen as small-scale efforts to apply the principles of "managed competition," a topic noted below. Finally, in addition to enriching their various programs for helping the uninsured by assisting hospitals in the provision of uncompensated care, a number of states have provided subsidies for small employers or for state-sponsored risk pools which serve as the insurer of last resort for persons otherwise uninsurable.

As the uninsured became an object of heightened public concern in the 1990s, it began to appear that major health care reform might be possible at the federal level—just as in the 1960s, when comparable shortcomings of private insurance and public charity in protecting the elderly led to the creation of the Medicare program. Although the health reform movement of 1993–94 ultimately failed, the problems surrounding the uninsured remained on the table in the ensuing Congress, which adopted the Health Insurance Portability and Accountability Act, Pub. L. No. 104–191, 110 Stat. 1936 (1996) (the so-called Kassebaum–Kennedy Act, or HIPAA). This legislation, resembling measures already in place in some states, was a significant effort to make health coverage easier to obtain and harder to lose. It requires insurers to provide coverage that an individual can retain even though he or she loses or switches employment. The act also prohibits group health plans or issuers of group health coverage from setting special conditions for eligibility and from singling out individuals for higher premiums because of their health status, claims experience, medical history, disability, or other factors that might correlate with higher health care costs. Exclusions of care needed for pre-existing conditions may apply only to conditions for which medical advice, diagnosis, or treatment was recommended or received within a six-month period ending on the enrollment date, and such exclusions may not apply for more than twelve months. And a prior period of continuous coverage with one insurer, if uninterrupted for more than 63 days, counts toward the waiting period with another. Finally, limitations for pre-existing conditions generally may not be applied to newborns or to newly adopted children.

The HIPAA also guarantees employers renewability of coverage; requires insurers to make conversion to an individual policy available as an option to participants in group health plans after 18 months; requires plan sponsors to notify participants of reductions in covered services; and amends COBRA to extend coverage for certain disabled persons and to include as qualified beneficiaries children born to or adopted by a covered employee during the continuation period.

Whether the Kassebaum–Kennedy legislation will greatly reduce the number of uninsured Americans may be doubted, since reforms in the market for health coverage will only marginally affect the willingness of employers to offer it or of individuals to purchase it. See Hall, supra (suggesting limited potential of insurance reforms). Even significant subsidies for small employers would not necessarily represent a major step toward universal coverage. See Thorpe et al., Reducing the Number of Uninsured by Subsidizing Employment-based Health Insurance, 267 J.A.M.A. 945 (1992) (estimating that substantial subsidies would not induce more than 16.5% of small uninsured employers to purchase coverage).

SECTION C: INTRODUCTION TO PUBLIC PROGRAMS FOR FINANCING HEALTH CARE

NOTE ON THE SUPPOSITIONAL CONSTITUTIONAL "RIGHT TO HEALTH CARE"

It is sometimes asserted in policy debates that there is a "right to health care." This assertion is usually made in support of proposals to establish a program of national or universal health insurance under which all citizens would be assured the financial means to obtain needed services. Although such a program would create a statutory entitlement to care, some observers in the 1970s hoped to persuade courts to discover a nonstatutory (constitutional) right to receive medical services at public expense.

These observers saw some potential support in the abortion cases, Roe v. Wade, 410 U.S. 113 (1973), and Doe v. Bolton, 410 U.S. 179 (1973). Although these decisions held only that a state could not prohibit a patient from receiving a medically accepted form of treatment, the Court's emphasis on the patient's right to receive a medical service and the physician's right to provide it without governmental interference seemed to raise medical care to a high position in the hierarchy of societal values.

In a few cases, the supposed right of patients to health care was coupled with the physician's alleged right "to administer medical treatment according to his professional judgment" (*Roe v. Wade*, supra, at 165) in order to contest government cost-control measures that had the effect of limiting alleged entitlements under Medicare and Medicaid. A constitutional challenge to the statute creating Professional Standards Review Organizations (PSROs), which were charged with preventing wasteful Medicare spending, was rejected in Association of American Physicians and Surgeons v. Weinberger, 395 F.Supp. 125, 136 (N.D.Ill.1975) (distinguishing the abortion cases), affirmed mem. 423 U.S. 975 (1975). However, in another case, brought by the AMA to challenge earlier regulations adopted for a similar cost-containment purpose, a preliminary injunction was issued and upheld on appeal because the court had the "impression that plaintiffs could ultimately succeed" in proving that the regulations interfered with the practice of medicine, perhaps constituting a violation of "constitutional rights of patients and doctors." AMA v. Weinberger, 522 F.2d 921, 927 (7th Cir.1975).

The constitutional issue arises in the context of both substantive due process and equal protection. *Roe* itself was decided on substantive due process grounds. It held that the protection of "liberty" in the Fourteenth Amendment extended to a woman's right to choose whether or not to carry a pregnancy to term. The next substantive due process question was whether that right to be free from a governmental ban on abortion would be extended to include an affirmative right to receive governmental funding for that procedure.

Although substantive due process cases have typically focused on the right of an individual to be free from a particular governmental restraint unless special justifications for government action exist, there is a line of "right-to" substantive due process cases that establish affirmative claims to governmental payments for certain benefits. See, e.g., Little v. Streater, 452 U.S. 1 (1981) (state has duty to provide indigent litigant access to a blood test in a paternity proceeding); Boddie v. Connecticut, 401 U.S. 371 (1971) (right of indigents to access to the courts in context of divorce proceeding). The Supreme Court, however, has never extended such "right-to" cases to provide protection against economic and social deprivations, at least outside the prison context. See, e.g., United States v. Kras, 409 U.S. 434 (1973) (declining to extend the "right-to" concept to bankruptcy filing fees); but see Estelle v. Gamble, 429 U.S. 97 (1976) (establishing a duty of prisons not to deny necessary medical treatment with deliberate indifference to the suffering of prisoners). The Court has focused on three factors in determining whether to extend the "right-to" cases to a particular area: (*a*) the importance and constitutional connections of the interest at stake; (*b*) whether (as in prisons and in the courts) the state has monopolized access to a particular service; and (*c*) whether there has been an absolute deprivation of the service in question. For a general discussion of these issues, see Blumstein, Constitutional Perspectives On Governmental Decisions Affecting Human Life and Health, Law & Contemp. Probs., Autumn 1976, p. 231, 256–70.

In Maher v. Roe, 432 U.S. 464 (1977), involving a challenge to a Connecticut regulation that forbade state funding for nontherapeutic abortions, the Supreme Court refused to find that an indigent person had a constitutional right to state-funded medical care. The Court noted that the "Constitution imposes no obligation on the states to pay the pregnancy-related medical expenses of indigent women, or indeed to pay any of the medical expenses of indigents." Id. at 469. *Roe* protects a woman "from unduly burdensome interference with her freedom to decide whether to terminate her pregnancy," but it does not limit the "authority of a State to make a value judgment favoring childbirth over abortion, and to implement that judgment by the allocation of public funds." Id. at 473–74. Since, outside of prisons, government does not absolutely control access to medical resources, the Court declined to hold that individuals have a constitutional entitlement to governmentally-provided medical services.

"Since *Maher* involved nontherapeutic abortions, some believed that the Supreme Court would treat medically necessary abortions in a different way. The Court in *Harris v. McRae* [448 U.S. 297 (1980)] declined to adopt that distinction." Blumstein, Rationing Medical Resources: A Constitutional, Legal, and Policy Analysis, 59 Tex. L. Rev. 1345, 1379 (1981). In *Harris*, the Court noted that a woman's freedom of choice does not carry with it a "constitutional entitlement to the financial resources to avail herself of the full range of protected choices." 448 U.S. at 316. While "[g]overnment may not impose unnecessary obstacles in the path of a woman's abortion decision, * * * it has no affirmative obligation to eliminate preexisting obstacles such as poverty, which the government did not cause." Blumstein, supra, 59 Tex. L. Rev. at 1379, citing *Harris*, 448 U.S. at 316.

In addition to the substantive due process issue, the question of public funding for medical care raises equal protection considerations. Equal protection establishes a norm of evenhanded treatment for persons similarly situated. When it allocates scarce public medical care funds, government makes choices among beneficiaries by determining who is eligible for a benefit and what services to pay for and in what amounts. These determinations result in classifications among persons and are subject to review under equal protection. "The essential equal protection inquiry is the determination of the content of the state's burden of justification." Blumstein, supra, 59 Tex. L. Rev. at 1381. Traditionally, such classifications are given a presumption of validity and will survive equal protection scrutiny if they are rationally related to a legitimate governmental interest. The "range of legitimate interests is broad, and the Court will not examine the weight of the interest." Id. Only when a classification impinges on a fundamental interest or involves a suspect (e.g., race) or otherwise disfavored (e.g., gender) classification will the Court (at least in theory) apply a more rigorous degree of scrutiny under equal protection. The Court has been unwilling to apply more rigorous review in the area of "economics and social welfare" generally. E.g., Dandridge v. Williams, 397 U.S. 471, 485 (1970) (welfare); San Antonio Independent School Dist. v. Rodriguez, 411 U.S. 1, 20–25 (1973) (education); Lindsey v. Normet, 405 U.S. 56 (1972) (housing). And it has expressly declined to find medical care to be a fundamental interest and therefore to apply heightened scrutiny to medical funding issues. *Harris v. McRae*, 448 U.S. at 318; *Maher v. Roe*, 432 U.S. at 469. Similarly, the Court declined in the cited cases to invoke heightened scrutiny because of the nature of the classification—that the putative beneficiaries were indigent. For an exchange of views on the constitutional and other ramifications of publicly providing and rationing medical care, see the series of four articles authored, alternately, by Professors James F. Blumstein and Rand Rosenblatt, 59 Tex.L.Rev. 1345, 1401 (1981); 60 Tex.L.Rev. 899, 919 (1982).

Should Health Care Be Distributed Equally?

Paul Starr, Ph.D., The New Critics of Medical Care: The Politics of Therapeutic Nihilism

Hastings Center Rep., Oct. 1976, at 24.

For most of this century, indeed until just the past several years, liberals and socialists had a relatively uncomplicated perception of medicine as a political question. There was one fundamental issue: equal access to medical services. No one doubted that medical care was a good thing; the trouble was that poor people were denied attention or went broke trying to pay for it. Some also thought doctors ought to be concerned with "community" medicine, and expand their concerns to include all manner of behavioral and social problems. The advantages of professional competence in medical matters, and the necessity of professional authority, seemed self-evident.

This was not always so. In the nineteenth century, many people, even some leading physicians, believed that most medical practice was completely ineffective, or even harmful. Critics, particularly during the Jacksonian period, attacked professional competence as illusory, denounced medicine as a "privileged monopoly," and sought the democratization of useful medical knowledge, so that every man (as the slogan then went) might be his own physician. Political and medical dissent had a close kinship. In the late nineteenth century, populists and others resisted giving the medical profession licensing powers that would enable it to exclude various forms of unorthodox practice. As earlier radicals had taken an interest in mesmerism or botanic medicine, so the populists had an affinity for faith-healers and other "irregular" practitioners. In the twentieth century the left, like the larger society, repudiated these tendencies. Rather than challenging the actual content of medical practice or the structure of professional authority, socialists and liberals gave their attention almost exclusively to the problem of health insurance—to the financing and rationalizing of institutions whose value was beyond debate.

Old Questions Reopened

However, in the past few years, almost all the questions about medicine that had been closed since the nineteenth century have been reopened. There has been a renewed interest in the democratization of medical knowledge, particularly in the women's movement. Professional authority has again come under attack. So has the actual content of medical practice, especially its technological character. But most important, there is, once more, widespread questioning of the ultimate value and effectiveness of medicine. Medical care, it turns out, may not be an unambiguously good thing. In the nineteenth century, some leading scientists held that virtually all existing drugs and treatments were of no use, and that the sick had no other hope than the healing power of nature. This doctrine was known as therapeutic nihilism. Today disbelief has returned in a new form: now the net effectiveness of the medical system as a whole, rather than particular treatments, is called into question. The most serious critics of the system now doubt that it does much good for our health. Instead of suggesting that medicine expand its concerns into behavioral and social matters, many people think the "medicalization" of experience has gone too far, and that childbirth, sickness, anxiety, aging, and death should be reclaimed from professional hegemony.

This recent attack on medicine seems to have begun in the 1960s with the mounting criticism of psychiatry and psychiatric institutions. The books of Thomas Szasz, R.D. Laing, and Erving Goffman, all widely read in the past decade, have portrayed medicine as an instrument primarily of social control rather than therapeutic assistance. The great recent successes of the play Equus and of One Flew Over the Cuckoo's Nest as a novel, play, and movie testify to the temper of public sentiment. In both Equus and Cuckoo's Nest, medicine is the force of oppression and conformity, called upon by society to domesticate the passion and spontaneity of patients caged against their will. One is given to understand, of course, that the settings and characters are symbolic (even allegorical!), but it is significant nonetheless what symbols writers select, at a particular moment in history, of all those that are potentially available.

From psychiatry, doubts and criticism have spread to medicine at large. Students of public health have long observed, without anyone's paying much attention, that the effect of environment and behavior on the health of populations is much greater than that of medical care. Suddenly this point is being treated, in influential circles, as if it were a major discovery. People ask, and none too soon, why medicine commands so much of our resources if it makes so little difference in health and life expectancy. In a book given widespread and serious attention in Europe last year and more recently in the United States, Ivan Illich has suggested that the entire medical system has become counterproductive, and now causes more illness than it relieves.[1] I will go into the details of the argument later. One point interests me here. By taking the doubts about medicine to the extreme, Illich has brought out the latent implications of the new criticism of the value of medicine. If the attack is justified, then the traditional concern of the left for equality in medical care no longer makes any sense. To give the lower classes greater access to health services, Illich writes in Medical Nemesis, "would only equalize the delivery of professional illusions and torts." In the earlier English edition of his book, he put the point even more bluntly: "Less access to the present health system would, contrary to political rhetoric, *benefit* the poor." (Emphasis added) This is, I believe, an indefensible statement, but it is just as well Illich has laid the issue open, for it underlies a more general problem in contemporary political argument.

The Tensions of Criticism

Two antagonistic impulses now dominate criticism of social policy. The first and more familiar impulse of the left is to argue that the poor and minorities receive inadequate services from schools, hospitals, public welfare agencies, and other institutions. The second, more novel, and in a sense more radical impulse is to call into question the value and efficacy (particularly the long-range effects) of the services themselves. Yet this second impulse undercuts the first. For if the services are worthless or in some way destructive, why worry about the poor—or, for that matter, anyone—not getting enough of them?

* * *

Distributive justice is a morally compelling concern only when what there is to distribute, or redistribute, is genuinely important and valuable. If it is irrelevant or harmful to human welfare, then the poor would clearly be better off without it. At a time of fiscal austerity, when public services to the poor are frequently in jeopardy, it becomes extremely difficult to resist cutbacks if one simultaneously concedes that schools and hospitals, welfare programs and mental health centers, legal services and employment bureaus don't make much difference in the long run, or are positively damaging to the interests of the poor. The more one questions the ultimate value of the social services, the less urgent, the less vital equal access to them appears; furthermore, the more difficult it becomes to argue persuasively that the government should spend more on domestic needs.

This is precisely the situation that confronts us today. In addition to the current fiscal crisis, the social services are in the midst of an intellectual crisis that has sapped their legitimacy and prepared the ground for

1. Ivan Illich, Medical Nemesis: The Expropriation of Health (London: Calder & Boyars, 1975; New York: Pantheon, 1976). The literature of therapeutic nihilism and disenchantment has grown rapidly in the past few years, and varies in political outlook and certainty of judgment. Some observers are more guarded and qualified than others, but there is a common ground of skepticism about the value of medical services. [References omitted.]

retrenchment. Ironically, the left has played a part in the process of delegitimation. The effect, unintended but no less real, has been to facilitate cutbacks in services that are likely to affect those groups least able to defend themselves politically.

Under these circumstances, those who fault the social services for being ineffective or harmful should at least be careful and deliberate about their claims. They ought to be clear about what the evidence says and what it doesn't say. They ought to be wary of diagnosing failure from fragmentary data that refer only to one of several functions that institutions and programs usefully perform.

I do not propose to deal with these issues in a general fashion here, but only to address the question as it has arisen in medical care. What I would like to do is to review the argument about the effectiveness and dangers of medicine, as well as the evidence regarding inequalities in health and life expectancy and in access to medical services. Does the traditional concern of the left for equality in medical care still make sense, particularly if it is not the way to achieve equality in health?

The Case Against Medicine

Those, like Ivan Illich, who argue that medicine has a negligible or deleterious effect on health typically rest their case on a series of distinct points. The following seem to me to be the most important:

1. *Historical record.* Great advances in health and life expectancy during the past several centuries have come from improvements in the standard of living, particularly in nutrition, and from public health measures, such as improved sanitation. Improvements in the treatment of individual illness do not seem to have been a major factor in decreased rates of mortality.

2. *Geographic variation.* Regional differences in the ratio of doctors or hospital beds to population, or in any other index of health services, seem to have no measurable relation to variations in mortality or life expectancy.

3. *Marginal returns.* In recent decades, national expenditures, measured either absolutely or as a proportion of gross national product, have increased enormously throughout most of the industrial world, but there has been no corresponding improvement in health. Life expectancy at ages beyond infancy has reached a plateau. In fact, in the United States, mortality rates for adult males at most ages have been increasing rather than declining.

4. *Empirical analysis of health services.* A few careful studies ("randomized controlled trials") of the effectiveness of specific procedures and treatments, such as intensive care, have cast doubt as to whether they have any positive value. The returns in health and extended life from technologically complex services, even when successfully used, are rather small. Typically, the most expensive medical technology, absorbing huge investments, is used to treat patients who have multiple problems and short life expectancies even if cured of the immediate problem at hand.

5. *Excess capacity.* A great deal of evidence suggests that there are too many hospital beds, too many surgeons, and much unnecessary surgery in the United States; that antibiotics, psychoactive drugs and other medications are vastly overprescribed; and that these overuses of medicine lead to adverse, often fatal complications.

6. *Iatrogenic (doctor-caused) injuries.* Good statistics are unavailable, but some studies suggest there may be several million every year. Malpractice suits touch a small fraction of the total.

7. *Medicine as an epidemic.* Illich argues that in addition to *clinical* iatrogenesis, medicine has created even more illness by redefining normal human experience as sickness. This "medicalization" of life he calls *social* iatrogenesis. Medical institutions, he suggests, have also helped create illness by weakening individual autonomy and the capacity of people to "suffer their reality." In other words, whereas in simpler times, people steadfastly endured pain, anxiety, and death, now they feel *sick* and expect to be made well. This Illich calls *cultural* iatrogenesis.

What ought we to conclude from these arguments? Is medical care worthless or even, as Illich maintains, destructive of health? Illich sees health as the autonomous ability of an individual organism to cope with its internal experience and external environment, and he argues that we ought to turn away from professionals toward self-care. But on what grounds are we to believe that self-care would be harmless? Especially when sick, people are fully capable of doing great harm to themselves. That is exactly why they seek out professional assistance. Such assistance need not destroy their autonomous ability to cope with the world; it may help them to regain it. Sickness itself creates dependency; medicine often relieves it. The ideal of pure autonomy that Illich offers is a romantic myth as illusory as the omnipotence of science.

Both clinical and social iatrogenesis I take to be serious problems, but one need not conclude they outweigh the positive effects of medicine. "Among murderous institutional torts," Illich writes, "only modern malnutrition injures more people than iatrogenic disease in its various manifestations." This is typical of Illich's rhetoric, but there is, as far as I know, no evidence that could possibly sustain this assertion.

Still, if it is true, as the historical and empirical data indicate, that medicine has had a relatively small effect on mortality rates and life expectancy, why do we bother with it? First of all, we are talking about only the most gross index of the outcome of medical services—mortality rates, which are governed by numerous other variables. Most medical care involves the relief of discomfort, disability, and uncertainty. Only a small part makes the difference between life and death (and almost all of that must be used for television melodramas). Most of us at some point have suffered injuries that might have left us disabled or disfigured had it not been for quick medical intervention. The more emotional functions of medicine should also not be slighted. People consult physicians not just for remedies, but also for clarification of the nature and meaning of their internal experience. "Am I sick?" we ask. "Is what I feel significant, or should I ignore it?" The resolution of ambiguity has a value in itself. Medicine, like most institutions, has a variety of legitimate functions, not only for the sick but for their families. Hospitals, for example, have grown in the last century not only because of their advantages for treatment, but because they help reduce the physical and emotional burden confronted by families when one member becomes acutely ill.

I do not wish to minimize the lifesaving aspect of medicine. The statistical effect on overall mortality rates is a poor measure of its psychological and moral importance. Consider the following figures: in the United States in 1940, nearly 9,000 women died in childbirth. In 1973, with 99 percent of all births occurring in hospitals (compared with about half in 1940), fewer than 500 women died. This decline has had some effect on female mortality rates, * * *. But the real point is the greater sense of security that such diminished risks afford. Illich and others lament the "medicalization" of normal aspects of human development like childbirth, but it seems quite plausible that women have made an entirely rational decision in seeking out medical attention. People may intelligently conclude that the reduction of risks, even at the margin, is worth the cost and the loss of autonomy they endure from consulting a physician.

The general plateau in mortality rates during the past few decades conceals changes in deaths from specific diseases that have been responsive to medicine. Among Americans aged fifteen to forty-four, for example, there were about 30,000 deaths from tuberculosis in 1940, but in 1973 only 407. Influenza and pneumonia took the lives of 11,600 young adults in 1940; in 1973, only 3,200. It happens, however, these declines have been partially offset, particularly among males, by increasing rates of deaths from violence and accidents. Yet it would be absurd to conclude from such facts that medicine has been ineffective. Had it not been for good medical care, the situation might have been worse.

There is no question but that the medical system in America is overextended in many areas. But along with excess capacity, there are shortages and inadequacies in needed services. There are too many surgeons, but too few "primary care" physicians; too many hospital beds in some communities, but too few neighborhood clinics in others. All this shows is that there are problems in allocating and organizing resources. While the system overproduces facilities and services whose costs can be covered by insurance, it underproduces them where coverage is weak. Recently Aaron Wildavsky wrote that "the marginal value of one, or one billion dollars spent on medical care would be close to zero in improving health." Given the current structure of incentives, this may be so, but it need not be. Large socioeconomic differences remain in diseases and deaths that ought to be therapeutically preventable. Medical care for mothers and young children, for example, has historically had a significant effect in improving their health. Were additional funds spent on maternal, infant, and child care, the marginal returns in improving health might be substantial. By concentrating on children, one might also affect the health of the future adult population. Such considerations have not traditionally governed medical policy. The nation has tended to invest resources in the treatment of diseases for which no effective therapy exists.[4]

Under the circumstances, it should not be surprising that the results of government expenditures have been unimpressive. A critic like Illich argues that because medical care has made no difference in health, we should not be particularly concerned about inequalities of access. He has the point turned around. We will have to be especially concerned about inequalities if we are to make future investments in medical care effective. Precisely because there is excess capacity in the medical system, the persistence of inadequacies in basic services is not merely unjust, but gratuitous.

The Dimensions of Inequality

For reasons that have nothing to do with deliberate social policy, we are probably in a period of increasing equality in health and life expectancy. As Anton Antonovsky has shown in an examination of the history of class differences in average length of life, the most dramatic contrasts appeared in the eighteenth and nineteenth centuries. In the preindustrial era, mortality rates were universally high, and the differences between upper and lower classes seem to have been relatively limited. But with industrialization, a substantial gap opened up: life expectancy increased much faster for the upper than for the lower classes. The ratio in average life span between rich and poor seems to have been on the order of two to one. In the twentieth century, that ratio has declined in industrialized countries to about 1.3 to one, or less, as the lower classes have caught up.

Not all countries have done equally well. While socioeconomic differences in mortality rates are low in Britain, they continue to be relatively high in the United States. * * *

Are the poor in worse health than the rich? * * * Rates of chronic illness * * * show strong socioeconomic differences. * * * Some of this relationship is explained by the reverse causal linkage—the effect that disability has on income. But we find the association between low income and ill health even among children, and in that case poverty is clearly the independent variable.

How much of this inequality in health could be eliminated by equalizing access to medical care? Probably not much. The last decade has already seen a very significant movement toward equalization in the use of medical services. In fact, the overall rate of physician visits is now higher for the

4. A good case in point: President Johnson's regional medical program, which in the mid–1960s established centers for the treatment of heart disease, cancer, and stroke. Elizabeth Drew, writing in The Atlantic in 1967, raised the questions that ought to have been asked before the program was enacted: "If the federal government is going to provide centers for certain diseases, would it be better to provide them for diseases which can be cured or for those which cannot yet be cured? Similarly, if such a departure is to be made, should it focus on diseases which affect primarily the elderly, as these do, or on diseases which affect primarily the young? These kinds of policy considerations should have preceded a decision to initiate a program of centers for heart disease, cancer and stroke, but they did not."

poor than for higher-income families. * * * This was not so in 1964, before Medicaid, and it continues not to be true for both children and the aged. At all ages, rates of hospitalization are today higher for the poor, reversing the dominant pattern of a decade ago. * * *

One must emphasize that these are measures of utilization, not access. Since the poor are less healthy and more prone to chronic illness—indeed, many are poor precisely because they are disabled—they probably require greater medical attention. Genuine equality of access might lead to higher utilization by the poor than is now observed: we have no way of knowing. There is some scattered evidence suggesting that when the poor receive medical attention, they do so at more severe stages of illness. This suggests either less access to care, or less inclination to use it. * * * The families of low-income workers, particularly in the "secondary" labor force, have less insurance coverage for medical costs. The newly unemployed often have no coverage at all. Families on welfare find their eligibility for Medicaid is constantly changing, because of changes in employment status or new welfare regulations.

Cutbacks in public support for medical care will probably not restrict expensive medical technology of dubious value. Costs of that sort will continue to be absorbed by third-party insurance. Retrenchment will more likely increase financial insecurity among low-income patients, and promote the deterioration of public hospitals and clinics. With inadequate staffing, a declining physical plant, and delays in service, all the iatrogenic aspects of medicine will be magnified. That, in fact, is the irony of Illich's jeremiad. Retrenchment in medical services would almost surely aggravate the very qualities in the system that he deplores.

Rationing Medical Care

The facts seem to support these conclusions:

1. Environment and behavior are the principal determinants of health and life expectancy; medical care plays a relatively small part. The medical services that seem to have the most impact, like vaccinations, tend to be relatively simple. No one familiar with the evidence disagrees with that. If one wishes to equalize health, equalizing medical care is probably not the most effective strategy.

2. On the other hand, the expansion and improvement of medical services probably have had a positive effect on health. The reduction of risks at the margin has enhanced personal security. Had it not been for medical care, mortality rates might be higher. Medicine has useful functions other than saving lives, such as relieving discomfort and disability and making sickness more bearable for patients and their families. Further investments in certain areas of medical care, such as maternal and child health, may continue to yield positive returns.

3. There has been a substantial equalization in the use of physicians' and hospital services during the past decade. In some categories, the poor now appear to have higher rates of utilization than other classes. The

enactment of Medicare and Medicaid probably played a major role in this development.

4. Because the poor have higher rates of disability and chronic illness, they probably require more medical services. Equal utilization, therefore, may not prove equal access to services. Furthermore, there are persistent inequalities in the conditions under which treatment is received and in the security and degree of financial coverage. The chief effect of cutbacks in public support would be to exacerbate these problems.

5. The hard and discriminating eye that distinguishes useless from effective practices in medicine, or other fields, need not be unfriendly to the concern for equality. To improve the effectiveness of social services, we will have to be especially attentive to inequalities. It makes no sense to add more where there is already too much.

6. Some means must be found to put firm limits on the funds the medical system absorbs. But while such limits are necessary, the rationing of services under the present medical system would almost certainly be neither just nor efficient, given the incentives that now govern the allocation of resources. If limits are to be placed on the system, this means challenging the authority of physicians and the structure of the medical market.

The recent debate over medicine has failed to address a central issue. Is it the purpose of national medical policy to maximize the health of the country, or is it to underwrite the services that individual physicians believe are warranted for their individual patients? The two are very different. If we continue to follow the second policy, we should not try to measure it by the standard of the first. It will always be found wanting.

The therapeutic nihilism of the nineteenth century had its justification in objective fact. We now know that it was correct: most medical treatment of the day was absolutely useless. Much of it—the bleeding, blistering, and purging of patients—was lethal. By helping to rid medicine of such techniques, therapeutic nihilism contributed to the liberation of medicine from the dead hand of the past. Today, medical institutions are often as ineffective as specific treatments were then. Let us hope that the new therapeutic nihilism, which questions the medical system in its totality, will have the same liberating effect.

NOTES

1. *Mortality Trends and Medical Care.* Some recent improvements in mortality trends, not observed by Starr, also suggest that the "nihilists" may have been too critical and that we may be doing something right. Overall death rates (age-adjusted) declined slightly more in the ten years from 1970 to 1980 (from 714.3 to 585.8 per 100,000) than they had in the previous twenty years. This decline continued to 520.2 in 1990. Life expectancy at birth for all Americans rose from 68.2 years in 1950 to 75.4 years in 1990. Infant mortality rates (deaths per 1000 live births) dropped

from 29.2 in 1950 to 9.2 in 1990. Despite this favorable evidence, it can still be debated how much of the improvement in mortality rates is attributable to medical care. Although the "therapeutic nihilists" are not so prominent today, some later writers have also been somewhat pessimistic concerning the efficacy of medical care. E.g., T. McKeown, The Origins of Human Disease (1988); B. Inglis, The Diseases of Civilization (1981) (reviewing medical progress in treating specific diseases); T. McKeown, The Role of Medicine: Dreams, Mirage or Nemesis? (1979).

Mortality experience with coronary heart disease has been especially encouraging. According to a 1993 report, "acute myocardial infarction fatality rates continued a long-term decline. In 1984, the U.S. acute myocardial infarction fatality rate was 7.7% for age <65 years and 22.4% for age >65 years. In * * * 1990 [the rates] were 5.0% and 17.6%, respectively." Gillum, Trends in Acute Myocardial Infarction and Coronary Heart Disease Death in the United States, 23 J.Am.Coll.Cardiol. 1273 (1993). Although the record with respect to heart disease suggests that medical care is helping people, there is also evidence that changed life-style (exercise, less smoking, better diet) is a major source of the improvement. The medical care system can claim some credit, however, for its role in promoting these changes and for monitoring and controlling hypertension, a factor contributing to heart disease. A recent study concludes "that risk factor reduction has resulted in a reduced incidence of acute myocardial infarction and sudden coronary death and that improvements in medical care have resulted in a continued decrease in acute myocardial infarction fatalities and overall coronary heart disease mortality." Id. at 1274. See also Braunwald, Stattuck Lecture—Cardiovascular Medicine at the Turn of the Century: Triumphs, Concerns, and Opportunities, 337 New Eng. J. Med. 1360 (1997); Hunink et al., The Recent Decline in Mortality from Coronary Heart Disease, 1980–1990: The Effect of Secular Trends in Risk Factors and Treatment, 277 J.A.M.A. 535 (1997); Stamler, Coronary Heart Disease: Doing the "Right Things," 312 New Eng. J. Med. 1053 (1985). Compare Starr's footnote 4.

Between the periods 1975–79 and 1987–91, total cancer death rates rose slightly from 131.3 to 139.6 (per 100,000) for white women and 206.9 to 213.3 for white men. Devesa et al., Recent Cancer Trends in the United States, 87 J. Natl. Cancer Inst. 175 (1995). These increases are not alarming, however, because an aging population, escaping other health hazards, can expect a higher incidence of cancer. Thus, according to the cited study (id. at 181),

> Increases were apparent across all broad age groups, but the specific cancers responsible varied by age and sex. Total cancer mortality rates increased less than incidence rates and, in fact, decreased for both males and females under the age of 55. Improvements in diagnosis or changes in classification contribute to much of the increases in some tumors, although improvements in treatment and survival influence the incidence/mortality differentials for certain cancers.

See also Bailar & Gornik, Cancer Undefeated, 336 New Eng. J. Med. 1569 (1997) (pessimistic assessment; modest very recent improvement in death rates from cancer attributed to "improved prevention and earlier detection"; "effect of new treatments for cancer on mortality have been largely disappointing"). See also Kramer & Klausner, Grappling with Cancer—Defeatism versus the Reality of Progress, 337 New Eng. J. Med. 931 (1997).

2. *Socioeconomic Variations in Health Status.* Despite Starr's statement in 1976 that "we are probably in a period of increasing equality in health and life expectancy," a more recent study found increasing inverse correlations between mortality and education and between mortality and income. Pappas, The Increasing Disparity in Mortality Between Socioeconomic Groups in the United States, 1960 and 1986, 329 N.Eng.J.Med. 103, 105 (1993) ("poor or poorly educated persons have higher death rates than wealthier or better educated persons, and these differences increased from 1960 through 1986"). Other inequalities also remain. For example, data for 1990 show blacks having a life expectancy of 69.1 years as compared to 76.1 years for whites. Data for 1990 also show a substantially higher infant mortality rate (deaths per 1,000 live births) for blacks (17.0) than for whites (7.7). National Center for Health Statistics, Advance Report of Final Mortality Statistics, 1989, 40 Monthly Vital Stat.Rep. (Supp. 2) (1990).

Socioeconomic inequalities in health status are difficult to interpret. Although the evidence might be read to imply that low income condemns individuals to poor health, the causal relationship may also run in the opposite direction to some extent. Racial differences in health status may be attributable to socioeconomic factors, not discrimination. Cultural factors may also be reflected. For example, although the improvement in death rates from coronary heart disease has been substantially greater in groups with higher socioeconomic status, this result may have had little or nothing to do with access to medical care. Thus, a discrepancy in reductions in death rates was noticeable between salaried (38%) and hourly (18%) workers in the same insured employment group (with identical insurance), suggesting that persons with more education may have changed their lifestyles more than persons with less education. See Stamler, supra, at 1054.

3. *Accessibility of Care.* Despite findings reported by Starr of improved access to care by the poor and minorities, there is still substantial evidence that significant health care needs are going unmet. Thus, 6% of representative individuals surveyed in one study reported an inability to obtain needed medical or surgical treatment in 1994, and 16% reported an unmet need for at least one service, such as prescription drugs, eyeglasses, dental care, or mental health care, that is frequently not covered by public or private health insurance. Berk et al., Ability to Obtain Health Care: Recent Estimates From the Robert Wood Johnson Foundation National Access to Care Survey, Health Affairs, Fall 1995, at 139.

Even when public financing is equally available to everyone, it appears, substantial inequalities in health outcomes and in the receipt of services still persist. See Gornick et al., Effects of Race and Income on Mortality and Use of Services Among Medicare Beneficiaries, 335 New Eng.J.Med. 791 (1996) (government study showing numerous inequalities, including findings that 51% of white beneficiaries received flu shots versus 31% of blacks and that blacks were 40% less likely to have coronary bypass surgery).

President's Commission for the Study of Ethical Problems in Medicine and Biomedical and Behavioral Research, Securing Access to Health Care: The Ethical Implications of Differences in the Availability of Health Services

Pp. 1–6 (1983).

The prevention of death and disability, the relief of pain and suffering, the restoration of functioning: these are the aims of health care. Beyond its tangible benefits, health care touches on countless important and in some ways mysterious aspects of personal life that invest it with significant value as a thing in itself. In recognition of these special features, the President's Commission was mandated to study the ethical and legal implications of differences in the availability of health services. In this Report to the President and Congress, the Commission sets forth an ethical standard: access for all to an adequate level of care without the imposition of excessive burdens. It believes that this is the standard against which proposals for legislation and regulation in this field ought to be measured.

In fulfilling its mandate from Congress, the Commission discusses an ethical response to differences in people's access to health care. To do so, it is necessary both to examine the extent of those differences and to try to understand how they arise. This focus on the problems of access ought not to obscure the great strengths of the American health care system. The matchless contributions made by America's biomedical scientists to medical knowledge and techniques, the high skill and compassionate devotion of countless physicians and other health professionals, the extensive financial protection against health care costs available to most people, the great generosity with time and funds of many individuals and organizations—these are the hallmarks of health care in the United States. Therefore, the objective here is not to disparage the system but merely to encourage responsible decisionmakers—in the private sector and at all levels of government—to strive to ensure that every American has a fair opportunity to benefit from it.

Health care is a field in which two important American traditions are manifested: the responsibility of each individual for his or her own welfare and the obligations of the community to its members. These two values are complementary rather than conflicting; the emphasis on one or the other varies with the facts of a particular situation. In the field of health care, personal responsibility is a corollary of personal self-determination, which the Commission discussed in its recent report on informed consent. At the same time, ill health is often a matter of chance that can have devastating consequences; thus, concern has long been expressed that health care be widely available and not unfairly denied to those in need.

Since the nineteenth century, the United States has acted—through the founding of the Public Health Service and of hospitals for seamen, veterans, and native Americans, and through special health programs for mothers and infants, children, the elderly, the disabled, and the poor—to reaffirm the special place of health care in American society. With the greatly increased powers of biomedical science to cure as well as to relieve suffering, these traditional concerns about the special importance of health care have been magnified.

In both their means and their particular objectives, public programs in health care have varied over the years. Some have been aimed at assuring the productivity of the work force, others at protecting particularly vulnerable or deserving groups, still others at manifesting the country's commitment to equality of opportunity. Nonetheless, most programs have rested on a common rationale: to ensure that care be made accessible to a group whose health needs would otherwise not be adequately met.[3]

The consequence of leaving health care solely to market forces—the mechanism by which most things are allocated in American society—is not viewed as acceptable when a significant portion of the population lacks access to health services. Of course, government financing programs, such as Medicare and Medicaid as well as public programs that provide care directly to veterans and the military and through local public hospitals, have greatly improved access to health care. These efforts, coupled with the expanded availability of private health insurance, have resulted in almost 90% of Americans having some form of health insurance coverage. Yet the patchwork of government programs and the uneven availability of private health insurance through the workplace have excluded millions of people. The Surgeon General has stated that "with rising unemployment, the numbers are shifting rapidly. We estimate that from 18 to 25 million Americans—8 to 11 percent of the population—have no health-insurance coverage at all." Many of these people lack effective access to health care, and many more who have some form of insurance are unprotected from the severe financial burdens of sickness.

Nor is this a problem only for the moment. The Secretary of Health and Human Services recently observed that despite the excellence of American medical care, "we do have this perennial problem of about 10% of the population falling through the cracks." What is needed now are ethical principles that offer practical guidance so that health policymakers in Federal, state, and local governments can act responsibly in an era of fiscal belt tightening without abandoning society's commitment to fair and adequate health care.

3. Although public programs have generally rested on this rationale, some have been structured so as to include people who could obtain adequate care on their own without excessive burdens. Medicare, for example, covers virtually all of the elderly, not only those who cannot afford the cost of care.

Summary of Conclusions

In this Report, the President's Commission does not propose any new policy initiatives, for its mandate lies in ethics not in health policy development. But it has tried to provide a framework within which debates about health policy might take place, and on the basis of which policymakers can ascertain whether some proposals do a better job than others of securing health care on an equitable basis.

In 1952, the President's Commission on the Health Needs of the Nation concluded that "access to the means for the attainment and preservation of health is a basic human right." Instead of speaking in terms of "rights," however, the current Commission believes its conclusions are better expressed in terms of "ethical obligations."

The Commission concludes that society has an ethical obligation to ensure equitable access to health care for all. This obligation rests on the special importance of health care: its role in relieving suffering, preventing premature death, restoring functioning, increasing opportunity, providing information about an individual's condition, and giving evidence of mutual empathy and compassion. Furthermore, although life-style and the environment can affect health status, differences in the need for health care are for the most part undeserved and not within an individual's control.

In speaking of society, the Commission uses the term in its broadest sense to mean the collective American community. The community is made up of individuals who are in turn members of many other, overlapping groups, both public and private: local, state, regional, and national units; professional and workplace organizations; religious, educational, and charitable institutions; and family, kinship, and ethnic groups. All these entities play a role in discharging societal obligations.

The societal obligation is balanced by individual obligations. Individuals ought to pay a fair share of the cost of their own health care and take reasonable steps to provide for such care when they can do so without excessive burdens. Nevertheless, the origins of health needs are too complex, and their manifestation too acute and severe, to permit care to be regularly denied on the grounds that individuals are solely responsible for their own health.

Equitable access to health care requires that all citizens be able to secure an adequate level of care without excessive burdens. Discussions of a right to health care have frequently been premised on offering patients access to all beneficial care, to all care that others are receiving, or to all that they need—or want. By creating impossible demands on society's resources for health care, such formulations have risked negating the entire notion of a moral obligation to secure care for those who lack it. In their place, the Commission proposes a standard of "an adequate level of care," which should be thought of as a floor below which no one ought to fall, not a ceiling above which no one may rise.

A determination of this level will take into account the value of various types of health care in relation to each other as well as the value of health care in relation to other important goods for which societal resources are needed. Consequently, changes in the availability of resources, in the effectiveness of different forms of health care, or in society's priorities may result in a revision of what is considered "adequate."

Equitable access also means that the burdens borne by individuals in obtaining adequate care (the financial impact of the cost of care, travel to the health care provider, and so forth) ought not to be excessive or to fall disproportionately on particular individuals.

When equity occurs through the operation of private forces, there is no need for government involvement, but the ultimate responsibility for ensuring that society's obligation is met, through a combination of public and private sector arrangements, rests with the Federal government. Private health care providers and insurers, charitable bodies, and local and state governments all have roles to play in the health care system in the United States. Yet the Federal government has the ultimate responsibility for seeing that health care is available to all when the market, private charity, and government efforts at the state and local level are insufficient in achieving equity.

The cost of achieving equitable access to health care ought to be shared fairly. The cost of securing health care for those unable to pay ought to be spread equitably at the national level and not allowed to fall more heavily on the shoulders of particular practitioners, institutions, or residents of different localities. In generating the resources needed to achieve equity of access, those with greater financial resources should shoulder a greater proportion of the costs. Also, priority in the use of public subsidies should be given to achieving equitable access for all before government resources are devoted to securing more care for people who already receive an adequate level.[7]

Efforts to contain rising health care costs are important but should not focus on limiting the attainment of equitable access for the least well served portion of the public. The achievement of equitable access is an obligation of sufficient moral urgency to warrant devoting the necessary resources to it. However, the nature of the task means that it will not be achieved immediately. While striving to meet this ethical obligation, society may also engage in efforts to contain total health costs—efforts that themselves are likely to be difficult and time-consuming. Indeed, the Commission recognizes that efforts to rein in currently escalating health care costs have an ethical aspect because the call for adequate health care for all may not be heeded until such efforts are undertaken. If the nation concludes that too much is being spent on health care, it is appropriate to eliminate expenditures that are wasteful or that do not produce benefits comparable to those that would flow from alternate uses of these funds. But measures designed to contain health care costs that exacerbate existing

7. Although the Commission does not endorse devoting public resources to individuals who already receive adequate care, exceptions arise for particular groups with special ethical claims, such as soldiers injured in combat, to whom the nation owes a special debt of gratitude.

inequities or impede the achievement of equity are unacceptable from a moral standpoint. Moreover, they are unlikely by themselves to be successful since they will probably lead to a shifting of costs to other entities, rather than to a reduction of total expenditures.

NOTES AND QUESTIONS

1. *The President's Commission.* The foregoing excerpt is taken from one of a series of provocative volumes prepared by the commission, which functioned pursuant to federal legislation from 1980 to 1983. For discussions of the commission's work, see Symposium, 6 Cardozo L. Rev. 223 (1984). One critique of the report excerpted above concluded as follows:

> The ethical minimalism, the antagonism toward governmental and especially federal action, and the rejection of a right to health care must be viewed as of a piece. Securing Access to Health Care is addressed to those who would hope to remedy the current patterns of inequity in the health care system without fundamental changes in the structure of delivery and financing of American medicine. Its effort to accommodate the prevailing political climate accounts for its timidity. Lacking a sharp, critical thrust, it will fail to capture the attention of those in search of a vision to guide the reform of the American health care system. The end result is an ethics in the service of the status quo.

Bayer, Ethics, Politics, and Access to Health Care: A Critical Analysis of the President's Commission, in id. at 303, 320. Another philosopher-commentator examined and rejected "the various arguments advanced by the Commission against individual rights and in favor of a certain conception of societal duty as the moral basis for political debate about access to health care." Arras, Retreat from the Right to Health Care: The President's Commission and Access to Health Care, in id. at 321, 322.

For early articles advocating adequacy rather than equality as the appropriate standard, see Blumstein & Zubkoff, Perspectives on Government Policy in the Health Sector, 51 Milbank Mem. Fund Q.: Health & Soc'y 395, 407–12 (1973); Blumstein & Zubkoff, Public Choice in Health: Problems, Politics and Perspectives on Formulating National Health Policy, 4 J. Health Pol., Pol'y & L. 382, 383–87, 403–05 (1979). See also Blumstein, Rationing Medical Resources: A Constitutional, Legal, and Policy Analysis, 59 Tex. L. Rev. 1345, 1346–56 (1981) (article commissioned by President's Commission, presented initially in testimony to Commission, and advocating adequacy standard).

2. *Policy Issues.* The provision of health care for "the poor" is, of course, a major social issue. The student should ponder at this point the arguments for and against a policy guaranteeing absolute equality of access (financial, geographic, etc.) to health services of equal quality. Consider also whether it would be a better policy for government to provide its disadvantaged citizens a guaranteed minimum income rather than to grant subsidies specifically earmarked for health care. Aside from the paternalistic argument that the poor cannot be trusted to spend their government stipends wisely (or that taxpayers should not be asked to support profligacy), what else can be said for addressing the health needs of the poor specifically—by providing either health services in kind, government payment for services received, or nontransferable vouchers convertible only into coverage in a private health care plan? Consider what would probably happen when a poor person who had failed to purchase health insurance with his cash allowance had a medical emergency.

3. *The Issue of "Rationing."* Proposals to give individuals less than equal health care are sometimes criticized for contemplating the "rationing" of care. Ironically, proposals to equalize care are also subject to the rationing charge insofar as they incorporate cost controls that would deny individuals services they could expect to receive under their current arrangements. Thus,

> [t]he health policy debate in the United States frequently goes like this:
>
> First debater: Your plan would lead to the rationing of care!
>
> Second debater: We're rationing care already!
>
> * * * Obviously, [the first debater] wants to talk about the effects of reform on those who currently benefit from mainstream medical care (either as patients or as providers), while the other is principally concerned about the underserved.

Havighurst, Prospective Self–Denial: Can Consumers Contract Today to Accept Health Care Rationing Tomorrow?, 140 U. Pa. L. Rev. 1755, 1758 (1992). See generally Symposium, The Law and Policy of Health Care Rationing: Models and Accountability, 140 U. Pa. L. Rev. 1505–1998 (1992). For an especially thoughtful critique of the contributions of medical ethicists to the debate over equality and rationing, see Elhauge, Allocating Health Care Morally, 82 Calif. L. Rev. 1449 (1994). Elhauge challenges the apparent assumption by many ethicists that society must somehow settle (by what process they rarely consider) on a single, ethically correct rule by which to direct societal resources to health care uses. He concludes, in a spirit like Starr's, that room must (and can) be left for "diversity of moral choice."

4. *Designing a Minimum Benefits Package: The Oregon Experiment.* The State of Oregon launched virtually the only official attempt by government to define—in the President's Commission's words—an "adequate level of care" for low-income persons when its legislature adopted that state's Basic Health Services Act in 1989. Or. Rev. Stat. §§ 414.025, .036, .720 (1989). This law provided for an unprecedented expansion of Medicaid to cover all individuals below the federal poverty line. In order to make this expansion feasible, however, the legislature launched a major effort to draw new lines significantly limiting the specific services that Medicaid would pay for. In 1991, a special commission established under the act released a list purporting to rank 709 different medical procedures and services in order of relative importance to the individual and society. Diseases appearing high on the list included pneumonia and tuberculosis, while terminal or incurable ailments ranked in the bottom ten. Following the commission's report, the Oregon legislature drew a line at #587 (a "painful swelling of the esophagus"). Below that line were items for which Medicaid would not pay in the current fiscal year. Thus, anyone needing disk surgery would have to look elsewhere; it ranked #588.

Although the Oregon plan reflected a high degree of cost-consciousness driven by state budgetary concerns, the rankings of procedures and conditions did not themselves purport to take the relative costs of different treatments into account. To some, the rankings seemed arbitrary in drawing lines, prompting strong criticism that the state was engaged in "rationing" care to the poor. (Can you see a way to minimize this criticism, or at least to reduce the arbitrariness of the lines drawn?) In addition, some critics of the act claimed that it was unfair because it sought to finance care for the previously uninsured working poor by reducing entitlements previously enjoyed by women and children who were poorer yet. (Was this a fair criticism?) Others objected that it would jeopardize physician autonomy in caring for poor patients.

The Oregon plan attracted national attention among health policy experts but also came to the attention of many ordinary citizens through extensive media coverage and served to heighten awareness of the need to prioritize medical care in order to make limited resources stretch further. See generally Blumstein, The Oregon Experiment: The Role of Cost–Benefit Analysis in the Allocation of Medicaid Funds, 45 Soc. Sci. & Med. 545 (1997); Bodenheimer, The Oregon Health Plan—Lesson for the Nation (pts. 1 & 2), 337 New Eng. J. Med. 651, 720 (1997); Crossley, As We Lay Dying: Medical Futility and Disability Discrimination, 81 Iowa L. Rev. 179 (1995); Astrue, Pseudoscience and the Law: The Case of the Oregon Medicaid Rationing Experiment, 9 Issues L. & Med. 375 (1993–94); Capron, Oregon's Disability: Principles or Politics?, 22 Hastings Center Rep., Nov.-Dec. 1992, p. 18; Eddy, Oregon's Methods: Did Cost–Effectiveness Fail?, 266 J.A.M.A. 2135 (1991) ("Oregon's plan * * * is performing an important national service"); Hadorn, Setting Health Care Priorities in Oregon, 265 J.A.M.A. 2218 (1991); Fox & Leichter, Rationing Care in Oregon: The New Accountability, 10 Health Affairs 7 (1991); Brown, The National Politics of Oregon's Rationing Plan, id. at 28.

Because the Oregon plan would have violated federal Medicaid rules, Oregon had to obtain federal approval of it, either from Congress or in the form of a waiver by the Secretary of HHS. The Bush administration withheld a waiver on the ground that the process of ranking procedures and conditions discriminated against the disabled in violation of the ADA. Do you agree that the Oregon plan violated the ADA? At times, administration officials merely seemed concerned that a telephone survey in which "each respondent was asked to compare the health state described by the surveyor to death (given a score of zero) or to perfect health (given a score of one)" did not adequately reflect the views of persons with disabilities. Blumstein, supra, at 547. At other times, however, the administration seemed to advance the more radical proposition that the ADA prohibits states from valuing life in an asymptomatic state more highly than life in a symptomatic (i.e., disabled) state. See id.

Oregon eventually submitted a revised plan to the Clinton administration. In revising the plan, the planners disregarded the results of the telephone survey and instead "evaluated the relative effectiveness of a treatment primarily on the basis of three 'objective' criteria: (1) probability of death; (2) probability of return to an asymptomatic state; and (3) cost of avoiding death." Id. at 547–48. In so acting, the planners evinced their belief that the Bush administration's main objection to the plan had been the perceived bias of the telephone survey and not the inclusion of quality-of-life considerations in establishing the priority scheme. The Clinton administration approved the revised plan subject to the condition that "Oregon eliminate[] from consideration * * * the factor regarding the probability of a course of treatment leading to a return to an asymptomatic state." Id. at 548. In requiring that Oregon disregard this factor, the Clinton administration implicitly adopted the more radical of the two views of the ADA evinced by the Bush administration—namely, that it prohibits a state from preferring interventions that are "more likely to result in a return to an asymptomatic state to interventions that would leave a patient with residual symptomatic conditions." Id. at 553. (Note that the discrimination to which this interpretation of the act is addressed is not discrimination against individuals with particular conditions but discrimination against certain medical treatments and procedures on the ground that they, unlike other treatments or procedures, might leave persons with a disability.) Will this interpretation of the ADA advance the welfare of Medicaid recipients or of persons who are possible candidates for extended Medicaid coverage?

As it finally implemented its reforms, Oregon stopped well short of taking anything like the radical approach to prioritizing health care spending that it originally contemplated.

5. *The "Comprehensive Benefit Package" in the Clinton Health Security Act.* The health reforms proposed by the Clinton administration in 1993–94, although not adopted by Congress, are of interest in the present context:

> The opening section of the Health Security Act declared that "each eligible individual is entitled to the comprehensive benefit package [specified in the act] through the applicable health plan in which the individual is enrolled." Although this language would certainly have created a statutory entitlement, it would arguably have been an entitlement only to a "benefit package," not an independent entitlement to particular health services. The act also purported, however, to enumerate "the items and services" of which "the comprehensive benefit package shall consist." Yet most of the items and services it enumerated were defined only in the most general terms. Thus, "hospital services" were described only as inpatient, outpatient, and emergency services rendered by certain institutions. Many other mandated benefits were also merely listed and minimally defined, rather than being specified in detail. In these cases, there was an obvious need for further specification. It was not clear whether the needed clarifica-

tions could have come only from the government and the courts or whether they might also have been supplied in contracts between health plans and their subscribers.

Although the comprehensive benefit package was undefined in many respects, there were several instances in which the act approached regulatory specificity in defining what health plans must commit themselves to pay for, thus seeming to create a statutory entitlement to particular care. It did this sometimes by cross-referencing the Medicare benefits outlined in § 1861 of the Social Security Act and other times by supplying a specific [often quite generous] standard for determining coverage. The act, for example, seemed to * * * create an entitlement to coverage of any durable medical equipment that "improves functional ability" * * *.[6] The drafting of the mental health benefit was also unfortunate in seeming to create an entitlement to care for any "diagnosable mental or substance abuse disorder" accompanied by a "functional impairment"—criteria that seemingly invite psychiatrists to define a vast number of human frailties as diseases that health plans are obligated to treat.[7]

Even though some parts of the comprehensive benefit package might have seemed to create a generous entitlement to specific services, however, the act qualified all of its definitions of covered services by a blanket exclusion of any "item or service ... that is not medically necessary or appropriate." These qualifying terms were generally undefined, although the act's new National Health Board was to have the power to issue regulations or guidelines to "interpret the comprehensive benefit package" and to classify particular items or services as unnecessary or inappropriate. The board's authority to define what was and was not covered did not appear to be plenary, however. Indeed, the drafters probably anticipated that the specific obligations of health plans and providers would in most instances continue to be determined as they have generally been in the past—by the legal system, having reference to contracts where they are unambiguous but mostly to professional norms, customary practices, and other generally applicable, centrally defined standards. Although centrally defined standards would include any applicable determinations by the National Health Board, the act did not make the board solely responsible for deciding which services were covered by the benefit package. In fact, the board was given no role in administratively adjudicating coverage disputes, such as it would have had if it were the ultimate arbiter of such matters. Instead, such disputes were to be resolved through an administrative system operated by the states and the Department of Labor. In various ways, therefore, the act appeared to treat the specific duty of providers and

6. Another mandatory benefit, "clinical preventive services," was also spelled out in enough detail to approximate a seeming entitlement to specific care. Here, however, the act's mandate could be explained by specific market-failure (public health) considerations that are lacking with respect to most other services. The somewhat exceptional character of this mandate thus helps to prove the general rule that, as to most clinical matters, the act was intended to leave health plans and providers significant discretion.

7. A contractual limit on such liberality in treating mental illness should be permissible, it would seem, if the plan takes a comparably conservative (nondiscriminatory) attitude toward all other medical problems. * * *

health plans to patients as still a legal and contractual matter rather than as a purely regulatory issue. It might thus have avoided finally displacing contracts as a possible source of definitions of patient entitlements to actual services.

At several points, however, the Health Security Act clearly discouraged the use of contracts to particularize entitlements. Thus, it stated that "the items and services in the comprehensive benefit package shall not be subject to any duration or scope limitation ... not required or authorized under this Act." The act also authorized the National Health Board to adopt such regulations or guidelines "as may be necessary to assure uniformity in the application of the comprehensive benefit package across all health plans." Finally, "the Board shall interpret the comprehensive benefit package ... and take such steps as may be necessary to assure that the comprehensive benefit package is available on a uniform national basis to all eligible individuals." These last two provisions, seemingly empowering the board to homogenize all medical care, revealed the egalitarian concerns and regulatory impulses of the drafters and suggested that such concerns and impulses had trumped such other values as freedom, responsibility, diversity, efficiency, and choice.

Thus, even though the act did not expressly rule out contracts as instruments for expanding the range of consumer choice, it is possible that it would have created an environment in which innovative contractual definitions of rights and obligations would not have been well received, especially if they seemed intended to save money for the plan. The act, however, clearly left room for qualitative differences among health plans. Thus, plans could have offered the comprehensive benefit package at different prices. Although price differences were permitted only within a limited range dictated by egalitarian concerns, the potential for variation remained significant. Thus, a regional health alliance would have been required to allow plans pricing freedom within a range up to 120 percent of the weighted average of premiums in the area. To the extent that the act encouraged competition on both price and quality, it validated the qualitative differences that may exist among different providers and among different organizational and compensation arrangements under which care is delivered. The interesting question * * * is whether it would also have been both tolerable and feasible, following Clinton-style health reform, for health plans to differentiate themselves by contract.

C. Havighurst, Health Care Choices: Private Contracts as Instruments of Health Reform 46–48 (1995) (references to sections of the bill omitted). For a critique of the "comprehensive" benefits approach in the Clinton proposal, leading to doubts about the proposal's political viability, see Blumstein, Health Care Reform: The Policy Context, 29 Wake Forest L. Rev. 15, 34–38 (1994).

Public Programs and Policies

NOTES ON FEDERAL HEALTH CARE PROGRAMS FOR THE ELDERLY AND THE POOR

1. *Medicare.* The largest public program for financing individuals' health care is the federal Medicare program (Title XVIII of the Social Security

Act). As a program of social insurance (rather than a welfare program benefitting only a means-tested minority of the population), Medicare is politically popular. As an entitlement program not subject to the congressional appropriation process, however, its high and rapidly rising cost ($156.5 billion in 1995, up from $70.7 billion in 1985 and $7.1 billion in 1970) makes it a perennial problem for Congress and federal budget makers. Indeed, Medicare accounts for more than 10 percent of the entire federal operating budget (excluding interest on the federal debt), and its annual surpluses or deficits are now counted in calculating the federal budget deficit.

(a) *Parts A and B*. The basic Medicare program has two complementary parts: *hospital insurance* (HI), known as Part A, and *supplementary medical insurance* (SMI), known as Part B. Part A, the HI program, covers not only hospital inpatient services but also inpatient services furnished by other institutional providers, such as nursing homes, home health agencies, and hospices. It is paid for exclusively out of Social Security (FICA) payroll taxes. Its coverage extends to all persons 65 and over who receive old-age benefits under Social Security or the railroad retirement system—nearly the entire elderly population. (In 1998, the Clinton administration proposed expanding Medicare so that the "near-elderly" between 55 and 65 could voluntarily enroll in the program at their own expense.) In addition to covering the elderly, the HI program also covers persons under 65 who have qualified (after a 24–month waiting period) for Social Security disability benefits and all persons with end-stage renal (kidney) disease (ESRD). In 1982, Congress passed legislation to control Medicare costs by requiring employers with health benefit plans to extend plan coverage to employees age 65 and over. Thus, Medicare coverage is often secondary to employer-provided insurance.

The Medicare SMI program pays for the services of doctors and for a wide variety of outpatient services. Participation in it is voluntary, however, and requires payment of a monthly premium ($42.50 in 1996). Premiums, however, are nominal in relation to the actuarial value of the coverage, with the difference made up out of general revenues. SMI is open to anyone eligible for Part A benefits and also to aged persons who for some reason are not enrolled under Part A.

(b) *Costs and Financing*. Medicare spending is concentrated on a relatively small percentage of beneficiaries with serious health problems. Thus, in 1993, about 10% of all Medicare enrollees accounted for 70% of all payments. On a per-beneficiary basis, Medicare payments in that year amounted to $3,385 for each of the 32.4 million aged beneficiaries and $3,174 for the 3.7 million under–65 disabled ones; 237,000 ESRD patients (some of them elderly or disabled) cost the program an average of $30,296 each.

The burden of paying Medicare's rising costs year after year has been a consistent irritant to federal policymakers. To be sure, Medicare was set up to be largely self-supporting through payroll taxes, premiums, and beneficiary cost sharing, with only limited support from general tax revenues of the federal government. Nevertheless, like the Social Security program itself, Medicare was not designed as a true insurance system, financed by actuarially determined contributions by prospective participants, and it was never intended to have reserves approximating the program's expected liabilities. Instead, current benefits under Part A are financed out of payroll taxes on virtually a pay-as-you-go basis. To the extent there is any excess revenue in a given year, it is set aside in a trust fund for use in future years when increasing outlays eventually exceed revenues.

Congress has had to increase payroll taxes from time to time over the years to finance Part A benefits and to prevent a deficit in the trust fund. In 1996, Medicare outlays under Part A began once again to surpass income. The Part A trust fund is predicted to be exhausted as early as 2001 unless Congress takes measures to head off that event.

Although Part B is financed in part by beneficiary premiums, those premiums have never covered the full cost of SMI. Currently, 68.5% of the cost of SMI is paid for out of general federal revenues. In 1995, President Clinton threatened to veto a congressional proposal to increase the beneficiary's share beyond 31.5%. The burden of these premiums on low-income persons is mitigated by the practice of state governments of paying SMI premiums for its elderly Medicaid beneficiaries.

(c) *Administration*. The Medicare program is overseen by the Health Care Financing Administration (HCFA) in the Department of Health and Human Services (DHHS), the budget of which exceeds that of all but a few nations of the world. Congress, however, closely oversees—some would say, micromanages—the program, particularly when different political parties control the legislative and executive branches. On a daily basis, Medicare is for the most part administered like private health insurance through private contractors, which are called "intermediaries" under Part A and "carriers" under Part B. The program's methods of paying providers are outlined in chapter 2(§D).

Recent data showing that private-sector health spending is growing more slowly than Medicare expenditures suggest not only that greater discipline in spending is possible without threatening access or quality of care but also that Medicare needs to respond to the changing nature of the U.S. health care system, with its growing emphasis on cost-containment incentives and competition among integrated systems of care. An increasing trend is the encouragement of beneficiaries to enroll in HMOs and other managed care plans. These plans generally receive a payment from the federal government intended to reflect the actuarially expected cost of caring for each individual so enrolled and thereafter assume legal and administrative responsibility for providing needed care.

(d) *Benefits*. Despite its high cost and generosity in covering medical and acute hospital care, Medicare's benefit package has been far from comprehensive. Because the program imposes substantial deductibles and coinsurance requirements and strictly limits its coverage of such things as nursing-home care and outpatient prescription drugs, the program has not entirely relieved the elderly of their health care cost burdens. Indeed,

Medicare paid only 45% of the personal health care expenses of the elderly in 1987. Moreover, the mean out-of-pocket burden of such expenses (including SMI and private insurance premiums), measured as a percentage of mean income, was approximately the same (15%) for the elderly in 1987 as it had been before Medicare and Medicaid took effect. See Waldo et al., Health Expenditures by Age Group, 1977 and 1987, Health Care Fin.Rev., Summer 1989, at 111, 114. Some beneficiaries have obtained additional financial protection by purchasing private "Medi-gap" insurance covering Medicare deductibles, copayments, and some noncovered expenses. As previously noted, low-income elderly have their Medicare benefits supplemented by Medicaid.

Partly in recognition of inadequacies in Medicare coverage, Congress in 1988 enacted legislation known as the Medicare Catastrophic Loss Prevention Act to expand benefits and cover so-called "catastrophic" expenses. This legislation set a maximum limit on beneficiaries' annual outlays for deductibles and copayments on covered services, with Medicare to pay all costs above this "cap." It also expanded coverage of nursing-home and home health care and provided new coverage of outpatient prescription drugs. These new benefits were to be financed by the beneficiaries themselves, however, through some combination of increased Part B premiums and a new "supplemental" premium to be paid only by higher-income elderly. The latter tax proved to be the legislation's undoing. In response to a backlash by upper-income elderly, Congress almost immediately repealed major portions of the 1988 legislation. Medicare Catastrophic Coverage Repeal Act of 1989, P.L. No. 101–234 (Dec. 13, 1989). Some new preventive care benefits were added to the program in the Balanced Budget Act of 1997.

The ESRD program is an anomaly in American public policy. Although technically a part of a public program designed principally for the elderly, it represents a national health insurance program for victims (of any age) of a particular disease and is viewed by many as a model for a national system of universal coverage. See, e.g., Friedman, End–Stage Renal Disease Therapy: An American Success Story, 275 J.A.M.A. 1118 (1996).

(e) *Medicare's New Part C.* In the Balanced Budget Act of 1997, Congress added a new Part C to the Medicare statute, creating a new program entitled Medicare + Choice. The object of the new program, which will be discussed more fully in chapter 2(§D), was to give beneficiaries more options with respect to the way they receive their federally financed benefits. A beneficiary who takes no affirmative action will remain in the traditional fee-for-service Medicare program under Parts A and B. In creating Part C, however, Congress aimed to make it easier for beneficiaries to enroll at federal expense in a private managed-care plan of some kind. Alternatively, a beneficiary (or at least the first 390,000 who apply) can elect to have the federal government contribute to a so-called Medical Savings Account (MSA), from which major health expenses can be paid once the individual has satisfied a high deductible. Part C also allows the beneficiary to purchase conventional fee-for-service coverage of a kind that has become less and less available in the private market as a whole and that is likely to be quite costly to beneficiaries over and above the federal contribution. The 1997 legislation represented a major overhaul of Medicare, the most extensive since its enactment in 1965. More changes in this hugely expensive and highly symbolic program undoubtedly lie ahead. See generally Medicare Payment Advisory Commission, Report to the Congress: Context for a Changing Medicare Program (June 1998) (highlighting outstanding technical and policy issues in wake of Balanced Budget Act of 1997); R. Reischauer et al., Medicare: Preparing for the Challengers of the 21st Century (1998).

2. *Medicaid.* Medicaid (Title XIX of the Social Security Act) is the other major federal entitlement program for health care and represents the primary effort of government to meet the medical needs of low-income individuals. Although fundamentally a federal program, Medicaid is administered in each state under a "State Plan" created by the state in accordance with extensive federal requirements. A state has significant discretion, however, in establishing eligibility and benefits and in making purchasing arrangements with providers. The federal statute has been judicially described as "almost unintelligible to the uninitiated," Friedman v. Berger, 547 F.2d 724, 727 n. 7 (2d Cir.1976), and, although more information is provided in chapter 2(§D), these materials cannot address the myriad technical issues that arise in administering the program. Valuable technical explanations of the Medicaid program, especially for lawyers, are provided in publications of the National Health Law Program. E.g., An Advocate's Guide to the Medicaid Program (1993). See generally 3 Medicare & Medicaid Guide (CCH) ¶ 14,000 *et seq.* (looseleaf).

Medicaid was enacted simultaneously with Medicare in 1965, though without adequate appreciation of its huge potential significance or its huge potential cost. See generally R. Stevens & R. Stevens, Welfare Medicine in America (1974). "Today, Medicaid's role as a health insurer and safety net for vulnerable Americans is visible throughout the health care system. Medicaid finances care for one in four American children, pays for one third of the nation's births, assists 60% of people living in poverty, pays for half of all nursing home care, and accounts for 13% of all health care spending." Rowland, Medicaid at 30: New Challenges for the Nation's Health Safety Net, 274 J.A.M.A. 271 (1995). The Medicaid program has significantly increased the use of physicians and hospital care by the poor. Between 1963 and 1974, for example, the proportion of low-income persons seeing a physician during the year rose 30%, and the proportion of low-income persons using hospitals rose 35%; in contrast, use of physicians and hospitals by the nonpoor rose by only 4% and 2%, respectively, during the same period. Freeman & Corey, Insurance Status and Access to Health Services Among Poor Persons, 28 Health Services Res. 531 (1993).

The Medicaid program's notoriously high and rising costs ($167.6 billion in FY 1996) pose perennial problems for the federal government and the states, which continuously struggle both to control them and to cover them out of general revenues. Indeed, Medicaid is the second largest item in most states' budgets, accounting on average for roughly 20% of general revenue spending. The political vulnerability of Medicaid at both the federal and state levels stems not only from its high cost but especially from its character (in contrast to Medicare) as a welfare program targeted at a relatively powerless segment of the population.

(a) *Eligibility*. Medicaid was originally conceived, and is still largely maintained, as a supplement to federal welfare programs for the "deserving" poor. As a consequence, federal law requires participating states to provide coverage to such specified groups (the "categorically needy") as poor families receiving cash assistance and aged, blind, or disabled persons receiving assistance under the Supplemental Security Income (SSI) program. Welfare reform legislation in 1996 discontinued the Aid to Families with Dependent Children (AFDC) program, to which mandatory Medicaid coverage had previously been linked. A last-minute change provided, however, that states cannot terminate Medicaid eligibility for persons whose welfare entitlement is exhausted. See generally National Health Law Program, Inc. (NHeLP), An Analysis of the New Welfare Law and Its Effects on Medicaid Recipients (joint special edition newsletter, Aug. 1996).

In addition to the categories of individuals that states must cover under federal law, states are authorized, at their option, to extend federally-subsidized coverage to certain other groups. These include (*a*) low-income persons who do not receive cash assistance but who have the same demographic characteristics as those covered by welfare or SSI and (*b*) the so-called "medically needy"—those whose status and incomes after deducting their medical expenses would qualify them for welfare or SSI assistance. The various categories of mandatory and optionally coverable individuals are listed in 3 Medicare & Medicaid Guide (CCH) ¶ ¶ 14,231, 14,251. Because Medicaid is "means-tested," serious complexity, seemingly exceeding that of the personal income tax, is encountered in deciding who is eligible for benefits; moreover, eligibility of a single individual can fluctuate monthly. See, e.g., Atkins v. Rivera, 477 U.S. 154 (1986) (resolving complex issue concerning how a state could, under federal law, calculate individual income in determining who qualifies for Medicaid as "medically needy"); Mitchell v. Lipscomb, 851 F.2d 734 (4th Cir.1988) (treatment of sibling income in determining eligibility of "family unit").

Variations in state eligibility rules mean that, nationally, Medicaid does not provide uniform coverage to the poor. For example, between 1990 and 1992, Nevada covered slightly under 29% of the nonelderly poor, while over 60% were covered in the District of Columbia. In general, wealthier states have more generous programs. Even though budget constraints make expansions of state Medicaid programs difficult, there have been advances in some areas. Most notably, states have made particular efforts to extend coverage for pregnant women and children. See National Governors' Ass'n, State Coverage of Pregnant Women and Children (periodic updates). In addition, federal Medicaid requirements were amended in 1990 and again in 1993 to extend coverage to pregnant women and children in households with incomes up to 133% of the federally recognized poverty line. See 55 Fed.Reg. 48601 (Nov. 21, 1990); 58 Fed.Reg. 48612 (Sept. 17, 1993). A special requirement that states provide "early and periodic screening, diagnosis, and treatment" (EPSDT) extends protection to children up to the age of 21. See 42 C.F.R. § 441.50 (1993).

The population covered by Medicaid has fluctuated substantially over time. Between 1977 and 1983, for example, federal and state budget problems led to cutbacks reducing the population covered by Medicaid from 27 million to 22 million so that, by 1984, the percentage of persons below the poverty line covered by Medicaid had fallen from around 65% in 1976 to 38%. This figure again rose to approximately 58% in 1995.

In any event, the Medicaid program serves as only a partial guarantee of care to low-income persons, especially the working poor. From its enactment, the program has reflected the traditional concern for the truly helpless or "deserving" poor, with the result that eligibility was closely linked to to actual or potential receipt of cash assistance under a federally sponsored welfare program (i.e. SSI or AFDC). This meant that states were not generally free to extend federally supported Medicaid eligibility to single individuals, childless couples, families with two resident parents, or others who were not within the reach of traditional welfare programs. (States could cover such individuals at their own expense, however.) The program's welfare link also meant that states would have to raise their eligibility levels for cash assistance in order to expand Medicaid coverage, something many states were unwilling to do. Recently, however, Congress has provided for administratively granted waivers of the usual statutory requirements in order that states can experiment with new ways of operating their Medicaid programs; in most cases, these waivers have been conditioned on the state's extension of coverage to otherwise ineligible low-income groups. These changes have substantially increased Medicaid coverage in some states. In addition, the 1996 welfare reform further attenuated the federal link between welfare and Medicaid, making eligibility for the latter program more extensive than eligibility for welfare.

An important feature of the Medicaid program is the extent to which it covers nursing home care. Many retired persons, struck by heavy medical expenses not covered by Medicare, eventually use up their income and assets and thus qualify for Medicaid. Such "spending down" helps to explain the high percentage (over half) of nursing home patients who are supported by state Medicaid programs. In effect, Medicaid provides a kind of universal coverage of long-term care and other catastrophic expenses, but does so only with a deductible equivalent to most of an individual's personal resources. This feature of the program has led Congress to legislate to prevent the states from making "spousal impoverishment" a precondition to receiving Medicaid nursing home benefits. In this area, Medicaid benefits many citizens not normally thought of as "the poor." See National Health Policy Forum, Eligibility for Medicaid in Nursing Homes: Coverage for Indigent or Well-off Older Americans? (Issue Brief No. 688, 1996). Medicaid: New Data on the Role of Medicaid in Paying for Nursing Home Care (AARP Public Policy Inst. 1996).

(b) *Administration.* States are understandably frustrated by federal Medicaid requirements that they must follow in order to receive federal matching funds despite their belief that the resulting costs are not justified. In addition, both HCFA and the states face continuing uncertainties because of congressional micromanagement of the program. The Administrative Conference of the United States (ACUS) sponsored studies of these administrative problems, resulting in a valuable description and discussion of the dynamics of the Medicaid program. Kinney, Rule and Policy Making for the Medicaid Program: A Challenge to Federalism, 51 Ohio St. L.J. 855 (1990). See also Recommendation 90–8, 1990 ACUS 35. The waiver program mentioned above allows states unprecedented flexibility and has been administered liberally in response to the concerns of states and governors.

(c) *Financing and Costs.* Medicaid is financed in large part by federal matching grants to states that maintain qualifying programs. "Federal financial participation" ranges from 50% to 83% of state program costs, with a higher percentage of matching funds going to states with lower per capita incomes. Total expenditures for Medicaid have more than quadrupled since 1975. Federal expenditures (in 1994 dollars) grew from $19 billion in 1975 to $82 billion in 1993, while state expenditures rose from $15 billion to $66 billion. Medicaid constitutes about 6 percent of the federal operating budget and accounted for about 42% of all federal funds allocated to the states in 1994, up from about 14% in 1975. In general, states can control their Medicaid costs only by varying eligibility and benefits within ranges permitted by federal law and by more prudent purchasing efforts permitted for the first time by federal legislation in 1981 and more recently by a highly liberal policy in waiving federal requirements for so-called "demonstration" projects undertaken by individual states. See chapter 2(§D); Coughlin et al., State Responses to the Medicaid Spending Crisis, 1988 to 1992, 19 J. Health Pol., Pol'y & L. 837 (1994).

The program is a prime candidate for major federal reform. In November 1995, for example, Congress passed legislation that would have converted Medicaid from a federal entitlement program to a program of block grants to the states. This legislation was vetoed by President Clinton, whose administration offered its own approaches to reform. Medicaid reform regularly appears on the congressional agenda.

3. *State Children's Health Insurance Program.* In the Balanced Budget Act of 1997, Congress allocated $24 billion over five years to create the State Children's Health Insurance Program ("SCHIP"), the largest expansion of public health coverage since Medicaid itself. Under SCHIP, the federal government makes matching grants to enable states to provide health insurance to children under 19 years of age in families with incomes up to twice the federal poverty line. States may spend the SCHIP money to expand existing Medicaid programs, to develop special insurance programs already in place, or to adopt a new plan for children's health needs. A significant concern in enacting the program was that new public funding would cause many persons with private coverage for their children to drop it in favor of the new subsidized coverage, thus raising the public cost of reaching the goal of covering half of the ten million previously uninsured children. To reduce the incidence of such "crowding-out," states are allowed to impose waiting periods (without coverage) and to require premiums or other types of cost-sharing from families with higher incomes, who are the most likely to have private health insurance coverage.

The design and implementation of state programs under SCHIP will vary from state to state, since Congress has not closely prescribed how the funds will be spent. While some states are expanding their Medicaid programs, others prefer another approach, such as subsidizing the purchase of private coverage or even providing vouchers that allow the parent to select from a full range of options. Questions exist as to which existing program expenditures may be counted by states in qualifying for matching funds.

4. *Other Federal Programs.* Medicare and Medicaid are both "entitlement" programs, meaning that the federal government is committed by law to pay the full cost of providing statutory benefits whatever that cost may turn out to be. In contrast, there are a number of "discretionary" health programs, the cost to the federal government of which is determined by annual budgetary appropriations. Such programs may retain their statutory authorization but be unfunded or funded at low levels in any particular year. In recent years, the government's relative inability to control the costs of entitlement programs has led to deep cuts in discretionary programs.

Discretionary programs that have been helpful in providing health services to the medically underserved include the Veterans Administration (VA), the National Health Services Corps, the Indian Health Service, and programs for migrant health, family planning, and community health centers. The VA operates an extensive system of hospitals for veterans, many of whom would otherwise be underserved. The National Health Services Corps employs physicians to work in medically underserved areas. The program provides medical school scholarships to recipients who agree to serve in the program for a certain number of years.

In the 1980s, a large number of discrete federal programs were folded into a series of block grants which Congress now makes annually to the states without closely specifying how the funds will be allocated among the various authorized uses. Block grants for the provision of health care services now include: Prevention and Treatment of Substance Abuse; Community Mental Health Services; Preventive Health and Health Services; and Maternal and Child Health. By way of example, the latter block grant may be used by the states for such purposes (among others) as maternal and child health services, hemophilia, genetic diseases, adolescent health services, and SSI disabled children's services; each of these was formerly a federal categorical program in which public and private organizations could participate by applying for federal grants.

For critical overviews of experience with the entire miscellany of federal health programs, see U.S. General Accounting Office, Block Grants: Characteristics, Experience, and Lessons Learned (1995); Blumenthal,

Right Turns, Wrong Turns and Roads Untaken: The Discretionary Federal Health Budget, in Center for National Policy, Health Care: How to Improve It and Pay for It (1985).

An array of special federal or state programs to subsidize or provide particular services in particular places would almost certainly be necessary even if government universally guaranteed health coverage. Rural and inner-city residents and persons with chronic health problems would undoubtedly continue to require some special attention, and numerous public health responsibilities could not be readily folded into a program concerned principally with ensuring access to personal health care.

NOTES AND QUESTIONS ON MOVEMENTS FOR FUNDAMENTAL HEALTH CARE REFORM

1. *Momentum for Federal Reform.* Apparent windows of opportunity for fundamental reform of the American health care system occur from time to time, but only rarely—as in 1965, when Medicare and Medicaid were enacted—do the political stars line up in a way that permits the enactment of revolutionizing legislation. Several times in the 1970s it seemed inevitable that Congress would enact a version of "national health insurance." Nevertheless, cost and other factors made designing an acceptable plan very difficult. In addition, proponents of a government solution seemed unwilling or unable to compromise enough to enact a program less grandiose than their initial vision. Thus, when President Nixon proposed a version of national health insurance (together with a guaranteed family income) in 1970, congressional Democrats raised the ante rather than let a Republican president get credit for the measure. Thereafter in the 1970s, legislative efforts were directed at laying the groundwork for national health insurance—by passing HMO and national health planning legislation, for example. The effort to construct an infrastructure for a national health system came to an end, however, with the defeat in 1979 of President Carter's proposal to regulate hospital revenues. After that watershed event, Congress for more than a decade addressed health care issues largely within the context of a market paradigm and paid relatively little attention to redistributive goals.

The 1990s, however, saw a substantial renewal of interest in major health care reform at the federal level. Indeed, some observers viewed the political prognosis for major reform as brighter then than ever before. In their view, costs were rising so rapidly that the business community would finally be receptive to extensive government intervention. In addition, physicians and hospitals were being squeezed in every direction and might, it was thought, support reforms that ensured additional public funding. Most important, it was believed that middle-class voters finally had reasons of their own to back major changes in the health care system. In 1991, Paul Starr described this new development and its political significance as follows:

> [A]s private insurance companies have refined their methods for rating groups and avoiding the highest health risks, they have put in jeopardy the security of many people who once thought the system protected them. Groups with older employees, particularly small businesses, and even whole industries and occupations find today that they have been red-lined as uninsurable. Millions of people, even with insurance, discover they have no coverage for pre-existing conditions, and others are reluctant to change jobs for fear of losing coverage. In principle, insurance is supposed to spread the costs of sickness among the healthy, but the practices of the insurance industry now run in the opposite direction: concentrating the costs of sickness among those most at risk.
>
> This "desocialization" of health insurance increasingly exposes the middle class to the insecurity of the uninsured poor. * * * In effect, the market-driven responses of employers and private insurers are undoing some of the middle-class insulation from health costs that made it so difficult to construct an alliance for health insurance reform across class lines.

Starr, The Middle Class and National Health Reform, Am. Prospect, Summer 1991, p. 7, 9.

2. *Policy Options*. But even though there may have been some consensus on the need for reform in the early 1990s, there was little agreement on a reform strategy. Indeed, the numerous bills introduced in Congress to increase the financial accessibility of care reflected a very wide range of policy options. Possible approaches to fundamental reform fall more or less into the following categories:

(a) *"Single-payer" plans*. Several proposals would have created a monolithic, government-managed purchaser of health care for all Americans. These plans would have resembled either the Medicare program (extended to cover the entire population), the widely admired system adopted in Canada in the 1970s, or the government-run health care systems featured in the welfare states of several European countries. Most proposals, however, would have avoided the costly entitlement feature of Medicare, setting instead a "global" annual budget within which administrators would have to operate the plan. In addition to allowing Congress to control costs by prospective budgeting, the single-payer approach also promised to yield significant savings in administrative costs over the private financing system. See U.S. General Accounting Office, Canadian Health Insurance: Lessons for the United States (1991) (estimating that eliminating private health insurance would result in savings of $75 billion a year). Obviously, this strategy, which lends itself to financing through progressive taxation as well as to equalizing benefits, appeals most strongly to those with egalitarian preferences. Most proposals, however, would leave some room (how much is always controversial) for individuals who are able to do so to opt out of the program entirely (as some families patronize private schools) or to pay additional amounts for more or better care than the plan entitles them to receive.

(b) *Employer mandates; "play-or-pay" plans.* This approach would preserve private health coverage but mandate that employers (or at least all employers over a certain size) provide health insurance for their workers. A variation on this theme would give an employer the option of either insuring its employees or paying a tax to finance public coverage of their workers. Although ostensibly intended to be less intrusive than a direct "employer mandate," some such "play-or-pay" plans would have made public coverage so much more attractive to employers that most would elect the government-run plan, leading in the long run to a single-payer model. E.g., Pepper Commission (U.S. Bipartisan Commission on Comprehensive Health Care), Access to Health Care and Long-term Care for All Americans, Medicare & Medicaid Guide (CCH) ¶ 38,402 (Mar. 2, 1990).

(c) *"Market reform" efforts.* This heading embraces all strategies (such as those noted previously) for making health insurance more accessible and affordable by correcting problems in the market for small-group and individual coverage and by eliminating regulatory requirements that allegedly make coverage unnecessarily costly. Most proposals of this kind would have included new subsidies in the form of tax credits or otherwise as an incentive to induce more people to procure private coverage. But for the most part such proposals were incremental rather than revolutionary in nature. The Health Insurance Association of America (HIAA), in particular, has sought to keep the discussion of health care reforms focused on incremental measures to improve the affordability, availability, and security of private coverage, especially for small employers. See, e.g., HIAA, Health Care Financing For All Americans: Private Market Reform and Public Responsibility (1991). The Health Insurance Portability and Accountability Act of 1996 (Kassebaum–Kennedy) is a good illustration of such an incremental measure.

(d) *"Managed-competition" plans.* This market-oriented approach to health care reform concentrates on facilitating effective purchasing of health coverage by small employment groups and individuals. Its objective is to rectify serious shortcomings of the market for health care by reshaping fundamentally the framework in which consumers choose their health coverage. It would do this by encouraging or mandating the creation of so-called "sponsors" to perform for participating consumers the same functions that large employers frequently perform for their employees in searching the market and structuring purchasing options. Thus, rather than simply purchasing coverage for the group, the manager of competition would prepare a menu of health plan options from which the participating consumers, with information specially provided, would choose the plan that best fits their individual needs. A key feature of the strategy is enough standardization of benefit packages and cost sharing that price differences would serve as a fairly reliable (though not the exclusive) indicator of the value of what is being purchased, so that individual consumers could give better effect to their preferences for different combinations of cost and quality. Standardizing benefits would also help in the prevention of "risk selection"—that is, efforts by competing health plans to attract only healthier subscribers. (It is observed that plans may manipulate their benefits for this purpose, such as by appealing to younger families by offering attractive maternity and well-child benefits or by deterring the less healthy by offering poor coverage for chronic diseases.) Managed-competition sponsors might also fight risk selection by requiring open enrollment, coverage of pre-existing conditions, and indefinite renewability of coverage. See generally A. Enthoven, The Theory and Practice of Managed Competition in Health Care Finance (1988); Ellwood et al., The Jackson Hole Initiatives for a Twenty–First Century American Health Care System, 1 Health Econ. 149 (1992); Enthoven & Kronick, A Consumer–Choice Health Plan for the 1990s: Universal Health Insurance in a System Designed to Promote Quality and Economy (pts. 1 & 2), 320 New Eng. J. Med. 29, 94 (1989).

(e) *Medicaid expansion.* Some reform plans contemplated reducing the number of uninsured Americans by expanding Medicaid coverage and allowing "buy-in" by lower-income working persons.

(f) *"Medical Savings Accounts."* A relatively recent reform idea, popular with congressional conservatives, involves so-called "medical savings accounts" (MSAs), which are being given an experimental demonstration (limited to 750,000 employees of small businesses and self-insured individuals) under the Health Insurance Portability and Accountability Act. (A similar experiment with MSAs for Medicare beneficiaries was launched in the Balanced Budget Act of 1997, discussed in chapter 2(§D).) Tax incentives comparable to those offered for the purchase of ordinary health coverage would encourage individuals to set funds aside in MSAs for future use in defraying routine health bills while maintaining "catastrophic" coverage to take care of expenses beyond a certain (deductible) amount. Expenditures below the deductible would come from the MSA, but funds deposited in the MSA and not spent on health services would eventually be returned tax-free to the consumer. The theory behind the MSA strategy is that consumers spending their own money on health care (assuming that they perceive funds in MSAs as being fungible with their other assets) would be more cost-conscious than insured individuals in selecting providers and in deciding to consume services. This proposal reflects some nostalgia for an earlier era when physicians and patients could decide on treatments without any involvement of a third party. It is therefore highly attractive to some providers and highly threatening to managed-care plans. Issues include the risk of adverse selection, which would occur if, as seems likely, healthier people opted to create MSAs and left the less healthy to be covered by conventional health insurance and managed-care plans. See generally American Soc'y of Actuaries, Medical Savings Accounts: Cost Implications and Design Issues (Public Policy Monograph #1, 1995).

3. *The Clinton Proposals.* The most notable reform proposal of the early 1990s was, of course, the one advanced by the Clinton administration in 1993, the so-called Health Security Act, S. 1757, H.R. 3600, 103d Cong., 1st Sess. (1993). That ill-fated proposal combined elements of the "global-budget" and "managed-competition" strategies. Nevertheless, even though it was promoted by such claims as that it would "put consumers in the driver's seat [by] unleashing the market forces that will lower costs and improve quality," the Clinton bill visualized a much more prominent and prescriptive role for government than was contemplated by the original advocates of managed competition. For example, the monolithic, government-sponsored "regional health alliances" provided for in the Health Security Act were only distant cousins of the sponsors visualized by managed-competition theorists.

The reasons for the defeat of the Clinton bill in Congress will be debated for a long time. See, e.g., H. Johnson & D. Broder, The System: The American Way of Politics at the Breaking Point (1996) (leading journalists' assessment, attributing outcome to political forces and miscalculations); T. Skocpol, Boomerang: Clinton's Health Security Effort and the Turn against Government in U.S. Politics (1995); Symposium, Health Reform: Past and Future, Health Affs., Spring 1995; Roundtable on the Defeat of Reform, J. Health Pol., Pol'y & L., Summer 1995. Some of the explanation for the failure of the Clinton reforms certainly lies, however, in the failure of a young administration to appreciate the limits of its political mandate and its indulgence of insiders who preferred a heavier involvement of government than Congress and the nation were prepared to endorse. The following assessment, though strongly worded, offers a perspective on the Clinton bill that connects directly to some of the themes of this chapter, while also offering some insights regarding the difficult political environment in which health care reform must be essayed:

> Much of the regulatory complexity of the Clinton Health Security Act stemmed from an underlying egalitarian agenda. Seeking to achieve a strongly egalitarian result in a political environment hostile to new taxes and redistributive schemes, the drafters of the proposal faced the task of moving very substantial resources from "haves" to "have-nots" without revealing the full magnitude or the radical purpose of the transfers involved. This was done in the act through a kind of shell game by which funds would have been appropriated from employers and others, pooled by health alliances, and then redistributed in ways that effectively broke any link between the amount an individual pays in and the value of the coverage he receives in return. The persons whose resources were to be tapped in this manner were not so much well-to-do taxpayers * * * as ordinary working people. Through a process not labeled as taxation, a substantial portion of workers' wages were to be captured and applied to doing good as the program drafters defined it—giving health care more or less equally to everyone without regard to contribution or desert. Even if a majority of voters would agree that some redistribution of incomes is warranted to ensure more systematic meeting of significant health needs, many of those voters, if they knew what was happening, would probably find the act's egalitarianism excessively gratuitous.
>
> Partly for the same political reasons that caused the administration not to propose a national single-payer system, the Health Security Act did not wear its egalitarianism on its sleeve. Although it would have created a clear entitlement to a comprehensive benefit package, it nowhere declared

a fully fleshed out statutory right to health care. * * * The act's egalitarian aims appeared clearly, however, in provisions contemplating enforced "uniformity" in the provision of benefits.

* * * One sign of the political astuteness of the act's drafters was their success in not revealing on the face of the bill how the extension, expansion, and equalization of benefits, with only limited new funding, would necessitate the involuntary rationing of arguably beneficial care. Because the administration could claim that only wasteful, "inappropriate" care would be squeezed out, those who paid good money into the system could not prove what they might suspect—that the drafters intended to deprive them of beneficial services so that others would receive equal treatment. * * *

Although the act's egalitarian agenda was fairly well disguised in its complex machinery, its drafters revealed their ideology in the unofficial (but widely circulated) "preliminary working group draft" of September 7, 1993. That document declared one of the "ethical foundations" of the plan to be "EQUALITY OF CARE: The system should avoid the creation of a tiered system[,] providing care based only on differences of need, not individual or group characteristics." Judging from the comprehensiveness of the benefit package and the manner in which its requirements were to be fleshed out, the drafters did indeed intend to give to each according to his needs. * * *

Although the Clinton program appeared dedicated to giving to each according to his needs, it did not propose to take from each worker according to his means. Instead, it would have imposed the equivalent of a regressive payroll tax. It was no accident that working people had trouble recognizing the taxlike character of the contributions to be made on their behalf to the health security system. For one thing, the burden appeared to fall mostly on employers. It is common knowledge among economists, however, that any cost that an employer is required to incur for an individual worker ultimately reduces that worker's other compensation. In addition, although the tax was disguised as a "premium" such as most workers were already accustomed to paying, the payments were largely mandatory. Moreover, they were not earmarked for the employee's direct benefit but instead were to be channeled by law into a central fund. Although that fund might have been collected by a private rather than a public entity (an alliance), it was to be applied to publicly defined purposes according to statutory rules. It could be argued, perhaps, that taxpayers who have hitherto neglected the needs of the poor and uninsured are fair game for such stealth taxes if the revenue is needed to finance some form of universal coverage. Nevertheless, it is fair to question the use of deception to finance a system that is driven by an egalitarian ideology that few voters (other than potential beneficiaries) probably share. Because of its hidden egalitarian agenda, the Clinton program would cost working persons a great deal more—in marginal jobs lost, in reduced take-home pay, and in beneficial health services rationed away—than universal coverage has to cost.

The Clinton program, in trying to bridge the gulf between true egalitarianism and a system based on market choices, was true to the principles of neither and suffered the shortcomings of both. Shrinking from imposing a single-payer system, it would * * * have incurred the high transaction and administrative costs of operating and regulating a seemingly pluralistic system. The * * * egalitarianism it embodied, though, would have tied the hands of competing health plans in writing their contracts[, thus denying] them the only means by which they could explicitly tailor their offerings to meet the various preferences and needs of consumers. * * *

In any event, the political problems that the Clinton program encountered were traceable in large measure to its egalitarian thrust. The high financial cost of leveling up—equalizing care at current levels of utilization—and the strong political resistance to leveling down—rationing care to bring everyone down to the level that government deems affordable for its clients—suggest the magnitude of the political challenge of bringing a strongly egalitarian system into being. In view of these political obstacles, the Clinton plan attempted to level up and down simultaneously without resembling a purely egalitarian single-payer system too closely. Yet its leanings toward an egalitarian outcome were so strong, and ultimately so poorly disguised and so costly, as to carry with them the seeds of political defeat.

C. Havighurst, Health Care Choices: Private Contracts as Instruments of Health Reform 75–80 (1995).

4. *Public or Private Financing?* What are the arguments for and against retaining private intermediaries in health care financing? As noted above, some have claimed that the administrative costs of American health care financing are extremely high relative to those of government-run systems. See also Woolhandler & Himmelstein, The Deteriorating Administrative Efficiency of the U.S. Health Care System, 324 New Eng. J. Med. 1253 (1991). Do Americans get anything in return for the added costs of private financing? Is it relevant that they already have the option of buying (through certain types of HMO) private protection that does not entail all the administrative costs of insured fee-for-service medicine? Note that HMOs operate on a predetermined "global" budget, very much as the Canadian system does, and can avoid numerous transaction costs simply by employing physicians on a salary.

To be sure, a single-payer scheme would avoid many of the costs associated with marketing competing health plans (although some provider marketing efforts would probably continue under a single-payer system). But are such costs pure waste? Medicare and most state Medicaid programs are relying increasingly on competing managed-care plans to provide services. Does this suggest that competition yields benefits offsetting the marketing and other costs it inevitably entails?

Under what handicaps does a public program such as Medicare or Medicaid operate, in comparison with a private health plan, in refusing to deal with certain providers or in denying payment for certain services that it regards as inappropriate but that patients might demand? (Students who have studied administrative law will be better positioned to answer this question.) What advantages might it have in setting prices?

Some of the added costs associated with private coverage are so-called "underwriting" costs, incurred to protect the health plan against adverse selection. Could these costs be reduced by regulations prescribing who must be covered and the nature of coverage (precluding exclusion of pre-existing conditions, for example)? (Regulation of this kind, typified by the Kassebaum–Kennedy Health Insurance Portability and Accountability Act of 1996, might also make it easier for individuals to obtain coverage or to retain it.) Could underwriting costs also be minimized by adopting a variant of managed competition, under which a sponsor or manager would create the framework for consumer choice and prescribe rules by which the players must play? Is it clear that health plans could be effectively prevented from engaging in all forms of "risk selection"? The case against private coverage rests heavily on *(a)* the perceived difficulty of getting competitors to focus on efficiently delivering services of the kind and quality consumers desire rather than on trying to select better risks and *(b)* the perceived inequity in letting healthier people pay lower premiums than those who present greater risks to the insurer.

A fundamental question, unanswerable at this point, is whether competing private insurers and organized health plans are both willing and able to offer a full range of clear, meaningful choices to American consumers. If competing health plans do not in fact offer meaningful options, where is the pluralism that competition is presumed to foster? In other words, if consumers' choices are limited in practice (or prescribed by law), why cling to the belief that the market serves consumers better in this field than government would? On these large questions, see Havighurst, Why Preserve Private Health Care Financing?, in R. Helms, ed., American Health Policy: Critical Issues for Reform (1992).

There is in fact some reason to question whether the market for health care is catering to the full range of consumer needs. For example, it was observed earlier that there may be something seriously wrong with a market in which some 40 million people are unable to find a product within their means. Similarly, if Canadian-style medical care is as good a value as many say, why is something like it not already a popular option in the American market? A possible hypothesis is that the American market essentially gives consumers only two choices: They must either purchase an entitlement to first-class, state-of-the-art, American-style medical care or take their chances with the safety net that more or less exists for those without health coverage. If this hypothesis is valid (and it is essentially a legal question that the student should keep in mind for later consideration), then Canadian-style options are effectively precluded because U.S. health care plans and providers are not free to economize in all the ways Canada does—such as by delaying elective procedures and limiting use of high-tech diagnostic tests. Thus, the American legal system may be one reason why American purchasers seeking good, economical health care (such as Canada allegedly provides) have a hard time finding it. Although it would be premature to try to validate this diagnosis at this point, posing the policy issue in this way is a good way to keep the forest in view while studying the individual legal trees that constitute it.

5. *Mandating Private Coverage?* Given the difficulty of imposing new taxes to finance new subsidies for lower-income persons and the uninsured, the most promising strategy available to policymakers at the moment is probably to mandate that private parties purchase the coverage that government wishes to see provided. See generally Symposium, Mandates: The Road to Reform?, Health Affairs, Spring 1994.

The most likely approach is some form of employer mandate. As happened in the case of the Clinton bill of 1993–94, proposals for such mandates meet intense resistance from small employers and employers in low-wage industries. Large employers, on the other hand, often support the imposition of mandates on others, particularly their competitors. As a policy matter, all proposals to require employers to bear the cost of coverage must face the objection that they would have adverse effects on the employability and wages of marginal workers. There should be no illusion that anyone other than the workers themselves bear most of the cost of mandated coverage.

Another way to achieve universal coverage would be to require that each individual obtain a minimum level of health coverage for himself. Interestingly, a proposal of this kind was put forward by a prominent conservative think tank. See Heritage Foundation, A National Health System for America (1989). Rather than predicating the case for universal health insurance on any suppositional "right to health care," this proposal stressed the obligation of individuals to provide for themselves and not to freeload on the community's good will by going without coverage, while counting on health care providers to care for them without charge when a serious need arises. The proposal contemplated some public assistance for lower-income persons complying with the mandate. For another proposal that would mandate individual coverage with tax credits, see M. Pauly et al., Responsible National Health Insurance (1992). What problems would you anticipate in in mandating that all individuals obtain a minimum measure of health coverage?

6. *State Reform Initiatives*. Even before the failure of the Clinton reforms, major reform efforts were being actively pursued in many states. See Iglehart, Health Care Reform: The States, 320 New Eng.J.Med. 75 (1994); Symposium, Health Affs., Summer 1993; U.S. GAO, Access to Health Care: States Respond to Growing Crisis (1992). Following the defeat of the Health Security Act, the states became even more the focus of attention. Nevertheless, even though the states have a great deal of responsibility for regulating American health care, they are significantly limited in their ability to effectuate fundamental reform of health care financing. See generally Moon & Holohan, Can States Take the Lead in Health Care Reform?, 268 J.A.M.A. 1588 (1992). Perhaps the most fundamental problem is that states, which inevitably compete to attract and retain investment and employment opportunities for their citizens, are significantly con-

strained in imposing costly mandates or heavy taxes on employers. Likewise, they must be careful not to repel productive, tax-paying citizens or to attract from other states an undue number of persons unwilling or unable to insure themselves. See M. Sparer, Medicaid and the Limits of State Health Reform (1996). Do these observations suggest a possible reason why Hawaii has come closer to achieving universal coverage than any other state (see discussion below)?

State authority to control health care within their borders is also limited by federal dominance in some areas. Thus, Medicare, a major purchaser, is amenable to state control only in limited ways, and the Medicaid program is run in substantial respects from Washington rather than state capitals. On the other hand, states have—and have aggressively used—substantial power to influence the health care system through the arrangements they make to provide health coverage for state employees.

Perhaps the most frustrating federal barrier to state reform efforts has been ERISA. As seen in § B of this chapter, ERISA substantially curbs the power of states to mandate, regulate, and tax employee benefit plans. The exception that proves the rule here is Hawaii, which obtained a congressional waiver of ERISA in the 1970s allowing it to impose the heavy duties on employers that are necessary to effectuate near-universal coverage. 29 U.S.C. § 1144(b)(5) (1994). See Standard Oil Co. of California v. Agsalud, 633 F.2d 760 (9th Cir.1980), affirmed mem. 454 U.S. 801 (1981) (invalidating Hawaii Prepaid Health Care Act, necessitating special exception). (Could a state achieve a result similar to that in Hawaii by adopting the "play-or-pay" strategy?) Among other state legislative reforms that have been held under ERISA not to bind self-insured employers are provisions regulating conversion privileges (to individual from group coverage after leaving employment) and requirements of participation in insurance pools extending coverage to uninsurables. See generally Jordan, *Travelers Insurance*: New Support for the Argument to Restrain ERISA Pre-emption, 13 Yale J. Reg. 3 (1996). Does *Travelers* suggest that state regulation of entities that merely do business with employee benefit plans is now unlikely to be preempted despite the impact that such regulation may have on the cost of such plans?

7. *The Prospects for Fundamental Reform.* Many continue to believe that some kind of fundamental health care reform is necessary in the United States. See, e.g., H. Aaron, ed., The Problem That Won't Go Away: Reforming U.S. Health Care Financing (1996). Nevertheless, significant problems continue to exist in shaping the political coalition necessary for any reform featuring significant redistribution of income. Moreover, government's budgetary constraints and voter resistance to higher taxes make it difficult to imagine putting much additional public money into health care anytime soon. Although some expansion in insurance coverage might be financed out of savings in administrative and marketing costs that could be achieved by centralizing financing and decision making, there is resistance to centralizing this amount of control and buying power in government hands. Finally, whatever type of reform is attempted, there will have to be a strong emphasis on controlling costs—by means yet to be fully specified or accepted by either consumers or providers of care.

A particular difficulty with reform scenarios is that, even though many observers have long believed that giving all Americans a public guarantee of health coverage was only a matter of time, the target (as some would define it) is receding, rather than getting easier to hit. Despite some recent moderation in the trend, the cost of state-of-the-art health care still rises significantly faster each year than does the nation's ability to pay—as measured, for example, by GDP. Thus, the incremental public cost of giving everyone an entitlement to mainstream medical care increases each year it is not done. By the same token, creating an entitlement today commits government and society to coming up with new money each year to cover its increasing cost—unless an effective and acceptable method of limiting the entitlement can be devised.

But limiting entitlements requires some centralized method of rationing future care so that financing for certain desirable services will not be available. For this reason, "rationing" is a buzz word in political debates. The idea is unpopular because it would interfere with physicians' clinical freedom, which patients regard as a vital protection of their own interests, and would arbitrarily deny services to those who wish and can afford to purchase them. An alternative strategy, suggested by the President's Commission report, supra, is to find a way to define basic benefits that will be guaranteed to all but that will not also be a ceiling on what others may have. But financing of these basic benefits for all would have have to come either from employers under mandates to provide them or from explicit new taxes. The expedient of financing expanded coverage out of savings in administrative costs and new rationing would not be available in any system that preserves voluntary private insurance for some and provides public or mandated coverage for everyone else.

One way of approaching and conceptualizing cost controls is as a redistribution, not of income, but of health care in kind. In a single-payer system, for example, it would theoretically be possible, while keeping everyone's contributions essentially the same, to deny today's well-insured patients marginal services that they currently enjoy and to use the savings to increase services to those who have heretofore lacked insurance. The idea of generating funds by "taxing" away some of the unnecessary or marginally beneficial health care enjoyed by overinsured consumers is not a bad one and was in fact implicit in the Clinton proposal. But once again, as the Clinton bill demonstrated, such cost control would require a large role for government, arbitrary rationing of services, and arbitrary price controls. These measures will be threatening to many consumer and provider interests that might otherwise support reform.

A basic ideological problem is also present—whether to break with the egalitarian ideal and acknowledge that public policy can explicitly tolerate some marginal differences in the level of health care enjoyed by individuals in different income categories. The idea of rationing only publicly financed care was faced momentarily in the late 1980s, in the widely discussed effort to redesign the Medicaid program in Oregon. That initiative, described earlier in this section, seemed to challenge some basic assumptions about medical care entitlements and might have yielded the political key to finally solving, through compromise of the egalitarian ideal, the problem of universal access. The final outcome in Oregon was inconclusive, however, on the question whether egalitarian sentiments are so strong or so widespread as finally to preclude explicit acceptance of "two-tier" or "multi-tier" medical care. The 1997 Balanced Budget Act, which made major changes in the Medicare program, included a number of provisions allowing higher-income elderly persons to obtain care through different channels, possibly enhancing the quality of care they receive. See chapter 2(§D).

Recent experience with health care reform offers little reason to expect anything other than continued political gridlock when it comes to sweeping measures to achieve universal coverage. As the recent child health initiative (SCHIP) illustrates, however, there may be room for further incremental reforms targeting various subsets of the uninsured. See, e.g., Thorpe, Incremental Strategies for Providing Health Insurance for the Uninsured, 278 J.A.M.A. 329 (1997). (A new proposal on the national agenda in 1998 would expand Medicare to allow persons 55–65, who are perhaps disproportionately exposed to losing their private coverage, to enroll voluntarily and pay for the cost of coverage. What effect does the guaranteed-issue provision of the Kassebaum–Kennedy legislation have on the need for or desirability of this proposal? What does it suggest about the notion that the Medicare buy-in option would be fully paid for by those who choose to purchase Medicare coverage?) Whether the absolute number of uninsured persons can be significantly reduced by such measures remains doubtful, however, as long as the market for unskilled workers does not induce employers to offer them coverage or as long as low-income persons decline available coverage in order to maintain their take-home pay. Recent research indicates that, although more employers are offering coverage (75% of workers now have it available to them), more employees, especially younger and lower-paid ones, are declining it.

8. *The Status Quo as a Policy Option.* The full set of policy options available to the American public necessarily includes continuing in some measure the current practice of letting the uninsured rely upon local government and public or private institutions as payers or providers of last resort. Such a "policy" is unsatisfying in many respects, especially because evidence suggests that, in general, persons dependent on such local "systems" suffer some adverse health effects. Nevertheless, in the absence of political support for more fundamental reform, realism may counsel trying to improve local back-up systems by (*a*) providing the most cost-effective services (e.g., prenatal care and hypertension management) through "outreach" public health programs and (*b*) ensuring that adequate public resources are available to those institutions that assume responsibility for the uninsured. Ironically, however, creating a better back-up system would induce *more* persons rationally to forgo the purchase of insurance and to rely instead on the publicly provided minimal system. Although the appearance of more individuals without insurance could trigger more comprehensive public financing, political and budgetary considerations may dictate continued adherence to the approach of incrementally improving the system and occasionally plugging financial gaps. Query whether such "muddling through" could ever satisfy the societal obligation outlined by the President's Commission.

CHAPTER 2

Purchasing Health Care

Section A: The Nature of the Product

Medical Care as a "Good"

Paul Starr, Ph.D., A National Health Program: Organizing Diversity

Hastings Center Rep., Feb. 1975, at 11.

The pivotal long-range question in medical reform is whether medicine should be viewed as a technical activity with occasional moral and social overtones or, alternatively, as a social and moral activity with a technical substratum. Is the "delivery" of medical care, to use the current phrase, more like the supply of water or the provision of education?

If medical care is ultimately a technical activity like water supply, its management can be safely entrusted to experts in the field. We do not ordinarily worry about democratic participation in our local waterworks or seek to create competitive systems of reservoirs because there are usually no serious differences of opinion that technical knowledge cannot resolve. So long as clean water comes out of the tap, hot and cold, we are happy to be ignorant about how it got there. * * *

If, on the other hand, medical care is primarily a moral and social activity like education, the situation is quite different. In that case, we cannot entirely cede decisions to experts since there are questions of purpose and value that cannot be resolved by expert knowledge, however refined. Consequently, in organizing our institutions, we have good reason to provide for both participation and diversity. We may also wish to sacrifice some of the "efficiency" of a single, professionally run system for the relative inefficiency of variegated institutions sometimes in conflict with one another.

Let me illustrate this fundamental issue by referring to David Rutstein's very useful book, Blueprint for Medical Care (M.I.T.Press, 1974). Dr. Rutstein, who teaches social medicine at Harvard, treats the provision of medical services primarily as a technical activity like the supply of water, whereas I think of it more as a moral and social activity like education. He believes that the major questions of institutional organization can be resolved on the basis of unambiguous considerations of efficiency. I see no way to escape moral and political choices, and suspect that the ideal of maximizing "efficiency" obscures them. He is willing to consolidate medical services into a single system while I would prefer to leave room for diversity and competition.

Unlike most other current writers on social policy and medicine, Dr. Rutstein wastes little time describing the present chaos of America's health-care industry or debating the various proposals for national health insurance. Taking the long view, he concerns himself instead with how medicine should be organized under a national health program that goes considerably beyond insurance.

Rutstein would put physicians on salary (with incentives), largely eliminating the fee-for-service system and solo practice. He would integrate all ambulatory, emergency, inpatient, and preventive care into a comprehensive health system, regionally organized. Each region would have (1) a central, university-affiliated hospital for specialized services ("the focus of decentralization for the national medical care program at the same time that it serves as the focus of centralization for its own region"); (2) a number of community hospitals that would provide most inpatient care and house ambulatory treatment centers with offices for general practitioners; and (3) an array of dispersed neighborhood "reception centers" staffed by nurses and paraprofessionals to attend minor medical problems and select more difficult cases for referral.

For each region (one to three million people), there would also be a coordinated emergency care system, based on military battlefield experience, with centralized communications and transport. Preventive services such as well-baby care would be conducted at local reception centers, which would simultaneously serve as the initial point of entry into the medical system for all patients. Nurses and physician's assistants on duty would make only minimal decisions ("triage," i.e., to treat in minor cases, to refer for treatment in serious ones, or to seek advice from a physician by telephone in ambiguous ones); diagnosis would remain the doctor's responsibility. The reception centers would also function as the base for home visiting services and the site for meetings between staff and community representatives.

Manpower problems would be resolved in several ways. First, the general shortage of physicians would be met by reevaluating the division of medical labor and reassigning specialized tasks to allied professions and paraprofessions. Second, the difficulty in attracting physicians to general practice would be handled by rewarding general practitioners equally well as specialists, both in salary and status, and giving them a central role in the medical system. (This is one reason, Rutstein suggests, for locating GPs' offices at a hospital clinic; the current isolation of general practice discourages young physicians from entering it.) Third, problems of geographical maldistribution, particularly shortages in rural areas, would be met by affiliating each outlying hospital with an urban center, employing more paraprofessionals and new technology permitting "consultation at a distance," and encouraging physicians through salary incentives to practice in understaffed areas.

As for medical education, Rutstein would abolish the single four-year program in favor of a "multi-channel curriculum" that would vary in duration and content from one "pathway" to another. * * *

At the federal level, the system would be administered by the Department of Health, Education and Welfare, but there would also be an independent Federal Health Board. The board, staffed professionally and modeled after the Federal Reserve Board, would maintain a quality control system * * *.

Technocratic and/or Utopian

Throughout the book, Rutstein emphasizes the need for engineering competence, controlled use of new technologies such as information processing, continuous evaluation research, and cost-benefit analysis. There is no question that the plan he sets forth is highly technocratic; it bears the clear impress of industrial engineering, though in a social democratic vein. The "blueprint" is progressive in a traditional sense, and for this reason many radicals will find it unsatisfactory. They will miss any emphasis on internal democracy within medical institutions, or a sustained concern with such issues as patients' rights and the special health problems of women. These shortcomings, such as they are, involve matters of emphasis rather than fundamental contradictions. There is no reason why those concerns could not be reconciled with Rutstein's program.

Pragmatic liberals, in contrast, will argue that the plan is completely utopian given existing political and economic arrangements. Though Dr. Rutstein's language is precise, his ideas are occasionally vague and visionary, taking little account of mundane political realities like the American Medical Association, the insurance industry, or hospital interests. In what relation would the federal government, not to mention the states, stand to the medical care regions? We are not told. It seems at times that the book was written for an imaginary society rather than the United States, which, however regrettably, already has a federal system. The blueprint, in short, seems not to have been conceived with our particular landscape in mind.

But this is far from a fatal objection. There is a point in trying to figure out where we want to go, even if it may be impossible to go all the way. Rutstein's plan, moreover, is not as utopian as it first seems. Simply because of rising costs, medical care is likely to undergo major organizational change in the next few decades. Parts of his program—such as the emergency care system, which steps on the fewest toes—are quite feasible.

The chief defect of the "blueprint," as I see it, lies in neither its putative technocratic nor its utopian aspects, but rather in the basic postulate of a single and unified system. The danger in such a plan is that it creates a network of local monopolies; each district has one institutional system available for health care. For water supply that is convenient and logical; for medical care, it is not. Rutstein's argument for constructing such a system is that it would be more efficient because it eliminates duplication, permits long-run planning and budgeting, and cuts administrative costs. All of this may be true, but the system would nonetheless provide limited alternatives for those who become dissatisfied with the care they receive. In favoring short-run considerations of efficiency, Rutstein has sacrificed noneconomic considerations of choice. Furthermore, by protecting local systems against competition, he may in the long run have sacrificed efficiency as well, since it may be possible for very inefficient local programs to continue without challenge.

To be sure, Rutstein has incorporated safeguards into his plan. Under its quality control system, the Federal Health Board would take readings of "unnecessary disease, unnecessary disability and untimely death" in each region. But exactly how such data would be translated into institutional change—how this quality control system would actually control quality—remains unclear. Also, the board may be more responsive to professional than patient complaints as a result of an almost inevitable hierarchy of credibility. The history of other regulatory agencies, which have generally come under the influence of the industries they are supposed to regulate, does not inspire confidence.

The remedy many on the left would propose is community control. But participation in specialized institutions like medicine tends to be undependable and irregular. Community representatives are easily co-opted, deferring to the superior technical knowledge of professional staff. Community representation is desirable and ought to be required, but its effects are modest. It certainly offers no solution for the individual family in distress that finds service unsatisfactory.

Yet another safeguard would be that people could buy out of the system by consulting physicians who continue to practice in a fee-for-service arrangement. Indeed, it is difficult to see how this possibility could be foreclosed in a society such as ours, yet it opens the prospect of large numbers of upper-middle-class families deserting the national health service and thereby reestablishing a two-class system. If this penumbra of independent practitioners proved to be substantial, as I think it would, the attempt at creating a unified program would be to no avail. Furthermore, a centralized system, however efficient, could not easily embrace all the religious, ethnic, and social differences in America that find expression in health care as in other facets of life. Rather than insisting on a degree of consolidation that is socially unenforceable, I think it would be more wise and realistic to build diversity into the medical system itself.

That could be accomplished through a system of competing prepaid health care programs, or "health maintenance organizations" (HMOs), operating within a regional framework such as Rutstein proposes. Some of these programs would choose to have physicians immediately available; others would make greater use of nurse practitioners and physician's assistants. Some would be heavily computerized and terribly efficient; others would emphasize personal care and be disarmingly unorganized. Some would be based on religious ties; others would be secular. Some would cover unlimited psychiatric visits and premarital sex therapy; others would frown on such extravagances, but offer cosmetic surgery and home nursing. Rather than insisting on a uniform definition of the limits of health care, the system would encourage a varied set of programs in a community, each offering different services at somewhat different prices.

As in a voucher system in education, the government would pay the basic annual cost, although families could choose to spend more for additional services. This would produce some class differences in health care, but if the base support covered the cost of major medical services, the differences would be minimal. The retention of a price system for marginal services would provide a curb against overinvestment in that area. Moreover, were the government to provide automatic support of these services—and I am thinking mainly of the various psychotherapies—it would only encourage the increasing tendency in our society to redefine social and psychological problems as problems of medicine. The unlimited subsidy of medical treatment, though attractive as an ideal, would unfortunately create financial incentives for the mistaken use of the "medical model" to deal with grief, anxiety, compulsions, and various kinds of nonconformity.

A system along the lines I have described would work best if many of the elements of Rutstein's blueprint were incorporated into it. The conversion of physician payment from fee-for-service to salary, the redefinition of the division of medical labor, the incentives for general practice and service in under-doctored areas, the creation of regional emergency care systems, even the reforms of medical education and the establishment of a Federal Health Board, by and large, make good sense. * * *

Such a system would transfer important decisions from the federal government to a level at which people might have more direct control and a clearer understanding of the consequences. Various religious groups, for example, hold distinct positions on the use of certain medical procedures or on questions like the desirability of prolonging dying patients' lives. Rather than seek a false social consensus, it may be easier and wiser to allow different groups to reach their own conclusions and bear the consequences themselves. Such questions are likely to become progressively more acute as biomedical technology expands our capacity to maintain life after health and to rearrange genetic and physiological processes previously beyond our reach.

The challenge is not just to provide good health care at reasonable cost, though that is difficult enough, but to do it in a way that preserves free choice and accommodates cultural diversity. The disorganization in health care that today goes by the name of pluralism—entrepreneurial professional practice, hospital empires, incomplete and complicated insurance coverage, categorical federal benefits and projects, overlapping federal, state and local programs, unintegrated public health services and disjointed emergency measures—serves none of us well. What I am proposing here is an organized system that uses competition in a premeditated fashion: competition under constraint.

* * *

QUESTIONS

1. In the 1970s, it was common for persons interested in the field of public health to speak of the "health care delivery system." The term, which was most often used by critics of existing health care arrangements, has some interesting implications. Why interject the word *delivery?* What word might have been employed instead of *system?* What tensions do the terms set up?

2. Consider some other terminology. Who are "providers," and what do you think of the term? What can you say about the term "provider reimbursement," which is commonly used to describe payments by public and private financing mechanisms to "providers"? Does frequent reference to "consumers" in health policy discussions imply a more commercial perspective than the other terms canvassed here?

3. Early policy discussions also made frequent reference to "third-party payers." Who were they, and what was the point of referring to them as third parties? Might they be characterized in some way other than as "payers"? Are they still with us today? How do they differ from "HMOs" or "managed-care" plans?

4. Note how Rutstein's "Blueprint," as described by Starr, concentrates on reforming the supply side of the market for health services. Just how would policymakers proceed if they decided to implement Rutstein's proposals or otherwise to make the "delivery system" conform to a foreordained model? Is the American political system likely to embrace such a reform strategy? What alternative is there to a "supply-side" approach to health policy?

5. This chapter, focusing principally on the purchasing of health care rather than its delivery, conveys how far the industry has evolved since the time when Starr wrote. As you learn more, however, consider whether we have realized, or are likely to realize, Starr's vision of a system that, "rather than insisting on a uniform definition of the limits of health care, * * * encourage[s] a varied set of programs in a community" and "preserves free choice and accommodates cultural diversity."

Alain Enthoven, Ph.D., What Medical Care Is and Isn't

Excerpt from A. Enthoven, Health Plan: The Only Practical Solution to the Soaring Costs of Health Care 1–9 (1980).

Most people think of the need for medical care as an insurable event, very similar to insured hurricane or automobile collision damage. You are either sick or well. If you are sick, you go to the doctor. The doctor diagnoses your illness, applies the standard treatment, and sends the bill for his or her "usual, customary, and reasonable fee," all or most of which is paid by your insurance company. Our entire Blue Cross–Blue Shield and commercial insurance system was built on that view of the problem. Medicare and Medicaid, the public insurance systems for the elderly and poor, were built on the same model. The consequence is a financial disaster.

Our society has accepted the casualty insurance model for health care financing, only to find that it contributes to excessive and excessively costly care.

Some people think of medical care as a kind of public utility. It does respond to a vital need, and many people think of it as inherently a monopoly—or at least as unsuitable for competitive private enterprise. As a consequence, we are now [in the late 1970s] in the process of accepting the public-utility model of health care regulation, only to find that it is ineffective. The instruments of public-utility regulation are too blunt to grasp something as variable and imprecise as medical care.

[Some] Misconceptions About Medical Care

How is it that models that fit medical care so poorly could be so widely accepted? One reason, I believe, is that many people hold some basic misconceptions about medical care. * * *

1. *"The doctor should be able to know what condition the patient has, be able to answer the patient's questions precisely, and prescribe the right treatment. If the doctor doesn't, that is incompetence or even malpractice."*

Of course, in many cases the diagnosis is clear-cut. But in many others there is a great deal of *uncertainty* in each step of medical care. Doctors are confronted with patients who have symptoms and syndromes, not labels with their diseases. A set of symptoms can be associated with any of several diseases. The chest pains produced by a gall bladder attack and by a heart attack can be confused by excellent doctors. Diagnostic tests are not 100 percent reliable. Consider a young woman with a painless lump in her breast. Is it cancer? There is a significant probability that a breast X-ray (mammogram), will produce a false result; that is, it will say that she does have cancer when she does not, or vice versa. There is less chance of error if a piece of the tissue is removed surgically (biopsy) and examined under a microscope by a pathologist. But even pathologists may reach different conclusions in some cases.

There are often no clear links between treatment and outcome. * * * Because of these uncertainties, there is wide variation among doctors in the tests ordered for similar cases and in the treatments prescribed. * * *

2. *"For each medical condition, there is a 'best' treatment. It is up to the doctor to know about that treatment and to use it. Anything else is unnecessary surgery, waste, fraud, or underservice."*

Of course, in many cases there is a clearly indicated treatment. But for many other medical conditions there are *several possible treatments,* each of which is legitimate and associated with different benefits, risks, and costs. * * *

What is "best" in a particular case will depend on the values and needs of the patient, the skills of the doctor, and the other resources available. The quality of the outcome depends a great deal on how the patient feels about it. What is an annoyance for one patient may mean the inability to keep a job for another with the same condition. There is nothing wrong with the fact that doctors disagree. There is plenty of room for honest differences based on these and other factors. There are more and less costly treatments, practice patterns, and styles of medical care that produce substantially equivalent medical outcomes.

Medical care differs in important ways from repair of collision damage to your car. If you have a smashed fender, you can get three bids and make a deal to have it fixed. You can tell when it is fixed. There is one "correct treatment." Ordinarily, it should not be an open-ended task. But caring for a patient can be open-ended, especially when there is a great deal of uncertainty or when the patient has a chronic disease. Walter McClure, an analyst with InterStudy, a leading health policy research institute, put the point effectively when he wrote:

> The medical care system can legitimately absorb every dollar society will give it. If health insurance is expanded without seriously addressing the medical care system itself, cost escalation is likely to be severe and chronic. For example, why provide $50 of tests to be 95% certain of a diagnosis, if $250 of tests will provide 97% certainty?

Although there are generally accepted treatments for many diseases, and doctors can agree that there has been bad care in some cases, for many others there are no generally agreed standards of what is "the best" care. Physicians reject suggestions of what they refer to as "cookbook medicine"; recognizing the infinite variety of conditions, values, and uncertainties, they are understandably reluctant to impose such standards on one another.

The misconception that best-treatment standards exist for most cases underlies much of the belief in the feasibility of an insurance system like Medicare and the hope that regulatory schemes such as Professional Standards Review Organizations can control costs. If we understand that often there is no clear-cut best course of action in medical care, we will think in terms of alternatives, value judgments, and incentives rather than numerical standards.

3. "Medicine is an exact science. Unlike 50 or 100 years ago, there is now a firm scientific base for what the doctor does. Standard treatments are supported by scientific proof of efficacy."

In fact, medicine remains more of an art than a science. To be sure, it uses and applies scientific knowledge, and to become a physician, one must have command of a great deal of scientific information. But the application of this knowledge is a matter of judgment.

To prove beyond reasonable doubt that a medical treatment is effective often requires what is called a "randomized clinical trial (RCT)." In an RCT a large sample of patients is assigned randomly to two or more treatment groups. Each group is given one of the alternative treatments and then is evaluated by unbiased observers to see which treatment produced the better results. One of the "treatments" may be no treatment. (Of course, RCTs may not be needed in the case of "clear winners" such as penicillin, treatment of fractures, and congenital anomalies.) However, many practical difficulties stand in the way of doing a satisfactory clinical trial. As a result, RCTs are the exception, not the rule.

When medical or surgical innovations have been evaluated in this way, more often than not the innovation has been found to yield no benefit or even to be inferior to previous methods of treatment. Even when a clinical trial has established the value of a given treatment, judgment must be used in deciding whether a particular patient or set of circumstances is enough like those in the trial that the same good results can be expected in this particular case.

There are shifting opinions in medical care. Many operations have been invented and enjoyed popularity, only to be subsequently discarded when systematic testing failed to demonstrate their value. Benjamin Barnes, M.D., professor of surgery at Tufts University Medical School, provided numerous examples in his history of discarded operations between 1880 and 1942. More recent examples include gastric freezing as a treatment for duodenal ulcer and internal mammary artery ligation as a treatment of angina pectoris. Whether or not the coronary artery bypass graft operation that has recently become a billion-dollar-a-year industry will continue indefinitely at its present scale is uncertain. One good reason for not having national standards of care established by government is to avoid either imposing unsubstantiated treatments or freezing them into current practice.

Scientific and balanced analysis of the costs, risks, and benefits of different treatments is still the exception, not the rule.

4. *"Medical care consists of standard products that can be described precisely and measured meaningfully in standard units such as 'inpatient days,' 'outpatient visits,' or 'doctor office visits.'"*

In fact, medical care is usually anything but a standard product. Much of it is a uniquely personal interaction between two people. The elements of personal trust and confidence are an integral part of the process. Much of the process consists of reassurance and support—*caring* rather than *curing*. What doctors do ranges from the technical marvels of the heart surgeon to marriage counseling by the family doctor, each of which may fill a legitimate human need. A "doctor office visit" might last a few minutes or more than an hour. An "inpatient day" might be accompanied by the use of the most costly and complex technology or be merely a quiet day of rest, with an occasional visit by a nurse.

It is important to correct the misconception that medical care consists of standard products, because it underlies much of the thinking about costs and regulation. People will decry the rapid increase in hospital cost per day without giving recognition to the fact that the services provided during a typical hospital day now are much more complex and use much more elaborate technology than they did a decade ago. Proposals to regulate cost per day or cost per case assume that days or cases are more or less standard, so that the costs of a day in two different hospitals can be compared meaningfully. In fact, before one can make a meaningful comparison, one must specify many conditions, such as severity of illness, the length of stay, and the services provided. The belief that controls on physician fees are a feasible method of controlling the cost of physician services rests on the assumption that "doctor office visits" are more or less standard. They aren't.

Quality of medical care has many different dimensions: accessibility, convenience, style, and effectiveness. There are different systems and styles of care. This variability is desirable. It allows the medical care system to accommodate the preferences and needs of different patients and doctors. But it defies the public-utility regulators, who need standard units, such as passenger miles and kilowatt-hours.

5. "Much of medical care is a matter of life and death or serious pain or disability."

This view may come from watching television programs that emphasize the dramatic side of medicine. It is a foundation for the assertion that "health care is a right." As a society, we have agreed that all people should have access to life-saving care without regard to income, race, or social status.

Of course some medical care is life-saving, and its benefits are obvious and clear-cut. But most medical care is not a life-or-death matter at all. Even in the case of care for life-threatening diseases, the effectiveness of much care is measured in terms of small changes in life expectancy (for example, changes in the probability of surviving another year), as opposed to complete cures. Most medical care is a matter of "quality of life." Much of it is concerned with the relief of pain or dysfunction, with caring and reassurance.

All this is not to diminish the importance or value of medical care. But it does suggest that we are dealing with matters of darker or lighter shades of grey, conflicting values, and not clear-cut cases of life or death. Recognizing this makes it much less clear what it is that people have a "right" to or what is "necessary" as opposed to "unnecessary."

6. "More medical care is better than less care."

There is a tremendous amount of bias in favor of more care versus less. For example, the observation that physicians in group practices hospitalize their patients much less than do their fellow doctors in traditional solo practice is much more likely to cause suspicion that they are denying their patients necessary care than that the solo-practice doctors are providing too much care.

A.L. Cochrane, a British physician, supplied a nice example of this bias. Dr. H.G. Mather and colleagues in the National Health Service in Bristol did a randomized clinical trial comparing home and hospital treatment of uncomplicated heart attack (acute myocardial infarction) victims. They found that patients cared for in the coronary care units (CCUs) of hospitals survived in no greater proportion than did those cared for at home. Cochrane wrote:

> There is a great deal of bias, and a considerable amount of vested interest. The bias is beautifully illustrated by a story of the early days of Mather's trial. The first report after a few months of the trial showed a slightly greater death-rate in those treated in hospital than those treated at home. Some one reversed the figures and showed them to a CCU enthusiast who immediately declared that the trial was unethical and must be stopped at once. When, however, he was shown the table the correct way round he could not be persuaded to declare CCUs unethical![7]

In fact, more care may not be better than less care. More care may just be useless. Drs. Hill, Hampton, and Mitchell of Nottingham General Hospital recently repeated Dr. Mather's trial and got a similar result. Of 500 patients whose general practitioners called for the mobile coronary-care unit (a specially equipped ambulance with a doctor), 70 percent were suspected of having a myocardial infarction. Of these, 24 percent were excluded from the trial and were hospitalized because of their medical condition or lack of suitable home environment. The rest were assigned by random method to home or hospital. The result for these patients was no discernible benefit from costly coronary-care units compared with less costly home care. In many cases there may be nothing the medical care can do other than to relieve the patient's discomfort, and this relief may be accomplished as well or better at home as in a costly hospital bed.

Of course, in some cases more care will be better than less. But not in all cases. Above some minimum level that might be provided at a much lower per capita cost, more medical care may yield little, if any, discernible health benefit. This view is supported by two studies of the relationship of health resources to health indicators in different parts of the United States. One study looked at the health status of people living in different places as measured by such things as blood pressure, cholesterol concentration, abnormal electrocardiogram, and abnormal chest X-rays. The other looked at infant mortality and age-adjusted overall mortality. Each attempted to correlate these indicators with such measures of health resources as numbers and variables such as income, education, and occupation. Both found little or no significant relationship between health resources and health status.

More medical care may actually be harmful. There is such a thing as physician-caused (known as "iatrogenic") disease. People do die or are seriously injured on the operating table, and some are injured or die from the complications of anesthesia. * * *

Philip R. Lee, M.D., former Assistant Secretary of HEW for Health, has determined that excessive medical care may be harmful to your health. In a study with Milton Silverman, Ph.D., he estimated that "adverse drug reactions," that is, seriously harmful unintended effects of legally available drugs administered in normal doses for the diagnosis, prevention, or treatment of a disease

7. A.L. Cochrane, Effectiveness and Efficiency: Random Reflections on Health Services, London: Burgess & Son (Abingdon) Ltd. for the Nuffield Provincial Hospital Trust, 1972.

occur by the thousands or tens of thousands every day. They kill more victims than does cancer of the breast. They rank among the top ten causes of hospitalization. In the United States alone, they are held accountable for as many as fifty million hospital patient-days a year.[13]

Excessive antibiotics can encourage the development of resistant strains of bacteria. X-rays can cause harm. These and many other examples suggest that a financing system that motivates giving more rather than less care is not necessarily leading doctors to give better care or to produce better health.

QUESTIONS

1. Enthoven observes the difficulty of defining discrete, uniform units of service in the health care industry. In fact, many of the policy and practical problems to be explored in this chapter are traceable to this difficulty. Can you see why the difficulty of specifying measurable units of service creates a serious problem of public policy? For what specific purposes must units of service be defined? What problems arise if definitions are indefinite?

2. What different measures of providers' output can you propose? Consider how an HMO, as opposed to a fee-for-service provider, defines its units of service? As you will see later in this chapter, the Medicare program redefined the units of service for which it would pay hospitals in the early 1980s (adopting payment by "diagnosis-related group" for each admission in place of retrospective cost reimbursement). What are the strengths and weaknesses of the various measures of output observed in this paragraph?

3. What is the difference between health care and medical care? What is the relation of health care or medical care to health? The constitution of the World Health Organization defines "health" as "a state of complete physical, mental and social well being and not merely the absence of disease and infirmity." Consider the policy implications of such a definition. How else can "health" be produced other than through the provision of health and medical services?

4. Is medical care consumed for its own sake? For most goods and services, we presume that a consumer's purchasing decision reflects value received. Should we similarly presume that the consumption of health services evidences consumer satisfaction? If not, why not? Why is this question relevant to policy debates?

What Can Health Services Research Tell Us?

NOTES ON VARIATIONS IN MEDICAL PRACTICE

1. *Small–Area Variations.* In the 1980s, John Wennberg, M.D., and his colleagues reported significant differences in clinical practices between

13. Milton Silverman and Philip R. Lee, Pills, Profits and Politics, Berkeley: University of California Press, 1974.

areas that were otherwise similar: (*a*) In one area of Vermont, for example, only 8% of children had undergone tonsillectomies, as compared to 70% of the children in another area of the same state. (*b*) In two areas of Maine, the percentages of women aged 70 who had had hysterectomies were 20% and 70%, respectively. (*c*) The overall rate of surgery varied more than two-fold between areas and was more a function of the number of surgeons and hospital beds than of the population's health status. Wennberg reflected on his findings as follows:

> Most people view the medical care they receive as a necessity provided by doctors who adhere to scientific norms based on previously tested and proven treatments. When the contents of the medical care "black box" are examined more closely, however, the type of medical service provided is often found to be as strongly influenced by subjective factors related to the attitudes of individual physicians as by science. These subjective considerations, which I call collectively the "practice style factor," can play a decisive role in determining what specific services are provided a given patient as well as whether treatment occurs in the ambulatory or the inpatient setting.

Wennberg, Dealing with Medical Practice Variations: A Proposal for Action, Health Affs., Summer 1984, at 6, 7.

Wennberg also found that, for some conditions, people were hospitalized much more often in some areas than in others but that the degree of variation was much greater for some procedures than for others. (See table, adapted from id. at 13.) He explained the latter variation on the ground that the degree of medical consensus on the indications for hospitalization and surgery varied substantially for particular procedures. Wennberg made no effort to determine the optimal level of use of different procedures. For full discussion of the data on regional variations in physician practice patterns and their significance, see Symposium, Health Affs., Summer 1984, at 6. See also J. Eisenberg, Doctors' Decisions and the Cost of Medical Care: The Reasons for Doctors' Practice Patterns and Ways to Change Them (1986) (a physician's thoughtful examination of the problem, possible solutions, and the literature concerning both). Twenty years of Wennberg's findings on geographical variations are captured in J. Wennberg et al., The Dartmouth Atlas of Health Care in the United States (1996).

2. *Variations in Treating Medicare Patients.* Work by personnel of The RAND Corporation in the 1980s showed significant variations in the treatment of Medicare beneficiaries among thirteen large areas having an average of 340,000 beneficiaries:

> Of 123 procedures studied, * * * 67 had at least threefold differences between the highest and lowest rates. * * *
>
> * * * [T]he differences were not produced simply by one or two atypical sites: rather, for almost all the procedures, there was a distribution of rates that spanned the range between the sites with the highest rates of use and those with the lowest rates. Second, individual sites did

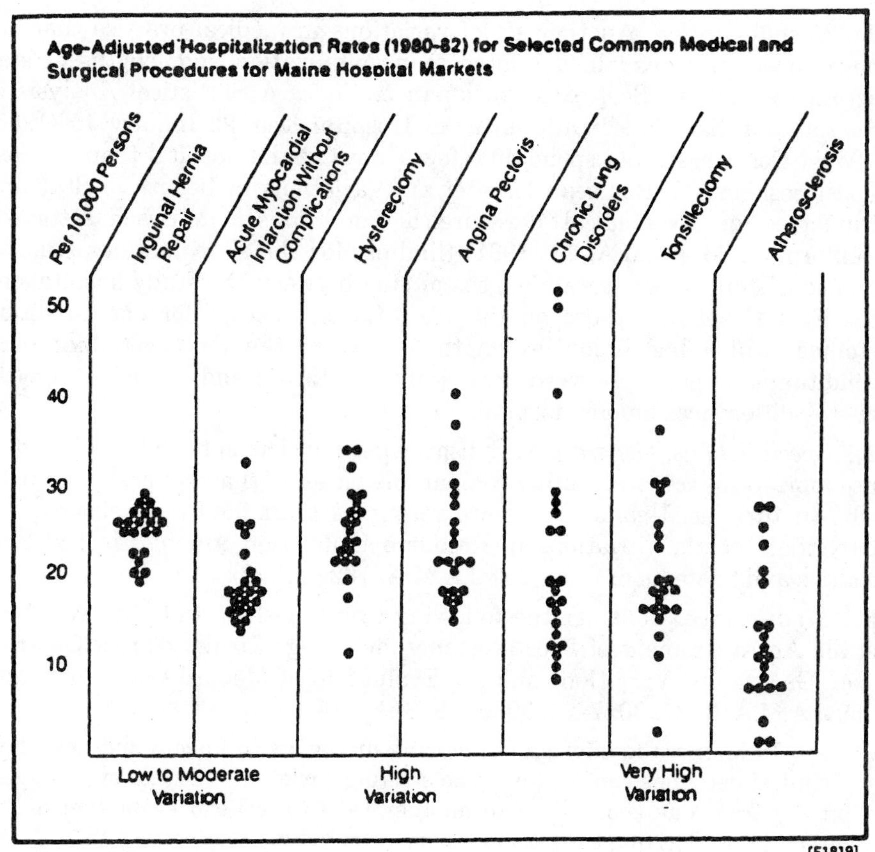

not exhibit the highest or lowest rates with any degree of consistency. Instead, the same site often had a high rate for one procedure and a low rate for another. * * *

Third, the use of procedures employed to diagnose and treat the same disorder usually varied together. * * *

The rates of use of procedures that can be employed as alternative treatments for the same condition also varied together. Table 4 [omitted] includes two such procedures—injection of hemorrhoids and hemorrhoidectomy. Geographic differences in the use of either of these procedures might be interpreted as a simple reflection of a preference for one of them by particular communities of physicians. In fact, however, areas with a high rate of use of either of these procedures also had a high rate of use of the other.

Chassin et al., Variations in the Use of Medical and Surgical Services by the Medicare Population, 314 New Eng.J.Med. 285, 286–87 (1986). The researchers, while observing the cost implications of their findings, were careful to state that they did not know the "correct" use rate of the various procedures.

3. *Hospitalization.* Another set of variations in medical practice that has never been fully explained related to hospitalization and lengths of stay across the nation. See, e.g., Knickman & Foltz, A Statistical Analysis of Reasons for East–West Differences in Hospital Use, 22 Inquiry 45 (1985) ("West Coast residents spend 40% fewer days in the hospital than do East Coast residents"). But see Cleary et al., Variations in Length of Stay and Outcomes for Six Medical and Surgical Conditions in Massachusetts and California, 266 J.A.M.A. 73 (1991) (finding, for the six conditions studied, "no consistent difference in lengths of stay between the study hospitals on the East Coast and those on the West Coast," except for one condition studied, which had a longer length of stay in the East; yet, "for each condition studied, there were statistically significant and important length-of-stay differences among hospitals.")

4. *Specialists vs. Generalists.* Subspecialist physicians have been found to use more resources in treating comparable patients than general internists, who in turn used somewhat more resources than family physicians. See Greenfield et al., Variations in Resource Utilization Among Medical Specialties and Systems of Care, 267 J.A.M.A. 1624 (1992).

5. *Significance.* Consider the following from another study by Wennberg et al., An Assessment of Prostatectomy for Benign Urinary Tract Obstruction: Geographic Variations and the Evaluation of Medical Care Outcomes, 259 J.A.M.A. 3027, 3027–28, 3030 (1988):

> In Maine, the efforts of practicing urologists to understand how their clinical decisions contribute to the striking variations in rates of prostatectomy from one community to another led to a critical evaluation of the theories underlying the decision to operate. * * *
>
> * * * Striking geographic variations in use are characteristic of many operations, diagnostic procedures, and causes of hospitalization. The policy implications of these variations for the cost, quality, and equitable allocation of medical care have aroused considerable interest. A variety of factors such as specialty training, clinical experience, economic motivation, and the personal characteristics of the physician and patient may influence the clinical decision in an individual situation, particularly when there is no consensus among expert physicians on the correct way to diagnose or treat the condition. In this setting [prostatectomy], where the optimal choice is unclear, it is inevitable that ethical, well-trained physicians will reach different conclusions about appropriate care and thus exercise a strong and variable influence on utilization. The evidence for a lack of consensus among expert physicians is amply illustrated by the controversies uncovered in almost any critical review of the medical literature and the inability of committees of experts to agree on the effects of treatment or on what constitutes correct practice.
>
> The dilemmas posed by physician uncertainty for the policies, economics and ethics of health care are increasingly evident to policymakers as well as to physicians and their patients. Physicians and patients want resource-allocation decisions to be based on the ethical imperatives of the medical model: to provide services based on correct theory and to optimize the outcome for patients. Often, however, there is an insufficient scientific

basis to guide physicians and their patients; the necessary assessments to identify correct practice have not been done. In this arena of uncertainty, and faced with ever-increasing medical care costs, policymakers are forced by their constituencies to intervene in the clinical decision process to save money. Everyone wants savings to come from reducing unnecessary services. Lacking standards for care that are based on scientifically valid assessments of outcomes, however, the tendency is to base services cuts on statistical norms or to contract selectively with physicians (or organizations, such as health maintenance organizations) who have low-use practice patterns, even though the implications for costs and the quality of care defined in terms of patient outcomes or costs are unclear over the long term.

An essential step for resolving these dilemmas is to learn which treatment theories are correct in terms of optimal outcomes for patients. Inattention to assessment of the outcome of medical care is not inevitable: regulatory rules require that the efficacy of new drugs must be established prior to their widespread use in medical practice. But the assessment of the efficacy of other elements of medical practice cannot so easily be subjected to regulation. These include diagnostic and surgical procedures, the decision to use hospitals as the place of treatment, and the novel uses physicians make of drugs for indications not covered in the original new drug assessment. Theories concerning efficacy for these practices arise within the context of practice itself, as part of the clinical problem-solving process. Strategies for evaluating these theories must be close to practice and based on acceptable and appropriate assessment methods, and they must involve physicians with the varying points of view who agree to assess their differences.

The Maine Medical Assessment Program provided a forum for discussion of differences in practice styles and the underlying clinical theories. Among Maine urologists, the major controversies about prostatectomy concerned the likelihood for symptom relief and complications following the operation as well as the reasons for performing it in patients without evidence of chronic obstruction. Some physicians advocate surgical intervention in such patients, believing that life expectancy is improved by avoiding the need for operation at a later date. Other physicians believe that the operation does not extend life expectancy in patients without obstruction. They reason that the competing causes of death, the relatively low risk of significant chronic obstruction, and death associated with the operation even in younger patients together mean that the initial loss in life expectancy due to the operation is never regained. For these physicians, the operation in patients without evidence of chronic obstruction is justifiable only on the basis of reduced symptoms and improved quality of life.

Although not controversial at the time of our study, another issue concerned the relative merits of the open prostatectomy vs the transurethral prostatectomy (TURP) for improving urinary stasis. Maine physicians (and those elsewhere in North America and in most places in Europe) now favor the TURP over the open procedure in most clinical situations. For example, our Medicare data for New England show that 95% of prostatectomies were TURPs in 1985. In the mid 1970s, however, the period covered by the assessment protocol, about 25% of operations were still done using open methods, and we could assess the relative advantages of the two approaches as they were used at that time.

* * *

Several lessons were learned [in the Maine assessment]. First, physicians, when faced with the dilemmas that stem from a lack of understanding of the outcome implications of their daily practices, are willing to recognize their uncertainties and take the necessary steps to clarify the implications of unassessed theory. Second, at relatively low costs—much less than for most RCTs—it is possible to complete studies similar in intent to the phase II assessments now routinely undertaken for new drugs. [Drug studies are discussed in the materials below.] Third, alternative technical approaches to a surgical problem can be identified and assessed retrospectively to obtain some evidence for efficacy: we found evidence for possible advantages of open prostatectomy, even though this operation has been largely replaced by TURPs. Fourth, conclusions useful for improving decision making and for reducing unwanted variations can be reached: the assessment shows that early operation does not extend live expectancy, so the primary therapeutic objective for the many patients without chronic obstruction should be the reduction of symptoms and the improvement in quality of life. The assessment thus focuses attention on the need for new methods to inform patients of their options and to assess treatments according to the patients' initial preference for possible outcomes of the alternative choices.

Adaptations of the nonexperimental assessment strategies we pursued for prostatectomy may be applicable to a broad number of assessment problems. In many cases, these assessments will identify scientific uncertainties that are best resolved through an RCT. In other cases, nonexperimental assessments may show that clinical experimental studies are so difficult to organize or so costly as to be impractical. When the condition is so rare that large centers see very few cases, such as the assessment of medical treatment vs surgery for endocarditis, large-claims databases may be the only feasible source of information. Also, when the treatment decision and the relevant outcomes are separated by many years, an RCT may be impossible. Examples include the assessment of failure rates for various alternative technologies for replacing lenses, knees, hips, and heart valves with mechanical or tissue prostheses. Claims data may prove particularly useful for following cohorts of patients to identify the incidence of failure according to the characteristics of patients and the prosthesis used.

Finally, there are the situations where the objective of a surgical procedure proves to be the reduction of symptoms and the improvement in the quality of life. Many operations appear to fit this class. For example, among the Medicare population, coronary bypass operations, angioplasty, cholecystectomy, hysterectomy, peripheral vascular surgery, total knee and hip replacement, and lens extraction stand out as operations where the primary (if not the exclusive) objective is improvement in the quality of life. Strategies similar to those we developed in the assessment of prostatectomy may be particularly appropriate for evaluating these procedures.

6. *Research Techniques and Agendas.* Wennberg's empirical studies of physicians' clinical decisions are good examples of health services research (as distinguished from pure biomedical research and applied clinical research). Health services research, employing empirical and statistical techniques, has also been employed to particular advantage in investigating the effects of organizing, financing, and regulating health care in different ways. Where such research is cited in this text, note not only the conclusions but also the nature of the studies and their limitations. Such studies, though difficult to do well, are numerous and are often influential in thinking about health policy.

Note Enthoven's call for "RCTs"—controlled clinical investigations of the safety and efficacy of particular clinical interventions. Note also the suggestion by Wennberg et al. that such studies are not always feasible or necessary. Why? What are the alternatives? One study compared the results of large RCTs with the results of earlier "meta-analyses," deductions from previously published studies and found poor correlation. LeLorier et al., Discrepancies Between Meta–Analyses and Subsequent Large Randomized, Controlled Trials, 337 New Eng. J. Med. 536 (1997) ("if there had been no subsequent [RCT], the meta-analysis would have led to the adoption of an ineffective treatment in 32 percent of cases * * * and to the rejection of a useful treatment in 33 percent of cases").

Would RCTs of established therapies be ethical? Such studies involve denying the accepted therapy to a control group and perhaps the use of placebos in order to see if there is a statistically significant association of a particular therapy with beneficial results. Should the trial be discontinued as soon as the conventional threshold of "statistical significance" is passed? In other words, do tests of statistical significance have ethical or legal implications? Consider in particular the complex problem of obtaining patients' informed consent to possibly risky experimentation. On the ethics and other issues surrounding randomized clinical trials, see, e.g., Hellman & Hellman, Of Mice but Not Men, 324 New Eng.J.Med. 1585 (1991); Passamani, Clinical Trials—Are They Ethical?, 324 New Eng.J.Med. 1589 (1991).

In the 1980s, a consensus developed on the need to increase clinical and other research on the "outcomes" and "effectiveness" of medical care and to use the findings of this research to develop "evidence-based" diagnostic and therapeutic recommendations for each medical condition. See, e.g., D. Eddy, Clinical Decision Making: From Theory to Practice (1996); D. Eddy, A Manual for Assessing Health Practices and Designing Practice Policies: The Explicit Approach (American College of Physicians, 1992); Roper et al., Effectiveness in Health Care: An Initiative to Evaluate and Improve Medical Practice, 319 New Eng.J.Med. 1197 (1988) (proposal by HCFA officials to increase public support for research efforts to rationalize clinical practice).

An area of particular interest has been the use of screening tests to detect disease at an early stage. Although intuition suggests the desirability of such measures, questions about the effectiveness of the test in real-world circumstances, about the cost of testing and of false positives, and about the cost and efficacy of treatment of the disease once discovered make it difficult to know in many cases whether and which populations to test. See generally L. Russell, Educated Guesses: Making Policy About Medical Screening Tests (1994).

NOTES AND QUESTIONS ON CLINICAL DECISION MAKING

1. *Science or Art?* How should the findings from clinical and outcomes/effectiveness research be implemented in clinical practice? It is frequently observed that clinical decision making in medicine is an art as well as a science. One reason for this characterization is the extraordinary degree to which a physician must extrapolate from what is known to determine what is best for a given patient. The first problem, of course, is in knowing what is known and in recognizing the limitations of knowledge that is based on studies of variable quality often using selected, possibly atypical patients. Many physicians do not start from first-hand knowledge and appraisal of the studies supporting clinical practice but instead rely upon article abstracts, formal and grapevine reports by colleagues, representations by drug company salesmen ("detail men"), and other sources. Another problem may be that physicians are predisposed—perhaps by economic self-interest but also by intellectual leaning—to accept some findings more readily than others.

What should physicians do when confronted with patients who do not fit neatly into categories for which data on efficacy of treatment exist? In practice what happens is that individual physicians decide on a case-by-case basis either that individual patients vary so much from studied groups that the study results do not apply or that the differences are not significant and the results are therefore applicable. This process is not usually carried out explicitly. For the individual physician it rapidly becomes a habit or an implicit algorithm that becomes the basis of that physician's approach to patient care. Medical decision making is thus often a matter of "feel" rather than the explicit application of scientific learning.

Note how the ad hoc, intuitive elements of clinical decisions complicate the task of evaluating and improving physician performance. These problems confront not only the legal system in enforcing some kind of accountability but also institutions such as hospitals or health plans that bear some responsibility for selecting physicians and overseeing their work. In fact, physicians make many errors resulting in iatrogenic injuries to patients, and leaders of the profession are troubled by the difficulty of raising the level of quality in an industry where individualism—justified by overbroad claims that medicine is an art and each patient is unique—is rampant. For a leading article on this theme, see Leape, Error in Medicine, 272 J.A.M.A. 1851 (1994). For a readable, constructive journalistic appraisal of current efforts to shift the emphasis from art to science and to improve the implementation of medical knowledge, M. Millenson, Demanding Medical

Excellence: Doctors and Accountability in the Information Age (1997). Quality issues will be addressed in due course in these materials.

2. *Cost as a Constraint.* The student will shortly confront the additional dilemmas that arise in medical decisions when cost considerations are introduced. Should a physician be expected to be "socially responsible" in making treatment decisions, taking costs borne by third parties (including government) as well as benefits to the individual patient into account? Would a physician who conscientiously rationed services to patients be successful in traditional medical practice?

What stance should conscientious physicians adopt when they confront resource constraints that impair their ability to realize the professional ideal that previously guided their work? Many physicians are frustrated by such constraints today and express moral uneasiness about having to practice under them. Recall the discussion of the physician's decision-making role in connection with the *Muse* case in chapter 1(§A). Consider also the position of physicians practicing in an HMO or other managed-care plan that systematically limits their options or introduces financial incentives to induce them to make economizing choices. These issues are increasingly encountered in modern health care and will reappear at many later points in these materials.

3. *Clinical Practice Guidelines.* The following excerpt describes an important development in the effort to rationalize medical practice:

> "Practice guidelines"—systematic, scientifically derived statements of appropriate measures to be taken by physicians in the diagnosis and treatment of disease—are widely viewed as a potential panacea for many of the health care industry's most pressing problems.[1] In addition to helping physicians obtain better medical results for their patients, practice guidelines are expected to give public and private financers of health services better tools with which to resist paying for (and thus discourage) inappropriate care. They are also being viewed hopefully as a way to ameliorate the problems associated with the law governing medical malpractice. * * *
>
> Practice guidelines have emerged rapidly in the last several years as the medical profession's main answer to revelations of significant shortcomings in prevailing medical practice. During the 1980s, health services research produced increasing evidence of inexplicably wide variations in physicians' diagnostic and treatment methods, of serious weaknesses in the scientific underpinnings of many customary practices,[6] and of substantial

1. See generally Institute of Medicine, Clinical Practice Guidelines: Directions for a New Program (Nat'l Acad. Press, 1990) (edited by Marilyn Field & Kathleen Lohr); Am. Med. Ass'n [AMA], Legal Implications of Practice Parameters (1990); * * * Clark Havighurst, Practice Guidelines for Medical Care: The Policy Rationale, 34 St. Louis U.L.J. 777 (1990); * * *. [See also Institute of Medicine, Guidelines for Clinical Practice: From Development to Use (Nat'l Acad. Press, 1992).]

6. See, for example, David Eddy & John Billings, The Quality of Medical Evidence: Implications for the Quality of Care, Health Affairs 19, 20 (Spring 1988) ("for at least some important practices, the existing evidence is of such poor quality that it is virtually impossible to determine even what effect the practice has on patients, much less

overuse of many medical and surgical procedures.[7] These revelations undermined one of the crucial premises on which the health care industry has long operated—namely, the assumption that, by and large, individual physicians are guided by medical science and the norms and standards of their profession to pursue appropriate courses of diagnosis and treatment. In addition to raising general concerns about the quality of medical care, the researchers' look inside the "black box" of medical practice gave those who are responsible for paying for health services in both the public and private sectors good reason to question whether there are any reliable hands at all on the controls governing the direction and rate of health care spending.

With payers, politicians, and other representatives of the general public questioning its collective performance as well as the judgment and integrity of individual physicians, the medical profession launched major new initiatives to develop and disseminate practice guidelines. The Clinical Efficacy Assessment Project of the American College of Physicians was one of the first and most extensive efforts. Other medical specialty societies have also taken concrete steps, increasingly going beyond simply sampling professional opinion and instead seeking to place medical practice on a firmer scientific base. The American Medical Association (AMA) has actively encouraged professional groups to promulgate what it prefers to call "practice parameters" and has laid down criteria and procedures for their development. Although these initiatives represent a sincere effort by the medical profession to improve its stewardship of the health care system, they may also be interpreted as an attempt to preserve professional dominance over medical decision making and to head off further interference by payers and other intermediaries that are increasingly distrustful of professionalism as a control mechanism. Indeed, physicians appear to hope that by voluntarily supplying better professional standards, they will be able to prevent the collapse of their preferred paradigm of medical care, under which they are held accountable only under norms and standards that they themselves develop.

The movement to develop authoritative practice guidelines received important new impetus in the budget reconciliation legislation adopted in the Fall of 1989.[13] In that law, Congress created a new Agency for Health

whether that effect is preferable to the outcomes that would have occurred with other options"); David Eddy, Clinical Policies and the Quality of Clinical Practice, 307 New Eng.J.Med. 343 (1982) ("[T]here is reason to believe that there are flaws in the process by which the profession generates clinical policies.").

7. See, for example, Robert Brook et al., Predicting the Appropriate Use of Carotid Endarterectomy, Upper Gastrointestinal Endoscopy, and Coronary Angiography, 323 New Eng. J. Med. 1173 (1990) ("[W]e concluded that 17 percent of coronary angiographies, 17 percent of endoscopies, and 32 percent of endarterectomies represented inappropriate overuse [using a liberal standard]. In addition, we considered that the use of the procedure was equivocal (that is, the health benefit and risk were approximately equal) in 9, 11, and 32 percent of the procedures, respectively.").

13. Omnibus Budget Reconciliation Act of 1989, P.L. 101–239, § 6103, to be codified in 42 U.S.C. §§ 299, adding Title IX to the Public Health Service Act and section 1142 to the Social Security Act. Hereinafter, this legislation is referred to by citing the affected acts.

Care Policy and Research (AHCPR) in the Public Health Service (PHS) and assigned it specific responsibilities for conducting and commissioning research focusing on the actual outcomes and effectiveness of medical treatments. The legislation also created a separate office within the AHCPR, called the Forum for Quality and Effectiveness in Health Care (the Forum), and expressly charged it with appointing panels of physician experts and consumer representatives to preside over the development of practice guidelines based to the greatest extent possible on the findings of outcomes and effectiveness research. * * *

It is notable that Congress carefully provided that panels of private citizens, rather the Forum as such, would formally adopt the practice guidelines to be produced. Although the panels are to follow the Forum's criteria and standards in their work, Congress clearly wished the guidelines produced to have only advisory, not official, status. On the other hand, Congress took special steps to give the panels a high degree of political legitimacy by providing that a variety of interests would be represented in their membership. One interpretation of these provisions is that Congress wanted the guidelines emanating from the program to be politically as well as technically authoritative, facilitating their use for quality-assurance and cost-containment purposes in public programs such as Medicare and Medicaid. In this same political spirit, Congress located the guidelines project in the PHS rather than in the Health Care Financing Administration, hoping thus to allay concerns that guidelines would be driven primarily by budgetary rather than medical considerations. Although Forum-generated guidelines will not be incorporated automatically in the Medicare program, the legislation lays political groundwork that will ease their adoption at a later date.

Some tension exists between the purely professional model within which organized medicine is pursuing the development of practice guidelines and the political model that is implicit in the federal program. Although conflict between the two ways of generating guidelines remained latent as the consensus on the need for guidelines was building, some controversy is likely as the Forum selects its panels and contractors and as guidelines are developed under different auspices and put into use. Guidelines produced under the respective models will differ most with respect to their prescriptiveness. Profession-sponsored guidelines will focus primarily on establishing floors (below which care may be deemed inadequate or incompetent) and ceilings (above which care may be deemed unnecessary and unreimbursable). The range between these boundaries—or "parameters," as the AMA calls them—will tend to be fairly wide except where the scientific evidence supporting a particular course is very clear. Not only would a professional organization be reluctant to rule out any practice supported by an appreciable number of its members, but one of its prime goals would be to protect the clinical freedom of practitioners. Although professionally promulgated boundaries of acceptable practice would be of some help in detecting overuse, underservice, and professional negligence, such guidelines would usually be more permissive than guidelines developed with input from consumer interests concerned only about raising quality and containing costs.

The potential differences between the two models of practice guidelines may be less important, however, than the common ground they share. Both models visualize guidelines in the same essentially regulatory way—as the sole authoritative source to which physicians, public financing programs, private insurers and other payers, physician peer reviewers, public disciplinary bodies, malpractice courts, and indeed the entire society should look for benchmarks establishing the appropriateness or inappropriateness of medical treatments. Therefore, any tension that exists between the two models concerns, not whether medical care requires some form of centralized, prescriptive regulation, but only the degree of flexibility that is appropriate in prescribing for a highly diverse health care system.[18] The issues are thus no different than those surrounding any program of command-and-control regulation: Who should set the regulatory standards, and how liberal or restrictive should they be? Moreover, one should not confuse the adoption of more permissive standards, such as the medical profession prefers, with responsible deregulation. Unless a market exists in which people can effectively express alternative preferences concerning how their funds are spent, a laissez-faire regulatory policy may be only an exemption from any accountability. Precisely because a consumer-driven market remains elusive in health care, the coming battle to capture the machinery for making practice guidelines may be little more than another skirmish in the long war between the medical profession and political institutions for control of the health care system's regulatory apparatus. Neither side contending in this war questions the assumption that practice guidelines are to serve as a kind of prescriptive regulation governing medical practice.

* * *

The regulatory scenario is not, however, the only possible one. Despite all the centralizing tendencies inherent in the professional, political, and legal paradigms of medical care, pluralism may still survive. One possibility is that the various parties interested in the substance of practice guidelines in particular areas of practice will not be able to agree upon a single set of specifications, even of the unrestrictive "boundary" variety.[21] Another possibility is that the federal guidelines program will take affirmative steps to foster pluralism, not as an end in itself, but to supply decision makers with verified facts and a variety of analyses that could facilitate the design and administration of health plans and the exercise of consumer choice. If

18. Even politically developed guidelines would have to make allowances for the wide differences in practice settings, in schools of medical thought, and in patients' basic health, prospects, preferences, and economic circumstances. There are also powerful pressures to leave room for the "art" as well as the science of medicine. Although professional interests would probably be more tolerant at both ends of the scale than consumer-oriented decision makers would be, the difference would be only one of degree, not fundamental conception.

21. True pluralism requires more than boundary guidelines (or parameters) that leave physicians room to exercise clinical judgment. "Flexibility allowed in a single set of practice guidelines is not the same thing ... as the pluralism that would result from the ability of users to choose among a number of competing guidelines each expressing a slightly different (but internally consistent) valuation of medical care and degree of risk aversion." Havighurst, 34 St. Louis U.L.J. at 800 (cited in note 1).

> in fact practice guidelines develop pluralistically, a very different scenario might evolve. Indeed, the health care industry might rather quickly be weaned from its exclusive dependence on professional norms and standards. Such "deregulation" of medical care could occur if the guidelines movement gave payers, physicians, and consumers clear-cut opportunities to choose alternative standards to govern their relationships.

Havighurst, Practice Guidelines as Legal Standards Governing Physician Liability, Law & Contemp. Probs., Spring 1991, at 87, 87–93.

The prospect that practice guidelines would come to serve essentially regulatory functions in the U.S. health care system have not been realized. Indeed, the AHCPR program was modified in the mid–1990s to support private guideline development rather than public efforts. The new approach was reportedly adopted following political backlash from AHCPR-sponsored guidelines approving chiropractic treatment for low back pain. Guidelines or their equivalent have been produced by many organizations and have been put to various uses, usually of an informal kind. See U.S. General Accounting Office, Managed Care Plans Customize Guidelines to Meet Local Interests (GAO/HEHS–96–95 1996).

What legal effect practice guidelines may have is still uncertain (and will be the subject of speculation at later points in these materials). See generally National Health Lawyers Association, Colloquium Report on Legal Issues Related to Clinical Practice Guidelines (1995).

4. *Policies to Ensure Appropriateness in Medical Care.* Should the medical profession as a whole assume responsibility for prescribing appropriate clinical practices and for controlling health care costs? Or should government exercise regulatory authority to constrain or prescribe clinical decisions? Consider the following description of how some of the larger issues in health policy have evolved in the last two decades:

> Until [the late 1970s], little in the health policy debate challenged the prevalent assumption that the health care system must operate under prescriptive standards of acceptable care and appropriate spending. Instead, the issue debated was whether the medical profession alone should define these performance limits or whether government should exert an influence. When the advocates of competition entered the discussion, however, they rejected both professional self-regulation and government command-and-control methods as mechanisms for resolving medical-economic issues. Their scenario opened the possibility that consumers would have a chance to decide for themselves in the marketplace what standards of medical practice best suited their preferences and pocketbooks. In essence, the market reformers contemplated that decision making responsibility could be shifted to the numerous actors on the demand side of the market and that consumers could safely be encouraged to do business with health plans and providers whose practices departed from accepted norms. In particular, procompetition strategists anticipated that cost considerations would be given greater weight in medical decision making if those paying the bills were given a wider range of choice.

Havighurst, Decentralizing Decision Making: Private Contract versus Professional Norms, in Jack Meyer, ed., Market Reforms in Health Care 22 (1983). In examining later materials, consider whether the scenario visualized by "advocates of competition" has been realized in fact, is potentially realizable if the right conditions (what conditions?) can be created, or was unrealistic from the outset.

5. *The Patient's Role in Clinical Decisions.* In an excerpt reproduced above, Wennberg et al. emphasized the importance of patient involvement in clinical decision making. Is it realistic to expect a patient to participate intelligently in decisions concerning treatment? Does the legal doctrine of "informed consent" (see chapter 7(§C)) presume that the answer to this question is "yes"? Would it make sense to require informed consent even if one doubted that patients are generally reliable decision makers? See generally J. Katz, The Silent World of Doctor and Patient (1984).

The foregoing questions open important issues relating to clinical practice and the physician/patient relationship. Jay Katz, a psychiatrist on the faculty of the Yale Law School, has offered the following observations (id. at 169):

> [T]hree problems that uncertainty of medical knowledge poses for physician-patient decision making deserve separate attention. One is engendered by the interrelationship between certainty and uncertainty inherent in medical knowledge itself. Uncertainty here raises the question: Is medicine sufficiently advanced so that doctors can be aware of, and distinguish between, opinions and recommendations based on certainty, uncertainty, or a mixture of both? The second problem is created by disclosures of uncertainties to patients. Disclosure of uncertainty here raises two questions: Can patients comprehend medicine's "esoteric" knowledge, in general, and its accompanying certainties and uncertainties, in particular? And is the impact on patients of such disclosures ultimately beneficial or detrimental? The third problem is created by the impact on physicians of a greater awareness of uncertainty. Awareness of uncertainty here raises the question: Would contemplation of medical uncertainties diminish physicians' effectiveness as healers? The fear is that doctors might become so obsessed by questions and doubts that they could no longer act with the necessary dispatch and conviction.

Note that patients have professional help in making decisions concerning their health care. Significant questions arise concerning the ability of patients to select physicians who are competent and reliable in this role, however. Once the physician/patient relationship is established, is it the physician's role to decide on the patient's behalf or only to advise the patient how to decide for himself? Bioethicists place great emphasis on the need to honor patient autonomy, but professionals often doubt the ability of patients to make sensible choices.

6. *Decisions at the End of Life.* By adopting the Patient Self-Determination Act in 1990, 42 U.S.C. § 1395cc(f) (1994), Congress sought to increase the number of Americans who execute living wills, durable powers of attorney, or other advance directives controlling their medical care in the event they become terminally ill and unable to direct their own treatment. The act requires hospitals, nursing homes, hospices, managed health care organizations (HMOs, etc.), and home health care agencies, as a condition of participating in Medicare, to inform all patients at admission of their right to refuse medical care and to control it by advance directives. The statute includes documentation and education requirements. Final regulations were published in 1995. 60 Fed. Reg. 33262 (1995) (codified in scattered sections of 42 C.F.R.). See generally Larson & Eaton, The Limits of Advance Directives: A History and Assessment of the Patient Self–Determination Act, 32 Wake Forest L. Rev. 24 (1997) (concluding that act has not significantly increased use of advance directives and that greater reliance on surrogate decision making will be required).

Decision making on ending treatment or withdrawing life support is a collaborative effort, involving patients (where competent), families, physicians, nurses, other health care personnel, chaplains, hospital ethics committees, and others. Although such decisions are made sensitively in most cases, it is thought that processes could be improved and that patients could be given more and better options than are usually available. See generally Institute of Medicine, Approaching Death: Improving Care at the End of Life (1997). For a critique of the role of hospital ethics committees, see Wilson, Hospital Ethics Committees as the Forum of Last Resort: An Idea Whose Time Has Not Come, 76 N.C. L. Rev. 353 (1998) (arguing that courts must retain ultimate responsibility for overseeing decisions hastening the end of life). The legal issues surrounding end-of-life decisions and the treatment of severely afflicted newborns, while important, are not covered systematically in these materials. See, however, the *Baby K* cases reproduced in chapter 1(§B).

The objective of the Patient Self–Determination Act was simply to encourage patients to make decisions to forgo life-prolonging care when such care would do nothing to improve the quality of life. In a later, more radical development, advocates urged not only letting a patient refuse heroic measures or continued life-supporting services but also allowing him to enlist medical assistance in cutting life short when the burden of incurable illness was too great. "Physician-assisted suicide," popularized by "Dr." Jack Kevorkian (this famous assistant in numerous suicides had in fact surrendered his medical license some years earlier), became a cause celebre in the mid–1990s. Because state law generally did not permit physicians to administer death-inducing drugs, etc., however, advocates for patients' right to die argued that the Constitution protects not only an individual's right to choose death but also his right to obtain medical assistance in exercising that choice. Two Supreme Court decisions rejected their arguments. Washington v. Glucksberg, 117 S.Ct. 2258 (1997) (holding state law against assisting in suicide did not violate fourteenth amendment due process clause); Vacco v. Quill, 117 S.Ct. 2293 (1997) (holding that equal protection clause is not violated by legal distinction drawn between actively assisting suicide and withdrawing life support on request). Although the constitutional arguments failed, state legislatures are considering the matter, and Oregon has passed an initiative approving a state law permitting physician-assisted suicide. One benefit of the national debate has been greater attention to palliative measures for dying patients. See Institute of Medicine, supra. The issue of assisted suicide is certain to remain on the public agenda.

7. *The Choices of Consumers Qua Consumers.* Is individual autonomy adequately preserved and protected by ethical and legal precepts binding professionals to give patients a role in selecting a therapy? Or should patients also be offered choices at an earlier stage in the care-seeking process—when they are still merely "consumers," not patients in need of specific services? How wide a range of choice should be offered? For example, should consumers be allowed to choose among competing providers of care who are not all stamped from the same mold or regulated to eliminate as many distinctions as possible? Should consumers be offered choices between different practice styles and philosophies? Should consumers' choice of a health insurance package or a health plan determine the care they ultimately receive when they get sick? Or should health care be provided by a monolithic or highly regulated system offering an essentially uniform product?

Is a consumer likely to be aware of his inability to choose well and therefore to seek assistance if it is available? What assistance is available in selecting a hospital, a specialist, or a nonphysician provider? Is comparable assistance available in choosing a health plan or insurance package? Does consumer ignorance pose an insurmountable obstacle to the maintenance of a health care system based primarily on competition and consumer choice? The questions posed here obviously lie at the heart of health policy and of many of the legal issues that arise. It is probably too early to attempt to answer them even tentatively, but the student should be alert to their significance.

NOTES AND QUESTIONS ON TECHNOLOGY ASSESSMENT AND THE REGULATION OF MEDICAL TECHNOLOGY

1. *Technology Assessment vs. Regulation.* The term "technology assessment" refers to any formal process of deciding on the appropriate uses of a new (or perhaps an old) diagnostic or treatment technology or method. According to one formulation, technology assessment has three elements: (1) knowledge development (the generation of new data and understanding through clinical trials, ethical and other assessments, and other means); (2) knowledge processing (gathering, validating, interpreting, and disseminating existing data and insights); and (3) regulation (centralized decision making and direct control of the development and implementation of technology). See Foote, Assessing Medical Technology Assessment: Past, Present, and Future, 65 Milbank Q. 59 (1987). This breakdown might be criticized, however, for seeming to point toward public regulation as the final objective. In reality, the public role in technology assessment might logically stop with the first or second step, leaving ultimate decisions on the acceptability of particular technologies to be made on a decentralized basis (with reliable, publicly developed information) by various public and private decision makers. It does not appear that the economics of information—which point strongly toward major public investment in the development of medical knowledge (a public good that will be underproduced without public involvement)—necessarily call for public regulation in this field. Note how the movement to develop clinical practice guidelines, as described above, featured this same tension between the collective generation and synthesis of information, on the one hand, and collective decision making, on the other. See generally Elhauge, The Limited Regulatory Potential of Medical Technology Assessment, 82 Va.L.Rev. 1525 (1996).

2. *Drug Regulation by the FDA.* Pharmaceutical products are screened for "safety and efficacy" by the the federal Food and Drug Administration (FDA) under the Federal Food, Drug and Cosmetic Act of 1938, as amended, 21 U.S.C. § 301 et seq. (1994). The requirement of advance proof of efficacy (as well as safety) was added to the act in 1962 as a direct political reaction to the tragedies resulting from thalidomide, a sleep-inducing drug that caused severe birth defects when taken by pregnant women. (Interestingly, there was no question about the efficacy of thalidomide itself; moreover, the drug had caused few injuries to U.S. citizens because the FDA had not yet approved its sale when its unsafe characteristics were revealed abroad.)

A major report on technology assessment prepared by a committee of the Institute of Medicine (IOM) describes the FDA and its functions as follows:

> The Food and Drug Administration is primarily a scientific regulatory agency for the development of regulations and product standards; development of methodologies and protocols for evaluation of product safety and efficacy; and approval of drugs, medical devices, and other products prior to marketing. Although the FDA reviews evidence accumulated in assessments directed by product sponsors, the agency does not conduct clinical trials of medical products. FDA assessment requirements address safety and efficacy but not cost, cost-effectiveness, or broader social issues. Sponsors must show that their products are safe and efficacious as claimed in their labeling, but they are not required to show safety and efficacy relative to similar products. Thus, FDA-required assessments do not generally produce comparative safety, efficacy, or cost-effectiveness information that may be useful to providers for choosing among alternative products, e.g., different drug treatments, or alternative technologies, e.g., treatment with drugs versus surgical treatment.

Institute of Medicine, Assessing Medical Technologies 41 (1985). Query how, if the FDA does not concern itself with economic efficiency in its assessments, efficiency considerations should be introduced.

The FDA has been accused of excessive regulatory caution, adhering to its scientific requirements even at the cost of denying patients valuable new drugs. Specifically, it is alleged that the agency is so fearful of the political backlash of "Type I" errors (of commission)—e.g., medical calamities, like thalidomide, that affect identified lives—that it commits the "Type II" error of inaction on potentially beneficial products. See, e.g., H. Grabowski & J. Vernon, The Regulation of Pharmaceuticals; Balancing the Benefits and Risks (1983); Richard & Lasagna, Drug Regulation in the United States and the United Kingdom: The Depo–Provera Story, 106 Annals of Internal Med. 886 (1987) (citing different regulatory treatment of the same drug as further evidence of U.S. "drug lag").

The IOM report, supra, at 47–48, describes the FDA's assessment of prescription drugs as follows:

> Following basic research and discovery, drug evaluation largely is guided by the regulatory process administered by the FDA. FDA involvement begins when a sponsor seeks to investigate a drug's safety and efficacy using clinical testing in humans. The FDA has established a two-part process for premarketing drug evaluation: (1) the investigational new drug (IND) application process and (2) the new drug application (NDA) process. In an IND application, a drug sponsor describes the proposed clinical studies, the qualifications of the investigators, the chemical description of the drug, and available data on its pharmacology and toxicity gained from studies in animals (and humans when available, usually from foreign studies). If the IND application is approved by the FDA, the sponsor may proceed with a three-phase clinical investigation of the drug. Following completion of testing under the approved IND application, a sponsor may file an NDA, which is a request for FDA permission to market the drug. About 1 in 10 drugs for which INDs are issued complete all phases of clinical investigation and receive NDA approval by the FDA.
>
> Premarketing clinical studies do not provide an adequate picture of a drug's potential adverse effects or indications. The total drug-exposed populations in such studies are relatively small (usually 700–3,000 patients) and do not permit detection of uncommon effects, such as those occurring less often than in 1 in 1,000 patients. Many types of patients who ultimately will use the drug are excluded from the premarketing study (e.g., certain age groups, pregnant women, patients with diseases other than the one being studied, patients taking concomitant medications, specific degrees of severity of disease), which may preclude identification of effects that occur only in other types of patients or effects that result from drug-drug interactions. The duration of premarketing studies is limited, usually 1 to 2 years, and thus may not enable identification of long-term effects. The conduct of premarketing studies often is limited to specialists affiliated with major medical centers and so may not permit assessment of effects of a drug as used by the average physician engaged in clinical practice. New indications for a drug may be found after marketing, raising efficacy issues not previously addressed.
>
> Although the FDA closely regulates the introduction and labeling of new drugs, the use of legally marketed drugs in practice is not regulated. The agency approves of what the manufacturer may recommend about uses in its labeling and advertising, but it cannot approve or disapprove of how a legally marketed drug is used by a physician in practice. Industry and the FDA conduct postmarketing studies of drugs which address some of the needs left unfilled by the premarketing study. However, compared

> with the volume of data that is collected prior to marketing, far fewer data are collected in the United States on drugs after they are approved for marketing. * * *
>
> The FDA conducts, coordinates, or sponsors a number of surveillance programs, including spontaneous reaction reporting programs, adverse reaction registries, and research programs.

For a revealing discussion of the extensive use of cancer drugs in ways not approved by the FDA and the problems posed for and by third-party payers, see Laetz & Silberman, Reimbursement Policies Constrain the Practice of Oncology, 266 J.A.M.A. 3023 (1991).

3. *Medical Devices*. Legislation in 1976 extended the FDA's jurisdiction to medical devices. The IOM report (supra at 50) described this legislation as follows:

> [T]he Medical Device Amendments of 1976 * * * gave the FDA significant authority to regulate the testing and marketing of medical devices to ensure their safety and efficacy. Congress required classification of all devices into one of three regulatory classes differentiated according to the extent of control necessary to ensure their safety and efficacy: class I, general controls; class II, performance standards; and class III, premarket approval. The amendments instituted systematic premarket notification and screening procedures rather than continued reliance on postmarket regulatory actions on a case-by-case basis. The FDA does not regulate the use of approved medical devices in clinical practice, but has the power to ban devices of any classification that present substantial deception or unreasonable and substantial risk of illness or injury that is not correctable by labeling.

See also Kessler, Pape & Sundwall, The Federal Regulation of Medical Devices, 317 New Eng.J.Med. 357 (1987). The Safe Medical Devices Act of 1990, Pub. L. No. 101–629, 104 Stat. 4511, imposed new regulatory and reporting burdens on manufacturers, users, and distributors of devices and introduced new penalties for noncompliance. See Symposium, 46 Food, Drug & Cosm. L.J. 129 (1991).

4. *FDA Update*. Major reforms of FDA regulation were enacted in 1997. Pub. L. No. 105–115, 105th Cong., 1st Sess. (1997). Among other things, the bill extended a pilot program under which annual and application-specific user fees charged to the regulated firms had already enabled the agency to add employees and significantly speed the approval process. The new law also allows drug and device manufacturers to distribute information from the scientific literature concerning uses of their products that have not yet received agency approval (if the manufacturer undertakes to seek such approval). Approval of medical devices of a less risky kind—this is, those outside class III and with "substantial equivalents" already on the market—may now be approved on the basis of reviews by outside (e.g., university-based) reviewers certified by the agency. Some other measures to reduce the burdens of device regulation were also included. A particularly striking provision in the 1997 law permits a physician to apply to use unapproved drugs or devices in individual cases where the patient has no reasonable alternative and the physician certifies that the patient faces greater risk from the disease than from the proposed treatment.

5. *Should Regulation Be Extended?* Consider the pros and cons of FDA-type regulation as way of controlling the overall performance of the health services industry. There is at present no comparable regulation of new technologies that do not require a new drug or specialized equipment—e.g., new surgical techniques. Do you think that the jurisdiction of the FDA (or some other agency) should be extended to allow it to regulate new procedures? Is it relevant that the latter originate with physicians rather than proprietary business enterprises? Is not the decision to adopt and use any new drug or medical device largely a medical decision? Is there any reason to entrust physicians with decisions to use new surgical procedures but to regulate the availability of new drugs and equipment? How might the law of medical malpractice and products liability be relevant to your thinking on these questions? Should there be some explicit attempt to coordinate liability rules and regulation?

The Clinton Health Security Act, as proposed in 1993, would have made either FDA approval or acceptance by the medical profession a binding criterion for deciding whether a health plan must pay for a prescription drug for a particular use. Would this have been wise policy?

6. *Private Technology Assessment.* Technology assessment also occurs in the private sector through a wide variety of professional and payer-supported collaborations. See IOM report, supra at 2–5, 13 (endorsing "this pluralism, [in the belief] that it contributes to the richness and variety of assessment activities and [that] it serves as a system of checks and balances"). The latest manifestation of voluntary private technology assessment is the movement to develop clinical practice guidelines. Should guidelines, which are themselves in some sense a new technology, be subject to regulatory approval?

7. *Incentives.* The IOM report called for additional public funds to be invested in the technology assessment effort—a proposal to which the new user fees are a response. Why would the private sector alone not adequately support medical technology assessment and related information-generating activities? Can public and philanthropic funding be counted on to fill the gap? Or might publicly or philanthropically supported research focus unduly on projects that the scientific community alone regards as important or that the researchers themselves deem scientifically exciting or career-enhancing?

SECTION B: INTRODUCTION TO HEALTH ECONOMICS

Should Money Matter?

Alain Enthoven, Ph.D., Why Financial Incentives Make a Difference

Excerpt from A. Enthoven, Health Plan: The Only Practical Solution to the Soaring Costs of Medical Care 9–11 (1980)

If medical diagnoses were always clear-cut, if the best treatment were always obvious, if the element of science were large, if the timing of care were determined by medical necessity, and especially if medical care were mostly a matter of life and death, it would be easier to understand how people could believe that the institutional arrangements for providing medical care, including the financial incentives, would be irrelevant to the amounts and kinds of care provided. This kind of medicine would fit into both the casualty-insurance and public-utility models. Making it free at the time of service would not lead patients to demand more of it. Every medical treatment would be "necessary" or "unnecessary," and medical review boards could audit physician performance if unnecessary care were suspected.

Making the decision to use medical care free or almost free to consumers is bound to lead them to resolve their doubts in favor of more, and more costly, care than if they had to pay for it themselves. And think of the physicians, with their concern for the patient and a humanitarian desire to do everything possible to help alleviate suffering, professional standards that emphasize the most advanced technology, and concern over the threat of malpractice suits in a society that believes that more care is always better than less. If in addition to all that, the financing arrangements make the care free to the patient and also yield more revenue to the doctor for giving more, and more costly, care, it should not be difficult to see how fee-for-service payment contributes to ever more costly care.

Studies show that institutional settings and financial incentives do make a difference in the behavior of patients and doctors. For example, Anne Scitovsky, a leading health services researcher, did a study of visits to the doctor by Stanford University employees and their families cared for under a prepaid plan with the Palo Alto Medical Clinic. In 1966 such visits were fully paid in advance by the monthly premiums. This led to such high use of services and costs that in 1967, the plan was changed to require the families to pay one-quarter of each doctor bill. In 1968 the same people's visits to the doctor's office decreased by 25 percent. (The decline in hospital visits was by only 3 percent.) As far as Mrs. Scitovsky and other investigators could tell, the introduction of this financial disincentive was the only thing that had changed between the two years.

Incentives for the physicians can also be important; indeed, they are much more important than patient incentives from an economic point of view, because physicians make the costly decisions. George Monsma, Jr., an economist at Amherst College, highlighted this by comparing the number of operations per capita in groups of employees and their families, some of whom were cared for under group-practice prepayment plans [i.e., HMOs], and some of whom were cared for under traditional insured fee-for-service plans. In the group-practice prepayment plans the surgery is free to the beneficiary, and the doctors get no more money for doing the surgery, because they are paid on the basis of a monthly per capita payment that is independent of the number of services performed. Under the traditional insured fee-for-service plans, the beneficiary pays 20 to 25 percent of the doctor bill, and the doctor gets more money for doing the operation than for not doing it.

The consumer incentive would be to have less surgery under the insured plan. But Monsma found significantly higher rates of surgery under the insured plan, thus lending support to the view that the physicians' incentives (which are in turn a function of how the physicians are organized and paid) dominate decision making on use of surgery. Numerous other comparative studies have reached similar conclusions.

To observe that financial incentives play an important role in the use of medical services is not to imply that they are the only, or even the most important, factor. Physicians are concerned primarily with curing their sick patients, regardless of the cost. That ethic has been instilled in them through years of arduous training. Many take a failure to cure a sick patient as a personal defeat. When we are sick, we want our doctors to be concerned with curing us and nothing else. Physicians and other health professionals are also motivated by a desire to achieve professional excellence and the esteem of their peers and the public. But their use of resources is inevitably shaped by financial incentives. Physicians who survive and prosper must ultimately do what brings in money and curtail those activities that lose money.

* * *

These insights also help explain why qualitative distinctions such as one finds in legal usage are not very helpful. One simply cannot divide all medical care into the categories "necessary" and "unnecessary." What is "necessary" care? Is "necessary" care limited to treatment of serious pain or life-threatening conditions? If it were, a great deal of care would not be "necessary." Even in life-and-death cases, the concept of "necessary" poorly describes many situations. Suppose that a patient with terminal cancer has 99–to–1 odds of dying within a year. Suppose that treatment costing $20,000 will reduce those odds to 97 to 1. Would that be "necessary" or "unnecessary" care? There are doubtless examples that most observers would judge to be "unnecessary." But the fact that two doctors disagree and that the doctor offering the "second opinion" says that the operation is "unnecessary" does not make it so.

Similarly, forceful assertions that "health care is a right" do not help in this large grey zone. In view of the variety of systems and styles of care and treatments, exactly what is a *right*? A *right* to *anything* health care providers can do to make you feel better? That interpretation would make "health care is a right" mean "money is no object." Our society cannot afford and will not support such a generous definition.

The concepts and language most useful for analyzing the problem of health care costs are concepts that have been developed for decision making under uncertainty and for choices of "a little more or a little less." We need to think in terms of judgments about probabilities and in terms of the balancing of various costs, risks, and benefits. The issues are not, for example, "complete care vs. no care for a heart-attack patient." Rather, they are more of the character "seven vs. fourteen or twenty-one days in the hospital after a heart attack." What is the medical value of the extra days? How do they affect the probability that the patient will be alive a year later? What do they cost, not only in resources measured in money, but also in other terms? Are the extra benefits worth the extra costs? These are the kinds of questions we must keep asking if we want to make sense out of the problem and to get good value for the money we spend on health care. They are matters of judgment, possibly aided by calculation.

NOTES ON ECONOMIC THEORY

1. *Welfare Economics*. The discipline of microeconomics is primarily concerned with the economy's ability to achieve "allocative" efficiency. Distinguishable from productive efficiency (inputs per unit of output), this type of efficiency concerns the degree to which society uses its scarce natural, capital, and human resources in the manner that yields the greatest overall consumer satisfaction given the purchasing power that each consumer possesses. The economist's textbook model of the free market yields allocative efficiency by letting well-informed consumers and producers engage in mutually advantageous transactions until the economy reaches "Pareto optimality," the equilibrium point at which no further voluntary exchanges are possible because no one's welfare can be improved without making someone else worse off. The abstractness of notions of Pareto optimality should not obscure the immense practical importance of putting society's limited resources to those uses that benefit consumers most. Can you state the problems facing health policy makers in terms of allocative efficiency?

It is customary in economics to treat issues of efficiency separately from issues involving the distribution of wealth, incomes, and purchasing power. The view commonly taken is that, whereas allocative and productive efficiency can be pursued primarily through market mechanisms, inequities in the distribution of income must be corrected, if at all, through government redistributive programs. Redistribution programs assume (with the Utilitarian philosophers) that it is possible (and morally just) to enhance aggregate welfare still further by making involuntary transfers from those who will not miss it much to those who need it more. As we will see, it is not always easy or appealing to treat efficiency issues and equity issues separately. As one economist has observed, "a society or an economy can be Pareto-optimal and still be perfectly disgusting." A. Sen, Collective Choice and Social Welfare 22 (1970), quoted in Rice, Can Markets Give Us the Health System We Want to Have?, 22 J. Health Pol., Pol'y & L. 383, 387 (1997).

National and state policies toward the U.S. health care industry remain unsettled and often incoherent in many respects in the 1990s. Debates have frequently focused on the need for government intervention in the market to protect the quality of care and to control rising costs. The desirability of such interventions depends upon an understanding of some peculiar features of the market for health services and ultimately upon whether the undeniable departures from the textbook model of smoothly functioning markets constitute such a serious "market failure" that government intervention can realistically be expected to make things better (in some generally accepted sense). The design of beneficial legal rules (statutes and judicial doctrine) and regulatory institutions depends fundamentally upon an understanding of the economics of health care.

2. *Market Failures: Adverse Selection and Moral Hazard.* Unfortunately, economic theory gives no clear guidance to policy. The theory of welfare economics, which leads many to the faith that free markets generally allocate scarce resources efficiently, has been found to be based on assumptions that are generally unfulfilled in the real world. For example, theorist Joseph Stiglitz has observed that recent developments in economic theory

> have raised the possibility that Adam Smith's invisible hand may be something akin to the Emperor's New Clothes: The Invisible Hand may be invisible because it simply is not there. But that, I think, underrates Smith's insight (and overrates the recent criticisms): I prefer to think of the Invisible Hand as being slightly palsied.

Stiglitz, Information and Economic Analysis: A Perspective, 95 Econ.J. 21, 26 (Supp.1985). Two particular problems that Stiglitz cites as damaging to the theory of free markets operate with particular force in the health care sector. Both have to do with information and threaten the efficient operation of markets for allocating risk.

The problem of *adverse selection* arises because of the unequal distribution of information between a party facing a risk and another party negotiating to assume it. Although insurers are most obviously plagued by customers who conceal the actual hazard that they present, the adverse selection problem is present in the allocation of other risks as well. Thus, it affects credit markets because a lender cannot know the riskiness of a loan as well as the borrower. Markets for complex goods and services are also affected because a buyer knows less than the seller about the risks of poor quality or poor performance (though more about whether he intends to act in a risk-enhancing way). Obviously, private insurance of health risks presents some possibly severe adverse selection problems, about which more will be said later in these materials. We will also encounter the correlative problem of *risk* selection by insurers seeking to insure only those whose risks are relatively small.

Although these materials will do no more than acknowledge them, new problems in spreading health risks by private insurance mechanisms and market choices can be expected to emerge in the not-too-distant future as consumers or insurers, as the case may be, become better informed about the health risks that individuals present. In particular, the efforts now under way to map the so-called human genome, the array of chromosomes in human cells, are expected in time to increase dramatically the quantum of knowledge concerning everyone's genetic makeup and of its implications for the individual's future need for health services. Whether private health coverage will continue to serve as satisfactorily for as much of the public as it currently serves remains to be seen. See generally T. Murray et al., eds., The Human Genome project and the Future of Health Care (1996); Berry, The Human Genome Project and the End of Insurance, U. Fla. J.L. & Pub.

Pol'y 205 (1996). Many legal issues related to these trends are just beginning to appear on the horizon.

Of more immediate significance for the student of health care law is the problem of *moral hazard.* This, too, may be seen as a problem of information—about the risk-affecting behavior of individuals who have laid off risks on another. Essentially, the difficulty arises because the presence of insurance (or risk sharing of any other kind) reduces the care taken by the insured individual to avert the hazard. Where insurance covers the costs of repairing the possible damage, the moral hazard also encompasses the tendency of the party seeking repair not to economize. The obvious relevance of the moral hazard for health insurance is more fully developed (in nontechnical terms) in the next selection, which also suggests that there may be other reasons why the health care market fails to yield efficient outcomes.

What should be made of market failures that undermine the reliability of economic theory as a guide to policy? Stiglitz observes, "Whenever there are information problems (whether of the adverse selection or moral hazard form) there are government interventions * * * which could make everyone better off." "But," he asks, "why should we believe that such improvements would evolve out of our political processes?" Id. at 26, 28. So, while economic theory is no sure guide to policy regarding the reliance to be placed on market forces, economic analysis may help to define and clarify the problems that policy makers and private actors must address.

An interesting exchange of views concerning the relevance of economics to the study of health policy, appearing in the *Journal of Health Politics, Policy and Law*, illuminates some of the problems of using economic theory to arrive at normative policy conclusions. According to Professor Thomas Rice, uncritical application of economic theory "based on a large set of assumptions that are not and cannot be met in the health care sector" causes some "advocates to champion a number of policies, including:

- Providing low-income people with subsidies to allow them to purchase health insurance, rather than paying directly for the services they use.
- Having people pay more money out-of-pocket in order to receive health care services, especially for services whose demand is most responsive to price.
- Also requiring that they pay more in premiums to obtain more extensive health insurance coverage.
- Letting the market determine the number and distribution of hospitals and what services they provide, as well as the total number of physicians and their distribution among specialties.
- Removing regulations to control the development and diffusion of medical technologies.
- Eschewing government involvement in determining how much a country spends on health care services."

Rice, supra, at 384. Responses by other economists to Rice's critique raise the question whether such policy proposals are in fact supported by theory alone or are reinforced by pragmatic judgments about the comparative virtues and efficacy of markets and government. See Pauly, Commentary—Who Was That Straw Man Anyway?, 22 J. Health Pol., Pol'y & L. 467 (1997); Gaynor & Vogt, Commentary—What Does Economics Have to Say about Health Policy Anyway?, id. at 475. While students should be alert to possible instances in which misplaced economic theory (and value judgments that may be implicit therein) may be driving policies, proposals, analyses, and arguments to be encountered in the pages ahead, one should always bear in mind Stiglitz's reminder of the second-best problem that arises when theory is not a reliable analytic tool.

3. *Consumers as Decision Makers.* A widely recognized problem with market theory in general is the ignorance of consumers about the technical qualities of goods and services and their inability to evaluate the quality or appropriateness of services, even after repeated experiences. In addition, psychological research has shown consumers to be unreliable decision makers on questions concerning risk, easily influenced by the way questions are presented and apparently unable to interpret and integrate information items, to form consistent preferences, or to make rational trade-offs. See, e.g., Hibbard, Slovic & Jewett, Informing Consumer Decisions in Health Care: Implications from Decision–Making Research, 75 Milbank Q. 395 (1997); Fischoff, Judgment and Decision Making, in R. Sternberg & E. Smith eds., The Psychology of Human Thought 153 (1988); Slovic, Perception of Risk, 236 Science 280 (1987); Kahneman & Tversky, The Psychology of Preferences, 246 Scientific American 12 (1982); Tversky & Kahneman, The Framing of Decisions and the Psychology of Choice, 211 Science 453 (1981). Do consumer ignorance and irrationality fatally undermine the market paradigm where risk and uncertainty are concerned? Indeed, is democratic government possible if voters are irrational about such matters? Or does the validity of both the market and the democratic paradigms depend more on the legitimizing power of the accountability feature than on the assumption that citizens make well-informed, consistent, and rational choices?

While not unique to health care, consumer ignorance and irrationality justify concern about the efficiency of the health care marketplace and invite consideration of policy moves by government either to improve the quality of information available or to prescribe certain features of health care transactions. On the other hand, relying on government to improve a questionable situation itself depends on some debatable assumptions—about the decision-making capacities of public officials, who, after all, do not always have all the information they need to make choices for the electorate and who, indeed, are elected by, or accountable to, the same public whose information, sophistication, and rationality are in doubt. As always, whether market failures justify particular government actions in the health care sector depends upon empirical judgments about which strategy is likely to work best in practice to correct a given problem.

Fortunately, the situation in health care is not as bleak as it would seem if individual consumers were forced to make their choices (take their chances) without help in an unfriendly world. Despite the obvious shortcomings of consumers and patients as decision makers, the private market makes available to them a variety of agents, both professional and corporate ones, who can assist them in making crucial choices. Although informational problems also complicate the selection and monitoring of agents, here again other agents and a variety of indicia and information sources ameliorate the problem of consumer ignorance. Moreover, because sellers respond mostly to decision makers at the margin, markets can often work efficiently to promote quality if only a modest percentage of buyers make informed choices. (As economist Mark Pauly has observed, a consumer's best strategy may be simply to say, "I'll have whatever he's having.") Finally, legal rules can create appropriate incentives to deter both bad outcomes and opportunistic behavior by sellers. Even though consumer ignorance and irrationality are prominent features of the health care landscape, it is not clear that they represent insuperable impediments to maintaining a tolerable marketplace.

4. *The Problem of Health Care Costs*. It has long been generally believed that the market fails to allocate resources efficiently to health care uses in the United States. Over many years, health care spending in the U.S. came to exceed by a truly startling margin—four whole percentage points of GDP and more—comparable levels of spending in other developed nations. To be sure, Americans normally applaud a "growth industry" and the new employment opportunities and technological miracles it makes available to the American people. But health care's increasing claims on GDP were long regarded as evidence of a crisis requiring a national solution. Even though cost escalation has moderated somewhat in the mid-1990s under the influence of managed care and other market developments (costs have even declined slightly in some circumstances), it is useful to consider whether or not U.S. health care costs, still by far the highest in the world, are in fact higher than they "should be" as a matter of allocative efficiency. The next selection takes a rigorous look at the staggering cost of health care in the United States, eventually concluding that they are indeed socially excessive—but not for the reasons usually given.

Trade-Offs Between Costs and Benefits

Clark C. Havighurst, The Rising Cost of Health Care: Growing Pains or Something Worse?

Excerpt from C. Havighurst, Health Care Choices: Private Contracts as Instruments of Health Reform 90–109 (1995)

* * * As nations (and individuals) become wealthier, they naturally tend to spend greater percentages of their income on personal health services. Thus, one should not be surprised or alarmed when, as GDP grows, more of it is allocated to health care. Moreover, because the United States has been richer than other nations, international comparisons, while

suggestive, do not confirm the belief that it spends too much in trying to restore health. Not only would the United States be expected to spend more, but other nations have government-controlled health care systems that may be systematically denying their citizens some benefits that Americans want for themselves.

Other explanations for increasing spending on health services demonstrate even more convincingly that the upward trend alone does not signify a fundamental problem. The U.S. population is aging, partly as a consequence of medical successes. In addition to the increasing medical needs of older citizens, the demand for health care has increased in recent years because of three severe epidemics: AIDS, drug abuse, and violence. Environmental hazards may (or may not) also be taking an increasing toll. These developments on the demand side of the market for medical care explain much of the increased spending on health services that we witness year after year and should give us pause in condemning the upward trend.

Perhaps the most important factor contributing to continual increases in health spending is the proliferation of new medical technologies. Just as modern technology is yielding dramatic breakthroughs in other areas (such as cellular telephones), biomedical research makes each year's health care significantly different from the previous year's. Price and cost comparisons quickly become meaningless. Indeed, the nation is really buying not an unchanging product called health care but a rapidly changing mix of discrete services. Although it is possible to question the desirability of some new technologies, many benefit patients enormously. Without knowing a great deal more, one cannot conclude that spending on new technologies is out of control or that cost increases attributable to them represent poor social or personal investments.

Because health care costs may naturally rise faster than other components of the cost of living, one cannot readily dismiss the argument that growth in the health care sector reflects simply consumer needs and preferences for more and better medical care. There may be—and probably is, for reasons that will appear—a great deal of inefficiency and inappropriate spending embedded in the base from which the health care industry grows each year. Yet it is cost increases, not the attained level or character of spending, that occasion most complaints and most political pressures for government intervention to control costs. Even if all spending were undeniably appropriate, the complaints about rising costs might be no less loud. Conversely, if costs were stabilized, there might be no overt complaints, even if the industry were wasting a significant portion of its GDP on activities yielding too few benefits to justify their costs.

What political figures identify as a severe national problem may therefore not be a significant problem at all from the standpoint of aggregate social welfare. Indeed, those who complain most loudly about rising health care costs—government officials and employers—may be merely special pleaders whose complaints, reflecting mostly their own difficulty in paying the increasing costs of established programs, misrepresent the situation of society as a whole. Health care entitlement programs, for example, present politicians with highly stressful options: either to increase taxes without anything new to show the voters or to reduce the entitlement in some way. It is no wonder that politicians think that health care cost increases should be controlled or rolled back, especially when they are hoping to introduce, and take political credit for, new programs to ensure universal access. But cost-control measures designed merely to satisfy such concerns could easily be mistaken or unfair. We must therefore develop an independent view of the nature and source of whatever malfunctions do occur in the market for health care.

Too Much of a Good Thing?

* * *

The explanation most often given for wasteful health care spending is the externalization of costs that results from financing care through private health insurance and public programs. Relatively little health care in America is paid for directly and in full by the patient who decides (with a doctor's advice) to purchase the particular service. Whether the entity actually incurring the cost is a private health insurer, an HMO, or a public financing program, the patient and, in many cases, the treating physician have no appreciable reason to consider whether the benefit of some expenditure, large or small, is likely to be worth its cost. Whenever a person is in a position to spend or risk funds belonging to someone else, he will calculate differently from the way he would if the money were his own. While all forms of insurance create distortions of this variety—the result of what economists call moral hazard—health coverage presents the problem with special force because so much health care spending is essentially discretionary.

The insurance-induced divorce of consumption decisions from the obligation to pay undoubtedly justifies concern that increased spending on health care does not truly reflect the preferences of consumers as to how their money should be spent. * * *

The Benefit–Cost No Man's Land. The nature of the challenge posed by health care costs can be appreciated best by seeing the graphic demonstration in figure 4–1. By illustrating the potential targets for attack in the war against excessive spending, figure 4–1 should be helpful in discovering whether that war is being won or lost. * * *

The "benefits" curve in figure 4–1 shows heuristically the probable relationships between the benefits of health care (measured in dollars on the vertical axis) and the inputs needed to obtain them. It is assumed that "inputs" are all uniform and that they will be added in a sequence dictated by their ability to yield benefits. Thus, at low input levels, the benefits curve rises steeply, reflecting the true miracles of modern medical science. The curve rises more and more gradually, however, as the inputs being added yield either cures at increasingly higher cost or benefits of increasingly equivocal kinds. The curve is flat after point *x*, as added inputs yield

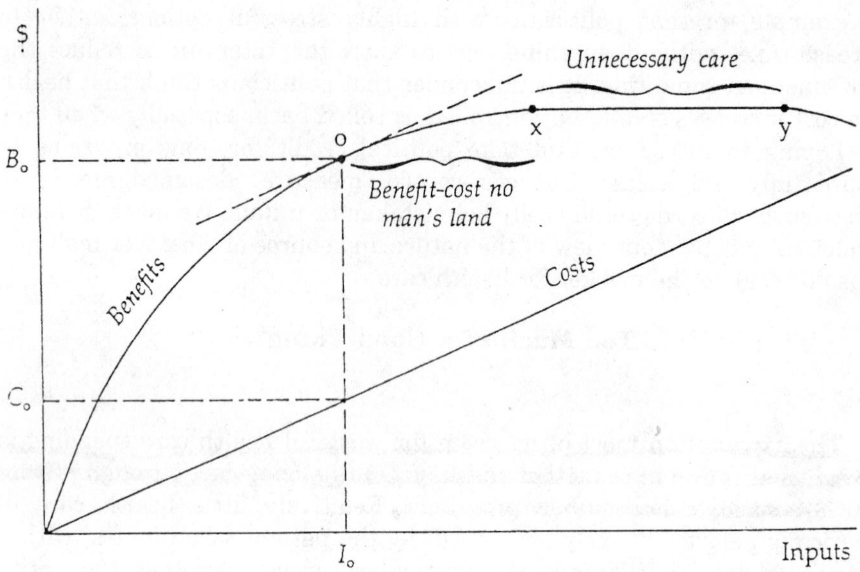

no benefit, illustrating the notion of unnecessary care. (The curve actually falls after point *y*, showing that some medical care is positively harmful.)

The benefits curve alone cannot reveal where society or any given purchaser should stop adding inputs. Although no care should be purchased beyond point *x*, cost-containment efforts that stop there would not ensure an efficient level of consumption. Efficiency demands that costs be taken into account. The diagram therefore introduces a cost curve, a straight line illustrating the cumulative dollar cost of adding uniform inputs. The critical feature of this line for present purposes is its slope (rate of increase), which is reflected in the dotted parallel line having a point of tangency with the benefits curve at point *o*. At that point, the benefits curve is rising at exactly the same rate as the cost line. Up to that point, the inputs added yield benefits that exceed the costs incurred. Beyond point *o*, however, the benefits obtainable by adding additional inputs are no longer as great as the cost of those inputs. In other words, marginal costs exceed marginal benefits. I_0 then represents—only provisionally, however (for reasons that shortly appear)—the optimal (efficient) level of inputs, and C_0 represents the (provisionally) optimal level of spending.

The first crucial point in this demonstration is that even though adding inputs and expenditures beyond point *o* would improve aggregate health, that fact does not justify such additional spending; employing the same resources in other ways, dedicating them to nonhealth purposes, would increase welfare even more. This conclusion, while theoretically correct, may be hard to accept because of doubts about valuing the health benefits of individuals in dollars and trading them off against other things beneficial to other individuals. It is not proposed, however, to operationalize this calculus in making social decisions or in rationing care. Instead, the analysis here is offered simply to make the point that it is almost certainly socially wrong—in the sense that it reduces aggregate welfare—to pay for every health service that yields some benefit. This point, however, is the beginning, not the end, of the discussion.

An equally important implication of the foregoing demonstration is the obvious practical difficulty of deciding what specific services to omit and of preventing them from being rendered in particular cases. This difficulty will be encountered at whatever level the requisite actions must be taken, whether by society as a whole acting through government, by financing intermediaries, by providers of care, or by individual patients. To highlight this aspect of the problem we are setting for ourselves, the diagram labels the portion of the benefits curve between point *o* and point *x* as the benefit-cost no man's land. In this area, health care, being beneficial, will seem desirable as long as the decision maker—public or private, as the case may be—does not consider the true cost of providing it. The potential for conflict is clear. Precisely because anyone venturing to fight the battle for cost containment in this range is likely to draw criticism of the most intense kind, including lawsuits, the no-man's-land metaphor seems apt. * * *

To draw figure 4–1 is not to prove that an excessive amount of care beyond point *o* on the benefits curve is actually being rendered or that society is wasting resources on medical care. In fact, it is not possible to know where as a society we fall on the benefits curve. Indeed, there is no reason to assume that, in the real world, inputs are added in the orderly fashion assumed in the diagram. A great deal of highly cost-effective care (to the left of point *o*) may not be currently provided. One challenge in making provision for the uninsured is to find methods that, while ensuring the provision of all care to the left of point *o*, protect the public in some measure against paying for care to the right of that point. Thus, the nation's ability to wage war in the no man's land directly affects its ability to guarantee all Americans financial access to basic care.

With respect to the larger, insured portion of the population, the main challenges lie to the right of point *o*. But, as shown later, the battle has been joined for the most part only around point *x*. Indeed, this demonstration will finally allow us to conclude that the United States is indeed wasting resources on medical care.

How Much Apparent Inefficiency in Health Insurance Is Efficient? In figure 4–1, point *o* was labeled optimal on only a provisional basis. Taking that label literally would call into question the entire system of health care financing, which almost inevitably—because of moral hazard—causes a great deal of consumption beyond that point. But even though public financing and private health insurance undeniably contribute to increased spending on health services, that fact alone does not establish that society is spending too much. The inefficiencies apparent in this naive diagram do not invalidate health insurance as an institution. The vital financial protection that insurance provides may more than justify the higher costs that it induces people to incur.

It is important in judging the performance of the health care market to recognize that two objectives are at war with each other: (1) protection of individuals against unpredictable medical costs and (2) efficiency in the allocation of resources to and within the health care sector. Both are desirable goals, but neither can be obtained without some sacrifice of the other. Because of this trade-off, some overconsumption is an inevitable, and therefore tolerable, part of the cost of pooling financial risks. This insight is important in making policy. Private insurance and public third-party financing may be efficient even if they cause substantial apparent inefficiency in the market for health services. The search for a reason to fear serious inefficiency in the market for health care thus requires a closer look at the intermediaries through which the national health care bill is paid.

In the search for still elusive evidence that health care costs are in fact out of control, it is necessary to ask whether public and private payers are doing all that efficiency demands to counter the distortions that third-party payment introduces. If they are, it could be strongly argued that there is no problem after all and that rising spending on health care should be no more alarming than increased spending on cellular telephones. If they are not, however, we may be on the trail not only of a final definition of the cost problem but of some solutions as well.

In theory, payers could do many things to ensure that only economically justified services are rendered at the expense of the common fund and that the prices paid for these services are competitive prices. In practice, however, many things that might be done may not be worth doing, because they cost more than they save or because they have unwanted consequences. Nevertheless, at least until recently, the prevalent perception of waste and overspending in the health care system was based in large part on a sense that payers were unduly passive or ineffective in confronting their cost-containment task. A crucial issue is therefore the performance of financing intermediaries. Do they have the incentives and the cost-containment tools they need to act as effective agents of their customers or of the public in seeking the optimal mix of financial protection, quality care, and administrative safeguards of the funds entrusted to them?

The health care sector experienced some deregulation in the early 1980s, partly in response to policy arguments supporting market reforms, increased competition, and decentralized decision making in health care. Advocates for these policies argued that payers could be activated and empowered to perform the cost-containment task more effectively. Until almost the end of the 1970s, however, nearly everyone considered health care cost control a job for government. Public regulation was used in an effort to limit the growth of hospitals and the proliferation of unnecessary services; additional types of regulation, most notably federal restrictions on the rate at which hospital revenues could grow, were proposed. It was also generally assumed throughout this period that government would shortly adopt some form of national health insurance with universal cost controls. Because government's initiatives, actual and proposed, appeared to obviate the need for cost-containment efforts by private purchasers of health care, the private sector—employers and insurers—simply waited for government to act. Legal obstacles and the medical profession's opposition to many of the most promising potential innovations also prevented third-party payers from assuming the duty of discouraging wasteful spending.

Beginning in the late 1970s, however, federal policy changed dramatically. Stepped-up antitrust enforcement made it more difficult for providers to suppress competition and to resist by collective action cost-control initiatives that they did not like. In 1979, the Carter administration's hospital-revenue controls were defeated in Congress, and a spate of bills designed to encourage private-sector initiatives were introduced. The 1980s brought to Washington a new administration that disclaimed any interest in regulating privately financed medical care or in imposing national health insurance. Nevertheless, the Reagan administration did direct its attention to controlling the costs of the federal government's own health care programs. Among other things, it got Congress to stop paying hospitals on the basis of their costs, to allow Medicare beneficiaries to join HMOs at program expense, and to give state Medicaid programs new freedom to innovate in controlling costs. Its policy toward the private sector, however, was one of benign neglect, on the premise that private health care costs are a private, not a public, responsibility.

As intended, these changes in federal policy triggered significant innovation in health care delivery and financing. Employers, recognizing the need to fend for themselves in cost containment, began to offer more health plan choices to their workers, on the theory that competition would stimulate efficiency. As a result, HMOs enjoyed much faster growth than in the 1970s, when, although federal subsidies were available, regulation kept their costs high and most employers chose to wait for the government to tell them what to do. Traditional insurers responded to the new competitive pressures by offering opportunities and incentives for consumers to patronize lower-cost preferred providers. For the first time, payers began to contract selectively with providers and to steer patients to those who granted price discounts and cooperated in cost-control efforts. New techniques for managing the utilization of services were introduced by payers. The term *managed care* was coined to describe the wide variety of techniques that developed to ensure that, even though price was not a central consideration in the decision to consume services, inappropriate services were not provided. Although trial and error produced some frustrations, it could no longer be said with assurance that payers were simply conduits for transferring funds from taxpayers or consumers to providers without appreciable oversight. The moral hazard enemy had at least come under attack, whether or not it was actually subdued.

In many people's judgment, the policy of relying less on government regulation and more on market forces failed to have the desired effect of controlling costs. Nevertheless, introducing new forms of price competition and utilization management and new incentives for consumers to patronize preferred providers did lower some unit prices and impose some discipline on providers. * * * It is * * * possible that the new cost-containment tools that became available to purchasers in the 1980s are now controlling utilization of services to the optimal extent. Until we know otherwise, at least, we cannot conclude that health care costs * * * are not under appropriate control.

An ironic development has been the recent outcry about the high administrative costs incurred in the U.S. health care system. A large fraction of these costs is incurred by payers in efforts to bargain with providers and manage utilization. Such efforts, although precisely the kind of cost-containment actions that the policies of the 1980s were designed to stimulate, are necessarily costly. The complaints being heard today about the magnitude of these costs and the burdens they impose on providers suggest that some kind of equilibrium may have been reached and that additional administrative efforts by payers would not yield savings exceeding their costs. In addition, the market is now relatively open to the formation and growth of integrated health plans—staff-model and group-model HMOs—that depend for cost control less on enforcing bureaucratic rules against providers and their patients and more on consensus and cooperation among plan physicians. Because consumers have not widely demanded these alternatives to [more] conventional [health care financing], they may not find the administrative costs of the latter * * * to be too high a price to pay for the freedom of choice and more personalized care that it provides.

Under the hypothesis that a certain amount of apparent inefficiency is efficient, it might be claimed that because payers appear to be doing everything administratively feasible to control costs, the remaining spending on apparently wasteful care (that is, care to the right of point *o*) is no cause for concern. The current level of spending could be deemed optimal, however, only if payers do indeed have all the tools needed to control costs and if they operate without inappropriate legal or practical constraints on their freedom of action. In addition, the incentives of consumers in making the choices they do all must be in proper order. * * * [In the latter connection,] we should focus on a significant problem affecting incentives on the demand side of the market for health coverage. Here we find the first solid basis for concluding that the United States does indeed engage in a great deal of unnecessarily wasteful spending on health care.

The Problem of Tax Subsidies

For many years, federal and state tax law has allowed employees to escape income and payroll taxes on group health insurance premiums paid on their behalf by their employers. The exclusion of such premiums from taxable income has been a valuable tax break for consumers. More important, it has given them a strong inducement to pay as many of their health bills as possible through employer-provided insurance rather than out of pocket. Purchasing services in this way allows them to be paid for with untaxed dollars, representing a large discount—more than 40 percent for much of the population—from the cost of paying for that care from aftertax income. Consumers have therefore purchased health coverage not just for the limited purpose of protecting themselves against catastrophic expenses (the usual object of insurance) but to get government help in paying routine health bills.

In taking optimal advantage of this tax loophole, consumers have substantially overinsured themselves. Tax considerations have excessively deterred them, for example, from accepting coverage with large deductibles and substantial coinsurance, which would have to be paid with aftertax dollars. The generous coverage thus chosen lacks vital constraints on inappropriate consumption. Consumers seeking tax relief have likewise purchased coverage that is much more comprehensive than would otherwise be optimal. By insuring against such relatively predictable and manageable expenses as routine doctor visits and routine dental care, they have appreciably widened the realm in which the moral hazard associated with health insurance holds sway and invited spending that would not otherwise occur.

The tax subsidy has distorted the nature of health insurance coverage in other ways. Although health plans are employing managed-care techniques more than ever before, they still have good reasons not to control as rigorously as they might the spending of the funds that consumers entrust to them. Indeed, any dollar saved by an employer's health plan is nowhere near a dollar earned once it is shared with the employees in the form of taxable wages. With incentives for effective cost containment thus systematically diluted, payers are certainly doing less than they should—though not necessarily less than their customers want them to do—to offset the effects of moral hazard.

Thus, with unwise, unlimited tax subsidies distorting the design of private health insurance in cost-increasing ways, a great deal of preventable overspending on health care does indeed occur in the United States. In addition to its specific effects on the kinds of insurance people purchase, the tax subsidy has also had adverse consequences of a more general kind. The long experience with employee health benefits as a tax-favored form of compensation, rather than as essential protection against unbearable risks, has contributed in some measure to the creation of a pervasive entitlement mentality among American consumers of health care. The prevalent attitude that apparently views state-of-the-art medical care—however it evolves and whatever it costs—as a virtual birthright of every citizen severely hampers both public and private actions to address the problems of the health care sector. To the extent that tax policy has helped to create a political, institutional, and legal climate hostile to economizing on health care, it has contributed to problems in the health care marketplace that are more fundamental than any we have yet discovered. Certainly, it has complicated the political task of making sensible health policy.

Proposals to cap the tax subsidy at an appropriate level have not fared well over the years. (Such a tax cap is the most obvious and widely advocated reform idea even though income-related tax credits or vouchers would probably be a wiser and more progressive way to subsidize basic coverage.) The current movement for health reform, however, would seem to offer a new opportunity to correct this fundamental flaw in national health policy, thus at one stroke eliminating incentives to overinsure and generating new tax revenues with which to extend coverage to the uninsured. Nevertheless, even though health insurers and some important business groups have recently dropped their opposition to limiting the subsidy, consumers still object to "taxing" health benefits. Indeed, most voters probably expect health reform to make it easier, not harder, for them to afford the generous benefits to which they have become accustomed. Whether the tax subsidy will be altered therefore remains doubtful. [T]he Clinton administration failed to address the tax subsidy in a serious way, recommending its repeal (with a substantial time lag for collectively bargained plans) only insofar as it applies to coverage outside the statutory comprehensive benefit package.

If changing the tax subsidy proves politically infeasible, must the nation by necessity then turn to government regulation, global budgets, or other centrally imposed remedies for overspending? What we have uncovered here is a political failure, not a market failure, and it might strike some people as unseemly for government to use its own ineptitude in making tax policy as an excuse for expanding its regulatory authority. Moreover, there is no political reason why the nation should not simply accept the higher spending resulting from an unwise tax policy. After all, people live quite comfortably (literally) with the excess spending that results from heavy tax subsidies for home ownership. The deductibility of home-mortgage interest and the nontaxability of nonmonetary returns from investments in owner-occupied dwellings, though offset somewhat by local property taxes, divert substantial resources from higher-valued uses to overly spacious and lavish housing; yet no move has been made to curb that overspending by regulatory means. On the contrary, growth in the housing market is universally regarded as a good thing because of the jobs and shelter it creates. Why shouldn't tax-subsidized growth in the health care sector be regarded with similar equanimity?

One thing seems clear: however socially destructive the tax subsidy for private health insurance may be, something other than the subsidy itself or its immediate consequences is causing the current political discontent about the cost of health care in the United States. Indeed, as the case of residential housing tellingly illustrates, a tax subsidy is insidious precisely because, in addition to being an off-budget public expenditure, it can misallocate huge amounts of society's resources, yet be entirely painless at the level of individual producers and consumers. Since the affected interests simply adjust their behavior to the incentives created, they have no occasion to complain or call for political attention.

Thus, in the abstract, capping the tax subsidy is a notion that only a policy wonk could love, a meritorious policy idea with no natural political constituency. Even so, some important insurer, employer, and provider interests reversed their position and actively advocated a tax cap in the * * * health reform debate. Ironically, their reason for doing so was not unhappiness with the tax subsidy as such. Indeed, they are among its main beneficiaries. Having been forced into a larger political game, however, they embraced a tax cap as a policy alternative preferable to other measures that government might take in response to the political pressures to do something about the high cost of health care. That the tax subsidy itself is not the source of these pressures suggests that people's grievances, and perhaps the cost crisis itself, may have some other root cause. * * *

Is Health Care Spending Out of (Purchasers') Control?

Although the tax subsidy undoubtedly induces more inappropriate spending on health care than consumers would tolerate merely as one cost of health insurance, the private sector may be reasonably efficient in controlling for moral hazard after discounting for tax effects. Because many elements of an efficient market are now in place, we must ask whether there is any good nontax reason to doubt that the nation is putting increasing resources into health care * * * simply because people like what they are getting in return. * * *

* * * A possible hypothesis * * * is that the nation overspends on health services because the marketplace offers an inadequate range of options to purchasers of all kinds, preventing them from choosing anything other than first-class, state-of-the-art, American-style medical care. Instead of being able to choose among a variety of offerings designed to appeal to persons in different economic circumstances, consumers and taxpayers may be the victims of a kind of tying arrangement under which, in order to obtain vital basic services, they must buy additional, unwanted services as well. Although purchasers of health care can reject some frills and can exclude some categories of service altogether, employers and employees may be unable to respond to the rising cost of health care as they normally respond when other costs increase—by cutting back on the quantity purchased, by making small compromises on content and quality, or by assuming slightly greater risks. Similarly, when government is forced to make cuts in its health programs, it may have to be arbitrary because it lacks the means to be selective.

Whether health care spending is as voluntary as efficiency would require is ultimately an empirical question. There is at least some factual support, however, for the hypothesis that the U.S. health care system offers only a kind of Hobson's choice, requiring consumers either to purchase some version of a health care Cadillac or to take their chances with the safety net that more or less exists for those without health insurance. Whereas most people simply pay the price of one of the Cadillac models available in the marketplace, the many people who have chosen to go without health coverage would appear to be some evidence that the market has failed to meet consumer demand for low-cost care. Government's longstanding unwillingness to finance universal coverage is also in part a function of the market's lack of low-cost options, which, however inadequate they might seem in the abstract, would certainly be preferable to no coverage at all. * * *

* * * The exact nature of the market's apparent failure in offering economizing options can be forcefully demonstrated by referring again to figure 4–1. Recall that no consumption to the right of point *o* in that diagram is justified solely on the basis of the medical benefit derived. (After that point, derived from the slope of the cost curve, the benefits of adding inputs are less than the cost of those inputs.) Most spending beyond point *o* is thus an artifact not of the strength of people's preferences but of the moral hazard associated with health insurance. All such care is therefore a legitimate potential target for cost-containment efforts.

Recall also that some care falling to the right of point *o* in figure 4–1 may be (despite its inappropriateness in benefit-cost terms) a necessary cost of the valuable financial protection that health insurance provides. Because the costs that would have to be incurred to prevent or deter such spending would in many cases exceed the net saving, it would often be better—more efficient—to incur the costs of such marginally beneficial care than to strive to stamp it out. Nevertheless, all health services falling to the right of point *o* should be regarded as legitimate targets for economizing efforts if a health plan can devise cost-effective measures to attack them. Indeed, if health plans are not taking such measures, then the market can be judged to be malfunctioning and allocating excessive resources to health care.

[An] examination * * * of health plan contracts in use today reveals that all plans (including HMOs) generally commit themselves, explicitly or implicitly, to paying for all care to the left of point *x*, rather than covering only care up to point *o* (even as plan subscribers, rather than society as a whole, might value the benefits of that care). These contractual undertakings reflect in part a natural disinclination to fight the cost battle in the metaphorical benefit-cost no man's land, where the cost controllers would come under heavy fire—including possible legal liability for denying medically beneficial care. This reluctance to economize even where it would be efficient to do so is partly a consequence of the tax subsidy, which weakens economizing incentives. [H]owever, it is also a consequence of a legal system whose unrealistic expectations of payers and providers artificially raise the costs of economizing in the treacherous territory of benefit-cost trade-offs. There are thus some good reasons for taking seriously the possibility that because consumers are systematically denied desirable opportunities to economize, the market as a whole is failing to control costs optimally.

Many observers might disagree with the hypothesis that the health care market does not offer consumers an adequate range of choice. In their view, employers, particularly self-insured ones, have many options for providing bare-bones coverage to their workers. These skeptics would point to increased use of substantial patient cost sharing and to recent shifts by employers from open-panel fee-for-service plans to closed-panel HMOs in which utilization management, gatekeeper arrangements, and financial incentives discourage inappropriate spending. Proponents of the managed-competition strategy are among those who are apparently satisfied with the range of cost-containment tools available in the current market. In their view, all that is needed to facilitate all the economizing that consumers should want is more of the same: more integration of financing and delivery in cost-conscious HMOs. The Clinton administration's proposed Health Security Act reflect[ed] a similar premise.

Many of those who profess unconcern about consumers' lack of choice are not, however, merely making an empirical judgment about the efficacy of the cost-containment tools currently available. Instead, they are making an essentially political judgment that it is not necessary or feasible or desirable to carry the battle into the benefit-cost no man's land. Paul Starr, a prominent health policy advisor to President Clinton, has written, "The challenge of health reform is not to persuade the public to give up beneficial care but to reduce the costs that have no benefit, thereby freeing up the resources needed to include the uninsured within a mainstream standard of health coverage."[4] Other commentators similarly seek voter support for impending reforms by denying that the time for "rationing" health care has arrived. Thus, * * * Dr. Robert Brook, whose research leads him to believe that as much as a third of the care we consume lies, in effect, beyond point x in figure 4–1, thinks "we have at least 10 years before we have to think about rationing."[7]

Other influential observers, including economist Victor Fuchs and William Schwartz, are more candid and insist on getting away from the any-benefit test that point x symbolizes. Schwartz identifies specific targets to the left of point x that should be addressed immediately, such as a policy in prescribing magnetic resonance imaging for head injuries that clearly saves an occasional life but at a cost of about $2 million dollars each time.[8] Even these observers are quite vague, however, about the specific mechanisms that should be deployed to attack targets in the no man's land. Indeed, in virtually all discussions, rationing implies some form of government control and at least implicit valuation of the lives of individual citizens. Understandably, few commentators are willing to embrace it. The question under consideration here is, however, only whether consumers have, or should be given, opportunities to economize in purchasing their own care—with whatever subsidies the government provides to ensure that they are not forced to make unacceptable choices. Essentially, the question is whether consumers can consent today to some limits on their entitle-

4. Paul Starr, *The Logic of Health–Care Reform* (Knoxville, Tenn.: Grand Rapids Press, 1992), p. 43.

7. ["Those Who Pay Health Costs Think About Drawing Lines," *New York Times*, Mar. 28, 1993, § 4, at 1.]

8. See ibid. See also William Schwartz, "The Inevitable Failure of Current Cost–Containment Strategies: Why They Can Provide Only Temporary Relief," *Journal of the American Medical Association*, vol. 257 (1987) *p.* 220. [Ed.—Is $2 million too much to pay to save a life (as Schwartz implies)? How should one answer this question, assuming it is a matter of public policy? See, e.g., K. Viscusi, Fatal Tradeoffs: Public and Private Responsibilities for Risk (1992) (analyzing values imputed to human life in various market and regulatory contexts). Are consumers and their agents capable of making such tradeoffs in their purchasing decisions? Is anyone else likely to make wiser choices?]

ment to marginally beneficial services that they may arguably need tomorrow.

Those who believe that only unnecessary, nonefficacious care needs be targeted immediately in the war against health care costs are making a grave miscalculation in at least one respect. Those targets that they are prepared to attack will be much harder to attack successfully if the benefit-cost no man's land remains a privileged sanctuary rather than being viewed as a legitimate part of the battlefield. As long as the appropriateness of a service is deemed to turn on whether it is beneficial at all (that is, falls to the left or right of point x) rather than on whether it is likely to be worth its cost (that is, falls to the left or right of point o), the burden of proof in challenging a particular expenditure will be much harder to meet than it should be. Many battles that should be won will be lost, including many battles against spending on the flat of the curve.

Another reason that some observers give for not worrying about consumers' economizing opportunities is their doubt that consumers would enroll in health plans that threaten to deny them beneficial care. This empirical judgment is based on nothing more than consumer behavior in the present market and the assumed immutability of the entitlement mentality apparent in opinion polls and labor-management disputes. There is no empirical basis for skepticism about a policy of capping the tax subsidy, exposing consumers directly to cost burdens now borne by their employers, and ensuring that the market is not artificially prevented from offering an adequate range of choice. Sooner or later, such a policy would induce the economizing that consumers now resist.

Still other resistance to expanding consumers' market options is rooted in a preference for the any-benefit test (point x) as the criterion for making health care choices. Industry interests naturally prefer this liberal standard. Public officials give it at least lip service because they are hesitant to deny, in the face of public opinion, the government's responsibility to ensure that everything feasible is done for the health of every individual. Most academic observers similarly prefer not to be associated with politically unpopular ideas. In the political world inhabited by these influential players, point x represents the moral high ground, a position that conveniently spares them both criticism for being insensitive and the need for long explanations about trade-offs. Yet, despite its safety overlooking the benefit-cost no man's land, point x cannot be morally defended, even under the moral assumptions of those who occupy it. A policy that puts excessive public and private resources into financing Cadillac-style care for everyone has only symbolic merit. It is likely to result, in reality, in the continued neglect of other, more pressing national needs in such fields as education, housing, nutrition, crime control, and environmental protection. Because the aggregate cost of avoiding cost-containment skirmishes in the benefit-cost no man's land could exceed one or more whole percentage points of the nation's GDP, it is irresponsible to deny consumers the means to carry on the battle against wasteful spending wherever the enemy is found.

If we can conclusively establish that the market for health care systematically denies consumers opportunities to economize in reasonable ways, we will finally have a solid basis for concluding that U.S. health care costs are out of control—in the literal sense of being beyond the influence of those who ultimately pay them. If a substantial amount of health care spending is involuntary in the sense that consumers (or taxpayers) do not assume the payment burden willingly, then rising societal investments in health care can be clearly distinguished from healthy economic growth. Society could not then reasonably presume—as it does in the case of * * * other commodities—that people buying increasing amounts of ever more costly goods and services derive benefits from their purchases at least equal to their outlays, justifying the increase in aggregate spending.

QUESTIONS ON THE PROBLEM OF HEALTH CARE COSTS

1. Are you yet satisfied that U.S. health care spending, which currently totals over one trillion dollars per year (having doubled since about 1987), is excessive in some relevant sense? Is it significant that health care's claim on the nation's GDP, which stabilized at 13.6% in 1993–96, rose to that level from 10.7% in 1985, 8.6% in 1975, and 6.0% in 1965? Is it relevant that no other developed nation spends more than 10% of its GDP this way? E.g., in 1991, Canada 10.0%, France 9.1%, Germany 8.5%, Finland, 8.9%. Do Wennberg's studies show wasteful spending? Do findings that many specific services provided to patients are deemed "inappropriate" settle the question whether the nation is spending "too much" on health care?

In the mid–1990s, the cost of health care in the U.S. ceased to rise at rates far in excess of the growth of national income. Not only did the overall rate of increase moderate, but some (large) employers experienced a stabilization or even modest declines in the annual cost of care for their employees. What conclusions do you draw from this historic development? Is the health care cost "crisis" over? In fact, projections for 1997 indicated that overall costs were likely to rise at a faster rate than previously (6.4% in 1997 versus 5.3% in the two years from 1993 to 1995). Some contend that the introduction of managed care will yield only a one-time saving and that costs will resume their previous trend, reaching $1.5 trillion around 2002. Is this undesirable? It is inevitable?

2. What grounds are there for believing that the market mechanism that has gotten health care spending to its present levels is unreliable in accurately registering the preferences of consumers with respect to how their resources are spent? How do you respond to the argument that health care is just another growth industry and that consumers are simply voting with their dollars to have more of it produced?

3. Are you yet able to identify a particular "market failure" that systematically causes U.S. consumers to spend more on personal health care than they actually "want" to spend? What about "moral hazard"? Consider the various ways in which it may manifest itself in health care. Remember that moral hazard is a problem inherent in insurance of all kinds and, indeed, arises whenever normal economizing incentives are diluted by the opportunity to risk or spend another's funds. If the moral hazard attendant on third-party payment for health services is a serious problem, why do we tolerate the latter? Does the problem lie in third-party payment as such or in the way in which it is administered? Would the problem disappear if government were to assume responsibility for health care financing as a "single payer"? Could government regulation be expected to solve the problem any better than an insurer can solve it for itself—as a service to its insureds, who presumably want the fund to which they contribute protected against excessive claims?

4. What other factor present in the marketplace clearly warrants the conclusion that the market for health services in the U.S. is not accurately resolving trade-offs between quantity, quality, and cost? Is this factor correctable by public policy measures? Is government likely to take the measures necessary to make the market a better vehicle for translating consumer preferences into wise spending decisions by health care providers? If not, what should policymakers do instead?

The foregoing questions are intended to highlight the effects of tax policy on health spending. See generally J. Gruber & J. Poterba, Tax Subsidies to Employer–Provided Health Insurance (NBER Working Paper No. 5147, 1995). Legislation in 1996 and 1997 mildly exacerbated the problem by providing that self-employed persons can deduct (in amounts increasing to full deductibility in 2007) the premiums they pay for health coverage in calculating their income taxes. Do the distortions introduced by an unwise tax policy render the market useless as an instrument for guiding health care spending?

5. Havighurst advances the hypothesis that, even putting the tax subsidy aside, the market does not offer consumers economizing options, forcing many of them to go without any protection other than the safety net provided by a combination of public programs and private charity. Where does he suggest the causes of this possible problem may lie? Some possible constraints on the freedom of health plans and providers to economize in the interest of consumers will be suggested in the materials that follow and will reappear throughout the book.

6. Current controversies surrounding managed care tend to focus on allegations of excessive economizing rather than excessive spending. See, e.g., George Anders, Health Against Wealth: HMOs and the Breakdown of Medical Trust (1996); Bodenheimer, The HMO Backlash—Righteous or Reactionary?, 335 New Eng. J. Med. 1601 (1996); Freudenheim, HMOs Cope with a Backlash on Cost Cutting, N.Y. Times, May 19, 1996, at A1?. Do you conclude that Havighurst's emphasis on overspending is misplaced?

7. Bear in mind the significance of "point o" and "point x" in the diagram included in the foregoing excerpt. Those points (and the "no man's land" between them) will be referred to in later discussion. For some concrete examples of the kinds of issues illustrated in the diagram, consider the following:

(a) "Two drugs for treating people with heart attacks are equally effective in saving lives, according to two important studies. One drug [TPA] costs $2,200 a dose, and the other [streptokinase] $76 to $300." Pollack, The Battle of the Heart Drugs/A Special report; Two Remedies That Save Lives: Doctors Prescribe the Costly One, N.Y. Times, June 30, 1991, p. A1. Two thirds of patients treated in 1990 received TPA, at a cost of $210 million—versus $5 million spent on the remaining patients. TPA was heavily promoted by its maker (Genentech), and doctors purported to find "theoretical" reasons to prefer it and to doubt the studies showing clinical equivalence. What, if anything, should be done to make doctors to accept the studies' findings? What should be done if studies show (as later ones in fact do) that TPA is marginally better?

(b) Although there are certain clinical advantages in using low-rather than high-osmolality intravascular contrast agents in x-ray studies, "the clinical importance of these differences is small." Hirshfeld, Low–Osmolality Contrast Agents—Who Needs Them?, 326 New Eng. J. Med. 482 (1992). Such agents cost about 25 times as much, however, a difference not offset by the cost of managing the occasional side effects. Studies suggest that patients might be categorized with respect to the risk of side effects but are in conflict. What should be done? How should physicians' clinical decisions be influenced—by professional education, by professional peer review, by payer oversight, or in some other way?

(c) A hospital study found that when prehospital efforts to resuscitate victims of cardiopulmonary arrest had failed, further efforts in the emergency room succeeded in only 9 percent of cases. Although admitted to the hospital, none of these patients was discharged alive, and 15 of the 16 remained comatose until death. The total hospital bill for the 16 was $180,000. Should the hospital cease attempting to resuscitate such patients? How could such a policy change be legitimized? Should payers have any role in the determination?

SECTION C: HEALTH PLANS TODAY

NOTE ON THE HISTORY OF HEALTH INSURERS' COST–CONTAINMENT EFFORTS

You will be asked below to consider the question, raised by Havighurst, whether today's health plans are doing all they might reasonably be expected to do to curb the impact of moral hazard and to control health care spending in accordance with the wishes of their subscribers. Whatever the case today, however, it is clear that health plans began to tackle the problem of health care costs in earnest only in the early 1980s. In the 1970s, observers outside the health insurance industry criticized insurers' slowness in adopting aggressive cost-containment measures. E.g., Havighurst, The Questionable Cost–Containment Record of Commercial Health Insurers, in H. Frech, ed., Health Care in America: The Political Economy of Hospitals and Health Insurance 221 (1988). Some possible explanations for insurers' passivity and failure to innovate during that earlier era are offered here for your evaluation:

—*Demand for cost containment was weak.* In addition to the tax subsidy, other factors seemed to dilute the interest of insurance purchasers in effective cost containment. In particular, employers appeared fearful of appearing to short-change the workers. The significance of a health benefits program as a symbol of an employer's (or a union's) commitment to employee welfare was for a long time an important impediment to many reforms that might have been in the workers' true interest but were not easily perceived as being so.

—*Insurers were too small to act alone.* Insurers claimed to lack the bargaining power needed to confront providers and even asked for an antitrust exemption to allow them to bargain collectively. But even a large plan could not hope to get the attention of a high-priced or uncooperative provider if it could not steer insured patients away from that provider. Critics observed that few plans had developed that capability, which (as noted below) rapidly appeared in the 1980s to be the most crucial of the innovations available to insurers.

—*Costs incurred in innovating were not recoverable.* If an insurer's competitors could free-ride on his innovations, he had no incentive to undertake them. Thus, if a change was difficult or risky to introduce but easily imitated if it was successful, an insurer would be unlikely to adopt it. Similarly, an insurer that succeeded in changing provider behavior toward all patients, not just its own insureds, could hope to gain little competitive advantage and might therefore choose to leave well enough alone.

—*Law and regulation limited what insurers could do.* Although there were certainly some significant regulatory restraints on insurer innovation, the insurance industry sometimes seemed to construe legal restrictions very narrowly, perhaps to suit a collective preference in the industry for not competing in the difficult and risky business of cost containment. Moreover, insurers appeared to struggle significantly against such anticompetitive regulation by legal or political action only in situations where their competitors, such as HMOs and self-insured groups, were not subject to the same restraints.

—*Collusion inhibited change.* Even though commercial health insurers regularly consulted one another through their trade association (the Health Insurance Association of America) and seemed to have a strong concern for their collective welfare, collusion to limit competitive innovation, which would probably be illegal under the antitrust laws, would have been difficult to prove. The structure of the industry (which featured many firms and conditions making entry relatively easy) seemed not conducive to effective collusion.

—*Innovation was restrained by organized medicine.* Some evidence of such restraints will appear in chapters 4 and 9. Nevertheless, a cynical observer might suggest that insurers acquiesced too readily to physician pressure in refraining from conduct that would have benefitted consumers.

—*Blue Cross and Blue Shield plans set the tone for all insurers.* Originating under provider control, the "Blues" did indeed fail to challenge providers for a long time. In the 1980s, however, the Blues began to take a more active interest in cost containment and a more adversarial stance toward providers. Materials in chapter 9 will suggest some reasons why commercial carriers did not assume the pace-setting role.

Another possible explanation for the lack of innovation in the 1970s was the general expectation throughout that period that government would shortly take aggressive actions to remedy the problem of health care costs, possibly implementing some form of national health insurance. The expectation of government action may have caused private actors—employers as well as insurers—to sit on their hands rather than addressing the cost problem aggressively for themselves. Another factor may have been the general encouragement that federal policy makers in those years gave to HMOs—but not to other potential innovations in health care financing, which were therefore rendered riskier. (What events arguably finally unleashed the creative energies of the private sector? Note that the private sector has only been working actively on addressing this extraordinarily difficult problem for a relatively short time. Are you more impressed by how much progress has been made or by the steepness and length of the learning curve?)

Coping With the Trade-Offs

NOTES AND QUESTIONS ON WRITING HEALTH CARE CONTRACTS TO COUNTERACT MORAL HAZARD

1. Although moral hazard certainly represents a serious theoretical weakness in policy proposals based on the supposed efficiency of unregulated markets for health care, it can also be thought of as a challenge that competing insurers and other health plans must attempt to meet in order to keep their costs down and their premiums competitive. Indeed, whether moral hazard represents a market failure serious enough to require some kind of public action (such as the imposition of a politically determined global budget) depends on how manageable it is in practice by independent private actors. Thus, you are invited to imagine that you have been charged with designing a health care financing plan capable of giving beneficiaries effective financial protection at a reasonable cost. (Alternatively, put yourself in the position of a private firm's employee benefits manager designing a self-insured health plan or searching the market for an appropriate offering.) The following notes examine various strategies that are in use today. In considering the various approaches and particularly the various contractual formulations of the obligations of health plans to their subscribers, look for indications that payers are anything but comfortable with the any-benefit criterion symbolized by "point x" in Havighurst's Figure 4–1. Is it possible that today's health plans are capable of systematically engaging the cost problem only on the least controversial ground? See generally Frech, Health Insurance: Designing Products to Reduce Costs, in L. Deutch, ed., Industry Studies 307 (1993).

2. *Optimal Insurance.* What are the considerations that influence a consumer's decision to purchase financial protection against a particular risk? Economic theory (recall Professor Rice's reservations about its relevance on such matters) suggests that optimal insurance coverage for an individual is a function of four things: the degree of risk, the individual's preferences with respect to bearing risk, the elasticity of consumer demand for the service in question (that is, the responsiveness of demand to price changes), and the administrative costs of insurance. Elasticity of demand, not for medical care in general but for each specific medical service, reveals the importance attached to the service by consumers and physicians and thus signifies both the medical need for it and the value of insuring against that need. Consider the following illustration:

> [W]here demand is "inelastic," as in figure 1, a price reduction from p_1 (equal to 100 percent of cost) to p_2 (equal to 20 percent of p_1 due to insurance covering 80 percent of the cost) increases the quantity of the service rendered only from q_1 to q_2 and yields a "welfare" loss (deduced from some patients' unwillingness to pay as much as the full price, p_1) equal to the area of the shaded triangle. In contrast, where demand is "elastic," as in figure 2, the same insurance causes a much greater welfare loss as societal resources are employed to provide services that are valued at less than their cost. Other things being equal, insurance would be more sensible from the consumer's standpoint, and more socially efficient, for those essential services whose demand approximates that shown in figure 1.[10]
>
> It should be obvious that defining covered medical services with greater particularity would allow more discriminating judgments to be made about whether or not to insure. For example, the overall demand for hysterectomies may look like figure 2, making insurance inappropriate, but, in a few cases with certain medical indications, the need for the service would be so clear that demand would not be significantly affected by price. If insurance coverage could be readily restricted to such medically necessary services, it would be appropriate for many people to purchase only this limited coverage. The administrative costs which obviously limit the feasi-

10. Demand curves reflect not only variations in preferences but also income differences, since some of the fall-off at higher prices may be said to reflect consumers' inability, not their unwillingness, to pay. The relevance of this observation for social policy is not clear. On the one hand, some observers would completely reject demand elasticity as a relevant consideration, endorsing proposals for comprehensive coverage and contending, in effect, that the "welfare-loss triangle" reflects inequality, not inefficiency. On the other hand, it can be argued that demand elasticities provide a good index of relative medical necessity despite income differences, which probably affect the slope of all demand curves to about the same degree. [Professor Rice's reservations, cited earlier, about a policy of not insuring discretionary health services go mostly to preventive ones, which, he suggests, consumers may unwisely forgo if they have to pay for them.—Eds.]

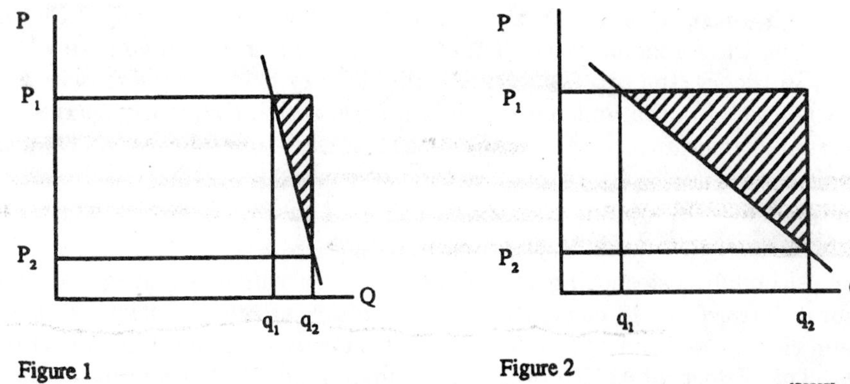

Figure 1

Figure 2

bility of minute specification of coverage do not invalidate the basic point that highly selective coverage could well make very good sense.

Havighurst, The Role of Competition in Cost Containment, in W. Greenberg, ed., Competition in the Health Care Sector: Past, Present, and Future 359, 362–63 (FTC 1978). The following notes address the feasibility of defining coverage with the particularity required to achieve optimal coverage.

3. *Cost Sharing.* Cost sharing—that is, requiring patients to pay deductibles and coinsurance—is the most common example of a coverage limitation used by insurers of all kinds (not just health insurers) to combat moral hazard. Because of its administrative simplicity and its potential for dampening insurance-subsidized demand, cost sharing should be part of any program of health care financing except perhaps one serving the poorest of the poor. Most health care contracts in use today, however, set deductibles (that is, levels of expenditure that must be reached before the plan has any responsibility) at levels so low—generally $100 or $200—as to signify a desire only to save paperwork and shift some basic costs to insureds, not to use price to curb moral hazard. What accounts for this preference for "first-dollar" coverage? What is the logic of proposals to encourage "medical savings accounts"?

Today's health care contracts also reveal that health plans make little effort to optimize coverage by fine-tuning coinsurance (that is, the percentage of a covered expense that the subscriber must pay) in pursuit of microefficiency in health care spending. Many contracts, particularly those of an increasing number of HMOs, require subscribers to pay small per-visit charges, which may be waived or reduced when cost-effective preventive care is sought. Contracts also impose special charges when a subscriber seeks care from a hospital emergency room, where costs cannot be effectively monitored by the plan.

Pure indemnity plans, which reimburse insureds for bills incurred on a fee-for-service basis, are the most likely to employ coinsurance to discourage overconsumption—usually at an across-the-board rate of 20 or 25 percent. Such across-the-board coinsurance requirements are clumsy tools, however. While underdeterring consumption of highly discretionary services, they unduly penalize the patient who obtains only truly vital care. Based on the foregoing discussion of optimal insurance, can you see why, at least in theory, the coinsurance rate should vary from service to service (as in the case of outpatient mental health care, which frequently carries a 50 percent coinsurance rate)? In practice, of course, varying cost sharing to reflect precisely the benefits and costs of covering each service more or less comprehensively would severely challenge the drafters of health plan contracts and complicate plan administration.

Although cost sharing would seem to be a valuable tool for offsetting moral hazard, is it clear that it will often affect physician decisions? Empirical evidence on the effects of cost sharing is mixed. E.g., Cherkin et al., The Effect of Office Visit Copayments on Utilization in a Health Maintenance Organization, 27 Med. Care 1036 (1989) (finding significant reductions in physician visits); Siu et al., Inappropriate Use of Hospitals in a Randomized Trial of Health Insurance Plans, 315 New Eng.J.Med. 1259 (1986) ("cost sharing did not selectively reduce inappropriate hospitalization"). For an antitrust case upholding a Delta Dental plan's refusal to allow payments under supplemental insurance to count toward a patient's copayment, see SmileCare Dental Group v. Delta Dental Plan of California, Inc., 88 F.3d 780 (9th Cir.) (recognizing utilization discouragement as business justification for practice), cert. denied, 117 S.Ct. 583 (1996).

4. *Categorical Exclusions*. Another strategy for reducing health insurance costs is to exclude certain categories of disease or treatment from coverage altogether. Even relatively comprehensive contracts are likely to exclude, for example, dental care, sexual reassignment surgery, in vitro fertilization, reversal of voluntary sterilization, treatment for morbid obesity, and cosmetic surgery undertaken solely for purposes of beautification—all items of arguably low priority (either as health needs or as candidates for insurance coverage) compared to covered services. Other, less common exclusions found in health plan contracts include self-administered drugs, enteral feeding, examinations for learning disorders or developmental delay, cytotoxicity testing, bionics, cochlear implants, temporomandibular ("TMJ") disease, nonhuman and other radical organ transplants, and surgery to correct nearsightedness. A particularly common approach is to provide that coverage of prescription drugs is limited to those included in a formulary maintained by the plan, with the result that a physician's or patient's drug of choice may not be covered. See generally AMA Council on Ethical and Judicial Affairs, Managed Care Cost Containment Involving Prescription Drugs, 53 Food & Drugs L.J. 25 (1998) (policy statement raising issues concerning formularies restricting physicians' prescribing freedom).

By their nature, categorical exclusions are poor rationing tools, incapable of reliably directing money to meeting only essential needs. Some highly beneficial services in the excluded categories are inevitably excised from coverage, while some questionable services in covered categories continue to be financed because contract language is not precise enough to exclude them. On the other hand, categorical approaches might be helpful in imposing cost sharing and other refinements in the scope of coverage. For example, a plan might exclude hospital stays beyond stated maximums for particular categories of treatment (barring special complications). But see Declercq & Simmes, The Politics of "Drive–Through Deliveries": Putting Early Postpartum Discharge on the Legislative Agenda, 75 Milbank Q. 175 (1997) (discussing rapid enactment of state and federal legislation to reverse plan policies setting strict limits on hospital stays after childbirth).

5. *Selective Coverage.* Some contract drafters have tried to be selective rather than categorical with respect to certain services. For example, while physical, occupational, and speech therapy are rarely wholly excluded from coverage, such services usually are subject to certain limitations. Thus, one HMO covers rehabilitative therapy only "when the personal care physician [gatekeeper] determines that significant improvement of a member's condition can be expected within a period of two months." Another contract excludes physical, occupational, and speech therapy "when there is no reasonable expectation that the member's condition will improve over a predictable period of time as determined by [the plan]." To what extent do the quoted provisions represent efforts to economize in the "no man's land" of benefit/cost trade-offs?

Mental health care has been another milieu in which health plans have sought more sensitive instruments for rationing financing. One HMO excludes coverage for "services for mental disorders which [the plan] determines cannot be improved with treatment." Other plans, apparently acknowledging that efficacy will prove exceedingly difficult to deny with respect to care of this kind, venture into more treacherous territory. Thus, another HMO excludes mental health services, after diagnosis, "for conditions which, in the professional judgment of a physician, are not subject to significant improvement through relatively short-term therapy."

6. *Selective Coverage vs. Antidiscrimination Legislation.* Would a health plan that places coverage limits on mental health benefits that are more restrictive than those imposed on benefits of other kinds violate the Americans with Disabilities Act? Although the ADA broadly prohibits discrimination against disabled persons, it creates a qualified safe harbor for insurance plans, stating that it should not be construed to prohibit a covered entity "from establishing, sponsoring, observing or administering the terms of a bona fide benefit plan that are based on underwriting risks, classifying risks, or administering such risks that are based on and not inconsistent with state law," provided that the plan is not "used as a subterfuge to evade the purposes" of the ADA. 42 U.S.C. § 12201(c) (1995). Whether an insurance plan violates the ADA thus appears to turn on a three-part inquiry: (1) at the threshold, whether a provision draws a disability-based distinction (if no disability-based distinction is found, the plan will be upheld); (2) whether the plan is "bona fide" and "not inconsistent with state law"; and (3) whether the distinction is being used as a "subterfuge." See Equal Employment Opportunity Comm'n (EEOC), Interim Guidance on Application of ADA to Disability–Based Distinctions in Employer Provided Health Insurance, EEOC Compl. Man. (CCH) ¶ 6902, at 5355 (June 8, 1993).

Courts have held that an insurance plan that provides broader health benefits for physical ailments than for mental ailments does not draw a disability-based distinction because the "mental ailment" group includes persons without a "disability" (defined in part as a condition that substantially limits a major life function). Modderno v. King, 82 F.3d 1059, 1062 (D.C.Cir.1996) (generalized across-the-board limits are permissible, and "distinctions between mental and physical care are no more vulnerable * * * than are completely generalized limits"); EEOC v. CNA Ins. Cos., 96 F.3d 1039 (7th Cir.1996) ("all employees—the perfectly healthy, the physically disabled, and the mentally disabled—had a plan that promised them long-term benefits * * * until age 65 if their problem was physical, and long-term benefits for two years if the problem was mental or nervous"). Accord, Parker v. Metropolitan Life Ins. Co., 121 F.3d 1006, 1015 (6th Cir.1997) (en banc) ("the ADA prohibits discrimination between the disabled and the non-disabled" but does not mandate "equality between individuals with different disabilities"; if all employees, "whether disabled or not," receive the "same access to [a] long-term disability plan," there is no discrimination in violation of the ADA); Krauel v. Iowa Methodist Med. Center, 95 F.3d 674, 678 (8th Cir.1996) (holding that "insurance distinctions that apply equally to * * * individuals with disabilities and to those who are not disabled, do not discriminate on the basis of disability"). The EEOC has also taken the position that benefit provisions that provide greater coverage for physical ailments "are not distinctions based on disability." EEOC, supra, at 5355. If there is no disability-based distinction, there is no ADA discrimination claim at the threshold.

If a plan were found to draw a disability-based distinction, the next question would be whether it was "bona fide" and consistent with state law and not a "subterfuge" to avoid compliance with the ADA. The EEOC has taken the position that the employer will satisfy the "bona fide and consistent with state law" requirement by showing that the plan exists and pays benefits, that the terms of the plan have been accurately communicated to eligible employees, and that the plan's "terms are not inconsistent with applicable state law as interpreted by the appropriate state authorities." Id. at 5356; accord, *Krauel,* 95 F.3d. at 678.

As to "subterfuge," the Department of Justice and the EEOC have taken the position that, in order not to be a "subterfuge," disparities in insurance policies must be based on "sound actuarial principles." The EEOC allows an employer to justify a disability-based distinction by showing that the disparate treatment is "attributable to the application of legitimate risk classification and underwriting procedures (and thus increased cost to the health insurance plan) of the disability, and not to the disability per se." EEOC, supra, at 5357. Similarly, the employer may prove that the "disparate treatment is necessary * * * to ensure that the challenged health insurance plan satisfies the commonly accepted or legally required standards for fiscal soundness of such a plan" or that the challenged practice is "necessary to prevent the occurrence of an unacceptable change either in the coverage of the health insurance plan, or in the premiums charged for the health insurance plan." Id. at 5357–58.

A panel of the Sixth Circuit court of appeals sustained the EEOC position allowing actuarially justified distinctions. Parker v. Metropolitan Life Ins. Co., 99 F.3d 181, 191 (6th Cir.1996) (stating that "insurance practices are protected by the safe-harbor provision * * * only to the extent that they are consistent with 'sound actuarial principles,' 'actual reasonably anticipated experience' and 'bona fide risk classification.' "). The court of appeals sitting en banc, however, reversed the panel's decision. Parker v. Metropolitan Life Ins. Co., 121 F.3d 1006 (6th Cir.1997) (en banc). Although the court left open the question of the proper definition of "subterfuge" under the ADA, it noted that the "sound actuarial principles" approach is "inconsistent with the Supreme Court's definition of the term subterfuge in the Age Discrimination in Employment Act ["ADEA"]." Id. at 1013 n.7. In the ADEA context, the Supreme Court has held that, for "subterfuge" to be established, there must be an intent to evade the purposes of the act. Public Employees Retirement System v. Betts, 492 U.S. 158, 167 (1989). In *Modderno*, supra, 82 F.3d at 1065, the D.C. Circuit applied the *Betts* approach to the "subterfuge" language of the ADA, noting that insurance plans adopted before the enactment of the ADA could not have been adopted with the intent to evade the purposes of the act.

In the Mental Health Parity Act of 1996, 42 U.S.C. § 300gg–5 (Supp. 1997), Congress prohibited group health plans maintained by larger employers from setting annual or lifetime dollar maximums for mental health benefits at levels lower than the limits set for physical illness. However, nothing in the act requires plans to offer such benefits, and plans are still free to make distinctions in setting deductible and copayment levels and in limiting the number of covered visits or inpatient days. The act also makes exceptions where adherence to the requirement would result in "an increase in the cost under the plan of at least one percent" and specifically exempts limits on the treatment of alcohol and drug problems. Should the one-percent exception be based on projections of prospective cost increases resulting from the act or on retrospective analysis of actual results? In late 1997, that issue raised a significant controversy. The interim rules effective January 1, 1998, called for a "modified" retrospective approach, using a six-month base period rather than a longer one-year period. Thus, companies offering mental health benefits seemingly must demonstrate some actual experience in order to qualify for the exception. See Interim Rules for Mental Health Parity, 62 Fed. Reg. 66932 (Dec. 22, 1997).

7. *Medical Necessity, etc.* "Medical necessity" is ubiquitous as a contractual criterion governing the obligation of a health plan to pay for particular services. See generally Agency for Health Care Policy and Research & National Institute for Health Care Management, Medical Necessity (Proceedings of a Symposium on Policy Issues, Implementation Challenges and Tough Choices, April 28, 1995). Use of this criterion again reflects the difficulty that contract drafters face in precisely defining the limits of plan coverage. Because of this difficulty and perhaps also because of the continuing influence of the professional paradigm of medical care, drafters have adopted the expedient of defining coverage by explicit or implied reference to a purely medical criterion. How is medical necessity determined? Most health care contracts define medically necessary services in part as those rendered "in accordance with generally accepted medical practice," "widely accepted standards," or "the medical standard of the community." Was it wise thus to incorporate standards prevailing in the medical profession? If it was efficient to incorporate professional standards by reference as contractual default rules in the first instance, is it necessarily a wise tactic today? What has changed since the first policies incorporating professional standards were written?

Some contract drafters have tried to reduce the extent to which payment obligations turn solely on the collective judgment of medical practitioners by including language to ensure that the standard is not solely a professional one. One term occasionally employed as a modifier of services that qualify for coverage is *essential*. Thus, one plan defines medically necessary services as those "essential for the treatment of a Member's medical condition." Although the focus here remains on the patient's medical needs, the notion of essentiality betokens a desire to omit from coverage at least some services to the left of "point x." Another term conveying the impression that any benefit is not enough is *adequate*, which is occasionally employed. Indeed, one contract uses *adequately* together with *sufficient* in a clause conveying a rather clear economizing intent. That plan stipulates that it will not pay more than an amount that "would have been sufficient to safely and adequately diagnose or treat a [patient]." The use of the word *safely* in this clause is also of interest. Should it be interpreted as an absolute or only a relative value?

Another term frequently appearing in health plan contracts is *appropriate*. Although this term has no fixed meaning in medical contexts, it can be read as requiring some attention to trade-offs. Mostly, however, its use is substantively significant because it so pointedly avoids explicit reference to prevailing professional standards. Therefore, litigation focusing on appropriateness would probably not be resolved solely by reference to what is customary or standard in medical practice. Instead, a plan should be able to present evidence, perhaps drawn from health services research, on such issues as cost-effectiveness. In your view, would making appropriateness a criterion of coverage facilitate effective resistance to expenditures in the benefit/cost no man's land? Interestingly, some studies undertaken by The RAND Corporation revealed startling differences in physician assessments of surgical and medical procedures when, instead of "appropriateness," they were asked to consider "cruciality"; in these same studies, the notion of "necessity" was found to be too confusing to elicit clear and consistent assessments. See Havighurst, Health Care Choices, supra, at 254–59.

Why would contract drafters, in their effort to enable plans better to control costs, seize upon terms as imprecise and ambiguous as *essential*, *adequate*, *safely*, and *appropriate*? Although begging virtually every relevant question, such terms have at least the merit of releasing the plan from a duty to accept professional standards unquestioningly as the measure of its obligations to patients. (What other term might lawyers be expected to employ to achieve the same purpose?) Their lameness as alternative standards, however, illustrates that contract drafters have not yet hit upon an effective way to exercise the independence thus declared. Indeed, it is a sign of the dangers attending forays in the no man's land of benefit/cost trade-offs that such terms, although capable of being read as rejections of the any-benefit test symbolized by "point x," are at the same time vague and question-begging enough to allay apprehension and avert criticism. It is possible, nevertheless, that these terms succeed at some level in communicating to providers, plan administrators, subscribers, and courts the drafters' intention that trade-offs should matter. Note, however, how difficult it is, both linguistically and as a matter of public relations, to be explicit about such things. Chapter 8(§C) includes material on the interpretation and administration of coverage limits in health care contracts.

In general, what do you think of the medical necessity standard? For a study, based on interviews, of how medical necessity works in practice as a basis for constraining medical and insurer decision making, see Jacobson et al., Defining and Implementing Medical Necessity in Washington State and Oregon, 34 Inquiry 143 (1996) (concluding that "medical necessity as an organizing principle for clinical practice decision making is likely to continue to erode in a managed care environment"). Can you imagine other ways of formulating enrollees' entitlements? For some proposed language aimed at differentiating health plans in terms of their aggressiveness in attacking targets in the benefit/cost no-man's-land, see Havighurst, Health Care Choices, supra, at 178–95. See also Eddy, Benefit Language: Criteria That Will Improve Quality While Reducing Costs, 275 J.A.M.A. 650 (1996) (proposing specific "benefit language that will have the greatest effect on the day-to-day practice of medicine"). What about the possibility of incorporating "practice guidelines," particularly those of a more prescriptive kind, by reference in a plan/subscriber contract? See id. at 222–64. For a formal proposal of a scheme in which consumers would face explicit choices based on their respective valuations of "quality-adjusted life years" (or "QALYs"), see Rai, Rationing Through Choice: A New Approach to Cost–Effectiveness Analysis in Health Care, 72 Ind. L.J. 1015 (1997) ("Choice is desirable for the following reasons: first, moral theory does not provide a determinate answer to the question of how we should ration care; second, the most commonly prescribed alternative to moral theory—the democratic political process—does not respect the diversity of individual health and allocational preferences, and hence individual autonomy, to the same extent as does choice; and third, choice can be implemented in a manner that not only respects individual autonomy but also attends to other important moral principles, such as justice and beneficence.").

8. *Administering Selective Coverage*. Consider the practical difficulties of giving effect to contractual limitations on coverage in day-to-day decision making by clinicians and plan administrators. Indemnity coverage presents particular difficulties. For example, would a tough policy toward all claims submitted for reimbursement be a good idea? Or would careful scrutiny of medical necessity cost too much, upset patients whose claims are rejected (leaving them liable to the provider for the costs incurred), and anger physicians whose clinical decisions are second-guessed?

What are the alternatives to retrospective claims review? What about writing the policy to require an insured to obtain a second (confirming?) opinion before certain costly procedures will be paid for by the plan? Why do you suppose this approach was among the first experimented with, coming into limited use even in the 1970s? What drawbacks can you see?

What would be the advantages and disadvantages of an insurer's requiring advance submission of nonemergency treatment plans (for hospitalization, for example) for prior determination of its coverage responsibilities? Such prior authorization is now in widespread use; originally referred to as "predetermination of benefits," it is now commonly described as "utilization management." For a case examining and upholding (under federal law) prior authorization requirements in California's Medicaid program, see Cowan v. Myers, 187 Cal.App.3d 968, 232 Cal.Rptr. 299 (1986), cert. denied 484 U.S. 846 (1987). A prior-authorization requirement allows the plan, or a utilization manager it employs, to make coverage determinations prior to treatment rather than denying payment for services already rendered. The ability to interpret and apply contractual criteria at this early stage obviously strengthens the plan's negotiating position, often allowing an alternative course of treatment to be arranged. Some contracts provide for appeals from adverse initial decisions, and a few provide for submission of disputes to arbitration if the issue cannot be resolved internally. What should be the duty of the physician confronting an obstinate utilization manager? See the *Wickline* case, reproduced in chapter 8(§B).

Will insureds appreciate an insurer's efforts to enforce contractual limitations on coverage? Or will they perceive them only as attempts by an unfeeling, profit-oriented corporation to renege on its obligations? Would entrusting decisions to the plan's medical director or to an independent utilization management company solve the problem? How different would the problem be if the plan was maintained by a self-insured employer, perhaps under an administrative-services-only (ASO) arrangement with an insurer? Avoiding actual or apparent conflicts of interests is not easy.

How would a plan engaged in utilization management answer the charge that it is engaged in "rationing" care? Conceptually, an insurer can be seen as the executor of the wishes of the plan subscribers, who, having entered into a mutual bargain to pool their risks, rely upon the plan administrator to enforce that bargain fairly and consistently. Query, however, whether a health plan could convincingly portray itself in a real dispute as only a stakeholder. Note how the imprecision and ambiguity of the contractual obligation ("medical necessity") is a large part of the problem here.

Should a health plan or utilization manager be required to disclose the standards, protocols, algorithms, or clinical practice guidelines it employs in making coverage decisions? This has been a matter of some controversy. Can you see the arguments for not disclosing the plan's criteria? Should those criteria have been incorporated in the original plan/subscriber contract? If they are not, what legal status do they have? The question of plan accountability—specifically, liability for injuries caused by overly restrictive utilization decisions—will be examined in chapter 8(§B).

In many respects, the procedures that plans establish for giving effect to contractual coverage criteria may be more important than the literal criteria themselves in determining the plan's overall ability to control costs. For example, the opportunity for the plan and the patient's physician to discuss and even negotiate the patient's future treatment could well yield near-optimal decisions in many cases. It is an open question, however, whether utilization management, conducted without more precise contractual authority than is generally found in health care contracts today, is capable of ensuring uniform treatment of like cases or of making significant inroads in the benefit/cost no man's land. On the other hand, it is reported that even the appearance of utilization management can affect utilization by means of the so-called "sentinel effect." See Rosenberg et al., Effect of Utilization Review in a Fee-for-Service Health Insurance Plan, 333 New Eng. J. Med. 1326 (1995).

9. *Are Health Care Contracts Up to the Task?* What do you conclude from the foregoing about the utility of private contracts between health plans and their subscribers as instruments for defining predictable, enforceable entitlements and for giving consumers an appropriate range of choices in the market for health coverage? Consider the following:

> Ordinarily, when purchasers contract for the future delivery of complex goods or services, the sales contract contains detailed specifications of the purchaser's requirements. Health care contracts, however, are not remotely of this kind. Thus, contracts between patients and the actual providers of care are usually unwritten and rarely say anything specific about the provider's undertaking. Even more significantly, the subscriber contracts of private health plans employ only the most general terms in defining the services that subscribers are, in effect, purchasing on a prepaid, pre-need basis. * * *
>
> Of course, most health plan contracts are more in the nature of insurance policies than contracts for the future delivery of services. As such, their actual function is not to prescribe the services that providers will eventually supply. Instead, it is to curb moral hazard—by limiting the services that insureds can purchase at plan expense. [It can be demonstrated], however, that today's health plan contracts are crafted to counteract moral hazard only on the fringes of the problem. Thus, they impose few explicit limitations (other than categorical exclusions and limited cost-sharing requirements) on the obligation of the plan to pay for whatever services a physician prescribes. Under the test of "medical necessity," which serves almost universally as the contractual touchstone of plan coverage, the criteria used to check the spending discretion of providers are almost exclusively medical, not economic. Omission of cost considerations from the coverage calculus obviously neglects a principal concern of consumers.
>
> More ominously, the medical-necessity test perpetuates the values and preferences of health care providers, whose imperative is to prescribe for patients everything that may be beneficial—and nothing but the best.

Thus, today's health plan contracts are generally shaped in accordance with a convention, or paradigm, under which health care is not regarded, even at the margin, as a consumer good that people are free to purchase according to their preferences and economic circumstances. Written primarily to create individual entitlements to whatever providers competently and in good faith prescribe, health care contracts are simply never thought of as mutual undertakings by which individuals pool their funds to cover their future health needs and, in so doing, accept reciprocal limitations on their future right to make claims on the common fund.

* * *

Serious consequences have flowed from the ineffectiveness of health care contracts as instruments either for dictating terms to providers or for combating moral hazard in the benefit-cost no man's land. The inadequacy or absence of crucial terms in such contracts has meant that all concerned—patients, providers, plan administrators, and courts—have had to look elsewhere for rules and definitive decisions concerning the specific services to be provided in each case. Much of the content of the bundle of rights belonging to each consumer of health services is therefore ultimately established by judges, juries, and medical expert witnesses—arbiters unlikely to share, or implement, consumers' concerns about costs. As so construed, patients' entitlements include the right to demand, at little or no direct cost, many health services that are of dubious benefit or marginal value. Among the entitlements implicitly conferred on patients is the right—also of questionable value—to obtain a particular kind of legal redress for whatever the law (not the contract) defines as medical malpractice. * * *

The adverse cost and legal consequences of inadequate health care contracts have become increasingly serious over time. With consumers and their agents poorly armed in the fight against overspending, the nation's physicians, technology suppliers, and hospitals have been free for nearly a generation (certainly since Medicare and Medicaid) to invent and sell ever more expensive goods and services with little reference to cost considerations. * * * At the same time, the courts * * * picked up the costly professional standards and customary practices that evolved in the dysfunctional marketplace and used them to define the specific coverage obligations of health plans and to detect substandard care in malpractice suits. The health care industry has thus operated for many years under a legal regime that threatens physicians, hospitals, and health plans with severe sanctions if they are caught violating standards that have increasingly lost touch with economic reality. * * *

Because it operates to a large extent under centrally prescribed rather than privately prescribed standards, the health care industry can usefully be thought of as a regulated industry. Whatever one thinks of government regulation in general, public regulators are at least accountable to elected officials and potentially capable of serving the general public interest by balancing competing values such as benefits and costs. Unfortunately, the same cannot be said about the regulatory regime under which the health care industry operates. Neither the courts nor the professional sources from which they borrow standards are accountable to either voters or consumers. Moreover, they tend to focus on individual cases, not on issues of public policy, and to consider only benefits to individuals, not costs to consumers or to the economy as a whole. Although government regulation is often faulted for falling too much into the hands of the interests being regulated, actual industry capture of a regulatory program is presumably exceptional. The health care industry, conversely, has been effectively empowered to regulate itself. Under industry conventions strongly supported by the legal system, health care providers have broad powers, both individually and collectively, to decide without substantial cost constraints or effective oversight what services patients should receive at society's expense. [R]ecent innovations in managed care and utilization management, though significant, do not invalidate these assertions. Without contracts that expressly authorize their cost-control efforts * * *, [HMOs] and other managed-care plans can economize only sub rosa and not—because of legal constraints—to the full extent that cost-conscious consumers might approve.

For present purposes, the most important consequence of the defective regulatory regime under which the health care industry currently operates is that consumer choice is largely illusory in health care markets. Although the marketplace offers many apparent options, including a variety of managed-care plans, the real range of consumer choice is limited by the need for all plans to conform to ill-considered, often vague, but potentially demanding standards emanating from the same central source—the legal system, borrowing standards wherever necessary from providers themselves. Consumers are thus denied, beyond a certain point, the freedom to benefit themselves by economizing choices. Specifically, they lack opportunities for prospective self-denial—that is, they are not free to contract voluntarily today to accept a degree of health care rationing tomorrow. Thus, the same consumers who are free to buy small, arguably less safe cars (or used cars or cars without air bags or antilock brakes) cannot make comparable economizing choices in purchasing health care. Unable to save money for other uses by assuming a small degree of risk—risks that would almost certainly be near-negligible, judging from the doubtful value of so much of today's health care spending—purchasers of health coverage face essentially a Hobson's choice between different versions of the same health care Cadillac. Of course, American consumers have always had the option of going without health care coverage altogether. The very large number of persons who have made that choice, however, is itself mute testimony to the need for intermediate alternatives.

In sum, the reason for the huge margin by which the United States leads other nations in per capita health care spending is that its political and legal institutions have given it the worst of both worlds—regulation and the free market. On the one hand, the centrally prescribed, legally enforced standards that the nation has allowed to guide health care spending have never been evaluated as public policy or formally adopted as such. On the other hand, the private health plans to which the nation has entrusted great responsibilities have been either unwilling or unable to define private rights and obligations effectively by contract. Not only have the good intentions underlying the medical-legal system's insistence on high standards for everyone undercut the ability of market forces to determine the appropriate level of spending on health services, but they also have tragically impeded efforts to guarantee universal access to health care. The same regulatory system that has priced so many individuals out of the health insurance market has also made prohibitive the cost of providing for them at public expense. Once again, the best has proved an enemy of the good.

* * *

[E]ven though the health care industry has long operated under centrally prescribed rules and standards, its status as a regulated industry restricting consumer choice is in fact more de facto than de jure. Adherence to professional standards or industry custom is rarely mandatory in the sense that the law specifically prohibits health plans from varying the law's own requirements by contract. Instead, the general uniformity that one finds in today's contracts is arguably more a product of convenience and convention than of positive law or government regulation of the command-and-control variety. To be sure, health plans would certainly encounter some judicial resistance if they set out independently to define patient rights and provider obligations differing appreciably from those that have become customary. But even though legal scholars have frequently mourned, applauded, or otherwise noted the "death of contract," well-drafted health care contracts that were fairly marketed and not manifestly unfair to consumers would stand a good chance of being enforced more or less according to their terms. Although the caution of lawyers in proposing such contracts is understandable, there is almost certainly more room for contractual innovation than they have sought to exploit.

Havighurst, Health Care Choices, supra, at 14–19, 22. Are you persuaded by the above diagnosis of the health care industry's problems? Is it realistic to think that entitlements to health care could ever be more than nominally a matter of contract? If not, why not? (Some legal issues concerning the enforcement and interpretation of health care contracts will be examined in chapter 8(§B).) Precisely why have health care contracts been unused in the past as tools for particularizing entitlements? Has anything changed to make make contracts more promising as instruments for giving consumers a fuller range of explicit options in the health care marketplace?

Few observers define the market failure afflicting the health care sector as one of contract failure. The more conventional approach to the problem of health care costs is to advocate modification of prevailing standards of medical practice to incorporate greater concern about costs. A prominent spokesman for this approach is David Eddy, M.D., perhaps the leading national expert on the the quality of evidence supporting the use of medical technologies. Eddy views the strategy of modifying standards across the profession, rather than in individual health plans, as the only available answer to the "strong taboo against explicitly taking costs into account when determining the appropriate use of a treatment[, which taboo] creates a huge limitation on how any type of system[, fee-for-service or managed care,] can trade off cost and quality." Eddy, Balancing Cost and Quality in Fee–For–Service Versus Managed Care, Health Affs., May–June 1997, p. 162, 162–63. Eddy further observes (id. at 165),

Neither system, nor any of the variations (with very rare exceptions), approaches the trade-offs systematically or explicitly. To do so would violate the cost taboo and expose the party to charges of rationing. Thus, the superficial answer from fee-for-service and managed care plans on how they trade off cost and quality is, "We don't!" A search of mission statements, benefit language, instructions for designing guidelines, criteria for covering new treatments, or algorithms for developing care paths has not turned up any explicit policies about how costs should be incorporated in treatment decisions.

Eddy goes on to argue, however, that the standards of medical practice have always incorporated implicit cost concerns:

> There have always been trade-offs between cost and quality [even in traditional fee-for-service medicine]. * * * If *rationing* is defined as withholding coverage, because of its cost, for a treatment that is known to be effective, then fee-for-service medicine has always rationed. [I]t is important to recognize that in fee-for-service, the standard practices that most people believe are free of any tainting by costs are, in fact, implicitly constrained by costs.

Id. at 166. Eddy concludes that, given the taboo chilling explicit benefit/cost trade-offs in both fee-for-service practice and managed care, the parties in the best position to incorporate cost considerations into medical practice standards are the medical specialty societies in developing practice guidelines, protocols, and recommendations. Do you believe that it is realistic to expect the medical profession to address this problem? Do you think there is an additional problem, which Eddy identifies as the ethical principle of "equality," meaning that "if two essentially identical patients seek treatment for the same health problem, they should get the same treatment"? Is the more serious "taboo" the one that appears to preclude treating health care as an ordinary consumer good of which people (some with public subsidies) can buy more or less, as they choose? Discussion in chapter 3(§A) will raise the question whether health care can be simultaneously a consumer good and a so-called "merit" good—that is, one that is not rationed exclusively by price.

10. *Questions*. A natural argument against relying on private contracts to determine coverage matters is the difficulty consumers have in knowing their future needs and the further difficulty they would have in picking the plan whose contract promises most clearly that they will be met. Can you see why this argument might be regarded as a red herring?

Are you concerned that the foregoing materials reflect undue concern with health care costs and inadequate concern about quality? Later materials will consider the various mechanisms, particularly legal mechanisms, for ensuring quality, asking at each point not only whether quality might be overvalued at the margin but also whether it is in danger of undue neglect.

Bradley v. Empire Blue Cross and Blue Shield

Supreme Court, New York County, New York.
149 Misc.2d 20, 562 N.Y.S.2d 908 (1990).

■ ELLIOTT WILK, JUDGE.

This is an action to compel Empire Blue Cross and Blue Shield to provide insurance coverage to Thomas Bradley for a medical procedure to be performed at Johns Hopkins Hospital in Baltimore, Maryland. Plaintiff has moved to enjoin defendant from refusing coverage. Although the courts are generally disinclined to favor preliminary injunctions which mirror the ultimate relief sought, because of the unique circumstances of this case, it is appropriate that this motion be granted. * * * An expedited hearing was ordered, at the conclusion of which I make the following findings.

Plaintiff, Thomas J. Bradley, is a 47 year old male who is infected with Human Immunodeficiency Virus (HIV), which is a principal cause of Acquired Immunodeficiency Syndrome (AIDS). As a result, he has a dangerously low T-cell lymphocyte count which compromises his immune system and exposes him to severe opportunistic infections which afflict AIDS victims. He has experienced numerous symptoms associated with HIV infection.

Mr. Bradley's treating physician, Dr. James D. Lax, referred him to Dr. H. Kent Holland, who is affiliated with Johns Hopkins Hospital, to evaluate his candidacy for a bone marrow transplant. Both doctors believe Mr. Bradley to be terminally ill.

After a thorough examination of Mr. Bradley's medical and emotional condition and with the approval of the Hospital, Dr. Holland and his staff concluded that Mr. Bradley is a suitable candidate for treatment.

The procedure contemplated by Dr. Holland is the administration of high doses of chemotherapy and whole body radiation to destroy the cells in the bone marrow. Mr. Bradley's immune system will then be reconstituted by the introduction of bone marrow donated by his identical twin brother. After the transplant, to protect donor cells from infection, Mr. Bradley will continue with the antiviral drug AZT, which will be administered intravenously.

The pre-transplant treatment of heavy doses of highly toxic drugs requires that Mr. Bradley be reasonably healthy. Should he develop any of the more severe opportunistic infections associated with AIDS, which could happen at any time, he would become ineligible for this treatment.

The proposed bone marrow transplant is to be followed by long term hospitalization and extensive follow-up with antibiotic treatment, transfusion, parenteral nutrition and monitoring of organs for toxic effects.

Empire Blue Cross and Blue Shield has moved to dismiss the complaint on the ground that the treatment described is outside of the scope of its contractual obligation to Mr. Bradley.

The "Empire Plan" provides that "Blue Cross will not pay for services which are deemed experimental or investigative according to guidelines established jointly for the Empire Plan by the State of New York, Blue Cross and Metropolitan Life Insurance Company." Apparently, the guidelines have never been drawn.

In an affidavit submitted in support of the cross motion, Dr. Arthur Levin, associate medical director of Empire, states that "[a]s an aid in determining whether a new procedure not previously evaluated by the Empire Plan is experimental or investigative in treating a particular diagnosis, Empire uses the criteria established by the Blue Cross and Blue Shield Association." He concludes that the proposed treatment meets none of the criteria.

Dr. David M. Eddy is a professor at Duke University, who specializes in the evaluation of medical practices. He, too, is affiliated with Empire Blue Cross and Blue Shield. He has done an analysis of the literature concerning the use of high-dose chemotherapy with autologous bone marrow transplant for the treatment of metastatic breast cancer. He is not an oncologist, a hematologist or a bone marrow transplant expert and has no expertise in the treatment of HIV or AIDS infected people. At the hearing, he was unable to provide an opinion about the potential benefits of the treatment proposed by Dr. Holland.

Dr. Eddy, in his affidavit, contends that the proposed treatment is investigative. He states that:

> [i]n order to be considered noninvestigational, two tests must be met: (1) there must be evidence that the procedure causes benefit, and (2) there must be evidence that, to patients, the benefits of the procedure outweigh its harms.

According to Dr. Eddy, the first test is met when it is determined that the treatment provides greater improvement in health outcomes than alternative treatments. He recognizes only AZT as an alternative available to Mr. Bradley. He distinguishes ultimate from intermediate health outcomes. He then considers (1) survival, (2) relief of symptoms, (3) prevention of complications, (4) risks of treatment and (5) side effects of treatment such as hair loss, nausea, vomiting, diarrhea and anxiety.

The thrust of Dr. Eddy's testimony was that medical treatment may not be considered non-investigative until controlled studies have shown it to be effective and beneficial. Subjective clinical judgments of practitioners do not determine whether a treatment is investigative. Dr. Eddy maintains that because only six of these procedures have been performed, all by Dr. Holland, the proposed treatment must be viewed as investigative.

Dr. Holland is a well credentialed oncologist, hematologist and bone marrow transplant expert who is a faculty member of Johns Hopkins University School of Medicine and a staff member at Johns Hopkins Hospital. I found his testimony to be clear, informed, insightful and persuasive. He testified that Dr. Eddy's mechanical definition of "investigative" is inadequate and inappropriate to the facts of this case. I agree.

The testimony made clear that both chemotherapy and bone marrow transplants have a sufficient history to support the medical community's conclusion that they are not investigative treatments. This is true notwithstanding the severe side effects of chemotherapy, the significant risk of death from bone marrow transplants and the uncertainty of the results. The consequences of the absence of these treatments is more certain.

The combination of chemotherapy and bone marrow transplant is also accepted by the medical community and has been used with varying success to treat, among other things, metastatic breast cancer, leukemia and aplastic anemia.

The third component of Dr. Holland's procedure, AZT, has gained wide acceptance in the medical community for the treatment of people infected with HIV and AIDS.

Dr. Holland believes that the chemotherapy, radiation, bone marrow transplant combination will be just as effective in treating Mr. Bradley's immunodeficiency as it has been with non-HIV related medical problems.

The availability of the non-infected bone marrow of Mr. Bradley's twin brother removes the most serious obstacle to a successful transplant—"graft-versus-host" disease—and substantially increases his chance of survival. Although Dr. Holland is no more able to guarantee success or to predict results than are physicians using similar methods to attack other diseases, I find the logic of his analysis, which stands unrefuted, to be compelling. The addition of AZT to the procedure provides another guard against reinfection. Its inclusion does not transform what is already accepted medical protocol into experimental treatment.

The only other witness called was Dr. Robert Geller, a well-credentialed expert in oncology, hematology and bone marrow transplants. He is a member of the faculty of the University of Chicago School of Medicine and is affiliated with the University of Chicago Medical Center. His testimony confirmed that of Dr. Holland. Dr. Geller stated that he expects to be performing similar procedures at the University of Chicago Medical Center within six to twelve months.

Hopkins will require that Mr. Bradley sign a "clinical investigation consent form" which emphasizes the research aspect of the procedure. A similar consent form is required in every bone marrow transplant procedure. The defensive and cautionary language of the form is, no doubt, the bar's contribution to the defense of potential medical malpractice litigation. I do not believe that the form accurately characterizes the nature of the treatment and I have given little weight to it.

In this motion for a preliminary injunction, Mr. Bradley must demonstrate a likelihood of success on the merits, irreparable harm in the absence of the injunction and a balancing of the equities in his favor. The likelihood of success is strong, the irreparable harm is, unfortunately, obvious, and the equities lie in his favor. Accordingly, the motion for injunctive relief is granted and Empire is directed to discontinue its refusal to approve payment for the hospitalization costs associated with Mr. Bradley's bone marrow transplant at Johns Hopkins Hospital and is directed to notify Hopkins forthwith that it will cover this procedure. Empire's cross motion to dismiss is denied.

NOTES AND QUESTIONS ON COVERAGE OF EMERGING MEDICAL TECHNOLOGIES

1. New medical procedures, drugs, and devices pose especially vexing problems for health plans because they usually become available well before careful research establishes their efficacy, either in general or in particular circumstances. Moreover, such innovations tend to attract entrepreneurial providers, to be demanded by patients in desperate need, and to be very costly, especially when first introduced. Health care contracts have long expressly excluded experimental treatments from coverage. The *Bradley* case illustrates the kind of disputes that such exclusions regularly trigger. These and other coverage disputes will be examined more fully in chapter 8(§B).

Why do you suppose experimental technologies are treated by contract drafters as a special problem rather than handled under the general language excluding from coverage any service not deemed "medically necessary"? Do you see here an artifact of the professional paradigm of medical care as it is embodied in the medical-necessity standard? Under the medical-necessity test, emerging technologies present a special problem precisely because, by hypothesis, they are not yet the subject of a professional standard or consensus on which a health plan can rely. Thus, in any case (such as *Bradley*) in which a physician witness professes confidence in a new technology for treating a patient *in extremis*, a health plan would face a heavy burden in establishing that the service was not medically necessary. It is no surprise, therefore, that health plans sought to develop a special contractual defense against paying for costly new procedures promising only a highly uncertain benefit. Nevertheless, it has been suggested that, instead of maintaining special rules for therapies on which the profession has not yet had an opportunity to develop standards or a reliable opinion, contract drafters should challenge the professional paradigm by creating a new general definition of covered services and applying it to all unproved and marginally beneficial therapies, established as well as "experimental." See C. Havighurst, Health Care Choices, supra, at 195–200 (discussing "The (Not So) Special Problem of New Medical Technologies" and arguing, "It is not only new medical technologies, after all, that lack a solid foundation in health services research while enjoying a significant degree of professional support.").

2. *Questions on the Bradley Case.* Which of the many policy problems developed earlier in this chapter does this case illustrate? What is your opinion of the test proposed by Dr. Eddy (whose path-breaking work was cited several times earlier in this chapter)? Are judges appropriate arbiters of issues of this kind? It is common for such cases to be resolved, as this one was, at the preliminary injunction stage and not to become the subject of a definitive legal ruling or of a decision on appeal.

3. *Conflicts of Interests?* What do you think of the *Bradley* court's treatment of Dr. Eddy's testimony? Is there an aspersion on his objectivity in the observation that he, like Dr. Levin, "is affiliated with Empire Blue Cross"? Courts frequently distrust economizing decisions by health plan personnel because they sense a conflict of interests. See, e.g., Reilly v. Blue Cross and Blue Shield United, 846 F.2d 416 (7th Cir.), cert. denied, 488 U.S. 856 (1988) (held arbitrary for Blue plan, acting as third-party administrator, to find in vitro fertilization an uncovered "experimental" procedure on the basis of standards that were developed by association of Blue plans in their capacity as self-interested insurers and that used a 50% success rate as an arbitrary rule of thumb in deciding on the acceptability of costly new procedures). Whether or not there was a problem of this kind in the *Bradley* case, was there any doubt about the objectivity of Drs. Holland and Geller?

A widely cited article purported to show that health plan decisions on a particularly controversial new procedure were "arbitrary and capricious." Peters & Rogers, Variation in Approval by Insurance Companies of Coverage for Autologous Bone Marrow Transplantation for Breast Cancer, 330 New Eng. J. Med. 473 (1994). The authors were, respectively, the head of the transplant program and chief operating officer of a leading academic medical center. In light of this apparent conflict of interests, should the *New England Journal of Medicine* have refused to publish their findings? It has been suggested that the inconsistencies detected by Peters and Rogers may have resulted in part from the widespread publicity given to individual lawsuits over the treatment in question and the resulting sensitivity of plans to the litigation risks presented by some patients. Light, Life, Death, and the Insurance Companies, 330 New Eng. J. Med. 498 (1994) (hypothesizing that "companies reversed their denials of coverage after they found themselves facing a lawyer"). If you had counseled the insurer in *Bradley*, would you have recommended litigation?

4. *Drafting Alternatives*. Knowing that courts, seeking to avert allegedly avoidable tragedies, are likely to construe contractual limitations generously in favor of patients, how would you go about writing a reasonable exclusion for new technologies? Some contracts appear to reflect the efforts of drafters, returning to the drawing board after a court has ignored their past efforts, to develop more sophisticated coverage criteria. Nevertheless, most contracts still link their coverage of experimental procedures to "generally accepted standards of medical practice" or the equivalent. One contract, for example, includes in its definition of experimental procedures those "not generally accepted by informed health care professionals." Another plan meets professional standards halfway, defining experimental treatments as services that "are not generally accepted medical practice in [the state] as determined by [the plan] in consultation with medical advisors." See also Adams v. Blue Cross/Blue Shield, 757 F.Supp. 661 (D.Md.1991) (defining experimental treatment as "any treatment ... not generally acknowledged as accepted medical practice by the suitable medical specialty practicing in Maryland, as decided by us"). Would any of these clauses have yielded a different result in *Bradley*?

5. *FDA Approval*. Definitions of experimental procedures in health care contracts frequently provide alternative grounds, besides lack of professional acceptance, on which exclusion can occur. The most common additional condition that must be met, where applicable, is approval by the FDA. Of course, the FDA has no power over surgical procedures unless new prescription drugs or medical devices happen to be required in performing them. In addition, the FDA's approval of a drug or device may be based on its demonstrated safety and efficacy in only one use, yet physicians may legally prescribe approved drugs or devices for numerous "off-label" uses, which may themselves still be experimental in fact. Why else might FDA approval be an insufficient condition of coverage by a health plan seeking to economize to the left of point x?

Organizational Responses to the Cost Problem

NOTES AND QUESTIONS ON LIMITING PATIENT CHOICE OF PROVIDER AND SELECTIVE CONTRACTING

1. *Limiting Enrollees' Choices*. Continuing your effort to design an efficient health plan, consider the alternative of expressly limiting, not benefits and coverage, but the providers whom a plan subscriber can patronize at the plan's expense. Consumers naturally value the freedom to patronize any physician (or hospital) in the community. Are there nevertheless reasons for restricting their options? Can you see how selecting certain providers and making them alone eligible to provide covered care (at least in the absence of a true emergency) could be helpful in addressing the moral hazard problem?

How might this strategy be practically superior to the strategy of closely specifying benefits and administering coverage through utilization managers? For one thing, limitations on the providers an enrollee may patronize are not facially controversial, since they do not purport to affect the quality or quantity of care that an individual will receive. Another advantage is the avoidance of ambiguity in the contractual limitation itself. (As will be seen in chapter 8(§B), ambiguous coverage limitations invite legal challenges by patients and generous interpretation by courts.) Is it another advantage that the providers selected by the plan will be in some measure beholden to it—not to say co-opted—and therefore less likely to take the patient's side in spending plan resources? As a policy analyst, would you be concerned by the absence in the contract of any acknowledgment that providers selected by the plan might actively ration care?

2. *The Costs of Unlimited Choice*. For many years, the medical profession steadfastly (and effectively) maintained that no one—neither government nor a corporate middleman—should be permitted to interfere with a patient's right freely to select any available physician. Because of the political and market power wielded by organized medicine in the earlier era, private health care financing—and, later, Medicare in its original form—almost universally took the form of indemnity insurance reimbursing patients for reasonable health care costs incurred anywhere in the community. Under this form of coverage, beneficiaries were insensitive both to provider prices and to the benefit/cost ratios of desirable services, and competition focused on quality and amenities, not value received.

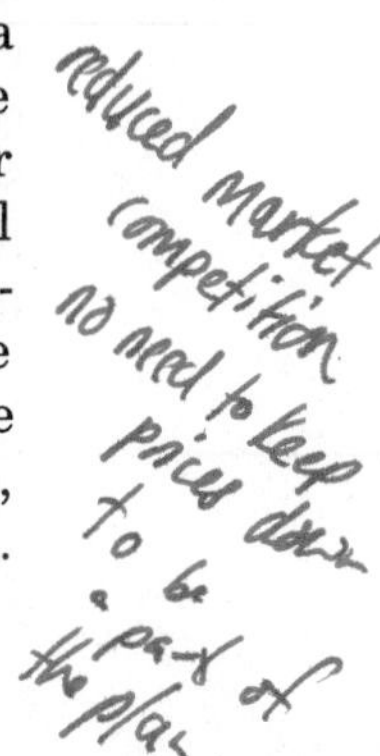

ironically, gives consumers bargaining power

Although free choice of physician appeared to preserve consumer sovereignty, it deprived consumers of the freedom to select a sophisticated corporate agent to purchase services on their behalf with costs, as well as need and quality, in view. Moreover, as long as free choice prevailed, financing plans were unable to control moral hazard by selecting low-cost, efficient providers. They also had no way to reward providers for discounting their prices or for cooperating with the plan in other respects. Thus, providers could not be required to compete for patients on the basis of price. As ironic as it may seem, therefore, restricting the freedom of consumers to choose a provider is necessary to give them effective bargaining power vis-a-vis providers. For the argument that free choice strengthened the market power of physicians, see Weller, "Free Choice" as a Restraint of Trade in American Health Care Delivery and Insurance, 69 Iowa L.Rev. 1351, 1352 (1984) ("[T]he AMA's free choice ethics, consistent with guild precepts, prevents providers from being split into groups competing over price. Market free choice, consistent with market principles, permits price as well as nonprice competition among providers.").

Can you now see how selective contracting with health care providers—hospitals and other providers as well as physicians—is the key to the current policy of relying principally on market forces and competition to control the cost and quality of health care? Are there any risks in the allowing corporate health plans, concerned about competing on price and paying dividends to investors (in the case of for-profit plans), to refuse to deal with providers whose terms or style of practice they find unacceptable?

3. *HMOs*. Health maintenance organizations (which are discussed extensively in the next set of notes) are the most obvious examples of "closed-panel" (choice-limiting) health plans. HMOs differ, however, with respect to their relations with providers. In the most tightly integrated plans, the participating physicians are fully dedicated to caring for the enrolled population, and the plan may even own its own hospital. In other HMOs, the physicians on the plan's panel may (and do) treat non-HMO patients and may participate in other managed care plans. Likewise, the plan contracts with selected hospitals and other nonphysician providers available in the community. In all cases, HMOs are well positioned to obtain providers' services on competitive terms and to insist on cooperation in their cost-containment efforts.

4. *Preferred-Provider Arrangements*. Is there a way to design a health plan to realize some of the benefits of restricted choice without denying choice altogether? A popular strategy has been to offer more favorable coverage (say, significantly reduced cost sharing) if the patient obtains a service from a physician or hospital that has agreed in advance—perhaps through a so-called "preferred-provider organization" (PPO)—to charge low prices or to cooperate with the plan's other cost-control measures. Although "PPO" is the more common term, "preferred-provider *arrangement*" (PPA) may be a more accurate generic term since it is not necessary that providers be organized. Thus, an insurer might simply negotiate direct contracts with individual hospitals, physicians, or physician groups. (Indeed, even this degree of formality is not essential, since an insurer might simply undertake to pay more liberally for care rendered by providers whose efficiency and fair prices it has admired from afar.)

The PPO concept got a surprising boost in the early 1980s when the California legislature, at the same time it first authorized Medi–Cal (the state's Medicaid program) to engage in selective contracting with hospitals, also passed an unheralded amendment to the insurance statutes, allowing private insurers to engage in similar selectivity. See Cal. Ins. Code §§ 10133, 10401 (West 1993 & Supp. 1998); Cal. Welf. & Inst. Code § 14165 et seq. (West 1991). Thereafter, other states also moved to clarify the legal status of insurer efforts to influence their insureds' choices of provider. E.g., Colo. Rev. Stat. Ann. § 24–51–1203 (1997) (public employees); Ga. Code Ann. § 33–30–21 (1996). The PPO movement made dramatic strides in a short time.

Can you explain to your own satisfaction why PPAs only developed as a useful force in the 1980s? Do you suppose that restrictions in state law were the only reason why PPAs, unlike HMOs, hardly appeared at all in the 1970s?

5. *Criteria for Selecting Providers*. If you were designing an HMO or PPO, how would you advise the plan to select providers? Would you recommend making price and willingness to cooperate with the payer's utilization controls and administrative requirements the only considerations? Would your policy toward providers depend on which type of plan you were developing? For example, should an HMO seeking to restrict its enrollees' choices as little as possible avoid making qualitative judgments about the providers it enlists? Should a PPO attempt to judge or to monitor the quality of services provided by hospitals and physicians to whom it seeks to steer patients? Are low-price physicians or hospitals necessarily less costly to the plan? How would you determine a physician's relative efficiency? How would you deal with a physician whose style of practice, monitored over time, appeared more costly than that of other providers? In due course, we will consider how legal rules and doctrines influence plan conduct in these respects.

Is there any legal obligation to offer participation to all providers who accept the plan's terms or to treat all participating providers equally? Some states have created such a duty by statute (sometimes called "any-willing-provider" laws), while others have imposed procedural and other obstacles to terminating a participating provider. Do you agree with the policy behind such laws, which seem premised on the notion that the plan is a kind of public utility with a duty to accommodate all whom it cannot justify rejecting? Or do you think plans should be free to select or reject providers without explaining their actions and, in the absence of a contractual commitment, to terminate a relationship at will? These issues will be examined in chapter 8(§C).

6. *Point-of-Service Plans*. In recent years, some HMOs have responded to employer and consumer desires for wider choice by giving enrollees the option, at the point when a particular service is needed, of getting the care either through the HMO's closed panel (at no or minimal out-of-pocket cost) or through any community physician (with a substantial copayment obligation). Such "point-of-service" (POS) plans blend HMO and conventional indemnity coverage, thereby both responding to consumers' and employers' desire for freedom of choice and capturing cost savings realizable by steering patients to low-cost, efficient providers. For an overview of the variety of arrangements offered by modern health plans, see Gold & Hurley, The Role of Managed Care "Products" in Managed Care Plans, 34 Inquiry 29 (1997) (finding that plans have multiple product offerings, with different opportunities for choice).

7. *Integrated Delivery Systems.* An option in designing an efficient health plan is to contract for services from a provider entity capable of providing a wide range of provider services, perhaps carving out such services as mental and behavioral health for coverage under a separate arrangement. A number of such integrated delivery systems (IDSs) have been organized by community providers in various locales. Some have a hospital at the center, some have a large physician network as the core element, while others have attempted to combine a hospital and members of its medical staff into a so-called physician-hospital organization (PHO). These entities are organized for the express purpose of contracting with various financing entities and bearing financial risk in providing care for specific populations. Would you visualize that these IDSs would become effectively integrated in fact, so that they provide a consistent, well-conceived style of medical care differentiated from other options in the community? Or would you anticipate that they will have difficulty integrating a cohort of independent medical practitioners into a coherent unit capable of centralizing decision making and coordinating practices? Some observations on these questions will appear at a later point,

8. *Combining Strategies for Combating Moral Hazard.* The most promising techniques for giving the desired quantity and quality of health care at competitive prices probably involve combining as much precision as possible in the definition of benefits with a program for selecting providers who will provide care of good quality, charge reasonable prices, and cooperate in the effort to achieve efficiency and to ensure that the plan pays for only the services it has contracted to provide. It has been observed, however, that the subscriber contracts employed by highly integrated HMOs—those that offer less freedom of choice with respect to providers whom enrollees can patronize at plan expense—contain relatively little language closely specifying and limiting the entitlements of enrollees. Havighurst, Health Care Choices, supra, at 126–27 ("More extensive definitions of medical necessity tend to be employed by plans in which the providers are relatively independent—traditional indemnity plans, PPOs, and [less integrated] HMOs.") Can you explain why the extent to which a health plan particularizes and qualifies its undertakings to subscribers might vary inversely with the degree to which physicians are integrated into the plan? What do you conclude about the utility of subscriber contracts as a instruments for defining in advance what consumers enrolling in the plan can expect to receive? Consider the implications of the finding that plans in the best

position to induce economizing by participating physicians (because they are more closely integrated) are generally less explicit in defining the standards employed in such economizing. Does it trouble you that plans that seem to promise more may actually deliver less?

9. *Compensating Participating Providers.* Now consider the compensation arrangements that might be made with selected providers. Should participating physicians be (1) paid a salary (possibly with bonuses based on plan or individual performance); (2) compensated on a fee-for-service basis under a negotiated fee schedule (perhaps with a "withhold" of some substantial fraction of fees, to be distributed at year end only if certain costs and utilization targets for physician, hospital, or other services are met); or (3) given a fixed amount per member per month—a so-called "capitation" payment? Capitation payments might be made to a large group practice, a network, or an IDS, which could in turn pay its member physicians any way it chooses. Although individual physicians might also be "capitated," this is usually done only with stop-loss provisions or some other protection against unusual experience. Other arrangements for putting providers "at risk," thus inducing them to economize, can also be imagined. What are the respective strengths or weaknesses of each method of payment in curbing moral hazard?

Do certain arrangements introduce a new kind of moral hazard—a risk of *over*economizing at patients' expense? Consider the so-called "gatekeeper" strategy widely used in network-and IPA-type HMOs:

> [M]ost of the new HMOs have no central facility. Instead, they contract with private physicians to care for HMO patients in their own offices along with their other patients. Although some of these HMOs pay physicians on a modified fee-for-service basis, the more successful ones operate "risk" physician payment systems.
>
> Here's how it works. As a private practitioner, I contract with the HMO to provide services to enrollees who select me as their primary care physician "gatekeeper." I get a monthly fee, called a "capitation" (payment by the head), for each HMO enrollee who signs on with me. The capitation payment averages about ten dollars a month [in 1987], with some variation based on the age and sex of the enrollee. Whether the enrollee comes in once during the year or 20 times, my payment from the HMO remains constant at ten dollars a month for that person. It is all supposed to average out.
>
> Now comes the "risk" part. For every ten dollars in capitation I receive, the HMO sets aside another $40 or so in a separate account. This account pays the hospital bills, fees for specialist care, laboratory and X-rays, and other services performed outside of my office. Every time one of the patients on my panel receives a specialty service, my separate account is debited. But I am the one who decides if they need this special attention. As gatekeeper, I must give permission for all non-emergency referrals.
>
> The HMO audits my account annually. If it shows a surplus, I receive a bonus, usually 30 percent to 50 percent of the total surplus in my account. If it shows a deficit, I have to forfeit a portion of my monthly

capitations, as much as 25 percent. In essence, I am paying for part of every specialty consultation, every hospital day, every ancillary service that the patient receives. The economic incentives are clear: keep the patient away from consultants, out of the hospital, and out of the office.

Berenson, In a Doctor's Wallet, New Republic, May 18, 1987, at 11, 12.

Shea v. Esensten

United States Court of Appeals, Eighth Circuit, 1997.
107 F.3d 625, cert. denied, 118 S.Ct. 297 (1997).

■ FAGG, CIRCUIT JUDGE.

After being hospitalized for severe chest pains during an overseas business trip, Patrick Shea made several visits to his long-time family doctor. During these visits, Mr. Shea discussed his extensive family history of heart disease, and indicated he was suffering from chest pains, shortness of breath, muscle tingling, and dizziness. Despite all the warning signs, Mr. Shea's doctor said a referral to a cardiologist was unnecessary. When Mr. Shea's symptoms did not improve, he offered to pay for the cardiologist himself. At that point, Mr. Shea's doctor persuaded Mr. Shea, who was then forty years old, that he was too young and did not have enough symptoms to justify a visit to a cardiologist. A few months later, Mr. Shea died of heart failure.

Mr. Shea had been an employee of Seagate Technologies, Inc. (Seagate) for many years. Seagate provided health care benefits to its employees by contracting with [an HMO] known as Medica. As part of its managed care product, Medica required Seagate's employees to select one of Medica's authorized primary care doctors. Mr. Shea chose his family doctor, who was on Medica's list of preferred doctors. Under the terms of Medica's policy, Mr. Shea was insured for all of his medically necessary care, including cardiac care. Before Mr. Shea could see a specialist, however, Medica required Mr. Shea to get a written referral from his primary care doctor. Unknown to Mr. Shea, Medica's contracts with its preferred doctors created financial incentives that were designed to minimize referrals. Specifically, the primary care doctors were rewarded for not making covered referrals to specialists, and were docked a portion of their fees if they made too many. According to Mr. Shea's widow Dianne, if her husband would have known his doctor could earn a bonus for treating less, he would have disregarded his doctor's advice, sought a cardiologist's opinion at his own expense, and would still be alive today.

Initially, Mrs. Shea brought a wrongful death action in Minnesota state court. Mrs. Shea alleged Medica's fraudulent nondisclosure and misrepresentation about its doctor incentive programs limited Mr. Shea's ability to make an informed choice about his life-saving health care. Medica removed the case to federal court, contending Mrs. Shea's tort claims were preempted by [ERISA]. Mrs. Shea filed a motion to remand, but the district court denied the motion. Mrs. Shea then amended her complaint to assert Medica's behind-the-scenes efforts to reduce covered referrals violated

Medica's fiduciary duties under ERISA. Believing ERISA does not require an HMO to disclose its doctor compensation arrangements because they are not "material facts affecting a beneficiary's interests," the district court dismissed Mrs. Shea's amended complaint for failing to state a claim. Mrs. Shea appeals. Having construed the pleaded facts in the light most favorable to Mrs. Shea, we reverse the judgment of the district court.

Because our removal jurisdiction is intertwined with the district court's preemption ruling, we must first consider whether ERISA displaces Mrs. Shea's tort claims against Medica. ERISA supersedes state laws insofar as they "relate to any employee benefit plan." To this end, the language of ERISA's preemption clause sweeps broadly, embracing common law causes of action if they have a connection with or a reference to an ERISA plan. See Pilot Life Ins. Co. v. Dedeaux, 481 U.S. 41, 47–48 (1987). Here, Medica administered Seagate's employee benefit plan, and Mrs. Shea maintains Medica wrongfully failed to disclose a major limitation on her husband's health care benefits. Along these lines, we have held that claims of misconduct against the administrator of an employer's health plan fall comfortably within ERISA's broad preemption provision. See Kuhl v. Lincoln Nat'l Health Plan of Kansas City, Inc., 999 F.2d 298, 301–04 (8th Cir.1993).

After considering the factors that guide our inquiry, we conclude the district court correctly decided that ERISA preempts Mrs. Shea's state-law claims. The outcome of Mrs. Shea's lawsuit would clearly affect how Seagate's ERISA-regulated benefit plan is administered, and if similar cases are brought in state courts across the country, ERISA plan administrators will inevitably be forced to tailor their plan disclosures to meet each state's unique requirements. This result would be at odds with Congress's intent to ensure "the nationally uniform administration of employee benefit plans." New York State Conference of Blue Cross & Blue Shield Plans v. Travelers Ins. Co., 115 S.Ct. 1671, 1677–78 (1995). Thus, we agree with the district court that Mrs. Shea's case was removable to federal court. See Anderson v. Humana, Inc., 24 F.3d 889, 891 (7th Cir.1994) (plan participant's attacks on HMO's incentive structure were both preempted and removable); Rodriguez v. Pacificare of Texas, Inc., 980 F.2d 1014, 1016–17 (5th Cir.1993) (state-law claims based on HMO's refusal to provide referral letter were properly preempted and removed).

* * *

[W]e next consider whether Medica had a duty to disclose its referral-discouraging approach to health care. ERISA requires plan fiduciaries to "discharge [their] duties with respect to a plan solely in the interest of the participants and beneficiaries." 29 U.S.C. § 1104(a)(1). In addition to ERISA's express disclosure requirements, " 'Congress invoked the common law of trusts to define the general scope of [a fiduciary's] ... responsibility.' " Varity Corp., 116 S.Ct. at 1070 (quoting H.R.Rep. No. 93–533, at 3–5, 11–13 (1973)). In affirming our decision in *Varity Corp.*, the Supreme Court concluded that ERISA fiduciaries must comply with the common law duty of loyalty, which includes the obligation to deal fairly and honestly with all

plan members. Although the Supreme Court found it unnecessary to reach the issue, our earlier opinion made clear that the duty of loyalty requires an ERISA fiduciary to communicate any material facts which could adversely affect a plan member's interests. "The duty to disclose material information is the core of a fiduciary's responsibility, animating the common law of trusts long before the enactment of ERISA." Eddy v. Colonial Life Ins. Co. of Am., 919 F.2d 747, 750 (D.C.Cir.1990).

Although the district court acknowledged Medica's duty of loyalty, the court felt the compensation arrangements between Medica and its doctors were not material facts requiring disclosure. We disagree. From the patient's point of view, a financial incentive scheme put in place to influence a treating doctor's referral practices when the patient needs specialized care is certainly a material piece of information. This kind of patient necessarily relies on the doctor's advice about treatment options, and the patient must know whether the advice is influenced by selfserving financial considerations created by the health insurance provider. The district court believed Seagate's employees already realized their doctors' pocketbooks would be adversely affected by making referrals to outside specialists. Even if the district court is right, Seagate's employees still would not have known their doctors were penalized for making too many referrals and could earn a bonus by skimping on specialized care. Thus, we conclude Mr. Shea had the right to know Medica was offering financial incentives that could have colored his doctor's medical judgment about the urgency for a cardiac referral. * * * If Mr. Shea had been aware of his doctor's financial stakes, he could have made a fully informed decision about whether to trust his doctor's recommendation that a cardiologist's examination was unnecessary.

In sum, we believe Mrs. Shea has stated a claim against Medica for breaching the fiduciary obligation to disclose all the material facts affecting her husband's health care interests. When an HMO's financial incentives discourage a treating doctor from providing essential health care referrals for conditions covered under the plan benefit structure, the incentives must be disclosed and the failure to do so is a breach of ERISA's fiduciary duties. We thus reverse the district court's order dismissing Mrs. Shea's amended complaint for failure to state a claim on which relief can be granted and remand the case to the district court for further proceedings. We decline Medica's invitation to consider several remedy-related issues that were not addressed in the district court's ruling.

NOTES AND QUESTIONS

1. Although the court in the *Shea* case found a violation of ERISA, the final sentence in the opinion calls attention to some unanswered questions concerning the remedy for that violation. In fact, ERISA, although it preempts state remedies for many supposed wrongs, makes no provision under which a federal court can award damages for personal injuries of the kinds complained of in *Shea*. See chapter 8(§B).

2. Consider the effect on the doctor/patient relationship of the incentives used by the plan in the *Shea* case. Such incentive arrangements have prompted considerable concern among scholars and calls for disclosure or possibly regulation. See, e.g., M. Hall, Making Medical Spending Decisions: The Law, Ethics, and Economics of Rationing Mechanisms 171–92 (1997) (accepting inevitability of physician interest conflicts of one kind or another and focusing on disclosure and informed-consent issues); M. Rodwin, Medicine, Money & Morals: Physicians' Conflicts of Interest 135–75 (1993); H. Morreim, Balancing Act: The New Medical Ethics of Medicine's New Economics (1991); Orentlicher, Paying Patients More to Do Less: Financial Incentives to Limit Care, 30 U. Rich. L. Rev. 155 (1996) ("As long as the level of incentives is not allowed to become too high and there are other safeguards to protect patient welfare, financial incentives can serve an important role in cost containment."); Mechanic & Schlesinger, The Impact of Managed Care on Patients' Trust in Medical Care and Their Physicians, 275 J.A.M.A. 1693 (1996) (arguing "that managed care plans rather than physicians should be required to disclose financial arrangements, that limits be placed on incentives that put physicians at financial risk, and that professional norms and public policies should encourage clear separation of interests of physicians from health plan organization and finance"); Hillman et al., HMO Managers' Views on Financial Incentives and Quality, Health Affs., Winter 1991, p. 207 (suggesting, in view of the need for cost control, that a pragmatic view be taken of incentives). Physician conflict-of-interests issues will be considered again in chapter 3(§D).

An unsuccessful initiative on the ballot in Oregon in 1996 would have barred the use of capitation payments to compensate physicians. See Wynia, The Oregon Capitation Initiative: Lessons and Warnings, From the Forefront of the Backlash, 276 J.A.M.A. 1441 (1996).

3. Should the physician have a duty to disclose any conflict of interests to patients? Or would discharge of that duty (as some, e.g., Mechanic & Schlesinger, supra, have argued) put the physician/patient relationship on a troublesome basis from the outset? How else might a patient consent to being treated by a physician who has some incentive to withhold services?

4. What significance do you attach to the fact that the physician in *Shea v. Esensten* discouraged Mr. Shea from seeking a cardiologist's services at his own expense? Does this fact establish that the doctor truly believed that Mr. Shea was not at risk? Or is there a more ominous possibility? In what respect was the doctor's advice here possibly similar to that of the doctor in the *Muse* case, reproduced in chapter 1(§A)? What does a careful comparison of the two cases suggest with respect to the choice between imposing cost-saving incentives on institutional providers or organized physician groups and using them to motivate individual physicians?

NOTES AND QUESTIONS ON HMOS

1. *HMO Types*. Although HMOs vary widely, the essential feature that distinguishes them from conventional health insurance is a contractual

commitment to provide or arrange for care, not just to indemnify the subscriber for costs he or she reasonably incurs. Although the HMO entity itself contracts directly with subscribers (or with an employer acting on behalf of its employees), its arrangements with providers can take several forms. Thus, there are four reasonably distinct types of HMO: (1) A so-called "staff-model" HMO employs its doctors on a salary. (2) "Group-model" HMOs contract with one or a few large multi-specialty physician group practices to provide services to the plan's members, usually for a negotiated capitation payment. (3) HMOs of the so-called "network" variety contract directly with an array of individual physicians and small physician groups practicing in their own offices. (4) Finally, an "IPA-model" HMO contracts with a physician-sponsored "individual practice association" (IPA), a loose organization of physicians in private practice throughout the community.

Consider, with respect each of the four HMO types, the contractual and other legal relationships between and among the various parties—the HMO entity, the individual physicians, other providers, and the subscriber-patients. How are the various functions that must be performed—financing, risk bearing, the provision of services, utilization management, performance monitoring, marketing, administration, and so forth—allocated and integrated in the various models? Much of the work of many health care lawyers is negotiating, drafting, and reviewing contracts between health plans and providers. What matters must be covered in the various contracts that must be drafted? What are the crucial issues that must be negotiated? Who are the negotiating parties? Where are the sticking points likely to be?

What are the respective virtues of the various types of HMO? Which types seem to integrate financing and delivery most effectively and to be most capable of discovering and implementing a particular style of medical practice in response to particular consumer desires with respect to cost and quality? Note the following from an assessment of the practical differences between group-and IPA-model HMOs:

> The group practice can take advantage of close physician proximity to foster a strong social structure and communication network. This in turn permits interactions to be more informal and norms to be established by example rather than by fiat, though the impact of hierarchy and a powerful medical director must not be discounted. The IPA, however, must rely more heavily upon formal processes, meetings, and rules.

Palay, Organizing an HMO by Contract: Some Transaction Cost Considerations, 65 Neb.L.Rev. 728, 746 (1986). The implication here is that arrangements featuring closer integration of physicians may be more efficient because they can rely on professionalism, collegiality, and consensus rather than on enforcement of rules in a hierarchical enterprise. An important empirical question is whether network-and IPA-type HMOs have in fact employed rules and prescriptions to modify physician behavior. In reading the material below, consider which types of HMOs are most promising as instrumentalities for offering consumers an appropriate range of choices in the marketplace. Also note which models are emerging in practice. See generally Weiner & deLissovoy, Razing the Tower of Babel: A Taxonomy for Managed Care and Health Insurance Plans, 18 J. Health Pol., Pol'y & L. 75 (1993); Welch, The New Structure of Individual Practice Associations, 12 J.Health Pol., Pol'y & L. 723 (1987).

2. *History*. Forerunners of the various entities now known as HMOs can be found in arrangements for medical care made by early fraternal societies and by employers for employees in remote locations, such as mining and logging camps. See generally P. Starr, The Social Transformation of American Medicine 200–09 (1982). During World War II, Henry J. Kaiser offered a group practice prepayment plan to his firm's shipyard workers on the West Coast—from which beginning came the nonprofit Kaiser Foundation Health Plan, Inc., now an industry leader. The concept also attracted the attention of consumer groups, including government employees (Group Health Association, Inc., of Washington, D.C., and the Health Insurance Plan (HIP) of Greater New York) and the cooperative movement, which organized the highly successful Group Health Cooperative of Puget Sound (which recently merged with Kaiser). The common thread linking these developments was the replacement of fee-for-service compensation of independent medical practitioners by a fixed payment to an entity responsible for providing or procuring care.

The concept of "prepaid group practice" was endorsed by the prestigious Committee on the Costs of Medical Care in a famous 1932 report entitled *Medical Care for the American People*. That report inspired organized medicine to object to the ethical and economic effects of so-called "contract practice" and to defend the fee-for-service method of payment. In the ensuing years, organized professional resistance to HMOs led to some noteworthy antitrust showdowns. E.g., AMA v. United States, 130 F.2d 233 (D.C.Cir.1942), affirmed, 317 U.S. 519 (1943) (summarized in chapter 4(§A)); Group Health Coop. v. King County Med. Soc'y, 237 P.2d 737 (Wash.1951). Professional opposition helped to make HMO development in particular markets slow and uncertain even into the 1980s, when antitrust enforcement significantly lowered barriers to innovation. See P. Starr, supra, at 215–32, 290–334; Havighurst, Professional Restraints on Innovation in Health Care Financing, 1978 Duke L.J. 303, 306–19.

In the late 1960s, Paul Ellwood, M.D., coined the name "health maintenance organization" and brought the idea of encouraging prepaid "alternative delivery systems" to the attention of the Nixon administration. Although HMOs were attractive simply as mechanisms for delivering good care at reasonable prices, Ellwood and others also saw them as vehicles for introducing competitive forces into the health care market as a whole. E.g., P. Ellwood et al., The Health Maintenance Strategy (Institute for Interdisciplinary Studies 1970); Havighurst, Health Maintenance Organizations and the Market for Health Services, 35 Law & Contemp. Prob. 716 (1970). The federal Health Maintenance Organization Act of 1973 (currently codified at 42 U.S.C. § 300e (1994 & Supp. I 1995)), however, was principally a congressional effort to encourage and subsidize a particular vision of how health care should be delivered, not an invitation to entrepreneurs to submit innovative ways of packaging and paying for health care to a market test. See generally Institute of Medicine, Health Maintenance Organizations: Toward a Fair Market Test (1974). (The act's later evolution is described in chapter 8(§C).) Indeed, policy toward HMOs in the 1970s reflected, sometimes obscurely, a tension between those who viewed HMOs as a desirable option—a dash of pluralism, as it were—in a generally monolithic health care system and those who saw them as the vanguard of competition and decentralization.

As a practical matter, the HMO Act did not do as much to assist the progress of HMOs as might have been expected. Indeed, it may even have interrupted a promising movement that was just beginning to emerge as states enacted HMO enabling legislation that was less restrictive than the federal law turned out to be. To be sure, the federal statute did not preclude an HMO authorized under state law from avoiding the regulatory requirements for federally qualified status by forgoing the benefits of that status. Nevertheless, many employers were reluctant to contract with nonqualified plans because they anticipated being required, under the mandatory "dual-choice" provisions of the federal act, also to offer a federally qualified plan once one became available. In addition, many employers, even some attracted by the HMO concept, were reluctant to do anything at all until their federal obligations were clarified in regulations, a process that took several years—during which time some federal appropriations for HMO subsidies went unused. Finally, many of the HMO Act's requirements raised the costs of federally qualified HMOs to the point where they had to be priced out of the reach of many consumers. For a telling account of the contradictions and inconsistencies in the federal effort on behalf of HMOs, see Starr, The Undelivered Health System, Pub. Interest, Winter 1976, p. 66 (advancing the "intriguing hypothesis" that the HMO Act's shortcomings reflected encouragement given to the regulatory impulses of pro-HMO congressional liberals by lobbyists for organized medicine). For a view more favorable to the political process and more critical of the policy itself, see L. Brown, Politics and Health Care Organization: HMOs as Federal Policy (1983). The most rapid growth of HMOs did not occur until the 1980s, after federal subsidies for HMO development had been terminated.

Despite the obstacles they faced, HMOs continued as the centerpiece of policy prescriptions calling for increased competition and less government involvement in health care. A major event in focusing the policy debate on HMOs and competition was Professor Alain Enthoven's Consumer Choice Health Plan, a late–1970s blueprint for a program offering all citizens the opportunity to choose from a government-maintained menu of competitive health plans, along the lines of the Federal Employees Health Benefits Program (FEHBP). See A. Enthoven, Health Plan (1980). (This plan was the forerunner of what was later called "managed competition.") HMOs provided essential evidence for Enthoven's proposition that alternatives to the dominant delivery system were feasible and potentially desirable and that significant reform of the health care system might be accomplished through competition and consumer choice rather than by increasingly tightening regulatory screws. For differing early views on this policy prescription, see Havighurst, Competition in Health Services: Overview, Issues and Answers, 34 Vand.L.Rev. 1117 (1981), and Rosenblatt, Health Care, Markets, and Democratic Values, 34 Vand.L.Rev. 1067 (1981). Obviously, national health policy has moved dramatically to embrace the idea that competition among managed care organizations can ensure that consumers get the health care they want (and are prepared to pay for) at competitive prices. Had HMOs not developed and survived under antitrust protection, this policy option would have been effectively foreclosed.

3. In what respects do HMOs represent a potential improvement over the traditional model of third-party financing? In what respects might the traditional system be superior? Is there an ideal system for organizing, delivering, and financing medical services? In the absence of a clear path to follow, is the best strategy to leave the matter to the marketplace, trusting interactions of consumer, providers, and health plans to find workable solutions to the many dilemmas presented?

NOTES AND QUESTIONS ON THE EMERGING HEALTH CARE MARKETPLACE

1. Although the foregoing conceptual and descriptive material should be helpful to the student in observing the modern health care scene, it is practically impossible to provide a complete and accurate picture of the way things actually are in the real world of health care, let alone of where they are headed. For recent descriptions of the fast-changing scene, see M. Morrisey, ed., Managed Care & Changing Health Care Markets (1998); Center for Studying Health System Change, Health System Change in Twelve Communities (1997) (presenting illuminating case studies of change in representative markets, revealing that "although communities face many common forces for change, the effects of those forces vary based on local conditions and the history of the local health system"); W. Zelman, The Changing Health Care Marketplace: Private Ventures, Public Interests (1996); S. Shortell et al., Remaking Health Care in America: Building Organized Delivery Systems (1996). To be sure, we are in the era of so-called "managed care," signifying that financing entities are shifting away from free-choice indemnity coverage and are actively striving in various ways to control moral hazard. But the concept of managed care encompasses a wide variety of arrangements, ranging from, at one extreme, traditional insurance with predetermination of benefits to, at the other extreme, staff-model and group-model HMOs. The following notes attempt to highlight essential features of the emerging marketplace, the forces that are shaping them, and some issues that remain to be resolved.

2. *The Purchasers*. The central reality of today's market for health care is the cost-consciousness and aggressiveness of employers as purchasers of health benefits for their employees:

> Private-sector employers have become key drivers of health system change. They have achieved this influence by shifting their purchasing

power from paying for open-ended, fee-for-service health insurance benefits to buying health care, on a capitated basis, from managed care plans. The percentage of workers in private firms who are enrolled in some form of managed care grew from 29 percent in 1988 to 70 percent in 1995. Employers now have a firm conviction that enormous savings are possible in health spending without reducing quality of care. They now expect (and demand) that rather than the annual doubledigit premium increases of the insurance era, managed care premiums should fall, or rise only modestly. This strategy has succeeded in slowing the rise of national health care costs to its lowest rate in three decades.

HEALTH PLAN PURCHASING STRATEGIES. Employers drive the health care market through a tough, price-focused competitive process to select the plans offered to workers. Most employees (48 percent) have only a single plan available or may choose among only two plans (23 percent) or three plans (12 percent). In this environment, health plans must control their health care spending; price competition is intense and effective. * * *

EMPLOYEE SATISFACTION. Employers seek, through a number of strategies, to allay workers' concerns about plans that are too restrictive. Many employers select health plans with out-of-network options, which has made such plans the fastest-growing insurance product. Larger employers, with more geographically dispersed and diverse employees, also tend to offer a greater choice of plans; smaller employers offer fewer choices. The need for cost control has driven employers away from purchasing fee-for service insurance, while the need to satisfy their workers is driving them away from purchasing tight, closed-panel [HMO] plans. * * *

* * *

FUTURE INFLUENCES. We expect price (premium)-driven purchasing by employers to dominate the health care system for the foreseeable future. Employers also will make use of better information and watch the effectiveness of new purchasing strategies.

First, better information for employers will give them a basis for more sophisticated purchasing of health care. Employers would like to go beyond price-based comparisons to purchase health plans on the basis of value added, such as improved health and productivity of their workforce. The National Committee for Quality Assurance's (NCQA's) accreditation and the Health Plan Employer Data and Information Set (HEDIS) are widely viewed as steps in the right direction. But these indicators still leave many aspects of quality unmeasured and a large burden for consumers and purchasers to carry in trying to assess quality. Only as better measures of value are available will employers have a persuasive basis for purchasing health care other than by price comparisons.

Second, pragmatism may lead to new purchasing arrangements. Employers have evolved their purchasing strategies mostly by emulating the successes of leading companies. In many areas, excessive hospital overuse and excessive specialists' incomes remain a problem. In other areas, employers are already questioning whether there is much value added from health plans beyond their ability to aggregate purchasing power and impose unsophisticated utilization controls.

Employer initiatives that will be watched include direct contracting and health care purchasing alliances. Large employers in the Twin Cities market [historically, a bellwether region—Eds.] are now aggregating their purchasing power through a business purchasing coalition and are seeking direct contracts with organized delivery systems; this purchasing strategy bypasses managed care plans, with their large overheads and profits. * * * Most large employers already "carve out" mental health and pharmacy services to specialized benefit management firms.

Employers also are evolving ways to make better use of purchasing alliances and multiemployer purchasing arrangements. These organizations offer greater purchasing power than individual companies offer alone; they can be particularly attractive options for small firms. Larger firms, if they judge that a more effective health plan market has been created by such mechanisms, may disengage from their own purchasing efforts and allow workers to purchase through such arrangements.

Etheredge, Jones & Lewin, What Is Driving Health System Change?, Health Affs., Winter 1996, p. 93, 94–95.

Consider the implications of relying upon employers to act as consumers' agents in purchasing health care. Do employers help to overcome some of the disabilities of consumer themselves as makers of complex decisions? What new problems do they introduce? See generally M. Pauly, Health Benefits at Work: An Economic and Political Analysis of Employment–Based Health Insurance (1997).

3. *Self-insurance*. Largely because of ERISA, most large employers self-insure their employees' benefits, often employing an insurer or HMO to administer the plan under an administrative-services-only (ASO) contract. The following excerpt suggests how ERISA has influenced employer purchasing practices, which in turn have failed to encourage the development of closely integrated health plans (which the author believes offer the best prospects for achieving efficiency in the use of resources):

Employer self-insurance, fostered by [ERISA], permits employers to avoid state insurance premium taxes, state benefits mandates, and other [special taxes] used to subsidize uncompensated care and high-risk pools. Interstate differences in mandated benefits and other regulatory requirements drove large, multistate firms to self-insure in the first place. Self-insured plans need not hold reserves or meet solvency standards, and, under ERISA, workers have less recourse to redress grievances about plan administration. Recent surveys indicate that 32 to 42 percent of workers who enroll for employer-sponsored health benefits are in a self-insured plan.

To avoid state insurance regulations [which arguably apply to risk-bearing (capitated) provider networks with which employers contract], self-insured plans are particularly likely to use fee-for-service reimbursement, increasingly with a [PPO] arrangement. Although some PPOs have attempted to build in innovations that are associated with [HMOs] (for example, gatekeepers), they have avoided a core component of HMOs' cost containment efforts—risk sharing with physicians—that would subject them to state insurance regulations. Whatever their merits as a gentle form of managed care, PPOs tend to perpetuate provider fragmentation and work against the alliance of delivery system and insurer. Employer-sponsored plans have idiosyncracies related to patient cost-sharing formulas, benefit exclusions, and the process for making coverage decisions. Thus, in an HMO-dominated, capitated environment, PPOs actually impede reorganization of the delivery system.

In addition, to attract the self-insured market, even health plans with integrated delivery systems, such as Kaiser Permanente, are learning how to bill third-party administrators for ERISA plans on a fee-for-service basis. Thus at the same time that traditional fee-for-service providers are being asked to assume financial risk, organizations steeped in cultures of cost effectiveness are being given incentives to regress to cost-based reimbursement.

Berenson, Beyond Competition, Health Affs., March–April 1997, p. 171, 172.

4. *Competition.* Competition among managed care organizations (MCOs) is clearly a fact of life today. Is it making things better? Is it addressing the right things? Consider the following:

Most managed care plans now use the aggregated purchasing power of employer and worker premiums, through contracted networks, to leverage price discounts from the oversupplied hospital sector and specialists. They also use various "triage" approaches to control utilization through tighter controls over specialist referrals and hospital use. Only a few companies thus far are actively managing clinical care quality through improved disease management.

In the face of tough market pressures, leading plans are quite confident that in most markets they will be able to realize economies for years to come. This confidence * * * is based on a track record of realizing large economies while still having high consumer ratings, particularly through reducing hospital use. Both health plans and employers cite hospital use rates achieved by managed care (days of care per thousand population), compared with much higher levels that prevail in most markets, as the single most persuasive predictor for future savings. Other major savings opportunities are seen in reducing specialists' fees and use in oversupplied fields. Such easy savings mean that health plans could prosper without having to take on more challenging issues, such as improving health status, unless purchasers and competitors forced them to do so.

* * *

Today's health plan strategies also are driven by risk selection, particularly in markets for small-group and individual coverage. It is much easier for health plans to price their premiums competitively by avoiding high-risk populations than by achieving real economies. About 10 percent of the population uses 70 percent of health care. Marketing strategies are usually designed primarily to attract good risks and to avoid patients on whom a plan would lose money. Why do health plan ads show happy, healthy babies? Will we ever see health plans advertising for patients with congestive heart failure, cancer, or cerebral palsy on the grounds of their clinical excellence in treating them?

Etheredge et al., supra, at 95–96.

5. *Information on Quality.* Note the emphasis placed on quality information in the first excerpt from the article by Etheredge et al. (This is a constant theme among observers concerned about the performance of the health care market. See generally Symposium, Quality in a Changing System, Health Affs., May–June 1997, p. 7ff.) What kinds of information are available? What kinds are desired? What features and outcomes need to be measured and compared? Will reliable information of the right kinds ever be forthcoming? Why is information so crucial? If contracts between health plans and their subscribers accurately defined the obligations of the former and their participating providers and were readily enforced in practice, would information on the past performance of plans be so crucial?

6. *Health Plans in the Current Competitive Environment.* Today's health plans are increasingly operated by for-profit corporations. For-profit plans increased their enrollment by 91.6% from 1988 to 1994, compared to 24.9% growth by nonprofits. In 1994, for-profit plans enrolled 58% of HMO members, whereas in 1988 a majority (53%) of HMO enrollees were in nonprofit plans (a few of which converted to for-profit status during the period in question). For-profit HMOs, perhaps quicker to detect and respond to employer preferences, more often provide care through an IPA or provider network, whereas nonprofits are more likely to adopt more integrated forms of organization. Gabel, Ten Ways HMOs Have Changed During the 1990s, Health Affs., May–June 1997, p. 134. Does the preference of nonprofits for greater integration of providers reflect a search for organizational forms that emphasize the quality as well as the cost of care? (Materials in chapter 3(§B) will address in some depth the distinctions between for-profit and nonprofit firms, at which point it would be interesting to return to this question.) If so, why have they not been more successful in the marketplace?

It has been observed that today's health plans, evolving under intensified competition for employers' business, are not fully bearing out the predictions of earlier informed observers about the way health care would be organized and delivered in the future. Judging from the observations quoted below, how (and why) do today's plans differ from the plan you would have designed on the basis of your earlier reading?

> Today's health plans include many new hybrid models of varied structure, sponsorship, financial relationships, out-of-plan options, and other features. Old verities, such as that Kaiser-type organizations will be the most successful, are being challenged with views that such organizations are, for now, at a disadvantage because of their ownership of hospitals and salaried physicians, and that service capacity can be purchased less expensively in the market. In a rapidly changing marketplace, health plans recognize the need to be nimble, operate through many contractual and other relationships, and be ready to change rapidly.

Etheredge et al., supra, at 95. Another observer reports as follows:

> Increasingly, HMOs are "virtual organizations" or "organizations without walls," built on contractual relationships with community provid-

ers. The traditional group-or staff-model HMO is a vertically integrated organization, which operates its own physical facilities in different geographic locations, and whose physicians work solely for the HMO. In 1988 group and staff models constituted about 42 percent of HMO membership. By the end of 1994 they constituted only 31 percent.

Why the greater appeal of IPAs and network models? First, virtual organizations needed less capital to enter new geographic markets than vertically integrated organizations needed. Second, employees could switch to an IPA or a network plan and, in many cases, retain their family physician and specialist. Third, many group and staff models, which were more likely to be owned by a non-profit organization, were not as aggressive in increasing market share as were IPAs or network plans. For example, in the early 1990s, Kaiser plans in California suspended new enrollment during a period when the plans could not keep up with demand. Many Kaiser physicians regarded the expansion as a burden, and they resisted adding new facilities and physicians.

Gabel, supra, at 136.

Yet another observer (a physician) has speculated as follows on why more integrated plans, seemingly the most capable of efficiently allocating scarce resources to their best uses, have not developed and prospered as predicted:

Stephen Shortell has identified a number of barriers to the success of hospital-based integrated delivery systems: the contradictory financial incentives that providers face; the embryonic development of clinical information systems; the lack of adequate geographic concentration of facilities; ambiguous roles and responsibilities; and overemphasis on the acute hospital paradigm (that is, filling beds and satisfying the needs of specialists); the lack of strategic alignment; and the inability to "manage" managed care.[14] Other critics have focused on hospitals' and physicians' inability to set aside their historic suspicions, the poor interpersonal skills of the participants, and the deteriorating moral climate of medical practice in many communities, which leads many physicians to attempt to achieve the maximum economic value from their franchises before they become worthless. Hundreds of PHOs have formed; most lie dormant.

Physician organizations have been relatively late in forming, partly because of lack of access to the capital needed to build organizations and the relative lack of physician leaders and managers. Some argue that legal barriers, especially antitrust issues, have interfered with physician-based integrated delivery systems. Nevertheless, a few successful physician organizations have formed despite these legal barriers.

Provider Resistance. Perhaps the fundamental reason that integration has been slow is that neither health plans nor providers have wanted it to proceed—the former for sound business reasons, the latter for emotional and ideological ones. The basis for the opposition of most health plans to integration efforts has been well described: The better job provid-

14. Shortell et al., "The New World of Managed Care[: Creating Organized Delivery Systems," *Health Affairs* (Winter 1994): 46–64.]

> ers do of organizing the delivery system, the more of the premium dollar they can demand in the form of risk contracts, thereby limiting plan profits, and the better case the provider system can make to purchasers that they should contract directly, without the health plan intermediary.
>
> Less often discussed is the reason that providers, especially physicians, resist integration. As many have pointed out, Americans have been upset chiefly by the cost of their care, not by the health care delivery system or the quality of their care. The corollary is this: Physicians are not upset about either the cost or the quality of care, and they are not interested in remaking the health care system.
>
> In their training, physicians learn to become patient-centered, not population-oriented. (A hallmark of an integrated delivery system is its focus on populations.) Most physicians believe that patients who seek care deserve greater claims on their time and attention than those who do not. At the same time, physicians seem unsympathetic to the fact that patient cost sharing creates a barrier to care, as evidenced by broad physician support for medical savings accounts. They value choice of physicians for their own families and are in a unique position to benefit from direct access to specialists. They generally are individualistic, strive for personal achievement, and resist management techniques that reduce their authority and autonomy, even if these approaches have more promise for improving quality. Finally, physicians work remarkably hard, often in stressful circumstances, and therefore have difficulty accepting criticism that their work is not as effective as it might be.
>
> In my own experience with trying to motivate physicians to organize individual practice associations (IPAs) or, now, integrated delivery systems, the argument that they will be able to practice a higher-quality, more efficient style of care tends to fall on deaf ears. A far more important stimulus for physician action has been publicity about the extraordinarily low medical loss ratios of some for-profit HMOs and about exorbitant executive salaries. Physicians get involved in integrated delivery system activities or sell their practices for defensive reasons: to take back some of the control they have ceded to managed care or to "cash out" while they can. They do not have a vision of better health care resulting from these activities.

Berenson, Beyond Competition, Health Affs., March–April 1997, p. 171, 174–75. See also Berenson, Do Physicians Recognize Their Own Best Interests?, Health Affs., Spring 1994, p. 185 (arguing that "systems that pit managers against affiliated physicians are inherently dysfunctional and will fail"; favoring instead "development of responsible corporate practice of medicine").

Finally, the same physician observer comments as follows on how the path that managed care has actually taken deviates from that predicted by proponents of managed competition:

> The logic of managed competition suggests that within each health care market, networks with different and distinct organizational characteristics and internal cultures will form and compete, initially on price and style of care and later on quality and value. Individual consumers will be

able to recognize the differences among plans and make plan selections based on their own assessment of comparative value. Assuming competition based on clear-cut organizational differentiation at the health plan and delivery system levels, some have envisioned competition even over standards of care.[1]

Health care markets have not evolved that way. The structures of most markets do not encourage consumer choice because of the paucity of employer-based purchasing coalitions, the lack of standardized benefit packages, and the relative lack of financial incentives to encourage value purchasing. It appears that, at least for now, purchasers' success in forcing premiums down through direct bargaining has obviated the need for enrollee incentives to choose lower-cost plans.

Risk-adjusted premiums and capitation rates are not being used to [counter the tendency of plans to engage in risk selection by rewarding] plans and providers who care for sicker patients. Quality measurement remains in an early, developmental stage. Tight partnerships between health plans and providers have not emerged. Indeed, it appears that vertically integrated systems are dissolving into their constituent parts, and that "virtually" integrated organizations and lack of exclusivity have proved more flexible and efficient for plan and provider managers and more attractive to the market.

Berenson, Beyond Competition, supra, at 171.

Why, precisely, have HMOs not become the integrated, differentiated delivery systems visualized by early proponents, each offering a distinct quality and style of care and thus giving consumers opportunities to select the combination of cost and quality best suited to their needs and pocketbooks? Why have they instead evolved into larger plans that are less selective with respect to providers and more difficult to distinguish conceptually from conventional health insurers (except insofar as they retain the ability to set provider compensation)? Does Berenson's account fully explain the path that change has taken? Later materials will provide opportunities to consider the role of the legal system in shaping market developments. Nothing is more important for our study of health care law and policy than trying to understand the influences that are driving developments in the emerging health care marketplace. Health care lawyers should not only appreciate the business considerations underlying the transactions in which they participate, but should also be aware of any ways in which the legal system fails to guide the industry and individual health plans and providers to appropriate goals.

NOTE AND QUESTIONS ON "PROVIDER-SPONSORED ORGANIZATIONS" (PSOS)

In the Balanced Budget Act of 1997 (BBA), Pub. L. No. 105-33, Stat. (1997), Congress authorized the Medicare program to contract with so-

1. C.C. Havighurst, *Health Care Choices: Private Contracts as Instruments of Health Reform* (Washington: The AEI Press, 1995).

called "provider-sponsored organizations" (PSOs) to provide prepaid care to Medicare beneficiaries. Although Medicare had for some time allowed beneficiaries to enroll at public expense in more conventional managed-care organizations—HMOS and so-called "competitive medical plans"—, the BBA was designed to further the privatization of the Medicare program under a new name, "Medicare+Choice." The 1997 legislation will be explained in more detail in the next section of this chapter.

The BBA defines a PSO as an entity that is "established or organized, and operated, by a health care provider, or group of affiliated providers." The providers operating the PSO must themselves provide a "substantial proportion" (as defined in regulations) of the services they undertake to finance—as opposed to having them provided by other providers. Although the sponsoring providers must assume direct or indirect financial responsibility for the services promised to beneficiaries, they are free to arrange for the actual providers of care to bear some of the risk. Unlike Medicare HMOs and competitive medical plans, a PSO may be organized solely for the purpose of contracting with Medicare and is not required to participate in the privately financed market as well. As will appear more fully in the next section and in chapter 9(§A), a Medicare-only PSO can obtain an exemption from state insurance regulation for the first three years of its existence if it complies with federal capital and solvency requirements. Obviously, a PHO, having a hospital as one of the sponsoring providers, can qualify as a PSO. A physician group could organize a PSO alone, however, only if HCFA defines the term *substantial proportion* so that the PSO is not forced (by the numbers) to include a hospital among the affiliated providers.

Recognition of PSOs followed intense lobbying by organized medicine, which argued that physician-controlled plans—or at least provider-controlled ones—would be more attuned to patient interests than lay-sponsored entities. Temporary relief from state insurance regulation was consciously designed by Congress to facilitate start-ups by physicians and other providers, who might find it difficult to comply with state capital and other requirements before they had mastered all the business problems that risk-bearing delivery systems inevitably encounter.

At this writing, the Medicare+Choice program was only getting under way, and final regulations had not been issued. Although you have little to go on, do you think PSOs are likely to be a useful addition to the health care marketplace? Are they likely, for example, to offer consumers opportunities to economize on medical care? Would it be reasonable to expect them to be any more adept than today's other health plans at achieving efficiency in delivering and allocating resources to health care? Should such plans include hospitals as equal partners with physicians? Or would physician-only plans be better able to manage the care required? Students should keep PSOs in mind as new players in the marketplace as they encounter legal issues affecting managed care in the materials ahead.

SECTION D: PRUDENT PURCHASING IN PUBLIC PROGRAMS

Medicare as a Third-Party Payer

NOTES ON MEDICARE COST REIMBURSEMENT

1. *History*. Part A of the Medicare program provides federal payments to providers for inpatient hospital care and for services that are a direct continuation of or directly related to hospitalization, such as convalescent care provided in a nursing home or by a home health agency. From the Medicare program's inception in 1965 until the adoption of a new, prospective system of payment in 1983, it followed under Part A the practice, long common among Blue Cross plans, of reimbursing participating providers for the "reasonable costs" of services rendered. Although virtually no one objected to it when the program was being established, this practice contained the seeds of subsequent cost problems. Not only did cost reimbursement create disincentives for cost containment by providers, but it also eliminated any reason (other than modest deductibles and coinsurance) for program beneficiaries to seek care from lower-cost providers.

The specific principles of cost-based reimbursement that were developed in the early days of Medicare reflected a political compromise between hospitals and the government, which needed providers' cooperation in order to implement the complex new program. Thus, the Johnson administration gave in to hospital demands on a number of crucial points, granting liberal allowances for depreciation, a return on equity to both for-profit and nonprofit hospitals, and a 2 percent allowance for unspecified extra costs. See J. Feder, Medicare: The Politics of Federal Hospital Insurance 53–142 (1977). Although this early liberality was reneged upon in later years, the principle of cost reimbursement remained strongly entrenched, in part because of the belief that there should be no potential for profit in caring for federal beneficiaries.

The inflationary possibilities of cost reimbursement materialized between 1967 and 1983, as annual Medicare hospital expenditures increased from $3 billion to $33 billion. In 1972, Congress attempted to contain this growth by imposing, in section 223 of the Social Security Amendments of that year, a new reasonableness requirement. See 42 U.S.C. § 1395x(v) (1994); 42 C.F.R. § 413.30 (1996). But the "section 223" limit was hard to administer. See, e.g., Regents of the Univ. of Calif. v. Heckler, 771 F.2d 1182 (9th Cir.1985) (invalidating regulation setting absolute reimbursement limits based on general cost estimates; reasonableness of incurred costs could therefore be challenged only hospital by hospital). Later, a ceiling on the allowable rate of increase of operating costs per case was imposed. See 42 U.S.C. § 1395ww(b)(3)(B) (1994); 42 C.F.R. § 413.40 (1996).

Following the defeat in 1979 of the Carter administration's attempt to cap hospitals' revenue increases across the board, the federal government began to study alternative reimbursement methods for Medicare. In 1982, Congress borrowed an approach to hospital payment developed at Yale University (and implemented in a state rate-setting program in New Jersey) and enacted the so-called prospective payment system (PPS), based primarily on diagnosis-related groups (DRGs). Despite the adoption of prospective payment for hospitals, however, cost-based reimbursement continues for psychiatric, rehabilitation, children's, and long-term hospitals (as well as psychiatric and rehabilitation units that are "distinct parts" of short-term general hospitals). See 42 C.F.R. §§ 412.23–.30, 413.1(d)(2)(ii) (1996). Finally, cost reimbursement is still employed by Medicare (to varying degrees) in paying skilled nursing facilities (SNFs), home health agencies (HHAs), comprehensive outpatient rehabilitation facilities (CORFs), end-stage renal disease (ESRD) facilities, and a few other providers and suppliers.

Medicare's experience with cost reimbursement raised enormous accounting and other issues, revealing the complexity of hospitals, of their financial management, and of any program that undertakes to control their revenues. Federal regulations governing cost reimbursement state a number of principles and policies governing the determination of a facility's reasonable costs. See 42 C.F.R. §§ 413.5, 413.9 (1996). For an example of the difficult accounting and definitional problems to which cost reimbursement gave rise, see Charter Peachford Hosp., Inc. v. Bowen, 803 F.2d 1541 (11th Cir.1986) (dealing with the apportionment of costs between Medicare and non-Medicare patients). The PPS, by its nature, has produced many fewer litigable issues.

2. *A Typical Medicare Cost Issue.* As an example of a specific cost-reimbursement issue, consider Medicare's treatment of hospitals' malpractice costs. Before 1979, malpractice insurance premiums and self-insurance costs were lumped under "general and administrative" costs and reimbursed in proportion to beneficiaries' use of the facility. On the basis of a study purporting to show that Medicare patients brought fewer malpractice suits and won smaller verdicts, the Secretary sought in 1979 to reduce the government's share of liability insurance costs. By regulation, the government undertook to pay only the fraction of a hospital's malpractice premiums that equaled the ratio of losses on beneficiaries' claims to total losses.

Many courts invalidated the Secretary's rule. E.g., Cumberland Med. Center v. Secretary of Health and Human Services, 781 F.2d 536, 537 (6th Cir.1986); St. James Hosp. v. Heckler, 760 F.2d 1460 (7th Cir.), cert. denied, 474 U.S. 902 (1985). The courts found the rule invalid for various reasons, including weaknesses in the supporting study, absence of proof that insurers charged lower premiums to hospitals with more Medicare patients, the Secretary's failure to respond to critical public comments on the proposed rule, the program's failure to cover reasonable costs, and the rule's tendency to shift Medicare costs to non–Medicare patients.

In 1986, the Secretary promulgated a new rule that sought to achieve much the same objective as the old one but featured many of the same defects. An immediate controversy arose from the Secretary's attempt to make the 1986 rule retroactive and to use it to dispose of the earlier cases. The courts split on the issue of retroactivity. The Supreme Court, however, in the context of another Medicare cost dispute, invalidated all retroactive rulemaking under the Administrative Procedure Act as well as under the Medicare statute. Bowen v. Georgetown Univ. Hosp., 488 U.S. 204 (1988). Ultimately, the 1986 malpractice rule was itself invalidated and withdrawn. Cf. Swedish Hosp. Corp. v. Shalala, 845 F.Supp. 894 (D.D.C.1993) (awarding attorney's fees to parties successfully challenging rule, on ground DHHS was not "substantially justified" in defending it).

3. *Treatment of Free-care Costs.* Recall the issue adverted to in chapter 1(§B) of the reimbursability under Medicare of Hill–Burton free-care costs. See also Baptist Hosp. East v. Secretary of Health and Human Services, 802 F.2d 860, 866–70 (6th Cir.1986) (rejecting claim that Medicare should bear fair share of non–Hill–Burton charity care and bad debt losses).

4. *Depreciation of Assets Purchased with Public Funds.* Consider whether Medicare should pay depreciation allowances on assets purchased with Hill–Burton or other publicly contributed funds. It does so:

> Like other assets (including other donated depreciable assets), assets financed with Hill–Burton or other Federal or public funds become a part of the provider institution's plant and equipment to be used in furnishing services. It is the function of payment of depreciation to provide funds that make it possible to maintain the assets and preserve the capital employed in the production of services. Therefore, irrespective of the source of financing of an asset, if it is used in the providing of services for beneficiaries of the program, payment for depreciation of the asset is, in fact, a cost of the production of those services.

42 C.F.R. § 413.149 (1996). (What would be the argument for the opposite result?)

NOTES AND QUESTIONS ON MEDICARE'S PROSPECTIVE PAYMENT SYSTEM FOR HOSPITALS

1. *Significance.* The enactment of the PPS in 1983 represented a true revolution in the way the federal government purchases hospital care for beneficiaries of public programs. Under the PPS, Medicare departed for the first time from individualizing the prices paid to each hospital (according to its retrospectively determined costs) in favor of paying preset (prospective) prices to all hospitals within a limited set of classifications. Suddenly, under the new system, it was possible, and acceptable, for a hospital to earn an explicit profit under a public health program. The reform also defined new units of service for which the government would pay, keying payments not to the cost of itemized services rendered to program beneficiaries but to each covered patient's diagnosis. Thus, the government for the first time subscribed to the idea that financial incentives akin to capitation could be used to restrain cost escalation.

An important consequence of the government's decision to act more prudently and aggressively in purchasing hospital services for Medicare beneficiaries was the severance of Medicare from the larger market for health services for policy-making purposes:

> Unlike the Carter administration, which sought to control the hospital expenditures of all payers, the Reagan government, from the outset, concentrated its efforts on making Medicare and Medicaid "prudent" buyers of medical care. The administration * * * ignored the plea of the commercial health-insurance industry that hospitals would simply shift costs in any scheme that did not apply to all payers.

Iglehart, Medicare Begins Prospective Payment of Hospitals, 308 New Eng. J. Med. 1428, 1430 (1983). One result of government's separately addressing the costs of public programs (Medicare and Medicaid) was that purchasers in the private sector had to attend to their own cost problems rather than counting on government to solve the problem globally by regulation or otherwise. Because many private purchasers did not immediately take up the challenge to purchase health services more prudently (as the federal government was now doing), some "cost shifting" undoubtedly occurred. But the pressure on private employers and other bulk purchasers to avoid becoming the hospitals' payers of last resort helped to inspire the managed-care revolution. The consequences of prudent purchasing in the private sector are still unfolding.

One theme of the treatment of government programs in this section is the similarities, as well as the differences, between public and private purchasers of health care for defined populations. Students should consider how the challenges facing the Medicare program differ from the challenges facing a private employer or an HMO committed to meeting the health care needs of an employment group for a fixed period of time. What tools available to private purchasers does government have, or lack, in attempting to get good value for the money it spends? What additional powers or advantages does it have? Any handicaps?

Government's decision to tackle Medicare costs independently of health care costs in the private sector carried with it the implication that patients in different health plans, public or private, would not necessarily receive identical care. Although there still has been little explicit acceptance of the idea that entitlements can vary between financing systems, in practice there has been increasing recognition, if not increasing acceptance, of de facto differences between health plans. Thus, the 1983 Medicare reforms can be seen as a giant step away from the old paradigm's premises that the need for health care is an on/off variable, that health care costs what it costs, and that society should pay whatever those costs (as the cumulative result of myriad scientific judgments by competent, ethical professionals) turn out to be.

Did the Reagan administration's initiation and aggressive implementation of the PPS to control Medicare costs represent (as some alleged at the time) a deviation from its antiregulation ideology? Conceptually, is the PPS system "regulation"? Is it likely to feel like "regulation" to hospitals? To be sure, the strategy adopted allowed the federal government, for the first time, to exercise its considerable buying (monopsony) power over providers on behalf of taxpayers and beneficiaries. But did this make it the equivalent of hospital rate-setting regulation such as the Carter administration sought to impose? Do you approve of this method of controlling health care costs? Would you support a national single-payer system on the ground that it could exercise even more monopsony power?

2. *Overview of the PPS.* In a case involving an early challenge to the methodology employed in putting the PPS in place, a federal appeals court provided the following outline of the PPS and of the transition from highly individualized cost-based reimbursement to national prospective pricing:

> In 1965, Congress enacted the Medicare statute which provides a system of health insurance for the aged and disabled. 42 U.S.C. § 1395. In 1983, Congress created a Prospective Payment System (PPS) which "completely changed the method of reimbursing a hospital's Medicare costs...." Charter Medical Corp. v. Bowen, 788 F.2d 728, 731 (11th Cir.1986). For cost reporting years beginning prior to October 1, 1983, participating hospitals were reimbursed for the actual "reasonable costs" of in-patient hospital services furnished to Medicare patients. Under the PPS, hospitals are to be reimbursed a fixed amount for each patient treated, regardless of the actual cost of treatment. By enacting the PPS, which applies to all but a few limited classes of hospitals and limited types of costs, Congress sought "to reform the financial incentives hospitals face, promoting efficiency in the provision of services by rewarding cost-effective hospital practices." H.R.Rep. No. 25, 98th Cong., 1st Sess. 132. By informing hospitals in advance of the payments they will receive per patient for various types of treatment, Congress thus sought to induce hospitals to lower actual costs in treating patients.
>
> 
>
> Under the PPS, Medicare will ultimately pay hospitals for in-patient operating services based on a standard national rate for each of approximately 470 diagnosis-related groups (DRG's). A DRG is a grouping of comparable types of patients and illnesses whose cost of treatment is expected to be similar. Each DRG is assigned a weight which varies with the severity of the illness. This number is then multiplied by one specific dollar figure which represents the national average per patient cost of medical treatment. Congress provided for a four-year "phase-in period to minimize disruptions that might otherwise occur because of a sudden change in reimbursement policy." H.R.Rep. No. 25 at 136. During this phase-in period, the dollar figure portion of the PPS payment formula is to be based on a blend of two components: a "hospital-specific rate" based on the hospital's actual cost during a designated "base year" and a standardized national cost figure. This average cost of treatment in the base year is adjusted upwards based for various factors including the Secretary's estimates of anticipated inflation. 42 C.F.R. § 412.71(a). Over the course of the transition period, the proportion of the payment based upon the hospital's costs decreases until it is finally eliminated, while the proportion based on the national figure increases accordingly.

Doctors Hosp., Inc. of Plantation v. Bowen, 811 F.2d 1448, 1449–50 (11th Cir.1987) (allowing hospitals to challenge Secretary's determination of hospital-specific rates in transition period). The phase-in of payment under two national, DRG-based rates (urban and rural) was completed by October 1987. As noted below, capital costs were handled separately. The number of DRGs had increased to 492 by the mid–1990s.

A 1996 report to Congress by the Prospective Payment Assessment Commission (a legislative-branch agency known, and referred to hereinafter, as "ProPAC") provides a fuller, more current description of the PPS:

> Under PPS, each hospital receives a fixed payment to cover the operating costs associated with each discharge. The hospital's basic payment rate is based on a national standardized payment amount, which is higher for hospitals in large urban areas (metropolitan statistical areas, or MSAs, with a population of more than one million) than for other hospitals. To account for differences in hospital wage rates across areas, the standardized payment amount is adjusted by a wage index for each MSA and for the rural areas in each state. The wage index measures the relative level of wages for hospital workers in each labor market compared with the national average.
>
> Payment also depends on the relative costliness of the case, based on the diagnosis-related group (DRG) to which the patient is assigned. For each DRG, a relative weight is computed that represents the average standardized charges for discharges in that DRG compared with the national average for all Medicare discharges. The wage-adjusted standardized payment amount is multiplied by the relative weight for each DRG to obtain the basic DRG payment rate for that type of case.
>
> A hospital's basic DRG payments thus reflect its location, local wage rates, and mix of Medicare cases. These factors partly explain why PPS payments are higher for some types of hospitals than for others. For example, hospitals in urban areas receive greater payments per discharge than those in rural areas, reflecting historical and continuing differences in costs. Wage rates in urban labor market areas generally exceed those in rural areas. In addition, urban hospitals are likely to treat a more complex and costly mix of Medicare cases, and to provide care that is more resource-intensive.
>
> Besides the basic DRG rates, hospitals receive extra payments under PPS for cases with extraordinarily high costs or unusually long stays (outliers). Payments are also adjusted for hospitals that operate graduate medical education programs to train residents or that serve a disproportionate share of low-income patients. These factors further increase the amounts paid to urban hospitals compared with rural facilities. Hospitals in urban areas are much more likely to have outlier cases, and most teaching and disproportionate share (DSH) hospitals are urban.
>
> * * * Policy changes enacted in the Omnibus Budget Reconciliation Acts (OBRA) of 1989 and 1990 had a major effect on both the aggregate level and distribution of PPS payments. One of the most important was the gradual elimination of the difference in the standardized amounts for rural and other urban hospitals. In addition, the number of rural hospitals receiving the DSH adjustment was expanded and the size of the adjustment was increased for many urban hospitals. Another major change was the basis of payment for sole community hospitals (geographically isolated

> facilities considered to be the only available source of inpatient care for the community). These hospitals now receive payment based on their updated 1982 or 1987 costs or the PPS rate, whichever is the greatest.
>
> For payment purposes, OBRA 1989 allows hospitals to request reclassification from the geographic area in which they are located to another one that is more advantageous. This reclassification, which must be approved by the Medicare Geographic Classification Review Board (MGCRB) each year, can change the hospital's standardized payment amount or wage index, or both. While slightly more than 1,200 hospitals were reclassified for fiscal year 1993, the criteria were modified the following year, significantly reducing the number eligible for reclassification. Only about 700 hospitals were reclassified for fiscal year 1995, and about 600 for fiscal year 1996.

ProPAC, Medicare and the American Health Care System, Report to Congress 60–61, reprinted in Medicare & Medicaid Guide (CCH) No. 911 (June 1996). (Prior to its merger with the Physician Payment Review Commission in 1997 to form the Medicare Payment Advisory Commission, or "MedPAC," ProPAC issued similar reports to Congress each year bearing the same name, which provided useful updates on the Medicare program and are cited hereinafter as, e.g., ProPAC 1996.) See also L. Russell, Medicare's Hospital Payment System: Is It Working? (1989). See generally Frankford, The Complexity of Medicare's Hospital Reimbursement System: Paradoxes of Averaging, 78 Iowa L. Rev. 517 (1993) (extensive descriptive and critical review of Medicare's policy toward purchasing hospital care); Frankford, The Medicare DRGs: Efficiency and Organizational Rationality, 10 Yale J. Reg. 273 (1993) (critique of DRG-based payment).

The PPS created new problems, of course, as hospitals behaved opportunistically to maximize their revenues and minimize their risks. One example that had to be addressed was the transfer of patients between hospitals. Why might transfers from one hospital to another during a course of treatment, especially in potentially costly cases, be common under the PPS? Under 42 C.F.R. § 412.4 (1996), a transferring hospital is paid (up to the full DRG allowance) at a per diem rate based on the average per diem cost to the government of patients in the same DRG. On the other hand, the transferee hospital receives the usual DRG payment in full. (Public hospitals reportedly received more transfers after the PPS was implemented.) The government set up a monitoring system to investigate transfers to ensure that the PPS was not being exploited. Numerous other potential loopholes were dealt with in similar fashion.

3. *Capital Costs.* When Congress chose prospective payment for inpatient hospital services in 1983, it elected to continue reimbursing capital costs on the old basis to allow time to study methods for incorporating allowances for such costs into prospective payments. On August 30, 1991, HCFA adopted a plan under which Medicare would pay most hospitals for capital costs on a prospective rather than a retrospective basis. See 42 C.F.R. § 412.300 (1996).

Under the old system, the capital expenses of a hospital, such as the cost of construction, equipment, and borrowing to purchase assets, were reimbursed by Medicare (with adjustments for the percentage of days that Medicare patients used the facility and for a statutory 15 percent discount) when those costs were recognized under general accounting principles. Among other things, this system failed to distinguish how much of a hospital's capital investment was actually necessary to treat Medicare patients and supported some hospitals with low occupancy rates. By helping to pay for unneeded capacity, the old system fueled a costly "medical arms race" in which competing hospitals scrambled to buy costly technologies that were then often underutilized.

Under the new system, Medicare adds a new component for capital costs to PPS payments to hospitals based on DRGs. Initially, the program uses (for most hospitals) a combination of industry-wide averages (federal rate) and the specific characteristics of the individual hospital (hospital-specific rate) to determine each hospital's payment. The federal rate reflects such things as a geographic adjustment for variations in wages and other costs and an adjustment for hospitals in urban areas for the higher costs of serving low-income patients. The hospital-specific rate considers an individual hospital's actual inpatient capital costs per discharge over a base period and includes multiple "hold-harmless" features to protect hospitals that currently have large "old capital" obligations.

Eventually hospitals will be paid solely on the basis of the federal rate, so that actual capital expenditures made by a hospital, historically or concurrently, will not figure into the calculation at all. To ease the transition, however, the federal rate is being phased in over a 10–year period, during which the proportionate weight of the federal rate will increase by 10 percent each year until finally, in the year 2001, only the federal rate will remain.

Paying for capital costs under a prospective system is expected to result in more prudent capital spending. See generally Kauer, Silvers & Teplensky, The Effect of Fixed Payment on Hospital Costs, 20 J. Health Pol., Pol'y & L. 305 (1995); U.S.General Accounting Office, Alternatives for Paying Hospital Capital Costs (Rep. No. GAO/HRO 86B93) (1986). In particular, it is expected that hospitals will no longer be biased in choosing between capital and noncapital inputs. Researchers have found evidence to confirm their theory-derived hypothesis that, because retaining cost-based reimbursement for capital costs alone had the effect of increasing labor and supply costs relative to capital, the ratio of capital to operating expenses for inpatient care should have increased under the original PPS. They concluded, "With the advent of capital PPS, the * * * theory would predict a greater balance of capital to operating cost according to the most appropriate production function to provide hospital service efficiently." Kauer et al., supra, at 315–16.

It seems certain that, as prospective payment replaces reimbursement of capital costs, hospitals will have to exercise more self-discipline in capital spending, set aside capital funds out of general revenues, and plan prudently to replace facilities as they wear out. Lenders, already perceiving greater risk in loans to hospitals since the advent of the PPS and of price competition for private business, may become even more skeptical toward hospital borrowers. On the question whether hospitals' capital spending will in fact become more efficient, given the state of the overall market for hospital care, see Kauer et al., supra.

4. *DRGs.* How might physicians, concerned about their hospitals' financial condition, alter their diagnostic practices under a DRG-based payment system? DRG 72 covers "nasal trauma and deformity." There is also, however, a separate category (73) for "other ear, nose, mouth and throat diagnoses." A higher weight is attached to the "other" classification than to the specific diagnosis. Can you see the temptation that would arise in this situation?

Each hospital has a unique case-mix index (CMI), reflecting the severity of the condition of its average Medicare patient. An increase in hospitals' average CMI was expected with the PPS, as a result of either more accurate coding or "DRG creep" or a combination of the two. An unanticipated further increase in CMIs occurred because many less profitable cases were shifted to outpatient settings, where more liberal payments could be obtained. Experience in New York and Massachusetts illustrated how strongly CMIs were affected by the PPS: In 1986, waivers exempting hospitals in both states from the PPS expired; those hospitals' CMIs promptly increased, uncharacteristically, by more than 6 percent. For a discussion of the coding problem, see Steinwald & Dummit, Hospital Case-mix Change: Sicker Patients or DRG Creep?, 8 Health Affs. 35 (1988).

What is the logic of setting a single price for treating all individuals in what can never be a totally homogeneous group of patients? How safe is the apparent assumption that things will "average out"? Some provision was made to soften the burden of costly "outliers" (individual cases involving unusual treatment costs or lengths of stay), 42 C.F.R. § 412.80–.86 (1996), but the additional payments provided for are inadequate to cover the actual cost of difficult cases. Proposals have been made to introduce a "severity index" or other adjustment to reduce inequities further. See Edwards et al., Refinement of the Medicare Diagnosis–Related Groups to Incorporate a Measure of Severity, Health Care Fin. Rev., Summer 1994, p. 45 (describing HCFA proposal to incorporate a severity factor that captures differences between patients that substantially affect resource use). Questions have also been raised concerning the DRG categories themselves. See, e.g., Horn et al., Misclassification Problems in Diagnosis–Related Groups: Cystic Fibrosis as an Example, 314 New Eng. J.Med. 484 (1986).

How might once-accurate DRG weights (multipliers) become outdated? Technological changes and new treatment methods may either lower the cost of efficacious treatment or increase both the efficacy and the cost of treatment. In either event, the original weights must be recalculated. Although recalibration occurs under the oversight of ProPAC (now MedPAC), there is always a question whether the government is paying an appropriate price for appropriate treatment. ProPAC found that the PPS had no adverse effect on the dispersion of such emerging technologies as cardiac catheterization, CT scanning, lithotripsy, MRI, open-heart surgery, and organ transplantation. ProPAC 1991, at 91. One efficacious new technology did not fare well, however. Cochlear implants (to improve hearing) are expensive relative to pre-existing technology, and HCFA was slow to raise the allowance for the relevant DRG. See Kane & Manoukian, The Effect of the Medicare Prospective Payment System on the Adoption of New Technology: The Case of Cochlear Implants, 321 New Eng. J. Med. 1378 (1989) ("the failure of cochlear implants to be widely accepted is due to the fact that physicians wanting to perform the procedure had to overcome the hospital's strong financial disincentives").

Annual inflation adjustments in the multipliers used with DRGs were implicitly promised when the PPS was introduced. Indeed, Congress expressly provided that the shift to the PPS should be budget-neutral in the early years, leaving hospitals' total revenue from Medicare unaffected. Later, however, the government became slow to increase allowances, imposing freezes on real increases and chipping away at the formula in other ways. Is the PPS viable for the long haul? Will DRG weights become increasingly artificial as technology changes? Will the budget-conscious federal government be hesitant to increase payments under the system enough to prevent quality and access problems from intensifying?

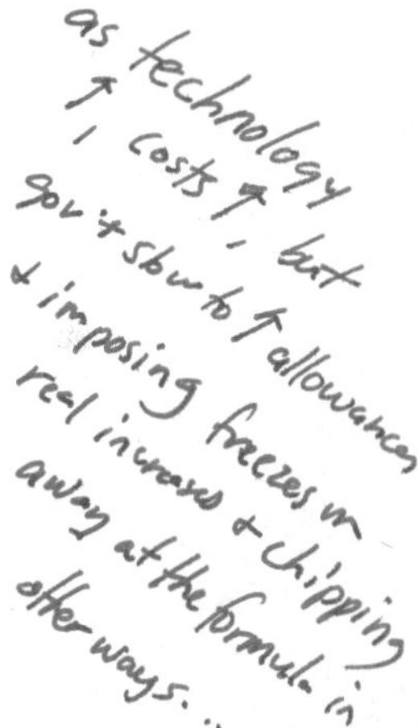
as technology
costs
gov't slow to allowances
imposing freezes on
real increases & chipping
away at the formula in
other ways..

5. *Effects on the Quality of Care*. What dangers might patients face under the PPS? Although the shift to fixed payment by diagnosis was intended to induce economizing, it might also induce profiteering at the expense of patient welfare. Abuse is, unfortunately, often in the eye of the beholder. Nevertheless, there were a number of specific risks: omission of necessary services, premature discharges, inappropriate readmissions and transfers to generate additional payments, and avoidance of potentially high-cost patients.

There were early reports of Medicare patients' being discharged too early under the PPS and of other corner-cutting, but no convincing proof of overall quality reductions has been forthcoming. One early study found no reduction under the PPS in the quality of care as detectable in the rates of in-hospital consultation, in-hospital mortality, or readmission. DesHarnais et al., The Early Effects of the Prospective Payment System on Inpatient Utilization and the Quality of Care, 24 Inquiry 7 (1987).

Also on quality issues, see the series of studies by The RAND Corporation compiled in Kahn et al., The Effects of the DRG–Based Prospective Payment System on Quality of Care for Hospitalized Medicare Patients (RAND Corp. 1992). Although the RAND findings are interesting, the last year looked at was 1986, before full implementation. The sickness of patients at initial admission was found to have increased significantly since 1983, but processes of care (what is done, not the patient outcome) appeared improved for both nursing care and physician cognitive performance. "[T]he implementation of the PPS was not associated with a deterioration in care, even in those areas that were most sensitive to the financial incentives provided * * *, such as nursing activities and the use of intensive care units." Id. at 72. The RAND studies also found, however, that more patients were being discharged in unstable condition, up from 10% to 15%; nevertheless, even though Medicare patient lengths of stay had dropped 24% since PPS, from 14.4 to 11.0 days, no change in 30–day and 180–day mortality rates was found. A study of practitioners' opinions on quality of care showed that the percent of patients considered to be receiving poor or very poor care dropped from 25% before PPS to 12% after. Id. at 82.

Although the various studies suggest that the PPS financial incentive for hospitals to limit care has not resulted in patient harm, a decline in quality may have been masked by changes in diagnostic practices. Thus, if the PPS encouraged physicians or administrative staffs to assign more severe DRG codes to patients to obtain higher Medicare reimbursement, unsatisfactory outcomes might be erroneously attributed to patients' more severe diagnoses rather than to a decline in the quality of care. See Orentlicher, Health Care Reform and the Patient–Physician Relationship, 5 Health Matrix 141, 165–66 (1995).

A 1990 Institute of Medicine (IOM) study of quality assurance in the Medicare program concluded that, although data were scattered, inconclusive, and only occasionally indicative of quality problems ("underuse"), "findings today do not indicate that Medicare PPS has had demonstrable negative effects on the quality of care or the health of the elderly population." 1 IOM, Medicare: A Strategy for Quality Assurance 230 (1990). In accordance with IOM recommendations, HCFA has launched a variety of initiatives to monitor and improve the quality of care received by Medicare and Medicaid beneficiaries. See, e.g., Gagel, Health Care Quality Improvement Program: A New Approach, Health Care Fin. Rev., Summer 1995, p. 15; Jencks, Measuring Quality of Care Under Medicare and Medicaid, id. at 39.

How might the risk of lowered quality be minimized? Who would most effectively and zealously monitor hospitals and providers to ensure quality of care—government agencies, private contractors, or consumer organizations? So-called peer review organizations (PROs) were assigned oversight responsibilities to prevent premature discharge of Medicare patients, other reductions in the quality of care, and such other abuses of the PPS as inappropriate transfers and imaginative DRG coding. These private organizations operate under contracts with HCFA. Because they are often closely associated with the organized medical profession, they are described in these materials in a note in chapter 4(§B), dealing with antitrust issues in profession-sponsored peer review. PROs will also be encountered in chapter 6(§B) as a mechanism for policing the medical profession. See generally Rubin et al., Watching the Doctor–Watchers: How Well Do Peer Review Organization Methods Detect Quality Problems?, 267 J.A.M.A. 2349 (1992).

6. *Effects on Hospitals.* Although Medicare may have ameliorated the growth of program costs by shifting to prospective payment, hospital costs themselves continued to rise, eventually leaving some hospitals in financial difficulty. To be sure, most hospitals operated quite profitably in the early years under the PPS, but that windfall ended fairly soon as Congress tightened the program. In the seventh year of the PPS, hospitals' overall average PPS margin fell below zero for the first time. However, PPS margins began to rise again after 1991, as the growth of hospital costs ameliorated. ProPAC estimated that the PPS inpatient margin in 1997 would be 12.7 percent. See ProPAC 1997, at 77–78.

Although the theory of the PPS–DRG system is that all hospitals should be equally capable of providing good care to beneficiaries for the federal payment, it is far from clear that this is the case. Indeed, the PPS has had quite different impacts on different hospitals, an effect that could be objected to not only on equity grounds but also because the hardship to some hospitals may be translated into hardships for their patients. See generally Bray et al., An Examination of Winners and Losers Under Medicare's Prospective Payment System, 19 Health Care Mgmt. Rev. 44 (1994). Most hospitals that do well under the PPS also do well overall. The hospitals considered "winners" included not only those with lower costs per case but also teaching hospitals and others qualifying for special treatment. "Losers" tended to be smaller hospitals and others having higher costs due to weaker financial control and management systems, poor utilization control procedures, less aggressive coding practices, and lower volumes overall. Hospital closures have been particularly common in rural areas, raising the problem of decreased access to care for Medicare beneficiaries as well as the population as a whole. Under the national PPS rates, some (lower-cost) regions profited more handsomely than others despite adjustments to account for cost differences.

The PPS has been open to applications for exceptional treatment and to continued tinkering and political manipulation on behalf of institutions that claim to be specially vulnerable. "Those hospitals with the best relative performance * * * tend to be hospitals that receive special consideration under PPS." Altman & Young, A Decade of Medicare's Prospective Payment System—Success or Failure?, J. Am. Health Pol'y, March–April 1993, p. 11, 16. Because the PPS threatened to deprive some hospitals of essential revenues that had cross-subsidized indigent care, temporary provision was made in 1986 for upward adjustment of rates payable to hospitals serving a "disproportionate share" (as determined by formula) of low-income patients and for other hospitals having heavy public responsibilities. 42 U.S.C. § 1395ww(d)(5)(F) (1994). The disproportionate-share adjustment (DSA) has been vital in keeping some hospitals solvent. Whether DSAs are meant to offset real, uncompensated costs of treating Medicare and Medicaid patients or are meant instead to subsidize care for a larger indigent population is an important question. In general, DSAs have favored large urban hospitals, which get the lion's share of all DSA payments even after adjustments for sole community hospitals and rural hospitals and referral centers. Urban hospitals obviously get a high percentage of AIDS, substance abuse, and trauma cases. The Balanced Budget Act of 1997 introduced new state-specific caps on DSAs.

Teaching hospitals feared the shift to prospective payment because they believed that their educational function increased their costs and that the treatment needs of their patients were systematically above average. In answer to these fears, such hospitals were granted reimbursement for two kinds of educational costs. Indirect reimbursement, which is explicitly intended to cover teaching costs, was also an implicit recognition of indigent care burdens (and was accordingly reduced when Congress provided relief to disproportionate-share hospitals). Direct reimbursement of educational costs includes a pass-through of the compensation of interns and residents. 42 C.F.R. §§ 412.2(e)(2)–(3), 413.85–.86 (1996). These provisions yielded quite favorable operating results for teaching hospitals that did not have large indigent care burdens. They are subject of course to periodic adjustment, and (as mentioned briefly below) the Balanced Budget Act of 1997 made significant reforms in this area.

7. *Was the PPS a "Success"?* Experience under the PPS is difficult to summarize and assess, but some observations are possible. In the five years before and the five years after its implementation, Medicare costs for inpatient hospital care, adjusted for inflation, rose 45 percent and 3 percent, respectively, suggesting that the program was successful in slowing the growth of federal outlays.

One reason Medicare hospital costs declined in the early years of the PPS was that there were significant decreases in the total number of Medicare hospital admissions after the inception of the PPS. (Having risen 12 percent, to 431 per 1000, between 1980 and 1983, Medicare admissions fell to 363 per 1000 in 1987.) Should this result be attributed to the PPS? (In fact, the designers of the PPS feared that it would cause hospitals to admit *more* patients, with less pressing needs.) It was unclear whether the reduction in admissions was indicative of more efficient treatment decisions and advances in technology or of less willingness to treat Medicare patients. One explanation may have been that, following implementation of the PPS, it was more profitable for hospitals to treat some Medicare patients on an outpatient basis. Interestingly, however, significant though less dramatic reductions were simultaneously occurring in admissions and lengths of stay of non-Medicare patients. See generally DesHarnais et al., supra. It appeared that, to some extent at least, Medicare benefitted from changing practice patterns unrelated to the PPS.

Although admissions declined under the PPS, Medicare costs per admission and total hospital costs paid by the program continued to rise even though Congress intervened to keep annual updates of PPS allowances below increases in the hospital "market basket" (the cost of goods and services that hospitals use), which was originally intended to determine updates. ProPAC officials reported as follows in 1993:

> The PPS was intended to control the growth in hospital costs through improved productivity and efficiency. Initially, productivity improved as hospitals reduced the quantity of services they furnished, especially length of stay. In the first year of PPS, operating costs per discharge increased only 1.9 percent. * * *

> Between 1985 and 1989, [however,] hospital operating costs per admission grew at an average annual rate of 8.9 percent. General inflation accounted for about 40 percent of the increase. Hospitals also treated a more complex mix of patients, accounting for an additional 21 percent of the growth. While these factors are generally regarded as beyond the control of hospitals, other contributors to the cost growth are at least partially controllable. These include the intensity of services furnished and hospital-specific price inflation that were responsible for a combined 37 percent of cost increases. Productivity is also within hospitals' control. Labor productivity improvements, however, have been modest, reducing the average annual increase in costs only 7 percent.

Altman & Young, supra, at 14–15.

One rap against the PPS was that it simply encouraged "cost shifting." See id. at 18 ("Critics argue * * * that Medicare has become an administered price system, allowing the government to control its spending by shifting its responsibilities to private payers."). On the other hand, early experience under the PPS suggested that private insurers, rather than being victimized by a cost shift, were themselves benefitting from cost-reduction efforts by hospitals seeking to accommodate to the new payment system. In any event, how much cost shifting could hospitals hope to get away with in the changing marketplace? If indeed some cost shifting did occur, it may only have increased pressure on private payers to engage in prudent purchasing themselves, triggering selective purchasing and the managed care revolution. Although ProPAC officials opined in 1993 that "the Medicare program is paying less than the costs of furnishing care to its beneficiaries while private payers are paying more," id., rising profit margins under the PPS suggest the problem, if it was one, has gone away, at least for the time being.

Even though the PPS effectively controlled one component of Medicare costs, spending for other components grew dramatically, as hospitals shifted some patients to other settings and as utilization of other services increased. The PPS expedient may therefore be seen as an attempt to deal with only one part of a much larger problem. The materials that follow show how the Medicare program adapted its purchasing of other health services and began to move toward a more coordinated approach. See generally MedPAC, Report to Congress: Medicare Payment Policy (March 1998) (2 vols., including background papers) (providing descriptions of, and policy recommendations on, wide variety of payment issues, particularly new ones arising under Balanced Budget Act, next discussed).

8. *The Balanced Budget Act of 1997.* This legislation (the BBA), Pub. L. No. 105–33 (1997), included the most extensive reforms of the Medicare program since its enactment in 1965. Medicare was a major target as the federal government moved to eliminate the budget deficit by 2002, and Congress set a goal of reducing Medicare costs by $115 billion over five years. All of the more than 200 changes in the program are highly technical, but some specific measures and themes can be observed here and at later points.

Hospitals were a tempting target for cost savings precisely because they had learned to live profitably under the PPS by cutting costs and, more importantly, by moving many Medicare services and costs out of the reach of the price controls—into outpatient surgical facilities, nursing homes, rehabilitation services, and patients' homes. (The latest estimates projected a 17% profit margin for hospitals on PPS business in 1998.) Congress therefore froze PPS rates for one year and set annual update factors one to two percentage points below the increase in the so-called "market basket" for each year until 2003. Only small reductions were made in the special allowance for hospitals serving a disproportionate share of low-income persons. Capital payments under the PPS were reduced by complex changes in formulas, resulting in a 17.8% cut in both the federal and the hospital-specific portions of the rate in 1998; in order to curb efforts to obtain reimbursement for costs incurred only on paper, changes were made in the manner of calculating depreciation and interest on capital debt when an asset changes hands.

Teaching hospitals faced reductions in allowances for graduate medical education. In order to reduce incentives to train too many physicians, indirect medical education (IME) adjustments were reduced, and ceilings were set on the number of interns and residents for whom IME or direct educational payments would be made. Most significantly, the BBA included provision for a complex five-year program of incentive payments to hospitals that voluntarily reduce by more than 5% the number of residents they train. Although the policy of giving subsidies for not producing new doctors has been likened to farm programs that reward cutbacks in output, the payments may be seen as compensation for employing doctors no longer in training to provide vital services in hospitals.

PPS-exempt hospitals and units (e.g., psychiatric, rehab) experienced a variety of changes in the manner in which Medicare calculates their costs for reimbursement purposes, including reductions in the percentage of capital costs to be reimbursed and reduced updates and a new cap on so-called target rates for individual hospitals. In 2000, Medicare will inaugurate a prospective payment system for rehabilitation hospitals or units, which will be phased in over three years.

When faced with cutbacks such as those in the BBA, hospitals naturally complain that the budget is being balanced on their backs. Nevertheless, hospitals may be viewed as fortunate that the policy problem facing government continues to be defined as providing funds to meet the industry's future needs for revenue. Unlike market prices, which can easily fall to ruinous levels if supply outstrips demand, government payment rates are guaranteed (at least for a time), thus allowing a hospital under clever management to earn positive profits even when there are unfilled beds in the community. As noted below, the federal government is inexorably moving to embrace a market-oriented approach to meeting the needs of Medicare beneficiaries, creating competition for the government's own program.

Physician Payment Review Commission, [Reforming the Payment of Physicians under Medicare]

Excerpt from Physician Payment Review Commission (PPRC), 1995 Annual Report to Congress, pp. 1–15.

In the late 1980s, consensus was building among physicians, beneficiaries, and policy makers that a major restructuring of physician payment under Medicare was needed to replace what many considered an inequitable and inflationary system. In 1983, Medicare's method of paying hospitals under Part A had been significantly overhauled to address rising costs. It was clear that it was time to bring Medicare's spending for physicians' services—which then made up more than 25 percent of total Medicare expenditures—under control as well. The lack of a rational basis for determining fees, acceleration of program outlays, and increasing financial liability of beneficiaries were issues that had to be addressed.

Distortions in Payments to Physicians

Pressure for payment reform arose in part from criticisms that Medicare's method of paying physicians, referred to as customary, prevailing, and reasonable (CPR), had created wide variations in payments among types of procedures, localities, and specialties that could not be attributed to differences in costs of practice. Under the CPR method, the payment for each service was determined by what the physician had charged in the past (customary) and what other physicians in the locality and specialty charged (prevailing).

The CPR payment method was under fire because it was inequitable, inflationary, and excessively complicated. First, because the fees were based on individual physicians' historical charges, two physicians who provided identical services could receive considerably different payments. Second, the differential in payments across geographic areas exceeded that which could be explained by differences in costs. Third, surgical and technical procedures had become increasingly overvalued relative to visits and consultations, reflecting the higher fees paid for newer services.[1] This distortion contributed to the marked disparity between the incomes of primary care practitioners and other physicians and perhaps also contributed to more rapid growth in the provision of technical services than justified by standards of appropriateness. Finally, administration of the system, which required maintaining individual charge profiles for every physician for every service, was complex, time-consuming, and costly.

Growth in Expenditures

Also troubling were double-digit growth rates in expenditures for physicians' services. Between 1965 when the Medicare program was enacted and the mid–1980s, spending for physicians' services increased at an

1. Although productivity for many of these services improved over the time, under CPR, their fees were not adjusted downward to reflect this change.

average annual rate of more than 13 percent [not adjusted for inflation]. * * *

Increased Medicare outlays can result from two sources: increases in payment rates and increases in the quantity or the mix of services provided per beneficiary (also referred to as volume and intensity). Increases in services can be separated further into two components: those due to growth and aging of the population and those due to changes in the practice of medicine. While population growth is often mentioned as being a major cause of rising physician expenditures, in fact, its impact on growth in Medicare physician spending has been relatively small (about 1.5 percent to 2.0 percent annually). More important are the impact of volume and price which together accounted for increases of 15.6 percent between 1980 and 1984, and 9.1 percent between 1984 and 1988.

* * * During the 1970s and 1980s, the primary policy levers to restrain Medicare expenditure growth were restraints on price. These took the form of limiting increases in prevailing charges to increases in the Medicare Economic Index, across-the-board fee freezes, and fee cuts for procedures that the Congress specified as overvalued. While these price constraints were effective in slowing expenditure growth, there was consensus that growth could not be held down over the long term without a mechanism to control volume and intensity.

Increasing Financial Liability of Beneficiaries

A third force motivating the push for payment reform was concern about the impact of rising program costs on Medicare beneficiaries. Increases in out-of-pocket costs including monthly premiums for Medicare Part B, deductibles, copayments, and liabilities for balance bills, were outpacing increases in Social–Security benefits. These came on top of other expenditures borne by older Americans including cost sharing for Part A, premiums for supplemental insurance, and expenses for services not covered by Medicare such as prescription drugs, eyeglasses, and long-term care.

During the mid–1980s, Medicare beneficiaries were provided with some relief from rising costs as a result of the Participating Physician and Supplier (PAR) program. Like physicians participating in private insurer networks, PAR physicians agree to accept the Medicare allowed charge as a payment in full on all claims, forgoing the opportunity to bill patients any additional amount. In return, they are listed in a directory available to beneficiaries and receive expedited claims processing. In addition, they were permitted to raise fees during a period of price constraints for other doctors.

Beneficiaries also benefited from the limits on maximum allowable actual charges (MAACs), the amount physicians who did not sign PAR agreements could charge patients above the Medicare fee. These limits were heavily criticized, however, because they were complex to administer (the limits varied from physician to physician and service to service) and virtually impossible for beneficiaries and physicians to understand.

THE POLICY RESPONSE

After taking a series of incremental steps to address problems within the Medicare program, the Congress enacted a comprehensive reform in OBRA89. The major features of the payment system created in that law are described below.

The Medicare Fee Schedule

The Medicare Fee Schedule was designed to introduce predictability and equity into Medicare physician payment by basing payments on the relative resources used to provide different services. At its heart is a relative value scale (RVS) consisting of three components:

- a physician work component that reflects the time and intensity of the physician's effort in providing a service;
- a practice expense component that includes costs such as office rent, salaries, equipment, and supplies; and
- a separate professional liability insurance component that reflects premium expenses.

The RVS is translated into a schedule of fees when the weighted sum of the three components is multiplied by a monetary conversion factor. A geographic adjustment factor is also applied to each of the components to allow payments to vary from one locality to another, reflecting differences in costs of practicing medicine. * * *

* * * As anticipated, payment levels have increased for evaluation and management services and for services delivered in rural areas; levels have decreased for surgical and technical procedures and for services delivered in metropolitan areas. Family and general practitioners have seen the largest increase in payments per service at 7.6 percent annually over the two-year period from 1991 to 1993 for a cumulative increase of close to 16 percent. * * *

In the future, the shift toward primary care is expected to become even more pronounced as practice expense relative values, now based on historical charges, are replaced with those based on resource costs. Under the technical amendments bill passed at the end of [1994], the Health Care Financing Administration was directed to develop resource-based practice expense relative values for implementation in 1998. * * *

Volume Performance Standards

The experience of the 1980s, when increased service use was the principal force driving up expenditures for physicians' services, suggested that a mechanism with the explicit aim of containing volume and intensity was needed to maintain spending at a sustainable level. OBRA89 created such a mechanism in the system of Volume Performance Standards.

* * *

Under OBRA89, a performance standard (essentially a target rate of expenditure growth) is to be set annually either by the Congress, after consulting with the Commission and the Secretary of Health and Human Services (HHS), or by a default formula specified in law.[4] Then payment rates are adjusted in subsequent years as actual expenditure growth exceeds or falls below these standards. Performance standards were first applied to physicians' services in 1990; fee updates based on physicians' performance in meeting these standards were first applied in 1992.

In the years since passage of OBRA89, annual growth in expenditures for physicians' services has slowed considerably relative to the historical trend. Between 1986 and 1991, expenditures grew at an annual rate of 10.5 percent, compared with inflation in the general economy of about 4 percent. By contrast, between 1991 and 1993, estimated expenditure growth slowed to an average rate of 3.8 percent.[5] Because performance standards were set with the expectation of higher growth, Medicare fee updates for 1994 and 1995 were much larger than had previously been anticipated.

The reasons for this slowdown in growth are unclear. Possible explanations include responses to the incentives created by the VPS and secular changes in the practice of medicine. The latter include slowed growth in technologies introduced during the mid-to late–1980s, such as cataract surgery and magnetic resonance imaging, and more efficient practice styles spilling over into Medicare as a result of the increasing percentage of physicians' other patients enrolled in managed care. Another explanation is that low volume growth in recent years merely reflects its inherent volatility. In fact, the trend probably reflects a combination of these factors.

Even at this rate, however, policy makers continue to be concerned about both the high level of spending and uncertain prospects about growth rates in the future. Physicians' services account for about 50 percent of spending under Medicare Part B and, in fiscal year 1994, amounted to almost $30 billion.[6]

Despite the moderating trend in physicians' services in recent years, growth in total Medicare expenditures continues to exceed growth in the GDP, raising questions about how much of the nation's income should be spent on health services. Moreover, Medicare expenditures as a whole are outpacing growth in private sector health spending (11.5 percent growth in Medicare versus 8.6 percent growth for private health insurance expenditures between 1992 and 1993).[7] * * *

As the VPS system has evolved, several other problems have emerged. First, despite recent high updates in Medicare fees, weaknesses in the design of the default formula will result in substantial reductions in the

4. In fact, the default formula has been used in most years.

5. General inflation during this period was about 3 percent annually.

6. Other services covered under Part B include outpatient hospital services, laboratory services, home health services, artificial devices, speech and physical therapy, and ambulance services.

7. Among the components of Medicare spending, inpatient hospital services and physicians' services account for nearly three-quarters of spending. Growth rates are much higher, however, for other types of services including home health and hospice services.

conversion factor over the next five years. Second, the existence of three performance standards is introducing serious distortions in the patterns of relative payment, the very problem the Medicare Fee Schedule was intended to correct. Although the Commission had recommended a single performance standard, OBRA89 created a system with two: one for surgical services and one for nonsurgical services. A third standard (primary care services) was added under OBRA93 in response to concerns that growth in volume for technical procedures in the nonsurgical service category was depressing payment levels for primary care. Even though this has resulted in larger fee updates for primary care services than under the two-standard system, surgical services have received even higher updates.

* * *

Beneficiary Liability

OBRA89 responded to beneficiary and physician frustration with MAAC limits by replacing them with straight percentage limits on balance billing. Phased in over a three-year period beginning in 1991, physicians may now charge beneficiaries no more than 115 percent of the fee schedule amount.[9] The legislation also set in place a process for monitoring trends in beneficiary liability and access to care. * * *

Since passage of OBRA89, the three indicators of changes in beneficiary liability—participation rates, assignment rates, and the level of balance billing—have all signaled improvement.[10] Participation rates (the percentage of physicians signing PAR agreements) have increased, rising from 70 percent in 1991 to 83 percent in 1993. Assignment rates (the percentage of allowed charges for which physicians accept the Medicare fee as payment in full) have gone up, rising from 85 percent in 1991 to 92 percent two years later. Balance billing has declined substantially as well: once amounting to 7 percent of allowed charges, balance bills now total less than 1.5 percent of allowed charges. * * *

The Commission has cautioned that reductions in Medicare payment rates, necessitated by efforts to reduce the federal deficit, must be balanced with consideration of their impact on access. Medicare payment rates are now 68 percent of those of private payers. This is slightly lower than the ratio in 1990; the ratio fell in the early 1990s due to Medicare payment reductions and rose more recently due to a combination of high Medicare updates and moderation of payment increases among private payers.

Larger differentials in payment between Medicare and private payers, coupled with discontent about Medicare's level of payment, could compromise access to care. Although the Commission has found no evidence that the current gap is causing an access barrier, it is possible that a substantially larger gap could affect physicians' willingness to care for Medicare patients.

9. Because nonparticipating physicians are paid 95 percent of the fee schedule amount, the effective charge limit is 109.25 percent.

10. Assignment and participation were both increasing prior to 1989 so it is difficult to know how much of the recent increase can be attributed to the legislation

NOTES AND QUESTIONS ON PHYSICIAN PAYMENT UNDER MEDICARE

1. *Payment Reform.* The reform legislation described by the PPRC (another arm of Congress that was merged with ProPAC in 1997 to become MedPAC) was OBRA '89 § 6102, which added § 1848 to the Social Security Act. For additional description and background, see, in addition to the PPRC's annual reports, H. Frech, ed., Regulating Doctors' Fees: Competition, Benefits, and Controls Under Medicare (American Enterprise Inst. 1991); Congressional Budget Office, Physician Payment Reform under Medicare (April 1990); Iglehart, The Struggle Over Physician–Payment Reform, 325 New Eng. J. Med. 823 (1991). As noted below, the 1997 BBA made significant, but not fundamental, changes in Medicare's methods of compensating physicians.

An additional feature of the 1989 reforms was a requirement for "global" surgical billing, under which surgeons bill a single fee for all their services associated with a single procedure, including preoperative and post-operative care, and are not paid for some additional services necessitated by complications. In addition, with respect to some surgical procedures (specifically, coronary artery by-pass grafts), HCFA has experimented with paying hospitals a single package price covering both the hospital's and the surgeon's services.

2. *The RBRVS.* The new Medicare fee schedule is based on a complex table of weights that purports to relate each medical service to every other (there about 5500 different codes) in terms of the actual resources employed in providing the service (hence the commonly used acronym RBRVS, for "resource-based" relative value scale). The fee schedule also incorporates adjustments for differences in costs among some 230 localities. One interesting aspect of the reform debate was the intraprofessional tensions that resulted from the goal of reducing surgeons' incomes while increasing the incomes of internists and primary care doctors.

As will be mentioned again in chapter 8(§A), relative value scales produced by organized medicine were attacked at one time under the antitrust laws because of their tendency to foster uniform cartel pricing. (It was only necessary to agree upon a single conversion factor to achieve effective price fixing.) Is it more appropriate for government to employ them? Might an authoritative RVS, coupled with restrictions on balance billing, facilitate the exercise of market power by buyers rather than by sellers? See generally McCormick & Burge, Diffusion of Medicare's RBRVS and Related Physician Payment Policies, Health Care Fin. Rev., Winter 1994, p. 159 (analyzing the extent to which private payers employ Medicare's RBRVS and fee schedule).

In accordance with 1994 instructions from Congress (mentioned by the PPRC), HCFA proposed in 1997 a new method for calculating the practice expense component of the RBRVS, a new formula that would have benefitted primary care physicians and reduced payments to specialists. In the Balanced Budget Act (BBA), however, Congress ordered HCFA to consult with physician organizations and to employ generally accepted accounting principles, actual practice expenses, and actual utilization data in developing its methodology, which was to be phased in over four years beginning in 1999. BBA § 4505. Again, the issue creates political divisions among the various medical specialties.

3. *Conversion Factor*. Once determined from the RVS, the relative value weight is converted into a dollar figure by using a "conversion factor." Congress required that the initial conversion factor be set in such a way as to be budget-neutral, in order to allay the medical profession's fear that its members would suffer a net loss under the new program. A substantial dispute arose when HCFA proposed a conversion factor reflecting the assumption that utilization would increase sharply under the fee schedule as physicians attempted to maintain their incomes by increasing volume. The medical profession was offended by HCFA's belief that physicians would prescribe services just to generate income. But one study has shown that utilization increased more for poorly compensated services. Trude & Colby, Monitoring the Impact of the Medicare Fee Schedule on Access to Care for Vulnerable Populations, 22 J. Health Pol., Pol'y & L. 49 (1997). Is this a surprising result, contrary to the assumption that supply curves slope upward to the right? Or would you have predicted that physicians would compensate for low fees by increasing volume (and possibly diluting the scope of the service)? For a legal challenge based on a claim that the assumption used in setting the low conversion factor had proved erroneous and seeking retroactive adjustment, see Painter v. Shalala, 97 F.3d 1351 (10th Cir.1996) (holding setting of conversion factor is not reviewable).

4. *Volume Performance Standards*. As noted by the PPRC, annual updates in the conversion factor are based on the "volume performance standard rate of increase" (VPS)—essentially a prospective estimate of how much Medicare spending on physician services should increase nationwide. This national approach was adopted in lieu of the Reagan administration's original proposal for local "expenditure targets." That approach would have set community targets and imposed automatic penalties, in the form of out-year reductions in the conversion factor used in the area, if they were not met. In effect, the Reagan plan would have made doctors in each area responsible for the costs they generate—just as they are in HMOs of the IPA variety. One object, which was not widely advertised, was to induce those physicians who did not want to be penalized for what some of their less responsible or less efficient colleagues were doing to opt out of the larger community of physicians into discrete HMOs or physician-sponsored networks, which would be paid on a different (capitation) basis. The implicit goal was to split the physician community into competing risk-bearing groups, thus creating desirable competition within the Medicare program. Note that leaving the standard national dilutes the incentive of physicians to cooperate locally, where progress is more likely to be made.

5. *The Balanced Budget Act and the Fee Schedule*. Problems encountered in administering the VPS led to a proposal to substitute a "sustainable growth rate" system tied to the growth of per-capita GDP rather than to medical inflation. See PPRC, 1997 Annual Report to Congress 249–55 (1997). This proposal dropped the pretense in the statutory criteria used in adopting a VPS that the goal in establishing an annual target was to estimate a reasonable level of spending that the medical profession should collectively achieve. Instead, it would set instead a highly, though not completely, arbitrary national ceiling on Medicare spending, with any overruns subject to recoupment (by modifying the national conversion factor) from the following year's payments to physicians. The 1997 BBA essentially adopted the PPRC proposal, eliminating the separate conversion factors for surgical, primary physician services, and other nonsurgical services. (A separate conversion factor is created for anesthesia services, however.) The new single conversion factor will be updated annually by a new formula incorporating both the Medical Economic Index (a measure of inflation) and a new factor, the Sustainable Growth Rate, which reflects growth in the overall economy and replaces the VPS.

6. *Balance Billing.* Balance billing is the provider practice of billing a patient for the amount by which the provider's charge exceeds what the Medicare program has determined to be allowable. Hospitals are not allowed to balance-bill Medicare beneficiaries except to the extent of deductibles and coinsurance expressly provided for. 42 U.S.C. § 1395cc(a)(1) (1994); 42 C.F.R. §§ 412.42, 413.35 (1996). Exceptions are made, however, for certain noncovered items and for luxury services whose costs exceed reasonable costs. Under the PPS, a patient may be charged for custodial care after an official determination that the patient no longer needs inpatient care (and a number of other requirements are satisfied, justifying charging the patient for an extended stay).

Medicare's Part B allows balance billing by physicians, but only to an increasingly limited extent. As to voluntarily "participating" physicians, it prohibits balance billing of beneficiaries (except for copayments). As to nonparticipating physicians, it sets a "limiting charge" (currently 115 percent of the maximum) on the amounts that beneficiaries can be required to pay over Medicare's allowed charge for the service. The restriction on nonparticipating physicians' freedom to balance-bill beneficiaries easily withstood a constitutional challenge in Garelick v. Sullivan, 987 F.2d 913 (2d Cir.1993), cert. denied, 510 U.S. 821 (1993) (rejecting anesthesiologists' claim of unconstitutional "taking" on ground they are not compelled to serve Medicare patients and must therefore accept any federal limits on what they can charge).

Medicare has developed several policies in recent years to encourage physicians to become participating providers, accepting "assignment" of the beneficiary's claim against Medicare and receiving payment directly from the government rather than from the patient. Participating providers are listed in a directory available to beneficiaries and receive expedited claims processing. From 1986 to 1995, the percentage of Medicare expenditures for physician services on assigned as opposed to unassigned claims increased from 60 percent to 96 percent. See Colby et al., Balance Billing

Under Medicare: Protecting Beneficiaries and Preserving Physician Participation, 20 J. Health Pol., Pol'y & L. 49 (1995).

Several states have enacted their own restrictions on providers' balance billing of Medicare beneficiaries. In Massachusetts Med. Soc'y v. Dukakis, 815 F.2d 790 (1st Cir. 1987), cert. denied, (484 U.S. 896 (1987)), the court held that Massachusetts's requirement that physicians foreswear balance billing (as a condition of state licensure) was not preempted by the federal Medicare Act and that Congress, in allowing physicians to balance-bill, had not intended to create a federal right to do so. See also Downhour v. Somani, 85 F.3d 261 (6th Cir.), cert. denied, 117 S.Ct. 389 (1996) (upholding Ohio law against balance billing).

The 1997 BBA § 4507(a)(1) resolved a legal issue that, while technically minor, was nevertheless of immense symbolic interest to some physicians and to many conservative critics of Medicare C whether a patient and a physician could, by contract, forgo Medicare financing for a particular transaction, thus escaping Medicare limits on clinical choices and fees. Litigation on this subject was dismissed for lack of ripeness in 1992 because HCFA had not unambiguously declared its opposition to such contracts. Stewart v. Sullivan, 816 F.Supp. 281 (D.N.J.1992); see McCormick, AMA Enters Doctor's Lawsuit to "Opt Out" of Medicare, Am. Med. News, July 27, 1992, at 6. HCFA then issued clear instructions prohibiting such contracts. See Effect of Beneficiary Agreements Not to Use Medicare Coverage, in HCFA, Medicare Claims Manual § 3044 (rev. June 1993); see generally Coleman & Shellow, Privacy and Autonomy in the Physician–Patient Relationship, 16 J. Leg. Med. 509 (1995). In the 1997 Medicare reforms, however, Congress allowed such private arrangements but only if the contract meets certain requirements and the physician agrees not to participate in the Medicare program for two years. Few believe more than a handful of physicians will utilize this opportunity to declare their independence from public financing.

7. *Effects.* How might the ability of beneficiaries to obtain care to which they are legally entitled be compromised by the Medicare fee schedule? Will the sheer number of Medicare beneficiaries and the dependence of physicians on Medicare for income be enough to prevent access from becoming a significant problem? How is the access problem of Medicare beneficiaries connected to what goes on in the private sector? The PPRC has reported that, while some vulnerable groups experience some difficulties, access remains generally good. PPRC, 1997 Annual Report, supra, at xl. See also Trude & Colby, supra.

NOTES AND QUESTIONS ON MEDICARE AS A PURCHASER OF OTHER SERVICES

1. Controlling its cost of hospitalization and physician services, although substantially more than half the battle in quantitative terms (hospital care absorbs around 60 cents of each Medicare dollar and physicians receive about 21 cents), is not all that Medicare has to worry about. Indeed, as

Medicare has implemented increasingly effective controls on what it pays for acute hospital care, its costs for other services have risen more rapidly:

> Among spending categories, * * * growth rates differ markedly. * * * Since 1991, annual Medicare hospital spending has increased at an average of 9.2 percent, while that for physicians' services has risen 6.0 percent, on average. By contrast, spending in other categories has grown more dramatically. For example, since 1985 outpatient, Part B home health, and laboratory care expenditures have all increased by more than 13 percent annually. Annual spending for skilled nursing facility care has grown, on average, about 33 percent, while Part A home health care costs have increased by roughly 23 percent, making these areas the focus of many recent proposals to reform Medicare.

PPRC, 1997 Annual Report, supra, at 11. Obviously, the shortening of hospital stays under the incentives introduced by the PPS increased reliance on other, post-acute care providers (also including hospices and rehabilitation hospitals). See also ProPAC 1997, at 103–20.

Substituting these other providers for hospitals may (or may not) be efficient. But even though removing cost reimbursement as an inducement to provide inpatient services undoubtedly produced some clear gains, it is unlikely that Medicare has found a way to ensure that only the trade-off between quality and cost dictates choices about the locus of care. Instead, providers are driven to some degree by relative profitability, which is a function of the different ways in which the various services are paid for. Again, Medicare's challenge is to design methods of payment that ensure appropriate utilization and quality at a reasonable cost—hardly an easy task. In the Balanced Budget Act of 1997, Congress made—or directed HCFA to make—revolutionary changes in Medicare's methods in paying for these services.

The potential for abuse of Medicare's current payment systems for post-acute institutional care and for outpatient services is enormous. The problems of fraud and abuse to be encountered in chapter 3(§D) will reveal some of the specific difficulties.

2. *Payment Methods.* The following list shows both (1) how Medicare paid for certain types of services other than in patient hospital care and physicians' services prior to implementation of the BBA and (2) how the BBA, usually in striking fashion, altered the payment method used:

Skilled nursing facility (SNF) (the services of which are covered by Medicare, up to 100 days per "spell of illness," only when incident to a covered hospital stay): (1) Part A, cost-based reimbursement; routine costs are subject to limits that vary for free-standing and hospital-based urban and rural facilities; allowable capital and ancillary costs are fully reimbursed. (2) Prospective payment for SNF services on a per diem basis will be phased in over four years beginning in 1998; the federal rate will cover a bundled set of all but physician and similar services and will be adjusted for case mix and geographic area. In 1997, ProPAC, although proposing that "a case-mix adjusted prospective payment system system for [SNFs] be implemented as soon as possible," observed that "a case-mix system that can account for differences in resource use on an admission basis has not yet been developed." Id. at 50–51. A special concern was ancillary services (e.g., occupational and speech therapy) provided in SNFs. Id. at 51.

Rehabilitation hospital or unit: (1) Part A, cost-based reimbursement; operating costs are subject to ceilings and incentive payments; allowable capital costs are fully reimbursed. (2) Prospective payment will begin in 2000; the unit of service for which payment will be made has yet to be determined as has the definition of "case mix groups."

Long-term care hospital: (1) (same as rehab hospitals). (2) The Secretary is to submit a proposal for prospective payment in 1999.

Home health agency: (1) Part A or B, cost-based reimbursement; limits for different types of visits; limits vary for free-standing and hospital-based urban and rural agencies. (2) Immediate reductions in cost limits in view of exploding cost and suspected abuses in the home health field, followed by a prospective payment system to be created and introduced by late 1999; service to become covered under Part B exclusively, opening the possibility that copayments will be introduced. A requirement that a home health agency post surety bond of $50,000 or 15% of its Medicare revenues, whichever is greater, has been controversial. Small agencies claim they will be put out of business because, in addition to being underpaid for the services they provide, they lack hard assets to pledge as collateral for the bond; HCFA's position is that the bond is helpful in keeping "fly–by–night providers" out of fraud–prone industry.

Hospice: (1) Part A, per diem payments; separate rates for routine home care, continuous home care, inpatient respite care, and general inpatient care. (2) Various minor changes.

Hospital, outpatient: (1) Part B, cost-or charge-based for some services; fee schedule for others. (2) A new prospective payment system for newly classified services—a fee schedule for ambulatory patient groups—is to be developed by the Secretary, beginning in 1999; no judicial review will be permitted of the classifications, relative payment weights, wage adjustments, conversion factors, etc. Some further background on the challenges facing Medicare in compensating providers of these services is provided in ProPAC 1997, at 39–40:

> HCFA estimates that about 70 percent of [payments for ambulatory services other than physician services] were made to hospitals for services provided in outpatient departments.
>
> Payment for hospital outpatient services is extremely fragmented. While some services are paid using prospective rates, most are paid on the basis of costs or charges, or a blend of costs or charges, or a blend of costs or charges and prospective rates. When payments are based on costs or charges, there is little financial incentive to provide care in the most efficient fashion, since lower costs or charges result in correspondingly lower payments. In addition, the multiple payment methods across services create conflicting financial incentives and undermine the effectiveness of any one set of incentives. At the same time, the existence of multiple

ambulatory settings complicates the issue of outpatient payment reform. Medicare's payment for a given service can vary substantially across these different providers. This may result in various payment amounts for the same service depending on where it was provided, and also may inappropriately affect the choice of treatment site.

Two additional problems arise with respect to Medicare's payment for hospital outpatient services. First, unlike in other settings where beneficiary cost sharing is 20 percent of the total payment, beneficiary liability for services provided in the hospital outpatient department is set at 20 percent of charges. Because charges are much higher than payments, beneficiaries using hospital outpatient services are responsible for significantly more than 20 percent of the total payment. * * *

Second, a flaw in Medicare' payment method for most hospital outpatient surgeries, radiology procedures, and selected diagnostic services systematically pays hospitals more than the Congress intended. Medicare's share of payment for these services is supposed to be the total amount minus the beneficiary copayment. For facilities paid a blend of cost or charges and prospective rates, however, program payments are not reduced by the entire copayment, because the payment formula written in statute was incorrectly specified.

The BBA attempts to address the problems noted.

Freestanding clinical diagnostic laboratories (as opposed to providers' own in-house labs serving their own inpatients). (1) Reimbursed on a fee-for-service basis under Part B according to areawide fee schedules; each fee schedule was originally set at 60 percent of the prevailing charge levels in each area in 1984, adjusted annually for inflation, and subject to a national ceiling based on the median of all the fee schedules for each particular test. (2) The Institute of Medicine is to study the method of paying labs, leading to recommendations for further legislation.

Reinventing Medicare

Lynn Etheredge, Reengineering Medicare: From Bill–Paying Insurer to Accountable Purchaser

Health Insurance Reform Project, George Washington University (June 1995)

At the time of its enactment 30 years ago, Medicare was patterned on the health insurance models widely used by private employers and insurers for the under–65 population. In this model, the primary administrative function of insurance companies and of the Medicare program was simply to pay bills. Today, Medicare remains essentially a bill-paying insurance program, with the addition of national formulas for hospital and physician payment rates.

In recent years, the private sector has moved beyond this traditional insurance model. Private-sector payers are no longer simply paying bills but are using a variety of evolving *purchasing* techniques, in a competitive marketplace, to restrain costs and improve quality and service. Among these purchasing strategies are many forms of selective, competitive contracting; capitation and risk-sharing arrangements; provider performance standards, with incentives, penalties, and continuous quality improvement goals; management of high-cost cases; centers of excellence for transplants, heart surgery, cancer care, and other treatment; prevention and chronic disease management initiatives; consumer information and incentives; specialized contracting for pharmaceutical benefits, substance abuse, mental health, and other services; and specialized claims-auditing firms to deal with fraud. Individuals with benefits offered by large employers—including, through the Federal Employees Health Benefits Program (FEHBP), the nation's political leaders and federal workers—are usually able to make choices among a number of health plans on the basis of provider networks, cost, quality, service performance, and other features.

In this new purchasing environment, private-sector employers and consumers are increasingly able to make informed choices—to hold providers (and the plans that contract with them) *accountable*—through the use of tools such athe National Committee on Quality Assurance's (NCQA's) "report cards," which are based on the Health Plan Empoyer Data and Information Set (HEDIS), and other quality measures, such as health outcomes. The HEDIS data set includes more than 60 quality, service access, patient satisfaction, outcomes, and other performance measures * * *.

In the current political climate, there is great interest in the federal government's making available to the Medicare population a broader choice of competing private health plans that use such purchasing technologies. Today, [HMOs] and other private plans enroll only about 10% of the Medicare population. Among the many measures that could open up more plan options are [a] "managed competition" approach [modeled on the FEHBP] that would allow Medicare beneficiaries to make informed choices among a wide range of HMO, preferred provider organization (PPO), Medicare Select, medigap, and other plans during an annual open season. * * * Much of the attention in Congress now centers on the policy questions involved in structuring new options for Medicare enrollees.

As a complete reform strategy, such options would fall short. They do not reform the basic Medicare program. Over 90% of Medicare's spending is through the fee-for-service model. As of January 1, 1995, 19 states had no Medicare HMO enrollees and 32 states had 1% or fewer of their Medicare-eligible populations enrolled in HMOs. * * * Even with an FEHBP-type arrangement and optimistic growth assumptions about private plan enrollments, many factors make it likely that most Medicare eligibles in most states will still be in the program for the rest of the decade and beyond. In its traditional bill-paying mode, the Medicare program has very few tools for dealing with the volume, intensity, and quality issues that are its major cost-drivers. Thus, devising a strategy for fundamental reform of the basic Medicare program—"reengineering" Medicare—is essential not only to deal with budget issues but also to achieve improvements for the 37 million people who depend on the program.

What should be done about the basic Medicare program? What would be in the best interest of its 37 million elderly and disabled enrollees?

This paper considers the question of whether Congress should give Medicare the same types of authorities that are available to its private-sector competitors—particularly authorities to use new purchasing techniques—and require performance accountabilities for their use * * *. If this approach were adopted, Medicare-eligible individuals would be able to enroll either in a Medicare program that is working hard to provide the best economy, quality, and services or in competing private-sector health plans that are paid equivalent (risk-adjusted) capitation amounts. One might expect that, over the long term, both taxpayers and Medicare-eligible persons would benefit by such competition.

At the most general level, reforming the Medicare program in this way would start with three fundamental changes:

- *A revised mission philosophy that emphasizes Medicare as a health plan.* Most importantly, Medicare would need to become accountable, not just for insurance to pay bills and protect financial assets, but for improving the health of its enrollees, by providing preventive health measures and quality medical care.
- *The adoption of "report cards" that assess Medicare's performance on the basis of cost, quality, outcomes, and service so that it can be held* accountable *by enrollees and policymakers.* These measures * * * should also apply to competing private health plans. * * *
- *Medicare should have new authorities to purchase health care on the basis of explicit quality and other criteria and competitive performance.* Within the many statutory constraints Medicare has to operate under as a government program, it has generally been run effectively, efficiently, and with continuing improvement and innovation. Given its constraints, Medicare is now about as good a program as it can be. But, in nearly every area—such as three-year-long rule-making processes, volume increases and quality assurance issues, fraud and abuse, and rapidly rising budget costs—it is clear that Medicare cannot deal as effectively as it needs to with the complexity and pace of change in today's health system, nor can it hold physicians, hospitals, and other providers accountable for improving their performance. To improve Medicare's performance, Congress needs to provide authority to move beyond the limits of regulatory rule-making and price-setting so that Medicare can adopt the same types of successful purchasing techniques pioneered by private-sector payers. Such evolution could build incrementally through many [HCFA] initiatives, but, if fully reengineered, the Medicare program would be quite different a decade hence. Such changes will require a new bipartisan political consensus.

[In discussing "the challenge of Medicare management," the author observes the sheer magnitude of the program—more revenue than General Motors—and the huge regional variability in the way Medicare beneficiaries use services—twice as many hospital days per 1000 (3455) in the northeast as in the west, six times as much use of nursing homes in Minnesota as in Maine, and seventeen times more home health visits in Mississippi than in Hawaii. He also notes dramatic increases and declines in hospitalizations in different DRGs as a way of exploding the "misperception" or "myth of uniformity, predictability, and gradual change."]

If Medicare were to be operated in a more business-like way, what important changes should Congress consider making in the Medicare program's authorities? Many government-sponsored activities do have flexibility similar to that found in private-sector businesses; these activities include the Tennessee Valley Authority and other power marketing authorities, the Government National Mortgage Association, and the Federal Reserve Board. But granting Medicare, with $175 billion in purchasing power and 37 million enrollees, a freer rein will need to be done carefully and watched vigilantly.

In general terms, *Medicare needs the authority to select providers based on quantifiable measures of quality, outcomes, and service and to use competitive purchasing.* The heart of a private-sector plan's ability to improve quality and assure accountability is its capacity to decline to do business with poor performers and to move business toward better performers. In contrast, Medicare is the prime remaining example of the traditional insurance "any willing provider" philosophy. To be certified as a Medicare provider usually requires little more than state licensure or accreditation by certifying organizations that are provider-dominated. Congress has created a virtual entitlement for health care providers to participate in Medicare. Competitive procurement is a standard business method for assuring good quality, cost, and service, and it should also be available for Medicare administrators.

Among the areas for possible use of such authorities are:

- *Competitive purchasing of standardized services and supplies*, including durable medical equipment, laboratory testing, radiology, and outpatient surgery
- *Establishment of explicit quality and service performance standards and refusal to do business with providers that do not measure up.* For the welfare of its beneficiaries, Medicare needs to move beyond the minimal participation requirements that are now set in legislation. * * *
- *Development and use of centers of excellence and specialized services contracting.* Medicare now uses such concepts in its coverage for transplant services; private-sector plans use selective contracting even more widely for many forms of surgery, cancer care, mental health and so forth. Major expansions may be possible to develop disease management and preventive services for patients with chronic or high-expense illnesses and for disabled enrollees. Intelligent purchasing by Medicare could call forth better quality, cost, and service competition among providers. To preserve Medicare's role in

assuring a broad choice of providers, Medicare enrollees might still be able to go to non-preferred providers, but with higher copayment rates.

- *Use of case management for high-cost patients.* Most private-sector health plans have the flexibility to work with high-cost patients to develop service packages, such as home care, that can better meet their needs. The Medicare statute does not permit such flexibility * * *.
- *Elimination of notice of proposed rule-making process for purchasing.* Like Gulliver tethered by many bonds, the Medicare program's effective use of its purchasing power is held back by numerous technical constraints, some of which are appropriate to a rule-making administrative style but not to a business-type operation. Most important of these is the Notice of Proposed Rule Making requirements that now involve at least a three-year process for major Medicare policy initiatives or changes. Such rule-making is frequently, in essence, simply a statement of contractual terms, that is, what Medicare will and will not pay for, under what terms, and in what circumstances. A private business that had to go through a three-year process any time it wanted to write or revise a contract with its suppliers would probably be in the same financial predicament as the Medicare program.
- *Authorization for Medicare simply to drop providers in the best interests of the program to deal with fraud and abuse.* In recent testimony, a General Accounting Office (GAO) official noted that the Medicare program is "overwhelmed" by fraud and abuse and that it is a "particularly rich environment for profiteers." Among Medicare's many problems are the difficulties of kicking providers out of the program and the limited resources made available by the Department of Justice. A recent GAO study based on studies of claims denial rates for 74 services across 6 carriers noted that one-half of denied claims were submitted by between 2% and 11% of providers. Acting as a business-type purchaser, Medicare would have authority to simply stop doing business with any supplier, at its discretion. * * *
- *Authorization for Medicare to organize and contract for quality assurance at its discretion.* Since 1965, the major initiative to improve Medicare quality has been enactment of the PRO system. It is an expensive program (costing some $325 million in 1994), deals almost exclusively with inpatient hospital care, and has been of questioned effectiveness. The 53 PROs are provider-dominated organizations. Most are physician-sponsored, for example, by local medical societies, and typically have a board of directors composed primarily of physicians and other provider representatives. Medicare Part B services are largely subject to quality review by the claims-paying carriers. As noted in an Institute of Medicine report on Medicare quality improvement, the implementation of a new health-

oriented mission for the Medicare program will require far-reaching administrative, contractual, and other changes that include reconsideration of PRO, carrier, and HCFA roles. Would a private-sector purchaser, intent on improving quality of care, want to be constrained to contracting with a medical society or provider-dominated organization?

- *Publicity about data on quality and service.* With the advent of HEDIS and buyers insisting on accountability, provider secrecy about quality problems is being replaced by publicized reporting in the private sector. Statutory change should also allow this approach to be adopted by the Medicare program. Such publicity about where physicians and hospitals stand compared to professional benchmarks and guidelines can be important acts in themselves to encourage better patterns of care and service.
- *Improvement of customer service.* * * * Customer service is an area in which Medicare is at a competitive disadvantage vis-á-vis competing private health plans.
- *Enactment of special authorities for Medicare in the hiring, promotion, and compensation of employees.* * * * Today, Medicare is bound by government-wide civil service procedures, promotion, firing, compensation levels, and personnel ceilings. In business-type operations, such as the Federal Reserve Board, Congress has been willing to make exceptions so that federal activities can be carried out with the required professional expertise. In particular, the Medicare program may need such flexibility if it is to compete with private-sector plans.

Certainly some health care providers—and competing health plans—will question the wisdom of such new Medicare authorities. But why would beneficiaries and taxpayers want to keep Medicare from being as good a program as it can be? If Medicare is expected to compete with private plans for enrollees, why should it not have comparable purchasing flexibility?

* * *

Given new accountabilities, new management authority to purchase health care, and a strategic plan for its future, can Medicare compete successfully with private health plans for the benefit of the elderly and disabled? Why not just leave Medicare alone as a traditional bill-payer and hope that it will wither away as beneficiaries choose better-managed private health plans? There will be those who believe that privately managed health care plans will out-perform any new-model, government-run Medicare program in head-to-head competition and that trying to manage Medicare as a competitive health program is hopeless or unwise.

Nevertheless, * * * it would be a high-stakes risk to ignore upgrading Medicare and place all of the nation's Medicare budgetary bets on presumptions about the success of private-sector plans that may prove to be wishful thinking. In addition, the federal government has a number of strengths to build on in trying to make Medicare a better program. Among these strengths are:

- *Good track record.* It is fashionable to disparage government competence, but, compared to much of the private insurance industry, the Medicare program has an excellent track record for innovation and efficiency, within its statutory constraints. Through the use of DRGs and RBRVS, Medicare has led private payers in reducing payments for overpriced procedures and using purchasing power to restrain inflation and rationalize payment rates. Medicare has also led in investing in medical efficacy studies and protocol development to improve clinical practices reflecting outcomes research (through the Agency for Health Care Policy and Research); publicizing information on comparative provider quality, for example, hospital mortality rates and nursing home reviews; setting up standardized data systems; establishing electronic submission of claims; and overall administrative efficiency. * * * Among recent innovative steps are beneficiary surveys, a consumer information strategy (immunizations, mammography), a coronary bypass surgery demonstration with bundled payment rates, Medicare Select demonstrations, and performance contracts with PROs. With a new statutory mandate and authorities, Medicare may also excel in new competition vis-á-vis private health insurance plans.

- *Flexible administrative structure.* Medicare is normally thought of as a government-run program, but, in fact, no federal employees actually pay claims. Federal employees oversee a system of some 74 private contractors (called intermediaries and carriers—mostly Blue Cross/Blue Shield plans or commercial insurers) that actually run the program on a day-to-day basis. * * * Medicare might be able to cross-fertilize between HCFA's rule-making and bill-paying culture and the private payers' purchasing culture to produce hybrid plans through joint efforts with its primary contractors.

- *Public trust and freedom of choice.* While government, in general, may be viewed with distrust and suspicion by many voters, the Medicare and Social Security programs retain strong senior citizen support. * * *

- *Enormous purchasing power.* * * * The price discounts Medicare has been able to achieve though DRGs and RBVS alone—although now undercut by HMOs in some markets—and its high assignment rate (over 96%) suggest a reasonable amount of optimism should be in order about the success of future purchasing strategies. If managed purposively, Medicare should be able to strike economic terms that are at least as favorable as its competing health insurance plans, as well as use its purchasing discretion for upgrading quality and service standards.

- *Data and research capacity.* Finally, Medicare has an unsurpassed data system, including claims records on medical services use by some 37 million enrollees and a potential for service-profiling and quality-auditing most of the nation's health care providers. * * *

NOTES AND QUESTIONS ON BRINGING MANAGED CARE TO MEDICARE

1. *Would Privatization Make Sense?* The low administrative costs of the Medicare program have often been admired and, indeed, have been touted as evidence in favor of establishing a single-payer system for all Americans. Yet Medicare has also been found to harbor a disturbing amount of waste, error, fraud, and abuse. See Pear, Audit of Medicare Finds $23 Billion in Overpayments, N.Y. Times, July 17, 1997, p.1 (about one Medicare dollar in seven found to be misspent); Editorial, N.Y. Times, Aug. 1, 1997, p. 18 ("recent reports suggest that Medicare's administrative costs are shockingly low, below 2 percent of costs, because Medicare is shockingly unsupervised"). The problem of fraud and abuse will be addressed in chapter 3(§D), where it may appear that the federal government has rather liberally defined as fraud any effort to take advantage of a poorly administered program. Does reading Etheredge suggest some arguments for privatizing the Medicare program? How does he suggest Medicare ought to deal with fraud and abuse—besides criminalizing it? For another thoughtful article on the same theme as Etheredge's, see Fox, Applying Managed Care Techniques in Traditional Medicare, Health Affs., Sept.-Oct. 1997, p. 44.

Etheredge observes that Medicare has made some progress in enrolling beneficiaries at public expense in prepaid (capitated) private health plans. What are the possible advantages of shifting to capitation as the method of purchasing health services for federal beneficiaries? Compare the probable effectiveness of managed care plans and traditional Medicare (perhaps as modified along the lines suggested by Etheredge) in controlling costs in the following categories: hospital admissions; hospital resources used per admission; hospital price per unit of resources used; the quantity of physicians' services; physicians' fees or other remuneration; the purchasing of post-acute services, outpatient surgery, clinical laboratory services, and so forth. Would private plans enjoy the same comparative advantages over any other single-payer plan that might be devised? What if Medicare were itself "capitated" by giving it a fixed budget to work with in caring for the beneficiaries for which it was responsible?

What cost disadvantages do managed care plans face? One potentially important one is the cost of marketing, which might be very great where many plans are dealing, as in the case of Medicare, with individuals rather than with employers screening options for large numbers of employees. The Federal Employees Health Benefits Plan (FEHBP), however, facilitates the low-cost marketing of competing plans to federal employees by distributing informative brochures meeting program specifications. Unexplored possibilities may also exist for efficient group purchasing by Medicare beneficiaries, perhaps through retirement communities or through retiree health plans maintained by former employers.

Consider whether the Medicare program should be fully "voucherized"—that is, cashed out so that beneficiaries can convert the actuarial value of their public coverage into private coverage. What are the arguments against thus abandoning the program's entitlement character?

2. *Background.* The following excerpt recounts the background and extent of Medicare's involvement with managed care as of the mid–1990s:

> Since the early 1970s the federal government has supported the voluntary enrollment of Medicare beneficiaries in managed care programs through a number of demonstration projects. The 1982 Tax Equity and Financial Responsibility Act, which became operational in 1985, gave Medicare beneficiaries the option to enroll in federally-qualified [HMOs] and competitive medical plans, all of which offer Medicare-covered benefits and the majority of which also offer coverage of cost sharing and supplemental services that replace Medigap policies. Beneficiaries may choose to enroll in an HMO when they become eligible for Medicare or at other times that Medicare HMOs offer open enrollment. Plans must have at least one 30–day open season each year and may offer additional open enrollment periods. Furthermore, they must allow enrollment at other times to beneficiaries who have been enrolled because of contract termination or nonrenewal by another managed care plan. Medicare beneficiaries can disenroll from their plans at the end of any month.
>
> The [HCFA's] managed care program has different types of contracts. Until recently, the only private health plans (risk contracts or risk plans) available to Medicare beneficiaries were HMOs, under which plans receive capitated payments for the beneficiaries whom they enroll. In general enrollees who select a risk plan are required to use the plan's network of providers and to agree to obtain all covered services through the plan, except in emergencies.
>
> Capitation payments to the plans are based on an estimate of local fee-for-service costs and are established for each county at 95 percent of the adjusted average per capita cost (AAPCC) for Medicare fee-for-service beneficiaries. HCFA adjusts the AAPCC for enrollees' demographic characteristics such as age, sex, Medicaid eligibility, and residence in an institution such as a nursing home. The "risk adjustment" attempts to prevent HMOs from benefitting from favorable selection of health risk, which occurs when HMOs enroll beneficiaries who are healthier (and therefore less costly to care for) than those in the fee-for-service sector. In 1995 AAPCC monthly rates [by county] ranged from a low of $177.32 to a high of $678.90.
>
> Under current law risk contract HMOs can retain profits up to the level earned on non-Medicare business. Profits that exceed this amount must be returned to enrollees either in out-of-payment reductions or enhanced benefits. On the basis of guidelines issued in October 1995, selected risk contracts will now be able to include a point-of-service option, upon HCFA's approval, which will allow beneficiaries to use providers outside a plan's network. HCFA expects that the point-of-service benefit may encourage more beneficiaries to join managed care plans.

Plans also can enter into cost contracts under which they are paid on a fee-for-service basis for the reasonable costs of services provided to their enrolled Medicare beneficiaries. Medicare beneficiaries in cost contract HMOs may seek care outside of the HMO at Medicare's expense—a benefit that is not available under risk contracts.

Medicare SELECT, another plan option, offers a network-based supplemental insurance (Medigap) policy that provides coverage for Medicare cost sharing. Medicare SELECT was created as a demonstration project in 1990 to offer beneficiaries in up to 15 states a new Medigap insurance option. In 1995 it was authorized to expand to all states. It could be made permanent in 1998.

Under its demonstration authority, HCFA also has operated a number of social HMO (SHMO) pilot projects with the purpose of providing a broad spectrum of acute-and long-term-care services to the frail elderly under a managed care system. In these types of projects HMOs receive higher reimbursements in exchange for providing home-based custodial care. The SHMO demonstrations also receive Medicaid funding.

* * *

In 1995 HCFA announced the Medicare Choices demonstration project, which would allow non-HMO managed care plans such as provider networks and POS plans to enroll Medicare patients for the first time, using a variety of payment mechanisms. The project was intended to test beneficiaries' responses to a range of health care delivery system options and to evaluate the suitability of those options for Medicare. The request for proposals explicitly encouraged a range of organizations, in addition to traditional HMOs, to submit applications, and it solicited applications from organizations in markets where Medicare managed care participation was relatively low. * * *

Although there is general agreement on the need to reduce Medicare spending and even on the potential merit and value of providing Medicare beneficiaries with the same array of health plan options available to the population under age 65, questions continue to be raised about the scope and pace of change being proposed and whether the necessary infrastructure for providing information, protections, and accountability are in place to enable Medicare beneficiaries to move safely and responsibly into what is for the vast majority of them a new frontier of health care delivery for this population: managed care. Although managed care has become the norm for the employed population, for most elderly individuals it represents uncharted waters, even with today's dramatic growth in the level of Medicare HMO enrollment.

Institute of Medicine, Improving the Medicare Market 13–15, 22–23 (1996).

3. *Paying Health Plans on the Basis of AAPCC.* Note the method of calculating the federal payment to risk-bearing managed care plans and the problems it is intended to solve. Unfortunately, the methodology for calculating payment rates using the AAPCC is highly imperfect. Moreover, the rationale for requiring plans to discount the AAPCC by 5 percent was unclear. ProPAC explained some of the problems with the AAPCC approach as follows:

There are two fundamental problems with Medicare's risk contracting program payment policies. First, the capitation payments are not adequately adjusted to account for differences in the expected costliness of enrollees in risk plans. In addition, the payment amounts reflect fee-for-service program spending at the county level. This approach has led to a number of problems with the payment rates, among them volatility and possible bias in the capitation amounts.

Medicare risk plans have attracted enrollees who are healthier, on average, than those in the fee-for-service option. This phenomenon is called favorable risk selection. The risk adjustment to the capitation amounts does not adequately account for these differences. Thus, Medicare outlays for beneficiaries who join risk plans are higher than they would have been if the enrollees had not joined such plans. It is estimated that favorable risk selection to plans and inadequate risk adjustment to payments together have increased Medicare spending for 5 percent to 7 percent for each beneficiary currently enrolled in a risk plan.

Medicare's capitation rates reflect variation in fee-for-service prices and practice patterns. Expensive providers, high utilization rates, or both have driven up fee-for-service spending in some areas. In these markets, plans may have considerable opportunities to furnish care more efficiently than under fee-for-service arrangements. For example, plans often can contract selectively with lower-priced or more efficient providers. Physicians, hospitals, and others may be willing to accept discounted payment rates in areas with many providers. Plans can sometimes shift patients from more expensive settings to less costly ones. But because Medicare capitation payments are tied to fee-for-service spending, Medicare has limited ability to share in these savings. Instead, plans convert most of the savings into extra benefits for their enrollees.

By contrast, capitation rates based on fee-for-service spending sometimes are not high enough to cover the service cost plus administration and profit requirements of the HMO. This is most likely to occur in the predominantly rural counties that have the lowest capitation rates. The rates may be low because of efficient patterns of care or inadequate access to care. In these counties, plans have fewer opportunities to reduce health care spending.

But these are not the only problems resulting from basing capitation rates on fee-for-service spending. Another is that, in some areas, changes in the amount of the capitation payments are volatile from year to year. This is the case particularly in counties with few Medicare beneficiaries. Additionally, base payment rates may be too high in areas where plans enjoy favorable selection. With less costly beneficiaries in risk plans, the payment rates there will reflect the higher-than-average spending for Medicare beneficiaries remaining in the fee-for-service option.

ProPAC, Report and Recommendations to the Congress 66–67, reprinted in Medicare & Medicaid Guide (CCH) No. 946 (March 1997). See also Rossiter et al., Strengths and Weaknesses of the AAPCC, in H. Luft, ed., HMOs and the Elderly (1994).

In order to strengthen the Medicare risk contracting program, ProPAC recommended a number of specific reforms. See id. at 67–71. A high priority, and a difficult technical challenge, was inventing better risk-adjusters—factors that explain more of the variation in spending on different populations and permit finer tuning of payments to health plans. One idea was to introduce prior use of services, prior diagnoses, and other health status indicators as factors supplementing demographic data (e.g., age and sex). It was also proposed that, in calculating local AAPCCs, Medicare costs be calculated after excluding special allowances paid to hospitals engaged in graduate medical training and in treating a "disproportionate share" of low-income and uninsured persons. Further, ProPAC proposed that differences between counties should be narrowed by establishing ceilings and floors and that year-to-year variations in local Medicare costs should be eliminated as contributors to fluctuations in AAPCCs by going to a national annual "update" formula keyed to general inflation. ProPAC also suggested "exploring alternative methods for setting capitation rates, such as competitive bidding and negotiation."

4. *Profits?* Is it risky for the government to allow private health plans, paid prospectively to care for seniors, to earn a profit from economizing on their care? As noted in the IOM report, there is a provision for limiting profits, which was described by ProPAC as follows:

> Medicare * * * requires each plan to submit what it calls an adjusted community rate (ACR) proposal to calculate how much plan payments will exceed projected costs. The annual proposal documents a plan's expected costs for Medicare-covered benefits. These costs are estimated from the spending experience of the plan's commercial (non-Medicare and non-Medicaid) enrollees, adjusted for higher expected use by Medicare beneficiaries. A plan includes in these calculations its administration and profit requirements, which are also based on its commercial experience.
>
> If a plan's expected payments [under the AAPCC] exceed its projected costs, the difference must be returned to Medicare, credited to future years, or used to provide additional benefits to enrollees. Most plans choose to offer the additional benefits in the form of more services, lower cost sharing, or coverage for out-of-network providers. To further attract Medicare enrollees, plans may include even more benefits than required to make up the difference between [AAPCC] payment and expected costs. Though plans can charge a premium for this coverage, many choose to waive some or part of this amount. Greater benefits and lower out-of-pocket spending generally make joining a risk plan an attractive option for beneficiaries.

ProPAC, Report and Recommendations, supra, at 66. Note how managed care plans, despite their limitations on choice of provider, can make themselves more attractive to Medicare beneficiaries than Medicare itself, which still offers relatively unconstrained fee-for-service medicine. Is it the case that the ability of managed care plans to compete effectively with Medicare proves that they are more efficient than the federal program? Or is it more complicated than that?

5. *Quality*. Whether managed-care plans are likely to offer good-quality care or to sacrifice quality in the name of profits is a natural concern, and researchers have identified some problems. See, e.g., Oberlander, Managed Care and Medicare Reform, 22 J. Health Pol., Pol'y & L. 595 (1997) (questioning, among other things, the ability of HMOs to care adequately for the chronically ill); Ware et al., Differences in Four–Year Health Outcomes for Elderly and Poor, Chronically Ill Patients Treated in HMO and Fee-for-service Systems, 276 J.A.M.A. 1039 (1996); Clement et al., Outcomes and Access of Elderly Patients Enrolled in Managed Care, 271 New Eng. J. Med. 1487 (1994); Retchin et al., Care of Patients Hospitalized with Strokes under the Medicare Risk Program, in H. Luft, ed., HMOs and the Elderly (1994).

NOTES ON ADVERSE SELECTION (RISK SELECTION)

1. *In General*. Adverse selection (together with its reciprocal, risk selection) is potentially the Achilles heel of a health policy relying on consumer choice to stimulate efficiency and needed reform in health care. Although the context in which adverse selection and risk selection are encountered here is Medicare reform, the theoretical problem they present was mentioned in the discussion of health economics in § B of this chapter and exists with any market-oriented reform strategy in health care. Thus, the selection possibilities that plague all insurance schemes were a principal concern underlying reform proposals based on the notion of "managed competition" that were described in chapter 1(§C). Nevertheless, even though adverse selection and risk selection are ubiquitous theoretical problems in health care markets, they are also intensely practical problems that may be amenable to practical solutions. An appreciation of the challenge they present can help the student better understand not only certain behavior of competing health plans and their customers but also important aspects of health policy debates. See generally Newhouse et al., Risk Adjustment and Medicare: Taking a Closer Look, Health Affs., Sept.-Oct. 1997, p. 26; Gauthier et al., Risk Selection in the Health Care Market: A Workshop Overview, 32 Inquiry 14 (1995), and three accompanying articles. See also Cutler & Zeckhauser, Adverse Selection in Health Insurance (NBER Working Paper 6107, 1997) (reporting real-world experiences with adverse selection and suggesting possible responses by employers in pricing coverage to individuals).

Adverse selection occurs in a multiple-choice system both because insurers seek to attract only good risks (risk selection) and because consumers use their inevitably superior knowledge of their own preferences and probable prospective needs to obtain insurance bargains (causing plans to experience adverse selection). In addition to creating artificial market segmentation and frequent plan switching, the parties' efforts to "game" the system create a general tendency for the better risks to isolate themselves in limited-coverage (low-option) plans and for high utilizers to congregate in more comprehensive (high-option) ones. Theoreticians suggest that this tendency creates a vicious cycle of price adjustments and responses that can destroy the market for insurance. See, e.g., Newhouse, Is Competition the Answer?, 1 J. Health Econ. 109 (1982). Although each health plan will want to avoid being selected against, there is only so much it can do, especially since other plans will likewise be seeking to avoid bad risks and to accept only good ones.

Risk selection is apt to be a factor in competition between HMOs and traditional carriers. Depending upon its character and the available alternatives, an HMO might be viewed as either a high-or a low-option plan, repelling or attracting healthier persons. Group-model and staff-model plans may tend to attract low-utilizers, however, because of their limitations on choice and their reputations for economizing. IPAs, on the other hand, may be prone to attracting poorer risks because patients can enroll without changing doctors. See generally Wilensky & Rossiter, Patient Self–Selection in HMOs, Health Affs., Spring 1986, at 66 (citing other studies). An especially troubling possibility is the ability of capitated providers to discourage the continued enrollment of persons who have contracted a disease that is costly to treat—e.g., AIDS or some forms of cancer. (Economist Harold Luft has compared the situation to the game of Hearts, in which one seeks to dump the Queen of Spades on an opponent.)

In addition to rendering the market for health coverage potentially unstable, adverse selection can also create specific problems for employers in situations where employees are offered a choice of plans. Thus, an employer may find that, as poor risks become concentrated in a high-option plan, the premium needed to maintain their coverage rises. Even if the employer is not bound to make equal contributions to alternative plans, it may be contractually or politically difficult to reallocate contributions, reducing those on behalf of healthier employees who have opted for an HMO or low-option insurance. The threat of adverse selection and the problems it creates in compensation arrangements may thus discourage employers, private or public, from offering a meaningful range of alternatives to their employees.

2. *Medicare's Experience*. Medicare, which is committed to funding benefits and not merely to making a dollar contribution on each beneficiary's behalf, faces essentially the same problem as the aforementioned private employer. The problem exists precisely to the extent that the AAPCC calculation does not accurately predict future utilization and therefore results in overpaying an HMO for caring for a population of low utilizers. While Medicare must still cover the full costs of caring for the sicker-than-average population left behind, other beneficiaries may receive from the HMO, as an inducement to enroll, extra services that Medicare, as such, does not ordinarily cover. The net result can be higher total Medicare costs. ProPAC suggested that this theoretical danger has been realized in practice and has not been fully offset by the 5 percent discount. See also R. Brown et al., Does Managed Care Work for Medicare? An Evaluation of the Medicare Risk Program for HMOs (Mathematica Policy Research, Inc., 1993); J. Buchanan et al., Cost and Use of Capitated Medical Services: Evaluation of the Program for Prepaid Managed Health Care (RAND 1992).

The IOM report suggests why Medicare confronts a particularly serious problem of adverse selection.

> The problem of risk selection is greater under Medicare both because beneficiaries enroll as individuals and because variability in health care expenditures among elderly and disabled enrollees is far greater than among the general population. In addition, opportunities for biased selection are shaped by the rules and practices of the present market. For example, the current ability of Medicare beneficiaries to change health plans every month, unlike the typical annual open enrollment seasons for employees, enhances the opportunities for biased selection, as does the ability of an HMO to decide whether or not to enter the Medicare market and the type of contract options it will make available to beneficiaries.

IOM, supra, at 26–27.

It is notable that, even recognizing this danger in the early 1980s, HCFA still proceeded to implement the HMO option, believing that the benefits of stimulating competition would eventually outweigh the costs. Although the evidence suggests that offering choice has yet to save the government money, it is possible that Medicare's encouragement of the growth of managed care has contributed to changes in the overall standard and style of medical care and in this manner generated savings for both the public and private sectors. In any event, the federal government is currently committed to continuing the movement toward privatization.

3. *Managing Adverse Selection*. Although Medicare and many employers (including the federal government under the FEHBP) have encountered adverse selection when offering choices, significant efforts have been made to curb its effects. Adverse selection can be managed to some degree—at least in a group insurance context—by premium adjustments and other measures, such as penalties for plan switching and exclusions of preexisting conditions. (Would it be feasible to permit a health plan, rather than refusing all coverage for a preexisting condition, to invoke for a period of time in the case of a new enrollee any contractual limits in the enrollee's previous plan?) (How would you propose to solve the "Queen of Spades" problem?) Once these measures are taken, any remaining adverse selection may not be intolerable. After all, it is not necessarily inappropriate—unless one is thinking purely in social-insurance terms—for people with generally similar risks to be grouped together for insurance (risk-pooling) purposes. Although there is room here for value differences and empirical disputes, it is not obvious that intelligent shopping by consumers is more harmful than beneficial.

The special problems faced by entities sponsoring multiple choice are a different matter. Such sponsors—private or public employers or government health plans—face potentially higher overall costs if individual employees or beneficiaries enroll in plans that best suit their anticipated needs. Nevertheless, sponsors should be able to manage these problems, too, by structuring and pricing each employee's or beneficiary's options so that opportunities for profitable self-selection are effectively minimized. Because sponsors can control the terms of the plans offered, can cause the dollar costs that some employees or beneficiaries face to differ from the premium that the plan actually receives, and can tinker with the system in other ways, the adverse selection problem should be reducible to tolerable proportions. The managed-competition strategy of health care reform is premised on the need to provide structural protections against risk selection by health plans and opportunistic choices by consumers knowing their probable health care needs better than the health plans offering to enroll them.

The goal of a procompetitive health policy must be to ensure that the competitive endeavors of competing health plans focus principally on achieving efficiency in the delivery of health care rather than on finding new and subtler ways of selecting risks and segmenting markets (that is, appealing to distinctive subsets of the population, thus avoiding head-on price competition with other insurers). See Swartz, Reducing Risk Selection Requires More Than Risk Adjustments, 32 Inquiry 6, 7 (1995) ("we want [Medicare beneficiaries] to face prices based on plan efficiency and style of care, and not the case mix of people within the plan"). Whether this goal can be achieved remains to be seen. One should not underestimate, after all, the ability of HMOs, for example, to compete by locating their facilities near the healthier segments of the population (or up two flights of stairs) or by advertising a "stay-well" philosophy that subtly stigmatizes the sick. On the other hand, some tools are available for overcoming these difficult problems, and other tools can be developed. Some observers believe that the solution can be found in government regulation—such as guaranteed issuance and guaranteed renewal of insurance, limits on medical underwriting, strategic use of exclusions for preexisting medical conditions, standardization of benefit packages, and community rating of premiums. Others, such as Professor Enthoven have argued, however, that sponsors of arrangements in which consumers exercise choice can manage competition with a view to limiting opportunities for risk selection by plans and opportunistic moves by consumers. See, e.g., A. Enthoven, Theory and Practice of Managed Competition in Health Care Finance 75–118 (1988). In particular, government, private employers, and other middleman-sponsors of consumer choice systems, in addition to developing appropriate risk adjusters, can take on their own initiative most of the antiselection measures proposed by regulation advocates, thereby forcing alternative health plans to compete primarily on the merits and price of their services.

Robert P. Charrow, David C. Main & Joseph N. Onek, Esqs., Retooling Medicine Through PSOs and Medicare + Choice Plans: Can Providers Catch the Brass Ring?

NHLA/AAHA Health Law Digest, Oct. 1997, p. 3 (Digest Analysis).

I. INTRODUCTION

The Balanced Budget Act of 1997 ("BBA") * * * is likely to have a profound effect on the fundamental nature of Medicare. The BBA adds a new Part C, aptly entitled "Medicare+Choice Program," to Title XVIII of the Social Security Act ("SSA"). Part C greatly expands the options available to Medicare beneficiaries and "enable[s] the Medicare program to utilize innovations that have helped the private market contain costs and expand health care delivery options." H. Rep. 105–217, 105th Cong., 1st Sess. (1997); *see* Social Security Act §§ 1851 *et seq.* * * *

In this *Analysis*, we summarize the newly-created Medicare+Choice Program, highlight some of the various regulatory actions that must be taken before implementation and analyze the potential impact of the new Part C of Medicare from the provider's and beneficiary's perspectives.

II. OVERVIEW OF MEDICARE+CHOICE PROGRAM (BBA §§ 4001—4006)

As a result of the BBA, eligible Medicare beneficiaries may elect to participate in a Medicare+Choice Program or, absent an election, will remain in the traditional fee-for-service programs under Parts A and B.

The Medicare+Choice Program ("MCP" or "Part C") is actually a menu of three basic options: (i) coordinated care plans offered by a traditional health maintenance organization ("HMO"), a competitive medical plan, * * * a preferred provider organization ("PPO"), [or] the newly-established provider sponsored organization ("PSO"); (ii) a Medical Savings Account ("MSA") plan; and (iii) an MCP fee-for-service plan. Except for the creation of PSOs, the coordinated care plans will be much the same as those that have been operating under § 1876. As noted below, payment rates will be adjusted to minimize adverse selection. The MCP's MSA plan replaces traditional Medicare with a catastrophic health insurance plan (i.e., high deductible) and allows the beneficiary to bear the risk of amounts under the high deductible. The MCP fee-for-service plan attempts to roll back the clock to the early days of Medicare when physicians could balance bill patients and operated outside a managed care environment. Given the fact that these plans may well reimburse physicians more than they could receive under other Medicare options, but are precluded from "managing care," it is difficult to see how MCP fee-for-service plans will effectively compete.

Each MCP plan, irrespective of type, will receive a specified monthly payment from Medicare, per enrollee, based on a phased-in blend of local and national "average adjusted per capita cost" ("AAPCC") payment rates. This will be updated by the rate of growth in national Medicare fee-for-service spending minus 0.5%. The new payment scheme is aimed at reducing disparity in the payment rates between urban and rural areas and reducing the growth of Medicare payments. For example, under the BBA methodology, an HMO in Dade County, Florida, (the county with one of the highest AAPCC rates in the country), according to a Congressional Research Service study, would be expected to receive $826 per patient per month in 2002 in comparison to $1,173 under the current AAPCC methodology. In short, the annual per patient savings in medically expensive counties could average approximately $4,100, a 42% savings.

Interestingly, though, in the short run, the transition methodology will actually result in an increase in payments to HMOs and competitive medical plans. * * *

The BBA also attempts to reduce the disparity in patient mix between those beneficiaries enrolling in a coordinated care plan and those in traditional fee-for-service. A recent General Accounting Office report prepared for House Ways and Means Health Subcommittee Chairman William M. Thomas (R–Cal) revealed that, for California Medicare beneficiaries, the average cost of new HMO enrollees was 29% lower than the cost of average fee-for-service beneficiaries. The BBA addresses this problem in two ways. First, monthly payments to providers under an MCP plan will be adjusted by factoring in the provider's patient mix (e.g., age, sex, health status). Second, beneficiaries will be restricted on when they can opt out of a coordinated care plan. Under existing law, a beneficiary is free to terminate his or her enrollment by giving a maximum of thirty days' notice. Under the BBA, a beneficiary's ability to "game the system" by freely moving in and out of a coordinated care plan will be curtailed, effective in year 2002, so that a beneficiary may only disenroll during the first six months of that year and in years thereafter may disenroll only during the first three months, barring special circumstances.

Each MCP plan would be required to pay an annual fee to the Secretary of Health and Human Services ("Secretary") that can be used only for purposes relating to enrollment and dissemination of relevant information to the Medicare beneficiaries. * * * Finally, a bevy of new civil monetary penalties have been enacted to ensure that MCP plans and organizations comply with the BBA.

III. PLANS AVAILABLE UNDER MEDICARE + CHOICE

A. Coordinated Care Providers

1. *Traditional Managed Care Entities.* As noted above, the BBA eliminates all cost reimbursement and risk-sharing contracts under SSA § 1876 and replaces them with Medicare + Choice Program contracts. The transition for most HMOs, competitive medical plans and their participants is supposed to be "seamless." * * *

2. *PSOs.* The major change in the coordinated care market will be the introduction of new competition in the form of PSOs. Although many HMOs are, in essence, insurers that have become healthcare providers, PSOs are the reverse—providers who seek to become insurers. PSOs will operate much like traditional managed care entities in that they would receive the same monthly payments from the Secretary and, in exchange, would bear the risk of providing full Medicare coverage to beneficiaries who enroll in the plan. PSOs, however, differ in certain salient respects from a traditional HMO, the most significant of which is the ability to operate without state licensure. These differences have generated significant controversy within the healthcare community and, as a result, the regulations implementing the PSO provisions will warrant close scrutiny.

Under the BBA, providers (e.g., physicians, hospitals) can form a PSO as a separate corporate entity and can operate for three years as a risk-based Medicare "HMO" without receiving or meeting state solvency or related insurance requirements, provided they satisfy the statutory criteria and federal solvency requirements. Many physician and hospital groups had argued that they could not effectively compete with traditional managed care entities because state solvency requirements were an insurmountable obstacle to market entry. In response, the insurance industry countered that it would be fiscally irresponsible to permit thinly capitalized risk-based entities to operate outside of state insurance laws. In the end, Congress compromised by imposing limiting conditions on the formation of MCP PSOs and by interjecting (for a limited time) federal solvency requirements in lieu of state requirements.

a. Structure of PSOs. The BBA defines a PSO as any entity that is "established or organized, and operated, by a health care provider or group of affiliated health care providers." Moreover, the healthcare providers that operate the PSO must directly provide a "substantial portion" of the healthcare and "have at least a majority financial interest in the entity." There is nothing in the statute that would preclude the formation of a nonprofit PSO. However, absent a well-endowed hospital to anchor the PSO, a nonprofit's inability to tap the equity market would make it difficult for it to raise the funds necessary to satisfy solvency and capital requirements.

A PSO is authorized under the BBA to enter into contracts with physicians and other providers who are not stakeholders in the PSO, but the relative dollar volume of those contracts will be limited by regulation. This provision was inserted to ensure that healthcare providers would not establish what amounts to a full blown HMO while avoiding state insurance regulation. Indeed, the rule for defining the phrase "substantial portion" is likely to be controversial and the subject of keen industry interest. A *de minimis* reading of the phrase (e.g., "substantial" as 5%) could well eviscerate the provider-character of a PSO, whereas a broad reading (e.g., "substantial" as 85%) may require an organization that is extremely large and, thus, difficult to organize and operate.

b. Solvency Requirements and Negotiated Rule Making. Clearly, the most controversial aspect of all PSO provisions relates to state solvency requirements. Under the compromise, a PSO would be required, like all other MCPs, to be licensed as a health insurance entity or HMO in the state where it intends to operate. However, if the PSO has filed an application for licensure with the state and the state has either not acted in a timely manner (i.e., ninety days) or has denied the application because the PSO did not meet the state's solvency requirements and the PSO meets the Secretary's yet-to-be adopted solvency and capitalization requirements, then a PSO may seek and obtain a three-year waiver of the state licensing requirement from the Secretary. [This waiver-granting authority is scheduled to expire in 2002.—Eds.] The Secretary must act on the waiver application within sixty days of receipt. Exactly how the waiver process will operate and what the reactions of the state insurance commissions to PSO applications will be, will depend on the Secretary's solvency requirements. Until that rule and the waiver process is in place, PSOs will only be able to operate if they can obtain state licensure.

Thus, whether PSOs will in fact become competitive in the MCP market will largely turn on the Secretary's solvency and capitalization rule. Given the importance of the rule, Congress mandated that it be issued by April 1, 1998, through the negotiated rule making ("reg neg") provisions of the Administrative Procedure Act (5 U.S.C. §§ 561–570). The theory underlying negotiated rule making is that if the proposed rule is developed by the agency and affected parties working together, then the likelihood that all concerned would find the rule more palatable than otherwise is greater, and the probability of judicial challenge is less. However, in general, negotiated rule making tends to be a time-consuming process, frequently taking longer than informal notice-and-comment rule making under 5 U.S.C. § 553. Accordingly, Congress authorized the Secretary to adopt abbreviated procedures and to abandon the process altogether, in favor of an interim final rule, if the Secretary believes a compromise is unlikely.

* * * Inasmuch as the [reg neg] negotiating committee is established as a Federal Advisory Committee, the Secretary is not obligated to issue the committee's proposed rule, but rather is free to adopt a rule of her choosing. In short, the reg neg process actually provides the Secretary with rule making authority without the need for notice and comment.

c. PSOs in the Market. The contours of the interim final rule on solvency will dictate the ease with which PSOs can be established. In addition, many issues have been raised concerning the viability of these entities, their status as "insurance companies," and what will occur when the three-year "non-renewable" waivers end. Some have questioned whether a typical PSO, which almost certainly would include a hospital as its anchor, can succeed. The lure of the PSO to the provider community is precisely the factor that could undermine its viability. Indeed, some providers have viewed PSOs as a vehicle for providing healthcare services without the burden of managed care; the theory is that by underwriting the risk, and thus acting as insurers, providers can forgo the profit of the insurer in exchange for a freer hand in treating patients. Whether this view is realistic remains to be seen. However, because PSOs are required to provide a substantial portion of the services to their beneficiaries, it is almost certain that each PSO will have at least one, and probably multiple, hospital investors. Hospitals tend to be more in favor of managed care than individual medical practitioners, thus giving rise to potential tension between the two groups. In fact, in the past, physicians have often been reluctant to participate in managed care arrangements with hospitals unless the physicians held the controlling stake in the venture. Thus, it remains to be seen whether physicians and hospitals can effectively join forces in a PSO.

PSOs that prominently feature their hospital members or otherwise market on the basis of the excellence of their hospital members could be burdened with less healthy patients than the typical HMO. This is so because many who choose their PSO based on the hospital will do so because they have had prior experience as a patient in that hospital. In short, they have been previously hospitalized, which is itself an adverse risk factor. Yet, as noted above, it is unlikely, given the limiting provisions in the BBA, that a PSO could be established without a hospital as a significant investor and provider.

d. Whether Physician Hospital Organizations Will Qualify as PSOs. An intriguing question is whether physician hospital organizations ("PHOs"), which have proliferated in recent years with mixed results, will be eligible to become PSOs and thus to receive the benefit of renewed interest and market potential. It does appear that many PHOs will meet the organizational requirements for a PSO and would be eligible to apply for PSO certification. Moreover, if a primary failing of PHOs has been a lack of market focus around which to rally disparate physician and hospital participants, the prospect of a Medicare revenue stream might provide the missing ingredient to many stagnant PHO efforts. However, the financial and administrative challenges facing PSOs are daunting, and it is hard to imagine that immediate capital and management resources will be available to support the risks and day-to-day operating needs of hospital-based PSOs, not to mention the legal, consulting and actuarial costs of the application process itself. However, where a hospital system decides to seek greater control over a payment source that may represent more than half of its revenues, the PSO challenge may be worth undertaking.

e. Legal Status of a PSO. The BBA provision relating to the solvency requirements for PSOs expressly pre-empts state law to the contrary. *See United States v. Rhode Island Insurers' Insolvency Fund*, 80 F.3d 616 (1st Cir.1996) (holding that [Medicare Secondary–Payer Act] regulation pre-empted state rule to the contrary notwithstanding the McCarran–Ferguson Act, 15 U.S.C. §§ 1011–1015). Indeed, the law permits an unlicensed PSO to operate in the state, if it is acting under a federal waiver. What is less clear, though, is whether the lack of a state license, coupled with the federal regulation, is sufficient to undermine a PSO's character as an "insurance company." Determining whether a PSO is an insurance company is important in two respects. First, insurance companies cannot avail themselves of bankruptcy protection, but instead can only seek protection through state receivership proceedings. *See* 11 U.S.C. § 109(b)(2); *In re Estate of Medcare HMO*, 998 F.2d 436, 446–47 (7th Cir.1993) (holding that an HMO is a "domestic insurance company" that is ineligible for relief under the Bankruptcy Code); *but see In re Affiliated Food Stores, Inc. Group Benefit Trust*, 134 B.R. 215, 224 (Bankr.N.D.Tex.1991) (holding that a trust established by a corporation to provide low-cost group medical benefits is not a "domestic insurance company" and is eligible for bankruptcy protection). Second, of less concern, is the fact that the federal antitrust laws do not apply to insurance companies in certain settings. *See* McCarran–Ferguson Act, 15 U.S.C. §§ 1011–15 (1994).

f. After the Waiver Period Ends. The three-year waiver from state solvency requirements provides a jump-start to a new form of healthcare provider. One of the more intriguing questions is what will occur after the three-year waiver period ends. This will depend on the character of the PSOs that exist, which in turn will depend in part on how closely the Secretary's regulation mirrors stringent state requirements. If only well-capitalized entities are permitted market entry from the outset, then the waiver provision will have little effect and the end of the waiver period will go unnoticed. However, if the solvency regulation incorporates flexible requirements that allow market entry by those entities unable to come close to meeting state requirements, then the end of the waiver period will have significance. In such an environment, successful PSOs that are unable to meet the state requirements will either merge with or be purchased by other coordinated care organizations. Other PSOs are likely to lobby Congress for an extension of the waiver period. If the number of PSOs and their respective Medicare membership is sizable, then there is a realistic probability that Congress would grant such an extension.

B. MCP Medical Saving Account Plan

While PSO provisions enable providers to act as insurers, the MSA provision enables a beneficiary to engage in limited self-insurance. Under the program, a beneficiary purchases a high deductible, private health insurance policy from an organization that has an MCP contract with the Secretary. The insurance policy must cover all services that would otherwise be covered under Parts A and B, although the aggregate deductible can be far higher than under traditional Medicare (more than $6,000 in 1999). Thereafter, the MSA plan must pay all of the medical expenses covered by Medicare "without regard to any deductibles or coinsurance."

The Secretary will deposit into the beneficiary's MSA the difference between the per capita rate that would otherwise be paid and the premium for the high deductible health insurance policy referenced above. The Secretary will remit the premiums to the carrier. Thus, by way of example, if the per capita rate is $9,200 and the premium for the policy is $5,200, the Secretary will deposit the difference ($4,000) into the beneficiary's MSA. If the beneficiary incurs limited medical expenses (e.g., $1,000) during the year, then the beneficiary's MSA will retain the remaining $3,000. If, on the other hand, the beneficiary incurs medical expenses in excess of $6,000 then the beneficiary will lose $2,000 ($6,000 deductible minus $4,000 in MSA).

There was significant concern that an unfettered MSA program would attract the healthiest Medicare beneficiaries and would leave those at higher risk in the traditional programs. This would undermine the cost and risk-spreading notions inherent in Medicare. As a result, Congress created the MSA program as a small demonstration project limited to 390,000 enrollees, on a "first come, first served" basis and for which there can be no further enrollment after December 31, 2002. Those already enrolled in an MSA plan could remain, but whether Congress would extend the date for new enrollment or raise the ceiling above the 390,000 will depend on the effect of the MSA program on traditional Medicare. The Secretary is required to carefully monitor the MSA program to determine what effect, if any, extending the program would have on adverse selection, access to care, and the financial status of the Medicare Trust Fund.

C. MCP Fee-for-Service Plans

One of the new plans available to beneficiaries under MCP is a private fee-for-service plan. A private fee-for-service plan is an MCP plan that:

> (A) reimburses hospitals, physicians and other providers at a rate determined by the plan on a fee-for-service basis without placing the provider at financial risk; (B) does not vary rates for such a provider based on utilization relating to such provider; and (C) does not restrict the selection of providers among those who are lawfully authorized to provide the covered services and agree to accept the terms and conditions established by the plan.

From a provider standpoint, the private fee-for-service plan is potentially better than traditional Medicare fee-for-service. First, the provider may be able to negotiate higher payment rates from the plan than Medicare currently provides. Second, unlike under traditional Medicare, the provider is entitled to bill patients up to 115% of the payment amount established by the plan.

A fee-for-service plan will presumably be more expensive for beneficiaries. First, providers are permitted to engage in limited balance billing. Second, the BBA places no limit on the premiums that a fee-for-service MCP plan can charge. Some wealthier beneficiaries may nonetheless find such a plan attractive. The plan assures them of getting "unmanaged care" from their providers. Moreover, beneficiaries may believe they will get special attention from providers who are being paid more than under traditional Medicare.

Whether such a plan can possibly succeed in the marketplace will depend on the issue of adverse selection. If the plan appeals primarily to the wealthy worried well, it can be financially successful. If the plan appeals primarily to those beneficiaries who are sicker than average, it will fail.[6]

Private fee-for-service plans, particularly taken in conjunction with MSA plans (currently limited to 390,000 enrollees), raise the likelihood that the Medicare program will increasingly be segmented by income. This parallels developments in the private market and is to be expected from legislation that seeks to make Medicare function more like the private market.

IV. CONCLUSION

The MCP will open up Medicare. For beneficiaries, this means a dazzling and potentially confusing array of new choices. In fact, it is

6. The BBA charges the Secretary with developing a risk adjustment system that would pay more to plans with sicker enrollees. It will be a long time, however, before such a system is effectively implemented.

difficult to see how the Secretary will be able to effectively communicate those choices and describe the plans under each choice to all Medicare beneficiaries, as required by the statute. In the past, Medicare has had difficulty explaining the complexities of the system to the general population. From that perspective, the BBA further complicates an already complex system.

From the providers' perspective, the MCP injects new flexibility into the Medicare program. Certain aspects of the MCP theoretically will enable physicians to operate with less control from managed care providers (e.g., MCP fee-for-service) and other aspects will enable physicians and hospitals to compete with large insurers (e.g., PSOs). For providers and others who venture into the MCP-market, the BBA contains some traps for the unwary. In particular, the civil monetary penalty provisions of the Social Security Act have been expanded to govern MCP plans and permit the Secretary to impose large penalties (e.g., $100,000), on what appears to be a no fault basis, on providers and plans that violate various terms or conditions of the BBA. In essence, the BBA applies the civil monetary penalty provisions more like a parking fine and less as a punishment for misconduct.

From the government's perspective, the MCP establishes two new advisory committees—one for long-term strategic planning and other for short-term planning. The National Bipartisan Commission on the Future of Medicare is supposed to identify problems that threaten the long-term viability of the Medicare trust funds and present Congress with solutions to those problems. * * *

The newly established Medicare Payment Advisory Commission ("MedPAC") replaces both the Prospective Payment Assessment Commission ("ProPAC") and the Physician Payment Review Commission ("PPRC") and as such, is charged with providing Congress with yearly reports and recommendations concerning physician and hospital payments. The fifteen members of MedPAC are to be selected by the Comptroller General to advise the Congress. Consolidating the jurisdictions of both ProPAC and PPRC into a single commission reflects Congress' philosophy, as exemplified in MCP, of treating hospital and physician payments as fungible. Indeed, the new Part C represents a dramatic turning point in the basic philosophy underlying Medicare, namely eliminating the artificial, although convenient, distinction between Parts A and B. As the Congress and HCFA have found, it is virtually impossible to control costs and quality of integrated delivery systems if those systems receive separate payment from separate funds. In essence, Part C and MCP may mark the beginning of the ends of Parts A and B.

NOTES AND QUESTIONS ON THE MEDICARE + CHOICE PROGRAM

1. The BBA is truly revolutionary in its potential impact. Although the outlines of the new program are fairly clear, many decisions have yet to be made, having been left to be made by HCFA or scheduled for revisitation by Congress after various mandatory studies are completed or after detailed proposals are developed. In general, the BBA moves strongly in the direction of privatizing care of the elderly (at present only about 12% of Medicare beneficiaries are enrolled in managed care), thereby shifting many administrative burdens and decision-making responsibilities from HCFA to the private sector. There are many reasons, to be sure, why Congress might have gone slower in this direction than it has. See, e.g., Oberlander, Managed Care and Medicare Reform, 22 J. Health Pol., Pol'y & L. 595 (1997) (questioning, among other things, the ability of HMOs to care adequately for the chronically ill). But the Medicare program has had huge problems, perhaps justifying radical surgery of a still experimental kind. In any event, the program has been launched in new directions. On the policy issues and past experience, see generally H. Luft, ed., HMOs and the Elderly (1994).

Is a market-oriented strategy likely to lower costs and maintain appropriate quality of care for Medicate patients? Although all managed-care plans participating in the Medicare+Choice program are required to provide Medicare's standard benefits, each plan will administer its own coverage. Thus, while subject to some regulatory and judicial oversight, they will be in positions to pursue many of their their own policies and to foster their own styles of practice. But see Grijalva v. Shalala, 946 F.Supp. 747 (D.Ariz.1996) (under prior law, requiring HCFA to adopt and enforce requirement that Medicare HMOs provide notice and appeal in all coverage denials, terminating plans that breach duty). Are costs likely to be optimally controlled in a system driven by statutory entitlements, not by private contract? Are quality concerns likely to be adequately addressed by the regulatory and other machinery to be installed? Will health plans have appropriate freedom to select only those providers whose style of practice they find acceptable?

2. *Consumer Choice.* Congressional enthusiasm for widening consumer choice may have been premature, given the difficulty that individual beneficiaries will have in making the choices required of them. (The Medicare+Choice program provides for no less than eight types of plan that beneficiaries may choose—can you identify them all on the basis of what you have read?—and there will be multiple sellers offering most types.) To be sure, the option of remaining in the traditional program is preserved, and inertia, strengthened by uncertainty, will undoubtedly lead most beneficiaries to elect this option by default. But seniors are going to be deluged with new, confusing information and marketing pleas, and complaints can be expected, especially since new "lock-in" provisions mean that choices will not be as easily reversible as in the past. Although major efforts will be undertaken to obtain useful information from providers and to make it available to beneficiaries, individual choice of health plan is notoriously difficult, and marketing abuses will be possible even with government oversight of enrollment procedures. Whether consumers will be well enough informed to stimulate appropriate attention to quality remains to be seen. Many economists believe, of course, that only a small subset of consumers needs to be well-informed in order for markets to work reasonably well.

3. *Regulating Managed Care.* The new law, embroidering on provisions in earlier law, includes a variety of requirements binding on health plans that enroll Medicare beneficiaries. These requirements track many provisions that are already present, or being considered for inclusion, in state law. See chapter 8(§C). The topics touched upon in federal law include (in addition to the new federal capital and solvency requirements for PSOs): open enrollment; provider participation rights; physician incentive arrangements (see chapter 3(§D)); capacity and accessibility of care; coverage of care in emergency departments; quality assurance; confidentiality; grievance and appeal mechanisms; advance directives concerning heroic measures in terminal cases; anti-gag clauses; and discrimination based on "health status." The prohibition on discrimination on the basis of health status applies not only to eligibility and premiums but also to "coverage and provision of benefits" and could therefore raise serious issues in benefit administration—i.e., in determining medical necessity in cases where elderly patients have various disabilities affecting their potential quality of life.

4. *Payment Formula.* By 2000, the Secretary is to develop and implement a new method of risk-adjusting Medicare payments to managed-care plans as a way of minimizing selection problems. The necessary methodology has not been developed, however, and it is doubtful that a wholly satisfactory approach can be devised. See, e.g., Newhouse et al., Risk Adjustment and Medicare: Taking a Closer Look, Health Affs., Sept.-Oct. 1997, p. 26. It therefore remains to be seen when, if ever, Medicare will enjoy net savings from offering beneficiaries the chance to use their "defined contribution" to enroll in an HMO (with or without a POS option), a PPO, or a PSO, to open a Medical Savings Account, or to obtain conventional fee-for-service insurance in the private sector.

Reforming Medicaid

NOTES AND QUESTIONS ON PURCHASING STRATEGIES IN STATE MEDICAID PROGRAMS

1. *Paying Hospitals.* Although the Medicaid program is financed jointly by the federal and state governments, it is administered by the states, which must nevertheless meet any requirements set forth in federal law. In their efforts to control Medicaid spending, most states have implemented prospective payment systems for institutional providers.

Prior to 1981, however, unless a state was granted a special federal waiver, its Medicaid program was required to pay hospitals in the same way as the Medicare program, which at that time reimbursed hospitals retrospectively for costs incurred. States could therefore control costs only by imposing prior authorization requirements or by limiting the number of hospital days that Medicaid would cover in a given case (a strategy that some states still employ). See, e.g, Alexander v. Choate, 469 U.S. 287 (1985) (rejecting challenge, based on Rehabilitation Act discrimination-against-the-handicapped theory, to Tennessee Medicaid's 14-day limit on payment for hospitalization); Charleston Mem. Hosp. v. Conrad, 693 F.2d 324 (4th Cir.1982) (reduction of covered inpatient days per year from 40 to 18, with some exceptions, held still a reasonable level of coverage). Note that limits of the latter kind work no appreciable hardships only because most hospitals would be willing, or be legally compelled, to continue to provide needed services after the state's payment obligation expired.

Changes in federal law in 1981 greatly increased the flexibility of states in controlling payments to hospitals under their Medicaid programs. Under the so-called Boren amendment attached to that legislation, however, the states were still bound to establish payment rates to institutional providers that were "reasonable and adequate to meet the costs which must be incurred by efficiently and economically operated facilities in order to provide care and services in conformity with applicable State and Federal laws, regulations, and quality and safety standards." Although the choice of payment methodology was otherwise largely within each state's discretion, states had to obtain HCFA approval of changes in their state Medicaid plans and to provide "assurances" that this and a few other federal requirements were complied with. See generally Burman, Judicial Review of Medicaid Hospital and Nursing Home Reimbursement Methodologies Under the Boren Amendment, 3 Annals Health L. 55 (1994).

The prospective reimbursement systems used by states in paying for Medicaid inpatient hospital services vary considerably. The majority of states established prospective systems that based rates on individual hospitals' historical costs as updated under some index of inflation. Under these systems, a maximum payment level might be set by reference to costs at peer hospitals. Adjustments might be made to reflect changes in volume (to reduce the incentive to increase admissions) and changes in case mix. Units of payment may also differ, with some states paying per diem rates and others paying a certain amount per discharge. Many refinements are possible, including variations on Medicare's DRG payment methodology.

In addition to granting state Medicaid programs greater latitude in designing hospital reimbursement systems, the Omnibus Budget Reconciliation Act of 1981 also authorized the granting of federal waivers to states that wished to require Medicaid recipients to receive nonemergency services only from selected providers. Without a federal waiver permitting selective contracting with cost-effective providers, Medicaid recipients would have been entitled to "freedom of choice," the right to receive care from any qualified provider willing to accept what the program would pay. On the other hand, selective contracting, either through competitive bidding or through negotiation, can achieve savings both by moving patients to lower-cost providers and by extracting discounts from providers with excess capacity. California pioneered selective contracting for its Medicaid program and realized substantial savings without dramatically altering where Medicaid recipients received their care. Partly because hospitals with large Medicaid caseloads were willing to lower their charges to the state in order to retain those patients, the state's total expenditures for inpatient hospital services fell from approximately $2.0 billion in 1982 to $1.6 billion in 1985. The waiver provision allowed the federal government to require a state engaging in selective contracting with hospitals to provide certain assurances that access to quality care was preserved.

2. *Payments to Nursing Facilities.* Nursing home care is a mandatory Medicaid service, and its cost to the states was $27 billion in 1994. States have substantial discretion in determining the methods and standards under which they pay for nursing home services. Most, however, pay nursing homes a prospective per diem rate based on the facility's historical costs. Such rates and periodic updates and adjustments were subject to the "efficiency and economy" test of the original Boren amendment. Under 1987 and 1990 amendments to 42 U.S.C. § 1396a(a)(13)(A), they were also required to "take into account the costs (including the costs of services required to attain or maintain the highest practicable physical, mental, and psychosocial well-being of each resident eligible for Medicaid benefits) of complying with" reforms enacted in 1987 to strengthen federal oversight of nursing homes. (See chapter 6 § (D).) Another federal requirement, first enacted in 1989 but amended since, is that states must "provide such methods and procedures relating to the utilization of, and the payment for, care and services available under the plan * * * as may be necessary * * * to assure that payments are consistent with efficiency, economy, and the quality of care and are sufficient to enlist enough providers so that care and services are available under the plan at least to the extent that such care and services are available to the general population in the geographic area." 42 U.S.C.A. § 1396a(a)(30) (A) (Supp. 1997).

3. *The Wilder Case.* In 1990, the Supreme Court removed a major obstacle to lawsuits by hospitals and other institutional providers (e.g., nursing homes) seeking to challenge habitually low Medicaid payments by state governments. In Wilder v. Virginia Hosp. Ass'n, 496 U.S. 498 (1990), the Court recognized the existence under the federal Medicaid law of an affirmative federal right on the part of providers to receive adequate payment for services to Medicaid beneficiaries. This right, it held, could be enforced in federal courts under 42 U.S.C. § 1983 (1994) (Civil War-era statute allowing suit against any person who, "under color of" state law, deprives another of a federally guaranteed right.) Note that only state officials, not the state itself, can be sued under § 1983 and that only prospective relief is available.

The hospital association in *Wilder* sought to bring suit under § 1983 to enforce its members' rights allegedly established by the 1981 Boren amendment. The Court had to determine whether, in addition to laying down procedures for obtaining state assurances of the adequacy of rates and access, the legislation also established an implied right to adequate reimbursement that providers could enforce in federal court. Do you agree with its view that "there can be little doubt that health care providers are the intended beneficiaries of the Boren Amendment"? 496 U.S. at 510. Is it relevant that Congress's primary concern was not the welfare of hospitals but the ability of beneficiaries to obtain adequate care? The four dissenting justices noted the "absence in the statute of any express 'focus' on providers as a beneficiary class of the provision." Id. at 527. The case presented an extremely interesting problem of statutory interpretation, raising the question whether Congress must be explicit in creating a federal right or whether courts may take their cue from legislation's general policy. For a later case declining to follow the *Wilder* rationale, see Suter v. Artist M., 503 U.S. 347 (1992) (holding that a similar "reasonable efforts" clause of the Adoption Assistance and Child Welfare Act did not create rights enforceable under § 1983 because Congress must unambiguously confer enforceable rights, privileges, or immunities if it intends to create such).

For a case showing the extent of state abuses for which *Wilder* provided a federal remedy, see Amisub (PSL), Inc. v. Colorado Dep't of Social Services, 879 F.2d 789 (10th Cir.1989) (invalidating state payment rate calculated by carefully adjusting DRG allowances and then subtracting an arbitrary 46% as a "budget adjustment" factor), cert. denied 496 U.S. 935 (1990). See also Kansas Health Care Ass'n v. Kansas Dep't of Social and Rehabilitation Services, 31 F.3d 1536, 1539–40 (10th Cir.1994) (nursing homes granted preliminary injunction because likely to prevail on claim that Kansas procedurally and substantively violated the Boren amendment when it changed the method of calculating the estimated inflation component of Medicaid reimbursement rates). For an overview of the issues raised by *Wilder*, see Ratcliff, The Mistakes of Medicaid: Provider Payment During the Past Decade and Lessons for Health Care Reform in the 21st Century, 35 B.C. L. Rev. 141 (1993); Anderson & Hall, The Adequacy of Hospital Reimbursement Under Medicaid's Boren Amendment, 13 J. Legal Med. 205 (1992).

It is questionable whether the higher reimbursement rates that *Wilder* forced states to pay achieved a net increase in access to care. *Wilder*, by forcing states to pay more for services already being provided, may actually have caused a reduction in Medicaid benefits and access to care. See Pear, Suits Force U.S. and States to Pay More for Medicaid, N.Y. Times, Oct. 29, 1991, at p. 1, col. 1.

4. *Repeal of the Boren Amendment.* In section 4711 of the Balanced Budget Act of 1997, Congress repealed the Boren amendment, replacing it with a mild requirement that each state Medicaid plan provide for a "public process for determination of rates of payment under the plan for hospital services [and] nursing facility services * * *." The Secretary of HHS is directed to "study the effect on access to, and quality of, services provided to beneficiaries of the rate-setting methods used by States pursuant to" the amended statute. Since Boren amendment litigation aimed only at prospective relief and not at recovering alleged underpayments of the past, the 1997 legislation essentially dried up an active area of health care law practice. Providers may still, however, bring suit to increase allowances under 42 U.S.C.A. § 1396a(a)(30)(A) (Supp. 1997), which requires provider compensation to be sufficient to ensure that recipients' access to care is not impaired. But query whether this right is enforceable under § 1983. See Minnesota HomeCare Ass'n v. Gomez, 108 F.3d 917, 918 (8th Cir.1997) (concurring opinion questioning applicability of § 1983 in case upholding methodology for paying for home health care).

The loss of Boren protection may be more serious for nursing homes than for hospitals, since the latter were already facing the loss of Medicaid revenues as a result of the shift in many states to managed care. (Hospitals contracting with managed care plans enrolling Medicaid recipients had no recourse to the courts to ensure adequate compensation for their services.) Nursing homes will once again be at the mercy of state legislatures facing tight Medicaid budgets.

5. *Physician Payment.* In order to encourage physician participation in the Medicaid program, early regulations required states to pay physicians' "usual and customary" fees. This requirement did not last long, however, since it led to spectacular increases in Medicaid program costs. As states took advantage of their new freedom to underpay physicians for treating Medicaid patients, many physicians became unwilling to accept such patients, and concern grew about their access to care. This concern led in turn to the enactment of the aforementioned 42 U.S.C.A. § 1396a(a)(30)(A) (Supp. 1997), requiring provider payments of all kinds to ensure equal access to care. Although states increased their Medicaid fee-for-service payments to physicians by an average of 15% between 1990 and 1993, Medicaid fees were still reported in 1994 to average only about 47% of private fees and only about 73% of Medicare fees. PPRC, 1994 Annual Report to Congress 352 (1994). See generally Watson, Medicaid Physician Participation: Patients, Poverty, and Physician Self–Interest, 21 Am. J. L. & Med. 191 (1995).

6. *Pharmaceuticals.* Every state's Medicaid program covers prescription drugs even though coverage is optional under federal law. States have opted to cover pharmaceuticals because use of medications often provides an alternative to more expensive therapy, results in shorter hospital stays, and prevents illness. Nevertheless, prescription drugs can be costly, and a number of cost-containment mechanisms have been established on both federal and state levels. In 1994, spending for pharmaceutical benefits accounted for 9.7 percent of Medicaid service expenditures (excluding disproportionate share hospital costs). In contrast, payments for physicians' services constituted 7.9 percent of program spending. States have limited spending under Medicaid through prescription caps (limits on the number of prescriptions that may be filled or refilled per beneficiary within a certain time period), prior authorization requirements, and drug-utilization review. Most states do not yet have on-line drug-utilization review and billing, however, and some have considered farming out management of the prescription drug benefit to private pharmacy-benefit management companies (PBMs). As states move to managed-care arrangements for their Medicaid populations, the pharmacy benefit may be either "carved out" for separate management or made the responsibility of the managed-care plan.

Federal cost-containment measures include limits on pharmacy reimbursement. For multiple source drugs meeting certain requirements (generics), a set maximum allowable cost (MAC) is paid to the pharmacy. For all other drugs, state payments may not exceed the lesser of the pharmacy's usual and customary charge or the estimated acquisition cost. States are allowed to pay pharmacists a reasonable "dispensing fee" to cover pharmaçy overhead and profit. See 42 C.F.R. §§ 447.301, 447.331–34 (1996). Legislation in 1990 included a most-favored-nation provision requiring a drug manufacturer to give Medicaid a price equal to its best price to any buyer. This provision had the unexpected (why?) effect of raising the cost of drugs to the Veterans Administration and the Public Health Service as well as to many buyers in the private sector—as manufacturers found the cost of giving a discount to anyone much higher than it had been. See Morton, The Strategic Response of Pharmaceutical Firms to the Medicaid Most–Favored–Customer Rules, 28 RAND J. Econ. 269 (1997).

NOTES AND QUESTIONS ON MEDICAID MANAGED CARE

1. The PPRC's 1997 Annual Report to Congress (pp. 424–27) described as follows the shift by states from fee-for-service payment to contracting out their Medicaid business to managed-care plans:

> Most Medicaid services traditionally have been provided under fee-for-service arrangements. But the use of managed care has been rapidly expanding. * * * Managed care has accelerated in Medicaid during the last few years—from only about 282,000 beneficiaries in HMOs in 1981 to about 13 million beneficiaries in a variety of managed-care arrangements in 1996. * * *
>
> * * *
>
> Medicaid managed-care arrangements vary widely in the amount of utilization management involved and the degree to which plans are at risk. HCFA classifies arrangements into four categories: HMOs, prepaid health plans (PHPs), health insuring organizations (HIOs), and PCCM [primary care case management] arrangements. For most purposes, however, it is more useful to distinguish between entities at full risk for a comprehensive range of services (generally HMOs, HIOs, and some PHPs); entities at risk for a more limited range of services (some PHPs); and programs that operate on a fee-for-service basis (PCCM arrangements). * * *
>
> HMOs provide comprehensive health services to Medicaid beneficiaries in return for a capitated payment that is based on expenditures for comparable beneficiaries in fee-for-service Medicaid. Of the 511 entities participating in some type of Medicaid managed care in 1996, well over half (349) were HMOs.
>
> Prepaid health plans have several variants. They include certain community, migrant, or Appalachian health centers located in medically underserved areas; organizations that contract with the state Medicaid agency for a specific list of services (e.g. behavioral health) or on a nonrisk basis; and comprehensive at-risk organizations that are statutorily exempt from HMO requirements. There were 89 PHPs contracting with Medicaid in 1996.

HIOs pay for services of subcontracting providers and plans and assume all financial risk in exchange for a premium. The HIO organizes a provider network and establishes preauthorization and utilization review to control the volume of services. Network providers serve as case managers and, in some HIOs, receive capitated payments. * * * There are only seven HIOs.

Primary care case management arrangements are different from HMOs PHPs, and HIOs in that they operate on a fee-for-service basis and are typically created and run by the states. Under these arrangements, a primary care physician coordinates and approves an array of services in addition to providing primary care services. In most PCCM systems, physicians are paid case-management fees (typically $3 per beneficiary per month) in addition to their regular fee-for-service payments for the primary care services they provide. In others, physicians are placed at financial risk for some services (usually ambulatory care). Physicians may determine the level of their Medicaid caseloads, up to a state-specified limit. PCCM arrangements operate in 31 states and the District of Columbia; a few states operate multiple programs.

2. *The BBA.* Continuing the trend to increase states' flexibility in controlling the cost of their Medicaid programs, the 1997 BBA made several changes that together make it easier for states to move Medicaid recipients into managed-care organizations (MCOs). It is no longer necessary, for example, for a state to obtain from HCFA a waiver allowing it require its Medicaid recipients to enroll in an MCO. Previously, the state would have needed either a waiver under Social Security Act (SSA) § 1915(b) of the federal freedom-of-choice requirement or approval under SSA § 1115 of a "demonstration" of an innovative program. Waivers remain available as a way of obtaining authorization for demonstrations, and waivers must be obtained if a state undertakes to force children with special needs into MCOs.

The significance of eliminating the waiver requirement is less than it might seem since HCFA had become very quick to grant waivers—even getting criticized for letting states have demonstration waivers when they were merely replicating methods that had already been tried and evaluated in other states rather than trying out a new idea or approach. But the new freedom to innovate, coupled with relief from other previous requirements, will undoubtedly facilitate the expanded use of managed care in state programs. States will still have to amend their state Medicaid plan before implementing their changes, however, and this process may allow public input and public criticism of the plan at the state level even if the federal government's formal approval is no longer required. States still must obtain federal approval of their specific contracts with MCOs.

Other relaxations of federal standards include the dropping of the previous requirement that a plan enrolling Medicaid beneficiaries also enroll a fraction of commercial enrollees; under the new program, Medicaid-only HMOs, etc., will be permitted. States now need offer recipients no more than two plans—one is enough in a rural area—and can require that the enrollee remain in the plan for at least a year, unless a specific reason justifies disenrollment. The various consumer protections that are provided (see earlier note on regulating managed care under the BBA) depend heavily on state or federal oversight, which overburdened bureaucracies may not be able to supply.

3. *TennCare.* In 1993, Tennessee applied for and was granted a § 1115 waiver under which the state was allowed to withdraw abruptly from traditional Medicaid and, on very short notice, to introduce an ambitious new managed care program, called "TennCare," on January 1, 1994. TennCare was designed not only to cover the entire Medicaid-eligible population but also to extend coverage to a new class of uninsured/uninsurable individuals. See generally U.S. General Accounting Office, Medicaid—Tennessee's Program Broadens Coverage But Faces Uncertain Future (GAO /HEHS 95–186, 1995); Bonnyman, Stealth Reform: Market–Based Medicaid in Tennessee, Health Affs., Summer 1996, p. 306. The TennCare program is slightly more generous than traditional Medicaid, covering inpatient and outpatient hospital care, physician services, prescriptions, lab and x-ray services, medical supplies, home health care, hospice, and ambulance transportation. Excluded from TennCare managed care, however, was long-term care, which the state still pays for on a fee-for-service basis.

TennCare contracted with 12 MCOs, including HMOs and PPOs, paying them a capitated monthly rate per enrollee in return for their commitment to deliver the covered care. MCOs received additional payments for enrollees having high-cost chronic conditions and higher than average utilization rates. MCOs are responsible for negotiating the compensation of their own providers. TennCare's original capitation rate was set at $101 per month per beneficiary, a third below the national Medicaid average. Tennessee relied on its purchasing power, including a threat to exclude plans and providers from treating state employees, to induce MCO and provider participation. The state proved correct in its assumption that its low capitation rate would be sufficient to attract an adequate number of provider networks, including Blue Cross/Blue Shield, TennCare's largest. See Watson, Medicaid Physician Participation: Patients, Poverty, and Physician Self–Interest, 21 Am. J.L. & Med. 191 (1995) (describing how TennCare expanded physician participation in Medicaid). Many participating physicians limit the number of Medicaid patients they will treat, however, so that the access problem has not been entirely solved.

Although TennCare succeeded in expanding coverage to include a larger population while remaining budget-neutral (as required by its HCFA Medicaid waiver), there were concerns about the program's effectiveness, at least during the sudden start-up phase. Primary concerns were access to quality care, accuracy and fairness in administering benefits, and the financial viability and continued participation of MCOs. See Daniels v. Wadley, 926 F.Supp. 1305 (M.D.Tenn.1996) (modifying, to accommodate TennCare, earlier consent decree governing administration of Tennessee Medicaid program). Beneficiaries expressed some dissatisfaction with the care they received under TennCare, and the state lacked adequate monitoring systems to evaluate access and quality of care. Overall, the MCOs lost money in the first year of the program, with the Blue Cross plan reporting almost a $9 million dollar loss. Capitation rates were raised somewhat thereafter, and the program continues to achieve its basic objectives. See Bonnyman, supra. For a discussion of the politics of TennCare, see Gold, Markets and Public Programs: Insights from Oregon and Tennessee, 22 J. Health Pol., Pol'y & L. 633, 649–59 (1997).

4. *Policy Concerns*. Obviously, the stampede of the states, now with strong federal encouragement, to enroll Medicaid populations in MCOs is highly debatable as a matter of policy. See, e.g., D. Rowland et al., Medicaid and Managed Care: Lessons from the Literature (Kaiser Commission on the Future of Medicaid, 1995); Sisk et al., Evaluation of Medicaid Managed Care: Satisfaction, Access, and Use, 276 J.A.M.A. 50 (1996); Sparer, Medicaid Managed Care and the Health Reform Debate: Lessons from New York and California, 21 J. Health Pol., Pol'y & L. 433 (1996); Note, The Impact of Medicaid Managed Care on the Uninsured, 110 Harv. L. Rev. 751 (1997) ("programs succeed marginally in containing costs and improving care"); Manski et al., Medicaid, Managed Care, and America's Health Safety Net, 25 J.L., Med. & Ethics 30 (1997) ("Managed care was never designed to address the needs of a population with higher than average incidence of chronic conditions and poor health."). Nevertheless, the issue now appears to be not whether, but how, to make managed care serve the needs of the Medicaid population.

*

PART II

Shifting Paradigms in American Health Care

CHAPTER 3

Commercialism Versus Professionalism

Section A: Tensions and Conflict

The Nature of a Profession

William J. Goode, Ph.D., Community Within A Community: The Professions

22 Am.Soc.Rev. 194 (1957).

This paper is concerned with a little explored area of social theory: the structural strains and supports between a contained community and the larger society of which it is a part and on which it is dependent. * * *

Characteristic of each of the established professions, and a goal of each aspiring occupation, is the "community of profession." * * *

Many of the traits that make the professions sociologically interesting grow from the dimension of community. Typically a profession, through its association and its members, controls admission to training and requires far more education from its trainees than the containing community demands. Although the occupational behavior of members is regulated by law, the professional community exacts a higher standard of behavior than does the law. Both of the foregoing characteristics allow the professions to enjoy more prestige from the containing community than can other occupations. Thus, professionals stand at the apex of prestige in the occupational system. Because of the controls over entrance and over professional behavior, and the possession of a monopoly of particular skills, the professional communities obtain incomes higher than those of other occupations. Moreover, since each professional community has a monopoly over its skills, it must be consulted by the containing community and thus the professions generally hold a disproportionate share of seats in state and national legislative houses, on boards of directors, on advisory and technical commissions, and so on. Little legislation relating to any profession is passed without being largely shaped by that profession. * * *

"Community" alone would not give so much power, of course, but each community of practitioners also demands high education of its members. This education is evaluated by the larger society as crucial in both individual and societal matters: disease and death, liberty and property, the problem of evil, construction and production, war, and so on. It is this last factor, the values of the larger society, in interaction with the prior two, which gives rise to the power of the professional community. No such power would be given, however, if there were not a professional community to demand it and be responsible for its use. As a consequence of the rewards given by the larger society, the community of profession can also demand higher talent in its recruits and require that they go through a considerable adult socialization process.

The advantages enjoyed by professionals thus rest on evaluations made by the larger society, for the professional community could not grant these advantages to itself. That is, they represent structured relations between the larger society and the professional community.

Socialization and Social Control

Socialization and social control in the professions are made important by the peculiarly exploitative opportunities the professions enjoy. The problems brought to the professional are usually those the client cannot solve, and only the professional can solve. The client does not usually choose his professional by a measurable criterion of competence, and after the work is done, the client is not usually competent to judge if it was properly done. In the face of these opportunities to exploit the larger society, the professional community is nevertheless given considerable discretion and power.

Indeed, the very great prestige of the professions is a response of the society to their apparent self-denial, i.e., they can, but typically do not, exploit. This is not to say that professionals are nobler than lay citizens. Instead, the professional community holds that exploitation would inevitably lower the prestige of the professional community and subject it to stricter lay controls. It is at least clear that if individual clients believed that their practitioners were seeking to exploit them, they would not trust them so far as they do. More fundamentally, as in any other community, the highest rewards of prestige and money are most likely to be granted to the practitioners who actually live up to the professional role obligations. The practitioner who tried to live by the doctrine of *caveat emptor* might, unlike the business man, find himself expelled from his community, either informally or formally.

These larger forces operating on the two communities are implemented by the specific role definitions of the professional *vis-à-vis* his client. This means, in turn, that to the extent that community of profession is strong, its members face real temptations, and its behavioral demands are different from the demands of the lay world—to that extent it must put its recruits through a set of adult socialization processes and maintain procedures for continuing social controls over the practicing professional. Three professions—the clergy, the military, and medicine—almost isolate their recruits from important lay contacts for several years, furnish new ego ideals and reference groups, impress upon the recruit his absolute social dependence upon the profession for his further advancement, and punish him for inappropriate attitudes or behavior. * * *

Social controls buttress the effects of socialization, and here again the larger society and the professional community interact in a complex way. There is probably a correlation between the degree of community of the profession and the extent of difference between the values of the practitioners and those of the larger society or of clients. However, in its bid for respect from the larger society, the professional community must justify each provision in its code of ethics or etiquette by invoking ethical notions that are also accepted by the larger society, even when certain provisions seem to the lay eye at least potentially exploitative. As an additional complexity, the client may be only partially aware of the provisions that guard him, and is himself not bound to do much in order to be protected by them. It is the professional who must abide by them.

Corresponding to these potential strains, the "working codes" of ethics—written or unwritten—largely define appropriate professional behavior with respect to four categories of people: the larger community, fellow practitioners, unauthorized practitioners, and clients. The lawyer must control his own client in court. The physician must not refer a patient to an unauthorized practitioner, and the professional community puts pressure on the lay society to enforce legislation against the unauthorized. Obviously, codes can demand conformity from only one of these, professional colleagues. On the other hand, colleagues control each other's behavior with respect to the other categories.

In turn *each* of the four categories of persons possesses some measures of social control: the larger community through the legal agencies of the state; the client through his choice or rejection of the professional; the professional community, or colleagues, through their control over prestige and career advancement, as well as over the legal agencies of the state, such as licensing boards; and unauthorized practitioners by offering services to clients who are not satisfied with the profession.

But professions vary in the degree to which they rely upon one of these controls rather than another. None seems to rely greatly upon state control agencies, which in any event are largely staffed by professionals. The professional community exercises less control itself, when *client* economic controls are based on criteria that are accepted by the profession. Indeed, the professional group requires its control over its own members precisely *because* its judgments do not coincide generally with those of clients. As a consequence, its members *need* the protection of the professional community and will submit to its demands. A negative case is engineering, where the client is usually experienced, has mainly a contractual relationship with his engineer, and demands from the engineer what the profession itself would demand. As a result, compared with other professions, the engineering community has relatively less control over individual members. At the other extreme are professions dealing in human relations, such as the clergy or medicine, where the client is thought to be a poor judge of the professional product. Consequently, his choices would not reflect the judgment of the professional community, and the latter exercises strong moral control over the practitioner. The unauthorized practitioner is most successful where the profession has poor technical control over a given problem.

Bureaucracy opens a further range of structural relationships. The professional who is also a bureaucrat becomes less *directly* dependent on the professional community for his career advancement, so that the ordinary sanctions of that community may have less impact. Nevertheless, the bureaucracy usually hires, fires, or advances him upon the advice of peer or superior professionals, who in turn may feel themselves to be part of the professional community. Correlatively, the bureaucracy makes and enforces rules for the professional, and thus becomes—like the professional community from which it derived most of those rules—a responsible control agent for the larger society. In turn, of course, the professional community is responsible to the bureaucracy for proper staffing.

By way of compensation, the professional community offers two main kinds of protection to its members. It protects the professional against client or lay community charges that it considers inappropriate or irrelevant. For example, * * * it takes a statistical view of professional errors of judgment. It also offers advantages to those who are part of this community, by structuring professional practice so that the insiders will generally fare better than outsiders, in spite of erroneous judgments that clients tend to make about professionals. Thus, in exchange for protection against the larger lay society, the professional accepts the social control of the professional community.

As a consequence, the larger society has obtained an *indirect* social control by yielding *direct* social control to the professional community, which thus can make judgments according to its own norms. As a corollary, the normative structure of the professional community is reinforced, while this community can avoid the loss of prestige that non-punishment of offenders would eventually cause. Professionals assert this relationship in their literature, and claim that their community is judged in lay society by their worst members. Moreover, they frequently argue that the most effective technique for avoiding lay control over the professional community is to maintain strong control over its members. Thus it is that the social control of the professional community over its members may be seen as a response to the threat of the larger lay society to control it. Failure to discipline would mean both a loss of prestige in the society, and a loss of community autonomy

Client Choice and Public Rankings

Client choices are a form of social control. They determine the survival of a profession or a specialty, as well as the career success of particular professionals. In turn, these choices determine the kind of professional help the society gets.

Almost no client *willingly* goes to an unethical or incompetent practitioner, and clients almost always claim that their own professionals are excellent. Yet, both informally and in their literature, professionals express a generally poor opinion of these choices. But, if these are *not* wise decisions, and the professional community is the only body that is competent to judge correctly, it would seem to be a violation of the professional ideal of service not to inform the larger society of its judgments. That is, if the larger society were to gain the benefit of professional knowledge, the professional community would publish evaluations of its members. Thereby, the larger society would benefit from better professional help, and the professional community might make individual practitioners more dependent on its approval.

Of course, professions are accustomed to ratings. In numerous professional schools, students are ranked. Examinations for entrance into the professions yield rankings that are sometimes made known. There are prizes for outstanding work. Professional associations place their honored members on boards and commissions. There are continuous professional judgments of high or low achievement. To the extent that any community exists, it evaluates the behavior of its members. Professional life is so fundamentally based on achievement, that such judgments of rank are made constantly. Indeed, rankings within the profession are a mode of social control.

However, such data are not generally available to the public, and are not widely known, even when not secret. The professional community will not rank its members for the larger society; and the latter cannot do so. In fact, the existing intra-professional evaluations create hostilities within the community, and the limitless challenge of professional life, for instance in the sciences, creates strong anxieties. The most successful practitioner, loaded with honors, worries about his failures and ineptness. The protective walls of the professional community keep these hostilities and anxieties within bounds by defining, for a given level of age, experience, training, and type of practice, what is a *passable* competence and achievement; and by forbidding the expression of such hostilities before the larger society. The guild asserts essentially that all, or nearly all, are colleagues, and that if reasonable allowances are made, they are all wiser in their craft than outsiders can be. As a corollary, these definitions protect the individual practitioner against impossible demands of the larger society, e.g., that he not make any errors in judgment, that he know all the latest discoveries and techniques, etc. Thus, colleague criticism is rarely permitted before laymen, and the professions justify the rule by asserting that such criticism would lower the standing of the profession in the larger society. A closely related sociological proposition is also offered as a justification—that such criticisms, and presumably public rankings, would weaken the ties of the professional community, while it is the strength of these ties that makes possible *any* achievements of this community. That is, it cannot achieve its other, more important, goals if it ceases to be a community.

Structurally, to evaluate *colleagues* publicly is different from evaluating *trainees*. The latter are not yet community members. That is, the very process of evaluation denies or questions status inside the community, even if the ultimate judgment is favorable. Moreover, such evaluations would have to be made continuously, so that no practitioner could be certain of his membership—yet, it is this certainty of a shared identity, a common career, that is the central element in any community. An empirical approximation of this interaction occurs when the standards for entrance are raised substantially. This is, in effect, an announcement to the public that certain older members of the professional community have not been adequately trained. However, allegiance to the professional collectivity outweighs the service obligation to the public, and "grandfather clauses" lessen the severity of that indictment.

* * * Although public rankings might seem to increase the power of the community, in fact they would give over social controls to the larger society. For, even if the rankings were broken down into classes of practitioners, by specialization, rural-urban location, or experience, the economic effect on those toward the bottom of *any* list would be catastrophic. The result, then, would be that the utilization of such evaluations would be in the hands of the clients or lay public—and this would be a denial of the primacy of the professional community in affairs of social control. Rankings would then have little independent potency within the community.

* * *

These structural factors in the interaction between the professional community and the larger society suggest that the evaluations, which are the daily experience of all professionals, cannot and will not be formalized and made public. On the other hand, to leave the client—whether a bureaucracy or an individual—without any guidance is to put the professional community entirely at the mercy of the untutored client. Consequently, there are community patterns and processes that give at least indirect guidance to the larger society. Among these are: (1) institutional advertising, (2) professional referrals, (3) various types of reference plans, such as the Legal Reference Plan, or the emergency medical referral system, (4) the informal association of specialists within physically contiguous offices, (5) formal lists and directories, (6) positions in bureaucracies, (7) awards and prizes, etc.

These are but rough and indirect guides, but they do serve to reduce the randomness of the choices made by the larger society without weakening the essential bonds within each professional community. It does not seem likely, on the other hand, that each professional community has found, unaided, the sociologically correct point of optimum balance between these two.

NOTES

1. A dictionary defines a "profession" as

> a calling requiring specialized knowledge and often long and intensive preparation including instruction in skills and methods as well as in the scientific, historical, or scholarly principles underlying such skills and methods, maintaining by force of organization or concerted opinion

> high standards of achievement and conduct, and committing its members to continued study and to a kind of work which has for its prime purpose the rendering of a public service.

Webster's Third New International Dictionary 1811 (1986). Sociologist Eliot Freidson defines a "professional" as "a person involved in an occupation which has assumed a dominant position in a division of labor so that it gains control over the determination of the substance of its own work." E. Freidson, Profession of Medicine xvii (1970). He distinguishes a profession from other occupations by noting that it is autonomous or self-directing and gives the individual practitioner substantial "control over the content and the terms of work." E. Freidson, Professional Dominance: The Social Structure of Medical Care 134 (1970).

2. The student should find Goode's article even more meaningful on rereading after becoming familiar with the medical profession and able to recognize how his general observations about professions apply to physicians. For example, chapter 5(§C) shows how a physician who belongs to a hospital medical staff qualifies as "a professional who is also a bureaucrat." Materials in chapter 6 will suggest how distinctions created by the medical profession may obscure more qualitative differences among physicians than they reveal.

3. Other sociologists have also supplied penetrating, though often conflicting, insights into the nature of the medical profession and its function in society. In addition to the works of Freidson, supra, see e.g., P. Starr, The Social Transformation of American Medicine (1982) (tracing the profession's rise and the emergence of threats to its high status in recent years); M. Larson, The Rise of Professionalism ch. 3 (1977) (a general critique of professions from a Marxist perspective); J. Berlant, Profession and Monopoly: A Study of Medicine in the United States and Great Britain (1975) (criticizing Talcott Parsons' "functionalist theory" of the medical profession and applying Max Weber's "theory of monopolization"); T. Parsons, The Social System 428–79 (1951) (viewing the organization of medicine as a functional societal response to the problem of disease).

4. There are many ways in which the legal system supports, or undermines, the concept of a self-governing professional community of physicians. The student will be asked at various points throughout these materials to consider the merits and consistency of legal rules expressing society's somewhat ambivalent attitude toward the medical profession as an instrument of social control.

Professional Values in a Changing Market

NOTES AND QUESTIONS ON PROFESSIONALISM AS A RESPONSE TO MARKET FAILURE

1. *"The New Industrial Complex."* Arnold S. Relman, M.D., was until 1991 the influential editor of the prestigious *New England Journal of Medicine* and a leading exponent of traditional professional values. In the article from which the following quotation is taken, he triggered an important national debate concerning the role of for-profit firms in the hospital and health care field:

> * * * In our country we are used to the notion that private enterprise should supply most of the goods and services that our society requires. With the growing demand for all kinds of health care over the past two decades and the increasing complexity and cost of the services and facilities required, wasn't it inevitable that businesses were attracted to this new market? Modern health-care technology needs massive investment of capital—a problem that has become more and more difficult for the voluntary nonprofit institutions. How appropriate, then, for private entrepreneurs to come forward with the capital needed to build and equip new hospitals, nursing homes, and laboratories, and to start new health-care businesses. The market was there and a good profit ensured; the challenge was simply to provide the necessary services efficiently and at an acceptable level of quality.
>
> In theory, the free market should operate to improve the efficiency and quality of health care. Given the spur of competition and the discipline exerted by consumer choice, private enterprise should be expected to respond to demand by offering better and more varied services and products, at lower unit costs, than could be provided by nonprofit voluntary or governmental institutions. Large corporations ought to be better managed than public or voluntary institutions; they have a greater incentive to control costs, and they are in a better position to benefit from economies of scale. We Americans believe in private enterprise and the profit motive. How logical, then, to extend these concepts to the health-care sector at a time when costs seem to be getting out of control, voluntary institutions are faltering, and the only other alternative appears to be more government regulation.
>
> That, at least, is the theory. Whether the new medical-industrial complex is in fact improving quality and lowering unit cost in comparison with the public or private voluntary sectors remains to be determined. There are no adequate studies of this important question, and we will have to suspend judgment until there are some good data. But even without such information, I think that there are reasons to be concerned about this new direction in health care.
>
> * * *
>
> There are [many] unique features of the medical marketplace, not the least of which is the heavy, often total, dependence of the consumer (patient) on the advice and judgment of the physician. Kenneth Arrow, in explaining why some of the economist's usual assumptions about the competitive free market do not apply to medical care, referred to this phenomenon as the "informational inequality" between patient and physician. Unlike consumers shopping for most ordinary commodities, patients do not often decide what medical services they need—doctors usually do that for them. Probably more than 70 per cent of all expenditures for personal health care are the result of decisions of doctors.

All these special characteristics of the medical market conspire to produce an anomalous situation when private business enters the scene. A private corporation in the health-care business uses technology often developed at public expense, and it sells services that most Americans regard as their basic right—services that are heavily subsidized by public funds, largely allocated through the decisions of physicians rather than consumers, and almost entirely paid for through third-party insurance. The possibilities for abuse and for distortion of social purposes in such a market are obvious.

Health care has experienced an extraordinary inflation during the past few decades, not just in prices but in the use of services. A major challenge—in fact, *the* major challenge—facing the health-care establishment today is to moderate use of our medical resources and yet protect equity, access, and quality. The resources that can be allocated to medical care are limited. With health-care expenditures now approaching 10 per cent of the gross national product, it is clear that costs cannot continue to rise at anything near their present rate unless other important social goals are sacrificed. We need to use our health-care dollars more effectively, by curbing procedures that are unnecessary or inefficient and developing and identifying those that are the best. Overuse, where it exists, can be eliminated only by taking a more critical view of what we do and of how we use our health-care resources.

How will the private health-care industry affect our ability to achieve these objectives? In an ideal free competitive market, private enterprise may be good at controlling unit costs, and even at improving the quality of its products, but private businesses certainly do not allocate their own services or restrict the use of them. On the contrary, they "market" their services; they sell as many units as the market will bear. They may have to trim their prices to sell more, but the fact remains that they are in business to increase their total sales.

If private enterprise is going to take an increasing share of the health-care market, it will therefore have to be appropriately regulated. We will have to find some way of preserving the advantages of a private health-care industry without giving it free rein and inviting gross commercial exploitation. Otherwise, we can expect the use of health services to continue to increase until government is forced to intervene.

The Role of the Medical Profession

It seems to me that the key to the problem of overuse is in the hands of the medical profession. With the consent of their patients, physicians act in their behalf, deciding which services are needed and which are not, in effect serving as trustees. The best kind of regulation of the health-care marketplace should therefore come from the informed judgments of physicians working in the interests of their patients. In other words, physicians should supply the discipline that is provided in commercial markets by the informed choices of prudent consumers, who shop for the goods and services they want, at prices that they are willing to pay.

Relman, The New Medical–Industrial Complex, 303 New Eng.J.Med. 963, 966–67 (1980).

2. *The Market Paradigm.* Another perspective on the conflict between professional values and the emerging market paradigm of medical care is provided in the following excerpt:

Thoughtful observers worry these days that the competitive model commercial interests are introducing into medical care will compromise the quality of care that has been upheld by the medical profession during this century. Yet the relations between quality and the underlying paradigms of competition and profession have not been carefully examined.

The fundamental nature of a profession is indicated by the original meaning of the word: a vow—solemn, altruistic, and honorable—made upon entering a religious order. * * * [P]rofessionals have claimed exclusive rights to practice the skills they profess to know, to act objectively on behalf of their clients, and to demand trust in return. Thus, underlying a profession is a social contract that grants it license and monopoly over an esoteric and valued calling in return for high quality and altruistic service. In the British tradition that we have inherited, the professional was not to take a salary or to negotiate fees (as might a businessman) but to charge what he thought reasonable and fair. It is this contract that Relman fears will be lost in the commercial age of the medical-industrial complex.

Unanticipated consequences, however, have emanated from the medical-social contract. The best observers of American medicine have described in detail how the monopoly established by the medical profession earlier in this century has led to its promoting the most profitable lines of work, organizational arrangements, and financing schemes while denigrating public health, preventive medicine, primary care, prepaid programs, and other approaches that have contributed to better health in other advanced societies. There is a fundamental conflict of interest inherent in the physician's receiving fees for the services he decides should be rendered—a conflict that ranges from running a private practice to managing a medical corporation. Physicians have long been entrepreneurs. What has made the medical-industrial complex so awesome—and profitable—is that it has operated not in a competitive marketplace but rather in a "cost-plus" reimbursement system in which third-party insurers (and the public) pay for whatever is ordered by physicians.

* * *

The Consequences of Competition and Commerce

There has always been competition within the medical profession: for admission to good teaching programs, for clinical distinction, and for various forms of prestige. What seems like a new element is the rather commercial competition for patients, though that too has been present before. In fact, it is medicine's recent period, characterized by the umbrella of cost-plus insurance, that has been unique in its protection of physicians from the commercial aspects of practicing medicine. Thus, the reemergence of commerce in medicine represents a cultural shift from the myths of professional purity that found their fullest expression in an era characterized by a protected and subsidized market over which the profession ruled. We can gain some perspective on the current swirl of events by looking at what 18th-century philosophers wrote about the nature and consequences of commercial competition in ways that are directly pertinent to American medicine today.

Montesquieu agreed with Hobbes that "every man who has power tends to abuse that power; he will go up to the point where he meets with barriers." Precisely for that reason, Montesquieu argued vigorously for the competition that commerce brings; for as each man pursues his interests he will be a countervailing force to others. * * *

Competition could not only check unbridled excesses among competitors, but competitors could also make up a coalition against the excesses of a ruling elite. Particularly astute were Sir James Steuart's observations of how the princes who promoted commerce to enhance their own wealth created thereby a class of affluent and wealthy entrepreneurs who limited princely authority. In a subtle way, this is what has happened in American medicine over the past 30 years. It is not that today's commercial health-care corporations and commercial competition are a new element; the entrepreneurial thrust has been there all along. Now, however, they have become an important force in limiting and altering the politics of organized medicine.

Competition lies at the heart of the philosophy of capitalism, for without it one would not have a network of mutual obligations or a balance of countervailing interests but new forms of despotism through monopoly. It is just for this reason that antitrust laws were passed. The excesses of capital accumulation, just like the excesses of professional dominance, can by another route reduce the quality of services. By extension, philosophers like Montesquieu * * * were arguing for professionally regulated competition, with the profession establishing standards of care, quality, and ethics under which providers would compete for business.

Examining the impact of competition on the three kinds of quality leads to some interesting results. Clinical quality can be high if it is professionally regulated and if it is commercially attractive. To date, there have been no studies that have rigorously compared clinical quality in proprietary and nonprofit institutions. Competition introduces another kind of quality at the individual level that the professional model does not recognize—namely, quality as measured by consumer satisfaction. In reality, the medical profession has been ambivalent about consumer satisfaction. On the one hand it disdains the way patients judge quality on medically irrelevant grounds; on the other hand it uses those grounds as a way of attracting patients. This is the unstated commercial side of professional behavior that in competition becomes a central tenet. As a consequence, consumer quality is by definition high when competitive providers give patients what they want. In the process they could give clinically inferior care, though no studies show this yet to be a serious problem. The widespread fear of inferior care is itself the most effective safeguard. In addition, a new class of consumers is growing rapidly—the expert, experienced, well-informed medical directors who negotiate large service contracts for corporations and institutions. As for social quality, competitive health care is more likely to match the level of care to the problems being treated, emphasize primary care, reduce the number of hospital days, and develop health-promotion programs. Social needs that are unprofitable, such as immunizations and primary care among the poor, will continue to be ignored until they are made economically attractive. Herein lies the principal danger of commercial medicine—that its world view pushes aside the moral language that deals with caring for what Edmund Pellegrino calls "the casualties of our new competitive ethos." Regarding relative quality, competitive medicine sometimes provides more for less and sometimes not. However, the benefits of competitive medicine depend on competitive conditions, and many barriers remain.

The Future of Professional Competition

Competition in medical care is likely to grow, not only because the increasing surplus of physicians and the concern about costs will endure, but also because powerful groups of "consumers" are coming into being for the first time who will "shop" for cost-effective care. These consumers include corporations, unions, and state and federal governments. In this new field of forces, some physicians will win and some will lose. The winners will be those who understand the nature of competition and know how to use resources efficiently. A key to using resources efficiently is understanding that whereas the professional model advocates providing the best possible care at any price, the competitive model advocates providing good care at the best price. Moreover, quality of care is measured in terms of procedures or outcome. It will not be long before organized consumers and enterprising physicians will challenge the fixed boundaries established by medical licenses and rules of certification so that they can match training with task in the most cost-effective way.

* * *

The next few years may see enterprising physicians and health administrators shift from the professional model, with its hallowed traditions and monopolistic tendencies to one of professionally regulated competition. They will use delegation, substitution, preset criteria for quality, and management skills to improve the social and relative

> quality of care. The extent to which organized medicine at the state and national level defends anticompetitive barriers or facilitates a responsible transition remains to be seen. But the 18th-century philosophers and economists noted that competition makes the prince rule more wisely than "his wishes alone intend."

Light, Is Competition Bad?, 309 New Eng.J.Med. 1315 (1983).

3. *Relman's Economics.* Consider Dr. Relman's economic analysis and conclusions:

(a) *A "Public Good"?* At one point in his article (Relman, supra, at 966), Relman describes health care as "a public rather than a private good." Is this an accurate characterization? Hansmann, in an article reproduced in the next section of this chapter, defines a public good as follows: "a good or service such that (1) the cost of providing the good to many persons is not appreciably more than the cost of providing it to one; and (2) once the good has been provided to one person, it is difficult to prevent others from enjoying it as well." Examples include national defense and information that, once published, is widely available to persons who need not pay for its use. An example of a mixed public/private good in the medical field is biomedical research, which is heavily supported by government subsidies but which is also carried out for private profit in fields (such as pharmaceuticals) where patent protection is available.

When might personal health care be a public good? Presumably, Relman's idea was that health care, while not a "public good" in the foregoing technical sense, is a "merit good"—that is, something that society generally does not want rationed strictly in accordance with willingness or ability to pay. If government is willing to classify something as a merit good and to subsidize its production and distribution, is there any reason why commercial firms should be excluded from providing it?

(b) *Third–Party Payment.* Arguing that "health insurance converts patients from consumers to claimants who want medical care virtually without concern for price," Relman asserts that "the classic laws of supply and demand do not operate because health-care consumers do not have the usual incentives to be prudent, discriminating purchasers." Is his conception of the effects of third-party payment accurate? Has he adequately allowed for the possibility of alterations in the way financial protection is provided? Can "the market" solve the problems he identifies? If not, why not?

(c) *Information.* In what other ways (besides the prevalence of insurance) does the market for health care differ from other markets? Is the information problem remediable? A consumer employs a personal physician precisely because the latter is expert on subjects about which the former is ignorant. These subjects include not only medical facts but also the quality of, and the necessity for, various inputs that might be employed in his treatment, such as specialists, hospitals, and pharmaceutical agents. Is comparable help available to the consumer in choosing a primary physician or an insurance plan? Does Light suggest some ways in which consumers might overcome their ignorance in such matters? The problem of "informational inequality" or "information asymmetry" is a common problem in all markets but is particularly serious in health care. Many institutional and regulatory features of the health care industry are traceable to information problems, which will be referred to at many points in the materials ahead. Although professionalism is one response to these problems, is it the best or only answer that society can find?

(d) *Agency Issues*. Relman appears to believe that physicians and the organized medical profession are the only agents whom consumers can trust to assist them in making difficult choices affecting their own health. What other agents might the consumer rely upon? What forces keep the various possible agents responsive to the full range of consumer concerns? Is professionalism the best or only source of the assurances that consumers require?

(e) Is Relman right when he says that commercial firms seek to maximize total sales and output? For his later views, see Relman, Shattuck Lecture—The Health Care Industry: Where Is It Taking Us?, 325 New Eng.J.Med. 854 (1991) ("We cannot afford all the care a market-driven system is capable of giving"). See also responsive Letters to Editor, 326 New Eng.J.Med. 205 (1992), including the suggestion by an official of a trade association of for-profit hospitals that "were we to impose limits on the tax subsidy for health insurance, enact laws to help small businesses obtain insurance, reform the malpractice laws, and accelerate the development of treatment protocols, the marketplace would respond with incentives against inappropriate care."

4. *Some History of Medical Ethics.* Light's historical references suggest how timeless are the issues confronted in medicine in recent years. Indeed, as the following discussion shows, these issues were current at the time of Adam Smith:

> One of the most conspicuous themes in [Thomas] Percival's medical ethics [written in 1794 and borrowed from extensively by the American Medical Association in its first Code of Ethics adopted in 1847] is his opposition to any form of competition. He opposes price competition and any claims which might distinguish one physician from another, i.e., quality competition. This is in marked contrast to the deep interest in competitive devices of one of Percival's contemporaries, the liberal Adam Smith. Since Smith's *Wealth of Nations* was published in 1776, one would expect that an educated man such as Percival was familiar with the arguments of Smith. Even though Percival never mentions Smith, he appears to have responded to liberalism in his code of ethics. Unlike Smith, Percival also opposes individualizing tendencies in social organization. Seeing dangers such as unchecked exploitation by individual practitioners, Percival favors the idea of a principled honorable fraternity of self-denying practitioners. * * *
>
> When the Enlightenment began in England, the question of the rationality of the corporation system, typified by the RCP [Royal

College of Physicians], arose. One major system of medical ethics, John Gregory's, specifically attacked the monopolistic medical corporations. John Gregory was a professor at the great medical school at Edinburgh, and presumably his independent position there influenced his conclusions about the problem with organized practitioners. His ethics found considerable following. * * *

Gregory's writings on the obligations of the physician to the patient are similar to those Percival later wrote. * * * Unlike Percival, he suggests few regulations for intraprofessional relations, the so-called "medical etiquette," except for consultations even with nonregular physicians and no "arrangements with apothecaries," such as kickbacks and fee splitting.

Gregory's ethical code, however, stands in opposition to the monopolistic codes of the RCP and of the later Percivalean work. Percival saw the forces binding the profession into a group—esprit de corps, a common academic training, and support of each other's reputations—as the source of the best in medicine, as something to be encouraged. Without this group basis, medicine would lose its professionality and hence its excellence. Gregory challenged this central presumption and thereby also the medical profession's elitist autonomy as an independent institutional body. The domination of medical thought by men of the practicing profession, he explained, distorted the pursuit of medical knowledge and blocked the development and delivery of medical care. * * *

Gregory's * * * criticism struck * * * directly at the type of professional organization Percival and other conservatives advocated: an autonomous, self-regulating body of elitist experts who made a living by treating patients and who sought to maximize the distance between medical man and patient, using secrecy and systematic ignorance to accentuate the disadvantageous position of the patient. Gregory believed, however, that confining practice "entirely to a class of men who live by it as a profession, is unfavorable to the progress of the art." The love of and devotion to medicine as an art, differentially distributed among physicians, "is often checked by a necessary attention to private interest." In most arts compromise by private interest is acceptable because "all mankind are judges." But in the case of medicine and of medicine alone, the public is in no position to judge the merit of a practitioner; medical practice is too private and medical science kept too secret. A physician with an acquaintance with "the outlines of practice," good presence, and good sense can persuade the public of his merit and become successful, for the public assumes that a physician clever in nonmedical matters will also be good in medicine. Gregory was taken aback, however, by the success of some incompetents who had little to recommend them even outside of medicine. The public could not seem to judge good physicians even by analogy. Like the conservative, then, Gregory concluded that the public could not judge accurately the technical merit of a physician.

Gregory posed for himself this problem: granted, the public cannot evaluate physicians accurately and so cannot direct itself to the best doctors; only the physician's own profession can judge his merit and direct patients to men of superior merit; *but* the collective interests of the practicing profession require that superior merit be concealed so that competition not occur. Therefore, the private interests of the profession led to the concealment of information which might benefit the medical interests of patients.

* * *

The division between Percival's conservative and Gregory's liberal versions of Enlightenment medicine is best captured in Gregory's concluding comments. For Percival, the Enlightenment and rationality were available only to elites paternalistically bound to assuming the burden of protecting the public. For him, the only conceivable authority in medical matters was the practicing medical profession as represented by the licensing bodies of the Royal Colleges. In his perspective, if physicians would only rise above the temptations of personal interest, society would be well served. Gregory rejected much of this formulation, claiming that the public was capable of assuming more responsibility for its own medical welfare than Percival would allow, and that the medical practitioner compromised some of the goals of the profession.

J. Berlant, Profession and Monopoly: A Study of Medicine in the United States and Great Britain 82, 87–88, 91–94 (1975).

5. *Arrow's and Starr's Views on Professionalism.* In a classic 1963 article, referenced by Relman, the distinguished economist Kenneth Arrow sought to explain the pervasive presence in the health care marketplace of practices and institutions that deviate from the classical competitive model. Arrow, Uncertainty and the Welfare Economics of Medical Care, 53 Am. Econ.Rev. 941 (1963). Specifically, Arrow sought to discover an economic rationale for such special features of the (then-existing) health care market as (*a*) widespread price discrimination, including not only use of sliding fee scales based on ability to pay but even the provision of some free care; (*b*) the equalization of insurance premiums through the use of "community rating," which has a redistributive tendency, rather than "experience rating," which is based strictly on actuarial (cost) factors; (*c*) the ubiquity of nonprofit corporations; (*d*) the simultaneous subsidization of medical education and restriction of access to it; (*e*) the predominance of fee-for-service payment; (*f*) the absence of overt price competition; and (*g*) ethical and legal restrictions on such things as professional advertising, prepayment for medical care, and HMO-type "closed-panel practice (contractual arrangements which [eliminate free choice and] bind the patient to a particular group of physicians)." Id. at 954.

Arrow posited that the phenomena, policies, and practices fostered by the medical profession—which he characterized as "nonmarket social institutions"—arose because optimality could not be achieved by market forces. He argued that, when the market does not work and government has not acted to solve the problem, "other social institutions will step into the optimality gap, and that the medical-care industry, with its variety of special institutions, some ancient, some modern, exemplifies this tendency." Id. at 947. Arrow, in other words, sensed the operation of some kind of nonmarket "invisible hand."

According to Arrow, the market for health care fails because of the unpredictable nature of the need for medical care, the vast difference in the information possessed by doctor and patient, and the consumer's ignorance concerning the quality of health care he was receiving, had received, or could expect to receive. In Arrow's view, these barriers to the proper functioning of the market had inspired what sociologist Talcott Parsons had called "a 'collectivity orientation,' which distinguishes medicine and other professions from business, where self-interest on the part of the participants is the accepted norm." Id. at 949. The impossibility of both fully informed purchasing and "ideal insurance" against the consequences of uncertainty and ignorance led, Arrow believed, "to the setting up of a relationship of trust and confidence, one which the physician has a social obligation to live up to." Id. at 965. Arrow's views, emphasizing both the collective and the individual responsibilities of physicians, seem directly reflected in Relman's appeals for continued reliance on nonmarket mechanisms in health care.

In a 1982 book, sociologist Paul Starr, although agreeing with Arrow about the problems confronting consumers in the health care marketplace, suggested that professionalism, which Arrow views as a response to inherent market failure, may in fact be a cause of some of the market's difficulties. Describing Arrow's article as "perhaps the single most influential neoclassical treatment" of "the political economy of American medicine," Starr wrote,

> Arrow suggests that these various structural features are attempts to compensate for imperfections in the medical market. His point of departure is the concept of "market failure"; as he puts it: "[W]hen the market fails to achieve an optimal state, society will, to some extent at least, recognize the gap, and nonmarket social institutions will arise to bridge it." The medical care market fails to perform efficiently because patients cannot assess the value of treatment, nor obtain insurance that would compensate them for any imperfect outcome. "The value of information is frequently not known in any meaningful sense to the buyer; if, indeed, he knew enough to measure the value of information, he would know the information itself." Patients are utterly dependent on physicians in ways that buyers are not normally dependent on sellers. Consequently, according to Arrow, other safeguards, such as ethical restrictions on physicians' behavior and licensing restrictions on entry into the market, arise to protect patients.
>
> Unfortunately, Arrow leaves unexplained the connection between the prevalence of uncertainty and the insistence of physicians on fee-for-service payment. Prepayment is itself an adaptation to uncertainty

in the incidence of disease and the costs of treatment; if anything, the profession's opposition to contract practice (and later to health insurance, medical cooperatives, and other prepaid health plans) increased the burden of uncertainty that patients had to bear.

This missing link in Arrow's argument is related to more fundamental difficulties. Uncertainty in medical care is partly a product of the way the market is organized. If the purchaser of medical services were the state or some collective agency, such as a fraternal society, it could employ knowledgeable agents to choose among physicians and medical facilities. Uncertainty has also been enhanced by the medical profession—in fact, by some of the features Arrow discusses, such as codes of professional ethics that require doctors called in on consultations to withhold from patients information that would discredit a colleague. Of course, most uncertainty is not artificially manufactured. Uncertainty reflects more general cultural beliefs. Democratic thought in the early 1800s held that all that was useful in medicine was within the reach of ordinary men. * * * [T]he advance of science and decline of confidence in common sense between the Jacksonian and Progressive eras helped restore a belief in the legitimate complexity of medicine. An increased sense of uncertainty (as was evident in the Supreme Court decision in Dent v. West Virginia [129 U.S. 114 (1889), upholding physician licensure against constitutional attack]) favored the reinstitution of licensing at the end of the nineteenth century.

But while the growth of uncertainty may explain why there were departures from the competitive market, it cannot explain the form the departures took. Other institutional arrangements, besides the restrictive practices adopted by the profession or enacted at its behest, would also have been adaptations to uncertainty, but they met resistance and were defeated. The particular alternative to the competitive market that developed in America cannot be derived from a purely abstract analysis; it requires an analysis that is both structural and historical. The structural features Arrow discusses have a history. He writes that when the market fails, "society" will make adjustments. This is too abstract. It is as if some inner dynamic were pushing the world toward Pareto optimality. One has to ask: For whom did the market fail, and how did "society" make these adjustments? The competitive market was failing no one more than the medical profession, and it was the profession that organized to change it—that barred advertising and price competition, lobbied for licensing laws, engaged in price discrimination, and fought against prepaid health plans.

Yet there is a still deeper problem. Arrow looks at the structure of the medical market as a rational adaptation to certain inherent characteristics of medical care; he attempts to explain the particulars of the system at a given moment in history in terms of universal features of medicine. There is the presumption that what is real is rational or, as the economists say, "optimal." * * * The result is not so much to explain as to explain away the particular institutional structure medical care has assumed in the United States.

P. Starr, The Social Transformation of American Medicine 226–27 (1982).

6. *The Professional Paradigm.* Blumstein, in an article examining "the competing visions of medical care represented by the professional paradigm and the market-based economic paradigm," describes the former paradigm as follows:

A. The Premises Underlying the Professional Paradigm

Under traditional economic theory, a smoothly functioning market requires adequate information so that economic actors can behave in an economically rational manner. Perhaps the most important rationale advanced by proponents of the professional model is the asymmetry of information held by doctors and patients. Critics of the market model in medical care contend that patients are essentially ignorant, whereas doctors are extremely well trained and expert. For advocates of the professional paradigm, what follows from that asymmetry is a justification for disempowering the market model's sovereign consumer. Instead of pursuing a strategy of market improvement—that is, improving the flow of understandable information or otherwise improving the functioning of the market—proponents of the professional model embrace a strategy of market substitution, in which the judgement of the physician is substituted for that of the patient.

The doctor's claim of expertise arises from scientific training. The scientific basis of medical training and practice legitimizes professional empowerment. Adoption of the professional model places the professional in a fiduciary relationship with the patient, for whom the professional makes decisions. But it also shifts a power between purchaser and service provider. Surrogate (and necessarily paternalistic) decisionmaking replaces consumer sovereignty. This confers upon the professional the authority to decide important economic questions concerning the demand for services and standards of quality. In an environment characterized by third-party financing, professional control of decisionmaking has led to ever-increasing expenditures in the name of quality, which is the professionals' watchword in combating efforts to rein in escalating costs.

Concomitant with the professional model are the duty of professional self-regulation, the commitment to promote and monitor high standards of quality, and the de-emphasis on economic issues. The de-emphasis on economic issues reinforces the professional paradigm by directing attention away from the economic characteristics of medical care service delivery.

Historically, advocates for improved access to care have linked up with the professions. For example, in 1965 this alliance resulted in the enactment of Medicare and Medicaid. The deal assured unrestricted, tax-generated public money to support access for the poor and the elderly in exchange for greater physician autonomy through institutionalized deference to physicians' clinical authority. The doctors were assured that their professional and economic autonomy would be respected, and public dollars would flow to provide medical benefits to undeserved groups. The Medicare and Medicaid deal adopted a blank check approach that virtually guaranteed, as commentators predicted, that cost escalation would ensue.

The professional paradigm places power paternalistically in physician hands. Physicians perceive themselves as controlling decisionmaking, and that perception is an important part of the professional paradigm, Physicians as professionals also control quality through peer review mechanisms that are part of the professional paradigm. Because of their expertise and professionalism, physicians look within the professional for their frame of reference regarding quality assurance.

This professional decisionmaking hegemony leads to physician control of costs and output. By shifting control from consumers to physician fiduciaries, the professional model insulates the medical services market from economic trade offs. In the traditional economic marketplace, consumers trade off increments of quality because of cost. Once decisionmaking authority is ceded to professionals, professional standards govern. Decisions are seen as technical and scientific so that consensus in decisionmaking is professionally oriented. Quality-cost trade offs are attenuated, and trade offs between medical care an other goods or services are precluded by dedicated medical care financing through nontransferable third-party insurance. Under the professional model, economics and trade offs become marginalized in the policy debate. Medical care thus becomes an exclusively technical-scientific enterprise.

B. Techniques for Promoting the Professional Paradigm

This Part identifies four techniques that have been used to promote the professional paradigm. First is freedom of choice of physician for patients, a phenomenon that has been paired with third party payment. Clearly the idea is to keep financial considerations out of the patients' deliberative process. The only thing that matters from a policy perspective is guaranteeing the right of patients to choose their professional provider, who faces minimal resource constraints because of third-party payment. That traditionally has meant that no expense is spared. The medical profession historically has opposed trading off limited physician choice for economic benefits, a hallmark of managed care.

Second, the professional paradigm has been bolstered by arguments that the imposition of resource constraints and containment of medical care expenditures will lead to lower quality. The treat to quality is perceived as the physicians' silver bullet in the debate about health care policy. In the market, however, the threat of lower quality should not ring the death knell for proposed policy shifts. Cost-benefit and risk-benefit calculations occur constantly and are and integral part of the economic marketplace. If lower quality were the death knell, we would not have different segments in the automobile industry—only the Lexus, the Infiniti, and the Mercedes would be manufactured.

In short, policies that lower the quality of care may be rational if higher levels of quality can be achieved only at extremely high costs. Intuitively, we all engage in such balancing. We take prudent (and sometimes even imprudent) risks to achieve objectives that are important to us, or because we believe that the cost of safety is excessive in that it would cause us to forgo other favorable benefits. Indeed, these kinds of economic trade-offs are routinely made in the medical care marketplace, but usually out of the public's sight. But only academic types, who are not running for public office, are prepared to state what should be obvious—that it might be socially optimal to have lower quality medical care, at least in some circumstances, if the cost of the highest quality care is too high. In no other marketplace do we say "spare no expense, cost is irrelevant." It is not radical to suggest that the highest levels of quality might be sub-optimal and that the diminution-of-quality argument should not be checkmate in health policy debates.

The third technique often used to promote and protect the professional paradigm is opposition to rationing. This is a great rhetorical ploy. We are told rationing is a terrible thing. "Rationing is a bad idea." But in the economic marketplace scarce resources are always allocated to their most beneficial use.

Use of the term "rationing" implies that someone is doing the choosing. But opponents of rationing do not always focus on that technical issue. Instead, they employ the term synonymously with the concept of allocating scarce resources. Yet, the need to allocate resources is a fundamental reality of economic life. Consumers constantly choose among alternatives based upon sensitive consideration of costs, risks, and benefits.

The rhetoric of rationing and denigration of its use suggest that economic trade-offs are inappropriate when it comes to health care. Rationing connotes government control over consumer expenditures. In the private economic marketplace, resources are allocated not by government but by the private choice of atomistic decisionmakers—households and firms. By failing to recognize that resource allocation is a normal market function, opponents of rationing impliedly suggest that private choice plays no part in the medical care marketplace. That form of rhetoric reinforces the tenet of the professional paradigm that medical care service decisions are scientific and technical in character, without a substantial economic dimension.

Fourth and finally in this regard, proponents of the professional model have advocated a unitary standard of practice in the medical services marketplace. In opposing policy proposals to restrain costs, they war against a two-tier or multi-tier medical system. But in the typical economic marketplace there is nothing unusual about the existence of multiple tiers, which may conform to consumer preferences. In the absence of special egalitarian claims, there is nothing inherently wrong with multiple levels of quality or multiply styles of practice. Presented honestly, the debate is about what degrees of difference society will allow, what obligation society has to finance care for those unable to pay, and who should benefit from public subsidy and in what magnitude. The truth is that serious analysts cannot persuasively defend the principle of total equality of end result. There are only two ways to achieve that kind of end-result equality—leveling up or leveling down (or some hybrid of the two approaches).

To achieve single tier equality, one must first establish the level of care required. Will society make it illegal for those seeking a higher standard to purchase additional medical care with their own resources, or for providers to sell those services in the marketplace? Is that the goal? That would be a leveling down scenario, and some coercion would be required to achieve quality given the differences in preferences and income/wealth in the nation. When unpacked, the ostensible ideal or a single tier becomes little more than a politically appealing but analytically vapid rhetorical flourish. But facing up to the real debate—what degree of difference in medical services should society accept—poses tough ethical and economic questions that direct attention away from the professional solution, which is to leave the level of services to the discretion of the profession with unlimited public payment.

Blumstein, Health Care Reform and Competing Visions of Medical Care: Antitrust and State Provider Cooperation Legislation, 79 Cornell L. Rev. 1459, 1464–69 (1994).

For a strong counterattack against the commercialization of medicine based on the professional paradigm, see McArthur & Moore, The Two Cultures and the Health Care Revolution: Commerce and Professionalism in Medical Care, 277 J.A.M.A. 985 (1997). Understandably, the new pressures on physicians have called forth much commentary (too extensive to be referenced here). Although much of this commentary has been merely reactionary, the insights of some professional commentators have been thoughtful, realistic, and constructive. See, e.g., Blumenthal, The Vital Role of Professionalism in Health Care Reform, Health Affairs, Spring (I) 1994, p. 252 ("Many doctors equate professionalism with autonomy—to be left alone to do what they want, not only medically but financially. Autonomy, however, is not a divine right of medical or other professionals."); Berenson, Do Physicians Recognize Their Own Best Interests?, Health Affs., Spring 1994, p. 185. The latter author blames the professional paradigm of medical care for obscuring for physicians the potential for ethical, professionally satisfying practice in a corporate health plan:

There remains a fundamental disagreement on the role of professionalism in the corporate practice environment. One view holds that physicians should be immunized from the commercial interests and many of the policies of managed care administrators, thereby ensuring that physicians continue to work for patients, not plans. The contrary view, which I endorse, holds that systems that pit managers against affiliated physicians are inherently dysfunctional, inhibit the full integration of financing and delivery, and will fail. Rather than pretending that the professional paradigm should reign supreme even in competitive markets, this view looks toward development of responsible corporate practice of medicine * * *. Instead of confronting the dictates of managers, physicians should become the managers.

Thus, physician autonomy should be promoted not because it adheres to the professional paradigm, but rather because patients generally prefer an unencumbered relationship with a caring and skilled physician.

Although observing that "physicians [understandably] feel threatened by the paradigm shift from professional practice to corporate practice," Berenson argues that skilled and conscientious physicians would find much to approve in a world in which corporate health plans rather than individual practitioners were primarily accountable for the quality as well as the cost of health care. Is Berenson's view realistic? Recall the discussion of today's health plans in chapter 2(§C).

7. *Questions.* (a) State as precisely as you can the concerns that Relman and Arrow might have about increasing commercialism in the health care sector? Are their concerns similar to Percival's? What is the argument against their position? Is it similar to Gregory's argument?

(b) Can you state the tenets of the professional paradigm of medical decision making? What are the tenets of the opposing market paradigm? What are the implications of each paradigm for the handling of information concerning the quality and appropriateness of health care?

(c) What might be lost in a competitive health care system? Is professionalism likely to be a casualty? In what sense? Will the element of trust be lost in the doctor-patient relationship? Will quality suffer? Be as precise as possible in your assessments.

(d) Will commercialism undermine the scientific tradition of sharing valuable information—through publication in journals, etc.? Are there possible offsetting benefits in the form of strengthened private incentives to generate new knowledge? Note how the concern here is with information and its character as a public or private good.

(e) Can one argue that professionalism ensures a higher degree of scientific rationality than is possible in a system driven primarily by consumer choice? In this connection, recall the findings in psychological research, referenced in chapter 2(§B), that individuals are easily influenced by the way choices are framed and indeed are systematically inconsistent and incoherent both in their weighing and treatment of risks and in their valuations of alternative outcomes. If the market is a poor vehicle for introducing rationality, should the medical profession be accorded ultimate decision-making authority? (The third alternative is, of course, government control through central planning or regulation, a subject considered at other points.) Consider the proposal, embodied in Senator Edward Kennedy's Health Security proposals of the 1970s and reappearing periodically since, to establish a fixed budget for the health care system, thus eliminating the openended financing of the past but leaving the allocation of the budget to some combination of political, planning, and professional processes. Would this approach strike the right balance between reliance on professionalism and political oversight? Or would political struggles over the size and division of the "pie" disappoint expectations?

Relman advocates a central decision-making role for the medical profession. Would reliance on professionalism ensure rationality? How closely do professionally developed norms and practice standards reflect scientific findings? Consider Wennberg's findings and the other observations on the state of medical practice, medical science, and clinical practice guidelines presented in chapter 2(§A).

(f) Is it possible that consumers are just rational enough to appreciate the need to seek the help of informed, rational persons who are in some way accountable to them for the quality of the services that they either provide or obtain on the consumer's behalf? The possibility that consumers might rely on agents, including lay-controlled middlemen, to assist them in purchasing health care is an important theme throughout this text. Especially in this and the following chapter, we shall see how ethical considerations were at one time used to justify collective professional actions and legal barriers designed to prevent anyone from interceding in the doctor/patient relationship.

SECTION B: THE EMERGENCE OF THE CORPORATION

Introduction to the For-Profit/Nonprofit Debate

NOTE ON FOR-PROFIT ENTERPRISE IN THE HEALTH CARE SECTOR

1. The debate touched off by the Relman article, supra, was carried on in many places. See, e.g., Institute of Medicine, For-profit Enterprise in Health Care (1986). A summary of the cited study presented the development this way:

> With little initial public notice, a vigorous and varied for-profit sector has developed in the predominantly not-for-profit world of medical care. Health services are now being provided by thousands of for-profit organizations that range from large investor-owned hospital and nursing home chains, whose stock has rapidly appreciated on the New York Stock Exchange, to various types of independent medical facilities—such as ambulatory surgery centers, cardiopulmonary testing centers, etc.—owned by local investors who often are also physicians. Sometimes the physician-owners generate revenues for the facilities by referring patients for services.
>
> Health care has long included a mixture of for-profit and not-for-profit activities. The manufacture and marketing of pharmaceuticals and medical equipment have always been predominantly organized on

a for-profit basis. The health insurance industry has included both for-profit and not-for-profit organizations. Not-for-profit forms have been more typical of the organizations that provide medical services to patients. This is because of the origins and evolution of the hospital as a charity institution providing care to the poor and not because of any organized social policy decision regarding appropriateness of different organizational forms. The availability and predictability of revenues that came with the rise of large-scale governmental payment for health services has opened up profit-making opportunities that did not previously exist.

* * *

Some analogous changes are also taking place in the not-for-profit health care sector. Not-for-profit health institutions (the survival of which also requires an excess of revenues over expenses) have variously been forming chains, establishing for-profit subsidiaries, selling services to other hospitals for profit, and taking on other attributes of the for-profit enterprises. There has been at least a short-term boom in the activities of attorneys and accountants who advise on reorganizing and incorporating various services to maximize revenues and reduce taxes. Even the language used today in hospital journals—such as "lines of business," "market shares," and "profit centers"—would have seemed foreign in the health policy world of only a few years ago.

* * *

Although knowledgeable observers agree that the growth of the for-profit sector is a development of major significance, there is as yet little agreement and few facts about the meaning and implications of that growth. Does the development of for-profit medical care represent a change in the goals pursued by medical professionals and institutions, or is it only a change in the methods by which the traditional goals of service are pursued? Does the growth in for-profit health care represent a decline in the ideals that morally anchored a powerful profession and facilitated necessary patient trust, or does it embody a more honest acknowledgment of realities that have always been present? Or is it a neutral development?

Gray, The New Health Care for Profit, National Research Council News Report, July–Aug., 1983, at 16–17, 21.

For a further examination of how increasing commercialization has affected hospitals and physician/patient relationships, see B. Gray, The Profit Motive and Patient Care: The Changing Accountability of Doctors and Hospitals (1991). Gray concludes that "nonprofit organizations and medical professionalism should continue as key elements in the structure of accountability of American health care." Although recognizing that economic pressures have lessened the distinction between nonprofit and for-profit hospitals, Gray stresses the importance of preserving the former, which he contends "conform more closely to a service ethic that remains central." See also S. Lutz & P. Gee, The For-profit Healthcare Revolution:

The Growing Impact of Investor-owned Health Systems in America (1995) (focusing on health care systems as well as hospitals); J. Seay & B. Vladeck, eds., In Sickness and in Health: The Mission of Voluntary Health Care Institutions (1988); Schlesinger et al., Nonprofit and For-profit Medical Care: Shifting Roles and Implications for Health Policy, 12 J. Health Pol., Pol'y & Law 427 (1987). (Lutz and Gee were reportedly planning to publish a more extensive history of the for-profit hospital industry in 1998.)

Legal scholars have pondered the policy implications of the increasing role of commercialism in medical care and of for-profit enterprise in the provision of hospital and health care. See, e.g., Blumstein, Health Care Reform and Competing Visions of Medical Care: Antitrust and State Provider Cooperation Legislation, 79 Cornell L.Rev. 1459, 1473–86 (1994); Frankford, Privatizing Health Care: Economic Magic to Cure Legal Medicine, 66 S.Cal.L.Rev. 1 (1992); Bloche, Corporate Takeover of Teaching Hospitals, 65 S.Cal.L.Rev. 1035 (1992).

2. A definite shift toward investor-owned enterprises in the health care industry is occurring. Between the first quarter of 1994 and the third quarter of 1995, for example, for-profit organizations gained 21,840 hospital beds, while nonprofits lost 16,827. Nevertheless, nonprofits still predominate, and the trend, while steady, is not as dramatic as the panic inspired in some circles has suggested. According to American Hospital Association statistics, the 5,256 nonfederal acute-care hospitals in the nation in 1994 broke down as follows: 3,139 nonprofits (59.7%), 719 investor-owned (13.7%), and 1398 public institutions (26.6%). When specialty hospitals are factored in, 17% of all nonfederal hospitals were owned by for-profit chains (owning 3 or more hospitals). An additional 363 hospitals (5.7%) were managed by investor-owned management companies. From 1982 to 1994, the percentage of acute-care hospitals owned by for-profit chains grew from 10% to 13.7%, and the percentage managed by for-profit companies grew from 4% to 5.7%.

3. Among the issues in the debate is the relative performance in terms of cost and quality of for-profit hospitals and other health care institutions. Before considering these empirical issues, the student must be introduced to the nature, legal character, and status of nonprofit, tax-exempt corporations. See generally M. Phelan, Nonprofit Enterprises: Law and Taxation (1996 looseleaf); B. Hopkins, The Law of Tax–Exempt Organizations (6th ed. 1992 & Supp. 1996); Brody, Charitable Endowments and the Democratization of Dynasty, 39 Ariz. L. Rev. 873 (1997) (examining historical roots and other features of charitable institutions); Developments in the Law—Nonprofit Corporations, 105 Harv. L. Rev. 1581 (1992).

NOTE: TRUSTEES OF DARTMOUTH COLLEGE v. WOODWARD, 17 U.S. (4 WHEAT) 518 (1819)

The New Hampshire legislature passed three acts "to amend the charter, and enlarge and improve the corporation of Dartmouth College," and the trustees challenged the legislation, arguing the inviolability of the corporation's charter under the Contracts Clause of the Constitution. The Supreme Court (Chief Justice Marshall) rejected the idea "that Dartmouth College has become a public institution, and its trustees public officers, exercising powers conferred by the public for public objects." (Id. at 635.) The nonprofit character of the corporation raised an additional problem, however:

> From this review of the charter, it appears, that Dartmouth College is an eleemosynary institution, incorporated for the purpose of perpetuating the application of the bounty of the donors, to the specified objects of that bounty; that its trustees or governors were originally named by the founder, and invested with the power of perpetuating themselves; that they are not public officers, nor is it a civil institution, participating in the administration of government; but a charity-school, or a seminary of education, incorporated for the preservation of its property, and the perpetual application of that property to the objects of its creation.
>
> Yet a question remains to be considered, of more real difficulty, on which more doubt has been entertained, than on all that have been discussed. The founders of the college, at least, those whose contributions were in money, have parted with the property bestowed upon it, and their representatives have no interest in that property. The donors of land are equally without interest, so long as the corporation shall exist. Could they be found, they are unaffected by any alteration in its constitution, and probably regardless of its form, or even of its existence. The students are fluctuating, and no individual among our youth has a vested interest in the institution, which can be asserted in a court of justice. Neither the founders of the college, nor the youth for whose benefit it was founded, complain of the alteration made in its charter, or think themselves injured by it. The trustees alone complain, and the trustees have no beneficial interest to be protected. Can this be such a contract, as the constitution intended to withdraw from the power of state legislation? Contracts, the parties to which have a vested beneficial interest, and those only, it has been said, are the objects about which the constitution is solicitous, and to which its protection is extended.
>
> The court has bestowed on this argument the most deliberate consideration, and the result will be stated. Dr. Wheelock, acting for himself, and for those who, at his solicitation, had made contributions to his school, applied for this charter, as the instrument which should enable him, and them, to perpetuate their beneficent intention. It was granted. An artificial, immortal being, was created by the crown, capable of receiving and distributing for-ever, according to the will of the donors, the donations which should be made to it. On this being, the contributions which had been collected were immediately bestowed. These gifts were made, not indeed to make a profit for the donors, or their posterity, but for something, in their opinion, of inestimable value; for something which they deemed a full equivalent for the

> money with which it was purchased. The consideration for which they stipulated, is the perpetual application of the fund to its object, in the mode prescribed by themselves. Their descendants may take no interest in the preservation of this consideration. But in this respect their descendants are not their representatives; they are represented by the corporation. The corporation is the assignee of their rights, stands in their place, and distributes their bounty, as they would themselves have distributed it, had they been immortal. So, with respect to the students who are to derive learning from this source; the corporation is a trustee for them also. Their potential rights, which, taken distributively, are imperceptible, amount collectively to a most important interest. These are, in the aggregate, to be exercised, asserted and protected, by the corporation.

Id. at 640–43.

The Court proceeded to consider whether the expectations of Dartmouth's donors were weighty enough to be given constitutional protection:

> It requires no very critical examination of the human mind, to enable us to determine, that one great inducement to these gifts is the conviction felt by the giver, that the disposition he makes of them is immutable. It is probable, that no man ever was, and that no man ever will be, the founder of a college, believing at the time, that an act of incorporation constitutes no security for the institution; believing, that it is immediately to be deemed a public institution, whose funds are to be governed and applied, not by the will of the donor, but by the will of the legislature.

Id. at 647. The Court concluded that a nonprofit corporation does indeed enjoy constitutional protection against legislative efforts to direct how its resources will be used.

Query whether a modern nonprofit hospital should enjoy the same constitutional protection. Would it be relevant, for example, that only a very small proportion (or none) of the hospital's assets were acquired by gift, as opposed to borrowing, unconditional government grants, and reinvestment of earnings?

Henry B. Hansmann, Reforming Nonprofit Corporation Law

129 U.Pa.L.Rev. 497, 501–11 (1981).

A. Characteristics and Classification

The defining characteristic of a nonprofit organization is that it is barred from distributing profits, or net earnings, to individuals who exercise control over it, such as its directors, officers, or members. This does not mean that a nonprofit organization is prohibited from *earning* a profit. Rather, it is only the *distribution* of profits that is prohibited; net income, if any, must be retained and devoted to the purposes for which the organization was formed. Moreover, it is only net income, or pure profits, that may not be distributed; nonprofits are generally free to pay reasonable compensation to individuals, including controlling individuals, for labor, services, or capital provided to the organization. For simplicity, I shall refer to this prohibition on the distribution of profits as the "nondistribution constraint."

In the United States, most nonprofits of any consequence are incorporated. * * *

Because of the nondistribution constraint, a nonprofit corporation, unlike a business corporation, cannot issue shares of stock that grant their owners a simultaneous right to participate in both profits and control. Some other device for allocating ultimate control over the organization must therefore be employed. The nonprofit corporation statutes are typically quite flexible in this regard. If the articles of incorporation so provide, the right to elect the board of directors, and to vote on other fundamental issues, can be lodged in a group of individuals designated as the organization's members. Alternatively, the power to appoint the directors can be given to other specified individuals or organizations, or the board can simply be made autonomous and self-perpetuating.

Given the variety of forms and functions common among nonprofits, it simplifies reference and analysis to categorize nonprofit organizations both according to the sources of their income and according to the way in which they are controlled.

Those organizations that receive the bulk of their income from relatively unrestricted donations and contributions I shall call *donative* nonprofits; typical examples are CARE, the American Red Cross, and the American Heart Association. Those organizations that, on the other hand, obtain most of their income from prices charged for goods or services they produce I shall call *commercial* nonprofits; this category includes many nonprofit day care centers, nursing homes, and hospitals, as well as the American Automobile Association and Consumers Union (publisher of Consumer Reports). Whether a nonprofit is donative or commercial, I shall refer to the individuals who are the ultimate source of its income as its *patrons*. The patrons of a donative nonprofit, therefore, are its donors, while the patrons of a commercial nonprofit are its customers. With an organization that has both donors and customers—as in the case of a college that receives alumni contributions as well as student tuition, and therefore combines both donative and commercial elements—the term *patron* will be used to include both groups.

Organizations that are controlled by their patrons I shall refer to as *mutual* nonprofits. Social clubs, which are controlled by their customers, provide one typical example; Common Cause, the citizens' lobby, which is controlled by its contributors, provides another. Those organizations that, on the other hand, are not controlled by their patrons I shall call *entrepreneurial* nonprofits. Most hospitals, for example, are in this latter category, as are many organizations for the relief of the poor and distressed, such as the Salvation Army.

The intersection of these two dichotomous classifications yields four categories of nonprofits: donative mutual, donative entrepreneurial, commercial mutual, and commercial entrepreneurial. Figure 1 below arrays common examples of the types of organizations that fall within these categories.

Figure 1

	mutual	entrepreneurial
donative	Common Cause National Audubon Society political clubs	CARE March of Dimes art museums
commercial	American Automobile Association Consumers Union country clubs	National Geographic Society Educational Testing Service community hospitals nursing homes

These four categories, it should be emphasized, merely describe polar or "ideal" types—extreme points on a continuum—rather than discrete forms of organization. Many nonprofit organizations cannot clearly be assigned to one type or another. Universities, for example, often combine elements of all four types: as already noted, they typically have both donative and commercial aspects; moreover, their boards of trustees are often elected in part by the alumni (who comprise the bulk of the former customers and current donors), and in part are self-perpetuating, so that they are neither clearly mutual nor clearly entrepreneurial nonprofits.

It should also be emphasized that this categorization is offered simply for ease of description and reference, and not because I believe that these descriptive categories should be given legal significance. Indeed, one of the major themes of this Article is that, contrary to current trends, nonprofit corporation law should be unitary, applying essentially the same rules and standards to all nonprofit corporations regardless of classification.

B. The Role of Nonprofit Organizations

To understand the unique functions served by the nonprofit form of organization, it is helpful to compare the role of nonprofits with that of profit-seeking (or "for-profit" or "business") organizations.

Like for-profit organizations, virtually all nonprofit organizations are, in a sense, engaged in the sale of services. This is, of course, true by definition for commercial nonprofits. Yet donative nonprofits, too, "sell" their services—and it is the donors who are the purchasers. For example, when an individual makes a contribution to the American Red Cross, or to the Metropolitan Opera, it is not quite a pure gift in the sense that the directors of the organization are free to do anything that they wish with the money. Rather, the contribution is a payment made with the understanding that it is to be devoted entirely to assisting disaster victims, or to presenting more and better opera productions. That is, such contributions are essentially efforts to "buy" disaster relief, or opera, and this is what the organizations in question exist to produce and "sell."

Why is it necessary that organizations such as these be nonprofit? In particular, why could not a for-profit firm provide the same services? The reason, in most cases, appears to be that either the nature of the service in question, or the circumstances under which it is provided, render ordinary contractual devices inadequate to provide the purchaser of the service with sufficient assurance that the service was in fact performed as desired. The advantage of the nonprofit form in such circumstances is that it makes the producer a fiduciary for its purchasers, and thus gives them greater assurance that the services they desire will in fact be performed as they wish.

1. Clarifying Examples

Some examples may help to make this clear.

a. Third Party Payment

Consider, initially, those donative nonprofits, such as CARE, the Salvation Army, and the American Red Cross, that collect contributions with which to provide relief to the poor and distressed. Why is it necessary that these organizations be nonprofit? Could not profit-seeking firms instead provide the same service—whether dried milk for hungry children in Africa, or bandages for disaster victims, or food for derelicts—in return for payments from philanthropically inclined individuals?

The answer, in considerable part, apparently lies in the fact that the individuals who receive the services in question have no connection with the individuals who pay for them. Thus, for example, suppose that a profit-seeking counterpart to CARE were to promise to provide one hundred pounds of dried milk to hungry children in Africa in return for a payment of ten dollars. Because the patron has no contact with the intended recipients, he or she would have no simple way of knowing whether the promised service was ever performed, much less performed well. Consequently, the owners of the firm would have both the incentive and the opportunity to provide inadequate service and to divert the money thus saved to themselves.

The advantage of the nonprofit form in such circumstances is that, because the nondistribution constraint prohibits those who control the organization from distributing to themselves out of the organization's income anything beyond reasonable compensation for services they render to the organization, they have less opportunity and incentive than would the managers of a for-profit firm to use the organization's income for anything other than what the organization's patrons intend it to be used for. In these circumstances, therefore, an individual would presumably much prefer to patronize a nonprofit organization than a for-profit organization. Consequently, it is not surprising that such redistributive services are provided almost exclusively by nonprofit firms.

b. Public Goods

Similar reasoning applies to the provision of what economists term a "public good"—that is, a good or service such that (1) the cost of providing the good to many persons is not appreciably more than the cost of providing it to one; and (2) once the good has been provided to one person, it is difficult to prevent others from enjoying it as well. Typical examples are noncommercial broadcasting, public monuments, and scientific research.

Even if individual consumers are willing to contribute to the cost of such services, rather than yielding to the incentive to be "free-riders" on the contributions of others, it is likely that they will do so only if the services are provided by a nonprofit. The reason for this is simply that, owing to the indivisible nature of the service involved, the consumer generally has no simple means of observing whether his or her contribution has increased the level of the service provided. Rather, the consumer must take the producer's word that the contribution will be used to purchase more of the good, rather than simply going into someone's pocket. Such a promise will be easier to believe if the producing firm is subject to the nondistribution constraint. Thus, listener-supported radio, tax reform lobbying, and heart research are all typically financed through nonprofit organizations.

c. Complex Personal Services

Those organizations—most of which we would classify as commercial nonprofits—that provide complex and vital personal services, such as nursing care, day care, education, and hospital care, offer yet another example. The patients at a nursing home, for example, are often too feeble or ill to be competent judges of the care they receive. Likewise, hospital patients and consumers of day care, owing to the difficulty of making an accurate personal appraisal of the kind and quality of services they need and receive, must necessarily entrust a great deal of discretion to the suppliers of those services. The nondistribution constraint reduces a nonprofit supplier's incentive to abuse that discretion, and, consequently, consumers might reasonably prefer to obtain these services from a nonprofit firm.

2. "Contract Failure"

In short, nonprofit firms serve particularly well in situations characterized by what I shall refer to, for simplicity, as "contract failure"—that is, situations in which, owing either to the nature of the service in question or to the circumstances under which it is produced and consumed, ordinary contractual devices in themselves do not provide consumers with adequate means for policing the performance of producers. In such situations, the nonprofit form offers consumers the protection of another, broader "contract"—namely, the organization's commitment, through its nonprofit charter, to devote all of its income to the services it was formed to provide.

It follows that the charter of a nonprofit corporation serves a rather different purpose than does the charter of a business corporation. In a business corporation, the charter, and the statutory and decisional law in which it is embedded, serves primarily to protect the interests of the corporation's shareholders from invasion by those immediately in control of the corporation, including management and other shareholders. In a nonprofit corporation, on the other hand, the restrictions imposed on controlling individuals by the charter and the law are primarily for the benefit of the organization's patrons. As a consequence, business corporation law is often a poor model for nonprofit corporation law. Unfortunately, as will be seen below, this is a point that has often been missed by those who draft and interpret the law of nonprofit corporations.

3. Countervailing Considerations

The nonprofit form brings with it costs as well as benefits. The curtailment of the profit motive that results from the nondistribution constraint can reduce incentives for cost efficiency, for responsiveness to consumers, and for expansion or creation of new firms in the presence of increasing demand. Moreover, the inability of nonprofits to raise equity capital through the issuance of stock can severely hamper their ability to meet needs for new capital. Only when contract failure is relatively severe is it likely that the advantages of nonprofits as fiduciaries will clearly outweigh these corresponding disadvantages, and thus give the nonprofit firm a net advantage over its for-profit counterpart.

Further, the nondistribution constraint is obviously not airtight. Indeed, as will be emphasized below, the constraint is often poorly policed and even, in many cases, poorly defined. As a consequence, the managers of nonprofits often find, and take advantage of, the opportunity to profit at the expense of the organization. Such behavior, of course, further reduces the advantages offered to patrons by nonprofit as opposed to for-profit firms in situations of contract failure.

In the case of services for the needy, public goods, and other services commonly provided by donative nonprofits, the need for a fiduciary organization is so obvious that for-profit firms are virtually unheard of. On the other hand, contract failure is not so obviously a critical problem for many consumers of the services that are often provided by commercial nonprofits, such as day care, nursing care, hospital care, and education. As a consequence, these services are commonly provided by for-profit as well as nonprofit firms. * * *

D. Summary

In sum, I am suggesting that the essential role of the nonprofit organization is to serve as a fiduciary for its patrons in situations of contract failure. This statement, it should be emphasized, has both a positive (descriptive) and a normative aspect. Taken descriptively, it is an assertion that nonprofit organizations tend to arise in situations in which there is evidence of contract failure and not in cases in which contract failure is absent. Casual empiricism appears to support this conclusion, at least in its broad contours. More important for the purposes at hand, however, is the normative aspect of this analysis—namely, the assertion that the fiduciary role described here is the *appropriate* role for nonprofit organizations. It follows from this assumption that the law should be designed to make the nonprofit form as effective as possible in performing this role.

NOTES

1. Hansmann's work on nonprofits helpfully brings economic theory into the discussion of legal issues. Other economists have also written on the nature of nonprofit firms. See, e.g., B. Weisbrod, The Nonprofit Economy (1988); E. James & S. Rose–Ackerman, The Nonprofit Enterprise in Market Economics (1986); S. Rose–Ackerman, ed., The Economics of Nonprofit Insitutions: Studies in Structure and Policy (1986); B. Weisbrod, The Voluntary Nonprofit Sector: An Economic Analysis (1977). Legal articles raising analytical issues about nonprofits have often focused on the issue of tax exemption for such firms. See, e.g., Bloche, Health Policy Below the Waterline: Medical Care and the Charitable Exemption, 80 Minn.L.Rev. 199 (1995); Atkinson, Altruism in Nonprofit Organizations, 31 B.C.L.Rev. 501 (1990) (critique of Hansmann's market-oriented analysis of nonprofits, with specific emphasis on the federal tax exemption). See also Brody, Agents Without Principals: The Economic Convergence of the Nonprofit and For-profit Organizational Forms, 40 N.Y.L.Sch.L.Rev. 457 (1996); Ellman, Another Theory of Nonprofit Corporations, 80 Mich.L.Rev. 999 (1982).

2. Note the place that Hansmann assigns to hospitals in his matrix. Only a small percentage of the total revenue of hospitals comes from philanthropy (less than 1.3% in 1985). Teaching and research institutions, however, are more dependent than community hospitals on grants and gifts, which they receive in significant volume. One might question why ordinary community hospitals, if they are indeed "entrepreneurial/commercial" in nature, are allowed special tax exemptions (as shown in the following materials). Indeed, Hansmann argues against favorable tax treatment for such hospitals. Hansmann, supra, at 866–68; see also Hansmann, The Rationale for Exempting Nonprofit Organizations from Corporate Income Taxation, 91 Yale L.J. 54, 87–89 (1981). Although noting that the inability of hospital patients to monitor quality and the use of funds might seem to justify encouraging use of the nonprofit form, Hansmann argues that physicians serve their patients as knowledgeable purchasing agents in obtaining hospital care, thus preventing a market failure that might warrant a tax subsidy. (Note how the issue of hospital tax exemption is made to turn ultimately on the professionalism and fiduciary role of individual physicians, a crucial issue in this chapter.) For the view that "Hansmann's disinclination to extend the exemption to nonprofit hospitals may reflect a misplaced confidence in the ability and inclination of physicians to act as knowledgeable and loyal purchasing agents for their patients," see Bloche, supra, at 324–36 (arguing that physicians lack the knowledge of outcomes necessary to serve as effective agents and are, in addition, subject both to divided loyalties and to manipulation by the hospitals themselves).

State and Federal Tax Exemptions

Utah County v. Intermountain Health Care, Inc.

Supreme Court of Utah, 1985.
709 P.2d 265.

■ DURHAM, JUSTICE:

Utah County seeks review of a decision of the Utah State Tax Commission reversing a ruling of the Utah County Board of Equalization. The Tax Commission exempted Utah Valley Hospital, owned and operated by Intermountain Health Care (IHC), and American Fork Hospital, leased and operated by IHC, from *ad valorem* property taxes. At issue is whether such a tax exemption is constitutionally permissible. We hold that, on the facts in this record, it is not, and we reverse.

* * *

Utah County seeks the resolution of two issues: (1) whether U.C.A., 1953, §§ 59–2–30 (1974) and 59–2–31 (1974), which exempt from taxation hospitals meeting certain requirements, constitute an unconstitutional expansion of the charitable exemption in article XIII, section 2 of the Utah Constitution; and (2) whether Utah Valley Hospital and American Fork Hospital are exempt from taxation under article XIII, section 2 of the Utah Constitution.

Utah County does not seriously dispute that the two hospitals in this case comply with sections 59–2–30 and 59–2–31, but contends instead that these statutes unlawfully expand the charitable exemption granted by article XIII, section 2 of the Utah Constitution (1895, amended 1982), which provides in pertinent part:

> The property of the state, cities, counties, towns, school districts, municipal corporations and public libraries, lots with the buildings thereon used exclusively for either religious worship or charitable purposes, . . . shall be exempt from taxation.

* * *

The power of state and local governments to levy property taxes has traditionally been limited by constitutional and statutory provisions such as those at issue in this case that exempt certain property from taxation. These exemptions confer an indirect subsidy and are usually justified as the *quid pro quo* for charitable entities undertaking functions and services that the state would otherwise be required to perform. A concurrent rationale, used by some courts, is the assertion that the exemptions are granted not only because charitable entities relieve government of a burden, but also because their activities enhance beneficial community values or goals. Under this theory, the benefits received by the community are believed to offset the revenue lost by reason of the exemption.

* * *

An entity may be granted a charitable tax exemption for its property under the Utah Constitution only if it meets the definition of a "charity" or if its property is used exclusively for "charitable" purposes. Essential to this definition is the element of gift to the community. * * * A gift to the community can be identified either by a substantial imbalance in the exchange between the charity and the recipient of its services or in the lessening of a government burden through the charity's operation. * * *

Given the complexities of institutional organization, financing, and impact on modern community life, there are a number of factors which must be weighed in determining whether a particular institution is in fact using its property "exclusively for ... charitable purposes." These factors are: (1) whether the stated purpose of the entity is to provide a significant service to others without immediate expectation of material reward; (2) whether the entity is supported, and to what extent, by donations and gifts; (3) whether the recipients of the "charity" are required to pay for the assistance received, in whole or in part; (4) whether the income received from all sources (gifts, donations, and payment from recipients) produces a "profit" to the entity in the sense that the income exceeds operating and long-term maintenance expenses; (5) whether the beneficiaries of the "charity" are restricted or unrestricted and, if restricted, whether the restriction bears a reasonable relationship to the entity's charitable objectives; and (6) whether dividends or some other form of financial benefit, or assets upon dissolution, are available to private interests, and whether the entity is organized and operated so that any commercial activities are subordinate or incidental to charitable ones. * * *

Because the "care of the sick" has traditionally been an activity regarded as charitable in American law, and because the dissenting opinions rely upon decisions from other jurisdictions that in turn incorporate unexamined assumptions about the fundamental nature of hospital-based medical care, we deem it important to scrutinize the contemporary social and economic context of such care. We are convinced that traditional assumptions bear little relationship to the economics of the medical-industrial complex of the 1980's. Nonprofit hospitals were traditionally treated as tax-exempt charitable institutions because, until late in the 19th century, they were true charities providing custodial care for those who were both sick and poor. The hospitals' income was derived largely or entirely from voluntary charitable donations, not government subsidies, taxes, or patient fees.[7] The function and status of hospitals began to change

7. Paul Starr, The Social Transformation of American Medicine at 150 (1982).
* * *

in the late 19th century; the transformation was substantially completed by the 1920's. "From charities, dependent on voluntary gifts, [hospitals] developed into market institutions financed increasingly out of payments from patients."[8] The transformation was multidimensional: hospitals were redefined from social welfare to medical treatment institutions; their charitable foundation was replaced by a business basis; and their orientation shifted to "professionals, and their patients," away from "patrons and the poor."[9]

* * *

Also of considerable significance to our review is the increasing irrelevance of the distinction between nonprofit and for-profit hospitals for purposes of discovering the element of charity in their operations. The literature indicates that two models, described below, appear to describe a large number of nonprofit hospitals as they function today.[10]

(1) The "physicians' cooperative" model describes nonprofit hospitals that operate primarily for the benefit of the participating physicians. Physicians, pursuant to this model, enjoy power and high income through their direct or indirect control over the nonprofit hospitals to which they bring their patients. The nonprofit form is believed to facilitate the control by physicians better than the for-profit form. Pauly & Redisch, The Not–For–Profit Hospital as a Physicians' Co-operative, 63 Am.Econ.Rev. 87, 88–89 (1973). This model has also been called the "exploitation hypothesis" because the physician "income maximizing" system is hidden behind the nonprofit facade of the hospital. Clark, Does the Nonprofit Form Fit the Hospital Industry?, 93 Harv.L.Rev. 1416, 1436–37 (1980). A minor variation of the above theory is the argument that many nonprofit hospitals operate as "shelters" within which physicians operate profitable businesses, such as laboratories. Starr, supra, at 438.

(2) The "polycorporate enterprise" model describes the increasing number of nonprofit hospital chains. Here, power is largely in the hands of administrators, not physicians. Through the creation of holding companies, nonprofit hospitals have grown into large groups of medical enterprises, containing both for-profit and nonprofit corporate entities. Nonprofit corporations can own for-profit corporations without losing their federal nonprofit tax status as long as the profits of the for-profit corporations are used to further the nonprofit purposes of the parent organization. (IHC owns at least one for-profit subsidiary.) The emergence of hospital organizations with both for-profit and nonprofit components has increasingly destroyed the charitable pretensions of nonprofit organizations: "The extension of the voluntary hospital into profit-making businesses and the penetration of

8. Id. at 146.

9. Id. at 147–48. * * *

10. The dissents attempt to characterize this opinion as "equating" profit and nonprofit enterprises. We disavow any such purpose. The point of * * * this opinion is to reiterate the essential requirement of the Utah Constitution that any entity claiming a charitable use exemption must *demonstrate* its entitlement and not rely upon unexamined and anachronistic assumptions about its status.

other corporations into the hospital signal the break-down of the traditional boundaries of voluntarism. Increasingly, the polycorporate hospitals are likely to become multihospital systems and competitors with profit-making chains, HMO's and other health care corporations." Id. at 438.

The foregoing discussion of the economic environment in which modern hospitals function is critical to our analysis in this case because it is an analysis which is generally not present in any of the cases relied upon by the dissenting opinions. Those cases, in our view, do not take into account the revolution in health care that has transformed a "healing profession" into an enormous and complex industry, employing millions of people and accounting for a substantial proportion of our gross national product. Dramatic advances in medical knowledge and technology have resulted in an equally dramatic rise in the cost of medical services. At the same time, elaborate and comprehensive organizations of third-party payers have evolved. Most recently, perhaps as a further evolutionary response to the unceasing rise in the cost of medical services, the provision of such services has become a highly competitive business. Furthermore, even the more recent cases cited by the dissenting opinions contradict the rule this Court has adopted strictly construing our constitutional provision, and requiring every charity to show an element of gift. Community Memorial Hospital v. City of Moberly, Mo., 422 S.W.2d 290 (1967), as an example, contains no mention of the element of gift that this Court has held crucial to the meaning of charity. It appears that the hospital in *Moberly* was granted its tax exemption largely on the basis of its nonprofit structure, for the Missouri court held it of no account that the hospital gave charity in an amount less than 1.4 percent of the amount collected from paying patients, that this so-called "charity" included some bad debts, and that for four of the eight years at issue no charity at all was given by the hospital. * * *

Having discussed the standards for the application of Utah's constitutional exemption for property used for charitable purposes, and the economic and historic context in which we conduct this review, we now examine the record respecting the two hospitals ("the defendants") whose eligibility has been challenged by Utah County. * * *

The stated purpose of IHC regarding the operation of both hospitals clearly meets at least part of the first criterion we have articulated for determining the existence of a charitable use. Its articles of incorporation identify as "corporate purposes," among other things, the provision of "care and treatment of the sick, afflicted, infirm, aged or injured within and/or without the State of Utah." The same section prevents any "part of the net earnings of this Corporation" to inure to the private benefit of any individual. Furthermore, under another section, the assets of the corporation upon dissolution likewise may not be distributed to benefit any private interest.

The second factor we examine is whether the hospitals are supported, and to what extent, by donations and gifts. * * * The evidence was that both hospitals charge rates for their services comparable to rates being charged by other similar entities, and no showing was made that the donations identified resulted in charges to patients below prevailing market rates. * * *

One of the most significant of the factors to be considered in review of a claimed exemption is the third we identified: whether the recipients of the services of an entity are required to pay for that assistance, in whole or in part. The Tax Commission in this case found as follows:

> The policy of [IHC's hospitals] is to collect hospital charges from patients whenever it is reasonable and possible to do so; however, no person in need of medical attention is denied care solely on the basis of a lack of funds.

* * * Between 1978 and 1980, the value of the services given away as charity by these two hospitals constituted less than one percent of their gross revenues. Furthermore, the record also shows that such free service as did exist was deliberately not advertised out of fear of a "deluge of people" trying to take advantage of it. Instead, every effort was made to recover payment for services rendered. Utah Valley Hospital even offered assistance to patients who claimed inability to pay to enter into bank loan agreements to finance their hospital expenses.

The defendants argue that the great expense of modern hospital care and the universal availability of insurance and government health care subsidies make the idea of a hospital solely supported by philanthropy an anachronism. We believe this argument itself exposes the weakness in the defendants' position. It is precisely because such a vast system of third-party payers has developed to meet the expense of modern hospital care that the historical distinction between for-profit and nonprofit hospitals has eroded. For-profit hospitals provide many of the same primary care services as do those hospitals organized as nonprofit entities.[14] They do so at similar rates as those charged by defendants. The doctors and administrators of nonprofit hospitals have the same opportunity for personal remuneration for their services as do their counterparts in for-profit hospitals.

The dissent of Justice Stewart suggests that the fact that "ability to pay" is not a criterion for admission to IHC's facilities is dispositive of the question of "charitable purpose," regardless of the actual amount of free care provided therein. This argument overlooks the fact that for-profit institutions may well implement similar policies, either for public relations reasons or by virtue of regulations mandated by their receipt of federal-or state-funded payments. * * *

14. The record does reflect that Utah Valley Hospital is the sole provider of tertiary care for a large geographic region. Because of the unique character of this sophisticated medical care, it may well be possible to identify a substantial imbalance in the exchange between Utah Valley Hospital and the recipients of its tertiary care, or a lessening of a government burden through the offering of such care. In light of our statement in Loyal Order of Moose [v. County Bd. of Equalization, 657 P.2d 257, 264 (Utah 1982)] the provision of tertiary care services could qualify as a charity if the requisite gift to the community were to be demonstrated. * * *

The fourth question we consider is whether the income received from all sources by these IHC hospitals is in excess of their operating and maintenance expenses. Because the vast majority of their services are paid for, the nonprofit hospitals in this case accumulate capital as do their profit-seeking counterparts. The record indicates that this accumulated capital is used for the construction of additional hospitals and other facilities throughout the IHC system and the provision of expanded services. The record before us is undeveloped on this point, but there is nothing therein to indicate that the capital accumulated by either of the defendant hospitals is even earmarked in any way for use in their facilities or even in Utah County. In view of the fact that Intermountain Health Care owns and operates facilities, for-profit and nonprofit, throughout this state and in other states, we are particularly concerned that there is no showing on the record that surplus funds generated by one hospital in the system will not be utilized for the benefit of facilities in other counties, outside the state of Utah, or purely for administrative costs of the system itself.

* * *

A large portion of the profits of most for-profit entities is used for capital improvements and new, updated equipment, and the defendant hospitals here similarly expend their revenues in excess of operational expenses. There can be no doubt, in reviewing the references in the record by members of IHC's administrative staff, that the IHC system, as well as the two hospitals in question, has consistently generated sufficient funds in excess of operating costs to contribute to rapid and extensive growth, building, competitive employee and professional salaries and benefits, and a very sophisticated management structure. While it is true that no financial benefits or profits are available to private interests in the form of stockholder distributions or ownership advantages, the user *entity* in this case clearly generates substantial "profits" in the sense of income that exceeds expenses. This observation is not intended to imply that an institution must consume its assets in order to be eligible for tax exemption—the requirement of charitable giving may obviously be met before that point is reached. However, there is a serious question regarding the constitutional propriety of subsidies from Utah County taxpayers being used to give certain entities a substantial competitive edge in what is essentially a commercial marketplace. None of the defendants in this case made any effort to demonstrate that they would suffer any operating losses or have to discontinue any services if they are ineligible for exemption from property taxes. Justice Stewart's assertion that the taxes levied by the county would have to be passed on to patients in the form of higher charges is without any foundation in the evidence. The far more logical assumption is that *growth of the IHC system* would possibly be slowed, but there is no indication of a likelihood that current and future levels of care would be jeopardized.

The final two factors we address are whether the beneficiaries of the services of the defendants are "restricted" in any way and whether private interests are benefited by the organization or operation of the defendants. Although the policy of IHC is to impose no restrictions, there were some incidents recounted in the testimony which suggested that these institutions do not see themselves as being in the business of providing hospital care "for the poor," an activity which was certainly at the heart of the original rationale for tax exemptions for charitable hospitals. Otherwise, it appears that they meet this criterion. On the question of benefits to private interests, certainly it appears that no individuals who are employed by or administer the defendants receive any distribution of assets or income, and some, such as IHC's board of trustees members, volunteer their services. We have noted, however, that IHC owns a for-profit entity, as well as nonprofit subsidiaries, and there is in addition the consideration that numerous forms of private commercial enterprise, such as pharmacies, laboratories, and contracts for medical services, are conducted as a necessary part of the defendants' hospital operations. The burden being on the taxpayer to demonstrate eligibility for the exemption, the inadequacies in the record on these questions cannot be remedied by speculation in the defendants' favor.

In summary, after reviewing the facts in this case in light of the factors we have identified, we believe that the defendants in this case confuse the element of gift to the community, which an entity must demonstrate in order to qualify as a charity under our Constitution, with the concept of community benefit, which any of countless private enterprises might provide. We have no quarrel with the assertion that Utah Valley Hospital and American Fork Hospital meet great and important needs of persons within their communities for medical care. Yet this meeting of a public need by a provision of services cannot be the sole distinguishing characteristic that leads to an automatic property tax exemption. "[T]he usefulness of an enterprise is not sufficient basis for relief from the burden of sharing essential costs of local government." In re Marple Newtown School District, 39 Pa.Cmwlth. 326, 336, 395 A.2d 1023, 1028 (1978). Such a "usefulness" rule would have to be equally applied to for-profit hospitals and privately owned health care entities, which also provide medical services to their patients. We note, for example, that the increasing emphasis on competition in health care services is resulting in significant expansion of the activities and roles of health care providers generally, including hospitals, both for-profit and nonprofit. Laboratory services, pharmaceutical services, "birthing" centers, and outpatient surgical units are becoming common adjuncts to traditional hospital care. It would be impossible to justify a distinction, within the constitutional boundaries of "charitable" activities, between outpatient surgical services, for example, provided on property owned by an IHC hospital and those provided on privately owned property, where both are identical and are remunerated at the same rate. As we have pointed out, there was no showing in the record that either of the hospitals in question uses billing rates which differ materially from rates charged for the same services by for-profit hospital, or that the defendants' rates or services would change if they were required to pay county property taxes.

* * *

Neither can we find on this record that the burdens of government are substantially lessened as a result of the defendants' provision of services. The record indicates that Utah County budgets approximately $50,000 annually for the payment of hospital care for indigents. Furthermore, the evidence described two instances within a three-month period where, after a Utah County official had declined to authorize payment for a person in the emergency room, Utah Valley Hospital refused to admit the injured person on the basis of that person's inability to pay. The county official was told in these instances to either authorize payment or to "come and get" the person. Such behavior on the hospital's part is inconsistent with its argument that it functions to relieve government of a burden. * * *

As we noted in the introduction to this opinion, the "burden" theory of tax exemptions has been traditionally based on the notion that a charitable organization should be eligible for exemption because it performs a task which the government would otherwise have to perform. The basis for the tax exemption is a *quid pro quo:* "private charities perform functions that the state would be required to undertake and tax exemption is granted as a quid pro quo for the performance of these functions and services." E. Fisch, D. Freed & E. Schacter, Charities and Charitable Foundations § 787, at 602 (1974) (footnote omitted). * * *

While the practice of courts has often deviated from the strict logic of the "burden" theory, the general pattern is that "burden" jurisdictions generally require some degree of almsgiving or unpaid services for the granting of a charitable tax exemption. "Consequently in these states operations financed primarily or entirely with funds supplied by the beneficiaries are classified as noncharitable." E. Fisch, *Charities,* supra, § 791, at 610.

We cannot find, on this record, the essential element of gift to the community, either through the nonreciprocal provision of services or through the alleviation of a government burden, and consequently we hold that the defendants have not demonstrated that their property is being used exclusively for charitable purposes under the Utah Constitution.

Because we so hold, it follows that U.C.A., 1953, § 59–2–31 provides no safe harbor for defendants. * * * [O]ur statutes cannot expand the scope of the tax exemption granted by article XIII, section 2 of our Constitution. * * *

We reverse the Tax Commission's grant of an *ad valorem* property tax exemption to defendants as being unconstitutional. We emphasize, contrary to the assertions of the dissents, that this opinion is no more than an extension of the principles of strict construction * * *. This is a "record" case, and we make no judgment as to the ability of these hospitals or any others to demonstrate their eligibility for constitutionally permissible tax exemptions in the future. We note, however, that reliance on automatic exemptions granted heretofore, and on the kind of minimal efforts to show charity reflected in this record, will no longer suffice.

* * *

[Two dissenting opinions omitted.]

NOTES AND QUESTIONS ON THE FEDERAL TAX TREATMENT OF NONPROFIT ENTERPRISES

1. *IRC § 501(c)(3).* Nonprofit corporations, including hospitals, may qualify for federal tax-exempt status under section 501(c)(3) of the Internal Revenue Code. This status not only exempts organizations from the federal income tax but also allows them to engage, with state assistance, in tax-exempt bond financing and to receive grants from tax-exempt private foundations and the federal government. (A 501(c)(3) corporation will also generally qualify under IRC § 170 to receive tax-deductible donations from individuals and other tax-paying entities.) To be eligible for a 501(c)(3) exemption, a nonprofit corporation must be "organized and operated exclusively for religious, charitable, scientific * * *, or educational purposes," must restrict its political activities, and must be an entity "no part of the net earnings of which inures to the benefit of any private shareholder or individual." IRC § 501(c)(3) (1994). See generally M. Phelan, Nonprofit Enterprises: Law and Taxation (1996 looseleaf); B. Hopkins, The Law of Tax–Exempt Organizations (6th ed. 1992 & Supp. 1996); T. Hyatt & B. Hopkins, The Law of Tax–Exempt Healthcare Organizations (1995 & Supp. 1996).

The requirements for 501(c)(3) tax exemption have been summarized under six headings: (1) an organizational test (relating to the corporation's charter, its not-for-profit status, and the appropriateness of its corporate purposes); (2) an operational test (relating to its adherence to its mission and compliance with the "exclusivity" requirement, which in practice means that nonexempt purposes may be pursued only incidentally or in aid of the organization's primary purpose); (3) the noninurement requirement (discussed below); (4) the requirement that benefits not be conferred on private individuals except as necessary to realize a public benefit (also discussed below); (5) the prohibition against lobbying and other political activities; and (6) a requirement that the organization conduct itself in accord with other public policies (e.g., accept Medicare and Medicaid patients, avoid dumping of nonpaying patients, and comply with statutes prohibiting "fraud and abuse"). See Crimm, Evolutionary Forces: Changes in For-profit and Not-for-profit Health Care Delivery Structures; A Regeneration of Tax Exemption Standards, 37 B.C.L.Rev. 1, 33–101 (1995).

On the policy rationale underlying the tax exemption of nonprofits, particularly as applicable to hospitals and other health care organizations, see J. Colombo & M. Hall, The Charitable Tax Exemption (1995); Bloche, Health Policy Below the Waterline: Medical Care and the Charitable Exemption, 80 Minn.L.Rev. 299 (1995) (a critical evaluation of the federal tax exemption for nonprofit hospitals, finding it "neither explicable nor justifiable in terms of the logic of efficiency or reward for virtue"); Crimm, supra; Colombo, Health Care Reform and Federal Tax Exemption: Rethinking the Issues, 29 Wake Forest L.Rev. 215 (1994); Simpson & Strum, How

Good a Samaritan? Federal Income Tax Exemption for Charitable Hospitals Reconsidered, 14 U. Puget Sound L.Rev. 633 (1991); Hansmann, The Rationale for Exempting Nonprofit Organizations from Corporate Income Taxation, 91 Yale L.J. 54, 87–89 (1981).

In reading the following notes, consider whether the IHC system, as described in the *Utah County* case, would qualify for tax exemption under section 501(c)(3).

2. *Noninurement; Private Benefit.* The noninurement provision of section 501(c)(3) obviously supplements the "nondistribution constraint" in state nonprofit corporation acts. Although somewhat vague, it generally prevents persons controlling a nonprofit organization from receiving excessive compensation from it in any form, such as through lucrative business contracts between the organization and enterprises controlled by its directors, trustees, managers, controlling physicians, etc. See, e.g., Church of Scientology of California v. Commissioner, 823 F.2d 1310 (9th Cir.1987) (inurement found where church paid its founder excessive royalties from sale of books and repaid his debt); Maynard Hosp. Inc. v. Commissioner, 52 T.C. 1006 (1969) (hospital spun off pharmacy to trustee-shareholders; hospital's payment for prescription drugs at marked-up rates held to constitute inurement); Sonora Community Hosp. v. Commissioner, 46 T.C. 519 (1966), affirmed per curiam, 397 F.2d 814 (9th Cir.1968) (hospital converted from for-profit to nonprofit form, but prior owners diverted profits from leased radiology service to themselves). The obvious purpose of the rule against "inurement" is to encourage trustees or other managers of a nonprofit hospital or other charitable institution to observe their fiduciary responsibilities. The tax law thus provides some assurance that the public subsidy implicit in the tax exemption of the institution and in the deductibility of gifts to it will benefit patients or other intended beneficiaries in the form of more or higher-quality services or lower prices.

In 1992, the IRS issued new guidelines for examiners reviewing the tax-exempt status of hospitals, including the effects of various hospital/physician relationships. Announcement 92–83, 1992–22 I.R.B. 59. The IRS observed that, by hypothesis, inurement can accrue only to "insiders (individuals whose relationship with an organization offers them an opportunity to make use of the organization's income or assets for personal gain)." The guidelines went on to state, however, "Physicians are considered insiders and in their dealings with the hospital are subject to the inurement prohibition. All contracts with the insiders should be reviewed to determine if they were negotiated at arms-length." Do you agree with this characterization of hospital/physician relations?

Manifestly, the IRS has used the noninurement requirement not merely to prevent the distribution of profits to true insiders but also to ensure that the organization's purposes are truly charitable—in the sense that the general public rather than some select group is benefitted. Indeed, a coupling of the noninurement requirement with the the requirement of section 501(c)(3) that the hospital be operated for a "charitable purpose" has yielded a general principle that a tax-exempt entity must not be operated for anyone's private gain. The statutory language, quoted above, would appear amenable to the IRS construction that imposes not only a form of nondistribution constraint but also a limitation on the conferral of "private benefit." Although this construction might seem to obviate disputes over who is and who is not an "insider," the prohibition against inurement is absolute, whereas the rule against conferring private benefits is not. Obviously, many persons benefit privately from their dealings with hospitals. Thus, only arrangements suggesting that the enterprise is being operated for a noncharitable purpose will jeopardize its tax exemption. Arrangements that advance the hospital's legitimate purposes are acceptable even if some private party also benefits. The difficulty of identifying (and avoiding) problematic transactions should be apparent.

As noted in the *Utah County* case, some nonprofit hospitals have been characterized as "physicians' cooperatives." Does this characterization suggest a basis for denying their federal tax exemption? Are the benefits that physicians derive from practicing in nonprofit hospitals incidental, both qualitatively and quantitatively, to the achievement of the purposes that justify the hospital's tax exemption?

Various relationships between hospitals and physicians are open to scrutiny under the rules against inurement and excessive private benefit. The issues are best illustrated by Gen.Couns.Mem. 39,862 (Dec. 2, 1991), which is reproduced later in this section. See also Gen.Couns.Mem. 39,598 (Feb. 4, 1987) (office lease between hospital and physicians to retain latter's services must be either negotiated at arm's length or shown to be the only way public benefit could be achieved); Gen.Couns.Mem. 39,674 (June 17, 1987) (incentive profit-sharing arrangement does not necessarily jeopardize hospital's tax-exempt status). The rule against conferring a private benefit has been particularly troublesome with respect to incentives offered by some hospitals to physicians they are trying to recruit to work in the hospital or in the community it serves. ("Physician recruitment" is the subject of a problem following GCM 39,862, infra.)

For some practical insights on the application of the rule against conferring private benefits, see the following comments by a practitioner on the above-referenced 1992 IRS guidelines for examiners:

> As to private benefit, the IRS also notes that "Some private benefit is *always present* in hospital-physician relationships since physicians use hospital facilities to treat paying patients. All private benefit must be incidental to accomplishment of the public benefits involved. This prohibition on excessive private benefit is not restricted to insiders."
>
> * * *
>
> [T]he Guidelines * * * alert IRS employees to review carefully many of the typical hospital-physician arrangements. These include: guarantee of private incomes, rent subsidies, the provision of hospital employees as support staff for physicians providing services in the hospital, joint venture arrangements, practice purchase arrangements,

and loans or other recruiting incentives. [Yet] the Guidelines lack specifics concerning how to determine whether these arrangements are violations of the private benefit and inurement rules. This lack of specificity has caused overconcern in the industry that such arrangements are therefore presumptively improper.

While the characterization of physicians as insiders and of the hospital-physician relationship as "always" resulting in private benefit, together with the simple listing of suspect activities, combine to create an unfortunate impression of impropriety, the basic test for whether inurement or improper private benefit occur is still a reasonableness test. That is, hospitals must demonstrate that the arrangements in these question areas that involve medical staff members are reasonable in light of the marketplace, the hospital's needs, and the community's needs.

Under these standards, I believe that the overwhelming majority of arrangements will be deemed to be proper. To the extent the Guidelines attempt to characterize (or perhaps simply give the impression) that contracts between physicians and hospitals are not negotiated at arms length, I think they are wrong. For a variety of reasons, hospital executives are concerned about the reasonableness of arrangements with their medical staff members. Your typical hospital board member is no more anxious to provide excessive benefits to physicians than is your typical IRS agent. Lengthy negotiations between hospitals and recruited physicians are common, as are failures to consummate transactions because of unwillingness to meet demands.

In this era of increasing scrutiny from a variety of sources, it is more necessary for the health care industry to be able to justify hospital-physician transactions and to document that justification. Evidence of advertising, of rejected offers, of extended negotiations, of community need, of comparable transactions between other providers, of appraisals for equipment and real estate ventures and similar documentation should be the norm. From a legal standpoint, these efforts should result in safer transactions and, who knows, from a business standpoint, that may result in better transactions.

Manson, Chairman's Corner, Health Lawyer, Summer 1992, p. 2 (ABA Forum on Health Law).

3. *Sanctions.* Until 1996, the only sanction for violating one of the requirements for tax exemption was revocation of the offending entity's exemption. This remedy was almost never invoked, however, because of its drastic nature and because most of its effects would be felt by innocent parties, such as donors, holders of tax-exempt bonds, employees, and the community benefitted by the entity's activities. Although the possibility that an exemption might be lost may have helped to induce good behavior in most cases and enabled the IRS to obtain prospective corrective action where it detected abuses, the lack of alternative, less draconian sanctions was widely noted as a shortcoming in the law.

In an important development, legislation in 1996, known as the Taxpayer Bill of Rights 2, Pub. L. No. 104–168, 110 Stat. 1452 (codified at IRC § 4958 (1996)), introduced so-called "intermediate sanctions" for violations of the requirements of tax exemption. Under the new law, so-called "disqualified persons" who benefit improperly from transactions with tax-exempt entities face a new excise tax on the proceeds therefrom. Another, perhaps surprising feature of the new law was the imposition of new penalties (another excise tax), not on the tax-exempt entity itself, but on its personnel—"organization managers"—who knowingly approve or participate in an "excess benefit transaction." Because of these new sanctions, managers of exempt organizations must now be personally concerned that IRS officials will second-guess their business judgments concerning compensation and other matters. New preventive measures are therefore advisable, raising administrative costs but possibly improving the husbanding of charitable assets. Fortunately, the law makes provision for a "rebuttable presumption of reasonableness" where a transaction with an insider is approved by a disinterested, informed board of directors or trustees. It also contemplates abatement of the penalties when no bad faith appears and the situation is promptly corrected once a deficiency notice is received. See generally B. Hopkins, Intermediate Sanctions: Curbing Nonprofit Abuse (1997).

4. *Unrelated Business Income.* The federal tax code permits an exempt organization to pursue purposes other than charitable ones (to a limited extent) but taxes the income from such "unrelated trade or business activities regularly carried on." IRC §§ 511–13 (1994). See generally Hansmann, Unfair Competition and the Unrelated Business Income Tax, 75 Va. L. Rev. 605 (1989) ("The truly difficult and important issue involving the tax treatment of nonprofits concerns not the UBIT but rather the scope of the basic exemption that underlies it, and that is where future debate should focus.") On the technical issues of the UBIT in health care contexts, see T. Hyatt & B. Hopkins, supra, at 343–97.

Unrelated trade or business activities are defined to include activities that do not contribute importantly to accomplishing the purpose for which the exemption was granted. Treas.Reg. § 1.513–1(d)(2) & (3) (as amended in 1983). Examples include: the sale of drug advertising in a journal published by a nonprofit professional organization, United States v. American College of Physicians, 475 U.S. 834 (1986) (rejecting argument that ads were educational); pharmacy sales by a hospital to the general public but not, under some circumstances, to private patients of staff doctors, Hi-Plains Hosp. v. United States, 670 F.2d 528 (5th Cir.1982); sale by a hospital of laboratory services to unhospitalized patients of staff physicians, Rev.Ruls. 85–109 and 85–110, 1985–2 C.B. 165, 166 (refusing to follow a case holding that such lab tests are necessarily for the convenience of "members" of the hospital even if available elsewhere); pharmacy sales to unrelated corporations but not to related corporations, Priv.Ltr.Rul. 92–41–055 (July 16, 1992); provision of management and consulting services by one HMO to another, Tech.Adv.Mem. 92–32–003 (Feb. 12, 1992) (holding that an HMO providing managerial and consulting services "is virtually indistinguishable from an ordinary commercial trade or business"); and use of excess capacity to sell nonhealth (e.g., laundry) services to the general public. IRC § 13(e) (1994); Priv.Ltr.Rul. 86–15–048 (Jan. 10, 1986). Because a substantial volume of unrelated services could destroy a 501(c)(3) exemption, a hospital or other nonprofit firm is limited in its ability to support its charitable objects by profit-seeking activities. See also Priv. Ltr.Rul. 87–36–046 (June 10, 1987).

By these restrictions on tax-exempt activity, the tax law encourages hospitals and other nonprofit organizations to concentrate on their charitable functions rather than providing other services for profit. It also protects taxable entities against unfair competition by tax-exempt entities in those activities not imbued with a charitable purpose. The increasing aggressiveness of some nonprofits has nevertheless prompted periodic complaints from the small-business community. See Unfair Competition from the Public Sector and Government Supported Entities (Nonprofits): Hearings before the Subcommittee on Procurement, Taxation and Tourism of the House Committee on Small Business, 103d Cong., 2d Sess. (1994); Note, Making Tax–Exempts Pay: The Unrelated Business Income Tax and the Need for Reform, 4 Admin.L.J. 527 (1991).

5. *Charitable Purpose.* What constitutes a "charitable purpose" of a hospital has been a controversial issue. Clearly the hospital must serve public rather than private interests. At one time, serving the public meant that a hospital "must be operated to the extent of its financial ability for those not able to pay for the services rendered and not exclusively for those who are able and expected to pay." Rev.Rul. 56–185, 1956–1 C.B. 202. A 1969 revenue ruling, however, removed the requirement of caring for indigent patients and held that the "promotion of health" is a sufficient charitable purpose that benefits the community as a whole. Rev.Rul. 69–545, 1969–2 C.B. 117. The IRS gave the following example to demonstrate when a nonprofit hospital is serving public interests:

> Since the purpose and activity of Hospital *A*, apart from its related educational and research activities and purposes, are providing hospital care on a nonprofit basis for members of its community, it is organized and operated in furtherance of a purpose considered "charitable" in the generally accepted legal sense of that term. The promotion of health, like the relief of poverty and the advancement of education and religion, is one of the purposes in the general law of charity that is deemed beneficial to the community as a whole even though the class of beneficiaries eligible to receive a direct benefit from its activities does not include all members of the community, such as indigent members of the community, provided that the class is not so small that its relief is not of benefit to the community. Restatement (Second), Trusts, sec. 368, comment (b) and sec. 372, comments (b) and (c); IV Scott on Trusts (3rd ed. 1967), sec. 368 and sec. 372.2. By operating an emergency room open to all persons and by providing hospital care for all those persons in the community able to pay the cost thereof either directly or through third party reimbursement, Hospital *A* is promot-

ing the health of a class of persons that is broad enough to benefit the community.

Legislation confirming this interpretation was proposed in the same year but not adopted. See S.Rep. No. 552, 91st Cong., 1st Sess. 61 (1969). Although Congress let the ruling stand, it was subsequently criticized by congressional staff. Staff of the Senate Comm. on Finance, Medicare and Medicaid—Problems, Issues, and Alternatives 58 (Comm. Print 1970). The IRS position with respect to hospitals that serve only paying patients is inconsistent with its treatment of other health care entities, which can qualify for an exemption only by demonstrating that they provide free or below-cost services. Federation Pharmacy Servs. v. Commissioner, 625 F.2d 804 (8th Cir.1980) (denying tax exemption to pharmacy claiming to be engaged in the "promotion of health").

In Rev.Rul. 83–157, 1983–1 C.B. 94, the IRS amplified the examples set out in Rev.Rul. 69–545 to clarify that a hospital's operation of an emergency room was not an essential requirement. Hypothesizing a state planning agency decision that an ER would duplicate nearby facilities, the IRS indicated that it would be satisfied by such other factors as "a board of directors drawn from the community, an open medical staff policy, treatment of persons paying their bills with the aid of public programs like medicare and medicaid, and the application of any surplus to improving facilities, equipment, patient care, and medical training, education and research." Long-term care facilities need not provide free care to the poor to qualify for 501(c)(3) status but must not evict patients who become unable to pay. Rev.Rul. 72–124, 1972–1 C.B. 145.

Several suits brought on behalf of indigents challenged, unsuccessfully, the IRS's 1969 relaxation of exemption requirements for hospitals. In Simon v. Eastern Kentucky Welfare Rights Org., 426 U.S. 26 (1976), a class of indigents brought suit against Treasury officials, claiming that Rev.Rul. 69–545 impaired their "opportunity and ability" to obtain medical services and was a misinterpretation of the term "charitable" in the Code. The Supreme Court found no case or controversy because the class failed to show that the hospitals which denied them services were covered by the ruling. The Court also found that the class lacked standing to sue because they failed to show that their injury would be redressed by a favorable decision. In a case with similar facts, a court of appeals found that, even though the hospitals that denied service to the plaintiffs were covered by Rev.Rul. 69–545, the indigents still lacked standing because they had failed to show that their failure to receive services was a direct result of the IRS ruling and not of other concerns and policies of the hospital. Lugo v. Miller, 640 F.2d 823 (6th Cir.1981). See also Barrette v. Phoenix Gen. Hosp., Inc., 58 A.F.T.R.2d (P–H) 86–5685 (D.Ariz. 1986) (challenge to hospital's tax-exempt status dismissed because plaintiff lacked personal stake in the outcome necessary for standing).

As long as indigent patients who might hope to benefit from an enforced charitable impulse of the hospital cannot bring suit to change the IRS interpretation, the issue would appear to be left to administrative discretion. For a later case also limiting the standing of parties alleging harm from IRS policies, see Allen v. Wright, 468 U.S. 737 (1984) (challenge to tax exemptions for segregated private schools).

What is your view, finally, of allowing charitable exemptions for nonprofit hospitals without any more showing of charitable purpose than the IRS has required? A GAO study in 1990 found that 15% of exempt hospitals enjoyed a net profit from their exemption, providing less charity care than the exemption was worth. GAO, Nonprofit Hospitals: Better Standards Needed for Exemption (May 1990). All the articles cited in paragraph (1), supra, question in some way the IRS's favoritism for community hospitals. For a wide-ranging overview, see National Health Lawyers Ass'n, Colloquium Report on Legal Issues Related to Tax Exemption and Community Benefit (1996) (breaking issues down into four categories: policy; measurement, reporting, and enforcement; jurisdiction; and accountability).

6. *Tax-exempt Financing.* Financing through tax-exempt bonds is one of the principal benefits of qualifying as a 501(c)(3) organization. See generally Rev. Proc. 97–13, 1997–15 I.R.B. 18; T. Hyatt & B. Hopkins, supra, at 477–95. Most 501(c)(3)'s, including hospitals, can issue tax-exempt bonds with state assistance. Hospitals are not subjected to the volume cap imposed in 1986 on individual states' use of tax-exempt financing, and interest on their bonds is not subjected to the alternative minimum tax. Restrictions on private nonprofit hospital bonds include a requirement that 95% of proceeds be used strictly for tax-exempt purposes. (Query whether allowing radiologists, pathologists, etc., to conduct private practices in the hospital could jeopardize compliance with this limitation.)

Prior to 1997, HMOs and other nonhospital 501(c)(3)'s were limited to $150 million in bonds outstanding. (Hospital financing was not subject to this limit, which became more significant for other nonprofits—e.g., exempt managed-care organizations, long-term care and retirement facilities, ambulatory care facilities, etc.—as they grew in size and scope, merged, or otherwise consolidated their operations.) In 1997, a new provision, IRC § 145(b)(5), was added to the Code to remove the $150 million limit for financings meeting certain conditions, most particularly a requirement that at least 95% of the proceeds be used for new capital expenditures, not working capital or refinancing of earlier projects.

7. *New Attention to Hospitals' Federal Tax Exemption.* Facing more cost-conscious purchasers and increased competition in the 1980s, many nonprofit hospitals adopted more commercial attitudes and practices, cutting back their charitable activities and becoming less distinguishable from their for-profit counterparts. These developments naturally invited new attention to the eligibility of all nonprofit hospitals for federal tax exemption. See generally U.S. General Accounting Office, Nonprofit Hospitals: Better Standards Needed for Tax Exemption (GAO/HRD–90–84, 1990) (suggesting that the tax exemption could be "directly linked to a certain level of (1) care provided to Medicaid patients, (2) free care provided to the poor, or (3) efforts to improve the health status of underserved portions of the community"). In response to these concerns, the IRS expanded the disclosure requirements of Form 990, the annual tax return that tax-exempt hospitals must file.

The 102d Congress seriously considered two bills that would have placed further conditions on a hospital wishing to retain its tax-exemption. Representative Roybal's Charity Care and Hospital Tax–Exempt Status Reform Act of 1991 (H.R. 790) would have required a tax-exempt hospital to (1) adopt an open-door policy toward Medicaid and Medicare patients, (2) serve a reasonable number of them without discrimination, (3) provide "qualified charity care" in an amount equal to 50% of the value of its tax exemption (calculated by a complex formula), and (4) provide "qualified community benefits" costing at least 35% of the exemption's value. Failure to meet the latter two tests would have resulted, after a one-year grace period, in a tax equal to 100% of any later shortfall, the revenue from which would be earmarked for additional Medicaid cost sharing in the state where the hospital is located. See also H.R. 1374, 102d Cong., 1st Sess. (1991). These bills are examined in Colombo & Hall, supra, at 10–28. Late in the consideration of health care reform in 1994, the House Ways and Means Committee reported a bill that would have required an exempt hospital, among other things, to provide (without discrimination on the basis of ability to pay) "medically necessary" care "to the extent of its financial ability." See H.R. Rep. No. 601, 103d Cong., 2d Sess., pt. 1, at 314 (1994).

In the 1991 debates, the Bush administration supported continuing the community-benefit standard for tax exemption, stressing (consistent with its "thousand points of light" philosophy) that hospitals operated by state and local governments are exempt in any event and that the community-benefit standard therefore "encourages pluralistic alternatives to government activity—the raison d'etre for tax exemption." See Tax-exempt Status of Hospitals and Establishment of Charity Care Standards: Hearings before the House Comm. on Ways and Means, 102d Cong., 1st Sess. 34 (1991) (statement of Michael J. Graetz, Deputy Assistant Secretary of the Treasury for Tax Policy).

NOTE AND QUESTIONS ON STATE AND LOCAL TAX EXEMPTIONS

As shown by the *Utah County* case, nonprofit hospitals may qualify for exemption not only from federal taxes but also from state and local property, sales, and other taxes. These exemptions confer substantial cost advantages on their recipients and are increasingly controversial not only because of the revenue loss to local governments but also because many nonprofit entities compete with taxpaying enterprises in either their primary or secondary lines of business.

A later decision in Utah restored the tax exemption withheld in *Utah County* because IHC demonstrated compliance with six new standards developed by the state tax commission for determining whether a hospital had bestowed "a gift to the community." Howell v. County Bd. of Equalization of Cache County ex rel. IHC Hospitals, Inc., 881 P.2d 880 (Utah 1994). The state supreme court found that the new standards were consistent with its holding in the earlier decision. The most striking of the six standards was the fifth, under which the hospital must list and total the uncompensated services it provides to the community; the total for the year must exceed what would otherwise be the hospital's property tax liability.

Some states follow the IRS's 501(c)(3) determinations in granting state tax exemptions to hospitals or adopt a similar community-purpose rationale for conferring exempt status. Others, however, like Utah, are apt to be more demanding than is the IRS that tax-exempt hospitals provide services to indigents. See generally Potter & Longest, The Divergence of Federal and State Policies on the Charitable Tax Exemption of Nonprofit Hospitals, 19 J.Health Pol., Pol'y & Law 393 (1994). For a more traditional holding than *Utah County*, see Medical Center Hosp. of Vermont v. City of Burlington, 566 A.2d 1352 (Vt.1989) (holding that availability of services without regard to ability to pay is enough for purposes of property tax exemption). For a discussion of profitability as a criterion for property tax exemption under California law, see Rideout Hosp. Found. v. County of Yuba, 10 Cal.Rptr.2d 141 (Cal.App.1992) (holding that 24% net revenues do not automatically bar exemption where hospital can show it is not organized or operated for profit).

Additional examples of stricter state policies include Tex. Tax Code Ann. § 11.18, Tex. Health & Safety Code § 311.045 (West 1992 & Supp. 1996) (mandating that exempt hospitals spend at least 4% of net revenue on charity care and meet extensive reporting requirements); Office of the Massachusetts Attorney General, Community Benefit Guidelines for Nonprofit Acute Care Hospitals (June 1994) (requiring mission statements and reporting by all exempt institutions but deferring quantification of obligations). Many states have reexamined their policies in recent years.

Pennsylvania has been the site of much controversy over tax exemptions, with hospitals in two-thirds of 67 counties facing challenges to their favorable tax treatment and many more institutions making voluntary payments to, or service agreements with, local governments to avoid such challenges. A particularly interesting case was School Dist. v. Hamot Med. Center, 602 A.2d 407 (Pa.Commw.1992). Hamot (HMC), together with its nonprofit parent (HHSI), had assets tied up in a marina, country clubs, and health spas; several of its executives had access to these as part of incentive plans. HMC claimed that these properties improved the neighborhood around the hospital, and thus did not prevent it from meeting the commonwealth's "purely public charity" test for property tax exemption. The lower court rejected this argument, finding that "HMC is merely the money tree of HHSI's corporate forest." The Commonwealth court found several indicia of charitable purposes lacking in one of the many showdowns between hospitals and local communities. In 1997, Pennsylvania entered a new era when the legislature spelled out some new (and clearer) requirements for local tax exemption, including relief of government from a burden it would otherwise bear; a quantitative test (the value of uncompensated services must be no less than 75% of net operating income or 3% of total operating expense); and compensation arrangements not substantially linked to profits.

Health care providers other than hospitals may also qualify for state tax exemptions. See, e.g., In re St. Margaret Seneca Place v. Board of Property Assessment, Allegheny County, 640 A.2d 380 (1994) (applying Pennsylvania's strict criteria in upholding tax exemption of nursing home); Sebastian County Equalization Board v. Western Arkansas Counseling & Guidance Center, 752 S.W.2d 755 (Ark.1988) (mental health center held exempt from property tax despite having some paying patients). See also Annot., 37 A.L.R.3d 1191 (1971 & Supp. 1995); Rothermich, Defining "Charitable" in the Context of State Property Tax Exemption for Nonprofit Nursing Homes, 34 St. Louis U.L.J. 1109 (1990).

An interesting question is whether, like the federal government, a state applies different standards to hospitals than to other providers. In two states, the question arose whether an ambulatory surgical facility fit the definition of a "hospital" and could therefore seek to qualify for the same tax-exempt status as its hospital competitor. See Department of Revenue v. Gallatin Outpatient Clinic, Inc., 763 P.2d 1128 (Mont.1988) (comparable functions not enough); In re Foundation Health Systems Corp., 386 S.E.2d 588 (N.C.App.1989), app. dismissed, 401 S.E.2d 358 (N.C.1991) (adopting broad definition instead of that in hospital licensing law).

Most states require that property exempt from property taxes be used exclusively for charitable purposes. E.g., Appeal of Northwestern Corp., 665 A.2d 856 (Pa.Commw.1995) (denying real estate tax exemption for a mental health facility of an otherwise tax-exempt health corporation); Chisago Health Services v. Comm'r of Revenue, 462 N.W.2d 386 (Minn.1990) (hospital auxiliary facilities must be "reasonably necessary to accomplish the hospital's objectives" in order to qualify for property tax exemption; "reasonably necessary" defined in terms of functional, not financial, dependence). Some states, however, require only that the dominant use be exempt, and a few states allow substantial nonexempt use, taxing the portion of the property used for such purposes. Norwegian Amer. Hosp. v. Illinois Dept. of Revenue, 569 N.E.2d 83 (Ill.App.1991) (property of charitable institutions exempt from taxation if "primarily used for purposes reasonably necessary for the accomplishment and fulfillment of the institution's objectives and administration;" property "need not be absolutely indispensable for carrying out [institution's] purposes"); Barnes Hosp. v. Leggett, 646 S.W.2d 889 (Mo.App.1983) (held hospital used exclusively for charitable purposes even though some office space was used by faculty members in connection with their part-time practices); Lynn Hosp. v. Board of Assessors, 417 N.E.2d 14 (Mass.1981) (hospital parking lot used by medical staff, patients, and public; tax exemption permitted only for medically related use).

The Oregon Supreme Court has ruled that a for-profit competitor has standing to challenge a nonprofit's tax-exempt status. Northwest Med. Laboratories v. Good Samaritan Hosp. & Med. Center, 786 P.2d 718

(Ore.1990). Are indigents entitled to enforce the obligations incurred by providers in return for a state tax exemption? Or do state tax collectors offer the only enforcement mechanism? In State ex rel. Cook v. Rose, 299 S.E.2d 3 (W.Va.1982), advocates for the poor succeeded in getting an order compelling the tax commissioner to issue regulations clarifying the duty of tax-exempt hospitals to provide free or below-cost services to patients unable to pay.

Is relief from tax burdens a sufficient quid pro quo to warrant imposing by statute or judicial ruling an affirmative obligation to provide uncompensated care to any patient seeking it? If so, where does this leave taxpaying institutions with respect to such obligations? Should states be more demanding of tax-exempt facilities than the federal government is in EMTALA?

General Counsel Memorandum 39862

Internal Revenue Service, Dec. 2, 1991

* * *

ISSUE

Whether a hospital, tax exempt because it is described in section 501(c)(3), jeopardizes its exempt status by forming a joint venture with members of its medical staff and selling to the joint venture the gross or net revenue stream derived from operation of an existing hospital department or service for a defined period of time.

CONCLUSION

A hospital entering into such a transaction jeopardizes its tax exempt status for at least three reasons. First, the transaction causes the hospital's net earnings to inure to the benefit of private individuals. Second, the private benefit stemming from such a transaction cannot be considered incidental to the public benefits achieved. Third, such a transaction may violate federal law. * * *

FACTS

[One of the three fact situations addressed in the Memorandum involved X–Corp, a not-for-profit subsidiary of X–Hospital. Both corporations are tax-exempt under section 501(c)(3) and have identical boards. X–Corp serves as the sole corporate general partner of LP, a limited partnership formed to purchase the net revenue stream of X–Hospital's outpatient surgical program and gastroenterology laboratory. These services represent about 4% of X–Hospital's gross receipts. The purchase price paid to the hospital for the revenue stream was established at fair market value after arm's length negotiations.

[X–Corp holds a 10% interest in LP as the general partner and planned initially to hold 40% as a limited partner. X–Hospital donated to X–Corp funds sufficient to purchase its interest in X–LP and establish a loss reserve. The limited partners, all physicians who are members of X–Hospital's medical staff, hold the remaining 50% of LP initially and ultimately may hold 90%. Various provisions ensure that limited partnership interests will never be held by persons other than medical staff physicians—"which would impede accomplishment of the objectives of this transaction."

[X–Hospital continues to own and operate the subject facilities and continues to establish the amounts charged patients for their use. Each quarter, X–Hospital is to pay to LP the net revenue (after deducting the hospital's expenses) from operation of those facilities. X–Corp represented that the surgical facility was only 54% utilized at the time of its ruling request. X–Corp stated that the arrangement was undertaken to allow X–Hospital's medical staff physicians to participate, on an investment basis, in the technical or facility charge component of the outpatient surgery program and gastroenterology lab. X–Corp told the Service that this would offer a financial incentive to the physicians to increase usage of its facilities.

[On April 30, 1986, X–Corp applied for a ruling that participation in the transaction would not jeopardize its exemption and that income received from LP would not be taxable as unrelated business income.]

ANALYSIS

Background

The joint venture arrangements * * * are just one variety of an increasingly common type of competitive behavior engaged in by hospitals in response to significant changes in their operating environment. Many medical and surgical procedures once requiring inpatient care, still the exclusive province of hospitals, now are performed on an outpatient basis, where every private physician is a potential competitor. The marked shift in governmental policy from regulatory cost controls to competition has fundamentally changed the way all hospitals, for-profit and not, do business.

A driving force behind the new hospital operating environment was the federal Medicare Program's 1983 shift from cost-based reimbursement for covered inpatient hospital services to fixed, per-case, prospective payments. This change to a diagnosis-related prospective payment system ("PPS") dramatically altered hospital financial incentives. PPS severed the link between longer hospital stays with more services provided each patient and higher reimbursement. It substituted strong incentives to control the costs of each individual inpatient's care while attracting a greater number of admissions. Medicare policies are highly influential; the program accounts for nearly 40% of the average hospital's revenues.

The need to increase admission volume was accompanied by a perceived need to influence physician treatment decisions which, by and large, were unaffected by the change to PPS. Hospitals realized that, in addition to attracting more patients, they needed to control utilization of ancillary hospital services, discharge Medicare beneficiaries as quickly as is medically appropriate, and operate more efficiently. Traditionally, physicians treating their private patients at a hospital had enjoyed nearly complete independence of professional judgement. Since they are paid separately by Medicare and other third party payers on the basis of billed charges, they still have an incentive to render more services to each patient over a longer period in order to enhance their own earnings. Once hospital and physician economic incentives diverged, hospitals began seeking ways to stimulate loyalty among members of their medical staffs and to encourage or reward physician behaviors deemed desirable.

Despite the presence of professional managers, a hospital's medical staff physicians hold the key to maintaining or improving its utilization, revenue, and expense profile (i.e., the "bottom line"). Of course, patients actually bring revenues to a facility, but they rarely decide for themselves when or where to be hospitalized or what tests to order. Recent studies suggest that individual practitioners control from 70–90 percent of health care expenditures. Since most medical staff physicians are not hospital employees, and typically do not provide services to or receive direct compensation from the hospitals at which they practice, managers have had to look for innovative ways to influence their behavior.

As in the present cases, there often are multiple reasons why hospitals are willing to engage in joint ventures and other sophisticated financial arrangements with physicians. In seeking Service approvals for transactions, hospitals frequently cite the need to raise capital and to give physicians a stake in the success of a new enterprise or service. * * *

I. SALE OF THE REVENUE STREAM FROM A HOSPITAL ACTIVITY ALLOWS NET PROFITS TO INURE TO THE BENEFIT OF PHYSICIAN-INVESTORS.

* * *

Protecting charitable organizations against private inurement serves important purposes. A charitable organization is viewed under the common law and the Internal Revenue Code as a trust whose assets must irrevocably be dedicated to achieving charitable purposes. The inurement prohibition serves to prevent anyone in a position to do so from siphoning off any of a charity's income or assets for personal use.

The proscription against inurement generally applies to a distinct class of private interests—typically persons who, because of their particular relationship with an organization, have an opportunity to control or influence its activities. Thus, regulations interpreting section 501(a) of the Code make clear that the words "private shareholder or individual" in section 501(c)(3) refer to persons having a personal and private interest in the activities of the organization, as opposed to members of the general public or the organization's intended beneficiaries. These individuals are often referred to informally as "insiders."

Despite this limitation, the class of persons properly viewed as private shareholders and individuals (i.e. insiders) can, under certain circumstances, be sizeable. In GCM 39498 (Jan. 28, 1986), this Office stated that all physicians on the medical staff of a hospital, as employees or persons with a close professional working association with the hospital, are persons who have a personal and private interest in the activities of the hospital, and are subject to the inurement proscription. * * *

That previously stated position clearly fits the facts in the present cases. While most physicians on the medical staffs of the subject hospitals presumably are not employees and do not provide any compensable services directly to the hospitals, they do have a close professional working relationship with the hospitals. The physicians have applied for and been granted privileges to admit and treat their private patients at the hospital. They are bound by the medical staff bylaws, which may be viewed as a constructive contract between them and the hospital. Individually, and as a group, they largely control the flow of patients to and from the hospital and patients' utilization of hospital services while there. Some may serve other roles at the hospital, such as that of part-time employee, department head, Board member, etc. Moreover, once the arrangements at issue commenced, each physician-investor became a joint venture partner of the hospital or an affiliate.

Even though medical staff physicians are subject to the inurement proscription, that does not mean there can be no economic dealings between them and the hospitals. The inurement proscription does not prevent the payment of reasonable compensation for goods or services. It is aimed at preventing dividend-like distributions of charitable assets or expenditures to benefit a private interest. This Office has stated "inurement is likely to arise where the financial benefit represents a transfer of the organization's financial resources to an individual solely by virtue of the individual's relationship with the organization, and without regard to the accomplishment of exempt purposes." GCM 38459 (July 31, 1980).

* * *

The proper starting point for our analysis of the net revenue stream arrangements is to ask what the hospital gets in return for the benefit conferred on the physician-investors. Put another way, we ask whether and how engaging in the transaction furthers the hospital's exempt purposes. Here, there appears to be little accomplished that directly furthers the hospitals' charitable purposes of promoting health. No expansion of health care resources results; no new provider is created. No improvement in treatment modalities or reduction in cost is foreseeable. We have to look very carefully for any reason why a hospital would want to engage in this sort of arrangement.

X–Hospital explained in its ruling request that it would have the benefit of receiving the discounted cash value of its expected revenue stream in advance and would experience greater utilization of ancillary and inpatient services. * * *

Assuming, arguendo, that X–Hospital [had] a pressing need for an advance of cash, we could examine this type of transaction strictly as a financing mechanism. It certainly is permissible for a section 501(c)(3) hospital to borrow funds against future earnings; in fact, they often use tax exempt bonds to borrow at favorable interest rates. Nevertheless, we do not believe it would be proper under most circumstances for a charitable organization to borrow funds under an agreement, even with an outside commercial lender, where the organization would pay as interest a stated percentage of its earnings. While doing so might not constitute inurement if an outside lender were involved (but see discussion of private benefit, below), it would if the lender were, as here, an insider. In any event, we do not believe these transactions were undertaken to raise needed cash.

Whether admitted or not, we believe the hospitals engaged in these ventures largely as a means to retain and reward members of their medical staffs; to attract their admissions and referrals; and to pre-empt the physicians from investing in or creating a competing provider. Even putting aside any legality issues, discussed in Section III, below, the structure of these transactions is problematic. Giving (or selling) medical staff physicians a proprietary interest in the net profits of a hospital under these circumstances creates a result that is indistinguishable from paying dividends on stock. Profit distributions are made to persons having a personal and private interest in the activities of the organization and are made out of the net earnings of the organization. Thus, the arrangements confer a benefit which violates the inurement proscription of section 501(c)(3).

* * *

II. SALE OF THE REVENUE STREAM FROM A HOSPITAL ACTIVITY BENEFITS PRIVATE INTERESTS MORE THAN INCIDENTALLY.

Another key principle in the law of tax exempt organizations is that an entity is not organized and operated exclusively for exempt purposes unless it serves a public rather than a private interest. Thus, in order to be exempt, an organization must establish that it is not organized or operated for the benefit of private interests such as designated individuals, the creator or his family, shareholders of the organization, or persons controlled, directly or indirectly, by such private interests. Treas. Reg. section 1.501(c)(3)–1(d)(1). However, this private benefit prohibition applies to all kinds of persons and groups, not just to those "insiders" subject to the more strict inurement proscription.

* * *

In our view, some private benefit is present in all typical hospital-physician relationships. Physicians generally use hospital facilities at no cost to themselves to provide services to private patients for which they earn a fee. The private benefit accruing to the physicians generally can be considered incidental to the overwhelming public benefit resulting from having the combined resources of the hospital and its professional staff available to serve the public. Though the private benefit is compounded in the case of certain specialists, such as heart transplant surgeons, who depend heavily on highly specialized hospital facilities, that fact alone will not make the private benefit more than incidental.

In contrast, the private benefits conferred on the physician-investors by the instant revenue stream joint ventures are direct and substantial, not incidental. If for any reason these benefits should be found not to constitute inurement, they nonetheless exceed the bounds of prohibited private benefit. Whether viewed as giving the physicians a substantial share in the profits of the hospital or simply as allowing them an extremely profitable investment, the arrangements confer a significant benefit on them. Against this, we must balance the public benefit achieved by the hospitals in entering into the arrangements. The public benefit expected to result from these transactions—enhanced hospital financial health or greater efficiency achieved through improved utilization of their facilities—bears only the most tenuous relationship to the hospitals' charitable purposes of promoting the health of their communities. Obtaining referrals or avoiding new competition may improve the competitive position of an individual hospital, but that is not necessarily the same as benefitting its community.

* * *

Thus far, our discussion has focussed principally on the sales of the revenue streams involved in the instant arrangements. We also need to address the joint venture aspect. * * *

* * *

GCM 39005 (Dec. 17, 1982) sets forth the required analysis in testing an exempt organization's participation as a general partner in a limited partnership. This Office stated that participation by a section 501(c)(3) organization as a general partner in a limited partnership would not per se endanger its exempt status. However, close scrutiny is necessary to ensure that the obligations of the exempt organization as general partner do not conflict with its ability to pursue exclusively charitable goals. Thus, in all partnership cases, the initial focus should be on whether the joint venture organization furthers a charitable purpose. Once charitability is established, the partnership agreement itself should be examined to see whether the arrangement permits the exempt party to act exclusively in furtherance of the purposes for which exemption is granted, and not for the benefit of the limited partners. This requires a finding that the benefits received by the limited partners are incidental to the public purposes served by the partnership. Hospital participation in a joint venture is inconsistent with exemption, then, if it does not further a charitable purpose or if there is inadequate protection against financial loss by the hospital or improper financial gain by the physician-investors.

* * *

In each of the cases at issue, the hospital has stated that its reasons for participating in the joint venture were to maintain or enhance utilization of its facilities. Applying the close scrutiny standard suggested by GCM 39005 to these transactions, we are unable to conclude that the partnerships serve charitable purposes or that hospital participation furthers their exempt purposes. Thus, the arrangements fail the first part of the analysis. All three arrangements are similar in this regard, so we will concentrate on the facts [relating to X–Corp.]

X–Corp appears to argue that participation does further its exempt purposes by improving utilization of its outpatient surgery program and other facilities, thereby improving its efficiency and financial results. While recognizing that hospitals are under pressure to operate efficiently, we are unwilling to accept on these facts such a tenuous connection with X–Hospital's health promotion or patient care objectives. In our view, there are a fixed number of individuals in a community legitimately needing hospital services at any one time. Paying doctors to steer patients to one particular hospital merely to improve its efficiency seems distant from a mission of providing needed care. We question whether the Service should ever recognize enhancing a hospital's market share vis-a-vis other providers, in and of itself, as furthering a charitable purpose. In many cases, doing so might hamper another charitable hospital's ability to promote the health of the same community. The only direct benefit expected here, increased net income that might have been used to further an exempt purpose, will actually flow in large part to the limited partner physician-investors.

* * *

III. SALE OF THE REVENUE STREAM FROM A HOSPITAL ACTIVITY TO REFERRING PHYSICIAN–INVESTORS MAY VIOLATE FEDERAL LAW.

Nearly every hospital that is exempt as an organization described in section 501(c)(3) participates in the Medicare and Medicaid programs. In the usual case, doing so is a virtual requirement for exemption. These hospitals thus are subject to a comprehensive body of law found in the Social Security Act. Of particular importance here is a part of the Medicare and Medicaid Anti–Fraud and Abuse Law commonly referred to as the anti-kickback statute. This law prohibits the offer, solicitation, payment, or receipt of *any remuneration*, in cash or in kind, in return for, or to induce, the referral of a patient for any service that may be paid for by Medicare or Medicaid. As discussed below, where a tax exempt hospital engages in activities or arrangements that violate the anti-kickback statute, its exemption may be jeopardized.

* * *

NOTES AND QUESTIONS ON THE TAX IMPLICATIONS OF HOSPITAL/PHYSICIAN JOINT VENTURES

1. The foregoing ruling notes how, in recent years, tax-exempt hospitals have increasingly engaged in joint ventures with taxable entities, including members of their medical staffs. Such ventures do not give rise to unrelated business income if they further the institution's charitable purposes. As indicated in GCM 39,862, however, a hospital's participation as a general partner in a limited partnership may threaten its tax-exempt status by giving rise to a risk of private benefit—that is, the conferral of nonincidental benefits on private individuals. One expert practitioner called GCM 39,862 "probably the most important position statement issued by the IRS in the last decade." See generally M. Sanders, Partnerships & Joint Ventures Involving Tax–Exempt Organizations (1994 & Supp. 1996).

In a subsequent development, the IRS offered to consult with and not to penalize hospitals that undertook to terminate offending arrangements at an early date. Announcement 92–70, 1992–37 I.R.B. 4. Query how the IRS would regard payments made by exempt hospitals to their co-venturers as the price of withdrawing from their contracts. Cf. Priv.Ltr.Rul. 93–23–035 (Mar. 17, 1993) (approving, as reconstitution of transaction condemned under GCM 39,862, an arrangement under which hospital would rent trailer at fair market value to physicians owning only CT scanner in the community, provide incidental services, and have use of scanner in return for payment at fair market value).

2. It should be noted that GCM 39,862 relates only to arrangements affecting existing, underutilized hospital departments that a hospital hopes to expand by strengthening physician incentives to refer patients. Thus, joint ventures to add to a hospital's facilities may be viewed more favorably. See, e.g., Priv. Ltr. Rul. 91–05–031 (Feb.1, 1991) (participation by exempt hospital as a general partner in a joint venture to purchase essential scanner found to be in furtherance of hospital's exempt purpose); Priv. Ltr. Rul. 90–24–085 (Mar. 22, 1990) (favorable ruling on a carefully designed hospital/physician joint venture to procure magnetic resonance imaging equipment).

GCM 39,862 may also apply only where the hospital continues to own and operate the property, sharing revenue from it with physicians. Other arrangements may be tolerable if the terms are fair and the transaction advances the hospital's exempt purpose. See Priv.Ltr.Rul. 94–07–022 (Nov. 22, 1993) (allowing hospital to sell a 50% interest in its surgical center to physicians and to form a joint venture with the physicians to operate the center; proceeds of sale allowed hospital to build new cardiac care center); Priv.Ltr.Rul. 93–45–057 (Aug. 20, 1993) (allowing hospital/physician venture that would purchase the hospital's ambulatory surgery facility, expand it with capital supplied by doctors, and lease it to the hospital at fair market value).

3. The final section of GCM 39,862 calls attention to the so-called "anti-kickback statute" and its pertinence for hospitals' tax exemptions. This legislation will be examined in § D of this chapter. It appears, however, that the IRS has joined DHHS in seeking to stamp out arrangements that create arguable conflicts of interests and incentives for providing unnecessary care.

4. Are you satisfied by the GCM's explanation of why hospitals have historically been allowed tax exemptions despite the huge "private benefits" that physicians derive from their use? (Note, for example, the reference in the GCM to "heart transplant surgeons, who depend heavily on highly specialized hospital facilities.") Recognize that, by virtue of certain legal constraints on the kinds of relationships hospitals might have with physicians (to be studied later in this chapter), a hospital may be able to function only by forming some kind of joint venture with a medical staff comprising physicians who bring patients to the hospital and perform many important managerial functions for the institution. The inducement for physicians to join a medical staff is obviously the opportunity to use the hospital's facilities at no charge and to bill patients for services rendered on the hospital's premises. How does the limited partnership described in the GCM differ from the conventional, mutually advantageous relationship between doctors and hospitals? Is the difference one of substance or only of the form of the benefits conferred on the physicians?

5. When might the IRS listen to a claim that a joint venture aimed at increasing utilization of an existing hospital department is in furtherance of an exempt purpose? What if the hospital could show that it was on the brink of insolvency, that its uncompensated care burden could only be met by increasing the profitability of existing departments, and that only for-profit hospitals would suffer a diversion of patients as a consequence of the hospital's competitive move? Cf. Priv.Ltr.Rul. 92–33–037 (May 20, 1992) (rejecting argument that competition necessitated hospital's joint venture with its physicians).

PROBLEM ON PHYSICIAN RECRUITMENT

Nirvana Memorial Hospital ("NMH") is a tax-exempt nonprofit hospital serving a large Medicaid and uninsured population in rural Nirvana, West Carolina. With relatively few paying patients, it has been in danger of closing from time to time. NMH's management now sees hope, however, in the elderly population moving into retirement communities being constructed in the Nirvana area. Nevertheless, the hospital's prospects depend heavily on its ability to retain Dr. Johanna Jost on the hospital's staff as an internist specializing in gerontology.

Dr. Jost has recently received an attractive offer to join a group practice in East Carolina, and she is willing to continue her practice in Nirvana only if the terms are right. The hospital administration has advertised widely for a replacement for Dr. Jost without finding anyone equally capable of filling the need it sees for a gerontologist in Nirvana. It is therefore proposing to offer to supplement her income for three years if she fails to earn less than a predetermined amount (fixed on the basis of a national survey of income of physicians in the same specialty). After that time, it is expected that the retirement communities around Nirvana will generate enough income that she will remain in the community.

One of NMH's concerns is that a new wing it recently opened is underutilized. Although it obtained from the state health planning agency a "certificate of need" (CON) authorizing the construction of the new space on the basis of the expanding elderly population, the projected demand for the new beds has not yet fully materialized. In addition, NMH management fears that if the community loses Dr. Jost as a physician experienced in treating problems of the elderly, many of the patients it currently serves will turn for care to physicians in nearby towns, some of whom hospitalize their patients in other institutions. Dr. Jost has privileges only at NMH.

What are the legal issues involved in the proposed offer to Dr. Jost?

1. *Inurement?* Many hospitals recruit physicians by offering a variety of financial incentives, and the rule against inurement/private benefit has been deemed to apply to such arrangements. Is inurement a concern under the facts stated?

2. *Revenue Ruling 97–21.* In Rev.Rul. 97–21, 1997–18 I.R.B. (April 21, 1997), the IRS set forth five fact situations illustrating the application of § 501(c)(3) and § 4958 (the "intermediate sanctions" provision) in cases of physician recruitment. It appears that the Service will insist, as a minimum, that recruitment incentives be entirely reflected in a written agreement negotiated at arm's length and under effective oversight by the hospital's governing board. Permissible incentives—which in any event must be reasonable, both individually and in the aggregate—include signing bonuses, income guarantees for "a limited number of years," moving expense reimbursement, reimbursement of liability insurance premiums (including coverage for the "long tail" of claims attributable to a previous practice), provision of office space on favorable terms, and loans or loan guarantees for a personal residence or practice start-up.

3. *Exempt Purpose?* Is it enough to ensure NMH's continued tax exemption that the arrangement with Dr. Jost will benefit a nonprofit institution committed to caring for Medicaid (and Medicare) recipients and for patients unable to pay? In three of the hypotheticals in Rev.Rul. 97–21, the IRS observes that the physician being recruited will fill a community need documented by a "community needs assessment" or by the area's designation by the U.S. Public Health Service as a Health Professional Shortage Area for primary care physicians. How does the recruitment of Dr. Jost compare with these cases?

4. *"Insider" or "Disqualified Person"?* Is Dr. Jost an "insider" subject to the noninurement requirement? What is your conclusion based on GCM 39,862? Rev.Rul. 97–21 states that the physicians in the hypothetical cases it examined did "not have substantial influence over the affairs of the hospitals that are recruiting them." Presumably, a physician being recruited from another community would rarely have such "influence." In one of the hypotheticals, however, the hospital was allowed to employ modest incentives to recruit an obstetrician from its own medical staff to serve Medicaid and charity patients.

Section 4958 defines a "disqualified person" as one "who was [during the five years preceding the transaction] in a position to exercise substantial influence over the affairs of the organization." Does Dr. Jost meet this test (Which the IRS appears to have incorporated into its definition of "insider")?

Is Dr. Jost's obvious bargaining power in dealing with the hospital enough to qualify her as an insider or disqualified person? If so, does this change the analysis of new recruits who are uniquely positioned to bargain with the institution?

5. *Retention vs. Recruitment?* Should it matter that NMH is trying to retain Dr. Jost rather than to attract her from another community? If the hospital loses Dr. Jost, won't it have to use similar incentives to attract a replacement for her? Make the best case you can for letting NMH strike a deal to retain Dr. Jost.

6. *"Cross-town" Recruitment.* Suppose that Dr. Jost was on the staff of a hospital in a nearby town, with or without privileges at NMH. In one of the hypotheticals in Rev.Rul. 97–21, the recruited physician was a diagnostic radiologist needed to "ensure adequate coverage and high quality care for [the hospital's] radiology department." Does this case help in Dr. Jost's situation? (In approving the recruitment, the Service noted that the radiologist, in the nature of the specialty, "does not refer patients to Hospital E or any other hospital in City Y.")

7. A question might be raised concerning NMH's compliance with the "anti-kickback" statute. You will be asked later to reconsider physician recruitment in connection with that legislation.

Tax Status of New and Complex Health Care Enterprises

Geisinger Health Plan v. Commissioner

("Geisinger I")

United States Court of Appeals, Third Circuit, 1993.

985 F.2d 1210.

■ LEWIS, CIRCUIT JUDGE.

* * * This case requires us to decide whether a health maintenance organization (an "HMO") which serves a predominantly rural population, enrolls some Medicare subscribers, and which intends to subsidize some needy subscribers but, at present, serves only its paying subscribers, qualifies for exemption from federal income taxation under 26 U.S.C. § 501(c)(3). We hold that it does not.

* * *

I.

GHP, which qualifies as an HMO under both Pennsylvania and federal law, operates as part of a system of health care organizations in northeastern and northcentral Pennsylvania (the "Geisinger system"). * * *

The Geisinger System consists of GHP and eight other nonprofit entities. All are involved in some way in promoting health care in 27 counties in northeastern and northcentral Pennsylvania. They include: the Geisinger Foundation (the "Foundation"); Geisinger Medical Center ("GMC"); the Geisinger Clinic (the "Clinic"); Geisinger Wyoming Valley Medical Center ("GWV"); Marworth; Geisinger System Services ("GSS") and two professional liability trusts. Each of these entities is exempt from federal income taxation under one or more sections of the Internal Revenue Code (the "Code").

* * * GHP's service area encompasses 17 predominantly rural counties within the area served by the Geisinger System. As of November 30, 1987, according to a finding of a bureau of the federal Department of Health and Human Services, 23 percent of GHP's subscribers resided in medically underserved areas while 65 percent resided in counties containing medically underserved areas.

* * *

GHP has two types of subscribers. First, it is open to all adult individuals who reside in its service area and satisfactorily complete a routine questionnaire regarding their medical history. From its inception through June 30, 1987, GHP accepted all but 11 percent of its individual applicants. Second, it enrolls group subscribers. Any individual who resides in GHP's service area and belongs to a group of at least 100 eligible enrollees may enroll as a group subscriber without completing a health questionnaire. * * *

GHP describes itself as "providing health services." In reality, it contracts with other entities in the Geisinger System (at least one of which will contract with physicians from outside the Geisinger System) to provide services to GHP's subscribers. It also contracts with entities such as pharmacies to provide medical and hospital services to its subscribers in exchange for compensation. Under the terms of these contracts, GHP reimburses the hospitals and clinics by paying a negotiated per diem charge for inpatient services and a discounted percentage of billed charges for outpatient services. For the fiscal year ended June 30, 1987, the Clinic and GWV provided 80 percent of all hospital services to GHP subscribers. The remaining 20 percent were provided by other hospitals.

All physician services are provided to GHP subscribers pursuant to a contract between GHP and the Clinic. The contract requires the Clinic to open its emergency rooms to all GHP subscribers, regardless of ability to pay, just as the Clinic's emergency rooms are open to all members of the public, regardless of ability to pay. The Clinic will contract with unaffiliated physicians to provide required services, but for the year ended June 30, 1987, more than 84 percent of the physician services which the Clinic provided to GHP's subscribers were performed by physicians who were employees of the Clinic. GHP compensates the Clinic for the physicians' services by paying a fixed amount per subscriber.

Generally, both GHP's group and individual subscribers are required to pay for hospital services on the basis of a community rating system. This system balances high-risk subscribers against low-risk subscribers. The subscribers must also make copayments for certain goods and services. Individual subscribers pay an additional amount which group subscribers do not pay. This amount covers the additional costs associated with handling individual subscriberships. If a subscriber fails to pay an amount due to GHP or fails to make a required copayment, the subscriber's coverage is terminated upon 30 days written notice, unless payment is made within the 30 days.

GHP has adopted a subsidized dues program which has not yet been implemented. The program would establish a fund comprised of charitable donations and operating funds to subsidize GHP subscribers who are unable to pay their premiums. The fund would, in GHP's view, "add to the security of [subscribers], any of whom may at some time suffer financial misfortune due to loss of employment, physical or mental disability or other causes beyond their control and which impute no dishonor to the [subscriber]." Although the program makes reference to subsidizing people who are already subscribers, GHP's submissions indicate that it also intends to admit people who require subsidization at the time they apply.

Despite GHP's initial projection that it would fund the program by raising $125,000 in contributions over its first three years of operation, it has been unable to do so, it claims, because potential donors cannot be assured that contributions will be deductible on their federal income tax returns until GHP receives recognition of tax-exempt status under section 501(c)(3). GHP has likewise been unable to support the program with operating funds because it operated at a loss from its inception through the time the record in this case closed.

GHP enrolls some subscribers who are covered by Medicare and Medicaid. As of March 31, 1988, it had enrolled 1,064 Medicare recipients at a reduced rate on a wraparound basis, meaning that it will cover what Medicare does not. It also has enrolled a small number of Medicaid recipients in a few exceptional situations. Generally, however, GHP cannot offer coverage to Medicaid recipients until and unless it contracts with the Pennsylvania Department of Welfare, which administers Pennsylvania's Medicaid program. GHP has negotiated with the Department to obtain such a contract, but efforts to reach agreement have thus far been unsuccessful.

II.

Shortly after its incorporation, GHP applied to the IRS for recognition of exemption. The Commissioner ruled that GHP was not exempt because (1) it was not operated exclusively for exempt purposes under section 501(c)(3); and (2) it could not vicariously qualify for exemption as an "integral part" of the Geisinger System.

GHP filed suit in Tax Court, [which] reversed the Commissioner's ruling[, and] the Commissioner appealed.

III.

The first issue is whether GHP, standing alone, is entitled to tax-exempt status under section 501(c)(3).

* * *

GHP argues that it qualifies for exemption because it serves the charitable purpose of promoting health in the communities it serves. There are no published revenue rulings and only one previously litigated case addressing whether an HMO may qualify for exemption under section 501(c)(3). The sole case on this issue is a Tax Court case, Sound Health Association v. Commissioner, 71 T.C. 158 (1978).

* * *

A. The Appropriate Test

[I]n light of the parties' and the Tax Court's reliance on the law regarding the tax-exempt status of nonprofit hospitals in formulating the test to be applied to HMOs seeking exemption under section 501(c)(3), we will measure GHP's tax-exempt status against that standard. In doing so, we recognize that courts are to give weight to IRS revenue rulings but may disregard them if they conflict with the statute they purport to interpret or its legislative history, or if they are otherwise unreasonable.

1. Nonprofit Hospitals as Tax-Exempt Entities

* * * [N]o clear test has emerged to apply to nonprofit hospitals seeking tax exemptions. Instead, a nonprofit hospital will qualify for tax-exempt status if it primarily benefits the community. One way to qualify is to provide emergency room services without regard to patients' ability to pay; another is to provide free care to indigents. A hospital may also benefit the community by serving those who pay their bills through public programs such as Medicaid or Medicare. For the most part, however, hospitals must meet a flexible "community benefit" test based upon a variety of indicia.

2. HMOs as Tax-Exempt Entities

Overlaid against this background is Sound Health. In Sound Health, the Tax Court applied the hospital precedents in ruling that an HMO was exempt from taxation.

The Sound Health HMO resembled GHP in many ways. Its articles of incorporation listed a number of charitable purposes relating to the promotion of health. Like GHP's subscribers, its subscribers paid for services based upon a community rating system, and a subsidized dues program assisted those who could not afford subscribership. Subscribers also had to satisfy eligibility requirements similar to GHP's.

Unlike GHP, however, the Sound Health HMO provided health care services itself rather than simply arranging for others to provide them to its subscribers.[4] It also employed doctors, health care providers and medical

4. GHP is, in fact, a different type of HMO than the HMO in Sound Health. HMOs had traditionally owned or provided hospital services themselves for a set, prepaid fee. In the late 1970's and early 1980's, however, Individual Practice Association (IPA) HMOs proliferated. "Unlike the traditional group practice or staff model HMOs, IPA-type HMOs do not directly own or provide hospital services. Rather, they arrange for the provision of hospital services by contracting with existing hospitals on a fee for service, capitation, per diem, or other basis." Douglas M. Mancino, Income Tax Exemption of the Con-

personnel who were not affiliated with the HMO to provide health care to its subscribers. Significantly, the Sound Health HMO provided services to both subscribers and members of the general public through an outpatient clinic which it operated and at which it treated all emergency patients, subscribers or not, and regardless of ability to pay. It also adjusted rates for and provided some free care to patients who were not subscribers. It offered public educational programs regarding health.

* * *

The Sound Health court went to great lengths to find a benefit to the community rather than simply a benefit to the HMO's subscribers. It rejected the argument that the HMO at issue benefited only its subscribers, finding:

> The most important feature of the Association's [subscribership] form of organization is that the class of persons eligible for [subscribership], and hence eligible to benefit from the Association's activities, is practically unlimited. The class of possible [subscribers] of the Association is, for all practical purposes, the class of members of the community itself. The major barrier to [subscribership] is lack of money, but a subsidized dues program demonstrates that even this barrier is not intended to be absolute.... It is safe to say that the class of persons potentially benefitted [sic] by the Association is not so small that its relief is of no benefit to the community. Id. at 185.

As we have observed, however, the court listed several factors in addition to open subscribership as indications that the Sound Health HMO was operated for charitable purposes. Chief among these were the HMO's operation of an emergency room open to all persons, subscribers or not, and regardless of ability to pay; rendering some free care to both subscribers and those who did not subscribe; conducting research; and offering an educational program. * * *

additional factors

Thus, the Sound Health court did not entirely dispense with the requirement that an entity seeking tax exemption must benefit the community, either by providing services to those who cannot afford to pay or otherwise. Sound Health was decided before Rev.Rul. 83–157 was issued [ruling that "a nonprofit hospital need not even maintain an emergency room open to all, regardless of ability to pay, if doing so would result in needless duplication of services in the area"], but provision of emergency care was only one of the factors relied upon in holding that the HMO was exempt from taxation under section 501(c)(3). The HMO in Sound Health demonstrated that it benefited the community in several ways beyond merely providing emergency services regardless of ability to pay.

temporary Nonprofit Hospital, 32 St. Louis U.L.J. 1015, 1034 (1988). GHP appears to fall within the IPA–HMO category. Also in the 1980's, nonprofit hospitals themselves began to form, purchase and contract with alternative delivery systems such as HMOs to vertically integrate and to maintain control over patient admissions. The Geisinger System's formation of GHP fits perfectly into this pattern.

3. The Resulting Test

In administrative proceedings in this case, the IRS contended that GHP had to meet a strict, fourteen-factor test based upon the facts of Sound Health in order to qualify for tax-exempt status. Upon review, we cannot agree that any strict, multi-factor test is appropriate when determining whether an HMO qualifies for tax-exempt status under section 501(c)(3). Rather, the determination must be based upon the totality of the circumstances, with an eye toward discerning whether the HMO in question benefits the community in addition to its subscribers.

B. GHP's Status as a Tax–Exempt Entity

Viewed in this light, GHP standing alone does not merit tax-exempt status under section 501(c)(3). GHP cannot say that it provides any health care services itself. Nor does it ensure that people who are not GHP subscribers have access to health care or information about health care. According to the record, it neither conducts research nor offers educational programs, much less educational programs open to the public. It benefits no one but its subscribers.

* * *

It is true that GHP is open to anyone who can afford to pay and that, like the HMO in Sound Health, GHP apparently intends to lower, or even to remove, this potential economic barrier to subscribing through its subsidized dues program. As we explain below, however, the mere presence of the subsidized dues program does not necessarily invite a conclusion that GHP benefits the community.

First, the Sound Health court ventured too far when it reasoned that the presence of a subsidized dues program meant that the HMO in question served a large enough class that it benefited the community. The court ruled that because there was no economic barrier to subscribership, "the class of persons potentially benefitted [sic] by the Association is not so small that its relief is of no benefit to the community." In doing so, however, the court misconstrued the relevant inquiry by focusing on whether the HMO benefited the community at all rather than whether it primarily benefited the community, as an entity must in order to qualify for tax-exempt status.

The mere fact that a person need not pay to belong does not necessarily mean that GHP, which provides services only to those who do belong, serves a public purpose which primarily benefits the community. The community benefited is, in fact, limited to those who belong to GHP since the requirement of subscribership remains a condition precedent to any service. Absent any additional indicia of a charitable purpose, this self-imposed precondition suggests that GHP is primarily benefiting itself (and, perhaps, secondarily benefiting the community) by promoting subscribership throughout the areas it serves.

* * *

Second, the Sound Health court need not have gone as far as it did. The presence of a subsidized dues program was not the only factor it considered when deciding that the HMO in question qualified for tax-exempt status. For example, the HMO in Sound Health "in effect, [ran] a substantial outpatient clinic as an important ingredient of its medical care services." Id. It also provided free care even to persons who did not subscribe and offered educational programs to the public.

Finally, even considering the subsidized dues program, the amount of benefit GHP intends to confer on people other than paying subscribers is minuscule. GHP anticipates subsidizing approximately 35 people. We cannot say that GHP operates primarily to benefit the community at large rather than its subscribers by arranging for health care for only 35 people, who would not otherwise belong, as compared to more than 70,000 paying subscribers. GHP argues that the HMO in Sound Health had provided only $158.50 in subsidies when it was granted tax-exempt status. This is true, but, as previously noted, the HMO in that case also benefited the community in other ways, most notably by providing free or reduced-cost care to people who were not subscribers. An HMO must primarily benefit the community, not its subscribers plus a few people, in order to qualify for tax-exempt status under section 501(c)(3).

In sum, GHP does not qualify for tax-exempt status under section 501(c)(3) since it does no more than arrange for its subscribers, many of whom are medically underserved, to receive health care services from health care providers. This is so even though it has a program designed to subsidize the subscribership of those who might not be able to afford the fees required of all other subscribers. Arranging for the provision of medical services only to those who "belong" is not necessarily charitable, particularly where, as here, the HMO has arranged to subsidize only a small number of such persons. GHP, standing alone, is not entitled to tax-exempt status under section 501(c)(3).

IV.

Alternatively, GHP argues that it is entitled to tax-exempt status under section 501(c)(3) because it is an integral part of the Geisinger System. The integral part doctrine provides a means by which organizations may qualify for exemption vicariously through related organizations, as long as they are engaged in activities which would be exempt if the related organizations engaged in them, and as long as those activities are furthering the exempt purposes of the related organizations. * * *

We decline to address the merits of the integral part doctrine at this stage, and instead remand the question of its application to this case to the Tax Court for clarification. * * *

NOTES AND QUESTIONS ON TAX EXEMPTIONS FOR HMOS AND HEALTH INSURERS

1. *Staff-model vs. Other HMOs.* Does it appear from the foregoing case and its discussion of the earlier *Sound Health* case that only staff-model

HMOs are eligible for 501(c)(3) status? Why might HMOs be treated differently based on their organizational structure? Consider separately "group models," in which treatment is provided by physicians in a group practice; "individual practice association (IPA) models," in which treatment is provided by individual physicians in their individual facilities; and "network models," in which treatment is provided by multiple independent physician groups. In Gen.Couns.Mem. 39,057 (Nov. 9, 1983), the IRS distinguished between an HMO that was merely an arranger of care and one that actually provided it. Signs of the same preference appeared in Gen.Couns.Mem. 39,828 (Aug. 30, 1990), which emphasized not only direct provision of care but also open enrollment, community rating of premiums (as opposed to premiums based on the anticipated costs of caring for particular covered groups), and reduced rates for the indigent as characteristics to be looked for in HMOs seeking 501(c)(3) status.

2. *Section 501(c)(4).* Although special circumstances can qualify an HMO for exemption under section 501(c)(3) (as in the *Sound Health* case), most nonprofit HMOs (a greater number of HMOs are for-profit enterprises) are exempt from income taxation under another provision, IRC § 501(c)(4) (1994). This provision, which confers none of the other benefits of section 501(c)(3), exempts "organizations not organized for profit but operated exclusively for the promotion of social welfare, * * * the net earnings of which are devoted exclusively to charitable, educational, or recreational purposes."

In Gen.Couns.Mem. 38,894 (Sept. 9, 1982), the IRS denied 501(c)(4) exempt status to an IPA-type HMO because HMO was controlled by its physician members, whom it served mainly as a marketing agent. The IRS indicated that a health care entity seeking exemption as a "social welfare" organization under section 501(c)(4) would have to address a bona fide community need and not simply duplicate services offered by commercial entities. Further criteria include whether the organization allows consumer input and whether the organization provides benefits for elderly, handicapped, or indigent individuals. The usual rules against inurement and conferral of private benefits apply.

3. *Blue Cross/Blue Shield Plans.* Section 1012 of the Tax Reform Act of 1986, Pub.L. No. 99–514, 100 Stat. 2085, denied exemption under sections 501(c)(3) and 501(c)(4) to nonprofit organizations substantially engaged in "providing commercial-type insurance." IRC § 501(m) (1994). This provision was designed specifically to make Blue Cross and Blue Shield plans subject to the federal income tax for the first time. Congress was moved to repeal the Blues' previous 501(c)(4) exemption by a study by the General Accounting Office finding that Blue plans are not materially more receptive to underwriting high-risk individuals than commercial carriers. U.S. Comptroller General, Health Insurance: Comparing Blue Cross and Blue Shield Plans With Commercial Insurers (General Accounting Office 1986). As serious as loss of the federal exemption was for Blue plans, plan officials were more concerned about the possibility, enhanced by the GAO study, of losing state-conferred exemptions from premium taxes. These taxes, typi-

cally 2% of gross premiums, are still in effect in some 30 states, where they put the Blues' commercial competitors at a distinct cost disadvantage.

4. *HMOs and Section 501(m).* Because HMOs of the non-staff variety resemble Blue Shield plans in many respects, the 1986 legislation revoking the Blues' 501(c)(4) exemption prompted the IRS to revisit the question of 501(c)(4) treatment for such HMOs. Under IRC § 501(m), an organization can qualify for exemption only if "no substantial part" of its activities consists of "providing commercial-type insurance." In Gen.Couns.Mem. 39,829 (Aug. 30, 1990), the IRS outlined the effects of section 501(m) on HMOs. Defining insurance as an activity involving "risk-shifting and risk-distributing," the Service first concluded that prepaid health plans such as HMOs do indeed provide "commercial-type insurance." Nevertheless, a HMO might still qualify for exemption because of IRC § 501(m)(3)(B), a special provision that permits HMOs to provide such insurance as long as it is "incidental health insurance * * * of a kind customarily provided by such organizations." In GCM 39,829, the Service listed several factors to consider in determining whether the insurance aspect of an HMO is "incidental." Among these factors were whether, and to what extent, the HMO provides health care services directly (as in a staff-model HMO) and whether, and to what extent, the HMO shifts risks of loss to the providers of care through capitation arrangements or otherwise. Only if the HMO entity itself bears substantial insurance risk will it be denied a 501(c)(3) or 501(c)(4) exemption under section 501(m).

5. *State and Local Taxation of HMOs.* States have taken different positions on the eligibility of HMOs for tax exemptions. E.g., Healthguard Services, Inc. v. Department of Revenue, 13 Or. Tax 415 (Or.Tax.1995) (HMO with 501(c)(4) exemption denied state corporate excise tax exemption); Supervisor of Assessments v. Group Health Ass'n, Inc., 308 Md. 151, 517 A.2d 1076 (1986) (HMO with 501(c)(3) exemption denied state property tax exemption); SHARE v. Commissioner of Revenue, 363 N.W.2d 47 (Minn.1985) (HMO providing services for compensation to cross section of community held not exempt as "public charity" from sales and use taxes); Harvard Community Health Plan, Inc. v. Board of Assessors of Cambridge, 384 Mass. 536, 427 N.E.2d 1159 (1981) (promotion of health for a sufficiently large or indefinite class establishes charitable purpose and qualifies HMO for property tax exemption).

Geisinger Health Plan v. Commissioner

("Geisinger II")

United States Court of Appeals, Third Circuit, 1994.
30 F.3d 494.

■ LEWIS, CIRCUIT JUDGE.

In [*Geisinger I*], we * * * remanded the case for determination of whether GHP was entitled to exemption from taxation by virtue of being an integral part of the Geisinger System. * * * We will affirm the Tax Court's decision that it is not exempt as an integral part of the System.

reason for present case

← App Ct affirms Tax Ct's decision → GHP not exempt

I.

GHP is a prepaid health care plan which contracts with health care providers to provide services to its subscribers. The facts relevant to GHP's function are detailed in our opinion in *Geisinger I*, and we need not repeat them here. Instead, far more relevant to this appeal is GHP's relationship with the Geisinger System and its other constituent entities, a relationship which we must examine in some detail to decide the issue before us.

The Geisinger System consists of GHP and eight other entities, all involved in some way in promoting health care in 27 counties in northeastern and northcentral Pennsylvania. * * *

The Foundation controls all these entities, as well as three for-profit corporations. It has the power to appoint the corporate members of GHP, GMC, GWV, GSS, the Clinic and Marworth, and those members elect the boards of directors of those entities. The Foundation also raises funds for the Geisinger System. Its board of directors is composed of civic and business leaders in the area.

GMC operates a 569–bed regional medical center. * * * It accepts patients without regard to ability to pay, including Medicare, Medicaid and charity patients. It operates a full-time emergency room open to all, regardless of ability to pay. It also serves as a teaching hospital.

GWV is a 230–bed hospital located in Wilkes–Barre, Pennsylvania. It accepts patients regardless of ability to pay, and it operates a full-time emergency room open to all, regardless of ability to pay.

The Clinic provides medical services to patients at 43 locations throughout the System's service area. It also conducts extensive medical research in conjunction with GMC and physicians who perform medical services for GMC, GWV and other entities in the Geisinger System. As of March 31, 1988, it employed 401 physicians. It accepts patients without regard to their ability to pay.

Marworth operates two alcohol detoxification and rehabilitation centers and offers educational programs to prevent alcohol and substance abuse.

GSS employs management and other personnel who provide services to entities in the Geisinger System.

* * *

[The Geisinger System] organized GHP as a separate entity within the System (as opposed to operating it from within the Clinic, GMC or GWV) for three reasons. First, HMOs in Pennsylvania are subject to extensive regulation by the Commonwealth's Departments of Health and Insurance. Operating GHP separately enables other entities in the System to avoid having to comply with the burdensome requirements associated with that regulation. Second, those administering the System believe it preferable for GHP's organization and management to remain separate from those of the System's other entities because it serves a wider geographic area than any of those other entities. Finally, under Pennsylvania law at least one-third of

GHP's directors must be subscribers. Establishing GHP as a separate entity avoids disrupting the governance of the other Geisinger System entities to comply with this requirement. * * *

For the year which ended June 30, 1987, GHP generated 8.8 percent of the aggregate gross receipts of the five health care providers in the Geisinger System. At the time this case was first submitted to the Tax Court, projections indicated that by June 30, 1991, GHP would generate 14.35 percent of the System's aggregate gross receipts.

GHP's interaction with other Geisinger System entities is varied. Its most significant contact is with the Clinic, from which it purchases the physician services its subscribers require by paying a fixed amount per member per month, as set forth in a Medical Services Agreement. Eighty-four percent of physician services are provided by doctors who are employees of the Clinic; the remaining 16 percent are provided by doctors who are not affiliated with the Clinic but who have contracted with the Clinic to provide services to GHP subscribers. GHP has similarly entered into contracts with GMC and GWV, as well as 20 non-related hospitals. When GHP's subscribers require hospital care, these hospitals provide it pursuant to the terms of their contracts, for either a negotiated per diem charge or a discounted percentage of billed charges. GHP has also contracted with GSS to purchase office space, supplies and administrative services.

* * *

The Tax Court considered GHP's role in the Geisinger System when, on remand from *Geisinger I*, it decided that GHP did not qualify for exempt status under the integral part doctrine. The court first distinguished a series of "group practice cases," in which incorporated groups of doctors on hospital or faculty medical staffs were held to be exempt from taxation as integral parts of the tax-exempt hospitals or medical schools with which they were associated. The Tax Court found that those cases did not control its decision because "[f]or [them] to apply here, the population of [GHP's] subscribers would have to overlap substantially with the patients of the related exempt entities [and t]he facts indicated that it does not." Moreover, it held, GHP was not entitled to tax-exempt status as an integral part of the System because it would produce unrelated business income for the Clinic, GMC or GWV if one of those entities were to absorb its activities. A timely appeal followed; as noted previously, we will affirm, although we will do so on grounds which differ from those on which the Tax Court rested. Specifically, because we deem it unnecessary to decide, we will not reach the issue whether GHP would produce unrelated business income if it were part of some entity created by merging its operations with one of the other Geisinger System entities.

II.

* * *

In *Geisinger I*, we described the integral part doctrine as follows: The integral part doctrine provides a means by which organizations may qualify for exemption vicariously through related organizations, as long as they are engaged in activities which would be exempt if the related organizations engaged in them, and as long as those activities are furthering the exempt purposes of the related organizations. The Tax Court on remand stated: The parties agree that an organization is entitled to exemption as an integral part of a tax-exempt affiliate if its activities are carried out under the supervision or control of an exempt organization and could be carried out by the exempt organization without constituting an unrelated trade or business.

GHP argues that these statements require us to examine whether the Clinic or GMC could retain tax-exempt status if it were to absorb GHP. It thus compares the attributes of a hypothetically merged Clinic/GHP or GMC/GHP entity to the attributes of the HMO held to be exempt in Sound Health Association v. Commissioner. Concluding that the merged entity would display more indicia of entitlement to exemption than the Sound Health HMO, GHP urges that it is exempt because of the characteristics of the hypothetical merged entity. Despite its superficial appeal, we reject this argument and hold that the integral part doctrine does not mean that GHP would be exempt solely because either GMC or the Clinic could absorb it while retaining its tax-exempt status. While this is a necessary condition to applying the doctrine, it is not the only condition. GHP is separately incorporated for reasons it found administratively and politically advantageous. While it may certainly benefit from that separate incorporation, it must also cope with the consequences flowing from it.

We acknowledge that interpreting the integral part doctrine in the manner GHP urges might enable entities to choose their organizational structures based on efficiency concerns rather than perverting those concerns by making tax considerations relevant. In our view, however, there are countervailing policy concerns which justify determining each entity's tax status based upon its own organizational structure. It is less complex and more certain for courts and administrators to assess an entity's tax status in light of its unique organizational composition and its association with another entity, and only to have to take into account some hypothetical combination of organizations as a second step in those relatively rare instances when an organization meets the other precondition of integral part status we set forth below. We recognize that it may appear overly technical to tax GHP differently from a GMC/GHP or a Clinic/GHP combination, for instance, merely because it is incorporated separately. On the other hand, to tax GHP differently merely because it is related to those entities, without searching for indicia that its association with them enhances its own tax-exempt characteristics, would be inconsistent with the narrow construction generally accorded tax exemptions. * * *

Accordingly, we will determine whether GHP is exempt from taxation when examined not only in the context of its relationship with the other entities in the System, but also based upon its own organizational structure. * * *

[We] conclude that a subsidiary which is not entitled to exempt status on its own may only receive such status as an integral part of its § 501(c)(3) qualified parent if (i) it is not carrying on a trade or business which would be an unrelated trade or business (that is, unrelated to exempt activities) if regularly carried on by the parent, and (ii) its relationship to its parent somehow enhances the subsidiary's own exempt character to the point that, when the boost provided by the parent is added to the contribution made by the subsidiary itself, the subsidiary would be entitled to s 501(c)(3) status.

* * *

In considering whether the boost received by GHP from its association with GMC or the Clinic might be sufficient, when added to its own contribution, to merit § 501(c)(3) treatment, we must first look at the nature of the boost which was sufficient in those instances where the integral part doctrine has been applied. The electric company [owned by Harvard University] discussed in 26 C.F.R. § 502–1(b), for example, would not be entitled to an exemption standing alone, because the provision of electric power to others is not a charitable purpose.

However, [a]s a subsidiary of the university, the electric company acquires the purpose of the university—it produces electricity solely for the purpose of allowing education to occur. The "boost" it receives from its association with the educational institution transforms it from a company without to a company with a charitable purpose and thus enables it to qualify for tax-exempt status as an integral part of that institution. * * * Absent receipt of such a "boost," we do not think that an institution is entitled to a tax exemption as an integral part. To hold otherwise might enable an organization that is not entitled to an exemption on its own to become tax-exempt merely because it happens to be controlled by an organization that is itself exempt.

Here, we do not think that GHP receives any "boost" from its association with the Geisinger System. In *Geisinger I*, we determined that while GHP helps to promote health, it does not do so for a significant enough portion of the community to qualify for tax-exempt status on its own. And, unlike the electric company * * *, the contribution that GHP makes to community health is not increased at all by the fact that GHP is a subsidiary of the System rather than being an independent organization which sends its subscribers to a variety of hospitals and clinics.

As our examination of the manner in which GHP interacts with other entities in the System makes clear, its association with those entities does nothing to increase the portion of the community for which GHP promotes health—it serves no more people as a part of the System than it would serve otherwise. It may contribute to the System by providing more patients than the System might otherwise have served, thus arguably allowing the System to promote health among a broader segment of the community than could be served without it, but its provision of patients to the System does not enhance its own promotion of health; the patients it provides—its subscribers—are the same patients it serves without its association with the System. To the extent it promotes health among non-GHP-subscriber patients of the System, it does so only because GHP subscribers' payments to the System help finance the provision of health care to others. An entity's mere financing of the exempt purposes of a related organization does not constitute furtherance of that organization's purpose so as to justify exemption. * * * Thus, it is apparent that GHP merely seeks to "piggyback" off of the other entities in the System, taking on their charitable characteristics in an effort to gain exemption without demonstrating that it is rendered "more charitable" by virtue of its association with them.

* * *

III.

In sum, GHP does not qualify for exemption as an integral part of the Geisinger System because its charitable character is not enhanced by virtue of its association with the System. We will affirm the decision of the Tax Court.

NOTES AND QUESTIONS ON COMPLEX CORPORATE STRUCTURES INVOLVING NONPROFIT FIRMS

1. The foregoing case illustrates the kind of corporate empires that have become commonplace in the nonprofit world in recent years and the tax issues that such empires present. The main object of such complex corporate structures is to avoid the strictures imposed on 501(c)(3) organizations in pursuing profit opportunities and to allow the profits from such ventures to support the nonprofit's general objectives. In addition, an affiliated, taxpaying corporation may often deduct expenses that would be disallowed in calculating unrelated business income. Limitation of liability and some advantages in obtaining capital are other benefits of segregating some activities of the enterprise. See Sawyer, How Tax–Exempt Hospitals Should Weigh the Risks of Strategic Restructuring, Journal of Taxation of Exempt Organizations, May–June 1993, at 32. See generally M. Sanders, Partnerships and Joint Ventures Involving Tax–Exempt Organizations (1994 and Supp. 1996); T. Hyatt & B. Hopkins, The Law of Tax-exempt Healthcare Organizations (1995).

It is common in hospital systems for separate for-profit or nonprofit affiliates to provide such outpatient services as ambulatory surgery, renal dialysis, and rehabilitation and to sell supplies, laundry, lab, and other services. A real estate affiliate might engage in the development of medical offices and space for outpatient services, perhaps as a general partner in a limited partnership with members of the medical staff.

2. *Parent Holding Corporations and "Supporting Organizations."* In order to seize market opportunities without jeopardizing its 501(c)(3) tax exemption, a nonprofit hospital might attempt to segregate its noncharitable from its charitable activities in separate but affiliated corporations. A common pattern in corporate restructurings is to set up a parent holding company, exempt under 501(c)(3), to control the hospital subsidiary corporation (by appointing its governing board) and perhaps other subsidiaries, for-profit as well as nonprofit. The parent's ability to operate this network and to subsidize the hospital from its earnings is ensured by applying, as a "supporting organization" of the hospital, for the status of a nonprivate foundation, or public charity, under IRC § 509(a) (1994). IRS policy allows a hospital's controlling parent as well as a controlled subsidiary to qualify as a "supporting organization" but only if there is such an overlap in board membership to ensure the supporting organization's responsiveness to the hospital's interests. Gen.Couns.Mem. 39,508 (May 28, 1986). See, e.g., Priv. Ltr. Rul. 95–04–029 (Oct. 30, 1994) (approving a reorganization plan involving creation of a separately incorporated parent holding company).

3. *For-Profit Subsidiaries.* A tax-exempt hospital or other parent corporation may also create a for-profit (taxable) subsidiary without jeopardizing its tax-exempt status if there is a bona fide business purpose and sufficient separation of management. Gen.Couns.Mem. 39,326 (Jan. 17, 1985). Although the IRS appears reluctant to "pierce the corporate veil" and attribute the conduct of the for-profit subsidiary to the nonprofit parent, the rule against inurement to private individuals must still be satisfied. Corporate restructuring instituted merely as a means to channel funds through subsidiaries to private individuals will result in a loss of tax exempt status. Gen.Couns.Mem. 39,646 (June 30, 1987). Thus, an exempt hospital or other parent will need to insure that its contracts with its for-profit subsidiaries are at arms length (hence, the requirement that management of the two entities not overlap appreciably) and that services are paid for at market rates. See generally B. Hopkins, The Law of Tax–Exempt Organizations 993–1002 (6th ed. 1992 and Supp. 1996).

4. *"Whole-Hospital" Joint Ventures.* Assume that a tax–exempt hospital entity contributes assets including the hospital to a joint venture company that it jointly owns with a for–profit firm, which firm contributes assets of equal value. The IRS would view the arrangement for operating the hospital favorably if the nonprofit entity retains effective corporate control (a veto of some kind), if profits are shared equally, and if no inurement problems appear (in management contracts, etc.). See Rev. Rul. 98–15, 1998–12 I.R.B. (Mar. 23, 1998) (setting forth safe harbor and illustrating potential pitfalls).

5. With nonprofit hospital systems looking more and more like commercial enterprises, are tax exemptions still appropriate? The issue continues to be argued, as references cited earlier demonstrate. See generally T. Hyatt & B. Hopkins, supra, at 29–51 (discussing among other things the so-called "*commerciality doctrine,*" which is described as "the singlemost [*sic*] important general element of the law of tax-exempt organizations today," and specifically the question "whether the typical nonprofit hospital or other healthcare provider is operating in a *commercial* manner—that is, looks and functions too much like its for-profit counterparts"). Perhaps the groundwork is being laid for a return to a strict charity-care standard. Nevertheless, are you persuaded that hospitals that cross-subsidize otherwise uncompensated care are engaged in truly charitable activity? The resources they expend are mostly raised, after all, from private payers that lack charitable intent but are forced by market conditions to pay prices in excess of marginal cost for the hospital's services. On the other hand, could (should) the public condition the tax exemption in such a way as to induce at least some firms enjoying a degree of monopoly power to devote a significant share of their profits to conferring benefits, not on the private persons who would otherwise benefit incidentally from the firm's discretionary spending, but on a specific class of beneficiaries—those who cannot pay for the health care they require?

6. Does a nonprofit community hospital violate any trust in associating itself with a nonprofit health care system serving a wider region? In the *Utah County* case, there was an inevitable tension between the interests of the local taxing jurisdiction and the interests of the nonprofit (but far-flung) IHC system. Similar tensions can arise as a matter of trust law or nonprofit corporation law if the larger system appears able to override the interests of local donors or other contributors to the local institution or to divert resources to system uses from designated charitable uses in the hospital's own community. Although such questions have been raised only rarely (see Peregrine & Makos, "Community Asset" Concept Threatens Nonprofit Healthcare System Control, Health L. Dig., July 1997, p. 3), they cannot be easily dismissed.

NOTES ON THE TAX TREATMENT OF INTEGRATED DELIVERY SYSTEMS

1. *Tax Treatment of the (Unintegrated) Geisinger System.* In *Geisinger II,* an HMO that could not qualify for a 501(c)(3) exemption on its own sought to qualify by virtue of its affiliation with a larger system that arguably supplied the elements it lacked. The court held, however, that as a general rule each component of a multicorporate system must meet the requirements for tax exemption on its own bottom. To be sure, it recognized the "boost" doctrine, under which a component can qualify by showing its contributions to the exempt activities of other constituents in the system. But a boost will be recognized, apparently, only if it comes *from*, not *to*, the component seeking exemption.

The notes below address what might be seen as the other side of the *Geisinger* coin: When can an *integrated* delivery system (IDS)—that is, one comprising many elements and activities under a single corporate umbrella—attain 501(c)(3) status?

2. *The Variety of Integrated Systems.* As noted in chapter 2(§C), IDSs are being formed in large numbers as health care providers seek to establish structures capable of coordinating the delivery of appropriate health care to defined populations and of managing the financial risks that many purchasers want them to assume. Although many of the new organizations may involve only minimal integration of providers, they may represent first steps toward effective integration. See generally Hitchner et al., Integrated

Delivery Systems: A Survey of Organizational Models, 29 Wake Forest L.Rev. 273 (1994). Favorable tax treatment should presumably be withheld from such arrangements until they can demonstrate that they are more than the sum of their parts. Although conventional wisdom holds that integration is the wave of the future, some IDSs may have been formed more in desperation—by providers seeking not to be left out or to follow the latest trend—rather than because the collaborators have discovered a way to give better value to purchasers. See Goldsmith, The Illusive Logic of Integration, Healthcare Forum J., Sept.-Oct. 1994, at 26 (questioning the presumed benefits of much of the organizational integration sweeping the health care industry).

3. *Tax Issues.* Certain IDSs can satisfy the community-benefit requirement for 501(c)(3) tax exemption. See generally T. Hyatt & B. Hopkins, The Law of Tax–Exempt Healthcare Organizations § 23 (1995 & Supp. 1996); Choi, Tax–Exempt Status and Integrated Delivery Systems, 23 J.L., Med. & Ethics 403 (1995). In scrutinizing an IDS, the IRS apparently demands more evidence of a commitment to the poor than it has required of hospitals. In one widely noted instance, an IDS was granted an exemption upon a showing that it operated an emergency room without regard to ability to pay, maintained open medical staffs in affiliated hospitals (though not necessarily in the constituent medical groups), served Medicare and Medicaid patients, and provided charity care; in addition, the IDS was affiliated with a university medical center and promised to engage in research and education as well as providing health services. See IRS Determination Ltr. to Friendly Hills Health Care Network, in 7 Exempt Orgs. Tax Rev. 490 (1993). A crucial issue in the *Friendly Hills* ruling was whether, in paying $120 million to acquire physician practices and other components of the IDS, the Friendly Hills network had conferred prohibited private benefits.

In its *Friendly Hills* ruling, the IRS also gave effect to its customary requirement that a 501(c)(3) organization must be governed by a board that is "representative of the community." Thus, the Service specified that no more than 20% of the Friendly Hills board could be physicians who provided services through the organization or other interested parties. Although the IRS had established the 20% requirement in earlier interpretations of the "community board" requirement and later indicated that the 20%-physicians rule could be regarded as a safe harbor, it has since relaxed its governance requirement for all 501(c)(3)'s. Thus, in what has been viewed as a major policy concession helpful to the formation of new IDSs, the Service now takes the position that physicians (or other interested persons) may constitute as much as 49% of the board of a tax-exempt organization (as long as other steps are taken to avoid private inurement or conferral of private benefits). See Mills, The IRS Prepares a New Position on Governance for Exempt Health Care Organizations, 8 J. Taxation of Exempt Orgs. 124 (1996).

The IRS has granted tax exemptions to other fully integrated IDSs. E.g., IRS Determination Ltr. to Tobey Med. Assocs., Inc., in 12 Exempt

Orgs. Tax Rev. 349 (1995). IDSs that are less than fully integrated are unlikely to satisfy the IRS's community-benefit standard since, like the HMO in *Geisinger I*, they may not provide health services directly but be only marketing and negotiating mechanisms for the providers involved. One physician-hospital organization (PHO) was found exempt, however, because it was comprised solely of organizations already exempt under 501(c)(3). IRS Determination Ltr. to University Affiliated Health Care, Inc., in 11 Exempt Orgs. Tax Rev. 825 (1995). A more complex inquiry is whether a tax-exempt hospital's participation in a PHO will jeopardize its exemption. To retain its exemption, the hospital must ensure that there is no sharing of the hospital's income with physicians and that its expenses are shared in proportion to the benefits derived. IRS Determination Ltr. to Williamsburg Community Hosp., in 9 Exempt Orgs. Tax Rev. 1323 (1994).

The Balanced Budget Act of 1997 added a new provision to the Code (IRC § 501(*o*)), which states that an exempt organization will not lose its exemption under § 501(c)(3) "solely because a hospital which is owned and operated by such organization participates in a provider-sponsored organization, whether or not the provider-sponsored organization is exempt from tax." Apparently, PSOs (see chapter 2(§D)) themselves may be tax-exempt if they meet the usual requirements. The new provision would be significant only if it allows a hospital to share financial risk with non-exempt entities in a PSO without affecting its exemption. It seems unlikely, however, that Congress intended to relax the private benefit/inurement rules. See generally Mills, Participation in Provider–Sponsored Organizations Does Not Affect Hospitals' Tax–Exempt Status, 9 J. Taxation of Exempt Orgs. 136 (1997).

4. *Joint Operating Agreements*. A nonprofit hospital might seek to realize scale and other economies while retaining some independence, individuality, and responsiveness to local interests by entering into a so-called joint operating agreement (JOA) with one more other nonprofit hospitals. Such transactions, which are becoming increasingly common, are sometimes referred to as "virtual mergers" and achieve some of the benefits of merger or consolidation without entirely depriving communities of their "own" hospitals. The transaction usually involves the creation of a joint operating company (JOC) that operates the cooperating hospitals and is controlled jointly by their boards.

The JOC may enjoy 501(c)(3) status as an "integral part" of the charitable operations of its parents if it performs essential services and if its activities would not constitute an unrelated trade or business if carried on by the hospitals themselves. The key issue, however, appears to be control. Thus, the JOC must be more than a mechanism for merely sharing income and eliminating competition. Instead, it must have and exercise authority to make crucial decisions for the joint enterprise, including approving budgets, setting prices, and hiring and firing key personnel. More complex issues would arise where a JOA involved a for-profit as well as a nonprofit enterprise. See generally Louthian, Meeting the IRS Benchmarks for Joint Operating Agreements, 8 J. Taxation of Exempt Orgs. 170 (1997).

Conversion to For-Profit Status

Memorandum of the Attorney General, Burson v. Nashville Memorial Hospital, Inc., Et Al.

Chancery Court, Davidson County, Tennessee, No. 94–744–I, March 17, 1994

I. Introduction

* * * The cause at issue relates to the sale of substantially all of the operating assets of Nashville Memorial Hospital (a nonprofit hospital) to HealthTrust (a for profit company). The Attorney General would advise the Court that his Office has investigated these transactions and is of the opinion, subject to entry of the Consent Decree [submitted by the Attorney General and the corporate defendants for the Court's approval], that a challenge to the sale is not warranted, in that the proposed sale is not injurious to the public interest.

* * *

IV. The Attorney General's Authority Over Nonprofit Corporations

The State Attorney General has broad discretion and authority to act in the public interest in nonprofit matters. [Under s]ection 48–51–701(b) and (c)(5) of Tennessee Code Annotated, the Tennessee Nonprofit Corporation Act * * *, it is [his or her function] to protect the public interest and the public beneficiaries in the transaction between Memorial Hospital and HealthTrust. Under Tennessee law governing not for profit corporations, the Attorney General is of the opinion that the valid public interests are (1) guarding against self interest and self dealing by those involved in the transaction, (2) ensuring proper disposition of nonprofit assets, and (3) ensuring that a fair and realistic market based price is obtained for the assets being sold. In essence, these factors indicate whether the hospital's directors were motivated by and acted in good faith for the interests of the nonprofit entity, its purposes, and the public beneficiaries.

* * *

V. The Sale Results in a $108 Million Foundation

The sale of Nashville Memorial Hospital's assets and the retention and transfer of certain existing properties or monies will result in an independent charitable foundation endowed with about $108 million dollars, the effective purchase price.

VIII. The Relevant Facts As Ascertained by the Attorney General

A. Strategic Considerations of the Nashville Memorial Board

In late 1990 and early 1991, the Nashville Memorial Hospital undertook to shape the vision and strategic direction for the hospital in the changing healthcare environment. The centerpiece of that process was a [consultant's report which] noted the Hospital's declining inpatient population, the lack of primary care referrals, the aging population of the service area, and the increasing Medicare population. * * *

In short, serious problems confronted the hospital and its governing boards. [An independent consultant's report prepared for the Attorney General described the hospital's environment as follows]:

> The healthcare industry can be considered to be in a major transition phase at the present time. The industry, driven by national healthcare reform initiatives, is adjusting to a new, more competitive, managed care environment in which larger and larger pools of potential patients will be represented by increasingly powerful "buyer groups." Hospitals are creating healthcare systems ranging from the basic, primary care physician network to more highly specialized physicians, as well as developing the ability to handle patient needs on both an inpatient and an outpatient basis.
>
> Like other industries in structural change, the hospital industry is in the midst of a consolidation phase that has been underway for many years. Initially, the for-profit healthcare companies acquired hospitals around the nation with the purpose of deriving purchasing and other management efficiencies. More recently, the industry has been driven by the need for acquisitions that "fill in" and complete systems.
>
> Smaller, independent hospitals are increasingly facing cost pressures in an environment where admissions and occupancy rates are declining. As a result, hospitals everywhere are beginning a process of "networking," (joining groups of hospitals that can provide pools of potential patients or referrals) giving them the ability to "sell" their services. In the midst of this, there is pressure on revenues, not only from declining admissions, but also from more intensive review by Medicare, Medicaid and private insurers. There is also emerging competition between the various hospital systems and the growing alliances of buying groups representing pools of patients. The result is that historical profitability is under pressure or deteriorating for many independent hospitals.
>
> Based upon the substantial record developed in the examination, testimony in the confidential hearing and our review of the healthcare industry, this is the broad environment in which Memorial finds itself at the present time.
>
> * * *

IX. Community Concerns

The Attorney General has met with and received the views of some members of the community who have no interests in this transaction, except to preserve what they regard as the community's hospital. * * *

The feelings and views of the community in part reflect certain misunderstandings or misperceptions about the proposed sale and the events surrounding it. * * *

Established legal principles generally recognize the community and state interests in nonprofit or charitable contributions by (1) prohibiting anyone from personally profiting from the nonprofit's activities and (2) ensuring that the assets remain committed to charitable purposes. The Attorney General found no evidence that any board member stood to personally profit from the transaction. Only [the hospital's CEO] may receive compensation from the resulting foundation and then only if he is hired. [The Attorney General insisted that the consent decree provide that the selection process for the foundation CEO be "open and not tailored for any particular person."]

Some in the community * * * have advanced the argument that the community supported the hospital throughout its existence by volunteering time, effort, and energy, by donating monies, and by utilizing the facility itself. No doubt, both the hospital and the community have benefitted thereby. It is true that the hospital's nonprofit corporate status allowed it to conduct most of its activities in past years without paying taxes. The hospital was thus built, developed, and maintained in a tax exempt environment. The monies obtained by or for the resulting foundation, however, will be used to further charitable purposes in the hospital's service area. These monies (foundation monies) are still held by a nonprofit corporation and are still tax exempt.

Certain members of the community voiced the concern that if Health-Trust acquires Memorial, their health care costs will escalate. They contend that they will be forced to pay for the hospital again. In today's health care market, however, * * * market forces are bringing competition and the real prospect of lower prices * * *. The unleashing of these market forces will require hospitals to become lean, efficient, and driven to reduce costs and pass [the savings] on to consumers. The hospital's move from tax exempt to taxpayer will not change the fundamental market reality. Thus, this community concern does not reflect today's market reality.

* * * Many hospitals will not survive the coming competitive storms and will close their doors. As a result of the sale, Memorial's directors believe that the hospital will continue its operations and benefit the public. At the same time, the directors believe that they have sold at the time when they could obtain the highest practical value for the charitable assets and are thus able to redirect them to other charitable endeavors as set forth in their foundation plans. * * *

* * * Not only does [the transaction] reasonably ensure for the community the preservation of the hospital in an increasingly competitive environment, but it also provides for an independent nonprofit foundation with assets of approximately $108 million dedicated to enhancing the health and welfare of the community. The Attorney General finds, after substantial inquiry and examination, that the directors have acted in good faith and with no view to personally profit, directly or indirectly, from this sale. In any event, the terms of the Consent Decree and existing state law protect against that possibility.

X. Attorney General's Opinion of Duties of Nonprofit Corporations in Conjunction with Asset Sales

A. Standard of Care for Directors of Nonprofit Corporations

Originally, the standard of care for a director of a nonprofit corporation was held to be more demanding than that for a director of a for profit business. See Louisiana World Exposition v. Federal Ins. Co., 864 F.2d 1147, 1152 (5th Cir.1989). The theory was that a nonprofit corporation was analogous to a public trust, and its directors were deemed trustees. However, modern statutes, including Tennessee's, Tenn. Code Ann. § 48–58–101(e), and case law have altered that theory. The current accepted standard for nonprofit corporate directors is the same as that of their for profit counterparts. See Oberly v. Kirby, 592 A.2d 445, 466–67 (Del.1991). * * * However, the courts have continued to discern some difference by recognizing that charitable corporations are created for a limited charitable purpose rather than a generalized business purpose. It follows therefore that those who control charitable corporations have a special duty to advance the charitable goals and protect charitable assets.

One theory of corporate law holds that once a sale of corporate assets is inevitable, the duty of the directors shifts from that of defenders of the corporate mission to auctioneers charged with getting the best price for their assets. However, in viewing the standard from the perspective of the public interest, it seems that the more appropriate standard for directors of nonprofits is to recognize their duty to advance charitable goals and to protect their assets by ensuring that a realistic market price is realized in the transaction.

* * * [T]he directors would not have approved this sale unless assured by independent and reliable sources that in fact they received fair market value of the hospital as an operating business concern. [D]uring the period from the signing of the letter of intent to the date that the boards voted to close the sale, the boards, through certain of its members, canvassed the market or suitably tried to identify prospective purchasers, looked critically at the HealthTrust offer and sought the particulars of the Tennessee Christian proposal, and read market conditions. Based upon the analysis by the Attorney General's independent expert, the price paid is a favorable price.

B. The Attorney General's Opinion Regarding Duty of Board to be Informed Prior to Decision–Making

The business judgment rule, under principles of corporate law, establishes a "presumption that in making a business decision the directors of a corporation acted on an informed basis, in good faith and in honest belief that the action taken was in the best interest of the company." Revlon, Inc. v. MacAndrews & Forbes Holdings, Inc., 506 A.2d 173, 180 (Del.Supr.1985). The rule is founded on the core principles of "care, duty, and loyalty." The business judgment rule serves to protect corporate boards' decisions, where the decisions meet its requirements, namely: (1) they are fully informed about the available options and consequences flowing from electing the option selected; (2) they have exercised their fiduciary duties of care and loyalty; (3) and the decisions are in fact rational and made with no self interest. Tennessee law generally applies this rule.

C. Fiduciary Responsibilities and Conflicts of Interest

In carrying out their managerial roles, directors of nonprofit or charitable corporations have fiduciary responsibilities comparable to those owed shareholders by a corporation, to act with fairness and loyalty devoid of considerations of self interest. * * *

Certain critical rules apply to nonprofit corporations: there are no shareholders; the board members are not the owners. Directors of nonprofit corporate boards are required to fulfill their fiduciary duties to the nonprofit corporation and the public beneficiaries they serve. [The Attorney General concluded that the directors did in fact fulfill their fiduciary duties to the patients, employees, physicians, and the community itself.]

D. Detailed Plan for Preservation and Protection of Nonprofit Assets Must be Submitted to Attorney General

It is also the position of the Attorney General that prior to the execution of any contract for sale of nonprofit assets, the Attorney General must be provided with a *detailed* written plan for the preservation, protection, and use of any and all nonprofit proceeds. * * *

E. Contract for Sale May Not Include Restrictions on Future Use of Non–Profit Assets.

* * *

In the proposed sale to HealthTrust, the term sheet * * * required that HealthTrust directed charities would receive twenty percent (20%) of the foundation's annual earnings for an eight (8) year period. The investigation disclosed that this type of provision may not be uncommon. * * * The Attorney General views any such future restriction on charitable funds by a for profit entity, as explained, as a violation of state law. * * * The provision has been stricken, and the foundation will have additional millions of dollars of unrestricted funds for use and needs in the community.

F. The Legal Requirements to Sell Nonprofit Assets

Prior to considering a sale of nonprofit corporate assets to a particular firm, the directors first must carefully consider the practically available options: whether the corporation or its assets should merge or acquire or be acquired; whether other structured transactions are available and to what extent; and whether the options further charitable or nonprofit interests. If the analysis leads to the option of an asset sale, the nonprofit corporation should canvas the market or use realistic market based tests to establish the value of the assets to be sold and identify candidates to acquire the assets. The nonprofit corporation should then examine the impact of the sale and the terms upon the nonprofit assets and their identifiable constituencies or public beneficiaries, and make an independent and informed decision. The directors' examination of the terms of the sale must focus upon price, effective price, the risks involved, the conditions of sale, the effect of the terms of the sale, and the impact on the community. The directors must stay attuned to the public beneficiaries and promote or advance their interests. * * *

XI. The Attorney General's View of Nashville Memorial/HealthTrust Proposed Transaction

Although each member of the boards was generally familiar with the value of the hospital and with the options that were being pursued by the boards' key members, they were not adequately advised of these matters at the time they voted in favor of entering into the HealthTrust letter of intent. The boards had not made a fully informed decision. In considering the sale initially, the boards members' primary goal was the continuation of the hospital as a viable health care resource for the community and not necessarily in maximizing the amount of money they received from the sale.

The Board members * * * did not have sufficient information to approve the letter of intent to trigger the protection afforded by the business judgment rule. * * * [The Attorney General concluded that, although the initial process in signing the letter of intent was flawed, the board's subsequent actions in informing themselves on the impact of the sale upon the various constituencies and beneficiaries rectified the situation.]

* * * [T]his Office is of the opinion that the directors are entitled to the presumptions of the "business judgment rule." In spite of the initial flawed process the transaction has yielded a favorable price for the hospital and that premium will inure to the benefit of the community through the proposed foundation. The Attorney General does not believe a challenge is warranted under the total facts of this transaction.

NOTES AND QUESTIONS ON THE SALE OR CONVERSION OF NONPROFIT ENTITIES

1. *The Growth of Columbia/HCA and Its Policy Implications.* The following lengthy excerpt from an important and informative article by Robert Kuttner, the editor of the *American Prospect*, uses the emergence of a powerful and particularly aggressive for-profit hospital chain as the occasion for reviewing important policy and legal issues presented by the introduction of the profit motive in the health care sector:

> Hospitals, surprisingly, have emerged as a prime growth industry attractive to entrepreneurs. Seemingly, a legacy of overbuilding combined with competitive cost-cutting pressures should reduce the earnings of nonprofit and for-profit hospitals alike, making them unattractive investment candidates. Yet in the 1990s, for-profit hospital chains on a buying binge have outpaced the stock market. Conversions of

nonprofit to investor-owned hospitals have accelerated, reaching a level of 58 in 1995, up from 34 in 1994.

This * * * article addresses the medical, ethical, and public-policy issues posed by the resurgence of for-profit chains and their acquisition of nonprofit community hospitals. The prime case in point is Columbia/HCA Healthcare Corporation, the largest and most aggressive of the for-profit chains, the product of three large and several smaller mergers. With 340 hospitals, 135 outpatient-surgery offices, and 200 home health care agencies in 38 states, Columbia/HCA now controls nearly half the for-profit beds, and 7 percent of all hospital beds, in the United States. The company's gross earnings exceed 20 percent of revenues, and its 1995 profits were just under $1 billion, with $20 billion in assets. It is now the nation's 10th largest employer, with 240,000 employees.

There are four broad explanations for the surprising profitability of the proprietary chains. First, the chains, as claimed, are generally more cost-conscious than voluntary and public hospitals, which have goals outside the market. Second, in their business strategy, for-profits tend to avoid unprofitable services and unprofitable patients, displacing these costs onto the rest of the health care system. Third, for-profits sometimes "re-engineer" or downgrade their staffing, administration, and supplies. Finally, large for-profit chains offer financial incentives for doctors to use their hospitals, even though competing hospitals may actually have lower costs and charges.

Columbia/HCA, for example, invites doctors to become shareholders in its local ventures, which often include several hospitals, ambulatory surgical centers, diagnostic facilities, a home care affiliate, and rehabilitation and physical therapy facilities. The company invests heavily in medical data systems that are available at both the hospital and the doctor's office. In many localities Columbia/HCA offers convenient office space at competitive rents. All these efforts are intended to make the doctor a partner (or happy captive) and an enthusiastic source of patients.

This strategy builds a powerful referral network and a source of market power. In addition, by bringing the doctor into an integrated network, Columbia/HCA neatly sidesteps ethical and legal conflict-of-interest constraints. Under the ethical guidelines of the American Medical Association, as well as federal and state anti-kickback laws, a doctor (with some exceptions) may not refer a patient to a facility in which he or she has a direct financial interest. Under federal "safe harbor" regulations, however, the most notable exception is a hospital or integrated delivery system owned by a public company worth at least $50 million in which the doctor is a shareholder. A clinical laboratory to which a doctor-owner cannot legally refer patients becomes a legal referral facility if it is part of a large, integrated entity in which the doctor holds stock. Though this maneuver creates a legal loophole, the ethical issue of whether self-referral distorts clinical judgment remains. * * *

Recent History

After a near-demise in the late 1980s, for-profit hospital chains are in a second phase of robust growth. In the 1920s, proprietary hospitals, often founded by local doctors, were a fixture of the health care system, accounting for some 36 percent of U.S. hospitals. With the rise of voluntary and public hospitals after World War II, however, the proprietary sector dwindled. Shareholder-owned chains date only to 1960, when American Medical International (AMI), a West Coast laboratory company, purchased its first two hospitals. Investor-owned chains grew rapidly after most people became insured with the enactment of Medicare and Medicaid in 1965. By 1971 there were 38 for-profit chains. At their postwar peak in 1986, for-profit companies owned 838 hospitals and 107,000 beds, or about 14 percent of general acute care hospital facilities in the United States.

In the late 1980s, shareholder-owned chains seemed likely to become casualties of cost-containment, overbuilding, and scandal. Reimbursement according to diagnosis-related group for Medicare patients and the rise of managed care undercut the economics of cost-plus billing. The two largest for-profit chains, Hospital Corporation of America (HCA) and Humana, stumbled in their attempt to operate both hospitals and health maintenance organizations (HMOs). HCA, after expanding to encompass more than 200 hospitals and launching a managed-care company, sold off 104 of its hospitals in 1987 to the newly created company Healthtrust (owned by former HCA executives). Humana, then the largest chain, launched its HMO subsidiary, Care Plus, in 1983 but was soon whipsawed between doctors and competing HMOs. Physicians affiliated with Humana Care Plus chafed under the constraints of managed care and would not reliably patronize Humana hospitals, whereas rival HMOs avoided them. Humana's hospitals were then spun off to the newly created Galen Health Care Corporation. Galen, in turn, was absorbed by Columbia/HCA in 1993.

Another major chain, National Medical Enterprises (NME), was fined $379 million on criminal charges that its psychiatric hospitals had paid for referrals and kept patients incarcerated until their insurance ran out. NME then raised over $3 billion in junk-bond and bank financing, bought AMI, and was reborn as the Tenet Corporation. * * *

Remarkably enough, the instability, bankruptcies, and falling profits of the 1980s have given way to a new wave of lucrative consolidations in the 1990s. In 1995 alone, there were 447 community hospitals in play in takeover negotiations, as well as several hundred more that had been sold in four large corporate mergers. In a sense, this process is not unlike the reorganizations of the steel, airline, and banking industries, in which well-capitalized entrepreneurs buy underperforming assets, consolidate, increase market power, cut costs, restore profitability, and reap the rewards. Richard L. Scott, the 43-year-old chief executive and architect of Columbia/HCA, has written that "free market, competitive forces should be the driver" to reform the health system.

Ethics, Cross-Subsidies, and Markets

* * *

Entrepreneurs, by directly imposing market principles on hospitals, overturn the explicit and implicit understandings that have allowed doctors and hospitals to balance professionalism, profitability, and service. Conceiving of a hospital as just another business undermines the service mission by eliminating the tacit cross-subsidies. In the logic of the marketplace, each investment must pursue profit. Temporary losses are defensible only as investments in future profits, so cross-subsidy must be avoided. Thus, in a purely for-profit enterprise or system, there is no place for uncompensated care, unprofitable admissions, research, education, or public health activities—all chronic money losers from a strictly business viewpoint. By definition, the value of public goods is not recognized by profit-maximizing private markets. * * *

Furthermore, by weakening the professionalism that has traditionally served as a counterweight to the profit motive in medicine, the investor-owned chains risk undercutting clinical care as they relentlessly pursue cost savings. In theory, the competitive marketplace prevents any deterioration in quality, because dissatisfied customers are free to take their business elsewhere. But the health care system is rife with well-known asymmetries of information and "customers" who are essentially captive. By attracting the doctor and the insurance plan or HMO, the for-profit chain brings along the patient. Insofar as the investor-owned chains initiate a cost-cutting "race to the bottom" among hospitals, effective consumer choice is precluded, because rival hospitals pursue essentially similar economies.

Columbia/HCA

Leading the race is Columbia/HCA, the result of a merger of two of the most aggressively entrepreneurial companies. * * *

Columbia/HCA's basic plan has been to acquire hospitals at the lowest possible cost, invest in upgrading where necessary, close or consolidate duplicative facilities, cut staff, increase administrative efficiencies, take advantage of economies of scale, integrate vertically and horizontally, and develop powerful local referral networks. The company's era of very rapid growth through the wholesale acquisition of other large for-profit chains is probably over. If Columbia/HCA attempted to merge with any of the other surviving large chains, such as Tenet * * *, it would probably face antitrust action.

Columbia's strategy differs strikingly from that of Humana and HCA in the 1980s. It does not, for the most part, build new hospitals. Rather, it buys existing hospitals cheaply, upgrading some acquisitions and closing or consolidating others. Despite the gradual shift to full capitation contracts with managed-care payers (in which hospitals are paid a flat fee), Columbia/HCA resists such contracts, except in markets where it can trade them for very substantial volume. Columbia will also buy new business from payers by pricing below its average cost, then seek compensating ways to raise charges. Unlike some of its competitors, purchasing physicians' practices has not been central to Columbia/HCA's strategy of creating alliances with doctors. Nonetheless, Columbia/HCA has absorbed over 1400 doctors' practices merely through its acquisitions of other corporations and occasionally buys practices to complement a local market strategy. The company's strategy is instead to rely on its referral networks to attract patients, despite the fact that it is often not the low-charge provider. If it controls enough market share in a given locale, insurers have no choice but to deal with Columbia/HCA. And, as hospital reimbursements are squeezed, its control of an integrated network gives the company access to profitable outpatient venues to treat patients. * * *

Columbia/HCA is extremely aggressive with vendors, offering all its business to the supplier who offers the best deal. Scott has claimed that his negotiating tactics save Columbia/HCA $300 million a year on supplies. General Electric, for example, has a five-year contract as the sole supplier and repairer of all the company's high-technology diagnostic equipment. In return for a favorable price, Columbia/HCA buys all its computed tomographic scanners and magnetic resonance imaging units from General Electric.

The company has targeted and achieved a formidable corporate goal of a 20 percent gross return on revenues. I was told by a Columbia/HCA executive that chief executives of company hospitals who fall short of this goal are regularly called to corporate headquarters in Nashville to explain and are ordered to redouble their efforts. Further economies at the local hospital usually follow.

Columbia/HCA markets [and advertises] aggressively [and] has waged strident campaigns to discredit nonprofits, as HCA did before it. Columbia/HCA has hired research firms to show that when the value of tax exemption and uncompensated care are aggregated, for-profit companies return more to the community than nonprofits. A 1995 report for Columbia/HCA by Healthcare Management Decisions, Inc., characterized five of six nonprofits that compete with the company in central Florida as providing "negative community benefits" and creating a "net community burden," because the value of their tax exemption exceeded that of their charity care. In a 1994 Virginia study financed by HCA, Nancy Kane, on the faculty of the Harvard School of Public Health, calculated that nonprofit hospitals provided more than double the free care provided by for-profits (3.7 percent of revenues vs.

1.7 percent) and contributed 1.1 percent of their revenues to medical education, as compared with effectively nothing in the case of for-profits. But Kane concluded that when the cost of tax exemption (8.4 percent of operating revenues) is included, for-profits return more, on balance, to society. Her method, however, assumes that tax payments to federal, state, and local government are equivalent to direct outlays for health care.

Comparing For-Profit and Nonprofit Hospitals

Researchers who systematically studied for-profit chains in the 1970s and 1980s generally found that the for-profits had slightly higher average costs and charges than nonprofits, that they provided below-average rates of uncompensated and charity care, and that their clinical outcomes were not significantly different from those of comparable nonprofits. But enormous changes have occurred in the hospital sector over the past decade. For-profit chains are no longer buying mainly independent proprietary hospitals or merging with each other: they are now acquiring community nonprofit hospitals. Cost-cutting pressures have intensified. Most important, hospitals are no longer paid predominantly on a fee-for-service basis, so profits must be made by cutting costs and services, not by increasing them.

The latest wave of for-profit consolidations and acquisitions is too recent to have been the subject of similar comprehensive studies. However, scattered evidence suggests that for-profits still provide relatively less charity care than their public and nonprofit counterparts and that they "cherry-pick" profitable admissions. One recent study, relying on data from the Health Care Financing Administration, concluded, "In summary, Columbia/HCA hospitals served fewer Medicaid patients, treated more complex cases, offered fewer services, incurred lower salary expenses per discharge, and had fewer occupied beds than local competing hospitals."[25] Florida's Agency for Health Care Administration, in a review of admissions at Victoria Hospital, a Columbia-owned facility in Miami, found that Medicare patients referred by Columbia-affiliated doctors stayed an average of 8.48 days. Patients sent by the same doctors to other area hospitals stayed 13.5 days. This pattern maximizes Columbia's profits, because of the system of Medicare reimbursement based on diagnosis-related groups. The Florida agency, in a draft report that was never officially released, concluded that the statistics "point to the possibility of cream-skimming," as well as "the possible adverse effects on a market of physician ownership in a hospital." * * *

In one of the most comprehensive tabulations of comparative charges, VHA, Inc. (formerly Voluntary Hospitals of America), used inpatient claims data supplied to the Florida Agency for Health Care

25. McCue MJ. A premerger profile of Columbia and HCA hospitals. Health Care Manage Rev 1996: 21(2):38–45.

Administration to compare for-profits and nonprofits. The VHA study found that investor-owned hospitals in 1994 were 13.7 percent more expensive on a charge basis than nonprofit and public hospitals. Charges by nonprofits, the report calculated, would have been even lower if the nonprofits had not been absorbing a disproportionate share of Medicaid and charity care. Medicaid patients accounted for 12.3 percent of the case mix among nonprofits, as compared with 6.3 percent among for-profits. * * *

The trouble with these dueling consultants' reports is that all the parties are self-interested. The comparisons * * * by VHA are based on public data and are seemingly accurate. But the question of the comparative performance of nonprofits and for-profit chains cries out for a second wave of disinterested scholarly research to examine such issues as charity and uncompensated care and costs and charges.

An even thornier question is whether the for-profits, in a much more stringent cost-cutting environment than the 1980s, are degrading clinical care. Although Columbia/HCA prides itself on scoring well on formal paperwork evaluations, and although it insists that its commitment to quality includes, above all, patient care, it is also strongly committed to reducing staff costs and outlays for equipment. In general, for-profits have continued to have a slightly lower overall ratio of staff to patients than nonprofits. Although in part, this reflects laudable "delayering" and economies of scale, Columbia/HCA has also been bitterly criticized by some of its own staff members for replacing licensed personnel such as registered nurses with "multi-skilled" employees trained by the company, for "short-staffing" nursing shifts, and for introducing inferior supplies.

* * * In fairness, "re-engineering" is pervasive among hospitals, and nurses' groups have objected to essentially similar staffing changes at public and voluntary hospitals.

In the further pursuit of economies, Columbia/HCA has merged traditional departments such as social work, which are seen as cost centers, with discharge planning. With the growing shift to Medicaid HMOs and the competition for Medicaid managed-care contracts, as well as increasing pressure for cost containment from other payers, the temptation will be great to further ratchet down staffing and, perhaps, care.

The Market Speaks

For-profit chains are ultimately accountable to shareholders, not to communities. And the stock market is certainly bullish on Columbia/HCA, whose stock price since 1990 has risen at more than twice the rate of the Standard and Poor's 500. * * * When it buys a hospital or hospital chain with a shakier balance sheet, Columbia/HCA refinances the target hospital's debt at its own more favorable interest rates, producing an instant savings. Leading financial analysts currently rate Columbia's stock as a "buy."

Some critics in the hospital industry argue that Columbia's expansion strategy is a kind of Ponzi scheme that works only as long as Columbia/HCA keeps acquiring underperforming hospitals. Its very high profit rate is driven in part by the creation of one-time economies that are not repeated year after year, except through the acquisition of other new hospitals. Yet with nearly 5000 nonprofit and public hospitals in the United States, many of them reeling from the financial pressures of managed care, there is no shortage of targets. * * *

Columbia/HCA's drive to increase its market power by purchasing not-for-profit community hospitals has raised thorny questions. Lately, it has also met escalating resistance. Columbia's deals are notable for the speed, secrecy, and legal ingenuity with which they are accomplished. The company has flying squads of acquisition specialists backed by financial analysts, accountants, lawyers, and consultants and can negotiate a binding letter of intent with a hospital's board of trustees in a matter of weeks. To a town with fiscal strains and a money-losing hospital, Columbia/HCA can look like a white knight. A tax-exempt institution stands to become a tax-paying one. A strapped hospital can gain millions of dollars in capital improvements. The company's acquisitions run the gamut from the hard-pressed local hospital genuinely needing rescue to the robust institution whose executives received an offer they couldn't refuse.

The issues posed by these acquisitions are multiple. Should nonprofit, charitable institutions be sold to for-profit chains at all? Often, land was deeded in perpetuity or a hospital was endowed explicitly to provide charity care. Moreover, the present worth of the hospital represents many decades of philanthropy, foregone taxes, other public outlays, and the contributions of staff members who may have worked at below-market salaries.

Without independent valuation, the conversion to for-profit status can produce a one-time windfall for the acquiring company, which seizes the capitalized value of an institution not previously considered a commodity. From the perspective of Columbia/HCA, the acquiring company takes under-performing assets, connects them to a network, and through the application of entrepreneurial skill, increases their worth. But by removing a key nonprofit institution, the conversion irrevocably diminishes the local stock of noncommercial community health care facilities and fuels the impression that the full commercialization of health care is both desirable and inevitable.

Conversions and the Law

A conversion usually circumvents the restrictions in a hospital charter, deed, or will by creating a new charitable foundation ostensibly to carry on the hospital's charity mission. The pertinent legal doctrine, known as Cy Pres, allows the original form of a public charity to be changed, subject to court approval, but requires the substantive charitable purpose to endure. Typically, Columbia/HCA negotiates a purchase price, obtains control of the hospital assets, sometimes by purchasing as little as 50 percent ownership, and uses part of the proceeds from the sale to set up the new foundation. This action, however, raises other issues: Who should control the foundation? Can it pursue purposes other than health care? Will the foundation, formally or tacitly, be part of the Columbia/HCA family? Does the hospital (now a profit-maximizing company) retain any obligation to provide money-losing community services? What aspects of the deal should be subject to ongoing government supervision? Was the selling price too low, and did trustees or executives of the hospital get excessive financial inducements to promote the sale? Under state and federal law, improper personal gain by trustees of charitable assets, known as "inurement," is illegal.

Columbia/HCA, understandably, seeks to buy these hospitals as cheaply as possible and goes to great lengths to discourage competitive bids. Its letters of intent require secrecy and may mandate severe penalties if the target hospital entertains other offers. This is somewhat ironic, since in a free market the best way to determine an asset's worth is to see what competing buyers will pay. * * *

In practice, not all state attorneys general strictly apply the Cy Pres doctrine to hospital conversions. In Massachusetts, MetroWest Health, the operator of two community hospitals in Framingham and Natick, was in distress and seeking a partner. Rebuffed by local nonprofit hospitals, a new chief executive, Lawrence Kaplan, negotiated an 80 percent sale to Columbia/HCA. In late 1995, Attorney General Scott Harshbarger intervened to supervise the sale. (Most financial details, however, were not made public. Harshbarger, according to a key aide, accepts the argument that such details are trade secrets.) The attorney general held a public hearing, retained an accounting firm to establish fair market value, extracted from Columbia/HCA a commitment to keep both emergency rooms open for at least three years, and improved other community benefits, including the terms of the foundation.

* * * In Dickson, Tennessee, where Goodlark Hospital was sold in 1995 to Columbia/HCA, the local state representative, Douglas Jackson, served both as a trustee of Goodlark and as its lawyer before its sale and as head of the new foundation afterward. The foundation's first outlay was to book the Nashville Symphony for a free local concert.

When HealthONE, a six-hospital system in Denver, put most of its $550 million in assets into a joint venture with Columbia/HCA, $350 million went to pay off HealthONE's huge debt, the hangover from a previous buyout deal. No money went into a foundation, and Colorado authorities let the deal stand. According to Deputy Attorney General Jan Zavislan, Colorado has no statutory authority to review hospital conversions.

California Deputy Attorney General James Schwartz, in contrast, routinely reviews and modifies terms of sale. Unlike Massachusetts and most other states, California makes all the financial details of such sales part of the public record. Schwartz told me, "We find it highly questionable that anybody would consider these other than public assets open to the public." However, in contrast to Harshbarger, Schwartz claims jurisdiction only over the new foundation, not over the newly converted hospital—which is then free to shift the burden of charity care to the foundation.

The conversion issue has gained particular visibility in California because of the controversial sales of other health care organizations in leveraged buyouts, at sums far below market value. HealthNet, a nonprofit health maintenance organization (HMO), was converted in 1992 to the for-profit Health Systems International at a price widely considered too low. Thirty-three executives of the nonprofit purchased 20 percent ownership of the new company for just $1.5 million. By April 1996 their shares were worth $315 million. Blue Cross of California contrived a conversion in July 1991 through a new for-profit subsidiary, WellPoint Health Networks, which would hold 90 percent of its assets. Since the nonprofit parent company would technically continue to exist, no charitable foundation would be necessary. Blue Cross, whose WellPoint subsidiary soon attained a market value of $2.7 billion, initially offered just $5 million in annual charitable donations. After more than three years of investigation and negotiation, the California corporations commissioner, prodded by Assemblyman Phillip Isenberg, other key legislators, Consumers Union, and the local press, compelled Blue Cross/WellPoint to fund two new public foundations—with assets of $3.2 billion.

A Growing Backlash

The growing resentment of hospital takeovers is part of a broader consumer backlash against other market intrusions into health care, most notably the practice of many HMOs of giving doctors financial inducements to withhold care. In the past year, at least 30 pending deals with Columbia/HCA have been killed or revised by regulatory, civic, physician, or community opposition.

In California, pending bipartisan legislation sponsored by Assemblyman Isenberg would give the state attorney general power to block conversions if he or she found the terms unfair or found that the sale might "create a significant effect on the availability or accessibility of health care services to the affected community." Other state regulators and legislatures have lately become more assertive, as well. * * * Nebraska enacted a law empowering the attorney general to block the conversion of a nonprofit hospital on the basis of any of nine criteria, including conflicts of interest involving board members, whether the proposed sale reflected fair market value, and "whether the purchaser has made a commitment to provide care to the disadvantaged, the uninsured, and the underinsured and to provide benefits to the affected community to promote improved health care." Thus, in Nebraska even a for-profit hospital is required by law to have other than profit-maximizing goals. In June, Michigan Attorney General Frank J. Kelley sued to block Columbia's proposed acquisition of 50 percent of Michigan Capital Medical Center in Lansing, asserting his general "supervisory power over charitable trusts." And in Houston, Attorney General Dan Morales recently joined a lawsuit filed by the Texas Medical Center, seeking to block a complex deal pending between Columbia/HCA and St. Luke's Episcopal Hospital, on the grounds that it violates deed restrictions that limit the use of most Texas Medical Center property to nonprofit institutions.

Columbia/HCA's most audacious recent foray, in Ohio, breaks its tradition of avoiding the insurance business. In March, Blue Cross and Blue Shield of Ohio, the state's largest insurer, with annual revenues of some $2 billion, agreed to sell 85 percent ownership to Columbia for $299.5 million through a complex venture called BlueCo, legally crafted to avoid the form of a conversion, thus eliminating a payout obligation to policyholders or a charitable foundation. Because $223 million of Blue Cross and Blue Shield reserves would go to the new venture, Columbia/HCA would be buying Blue Cross and Blue Shield largely with the latter's own assets. The National Blue Cross and Blue Shield Association voted on June 13 to revoke the license of the Ohio affiliate to use the famous trademark if the deal goes through. Under the proposed acquisition, Columbia/HCA will pay three top executives of Ohio Blue Cross and Blue Shield over $15 million in severance payments characterized as consulting fees and agreements not to compete, with millions more going as a consulting fee to the Blues' outside lawyer.

On July 11, Ohio Attorney General Betty Montgomery sued to block the transaction pending review by the Ohio insurance commissioner, who regulates mutual insurance companies. Montgomery requested an independent valuation and assurance that the Blue Cross and Blue Shield assets would go to policyholders or for charitable purposes, and she began an antitrust investigation. According to Montgomery, "Fifteen million dollars in severance packages for three officials of an organization founded as a charity, and operated to help the sick and the needy, strikes me as both inappropriate and excessive." Montgomery said she thought Blue Cross and Blue Shield was being sold at "pennies on the dollar."

An earlier class-action suit filed in April on behalf of Blue Cross and Blue Shield policyholders by former U.S. Senator Howard Metzenbaum, chairman of the Consumer Federation of America, characterized the deal as a disguised conversion of Blue Cross and Blue Shield and contended that its entire $302.5 million in reserves properly belongs to policyholders. In reply, attorney Kenneth F. Seminatore, for Blue Cross and Blue Shield, oddly accused Metzenbaum of "advocating the theft of policyholder money." Under the agreement between Columbia/HCA and the Ohio Blues, lawyer Seminatore will collect $3.5 million if the deal goes through.

Commercial and Political Hardball

Columbia/HCA has become a lightning rod for criticism not just because of its prodigious growth and scale, but also because of the ferocity of its tactics. When Columbia/HCA began entering markets in earnest, it did not just compete vigorously; it mounted a public-relations campaign to portray nonprofits as social parasites. On at least one occasion, chief executive officer Richard Scott flatly declared that "Nontaxpaying hospitals shouldn't be in business."

The political muscle of Columbia/HCA is legendary. When it enters a community in pursuit of an acquisition, Columbia/HCA lines up blue-chip legal talent, identifies allies among local civic, political, and medical leaders, and spreads around lots of money. In 1995, for example, Columbia/HCA had 33 lobbyists in Tallahassee, Florida. It also leads the list of corporate campaign contributors in Florida. Nationally, its staff is regularly solicited to donate to one of its political-action committees. Legally, the political-action committees are independent of the corporation, but employees of the company solicit their subordinates.

* * * In 1994, Columbia/HCA took over as sole provider for the health plan of the Lee County government. It won the business by underbidding Lee Memorial, despite the fact that Lee Memorial's average charges per discharge were about 25 percent below Columbia's, according to data cited in the Wall Street Journal. After the St. Petersburg Times ran an editorial advocating an antitrust investigation of Columbia/HCA's local acquisitions (amounting to nearly a third of hospital beds in the Tampa Bay area), the chain not only pulled an estimated $800,000 to $1 million worth of advertising from the newspaper, but also pulled the newspaper's sales racks from its area hospitals and refused to permit its sale in hospital gift shops. [The author recounts several other examples of "commercial hardball."]

Efficiency and Convergence

From Columbia/HCA's perspective, the company is performing a national service by at last creating a rational and efficient health care system that relies on the discipline of the market. The competitive hardball is just the free market at work. According to Dr. David Manning, a Columbia/HCA executive and previously architect of the TennCare Medicaid system, "Columbia is bringing an efficiency to the market in hospitals that can never be gained by an organization that does not seek to fully integrate the health system. We are well ahead of everyone else in getting our costs under control." Manning insists that such efficiencies do not compromise clinical care. "You don't get the kind of levels of Joint Commission on Accreditation of Healthcare

Organizations commendation that Columbia gets by skimping on patient care."

According to Dr. Frank Houser, a one-time Georgia public health commissioner who recently became coordinator of Columbia/HCA's physician relations, "We probably measure more things than anybody else in the industry." As Houser explains, Columbia's Meditech data system not only gives primary care doctors and financial planners computerized access to medical records, but also allows sophisticated tabulations and analysis, at the corporate level, to track clinical outcomes and control quality. Houser points to the company's Gallup-poll data on patient satisfaction as further evidence that Columbia/HCA does not skimp on quality.

* * *

Today, all hospitals, whether corporate or voluntary, operate in an environment increasingly contoured by for-profit institutions. A nonprofit hospital negotiates with for-profit insurers, HMOs, and corporations. To fill beds, it competes with other hospitals—nonprofit and public as well as corporate. It may well have for-profit subsidiaries and coventurers. A market culture and market idiom are becoming pervasive, even among nonprofits. Within living memory, service areas were not called markets; heads of hospitals were administrators, not chief executive officers; hospitals did not advertise for patients; and few hospital administrators spoke of market share, let alone EBITDA (earnings before interest, taxes, depreciation, and amortization). All this has changed, perhaps irrevocably. But if nonprofit hospitals defensively emulate for-profits, their claim to the ethical high ground rings hollow.

VHA, with some 1300 nonprofit hospital affiliates, is leading a public-relations counteroffensive against for-profits, but it also advises nonprofits on how to build integrated systems and win market share ("Are your physician relationships attracting primary care physicians to your system and aligning their incentives with yours?"). The nonprofits, however, have an offsetting advantage, in that for-profits have to pay dividends and taxes and often have higher corporate and marketing costs. Yet the competitive game is being played in increasingly convergent ways.

* * *

In *Animal Farm*, George Orwell concluded his allegory with the words, "The creatures outside looked from pig to man, and from man to pig, and from pig to man again; but already it was impossible to say which was which." Columbia/HCA insists that medicine is a business, and increasingly imposes its rules on the competitive game. If nonprofits are to retain their claim to fiscal and moral difference, they will need not only to match the chains lawyer for lawyer, ad for ad, market strategy for market strategy, and cost saving for cost saving, but also to be clearer about their own mission. And society, through better regulation and disclosure, will need to fashion clearer ground rules—or cede them to the market.

Kuttner, Columbia/HCA and the Resurgence of the For–Profit Hospital Business, 335 New Eng.J.Med. 362–367, 446–51 (1996).

2. *Hospitals.* The sale of Nashville Memorial Hospital illustrates the trend, noted by Kuttner, toward the sale of nonprofit hospitals, including teaching hospitals, to for-profit hospital chains. Such transactions are controversial but also potentially lucrative for the affected community. See, e.g., J. Bell et al., The Public Interest in Conversions of Nonprofit Health Charities (Millbank Mem. Fund 1997); Claxton et al., Public Policy Issues in Nonprofit Conversions: An Overview, Health Affs., Mar.-April 1997, p. 9; Lutz, How Much? Price is Becoming a Contentious Issue in Sales of Not–For–Profit Hospitals, as Communities Seek Fair Value and Challenge Secrecy, Mod. Healthcare, Feb. 12, 1996, p. 85; Hamburger et. al., The Pot of Gold: Monitoring Health Care Conversion Can Yield Billions of Dollars for Health Care, 29 Clearinghouse Rev. 473 (1995). For discussions of the legal issues surrounding such transactions, see Singer, The Conversion Conundrum: The State and Federal Response to Hospitals' Changes of Charitable Status, 23 Am. J.L. & Med. 221 (1997) ("state and federal law are coalescing quickly toward a view of approaching conversions with strong suspicion"); Bloche, Corporate Takeover of Teaching Hospitals, 65 S.Cal.L.Rev. 1035 (1992); Coyne & Kas, The Not–For–Profit Hospital as a Charitable Trust: To Whom Does Its Value Belong?, 24 J. Health & Hosp. L. 48 (1991). As Kuttner notes, many states are taking a greater interest in these transactions. On the experience in these states, see Singer, supra; Shriber, State Experience in Regulating a Changing Health Care System, Health Affs., Mar.-April 1997, p. 48; Peregrine, State Attorneys General Increase Enforcement of Charitable Trust and Fiduciary Duty Laws, Health L. Dig., Dec. 1996, p. 3 (Digest Analysis). On issues raised by changes in the nonprofit sector generally, see Symposium, The Commercialism Dilemma of the Nonprofit Sector, 17 J. Pol'y Analysis & Mgt. 165ff (1998) (to be published in a book entitled To Profit or Not to Profit: The Commercial Transformation of the Nonprofit Sector).

As an illustration of the cy pres doctrine, mentioned by Kuttner, see Attorney General v. Hahnemann Hosp., 397 Mass. 820, 494 N.E.2d 1011 (1986), where the court indicated that the power of hospital trustees to sell the nonprofit hospital depended on the terms of the original trust. An amendment to the corporation's charter permitting the sale proceeds to be used "to promote the health of the general public" was held not permissible, but support of another hospital or institutional provider was found compatible with the donors' intent. As noted, these transactions most often end up under the scrutiny of the state attorney general. What aspects of the Nashville transaction were most troubling?

Sale of a nonprofit hospital that is subject to free-care obligations under the Hill–Burton Act to a for-profit firm creates special problems. See 42 C.F.R. §§ 124.701–124.709 (1995) (waiving government's right to recover portions of Hill–Burton grant upon creation of an irrevocable trust to support uncompensated care).

Public hospitals have also been privatized in a similar manner. E.g., Richmond County Hosp. Auth. v. Richmond County, 255 Ga. 183, 336 S.E.2d 562 (1985) (allowing lease of county hospital to prevent its becoming a deficit-ridden, indigent-only hospital). See two articles under the heading "Public Facilities Going Private," Mod. Healthcare, Sept. 9, 1996, p. 32 (recounting experience in Los Angeles County and New York City).

3. *HMO Conversions.* As Kuttner states, a number of HMOs that began as nonprofit entities have converted to for-profit status, often in transactions that proved highly beneficial to insiders when the HMO or its common stock was thereafter sold to a larger for-profit chain or in a public offering. Bailey, Charities, Win, Lose in Health Shuffle, Chron. of Philanthropy, June 14, 1994, at 1 (reporting a number of lucrative resales yielding 10–fold markups over original purchase price). See also McMahon, Fair Value? The Conversion of Nonprofit HMOs, 30 U.S.F.L.Rev. 355 (1996); Levy, The Conversion of Nonprofit Health Maintenance Organizations to For–Profit Status, 16 N. Kentucky L.Rev. 361 (1988).

4. *Conversion of Blue Cross/Blue Shield Plans.* Blue Cross and Blue Shield health insurance plans have not escaped the trend towards conversion. In the aftermath of the Blues' loss of favorable federal tax treatment, the national Blue Cross Blue Shield Association first authorized plans licensing its trademarks to surrender their original nonprofit status in 1994. Plans in Georgia and California plans have already converted to investor-owned status, while several other plans are moving in that direction. An issue in every case is the ownership of reserves and the disposition of sale proceeds. See Tokarski, Mergers, Conversions: Blues' Survival Strategies, Am.Med. News, May 20, 1996, at 9; Page, Insurance Regulators Follow Blues' Money Trail, Am.Med.l News, May 20, 1996, at 9.

5. *Legislative Responses.* Several states have considered or enacted legislation giving the state attorney general more authority over these transactions. See generally Volunteer Trustees Found. A State–by–Profit Hospital: A State–by–State Analysis of New Legislation (1998). Tennessee, for example, formed a special committee to study the sale of not-for-profit hospitals. H.Res. 13, 99th Tenn. Gen. Assembly, 1st Sess. (1995). The Nebraska law referred to by Kuttner that sets forth criteria for attorney general approval of any sale of a nonprofit hospital is L.B. 1188, Neb. 94th Leg., 2d Sess. (1995) (enacted April 15, 1996). See also Act of June 19, 1997, ch. 280, 1997 N.H. Laws 1098 (titled "Standards for Acquisition Transactions Involving Health Care Charitable Trusts and Review by Director of Charitable Trust").

6. *Tax Implications.* What are the tax implications of transactions such as the one in Nashville? See, e.g., Priv.Ltr.Rul. 85–19–039 (Feb. 12, 1985) (approving sale of teaching hospital to for-profit enterprise with superior "financial resources and management systems"; sale yielded a fund the income from which was to support medical education and research).

NOTES AND QUESTIONS ON SPECIAL LEGAL TREATMENT OF NONPROFIT FIRMS

1. *Directors' Duties.* By analogy to the law of trusts and the fiduciary duties of trustees, directors of nonprofit corporations were at one time thought to be subject to a higher standard of care than directors of for-profit firms. As noted by the Tennessee Attorney General, this distinction probably no longer holds, at least in such business-like institutions as hospitals. (Paradoxically, hospital board members are reputed to be carrying much greater work loads and responsibilities today than ever before.) In the management of charitable funds, however, conflict-of-interests rules may be somewhat stricter than the rules applicable to corporate directors, in part because of the lack of shareholder oversight. In Stern v. Lucy Webb Hayes Training School for Deaconesses and Missionaries, 381 F.Supp. 1003 (D.D.C.1974), a class of patients sued the hospital's directors for placing funds in non-interest-bearing accounts in banks with which some of them were associated. Breaches of duties of care and loyalty were found. Unlike the court in *Stern*, most courts deny standing to beneficiaries of the nonprofit corporation, leaving enforcement of director duties to members or directors of the corporation and the state attorney general. See e.g. O'Donnell v. Sardegna, 336 Md. 18, 646 A.2d 398 (Md. 1994) (subscribers to nonprofit Blue Cross plan held to lack standing to sue officers and directors for mismanagement). See Blasko et al., Standing to Sue in the Charitable Sector, 28 U.S.F.L.Rev. 37 (1993).

See generally DeMott, Self–Dealing Transactions in Nonprofit Corporations, 59 Brook. L. Rev. 131 (1993); Developments in the Law—Nonprofit Corporations, 105 Harv. L. Rev. 1590 (1992).

2. *FTC Act Exemption.* Section 5 of the Federal Trade Commission Act, 15 U.S.C. § 45 (1994), grants the FTC jurisdiction to enforce the antitrust laws against "corporations." However, the definition of *corporation* in section 4 of the Act includes only corporations "organized to carry on business for its own profit or that of its members." 15 U.S.C. § 44 (1994). In Community Blood Bank of Kansas City Area, Inc. v. FTC, 405 F.2d 1011 (8th Cir.1969) (the facts of which are discussed infra and in chapter 4(§B)), the court of appeals dismissed for lack of jurisdiction an FTC action against a nonprofit blood bank and several nonprofit hospitals, all enjoying 501(c)(3) exemptions. What rationale might be offered for exempting nonprofits from FTC jurisdiction? Are nonprofit corporations such as hospitals or educational institutions unlikely to engage in anticompetitive practices? Do you agree that the FTC Act language must be construed to prevent the FTC from policing nonprofit firms?

Other cases have raised the question of FTC jurisdiction over nonprofit trade and professional organizations having "members" who benefit from the organization's activities. E.g., California Dental Ass'n, FTC Dkt. 9259 (Mar. 26, 1996), aff'd, 128 F.3d 720 (9th Cir.1997), in which the Commission opined as follows:

The statute does not [fully] specify the boundary of the for-profit limit to our jurisdiction (or nonprofit exemption as it is alternatively known), and the test we apply was first articulated in [the *Community Blood Bank* case]. In that case, the Eighth Circuit rejected the notion that a corporation's nonprofit organizational form places it beyond the Commission's jurisdiction. An examination of the legislative history of the Act led the court to conclude that "Congress did not intend to provide a blanket exclusion of all non-profit corporations, for it was also aware that corporations ostensibly organized not-for-profit, such as trade associations, were merely vehicles through which a pecuniary profit could be realized for themselves or their members." The Eighth Circuit explained that the nonprofit exemption extends only to corporations that are "in law and in fact charitable," and concluded:

> "[U]nder § 4 the Commission lacks jurisdiction over nonprofit corporations without shares of capital which are organized for and actually engaged in business for only charitable purposes, and do not derive any 'profit' for themselves or their members within the meaning of the word 'profit' as attributed to corporations having shares of capital."

We applied this standard in [*AMA v. FTC,* the appellate opinion in which is reproduced in chapter 4(§B)], where we [agreed] with the ALJ, who had decided that the Commission can "assert jurisdiction over nonprofit organizations whose activities engender a pecuniary benefit to its members if [those] activit[ies are] a substantial part of the total activities of the organization, rather than merely incidental to some non-commercial activity." We have since adhered to that formulation of the reach of our jurisdiction over nonprofit organizations.

* * *

CDA falls within our jurisdiction for the same reasons the AMA did * * *. CDA, like the AMA, is organized as a nonprofit corporation under state law and is exempt from federal income taxes under Internal Revenue Code § 501(c)(6), which applies to "business leagues, chambers of commerce, real estate boards and boards of trade" consisting of members that share common business interests. It thus apparently does not qualify for exemption under I.R.C. § 501(c)(3) * * *. This status is pertinent to our jurisdictional analysis, but in applying the *AMA* test, we nonetheless review for ourselves whether CDA confers pecuniary benefits upon its members as a substantial part of its activities.

* * *

[T]he last time CDA made a comprehensive accounting of the allocation of its resources, only 7 percent was spent on "[s]ervices to the [p]ublic," while 65 percent funded "[d]irect [m]ember [s]ervices," 20 percent was used for "[a]ssociation [a]dministration & [i]ndirect [m]ember [s]ervices," and 8 percent went to defray the costs of "[m]embership [m]aintenance." In sum, without questioning whether

CDA engages in activities that benefit the public, we agree with the ALJ that the services CDA provides to its members satisfy the jurisdictional threshold of the Act.

The court of appeals essentially approved this reasoning. 128 F.3d at 725–26.

3. *Robinson–Patman.* Section 2(a) of the Robinson–Patman Act, 15 U.S.C. § 13(a) (1994), a 1936 amendment to the Clayton Antitrust Act, was enacted to limit "price discrimination," particularly a seller's price favoritism that gives one customer a material competitive advantage over other customers. The dominant concern prompting the legislation was the ability of newly emerging grocery chains to get better prices from suppliers than small, independent stores could get. Retail pharmacists see high-volume hospital pharmacies and HMOs as a similar competitive threat. The Nonprofit Institutions Act, however, provides that the Robinson–Patman prohibitions do not apply "to purchases of their supplies for their own use by schools, * * * hospitals, and charitable institutions not operated for profit." 15 U.S.C. § 13(c) (1994).

The question that arises is when nonprofit and governmental health care providers, which frequently buy pharmaceuticals at low prices, can resell them without violating the condition that their purchase be "for their own use." The Supreme Court has held that the exemption applies for sales to hospitals as long as the resale "is a part of and promotes the hospital's intended institutional operation in the care of persons who are its patients." Abbott Laboratories v. Portland Retail Druggists Ass'n, 425 U.S. 1, 14 (1976). Thus, a nonprofit hospital forfeits its exemption if it supplies drugs to outpatients, former inpatients, or nonhospitalized patients of their staff physicians. An HMO has been held free to resell discounted drugs to its own members but not to the general public. DeModena v. Kaiser Found. Health Plan, Inc., 743 F.2d 1388 (9th Cir. 1984), cert. denied, 469 U.S. 1229 (1985). See also In re Brand Name Prescription Drugs Antitrust Litigation, No. 94 C 897, 1995 WL 715848 (N.D.Ill.1995) following and approving *DeModena*'s extension of *Abbott* test to HMOs because "institutional function" of latter, unlike hospitals, includes "continuing and preventative care"; rejecting protection of retail pharmacies as key to act's interpretation because "such a 'competitive injury' exception * * * would render the exemption 'practically meaningless' ". It should be observed that, even if no exemption is available, a Robinson–Patman violation may not be easy to prove because some adverse effect on competition must be shown.

Reflecting in part concern about unfair competition, new prohibitions on the resale of pharmaceuticals by health care entities of all kinds (not just nonprofit) were enacted in the Prescription Drug Marketing Act of 1987, Pub. L. No. 100–293, 102 Stat. 95 (1988), codified at 21 U.S.C. §§ 331, 333, 353, 381 (1994).

4. *Labor Laws.* Until 1974, nonprofit hospitals were exempt from the federal laws governing labor-management relations. Government hospitals still remain exempt. The Senate committee explained the 1974 legislation as follows:

> The Committee could find no acceptable reason why 1,427,012 employees of these nonprofit, nonpublic hospitals, representing 56% of all hospital employees, should continue to be excluded from the coverage and protections of the Act. In the Committee's deliberations on this measure, it was recognized that the needs of patients in health care institutions required special consideration in the Act including a provision requiring hospitals to have sufficient notice of any strike or picketing to allow for appropriate arrangements to be made for the continuance of patient care in the event of a work stoppage. In this respect the Committee believed that the special notice requirements should be extended to all proprietary and nonprofit hospitals, convalescent hospitals, health maintenance organizations, health or medical clinics, nursing homes, extended care facilities or other institutions devoted to the care of sick, infirm or aged persons. Accordingly this bill will provide the same procedures for employees of all health care institutions.

S.Rep. No. 766, 93d Cong., 2d Sess. 3 (1974). See 29 U.S.C. §§ 152(2), 158, 169 (1994). See generally A. Rutkowski & B. Rutkowski, Labor Relations in Hospitals 15–26 (1984). Some discussion of bargaining units appears in chapter 5(§A).

5. *Charitable Immunity.* At one time, the rule of charitable immunity generally protected nonprofit hospitals against tort actions for personal injuries resulting from the negligence of their employees. Largely abrogated in the late 1950s in most jurisdictions, it survives in only limited forms today. See generally Nonprofit Risk Management Center, State Liability for Charitable Organizations and Volunteers (2d ed. 1993); C. Tremper, Reconsidering Legal Liability and Insurance for Non–Profit Organizations 187–201 (1989) (summarizing state statutes and case law on charitable immunity); Annot., 25 A.L.R.4th 517 (1983 & Supp. 1995). (See further discussion in chapter 5(§B).) Do you suppose that charitable immunity provided a significant inducement to the formation of hospitals as nonprofit rather than for-profit corporations? To what extent, in your estimation, did the shift away from charitable immunity contribute to the "secularization" and commercialization of the hospital business?

6. *Corporate Practice of Medicine.* As § C of this chapter shows, corporations are under some inhibitions in providing professional services through their own employees. In some states, nonprofit corporations, including hospitals, are allowed more leeway than for-profits, and in a few places for-profits are barred altogether from performing certain functions. The historical predominance of nonprofits in the hospital sphere and elsewhere may have owed something to these legal restrictions. Is the law right to discriminate in this fashion?

NOTES AND QUESTIONS ON THE CHOICE BETWEEN THE NONPROFIT AND FOR–PROFIT FORMS

1. What accounts for the historical predominance of nonprofit corporations in the hospital field? What factors other than contract failure (Hansmann's term) may have contributed?

2. How might physician preferences affect the choice of corporate form? Which kind of hospital would physicians prefer? A study in the early 1980s suggested that for-profit hospitals were slightly less likely to impose oversight restricting their physicians' practice styles. AMA Center for Health Policy Research, Profit in Medicine: The Impact on Hospital Staffing Patterns and Physician Practice Behavior (3 SMS Report No. 4, June 1984), reported in Am.Med.News, Aug. 3, 1984, at 12. In light of this evidence, how do you account for physicians' historic preference for nonprofit hospitals? See Majone, Professionalism and Nonprofit Organizations, 8 J. Health Pol., Pol'y & Law 639 (1984); Bays, Why Most Private Hospitals Are Nonprofit, 2 J. Pol'y Anal. & Mgt. 366 (1983); Pauly & Redisch, The Not-for-Profit Hospital as a Physicians' Cooperative, 63 Am.Econ.Rev. 87 (1973). Note the date of the cited study. Had it been necessary theretofore for hospitals to oversee physicians' spending proclivities?

3. By extending your analysis, can you speculate on why the hospital industry and the medical profession adopted the nonprofit form when they entered the health insurance field by creating, respectively, Blue Cross plans covering hospital care and Blue Shield plans covering medical services?

4. What factors explain the expanding role of for-profits in the hospital field? Has the industry's source of capital changed? What advantages do for-profits enjoy in raising and directing capital? What other factors may have influenced the infiltration of for-profit firms, despite the tax disadvantages under which they operate? What development in tort law may have reduced the desirability of operating a hospital as a charitable undertaking? What changes in the financing of hospital care made the field more attractive to for-profit firms? Consider all the relevant advantages and disadvantages of for-profit and nonprofit firms in providing various health care services.

5. *Relative Performance of For-profit Firms.* As noted by Kuttner, most research on relative performance of for-profits and nonprofits is dated and occurred in markets quite different from today's. In 1986, an Institute of Medicine (IOM) committee report summarized the then-existing evidence on for-profit and nonprofit organizations, concluding that it was "not sufficient to justify a recommendation that investor ownership be either opposed or supported by public policy." IOM, For-profit Enterprise in Health Care 191 (1986). Findings were not generally favorable to for-profit providers, however, especially on the questions of cost and access. See also B. Gray, The Profit Motive and Patient Care: The Changing Accountability of Doctors and Hospitals, ch. 5 (1991); Clark, Does the Nonprofit Form Fit the Hospital Industry?, 93 Harv.L.Rev. 1416 (1980).

(a) *Access.* For a report of a study finding that "not-for-profit hospitals frequently provide much more care to the low-income uninsured than do investor-owned facilities," see Lewin & Eckels, Setting the Record Straight: The Provision of Uncompensated Care by Not-for-Profit Hospitals, 318 New Eng.J.Med. 1212 (1988). See also Frank & Salkever, The Supply of Charity Services by Nonprofit Hospitals: Motives and Market Structures,

22 RAND J.Econ. 430 (1991). The IOM committee found that for-profits although providing proportionately less uncompensated care, have had some beneficial effects on the accessibility of care. "[T]hey have tended to locate in areas of relatively rapid population growth * * * and at least some of the hospitals they have acquired were not in sound financial condition." IOM, supra, at 187. It also found that "Medicaid patients, who are generally less lucrative * * *, are served in disproportionately larger numbers by for-profit [nursing] homes." Id. at 189.

(b) *Prices, Profits, and Efficiency*. Some evidence supports the assertion that for-profit hospitals have charged higher prices and earned higher profits than comparable not-for-profit hospitals. See IOM, supra, at 74–96. This finding was disputed, however, and may simply reflect higher costs associated with newer facilities or higher quality. See, e.g., Becker & Sloan, Hospital Ownership and Performance, 21 Econ.Inquiry 21, 31 (1985) (concluding from a sample of several thousand that "profitability is no higher for the for-profit hospitals than for their nonprofit counterparts"). On relative efficiency, see Register et al., Profit Incentives and the Hospital Industry: Are We Expecting Too Much? 20 Health Services Res. 225 (1985) (reporting empirical study finding the two hospital types equally efficient). The IOM study, supra, at 186–87, found that "the expected ability of investor-owned for-profit organizations to produce the same services at lower cost * * * has not been demonstrated."

(c) *Quality*. Some evidence suggests that for-profit hospitals are generally comparable to nonprofits in rates of accreditation, facilities, incidence of malpractice, and the like. IOM, supra, at 127–41, 189–90; Clark, supra, at 1455 ("such evidence as exists does not show nonprofit hospitals to differ from for-profits in quality").

6. *Incentives*. Consider the operative incentives and motives of for-profit and nonprofit firms. Is there any reason *a priori* to expect one or the other to fall short in the areas of cost containment or quality of care? For a summary of the literature, concluding that nonprofits face generally similar market conditions and incentives and do not behave very differently than their for-profit counterparts. Brody, Agents Without Principals: The Economic Convergence of the Nonprofit And For–Profit Organizational Forms, 40 N.Y.L.Sch.L.Rev. 457 (1996). Economists tend to believe that nonprofits pursue nonpecuniary goals, in particular the gratifications that come from providing higher quality health care, charity care, education, and research, and that they tolerate more administrative slack and conferral of private benefits than for-profit firms. See, e.g., Clark, supra, at 1462 ("*ceteris paribus,* managerial discretion (or 'slack') is greater than in for-profits because of the absence of comparable capital-market controls—that is, controls exerted by capital suppliers as opposed to customers—and it results in organizational practices that increase the managers' utility"). Is it significant that nonprofit firms have not, until recently at least, been vulnerable to takeover bids or to acquisition by interests likely to dislodge existing management?

One theoretical hypothesis about nonprofits is that they maximize output (or their budgets), rather than profits, by pursuing price discrimination even to the extent of cross-subsidization, pricing some services above and others below costs in order to sell as much as possible while at least breaking even. See W. Niskanen, Bureaucracy and Representative Government 81–86, 102–04 (1971). An empirical study of Red Cross blood service units finds pricing to be consistent with this output-maximization hypothesis. Jacobs & Wilder, Pricing Behavior of Non-profit Agencies: The Case of Blood Products, 3 J. Health Econ. 49 (1984). Given these findings, what are the implications of nonprofits for allocative efficiency and health care cost containment? Is it socially preferable for firms to plow profits back into providing services at prices below cost or to distribute them to shareholders? How is one to know? What would Kuttner say?

A possible explanation for any higher charges and cost reimbursements earned by for-profits in the 1980s may have been simply their greater ability (or willingness) to exploit poorly designed financing mechanisms. If this hypothesis is true, what policy implications should be drawn? Does the fault lie in the profit motive or in the financing system? What is the significance of findings that for-profit nursing home chains have lower costs and serve a higher proportion of Medicaid patients? See Arling et al., Nursing Home Cost and Ownership Type: Evidence of Interaction Effects, 22 Health Services Research 255 (1987). Is it reasonable to expect for-profit firms to show up better in cost comparisons now that the financing system is beginning to reward cost savings?

How valid are Kuttner's fears about possible sacrifices of quality in hospital care? Can market forces be expected to reward quality as well as cost cutting? To be sure, a for-profit enterprise might sometimes find it advantageous to sacrifice the quality of care it provides in order to increase profitability. But simplistic thinking can easily exaggerate this risk, since there are many influences that limit the discretion that may in fact be exercised. Competition is only one of these influences. Certainly, if the for-profit provider plans to be in the market permanently (as a hospital almost certainly does), it cannot afford to jeopardize its reputation by skimping on quality, to risk liability, or otherwise to cause patients (or physicians) to doubt its commitment to quality care. On the other hand, a provider with a shorter time horizon would have fewer constraints and, in certain circumstances, may dupe consumers long enough to make a rapid and unconscionable profit at the expense of its patients' health—a "quick killing," so to speak.

An example of a market that proved inviting to the unscrupulous was that served in the 1970s by prepaid health plans (PHPs) under the California Medicaid program—Medi–Cal. That program, by funding a number of low-quality plans, created a scandal that strengthened fears concerning proprietary HMOs and proprietary providers in general. See generally Chavkin & Treseder, California's Prepaid Health Plan Program: Can the Patient Be Saved?, 28 Hastings L.J. 685 (1977). However, many of the PHPs contributing to this scandal were in fact organized as nonprofit plans that funneled cash to for-profit enterprises offering physician services, management services, and the like. Moreover, the "Medicaid-only" character of the PHPs, the medical profession's opposition to the plan (deterring involvement by ethical providers), and long-term uncertainty about the program (and about state and federal policy generally) contributed to the problems. In addition, the state appeared to be at fault in its haste to implement the PHP program, in its lack of attention to assuring meaningful consumer choice, and in its failure to monitor the quality of care. Finally, the scandals in California erupted before the competitive market had a chance to weed out the worst plans, whose initial success may have been possible only because the target population had not yet gained experience and sophistication and because demand temporarily exceeded supply. Concerns of this kind naturally arise as states increasingly turn to managed care plans to provide Medicaid services.

Another market in which poor quality has been associated with proprietary institutions is the nursing home industry. See, e.g., Hawes & Phillips, The Changing Structure of the Nursing Home Industry and the Impact of Ownership on Quality, Cost, and Access, in IOM, supra, at 492. A study of nursing homes in New York in the 1950s suggested that some of the quality problems may have been attributable to factors other than the profit motive. W. Thomas, Nursing Homes and Public Policy: Drift and Decision in New York State 155–58, 175, 261 (1969). Rapid growth of the proprietary sector occurred while the voluntary sector was unable to obtain the capital needed to meet the emerging demand attributable to the expanding state welfare program. Very uneven quality persisted while demand exceeded supply, but quality and efficiency began to improve as increased supply allowed competition to be effective in eliminating the poorer facilities. Although this experience was cited by Thomas as a demonstration of the proprietaries' quality failings, it also suggests that free entry and competition have virtues of their own. A question of central interest is whether weeding out unneeded, poor-quality nursing home beds could be left, within wide ranges established by limited regulation, to the market under a liberal regulatory policy toward nursing home entry and expansion. Admittedly, however, this market presents extremely difficult quality problems. See chapter 6(§D).

7. *Columbia/HCA: The Sequel.* Not long after Kuttner wrote, the Columbia/HCA empire began to disintegrate. First, a series of raids on Columbia hospitals by federal fraud investigators shook the company and investors. These were followed in due course by a handful of indictments of mid-level managers in Florida. Although these indictments alleged only some mundane fraudulent billing and cost accounting for Medicare services, they were accompanied by warnings that other investigations were ongoing. Earnings projections were drastically reduced, and the company's stock price fell substantially. These events set the stage for more drastic developments.

Within the company, there had been growing dissatisfaction with the aggressive style and methods of CEO Rick Scott, whose responses to the investigations and other public criticism caused further doubts about his management. The leader of the internal resistance, board member and former HCA chief executive Thomas Frist, M.D., eventually engineered the resignation of Scott and several of his lieutenants. Elected to fill Scott's post as CEO, Frist quickly promised to cooperate with the government's ongoing investigations and hired a high-profile ethics consultant. On the strategic side, he reversed Scott's commitment to fully integrated systems of care, putting the company's home care business and physician practices up for sale and cutting the number of operating divisions roughly in half. He also appeared poised to sell as many as a third of the company's acute care hospitals and to stop using the Columbia trade name, in which Scott had invested so heavily. As of this writing, Columbia/HCA had only begun to atone for its violations of health care market etiquette and, perhaps, of federal law. (See § D of this chapter.) Although the company would almost certainly survive in some form, the new leader among for-profit hospital companies was likely to be Tenet Healthcare of Santa Barbara, California, with some 130 hospitals nationwide.

The lessons to be learned from the Columbia/HCA story will be debated for years to come. Kuttner's view is obviously that for-profit health care of any kind is inherently corrupt or corrupting. In response, it might be variously argued that the Columbia/HCA case was overblown (lots of smoke, relatively little fire), that some nonprofits have been guilty of similar, less widely publicized abuses, and that, while a number of other investor-owned health care companies have also paid large fines for engaging in activities comparable to those of which Columbia is accused, hundreds of others are innovating and bringing costs down without seriously misbehaving. Another possible hypothesis is that the Columbia/HCA experience proves that the system works—that fraud or excesses in dealing with public programs are appropriately deterred because they will eventually be detected and punished, both by the legal system and in the marketplace. Still another possible conclusion is that, at least at the corporate level, Columbia/HCA was guilty of little more than taking maximum advantage of arguable loopholes in the Medicare/Medicaid payment systems. Under this premise, the government made the company a scapegoat for its own inability to manage its programs and to keep up with rapid changes in delivery and financing. For a critique of the case that finds as much fault on the government's side as on Columbia/HCA's, see Kleinke, Deconstructing the Columbia/HCA Investigation, Health Affs., Mar.–Apr. 1998, p.7 (with commentaries).

SECTION C: PROHIBITIONS ON CORPORATE PRACTICE AND COMMERCIALISM

Legislation Mandating Professional Control; Judicial Review of Economic Regulation

North Dakota State Board of Pharmacy v. Snyder's Drug Stores, Inc.

Supreme Court of the United States, 1973.
414 U.S. 156, 94 S.Ct. 407, 38 L.Ed.2d 379.

■ MR. JUSTICE DOUGLAS delivered the opinion of the Court.

North Dakota passed a statute that requires that the applicant for a permit to operate a pharmacy be "a registered pharmacist in good standing" or "a corporation or association, the majority stock in which is owned by registered pharmacists in good standing, actively and regularly employed in and responsible for the management, supervision, and operation of such pharmacy."

Petitioner Board denied a permit to Snyder's Drug Stores, Inc., because it did not comply with the stock-ownership requirements of the statute, it appearing that all the common stock of Snyder's was owned by Red Owl Stores and it not being shown if any Red Owl shareholders were pharmacists registered and in good standing in North Dakota. * * * [T]he Supreme Court of North Dakota * * * held that the North Dakota statute was unconstitutional by reason of our decision in 1928 in Liggett Co. v. Baldridge, 278 U.S. 105. That case involved a Pennsylvania statute that required that 100% of the stock of the corporation be owned by pharmacists. The North Dakota statute, however, requires only that a majority of the stock be owned by pharmacists. But the North Dakota Supreme Court held that the difference did not take this case out from under the *Liggett* case because under both statutes control of the corporation having a pharmacy license had to be in the hands of pharmacists responsible for the management and operation of the pharmacy. * * *

The case is here on a petition for certiorari which we granted.

* * *

Liggett, decided in 1928, belongs to that vintage of decisions which exalted substantive due process by striking down state legislation which a majority of the Court deemed unwise. *Liggett* has to date not been expressly overruled. We commented on it disparagingly, however, in Daniel v. Family Security Life Ins. Co., 336 U.S. 220 * * *. We noted that *Liggett* held that it was "clear" that "mere stock ownership in a corporation, owning and operating a drug store, can have no real or substantial relation to the public health; and that the act in question creates an unreasonable and unnecessary restriction upon private business," 278 U.S., at 113. In *Daniel*, however, we stated that "a pronounced shift of emphasis since the *Liggett* case," 336 U.S., at 225, had deprived the words "unreasonable" and "arbitrary" of the meaning which *Liggett* ascribed to them. * * *

[To show the change in the Court's philosophy since 1928, the Court quoted its 1963 opinion in] Ferguson v. Skrupa, 372 U.S. 726, where we sustained the constitutionality of a state law prohibiting persons other than lawyers from engaging in the business of debt adjusting and debt pooling. We said:

> "We conclude that the Kansas Legislature was free to decide for itself that legislation was needed to deal with the business of debt adjusting. Unquestionably, there are arguments showing that the business of debt adjusting has social utility, but such arguments are properly addressed to the legislature, not to us. We refuse to sit as a 'superlegislature to weigh the wisdom of legislation,' and we emphati-

cally refuse to go back to the time when courts used the Due Process Clause 'to strike down state laws, regulatory of business and industrial conditions, because they may be unwise, improvident, or out of harmony with a particular school of thought.' Nor are we able or willing to draw lines by calling a law 'prohibitory' or 'regulatory.' Whether the legislature takes for its textbook Adam Smith, Herbert Spencer, Lord Keynes, or some other is no concern of ours. The Kansas debt adjusting statute may be wise or unwise. But relief, if any is needed, lies not with us but with the body constituted to pass laws for the State of Kansas." Id., at 731B732 (footnotes omitted).

The majority of the Court in *Liggett* for which Mr. Justice Sutherland spoke held that business or property rights could be regulated under the Fourteenth Amendment only if the "legislation bears a real and substantial relation to the public health, safety, morals, or some other phase of the general welfare," 278 U.S., at 111B112. The majority held the Act governing pharmacies "creates an unreasonable and unnecessary restriction upon private business." Id., at 113. The opposed view stated by Mr. Justice Holmes, and concurred in by Mr. Justice Brandeis, was:

"A standing criticism of the use of corporations in business is that it causes such business to be owned by people who do not know anything about it. Argument has not been supposed to be necessary in order to show that the divorce between the power of control and knowledge is an evil. The selling of drugs and poisons calls for knowledge in a high degree, and Pennsylvania after enacting a series of other safeguards has provided that in that matter the divorce shall not be allowed. Of course, notwithstanding the requirement that in corporations hereafter formed all the stockholders shall be licensed pharmacists, it still would be possible for a stockholder to content himself with drawing dividends and to take no hand in the company's affairs. But obviously he would be more likely to observe the business with an intelligent eye than a casual investor who looked only to the standing of the stock in the market. The Constitution does not make it a condition of preventive legislation that it should work a perfect cure. It is enough if the questioned act has a manifest tendency to cure or at least to make the evil less." Id., at 114B115.

Those two opposed views of public policy are considerations for the legislative choice. The *Liggett* case was a creation at war with the earlier constitutional view of legislative power. The *Liggett* case, being a derelict in the stream of the law, is hereby overruled. We reverse and remand the judgment below and free the courts and agencies in North Dakota from what the State Supreme Court deemed to be the mandate of *Liggett*.

NOTES AND QUESTIONS ON STATE LEGISLATION REGULATING PROFESSIONAL SERVICES

1. *Judicial Review of Economic Regulation.* The appropriate standard of federal judicial review of economic regulation by the states is, of course, an issue of long standing in constitutional law. The laissez-faire attitude toward such legislation of the post New Deal Supreme Court has been reflected in numerous decisions sustaining regulation of professional services against charges that they violated the due process clause of the fourteenth amendment. E.g., Williamson v. Lee Optical of Oklahoma Inc., 348 U.S. 483 (1955) (upholding statutory prohibition of sale of eyeglass frames without a new prescription for lenses because the Court could imagine a public health rationale for such legislation). See also Brandwein v. California Board of Osteopathic Examiners, 708 F.2d 1466 (9th Cir.1983) (finding no denial of equal protection in state law requiring that certain osteopaths use "DO" label despite having training equivalent to some practitioners permitted to designate themselves as "MDs").

Although federal courts are highly deferential to state legislatures, some state courts appear willing to review state legislation under meaningful substantive due process (or equivalent) requirements. E.g., In re Certificate of Need for Aston Park Hosp., Inc., 282 N.C. 542, 193 S.E.2d 729 (1973) (striking down early "certificate-of-need" law aimed at limiting hospital growth); Pennsylvania State Board of Pharmacy v. Pastor, 441 Pa. 186, 272 A.2d 487 (1971) (invalidating under due process requirements a law prohibiting advertising of prescription drug prices); Blumenthal v. Board of Med. Examiners, 57 Cal.2d 228, 18 Cal.Rptr. 501, 368 P.2d 101 (1962) (invalidating 5-year apprenticeship requirement for dispensing opticians). Thus, in some jurisdictions at least, judicial review of regulatory legislation may still operate in the health care field.

An enlightening debate on the appropriate scrutiny to be given by courts to economic regulation appeared in 1985 under the heading "Economic Liberties and the Judiciary." The debaters were Judge (later Justice) Antonin Scalia and Professor Richard Epstein of the University of Chicago Law School. Scalia, On the Merits of the Frying Pan, Regulation, Jan.–Feb. 1985, at 10; Epstein, The Active Virtues, id., at 14. In pleading for restraint by unelected judges, Scalia stressed the superior political legitimacy of the legislative and executive branches of government as well as the administrative agencies they create. Epstein, however, noting that under this view "only political checks are available to ensure that national policy does not stray too far from the social consensus," replied as follows:

> Scalia's position represents the mainstream of American constitutional theory today. My purpose is to take issue with the conventional wisdom. * * *
>
> In my view, Scalia has addressed only one side of a two-sided problem. He has pointed out the weaknesses of judicial action. But he has not paid sufficient attention to the errors and dangers in unchanneled legislative behavior. The only way to reach a balanced, informed judgment on the intrinsic desirability of judicial control of economic liberties is to consider the *relative* shortcomings of the two institutions—judicial and legislative—that compete for the crown of final authority. * * *

> What are the problems with legislation? When we put someone in charge of the collective purse or the police force, we in effect give him a spigot that allows him to tap into other people's property, money, and liberty. The legislator that casts a vote on an appropriations bill is spending not only his own wealth, but everyone else's. When the power of coalition, the power of factions, the power of artifice and strategy come into play, it often turns out that legislatures reach results that (in the long as well as the short run) are far from the social optimum.

Id. at 40. Epstein's idea was essentially that courts should step in to prevent the worst effects of "legislative failure" just as regulatory legislation may sometimes be needed to overcome or minimize the effects of severe market failure.

Because legislative struggles and judicial review of legislation are constant features of health care law, it is pertinent to consider the politics of legislation in this field and to ask whether legislatures are always primarily concerned with protecting the public interest and the public health. For example, was the legislation in *Snyder's Drug Stores* in the public interest? Who probably lobbied for the prohibition of lay-controlled pharmacies? Who probably lobbied against it? Who were the winners? the losers? Was the Supreme Court right to eschew significant oversight of the "black box" of the North Dakota legislature?

2. *Public Choice Theory.* How does the political process sometimes fail? The problem of majoritarian exploitation of minorities is well recognized. See, e.g., Ackerman, Beyond Carolene Products, 98 Harv.L.Rev. 713 (1985). (Unlike Ackerman, Epstein's article, supra, especially stresses the danger that property rights will be invaded by democratic majorities. See also R. Epstein, Takings: Private Property and the Power of Eminent Domain (1985).) Other theoretical defects of the political process may be identified, however. The "public choice" school of economics (or "interest group" theory) has applied standard economic analysis to the political "marketplace," arriving at conclusions useful in understanding how the public's representatives may sometimes act against the interests of the larger public and in favor of a small but well organized interest group. The classic work in this field is M. Olson, The Logic of Collective Action (1965). The following excerpt is an excellent introduction to public choice theory (here called the "interest group theory of lawmaking"):

> The defining theme of the interest group theory of lawmaking is its rejection of the presumption that the government endeavors to further the public interest. Rather, under interest group theory, all the participants in the political process act to further their self-interest. Legislators seek to maximize their chances of reelection. Voters and interest groups seek to maximize their own well-being at the expense of others. Moreover, regulation is a commodity, subject to supply and demand like any other commodity. Voters and interest groups demand the regulatory results that benefit them, and legislators and agencies supply regulatory results to the highest bidder. The results need not further the public interest.

Indeed, fundamental distortions in the political process may lead to systematic divergences from the public interest. Most economic models focus on "demand side" distortions. Under these models, interest groups influence the political process (and thus exhibit "demand" for legislation) in a variety of ways: by voting or mobilizing voters; by undertaking volunteer work for political candidates; by paying lawmakers in the form of bribes, speaking fees, supportive advertising, campaign contributions, or offers of future employment; by pressuring political officials to support or oppose the appointment, promotion, removal, or budget of regulators; and by influencing the information that reaches legislators, regulators, and the voting public.

All this activity requires resources of time or money. * * *

An interest group's willingness to expend resources of time and money is thus an important determinant of its political influence. This might not seem troubling: if one assumes that skewed distributions of leisure time and money do not excessively distort a group's willingness to expend time and money, then such a willingness could be taken as an appropriate proxy for the degree of a group's interest. The result would be a political process that better balanced conflicting interests (and better curbed majoritarian exploitation) than one which simply favored the group having a larger membership. This appears to have been the premise of earlier political theory that emphasized the value of pluralism.

However, all groups face a collective action problem that may make a willingness to expend resources an inaccurate proxy for the degree of group interest. The problem occurs because laws tend to confer benefits on groups of persons whether or not those persons contribute to the enactment (or retention) of the law. Consequently, even if the total benefits the law would confer on the group exceed the petitioning costs of seeking (or opposing) the relevant legal change, group members acting rationally but individually may refuse to incur those petitioning costs. No individual member may be willing to incur all the costs of petitioning activities that would confer net benefits on the group because each member receives only part of the group benefits. Further, each member may be unwilling to volunteer her [*sic*] share of petitioning costs both because her failure to contribute will not exclude her from the benefits of successful group efforts and because any individual contribution would have little effect on the probability of group success. Individual members thus have an incentive to take a free ride on the efforts of others.

The result is that individual decisionmaking may not lead to group action even though each individual member would be better off if it did. A group may be able to overcome such free-riding problems if it can reach a collective agreement to share costs and to monitor and punish members' failures to contribute. However, such collective efforts to police free riding will themselves require resources, which may be difficult to raise because of free-riding problems. Further, where cost assessments are based on members' individual benefits, collective cost-sharing efforts will also be plagued by each member's incentive to understate her share of the benefits of group action.

These collective action problems mean that every group is likely to invest less in petitioning efforts than would be necessary to maximize the group's net gains from petitioning. But small groups with concentrated (high per capita) interests in lawmaking will come closer to their optimal level of petitioning than large groups with diffuse (low per capita) interests. The reason is that large diffuse groups face greater collective action obstacles to group petitioning in three respects.

First, * * * small intense groups trying to curb free riding will generally be able to do so with smaller penalties and less frequent detection than large diffuse groups.

Second, [i]n small groups, free riding will be easier to detect because it has a proportionally larger effect. Small groups also generally have lower organizational costs, and their members are more likely to have ongoing personal contact, making monitoring easier and making social sanctions, in particular, more effective.

Finally, * * * large groups are not just less effective in their own right; they also generally face more effective opposition than small groups. * * *

Large diffusely interested groups will thus tend to be underrepresented. They will have a harder time collecting the resources necessary to monitor and evaluate developing issues, make campaign contributions, present information to voters or officials, and keep group members informed. Their members may also rationally decide that their diffuse interests are not worth the effort of reading and writing about, or voting on, the issues. Indeed, their collective action difficulties may be so great that they fail to invest any resources in pursuing collectively beneficial legal change. Smaller groups with intensely interested members, while facing collective action problems themselves, are likely to invest more resources in influencing the government and are thus more likely to secure favorable governmental action.

To be sure, enlarging the size of a group does have some advantages that tend to offset the disadvantages of increased size: (1) more votes, (2) some economies of scale, and (3) perhaps more total resources. The confluence of these advantages and disadvantages may not benefit small groups per se. Rather, it may benefit those small to medium-sized groups that enjoy optimal combinations of free-riding avoidance, weak opposition, voting power, resources, and economies of scale. [Note how professional and occupational groups satisfy these criteria for optimal political effectiveness.—Ed.] This refines one's understanding of the problem but renders it no less disturbing. Medium-sized groups with organizational advantages will still have a disturbing ability to exercise disproportionate influence. They can use that power to exploit not only groups that are too large to be cohesive but also groups that are cohesive but too small to have significant resources, scale economies, or voting power. Exploitation of the latter groups is no less disturbing than exploitation of the former. After all, one might think of "the general public" as the collection of all groups too small (such as the typical family) or too large (such as consumers) to form effective interest groups.

The results are little better when one considers the supply side. Considering the supply side does help explain one thing: how very large diffuse groups sometimes manage to overcome free-riding problems. Political leaders, theorists argue, can act as "entrepreneurs" who organize large groups. But such political entrepreneurs must overcome the same information problems facing self-starting groups: it will be harder to get diffusely interested persons to pay attention. This will generally make it easier to build political support by appealing to groups whose members have high per capita interests in governmental action than by attempting to stir the rationally apathetic general public. The supply side theory thus adds nuance to the explanation of how groups become organized, but does not contradict the theory that certain interest groups will exercise disproportionate influence.

Moreover, the structure of the supply side creates some additional problems. First, supply structure creates the problem of issue bundling. Voting normally requires a choice among a limited set of candidates, each of whom offers a package of positions. Thus, even a perfectly informed voter can often do no better than to choose between candidates based on the issues that intensely interest the voter, even though a candidate's positions on other issues harm the voter in more diffuse ways. To the extent this happens, the diffuse interests can be systematically underrepresented even if voters face no collective action problem in informing themselves and taking the time to vote.

Second, territorial representation furthers "pork barrel" politics. Each representative has an incentive to support legislation favoring her district. The concentrated benefits to that district's constituents will be larger and easier to communicate than the diffuse costs inflicted on other districts. It will also be relatively easy for a district representative to claim credit for legislation conferring localized benefits: who else could have been behind it? It will be harder for any single legislator to claim—or be tagged with—responsibility for legislation when its benefits or costs are spread throughout all districts. In effect, each district will be an interest group that, compared to the group encompassing all other districts, is relatively small and intensely interested in its own local projects.

Third, committee structure can exacerbate interest group influence. Committee membership rarely represents a cross-section of the legislature. Instead, legislators tend to self-select into those committees in which their supporters have the greatest stakes. * * *

Fourth, legislative oversight of agencies means that, to some extent, unelected regulators are accountable to the legislature, and are thus indirectly influenced by the interest groups that influence legislators. Indeed, because the oversight committee will likely consist of those legislators supported by the relevant special interest groups, the agency may be influenced more disproportionately than the legislature as a whole. Further, delegating authority to agencies may, in some instances, exacerbate interest group problems by helping legislators avoid the public perception that the legislators are responsible for the regulatory costs.

As a result, certain groups enjoy organizational advantages that enable them to exercise "disproportionate" influence on politicians and regulators and thus secure laws favoring their interests even when those laws injure large groups with diffuse interests (e.g., the general public) and impose a net loss on society. This means that many statutes and regulations are enacted (or defeated) not to benefit the general public, but to help a special interest group exact economic rents from the larger society.

To be sure, the literature also suggests that "capture" by one group will never be complete. Interest groups always face some opposition, even if relatively underrepresented, and efforts to garner income through increased political pressure face declining marginal benefits and rising marginal costs. Consequently, interest group theory predicts that regulations will reflect compromises through which regulatory benefits are distributed among various groups depending on the marginal returns the groups can offer the legislators or regulators.

Nonetheless, the disproportionate influence of well-organized interest groups is disturbing. It suggests that legal change is likely to harm the general public when the benefits of the change are concentrated and the costs are diffuse. Similarly, it suggests that opposition to legal change (or to implementation of a change) is likely to harm the general public when the change confers diffuse benefits and concentrated costs. Not only do the regulatory outcomes in such situations seem suspect, but the "rent-seeking" activity encouraged by the political system seems socially wasteful.

Of course, this picture of the political process is hardly uncontroversial. Others have argued that interest group theory offers a simplistic and often inaccurate account of the political process. These scholars convincingly demonstrate that noneconomic factors such as altruism and ideology play at least some role in political participation and decisionmaking, and that the preferences of regulators and the general public sometimes prevail over the preferences of interest groups. Their analysis thus suggests that interest group theory, even if qualified to account for "incomplete" capture, cannot offer a complete theory of regulation. Still, these scholars do not disprove the point that the economic benefits and costs of political organization play a strong role and that special interest groups often take advantage of these economic factors to exercise disproportionate political influence.

> In any event, I do not wish to enter the empirical debate about the extent to which economic versus noneconomic factors play a role in political decisionmaking. My purpose is rather to address the normative question whether, assuming one accepts its empirical claims, interest group theory justifies more intrusive judicial review. For that purpose, I assume that to a substantial extent interest group theory accurately describes the political process.

Elhauge, Does Interest Group Theory Justify More Intrusive Judicial Review?, 101 Yale L.J. 31, 35–44 (1991). In answer to the question posed in his title, Professor Elhauge concludes that, "when one makes the necessary comparative assessment, interest group theory does not establish * * * that the litigation process is, overall, less defective than the political process." Other scholars have argued that more intrusive judicial review is justified. E.g., Chemerinsky, The Supreme Court, 1988 Term—Foreword: The Vanishing Constitution, 103 Harv.L.Rev. 43 (1989); Gunther, Foreword—In Search of Evolving Doctrine in a Changing Court: A Model for a Newer Equal Protection, 86 Harv.L.Rev. 1 (1972) (advocating use of the equal protection clause as a basis for judicial review of state regulatory legislation). Still others have suggested that courts should narrowly construe statutes that appear to represent interest group transfers. See Sunstein, Interpreting Statutes in the Regulatory State, 103 Harv.L Rev. 405 (1989); Easterbrook, The Supreme Court, 1983 Term—Foreword: The Court and the Economic System, 98 Harv.L.Rev. 4 (1984).

3. *State-Imposed Restrictions on Optometrists and Opticians*. On January 4, 1985, the Federal Trade Commission (FTC) issued a Notice of Proposed Rulemaking, 50 Fed.Reg. 598, proposing a trade regulation rule aimed at certain state-imposed bans on certain forms of ophthalmic practice. The FTC described its action as follows (id. at 598–600):

> The proposed rule would remove four major restraints imposed by state law on permissible forms of commercial practice: (1) Restrictions on employer-employee or other business relationships between optometrists or opticians and non-professional corporations or unlicensed persons; (2) limitations on the number of branch offices an optometrist or optician may operate; (3) restrictions on the practice of optometry on the premises of mercantile establishments (such as department stores); and (4) bans on the practice of optometry under a trade name.
>
> The proposed rule would only prevent state or local governments from enforcing total bans on these forms of commercial ophthalmic practice; it would not interfere with the states' ability to regulate specific harmful practices as long as commercial practice itself is not directly or indirectly prohibited.
>
> "Commercial practice" in the retail optical market is generally understood to refer to large-scale, high-volume providers. "Non-commercial practice," on the other hand, describes small firms or independent "solo" practitioners.

Legal impediments to the practice of optometry and opticianry in commercial settings restrain the growth and development of retail optical firms that offer optometric services and also restrain other high-volume "commercial" businesses, which, through managerial efficiencies and economies of scale, are often able to charge lower prices for ophthalmic goods and services than small "noncommercial" practitioners. These restrictions also prevent commercial firms, as well as opticians and non-dispensing optometrists, from competing effectively with dispensing optometrists and ophthalmologists who offer both examination and dispensing services. Individual practitioners are also precluded from establishing practices in mercantile locations such as shopping centers or department stores, where the potential for high-volume business exists.

Proponents of commercial practice restraints justify them as necessary to protect the public health, safety and welfare. * * *

With respect to the proposed rule provisions concerning commercial practice restrictions, the staff report presents evidence that state laws which restrict the ability of optometrists to practice in commercial settings raise consumer prices but do not maintain or enhance the quality of vision care. Results obtained from the 1980 Bureau of Economics study ("BE Study") indicate that: (1) Prices of eyeglasses and eye examinations are significantly lower in cities where commercial practice is not restricted and in cities where advertising is not restricted; (2) commercial optometrists charge lower prices than non-commercial optometrists; (3) non-commercial providers who operate in markets where commercial practice is permitted charge less than their counterparts in cities where commercial practice is proscribed; and (4) there is no difference in overall quality of care between cities where commercial practice is permitted and cities where commercial practice is restricted. To assess quality, the study evaluated the accuracy of the prescriptions written by the sampled optometrists, the accuracy and workmanship of the eyeglasses dispensed by the examining optometrist, the thoroughness of the eye examination, and the extent of unnecessary prescribing of eyeglasses. * * *

The 1983 Bureau of Consumer Protection and Bureau of Economics study of contact lens wearers concluded that: (1) The quality of cosmetic contact lens fitting provided by opticians and commercial optometrists was not lower than that provided by ophthalmologists and non-commercial optometrists, and (2) commercial optometrists charged significantly less for contact lenses than did any other group. To assess the quality of contact lens fitting, the study evaluated the relative presence or absence of several potentially pathological corneal conditions related to contact lens wear. * * *

The staff recommendation that the Commission engage in rule-making proceedings regarding commercial practice restrictions is based primarily on the results of these studies, which contradict the claim that the entry of commercial firms into the market lowers the overall level of quality of vision care. At the same time, the results show that the average prices are significantly higher where commercial practice is restricted. Therefore, the Commission has reason to believe that these restrictions may be unfair acts or practices within the meaning of Section 5 of the FTC Act.

In 1986, a hearing officer recommended against issuance of the proposed rule, finding it impossible to conclude that the harms to consumers were not, "in some manner, counterbalanced by quality of care considerations." 51 Antitrust & Trade Reg. Rep. (BNA) 818 (1986). Nevertheless, the FTC issued its so-called "Eyeglass II" rule in 1989, only to have it invalidated on jurisdictional grounds in California State Bd. of Optometry v. FTC, 910 F.2d 976 (D.C.Cir.1990) (holding a state acting in its sovereign capacity is not a "person" subject to the FTC Act). Despite this unexceptionable holding, would you wish to see the FTC, a federal administrative agency, endowed with authority to declare the products anticonsumer actions by state legislatures invalid? (Would close congressional oversight of FTC rules make it easier, constitutionally, to tolerate actions by federal bureaucrats that override the actions of state legislatures?) See generally Pierce, Regulation, Deregulation, Federalism, and Administrative Law: Agency Power to Preempt State Regulation, 46 U.Pitt.L.Rev. 607 (1985).

For an interesting study of the politics of economic regulation in the field of optometry, see J. Begun & R. Feldman, A Social and Economic Analysis of Professional Regulation in Optometry (DHSS Pub. No. (PHS) 81–3292, 1981). This study sought to explain the different regulatory experience in four states with respect to restrictions on commercial practice and optometrists' right to use diagnostic drugs. The study's findings were summarized as follows (id. at 54–55):

> The four states vary substantially in the degree of regulatory success achieved by professional optometry. Optometry's efforts have been highly successful in North Carolina and Florida, although recently in Florida opposing interest groups have been gaining power. Optometry has been much less successful in Texas and Maryland, although in Texas professional optometry has shown signs of increasing strength.
>
> The political environment for the drug use and commercialism issues in North Carolina, Texas, Florida, and Maryland can be depicted in general terms as follows: competing groups are few in number and strong in commitment. They consist of the professional and commercial segments of the occupation, economic competitors, and client groups. The professional segment is represented by the state professional association and has no allies among the competing groups. The arena for political activity is the state legislature. Legislators receive most of their information from the competing groups and dislike the issues because they are volatile and often esoteric. Political parties are irrelevant in the controversies.
>
> Rarely were consumer interests directly represented in the political arena. Interest group activity determined outcomes of policy-decisions and in only one instance (senior citizens in Florida) were consum-

ers sufficiently concentrated to motivate organization of an effective interest group.

Competing interest groups were few in number. In all four states there were only two major combatants in the battles over drug use—professional optometry and medicine. The major participants in each state on the commercial practice issues were the professional and commercial segments within optometry. Allied with commercial optometry were businesses which employ optometrists or sell eyeglasses, newspaper publishers who benefit from advertising, and client groups interested in introducing more competition into the market. It is notable that in no instance did professional optometry have a major ally in its legislative battles—it functioned on its own in the political environment.

In explaining optometry's varying success in the four states, we found that internal segmentation of optometry reduced its political effectiveness, while size, geographic distribution, income, social status, and leadership resources aided optometry's efforts to secure professional regulations. But these factors did not guarantee political success, because they are all relative to similar characteristics of opposing groups. Thus the presence and political participation of opposing groups was important. In two of the states, Maryland and Texas, professional optometry faced significant opposition to most of its political goals; in Florida, some opposition was present; and in North Carolina, opponents were few and relatively weak. We found that the following hypothesis best explains why variation in the political opposition to optometry exists:

> The greater the degree to which other groups perceive their economic interests to be affected by the policy goals of the professionalizing occupation, the greater the degree to which other groups will participate in the political environment.

Evidence from the four states indicated that ophthalmology's opposition to drug use by optometry varied with the degree to which ophthalmology perceived its economic interests to be affected by professional optometry's efforts to expand. Similarly, political opposition from commercial interests to optometry's professionalizing movement was highest in the states where more commercial competitors were present. In turn, the presence of political opponents to professional optometry was found to be related to the degree of urbanization of the state. Urbanization leads to the growth of high volume practices and businesses, whose owners resist restrictions on commercial activity. Also, urban areas are more likely to harbor the specialized occupations whose economic survival is threatened by the monopoly of a work domain by the professionalizing occupation.

The authors of the study drew the following broader conclusions (id. at 56):

> At issue here has been the "public interest" model of regulation, and in particular its assertion that professional regulation is necessary to

protect the public welfare. Proponents of this argument have claimed that professions seek autonomy in order to better serve the public at large. In this view, regulation enhances the quality of services, a benefit presumed to outweigh any possible adverse consequences.

This perspective has been challenged by advocates of a "self-interest" theory of the regulatory process, which asserts that professions actively seek regulation to protect and add to their status, power and income. These conflicting arguments were tested by analyzing how professional regulatory power is gained by an occupation, and scrutinizing the costs and benefits of professional regulation to consumers.

We found strong support for the self-interest or economic theory of regulation. Not only is the growth of professional regulation a political process, but the socioeconomic and political resources of professionalizing occupations determine their success in obtaining favorable regulatory outcomes. These factors are constrained somewhat by political system and environmental characteristics.

This analysis of professional regulation in optometry refutes the public interest theory in all respects. Although we did find that regulation is associated with higher quality in service delivery (as measured by examination length and procedures employed), the increased quality is not valued by consumers at its marginal cost. Apparently, the regulated occupation actively seeks regulations to enhance its status, income and power, even as those anticompetitive regulations have adverse consequences to consumers.

See also Maurizi, Moore & Shepard, Competing for Professional Control: Professional Mix in the Eyeglass Industry, 24 J. Law & Econ. 351 (1981) (evaluating the California market). For cases sustaining limits on the corporate practice of optometry, see Lens Express, Inc. v. Ewald, 907 S.W.2d 64 (Tex.App.1995); California Ass'n of Dispensing Opticians v. Pearle Vision Center, Inc., 143 Cal.App.3d 419, 191 Cal.Rptr. 762 (1983).

4. *Judicial Review of State Regulation under First–Amendment Principles; the "Commercial Speech" Doctrine.* The next principal case involves judicial review of restrictive Texas legislation affecting optometrists under norms derived, not from the due process clause, but from the first amendment. In the earlier case of Virginia State Bd. of Pharmacy v. Virginia Citizens Consumer Council, Inc., 425 U.S. 748 (1976), the Supreme Court had overturned, as violations of the first (and fourteenth) amendments, prohibitions in Virginia legislation against advertising the prices of prescription drugs, legislation justified by the state as a means of ensuring the professionalism of pharmacists. In so doing, the Court essentially overruled prior cases that had seemingly excluded "purely commercial advertising" altogether from the realm of constitutionally protected speech. Breard v. Alexandria, 341 U.S. 622 (1951); Valentine v. Chrestensen, 316 U.S. 52, 54–55 (1942). Noting that the plaintiffs challenging the Virginia statute represented consumers rather than would-be advertisers, the Court underscored earlier decisions in which it had recognized that the first amendment protects not only the right to speak freely but also the right to receive information that others wish to provide. Carrying that notion over to the commercial context, it observed that a "particular consumer's interest in the free flow of commercial information * * * may be as keen, if not keener by far, than his interest in the day's most urgent political debate." 425 U.S. at 763. Although noting that certain "entirely 'commercial' " ads "may be of general public interest" (id. at 764), the Court's opinion (by Justice Blackmun) rejected the idea of drawing a

> line between publicly "interesting" or "important" commercial advertising and the opposite kind * * *. Advertising, however tasteless and excessive it sometimes may seem, is nonetheless dissemination of information as to who is producing and selling what product, for what reason, and at what price. So long as we preserve a predominantly free enterprise economy, the allocation of our resources in large measure will be made through numerous private economic decisions. It is a matter of public interest that those decisions, in the aggregate, be intelligent and well informed. To this end, the free flow of commercial information is indispensable.

Id. at 765.

In answer to the state's claim that its policy against price advertising protected consumers in various ways, the Court observed (id. at 768) that "the State's protectiveness of its citizens rests in large measure on the advantages of their being kept in ignorance" and stated (id. at 770):

> There is, of course, an alternative to this highly paternalistic approach. That alternative is to assume that this information is not in itself harmful, that people will perceive their own best interests if only they are well enough informed, and that the best means to that end is to open the channels of communication rather than to close them. If they are truly open, nothing prevents the "professional" pharmacist from marketing his own assertedly superior product, and contrasting it with that of the low-cost, high-volume prescription drug retailer. But the choice among these alternative approaches is not ours to make or the Virginia General Assembly's. It is precisely this kind of choice, between the dangers of suppressing information, and the dangers of its misuse if it is freely available, that the First Amendment makes for us.

The Court took a similar position in invoking the first amendment to reject, 5–4, overbroad state restrictions on advertising by lawyers in Bates v. State Bar of Arizona, 433 U.S. 350, 375 (1977) ("the preferred remedy is more disclosure, rather than less"). In *Bates*, as in *Virginia Pharmacy*, a majority of the Court (again speaking through Justice Blackmun) was ultimately unimpressed by the state's policy concerns on behalf of sweeping restrictions—e.g., the adverse effects of advertising on the professionalism of lawyers, the allegedly inherent misleading nature of attorney advertising, and the potentially adverse effects of price advertising on the quality of legal services. Justice Powell's dissent endorsed the traditional view of the legal profession that strict regulation of advertising, together with the system of professional self-regulation of which it was an integral part, was in the overall public interest.

Both in *Virginia Pharmacy* and in *Bates*, the Supreme Court made clear that, while commercial speech enjoys some constitutional protection, it is also subject to state regulation with respect to such things as time, place, manner and truthfulness. Some further issues with respect to the regulation of commercial speech are addressed in the text following the *Friedman* case, infra.

Is the Court's willingness to scrutinize and invalidate state regulation under the first amendment consistent with the judicial philosophy apparent in *Snyder's Drug Stores*? Are not the interests seeking protection essentially the same in the two cases? (Would it have made any difference in *Snyder's Drug Stores* if, as in *Virginia Pharmacy*, the challenge to the statute had been mounted by a consumer group?) Was not the Court's previous refusal to protect commercial speech a manifestation of the identical impulse that led to the demise of substantive due process in the economic realm?

5. *The Future of Federal Judicial Oversight of Economic Regulation by the States*. At one point, it appeared that the Supreme Court was moving in the direction of closer scrutiny of state regulatory legislation—at least, if it could find a legal basis for such scrutiny other than substantive due process (such as the first amendment). See also Gibson v. Berryhill, 411 U.S. 564 (1973) (procedural due process denied by regulatory scheme controlled by "professional" optometrists when invoked against optometrists employed by corporations); California Retail Liquor Dealers Ass'n v. Midcal Aluminum, Inc., 445 U.S. 97 (1980) (federal antitrust law, requiring competition, held to preempt the field against certain anticompetitive state legislation); Community Communications Co., Inc. v. Boulder, 455 U.S. 40 (1982) (application of federal antitrust law, requiring competition, to anticompetitive actions of local government). The Supreme Court of the 1990s, however, seems unlikely to take an active role vis-a-vis state economic regulation.

Regulating Commercial Speech—Use of Trade Names

Friedman v. Rogers

Supreme Court of the United States, 1979.
440 U.S. 1, 99 S.Ct. 887, 59 L.Ed.2d 100.

■ MR. JUSTICE POWELL delivered the opinion of the Court.

* * *

I

The Texas Legislature approved the Texas Optometry Act (Act) in 1969, repealing an earlier law governing the practice of optometry in the State. Section 2.01 of the Act establishes the Texas Optometry Board (Board) and § 2.02 prescribes the qualifications for Board members. The Board is responsible for the administration of the Act, and has the authority to grant, renew, suspend, and revoke licenses to practice optometry in the State. The Act imposes numerous regulations on the practice of optometry, and on several aspects of the business of optometry.[5] Many of the Act's business regulations are contained in § 5.13, which restricts fee splitting by optometrists and forbids an optometrist to allow his name to be associated with any optometrical office unless he is present and practicing there at least half of the hours that the office is open or half of the hours that he practices, whichever is less. Section 5.13(d), at issue here, prohibits the practice of optometry under an assumed name, trade name, or corporate name.

F

The dispute in this case grows out of the schism between "professional" and "commercial" optometrists in Texas. Although all optometrists in the State must meet the same licensing requirements and are subject to the same laws regulating their practices, they have divided themselves informally into two groups according to their divergent approaches to the practice of optometry.[7] Rogers, an advocate of the commercial practice of optometry and a member of the Board, commenced this action by filing a suit against the other five members of the Board. He sought declaratory and injunctive relief from the enforcement of * * * § 5.13(d) of the Act, prohibiting the practice of optometry under a trade name.

* * *

II

PH

In holding that § 5.13(d) infringes First Amendment rights, the District Court relied primarily on this Court's decisions in [*Bates* and *Virginia Pharmacy Board*]. A trade name is a form of advertising, it concluded, because after the name has been used for some time, people "identify the name with a certain quality of service and goods." It found specifically "that the Texas State Optical [TSO] name has come to communicate to the consuming public information as to certain standards of price and quality, and availability of particular routine services," and rejected the argument that the TSO name misleads the public as to the identity of the optometrists with whom it deals. Balancing the constitutional interests in the commercial speech in question against the State's interest in regulating it, the District Court held that the prohibition of the use of trade names by

5. An optometrist must display his license in his office; when practicing away from his office, he must include his name and license number on a receipt given to each patient. § 5.01. Fraudulent, deceitful, and misleading advertising is proscribed by § 5.09, though the ban placed by that section on truthful price advertising has been nullified by the decision of the District Court in this case[, a holding that was not appealed]. An optometrist is forbidden to advertise in his office windows or reception rooms, and to use certain types of signs to advertise his practice. § 5.11. The practice of optometry on the premises of mercantile establishments is regulated, § 5.14, and relationships between optometrists and opticians are restricted. § 5.15.

7. The dissenting opinion minimizes the professional character of an optometrist's services, stating that his duties are "confined ... to measuring the powers of vision of the eye and fitting corrective lenses." But it is clear from the requirements for licensing imposed by the Act that the Texas Legislature considers optometry to be a professional service requiring in the public interest a high level of knowledge and training.

§ 5.13(d) is an unconstitutional restriction of the "free flow of commercial information."

* * *

Once a trade name has been in use for some time, it may serve to identify an optometrical practice and also to convey information about the type, price, and quality of services offered for sale in that practice. In each role, the trade name is used as part of a proposal of a commercial transaction. Like the pharmacist who desired to advertise his prices in *Virginia Pharmacy,* the optometrist who uses a trade name "does not wish to editorialize on any subject, cultural, philosophical, or political. He does not wish to report any particularly newsworthy fact, or to make generalized observations even about commercial matters." His purpose is strictly business. The use of trade names in connection with optometrical practice, then, is a form of commercial speech and nothing more.

A trade name is, however, a significantly different form of commercial speech from that considered in *Virginia Pharmacy* and *Bates.* In those cases, the State had proscribed advertising by pharmacists and lawyers that contained statements about the products or services offered and their prices. These statements were self-contained and self-explanatory. Here, we are concerned with a form of commercial speech that has no intrinsic meaning. A trade name conveys no information about the price and nature of the services offered by an optometrist until it acquires meaning over a period of time by associations formed in the minds of the public between the name and some standard of price or quality. Because these ill-defined associations of trade names with price and quality information can be manipulated by the users of trade names, there is a significant possibility that trade names will be used to mislead the public.

[The Court discussed several possibilities for deception involving the use of trade names.]

The concerns of the Texas Legislature about the deceptive and misleading uses of optometrical trade names were not speculative or hypothetical, but were based on experience in Texas with which the legislature was familiar when in 1969 it enacted § 5.13(d). * * * In a decision upholding the validity of the Rule, the Texas Supreme Court reviewed some of the practices that had prompted its adoption. Texas State Bd. of Examiners in Optometry v. Carp, 412 S.W.2d 307, appeal dismissed and cert. denied, 389 U.S. 52 (1967). One of the plaintiffs in that case, Carp, operated 71 optometrical offices in Texas under at least 10 different trade names. From time to time, he changed the trade names of various shops, though the licensed optometrists practicing in each shop remained the same. He purchased the practices of other optometrists and continued to practice under their names, even though they were no longer associated with the practice. In several instances, Carp used different trade names on offices located in close proximity to one another and selling the same optical goods and services. The offices were under common management, and had a common staff of optometrists, but the use of different trade names facilitated advertising that gave the impression of competition among the offices.

The Texas court found that Carp used trade names to give a misleading impression of competitive ownership and management of his shops. It also found that Rogers, a party to this suit and a plaintiff in *Carp,* had used a trade name to convey the impression of standardized optometrical care. All 82 of his shops went under the trade name "Texas State Optical" or "TSO," and he advertised "scientific TSO eye examination[s]" available in every shop. The TSO advertising was calculated as well, the court found, to give "the impression that [Rogers or one of his brothers] is present at a particular office. Actually they have neither been inside nor seen some of their eighty-two offices distributed generally over Texas." Even if Rogers' use and advertising of the trade name were not in fact misleading, they were an example of the use of a trade name to facilitate the large-scale commercialization which enhances the opportunity for misleading practices.[13]

It is clear that the State's interest in protecting the public from the deceptive and misleading use of optometrical trade names is substantial and well demonstrated. We are convinced that § 5.13(d) is a constitutionally permissible state regulation in furtherance of this interest. We emphasize, in so holding, that the restriction on the use of trade names has only the most incidental effect on the content of the commercial speech of Texas optometrists. As noted above, a trade name conveys information only because of the associations that grow up over time between the name and a certain level of price and quality of service. Moreover, the information associated with a trade name is largely factual, concerning the kind and price of the services offered for sale. Since the Act does not prohibit or limit the type of informational advertising held to be protected in *Virginia Pharmacy* and *Bates,* the factual information associated with trade names may be communicated freely and explicitly to the public. An optometrist may advertise the type of service he offers, the prices he charges, and whether he practices as a partner, associate, or employee with other optometrists. Rather than stifling commercial speech, § 5.13(d) ensures that information regarding optometrical services will be communicated more fully and accurately to consumers than it had been in the past when optometrists were allowed to convey the information through unstated and ambiguous associations with a trade name. In sum, Texas has done no more than require that commercial information about optometrical services "appear in such a form . . . as [is] necessary to prevent its being deceptive." Virginia Pharmacy, 425 U.S., at 772 n. 24.

13. * * * Rogers' testimony showed that the "Texas State Optical" name was used by offices wholly owned by him, partly owned by him, and by offices in which he had no ownership interest. The dissenting opinion states that the "Rogers organization is able to offer and enforce a degree of uniformity in care at all its offices. . . ." This was not Rogers' testimony. He stated that he exercised "no control whatsoever" over "office policy routines" in those TSO offices in which he owned no interest. It appears from Rogers' testimony that his primary business relationship with such offices was their participation in the TSO advertising and their purchase of materials and equipment from his supply house.

* * * The case is remanded with instructions to dissolve the injunction against the enforcement of § 5.13(d).

■ MR. JUSTICE BLACKMUN, with whom MR. JUSTICE MARSHALL joins, concurring in part and dissenting in part.

* * *

I do not agree with the Court's holding that the Texas Optometry Act's § 5.13(d), which bans the use of a trade name "in connection with" the practice of optometry in the State, is constitutional. In my view, the Court's restricted analysis of the nature of a trade name overestimates the potential for deception and underestimates the harmful impact of the broad sweep of § 5.13(d). * * *

II

The Court characterizes as "substantial and well demonstrated" the state interests offered to support suppression of this valuable information. It first contends that because a trade name has no intrinsic meaning, it can cause deception. The name may remain unchanged, it is pointed out, despite a change in the identities of the optometrists who employ it. Secondly, the Court says that the State may ban trade names to discourage commercial optometry while stopping short of prohibiting it altogether. Neither of these interests justifies a statute so sweeping as § 5.13(d).

A

Because a trade name has no intrinsic meaning, it cannot by itself be deceptive. A trade name will deceive only if it is used in a misleading context. The hypotheticals posed by the Court, and the facts of *Texas State Bd. of Examiners in Optometry v. Carp,* concern the use of optometric trade names in situations where the name of the practicing optometrist is kept concealed. The deception lies not in the use of the trade name, but in the failure simultaneously to disclose the name of the optometrist. In the present case, counsel for the State conceded at oral argument that § 5.13(d) prohibits the use of a trade name even when the optometrist's name is also prominently displayed. It thus prohibits wholly truthful speech that is entirely removed from the justification on which the Court most heavily relies to support the statute.

* * * By disclosing his individual name along with his trade name, the commercial optometrist acts in the spirit of our First Amendment jurisprudence, where traditionally "the remedy to be applied is more speech, not enforced silence." Whitney v. California, 274 U.S. 357, 377 (1927) (Brandeis, J., concurring). The ultimate irony of the Court's analysis is that § 5.13(d), because of its broad sweep, actually encourages deception. That statute, in conjunction with § 5.13(e), prevents the consumer from ever discovering that Rogers controls and in some cases employs the optometrist upon whom the patient has relied for care. In effect, the statute conceals the fact that a particular practitioner is engaged in commercial rather than professional optometry, and so deprives consumers of information that may well be thought relevant to the selection of an optometrist.

B

The second justification proffered by the Court is that a State, while not prohibiting commercial optometry practice altogether, could ban the use of trade names in order to discourage commercial optometry. * * * [T]his justification ignores the substantial First Amendment interest in the dissemination of truthful information about legally available professional services. It is not without significance that most of the persons influenced by a trade name are those who, by experience or by reputation, know the quality of service for which the trade name stands. The determination that banning trade names would discourage commercial optometry, therefore, necessarily relies on an assumption that persons previously served thought that the trade-name practitioner had performed an acceptable service. If the prior experience had been bad, the consumer would want to know the trade name in order to avoid those who practice under it. The first and second stated purposes of § 5.13 are "to protect the public in the practice of optometry," and to "better enable members of the public to fix professional responsibility." These purposes are ill-served by a statute that hinders consumers from enlisting the services of an organization they have found helpful, and so, in effect, prevents consumers from protecting themselves.

The Court repeatedly has rejected the "highly paternalistic" approach implicit in this justification. There is nothing about the nature of an optometrist's services that justifies adopting an approach of this kind here. An optometrist's duties are confined by the statute, § 1.02(1), to measuring the powers of vision of the eye and fitting corrective lenses. The optometrist does not treat disease. His service is highly standardized. Each step is controlled by statute. § 5.12. Many of his functions are so mechanical that they can be duplicated by machines that would enable a patient to measure his own vision. Patients participate in the refraction process, and they frequently can easily assess the quality of service rendered. The cost per visit is low enough—$15 to $35—that comparison shopping is sometimes possible. Because more than half the Nation's population uses eyeglasses, reputation information is readily available. In this context, the First Amendment forbids the choice which Texas has made to shut off entirely the flow of commercial information to consumers who, we have assumed, "will perceive their own best interests if only they are well enough informed." Virginia Pharmacy Board, 425 U.S., at 770.

Because § 5.13(d) absolutely prohibits the dissemination of truthful information about Rogers' wholly legal commercial conduct to consumers and a public who have a strong interest in hearing it, I would affirm the District Court's judgment holding that § 5.13(d) is unconstitutional.

NOTES AND QUESTIONS ON COMMERCIAL SPEECH

1. *How Much Protection for "Commercial" Speech?* In In re R.M.J., 455 U.S. 191 (1982), the Supreme Court unanimously reversed disciplinary action taken against a lawyer by the Missouri courts. Justice Powell's opinion for the Court stated,

> Commercial speech doctrine, in the context of advertising for professional services, may be summarized generally as follows: Truthful advertising related to lawful activities is entitled to the protections of the First Amendment. But when the particular content or method of the advertising suggests that it is inherently misleading or when experience has proven that in fact such advertising is subject to abuse, the states may impose appropriate restrictions. Misleading advertising may be prohibited entirely. But the states may not place an absolute prohibition on certain types of potentially misleading information, e.g., a listing of areas of practice, if the information also may be presented in a way that is not deceptive. Thus, the Court in *Bates* suggested that the remedy in the first instance is not necessarily a prohibition but preferably a requirement of disclaimers or explanation. Although the potential for deception and confusion is particularly strong in the context of advertising professional services, restrictions upon such advertising may be no broader than reasonably necessary to prevent the deception.
>
> Even when a communication is not misleading, the state retains some authority to regulate. But the state must assert a substantial interest and the interference with speech must be in proportion to the interest served.[15] Restrictions must be narrowly drawn, and the state lawfully may regulate only to the extent regulation furthers the state's substantial interest. Thus, in *Bates*, the Court found that the potentially adverse effect of advertising on professionalism and the quality of legal services was not sufficiently related to a substantial state interest to justify so great an interference with speech.

The rule violations charged against the appellant in *R.M.J.* included "listing the areas of his practice in language or in terms other than that provided by the rule, * * *, listing the courts and States in which he had been admitted to practice, and mailing announcement cards to persons other than lawyers, clients, former clients, personal friends, and relatives." Id. at 204. The Court had the greatest problem with appellant's listing, in large boldface type, that "he was a member of the bar of the Supreme

15. See Central Hudson Gas & Electric Corp. v. Public Service Comm'n, 447 U.S. [557, 566 (1980)]:

> "In commercial speech cases, then, a four-part analysis has developed. At the outset, we must determine whether the expression is protected by the First Amendment. For commercial speech to come within that provision, it at least must concern lawful activity and not be misleading. Next, we ask whether the asserted governmental interest is substantial. If both inquiries yield positive answers, we must determine whether the regulation directly advances the governmental interest asserted, and whether it is not more extensive than is necessary to serve that interest."

As the discussion in the text above indicates, the *Central Hudson* formulation must be applied to advertising for professional services with the understanding that the special characteristics of such services afford opportunities to mislead and confuse that are not present when standardized products or services are offered to the public.

Court of the United States." Id. at 205. Although the Court thought that this claim reflected "bad taste" and was of dubious informational value (in view of the Court's own minimal standards for admission to practice before it), it reversed the Missouri court because this claim, like the others challenged, had not been expressly found misleading.

What restrictions should courts allow states to impose on advertising by health care professionals? The court in Baker v. Registered Dentists of Oklahoma, 543 F.Supp. 1177, 1180–82 (W.D.Okl.1982), examining Oklahoma's prohibitions on advertising by dentists, was impressed that radio and TV ads might reach that half of the state's population that was not receiving dental care and concluded that "while the special problems inherent in radio and television advertising may warrant carefully delineated guidelines, an absolute bar is not permissible." The court believed, however, that "the misleading potential of these media could be reduced by prohibiting celebrity or personality endorsements[, which] might tend to subconsciously persuade listeners or viewers that the dentist advertising through the popular personality or recognizable voice was a better qualified dentist." As to attempts by the state to regulate the appearance of display ads, the court asked "what good are advertisements that do *not* catch the public's eye?" The court also invalidated a blanket prohibition on the use of billboards and off-site signs. The Illinois Supreme Court has upheld restrictions on telemarketing by an ophthalmologist, who used it to offer Medicare beneficiaries free eye exams and transportation to his clinic. Desnick v. Department of Professional Regulation, 665 N.E.2d 1346 (Ill.1996), cert. denied, 117 S.Ct. 390 (1996).

2. *Identifying Commercial Speech.* What, in your view, should be the crucial element in determining which speech is "commercial" and thus subject to some state regulation? In Bolger v. Youngs Drug Prods. Corp., 463 U.S. 60, 66–67 (1983), the Court listed three factors: whether the speech in question is advertising, whether it refers to a specific product, and whether it is economically motivated. Do these factors adequately isolate all the forms of speech that require not only some protection in the interest of the dissemination of information and ideas but also some policing in the interest of consumers? In other words, are there other kinds of speech that might be subject to some regulation under principles similar to those that warrant granting only limited protection to advertising? Consider, for example, the various kinds of "speech" in which a professional association might engage. Are there constitutional limitations on the power of government to regulate—under antitrust law, for example—professional codes of ethics, conversations at professional meetings, and resolutions adopted by medical societies that induce professionals to act in parallel fashion? Could some such speech be regulated as commercial speech?

3. The creation of limited protection for commercial speech also created considerable legal uncertainty, requiring the Supreme Court to revisit the area at least nine times between *Virginia Pharmacy* and 1985. Noting the confusion produced by the doctrine, one commentator wondered "whether the gain, if any, is worth the cost." Emerson, First Amendment Doctrine and the Burger Court, 68 Calif.L.Rev. 422, 460 (1980). What do you think? The area remains an active one today. See, e.g., Florida Bar v. Went For It, Inc., 515 U.S. 618 (1995) (upholding ban on direct-mail solicitation of accident victims); Ibanez v. Florida Dep't of Business and Professional Regulation, 512 U.S. 136 (1994) (allowing lawyer/CPA to advertise certification as "Certified Financial Planner"). In 44 Liquormart, Inc. v. Rhode Island, 517 U.S. 484 (1996), the Supreme Court revisited the foundations of the commercial speech doctrine, introducing new complexity as the justices split in several directions in analyzing the doctrine's application to—and in striking down—a restriction on price advertising of alcoholic beverages.

NOTES AND QUESTIONS ON ADVERTISING AND INFORMATION PROBLEMS IN HEALTH CARE MARKETS

1. Why might physicians and other health care providers advertise? Would their purposes in advertising differ from the purposes of other businesses? What kinds of health care and physician services are most likely to be extensively advertised? Among physicians, plastic surgeons are among the most aggressive advertisers. Why?

What are the likely effects of advertising by health professionals? Is such advertising desirable? Are the arguments against physician advertising similar to or different from the arguments that might be made against attorney advertising? What are the arguments and how might they be answered? See generally the *Bates* case.

2. *Advertising Quality.* A California hospital advertised as follows in a national newspaper: "We Mend Broken Hearts: Very Successfully. Eisenhower Medical Center has the lowest * * * mortality rates for heart bypass surgery in U.S. hospitals." The ad (reproduced in Hosps., Mar 5, 1987, at 36) set forth data compiled and publicized by HCFA showing only one death in 161 cases and comparative results in other hospitals. Health care professionals would argue that such data are not a reliable guide to quality because the samples were small and because results depend on severity, comorbidity, etc. Should such advertising be permitted (by the FTC or other agency)? Should physicians be allowed to make comparable claims with comparable support? The FTC has successfully challenged advertising containing unsubstantiated claims of cure rates, treatment effectiveness, etc., and patient testimonials lacking disclaimers that the patient's experience may not be typical. E.g., Cancer Treatment Centers of America, Inc., 61 Fed. Reg. 13197 (Mar. 26, 1996) (proposed consent order). See generally J. Calfee, Fear of Persuasion: A New Perspective on Advertising and Regulation (1997) (arguing that advertising improves consumer welfare more than is generally appreciated and is generally self-correcting); Schramm, Constitutional Protection of Commercial Speech under the Central Hudson Test as Applied to Health Claims, 51 Food & Drug L.J. 323 (1996).

3. *Search Information, Experience Goods, etc.* How restrictive should the regulation of advertising content be? Consider the following:

> [A]lthough new antitrust and constitutional protections for professional advertising now exist, they are unlikely to prevent private or public regulators from denying consumers a great deal of important but not readily verifiable information. Instead, the emphasis will be on permitting disclosure of basic, objective facts, such as price, location, and hours of operation—what economists have called "search" information. Professional advertising that features quality claims, asserts opinions, or contains arguable half truths is likely to be rare.
>
> The value of advertising search information to consumers depends upon the extent to which products or services can be adequately described thereby. Almost all necessary information about a familiar or standardized product or service, such as the services of a notary public, can be conveyed as search information, whereas other things, such as a restaurant, cannot be described fully in those terms alone. Although many professional services defy adequate description in terms classifiable as search information, there are some professional fields where search information, particularly price information, can be very important. For example, in the field of optometry, state laws restricting price advertising have been shown to be costly to consumers,[45] and professional claims that advertising significantly impairs quality have been found to be essentially frivolous.[46] Fortunately, even though it has long been an important goal of all freestanding professions to curb their members' advertising, recent antitrust and first amendment developments have eliminated the most restrictive private and public inhibitions on the advertising of search information by professionals.
>
> Because many professional services—notably legal and medical services—are extremely difficult to evaluate, it would probably be unrealistic to expect consumers of such services to benefit much from advertising that attempts to do more than convey search information.

45. Benham, The Effect of Advertising on the Price of Eyeglasses, 15 J.L. & Econ. 337 (1972); FTC, Staff Report, Advertising Ophthalmic Goods and Services (1976). * * *

46. FTC, supra note 45. Quality concerns should not be dismissed out of hand; if the consumer can evaluate price information but cannot make judgments concerning quality, less scrupulous providers might perceive opportunities to attract patients without loss of income by imperceptibly reducing quality as well as lowering price, thereby forcing others to do so as well. On the other hand, it is frequently alleged that some risk-averse consumers of medical care rely on price as an indication of quality, suggesting problems with the foregoing scenario and the conclusion that price competition in professional fields leads to suboptimal quality. In addition, in one study more information was found to influence consumers to buy higher quality consumer goods. Sproles, et al., Informational Inputs as Influences on Efficient Consumer Decisionmaking, 12 J. Consumer Aff. 88 (1978), discussed in Wilde & Schwartz, Intervening in Markets on the Basis of Imperfect Information: A Legal and Economic Analysis, 127 U.Pa.L.Rev. 630, 675 n. 100 (1979). Although this was not a health care study, it suggests that increasing the supply of information should help consumers address quality/price trade-offs more effectively even in health care, where consumer ignorance can be reduced even though it cannot be eliminated.

> It has been convincingly argued that where consumer goods can be evaluated only on the basis of experience, heavy advertising, however uninformative, is itself a reliable indicator of a business's ability to satisfy its customers.[49] Nevertheless, it seems unlikely that such "image" advertising, arguably valuable to consumers in purchasing so-called experience goods, would serve consumers well in choosing an individual health care provider. The problem lies in the difficulty that consumers have in evaluating many health care services even after extensive experience. Although consumers can gather, pool, and share opinions and results of their experiences with hard-to-evaluate services, such reputation information is only an imperfect protection against the harm that might be caused by certain kinds of advertising.
>
> For these reasons, a policy of limiting professional advertising of complex services to disclosure of verifiable facts may not be unduly harmful to the competitive process. * * * Even so, regulatory oversight of professional advertising, * * * should be strictly limited * * * to preventing overt misrepresentations and advertisements calculated to deceive the proverbial reasonable man. As to other questionable advertising, consumer skepticism should serve as an important protection against acceptance of excessive and unsubstantiated claims, and professional organizations, concerned about competitive inroads, are always free to employ counteradvertising containing warnings and useful substantive information. The main reason for rejecting regulation that chills the making of controversial claims should be clear: Without a dynamic marketplace of ideas, consumers will continue to be uninformed about health care issues that fundamentally concern them and thus be denied access to alternatives that might better satisfy their needs and preferences.

Havighurst & King, Private Credentialing of Health Care Personnel: An Antitrust Perspective (pt. 2), 9 Am.J.L. & Med. 263, 278–80 (1983).

4. What is your view of the Supreme Court's ruling in *Friedman v. Rogers*? An article by Pauly & Satterthwaite, The Pricing of Physicians' Services: A Test of the Role of Consumer Information, 12 Bell J.Econ. 488 (1981), demonstrates that, contrary to simple theory, physicians tend to have more market power in markets where they are numerous than where they are few, because of the consumer's greater difficulty in getting comparative information. For example, in a town with three physicians, everyone is likely to know a great deal about the relative merits of each; in a city with 1000 physicians, consumer ignorance makes competition less effective. Can you see why, in the past, the medical profession vigorously opposed group medical practice? How do these observations bear on the desirability of quality claims in advertising and the issue in *Friedman*?

49. See Nelson, Advertising as Information Once More, in Issues in Advertising: The Economics of Persuasion (D. Tureck ed. 1978); Nelson, Advertising as Information, 82 J.Pol.Econ. 729 (1974).

Implied Prohibitions Against Corporate Practice, Referral Agencies, etc.

Berlin v. Sarah Bush Lincoln Health Center

Supreme Court of Illinois, 1997.
688 N.E.2d 106.

■ JUSTICE NICKELS delivered the opinion of the court:

Plaintiff, Richard Berlin, Jr., M.D., filed a complaint for declaratory judgment and a motion for summary judgment seeking to have a restrictive covenant contained in an employment agreement with defendant, Sara Bush Lincoln Health Center (the Health Center), declared unenforceable. The circuit court of Coles County, finding the entire employment agreement unenforceable, granted summary judgment in favor of Dr. Berlin. The circuit court reasoned that the Health Center, as a nonprofit corporation employing a physician, was practicing medicine in violation of the prohibition on the corporate practice of medicine. A divided appellate court affirmed, and this court granted the Health Center's petition for leave to appeal.

The central issue involved in this appeal is whether the "corporate practice doctrine" prohibits corporations which are licensed hospitals from employing physicians to provide medical services. We find the doctrine inapplicable to licensed hospitals and accordingly reverse.

[In 1992 Dr. Berlin and the Health Center, a licensed hospital, "entered into a written agreement whereby the Health Center employed Dr. Berlin to practice medicine for the hospital for five years." The agreement was terminable on six months' notice and contained a restrictive covenant prohibiting Dr. Berlin from competing with the hospital by providing health services within a 50–mile radius of the Health Center for two years after the end of the employment agreement. 1n 1994, Dr. Berlin resigned his position with the Health Center and immediately began working for the Carle Clinic at a facility one mile from the Health Center. The Health Center sought a preliminary injunction to enforce the restrictive covenant, but the lower courts ruled the entire employment agreement unenforceable on the ground that the Health Center, by hiring Dr. Berlin to practice medicine as its employee, violated the prohibition against corporations practicing medicine.]

This court granted the Health Center's petition for leave to appeal. We granted the County of Cook, the Illinois Hospital and Healthsystems Association, the Metropolitan Chicago Healthcare Council, the American Hospital Association, and OSF HealthCare System leave to file amicus curiae briefs in support of the Health Center. We granted leave to the American Medical Association, the Illinois State Medical Society, the Illinois State Dental Society, and several regional medical societies to file amicus curiae briefs in support of Dr. Berlin's position.

Hospital Employment of Physicians

The Health Center and its supporting amicus curiae contend that no judicial determination exists which prohibits hospitals from employing physicians. In support of this contention, the Health Center argues that this court has acknowledged the legitimacy of such employment practices in past decisions. In the alternative, the Health Center contends that if a judicial prohibition on hospital employment of physicians does exist, it should be overruled. In support of this contention, the Health Center argues that the public policies behind such a prohibition are inapplicable to licensed hospitals, particularly nonprofit hospitals.

The Health Center also contends that there is no statutory prohibition on the corporate employment of physicians. The Health Center notes that no statute has ever expressly stated that physicians cannot be employed by corporations. To the contrary, the Health Center argues that other legislative actions recognize that hospitals can indeed employ physicians.

Dr. Berlin and supporting amicus curiae contend that this court, in People ex rel. Kerner v. United Medical Service, Inc., 362 Ill. 442, 200 N.E. 157 (1936), adopted the corporate practice of medicine doctrine, which prohibits corporations from employing physicians. Dr. Berlin concludes that the Health Center, as a nonprofit corporation, is prohibited by the *Kerner* rule from entering into employment agreements with physicians.

Dr. Berlin also disputes the Health Center's contention that public policy supports creating an exception to the *Kerner* rule for hospitals. He argues that, because no legislative enactment subsequent to the *Kerner* case expressly grants hospitals the authority to employ physicians, the legislature has ratified the corporate practice of medicine doctrine as the public policy of Illinois. At this point, a review of the corporate practice of medicine doctrine is appropriate.

Corporate Practice of Medicine Doctrine

The corporate practice of medicine doctrine prohibits corporations from providing professional medical services. Although a few states have codified the doctrine, the prohibition is primarily inferred from state medical licensure acts, which regulate the profession of medicine and forbid its practice by unlicensed individuals. See A. Rosoff, The Business of Medicine: Problems with the Corporate Practice Doctrine, 17 Cumb. L.Rev. 485, 490 (1987). The rationale behind the doctrine is that a corporation cannot be licensed to practice medicine because only a human being can sustain the education, training, and character-screening which are prerequisites to receiving a professional license. Since a corporation cannot receive a medical license, it follows that a corporation cannot legally practice the profession.

The rationale of the doctrine concludes that the employment of physicians by corporations is illegal because the acts of the physicians are attributable to the corporate employer, which cannot obtain a medical license. See M. Hall, Institutional Control of Physician Behavior: Legal

Barriers to Health Care Cost Containment, 137 U. Pa. L.Rev. 431, 509–10 (1988). The prohibition on the corporate employment of physicians is invariably supported by several public policy arguments which espouse the dangers of lay control over professional judgment, the division of the physician's loyalty between his patient and his profitmaking employer, and the commercialization of the profession. See A. Willcox, Hospitals and the Corporate Practice of Medicine, 45 Cornell L.Q. 432, 442–43 (1960).

Application of Doctrine in Illinois

This court first encountered the corporate practice doctrine in Dr. Allison, Dentist, Inc. v. Allison, 360 Ill. 638, 196 N.E. 799 (1935). In *Allison*, the plaintiff corporation owned and operated a dental practice. When defendant, a dentist formerly employed by plaintiff, opened a dental office across the street from plaintiff's location, plaintiff brought an action to enforce a restrictive covenant contained in defendant's employment contract. Defendant's motion to dismiss the action was granted on the grounds that plaintiff was practicing dentistry in violation of section 18a of the Dental Practice Act of 1933 (Ill.Rev.Stat.1935, ch. 91, par. 88(1)). In affirming the judgment of the lower court, this court stated:

> "To practice a profession requires something more than the financial ability to hire competent persons to do the actual work. It can be done only by a duly qualified human being, and to qualify something more than mere knowledge or skill is essential. The qualifications include personal characteristics, such as honesty, guided by an upright conscience and a sense of loyalty to clients or patients, even to the extent of sacrificing pecuniary profit, if necessary. These requirements are spoken of generically as that good moral character which is a prerequisite to the licensing of any professional man. No corporation can qualify." *Allison*, 360 Ill. at 641–42, 196 N.E. 799.

* * *

The year following the *Allison* [decision], this court addressed the corporate practice doctrine as it pertained to medicine. [The 1936 *Kerner* case] involved a corporation which operated a low-cost health clinic in which all medical services were rendered by duly-licensed physicians. The State brought a quo warranto action against the corporation, alleging it was illegally engaged in the practice of medicine in violation of the Medical Practice Act. The lower court found the corporation guilty and rendered the judgment of ouster against it.

In affirming, this court rejected defendant's contention that the practice of medicine does not encompass the corporate ownership of a health clinic where treatment is rendered solely by licensed physician employees. * * * The court stated that "[t]he legislative intent manifest from a view of the entire [Medical Practice Act] is that only individuals may obtain a license thereunder. No corporation can meet the requirements of the statute essential to the issuance of a license."

Prior to the instant action, apparently no Illinois court has applied the corporate practice of medicine rule set out in *[Kerner]* or specifically addressed the issue of whether licensed hospitals are prohibited from employing physicians. We therefore look to other jurisdictions with reference to the application of the corporate practice of medicine doctrine to hospitals.

Applicability of Doctrine to Hospitals in Other Jurisdictions

Although the corporate practice of medicine doctrine has long been recognized by a number of jurisdictions, the important role hospitals serve in the health care field has also been increasingly recognized. Accordingly, numerous jurisdictions have recognized either judicial or statutory exceptions to the corporate practice of medicine doctrine which allow hospitals to employ physicians and other health care professionals. See, e.g., Cal. Bus. & Prof.Code § 2400 (West 1990) (exception for charitable hospitals); Colo. Rev.Stat. § 25–3–103.7(2) (West Supp.1997) (hospitals may employ physicians); Rush v. City of St. Petersburg, 205 So.2d 11 (Fla.App.1967); St. Francis Regional Medical Center, Inc. v. Weiss, 254 Kan. 728, 869 P.2d 606 (1994); People v. John H. Woodbury Dermatological Institute, 192 N.Y. 454, 85 N.E. 697 (1908). A review of this authority reveals that there are primarily three approaches utilized in determining that the corporate practice of medicine doctrine is inapplicable to hospitals.

First, some states refused to adopt the corporate practice of medicine doctrine altogether when initially interpreting their respective medical practice act. These states generally determined that a hospital corporation which employs a physician is not practicing medicine, but rather is merely making medical treatment available. See, e.g., State ex rel. Sager v. Lewin, 128 Mo.App. 149, 155, 106 S.W. 581, 583 (1907) ("[H]ospitals are maintained by private corporations, incorporated for the purpose of furnishing medical and surgical treatment to the sick and wounded. These corporations do not practice medicine but they receive patients and employ physicians and surgeons to give them treatment.") * * *.

Under the second approach, the courts of some jurisdictions determined that the corporate practice doctrine is inapplicable to nonprofit hospitals and health associations. These courts reasoned that the public policy arguments supporting the corporate practice doctrine do not apply to physicians employed by charitable institutions. See, e.g., Group Health Ass'n v. Moor, 24 F.Supp. 445, 446 (D.D.C.1938) (actions of nonprofit association which contracts with licensed physicians to provide medical treatment to its members in no way commercializes medicine and is not the practice of medicine), aff'd, 107 F.2d 239 (D.C.Cir.1939); * * *.

In the third approach, the courts of several states have determined that the corporate practice doctrine is not applicable to hospitals which employ physicians because hospitals are authorized by other laws to provide medical treatment to patients. See, e.g., *St. Francis Regional Medical Center, Inc. v. Weiss*, 254 Kan. 728, 869 P.2d 606; * * *.

We find the rationale of the latter two approaches persuasive. We decline to apply the corporate practice of medicine doctrine to licensed hospitals. The instant cause is distinguishable from *Kerner* [and] *Allison*, [neither of which] specifically involved the employment of physicians by a hospital. More important, none of those cases involved a corporation licensed to provide health care services to the general public. See *Weiss*, 254 Kan. at 746, 869 P.2d at 618. Accordingly, we decline to extend the *Kerner* corporate practice rule to licensed hospitals.

The corporate practice of medicine doctrine set forth in *Kerner* was not an interpretation of the plain language of the Medical Practice Act. The Medical Practice Act contains no express prohibition on the corporate employment of physicians. Rather, the corporate practice of medicine doctrine was inferred from the general policies behind the Medical Practice Act. Such a prohibition is entirely appropriate to a general corporation possessing no licensed authority to offer medical services to the public, such as the appellant in *Kerner*. However, when a corporation has been sanctioned by the laws of this state to operate a hospital, such a prohibition is inapplicable.[2] Accord *Weiss* * * *.

The legislative enactments pertaining to hospitals provide ample support for this conclusion. [See footnote 2.] In addition, * * * the Hospital Emergency Service Act (210 ILCS 80/0.01 et seq. (West 1994)) requires "[e]very hospital * * * which provides general medical and surgical hospital services" to also provide emergency services; see also 210 ILCS 70/1 (West 1994) (requires licensed providers of professional health care, including hospitals, to provide emergency medical treatment in life-threatening situations, regardless of patient's ability to pay).

The foregoing statutes clearly authorize, and at times mandate, licensed hospital corporations to provide medical services. We believe that the authority to employ duly-licensed physicians for that purpose is reasonably implied from these legislative enactments. We further see no justification for distinguishing between nonprofit and for-profit hospitals in this regard. The authorities and duties of licensed hospitals are conferred equally upon both entities. Accord *Weiss*.

In addition, we find the public policy concerns which support the corporate practice doctrine inapplicable to a licensed hospital in the modern health care industry. The concern for lay control over professional judgment is alleviated in a licensed hospital, where generally a separate professional medical staff is responsible for the quality of medical services

2. It is noteworthy that this court in *Kerner* observed that the defendant corporation's activities violated section 24 of the Medical Practice Act, which prohibited "the maintenance of an office for the examination and treatment of" afflicted persons without a medical license. In contrast, this same activity by a licensed hospital is expressly sanctioned. See 210 ILCS 85/3(A) (West 1994) (hospital is an institution "devoted primarily to the maintenance and operation of facilities for the diagnosis and treatment or care" of afflicted persons).

rendered in the facility. See 210 ILCS 85/4.5 (West Supp.1995); 77 Ill. Adm.Code §§ 250.150, 250.310 (1997).[5]

Furthermore, we believe that extensive changes in the health care industry since the time of the *Kerner* decision, including the emergence of corporate health maintenance organizations (see 215 ILCS 125/1–1 et seq. (West 1994) (Health Maintenance Organization Act)), have greatly altered the concern over the commercialization of health care. In addition, such concerns are relieved when a licensed hospital is the physician's employer. Hospitals have an independent duty to provide for the patient's health and welfare. See [Gilbert v. Sycamore Munic. Hosp., 622 N.E.2d 788 (Ill.1993)] (recognizing hospital's duty to review and supervise the medical treatment of a patient); [Darling v. Charleston Comm. Mem. Hosp., 211 N.E.2d 253 (Ill.1965) (reproduced in chapter 5(§B))] (recognizing hospital's duty to assume responsibility for the care of its patients); see also 410 ILCS 50/0.01 et seq. (West 1994) (Medical Patient Rights Act) (establishing right of patient to receive health care from hospital which is consistent with sound medical practices).

We find particularly appropriate the statement of the Kansas Supreme Court that "[i]t would be incongruous to conclude that the legislature intended a hospital to accomplish what it is licensed to do without utilizing physicians as independent contractors or employees.... To conclude that a hospital must do so without employing physicians is not only illogical but ignores reality." *Weiss*, 869 P.2d at 618. Accordingly, we conclude that a duly-licensed hospital possesses legislative authority to practice medicine by means of its staff of licensed physicians and is excepted from the operation of the corporate practice of medicine doctrine.

Consequently, the employment agreement between the Health Center and Dr. Berlin is not unenforceable merely because the Health Center is a corporate entity. The circuit court has not yet adjudicated the substantive merits of the instant employment agreement. Therefore, we remand this cause to the circuit court to proceed with the original action in a manner consistent herewith.

CONCLUSION

For the reasons stated, the judgment of the appellate court affirming the circuit court's award of summary judgment for plaintiff is reversed. The judgment of the circuit court is reversed and the cause is remanded to the circuit court for further proceedings not inconsistent with this opinion.

■ JUSTICE HARRISON, dissenting:

* * *

5. Moreover, in the instant case, the employment agreement expressly provided that the Health Center had no control or direction over Dr. Berlin's medical judgment and practice, other than that control exercised by the professional medical staff. Dr. Berlin has never contended that the Health Center's lay management attempted to control his practice of medicine.

More than 60 years have passed since *Kerner* was decided. If the legislature believed that our construction of the Act was erroneous or that the rule announced in *Kerner* should be changed, it could have amended the law to authorize the practice of medicine by entities other than individuals. With limited exceptions not applicable here, it has not done so. * * *

That the legislature has acquiesced in the judiciary's construction of the Medical Practice Act is especially clear given recent developments in the law. Under section 4.9 of the Regulatory Agency Sunset Act (5 ILCS 80/4.9 (West 1994)), the Medical Practice Act was scheduled for repeal on December 31, 1997, unless the General Assembly enacted legislation providing for its continuation (5 ILCS 80/4 (West 1994)). On April 12, 1996, the appellate court filed its opinion in this case, holding under *Kerner* that the Medical Practice Act bars the corporate practice of medicine by hospitals. Subsequent to that decision, the General Assembly passed and the Governor signed new legislation extending the Medical Practice Act until January 1, year 2007. The new legislation made no substantive changes to the licensing requirements and included no provisions contrary to the appellate court's holding. See 225 ILCS 60/1 et seq. (West 1996). Because the legislature is presumed to know the construction the statute has been given by the courts, its reenactment of the law can only be understood as an endorsement of the construction followed by the appellate court here. * * *

[N]one of the other statutes invoked by my colleagues supports their position. The most that can be said of those statutes is that they authorize hospitals to operate facilities for the diagnosis and care of patients and to make emergency service available regardless of ability to pay. Hospitals may also employ physician's assistants, provided such assistants function under the supervision of a licensed physician. 225 ILCS 95/7 (West 1994). None of those endeavors, however, requires that hospitals have the power to employ physicians directly or to charge patients for the physicians' services. All may be accomplished by granting staff privileges to duly licensed private physicians, and the Hospital Licensing Act presumes that hospitals will staff their facilities in precisely that way.

As noted earlier, the Medical Practice Act provides that it is inapplicable to "persons lawfully carrying on their particular profession or business under any valid existing regulatory Act of this State." 225 ILCS 60/4 (West 1994). Through this exemption, the statute recognizes that activities and enterprises otherwise in violation of the Medical Practice Act may be sanctioned by the General Assembly through separate enactments. In accordance with the exemption, the General Assembly has expressly authorized the employment of physicians by Health Maintenance Organizations (HMOs) under the Health Maintenance Organization Act (215 ILCS 125/1–1 et seq. (West 1994)). If the General Assembly had intended to grant the same authority to hospitals, I believe that it would have been similarly straightforward and unambiguous in doing so.

In addition to creating special rules for HMOs, the General Assembly has also decided to allow physicians to employ various forms of business organizations in practicing their profession. Physicians may incorporate in accordance with the Professional Service Corporation Act (805 ILCS 10/1 et seq. (West 1994)), they may form corporations to provide medical services under the Medical Corporation Act (805 ILCS 15/1 et seq. (West 1994)), they have the right to practice in a professional association organized pursuant to the Professional Association Act (805 ILCS 305/1 et seq. (West 1994)), and they can organize and operate limited liability companies to practice medicine under the recently amended Limited Liability Company Act (805 ILCS 180/1–1 et seq. (West 1996)). Again, however, none of these provisions pertains to hospitals, and no inference can be drawn from any of them that the General Assembly intended to alter the prohibition against the corporate practice of medicine by hospitals.

For the foregoing reasons, I agree with the appellate court that the corporate practice doctrine prohibited defendant, Sarah Bush Lincoln Health Center, from entering into an employment agreement with Dr. Berlin. * * *

■ MILLER, J., joins in this dissent.

California Attorney General, Opinion No. 81–1004

April 7, 1982.

* * * In recent months a number of general business corporations, not licensed as medical corporations but styled as "industrial medical corporations," have started to operate what are called "industrial medical centers." They lease space for operations and contract with licensed physicians to perform preemployment physicals on and to diagnose and treat employment-related injuries sustained by employees of the state, of local governmental agencies, and of large corporations or other entities with whom they also contract to furnish those services. The patient-employees do not themselves pay for the medical services rendered; consideration instead is paid by the employer to the industrial medical corporation for them. The contracting physicians in the operation are not employees of the industrial medical corporation but rather are independent contractors who are compensated on a fixed fee basis by it. * * *

We are asked about the legality of this endeavor and specifically whether the "industrial medical corporation," as a general business corporation not licensed as a medical corporation, may lawfully engage licensed physicians to perform preemployment physical examinations and to diagnose and treat employment-related injuries for another entity with whom it contracts to furnish those services. Since that activity clearly constitutes the "practice of medicine," its being undertaken by the industrial medical corporation would contravene the prohibition against a corporation engaging in that practice unless its so doing falls within a recognized exception to the general rule against corporate practice. * * *

* * * [A]s a general rule a corporation may neither engage in the practice of medicine directly, nor may it do so *indirectly* by "engaging [physicians] to perform professional services for those with whom the corporation contracts to furnish such services." (Pacific Employers Ins. Co. v. Carpenter (1935) 10 Cal.App.2d 592, 594). Basically, this prohibition is "designed to protect the public from possible abuses stemming from the commercial exploitation of the practice of medicine" (County of Los Angeles v. Ford (1953) 121 Cal.App.2d 407, 413) and it has been said "to be against public policy to permit a 'middleman' to intervene for profit in establishing the professional relationship between members of said profession and members of the public." (Pacific Employers Ins. Co. v. Carpenter, supra, 10 Cal.App.2d at 595.) * * * [T]he reasons underlying the proscription are two: first, that the presence of a corporate entity is incongruous in the workings of a professional regulatory licensing scheme which is based on *personal* qualification, responsibility and sanction, and second, that the interposition of a lay commercial entity between the professional and his/her patients would give rise to divided loyalties on the part of the professional and would destroy the professional relationship into which it was cast.

However, the general rule against corporate practice is not absolute as exceptions to it have been found which, basically put, permit (1) nonprofit corporations, (2) fraternal, religious, hospital, labor, educational, and similar organizations, [and] (3) corporations having an interest in the health of its employees to contract with physicians to provide medical services for *their* people at a reduced cost[. In addition,] certain licensed health care institutions [are permitted] to do the same as part of their delivery of health care. Essentially we are asked whether the activities of the industrial medical corporation/center described in the request falls within the exceptions, for most assuredly they appear to be embraced by the general prohibition on the corporate practice of medicine.

* * *

To begin with, [the "industrial medical corporation/center"] is a general business corporation that is *organized for profit,* which removes it from the latitude given *nonprofit* noneducational and nonhealth care delivery corporations to contract with physicians to provide professional services to their subscribers. Moreover, the fact that the industrial medical corporation is organized for profit, which *profit is to be derived from a commercial exploitation of the practice of medicine and more particularly from its establishing and administering the physician-patient relationship, makes its operation even more suspect and its interposition into the professional relationship between the physicians whom it engages and the patients whom it sends to them even more questionable.* * * *

Second, the "industrial medical corporation" is *not* an institution which is traditionally thought of as being within the health care delivery system as are hospitals and clinics, and therefore it cannot avail itself of the latitude provided those entities to contract with physicians to render services to others. * * *

* * *

While it is true that the industrial medical corporation does not actually solicit or offer the provision of medical services *to the public generally,* neither does it work with a meaningfully defined limitation on those to whom it will provide its services. We are told that it contracts to serve such diverse groups of prospective patients as employees of corporations and employees of governmental entities, and it appears that its services are available to *any* corporation or other entity, public or private, willing to avail itself of them. That general availability distinguishes the industrial medical corporation/center from the institution which makes medical services available to a "*limited and particular group* as a result of cooperative association" such as the members of a fraternal association, the infirm indigent at a county hospital, or the subscribers (be they legion) to a health plan or even the employees of a large corporation solicitous of their health. With respect to the last group too, inasmuch as the operation of the industrial medical corporation is directed toward providing medical services to the employees of *other* entities, it is a far cry from being "some corporation which has an interest in the health of *its* employees" contracting with physicians to do so. More important though, * * * the industrial medical corporation *actively solicits* clientele and in so doing plays a positive role in establishing the physician-patient relationship which the proscription against the corporate practice of medicine is designed to protect.

The industrial medical corporation is a lay commercial enterprise that is organized for profit which it expects to derive from creating and administering the professional relationship between physicians whom it engages and their patients who are employees of entities with whom it contracts to furnish medical services. It actively solicits corporations to permit it to become the "middleman" in establishing that professional relationship and to thereafter "administer" it (e.g., billings, etc.). The activity thus described, albeit a variation on the theme, clearly is of the type that has consistently been assailed as constituting the corporate practice of medicine.

We therefore conclude that the operation of the industrial medical corporation described herein is illegal, i.e., that a general business corporation that is not licensed as a medical corporation may not lawfully engage licensed physicians to perform preemployment physical examinations and to diagnose and treat employment-related injuries sustained by employees of another entity with whom it contracts to furnish such services even though the physicians performing them do so as independent contractors and not as employees of the general business corporation.

NOTES AND QUESTIONS ON THE CORPORATE PRACTICE OF MEDICINE

1. In jurisdictions where it exists, the corporate-practice rule varies significantly in its origins, its scope and impact, and its current status. For state-by-state surveys of the law, see NHLA Survey on State Restrictions on Physician Practice Organizations, Corporate Practice of Medicine, and Related Rules, Health Law Dig., Aug. 1996, p. 67 (Professional Rights) (reporting that some version of the corporate-practice rule exists in at least 38 states); Dobbins, Survey of State Laws Relating to the Corporate Practice of Medicine, Health Lawyer, vol. 9, no. 5, p. 18 (1997). Although the rule seems to many to be an anachronism in the modern health care marketplace, it enjoys the political support of both professional interests seeking to preserve their autonomy and ideological opponents of commercialism in medical care. In the State of Washington in 1997, the governor vetoed a bill that would have abrogated the doctrine, as set forth in Morelli v. Ehsan, 756 P.2d 129 (Wash.1988). Did the *Berlin* ruling abrogate the rule in Illinois, or does it still operate as a constraint on innovative arrangements for financing and delivering health services?

2. Enforcement of the corporate-practice doctrine, such as it is in particular jurisdictions, has been very uneven. For example, although it has rarely been directly invoked by state licensing boards against practitioners participating in arguably unethical, unlawful arrangements, California regulators have lately been employing it in this fashion. from time to time, the rule is applied by state attorneys general, whose opinions have been sought by legislators or state regulators, perhaps at the instigation of professional interests opposed to some arrangement. Otherwise, the nature of the prohibition is such that it may come into play when it is least expected, as in the *Berlin* case. Lawyers must therefore be wary of it in structuring relationships, even if there is little current guidance on the matter in the particular jurisdiction. Today, most arrangements between physicians and lay-controlled entities are crafted to preserve physicians' status as independent contractors and to avoid the appearance of letting nonphysicians control medical decisions. As will appear at later points, however, corporate middlemen often impose economic incentives on physicians in ways suggesting a reality substantially at odds with the appearance of physician independence. Indeed, the threat that an independent-contractor relationship might be terminated may make a physician as subject to control by the other party as an employee would be.

3. Between 1983 and 1994, the percentage of "nonfederal postresident patient care physicians" practicing as employees (in the sense that they had "no ownership interest in their practice") increased from 24.2% to 42.3%. Kletke et al., Current Trends in Physicians' Practice Arrangements: From Owners to Employees, 276 J.A.M.A. 555 (1996). Of these, 34.4% worked for other physicians, 15.9% for hospitals, 19.5% for a university or medical school, 7.5% for a state or local government, 9.7% for a staff-model HMO, and 1.8% for an emergency care center (plus 11.1% "other"). Id. at 557. Percentages did not vary much among four regions even though state law might be expected to be a factor in some categories. Which categories are most likely to require special legislation? University medical centers typically make the services of their salaried medical faculty available to the public on a fee-for-service basis, with the medical school retaining some portion of the income. Such a "faculty practice plan" was upheld in Albany

Medical College v. McShane, 66 N.Y.2d 982, 499 N.Y.S.2d 376, 489 N.E.2d 1278 (1985).

4. Consider the policy arguments supporting the corporate-practice doctrine. Is the rule outmoded? See, e.g., Patient Care and Professional Responsibility: Impact of the Corporate Practice of Medicine Doctrine and Related Laws and Regulations (NHLA/AAHA 1997) (reporting colloquium of practitioners and other legal authorities); Dowell, The Corporate Practice of Medicine Prohibition: A Dinosaur Awaiting Extinction, 27 J. Health & Hosp. L. 369 (1994); Note, The Corporate Practice of Medicine Doctrine: An Anachronism in the Modern Health Care Industry, 40 Vand.L.Rev. 445 (1987). If the corporate-practice rule is obsolete, how should it be changed? Were the Illinois appellate court and the dissenters in *Berlin* right to rely on the principle of stare decisis with respect to a statute that had not been applied aggressively for sixty years? See G. Calabresi, A Common Law for the Age of Statutes (1982) (arguing for construing older statutes in light of modern developments).

5. *Professional Corporations.* Legislation in every state (including Illinois, as reported in the dissenting opinion in *Berlin*) permits professionals to practice in professional corporations or in professional associations having many of the earmarks of corporations. These laws were drafted against a background of ethical and other concerns, however, and did not represent a significant departure from the traditional view that professional services are personal and should be rendered with full accountability and without lay interference. Note the similarity to statutes governing the provision of other professional services, such as the one in *Snyder's Drug Stores.*

The impetus for the legislation authorizing professional corporations and associations, most of which was adopted in the 1960s, came from professionals seeking to obtain tax advantages from use of the corporate form, particularly the opportunity to establish tax-favored retirement plans. Although most of the original tax advantages of professional corporations have been eliminated by subsequent tax legislation, the model remains popular for other reasons. Professional corporations differ significantly from general business corporations. For example, they generally are authorized to engage only in providing professional services, and only persons licensed to render such services can own stock, thus ensuring that lay persons will not participate in control. In addition, most states require that only professionals active in the firm's practice may hold stock and that employees must be under direct supervision and control of a licensed professional. Although limited liability is usually permitted with respect to ordinary business obligations, a primary requirement in professional corporations is that the professionals practicing within them remain personally liable for their torts. A typical statute provides:

> Every individual who renders professional services as an employee of a professional corporation shall be liable for any negligent or wrongful act or omission in which the individual personally participates to the same extent as if the individual rendered the services as a sole practitioner. An employee of a professional corporation shall not

be liable for the conduct of other employees unless the employee is at fault in appointing, supervising, or cooperating with the other employees.

Hawaii Rev.Stat. § 415A–11 (1993). A few states go further and hold all shareholders jointly and severally liable for the negligent acts of any other member of the corporation in the same way that a partner is liable for the tortious acts of other partners. Colo.Rev.Stat.Ann. § 12–36–134(1)(g) (West 1997).

Legislative permission to form a professional corporation amounts, in some states, to a strict prohibition (absent other statutory authorization) against practicing medicine through any corporate vehicle not exclusively under physician control. How should the IRS view an entity formed to comply with such a legal requirement for purposes of tax exemption? Specifically, could a clinic controlled exclusively by doctors avoid the private-benefit prohibition (it is, after all, formed to confer benefits on the physician owners) by claiming that it is an integral part of a larger network that itself meets the charitable-purpose test and that includes other components capable of checking the power of the doctor group? The IRS has issued a ruling to this effect for a clinic in Texas, where the corporate-practice rule requires such exclusive physician control. IRS Determination Ltr. re C.H. Wilkinson Phys. Network, 1996 WL 343384 (June 19, 1996). See also IRS Determination Ltr. re North Shore Med. Specialists, S.C., 1996 WL 688398 (Nov. 22, 1996) (Illinois for-profit professional corporation granted tax exemption in view of ties to exempt medical center and representation that appellate court's decision in *Berlin* case precluded nonprofit entities from practicing medicine).

6. *HMOs*. California courts made an early exception to the rule against corporate practice, permitting groups of interested persons to form a nonprofit corporation to secure medical services for themselves at low cost. See Complete Service Bureau v. San Diego Med. Soc'y, 43 Cal.2d 201, 272 P.2d 497 (1954) ("nonprofit medical service corporation," a kind of cooperative, allowed to contract with physician panel and to pay them on discounted basis for services rendered to its subscribers). In this way, California became open to the development of entities now known generically as HMOs.

In Texas in the 1970s, plaintiffs challenged the constitutionality of the state's refusal to charter a lay-controlled HMO-type "organization whose purpose is to provide medical and health care programs to the Mexican–American and black communities as well as other low-income groups in Bexar County, Texas." Garcia v. Texas St. Bd. of Med. Examiners, 384 F.Supp. 434 (W.D.Tex.1974) (three-judge court), aff'd mem. 421 U.S. 995 (1975). The court reasoned as follows:

> The Texas statutes clearly have a rational basis to justify the restrictions imposed. The Texas legislature seeks to preserve the vitally important doctor-patient relationship, and prevent possible abuses resulting from lay person control of a corporation employing licensed

physicians on a salaried basis. The Texas legislature could rationally believe that the statutes in question will accomplish these goals. * * *

The plaintiffs imply that the Texas Medical Practice Act promulgates an elitist, unreasonably restrictive and self-perpetuating monopoly by the medical profession to the detriment of the economically disadvantaged. While it is no doubt true that this nation faces a grave shortage of doctors, is the panacea to be found in the formation of non-profit layman corporations? We think not. It appears to the Court that not only is such a corporation fraught with practical and ethical considerations, but may well represent a backward step in the legislative protections it has taken so long to achieve. Without licensed, professional doctors on Boards of Directors, who and what criteria govern the selection of medical and paramedical staff members? To whom does the doctor owe his first duty—the patient or corporation? Who is to preserve the confidential nature of the doctor-patient relationship? What is to prevent or who is to control a private corporation from engaging in mass media advertising in the exaggerated fashion so familiar to every American? Who is to dictate the medical and administrative procedures to be followed? Where do budget considerations end and patient care begin?

There can be no doubt but that more medical care at a less expensive cost is needed today. However, where the health of the American citizen is at stake, Machiavellian rationale does not and should not apply. Should the Legislature in its wisdom find a necessity for the lay-medical corporation and the method for its proper administration, that is its prerogative and answer to the will of the electorate. Until such a time, this Court believes and so finds the existing statutes constitutionally permissible in all respects and will not endeavor or presume to retreat to the past at the potential expense of public health and welfare.

Like Illinois (as reported by the dissenters in *Berlin*), Texas subsequently enacted an HMO enabling act allowing the employment of physicians. Tex.Ins. Code Ann., §§ 20A.01–20A.33, 20A.06(a)(3) (1987 & Supp. 1996).

The federal HMO Act of 1973, 42 U.S.C. § 300e–10(a)(1)(B) (1994), preempted state law, for some purposes, in so far as it required that "physicians constitute all or a percentage of [an HMO's] governing body." Today, most state enabling acts clearly permit HMOs to employ physicians as well as permitting lay control.

7. *Hospital Employment of Physicians*. On the general issue addressed in the *Berlin* case, California law was interpreted at an early date to permit at least nonprofit hospitals to contract with physicians to provide certain medical services as long as professional independence was not infringed. 55 Ops.Cal.Att'y Gen. 103, 108–109 (1972) (proprietary hospital and physician director of its electroencephalography department); 54 Ops.Cal.Att'y Gen. 126, 128–129 (1971) (employment of licensed physician in emergency room); 11 Ops.Cal.Att'y Gen. 236, 239 (1948) (hospital and pathologist). Some other states, as reported in *Berlin*, have viewed the matter otherwise, whereas many others have statutes on the subject. E.g., Official Code Ga.Ann. § 43–34–37(a)(9) (1994 & Supp. 1996).

In Tennessee, a 1994 opinion of the Attorney General, Tenn.Op. Att'y Gen. No. 94–053 (1994), applied statutes more explicit than those in Illinois and a 1949 judicial decision, Loser v. National Optical Stores Co., 189 Tenn. 433, 225 S.W.2d 263 (1949) (professing concern that "professional standards would be practically destroyed, and professions requiring special training would be commercialized, to the public detriment"), to reach a result similar to the one rejected in *Berlin*. Shortly thereafter, the Tennessee legislature extensively revised the law, allowing hospitals to employ physicians other than radiologists, anesthesiologists, pathologists, and emergency specialists (what might explain these exceptions?) if diagnostic and treatment decisions are not interfered with, if limits on the doctor's freedom to refer patients to other hospitals are written and disclosed to patients, and if any restrictive covenants (such as the one in *Berlin*) meet statutory requirements. Tenn. Code Ann. §§ 68–11–205(b), 63–6–204(d) (1992 & Supp. 1996).

8. *Employee Health*. Can an employer hire a physician to provide preemployment physicals and other on-site health care for his employees (at no cost to the latter)? Once again, the Tennessee Attorney General has opined against corporate employment, even in these circumstances. Tenn.Op. Att'y Gen. No. 94–009 (1994). On the other hand, although California had long permitted such arrangements, its Attorney General drew the line at the "industrial medical corporation" described in the opinion reproduced above. Was the corporation practicing medicine? Where were the conflicts of interests, if any? Were the doctors' loyalties divided? What are the alternatives to involving such corporate middlemen?—consumers purchasing medical services on their own?—employers procuring physician services directly? Why is a small California employer trusted to choose a doctor to treat an employee but not trusted to choose a sophisticated agent to help him deal with physicians?

9. *Employee or Independent Contractor for Tax Purposes?* Professionals who are nominally independent contractors could be treated by the IRS as employees for purposes of collecting various employment taxes. Although there is a presumption that professionals are independent, new arrangements featuring closer control and oversight could invite reclassification in some cases. See generally Mustokoff & Sarner, Minimizing the Risks of Independent Contractor Status in the Health Care Industry, 8 J. Taxation of Exempt Orgs. 16 (1996).

10. *Effects of the Corporate–Practice Rule on Purchases of Physician Practices*. The Securities and Exchange Commission has suggested that firms acquiring and managing physician practices may be barred from treating the practices they purchase as acquisitions for accounting purposes if state law bars them from corporate practice. The investment value of so-called practice management companies could be adversely affected. The corporate-practice rule also affects both the form of purchases of physician practices and the attractiveness of such practices to potential purchasers—hospitals or practice management companies, as the case may be.

NOTES ON PROFESSIONAL ETHICS CONCERNING CONTRACT PRACTICE

1. In 1975, the FTC challenged as antitrust violations certain provisions of the AMA's then-current Principles of Medical Ethics, including prohibitions against so-called "contract practice"—essentially, corporate practice as seen from the physicians' side. In re AMA, 94 F.T.C. 701 (1979), modified and enforced, 638 F.2d 443 (2d Cir.1980), affirmed by an equally divided Court, 455 U.S. 676 (1982). Although the legal issues in this case are taken up in chapter 4(§B), the following excerpts from the FTC's factual discussion (94 F.T.C. at 1011–16) are of interest here:

> The Principles state that:
>
> > A physician should not dispose of his services under terms or conditions which tend to interfere with or impair the free and complete exercise of his medical judgment and skill or tend to cause a deterioration of the quality of medical care.
>
> * * * Though the Principles couch the ethical standard in terms of preventing impairment of medical judgment and deterioration of medical care, the interpretations, as reflected in the Opinions and Reports, bear little relation to those objectives. Whatever the extent to which quality of care concerns are cognizable under the antitrust laws * * * the restraints here go far beyond anything that might be reasonably related to the goal of preventing use of improper medical procedures. * * *
>
> Opinion 3 of Section 6 of the Opinions and Reports lists several contractual restrictions that are unfair or unethical. These are:
>
> > (1) When the compensation received is inadequate based on the usual fees paid for the same kind of service and class of people in the same community.
> >
> > (2) When the compensation is so low as to make it impossible for competent service to be rendered.
> >
> > (3) When there is underbidding by physicians in order to secure the contract.
> >
> > (4) When a reasonable degree of free choice of physicians is denied those cared for in a community where other competent physicians are readily available.
> >
> > (5) When there is solicitation of patients directly or indirectly.
>
> The use of the above-described standards for determining whether a contract is ethical received the approval of the House of Delegates in 1927. Although the record does not indicate the motivation for the 1927 action, AMA's anticompetitive purpose is evident in the Minority Report to a 1932 report of the Committee on the Costs of Medical Care,

entitled "Medical Care for the American People." The Minority Report, which was endorsed by the House of Delegates in 1933 as "expressive, in principle, of the collective opinion of the medical profession," provides a valuable insight into the thinking of the AMA at a point in time reasonably contemporaneous with incorporation of the five standards into the Opinions and Reports. After reiterating the five factors noted above, the Minority Report states:

> One of the strongest objections to industrial medical services, mutual benefit associations, so-called health and hospital associations, and other forms of contract practice is that there has been found no means of preventing destructive competition between individuals or groups concerned with these movements. This injects a type of commercialism into medical practice which is harmful to the public and the medical profession and results in inferior quality of medical service.
>
> One of the pernicious effects of contract practice schemes is that each of them stimulates the launching of other similar schemes until there are many in the field competing with each other. The first may have safeguards against many of the abuses of contract practices, but as new ones are formed the barriers are gradually broken down in order to secure business.
>
> * * *
>
> The minority recognizes the advantage of group practice under certain conditions, especially in communities where practically all of the physicians can be joined in one, or at the most, two groups.

With respect to the voluntary insurance systems operated through contracts with organized groups of the medical profession, the Minority Report stated that these systems were:

> ... giving rise to all the evils inherent in contract practice.... Wherever they are established there is solicitation of patients, destructive competition among professional groups, inferior medical service, loss of personal relationship of patient and physician, and demoralization of the professions. It is clear that all such schemes are contrary to sound public policy and that the shortest road to commercialization of the practice of medicine is through the supposedly rosy path of insurance.
>
> * * *

AMA's support of the fee-for-service method of compensation is extensively documented in the record of this proceeding. The 1971 Opinions and Reports state that:

> A physician should not dispose of his professional attainments or services to any hospital, corporation or lay body by whatever name called or however organized under terms or conditions which

permit the sale of the services of that physician by such agency for a fee.

While such a restriction does not have a direct impact on price, it clearly limits the ability of hospitals, prepaid health plans, and other lay organizations to dealing with physicians on the traditional basis of fee-for-service and precludes the use of salaries or other arrangements that may be more cost efficient. The purpose of this restriction is manifest: to retain for the physician the full profit generated by his or her services and to preclude competition by group health plans, hospitals and other organizations not directly under the control of physicians.[65]

2. The AMA's Principles were substantially rewritten in 1980, largely in response to the FTC attack. The current provision most in point states, "A physician shall * * * be free to choose * * * with whom to associate, and the environment in which to provide medical services." It is now clear that the medical profession is no longer in a position to oppose the growth of corporate medicine by collective action in the marketplace. Battles are still likely to be fought in legislative forums, however, over such matters as permitting hospitals to employ physicians (see, e.g., the fine print in the recent Tennessee legislation cited supra) and corporate interference in "medical" decisions.

State v. Abortion Information Agency, Inc.

Supreme Court, Appellate Division, First Department, 1971.
37 A.D.2d 142, 330 N.Y.S.2d 927, affirmed 30 N.Y.2d 779, 334 N.Y.S.2d 174, 285 N.E.2d 317 (1972).

■ PER CURIAM. We would affirm on the opinion at Special Term (ASCH, J.), but would add the following. Special Term's decision was based essentially on three findings. (1) It found as a matter of law, the public policy of the State "is opposed to the practice of acting as an intermediary or broker in the sale of professional services", and the Abortion Information Agency was so engaged. (2) The court found that A.I.A.'s practice amounted to fee splitting which "on its face violates" section 6514 of the Education Law and finally (3) that A.I.A.'s method of operation constituted the practice of

65. Respondent's purpose is set forth with unusual clarity in the 1971 Opinions and Reports:

> There are insurance companies administering workmen's compensation benefits wherein the salaries or fees paid to the physician by the insurance company are so much below the legal fees on which the premium paid by the industry is based as to furnish a large direct profit to the insurance company. Certain hospitals are forbidding their staffs of physicians to charge fees for their professional services to "house cases" but are themselves collecting such fees and absorbing them in hospital income. Some universities, by employing full-time hospital staffs and opening their doors to the general public, charging such fees for the professional care of the patients as to net the university no small profit, are in direct and unethical competition with the profession at large and their own graduates. They are making a direct profit by a practice of questionable legality, from the professional care.

medicine in violation of subdivision 1 of section 6501 of the Education Law. These findings were overwhelmingly supported by the incontrovertible proof submitted at Special Term.

As to the finding that the "public policy of the State is opposed to the practice of acting as an intermediary or broker in the sale of professional services", the court relied upon the case of Matter of Co-op. Law Co. (198 N.Y. 479, 484) where the court stated, "A corporation can neither practice law nor hire lawyers to carry on the business of practicing law for it any more than it can practice medicine or dentistry by hiring doctors or dentists to act for it." That case is applicable here, for the entire mode of operation so clearly established is that the defendants hire the hospital and make all arrangements with the hospital. It is the defendant corporation that is billed by the hospital, not the patient. As the record shows, the defendant and the hospital are clearly the contracting parties, and there is not even any indication that the patient herself undertakes any responsibility pursuant to contract insofar as her obligation to pay the hospital. This is A.I.A.'s responsibility, apparently agreed to by the hospital. While the Supreme Court in Railroad Trainmen v. Virginia Bar (377 U.S. 1) upheld a situation where a union channelled legal employment to particular lawyers in order to advise and protect union members, such is not analogous to the situation at bar, for in that case there is no indication that the union itself hired the attorneys—thus bypassing the ordinary attorney-client relationship. * * *

With relation to the finding that the practice of the defendants on its face violates section 6514(2)(f) of the Education Law, constituting illegal fee splitting, that finding too must be sustained. While the provision against fee splitting is particularly aimed against members of the medical profession, nevertheless, that section of the law prohibits payments in general (as a matter of public policy) for referring a client to a physician. The participation by the defendant in any arrangement which involves fee splitting by a physician is clearly against public policy. The affidavits disclosed the behind-the-scenes arrangements between A.I.A. and the cooperating doctors and hospital. In fact, the affidavit submitted by defendant John A. Settle admits that defendants were granted a discount in hospital charges amounting to their referral fees. That the discount may not have involved an increase in cost to the patient is irrelevant. What is clear from the affidavit, is that if the hospitals were contacted directly by the patient, a different fee would of necessity have been demanded. This is the logical conclusion from the admission that a discount was granted in an amount equal to the referral fee. The discount then quite clearly is the equivalent of fee splitting.

With respect to the admission that the defendants were able to obtain discounts at hospitals, and further taking into account the entire background of dealings between the defendants and hospitals, it is quite clear that plaintiff has made out a clear and convincing case concerning the inherent dangers to the public involved in this situation, considering the distinct probability of domination by the agency of the institutions. Contrary to the dissent's conclusion that such created only an issue of fact, in the circumstances of this case, the record being replete with the overwhelming probability that such is the situation, a temporary injunction was not only properly granted, but was mandated for the protection of the public.

Additionally, the finding that A.I.A.'s procedures constituted the practice of medicine in violation of section 6501 of the Education Law was correct. Subdivision 4 of section 6501 of the Education Law defines the practice of medicine as follows: "A person practices medicine within the meaning of this article . . . who holds himself out as being able to diagnose, treat, operate or prescribe for any human disease . . . or who shall either offer or undertake, by any means or method to diagnose, treat, operate or prescribe for any human disease". It is quite clear under the facts developed in the record that the defendants did engage in diagnosing a human or physical condition. Defendants' employees were specifically instructed to interrogate women making inquiries upon a variety of matters pertinent to determination of the type of operation required and to inform the prospective patient as to the type of operation for which the caller qualified. This constitutes an attempt at a diagnosis by one not qualified to act as a physician, or acting under the direction and supervision of a physician. Moreover, A.I.A. also engaged in giving preadmission directives, which is also violative of the statute.

In addition to the grounds upon which Special Term reached its conclusion, there is yet another reason which justifies affirmance of the order. The record shows that a comprehensive fee is charged and that such "is a guaranteed flat charge that covers everything. . . . Even if minor complications . . . require an extra stay in the hospital, blood, special laboratory work or medications, you never pay anything more. . . . All extra charges not defrayed by [the patient's] insurance coverage (if any) would be borne by the hospital and/or A.I.A." Such practice would appear to constitute the practice of the business of insurance (Insurance Law, § 41), and the defendants not being licensed to conduct an insurance business, their activities were illegal (Insurance Law, § 40, subd. 1).

Finally, we would like to add these final comments. From the beginning to end, A.I.A.'s operation has the appearance of one conceived in fraud. The certificate of incorporation for example provides that the purpose of the corporation is: "To provide general information concerning legal abortions to the public and to women with problem pregnancies. The corporation, nor its agents, shall not undertake to diagnose pregnancy, or any other physical or mental condition of a client. The corporation shall not undertake to advise a client on the medical desirability of obtaining an abortion, nor shall it provide any information or perform any act which may constitute the practice of medicine."

The appearance then was the creation of an informational agency, not a business which would engage so extensively in the procurement of hospital services and make all arrangements for abortions. This combined with the manner in which the corporation functioned demonstrates an undisclosed intent to conceal the real nature of defendants' business.

Also to be noted is the manner of contact between the patient and defendants. The overwhelming contacts were made over the telephone. Although the defendants' advertising gives the impression of having trained counselors, they were without any real training in the field and operated without any proper supervision. Moreover, affidavits of various former employees indicate the extent to which the caller would be discouraged from seeking other aid, and encouraged to register with the appellant corporation.

We do not dispute that those women desiring abortions are entitled under the law to have them. But, that does not mean that we should countenance an operation where under the guise of providing information, women are instead solicited and encouraged to seek out abortions. That the initial inquiry concerning the abortion is made by the patient does not negate the fact the defendants' methodology once a patient contacted it was to further encourage the abortion, for the sole motive of financial gain to defendants, rather than to aid in giving objective and concerned advice to the patient. The nature of the business we are dealing with requires the court to give close scrutiny to the facts in an attempt to provide maximum assurance that those who are merely inquiring as to information concerning abortions are not improperly influenced or induced to have such abortion. This is all the more necessary when we are dealing with unlicensed people entering a field where generally, licensing and supervision are necessary.

Despite the fact that the appeal is from an order which granted drastic relief, we find as did the court below, that the evidence overwhelmingly justifies the granting of such relief. Unquestionably, defendants' operation presents a superficial aspect of legality and regularity. But it is the duty of the Attorney–General and of the courts, to penetrate below the surface and to reach the essence of what defendants are doing. When that is done, there emerges a clear picture of the practice of medicine, fee splitting, a measure of insurance and a totality of procedure which violates the public policy of the State. That conclusion cannot be dissipated by sophistical argument.

Accordingly, the order entered May 20, 1971, granting petitioner's application, should be affirmed with costs and disbursements.

■ STEUER, J. (dissenting). A temporary injunction has been granted against defendants preventing them from conducting an abortion referral agency and from collecting fees in connection therewith. A temporary receiver has been appointed. The conceded purpose is to prevent the defendant from continuing its business, and this has effectually been done without any trial. It is almost inconceivable that such drastic action could be had and countenanced where determination rests solely upon inferences drawn from facts. The only possible explanation is that when abortion at the pleasure of the woman involved was legalized, thereby abolishing a deep rooted public antipathy, it was not contemplated that the local response to the lifting of the ban would be anything like as great as it proved to be, or that women throughout the nation would seek to take advantage of our laws and our facilities for this purpose. The volume appalled the public mind, and any service or facility which made the practice more available became an obvious target. When the service reached sizable proportions the reaction became hysterical, which hysteria is typified by the * * * Special Term's opinion, and the continued iteration of the size and financial success of defendant's operation as proof that such operation is illegal.

While every imaginable make weight argument is advanced to support the determination, the grounds of decision below are the claim that the defendant has been practicing medicine; that it is engaged in fee splitting; and that its operation is against public policy. [The opinion found these claims inadequately supported.]

NOTES AND QUESTIONS ON THE AIA CASE

1. The New York legislature, finding violations of "the standards of medical ethics and public policy applicable to the practice of medicine," prohibited for-profit medical referral centers in 1971. N.Y.Pub.Health Law §§ 4500–03 (1995). Do you agree that the profit motive was harmful here?

2. Note that the *AIA* case preceded the Supreme Court's invalidation of state antiabortion statutes in Roe v. Wade, 410 U.S. 113 (1973). Do you see in the politics surrounding *AIA* and the subsequent legislation a preview of the national debate that followed the Supreme Court's action?

3. What "sophistical argument" can you make in support of AIA's activities? How would this decision stand following *Roe v. Wade?* Cf. Bigelow v. Virginia, 421 U.S. 809 (1975) (state law prohibiting advertising of abortion services held invalid under first amendment).

4. In a New Jersey case, state regulators contended that the state certificate-of-need law, which controlled the location and growth of health care facilities but not of physician offices, should apply to an abortion clinic because it was managed by a lay-controlled corporation and allegedly engaged in fee-splitting and undue influence over professionals. The argument was rejected. Women's Med. Center v. Finley, 192 N.J.Super. 44, 469 A.2d 65 (1983). How would you argue this case, both ways?

SECTION D: HEALTH CARE "FRAUD AND ABUSE"

NOTES AND QUESTIONS ON PHYSICIAN SELF-REFERRAL, FEE SPLITTING, ETC.

1. *Physician Entrepreneurship; Self-referral.* Relman's article on the "medical-industrial complex," excerpted in § A of this chapter, addressed another aspect of physician involvement in commercial enterprise—as investors in hospitals or other businesses whose commercial welfare they can enhance by their professional actions. In Relman's view, physicians

"should have no economic conflict of interest and therefore no pecuniary association with the medical-industrial complex." Relman, supra, at 967. He observed that, although the AMA's pre–1980 Principles of Medical Ethics included a declaration on physicians' financial interests, it was directed primarily at fee-splitting and rebates. Thus, the old principles stated (italics Relman's): "*In the practice of medicine* a physician should limit the source of his *professional* income to medical services actually rendered by him, or under his supervision, to his patients." The italicized words were deemed to make the principle inapplicable to income derived other than directly from the care of a physician's own patients. Relman noted that the AMA Judicial Council had opined that "it is not in itself unethical for a physician to own a for-profit hospital or interest therein," provided that the physician does not make unethical use of that ownership. In 1987, Dr. Relman supported federal legislation—which was never passed, despite support from retail pharmacists—to bar physicians from dispensing drugs they prescribed to their patients. Relman, Doctors and the Dispensing of Drugs, 317 New Eng. J. Med. 311 (1987). Is legislation of this type needed to protect consumers?

The issue of physician entrepreneurship and its effects on the utilization of services attracted increasing interest in the late 1980s and became the subject of intense legislative activity (including federal legislation). A comprehensive study of Florida physicians found that 40% of physicians involved in direct patient care had a proprietary interest in some freestanding service to which they referred patients. Mitchell & Scott, New Evidence of the Prevalence and Scope of Physician Joint Ventures, 268 J.A.M.A. 80, 83 (1992) ("More than 75% of the responding ambulatory surgical facilities and 90% of the diagnostic imaging centers are owned wholly or in part by referring physicians."). Utilization rates and charges were found higher where referring physicians had an investment interest. See also Mitchell & Scott, Physician Ownership of Physical Therapy Services, 268 J.AM.A. 2055 (1992) (utilization, charges, and profits were higher, and time spent with patients was lower, when facilities were owned by referring physicians); Hillman et al., Physicians' Utilization and Charges for Outpatient Diagnostic Imaging in a Medicare Population, 268 J.AM.A. 2050 (1992) (finding that physicians with x-ray equipment in their offices use imaging examinations more often than those who refer their patients to radiologists and that charges are generally higher when the procedure is done by the self-referring physician); Swedlow et al., Increased Costs and Rates of Use in the California Workers' Compensation Program as a Result of Self–Referral by Physicians, 327 New Eng. J. Med. 1502, 1504 (1992) (finding self-referral increases "the percentage of injured workers who receive physical therapy (which more than offsets the slight decrease in the cost per case); * * * the number of psychometric tests and the cost of psychiatric-evaluation reports; and * * * the frequency of requests for clinically inappropriate MRI scans"). Although the results of these studies were certainly suggestive of significant demand inducement, issues could still be raised as to what levels of utilization were medically or economically appropriate (because of the lack of definitive data).

For a revised ethical pronouncement by the AMA on physician self-referral and entrepreneurship, see AMA Council on Ethical and Judicial Affairs, Conflicts of Interest: Physician Ownership of Medical Facilities, 267 J.A.M.A. 2366 (1992). Acknowledging a lack of professionalism on the part of some physicians, the Council insists that most physicians can be trusted to make self-referrals and that such referrals can benefit patients. Nevertheless, says the AMA, physicians should not make referrals outside their office to facilities where they do not directly provide services but merely have an investment interest. Physicians may make such referrals, however, if there is a community need for the facility and if financing for it is not forthcoming from other sources. (The latter loophole could be a large one, given, for example, the situation in Florida described above.)

2. *Fee Splitting, Kickbacks, etc.* Professional ethics prohibit physicians and other professionals from splitting fees with and getting rebates from other professionals. The AMA's Judicial Council has officially declared that "[c]linics, laboratories, hospitals, or other health care facilities that compensate physicians for referral of patients are engaged in fee splitting, which is unethical." AMA Council on Ethical and Judicial Affairs, Code of Medical Ethics: Current Opinions on Ethical and Judicial Affairs § 6.03 (1996–97). The obvious concern is that such kickbacks introduce inappropriate considerations in the making of referrals. Similar principles govern a physician's receipt of any benefit for prescribing pharmaceutical or other products or for referring patients to a particular source of goods or services. Contract practice—the other side of the corporate-practice coin—can be seen as a fee-splitting problem, with the physician allowing an intermediary to earn a portion of his fee in return for supplying the patient.

Although the basic ethical rules are clear, competition for patients can lead specialists to test their limits by accommodating the interests of referring physicians in various ways short of paying actual commissions. Allowing the referring physician to assist in surgery is a common practice and is ethically permissible if the bill for such service is separate and independently justifiable. Id. § 6.09. Reciprocal referral is another practice generally believed to be a common inducement in the choice of a consultant. Specialists and the large medical centers in which they frequently practice are paying increasing attention to the cultivation of community physicians as potential sources of referrals. Moreover, new organizational arrangements (e.g., income-sharing multispecialty group practices, hospital/physician joint ventures, and closer integration of financing and delivery) are often launched specifically to ensure patient flows. See generally Schaffer & Holloman, Consultation and Referral Between Physicians in New Medical Practice Environments, 103 Annals of Internal Med. 600 (1985).

May a manufacturer of medical devices offer gifts or educational programs in exotic locations to physicians who prescribe its products? For AMA guidelines concerning physicians' acceptance of gifts from pharmaceutical companies, see AMA Council on Ethical and Judicial Affairs, Gifts to Physicians from Industry, 256 J.A.M.A. 440 (1991) (gifts cannot be related to physician prescribing practices, must primarily concern a benefit to patients, and cannot be of substantial value). The Pharmaceutical Manufacturers Association adopted identical guidelines two days later. (At a later point, consider whether the antitrust laws were violated by either set of guidelines.)

3. *State Laws*. State statutes frequently prohibit fee-splitting and similar abuses. California prohibits "the offer, delivery, receipt, or acceptance by any person licensed under this division of any rebate, refund, commission, * * * or other consideration * * * as compensation or inducement for referring patients, clients, or customers * * *." Cal.Bus. & Prof.Code § 650 (West Supp. 1990). In 1990, this provision was amended to provide an exemption for receipt of a percentage of gross revenues for services other than referrals if that amount is "commensurate with the value of the services furnished." Id. This law allows California physicians to split fees as long as the fee received accurately represents the services performed. See 73 Ops.Cal. Att'y Gen. 204 (1993) (physicians referring patients to a pharmaceutical company's clinical research program may not receive referral fees from the company but may receive evaluation fees for legitimately performed evaluations of the results of the program; "the purposes of section 650 are to protect the public from excessive health care costs, referrals based upon considerations other than the best interests of the patients, deceit and fraud, and payment to a licensee where professional services have not been rendered"). Where a physician has a proprietary interest in a laboratory or other facility, California imposes a disclosure requirement. Cal.Bus. & Prof.Code § 654.2 (1990).

New York law broadly prohibits a licensed professional from requesting, receiving, or profiting from a fee split, commission, discount or gratuity "for or in connection with the furnishing of professional care, or service," or "the sale, rental, supplying or furnishing" of numerous specified and unspecified "goods, services or supplies prescribed for medical diagnosis, care or treatment"; an exception is made for the pooling of income in partnerships, group practices, professional corporations (except "with respect to care and treatment under the workmen's compensation law") and university faculty practices. N.Y. Educ. Law § 6509–a (McKinney Supp. 1998). This broad prohibition has been held to regulate only Medicaid providers—so-called "Medicaid mills"—and thus not to permit a suit by a private purchaser of services (an HMO) against fee-splitting audiologists. Deutsch v. Health Ins. Plan of Greater New York, 573 F.Supp. 1443 (S.D.N.Y.1983). If this interpretation is sound, New York law lacks a general prohibition of fee-splitting. But see Necula v. Glass, 647 N.Y.S.2d 501 (App. Div. 1996) (arrangement with a management company for facilities and staff in exchange for fixed percentage of physicians' receipts held to constitute illegal fee splitting). See also Maleki v. Fine–Lando Clinic Chartered, S.C., 469 N.W.2d 629, 635–36 (Wis.1991) (Wisconsin prohibition against fee-splitting, though violated, held not enforceable by competing physician adversely affected by illegal arrangement).

In Michigan, a physician who splits fees or pays commissions to attract patients is guilty of a misdemeanor. Mich. Penal Code § 750.428 (1991). Moreover, this provision empowers the board of registration to revoke the physician's license following a first offense and requires revocation following any subsequent violations. Receipt of a fee for submitting specimens for testing by a clinical lab is expressly prohibited in Michigan. Mich. Comp. Laws Ann. § 445.162 (1989).

In Lieberman & Kraff v. Desnick, 614 N.E.2d 379 (Ill.App.1993), two physicians who tried to sell their practice to a young physician on an amortized payment plan were held to have violated the fee splitting prohibition and thus the contract was voided. Because the purchaser did not have the capital necessary to purchase a practice, the sales price was measured by a percentage of the purchaser's gross revenue; he agreed to pay 10% of his gross billings for the first ten years and 5% of his gross billings for the following ten years. Do you agree that this arrangement—or any other involving the sale of a practice (including "goodwill")—should be challengeable under the principles found in anti-kickback ethics or legislation? Does a physician owe an ethical or legal duty to his patients to pass them on to anyone other than the highest bidder? Should disclosure of the financial arrangements satisfy a physician's obligation to his patients?

In 1992, Florida adopted what appeared at the time to be the most comprehensive and restrictive state law dealing with the self-referral problem. Patient Self–Referral Act of 1992, Fla. Stat. Ann. § 455.654 (West Supp. 1997). Under it, referrals by interested physicians for certain "designated" services are absolutely prohibited. In other cases, referring physicians and entities to whom patients are referred must disclose investment interests and supply names of alternative providers of the service. Cross-referrals aimed at circumventing the law and kickbacks are also prohibited. For a 1989 Pennsylvania law requiring physicians to disclose financial interests before referring the patient, see 35 Pa. Cons. Stat. Ann. § 449.22 (West 1993). See also Tenn. Code Ann. § 63–6–602(a) (1997), stating that a physician who has an investment interest in a health care entity cannot refer his or her patients to that entity unless certain requirements are met. See generally T. Mayo, State Illegal–Remuneration and Self–Referral Laws (1996). The federal antireferral legislation (known as Stark I and Stark II) is discussed below, after consideration of the federal fraud and abuse legislation.

4. Can law and professional ethics effectively eliminate or counteract conflicts of interests? Can they, for example, deal with situations where referrals or prescriptions are induced by cultivating goodwill through entertainment, gifts, drug samples, and other means? An AMA official, while acknowledging abuses in self-referral by some physicians, has commented, "There is no known method of physician reward that dissolves conflict of interest. The trick is to tilt that conflict toward the patient, and most physicians do." Todd, Must the Law Assure Ethical Behavior?, 268 J.A.M.A. 98 (1992). How would you answer the question posed in the title of Dr. Todd's article? For articles skeptical of the effort to rectify conflicts

of interests by legal prohibitions, see Frankford, Creating and Dividing the Fruits of Collective Economic Activity: Referrals Among Health Care Providers, 89 Colum. L. Rev. 1861 (1989); Hall, Making Sense of Referral Fee Statutes, 13 J. Health Pol., Pol'y & L. 623 (1988).

5. *Problem*. Extracorporeal shock-wave lithotripsy (ESWL) is a technological procedure introduced in the mid–1980s for shattering kidney stones, allowing the fragments to pass easily from the body through the urinary tract. Because a "lithotripter" can treat many patients and costs over $2 million installed, the introduction of this technology meant that very few centers would now treat a condition that previously occupied up to 20 percent of the practice time of independent urologists. ESWL is generally recognized not only as safe and effective new technology but also as a cheaper alternative to the surgical treatments previously customary in many cases.

The Little Rock Treatment Center, Ltd., is a limited partnership, comprised of 32 urologists in the eastern part of your state. These physicians contributed the capital needed to install a lithotripter in a freestanding unit adjacent to Community Hospital. Patients are referred to the Center for ESWL by urologists throughout the state. The Center customarily pays a $250 fee to the referring urologist for "follow-up" care, although little such care is required. The other four ESWL centers in the state regard such fees unethical and do not pay them, although they are careful to prescribe a return visit to the referring doctor. One center allows the referring urologist to accompany the patient and to participate in the treatment, which is mostly performed by the technicians.

(a) Consider first the ethical appropriateness of physician entrepreneurship in this field. Will the Center's partners refer patients for ESWL solely on the basis of quality, cost, and the patient's convenience? Do you agree with Dr. Relman that physicians should refrain from participating in such ventures? Under what alternative auspices might ESWL then be offered? How is the situation different from that of an HMO that uses its own specialists and hospital to treat nearly all of its subscribers? Is such vertical integration objectionable per se? What guidelines can you suggest to improve the ethical position of the Center? (You will be asked below about the legal risks and what can be done about them.)

(b) Consider now the "follow-up" fee. What is the precise objection to it? If it is prohibited as a "kickback," is the community urologist's conflict of interest eliminated? Is it clear that the fee split impedes optimal treatment?

(c) Is the fee split simply a manifestation of the price competition among specialists? Why does competition for patients take this form? Should this form of competition be prohibited because it benefits the referring physician rather than the patient? Is it clear that such price competition will not benefit patients? Is it clear that the medical profession's opposition to fee splitting is based only on ethical concerns?

(d) Consider the referral fee in the *AIA* case. Did it raise the overall price? Were patients otherwise harmed?

(e) For discussion of these issues, see Havighurst & McDonough, The Lithotripsy Game in North Carolina: A New Technology under Regulation and Deregulation, 19 Ind.L.Rev. 989, 1004–07 (1986). See also Blumstein, The Fraud and Abuse Statute in an Evolving Health Care Marketplace: Life in the Health Care Speakeasy, 22 Am. J.L. & Med. 205 (1996); Pauly, The Ethics and Economics of Kickbacks and Fee Splitting, 10 Bell J. Econ. 344 (1979). Pauly's article, showing in a medical context how "it is possible for fee splitting to offer incentives which actually improve patient welfare" and to erode "specialist monopoly power," is particularly striking in the present context. Can you reconstruct the line of reasoning that might lead to Pauly's conclusion that fee splitting may do more good than harm?

Paying or Receiving "Remuneration" for Medicare/Medicaid Referrals

United States v. Greber

United States Court of Appeals, Third Circuit, 1985.
760 F.2d 68, cert. denied, 474 U.S. 988 (1985).

■ WEIS, CIRCUIT JUDGE

In this appeal, defendant argues that payments made to a physician for professional services in connection with tests performed by a laboratory cannot be the basis of medicare fraud. We do not agree and hold that if one purpose of the payment was to induce future referrals, the medicare statute has been violated. * * *

Defendant is an osteopathic physician who is board certified in cardiology. In addition to hospital staff and teaching positions, he was the president of Cardio–Med, Inc., an organization which he formed. The company provides physicians with diagnostic services, one of which uses a Holter-monitor. This device, worn for approximately 24 hours, records the patient's cardiac activity on a tape. A computer operated by a cardiac technician scans the tape, and the data is later correlated with an activity diary the patient maintains while wearing the monitor.

Cardio–Med billed Medicare for the monitor service and, when payment was received, forwarded a portion to the referring physician. The government charged that the referral fee was 40 percent of the Medicare payment, not to exceed $65 per patient.

* * *

The proof as to the Medicare fraud counts (18–23) was that defendant had paid a Dr. Avallone and other physicians "interpretation fees" for the doctors' initial consultation services, as well as for explaining the test results to the patients. There was evidence that physicians received "interpretation fees" even though defendant had actually evaluated the monitoring data. Moreover, the fixed percentage paid to the referring physician was more than Medicare allowed for such services.

The government also introduced testimony defendant had given in an earlier civil proceeding. In that case, he had testified that " ... if the doctor didn't get his consulting fee, he wouldn't be using our service. So the doctor got a consulting fee." In addition, defendant told physicians at a hospital that the Board of Censors of the Philadelphia County Medical Society had said the referral fee was legitimate if the physician shared the responsibility for the report. Actually, the Society had stated that there should be separate bills because "for the monitor company to offer payment to the physicians ... is not considered to be the method of choice."

* * *

The Medicare fraud statute was amended by P.L. 95–142, 91 Stat. 1183 (1977). Congress, concerned with the growing problem of fraud and abuse in the system, wished to strengthen the penalties to enhance the deterrent effect of the statute. To achieve this purpose, the crime was upgraded from a misdemeanor to a felony.

Another aim of the amendments was to address the complaints of the United States Attorneys who were responsible for prosecuting fraud cases. They informed Congress that the language of the predecessor statute was "unclear and needed clarification." H.Rep. No. 393, PART II, 95 Cong., 1st Sess. 53, reprinted in 1977 U.S.CODE CONG. & AD.NEWS 3039, 3055.

A particular concern was the practice of giving "kickbacks" to encourage the referral of work. Testimony before the Congressional committee was that "physicians often determine which laboratories would do the test work for their medicaid patients by the amount of the kickbacks and rebates offered by the laboratory.... Kickbacks take a number of forms including cash, long-term credit arrangements, gifts, supplies and equipment, and the furnishing of business machines." Id. at 3048–3049.

To remedy the deficiencies in the statute and achieve more certainty, the present version of [42 U.S.C. § 1395nn(b)(2), now 42 U.S.C. § 1320a–7(b)(2)] was enacted. It provides:

> "whoever knowingly and willfully offers or pays any remuneration (including any kickback, bribe or rebate) directly or indirectly, overtly or covertly in cash or in kind to induce such person—
>
> . . .
>
> (B) to purchase, lease, order, or arrange for or recommend purchasing ... or ordering any ... service or item for which payment may be made ... under this title,
>
> shall be guilty of a felony."

The district judge instructed the jury that the government was required to prove that Cardio–Med paid to Dr. Avallone some part of the amount received from Medicare; that defendant caused Cardio–Med to make the payment; and did so knowingly and willfully as well as with the intent to induce Dr. Avallone to use Cardio–Med's services for patients covered by Medicare. The judge further charged that even if the physician interpreting the test did so as a consultant to Cardio–Med, that fact was immaterial if a purpose of the fee was to induce the ordering of services from Cardio–Med.

Defendant contends that the charge was erroneous. He insists that absent a showing that the only purpose behind the fee was to improperly induce future services, compensating a physician for services actually rendered could not be a violation of the statute.

The government argues that Congress intended to combat financial incentives to physicians for ordering particular services patients did not require.

The language and purpose of the statute support the government's view. Even if the physician performs some service for the money received, the potential for unnecessary drain on the Medicare system remains. The statute is aimed at the inducement factor.

The text refers to "any remuneration." That includes not only sums for which no actual service was performed but also those amounts for which some professional time was expended. "Remunerates" is defined as "to pay an equivalent for service." Webster Third New International Dictionary (1966). By including such items as kickbacks and bribes, the statute expands "remuneration" to cover situations where no service is performed. That a particular payment was a remuneration (which implies that a service was rendered) rather than a kickback, does not foreclose the possibility that a violation nevertheless could exist.

In United States v. Hancock, 604 F.2d 999 (7th Cir.1979), the court applied the term "kickback" found in the predecessor statute to payments made to chiropractors by laboratories which performed blood tests. The chiropractors contended that the amounts they received were legitimate handling fees for their services in obtaining, packaging, and delivering the specimens to the laboratories and then interpreting the results. The court rejected that contention and noted, "The potential for increased costs to the Medicare–Medicaid system and misapplication of federal funds is plain, where payments for the exercise of such judgments are added to the legitimate cost of the transaction ... [T]hese are among the evils Congress sought to prevent by enacting the kickback statutes...." Id at 1001.

Hancock strongly supports the government's position here, because the statute in that case did not contain the word "remuneration." The court nevertheless held that "kickback" sufficiently described the defendants' criminal activity. By adding "remuneration" to the statute in the 1977 amendment, Congress sought to make it clear that even if the transaction was not considered to be a "kickback" for which no service had been rendered, payment nevertheless violated the Act.

* * *

We conclude that the more expansive reading is consistent with the impetus for the 1977 amendments and therefore hold that the district court correctly instructed the jury. If the payments were intended to induce the physician to use Cardio–Med's services, the statute was violated, even if the payments were also intended to compensate for professional services.

A review of the record also convinces us that there was sufficient evidence to sustain the jury's verdict.

* * *

Medical Development Network, Inc. v. Professional Respiratory Care/Home Medical Equipment Services, Inc.

District Court of Appeal of Florida, Fourth District, 1996.
673 So.2d 565.

■ WARNER, JUDGE.

The issue in this appeal from a summary final judgment is whether the "Public Relations Agreement" between appellant, Medical Development Network, Inc. (MDN), and appellee, Professional Respiratory Care/Home Medical Equipment Services, Inc. (PRC), violates the Medicare/Medicaid Anti-Kickback Statute, thereby rendering the agreement void and unenforceable as a matter of law. We hold that the agreement is void and unenforceable as a matter of law, and affirm the summary final judgment.

MDN and PRC entered into a consulting agreement wherein PRC agreed to pay MDN a percentage of all business developed by MDN's marketing of PRC's durable medical supplies to clients, which included physicians, nursing homes, retirement homes, and individual patients. MDN would contact various users of medical equipment, such as nursing homes and physicians, and promote the use of PRC's equipment. Nursing homes would order supplies directly from PRC. Physicians would refer their patients to PRC for lease or sale of needed medical equipment, such as wheelchairs. As many of the patients served were covered by Medicare or Medicaid, PRC's supplies were paid for by these federal funds in large part. PRC would pay MDN a percentage of its sales generated from clients contacted and serviced by MDN.

When PRC breached the agreement, MDN filed suit, and PRC defended on the ground that the agreement was illegal under the Anti-Kickback Statute. The trial court agreed and entered summary judgment in favor of PRC.

To correct the problem of fraud and abuse in the Medicare system, the Medicare fraud statute was amended by Pub.L. No. 95–142, 91 Stat. 1183 (1977), to strengthen penalties and to enhance the deterrent effect of the statute. A specific concern was the practice of giving "kickbacks" to encourage the referral of work. Such practices not only deterred price competition but also tended to encourage overutilization of goods and services within the system. In 1977, Congress amended the act adding the language prohibiting "any remuneration," including kickbacks.

* * *

MDN contends that the act does not apply to the arrangement it had with PRC, because the act applies only to health care providers. However, none of the cases cited by MDN support its contention that only health care providers may violate the act. Moreover, the federal regulations show that an arrangement such as the one between MDN and PRC is within the contemplation of the statute. The Department of Health and Human Services was charged with designing [so-called "safe-harbor"] regulations to specify various payment practices which would not be considered kickbacks for purposes of the act. One statutory exemption provides that payments by an employer to an employee would not be violative of the act. The commentary of the Department noted:

exemptions do not apply to independent contractors

> In response to the October 21, 1987, request for comments, many commentators suggested that we broaden the exemption to apply to independent contractors paid on a commission basis. We have declined to adopt this approach because we are aware of many examples of abusive practices by sales personnel who are paid as independent contractors and who are not under appropriate supervision. We believe that if individuals and entities desire to pay a salesperson on the basis of the amount of business they generate, then to be exempt from civil or criminal prosecution, they should make these salespersons employees where they can and should exert appropriate supervision for the individual's acts.

54 Fed.Reg. 3088, 3093 (1989). This commentary clearly contemplates that an arrangement whereby MDN is paid a percentage of the sales it generates for PRC is violative of the act.

* * *

We * * * therefore affirm the summary final judgment.

NOTES AND QUESTIONS ON THE MEDICARE/MEDICAID ANTI-KICKBACK LEGISLATION

1. To address the problem of overutilization in the Medicare and Medicaid programs, Congress enacted the original "fraud and abuse" law in 1977. "The antikickback section was originally passed in 1972 as a part of two separate statutes, one for Medicare and one for Medicaid. In 1977, the present remuneration language replaced previous kickback, bribe, and rebate language, and the penalty changed from a misdemeanor to a felony. In 1980, the knowing and willful scienter requirement was added. In 1987 the two separate statutes were combined into the present one." Blumstein, The Fraud and Abuse Law in an Evolving Health Care Marketplace: Life in the Health Care Speakeasy, 22 Am. J.L. & Med. 205, 206–07 (1996) [hereinafter, "The Health Care Speakeasy"]. The *Greber* case deals with the law as it was amended in 1980 (as described above). In 1987, the prohibition was moved to a different section of the Social Security Act, § 1128B(b), and of the Code, 42 U.S.C. § 1320a–7b.

The other operative provision of the anti-kickback statute appears in footnote 19 in the next principal case (*Hanlester*), which you should consult at this point. Note that, in addition to prohibiting the offer or payment of illegal "remuneration," the statute also prohibits the solicitation or receipt of payments "in return for" referrals. It thus governs referring professionals as well as institutional providers and commercial enterprises that seek to attract business by offering prohibited inducements. The *MDN* case, reproduced above, illustrates how far the statute reaches into ordinary commercial arrangements.

2. *Sanctions*. In addition to criminal penalties for felonious conduct, the sanctions provided in the anti-kickback law for improperly filed claims include "a civil money penalty of not more than $10,000 for each item or service" in addition to an "assessment of not more than three times the amount claimed for each item or service in lieu of damages sustained by the United States or a State agency because of such a claim." 42 U.S.C.A. § 1320a–7a (West Supp. 1998). Further, "the Secretary may make a determination in the same proceeding to exclude the person from participation in the Federal health care programs * * * and to direct the appropriate State agency to exclude the person from participation in any State health care program."

As a practical matter, the statute's sanctions do not stop there—as the *MDN* case illustrates. Consider also the potential effect of a violation of the anti-kickback statute on the tax-exempt status of a nonprofit health care institution. (Note that fraud and abuse allegations are not directed exclusively at for-profit providers.) Recall GCM 39,862 (reproduced in § B of this chapter), which indicated that a violation of the anti-kickback provision is inconsistent with exempt status. See also Colombo, Health Care Reform and Federal Tax Exemption: Rethinking the Issues, 29 Wake Forest L. Rev. 215, 228–31(1994). Cf. Bob Jones Univ. v. United States, 461 U.S. 574, 588 (1983) (tax-exempt status can be maintained as long as non-profit organization does not run afoul of local laws and public policy).

3. Courts have generally followed the *Greber* court's broad reading of the anti-kickback law. See, e.g., United States v. Bay State Ambulance & Hosp. Rental Serv., Inc., 874 F.2d 20 (1st Cir.1989) (upholding conviction of ambulance company and hospital contracting officer for payments made by former to latter as consultant; court indicated that instruction to the effect that illegal payment must have been made primarily to influence award of contract was more favorable to defendant than required by *Greber*, that the *Greber* reading of the statute was implicitly approved by Congress in passing later legislation, and that it was irrelevant whether payments were reasonable compensation for consultant's services); United States v. Kats, 871 F.2d 105 (9th Cir.1989) (adopting *Greber* reasoning and holding statute violated unless payments were only incidentally intended to induce referrals).

4. *Safe-Harbor Regulations*. Because the *Greber* reading of the fraud and abuse law potentially criminalized a great deal of possibly benign behavior, Congress in the Medicare and Medicaid Patient and Program Protection Act of 1987, Pub. L. No. 100–93, § 14(a), authorized DHHS to promulgate so-called "safe-harbor" regulations specifying business practices that would not be deemed unlawful even though they could easily be interpreted as involving "remuneration" and might have been designed, at least in part,

to induce referrals. 42 U.S.C. § 1320a–7b note (1991). The resulting regulations appear at 42 C.F.R. § 1001.952 (1997).

The idea behind the safe-harbor regulations was to preserve the sweeping prohibition manifested in the *Greber* case while authorizing DHHS to declare administratively that certain conduct falling within the letter of the law would nevertheless be deemed acceptable and shielded from liability. The DHHS Office of the Inspector General (OIG) has emphasized that the regulations are intended only to identify behavior that is clearly lawful and not to state what behavior is actually illegal. Thus, if behavior does not fall within the four corners of a safe harbor, it will be analyzed under *Greber*. As drafted by DHHS, the safe harbors are narrowly defined and leave unimmunized many transactions that, if not efficiency-enhancing, seem relatively innocuous. To be sure, behavior falling outside a safe harbor may nevertheless pass muster, but the prevailing test, as enunciated in *Greber* and other cases noted here, leaves little room for maneuver.

See if you can begin to imagine the large number of possible business arrangements and transactions between health care providers and suppliers of goods and services that naturally include the essential elements of a fraud and abuse violation—"remuneration" plus the intent to attract business financed by Medicare/Medicaid. To be sure, the safe-harbor regulations remove many of these transactions and relationships from legal jeopardy if highly specified conditions are met in each case. But just listing the types of practices, transactions and relationships to which the safe harbors apply forcefully illustrates the statute's impressive reach: investment interests; space and equipment rentals; personal services and management contracts; sale of a practice to another practitioner; referral services; discounts or payments under a warranty by a seller to a buyer of an item the cost of which may be reimbursed under a federal health program; bona fide employment relationships; group purchasing organizations; waivers of beneficiary deductibles and coinsurance (which may induce utilization of unnecessary services); increased coverage, reduced cost-sharing amounts, or reduced premium amounts offered by health plans to beneficiaries in health plans participating in a federal health program; and price reductions given by a contract provider to an organized health plan to attract patients. Some of these transactions and relationships are examined in notes at the end of this section.

More safe harbors may be developed in time. Legislation in 1996 (the Kassebaum–Kennedy act, discussed further below)

> establishe[d] a formalized process of accountability in the development of additional safe harbors. HHS is required to solicit proposals for new safe harbors or revisions of existing ones. If the government does not accept a recommendation, it is obliged to explain its rationale in an annual report to Congress. That procedure, in turn, provides a potential vehicle for further refinements of the fraud and abuse law. Possible new safe harbors could specify (1) that inducing future referrals must be a "significant" (and not just any) purpose in the financial arrangements among providers; (2) that

reducing Medicare or Medicaid costs is a defense to a prospective fraud and abuse violation in the absence of significant, unacceptable decreases in the level of quality; and (3) that a defense to a prospective fraud and abuse violation is established when improved quality or choice is provided to the program beneficiaries at no increased costs.

Blumstein, Rationalizing the Fraud and Abuse Statute, Health Affs., Winter 1996, p. 118, 126. As noted further below, the 1996 legislation also required DHHS, on request, to issue advisory opinions on fraud and abuse matters, so that providers would be better able to comply with the law.

5. What is the precise concern prompting the federal government's opposition to kickbacks, etc.? Why should the government care how the profits from treating federal beneficiaries are divided? Although the government has a legitimate concern about inducements to provide unneeded or inappropriate services and about adverse effects on the quality of care, is it clear how the elimination of payments to induce referrals will affect the quality of care, access to services, or program costs? What are (and what is the significance of) the possible effects on system efficiency, including realization of economies of scale? In answering these questions, it may be helpful to consider why fraud and abuse issues loom so large in care financed by the Medicare and Medicaid programs yet seem entirely manageable in privately financed care.

In reading the following materials, consider whether Congress may have criminalized conduct simply because it exploits weaknesses in the design and administration of the Medicare and Medicaid programs and not because it is reprehensible in any objective sense. Indeed, some of the conduct subject to penalty under the anti-kickback law appears fairly well sanctioned in common practice in the private sector, thus passing muster under, at least, the morals of the marketplace. To be sure, some providers are unduly opportunistic, even venal and guilty of undeniable fraud on the government. But does the federal government seem to be using the threat of criminal prosecution also against providers and entrepreneurs who are merely adapting to a more entrepreneurial, incentive-driven health care marketplace? See Blumstein, Health Care Reform and Competing Visions of Medical Care: Antitrust and State Provider Cooperation Legislation, 79 Cornell L. Rev. 1459, 1472 (1994) (arguing that the anti-kickback crusade manifests a "clash of cultures," has created "significant barriers to market-oriented attempts to rationalize the medical care marketplace," and "must be reexamined if market incentives are to succeed within the medical care system"). How objectionable is it, after all, for providers and entrepreneurs to pursue their economic advantage (i.e., profits or market share) by seeking lucrative opportunities to care for beneficiaries of a poorly administered public program? See, e.g., Kleinke, Deconstructing the Columbia/HCA Investigation, Health Affs., Mar.-Apr. 1998, p. 7 (suggesting that Columbia/HCA was in some respects ahead of its time in consolidating and reorganizing health services and was singled out for investigation and prosecution because it was particularly adept at beating the government at its own game; "it is easy to view the [Columbia/HCA] investigation as a public policy drama, a battle over the philosophy and pace of market-driven reform"); but see critiques of Kleinke article by Goldsmith, Reinhardt, and Vladeck, in id. at 27, 30, & 37.

It is notable that, even with the safe-harbor regulations in place, a recent audit of the Medicare program by DHHS and the U.S. General Accounting Office still found rampant fraud and abuse—$23 billion of waste and improper payments by HCFA (roughly 14% of program costs) in the single year of 1996. See Medicare Audit: Hearing Before the House Comm. on Ways and Means, Subcomm. on Health, 105th Cong., 1st Sess. (1997) (statement of June Gibbs Brown, DHHS Inspector General). See generally Mashaw & Marmor, Conceptualizing, Estimating, and Reforming Fraud, Waste, and Abuse in Healthcare Spending, 11 Yale J. on Reg. 455, 463–70 (1994). Based on your reading of chapter 2(§D), how might the federal government's efforts be directed toward reforming Medicare payment methods and program design—in lieu of attempting to suppress providers' opportunistic behavior by criminalizing it, by using increased sanctions to raise providers' stakes in the game, and by maintaining blurry or irrational lines to deter efforts to exploit system loopholes?

NOTES AND QUESTIONS ON IDENTIFYING FRAUD IN HEALTH CARE TRANSACTIONS AND RELATIONSHIPS

1. *The Different Faces of Fraud.* You should realize by now that significant conflicts of interests pervade the health care industry, are largely unavoidable (except by creating new ones), and manifest themselves in many ways, not all of them deserving the pejorative label of "fraud." Indeed, health care fraud is not a monolithic issue. Instead, it has at least two faces. On one hand, there is "raw fraud" (or "layman's fraud"), which is what naturally comes to mind whenever fraud is mentioned. Examples include billing for services not provided, providing and billing for services known to be medically inappropriate, and intentionally providing services of inferior quality. For a particularly egregious instance of such fraudulent conduct, see United States v. Hughes, 895 F.2d 1135 (6th Cir.1990) (clinic routinely prescribed controlled substances for drug addicts in return for blood samples, billing Medicaid for testing same and collecting kickbacks in the form of disguised rental payments from pharmacy filling prescriptions).

Fraud of these conventional kinds can be distinguished from the kinds of conduct characterized as fraud in anti-kickback cases like *Greber*. Some of the problems created by extending the definition of fraud to reach more ambiguous conduct appear in the following excerpt:

> The so-called antikickback provision bars the knowing and willful use of "remuneration," direct or indirect, to induce or solicit referrals. This provision is designed to eliminate incentives for the overutilization of services. In a world of fee-for-service payments and cost-based reimbursements of expenses, there is much to be said for outlawing measures that can cost the federal programs money that might not be appropriately spent. However, as the market has evolved and financial incentives have become part of the fabric of the health care industry, the antikickback law

has had unfortunate consequences. Doing a good job for the purpose of encouraging repeat Medicare business can be a technical violation. Arrangements among providers designed to promote high quality in exchange for referrals (for example, encouraging a group of physicians to invest in new equipment in exchange for a promise of referrals) can run afoul of the law. Indeed, a hospital's provision of free doughnuts in a physician lounge can be "fraud" if it's intended—even in small part—to induce physicians to refer Medicare or Medicaid patients. In short, market-driven activities aimed at improving efficiency or market share may be labeled fraud if the intent is to achieve a future flow of business.

Blumstein, What Precisely is "Fraud" in the Health Care Industry?, Wall St. J., Dec. 8, 1997, p. A25.

May physicians accept gifts or entertainment from professional colleagues to whom they refer Medicare or Medicaid beneficiaries? May a manufacturer of medical devices offer gifts or educational programs in exotic locations to physicians who prescribe its products? May a hospital provide preferred parking (or any other amenities) to staff physicians? (Is it not likely that some part of the hospital's motivation is a desire to ensure continued referrals of federal program beneficiaries?)

2. Recall the ESWL problem preceding the *Greber* case. Would a payment for follow-up care to a urologist referring a patient for lithotripsy, as contemplated in the problem, violate federal law if the patient were a Medicare beneficiary? How would you defend the lithotripsy center if it were charged with such a violation? Were either the patients or the government harmed by the practices in question? Is a demonstrated or demonstrable harm to patients or harm to the government as a payer a necessary element of the offense? Would it be appropriate, as has been suggested, to allow defendants to defend their conduct by showing that it was not harmful either to the government or to public beneficiaries? See Blumstein, Rationalizing the Fraud and Abuse Statute, Health Affs., Winter 1996, p. 118. See also Hall, Making Sense of Referral Fee Statutes, 13 J. Health Pol., Pol'y & L. 623, 629 (1988) (recommending that fees "incidentally related to a referral [be considered valid] if they are fully earned by legitimate nonreferral services—that is, if they do not exceed the fair market value of necessary services bargained for at arm's length").

How can health care providers (e.g., in the ESWL problem and in *Greber*) afford to pay kickbacks? There are several possible explanations, but one possibility is that the federal government is regularly paying too much for services of the type in question, inducing an unseemly scramble for the lucrative business. Indeed, it has been suggested that evidence that "remuneration" was being paid for referrals could serve as an "enforcement cuing mechanism" that "could (and probably should) trigger review of payment levels." Blumstein, "The Health Care Speakeasy," 22 Am. J.L. & Med. at 229 n.202. Of course, if kickbacks are effectively suppressed, they cannot serve this function, leaving the government to continue paying excessive fees for the services in question. Thus, Blumstein (id.) advocates that, "[i]nstead of suppressing payments," the law "could require disclosure as a market-driven way of triggering review of payment levels." Disclosure might also invite attention to the possibility of inappropriate, cost-increasing referrals or sacrifices of quality.

3. *The MDN Case.* Were you surprised, in reading the *MDN* case, to see the anti-fraud law applied to prohibit ordinary commission arrangements with sales agents selling health care products to health care providers? For another case to the same effect as *MDN*, see Nursing Home Consultants, Inc. v. Quantum Health Services, Inc., 926 F.Supp. 835 (E.D.Ark.1996), aff'd per curiam, 112 F.3d 513 (8th Cir.1997). In that case, the court denied enforcement of a contract (as well as recovery under quantum meruit) for services in identifying nursing home residents who were potential users of defendant's products; the plaintiff was to be compensated according to the volume of sales to the individuals identified. In finding a violation, the district court noted that, while there is a regulatory safe harbor for contracts for sales effort, it applies only if "the aggregate compensation paid to the agent over the term of the [written] agreement is set in advance, is consistent with fair market value in arm's-length transactions and is not determined in a manner that takes into account the volume or value of any referrals or business otherwise generated between the parties for which payment may be made in whole or in part under Medicare [or any other federal health care program]." See 42 C.F.R. § 1001.952(d)(5) (1997). Interestingly, there is a statutory safe harbor authorizing commission arrangements in some circumstances, but only where there is a written contract between an agent and a provider under a federal health program (not between an agent and a supplier). 42 U.S.C.A. § 1320a–7b(b)(3)(C) (West Supp. 1998). See *Nursing Home Consultants*, 926 F. Supp. at 843 n.19.

4. *Physicians and Institutional Providers.* Consider a hospital emergency department, from which many patients are admitted to hospital beds. Might any compensation paid by the hospital to ED physicians be deemed a payment for referrals? If the ED is staffed by physicians who are salaried employees of the hospital, the case falls within an exception (safe harbor) for amounts paid to bona fide employees by employers. 42 C.F.R. § 1001.952(i) (1997). If the emergency room is run on a contract basis by an independent firm, however, fraud and abuse law may be implicated. Although another safe harbor—for "personal services"—might permit the payment from the hospital to the physician, it would not clearly protect the physician who uses remuneration (referrals to the hospital) to retain the emergency room contract with the hospital. 42 C.F.R. § 1001.952(d) (1997). Thus, an emergency room doctor or firm hired as an independent contractor to work in or operate the ED may be in some jeopardy for referring even medically appropriate cases to the hospital if it ever crosses the contractor's mind that failure to hospitalize to the hospital might result in termination of his or her contract. Obviating much of this discussion is, of course, EMTALA (see chapter 1(§B)), which imposes enough barriers to transfers to other hospitals to ensure that the hospital maintaining the ED will retain all the patients it is arguably capable of treating. On the other hand, what about decisions not to hospitalize federal beneficiaries coming

to the ED with conditions for which further "observation" might reasonably be prescribed. (In such a case, which side is Medicare on?)

It is apparently common for radiologists, anesthesiologists, and pathologists to make payments, perhaps a percentage of their gross, to the hospitals in which they work. These payments, which sometimes exceed the fair value of benefits conferred on the physicians by the hospital, may be interpreted as unlawful remuneration paid in return for referrals of Medicare or Medicaid business from other physicians on the hospital staff. The DHHS Office of the Inspector General (OIG) once warned that it was inclined to adopt that interpretation. OIG, Financial Arrangements Between Hospitals and Hospital-Based Physicians (Management Advisory Report 1991). At present, no safe harbor appears to protect such arrangements.

For a general discussion regarding the concerns that fraud and abuse law raises with regard to the relationships between physicians and institutional providers, see Hitchner, et al., Integrated Delivery Systems: A Survey of Organizational Models, 29 Wake Forest L. Rev. 273 (1994).

5. *Physician Recruitment.* Recall the problem on physician recruitment in § B of this chapter (where tax issues were principally under discussion). Would the arrangement contemplated there—retention on a hospital's staff of a highly valued physician treating mostly Medicare patients—violate the anti-kickback statute as construed in *Greber*? What difference would it make, if any, if the physician were being attracted from a distant location? As a legal matter, is it relevant that a recruited physician would bring skills that the community or the hospital needs as long as the hospital is partly motivated by a desire to retain or expand its Medicare clientele?

In Polk County v. Peters, 800 F.Supp. 1451, 1456 (E.D.Tex.1992), a physician who failed to repay money advanced to him by a hospital under a physician recruitment agreement prevailed in a breach of contract action filed against him because the court found that "there can be no doubt that the benefits extended to Defendant were, in part, an inducement for him to refer patients to the hospital." Note that the physician, seeking to escape his contract obligation, essentially admitted having committed a felony. (Would you have recommended this strategy to your client?)

Physician recruitment issues also arise under the more recent federal anti-referral legislation, 42 U.S.C.A. § 1395nn (West Supp. 1998) (popularly known, after its principal congressional sponsor, as Stark I and Stark II). This legislation, which will be discussed at greater length later in this section, flatly bars certain "financial relationship[s]" between a physician and a health care entity, including a "compensation arrangement." A compensation arrangement exists whenever "remuneration" is provided, so that any payment by a hospital to a physician it recruits is open to question. The Stark law makes an explicit exception for physician recruitment situations, however, if the physician is not "precluded from establishing staff privileges at another hospital or referring business to another entity." 42 U.S.C.A. § 1395nn(e)(5) (West Supp. 1998); 42 C.F.R.

§ 411.357(e) (1996). Of course, it is not clear that the arrangement in the § B problem would qualify as a "recruitment."

NOTES AND QUESTIONS ON THE ADMINISTRATION AND ENFORCEMENT OF THE FEDERAL ANTI-FRAUD LEGISLATION

1. *Counseling on Fraud and Abuse Issues.* As a way of appreciating why fraud and abuse issues have generated so much business for lawyers, consider the difficulty of complying with the statute, as interpreted, in a complex commercial world in which competition and commercial advantage practically demand that paying patients be attracted and in which such patients can be gained only by attracting physicians themselves (enlisting them in a vertically integrated arrangement) or by attracting their referrals. Unless the transaction falls within the precise contours of a so-called safe harbor, could you as a private lawyer give a "clean" opinion on any joint venture, financial arrangement, or physician recruitment scheme in which you sensed a possible inducement motivation? Might your client, seeing similar things going on all around it, look elsewhere for an attorney who is not "overly technical"? Within a law firm environment, how would you as an associate handle these issues? How should a partner in the firm deal with these questions with respect to clients or with respect to other lawyers in the firm?

2. *Advisory Opinions.* Practicing lawyers, frustrated by their inability to give definitive, reliable opinions on innovative arrangements in a rapidly changing marketplace, unsuccessfully urged DHHS to issue authoritative advisory opinions on proposed transactions. In the Health Insurance Portability and Accountability Act of 1996 (the Kassebaum–Kennedy act), Congress (over the objections of the Clinton administration) required that DHHS render advisory opinions on proposed arrangements on request and within 60 days—much as the IRS does on tax questions. See 42 U.S.C.A. § 1320a–7d(b) (West Supp. 1998); 42 C.F.R. § 1008 (1997). Unlike IRS advisory opinions, however, opinions issued by DHHS/OIG are binding, but only with respect to the parties and the transactions in question (assuming full disclosure). The government is free to object to and challenge other comparable transactions.

In Blumstein's view, provision for advisory opinions

> reestablishes the rule of law and provides a case-by-case opportunity for the government to determine what structures and organizational arrangements are beneficial. The government then will be in a better position to develop broader, generalized rules that are more widely applicable. This is the familiar common-law process, whereby rules or principles are derived by examining the rationales used over time in deciding on the merits of specific situations.

Blumstein, Rationalizing the Fraud and Abuse Statute, Health Affs., Winter 1996, p. 118, 126.

Do you agree that DHHS should issue advisory opinions under the anti-kickback law, at least on a selective basis? Is such a practice unduly burdensome to the agency, detracting from its enforcement effort, or is it an efficient way to obtain voluntary compliance with the statute's primary objectives? Is it ever proper, under separation-of-powers principles, for a prosecutor to announce that he or she will not prosecute certain violations of a statute, particularly a statute laying down an intent-based "per se" rule such as the one articulated in *Greber*? In opposing the provision for advisory opinions, Attorney General Janet Reno expressed the concern that physicians would use the opinions as "a shield for fraudulent activities that rob the Medicare system and cause real harm to patients." Janet Reno, letter to Speaker of the House Gingrich, June 8, 1996. She also argued that conduct should be deemed criminal (or not) only after an independent investigation, not after a review of information provided by the potential defendant. Despite this early opposition (President Clinton's fiscal 1998 budget submission proposed repeal of the advisory opinion procedure), DHHS/OIG now appears to accept advisory opinions, describing them as " 'Case Specific' Safe Harbors":

> The OIG views the advisory opinion process with a means of analysis similar to the safe harbor provisions, with one major exception. Where safe harbors describe generalized, hypothetical arrangements which are protected, we view an advisory opinion as a means of relating the antikickback statute to the particular facts of a specific arrangement.

62 Fed. Reg. 7350, 7351 (Feb. 17, 1997).

The Balanced Budget Act of 1997 established a comparable process for the issuance of binding advisory opinions in administering the Stark anti-self-referral laws, discussed infra. See 42 U.S.C.A. § 1395nn(g)(6) (West Supp. 1998).

3. *Encouraging Voluntary Compliance.* The OIG has sought to encourage voluntary compliance and self-reporting as a way of cleaning up arrangements that were previously commonplace but are now regarded as unlawful. Beginning in 1995, a pilot Voluntary Disclosure Program launched as part of "Operation Restore Trust" was offered to corporate providers of nursing home and home health care and of durable medical equipment in five major states. (The program was later expanded to additional states.) Providers were given a chance to come forward and disclose violations of the anti-fraud act in exchange for the opportunity "to minimize the potential cost and disruption of a full scale Federal audit and investigation; to negotiate a monetary settlement * * *, and to reduce or avoid an OIG permissive exclusion [from Medicare and Medicaid]." The program attracted few volunteers, however, perhaps because the information disclosed might provide a basis for excluding the volunteer from the federal health programs, at the OIG's discretion. In addition, there was no guarantee that the sensitive information would not be disclosed to the Department of Justice or to private parties—whom the program did not preclude from acting under other criminal or civil laws.

An example of a more successful compliance program was called "Physicians at Teaching Hospitals" (PATH). PATH encouraged independent audits of teaching physicians' billing practices under procedures established by DHHS.

4. *Civil Penalties.* In addition to criminal prohibitions such those enforced in *Greber,* there are civil remedies for fraud and abuse in federal health programs. The potential for large cash recoveries makes active enforcement profitable for the government. The Kassebaum–Kennedy legislation in 1996 required the DHHS Inspector General to set up a new program with the Department of Justice to coordinate federal, state, and local enforcement programs in the area of health care fraud and abuse. The Health Care Fraud and Abuse Account provides substantial funding (in excess of $100 million, with increments of 15% for the first few years) to DHHS and DOJ for such enforcement. See 42 U.S.C.A. § 1395i(k) (West Supp. 1998). This fund includes money recovered from civil monetary penalties as provided in the Kassebaum–Kennedy legislation. 42 U.S.C.A. § 1320a–7c (West Supp. 1998).

The Civil Monetary Penalties Law (CMPL), 42 U.S.C.A. § 1320a–7a (West Supp. 1998), provides for the enforcement by civil penalties of a wide variety of statutory rules under federal health programs, including rules aimed at fraud and abuse. See Bernstein v. Sullivan, 914 F.2d 1395 (10th Cir.1990) (upholding the constitutionality of civil penalties if the sanction serves the goal of making the government whole rather than of punishing the offender); Chapman v. DHHS, 821 F.2d 523 (10th Cir.1987) (resolving the dispute over proper calculation of penalty, which may equal twice the amount falsely claimed whether or not the claim was paid). Actions are initiated by DHHS rather than the Justice Department, and penalties may also include exclusion from participation in federal health programs. The 1996 Kassebaum–Kennedy amendments to the CMPL included an increase of the penalty amount to $10,000 per item or service. The Balanced Budget Act of 1997 established a $50,000 civil monetary penalty for a knowing or willful false statement or representation of a material fact in any application for any benefit or payment under a federal health care program—that is, for any violation of 42 U.S.C.A. § 1320a–7b(a)(1), (2) (West Supp. 1998).

The CMPL makes it illegal for any person (which includes an organization, agency, or other entity but does not include a beneficiary) "knowingly" to present a claim that the person "knows or should know" was not provided or is otherwise fraudulent. 42 U.S.C.A. § 1320a–7a(a)(1)(A), (B) (West Supp. 1998). The Kassebaum–Kennedy legislation clarified the knowledge standard required for a CMPL violation. The law now defines "should know" as involving "deliberate ignorance * * * or reckless disregard of the truth or falsity of * * * information," but "no proof of specific intent to defraud is required." 42 U.S.C.A. § 1320a–7a(i)(7) (West Supp. 1998). This scienter requirement is borrowed from that found in the False Claims Act, 31 U.S.C.A. § 3729(b) (West Supp. 1998), considered below.

Self–Referral Under the Anti–Kickback Law

Hanlester Network v. Shalala

United States Court of Appeals, Ninth Circuit, 1995.
51 F.3d 1390.

■ TANNER, SENIOR DISTRICT JUDGE [sitting by designation]:

Plaintiffs/appellants appeal the district court's grant of summary judgment in favor of the Secretary, and denial of plaintiffs/appellants motion for summary judgment.

The issues presented are whether appellants violated the provisions of the Medicare–Medicaid antikickback statute by (1) offering or paying remuneration to physician limited partners to induce the referral of program-related business to limited partnership laboratories, or (2) soliciting or receiving remuneration "in return for" referrals by virtue of their management agreement with Smithkline BioScience Laboratories (SKBL) * * *.

[In 1987 and 1988, The Hanlester Network (Hanlester), a California general partnership, offered limited partnerships in three clinical laboratories (PPCL, Placer, and Omni) to physician investors—the minimum investment was $1500. Each lab entered into a laboratory management agreement with SKBL under which SKBL, in return for a percentage (80% or so) of net cash receipts, supervised the labs' administration and operations, employed the necessary personnel, provided some lab equipment not provided by the labs themselves, and conducted billing and collection activities for them. Under a "laboratory support services agreement" with SKBL, Hanlester set up and serviced client accounts for the labs.]

Hanlester was notified by the Inspector General (I.G.) of the Department of Health and Human Services (DHHS) in December 1989 that he had determined that the Hanlester respondents (hereafter referred to as appellants) had violated § 1128B(b)(2) of the Social Security Act (the Act) by offering and paying remuneration to physician-investors to induce them to refer laboratory tests to the three Hanlester laboratories. The Hanlester appellants were also told they had violated § 1128B(b)(1) of the Act by soliciting and receiving payments from SKBL in return for referrals of lab tests, and that it would be proposed that all of the appellants be excluded from the Medicare and state health care programs under § 1128(b)(7) for varying periods of time. * * *

[T]he ALJ found that all nine appellants had violated § 1128B(b)(2) of the Social Security Act by knowingly and willfully offering or paying remuneration to physicians to induce them to refer program-related business. The ALJ also found that all appellants except Welsh and Huntsinger violated § 1128B(b)(1) by knowingly and willfully soliciting or receiving remuneration in return for referring program-related business. The ALJ further concluded that permissive exclusions under § 1128(b)(7) were necessary for some, but not all appellants.

[The Departmental Appeals Board (DAB)] affirmed the ALJ's findings and conclusions with respect to the violations by appellants, but vacated his decision not to impose exclusions on all appellants. Hanlester appealed to the district court * * *. The district court granted the Secretary's motion for summary judgment, and denied appellants' motion for summary judgment. Appellants timely appealed.

* * *

This is the first instance in which physician self-referral joint ventures have been challenged under the Act, and in which the Act has been applied to arrangements other than kickbacks, bribes, or rebates, as a basis for excluding persons from participation in Medicare/Medicaid programs.

Nothing in the language of the statute itself prohibits joint venture arrangements. We must, therefore, look to the legislative history, the Act's purpose and context to determine whether such arrangements violate the statute.

The Statute

Congress, concerned with escalating fraud and abuse in the Medicare-Medicaid system, amended the misdemeanor antikickback statute in 1977 to strengthen the government's ability to prosecute and punish fraud in the system. Language was added prohibiting (1) the solicitation or receipt of "any remuneration (including any kickback, bribe, or rebate) directly or indirectly, overtly or covertly, in cash or in kind," in return for referrals, and (2) the offer or payment of such remuneration to "induce" referrals. Congress also upgraded the violation to a felony.

In 1987, Congress consolidated the antikickback laws for Medicare and state health care programs into § 1128B(b) of the Social Security Act, 42 U.S.C. § 1320a–7b. Also through amendment, Congress authorized the exclusion from Medicare or Medicaid program participation of individuals or entities found by the Secretary to have committed an act proscribed by § 1128B(b) of the Act.

Both § 1128B(b)(1), which prohibits solicitation or receipt of remuneration "in return for" the referral of program-related business, and (b)(2), which proscribes offers or payments of remuneration "to induce" referrals of program-related business, are implicated here.

Proof of Agreement

We first address the threshold question of whether proof of an agreement is required to establish a violation of either subsection of the antikickback statute.

[The court held that proof of existence of an agreement to refer program-related business is not required to establish violation of § 1128B and then ruled that the statute is not unconstitutionally vague.]

Offer or Payment to Induce Referrals

The Secretary claims that appellants knowingly and willfully engaged in conduct which violated the antikickback laws. We address the subsection (b)(2) violation first.

In order to find a violation of section 1128B(b)(2) of the Social Security Act, we must conclude that appellants knowingly and willfully offered or paid remuneration to induce referrals of program-related business.[13]

13. The relevant portions of § 1128B(b)(2) [42 U.S.C. § 1320a–7b(b)(2)] read:

(2) whoever knowingly and willfully offers or pays any remuneration (includ-

Remuneration

Congress introduced the broad term "remuneration" in the 1977 amendment of the statute to clarify the types of financial arrangements and conduct to be classified as illegal under Medicare and Medicaid. The phrase "any remuneration" was intended to broaden the reach of the law which previously referred only to kickbacks, bribes, and rebates.

Inducement

Appellants argue that the term "induce" is synonymous with "to encourage," and that encouragement is not prohibited by the statute. Appellants are correct that mere encouragement would not violate the statute. However, the term "induce" is not defined simply by reference to influence or encouragement.

The term "induce" has been defined as follows: to bring on or about, to affect, cause, to influence to an act or course of conduct, lead by persuasion or reasoning, incite by motives, prevail on. Black's Law Dictionary, 697 (6th ed. 1990).

The Secretary determined that the phrase "to induce" in § 1128B(b)(2) of the Act connotes "an intent to exercise influence over the reason or judgment of another in an effort to cause the referral of program-related business". We agree with this interpretation. We now look to the conduct of the parties to determine whether the statute was violated.

Hanlester Appellants

The I.G. argued that appellants unlawfully induced referrals in the way in which they marketed the limited partnerships. [The marketing strategy was to enlist physician investors who were in a position to refer substantial quantities of tests to joint venture labs.]

At the time appellants entered into the management agreements, these types of arrangements were fairly common. Health care joint ventures such as that entered into by appellants were not per se unlawful. The evidence shows that Hanlester desired to comply with the law and structured its business operation in a manner which it believed to be lawful. There is ample evidence that appellants intended to encourage limited partners to refer business to the joint venture laboratories. The appellants offered physicians the opportunity to profit indirectly from referrals when they could not profit directly. Potential partners were told that the success of the limited partnerships depended on referrals from the limited partners.

ing any kickback, bribe, or rebate) directly or indirectly, overtly or covertly, in cash or in kind to any person to induce such person—

* * *

(B) to purchase, lease, order or arrange for or recommend purchasing, leasing, or ordering any good, facility, service, or item for which payment may be made in whole or in part under [Medicare or Medicaid], shall be guilty of a felony....

While substantial cash distributions were made to limited partners by the joint venture labs, dividends were paid to limited partners based on each individual's ownership share of profits, and not on the volume of their referrals. Payments were made to limited partners whether or not they referred business to the joint venture labs.

The fact that a large number of referrals resulted in the potential for a high return on investment, or that the practical effect of low referral rates was failure for the labs, is insufficient to prove that appellants offered or paid remuneration to induce referrals. The conduct of Patricia Hitchcock, however, is another matter.

Hanlester told prospective limited partners of the joint venture labs that the private placement memoranda issued for the limited partnerships were the only sales material which could be used in connection with the sale of shares. In spite of this, Ms. Hitchcock implied that eligibility to purchase shares depended on an agreement to refer program-related business; told prospective limited partners that the number of shares they would be permitted to purchase in PPCL, Omni, and Placer would depend on the volume of business that they referred to the labs; and stated that partners who did not refer business would be pressured to leave the partnerships. Hitchcock also told potential investors that the partners' return on their investment would be virtually guaranteed. Hitchcock's representations to limited partners constitutes offers of payment to induce referrals of program-related business.

The ALJ found that Patricia Hitchcock, acting as an agent of the Hanlester Network and the joint venture laboratories, violated section 1128B(b)(2), and held the Hanlester Network, PPCL, Omni, and Placer liable for her acts on the theory of respondeat superior.

In order to prove that appellants violated the antikickback statute, the government must also prove that appellants' conduct was knowing and willful.

The Scienter Requirement

* * * The Supreme Court has defined "Willfully" as "a voluntary, intentional violation of a known legal duty". Most recently, the Supreme Court has ruled that to establish willfulness, the Government must prove that defendants knew their conduct was unlawful. Ratzlaf v. United States, 510 U.S. 135, 137, 114 S.Ct. 655, 657, 126 L.Ed.2d 615 (1994). * * *

We construe "knowingly and willfully" in § 1128B(b)(2) of the antikickback statute as requiring appellants to (1) know that § 1128B prohibits offering or paying remuneration to induce referrals, and (2) engage in prohibited conduct with the specific intent to disobey the law.

Liability of the Hanlester Network and Joint Venture Labs

Patricia Hitchcock's representations to limited partners exceeded the parameters of the private placement memorandum issued by the Hanlester Network. Her actions reflect both knowledge that her conduct was unlawful, and a specific intent to disobey the law. Her conduct was knowing and willful.

Because Hitchcock was acting as an agent for Hanlester and the joint venture labs, these corporate entities may be held vicariously liable for her actions. Moreover, the fact that Hitchcock acted contrary to the corporations' stated policy does not absolve them of liability. * * * The ALJ determined that Hanlester and the joint venture labs permitted Hitchcock to engage in conduct violative of § 1128B within the scope of her employment. Thus, the Secretary's finding that Respondents Hanlester, Placer, Omni and PPCL "knowingly and willfully" violated § 1128B(b)(2) through the conduct of their agent, Ms. Hitchcock, is supported by substantial evidence in the record.

Vicarious liability, however, does not extend to the partners individually.

* * *

There is no evidence that Lewand, Tasha, Welsh, Huntsinger or Keorle either directed or approved of the unauthorized representations made by Patricia Hitchcock in any way. In fact, Ms. Hitchcock's actions were contrary to their directions.

The I.G. did not prove that any of the individual appellants conditioned the purchase of shares on an agreement to order tests; or that they conditioned the number of shares sold on the amount of business that the physicians agreed to refer; or authorized the ouster of partners who failed to refer business. Therefore, these appellants are not personally liable for the unlawful conduct of Hanlester, PPCL, Omni, and Placer, which resulted from Ms. Hitchcock's unlawful acts. To the extent that the Secretary now contends that appellants' conduct was unlawful, any illegality was not intentional.

We now consider whether appellants violated § 1128B(b)(1). Solicitation or Receipt of Remuneration in Return for Referrals Subsection (b)(1) prohibits the receipt of remuneration in return for referrals.[19]

The Secretary characterized the joint venture labs as "sham" operations which served as mere conduits for the payment of monies to physicians in return for the referral of tests from the labs to SKBL.

The antikickback statute proscribes solicitation or receipt of remuneration directly or indirectly, overtly or covertly, in cash or in kind.

19. The relevant text of section § 1128B(b)(1) [42 U.S.C. § 1320a–7b(b)(1)] states:

> (1) whoever knowingly and willfully solicits or receives any remuneration (including any kickback, bribe, or rebate) directly or indirectly, overtly or covertly, in cash or in kind—
>
> * * *
>
> (B) in return for purchasing, leasing, ordering, or arranging for or recommending purchasing, leasing, or ordering any good, facility, service, or item for which payment may be made in whole or in part under [Medicare or Medicaid],
>
> shall be guilty of a felony.

In [United States v. Bay State Ambulance, 874 F.2d 20 (1st Cir.1989)], the court held that "remuneration" encompasses both sums for which no actual service was performed, and sums for which some service was performed.

The master laboratory services agreement between Hanlester and SKBL specified that PPCL, Omni, and Placer were required to provide facilities and equipment necessary for the operation of the clinical labs, and to repair and maintain lab space and pay utility charges. SKBL had a duty to staff, operate, and supervise the labs, and to conduct all billing and collection activities on their behalf. SKBL was to receive a fee of 76% of the laboratories' net revenues. The appellants received 24% of net revenues.

There is no question that appellants received substantial economic benefit from their relationship with SKBL. In addition to a net profit, appellants received benefits in the form of (1) SKBL's assumption of the operating risks and management responsibilities for the laboratories and appellants' corresponding relief from those duties, (2) SKBL's payment of anticipated receipts in advance, and (3) the use of SKBL's name and reputation as an enticement for enlisting potential limited partners.

The management services agreement between SKBL and appellants reflects a relatively common practice in the clinical laboratory field. There is no evidence that appellants intended to conceal payments from SKBL to physicians in return for referrals.

The Hanlester appellants believed their conduct to be lawful. The evidence shows that no payments were made to appellants, and that payments actually flowed from PPCL, Omni, and Placer to SKBL in the form of fees for its management services. The I.G. did not prove that any of the appellants intentionally solicited or received remuneration from SKBL in return for referrals. Therefore, the Secretary's finding that appellants "knowingly and willfully" solicited and received remuneration in return for referrals is not supported by substantial evidence.

Permissive Program Exclusions

The Secretary's authority to impose a civil remedy against parties who violate § 1128B(b) derives from § 1128(b)(7), which applies to "any individual or entity" whom the Secretary determines has committed an act described in § 1128B.

The remedial purpose of § 1128(b) is to enable the Secretary to protect federally-funded health care programs and their beneficiaries and recipients from future conduct which is or might be harmful.

There is no evidence that Hanlester, PPCL, Omni, or Placer caused harm to the Medicare or Medicaid programs. Because liability is strictly vicarious, emanating totally from the conduct of Ms. Hitchcock, any untrustworthiness on the part of the Hanlester appellants which existed while Hitchcock represented them ceased to exist once Hitchcock left the employ of Hanlester. Exclusion of these appellants is therefore unnecessary to meet the remedial purposes of the Act.

Individual Appellants

Since we find that Lewand, Tasha, Huntsinger, Keorle, and Welsh did not violate either subsection of § 1128B, no remedial purpose would be served by excluding these appellants. Based on the foregoing, we AFFIRM the Secretary's conclusion that appellants Hanlester, Omni, Placer and PPCL violated subsection (b)(2) of § 1128B. We REVERSE the Secretary's conclusion that any of appellants violated subsection (b)(1) of § 1128B, and REVERSE the imposition of permissive exclusions on appellants.

NOTES AND QUESTIONS ON SELF-REFERRAL AND THE QUESTION OF INTENT

1. *Joint Ventures and the Anti-Kickback Law*. Consider the physician joint venture for the provision of lithotripsy services described in the problem preceding the *Greber* case. Could the government argue that, simply by participating in the profits of an enterprise to which they refer patients, the limited partners were receiving "remuneration * * * in return for" referrals? How would you advise the joint venturers to arrange their affairs to weaken the force of such an argument? Could creative lawyering eliminate the problem entirely? If not, how would you counsel your client? (Reconsider these questions once you have read about the Stark legislation and the relevant safe harbors at the end of this section.)

2. *Mens Rea?* Is corrupt intent an essential element for a conviction in a kickback case? Is it enough that inducement of a future flow of business was a significant or substantial factor in the defendant's thinking? Must it be the dominant or predominant factor? What if it is just one factor among several weighing in the decision?

Prior to 1980 amendments to the anti-kickback statute, courts applied a relaxed version of the mens rea requirement. Thus, when physicians charged with violating the statute challenged their indictments claiming they lacked the requisite criminal intent, courts held that the mere presence of corruption in the deals satisfied the intent requirement. Corruption, in turn, could be found in "[t]he potential for increased costs to the Medicare–Medicaid system and misapplication of federal funds." United States v. Hancock, 604 F.2d 999, 1001 (7th Cir.1979) (cited in *Greber*) (chiropractors found guilty of fraud and abuse in sending blood and tissue specimens to lab which then split Medicaid payment with them). See also United States v. Ruttenberg, 625 F.2d 173 (7th Cir.1980) (paying monthly fee to nursing home for opportunity to provide drugs and pharmaceutical services and solicitation of such fees violate federal anti-kickback law whether or not payments are from federal funds); United States v. Perlstein, 632 F.2d 661 (6th Cir.1980) (nursing home administrator found guilty of fraud and abuse in selecting pharmaceutical supplier to service Medicaid recipients in return for alcoholic beverages worth $416 per month).

The requirement that the challenged acts be shown to have been taken "knowingly and willfully" was added to the statute in 1980 to reflect congressional concern that "criminal penalties may be imposed under current law to [*sic*] an individual whose conduct, while improper, was inadvertent." H.R. Rep. No. 96–1167, 96th Cong., 2d Sess. 59 (1980). *Hanlester* deals with the effect of that statutory change. Thus, the principal issue in *Hanlester* was not the inducement element but whether remuneration was "knowingly and willfully" paid or received. The court's reading of the scienter requirement was a somewhat heroic attempt to ameliorate the consequences of the *Greber* interpretation of other statutory terms.

3. *The Requisite Intent.* How did *Hanlester* affect the level of proof required by the *Greber* holding? Normally, ignorance of the law is not a defense to a criminal charge; a prosecutor need only show that the defendant purposely committed the act with which he or she is charged. Even though *Hanlester* was an administrative enforcement action and not a criminal case, the court of appeals appeared to read the phrase "knowingly and willfully" in such a way that a respondent could plead that he did not know that his activities were illegal. For later authority on the question of the requisite intent, see United States v. Jain, 93 F.3d 436 (8th Cir.1996), cert. denied, 117 S.Ct. 2452 (1997), in which a psychologist and a clinic he controlled appealed a conviction for soliciting and receiving "remuneration" for referring patients to a psychiatric hospital. The court upheld the conviction, reasoning as follows:

> Defendants argue that the district court's instructions incorrectly defined the term "willfully" in the Medicare anti-kickback statute. * * *
>
> The parties assert radically different positions on this issue of statutory construction. Based upon the traditional principle that ignorance of the law is no defense, the government urges us to apply the general rule that "willfully" in a criminal statute "refers to consciousness of the act but not to consciousness that the act is unlawful." Cheek v. United States, 498 U.S. 192, 209 (1991) (Scalia, J., concurring). * * * Defendants rely most heavily upon Ratzlaf v. United States [cited and discussed in *Hanlester*].
>
> The district court adopted a middle ground. The court declined to instruct the jury that Jain must have intentionally violated a known legal duty because the anti-kickback statute prohibits willful conduct—receiving remuneration for referring patients to a Medicare provider—rather than the willful violation of a statute, as in *Ratzlaf*. But the court also concluded that a mens rea instruction more rigorous than the traditional rule was appropriate because the literal language of this statute might otherwise encompass some types of innocent conduct. Accordingly, * * * the court instructed the jury that "the word 'willfully' means unjustifiably and wrongfully, known to be such by the defendant Swaran Jain." It also instructed that "good faith" was a defense to this charge, explaining that Dr. Jain acted in good faith if he believed he was being paid for promoting North Hills, not for referring patients.

We agree with the district court's resolution of this issue. The word "willful" has many meanings and must be construed in light of its statutory context. Here, the elements "knowingly and willfully" were added to the statute in 1980 to reflect congressional concern "that criminal penalties may be imposed under current law to an individual whose conduct, while improper, was inadvertent." H.R.Rep. No. 1167, 96th Cong., 2d Sess. 59 (1980). * * * [T]he statute also has elaborate "safe harbor" provisions, provisions which have prompted pages of administrative agency explication. This confirms that a broad "illegal remunerations" statute is like the statute at issue in *Ratzlaf* in that it potentially includes conduct that is not "inevitably nefarious." Only conduct that is inevitably nefarious, that is, "obviously 'evil' or inherently 'bad,'" warrants the traditional presumption that anyone consciously engaging in it has fair warning of a criminal violation. *Ratzlaf*, 510 U.S. at 146–48. Thus, we agree with the district court's decision to instruct the jury that the government must meet a heightened mens rea burden.

But that does not mean that the specific instruction adopted in *Ratzlaf* and the criminal tax cases is appropriate in this case. The statute at issue in *Ratzlaf*, [31 U.S.C § 5322(a)], made criminal a willful violation of another anti-structuring statute [31 U.S.C. § 5324]. Because one cannot willfully violate a statute without knowing what the statute prohibits, the Supreme Court required proof that defendant intentionally violated a "known legal duty." By contrast, in the Medicare anti-kickback statute, the word "willfully" modifies a series of prohibited acts. Both the plain language of that statute, and respect for the traditional principle that ignorance of the law is no defense, suggest that a heightened mens rea standard should only require proof that Dr. Jain knew that his conduct was wrongful, rather than proof that he knew it violated "a known legal duty." Therefore, the district court's definition of "willfully" correctly construed the 1980 amendment to § 1320a–7b. [*Hanlester*] does not persuade us to adopt defendants' position. That case is distinguishable because it involved an administrative debarment proceeding. In addition, the court adopted *Ratzlaf*'s heightened mens rea standard without considering other alternatives to the general rule.

Alternatively, we conclude that the district court's refusal to give an instruction using the *Ratzlaf* definition of *willfully* was harmless error. Dr. Jain's defense was that he did not take money from North Hills for referring patients. On direct examination, he testified that payments for patient referrals are not only "unethical" and "wrong," they are "illegal." That testimony effectively took mens rea out of the case, for Dr. Jain acknowledged that, if the jury disbelieved his denials, he would be guilty under his own requested instruction as well as the instruction given by the district court.

93 F.3d at 431–41.

How does the *Jain* court's reading of *Ratzlaf* and the mens rea requirement differ from the court's in *Hanlester*? In the *MDN* case, reproduced supra, the court reflected as follows (at the point marked by an ellipsis near the end of the opinion) on *Hanlester* and the issue of intent in kickback cases:

> Although not raised as an issue by the appellant in its brief, the appellee has called our attention [N.B.—Eds.] to *Hanlester*, which created a two-prong test for the interpretation of the words "knowingly and willfully" in the Anti-Kickback Statute. First, the individual must know that the statute prohibits offering or paying remuneration to induce referrals and, second, the individual must engage in conduct with the specific intent to violate the law. The *Hanlester* court relied on Ratzlaf v. United States, 510 U.S. 135 (1994), for its interpretation of the terms "knowing and willful." In *Ratzlaf*, the United States Supreme Court dealt with a banking statute which provided criminal penalties against persons who "willfully violate the Reporting Act." According to *Ratzlaf*, what must be willful is the violation and, thus, the person must know that the statute prohibits the conduct and intend to violate the law by engaging in such conduct. In contrast, the Anti–Kickback Statute provides for criminal penalties for whoever "knowingly and willfully" pays or receives remuneration for a referral. Thus, the Anti–Kickback Statute is textually distinguishable from the statute that was considered in *Ratzlaf*. The Anti–Kickback Statute is directed at punishment of those who perform specific acts and does not require that one engage in the prohibited conduct with the specific intent to violate the statute. We therefore decline to follow the *Hanlester* interpretation of the Anti–Kickback Statute. Therefore, we affirm the trial court's conclusion that the agreement between MDN and PRC is violative of the Anti–Kickback Statute.

See generally Note, Toward a Fair and Practical Definition of "Willfully" in the Medicare/Medicaid Anti–Kickback Statute, 50 Vand. L. Rev. 1029 (1997). See also United States v. Neufeld, 908 F.Supp. 491 (S.D.Ohio 1995) (adopting intent standard similar to that in *Jain*).

4. Assume that *Hanlester* were the rule in your circuit, so that ignorance of the law might serve as an excuse for engaging in joint ventures involving self-referrals. How would you counsel a client who, lacking your advice, is unaware that a particular commercial arrangement, of a type common in other industries, might not be lawful when Medicare or Medicaid is paying the bill? See Blumstein, "The Health Care Speakeasy," 22 Am. J.L. & Med. at 226 n.175 (1996) ("This scienter requirement standard places lawyers in an extraordinary ethical dilemma because their provision of advice to clients, in accordance with their normal professional responsibility, could have the effect of transforming innocent into criminal conduct"). See generally Pepper, Counseling at the Limits of the Law: An Exercise in the Jurisprudence and Ethics of Lawyering, 104 Yale L.J. 1545 (1995).

5. In your view, did the physicians who responded to Hanlester's offers likewise violate the anti-fraud law, warranting their exclusion from Medi-

care participation? (Only Hanlester itself was finally sanctioned.) Might it depend on whether they did in fact make referrals to Hanlester or on the volume of those referrals? Or might it turn on something else? How would you defend them? Were they, as participants in joint ventures expressly designed to attract their referrals, any more or less innocent than Dr. Jain, who received fees for services arguably rendered?

By the same token, would the hospital in *Jain* be entitled to plead "good faith" and a lack of wrongful intent? In other words, should the intent requirement applicable to the payers of referral fees differ from the requirement applied to the recipients of those fees? Why might one apply a more permissive test to a professional (who has well-recognized ethical responsibilities, after all) than to a commercial enterprise that employs methods common in other industries and not generally thought to be illegal or unethical? (Note that the court in *Jain* observed that Dr. Jain's conduct was unethical and presumably could be sanctioned under the state licensure law.) Why were the individual physician entrepreneurs who helped put the *Hanlester* deal together not sanctioned?

Should the test for discovering an unlawful kickback differ between criminal proceedings (as in *Jain*), administrative enforcement proceedings (as in *Hanlester*), and cases involving the enforcement of contracts under principles of public policy (as in *MDN*)?

6. *Mail Fraud.* In the *Jain* case, supra, the defendant physician was also prosecuted under the mail fraud statute, 18 U.S.C. § 1341 (1994), which prohibits the use of the mails to execute "any scheme or artifice to defraud." Because the submission of claims under federal health care programs and the receipt of payments under those programs inevitably involve the use of the mail, it is common to find mail fraud charges included along with charges of fraud and abuse. But because a conviction for mail fraud requires that the accused possess "fraudulent intent" to use the mails to cause some harm or injury, *Jain,* 93 F.3d at 441, an essential ingredient of the charge is some demonstrable harm or injury to the government, a federal beneficiary, or someone else. Thus, while Dr. Jain's conviction for Medicare/Medicaid fraud and abuse was upheld without evidence of harm or injury, his conviction for mail fraud was reversed. The court found that "there was no evidence that any patient suffered tangible harm. * * * Dr. Jain provided quality psychological services. Each hospitalized patient required hospitalization." The facility to which Dr. Jain referred his patients "was as good as or better than any alternative facility and provided his patients with proper care." Further, "no patient was financially harmed." Id. at 442. Because the evidence indicated that "Dr. Jain intended to provide and did in fact provide his patients with the highest quality psychological services," the appeals court reversed his conviction for mail fraud. The *Jain* case therefore nicely underscores the unusual notion of fraud under the anti-kickback law.

For a criticism of the *Jain* case, see Note, Primum Non Nocere: The Expanding "Honest Services" Mail Fraud Statute and the Physician–Patient Fiduciary Relationship, 51 Vand. L. Rev. 139 (1998) (arguing that a breach of a physician's fiduciary relationship to a patient occurs when the physician fails to disclose an economic conflict of interest, such as a kickback, that could influence a medical decision, and that such a breach of fiduciary duty, in depriving the patient's right to "honest services," causes harm enough to trigger a violation of the mail fraud statute).

7. *Effect of the Subsequent Stark Legislation.* As will appear more fully below, later federal legislation known as "Stark I" (passed in 1989) flatly prohibited a wide range of financial relationships between physicians and clinical laboratories to which they directed business. These same prohibitions were subsequently extended (in "Stark II," 1993, effective 1995) to physician relationships with most other types of service providers. Thus, arrangements of the type encountered in *Hanlester* (as well as in the lithotripsy problem) are now subject to a statutory "per se" rule. The Stark legislation is not enforced by criminal sanctions, however. An arrangement offending it may therefore be the subject of a prosecution under the older criminal statute (as well as under the mail fraud statute). Presumably, however, criminal sanctions would be invoked only in cases of knowing and willful evasion of the Stark prohibition, which incorporates the requirement of criminal intent.

The False Claims Act

United States ex rel. Thompson v. Columbia/HCA Healthcare Corporation

United States Court of Appeals, Fifth Circuit, 1997.
125 F.3d 899.

■ W. EUGENE DAVIS, CIRCUIT JUDGE.

Relator, James M. Thompson, M.D., a physician in private practice in Corpus Christi, Texas, brought this qui tam action pursuant to the federal False Claims Act ("FCA"), 31 U.S.C. §§ 3729 et seq., against defendants Columbia/HCA Healthcare Corporation and certain affiliated entities (collectively, "Columbia/HCA") and Corpus Christi Bay “rea Surgery, Ltd. The district court dismissed Thompson's complaint for failure to state a claim under Rule 12(b)(6) of the Federal Rules of Civil Procedure. For the reasons set out below, we affirm in part, vacate in part, and remand for further proceedings.

I.

In his second amended complaint, at issue in this appeal, Thompson alleged that defendants submitted false or fraudulent claims under the FCA by submitting Medicare claims for services rendered in violation of the Medicare anti-kickback statute,[1] 42 U.S.C. § 1320a–7b, and two versions of

1. Thompson alleged that defendants violated the Medicare anti-kickback statute by inducing physicians to refer Medicare patients to Columbia/HCA hospitals in the following ways:

(1) Offering physicians preferential opportunities not available to the general

a self-referral statute, 42 U.S.C. § 1395nn, commonly known as the "Stark" laws after the statute's congressional sponsor, United States Representative Fortney H. "Pete" Stark. He further alleged that defendants made false statements to obtain payment of false or fraudulent claims in violation of the FCA by falsely certifying in annual cost reports that the Medicare services identified therein were provided in compliance with the laws and regulations regarding the provision of healthcare services. Finally, Thompson alleged that defendants violated the FCA by submitting Medicare claims for medically unnecessary services.

The district court granted defendants' motions to dismiss Thompson's second amended complaint for failure to state a claim. The court held that Thompson's allegations that defendants submitted Medicare claims for services rendered in violation of the anti-kickback statute and the Stark laws were insufficient, by themselves, to state a claim for relief under the FCA. The court also held that Thompson's allegations that defendants falsely certified in annual cost reports that the Medicare services identified therein were provided in compliance with the laws and regulations regarding the provision of healthcare services were insufficient to state a claim for relief under the FCA. The court concluded that these allegations were insufficient because Thompson had not alleged that defendants submitted false certifications to obtain payment of false or fraudulent claims, i.e., claims or claim amounts that the government would not have paid but for the alleged fraud. Finally, the court held that Thompson's allegations that defendants submitted claims for medically unnecessary services were insufficient to state a claim because he failed to plead his allegations with particularity as required by Rule 9(b) of the Federal Rules of Civil Procedure.

II.

* * *

The FCA provides, in relevant part:

(a) Liability for certain acts.—Any person who—

public to obtain equity interests in Columbia/HCA healthcare operations through partnership or corporate structure arrangements;

(2) Offering loans or assistance in obtaining loans to physicians to finance capital investments in equity interests in Columbia/HCA entities;

(3) Making payments disguised as "consultation fees" to physicians in order to guarantee on a risk-free basis their capital investments in equity interests in Columbia/HCA entities;

(4) Paying physicians "consultation fees," "rent" or other monies;

(5) Providing physicians with free or reduced rent for office space near Columbia/HCA hospitals in facilities owned or operated by Columbia/HCA;

(6) Offering physicians free or reduced-rate vacations and other recreational opportunities;

(7) Offering physicians free or reduced-cost medical training;

(8) Providing physicians with income guarantees; and

(9) Granting physicians superior or exclusive rights to perform procedures in particular fields of practice.

> (1) knowingly presents, or causes to be presented, to an officer or employee of the United States Government . . . a false or fraudulent claim for payment or approval . . .; [or]
>
> (2) knowingly makes, uses, or causes to be made or used, a false record or statement to get a false or fraudulent claim paid or approved by the Government . . .
>
> * * *
>
> is liable to the United States Government for a civil penalty of not less than $5,000 and not more than $10,000, plus 3 times the amount of damages which the Government sustains because of the act of that person. . . .

31 U.S.C. § 3729(a)(1), (2).

A. Thompson's Claims Predicated on Statutory Violations

Thompson alleged that defendants violated the FCA by submitting Medicare claims for services rendered in violation of the Medicare anti-kickback statute and the Stark laws. The Medicare anti-kickback statute prohibits (1) the solicitation or receipt of remuneration in return for referrals of Medicare patients, and (2) the offer or payment of remuneration to induce such referrals.

The first Stark law, commonly known as "Stark I," was in effect between January 1, 1992 and December 31, 1994. Stark I prohibited physicians from referring Medicare patients to an entity for clinical laboratory services if the referring physician had a nonexempt "financial relationship" with such entity. Stark I also prohibited the entity from presenting or causing to be presented a Medicare claim for services furnished pursuant to a prohibited referral. With certain exceptions, "financial relationship" was defined as (1) an ownership or investment interest in the entity, or (2) a compensation arrangement with the entity. Stark I expressly prohibited payment of Medicare claims for services rendered in violation of its provisions.

Stark II became effective January 1, 1995, and prohibits physicians from referring Medicare patients to an entity for certain "designated health services," including inpatient and outpatient hospital services, if the referring physician has a nonexempt "financial relationship" with such entity. Like its predecessor, Stark II provides that the entity may not present or cause to be presented a Medicare claim for services furnished pursuant to a prohibited referral, and expressly prohibits payment of Medicare claims for services rendered in violation of its provisions.

We agree with the district court that claims for services rendered in violation of a statute do not necessarily constitute false or fraudulent claims under the FCA. In United States ex rel. Weinberger v. Equifax, Inc., 557 F.2d 456, 460–61 (5th Cir.1977), we held that claims submitted by a government contractor who allegedly violated the Anti–Pinkerton Act did not necessarily constitute false or fraudulent claims under the FCA. In so holding, we observed that the FCA is not an enforcement device for the

Anti–Pinkerton Act. We recognized, however, that the FCA "interdicts material misrepresentations made to qualify for government privileges or services."

The Ninth Circuit has taken a similar approach concerning the scope of the FCA. In United States ex rel. Hopper v. Anton, 91 F.3d 1261, 1266 (9th Cir.1996), the court held that "violations of laws, rules, or regulations alone do not create a cause of action under the FCA." The court concluded, however, that false certifications of compliance create liability under the FCA when certification is a prerequisite to obtaining a government benefit.

Thus, where the government has conditioned payment of a claim upon a claimant's certification of compliance with, for example, a statute or regulation, a claimant submits a false or fraudulent claim when he or she falsely certifies compliance with that statute or regulation.

Thompson alleged that, as a condition of their participation in the Medicare program, defendants were required to certify in annual cost reports that the services identified therein were provided in compliance with the laws and regulations regarding the provision of healthcare services. He further alleged that defendants falsely certified that the services identified in their annual cost reports were provided in compliance with such laws and regulations. Thus, Thompson fairly alleged that the government's payment of Medicare claims is conditioned upon certification of compliance with the laws and regulations regarding the provision of healthcare services, including the anti-kickback statute and the Stark laws, and that defendants submitted false claims by falsely certifying that the services identified in their annual cost reports were rendered in compliance with such laws and regulations.

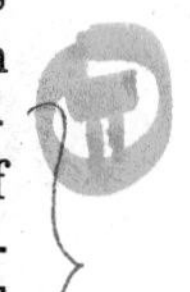

Columbia/HCA argues that the certifications of compliance contained in annual cost reports are not a prerequisite to payment of Medicare claims because Medicare claims are submitted for payment shortly after services have been rendered and well before annual cost reports are filed. Thompson contends that such certifications are indeed a prerequisite to payment because the retention of any payment received prior to the submission of an annual cost report is conditioned on the certification of compliance contained therein. We are unable to determine from the record before us whether, or to what extent, payment for services identified in defendants' annual cost reports was conditioned on defendants' certifications of compliance. We therefore deny defendants' 12(b)(6) motions as they relate to this issue and remand to the district court for further factual development.

Thompson also contends that, in any event, claims for services rendered in violation of the Stark laws are, in and of themselves, false or fraudulent claims under the FCA. Thompson bases his contention on provisions in the Stark laws expressly prohibiting payment for services rendered in violation of their terms. In holding that Thompson failed to allege a violation of the FCA, the district court did not specifically consider this contention. Because the district court must determine whether the government's payment of defendants' Medicare claims was conditioned on defendants' certifications of compliance in their annual cost reports, we will

give the district court the opportunity to consider this argument on remand as well.

B. Thompson's False Statement Claims

As discussed above, the FCA imposes liability not only on any person who submits a false or fraudulent claim for payment, but also on any person who knowingly makes a false statement in order to get a false or fraudulent claim paid. If the district court determines on remand that claims for services rendered in violation of the Stark laws are, in and of themselves, false or fraudulent claims under the FCA, then the court should also consider whether Thompson has sufficiently alleged that defendants committed separate and independent violations of the FCA by making false statements to obtain payment of false or fraudulent claims.

C. Thompson's Claims Based on Medically Unnecessary Services

Thompson alleged that "in reasonable probability, based on statistical studies performed by the Government and others" approximately 40 percent of claims submitted by defendants for services rendered in violation of the anti-kickback statute or the Stark laws were for services that were not medically necessary. Thompson made no further allegations in support of his claim. The district court held that Thompson failed to satisfy Rule 9(b) of the Federal Rules of Civil Procedure, which requires that all averments of fraud be pled with particularity. The court concluded that Thompson failed to meet the pleading requirements of Rule 9(b) because he did not identify any specific physicians who referred patients for medically unnecessary services or any specific claims for medically unnecessary services that were submitted by defendants.

Claims brought under the FCA must comply with Rule 9(b). Gold v. Morrison–Knudsen Co., 68 F.3d 1475, 1476–77 (2d Cir.1995), cert. denied, 116 S. Ct. 1836 (1996). At a minimum, Rule 9(b) requires that a plaintiff set forth the "who, what, when, where, and how" of the alleged fraud. Williams v. WMX Tech., Inc., 112 F.3d 175, 179 (5th Cir.1997). Thompson argues, however, that the pleading requirements of Rule 9(b) are relaxed where, as here, the facts relating to the alleged fraud are peculiarly within the perpetrator's knowledge. Although we have held that fraud may be pled on information and belief under such circumstances, we have also warned that this exception "must not be mistaken for license to base claims of fraud on speculation and conclusory allegations." In addition, even where allegations are based on information and belief, the complaint must set forth a factual basis for such belief.

In his complaint, Thompson provided no factual basis for his belief that defendants submitted claims for medically unnecessary services other than his reference to statistical studies. There is no indication, however, that these studies directly implicate defendants. Thompson's allegations, therefore, amount to nothing more than speculation, and thus fail to satisfy Rule 9(b).

* * *

AFFIRMED in part; VACATED and REMANDED in part.

NOTES AND QUESTIONS ON THE FALSE CLAIMS ACT

1. *Remedies under the FCA; Qui Tam Actions.* The False Claims Act, 31 U.S.C.A. § 3729 (West Supp. 1998) (FCA), provides another tool for the pursuit of remedies against health care fraud. Claims under the FCA can be brought by the Department of Justice or by private whistleblowers in so-called qui tam actions.

The Justice Department has achieved a number of notable health care recoveries under the FCA. In United States v. Lorenzo, 768 F.Supp. 1127 (E.D.Pa.1991), for example, a dentist submitted claims for cancer examinations of the oral cavity as "limited consultations" even though such exams were part of a routine dental examination, which Medicare does not cover. In addition to recovering $392,157 in treble damages allowable under the FCA, the government was also entitled to recover a civil penalty under the act of $5000 for each of the 3683 false claims filed, or $18,415,000. The court noted that its discretion to reduce this penalty was limited. See also United States v. Krizek, 111 F.3d 934 (D.C.Cir.1997) (doctor charged with "upcoding," or routinely using the payment code for 45–50 minute sessions when code for 20–30 minute period was more appropriate; government had sought $80 million in damages, but court declined to impose a monetary penalty for each coding error, instead treating the form submitted as the "claim").

The government has achieved especially impressive recoveries against corporate providers. For example, when Caremark pleaded guilty to charges of fraud and abuse in the operation of its home infusion, oncology, hemophilia, and growth hormone business, it paid $161 million in criminal fines, civil restitution, and damages. See Medicare and Medicaid Guide (CCH) & 43,406. A 1997 settlement between DHHS and SmithKline Beecham required the company to pay $325 million in fines for false billing of medical laboratory services and payment of kickbacks to providers. See 6 Health L. Rep. 328 (Feb. 27, 1997).

A particularly striking development under the FCA (illustrated in the principal case) is its frequent use by private plaintiffs in qui tam (or "whistleblower") actions, in which a private party (a "relator") is authorized to sue on behalf of the government and can expect to share in the (possibly very large) recovery. Although neither the anti-kickback law nor the anti-self-referral law (Stark I & II) provides for a private cause of action by private parties, some private plaintiffs have succeeded in using the FCA to prosecute alleged violations of both statutes. In considering the following material, focus on the standard of proof under the FCA. Although the anti-kickback law has been interpreted not to require a finding of specific harm flowing from the alleged fraud, does (or should) this less demanding standard of proof apply under the FCA? (The Supreme Court recently heard a case on this issue but left the question open, deciding the case on other grounds. Hughes Aircraft Co. v. United States ex rel. Schumer, 117 S.Ct. 1871 (1997).)

2. *Proof Requirements under the FCA*. In United States ex rel. Pogue v. American Healthcorp, Inc., 914 F.Supp. 1507, 1509 (M.D.Tenn.1996), a qui tam action with facts similar to those in *Thompson*, the court concluded that "a violation of Medicare antikickback and self-referral laws constitutes a violation of the False Claims Act." Thus, a private party bringing an FCA qui tam action would have to allege not actual damage to the government, only a technical violation. The *Pogue* court reasoned that the FCA was "intended to govern not only fraudulent acts that create a loss to the government but also those fraudulent acts that cause the government to pay out sums of money to claimants it did not intend to benefit." Id. at 1513.

The district court in *Thompson* rejected the *Pogue* reasoning, concluding that "a claim itself [must] be false or fraudulent in order for liability under the FCA to exist." 938 F.Supp. 399, 405 (S.D.Tex.1996). Since the defendants' claims in *Thompson* represented requests for services actually rendered and would have qualified for government payment in the absence of a violation of the anti-kickback or Stark laws, the district court would have rejected relator's FCA claim. In other words, the district court in *Thompson* would have required a showing of some harm or injury to the government in order to sustain an FCA claim.

On which side of the argument did the court of appeals in *Thompson* come down? While agreeing with the district court "that claims for services rendered in violation of a statute do not necessarily constitute false or fraudulent claims under the FCA," the court stated that "where the government has conditioned payment of a claim upon a claimant's certification of compliance with, for example, a statute or regulation, a claimant submits a false or fraudulent claim when he or she falsely certifies compliance with that statute or regulation." Thus, in some situations—it seems to depend on the nature of the certification required for payment—a claim may be the subject of a recovery in an FCA action even though made for services appropriately rendered to program beneficiaries.

3. *Effect of Noncompliance with State Regulatory Requirements*. For an illustration of how far FCA qui tam actions can reach, see United States ex rel. Sanders v. East Alabama Healthcare Authority, 953 F.Supp. 1404, 1411 (M.D.Ala.1996) (plaintiff/relator successfully alleged FCA violation on ground that defendant had improperly obtained a state "certificate of need" to operate additional beds; "knowing submission of a claim that falsely represented attainment of state licensing requirements is enough to constitute a false claim").

Other cases do not go so far. For example, the defendants in United States ex rel. Joslin v. Community Home Health of Maryland, Inc., 984 F.Supp. 374 (D.Md.1997), allegedly submitted claims without complying with a state licensing requirement (as in *Sanders*). The court, while acknowledging that false certification of regulatory compliance may create a false claim (citing *Thompson*), rejected the view that the "mere submission of a claim for payment, without more, always constitutes an 'implied certification' of compliance with the conditions of the Government program." The court emphasized the scienter requirement of the FCA and expressed concern lest "FCA liability * * * attach every time a document or request for payment is submitted to the Government, regardless of whether the submitting party is aware of its noncompliance."

4. *Scienter.* Although it was not yet a factor in *Thompson*, the FCA has a scienter requirement, so that a violation is established only if a person "knowingly" presents a false claim to government. Moreover, "knowing" and "knowingly" are specifically defined to mean that a person "(1) has actual knowledge of the information; (2) acts in deliberate ignorance of the truth or falsity of the information; or (3) acts in reckless disregard of the truth or falsity of the information, and no proof of specific intent to defraud is required." 31 U.S.C.A. § 3729(b) (West Supp. 1998). (This is the same standard that, since the enactment of the Kassebaum–Kennedy legislation in 1996, applies to civil monetary penalties.)

What must the qui tam plaintiff in *Thompson* establish on remand in order to satisfy the FCA requirement that the hospital defendants "knowingly" filed a false claim? Will satisfaction of the underlying fraud and abuse intent standard under either *Hanlester* or *Jain* be sufficient, or is an independent showing required under the FCA? Note that the statutory definition of "knowingly" in the FCA focuses on the "truth or falsity" of the information presented to government. The truth or falsity of what information will form the crux of the plaintiff/relator's showing on remand in *Thompson*? In the case of corporate defendants such as the affiliated entities in *Thompson*, just whose knowledge (or ignorance) and intent will determine corporate liability?

5. Under a broad reading of the FCA (as in the *Pogue* case, supra), a private whistleblower (and, of course, his attorney) could recover a huge bounty as a windfall from a provider even if the Medicare-covered services in question were medically necessary and provided at the lowest price. Indeed, a provider could be liable to the government and to a qui tam plaintiff for anti-kickback or Stark violations that save the government money or enhance the quality of service. To be sure, the principle that wrongdoing may be punished even if there is no harm is found in the law of trusts. Restatement (Second) of Trusts § 205 (1992) (fiduciary who breaches duty to beneficiary will be held liable to beneficiary even if breach results in gain to trust). But are qui tam actions under the Medicare/Medicaid anti-fraud law and the FCA good occasions for applying this principle? In any event, what is significant about the attempt to import principles of trust law into the law governing health care providers dealing with the government? If a private payer rather than the government were the purchaser, should the same principles apply?

Although the need to deter fraud is obvious, the complexity of the law in the health care field is such that many violations may be essentially technical and inadvertent as well as harmless. Do the civil monetary penalty and FCA provisions, which have scienter requirements, extend to inadvertent behavior? How important is it to send messages that lack of harm is no excuse? To be sure, if the goal is to roll back the commercialization of health care in the United States and to penalize those who are especially successful in doing business with government health programs, then the impulse to punish conduct that crosses the line is understandable. How would you rule with respect to the critical issue in *Pogue*?

Should claims brought under the FCA be barred in light of other, more specific remedies available? Might one argue that, when Congress adopted a comprehensive, fully articulated scheme for defining and policing fraud and abuse in dealing with government health care programs, it foreclosed by implication the use of other, more generally available remedies for fraud in dealings with the government—such as those provided in the FCA? Cf. Middlesex County Sewerage Auth. v. Nat'l Sea Clammers Ass'n, 453 U.S. 1 (1981) (existence of express remedies in the Federal Water Pollution Control Act and the Marine Protection, Research, and Sanctuaries Act demonstrated Congress' intent to supplant other more generalized remedies available under the Civil Rights Act, 42 U.S.C. § 1983).

6. *"Life in the Health Care Speakeasy."* The ubiquity of technical violations of the anti-kickback law (as interpreted in *Greber*) or of the "Stark" legislation (about which more is said below) is widely recognized. As Blumstein notes, "[i]n the current environment, it is a truism that the fraud and abuse law is being violated routinely but that those violations are acknowledged as not threatening the public interest." Blumstein, "The Health Care Speakeasy," 22 Am. J.L. & Med. at 218. Indeed, he analogizes "the modern American health care industry * * * to a speakeasy—conduct that is illegal is rampant and countenanced by enforcement officials because the law is so out of sync with the * * * realities of the marketplace" and argues that activity that is technically illegal is nevertheless "desirable in improving the functioning of the market." Despite the due process and civil liberties implications of a "trust us" approach to implementation of a very broad statute, prosecutorial discretion has been exercised to yield relative stability in the fast-changing health care marketplace; as Blumstein would put it, only loud and obnoxious drunks in the speakeasy have been prosecuted.

What are the implications of qui tam suits in a "speakeasy" environment? If prosecutorial discretion has restrained the use of the anti-fraud law and the FCA as hunting licenses rather than to protect the public fisc and public beneficiaries, is it wise to invite private whistleblower lawsuits in the name of the government? Note that a private relator need not secure approval from government officials in order to bring an FCA claim to court. Incidentally, note also that the Kassebaum–Kennedy legislation in 1996 eroded governmental restraint in prosecuting these violations in another way—by creating positive incentives for government prosecutors to bring more lawsuits; money recovered in fraud and abuse actions goes back into the enforcement program to fund further prosecutions. Observing these new developments and the prevalence of technically questionable practices that are both well entrenched and usually innocuous but still provoke moral outrage in some circles, Blumstein decries the new "bounty hunter scenario for public-spirited whistleblowers" and warns, "Even those sipping sherry in the speakeasy will be at risk." Id. at 219.

7. *Limits on Qui Tam Actions*. What, if anything, limits the ability of a plaintiff to bring a qui tam action? One important limitation is that a qui tam lawsuit cannot be based on publicly disclosed facts and that the whistleblower/relator must be the "original source" of the information upon which the FCA claim is based. 31 U.S.C.A. § 3730(e)(4)(A) (West Supp. 1998). An "original source" is an "individual who has direct and independent knowledge of the information on which the allegations are based and has voluntarily provided the information to the Government before filing an action." Id. § 3730(e)(4)(B). Some courts have been quite permissive in determining who qualifies under this provision as a qui tam plaintiff/relator. See, e.g., United States ex rel. Schumer v. Hughes Aircraft Co., 63 F.3d 1512, 1518 (9th Cir.1995), rev'd on other grounds, 117 S.Ct. 1871 (1997) (information disclosed to employees or already known by the government does not constitute "public disclosure" and thus does not bar qui tam actions by company insiders). Some courts have been more restrictive. See, e.g., United States ex rel. Doe v. John Doe Corp., 960 F.2d 318, 326 (2d Cir.1992) (government investigation or government possession of information relating to fraud constitutes public disclosure and precludes qui tam suits).

8. *Constitutionality of Qui Tam Actions under the False Claims Act.* Contrary to opinions by the Ninth Circuit court of appeals consistently upholding the constitutionality of the qui tam provisions of the FCA (e.g., *Hughes Aircraft*, supra), one district court has held that the case or controversy requirement of article III of the Constitution does not permit Congress to confer standing upon a qui tam plaintiff bringing an FCA suit if that plaintiff has not suffered some particularized cognizable injury. United States ex rel. Riley v. St. Luke's Hosp., 982 F.Supp. 1261 (S.D.Tex. 1997) (court found plaintiff/relator who alleged defendant had filed false claims for Medicare and Medicaid reimbursement during her employment had suffered no injury-in-fact and thus had not met the "irreducible constitutional minimum" requirement for standing; court stated that allowing "an unnamed, theoretical plaintiff who has suffered no injury" to pursue a fraud claim "allows Congress to circumvent Article III's standing requirements, which are essential to the principle of a limited judicial role under our separation of powers").

Overview of Federal Prohibitions and Safe Harbors Relating to Fraud and Abuse

NOTES ON THE STARK ANTI-SELF-REFERRAL LEGISLATION

1. *Stark I and Stark II*. The Stark legislation was a direct response to findings, cited near the beginning of this section, that physicians having an ownership interest in, or some other financial relationship with, certain health care facilities tend to utilize those facilities at higher levels than comparably situated physicians having no such relationship. See also DHHS/OIG, Financial Arrangements Between Physicians and Health Care Businesses, OIG Rep. No. OA–12–88–01410 (May 1989), reprinted in Medicare & Medicaid Guide (CCH) ¶ 37,838. This evidence was commonly interpreted as proof of "overutilization" despite the existence of uncertainty about medically and economically appropriate utilization levels. Whatever the merits on the question of efficiency, however, the perception that physicians were abusing public programs naturally attracted congressional interest.

The Stark legislation (Stark I & Stark II or, collectively, Stark) flatly prohibits physicians from referring Medicare or Medicaid patients to certain entities with which they or their family members have a "financial relationship." Stark I (1989) applied only to physician interests in clinical laboratories. Stark II (effective 1995) expanded the coverage of Stark I to encompass a wide range of other "designated health services" as well—specifically, physical therapy services; occupational therapy services; radiology and other diagnostic services; radiation therapy; the provision of durable medical equipment, prosthetic and other devices, and other supplies; home health services; outpatient prescription drugs; and inpatient and outpatient hospital services. In these and the following notes, the Stark legislation, 42 U.S.C.A. § 1395nn (West Supp. 1998), is cited simply as Stark, and the proposed regulations under Stark (and related commentary), 63 Fed. Reg. 1659 (Jan. 9, 1998), are cited to pages in the Federal Register.

The basic prohibition of the Stark legislation reads as follows:

> (1) [With numerous highly specified exceptions,] if a physician (or an immediate family member of such physician) has a financial relationship with [a specified] entity * * * then—
>
> (A) the physician may not make a referral to the entity for the furnishing of designated health services for which payment may be made under this title, and
>
> (B) the entity may not present or cause to be presented a claim under this title or bill to any individual, third party payor, or other entity for designated health services furnished pursuant to a referral prohibited under subparagraph (A).

Stark § 1395nn(a)(1). The statute defines "financial relationship" as either (1) an ownership or investment interest or (2) a "compensation arrangement," very broadly defined. Although this prohibition is very broad, it is the numerous exceptions from it that form the heart of the Stark law. Thus, although Stark starts from the basic anti-self-referral prohibition just quoted, it proceeds by exception, painstakingly identifying, defining, and expressly authorizing a large number of investment relationships, compensation arrangements, and practices that would otherwise be prohibited by the statute's "per se" rule. Later notes review the exceptional categories.

2. *The Stark and Anti-Kickback Laws Compared.* Some of the statutory exceptions to the basic prohibition of the Stark law resemble safe harbors created by regulations under the anti-kickback statute. There are important analytical distinctions, however, between the Stark exceptions and the anti-kickback safe harbors. Stark prohibits certain referrals outright, so that, if a transaction comes within its per se proscription, it is automatically barred unless the terms of a specific exception have been complied with. The anti-kickback statute, on the other hand, is not a categorical bar but rather a ban on the knowing and willful use of remuneration to induce or solicit referrals; intent is a critical ingredient of a violation, and case-by-case analysis is required. Thus, unlike the case with Stark, a failure to comply with an anti-kickback safe harbor rule does not automatically result in a violation. See 63 Fed. Reg. at 1662 ("Although the purposes behind the anti-kickback statute and [Stark] are similar, it is important to analyze them separately. * * * [T]o operate lawfully under Medicare and Medicaid, one must comply with both statutes.").

It will also be noted that Stark focuses on objective structural relationships and only on those involving physicians, whereas the anti-kickback law is principally concerned with conduct and motive and covers not just physicians and others seeking their referrals but also anyone providing goods or services financed under Medicare or Medicaid. Thus, Stark is broader than the anti-kickback statute in some respects and narrower in others.

3. *Sanctions; Administration*. Whereas § 1320a–7b is a criminal law (with attendant civil remedies, such as debarment from participation in federal health programs), Stark is exclusively civil legislation that establishes its own sanctions where a prohibited referral occurs. The Stark sanctions include denial of payment for services improperly rendered (even when the treatment was medically necessary), civil money penalties (up to $15,000 for each improper service and up to $100,000 for each scheme to circumvent the nonreferral rules), nonliability of the patient for the services provided by virtue of an unlawful referral, and exclusion from participation in Medicare. Additionally, failure to report one's ownership interest, as the act requires, could result in a civil penalty of up to $10,000 per day for each day a proper report is not made. Stark § 1395nn(g)(1)-(5). The Balanced Budget Act of 1997 established a binding advisory opinion process for the Stark law. See Stark § 1395nn(g)(6); 63 Fed. Reg. 1646.

remedy/ punishment ! Stark

Interestingly, HCFA has taken the position that the Stark sanctions do not apply to physicians and providers when the referral involves Medicaid services. In HCFA's view, states, which administer their own Medicaid programs under HCFA's general supervision, may choose to pay for self-referrals of Medicaid beneficiaries (or to develop their own sanctions against such referrals). However, the federal government will not provide federal Medicaid matching funds (federal financial participation or FFP) where a state has paid for services rendered in violation of Stark. 63 Fed. Reg. at 1704, 1727.

NOTES AND QUESTIONS ON SPECIFIC RELATIONSHIPS AND TRANSACTIONS UNDER THE ANTI–SELF–REFERRAL AND ANTI–KICKBACK LAWS

1. Even though Stark and the anti-kickback law address many different situations and approach matters in very different ways, there is substantial overlap between them. The following notes address some of the transactions, relationships, and practices to which one or the other law applies, not always differentiating between them. The goal here is not to state definitive legal rules, however, but to introduce the many types of transactions and relationships that raise issues of the kind the two laws undertake to address. The student should consider whether the law is succeeding in eliminating economic biases in referrals and in other health care decisions and, indeed, whether it is realistic to seek to prevent economic considerations and self-interest from influencing the flow of health care business.

In these and the following notes, the safe-harbor regulations under the anti-kickback law, 42 C.F.R. § 1001.952 (1997), are cited as S.H. Regs.

2. *Investment Interests in General.* The anti-kickback safe harbor regulations immunize provider investments in large entities—publicly held companies with over $50 million in health care-related assets in the previous year—or in smaller entities that have a clear majority of investors not in a position to refer patients. S.H. Regs. § 1001.952(a)(1). The Stark law, on the other hand, exempts investments in publicly-held companies with at least $75 million in equity in either the previous fiscal year or on average over the past three fiscal years. Stark § 1395nn(c)(1)(B).

If an entity does not qualify for the large-entity component of the investment interest safe harbor, then it must come within the small-entity component—under the so-called "60/40 rules." These twin rules are termed the investment rule and the revenue rule. The 60/40 investment rule states that no more than 40% of the value of the investments can have been held in the past year by persons in a position to make or influence referrals to the entity. S.H. Regs. § 1001.952(a)(2)(i). The 60/40 revenue rule states that no more than 40% of the entity's total revenue in the past year can have come from referrals or in other ways from such investors, and the investment return must bear no relation to the amount of referrals or other business generated by an investor. S.H. Regs. § 1001.952(a)(2)(vi) & (viii). Both rules must be met in order to gain immunization under the safe harbor. Query how a physician considering investment in an entity to which he might refer patients can know for certain whether all of these conditions are met or will continue to be met.

3. *Physician Investments in Hospitals.* Stark permits a physician to have an ownership or investment interest in a hospital to which he or she refers patients (as opposed to an interest in some subdivision of that hospital) if the physician has admitting privileges at the hospital. Stark § 1395nn(d)(3). This so-called "whole-hospital" exception to the anti-self-referral proscription reflects a judgment that self-interest will not unduly affect physician decision making when an investment is in an entire institution rather than in a particular component or department (where financial pressures on individual physicians would be stronger). At the same time, physician investment in hospitals might have some advantages in resolving the ancient conflict between physicians and hospitals and giving physicians a stake in the smooth running and economic success of the institution.

Columbia/HCA, the largest investor-owned hospital company, came under attack for offering physicians investment interests in local Columbia-owned hospitals (a practice it subsequently discontinued under new management):

> U.S. Rep. Fortney (Pete) Stark, D–Calif., who sponsored laws banning physicians from referring Medicare and Medicaid patients to certain entities in which they've invested, * * * last year asked the federal government to investigate whether Columbia's deals violate the so-called Stark laws by marketing the investments [in hospitals] to physicians only. * * * The inspector general's office doesn't confirm or deny investigations, but Stark says one is ongoing. * * * [Stark] calls the deals "immoral, indecent, unethical." He also believes they're illegal, despite an exemption in the federal law that appears to allow physician investments in entire hospitals.

Bell, As Hospitals Cut Doctors in on Profits, Do Patients Lose?, Nashville Tennessean, Oct. 13, 1996, p. A1. (Had Rep. Stark read his own statute?) Columbia/HCA countered the allegation by Rep. Stark by pointing to an (unverified) study showing no significant change in referral patterns of Columbia staff physicians in the two years before and the two years after they became investors in their hospitals.

What do you think of Columbia's strategy of tightening relationships between its hospitals and their staff doctors? See Kleinke, Deconstructing the Columbia/HCA Investigation, Health Affs., Mar.-Apr. 1998, p. 7, 13 ("Another of Columbia/HCA's core strategies has been its attempt to resolve, for its own commercial benefit, the historical antagonism and conflicting economic interests of physicians and hospitals. * * * It sold equity stakes in its local hospital systems to physicians, seeking not only to capture referrals (the cause of much criticism of the strategy) but also to turn these adversaries into economic allies."). But see Reinhardt, Columbia/HCA: Victim or Villain?, id. at 30, 33 ("Kleinke salutes Columbia/HCA's unique method of aligning the financial incentives of physicians and hospitals as the *sine qua non* of an efficient health care system. Other observers decry that approach as a distortion of the doctor/patient relationship.").

How might Medicare be adversely affected by the strategy adopted by Columbia/HCA? It is arguably ironic that HCFA is itself moving (slowly, with much resistance) toward contracting with so-called " 'centers of excellence' * * * allowing hospitals and physicians to 'partner' in return for global fees" and toward "a program for 'global package pricing,' whereby physicians and hospitals receive bundled reimbursements for care for Medicare inpatients." Kleinke, supra, at 15. See also id. at 16 (arguing that, although Columbia/HCA anticipated the eventual widespread adoption of such methods of bundling services, "[t]his strategy has proved to be wholly premature, or so it now seems"). But see Reinhardt, supra, at 32–33 (noting that Kleinke "provides no evidence that Columbia/HCA ever derived a significant fraction of its total revenue from global capitation, in exchange for assuming full financial risk for the comprehensive, clinically integrated care of enrolled populations").

4. *Vertical Integration by Hospitals*. The linking of an acute care hospital with providers of post-acute care services promises some efficiencies but runs afoul of notions based on the paradigm of a disaggregated system in which consumers and physicians select providers of each discrete service:

> Columbia/HCA and the other national health care companies have sought to integrate care vertically because they spotted a market opportunity. As with the integration of physicians, the operation of a full continuum of care addresses another structural flaw that has plagued the U.S. health care system from the start: the balkanization of care settings and fragmentation of medical delivery. * * * One of the best methods to resolve this enormous "continuity and transition" problem—one that would be intolerable in any other industry from the consumer's viewpoint—is the vertical integration of medical care. Control of the continuum allows for the coordination, timing, and management of postdischarge care, rehabilitation, drug compliance, and other services.

Kleinke, supra, at 17. But see Vladeck, Market Realities Meet Balanced Government: Another Look at Columbia/HCA, Health Affs., Mar.-Apr. 1998, p. 37, 38 ("There is no evidence whatsoever that Columbia/HCA's profit-maximizing behavior in home care referrals produced any clinical benefit for patients or indeed that the integration had any clinical reality to it.").

Does the "whole-hospital" exception in the Stark law apply when a hospital vertically integrates by purchasing or otherwise establishing units or services to which hospital patients might be referred or discharged? For example, if a hospital owns a pharmaceutical benefits company, a nursing home, a home health agency, and a durable medical equipment firm, are the physician's increased opportunities to refer patients to an affiliated or captive provider a matter for public concern? Does the rationale underlying the whole-hospital exception—namely, that the incentive to refer is not of overriding importance because staff physicians cannot profit greatly by their own referrals—become more difficult to sustain as the hospital owns more and more ancillary and post-acute services? Was this the nub of the complaint that Rep. Stark was leveling against Columbia/HCA? Nevertheless, is there anything in the whole-hospital exception to prevent its application to the case of the aggressively vertically integrated hospital? The proposed Stark rules did not seem to restrict application of the whole-hospital exception in the case of vertically integrated institutions. 63 Fed. Reg. at 1713.

With regard to the anti-kickback law, on the other hand, vertical integration issues arise because of the potential for the illegal use of remuneration to induce or solicit referrals between the hospital and the various ancillary services. If a hospital purchases or establishes a service such as home care and integrates it fully into the hospital itself with staff employed as employees of the hospital, anti-kickback issues will not arise because of the safe harbor regarding referrals by employees. But what happens if a hospital seeks to integrate vertically by acquiring an interest in, say, a freestanding home health agency or supplier of durable medical equipment (DME) for use by formerly hospitalized patients? Hospitals may be in a position to influence the consumption decisions of patients needing post-hospital care. Cf. Key Enterprises of Delaware, Inc. v. Venice Hosp., 919 F.2d 1550 (11th Cir.1990) (antitrust case challenging hospital efforts to induce home health nurses engaged in predischarge planning to recommend affiliated DME supplier). May a hospital own a 50% interest in such a facility or service? The relevant safe harbor (the "60/40 investment rule") provides a bright line rule that protects investments by potential referring persons or entities only to the point of allowing 40% ownership by investors in a position to influence referrals. Failure of a hospital to adhere to the 60/40 rule would subject a transaction to analysis under the *Greber* interpretation, in which the presence of some intent to induce referrals would be the critical issue.

5. *Space and Equipment Rental, Personal Services, and Management Contracts.* Transactions and contracts such as these put health care facilities in a position to make payments to providers who can refer patients to them in return. The anti-kickback safe-harbor regulations, S.H. Regs. § 1001.952(b), (c) & (d), and Stark, Stark § 1395nn(e)(1), (3), permit such payments, however, only if the contracts are written and bona fide, if the terms are set out in advance, and if payments are reasonable in light of market conditions and in no way contingent on referrals.

6. *Sale of a Physician's Practice.* Note that a physician selling a practice to another physician is, in effect, referring patients to that physician in return for "remuneration." Should the government try to ensure that payments do not exceed the value of the assets transferred—that is, do not contain an element of "goodwill"—because of the risk of inducing referrals? The safe-harbor regulations provide some protection for the sale of a physician practice but contemplate sales only to another practitioner, not to an institution such as a hospital. To qualify for protection, the sale must be complete within a year, and the selling physician cannot be in a professional position to generate business for the purchasing physician. S.H. Regs. § 1001.952(e)(1), (2).

It has been common in recent years for hospitals to purchase physician practices in the obvious hope that ownership will ensure referrals. The safe-harbor regulations do not protect these transactions directly. They do make exceptions from the anti-kickback rules for bona fide employees, so that if the physician becomes an employee of the purchasing institution, there would seem to be no problem for that employee to refer to the hospital once the deal is consummated. S.H. Regs. § 1001.952(i). But does this result make sense under the rationale of the laws under consideration? Has not the hospital rather obviously paid the physician the purchase price largely in the hope of inducing future referrals? What if the state corporate-practice doctrine prevents an employment arrangement? Does the safe harbor for personal services and management contracts provide a basis for protection? See S.H. Regs. § 1001.952(d).

7. *Waiver of Beneficiary Cost Sharing.* Why might a hospital or physician be questioned for waiving a Medicare beneficiary's copayment? Has the provider offered "remuneration (including any kickback * * * or rebate) * * * to any person to induce" the patient to "order * * * any * * * service * * * for which payment may be made in whole or in part under [Medicare]"? How would you have written the relevant safe-harbor regulation? See S.H. Regs. § 1001.952(k).

8. *Nonreferral; Referrals within a Group Practice.* Should there be an exception under Stark for self-referral in the sense of not referring the patient to an independent specialist? After all, physicians have an obvious "ownership or investment interest" in their own practices, solo or group as the case may be. Moreover, they often have an incentive to provide particular services themselves (especially if no rebates or kickbacks can be earned by referring the patient), may not be wholly objective in evaluating the options, and may hope to capture substantial producer surplus in dealing with the government.

Stark makes an exception from its general ban on self-referral for ancillary "designated health services" provided personally by the referring physician, personally by a member of the same group practice as the referring physician, or personally by individuals who are directly supervised by the referring physician or by another physician in the group practice. This exception is limited, however, to services provided in specific locations: (a) the same building in which the referring physician or another physician in the same group practice furnishes services "unrelated to the furnishing of designated health services," or (b) a building used by the referring physician's group practice for the group's clinical laboratory services, or (c) a building used by the group for the centralized provision of the group's non-laboratory "designated health services." A further limitation of this exception is a requirement involving billing for the services provided. To qualify for the ancillary services exception, the services must be billed by the physician performing or supervising the service, by the group practice, or by an entity "wholly owned" by the physician or the group practice. Stark § 1395nn(b)(2). The flavor of the regulatory detail here is reflected in a HCFA proposal to define "same building" as "the same physical structure, with one address, and not multiple structures connected by tunnels or walkways." 63 Fed. Reg. at 1723.

Can you identify the rationale for this Stark exception? How does this exception reflect a balance between convenience to the patient (one-stop shopping) and concerns about overutilization associated with physician self-referral? At what possible abuse is the proposed regulation defining "same building" aimed?

Stark protects a physician's referrals to his or her own group practice not only for in-office ancillary services but also for physicians' services generally. Thus, physicians' services "furnished personally by (or under the personal supervision of) another physician in the same group practice * * * as the referring physician" are not covered by the general Stark ban on self-referrals. Stark § 1395nn(b)(1). This seemingly straightforward provision raises intricate issues and potential practical pitfalls, however, because of convolutions in the Stark definition of what constitutes a "group practice." The next note considers some of these regulatory issues and pitfalls both to illustrate the statute's extraordinary focus on minutiae and to introduce the student to the complex relationships in medical groups.

9. *Group Practices Defined for Stark Purposes.* A group practice is defined in Stark as a group of two or more physicians legally organized as a partnership, professional corporation, or similar association in which each physician in the group provides "substantially the full range of patient care services" (such as medical care, consultation, diagnosis, or treatment) which that physician would routinely provide, and provides those services "through the joint use of shared office space, facilities, equipment, and personnel." Additionally, "substantially all" (i.e., 75%) of the patient care services of the physician members of a group must be "provided through the group" and billed in the name of the group; income must be treated as receipts of the group. Further, members of the group must personally conduct no less than 75% of the physician/patient encounters of the group practice. See Stark § 1395nn(h)(4)(A)(i), (ii); 42 C.F.R. § 411.351 (1997). A proposed rule revision goes further by requiring that income and overhead of the group be distributed according to methods that "indicate that the practice is a unified business," reflecting "centralized decision making, a pooling of expenses and revenues, and a distribution system that is not based on each satellite office operating as if it were a separate enterprise." 63 Fed. Reg. at 1721.

What is the rationale for the 75% rules? They suggest the goal of barring a proliferation of part-time members. Why might that be important in terms of guarding against rampant abuse of the group practice exception to the broad Stark prohibitions on self-referral? How should it be determined whether 75% of a physician's services are provided through the group? Should the yardstick be financial (e.g., percentage of billings) or temporal (e.g., percentage of time)? The Stark regulations use the temporal measure (percentage of total "patient care time" a physician spends on delivering "patient care services"). 42 C.F.R. § 411.351 (1997). Does this requirement apply to every member of the group, or can it be satisfied by viewing the percentages in the aggregate? What policy considerations would cause you to lean in either direction?

Who count as "members of the group"? Why is this definition of great potential significance to some group practices, especially those that contract with part-time specialists? Proposed regulations provide that independent contractor physicians do not qualify as constituting "members of the group." 63 Fed. Reg. at 1687, 1722. What justifies that proposed restriction? What are the consequences for the ability of a group to qualify for group practice status under Stark? How might this proposed restriction affect an independent contractor physician specialist who refers patients to the group with whom he has a consulting contract? Would the Stark exception for personal service arrangements between an entity that provides designated health services and a referring physician be useful here? To qualify, such an arrangement must include all services provided to the entity by the physician, and compensation must not be determined in a manner that takes into account the volume or value of any referrals or other business generated between the parties. Stark § 1395nn(e)(3). Note that HCFA has proposed a new regulatory exception (for "fair market value compensation") that might also be useful here. It is a generic exception for compensation arrangements that are based on fair market value and, among other requirements, comply with the anti-kickback law. 63 Fed. Reg. at 1725–26. This generic regulatory exception reflects a considerable change in HCFA's approach. The proposed exception, which provides some structural flexibility, is ostensibly driven by HCFA's awareness that the Stark statutory exceptions are too specific and narrowly circumscribed to permit some arrangements that might in fact be reasonable or beneficial to the federal health programs. Id. at 1699.

Can a multi-specialty group practice reward a primary care provider (PCP) who generates considerable business for the specialists within the practice? Tensions sometime develop in multi-specialty group practice contexts because specialists typically have been more highly paid than PCPs (e.g., internists, pediatricians, or family physicians), yet PCPs often generate the bulk of the business for the practice and, through referrals, for the group's specialists. The Stark definition of a "group practice" would bar any member of a group from directly or indirectly receiving compensation "based on the volume or value of referrals by the physician." Stark § 1395nn(h)(4)(A)(iv). Does a group practice physician's referral to a partner in a multi-specialty group practice nevertheless give rise to a concern of the kind that prompted the Stark legislation? If so, why does the statute create an exception for referrals to "another physician within the same group practice"? Should the patient be concerned that such referrals may not be taken with his welfare as the sole consideration? What are the competing policies and values at stake? Would mandating disclosure be helpful in providing notice to patients of possible conflicts?

10. *Summing Up*. Has the law succeeded in equalizing pressures on health care decision makers so that all referral (and nonreferral) decisions will be made with only the patient's welfare in mind and with no thought, conscious or unconscious, to the decision maker's short-term or long-term economic advantage? If not, has the regulatory effort been a failure? Are there at least some benefits that can be weighed against the costs of anti-fraud-and-abuse regulation (which must include substantial expenditures for legal advice and services)? Should policy makers have been concerned about perpetuating old, familiar organizational structures and patterns and about precluding the emergence of new arrangements that might be more efficient or more responsive to patient needs? Were there alternative policies that might have served the nation better? Could government, realistically, be expected to discover those policies?

NOTES AND QUESTIONS ON FRAUD AND ABUSE AND MANAGED CARE

1. The principal concern behind the enactment of the anti-kickback and Stark laws was obviously the possibility that Medicare and Medicaid costs would be inflated by inappropriate referrals. Although a secondary concern was perhaps that referrals not be based on concerns other than the welfare of the patient, the law seems incapable of ensuring patient welfare in this respect through regulation of the kind enacted. In any event, as fee-for-service practice gives way to capitation and other risk-shifting, demand-suppressing methods of payment, the former concern for the public fisc practically disappears. Are any of the anti-fraud statutes examined in this section well designed to deal with the kinds of referral abuses that might occur where capitation, global fees, and other payment innovations have replaced fee-for-service payments and radically altered the operative incentives? See generally Davies & Jost, Managed Care: Placebo or Wonder Drug for Health Care Fraud and Abuse?, 31 Ga. L. Rev. 373 (1997) (noting inadequacy of existing regulatory controls to address the concern "that managed care organizations will inappropriately deny necessary care or provide substandard care, thus defrauding and abusing consumers, purchasers, and intermediaries").

2. *Anti-Kickback Issues.* In general, the shift to risk-based contracting for Medicare and Medicaid services seems certain in time to render the main concerns behind the anti-kickback law largely moot. Nevertheless, because the prohibitions in the anti-kickback law are not conditioned on the existence of economic injury to the government, they do not automatically cease to apply just because enhancement of fee-for-service revenue from the federal government is no longer an arguable incentive driving a referral. Moreover, managed-care plans rely heavily on using the lure of future business (referrals) to induce providers to shade their fees or charges and to make other concessions in order to secure contracts, and it would be hard to argue that the discounts they obtain do not constitute "remuneration * * * to induce" referrals, etc. Precisely because of the carryover of the concern that referrals will be made on the basis of considerations other than the physical welfare of patients, the anti-kickback law might still be thought applicable whether or not there is any incentive to overutilize services. Indeed, because the previous incentive to overutilize has been replaced not by an optimal incentive regime but by incentives to do less and possibly to undertreat patients, the need for legal supervision may be felt even more strongly. See, e.g., Davies and Jost, supra.

On the other hand, where an at-risk purchaser—e.g., a Medicare risk contractor—contracts for providers' services, could you argue that the services are not such that "payment [for them] may be made in whole or in part under a federal health program"? This and related issues were largely resolved by the 1996 Kassebaum–Kennedy law, in which Congress provided a statutory safe harbor under the anti-kickback law for arrangements in which providers assume significant financial risk through capitation or other arrangements for their treatment decisions. That legislation creates an express exception for

> any remuneration between an organization and an individual or entity providing items or services * * * pursuant to a written agreement between the organization and the individual or entity if the organization is [a

> Medicare risk contractor] or if the written agreement, through a risk-sharing arrangement places the individual or entity at substantial financial risk for the cost or utilization of the items or services * * * which the individual or entity is obligated to provide.

42 U.S.C.A. § 1320a–7b(3)(F) (West Supp. 1998). Enactment of this statutory safe harbor was a necessary step in removing the aforementioned anomaly in fraud and abuse law in managed-care contexts. Congress mandated fast-track regulatory implementation of this provision through a negotiated rulemaking process. The result was agreement on two new safe-harbor regulations—one to deal with managed-care organizations (MCOs) that are capitated under Medicare and one that concerns MCOs that bill Medicare on a FFS basis.

For discussions of the changing nature of health care financing and its implications for the problem of fraud and abuse, see Blumstein, "Life in the Health Care Speakeasy," 22 Am. J.L. & Med. at 207–11; Frankford, Creating and Dividing the Fruits of Collective Activity: Referrals Among Health Care Providers, 89 Colum. L. Rev. 1861 (1989); Hyman & Williamson, Fraud and Abuse: Regulatory Alternatives in a "Competitive" Health Care Era, 19 Loyola U. Chi. L.J. 1133 (1988); McDowell, The Medicare–Medicaid Anti–Fraud and Abuse Amendments: Their Impact on the Present Health Care System, 36 Emory L. Rev. 691 (1987).

3. *Problem*. Consider the following scenario: Eldercare Associates is a Medicare risk-contracting MCO. It receives a capitated payment per enrollee from the government for each of its Medicare patients. In turn, Eldercare contracts with a number of primary care physician (PCP) groups from which Eldercare enrollees may choose for the provision of primary care. Golden Years Physician Group is a provider of primary care services to Eldercare enrollees. Many physicians at Golden Years have traditionally referred patients to the New Age Radiology Group for x-rays and other radiology services. Patients at Golden Years complain to their PCPs that, while providing friendly and competent services, New Age Radiology keeps them waiting for as long as four hours for services, even though Golden Years patients have definitive appointment times established in advance. Concerned about these complaints (because of professional considerations of providing good quality services to their patients but also because of their fear of losing patients to other competitor PCP groups in the Eldercare network), Golden Years physicians contact New Age Radiology to see whether something can be worked out so that Golden Years patients can be treated within thirty minutes of their arrival at the New Age facility. New Age doctors explain to the PCPs from Golden Years that assuring a maximum of a thirty-minute wait at New Age for Golden Years patients would require a substantial investment in new equipment and a significant increase in staffing levels (thereby also raising operational expenses). New Age expresses its willingness to incur these expenses but only if Golden Years guarantees that its PCPs will refer all radiology business to New Age for a period of five years (assuming that quality standards are otherwise maintained). Golden Years PCPs believe this to be a reasonable proposal

and are willing to accept the New Age plan. Assuming that the transaction cannot be crafted to fit within a safe harbor (e.g., the personal services and management contracts provision of 42 C.F.R. § 1001.952(d)), how would you advise Golden Years if it sought your advice? Explain your thinking. From a policy perspective, are you satisfied with the legal advice that you might feel constrained to give?

4. *Stark Issues; Physician Incentive Plans.* While the Kassebaum–Kennedy shared-risk safe harbor under the anti-kickback law was adopted only in 1996, the Stark law has included provisions focused on managed care from its inception. Thus, Stark's broad anti-self-referral provisions do not apply where a Medicare risk-contracting entity furnishes services to Medicare enrollees through various kinds of affiliated providers. Stark § 1395nn(b)(3). On the other hand, the Stark law does purport to govern certain "compensation" arrangements between at-risk organizations paying for services and the individual or entities providing those services. Although the numerous exceptions to the broad Stark prohibitions that were reviewed earlier typically required that a referring physician's compensation not be based on the "volume or value" of referrals, the Stark exception for so-called physician incentive plans (PIPs) can in certain carefully delineated circumstances result in physician compensation that is to some extent related to the volume or value of referrals. Stark § 1395nn(e)(3)(B). The concern here is to allow incentive arrangements that discourage overutilization of services—a major raison d'etre of managed care—but also to protect against arrangements that threaten to result in undertreatment or the denial of necessary care.

A PIP is "any compensation arrangement between an entity and a physician or physician group that may directly or indirectly have the effect of reducing or limiting services provided with respect to individuals enrolled with the entity." Stark § 1395nn(e)(3)(B)(ii). Thus, the law applies to any situation where a physician is paid on a capitated basis, through bonuses or penalties, under a withhold arrangement, or in any other manner that gives the physician a financial incentive to reduce or withhold services that might otherwise be provided or prescribed or to deny a referral to a specialist or to a provider of designated health services. PIPs are of course recognized as being integral to any MCO's utilization control program, and MCOs with Medicare risk contracts are expressly authorized to employ PIPs meeting regulatory standards. 42 U.S.C. § 1395mm(i)(8) (West Supp. 1998).

PIPs do not violate Stark as long as "[n]o specific payment is made directly or indirectly under the plan to a physician or physician group as an inducement to reduce or limit medically necessary services provided with respect to a specific individual enrolled with the entity." Stark § 1395nn(e)(3)(B)(i)(I). The same standard also applies specifically to Medicare risk-contracting MCOs, 42 U.S.C. § 1395mm(i)(8)(A)(i) (West Supp. 1998). Stark also requires such plans to comply with other regulatory requirements promulgated under the latter legislation. Stark § 1395nn(e)(3)(B)(i)(II). If a PIP places a physician or physician group at substantial risk for services provided by the physician or physician group, then the MCO must ensure that all such physicians or physician groups have "stop-loss" (high-deductible) insurance to minimize the impact of bad experience. It must also conduct periodic surveys of the experience of past and present enrollees to determine how much access to services an MCO provides to enrollees and whether such services are satisfactory. Id. at § 1395mm(i)(8)(A)(ii). In addition, an MCO must provide DHHS with descriptive information regarding the PIP to ensure that the plan is in compliance with the above requirements. 42 U.S.C.A. § 1395mm(i)(8)(A)(iii) (West Supp. 1998); see also Stark § 1395nn(e)(3)(B)(i)(III). For regulations implementing the PIP requirements, see 42 C.F.R. § 417.479 (1997).

Note that under a PIP a physician can benefit from his or his group's general reduction in costs (e.g., from lower levels of referrals) but not from a payment to induce lower levels of care for a specific individual in the plan. What is the judgment that underlies that standard? What are the competing values and policies that are being balanced? What assumptions underlie the compromise (between reducing costs and maintaining quality) that is reached in the foregoing standard? For a discussion of some of these issues, see 61 Fed. Reg. 13430, 13432–33 (Mar. 27, 1996). How do you evaluate the Stark exception for PIPs (and, more generally, Medicare's allowing its MCO risk contractors to have PIPs)? Do you view the acceptance of PIPs as a positive step in balancing the goals of cost containment and quality assurance? If you object, describe and characterize your concerns. Has the regulatory system left appropriate room for MCOs to address the cost problem by shifting risks to health care providers?

CHAPTER 4

THE ANTITRUST CHALLENGE TO PROFESSIONAL DOMINANCE

SECTION A: THE SHERMAN ACT AND PROFESSIONAL SERVICES

NOTE ON THE SIGNIFICANCE OF ANTITRUST LAW IN THE HEALTH CARE SECTOR

Extending our examination of the paradigm shifts that underlie recent changes in American health care, this chapter tells how the antitrust laws came to be applied to the "learned" professions, and particularly to organized medicine. In so doing, it introduces students to an important body of public law that they may not encounter elsewhere in their studies. Most of the antitrust issues covered in this book (antitrust matters are not confined to this chapter alone) arise under section 1 of the Sherman Act, which prohibits "every contract, combination * * *, or conspiracy in restraint of trade * * *." 15 U.S.C. § 1 (1994). Although this statute provides a warrant for scrutinizing concerted action by competitors of all kinds, study of its application to the collaborative activities of competing professionals provides an excellent introduction to some of the most basic principles of antitrust law. Equally important, studying antitrust cases arising in the health care field is highly instructive about the health care industry, about how certain private interests dominated it in the past, about the nature and origins of the forces that are rapidly reshaping the industry today, and about possible unfinished legal business in making competition work to the advantage of health care consumers. The student of health care law is encouraged to think about antitrust law as one of the foremost expressions of current public policy toward the health care sector—and not merely as a sophisticated subspecialty in health care law or as a subject of interest only to afficionados of free-market economics.

The first element of a violation of section 1 of the Sherman Act—concerted action by multiple actors—is usually satisfied whenever independent professionals or other independent entities cooperate for some purpose. The crucial question in applying the statute is therefore likely to be whether there is in fact a "restraint of trade"—that is, whether the concerted conduct in question is or is not compatible with the maintenance of competition as a guarantor of consumer welfare. For these purposes, competition is best thought of as a dynamic process featuring voluntary transactions between, and independent decisions by, mutually accountable buyers and sellers. As materials in this chapter will demonstrate, the statute is deemed by most courts to incorporate a virtually conclusive presumption that consumers benefit from maintaining competition and its attendant incentives, checks, and balances. Thus, even plausible claims that competition may be impeded because it serves consumers badly in a particular market will generally be rejected on the basis of this statutory presumption and the inappropriateness of letting courts rather than a legislative body decide as a policy matter whether competition should be displaced in one part of the economy. Although case law has never declared that concerted action destructive of competition can *never* be redeemed by a claim that the public interest would be better served by permitting the restraint, antitrust counsellors should probably consider only competitive effects in appraising concerted action by professionals even though the collaborators' motives might be regarded as noncommercial or even altruistic. This chapter focuses at some length on the validity of using policy arguments, claims of "reasonableness," or (in health care contexts) quality-of-care considerations to justify a true restraint of trade. Although courts are certainly influenced by perceptions that the collaborators' objectives were laudable, antitrust doctrine does not easily permit worthy (as opposed to procompetitive) purposes to be raised as a defense. Thus, private interests are generally not permitted to restrict competition to achieve another social objective, such as consumer protection.

The so-called Rule of Reason, explicated in a note later in this chapter, is typically employed in deciding whether certain concerted action constitutes a restraint of trade. Certain categories of concerted action—such as price fixing, market division, and some group boycotts—are so certain to restrain trade that they have been classified as "per se" offenses, meaning essentially that it is no defense that no harm was actually done in the particular case; indeed, when such conduct is encountered, courts conclusively presume that a restraint occurred—that is, that the competitive process was interfered with. In other cases, the question whether competition was harmed can be answered only after a more extensive factual inquiry. Antitrust lawyers are often highly concerned whether a per se rule or the Rule of Reason applies to a case in question. This chapter provides examples of offenses found under both analytical approaches. Particular attention is paid to so-called group boycotts (or concerted refusals to deal) in which professionals have engaged. In these cases, terminology can be misleading, and harms to competition may lie somewhere other than where courts and analysts tend to look for them.

Whether or not students are to study this chapter in full, they should appreciate what fundamental changes have been triggered in the health care sector as a direct result of the enforcement of the antitrust laws in the health care sector since the mid-1970s. The control exercised by the medical profession over the economic environment of physicians from the 1930s to the 1980s—particularly in delaying the emergence of corporate middlemen able and willing to act as purchasing agents for consumers in procuring physician services on competitive terms—may have been the most successful restraint of trade ever perpetrated by private interests in the American economy. By the same token, the antitrust battles that hastened the breakdown of medical control of health care delivery and financing paved the way for the revolution that is occurring in the health care industry today. Indeed, without uncompromising antitrust enforcement against physicians, the nation would have had to wait much longer for private innovations that make providers appreciably accountable to consumers for the cost as well as the quality of medical care. More likely, without antitrust enforcement clearing the way for private innovation, government would have assumed a dominant role in American health care, as it has in other countries.

In studying antitrust materials in the health care field, students should focus not only on the evolution of legal doctrine but also on the history of the health care industry itself. Earlier materials have already provided evidence of how health care markets have evolved under antitrust protection so that they now feature a variety of financing entities that are not only independent of professional control but also highly aggressive in forcing physicians to sell their services on competitive terms. The student should consider whether competition has yet come to every market for health services or whether concerted action by physicians may still be an obstacle to its emergence in some places. Another issue for consideration is the role that competitor collaboration may continue to play under an antitrust regime.

Are the "Learned Professions" Exempt?

Goldfarb v. Virginia State Bar

Supreme Court of the United States, 1975.
421 U.S. 773, 95 S.Ct. 2004, 44 L.Ed.2d 572.

■ MR. CHIEF JUSTICE BURGER delivered the opinion of the Court.

We granted certiorari to decide whether a minimum-fee schedule for lawyers published by the Fairfax County Bar Association and enforced by the Virginia State Bar violates § 1 of the Sherman Act, [which prohibits "every contract, combination * * *, or conspiracy, in restraint of trade or commerce among the several states * * * "]. The Court of Appeals held that, although the fee schedule and enforcement mechanism substantially restrained competition among lawyers, publication of the schedule by the County Bar was outside the scope of the Act because the practice of law is not "trade or commerce," * * *.

In 1971 petitioners, husband and wife, contracted to buy a home in Fairfax County, Va. The financing agency required them to secure title insurance; this required a title examination, and only a member of the Virginia State Bar could legally perform that service. Petitioners therefore contacted a lawyer who quoted them the precise fee suggested in a minimum-fee schedule published by respondent Fairfax County Bar Association * * *. Petitioners then * * * sent letters to 36 other Fairfax County lawyers requesting their fees. Nineteen replied, and none indicated that he would charge less than the rate fixed by the schedule; several stated that they knew of no attorney who would do so.

The fee schedule the lawyers referred to is a list of recommended minimum prices for common legal services. Respondent Fairfax County Bar Association published the fee schedule although, as a purely voluntary association of attorneys, the County Bar has no formal power to enforce it. Enforcement has been provided by respondent Virginia State Bar which is the administrative agency through which the Virginia Supreme Court regulates the practice of law in that State; membership in the State Bar is required in order to practice in Virginia. Although the State Bar has never taken formal disciplinary action to compel adherence to any fee schedule, it has published reports condoning fee schedules, and has issued two ethical opinions indicating that fee schedules cannot be ignored. The most recent opinion states that "evidence that an attorney *habitually* charges less than the suggested minimum fee schedule adopted by his local bar Association, raises a presumption that such lawyer is guilty of misconduct.... "

* * * [Petitioners] then brought this class action against the State Bar and the County Bar alleging that the operation of the minimum-fee schedule, as applied to fees for legal services relating to residential real estate transactions, constitutes price fixing in violation of § 1 of the Sherman Act. * * *

A purely advisory fee schedule issued to provide guidelines, or an exchange of price information without a showing of an actual restraint on trade, would present us with a different question. The record here, however, reveals a situation quite different from what would occur under a purely advisory fee schedule. Here * * * a naked agreement was clearly shown, and the effect on prices is plain.

* * * On this record respondents' activities constitute a classic illustration of price fixing.

[The Court first considered the respondents' argument that "any effect on interstate commerce caused by the fee schedule's restraint on legal services was incidental and remote," concluding as follows:] Given the substantial volume of commerce involved, and the inseparability of this particular legal service [title searches] from the interstate aspects of real estate transactions, we conclude that interstate commerce has been sufficiently affected.

* * *

Where, as a matter of law or practical necessity, legal services are an integral part of an interstate transaction, a restraint on those services may substantially affect commerce for Sherman Act purposes. Of course, there may be legal services that involve interstate commerce in other fashions, just as there may be legal services that have no nexus with interstate commerce and thus are beyond the reach of the Sherman Act.

The County Bar [next] argues that Congress never intended to include the learned professions within the terms "trade or commerce" in § 1 of the

Sherman Act,[15] and therefore the sale of professional services is exempt from the Act. No explicit exemption or legislative history is provided to support this contention; rather, the existence of state regulation seems to be its primary basis. Also, the County Bar maintains that competition is inconsistent with the practice of a profession because enhancing profit is not the goal of professional activities; the goal is to provide services necessary to the community.[16] That, indeed, is the classic basis traditionally advanced to distinguish professions from trades, businesses, and other occupations, but it loses some of its force when used to support the fee control activities involved here.

In arguing that learned professions are not "trade or commerce" the County Bar seeks a total exclusion from antitrust regulation. Whether state regulation is active or dormant, real or theoretical, lawyers would be able to adopt anticompetitive practices with impunity. We cannot find support for the proposition that Congress intended any such sweeping exclusion. The nature of an occupation, standing alone, does not provide sanctuary from the Sherman Act, nor is the public-service aspect of professional practice controlling in determining whether § 1 includes professions. United States v. National Assn. of Real Estate Boards, 339 U.S., at 489. Congress intended to strike as broadly as it could in § 1 of the Sherman Act, and to read into it so wide an exemption as that urged on us would be at odds with that purpose.

The language of § 1 of the Sherman Act, of course, contains no exception. * * * And our cases have repeatedly established that there is a heavy presumption against implicit exemptions. Indeed, our cases have specifically included the sale of services within § 1. E.g., American Medical Assn. v. United States, 317 U.S. 519 (1943). Whatever else it may be, the examination of a land title is a service; the exchange of such a service for money is "commerce" in the most common usage of that word. It is no disparagement of the practice of law as a profession to acknowledge that it has this business aspect,[17] and § 1 of the Sherman Act "[o]n its face ...

15. The County Bar cites phrases in several cases that implied the practice of a learned profession is not "trade or commerce" under the antitrust laws. E.g., Federal Club v. National League, 259 U.S. 200, 209 (1922) ("a firm of lawyers sending out a member to argue a case ... does not engage in ... commerce because the lawyer ... goes to another State"); FTC v. Raladam Co., 283 U.S. 643, 653 (1931) ("medical practitioners ... follow a profession and not a trade ..."); Atlantic Cleaners & Dyers v. United States, 286 U.S. 427, 436 (1932); United States v. National Assn. of Real Estate Boards, 339 U.S. 485, 490 (1950). These citations are to passing references in cases concerned with other issues; and, more important, until the present case it is clear that we have not attempted to decide whether the practice of a learned profession falls within § 1 of the Sherman Act. In National Assn. of Real Estate Boards, we specifically stated that the question was still open, 339 U.S., at 492, as we had done earlier in American Medical Assn. v. United States, 317 U.S. 519, 528 (1943).

16. The reason for adopting the fee schedule does not appear to have been wholly altruistic. The first sentence in respondent State Bar's 1962 Minimum Fee Schedule Report states: " 'The lawyers have slowly, but surely, been committing economic suicide as a profession.' "

17. The fact that a restraint operates upon a profession as distinguished from a business is, of course, relevant in determin-

shows a carefully studied attempt to bring within the Act every person engaged in business whose activities might restrain or monopolize commercial intercourse among the states." United States v. South–Eastern Underwriters Assn., 322 U.S. 533, 553. In the modern world it cannot be denied that the activities of lawyers play an important part in commercial intercourse, and that anticompetitive activities by lawyers may exert a restraint on commerce.

[The Court also rejected arguments that the State Bar was immune from suit because it was acting as a state agency and that the County Bar, having been "prompted" to act by the State Bar, enjoyed the same implied exemption.]

Reversed and remanded.

■ MR. JUSTICE POWELL took no part in the consideration or decision of this case.

NOTES AND QUESTIONS ON THE APPLICABILITY OF ANTITRUST STATUTES TO PROFESSIONALS

1. *Interstate Commerce*. It has long been the rule that the Sherman Act's interstate commerce requirement is met if a restraint occurs "in" or has a "substantial effect on" interstate commerce. Burke v. Ford, 389 U.S. 320 (1967). Traditionally, professional activities such as medicine, law, engineering, and teaching were seen as localized and unlikely to meet either of these tests. In *Goldfarb,* however, the Court held the interstate commerce requirement satisfied by a showing that the local activity was an inseparable part of a larger transaction involving interstate commerce. For a slightly later decision extending the reach of the Sherman Act in the health care industry, see Hospital Building Co. v. Trustees of Rex Hospital, 425 U.S. 738 (1976) (interstate commerce requirement held satisfied because the hospital plaintiff, allegedly the victim of an "attempt to monopolize," made out-of-state purchases of medicines and supplies, derived revenues from out-of-state insurance companies, made payments to an out-of-state management company, and obtained financing for its expansion from out-of-state sources).

In McLain v. Real Estate Board of New Orleans, Inc., 444 U.S. 232, 240 (1980), the Supreme Court held that jurisdiction over real estate brokers could be established even if the challenged local activity—commission fixing—was not "an essential, integral, part of the transaction and inseparable from its interstate aspects." The Court stated, "To establish federal jurisdiction in this case, there remains only the requirement that

ing whether that particular restraint violates the Sherman Act. It would be unrealistic to view the practice of professions as interchangeable with other business activities, and automatically to apply to the professions antitrust concepts which originated in other areas. The public service aspect, and other features of the professions, may require that a particular practice, which could properly be viewed as a violation of the Sherman Act in another context, be treated differently. We intimate no view on any other situation than the one with which we are confronted today.

respondents' activities which allegedly have been infected by a price-fixing conspiracy be shown 'as a matter of practical economics' to have a not insubstantial effect on the interstate commerce involved." Id. at 246 (quoting *Rex Hospital*, 425 U.S. at 745). In a passage linking the substantive aspects of the Sherman Act offense with the jurisdictional requirement, the Court said (id. at 242–43):

> To establish the jurisdictional element of a Sherman Act violation it would be sufficient for petitioners to demonstrate a substantial effect on interstate commerce generated by respondents' brokerage activity. Petitioners need not make the more particularized showing of an effect on interstate commerce caused by the alleged conspiracy to fix commission rates, or by those other aspects of respondents' activity that are alleged to be unlawful * * *. If establishing jurisdiction required a showing that the unlawful conduct itself had an effect on interstate commerce, jurisdiction would be defeated by a demonstration that the alleged restraint failed to have its intended effect. This is not the rule of our cases.

It is notable that price fixing is a so-called per se antitrust offense, meaning that a plaintiff need prove only that price fixing occurred, not that it had any particular effect in raising or stabilizing prices. It would obviously be anomalous if a plaintiff, in order to establish jurisdiction, had to prove effects that he did not have to prove to establish the substantive violation.

The quoted passages from the *McLain* opinion led lower courts to split on the test to be applied to large entities, such as hospitals. Does a plaintiff alleging that a hospital has violated the federal antitrust laws have to show only that the hospital's general activities affect interstate commerce, or must he show that the particular activity alleged to be illegal (a denial of admitting privileges to a single physician, for example) had the required impact? In Summit Health, Ltd. v. Pinhas, 500 U.S. 322 (1991), the Supreme Court, seeking to resolve this split, held (5–4) that the plaintiff physician, in a case challenging a hospital's actions with respect to his staff privileges, did not have to allege or prove that the unlawful action that caused his harm also had an actual effect on interstate commerce. It would be sufficient if the restraint alleged was potentially capable of affecting commerce. (This issue will be returned to briefly in chapter 5(§C).) An interesting feature of *Pinhas* was Justice Scalia's dissent, which would have rejected the time-honored axiom—not well supported by the statutory language—that Congress intended the Sherman Act to reach as far as Congress is constitutionally empowered to reach.

2. *State Antitrust Laws.* Most states have their own antitrust laws. These laws are frequently modeled on the federal statutes and interpreted in similar fashion. New York's Donnelly Act, however, has been interpreted as inapplicable to combinations of licensed professionals affecting the provision of professional services. People v. Roth, 52 N.Y.2d 440, 438 N.Y.S.2d 737, 420 N.E.2d 929 (1981). In 1985, the California Supreme Court, expressly adopting the reasoning of the *Goldfarb* case, reversed an earlier holding that the professions were not governed by that state's Cartwright

Act. Cianci v. Superior Court, 40 Cal.3d 903, 221 Cal.Rptr. 575, 710 P.2d 375 (1985).

3. Why did it take 85 years, from the enactment of the Sherman Act in 1890 to the *Goldfarb* case, to settle whether the "learned professions" were bound by the basic rule that competitors may not restrain trade? Consider note 15 in *Goldfarb,* supra, and the cases in the following notes.

4. *Atlantic Cleaners & Dyers, Inc., v. United States*, 286 U.S. 427 (1932). The United States sued launderers in Washington, D.C., under section 3 of the Sherman Act, which extends the prohibitions of section 1 to activities in the District of Columbia. The launderers claimed that their services—cleaning, dyeing, and renovating clothing—were exempt from the antitrust laws under section 6 of the Clayton Act, 15 U.S.C. § 17 (1982), which declares that "[t]he labor of a human being is not a commodity or article of commerce." Construing this "labor exemption" narrowly, the Court confined it to protecting the legitimate concerted activities of employees organized in labor unions and the like. The Court also rejected the defendants' argument that their services did not involve "trade," quoting an 1834 opinion by Justice Story: "Wherever any occupation, employment, or business is carried on for the purpose of profit, or gain, or a livelihood, not in the liberal arts or in the learned professions, it is constantly called a *trade.*" 286 U.S. at 436 [quoting The Schooner Nymph, 18 F.Cas. 506 (C.C.D.Me.1834) (No. 10,388)].

5. *United States v. National Association of Real Estate Boards*, 339 U.S. 485 (1950). In another action under section 3, the Court held that District of Columbia real estate brokers were engaged in "trade" for Sherman Act purposes. The Court cautioned, however, that "[w]e do not intimate an opinion on the correctness of the application of the term to the professions." Id. at 491–92.

6. *AMA v. United States*, 130 F.2d 233 (D.C.Cir.1942), affirmed 317 U.S. 519 (1943). The AMA and its Washington, D.C., affiliate society were convicted of a criminal violation of section 3 of the Sherman Act. The defendants conspired to prevent Group Health Association, an early health maintenance organization, from obtaining and keeping staff doctors. Citing ethical objections to contract practice and prepayment, the defendants threatened HMO doctors and doctors who consulted with them with expulsion from society membership, which was usually a prerequisite for obtaining staff privileges in local hospitals. The defendants circulated a "white list" of approved providers, which presumably served as an invitation to boycott those not listed; one specialist was challenged for accepting a Group Health check after treating a referred patient. (For a fuller statement of the facts, see the earlier opinion in the case, United States v. AMA, 110 F.2d 703 (D.C.Cir.1940).)

On appeal, the defendants argued that the practice of medicine was not trade or commerce within the meaning of the Sherman Act and that their actions were reasonable attempts to regulate the practice of medicine. The court of appeals affirmed the convictions. At common law, the court said, the practice of medicine was a trade, and the Sherman Act's use of the common law phrase "in restraint of trade" revealed a congressional intent to make the statute coextensive with the common law. Moreover, although the defendants had traditionally regulated the practice of medicine, that regulation could not take the form of illegal acts. The defendants had no public mandate to dictate how physicians should organize their practices or to whom hospitals should grant staff privileges. The court suggested that the defendant associations could discipline their own members: "[Defendants] were permitted to organize to establish standards of professional conduct, to effect agreements for *self-discipline and control.* There is a very real difference between the use of such self-disciplines and an effort upon the part of such associations to destroy competing professional or business groups or organizations." 130 F.2d at 248. If the defendants did not like HMOs or how hospitals made staff privileges decisions, they had "open to them always the safer and more kindly weapons of legitimate persuasion and reasoned argument as a means of preserving professional esprit de corps, winning public sentiment to their point of view or securing legislation." Id.

The court of appeals majority in *Goldfarb* attempted to distinguish *AMA* by arguing that, while restrictions imposed by professionals on fellow professionals are exempt, restrictions imposed upon outsiders, such as insurers and corporate health plans like the HMO, would not be; thus, a doctors' conspiracy "to obstruct the interstate sale of health insurance" was said in dicta not to be exempt. 497 F.2d at 15.

7. *Group Health Cooperative of Puget Sound v. King County Medical Society*, 39 Wash.2d 586, 237 P.2d 737 (1951). Decided under a state antitrust law, this case involved facts strikingly similar to those in *AMA v. United States* and resulted in the vindication of another early HMO.

8. *United States v. Oregon State Medical Society*, 343 U.S. 326 (1952) (discussed more fully later in this chapter and reproduced in chapter 8(§A)). The Court reviewed the evidence and found no reason to overturn the district court's finding that the society had not, as alleged by the government, organized a boycott to stamp out certain health insurers that undertook cost-containment efforts of which the society and its members disapproved. Despite finding that a boycott (normally a per se violation) had not been proved, the Court uttered the following dictum:

> We might observe in passing, however, that there are ethical considerations where the historic relationship between patient and physician is involved which are quite different than the usual considerations prevailing in ordinary commercial matters. This Court has recognized that forms of competition usual in the business world may be demoralizing to the ethical standards of a profession.

343 U.S. at 336, citing Semler v. Oregon State Board of Dental Examiners, 294 U.S. 608 (1935) (upholding, against constitutional attack, state restrictions on advertising by dentists).

9. Antitrust law is concerned with many things, including single-firm monopolization, certain arguably exclusionary business practices, restrictive arrangements between firms "vertically" related in the chain of distribution, and price discrimination. But its principal focus is on so-called "horizontal" restraints, a category comprising complete mergers of competitors as well as loose collaboration among them. Most of the antitrust issues that have arisen in the health care industry have involved competitor collaboration. During the long era when the industry enjoyed a de facto (or was it de jure?) exemption from antitrust scrutiny, industry groups became accustomed to making many decisions collectively, thus depriving consumers of opportunities to choose for themselves. A question throughout these materials is the extent to which decision making in health care can and should be decentralized. The antitrust laws are the primary vehicle by which decision-making authority might be kept in consumers' hands.

The materials in the remainder of this chapter deal with basic antitrust principles applicable to competitor collaboration and with the application of these principles to the activities of health care professionals. See generally H. Feller, Antitrust Developments in Evolving Health Care Markets (1996); T. Walters & R. Morse, Antitrust & Trade Associations: How Trade Regulation Laws Apply to Trade and Professional Associations (1996); J. Miles, Health Care and Antitrust Law: Principles and Practices (3 vols. 1992 & supps.).

10. *Criminal Prosecutions of Professionals*. As the old *AMA* case shows, the Sherman Act can be enforced by criminal as well as civil sanctions. In the recent era, the government initiated only civil actions against professionals until quite recently. Now, however, the Department of Justice has begun to make it clear to physicians and other professionals that their professional status will not protect them from criminal prosecution if they engage in hard-core antitrust violations. See Remarks of Robert E. Bloch, Chief, Professions and Intellectual Property Section, Antitrust Division, Los Angeles, Oct. 25, 1989 (mentioning, as possible targets of criminal investigations and grand juries, agreements with respect to price; use of fee schedules or boycott threats in negotiations with payers; boycotts aimed at excluding HMOs from the marketplace; and the formation of sham organizations ostensibly to provide services but in actuality to engage in collective negotiation of fees). Several criminal investigations have been commenced. One criminal prosecution of three Arizona dentists resulted in convictions that were overturned on appeal. United States v. A. Lanoy Alston, D.M.D., P.C., 974 F.2d 1206 (9th Cir.1992).

NOTES AND QUESTIONS ON TRADE UNIONISM FOR PHYSICIANS

1. Under what circumstances would physicians engaged in concerted action be protected by the labor exemption from the antitrust laws referred to in the *Atlantic Cleaners* case, noted supra? The usual antitrust rule is that independent contractors, because they are not common-law employees, do not qualify for the exemption, which, like other antitrust exemptions, is narrowly construed. The argument has been made, however, that fee-for-service physicians should be allowed to organize for collective bargaining on the theory that they are de facto employees needing protection against monopsonistic purchasers of their services. The nonlegal case for unionization is presented in Marcus, Trade Unionism for Doctors—An Idea Whose Time Has Come, 311 New Eng.J.Med. 1508 (1984). A letter to the editor in response to the Marcus article stated as follows: "If we [doctors] continue to act as individuals and attend only to our personal interests, we may, ironically, be forced to practice medicine in a style dictated by business or government or both. Dr. Marcus seems to offer a viable alternative in proposing a trade union for physicians. As a united force, we could have a large impact on policies that would affect the day-to-day practice of medicine." 312 New Eng.J.Med. 925–26 (1985).

2. As many as 20,000 physicians are reported to have joined one of eight labor unions that have been formed to represent their interests. See Jaklevic, Physicians Find Power in Unions, Mod. Healthcare, Oct. 6, 1997, p. 99. See generally G. Budrys, Why Doctors Join Unions (1997); Ile, From the Office of the [AMA] General Counsel: Collective Negotiation and Physician Unions, 262 J.A.M.A. 2444 (1989) (discussing the limited freedom of doctors to engage in collective bargaining).

3. The right to organize, bargain collectively, and strike is governed by the federal labor laws. Physicians employed by Group Health Association, the same HMO that was victimized by the defendants in the early *AMA* case, eventually unionized under federal law and even engaged in a strike in the 1980s. However, the National Labor Relations Board (NLRB) has since held that HMO physicians are managerial employees and thus not entitled to the protections of the National Labor Relations Act. FHP, Inc. v. Union of American Physicians and Dentists, 274 N.L.R.B. 1141, 1985–86 NLRB Dec. (CCH) ¶ 17,229 (1985). In the *FHP* case, the NLRB ruled that full-time physicians were members of FHP's management because they served on various committees concerned with controlling the quality of services offered by the HMO. Although these committee activities were not managerial in the day-to-day sense, the NLRB concluded that the duties of committee members fell "outside the scope of decision-making routinely performed by health care professionals." What is the significance of this decision for professionalism and professional autonomy? The *FHP* ruling is being questioned in a case pending before the Ninth Circuit court of appeals, but the Supreme Court has ruled more recently that licensed practical nurses working in a nursing home were supervisors and not entitled to organize. NLRB v. Health Care & Retirement Corp., 511 U.S. 571 (1994).

4. Resident physicians undergoing postgraduate medical training have been held ineligible for unionization under the federal labor laws because they were students, not employees. Cedars–Sinai Medical Center, 223 N.L.R.B. 251 (1976), motion denied, 224 N.L.R.B. 626 (1976). In California and some other states, however, house staffs of public hospitals are entitled to union representation. See, e.g., Regents of the University of California v. Public Employment Relations Board, 715 P.2d 590 (Cal.1986). The *Cedars-Sinai* ruling is being challenged in a Boston case.

Applying the Sherman Act to Professionals

National Society of Professional Engineers v. United States

Supreme Court of the United States, 1978.
435 U.S. 679, 98 S.Ct. 1355, 55 L.Ed.2d 637.

■ MR. JUSTICE STEVENS delivered the opinion of the Court.

This is a civil antitrust case brought by the United States to nullify an association's canon of ethics prohibiting competitive bidding by its members. The question is whether the canon may be justified under the Sherman Act because it was adopted by members of a learned profession for the purpose of minimizing the risk that competition would produce inferior engineering work endangering the public safety. The District Court rejected this justification without making any findings on the likelihood that competition would produce the dire consequences foreseen by the association. The Court of Appeals affirmed. We granted certiorari to decide whether the District Court should have considered the factual basis for the proffered justification before rejecting it. Because we are satisfied that the asserted defense rests on a fundamental misunderstanding of the Rule of Reason frequently applied in antitrust litigation, we affirm.

I

* * *

The National Society of Professional Engineers (Society) was organized in 1935 to deal with the nontechnical aspects of engineering practice, including the promotion of the professional, social, and economic interests of its members. Its present membership of 69,000 resides throughout the United States and in some foreign countries. Approximately 12,000 members are consulting engineers who offer their services to governmental, industrial, and private clients. * * *

The charges of a consulting engineer may be computed in different ways. He may charge the client a percentage of the cost of the project, may set his fee at his actual cost plus overhead plus a reasonable profit, may charge fixed rates per hour for different types of work, may perform an assignment for a specific sum, or he may combine one or more of these approaches. Suggested fee schedules for particular types of services in certain areas have been promulgated from time to time by various local societies. This case does not, however, involve any claim that the National Society has tried to fix specific fees, or even a specific method of calculating fees. It involves a charge that the members of the Society have unlawfully agreed to refuse to negotiate or even to discuss the question of fees until after a prospective client has selected the engineer for a particular project. Evidence of this agreement is found in § 11(c) of the Society's Code of Ethics, adopted in July 1964.

The District Court found that the Society's Board of Ethical Review has uniformly interpreted the "ethical rules against competitive bidding for engineering services as prohibiting the submission of any form of price information to a prospective customer which would enable that customer to make a price comparison on engineering services." If the client requires that such information be provided, then § 11(c) imposes an obligation upon the engineering firm to withdraw from consideration for that job. * * * Under the traditional method, the client initially selects an engineer on the basis of background and reputation, not price.[6]

In 1972 the Government filed its complaint against the Society alleging that members had agreed to abide by canons of ethics prohibiting the submission of competitive bids for engineering services and that, in consequence, price competition among the members had been suppressed and customers had been deprived of the benefits of free and open competition. * * *

In its answer the Society admitted the essential facts alleged by the Government and pleaded a series of affirmative defenses, only one of which remains in issue. In that defense, the Society averred that the standard set out in the Code of Ethics was reasonable because competition among professional engineers was contrary to the public interest. It was averred that it would be cheaper and easier for an engineer "to design and specify inefficient and unnecessarily expensive structures and methods of construction." Accordingly, competitive pressure to offer engineering services at the lowest possible price would adversely affect the quality of engineering. Moreover, the practice of awarding engineering contracts to the lowest bidder, regardless of quality, would be dangerous to the public health, safety, and welfare. For these reasons, the Society claimed that its Code of Ethics was not an "unreasonable restraint of interstate trade or commerce."

The parties compiled a voluminous discovery and trial record. The District Court made detailed findings about the engineering profession, the Society, its members' participation in interstate commerce, the history of the ban on competitive bidding, and certain incidents in which the ban appears to have been violated or enforced. The District Court did not, however, make any finding on the question whether, or to what extent, competition had led to inferior engineering work which, in turn, had adversely affected the public health, safety, or welfare. That inquiry was considered unnecessary because the court was convinced that the ethical prohibition against competitive bidding was "on its face a tampering with the price structure of engineering fees in violation of § 1 of the Sherman Act."

Although it modified the injunction entered by the District Court, the Court of Appeals affirmed its conclusion that the agreement was unlawful on its face and therefore "illegal without regard to claimed or possible benefits."

6. Having been selected, the engineer may then, in accordance with the Society's canons of ethics, negotiate a satisfactory fee arrangement with the client. If the negotiations are unsuccessful, then the client may withdraw his selection and approach a new engineer. Id., at 1215.

II

In Goldfarb v. Virginia State Bar, 421 U.S. 773, the Court held that a bar association's rule prescribing minimum fees for legal services violated § 1 of the Sherman Act. In that opinion [footnote 17] the Court noted that certain practices by members of a learned profession might survive scrutiny under the Rule of Reason even though they would be viewed as a violation of the Sherman Act in another context. * * *

Relying heavily on this footnote, and on some of the major cases applying a Rule of Reason, petitioner argues that its attempt to preserve the profession's traditional method of setting fees for engineering services is a reasonable method of forestalling the public harm which might be produced by unrestrained competitive bidding. To evaluate this argument it is necessary to identify the contours of the Rule of Reason and to discuss its application to the kind of justification asserted by petitioner.

A. The Rule of Reason

One problem presented by the language of § 1 of the Sherman Act is that it cannot mean what it says. The statute says that "every" contract that restrains trade is unlawful. But restraint is the very essence of every contract; read literally, § 1 would outlaw the entire body of private contract law. Yet it is that body of law that establishes the enforceability of commercial agreements and enables competitive markets—indeed, a competitive economy—to function effectively.

Congress, however, did not intend the text of the Sherman Act to delineate the full meaning of the statute or its application in concrete situations. The legislative history makes it perfectly clear that it expected the courts to give shape to the statute's broad mandate by drawing on common-law tradition. The Rule of Reason, with its origins in common-law precedents long antedating the Sherman Act, has served that purpose. It has been used to give the Act both flexibility and definition, and its central principle of antitrust analysis has remained constant. Contrary to its name, the Rule does not open the field of antitrust inquiry to any argument in favor of a challenged restraint that may fall within the realm of reason. Instead, it focuses directly on the challenged restraint's impact on competitive conditions.

* * *

The Rule of Reason * * * has been regarded as a standard for testing the enforceability of covenants in restraint of trade which are ancillary to a legitimate transaction, such as an employment contract or the sale of a going business. Judge (later Mr. Chief Justice) Taft so interpreted the Rule in his classic rejection of the argument that competitors may lawfully agree to sell their goods at the same price as long as the agreed-upon price is reasonable. United States v. Addyston Pipe & Steel Co., 85 F. 271, 282–283 (C.A.6 1898), aff'd, 175 U.S. 211. That case, and subsequent decisions by this Court, unequivocally foreclose an interpretation of the Rule as permitting an inquiry into the reasonableness of the prices set by private agreement.

The early cases also foreclose the argument that because of the special characteristics of a particular industry, monopolistic arrangements will better promote trade and commerce than competition. That kind of argument is properly addressed to Congress and may justify an exemption from the statute for specific industries, but it is not permitted by the Rule of Reason. * * *

The [Rule-of-Reason test] is whether the challenged contracts or acts "were unreasonably restrictive of competitive conditions." Unreasonableness under that test could be based either (1) on the nature or character of the contracts, or (2) on surrounding circumstances giving rise to the inference or presumption that they were intended to restrain trade and enhance prices. Under either branch of the test, the inquiry is confined to a consideration of impact on competitive conditions.

In this respect the Rule of Reason has remained faithful to its origins. * * * [T]he Court has adhered to the position that the inquiry mandated by the Rule of Reason is whether the challenged agreement is one that promotes competition or one that suppresses competition. * * *

There are, thus, two complementary categories of antitrust analysis. In the first category are agreements whose nature and necessary effect are so plainly anticompetitive that no elaborate study of the industry is needed to establish their illegality—they are "illegal *per se*." In the second category are agreements whose competitive effect can only be evaluated by analyzing the facts peculiar to the business, the history of the restraint, and the reasons why it was imposed. In either event, the purpose of the analysis is to form a judgment about the competitive significance of the restraint; it is not to decide whether a policy favoring competition is in the public interest, or in the interest of the members of an industry. Subject to exceptions defined by statute, that policy decision has been made by the Congress.

B. The Ban on Competitive Bidding

Price is the "central nervous system of the economy," and an agreement that "interfere[s] with the setting of price by free market forces" is illegal on its face. In this case we are presented with an agreement among competitors to refuse to discuss prices with potential customers until after negotiations have resulted in the initial selection of an engineer. While this is not price fixing as such, no elaborate industry analysis is required to demonstrate the anticompetitive character of such an agreement. It operates as an absolute ban on competitive bidding, applying with equal force to both complicated and simple projects and to both inexperienced and sophisticated customers. As the District Court found, the ban "impedes the ordinary give and take of the market place," and substantially deprives the customer of "the ability to utilize and compare prices in selecting engineering services." On its face, this agreement restrains trade within the meaning of § 1 of the Sherman Act.

The Society's affirmative defense confirms rather than refutes the anticompetitive purpose and effect of its agreement. The Society argues that the restraint is justified because bidding on engineering services is inherently imprecise, would lead to deceptively low bids, and would thereby tempt individual engineers to do inferior work with consequent risk to public safety and health. The logic of this argument rests on the assumption that the agreement will tend to maintain the price level; if it had no such effect, it would not serve its intended purpose. The Society nonetheless invokes the Rule of Reason, arguing that its restraint on price competition ultimately inures to the public benefit by preventing the production of inferior work and by insuring ethical behavior. As the preceding discussion of the Rule of Reason reveals, this Court has never accepted such an argument.

It may be, as petitioner argues, that competition tends to force prices down and that an inexpensive item may be inferior to one that is more costly. There is some risk, therefore, that competition will cause some suppliers to market a defective product. Similarly, competitive bidding for engineering projects may be inherently imprecise and incapable of taking into account all the variables which will be involved in the actual performance of the project. Based on these considerations, a purchaser might conclude that his interest in quality—which may embrace the safety of the end product—outweighs the advantages of achieving cost savings by pitting one competitor against another. Or an individual vendor might independently refrain from price negotiation until he has satisfied himself that he fully understands the scope of his customers' needs. These decisions might be reasonable; indeed, petitioner has provided ample documentation for that thesis. But these are not reasons that satisfy the Rule; nor are such individual decisions subject to antitrust attack.

The Sherman Act does not require competitive bidding,[21] it prohibits unreasonable restraints on competition. Petitioner's ban on competitive bidding prevents all customers from making price comparisons in the initial selection of an engineer, and imposes the Society's views of the costs and benefits of competition on the entire marketplace. It is this restraint that must be justified under the Rule of Reason, and petitioner's attempt to do so on the basis of the potential threat that competition poses to the public safety and the ethics of its profession is nothing less than a frontal assault on the basic policy of the Sherman Act.

The Sherman Act reflects a legislative judgment that ultimately competition will produce not only lower prices, but also better goods and services.

21. Indeed, Congress has decided not to require competitive bidding for Government purchases of engineering services. The Brooks Act, 40 U.S.C. §§ 541–544 (1970 ed., Supp. V), requires the Government to use a method of selecting engineers similar to the Society's "traditional method." See n. 6, supra. The Society relies heavily on the Brooks Act as evidence that its ban on competitive bidding is reasonable. The argument is without merit. The Brooks Act does not even purport to exempt engineering services from the antitrust laws, and the reasonableness of an individual purchaser's decision not to seek lower prices through competition does not authorize the vendors to conspire to impose that same decision on all other purchasers.

The assumption that competition is the best method of allocating resources in a free market recognizes that all elements of a bargain—quality, service, safety, and durability—and not just the immediate cost, are favorably affected by the free opportunity to select among alternative offers. Even assuming occasional exceptions to the presumed consequences of competition, the statutory policy precludes inquiry into the question whether competition is good or bad.

The fact that engineers are often involved in large-scale projects significantly affecting the public safety does not alter our analysis. Exceptions to the Sherman Act for potentially dangerous goods and services would be tantamount to a repeal of the statute. In our complex economy the number of items that may cause serious harm is almost endless—automobiles, drugs, foods, aircraft components, heavy equipment, and countless others, cause serious harm to individuals or to the public at large if defectively made. The judiciary cannot indirectly protect the public against this harm by conferring monopoly privileges on the manufacturers.

By the same token, the cautionary footnote in *Goldfarb* cannot be read as fashioning a broad exemption under the Rule of Reason for learned professions. We adhere to the view expressed in *Goldfarb* that, by their nature, professional services may differ significantly from other business services, and, accordingly, the nature of the competition in such services may vary. Ethical norms may serve to regulate and promote this competition, and thus fall within the Rule of Reason. But the Society's argument in this case is a far cry from such a position. We are faced with a contention that a total ban on competitive bidding is necessary because otherwise engineers will be tempted to submit deceptively low bids. Certainly, the problem of professional deception is a proper subject of an ethical canon. But, once again, the equation of competition with deception, like the similar equation with safety hazards, is simply too broad; we may assume that competition is not entirely conducive to ethical behavior, but that is not a reason, cognizable under the Sherman Act, for doing away with competition.

In sum, the Rule of Reason does not support a defense based on the assumption that competition itself is unreasonable. Such a view of the Rule would create the "sea of doubt" on which Judge Taft refused to embark in Addyston, 85 F., at 284, and which this Court has firmly avoided ever since.

III

The judgment entered by the District Court, as modified by the Court of Appeals, prohibits the Society from adopting any official opinion, policy statement, or guideline stating or implying that competitive bidding is unethical. Petitioner argues that this judgment abridges its First Amendment rights.[25] We find no merit in this contention.

25. Petitioner contends the judgment is both an unconstitutional prior restraint on speech and an unconstitutional prohibition against free association.

Having found the Society guilty of a violation of the Sherman Act, the District Court was empowered to fashion appropriate restraints on the Society's future activities both to avoid a recurrence of the violation and to eliminate its consequences. While the resulting order may curtail the exercise of liberties that the Society might otherwise enjoy, that is a necessary and, in cases such as this, unavoidable consequence of the violation. Just as an injunction against price fixing abridges the freedom of businessmen to talk to one another about prices, so too the injunction in this case must restrict the Society's range of expression on the ethics of competitive bidding. In fashioning a remedy, the District Court may, of course, consider the fact that its injunction may impinge upon rights that would otherwise be constitutionally protected, but these protections do not prevent it from remedying the antitrust violations.

* * *

The Society apparently fears that the District Court's injunction, if broadly read, will block legitimate paths of expression on all ethical matters relating to bidding. But the answer to these fears is that the burden is upon the proved transgressor "to bring any proper claims for relief to the court's attention." In this case, the Court of Appeals specifically stated that "[i]f the Society wishes to adopt some other ethical guideline more closely confined to the legitimate objective of preventing deceptively low bids, it may move the district court for modification of the decree." This is, we believe, a proper approach, adequately protecting the Society's interests. We therefore reject petitioner's attack on the District Court's order.

The judgment of the Court of Appeals is

Affirmed.

■ MR. JUSTICE BRENNAN took no part in the consideration or decision of this case.

■ MR. JUSTICE BLACKMUN, with whom MR. JUSTICE REHNQUIST joins, concurring in part and concurring in the judgment.

I join Parts I and III of the Court's opinion and concur in the judgment. I do not join Part II because I would not, at least for the moment, reach as far as the Court appears to me to do in intimating that any ethical rule with an overall anticompetitive effect promulgated by a professional society is forbidden under the Sherman Act. In my view, the decision in *Goldfarb* properly left to the Court some flexibility in considering how to apply traditional Sherman Act concepts to professions long consigned to self-regulation. Certainly, this case does not require us to decide whether the "Rule of Reason" as applied to the professions ever could take account of benefits other than increased competition. For even accepting petitioner's assertion that product quality is one such benefit, and that maintenance of the quality of engineering services requires that an engineer not bid before he has made full acquaintance with the scope of a client's desired project, petitioner Society's rule is still grossly overbroad.

* * *

My skepticism about going further in this case by shaping the Rule of Reason to such a narrow last as does the majority, arises from the fact that there may be ethical rules which have a more than *de minimis* anticompetitive effect and yet are important in a profession's proper ordering. A medical association's prescription of standards of minimum competence for licensing or certification may lessen the number of entrants. A bar association's regulation of the permissible forms of price advertising for nonroutine legal services or limitation of in-person solicitation, see Bates v. State Bar of Arizona, 433 U.S. 350 (1977), may also have the effect of reducing price competition. In acknowledging that "professional services may differ significantly from other business services" and that the "nature of the competition in such services may vary," ante, at 696, but then holding that ethical norms can pass muster under the Rule of Reason only if they promote competition, I am not at all certain that the Court leaves enough elbowroom for realistic application of the Sherman Act to professional services.

■ MR. CHIEF JUSTICE BURGER, concurring in part and dissenting in part.

I * * * dissent from that portion of the judgment prohibiting petitioner from stating in its published standards of ethics the view that competitive bidding is unethical. The First Amendment guarantees the right to express such a position * * *.

NOTES AND QUESTIONS ON GOLDFARB, PROFESSIONAL ENGINEERS, AND "PER SE" RULES

1. What was the status of the "learned professions" exemption after *Goldfarb* and *Professional Engineers*? Was the dictum in the *Oregon State Medical Society* case still valid? Later portions of this chapter consider further whether the antitrust laws do or should apply to the professions in the same way that they apply to other businesses.

2. If the Court in *Goldfarb* had accepted the idea that the "learned professions" were exempt, which occupations would qualify? Engineers? Real estate brokers? Chiropractors? Plumbers? Any occupational group claiming an ethical motivation? Would the difficulty of answering this question be a reason for not finding an exemption? Do similar considerations counsel against developing "soft" antitrust rules for professionals?

3. What defense did the engineers assert? Why was it rejected? According to the Court, what is the ultimate touchstone for testing the legality of an agreement under the Sherman Act?

4. What are the two distinct ways in which courts analyze agreements between competitors? Which method did the Court employ in *Professional Engineers*? It is possible to read the Court as suggesting that a bidding rule protecting "inexperienced" buyers in "complex" transactions would have been treated differently. Should the law allow sellers to establish ethical rules that diminish competition in the name of consumer protection?

Assume that a powerful medical society adopted a rule against accepting a predetermined price in return for either (*a*) treating a given patient for a fixed period of time (i.e., a rule prohibiting acceptance of "capitation" payments, such as HMOs receive and sometimes employ in obtaining physician services) or (*b*) treating a given condition (i.e., a rule prohibiting acceptance of payment by DRG). What arguments could be offered to support this rule and to distinguish *Professional Engineers*? Does the Rule of Reason permit such arguments? Or would they amount to a "frontal assault on the basic policy of the Sherman Act"? Does the statute demand competition for better or for worse—so that it is blind to circumstances where competition may be harmful to consumer interests? In reading the textual discussion of the Rule of Reason below, consider whether there is any basis for principled exceptions to the law's requirement of competition. Is the medical society rule hypothesized here a good candidate for such an exception?

5. *The Rationale for Per Se Rules.* A classic summary of the justifications for antitrust rules establishing the "per se" illegality of some practices is found in Northern Pacific Ry. Co. v. United States, 356 U.S. 1, 5 (1958):

> [T]here are certain agreements or practices which because of their pernicious effect on competition and lack of any redeeming virtue are conclusively presumed to be unreasonable and therefore illegal without elaborate inquiry as to the precise harm they have caused or the business excuse for their use. This principle of *per se* unreasonableness not only makes the type of restraints which are proscribed by the Sherman Act more certain to the benefit of everyone concerned, but it also avoids the necessity for an incredibly complicated and prolonged economic investigation into the entire history of the industry involved, as well as related industries, in an effort to determine at large whether a particular restraint has been unreasonable—an inquiry so often wholly fruitless when undertaken. Among the practices which the courts have heretofore deemed to be unlawful in and of themselves are price fixing, division of markets, group boycotts, and tying arrangements.

A particular advantage of per se rules is their "bright-line" quality. The Sherman Act is enforced with criminal penalties whenever the prosecutor (the Antitrust Division of the Justice Department) believes that the violation was clear and that the parties exhibited a criminal intent. Not only does the absence of a "grey area" make criminal prosecution easier, but it also increases the law's deterrent effect. If colorable defenses were available for price fixing and similar restraints, there would be a greater temptation for business persons to ignore legal advice, to pursue a profitable strategy, and to take their chances on an antitrust suit. The importance of deterrence in antitrust law is apparent in the treble-damage remedy available in private civil suits. There have been proposals to limit this remedy to cases involving the so-called "per se" offenses.

6. Consider carefully the various justifications for per se rules. Do they justify per se rules against the establishment of minimum professional fee schedules, as in *Goldfarb,* and ethical canons like that in *Professional Engineers*? Or should activities of professionals be generally spared treatment under per se rules? In Arizona v. Maricopa County Medical Society, 457 U.S. 332 (1982), the Supreme Court held that the per se rules do not have to be rejustified before applying them in the health care field and that a medical organization's schedule of *maximum* fees was subject to the usual per se rule against price fixing. The Court also intimated, however, that professional restraints "premised on public service or ethical norms" might escape automatic condemnation and be entitled to more sympathetic scrutiny under the Rule of Reason. This opinion, controversial because it seemed to extend the per se rule so far, is reproduced in chapter 9(§A).

NOTE ON THE ANTITRUST RULE OF REASON

Antitrust lawyers frequently dichotomize between per se rules and the Rule of Reason. The *Professional Engineers* case makes clear, however, that per se rules do not stand in contradistinction to the Rule of Reason but are a subcategory of it, resulting from the Rule's application to particular conduct. Thus, the Rule of Reason is an all-pervasive technique that courts are to employ in determining whether particular collaborative arrangements frustrate, or advance, the consumer-welfare objectives of the statute's procompetition mandate. Unfortunately, antitrust analysis is confused as often as it is helped by these special formulations of its tests, and the student may be well advised not to look for anything especially mysterious here. Indeed, one can stay on reasonably solid ground by viewing per se rules simply as common-law-like rules supported by the principle of *stare decisis* and the Rule of Reason simply as an invitation to apply the lawyer's usual technique of viewing precedent as binding unless it can be distinguished on policy-relevant grounds. Thus, the first step in applying the Rule of Reason to particular facts is to decide whether an established per se rule applies, whether policy requires the modification or extension of an existing rule, or whether a new per se rule should be declared to guide future conduct. This task should be approached without primary concern for labels and categories. Many judicial mistakes in antitrust law appear to flow from neglect of traditional lawyerly analysis.

When seeking to distinguish lawful from unlawful collective action by competitors, antitrust courts seem to consider the *purpose* of the particular arrangement, the *market power* of the parties, whether a *less restrictive alternative* is available, and the arrangement's procompetitive and anticompetitive *effects*. See generally 7 P. Areeda, Antitrust Law §§ 1500–11 (1986); P. Areeda, The "Rule of Reason" in Antitrust Analysis: General Issues 2–13 (Federal Judicial Center 1981). Although the analytical framework set forth here is not the only possible way to formulate the tests for section 1 violations, it will help the student understand the issues and appreciate the significance of introducing antitrust law in the health care field.

Purpose: "Naked" Restraints. A good way to start a Rule of Reason analysis is to ask whether the purpose of the collective action is compatible with the maintenance of competition as the guarantor of consumer welfare. If the stated or obvious purpose of the restraint was such that it could only be achieved by suppressing the general vigor of competition in the market as a whole, it is a so-called "naked" restraint and thus a poor candidate to survive antitrust scrutiny. For example, an agreement among competitors for the purpose of stabilizing their troubled industry would be classed as a naked restraint because it explicitly contemplates the attenuation of market forces; even though such an agreement might yield some real social benefits, it would almost certainly be illegal because it diminishes competition, which the law presumes to be in the public interest.

The *Professional Engineers* case reiterates the law's traditional insistence that competition be maintained even in the face of a claim that it was curtailed for a worthy purpose. The classic statement of this principle appears in the 1898 *Addyston Pipe* case, cited in *Professional Engineers.* To then Judge William Howard Taft, to allow a worthy-purpose defense for a naked restraint (in that case an agreement to fix "reasonable" prices) would be "to set sail on a sea of doubt" and to rely upon "the vague and varying opinion of judges as to how much, on principles of political economy, men ought to be allowed to restrain competition." 85 Fed. at 283–84. See also United States v. Socony–Vacuum Oil Co., 310 U.S. 150 (1940) (condemning virtually all agreements aimed at affecting prices, "the central nervous system of the economy"); United States v. Trenton Potteries, 273 U.S. 392 (1927) (condemning price fixing as a per se restraint without regard to the reasonableness of the prices fixed). As will appear below, Judge Taft's advice to avoid balancing competition against other values has been particularly difficult to adhere to in cases involving professional providers of health services.

Although naked restraints will very often be illegal, the courts have never said that all naked restraints are illegal per se. Instead, they have reserved that classification for agreements of certain specific types. A typical listing of the per se offenses appears in the earlier quotation from the *Northern Pacific* case. In a recent decision, a bare majority of the FTC attempted to add agreements among competitors to restrain the truthful, nondeceptive advertising of professional fees or prices to the list of per se violations. California Dental Ass'n, FTC Dkt. 9259 (Mar. 26, 1996). The court of appeals, however, characterizing the restriction in question as "a fairly 'naked' restraint on price competition itself," said,

> It may be correct that some types of price advertising restrictions amount to bans on price competition that warrant per se condemnation. But we cannot endorse the use of per se analysis in this case, which concerns a set of ethical guidelines promulgated by a professional organization for the apparent purpose of preventing false and misleading advertising.

California Dental Ass'n v. FTC, 128 F.3d 720, 727 (9th Cir.1997) (affirming FTC order on other grounds).

Some naked restraints might be permitted because they seem minor or de minimis or because they affect only the nonprice dimensions of competition. (Query whether price should be viewed as the law's only significant concern, especially in the area of professional services.) Other naked restraints might be regarded favorably because they are ostensibly intended to produce results closer to the results that would be yielded in a perfectly competitive market (that is, where consumers have good information and the other assumptions underlying economists' textbook models are also satisfied). In other words, there may be room for a "market failure" defense under which the law tolerates attenuation of rivalry that can be shown not to serve the public well. Although the defendants in *Professional Engineers* claimed that their restraint yielded a level of safety more consistent with the public interest than would result under unbridled competition, the Supreme Court apparently thought either that there was no market failure or that the restraint went further than was necessary to correct for it. Do you think competitors should be allowed to assert such market failure defenses? Or should all naked restraints be illegal? Can one argue that leaving room for a market failure defense would not violate Judge Taft's precepts because it leaves the competitive paradigm conceptually intact? Can an especially appealing case for a market failure defense be made in situations involving professional services? Consider these questions again in light of *AMA v. FTC, Wilk v. AMA,* and *FTC v. Indiana Federation of Dentists,* infra.

Purpose: "Ancillary" Restraints. An agreement may eliminate competition among the parties thereto but escape classification as a naked restraint because its purpose can be achieved even though the market as a whole remains vigorously competitive. For example, in forming a partnership, a group of engineers or lawyers would probably agree among themselves not to submit bids individually for work on which the partnership had bid. Although such an agreement eliminates competition among the partners, it is essential to the formation of a new business entity, the partnership.*

* A common legal problem is the enforceability under state law of restrictive covenants binding an individual physician not to enter into competition with a medical practice with which he was formerly affiliated. Such noncompetition clauses are typical in partnership and employment agreements and in agreements to sell an established practice. Although such covenants may be analyzed under antitrust law (query how they would be treated under the principles stated in the text), they are more often evaluated as common-law restraints of trade and, typically, are enforced only if they are judged (by uncertain standards) to be reasonable in scope and duration. See, e.g., Weber v. Tillman, 913 P.2d 84 (Kan.1996) (enforcing covenant despite argument that rural area had too few dermatologists, a specialty that court did not view as "medically necessary"); Statesville Med. Group, P.A. v. Dickey, 418 S.E.2d 256 (N.C.App.1992) (refusing enforcement on public policy grounds because of shortage of endocrinologists in area); Total Health Physicians v. Barrientos, 502 N.E.2d 1240 (Ill.App. 1986) (enforcing 3-year restrictions in limited area; physician had option of paying $50,000 to former employer). Cf. Humana Medical Plan, Inc. v. Jacobson, 614 So.2d 520 (Fla.App.1992) (invalidating on policy grounds, as interfering with doctor/patient relationship, contractual provision whereby doctor leaving HMO would pay plan, as liquidated damages, $700 per patient whom he continued treat under other auspices). See generally Levy, Because Judges Went to Law School, Not Medical School: Restrictive Covenants in the Practices of Law and Medicine,

Similarly restrictive agreements may be needed to effectuate looser collaborative arrangements—so-called joint ventures—by which the parties, though retaining their competitive independence for most purposes, pool their efforts or complementary resources to produce new or better goods or services, realize production or other economies, or accomplish some other constructive purpose.

Because the formation of new entities and other joint undertakings may yield consumer benefits and efficiency and because other competition may exist to prevent higher prices, any restraints incidental to achieving these objectives ought never to be subjected to per se antitrust rules. Instead, such so-called "ancillary" restraints are appropriately viewed as sui generis and judged under the Rule of Reason to see whether their net effects are harmful to competition. It is notable that the purposes that may justify ancillary restraints are those that manifest a desire to compete and to realize business efficiencies—a procompetitive purpose—and not a desire to curb general market forces to achieve some arguable social benefit. Most of the restraints of trade examined in this chapter are not of the ancillary variety, but questions concerning the antitrust status of arguably procompetitive collaboration will arise at later points.

Market Power. Market power—that is, the ability of the parties to a restraint, acting collectively, to raise prices or otherwise set the terms of trade in the market as a whole—is an essential element in any violation of section 1 of the Sherman Act. Measurement of market power is often technically difficult. It suffices here, however, to say only that it requires (*a*) defining a "relevant market"—that is, a geographic area and a set of products or services that together constitute a distinct competitive arena; (*b*) estimating the parties' market share and overall market concentration—that is, the fewness of firms, which may facilitate collusion or tacit coordination of business policies; and (*c*) identifying other factors—product characteristics, the ease with which new competitors can enter the market, etc.—that may affect the likelihood that competition will be diminished. See generally Landes & Posner, Market Power in Antitrust Cases, 94 Harv.L.Rev. 937 (1981).

Although market power is always an element in a section 1 case, the proof requirement may vary, depending upon whether the conduct in question is clearly anticompetitive, ambiguous, or clearly procompetitive. For example, the market power possessed by the collaborators will normally not have to be proved in a case involving a naked restraint because the power element is implicit in the anticompetitive purpose of such restraints and can therefore be presumed. If the purpose of a restraint is in dispute, however, the inability of the joint venturers to affect appreciably the market's overall vigor would suggest an innocent purpose as well as the absence of any threat to the public interest.

30 J. Health & Hosp. L. 89 (1997). Several states have statutes limiting the use of covenants not to compete with respect to physician services. E.g. Colo. Rev. Stat. Ann. § 8–2–113(3) (West 1997) (such covenants "shall be void").

If a restraint can be shown to be ancillary to achieving a procompetitive purpose, should that be a complete defense? What if, even though their purpose is one that could be achieved without market power, the parties appear to possess market power in fact? For example, what if a newly formed professional partnership comprised a substantial percentage of local practitioners or of the practitioners in a particular specialty? In circumstances such as these, the economic benefits of the procompetitive joint action—by hypothesis, an entrepreneurial initiative of the kind that should normally be welcomed—must be compared to the welfare losses associated with reduced competition and higher prices (which transfer wealth and reduce output, creating allocative inefficiency). Unfortunately, the law becomes murky at the point where such balancing becomes necessary. Nevertheless, a few observations are possible.

Less Restrictive Alternatives. Before undertaking to balance a joint venture's benefits to competition and efficiency against its likely harms to competition's vigor, it is appropriate first to consider whether the collaborators could have achieved their declared procompetitive purpose by some means less threatening to competition. If such a less restrictive alternative was available and was not adopted, a government prosecutor or a court might judge either (*a*) that the collaborators' true purpose was not what they claimed or (*b*) that their conduct was unreasonably restrictive and therefore illegal.

Although search for such a "less restrictive alternative" can sometimes produce a satisfactory result, courts and law enforcers should be careful not to be unreasonably demanding in their exercise of hindsight. It has been observed that "the key difficulty in examining less restrictive alternatives lies in deciding how refined a distinction to make among the possible alternatives available to the defendants." P. Areeda, The "Rule of Reason," supra, at 9. The need for a "rule of reason" is particularly clear here because a policy of closely second-guessing the collaborators' structuring of their relationship would create liability risks that could easily dampen their competitive impulse and deprive the public of the benefits of useful joint activities.

Balancing Procompetitive and Anticompetitive Effects. If the collaborators' purposes are acceptable but the parties appear to possess market power and no less restrictive alternative to their ancillary restraint is reasonably available, the court's task becomes complicated. Unfortunately, courts have not always fully appreciated the need for careful balancing of procompetitive benefits and anticompetitive risks. See, e.g., United States v. Topco Associates, Inc., 405 U.S. 596 (1972) (applying per se rule to restrictions seemingly necessary to facilitate a joint venture to develop a new trademark; absence of market power ignored, or evidence misinterpreted); Broadcast Music, Inc. v. Columbia Broadcasting System, Inc., 441 U.S. 1 (1979) (marketing practices of "performing rights societies" upheld; such joint selling arrangements viewed as efficiency-enhancing ancillary restraints despite facts that only two societies constituted virtually the entire market, economies of scale did not clearly dictate such concentration, and two entities used identical, price-discriminating methods in marketing their music).

Because issues have been cloudy in courts' minds, the techniques for the necessary balancing have not been well developed. The analysis required in joint venture cases, however, should be similar to that employed in the law governing horizontal mergers. In each case, the law should allow competitors to combine or act in concert unless the threat to the competitive process from increased concentration or otherwise seems to outweigh the potential for increased efficiency. For example, the formation of a partnership by erstwhile professional competitors is analogous to a corporate merger and should be condemned only if it seems likely to create a firm with market power or to increase market concentration to a point where actual or tacit collusion is a danger. Likewise, where independent entities collaborate in a joint venture for some procompetitive purpose, analysis of any restrictions on competition among them as ancillary restraints should not frustrate the venture without good reason. For critiques of current antitrust policy regarding competitor collaboration and a call for clarification, see FTC Staff, Anticipating the 21st Century: Competition Policy in the New High–Tech, Global Marketplace, ch. 10 (1996) (summarizing FTC informational hearings on competition policy with respect to joint ventures). On the analysis of corporate mergers, see generally U.S. Department of Justice & FTC, Horizontal Merger Guidelines (1992). Enforcement policies toward various arrangements and transactions in the health care field are set forth in U.S. Department of Justice & FTC, Statements of Enforcement Policy and Analytical Principles Relating to Health Care and Antitrust (August, 1996).

The Rule of Reason analysis called for in cases of competitor collaboration will not always be exhaustive but may often be accomplished by a so-called "quick look" that satisfies the court concerning the probable purpose of the collaboration, the parties' market power, and the restraint's likely net effect. See, e.g., *Professional Engineers*, 435 U.S. at 692 ("no elaborate industry analysis is required to demonstrate the anticompetitive character of [the] agreement"); *California Dental Ass'n v. FTC*, 128 F.3d at 727–30 (rejecting FTC's per se analysis of restrictions on price advertising but upholding its "abbreviated, or 'quick look,' rule of reason analysis designed for restraints that are not per se unlawful but are sufficiently anticompetitive on their face that they do not require a full-blown rule of reason inquiry"). Sometimes, where a court employs a "quick look" to find a violation, it may be difficult to discern that it did not in fact apply a per se rule. Likewise, an extensive inquiry may not be needed to detect that a challenged restraint is a lawful ancillary one.

Although evidence will be taken on the various effects of a particular joint action, one should have no illusions that these effects can or will be isolated, measured, and balanced with any precision in a particular case. Courts continually slip back into sympathizing with collaborators whose purpose is deemed worthy, even if it was not procompetitive. See, e.g., United States v. Brown Univ., 5 F.3d 658 (3d Cir.1993) (refusing to treat as a per se violation an agreement by prestigious universities not to compete for outstanding students by increasing financial aid beyond agreed-upon "need"). They also have trouble distinguishing procompetitive from anticompetitive behavior and often confuse actions harmful to competitors or to competition between the parties *inter se* with harm to competition itself. E.g., *Topco*, supra. It has been difficult for many courts to appreciate that an intent by one group to succeed at the expense of their competitors does not signal an antitrust violation as long as the parties confine their efforts to offering better products or attractive terms and otherwise competing on the merits.

In recent years, major controversy has surrounded the question whether courts should use antitrust law, not exclusively to foster consumer welfare as served by competition, but also to promote fairness and other noneconomic values and to protect small business or individual competitors against hard competition by those better situated in the market. Although the 1970s and 1980s saw some shifts in the less protectionist, more "conservative" direction pointed by so-called "Chicago School" theorists, some observers believe that antitrust law has lately entered a "post-Chicago" phase of somewhat stricter enforcement.

Another Formulation. In Massachusetts Board of Registration in Optometry, 110 F.T.C. 549 (1988) (reproduced in § C of this chapter), the FTC recognized the blurring of the distinction between the per se rule and the Rule of Reason by the Supreme Court in *FTC v. Indiana Federation of Dentists*, reproduced later in this chapter, and in the *NCAA* and *BMI* cases cited therein. The FTC attempted to state (id. at 604) a new, less categorical test for the legality of collaborative arrangements under section 1:

> First, we ask whether the restraint is "inherently suspect." In other words, is the practice the kind that appears likely, absent an efficiency justification, to "restrict competition and decrease output." * * * [I]f it is inherently suspect, we must pose a *second* question: Is there a plausible efficiency justification for the practice? That is, does the practice seem capable of creating or enhancing competition (e.g., by reducing the costs of producing or marketing the product, creating a new product, or improving the operation of the market)? Such an efficiency defense is plausible if it cannot be rejected without extensive factual inquiry. If it is not plausible, then the restraint can be quickly condemned. But if the efficiency justification is plausible, further inquiry—a *third inquiry*—is needed to determine whether the justification is really valid. If it is, it must be assessed under the full balancing test of the rule of reason. But if the justification is, on examination, not valid, then the practice is unreasonable and unlawful under the rule of reason without further inquiry—there are no likely benefits to offset the threat to competition.

When it was announced, this formulation of the Rule of Reason was heralded as breaking with the traditional dichotomy between per se rules and the Rule of Reason. And, indeed, it has much to recommend it over efforts to decide cases by applying labels. Nevertheless, can you see ways in which the *Mass. Board* approach might yield different results than the analytical approach outlined above? It appears, for one thing, to create a presumption against certain practices that can be overcome only by an acceptable demonstration of efficiencies. The analysis offered earlier, on the other hand, places the burden on the plaintiff or prosecutor once a legitimate, procompetitive purpose appears. This burden does not shift until some degree of market power is demonstrated, at which point the reasonableness of the restraint comes into question. A full investigation and balancing of procompetitive and anticompetitive effects is triggered only when it appears that the restraint is well tailored to achieve a procompetitive purpose but still poses some threat to competition in the market as a whole. Under the *Mass. Board* analysis, by contrast, the power issue never seems to arise. The conduct apparently can be condemned if the conduct is of a certain kind (characterizable as price fixing, a boycott, etc.) and if efficiencies are not proven to the agency's satisfaction. Do you think a "power screen"—requiring at least a quick look at the likelihood the parties could effectively restrain trade—should be employed in all section 1 cases? If the market is vigorously competitive and likely to remain so, is there any basis for antitrust agencies or courts to become involved?

A more recent FTC decision, *California Dental Ass'n*, supra, has called into question the FTC's continued adherence to the *Mass. Board* analysis. In that case, the Commission found unlawful certain restrictions imposed by the dental society on advertising by its members. One commissioner, dissenting on the ground that efficiencies and entry possibilities should have been weighed more carefully, said that the majority had implicitly overruled *Mass. Board*, returning to a labeling approach. Another commissioner agreed but concurred in the result on the ground that the *Mass. Board* test was easily satisfied. In affirming the FTC order, the court of appeals upheld the finding of a violation based on a quick-look assessment of association's intent, the aggregate market power of the dentists, and the probable effect of the restrictions on price advertising. 128 F.2d at 727–30.

It is of interest that the technique of analyzing horizontal restraints under the Sherman Act remains unsettled after more than 100 years.

PROBLEM

Responding to a crisis in the availability of malpractice liability insurance in the 1980s, the AOA, the leading (fictitious) national organization of ophthalmologists ("O's"), established a physician-owned liability insurance company. This company, Ophthalmologists' Mutual (OMu), is incorporated in Bermuda, is controlled by a board initially appointed by the AOA and thereafter elected periodically by policyholders, and is qualified to offer coverage in every state. Coverage is available to all O's, including nonmembers of the AOA. Nationwide, about 35% of O's are insured through OMu, whose rates vary by state. In a few locations, OMu is a much larger factor. For example, in Colorado, 77% of O's have their coverage through OMu.

The OMu policy contains certain coverage limitations, including one that excludes coverage for "any alleged post-operative act or omission where the post-operative care is rendered by anyone other than a licensed ophthalmologist" (e.g., an optometrist). In addition, one of OMu's Underwriting Guidelines instructs its agents not to issue policies to O's who follow the practice of referring post-operative patients to anyone other than another O. The coverage limitation and the Underwriting Guideline appear to reflect the traditional distrust by O's of the quality of eye care provided by nonphysicians. In addition, there is some antipathy in the specialty toward those O's who follow the allegedly unethical practice of inducing optometrists to refer patients to them for eye surgery by promising to allow the referring optometrist to provide the needed post-operative observation.

Your law firm has been consulted by the AOA and OMu concerning their possible exposure to antitrust actions. In light of the analytical methods suggested in the reading, consider the risks they face. (Note that the coverage limit and the refusal to insure O's who cooperate with optometrists should be analyzed separately.) An attorney for an organization of Colorado optometrists has made threatening noises against the AOA and OMu, and both are nervous not only about being found guilty of a violation but also about the prospect of a long and costly lawsuit. Consider the prospects for summary judgment in any case that might be brought.

Cf. Nurse Midwifery Assocs. v. Hibbett, 918 F.2d 605, 615–17 (6th Cir.1990) (upholding claim that physician-owned malpractice insurer was a combination of its members and could be charged with conspiring against obstetricians who cooperated with nurse midwives); Kiepfer v. Beller, 944 F.2d 1213 (5th Cir.1991) (physician-owned insurer dropped plaintiff for testifying for malpractice plaintiff; no anticompetitive effect found because "no indication that defendants' conspiracy made it any more difficult to get local doctors to testify").

SECTION B: PROFESSIONAL SELF-REGULATION?

The Antitrust Laws and the Ethics of a Profession

AMA v. FTC

United States Court of Appeals, Second Circuit, 1980.
638 F.2d 443, affirmed by an equally divided Court 455 U.S. 676, 102 S.Ct. 1744, 71 L.Ed.2d 546 (1982), rehearing denied 456 U.S. 966, 102 S.Ct. 2048, 72 L.Ed.2d 491 (1982).

■ BONSAL, DISTRICT JUDGE:

[The AMA and two other medical societies petitioned for review of an FTC cease and desist order based on the agency's finding that provisions in the AMA's code of ethics governing contract practice and physician advertising violated section 5 of the Federal Trade Commission Act, 15 U.S.C. § 45(a)(1) (1994), which prohibits "unfair methods of competition in or affecting commerce, and unfair or deceptive acts or practices in or affecting commerce." (Eds.—Although the FTC is not empowered to enforce the

Sherman Act as such, any conduct violating the Sherman Act also violates section 5. Using this authority as well its independent authority to enforce the Clayton Act (the other main antitrust statute), the FTC shares the task of antitrust enforcement with the Department of Justice, acting particularly in cases in which prospective relief alone—i.e., a Commission cease and desist order—is deemed to be sufficient to rectify the problem. In most antitrust cases it initiates, the FTC applies ordinary Sherman Act principles.)

[In this case, the FTC also cross-petitioned for enforcement of its order. The challenged ethical principles and related conduct were previously described in notes on contract practice and on professional advertising in chapter 3(§C).]

* * * The Final Order requires AMA to cease and desist from promulgating, implementing and enforcing restraints on advertising, solicitation and contract practices by physicians and on the contractual arrangements between physicians and non-physicians. Exception is made with respect to "false or deceptive" practices, and the Order provides that nothing contained therein prohibits AMA from

> "formulating, adopting, disseminating to its constituent and component medical organizations and to its members, and enforcing reasonable ethical guidelines governing the conduct of its members with respect to representations, including unsubstantiated representations, that would be false or deceptive within the meaning of Section 5 of the Federal Trade Commission Act, or with respect to uninvited, in-person solicitation of actual or potential patients, who, because of their particular circumstances, are vulnerable to undue influence."

The Order also requires AMA to disassociate itself from any state or local society that violates the terms of the Order.

[The court first held that the AMA's status as a not-for-profit corporation did not shield it from the FTC's jurisdiction, the scope of which was examined in chapter 3(§B).]

Liability

At the time the FTC filed its complaint in this action on December 19, 1975, AMA's authoritative interpretation of the ethical restraints that are the subject of this action were contained in the 1971 edition of Opinions and Reports. Both the administrative law judge and the Commission detailed numerous examples of applications of the ethical restraints evidencing an anticompetitive purpose and effect. These included restrictions upon the dissemination of price information, bans upon advertisement of individual physicians' services and alternative forms of medical care, and restraints upon particular forms of advertising. The Commission concluded that this evidence "is susceptible to no interpretation other than that ethical principles of the medical profession have prevented doctors and medical organizations from disseminating information on the prices and services they offer, severely inhibiting competition among health care providers." The Commission further found that AMA's contract practice restrictions had the purpose and effect of restraining competition by group health plans, hospitals, and similar organizations, and restricted physicians from developing business structures of their own choice. Based upon our own review of the record, we conclude that these findings are supported by substantial evidence.

Petitioners contend that the ethical guidelines are merely to assist the state societies and the local associations; in other words, that they are advisory only. They point out that no formal action has been taken by AMA in these matters since 1955 * * *

* * * [T]he issue here is not whether AMA has specific power or authority over the state societies and local associations or, if it has, whether it exercises it. The issue is whether these groups have acted in concert to effectuate restraints on advertising and solicitation in violation of the Federal Trade Commission Act. It is this concerted activity for a common purpose that constitutes the violation.

The record satisfies us that AMA intended and expected that the state and local medical groups would enforce the limitations on advertising and solicitation and, indeed, advised them as to how to do it. In other words, AMA limitations "provided the impetus" for the actions taken, and individual physicians "could be expected to comply in order to assure that they did not discredit themselves by departing from professional norms, and perhaps betraying their professional oaths." *Goldfarb v. Virginia State Bar*, 421 U.S. at 791.

Remedy

The Final Order of the Commission consists of six Parts, the first two being the Cease and Desist Orders, and the third and fourth being the notice and disaffiliation provisions. The Final Order is directed only to AMA, and not to [the state and local society respondents].

Part I of the Order directs AMA to cease and desist from (A) restricting the advertising of services, facilities, or prices by physicians or organizations with which physicians are affiliated; (B) restricting the operation of any organization that offers physicians' services to the public, by means of representations concerning the ethical propriety of medical service arrangements that limit the patients' choice of a physician; and (C) inducing any physician or nongovernmental medical organization to take any of the prohibited restrictive actions. Part I expressly excludes from its prohibitions the dissemination by AMA of reasonable ethical guidelines concerning false and deceptive advertising and solicitation.

Part II of the Order directs AMA to cease and desist from (A) restricting or interfering with the consideration offered or provided physicians in return for the sale or distribution of their professional services; (B) restricting any organization that offers physicians' services by means of representations concerning the ethical propriety of medical service arrangements that limit the patients' choice of a physician; (C) restricting participation by non-physicians in the ownership or management of such organizations; and (D) inducing physicians or any organization from taking any of the actions prohibited by Part II.

Part III of the Order requires AMA in any proceeding involving violations of its ethical standards to provide (A) reasonable notice, (B) a hearing, and (C) written findings and conclusions.

Part IV of the Order requires AMA to (A) give written notice of the order to its members and affiliate societies; (B) provide all new members and affiliate societies with a copy of the Order for a period of ten years; (C) remove from all of its publications and policy statements any provisions inconsistent with the Order; (D) require that all affiliate organizations, as a condition of affiliation, agree to adhere to the Order; and (E) disaffiliate for one year any constituent organization that engages in any act or practice prohibited by the Order.

Post–Complaint Activities of AMA

Petitioners contend that the revisions of the ethical standards contained in the 1977 Opinions and Reports obviate any need to enter the Order herein. However, this does not constitute grounds for denying enforcement of an FTC order, especially since the publication of the revisions occurred "only after the filing of the FTC complaint." In any event, the Commission can properly find, as it did here,[6] that the revisions were insufficient.

Additionally, it is not clear that the 1977 revisions rescinded prior ethical standards.[7] AMA has never announced to its members or affiliate societies that the 1971 ethical standards are no longer in effect. Moreover, nothing in the 1977 version of the Opinions and Reports indicates that it was intended to disavow prior standards. Rather, it refers with approval to the "long standing policy of the Judicial Council on advertising and solicitation by physicians." By referring to the established policies, AMA indicated that its positions may not have changed and that the restraints, "if abandoned at all, may be resumed." Finally, it is well established law that it is within the discretion of the FTC to determine whether an order is "necessary to cope with the unfair practices found." We have determined that the FTC considered the changes and rationally assessed their significance in concluding that a cease and desist order was warranted.

6. For example, the ban on "solicitation" in the "Principles of Medical Ethics" was left unchanged, and the definition of that term incorporates many of the catchwords of earlier restraints. One instance of this is the retained condemnation of "self-laudatory" advertisements, even if fully accurate. In addition, the list of "accepted local media" fails to include newspapers, radio, or television. Publication of fees is mentioned only in connection with "reputable directories."

7. The record is mixed with regard to the impression of the average physician regarding the effect of the 1977 edition of Opinions and Reports on earlier versions. One witness testified that it was well accepted in the medical community that publication of a new edition rescinds previous editions. Other evidence, however, indicated that pre–1977 standards are still viewed as binding by physicians.

On July 22, 1980, AMA's House of Delegates adopted a new version of the Principles of Medical Ethics [reproduced in chapter 3(§A)]. The most notable change is the removal of the ban on "solicitation" previously found in Section 5 of the Principles. The 1980 Principles instead require a physician to deal "honestly," to expose doctors "deficient in character or competence," and "to respect the rights ... of other health professionals."

The elimination of the ban on solicitation which appeared in the 1957 version of the Principles reflects a significant and commendable effort to comply with the terms of the FTC order here under review. AMA does not, however, concede any legal obligation to make such changes, since it still denies any involvement in the unlawful restraints found by the FTC.

The language of the 1980 Principles is general and imprecise in nature. Moreover, the various written interpretations of the 1957 Principles previously promulgated by AMA remain in effect. In the absence of any interpretation of the 1980 Principles in AMA's Opinions and Reports, we cannot find that the FTC's claims are moot.

First Amendment

Petitioners contend that Part II of the Cease and Desist Order constitutes a prior restraint upon speech and impermissibly interferes with the right to freedom of association under the First Amendment. We disagree. The FTC determined that various restrictions which AMA imposed upon contract practices of physicians violated the FTC Act. These included ethical restraints upon so-called "closed panel" arrangements, upon the consideration paid physicians by health care organizations, and upon physicians' arrangements with non-physicians. By its terms, the Order applies solely to "ethical" restraints, and thus does not affect any speech or other First Amendment rights except insofar as it applies to statements officially condemning contract practices. "Just as an injunction against price fixing abridges the freedom of businessmen to talk to one another about prices, so too the injunction in this case must restrict [AMA's] range of expression on the ethics of [contract practices of physicians]." National Society of Professional Engineers v. United States, 435 U.S. 679, 697 (1978).

Overbreadth and Vagueness

Petitioners assert that the proviso at the end of Part I, which permits AMA to adopt "reasonable ethical guidelines governing the conduct of its members with respect to representations, including unsubstantiated representations, that would be false or deceptive within the meaning of Section 5 of the Federal Trade Commission Act," is overbroad and vague. The proviso was inserted in the Final Order at the request of AMA because of the Commission's "conviction that the AMA has a valuable and unique role to play with respect to deceptive advertising and oppressive forms of solicitation by physicians." AMA asks that it be granted more leeway in determining what kinds of claims are deceptive and misleading without the chilling effect that the threat of fines and penalties could have on its regulation of false and deceptive advertising. The Commission recognizes the " 'special role' of organized medicine . . . [that] necessarily confers on AMA a measure of discretion to develop 'principles of conduct.' " FTC Brief at 109, quoting Bates v. State Bar of Arizona, 433 U.S. 350, 384 (1977). In view of the foregoing, we will amend the proviso by inserting the words "respondent reasonably believes" so that the concluding paragraph of Part I will read as follows:

> "Nothing contained in this Part shall prohibit respondent from formulating, adopting, disseminating to its constituent and component medical organizations and to its members, and enforcing reasonable ethical guidelines governing the conduct of its members with respect to representations, including unsubstantiated representations, that *respondent reasonably believes* would be false or deceptive within the meaning of Section 5 of the Federal Trade Commission Act, or with respect to uninvited, in-person solicitation of actual or potential patients, who, because of their particular circumstances, are vulnerable to undue influence."[11] (modification emphasized)

* * *

The Disaffiliation Provision

Part IV of the Order requires AMA to disaffiliate for one year any state or local medical society that engages in acts or practices that would violate the Order if engaged in by AMA, and requires as a condition to affiliation that the state and local societies agree to adhere to the provision of the Order. Petitioners contend that this violates due process. However, this provision finds support in National Society of Professional Engineers v. United States, 435 U.S. at 697. The Order does not violate AMA's right to due process since it bears a reasonable relationship to the unlawful practices found to exist. The Commission "must be allowed effectively to close all roads to the prohibited goal, so that its orders may not be bypassed with impunity," FTC v. Ruberoid Co., 343 U.S. 470, 473 (1952), by the state and local medical societies.

The Final Order of the FTC is MODIFIED as indicated herein. As so modified, the Order is ENFORCED.

■ MANSFIELD, CIRCUIT JUDGE (dissenting):

* * * [A] review of the 1977 Opinions and Reports, considered in the light of the other record evidence, demonstrates that the Association, long prior to any order in this case, had changed its ethical standards to insure reasonable compliance with the law and at the same time properly to "discourage abusive practices that exploit patients and the public and

11. In addition, we refer petitioners to the opinion of the FTC herein, in which they are provided certain guidelines, to wit, where ads merely state the price of routine and standardized services, there is little need for further ethical restrictions to prevent deception; where restrictions are justified, they should be reasonably related to goal of preventing deception; and across-the-board bans to broad categories of representations, or general restrictions applicable to any representation made through a specific medium, are highly suspect. FTC Opinion, at 59.

interfere with freedom in making an informed choice of physician and free competition among physicians." * * *

Any possible lingering doubt about the Association's independent voluntary compliance with the law is dispelled by the adoption by its House of Delegates on July 22, 1980, of new "Principles of Medical Ethics" which completely eliminate the controversial former provisions attacked by the FTC despite their reasonableness as construed by the Association's Opinions and Reports. The new ethics code * * * omits Section 5 of the former Principles of Ethics which provided that a physician "should not solicit patients" and Section 6 * * *. Thus the Commission's order deals with practices that are now ancient history rather than with the facts as they now exist. Instead of facing reality it has set up the equivalent of a "straw man" to accommodate its desire to regulate the Association.

American Medical Association, Principles of Medical Ethics

Adopted July 22, 1980.

PREAMBLE:

The medical profession has long subscribed to a body of ethical statements developed primarily for the benefit of the patient. As a member of this profession, a physician must recognize responsibility not only to patients, but also to society, to other health professionals, and to self. The following Principles adopted by the American Medical Association are not laws, but standards of conduct which define the essentials of honorable behavior for the physician.

I. A physician shall be dedicated to providing competent medical service with compassion and respect for human dignity.

II. A physician shall deal honestly with patients and colleagues, and strive to expose those physicians deficient in character or competence, or who engage in fraud or deception.

III. A physician shall respect the law and also recognize a responsibility to seek changes in those requirements which are contrary to the best interests of the patient.

IV. A physician shall respect the rights of patients, of colleagues, and of other health professionals, and shall safeguard patient confidences within the constraints of the law.

V. A physician shall continue to study, apply and advance scientific knowledge, make relevant information available to patients, colleagues, and the public, obtain consultation, and use the talents of other health professionals when indicated.

VI. A physician shall, in the provision of appropriate patient care, except in emergencies, be free to choose whom to serve, with whom to associate, and the environment in which to provide medical services.

VII. A physician shall recognize a responsibility to participate in activities contributing to an improved community.

NOTES AND QUESTIONS ON AMA v. FTC AND PRIVATE RESTRAINTS ON PROFESSIONAL ADVERTISING

1. The FTC stated the AMA's position on advertising as of the mid–1970s as follows (94 F.T.C. at 1004–05):

> The *Principles* make clear that physicians should "uphold the dignity and honor of the profession" and "should not solicit patients." All solicitation, whether direct or indirect, is forbidden, and "solicitation" is defined in the 1971 Opinions and Reports as any "attempt to obtain patients or patronage by persuasion or influence." Hence, it is fair to say that almost all advertising and promotional activity is proscribed, with a few narrowly circumscribed exceptions. A doctor may only furnish the public with information regarding his or her name, type of practice, location of office and office hours, and this information must be communicated through the "accepted local media," which includes "telephone listings, office signs, professional cards, and dignified announcements." Although the guidelines in theory permit listing in a physician or telephone directory, or the sending of announcements regarding follow-up treatments or the opening or removal of an office the AMA has strictly limited the manner in which its members may utilize these media for solicitation of new patients.

As noted by Judge Mansfield, the AMA issued a new interpretation of its policy against solicitation while the FTC's case against it was pending. This interpretation read as follows (see id. at 1034–35):

> This statement reaffirms the long-standing policy of the Judicial Council on advertising and solicitation by physicians. The Principles of Medical Ethics are intended to discourage abusive practices that exploit patients and the public and interfere with freedom in making an informed choice of physicians and free competition among physicians.
>
> *Advertising.* The Principles do not proscribe advertising; they proscribe the solicitation of patients. Advertising means the action of making information or intention known to the public. The public is entitled to know the names of physicians, the type of their practices, the location of their offices, their office hours, and other useful information that will enable people to make a more informed choice of physician.
>
> The physician may furnish this information through the accepted local media for advertising or communication, which are open to all physicians on like conditions. Office signs, professional cards, dignified announcements, telephone directory listings, and reputable directories are examples of acceptable media for making information available to the public.

A physician may give biographical and other relevant data for listing in a reputable directory. A directory is not reputable if its contents are false, misleading, or deceptive or if it is promoted through fraud or misrepresentation. If the physician, at his option, chooses to supply fee information, the published data may include his charge for a standard office visit or his fee or range of fees for specific types of services, provided disclosure is made of the variable and other pertinent factors affecting the amount of the fee specified. The published data may include other relevant facts about the physician, but false, misleading, or deceptive statements or claims should be avoided.

Local, state, or specialty medical associations, as autonomous organizations, may have ethical restrictions on advertising, solicitation of patients, or other professional conduct of physicians that exceed the Principles of Medical Ethics. Furthermore, specific legal restrictions on advertising or solicitation of patients exist in the medical licensure laws of at least 34 states. Other states provide regulation through statutory authority to impose penalties for unprofessional conduct.

Solicitation. The term "solicitation" in the Principles means the attempt to obtain patients by persuasion or influence, using statements or claims that (1) contain testimonials, (2) are intended or likely to create inflated or unjustified expectations of favorable results, (3) are self-laudatory and imply that the physician has skills superior to other physicians engaged in his field or specialty of practice, or (4) contain incorrect or incomplete facts, or representations or implications that are likely to cause the average person to misunderstand or be deceived.

Competition. Some competitive practices accepted in ordinary commercial and industrial enterprises—where profit-making is the primary objective—are inappropriate among physicians. Commercial enterprises, for example, are free to solicit business by paying commissions. They have no duty to lower prices to the poor. Commercial enterprises are generally free to engage in advertising "puffery," to be boldly self-laudatory in making claims of superiority, and to emphasize favorable features without disclosing unfavorable information.

Physicians, by contrast, have an ethical duty to subordinate financial reward to social responsibility. A physician should not engage in practices for pecuniary gain that interfere with his medical judgment and skill or cause a deterioration of the quality of medical care. Ability to pay should be considered in reducing fees, and excessive fees are unethical.

Physicians should not pay commissions or rebates or give kickbacks for referral of patients. Likewise, they should not make extravagant claims or proclaim extraordinary skills. Such practices, however, common they may be in the commercial world, are unethical in the practice of medicine because they are injurious to the public.

Freedom of choice of physician and free competition among physicians are prerequisites of optimal medical care. The Principles of

Medical Ethics are intended to curtail abusive practices that impinge on these freedoms and exploit patients and the public.

The FTC concluded that, partly because this new statement did not specifically retract old positions, it did not represent an abandonment of the challenged practices.

Note that the current AMA Principles of Medical Ethics, which were revised in 1980 in response to the FTC challenge, omit all reference to advertising and solicitation.

2. The decision in *AMA v. FTC* was affirmed by an equally divided Supreme Court, Justice Blackmun not participating. Can you speculate on what might have led four justices to vote for reversal? The AMA, in subsequently seeking a statutory exemption of state-regulated professions from the jurisdiction of the FTC, suggested that the Court had split on the jurisdiction issue. Is that likely?

3. A legislative exemption of professional activities from FTC jurisdiction was defeated in a dramatic Senate vote in December 1983, and a later "compromise" bill agreed to by the FTC and the AMA was never adopted. Note that these measures would have exempted professional organizations only from FTC oversight, not from the antitrust laws as such. Although it was not taken very seriously in Congress, a very broad antitrust exemption for "medical self-regulatory entities," including professional societies, was included in a Republican Medicare reform bill in 1995. H.R.2425, 104th Cong., 1st Sess. § 15221 (1995).

4. Consider the leeway left for professional regulation of deceptive advertising in *AMA v. FTC*. In California Dental Ass'n, FTC Dkt. 9259 (Mar. 26, 1996), aff'd, 128 F.3d 720 (9th Cir.1997), the FTC again allowed a professional society that had unlawfully suppressed truthful advertising of the price, quality, and availability of services to continue regulating false and misleading advertising. How could the Commission justify allowing the professional respondents even this much self-regulatory power? Is not an agreement by AMA (or CDA) members not to advertise deceptively an agreement not to compete in a certain way? Would it be a "naked" or an "ancillary" restraint? Based on the preceding discussion of these matters, can you state a rationale for upholding such a restraint under the Sherman Act? Are you entirely satisfied that the exception you have identified is appropriately invoked in these cases? (In the *CDA* case, the FTC found no "efficiency" justification for the restraints it condemned but stated that "the prevention of false and misleading advertising is indeed a laudable purpose." How do you argue that it is also a procompetitive purpose?)

5. The American Academy of Ophthalmology maintains a Code of Ethics that addresses advertising. The Code is divided into unenforceable Principles of Ethics, which set goals for behavior; enforceable Rules of Ethics, which require certain behavior and prohibit other behavior; and Administrative Procedures, which explain how the Code will be enforced. The longest Rule in the Code, Rule 13, concerns communications to the public:

> Communications to the public must be accurate. They must not convey false, untrue, deceptive, or misleading information through statements, testimonials, photographs, graphics or other means. They must not omit material information without which the communications would be deceptive. Communications must not appeal to an individual's anxiety in an excessive or unfair way; and they must not create unjustified expectations of results. If communications refer to benefits or other attributes of ophthalmic procedures that involve significant risks, realistic assessments of their safety and efficacy must also be included, as well as the availability of alternatives and, where necessary to avoid deception, descriptions and/or assessments of the benefits or other attributes of those alternatives. Communications must not misrepresent an ophthalmologist's credentials, training, experience or ability, and must not contain material claims of superiority that cannot be substantiated. * * *

In some ways, the AAO Code is less restrictive than the version of the Principles of Medical Ethics that was at issue in *AMA v. FTC.* The Code allows solicitation of patients and does not prohibit "self-laudatory" or "self-aggrandizing" statements. The Code only requires that claims of superiority be capable of substantiation, rather than banning them altogether. Finally, the Code focuses on the likely effect of a communication on the receiver rather than on the media employed or the information provided; information may be communicated in any way so long as it is not false or deceptive, either as a result of what is included or of what is excluded.

In an advisory opinion approving Rule 13, the FTC stated that "[r]ules that are tailored to prevent false or deceptive advertising serve to enhance the competitive process and provide valuable consumer protection." American Academy of Ophthalmology, FTC advisory opinion, 3 Trade Reg. Rep. (CCH) ¶ 22,037 (June 24, 1983). Was the FTC right to approve the Code? Is the Code's effect likely to be to enhance or restrict the flow of information? Will it improve the quality of information? Should the FTC itself police professional advertising under its power to prevent "unfair or deceptive acts or practices"?

6. *The CDA Case.* In the *CDA* case, supra, the FTC condemned ethical restrictions on price advertising that, while not barring such advertising outright, required that any price claims be "exact, without omissions," and that any discounts offered be accompanied by detailed information concerning the standard price prior to discount. The Commission found that, as a practical matter, the "CDA's restrictions on advertising 'low' or 'reasonable' fees, and its extensive disclosure requirement for discount advertising, effectively preclude its members from making low fee and across-the-board discount claims regardless of their truthfulness." Although the Commission applied the Rule of Reason (utilizing a "quick look" approach) in condemning both the restrictions on price advertising and the CDA's restrictions on advertising of other kinds (e.g., claims about the quality or superiority of services), a majority of the commissioners also held that the restriction on price advertising was a per se violation, thus creating a new category of per se offense. The court of appeals rejected this effort to extend per se analysis to a new category of restraint but affirmed the finding of a violation under the Rule of Reason. 128 F.3d at 726–28.

NOTES AND QUESTIONS ON CODES OF PROFESSIONAL ETHICS

1. In *AMA v. FTC,* was it necessary for the FTC to find concerted action? (Answer: Although the FTC Act makes no reference to concerted action, the FTC usually applies the legal standards of the Sherman Act in finding "unfair methods of competition.") What concerted action was alleged and found? Can a single professional association establish a code of ethics without facing antitrust scrutiny? Professional associations are "routinely treated as continuing conspiracies of their members." 7 P. Areeda, Antitrust Law ¶ 1477, at 343 (1986).

2. Does a professional society's declaration that certain conduct is unethical constitute a naked agreement by the society's members not to engage in such conduct? In *CDA*, the FTC stated, "CDA clearly promulgated the Code of Ethics, which, as we noted in *AMA*, by itself 'implies agreement among the members of [the] organization to adhere to the norms of conduct set forth in the code.'" Should it matter that the society maintains no enforcement machinery (such as threatening, as did the CDA, to revoke the membership of violators)? See United States v. National Association of Real Estate Boards, 339 U.S. 485, 489 (1950) ("Subtle influences may be just as effective as the threat or use of formal sanctions to hold people in line"); American Column & Lumber Co. v. United States, 257 U.S. 377, 411 (1921) (parties said "to rely for maintenance of concerted action * * *, not upon fines and forfeitures as in earlier days, but upon what experience has shown to be the more potent and dependable restraints, of business honor and social penalties").

3. What defenses are available for an ethical canon? Assume that a surgical specialty society resolves that surgery of a certain kind should not be undertaken without first procuring in person the patient's fully informed and written consent. Is this a naked agreement not to compete by offering hasty and possibly cheaper service? Does it preclude the offering of one variety of service that some patients—e.g., those willing to put themselves entirely in the surgeon's hands—might want? Is it relevant that the law already requires "informed consent" and, in many states, defines its disclosure requirement by reference to the disclosure practices of other physicians? Would it make a difference whether the canon appeared to expand or contract the surgeons' disclosure obligations under existing law? In what sense does the hypothetical canon restrain trade?

In the *CDA* case, the FTC found it irrelevant that state law contained restrictions similar to the CDA's own. Why is a private agreement in restraint of trade not saved because state law arguably imposes the same restraint?

4. Is the canon hypothesized above a "naked restraint"? Although it does somewhat limit surgeons' competitive independence, its purpose may be only to establish a professional ideal, a purpose that may be accomplished even though those promulgating the canon lack market power and even though the canon is not universally obeyed. Thus, the strict test for a naked restraint suggested above is not satisfied. Moreover, one can interpret the canon as serving such procompetitive purposes as overcoming a market failure (consumer ignorance) and differentiating practitioners who adhere to the canon from those who may not.

5. Should the hypothetical canon be unlawful, despite its arguable ancillarity to a procompetitive purpose, if the society succeeded (either because of the law of informed consent or because the society conditioned valuable membership on adherence to the canon) in controlling the behavior of the large majority of surgeons? Do the *procompetitive* benefits of the canon outweigh its anticompetitive effects? Can these issues be resolved without finally relying on "the vague and varying opinion of judges as to how much, on principles of political economy, men ought to be allowed to restrain competition"?

In the *CDA* case, the FTC's invalidation under the Rule of Reason of the CDA's ban on price and other advertising included a conclusion that entry into the market for dental services in California as a nonmember of the CDA was not sufficiently easy to ensure that consumers would have the benefits of price competition despite the CDA's restraints. The Commission stated,

> [I]f alternative sources for the service offered by the association's members are so prevalent as to permit consumers easily to switch to providers who are unfettered by the rule, even a well-enforced restraint should cause no harm to the efficient functioning of the market. * * * If, on the other hand, consumers' abilities to turn elsewhere are limited, the association is in a position to harm consumers by adopting restrictive rules. This turns out to be the case here.

In fact, the CDA included 75% of the state's dentists and had an even higher percentage in some localities.

6. In order to avoid the kind of close analysis attempted here, many courts would declare that the canon hypothesized above is "reasonable" or serves a "noncommercial purpose" and is therefore outside the reach of the Sherman Act. Query, however, whether an agreement defining the precise service the collaborators will offer consumers and denying consumers other options should be dismissed so quickly from scrutiny under the antitrust laws, which have as an important policy objective the preservation of sellers' independence and the decentralization of decision making. Later materials develop more fully the status of the "noncommercial purpose" defense.

7. An analysis somewhat along the lines suggested in paragraph (4) above appears to have been accepted in principle in Koefoot v. American College of Surgeons, 652 F.Supp. 882 (N.D.Ill.1986). The plaintiff lost his designation as a Fellow of the prestigious American College of Surgeons (ACS) because he practiced "itinerant surgery," which entailed his leaving his patients' postsurgical care to general practitioners in rural Nebraska hospitals. The ACS rule against delegating postsurgical care to nonsurgeons might have been viewed as a naked agreement among the fellows (60% of board-certified surgeons) to practice surgery (i.e., to compete) in only one way, thus boycotting general practitioners, enhancing the demand for surgeons, and denying consumers an option that they might prefer for personal or cost reasons. The court, however, refused to apply a per se rule. Although it cited *Professional Engineers* to bar proof of the dangers of itinerant surgery and the medical merits of the rule, the court did allow the College to defend by proving that its seal of approval "provides consumers with a shorthand method of locating something they already desire, which in this case would be post-operative care rendered by a surgeon." Id. at 904. By saying that consumers must have arrived at a particular preference independently before it can be incorporated in a professional association's standards, did the court unduly restrict the ACS's freedom to set high standards of its own choosing. Materials on "private credentialing and accrediting" in chapter 6(§§ C & D) will also explore the informational value of private standard-setting programs similar to that maintained by the ACS.

Does the *Koefoot* case cast doubt on the FTC's attempt to rule in the *CDA* case that restrictions of price advertising are illegal per se? *Koefoot* also raises questions concerning the interaction of quality-of-care considerations and antitrust law. For the view that quality concerns in the health care field do not require special antitrust rules but can be adequately accommodated in traditional analysis focusing on competitive effects, see Kauper, The Role of Quality of Health Care Considerations in Antitrust Analysis, 51 Law & Contemp. Probs. 273 (Spring 1988). See also Greaney, Quality of Care and Market Failure Defenses in Antitrust Health Care Litigation, 21 Conn. L. Rev. 605, 659–61 (1989).

8. *Problem*. The Noah County Medical Society has resolved that it is never ethical or appropriate for a physician to assist a patient in committing suicide, even when the patient is terminally ill, in severe, untreatable pain, or wholly and permanently incapacitated. The society's resolution states, "A physician should be dedicated solely to healing and the preservation of life and should never take measures intended to bring about an unnatural death. The medical community of Noah County will view any violation of this tenet as a grave violation of medical ethics and as a threat to the integrity and public standing of the medical profession." In support of its position, the society cites Orentlicher, Physician Participation in Assisted Suicide, 262 J.A.M.A. 1844 (1989) (arguing physicians should have no role in treatments primarily directed at causing death; such treatments necessarily violate fundamental premise of the patient/physician relationship); Kass, Neither for Love nor Money: Why Doctors Must Not Kill, 94 Public Interest 25 (1989) (noted medical ethicist argues that physicians should all agree to observe a norm that the medical profession will not engage in euthanasia). For the AMA position on this and related issues, see Council on Ethical and Judicial Affairs, AMA, Decisions Near the End of Life, 267 J.A.M.A. 2229 (1992) (and other statements cited therein).

How should the ethical propriety of physician actions be determined—by legislation, by courts, by professional bodies, or in some other way? Or should the matter be left to the patient alone? Two federal courts of appeals ruled in 1996 that states cannot constitutionally bar physicians from participating in "assisted suicide." But the Supreme Court overturned both rulings. Washington v. Glucksberg, 117 S.Ct. 2258 (1997) (holding state law against assisting in suicide did not violate patient's fourteenth amendment due process rights); Vacco v. Quill, 117 S.Ct. 2293 (1997) (holding that patient's right to equal protection is not violated by legal distinction drawn between actively assisting suicide and withdrawing life support on request). Do you agree with Drs. Orentlicher and Kass that a profession should be free to define itself in such a way as to deny its clients certain services that they might demand and that professionals are best equipped to provide? Is the action of the Noah County Medical Society an unlawful restraint of trade? Is the *Koefoot* holding relevant to your conclusion?

Professional Boycotts

NOTE: KLOR'S, INC. v. BROADWAY-HALE STORES, INC., 359 U.S. 207 (1959)

In this leading case on the law of group boycotts, the Supreme Court evaluated a complaint alleging that a retailer (BH) had induced several manufacturers of electrical appliances to agree among themselves not to deal with a second retailer, Klor's—apparently a discounter whose proximity to BH allowed him to free-ride on BH's sales efforts in demonstrating merchandise that the customer could then buy from Klor's at a lower price. In holding that the complaint stated a cause of action even though it alleged no specific injury to competition in the retail market or to consumers, the Court noted (id. at 211–12):

> In the landmark case Standard Oil Co. v. United States, 221 U.S. 1 [1911], this Court read § 1 to prohibit those classes of contract or acts which the common law had deemed to be undue restraints of trade and those which new times and economic conditions would make unreasonable. * * * The Court recognized that there were some agreements whose validity depended on the surrounding circumstances. It emphasized, however, that there were classes of restraints which from their "nature or character" were unduly restrictive, and hence forbidden by both the common law and the statute. * * *
>
> Group boycotts, or concerted refusals by traders to deal with other traders, have long been held to be in the forbidden category. They have not been saved by allegations that they were reasonable in the specific circumstances, nor by a failure to show that they "fixed or regulated prices, parcelled out or limited production, or brought about a deterioration in quality." Fashion Originators' Guild v. Federal Trade Commission, 312 U.S. 457, 466, 467–468 [1941]. * * * Even when they

> operated to lower prices or temporarily to stimulate competition they were banned.

The *Klor's* Court saw several types of harms in the boycott (id. at 213):

> This combination takes from Klor's its freedom to buy appliances in an open competitive market and drives it out of business as a dealer in the defendants' products. It deprives the manufacturers and distributors of their freedom to sell to Klor's at the same prices and conditions made available to Broadway–Hale, and in some instances forbids them from selling to it on any terms whatsoever. It interferes with the natural flow of interstate commerce. It clearly has, by its "nature" and "character," a "monopolistic tendency."

Finally, the Court held it irrelevant that the boycott had no effect on competition because of Klor's small size and the presence of many other retailers in the neighborhood. A boycott "is not to be tolerated merely because the victim is just one merchant whose business is so small that his destruction makes little difference to the economy. Monopoly can as surely thrive by the elimination of such small businessmen, one at a time, as it can by driving them out in large groups." Id. at 213.

1. If the destruction of Klor's made "little difference to the economy," how was the interstate commerce requirement met?

2. What did the Court in *Klor's* mean when it held that group boycotts are unduly restrictive because of their "nature or character"?

3. In antitrust terms, what harms justify condemning a group boycott? Is it the harm to the direct or individual victim of the boycott that matters most? What other harm is there? What is the significance of the commonly cited dictum that antitrust law is intended to protect "competition, not competitors"? Brunswick Corp. v. Pueblo Bowl–O–Mat, Inc., 429 U.S. 477, 488 (1977). Are the antitrust laws primarily concerned with the unfairness of "ganging up" on a victim or with the impairment of independent decision making? Courts uniformly observe the harmful effects of boycotts on their targets, especially if the impact is felt directly or indirectly by a competitor of the boycotting group, but the more basic concern may lie elsewhere. Reconsider the 1942 *AMA* case, discussed earlier, as a case in point.

4. The terms "group boycott" and "concerted refusal to deal" (the quoted language from *Klor's* suggests that these terms are synonymous) have been applied to denials of membership in competitor-sponsored organizations and to refusals by such organizations to accredit or otherwise certify the quality of a competitor or of a competitor's products or services. We will see cases of this kind in chapter 6(§§ C & D), but it should be asked here how such boycotts differ from the boycotts in *Klor's* and in the cases that follow. To be sure, both kinds of boycott involve concerted action by competitors. A true or classic boycott of the kind in *Klor's,* however, restricts the decision-making freedom of a multiplicity of independent actors and is likely to be a naked restraint, having no purpose other than to foreclose the boycotters' independence, thus impairing the market opportunities and independence of the boycott's targets. Such boycotts seem appropriately treated as per se violations—at least if they are commercially motivated (a qualification explored in the following notes and questions).

The second type of "group boycott" or "concerted refusal to deal" presents a very different aspect. Here, the decisions of a single entity, albeit a competitor-controlled one, are involved. Although courts, by using the same labels for both types of concerted action, have blurred the seemingly obvious distinction between a naked restraint and a useful joint venture, it is becoming clearer that per se rules are appropriate only for classic boycotts and that joint ventures are entitled to a complete hearing under the Rule of Reason. See Northwest Wholesale Stationers, Inc. v. Pacific Stationery and Printing Co., 472 U.S. 284 (1985).

The need for a sharp distinction between these different types of "group boycott," if not for a better nomenclature as well, seems clear. The essential vice of naked concerted refusals to deal by competitors, which justifies their condemnation as per se violations, is their abrogation of the independent decision making that is the norm in competitive markets. The harms complained of in joint ventures of the kinds considered here, however, lie, if anywhere, not in their effects on competition among the joint venturers themselves but in their effects on excluded competitors of the venture's sponsors. It would appear that the actions of a useful joint venture should be subjected to only limited judicial scrutiny to ensure that their procompetitive purposes are accomplished without unreasonable risk of anticompetitive abuse. Later examination of the legal treatment of competitor-sponsored accreditation and credentialing programs and of organized hospital medical staffs will suggest that courts, by failing to draw appropriate distinctions, may be stifling legitimate collective action in the interest of protecting competitors, not competition itself.

5. The *Klor's* defendants offered no explanation for their concerted action against the plaintiff. Assume, however, that at the trial on remand they allege that Klor was an unethical businessman, free-riding on BH's product demonstrations (which are valuable to both manufacturers and consumers) or, worse, engaging in unconscionable consumer credit practices. Should competitors be allowed collectively to police the morals of the marketplace? What does *Professional Engineers* contribute to this discussion? The cases noted below consider these issues further in the context of professional services. Should a special rule prevail in such cases?

NOTES ON CASES INVOLVING PROFESSIONAL BOYCOTTS

1. *AMA v. United States*, 130 F.2d 233 (D.C.Cir.1942), affirmed 317 U.S. 519 (1943). This case, several aspects of which are discussed supra, involved a variety of efforts by two medical societies to suppress an early HMO by a series of actions that included concerted refusals by physicians to accept referrals or payments from, or to consult with, HMOs or HMO physicians. Although the court of appeals acknowledged that the defendants were entitled to establish standards of conduct, to engage in self-discipline, and to maintain "professional esprit de corps" (see earlier note), it held that the doctor conspiracy to boycott Group Health and its participating doctors could not be defended on the basis that it was "intended to promote the public welfare" or "designed to eliminate unfair, fraudulent and unlawful practices." 130 F.2d at 249. Underscoring its view concerning the limits of professional power, the court of appeals observed the "[A]ppellants are not law enforcement agencies . . . and although persons who reason superficially concerning such matters may find justification for extra-legal action to secure what seems to them desirable ends[,] this is not the American way of life." Id.

2. *United States v. Oregon State Medical Society*, 343 U.S. 326 (1952). The government charged the medical society with organizing a physician boycott of certain private "hospital associations"—embryonic managed care plans—that were objectionable to physicians because they attempted to impose certain cost controls. (These will be examined in chapter 9(§A).) The district court found that no boycott had been proved, and the Supreme Court affirmed, having this to say about the evidence:

> The record contains a number of letters from doctors to private associations refusing to accept checks directly from them. Some base refusal on a policy of their local medical society, others are silent as to reasons. Some may be attributed to the writers' personal resistance to dealing directly with the private health associations, for it is clear that many doctors objected to filling out the company forms and supplying details required by the associations, and preferred to confine themselves to direct dealing with the patient and leaving the patient to deal with the associations. Some writers may have mistaken or misunderstood the policy of local associations. Others may have avoided disclosure of personal opposition by the handy and impersonal excuse of association "policy." The letters have some evidentiary value, but it is not compelling and, weighed against the other post–1941 evidence, does not satisfy us that the trial court's findings are "clearly erroneous."
>
> [A paragraph omitted here contained language quoted earlier in this chapter.]
>
> Appellees' evidence to disprove conspiracy is not conclusive, is necessarily largely negative, but is too persuasive for us to say it was clear error to accept it. In 1948, 1,210 of the 1,660 licensed physicians in Oregon were members of the Oregon State Medical Society, and between January 1, 1947, and June 30, 1948, 1,085 Oregon doctors billed and received payment directly from the Industrial Hospital Association, only one of the several private plans operating in the State. Surely there was no effective boycott, and ineffectiveness, in view of the power over its members which the Government attributes to the Society, strongly suggests the lack of an attempt to boycott these private associations. A parade of local medical society members from all parts of the State, apparently reputable, credible, and informed professional men, testified that their societies now have no policy of discrimi-

nation against private health associations, and that no attempts are made to prevent individual doctors from cooperating with them. Members of the governing councils of the State and Multnomah County Societies testified that since 1940 there have been no suggestions in their meetings of attempts to prevent individual doctors from serving private associations. The manager of Oregon Physicians' Service testified that at none of the many meetings and conferences of local societies attended by him did he hear any proposal to prevent doctors from cooperation with private plans.

If the testimony of these many responsible witnesses is given credit, no finding of conspiracy to restrain or monopolize this business could be sustained. Certainly we cannot say that the trial court's refusal to find such a conspiracy was clearly erroneous.

3. *Community Blood Bank of Kansas City, Inc. v. FTC*, 70 F.T.C. 894 (1966), reversed for lack of jurisdiction, 405 F.2d 1011 (8th Cir.1969). (Recall that the important jurisdictional issue in this case was discussed in chapter 3(§B).) The FTC, in a 3–2 decision, found that, although there was no direct evidence of an actual agreement to refuse to deal, circumstantial evidence supported a finding of a conspiracy to boycott. Specifically, the majority found (70 F.T.C. at 913) that the respondents

> possessed a motive for joint action—their belief that commercial blood banking was morally wrong or their opinion that commercial blood banks did not supply blood of equal quality with nonprofit banks. There was ample opportunity for discussion and agreement at the various meetings of the Society of Pathologists, the Hospital Association, the meetings of the corporate body of the proposed Community bank, and the joint meetings of representatives of those groups. The commercial blood banks were discussed at some of these meetings. Several affirmative steps by individuals and groups were taken to prevent the commercial banks from establishing donor clubs and otherwise to inhibit their growth. There was a consistent pattern of reaction to the commercial banks' efforts to expand and a universal reluctance to use blood supplied by them.

The Commission considered the respondents' argument "that the evidence of record establishes at most parallel action by each respondent explainable by reference to individual beliefs and personal preferences." Id. at 938. Without considering whether the respondents' own commercial motives might have influenced their views on proprietary blood banking, the majority held that "the individual beliefs and preferences of the various respondents, rather than negating the inference of joint action, provide a motive therefor." Id. at 942.

The FTC majority further elaborated their views on the boycott's alleged motives as follows (id. at 943–44):

> A group of private citizens, no matter how public spirited or altruistically motivated, may not relegate to themselves the essentially governmental function of determining the standards which will be

> applied in the interstate operation of blood banks and band together to inhibit the development of licensed commercial banks which meet governmental but not their own self-imposed standards. Nor may they take such action because they hold the opinion that the buying and selling of human blood is morally wrong. While the Commission applauds public-sponsored projects, such as Community, and encourages public participation in such projects, it cannot ignore a combination having the effect of limiting the growth of legitimate private competitors to such organizations. As long as commercial blood banks are authorized by law, they are entitled to protection from such a combination or conspiracy, whether inspired by a good faith, but overzealous, effort to insure the success of a community-sponsored bank, a desire to impose more rigid standards upon blood banks than those now existing, or a belief that human blood should not be bought and sold.

Commissioner Elman, dissenting, expressed the following views (id. at 953–58):

> As I read the record, that refusal to deal [with the commercial blood banks], which is the crux of the Commission's case, was not collusive, and not the product of agreement or conspiracy, but stemmed from the unanimously and strongly held views of individual pathologists about the medical and ethical propriety of selling human blood for profit and their concern with the safety of the blood banked by the commercial blood banks.
>
> * * *
>
> To be sure, even where individual self-interest dictates a uniform response by members of a group, the members may enter into an agreement or combination to effectuate their common purpose. If the pathologists in the Kansas City area entered into a solemn pact to have no truck with commercial blood banking, there would obviously be an element of agreement or conspiracy, as well as of individual decision, in their refusal to deal with such banks. But they testified unequivocally to the contrary; there is no direct evidence of any agreement or conspiracy; and the theory on which the Commission is forced to rely is singularly unpersuasive. [The] evidence consists of facts whose significance (whether considered singly or in combination) is wholly indeterminate. The first is that respondents had frequent communication among themselves with regard to the blood banking problem. This was inevitable, of course, and hardly sinister, since all of the individual respondents are pathologists or hospital officials directly concerned with blood banking and participants in the Community Blood Bank project. The second is the fact that Community Blood Bank was apparently organized in order to enable respondents to do without the services of commercial blood banks. But if a group of persons are not satisfied with the services rendered them by existing firms, they are surely free—without being stigmatized as conspirators against the outside firms—to organize their own enterprise to provide these ser-

vices. The third is the fact that the hospitals and pathologists in the Kansas City area did refuse (though not without exception) to deal with the commercial blood banks after Community Blood Bank was organized. But their refusal to deal, as I have indicated, was the natural outgrowth of respondents' feelings toward commercial blood banking and of the formation of Community. The rest of the Commission's case seems to me mere bits and scraps of completely inconclusive, wholly speculative, circumstantial evidence.

* * * The harsh treatment accorded boycotts under the antitrust laws stems in part from recognition that in the hands of businessmen they are typically a potent and completely unjustifiable method for stifling competition, but even more, perhaps, from a conviction that to allow private groups to wield coercive powers is inconsistent with a free, democratic society.

Suppose that the members of an industry got together and agreed to blacklist any member who deviated from certain standards established by the industry. The agreement would be illegal even if violations of the standards would be unlawful, even if the only competition suppressed by the boycott would be unfair competition. For, it is felt, the application of sanctions to unethical and even unlawful business conduct should be left to the orderly processes of the law, not to vigilante action—however justifiable such action may seem in the circumstances—by private individuals or firms who, acting concertedly, enjoy great power.

The principle that boycotts are forbidden without inquiry into either competitive effects or possible justifications is sound. But, like all principles, there are limits beyond which it should not be pushed. The antitrust laws are concerned with the regulation of business behavior and most boycott cases have involved such behavior. In the typical case, what is challenged is the conduct of some businessmen in refusing, for business reasons, to deal with other businessmen. This was essentially the situation in the famous group-health case, which involved the efforts of medical societies to frustrate a plan to provide low-cost medical services to government employees. American Medical Assn. v. United States, 130 F.2d 233 (D.C.Cir.1942), affirmed 317 U.S. 519. Doctors are not businessmen, strictly speaking, and the boycott was not a typical restraint of trade; but the motives and purposes of the medical societies were commercial and pecuniary: to discourage a method of price competition in the furnishing of medical services. The issues in the case were basically economic.

Much can be said for confining the reach of the antitrust laws to boycotts that are economic in origin, as in the group-health case. I recognize, however, that courts have occasionally enjoined under the antitrust laws boycotts whose origin was ideological rather than economic. An example is the case of the "Hollywood Ten," who were blacklisted by the motion picture industry because they were allegedly Communists. Young v. Motion Picture Assn., Inc., 299 F.2d 119

(D.C.Cir.1962). But though there is precedent for applying the antitrust laws to boycotts growing out of other than commercial or competitive problems or conflicts, we should be cautious in assuming that the same *per se* rule of illegality that is applied to the more usual business boycott is applicable here. Suppose that a group of Negroes, in protest against segregated busses, boycotted the bus system. Assuming that the jurisdictional obstacles to bringing a federal antitrust suit could be overcome, I still would not be prepared to say that such conduct was illegal *per se*. Or suppose that the doctors in a medical society agreed among themselves not to prescribe thalidomide to pregnant women, or not to use a certain scalpel because it was made of inferior steel, or not to send their patients to a substandard private hospital or to one which excluded Negroes from its professional staff. In all these cases, too, I would have difficulty with invoking the *per se* rule of *Klor's* and *Fashion Originators' Guild*.

While we are on safe ground in assuming that the public policy of this country is opposed to permitting purely economic or business judgments to be delegated to private groups armed with the sanction of a concerted refusal to deal, we are on more tenuous ground in assuming a like public policy where professional and other noncommercial judgments and issues are concerned. For purposes of the present case, it is the professional judgment that is relevant. Professional self-regulation is prevalent in our society. Bar associations and medical societies are permitted to regulate the professional conduct of lawyers and doctors in ways that society does not tolerate in the business sphere. Where challenged group conduct that in other contexts would be struck down out of hand as an illegal boycott is the product of a professional judgment, it should, in my opinion, be given a fuller analysis.

This brings me to the facts of the present case. It is undisputed that respondents' activities did not have a business motive or objective. The aims and purposes of all the respondents were professional rather than commercial or economic in character.

Two types of professional judgment are disclosed in this record. The first includes such reasons for opposing the commercial blood banks as respondents' strongly held view that it is immoral to make money from the sale of human blood. Such reasons are not purely "medical" judgments in the strict sense of a judgment based exclusively on concern for what is in the patient's best interest. However, in addition to these ethical or moral reasons involved in respondents' unwillingness to use the blood of commercial blood banks, there was clearly a professional medical basis for their conduct. Respondents believed, and I find no basis in this record for doubting their sincerity, that the blood supplied by the commercial blood banks in the Kansas City area was unsafe. They feared that because these blood banks paid for the blood they banked and, respondents thought, were none too careful about whom they bought it from, and because they lacked (in respondents' view) adequate qualified personnel, their blood was medically unsafe, and created an undue risk of causing hepatitis in users. Respondents—whose professional duty was to protect the health and safety of their patients—did not have confidence in the safety and soundness of the commercial blood banks' operations.

Much of complaint counsel's case was given over to attempting to refute the views of the respondents and prove that the blood of the commercial blood banks was perfectly good and safe—for example, because they met the minimum standards promulgated by the National Institutes of Health. But it is not for us to decide whether the respondents were exercising sound medical judgment in insisting on higher standards for the blood to be used in treating *their* patients. If a group of doctors have concluded not to use certain blood because of genuine doubts as to its safety and reliability, they should not be compelled by order of the Federal Trade Commission to accept such blood. This Commission was not established to sit as a board of review over professional medical judgments made by doctors in the course of their practice. There is no question in my mind that the respondents believe, sincerely and honestly, that their professional responsibility as doctors requires that they not dispense to their patients blood bought from these commercial blood banks. * * * Unless we are prepared to say, as I am not, that the testimony given by the doctors in this proceeding was false and is not to be believed, their attitude towards the commercial blood banks was shaped by professional medical considerations and nothing else. This case ought to be decided by the Commission on that basis, and not on the basis that these doctors were lying to us or were acting irresponsibly and unprofessionally.

Under the Commission's order in this case the respondent doctors will *not* be free to exercise their own professional medical judgment, as they see fit, in accepting or rejecting blood from commercial blood banks. They will *not* be free to meet, discuss, and recommend the use or non-use of such blood. If there should be any such meetings or discussions and if any doctor should refuse to accept blood from a commercial blood bank, he will be subject to $5,000–a–day penalties for violation of the order. The right of the respondent doctors to practice medicine is thus seriously restricted by the order, which deprives them, individually and collectively, of the freedom to exercise a professional medical choice in accepting or rejecting blood to be used in treating their patients. [What kind of order should the FTC have issued, given the nature of the violation it found and the need to restore competition?—Eds.]

This case is atypical, to the point of freakishness, of the kind of proceedings this Commission is equipped to bring in the restraint of trade area. It does not involve monopoly or competition in the usual sense. It does not involve conduct having commercial motives or ends; the participants are not business concerns actuated by the profit motive. What this case really involves is an acrimonious private contro-

> versy, professional and personal in character and origin, between the pathologists and the commercial blood bankers in Kansas City. * * * We should stick to our own job: the elimination of unfair methods of competition in interstate commerce. Regulating the professional conduct of doctors is not our business.

4. *Wilk v. AMA,* 719 F.2d 207 (7th Cir.1983), cert. denied 467 U.S. 1210 (1984). Plaintiff chiropractors alleged that the AMA and several other medical groups, including the American Hospital Association, the American College of Surgeons, the American College of Physicians, and the Joint Commission on Accreditation of Hospitals, had

> engaged in a combination and conspiracy to eliminate the chiropractic profession through refusing to deal with plaintiffs and other chiropractors. Plaintiffs alleged defendants implemented the group boycott by agreeing to induce individual medical doctors to forego any form of professional, research, or educational association with chiropractors, to induce hospital and other health care facilities to deny access to chiropractors, and to induce actual and prospective patients of chiropractors to avoid seeking chiropractic services.

719 F.2d at 211. At issue was a provision of the AMA Principles of Medical Ethics which then provided: "A physician should practice a method of healing founded on a scientific basis; and he should not voluntarily professionally associate with anyone who violates this principle." In line with this principle, the AMA had established in 1963 a "Committee on Quackery," which "considered 'its prime mission to be, first, the containment of chiropractic and ultimately the elimination of chiropractic'." Id. at 213. In addition the AMA House of Delegates, in a 1966 resolution, stated, "It is the position of the medical profession that chiropractic is an unscientific cult whose practitioners lack the necessary training and background to diagnose and treat human disease." Id.

Though noting that the Supreme Court had been "persistent and firm in its support of the *per se* doctrine" (id. at 221), the court of appeals refused to allow the jury to treat the physician boycott of chiropractors as a *per se* violation. Observing that the Court had "taken pains to preserve the possibility that a particular practice which could be viewed as a violation of the Sherman Act in another context, should be treated differently in the circumstances peculiar to a learned profession," the court said that "a canon of medical ethics purporting, surely not frivolously, to address the importance of scientific method gives rise to questions of sufficient delicacy and novelty at least to escape *per se* treatment." Id. at 222.

Acknowledging but refusing to follow the Rule of Reason test laid down in *Professional Engineers*—focusing exclusively on whether the challenged agreement promoted or suppressed competition—, the court of appeals declared itself "free to modify the rule of reason test in a case involving a certain kind of question of ethics for the medical profession." Id. at 226. The court thought the defendants could have behaved as they did toward chiropractors for any (or a combination) of three reasons (id. at 219):

> (1) because they believed that it would permit them to make more money than they would make if they did not do it; or (2) because they believed they were performing a public service in applying economic pressure to diminish or eliminate the general threat posed by chiropractic to public health, safety and welfare; or (3) because defendants respected scientific method as the basis for diagnosis and treatment and were unwilling to risk the health and lives of their patients by associating professionally in the care of patients with persons who (so defendants thought) do not share respect for scientific method; or (4) because of some combination of (1), (2) and (3). For brevity and convenience, we will refer to (1) as a money motive, (2) as a public interest motive, and (3) as a patient care motive.

The court found that the jury, which had decided for the defendants, had been given erroneous instructions. One problem was that the instructions led the jury "to believe that if the money motive was present but was not 'primary' or 'principal,' even the most classical anti-competitive conduct would not constitute a *per se* violation." Id. at 220. The court also found (id. at 228)

> that a generalized public interest motive affords no legal excuse for such economic warfare.
>
> Since at least as early as 1941 when *Fashion Originators' Guild of America, Inc. v. FTC*, was decided it has been clear that private persons and entities may not presume to function as "an extra-governmental agency, which prescribes rules for the regulation and restraint of interstate commerce." It is true that medical doctors are better qualified than most members of the public to form an opinion whether chiropractic poses a threat to public health, safety and welfare. They are free to attempt to persuade legislatures and administrative agencies. But a generalized concern for the health, safety and welfare of members of the public as to whom a medical doctor has assumed no specific professional responsibility, however genuine and well-informed such a concern may be, affords no legal justification for economic measures to diminish competition with some medical doctors by chiropractors.
>
> The jury was instructed that chiropractic was lawful within the limits imposed by Congress and state legislatures; that whether chiropractic poses an impermissible hazard to the health and welfare of the public is for Congress and state legislatures to resolve and not for the defendants; and that the law will not allow the legislative decision to be overturned. The jury was then told that it is a different question whether medical doctors may limit their own relationships with chiropractors.
>
> Had the jury been instructed that the sole test under the rule of reason was the effect of defendants' conduct on competition and that the jury must disregard evidence both of defendants' public interest motive and of their patient care motive, plaintiffs would have suffered no prejudice, of course. But when the district court ventured to

> instruct that defendants' concerns with the perceived threat of chiropractic were relevant to the jury's task, it was essential that a line be drawn sharply and unmistakably between evidence of the public interest motive and evidence of the patient care motive. We conclude that such a line was not drawn with sufficient emphasis and clarity.

Concluding that the jury had not been correctly instructed, the court (id. at 227) remanded the case for a new trial in which the defendants would be given the opportunity to show

> (1) that they genuinely entertained a concern for what they perceive as scientific method in the case of each person with whom they have entered into a doctor-patient relationship; (2) that this concern is objectively reasonable; (3) that this concern has been the dominant motivating factor in defendants' promulgation of Principle 3 and in the conduct intended to implement it; and (4) that this concern for scientific method in patient care could not have been adequately satisfied in a manner less restrictive of competition.

On remand after plaintiffs dropped their damage claim, a bench trial resulted in a finding of a conspiracy by the AMA and its members and injunctive relief. Wilk v. AMA, 671 F.Supp. 1465 (N.D.Ill.1987), affirmed, 895 F.2d 352 (7th Cir.1990). The trial court's injunction, including its findings on the "patient care" defense, are published in 259 J.A.M.A. 81 (1988).

QUESTIONS ON BOYCOTTS FOR NONCOMMERCIAL PURPOSES

1. Do you agree with Commissioner Elman in the *Blood Bank* case that an explicit boycott of the commercial banks should have been permitted? Is it relevant that the nonprofit Community Blood Bank, though long discussed, was only put into operation after the commercial banks opened their doors? Do the *Goldfarb* and *Professional Engineers* decisions and other subsequent events resolve the issue here against Commissioner Elman's position?

2. Are you satisfied that the boycott in the *Blood Bank* case—if there was one—was inspired by a noncommercial purpose? Do you agree with Commissioner Elman that the respondents' behavior was "shaped by professional medical considerations and nothing else"? Could one say the same thing about the conduct of the Oregon medical society and of the AMA in *Wilk*?

3. What do you think of the distinction drawn in the *Wilk* case between a "public interest" motive and a "patient care" motive? Can you state and justify the distinction in your own words? Would you advise a medical organization in the Seventh Circuit that an explicit boycott harmful to physicians' competitors—for example, nurse midwives willing to preside over home births—could be safely organized if the physicians were morally certain that their patients would be endangered by the competitors' care?

4. Commissioner Elman opined that "grave constitutional problems would be raised if the Commission tried to enjoin communications among medical personnel on professional questions" of the kind presented by commercial blood banking. Are such problems also raised by the FTC majority's willingness to infer the existence of an explicit boycott on the basis of the evidence presented? How much constitutional protection should professionals enjoy in discussing matters of mutual concern? How should the speech in question in the *Blood Bank* case be characterized for purposes of answering this question?

5. Are there other reasons (besides constitutional considerations) to be concerned about the chilling effects of the majority's approach in the *Blood Bank* case? Surely there are significant public benefits to be gained from allowing professionals to discuss shared ethical and quality concerns freely among themselves. Would a rule that prohibited professional boycotts be more acceptable if courts were not quick to infer the existence of a conspiracy on the basis of parallel conduct, shared concerns, and close communication? What do you think of the Court's appraisal of the evidence in *Oregon State Medical Society?*

6. *Problem.* Imagine a county medical society concerned about the excesses of managed care. Its officers believe that these excesses are especially exemplified by Val–U–Care, an IPA-type HMO that is currently scouting the county for participating doctors with the intention of competing for employer contracts in the area. Recent meetings of the medical society have featured speeches attacking Val–U–Care for being a stock-market high flier, for earning high profits, and for paying its CEO over $6 million in salary and bonuses last year. Speakers have also recounted anecdotes, obtained from doctors in other communities, illustrating how Val–U–Care has overridden medical judgments and withheld necessary care from patients. One speaker emphasized that physicians may expose themselves to malpractice suits if they practice according to the standards of Val–U–Care rather than according to prevailing community standards.

There has been particular comment on the presence of so-called "gag" clauses in Val–U–Care's contracts with its participating physicians. Such clauses bind the doctor not to disparage the plan to patients, to colleagues, to the media, or to anyone else and not to advise patients of the availability of treatment options that Val–U–Care does not cover. The society recently adopted a resolution condemning gag clauses in general as "unethical and unconscionable." In addition, a recent speaker advised the members to "consult your consciences before cooperating with this wealthy company's effort to enrich itself at the expense of your patients and yourselves." On gag clauses in general, see Gianelli, Bound and Gagged, Am.Med. News, Feb. 5, 1996, at 1; Woolhandler & Himmelstein, Extreme Risk—The New Corporate Proposition for Physicians, 333 New Eng.J.Med. 1706 (995).

Val–U–Care reports that it is meeting more than the usual resistance in its effort to recruit physicians. Although it is offering terms that should be attractive to physicians, it is still not clear that it will be able to obtain physicians in all the specialties it must cover in order to open its doors in the county. Would you advise Val–U–Care that it might have an antitrust claim if its undertaking is ultimately unsuccessful?

(a) Is there a boycott here? Because there is no overt concerted refusal to deal, it is necessary to ask whether an unlawful conspiracy to boycott can fairly be inferred from the evidence of knowingly similar conduct by the competitors (so-called "conscious parallelism") coupled with other suspicious circumstances. In a 1914 case in which some retail lumber dealers' associations published a list of wholesalers who also traded at retail in competition with the associations' members, the Supreme Court said,

> when, in this case, by concerted action the names of wholesalers who were reported as having made sales to consumers were periodically reported to the other members of the associations, the conspiracy to accomplish that which was the natural consequence of such action [i.e., refusals to deal] may be readily inferred.

Eastern States Retail Lumber Dealers' Ass'n v. United States, 234 U.S. 600, 612 (1914). A conspiracy to boycott could not be inferred from an exchange of information and opinion, however, if that exchange had value other than as a signal for concerted action.

(b) Although true group boycotts are illegal per se, unilateral refusals to deal are normally not suspect. United States v. Colgate & Co., 250 U.S. 300 (1919). Indeed, the freedom to do business with whomever one chooses is part of that same "freedom of traders" that the rule announced in *Klor's* was itself designed to vindicate. Is it possible that the physicians in the problem had their own personal reasons for refusing to join Val–U–Care? Are malpractice fears their only reason? Normally, a conspiracy is inferrable only if the acts of the alleged conspirators, viewed independently, did not make sense from the point of view of their individual self-interest—that is, would be in their own interest only if their competitors acted in the same way. Is the fact that many physicians passed up seemingly lucrative offers of employment conclusive on the issue of agreement?

(c) Even if a conspiracy to boycott cannot be inferred in the problem, the actions of a medical society are still actions taken by competitors in concert and must be analyzed under antitrust principles to see if they are so unreasonable as themselves to be classed as restraints of trade. Could the medical society resolution condemning Val–U–Care's ethics be said to restrain unduly the HMO's freedom to act in accordance with its own business judgment concerning the public's desire for low-cost health care? See Pennsylvania Dental Ass'n v. Medical Serv. Ass'n, 815 F.2d 270 (3d Cir.1987) (extensive evidence of dentists' conspiracy to coerce Blue Shield plan included resolutions endorsing departicipation). Could a court hold that the medical society's provision of meeting time and leadership on the Val–U–Care issue unreasonably contributed to the ensuing trade-restraining activities of its members?

(d) Does the *Oregon State Medical Society* case suggest that the courts may not be quick to characterize as a boycott medical society activities of the sort found in the problem?

(e) Recall Commissioner Elman's discussion of the evidence of a concerted refusal to deal in the *Community Blood Bank* case. What is your final opinion on the FTC's decision in that case?

7. Outside the professional context, noncommercial purposes have occasionally received some recognition as a Sherman Act defense. The most prominent recent case, although not involving a boycott, is United States v. Brown Univ., 5 F.3d 658 (3d Cir.1993), in which the government challenged the practice by eight Ivy League colleges and the Massachusetts Institute of Technology (the "Ivy Overlap Group") of collectively determining the amount of financial aid that each would offer to commonly admitted students. Was this a price-fixing agreement? The court held that the agreement to limit the amount of "discount" the schools would offer to potential "customers" was a form of price fixing. It refused to apply a per se rule, however, overturned the lower court's finding of a violation based on a "truncated" Rule of Reason analysis, and ordered the court "to more fully investigate the procompetitive and noneconomic justifications proffered by MIT [the only defendant that had not agreed to a settlement of the case]." The court discussed MIT's justifications as follows (id. at 677–78):

> MIT argues that participation in the Overlap arrangement provided some consumers, the needy, with additional choices which an entirely free market would deny them. The facts and arguments before us may suggest some significant areas of distinction from those in *Professional Engineers* * * * in that MIT is asserting that Overlap not only serves a social benefit, but actually enhances consumer choice. Overlap is not an attempt to withhold a particular desirable service from customers, * * * but rather it purports only to seek to extend a service to qualified students who are financially "needy" and would not otherwise be able to afford the high cost education at MIT. Further, while Overlap resembles the ban on competitive bidding at issue in *Professional Engineers*, MIT alleges that Overlap enhances competition by broadening the socio-economic sphere of its potential student body. Thus, rather than suppress competition, Overlap may in fact merely regulate competition in order to enhance it, while also deriving certain social benefits. If the rule of reason analysis leads to this conclusion, then indeed Overlap will be beyond the scope of the prohibitions of the Sherman Act.
>
> We note the unfortunate fact that financial aid resources are limited even at the Ivy League schools. A trade-off may need to be made between providing some financial aid to a large number to the most needy students or allowing the free market to bestow the limited financial aid on the very few most talented who may not need financial aid to attain their academic goals. Under such circumstances, if this trade-off is proven to be worthy in terms of obtaining a more diverse student body (or other legitimate institutional goals), the limitation on the choices of the most talented students might not be so egregious as to trigger the obvious concerns which led the Court to reflect the "public interest" justification in *Professional Engineers* * * *. However, we leave it for the district court to decide whether full funding of need may be continued on an individual institutional basis, absent

Overlap, whether tuition could be lowered as a way to compete for qualified "needy" students, or whether there are other imaginable creative alternatives to implement MIT's professed social welfare goal.

* * *

It is most desirable that schools achieve equality of educational access and opportunity in order that more people enjoy the benefits of a worthy higher education. There is no doubt, too, that enhancing the quality of our educational system redounds to the general good. To the extent that higher education endeavors to foster vitality of the mind, to promote free exchange between bodies of thought and truths, and better communication among a broad spectrum of individuals, as well as prepares individuals for the intellectual demands of responsible citizenship, it is a common good that should be extended to as wide a range of individuals from as broad a range of socio-economic backgrounds as possible. It is with this in mind that the Overlap Agreement should be submitted to the rule of reason scrutiny under the Sherman Act.

Do you agree that the parties had a procompetitive as well as a worthy purpose? The dissenting judge would have held that the challenged practices were altogether outside the intended scope of the antitrust laws.

See generally Goldman, The Politically Correct Corporation: The Proper Treatment of Noneconomic or Social Welfare Justifications under Section One of the Sherman Act, 13 Yale L. & Policy Rev. 137 (1995); Beschle, Doing Well, Doing Good, and Doing Both: A Framework for the Analysis of Noncommercial Boycotts under the Antitrust Laws, 30 St. Louis U.L.J. 385 (1986). As noted by Commissioner Elman, there are a number of cases rejecting noncommercial purpose defenses for certain boycotts. Nevertheless, it seems reasonable to regard at least consumer boycotts for social or political objectives—racial or social justice, redress of consumer grievances, suppression of abortion or pornography, and so forth—as outside the ambit of the Sherman Act, which may be appropriately construed to protect only against concerted action that prevents the free market from resolving issues that are primarily economic in nature. Cf. NAACP v. Claiborne Hardware Co., 458 U.S. 886 (1982) (consumer boycott to improve employment and other opportunities for blacks held to enjoy first amendment protection against antitrust attack); Missouri v. National Organization for Women, 620 F.2d 1301 (8th Cir.), cert. denied 449 U.S. 842 (1980) (Sherman Act construed not to apply to NOW's boycott of state's convention facilities; boycott was aimed at getting state legislature to ratify proposed Equal Rights Amendment). This recognized defense is not broad enough, however, to protect coercive boycotts by professionals.

The Quality of Care as an Antitrust Defense

FTC v. Indiana Federation of Dentists

Supreme Court of the United States, 1986.
476 U.S. 447, 106 S.Ct. 2009, 90 L.Ed.2d 445.

■ JUSTICE WHITE delivered the opinion of the Court.

This case concerns commercial relations among certain Indiana dentists, their patients, and the patients' dental health care insurers. The question presented is whether the Federal Trade Commission correctly concluded that a conspiracy among dentists to refuse to submit x rays to dental insurers for use in benefits determinations constituted an "unfair method of competition" in violation of § 5 of the Federal Trade Commission Act.

I

Since the 1970's, dental health insurers, responding to the demands of their policyholders, have attempted to contain the cost of dental treatment by, among other devices, limiting payment of benefits to the cost of the "least expensive yet adequate treatment" suitable to the needs of individual patients. Implementation of such cost-containment measures, known as "alternative benefits" plans, requires evaluation by the insurer of the diagnosis and recommendation of the treating dentist, either in advance of or following the provision of care. In order to carry out such evaluation, insurers frequently request dentists to submit, along with insurance claim forms requesting payment of benefits, any dental x rays that have been used by the dentist in examining the patient as well as other information concerning their diagnoses and treatment recommendations. Typically, claim forms and accompanying x rays are reviewed by lay claims examiners, who either approve payment of claims or, if the materials submitted raise a question whether the recommended course of treatment is in fact necessary, refer claims to dental consultants, who are licensed dentists, for further review. On the basis of the materials available, supplemented where appropriate by further diagnostic aids, the dental consultant may recommend that the insurer approve a claim, deny it, or pay only for a less expensive course of treatment.

Such review of diagnostic and treatment decisions has been viewed by some dentists as a threat to their professional independence and economic well-being. In the early 1970's, the Indiana Dental Association, a professional organization comprising some 85% of practicing dentists in the State of Indiana, initiated an aggressive effort to hinder insurers' efforts to implement alternative benefits plans by enlisting member dentists to pledge not to submit x rays in conjunction with claim forms.[1] The Associa-

1. A presentation made in 1974 by Dr. David McClure, an Association official and later one of the founders of respondent Indiana Federation of Dentists, is revealing as to the motives underlying the dentists' resistance to the provision of x rays for use by insurers in making alternative benefits determinations:

> "* * * We are fighting an economic war where the very survival of our profession is at stake.
>
> "* * * The Delta Dental Plans have bedded down with the unions and have been a party to setting up the greatest controls that any profession has ever known in a free society. . . .
>
> "The name of the game is money. The government and labor are determined to reduce the cost of the dental health dollar at the expense of the dentist. There is no way a dental service can be rendered cheaper when the third party has to have its share of the dollar.

tion's efforts met considerable success: large numbers of dentists signed the pledge, and insurers operating in Indiana found it difficult to obtain compliance with their requests for x rays and accordingly had to choose either to employ more expensive means of making alternative benefits determinations (for example, visiting the office of the treating dentist or conducting an independent oral examination) or to abandon such efforts altogether.

By the mid–1970's, fears of possible antitrust liability had dampened the Association's enthusiasm for opposing the submission of x rays to insurers. In 1979, the Association and a number of its constituent societies consented to a Federal Trade Commission order requiring them to cease and desist from further efforts to prevent member dentists from submitting x rays. Not all Indiana dentists were content to leave the matter of submitting x rays to the individual dentist. In 1976, a group of such dentists formed the Indiana Federation of Dentists, respondent in this case, in order to continue to pursue the Association's policy of resisting insurers' requests for x rays. The Federation, which styled itself a "union" in the belief that this label would stave off antitrust liability,[2] immediately promulgated a "work rule" forbidding its members to submit x rays to dental insurers in conjunction with claim forms. Although the Federation's membership was small, numbering less than 100, its members were highly concentrated in and around three Indiana communities: Anderson, Lafayette, and Fort Wayne. The Federation succeeded in enlisting nearly 100% of the dental specialists in the Anderson area, and approximately 67% of the dentists in and around Lafayette. In the areas of its strength, the Federation was successful in continuing to enforce the Association's prior policy of refusal to submit x rays to dental insurers.

[The FTC] Commission ruled that the Federation's policy constituted a violation of § 5 and issued an order requiring the Federation to cease and desist from further efforts to organize dentists to refuse to submit x rays to insurers. The Commission based its ruling on the conclusion that the Federation's policy of requiring its members to withhold x rays amounted to a conspiracy in restraint of trade that was unreasonable and hence unlawful under the standards for judging such restraints developed in this Court's precedents interpreting § 1 of the Sherman Act. The Commission found that the Federation had conspired both with the Indiana Dental Association and with its own members to withhold cooperation with dental insurers' requests for x rays; that absent such a restraint, competition among dentists for patients would have tended to lead dentists to compete with respect to their policies in dealing with patients' insurers; and that in those areas where the Federation's membership was strong, the Federation's policy had had the actual effect of eliminating such competition among dentists and preventing insurers from obtaining access to x rays in

"Already we are locked into a fee freeze that could completely control the quality of dental care, if left on long enough."

2. Respondent no longer makes any pretense of arguing that it is immune from antitrust liability as a labor organization.

the desired manner. These findings of anticompetitive effect, the Commission concluded, were sufficient to establish that the restraint was unreasonable even absent proof that the Federation's policy had resulted in higher costs to the insurers and patients than would have occurred had the x rays been provided. Further, the Commission rejected the Federation's argument that its policy of withholding x rays was reasonable because the provision of x rays might lead the insurers to make inaccurate determinations of the proper level of care and thus injure the health of the insured patients: the Commission found no evidence that use of x rays by insurance companies in evaluating claims would result in inadequate dental care. Finally, the Commission rejected the Federation's contention that its actions were exempt from antitrust scrutiny because the withholding of x rays was consistent with the law and policy of the State of Indiana against the use of x rays in benefit determination by insurance companies. The Commission concluded that no such policy existed, and that in any event the existence of such a policy would not have justified the dentists' private and unsupervised conspiracy in restraint of trade.

The * * * Court of Appeals for the Seventh Circuit * * * vacated the order on the ground that it was not supported by substantial evidence. * * *

* * * We now reverse.

II

* * * In the case now before us, the sole basis of the FTC's finding of an unfair method of competition was the Commission's conclusion that the Federation's collective decision to withhold x rays from insurers was an unreasonable and conspiratorial restraint of trade in violation of § 1 of the Sherman Act. Accordingly, the legal question before us is whether the Commission's factual findings, if supported by evidence, make out a violation of Sherman Act § 1.

III

The relevant factual findings are that the members of the Federation conspired among themselves to withhold x rays requested by dental insurers for use in evaluating claims for benefits, and that this conspiracy had the effect of suppressing competition among dentists with respect to cooperation with the requests of the insurance companies. As to the first of these findings there can be no serious dispute: abundant evidence in the record reveals that one of the primary reasons—if not *the* primary reason—for the Federation's existence was the promulgation and enforcement of the so-called "work rule" against submission of x rays in conjunction with insurance claim forms.

As for the second crucial finding—that competition was actually suppressed—the * * * Commission's finding that "[i]n the absence of ... concerted behavior, individual dentists would have been subject to market forces of competition, creating incentives for them to ... comply with the requests of patients' third-party insurers," finds support not only in common sense and economic theory, upon both of which the FTC may reasonably rely, but also in record documents, including newsletters circulated among Indiana dentists, revealing that Indiana dentists themselves perceived that unrestrained competition tended to lead their colleagues to comply with insurers' requests for x rays. Moreover, there was evidence that outside of Indiana, in States where dentists had not collectively refused to submit x rays, insurance companies found little difficulty in obtaining compliance by dentists with their requests. A "reasonable mind" could conclude on the basis of this evidence that competition for patients, who have obvious incentives for seeking dentists who will cooperate with their insurers, would tend to lead dentists in Indiana (and elsewhere) to cooperate with requests for information by their patients' insurers.

The Commission's finding that such competition was actually diminished where the Federation held sway also finds adequate support in the record. The Commission found that in the areas where Federation membership among dentists was most significant (that is, in the vicinity of Anderson and Lafayette) insurance companies were unable to obtain compliance with their requests for submission of x rays in conjunction with claim forms and were forced to resort to other, more costly, means of reviewing diagnoses for the purpose of benefit determination. Neither the opinion of the Court of Appeals nor the brief of respondent identifies any evidence suggesting that the Commission's finding that the Federation's policy had an actual impact on the ability of insurers to obtain the x rays they requested was incorrect. The lower court's conclusion that this evidence is to be discounted because Federation members continued to cooperate with insurers by allowing them to use more costly—indeed, prohibitively costly—methods of reviewing treatment decisions is unpersuasive. The fact remains that the dentists' customers (that is, the patients and their insurers) sought a particular service: cooperation with the insurers' pretreatment review through the forwarding of x rays in conjunction with claim forms. The Federation's collective activities resulted in the denial of the information the customers requested in the form that they requested it, and forced them to choose between acquiring that information in a more costly manner or forgoing it altogether. To this extent, at least, competition among dentists with respect to cooperation with the requests of insurers was restrained.

IV

The question remains whether these findings are legally sufficient to establish a violation of § 1 of the Sherman Act—that is, whether the Federation's collective refusal to cooperate with insurers' requests for x rays constitutes an "unreasonable" restraint of trade. * * *

The policy of the Federation with respect to its members' dealings with third-party insurers resembles practices that have been labeled "group boycotts": the policy constitutes a concerted refusal to deal on particular terms with patients covered by group dental insurance. Although this Court has in the past stated that group boycotts are unlawful *per se*, we decline to resolve this case by forcing the Federation's policy into the "boycott" pigeonhole and invoking the *per se* rule. As we observed last Term in *Northwest Wholesale Stationers, Inc. v. Pacific Stationery and Printing Co.,* the category of restraints classed as group boycotts is not to be expanded indiscriminately, and the *per se* approach has generally been limited to cases in which firms with market power boycott suppliers or customers in order to discourage them from doing business with a competitor—a situation obviously not present here. Moreover, we have been slow to condemn rules adopted by professional associations as unreasonable *per se,* see *National Society of Professional Engineers v. United States,* and, in general, to extend *per se* analysis to restraints imposed in the context of business relationships where the economic impact of certain practices is not immediately obvious, see Broadcast Music, Inc. v. CBS, 441 U.S. 1 (1979). Thus, as did the FTC, we evaluate the restraint at issue in this case under the Rule of Reason rather than a rule of *per se* illegality.

Application of the Rule of Reason to these facts is not a matter of any great difficulty. The Federation's policy takes the form of a horizontal agreement among the participating dentists to withhold from their customers a particular service that they desire—the forwarding of x rays to insurance companies along with claim forms. "While this is not price fixing as such, no elaborate industry analysis is required to demonstrate the anticompetitive character of such an agreement." Society of Professional Engineers, 435 U.S. at 692. A refusal to compete with respect to the package of services offered to customers, no less than a refusal to compete with respect to the price term of an agreement, impairs the ability of the market to advance social welfare by ensuring the provision of desired goods and services to consumers at a price approximating the marginal cost of providing them. Absent some countervailing procompetitive virtue—such as, for example, the creation of efficiencies in the operation of a market or the provision of goods and services, NCAA v. Board of Regents of Univ. of Okla., 468 U.S. 85 (1984)—such an agreement limiting consumer choice by impeding the "ordinary give and take of the market place," Society of Professional Engineers, 435 U.S. at 692, cannot be sustained under the Rule of Reason. No credible argument has been advanced for the proposition that making it more costly for the insurers and patients who are the dentists' customers to obtain information needed for evaluating the dentists' diagnoses has any such procompetitive effect.

The Federation advances three principal arguments for the proposition that, notwithstanding its lack of competitive virtue, the Federation's policy of withholding x rays should not be deemed an unreasonable restraint of trade. First, as did the Court of Appeals, the Federation suggests that in the absence of specific findings by the Commission concerning the definition of the market in which the Federation allegedly restrained trade and the power of the Federation's members in that market, the conclusion that the Federation unreasonably restrained trade is erroneous as a matter of law, regardless of whether the challenged practices might be impermissibly anticompetitive if engaged in by persons who together possessed power in a specifically defined market. This contention, however, runs counter to the

Court's holding in *NCAA v. Board of Regents,* supra, that "[a]s a matter of law, the absence of proof of market power does not justify a naked restriction on price or output," and that such a restriction "requires some competitive justification even in the absence of a detailed market analysis." 468 U.S., at 109–110. Moreover, even if the restriction imposed by the Federation is not sufficiently "naked" to call this principle into play, the Commission's failure to engage in detailed market analysis is not fatal to its finding of a violation of the Rule of Reason. The Commission found that in two localities in the State of Indiana (the Anderson and Lafayette areas), Federation dentists constituted heavy majorities of the practicing dentists and that as a result of the efforts of the Federation, insurers in those areas were, over a period of years, actually unable to obtain compliance with their requests for submission of x rays. Since the purpose of the inquiries into market definition and market power is to determine whether an arrangement has the potential for genuine adverse effects on competition, "proof of actual detrimental effects, such as a reduction of output" can obviate the need for an inquiry into market power, which is but a "surrogate for detrimental effects." 7 P. Areeda, Antitrust Law ¶ 1511, p. 429 (1986). In this case, we conclude that the finding of actual, sustained adverse effects on competition in those areas where IFD dentists predominated, viewed in light of the reality that markets for dental services tend to be relatively localized, is legally sufficient to support a finding that the challenged restraint was unreasonable even in the absence of elaborate market analysis.

Second, the Federation, again following the lead of the Court of Appeals, argues that a holding that its policy of withholding x rays constituted an unreasonable restraint of trade is precluded by the Commission's failure to make any finding that the policy resulted in the provision of dental services that were more costly than those that the patients and their insurers would have chosen were they able to evaluate x rays in conjunction with claim forms. This argument, too, is unpersuasive. Although it is true that the goal of the insurers in seeking submission of x rays for use in their review of benefits claims was to minimize costs by choosing the least expensive adequate course of dental treatment, a showing that this goal was actually achieved through the means chosen is not an essential step in establishing that the dentists' attempt to thwart its achievement by collectively refusing to supply the requested information was an unreasonable restraint of trade. A concerted and effective effort to withhold (or make more costly) information desired by consumers for the purpose of determining whether a particular purchase is cost-justified is likely enough to disrupt the proper functioning of the price-setting mechanism of the market that it may be condemned even absent proof that it resulted in higher prices or, as here, the purchase of higher-priced services, than would occur in its absence. Moreover, even if the desired information were in fact completely useless to the insurers and their patients in making an informed choice regarding the least costly adequate course of treatment—or, to put it another way, if the costs of evaluating the information were far greater than the cost savings resulting from its use—the Federation would still not be justified in deciding on behalf of its members' customers that they did not need the information: presumably, if that were the case, the discipline of the market would itself soon result in the insurers' abandoning their requests for x rays. The Federation is not entitled to pre-empt the working of the market by deciding for itself that its customers do not need that which they demand.

Third, the Federation complains that the Commission erred in failing to consider, as relevant to its Rule of Reason analysis, noncompetitive "quality of care" justifications for the prohibition on provision of x rays to insurers in conjunction with claim forms. This claim reflects the Court of Appeals' repeated characterization of the Federation's policy as a "legal, moral, and ethical policy of quality dental care, requiring that insurers examine and review all diagnostic and clinical aids before formulating a proper course of dental treatment." The gist of the claim is that x rays, standing alone, are not adequate bases for diagnosis of dental problems or for the formulation of an acceptable course of treatment. Accordingly, if insurance companies are permitted to determine whether they will pay a claim for dental treatment on the basis of x rays as opposed to a full examination of all the diagnostic aids available to the examining dentist, there is a danger that they will erroneously decline to pay for treatment that is in fact in the interest of the patient, and that the patient will as a result be deprived of fully adequate care.

The Federation's argument is flawed both legally and factually. The premise of the argument is that, far from having no effect on the cost of dental services chosen by patients and their insurers, the provision of x rays will have too great an impact: it will lead to the reduction of costs through the selection of inadequate treatment. Precisely such a justification for withholding information from customers was rejected as illegitimate in the *Society of Professional Engineers* case. The argument is, in essence, that an unrestrained market in which consumers are given access to the information they believe to be relevant to their choices will lead them to make unwise and even dangerous choices. Such an argument amounts to "nothing less than a frontal assault on the basic policy of the Sherman Act." Society of Professional Engineers, 435 U.S. at 695. Moreover, there is no particular reason to believe that the provision of information will be more harmful to consumers in the market for dental services than in other markets. Insurers deciding what level of care to pay for are not themselves the recipients of those services, but it is by no means clear that they lack incentives to consider the welfare of the patient as well as the minimization of costs. They are themselves in competition for the patronage of the patients—or, in most cases, the unions or businesses that contract on their behalf for group insurance coverage—and must satisfy their potential customers not only that they will provide coverage at a reasonable cost, but also that that coverage will be adequate to meet their customers' dental needs. There is thus no more reason to expect dental insurance companies to sacrifice quality in return for cost savings than to believe this of consumers in, say, the market for engineering services. Accordingly, if noncompetitive quality-of-service justifications are inadmissible to justify the denial of information to consumers in the latter market, there is little reason to credit such justifications here.

In any event, the Commission did not, as the Federation suggests, refuse even to consider the quality of care justification for the withholding of x rays. Rather, the Commission held that the Federation had failed to introduce sufficient evidence to establish such a justification: "IFD has not pointed to any evidence—or even argued—that any consumers have in fact been harmed by alternative benefits determinations, or that actual determinations have been medically erroneous." The evidence before the Administrative Law Judge on this issue appears to have consisted entirely of expert opinion testimony, with the Federation's experts arguing that x rays generally provide an insufficient basis, standing alone, for dental diagnosis, and the Commission's experts testifying that x rays may be useful in assessing diagnosis of and appropriate treatment for a variety of dental complaints. The Commission was amply justified in concluding on the basis of this conflicting evidence that even if concern for the quality of patient care could under some circumstances serve as a justification for a restraint of the sort imposed here, the evidence did not support a finding that the careful use of x rays as a basis for evaluating insurance claims is in fact destructive of proper standards of dental care.[4]

In addition to arguing that its conspiracy did not effect an unreasonable restraint of trade, the Federation appears to renew its argument, pressed before both the Commission and the Court of Appeals, that the conspiracy to withhold x rays is immunized from antitrust scrutiny by virtue of a supposed policy of the State of Indiana against the evaluation of dental x rays by lay employees of insurance companies. Allegedly, such use of x rays by insurance companies—even where no claim was actually denied without examination of an x ray by a licensed dentist—would constitute unauthorized practice of dentistry by the insurance company and its employees. The Commission found that this claim had no basis in any authoritative source of Indiana law, and the Federation has not identified any adequate reason for rejecting the Commission's conclusion. Even if the Commission were incorrect in its reading of the law, however, the Federation's claim of immunity would fail. That a particular practice may be unlawful is not, in itself, a sufficient justification for collusion among competitors to prevent it. See Fashion Originators' Guild of America, Inc. v. FTC, 312 U.S. 457, 468 (1941). Anticompetitive collusion among private

4. It is undisputed that lay claims examiners employed by insurance companies have no authority to deny claims on the basis of examination of x rays; rather, initial screening of x rays serves only as a means of identifying cases that merit further scrutiny by the licensed dentists serving as consultants to the insurers. Any recommendation that benefits be denied or a less expensive course of treatment be pursued is based on the professional judgment of a licensed dentist that the materials available to him—x rays, claim forms, and whatever further diagnostic aids he chooses to consult—are sufficient to indicate that the treating dentist's recommendation is not necessary to the health of the patient. There is little basis for concluding that, where such a divergence of professional judgment exists, the treatment recommendation made by the patient's dentist should be assumed to be the one that in fact represents the best interests of the patient.

actors, even when its goal is consistent with state policy, acquires antitrust immunity only when it is actively supervised by the State. See Southern Motor Carriers Rate Conference, Inc. v. United States, 471 U.S. 48 (1985). There is no suggestion of any such active supervision here; accordingly, whether or not the policy that Federation has taken upon itself to advance is consistent with the policy of the State of Indiana, the Federation's activities are subject to Sherman Act condemnation.

V

The factual findings of the Commission regarding the effect of the Federation's policy of withholding x rays are supported by substantial evidence, and those findings are sufficient as a matter of law to establish a violation of § 1 of the Sherman Act, and, hence, § 5 of the Federal Trade Commission Act. Since there has been no suggestion that the cease-and-desist order entered by the Commission to remedy this violation is itself improper for any reason distinct from the claimed impropriety of the finding of a violation, the Commission's order must be sustained. The judgment of the Court of Appeals is accordingly reversed.

QUESTIONS ON THE IFD CASE

1. Is this a "boycott" case? How does the Court characterize the challenged practice? How might the restraint be characterized more precisely and accurately?

2. What reasons justify not applying a per se rule? Is there a naked restraint? (What does the Court say?) How great is the danger that, in the absence of a per se rule, plaintiffs will find cases like this one difficult to litigate and win, with the result that violations will be inadequately deterred?

3. Does the Court's holding and reasoning strengthen or weaken the *Wilk* case's ruling that a "patient-care motive" can justify a naked restraint?

4. Were the Indiana insurers engaged in the corporate practice of dentistry?

Competitor Collaboration in the Production of Information

Schachar v. American Academy of Ophthalmology, Inc.

United States Court of Appeals, Seventh Circuit, 1989.
870 F.2d 397

■ EASTERBROOK, CIRCUIT JUDGE.

There can be no restraint of trade without a restraint. That truism decides this case, in which eight ophthalmologists contend that the American Academy of Ophthalmology violated the antitrust laws by attaching the label "experimental" to radial keratotomy, a surgical procedure for correcting nearsightedness.

Nearsightedness (myopia) occurs when the cornea of the eye does not focus light on the retina. A thick cornea bends light excessively, so that the focal point falls short of the vision receptors. Glasses and contact lenses correct the problem by introducing an offsetting distortion; the net effect of the series of lenses is a proper focal point. Radial keratotomy corrects the problem surgically. The ophthalmologist makes shallow incisions along radii of the cornea; as the cornea heals it becomes flatter, and vision improves.

Svyatoslav Fyodorov of the Soviet Union devised radial keratotomy in 1973. American physicians, including some of the plaintiffs, started performing the operation in 1978. Even the most promising medical developments often turn out to have drawbacks, whose nature and magnitude should be determined. Many who have undergone radial keratotomy report improvement in their eyesight (sometimes so much change that they become farsighted). What are the long-run consequences? Most persons' visual acuity slowly changes with time. Does the eyesight of those who have had this operation change in different ways? Might the invasive procedure weaken the eye in a way that creates problems of a different kind? A surgical procedure used in Japan in the 1950s caused "corneal decompensation" about ten years later, a serious condition leading to blindness (avoidable with corneal transplants). Radial keratotomy is different, but once burned twice shy.

In January 1979 the National Advisory Eye Council, the principal advisory body to the National Eye Institute (part of the National Institutes of Health) called refractive keratoplasty (a group of surgical procedures that includes radial keratotomy) "experimental". In 1980 it applied this term to radial keratotomy specifically, calling on the profession to use restraint until more research could be done. As the federal government does not regulate surgical procedures, this was all a federal body could do. In June 1980 the board of directors of the American Academy of Ophthalmology—the largest association of ophthalmologists, with more than 9,400 members—endorsed the Eye Council's position. It issued a press release urging "patients, ophthalmologists and hospitals to approach [radial keratotomy] with caution until additional research is completed."

This suit under § 1 of the Sherman Act contends that the press release issued in 1980 was the upshot of a conspiracy among the Academy's members in restraint of trade. After a month of trial, the jury disagreed. The plaintiffs press objections to the jury instructions * * *. Mulling over the jury instructions would be pointless, however, for this case should not have gone to the jury; indeed it should not have gone to trial. All the Academy did is state as its position that radial keratotomy was "experimental" and issue a press release with a call for research. It did not require its members to desist from performing the operation or associating with those who do. It did not expel or discipline or even scowl at members who performed radial keratotomies. It did not induce hospitals to withhold permission to perform the procedure, or insurers to withhold payment; it has no authority over hospitals, insurers, state medical societies or licensing boards, and other persons who might be able to govern the performance of surgery.

Plaintiffs concede that the Academy did not attempt to coordinate activities with these groups, actors independent of the Academy. Although plaintiffs believe that the Academy's prestige influenced others' conduct, plaintiffs also concede that after the Academy's press release in 1980 hospitals still allowed them to perform radial keratotomies and many insurers reimbursed them for that work. In 1982 plaintiff Doyle Leslie performed 1,181 radial keratotomies; in 1983 he performed 1,314. Other plaintiffs performed fewer, and all believe that the demand for their services would have been greater if the Academy had not thrown its weight behind the position that their bread-and-butter was "experimental", but none maintains that the Academy prevented him from doing what he wished or imposed sanctions on those who facilitated the work. This uncontested fact required the district court to grant the Academy's motion for summary judgment and on this alternative ground we affirm the judgment in the Academy's favor.

* * *

Ophthalmologists are each others' rivals for custom. They offer competing procedures to cope with myopia—some surgical, some optical (glasses plus contact lenses of many kinds: hard, soft, extended wear). Plaintiffs say that the Academy is in the grip of professors and practitioners who favor conservative treatment, forever calling for more research (the better to justify the academics' requests for grants); plaintiffs portray themselves as the progressives, disdaining the Academy's fuddy-duddies in order to put the latest knowledge to work. Warfare among suppliers and their different products is competition. Antitrust law does not compel your competitor to praise your product or sponsor your work. To require cooperation or friendliness among rivals is to undercut the intellectual foundations of antitrust law. Unless one group of suppliers diminishes another's ability to peddle its wares * * *, there is not even the beginning of an antitrust case, no reason to investigate further to determine whether the restraint is "reasonable".

[W]hen a trade association provides information * * * but does not constrain others to follow its recommendations, it does not violate the antitrust laws. * * * An organization's towering reputation does not reduce its freedom to speak out. Speech informed, hence affected, demand for radial keratotomy, but the plaintiffs had no entitlement to consumers' favor. The Academy's declaration affected only the demand side of the market, and then only by appealing to consumers' (and third-party payors') better judgment. If such statements should be false or misleading or incomplete or just plain mistaken, the remedy is not antitrust litigation but more speech—the marketplace of ideas.

* * *

Plaintiffs' fundamental position, stated in its reply brief, is that: "Issuing such a statement [calling radial keratotomy 'experimental'] carried with it an obligation to the public, ophthalmologists, and third party payors to have studied the procedure and reached a considered opinion." Putting to one side the conundrum that once you have "studied" something it is no longer "experimental"—that the declaration of "experimental" status logically precedes the gathering of information—we do not perceive what this has to do with antitrust. * * * The Sherman Act is not a code of medical ethics or methodology, and whether radial keratotomy is "experimental" is a medical rather than a legal question.

AFFIRMED.

NOTES AND QUESTIONS ON THE SCHACHAR CASE

1. How did the actions of the professional group in *Schachar* differ from the actions of professionals penalized in the preceding cases? Are you satisfied that those cases are distinguishable? See generally Havighurst, Applying Antitrust Law to Collaboration in the Production of Information: The Case of Medical Technology Assessment, Law & Contemp. Probs., Spring 1988, p. 341.

Would the result have been different in *Schachar* if the Academy's position on radial keratotomy had been universally, or nearly universally, accepted by hospitals and health insurers, greatly reducing both the supply of the procedure and the demand for it—as well as the incomes of certain eye surgeons? Would it matter how this result was achieved? It so happened, see *Schachar*, 1988–1 Trade Cas. (CCH) ¶ 67,986, at 58,051 (N.D.Ill. 1988), that the Council of Medical Specialty Societies (of which the Academy was a member) routinely advised the Health Insurance Association of America (HIAA) of the status of new medical technologies. When the Academy declared radial keratotomy to be experimental, it was listed in an HIAA newsletter under the heading "Procedures Which Should Not Be Reimbursed Routinely by Third Party Payers Without Written Justification." Should the plaintiffs have made the Council and the HIAA (the leading trade association of health insurers) defendants in the case?

2. Judge Easterbrook apparently sees no sign of a restraint of trade when a private group merely publishes its opinion on a product or service being offered by competitors of its members. Would his view be the same in a case involving, not just a single pronouncement on a single surgical procedure, but a formal program for issuing authoritative pronouncements of a particular kind? In fact, many private standard-setting, certifying, credentialing, and accrediting bodies operate in the health care field, opining on such questions as the qualifications of individuals to perform various health care tasks, the acceptability of hospitals or other institutional providers of care, the adequacy of educational institutions or training programs of various kinds, and the necessity for or appropriateness of particular health services. These entities are frequently controlled by a dominant professional group (e.g., physicians), and the standards they set and apply (e.g., criteria for certification in a medical specialty or other occupational category, accrediting standards for hospitals or other institutional providers, or clinical practice guidelines) may enhance the welfare of the dominant group at the expense of other competitors. Although private standard setting and related activities are not unique to the health care field, such programs have been powerful tools by which professional interests have maintained their influence over their economic environment. See generally Havighurst & King, Private Credentialing of Health Care Personnel: An Antitrust Perspective (pts. 1 & 2), 9 Am.J.L. & Med. 131, 263 (1983).

Some analysts believe, contrary to the implication of Judge Easterbrook's opinion in *Schachar*, that the Sherman Act can and should be used to police private standard setting and accrediting programs. For example, a 1983 FTC study stated that a "standard is the product of joint action and restrains trade by diverting business from one competitor to another. * * * Standards activities by their nature restrain trade." Bureau of Consumer Protection, FTC, Standards and Certification 275–76 (Final Staff Report 1983). Do you agree? If so, what follows? If not, what can be done, legally, about private organizations that issue unfair or deceptive advice to consumers, thereby disadvantaging competitors and distorting market outcomes? Later materials—chapter 6(§§ C & D)—will address these questions in some depth.

3. *Problem on Antitrust Issues in Clinical Trials.* Imagine that the Academy in *Schachar*, concerned that radial keratotomy was giving ophthalmologists ("Os") a black eye (in fact, the procedure eventually proved moderately efficacious and reasonably safe), had launched a nationwide randomized clinical trial (RCT) to test the efficacy and cost-effectiveness of the procedure in treating a wide range of conditions. Imagine further: In order to bring as many patients as possible into the study and thus to speed the appearance of definitive results, the Academy declared it unethical for any O to undertake the procedure except as a participant in the RCT. In accordance with good scientific practice, participation in the RCT meant that a physician, after obtaining a patient's informed consent to participate in the experiment, had to consent to the patient's being randomly assigned to one of several groups that would receive different treatments. A patient refusing to give his consent to participate in the experiment could receive the treatment of his choice. According to the Academy, however, a physician could not ethically recommend the operation to a nonparticipant in the experiment, because there was as yet no scientific basis for preferring the treatment over ordinary eyeglasses or contact lenses. The Academy persuaded several private insurers and employers to reimburse the cost of the operation only if the O performing it was participating in the RCT or only if the insured himself agreed to participate in the experiment.

Next imagine that the Academy has been sued in a class action under the antitrust laws by Dr. I. Care, an early pioneer of radial keratotomy. Dr. Care alleges that, like other class members, she cannot participate in the RCT because she cannot ethically deny her patients a procedure in which she believes. She claims that her medical practice and the practices of other Os have been adversely affected because many of their private patients cannot obtain reimbursement for the operation. She further alleges that she and others like her have been coerced by the Academy's threat to terminate their memberships for unethical practices and that they have been denied the freedom to practice their profession in accordance with their state-granted licenses.

You have been asked to evaluate Dr. Care's antitrust case against the Academy. What are the precise harms to competition? Can you argue that the Academy's activities are procompetitive? Are its restraints defensible as ancillary restraints? How might the less-restrictive-alternative requirement apply? See Havighurst, *Law & Contemp. Probs.*, at 369–73.

NOTES AND QUESTIONS ON PROFESSION–SPONSORED PEER REVIEW PROGRAMS

1. In Union Labor Life Ins. Co. v. Pireno, 458 U.S. 119 (1982), the Supreme Court considered "an alleged conspiracy to eliminate price competition among chiropractors, by means of a 'peer review committee' that advised an insurance company whether particular chiropractors' treatments and fees were 'necessary' and 'reasonable.' " Although the Court ruled only on the narrow question "whether the alleged conspiracy is exempt from federal antitrust laws as part of the 'business of insurance' within the meaning of the McCarran–Ferguson Act," 15 U.S.C. §§ 1011–15 (1994), holding it was not, the substantive antitrust issues raised by profession-sponsored peer review programs are of great conceptual and historical interest. The chiropractic association's program that questioned the reasonableness of Dr. Pireno's fees and the necessity for certain professional services he rendered closely resembled similar peer review programs that were for many years instrumental in maintaining the medical profession's control of health care financing.

Was there more at stake in the *Pireno* case than Dr. Pireno's freedom to charge what he believed his services were worth and to adopt innovative methods in treating his patients? What was the interest of consumers? On what basis might the antitrust laws limit the right of the chiropractic organization to operate a peer review program? Note that the profession-appointed peer reviewers purported to perform tasks of the kind that the dental insurers in the *IFD* case undertook to perform for themselves. Whom would you prefer to have looking out for your interests—organized practitioners or your health insurer? Does antitrust law finally control who may perform this service in your case? How would you explain to a client, a chiropractor who had selflessly dedicated himself to developing the association's peer review program, why he is especially vulnerable to antitrust suits?

2. *Antitrust Law and Professional Peer Review.* How would you defend a peer review body against an antitrust suit? Partly because peer reviewers view themselves as engaging in professional self-regulation, their lawyers often defend them on general public interest grounds, asserting the "reasonableness" of their actions—as if a worthy purpose (or the fixing of "reasonable" prices) could justify a restraint of trade. Instead of conceding the main premise of the plaintiff's case, however, could you argue, much as Judge Easterbrook argued for the professional body in *Schachar*, that peer review does not restrain trade at all, is not private regulation, and indeed is procompetitive, not anticompetitive? In fact, if the program does no more than generate advice useful to independent decision makers in a competitive market, there is no obvious restraint. The issue must therefore be faced under the Rule of Reason.

What hazards might there be in allowing a powerful and influential organization of professionals to organize a peer review effort? What legal requirements flow from the existence of such hazards? What factual inquiries would you make to determine whether these hazards have materialized? Consider separately the cases of fee, utilization, and quality-oriented peer review by profession-sponsored committees. See generally Havighurst, Professional Peer Review and the Antitrust Laws, 36 Case W.Res.L.Rev. 1117 (1986).

3. *Fee Review.* Recall that the Supreme Court said in *Goldfarb* that "a purely advisory fee schedule issued to provide guidelines" would present "a different question." Even though there might be no obvious agreement to follow an advisory fee schedule, its promulgation could, like a standardized fee-setting formula, easily result in noncompetitive prices. Should the courts undertake to determine whether generally uniform adherence to the fee schedule ("conscious parallelism") reflected practitioners' unilateral choices or collective action? Or should they adopt a market-failure rationale for looking the other way? Is there a middle ground?

Under the antitrust requirement that actions of powerful competitor groups must be tailored to endanger competition as little as reasonably possible (that is, the less-restrictive-alternative requirement), antitrust authorities have insisted that peer reviewers not employ an announced maximum-fee schedule or pricing formula that might serve as an invitation to providers to raise below-ceiling prices. They have, however, approved profession-sponsored programs for reviewing fees on an ad hoc, retrospective basis as long as they do not publish their review standards and do nothing to force insurers or others to employ the peer reviewers instead of electing some other method of cost control. See, e.g., Iowa Dental Ass'n, 99 F.T.C. 648 (1982) (advisory opinion). Thus, peer review of practitioners' charges appears permissible (because procompetitive) if it is designed to give advice on pricing matters to payers but not if it is advisory to providers. See also Zinser v. Rose, 868 F.2d 938 (7th Cir.1989) (no unlawful vertical price-fixing conspiracy found between insurer and two chiropractors advising it concerning plaintiff chiropractors' fees).

4. *Utilization Review.* Utilization review is often undertaken in conjunction with fee review, as in *Pireno*. By itself, however, utilization review, even with published standards (appropriate lengths of stay, hospital admissions criteria, clinical practice guidelines, etc.), is less likely to trigger an antitrust suit. Nevertheless, there was at one time

> a substantial danger that private health insurers would unanimously embrace the medical profession's preferred methods of fee and utilization review, eschewing alternative methods of controlling their costs and in effect letting the profession dictate overall spending. Although this danger has diminished as competition has intensified, such unanimity could still appear in a given local market, warranting an antitrust investigation. If profession-sponsored peer review is instrumental in curbing insurers' competitive independence and thus protecting physicians from competitive pressures, antitrust law might be invoked to rectify the situation.

Havighurst, supra, at 1148–49. For a more sanguine view, see Rhode Island PSRO, 101 F.T.C. 1010 (1983) (advisory opinion).

5. *Quality-Oriented Peer Review.* Quality standards promulgated by a dominant professional organization also present the risk that provider performance will be dictated by professional fiat, contrary to the decentralization premise of the antitrust laws. The danger, however, is not so much that professionals will tacitly agree to adhere to the cartel's policies as that they will be coerced into following possibly inefficient standards by fear of malpractice suits, of action by licensing authorities, of collegial criticism, and of bad publicity. Nevertheless, protecting consumers against substandard providers or substandard practice may be a valuable social benefit that cannot be obtained without some risk of impairing practitioners' competitive independence and the industry's capacity for responsible innovation. The dilemma for antitrust analysis is similar to that presented by profession-sponsored accrediting and credentialing bodies, which are examined in chapter 6(§§ C & D). Discussion at that point may suggest an appropriate stance for courts to adopt in evaluating quality-assurance efforts of professional peer review bodies and the promulgation by professional societies of clinical practice guidelines.

6. *Peer Review in the Medicare Program.* In the Medicare program, major responsibility for assuring the medical appropriateness and quality of services to beneficiaries is currently borne by so-called Peer Review Organizations (PROs). PROs are statewide private organizations with which the federal government contracts for specified services pursuant to the Peer Review Improvement Act of 1982, Pub.L. No. 97–248, § 143, 96 Stat. 382, 385, 387 (codified at 42 U.S.C. § 1320c–3). Prior to 1982, similar functions were performed by similar entities called Professional Standards Review Organizations (PSROs), which were first set up under the Social Security Amendments of 1972. PSROs were intended to perform for Medicare tasks similar to those that profession-designated peer reviewers performed for private health insurers during that same era.

Under the PRO legislation, two types of statewide organizations are eligible for designation as a PRO. Special preference is given to "physician-sponsored organizations," which are defined in regulations as entities composed of at least 10% of the area's licensed practicing physicians. 42 C.F.R. § 462.102(b) (1995). The AMA sought to obtain a preference for organizations representing at least 25% of the area's physicians (as under the earlier PSRO law). See Editorial, Am.Med.News, Oct. 7, 1983, at 3. Although the action of HCFA in setting the lower percentage test for physician sponsorship may have somewhat attenuated the connection between physician-sponsored PROs and organized medicine, the cited regulations also require that such PROs be "representative" (in what sense do you suppose HCFA means? political or statistical?) of area physicians. Because the Peer Review Improvement Act provided that other entities, including a financial intermediary such as a Blue Cross plan, could be designated as the area PRO (as a "physician-access organization") if a physician-sponsored group could not be identified within six months, state medical societies had a strong incentive to organize a PRO of their own. Most PRO contracts have gone to groups organized with medical society support. Legislation in 1987 gave "in-state organizations" certain advantages in obtaining a PRO contract. Because both PSROs and PROs have been dominated by practicing physicians, it is appropriate to consider them in some depth in the current context. Government's delegation of important powers to these entities revealed not only the political strength of organized medicine but also the strength of the old paradigm of medical decision making, the same paradigm that long supported tolerance for collective professional action under the antitrust laws.

Although PROs emerged in 1982 as a result of some relatively minor modifications of the PSRO legislation, Congress's adoption in the following year of the DRG-based PPS for Medicare hospital payments substantially changed the specific functions that the Medicare program needed to have performed. Under cost reimbursement, PSROs were needed to police excessive lengths of stay and overutilization of in-hospital services; with prospective pricing based on DRGs, these things (except for the number of admissions) could be expected largely to take care of themselves. Simultaneously, however, because of the PPS's new economizing incentives, there developed a more urgent need to police underservice and overeconomizing—premature discharge, for example.

The duties of PROs are mostly statutory but are spelled out in detail, first, in the "scope of work" section of HCFA's periodic requests for contract proposals, then in the resulting HCFA/PRO contract, and most extensively in HCFA's periodically updated PRO Manual. See generally 2 Medicare & Medicaid Guide (CCH) ¶ 12,850 et seq.; K. Lohr, Peer Review Organizations: Quality Assurance in Medicare 22–41 (Rand Corp.1985). PRO functions are of several types. The PRO's primary task is to determine whether the government should pay for particular services. Review for this purpose focuses on such things as the medical necessity for and reasonableness of the treatment provided, the economic appropriateness of the treatment site (e.g., of hospital versus outpatient treatment), the medical appropriateness of hospital admissions and discharges, and the data provided to support the request for payment. A PRO's denial of payment on these or other grounds is conclusive, although limited provision is made for reconsideration and administrative appeal. PROs are also charged with monitoring the quality of care rendered to Medicare beneficiaries. See Greene v. Bowen, 639 F.Supp. 554 (E.D.Cal.1986) (reproduced in chapter 6(§B)).

The role and position of PROs in the Medicare system has been described by one court as follows:

> To receive payment under PPS, hospitals must have an agreement with a Utilization and Quality Control Peer Review Organization ("PRO"). 42 U.S.C. § 1395cc(a)(1)(F). The PRO generally is responsible for reviewing a hospital's administration of the Medicare Program: it determines whether the services provided to Medicare beneficiaries are medically necessary and allowable under the program, whether the quality of care meets professionally recognized standards, and whether proposed in-hospital care could be provided more economically on an out-patient basis. The PRO also is responsible for determining, based on its review, whether Medicare shall make payment for medical services. The PRO determination of whether payment shall be made generally is conclusive.
>
> HHS is directed to designate geographic areas corresponding to each state, to be served by individual PROs. HHS then must enter agreements, for an initial two-year term, with a PRO in each area. HHS has considerable discretion in negotiating each of these contracts. It may negotiate different agreements with each PRO; it may make agreements without regard to any federal laws regarding contracts which it determines to be inconsistent with the PRO program.
>
> To qualify as a PRO an entity must be composed of a sufficient number of physicians practicing in the PRO area to carry out the requisite review functions. The contract between the PRO and HHS must include negotiated objectives against which PROs will be judged and must contain negotiated specifications for use of regional norms, or modification of national norms, for performing review functions. The PRO must specify in its contract the types of cases it will review. HHS has entered into contracts with a PRO in each PRO area.
>
> To participate in the Medicare program, hospitals must enter into agreements with the PRO in its area. The agreement between the hospital and the PRO must allow PROs to review the validity of diagnostic information provided by the hospital, to review the completeness, adequacy and quality of care provided, to review the appropriateness of hospital admissions, and to review the appropriateness of care provided for which extra Medicare payments are sought.

AHA v. Bowen, 640 F.Supp. 453, 457 (D.D.C.1986). See generally K. Lohr, supra.

What do you think about the policy of turning major responsibilities in the administration of the Medicare program over to private organizations that are for the most part closely associated with organized medicine? The PSRO program raised this question most sharply, because PSROs were even more representative of local physicians than PROs and because they were asked even more pointedly to decide whether Medicare should pay for particular medical services. The duties of PSROs thus drew into sharp focus the trade-offs between cost and quality encountered in public financing of health care. The decision in 1972 to enlist profession-sponsored peer review bodies in the cost-containment effort revealed how deep-seated was the public's acceptance at that time of the medical profession as a source of wisdom on issues of intense societal concern—including the value to be placed on medical services in comparison with other things that might be purchased with scarce resources. What does the recent interest in capitation in public programs imply about how such resource-allocation decisions should be made? (Does the answer depend on how closely government chooses to specify the benefits and practices of the private plans that are authorized to compete for beneficiaries' business?) Are economizing choices more likely to be made wisely and efficiently in a privatized system, in a professionally managed system, or in a publicly administered or regulated system?

An illuminating question arose under the PSRO program as to whether PSROs were expected to focus primarily on controlling program costs or were instead to emphasize quality considerations. The statute and the legislative history focused rather clearly on cost and recognized quality of care only as a constraint on cost-containment efforts, not as an affirmative program goal. Nevertheless, when DHEW set out to enlist physician cooperation in forming PSROs, the program's emphasis was altered. "In the rhetoric of this highly politicized debate, 'quality of care' became something of a 'code word' for professional prerogatives, and 'cost control' was soft-pedaled, having become a 'buzz word' for government interference." Havighurst & Blumstein, Coping with Quality/Cost Trade-offs in Medical Care: The Role of PSROs, 70 Nw.U.L.Rev. 6, 41 (1975) (reviewing the legislative history and implementation of the program in light of the issues raised here). An AMA official made the following revealing recommendation to his professional colleagues:

> It seems apparent after examining the legislation that the primary, if not total intent of the program is to contain the cost of medical care. Despite the legislative intent of the program, however, the concern of health care providers and insurers should be to reassign priorities of the PSRO program to assure that maintenance of high quality care is the primary focus of PSROs.

Theodore, Towards a Strategy for Evaluating PSROs, Westchester Med. Bull., Nov. 1974. What do you think about the proposal to "reassign" Congress's priorities?

Although PROs primarily serve the Medicare program, they may also provide claims and utilization review services to private insurers and self-insured employers. Indeed, the federal statute requires that a PRO contracting with Medicare must "make available its facilities and resources for contracting with private and public entities paying for health care in its area for review, as feasible and appropriate, of services reimbursed by such entities." 42 U.S.C. § 1320c–3(a)(11) (1994). Would a PRO sponsored by professional interests (some may have other sponsorship) have to worry about antitrust risks in its private peer review activities? Despite the argument that such activities are expressly mandated by federal law and thus exempt, the statute says only that a PRO must make its "facilities and resources" available to the private sector. It may thus contemplate that private payers will delegate to PROs only the administrative task of applying the payer's own standards to particular cases and not the more crucial responsibility of establishing the standards themselves. It is at least arguable that Congress did not visualize that PROs would perform for private payers the same coverage definition functions that PSROs performed for Medicare under cost reimbursement.

7. *The Health Care Quality Improvement Act.* Congress passed this legislation in 1986 to reduce the threat of legal liability that, in Congress's view, "unreasonably discourage[d] physicians from participating in effective professional peer review." 42 U.S.C. § 11101(5) (1994). The Act somewhat increases the burden of proof of a plaintiff challenging a "professional review action" of "a professional review body," if certain statutory conditions are met. It will be examined in greater detail in chapter 5(§C).

SECTION C: ANTITRUST LAW AND ANTICOMPETITIVE GOVERNMENTAL ACTION

The State-Action Antitrust Defense

In re Massachusetts Board of Registration in Optometry

Federal Trade Commission, 1988
110 F.T.C. 549

■ By CALVANI, COMMISSIONER:

* * *

Respondent Massachusetts Board of Registration in Optometry is charged with engaging in practices constituting (1) unfair methods of competition and (2) unfair or deceptive acts or practices that violate Section 5 of the Federal Trade Commission Act, 15 U.S.C. § 45. The complaint alleges that respondent has restrained competition among optometrists in the Commonwealth of Massachusetts by unreasonably restricting truthful advertising.

Respondent is a state agency that regulates the practice of optometry in Massachusetts. But the Massachusetts Legislature has vested respondent with only limited authority to regulate advertising. Section 61 of Mass. Gen. Laws Ann., ch. 112, provides that:

> Except as otherwise provided in this chapter, no such board shall make any rule or regulation prohibiting the advertising or dissemination of truthful information concerning the price, nature and availability of goods and services to consumers, the effect of which would be to restrain trade or lessen competition.

In promulgating this law the Massachusetts Legislature declared that:

> any ordinance, rule or regulation promulgated by an agency of the commonwealth or political subdivision thereof which prohibits or limits competitive advertising relating to the price of consumer goods or services shall be void as against public policy.

These statutes apply to the regulations promulgated by the respondent.

Notwithstanding the determination by the Massachusetts Legislature limiting respondent's authority to issue regulations restricting truthful competitive advertising, on two occasions respondent promulgated regulations that are the subject of the challenge in this action. * * * Section 3.08 of respondent's regulations prohibited any optometrist from allowing "the use of his name or professional ability by an optical establishment for the financial gain of such establishment;" [in later regulations, the Board] replaced Section 3.12 of its regulations with an explicit restriction on discount advertising; and added two other explicit restrictions on advertising. Section 5.11(d) declared "advertising which uses testimonials" to be contrary to the public interest. Section 5.11(1)(a) prohibited advertising that appeared to be "sensational" or "flamboyant." * * *

After a three-week trial, Administrative Law Judge James P. Timony * * * found that respondent has attempted to slow the growth of "commercial" optometric practice through its restraints on truthful advertising, and that the result has been higher prices for eye care in Massachusetts. He found that respondent's actions were controlled by practicing optometrists who stood to benefit financially from the restraints on competition and ruled that respondent's conduct constituted a "combination or conspiracy." He further ruled that respondent's ban on discount advertising was per se unlawful, and that all of the restraints were unlawful under the rule of reason, finding no valid justification for respondent's suppression of broad categories of truthful information about prices and services offered by optometrists.

Judge Timony rejected respondent's state action defense and held that respondent's actions constituted unfair methods of competition and unfair acts or practices in violation of Section 5. * * *

[Reviewing recent precedents, the Commission, inter alia, set forth the test for the legality of competitor collaboration that was quoted near the end of the Note on the Antitrust Rule of Reason earlier in this chapter.]

B. The Commission's Jurisdiction

Respondent argued below that it was not a "person" within the meaning of Section 5 of the Federal Trade Commission Act. * * *

"Person" is not specifically defined within the Commission's organic statute. While defined in both the Sherman and Clayton Acts, state boards are not specifically included in the definitions. Nonetheless, local governments, as agents of the state, have been held to be persons within the meaning of the Sherman Act and Clayton Act. City of Lafayette v. Louisiana Power & Light Co., 435 U.S. 389, 394–97 (1978). There the Court relied on the presumption against implied exclusions from coverage to the antitrust laws. Id. at 398. State and county entities are persons within the meaning of the Robinson–Patman Act, 15 U.S.C. 2(a) (1982). Jefferson County Pharmaceutical Association v. Abbott Laboratories, 460 U.S. 150, 155–56 (1983). Terms in the Federal Trade Commission Act, the Sherman Act, and Clayton Act should be construed together. United States v. American Building Maintenance Industries, 422 U.S. 271, 277–78 (1975). Accordingly, we hold that respondent is a "person" for purposes of jurisdiction under the Federal Trade Commission Act. * * *

C. The Contract, Combination & Conspiracy Requirement

Respondent urges that complaint counsel has not satisfied the duality requirement of Section 1 of the Sherman Act [and] that respondent is a single entity incapable of conspiring with itself.

We disagree. The Supreme Court and lower courts have recently focused on whether there are separate economic entities in play in determining whether a contract, combination or conspiracy is present. In Copperweld Corp. v. Independence Tube Corp., 467 U.S. 752 (1984), the Court found that a parent corporation was incapable of conspiring with its wholly-owned subsidiary, stressing that economic reality and not formalism control in assessing whether "separate economic entities" engaged in a common course of action. Applying the *Copperweld* analysis, Judge Timony correctly found that respondent members have separate economic identities and thus engage in a combination when they act together on the Board. He noted that each optometrist on the Board is principally engaged in the private practice of optometry in the market that respondent regulates. Absent respondent members' agreement that imposed the regulations at issue, the members and all other optometrists in the Commonwealth would be free to compete with each other by individually deciding whether to advertise. It is precisely such combinations to suppress competition that are prohibited by Section 1 of the Sherman Act.

* * *

Our conclusion that the members of the Board are capable of conspiring is supported by the case law. The Supreme Court, in Hoover v. Ronwin, 466 U.S. 558, 575 (1984), acknowledged that the members of the Arizona committee of bar examiners—a state agency composed of practicing lawyers—could conspire with each other. In holding that their actions were immune under the state action doctrine because the challenged conduct was actually that of Arizona Supreme Court, the Court stated that "[c]onspire as they might," the committee members could not affect what was ultimately within the control of the Arizona Supreme Court. Thus the Supreme Court has recognized that state board members are capable of conspiring with each other.

* * *

D. State Action Immunity

The state action immunity doctrine is the vehicle created by the Supreme Court to resolve conflict between the national policy of competition embodied in the federal antitrust laws and state regulation in our federal system. State action immunity shields the activity challenged here if: (a) the party is acting as the sovereign state; or (b) the state elects to insulate the conduct by adhering to certain narrowly prescribed procedures.

1. Conduct by the State as Sovereign

If a State, acting as sovereign, restrains competition, its actions are ipso facto immune from federal antitrust laws. *Hoover v. Ronwin*, 466 U.S. at 567–68. Respondent argues that as a matter of state law, it exercises, sovereign, statewide authority over the practice of optometry and that it is therefore immune from prosecution.

We disagree. The Supreme Court has accorded only legislatures and courts status as sovereign. *Hoover v. Ronwin*, 466 U.S. at 568. The Court has not accorded other state subdivisions status as the sovereign. For example, although municipalities are state subdivisions, the Court has not accorded them status as the sovereign entity. Community Communications Co. v. Boulder, 455 U.S. 40, 44–50 (1982); *City of Lafayette v. Louisiana Power & Light Co.*, 435 U.S. at 411.

Further, federal appellate and district court rulings involving state regulatory boards have not held that such boards are, merely by virtue of their governmental status, "the state acting as sovereign" for purposes of immunity under Parker v. Brown, 317 U.S. 341 (1943). In Federal Trade Commission v. Monahan, 832 F.2d 688, 689 (1st Cir.1987), cert. denied, 108 S. Ct. 1289 (1988), the First Circuit declared that the Massachusetts Board of Registration in Pharmacy is not the sovereign, but "a subordinated governmental unit." In this and other cases, the courts have looked to state policy as articulated in enactments of the legislature. Employing the same method of analysis as used in these cases, we hold that the respondent is not entitled to immunity as the sovereign.

2. Conduct That Is Immunized by the State

Second, under the state action doctrine, a state may insulate a regulatory regime from federal antitrust scrutiny where two criteria are satisfied. California Retail Liquor Dealers Association v. Midcal Aluminum, Inc., 445 U.S. 97, 105 (1980). First, the challenged restraint must be "one clearly articulated and affirmatively expressed as state policy," and, second, the policy must be "actively supervised" by the state itself. Id. (quoting *City of Lafayette v. Louisiana Power & Light Co.*, 435 U.S. at 410). However, in Town of Hallie v. City of Eau Claire, 471 U.S. 34, 47 (1985), the Court held that the second prong of the Midcal test, i.e., active supervision, need not be satisfied in the context of local government regulation where the defendant is an organ of local government. We need not reach that question here as complaint counsel and respondent agree that the Commonwealth need not demonstrate active supervision to establish state action immunity in this case.

We now address the first, and determinative prong of the test. Is there a clear articulation of a state policy to displace competition by regulation in the case at bar? Massachusetts law provides the answer to this question. [The Commission again quotes the statutory language quoted earlier in its opinion.] Rather obviously, the Commonwealth articulated a policy favoring—not displacing—competition. * * * Finding no clear articulation to displace competition by state regulation, we find that the state action immunity doctrine is inapplicable to the instant case. * * *

[The Commission issued "an order prohibiting respondent from continuing to engage in the same or similar unlawful activities in the future."]

NOTES ON THE MAKEUP OF STATE REGULATORY BOARDS

1. *Board Composition.* According to the FTC's complaint in the preceding case, four of the five members of the respondent state agency were private optometrists who "may, and do, continue to engage in the business of providing optometric services for a fee." It is, in fact, common for state licensing boards to be controlled by practicing professionals in this fashion. Indeed, some states go as far as authorizing professional bodies to nominate the slates from which the governor must pick appointees to regulatory boards. The following paragraphs address some of the constitutional and administrative law issues raised by such regulatory schemes. The antitrust issues are addressed separately.

2. *Delegation.* In United Chiropractors of Washington, Inc. v. State, 90 Wash.2d 1, 578 P.2d 38 (1978) (en banc), the plaintiff organization complained that two other organizations of chiropractors were empowered to designate members of the licensing and disciplinary boards in the field, leaving its members at an arguable regulatory disadvantage. The court discussed the delegation of legislative and executive authority to private interests as follows (id. at 4–5):

> This court has previously held unconstitutional the legislature's delegation of authority to a private association to control licensing of physicians through granting or refusing accreditation to schools of medicine. State ex rel. Kirschner v. Urquhart, 50 Wn.2d 131, 310 P.2d 261 (1957). That decision rested upon the court's conclusion that "[l]egislative power is nondelegable." Since that time, however, we have recognized that this rule unreasonably restricts the alternatives available to the legislature in approaching a problem or issue. In place of the rule that legislative power is nondelegable, we have substituted a rule that delegation is permissible when (1) the legislature has provided standards or guidelines which define in general terms what is to be done and the instrumentality or administrative body which is to accomplish it; and (2) that procedural safeguards exist to control arbitrary administrative action and any administrative abuse of discretion. * * * However, this court has not had occasion since adopting this new standard to consider its applicability to legislation involving delegation to private parties.
>
> Delegation to a private organization raises concerns not present in the ordinary delegation of authority to a governmental administrative

agency. The courts of other states have found a violation of the basic governmental framework in such delegations.

Several state courts have indeed treated statutes giving a professional society a role in selecting licensing board members as instances of unconstitutional delegation. E.g., Rogers v. Medical Ass'n, 244 Ga. 151, 259 S.E.2d 85 (1979) (invalidating requirement that governor appoint physician members of board of medical examiners from society's list of nominees); Toussaint v. State Bd. of Med. Examiners, 285 S.C. 266, 329 S.E.2d 433 (1985) (invalidating requirement of membership in state society). The majority view, however, is apparently that such statutes are not unconstitutional delegations of the appointment power or legislative power to private interests. For example, a Mississippi statute similar to the one in the *Rogers* case, supra, was upheld both in Clark v. State ex rel. Mississippi State Med. Ass'n, 381 So.2d 1046 (Miss.1980), and in Finch v. Mississippi State Med. Ass'n, 594 F.2d 163 (5th Cir.1979) (under federal law). The latter decision relied in part on Friedman v. Rogers, 440 U.S. 1 (1979) (partially reproduced in chapter 3), where the Supreme Court held, inter alia, that a statute requiring that optometry board members be members of a certain professional association was "reasonably related to the State's legitimate purpose of securing a Board that will administer the Act faithfully." Id. at 17.

The excerpt from *United Chiropractors* cites an earlier decision invalidating state reliance on a profession-sponsored private accreditor to determine which schools' graduates are eligible for medical licensure. *Contra* Lucas v. Maine Comm'n of Pharmacy, 472 A.2d 904 (Me.1984). Materials in chapter 6(§§ C & D) will consider private accrediting and credentialing programs and the legal significance of reliance thereon by public agencies.

3. *Due Process*. The Washington court in the *United Chiropractors* case, supra, instead of invoking antidelegation principles as such, condemned the arrangement for licensing and disciplining chiropractors on the ground that "this delegation violates the constitutional due process rights of those chiropractors who do not belong to the legislatively favored organizations." The court explained (id. at 7–8),

> Our due process objection to these particular statutes is based on several factors. One such factor is the nature of the appointive power itself. The private organizations to which the appointment power is delegated are subject to few standards in selecting the members of the two boards. As a result, each legislatively favored organization may make its selections based solely upon its potential appointees' ability and inclination to advance that group's private interests and reflect only that group's opinions and beliefs regarding chiropractic practice. This may be accomplished without any effective power of elected officials to veto or disallow the selections made, and without providing nonmember chiropractors any means of objecting to or challenging the appointees who will govern their profession. Important also is the nature of the power exercised by the board once the private organizations have made the appointments. The statutes vest the boards with

> the power to make individualized, quasi-judicial decisions, rather than limiting their role to a generalized supervisory or advisory capacity. Appeals from the decisions of the boards are either not provided for or provided for under general administrative review standards, thus restricting judicial control and supervision of the boards. The boards may, without significant interference, advance the pecuniary interests of the members of the favored groups through their licensing and disciplinary practices and standards. In sum, the appointment powers of the favored groups, coupled with the power of the boards once appointments are made, constitute due process defects in the statutory procedures.

(Do you agree that the potential for denying due process to competitors of the favored chiropractors is the principal concern here? What other interests are at stake? What legal doctrines are available to protect these interests?)

The U.S. Supreme Court found sufficient risk of bias in the adjudications of an Alabama licensing board to constitute a denial of due process in Gibson v. Berryhill, 411 U.S. 564 (1973). The Alabama Optometric Association, whose membership was limited to independent (professional) optometrists, had filed a complaint before the Alabama Board of Optometry against optometrists employed by Lee Optical Company, a for-profit corporation. The charge was that acceptance of such employment by the optometrists constituted unethical contract practice and violated Alabama law. Noting that the Alabama Board of Optometry was composed entirely of Association members who had an economic stake in curbing the practice being challenged, the Court found that due process was denied in the administrative proceeding.

In Withrow v. Larkin, 421 U.S. 35 (1975), the Supreme Court held that procedural due process was not denied by a Wisconsin statute that empowered a state board composed of physicians both to investigate a physician's alleged professional misconduct and to conduct subsequent hearings to determine whether the physician's license should be suspended or revoked. A similar holding in a state court is Washington State Med. Discip. Bd. v. Johnston, 99 Wash.2d 466, 663 P.2d 457 (1983) ("appearance of fairness" doctrine did not require separation of investigative and adjudicative functions in case involving physician's use of "natural remedies" and unlicensed personnel).

NOTES AND QUESTIONS ON THE POTENTIAL ANTITRUST LIABILITY OF LICENSING AND REGULATORY BOARDS

1. *The Issues.* The student should have been surprised to learn, in the *Mass. Board* case, that the federal antitrust laws may apply to an agency of state government that was expressly created to regulate a licensed profession in the public interest. Is there a possible remedy here for the anticompetitive abuses that might be anticipated when a state legislature confers regulatory powers on a board composed of practicing professionals or of persons selected by or from the ranks of the dominant professional association? Note that, although the FTC's jurisdiction apparently extends to a "person" such as the respondent in *Mass. Board*, a state acting in its sovereign capacity is not deemed a "person" under the FTC Act. California State Bd. of Optometry v. FTC, 910 F.2d 976 (D.C.Cir.1990) (invalidating, for want of jurisdiction, the FTC's "Eyeglasses II" rule condemning certain state laws restricting practice of optometry).

Three somewhat separate issues may be identified, although courts do not always distinguish adequately between them. First, can a state agency itself violate the federal antitrust statutes? Second, when does state regulation confer federal antitrust immunity? Third, when might federal law preempt the field, rendering state requirements that are inconsistent with the policies of the Sherman Act unconstitutional under the Supremacy Clause?

2. *Action of the State Itself or State–Authorized Agency Action?* In Hoover v. Ronwin, 466 U.S. 558 (1984), discussed in *Mass. Board*, the Supreme Court held that the so-called state-action doctrine immunized from antitrust scrutiny the administration of bar examinations by a committee of practicing attorneys appointed by the Arizona Supreme Court. A candidate for admission to the bar claimed that the committee had set the passing grade on the bar exam with reference to the number of licensed new attorneys it thought desirable rather than with reference to some suitable level of minimum competence. The Court held that the practice was exempt from the Sherman Act under the state-action doctrine of Parker v. Brown, 317 U.S. 341 (1943), reasoning that the action challenged was in reality that of the Arizona Supreme Court itself and not a private body. "[A]lthough the Arizona Supreme Court necessarily delegated the administration of the admissions process to the Committee, the court itself approved the particular grading formula and retained the sole authority to determine who should be admitted to the practice of law in Arizona." 466 U.S. at 573.

Justice Stevens, dissenting, argued that the state-action doctrine was inapplicable because the challenged practice was not that of the Arizona Supreme Court but rather was that of private "market participants [who] are allegedly attempting to protect their competitive position through a misuse of their powers." Id. at 586. In his view, the law, in order to avoid the risk that public power will be exercised for private benefit when authority is delegated to market participants, requires (1) that state policies displacing competition must be "clearly articulated and affirmatively expressed" by the state legislature (or, in this case, by the state supreme court) and (2) that entities that do not qualify as the state itself must be actively supervised by the state in exercising the power to limit competition. Id. at 585 (citing Community Communications Co., Inc. v. Boulder, 455 U.S. 40 (1982); California Retail Liquor Dealers Ass'n v. Midcal Aluminum, Inc., 445 U.S. 97 (1980)). He concluded that the Arizona Supreme Court had directed the committee to employ only the criterion of competence.

The majority in *Hoover v. Ronwin* differed with Justice Stevens only over the status of the bar committee and its relationship with the Arizona Supreme Court. In dictum it reaffirmed the two-part test from the *Midcal Aluminum* case, supra (outlined by Justice Stevens) for determining whether *Parker* immunity applies to anticompetitive actions taken under state authority. The FTC opinion in *Mass. Board* restates this black-letter rule, holding the "first prong" of the test unsatisfied. It also notes, however, that the "second prong" of the test—the "active supervision" requirement, see generally FTC v. Ticor Title Ins. Co., 504 U.S. 621 (1992)—may be relaxed in the case of state agencies. (Can you see why?) This result is said to follow from the Supreme Court's decision in Town of Hallie v. City of Eau Claire, 471 U.S. 34 (1985) (active supervision requirement held inapplicable to municipalities). It seems likely that state agencies and their members will not be held liable for antitrust violations simply because their official actions were not supervised by the state in some specific fashion; general legislative, executive, and judicial oversight is probably sufficient.

As to the first prong of the *Midcal* test, subsequent decisions, most notably *Town of Hallie*, have held that political subdivisions need demonstrate no more than that anticompetitive results were "a foreseeable result of empowering" a municipality to engage in certain activities. Id. at 42 (clear articulation requirement held met because "it was clear that anticompetitive effects logically would result from this broad authority to regulate"). Do these modifications suggest that, if the Massachusetts legislature had not expressly barred restrictions on truthful professional advertising, the result in *Mass. Board* would have been different? In the *Midcal* case itself, 445 U.S. at 106, the Supreme Court expressed as follows its essential concern in enunciating the two-part test: "The national policy in favor of competition cannot be thwarted by casting * * * a gauzy cloak of state involvement over what is essentially a private price-fixing arrangement." In your view, should the liberalization of the first prong of the *Midcal* test in *Town of Hallie* be deemed to apply in antitrust cases against state licensing and regulatory boards?

3. *Liability for Unauthorized Anticompetitive Actions?* The *Massachusetts Board* case indicates that a state regulatory agency that stifles competition without a solid legislative warrant for so doing faces severe antitrust risks. See also United States v. Texas State Bd. of Public Accountancy, 464 F.Supp. 400 (W.D.Tex.1978) (antitrust action by Department of Justice; court held that *Parker* doctrine did not immunize a regulatory rule prohibiting competitive bidding by accountants), modified 592 F.2d 919 (5th Cir.1979), cert. denied 444 U.S. 925 (1979). In the cited case, the board, which consisted of nine licensed accountants who were appointed by the governor and approved by the state senate, was empowered by statute to promulgate rules of professional conduct, which became effective when approved by a majority of licensed accountants voting in a referendum. The district court observed the Supreme Court's conclusion that " 'the *Parker* doctrine exempts only anticompetitive conduct engaged in as an act of government by the State as sovereign, or, by its subdivisions, pursuant to a state policy to displace competition with regulation or monopoly public service.' " 464 F.Supp. at 404, quoting City of Lafayette v. Louisiana Power and Light Co., 435 U.S. 389, 413 (1978). The district court reasoned that the state statute did not mandate the rule against competitive bidding and contemplated rules requiring high standards of professional conduct, not rules limiting competitive freedom. See also Goldfarb v. Virginia State Bar, 421 U.S. 773 (1975) (state bar association's minimum fee schedule was not exempt from antitrust scrutiny because, although the state had an "integrated" bar, the fee schedules were not compelled by the state itself).

Query whether an allegation of "conspiracy" should be enough to raise an antitrust issue when public officials do not have—as they did have in the *Massachusetts Board* and *Texas State Board* cases—an independent competitor's stake in suppressing competition. Should, for example, the antitrust laws be used to punish certain kinds of official corruption? The Supreme Court ruled in 1991 that the state-action doctrine insulates municipal officials from suits under the antitrust laws when carrying out their legislatively authorized regulatory responsibilities even if they are charged with conspiring with one regulated enterprise against its competitors. City of Columbia v. Omni Outdoor Advertising, 499 U.S. 365 (1991). This ruling that there is no "conspiracy exception" to the state-action doctrine is significant in clarifying that official corruption is not to be policed under the antitrust laws. How should it affect suits against professional licensing boards having some members who have a commercial interest in anticompetitive rules?

Should the antitrust laws be available to challenge as anticompetitive a regulatory action that is arguably attributable to a policy bias (e.g., against proprietary hospitals)? See, e.g., Huron Valley Hospital, Inc. v. Pontiac, 612 F.Supp. 654 (E.D.Mich.1985) (holding that the *Parker* doctrine did not provide blanket antitrust immunity for the actions of officials of a state agency who recommended the denial of a certificate of need necessary to build a hospital, where plaintiff hospital alleged that the officials had exceeded their statutory authority by conspiring with existing hospitals to exclude it from the market), affirmed on other grounds, 792 F.2d 563 (6th Cir.1986) (state officials without legislative warrant could not claim eleventh amendment immunity from suit in federal court; state-action defense not ruled upon). A later ruling in the *Huron Valley* case indicated that state and federal health planning legislation provided enough of a warrant for cooperation between local hospitals and state health planners to warrant summary judgment on the claim of an anticompetitive conspiracy violating the antitrust laws. Huron Valley Hosp., Inc. v. Pontiac, 650 F.Supp. 1325 (E.D.Mich.1986), aff'd per curiam, 849 F.2d 262 (6th Cir.1988), cert. denied, 488 U.S. 942 (1988).

Consider the nature of the antitrust liability of a state agency that writes restrictive rules without statutory warrant. Is the state liable for treble damages? Note that the Local Government Antitrust Act of 1984, 15 U.S.C. §§ 34–36 (1994), exempts municipalities and their employees and private parties acting under their direction from liability for monetary antitrust damages resulting from official acts; injunctive relief may still be obtained. Should a similar exemption be provided for state boards and their members? In the absence of an explicit or implied exemption, are individual board members subject to personal liability? In assessing personal liability, should a court distinguish between those board members who are themselves engaged in practicing the regulated profession, those who are nominated to serve by the practicing profession, those who are members of the profession but not actively practicing, and those members who are lay persons appointed as "public representatives"? Would making such distinctions make a useful point? Should board members carry insurance against antitrust liability? Who should pay for it?

4. *Restrictions in Optometry.* The Maryland Attorney General once conducted a review of the "antitrust implications of the powers and conduct of Maryland's occupational licensing and regulatory boards." In a Report on the Maryland State Board of Examiners in Optometry (Oct. 8, 1985), he noted that the state had the third lowest ratio of optometrists to population, that five of six board members were practicing optometrists, and that "members of a licensing board who are members of the industry they regulate may be considered participants in a conspiracy to restrain trade if they adopt competition-restraining regulations that are neither explicitly authorized in their statutory mandate nor clearly necessary to fulfill the stated legislative policy." He recommended that the board, in order to reduce its liability risks, make changes in the following: (1) the requirement "that licensure applicants be graduates of [accredited] schools"; (2) a provision requiring "an examining optometrist when writing a lens prescription to record * * * fitting data regardless of whether the optometrist is dispensing the eyewear"; (3) a provision requiring "that any minimum patient examination include a tonometry examination [for glaucoma, which] should be amended to make it consistent with the Board's statutory authority[, which is limited to] requiring tonometry only when indicated or for patients over 40 years of age"; (4) a prohibition of "advertisements related to fees for specific types of services without fully disclosing all variables and relevant factors"; and (5) a proposed prohibition of "all advertising that does not include the name and address of the optometrist rendering the services advertised."

5. *Denturists Versus State Dental Boards.* A good example of the "turf battles" frequently fought by licensing boards on behalf of their regulated constituency appeared in litigation initiated by denturists—unlicensed operators of dental laboratories making dentures. In Brazil v. Arkansas Bd. of Dental Examiners, 593 F.Supp. 1354, 1357–58 (E.D.Ark.1984), affirmed per curiam, 759 F.2d 674 (8th Cir.1985), the plaintiff's allegations were summarized as follows:

> First, the Board and the Association have sought to protect the economic interests of dentists by requiring any procedure undertaken in a dental laboratory to be accompanied by a work order signed by a licensed dentist.
>
> Second, that the State, the Board and the Association have prohibited dentists from being employed by dental laboratories or being engaged

in an ownership capacity in the operation of dental laboratories with non-dentists.

Third, that the Board has expanded the definition of "the practice of dentistry" by promulgating rules that prohibit anyone other than a licensed dentist from making impressions for dentures.

Fourth, that certain restrictions applicable to the plaintiffs, which were established only after the plaintiffs started advertising their services, were designed to harass and intimidate the plaintiffs. In a related claim, plaintiffs assert that the Board has launched a campaign against the plaintiffs to drive them out of business. They cite numerous cases brought by the Board against several of the plaintiffs as examples of such harassment tactics.

Fifth, plaintiffs allege what might possibly be construed as an equal protection claim in connection with litigation instituted by the Board against several of the plaintiffs. Specifically, they claim that they have been singled out for prosecution for alleged violations of Ark.Stat.Ann. § 72–545 while other operators of dental laboratories, which are owned by dentists, have not been sued even though they have engaged in activities that are identical to those of the plaintiffs.

Sixth, the plaintiffs challenge the rule-making powers of the Dental Board. They specifically seek to enjoin enforcement of several rules adopted by the Board that prohibit the issuance of permits to providers of dental services unless the providers are entirely owned by licensed dentists. Plaintiffs also challenge the Board's rule that any licensed dentist who associates and advertises with unlicensed dental associations is guilty of unprofessional conduct. Plaintiffs assert that by taking these actions the defendants are attempting to monopolize the marketing and distribution of dental care services and in doing so have infringed upon the plaintiffs' rights to contract with licensed dentists.

Seventh, the plaintiffs challenge several rules adopted by the Board as unreasonable, arbitrary and capricious. They assert that the Rules are tainted heavily by the fact that all of the defendant members of the Board have a financial interest in restricting the opportunities of denturists to practice.

The court found the board to be a "state agency" that need not be "actively supervised" by the state. It also held that the state legislature " 'contemplated' the Board's challenged regulatory activities, and that the restraints emanating from such activities are necessary or reasonable outgrowths of the Board's engaging in those activities." Id. at 1363. See also Gambrel v. Kentucky Bd. of Dentistry, 689 F.2d 612, 619 (6th Cir.1982) (board's construction of statute to preclude giving prescriptions for dentures directly to patients so that they could be filled by a laboratory of the patient's choice—as opposed to having dentures made by a denturist selected by the dentist—held entitled to "great persuasive weight [as] the interpretation of the statute by the administrative body charged with enforcing it"). Do you agree with (approve of) these applications of the *Midcal* test, as modified by *Town of Hallie*?

6. *Attacking State Restrictions Under the Supremacy Clause.* Consider the difference, observed in paragraph (1), between a charge that a state agency has violated the Sherman Act and a challenge to the constitutionality of its regulations under the Supremacy Clause on the theory that they are inconsistent with federal antitrust policy. Cf. Schwegmann Bros. v. Calvert Distillers Corp., 341 U.S. 384 (1951) (state law facilitating resale price maintenance held invalid because of conflict with Sherman Act). Although the latter type of challenge to state regulation would be less disruptive of state government (because of differences in the remedy imposed), it might be too redolent of the era of substantive due process to be easily embraced. Perhaps most important, the former approach has evolved in such a way that the competition-limiting actions of state legislatures are not subject to antitrust challenge at all; only the excesses of licensing agencies, especially those controlled by the regulated occupation itself, are open to attack. The more serious federalism questions that would arise under the Supremacy Clause approach, which would open state legislation as well as administrative actions to attack, are therefore avoided.

Could federal antitrust policy be invoked to challenge the validity of a state law giving broad regulatory powers to a board that is composed (like those in the denturist cases) largely of practicing professionals? How would the argument go? Can the *Parker–Midcal* doctrine by itself adequately ensure that any anticompetitive policies emerging from such a regulatory scheme are legislatively approved and that consumer welfare (the prime concern of the antitrust laws) is being fostered?

Collective Action to Obtain Legislative Relief From Competition

NOTE ON THE NOERR–PENNINGTON DOCTRINE

1. Should the antitrust laws have anything to say about collective efforts by competitors to obtain legislation or other government action that favors their interests at the expense of competition, of consumers, or of their competitors or would-be competitors? As it happens, the Sherman Act has been authoritatively limited in its application to political activity. Under the so-called *Noerr–Pennington* doctrine, collective lobbying for anticompetitive legislation is not subject to antitrust challenge even if some misrepresentation is involved. See generally Elhauge, Making Sense of Antitrust Petitioning Immunity, 80 Cal.L.Rev. 1177 (1992). Although this principle may seem to derive from the first amendment, it is more accurately viewed as a narrow construction of the Sherman Act that attributes to Congress an intention to regulate only behavior in the marketplace, not political activity. Even though one might (under public choice theory) question the ability of political and legal processes to protect consumers against anticompetitive legislation or official action, it is hard to argue that antitrust law was intended by Congress to limit the political power of well-positioned interest groups. See Eastern R.R. Presidents Conf. v. Noerr Motor Freight, Inc., 365 U.S. 127 (1961) (rejecting antitrust claim by trucking firms based on railroads' publicity campaign "designed to foster the adoption and retention of laws * * * destructive of the trucking business"); Missouri v. National Organization for Women, 620 F.2d 1301 (8th Cir.), cert. denied 449 U.S. 842 (1980) (Sherman Act construed not to apply to NOW's boycott aimed at getting state legislature to ratify proposed Equal Rights Amendment).

Limitations on the *Noerr* principle include the so-called "sham" exception, which prevents competitors from casting their activities as calls for political action—"there ought to be a law"—when their true purpose is to inspire a boycott or other direct collective action. See Federal Prescription Service, Inc. v. American Pharmaceutical Ass'n, 663 F.2d 253 (D.C.Cir. 1981) (campaign against mail-order sales of prescription drugs, although disingenuous in its professed concern for the pharmacist-patient-physician relationship, held to have injured plaintiff only as a result of governmental action and thus not to violate the Sherman Act).

2. In one case, an association of truckers undertook to contest all applications to a state agency for new operating authority. California Motor Transport Co. v. Trucking Unlimited, 404 U.S. 508 (1972). Although this use of the administrative process to block competition was defended under the *Noerr* doctrine as collective recourse to governmental processes, the Supreme Court held that the sham exception might apply if the purpose was to raise entry barriers. The analogy to the tort of "abuse of process" suggests one way to think about such cases. Although initiating litigation allows a competitor to impose costs and uncertainty on a rival, the Supreme Court has held that attempting to assert one's legal rights against a competitor in an appropriate forum can be challenged as an exclusionary practice or attempt to monopolize only if the claim asserted is "objectively baseless." Professional Real Estate Investors v. Columbia Pictures, 508 U.S. 49 (1993).

3. *Problem*. Recall the "Val–U–Health" problem earlier in this chapter. What if the county medical society in that problem had couched all its discussions of "gag" clauses in HMOs' provider contracts in terms of the need for legislative relief against what the members agreed was an unconscionable practice? Alternatively, what if the AMA, objecting to such clauses, had gotten its state affiliates to bring lawsuits challenging their use by Val–U–Health in all the states where Val–U–Health does business?

4. In Michigan State Medical Society, 101 F.T.C. 191 (1983), the medical society had a series of disputes with the local Blue Cross plan and with the state Medicaid program. It organized an effective threat by its members to boycott the programs if they did not modify their tactics. The FTC held that both boycott threats were unlawful, stating as follows in answer to the claim that collective bargaining, backed by a threat to withdraw services, was justified by concern for the welfare of Medicaid beneficiaries:

> Even in the case of Medicaid reductions, where an argument might be made that arbitrary cuts could be counter-productive by impairing physicians' economic incentives to treat the poor, it is difficult to see how concerted agreements and refusals to deal can be sanctioned as a means of fighting proposed payment cutbacks. While granting MSMS'

> laudable concerns about the effects of physician withdrawal from Medicaid, we observe that respondent clearly had public forums (protected under the *Noerr–Pennington* doctrine * * *) available to it to correct perceived mistakes made by the state legislature or the administrators of Medicaid; it could have expressed its views in ways that fell well short of organized boycott threats.

Id. at 294–95 . See also id. at 296–301. In FTC v. Superior Court Trial Lawyers Ass'n, 493 U.S. 411 (1990), the Supreme Court condemned as a per se violation a lawyers' boycott of a trial court's program for assigning counsel to indigent criminal defendants despite the lawyers' claim that their purpose was to call the attention of government officials to the plight of their needy clients resulting from the inadequacy of the professional fees allowed. See also West Virginia Attorney General Opinion, 1980–81 Trade Cas. (CCH) ¶ 63,676 (1980) (distinguishing health care providers' concerted efforts to influence major policy decisions from boycotts to obtain higher reimbursement).

5. The question of the Sherman Act's application to "political" boycotts may not be finally settled. For an article arguing for a narrow construction in the case of Medicaid boycotts, see Raup, Medicaid Boycotts by Health Care Providers: A *Noerr–Pennington* Defense, 69 Iowa L.Rev. 1393 (1984). Observing that bid-rigging on state projects clearly violates the Sherman Act, Raup distinguishes the situation where the state, instead of relying on competitive bidding, dictates terms to providers who are in a position to be exploited by the state acting as a monopsonistic purchaser. His idea appears to be that where the state has removed the transaction from the competitive marketplace and made price and other terms a political issue, the Sherman Act should have no application. The potential for monopsonistic exploitation has been especially acute for nursing homes, which have substantial capital investments and are heavily dependent upon state Medicaid programs for patients. See, e.g., United States v. Montana Nursing Home Ass'n, 1982–2 Trade Cases ¶ 64,852 (D.Mont.1982) (consent judgment). For another case showing government acting as a powerful "prudent purchaser," see United States v. North Dakota Hosp. Ass'n, 640 F.Supp. 1028 (D.N.D.1986) (hospitals violated Sherman Act by collectively resisting efforts of the Indian Health Service to obtain discounts from individual hospitals).

Query in which of the cases cited above the government might be said, under Raup's analysis, to have purchased services noncompetitively. In the *Superior Court Trial Lawyers* case, supra, the FTC had expressly found that "the city's purchase of * * * legal services for indigents is based on competition." 107 F.T.C. 510, 570 (1986).

6. Many other nations rely upon formal or informal collective bargaining between government (or government-supervised "sick funds") and organized providers to set the terms on which health services will be provided. See W. Glaser, Health Insurance Bargaining: Foreign Lessons for Americans (1978). Should the antitrust laws be set aside (or interpreted) so that American providers can protect themselves against government-sponsored monopsony?

CHAPTER 5

Changing Institutional Providers

Section A: Power Relationships in Hospitals

Accrediting Requirements and the Organization of Hospitals

Joint Commission on Accreditation of Healthcare Organizations, Comprehensive Accreditation Manual and the Organization of Hospitals (1997)

Excerpts from 1997 Update 2

Governance

* * *

GO.2.1 The hospital's governing body or authority adopts by laws addressing its legal accountabilities and responsibility to the patient population served.

GO.2.2 The hospital's governing body or authority provides for appropriate medical staff participation in governance.

GO.2.2.1 The medical staff has the right to representation (through attendance and voice), by one or more medical staff members selected by the medical staff, at governing body meetings.

GO.2.2.2 Medical staff members are eligible for full membership in the hospital's governing body, unless legally prohibited.

* * *

GO.2.6 The hospital's governing body or authority provides for conflict resolution.

* * *

The Organized Medical Staff

Individual members of the medical staff care for patients within an organizational context. Within this context, members of the medical staff, as individuals and as a group, interface with, and actively participate in, important organization functions.

MS.1 One or more organized, self-governing medical staffs have overall responsibility for the quality of the professional services provided by individuals with clinical privileges,[1] as well as the responsibility of accounting therefore [*sic*] to the governing body.

MS.1.1 Each medical staff has the following characteristics:

MS.1.1.1 It includes fully licensed physicians and may include other licensed individuals permitted by law and by the hospital to provide patient care services independently in the hospital (both physicians and these other individuals are referred to as "licensed independent practitioners"[2]).

MS.1.1.2 All medical staff members have delineated clinical privileges that define the scope of patient care services they may provide independently in the hospital.

MS.1.1.3 All medical staff members and all others with delineated clinical privileges are subject to medical staff and departmental bylaws, rules and regulations, and policies and are subject to review as part of the organization's performance-improvement activities.

Documents Governing Activities of the Organized Medical Staff

Medical staff self-governance is delineated in documents that set out how the medical staff will organize and govern its affairs. * * * The medical staff bylaws, as adopted or amended by the medical staff and approved by the governing body, create a system of mutual rights and responsibilities between members of the medical staff and the hospital.

MS.2 Each medical staff develops and adopts bylaws and rules and regulations to establish a framework for self-governance of medical staff activities and accountability to the governing body.

MS.2.1 Medical staff bylaws and rules and regulations are adopted by the medical staff and approved by the governing body before becoming effective. Neither body may unilaterally amend the medical staff bylaws or rules and regulations.

* * *

MS 2.3 Medical staff bylaws include provisions for at least the following:

MS.2.3.1 An executive committee of the medical staff;

MS.2.3.2 Fair-hearing and appellate review mechanisms for medical staff members and other individuals holding clinical privileges;

1. **clinical privileges**—Authorization granted to a practitioner to provide specific patient care services in the hospital within well-defined limits, based on the following factors, as applicable: license, education, training, experience, competence, health status, and judgment.

2. **licensed independent practitioner**—Any individual permitted by law and by the hospital to provide patient care services without direction or supervision, within the scope of the individual's license and consistent with individually granted clinical privileges.

MS.2.3.3 Mechanisms for corrective action, including indications and procedures for automatic and summary suspension of an individual's medical staff membership or clinical privileges;

MS.2.3.4 A description of the medical staff's organization, including categories of medical staff membership, when such exist, and appropriate officer positions, with the stipulation that each officer is a medical staff member;

* * *

MS.2.3.7 A mechanism for adopting and amending the medical staff bylaws, rules and regulations, and policies; and

MS.2.3.8 Medical staff representation and participation in any hospital deliberation affecting the discharge of medical staff responsibilities.

* * *

MS.2.4.1 The medical staff bylaws, rules and regulations, and policies and the governing body's bylaws do not conflict.

* * *

Medical Staff Executive Function (Committee)

The medical staff executive committee has responsibilities, delegated by the medical staff, within the organization governance function. * * * The medical staff executive committee is delegated the primary authority over activities related to the functions of self-governance of the medical staff and over activities related to the functions of performance improvement of the professional services provided by individuals with clinical privileges. * * *

* * *

MS.3.1.1 The executive committee's function, size, and composition and the method of selecting its members are defined in the medical staff bylaws.

MS.3.1.2 The chief executive officer of the hospital or his or her designee attends each executive committee meeting on an ex-officio basis, with or without vote.

* * *

MS.3.1.6 The executive committee is responsible for making medical staff recommendations directly to the governing body for its approval.

MS.3.1.6.1 Such recommendations pertain to at least the following: [the medical staff's structure; the mechanism used to review credentials and delineate individual clinical privileges; recommendations of individuals for staff membership and for delineated clinical privileges; participation of the medical staff in organization performance-improvement activities; the mechanism by which membership may be terminated; and the mechanism for fair-hearing procedures].

MS.3.1.7 The executive committee receives and acts on reports and recommendations from medical staff committees, clinical departments, and assigned activity groups.

[Medical Staff Clinical] Department Leadership

* * *

MS.4.2 Medical staff department directors' responsibilities are specified in the medical staff bylaws and rules and regulations.

* * *

The Credentialing Process

The medical staff is responsible for a credentialing process. The credentialing process includes a series of activities designed to collect relevant data * * *. Although the specific information used to make decisions regarding appointments and reappointments is at the discretion of the individual organization, the range of information used should be explicit. In addition, within, and at the discretion of, an organization, the specific information required for appointment may differ from the information required for reappointment. The required information should include data on qualifications such as licensure and training or experience, and data on actual performance that is collected and assessed initially and in an ongoing process.

MS.5 The organization establishes mechanisms for hospital-specific appointment and reappointment of medical staff members and for granting and renewing or revising hospital-specific clinical privileges.

MS.5.1 The governing body appoints and reappoints to the medical staff and grants initial, renewed, or revised clinical privileges, based on medical staff recommendations, in accordance with the bylaws, rules and regulations, and policies of the medical staff and of the hospital.

* * *

MS.5.2 There are mechanisms, including a fair hearing and appeal process, for addressing adverse decisions for existing medical staff members and other individuals holding clinical privileges for renewal, revocation, or revision of clinical privileges.

* * *

MS.5.4 The mechanisms provide for professional criteria that are specified in the medical staff bylaws and uniformly applied to all applicants for medical staff membership, medical staff members, or applicant for delineated clinical privileges. These criteria constitute the basis for granting initial or continuing medical staff membership and for granting initial, renewed, or revised clinical privileges

* * *

MS.5.4.4 Decisions on reappointments or on revocation, revision, or renewal of clinical privileges must consider criteria that are directly related to the quality of care.

MS.5.4.4.1 Such decisions are subject to a fair hearing and appeal process.

MS.5.4.5 Decisions on appointments or on granting of clinical privileges must consider criteria that are directly related to the quality of care.

MS.5.5 The medical staff bylaws, rules and regulations, or policies define the information to be provided by each applicant for appointment or reappointment to the medical staff and initial, renewed, or revised clinical privileges, including at least

MS.5.5.1 previously successful or currently pending challenges to any licensure or registration (state or district, Drug Enforcement Administration) or the voluntary relinquishment of such licensure or registration;

MS.5.5.2 voluntary or involuntary termination of medical staff membership or voluntary or involuntary limitation, reduction, or loss of clinical privileges at another hospital; and

MS.5.5.3 involvement in a professional liability action under circumstances specified in the medical staff bylaws, rules and regulations, and policies.

MS.5.5.3.1 At a minimum, final judgments or settlements involving the individual are reported.

NOTES AND QUESTIONS ON THE JCAHO

1. The Joint Commission on Accreditation of Healthcare Organizations (JCAHO or Joint Commission) is a nonprofit organization headquartered in Chicago. Its stated mission is "to improve the quality of care provided to the public by offering of health care accreditation and related services that support performance improvement in health care organizations." For further information concerning the JCAHO, see http://www.jcaho.org

The immediate purpose of reproducing selections from the JCAHO's accrediting standards here is to assist the student's understanding of how hospitals are organized and operated in fact. Because virtually all hospitals of any size are accredited by the Joint Commission, they tend to resemble each other in important organizational respects. The JCAHO's standards thus provide a good guide to the power relationships in hospitals. The standards on credentialing will be useful in considering disputes over hospital staff privileges in § C of this chapter.

2. *History*. The original program to accredit hospitals in the United States was launched by the American College of Surgeons (ACS) in 1919. In 1951, hospital accrediting was taken over by the Joint Commission on Accreditation of Hospitals (JCAH), a joint venture of the American Medical Association (AMA), the American Hospital Association (AHA), the ACS, and the American College of Physicians. The name JCAHO was adopted in 1987 to reflect the fact that the organization had begun accrediting health care providers other than hospitals. See generally Jost, The Joint Commission on Accreditation of Hospitals: Private Regulation of Health Care and the Public Interest, 24 B.C. L.Rev. 835 (1983). Today, more than 15,000 health care organizations, including more than 5,200 hospitals are evaluated by the Joint Commission. As will appear in more detail in chapter 6(§D), over 40 states and the federal government (Medicare) use JCAHO accreditation as a proxy for compliance with licensing and regulatory requirements.

3. *Control.* The JCAHO's governing Board of Commissioners has always been dominated by nominees of the sponsoring organizations (seven nominated by the AMA and by the AHA and three each by the Colleges). The American Dental Association has had one representative since 1979, and an increasing number of so-called public representatives, selected by the board itself, have been included since 1982. Since 1994, there have been six public members, with the result that official representatives of organized medicine (the AMA and the Colleges) no longer constitute a majority of the board (13 of 27). If there ever was an antitrust problem in the way the JCAH(O) was constituted and controlled, has the problem been cured by the latest moves to reduce professional dominance? (You will be asked in chapter 6(§D) whether the JCAHO's accrediting activities give rise to antitrust issues, but your study of chapter 4(§B) should have prepared you at least to frame the relevant questions.)

NOTES AND QUESTIONS ON HOSPITAL ORGANIZATION

1. The allocation of responsibilities and power relationships under various management arrangements in hospitals were described as follows in 1983:

> Community hospitals, whether owned by local government or private associations, developed some unique features. The most important of these was sharing power in an arrangement called a triad. In this regard, the private, voluntary not-for-profit hospital is the foremost example. The triad includes the governing authority, chief executive officer or administrator and medical staff. Theoretically, this arrangement permits a sharing of power among the three participants, but it can best be characterized as an accommodation. The triad results from: the independent contractor status of staff physicians who care for their patients in the hospital, and the need for governing authorities to delegate responsibility for day-to-day operation of the facility to an administrator. Despite its many shortcomings and challenges to its efficiency and desirability, the triad continues to be the dominant organizational form of voluntary not-for-profit hospitals (see Figure I–1). And with no significant differences, this depiction shows the general organization of community hospitals, whether public or private, if they have not adopted the corporate structure.
>
> * * *
>
> Corporate structures of investor-owned hospitals tend to be different from not-for-profit in policy-making, and certain management

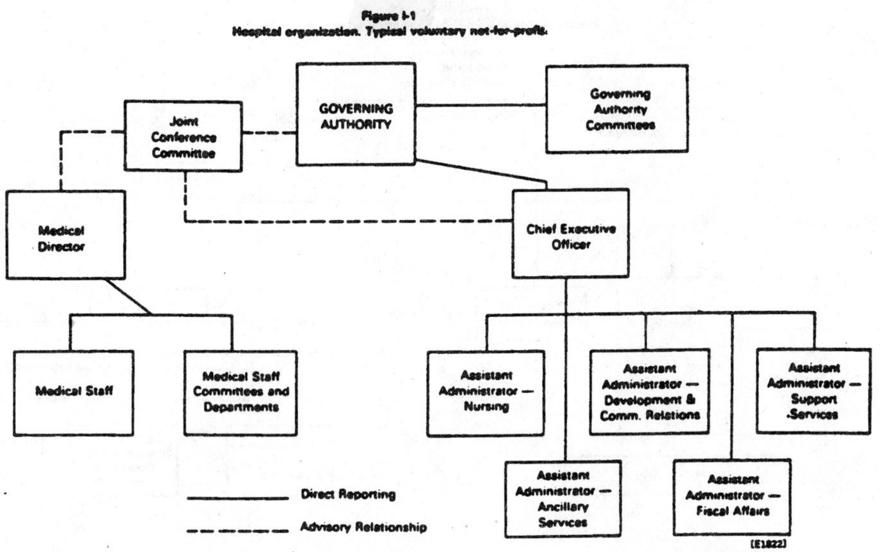

Figure I-1
Hospital organization. Typical voluntary not-for-profit.

functions, e.g., purchasing and planning, are often centralized. In some chains, each hospital has a governing authority which formulates local policy within the corporate policy framework. In this respect, investor-owned chains are not unlike hospital systems developing in the not-for-profit field; * * *

A typical model of a hospital which has not adopted the corporate structure is shown in Figure I–1. The corporate model is shown in Figure I–2. In the latter, which is far less common, the distinguishing features are the enhanced overall role played by the CEO and the extent of line accountability for medical staff activities. The American College of Hospital Administrators is on record as preferring the corporate structure through its endorsement of a 1974 ACHA task force report. This report recommended to the Joint Commission on Accreditation of Hospitals that there be direct line accountability between the medical staff and CEO through a medical director. In the intervening years, JCAH has stressed accountability of medical staff to a much greater extent, but has yet to interpose the CEO between the medical staff and governing authority. It is unlikely that the Joint Commission will include such a requirement in the near term: medical staffs continue to be extremely powerful and independent; and the Joint Commission tends to have a strong physician bias. It should be stressed, however, that even where physicians are independent contractors, their clinical practice is subject to peer review. Recommendations from this process are made to governing authorities who are increasingly aware of the peril in failing to act or acting contrary to them. * * *

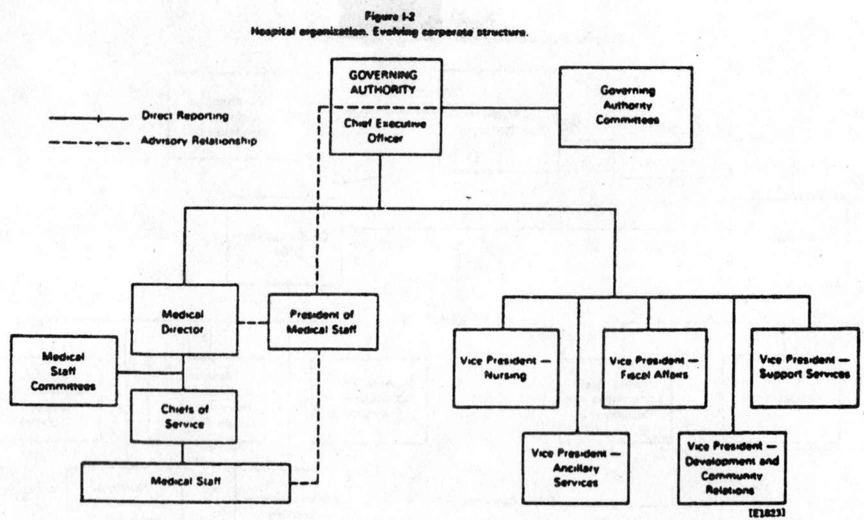

Figure I-2
Hospital organization. Evolving corporate structure.

> This raises a basic dilemma for hospitals, since by the very nature of a physician's education and professional activity, independence is a necessary and desirable trait. And, in most hospitals, medical staffs retain a high degree of independence. In these, significant reliance must be put on moral suasion. Increasingly, however, this may not be enough, and hospitals will have to take a much more aggressive position in dealing with medical staff problems. The courts have declared that even in the absence of an employment relationship, the hospital, through its governing authority, has corporate liability for substandard medical practice. The inevitable result will be increased control of physicians' activities and a greater willingness to use sanctions such as limitation on, or suspension of, hospital privileges. Attenuating or removing privileges is the most direct and drastic control point which hospitals have over physicians; however, this happens more rarely than anecdotes and incident reports suggest it should.

J. Rakich & K. Darr, Hospital Organization and Management: Text and Readings 25–29 (3d ed. 1983). These authors observed that hospitals were increasingly employing a salaried chief of the medical staff, sometimes called the medical director. Like the hospital's CEO, these physicians are often permitted to sit on the hospital's governing board, which the authors suggested "raises other problems." What problems do you see? Should the medical staff as such be represented on the board?

2. Why are hospitals organized as they are? Although some state licensing statutes require a "self-governing" medical staff (e.g., California), those statutes appear to have been enacted only after the bifurcated model of the hospital was well established—perhaps because professional interests were concerned about persistent deviations by smaller, unaccredited institutions from the favored model. What other legal restrictions that you have learned about may help to explain the way hospitals are organized? What organizational structures can you devise to meet legal requirements while giving the hospital board substantial authority over physicians? Would adoption of your proposals create questions about the institution's accreditation? Is this a conclusive argument for not adopting them?

3. Another source of requirements governing hospital organization is the Medicare and Medicaid Conditions of Participation of Hospitals. In extensively revising these regulations in 1986, 51 Fed.Reg. 22010 (1986), HCFA stated that it

> took into consideration the fact that, in addition to Federal regulations, hospitals are subject to substantial State inspection through licensure programs and that there are nationally recognized standards of practice that are well accepted and adhered to generally through a voluntary accreditation process. We maintained in the [notice of proposed rulemaking] the basic function of the conditions of protecting patient health and safety. In addition, we focused on: (1) Eliminating unnecessary regulations and providing hospitals with greater flexibility; (2) replacing prescriptive administrative requirements with language that is stated in terms of expected outcome; (3) in most cases, giving responsibility to the hospital for choosing its own staff and delineating staff responsibilities rather than specifying Federal requirements for credentials and qualifications; (4) replacing specific details on maintaining adequate and safe facilities with general comprehensive statements; and (5) clarifying the regulations to avoid any implied suggestion that hospitals should organize their services into formal departments.

On the subject of the hospital medical staff, the original proposal would have required the following:

> (a) a well-organized medical staff accountable to the governing body for the quality of medical care given to patients; (b) periodic appraisals of members of the staff; (c) the granting of clinical privileges only to those legally, professionally, and ethically qualified; and (d) an individual physician who is responsible for the organization and conduct of the medical staff. We proposed to maintain these requirements since there is evidence that a strong and responsible medical staff organization is related positively to the provision of quality care.

HCFA responded as follows to comments relating to governing board/staff relations:

> **Comments:** Commenters recommended that we continue the requirement for a joint committee to formalize liaison between the medical staff and the hospital's administration. The commenters argued that this committee is necessary to coordinate activities related to patient care and that without such a requirement coordination would falter.
>
> **Response:** We have not accepted this recommendation because we believe that the requirement that the medical staff be accountable to the governing body for the quality of care makes the governing body

responsible for assuring coordination of patient care services. We believe that how best to organize liaison and coordination of activities with the medical staff should be the internal decision of the hospital's management.

In 1997, HCFA proposed another extensive revision of the hospital conditions of participation in Medicare and Medicaid. 62 Fed. Reg. 66726 (Dec. 19, 1997) (to be codified at 42 C.F.R. pts. 416, 485, 489):

> The primary requirement under the proposed governing body COP is that a hospital's governing body * * * is legally responsible for the management and provision of all care furnished to hospital patients, including the structure needed to administer the hospital effectively. Thus, the governing body must create an environment that helps ensure the provision of high quality care that is consistent with patient needs and the effective administration of the hospital. In the proposed new condition, we emphasize the responsibility of the hospital governing body for the entire operation of the hospital, including care furnished under contracts and arrangements, the appointment of an administrator, the appointment of the medical staff and its bylaws, and the implementation of effective budgeting, accounting, and quality control programs.

Id. at 66745. HCFA made only minor editorial changes in the requirements concerning the governing body's responsibilities for the medical staff's bylaws.

4. In 1984, the AMA and the AHA convened a joint task force to address emerging tensions in hospital/staff relations. Among the causes of these increasing tensions were such factors as new financial and competitive pressures on hospitals, expansion in the number and types of practitioners (including nonphysicians) seeking hospital affiliation, and hospitals' expanding liability for "corporate negligence" in selecting staff physicians or overseeing their work (see § B of this chapter). In its 1985 report, the task force examined virtually the full range of policy issues that hospitals confront and expressed a consensus as to the way in which responsibility for each issue should be allocated between the hospital governing body and the medical staff. AMA & AHA, Report of the Joint Task Force on Hospital–Medical Staff Relationships (1985). On some issues, there was "no duty to consult" (in which case responsibility was declared to be "singular"); in other cases, formal consultation was expected (and responsibility was characterized as "shared"); in still other cases, there was to be informal consultation; and in one instance (the adoption of bylaws for the medical staff), the responsibility was declared to be "joint."

At one point, the task force stated as follows:

> The hospital governing board is responsible for the conduct of the institution as an institution, including oversight of the overall quality of care provided in the hospital and the allocation of resources. The ultimate legal responsibility of the hospital governing board for these functions necessitates that the medical staff be responsible to the hospital governing board for the performance of its own obligation to

carry out the range of activities requiring the exercise of professional skill and judgment possessed only by fully-licensed physicians.

What is the significance of referring here to the "governing board" and not to the "governing board/administration" (as the task force did elsewhere)? Is it possible that the report may have gone further than is appropriate in making the medical staff co-equal to the governing board despite its legal subservience?

The task force generally spoke in prescriptive terms even though it did not purport to be stating legal requirements. Was its report likely to have any legal effect? Should it have such effect? If it is assumed that the ideal hospital should indeed be organized and operated in accordance with the task force's prescriptions, does it follow that all hospitals should be so organized and operated? What characteristics of a hospital or medical staff might suggest that different arrangements would be preferable?

How Hospitals Operate

Jeffrey E. Harris, M.D., Ph.D., Regulation and Internal Control in Hospitals

55 Bull. N.Y. Acad. of Med. 88 (1979).

In all the recent [late 1970s] discussions of hospital regulation, one important question remains unanswered: How can hospitals comply with cost controls? Confronted by prospective reimbursement limits and investment "caps," hospital administrators and trustees must somehow eliminate underutilized beds, stop surgeons from performing too many hysterectomies, and force radiologists to go without tomographic scanners. Unfortunately, hospitals are not used to this sort of thing, nor are physicians accustomed to being cost conscious. Any regulatory intervention which merely sets limits on hospital costs in effect entrusts a great deal of institutional change to the hospital alone. If these internal changes are not forthcoming, cost controls may produce only long queues, litigation, cream skimming, and bad medical care.

Hospital cost containment, I shall argue, is ultimately a problem in internal management control. * * *

A growing body of literature has begun to question the clinical cost-effectiveness of much * * * medical care. We hear about too many laboratory tests, procedures with dubious indications, inappropriately long postoperative stays, and unwarranted hospital admissions. But we should hardly conclude from this evidence that there are just two types of hospital care: necessary and unnecessary, or that hospital-cost inflation resulted entirely from unnecessary treatment. On the contrary, physicians perceive these medical interventions as having an entire spectrum of benefits, ranging from life-saving treatments to marginally useful laboratory tests. The real difficulty is that under the present system of almost complete insurance coverage, physicians and their patients have not had to make the finely tuned distinctions necessary to balance the clinical benefits of these interventions against their actual costs.

* * * [A]s regulatory constraints progressively tighten, we have no obvious assurance that [the] layers of inefficiency will peel off cleanly and in the right order. There is a substantial danger, in fact, that truly beneficial medical care may be rationed away before the excess fat is gone. All this depends on how this internal rationing process actually works in hospitals.

THE CURRENT SYSTEM

All but the smallest hospitals in this country have a common characteristic: the hospital administration and medical staff are separate organizations. Physician members of the medical staff admit and treat their patients essentially without the administration's interference. The administrator manages an organization whose basic function is to make various resources available for the physician's use. Many hospitals, to be sure, have complicated physician staff rules, salaried chiefs of service, professional corporations, and joint medical staff-trustee committees. But the medical staff basically constitutes a distinct organizational unit, with its own bylaws, ethics, and disciplinary procedures.

* * *

This organizational separation between medical staff and administration is reflected in the hospital's product-pricing practices. Though cost reporting and reimbursement schemes are many, complex, and ever-changing, their common characteristic is separate payment for physician and hospital care. Physicians customarily bill for their services as individual entrepreneurs; and even in the case of hospital-based physician care, a "professional component" of hospital costs is separately accounted for and reimbursed. The administration receives its revenues from patient-care services which are delivered, such as drugs, laboratory tests, and daily room and board.

The resource-allocation scheme in this organization is basically a system of internal orders and deliveries. That is, physicians order tests and treatments for their patients and the administration supplies them. * * * In [the] example [of a gynecologist admitting a patient for a hysterectomy], the attending physician orders preoperative studies from the chemistry laboratory, reserves an operating room, orders intravenous solutions from central supply, transfuses blood provided by the blood bank, orders postoperative analgesics from the pharmacy, and so forth. These physician orders for particular tests or treatments in turn place indirect demands on the hospital's support services. For example, this gynecologist's use of an operating room places indirect demands on messenger and escort services, accounting, laundry, and so forth. * * *

The current system of cost accounting in hospitals is molded around these organizational characteristics. * * * Hospital-cost reporting, as currently conceived, allocates the expenses of nonrevenue cost centers [i.e., administrative support mechanisms which do not provide direct patient care services: accounting, admissions, laundry, etc.] to revenue centers [i.e. administrative support mechanisms that do provide patient care services: blood banks, pharmacies, labs, etc.]. The medical staff, organizationally and financially separate, is divorced from this cost-allocation scheme.

* * * On the same day that this gynecologist orders a unit of blood, thousands of other spot orders of many types may compete from many other physicians. Coordinating the delivery of all these resources in effect requires the solution of a complicated inventory-control problem. * * *

As long as the medical staff's demands do not exceed short-run capacity constraints, physicians continue to admit patients and to order tests, and the administration delivers. But when there is excess demand, a variety of rationing mechanisms come into play. * * * There are waiting lists, emergency priorities, negotiations among physicians, bed-juggling by interns, and sometimes crude arm twisting. Some of this rationing is undoubtedly purely random, but most of it is based on medical priorities, on the attending physician's status, or on the patient's ability to pay. Any physician who has pleaded with a laboratory technician to process his patient's blood sample with due speed knows that a great deal of this rationing is purely informal.

Most of the evidence about this rationing of excess demand is anecdotal, but available studies suggest that it is achieved primarily through entry control. It is apparently much easier to keep a patient out of the hospital than to affect a physician's orders once that patient is admitted. Admission rates, it has been found, are much more sensitive to bed scarcities than to inpatient length of stay. During peak loads the more serious cases are preferentially admitted. Because more serious cases will have longer hospital stays, the average length of stay may actually increase. But even when corrected for variations in case mix, length of stay and laboratory test orders apparently increase during periods of high capacity. Conditions of excess demand apparently induce physicians to take strong hedging positions. For example, additional diagnostic radiology and laboratory tests are ordered in advance merely to hedge against a long waiting line. Patient transfers from intensive-care units are deferred to hedge against the possibility of a relapse. In larger hospitals the motive to stay at the head of the queue can become so strong that each medical staff department demands its own technicians, laboratories, and intensive-care units.

Whatever their motivations, these complex physician responses to tight hospital capacity make the internal rationing process very costly. As a result, the administration opts for the least costly rationing method—guarding the front door. Physicians, of course, attempt to circumvent this bottleneck. Patients are sometimes admitted to other hospitals so that they can be transferred through the emergency ward. But the central point remains: Once you get your patient into the hospital, his treatment is up to you.

* * *

Let us attempt to characterize this internal control problem abstractly. The real difficulty is that the administration must comply with the restraints imposed by regulators, whereas physicians control the allocative decisions. Because administrators cannot directly intervene in patient care, we therefore need to devise some sort of information channel between these two sets of actors. Somehow, administrators must signal the scarcity values of its patient-care resources to the doctors. The clinical decisions of the medical staff, in turn, must respond to these scarcity values. Unfortunately, administrators have no method to flash these values to the doctors. And even if it could magically announce all the shadow prices of all its patient-care services, the medical staff has no real incentive to pay attention to them. Not only are their patients insulated by insurance coverage, but physicians themselves are paid separately from the hospital. * * *

This abstract characterization immediately helps us understand why the naive team-spirit solution to the control problem is unlikely to succeed. Imagine that the chiefs of the various medical staff departments met jointly with administrators and trustees and agreed to be more cost conscious. How, then, are they going to do this? If all of the useless medical care were embodied in one extremely expensive test, this task might be quite simple. Unfortunately, the benefit of any test varies tremendously with clinical circumstances. * * * [E]ven if we assume that some efficient judgments can be made, it is still not clear why individual physicians would be collectively motivated to respond to the cost-consciousness idea, especially when patients demand that everything possible be done for them. * * *

Physician participation in governing boards or administrative committees is frequently suggested as a solution to these difficulties. But it is simply not clear how such top-down control can effectively modulate all of the individual, decentralized cost-benefit decisions clinicians need to make. Although chiefs of service can issue selective admonitions such as "Let's stop ordering routine blood cultures on all intensive-care unit patients", available evidence suggests that the success of these pressure tactics is usually short-lived. Further, these medical staff-administration committees often are plagued by serious joint loyalty conflicts, as chiefs of service are torn between global hospital goals and local departmental peer pressure.

NOTES AND QUESTIONS ON THE HARRIS ARTICLE

1. Harris is both an M.D. and a Ph.D. economist. What advantages does he have in evaluating hospitals? Any disadvantages?

2. Harris's article discusses the effects of proposed regulation, but is it clear that his analysis of the dynamics of hospital management applies only to a regulated hospital? Would similar organizational and operational problems arise if hospitals faced a price-competitive marketplace? What effect would the introduction of the prospective payment system (PPS) under Medicare be likely to have on hospitals? See Glandon & Morrisey, Redefining the Hospital/Physician Relationship under Prospective Payment, 23 Inquiry 166 (1986) ("PPS fundamentally changed the financial incentives facing hospitals but left physician (and patient) incentives unaffected").

Are the problems of cost containment that Harris observes limited to hospitals? Consider the dynamic effects of imposing a budget constraint on any group of health care providers. For example, making a capitation payment to an HMO, group practice, physician network, or PHO creates major challenges to the decision-making mechanisms of the organization. Although the Harris article is offered here for the insights it provides into the operation of hospitals, the problem of getting physicians to cooperate with institutional or other cost-containment efforts and to achieve a consistent, rational allocation of resources is universal.

3. In considering the materials in this section, keep in mind the question *why* hospitals are organized as they are. Does Harris address this question or give a hint as to the answer? In another, more technical article covering much of the same ground and characterizing the hospital as "two firms in one," Harris considered this question more fully. Harris, The Internal Organization of Hospitals: Some Economic Implications, 8 Bell J. Econ. 467 (1977). Noting that "business as usual in hospitals is, after all, a continuous sequence of potential crises," he concludes that "the organization is set up to protect the doctor from behaving as economic man" (id. at 468) and "to eliminate the necessity for repeated cost calculations in the care of patients" (id. at 475). Harris observes, however, that the special organizational bifurcation of the hospital might also be regarded either "as a mere artifact of the insurance system" (id. at 468) or as "basically designed to perpetuate an organized medical monopoly" (id. at 474). Can you explain the thinking behind these alternative explanations? Which explanation do you find most plausible at this point?

4. What do you think of Harris's preferred explanation for the extreme separation of responsibilities in hospitals? Recall how economist Kenneth Arrow, in his well known 1963 article referenced in chapter 3(§A), attributed the noncompetitive character of the overall market for medical care to its special nature, particularly the unequal distribution of knowledge and information and the pervasive uncertainty about the possible need for and efficacy of medical treatment. Arrow, Uncertainty and the Welfare Economics of Medical Care, 53 Am.Econ.Rev. 941 (1963). Does Harris's analysis of the internal structure of hospitals reflect a similar view? Sociologist Paul Starr, in a discussion also quoted in chapter 3, criticized Arrow's earlier expression of admiration for the systematic subversion of market forces that he observed in medical care. Is Harris's view of hospital organization subject to a similar criticism?

The Legal Status of Hospital Medical Staffs

St. John's Hospital Medical Staff v. St. John Regional Medical Center, Inc.

Supreme Court of South Dakota, 1976.
90 S.D. 674, 245 N.W.2d 472.

■ MILLER, CIRCUIT JUDGE.

St. John's Hospital Medical Staff (hereinafter referred to as medical staff) is an unincorporated association whose members are physicians duly licensed to practice medicine in South Dakota, holding medical staff privileges at and utilizing the facilities of the St. John Regional Medical Center, Inc., of Huron, South Dakota. St. John Regional Medical Center (hereinafter referred to as medical center) is a South Dakota corporation, incorporated under the laws regulating nonprofit corporations and is authorized to operate in the State of South Dakota.

This is an action for declaratory judgment under SDCL 21–24–1 et seq. It was commenced by the medical staff on June 25, 1973, asking the trial court to determine the rights and duties of the parties under an agreement designated as the "Bylaws, Rules, and Regulations of St. John's Hospital Medical Staff" (hereinafter referred to as medical staff bylaws) as those bylaws relate to the corporate bylaws (hereinafter referred to as medical center bylaws) enacted by the defendant. Plaintiffs requested the trial court to compel the defendant to abide by the provisions of certain medical staff bylaws and to invalidate the purported changes unilaterally made by the medical center in such bylaws. The trial court granted the requested relief and the medical center appealed. On appeal, the medical center argues (1) that the trial court erred in holding that a legal contract existed between the medical staff and the medical center by reason of the medical staff bylaws, and (2) that the medical staff lacks the attributes of a legal entity necessary to commence this action.

In October 1947, the Sisters of the Franciscan Order proposed certain medical staff bylaws to regulate the affairs of the physicians wanting to use the hospital. These bylaws were taken from a book on hospital organization and management. They were printed and distributed to the doctors of the area who were considering association with the hospital. The proposed medical staff bylaws contained an "Amendment Article" and an "Equally Binding Article." The interpretation and effect of these articles formulate the main issues of this action. The "Amendment Article" provides:

> "Article VIII
>
> "These by-laws may be amended after notice given at any regular meeting of the staff. Such notices shall be laid on the table until the next regular meeting and shall require a two-thirds majority of those present for adoption. Amendments so made shall be effective when approved by the governing body."

The "Equally Binding" article provides:

> "Article IX
>
> "These by-laws shall be adopted at any regular meeting of the staff and shall become effective when approved by the governing body of the hospital. They shall when adopted and approved, be equally binding on the governing body and the staff."

After a great deal of discussion concerning these two provisions, as well as provisions relating to the internal rotation of staff, the medical staff bylaws were adopted by the medical staff and approved by the medical center.

These medical staff bylaws were in effect from 1947 until 1972. During that time, various amendments were made to them in accordance with the amendment procedure prescribed. In 1972, the medical center wished to make certain changes in the bylaws.[3] The attempted changes were unacceptable to the medical staff and an impasse developed. Out of this impasse springs the present lawsuit.

On November 24, 1972, the board of directors of the medical center unilaterally adopted new medical staff bylaws which were not approved by the medical staff. The medical center now insists that the medical staff is bound by the bylaws so adopted. The medical staff contends and the trial court held that the 1972 revised medical staff bylaws are null and void by reason of the fact that they were not enacted according to the provisions set out in the original 1947 medical staff bylaws.

The main issue raised in this appeal is whether the board of directors of the medical center has the power to amend the 1947 medical staff bylaws without the participation and approval of the medical staff as provided for in Article VIII of the medical staff bylaws. The medical center argues that the trial court erred in holding that a legal contract existed between the medical staff and the medical center by reason of the original 1947 medical staff bylaws. It raises two policy arguments in support of this contention: the power to amend the articles must be lodged in the directors in order (a) to avoid impending loss of accreditation, and (b) to avoid the possibility of independent hospital liability in some future case of malpractice. After a review of the record, we find these arguments to be without merit. The trial court specifically held that there was no evidence that the hospital would lose accreditation if it were not allowed to revise the medical staff bylaws. Further, the medical center's assertions regarding independent liability are premature and not vital to this appeal. We therefore decline to decide that issue.

The medical center additionally argues that the medical staff lacks the attributes of a legal entity necessary to commence this action. As stated above, the medical staff represents an unincorporated association of the individual physicians holding medical staff privileges at the medical center. SDCL 21–24–2 provides that:

> "The word 'person' wherever used in [the declaratory judgment chapter] shall be construed to mean any . . . unincorporated association, or society . . . of any character whatsoever."

Therefore, plaintiff medical staff is a proper party to bring this action.

---

3. E.g., one change would allow the Chief Executive Officer of the medical center to temporarily suspend the clinical privileges of a staff physician upon a determination that the action must be taken immediately in the best interests of the patient care in the medical center. Another change would require medical center approval of all officers of the medical staff. These examples are for illustrative purposes only.

The remaining question to be resolved is whether the trial court erred in holding that the medical staff bylaws adopted and approved by both the medical center and the medical staff constitute a contract.

As a general rule, the bylaws of a corporation, so long as adopted in conformity with state law, constitute a binding contract between the corporation and its shareholders.

An analogous rule in the area of medical staff bylaws is found in Berberian v. Lancaster Osteopathic Hospital Association, Inc., (1959), 395 Pa. 257, 149 A.2d 456, 458, where the court stated that "[t]he relationship between a hospital association and a member of the hospital's staff is based on contract...." * * * See also Joseph v. Passaic Hospital Ass'n, 26 N.J. 557, 141 A.2d 18. In the present case, we hold that the 1947 medical staff bylaws do constitute a contract which is, by its express terms, subject to amendment when the amendment is agreed to by both the medical staff and the medical center.

* * * SDCL 47–22–63[4] grants the corporation power to make or alter bylaws for the administration and regulation of corporate affairs, so long as such bylaws are not inconsistent with the corporate charter or state laws. SDCL 47–22–33 carries this power one additional step in that:

> "... The power to alter, amend or repeal the bylaws or adopt new bylaws shall be vested in the board of directors *unless otherwise provided in ... the bylaws.* The bylaws may contain any provisions for the regulation and management of the affairs of a corporation not inconsistent with law or the articles of incorporation." (emphasis supplied)

In the present case the medical staff bylaws did so otherwise provide.

Clearly, then, South Dakota statutes recognize the power in a corporation to delegate a voice in the adoption of new bylaws to another entity. Such is the case here. The original articles of incorporation and medical center bylaws authorize the medical staff to promulgate medical staff bylaws.[5] These medical staff bylaws call for a specific amendment procedure which must be followed. The medical center by ignoring the procedure set forth in Article VIII and by not including the medical staff in the attempted bylaws amendment has breached this contractual relationship with the medical staff.

It is therefore the holding of this court that the 1947 medical staff bylaws, after approval by the medical center, were binding upon the medical center and must be amended in accordance with Article VIII of

4. SDCL 47–22–63. "Each corporation shall have power to make and alter bylaws, not inconsistent with its articles of incorporation or with the laws of this state, for the administration and regulation of the affairs of the corporation."

5. The medical center bylaws provided, before amendment:

"There shall be By–Laws, rules and regulations for the Medical Staff setting forth its organization and government. Proposed By–Laws, rules and regulations may be recommended by the Medical Staff, but only those adopted by the Board of Directors shall become effective."

those bylaws. Therefore, the medical staff bylaws unilaterally adopted by the medical center are null and void.

Affirmed.

NOTES AND QUESTIONS ON MEDICAL STAFF BYLAWS

1. Who were the parties to the "contract" in the *St. John's* case? The staff bylaws may also be part of the hospital's contract with each individual doctor (see the *Berberian* case, cited in *St. John's*), but that is a distinct issue to be touched upon in § C of this chapter. You might consider, however, whether bylaw changes might be effective only with respect to new physicians or those accepting renewals of term appointments.

2. The last sentence of MS.2.1 in the 1997 JCAHO Manual, reproduced supra, was added in 1987. Should the JCAHO standard influence a court in judging a particular controversy? For an account of how a hospital board, in a showdown with a recalcitrant medical staff, suspended the staff's bylaws and appointed new staff officers, see Holoweiko, How Much Muscle Does a Hospital Board Have?, Med. Econ., Jan. 23, 1984, at 273. Would you advise a hospital to conform its bylaws to the JCAHO requirement? Does the hospital have any choice?

3. What is the best argument that might be made for the St. John Hospital? As a matter of corporate law, are there some powers and responsibilities that a corporate board cannot delegate to others? Might some provisions in medical staff bylaws be invalid because the board's acceptance of them was *ultra vires* or inconsistent with the model of corporate governance embodied in state corporation acts? What kinds of provisions might be deemed to exceed the board's inherent powers?

4. The provision of the 1984 and 1985 JCAH Manuals comparable to the JCAHO's current MS.2 provided that "the medical staff develops and adopts bylaws and rules and regulations to establish a framework for medical staff activities and accountability to the governing body." The 1983 Manual was similar to later versions (including MS.2 in the 1997 edition) in referring to "a framework of self-government." What do you suppose was the significance of dropping and then adding back the reference to self-governance?

5. The 1988 Manual (GB.1.18.1) provided, "The medical staff bylaws and rules and regulations that have been adopted by the medical staff are subject to, and effective upon, approval by the governing body; approval is not unreasonably withheld." Although the 1997 Manual contains no similarly explicit provision, MS.2.1 makes clear that hospitals should not act unilaterally with respect to the staff's bylaws.

6. The AMA–AHA Joint Task Force Report of 1985, in declaring that the governing board and the medical staff had to agree on the staff bylaws, stated (p. 19),

> Such an allocation of responsibility is not a test of the legal authority of either party, but rather acknowledges that the medical staff cannot

adequately perform its duties unless both the governing board and the medical staff agree to and support the bylaws that govern the medical staff's activities. If the hospital governing board and the organized medical staff do not agree * * * then the parties should act to achieve resolution of the impasse at an intra-institutional level.

7. Compare to the *St. John's* case the situation that arose, and the result, in Keane v. St. Francis Hosp., 522 N.W.2d 517 (Wis.App.1994). In that case, the court found that the governing board of a county hospital had acted improperly in peremptorily removing Dr. Keane as the elected president or chief of the medical staff (COS) despite the following provision in the medical staff's bylaws: "The Governing Board, by resolution, may remove an officer of the Medical/Dental Staff upon receipt of a recommendation of three-fourths (3/4) of the Active Medical/Dental Staff." The trial court had found that "the dynamic tension between the Chief of Staff and the Board has ripened into something beyond dynamic tension into some sort of warfare," id. at 525, and the board, of which Dr. Keane was an ex officio member, was told that his differences with the hospital's CEO were not personal but would "be the same towards any administration that stands up to him on what is right." Id. at 527. At a meeting where the medical staff voted to condemn the board's action, at least one physician was troubled, stating, "In thirty years there has never been a vote like this before in this hospital where the staff has rebelled against the Board. The Board is the authority." Id. at 529.

The court rejected all constructions of the bylaws that would have justified the board's action, ruled that "bylaws can constitute a contract between a hospital and its staff," id. at 522, and cited the *St. John's* case on the difficulty of amending the staff bylaws. Finally, the court disagreed with the hospital's argument that limiting the board's power to discharge the COS "would be incompatible with its legal responsibility for the overall operation of the hospital and its staff under various broadly-worded state and federal regulations." Id. In the final analysis, however, the court agreed with the trial judge's decision, on equitable grounds, not to issue an order of mandamus compelling the hospital to reinstate Dr. Keane. Id. at 525–30. The potential for renewed "warfare" and for adverse effects on the hospital's work, board, staff, and patients justified the trial court's exercise of its discretion not to provide the remedy that would normally follow from its legal conclusions. Should it have been necessary for the court to invoke principles of equity to ensure that the hospital board controls the work environment in the institution?

NOTES AND QUESTIONS ON THE NATURE AND LEGAL STATUS OF THE MEDICAL STAFF

1. *Amenability to Lawsuits.* Is a medical staff an independent legal entity capable of being sued for negligence in selecting or overseeing the work of a staff physician? In a case widely remarked at the time, a New Jersey court allowed a plaintiff to include the medical staff as well as the hospital as a defendant, where the allegation was that "they knew or should have known that Dr. McCracken was not competent to perform the surgical procedure on the decedent which he did, but they nevertheless permitted him to do so and allowed him to remain on the case when the situation was obviously beyond his control." Corleto v. Shore Memorial Hospital, 350 A.2d 534 (N.J. Super. 1975). The court thought the legislature had authorized suits against unincorporated associations (and could immunize medical staffs if it wished) and that suing the staff as an entity was more efficient than suing its individual members. It also speculated that "subjecting persons in the class to liability will serve to make them more aware of their responsibilities in assuring that only competent physicians practice within their hospitals, thereby raising the level of medical care within the State." Id. at 539.

The *Corleto* and *St. John's* decisions prompted two hospital law experts to argue that there is no legal basis for the notion that the medical staff is an independent legal entity and that the consequences of conceiving of it as such would be undesirable. Horty & Mulholland, The Legal Status of the Hospital Medical Staff, 22 St. Louis U.L.J. 485 (1978). In their view, "the hospital medical staff is not a legal entity at all" but is instead a "department" of the hospital, which means that "the staff cannot sue or be sued as a body." For further support for the proposition that the medical staff is an unincorporated association, capable of suing and being sued, see W. Isele, The Hospital Medical Staff 4 (1984).

2. *Antitrust Status*. A medical staff can be sued under the Sherman Act as a "combination" or joint venture of its members, who are for most purposes independent competitors. See, e.g., Weiss v. York Hosp., 745 F.2d 786, 814 (3d Cir.1984), cert. denied, 470 U.S. 1060 (1985) (concluding that, "as a matter of law, the medical staff is a combination of individual doctors and therefore that any action taken by the medical staff satisfies the 'contract, combination, or conspiracy' requirement of section 1"). How should staff actions be analyzed to determine whether they are in restraint of trade? This interesting question will be explored in § C of this chapter.

Consider here, however, whether a hospital medical staff can conspire with the hospital itself—as has frequently been alleged by individual physicians in cases brought to redress their loss of clinical privileges. In Nurse Midwifery Assocs. v. Hibbett, 918 F.2d 605 (6th Cir.1990), modified, 927 F.2d 904, cert. denied, 502 U.S. 952 (1991), the court held that the "intracorporate conspiracy doctrine" of Copperweld Corp. v. Independence Tube Corp., 467 U.S. 752 (1984)—under which separate parts of a single enterprise cannot be viewed as co-conspirators for antitrust purposes—precludes finding a conspiracy between a hospital and its medical staff. Because the hospital and staff are not competitors, the court could see no substantial antitrust concerns that would support a departure form traditional theories of agency. The court further refused to recognize the exception to the intracorporate conspiracy doctrine for cases in which an employee or other agent of the enterprise has an independent personal interest in achieving the object of the conspiracy. Several other courts of appeals have agreed with this reasoning. E.g., Pudlo v. Adamski, 2 F.3d 1153 (7th Cir.1993) (unpublished) (noting "our agreement with the position taken by the Third and Fourth Circuits"), cert. denied, 510 U.S. 1072 (1994); Oksanen v. Page Mem. Hosp., 945 F.2d 696 (4th Cir.1991) (en banc), cert. denied, 502 U.S. 1074 (1992); Nanavati v. Burdette Tomlin Mem. Hosp., 857 F.2d 96 (3d Cir.1988), cert. denied, 489 U.S. 1078 (1989) (holding that the hospital's medical staff "operated as an officer of the corporation would in relation to the corporation" and thus could not conspire with it). But at least two others circuits have not. See Bolt v. Halifax Hosp. Med. Ctr., 891 F.2d 810 (11th Cir.1990), cert. denied, 495 U.S. 924 (1990); Oltz v. St. Peter.s Community Hosp., 861 F.2d 1440 (9th Cir.1988).

As will be seen in § C, federal courts have been very quick (sometimes too quick) to find legal excuses—various immunities and exemptions, for example—to dismiss antitrust suits by individual doctors claiming to be victims of illegal conspiracies. How would you argue against those courts that have used the *Copperweld* doctrine to reduce their dockets? See generally Brewbaker, Antitrust Conspiracy Doctrine and the Hospital Enterprise, 74 B.U. L. Rev. 67 (1994). Should the Supreme Court have granted any of the numerous petitions for certiorari to resolve the conflict among the circuits on the application of *Copperweld* in these cases? Can you see a reason why the conflict may be of little moment as a practical matter?

3. *Having It Both Ways?* Consider the following from a statement issued by the office of the AMA general counsel:

> The contention that the powers of the medical staff in dealing with professional matters in the hospital are derived by delegation from the governing board is more symbolic than real. State law, or JCAH standards that have the practical effect of law, mandate an organized medical staff with self-governing authority. Furthermore, JCAH standards are recognized in the Medicare law for hospitals participating in providing reimbursable services to Medicare beneficiaries.
>
> Briefly stated, the organized medical staff is a legally separate entity, an unincorporated association representing the collective professional responsibility of its individual members in the management and administration of medical care within the hospital.
>
> When it functions in the name of and on behalf of the hospital, separate identity does not comport with public policy and is not relevant in dealing with third parties, as in negligence and antitrust litigation.
>
> Insofar as the medical staff in dealing with the hospital represents the interests of individual staff members, or patients whom they have brought to the hospital for treatment, or the collective interests of members in disputes with the hospital, the status of the medical staff as a separate entity is relevant.

Hospital Decision-makers Urged to Unify, Am.Med.News, Nov. 1, 1985, at 1, 26. Does it make sense to view the medical staff as a separate legal entity for some legal purposes but not for others? From the perspective of the medical staff, what is the most advantageous legal status? From the perspective of the hospital? Should a medical staff retain its own legal counsel? What are the possible risks of so doing?

4. *Medical Staff vs. Administration.* In Yarnell v. Sisters of St. Francis Health Services, 446 N.E.2d 359 (Ind.App.1983), the medical staff of the hospital recommended Dr. Yarnell's reappointment, but the hospital's CEO opposed it before the governing board on the basis that the doctor was "threatening and abusive of medical staff personnel and that he was generally disruptive of hospital procedures." Id. at 361. Dr. Yarnell filed suit to enjoin a hearing on his case scheduled by the governing board on the theory that the board had delegated its authority to make reappointments to the medical staff through certain bylaw provisions. The court disagreed with Dr. Yarnell's reading of the bylaws, finding that the governing board had final authority to make reappointments. The court also rejected a claim that the process was "unfairly tainted by the involvement of the administrator and executive director," commenting that "[t]he mere fact that officers in the Hospital were performing their duties in what they perceived as the best interests of the Hospital is not enough to prove that he [Yarnell] was prejudiced." Id. at 363.

In Ad Hoc Executive Committee v. Runyan, 716 P.2d 465 (Colo.1986), the executive committee of a public hospital's medical staff sought to challenge the decision of the hospital's trustees to reinstate the staff privileges of a doctor whom the staff had sought to suspend for violating a medical staff bylaw prohibiting a staff physician from telling patients about presumed deficiencies of another staff physician. The court found that the executive committee lacked standing to bring the suit because, by statute, "the medical staff operates pursuant to written bylaws approved by the governing board of the hospital" and because the Executive Committee was created by and answerable to and was, "in effect, an arm of the Trustees." Id. at 469–70. Although a state statute did encourage "disciplinary control of the practice of health care rendered by physicians" (in part by granting members of peer review committees immunity from lawsuits related to review functions), the court saw nothing in these provisions conferring standing to sue upon such committees and went on to find that a "reading of the entire statute suggests that the right to seek judicial review of an adverse decision of a governing board belongs only to the physician." Id.

For a revealing (but extreme) example of the conflicts that can arise between a hospital and its medical staff, see Carlova, Is This a Waterloo in the Privileges War?, Med.Econ., Jan. 7, 1985, p. 62. The medical staff had blocked 79 consecutive applicants for staff privileges, allegedly because staff members not only wanted no new competition in the area but also hoped eventually to buy the hospital (cheap). The hospital board, over strenuous staff objections, appointed a highly controversial surgeon who specialized in "bloodless" surgery, which was especially attractive to Jehovah's Witnesses (who oppose blood transfusions on religious grounds). The showdown ended in court, which ruled in favor of the hospital.

5. *Impasse.* A 1985 AMA–AHA joint task force report on relationships between hospitals and their medical staffs (referenced earlier in this section) suggested that hospitals maintain some form of intra-institutional "impasse resolution mechanism * * * to prevent potentially harmful discord and to avoid having to test the legal rights of the parties." The 1983 JCAH Manual provided that, where the governing board differed with the staff on a question of privileges, a combined committee of board and staff members should review the matter. Many hospitals were organized to meet this requirement (see Figure I–1 in the excerpt from Rakich & Darr, supra), although it was relaxed in later manuals. Standard GB.1.12 in the 1988 Manual, for example, provided simply that "any differences in recommendations concerning medical staff appointments [or] clinical privileges are resolved within a reasonable period of time by the governing body and the medical staff." Compare GO.2.6 in the 1997 Manual, supra.

In one case, the bylaws of a public (county) hospital provided that

> when the Executive Committee and the Board of Trustees disagree, the case is referred to a Joint Conference Committee consisting of four trustees and four physicians. In this case, three of the four committee physicians were the original complainants.

In re Zaman, 329 S.E.2d 436 (S.C.1985). The trustees initially rejected the staff's recommendation against Dr. Zaman but later reversed themselves. The court held, "Having three of respondent's original accusers sit also as his jury is a direct violation of respondent's right to a fair and meaningful hearing under the due process clause." Id. at 437. Where else does one find joint "conference committees" used to resolve differences between disagreeing bodies? Is the analogy illuminating?

Are you satisfied with the JCAHO requirements and the arrangement in the *Zaman* case? Or do they seem to subject governing boards to inappropriate accountability to the medical staff? Should this decision-making framework affect the view that antitrust courts, concerned about possible anticompetitive abuses by the medical staff, take of hospital decisions? Recall this question when considering the antitrust aspects of privilege decisions in § C.

6. How does a hospital medical staff differ from a labor union? Could the staff engage in collective bargaining with the hospital, using the strike threat as a sanction?

NOTES ON THE ORGANIZATION OF OTHER HOSPITAL PERSONNEL; COLLECTIVE BARGAINING

1. *The Nursing Service.* According to the 1997 JCAHO Manual, a hospital's nursing service should be "directed by a nurse executive who is a registered nurse qualified by advanced education and management experience" and who has "the authority and responsibility for establishing standards for nursing practice." (How and why are nursing professionals organized differently within the hospital than physicians?)

2. *Bargaining Units.* Unlike physicians, nurses and other hospital employees may organize labor unions for collective bargaining and are free, at least in private institutions, to strike. (Strikes have in fact become more common in recent years.) The 1974 legislation that removed the earlier exemption of nonprofit hospitals from the National Labor Relations Act (noted in chapter 3(§B)) indicated a congressional concern that unionization not divide the hospital work force into such a large number of bargaining units that hospital services would be frequently disrupted. Employers tend to prefer larger units with heterogeneous membership less likely to agree on collective action. See American Hosp. Ass'n v. NLRB, 899 F.2d 651, 654 (7th Cir. 1990) ("If the desirability (from the union standpoint) of homogeneous units is stressed, even a hospital of average size might have ten or twenty or even more units, each with a bare handful of workers. The cost of the institution's labor relations and the probability of work stoppages would soar."), aff'd, 499 U.S. 606 (1991). Naturally, questions have arisen over the years concerning the right of nurses and other workers to be organized separately from other professional and nonprofessional employees.

Until 1984, the National Labor Relations Board (NLRB), using its traditional "community-of-interests" test, recognized seven categories of hospital employees as presumptively appropriate bargaining units. Several federal courts took the view that the Board's approach failed to satisfy Congress's desire to avoid undue proliferation of bargaining units in the health care field. In 1984, the NLRB shifted to a case-by-case approach, starting with broad units (professionals and nonprofessionals) and allowing separate representation only for those groups that could demonstrate a "disparity of interests," but this approach was overturned in 1987. International Brotherhood of Elec. Workers, Local No. 474 v. NLRB, 814 F.2d 697 (D.C.Cir.1987). Differing from other courts, the court regarded the use of the disparity-of-interests approach as a departure from precedent that was not compelled by the 1974 legislation, as the Board had maintained.

Shortly after this ruling, the NLRB, long famous for preferring to make policy through case-by-case adjudication rather than through formal rulemaking, resolved to establish hospital bargaining units by the latter method. In 1988, it promulgated a rule creating the following eight distinct bargaining units for the health care industry: registered nurses, physicians, all other professionals, technical employees, business office clericals, skilled maintenance employees, all other nonprofessional employees, and security guards. Preexisting nonconforming units were exempted. 29 C.F.R. § 103.30 (1997). The rule was challenged in court, and finally upheld by the Supreme Court. American Hosp. Ass'n v. NLRB, 499 U.S. 606 (1991). The effect of the rule is to create more homogeneous bargaining units, generally considered easier to unionize than broadly defined units. See generally LeRoy et al., The Law and Economics of Collective Bargaining for Hospitals: An Empirical Public Policy Analysis of Bargaining Unit Determinations, 9 Yale J. on Reg. 1 (1992) (finding NLRB rule workable); Mandelman, NLRB Rulemaking on Health Care Collective Bargaining Units: Predictability, But At What Cost?, 9 Hofstra Labor L.J. (1992); Grunewald, The NLRB's First Rulemaking: An Experiment in Pragmatism, 41 Duke L.J. 274 (1992).

3. *Supervisory Employees.* In the NLRA, Congress extended protection only to nonsupervisory workers. A significant tension has developed between the NLRB's definition of a "supervisor" as someone who uses independent judgment in directing other workers and Congress's desire to extend the acts's protections to "professional employees"—nearly all of whom are likely to have some supervisory responsibilities. In NLRB v. Health Care & Retirement Corp., 511 U.S. 571 (1994), the issue was whether licensed practical nurses (LPNs) who were the highest-ranking staff members on duty in a nursing home during most of 24–hour day (and on weekends) were supervisors (as the nursing home contended) and therefore subject to termination or discipline "at will," without recourse to the NLRA's protections against "unfair labor practices." The Court set forth the factual tests for determining whether an individual employee is a supervisor. In answer to the argument that the LPNs, as professionals, were working on behalf of patients and not "in the interest of the employer," the Supreme Court stated that it "could see no basis for the Board's blanket assertion that supervisory authority exercised in connection with patient care is somehow not in the interest of the employer." Id. at 577–78. Federal appeals courts have reached differing conclusions in later, similar cases involving nurses. Compare Beverly Enters., W.Va., Inc. v. NLRB, 136 F.3d 353 (4th Cir.1998) (LPNs working as "charge nurses" in nursing homes held not supervisors precluded by NLRA from bargaining collectively); Beverly Enters.—Pa., Inc. v. NLRB, 129 F.3d 1269 (D.C.Cir. 1997) (LPNs not supervisors) with Caremore, Inc. v. NLRB, 129 F.3d 365 (6th Cir.1997) (LPNs held supervisors). See also Providence Alaska Med. Center v. NLRB, 121 F.3d 548 (9th Cir.1997) ("charge nurses," RNs who occasionally fill in for supervisory nurses in hospitals, held not supervisors under NLRA).

In the interest of economy, many hospitals have been modifying their staffing patterns to assign more patients, and more aides and other helpers, to a single registered nurse. In becoming supervisors with less contact with patients, are RNs losing (or gaining) professional status? Where must they look for job security if the federal labor laws are unavailable?

SECTION B: HOSPITAL LIABILITY

Corporate Responsibility for Professional Work

Bernardi v. Community Hospital Association

Supreme Court of Colorado, En Banc, 1968.
166 Colo. 280, 443 P.2d 708.

■ GROVES, JUSTICE.

This action was brought by the plaintiffs in error, Lisa Marie Bernardi and her father, against Community Hospital Association, a Colorado corpo-

ration, Dorothy Dravis [the Nurse] and Charles L. Aumiller [the Doctor].
* * *

Lisa, seven years of age, was a patient in the Hospital, having been the subject of surgery for the drainage of an abscessed appendix. The Doctor was her attending physician. He had left a written post-operative order at the Hospital that Lisa was to be given an injection of tetracycline every twelve hours. During the evening of the first day following surgery, the Nurse, employed by the Hospital and acting under this order, injected the dosage of tetracycline in Lisa's right gluteal region. It was alleged in the complaint that the Nurse negligently injected the tetracycline into or adjacent to the sciatic nerve, causing Lisa to have a "complete foot-drop" and to lose permanently the normal use of her right foot. For the purpose of this opinion the alleged negligence and resulting injury are assumed, although undoubtedly these will be issues at the trial.

* * *

The Hospital's motion for summary judgment was predicated on the following propositions: That the scope of the license of the Hospital did not contemplate "the practice of medicine" nor "the practice of professional nursing" under Colorado statutes; that the Nurse could act only under the direction of a licensed physician; that under the U.S. Food, Drug and Cosmetic Act the drug tetracycline was limited to "use under the professional supervision of a practitioner licensed by law to administer such drug"; and that the Nurse was "obeying instructions of a physician" and subserving "him in his ministrations to the patient" when she administered the injection of tetracycline.

I.

The trial court's order * * * did not state specifically the reason or theory underlying the judgment.

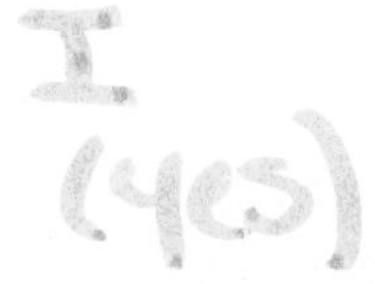

The principal argument of counsel for the plaintiffs and the Hospital are directed toward the question as to whether the doctrine of *respondeat superior* should be applied to the Hospital for the act of the Nurse. We have concluded that the rule of *respondeat superior* should be applied to the Hospital and to reverse so far as it is concerned. As a preface to our enunciation in this respect, it is well to review some of the decisions of this court relating to the liability of hospitals.

In St. Mary's Academy of Sisters of Loretto of City of Denver v. Solomon, 77 Colo. 463, 238 P. 22, it was held that judgment may be obtained against a charitable corporation for a tort, but that no property held in a charitable trust can be taken under execution upon the judgment.

* * * O'Connor v. Boulder Colorado Sanitarium Association, 105 Colo. 259, 96 P.2d 835, followed *St. Mary's Academy* [and held] that the charitable institution might be liable for the tortious acts of its agents and any

judgment would have to be satisfied from sources other than its trust funds, e.g., from insurance. * * *

We can, therefore, assume in the instant case that the trial court did not grant summary judgment in favor of the Hospital because of its finding that it is a charitable corporation.

In Rosane v. Senger, 112 Colo. 363, 149 P.2d 372, there was involved alleged negligence by surgeons in leaving a gauze pad inside the plaintiff. This court affirmed dismissal of the action insofar as it related to the hospital involved, stating that a hospital could not be licensed to practice medicine and surgery; that the relation between doctor and patient is personal; that a hospital is powerless to command or forbid any act by staff doctors it employs in the practice of their profession; and that, unless it employs those whose lack of skill is known or should be known to it or by some special conduct or neglect makes itself responsible for their malpractice, it cannot be held liable therefor. To the same effect are Beadles v. Metayka, 135 Colo. 366, 311 P.2d 711, and Moon v. Mercy Hospital, 150 Colo. 430, 373 P.2d 944. In *Beadles* the plaintiff, while under anesthetic and prior to commencement of surgery, fell off the operating table. It was held that the surgeon had assumed command and responsibility and that, therefore, the doctrine of *respondeat superior* did not apply to the hospital with respect to any negligence on the part of the hospital orderly who was in the operating room. In *Moon* it was pointed out that the respective licenses to practice medicine and to operate a hospital authorize related but different activities. It was held that the employment by a hospital of doctors on its staff does not make it liable for neglect in the discharge of their professional duty, as the hospital is powerless to command or forbid any act by them in the practice of their profession, and that a licensed physician is the principal when performing medical services in a hospital.

This brings us to St. Lukes Hospital Association v. Long, 125 Colo. 25, 240 P.2d 917. There, during the early morning hours of the day following a tonsilectomy and adenoidectomy, the body of a three-year-old boy slipped through the rails of his hospital bed, his head was caught, and he strangled. It was held that any negligent acts of the nurse employed by the hospital were administrative acts, as distinct from professional services, and might be the basis for liability of the hospital. * * *

It has been ably argued that, since this Court has held that *respondeat superior* does not apply to doctors for the reason that hospitals are not licensed to practice medicine, it follows that *respondeat superior* does not apply to professional acts of nurses since hospitals are not licensed to practice nursing. It appears that the matter of *respondeat superior* with respect to a nurse acting in professional capacity heretofore has not been before this Court. We feel that a distinction should be made between the "doctor" cases above mentioned and the "nurse" case, and a different rule applied.

Of particular interest are the 1914 opinion in Schloendorff v. Society of New York Hospital, 211 N.Y. 125, 105 N.E. 92, and the 1957 opinion in Bing v. Thunig, 2 N.Y.2d 656, 163 N.Y.S.2d 3, 143 N.E.2d 3, which overruled *Schloendorff*. In *Schloendorff* Judge Cardozo, speaking for the Court of Appeals of New York, ruled that nurses in treating a patient are carrying out the orders of physicians, to whose authority they are subject, and are not servants of the hospital.

In *Bing* hospital nurses were aware that tincture of zephiran, an alcoholic antiseptic painted on the patient's back prior to surgery, was potentially dangerous. They had been instructed to exercise care to see that none of this fluid dropped on linen, to inspect linen and to remove any that had become so stained. The fluid reached the sheeting underneath the patient, but the nurses did not discover or attempt to discover this and as a result the patient was severely burned when the sheeting caught fire from an electric cautery. It was there stated:

> "Following Schloendorff v. Society of New York Hosp., 211 N.Y. 125, 105 N.E. 92, a body of law has developed making the liability of a hospital for injuries suffered by a patient, through the negligence of its employees, depend on whether the injury-producing act was 'administrative' or 'medical.' The wisdom and workability of this rule exempting hospitals from the normal operation of the doctrine of *respondeat superior* have in recent years come under increasing attack. * * *
>
> "* * * The difficulty of differentiating between the 'medical' and the 'administrative' in this context * * * has long plagued the courts, and, indeed, as consideration of a few illustrative cases reveals, a consistent and clearly defined distinction between the terms has proved to be highly elusive. Placing an improperly capped hot water bottle on a patient's body is administrative, while keeping a hot water bottle too long on a patient's body is medical. Administering blood, by means of a transfusion, to the wrong patient is administrative, while administering the wrong blood to the right patient is medical. Employing an improperly sterilized needle for a hypodermic injection is administrative, while improperly administering a hypodermic injection is medical. Failing to place sideboards on a bed after a nurse decided that they were necessary is administrative, while failing to decide that sideboards should be used when the need does exist is medical. [The court cited cases in support of each proposition stated.—Eds.]
>
> "From distinctions such as these there is to be deduced neither guiding principle nor clear delineation of policy; they cannot help but cause confusion, cannot help but create doubt and uncertainty. And, while the failure of the nurses in the present case to inspect and remove the contaminated linen might, perhaps, be denominated an administrative default, we do not consider it either wise or necessary again to become embroiled in an overnice disputation as to whether it should be labeled administrative or medical. . . .
>
> ". . . For example, the nurse, regarded as an independent contractor when she injures a patient by an act characterized as medical, is considered an employee of the hospital, entitled to compensation, if she should happen to injure herself by that very same act. . . .

. . .

"The doctrine of *respondeat superior* is grounded on firm principles of law and justice. Liability is the rule, immunity the exception. It is not too much to expect that those who serve and minister to members of the public should do so, as do all others, subject to that principle and within the obligation not to injure through carelessness.

. . .

"Hospitals should, in short, shoulder the responsibilities borne by everyone else. There is no reason to continue their exemption from the universal rule of *respondeat superior*. The test should be, for these institutions, whether charitable or profit-making, as it is for every other employer, was the person who committed the negligent injury-producing act one of its employees, and, if he was, was he acting within the scope of his employment."

If we were to rule that *respondeat superior* does not apply because the hospital is not licensed as a Nurse, then it would seem to follow that an airline should not be liable for the negligence of its pilot because the airline is not licensed to fly an aircraft. This and other examples are given in Bing v. Thunig, supra. The Hospital was the employer of the Nurse. Only it had the right to hire and fire her. Only it could assign the Nurse to certain hours, certain areas and certain patients. There was no choice in the Doctor or the plaintiffs as to the identity of the nurses who would serve Lisa. In this day and age a hospital should be responsible for the acts of its nurses within the scope of their employment, irrespective of whether they are acting "administratively" or "professionally."

Some of the authorities mentioned, and others, make no distinction in application of the rule of *respondeat superior* to hospitals between employed nurses and employed doctors. Expressly, this opinion relates only to nurses. Also, it should be borne in mind that this decision relates only to the case in which the nurse acts out of the presence of the doctor.

* * *

III.

There is now considered the order dismissing the complaint as against the Doctor. The Doctor was a private physician. He left orders at the Hospital for post-operative injections to be given by any nurse on the staff of the Hospital. The plaintiffs alleged in the complaint that the Nurse gave the injection "while acting pursuant to Defendant Aumiller's directions and while under his control and supervision." However, the Nurse stated in her answers to interrogatories that she and Lisa were the only ones present in the room at the time of the injection and that Lisa's parents were standing just outside the room. The plaintiffs concede in their brief that the Doctor was not present at the time the injection was given.

* * *

It is apparent from the record that the Doctor did not have the control necessary to apply the doctrine of *respondeat superior* to him. He did not know what nurses would give the injection. The Nurse had been employed by the Hospital and was under its control and direction. The Doctor, not being present when the injection was given, had no opportunity to control its administration. His instructions that injections were to be given did not give rise to a master-servant relationship.

The Doctor's position here is vastly different from that in Beadle v. Metayka, supra, where it was held that in the operating room the surgeon is master, has the exclusive control of the acts of the orderly and nurse, and is responsible for their negligence during the time that the patient is in the operating room and the surgeon is present. * * *

IV.

The last assignment of error relates to the order of the trial court denying the plaintiffs' motion for production by the Hospital of an "Incident Report" prepared by the Nurse. The Hospital objected to production of the document on the ground that it was prepared for the Hospital's attorney and was protected by attorney-client privilege. After the Nurse prepared the Incident Report a copy was placed in Lisa's hospital chart, another copy went to the Hospital Administrator and a further copy went to the Director of Nurses at the Hospital. * * *

It well may be that the practice of making an incident report resulted from the advice of counsel, but it seems rather plain that these incident reports were not prepared for the attorney. Rather, they were prepared for certain administrative officials of the Hospital and they were available to the Hospital's attorney if he wished to see them. "To entitle the party to the protection accorded to privileged communications, the communications must have been made to the counsel, attorney, or solicitor acting, for the time being, in the character of legal adviser, and must be made by the client for the purpose of professional advice or aid upon the subject of his rights and liabilities." Caldwell v. Davis, 10 Colo. 481, 15 P. 696, 3 Am.St.Rep. 599. In our view the Court should have ordered the incident report to be produced, and now should do so.

The judgment of dismissal in favor of the [Doctor] * * * is affirmed. The judgment entered in favor of [the Hospital] * * * is reversed and the cause is remanded * * *.

NOTES AND QUESTIONS ON CHARITABLE AND GOVERNMENTAL IMMUNITIES

1. *Charitable Immunity.* A majority of states have abrogated the immunity previously enjoyed—under various rationales—by hospitals that could claim that they were operated for eleemosynary purposes. A number, however, like Colorado in the *Bernardi* case, preserve the immunity for assets held in trust or set it aside only to the extent of the institution's liability insurance. Other states have, by statute, set aside immunity only up to specified dollar amounts. The constitutionality of such caps on liability of charitable institutions was upheld in Lazerson v. Hilton Head

Hosp.,. 439 S.E.2d 836 (S.C.1994); Johnson v. Mountainside Hosp., 571 A.2d 318 (N.J. Super.A.D.1990), cert. denied, 584 A.2d 248 (N.J.1990); and English v. New England Med. Center, 541 N.E.2d 329 (Mass.1989), cert. denied, 493 U.S. 1056 (1990). See generally J. Smith, Hospital Liability § 2.06 (1997); Immunities from Liability ¶ 2, in 2A Hospital Law Manual (1991).

What were/are the policy justifications for charitable immunity in its various forms? In a Georgia case brought against a large public hospital treating a large volume of indigents, charitable immunity was upheld against an equal protection challenge. Ponder v. Fulton–DeKalb Hosp. Auth., 353 S.E.2d 515 (Ga.1987) ("The disadvantaged as a class, far from being discriminated against by the charitable institution, are its only beneficiaries. * * * The charitable immunity doctrine * * * protects the charitable assets available for their care.") The court also held that the hospital did not waive its immunity by maintaining a self-insurance fund to cover liabilities; the purchase of liability insurance would have amounted to a waiver, however. How much sense does this distinction make?

On the scope of charitable immunity, see Endres v. Greenville Hosp. System, 439 S.E.2d 261 (S.C.1993) (damage cap applicable to charities held not to apply to derivative action by parents of injured child, who had already recovered permissible maximum of $200,000); Fulton–DeKalb Hosp. Auth. v. Fanning, 396 S.E.2d 534 (Ga.App.1990) ("a charitable hospital may be liable for negligence to a paying patient"; however, patient who received hospital's charity but now claims he was able to pay and thus not technically a charity patient bears the burden of proving his claim); Harlow v. Chin, 545 N.E.2d 602, 612–13 (Mass.1989) (statutory cap applicable because, although ER patient was charged $26, tort was "committed in the course of [accomplishing] the charitable purposes of [charitable] corporation").

On the applicability of charitable immunity in Georgia to physicians employed by charitable hospitals, see Cutts v. Fulton–DeKalb Hosp. Auth., 385 S.E.2d 436 (Ga.App.1989) (physicians not protected, as doctrine's goal is to preserve funds for charitable uses); Ramey v. Hospital Auth., 462 S.E.2d 787 (Ga.App.1995) (hospital's medical staff and chief of staff held to share charitable immunity since they were not subject to suit independently of hospital authority). Note that physicians may be especially vulnerable to malpractice suits that would normally be brought against the hospital.

How did the decline of charitable immunity affect the character of American hospitals? Conversely, how did the changing character of hospitals affect the rationale for charitable immunity?

2. *Sovereign Immunity.* Government hospitals have also enjoyed immunity from tort actions. The federal government has waived its common-law immunity in the Federal Tort Claims Act. 28 U.S.C. §§ 1346, 2671 et seq. (1994). Indeed, it is exclusively liable for the torts of its employees (including physicians) providing health services within the scope of their employment. 38 U.S.C. § 7316 (1994) (immunizing health personnel from liability). Immunity is preserved against suits for the negligent performance of discretionary functions, for the acts of independent contractors, for intentional torts, and for punitive damages. See J. Smith, supra, at § 2.03; Immunities from Liability, supra, at ¶ 1. There is an exception to the FTCA for injuries sustained by members of the armed services while on active duty. Feres v. United States, 340 U.S. 135 (1950). But see C.R.S. v. United States, 761 F.Supp. 665 (D.C.Minn.1991) (holding that rationale underlying *Feres* doctrine does not apply to suit by national guardsman who contracted AIDS during surgery while in basic training).

Although state governments enjoy sovereign immunity, municipal and county governments have generally been treated as immune only for governmental activities, which have usually, but not always, been held to include the operation of a hospital. In varying degrees, most states have abrogated their own and local governments' immunities by statute. See, e.g, Moser v. Heistand, 681 A.2d 1322 (Pa.1996) (holding statute waiving sovereign immunity to permit suit against public hospitals for negligence on part of employees and agents did not extend to suits, permitted against private hospitals in state, for so-called "corporate negligence," discussed later in this chapter). As in the case of charitable immunity, carrying malpractice insurance or provision for self-insurance may constitute a waiver of sovereign immunity. For cases upholding the sovereign immunity of state university medical centers, see Withers v. University of Kentucky, 939 S.W.2d 340 (Ky.1997) (rejecting argument that statute authorizing university to establish malpractice compensation fund constituted waiver of sovereign immunity); Brennan v. Curators of the Univ. of Missouri, 942 S.W.2d 432 (Mo.App.1997) (holding that curators' adoption of self-insurance plan might operate as waiver of sovereign immunity but that plaintiffs' allegations failed to raise issue); Hyde v. University of Michigan Board of Regents, 393 N.W.2d 847 (Mich.1986) (court noted that later statute abrogated immunity).

For a case striking down a statute limiting liability of government-owned hospitals to $100,000, see Condemarin v. University Hosp., 775 P.2d 348 (Utah 1989). For a recent statute extending sovereign immunity to government-employed physicians, see S.C. Code Ann. § 15–78–20(g) (Supp. 1996).

NOTE ON ACCESS TO HOSPITAL RECORDS BY PLAINTIFFS IN MALPRACTICE ACTIONS

A party contemplating a malpractice suit against a physician or a hospital would naturally wish to have access to hospital records that might disclose negligent acts or even contain admissions of negligence by hospital personnel. The *Bernardi* case deals with the discoverability of incident reports, which are important features of hospital risk management programs. (How could a hospital seek to ensure the protection of such reports under the attorney-client privilege?) See Medical Records ¶ 4–5, in 2A Hospital Law Manual (1991).

The hospital record that is most important to a potential malpractice plaintiff is the medical record of the patient's case that is kept by the hospital in the ordinary course of business. This record contains detailed, candid information, much of it required by statute, regulation, or JCAHO standards. Although the medical record is technically the property of the hospital, about half the states now have statutes permitting a patient access to it under certain conditions. See generally id. at ¶ 3–1; J. Smith, Hospital Liability § 14.04[2][v][A] (1997). Although the merely curious patient, such as one still undergoing treatment in the hospital or being treated for a mental disorder, may not have an automatic right to see his record, a patient has an undoubted right to authorize his attorney or another health care provider to see it for professional purposes. A special process for discovering the record is likely to be available where a malpractice action is contemplated. Hospitals will normally be cooperative in granting access to medical records; however, a reasonable fee may be charged for duplication.

Although these matters are relatively clear, an interesting question is whether a prospective malpractice plaintiff is also entitled to review records of hospital committees and peer review bodies that have looked into his case or into related matters, such as the performance of the physician in question or other hospital personnel. Where no statute governs, the court must balance competing policy considerations. In one leading case, access to records of peer review meetings was denied on the following grounds:

> Confidentiality is essential to effective functioning of these staff meetings; and these meetings are essential to the continued improvement in the care and treatment of patients. Candid and conscientious evaluation of clinical practices is a sine qua non of adequate hospital care. To subject these discussions and deliberations to the discovery process, without a showing of exceptional necessity, would result in terminating such deliberations. Constructive professional criticism cannot occur in an atmosphere of apprehension that one doctor's suggestion will be used as a denunciation of a colleague's conduct in a malpractice suit.
>
> The purpose of these staff meetings is the improvement, through self-analysis, of the efficiency of medical procedures and techniques. They are not a part of current patient care but are in the nature of a retrospective review of the effectiveness of certain medical procedures. The value of these discussions and reviews in the education of the doctors who participate, and the medical students, who sit in, is undeniable. This value would be destroyed if the meetings and names of those participating were to be opened to the discovery process.

Bredice v. Doctors Hospital, Inc., 50 F.R.D. 249, 250 (D.D.C.1970), *affirmed* 479 F.2d 920 (D.C.Cir.1973). The holding in *Bredice* was arguably narrowed in Gillman v. United States, 53 F.R.D. 316 (S.D.N.Y.1971) (holding factual statements discoverable). For another case upholding a nonstatutory privilege, see Dade County Med. Ass'n v. Hlis, 372 So.2d 117 (Fla.App.1979).

Other cases have found no privilege for peer review records, emphasizing the importance of the information sought to the plaintiff and the judicial process. E.g., State ex rel. Chandra v. Sprinkle, 678 S.W.2d 804 (Mo.1984) (en banc) (viewing statutory immunity from personal liability enjoyed by peer review committee members as diminishing the chilling effect of discoverability of records on peer review activity); Wesley Med. Center v. Clark, 669 P.2d 209 (Kan.1983) (holding, in absence of statutory privilege, that peer review committee records are not protected unless physician-patient privilege applies; balancing test to be applied). See generally Note, The Privilege of Self–Critical Analysis, 96 Harv.L.Rev. 1083 (1983).

Responding to considerations similar to those that influenced the *Bredice* court, virtually all state legislatures have made the records of peer review committees immune from discovery by malpractice plaintiffs. See Medical Records, supra, at 85–117 (state-by-state analysis including statutes and cases). The 1986 Missouri statute is typical:

> Except as otherwise provided in this section, the proceedings, findings, deliberations, reports and minutes of peer review committees concerning the health care provided any patient are privileged and shall not be subject to discovery, subpoena, or other means of legal compulsion for their release to any person or entity or be admissible into evidence in any judicial or administrative action for failure to provide appropriate care.

Vernon's Ann.Mo.Stat. § 537.035 (1988 & Supp. 1997). This statute was adopted to reverse the result in *Chandra v. Sprinkle,* supra.

Statutes protecting peer review records from discovery raise many issues. See, e.g., Corrigan v. Methodist Hosp., 885 F.Supp. 127 (E.D.Pa. 1995) (peer review statute protected minutes of staff meeting where more than 300 people were present); Swatch v. Treat, 671 N.E.2d 1004 (Mass. App.1996) (voluntary national professional organization held to be a peer review committee whose proceedings enjoy statutory confidentiality; organization allowed to intervene to protect integrity of its proceedings); Spinks v. Children's Hosp. Nat'l Med. Center, 124 F.R.D. 9 (D.D.C.1989) (holding that, even if confidentiality statute did not apply, D.C. recognizes a common law qualified privilege in peer review proceedings); State ex rel. Grandview Hosp. & Med. Center v. Gorman, 554 N.E.2d 1297 (Ohio 1990) (upholding order to produce records for in camera review, since privilege statute contains "major exception" for records "otherwise available from original sources" and court must evaluate which parts of records are within scope of exception); Anderson v. Breda, 700 P.2d 737, 741 (Wash.1985) ("the fact that a physician's privileges are restricted, suspended, or revoked is not properly subject to the protection of the statute").

Where statutes are unclear, a question may be raised whether a hospital's records may be sought by a state licensing board looking into a physician's conduct. See, e.g., Arnett v. Dal Cielo, 56 Cal.Rptr.2d 706 (Cal. 1996) (board subpoena of peer review records concerning drug-addicted physician held distinguishable from "discovery"; records therefore not protected under statute); Commonwealth v. Choate–Symmes Health Serv., 545 N.E.2d 1167 (Mass.1989) (state statute allows board access to reports for administrative purposes, but not for investigation); In re Petition of Attorney General, 369 N.W.2d 826 (Mich.1985) (disclosure not compelled).

NOTES AND QUESTIONS ON THE "CAPTAIN-OF-THE-SHIP" AND "BORROWED–SERVANT" DOCTRINES

1. As briefly discussed in *Bernardi,* special agency rules sometimes govern liability for negligent acts of hospital employees (e.g., nurses or resident physicians), especially in the operating room. These rules, which are frequently labeled the "borrowed-servant" and "captain-of-the-ship" doctrines, have been described and discussed as follows:

> In a typical situation, the surgeon, or chief surgeon, is a private practitioner with staff membership at the hospital where the operation is performed. Legally, the surgeon's status is that of an independent contractor. Other physicians or specialists involved may also be independent contractors, or they may be employees of the hospital. The nurses and other attendants are usually employees of the hospital.
>
> 
>
> A long established, widely accepted rule of law is that a general employee of one employer may become a special employee or "borrowed servant" of another. (Under this rule, a nurse employed by a hospital may become a special employee of a physician or surgeon with staff privileges.) Is the special employer liable for the negligence of the borrowed servant? The proper test, under the doctrine of *respondeat superior,* is whether the special employer has the right to control the actions of the borrowed servant. The right to control is ordinarily a question of fact that must be determined by a jury.
>
> Depending on a state's common law, then, a servant may have one or more masters in a given situation. In surgical malpractice cases, the courts have had a hard time assigning responsibility for employees' acts. In some instances, surgeons have been subject to the standard rules that are applied to liability for borrowed servants. Some jurisdictions, however, have imposed on the medical profession stricter standards and more burdensome forms of vicarious liability, including the captain of the ship doctrine.
>
> The phrase was first used in a medical malpractice case by the Pennsylvania Supreme Court.[2] In maritime tradition and under admiralty law, the master of a vessel is in total command of the care and efficiency of the ship and has full responsibility for the welfare of all hands. The captain's authority over the ship's crew is supreme, and he is liable for damages caused by their negligence.
>
> In adopting the doctrine, the Pennsylvania court recognized that it was a legal fiction. At the time, the doctrine of charitable immunity eliminated any possibility of collecting damages from the hospital.

2. McConnell v. Williams, 361 Pa. 355, 65 A.2d 243 (1949).

Therefore, the court felt constrained to make a policy decision that would provide some way to reimburse an injured patient. Even so, the court did not impose liability on the surgeon but only ruled that it was a question of fact for the jury to decide whether a master-servant relationship existed between the surgeon and an intern in the operating room.

Later, when charitable immunity was abolished in Pennsylvania the captain of the ship doctrine was abrogated there.[3] In the meantime, however, other courts had picked up the phrase and applied it to make the surgeon liable for any negligence in the operating room.

In 1977, the Texas Supreme Court rejected the doctrine [in two cases in which] the alleged malpractice was the failure to remove all the sponges used during surgery before the incision was closed. * * *

* * * It said: "We now disapprove [of lower court cases using the doctrine] insofar as they suggest that a surgeon's mere presence in the operating room makes him liable as a matter of law for the negligence of other persons. We disapprove the captain-of-the-ship doctrine and hold that it is a false special rule of agency. Operating surgeons and hospitals are subject to the principles of agency law which apply to others."[10]

The Texas court added: "Similes help to explain a factual situation, but in legal writing, phrases have a way of being canonized and of growing until they can stand and walk independently of the usual general rules." This is what has happened with the captain of the ship doctrine. Some courts have allowed the phrase to become a separate and independent concept of agency that is specially applied in medical malpractice cases.

At best, it should be only a shorthand statement of some basic concepts of agency law. The built-in danger of even this "best" use, however, is that it tends to oversimplify the situation in the minds of judges. It allows an escape from the necessary reasoning and balancing of facts against accepted principles of agency law.

Such reasoning and balancing of facts is not immediately apparent in another 1977 case.[11] In it, the Kentucky Supreme Court held both the surgeon and the hospital responsible for the operating room nurses' failure to account for scalpel blades. One blade was left in the patient during a procedure for kidney stone removal. The court said the operating room staff members were primarily the "servants" of the hospital and continued to perform hospital duties but were also working for the surgeon. The court applied the doctrine of *respondeat*

3. Flagiello v. Pennsylvania Hosp., 417 Pa. 486, 208 A.2d 193 (1965); Tonsic v. Wagner, 458 Pa. 246, 329 A.2d 497 (1974).

10. Sparger v. Worley Hosp., Inc., 547 S.W.2d 582 (Tex.1977). See also Ramon v. Mani, 550 S.W.2d 270 (Tex.1977).

11. City of Somerset v. Hart, 549 S.W.2d 814 (Ky.1977).

> *superior* to both employers. The court did not discuss how the surgeon might supervise the count. Most significantly, it did not mention any evidence of negligence on his part.
>
> Similarly, the Georgia Court of Appeals in *Miller v. Atkins*[12] approved the dismissal of a complaint against a hospital. The court held that the surgeon was "in control of the operating room" and should be liable for the negligence of nurses who were working in his presence. Their alleged negligence was putting a stainless steel container of hot water between the patient's legs: this act resulted in severe burns. The court held that the nurses were the surgeon's "borrowed servants." Therefore, their negligence was to be imputed to him, not the hospital, under the doctrine of *respondeat superior.* The court apparently assumed that the surgeon could and did control the acts of the nurse employees.
>
> Certainly, a general employee of one employer may become a special employee or "borrowed servant" of another employer. But the true test of liability for that employee's acts should be whether the special employer could or did control the actions of the borrowed servant.

Hollowell, Has the "Captain of the Ship" Been Relieved of Command?, Legal Aspects of Med. Pract., July 1980, at 37–39.

2. For a judicial critique of the "captain of the ship" doctrine, see Truhitte v. French Hosp., 128 Cal.App.3d 332, 344–51, 180 Cal.Rptr. 152, 157–62 (1982). The court observed,

> A theory that the surgeon directly controls *all* activities of whatever nature in the operating room certainly is not realistic in present day medical care. Today's hospitals hire, fire, train and provide day-to-day supervision of their nurse-employees. Fortunately, hospitals can and do implement standards and regulations governing good surgery practices and techniques and are in the best position to enforce compliance; hospitals also are in a position to insure against the risk and pass the cost to consumers.

Id. at 348–49, 180 Cal.Rptr. at 160.

Many courts have declined to apply the "captain-of-the-ship" doctrine in recent cases, adopting the "borrowed-servant" doctrine in its place. See, e.g., Starcher v. Byrne, 687 So.2d 737 (Miss.1997) (surgeon not liable under borrowed-servant doctrine where nurse anesthetist was doing own job, was not specially employed by surgeon, and was not under surgeon's control); Oberzan v. Smith, 869 P.2d 682 (Kan.1994) (physician not responsible for negligence of x-ray technician assigned by hospital and not under physician's personal control or supervision); Franklin v. Gupta, 567 A.2d 524 (Md.1990) (holding the captain-of-the-ship doctrine no longer necessary to ensure patient compensation and adopting the borrowed-servant doctrine instead, so that a surgeon is only liable if he actually had the right to

12. Miller v. Atkins, 142 Ga.App. 618, 236 S.E.2d 838 (1977).

control the agent's work); Parker v. Vanderbilt Univ., 767 S.W.2d 412 (Tenn.App.1988) (captain-of-the-ship doctrine said to be unnecessarily confusing; borrowed-servant doctrine held more consistent with general principles of agency law). But see Ravi v. Williams, 536 So.2d 1374 (Ala.1988) (holding that surgeon is ultimately responsible for ensuring that all sponges are removed from incision and cannot avoid liability by delegating the task to a nurse). Although the court in Johnston v. Southwest Louisiana Ass'n, 693 So.2d 1195 (La.App.1997), held that "vicarious liability must be based on the surgeon's control of the hospital's employee, not merely on his status," it also held that a surgeon has a "nondelegable duty to remove all sponges from the patient's body" after surgery.

Despite their new emphasis on the borrowed-servant doctrine, courts have been slow to allow a hospital to escape liability by claiming that its employee was on loan to (borrowed by) the physician when the negligent act occurred. See, e.g., Brickner v. Normandy Osteopathic Hosp., 746 S.W.2d 108 (Mo.App.1988) (hospital may disclaim responsibility for its employees' actions only if it can show a complete relinquishment to the physician of any right to control the employee's conduct); Ross v. Chatham County Hosp. Auth., 367 S.E.2d 793 (Ga.1988) (conduct in question must involve professional skill; the hospital cannot escape vicarious liability for clerical or administrative tasks, such as a sponge count). But see Hoffman v. Southwest Community Hosp. & Med. Center, 397 S.E.2d 696 (Ga.1990) (although hospitals may be liable for negligently performed administrative tasks, borrowed-servant doctrine precludes recovery against a hospital for negligently performed medical procedures where doctor is in complete control).

For a full discussion of both the captain-of-the-ship and borrowed-servant doctrines, see Lisk, A Physician's Respondeat Superior Liability for the Negligent Acts of Other Medical Professionals—When the Captain Goes Down Without the Ship, 13 Ark.L.Rev. 183 (1991).

3. Do you agree with Hollowell that courts should focus in each case on who actually controlled the employee, taking evidence on the issue? Must liability for a nurse's negligence attach to either the surgeon or the hospital, or might the court treat liability as joint and several since each "employer" exercises some control? Compare Krane v. St. Anthony Hosp. Systems, 738 P.2d 75 (Colo.App.1987) (both could not be liable for nurse's acts during surgery), with Grubb v. Albert Einstein Med. Center, 255 Pa.Super. 381, 395–98, 387 A.2d 480, 487–88 (1978) (" 'both masters may be liable' ").

4. Is it fair to hold a surgeon liable for things not directly under his or her control? Is vicarious liability supposed to be fair? Or is it intended to inspire parties who could exercise some control, directly or indirectly, to do so? What could surgeons faced with vicarious liability do to ensure accurate sponge counts, etc.? Are they limited to acting individually, or might they, through the medical staff, influence the hospital's selection and supervision of nurses? If quality of care is the object, how should liability be assigned?

Vicarious Liability for Physician Torts?

Sword v. NKC Hospitals, Inc.

Court of Appeals of Indiana, 1996.
661 N.E.2d 10

■ BARTEAU, JUDGE.

Diana and Carl Sword appeal from the entry of summary judgment in favor of NKC Hospitals, Inc., Alliant Health System, Inc., d/b/a Norton's Children Hospital (hereinafter "Norton Hospital"), a Kentucky hospital.

* * *

The Swords seek to hold Norton Hospital liable for the negligence of Dr. Luna, an anesthesiologist who practices medicine at Norton Hospital. The parties do not dispute that Dr. Luna was not an employee of Norton Hospital, and practiced medicine at Norton Hospital as an independent contractor. The trial court granted Norton Hospital's motion for summary judgment based upon Indiana law that hospitals may not be held liable for the negligence of independent contractor doctors. See Iterman v. Baker (1938), 214 Ind. 308, 15 N.E.2d 365. * * *

The Swords argue that Norton Hospital should be held liable for the negligence of Dr. Luna, despite the fact that Dr. Luna is an independent contractor, under the doctrine of apparent agency. Many courts have recognized such liability based upon either or both of two theories arising under the specter of apparent agency, in some cases confusing the two and misapplying the analysis. The first theory is commonly referred to as ostensible agency, and is based upon Restatement (Second) of Torts, § 429, which states:

> One who employs an independent contractor to perform services for another which are accepted in the reasonable belief that the services are being rendered by the employer or by his servants, is subject to liability for physical harm caused by the negligence of the contractor in supplying such services, to the same extent as though the employer were supplying them himself or by his servants.

The second theory is commonly referred to as agency by estoppel, and is predicated on Restatement (Second) of Agency, § 267:

> One who represents that another is a servant or other agent and thereby causes a third person justifiably to rely upon the care or skill of such apparent agent is subject to liability to the third person for harm caused by the lack of care or skill of the one appearing to be a servant or other agent as if he were such.

The Swords invite us to adopt either of these Restatement provisions and find that Norton Hospital may be held liable for Dr. Luna's alleged negligence. While we decline to adopt either of the Restatement provisions at this time, we find that the Swords may state a claim against Norton Hospital under existing Indiana law.

Indiana recognizes the doctrine of apparent agency and follows the rule that a principal may be held liable by a third party for the negligence of one whom the principal holds out as its agent. * * * Still, no Indiana case has ever applied the doctrine of apparent agency and found that a hospital may be held liable for injuries sustained by a patient as the result of the negligence of an independent contractor.

Indiana hospitals' insulation against liability for the negligence of independent contractor doctors may be traced to our Supreme Court's [1938] decision in *Iterman*. Therein, the Court recognized that, while other jurisdictions held hospitals accountable for independent contractor doctors' negligence under apparent agency, such an approach was not viable in Indiana because Indiana statutes prohibited hospital corporations from practicing medicine.

> The right to practice medicine and surgery under a license by the state is a personal privilege. It cannot be delegated, and a corporation, or other unlicensed person, may not engage in the practice of medicine by employing one who is licensed to do the things which constitute practicing the profession. * * *

In other words, the *Iterman* Court concluded that because hospitals could not practice medicine under Indiana law, no patient could reasonably conclude that those who were practicing medicine in hospitals were the hospital's employees. This rationale has stood as a shield, protecting hospitals from liability for the negligence of health care professionals whom the hospitals hire as independent contractors.

However, cases and statutory changes subsequent to *Iterman* have opened Indiana hospitals to potential liability for the negligence of physicians practicing within hospitals' facilities, and have eroded the foundation for insulating hospitals from such liability. We now find that there is no reason under law or policy for shielding hospitals from liability for the negligence of their agents, and instead find several reasons justifying such liability.

* * * In Sloan v. Metro. Health Council (1987), Ind. App. 516 N.E.2d 1104, 1106–09, we recognized that the rationale for shielding hospitals from liability for their employees' negligence has eroded over time, and found that *Iterman*'s holding that hospital corporations could not be held liable for the malpractice of employee physicians is no longer viable. Indiana statutes now hold corporate entities such as hospitals liable for the negligent acts of employees. See Ind.Code 23–1.5–2–1 to I.C. 23–1.5–5–2. Thus, the rationale of *Iterman*—that patients could not reasonably conclude that doctors are agents or servants of the hospitals in which they practice because hospitals cannot practice medicine—is now without foundation in law or policy.

Under the nature of health care services today, it is entirely possible for a reasonable, prudent person to conclude from representations made by hospitals that the doctors and health care professionals that service patients within the hospitals's facilities are agents or servants of the hospitals. As the Supreme Court of Wisconsin recently noted in Kashishian v. Port (1992), 167 Wis.2d 24, 481 N.W.2d 277, [282,] reh'g denied:

> [H]ospitals increasingly hold themselves out to the public in expensive advertising campaigns as offering and rendering quality health services. One need only pick up a daily newspaper to see full and half page advertisements extolling the medical virtues of an individual hospital and the quality health care that the hospital is prepared to deliver in any number of medical areas. Modern hospitals have spent billions of dollars marketing themselves, nurturing the image with the consuming public that they are full-care modern health facilities. All of these expenditures have but one purpose: to persuade those in need of medical services to obtain those services at a specific hospital. In essence, hospitals have become big business, competing with each other for health care dollars.

* * * Because hospitals stand to profit from their representations concerning the quality of services provided by those hired to treat patients, either as employees or independent contractors, it would be anomalous for hospitals to escape liability if those same health care professionals delivered services below minimally accepted standards, let alone the heightened degree of quality often represented in the hospitals' advertisements.

We therefore find that hospitals may be held liable for the negligence of their apparent agents, notwithstanding the fact that the agents are independent contractors. For a hospital to be held liable for the negligence of a health care professional under the doctrine of apparent agency, a plaintiff must show that the hospital acted or communicated directly or indirectly to a patient in such a manner that would lead a reasonable person to conclude that the health care professional who was alleged to be negligent was an employee or agent of the hospital, and that the plaintiff justifiably acted in reliance upon the conduct of the hospital, consistent with ordinary care and prudence.[2] A hospital is not liable for the plaintiff's injuries if the plaintiff knew, or should have known, that the allegedly negligent health care professional is an independent contractor.

In support of their claim, the Swords point to * * * brochures [advertising that Norton's Women's Pavilion offers]:

2. The Restatement (Second) of Torts, § 429 does not require that a third party act in reliance upon the representations of the principal in order to establish liability. And, while the Restatement (Second) of Agency, § 267 does include reliance as an element of liability, Illustration 3 to that Restatement section indicates that reliance is not essential to the cause of action. * * * Many jurisdictions have found that under either Restatement provision a patient may hold a hospital liable without a showing that the patient relied upon representations made by the hospital, often in cases alleging negligence on the part of emergency room physicians.

As noted supra, we have declined to adopt either Restatement provision and instead have applied existing Indiana law on the doctrine of apparent agency. * * * Therefore, our analysis includes the requirement that the Swords demonstrate that they justifiably acted in reliance upon Norton Hospital's representations. * * *

> [I]nstant access to the specialized equipment and facilities, as well as to physician specialists in every area of pediatric medicine and surgery. Every maternity patient has a private room and the full availability of a special anesthesiology team, experienced and dedicated exclusively to OB patients.
>
> * * *
>
> The Women's Pavilion medical staff includes the only physicians in the region who specialize exclusively in obstetrical anesthesiology. They are immediately available within the unit 24 hours a day and are experts in administering continuous epidural anesthesia.
>
> * * *

Whether the representations made by Norton Hospital concerning its obstetrical anesthesiology team would lead a reasonable person to conclude that Dr. Luna was an agent of Norton Hospital, and whether the Swords exercised ordinary care and prudence and justifiably relied upon the representations of Norton Hospital, are genuine issues of material fact to be resolved by a jury after considering all of the circumstances in evidence. * * *

REVERSED.

■ RUCKER, JUDGE, dissenting.

* * * In our system of tort liability based upon fault, if a party is to be held liable for the acts of another, then the party should have the right or power to control the other's conduct. * * *

It is now clear that a hospital may be held liable for the acts of a physician performing services on the hospital's premises. However, * * * that is so only where the physician is an employee of the hospital and the hospital is aware that the care the physician is providing has deviated from normal practice. In this case there is no dispute that Doctor Luna was employed by Norton Hospital as an independent contractor. She could not therefore have also served as the hospital's agent, apparent or otherwise, because she was not an employee over whom the hospital exercised control * * *.

Grewe v. Mount Clemens General Hospital

Supreme Court of Michigan, 1978.
404 Mich. 240, 273 N.W.2d 429.

■ PER CURIAM.

This is a medical malpractice case. At approximately 11 p.m. on March 20, 1967, the plaintiff received an electrical shock while at work. This shock allegedly caused the plaintiff to suffer a dislocated shoulder. After initially visiting a clinic for treatment, the plaintiff went to the defendant Mt. Clemens General Hospital where he was admitted. He was initially examined by Dr. Gerald Hoffman, an internist, who sought to ascertain whether the plaintiff had suffered any cardiac damage. Dr. Hoffman sought consultation from Dr. Robert O. Fagen, an orthopedic surgeon with staff privileges at the hospital. Dr. Fagen's examination revealed, *inter alia,* that the plaintiff had sustained a dislocated right shoulder.

Dr. Fagen designated Dr. Michael Fugle, an orthopedic resident, to attempt to reduce, at least partially, the dislocation of plaintiff's shoulder. Therefore, Dr. Fugle made several unsuccessful attempts to do so.

After one of these unsuccessful attempts, Dr. A. Lewis Katzowitz, Dr. Hoffman's associate, who also had staff privileges at the hospital and who, like Dr. Hoffman, was also an internist, observed that the plaintiff was in considerable discomfort and himself attempted to reduce the dislocation by placing his foot on the plaintiff's chest and pulling his arm. He too was unsuccessful in reducing the dislocation. Significantly, Dr. Katzowitz testified that he did not view the X-rays before attempting the reduction.

The plaintiff was to argue at trial that these attempts at reducing his shoulder dislocation resulted in a brachial plexus injury and a fracture of the greater tuberosity. The plaintiff claimed that these injuries were the result of medical malpractice performed on him while he was in the hospital.

In any event, the plaintiff eventually had to undergo surgery for the removal of bone fragments in repair of the biceps tendon and joint capsule.

[In the lawsuit that followed, the jury found the hospital, but not Dr. Fugle, liable for negligence, raising the question how the hospital could be liable other than through its physician employee. The hospital argued that] there is no basis for concluding that Dr. Katzowitz was an agent of the hospital so as to render it vicariously liable for his negligent treatment of the plaintiff. The hospital vigorously contends that Dr. Katzowitz merely had staff privileges at the hospital, and was not in the employ of the hospital; and that therefore no agency relationship can be found to exist. The hospital further asserts that it exercised no control over Dr. Katzowitz' treatment of the plaintiff and should not be held accountable for his actions.

* * *

Generally speaking, a hospital is not vicariously liable for the negligence of a physician who is an independent contractor and merely uses the hospital's facilities to render treatment to his patients. However, if the individual looked to the hospital to provide him with medical treatment and there has been a representation by the hospital that medical treatment would be afforded by physicians working therein, an agency by estoppel can be found. See Howard v. Park, 37 Mich.App. 496, 195 N.W.2d 39 (1972), lv. dn. 387 Mich. 782 (1972).

In our view, the critical question is whether the plaintiff, at the time of his admission to the hospital, was looking to the hospital for treatment of his physical ailments or merely viewed the hospital as the situs where his physician would treat him for his problems. A relevant factor in this determination involves resolution of the question of whether the hospital provided the plaintiff with Dr. Katzowitz or whether the plaintiff and Dr.

Katzowitz had a patient-physician relationship independent of the hospital setting.

* * *

The relationship between a given physician and a hospital may well be that of an independent contractor performing services for, but not subject to, the direct control of the hospital. However, that is not of critical importance to the patient who is the ultimate victim of that physician's malpractice. In *Howard v. Park,* supra, the Court of Appeals quoted with approval from the opinion in Stanhope v. Los Angeles College of Chiropractic, 54 Cal.App.2d 141, 128 P.2d 705 (1942). We too find the California Court's analysis of this area enlightening:

> " 'An agency is ostensible when the principal intentionally, or by want of ordinary care, causes a third person to believe another to be his agent who is not really employed by him.' § 2300, Civ.Code. In this connection it is urged by appellant that 'before a recovery can be had against a principal for the alleged acts of an ostensible agent, three things must be proved, to wit:' (quoting from Hill v. Citizens National Tr. & Sav. Bank, 9 Cal.2d 172, 176, 69 P.2d 853, 855 [1937]); '[First] The person dealing with the agent must do so with belief in the agent's authority and this belief must be a reasonable one; [second] such belief must be generated by some act or neglect of the principal sought to be charged; [third] and the third person relying on the agent's apparent authority must not be guilty of negligence.'
>
> "An examination of the evidence hereinbefore referred to which was produced on the issue of agency convinces us that respondent has met the requirements enumerated in the *Hill* case. So far as the record reveals appellant did nothing to put respondent on notice that the X-ray laboratory was not an integral part of appellant institution, and it cannot seriously be contended that respondent, when he was being carried from room to room suffering excruciating pain, should have inquired whether the individual doctors who examined him are employees of the college or were independent contractors. Agency is always a question of fact for the jury. The evidence produced on this issue is sufficient to support the jury's implied finding that Dr. Joyant was the ostensible agent of appellant college." 54 Cal.App.2d 141, 146, 128 P.2d 705, 708.

Turning to the facts of the instant case, we see nothing in the record which should have put the plaintiff on notice that Dr. Katzowitz, when he attempted to reduce the plaintiff's shoulder separation, was an independent contractor as opposed to an employee of the hospital.

The plaintiff's testimony convincingly demonstrates that he went to the hospital for treatment and expected to be treated by the hospital:

> "*Q:* Mr. Grewe, when you went to the Mt. Clemens General Hospital that evening the 21st, or the morning of the 21st, did you know any doctor there that you were going to ask for treatment?

"*A:* I never knew of a doctor, D.O. doctor, before in my life that I can recall of.

"*Q:* Do you know how Dr. Hoffman happened to see you at the hospital?

"*A:* Well, no. I don't know who he assigned to me. The only thing that I know that somebody had said that the doctor the night before refused to take the case and the next thing I know, Dr. Hoffman was on the scene.

. . .

"*Q:* You didn't know Dr. Hoffman before you got there?

"*A:* No, I did not.

"*Q:* Did you know that Dr. Hoffman and Dr. Katzowitz were partners in the specialty of internal medicine?

"*A:* Not at this time, I didn't, no.

"*Q:* Did you subsequently find that out?

"*A:* Yes, I did.

"*Q:* Who provided you with Dr. Fugle, who did these reductions?

"*A:* That, I couldn't answer you.

* * *

We are convinced, as the jury must have been, that the plaintiff, when he entered the hospital, was seeking treatment from the hospital itself. There is no record of any preexisting patient-physician relationship with any of the medical personnel who treated the plaintiff at the hospital. In fact, Dr. Hoffman, the internist, did not see the plaintiff until approximately 12 hours after the plaintiff had been admitted to the hospital. Dr. Hoffman's relationship with the plaintiff comes into clear focus in Dr. Hoffman's testimony:

"*Q:* Do you know how he [plaintiff] happened to be referred to you or placed under your care for examination on this particular day?

"*A:* Yes, sir, I do.

"*Q:* And for what reason, Doctor?

"*A:* Mr. Grewe had presented himself to the emergency room there earlier that day with his particular problem, at which time the emergency room doctor had referred Mr. Grewe to myself for my particular investigation and management."

Dr. Katzowitz also testified:

"*Q:* Doctor, can you tell us as to what occurred during the course of that reduction on March 21, 1967?

"*A:* As I remember, I was told that Dr. Hoffman and I were in care of this patient. I don't recall who told me at the time, but it was years ago, but I was told."

It is abundantly clear on the strength of this record that the plaintiff looked to defendant hospital for his treatment and was treated by medical personnel who were the ostensible agents of defendant hospital. Accordingly, a jury verdict against defendant hospital on this theory is supported by the record. We make no intimation that the hospital would escape liability even if plaintiff knew or should have known the relationship of Dr. Katzowitz with the hospital.

* * *

Affirmed. * * *

NOTES AND QUESTIONS ON THE LIABILITY OF HOSPITALS FOR THE NEGLIGENCE OF HOSPITAL-BASED PHYSICIANS

1. *Respondeat Superior.* In McDonald v. Hampton Training School for Nurses, 486 S.E.2d 299 (Va.1997), the Virginia Supreme Court overturned old precedent holding that "a physician is an independent contractor solely because the nature of his profession prevents his employer from acquiring the requisite ability to control his medical activities." Id. at 302. The physician for whose negligence the plaintiff sought to hold the hospital liable under the doctrine of respondeat superior was not formally an employee of the hospital but had worked under contract for thirty-three years as its Director of Pathology. Citing various indicia of employment, the court held that whether the physician was an employee or an independent contractor should have been a question for the jury. For an earlier leading case treating radiologists' status as a factual question, see Beeck v. Tuscon Gen. Hosp., 500 P.2d 1153 (Ariz.App.1972) (hospital held liable as employer despite radiologist's nominal status as independent contractor). See also Rucker v. High Point Mem. Hosp., 202 S.E.2d 610 (N.C.App.1974), affirmed, 206 S.E.2d 196 (N.C.1974) (physicians treating patients in emergency room found to be hospital employees due to contract terms, including requirement that doctors call specialists when needed); Overstreet v. Doctors Hosp., 237 S.E.2d 213 (Ga.App.1977) (degree of control conferred by contract, including requirement to cooperate in the utilization of interns, held "not inconsistent with an independent contractor relationship").

Resident physicians, in training and paid a salary, are the responsibility of their employer but may be rotating through training in another institution. Which employer should be responsible for their torts? See Reuter, Professional Liability in Postgraduate Medical Education: Who Is Liable for Resident Negligence?, 15 J. Legal Med. 485 (1994).

2. *Emergency Room Physicians.* In the past, hospitals typically provided emergency services by requiring staff physicians, as a condition of enjoying admitting privileges, to take turns in the emergency room (ER). Should a hospital be allowed to argue that it is not liable for the torts of physicians treating patients under such circumstances on the ground that they are independent contractors? Today, it is more common for hospitals, if they do not directly employ emergency specialists, to contract with a physician group or a corporate entity to operate the institution's emergency department. See, e.g., Richmond County Hosp. Auth. v. Brown, 361 S.E.2d 164 (Ga.1987) (physicians were independent contractors retained by another independent contractor, which operated the ER and which appeals court found not liable because patient had not relied on it or its reputation; hospital held liable for negligence of ER doctor on apparent agency grounds); Gray v. Vaughn, 460 S.E.2d 86 (Ga.App.1995) (ER operator held vicariously liable for negligence of ER nurses, whom it contracted to supervise, but not for negligence of physician, who was deemed independent contractor); McClendon v. Crowder, 1997 WL 412120 (Tenn.App.1997) (suggesting ER operator might be liable to patient as third-party beneficiary of contract with hospital, which required services to meet prevailing medical standards).

Consider how the doctrines of apparent or ostensible agency and agency by estoppel—such as were applied in the *Sword* and *Grewe* cases—should apply to physician negligence in the ER. See, e.g., Clark v. Southview Hosp. & Family Health Ctr., 628 N.E.2d 46 (Ohio 1994) (agency by estoppel found on basis that hospital generally held itself out as provider of emergency care); Gilbert v. Sycamore Municipal Hosp., 622 N.E.2d 788 (Ill.1993) (adopting vicarious liability for hospitals based on the doctrine of apparent authority); Hardy v. Brantley, 471 So.2d 358 (Miss.1985) (when patient does not select physician, "hospital should be estopped to deny responsibility").

3. *Radiologists, Anesthesiologists, and Pathologists (RAPs).* These hospital-based physicians usually work under a special contract with the hospital. For cases permitting hospitals to be held liable for the negligence of non-employee RAPs under various agency theories, see *Sword*; White v. Methodist Hosp. South, 844 S.W.2d 642 (Tenn.App.1992); Doctors Hosp. v. Bonner, 392 S.E.2d 897 (Ga.App.1990) (holding hospital responsible for the malpractice of its independent anesthesiologists under actual and apparent agency theories; rejecting the argument that apparent agency principle applies only to ER doctors); Thomas v. Raleigh Gen. Hosp., 358 S.E.2d 222 (W.Va.1987) (anesthesiologist's negligence held attributable to hospital selecting him); Szortc v. Northwest Hosp., 496 N.E.2d 1200 (Ill.App.1986) (radiologists; hospital held potentially liable on ostensible agency theory).

4. *Agency or Policy?* Under theories of ostensible or apparent agency or agency by estoppel, a plaintiff is normally required to prove detrimental reliance (i.e., that the hospital's holding-out influenced the patient's choice of provider). See, e.g., *Sword*; Menzie v. Windham Community Mem. Hosp., 774 F.Supp. 91, 97 (D.Conn.1991) (requiring proof of reliance "[a]lthough plaintiff complains that a reliance requirement will preclude many plaintiffs from demonstrating that the hospital is liable under an agency theory"); *Gilbert*, 622 N.E.2d at 795 (holding that if "patient knows, or should have known, that the [ER] physician is an independent contractor," then the hospital will not be vicariously liable); Floyd v. Humana of Virginia, Inc., 787 S.W.2d 267 (Ky.App.1989) (rejecting ostensible agency theory in case of anesthesiologist since patient had signed form stating that her physicians were not agents of the hospital). In procuring the services of

RAPs, does the patient customarily exercise any choice? What would you conclude if a surgeon who had been selected by the patient chose the anesthesiologist? Cf. Milliron v. Francke, 793 P.2d 824 (Mont.1990) (rejecting ostensible agency theory where patient was referred by family physician to particular radiologist, as opposed to being provided with one by the hospital); Trapp v. Cayson, 471 So.2d 375 (Miss.1985) (finding no vicarious liability for radiologist's negligence where patient had received brochure indicating independence and personal physician ordered services).

Do you agree that these cases should turn on agency principles, particularly the individual plaintiff's probable impression of the hospital/physician relationship? (What was the *Grewe* court's position on this question?) Or do these issues simply raise the cost and uncertainty of litigation to no good purpose? In fact, a number of cases have found vicarious liability in circumstances where ordinary agency rules would seem to preclude it. One court held, for example, that a hospital is "estopped to deny" that its emergency room physicians are its agents even while observing that people seek emergency care under "crisis circumstances," suggesting that they have no opportunity to make a considered choice or to form an estoppel-triggering impression. Hannola v. City of Lakewood, 426 N.E.2d 1187, 1190 (Ohio App. 1980). See also Sampson v. Baptist Mem. Hosp. System, 940 S.W.2d 128, 134–38 (Tex.App.1996) (embracing vicarious liability as matter of policy and declaring that signs placed in emergency department are insufficient to defeat vicarious liability because ruling otherwise would only "lead to more far-reaching general notices by hospitals contained in advertisements"; also observing that "an injured party must rely on a hospital's emergency room because there is no other place to go"), rev'd, 1998 WL 253914 (Tex.1998); *Clark*, 628 N.E.2d at 53 (expressly dispensing with requirements of affirmative representations by hospital and proven reliance by patient in favor of generalized "agency by estoppel" theory based on hospital's generally holding itself out as provider of care).

5. *Nondelegable Duty?* Some courts appear to employ the principle of agency law under which certain functions are deemed to be so dangerous that they give rise to a "nondelegable duty" that cannot be escaped by employing an independent contractor. See, e.g., Restatement (Second) of Agency § 214 (1958): ("A * * * principal who is under a duty * * * to have care used to protect others * * * and who confides the performance of such duty to a servant or other person is subject to liability to such others for harm caused to them by the failure of such agent to perform the duty.") See also W. P. Keeton et al., Prosser and Keeton on the Law of Torts § 71, at 511–15 (5th ed. 1984) (discussing when employer's duty of care cannot be delegated to independent contractor).

The leading case applying the principle of nondelegable duty to hospitals is Jackson v. Power, 743 P.2d 1376 (Alaska 1987) (holding that acute care hospital had duty, under licensing statute and accrediting standards, to provide ER care and that duty was nondelegable because of importance of services to community). See also *Sampson*, 940 S.W.2d at 136 (for reasons of "public policy and fundamental fairness," court "encourage[d] the full leap-imposing a nondelegable duty on hospitals for the negligence of emergency room physicians"), rev'd, 1998 WL 253914 (Tex.1998); Simmons v. Tuomey Regional Med. Center, 498 S.E.2d 408 (S.C.App.1998) (holding hospital's duty to ER patients has evolved into nondelegable duty); Irving v. Doctors Hosp. of Lake Worth, Inc., 415 So.2d 55 (Fla.App.1982) (using ostensible agency principles to support jury instruction that hospital may not escape liability to patient injured in ER by delegating performance to an independent contractor). In addition, as Professors Abraham and Weiler have observed, those courts that have ignored agency law's strict requirement of hospital-induced reliance can be seen as implicitly employing a theory very much like that of nondelegable duty. See Abraham & Weiler, Enterprise Liability and the Evolution of the American Health Care System, 108 Harv. L. Rev. 381, 389 (1994). See, e.g., *Clark*, 628 N.E.2d at 53 (holding that public perception of ER as community medical center justifies hospital liability); *Beeck*, 500 P.2d at 1158 (imposing vicarious liability for radiologist's tort partly on ground of hospital's "high trust" and observation that radiologists' services are "an inherent function of the hospital, a function without which a hospital could not properly achieve its purpose").

Although several courts appear to view hospitals as unavoidably responsible for the quality of services provided by hospital-based physicians, some have expressly rejected the idea that providing medical services is enough of a hospital function or inherently dangerous enough to create a nondelegable duty. E.g., *Milliron*, 793 P.2d at 204 (finding nondelegable duty theory inapplicable because the physician, not the hospital, has the primary duty to provide adequate medical care); *Menzie*, 774 F. Supp. at 97–98; Kelly v. St. Luke's Hosp., 826 S.W.2d 391, 395–96 (Mo.App.1992). In addition, a number of the rulings recognizing the fruitlessness of continuing to follow agency rules prompted dissents protesting such judicial activism. For example, in the *Sampson* case, supra, the dissenting judge advocated "leav[ing] this difficult policy decision—with its far-reaching social and economic ramifications—to the Texas Legislature." 940 S.W.2d at 139. (This view apparently prevailed on appeal. 1998 WL 253914 (Tex.1998).) See also *Clark*, 628 N.E.2d at 56 (Moyer, C.J., dissenting) (observing "difference between the incremental development of the common law and judicial legislation," and warning that "[i]n a time of ever-increasing medical costs and potentially drastic changes to our health care system, this court would do well to take caution in its radical redistribution of liabilities for acts of medical malpractice"). Might the dissenters in the latter case be advised that at least equal danger may lie in *not* updating old notions to accommodate new developments?

6. *Corporate Practice vs. Vicarious Liability.* Note the problem that confronted the court in the *Sword* case as a result of its earlier decision in *Iterman*. What similar difficulty do courts face in applying the principle of nondelegable duty to hold hospitals vicariously liable for the torts of ER physicians and RAPs? Is there, for example, an arguable flaw in the following judicial logic?

> [P]ublic policy requires that the hospital not be able to artificially screen itself from liability for malpractice in the emergency room.
>
> [T]he hospital will be estopped to deny that the physicians and other medical personnel on duty providing treatment are its agents. Regardless of any contractual arrangements with so-called independent contractors, the hospital will be liable * * *.

Hannola, 426 N.E.2d at 1190.

The hospital in *Jackson v. Power*, supra, argued that "[p]hysicians, not hospitals, * * * have a duty to practice medicine non-negligently" and that "a hospital cannot be held to have delegated away a duty it never had." 743 P.2d at 1382. The Alaska Supreme Court, in finding vicarious liability, appeared to miss the hospital's point, however. Thus, it concluded, on the basis of regulations and accrediting standards requiring only that a hospital "provide emergency care physicians" and get its physicians to meet certain administrative standards, that "it cannot seriously be questioned that [the hospital] had a duty to provide" the emergency care itself. Id. at 1382–83. Although this leap from individual to corporate responsibility for medical services may be justified as a matter of policy, the court failed to confront the issue directly as other courts have done. See, e.g., Pamperin v. Trinity Mem. Hosp., 423 N.W.2d 848, 857–58 (Wis.1988) (court not convinced that hospital had nondelegable duty: "[W]e are not convinced that the duty to have a radiologist available is a duty which a hospital may not delegate to an independent contractor.").

Not only have numerous courts ruled clearly in favor of hospital vicarious liability despite the argument that hospitals cannot practice medicine, but several of them have justified their holdings by observing the changing character and expanding responsibilities of hospitals in the modern era and their increasing advertising of themselves as providers of high-quality care. E.g., *Jackson*, 743 P.2d at 1382–85 ("Not only is this [nondelegable duty] rule consonant with the public perception of the hospital as a multifaceted health care facility responsible for the quality of medical care and treatment rendered, it also treats tort liability in the medical arena in a manner that is consistent with the commercialization of American medicine."); *Clark*, 628 N.E.2d at 53; *Gilbert*, 622 N.E.2d at 794; Martell v. St. Charles Hosp., 523 N.Y.S.2d 342, 351–52 (App.Div.1987); *Clark*, 628 N.E.2d at 53; Capan v. Divine Providence Hosp., 430 A.2d 647, 649–50 (Pa. Super. Ct. 1980). See also Kashishian v. Port, 481 N.W.2d 277, 282 (Wis.1992) (including language emphasizing hospital advertising that has been widely quoted in subsequent cases, including *Sword*). For a case suggesting that hospital quality-assurance and utilization-review activities might constitute enough control to justify holding hospital vicariously liable for torts of independent physician, see Berel v. HCA Health Servs., Inc., 881 S.W.2d 21 (Tex.App.1994).

7. *Reference*. See generally McWilliams & Russell, Hospital Liability for Torts of Independent Contractor Physicians, 47 S.C. L. Rev. 431 (1996).

Corporate Negligence

Darling v. Charleston Community Memorial Hospital

Supreme Court of Illinois, 1965.
33 Ill.2d 326, 211 N.E.2d 253, cert. denied 383 U.S. 946 (1966).

■ SCHAEFER, JUSTICE.

* * *

On November 5, 1960, the plaintiff, who was 18 years old, broke his leg while playing in a college football game. He was taken to the emergency room at the defendant hospital where Dr. Alexander, who was on emergency call that day, treated him. Dr. Alexander, with the assistance of hospital personnel, applied traction and placed the leg in a plaster cast. A heat cradle was applied to dry the cast. Not long after the application of the cast plaintiff was in great pain and his toes, which protruded from the cast, became swollen and dark in color. They eventually became cold and insensitive. On the evening of November 6, Dr. Alexander "notched" the cast around the toes, and on the afternoon of the next day he cut the cast approximately three inches up from the foot. On November 8 he split the sides of the cast with a Stryker saw; in the course of cutting the cast the plaintiff's leg was cut on both sides. Blood and other seepage were observed by the nurses and others, and there was a stench in the room, which one witness said was the worst he had smelled since World War II. The plaintiff remained in Charleston Hospital until November 19, when he was transferred to Barnes Hospital in St. Louis and placed under the care of Dr. Fred Reynolds, head of orthopedic surgery at Washington University School of Medicine and Barnes Hospital. Dr. Reynolds found that the fractured leg contained a considerable amount of dead tissue which in his opinion resulted from interference with the circulation of blood in the limb caused by swelling or hemorrhaging of the leg against the construction of the cast. Dr. Reynolds performed several operations in a futile attempt to save the leg but ultimately it had to be amputated eight inches below the knee.

The evidence before the jury is set forth at length in the opinion of the Appellate Court and need not be stated in detail here. The plaintiff contends that it established that the defendant was negligent in permitting Dr. Alexander to do orthopedic work of the kind required in this case, and not requiring him to review his operative procedures to bring them up to date; in failing, through its medical staff, to exercise adequate supervision over the case, especially since Dr. Alexander had been placed on emergency duty by the hospital, and in not requiring consultation, particularly after complications had developed. Plaintiff contends also that in a case which developed as this one did, it was the duty of the nurses to watch the protruding toes constantly for changes of color, temperature and movement, and to check circulation every ten to twenty minutes, whereas the proof showed that these things were done only a few times a day. Plaintiff argues that it was the duty of the hospital staff to see that these procedures were followed, and that either the nurses were derelict in failing to report developments in the case to the hospital administrator, he was derelict in bringing them to the attention of the medical staff, or the staff was negligent in failing to take action. Defendant is a licensed and accredited hospital, and the plaintiff contends that the licensing regulations, accreditation standards, and its own bylaws define the hospital's duty, and that an infraction of them imposes liability for the resulting injury.

The defendant's position is stated in the following excerpts from its brief: "It is a fundamental rule of law that only an individual properly educated and licensed, and not a corporation, may practice medicine. ... Accordingly, a hospital is powerless under the law to forbid or command any act by a physician or surgeon in the practice of his profession. ... A hospital is not an insurer of the patient's recovery, but only owes the patient the duty to exercise such reasonable care as his known condition requires and that degree of care, skill and diligence used by hospitals generally in that community. ... Where the evidence shows that the hospital care was in accordance with standard practice obtaining in similar hospitals, and Plaintiff produces no evidence to the contrary, the jury cannot conclude that the opposite is true even if they disbelieve the hospital witnesses. ... A hospital is not liable for the torts of its nurse committed while the nurse was but executing the orders of the patient's physician, unless such order is so obviously negligent as to lead any reasonable person to anticipate that substantial injury would result to the patient from the execution of such order. ... The extent of the duty of a hospital with respect to actual medical care of a professional nature such as is furnished by a physician is to use reasonable care in selecting medical doctors. When such care in the selection of the staff is accomplished, and nothing indicates that a physician so selected is incompetent or that such incompetence should have been discovered, more cannot be expected from the hospital administration."

The basic dispute, as posed by the parties, centers upon the duty that rested upon the defendant hospital. That dispute involves the effect to be given to evidence concerning the community standard of care and diligence, and also the effect to be given to hospital regulations adopted by the State Department of Public Health under the Hospital Licensing Act to the Standards for Hospital Accreditation of the American Hospital Association, and to the bylaws of the defendant.

As has been seen, the defendant argues in this court that its duty is to be determined by the care customarily offered by hospitals generally in its community. Strictly speaking, the question is not one of duty, for "... in negligence cases, the duty is always the same, to conform to the legal standard of reasonable conduct in the light of the apparent risk. What the defendant must do, or must not do, is a question of the standard of conduct required to satisfy the duty." (Prosser on Torts, 3rd ed. at 331.) "By the great weight of modern American authority a custom either to take or to omit a precaution is generally admissible as bearing on what is proper conduct under the circumstances, but is not conclusive." (2 Harper and James, The Law of Torts, sec. 17.3, at 977–978.) Custom is relevant in determining the standard of care because it illustrates what is feasible, it suggests a body of knowledge of which the defendant should be aware, and it warns of the possibility of far-reaching consequences if a higher standard is required. (Morris, Custom and Negligence, 42 Colum.L.Rev. 1147 (1942); 2 Wigmore, Evidence, 3rd ed. secs. 459, 461.) But custom should never be conclusive. As Judge Learned Hand said, "There are, no doubt, cases where courts seem to make the general practice of the calling the standard of proper diligence; we have indeed given some currency to the notion ourselves. ... Indeed in most cases reasonable prudence is in fact common prudence; but strictly it is never its measure; a whole calling may have unduly lagged in the adoption of new and available devices. It never may set its own tests, however persuasive be its usages. Courts must in the end say what is required; there are precautions so imperative that even their universal disregard will not excuse their omission." The T.J. Hooper (2d Cir.1932), 60 F.2d 737, 740.

In the present case the regulations, standards, and bylaws which the plaintiff introduced into evidence, performed much the same function as did evidence of custom. This evidence aided the jury in deciding what was feasible and what the defendant knew or should have known. It did not conclusively determine the standard of care and the jury was not instructed that it did.

"The conception that the hospital does not undertake to treat the patient, does not undertake to act through its doctors and nurses, but undertakes instead simply to procure them to act upon their own responsibility, no longer reflects the fact. Present-day hospitals, as their manner of operation plainly demonstrates, do far more than furnish facilities for treatment. They regularly employ on a salary basis a large staff of physicians, nurses and interns, as well as administrative and manual workers, and they charge patients for medical care and treatment, collecting for such services, if necessary, by legal action. Certainly, the person who avails himself of 'hospital facilities' expects that the hospital will attempt to cure him, not that its nurses or other employes will act on their own responsibility." (Fuld, J., in Bing v. Thunig (1957), 2 N.Y.2d 656, 163 N.Y.S.2d 3, 11, 143 N.E.2d 3, 8.) The Standards for Hospital Accreditation, the state licensing regulations and the defendant's bylaws demonstrate that the medical profession and other responsible authorities regard it as both desirable and feasible that a hospital assume certain responsibilities for the care of the patient.

We now turn to an application of these considerations to this case. * * * Two of [the issues submitted to the jury] * * * were that the defendant had negligently: "5. Failed to have a sufficient number of trained nurses for bedside care of all patients at all times capable of recognizing the progressive gangrenous condition of the plaintiff's right leg, and of bringing the same to the attention of the hospital administration and to the medical staff so that adequate consultation could have been secured and such conditions rectified; ... 7. Failed to require consultation with or examination by members of the hospital surgical staff skilled in such treatment; or to review the treatment rendered to the plaintiff and to require consultants to be called in as needed."

We believe that the jury verdict is supportable on either of these grounds. On the basis of the evidence before it the jury could reasonably have concluded that the nurses did not test for circulation in the leg as frequently as necessary, that skilled nurses would have promptly recognized the conditions that signalled a dangerous impairment of circulation in the plaintiff's leg, and would have known that the condition would become irreversible in a matter of hours. At that point it became the nurses' duty to inform the attending physician, and if he failed to act, to advise the hospital authorities so that appropriate action might be taken. As to consultation, there is no dispute that the hospital failed to review Dr. Alexander's work or require a consultation; the only issue is whether its failure to do so was negligence. On the evidence before it the jury could reasonably have found that it was.

* * *

Judgment affirmed.

QUESTIONS ON THE DARLING CASE

1. What precisely were the duties of the hospital that were breached? Do these duties exist toward all patients treated in the hospital? Or did they arise from certain special circumstances? Should a hospital be held to have a duty to monitor routinely all care rendered by staff physicians? (Did the *Darling* court so hold?) Consider this question in reading the rest of this section. The last case, in particular, reopens the question.

2. Was the problem really that there was not "a sufficient number of trained nurses"? In fact, according to the appellate court, the nurses made many notations in the record of the patient's discomfort, etc. 200 N.E.2d 149, 159–60 (Ill.App.1964). Why did the court not hold simply that the nurses were negligent—and the hospital vicariously liable—for not reporting to higher authority Dr. Alexander's inept handling of the case? (Or did it so hold?) How should such a duty on the part of the nurses be established? See Hardy, When Doctrines Collide: Corporate Negligence, Respondeat Superior, and Hospital Liability When Employees Fail to Speak Up, 61 Tul.L.Rev. 85 (1986). What are the justifications in policy for imposing vicarious liability on employers for the torts of their employees without regard to the employer's own fault? Why did courts originally hesitate to invoke the doctrine of respondeat superior against hospitals? Does the *Darling* decision reflect any such hesitancy?

3. The *Darling* case is perhaps the most famous case in hospital law. Indeed, when it was decided, it prompted much comment and caused many hospitals to demand more cooperation in quality assurance by their medical staffs. But is there anything so revolutionary here? From all that appears, the result could have been reached simply by applying principles of ostensible agency and holding the hospital liable for Dr. Alexander's negligence in applying the cast in the ER and providing follow-up care. Would a decision on this ground have been particularly surprising? If not, how can you account for the case's notoriety and impact?

Elam v. College Park Hospital

Court of Appeals of California, 1982.
132 Cal.App.3d 332, 183 Cal.Rptr. 156.

■ WORK, ASSOCIATE JUSTICE.

The pivotal question presented by this appeal is whether a hospital is liable to a patient under the doctrine of corporate negligence for negligent conduct of independent physicians and surgeons who, as members of the hospital staff, avail themselves of the hospital facilities, but who are neither employees nor agents of the hospital. We answer this question in the affirmative and reverse the judgment.

Factual and Procedural Background

After Sophia Elam filed a complaint alleging medical malpractice against doctors Martin J. Schur, Merrill F. Cahn and Samuel Markarian, and College Park Hospital (Hospital), Hospital was granted summary judgment.

Elam complains Schur, a licensed podiatrist, performed negligent podiatric surgery at Hospital to correct bilateral bunions and bilateral hammer toes. She was admitted to Hospital for surgery by Schur and Markarian, a medical doctor, pursuant to a hospital co-admission procedure requiring concurrence of a medical doctor before admitting a podiatric patient and the physician's assumption of responsibility for the overall medical care of that patient, including the taking of a medical history and the performance of a physical examination to insure podiatric surgery is not contraindicated. The surgery was performed by Schur and Cahn.

Schur was always an independent contractor with Hospital and never an employee or agent. He was never paid by Hospital, as he operated his own office and billed Elam directly. She had personally selected him for medical treatment. In June 1974 he applied for appointment to Hospital's medical staff. After verifying his Doctor of Podiatric Medicine degree, state podiatric license, and podiatric surgery privileges at Hillside and Heartland Hospitals in San Diego, Hospital's governing board granted Schur podiatric surgery privileges on April 25, 1975.

Between April 25, 1975 and the date of surgery, Hospital's Medical Care Evaluation Committee (later renamed Patient Care Evaluation Committee), was responsible for evaluating and improving the quality of care rendered to patients treated at Hospital. The Committee met monthly, reviewing the medical charts of doctors and podiatrists treating patients at Hospital. On this routine basis, Schur's medical charts were reviewed along with the charts of other doctors and podiatrists. The Committee constituted a peer review mechanism designed to continually monitor, evaluate and improve the quality of medical care furnished patients at Hospital in compliance with the standards of the Joint Commission of Accreditation to Hospitals. The Committee never complained or reported to the Hospital's administration it considered or had reason to consider Schur incompetent or unqualified to practice podiatric surgery.

Elam's counsel has handled three other cases against Schur * * * Each case involved Schur's first seeing the patient less than a week before the operation. In its answers to interrogatories, Hospital *admits it learned of the Bailey malpractice suit against Schur approximately four and one-half months before Elam's surgery.*[3]

The Doctrine Of Corporate Hospital Liability

Elam asserts Hospital breached its duty to her of insuring the competence of its staff physicians. In other words, she contends a hospital owes a duty to the patient of selecting and reviewing the competency of its staff physicians carefully. California case precedent establishes a hospital may be held liable for a doctor's malpractice when the physician is actually employed by the hospital or is ostensibly the agent of the hospital but not absent such a relationship. However, we find no appellate decision of this state addressing precisely this application of the doctrine of corporate hospital liability nor "considering tort liability of a hospital for negligent selection or retention of staff practitioners" (Matchett v. Superior Court, 40 Cal.App.3d 623, 629, fn. 4, 115 Cal.Rptr. 317). Thus, we treat this matter as one of first impression.

* * *

Although not involving the determination of whether a hospital can be directly liable for the negligence of its staff physicians, case precedent establishes a hospital has a duty of reasonable care to protect patients from harm, including the discovery and treatment of their medical conditions. * * * We can perceive of no reason why this established duty of due care does not encompass the duty asserted by Elam; for, as a general principle, a hospital's failure to insure the competence of its medical staff through careful selection and review creates an unreasonable risk of harm to its patients.

Our conclusion accords with statutory authority recognizing hospital accountability for the quality of medical care provided and the competency of its medical staff. Health and Safety Code section 1250, subdivisions (a), (b), (f) and (g) define hospital in pertinent part as "a health facility having a duly constituted governing body with overall administrative and professional responsibility. . . ." More specifically, section 32125 confers upon the board of directors of a public hospital the responsibility of its operation in

3. In the *Bailey* case, plaintiff's initial complaint was of a callous on her left foot. Expert testimony confirmed, at an arbitration hearing in the presence of Hospital's counsel, Schur performed extensive surgery on both feet in Hospital and billed for operative procedures which were never done.

accordance with "the best interests of the public health," including the power to "make and enforce all rules, regulations and by-laws necessary for the administration, government, protection and maintenance" of the hospital, and to insure that minimum standards of operation required by statute are followed. Section 32128[11] and Business and Professions Code section 2282 set forth, at least by implication, the scope of public and private hospitals' duty of care. Regarding staff selection, although the medical staff is to be "self-governing," a hospital must provide procedures for selection and reappointment of the medical staff in accordance with JCAH standards, implying investigation of competency for initial appointment and periodic review of competency before reappointment. The hospital's duty to guard against physician's incompetency is further implied by requiring renewal of staff privileges at least every two years (implying a periodic competency review) and the periodic review of the medical records of hospital patients. Although these reviews are conducted by medical staff "peer" committees, the governing body of the hospital is responsible for establishing the review procedures. Finally, section 32128 provides that the hospital rules shall include "[s]uch limitations with respect to the practice of medicine and surgery in the hospital as the board of directors may find to be in the best interests of the public health and welfare...."

Sections 70701 and 70703 of Title 22, California Administrative Code, are even more explicit. Title 22, California Administrative Code, Section 70701, subdivision (6) mandates the hospital governing body "[r]equire that the medical staff establish controls that are designed to ensure the achievement and maintenance of high standards of professional ethical practices including provision that periodically all physicians may be required to demonstrate their ability to perform surgical and other procedures competently and to the satisfaction of an appropriate committee or committees of the staff." Moreover, title 22, California Administrative Code, section 70703, subdivision (a) requires each hospital to "have an

11. Section 32128 provides: "The rules of the hospital, established by the board of directors pursuant to this article, shall include: 1. Provision for the organization of physicians and surgeons, podiatrists, and dentists licensed to practice in this state who are permitted to practice in the hospital into a formal medical staff, with appropriate officers and bylaws and with staff appointments on an annual or biennial basis; 2. Provision for procedure for appointment and reappointment of medical staff as provided by the standards of the Joint Committee on Accreditation of Hospitals; 3. Provisions that the medical staff shall be self-governing with respect to the professional work performed in the hospital; that the medical staff shall meet in accordance with the minimum requirements of the Joint Committee on Accreditation of Hospitals; and that the medical records of the patients shall be the basis for such review and analysis; 4. Provision that accurate and complete medical records be prepared and maintained for all patients.... Such limitations with respect to the practice of medicine and surgery in the hospital as the board of directors may find to be in the best interests of the public health and welfare, including appropriate provision for proof of ability to respond in damages by applicants for staff membership; provided, that no duly licensed physician and surgeon shall be excluded from staff membership solely because he or she is licensed by the Board of Osteopathic Examiners.

"Said rules of the hospital shall, insofar as consistent herewith, be in accord with and contain, minimum standards not less than the rules and standards of private or voluntary hospitals operating within the district."

organized medical staff responsible to the governing body for the fitness, adequacy and quality of the medical care rendered to patients in the hospital."

Further, our conclusion is consonant with the public's perception of the modern hospital as a multi-faceted, healthcare facility responsible for the quality of medical care and treatment rendered. The community hospital has evolved into a corporate institution, assuming "the role of a comprehensive health center ultimately responsible for arranging and coordinating total health care." (Southwick, The Hospital as an Institution—Expanding Responsibilities Change Its Relationship with the Staff Physician (1973) 9 Cal.Western L.Rev. 429.) The patient treated in such a facility receives care from a number of individuals of varying capacities and not merely treated by a physician acting in isolation. (Ybarra v. Spangard, 25 Cal.2d 486, 491, 154 P.2d 687.) The patient relies upon the effectiveness of this "highly integrated system of activities. . . ." (Id., at p. 493, 154 P.2d 687.) Consequently,

> "[t]he concept that a hospital does not undertake to treat patients, does not undertake to act through its doctors and nurses, but only procures them to act solely upon their own responsibility, no longer reflects the fact. The complex manner of operation of the modern-day medical institution clearly demonstrates that they furnish far more than mere facilities for treatment. * * *" (Johnson v. Misericordia Community Hospital (1981), 99 Wis.2d 708, 301 N.W.2d 156, 163–164).

Moreover, imposing the duty of care upon a hospital should have the "prophylactic" effect of supplying the hospital with a greater incentive to assure the competence of its medical staff and the quality of medical care rendered within its walls. Otherwise stated, "[s]ince the corporate negligence theory focuses upon the hospital's own conduct in providing medical care, the spectre of liability based upon this theory should encourage the hospital to examine its conduct more carefully in order to prevent the occurrence of unreasonable harm to patients." (Comm., The Hospital's Responsibility for its Medical Staff: Prospects for Corporate Negligence in California, 8 Pac.L.J. 141, 149; but see, Piercing The Doctrine of Corporate Hospital Liability, 17 San Diego L.Rev. 383, 398–399; see generally, Southwick, The Hospital as an Institution—Expanding Responsibilities Change Its Relationship with the Staff Physician, supra, 9 Cal.Western L.Rev. 429, 466, regarding the mutual dependency of a hospital governing board and its medical staff.) Indeed, the hospital is in the best position to evaluate the competence of physicians it, in its discretion, allows to perform surgery and to practice within its premises, as it constitutes the only institutional "vehicle available to coordinate the delivery of health care of reasonable quality to large numbers of people, especially in urban areas." (Id., at p. 466).

Finally, our holding agrees with the decisions of courts in varying jurisdictions. It appears the proposition a hospital may be held liable to a patient under the doctrine of corporate negligence has its genesis in Darling v. Charleston Community Memorial Hospital (1965), 33 Ill.2d 326,

211 N.E.2d 253, where the court found hospital negligence in failing to require consultation with or examination by members of its medical staff and to review the treatment rendered plaintiff. From this beginning, the doctrine has been utilized and expanded by the courts of several jurisdictions to collectively impose upon a hospital a direct and independent responsibility to its patients of insuring the competency of its medical staff and the quality of medical care provided through the prudent selection, review and continuing evaluation of the physicians granted staff privileges.

In summary, we hold a hospital is accountable for negligently screening the competency of its medical staff to insure the adequacy of medical care rendered to patients at its facility. * * *

In light of our conclusion Hospital owes generally a duty to insure the competency of its medical staff and to evaluate the quality of medical treatment rendered on its premises, the filed papers pertaining to the motion for summary judgment are replete with triable issues of fact. For example, whether Hospital should have conducted an investigation through its peer review committee upon notice of the *Bailey* case? Whether the committee had conducted its periodic reviews of Schur in a non-negligent manner? Assuming a review was made after notice of the *Bailey* case, was it performed in a non-negligent manner? If it had been made in a careful and proper manner, would the committee have recommended revocation or suspension of Schur's staff privileges?

Disposition: Judgment reversed.

NOTES AND QUESTIONS ON CORPORATE NEGLIGENCE

1. *Direct vs. Vicarious Liability.* As noted in *Elam*, other jurisdictions have also recognized affirmative duties on the part of hospitals to patients. Thus, in Purcell v. Zimbelman, 500 P.2d 335 (Ariz.App.1972), the physician had twice been sued for committing similar negligence in performing the same surgical procedure that caused the plaintiff's injuries, but his operating privileges had not been curtailed. The hospital claimed that, while its medical staff had been aware of the earlier mishaps, the hospital itself had not been. The court (id. at 341) cited accrediting standards and the medical staff's bylaws as evidence that the "doctors themselves and other responsible authorities regard as both desirable and feasible that a hospital assume certain responsibilities for the care of its patients" and held,

> The hospital had assumed the duty of supervising the competence of its staff doctors. The Department of Surgery was acting for and on behalf of the hospital in fulfilling this duty and if the department was negligent in not taking any action against Purcell or recommending to the board of trustees that action be taken, then the hospital would also be negligent.

In another case, the hospital had appointed a physician to its staff without knowledge of his past problems and claimed that it had no duty in the absence of specific information revealing his incompetence. The court held that there was a duty to inquire and that, since it should have known what it could have learned, it was liable for injuries caused by the doctor's subsequent negligence. Johnson v. Misericordia Community Hosp., 301 N.W.2d 156 (Wis.1981). See also Butler v. South Fulton Med. Ctr., 452 S.E.2d 768 (Ga.App.1994) (affidavit opining that doctor lacked credentials required to perform neurolytic block held insufficient to overcome evidence that there was nothing in doctor's work history which should have put the hospital on notice); Humana Med. Corp. v. Traffanstedt, 597 So.2d 667 (Ala.1992) (holding that verdict against hospital under corporate negligence theory cannot stand where jury also found surgeon not negligent); Thompson v. Nason Hosp., 591 A.2d 703 (Pa.1991) (holding that corporate negligence doctrine creates nondelegable duty on part of hospital to ensure the patient's safety and well-being); Insinga v. LaBella, 543 So.2d 209 (Fla.1989) (holding that hospital has duty to select and retain only competent physicians on staff, even as regards independent contractors); Bell v. Sharp Cabrillo Hosp., 260 Cal.Rptr. 886 (Cal.App.1989) (holding that statute limiting damages for professional negligence applies to action against hospital for failure to use care in reviewing competence of medical staff).

The Kansas Supreme Court, faced with a state statute abrogating hospital liability for corporate negligence, ruled that the right of action, though newly recognized, was implicit in common-law negligence principles antedating the constitutional guarantee and therefore could be repealed only if the legislature acted for the general welfare and provided an adequate substitute remedy. Lemuz v. Fieser, 933 P.2d 134 (Kan. 1997). In upholding the law, the court found that it was enacted to "encourage hospitals to actively engage in the peer review of staff physicians, without the threat of liability from peer review." Id. at 144. Does this make sense? Or would the threat of liability be more likely to encourage hospitals to oversee their physicians? The court was impressed that the legislature had enacted "a requirement that hospitals engage in risk management to ensure that all incompetent physicians are discovered and denied staff privileges. With these statutes, the very purpose of the corporate negligence cause of action is fulfilled." Id. at 150. Would the court recognize an implied right of action if a hospital failed to fulfill its duties under the risk management legislation?

A Texas statute protecting participants in peer review actions against liability was construed to bar suits for negligent credentialing and, as so construed, was upheld against a constitutional challenge for abrogating a common-law cause of action. St. Luke's Episcopal Hosp. v. Agbor, 952 S.W.2d 503 (Tex.1997). Two dissenters, however, protested against construing the statute to eliminate claims for corporate negligence. How would you argue that an immunity statute should not bar suits against hospitals by patients injured by physicians whose privileges should have been restricted?

2. *Nature of the Cause of Action.* Is a claim against a hospital for corporate negligence a claim for "medical malpractice" and therefore subject to statutory limitations applicable to actions of the latter kind? See, e.g., Browning v. Burt, 613 N.E.2d 993 (Ohio 1993) (applying statute of limitations applicable to claims for ordinary, not professional, negligence); Sibley v. Board of Supervisors of Louisiana State Univ., 477 So.2d 1094 (La.1985) (statutory ceiling on damages in medical malpractice actions held not to apply to claim for corporate negligence).

3. *Sources of the Standard of Care.* An important feature of the *Darling* case was the court's reliance on regulations, standards, and bylaws rather than custom and practice to establish the hospital's duty to the plaintiff. See also *Purcell*, supra. What are the arguments for and against such prescriptive use of such sources? Violation of a clear regulation might be treated as negligence per se, but what about violation of a JCAHO standard? In Van Iperen v. Van Bramer, 392 N.W.2d 480 (Iowa 1986), the court held an accrediting standard requiring hospital pharmacies to monitor individual patients' drug usage to be insufficient, standing alone, to generate a jury issue; the standards were not viewed as "self-authenticating with respect to the standard of care."

Should expert testimony be necessary to establish the standard of care to which hospitals are held, as it usually is in the case of physicians? See, e.g., Welsh v. Bulger, 698 A.2d 581 (Pa.1997) (requiring expert testimony in case of alleged hospital negligence in authorizing physician to perform deliveries without the skill or backup needed to perform cesarian section, if necessary; dissenting opinion questioned whether testimony of plaintiff's expert, an obstetrician, had established a hospital standard of care or only his own opinion); Buckley v. Lovallo, 481 A.2d 1286 (Conn.App.1984) (requiring expert testimony to show standard of care at similar hospitals). What kind of experts are required—hospital administrators or physicians? Should hospitals be judged by the standards prevalent in their locality, in similar hospitals, or in the best hospitals? The *Shilkret* case reproduced in chapter 7(§B) will provide an occasion for raising these and a few further issues concerning the standard of care applicable to hospitals.

4. *Establishing Negligence in Credentialing.* Do hospitals risk a jury finding of corporate negligence whenever there is anything in the record (such as a PRO sanction) that might be interpreted as grounds for disciplinary or other action? Or may a hospital escape liability by showing that it maintains and follows appropriate procedures? In Sheffield v. Zilis, 316 S.E.2d 493 (Ga.App.1984), affidavits showing adherence to an accreditor's standards were held to justify summary judgment for the hospital, but the plaintiff had apparently offered no evidence suggesting that the hospital knew or should have known of any deficiency in the physician's performance. See also Lopez v. Central Plains Reg. Hosp., 859 S.W.2d 600 (Tex.App.1993) (summary judgment for hospital denied even though evidence showed only arguably sloppy procedures, not physician's past incompetence; nonphysician hospital administrator held qualified as expert on evaluation forms, procedures, and standard of care in credentialing of physicians). Should a plaintiff offering evidence of, say, past malpractice claims against a physician also have to show, by expert testimony, that the hospital and its medical staff acted unreasonably in resolving the question in the doctor's favor? Or should the jury be free to make its own judgment? Should the mere filing of a malpractice action naming the physician be enough to raise a factual issue for the jury?

5. *Using the Practitioner Data Bank.* How will the creation of the National Practitioner Data Bank (created under the federal Health Care Quality Improvement Act of 1986 and described in chapter 6(§B)) affect a hospital's liability for negligent acts of its staff? Presumably, a hospital has a responsibility to use the data bank and to investigate any "black marks" appearing on the record. How will a plaintiff discover what the data bank record revealed and what was done to follow up? (Data bank records are not available to the general public, including malpractice or other plaintiffs.)

6. *Access to Peer Review Records.* The court in the *Elam* case makes clear that peer review actions by a hospital with respect to a practitioner are relevant in establishing the hospital's liability. Are the records of such actions discoverable? (See earlier note on the privilege that such records frequently enjoy.) In California cases after the *Elam* decision, plaintiffs argued that the statutory privilege for peer review records was necessarily restricted by *Elam,* because access to such records was necessary to establish hospital liability for negligently reviewing and screening medical staff members. The courts dismissed this argument, however, stating that the *Elam* decision did not affect the legislature's "judgment call" in making the records "off limits." West Covina Hosp. v. Superior Court, 200 Cal.Rptr. 162, 165 (Cal.App.1984). See also Mt. Diablo Hosp. Med. Center v. Superior Court, 204 Cal.Rptr. 626 (Cal.App.1984).

A North Carolina case similarly denies access to peer review records in a case alleging corporate negligence in failing to restrict the surgical privileges of two physicians. Shelton v. Morehead Mem. Hosp., 347 S.E.2d 824 (N.C.1986). The plaintiff could, however, discover information in the hands of the governing board and the hospital administration if it was not originally generated through peer review. For additional cases protecting peer review records under state statutes see Toth v. Jensen, 649 N.E.2d 484 (Ill.App.1995) (materials that "served an integral function in the decision-making process" of the hospital's executive and credentials committees held protectable under peer review statute, despite absence of formal peer review committee); Adventist Health Systems v. Trude, 880 S.W.2d 539 (Ky.1994) (confidentiality statute applicable to "any civil action in any court" held to protect peer review records against discovery in physician suit against hospital despite possibility that harm to defendants of disclosure would not be irreparable if made under seal).

To whom does the privilege belong—the doctor, the hospital, or the peer reviewers themselves? Might hospitals sometimes voluntarily open their records in court in order to defend themselves? Will this prospect tend to inhibit or encourage effective peer review? The California Supreme Court has allowed an individual participant in the peer review process to testify *voluntarily* concerning it in a corporate negligence case. West Covina Hosp. v. Superior Court, 718 P.2d 119 (Cal.1986). But see Cedars–Sinai

Med. Center v. Superior Court, 16 Cal.Rptr.2d 253 (Cal.App.1993) (court held identities of members of peer review committees was privileged information in suit charging medical malpractice).

7. How does the law of hospital liability (*a*) reflect and (*b*) determine hospital/physician relationships? Why are hospitals becoming more prominent actors in the health care system? List your reasons and consider their implications for hospital liability. Keep these matters in mind in studying hospital staff privileges in the next section. Chapter 8 will address comparable issues with respect to managed-care organizations.

NOTES AND QUESTIONS ON HOSPITAL LIABILITY FOR THE TORTS OF STAFF PHYSICIANS

1. Where is the law on hospital responsibility for physician negligence headed? Is it only a matter of time before hospitals are liable for all negligent acts of physicians in the hospital? Would this be a sound principle? Can you define a reasonable stopping point short of such vicarious liability? Consider the following notes.

2. *Private Physicians.* As illustrated in the Colorado cases discussed in *Bernardi* (*Rosane, Beadles,* and *Moon*), the law generally does not impose vicarious hospital liability for the negligent acts of independent physicians on a hospital's medical staff where the patient, rather than the hospital, selected the physician in the first instance. Only if special facts are shown—e.g., that the patient reasonably "looked to" the hospital to provide the care—will an agency relationship be found. For example, in Kashishian v. Port, 481 N.W.2d 277 (Wis.1992), the court was willing to apply the doctrine of apparent agency outside ER context, but the jury was free to find vicarious liability for a cardiologist's negligence only because the patient was referred to the cardiology department rather than to an individual doctor, the hospital's letterhead was used for informed consent, and the hospital advertised its "international reputation" in cardiology. See also Porter v. Sisters of St. Mary, 756 F.2d 669 (8th Cir.1985) (rejecting ostensible agency theory where patient first encountered surgeon in ER but later elected to have him perform surgery); Schlotfeldt v. Charter Hosp., 910 P.2d 271 (Nev.1996) (in case where patient first encountered physician in hospital, court overturned trial court's instruction that independent contractor physician was hospital's agent); Cooper v. Curry, 589 P.2d 201 (N.M.App.1978) (holding that hospital could not be liable for physician's negligence under a joint venture theory in absence of mutual right of control or evidence that physician shared in hospital's losses or profits). But see id. at 208–11 (dissenting opinion favoring hospital liability for all in-hospital physician negligence); Strach v. St. John Hosp. Corp., 408 N.W.2d 441 (Mich.App.1987) (holding that preexisting physician/patient relationship did not preclude finding of ostensible agency where patient perceived surgeon as member of hospital's cardiac "team"); Simmons v. St. Clair Mem. Hosp., 481 A.2d 870 (Pa.Super.1984) ("on-call" staff psychiatrist treated patient for five months after admission; remand left open possibility that agency theory might apply).

To be sure, a hospital may be liable for injuries caused by a physician selected by the patient if it was somehow guilty of corporate negligence in overseeing the work of that physician. Once again, however, hospital liability requires a special showing of more than the physician's own negligence. Thus, the law maintains the distinction between hospital-selected and patient-selected physicians. While this is a fairly bright line, its long-term viability may depend on whether it has a strong policy rationale. Does it?

3. *Enterprise Liability?* There have been influential proposals to impose on hospitals exclusive enterprise liability for the negligence of all staff physicians. See generally 2 American Law Inst. Reporters Study, Enterprise Responsibility for Personal Injury 113–26 (1991); Abraham & Weiler, Enterprise Medical Liability and the Evolution of the American Health Care System, 108 Harv. L. Rev. 381 (1994). These proposals would make hospitals bear liability risks not only because they are convenient spreaders of losses but also because they are well-positioned to ensure the quality of care, either by taking direct action or by inducing others (e.g., their medical staffs) to do so. In addition, making them exclusively responsible would increase the overall efficiency of the compensation system. See id. at 406 (estimating as much as 30% savings in litigation costs from eliminating multiple defendants). In pursuit of these benefits, Abraham and Weiler have proposed extending hospital responsibility to encompass even out-of-hospital negligence by physicians affiliated with the institution, with a view to focusing responsibility for the quality of care, simplifying litigation and settlement negotiations, and eliminating the need for physicians to carry their own liability insurance.

Despite the expediency of proposals for enterprise liability, do you see reasons why a court or legislature should not impose liability on hospitals without regard to whether the patient initially selected the physician or the hospital as the party to be responsible for his or her care? Be prepared to encounter in chapter 8(§A) the analogous question whether various managed-care organizations, rather than hospitals, should face enterprise liability for the torts of their affiliated doctors.

Allocating Responsibilities Between Physicians and Hospitals

Alexander v. Gonser

Court of Appeals of Washington, Division 3, Panel Three, 1985.
42 Wn.App. 234, 711 P.2d 347, reh. den. Jan. 23, 1986.

■ THOMPSON, JUDGE.

* * *

On October 6, 1982, Nancy Alexander, who was at full term pregnancy, was brought to the Yakima Valley Memorial Hospital (hospital) emergency room following a 2–car collision. Mrs. Alexander was driving at the time of

the accident and suffered direct trauma to her abdomen when she struck the steering wheel. Mrs. Alexander's obstetrician, Dr. Figgs,[1] when notified of the accident, instructed the emergency room staff to perform a general examination. When he arrived, he personally gave Mrs. Alexander a gynecological examination in the emergency room. Thereafter, Mrs. Alexander was transferred to another area of the hospital for fetal heart monitoring.

The nurse who was monitoring the fetal heart tones called Dr. Figgs at his home to inform him the results were "equivocal" and that Mrs. Alexander continued to complain of numbness to her abdomen. Dr. Figgs instructed the nurse to send Mrs. Alexander home; however, after the nurse voiced her concern with the test results, Dr. Figgs agreed to have Mrs. Alexander return the following morning for additional monitoring. Mrs. Alexander and her husband were not informed of the "equivocal" results.

The following morning when Mrs. Alexander returned to the hospital, stress tests indicated fetal distress, and a Caesarean section was performed. A male infant was delivered suffering from asphyxia. The child has been diagnosed as permanently brain damaged.

Mrs. Alexander, as guardian ad litem for her child, and on her own behalf, brought suit against the hospital for negligence. The hospital moved for summary judgment which was partially granted May 25, 1984, on the issues of respondeat superior, failure of the hospital to inform Mrs. Alexander of the "equivocal" test results, and the alleged delay in monitoring. On June 8, 1984, the court granted summary judgment for the hospital on the remaining issues of corporate negligence and the alleged inaccurate medical history. Mrs. Alexander appeals the issues of informed consent [and] corporate negligence * * *

Mrs. Alexander interprets RCW 7.70 as imposing upon the hospital the same informed consent duties the statutes and case law impose upon Dr. Figgs. She contends that the hospital comes within the RCW 7.70.020 definition of a health care provider and since the hospital, through its employee, had become aware of a possible patient abnormality, it had a duty to relate this information to Mrs. Alexander. We disagree. Although the hospital did the monitoring and observed equivocal results, it did so at the direction of Mrs. Alexander's personal physician. The results and concerns were relayed to Dr. Figgs and the medical decision as to the significance of the test was his to make.

The fact the hospital comes within the definition of health care provider alone does not warrant the conclusion that every entity and every individual that falls within the definition has equal informed consent obligations. The logic of this conclusion is illustrated by a number of cases from other jurisdictions.

> [T]he relationship between the physician and his patient "is always one of great delicacy. And it is perhaps the most delicate matter, often

1. Although consulted by Mrs. Alexander as her private physician, Dr. Figgs also had hospital privileges at Yakima Valley Memorial Hospital.

with fluctuating indications, from time to time with the same patient, whether a physician should advise the patient (or his family), more or less, about a proposed procedure, the gruesome details, and the available alternatives. Such a decision is particularly one calling for the exercise of medical judgment. ... In the exercise of that discretion, involving as it does grave risks to the patient, a third party should not ordinarily meddle ..." Fiorentino v. Wenger, 19 N.Y.2d 407, 415–416, 280 N.Y.S.2d 373, 227 N.E.2d 296 (1967).

... Any other rule is inherently impossible under the circumstances.

Prooth v. Wallsh, 105 Misc.2d 603, 432 N.Y.S.2d 663, 665 (1980). Any duty to inform Mrs. Alexander of the test results would have been that of her privately retained physician, not the hospital or its personnel. To hold a hospital or its employees have a duty to intervene in the independent physician/patient relationship, unless the hospital is aware of circumstances more extraordinary than those in the record before this court, would be far more disruptive than beneficial to a patient. This is not a case wherein it is alleged the hospital is liable on the issue of informed consent because of vicarious liability for the failure of an employee physician to obtain consent. * * *

Next, Mrs. Alexander claims there is an issue of material fact regarding hospital liability for corporate negligence in the hiring and supervision of Dr. Figgs which precludes summary judgment. We disagree.

Corporate negligence was recently adopted in Washington. Pedroza v. Bryant, 101 Wash.2d 226, 677 P.2d 166 (1984). The doctrine is based on a nondelegable duty the hospital owes directly to the patient, and requires hospitals to exercise reasonable care to ensure that only competent physicians are selected as members of the hospital staff. The standard of care is generally defined by the accreditation standards of the Joint Commission on Accreditation of Hospitals (JCAH), and the hospital's own bylaws.

Corporate negligence has been extended to include placing a duty on the hospital to "intervene in the treatment of its patients if there is obvious negligence". Schoening v. Grays Harbor Community Hosp., 40 Wash.App. 331, 335, 698 P.2d 593, review denied, 104 Wash.2d 1008 (1985). This is in accord with other jurisdictions which find the hospital liable when its employees fail to recognize and report abnormalities in the treatment and condition of patients. See Poor Sisters of St. Francis Seraph of the Perpetual Adoration, Inc. v. Catron, 435 N.E.2d 305 (Ind.App.1982); Fridena v. Evans, 127 Ariz. 516, 622 P.2d 463 (Ariz.1980); Utter v. United Hosp. Ctr., Inc., 160 W.V. 703, 236 S.E.2d 213 (1977); Toth v. Community Hosp. at Glen Cove, 22 N.Y.2d 255, 292 N.Y.S.2d 440, 239 N.E.2d 368 (1968); Annot., Hospital's Liability For Negligence in Failing to Review or Supervise Treatment Given By Doctor, or to Require Consultation, 12 A.L.R.4th 57 (1982).

To prevail in an action for professional negligence against a hospital, the plaintiff must

> prove by a preponderance of the evidence that the defendant ... failed to exercise that degree of skill, care, and learning possessed at that time by other persons in the same profession, and that as a proximate result of such failure the plaintiff suffered damages ...

RCW 4.24.290. In resisting a motion for summary judgment, Mrs. Alexander had a duty to present some evidence that negligence on the part of the hospital in monitoring Dr. Figgs proximately caused her injuries. * * *

[The court examined the evidence tendered on the latter question and found that it did not preclude summary judgment.]

Affirmed.

NOTES AND QUESTIONS ON HOSPITALS' DUTIES TO PATIENTS UNDER A PHYSICIAN'S CARE

1. Many cases reject the argument that a hospital may be held liable for failing to obtain a patient's informed consent. E.g., Mele v. Sherman Hosp., 838 F.2d 923 (7th Cir.1988) (finding hospital has no duty under Illinois law to obtain informed consent for surgery done by independent staff physician; hospital bylaw requiring all staff physicians to obtain signed consent prior to surgery and provision of consent form reflected merely hospital's effort to increase likelihood that physicians would fulfill their obligation to patients); Giese v. Stice, 567 N.W.2d 156 (Neb.1997) (hospital held to have no duty to disclose risk of breast implants; concern expressed for doctor/patient relationship); Mathias v. St. Catherine's Hosp., 569 N.W.2d 330 (Wis.App.1997) (holding that, because duty to advise patient of risks of medical treatment lies with the physician, the physician, and not the hospital, has the duty to obtain patient consent; without knowledge of the absence of consent, hospital and its employees owe patients only a duty of ordinary care); Petriello v. Kalman, 576 A.2d 474 (Conn.1990) (duty of disclosure lies solely with physician; hospital consent form only assists physician, without shifting responsibility).

Even though the physician's legal duty to obtain informed consent is clear, should a hospital have an independent legal duty to establish procedures, etc., to ensure that the doctor's duty is performed? For cases rejecting such a duty, see (in addition to *Petriello*, supra) Femrite v. Abbott Northwestern Hosp., 568 N.W.2d 535 (Minn.App.1997) (holding hospital has no duty under doctrine of corporate negligence to ensure that consent is obtained); Kelly v. Methodist Hosp., 664 A.2d 148 (Pa.Super.1995) (no hospital duty to ensure that physician obtains consent); Boney v. Mother Frances Hosp., 880 S.W.2d 140 (1994) (hospital policy requiring patients to sign consent form held not to create duty to ensure that informed consent was obtained). But see Karibjanian v. Thomas Jefferson Univ. Hosp., 717 F.Supp. 1081 (E.D.Pa.1989) (hospital held to have duty to supervise care, including consent getting, by independent staff physicians under Pennsylvania doctrine of corporate negligence); Kenner v. Northern Ill. Med. Center, 517 N.E.2d 1137 (Ill.App.1987) (hospital liable for nurse's acts taken on doctor's authority without informed consent because hospital's duty of care extends to ensuring that doctors have obtained proper authority for nurses' actions).

2. What was the nature of the "corporate negligence" alleged by Mrs. Alexander and considered by the court? Did it involve Dr. Figgs' staff privileges or something else? How does this case compare to *Darling?* Was this a case of corporate negligence at all? What evidence should the plaintiff have offered?

Was the nurse in the *Alexander* case a "borrowed servant"? What would be the implications of so finding? What would be the implications of holding that a nurse may sometimes have a duty to second-guess a physician's judgment? A number of cases do hold that a nurse may have a duty to "speak up." See references cited by the court in *Alexander; Campbell* case, supra; Koeniguer v. Eckrich, 422 N.W.2d 600 (S.D.1988) (based on expert testimony concerning nurse's duty, hospital could be vicariously liable for nurse's failure to object to patient's discharge, ordered by physician). Similar reasoning has also been applied to hold a hospital liable where a resident physician failed to question the discharge order of an attending physician personally selected by the patient. Somoza v. St. Vincent's Hosp., 596 N.Y.S.2d 789 (N.Y.A.D.1993). See generally Hardy, When Doctrines Collide: Corporate Negligence, Respondeat Superior, and Hospital Liability When Employees Fail to Speak Up, 61 Tul.L.Rev. 85 (1986). The latter commentator convincingly argues for treating such cases as involving professional negligence, requiring expert testimony concerning the nursing standard of care, and as giving rise to hospital liability under principles of respondeat superior, not corporate negligence. Should the hospital also have an independent duty to establish procedures to ensure that its employees monitor physicians' performance?

SECTION C: HOSPITAL STAFF PRIVILEGES

Judicial Review of Hospital Actions and Policies on Admitting Privileges

Silver v. Castle Memorial Hospital

Supreme Court of Hawaii, 1972.
53 Haw. 475, 497 P.2d 564, cert. denied 409 U.S. 1048, 93 S.Ct. 517, 34 L.Ed.2d 500.

■ KOBAYASHI, JUSTICE.

* * * This case presents the issue of whether the administrative decision of a private hospital in refusing to grant licensed doctors staff privileges is subject to judicial review. This question has been decided in other jurisdictions on the basis of two distinctly divergent views.

Judicial Review of Private Hospital

The majority of jurisdictions have held that a private hospital, as opposed to a public hospital, has the absolute right to exclude any physician from practicing therein. * * * It is reasoned that even though a doctor may have exemplary qualifications, he has no vested right to practice in a private hospital but merely a privilege which may be granted or denied at the election of the private corporation in exercising its fundamental right to manage its own internal affairs.

We agree that the board of directors of a private hospital should have broad discretionary power in determining which doctors will be given staff privileges and on what basis. There are many justifications for such power aside from the general malpractice considerations. Apparently the state licensing procedure does not distinguish between general practitioners and specialists such as neurosurgeons. Nor does the state licensing system provide for adequate periodic review of a doctor's skill and performance, both of which are of primary importance to the beneficiaries of the services of the hospital and doctors involved, the patients themselves. When considering the interest of the patient, it is not enough that his doctor possess the necessary skills of his profession. The absence of a compatible team working together could impair the doctor's performance and consequently undermine the effectiveness of the treatment given the patient. All of the above criteria are and should be weighed by the board in granting staff privileges. This staff privileges determination is, as a system, the general method utilized by hospitals throughout the country for screening and reviewing applicants in terms of qualifications, current skills, performance, personality and character.

We cannot agree, however, that the discretionary power of a hospital is absolute or that a decision of a private hospital board in refusing to grant a licensed doctor staff privileges is not subject to judicial review. The better rule provides that such review be available as to whether the doctor excluded was afforded procedural due process, and as to whether an abuse of discretion by the hospital board occurred, resulting in an arbitrary, capricious or unreasonable exclusion. As to what constitutes such an abuse it has been held that "the managing authorities of a private hospital are vested with broad discretionary powers in the selection of its medical and surgical staffs. If the exclusion of a person from its medical or surgical staff is based on the sound and reasonable exercise of discretionary judgment, courts will not intervene, but if the exclusion stems from unreasonable, arbitrary, capricious or discriminatory considerations, equitable relief is available." Davidson v. Youngstown Hospital Association, 19 Ohio App.2d 246, 251, 250 N.E.2d 892, 896 (1969).

The basis for this departure from the traditional rule was first voiced in Greisman v. Newcomb Hospital, 40 N.J. 389, 402–404, 192 A.2d 817, 824–825 (1963).

> [W]hile the managing officials [of a private hospital] may have discretionary powers in the selection of the medical staff, those powers are deeply imbedded in public aspects, and are rightly viewed, for policy reasons . . . as fiduciary powers to be exercised reasonably and for the public good.
>
> . . . .

Hospital officials are properly vested with large measures of managing discretion and to the extent that they exert their efforts toward the elevation of hospital standards and higher medical care, they will receive broad judicial support. But they must never lose sight of the fact that the hospitals are operated not for private ends but for the benefit of the public, and that their existence is for the purpose of faithfully furnishing facilities to the members of the medical profession in aid of their service to the public. They must recognize that their powers, particularly those relating to the selection of staff members, are powers in trust which are always to be dealt with as such. While reasonable and constructive exercises of judgment should be honored, courts would indeed be remiss if they declined to intervene where, as here, the powers were invoked at the threshold to preclude an application for staff membership, not because of any lack of individual merit, but for a reason unrelated to sound hospital standards and not in furtherance of the common good.

Public Versus Private Hospital

* * * [R]ecently some courts have recognized another hospital classification falling between that of public and private. Such a status can be termed "quasi public" as distinguished from a hospital that is truly private. E.g., Sussman v. Overlook Hospital Association, 92 N.J.Super. 163, 168, 222 A.2d 530, 533 (1966), aff'd 95 N.J.Super. 418, 231 A.2d 389 (1967). The "quasi public" status is achieved if what would otherwise be a truly private hospital was constructed with public funds, is presently receiving public benefits or has been sufficiently incorporated into a governmental plan for providing hospital facilities to the public. It is not surprising that courts would be more readily willing to grant judicial review of a private hospital's administrative decision if it could be shown that the hospital in question was not a truly private institution. However, if the proposition that any hospital occupies a fiduciary trust relationship between itself, its staff and the public it seeks to serve is accepted, then the rationale for any distinction between public, "quasi public" and truly private breaks down and becomes meaningless, especially if the hospital's patients are considered to be of primary concern.

In holding that the actions of appellee hospital in this case are subject to judicial review we do not mean to characterize appellee as anything other than a private hospital. In relation to this point we are in concurrence with the reasoning that "a private nonprofit hospital, which receives part of its funds from public sources and through public solicitation, which receives tax benefits because of its nonprofit and nonprivate aspects and which constitutes a virtual monopoly in the area in which it functioned, is a 'private hospital' in the sense that it is nongovernmental, but that it is in no position to claim immunity from public supervision and control because of its private nature. The power of the staff of such a hospital to pass on staff membership applications is a fiduciary power which must be exercised reasonably and for the public good." Davidson v. Youngstown Hospital Association, 19 Ohio App.2d 246, 250, 250 N.E.2d 892, 895 (1969).

In the case before us we need not reach the issue of whether the decision of the board of a truly private hospital not to grant staff privileges is subject to judicial review. As indicated previously, appellee hospital was the recipient of state and federal funding during its construction. Our opinion today, therefore, is limited to those situations where the hospitals involved have had more than nominal governmental involvement in the form of funding. We leave the issue as to what other forms of governmental-public involvement are sufficient to constitute a basis for judicial review and the issue as to whether a truly completely private hospital is subject to such review to future cases wherein those questions are more adequately briefed by the litigants involved.

Procedural Due Process—Requirement of a Hearing

Compliance with the principle that a doctor applying for staff privileges at a private hospital, as well as at a public hospital, be afforded procedural due process requires a balancing process of the varying interests involved. The doctor has an interest in being able to pursue his profession which requires that the necessary facilities be available to him. The hospital is interested in preserving its autonomy and in maintaining quality control in its medical staff. The public's interest lies in the perpetuation of that quality control and, in the sense that its services are and remain available to those in need, in the productivity of the hospital.

The purposes and interests of everyone concerned would be defeated if hospitals were required to engage in excessively burdensome procedures in screening staff applicants. However, due process, in this context, requires that a fair and thorough consideration be made of a doctor's application for initial appointment or reappointment to the staff. Therefore, a hearing before the deciding board must be provided. It is not possible that such a hearing require all the aspects of a formal judicial or quasi judicial hearing. Although a hospital board does not have the power to subpoena witnesses or administer oaths, certain procedural safeguards must be provided. The doctor should be on notice that a hearing is available to him. He should be given timely notification sufficiently prior to the hearing for him to adequately prepare a defense. In conjunction with such notice, a doctor whose privileges are being revoked or who is being denied reappointment should be provided a written statement of the charges against him. Such statement should be sufficiently adequate to apprise him of the specific charges against him. A doctor who is being denied initial appointment to a hospital staff should be provided a written statement specifying the reasons his application is being denied.

Because a hospital board has no subpoena power, there can be no right to confront and cross-examine persons who have made adverse statements of a doctor unless such persons testify at the hearing. However, a doctor should have the right to call his own witnesses.

It should be within the discretion of the hospital board as to whether counsel may attend the hearing and participate in the proceedings. Participation of counsel would probably not be necessary unless the hospital's attorney is used in the proceedings or the extreme nature of the charges involved indicated that representation by an attorney would be advantageous. Such a limitation would not preclude a doctor from consulting an attorney prior to the hearing even though the attorney was not allowed to participate in the hearing itself.

The basis for the decision of the board must come from substantial evidence which was produced at the hearing. As such the board cannot rely on *ex parte* communications that were not made known to the doctor in question. The utilization of such material would render ineffective the doctor's right to answer the charges upon which the denial of his staff privileges are based.

The decision of the board should be written, including the basis for the decision, thus providing a record for judicial review.

Disposition of Present Case

In the present case appellant was granted staff privileges apparently on a probationary basis for a period of one year. At the end of that period it was decided that such privileges not be renewed. It is our opinion that appellant was not afforded procedural due process. Although a hearing was provided appellant, it was patently defective.

Presumably among the significant factors to be considered by a hospital board at a reappointment or revocation of privileges hearing would be included the previous performance of the doctor at the hospital. A year's time, as in this case, would appear to be a sufficiently long period for specific charges to develop against appellant if his denial of privileges were to be justified. And yet in this case, prior to the termination of appellant's privileges, appellant was never provided with specific written charges as to why his performance was not deemed acceptable. He was merely read an indictment of general allegations at the hearing. In order for appellant's right to a hearing to be effective he must have been apprised of the particulars of the specific claims against him prior to the hearing. In this case appellant had no opportunity to investigate the basis for his performance being questioned. As such his right to present a defense was rendered nugatory.

It is clear from the record of this case that the hospital board made its decision as to the renewal of appellant's privileges prior to the ineffective hearing granted appellant. Such a procedure cannot be considered satisfactory. A final decision to revoke privileges or not reappoint, made by the ultimate governing body, the hospital board, must come after the requisite hearing is provided. In order for the board to function as an objective decision making body in its capacity as grantor of staff privileges it must not be tainted by its own premature decisions prior to the hearing.

We do not reach the issue whether in this case the decision of the board, aside from the fact that the hearing was not adequate, was based on insubstantial evidence, resulting in an arbitrary, capricious or unreasonable exclusion amounting to an abuse of discretion. Appellant clearly was denied procedural due process. Although this case is appealed from the decision of the court in the jury trial below, equitable relief having been prayed for, it is appropriate to grant such a remedy. Therefore this case is remanded for the trial court to grant an injunction against appellee, reinstating appellant with his temporary staff privileges.

NOTES AND QUESTIONS ON THE REVIEWABILITY OF PRIVILEGES DECISIONS IN HOSPITALS

1. *State Action.* Overruling an earlier decision involving racial discrimination, a federal court of appeals in 1982, applying principles established by the Supreme Court in Jackson v. Metropolitan Edison Co., 419 U.S. 345 (1974), ruled that "the staff privileges decisions of a hospital which receives Hill–Burton Act funds, accepts Medicare and Medicaid patients and reports privileges revocations to state medical licensing authorities do not constitute 'state action.'" Modaber v. Culpeper Mem. Hosp., Inc., 674 F.2d 1023 (4th Cir.1982). Thus, a private institution was held not subject to constitutional norms of procedural and substantive due process or to suits to enforce constitutional rights under section 1983 of the Civil Rights Act, 42 U.S.C. § 1983 (1994) (prohibiting denial of constitutionally protected rights under color of state law). Since *Modaber* and Blum v. Yaretsky, 457 U.S. 991 (1982) (nursing homes' decisions to discharge Medicaid patients held not state action), the courts have been unanimous in not applying constitutional requirements to ordinary private hospitals. Some gray areas remain, however. See, e.g., Jatoi v. Hurst–Euless–Bedford Hosp. Auth., 807 F.2d 1214 (5th Cir.1987) (public authority leased hospital to private entity but its monitoring and fund-raising activities were enough to establish state action in a civil rights suit). See generally Annot., Action of Private Hospital as State Action Under 42 U.S.C.A. § 1983 or Fourteenth Amendment, 42 A.L.R.Fed. 463 (1979 & Supp. 1995).

Note that the factors cited by the *Silver* court to justify its holding are essentially the same factors that were not enough in *Modaber*. If not from the Constitution, where did the *Silver* court get the requirements it imposed on "quasi-public" hospitals?

2. *The Greisman Decision.* The 1963 case of Greisman v. Newcomb Hosp., 40 N.J. 389, 192 A.2d 817 (1963), relied upon in *Silver*, is the leading authority supporting judicial review of hospital staff privileges decisions without a specific constitutional, statutory, or contractual warrant. That case involved a private hospital that refused to entertain an osteopath's application for privileges because he lacked both AMA-approved training and membership in the local medical society. The court reasoned as follows (id. at 396–401, 192 A.2d 820–24):

> Broad judicial expressions may, of course, be found to the effect that hospitals such as Newcomb are private in nature and that their staff admission policies are entirely discretionary. They are private in the sense that they are nongovernmental but they are hardly private in other senses. Newcomb is a nonprofit organization dedicated by its certificate of incorpo-

ration to the vital public use of serving the sick and injured, its funds are in good measure received from public sources and through public solicitation, and its tax benefits are received because of its nonprofit and nonprivate aspects. It constitutes a virtual monopoly in the area in which it functions and it is in no position to claim immunity from public supervision and control because of its allegedly private nature. Indeed, in the development of the law, activities much less public than the hospital activities of Newcomb, have commonly been subjected to judicial (as well as legislative) supervision and control to the extent necessary to satisfy the felt needs of the times.

During the course of history, judges have often applied the common law so as to regulate private businesses and professions for the common good; perhaps the most notable illustration is the duty of serving all comers on reasonable terms which was imposed by the common law on innkeepers, carriers, farriers and the like. See Falcone v. Middlesex Co. Medical Soc., 34 N.J. 582, 170 A.2d 791 (1961); Messenger et al. v. Pennsylvania R.R. Co., 36 N.J.L. 407 (N.J.Sup.1873), aff'd, 37 N.J.L. 531 (N.J. E. & A.1874). In the *Messenger* case Chief Justice Beasley, speaking for the former Supreme Court, noted that a railroad, though a private corporation, is engaged in a "public employment," that it "owes a duty to the community" and that under considerations of public policy it must be held under obligation to serve without discrimination. On appeal, Justice Bedle, speaking for the Court of Errors and Appeals, expressed the view that although railroad corporations are private, they hold their property "as a quasi-public trust," and that as trustees they must conduct their operations in such manner so as to insure to every member of the community the equal enjoyment of the means of transportation.

Implemented by specific legislation, the supervision of private businesses and professions for the public good has gone far beyond the early common law fields. In Munn v. Illinois, 94 U.S. 113, 130 (1877), a state's imposition of maximum charges for the storage of grain in warehouses was sustained in an opinion which stressed that the private property was devoted "to a public use" and was therefore subject to public regulation; * * * and in Nebbia v. New York, 291 U.S. 502, 536–37 (1934), a state's extensive regulation of its milk industry was upheld in an opinion by Justice Roberts which frankly recognized that there is no closed class or category of businesses affected with a public interest, that the phrase means no more than that an industry, for adequate reason, is subject to control for the public good, and that "upon proper occasion and by appropriate measures the state may regulate a business in any of its aspects."

Consistent with the historic precedents in the common law and its valued principle of growth, and independent of any specific implementing legislation, this court in *Falcone v. Middlesex Co. Medical Soc.*, supra, recently exercised its judicial function to strike down an arbitrary membership requirement of a nonprofit organization engaged in activity of public concern. There the Middlesex County Medical Society sought to exclude Dr. Falcone from membership because, though fully licensed and otherwise qualified, he could not fulfill its requirement of four years of study at a medical college approved by the American Medical Association—most of his study was at the Philadelphia College of Osteopathy. * * *

In essence, *Falcone* declared, on strong policy grounds, that the Medical Society's authority to pass on membership applications by licensed physicians is a power which is fiduciary in nature, to be exercised accordingly, and it held that, under the evidence presented, Dr. Falcone was entitled to admission despite the Society's requirement * * *. It is evident that, though we are here concerned with a hospital rather than a medical society, similar policy considerations apply with equal strength and call for a declaration that the hospital's power to pass on staff membership applications is a fiduciary power, and a holding that Dr. Greisman is entitled to have his application evaluated on its own individual merits without regard to the bylaw requirement rejected by the Law Division.

Do you agree that the result in *Greisman* follows inevitably from the court's earlier (and widely heralded) decision in *Falcone*? Is there any basis for giving a hospital more (or less) freedom of action than a medical society? The result in *Falcone* turned in large part on the fact that local hospitals, like the one in *Greisman,* made medical society membership a prerequisite to staff appointments.

What is your opinion of the *Greisman* court's invocation of common-law cases allowing judicial regulation of innkeepers, common carriers, etc., and of later cases upholding regulatory legislation governing businesses "affected with a public interest"? Does the ancient common-law tradition cited by the court justify modern courts in extending regulation to activities that the legislature has not explicitly chosen to regulate?

Some states have regulated hospitals along lines similar to the regulation of public utilities. Such regulation usually takes the form of "comprehensive health planning," including certificate-of-need requirements for new services and new facilities, and may or may not also involve controls on hospital rates or revenues. Does entry regulation, which strengthens the "virtual monopoly" that many hospitals enjoy, strengthen the case for judicial review of privileges policies?

3. *Cases Following Greisman.* In the years following the *Greisman* decision in New Jersey, courts in a number of other states, in addition to Hawaii, abandoned the traditional rule of nonreview of privileges actions by private hospitals. E.g., Storrs v. Lutheran Hosp. and Homes Soc'y, 609 P.2d 24 (Alaska 1980), appeal after remand 661 P.2d 632 (1983); Peterson v. Tucson Gen. Hosp., Inc., 114 Ariz. 66, 559 P.2d 186 (Ariz.App.1976); Hawkins v. Kinsie, 540 P.2d 345 (Colo.App.1975); Rao v. Auburn Gen. Hosp., 10 Wn.App. 361, 517 P.2d 240 (1973), appeal after remand 19 Wn.App. 124, 573 P.2d 834 (1978); Bricker v. Sceva Speare Memorial Hosp., 281 A.2d 589, 592–593 (N.H.1971); Woodard v. Porter Hosp., Inc., 125 Vt. 419, 423, 217 A.2d 37, 40 (1966). See generally Annot., Exclusion of, or Discrimination Against, Physician or Surgeon by Hospital, 28 A.L.R.5th 107, 152–167 (1995).

Although, like *Silver*, most of the early decisions of this kind were based on findings that the particular hospital was "quasi-public" in some respect, that factual issue has increasingly been passed over, with the result that some courts now seem to treat all hospital actions affecting privileges as reviewable in some manner. But see Hottentot v. Mid–Maine Med. Center, 549 A.2d 365 (Me.1988) (private nonprofit hospitals' staffing decisions held not subject to judicial review unless the hospital has monopoly power in a geographic area). See also Kelly v. St. Vincent Hosp., 102 N.M. 201, 203, 692 P.2d 1350, 1352–1353 (N.M.App.1984), where the court said, "New Mexico is in a unique situation where, in many instances, only one hospital serves an isolated area. Because * * * there is no economic mechanism which encourages hospitals to make consumer-sensitive policy choices, some public oversight must be exercised over private hospitals. Accordingly, we hold * * * that we will review, under very limited circumstances, decisions made by a private hospital board." (Did the court mean it would review all such decisions or only those made under certain circumstances?)

4. *The Traditional Rule of Nonreview.* Although at one time there seemed to be a decided trend toward *Greisman*-type common-law review of hospital privileges decisions, a number of courts refused to adopt the *Greisman* rationale, electing to adhere to the traditional rule as stated in *Silver.* E.g., Pepple v. Parkview Mem. Hosp., 536 N.E.2d 274 (Ind.1989) (holding that, in absence of state action, a private hospital's decision to exclude a physician or surgeon from staff privileges is not subject to judicial review, even for arbitrariness or capriciousness); Bello v. South Shore Hosp., 384 Mass. 770, 777, 429 N.E.2d 1011, 1015 (1981) ("we decline to adopt the theory urged by the physicians, and apparently prevailing in a small minority of States, that a private hospital's actions are reviewable under a common law theory of judicial review apart from any finding of State action"); Hoffman v. Garden City Hosp.–Osteopathic, 115 Mich.App. 773, 778–779, 321 N.W.2d 810, 813 (1982) ("Plaintiffs * * * urge an explicit adoption of the *Greisman* rationale. * * * We * * * decline the invitation to review the defendant hospital's reasons for denying staff privileges to plaintiffs"). See also Eyring v. Fort Sanders Parkwest Med. Center, Inc., 1997 WL 294457 (Tenn.App.1997) (applying Tennessee peer-review immunity statute to preclude suit against hospital for termination of privileges).

Is there any basis for treating differently a physician who is applying for privileges for the first time (as in *Greisman*) and one whose privileges are being revoked, curtailed, or not renewed? Why might the latter have a better argument for invoking the hospital's own bylaws as the basis for a challenge to the hospital's action? The Illinois Supreme Court reversed a lower court's announcement that it would follow *Greisman* approach in privileges cases, holding that private hospitals' decisions to refuse privileges to initial applicant are not subject to judicial review. Barrows v. Northwestern Mem. Hosp., 525 N.E.2d 50 (Ill.1988). The same court has also held, however, that "there are certain basic protections that must be accorded a doctor subject to a disciplinary action which could seriously affect his or her ability or right to practice medicine." Adkins v. Sarah Bush Lincoln Health Center, 544 N.E.2d 733, 739 (Ill.1989).

Is the *Greisman* court's analysis and approach appropriate to the hospital industry today? What specific conditions have changed in the industry and its legal environment since 1963? What is the significance of these changes for the reviewability of hospitals' actions on privileges?

5. *California's Unique Approach.* Of the states following a *Greisman*-like approach, only California has expressly made all hospitals automatically subject to common-law review without regard to particular factors bearing on the question of the hospital's "quasi-public" nature. One judge has discussed the situation as follows:

> How in the world did the judiciary ever get into the business of Monday-morning quarterbacking the decisions of private hospitals about staff doctors? The answer is laid out in two footnotes [7 & 8] in a California Supreme Court case, Pinsker v. Pacific Coast Society of Orthodontists[, 526 P.2d 253 (Cal.1974), in which] Justice Tobriner explained that courts have imposed a right to "fair procedure" in the membership decisions of certain private associations, such as professional associations and labor unions, since late Victorian times.
>
> The initial theory was that these groups enjoyed monopoly power over the right of individuals to practice their trade or profession. By 1977, however, the Supreme Court thought it enough that association membership merely affect "an important economic interest." Ezekial v. Winkley, 20 Cal.3d 267, 277, 142 Cal.Rptr. 418, 572 P.2d 32 (1977) ("the application of the common law rule does not depend on the existence of 'monopoly' power.... The judicial inquiry, rather, has consistently been focused on the practical power of the entity in question to affect substantially an important economic interest."). Thus the California fair procedure cases began with a labor union's expulsion of a tailor who worked during a strike, progressed to black shipyard workers seeking membership in a labor union where there was a closed shop, and eventually found their way to an orthodontist seeking membership in a specialist medical society. Pinsker v. Pacific Coast Soc. of Orthodontists, 1 Cal.3d 160, 81 Cal.Rptr. 623, 460 P.2d 495 (1969).
>
> It was not until 1975, however, that this common law right of fair procedure was extended to applications for staff privileges in a hospital. Ascherman v. Saint Francis Memorial Hosp., 45 Cal.App.3d 507, 119 Cal.Rptr. 507 (1975). The theory was that the hospital enjoyed control over the physician's ability to "fully practice" his or her profession. The court reasoned the "mere existence of other hospitals" was not "a sufficient safety valve to prevent deprivation of substantial economic advantage with the advent of comprehensive health planning."

Oskooi v. Fountain Valley Hosp. & Med. Center, 49 Cal.Rptr.2d 769, 776–77 (Cal.App.1996) (concurring opinion).

Thus, the California courts, taking their cue from cases involving private membership associations rather than business enterprises, initially focused exclusively on the physician's personal stake in the action taken, neglecting countervailing considerations such as are encountered in the management of hospitals. The concurring judge in *Oskooi* especially noted, "When *Ascherman* was decided, no published [California] decision had held that a hospital might be liable for the negligent selection of physicians * * *." Id. Did the combination of *Ascherman* and the *Elam* case (reproduced in § B of this chapter) put California hospitals in an untenable position? If the policy underlying one decision or the other had to give way, which should it be? How do you state the problem that is presented so sharply in California but that is implicit in all restraints on hospital discretion in retaining or employing physicians?

The *Ascherman* case was an extreme example of California's protectiveness toward physicians, since the court invalidated a private hospital's substantive standard for admission to its medical staff even though the plaintiff doctor had privileges at four other hospitals and was seeking only greater convenience in his practice. See also Anton v. San Antonio Community Hosp., 567 P.2d 1162, 1168 (Cal.1977) (in light of *Pinsker*, "a physician may neither be refused admission to, nor expelled from, the staff of a hospital, *whether public or private,* in the absence of a procedure comporting with the minimum common law requirements of procedural due process"). In the latter case, the court went so far as to apply a state statute governing judicial review of administrative agencies to privileges actions of private hospitals. Although a subsequent statute relaxed the review standard—from independent judgment (de novo review) to a substantial-evidence requirement—in cases involving private institutions, West's Ann.Cal. Civ.Proc.Code § 1094.5(d) (1980 & Supp. 1996), California courts still treat private as well as public hospitals very much like administrative agencies. See Unterthiner v. Desert Hosp. Dist., 656 P.2d 554 (Cal. 1983), cert. denied, 464 U.S. 1068 (1984) (revocations of privileges by public hospitals held subject to independent-judgment review by courts; denial of initial applications held reviewable under a substantial-evidence test); Kumar v. National Med. Enterprises, Inc., 267 Cal.Rptr. 452 (Cal.App.1990) (requiring exhaustion of administrative remedies in private hospital as a prerequisite to seeking judicial review).

For a strong criticism of the California position, suggesting that only monopoly hospitals should be subject to review, see Miller v. Eisenhower Med. Center, 614 P.2d 258, 271–72 (Cal.1980) (Mosk, J., dissenting). For later cases indicating declining protectiveness of physicians' interests, see *Oskooi*, supra (failure of physician to disclose some past hospital affiliations when he applied for privileges held grounds for suspending him at later date even though omission was largely a technical and, under the bylaws, suspension of privileges was a remedy only where patient safety was jeopardized); Bonner v. Sisters of Providence Corp., 239 Cal.Rptr. 530 (Cal.App.1987) (physician exonerated by Board of Medical Quality Assurance could not persuade court to overturn revocation of privileges where substantial evidence supported private hospital's determination that its own, higher standards were not met). Cf. Potvin v. Metropolitan Life Ins. Co., 63 Cal.Rptr.2d 202 (Cal.App.1997) (extending reasoning of *Pinsker* and related cases to protect physician, despite "without cause" provision in contract, from termination by managed-care plan without due process), review granted, 941 P.2d 1121 (Cal.1997). The *Potvin* case will be briefly mentioned again in chapter 8(§C).

6. *Public Hospitals.* A true public hospital is, of course, subject to constitutional norms of due process and equal protection and to suits under section 1983 of the Civil Rights Act if some constitutionally protected interest is infringed. One federal court has stressed, however, that a physician is deprived of a "liberty" interest only if the decision is made in a way "likely to have severe repercussions *outside* of professional life." Stretten v. Wadsworth Veterans Hosp., 537 F.2d 361, 366 (9th Cir.1976). A "property" interest, on the other hand, is affected only if there is some actual entitlement, not merely an expectancy or a potential benefit. Id., citing Board of Regents v. Roth, 408 U.S. 564, 577 (1972) (stating principle in context of public employment generally). In Lowe v. Scott, 959 F.2d 323, 336 (1st Cir.1992), the court of appeals, in a general discussion, confirmed the latter principle, stating that "a public hospital creates a property interest * * * if, in granting hospital privileges to its staff physicians, [it] also fosters the understanding that these privileges will not be terminated without some form of process."

First amendment rights may also be invoked in challenging actions of public hospitals. For a colorful case holding that a hospital's termination of an outspoken physician violated his free-speech rights, see Smith v. Cleburne County Hosp., 667 F.Supp. 644 (E.D.Ark.1987), 607 F.Supp. 919 (E.D.Ark.1985). See also Caine v. Hardy, 943 F.2d 1406, 1411 (5th Cir. 1991) (en banc) (first amendment rights held not violated despite doctor's claim that his suspension was based on policy dispute and unsuccessful campaign for job of department chief). Employees of public hospitals other than physicians also enjoy some protection of their right to speak freely on matters of public concern, subject to government's interest as an employer in efficiently providing a public service. See Waters v. Churchill, 511 U.S. 661 (1994) (nurse could be discharged if hospital reasonably believed, after reasonable inquiry, that speech was disruptive).

Courts have been about equally deferential to public institutions as to private ones in reviewing privileges decisions. For example, in the early leading case of Sosa v. Board of Managers of Val Verde Mem. Hosp., 437 F.2d 173, 177 (5th Cir.1971), the court stated that "so long as staff selections are administered with fairness, geared by a rationale compatible with hospital responsibility, and unencumbered with irrelevant considerations, a court should not interfere. Courts must not attempt to take on the escutcheon of Caduceus."* See also Stern v. Tarrant County Hosp. District,

* Of the last sentence quoted, another court had this to say:

> The author * * * apparently mixed his metaphors because there is no escutcheon involved, but only the caduceus, carried by the messenger of the Gods in Roman mythology, Mercury. Mercury's wand, and caduceus, is winged with two serpents twined about it. It symbolized Mercury's power of inducing sleep. Milton calls it the "opiate rod." Another of the attributes of Mercury was the power of healing. Hence, the caduceus is now the emblem of physicians and the United States Army Medical Corps has adopted it as its symbol. What the author of the opinion apparently meant was that judges should not be flaunting the staff of Mercury and telling physicians how to run their profession.

778 F.2d 1052 (5th Cir.1985) (en banc) (limited-scrutiny constitutional test employed in upholding, against equal protection and substantive due process claims, a state hospital's discrimination against osteopaths; no fourteenth amendment violation found even though hospital had acted in defiance of a state statute expressly prohibiting such discrimination). In the latter case, the dissenting judges objected that the majority, by asking only whether the hospital's policy had a rational basis, "accords to the conclusions of a board of directors of a hospital district the same deference it extends to the enactments of a state legislature." Id. at 1061. Thus, except where discrimination on the basis of gender, race, or national origin is alleged, courts applying constitutional norms are unlikely either to require more than that a public hospital's standards or actions be rationally related to a proper hospital purpose or to look beyond the hospital actors' ostensible motives. Likewise, the constitutional requirement of due process will probably be applied with particular attention to the special circumstances encountered in operating a hospital. See, e.g., Everhart v. Jefferson Parish Hosp. Dist. No. 2, 757 F.2d 1567, 1571 (5th Cir.1985) (hospital's procedures deviated in several respects from its bylaws but were held "adequate and appropriate under the nature and circumstances of this case").

An issue arises whether public hospitals are subject to requirements imposed by law on other public agencies. In Hawaii, for example, a public hospital, although a state agency, is not bound to promulgate its rules and regulations governing staff appointments in accordance with the state administrative procedure act. Rose v. Oba, 717 P.2d 1029, 1031 (Haw. 1986). Public hospital boards may be subject to state "open meetings" laws, possibly compromising their ability to deal sensitively with staffing issues as well their ability to protect trade secrets from competitors in the modern era.

7. *Statutory and Other Remedies.* Some courts have found a warrant in state statutes and regulations for reviewing hospital decisions on staff privileges. For example, a Florida statute authorizing "the medical staff of any hospital * * * to suspend, deny, revoke, or curtail the staff privileges of any staff member for good cause" and foreclosing liability for actions "taken in good faith and without malice," was held to authorize appeals for procedural lapses but only if malice was alleged. Carida v. Holy Cross Hosp., Inc., 427 So.2d 803 (Fla.App.1983). (It is notable that the current Florida statute grants similar authority to "the governing board" rather than "the medical staff." Fla.Stat.Ann. § 395.0193 (West 1993 & Supp. 1996).) See also St. Mary's Hosp. v. Radiology Prof. Corp., 421 S.E.2d 731, 737 (Ga.App.1992) (statutory requirement to adopt staff bylaws held to imply right to sue for noncompliance therewith); Cohoes Mem. Hosp. v. Department of Health, 399 N.E.2d 1132 (N.Y.1979) (detailing New York procedures); Rosenberg v. Holy Redeemer Hosp., 506 A.2d 408, 412–13

Khan v. Suburban Community Hosp., 45 Ohio St.2d 39, 44, 340 N.E.2d 398, 402 (1976).

(Pa.Super.1986) (regulations provide basis for review for procedural fairness).

A physician whose staff privileges are denied or revoked might seek redress under tort law (e.g., for defamation or tortious interference with advantageous business relations) not only against the hospital but also against individuals perceived as instrumental in the process. See generally Annot., Liability for Interference with Physician–Patient Relationship, 87 A.L.R.4th 845, 877–884 (1991 & Supp. 1995).

8. *Title VII Actions Against Private Hospitals.* Is a physician seeking staff privileges entitled to the protections of Title VII of the Civil Rights Act of 1964, 42 U.S.C. § 2000e et seq. (1994), which prohibits private employers from engaging in employment discrimination on the basis of race, color, religion, sex, or national origin? Some courts that have considered the matter have found grounds for overlooking the fact that the position being sought by a health professional in a hospital is not strictly that of an employee. E.g., Christopher v. Stouder Memorial Hospital, 936 F.2d 870, 874–77 (6th Cir.1991) (hospital's "control over [plaintiff's] ability to practice as a private scrub nurse [employed by surgeons working in the hospital] sufficiently affected her employment opportunities"). But see Alexander v. Rush North Shore Med. Center, 101 F.3d 487 (7th Cir.1996) (reversing 1986 ruling allowing Korean doctor to sue for race discrimination despite independent contractor status); Diggs v. Harris Hospital–Methodist, Inc., 847 F.2d 270 (5th Cir.1988) (staff physician found to lack employer/employee relationship both with the hospital and with patients she sought to treat therein).

King v. Bartholomew County Hospital

Court of Appeals of Indiana, First District, 1985.
476 N.E.2d 877, rehearing denied May 23, 1985.

■ ROBERTSON, JUDGE.

* * * King sued on his own behalf and on behalf of all other physicians applying for medical staff privileges at BCH, to enjoin the hospital from requiring the applicants to execute a grant of absolute immunity and a release of liability to the hospital, its representatives, and any third party with respect to any and all civil liability which might arise from any acts, communications, reports, recommendations, or disclosures involving an applicant or appointee, performed, made, requested, or received by the hospital and its representatives to, from, or by any third party including other members of the medical staff concerning but not limited to certain specified activities implemented in the hospital credentialing process.

* * * In 1983, the hospital's Credentials Committee approved a new application form which set out in detail the absolute immunity and release of liability provisions [that had previously been contained only in the medical staff] by-laws. King refused to complete the form and instead

sought judicial process to enjoin the hospital from requiring an applicant to execute these provisions as prerequisite to staff membership.

No genuine issue as to a material fact is present in the record. Our next and final step then, is to determine whether the hospital was entitled to judgment as a matter of law. Ind. Code 34–4–12.6–3 provides immunity from civil liability to any persons or organizations, including peer review committees, who, in good faith, furnish records, information or assistance to a peer review committee, in regard to evaluation of qualifications of professional health care providers, or of patient care. Further, the personnel of a peer review committee shall be immune from any civil action arising from any determinations made in good faith in regard to evaluation of patient care. Ind. Code 34–4–12.6–3(d) specifically provides that no restraining order or injunction shall be issued against a peer review committee to interfere with the proper functions of the committee acting in good faith in regard to evaluation of patient care. A peer review committee is that committee which has the responsibility of evaluation of the qualifications of professional health care providers, (including licensed physicians) or of patient care rendered by professional health care providers. See, Ind. Code 34–4–12.6–1(c).

Further, county hospital legislation provides that the board, as the supreme authority in the hospital, shall have the power to determine appointments to the medical staff in accordance with Ind. Code 16–10–1–6.5 and Ind. Code 16–12.1–5–1 and the medical staff by-laws and rules approved by it. [The legislation also gives the medical staff of a county hospital "the responsibility of reviewing the professional practices in the hospital for the purpose of reducing morbidity and mortality, and for the improvement of the care of patients in the hospital" and confers on "members of any medical staff committee organized for the purpose of conducting medical review * * * an absolute immunity from civil liability for communications * * * and reports and recommendations * * *."]

Finally, Ind. Code 16–12.1–5.1 provides that all physicians possessing an unlimited license to practice medicine and surgery are eligible for membership on the medical staff, subject, however, to the power of the board to establish and enforce reasonable standards and rules concerning the qualifications for admission to the medical staff and to practice in the hospital and reasonable rules for retention of such membership and for the granting of medical staff privileges within the hospital. The statute specifically provides that:

> (b) Such reasonable standards and rules may not discriminate against practitioners of any school of medicine who hold an unlimited license but may, in the interest of good patient care, and without limiting the generality of the foregoing, consider the applicant's post graduate medical education, training, and experience and any other facts concerning the applicant which may reasonably be expected to affect his professional competence.

Ind. Code 16–12–.1–5–1(c) provides that the medical staff shall originate by-laws and rules for self-government which shall be subject to the approval of the board.

Pursuant to its by-laws, the hospital's yearly reevaluation of medical staff applicants, whether new or incumbent, provides a reasonable, systematic, and objective method geared at ensuring good patient care. * * * The documents on file, together with BCH's affidavit demonstrate the immunity granted those aiding in the re-evaluation process is intended to be a justifiable means in providing a complete, candid, up-to-date professional history of the applicants. King fails to demonstrate otherwise. When read together, the statutes cited fully support such endeavors and King fails to move us otherwise.

* * *

Accordingly, judgment is affirmed.

■ RATLIFF, PRESIDING JUDGE, concurring.

* * * [T]he hospital governing authority, its credentials committee, and persons furnishing information in regard to an applicant may well be clothed with a qualified privilege. A communication made in good faith on any subject matter in which the party making the communication has an interest or in reference to which such party has a duty, public or private, and either legal, moral, or social, if made to a person having a corresponding interest or duty is subject to a qualified privilege. * * * Statements made by a medical committee to a hospital with regard to physicians have been held clothed with qualified privilege. Likewise, a letter from the director of nurses at a hospital to a nurses' registry concerning a certain nurse was deemed privileged in [an Illinois case], where the court stated that the essential elements of a qualified privilege are good faith, an interest or duty to be upheld, a statement limited in its scope to that purpose, a proper occasion, and publication in a proper manner and to proper parties only.* * * *

* * * To hold that a hospital may require a physician-applicant to grant absolute immunity to the hospital, its representatives, and any third party, and to release them from any and all liability which might arise from any such acts, communications, reports, disclosures, or recommendations, without regard to whether such are made or given in good faith goes far beyond any legitimate privilege. Requiring a release and grant of immunity as a condition of applying for hospital privileges which is so broad as conceivably to include within its protection acts, statements, communications, or recommendations motivated by ill will, or done maliciously or capriciously, is unconscionable. In order to avoid unconscionability, the requirement of acting in good faith must be read into the release and grant of immunity. * * *

* The protection of a qualified privilege may be lost if the plaintiff shows that the speaker was primarily motivated by ill will, or if the privilege was abused by excessive publication of the defamatory statement, or if the statement was made without belief or grounds for belief in its truth (lack of good faith).

With the limitation that the release and grant of immunity, in order to escape being invalid for unconscionability, must be read to grant immunity and release from liability only to those communications in good faith requested and given, I concur in the decision in this case.

NOTES AND QUESTIONS

1. *State Immunity Statutes, etc.* The Indiana statutes cited by the court are similar to those in other states in immunizing participants in hospital-based peer review from tort and other claims. See, e.g., Cardwell v. Rockford Mem. Hosp. Ass'n, 555 N.E.2d 6 (Ill.1990) (holding statutes created absolute immunity against various tort claims, even for "willful and wanton" conduct). Likewise, the law of defamation generally recognizes qualified privileges for certain communications, such as those noted in the concurring opinion.

Statutes or case law protecting hospital peer-review records from discovery (see note on this subject in § B of this chapter) may or may not prevent physicians challenging denials or revocations of staff privileges from obtaining access to the hospital's files on their cases. Compare Jenkins v. Wu, 468 N.E.2d 1162, 1167–68 (Ill.1984) (upholding statutory exception permitting disclosure in staff privileges cases); Roseville Community Hosp. v. Superior Court, 139 Cal.Rptr. 170 (Cal.App.1977) (disclosure of medical staff records held required under exception to immunity statute), with Adventist Health Systems v. Trude, 880 S.W.2d 539 (Ky.1994) (peer-review actions held privileged in "any civil action in any court"); Holly v. Auld, 450 So.2d 217 (Fla.1984) (physician alleging defamation in peer-review process not permitted access to credentials committee records). See also Ray v. St. John's Health Care Corp., 582 N.E.2d 464 (Ind.App. 1991) (court recognized relevance of documents and held trial court should have scrutinized them to determine whether privileged). Because of the strength of the federal policy involved, peer-review records may be discovered in a federal civil rights action even if a state statute would make them confidential. Schafer v. Parkview Mem. Hosp., Inc., 593 F.Supp. 61 (N.D.Ind.1984) (holding plaintiff's need for discovery in an age discrimination claim outweighs Indiana's policy of privileging peer-review communications).

See generally Annot., Testimony Before or Communications to Private Professional Society's Judicial Commission, Ethics Committee, or the Like, as Privileged, 9 A.L.R.4th 807, 814–17 (1981 & Supp. 1995).

2. Was the majority in the *King* case entirely responsive to the plaintiff's objection to the hospital's insistence that he waive his right to challenge future decisions affecting his privileges? Note that the hospital was a public institution. Did the court rule on the legitimacy of making a waiver of (constitutional?) rights a prerequisite to the award of privileges? Would the contractual immunity sought by this public hospital effectively preclude judicial review of its actions in revoking privileges? Would it at least alter the standard of review?

3. What are the arguments for and against letting a private hospital impose limitations on physician rights such as those in the *King* case? The foregoing materials identify a variety of legal approaches to the reviewability of staff privileges. Which states would be most likely to tolerate waivers of the kind sought in *King*? Cf. Medical Center Hosps. v. Terzis, 367 S.E.2d 728 (Va.1988) (in state adhering to rule of nonreview, judicial review held inappropriate because, even if bylaws constituted a contract, they contained a provision that decisions of the governing board were not "subject to further hearing or appellate review").

4. *The Employment-at-Will Analogy.* Note that a contractual waiver of the kind questioned in the *King* case would put staff physicians in essentially the same position vis-a-vis the hospital as so-called "at-will" employees. Under the employment-at-will doctrine, employers, in the absence of an employment contract, are generally not required to justify firing an employee. See generally H. Perritt, Jr., Employee Dismissal Law and Practice 1–83 (3d ed., 1992 & Supp. 1996); Symposium, Individual Rights in the Workplace: The Employment-at-Will Issue, 16 U.Mich.J.L.Ref. 199 (1983); Gold & Hamilton, Employer Liability Grows for Discharging at-Will Employees, Hosps., July 16, 1984, at 121. For efficiency-oriented arguments against legal recognition of noncontractual vested rights in employment, see Epstein, In Defense of the Contract at Will, 51 U.Chi.L.Rev. 947 (1984). In one California case, a physician was allowed to overcome a statutory presumption that he was employed at will by introducing the hospital's statement that "we look forward to a long, pleasant, and mutually satisfactory relationship with you." Hillsman v. Sutter Community Hosps., 200 Cal.Rptr. 605 (Cal.App.1984).

Courts have created exceptions to the employment-at-will doctrine in cases where public policy considerations are deemed dominant. An example is Kirk v. Mercy Hosp. Tri–County, 851 S.W.2d 617 (Mo.App.1993), where the hospital fired a nurse for allegedly making false statements "detrimental to the hospital" but the nurse claimed that she had only spoken up on behalf of a patient whose condition she had diagnosed and whom she believed was being inadequately treated by the responsible physician. (She was told to "stay out of it," and the patient died.) The court allowed the nurse to sue for wrongful discharge, citing a public policy favoring nurse responsibility for patient welfare apparent in the state nursing practice act. But see Thompson v. Memorial Hosp., 925 F.Supp. 400 (D.Md.1996) (because plaintiff radiation physicist had no legal duty in the matter, "fact that [he] discovered 'operational illegalities' and was fired because he intended to 'blow the whistle' on his employer is simply not enough" to support wrongful discharge claim).

5. Should physicians be entitled to special help in surmounting marketplace barriers to their pursuit of a livelihood? If so, why? How should decisions on the extent of an individual's job security be made? What is the appropriate role for courts?

NOTES AND QUESTIONS ON PROCEDURAL AND SUBSTANTIVE ISSUES IN ADMINISTERING STAFF PRIVILEGES

1. Assume that you are assigned to draft a hospital's bylaws governing the administration of staff privileges and that you will henceforth oversee the operation of the process you help to create. If your state's courts recognize a common-law right to fair procedures, you must naturally concern yourself with meeting their procedural requirements and with anticipating the scope and standard of judicial review. On the other hand, your task may go beyond merely satisfying the courts concerning fundamental fairness. What nonlegal factors might influence your hospital's decision concerning the protections to be conferred on its staff physicians? Under what circumstances might a hospital wish to provide relatively little job security to its staff physicians?

Assuming that your object is to provide fair but not overly cumbersome procedures, what procedural guarantees would you provide? Subsequent materials will introduce a new set of drafting considerations based on federal law, particularly the antitrust laws and the Health Care Quality Improvement Act of 1986, 42 U.S.C. §§ 111101–52 (1994) (HCQIA). You will be asked at that point to reconsider your drafting efforts and to opine on the advisability of establishing procedures that would qualify the hospital peer-review program for the broad immunity from damage actions that Congress made available in the HCQIA.

In any event, you should recognize that the administration of admitting privileges is among the most sensitive and important tasks a hospital performs and that legal proceedings challenging hospital actions are both common and potentially costly to the institution. See generally C. Wilson & A. Dellinger, Staff Membership and Clinical Privileges, in A. Dellinger, ed., Health Care Facilities Law 34–36 (1991 & Supp. 1995). Can you visualize a role for "alternative dispute resolution" here? If so, what kind?

2. *Procedures.* Courts recognizing an independent legal duty on the part of hospitals to accord fair treatment to health professionals must decide what procedures are minimally sufficient. In so doing, they might borrow standards from constitutional or administrative law, adapting them to accommodate the practical necessities and competing interests encountered in the hospital context. Thus, in Garrow v. Elizabeth Gen. Hosp. and Dispensary, 401 A.2d 533, 538 (N.J.1979), the court stated, "Many of the rules which are applicable to judicial intervention in proceedings before administrative agencies would seem as a matter of principle to be equally applicable to appointment procedures before a hospital board." The *Garrow* case, a post-*Greisman* decision by the New Jersey Supreme Court, also provides a typical statement of the general legal standard governing procedures in privileges disputes: "Fundamental fairness dictates that the hospital apprise the physician of the specific charges and that the applicant be afforded the opportunity to appear and present witnesses and material in support of his position and to contradict or explain the bases asserted for the proposed denial." *Garrow*, supra, 401 A.2d at 541. See also Cipriotti v. Board of Directors of Northridge Hosp. Found. Med. Center, 196 Cal.Rptr.

367, 374 (Cal.App.1983): "So long as a fair hearing is provided, in disciplining or suspending those who do not meet its professional standards, the hospital should not be hampered by formalities not required by its bylaws nor by due process considerations. Fair hearing includes ample notice, opportunity to hear and cross-examine witnesses and to present evidence."

Among the procedural issues encountered in devising a system for awarding and withdrawing staff privileges are the following: (*a*) the right to be represented by counsel, *see Garrow*, supra, 401 A.2d at 542 ("we believe that the physician should have the right to have counsel present at mandated hospital hearings with respect to his application for admission to the staff"); (*b*) access to evidence prior to the hearing, see id. at 542 (holding that courts should not intervene to order prehearing discovery; "relevant and material underlying data upon which the Board of Trustees relied in arriving at its conclusions should be made available to plaintiff (at his expense) prior to the hearing so as to enable him to prepare adequately"); (*c*) the applicability of rules of evidence, see id. at 541 ("the record should contain sufficient reliable evidence, even though of a hearsay nature, to justify the result"); and (*d*) claims of confidentiality, see id. at 542 (recognizing hospital's "concern that disclosure of much of the information it receives will impede its ability to investigate a doctor's competence and temperament" but holding that "the fair solution calls for divulging the information"); Bock v. John C. Lincoln Hosp., 702 P.2d 253 (Ariz.App.1985) (due process held denied because hospital refused to allow plaintiff to review his evaluations by other staff members, citing a need to preserve the integrity of the peer-review process).

3. *Substantive Standards.* Is it necessary that hospital or staff bylaws declare in advance specific substantive criteria to be used in awarding or revoking privileges? If only general criteria are stated, what conduct would a court view as providing sufficient grounds for an adverse action? Would a common-law court feel any necessity, in view of the interests at stake, to be as deferential to the decision maker as is customary in judicial review of the work of public agencies?

A particularly rigorous standard of review was used by the California Supreme Court, over a vigorous dissent, to overturn a hospital's denial of privileges for inability to "work with others" because the court was not persuaded that the physician's problems in interpersonal relations posed a real threat to the quality of the hospital's services. Miller v. Eisenhower Med. Center, 614 P.2d 258 (Cal.1980). Other courts have been more willing to let hospitals reject individuals on the basis of an uncooperative attitude or disruptive personality. E.g., Silver v. Queen's Hosp., 629 P.2d 1116 (Haw.1981) (privileges properly denied due to the physician's disruptive personality and doubts as to his professional ethics). But see Mahmoodian v. United Hosp. Center, Inc., 404 S.E.2d 750, 758–63 (W.Va.1991) (finding evidence supported revocation of privileges but stating that irascibility, annoying conduct, or criticism of hospital or its personnel would be insufficient); Nanavati v. Burdette Tomlin Mem. Hosp., 526 A.2d 697 (N.J.1987) (disharmony could not be grounds for termination without "sufficient reliable evidence" of probable harm to patients; case notable for the number of administrative and judicial hearings and appeals, with more to come).

Other substantive standards that have been upheld by the courts include a hospital's requirement that its doctors carry acceptable malpractice insurance. E.g., Courtney v. Shore Mem. Hospital, 584 A.2d 817 (N.J. Super.1990); Kelly v. St. Vincent Hosp., 692 P.2d 1350 (N.M.App.1984). (What are the business justifications for such a requirement?) Distance from a hospital has been upheld as the sole reason for discontinuing staff privileges. Kennedy v. St. Joseph Mem. Hosp., 482 N.E.2d 268 (Ind.App. 1985) (rule promulgated by the hospital that physicians should live no more than 20 minutes' driving time from the hospital found in accordance with JCAHO standards and not arbitrary or capricious). Other courts have also upheld substantive grounds for denying privileges that do not relate specifically to the physician's competence. E.g., Tarleton v. Meharry Med. College, 717 F.2d 1523 (6th Cir.1983) (refusal to join a practice plan which would regulate patient fees of salaried faculty members conducting private practices in campus facilities); Oskooi v. Fountain Valley Regional Hosp. & Med. Center, 49 Cal.Rptr.2d 769 (Cal.App.1996) (failing to disclose past hospital affiliations).

4. *Closure of the Hospital to New Applicants.* A series of common-law cases in New Jersey address the question whether a private hospital may decide that it has enough physicians and therefore refuse to receive new applications or review them on the merits. In the earlier cases, the New Jersey courts appeared to allow a hospital to close the staff for its own reasons but not as an accommodation to its doctors. See. e.g., Walsky v. Pascack Valley Hosp., 367 A.2d 1204, 1206 (N.J. Super. 1976): "[T]he only significant effect of continuing the closure of staff appointments is to confine control of the institution's beds to its existing medical staff and to enhance their economic interests at the expense of other qualified physicians whose patients are excluded * * *. If there were any credible evidence that the continuation of the moratorium contributed or was related to the quality of patient care at PVH, this court would be both obligated and eager to sustain it."

In two 1986 cases, the New Jersey Supreme Court seemed even more demanding of private hospitals, reviewing decisions to limit new applications very much as it would review the actions of a state administrative agency. In Berman v. Valley Hosp., 510 A.2d 673 (N.J.1986), a hospital sought to protect against overcrowding and an influx of patients from outside its immediate service area by refusing to consider new applications for privileges from physicians who had practiced in the area for more than two years, using other hospitals. The court posed the question as "whether the restrictive hospital admissions policy with its discriminatory feature genuinely serves a legitimate public-health objective." Id. at 676. Although it was persuaded that the overcrowding problem was real and that the solution chosen was effective, the court nevertheless found the hospital policy arbitrary and unreasonable in comparison with other solutions that might have been adopted. In a companion case, the court similarly "concluded that the hospital's policy of admitting only those doctors joining the practices of doctors already on staff did not genuinely advance the professed objectives of providing better patient coverage while reducing occupancy." Id. at 680, citing Desai v. St. Barnabas Med. Center, 510 A.2d 662 (N.J.1986).

The New Jersey courts are apparently unique in their willingness to scrutinize the substantive basis for closing a hospital staff. In one North Carolina case, a statute entitling podiatrists to fair treatment was construed to allow closure of the staff to additional podiatrists subject to judicial review of the hospital's reasons for so doing. Claycomb v. HCA–Raleigh Community Hosp., 333 S.E.2d 333 (N.C.App.1985), pet. for review denied, 341 S.E.2d 23 (N.C.1986).

5. *"Economic Credentialing."* As hospitals have come under financial pressure, they have a greater interest in a physician's effect on the hospital's bottom line—either as a big admitter or as a drain on hospital resources. May a hospital deny or withdraw privileges not because of doubts concerning the physician's professional competence but because she is too demanding on behalf of her patients, thus imposing high costs on the institution? See, e.g., Blum, Evaluation of Medical Staff Using Fiscal Factors: Economic Credentialing, 26 J. Health & Hosp.L. 65 (1993). Is the issue one of contract or public policy?

A Florida trial court upheld a denial of privileges on economic grounds to a cardiac surgeon whom the hospital regarded as having a conflict of interest resulting from his position as head of the comparable department at a competing facility. Rosenblum v. Tallahassee Regional Med. Center, No. 91–589 (Fla. Cir. Ct. June 22, 1992). Although there appear to be no reported cases concerning privileging decisions based solely on economics, several courts have upheld actions where such considerations were present along with more conventional ones. E.g., Knapp v. Palos Community Hosp., 465 N.E.2d 554, 560 (Ill.App.1984) (noting plaintiff's use of hospital resulted in 50% longer stays and 31% higher costs than other staff members incurred); Friedman v. Delaware County Mem. Hosp., 672 F.Supp. 171, 178 (E.D.Pa.1987) (summary judgment for hospital terminating physician's privileges for overutilization and failure to amend practice after notice).

Admitting Privileges as a Matter of Contract

NOTES AND QUESTIONS ON THE LEGAL EFFECT OF HOSPITAL AND STAFF BYLAWS

1. The reviewability of hospital actions on staff privileges under either constitutional or common-law principles has become more or less a moot question in many jurisdictions because courts treat the hospital bylaws (or medical staff bylaws approved by the governing board) as part of the physician's contract with the hospital. Because bylaws customarily incorporate procedural and substantive protections for staff physicians, treating them as part of the underlying contract allows adverse actions to be challenged without regard to other legal doctrines. Note that this theory carries no weight in cases involving initial applications for privileges, leaving plaintiffs in those cases dependent on constitutional, common-law, or statutory rights.

2. The leading case allowing a physician to enforce the terms of medical staff bylaws under a contractual theory is Berberian v. Lancaster Osteopathic Hosp. Ass'n, 149 A.2d 456, 459 (Pa.1959), where the court stated:

> While there can be no doubt that the board of directors of the hospital has authority to deprive a physician of the privileges of the staff, it is equally clear that the board has agreed to follow certain specified procedures before determining whether to exercise its authority in a matter of a staff member's expulsion from the hospital. The procedure so approved by the board requires an "adequate hearing and thorough investigation" by the executive committee of the general staff and an "appeal, with legal counsel, before a joint meeting" of the staff's executive committee and the hospital's board of directors. When the board of directors approved the staff by-laws, they became an integral part of the contractual relation between the hospital and the members of its staff.

See also Lewisburg Community Hosp. v. Alfredson, 805 S.W.2d 756 (Tenn. 1991) (bylaws, adopted pursuant to statute, enforced as contract entitling plaintiff to fair procedures prior to termination of his exclusive contract to provide radiology services); Terre Haute Regional Hosp. v. El–Issa, 470 N.E.2d 1371, 1376–77 (Ind.App.1984).

Do you agree that staff bylaws should be deemed to be incorporated by reference in a physician's contract with the hospital? (Is this the same issue that was addressed in the *St. John's* case in § A of this chapter?) Is the hospital's agreement to the staff bylaws sufficiently voluntary—recall the role of the JCAHO and the organized medical staff—that the hospital should be bound by them in trying to control an incompetent physician?

3. An alternative to the view expressed in *Berberian* was stated in Weary v. Baylor Univ. Hosp., 360 S.W.2d 895, 897 (Tex.Civ.App.1962):

> Plaintiff contends that he has a contractual right to a "hearing" under the By Laws; and that he was not accorded such hearing; and that for such reason the Governing Board is legally precluded from failing to reappoint him.
>
> Under our view of the case, it is unnecessary to pass on the question of whether plaintiff was in fact accorded a hearing before the Medical Board.
>
> There is no question but that the various committees of the Medical Staff, including the Medical Board, could only *recommend and advise* on reappointments; and that the Governing Board has *final authority* on reappointments and is under no obligation to accept or reject the recommendations of the Medical Board. The Governing Board has the power to determine who shall practice in the hospital, and such power to make Staff appointments and reappointments is without restriction. Neither the results of a hearing, nor the provisions for a hearing before the Medical Board are binding on the Governing Board; and internal procedures set forth in the Medical Staff By–Laws, even though such By–Laws be approved and adopted by the Governing Board, cannot limit the power of the Governing Board of the Hospital to reappoint or not reappoint a Staff Doctor.

See also St. Mary's Hosp. v. Radiology Prof. Corp., 421 S.E.2d 731, 737 (Ga.App.1992) ("bylaws alone do not create any contractual right to continuation of staff privileges [since] hospitals are entitled to change the staff bylaws or the terms of appointment"; but bylaws held enforceable under statute unless physician has waived procedural rights); Sarin v. Samaritan Health Center, 440 N.W.2d 80 (Mich.App.1989) (stating that permitting challenge to termination of privileges on basis of hospital's alleged failure to follow its bylaws would "necessarily involve a review of the decision to terminate and the methods or reasons behind that decision, thus making a mockery of the rule that prohibits judicial review of such decisions by private hospitals"); Ponca City Hosp., Inc. v. Murphree, 545 P.2d 738, 742 (Okl.1976) ("The staff by-laws do not purport to be a contract and do not appear to be such on their face").

4. Several courts, although acknowledging the reviewability of privileges actions under a contract theory, have also made it clear that they believe that courts have responsibilities broader than this theory implies. E.g., Babcock v. Saint Francis Med. Center, 543 N.W.2d 749 (Neb.App.1996) ("the majority of the courts have held that the decision of a private hospital to revoke, suspend, or limit the privileges of a physician or other member of the medical staff is subject to limited judicial review to ensure that the hospital substantially complied with its medical staff bylaws, *as well as to ensure that the bylaws provide for basic notice and fair hearing procedures*") (emphasis added); Owens v. New Britain Gen. Hosp., 643 A.2d 233, 240 (Conn.1994) ("A hospital's duty to follow bylaws can stem from a contractual relationship[, from] a preexisting legal duty imposed by our state department of health regulations to adopt 'bylaws, rules and regulations, including medical staff bylaws,'* * * from the recognition of a 'fiduciary concept' [citing *Greisman*] [and] from the public's substantial interest in the operation of hospitals, public or private"); Mahmoodian v. United Hosp. Center, Inc., 404 S.E.2d 750, 755 (W.Va.1991) ("Utilizing breach of contract principles, most courts explicitly addressing the issue presented here have held, and we hereby hold, that [privileges revocations, etc., are] subject to limited judicial review to ensure that there was substantial compliance with hospital's medical staff bylaws, as well as to ensure that the medical staff bylaws afford basic notice and fair hearing procedures, including an impartial tribunal"). See also Murphy v. St. Agnes Hosp., 484 N.Y.S.2d 40, 43 (N.Y.A.D.1985) (invalidating a hospital's suspension of an anesthesiologist's privileges without deciding "whether the [hospital's] obligation to comply with * * * [its own] by-laws is grounded in concepts of fundamental fairness, principles of contract law or the law of associations").

Bartley v. Eastern Maine Medical Center

Supreme Judicial Court of Maine, 1992.
617 A.2d 1020.

■ CLIFFORD, JUSTICE.

Plaintiffs, four doctors who practice emergency medicine, * * * argue that they are entitled to a judgment as a matter of law because [the defendant hospital (EMMC)] breached its contract with them. Finding no error, we affirm the judgment [for the defendant].

For more than ten years the Plaintiffs provided physician services in EMMC's emergency department pursuant to a contract the hospital had with Bridges, Emmet & Rosenberg, a group with which each of the Plaintiffs was associated. In accordance with procedures established by the hospital's Medical Staff Bylaws, each Plaintiff was granted, and continues to hold, membership on the medical staff and each has staff privileges, enabling him to practice emergency medicine at EMMC. In 1989, in order to reduce its operating expenses, EMMC terminated its contract with Bridges, Emmet & Rosenberg after unsuccessfully attempting to negotiate an alternative compensation arrangement with them. EMMC contracted with a different group of emergency physicians resulting in a compensation arrangement more favorable to the hospital. Subsequently, the hospital decided to directly contract with emergency room physicians and notified Plaintiffs they could no longer work in the emergency department unless they negotiated employment contracts with EMMC. Plaintiffs' staff privileges, however, were not expressly terminated when the hospital made different arrangements for staffing the emergency department.

Plaintiffs filed suit in the Superior Court on the basis that the approval of their staff privileges established a contract between them and the hospital. They assert that this contract, arising from the staff privileges granted to them pursuant to the Medical Staff Bylaws, gives them a right to practice medicine in the emergency department, a right that is not contingent on a separate employment contract with EMMC. According to Plaintiffs, EMMC breached the contract arising out of their staff privileges when the hospital required them to enter into a separate employment contract in order to exercise their privileges in the emergency department. Plaintiffs allege that this requirement works a constructive revocation of their privileges.

* * *

We agree with Plaintiffs that the bylaws of a private medical center may constitute an enforceable contract between the medical center and its staff physicians. The Medical Staff Bylaws at issue here contain several provisions relied on by Plaintiffs to support their contention that EMMC has breached its contract with them. In a section describing the various categories of the medical staff, the bylaws define the "active medical staff" as those physicians "who have been selected to transact the business of the medical staff, including voting and holding office, as well as to attend service [patients] and private patients.... The active staff must maintain clinical privileges."[2] Another section of the bylaws discusses the terms of

2. Plaintiffs are members of the active medical staff with clinical privileges in the emergency department. A "service patient" is someone who does not have a physician on entering the hospital.

appointment to the medical staff. Here Plaintiffs point to the factors to be taken into account when a physician is under consideration for reappointment to the staff, including "maintenance of timely, accurate, and complete medical records" and "patterns of care as demonstrated by reviews and evaluations." They also refer to a provision which states that continuation of staff membership shall not be made contingent on the continuance of an employment contract.

The Plaintiffs use these isolated provisions in the bylaws to support the position that the grant to them of staff privileges confers on them an absolute right to practice in the emergency department. Viewed as a whole, however, as a contract must be construed, the bylaws confer no such right.

While it may be true that the Medical Staff Bylaws contemplate that the active staff will treat patients, the preamble to the bylaws clearly states that the medical staff assume their responsibilities "subject to the authority of the hospital board of trustees." The authority of the board is set forth in the Bylaws of the Eastern Maine Medical Center (hereinafter "corporate bylaws") which provide that "[t]he general management of the affairs of [EMMC] shall be vested in a board of trustees." The corporate bylaws also provide for a president who shall be the chief executive officer and "shall have the necessary authority and responsibility to operate [EMMC] in all of its activities." They further provide for a medical director, appointed by the board, who is responsible "for maintaining and improving the quality of medical practice at the medical center." In addition, the corporate bylaws require the board to appoint chiefs of service who, under the Medical Staff Bylaws, are given broad authority to supervise their individual departments. The emergency department is one of many departments that has a chief of service, reporting to the medical director.

It is clear from these bylaw provisions that the board of trustees, acting through the president and medical director, has the authority to manage all the affairs of the hospital. This would necessarily include decisions on how to operate individual departments in order to best serve the corporation's purposes of "car[ing] for ill or disabled persons . . . and . . . promot[ing] community health." The cost of such care and promotion of community health is vitally important to the community and a legitimate concern for the board. In the case of the emergency department, the board determined that the contract with the Plaintiffs' group was too costly and that directly employing physicians is the most cost efficient approach to providing emergency services. The bylaws confer authority on the board to make such a decision, and the bylaw provisions relied on by the Plaintiffs do not restrict that authority. Indeed, the Medical Staff Bylaws are subject to it.

We also do not agree with Plaintiffs' contention that their staff privileges have been constructively revoked by EMMC's requirement of an employment contract. The granting of privileges signifies that a doctor is qualified to practice at the hospital. EMMC has determined that each of the Plaintiffs is qualified, and that determination is embodied in the staff privileges they have been granted. The right to exercise the privileges, however, is a separate matter. For some physicians, such as general practitioners, the granting of staff privileges may be all that is necessary in order for the physician to treat his own patients in the hospital. For other doctors whose practice is entirely hospital-based, such as emergency room physicians, additional arrangements with the hospital may be required.

Because their staff privileges have not been constructively revoked or significantly reduced, Plaintiffs are not entitled to invoke the notice and hearing provisions of the Medical Staff Bylaws.[6] These procedures are available to a physician who is facing "major corrective action." Under the bylaws corrective action may be instituted when a doctor's conduct falls below an acceptable standard or when there is a recommendation that a physician's privileges be reduced. EMMC has never suggested that the professional conduct of any of the Plaintiffs is unacceptable nor has there been a recommendation that their privileges be reduced. Therefore, no corrective action has been initiated with respect to Plaintiffs, and the notice and hearing provisions of the bylaws do not apply.

Because the language of the Medical Staff Bylaws does not confer on the Plaintiffs any right to practice medicine in the EMMC emergency department, and because the Plaintiffs are not entitled to notice and a hearing under the bylaws, the Superior Court correctly concluded that EMMC did not breach the contract and is entitled to a judgment as a matter of law.

NOTES AND QUESTIONS ON EXCLUSIVE CONTRACTS WITH HOSPITAL–BASED PHYSICIANS

1. Certain physicians—specifically, hospital-based ones such as radiologists, anesthesiologists, pathologists, and emergency-care specialists—are dependent on the hospital for more than admitting and clinical privileges such as are sufficient for community-based practitioners. How should courts resolve issues involving hospital-based physicians whose staff privileges remain intact even though the hospital has made other arrangements to obtain services in the doctor's specialty? See also Mateo–Woodburn v. Fresno Community Hosp., 270 Cal.Rptr. 894 (Cal.App.1990) (no relief for anesthesiologists who lost business opportunities, but not privileges, when hospital entered into exclusive contract). In addition to the situation in the *Bartley* case, a hospital-based specialist might also lose lucrative opportunities (*a*) because the hospital enters into a new exclusive contract with another group, e.g., Holt v. Good Samaritan Hosp. & Health Center, 590 N.E.2d 1318 (Ohio App. 1990); (*b*) because he loses his position in a group having an exclusive contract with the hospital, e.g., Collins v. Associated Pathologists, Ltd., 844 F.2d 473 (7th Cir.1988) (antitrust case); or (*c*) because he loses his position as an at-will employee of the hospital itself,

6. Although there is authority to the contrary, we are unpersuaded by the reasoning of those cases. See, e.g., Lewisburg Community Hosp. v. Alfredson, 805 S.W.2d 756, 761 (Tenn.1991) (hospital's refusal to give doctor access significantly reduced his privileges and doctor entitled to hearing under bylaws).

e.g., Engelstad v. Virginia Munic. Hosp., 718 F.2d 262 (8th Cir.1983) (director of pathology department).

Presumably, as in *Bartley*, the issues should be viewed in contractual terms, with some recognition that the hospital has ultimate control of the services in question. For the view that "courts should rely on the [dependent] economic relationship between the parties as the best extrinsic evidence of the parties' intent," see Zellers & Poulin, Termination of Hospital Medical Staff Privileges for Economic Reasons: A Plea for Consistency, 46 Me.L.Rev. 67 (1994) (suggesting that bylaws should clarify that special procedural protections are extended only when privileges are withdrawn for disciplinary or quality-related reasons and that contracts with hospital-based physicians should specify that they supersede rights provided under the bylaws). The case criticized in *Bartley*, footnote 6, held that, under the staff bylaws, a radiologist had a contractual right to a hearing before being denied use of hospital equipment he had previously used under an exclusive contract that was terminated by the hospital according to its terms. See also St. Mary's Hosp. v. Radiology Prof. Corp., 421 S.E.2d 731, 737 (Ga.App.1992) (leaving open possibility that radiologist "acquiesced in the limitations St.Mary's placed upon * * * his staff privileges [in renewing his exclusive contract for radiology services] so as to waive his right to insist on compliance" with procedural requirements).

2. *Exclusive Dealing and the Antitrust Laws.* The use and antitrust status of hospitals' exclusive contracts for physician services have been described as follows:

> Hospitals must have the capacity to supply certain physician services that are regularly needed to supplement the services provided by attending physicians. Such services as anesthesia, radiology, and pathology are often provided by a physician group with whom the hospital has contracted on an exclusive basis. Although such exclusive contracts have often been challenged under the antitrust laws by physicians who are thereby excluded from access to the hospital's patients, they have generally been upheld in view of the hospital's vertical relationship to the excluded plaintiff and the sound business reasons for the arrangement.
>
> In examining exclusive hospital/physician contracts, courts have uniformly recognized that such contracts, which are renewable periodically on a competitive basis, give hospitals the opportunity to ensure the availability of services of good quality. Although the hospital/physician agreement has been alleged to create a conspiracy against the plaintiff, it has generally not been viewed with suspicion, but has instead been recognized as the natural result of a hospital decision to deal with one supplier rather than another. The physician group's successful foreclosure of competitors is likewise seen as a normal result of competition and of arm's-length bargaining resulting in an arrangement mutually advantageous to both parties as well as to consumers. In general, the law of exclusive dealing does not much threaten to impede efficient arrangements, providing as it does for judicial intervention only in rare and extreme situations in which a market is tightly and

unnecessarily closed to new entrants.[251]

Havighurst, Doctors and Hospitals: An Antitrust Perspective on Traditional Relationships, 1984 Duke L.J. 1071, 1148–49.

For cases rejecting antitrust attacks on hospitals' exclusive contracts with physicians, see Jefferson Parish Hosp. District v. Hyde, 466 U.S. 2 (1984) (upholding hospital's exclusive contract for anesthesiologists' services, but also declaring that forcing patients to patronize exclusive group, which paid hospital a share of its earnings, would constitute an unlawful "tying arrangement" if hospital has undue market power); Balaklaw v. Lovell, 14 F.3d 793 (2d Cir.1994) (finding anesthesiologist, excluded due to hospital's exclusive contract with a competitor, had not suffered antitrust injury or demonstrated a group boycott); Ezpeleta v. Sisters of Mercy Health Corp., 800 F.2d 119 (7th Cir.1986); Wright v. Southern Mono Hosp. Dist., 631 F.Supp. 1294 (E.D.Cal.1986). But see Oltz v. St. Peter's Community Hosp., 861 F.2d 1440 (9th Cir.1988) (hospital held to have conspired with anesthesiologists in terminating former arrangement with nurse anesthetists). Do hospitals act as reliable purchasers of professional services, so that they can be viewed as acting as the agents of consumers in procuring them?

Competition and Antitrust Issues in the Allocation of Admitting Privileges

NOTES AND QUESTIONS ON THE RIGHTS OF NONPHYSICIAN PRACTITIONERS

1. *JCAHO Standards, etc.* Prior to 1985, the JCAHO provided that "medical staff membership shall be limited, unless otherwise provided by law, to individuals who are currently fully licensed to practice medicine and, in addition, to licensed dentists." Its accreditation manual now provides (MS 1.1.1), however, that the staff "may include other licensed individuals permitted by law and by the hospital to provide patient care services independently in the hospital." The change to the current version was highly controversial. See, e.g., MD Control of Medical Staff Sought, Am.Med.News, Dec. 16, 1983, at 1.

In 1985, an AMA–AHA Joint Task Force on Hospital–Medical Staff Relationships made the following statement on the making of hospital policy toward limited-license practitioners:

251. See generally Tampa Elec. Co. v. Nashville Coal Co., 365 U.S. 320, 325–35 (1961) (twenty-year requirements contract affecting less than 1% of relevant market upheld); FTC v. Motion Picture Adv. Serv. Co., 344 U.S. 392, 395–98 (1953) (exclusive dealing contracts, with 40% of available outlets, limited to one-year duration); Standard Oil Co. v. United States, 337 U.S. 293, 299–320 (1949) (exclusive dealing contracts of six-month duration foreclosing 6.7% of relevant market found illegal). The later decisions appear to undercut the rigid rule of the *Standard Oil* case. See Twin City Sportservice Inc. v. Charles O. Finley & Co., 676 F.2d 1291, 1301–09 (9th Cir.), cert. denied, 459 U.S. 1009 (1982); Beltone Elecs., 100 F.T.C. 68, 204 (1982).

Decisions concerning access of categories of non-physicians (in contrast to applications of individual non-physicians) to the hospital should be a "shared" responsibility, since the governing board and the medical staff will undoubtedly have a variety of legitimate, yet possibly divergent interests, expectations and concerns. Both the governing board/administration and the medical staff will be concerned with quality of care, cost efficiency, resource allocation, consumer perception of need, and state statutes that mandate access for certain non-physicians; the individual medical staff member is likely to focus on potential exposure to tort liability for supervision of and consultation with non-physicians. The ultimate decision should be made by the governing board and be well documented in order to minimize potential antitrust exposure.

2. *Nondiscrimination Statutes.* Before the Joint Commission liberalized its policy in 1985, podiatrists and dentists had succeeded in many states in obtaining some legislative recognition of their need for access to hospital facilities. E.g., Colo.Rev.Stat. 25–3–103.5 (1997). Similar legislation has been passed on behalf of other limited-license practitioners and osteopaths. E.g., D.C.Code Ann. § 32–1307(c) (Supp. 1997) (certified nurse anesthetists, nurse-midwives, nurse practitioners, and psychologists); Official Code Ga.Ann. § 31–7–161 (1996 & Supp. 1997) (psychologists). An Ohio statute prohibiting discrimination "against a qualified person solely on the basis of whether such person is certified to practice medicine or osteopathic medicine, or podiatry, or dentistry" was held not to prohibit discrimination against chiropractors in Fort Hamilton–Hughes Mem. Hosp. Center v. Southard, 466 N.E.2d 903 (Ohio 1984). (Do you see how another reading might have been tenable?)

Most statutes in this area do not *guarantee* a practitioner access to a hospital but do have the effect of barring their categorical exclusion. A Florida statute, for example, allows osteopaths a chance to demonstrate that their training was equivalent to that of allopathic physicians. Fla. Stat. Ann. § 395.0191(3) (1996). Similarly, a Massachusetts statute provides that podiatrists' applications "shall be considered solely on the basis of the individual training, current competence, experience, ability, personal character and judgment of the applicant." Mass.Gen.Laws Ann. ch. 111, § 51C (Michie/Law Coop.1995). In Claycomb v. HCA–Raleigh Community Hosp., 333 S.E.2d 333 (N.C.App.1985), petition denied, 341 S.E.2d 23 (N.C.1986), a hospital was held free to close its staff to additional podiatrists if the board's decision was reasonably related to the operation of the hospital as a community hospital; the statute in question allowed the hospital to consider its "reasonable objectives" as well as the applicant's specific characteristics.

3. *Nonstatutory Rights.* In the absence of a statute, do limited-license practitioners have any right to hospital admitting privileges? Would a hospital's public, "quasi-public," or private status govern the extent of judicial review, if any? See, e.g., Samuel v. Curry County, 639 P.2d 687 (Or.App.1982) (no review of public hospital's policy denying privileges to chiropractors and naturopaths); Cameron v. New Hanover Mem. Hosp., 293 S.E.2d 901, 921–24 (N.C.App.1982), petition denied, 297 S.E.2d 399 (N.C.

1982) (public hospital's standards excluding podiatrists from surgical privileges held not arbitrary or capricious under statutory or constitutional standards). In New Jersey, a chiropractor has been held to have no claim to privileges where the hospital board had determined to exclude chiropractors as a class. Petrocco v. Dover Gen. Hosp. & Med. Center, 642 A.2d 1016 (N.J.Super.1994). How does this holding square with *Greisman* and *Falcone*? According to the court, those cases held only that hospitals, as "fiduciaries," must not "exercise their discretion over staff composition without considering the interests of the medical profession and the public." Should the interests of "the medical profession" be a factor in deciding the role of chiropractors in hospitals? Indeed, might taking those interests into account expose the hospital to antitrust risks?

4. *Antitrust Theories.* Limited-license practitioners have frequently invoked state and federal antitrust statutes, alleging that their exclusion from a hospital is attributable to a contract, combination, or conspiracy in restraint of trade. Instances involving the exclusion of an entire class of practitioners would seem more tenable as antitrust cases than cases brought by a single practitioner. Nevertheless, courts have been unreceptive to these claims in the absence of clear evidence of a threat by staff doctors to boycott the hospital if it decides to admit nonphysicians. For example, in Cooper v. Forsyth County Hosp. Auth., Inc., 789 F.2d 278 (4th Cir.1986), a summary judgment against plaintiff podiatrists was affirmed because evidence of the medical staff's categorical opposition to staff privileges for podiatrists and support for that view by the state association of orthopedists did not permit an inference of an anticompetitive medical conspiracy; the majority signified a willingness, if a conspiracy had been shown, to give the defendants "the opportunity to advance an affirmative defense of good faith or patient care motive." Id. at 282 n.14.* See also Bhan v. NME Hosps., Inc., 929 F.2d 1404 (9th Cir.1991) (hospital defended new physician-anesthetist-only policy against antitrust claim by certified registered nurse anesthetist by asserting its reasonable belief that policy reduced its malpractice risks and its reasonable desire for 24–hour physician coverage in case of complicated emergencies; court found no violation because plaintiff failed to demonstrate that hospital policy threatened competition in a relevant market); Flegel v. Christian, 4 F.3d 682 (8th Cir.1993) (denial of staff privileges to osteopathic urologists held not to violate antitrust laws because hospital lacked market power and there were no actual anticompetitive effects).

Consider the reasoning of the cited cases in light of the following materials, which, ironically, begin with an antitrust case involving an alleged conspiracy by osteopaths against an allopathic physician. (Be warned that this case was chosen, not as a model of antitrust reasoning, but as a test of the student's ability to read critically and to apply principles studied in chapter 4.)

* The state orthopedic association, however, accepted an FTC consent order barring it from certain antipodiatrist activities. North Carolina Orthopaedic Ass'n, 108 F.T.C. 116 (1986) (consent order).

Hackett v. Metropolitan General Hospital

District Court of Appeal of Florida, Second District, 1985.
465 So.2d 1246, rehearing denied March 22, 1985.

■ LEHAN, JUDGE.

I. Summary of Issues, Facts and Holding

In this antitrust case plaintiff, a doctor, appeals from a final judgment determining after a nonjury trial that no violation of section 542.18, Florida Statutes (1981) (the counterpart of section 1 of the Sherman Act) was established from the refusal by defendant, a hospital, to grant staff privileges at the hospital to plaintiff. We affirm.

* * * Plaintiff, who is a medical doctor specializing in urology, contended that he was refused staff privileges at the hospital "by reason of a conspiracy between the hospital through its board of trustees and the osteopathic physicians on the staff to perpetuate a monopoly for the one staff member practicing urology and to limit the staff to osteopathic physicians, thereby insulating them from competition by medical doctors." * * *

Plaintiff's application for staff privileges at the hospital was rejected by the hospital's staff and by the hospital's board of trustees. He was advised that the basis for his rejection was that the hospital already had adequate urology coverage. * * *

In its final judgment for the defendant the trial court disagreed with the hospital's initial basis for refusing staff privileges to plaintiff, finding that there was a need for a urologist with the qualifications of plaintiff at the hospital. Nonetheless, the trial court concluded that the board sincerely felt that the hospital's urology needs were being fulfilled and that the board was justified in finding that plaintiff would be a disruptive influence. The court found that the rejection of plaintiff's application was not based upon the fact that he was a medical doctor, noting that other medical doctors had been admitted to the staff. The court further found that the decision to deny plaintiff staff privileges was not based upon a desire to create a closed shop or to stifle competition.

Our reasoning for affirming the judgment for defendant can be summarized as follows: Although *per se* concepts of antitrust liability based upon the group boycott doctrine might on the surface seem to apply, we believe that doctrine is inapplicable here. It is inappropriate to strictly apply the group boycott doctrine, which was created with reference to commercial conduct, to determinations like those in this case involving the composition of a hospital's professional staff. Although there is authority stating that, to impose antitrust liability under the rule of reason, a showing of either anticompetitive purpose or unreasonable anticompetitive effect is sufficient, we believe that in a case like this there should not be liability without a clear showing that the dominant purpose of excluding a physician from a hospital's staff was anticompetitive. We conclude that the record does not establish the existence of a dominant anticompetitive purpose in the decision to exclude plaintiff in this case. In any event, even if a showing of unreasonable anticompetitive effect alone were sufficient to establish a rule of reason violation, we conclude that the record does not establish an unreasonable restraint on competition in the relevant market.

That reasoning is further explained below.

II. Background

This type of lawsuit has originated only in recent years. The genesis apparently was *Goldfarb v. Virginia State Bar,* to the effect that the learned professions are not exempt from the antitrust laws. In *Goldfarb* the Supreme Court in a footnote nonetheless indicated that certain practices on the part of those engaged in professions might be lawful even though the same practices would be unlawful in a commercial context. * * *

The case before us involves a number of aspects which are peculiar to the antitrust field. * * * For an extensive analysis of the ramifications of applying traditional antitrust concepts to decisions by hospitals to deny staff privileges to physicians, see Kissam, Webber, Bigus & Holzgraefe, Antitrust and Hospital Privileges: Testing the Conventional Wisdom, 70 Cal.L.Rev. 595 (1982). * * *

III. Reasoning

Since our approach to this case does not entirely conform to all traditional antitrust principles applied in commercial cases and in light of the increasing numbers of lawsuits of this type in recent years, we feel we should explain our reasoning in some depth. * * * We should particularly recognize that the discussion in the above-referenced California Law Review article is profound and thought provoking, whether or not one is in agreement with all views expressed in that article.

A. *All Traditional Commercial Antitrust Concepts Should Not Control a Case Like This Which Involves the Quality and Efficiency of Medical Services*

In the final analysis, resolution of disputes of this type must center largely upon decisions concerning the quality or efficiency of professional health care services. We feel those decisions usually are best left to members of those professions, absent more clearcut antitrust ramifications of the type involved, for example, in *Goldfarb* and *Professional Engineers* (price-fixing) * * *. We agree with the foregoing law review article that hospital staff decisions on the admission of doctors "typically will involve quality determinations by and about professionals that appear to have a substantially different nature than professional pricing choices."

Although we realize that plaintiff's medical skills were not questioned in this case and that the purpose of the rejection of plaintiff was, according to the trial court's findings, related to a lack of need for plaintiff's specialty at the hospital and plaintiff's perceived disrupting influence, cases involving a rejection of a physician's application to a hospital staff on the basis of an appraisal of the doctor's competence are not irrelevant. Those cases, like the present case, involve subjective decision-making. The court in Williams v. Kleaveland, 534 F.Supp. 912 (W.D.Mich.1981), observed that

> the determination of the medical competence of a physician is peculiarly within the domain of the medical profession. Although members of the public in general and of other professions, in particular, may effectively ascertain the effects of ethical codes prohibiting advertising, the establishment of fees, and other conduct which essentially concerns the economic aspects of the profession, it is my view that physicians themselves are best able to evaluate the competence and skill of another physician and to take appropriate action in the public interest.

Id. at 918–19. Those comments could apply to the types of determinations involved here relating to the needs of the hospital and the desired relationship between a doctor and others at the hospital. There may well be a legitimate concern with what the law review article suggests could, if traditional commercial antitrust concepts were strictly applied to this type of case, "turn antitrust courts and hospital attorneys into public utility regulators with the power to make these decisions for hospitals."

* * *

A physician's role in society depends more upon subjective, ethics-oriented factors, such as physical and mental skills and basic caring, than the more objective economic concepts which govern the commercial marketplace. Therefore, we believe the antitrust laws should be applied to physicians with circumspection.

The legal resolution of matters like this involving hospital staffing decisions involves a balancing of competing interests. We feel that the interests of society in the efficiency and quality of health care can best be served by not disturbing a hospital staff decision like that before us in this case and that those interests counter-balance any economic desirability of imposing all commercial standards of competition upon health care decisions of the type involved here. We do not believe that the U.S. Supreme Court, by saying that the learned professions are not exempt from the antitrust laws, meant to require a finding of antitrust liability in a case like this.

Plaintiff argues that the decision to exclude him from the hospital staff involved economic motivations to protect the income of the existing staff. It is a rather self-evident truth that some physicians may receive economic benefit from circumspect antitrust enforcement in this field. But that in itself does not provide to us under the facts of this case sufficient cause to make the courts, through the application of commercial antitrust principles, controlling participants in subjective decision-making processes concerning the composition of a hospital staff.

> Every appropriate application of conventional antitrust principles to the health care industry must account for great dissimilarities between the present day health care sector and the traditional commercial context in which classical antitrust doctrines developed. Because of the professional, social, and economic complexities of health

> care delivery, physicians and hospitals cannot be held to the same pro-competitive rules as the makers of cellophane and aluminum; our society is willing to tolerate large-scale production and consumption of cut-rate aluminum and cellophane, but is unwilling to tolerate the large-scale production and consumption of substandard health care services. Additionally, application of "rules of the marketplace" assumes that consumers can balance quality against cost, a dubious assumption in the context of health care.... Before the courts attempt to coerce health care providers into more competitive modes of behavior, they should be reasonably certain that more competitive behavior not only is possible, but is desirable as well.

7 Am.J. of Law & Medicine, vol. 1, 1981, at iii, as quoted in Williams v. Kleaveland, 534 F.Supp. at 919.

* * *

B. While Hospital Staffing Decisions Should Not Be Exempt From Antitrust Scrutiny, They Should Be Exempt From Antitrust Per Se Liability Concepts

* * *

C. Without a Dominant Anticompetitive Purpose the Decision to Exclude Plaintiff From Defendant's Staff Should Not Constitute an Antitrust Rule of Reason Violation

In considering the rule of reason we agree * * * that an anticompetitive purpose is a requisite for antitrust liability in a case like this. We go further and believe that the requisite is a *dominant* anticompetitive purpose which, as referred to further below, was not found to exist in this case. See Kissam, supra, at 660.

Our approach is consistent with the "purpose based approach" which is suggested by the foregoing article to resolve antitrust cases of this kind and which the authors believe would "promote important public policies" and yet at the same time "serve the central antitrust policies." Kissam, supra, at pp. 659–63, 670. "[P]roof that Defendants acted for the primary purpose of maintaining high quality patient care is a persuasive defense to an antitrust claim." Williams v. Kleaveland, 534 F.Supp. at 919.

D. The Evidence Does Not Require Reversing the Trial Court's Finding That the Purpose of Excluding Plaintiff From the Hospital's Staff Was Not Anticompetitive

The purposes which the trial court found the hospital had for rejecting plaintiff—good faith belief that there was no need for his services and the justified belief that he would be a disruptive influence—were, if supported by the evidence, related to the quality and efficiency of patient care at the hospital and were, therefore, not anticompetitive. Plaintiff argues that those purposes were not supported by the weight of the evidence and that therefore the trial court's findings in that regard constituted reversible error. We do not agree.

The basic question is not whether the hospital's beliefs were justified, e.g., whether, as the trial court found, the hospital was justified in believing that plaintiff would be a disruptive influence. The basic question is whether the hospital in good faith actually had that belief in forming its purpose to reject plaintiff's application. * * *

Plaintiff had the burden to show dominant anticompetitive purpose. The trial court saw and heard the witnesses. After weighing the evidence, the trial court found that the hospital board sincerely felt the hospital's urology needs were being fulfilled, that the board was justified in believing that plaintiff would be a disruptive influence, and that there was no anticompetitive purpose in denying plaintiff's application. The record does not justify a reversal of those findings.

E. Even if Antitrust Liability in This Case Could Exist Without Anticompetitive Purpose by the Hospital, No Unreasonable Anticompetitive Effect Was Established

In any event, we do not conclude that the record establishes that the effect of the hospital's conduct was an unreasonable restraint in the relevant market. The antitrust laws are primarily for the protection of competition, not an individual competitor. The fact that the exclusion of plaintiff in this case from the staff of one hospital caused him to practice medicine elsewhere does not establish an unreasonable restraint upon competition, especially where, as here, the evidence shows the availability of other hospitals in the area to plaintiff who, in fact, was on the staffs of four other hospitals. * * *

We have no doubt that procompetitive effects exist from hospital staffing decisions which improve or prevent erosion of a hospital's efficiency [or] the quality of its services.

* * *

NOTES AND QUESTIONS ON ANTITRUST ANALYSIS IN STAFF PRIVILEGES CASES

1. *Softer Antitrust Rules?* The *Hackett* court quotes one source to the effect that courts applying the antitrust laws "should be reasonably certain that more competitive behavior not only is possible, but is desirable as well." Should a court feel free to approve anticompetitive conduct because competition is not desirable? Was this in fact how *Hackett* was decided?

Do you agree with the *Hackett* court's concern about making courts the final decision makers on privileges questions? If so, do you also agree with the court's conclusion that the way to solve this problem is by subjecting physicians to softer antitrust rules than apply in "commercial" contexts? Many courts addressing privileges denials or revocations under the antitrust laws have suggested that professionals might be allowed some freedom to regulate themselves and their economic environment in anticompetitive ways—a privilege not permitted to other varieties of tradesmen. Is it in fact necessary to develop specially permissive antitrust rules to resolve these cases satisfactorily? Or do traditional antitrust principles leave ample room for hospital medical staffs to act on technical matters within the hospital? Is there a naked restraint here or only concerted action to accomplish a procompetitive purpose, which should, whatever the context, be analyzed sympathetically under the Rule of Reason?

Is the administration of staff privileges truly an instance of professional self-regulation (as the *Hackett* court implies in quoting approvingly from *Williams v. Kleaveland*)?

2. *A Group Boycott?* Do you agree that a denial of privileges might be viewed as a "group boycott" (whether lawful or unlawful)? Note that only a single entity (the hospital), not a group of independent competitors, is refusing to deal. The *Hackett* court's problem in confronting this terminology is a good illustration of the point made in connection with the *Klor's* case in chapter 4(§B) concerning the need to distinguish between true "concerted refusals to deal" and the actions of a single entity over which competitors exercise some control.

Assume that a medical staff threatens that its members will take their patients elsewhere if the hospital grants clinical privileges to limited-license practitioners or if it decides to admit a particular physician to the staff because, though questionable in some respects, she is a big admitter. Is there a true boycott here? Can the staff assert in defending an antitrust suit that its purposes were procompetitive or that its action was purely professional and taken in the interest of patients? How does this situation differ from the typical privileges case?

3. *What Level of Judicial Scrutiny?* Does the *Hackett* opinion (which is fairly typical of early judicial pronouncements on these problems) or the cited article by Kissam et al. lay out a consistent and satisfying approach for antitrust courts to use in reviewing the merits of the actions taken in privileges cases? What level of scrutiny is appropriate? Is there a difference between common-law and antitrust cases that might call for different levels of judicial scrutiny? (Consider the interests being vindicated, recalling that the antitrust laws are supposed to protect "competition, not competitors." What is "competition"? What, precisely, is the threat to it here? Is it great enough in each privileges case that the time and energies of courts are well spent in attempting to reconstruct precisely what happened and to discover the justification for the action taken?) Do you see ways, or situations, in which antitrust courts might appropriately limit their review of privileges decisions?

It has been suggested that what is sometimes called the "essential-facilities doctrine" provides antitrust principles appropriate for privileges cases. See Havighurst, Doctors and Hospitals: An Antitrust Perspective on Traditional Relationships, 1984 Duke L.J. 1071, 1108–39. As developed under section 1 of the Sherman Act (it has a more problematic existence under section 2 that can be ignored for present purposes), the essential facilities doctrine applies wherever a group of competitors collectively controls some resource to which other competitors need access in order to survive or compete effectively in the marketplace. Because such collective ventures appear procompetitive and efficiency-enhancing, they are generally not condemned outright. Instead, the courts have, under some circumstances (especially where the incentive to undertake similarly efficient activities would not be impaired), scrutinized the joint venture to ensure that it adopts evenhanded policies in dispensing its benefits.

If the essential-facilities doctrine were applied in privileges cases, it would necessitate close judicial scrutiny of a privileges decision only when two factual conditions were met. First, the hospital must be a truly essential facility. Second, the facility must be truly under the control of competitors of the disappointed applicant. Consider whether these conditions were satisfied in *Hackett.* Does the outcome square with the essential-facilities doctrine?

Assuming that the essential-facilities doctrine applies in a particular case, what standard of review should the court employ? As an embodiment of the Rule of Reason, the essential-facilities doctrine leaves room for judgment in tailoring the court's intervention in proportion to the risk of anticompetitive harm. Havighurst argues (id. at 1122–25) that antitrust law requires close scrutiny only of physician-dominated decisions:

> Under the rule of reason, [a joint venture should be viewed sympathetically] only if the collaborators have available to them no less restrictive alternative method to accomplish their valid purposes. Where a medical staff exercises de facto control over access to a hospital, there clearly exists another way—namely, submission to the authority of the hospital board—for the staff to accomplish its procompetitive [e.g., quality-assurance] purposes without the same danger to competition. Although a court should not condemn the staff's exercise of delegated powers on this ground alone, neither should it presume the regularity of the staff's decisions or accord any special deference to the action taken by it in a given case.
>
> Where the facts support application of the essential-facilities doctrine, a court would be justified in subjecting medical-staff actions on personnel matters to strict requirements and close oversight. Thus, it might reasonably require that fair procedures be followed and award treble damages where they are not. * * *
>
> In addition to insisting upon fair procedures, a court in an essential-facilities case should closely examine the medical staff's specific requirements for admitting privileges in order to ascertain whether they do in fact serve the hospital's business interests. Courts should also be willing to investigate in depth the circumstances surrounding each staffing and personnel decision and to judge the decision's merits under a fairly demanding standard of review.

Havighurst's argument is thus that antitrust courts should be intensely concerned whether a hospital and its medical staff have structured their collaboration in such a way as to minimize the danger that physicians' conflicts of interests and anticompetitive impulses will infect hospital decisions. In addition to advocating close scrutiny of physician-dominated decisions, he also argues that only limited scrutiny, under a rational-basis test, is appropriate for hospital decisions taken independently of, though perhaps in close cooperation with, the medical staff:

> [W]here a hospital [through its governing board and employees] participates independently in the making of a privileges decision, antitrust analysis should recognize how the vertical nature of the hospital's interest reduces the risk that consumer welfare will be harmed and thus reduces also the need for judicial oversight. Privileges decisions that are not dominated by a medical staff comprising competitors of those seeking access to the hospital should be subject to no more judicial scrutiny than can be exercised without exhaustive discovery or a full trial. Such a test, sparing the hospital undue burdens as it pursues its corporate goals, should apply even when the hospital possesses a clear monopoly because of the uniqueness of its facility, and thus exercises life-and-death power over a practitioner's right to practice in an area. More controversially, this test should apply even in the face of an allegation that the hospital, though acting independently, conspired with its medical staff.

Id. at 1125–26.

In a 1982 advisory opinion, the Maryland Attorney General stated, "The principal danger, in antitrust terms, inherent in the procedure for awarding hospital staff privileges is that doctors with privileges may combine to use their decision-making authority to exclude their competitors from access to essential hospital facilities. * * * [W]here the hospital itself decides to deny an application or to limit the size of its staff, the essential element of an agreement among competitors is lacking. Furthermore, when the hospital acts unilaterally, it presumably lacks the anticompetitive motive of excluding competitors." Letter from Stephen H. Sachs to Benson E. Legg (Feb. 10, 1982). Applying these insights, the Attorney General gave a clean bill of health to a particular hospital's process for administering staff privileges. How does the approach taken compare to the proposal to employ the essential-facilities doctrine?

4. *Queries.* (a) Assuming that you are persuaded that your hospital client would be better positioned to defend its privileges decisions if it could show that it acted independently and did not simply rubberstamp the medical staff's actions, how would you advise it to proceed? To put the issue in a slightly different light, how would you as a litigator seek to prove that a hospital's action was (or was not) taken independently of its medical staff? See, e.g., Todorov v. DCH Healthcare Authority, 921 F.2d 1438, 1459 n. 34 (11th Cir.1991) (reviewing evidence and concluding that "the hospital's board does more than simply 'rubber stamp' the recommendations of the medical staff. That the board is likely to follow [such recommendations] does not establish, or even reasonably suggest, the existence of a conspiracy.").

(b) If the medical staff was the true decision maker, should it matter that the physicians actually making the decision were not in fact competitors of (i.e., were not in the same specialty as) the plaintiff?

(c) In Boczar v. Manatee Hosps. & Health Systems, Inc., 993 F.2d 1514 (11th Cir.1993), the plaintiff physician was successful even though the jury finding a conspiracy exonerated all the named individual physician defendants. In addition to suggesting that there might have been unnamed co-

conspirators, the court of appeals approved the verdict because the jury might have inferred that "the hospital came to think that it would be better to lose [the plaintiff] and the revenue she generated than to keep her on staff and risk additional dissatisfaction and defections among her competitors." Although there were other hospitals in the community, the court was satisfied that competition had been harmed because the hospital's action, communicated to state licensing authorities, "effectively ended Dr. Boczar's ability to compete and to practice in Bradenton and burdened her ability to compete generally." Was this case correctly decided?

(d) If Havighurst's view of the law (or that of the Maryland Attorney General) were widely accepted, how would hospital/physician relations be affected? Would the changes in such relations be desirable from a policy standpoint? On balance, which line of antitrust analysis makes the most sense? What advantages (disadvantages) might the essential-facilities analysis have in comparison with the "purpose-based" test of Kissam et al. and the *Hackett* case?

(e) Most hospital medical staffs, acting in accordance with JCAHO standards, grant their members "delineated clinical privileges." Is there an antitrust problem? Recall that horizontal division of markets is normally a per se violation. How would you defend?

NOTES AND QUESTIONS ON ANTITRUST DEFENSES IN STAFF PRIVILEGES CASES

1. Trial judges have been receptive to a number of defenses offered by defendants in antitrust cases concerning staff privileges. (Speculate for a minute on the possible reasons why a busy federal district judge might be quick to find grounds for dismissing these cases without trial.) There has indeed been a series of such defenses, several of which (like the early notion that professionals were somehow exempt from ordinary antitrust rules) became popular for a while only to be rendered unavailable by subsequent judicial rulings. See generally Starling, Antitrust Defenses in Physician Peer Review Cases, 63 Antitrust L.J. 399 (1995). See also Hammack, The Antitrust Laws and the Medical Peer Review Process, 9 J. Contemp. Health L. & Pol'y 419 (1993); Annot., Denial by Hospital of Staff Privileges or Referrals to Physician or Other Health Care Practitioner as Violation of Sherman Act, 89 A.L.R.Fed. 419 (1988 & Supp. 1995).

2. *Concerted Action?* At this writing, a defense *du jour* in some circuits is the "intraenterprise conspiracy" defense already noted in § A of this chapter. See generally Brewbaker, Antitrust Conspiracy Doctrine and the Hospital Enterprise, 74 B.U.L.Rev. 67 (1994). The Supreme Court has declined several invitations to resolve the conflict in the circuits on this issue.

If courts are in fact unwilling or unable to recognize even the possibility of a conspiracy between the hospital and its medical staff (on the theory that they constitute a single enterprise), they will obviously have no occasion to scrutinize the structure of hospital/staff relationships or to apply the less-restrictive-alternative principle to determine whether the hospital maintains an independent check on staff activities that endanger competition. It is possible, however, to conceive of the relationship between a hospital and its medical staff as a "joint venture" by two essentially independent entities and to view it, not as a "conspiracy" (the pejorative term is unfortunate), but as a collaboration having a highly procompetitive purpose—the efficient operation of a modern hospital. This approach would leave room for the court to ensure that the joint venturers had allocated decision-making authority on sensitive issues in a manner consistent with the maintenance of competition. Arguably, as the Maryland Attorney General seemed to appreciate, the allocation of power within the hospital enterprise should be the principal concern in applying the antitrust laws.

From what you have learned about medical staffs, does it make sense to view them as agents serving only hospital interests? To be sure, most formulations of the intraenterprise conspiracy defense leave room for a plaintiff to rebut the presumption that the staff acted responsibly as an arm of the hospital enterprise. But this means that proof of an actual anticompetitive motive is required before a plaintiff can even get into court. A presumption of regularity in decision making that applies even though ultimate power resides in the medical staff rather than in the hospital board will be very hard for any plaintiff to overcome, especially given the reluctance of many judges to open the courthouse door to full trials in these cases.

Of course, the medical staff is itself a combination of competitors, and a plaintiff physician can easily sue it, alleging that it and its members conspired against him. Moreover, if the staff is deemed to be simply an arm of the hospital enterprise, any antitrust liability it incurs would presumably attach to the hospital under elementary principles of agency. Do you conclude, therefore, that whether the hospital and the staff can conspire with each other is a moot point?

Consider the possibilities for obtaining cost-saving summary judgment in these cases. Presumably, physician plaintiffs would find it relatively easy to raise factual questions (thus avoiding summary judgment) as long as the issue is defined as whether the medical staff was a co-conspirator pursuing an agenda other than the hospital's or as whether the staff was itself restraining the plaintiff's competitive freedom for an improper purpose. Thus, only if the evidence against the doctor was very strong—so that a jury could not find anticompetitive intent—could a hospital or medical staff reasonably hope to obtain summary judgment. Hospitals might therefore take action against questionable physicians only when the evidence was very clear. Is this the optimal outcome? Note that, under the essential-facilities theory outlined above, courts could dismiss cases upon a showing of the hospital board's independence; thus, the institution could act very much as it saw fit, subject only to constraints imposed by bylaws it had itself adopted. On the other hand, cases in which the medical staff, rather than the hospital board, was the true decision maker would have to go to trial if there was any factual question. Both hospitals and medical staffs would therefore have an incentive to arrange things so that the staff was subordinate to the hospital board. Would this result be desirable as a matter of policy? Would it serve the apparent objectives of antitrust law?

3. *Interstate Commerce.* In several early cases, the courts were not convinced that the exclusion of a single applicant from the staff of a single hospital had any significant bearing upon either interstate trade or consumer welfare, the focus of federal antitrust law. In several circuits, therefore, a plaintiff was required to establish jurisdiction by showing that the alleged illegal acts had some impact on interstate commerce. As noted in chapter 4(§A), however, the Supreme Court, in Summit Health Ltd. v. Pinhas, 500 U.S. 322 (1991), made it relatively easy for a single professional to meet the test for jurisdiction under the Sherman Act. The Court held (5–4) that the test for jurisdiction is simply the potential harm that the conspiracy might do. Thus, "the competitive significance of respondent's exclusion from the market must be measured, not just by a particularized evaluation of his own practice, but rather, by a general evaluation of the impact of the restraint on other participants and potential participants in the market from which he has been excluded." Id. at 332.

At first glance, it might appear that the courts should be more demanding. After all, as one court put it, a liberal test "would mean that virtually every physician who is ever temporarily denied hospital privileges for whatever reason could drag the hospital and members of its staff into costly antitrust litigation merely by alleging that the [hospital] receives payments, goods, or equipment in interstate commerce." Seglin v. Esau, 769 F.2d 1274, 1283 (7th Cir.1985). Could it be argued, however, that the more demanding view would place too much emphasis on the harm done to a particular competitor? Might it result in a failure of federal law to reach many situations in which hospitals and physicians, though engaged in a procompetitive activity, fail to structure their effort in a way that lessens the threat to the competitive process? Do the foregoing notes and questions suggest that there is more at stake in a privileges case than the public's interest in preserving an individual plaintiff as a competitor?

4. *Antitrust Injury.* Citing the axiom that antitrust law is intended to protect competition rather than competitors as such, some courts have lately begun to dismiss staff privileges cases on the ground that the physician is only a disappointed competitor and has not suffered so-called "antitrust injury." Thus, according to one court, injury to the doctor-victim of an alleged hospital/staff conspiracy "is really only harm to the individual doctor and not to competition within the marketplace." Robles v. Humana Hosp. Cartersville, 785 F.Supp. 989, 999 (N.D.Ga.1992). In that case, the court was impressed that additional obstetricians appeared in the market after the plaintiff was excluded and that "now patients have more choice concerning which doctor to visit." It discounted the plaintiff's allegations that the surviving doctors were affiliated with each other, had "financial ties" to the hospital, and had conspired with the hospital "to eliminate all the independent doctors in Bartow County." Is there a possible public harm here? Will managed care plans attempting to enter the marketplace find a competitive market in which to procure obstetrical services?

To be sure, a private plaintiff must allege acts that harm the competitive process as well as himself—that is, an "injury of the type the antitrust laws were intended to prevent." Brunswick Corp. v. Pueblo Bowl–O–Mat, Inc., 429 U.S. 477, 488 (1977) (the leading case establishing the antitrust-injury requirement). But, just as interstate commerce may be affected by unlawful practices even if it may not be affected by the fate of any particular victim of those practices, courts should not be too quick to find that antitrust injury has not been alleged. Of course, there are many cases in which the competitive process has not been interfered with and the plaintiff is indeed complaining only about the outcome of that process—e.g., about a hospital's decision that his services are not needed. But the antitrust-injury requirement should not be used to deny standing to all competitors seeking market opportunities. Instead, it should be used to screen complaints to ensure that the federal courts are being invoked in the public interest—that is, to protect the competitive process, which is presumed to benefit consumers and which contemplates that competing practitioners shall be free to sell their services in a market that has not been rigged against them.

5. *The State–Action Defense (Patrick v. Burget).* A number of courts dismissed early staff privileges cases brought under the federal antitrust laws because they found warrants in state law for hospital peer-review actions excluding physician-competitors from the marketplace. One such case was Patrick v. Burget, 800 F.2d 1498 (9th Cir.1986), rev'd 486 U.S. 94 (1988). In that case, the hospital was organized along traditional lines to carry out peer-review activities, which were mandated by Or.Rev.Stat. 441.055 (1987) in the following terms:

> (3) The governing body of each health care facility shall be responsible for the operation of the facility, the selection of the medical staff and the quality of care rendered in the facility. The governing body shall:
>
> * * *
>
> (c) Insure that procedures for granting, restricting and terminating privileges exist and that such procedures are regularly reviewed to assure their conformity to applicable law; and
>
> (d) Insure that physicians admitted to practice in the facility are organized into a medical staff in such a manner as to effectively review the professional practices of the facility for the purposes of reducing morbidity and mortality and for the improvement of patient care.

Oregon law also provided protection from liability resulting from participation in peer review: "A person serving on or communicating information to any [hospital committee in connection with peer review] shall not be subject to an action for civil damages for affirmative actions taken or statements made in good faith." Or.Rev.Stat. § 41.675(4) (1984). (Does the latter statute resolve the question? It is usually held that federal policy is strong enough to overcome state immunity statutes unless the terms of the *Midcal Aluminum* test are met. E.g., Tambone v. Mem. Hosp., Inc., 825 F.2d 1132 (7th Cir.1987).)

On the basis of the Oregon legislation mandating quality assurance and the selection of a medical staff, the court of appeals invoked the state-action doctrine: "The peer review process allows doctors to agree to eliminate a competitor from the market because they believe his or her product is substandard." 800 F.2d at 1506. It concluded its opinion as follows: "There is no doubt that the evidence, viewed in the light most favorable to Patrick, reveals shabby, unprincipled and unprofessional conduct on the part of the defendants. However, the State of Oregon regulates its health care industry through mandatory peer review and thereby immunizes much of the conduct complained of."

The Supreme Court reversed, holding that the "active supervision" requirement of the *Midcal* test was not satisfied. "The active supervision prong * * * requires that state officials have and exercise power to review particular anticompetitive acts of private parties and disapprove those that fail to accord with state policy. Absent such a program of supervision, there is no realistic assurance that a private party's anticompetitive conduct promotes state policy, rather than merely the party's individual interests." *Patrick*, 486 U.S. at 101. Judicial review of privileges decisions was relatively limited in Oregon. Would judicial review of the kind provided by state courts in, say, New Jersey provide enough protection to meet the second requirement of the *Midcal* test?

Because the Supreme Court chose to rest its decision only on the lack of active state supervision, it might be assumed that Oregon had met the first-prong requirement—that of a "clearly articulated and affirmatively expressed" state policy at odds with the general federal policy favoring competition. The Court did not so find, however, but jumped directly to the second prong. In your view, did the state statute quoted above satisfy the first-prong requirement? Indeed, is there anything at all about the policy expressed that is inconsistent with federal antitrust policy? For example, was the statute's purpose to enable *doctors* to remove competitors, or did the legislature intend only that *hospitals* would remove doctors whose performance was below the standards of the hospital?

6. *The State–Action Defense (Public Hospitals).* In Todorov v. DCH Healthcare Authority, 921 F.2d 1438 (11th Cir.1991), a public hospital was ruled immune from antitrust suits concerning staff privileges under the state-action doctrine. The Alabama statute under which the hospital operated expressly made it a "political subdivision of the state" and authorized it to exercise certain powers even if it thereby "engages in activities that may be deemed 'anticompetitive' within the contemplation of the antitrust laws." Recall that, under Town of Hallie v. Eau Claire, 471 U.S. 34 (1985), the active supervision requirement is relaxed for state agencies. Recall also that, under City of Columbia v. Omni Outdoor Advertising, Inc., 499 U.S. 365 (1991), there is no "conspiracy exception" to the state-action doctrine, implying that a hospital's overclose cooperation with its medical staff might not be subject to challenge (although ultra vires delegation of the hospital's power to the staff might forfeit immunity). See also Martin v. Memorial Hosp., 86 F.3d 1391 (5th Cir.1996) (immunity found for public hospital's exclusive contract to operate dialysis unit); Bolt v. Halifax Hosp. Med. Center, 891 F.2d 810, 825 (11th Cir.), cert. denied, 495 U.S. 924 (1990) (public hospital alleged to have conspired against plaintiff not only with its doctors but also, through them, with other hospitals in the community; court still found immunity, however, on ground that "when Florida's legislature authorized peer review * * *, it could foresee that [the hospital] would rely on recommendations made by a physician's peers and refuse to deal with (i.e., boycott) that physician").

Although public hospitals do not qualify for antitrust immunity solely on the basis of their status as public entities, the Local Government Antitrust Act of 1984, 15 U.S.C. §§ 34–36 (1994), has been held to insulate a county hospital and its medical staff against antitrust treble damage actions. E.g. Cohn v. Bond, 953 F.2d 154 (4th Cir.1991).

Federal Statutory Immunity for Peer-Review Actions, etc.

Smith v. Ricks

United States Court of Appeals, Ninth Circuit, 1994.
31 F.3d 1478.

■ TROTT, CIRCUIT JUDGE

Dr. John Smith, a cardiologist, was removed from the staff of Good Samaritan Hospital. After a lengthy peer review process, the reviewing doctors and the hospital concluded that Dr. Smith's performance was below acceptable standards of care and that removal from the hospital staff was necessary to ensure patient safety. Dr. Smith responded by filing a complaint in federal court alleging that the doctors and the hospital had engaged in an antitrust conspiracy against him and violated his due process rights.

The district court granted summary judgment and awarded attorneys' fees and costs in favor of defendants ("Good Samaritan"). The district court held that Good Samaritan was immune from federal antitrust liability pursuant to the Health Care Quality Improvement Act of 1986 ("HCQIA"), 42 U.S.C. §§ 11101–52, which shields peer review participants from liability if certain review standards are met. The district court also held that Good Samaritan was entitled to reasonable attorneys' fees and costs pursuant to 42 U.S.C. § 11113.* * * [W]e affirm.

II

Congress passed the HCQIA because it found the threat of liability under federal law "unreasonably discourages physicians from participating in effective professional peer review" and "[t]here is an overriding national need to provide incentive and protection for physicians engaging" in peer review. Good Samaritan is immune from antitrust damages under HCQIA if it demonstrates [that] its professional review actions complied with the fairness standards set out in 42 U.S.C. § 11112(a) * * * See Austin v. McNamara, 979 F.2d 728, 733 (9th Cir.1992).[5] * * *

> Section 11112(a) provides that a professional review action must be taken:
>
> > (1) in the reasonable belief that the action was in furtherance of quality health care,
> >
> > (2) after a reasonable effort to obtain the facts of the matter,
> >
> > (3) after adequate notice and hearing procedures are afforded to the physician involved or after such other procedures as are fair to the physician under the circumstances, and
> >
> > (4) in the reasonable belief that the action was warranted by the facts known after such reasonable effort to obtain facts and after meeting the requirement of paragraph (3).
>
> A professional review action shall be presumed to have met the preceding standards necessary for the protection set out in section 11111(a) of this title unless the presumption is rebutted by a preponderance of the evidence.

Because the "reasonableness" requirements of § 11112(a) were intended to create an objective standard, rather than a subjective standard, this inquiry may be resolved on summary judgment. See *Austin*, 979 F.2d at 734. The rebuttable presumption "creates a somewhat unusual standard" of review for summary judgment because the "inquiry focuses on whether [plaintiff] has provided sufficient evidence to permit a jury to find that he has overcome, by a preponderance of the evidence, the presumption that physicians in the defendants' position would reasonably have believed that their action was warranted by the facts." Id. The district court held that Dr. Smith could not rebut that presumption, and we affirm.

A. As the district court noted, Good Samaritan did not begin its review process until the [state Bureau of Medical Quality Assurance] notified Good Samaritan that Dr. Smith's staff privileges had been revoked at another hospital due to inadequate care. At all stages of the investigation, the peer review participants found that Dr. Smith's treatment was inadequate. Dr. Smith alleges a vague conspiracy by an "in-group" of doctors out to get him, but he never challenges the substance of their findings. * * *

B. Good Samaritan conducted a thorough review over the course of almost two years. Good Samaritan reviewed the O'Connor records as well

5. The *Austin* court lists [another] requirement that defendants "satisf[y] § 11112(b)'s requirement of adequate notice and hearing." Section 11112(b) lists a series of characteristics and requirements for conducting hearings and giving notice regarding professional review actions. However, § 11112(b) specifically provides: "A professional review body's failure to meet the conditions described in this subsection shall not, in itself, constitute failure to meet the standards of [adequate notice and hearing procedures as provided in] subsection (a)(3) of this section." In other words, § 11112(b) describes a "safe harbor" for immunity, but it is not necessary to satisfy § 11112(b) to receive immunity. * * *

as the Good Samaritan records. Dr. Smith's only challenge to Good Samaritan's investigation is that he was not permitted to discover or introduce evidence regarding the conduct of other doctors. Dr. Smith essentially claims he was not the worst doctor at Good Samaritan. However, nothing in the statute, legislative history, or case law suggests the competency of other doctors is relevant in evaluating whether Good Samaritan conducted a reasonable investigation into Dr. Smith's conduct. Thus, Dr. Smith cannot rebut the presumption that the termination of his staff privileges was made after a reasonable effort to obtain the facts.

C. Dr. Smith's primary challenge to the district court's grant of summary judgment is that the hearings Good Samaritan conducted were inadequate. Dr. Smith claims Good Samaritan is not entitled to immunity unless all the procedural requirements of § 11112(b)(3)(C) are met. However, as discussed previously, § 11112(b) describes a "safe harbor" provision. The statute expressly provides that hospitals need not meet all of the § 11112(b) requirements. The ultimate inquiry is whether the notice and hearing procedures were adequate. Nevertheless, Good Samaritan's hearing procedures satisfied the "safe harbor" provisions of § 11112(b)(3).[7]

During the hearing, the physician must have the right:

(i) to representation by an attorney or other person of the physician's choice,

(ii) to have a record made of the proceedings, copies of which may be obtained by the physician upon payment of any reasonable charges . . .,

(iii) to call, examine, and cross-examine witnesses,

(iv) to present evidence determined to be relevant by the hearing officer, regardless of its admissibility in a court of law, and

(v) to submit a written statement at the close of the hearing.

The district court found that Good Samaritan's proceedings satisfied those requirements. We agree. Dr. Smith raises a number of "procedural defects," but we reject his claims. * * *

Dr. Smith raises numerous other alleged defects. Essentially, he wants peer review proceedings to look like regular trials in a court of law. Whether or not that is a good suggestion, § 11112(b) does not pose such a requirement. Rather, § 11112(b) lists certain procedures, which, if satisfied, guarantee a shield from liability. Good Samaritan's procedures either fit into the § 11112(b)(3) "safe harbor," or are so close to the "safe harbor" that no reasonable jury could find Dr. Smith rebutted the presumption that the procedures were adequate.

7. Only the hearing procedures of § 11112(b)(3)(C) are at issue. Dr. Smith conceded below that the JRC hearing was held before a panel of physicians who were not in economic competition with him. Thus, the requirement of § 11112(b)(3)(A) was satisfied. Also, there is no question that Good Samaritan gave Dr. Smith a written statement describing the basis for its decision upon completion of the hearings, satisfying § 11112(b)(3)(D).

D. Based on the foregoing, we hold that the district court did not err in granting summary judgment in favor of Good Samaritan. Dr. Smith failed to rebut the presumption that, after a reasonable effort to obtain the facts and an adequate hearing, Good Samaritan reasonably believed its action was warranted.

III

If a defendant "substantially prevails" and satisfies the immunity requirements of § 11112(a), the HCQIA provides:

> [T]he court shall, at the conclusion of the action, award to a substantially prevailing party defending against any such claim the cost of the suit attributable to such claim, including reasonable attorney's fee, if the claim, or the claimant's conduct during the litigation of the claim, was frivolous, unreasonable, without foundation, or in bad faith.

42 U.S.C. § 11113. The policy behind this provision is clear: Congress wanted to encourage professional peer review by limiting the threat of unreasonable litigation expenses.

* * *

We review the district court's decision to award attorneys' fees and costs under the HCQIA for abuse of discretion, and we affirm. [The court also upheld $2000 in sanctions against Dr. Smith's attorney under Rule 11 of the Federal Rules of Civil Procedure.]

NOTES AND QUESTIONS ON THE HEALTH CARE QUALITY IMPROVEMENT ACT

1. The HCQIA included the following congressional findings:

> (1) The increasing occurrence of medical malpractice and the need to improve the quality of medical care have become nationwide problems that warrant greater efforts than those that can be undertaken by any individual State.
>
> (2) There is a national need to restrict the ability of incompetent physicians to move from State to State without disclosure or discovery of the physician's previous damaging or incompetent performance. [In this connection, another subchapter of the law, 42 U.S.C. §§ 11131–37 (1994), created the National Practitioner Data Bank, to which hospitals, professional bodies, and malpractice insurers must report disciplinary actions taken and malpractice awards and settlements affecting individual physicians.]
>
> (3) This nationwide problem can be remedied through effective professional peer review.
>
> (4) The threat of private money damage liability under Federal laws, including treble damage liability under Federal antitrust law, unreasonably discourages physicians from participating in effective professional peer review.

(5) There is an overriding national need to provide incentive and protection for physicians engaging in effective professional peer review.

These findings were prompted in significant part by the outcome in *Patrick v. Burget*, noted supra, which resulted in a large judgment against (and the virtual destruction of) the Astoria Clinic, a reputable medical group.

Precisely how does the HCQIA solve the problems to which it was addressed? Does it amend or modify any substantive law (e.g., the antitrust laws)? What are the conditions that must be met to qualify for the act's protections?

2. Exactly how much protection (and what kind) does the act provide? The operative provision, § 11111(a), reads as follows:

> If a professional review action (as defined * * *) of a professional review body meets all the standards specified in section 11112(a) of this title [various entities and individuals participating in such action] shall not be liable in damages under any law of the United States or of any State (or political subdivision thereof) with respect to the action. The preceding sentence shall not apply to damages under any law of the United States or any State relating to the civil rights of any person or persons. * * *

Note that the act forecloses damage actions under state law of all kinds as well as under federal antitrust law.

Assume that a physician is terminated for an economic reason, such as overuse of the hospital in treating Medicare patients. Does the HCQIA protect the hospital against suit? The statute defines a "professional review action" as one "based on the competence or professional conduct of an individual physician (which conduct affects or could affect adversely the health or welfare of a patient or patients)." Id. § 11151(9).

3. The act's safe-harbor protections extend to entities other than hospitals and their medical staffs. Thus, a "professional review action" eligible for the act's immunities may be taken by an HMO, a group medical practice, or "a professional society * * * of physicians or other licensed health care practitioners that follows a formal peer review process for the purpose of furthering quality health care." On the other hand, a "professional review action" is defined to include only actions aimed at physicians. Thus, the act has no bearing on "any provision of Federal or State law, with respect to activities of professional review bodies regarding nurses, other licensed health care practitioners, or other health professionals who are not physicians." HCQIA § 11115(c).

4. Could a county medical society, citing quality-of-care concerns, invoke the act to protect its expulsion of a member for "unethically" cooperating with a health insurer's requirement that x-rays or other documentation be submitted in advance to justify a patient's elective hospitalization? Cf. the *Indiana Federation of Dentists* case reproduced in chapter 4(§B). To prevent serious antitrust violations from being sheltered, the act provides (§ 11151(9)) that immunity does not extend to actions disciplining a physician for certain affiliations or associations, for advertising, for price cutting or other competitive acts (such as submitting x-rays?), or for relationships with other types of health care personnel. In addition, the act affects only damage actions and does not "prevent the United States or any Attorney General of a State from bringing an action * * * where such an action is otherwise authorized." HCQIA § 11111(a)(D).

5. How safe is the "safe harbor" created by the act? See, e.g., Brown v. Presbyterian Healthcare Servs., 101 F.3d 1324 (10th Cir.) (holding peer reviewers' investigation inadequate to satisfy requirement for immunity and exposing hospital administrator to suit for defamation for report to Data Bank), cert. denied sub nom. Miller v. Brown, 117 S.Ct. 1461 (1997); Mathews v. Lancaster Gen. Hosp., 87 F.3d 624 (3d Cir.1996) (upholding HCQIA immunity partly on basis that hospital board, obtaining advice from independent physician reviewer as well as medical staff committee, acted independently); Bryan v. James E. Holmes Regional Med. Center, 33 F.3d 1318 (11th Cir.1994) (overturning $4.2 million award; holding that "HCQIA immunity is a question of law for the court to decide and may be resolved whenever the record in a particular case becomes sufficiently developed").

Would you advise a hospital to try to meet the act's extensive procedural requirements in order to qualify for such protection as it provides against antitrust suits? See Pugsley, Implementing the Health Care Quality Improvement Act, 23 J. Health & Hosp.L. 42 (1990) (concluding that hospital compliance with the act's procedural requirements should ensure immunity and payment of the costs of defense). What alternative does a hospital have? What reasons might a hospital have for considering any alternative?

6. Was this legislation necessary or desirable? Clearly, antitrust lawsuits had become a serious problem for hospitals and physicians. Is there in fact, however, a fundamental conflict between the policy of promoting competition and the need for effective peer review in hospitals? Or did the courts simply confuse effects on competitors with effects on competition? Although this was certainly part of the problem, the matter was somewhat more complex. Consider the following:

> One serious problem is that defense costs are high even if the suit is eventually won. Antitrust actions in this area have most often been handled in ways that allow many motions, extensive discovery, and lengthy trials. Most cases involve multiple parties, each of whom requires independent counsel. In addition, physicians' liability and defense costs may not be covered by their malpractice insurance. Because [physicians whose privileges are threatened] know of these burdens and may be tempted to bring suits for strategic or vexatious purposes, it may be irrelevant that peer reviewers' risk of actual liability in these cases is small. Recognition of the high cost of defending against these challenges could easily inhibit peer-review actions that would be in the best interest of consumers. * * * A strong argument could therefore be made for more extensive, even automatic,

fee shifting instead of the conditional fee shifting provided for in the HCQIA.

Although it may seem desirable to reduce the ability of marginal practitioners to retaliate for legitimate actions taken against them, the other horn of the legal system's dilemma is the risk that [anticompetitive] conduct will be inadequately policed if statutory immunities reduce the threat of suit. The HCQIA's solution to this dilemma is not to grant a complete exemption but to specify conditions that must be satisfied before the exemption may be invoked. Although hard to criticize substantively, this approach may [by adding new issues to be litigated] make litigation even more complicated and costly and may in addition do a disservice to antitrust law by implying that the courts employing traditional doctrine are incapable of reaching sound results in these cases on their own; indeed, it may confirm the misinterpretations of [antitrust law that are the real restraint on] useful collective action. Because antitrust doctrine itself remains unaffected by the new law, there is still a need for courts to shape that doctrine so that entities that merely provide information [and advice] to independent decision makers [or] that stand in a truly vertical relationship to the plaintiff can have antitrust claims against them summarily dismissed without reference to the HCQIA. It would be ironic indeed if the solution to the problem of vexatious and burdensome litigation against professional peer review were ultimately found in antitrust principles themselves and not in the legislation that Congress devised specifically for the purpose.

Havighurst, Professional Peer Review and the Antitrust Laws, 36 Case W.Res.L.Rev. 1118, 1164–65 (1986).

7. See generally Annot., Construction and Application of Health Care Quality Improvement Act of 1986, 121 A.L.R.Fed. 255 (1994 & Supp. 1995); Adler, Stalking the Rogue Physician: An Analysis of the Health Care Quality Improvement Act, 28 Am.Bus.L.J. 683 (1991).

Section D: Controlling Institutional Growth Through Central Planning and Regulation

Introduction to Certificate-of-Need Regulation

St. Joseph Hospital and Health Care Center v. Department of Health

Supreme Court of Washington, 1995
125 Wash. 2d 733, 887 P.2d 891 (en banc).

■ Johnson, Justice.

This case requires us to analyze the administrative procedure act, RCW 34.05, along with the certificate of need statute, RCW 70.38, to determine the scope of statutory standing. Specifically, we must decide whether a competing health care provider has standing to seek review of a Department of Health (Department) decision granting a certificate of need, and if so, whether the Department followed proper procedures in granting the certificate.

The trial court found St. Joseph Hospital and Health Care Center [St. Joseph] had standing to challenge an order of the Department granting a certificate of need to Medical Ambulatory Care, Inc. [Care, Inc.], for the establishment of an outpatient kidney dialysis center. Additionally, the trial court found the Department had not given St. Joseph's proper notice and had improperly determined the need for dialysis services. [The Department and Care, Inc., appealed.]

* * *

In 1979, the Legislature enacted RCW 70.38, the State Health Planning and Resources Development Act, creating the certificate of need (CN) program. The Legislature acted in response to the National Health Planning and Resources Development Act of 1974, Pub.L. No. 93–641, 88 Stat. 2225 (repealed 1986).

One purpose of the federal law was to control health care costs. Congress was concerned "that marketplace forces in this industry failed to produce efficient investment in facilities and to minimize the costs of health care". National Gerimedical Hosp. & Gerontology Ctr. v. Blue Cross of Kansas City, 452 U.S. 378, 386 (1981). Congress endeavored to control costs by encouraging state and local health planning. It offered grants to state agencies provided the agencies met certain standards and performed certain functions. Among the specified functions was the administration of a CN program.

The CN program seeks to control costs by ensuring better utilization of existing institutional health services and major medical equipment. Those health care providers wishing to establish or expand facilities or acquire certain types of equipment are required to obtain a CN, which is a nonexclusive license.

* * *

[Care, Inc.], a wholly owned subsidiary of National Medical Enterprises, Inc., is a for-profit company headquartered in downtown Tacoma. On November 22, 1991, Care, Inc. filed a CN application for a 17–station outpatient kidney dialysis center to be located in the Lakewood area south of Tacoma. At the time of its application for a CN, Care, Inc. operated 35 Medicare certified centers in seven states, providing kidney dialysis services.

[In acknowledging receipt of Care, Inc.'s application, the] Department indicated its review criteria included [its published] general criteria for judging financial feasibility, structure and process of care, and cost containment. Only former WAC [Washington Administrative Code] 246–310–280 dealt specifically with kidney dialysis. The WAC detailed a 7–step methodology for determining the number of dialysis stations necessary for a given health service area.

* * * Because changes [to the WAC] were being considered, Care, Inc. sought additional written assurances that WAC 246–310–280 would be used to evaluate their proposal rather than any proposed changes. There is no response to Care, Inc.'s request in the administrative record.

Following Care, Inc.'s application for a CN, the Department notified "affected persons" as defined in WAC 246–310–010(2), including [St. Joseph], of their right to request a public hearing on the application. On January 13, 1992, St. Joseph requested a hearing[, following which the CN was denied on the ground that "there was not a need for additional stations based on actual area utilization rates rather than the formula in former WAC 246–310–280." The applicant's appeal was resolved by a stipulation of the Department and Care, Inc., under which the application was remanded for reconsideration. Without notifying St. Joseph, the Department changed its decision, indicating its willingness to issue a CN subject to certain conditions. The Department then denied a request by St. Joseph for reconsideration as neither "timely nor appropriate." St. Joseph petitioned for judicial review of the administrative action, and the Department moved to dismiss the petition on the ground St. Joseph lacked standing. The court denied the motion and remanded the matter to the Department for further proceedings in which St. Joseph would have an opportunity to be heard. This order was then appealed to the supreme court.]

* * *

The administrative procedure act, RCW 34.05, governs proceedings involving the issuance of a CN. Under RCW 34.05.530, only a person who is "aggrieved or adversely affected" by an agency action has standing to obtain judicial review of the action. To qualify as "aggrieved or adversely affected", a person must satisfy three conditions:

(1) The agency action has prejudiced or is likely to prejudice that person;

(2) That person's asserted interests are among those that the agency was required to consider when it engaged in the agency action challenged; and

(3) A judgment in favor of that person would substantially eliminate or redress the prejudice to that person caused or likely to be caused by the agency action.

These statutory conditions are drawn from federal case law. See Association of Data Processing Serv. Orgs., Inc., v. Camp, 397 U.S. 150, 153 (1970). The first and third conditions are often referred to as the injury-in-fact requirement. Appellants Care, Inc. and the Department have asked the court to assume for purposes of appeal these conditions are met.

Therefore, we look only at the second condition. We have not previously considered the second prong of the statutory standing test, which was enacted in 1988. The Legislature appears to have adopted this "zone of interest" test from the U.S. Supreme Court's decision in [the *Association of Data Processing* case]. The zone of interest test addresses the concern that mere injury-in-fact is not necessarily enough to confer standing because so many persons are potentially "aggrieved" by agency action. The test focuses on whether the Legislature intended the agency to protect the party's interests when taking the action at issue.

This case requires us to answer the question of whether the Legislature intended to protect the interests of competing health care providers when they enacted the certificate of need statute. The parties differ in their interpretations of the legislative purpose of the statute. The Department and Care, Inc. argue the Legislature intended the focus of the CN process to be on the public's interests, not the interests of providers. They point to RCW 70.38.015:

> It is declared to be the public policy of this state:
>
> (1) That health planning to promote, maintain, and assure the health of all citizens in the state, to provide accessible health services, health manpower, health facilities, and other resources while controlling excessive increases in costs, and to recognize prevention as a high priority in health programs, is essential to the health, safety, and welfare of the people of the state.... Involvement in health planning from both consumers and providers throughout the state should be encouraged;
>
> (2) That the development of health services and resources, including the construction, modernization, and conversion of health facilities, should be accomplished in a planned, orderly fashion, consistent with identified priorities and without unnecessary duplication or fragmentation;
>
> . . .
>
> (4) That the development of nonregulatory approaches to health care cost containment should be considered, including the strengthening of price competition; and
>
> (5) That health planning should be concerned with public health and health care financing, access, and quality, recognizing their close interrelationship and emphasizing cost control of health services, including cost-effectiveness and cost-benefit analysis.

Appellants claim neither this language nor any other language within RCW 70.38 even suggests economic or competitive interests of existing providers are to be considered in making certificate of need decisions.

Respondent St. Joseph argues this same language supports its position. It claims the focus on cost control through regulation of competition requires its economic interests be considered. St. Joseph also points to former RCW 70.38.115(2), which establishes criteria for the examination of CN applications:

> (2) Criteria for the review of [CN] applications ... shall include ...
>
> . . .

(b) The need that the population served or to be served by such services has for such services;

(c) The availability of less costly or more effective alternative methods of providing such services;

(d) The financial feasibility and the probable impact of the proposal on the cost of and charges for providing health services in the community to be served....

St. Joseph argues this analysis of need, costs, and financial feasibility necessarily involves assessing a proposed project's impact on existing providers.

We find St. Joseph's interpretation of legislative intent more persuasive. While the Legislature clearly wanted to control health care costs to the public, equally clear is its intention to accomplish that control by limiting competition within the health care industry. The U.S. Congress and our Legislature made the judgment that competition had a tendency to drive health care costs up rather than down and government therefore needed to restrain marketplace forces. The means and end here are inextricably tied. Because the Legislature intended to regulate competition as well as control costs, we hold competing service providers to be within the statutory zone of interest.

The Supreme Court of Kentucky reached the same conclusion in a similar case. See Humana of Kentucky, Inc. v. NKC Hosps., Inc., 751 S.W.2d 369 (Ky.1988). In Humana, a competing provider of pediatric cardiac services was held to have standing to challenge a decision by the certificate of need authority that another provider's expansion did not require a certificate of need. The court ruled the statutory scheme protected existing facilities from competition unless a need for additional services could be demonstrated in an administrative hearing subject to the review process. The court reasoned competitors' interests were parallel to the public's:

> The hospital is protected so it can maintain a quality, cost effective program. The hospital has the information available to assess the impact of a new program, and if it has no standing to challenge the agency's actions as arbitrary, as a practical matter no one will.

We agree with the Kentucky court. While an applicant who is denied a CN has both a motive and a statutory right to seek review of the Department's determination, no comparable motivation or statutory authority to seek review exists when the Department grants a CN. Practically, this review can only be achieved if competitors have standing.

[The court then reviewed the Department's action, holding that, under the state administrative procedure act, St. Joseph should have been given notice of the reopening of the CN proceeding pursuant to the stipulation resolving the earlier appeal. It refused to rule on St. Joseph's claim that the administrative rule dealing with dialysis, WAC 246–310–280, was outdated and therefore invalid as a basis for granting the CN to Care, Inc.]

NOTES ON THE HISTORY OF HEALTH PLANNING AND CERTIFICATE–OF–NEED REGULATION

1. *A Short History of Health Planning.* As early as the 1930s, the notion of voluntary "health planning" took root in some communities, where hospital planning councils composed of community leaders, including hospital trustees, undertook to coordinate the raising and allocation of community or charitable funds for hospital construction and modernization. Such efforts were generally approved because they reduced competition for scarce philanthropic and other resources and permitted service responsibilities to be allocated by agreement rather than left to the unmanaged marketplace. (Can health planning, as described here, be reconciled with antitrust law, as applied today? A note later in this chapter explores aspects of this question.)

The federal government gave new impetus to health planning in the Hill–Burton program (the 1946 Hospital Survey and Construction Act), which offered matching grants for the construction of hospitals and public health centers to states that had an approved planning apparatus to determine where needs existed. In the 1960s, a series of federal laws encouraged what came to be called "comprehensive" health planning, which states were to foster in order to receive and to allocate federal funds for a variety of uses. The idea of areawide planning for all health services appeared most prominently in the Community Health Planning Amendments of 1966, which assigned heavy responsibilities for a wide range of activities to a panoply of state and private nonprofit agencies. Although these programs were chronically underfunded, the concept had widespread support as a way of curbing the expense of unbridled (nonprice) competition in health care while also heading off price controls or a public takeover of hospitals. See generally Institute of Medicine, Health Planning in the United States (1980).

2. *The CON Movement.* Whereas health planning originally focused on the allocation of private gifts and public subsidies to hospitals and other health care institutions, the expansion of health insurance in the 1960s gave hospitals an infusion of discretionary resources that could be invested without consulting the health planners. As a result, some planners and others concerned about the unruliness of the emerging system began to yearn for a regulatory authority that could direct where hospitals could and could not make investments. To be sure, some planners, preferring to operate in their traditional nonadversarial manner, dissented from the movement to assign them a regulatory role. Nevertheless, the desire for "health planning with teeth" eventually gave rise to the movement for certificate-of need (CON) regulation.

Beginning with New York in 1964, a number of states moved to institute planning-oriented CON controls over new entry and new capital investments in health care. Thus, about half the states already had such laws in place in 1974, when Congress enacted the National Health Planning and Resources Development Act (commonly known as Public Law 93–641). This law, following on the heels of 1972 legislation that introduced (in section 1122 of the Social Security Act) a method for controlling Medicare reimbursement of expenditures for "unneeded" capital investment, required all states, as a condition of receiving funds under the Public Health Service Act, to put in place a highly specified program of health planning and CON regulation. See North Carolina ex rel. Morrow v. Califano, 445 F.Supp. 532 (E.D.N.C.1977), affirmed mem., 435 U.S. 962 (1978) (upholding constitutionality of federal compulsion as a use of the federal spending power). The national experiment with health planning and CON regulation dominated national and local health policy throughout the 1970s.

3. *Public Law 93–641.* Under the 1974 Act, the states were required not only to pass a CON law by 1980 but also to create a total of 213 consumer-controlled local "health systems agencies" (HSAs) and, in each state, a "statewide health coordinating council" (SHCC) and a "state health planning and development agency" (SHPDA) empowered to regulate expansion and capital expenditures by hospitals and other health care facilities. Under this law, the U.S. sought to achieve nationwide control of all capital expenditures over $150,000 (increased in the early 1980's to $600,000) by hospitals, nursing homes, kidney treatment centers, and ambulatory surgical centers, all changes in the number of beds, and all new health services these providers might introduce. Applications were to be reviewed, first, by the local planning bodies and then approved or disapproved by the SHPDA, the CON agency. States were to generate written comprehensive health plans and to take steps to see that all covered investments and construction projects conformed thereto.

The 1974 legislation was enacted at a time when some kind of national health insurance seemed inevitable, awaiting only the development of an effective infrastructure of cost-containment mechanisms. Thus, local health planning agencies and state regulatory programs created under Public Law 93–641 were expected to be cornerstones of the health care system of the future. In particular, the provisions governing HSAs represented a major experiment with consumer participation in the governance of the health care system. Indeed, the law was in many ways a search for a way of democratizing public control and weakening the power of providers, without overtly "socializing" medicine.

The key provisions of Public Law 93–641 aimed at involving consumers in the health planning effort were those mandating that HSA governing boards have a consumer majority (together with closely specified numbers and types of health care providers and public officials) and that the consumer membership be "broadly representative" of the population of the health service area (in terms of geography and social, economic, linguistic, and racial characteristics) and also of major purchasers of care (including labor unions). Much of the flavor of the policy and practical issues raised by these requirements can be gained by asking whether Congress used the term *representative* in a political or merely a statistical sense. Cf. Texas Acorn v. Texas Area 5 Health Systems Agency, Inc., 559 F.2d 1019, 1024 (5th Cir.1977) (rejecting the notions that HSA membership must "conform directly to the demographic breakdown of the area population" and that a member "must have an income equal to that of the constituency he or she represents").

HSAs were apparently constituted in an effort to structure decision-making in accordance with the theory of "interest-group liberalism," which contemplates that acceptable (efficient?) outcomes will emerge from forcing the affected interests to fight out their differences in a political arena. Political scientist Lawrence D. Brown has suggested, however, that the HSA effort lacked both a clear theoretical basis and practical merit. Brown, Some Structural Issues in the Health Planning Program, in 2 Health Planning in the United States: Selected Policy Issues 1, 20–28 (Institute of Medicine, National Academy of Sciences, 1981). He has described and commented upon the reality of local health planning as follows (id. at 24–25):

> Vast organizational anguish tends to accompany a "no" decision by an HSA on a question of genuine interest to a local health care institution. The many hours of negotiation; the charges of lay ignorance on one side and of provider dominance on another; the endless fiddling with formulas and ratios no one understands; the contrived public hearings at which a hospital displays its audiovisual aids to testify to the urgent needs of a venerated community institution and "the community" in attendance (three-fourths of it employed by or related to employees of the hospital) rises in long-winded support; the 4–3 vote finally taken at 1 a.m. in committee; the endless buttonholing and hand holding; the threat of appeal and legal redress; all of this, inherent in self-regulating localism, raises the personal and organizational costs of nay-saying very high. * * *
>
> Finally, consumers determined to fight for such cost containing measures as denied expansion or modernization projects, or for mergers or closures, may find that their success in persuading the HSA board carries little weight in the larger community. Tough HSA recommendations often come under sharp fire at public meetings from contingents of "average citizens," some speaking out spontaneously, others orchestrated by providers, and HSAs often back down under such fire. In short, cost-conscious consumer representatives may find themselves at odds with the sentiments of community participants—a predicament to which enthusiasts of "greater consumer representation and participation" have given too little thought.

Having questioned whether participatory health planning can impose spending discipline on a health care system with openended financing, Professor Brown went on to embrace central planning as a mechanism for allocating a centrally fixed budget for health services and for bargaining with providers in that context. As to the auspices of such planning, however, he also observed that "the community [already] has 'representatives'—elected officials—and it may be unwise to forget them or usurp their roles or complicate their lives without first giving careful attention to the character of the polyarchy one creates by devising such supplementary—or supplanting—structures as the HSAs."

Public Law 93–641 was somewhat schizophrenic in its approach to planning, sometimes emphasizing a technocratic approach calling for a high level of technical expertise in agency staffs and highly specified health systems plans and at other times emphasizing an interest-group bargaining approach to decision making. For Professor Brown's comments on "scientifically grounded planning," see id. at 35–37 (concluding, "Science will no more generate a planned solution than the market will yield an unplanned one."). See also Kansas Dep't of Health and Environment v. Banks, 630 P.2d 1131, 1133 (Kan.1981) (referring to the "inherently inexact science of determining how society's scarce health care resources might best be allocated").

4. *The 1979 Amendment of Public Law 93–641.* Congress's enthusiasm for regulating the health care sector began to wane in the late 1970s, reflecting both political trends and pragmatic assessments of regulation's achievements both in health care and in other regulated industries, most notably in transportation. The watershed year was 1979. In that year, Congress defeated the Carter administration's proposal to cap hospital revenues and amended Public Law 93–641 by adding provisions designed to make health planning-cum-regulation more sensitive to the possibilities and benefits of competition in health care. Health Planning and Resources Development Amendments of 1979, Pub. L. No. 96–79, 93 Stat. 592 (1979).

Because the Washington statute applied in the *St. Joseph Hospital* case was enacted prior to the 1979 federal legislation, the court's discussion reflects only federal policy circa 1974. This policy had changed significantly by 1979. Thus, in reporting the 1979 health planning amendments, the same Senate committee that in 1974 had said that "the health care industry does not respond to classic marketplace forces" revised its diagnosis to state that the industry "has not to date responded" to such forces. S.Rep. No. 96–96, 96th Cong., 1st Sess. 53 (1979). A further indication of the committee's perception that market forces might play a useful role after all was its recommendation that health planners and regulators "should encourage competitive forces * * * wherever competition and consumer choice can constructively serve to advance the purposes of quality assurance and cost effectiveness." Id. The 1979 amendments themselves traced the health sector's problems to "the *prevailing* methods of paying for health services," thus revealing a glimmer of congressional hope that payment methods might change and that cost problems could ultimately be resolved by nonregulatory means. It is notable that the trend away from regulation was well under way before the Reagan administration, with its deregulation agenda, took office in 1981.

It is notable that the state legislation in *St. Joseph* itself stressed the need to develop "nonregulatory approaches to health care cost containment * * *, including the strengthening of price competition." This language is a revision of language inserted in 1980 to set forth essentially the same policy objective as was added to the federal statute in 1979—namely "the strengthening of competitive forces in the health services industry, wherever competition and consumer choice can constructively serve to advance the purposes of quality assurance, cost-effectiveness, and access." Wash. Rev. Code Ann. § 70.38.015 (West 1992 & Supp. 1997) The significance of the 1979 federal amendments and their impact on state CON statutes are explored further in connection with the *Oregon Eye Associates* case, reproduced later in this section.

5. *Repeal of Public Law 93–641.* In the 1980s, a combination of factors led first to cutbacks of federal subsidies for state and local health planning and deferral of the deadline for state compliance with Public Law 93–641 and finally to outright repeal of the 1974 legislation in 1986. Act of Nov. 14, 1986, Pub. L. No. 99–660 §§ 701–816, 100 Stat. 3743, 3799–3802 (1986). This outcome reflected disappointment with the results of the planning effort, new views of federal-state relations, and second (more conservative) thoughts about the federal government's role in financing and regulating health care. President Reagan stated as follows in signing the repeal legislation:

> These authorities, while perhaps well-intentioned when they were enacted in the 1970s, have only served to insert the Federal government into a process that is best reserved to the marketplace. Health planning has proved to be a process that was costly to the Federal government, in the last analysis without benefit, and even detrimental to the rational allocation of economic resources for health care.

With the repeal of Public Law 93–641, CON regulation ceased to be a topic for public debate. Students of health care law and policy should nevertheless be aware of the federal government's failed experiment with central planning as a mechanism for controlling the health care industry's development. Moreover, it turns out, ironically, that CON regulation persists in many states despite the removal of the federal compulsion to maintain it.

6. *CON Regulation in the 1980s and 1990s.* Even though repeal of Public Law 93–641 brought to an end an important chapter in the history of federal involvement with the health care industry, only a minority of states (e.g., Ariz., Calif., Colo., Idaho, Ind., Kan., Minn., N. Dakota, N. Mex., Ohio, Tex., Utah, Wis., and Wyo.) have repealed all or major portions of their CON laws. Thus, many of the state certificate-of-need (CON) laws that were originally enacted or shaped under the federal mandate remain on the books today. It is notable that Congress, having compelled the states to adopt these laws, did not compel their repeal when it later changed its mind about their desirability.

Although there were a number of repeals following the repeal of Public Law 93–641, North Dakota, in 1995, became the first state in the 1990's to entirely terminate CON regulation. N.D. Cent. Code § 23–17.2 (1991), *repealed by* S.L. 1995, ch. 254, § 6 (Supp. 1995). During the same year, Ohio and Wisconsin enacted laws removing CON requirements from hospitals and other acute care facilities. Ohio's legislation set in motion a two-year plan to replace CON regulation with quality and safety standards. Ohio Rev. Code Ann. §§ 3702.511, 3702.57 (Banks–Baldwin 1995 and Supp. 1997). Proposed legislation deregulating entry and investment in health care became a hot topic in a number of other states during the mid–1990's (e.g., N.J., Pa., R.I., Conn.). See generally Leeds, Certificate of Need: Up For Revision, Health Systems Rev., Jan.-Feb. 1996, p. 26.

Numerous amendments have occurred in state CON laws. Many states have raised their statutory threshold for covered capital investments to the $1–2 million range. E.g., Fla. Stat. Ann. § 381.706(1)(c) (West Supp. 1991); N.H. Rev. Stat. Ann. § 151–C:5 (1990); Tenn. Code Ann. § 68–11–106(2) (Supp. 1991). Indeed, Massachusetts raised its threshold for acute care hospitals to seven million dollars. Mass. Gen. Laws Ann. ch. 111, § 25B (Supp. 1991). Some states have imposed outright moratoria on certain types of construction, however. E.g., Ark. Stat. Ann. § 20–8–106(a)(1) (Supp. 1990). Most states, besides raising monetary thresholds, have altered the mix of facilities to which CON requirements apply. Some limit CON requirements to very high-cost or cutting-edge facilities, while a few states have added CON requirements for outpatient, intermediate care, and substance abuse facilities, to which the original federal law did not apply.

The purpose of raising regulatory thresholds is apparently to focus regulatory efforts on truly consequential projects and to exclude review of modifications and renovations of existing facilities. Do you see any problems? Will providers simply invest in more but smaller projects? Salkever and Bice found that, although some early CON efforts controlled the hospital bed supply, there was no saving in aggregate capital expenditures—perhaps because of increased investments of types not subject to regulatory control. D. Salkever & T. Bice, Hospital Certificate–of–Need Controls 21–22, 35–51 (1979). Is the net effect of raised thresholds likely to be that existing providers may grow incrementally but new providers cannot enter the market?

Because hospitals' capital investments were closely regulated under the original legislation, some major medical equipment was installed in physicians' offices, thus escaping regulatory control. In order to plug this leak in the regulatory dike, federal law was amended to require the states to regulate purchases of such equipment (above a specified dollar threshold) where it was to be used to treat inpatients. Current state requirements vary with respect to physician-owned equipment and may be more or less extensive than the now-repealed federal requirement. Such laws have powerful, sometimes anomalous, effects on the location and ownership of particular facilities. See, e.g., Clifton Springs Sanitarium Co., Inc. v. Axelrod, 115 A.D.2d 949, (N.Y.App.Div.1985) (CAT scanner owned by staff radiologist and located in trailer eight feet from hospital held not subject to CON requirement). Consider why regulation did not cover physician practices more extensively. Are physician services properly distributed by market forces? Did the rationale for CON regulation (examined below) apply?

Like the Washington statute in the *St. Joseph* case, and the Oregon statute in the *OEA* case reproduced later in this section, CON laws that were originally enacted or shaped under the federal mandate are best understood in light of their legal and historical roots. Perpetuating the earlier tradition of planning-cum-regulation, the CON laws that remain on the books today stand in stark contrast to the now-dominant policy of relying on competitive markets to allocate resources to health care. For a thorough review of the history and status of federal and state law in this area just prior to the repeal of Public Law 93–641 in 1986, see Simpson, Full Circle: The Return of Certificate of Need Regulation of Health Facilities to State Control, 19 Ind.L.Rev. 1025 (1986) (hereinafter cited as Simpson).

NOTES AND QUESTIONS ON THE POLICY AND POLITICS OF CERTIFICATE-OF-NEED REGULATION

1. What concerns prompted enactment of laws requiring private interests to obtain state approval before making certain capital investments in health facilities or offering certain new health services? This requirement is similar to requirements for "certificates of public convenience and necessity" that are widely imposed on public utilities. Are hospitals and other health care providers public utilities? Why might they be treated as such?

2. *The Original Rationale for Entry and Investment Controls.* The predominant policy rationale for introducing entry and investment controls in health care was that "the health care industry does not respond to classic marketplace forces." S.Rep. No. 93–1285, 93d Cong., 2d Sess. (1974). This statement reflected the then-conventional view that public and private health care financing arrangements inevitably induce excessive capital investment, inefficient duplication of facilities and services, and the provision of nonessential care. Indeed, according to a principle known as "Roemer's law," the supply of hospital beds was deemed to be the main determinant of hospital use, far surpassing factors related to patients' health. Because of this belief that "supply creates its own demand" and that provider preferences rather than cost-conscious consumer choices drive the system, regulation constraining provider discretion was deemed necessary if costs were to be contained. In addition to being supported by this cost-containment rationale, CON laws were sometimes advocated as a way of improving quality—by promoting the development of a few specialized centers. See, e.g., Chassin, Assessing Strategies for Quality Improvement, Health Affs., May–June 1997, p. 151, 154–55 (observing correlation between improved cardiac surgery survival rates and N.Y. regulations limiting number of hospitals permitted to perform cardiac procedures). CON legislation was also thought to be helpful in ensuring access—both by better locating facilities and by preventing "cream-skimming" by new entrants from eroding the ability of existing hospitals to cross-subsidize indigent care.

The basic economic rationale for CON regulation has been discussed as follows:

> Certificate-of-need laws were conceived to restrain the perceived impulse of health care institutions of all kinds to overinvest in unneeded facilities and to provide unneeded services. Because of the preva-

lence of largely unquestioning third-party payment, the competitive market provides an inadequate deterrent to the creation of overcapacity, making direct public control arguably necessary. * * *

* * * However, third-party payment alone is not a sufficient explanation for regulation. Instead, the justification for intervention is provided by the common practice of paying on the basis of retrospective cost reimbursement (or on some other cost-related basis, including reimbursement of patients for bills incurred) and the payers' extreme deference toward physician decisions concerning utilization of services. These market characteristics have frequently made it possible for institutional providers to add facilities and raise costs without significant risk that the facilities will not be used or that revenue from their use will fail to cover costs (as they will in competitive markets with excess capacity). Furthermore, nonprofit firms, such as predominate in the health sector, have peculiar incentives inclining them toward growth as a means of gratifying their managers and of reinvesting profits and other funds that, under the restrictions usually applicable to nonprofit corporations, are neither distributable as dividends nor applicable to non-health-related activities. A nonprofit monopoly also tends to grow by plowing its excess earnings into the provision of nonremunerative services, including not only indigent care but also marginally productive undertakings, thereby assuming burdens that make it vulnerable to "cream skimming" by new and possibly less efficient competitors. Moreover, nonprofit firms are relatively slow to leave an overcrowded market because their managers have an incentive to stay in business even if salvageable capital is being eroded. Finally, nonprice competition, focused on attracting both doctors and insured patients, is also a force compelling investments that would otherwise not be made.

The foregoing arguments for regulation of entry are somewhat stronger than the usual arguments for [controls on entry] into potentially competitive industries [e.g., transportation]. This does not mean, however, that certificate-of-need laws are necessarily the best answer that public policy might find to deal with the problems presented. That depends on how well they work in practice as well as on how well alternative approaches would work. In addition to the empirical question about whether this form of regulation works well or poorly or not at all, a serious question exists as to whether this is theoretically the soundest approach that might be taken.

C. Havighurst, Deregulating the Health Care Industry 54–55 (1982).

What were the original causes of the excess capacity in the hospital industry that CON laws were intended to prevent? What was the contribution of early government-sponsored central planning (e.g., the Hill–Burton program)? How did the object of central planning change over time? Do you see any parallels to the government policy in the 1960s and 1970s of subsidizing medical education to increase the supply of physicians, thereby improving the chances that unmet needs would be met? Hospital occupancy rates have fallen dramatically in recent years, so that there is greater excess capacity than ever before. (What, incidentally, does this development say about "Roemer's law"?) This development has in turn caused unprecedented price competition among hospitals. What role have regulation and central planning played in these developments and in the development of a "physician glut," which has also contributed to the emergence of price competition? Do you see any ironies here?

3. *The Politics and Effectiveness of CON Regulation.* CON laws have been criticized on the basis that they were poorly designed to address to cost problem effectively:

> [CON] initiatives were unlikely to succeed * * * because they were based upon both a basic misconception of the cost problem and an overestimate of government's political ability to contest health care spending decisions taken in the private sector. Indeed, CON regulation was promoted by some industry interests precisely because it was limited to addressing certain symptoms of the cost problem and was more likely, because of the political context, to legitimize than to prevent high levels of health care spending.[34] Although the planning agencies that were expected to rationalize the system included consumers, few of the participants in the planning effort had any incentive to work for cost containment. Because consumer representatives were usually more interested in ensuring availability of services than in cost control, they could usually be co-opted or circumvented. Thus, there was no more than a minor shift in the locus of decision-making authority and no challenge at all to the dominant conception of a unitary, largely self-regulated system financed by payers committed to reimbursing all but demonstrably unreasonable costs. Because they did not seek to alter the monolithic character of the industry or to change payment ground rules, CON controls can be viewed in retrospect as highly conservative measures.[35]
>
> Several specific misconceptions of the cost problem were reflected in CON laws. Among other things, they neglected the likelihood that, as long as open-ended revenue sources were available to be exploited, costs incurred by providers and patients would, like a partially constrained balloon, simply expand in unregulated directions. Experience under these regulatory programs suggested that any savings achieved in capital and related costs were indeed offset by increases in labor costs and in capital spending that regulation did not reach.[36] Moreover, CON laws * * * were based upon the assumption that the cost prob-

34. See generally Payton & Powsner, Regulation through the Looking Glass: Hospitals, Blue Cross, and Certificate–of–Need, 79 Mich.L.Rev. 203 (1980).

35. They were so characterized in Havighurst, Regulation of Health Facilities and Services By "Certificate of Need," 59 Va. L.Rev. 1143, 1156 (1973).

36. See, e.g., D. Salkever & T. Bice, Hospital Certificate-of-Need Controls (1979); Sloan & Steinwald, Effects of Regulation on Hospital Costs and Input Use, 23 J.L. & Econ. 81 (1980). See also C. Havighurst, Deregulating the Health Care Industry 53–76 (1982).

lem is one of spending on facilities and services that are essentially worthless, both to society and to the patients being treated. Unfortunately, although some useless, "flat of the curve" spending does occur, the ultimate problem almost certainly lies in spending on services that, though arguably beneficial, are not enough so—given the small probability or slight value of the health benefits sought or the existence of offsetting risks—to justify the outlay.

* * * CON laws * * * also proceeded on the unexamined assumption that publicly designated experts could reliably determine on a case-by-case basis how society should spend its resources on health care services and on the additional assumption that they could make their official judgments stick. Unfortunately, policy makers underestimated the ability of providers to rationalize high levels of spending, either by ignoring the trade-off between benefits and costs or by exaggerating the likelihood or value of the health benefits to be obtained. Faced with professional justifications for particular spending, politically accountable health planners and regulators found it difficult to deprive patients of allegedly obtainable benefits or to veto any desirable capital project that was not clearly duplicative of existing facilities. In a political world where professing commitment to unstinting provision of health services is a useful way of demonstrating compassion, it is difficult for publicly accountable decision makers to challenge authoritative professional judgments and to insist upon close comparisons of benefits and costs.

Thus, even when government tried to impose specific checks on the industry's spending impulses, it found that it was politically impossible to make much difference. Professional advocacy for patient interests was too effective to resist in most close cases. Also, there was no room at all to challenge a professional consensus where it existed. Not only were the potential cost savings that might have helped offset the weight of industry opinion effectively hidden by the financing system, but there were severe questions about the basic legitimacy of economizing at the expense of a few sick persons for the benefit of the public treasury or an insurer's deep pocket. In short, government found it virtually impossible to assume decision-making responsibilities that had previously been entrusted to professional decision makers.

Havighurst, The Changing Locus of Decision Making in the Health Care Sector, 11 J.Health Pol., Pol'y & L. 697, 708–10 (1986). For additional insights into the politics of CON, see D. Altman, R. Greene & H. Sapolsky, Health Planning and Regulation: The Decision–Making Process (1981); Brown, Some Structural Issues in the Health Planning Program, in 2 Health Planning in the United States: Selected Policy Issues 1, 20–28 (Institute of Medicine, National Academy of Sciences, 1981).

4. *Measuring the Effects of CON Regulation.* Most empirical studies by economists have demonstrated little or no impact of CON regulation in slowing the growth of health care costs. See references in note 36 in the previously quoted source; see also P. Joskow, Controlling Hospital Costs

76–99, 138–68 (1981); Lanning et al., Endogenous Hospital Regulation and Its Effects on Hospital and Non–Hospital Expenditures, 3 J. Reg. Econ. 137 (1991) (concluding, in study of state rate-setting regulation, that CON regulation increases long-run hospital expenditures by 20.6%); Sloan, Containing Health Expenditures: Lessons Learned from Certificate of Need Programs, in Cost, Quality, and Access in Health Care: New Roles for Health Planning in a Competitive Environment, 44, 58–59 (F. Sloan et al. eds., 1988) (concluding that CON laws had "no influence on overall growth of expenditures for hospital care per capita"). But see Harrington et al., The Effect of Certificate of Need and Moratoria Policy on Change in Nursing Home Beds in the United States, 35 Med. Care 574 (1997) (finding effectiveness in constraining bed supply in nursing homes).

CON regulation has its defenders, of course:

> Those who support health planning and certificate-of-need requirements * * * suggest that the experience of the 1970s and early 1980s did not reflect the full potential for health planning and CON as a strategy for cost containment. They argue that CON was applied in most states in an erratic and politically motivated process that resulted in decisions about capital proposals that were not consistent with cost-conscious expansion of health facilities and orderly adoption of new technologies. In a few states where CON has been linked to hospital rate-setting and to statewide (rather than local area) health planning, proponents of CON suggest it has been much more effective in reducing growth in health care costs.

Congressional Budget Office, Rising Health Care Costs: Causes, Implications, and Strategies 48–49 (April 1991). Planner-regulators often point to the applications they turn down, arguing that the public would have had to pay for these costly projects if they had not been rejected. See, e.g., B. Lefkowitz, Health Planning: Lessons for the Future 34–38 (1983) (relying on studies of denial rates rather than cost trends and concluding that, although CON programs may have shown poor results in their early years, mature programs are more effective). (What are the possible pitfalls of denial-counting as a measure of regulatory success? Can you see how costs might rise an equal amount even if the regulators reject numerous applications?) Planners also claim that many proposals are modified substantially before they are approved, thus saving further costs. (Is it possible that applicants submit unrealistic proposals, anticipating a regulatory compromise?)

Perhaps the best evidence that CON is effective, at least in its primary mission of controlling capital spending, is the increase in new construction in several of the states that have lifted all controls. See Simpson, supra, at 1079–82. (This development will be evaluated at the conclusion of this section.) Even if CON regulation had some demonstrable cost-containment effects, however, one might still ask whether, if CON laws had not been in place, public and private financing programs might have evolved more quickly to introduce defenses against paying for unused facilities and to seize opportunities to purchase services cheaply in overstocked markets.

Finally, the proper comparison may not be between experience under a CON program and the probable consequences of a do-nothing state policy. For example, aggressive market reform efforts taken at the time CON laws were adopted might have yielded benefits greater than any associated with CON.

5. Of course, it can be argued that CON laws are supportable for reasons other than cost containment. What are those reasons? See Simpson, supra, at 1028–33. See also Campbell & Fournier, Certificate-of-Need Regulation and Indigent Hospital Care, 18 J. Health Pol., Pol'y & L. 905 (1993); Hackey, New Wine in Old Bottles: Certificate of Need Enters the 1990s, id. at 928. Be prepared, after studying the remainder of this section, to recommend whether CON statutes should be repealed.

NOTES AND QUESTIONS ON THE ROLE OF INCUMBENT COMPETITORS IN CERTIFICATE-OF-NEED PROCEEDINGS

1. *The Handling of Competing Applications.* In Huron Valley Hosp., Inc. v. Michigan State Health Facilities Comm'n, 312 N.W.2d 422 (Mich.App. 1981), a CON had been granted to an existing hospital desiring to replace its antiquated facility with a new one. Huron, a competing applicant, was a newly formed nonprofit corporation that likewise sought authority to build a new hospital in the area. The court found that the CON had been awarded under a criterion that gave "the highest priority * * * to existing facilities seeking a certificate of need to modernize or correct licensing deficiencies." Because this criterion had never been published as required by the state administrative procedure act, the courts invalidated the grant. The court rejected the claim that "a preference for existing facilities is inherent in the statute." Also in *Huron*, the agency had approved the incumbent institution's application before finally ruling on Huron's application, which had been filed first. The court found that Huron's application was not considered until after the decision had already been made to grant the incumbent's application. The court found a violation of due process, relying on the Supreme Court's decision in Ashbacker Radio Corp. v. FCC, 326 U.S. 327 (1945) (holding that "where two bona fide applications are mutually exclusive the grant of one without a hearing to both deprives the loser of the opportunity which Congress chose to give him"). The *Huron* case illustrates both the application of administrative law principles to CON regulation and a common tendency of CON regulators to accommodate existing providers and resist entry by new interests.

To solve the *Ashbacker* problem and introduce a kind of competition, most state CON programs have adopted the practice of "batching" competing proposals every three to six months for comparative evaluation. Should all applications stand on an equal footing in such a proceeding? Or should some priority be given to the first applicant to identify an existing need? (Consider, for example, the incentive effects of the following recommendation by a planning agency in rejecting an application because incumbent providers had moved to meet the identified need: "That the physician applicants be praised for creating pressures which encouraged Las Vegas area hospitals to upgrade and to lay plans for further upgrading health manpower, facilities and equipment for use in neurologic, thoracic, cardiovascular and orthopedic surgery procedures." Minutes of the Nevada State Comprehensive Health Planning Advisory Council, April 7, 1972.) On the other hand, what equities or other arguments might weigh in favor of an existing facility? See Arkansas Health Servs. Agency v. Desiderata, Inc., 958 S.W.2d 7 (Ark.1998) (preference for existing facility might be justified because "competition among hospitals, unlike competition in the market place, does not reduce the cost of in-patient hospital services to the consuming public"). What, if anything, might justify giving the nod, not to an existing facility, but to an existing corporate entity, such as the incumbent in the *Huron* case?

Alternatively, should state agencies, once they recognize an unmet need, issue a call for "bids" in anticipation of granting a CON? A few states have adopted this method to generate batches of competing applications, even going so far as to make a prior agency request for applications (RFA) a prerequisite for CON approval. See, e.g., Appeal of Nashua Brookside Hosp., 636 A.2d 57 (N.H.1993) (CON invalid despite agency determination of need because application not in response to RFA). Do you see an incentive problem with this arrangement? Or is this approach a desirable way of effectuating central planning and sparing the agency the burden of ruling on applications to fill needs that it has not independently recognized?

2. *Competitor Standing to Challenge CON Actions.* Now consider the specific issue in the *St. Joseph* case: whether the grant of a CON should be appealable by an existing competitor in the market. Obviously, if the competitor had itself submitted an expansion proposal that was turned down (perhaps following a comparative hearing), it could appeal that denial. But could it also argue that no CON should issue at all, on the ground that there is no need for a new facility or service? Could it, for example, contend that competition would be undesirable, weakening its financial condition and impairing its ability to provide good quality or uncompensated care? Although such a party can reasonably claim to be a person "adversely affected" by the decision (the operative undefined term in Public Law 93–641), a court might have reference—as did the *St. Joseph* court—to the policy underlying the federal and state statutes in deciding whether to allow an appeal by one seeking only to protect a market position.

Other courts have also held that incumbent providers, as such, have a legislatively conferred right to contest a CON award to a competitor. In fact, most state statutes provide for competitor standing, on the basis that federal regulations under Public Law 93–641 (though not the statute itself) did contemplate that appeal rights would be extended to providers that offered similar services in the same service area. See, e.g., In re Application for Certificate of Need by HCA Health Services of Wyoming, Inc., 689 P.2d 108 (Wyo.1984). But see Coastal Care Centers, Inc. v. Meeks, 184 Cal.

App.3d 85, 228 Cal.Rptr. 883 (1986) (federal requirements not finally determinative of construction of state law, which was held not to confer hearing and appeal rights on competitors).

Missouri is among the states adhering to a strict policy against competitor standing in CON case:

> [T]here is no right to be free of competition nor a private interest in preventing competition. There is no question that regulation of * * * medical facilities under the CON statutes is premised upon maintaining the business in healthy condition by reducing competition and thereby insuring that those providing * * * medical service are strong viable entities able to serve the public more effectively and efficiently at lower cost. The purpose of restricting competition through licensing is to benefit the public generally, not to protect the rights or interests of the regulated companies. As such, competitors may be the beneficiaries of the licensing procedures but those procedures do not directly affect their "private rights."
>
> * * * The nature of the CON law does not mandate a finding that it inherently requires an opportunity for appeal by a competitor.
>
> We conclude therefore that plaintiff * * * has not been accorded "aggrieved" status under the provisions of the CON legislation.

St. Joseph's Hill Infirmary, Inc. v. Mandl, 682 S.W.2d 821, 825–26 (Mo.App. 1984), appeal dismissed, 474 U.S. 801 (1985). See also Community Care Centers, Inc. v. Missouri Health Facilities Review Committee, 735 S.W.2d 13 (Mo.App.1987) (holding that R.S. Mo. § 197.335 expressly limits appeal rights to the applicant and the health systems agency in the area); John T. Finley, Inc. v. Missouri Health Facilities Review Committee, 904 S.W. 2d 1 (Mo. App. 1995) (competitors lack standing on taxpayer basis).

Can you suggest further arguments, based on the purposes of CON regulation, supporting the standing of competing institutions? Recall, for example, the practical consideration emphasized by the Kentucky court cited in *St. Joseph*. See also In re Valley Hosp., 573 A.2d 203 (N.J. Super.1990) (competitor held to have standing to challenge a grant of CON because of the strong public interest in efficient health care); New England Rehabilitation Hospital of Hartford, Inc. v. Comm'n on Hospitals and Health Care, 627 A.2d 1257 at 1282–86 (Conn.1993) (Berdon, J., dissenting) (arguing that "the majority uses aggrievement as a bolt on the doors of the courthouse to exclude the plaintiffs * * * and thereby deprives the public of a 'private attorney general' who could vindicate their rights by assuring that these health care services are delivered in a cost effective and efficient manner. The real losers today are the public.") [hereinafter *NERH*]. Would an HSA's right to appeal protect the public interest? What if HSAs no longer exist? See St. Joseph's Hill Infirmary, Inc. v. Mandl, 682 S.W.2d 821, 827 (Mo.App.1984), appeal dismissed 474 U.S. 801 (1985); Michigan Affiliated Healthcare System, Inc. v. Dep't of Public Health, 531 N.W.2d 722 (Mich.App.1994) (code section providing appellate standing to applicant, amended after elimination of HSAs, did not confer standing on competitor).

Competitors have frequently argued that their status as an intervenor or "affected party," in an earlier phase of the CON process necessarily satisfies standing requirements on appeal. See Missouri Health Care Ass'n v. Missouri Health Facilities Review Comm'n, 777 S.W.2d 241 (Mo.App. 1989) (although allowed, as an "affected person," to intervene in the administrative proceeding, competitor did not have standing to challenge decision that CON was not required for the project because it was being built with private funds); Home Health Servs., Inc. v. South Carolina Dep't of Health & Envtl. Control, 379 S.E.2d 734 (S.C.App.1989) (intervenor status necessary for standing to appeal; merely testifying insufficient). Cf. SHPDA v. AMI Brookwood Med. Center, 564 So.2d 54 (Ala.Civ.App.1989) (state administrative procedure act held to give competing hospital the right to challenge a CON as an "aggrieved party"), rev'd on other grounds, 564 So.2d 63 (Ala.1990); *NERH*, supra, 627 A.2d 1257, 1284 (Berdon, J., dissenting) ("common sense dictates that when CHHC acts upon competing proposals, granting one and denying the other, the party who is denied the [CON] is aggrieved. This is especially so when only one certificate will be awarded.")

3. *Antitrust Issues*. Can an applicant for a CON sue a competitor under the antitrust laws for fighting his entry to the market? The *Noerr–Pennington* doctrine, discussed in chapter 4(§C), provides an available defense for competitors who, singly or collectively, seek to influence planners and regulators to exclude a competitor. The theory of this defense is that political and administrative processes adequately ensure that any anticompetitive result is consistent with the public interest and that input from competitors improves the quality of decisions by making a more complete record. The "sham" exception, however, may allow antitrust courts to examine the conduct of competitors participating in the administrative process. See, e.g., St. Joseph's Hosp. v. Hospital Corp., 795 F.2d 948, 954–55 (11th Cir. 1986) (misrepresentations but not alleged delaying tactics before SHPDA could fall within exception); Hospital Building Co. v. Trustees of Rex Hosp., 691 F.2d 678, 687–88 (4th Cir.1982) (baseless appeal to delay approval could trigger liability).

Determining "Need" for New Facilities or Services

Sinai Hospital of Baltimore, Inc. v. Maryland Health Resources Planning Commission

Court of Appeals of Maryland, 1986.
306 Md. 472, 509 A.2d 1202.

■ RODOWSKY, JUDGE.

Appellants, Sinai Hospital of Baltimore, Inc. (Sinai) and North Charles General Hospital (North Charles), appeal from a judgment of the Circuit Court for Baltimore City affirming an order of the Maryland Health Resources Planning Commission (Commission) which had denied each hospital's separate application for a certificate of need (CON) to perform open heart surgery. Sinai and North Charles argue, in essence, that the

Commission failed to give controlling effect to the State Health Plan which they contend determines need under the circumstances here. For the reasons set forth below we shall affirm.

Md.Code (1982, 1985 Cum.Supp.), §§ 19–101 to –125 of the Health–General Article comprise the subtitle "Comprehensive Health Planning" of the title, "Health Care Facilities." * * * One of the Commission's duties is to adopt, at least every five years, a State Health Plan (SHP). Section 19–114(a)(2) in relevant part states that

> [t]he plan shall include:
>
> (i) A description of the components that should comprise the health care system;
>
> (ii) The goals and policies for Maryland's health care system;
>
> (iii) Identification of unmet needs, excess services, minimum access criteria, and services to be regionalized;
>
> (iv) An assessment of the financial resources required and available for the health care system; [and]
>
> (v) The methodologies, standards, and criteria for certificate of need review[.]

* * *

In September 1983, each appellant applied for a CON to conduct an open heart surgery program in the Central Maryland Health Service Area. * * * Because both applications sought approval for similar projects in the same area, they were subject to a comparative review. After the Central Maryland Health Systems Agency, a local health planning agency, had recommended Sinai, and the Commission's staff had recommended North Charles, the Commission designated one of its members to hold a hearing pursuant to § 19–118(d)(2). Appellee Saint Joseph Hospital (St. Joseph) participated in that hearing. During the pendency of these proceedings before the Commission, on September 10, 1984, the 1983–88 SHP went into effect and became the SHP applicable to this case. In a proposed decision of October 26, 1984, the hearing officer-commissioner recommended awarding the CON to Sinai. Despite her serious concern over the lack of excessive waiting times for CS procedures, she felt compelled under the SHP need methodology to find a need for one program.

The full Commission met on November 13 and voted to deny both applications. * * * The Commission found that at the three hospitals authorized for CS programs the times from registration for surgery to actual surgery were reasonable. Based largely on that finding the Commission further found that there was no present need for an additional cardiac surgery program, although the Commission recognized that the methodology adopted in the SHP predicted a need in 1986. In rejecting both applications the Commission basically gave determinative weight to a review criterion in Reg. 07.

Sinai and North Charles appealed to the Circuit Court for Baltimore City which affirmed the Commission. We issued the writ of certiorari before consideration of the matter by the Court of Special Appeals.

Code § 19–118(c)(1) requires the Commission to consider both the SHP and Reg. 07.

> All decisions of the Commission on an application for a certificate of need, except in emergency circumstances posing a threat to public health, shall be consistent with the State health plan *and* the standards for review established by the Commission. [Emphasis added.]

The SHP provides a formula for estimating the future utilization of adult (age 15 and above) cardiac surgery procedures. The projections are made two calendar years into the future from the time a CON review takes place. Under the formula the most recent national use rates as issued by the National Center for Health Statistics are multiplied by the projected population of the health service area as reported by the Department of State Planning. The existing total CS capacity of the area is then subtracted from the total number of procedures estimated to be required two years into the future to determine whether additional services are needed. Before the Commission can certify a new program to fill the future need, it must also find that at least 350 CS procedures per year are performed in each existing program. At the time of the CON review for Sinai and North Charles, Johns Hopkins was performing 780 procedures per year, the University of Maryland was performing 527 procedures, and under the SHP methodology St. Joseph was performing 350. The result of the formula calculations was that 420 additional procedures would be required in 1986. Under the SHP the Commission may grant only one CON at a time for open heart surgery, in order to allow the new program to develop without competition until it reaches 350 procedures per year.

It is to be noted that the SHP employs as the use factor in the cardiac surgery need formula a national rate as opposed to the historic rate for Central Maryland. The 1983–88 SHP, which was in effect as of September 10, 1984, was the first SHP to employ a national use factor for CS need projections. As explained by the Commission in the present case the national rate was chosen over the local rate because the latter " 'was felt [to] have been constrained.' The basis for this feeling [was] reports of unacceptable waiting times."

Code § 19–118(c)(1) also requires a decision on a CON application to be consistent with "the standards for review established by the Commission." These are set forth in Reg. 07. Reg. 07D, entitled "Criteria for Review of Application," provides in relevant part that

* * *

> (2) ... the review shall include consideration of the following criteria:
>
> ...
>
> (c) The need for the proposed health services of the population served or to be served, including an analysis of *present* and future *utilization*.... [Emphasis added.]

In considering "present ... utilization" in this case the Commission found that "current waiting times are reasonable when considered in light of the standard in the SHP. No additional need is currently shown when considering waiting times." The standard referred to by the Commission is thirty days from registration to surgery. The standard is based on a policy decision made by the Commission in the SHP and set forth in CS Standard 6, headed "Accessibility," which reads as follows:

> The maximum waiting time for elective cardiac catheterization or cardiac surgery services should not exceed one month from the date of registration. Facilities seeking to expand or establish cardiac catheterization or cardiac surgery capacity on the basis of waiting times must demonstrate that the standard has been exceeded, on average, for at least 6 consecutive months. In no case can the waiting time standard serve as justification for additional cardiac surgery or catheterization capacity in the absence of need for such capacity as based on the need methodology contained in this Plan.

This standard does not exclusively discuss "Accessibility." The second sentence of the standard recognizes that extended waiting times are relevant to the issue of additional capacity. Consequently in applying Reg. 07D(2)(c), the Commission appropriately considered waiting times in analyzing present utilization. The Commission found that waiting times did not exceed thirty days and concluded that there was no present need. This conclusion supports the Commission's order and the affirmance thereof by the circuit court.

In a nutshell the present case is one in which the Commission could have ruled as it did or it could have determined that there was a need for an additional CS program. It is the function of the Commission to decide whether or not a CON should be granted where, as here, there is substantial evidence to support either conclusion. * * *

Sinai and North Charles, however, argue that the Commission made an error of law. Appellants submit that the SHP determination of need is paramount because the legislative intent is that policy as established by the SHP controls in the grant or denial of a CON. But the comprehensive health planning statutes specify in § 19–118(c)(1) that decisions on CON applications must be consistent both with the SHP and with the standards for review which the Commission established in Reg. 07. Under the statute neither the SHP nor Reg. 07 predominates.

The principal thrust of the appellants' argument is premised on the existence of a conflict between the need projection developed under the SHP formula and the Commission's fact-finding that there is no present need. That perceived conflict leads appellants to urge us to apply a variety of statutory construction rules. We do not reach those rules because there is no conflict. The SHP deals with future need. It deals with projected need two years from the time a CON application is reviewed. Reg. 07D(2)(c) looks to available data reflecting actual utilization. The SHP neither provides a methodology for computing current need nor prohibits the Commission from establishing current need as one of the standards of review. The Commission's denial of the CON applications, therefore, was consistent with the SHP.

* * *

There was substantial evidence to support the Commission's finding that there was no present need for additional CS capacity. Dr. Robert Brawley, Chief of Cardiac Surgery at St. Joseph Hospital, stated that there was no waiting list for open heart surgery at St. Joseph and that he understood waiting times at Johns Hopkins Hospital and the University of Maryland Hospital had become shorter. In his opinion there was no need for an additional program. According to Dr. Bruce Reitz, Director of Cardiac Surgery at Johns Hopkins, overall waiting time for elective cardiac surgery at Johns Hopkins was three to four weeks. Chief of Cardiology at Sinai, Dr. Phillip Reid, stated that his most recent experience revealed that the waiting time at Johns Hopkins was two to four weeks. Finally, in a letter dated June 1, 1984, to Dr. Robert Mahon, Vice President of Medical Affairs at St. Joseph Hospital, Morton Rapoport, Chief Executive Officer of the University of Maryland Hospital, stated that in the first five months of 1984 there was a 17% reduction in caseload from the same period in 1983. University of Maryland could accommodate referrals within one week. Mr. Rapoport also stated that cardiac surgery in the United States had dropped by 25% overall, and in some areas by 40%. He listed as possible reasons for this decline:

1. The economic climate.
2. Indications from the CASS study that 25% of patients can be treated safely medically.
3. The more frequent use of balloon angioplasty.
4. The availability of newer drugs introduced in the last few years.

Indeed, the Commission found that waiting times were not only reasonable but that they were declining. This was also based on substantial evidence. Dr. Brawley attributed the declining waiting times at St. Joseph to an increase in the number of cardiac surgery procedures permitted by the overall decline in the occupancy rate of the hospital. Dr. Reitz testified that at Johns Hopkins waiting times had decreased while the number of procedures had increased as a result of providing more efficient services.

The Commission in addition found that without being required to obtain a CON the existing programs could, and were willing to, expand to the extent of providing 220 of the 420 future needed procedures, leaving a net 1986 need of 200 procedures. The appellants also represented that within only three months of approval each could be operating its proposed CS program. The Commission reasoned in part that since a new cardiac surgery program could be initiated quickly should there be evidence of a then present need for additional open heart surgery capacity in 1986, such capacity could be added at that time.

A reasonable mind could have reached the conclusion that there was no current need for an additional cardiac surgery program and that the applications of Sinai and North Charles, therefore, were both inconsistent with Reg. 07D(2)(c) and, ultimately, § 19–118(c)(1).

[Judgment affirmed.]

NOTES AND QUESTIONS ON DETERMINATIONS OF "NEED"

1. *Methodology.* How was "need" determined in the *Sinai Hospital* case? How precise was the methodology employed? Was the applicant unfairly surprised?

Was the methodology used in *Sinai Hospital* well calculated to solve the problem of provider-created demand that induced the enactment of CON laws in the first place? Or does it merely ensure that there will be no unused capacity? Which of the following is the better statement of the purpose of a CON law: (1) to eliminate duplication of services and save the costs of underutilized assets or (2) to limit the availability of facilities as a means of forcing providers to make hard choices about their use? Which of these purposes does the Maryland program, as administered, serve?

What is "need"? Can it be objectively determined? One commentator has stated, "Need is a medical concept, largely defined by professionals. It is subjective, rather than objective, and consequently not a limiting, but an expansive concept." Bovbjerg, Problems and Prospects for Health Planning: The Importance of Incentives, Standards, and Procedures in Certificate of Need, 1978 Utah L.Rev. 83, 90. He goes on to say,

> It is simply not true that experts know what constitutes desirable levels of health, what medical interventions can assure their attainment, or what pattern of facilities is needed to support those interventions. Planning is not a simple, value-free, quantitative endeavor that involves gathering all the data on institutional health services delivery and plugging them mechanistically into expert calculations to determine what we need. Rather, through planning we must decide how much health care is enough. Standards and processes must be developed to make and implement such decisions. In short, planning is as much or more a political activity than a scientific one.

Id. at 97. More recently, another commentator has suggested that "recent studies of the appropriate utilization of health care services [arising from a renewed emphasis on patient outcomes] offer improved guidance for regulators in determining the 'need' for new health care facilities." Hackey, New Wine in Old Bottles: Certificate of Need Enters the 1990's, 18 J. Health Pol., Pol'y & L. 927, 931 (1993). From what you have read so far, what are the chances that need determinations will be based on findings from health services research?

How would you feel if, as a candidate for open-heart surgery, you were told that the procedure could not be performed for thirty days because the government had limited the supply of services? What would be your reaction if, as a legislator, you found that one of your constituents had suffered a fatal heart attack while awaiting the procedure? Is CON regulation likely to prove a good way of forcing providers to ration services?

2. *Need Formulas and State Health Plans.* Formula approaches to need determination have been resisted by some courts as unduly arbitrary. E.g., Charter Med. of Cook County v. HCA Health Servs. of Midwest, 542 N.E.2d 82 (Ill. App.1989) (agency's grant of CONs to three competing psychiatric hospitals in the same planning area resulted in more approved beds than in need projections; action upheld against challenge by one of the three, citing agency's statutory discretion and expertise in matter); Balsam v. Department of Health and Rehab. Servs., 486 So.2d 1341 (Fla.App.1986) (denial of CON overturned for overreliance on mathematical formula and assumption that licensed and accredited psychiatric and substance abuse hospitals were fungible; applicant allowed to present evidence on unique treatment philosophy, specialized programs, accessibility to nonpaying patients, and research and training capability); Oak Park Manor v. State CON Review Board, 500 N.E.2d 895 (Ohio App.1985) (denial of CON for long-term care facility overturned for overreliance on Hill–Burton bed-demand formula). What are the relative virtues of formulas versus a long list of relevant criteria? Would an agency, by claiming that it has balanced all the competing factors, usually be able to write a judge-proof decision?

How binding should the state health plan (SHP)—with its quotas for each provider category and conclusions on the existence or nonexistence of need—be in decision making on particular CON applications? See West Bloomfield Hosp. v. Certificate of Need Board, 550 N.W.2d 223 (Mich.1996) (latest phase of CON proceeding that was subject of 1981 *Huron Valley* case, cited earlier in this section; holding that CON review could proceed without waiting for formal promulgation of state medical facilities plan). The 1979 federal health planning amendments introduced a specific requirement that, except in "emergency circumstances," decisions on CON applications should be "consistent with the State health plan." What are the arguments for and against making the SHP binding? In Lenoir Mem. Hosp. v. North Carolina Dep't of Human Resources, 390 S.E.2d 448 (N.C.App.1990), the court found that the agency acted arbitrarily and capriciously by (1) not adjusting the projected need to add beds that had been previously allocated but that were not going to be built and (2) focusing on numbers to the exclusion of policy considerations, including the increased efficiency anticipated when the hospital converted chronically underutilized acute-care beds to beds needed for psychiatric care. The North Carolina legislature responded by amending the statute to state that the State Medical Facilities Plan provides the last word on need determinations. N.C. Gen. Stat. § 131E–183(1) (1992).

Despite the existence of a definitive plan, some cases allow reliance on additional evidence concerning need or special circumstances. See, e.g., Roanoke Mem. Hosps. v. Kenley, 352 S.E.2d 525 (Va.App.1987) (upholding grant of CON for radiation therapy unit despite failure of one incumbent to provide minimum number of treatments contemplated in SHP; plan provision held only a guideline, and requirement of consistency with SHP held to confer discretion on agency); Perini Servs., Inc. v. Maryland Health Resources Planning Comm'n, 506 A.2d 1207 (Md. App.1986) (agency allowed to deny CON in reliance on new data, but not new policy, in new SHP not yet officially promulgated); the *Balsam* case, supra. Other courts have reversed CON actions that departed from the SHP. E.g., Ex parte Shelby Med. Center, 564 So.2d 63 (Ala.1990) (grant of CON for new hospital overturned on petition of six recently disappointed applicants, on ground of state health plan and unconvincing evidence of need); Statewide Health Coordinating Council v. General Hosps. of Humana, Inc., 660 S.W.2d 906 (Ark.1983) (grant of CON to hospital reversed where area already exceeded maximum ratio of 4 beds per 1000 residents provided in SHP and no special circumstances were shown).

Access as a Consideration in CON Regulation

Chambery v. Axelrod

Supreme Court, Appellate Division, Third Department, 1984.
101 A.D.2d 610, 474 N.Y.S.2d 865.

■ MEMORANDUM DECISION.

* * *

We are once again called upon to review a determination of the Commissioner of Health, who, in the underlying proceedings, denied an application made pursuant to section 2802 (subd. 2) of the Public Health Law for approval to construct a 48-bed addition to petitioners' nursing home.

Petitioners' initial argument that the denial was arbitrary and capricious and unsupported by substantial evidence is unpersuasive. They correctly argue that while respondent commissioner may enforce regulations which prohibit discriminatory sponsorship policies (i.e., preclude or limit the number of Medicaid supported patients either as initial admittees or as retention patients after exhaustion of private funds), he may do so "only if reimbursement rates are not lower than the fee charged other patients" (Matter of Blue v. Whalen, 57 A.D.2d 240, 243, 394 N.Y.S.2d 290). Equally correct and well settled is the principle that participation by a provider of health services in the Medicaid program is purely voluntary. These arguments, however well grounded, are of no moment in this proceeding where the commissioner's action under review is not an attempt to enforce or impose a mandatory Medicaid admission policy. Rather, our review is focused upon whether his denial of the application was violative of the applicable statute and regulations. Section 2802 (subd. 2, par. [b]) of the Public Health Law states, in pertinent part, that the commissioner shall not act upon an application for construction of a hospital (facility) unless he "is satisfied as to the public need for the construction, at the time and place and under the circumstances proposed".

The Department of Health's regulations set forth the factors which are relevant to the determinations of public need. 10 NYCRR 709.1(a) provides, in pertinent part:

> The factors for determining public need for health services and medical facilities shall include, but not be limited to: (1) the current and projected population characteristics of the service area, including relevant health status indicators and socio-economic conditions of the population.

Similarly, 10 NYCRR 709.1(b) provides, in relevant part:

> The evaluative procedure for review of public need pursuant to section 2802 of the Public Health Law shall include, but not be limited to: ... (3) identification of current and projected user population of the service area....

Additionally, section 123.412(a)(6)(iii) of title 42 of the Code of Federal Regulations provides that when a State agency reviews a proposal for expansion, it must consider "[t]he contribution of the proposed service in meeting the health related needs of members of medically underserved groups which have traditionally experienced difficulties in obtaining equal access to health services" and thus must consider "[t]he extent to which Medicare, Medicaid and medically indigent patients are served by the applicant".

These principles in mind, examination of the record demonstrates that petitioners historically had a low number of Medicaid admissions and that their admissions agreement reserves the right to terminate the stay of initially private paying patients who subsequently become Medicaid dependent upon exhaustion of private resources. Although at the time of filing the application and at the hearing between 42% and 50% of petitioners' patients had become Medicaid dependent, the admissions policy containing the reservation right continued in effect. Since the proof showed that the vast majority of persons in Monroe County needing long term care were Medicaid dependent, it cannot be said the commissioner erred in approving the application of another nursing home without admission reservations in preference to petitioners' application. Recognition of the characteristics and socio-economic conditions in the user population to be served, which demonstrated the need for Medicaid-sponsored beds, made the commissioner's determination both logical and reasonable. We find no defect in the regulations with respect to Medicaid admissions policy nor in the commissioner's methodology for determining the need for Medicaid-sponsored patient beds in 1980, the year of petitioners' application. We find that the record contains substantial evidence to support the determination.

* * *

Determination confirmed, and petition dismissed, without costs.

NOTES AND QUESTIONS

1. *CON and Access.* CON regulation has been widely used to foster access to care by nonpaying patients and public program beneficiaries, partly as a result of the (now repealed) federal regulations alluded to in *Chambery*. See, e.g., Collier Med. Center v. State, Department of Health and Rehab. Servs., 462 So.2d 83 (Fla.App.1985) (upholding denial of CON to new hospital to protect revenues of existing hospitals with heavy indigent care burdens); Doctors' Hosp. v. Maryland Health Resources Planning Comm'n, 501 A.2d 1324 (Md.App.1986) (disproportionately low Medicaid and indigent patient load held evidence justifying denial of CON to hospital); 65 Op.Att'y Gen. 659 (Calif. 1982) (state agency may attach express conditions to CON requiring facility to serve "negotiated quota" of Medi–Cal beneficiaries). But see Huntington Manor v. North Carolina Dep't of Human Resources, 393 S.E.2d 104 (N.C.App.1990) (overturning denial of CON based on agency's perception that low-income patients would lack access to the facility; facility's policy toward indigents found reasonable in not providing unlimited care to indigents at unfair cost to nonindigents). Note the limits observed in *Chambery* on the conditions that a state may impose on CON recipients in order to protect the interests of Medicaid beneficiaries.

For a while beginning in 1980, DHHS sought to induce the states to require a CON for *termination* of services. A few states do so. But see Capitol Hill Hosp. v. District of Columbia SHPDA, 600 A.2d 793 (D.C.1991) (100–year-old hospital allowed to close its acute care services without CON since no capital expenditure was involved). Obviously the object in requiring approval of closures would be to protect the access to such services of patients who lack the ability to pay for them. Can a health care facility be legally required to continue a money-losing service? Although many regulated utilities have such service obligations, they are legally guaranteed the right to charge rates on their overall business that should yield a fair return on their total investment. Most health care providers have no such guarantee.

2. *Cross-subsidization as a Rationale for CON.* The protectionism inherent in CON regulation is perhaps the clearest expression in law of a public policy favoring the cross-subsidization of health services for those unable to pay. Indeed, as the following excerpt suggests, the need to protect cross-subsidies may have been the principal barrier to deregulation in the 1980s:

> The 1980s have, of course, seen dramatic changes in the health care marketplace as Medicare and private payers have shed their old role as passive conduits for incurred costs and have become aggressive purchasers. The resulting changes in the prevailing methods of paying for health services have undercut the original rationale for CON laws so completely that those with vested interests in those laws have had to scurry to shore them up with a new theory. One argument occasionally heard is that a mix of regulation and competition is needed because payment mechanisms are still in transition and are not yet ready to sustain the full force of deregulation. But this point ignores the extent to which CON regulation and similar controls (of hospital rates, for example) actually shelter inefficient payers, the true causes of the cost problem, from the necessity of changing their methods and

addressing the cost problem for themselves, as a service to their customers. * * *

The argument for CON regulation * * * has only one remaining cornerstone, the arguable need to protect what is left of the health care industry's capacity to cross-subsidize desirable services, particularly uncompensated health care for the poor and underinsured. * * * [L]ifting such regulation would expose institutional providers to "cream-skimming" and loss of the revenues they need to support good works, particularly the provision of uncompensated care. Although these arguments have always been in the background in CON debates, they have become the crucial argument today. Indeed, the Florida CON Task Force concluded that deregulation of hospital facilities and [free-standing ambulatory surgical facilities] should not even be considered until "an effective hospital indigent care program [has been] fully implemented and funded by a broad-based revenue source." [Certificate of Need Task Force, A Final Report on Florida's Certificate of Need Program, p. i (1986).] This conclusion was reached even after the task force had clearly shown both how changing market conditions are invalidating the economic rationale for CON regulation of hospitals and why such regulation may have had both little effect on costs and some undesirable side effects.

* * * [P]rotectionist arguments for continued CON regulation [are not] palpably invalid. Given the nature of the interest at stake, health care for the poor, it cannot be adequate simply to reject such arguments as grounded in expediency and to argue puristically that redistribution issues should be dealt with by mechanisms that do not impair efficiency. Nevertheless, a policy of perpetuating regulation solely in the interest of the beneficiaries of cross-subsidies has some major costs and may not turn out to be in the long-run interest even of those whom it claims to benefit. Without launching into a full comparison of possible approaches to solving the health care problems of the poor, a few observations may be offered.

CON regulation cannot, when all is said and done, prevent serious and fairly rapid erosion of desirable cross-subsidies. Consumers are already rapidly shifting their custom away from institutions that overcharge for their services, and insurers are increasingly rewarding consumers who escape the "tax" that some institutions seek to levy to support their good deeds. Although CON laws may limit the availability of some substitutes, they cannot prevent all competition and all diversion of business to providers who lack a commitment to providing unremunerative services. * * *

There are other problems, too, with trying to meet the needs of the poor through cross-subsidization. One concern is that this method of financing distributes the burden inequitably, making it fall on those who fortuitously lack access to alternative providers. It also deprives society of effective oversight of the spending practices of institutions sheltered from competition. Although some of the excess revenues yielded by regulatory protectionism may be dedicated to indigent care, there is no guarantee that only worthy goals will be pursued. One danger is that protected hospitals will simply waste resources, using more than the optimal quantity needed to yield a given result. Another troublesome possibility is that the institution will pursue goals of its own, allocating a portion of the tax it levies to uses that the public would not approve, given other societal needs.

Finally, there is reason to fear that the care financed by internal subsidies in struggling institutions is not always of acceptable quality or adequately accessible to the populations that need it. A recent comparison of uncompensated care and care financed through public insurance concludes, on the basis of the number of visits by poor patients, that "the availability of uncompensated care at a small number of hospitals is not a substitute for some form of public insurance coverage." [Blendon et al., Uncompensated Care by Hospitals or Public Insurance for the Poor: Does It Make a Difference? 314 New Eng.J.Med. 1160, 1163 (1986).] If uncompensated care is indeed a poor substitute for better public subsidies, then using CON regulation to perpetuate dwindling cross-subsidies may be a self-defeating policy. It is at least possible that the poor would benefit more and in greater numbers if a crisis in public financing were allowed to develop and state legislatures were finally forced to guarantee a decent minimum level of health care to those who are unable to procure it for themselves.

Havighurst, Developing Noninstitutional Health Services: The Role of Certificate-of-Need Regulation, in Cost, Quality, and Access in Health Care: New Roles for Health Planning in a Competitive Environment 71, 87–89 (F. Sloan, J. Blumstein & J. Perrin eds., 1988). See also Campbell & Fournier, Certificate-of-Need Regulation and Indigent Hospital Care, 18 J. Health Pol., Pol'y & L. 905 (1993); Hackey, New Wine in Old Bottles: Certificate of Need Enters the 1990s, id. at 928.

3. *Nursing Homes and CON.* Consider the rationale for regulating the supply of long-term care facilities. Does the financing system induce overuse of long-term care? Is it relevant that Medicare and private health insurance cover only a very small portion of nursing home care? What is the role of the Medicaid program? Can you explain why a nursing home serving only private patients was preferred in South Carolina over a home with 65 percent of its beds dedicated to Medicaid beneficiaries? National Health Corp. v. South Carolina Dep't of Health & Envtl. Control, 380 S.E.2d 841 (S.C.App.1989). What explains the former provision in Virginia's CON statute that made it possible to obtain authority to build new nursing home beds, despite a moratorium, if "the provider agrees in writing not to seek certification for the use of such beds by persons eligible to receive medical assistance services pursuant to Title XIX of the United States Social Security Act." Va. Code Ann. § 32.1–102.3:2 (Michie 1992 & Supp. 1994), repealed by Act of April 10, 1996 Va. Acts ch. 901, H.B. 1302, 1996 Sess.

To understand the role of CON regulation in this special sector of the health care industry, consider the following:

> Nursing home controls seem a category unto themselves because the market is so heavily dominated by Medicaid. About half of revenues and an even larger share of patients are public, although these percentages have declined somewhat in recent years. The market is even more heavily public in that many patients who enter long-term nursing care as private patients end as Medicaid patients once they exhaust their resources. Under these circumstances, many state Medicaid agencies are very concerned to limit the number of nursing home beds. Such limits control utilization indirectly, with the result that there is considerable excess demand for Medicaid entry into a nursing home and very little excess capacity in the nursing home industry.
>
> This supply-side rationing also means that there are great numbers of people not in nursing homes who objectively resemble nursing home patients and who would qualify for admission if beds were available, yet who receive little or no public support because they are not institutionalized. There are problems with this approach, most notably that the quality of life for noninstitutionalized people is reduced. * * *
>
> Moreover, the quality of care for institutionalized patients is also a constant problem. * * * Where patients have very little effective choice among nursing homes because there are so few empty beds, Medicaid patients cannot promote quality by shopping for a better provider. * * *
>
> [T]he strategy of limiting nursing home beds remains a very important one for many Medicaid programs, and states may wish to retain it at least in part for the near future. Moratoria and ad hoc Medicaid planning are all that is truly needed, but a fuller, CON-style of proceeding helps provide political and legal legitimation. How far courts would accept limits on nursing home entry in an otherwise deregulated state is an open question.

Bovbjerg, New Directions for Health Planning, in Health Care: New Roles for Health Planning in Cost, Quality and Access a Competitive Environment 206, 214–16 (F. Sloan, J. Blumstein & J. Perrin eds., 1988). See also Arkansas Health Servs. Agency v. Desiderata, Inc., 958 S.W.2d 7 (Ark.1998) (CON agency allegedly gave preference to existing nursing home; court stated such a preference might be justified because "competition among hospitals, unlike competition in the market place, does not reduce the cost of in-patient hospital services to the consuming public"). Consider this rationale in reading the remainder of this section.

What do you think of the states' use of CON regulation to deny Medicaid recipients an entitlement to nursing home care that they enjoy (on paper, at least) under federal law? Would deregulation be feasible? Can you suggest alternative ways of solving the cost problem that states face? See generally Feder & Scanlon, Regulating the Bed Supply in Nursing

Homes, 58 Milbank Mem. Fund Q. 54 (1980); Scanlon, Possible Reforms for Financing Long–Term Care, J. Econ. Persp., Summer 1992, p. 43. On the issue of nursing home quality as it is affected by CON laws, see Zinn, Market Competition and the Quality of Nursing Home Care, 19 J. Health Pol., Pol'y & L. 555 (1994).

Reconciling CON Regulation With Policies Favoring Competition

Oregon Eye Associates v. State Health Planning and Development Agency

Court of Appeals of Oregon, 1987.
83 Or.App. 368, 732 P.2d 41.

■ WARDEN, PRESIDING JUDGE.

Oregon Eye Associates (OEA) seeks review of a final order of the State Health Planning and Development Agency (SHPDA) which denied OEA's application for a certificate of need to build an ambulatory surgical center (ASC) in Eugene for the performance of outpatient eye surgery. Sacred Heart General Hospital (SHGH) intervened before the agency to oppose the application and is a respondent on review. We affirm SHPDA.

OEA is a partnership of ophthalmologic surgeons who presently perform eye surgery at SHGH, the great majority on an outpatient basis at the hospital's short stay unit (SSU). OEA proposes to build an ASC at which its partners, and possibly other surgeons, would perform their outpatient surgery. Under ORS 442.320(1), OEA is required to have a certificate from SHPDA in order to construct the facility. SHPDA denied OEA's application, and OEA then requested a reconsideration hearing. The hearings officer recommended approval, but SHPDA's final order on reconsideration affirmed the original denial. OEA then sought judicial review.

OEA does not challenge most of the facts which SHPDA specifically found or the factual conclusions that it drew. Rather, it challenges the relevance of those facts and conclusions to the issues SHPDA had to decide. OEA's primary argument is that SHPDA erred by evaluating the proposed ASC according to traditional criteria, such as avoiding excessive capacity or planning to allocate health care resources in order to minimize total cost to the community. It argues that recent state and federal legislation has made the promotion of competition the overriding—and, possibly, the only—basis for determining whether to grant a certificate to an ASC. The reason, OEA states, is that ASCs provide an inexpensive alternative to hospitals and that they are necessary to achieve the statutory goal of reducing health care costs to patients. According to OEA, SHPDA should approve an ASC if it will produce lower costs to the patient than do existing facilities. Because competition cannot exist without some excess capacity, OEA argues, previous policies designed to limit capacity are no longer relevant.

OEA's position both misstates the role Congress and the Oregon legislature intend competition to play in the certificate process and fails to understand the kinds of competition which they had in mind. The legislature has declared that the overall purpose of the process is to achieve reasonable access to quality health care at a reasonable cost. The problems which the legislature identified and which the process must overcome include:

> "(a) The inability of many citizens to pay for necessary health care, being covered neither by private insurance nor by publicly funded programs such as Medicare and Medicaid;
>
> "(b) Rising costs of medical care which exceed substantially the general rate of inflation;
>
> "(c) Insufficient price competition in the delivery of health care services that would provide a greater cost consciousness among providers, payors and consumers;
>
> "(d) Inadequate incentives for the use of less costly and more appropriate alternative levels of health care;
>
> "(e) Insufficient or inappropriate use of existing capacity, duplicated services and failure to use less costly alternatives in meeting significant health needs; and
>
> "(f) Insufficient primary and emergency medical care services in some rural areas of the state." ORS 442.025(2).

Both insufficient price competition *and* duplicated services are included in the list.

The statute goes on to list several ways to attack these problems:

> "(4) To foster the cooperation of the separate industry forces, there is a need to compile and disseminate accurate and current data, including but not limited to price and utilization data, to meet the needs of the people of Oregon and improve the appropriate usage of health care services.
>
> "(5) It is the purpose of this chapter to establish area-wide and state planning for health services, staff and facilities in light of the findings of subsection (1) of this section and in furtherance of health planning policies of this state.
>
> "(6) It is further declared that hospital costs should be contained through improved competition between hospitals and improved competition between insurers and through financial incentives on behalf of providers, insurers and consumers to contain costs. As a safety net, it is the intent of the Legislative Assembly to monitor hospital performance during the 1985–1987 biennium so that controls over hospital operating and capital expenditures can be established in the event that competition-oriented methods do not adequately contain costs and the access of Oregonians to adequate hospital care becomes jeopardized because of unaffordable costs." ORS 442.025.

Subsection (5), calling for the planning of health facilities, was in the act as originally adopted in 1977. The 1985 legislature added subsections (4) and (6). Or.Laws 1985, ch. 747, § 1. OEA argues from that fact that the legislature has made competition the primary method of resolving the problems it identified. OEA ignores, first, the legislature's retention of subsection (5) with its emphasis on planning. It ignores, secondly, that subsection (6) speaks of improved competition *between hospitals* and *between insurers,* not of improved competition in general.[5] As OEA argues vigorously in other contexts, its proposed ASC is not a hospital.

Finally, OEA ignores that there are methods of promoting competition other than bringing in new competitors and that there are factors that impede competition other than inadequate capacity. Increased information about facilities and prices and increased advertising by hospitals and other existing health care institutions are obvious ways of increasing price competition. Subsection (4) appears to have been drafted, in part, to encourage that kind of competition. Other portions of the 1985 act also seem to have that goal. See, e.g., Or.Laws 1985, ch. 747, § 5 (amending ORS 442.045 to require the Oregon Health Council to act as a statewide data clearing house) and § 6 (amending ORS 442.155 to require health system agencies to serve as clearing houses for information on the enhancement of competition in the health care market place). As we discuss below, Congress was also concerned about deterrents to competition other than insufficient competition.

Before 1985, Oregon law required the planning and coordination of health facility construction in order to reduce overall health system costs. The 1985 changes encouraged competition among health care providers as a method of achieving that goal, but they do not suggest that constructing new facilities is the primary method of promoting competition or that competition is now the overriding state policy. Federal law, which is relevant because the state health planning system is, in large part, the result of federal enactments, does not suggest that Congress' intent was significantly different from that of the Oregon legislature.

In 1979, Congress amended the National Health Planning and Resources Development Act (NHPRDA) to adopt as a priority the "strengthening of competitive forces in the health services industry wherever competition and consumer choice can constructively serve, in accordance with subsection (b),[6] to advance the purposes of quality assurance, cost effectiveness, and access." NHPRDA § 1502(a)(17), 42 U.S.C. § 300k–2(a)(17). On the basis of that amendment OEA argues that "Congress chose free market economics as policy" to the exclusion of all other policies. It asserts that Congress permitted the allocation of supply only for institutional services (which OEA insists means inpatient hospital services, not ASCs) and required competition for other services. What Congress actually did is not as simple as OEA would make it.[7]

5. These purposes are consistent with the congressional concern that widespread payment by insurers rather than consumers was one of the major obstacles to effective competition. See H.R.Rep. No. 190, 96th Cong. 1st Sess (1979), 51–52.

6. We discuss subsection (b) below.

7. Oregon law explicitly treats ASCs as institutional health services. ORS 442.015(16)(e) includes them in the definition

In the same act in which it amended 42 U.S.C. § 300k–2 to add subsection (a)(17), Congress also added subsection (a)(12), which lists "the identification and discontinuance of duplicative or unneeded services and facilities" as another national health priority. It also adopted subsection (b), in which it found that, in certain kinds of services, competitive forces are diminished, primarily because public and private insurance has become the prevailing method of paying for those services. According to the statute, the state agencies which administer the health planning system should allocate the supply of those services which competition will not allocate appropriately and should make decisions which will strengthen competition for services where competition does allocate supply, *consistent with the appropriate regional and state plans.*[8] The statute does not describe all areas in which competition is inadequate, although it does include "inpatient health services and other institutional health services" in that category. 42 U.S.C. § 300k–2(b)(2).[9] Rather, as the legislative history makes clear, Congress left the determination of where competition could be encouraged to the state agencies.

The house committee which considered the 1979 amendments to NHPRDA noted in its report that

> "[p]rimarily because of ... third party reimbursement arrangements, individuals often make decisions regarding their use of institutional health services with almost no regard to the price of the services, and providers make decisions respecting the supply of institutional health services substantially unaffected by the usual financial incentives and risks which exist in other personal service industries."

It also pointed out that "the predominant role of the physician in making purchasing decisions on behalf of the patient" limited competition among facilities. H.R.Rep. No. 190, supra n 5, at 52. When Congress acted, it appears that it did not believe that there was competition among institutional health services. If, however, there was discovered some way to develop competition, Congress wished to encourage it. If new financing arrangements were developed which would *both* create incentives for patients to respond to prices charged *and* would place providers at financial risk for excess capacity, Congress expected agencies to take that fact into account in making their decisions. H.R.Rep. No. 190, supra n 5, at 53–54. Determining whether the requisite circumstances exist and how to take competition into account in a particular case are the agency's responsibility.

Both federal and state law, thus, treat competition as *one* method by which to achieve the goal of quality care at reasonable cost, and both place

of "health care facility." ORS 442.015(21) provides:

> " '[I]nstitutional health services' means health services provided in or through health care facilities and includes the entities in or through which such services are provided."

8. Thus Congress treats competition as one method of implementing health facility planning, not as a substitute for it.

9. ASCs are "institutional health services" under the statute. 42 U.S.C. § 300n(5); 42 CFR § 123.401.

the responsibility on SHPDA to determine the extent to which competition is appropriate in each situation. Neither makes competition the sole criterion for SHPDA to consider. In this light, OEA's assignment of error is simply an assertion that SHPDA did not adequately consider competition in deciding to deny the OEA application. Although the record indicates that ASCs are a recent development with a significant potential to reduce surgical costs, we do not see any basis for holding that SHPDA must evaluate OEA's proposal differently from how it evaluates proposals for other institutional services simply because it is for an ASC. The same criteria apply, with the nature of the proposal being one of the factors SHPDA must consider.

OEA's position is that the proposed ASC will promote competition, because Medicare will pay a fixed amount per patient, rather than reimbursing services on a cost basis.[10] Thus, OEA will be at risk for excess capacity. Because OEA intends to charge less than SHGH charges for the use of its SSU, and considerably less than another local hospital charges for its facilities, the ASC will, according to OEA, make a major contribution to keeping prices down. The law therefore required SHPDA to rely on market forces rather than regulation to control costs to the public. We believe that SHPDA's responsibility was to consider all the relevant criteria rather than relying solely on a single criterion.

In its order, SHPDA carefully considered all the statutory factors, including the effect that the OEA proposal would have on competition for outpatient eye surgery. In that respect it found that there was a significant surplus of facilities in the area and that so high a percentage of eye surgery was performed on an outpatient basis that a new facility was unlikely to produce a significant increase. There is substantial evidence in the record to support those findings. SHGH's facilities are not fully used, and the Northwest Eye Center (NEC), an existing ASC, has two operating rooms which are idle four working days a week. OEA's physicians refuse to use NEC, although it has been recently remodeled to eliminate the major architectural problems which were the basis for many of their complaints.

SHPDA found that the competitive pressure that NEC provided, despite its underutilization, was a major factor in SHGH's recent change in its method of billing Medicare patients, a change which eliminated out-of-pocket costs for most of them.[12] SHPDA also found that OEA had over-

10. Most of the surgery to be performed in the ASC will be cataract surgery, and most of the patients will be covered by Medicare. Medicare's method of payment will therefore be of major significance for the ASC's financial success.

12. OEA's members, and apparently other Eugene ophthalmologists, refuse to use NEC because of personal and professional disagreements with its owner. SHPDA did not have to take that refusal into account in determining if there were sufficient competitive pressures in the market. A physician's refusal to use a particular facility is precisely the kind of physician, rather than patient, choice among providers which Congress identified as one reason for the lack of competition for institutional health services. Its existence here indicates that ASCs do not meet the criteria which the Congressional committee identified for determining when competition could be the primary method of allocating resources. If groups of physicians, by refusing to use existing facilities, can restated its probable volume and underestimated its costs, making its financial viability questionable. By withdrawing a significant patient load from the SSU, it would increase SHGH's costs. The net effect, SHPDA found, was that the proposed ASC would represent a substantial loss to the community.

SHPDA's order is a carefully reasoned evaluation of the evidence and considers the statutory factors. It explains the agency's action. Its essential findings of fact are, if challenged, supported by substantial evidence. OEA's attack on the order is primarily a disagreement with SHPDA's view of the law. Because we have held that SHPDA's view is essentially correct, there is no basis for us to reverse the order.[14] In the light of our decision, SHGH's cross-petition is moot.

Affirmed on review and on cross-review.

NOTES AND QUESTIONS ON COMPETITION AND CERTIFICATE-OF-NEED REGULATION

1. *The 1979 Federal Legislation.* The *OEA* case summarizes the procompetition language introduced into Public Law 93–641 in the 1979 amendments. Although Public Law 93–641 was repealed before the mandate to embrace these new regulatory concepts became effective, some states did adopt similar language or procompetitive criteria in their CON statutes and regulations. As the *OEA* court observes, Congress was quite circumspect in endorsing competition in health care. It did, however, set up requirements under which the planner-regulators could no longer simply assume that competition is dysfunctional. Instead, they would have to make a threshold determination of the market's efficacy as an allocative mechanism (with respect to the particular service and market in question) before substituting their own judgments for those of the marketplace. For a history and analysis of the 1979 amendments, see C. Havighurst, Deregulating the Health Care Industry 125–378 (1982).

2. *Is Competition Likely to Yield Efficient Results?* Several early studies suggested that, where hospital competition is most intense, costly medical technology is most heavily employed, costs are higher, and quality is lower (due to inadequate specialization). E.g., Robinson, Garnick & McPhee, Market and Regulatory Influences on the Availability of Coronary Angioplasty and Bypass Surgery in U.S. Hospitals, 317 New Eng.J.Med. 85 (1987) ("in the period under consideration [1983], competition encouraged and [rate] regulation discouraged the proliferation of the cardiac services"); Robinson & Luft, Competition and the Cost of Hospital Care 1972 to 1982, 257 J.A.M.A. 3241 (1987). These studies suggest that appropriate regionali-

quire SHPDA to issue a certificate for an otherwise unnecessary facility, they will have effectively destroyed the legislature's and Congress' purposes in enacting the health planning acts.

14. SHPDA has adequately explained why it denied this application despite its stated support for ASCs generally and its favorable action on other ASC proposals. ORS 183.482(8)(b)(B). OEA has not made its case on its claim of disparate treatment.

zation, with services concentrated in the hands of low-cost, high-quality providers, may be more readily achieved under regulation than under competition.

Could CON regulation, perhaps in combination with hospital rate or revenue controls, reasonably be expected to yield greater efficiency than competition? What is competition? The foregoing studies measured it largely by reference to the number of hospitals in a geographic area. In your view, are emerging forms of competition—most notably that necessitated by prudent purchasing by public and private health plans and by such plans' selective contracting with preferred providers—likely to achieve an efficient allocation of resources? The federal 1979 amendments and state laws implementing the modified federal policy contemplated that health planners and regulators would answer this question market by market. Is it likely that health planners and regulators would often find the market superior to regulation as an allocative device?

Should the issue of competition's virtues be resolved in preparing the state health plan or on a case-by-case basis? If the former, how could an applicant or other interested party challenge the evidentiary support for the determinations made? Is judicial review available? See Havighurst, supra, at 274–77; Note, Judicial Review of State Health Plans After the Health Planning and Resources Development Amendments of 1979, 1981 Duke L.J. 404. Cf. Statewide Health Coord. Council v. Circuit Court, 287 Ark. 84, 696 S.W.2d 729 (1985) (refusal of SHCC to amend SHP to allow more hospital beds treated as "adjudication" subject to judicial review).

3. *Freestanding Ambulatory Surgical Facilities (FASFs).* Regulations under Public Law 93–641, as amended, specifically identified FASFs (such as the facility in *OEA*) as mandatory objects of state CON regulation. Consider the rationale for regulating market entry by FASFs. How does the policy question whether to cover FASFs differ from the regulatory issue posed in a particular case (assuming that the principles of the 1979 federal amendments are incorporated in state law, as they apparently were in Oregon)? Even if a state legislature has resolved to maintain regulatory oversight of a certain category of investments or services, the procompetition thrust of the 1979 amendments suggests that local market conditions must still be considered in deciding whether to bar entry on the basis that a need has not been demonstrated. Can one argue that there is a "need" for the competition that the new service would provide? What factors would enter into an evaluation of a particular market's ability to deter the construction of excess capacity for which the public (rather than private investors) must ultimately pay?

The following discussion of the appropriateness of deregulating FASFs may also provide some insight on how to address a specific regulatory decision:

> The economic argument for regulating FASFs turns in large measure on the methods used in paying for their services. * * * [T]reatment by an FASF is usually paid for by mechanisms that do not effectively discourage the creation of overcapacity. Not only can most

FASFs expect to recover their capital costs through cost-reimbursement formulas (such as Medicare's) or through charges to patients whose indemnity insurance covers their outlays, but they have also been able to count on the insurance system to obviate price cutting by hospitals as a competitive response. Indeed, because of the payment systems in place, hospitals seeking to offset the loss of surgical patients to FASFs are more likely to raise their charges than to lower them—spreading their overhead over fewer patients—and to seek new and profitable procedures to do. The planner-regulators are likely to see in this pattern not only an inadequate market deterrent to overexpansion by FASFs but also an invitation to cost-escalating demand creation by the FASFs' competitors. * * * FASFs are likely to be perceived as cream-skimmers, taking the profitable business from the hospitals and leaving the latter not only to care for indigents but also to provide occasionally needed, expensive backup for the FASFs themselves. The destruction of hospitals' cross-subsidization capability remains a powerful inducement to protectionist exclusion of innovative competitors.

As is usual with arguments for CON regulation, the case for regulating FASFs, however plausible on its face, is shortsighted. The weakness of the market's deterrent to the creation of excess capacity lies in a financing system that has lacked the ability to steer patients to lower-cost providers and has thus insulated providers from significant price competition. Planner-regulators have long viewed such payment systems as inevitable and immutable and thus as a permanent justification for regulation. Believing that the need for their regulatory services has been established once and for all, they have been slow to recognize that changing purchasing practices in both public and private health plans are fundamentally altering the conditions that may once have justified their intervention in the market. But if planners and regulators were committed to advancing the goals of efficiency and consumer welfare, they would see increasing FASF competition for hospitals as a desirable stimulus for change not only in the hospitals themselves but also in prevailing payment methods. Payers who faced an immediate and palpable threat of rising costs resulting from overcapacity would have a powerful incentive to change their reimbursement practices and act as prudent purchasers. In this role, they would force providers of surgical care into competition by offering to contract with one or a few efficient providers to take care of their beneficiaries for fixed fees and under utilization controls. To make such bargaining effective, of course, an insurer would have to be able to steer its insureds, by financial inducements or otherwise, to contracting or other preferred providers. In these ways, price competition could become a reality in the health care sector.

Some planner-regulators would be naturally reluctant to count on such competitive pressures to induce reform of payment systems that currently shelter both high-cost providers from price competition and creators of excess capacity from the losses that would normally result from unwise investments (as existing providers, ignoring their sunk costs, respond to competition by pricing on a variable-cost basis).

Regulators lacking faith in the market as a spur to needed change might, however, at least treat any FASF having long-term contracts to serve the beneficiaries of public or private health plans as having conclusively demonstrated a need for its services. A policy of favoring (deregulating) providers who have established such relationships with payers would put pressure on existing providers to enter into such contracts, thus introducing real price competition where it has long been absent. * * * Unfortunately, few planner-regulators have been quick to seek changes in the inefficient payment systems that provide the justification for their regulatory power.

The more popular strategy among planner-regulators is to define some numerical ideal as the needed ambulatory surgery capability in the area. Such a central-planning approach, however, requires planners to make the essential choices concerning which medical conditions should be treated in which setting. Even assuming that such choices would be made technocratically and not on political grounds, the effect would be to freeze technology and put the burden of proof on would-be innovators likely to be perceived as opportunists. The main danger is that the public will lose the benefits of nonprice competition in the development of the full potential of outpatient surgery. A possible concern of a different kind is that the planners will accept the conventional view that ambulatory surgery is always cheaper, neglecting the possibility that, because excess hospital capacity exists, the avoidable costs of hospital-based care may actually be less. Improving the market would induce hospital pricing responses that would obviate the risk of overcapacity.

The case for deregulating FASFs rests in part on some evidence of past discrimination against them by planners seizing on available regulatory rationales for curbing their growth and competitive effectiveness. Even where the regulators have been able to point to an expansion of ambulatory surgery, they may have forced the new entrants to accommodate themselves to the planners' preferences and their competitors' concerns, thus sacrificing efficiency, real change, and real competition. Another possibility is that the regulators, having been convinced that ambulatory surgery is desirable, decided to let the incumbent providers offer it rather than allowing an FASF to be established. Planners are apt to see this as a happy outcome, giving the public the benefit of ambulatory surgery while keeping the hospital at the center of the system and preserving its ability to generate resources to cross-subsidize other services. What is lost is, first, competition between providers with different strengths, interests, and perceptions and, second, much of the incentive for independent interests to file a CON application that will be "batched" with defensive applications from existing hospitals likely to enjoy a presumption in the planners' eyes.

Whether or not hospitals are left subject to CON requirements, FASFs should be deregulated. The benefits to the public of free entry into the provision of ambulatory surgery include not only improvements in the provision of surgical care but also the stimulation of new

> purchasing practices by payers. Overcapacity would be unlikely once payers were in a position to refuse support to a higher-priced facility and prices began to reflect marginal costs. Although it is well within the power of the regulators to stimulate these private reforms, deregulation by statute is a surer path to prompt and meaningful change.

Havighurst, Developing Noninstitutional Health Services, supra, at 78–81.

Note the emphasis in the foregoing excerpt on a "market-forcing" rationale for deregulation. Under this concept, proposed in C. Havighurst, Deregulating the Health Care Industry, supra, at 321–44, planner-regulators would focus on the financing system's *potential* for reform rather than on whether sufficient reform had already occurred to make deregulation safe. See also McGinley, Beyond Health Care Reform: Reconsidering Certificate of Need Laws in a "Managed Competition" System, 23 Fla. St. U.L. Rev. 141, 157–58 (1995).

4. *Has the Time Come for Deregulation?* Would you recommend repeal of CON? What empirical questions would you like to see answered more fully before making up your mind? See Conover & Sloan, Does Removing Certificate-of-Need Regulations Lead to a Surge in Health Care Spending?, 23 J. Health Pol., Pol'y & L. 455 (1998) (finding no significant reduction in total per capita spending on health care in states with mature CON programs and no surge in spending or acquisition of facilities when CON controls are lifted). What significance would you attach to evidence that states that repealed CON law in the 1980s (e.g., Arizona) experienced some increases in capital construction? See Simpson, supra, at 1079–82. (Why do you suppose the "market" did not deter the construction of new hospitals in Arizona? Did the Arizona legislature make a mistake?) What is the significance for the questions posed here of the Medicare program's practices in reimbursing hospitals for their capital costs and of recent changes in those practices? (See chapter 2(§D).) What alternatives are there to a "let-'er-rip" policy of deregulation?

5. *Problem on Home Health Care.* Your state is considering repeal of CON regulation of home health agencies (HHAs), and you are asked by the legislator who employs you as a legislative assistant to brief him on the issue. Although federal law never required states to apply CON requirements to HHAs, a majority of states did so. In rejecting a 1979 federal proposal to compel state CON regulation of HHAs, a House committee stated its "belief that those services would not be excessive if they were not regulated and that market forces of supply and demand may appropriately allocate them." H.R.Rep. No. 96–190, 96th Cong., 1st Sess. 53 (1979). In West–Mont Community Care, Inc. v. Board of Health and Environmental Sciences, 703 P.2d 850 (Mont.1985), the court cited some benefits of competition in upholding a grant of a CON to a second HHA despite the existing agency's claim that its services would be duplicated. A 1986 FTC staff economic study argued that CON regulation of HHAs is unnecessary. K. Anderson & D. Kass, Certificate of Need Regulation of Entry Into Home Health Care (FTC 1986).

Consider why HHAs have been regulated in some states. Does home health care, which is provided by visiting nurses employed by nonprofit and for-profit agencies, give rise to problems of the kind that prompted CON regulation of hospitals? What is the significance of the following facts? (1) A number of other states have recently repealed CON regulation of HHAs. (2) Private payers have gradually expanded their coverage of home health services as a way of inducing earlier hospital discharges. (3) Medicare has installed new conditions of participation for HHAs and new survey and enforcement procedures and is moving toward prospective payment for home health care (e.g., per case, per illness, or per episode). (4) Since your state adopted CON regulation, Medicare has shifted to prospective payment for hospital inpatient care. (How does this change affect the hospitals' and the public's stake in home health care and the political forces bearing on the regulatory issue?) (5) Your state currently maintains an administrative rule—"the rule of 300"—under which no CON will be issued for an HHA unless every existing HHA in the area is already seeing an average of at least 300 patients per day; exceptions are made when existing agencies are unable to meet demand or the new agency would lower community health care costs. See Department of Health and Rehab. Servs. v. Johnson & Johnson Home Health Care, Inc., 447 So.2d 361 (Fla.App.1984) (invalidating such a rule as arbitrary and inconsistent with statutory criteria despite claim that purpose was to achieve economies of scale). (6) In some states, a new HHA requires a CON, but expansion of an existing one does not. See, e.g., Total Care, Inc. v. Department of Human Resources, 393 S.E.2d 338 (N.C.App.1990). (7) A hospital operating a HHA might monopolize the care of its former inpatients. Is such vertical integration to be avoided, or does it promise certain efficiencies? Cf. Arkansas Health Planning and Devel. Agency v. Hot Springs County Mem. Hosp., 291 Ark. 186, 723 S.W.2d 363 (1987) (denial of hospital's CON for HHA upheld on evidence that four HHAs already existed, that needs were met, that duplication would be costly, and that better coordination with existing agencies would serve hospital's asserted need for convenience).

6. *CON and HMOs.* Public Law 93–641 required the states to adopt CON laws meeting extensive federal specifications, one of which was coverage of HMOs. Not only were HMOs' major capital investments in hospital services and facilities to be subject to the planners' oversight, but HMOs were to be required, unlike other primary care providers, to obtain CONs for their initial establishment and for any outpatient facilities they wished to build. Although the statute indicated that HMOs should receive sympathetic treatment by the health planners, the states were not given the option of not regulating HMOs at all. What do you suppose was the thinking behind the legislation? What arguments might have been offered for leaving HMOs outside the reach of CON regulation? Was it realistic to expect HSAs and SHPDAs to view HMOs favorably? Would HMOs' efficiency claims be likely to impress the various participants in the planning and regulatory process? What arguments might be advanced to persuade the planners to deny a CON to an HMO? What modifications or undertakings might planner-regulators insist upon before allowing an HMO to enter a market or build a facility?

There is some evidence, both anecdotal and empirical, that HMOs suffered some detriment at the hands of the planner-regulators. See Brandon & Lee, Evaluating Health Planning: Empirical Evidence on HSA Regulation of Prepaid Group Practices, 9 J. Health Pol., Pol'y & L. 103 (1984). Whatever the actual burdens of CON regulation on HMO development, Congress and DHEW saw fit on several occasions between 1974 and 1978 to amend the planning law and regulations to make it increasingly clear that HMOs were not to be reviewed under the same principles as other providers. Instead of considering the needs of the community as a whole, the planners were to consider only the needs of the HMO's subscribers. Thus, an HMO seeking to build a hospital should be allowed to do so if the enrollees needed beds, even if the community was overbedded. What would be the effect of giving an HMO the freedom to build a new facility? Can you see how, paradoxically, the freedom to build might obviate new construction by making existing hospitals more willing to make their underused facilities available to the HMO on favorable terms?

In the 1979 amendments to Public Law 93–641—just five years after compelling the states to regulate HMOs—Congress reversed itself. Indeed, instead of merely repealing the earlier requirement, it prohibited the states from requiring CONs for the creation of HMOs or for their construction of outpatient facilities; significantly, this exemption extended to a much broader class of entities than met the requirements of the HMO Act. Congress also required the states to provide exemptions for other capital construction projects by HMOs upon receipt of assurances that enrollees would constitute no less than 75% of the users of the new facility. Can you see why, instead of granting a blanket exemption, this last minimal showing was required? (Senator Kennedy wanted assurance that, "if you're going to call it a duck, it really is a duck." More broadly, is there any reason why HMO decision makers might give inadequate weight to the risk that their subscribers would not fully utilize a projected facility?) Might one draw any general lessons for CON regulation from Congress's willingness to allow HMOs, because they face fairly effective discipline by market forces, to escape regulatory oversight?

Because the federal mandate to the states in Public Law 93–641 was not taken very seriously after 1979 and was repealed altogether in 1986, the states did not all amend their CON laws to conform to Congress' newly permissive policy toward HMOs. Some states still subject HMOs to some CON regulation. How should the planner-regulators exercise their powers?

SECTION E: HORIZONTAL AND VERTICAL INTEGRATION

Analyzing Hospital Mergers Under the Antitrust Laws

Hospital Corporation of America

Federal Trade Commission, 1985.
106 F.T.C. 455.

■ By CALVANI, COMMISSIONER:

* * *

In August 1981, Respondent Hospital Corporation of America ("HCA"), the largest proprietary hospital chain in the United States, acquired Hospital Affiliates International ("HAI") in a stock transaction valued at approximately $650 million. * * * Some four months later HCA acquired yet another hospital corporation, Health Care Corporation ("HCC") in a stock transaction valued at approximately $30 million. * * *

As a result of the HCABHAI acquisition, Respondent increased its hospital operations in Chattanooga and its suburbs from ownership of one acute care hospital to ownership or management of four of the area's eleven acute care hospitals. Within the six-county Chattanooga Metropolitan Statistical Area ("Chattanooga MSA"), HCA changed its position from owner of one hospital to owner or manager of six of fourteen acute care hospitals. With the acquisition of HCC, HCA obtained yet another acute care hospital in Chattanooga. Thus, HCA became owner or manager of five of the eleven acute care hospitals within the Chattanooga urban area and seven of the fourteen in the Chattanooga MSA.

* * * [Administrative Law] Judge Parker issued his Initial Decision on October 30, 1984. He found that the acquisitions violated Section 7 of the Clayton Act and Section 5 of the Federal Trade Commission Act, and ordered HCA to divest two of the hospitals of which it had acquired ownership. * * *

* * * We affirm Judge Parker's finding of liability and modify his opinion only as stated below.

* * *

We are * * * confronted in this case with a very peculiar market indeed. Because of the uncertainty of illness and injury and the grossly imperfect information available to consumers of hospital services, patients generally rely on physicians to determine the nature and extent of the medical care they receive and on third-party payors to provide the financial assurances that such care will be paid for. Any analysis of hospital markets under Section 7 must bear in mind both the role that physicians play on behalf of patients and the role of the insurance market in financing hospital care. With this in mind, we now turn to the merits of the case before us.

* * *

III. The Product Market

An acquisition violates Section 7 of the Clayton Act "where in any line of commerce in any section of the country, the effect of such acquisition may be substantially to lessen competition, or to tend to create a monopoly." 15 U.S.C. 18 (1982). Accordingly, we now turn to the definition of the relevant "line of commerce" or "product market" in which to measure the likely competitive effects of these acquisitions. In measuring likely competitive effects, we seek to define a product or group of products sufficiently distinct that buyers could not defeat an attempted exercise of market power on the part of sellers of those products by shifting purchases to still different products. Sellers might exercise market power by raising prices, limiting output or lowering quality.

Complaint Counsel argued below that the product market was properly defined as the provision of acute inpatient hospital services and emergency hospital services provided to the critically ill. This definition would exclude non-hospital providers of outpatient services, e.g., free standing emergency centers, as well as non-hospital providers of inpatient services, e.g., nursing homes, from the product market. It would also exclude the outpatient business of hospitals, except for that provided to the critically ill in the emergency room. The rationale for excluding outpatient care is that inpatient services are the reason for being of acute care hospitals; inpatient services are needed by and consumed by patients in combination and therefore can be offered only by acute care hospitals. Inpatients in almost all cases will purchase a range of services and not just one test or procedure; they will typically consume a "cluster" of services involving 24–hour nursing, the services of specialized laboratory and X-ray equipment, the services of equipment needed to monitor vital functions or intervene in crises, and so forth. An acutely ill patient must be in a setting in which all of these various services can be provided together. According to this reasoning, outpatient services are not an integral part of this "cluster of services" offered by acute care hospitals, and therefore must be excluded.

Respondent, on the other hand, urged that the market be defined to include outpatient care as well as inpatient care. Respondent's expert witness, Dr. Jeffrey E. Harris, testified that outpatient care is growing rapidly for hospitals, as well as for free-standing facilities such as emergency care and one-day surgery centers, which compete with hospitals for outpatients. Moreover, because of substantial changes in medical technology, there are a growing number of procedures that can be provided on an outpatient basis that previously could have been done on only an inpatient basis.

Judge Parker agreed that the market should include outpatient services provided by hospitals but excluded outpatient services provided by non-hospital providers, holding that only hospitals can provide the "unique combination" of services which the acute care patient needs. He defined the relevant product market to be the cluster of services offered by acute care hospitals, including outpatient as well as inpatient care, "since acute care hospitals compete with each other in offering both kinds of care and since ... acute care outpatient facilities feed patients to the inpatient facilities."

Neither HCA nor Complaint Counsel appeal Judge Parker's product market definition. Accordingly, for purposes of this proceeding only we accept Judge Parker's finding on this issue.

However, we do note that Judge Parker's definition does not necessarily provide a very happy medium between the two competing positions; the evidence in this case tended to show *both* that free-standing outpatient facilities compete with hospitals for many outpatients and that hospitals offer and inpatients consume a cluster of services that bears little relation to outpatient care. If so, it may be that defining the cluster of hospital inpatient services as a separate market better reflects competitive reality in this case. In American Medical International, Inc., ("AMI") [104 F.T.C. 1 (1984)], we defined the relevant product market as the "cluster of general acute care hospital services" to the exclusion of outpatient substitutes for individual services that comprise the cluster, since the "benefit that accrues to patient and physician" is derived from the complementarity of those services. It may well be that in this case the proper product market excludes *all* outpatient care; perhaps outpatient care should be a separate relevant market or markets. In any case, it is clear from the evidence that the core and vast majority of an acute care hospital's business is acute inpatient care. Certainly, it is clear that anticompetitive behavior by hospital firms could significantly lessen competition for hospital inpatients that could not be defeated by competition from non-hospital outpatient providers. Our analysis will hence proceed with primary reference to the cluster of services provided to inpatients.

IV. The Geographic Market

We now turn our attention to the relevant geographic market or "section of the country" in which competition could be substantially lessened by these acquisitions. Because we are concerned only with an area in which competition could be harmed, the relevant geographic market must be broad enough that buyers would be unable to switch to alternative sellers in sufficient numbers to defeat an exercise of market power by firms in the area. Again, sellers may exercise market power by raising prices, reducing output or reducing quality. If an exercise of market power could be defeated by the entry of products produced in another area, both areas should be considered part of the same geographic market for Section 7 purposes, since competition could not be harmed in the smaller area. That is, the geographic market should determine not only the firms that constrain competitors' actions by currently selling to the same customers, but also those that would be a constraint because of their ability to sell to those customers should price or quality in the area change.

* * *

HCA would have us adopt Hamilton County, Tennessee, together with Walker, Dade and Catoosa counties in Georgia, the "Chattanooga urban area," as the relevant geographic market. HCA predicates its conclusion largely on an analysis of evidence concerning physician admitting patterns.

Dr. Harris, HCA's expert, testified that the relevant geographic market is determined to a great extent by physician admitting practice, because physician preference, rather than patient choice, decides what hospitals will be utilized. * * * With few exceptions, every physician who admitted to Chattanooga urban area hospitals admitted exclusively to other hospitals in the Chattanooga urban area. Conversely, physicians admitting and treating patients at hospitals outside the Chattanooga urban area rarely admitted and treated patients at hospitals in the Chattanooga urban area.

* * *

On appeal, Complaint Counsel agree that the Chattanooga urban area is an appropriate geographic area in which to assess the competitive effects of these acquisitions. However, they claim that a much more appropriate geographic market is the federally designated Metropolitan Statistical Area that includes Chattanooga. In effect, Complaint Counsel would have us add the Tennessee counties of Marion and Sequatchie to the market proffered by HCA and adopted by Judge Parker. By adding this area, three additional hospitals—South Pittsburg Municipal Hospital, Sequatchie General Hospital, and Whitwell Community Hospital—would be included in the relevant market. Both South Pittsburg and Sequatchie were acquired by HCA from HAI, and Complaint Counsel seek divestiture by HCA of its long-term lease arrangement with South Pittsburg.

* * * The fact is that use of the Chattanooga MSA as the relevant geographic market would exclude a large number of hospital beds that are equally as accessible to physicians and patients as the beds it would include. Certainly, the greater number of beds to the northeast and southeast would provide a greater constraint on the exercise of market power in the Chattanooga urban area, if at all. We therefore find Complaint Counsel's argument to be economically artificial.[9]

* * *

Since Complaint Counsel concede that the Chattanooga urban area is an appropriate market within which to assess the competitive effects of these acquisitions, we conclude that the Chattanooga urban area is the relevant "section of the country" for purposes of this case. However, we note that Complaint Counsel's criticism of the evidence offered by HCA is a valid one; HCA offered a static picture of the market without offering evidence or argument considering the likelihood or unlikelihood that physicians and their patients in Chattanooga would travel to outlying hospitals in the event of an exercise of market power by Chattanooga urban area hospitals.

A proper dynamic analysis might have considered some of the evidence in this case as follows: "The closest hospitals to the Chattanooga urban area are about 45 minutes driving time away. Chattanooga doctors try as much as possible to avoid travel, because it is time consuming and inconvenient. It is unlikely that doctors would be willing to make rounds that far away from home on a daily basis in response to a small but significant reduction in the quality of hospital services in Chattanooga. They therefore would be very unlikely to admit patients to outlying hospitals. It is also

9. Patient inflow into the Chattanooga urban area from outlying MSA counties cannot save Complaint Counsel's proposed market. First, * * * the weight of the evidence suggests that the great part of patient flow into Chattanooga hospitals from outlying areas is for specialized treatment not available in outlying hospitals. Thus, such inflow does not reflect well the ability of outlying hospitals to compete away those patients should Chattanooga hospitals behave anticompetitively. Second, the evidence shows in any case substantial inflow from Bradley County which lies to the east of Chattanooga. Indeed, Complaint Counsel's own expert, Dr. Salkever, rejected the Chattanooga MSA as the relevant geographic market in this case partly on that basis. The Chattanooga MSA thus cannot be distinguished on the basis of inflow data.

unlikely that patients themselves would seek hospitalization that far away from home even if they recognized a small but significant change in the quality or price of services in Chattanooga. The evidence suggests that family and friends do not like to commute far to visit patients. Proximity to family and friends is therefore very important to the hospital inpatient. Thus it is highly unlikely that many patients and their employers would agree to insurance coverage that required extensive travel for health care, even if insurance carriers had to increase premiums because of a small but significant exercise of market power by Chattanooga hospitals."

It is clear that the analysis offered by HCA and adopted by Judge Parker is incomplete. A review of patient flow data, physician admitting patterns, and other facts integral to a static analysis may all be important to a proper dynamic analysis, since a picture of current competition must be drawn before competitive responses to changes in that competitive pattern can properly be considered. But without looking at those facts in a framework considering potential competitive responses to the current market picture, a relevant geographic area in which competition may be substantially harmed will be extremely difficult to define. In any event, the Chattanooga urban area is the area within which we will assess the competitive effects of these acquisitions.

V. The Effect on Competition

A. The Effect of HCA–Managed Hospitals

One of the major dimensions of HCA's purchase of HAI was the acquisition of some 75 to 80 hospital management contracts. Two of these were management contracts HAI had with two hospitals in the Chattanooga urban area—Downtown General Hospital and Red Bank Community Hospital. * * * HCA argues, and Judge Parker agreed, that Downtown General and Red Bank hospitals should be treated as entities completely separate from HCA, incapable of being significantly influenced by HCA in its role as administrator. * * *

We conclude that treating the two managed hospitals as entities completely independent of HCA is contrary to the overwhelming weight of the evidence in this case. * * *

* * * We think it clear that the management relationships greatly enhance HCA's ability to coordinate behavior, since HCA personnel run the hospitals' competitive mechanisms and the hospital boards have hired managers for the very reason that the boards have neither the time nor the expertise to manage the variables of hospital competition themselves.

* * * Indeed, the evidence in this case indicates more than a symbiotic relationship between the two types of HCA hospitals. HCA's sister relationship program for coordination between HCA hospitals in the same local area includes both owned and managed hospitals. In Chattanooga, HCA held meetings for both owned and managed hospital administrators "to initiate them into the HCA philosophy." * * *

In short, we find that considering managed hospitals to be entities independent of HCA in examining an increased likelihood of competitive behavior in this market strains credulity. Doing so would seriously understate the likelihood of competitive harm in the Chattanooga urban area from HCA's acquisition of HAI. The evidence compels us to consider the market shares of Downtown General and Red Bank as part of HCA's market share in considering the effect on competition in this case. Even were the evidence not as compelling, we would consider HCA's management of the two hospitals to greatly enhance the likelihood of collusion in this market.

B. The Nature of Competition Among Chattanooga Hospitals

Traditionally, hospitals have competed for patients in three general ways: first, by competing for physicians to admit their patients; second, by competing directly for patients on the basis of amenities and comfort of surroundings; and third, by competing to a limited degree on the basis of price. The first two constitute "non-price" or "quality" competition, and by far have been in the past the most important of the three.

Non-price competition for physicians includes the provision of up-to-date equipment, a qualified and reliable nursing staff and other technically trained personnel, convenient office space to make it easier for the physician to concentrate both his ambulatory and inpatient work within the same location, a nice doctors' lounge with a good selection of journals—everything that will convince physicians that their patients are receiving the best care possible and make physicians' lives more comfortable. Competition directed at patients themselves has traditionally been through the provision of amenities, such as pleasant surroundings, attractive rooms, televisions and telephones, high nurse-to-patient ratios, convenient parking—everything that will make patients more comfortable.

* * *

Over the last decade, two major trends increasing competition among hospitals beyond its traditional limits have developed. First, both non-price and price competition are now being directed much more toward patients themselves than in the past. Second, beginning in the late 1970s the hospital industry has seen the clear emergence of direct price competition. At the same time, traditional non-price competition for patients on the basis of amenities has intensified somewhat, through the provision of such amenities as private rooms. Non-price competition for physicians remains pervasive, since physicians still largely determine the disposition and treatment of their patients.

Increasing competitive efforts aimed directly at patients include health education programs, CPR classes, community activities, and direct mass media advertising, such as on billboards and radio. The clear emergence of direct price competition is even more striking. Hospitals are now trying to attract the business of employers and insurers by offering price discounts.

The reason for this increase in price competition is a reaction in the health insurance market to rising costs.

* * *

The result of rising insurance costs has been a change in employer and employee concern that in turn has changed insurer behavior. Insurers realized that there was a market for cost containment and have reacted by providing new insurance packages and by marketing cost containment services.

* * *

In sum, this increasing concern of employers and employees with the costs of insurance means that differences in prices between hospitals matter to them and their third-party payors, since insurance will cost less when hospital care costs less. The result is that hospitals are now far more likely to present themselves to insurers, employers and employee groups as less costly than their competitors as one method of attracting more business. Price competition, fostered by these new insurance mechanisms, is therefore growing in the hospital industry.

HCA's claim that any increase in price competition among hospitals is insignificant is belied by its own records. HCA itself has predicted a "more price competitive environment" for hospitals because of increased pressure from private industry to reduce hospital expenses. HCA planners have noted the sensitivity of major purchasers of health care to rising costs, which should "stimulate considerable competition among health care providers." Another HCA document reflects the belief that "increasing competition in the health care sector ... will allow natural market forces to slow the price rise spiral."

* * *

Both the traditional forms of non-price and price competition are evident in Chattanooga, as well as the emerging trends, though changes such as the development of HMOs and PPOs are proceeding more slowly than elsewhere. The evidence is clear that Chattanooga hospitals compete for physician patronage and that they do so in a variety of ways. * * *

Moreover, the testimony of hospital administrators is overwhelming that Chattanooga area hospitals compete in some manner on the basis of price. The price competition that has traditionally existed in Chattanooga is meaningful enough that competition could be harmed substantially if it is restricted. For example, the Blue Cross participating hospital system is a form of this price competition that has existed for years. Under the plan, hospitals become members of Blue Cross and Blue Shield of Tennessee and agree to charge only Blue Cross-approved prices to Blue Cross subscribers in order to attract them as patients. Blue Cross has a large number of subscribers who receive higher amounts of reimbursement if they are treated at member hospitals. The result is a strong incentive for hospitals to participate in the program; indeed, all of the Chattanooga urban area hospitals are member hospitals. This is "price competition" because if a hospital unilaterally refuses to deal with Blue Cross at the desired rates, it will lose business to competing hospitals that are willing to charge lower rates for Blue Cross subscribers.

Moreover, the evidence shows that hospital rates in Chattanooga are established with at least some reference to the rates of other hospitals. Formal and informal rate surveys have been used by area hospitals to determine whether the surveyor's prices were within the range of prices offered by competing hospitals or to justify price increases to Blue Cross. * * *

Thus, it is obvious that price has been a competitively sensitive matter among Chattanooga hospitals. We do not here conclude that price has been the prime arena in which hospitals in Chattanooga compete. However, we do think it clear that even though rates are not constantly adjusted due to a changing price structure, they have been periodically set with some reference to what the market will bear in face of the prices of other hospitals.

It is clear that Section 7 protects whatever price competition exists in a market, however limited. * * *

There is, however, even more reason to conclude that price competition could be harmed by these acquisitions. The evidence shows that the industry-wide growth in price competition has taken root as a market phenomenon in the Chattanooga area. Price competition is increasing and appears likely to further increase significantly among Chattanooga hospitals.

Because employers and employee groups in the Chattanooga area are experiencing severe cost increases, they have been forced to make significant changes in their employee health benefit plans. For example, Provident Insurance Company's model insurance plan, which it both markets and uses for its own employees, calls for 20% coinsurance and a 100 to 150 dollar deductible that employees must pay out of their own pockets. * * * These changes are intended to encourage employees to become more cost conscious and therefore at least to some extent to be more sensitive to differences in the prices charged by different health care providers. In fact, the evidence shows some increased price sensitivity on the part of consumers. See, e.g., Lamb 179 ("Patients do comparisons. They shop around some ... [A]s insurance coverages change and patients become more a part of paying the cost of their own hospital bills they are becoming more concerned about their cost.").

Following the industry trend, some Chattanooga area employers have been counseling their employees in an effort to persuade them to seek health care from low cost providers. In response to Memorial's encouragement, various companies have urged their employees to utilize Memorial Hospital because of its low costs. Moreover, employers are developing data bases so that the prices of services provided by different health care providers can be more effectively compared.

As a result of these phenomena, Chattanooga hospitals are beginning to show the signs of more direct price competition. Memorial has encouraged employers to steer employees to it on the basis of its lower prices and concurrent high quality, and has disseminated newsletters to Chattanooga industries encouraging price shopping for health services and preadmission counseling of employees. Memorial has urged employers "to identify the hospital which is giving your employees the best service for the least dollar amount" and "to take a look at the price differential among hospitals. . . ." East Ridge has advertised emergency room price lists and its publications explain the pricing system at the hospital and urge prospective patients to inquire about hospital accommodations and rates when hospital-shopping.

In addition to increasing price competition, the evidence * * * shows that advertising is increasing in Chattanooga.[17]

Finally, we note that Chattanooga hospitals compete in the recruitment of qualified medical personnel, such as nurses and laboratory technicians. The evidence shows that they offer salaries and benefits competitive with other hospitals to retain their personnel. Therefore, any analysis of the likely effects on competition from these acquisitions may also consider competition for inputs.

C. Respondent's Market Share and Concentration in the Chattanooga Urban Area

Three ways to measure a hospital's share of the acute care hospital services market are by using: (1) bed capacity; (2) inpatient days; and (3) net revenues. Bed capacity and inpatient days measure a hospital's position with regard to the cluster of inpatient services, the heart of hospital care. Net revenues, on the other hand, account for both inpatient and outpatient services.

Naturally, because of their proposed market definitions, Complaint Counsel advocate use of inpatient measures, while HCA urges net revenues as the preferable measure since it accounts for outpatient services. We conclude, however, that the three measures are so similar in this case that they yield the same result whatever measure is used.

* * *

The Herfindahl–Hirschman Index ("HHI") of market concentration is calculated by summing the squares of the individual market shares of all the firms in the market. The HHI reflects the distribution of market shares

17. The importance to our analysis of the emerging competition in the health care industry is essentially acknowledged by HCA, we think, in its attempt to exclude relevant post-acquisition evidence in this case. HCA argues that these acquisitions should be judged by the facts as of the time the acquisitions occurred and that those facts indicate no likely lessening of competition.

We reject HCA's attempt to exclude this evidence [because], it presumes that this post-acquisition evidence does not "illuminate the validity of arguments relating to a possible lessening of competition based fundamentally upon market dynamics at the time of the acquisition." HCA is simply wrong. The record is conclusive that the trends * * * both nationwide and in Chattanooga toward greater price and non-price competition, advertising and other marketing, patient awareness, and the cost pressures that spawned those trends, were well underway before the 1981 acquisitions at issue here. * * *

between firms and gives proportionately greater weight to the market shares of the larger firms, which likely accords with their relative importance in any anticompetitive interaction. U.S. Department of Justice Merger Guidelines (June 14, 1984) ("DOJ Guidelines") § 3.1. * * * [U]sing any measure of market power the Herfindahl index was above 1900 before the acquisitions. Thus, the acquisitions occurred in a market already highly concentrated. Following HCA's acquisition of HAI, the HHI increased some 295 points using net patient revenues and over 300 using beds or patient days. With the acquisition of HCC, the HHI additionally increased well over 100 points using any measure. Again using any measure, the HHI at the very least rests at 2416 after the acquisitions. We consider such an increase in concentration in an already concentrated market to be of serious competitive concern, all other things being equal.

More traditional measures of market share also support this conclusion. For example, using patient days HCA's market share increased from 13.8% to 25.8% in the Chattanooga urban area, while four-firm concentration increased to almost 92% and two-firm concentration to 61%. The figures for approved beds and net patient revenues are almost identical. These figures support an inference of harm to competition, all other things equal.

Moreover, all other things being equal, an increase in market concentration through a reduction in the absolute number of competitive actors makes interdependent behavior more likely. These acquisitions decreased the number of independent firms in the market from 9 to 7. The costs of coordination or of policing any collusive agreement are less with fewer participants, and the elimination of competitive forces in this market facilitates joint anticompetitive behavior.

In sum, evidence of the increased concentration caused by these acquisitions points toward a finding of likely harm to competition, all other things being equal. HCA's acquisitions have made an already highly concentrated market more conducive to collusion by eliminating two of the healthiest sources of competition in the market and increasing concentration substantially. But all other things are not equal in this market, and statistical evidence is not the end of our inquiry. In the absence of barriers to entry, an exercise of market power can be defeated or deterred by the entry or potential entry of new firms regardless of the structure of the existing market. We now turn to the issue of entry barriers and conclude that they confirm and even magnify the inference to be drawn from the concentration evidence in this case.

D. Barriers to Entry

* * * [T]here is hardly free entry into the acute care hospital industry in either Tennessee or Georgia. Indeed, the CON laws at issue here create a classic "barrier to entry" under every definition of that term. In *Echlin Manufacturing Co.*, we defined a "barrier to entry" to include "additional long-run costs that must be incurred by an entrant relative to the long-run costs faced by incumbent firms." We explained that "[t]he rationale under-

lying this definition is that low-cost incumbent firms can keep prices above the competitive level as long as those prices remain below the level that would provide an incentive to higher-cost potential entrants."

If a potential entrant desires to build a new hospital in Chattanooga, he must incur all the costs in time and money associated with obtaining a CON. The cost of starting a new hospital includes not only the start-up costs that any firm would incur to enter the market but also the costs of surviving the administrative process. Incumbents in this market, however, did not incur such costs during initial construction. They have only had to incur those costs for additions made to bed capacity since the enactment of the CON laws a decade ago. Incumbents thus have a long run cost advantage over potential entrants. The result is that market power could be exercised by incumbents without attracting attempts at entry as long as supracompetitive profits are not high enough for a potential entrant to justify incurring all the ordinary costs of starting a hospital *plus* the significant costs of obtaining a CON.

The evidence is clear that those costs are significant in this market. We agree with Judge Parker that because incumbent hospitals can oppose new entry, even an unsuccessful opposition to a CON application may delay its disposition by several years. * * *

Thus the CON process provides existing hospitals in the Chattanooga urban area ample opportunity to significantly forestall the entry of a new hospital or the expansion of an existing hospital within the area. Indeed, the evidence shows that existing hospitals frequently oppose CON applications when they feel competitively threatened. * * *

Even this analysis presumes that a CON can be obtained if the costly process is followed through in this market. In fact, * * * the last three applications for new bed capacity in the Chattanooga area have all been denied, and the only application for a new hospital in the Chattanooga area since 1974 was denied. Only one CON for new beds in the Georgia portion of the Chattanooga health planning area has ever been approved. In fact, Judge Parker concluded that "[i]t is doubtful . . . whether health planning authorities in Tennessee and Georgia will find that any need for additional facilities in the HSA will exist in the foreseeable future."

* * *

Finally, HCA executives have in the past ascribed a "franchise value" to hospitals as a result of CON regulation. David G. Williamson, Jr., Executive Vice President of Domestic Development for HCA, has referred to the "franchise value" and "franchise type protection" of hospitals that is created by certificate of need regulation. The very existence of a "franchise value" is a tacit admission of the existence of barriers to entry.

Accordingly, we agree with Dr. Salkever that CON laws pose a very substantial obstacle to both new entry and expansion of bed capacity in the Chattanooga market. Indeed, the very purpose of the CON laws is to restrict entry. Existing Chattanooga area hospitals appear virtually insulated from new competition in the short term, and have an absolute cost advantage that extends into the long term. Therefore, any harm to competition that could be generated by profitable collusion or interdependent behavior in this market will unlikely be deterred by threatened or actual new entry.

E. The Nature and Likelihood of Anticompetitive Behavior in the Chattanooga Hospital Market

1. The Nature of Anticompetitive Behavior

Because HCA denies that anticompetitive behavior among Chattanooga urban area hospitals is likely, it is useful to consider the likely forms that any anticompetitive behavior would take. Profitable collusion could take a number of different forms and restrict price or non-price competition or both.

Some of the most likely forms of collusion between hospitals would involve collective resistance to emerging cost containment pressures from third-party payors and alternative providers. For example, joint refusals to deal with HMOs or PPOs may occur, or perhaps joint refusals to deal on the most favorable terms. Conspiracies to boycott certain insurance companies that are generating price competition may occur. Utilization review programs may be also be resisted. Hospitals could concertedly refuse to provide the information desired by third-party payors—information that would otherwise be provided as hospitals vie to attract the business of those payors and their subscribers. The result of any such boycott would be to raise prices, reduce quality of services or both.

* * *

Quality competition itself might also be restricted. For example, * * * hospitals could accomplish anticompetitive ends not only by fixing staff-patient ratios but by agreeing on wages or benefits to be paid certain personnel—for example, laboratory technicians. Indeed, wage and salary surveys are common in this market. The result would be the same—to hold the cost of inputs down with probable harm to the quality of output of health care services. Hospitals could also agree not to compete for each other's personnel or medical staff. Indeed, some Chattanooga urban area hospital firms have already engaged in such behavior.

Moreover, under certificate of need legislation, the addition of new services and purchases of certain kinds of new equipment require a demonstration of need for the expenditure, and the existence of need is determined in part by the facilities already provided in the community. It would thus be to the advantage of competing hospitals to enter into agreements among themselves as to which competitor will apply for which service or for which piece of equipment. New bed applications might also be allocated among existing hospitals. * * * In return for agreements not to file competing applications, administrators can support each other's CON applications, thereby assisting the applicant to demonstrate need. In fact, there is evidence that Chattanooga area hospitals have recognized the advantage of cooperating on CON matters and that this type of allocation has occurred in Chattanooga. Such market division by private agreement would save hospitals the expense of applying for numerous CONs but may harm the quality of care that would be available to patients were CON approval sought independently by each hospital with reference to its own merits and expertise.

Concerted opposition to the CON application of a potential new entrant is yet another manner in which Chattanooga hospitals could successfully collude. * * *

Hospitals could also successfully collude with respect to price by agreeing not to give discounts to businesses, insurers and other group purchasers such as HMOs and PPOs. Moreover, an agreement on the percentage discount to be offered or the group or groups of purchasers to receive a discount can be reached, even without an agreement on the base price to which the discount is applied. * * *

In sum, we conclude that hospitals compete in a myriad of ways that could be restricted anticompetitively through collusion. Thus, it appears that a merger analysis in this case need be no different than in any other case; market share and concentration figures, evidence of entry barriers and other market evidence taken together appear to yield as accurate a picture of competitive conditions as they do in other settings. Nevertheless, although HCA concedes that many of the above described forms of collusion *could* occur, the heart of HCA's case is that collusion in this market is inherently unlikely, and to that contention we now turn.

2. *The Likelihood of Anticompetitive Behavior*

Section 7 of the Clayton Act prohibits acquisitions that may have the effect of substantially lessening competition or tending to create a monopoly. Because Section 7 applies to "incipient" violations, actual anticompetitive effects need not be shown; an acquisition is unlawful if such an effect is reasonably probable.

The small absolute number of competitors in this market, the high concentration and the extremely high entry barriers indicate a market in which anticompetitive behavior is reasonably probable after the acquisitions. The fact that industry members recognize the enormity of entry barriers makes collusion even more probable. In addition, hospital markets have certain features that evidence a likelihood of collusion or other anticompetitive behavior when they become highly concentrated.

First, price elasticity of demand for hospital services is very low, which makes anticompetitive behavior extremely profitable and hence attractive. Second, because consumers of hospital services cannot arbitrage or resell them as is often possible with goods, discrimination among different groups of consumers is possible. That is, collusion may be directed at a certain group or certain groups of consumers, such as a particular insurance company, without the necessity of anticompetitive behavior toward other groups. Third, the traditions of limited price competition and disapproval of advertising provide an incentive for future anticompetitive restrictions of those activities. Fourth, and in the same vein, the advent of incentives to resist new cost containment pressures may create a substantial danger of hospital collusion to meet those pressures. Fifth, the hospital industry has a tradition of cooperative problem solving which makes collusive conduct in the future more likely. Hospitals have historically participated in voluntary health planning in a coordinated manner, and along with other professional organizations, such as medical societies, have participated in developing joint solutions to industry problems.

Moreover, the history of interaction among Chattanooga hospitals supports a conclusion that anticompetitive behavior, whether through interdependent behavior or express or tacit collusion, is reasonably probable in the highly concentrated market created by these acquisitions. The most convincing evidence of the facility with which such collusion could occur is a blatant market allocation agreement executed in 1981 between Red Bank Community Hospital and HCC. The parties actually *signed a contract* under which Red Bank agreed that for a period of three years it would not "file any application for a Certificate of Need for psychiatric facilities or nursing home facilities." Moreover, the parties agreed that they would not compete for each other's personnel and medical staff during that time period, and that they would not oppose each other's CON applications in certain areas. Such an overt agreement to refrain from competition at the very least demonstrates the predisposition of some firms in the market to collude when it is in their interest; at worst it shows a callous disregard for the antitrust laws.

* * *

Furthermore, a basis for collusion is provided by the exchanges of rate, salary and other competitively sensitive information that occur in this market. * * *

a. Non-profit Hospitals and the Likelihood of Collusion

HCA contends that the most fundamental difference between hospitals in Chattanooga is that several of the hospitals are "non-profit" institutions. Economic theory presumes that businesses in an industry are profit-maximizers and that output will be restricted in pursuit of profits. Non-profit hospitals, the argument goes, have no incentive to maximize profits; rather, they seek to maximize "output" or the number of patients treated. HCA contends that non-profit hospitals may have other goals as well, such as providing the most sophisticated and highest quality care possible, or pursuing religious or governmental goals. In short, HCA argues that collusion would not occur because the "for-profit" and "non-profit" competitors have no common goal.

We disagree that non-profit hospitals have no incentive to collude with each other or with proprietary hospitals to achieve anticompetitive ends. First, we note that non-profit status of market participants is no guarantee of competitive behavior. * * *

Dr. Salkever testified that non-profit hospitals "can find attractive ways from their point of view to make use of the monopoly rents which would appear as returns to stockholders in the case of the for-profit hospitals." Anticompetitive behavior effecting monopoly rents may permit non-profits to maximize other goals, such as quality of care, amount of unreimbursable care, experimentation, development of highly specialized services, prestige, and so forth. Our concern under Section 7 is not what economic profits would be used for by the parties exercising market power but simply the fact that such an exercise of market power would be to the detriment of consumers.

* * * We also find that even when the goals of non-profit hospitals diverge from profit-maximization, the evidence shows that they are not necessarily commensurate with the ends of competition that Section 7 is intended to protect. Divergent maximands between competitors can often produce the same anticompetitive ends. And lastly, the evidence shows that non-profits in this market have an incentive to collude and have engaged in cooperative behavior with other hospitals.

b. Purported Obstacles to Successful Coordination

Relying entirely upon the testimony of its expert, Dr. Harris, HCA argues that even if hospitals in Chattanooga were inclined to collude, the administrators of those hospitals would find it difficult to reach anticompetitive agreements or understandings, or to sustain them if they ever were reached. This is so because the ideal market circumstances for collusion are not present, *i.e.* where manufacturers are selling "some simple, relatively homogeneous good, well characterized by a single price." HCA contends that hospital services are heterogeneous and influenced by a variety of complicating factors. Hospitals provide a large number of varied medical tests and treatments and each patient receives unpredictable personalized service the extent of which is determined by physicians. Moreover, HCA claims, costs and demand vary between hospitals. And because the dominant avenues of competition relate to the quality of medical care and patient amenities, hospitals would have to agree on a whole host of things to eliminate competition in a manner sufficient to earn monopoly returns, it is alleged.

* * * HCA would have us believe that the world of possible collusion is limited to complicated formulae concerning every aspect of hospital competition—that market power can only be exercised with respect to the entire cluster of services that constitutes the acute care hospital market through a conspiracy fixing the overall quantity or quality of treatment running to each patient in the market. Rather than focus on the likely avenues of collusion among hospitals, HCA assumes into existence a world in which collusion is infeasible.

We reject this analysis. Neither Dr. Harris nor HCA in its briefs offer any explanation whatsoever for why hospitals would have to fix every aspect of competition between them to collude profitably. We see no reason why hospitals would have more difficulty reaching an understanding with respect to many of the different aspects of acute care hospital competition described above than competitors would in any other market that is equally concentrated. For example, boycotts of third-party payors or agreements not to advertise do not depend upon complex formulae.

VII. CONCLUSION

We hold that HCA's acquisitions of HAI and HCC may substantially lessen competition in the Chattanooga urban area acute care hospital market in violation of Section 7 of the Clayton Act and Section 5 of the Federal Trade Commission Act. * * *

[The Commission ordered appropriate divestiture.]

NOTES AND QUESTIONS ON THE ANTITRUST TREATMENT OF HOSPITAL MERGERS

1. Although the antitrust laws apply to horizontal mergers of all kinds, the discussion here is limited to hospital mergers. On mergers of physician practices, see HTI Health Services, Inc. v. Quorum Health Group, Inc., 960 F.Supp. 1104 (S.D.Miss.1997) (rejecting challenge by Columbia/HCA hospital chain to merger of dominant physician practices in Vicksburg, Miss.). Recent mergers of large managed care plans (e.g., Aetna/U.S. Healthcare, Cigna/Healthsource), although signifying increasing consolidation on the payer side of market, have nevertheless passed muster with federal and state enforcement agencies.

2. *Is Antitrust Law a Barrier to Desirable Change in Hospital Markets?* Because most hospital markets (except in the largest cities) are already highly concentrated, many hospital mergers will fail to pass scrutiny under the recently liberalized but still concentration-oriented tests employed by antitrust enforcers. It has been argued that, for this reason and because hospital mergers frequently yield efficiencies and facilitate control of health care costs, special tests should be used to assess mergers in this industry. See, e.g., Schramm & Renn, Hospital Mergers, Market Concentration and the Herfindahl–Hirschman Index, 33 Emory L.J. 869 (1984). Do you agree? HCA argued that factors other than effects on competition should be taken into account in weighing hospital mergers because price competition is not especially effective in the hospital field and because nonprice competition is cost-escalating at a time when cost containment is widely desired. How did the FTC respond? How should it have responded? In antitrust terms at least, a strong argument can be made that nonprice competition, because it stimulates attention to consumers' needs and preferences and induces the husbanding of resources to satisfy those needs and preferences better, is substantially better than no competition at all. What further answers are there to the argument in an antitrust merger case that, with hospitals, price competition is unreliable as a stimulus for efficiency and cost containment?

Hospitals currently suffer from a great deal of overcapacity as a result of the revolutionary changes sweeping the health care industry. They are also under intense competitive pressure to reduce costs, which may be possible only by eliminating some facilities and combining others. The necessary restructuring of the hospital industry might be effectuated more readily through mergers than through competition that leads eventually to hospital bankruptcy—at the brink of which antitrust law's so-called "failing company" doctrine might finally permit a hospital's rescue by a substantial competitor. Is there any way, consistent with the statutory command that competition must be preserved, that merger law can be prevented from being an obstacle to rationalization of an industry in a time of major upheaval and technological change? In the following paragraphs, look for ways in which the antitrust agencies and courts, consistent with antitrust doctrine, could facilitate desirable consolidation. In fact, both agencies and courts have become much more tolerant of hospital mergers since the *HCA* case. Has this tolerance come by bending antitrust rules or by applying them with greater insight?

3. *Antitrust Doctrine.* It is of course not possible here to explore in depth the antitrust principles applicable to corporate mergers and acquisitions. Nevertheless, it may be helpful to recognize that the basic issue in "horizontal" merger cases is essentially the same as that raised by any kind of competitor collaboration (such as that examined in chapter 4): Is the agreement between competitors compatible with the maintenance of competition as the chosen instrument for allocating resources, inducing efficiency, and advancing consumer welfare? Although mergers obviously eliminate competition between the parties, they are potentially procompetitive in combining complementary resources or facilitating the realization of economies of scale. If a combination might facilitate the exercise of substantial market power, however, the law may oppose it, preferring to see efficiencies, if any, realized in a way more compatible with the maintenance of vigorous competition. The crucial issue in evaluating a merger is therefore whether it will make it easier for the merged firm, acting alone or through coordination of prices or business practices with other firms in the market, to exercise market power. Judgments on this question, as well as on the likelihood and magnitude of procompetitive benefits, are necessarily quite speculative. Partly for this reason, the Clayton Act focuses not on actual effects, which may lie in the unknowable future, but on probabilities. Thus, the statute asks whether "the effect of such acquisition *may be* substantially to lessen competition."

Antitrust law went through a period of mergerphobia in the 1960s as the courts interpreted a 1950 amendment to the Clayton Act as signifying a congressional preference for protecting small business and for preserving large numbers of competitors, even at some cost in economic efficiency. The Supreme Court precedents of the 1960s, in which mergers were condemned without convincing proof that competitive forces were in any way jeopardized, have not been overruled, a fact observed by the court of appeals that affirmed the FTC's action in the *HCA* case. Hospital Corp. of America v. FTC, 807 F.2d 1381, 1387 (7th Cir.1986) (Posner, J.). In that decision, the court noted that the Commission, rather than taking its cue from these cases, had focused on "the economic concept of competition, rather than any desire to preserve rivals as such"; "this principle," the court stated, "requires the [Commission] to make a judgment whether the challenged acquisition is likely to hurt consumers, as by making it easier for the firms in the market to collude, expressly or tacitly, and thereby force price above or farther above the competitive level."

Considerable progress has been made in recent years in structuring the inquiry needed to appraise a merger's potential anticompetitive effects. The principal source of guidance is U.S. Dep't of Justice & FTC, Horizontal Merger Guidelines (1992). These jointly issued guidelines were a substantial revision of the Justice Department's 1984 guidelines, which are cited and relied upon by the FTC in *HCA*. Although the guidelines are not law but only a prosecutor's statement of enforcement policy, they are a powerful influence, since, as a practical matter, few mergers are likely to proceed in the face of a government challenge. In 1994 (and again in 1996) the DOJ and FTC released a series of nine joint statements of enforcement policy in the health care field, including one statement (#1) on hospital mergers. U.S. Dep't of Justice & FTC, Statements of Enforcement Policy and Analytical Principles Relating to Health Care and Antitrust (rev. ed. 1996). Although it establishes an antitrust "safety zone" for mergers involving hospitals with less than 100 licensed beds and an average daily census of fewer than 40 inpatients, the policy statement on mergers does little more than state that hospital mergers will be analyzed by the agencies according to the criteria set forth in the agencies' 1992 guidelines.

Although it is an early opinion on hospital mergers, the FTC's opinion in *HCA*, described by Judge Posner as a "model of lucidity," provides a good statement of merger law and of the issues encountered in evaluating hospital mergers. As will be seen in the notes below, however, the Commission did not fully anticipate the way in which markets for hospital care have evolved under the increasing influence of managed care organizations. See generally Greaney, Night Landings on an Aircraft Carrier: Hospital Mergers and Antitrust Law, 23 Am. J.L. & Med. 191 (1997) (observing that courts in hospital merger cases "are asked to make exceedingly fine-tuned appraisals of complex economic relationships [and] factual judgments regarding what the future may hold in an industry undergoing revolutionary change"); Bazzoli et al., Federal Antitrust Merger Enforcement Standards: A Good Fit for the Hospital Industry?, 20 J. Health Pol., Pol'y & L. 137 (1995) (with commentary); Vita et al., Economic Analysis in Health Care Antitrust, 7 J. Contemp. Health L. & Pol'y 73 (1991) (treatment of economic issues authored by FTC staff economists); Baker, Antitrust Analysis of Hospital Mergers and the Transformation of the Hospital Industry, Law & Contemp. Probs., Spring 1988, p. 93.

4. *Market Definition.* A crucial step in merger analysis is the definition of a "relevant market" in which the merger might jeopardize competition. A market is an economic phenomenon and has both a product (or service) and a geographical dimension. Market definition is especially complex in the case of hospital mergers because of the diverse range of services produced by hospitals, the expanding role of managed care organizations, and the effect of rapidly changing technology. See generally Dranove, Market Definition in Antitrust Analysis and Applications to Health Care, in Managed Care and Changing Health Care Markets 121, 139 (M. Morrisey, ed., 1998) (finding "reasons to believe that traditional methods [of market definition] may create a bias in favor of [hospital] mergers that will turn out to harm consumers"). Although the *HCA* case did not turn on market definition, the FTC's opinion gives some indication of how the issue is addressed.

(a) *Product Market.* Because a hospital provides a wide variety of discrete services and competes with providers of other kinds in many lines of business, a hospital merger might be evaluated in each of many markets. Alternatively, hospitals might be viewed as competing primarily with each other in providing a unique "cluster" of services. Courts tend to favor the "cluster market" approach in analyzing hospital mergers, defining the market as the provision of acute inpatient services, not individual hospital services. E.g., United States v. Rockford Mem'l Corp., 898 F.2d 1278 (7th Cir. 1990); FTC v. University Health, Inc., 938 F.2d 1206 (11th Cir. 1991).

Excluding all outpatient services from the analysis of a hospital merger (as suggested in *HCA*) makes sense under the following rationale:

> The defendants point out correctly that a growing number of services provided by acute-care hospitals are also available from nonhospital providers. But the force of the point eludes us. If a firm has a monopoly of product X, the fact that it produces another product, Y, for which the firm faces competition is irrelevant to its monopoly unless the prices of X and Y are linked. For many services provided by acute-care hospitals, there is no competition from other sorts of provider. If you need a kidney transplant, or a mastectomy, or if you have a stroke or a heart attack or a gunshot wound, you will go (or be taken) to an acute-care hospital for inpatient treatment. The fact that for other services you have a choice between inpatient care at such a hospital and outpatient care elsewhere places no check on the prices of the services we have listed, for their prices are not linked to the prices of services that are not substitutes or complements. If you need your hip replaced, you can't decide to have chemotherapy instead because it's available on an outpatient basis at a lower price. Nor are the prices of hip replacement and chemotherapy linked. The defendants' counsel correctly noted that diet soft drinks sold to diabetics are not a relevant product market, but that is because the manufacturers cannot separate their diabetic customers from their other customers and charge the former a higher price. Hospitals can and do distinguish between the patient who wants a coronary bypass and the patient who wants a wart removed from his foot; these services are not in the same product market merely because they have a common provider.

Rockford, supra, at 1284 (Posner, J.). The cluster market approach differs from ordinary merger analysis in grouping together products that are not substitutes for each other. Such a market may be justified, however, where the goods or services are in some way complementary in production, consumption, or distribution. See generally Ayres, Rationalizing Antitrust

Cluster Markets, 95 Yale L.J. 109 (1985). In the hospital context, the relevant cluster of services typically includes various medical and surgical services, pathology and diagnostics, pharmaceuticals, nursing care, and food service. Although these diverse services are used to treat patients with differing needs and different options in the marketplace, their integration in a single institution yields important economies of scale and scope. It therefore makes some sense to treat these hospital services, at least presumptively, as a discrete market without regard to whether some patients have the alternative of patronizing a nonhospital provider (e.g., an ambulatory surgical facility).

To some extent, using market share statistics derived by lumping all acute care services together and ignoring competing suppliers for some services compensates for another, even more misleading effect of using cluster markets. For some services, a given hospital (or pair of merging hospitals) will inevitably have a market share higher than for the cluster market as a whole, since the market share for the cluster of services is a weighted average that hides higher percentages for some, including some that hospitals alone provide. A court is always free, of course, to look behind the average at markets for discrete services (e.g., birthing services) if sound analysis requires it. Moreover, if unbundling the market discloses a threat to competition in any disaggregated market (after taking account of any nonhospital providers), the merger would have to be invalidated (unless the problem could be resolved by a strategic divestiture or otherwise), since the Clayton Act bars any merger having anticompetitive effects "in any line of commerce * * * in any section of the country." It is, after all, antitrust dogma (consistent with the principle that a worthy purpose or benign motive cannot be offered in defense of a restraint of trade) that a procompetitive effect in one market cannot justify anticompetitive effects in another. Given the formidable evidentiary problems which arise in attempting to define relevant markets, however, the cluster market approach is most often used in analyzing hospital mergers. Cf. HTI Health Services, Inc. v. Quorum Health Group, Inc., 960 F.Supp. 1104 (S.D.Miss.1997) (merger of two physician multispecialty groups analyzed in terms of a variety of specific services).

(b) *Geographic Market.* In communities outside the largest metropolitan areas, there are relatively few hospitals, so that, if the relevant market is limited to that community, a merger of any two hospitals is likely to yield market concentration (measured by the HHI) exceeding the usual threshold of antitrust concern. Is it reasonable to think that a hospital in a neighboring community could be a good enough substitute for a local hospital to check the latter's exercise of market power? In other words, should a hospital in a nearby town ever be counted "in" the market, diluting market share percentages and permitting a more tolerant view of the merger? How would you go about deciding this factual question? Using a methodology outlined in the Horizontal Merger Guidelines, the enforcement agencies would pose the question as whether a hypothetical monopolist at the first location could raise the prevailing price without inviting a competitive response from neighboring hospitals that would render the price increase unprofitable. Is this a realistic test in the hospital context? How would one get the information needed to apply it?

A widely used test for geographic markets in merger cases comes from an article by Elzinga & Hogarty, The Problem of Geographic Market Delineation in Antimerger Suits, 18 Antitrust Bull. 45 (1973). Their test focuses in part on the percentage of the output of local producers that is exported outside the putative market and the percentage of local consumption represented by imports. (How would such a test be applied to hospitals, which do not literally "export"?) A percentage of more than 25 percent for either the "LOFI" (little out from inside) or the "LIFO" (little in from outside) aspect of the Elzinga–Hogarty test defeats the case for a local market. (More demanding analysts use a 10 percent threshold before they will declare a geographic area self-sufficient and effectively insulated from outside competition.) Would this test be helpful in evaluating a merger of two hospitals in nearby communities? Assume that patient-origin data showing the number of patients from each postal zip code treated at each institution reveals little overlap in the catchment areas of the two hospitals. Is it clear that the two hospitals are in different markets?

Before giving your answer to the foregoing question, consider the following situation: Sisters of Mercy Health Systems, Inc. ("BigSys"), a nonprofit hospital chain in the State of Bliss, is considering acquisition of Little Sisters of Charity Hospital ("Little Sis"), located in Alpha, Bliss. Data concerning annual discharges of residents of Alpha and Bravo Counties from the various hospitals they patronize are provided in the accompanying table. Consider the legality of the merger, applying the appropriate tests and assuming that a plausible claim can be made that the merger will yield significant efficiencies. Do you see any reason not to rely on the following proposition, paraphrased from a 1988 speech by a Justice Department official?

> Many hospital mergers involve multi-hospital systems acquiring hospitals in markets where the acquiring system currently does no business. Such acquisitions merely substitute one owner for another and thus almost certainly have no competitive impact in the market served by either hospital. Such mergers therefore should not raise antitrust problems.

Firm	Hospital	Location	Dischgs. (Bravo)	Dischgs. (Alpha)
BigSys	BigSys Gen'l	Bravo	4200	120
Little Sisters	Little Sis	Alpha	600	3600
Kaiser Fdn. Health Plan	Kaiser Hosp.	Bravo	4200	1800
Queen	Queen Gen'l	Bravo	2400	300
X, Y and Z	3 other hospitals	Nearby	600	180
Totals			**12000**	**6000**

What powerful point, not apparent in the *HCA* case, emerges from the foregoing problem? Courts have recently stressed that the definition of a geographic market must take a dynamic rather than a static view, focusing not only on where consumers actually travel for hospital care but also on where they could practicably obtain alternative inpatient care if prices became noncompetitive. See FTC v. Freeman Hosp., 69 F.3d 260, 269 (8th Cir.1995) (affirming holding that "FTC failed to produce sufficient evidence on * * * where consumers of acute care inpatient hospital services could practicably turn for alternative services of that product"). To be sure, hospital services are usually thought of as local. See, e.g., *Rockford*, supra, at 1285 (opinion by Posner, J., characterizing as "ridiculous" the defendants' proposed geographic market: "a ten-county area in which it is assumed (without any evidence and contrary to common sense) that Rockford residents or third-party payors, will be searching out small, obscure hospitals in remote rural areas if the prices charged by the hospitals in Rockford rise above competitive levels"). But this perception results from the fact that, in the past, patients generally received hospital care wherever their physicians referred them, largely to suit the doctor's own convenience. What new element in modern health care markets, not observed in the *HCA* case, may alter the situation enough to widen markets significantly? One district court would have approved a merger between the only two general acute care hospitals in Dubuque, Iowa, reasoning that the ability and apparent willingness of consumers to travel to other regional hospitals if required by a managed care organization would defeat any attempt to raise prices. United States v. Mercy Health Services, 902 F.Supp. 968, 981–983 (N.D.Iowa 1995), vacated as moot, 107 F.3d 632 (8th Cir.1997).

What problems would you visualize in defining the geographic market if a court elected to unbundle the product market to consider effects on patients with particular conditions? Is it reasonable to expect that patients would travel farther for certain rarefied or complex procedures than for more routine treatments? Would the geographic market therefore be different depending on which service one is talking about? See *Freeman Hospital*, supra, at 270–71 (suggesting looking at individual DRGs in determining relevant geographic markets). Note how changing medical technology can affect market definition. As more and more procedures can be performed in outpatient clinics, the core cluster of hospital-exclusive inpatient services will be increasingly limited to complex procedures requiring highly specialized inpatient care—the very services for which consumers will be willing to travel farther.

5. *Entry Barriers and Potential Competition.* Note the attention paid by the FTC to "barriers to entry" as a factor in evaluating a merger that added significantly to concentration in a local hospital market. Entry barriers are important both because they foreclose the appearance of actual new competitors and because, by obviating the threat that higher prices will attract new capacity, they make it profitable for industry incumbents to collude, explicitly or tacitly. Indeed, barriers to entry have become an increasingly important part of merger analysis. On the other hand, economic evidence suggests that the barriers to entry in the hospital industry are large. What barriers loomed largest in *HCA*, strengthening the Commission's concerns regarding the merger's effect? What effect should a state's repeal of its CON law have on merger analysis?

6. *Nonprofit vs. For-profit Hospitals.* Note the way in which the significance of the nonprofit versus for-profit status of hospitals was raised in *HCA*. One court of appeals addressed the same issue as follows:

> Finally, the appellees argue, as the district court held, that University Hospital's nonprofit status supports their position that the proposed acquisition would not result in substantially less competition. We disagree.
>
> While "[d]ifferent ownership structures might reduce the likelihood of collusion, ... this possibility is conjectural." Hospital Corp. of Am., 807 F.2d at 1390. Indeed, the Supreme Court has rejected the notion that nonprofit corporations act under such a different set of incentives than for-profit corporations that they are entitled to an implicit exemption from the antitrust laws. See National Collegiate Athletic Ass'n v. Board of Regents, 468 U.S. 85, 100 n. 22 (1984). As the Seventh Circuit explained:
>
>> We are aware of no evidence—and the [appellees] present none, only argument—that nonprofit suppliers of goods or services are more likely to compete vigorously than profit-making suppliers.... If the managers of nonprofit enterprises are less likely to strain after that last penny of profit, they may be less prone to engage in profit-maximizing collusion but by the same token less prone to engage in profit-maximizing competition.
>
> Rockford Memorial Corp., 898 F.2d at 1285. Thus, the nonprofit status of the acquiring firm will not, by itself, help a defendant overcome the presumption of illegality that arises from the government's prima facie case.
>
> The appellees argue that University Hospital's prior history of service to the public and procompetitive behavior, added to its nonprofit status, removes their argument from the realm of speculation. We cannot agree. University Hospital's business decisions are not mandated by law; rather, its governing body is free to decide where to set prices and output. While University Hospital's prior practices may suggest its future conduct, such evidence has limited probative value. The appellees' self-serving declarations simply do little to undermine the impressive evidence the FTC has introduced to make its case. Furthermore, although public scrutiny may reduce University Hospital's ability to commit undetected violations of the antitrust laws, it would not eliminate altogether the risk that it might act anticompetitively. For example, while public pressure might inhibit it from raising prices, "similar pressure might inhibit [it] from expanding capacity to take on additional patients attracted by lower prices." Hospital Corp. of Am., 807 F.2d at 1391. * * * Accordingly, we conclude that the district court erred in relying on this argument to rebut the FTC's prima facie case.

University Health, supra, at 1223–24.

The language omitted by the *University Health* court from its quotation of Judge Posner's opinion in *Rockford* reads as follows: "Most people do not like to compete, and will seek ways of avoiding competition by agreement tacit or explicit, depending of course on the cost of agreeing. The ideology of nonprofit enterprise is cooperative rather than competitive." Do you agree? Or do you share the view that a private nonprofit hospital is akin to a consumer cooperative and that "if a nonprofit organization is controlled by the very people who depend on it for service, there is no rational economic incentive for such an organization to raise its prices to the monopoly level, even if it has the power to do so." *Freeman Hospital*, supra, 911 F. Supp. at 1222. See Lynk, Property Rights and the Presumptions of Merger Analysis, 39 Antitrust Bull. 363 (1994) (examining incentives of nonprofit hospitals and questioning applicability, where nonprofits are involved, of usual presumptions against mergers creating high levels of concentration).

How should a court evaluate the likely effects of a merger of nonprofits? One district court refused to grant a preliminary injunction against an otherwise objectionable merger of the two largest hospitals (with about 80 percent of the beds) in Grand Rapids, Michigan, partly on the ground that the board of the resulting nonprofit institution included strong representation of employers in the community, who had a strong interest in controlling the cost of their employees' health benefits. FTC v. Butterworth Health Corp., 946 F.Supp. 1285, 1296–97 (W.D.Mich.1996), affirmed, 121 F.3d 708 (6th Cir.1997). As a condition of its ruling, the court required the hospital to enter into a consent decree incorporating a so-called "Community Commitment," proposed by the hospitals, under which they agreed to freeze their prices and limit their profit margins for several years, to provide for the uninsured, and to maintain a board representative of community interests. The court relied heavily on testimony of an expert witness who purported to find that in Michigan "higher hospital concentration is associated with lower nonprofit hospital prices." Id. at 1295. See also Lynk, Nonprofit Hospital Mergers and the Exercise of Market Power, 38 J. Law & Econ. 437 (1995) (same expert's similar findings in California). Was the *Butterworth* court's ruling consistent with antitrust law as you understand it? Would you have expected that it would stand up on appeal? See also United States v. Carilion Health System, 707 F.Supp. 840 (W.D.Va.), affirmed, 892 F.2d 1042 (4th Cir.1989) (unpublished opinion) (hospital's nonprofit status held a factor weighing in favor of merger).

7. *Efficiencies.* Although the only reason for the law to tolerate mergers that eliminate competition and increase concentration in an industry is the prospect of efficiencies beneficial to consumers and to the economy as a whole, both the enforcement agencies and the courts have long been slow to accept efficiency claims offered in defense of mergers that were anticompetitive in any significant degree. Lately, however, they have become more receptive to such claims, particularly with respect to hospital mergers. See generally Mary Lou Steptoe, Acting Director, FTC Bureau of Competition, Efficiency Justifications for Hospital Mergers (Speech, San Francisco, June 17, 1994). Mergers are recognized as having the potential both to reduce excess capacity in hospital markets and to facilitate the realization of important economies of scale or scope that hospitals neglected when the market featured only passive payers, cost reimbursement, and nonprice competition. The high fixed and capital costs of hospitals may mean that lower prices, higher quality, and greater output are achievable by fewer firms rather than by many.

A 1997 amendment to the 1992 Horizontal Merger Guidelines clarified the role that efficiencies play in the agencies' exercise of their prosecutorial discretion with respect to particular mergers. The agencies, it appears, will take into account only merger-specific efficiencies—that is, those that can be achieved only through merger and not through another practical alternative. For example, claims of increased efficiency by consolidating data processing or laundry facilities or by group purchasing will not pass muster, since such efficiencies can be achieved through more limited collaboration. Moreover, the agencies will only consider efficiency claims that can be substantiated and will not consider claims that are "vague or speculative." The new 1997 guideline also acknowledged more clearly than ever before the existence of a trade-off: An efficiencies claim is more likely to deflect a challenge "when the likely adverse competitive effects, absent the efficiencies, are not great."

The new guideline on efficiencies seemed to recede from the agencies' customary position that, although they might take efficiencies into account in deciding as prosecutors whether to challenge a merger, efficiencies are not a legal defense to an otherwise anticompetitive combination. Although older Supreme Court cases can be cited for the proposition that efficiencies are not a cognizable legal defense, courts have recently become more receptive to efficiency arguments, particularly in the case of hospital mergers. See, e.g., United States v. Rockford Mem'l Corp. 717 F.Supp. 1251, 1289–91 (N.D.Ill.1989); *Carilion*, supra, 707 F. Supp. at 845–46, 849; *Butterworth*, supra, 946 F. Supp. At 1300–03. To be sure, an efficiency defense may not be easy to make out. Thus, in *University Health*, supra, 938 F.2d at 1223, the court of appeals stated that "a defendant who seeks to overcome a presumption that a proposed acquisition would substantially lessen competition must demonstrate that the intended acquisition would result in significant economies and that these economies would benefit competition and, hence, consumers" and explain how the alleged efficiencies "would be created and maintained." The court rejected the defendant's unsubstantiated claim that the acquisition would reduce "unnecessary duplication."

An important consideration in evaluating efficiency claims in the hospital context is the effect on quality of service. Because the courts and agencies focus only on net efficiencies, a reduction in costs which also results in a reduction in quality of service is not counted as a relevant efficiency. But an improvement in quality may count as an efficiency. According to an enforcement official (Steptoe, supra),

> We recognize, for example, that a hospital performing only one open-heart surgery a week is going to have trouble achieving normal quality levels and mortality rates, given the need for the surgical team to participate in such surgeries more frequently in order to keep their skills sharp. A consolidation of two such underutilized heart surgery programs would show at least substantial promise on the surface for significant, cognizable quality improvements for patients. Indeed, in some instances combining patient volumes may enable the post-merger hospital to offer new services which would expand consumers' competitive options. For example, combining two obstetrics units, each with only enough volume to support the equipment and staff to handle normal deliveries, may make possible the addition of capabilities to handle high-risk pregnancies.

8. *State Antitrust Enforcement.* In addition to the federal antitrust laws, health care providers must also contend with state antitrust law and enforcement authorities. Massachusetts, for example, has released its own guidelines relating to hospital mergers. Massachusetts Attorney General, Antitrust Guidelines for Mergers and Similar Transactions Among Hospitals (1993), reprinted in 4 Trade Reg. Rep. (CCH) ¶ 13,450. States mutually support each other's enforcement efforts through the National Association of Attorneys General (NAAG), which maintains a Multistate Antitrust Task Force and which has released its own horizontal merger guidelines. NAAG Horizontal Merger Guidelines (1993), reprinted in 4 Trade Reg. Rep (CCH) ¶ 13,406. In some cases, state attorneys general work with the federal agencies in investigating mergers and other possible antitrust violations. A widely noted example of such collaborative enforcement involved the Morton Plant Health System and another hospital in the Tampa–St. Petersburg area. United States v. Morton Plant Health System, Inc., 1994 WL 655199 (M.D.Fla.). In that case, federal and state authorities bargained for an innovative consent decree that barred a merger between two hospitals but allowed a limited joint venture for the provision of certain services on the condition that both hospitals maintain their institutional independence and make independent decisions as to marketing and pricing of the jointly produced services. Id. at *3. Enforcement officials took pride in this outcome because, in their view, it preserved the efficiencies sought through the proposed merger while reducing the potential for anticompetitive harm.

Normally, federal antitrust officials employ consent decrees (or consent orders, in the case of the FTC) to obtain appropriate relief without the burdens, costs, or uncertainties of litigation. Often, the agencies are able to negotiate a divestiture of certain assets or some other measure that cures or neutralizes the anticompetitive feature of the transaction as originally proposed. See, e.g., FTC, Columbia/HCA Healthcare Corp.; Proposed Consent Agreement With Analysis To Aid Public Comment, 60 Fed. Reg. 27292 (1995) (FTC proposal to settle merger case by requiring the divestiture of six acute care hospitals and the termination of joint ownership of a seventh, thus eliminating competitive overlaps in the respective service areas of the merging firms). Some state antitrust authorities, however, appear to have employed the threat of enforcement action, where federal officials have elected not to act or have to deferred to the state's authorities, to obtain relief that is highly regulatory in nature and difficult to reconcile with the usual procompetitive goals of antitrust law. An example is Commonwealth v. Capital Health System Services, 1995 WL 787534 (M.D.Pa.), where the Pennsylvania Attorney General approved a merger of two corporate parents of three hospitals in central Pennsylvania, subject to the condition that at least 80 percent of the $70 million projected as cost savings from the merger be passed on to community "in the form of low-cost or no-cost health care programs for the community or by reducing prices or by limiting actual price increases for existing services." Id. at *2. In the event that the projected savings are not realized, the decree provided that the merged entity would pay the state any shortfall. The decree also imposed a number of other regulatory terms, including limitations on exclusive dealing, caps on annual inpatient revenue, and restrictions on the number of physicians that could be employed. See also Commonwealth v. Providence Health System, Inc., 1994 WL 374424 (M.D.Pa.) (earlier settlement on similar terms); Physician Cap Resolves State's Concerns Over Merger of Massachusetts Hospitals, 70 Antitrust and Trade Reg. Rep. (BNA) 568 (1996) (Massachusetts hospital merger allowed on condition that merged entity not enter into employment or exclusive contracts with more than 40% of primary care physicians, pediatricians, and obstetricians in a 26–community area). One commentator, observing similar federal settlements, has lamented that the use of consent decrees has "contributed to a shift in focus from the wrong to the remedy and, thus, to the emergence of antitrust enforcement, not just as a traffic cop to ensure robust competition, but as a new form of government regulation." Melamed, Antitrust: The New Regulation, 10 Antitrust 13 (1995) at 15.

The Effect of Statutes Fostering Provider Cooperation

NOTES AND QUESTIONS ON IMMUNITIES FOR PROVIDER COOPERATION AND MERGERS

1. *Health Planning vs. Antitrust.* In 1980, the Justice Department took the position that a local health planning agency brokering an anticompetitive agreement between hospitals could not confer antitrust immunity on those hospitals, even if the agreement effectuated a carefully considered health plan promulgated pursuant to the federal health planning legislation. This ruling meant, for example, that two hospitals could not agree, even under the auspices of health planners designated pursuant to Public Law 93–641 (the federal health planning act), to concentrate respectively on providing maternity care and emergency medicine in order to achieve economies of scale and to eliminate costly duplication. In the Antitrust Division's view, this legal conclusion followed from the absence in Public Law 93–641 of both an explicit antitrust exemption for planner-approved agreements and any basis for finding an implied exemption. The enforcement agency believed that the issue of statutory construction was settled by authorities holding that a congressional intent to create an antitrust exemption will be inferred only where there is a "clear repugnancy" between the two statutes and then only to the extent necessary to make the regulatory statute work.

Proponents of health planning were naturally dismayed by the Justice Department's position, which undercut the whole idea of voluntary planning as a means of inspiring cooperative effort to improve the system's functioning. Critics of the Justice Department position observed that the legislative history of the planning act revealed a clear lack of congressional faith that competition was beneficial in health care. Moreover, the act itself was full of indications of Congress's desire to see duplication eliminated and agency plans realized. On the basis of impressions gained from these expressions of congressional purpose, several lower courts found that Congress did indeed intend blanket antitrust immunity for all actions taken in the name of health planning. Although the repeal of Public Law 93–641 in 1986 obviously rendered the legal issue moot, the controversy sharply highlighted the conflict between, on the one hand, a regulatory, central-planning approach to rationalizing the health care industry's development and, on the other hand, reliance upon independent, decentralized decision making in a competitive environment. The manner in which this policy conflict was viewed and addressed by Congress, the antitrust enforcers, and the courts reveals a great deal about the evolution of national health policy, the policy-making process, and the construction of inconsistent statutes.

Although there was a good argument that implied antitrust immunity was necessary to make congressionally-approved health planning work, the fact remained that Congress had not expressly conferred upon planning agencies the power to immunize anticompetitive (e.g., market allocation) agreements, as other regulatory agencies have frequently been authorized to do. Moreover, a careful reading of the legislative history revealed substantial congressional ambivalence concerning the legal effect to be given to the health planners' plans and the wisdom of conferring plan-implementing powers on the agencies. Thus, despite all the rhetoric in support of health planning, Congress had real policy doubts about making plans binding and real political doubts about extending the planners' and regulators' powers. It thus appears that the legislative process yielded a compromise under which some members were allowed to incorporate their aspirations in the statute but the agencies were not given the means to effectuate those aspirations. Congressional proponents of planning may have accepted that their expressed desire to reduce existing capacity and duplication might go unrealized unless and until it was implemented either in later amendments or in state laws. If this reading of Congress's thinking is correct, the Justice Department was justified in refusing to infer an intent to create an antitrust exemption for plan-implementing efforts.

The Justice Department's interpretation of Public Law 93–641 was seemingly confirmed by Congress in 1979, when it specifically refused to grant explicit exempting powers to planning agencies. In addition, the House committee wrote legislative history indicating that no implicit exemption was intended, stating that "agency acts which are not necessary to carry out [specific assigned] functions or which are outside the scope of title XV are not authorized and therefore not immune from the application of the antitrust laws." H.R.Rep. No. 190, 96th Cong., 1st Sess. 54–55 (1979). Finally, in 1981, the Supreme Court ruled that the planning legislation did not create "a 'pervasive' repeal of the antitrust laws as applied to every action taken in response to the health-care planning process." National Gerimedical Hosp. & Gerontology Center v. Blue Cross of Kansas City, 452 U.S. 378, 393 (1981).

Although the *National Gerimedical* decision and the 1979 amendments settled that the planning act did not create a blanket antitrust exemption, some dicta in *National Gerimedical* suggested that the Supreme Court might still have been willing, under some circumstances at least, to tolerate planner-brokered agreements implementing local health plans. Id. at 393 n.18. The Court was impressed by Congress's expressions of doubt that competition was a reliable vehicle for allocating all types of health resources. It also attached weight to a floor statement by the chairman of the House Subcommittee in charge of the planning legislation to the effect that, if the antitrust laws barred competitor collaboration in support of health planning objectives, "Public Law 93–641 simply could not be implemented." 124 Cong.Rec. H11,963 (daily ed. Oct. 10, 1978) (remarks of Rep. Rogers). On the basis of these impressions, the Court seemed willing to conclude that less rigorous antitrust rules should be used to evaluate naked anticompetitive agreements entered into under the planners' auspices. (How much weight should be given to a statement such as that of Rep. Rogers, which was made without regard to any pending legislation? Was the statement supportable?)

The *National Gerimedical* footnote, together with a similar holding in Hospital Building Co. v. Trustees of Rex Hosp., 691 F.2d 678 (4th Cir. 1982), cert. denied 464 U.S. 890 (1983), raises an interesting question: whether emanations from a regulatory statute and its legislative history, as opposed to clear statutory directives, can be the basis for inferring, not an implied repeal of or exemption from the antitrust laws, but an implied substantive amendment of those laws as previously interpreted by the courts. The idea that substantive amendments to antitrust principles can be inferred from apparent congressional reservations about the virtues of competition in particular settings raises further interesting questions about how policy on such issues is made and how far courts should go in supplementing incomplete or inconclusive congressional efforts. The following conclusion was drawn by one commentator after a lengthy review of the experience summarized here:

> In view of the impossibility of knowing what specific implications to draw from congressionally expressed doubt about competition's current value in a particular setting, the courts should adhere to their traditional insistence that Congress alone must declare those implications. If the

> courts instead undertake to make their own judgments about when an exemption or relaxation of substantive rules is or is not appropriate, they will have "set sail on a sea of doubt"[81] which ninety years of antitrust jurisprudence should have taught them to avoid.[82] The wisdom of the "clear repugnancy" test, rigorously applied, is revealed by the difficulty and subjective artificiality of trying first to guess what was in the back of Congress's collective mind and then to fashion a different, milder antitrust regime to fit a situation where competition has been declared a mixed blessing. Thus, an implied amendment doctrine has no place in antitrust law.

Havighurst, Health Planning and Antitrust Law: The Implied Amendment Doctrine of the *Rex Hospital* Case, 14 N.C.Cent.L.J. 45, 70–71 (1983). But see Bolze & Pennak, Reconciliation of the Sherman Act with Federal Health–Planning Legislation: Implied Antitrust Immunity in the Health Care Field, 29 Antitrust Bull. 225 (1984) (concluding that usual antitrust tests should be relaxed in the presence of publicly authorized health planning).

2. *Provider Cooperation Laws*. In recent years, some nineteen states have enacted so-called provider cooperation laws for the purpose of sheltering collaborative activities of certain health care providers from the requirements of federal antitrust law. See generally Blumstein, Assessing Hospital Cooperation Laws, 8 Loy. Cons. L. Rep. 98 (1995–96); Blumstein, Health Care Reform and Competing Visions of Medical Care: Antitrust and State Provider Cooperation Legislation, 79 Cornell L. Rev. 1459 (1994); Vance, Immunity for State–Sanctioned Provider Collaboration After *Ticor*, 62 Antitrust L.J. 409 (1994). Lack of clarity and predictability in antitrust law and inadequate appreciation of efficiency considerations by antitrust enforcers were often given as reasons for passing such laws. But it was clear that hospitals, in lobbying for such laws, desired relief from competition as well as from antitrust uncertainty. After reading this note, see if you can state a convincing public-interest rationale for these statutes. Or are they simply one more instance of special-interest legislation?

The North Carolina Hospital Cooperation Act of 1993, N.C. Gen. Stat. §§ 131E–192 (1996), declares (§192.1), among other things,

> (7) That competition as currently mandated by federal and State antitrust laws should be supplanted by a regulatory program to permit and encourage cooperative agreements between hospitals, or between hospitals and others, that are beneficial to North Carolina citizens when the benefits of cooperative agreements outweigh their disadvantages caused by their potential or actual adverse effects on competition.
>
> (8) That regulatory as well as judicial oversight of cooperative agreements should be provided to ensure that the benefits of cooperative agreements permitted and encouraged in North Carolina outweigh

81. United States v. Addyston Pipe & Steel Co., 85 Fed. 271, 284 (6th Cir.1898). * * *

82. See National Soc'y of Professional Eng'rs v. United States, 435 U.S. 679 (1978).

any disadvantages attributable to any reduction in competition likely to result from the agreements.

Substantively, the North Carolina law provides (§192.3) that

> A hospital and any person who is a party to a cooperative agreement with a hospital may negotiate, enter into, and conduct business pursuant to a cooperative agreement without being subject to damages, liability, or scrutiny under any State antitrust law if a certificate of public advantage is issued for the cooperative agreement, or in the case of activities to negotiate or enter into a cooperative agreement, if an application for a certificate of public advantage is filed in good faith. It is the intention of the General Assembly that immunity from federal antitrust laws shall also be conferred by this statute and the State regulatory program that it establishes.

A "certificate of public advantage" is to be issued by the North Carolina Department of Human Resources if "it determines that an applicant has demonstrated by clear and convincing evidence that the benefits likely to result from the agreement outweigh the disadvantages likely to result from a reduction of competition." Id. at § 192.4. However, the statute gives the Attorney General a veto over the issuance of any certificate. In addition, it requires periodic reports from the parties and permits revocation of certificates either for noncompliance with "conditions" contained therein or after a reassessment of the "benefits and disadvantages" that are to be weighed in approving the agreement. Among the "disadvantages" to be considered are the following:

> (3) The extent to which the agreement may reduce competition among the parties to the agreement and the likely effects thereof.
>
> (4) The extent to which the agreement may have an adverse impact on the ability of health maintenance organizations, preferred provider organizations, managed health care service agents, or other health care payors to negotiate optimal payment and service arrangements with hospitals, physicians, allied health care professionals, or other health care providers.
>
> (5) The extent to which the agreement may result in a reduction in competition among physicians, allied health professionals, other health care providers, or other persons furnishing goods or services to, or in competition with, hospitals.
>
> (6) The availability of arrangements that are less restrictive to competition and achieve the same benefits or a more favorable balance of benefits over disadvantages attributable to any reduction in competition.

Does the analysis to be conducted by the state agencies differ from antitrust analysis? If so, how? What "benefits" would count that would not count in an antitrust case?

The North Carolina act is regarded, in comparison to similar laws in other states, as among the most likely to pass muster under the state-action exemption from the federal antitrust laws examined in chapter 4(§C). Do you agree that it meets the requirements of the *Midcal* test for state-action immunity? In connection with the second-prong of the *Midcal* test, consider the Wisconsin statute, under which the state is presumed to consent to an anticompetitive agreement unless state officials act to invalidate it within a specified period. A similar "negative-option" provision in Wisconsin's scheme for regulating collectively set rates for title insurance was struck down in the leading case of FTC v. Ticor Title Ins. Co., 504 U.S. 621 (1992) (state's unexercised opportunity to review rates under negative option held inadequate to satisfy the "active supervision" requirement introduced in *Midcal*). Should the matter turn on what the state overseers do in fact, or should federal law require only that the state legislature gave regulators an opportunity to oversee the authorized conduct? Will the effectiveness of the immunity conferred by the North Carolina statute depend on how seriously the state administrators take their assigned responsibility to provide "active supervision"?

Would you advise a hospital thinking of merging with a competitor to avail itself of the protections provided by a provider cooperation act, even one as well crafted as North Carolina's? Why might you hesitate to do so? In fact, it is reported that few providers have taken advantage of these new laws. See Blumstein, Assessing Hospital Cooperation Laws, supra, at 105–08. At this writing, it appeared that only three hospital combinations—in North Carolina (Asheville), Minnesota (Twin Cities), and Montana (Great Falls)—had been authorized under provider cooperation acts. On the Minnesota merger, see Feldman, The Welfare Economics of a Health Plan Merger, 6 J. Reg. Econ. 67 (1994) (economist's estimate that merger would increase cost of hospital care 6%). Can you speculate on why this seeming loophole in the antitrust regime has not been more widely exploited?

3. *Acquisitions by Public Hospitals.* In FTC v. Hospital Board of Directors of Lee County, 38 F.3d 1184 (11th Cir.1994), Lee Memorial Hospital, a large public hospital, was held immune from federal antitrust law in its effort to acquire a competing nonprofit hospital. The governing board of Lee Memorial was a political subdivision of the State of Florida authorized by statute, in general terms, to establish and provide for the operation and maintenance of a public hospital and to acquire and operate additional hospital facilities. Relying on the legislative history of the enabling statute and on case law governing state-action immunity for municipal corporations (see chapter 4(§C)), the court of appeals rejected the FTC's argument that state action immunity requires an express articulation of an intent to displace competition and held that it was enough that "the acquisition of one of the three competing hospitals in Lee County was a foreseeable result of the Florida legislature's granting the Board the authority to add new facilities to its operation." Before the FTC could appeal the ruling, Lee Memorial terminated its acquisition plans. Greene, Health Management Wins Cape Coral, Modern Healthcare, Jan. 30, 1995, p. 3. How would you have ruled in the *Lee Memorial* case? See generally Harris, State Action

Immunity From Antitrust Law for Public Hospitals: The Hidden Time Bomb for Health Care Reform, 44 U. Kan. L. Rev. 459 (1996).

Other Business Strategies of Hospitals Today

NOTES ON HOSPITAL DIVERSIFICATION AND VERTICAL INTEGRATION

1. *Competition and Vertical Integration.* Horizontal integration, whether by merger or cooperative agreement with competitors, is not the only strategy hospitals are pursuing in response to the competitive and technological forces affecting the health care industry. Faced with stagnant revenues and declining admissions and lengths of stay in their traditional inpatient market, many hospitals are seeking to diversify into related health services or are pursuing strategies of vertical integration.

A firm vertically integrates when it combines with another firm, or expands its operations, to take over additional functions occurring earlier or later in the sequence of activities by which a final product is designed, produced, marketed, and delivered to the ultimate consumer. For example, a hospital might integrate backward by opening an outpatient clinic that brings more inpatients to the institution, by acquiring physician practices, or by forming a PHO with generalists and specialists on its medical staff. Such a strategy may be designed simply to protect referrals or to enable noncompetitive contracting with managed care plans or employers. (The latter motivation would raise restraint-of-trade issues, which will be examined in chapter 8(§A).) On the other hand, integrating medical and hospital services may be an effort to produce seamless or "total patient care" solutions, enabling the hospital to cater to a wider range of patients' needs. Thus, integration could increase efficiency by reducing transaction costs, centralizing control over the provision of care, and improving quality. If real integration is achieved, it can benefit both the consumer and the hospital.

Hospitals have also diversified into the provision of related services. For example, some have entered the business of renting or leasing durable medical equipment (DME), such as wheelchairs, oxygen equipment, convalescent beds. Others have developed or acquired their own home health-care services, providing nursing and ancillary services in patients' homes. Integrating these services with those of the hospital may yield efficiencies in discharge planning but may also be undertaken merely to supplement declining revenues from inpatient care. Such product extensions are perhaps more lucrative in markets where managed care plans have not yet become established or adept at contracting for such services at competitive prices.

Both types of vertical integration are also potential sources of antitrust liability. The courts have in the past been concerned about the effects on existing competitors that arise when a player with a significant advantage in one market decides to enter a related market. Such spillover effects may be unavoidable for hospitals that occupy powerful market positions. Antitrust law has not come to any clear view about how firms with dominant positions should be treated when their competitive moves harm smaller competitors. Although it is frequently stated that antitrust law is intended to protect competition and consumer welfare, not competitors as such, this principle is regularly in danger of being violated when private litigants cry "foul." See generally Kopit, Old Wine in New Bottles: The Increased Risk of Hospital Diversification, 26 Wake Forest L. Rev. 601 (1991).

2. *Types of Vertical Integration.* Vertical integration may be achieved by internal growth, by merger, by joint venture with an independent player, or by contracts imposing so-called "vertical restraints," such as a tying arrangement, reciprocity, or exclusive dealing. The antitrust analysis will differ according to which form of integration is adopted. For example, the law scrutinizes contractual restraints more strictly than it does integration by internal growth. Similarly, vertical mergers are only rarely questioned. Where contractual restraints are involved, the agreement between independent parties is scrutinized under section 1 of the Sherman Act, whereas section 2 (dealing with monopolization) is the primary concern when integration is achieved through internal growth or unilateral action. In each case, however, the law needs to determine whether adverse effects on the opportunities of competing providers affect competition in some way requiring antitrust redress.

3. *Monopoly Leveraging or Extension of Monopoly.* Various forms of vertical integration involving hospitals have been challenged in private antitrust suits on the ground that vertically integrated hospitals are abusing their position in the inpatient care market to obtain an unfair advantage, to restrain trade, or to gain a monopoly in a second market. These challenges are usually premised on some theory of monopoly leveraging or attempted monopolization. A good example is Key Enterprises of Delaware, Inc. v. Venice Hospital., 919 F.2d 1550 (11th Cir.1990), appeal dismissed and judgment vacated, 9 F.3d 893 (11th Cir.1993) (en banc), a case involving the entry of a hospital into the market for DME. The defendant hospital, which had an 80 percent market share, had encouraged its discharged patients to use DME supplied by a firm in which the hospital had a 50 percent interest. Although there was no coercion to use the hospital-owned supplier, an attempt to monopolize the DME market was found on the theory that the hospital was using its monopoly power in the hospital market to take business from DME suppliers. The court found a section 2 violation even though there was no chance that the practice would give the hospital a monopoly in the DME market since there were many customers for DME who were not referred by the hospital.

The power of "referral" that a hospital has over its patients is a natural, though not necessarily an appropriate, antitrust concern. For many ancillary medical services, customers may be ignorant or apathetic about what equipment they take or services they use, as they do not possess any personal knowledge or information about such specialized services or equipment. Moreover, the consumer may be insensitive to prices because Medicare or a private health insurer ultimately bears the cost.

Some courts have regarded exploitation of "captive referrals" as a basis for imposing antitrust liability. Advanced Health–Care Services, Inc. v. Radford Community Hospital, 910 F.2d 139 (4th Cir.1990) (allegations that hospital deliberately discouraged its patients from dealing with rival DME suppliers stated a claim for attempted monopolization). In the *Venice Hospital* case, for example, the court stated as follows:

> Much has been said about patient choice in this case. The district court noted that the parties stipulated that the patients had the freedom to choose any DME vendor. However, a patient's freedom to choose under these circumstances may be illusory. The evidence presented in this case shows that patients rarely have a preference for a DME vendor. The patients know very little about the equipment or the companies that rent the equipment. Thus, they are very susceptible to recommendations made by anyone who appears to be knowledgeable on the subject. It therefore becomes very easy to channel patient choice by limiting the patient's exposure to the competition.

Venice Hospital, supra, 919 F.2d at 1557.

This theory of liability based upon "channeling" is very debatable as a matter of antitrust law. To be sure, many hospitals do possess a competitive advantage in ancillary health services because of their access to and influence over patients. But this is a natural advantage flowing from their success in their primary business, something the law does not normally penalize if it was not gained by improper conduct. Even though a hospital's entry into an ancillary market may entail significant harm to their non-hospital competitors, that harm may be deemed to flow from effective competition, not from an impairment of competition itself. (Do you think the law should aim to prevent hospitals from exploiting their "power" over apathetic or ignorant patients? How are consumers likely to be harmed by such activities? Would it be wiser, instead of relying on courts to referee the competitive process, to rely on market developments, such as the appearance of managed care organizations as effective, price-conscious purchasers, to solve the problem?) In any event, it is not clear, under recent antitrust case law, that future courts will be concerned about spillover effects on smaller competitors. It is more likely that, to be successful, a plaintiff will have to show a significant likelihood that the defendant will achieve a true monopoly in the second market. See generally Kattan, The Decline of the Monopoly Leveraging Doctrine, 9 Antitrust 41 (1994).

4. *Vertical Restraints.* Exclusive dealing contracts and tying arrangements are also forms of vertical integration: They enable hospitals to control (by contract) processes occurring earlier or later in the continuum of patient care. They have also been the subject of antitrust challenges. For example, Collins v. Associated Pathologists, 844 F.2d 473 (7th Cir.1988), involved an exclusive contract requiring the hospital to use only members of an particular pathology group for pathology work. The court held that the arrangement did not violate section 1 of the Sherman Act, because the exclusive contract did not restrict competition in a substantial share of the relevant market—the nationwide market in which pathologists compete for jobs. The court also rejected the idea of an illegal tying agreement under section 1 because hospital services and pathology services are not two separate products.

A 1984 Supreme Court opinion also raised the issue of tying, as the following article excerpt explains:

> Another legal theory under which exclusive contracts might be attacked was recently considered by the Supreme Court in Jefferson Parish Hospital District No. 2 v. Hyde.[253] The plaintiff in that case, an anesthesiologist, alleged that the exclusive contract amounted to a tying arrangement, a type of vertical restraint that, in contrast to exclusive dealing contracts, has historically been treated as a per se violation.[254] Although refusing to overturn its earlier characterization of tying as a per se offense, the Supreme Court majority nevertheless held that the offense had not been established because the hospital lacked sufficient power in the market for hospital services to force patients accept the services of unwanted anaesthesiologists.[255] In other words, because there were other hospitals to which patients could go, the hospital's insistence that its patients use a particular physician group did not violate the law.
>
> * * *
>
> Although the *Hyde* decision should not affect a hospital's right to select physicians, it creates other severe problems for hospitals that do occupy powerful market positions, owing perhaps to the natural monopoly characteristics of their markets. Can such a hospital, for example, integrate vertically by employing its own anesthesiologists and excluding nonemployees? Can it require that patients accept the products or services of its own—or a contracting—food service, pharmacy, or clinical laboratory? Must the hospital avoid providing all tied goods and services itself and also eschew any contract or lease giving it a share in the earnings of those who enjoy its franchise? The *Hyde* opinion implies that these issues should be resolved in such a way that no hospital can exercise the power inherent in its middleman position in the market to foreclose some option that some consumer might wish to have available.[260] This idea, which fortunately is not well established in antitrust law, seems to miss entirely the great benefit that most ignorant consumers might derive from having a sophisticated middleman with bargaining power make choices on their behalf. The argument that hospitals can perform useful services to consumers in this regard * * * seems to have escaped Justice Stevens on this occasion.[261] The Court would have done better if—as the Federal Trade Commission, the Antitrust Division of the Justice Department, and the four concurring justices wanted—it had retracted the per se rule for tying arrangements

253. 466 U.S. 2 (1984).

254. Id. at 1556–68.

255. Id. at 1556–57.

260. See id., at 1565–66 (unlawful tying occurs wherever market power is used to "force" consumers to buy the tied product).

261. Justice Stevens has recognized elsewhere how selectivity practiced by health insurers can serve consumer interests. Arizona v. Maricopa County Medical Soc'y, 457 U.S. 332, 353 (1982) (citing Group Life & Health Ins. Co. v. Royal Drug Co., 440 U.S. 205 (1979)).

> and substituted instead the analytical tools employed in exclusive dealing cases.[262]

Havighurst, Doctors and Hospitals: An Antitrust Perspective on Traditional Relationships, 1984 Duke L.J. 1071, 1149–51.

6. A necessary element in any tying case is that the defendant have the power to coerce customers into purchasing the tied product. This will often require a demonstration that the hospital possesses market power in the tying product, that is, market power in the inpatient care market. To that extent, the evolving understanding of market definition which was discussed in relation to hospital mergers will be relevant to cases of vertical integration.

262. See supra note 252 and accompanying text. Amicus curiae briefs filed in *Hyde* by the FTC and the Solicitor General took positions similar to those taken in the concurring opinion of Justice O'Connor. See 104 S.Ct. at 1569–76.

*

PART III

Quality-Assurance Mechanisms in a Policy Perspective

CHAPTER 6

Public and Industry-Sponsored Quality Controls

Section A: Regulating Health Care Personnel

INTRODUCTORY NOTES AND QUESTIONS ON QUALITY AND QUALITY ASSURANCE IN MEDICAL CARE

1. Although there is no blueprint for it and much doubt about how well it works, a complex, socially maintained system of rewards and punishments operates, directly and indirectly, to protect and promote the quality of health care. The main elements of this system are direct government regulation, tort law, and consumer choice. Another instrument for ensuring the quality of care is professionalism, which operates at both the individual and the collective level. In addition to the influence of ethical impulses and professional norms on individual behavior, broadly based professional groups engaged in what is sometimes called "self-regulation" also affect the quality of care. The efforts of these groups may be seen either as another socially developed response to the quality problem—a fourth element in the larger network of social controls—or as vehicles by which professions preempt other decision makers and avoid both government regulation and exposure to market forces. The role and legal status of professional organizations and of professionally developed norms and quality standards are a continuing theme throughout this Part of the book.

2. *Quality Today.* Together with other, less identifiable influences, the incentives created by the aforementioned complementary instruments of social control induce individual practitioners and institutional providers to maintain the current level of quality. Whether that level approaches optimality is of course unknowable, but there are reasons to question the quality of medical care in the United States.

One source of concern has been the appearance of managed care, which is the subject of intensive attention in chapter 8. Much of the evidence of quality problems in MCOs is only anecdotal, however, appearing in journalistic accounts. E.g., G. Anders, Health Against Wealth: HMOs and the Breakdown of Medical Trust (1996) (describing alleged flaws in HMOs and occasional adverse consequences allegedly associated with new arrangements). In addition, much of the criticism is misdirected or misleading in failing to recognize the probabilistic nature of medical care or to take into account the cost side of benefit/cost trade-offs. Moreover, most empirical studies still suggest that managed care is both less costly and no more harmful to consumers than was the old, unmanaged health care system. See, e.g., Miller & Luft, Does Managed Care Lead to Better or Worse Quality of Care?, Health Affs., Sept.-Oct. 1997, p. 7 (reviewing recent empirical studies, finding inconclusive results on quality of care); Miller & Luft, Managed Care Plan Performance Since 1980: A Literature Analysis, 271 J.A.M.A. 1512, 1517 (1994) (suggesting "that HMOs provide care at lower cost than do indemnity plans" and citing evidence that care in HMOs and in indemnity plans results in roughly comparable health outcomes). To be sure, there is some evidence that chronically ill patients do slightly less well under managed care. See, e.g., Ware et al., Differences in Four–Year Health Outcomes for Elderly and Poor, Chronically Ill Patients Treated in HMO and Fee-for-service Systems, 276 J.AM.A. 1039 (1996). But managed care may not be the principal reason for quality concerns in American medicine. See Brook, Commentary: Managed Care Is Not the Problem, Quality Is, 278 J.A.M.A. 1612 (1997).

Despite widespread concern that the quality of care is declining under MCOs, anyone who is nostalgic for the way things used to be should be reminded of the major study by the Harvard School of Public Health of malpractice in New York hospitals in the early 1980s (before managed care made significant inroads). Harvard Medical Practice Study, Patients, Doctors, and Lawyers: Medical Injury, Malpractice Litigation, and Patient Compensation in New York (1990). That study found a huge iceberg of iatrogenic (treatment-caused) injuries, many of them attributable to actionable negligence that only rarely came to light in tort actions. See chapter 7(§A) for more on the "Harvard Study." The Harvard researchers have summarized their findings on "the epidemiology of medical injury" as follows:

> Securing accurate estimates of the incidence and patterns of medical injury or adverse events—or in health care parlance, iatrogenic injury—was the cornerstone of our research agenda * * *.
>
> The technique we employed for the studies of medical injury was an in-depth appraisal of the medical records of a carefully selected representative sample of 31,000 patients hospitalized in New York State in 1984. Through this record review we set out to identify which patients suffered iatrogenic injuries and which of these injuries were attributable to the negligence of a doctor or other health care provider.
>
> * * *
>
> Our results indicate that in New York in 1984 the incidence of adverse events suffered by hospitalized patients was 3.7 percent. Of these, 27.6 percent were due to negligence; that is, about 1 percent of all patients hospitalized suffered a negligent medical injury.
>
> These figures are similar to those compiled in California more than a decade earlier. While the California study reported a somewhat lower negligence rate and a somewhat higher injury rate, the differences are not practically significant. Thus, these two large-scale and independent studies indicate that in approximately 4 percent of all hospitalizations adverse events take place, and one-quarter of these involve substandard care.

> Our results are even more striking when the sample findings are weighted up to produce population estimates. Among the 2.6 million patients discharged from New York hospitals in 1984 we estimate that nearly 99,000 suffered disabling injuries. Of these, 56,000 produced minimal impairment, from which the individuals recovered within one month. Another 13,500 led to moderate impairment, with recovery in less than six months. More than 70 percent of the adverse events we identified, then, led to reasonably short-term disability. Still, there were large numbers of individuals who suffered more serious injuries. More than 3,800 adverse events produced *permanent* impairment causing a level of disability ranging up to 50 percent, and another 2,500 patients suffered severe to total disabilities as a result of their treatment. Most dramatically, 13,400 New York patients died in 1984 as a result of medical treatment.
>
> * * * If New York's adverse-event-related death total can be extrapolated to the U.S. population as a whole, one would estimate over 150,000 iatrogenic fatalities annually, more than half of which are due to negligence. Medical injury, then, accounts for more deaths than all other types of accidents combined, and dwarfs the mortality rates associated with motor vehicle accidents (50,000 death per year) and occupation-related mishaps (6,000 deaths per year).

P. Weiler et al., A Measure of Malpractice: Medical Injury, Malpractice Litigation, and Patient Compensation 33, 43–45, 55 (1993).

Although (as the researchers themselves observed) the extrapolations in the foregoing excerpt are open to some question (being based, for example, on non-unanimous subjective judgments of negligence in only 71 cases resulting in death), many experts share the view that the quality of health care in the U.S. has much room for improvement. One observer, for example, noting that "quality problems take three forms: underuse, overuse, and misuse," offers the following evidence:

> Rigorous clinical research has demonstrated that timely provision of a series of interventions can greatly reduce the likelihood of dying from a heart attack. The cumulative impact of thrombolytic therapy, aspirin, beta blockers, and angiotensin-converting enzyme inhibitors is approximately eighty lives saved for every thousand patients treated. Despite these data, all of the these treatments continue to be dramatically underused. One recent study showed that only 21 percent of eligible elderly patents were treated with beta blockers and that the subsequent mortality rate for those who did not receive this treatment was 75 percent higher than that for patients who did.
>
> * * * The efficacy research suggests that these therapies could avert nearly 18,000 deaths [each year] among this untreated group—and that is the toll for just one disease.

Chassin, Assessing Strategies for Quality Improvement, Health Affs., May–June 1997, p. 151 (also noting, among other evidence of quality problems, that, in both fee-for-service and managed-care settings, there were high levels of failure (ranging from 40% to 70%, with managed care doing somewhat better) to diagnose and treat depression, to control hypertension, to obtain recommended mammograms, and to provide appropriate eye care to patients with diabetes). See also Dubois & Brook, Preventable Deaths: Who, How Often, and Why?, 109 Annals Internal Med. 582, 588 (1988) (finding, in study of 182 in-hospital deaths, that 14% to 27% of deaths may have been preventable); Leape, Error in Medicine, 272 J.A.M.A. 1851 (1994) (classic article, quoted below, expressing concern that physicians are not more alarmed by the frequency of errors in treatment). See generally M. Millenson, Demanding Medical Excellence: Doctors and Accountability in the Information Age (1997) (constructive journalistic appraisal of weaknesses in the implementation of medical knowledge, expressing optimism concerning prospects for improvement).

Unfortunately, it is not obvious just what interventions would significantly reduce the incidence of human and other error in the inevitably dangerous and uncertain business of providing medical care. But see Marciniak et al., Improving the Quality of Care for Medicare Patients with Acute Myocardial Infarction, 279 J.A.M.A. 1351 (reporting modest success from PRO-sponsored educational campaign aimed at promoting use of beta blockers, etc.). In any event, study of the various mechanisms of quality assurance will illuminate numerous legal issues and suggest where some improvements might be possible. This chapter deals mostly with direct government regulation of health care personnel and institutions and with private organizations that engage in self-regulation or otherwise promote the quality of care. Chapter 5 has already examined health care institutions, especially hospitals, and how they are motivated and organized internally to maintain and improve the quality of care. Chapter 7 will consider the tort system as a deterrent to bad practice. (Regulatory and tort issues will also arise in chapter 8 in connection with managed care.) Although the primary focus in this Part is on the quality of care, many other values are also implicated and should be observed.

3. *Approaches to the Quality Problem.* Consider the various indicia of quality in medical care and the problems of evaluation and measurement. Medical experts have observed that quality may be assessed by looking at "inputs," "process," or "outcomes." As you consider specific examples of each of the complementary quality-assurance mechanisms identified above (regulation, the tort system, the market, and self-regulation), ask yourself which of these criteria for assessing quality—inputs, process, or outcomes—is being emphasized.

It is possible to identify several different approaches to health care quality improvement. See generally T. Brennan & D. Berwick, New Rules: Regulation, Markets, and the Quality of American Health Care (1996); Chassin, supra. One approach, which Brennan and Berwick label "repair," is the identification of quality failures after the fact, followed by aggressive action to prevent their recurrence. Another approach—"culling"—is the forceful removal of defective elements from a system. Culling may be done through public disciplinary actions against licensed professionals or institutions, by peer review in institutions or professional societies, or by excluding questionable providers from participation in public or private health programs. Coupled with licensure as an instrument for admitting only preapproved "inputs" to the system in the first place, culling is the principal tool used to regulate quality in the American health care industry. There is little evidence, however, that licensing and other boards make more than a minor contribution to the quality of health care. Id. at 356–59. Moreover, such traditional regulatory measures, which are usually rooted in the old paradigm under which medical care is viewed as a self-regulated professional activity, may frustrate more promising attacks on the quality problem by creating a public perception and professional presumption that any provider who has not been "culled" from the system practices at an acceptable level.

Other approaches that might be employed to raise the level of health care quality are more constructive and less police-like than regulatory and legal efforts to assign blame, point fingers, and remove "bad apples" from the barrel. One widely used strategy is to use public and professional resources to generate and circulate information—e.g., clinical practice guidelines—about how better quality can be achieved, in the hope that providers will be motivated to follow the guidance thus provided and to copy the innovations and breakthroughs thus publicized. While promising and certainly helpful in raising the level of quality, these strategies still assume, in accordance with the old paradigm, that professionals and institutions are sufficiently motivated to act on the information provided and can be counted on voluntarily to modify their practices in pursuit of quality improvement. A more recent strategy is to publish outcomes information, relying on the fear of bad publicity to stimulate improvements. See generally Longo et al., Consumer Reports in Health Care: Do They Make a Difference in Patient Care?, 278 J.A.M.A. 1579 (1997) (reporting improved hospital performance following circulation of consumer guides presenting comparative data); Chassin et al., Benefits and Hazards of Reporting Medical Outcomes Publicly, 334 New Eng. J. Med. 394 (1996) (reporting successes in N.Y. program of disclosing risk-adjusted mortality rates in heart surgery); O'Connor et al., A Regional Intervention of Improve the Hospital Mortality Associated with Coronary Bypass Graft Surgery, 275. J.A.M.A. 841 (1996) (similar program in 3 New England states). A related strategy involves giving purchasers of health services detailed information bearing on the quality of care delivered by different health plans and providers. See generally McGlynn, Six Challenges in Measuring the Quality of Health Care, Health Affs., May–June 1997, p. 7. Thus, a great deal of interest has focused on the provision of "report cards" and other comparative information to consumers and their agents, in the hope that purchasers will reward high quality as well as low cost. Regrettably, however, because cost is inevitably more visible and more easily measured than quality, the market may systematically fall short as a stimulus to optimize quality.

4. *Continuous Quality Improvement; Total Quality Management*. In recent years, discussions of the quality of health care in the United States have focused less on "quality assurance," with its emphasis on labeling substandard providers, and more on so-called "continuous quality improvement" (CQI) and "total quality management" (TQM). See generally T.

Brennan & D. Berwick, supra, at 297–333; D. Blumenthal & A. Scheck, eds., Total Quality Management and Physicians' Clinical Decisions (1995). The CQI/TQM movement represents an effort to import into the health care field methodologies similar to those employed in manufacturing industries to ensure product quality. This approach to the quality problem differs from traditional quality assurance in concentrating—constructively, it would seem—on prospective improvement rather than on assigning blame for past failings.

The following excerpt from a classic discussion of the quality problem sheds light on the difficulty of attacking it in ways that offend paradigms implicit in the current organization of health care:

> Physicians, nurses, and pharmacists are trained to be careful and to function at a high level of proficiency. Indeed, they probably are among the most careful professionals in our society. It is curious, therefore, that high error rates have not stimulated more concern and efforts at error prevention. One reason may be a lack of awareness of the severity of the problem. Hospital-acquired injuries are not reported in the newspapers like jumbo-jet crashes, for the simple reason that they occur one at a time in 5000 different locations across the country. Although error rates are substantial, serious injuries due to errors are not part of the everyday experience of physicians or nurses, but are perceived as isolated and unusual events—"outliers." Second, most errors do no harm. Either they are intercepted or the patient's defenses prevent injury. (Few children die from a single misdiagnosed or mistreated urinary infection, for example.)
>
> But the most important reason physicians and nurses have not developed more effective methods of error prevention is that they have a great deal of difficulty in dealing with human error when it does occur. The reasons are to be found in the culture of medical practice.
>
> Physicians are socialized in medical school and residency to strive for error-free practice. There is a powerful emphasis on perfection, both in diagnosis and treatment. In everyday hospital practice, the message is equally clear: mistakes are unacceptable. Physicians are expected to function without error, an expectation that physicians translate into the need to be infallible. * * *
>
> Cultivating a norm of high standards is, of course, highly desirable. It is the counterpart of another fundamental goal of medical education: developing the physician's sense of responsibility for the patient. If you are responsible for everything that happens to the patient, it follows that you are responsible for any errors that occur. While the logic may be sound, the conclusion is absurd, because physicians do not have the power to control all aspects of patient care. Nonetheless, the sense of duty to perform faultlessly is strongly internalized.
>
> * * * It has been suggested that this need to be infallible creates a strong pressure to intellectual dishonesty, to cover up mistakes rather than to admit them. The organization of medical practice, particularly in the hospital, perpetuates these norms. Errors are rarely admitted or discussed among physicians in private practice. Physicians typically feel, not without reason, that admission of error will lead to censure or increased surveil-

lance or, worse, that their colleagues will regard them as incompetent or careless. Far better to conceal a mistake or, if that is impossible, to try to shift the blame to another, even the patient.

Yet physicians are emotionally devastated by serious mistakes that harm or kill patients. Almost every physician who cares for patients has had that experience, usually more than once. * * *

The paradox is that although the standard of medical practice is perfection—error-free patient care—all physicians recognize that mistakes are inevitable. Most would like to examine their mistakes and learn from them. From an emotional standpoint, they need the support and understanding of their colleagues and patients when they make mistakes. Yet, they are denied both insight and support by misguided concepts of infallibility and by fear: fear of embarrassment by colleagues, fear of patient reaction, and fear of litigation. Although the notion of infallibility fails the reality test, the fears are well grounded.

The Medical Approach to Error Prevention

Efforts at error prevention in medicine have characteristically followed what might be called the perfectibility model: if physicians and nurses could be properly trained and motivated, then they would make no mistakes. The methods used to achieve this goal are training and punishment. Training is directed toward teaching people to do the right thing. In nursing, rigid adherence to protocols is emphasized. In medicine, the emphasis is less on rules and more on knowledge.

Punishment is through social opprobrium or peer disapproval. The professional cultures of medicine and nursing typically use blame to encourage proper performance. Errors are regarded as someone's fault, caused by a lack of sufficient attention or, worse, lack of caring enough to make sure you are correct. Punishment for egregious (negligent) errors is primarily (and capriciously) meted out through the malpractice tort litigation system.

Students of error and human performance reject this formulation. While the proximal error leading to an accident is, in fact, usually a "human error," the causes of that error are often well beyond the individual's control. All humans err frequently. Systems that rely on error-free performance are doomed to fail.

The medical approach to error prevention is also reactive. Errors are usually discovered only when there is an incident—an untoward effect or injury to the patient. Corrective measures are then directed toward preventing a recurrence of a similar error, often by attempting to prevent that individual from making a repeat error. Seldom are underlying causes explored.

* * *

It seems clear, and it is the thesis of this article, that if physicians, nurses, pharmacists, and administrators are to succeed in reducing errors in hospital care, they will need to fundamentally change the way they think about errors and why they occur. Fortunately, a great deal has been learned about error prevention in other disciplines, information that is relevant to the hospital practice of medicine.

* * *

[In the aviation industry, d]esigning for safety has led to a number of unique characteristics of aviation that could, with suitable modification, prove useful in improving hospital safety.

First, in terms of system design, aircraft designers assume that errors and failures are inevitable and design systems to "absorb" them, building in multiple buffers, automation, and redundancy. * * *

Second, procedures are standardized to the maximum extent possible. Specific protocols must be followed for trip planning, operations, and maintenance. Pilots go through a checklist before each takeoff. Required maintenance is specified in detail and must be performed on a regular (by flight hours) basis.

Third, the training, examination, and certification process is highly developed and rigidly, as well as frequently, enforced. Airline pilots take proficiency examinations every 6 months. Much of the content of examinations is directly concerned with procedures to enhance safety.

Pilots function well within this rigorously controlled system, although not flawlessly. For example, one study of cockpit crews observed that human errors or instrument malfunctions occurred on the average of one every 4 minutes during an overseas flight. Each event was promptly recognized and corrected with no untoward effects. Pilots also willingly submit to an external authority, the air traffic controller, when within the constrained air and ground space at a busy airport.

Finally, safety in aviation has been institutionalized. Two independent agencies have government-mandated responsibilities * * *. The FAA recognized long ago that pilots seldom reported an error if it led to disciplinary action. Accordingly, in 1975 the FAA established a confidential reporting system for safety infractions, the Air Safety Reporting System (ASRS). If pilots, controllers, or others promptly report a dangerous situation, such as a near-miss midair collision, they will not be penalized. This program dramatically increased reporting[.] * * *

By contrast, accident prevention has not been a primary focus of the practice of hospital medicine. It is not that errors are ignored. Mortality and morbidity conferences, incident reports, risk management activities, and quality assurance committees abound. But, as noted previously, these activities focus on incidents and individuals. When errors are examined, a problem-solving approach is usually used: the cause of the error is identified and corrected. Root causes, the underlying systems failures, are rarely sought. System designers do not assume that errors and failures are inevitable and design systems to prevent or absorb them. There are, of course, exceptions. * * * Nonetheless, the basic health care system approach is to rely on individuals not to make errors rather than to assume they will.

Second, standardization and task design vary widely. In the operating room, it has been refined to a high art. In patient care units, much more could be done, particularly to minimize reliance on short-term memory, one of the weakest aspects of cognition. On-time and correct delivery of medications, for example, is often contingent on a busy nurse remembering to do so, a nurse who is responsible for four or five patients at once and is repeatedly interrupted, a classic set up for a "loss-of-activation" error.

On the other hand, education and training in medicine and nursing far exceed that in aviation, both in breadth of content and in duration, and few professions compare with medicine in terms of the extent of continuing education. Although certification is essentially universal, including the recent introduction of periodic recertification, the idea of periodically testing performance has never been accepted. Thus, we place great emphasis on education and training, but shy away from demonstrating that it makes a difference.

Finally, unlike aviation, safety in medicine has never been institutionalized, in the sense of being a major focus of hospital medical activities. Investigation of accidents is often superficial, unless a malpractice action is likely; noninjurious error (a "near miss") is rarely examined at all. Incident reports are frequently perceived as punitive instruments. As a result, they are often not filed, and when they are, they almost invariably focus on the individual's misconduct.

One medical model is an exception and has proved quite successful in reducing accidents due to errors: anesthesia. Perhaps in part because the effects of serious anesthetic errors are potentially so dramatic—death or brain damage—and perhaps in part because the errors are frequently transparently clear and knowable to all, anesthesiologists have greatly emphasized safety. The success of these efforts has been dramatic. Whereas mortality from anesthesia was one in 10,000 to 20,000 just a decade or so ago, it is now estimated at less than one in 200,000. Anesthesiologists have led the medical profession in recognizing system factors as causes of errors, in designing failsafe systems, and in training to avoid errors.

Systems Changes to Reduce Hospital Injuries

Can the lessons from cognitive psychology and human factors research that have been successful in accident prevention in aviation and other industries be applied to the practice of hospital medicine? * * *

* * * Efficient, routine identification of errors needs to be part of hospital practice, as does routine investigation of all errors that cause injuries. The emphasis is on "routine." Only when errors are accepted as an inevitable, although manageable, part of everyday practice will it be possible for hospital personnel to shift from a punitive to a creative frame of mind that seeks out and identifies the underlying system failures.

Data collecting and investigatory activities are expensive, but so are the consequences of errors. Evidence from industry indicates that the savings from reduction of errors and accidents more than make up for the costs of data collection and investigation. While these calculations apply to "rework" and other operational inefficiencies resulting from errors, additional savings from reduced patient care costs and liability costs for hospitals and physicians could also be substantial.

* * *

Many of the principles described herein fit well within the teachings of total quality management. One of the basic tenets of total quality management, statistical quality control, requires data regarding variation in processes. In a generic sense, errors are but variations in processes. Total quality management also requires a culture in which errors and deviations are regarded not as human failures, but as opportunities to improve the system, "gems," as they are sometimes called. Finally, total quality management calls for grassroots participation to identify and develop system modifications to eliminate the underlying failures.

Like total quality management, systems changes to reduce errors require commitment of the organization's leadership. None of the aforementioned changes will be effective or, for that matter, even possible without support at the highest levels (hospital executives and departmental chiefs) for making safety a major goal of medical practice.

But it is apparent that the most fundamental change that will be needed if hospitals are to make meaningful progress in error reduction is a cultural one. Physicians and nurses need to accept the notion that error is an inevitable accompaniment of the human condition, even among conscientious professionals with high standards. Errors must be accepted as evidence of systems flaws not character flaws. Until and unless that happens, it is unlikely that any substantial progress will be made in reducing medical errors.

Leape, Error in Medicine, 272 J.A.M.A. 1851 *passim* (1994).

One pioneer in CQI, David Blumenthal, M.D., of the Massachusetts General Hospital, has observed that, although CQI methods have been employed with profit in some institutions, few, if any, health care organizations have built CQI methods into their infrastructures. Blumenthal, A Report Card on Continuous Quality Improvement (address at an Institute of Medicine conference on Integrating Strategies for Quality Improvement, Airlie, Va., Oct. 1997). Blumenthal noted the contrast between the revolutionary transformation of manufacturing methods that occurred in the American auto industry in response to competition from quality-oriented foreign makers and the slow movement to embrace CQI in the health care sector. Despite the promise shown by CQI in a few settings, he questioned whether health care organizations will ever undertake the radical changes required by the CQI approach if they do not face a comparable threat to their survival. Observing that it took a "near-death experience" to revolutionize American auto manufacturing, Blumenthal said he could see no comparable source of pressure on health care providers and institutions. See also Chassin, Improving the Quality of Health Care, 335 New Eng. J. Med. 1060 (1996) (observing physician distrust of quality-assurance efforts).

5. Having been introduced to managed-care organizations in chapter 2(§C) and having studied the legal and economic environment of hospitals in chapter 5, you may have some views concerning the kinds of changes that are needed to raise substantially the quality of American medicine. In studying the materials that follow, consider which definitions of quality are implicit in various approaches to quality assurance. For example, which mechanisms focus in some way on matters other than technical or clinical quality? Is adequate attention given to the "caring" as well as the "curing" function of medicine? Is the cost element factored in? Also keep in mind the question where, realistically, pressures to introduce radical quality improvements might come from. Are health care organizations likely to face the kind of "near-death experience" that is arguably required to induce adoption of CQI methods or other measures at odds with conventional ways of doing medical business?

Occupational Licensure and Nonphysician Health Workers

NOTES AND QUESTIONS ON THE ECONOMICS, POLITICS, AND EFFECTS OF OCCUPATIONAL LICENSURE

1. *History.* Occupational licensure laws became firmly established in the United States between 1890 and 1910. During this same period, public distrust of monopoly was given vigorous expression in the antitrust movement, giving rise to this question: How could the legislatures, without inconsistency, simultaneously attack big-business monopolies and enhance, through licensing laws, the market power of the incumbents in middle-class occupations and trades? Legal historian Lawrence Friedman has suggested that both developments reflected essentially middle-class values; certainly, during this period, the robust anti-elitism of the Jacksonian Era, which had produced the repeal of early laws licensing physicians, was long forgotten. See generally Friedman, Freedom of Contract and Occupational Licensing 1890–1910: A Legal and Social Study, 53 Calif.L.Rev. 487 (1965). During this era also, railroads, telephone companies, and other business interests found that utility-type regulation could solve both their economic and their political problems, strengthening their market position while also enhancing their political legitimacy and hence their security against more far-reaching political change. Voters, many of them caught up in a naive populism, were apparently readily convinced that their interests would be served by economic regulation and the upgrading of professional standards.

Occupational licensure began innocuously with such professions as dentistry and medicine before being gradually extended to additional trades which posed less serious risks to public health and safety. Early courts were likely to regard a new entry restriction as unconstitutional, however, unless the newly licensed occupation fit current conceptions of activities within the scope of the police power and could thus be differentiated from the so-called "ordinary callings." (On the invalidation of statutes regulating horseshoeing, for example, see id. at 518.) Nevertheless, once the principle of exclusionary licensure was accepted in the health occupations, there was no logical stopping point. Because there were always several additional callings that appeared to be no more "ordinary" than the last one whose licensure law had been upheld, the class of occupations that could be regulated under the police power steadily grew. In time, legislatures (and the courts) stopped insisting on a clear or persuasive health or safety rationale for supplying a licensure statute to any group which found it worthwhile to mount the necessary lobbying effort. Even if the group failed on the first attempt, pressure on the legislators usually worked in time. Not only was there no point at which a stand against occupational licensure could be made on principle, but the very ubiquity of licensure probably made it seem any group's right to have itself dignified as similar ones had been.

From time to time, occupational licensure has been challenged in the name of civil liberties. See, e.g., Gellhorn, The Abuse of Occupational Licensing, 44 U.Chi. L. Rev. 6 (1976). See also State v. Harris, 216 N.C. 746, 6 S.E.2d 854 (1940), where the court struck down a law licensing and regulating dry cleaners, holding it an "invasion of personal liberty and the freedom to choose and pursue one of the ordinary harmless callings of life"; the court rejected as pretexts certain police-power justifications offered in defense of the statute. Under modern interpretations of substantive due process, of course, legislative determinations of the necessity for licensure and for particular requirements are almost certain to be upheld. Some state courts, however, still demand more than a merely rational basis for a legislative infringement on personal freedom.

2. *Finding a Policy Rationale.* Can you state a convincing economic case for occupational licensure? What are the benefits to consumers? What are the costs? Be precise in your answers to these questions. How would you define the optimal level of restrictiveness in licensing? (A later note based on the work of Carroll and Gaston will help you in thinking about theses matters.) For overviews of occupational licensure, see C. Cox & S. Foster, The Costs and Benefits of Occupational Regulation (FTC Bureau of Economics 1990) (concluding that occupational licensing frequently imposes price increases and substantial costs on consumers while failing to realize the goal of enhancing quality); S. Young, The Rule of Experts: Occupational Licensing in America (Cato Inst. 1987); B. Shimberg, Occupational Licensing: A Public Perspective (Educational Testing Service 1982).

Of all occupations, medicine is probably the one that most people would be quickest to license. Consider how you as a consumer would select a doctor if the state provided no assurance that individual practitioners meet minimum standards? (At a later point you may consider to what extent the state in fact provides such assurance.) What would you do differently? What help would be available to you? Would the same help that is available to you personally also be available to other consumers? For critiques of medical licensure, see generally M. Cohen, Complementary and Alternative Medicine: Legal Boundaries and Regulatory Perspectives 15–38 (1998) (viewing medical licensure from point of view of healers left out of the dominant system of orthodox medicine); S. Blevins, The Medical Monopoly: Protecting Consumers or Limiting Competition?(Cato Inst. Policy Analysis No. 246, 1995); Baron, Licensure of Health Care Professionals: The Consumer's Case for Abolition, 9 Am.J.L. & Med. 348 (1983); Leffler, Physician Licensure: Competition and Monopoly in American Medicine, 21 J.L. & Econ. 165 (1978). See generally T. Jost, ed., Regulation of the Healthcare Professions (1997); Reforming Health Care Workforce Regulation: Policy Considerations for the 21st Century (Pew Health Professions

Comm'n, 1995); Reforming Health Care Workforce Regulation (Pew Health Professions Comm'n 1990).

3. *The "Allied" Health Professions.* Although they are difficult to count, there are more than 200 different occupations in the highly labor-intensive health services industry, only the most prominent of which are subject to some kind of licensure requirement. Ten categories—chiropractors, dental hygienists, dentists, optometrists, pharmacists, physical therapists, physicians (both MDs and osteopaths), podiatrists, and practical and professional nurses—are licensed in all states and the District of Columbia. Nearly all the states also license psychologists and nursing home administrators, while a significant number license clinical laboratory directors, medical technologists, opticians, physical therapy assistants, and speech pathologists and audiologists. Using an expansive definition—to include, for example, such categories as funeral directors and various public health workers—, it can be estimated that over thirty-five different health occupations are licensed in at least one state, with California licensing the most.

Most of the nonphysician occupations that have achieved legal recognition are referred to as the "allied" professions. The term is interesting because it implies that they have entered into some kind of alliance with medicine. The most prominent exception is, of course, chiropractors, with whom physicians remain at war. (Note how the following paragraph extends the metaphor of international relations.) On the legal and other problems faced by other practitioners of healing arts not recognized by the dominant system, see M. Cohen, Complementary and Alternative Medicine, supra.

4. *The Politics of Occupational Regulation.* Most occupational licensure proceeds by creating an exclusive province for physicians and then carving out narrow enclaves within that province for various other licensed occupations. The typical approach is for the state legislature to prescribe a statutory "scope of practice" for the occupation being licensed, defining in general terms the tasks that only an individual licensed in the field can perform. The legal recognition of the medical profession's sovereign sphere and the line-drawing between occupations that might otherwise overlap (i.e., compete) give rise to serious jurisdictional struggles which state legislatures must mediate. Because of the political sensitivity of such "turf" battles, legislators usually prefer to ratify peace treaties worked out among the various professional groups that are seeking to preserve or expand their domain. Thus, private negotiation is often the rule, and the consumer interest in having wider choice is frequently overwhelmed by the political exertions of the competing provider groups. See J. Kany, Developing Rational Health Professions Licensure, in The U.S. Health Workforce: Power, Politics, and Policy 114 (1996) (table showing substitutes for 26 different types of health professionals, including 8 types of personnel capable of providing services in lieu of registered nurses and 12 capable of substituting in for physicians in some cases).

Even if you are persuaded that occupational licensure can be justified, are real world legislatures and licensing boards likely to establish optimal restrictions? (Recall chapter 3(§C)'s examination of the politics of regulation directed at "commercial" practices in various health care occupations.) What are the stakes of the majority of consumer/voters in these debates? Are provider interests the only ones likely to set standards that unduly raise the cost of care? Note that the tendency to overregulate discovered here is encountered in many other health and safety contexts, including the regulation of managed care, which is discussed in chapter 8(§C).

5. *A Federal Critique of Occupational Licensing in Health Care.* In the 1970s, a series of reports issued by the U.S. Public Health Service criticized the states for their efforts in credentialing health care personnel. The final report, issued in 1977, recommended a moratorium on the creation of additional licensing categories and suggested some criteria for states to use in deciding whether to adopt new licensing schemes once the moratorium expired. Its recommendations were based on findings in earlier reports that

> State licensure of the health occupations had evolved into a system of varying requirements, responsibilities, and controls that tends, in many instances, to impede effective utilization of health personnel, to inhibit geographic and career mobility, and to foster variable licensure standards and procedures in different regions of the country. Furthermore, licensing agencies often tend to emphasize formal education and other requirements for entry into a profession but devote much less attention to assuring the continued competence of those who are licensed. In some cases, the involvement of professional associations in the activities of licensure boards raises questions about the independence and objectivity of the boards. * * *
>
> * * * [T]he rapidly growing number of health occupations seeking and obtaining State licensure * * * poses at least two problems: (1) a general proliferation of occupations and roles that is likely to contribute to inefficiencies in the health system; and (2) the adoption of arbitrary scopes of practice in fields that will be undergoing substantial evolution over the next five to ten years.

Public Health Service, U.S. Dep't of Health, Education and Welfare, Credentialing Health Manpower pp. 4–5 (1977) (hereinafter cited as 1977 DHEW Report).

Why was the federal government interested in credentialing issues at all? Isn't occupational licensure a purely local concern, a subject of the states' police power? Do you agree with the 1977 DHEW Report's implication that differences in licensing standards between states are undesirable?

6. *Certification vs. Licensure.* The 1977 DHEW Report recommended the creation of a private national certifying or accrediting body to oversee the issuance of credentials in the various allied health fields. Nobel economist Milton Friedman, in a well-known essay on occupational licensure in his book, Capitalism and Freedom ch. 9 (1962), had suggested public certification—sometimes called title licensure—as an intermediate form of government intervention that supplies useful information to consumers without restricting their access to other providers of the service; CPAs and architects are examples of persons who are legally authorized to use certain titles but are not protected by law against competition from uncertified personnel. Most licensure in the allied health professions is mandatory, but nonexclusionary title licensure prevails in some states for such occupations as nursing, so that nonlicensees, while they may engage in nursing, may not call themselves "registered nurses" (RN) or "licensed practical nurses" (LPN).

If certification is desirable as an alternative to licensure, should it be done publicly or privately? Private credentialing is common in health care occupations, and the 1977 DHEW Report called for its wider use and its regularization under an umbrella national commission. If certification can be done privately, why should government ever become involved? How might private credentialing programs be paid for? Who will control them? Will their standards be set with the consumer's interest primarily in mind? Is there any reason to think a public certification scheme would be preferable? Might it be worse? The next section of this chapter examines some issues surrounding private credentialing of health care personnel.

Although seeming to echo Milton Friedman's preference for informative certification over exclusionary licensing, the 1977 DHEW Report actually had a quite different situation and scenario in mind. The occupational groups seeking recognition through new licensure schemes were not after all, as they are in the usual case, trying to fence others out of territory they wished to claim for themselves. In many cases, they were simply trying to get into a field from which they were themselves fenced out by licensing laws that already blanketed the field of patient care. Thus, DHEW's concern was not that competent people were being excluded from practicing their skills but that too many different types of personnel were being licensed, fragmenting the industry, hampering efficient use of personnel, and complicating the federal government's decisions about whom to pay for particular services. In addition, the report did not contemplate (as Friedman did) a market featuring both certified and uncertified practitioners. Instead, it looked the other way—toward government reimbursement only of certified practitioners and ultimately to a national health insurance system, under which there would be little room for practitioners and other personnel not appropriately credentialed. Although DHEW's position favoring certification over licensing may have sounded like an endorsement of Friedmanesque free-market principles, the moratorium on new licensing programs that its report proposed was strongly endorsed by already-licensed groups, whom it protected against new competition.

7. *A State Legislative Reform.* Where in state government should decisions about the appropriateness and scope of occupational licensure be made? What benefits do you see in the following Virginia statute, Va. Code § 54.1–310(A)(6), –311 (Michie 1994), which was originally enacted in an effort to address the same problem of proliferating licensing schemes that was the subject of the 1977 DHEW Report. Under the legislation, a Board of Commerce consisting of nine part-time members was instructed as follows:

§ 54.1–310(A)(6). [The Board shall] evaluate constantly each profession and occupation in the Commonwealth not otherwise regulated for consideration as to whether such profession or occupation should be regulated and, if so, the degree of regulation that should be imposed. Whenever it determines that the public interest requires that a profession or occupation which is not regulated by law should be regulated, the Board shall recommend to the General Assembly next convened a regulatory system accompanied by comprehensive regulations necessary to conduct the degree of regulation required.

§ 54.1–311. Degrees of regulation.—

A. Whenever the Board determines that a particular profession or occupation should be regulated, or that a different degree of regulation should be imposed on a regulated profession or occupation, it shall consider the following degrees of regulation in the order provided in subdivisions 1 through 5. The Board shall regulate only to the degree, or degrees, of regulation that it finds necessary to fulfill the need for regulation and only upon approval by the General Assembly.

1. Private civil actions and criminal prosecutions.—Whenever existing common law and statutory causes of civil action or criminal prohibitions are not sufficient to eradicate existing harm or prevent potential harm, the Board may first consider the recommendation of statutory change to provide more strict causes for civil action and criminal prosecution.

2. Inspection and injunction.—Whenever current inspection and injunction procedures are not sufficient to eradicate existing harm, the Board may promulgate regulations consistent with the intent of this chapter to provide more adequate inspection procedures and to specify procedures whereby the appropriate regulatory board may enjoin an activity which is detrimental to the public well-being. The Board may recommend to the appropriate agency of the Commonwealth that such procedures be strengthened or it may recommend statutory changes in order to grant to the appropriate state agency the power to provide sufficient inspection and injunction procedures.

3. Registration.—Whenever it is necessary to determine the impact of the operation of a profession or occupation on the public, the Board may implement a system of registration.

4. Certification.—When the public requires a substantial basis for relying on the professional services of a practitioner, the Board may implement a system of certification.

5. Licensing.—Whenever adequate regulation cannot be achieved by means other than licensing, the Board may establish licensing procedures for any particular profession or occupation.

B. In determining the proper degree of regulation, if any, the Board shall determine the following:

1. Whether the practitioner, if unregulated, performs a service for individuals involving a hazard to the public health, safety or welfare.

2. The opinion of a substantial portion of the people who do not practice the particular profession, trade or occupation on the need for regulation.

3. The number of states which have regulatory provisions similar to those proposed.

4. Whether there is sufficient demand for the service for which there is no regulated substitute and this service is required by a substantial portion of the population.

5. Whether the profession or occupation requires high standards of public responsibility, character and performance of each individual engaged in the profession or occupation, as evidenced by established and published codes of ethics.

6. Whether the profession or occupation requires such skill that the public generally is not qualified to select a competent practitioner without some assurance that he has met minimum qualifications.

7. Whether the professional or occupational associations do not adequately protect the public from incompetent, unscrupulous or irresponsible members of the profession or occupation.

8. Whether current laws which pertain to public health, safety and welfare generally are ineffective or inadequate.

9. Whether the characteristics of the profession or occupation make it impractical or impossible to prohibit those practices of the profession or occupation which are detrimental to the public health, safety and welfare.

10. Whether the practitioner performs a service for others which may have a detrimental effect on third parties relying on the expert knowledge of the practitioner.

8. *"Sunset"?* It is notable that the 1977 DHEW Report, in setting forth criteria for use in creating new licensing programs, did not question any licensure scheme already in place. Is it plausible that, if proliferation of licensure was a problem, no rollback (deregulation) was in order? Does the Virginia statute contemplate any rollbacks? In recent years, many states have adopted so-called "sunset" statutes, requiring regulatory programs to be re-examined at intervals to ensure their continued utility.

9. *"Institutional Licensure."* The 1977 DHEW Report, after recalling that an earlier report in the series had expressed an interest in "the feasibility of a 'national certification system' and 'institutional licensure' as alternatives to the traditional model of occupational licensure in health," endorsed the private certification alternative to licensure but recommended that "the institutional licensure approach—because of the intense controversy that it generated—should not receive further consideration at this time." 1977 DHEW Report, at 5–6. The proposal thus rejected is of some conceptual interest and relevant to a variety of policy proposals afoot today.

Although the term *institutional licensure* can be understood simply as state licensing of institutions (e.g., hospitals), in the 1977 DHEW Report it referred to a proposal under which a licensed institution, instead of assigning state-licensed personnel to tasks within their state-defined competence, would be allowed to write job descriptions for the positions it needed filled, to establish criteria for personnel filling those positions, and to identify individuals to fill those slots. In effect, the institution would "license" individuals to perform particular tasks—subject to accountability to state authorities. See generally N. Hershey & W. Wheeler, Health Personnel Regulation in the Public Interest: Questions and Answers on Institutional Licensure (Calif. Hosp. Ass'n 1973). The objective of this proposal was to relate "the qualifications and experience of health workers to the tasks and functions they will be required to perform on the job." Id. at 12. The efficiency objective is fairly obvious. Who do you suppose objected, causing DHEW to drop the idea? Should the concept be rehabilitated? How does your learning from chapter 5 inform your views on this question? How does the role of hospitals vis-a-vis physicians compare with "institutional licensure" for other types of health care personnel?

10. *Does Licensing Ensure Quality?* For a helpful review of empirical studies of occupational licensure, see Carroll and Gaston, Occupational Licensing and the Quality of Service: An Overview, 7 Law & Human Behavior 139 (1983). These authors observe that occupational licensing can serve a useful function in markets with imperfect information by lowering "search costs" incurred by individuals seeking to protect themselves against poor-quality providers. They submit that even though exclusionary licensure increases prices and the incomes of practitioners (to compensate for added investments in training), the gains in improved quality could justify licensure of a certain level of restrictiveness.

Carroll and Gaston summarize several empirical studies that, although encountering difficult measurement problems, appear to demonstrate that the quality of the services provided by licensed practitioners is indeed higher when licensing practices are more stringent. For example, licensing restrictions on lawyers in different jurisdictions were analyzed using several indicia of quality: malpractice insurance rates, frequency of disciplinary actions, and ratings of lawyers in the Martindale–Hubbell Law Directory. For each of these quality measures, greater restrictiveness in licensure was associated with higher average quality of practitioner. Studies of optometrists and pharmacists yielded similar findings, leading Carroll and Gaston to state that "the argument that higher standards yield enhanced quality of practitioner is borne out of the evidence."

Carroll and Gaston go on to observe, however, that even though stringent occupational licensing may improve the quality of service delivered by licensed personnel, greater stringency does not necessarily translate into improved quality of service actually received by consumers—if one takes into account the substitutions induced by higher prices. Their article summarizes a number of studies that attempt to relate licensing standards to the quality of services actually enjoyed by consumers. A study of dental licensure revealed, for example, that licensing restrictions, such as citizenship requirements and lack of interstate reciprocity in the granting of licenses, are associated with fewer dentists per capita, which in turn is associated with poorer overall dental health. States with stringent licensing measures governing electricians were found, in another study, to have a greater number of accidental electrocutions. In plumbing, where unionization rather than licensing accounts for the limitation of supply, areas with fewer plumbers have higher retail sales of plumbing supplies, indicating the substitution of do-it-yourself service for professional service. Similar findings are reported in studies of optometrists and veterinarians. In the case of sanitarians, restrictive licensure was found to limit their numbers "in isolated rural areas and the inner city, while suburbia and small towns evidence no significant impact."

It thus appears that supply limitations and the resulting higher costs of higher-quality services affect the welfare of consumers in an unanticipated way and that considering only the quality of services rendered by licensed personnel is to miss an important cost of occupational licensing. Carroll and Gaston conclude that "the results * * * [are] consistent with the proposition that licensing has gone far enough to ensure adequate quality in most places and has gone too far in others." Leffler, supra, at 175, argues in defense of physician licensure that greater assurance of minimum quality could induce more patronage of licensed professionals.

Do the findings of Carroll and Gaston provide insights helpful in answering the earlier questions concerning the economics and politics of occupational licensure? See also M. Kleiner & R. Kudrle, Does Regulation Improve Outputs and Increase Prices?: The Case of Dentistry (NBER Working Paper No. 5869, 1997) (finding that restrictive licensing has no effect on dental health but does increase prices so that a state changing from low to high level of restrictiveness would experience 14–16% higher prices for dental services; also finding incomes of dentists in states with more restrictive regulation 10% higher than incomes of dentists in low-regulation states); B. Shimberg et al., Occupational Licensing: Practices and Policies 12–16 (1972); Hogan, The Effectiveness of Licensing: History, Evidence, and Recommendations, 7 Law & Human Behavior 117 (1983). How do the findings of Carrol and Gaston bear on debates on other regulatory issues, such as the requirements to be imposed on managed-care plans? See chapter 8(§C).

11. *Prospects for Improving Occupational Licensure in Health Care.* With specific regard to the regulation of health care personnel, the following conclusions were drawn in the mid 1980s from a review of empirical literature:

> Credentialing regulations * * * seem, in theory, to be the most comprehensive set of mechanisms for monitoring both initial and subsequent competence. Yet, the research on credentialing shows that contemporary credentialing procedures may not be reliably screening actual practice competence; they certainly are not effective in ensuring lifetime competence; and the current practice of credentialing can have undesirable consequences for access and health care costs.
>
> In addition to the liberalizing actions taken by the courts and the FTC, many states have begun to reform their credentialing practices, with the

general aim of making regulation more accountable to broad public interests and less responsive to the narrow interests of particular professions.

While reforms have tended to focus on relieving deleterious economic side effects of credentialing practices, the presumption of need to regulate competency remains. Little has been done to make credentialing practices more reliable in ensuring practice competence. One proposal being made to improve competency is mandatory relicensure. Mandatory relicensure at regular intervals focuses on lifetime (rather than initial) competence. The research * * * on competence and quality of care indicates that professional obsolescence is a real concern. There is a need for augmenting the knowledge base and clinical skills as technology changes and as encounters with particular case problems and clinical tools become less frequent as a result of specialization. * * * [T]he research [also] shows that current credentialing methods for assessing patient care competence (initial or periodic) are not reliable and that current techniques for disseminating new skills are not effective in altering actual behavior. The only demonstrably reliable way to monitor continued competence and remedy deficiencies is through the use of "output monitoring" and corresponding deficiency-oriented training. For these reasons, standards for relicensure are not likely to be effective in relieving the inadequacies of current licensing practices.

As noted above, most refinements in credentialing attempt to make regulators more accountable to public interests * * *. The most popular and politically acceptable change has been the use of sunset provisions for licensing boards. This attempt to extract accountability through periodic scrutiny has been employed in 35 states. Clearly, the purpose here is to regulate the regulators. Attempts to make licensing boards accountable for their actions, rather than assuming accountability because of their composition, may encourage higher rates of sanctions and possibly more evaluative research. However, there is no evidence to suggest that this form of scrutiny will constitute anything more than a resource allocation tool for state budgeting purposes. For sunset provisions to contribute the appropriate incentives, it will be essential to stipulate achievement of public objectives of accessible and cost-effective services as criteria to be met in the sunset performance evaluation. While the notion of accountability is laudable, the problems of measurement of board effectiveness on dimensions of access, cost, and quality are likely to be prohibitively large.

The second type of refinement that is being proposed for credentialing systems is an alteration of the structure of the licensing agency. One such approach is to change the locus of the licensing function to a state regulatory agency, providing a better opportunity for integrating the manpower and cost policies of the state into the competence control process. The problems of proliferation of credentialing, coordination of tasks across professions, and the continued threats of board control by the professions can be addressed through creation of a centralized administrative body within the state vested with legislative authority to license by regulation, rather than by statute. States such as California, Michigan, Virginia, and Minnesota have implemented such systems. Another variation of this approach is to group related professions together on boards, while continuing to license them separately (for example, physicians, physician assistants, and nurse practitioners). This administrative change will shift the disputes over roles and responsibilities from the legislature to the board.

Gaumer, Regulating Health Professionals: A Review of the Empirical Literature, 62 Milbank Mem. Fund Q. 380, 406–08 (1984). For a series of recommendations for reforming regulation of health workers, see L. Finnochio et al., Reforming Health Care Workforce Regulation: Policy Considerations for the 21st Century (Pew Health Professions Comm'n, 1995). See also Jost, Oversight of the Competence of Healthcare Professionals, in Regulation of the Healthcare Professions 17 (T. Jost, ed., 1997); S. Gross, Of Foxes and Hen Houses: Licensing and the Health Professions (1994).

Physician Extenders; Scope of Practice

Sermchief v. Gonzales

Supreme Court of Missouri, En Banc, 1983.
660 S.W.2d 683.

■ WELLIVER, JUDGE.

This is a petition for a declaratory judgment and injunction brought by two nurses and five physicians employed by the East Missouri Action Agency (Agency) wherein the plaintiff-appellants ask the Court to declare that the practices of the Agency nurses are authorized under the nursing law of this state, § 335.016.8, RSMo 1978 and that such practices do not constitute the unauthorized practice of medicine under Chapter 334 relating to the Missouri State Board of Registration For the Healing Arts (Board). The petition further requests that the Board be enjoined from taking any steps, either civil or criminal, to enforce the unauthorized practice of medicine provision of § 334.010 against these parties. The holding below was against appellants who make direct appeal to this Court alleging that the validity of the statutes is involved. Mo.Const. art. V, '3. While the case may involve no more than application of the statutes, we retain jurisdiction because of the general interest in this matter. Mo.Const. art. V, § 4. We reverse.

I

The facts are simple and for the most part undisputed. The Agency is a federally tax exempt Missouri not-for-profit corporation that maintains offices in Cape Girardeau (main office), Flat River, Ironton, and Fredericktown. The Agency provides medical services to the general public in fields of family planning, obstetrics and gynecology. The services are provided to an area that includes the counties of Bollinger, Cape Girardeau, Perry, St. Francis, Ste. Genevieve, Madison, Iron and Washington. Some thirty-five hundred persons utilized these services during the year prior to trial. The Agency is funded from federal grants, Medicaid reimbursements and patient fees. The programs are directed toward the lower income segment of the population. Similar programs exist both statewide and nationwide.

Appellant nurses Solari and Burgess are duly licensed professional nurses in Missouri pursuant to the provisions of Chapter 335 and are employed by the Agency. Both nurses have had post-graduate special training in the field of obstetrics and gynecology. Appellant physicians are also employees of the Agency and duly licensed to practice medicine (the healing arts) pursuant to Chapter 334. Respondents are the members and the executive secretary of the Missouri State Board of Registration for the Healing Arts (Board) and as such are charged with the enforcement, implementation, and administration of Chapter 334.

The services routinely provided by the nurses and complained of by the Board included, among others, the taking of history; breast and pelvic examinations; laboratory testing of Papanicolaou (PAP) smears, gonorrhea cultures, and blood serology; the providing of and giving of information about oral contraceptives, condoms, and intrauterine devices (IUD); the dispensing of certain designated medications; and counseling services and community education. If the nurses determined the possibility of a condition designated in the standing orders or protocols that would contraindicate the use of contraceptives until further examination and evaluation, they would refer the patients to one of the Agency physicians. No act by either nurse is alleged to have caused injury or damage to any person. All acts by the nurses were done pursuant to written standing orders and protocols signed by appellant physicians. The standing orders and protocols were directed to specifically named nurses and were not identical for all nurses.

The Board threatened to order the appellant nurses and physicians to show cause why the nurses should not be found guilty of the unauthorized practice of medicine and the physicians guilty of aiding and abetting such unauthorized practice. Appellants sought Court relief in this proceeding.

The trial can be capsulized by saying that the foregoing facts were either stipulated or agreed to by all parties. The appellants, in addition to the two nurses and the director of the Agency, called four witnesses who were permitted to express their opinion that the nurses' described acts were within § 335.016.8. * * * [Respondents' three witnesses] expressed the view that the acts of the nurses were outside the contemplation of § 335.016.8 and constituted the practice of medicine prohibited by § 334.010. Virtually all of the admitted testimony of these seven witnesses consisted of their opinion of what the trial court described in its memorandum opinion as the ultimate issues for determination:

> A. Does the conduct of plaintiff nurses Solari and Burgess constitute "Professional Nursing" as that term is defined in § 335.016.8, RSMo?
>
> B. If the Court finds and concludes that any act or acts of plaintiff nurses Solari and Burgess does not or do not constitute(s) "professional nursing" and, constitutes the unauthorized practice of medicine under § 334.010, RSMo the Court must then determine if § 334.010, RSMo is unconstitutionally vague and uncertain on its face and, thus, is in violation of the specificity requirements of the Fifth and Fourteenth Amendments to

the United States Constitution and of Article 1, § 10 of the Missouri Constitution.

All of appellants' offers to prove the general practices of nursing, national or other recognized guidelines and standards for nursing, or the legislative intent with reference to the 1975 revision of the Nursing Practice Act, Chapter 335, were overruled by the trial court.

In our opinion the trial court correctly defined the issues of the case, both of which we deem to be matters of law to be determined by the Court. The trial court then made extensive findings of fact, the first nine denominated as stipulated and undisputed facts and the last nine denominated as controverted facts. The last nine findings are:

10. Pursuant to the standing orders and protocols (Joint Exhibits 3, 4 and 5), plaintiffs Burgess and Solari provided oral contraceptives, IUD's and vaginal medications to their patients.

11. Providing oral contraceptives, IUD's and vaginal medications is the administration of medications and treatments.

12. Plaintiffs Burgess and Solari administered these medications and treatments which were not prescribed by a person licensed in this state to prescribe such medications and treatments.

13. Plaintiffs Burgess and Solari performed pelvic examinations and based upon their findings, attempted to diagnose the existence or nonexistence of contraindications to the use of oral contraceptives, IUD's and vaginal medications, set out in their standing orders and protocols (Joint Exhibits 3, 4 and 5).

14. Graduation from a school of medicine or a school of osteopathy is a prerequisite for one to be capable of interpreting the results of a pelvic examination.

15. The State Board of Nursing regulations do not require professional nursing programs to include courses in pathology or physical diagnosis.

16. The acts of plaintiffs Burgess and Solari in utilizing the findings derived from pelvic examinations which they performed to attempt to diagnose the existence or nonexistence of contraindications to the use of oral contraceptives, IUD's and vaginal medications, require an individual to draw upon education, judgment and skill based upon knowledge and application of principles in addition to and beyond biological, physical, social and nursing sciences.

17. The acts of plaintiffs Burgess and Solari in administering oral contraceptives, IUD's and vaginal medications, without the same being prescribed by a person licensed in this state to prescribe such medications and treatments, require an individual to draw upon education, judgment and skill based upon knowledge and application of principles in addition to and beyond biological, physical, social and nursing sciences.

18. The conduct of plaintiffs Burgess and Solari in utilizing the findings derived from pelvic examinations which they performed to attempt to diagnose the existence or nonexistence of contraindications to the use of oral contraceptives, IUD's and vaginal medications, as described in their standing orders and protocols (Joint Exhibits 3, 4 and 5), constitutes medical diagnosis and not nursing diagnosis.

* * *

II

The appeal of this case attracted amici briefs resembling a letter writing campaign directed at a legislative body. * * *

III

The statutes involved are:

It shall be unlawful for any person not now a registered physician within the meaning of the law to practice medicine or surgery in any of its departments, or to profess to cure and attempt to treat the sick and others afflicted with bodily or mental infirmities, or engage in the practice of midwifery in this state, except as herein provided.

Section 334.010.

This Chapter does not apply * * * *to nurses licensed and lawfully practicing their profession within the provisions of chapter 335, RSMo.*

* * *

Section 334.155, RSMo Supp.1982 (Emphasis Added).

Definitions.—As used in sections 335.011 to 335.096, unless the context clearly requires otherwise, the following words and terms shall have the meanings indicated:

. . .

(8) "Professional nursing" is the performance for compensation of any act which requires substantial specialized education, judgment and skill based on knowledge and application of principles derived from the biological, physical, social and nursing sciences, including, but not limited to:

(a) Responsibility for the teaching of health care and the prevention of illness to the patient and his family; or

(b) Assessment, nursing diagnosis, nursing care, and counsel of persons who are ill, injured or experiencing alterations in normal health processes; or

(c) The administration of medications and treatments as prescribed by a person licensed in this state to prescribe such medications and treatments; or

(d) The coordination and assistance in the delivery of a plan of health care with all members of the health team; or

(e) The teaching and supervision of other persons in the performance of any of the foregoing;

Section 335.016.8(A)b(e).

At the time of enactment of the Nursing Practice Act of 1975, the following statutes were repealed:

2. A person practices professional nursing who for compensation or personal profit performs, *under the supervision and direction of a practitioner authorized to sign birth and death certificates,* any professional services requiring the application of principles of the biological, physical or social sciences and nursing skills in the care of the sick, in the prevention of disease or in the conservation of health.

Section 335.010.2, RSMo 1969 (Emphasis Added).

Nothing contained in this chapter shall be construed as conferring any authority on any person to practice medicine or osteopathy or to undertake the treatment or cure of disease.

Section 335.190, RSMo 1969.

The parties on both sides request that in construing these statutes we define and draw that thin and elusive line that separates the practice of medicine and the practice of professional nursing in modern day delivery of health services. A response to this invitation, in our opinion, would result in an avalanche of both medical and nursing malpractice suits alleging infringement of that line and would hinder rather than help with the delivery of health services to the general public. Our consideration will be limited to the narrow question of whether the acts of these nurses were permissible under § 335.016.8 or were prohibited by Chapter 334.

In analyzing this question, we are guided by well-established rules of statutory construction. * * *

The legislature substantially revised the law affecting the nursing profession with enactment of the Nursing Practice Act of 1975.[5] Perhaps the most significant feature of the Act was the redefinition of the term "professional nursing," which appears in § 335.016.8. Even a facile reading of that section reveals a manifest legislative desire to expand the scope of authorized nursing practices. Every witness at trial testified that the new

5. The impetus for the legislation was the ongoing expansion of nursing responsibilities. Several national commissions investigated the causes of and the implications of this phenomenon during the early 1970's. One committee concluded: "Professional nursing ... is in a period of rapid and progressive change in response to the growth of biomedical knowledge, changes in patterns of demand for health services, and the evolution of professional relationships among nurses, physicians and other health professions." Secretary's Committee to Study Extended Roles for Nurses, Dep't. of Health, Education and Welfare, Pub. No. (HSM) 73–2037, "Extending the Scope of Nursing Practice: A Report of the Secretary's Committee to Study Extended Roles for Nurses" 8 (1971). The broadening of nursing roles necessitated altering existing nursing practice laws to reflect the changes in a nurse's professional duties. At the time the Missouri legislature acted, thirty states had amended their laws regulating the nursing profession. Forty states currently have broadened nursing practice statutes similar to § 335.016.8.

definition of professional nursing is a broader definition than that in the former statute. A comparison with the prior definition vividly demonstrates this fact. Most apparent is the elimination of the requirement that a physician directly supervise nursing functions. Equally significant is the legislature's formulation of an open-ended definition of professional nursing. The earlier statute limited nursing practice to "services . . . in the care of the sick, in the prevention of disease or in the conservation of health." § 335.010.2, RSMo 1969. The 1975 Act not only describes a much broader spectrum of nursing functions, it qualifies this description with the phrase "including, but not limited to." We believe this phrase evidences an intent to avoid statutory constraints on the evolution of new functions for nurses delivering health services. Under § 335.016.8, a nurse may be permitted to assume responsibilities heretofore not considered to be within the field of professional nursing so long as those responsibilities are consistent with her or his "specialized education, judgment and skill based on knowledge and application of principles derived from the biological, physical, social and nursing sciences." § 335.016.8.

The acts of the nurses herein clearly fall within this legislative standard. All acts were performed pursuant to standing orders and protocols approved by physicians. Physician prepared standing orders and protocols for nurses and other paramedical personnel were so well established and accepted at the time of the adoption of the statute that the legislature could not have been unaware of the use of such practices. We see nothing in the statute purporting to limit or restrict their continued use.

Respondents made no challenge of the nurses' level of training nor the degree of their skill. They challenge only the legal right of the nurses to undertake these acts. We believe the acts of the nurses are precisely the types of acts the legislature contemplated when it granted nurses the right to make assessments and nursing diagnoses. There can be no question that a nurse undertakes only a nursing diagnosis, as opposed to a medical diagnosis, when she or he finds or fails to find symptoms described by physicians in standing orders and protocols for the purpose of administering courses of treatment prescribed by the physician in such orders and protocols.

The Court believes that it is significant that while at least forty states have modernized and expanded their nursing practice laws during the past fifteen years neither counsel nor the Court have discovered any case challenging nurses' authority to act as the nurses herein acted.

The broadening of the field of practice of the nursing profession authorized by the legislature and here recognized by the Court carries with it the profession's responsibility for continuing high educational standards and the individual nurse's responsibility to conduct herself or himself in a professional manner. The hallmark of the professional is knowing the limits of one's professional knowledge. The nurse, either upon reaching the limit of her or his knowledge or upon reaching the limits prescribed for the nurse by the physician's standing orders and protocols, should refer the patient to the physician. There is no evidence that the assessments and diagnoses made by the nurses in this case exceeded such limits.

In preparing this opinion, the Court did considerable research and reading in medical libraries. We find nothing in our construction of the statutes that is incompatible with the history and development of the profession of nursing, the general standards of state and national nursing organizations and associations, the utilization of special nursing services by the Federal and State governments in the delivery of health services, or the utilization of nursing services by schools, factories, homes for the aging and our hospitals.

Having found that the nurses' acts were authorized by § 335.016.8, it follows that such acts do not constitute the unlawful practice of medicine for the reason that § 334.155 makes the provisions of Chapter 334 inapplicable "to nurses licensed and lawfully practicing their profession within the provisions of Chapter 335 RSMo."

This cause is reversed and remanded with instructions to enter judgment consistent with this opinion.

NOTES AND QUESTIONS ON PHYSICIAN ASSISTANTS AND NURSE PRACTITIONERS

1. *Expanded Roles for Nonphysicians?* The following excerpt from a 1967 article shows the interest in expanding the legal authority of nonphysician health care personnel at a time when physicians were in short supply:

> [H]ealth authorities now generally agree that the serious shortage of physicians can be overcome only by allocating certain tasks not requiring the judgment and ability of a physician to specialized personnel with fewer skills and less education. * * *
>
> What is the legal basis for these innovations? For example, do the medical and nursing practice acts permit specifically trained nurses, under standing orders from a physician, to administer cardiopulmonary resuscitation by means of a Pacemaker machine to patients suffering heart stoppages? For most jurisdictions there can be no certain answers to such questions because legal authorities have not yet resolved the underlying issues. In a few states, however, the answers have begun to emerge from court decisions, attorney general opinions, or legislative enactments. These initial efforts clearly indicate that the legality of delegations of medical functions involves not only mandatory licensure for the practice of medicine, as statutorily defined, but also the scope and effect to be given to (1) licenses of allied and auxiliary personnel, (2) prevailing customs of medical practitioners and institutions, and (3) physicians' supervision and control of assisting personnel.
>
> In most states the only official guidelines for delegation are the functional definitions of allied and auxiliary personnel in statutes which provide for their licensure. But these definitions are often difficult to interpret and apply to new or unforeseen situations—hence the many advisory opinions of state attorneys general on the scope of these licenses.

> Faced with such uncertainties, the medical and nursing professions have recently adopted interprofessional agreements to clarify accepted customs and practices. As a practical matter, delegation of health service functions is predominantly governed by prevailing custom and practice.

Forgotson et al., Licensure of Physicians, 1967 Wash.U.L.Q. 249, 253–54.

According to the foregoing, what are the various sources of "law" defining the scopes of practice of various categories of health care personnel? What weight should be accorded to custom? What is your opinion of "interprofessional agreements [between medicine and nursing] to clarify accepted customs and practices"?

2. *Physician Extenders.* Concerns such as those expressed above prompted interest in the 1960s and 1970s in training and employing so-called "physician extenders" (PEs). PEs are health care professionals who deliver medical services (such as history taking and well-baby examinations) that, while not requiring a physician's expertise, fall technically within the practice of medicine and outside the statutory scope of other licensed personnel. The term refers to both physician's assistants (PAs) and nurse practitioners (NP), which have in common the capability to perform a significant number of routine health care ordinarily performed by physicians. The training and use of PEs became widespread in the 1970s as a way to relieve what was perceived to be a shortage of physicians, especially in certain geographic areas and in primary care. The possibility that costs might be reduced by substituting less highly trained personnel for physicians was another factor inspiring the development of PEs. Although quality concerns were inevitably raised, one 1984 report stated, "Several well-calibrated studies of the quality of care by nurse practitioners have demonstrated equivalence with physicians. Superiority has been shown in some selected areas." Spitzer, The Nurse Practitioner Revisited: Slow Death of A Good Idea, 310 New Eng.J.Med. 1049 (1984) ("many other innovations mediated by medical practitioners have gained widespread acceptance with less rigorous prior evaluation than was given to the use of nurse practitioners and physician assistants"). For a full appraisal, see U.S. Office of Technology Assessment, Nurse Practitioners, Physician Assistants, and Certified Nurse–Midwives: A Policy Analysis (Health Technology Case Study No. 37, 1986).

Despite early good experience with physician assistants and nurse practitioners, enthusiasm for them waned in the late 1980s as the physician supply grew. The following commentary on nurse practitioners indicates some of the perceived problems:

> One might have expected rural communities to be highly favorable to nurse practitioners' influence on the control of basic primary-care services, but the barriers that keep physicians from such areas also affect nurses. Moreover, additional barriers, such as nonrecognition by third-party insurers, lack of legal status, inability to prescribe any medication, and inefficient access to medical support or referral coverage frustrate even the hardiest and most committed nurse practitioners in rural America * * *

> * * * The push by nurses for parity of remuneration with physicians providing primary-care services is a force of critical importance. If it succeeds, it will vitiate all the early research results on the cost effectiveness of nurses that were based on the assumption of a differential in income rates between nurses and physicians. The inevitable consequence would be much weaker support from governmental promoters of the nurse-practitioner concept * * *
>
> * * * At best, third-party payers are less than lukewarm about opening doors to new reimbursement methods for nurses; in general, they are strongly opposed.

Spitzer, supra, at 1050. What is your view on "parity of remuneration"?

In the 1990s, there has been an increasing demand for what have come to be known as "advanced practice" nurses (APNs)—nurses with special capabilities, such as nurse practitioners, nurse midwives, clinical nurse specialists and certified registered nurse anesthetists (CRNAs). Not only have cost pressures awakened renewed interest in PEs, but managed-care plans have grown and come to view nurses as capable of providing high-quality, cost-effective primary care and other services also provided by physicians. The nursing profession has seized some initiative in seeking expanded responsibilities and increased independence. See generally Andrews, The Shadow Health Care System: Regulation of Alternative Health Providers, 32 Hous. L. Rev. 1273 (1996); Safriet, Health Care Dollars and Regulatory Sense: The Role of Advanced Practice Nursing, 9 Yale J. Reg. 417 (1992); Aiken & Sage, Staffing National Health Care Reform: A Role for Advanced Practice Nurses, 26 Akron L. Rev. 187 (1992). These efforts by nurses to expand their functions have naturally met resistance from the medical profession. See, e.g., Freudenheim, Nurses Working Without Doctors Anger the Medical Establishment, N.Y. Times, Sept. 30, 1997, p. A1.

3. *The Legal Environment for Physician Extenders.* Consider the following assessment of the legal environment in which physician extenders—in this instance, advanced practice nurses—practice:

> [The legal issues APNs] face apply also to physician assistant, clinical psychologists, and often optometrists and other recognized providers.
>
> *Scope of practice.* The first concern for APNs is the scope of practice permitted by their license, which varies from state to state. Although a pediatric earache is the same in Washington as it is in Kentucky, nurse practitioners in Kentucky, unlike their colleagues in Washington, may not be able to treat that earache unless they are supervisee by a physician. Scopes of practice range from those fully independent of physicians, to those entirely dependent on physicians, to those entailing some degree of "collaborative" practice with physicians. At one end of the spectrum, APNs may practice on their own license and use their own professional judgment in diagnosing, treating, prescribing, and referring when appropriate, just as physicians do. At the other end, APNs' professional authority is entirely derivative or dependent upon physicians saying, "Ayes, do this."
>
> In between is a vast middle ground. Must APNs proceed with written protocols or practice standards? States vary. What about prescriptive

authority? Most states now specifically afford APNs some prescriptive authority, but the endlessly varied legal barriers embedded in these provision are enormous. Often, APNs may exercise such authority only if they obtain a counter signature by a supervising physician, or if they prescribe only those drugs on a specified formulary, which may or may not include controlled substances. They may be required to have continuously updated protocols or standardized procedures. * * *

Variation by practice setting. One of the most astonishing features of these various legal barriers is their geographic mutability. Under many state regulatory schemes, some APNs are afforded a more independent scope of practice and more prescriptive authority than others practicing in the same state. The difference depends not, as one might imagine, on the skill of the practitioners, but rather on their geographic or clinical setting. APNs who practice in rural areas, in long-term care facilities, or in community health clinics, for example, may by law prescribe more and do more things under their own scope of practice.

* * *

Some states have added a final twist by varying the scope of practice and prescriptive authority according to the financial nature of the clinics in which APNs practice. Those who are in nonprofit clinics can do more on their own license (with less supervision) and prescribe more than those in for-profit clinics. Clearly, there can be no competence-or quality of care-based rationale for such a distinction.

If these variations by practice setting are intended as an incentive to treat the underserved, the use of the licensure system to achieve such an outcome is troublesome at best. Rather, we would think, a rational incentive system would resemble the current federal Medicare payment scheme for physicians, who are offered a 10% bonus to practice in health personnel shortage areas.

Safriet, Impediments to Progress in Health Care Workforce Policy: License and Practice Laws, 31 Inquiry 310, 314–15 (1994). See also Safriet, Health Care Dollars and Regulatory Sense, supra; Kissam, Physician's Assistant and Nurse Practitioner Laws: A Study of Health Law Reform, 24 Kan. L.Rev. 1 (1975) (finding legislation unduly restrictive). For a survey ranking states in terms of receptivity to physician extenders (specifically, the licensing scheme, requirements or practices with respect to reimbursement for services, and authority to write prescriptions), see Sekscenski et al., State Practice Environments and the Supply of Physician Assistants, Nurse Practitioners, and Certified Nurse–Midwives, 331 New Eng. J. Med. 1266 (1994).

In legal contemplation, PAs are generally conceived as operating strictly under the direction, supervision, or authority of a physician and not as having any independent professional status. Although PAs aspire to recognition as professionals through state licensure, their legal authority to treat patients derives from the authority of the physicians they assist and is limited to carrying out tasks delegated to them by physicians in accordance with law, regulation, or professional custom. PAs themselves are generally comfortable in this more or less dependent, subordinate role, in which they nevertheless may exercise broad authority. Indeed, partly because they accept the dominance of physicians, their legal authority has been gradually been allowed to expand over time to serve the convenience and economic interest of the physicians who employ them. See, e.g., Ariz. Rev. Stat. Ann. § 32–1456B (West Supp. 1997) (allowing PAs to perform minor surgery with specific approval and under "direct supervision").

In contrast to PAs, nurses view themselves, and prefer to be viewed, as practicing on their own professional authority, as differently trained, skilled, and licensed practitioners and not merely as second-class stand-ins for physicians, always dependent for their legitimacy on the authority of a physician. Although nurses must work closely with physicians, they strongly desire to be seen as doing so as independent collaborators rather than as subordinate personnel. (Is it possible that the aspirations of nurses, the great majority of whom are women, are driven in some measure by gender politics and a desire to escape apparent domination by physicians, most of whom historically have been males?) Would you suppose that nurses are most comfortable with a licensing statute like the open-ended one in *Sermchief*, or would they prefer one giving explicit recognition to advanced practice nurses? Would an explicit statute be likely to give them more, or less, professional status and practical and symbolic independence in carrying out their professional tasks?

4. *Nurse Practice Acts*. In fact, the nursing statutes vary widely, with some states having only a basic nurse practice act while others provide special recognition for advanced practice nurses. The open-ended statute in Missouri exemplifies the former approach, while California provides an example of the more categorical approach. E.g., Cal. Bus. & Prof. Code § 2746.5 (West 1990) (nurse midwife must be supervised by obstetrician); id. § 2836.1(d) (West Supp. 1998) (authorizing nurse practitioner, under supervision, to prescribe drugs or devices). Maryland, on the other hand, recognizes nurse midwives as independent practitioners. Md. Code Ann., Health Occ. § 8–601 (1994).

5. *Physician Assistants*. The following from a 1975 GAO report indicates some of the ways in which states moved legally to accommodate physician assistants (PAs):

> Two distinct statutory forms are used by States to sanction [PAs]. The first is the general delegatory statute that amends the existing medical practices act to allow them to work under a supervising physician. The other is referred to as a regulatory authority statute and authorizes an agency—usually the State board of medical examiners—to establish rules and regulations concerning education and employment qualifications and functions. By January 1975, 30 States had enacted regulatory legislation and 7 States had enacted delegatory authority legislation. * * *
>
> Although some State laws sanction [PAs], at least one State regulatory agency's actions have had the effect of counteracting that intent of the State's law. In September 1976 the Governor of California approved legislation "* * * to provide that existing legal constraints should not be an unnecessary hindrance to the more effective provision of health care

services." One purpose of this law was to allow for innovative development of programs for educating [PAs]. The State board of medical examiners was charged with establishing standards for approving training programs and supervisory physicians in California.

The regulations developed by the California board require strict compliance with its (1) standards for training programs and student qualifications, (2) determinations of the professional qualifications of the [PA] and the employing physician, (3) prohibitions against [PAs] performing certain tasks, such as pelvic and endoscopic examinations, (4) requirement for written patient consent before a [PA] can provide nonemergency general medical services, and (5) requirement that an extender practice in close physical proximity to the supervising physician. The regulations specifically require that the supervising physician consult with the [PA] and the patient after the completion of a history taking and physical examination. He must also consult with both before and after the extender performs routine laboratory and screening techniques and therapeutic procedures outlined in the act, except when they are part of the history taking and physical examination or followup examination.

According to one program official, such strict requirements for physician consultation and supervision involving all treatment procedures would require the physician to spend almost all of his time consulting with patients and the extender. Coupled with the other regulations imposed by the board, these requirements may remove the incentive to employ a [PA].

U.S. General Accounting Office, Progress and Problems in Training and Use of Assistants to Primary Care Physicians ch. 3 (1975). While some PA statutes rely on the delegation model, other states adopt a more regulatory approach, requiring that PAs meet educational requirements and pass an examination prepared by the National Commission on Certification of Physician Assistants. Some states also require individual approval of each physician/PA relationship and approval of the specific tasks delegated. See, e.g., Md. Code Ann., Health Occ. § 15–302 (1994) (PA's "job description" subject to state board approval); W.Va. Code § 30–3–16(b), (g) (Supp. 1997). Some states have placed a limitation on the number of physician extenders employed in a medical practice. See, e.g., Arkansas St. Nurses Ass'n v. Arkansas State Med. Bd., 677 S.W.2d 293 (Ark.1984) (discounting danger that "a doctor might hire 20 R.N.P.'s in different areas of a city and let them do the practice while he was on the golf course").

6. *Task Delegation.* The idea that physicians could delegate tasks within their professional competence to unlicensed individuals (or licensed individuals whose authorized scopes of practice did not extend to the task in question) antedated the appearance of PAs and nurse practitioners. Some PA statutes attempted to preserve the custom of such delegation. North Carolina, for example, provides that its PA statute "shall not limit or prevent any physician from delegating to a qualified person any acts, tasks, and functions that are otherwise permitted by law or established by custom." N.C. Gen. Stat. § 90–18(13) (1997). See also Jacobs v. United States, 436 A.2d 1286 (D.C.App.1981) (considering whether, under a statute allowing the "accepted use of paramedical personnel," custom could justify letting office help issue prescriptions using pre-signed prescription forms).

On the legality of a physician's delegation of tasks to unlicensed persons, consider the case of Magit v. Board of Medical Ex'rs, 366 P.2d 816 (Cal.1961), in which an anesthesiologist was found guilty of unprofessional conduct in allowing three unlicensed foreign medical graduates (FMGs) to administer anesthesia under his supervision. Consider how this delegation might come out under a state regime taking a regulatory approach to PAs. Do you suppose that a state medical board would be likely to authorize FMGs to qualify as PAs? What factors might enter into the board's decision whether to authorize the use of FMGs as PAs in anesthesiology? What if the state has a statute expressly recognizing CRNAs?

Without specific approval of FMGs as PAs in anesthesiology, would provision similar to the one quoted from the N.C. law have allowed Dr. Magit to introduce evidence of custom in defense of his practice? The court in *Magit* discussed California law on delegation to FMGs as follows:

> The fact that * * * the unlicensed physicians had training enabling them to practice competently did not exculpate the physician who aided them in practicing. This is the necessary result of our statutory system which, in order to assure the protection of the public, requires that a person's competency be determined by the state and evidenced by a license.
>
> It is argued that in construing the provisions of the code we should take into consideration an asserted custom in California of permitting persons other than licensed physicians and surgeons to administer anesthetics. There was evidence from which it might be inferred that in California it was common practice to permit general anesthetics to be administered by registered nurses, who, as we have seen, are authorized by statute to perform some medical acts. However, there was no substantial evidence of a common practice in California to permit anesthetics to be given by persons who have no authority whatever to perform medical acts.

Id. at 821. Do you agree that the *Magit* court should have rejected as irrelevant the evidence of customary delegation to RNs, or is it significant that the FMGs, while arguably competent to perform the services assigned, had no license of any kind? Do you agree with the court that not allowing delegations to unlicensed personnel based on custom is the "necessary result" of the overall licensing scheme? Would the licensing statute in fact be left no substantial function to perform if it were read to allow licensed physicians to delegate tasks to unlicensed personnel pursuant to custom?

What are the arguments for and against permitting physicians to delegate tasks to unlicensed personnel? Why not allow physicians, whom we trust to do many things and who are liable for the torts of their employees and "borrowed servants," to delegate on their own responsibility? Is liability a sufficient protection against abuses? Do you see a parallel here to "institutional licensure," discussed earlier in this section? Consider the benefits and risks of allowing delegation to introduce flexibility in an overregulated system and the benefits to the employees themselves in allowing them to expand their skills and earning potential despite lacking formal credentials.

7. *"Turf" Battles over Task Delegation.* In a New Jersey case, physical therapists challenged a regulation of the state medical board authorizing physicians to delegate, under certain protective conditions, certain "physical modalities" to unlicensed employees. Matter of Promulgation of N.J.A.C. 13:35–6.14, 501 A.2d 547 (N.J. Super. 1985). In previous litigation described by the court, physicians had sought to prevent issuance of a regulation that, on the basis of an interpretation of the new Physical Therapy Act, would have prohibited "the use of simple physical therapy modalities within their offices by unlicensed assistants, a procedure that they claim had been used [customarily] throughout the state." Id. at 548–49. The regulation finally issued was satisfactory to the physicians but not to the physical therapists. The court upheld the regulations as being reasonably within the scope of the medical board's responsibilities and reconciled the legislative conflict as follows (id. at 549):

> Physical therapists provide treatment "upon the *direction* of a licensed physician, dentist or other health care practitioner authorized to prescribe treatment." (Emphasis added). The aide described in the regulation before us may utilize limited modalities for similar treatment, but only under the supervision of a physician or other health care provider. The physical therapist practices free of the controls specified in N.J.A.C. 13:35–6.14(d) and exercises independent discretion not permitted to the physician's aide.

In a similar Ohio case, licensed dental hygienists challenged a dental board's informal authorization of delegation by orthodontists of certain "intraoral" functions to "BQPs" (basic qualified personnel, "adjudged by the licensed dentist to be capable and competent * * * [to perform basic tasks] under his direct supervision and full responsibility"). Legislation expressly authorized such delegations only where the board, by rule, approved. The court held that, absent a formal rule authorizing it, the delegation in question was invalid. Ohio Dental Hygienists Ass'n v. Ohio State Dental Bd., 487 N.E.2d 301 (Ohio 1986).

8. *Supervision, Diagnosis, etc.* Issues in defining the scope of practice of physician extenders include the nature and intensity of the physician supervision required and the borderline between diagnosis, a medical function, and what physician extenders do. Supervision requirements usually specify that the physician need not be physically present. E.g., Wash. Rev. Code Ann. § 18.71A.020(b)(2)(ii) (West Supp. 1998). For a more detailed statutory prescription of supervision requirements, see Conn. Gen. Stat. Ann. § 20–12a(7) (West Supp. 1998). How did the *Sermchief* court resolve the question whether the nurses were engaged in diagnosis? Some states allow PAs to diagnose patients' conditions under the supervision and direction of the physician. E.g., S.D. Codified Laws § 36–4A–22(3) (Michie Supp. 1997). But see Va. Code Ann. § 54.1–2952 (Michie Supp. 1997) (PA not permitted to make "final" diagnosis).

9. *Problem.* P.A. Tient, having suffered a serious anesthesia-related injury during surgery, has initiated a malpractice action against the following five defendants:

General Hospital (GH), the nonprofit institution where the surgical procedure was performed;

Anesthesia Associates P.C. (AA), a professional corporation comprising eight anesthesiologists and designated by GH as the exclusive provider of anesthesia services at the hospital;

Rebecca Nertz, a licensed registered nurse (RN) and second-year student in the accredited training program for Certified Registered Nurse Anesthetists (CRNAs) operated by AA at GH;

Philip Asst, a physician's assistant (PA) trained in anesthesiology and employed by AA;

S.R. Geon, M.D., the surgeon who operated on Mr. Tient.

Plaintiff Tient alleges that all five defendants are liable for his injuries because Nertz administered his anesthesia in violation of state licensure laws. The relevant statutes govern the functions of health care personnel, including PAs and CRNAs (whose certification by the American Association of Nurse Anesthetists is expressly recognized). Section 33 of the state Professions Act provides:

> In any case where it is lawful for a duly licensed physician practicing medicine under the laws of this state to administer anesthesia, such anesthesia may also be lawfully administered by a CRNA under the direction and responsibility of a duly licensed physician with training or experience in anesthesiology.

Rule 7 of the State Board of Nursing creates an exception to the nurse anesthetist certification requirement in cases where the RN administering anesthesia "is duly enrolled in an accredited nurse anesthesia training program, if the administration of anesthesia serves an educational purpose and is under the direct supervision of an anesthesiologist or CRNA."

Section 44(a) of the Professions Act defines a PA as "a person qualified by academic or practical training to provide medical services under the personal direction and supervision of a physician." Section 44(b) states that a PA may perform, in addition to certain enumerated tasks, "any functions normally performed by the supervising physician that the physician's assistant is qualified to perform."

Tient suffered brain damage while Nertz was attending him during the surgical procedure. Asst had been present during the induction of anesthesia but had left the operating room for 15 minutes to see about another patient. When an emergency was detected, Asst was recalled, and Dr. Gass, one of the AA principals, was summoned from his office on another floor.

Consider and be prepared to discuss the plaintiff's theory of the case. You should assume that there is little additional evidence to suggest negligence in the administration of anesthesia or management of the patient.

(a) *Negligence Per Se?* Consider first whether violation of a licensing statute should be viewed in law as negligence per se. In Leahy by Heft v. Kenosha Mem. Hosp., 348 N.W.2d 607 (Wis.App.1984), the following jury instruction was found improper:

> If you find by virtue of this statute [defining professional nursing and practical nursing] that the Kenosha Memorial Hospital placed practical nurses or technicians in positions where they could not legally function, in positions that should have been staffed by professional registered nurses, or if the Kenosha Memorial Hospital permitted practical nurses to function as professional registered nurses, then the Kenosha Memorial Hospital would be negligent as that term has been defined for you.

The court stated the relevant principles as follows:

> For the violation of the statute to constitute negligence per se, it must be demonstrated that the harm inflicted was the type the statute was designed to prevent and that the person injured was in the class sought to be protected. Further, some expression of legislative intent that the statute was meant to become a basis for the imposition of civil liability must appear.
>
> * * * [T]he purpose of ch. 441, Stats., is to regulate the nursing profession through the creation of a board of nursing and to provide for the licensing of nurses. While these laws result in securing the safety and welfare of the public as an entity, nothing in ch. 441, directly or by implication, reveals a legislative intent to grant a private right of action for a violation of the statute. Dean Prosser has stated that:
>
> Most licensing statutes, such as those applicable to automobile drivers or physicians, have been construed as intended only for the protection of the public against injury at the hands of incompetents, and to create no liability where the actor is in fact competent but unlicensed.
>
> W. Prosser, Handbook of the Law of Torts § 36 at 196 (4th ed. 1971).

In the case which provided the basis for the foregoing problem, however, violation of a statute similar to "section 33" was held to constitute negligence per se:

> The purpose of OCGA § 43–26–9 is to protect patients from the dangers of improperly administered anesthesia by those unqualified by a lack of what public policy regards as minimum education in the field, and by a lack of specified supervision. Mrs. Worthy is one such patient the statute was intended to protect. So too is the harm incurred by Mrs. Worthy the harm the statute was intended to guard against. The statute set threshold qualifications which had to be met before a person would be permitted under the law to apply anesthesia. These qualifications do not establish how the anesthesia is to be administered, or what methods or instruments may be used, but rather who may do it with whose supervision. Thus it prohibits anyone not meeting these qualifications from performing, and it further prohibits even a statutorily qualified person from performing without prescribed supervision.

> For a violation of the statute to be negligence per se, the violation "must be capable of having a causal connection between it and the damage or injury inflicted upon the other persons." Etheridge v. Guest, 12 S.E.2d 483 (Ga.App.1940). This refers not to the proximate cause element of the negligence action, which the Worthys still must prove by a preponderance of the evidence, but rather to the character of the legal duty involved. Is this statutory duty one which, if breached, is capable of producing injury to an anesthetized person?
>
> It seems clear that it is. The unauthorized and unsupervised administration of anesthesia could indeed cause injury to the patient. Had the statute been followed, and had the anesthesia been administered by a CRNA under an anesthesia-qualified physician's supervision, it is possible that no injury or at least lesser injury would have resulted to Mrs. Worthy. Thus, the violation of O.C.G.A. § 43–26–9 constitutes negligence per se.

Central Anesthesia Assocs. P.C. v. Worthy, 325 S.E.2d 819, 823 (Ga.App. 1984), affirmed, 333 S.E.2d 829 (Ga.1985). Do you agree that violation of the licensing statute should be deemed negligence per se? After considering the following questions and in light of earlier reading, formulate some arguments for and against the use of licensure and scope of practice rules to define practice standards enforceable in tort actions.

(b) *How Clear Is the Statutory Violation?* Formulate and evaluate all of the possible arguments that state law was violated. Note that it would have been all right, under the nursing board's rule, for a CRNA to supervise Nertz. Was assigning Asst to supervise her a violation of state law? What if Asst's training in anesthesiology was at least as extensive as that of a CRNA? Even if there was a statutory violation, should it be treated as negligence or only as a technical violation, correctable by regulatory measures? If the nursing board's rule had been complied with but was found by the court to be an invalid relaxation of the statute, would a finding of negligence per se be justified?

(c) *Supervision, etc.* Note the different formulations of requirements for direction, supervision, etc. Which requirements were breached? (Statutory and regulatory formulations of supervision requirements are numerous and vary widely, with significant effects on the organization and cost of services.)

(d) *The Corporate Defendants.* Should AA or GH, or both, be liable for any statutory violations? for any negligence by the various individual defendants? Recall that you considered the liabilities of hospitals and surgeons in comparable situations in chapter 5(§B).

NOTES AND QUESTIONS ON SCOPE-OF-PRACTICE, SUPERVISION, AND PAYMENT ISSUES

1. So-called "turf" battles between competing or potentially competing occupational categories are ubiquitous in health care, and can only be sampled here. Most of these battles are fought in legislative forums, but many also end up in court. Note how, in several of the cases encountered in this section, competing professionals or licensing bodies regulating such competitors were allowed to challenge expansive scopes of practice established by regulators of another occupation. See also Oklahoma Bd. of Med. Licensure & Supervision v. Oklahoma Bd. of Ex'rs in Optometry, 893 P.2d 498 (Okla.1995) (medical board allowed, under statute, to challenge optometry board's position on laser use by optometrists).

2. *Prescribing Drugs*. A matter of continuing tension is the power to prescribe medications. A regulatory board's attempt to confer prescribing authority on physician assistants was struck down in New Mexico Bd. of Pharmacy v. New Mexico Bd. of Osteo. Med. Ex'rs, 626 P.2d 854 (N.M.App. 1981). This decision, like other legislative and judicial decisions affecting drug prescribing, reflected a concern about access to controlled substances. See also Va. Code Ann. § 54.1–2952.1 (Michie Supp. 1997); W.Va. Code § 30–3–16(*l*) (Supp. 1997) (authorizing PAs to prescribe drugs under certain circumstances). See generally Nuzzo, Independent Drug Prescribing Authority of Advanced Practice Nurses, 53 Food & Drug L.J. 35 (1998) (questioning movement to expand prescribing authority and recommending FDA action to preempt state laws facilitating it); Beck, Improving America's Health Care: Authorizing Independent Prescriptive Privileges for Advanced Practice Nurses, 29 U.S.F. L. Rev. 951 (1995); Hadley, Nurses and Prescriptive Authority: A Legal and Economic Analysis, 15 Am. J.L. & Med. 245 (1989).

In recent years, optometrists have fought—successfully in some states—for legislation authorizing them to prescribe and use drugs in the diagnosis of eye conditions; a few states also allow drug prescriptions for the treatment of such conditions. Physicians have opposed such legislation. See, e.g., Board of Optometry v. Florida Med. Ass'n, Inc., 463 So.2d 1213 (Fla.App.1985) (invalidating, as unauthorized by statute, a board rule allowing optometrists to use and prescribe drugs; physicians allowed standing to raise issue.)

3. *Pharmacists*. Nearly all states have now repealed or amended earlier drug anti-substitution laws that prevented pharmacists from dispensing a generic drug when the physician had prescribed by brand name. Detailed legislation frequently governs substitution, however. See Note, Consumer Protection and Prescription Drugs: The Generic Drug Substitution Laws, 67 Ky. L.J. 384 (1978–79).

Although an unusual Florida statute allows pharmacists actually to prescribe a limited set of drugs, Fla. Stat. Ann. § 465.186 (West Supp. 1998), the practice was reported to be uncommon because of record-keeping requirements, liability insurers' fears, and other factors. Ferber, What Happens When the Law Lets Pharmacists Prescribe?, Med. Econ., July 13, 1987, at 23.

4. *Podiatry*. When Medicare ruled that Connecticut podiatrists would not be paid for treating ankle problems because their jurisdiction was legally limited to the foot, the state podiatry board declared otherwise. The state medical society was held to have standing to challenge this invasion of physicians' province. Connecticut State Med. Soc'y v. Connecticut Bd. of Ex'rs in Podiatry, 524 A.2d 636 (Conn.1987).

5. *Dental Hygienists.* Continuing struggles between organized dentistry and dental hygienists reflect the oversupply of dentists and the desire of hygienists to provide a wider range of services and to practice independently, perhaps making low-cost services available to those who cannot afford a licensed dentist. See, e.g, In re DeLancy, 313 S.E.2d 880 (N.C.App.1984) (revoking hygienist's license for establishing "The Smile Clinic," an independent practice). Studies indicate that well trained auxiliaries can perform many dental services satisfactorily. See J. Liang & J. Ogur, Restrictions on Dental Auxiliaries (Staff Report, FTC Bureau of Economics 1987) (criticizing limitations on the number of hygienists a dentist may employ and restrictions on tasks to be performed); B. Shimberg et al., Occupational Licensing: A Public Perspective 87–91 (1982). An FTC investigation of the merits of independent practice by dental hygienists was terminated in 1980 because evidence concerning quality was unobtainable. See Trade Reg. Rep. (CCH) ¶ 10,535. (Was the FTC in politically sensitive terrain?) Colorado legislation allows hygienists to practice independently. Colo. Rev. Stat. § 12–35–122.5 (1997). On the constitutionality of supervision requirements, see Note, 30 Wayne L. Rev. 127 (1983).

6. *Independent Practice.* Like some dental hygienists, other limited-license health professionals also aspire to practice independently, and a few now enjoy that right. For example, physical therapists in a few states have obtained legislative permission to maintain their own offices and attract patients directly rather than by physician referral. See, e.g., Medical Soc'y v. New Jersey Dep't of Law and Public Safety, 575 A.2d 1348 (N.J.1990) (upholding physical therapy board's regulations, under new liberalizing legislation, allowing examinations, but not diagnosis, without physician direction or referral). See generally Annot., Licensing and Regulation of Practice of Physical Therapy, 8 A.L.R.5th 825 (1992). Some practitioners with independent practices may be required to perform services only pursuant to the prescription or direction of a professional higher in the hierarchy, limiting their freedom to exercise independent judgment. Physical therapists subject to such requirements contend that they are better able than most physicians to determine just what therapy a patient needs. The New Jersey statute in the case cited supra allows therapists to modify treatment plans consistently with the physician's original directive. Other practitioners may maintain independent practices but can legally serve patients only on referral. For example, occupational therapists in West Virginia may not serve a walk-in trade but must obtain their clients only by referral from other practitioners. W. Va. Code § 30–28–4 (1993). (What effect would such a restriction have on therapists' propensity to advertise and to offer inducements to potential referral sources?)

It is possible to view recent developments in health care as a kind of "deregulation," with professional controls being relaxed under antitrust prohibitions and consumers being given a wider range of choice (e.g.,

HMOs) in obtaining health care. What are the implications of this deregulation for statutory restrictions on the independence of health care practitioners? Recent developments have reduced the de facto independence of physicians by subjecting them to the demands of corporate intermediaries, such as HMOs, insurers, and hospitals. To the extent that the aspiration of allied health professionals to practice independently reflects only a desire to emulate the medical profession's ideal of solo fee-for-service practice with accountability to no one other than the individual patient, it is no more likely to be realized after deregulation than it was before. Nonphysician practitioners, in addition to obtaining the legal authority requisite to independent practice, must also satisfy employers purchasing health care coverage, third-party payers, and other independent decision makers concerning the desirability and costs of their services.

How has the deregulation movement, such as it is, improved the political prospect for relaxation of inappropriate regulatory restrictions on practitioner independence? Has the original consumer-ignorance rationale for exclusionary personnel licensure been devalued? Has the political climate changed in any way likely to enhance the prospects for a relaxation of restrictions? Does the new recognition that corporate middlemen may safely be given an expanded role provide any basis for revising prohibitions on independent practice that were grounded in concerns about the ability of consumers to evaluate services that they purchase directly?

7. *Mandated-Provider Laws*. Health insurers' decisions in designing coverage—the services they will pay for—are other important determinants of the market demand for the services of nonphysician health professionals, particularly those who practice or might practice independently and not as employees of physicians or institutions. As a result of political pressures brought to bear by such practitioners, nearly every state has one or more statutes requiring an insurer, if it covers a service when provided by a physician, also to cover that service when it is lawfully provided by some other type of licensed professional. The beneficiaries of these so-called "mandated-provider," "freedom-of-choice," "nondiscrimination," or "equalization" statutes differ widely from state to state but frequently include podiatrists, optometrists, psychologists, chiropractors, physical therapists, and nurse practitioners. For an earlier listing of such statutes, see Note, ERISA Preemption of State Mandated–Provider Laws, 1985 Duke L.J. 1194, 1194–96 n.8.

Mandated-provider laws have generally been upheld against constititutional challenges. E.g., Blue Cross v. Commonwealth, 269 S.E.2d 827 (Va.1980); Maryland Med. Serv., Inc. v. Carver, 209 A.2d 582 (Md.1965) (upholding law benefitting chiropodists). But see Ketcham v. King County Med. Serv. Corp., 81 Wn.2d 565, 502 P.2d 1197 (1972) (law requiring service-benefit plan to pay nonparticipating optometrists held to infringe freedom of contract). ERISA certainly blocks the application of such laws to self-insured employee benefit plans, but a question exists whether they constitute insurance regulation not preempted by ERISA. Cf. Metropolitan Life Ins. Co. v. Massachusetts, 471 U.S. 724 (1985) (mandated benefits held insurance regulation saved from preemption by so-called saving clause). It has been argued that mandated-*provider* laws (as opposed to mandated benefits) do not regulate "insurance" and thus should be held not to apply to any plan, insured or self-insured, governed by ERISA. Note, supra. But see Blue Cross & Blue Shield of Kansas City v. Bell, 798 F.2d 1331 (10th Cir.1986) (holding mandated-provider laws not preempted vis-a-vis insurers).

Mandated-provider laws are of obvious importance to the nonphysician professionals who lobby for them. They are opposed by insurers, who claim that they raise insurance costs and put traditional insurers at a disadvantage vis-a-vis HMOs and self-insurance, which is attractive in part because employers are not subject to regulations and taxes applicable to insurers. From the public's standpoint, mandated-provider laws are objectionable if they interfere with efficiency in coverage design and administration without offsetting benefits.

Mandated-provider statutes are frequently passed in the name of promoting competition, but they obviously substitute regulation for marketplace determinations of the scope of insurance coverage. Is there a policy justification for so doing? Because most health insurance is purchased on a group basis and not by individuals, individuals who would be willing to pay for coverage entitling them to patronize a particular class of providers may not have their preference honored if they constitute only a minority of the covered group. See, e.g., Michigan Ass'n of Psychotherapy Clinics v. Blue Cross & Blue Shield, 118 Mich.App. 505, 325 N.W.2d 471 (1982) (insurance coverage adopted by labor union was changed so as no longer to cover the services of certain mental health professionals who had been in demand by some beneficiaries). Such "market failures," traceable to majoritarian rule in employment groups, are rectifiable to some extent (and at some cost) by regulation. On the other hand, it can be argued that, in a deregulatory era, it is more reasonable to look to employers, unions, insurers, and other health plans to determine the role of nonphysician practitioners. Many employers are now offering alternative health plans to their employees, suggesting that minority preferences are more likely to be served today than in the past.

8. *Medicare Reimbursement.* The Balanced Budget Act of 1997 removed previous restrictions that allowed nurse practitioners to be reimbursed for serving Medicare beneficiaries only in rural areas or in skilled nursing facilities. Both NPs and PAs can now treat Medicare patients anywhere they are found and will be reimbursed at 80% of the lower of (a) the actual charge or (b) 85% of the amount provided for the service in the physician fee schedule.

NOTES AND QUESTIONS ON UNORTHODOX PRACTITIONERS AND PRACTICES

1. *Alternative Medicine.* So-called alternative medicine has always been a bigger business than is commonly appreciated. Indeed, it is reported that in

1990 Americans visited alternative practitioners more often than they visited family physicians and internists, paying $13.7 billion for the privilege (most of it out of pocket rather than through insurance). Eisenberg et al., Unconventional Medicine in the United States: Prevalence, Costs, and Patterns of Use, 328 New Eng. J. Med. 246 (1993). It has been predicted that the supply of alternative providers (chiropractors, naturopaths, and practitioners of Oriental medicine) will increase 88 percent between 1994 and 2005. Cooper & Stoflet, Trends in the Education and Practice of Alternative Medicine Clinicians, Health Affs., Fall 1996, p. 226.

New interest in alternative medicine is prompted in part by distrust of what is viewed as a monopoly enjoyed by proponents of biomedicine and in part by belief—ideological, empirical, or otherwise—in holistic approaches to healing. The subject is of growing interest to the medical establishment. In 1992, Congress created an Office of Complementary and Alternative Medicine in the National Institutes of Health to "facilitate the evaluation of alternative medical treatment modalities, including acupuncture and Oriental medicine, homeopathic medicine, and physical manipulation therapies." See generally M. Cohen, Complementary and Alternative Medicine: Legal Boundaries and Regulatory Perspectives (1998).

It is not unreasonable to be concerned about the dominance of a particular theory, analytical approach, school of thought, intellectual elite, or Zeitgeist, and supporters of alternative medicine make much of Thomas Kuhn's observations about the power of outmoded "paradigms" to retard intellectual progress. See T. Kuhn, The Structure of Scientific Revolutions (2d ed. 1970). Consider, for example, the following commentary by a Florida judge in holding that the state could not, constitutionally, enjoin a physician from using "chelation therapy," characterized as "a non-harmful mode of medical treatment," to treat arteriosclerosis after fully disclosing its unconventionality to the patient:

> History teaches us that virtually all progress in science and medicine has been accomplished as a result of the courageous efforts of those members of the profession willing to pursue their theories in the face of tremendous odds despite the criticism of fellow practitioners. Copernicus was thought to be a heretic when he theorized that the earth was not the center of the universe. * * * We can only wonder what would have been the condition of the world today and the field of medicine in particular had those in the midstream of their profession been permitted to prohibit continued treatment and thereby impede progress in those and other fields of science and the healing arts.

Rogers v. State Bd. of Med. Ex'rs, 371 So.2d 1037, 1041 (Fla.App.1979) (observing hearing officer's characterization of chelation therapy as "quackery under the guise of scientific medicine"), aff'd on other grounds, 387 So.2d 937 (Fla.1980).

Obviously, there is a great deal of room for conflict between alternative healers and laws and regulations ostensibly designed to protect consumers but often shaped or administered by dominant special interests to foreclose feasible and potentially valuable competition. For an interesting, well documented critique, see M. Cohen, supra, which is relevant and informative on most of the topics addressed below.

2. *Unorthodox Methods; Chelation Therapy*. Orthodoxy is enforced within the mainstream health care professions as well as against outsiders. An example is chelation therapy, the subject of the disciplinary action against a physician in the *Rogers* case, quoted supra. This treatment method, which (as a quick Internet search will show) has a strong following despite a lack of clinical evidence of efficacy, involves injecting a drug to remove excess calcium from blood vessels as a cure for arteriosclerosis and other circulatory ailments. Chelation therapy is not covered by Medicare. See Friedrich v. Secretary of HHS, 894 F.2d 829 (6th Cir.1990) (upholding HCFA's determination not to cover chelation therapy for arteriosclerosis; regulation was interpretive, not substantive, merely applying Medicare mandate to reimburse for "necessary and proper" treatments). An Oklahoma statute providing that physicians should be held to national standards of care also provides that it should not be construed to prohibit chelation therapy or any other lawful therapy or treatment. Okla. Stat. Ann. tit. 76, §§ 20.1–20.2 (West 1995). The *Rogers* case further illustrates both the controversial character of this therapy and the way in which dominant interests sometimes use the state's police power to enforce their beliefs against dissenters. In the notes below, notice how licensed, ethical mainstream practitioners are nevertheless barred from using methods borrowed from unapproved sources, such as alternative medicine.

3. *Osteopaths*. In a classic confrontation, observable at several points in chapter 5(§C) (e.g., the *Greisman* case), osteopaths were at sharply odds with allopathic physicians for many years. See generally N. Gevitz, The D.O.'s: Osteopathic Medicine in America (1982); Blackstone, The A.M.A. and the Osteopaths: A Study of the Power of Organized Medicine, 22 Antitrust Bull. 405 (1977). Today, the relationship between the two professions varies widely from state to state, with some states having obliterated the distinction while in other states practitioners of both persuasions actively compete with each other. Roughly five percent of American physicians are osteopaths.

The following excerpt from Brandwein v. California Bd. Of Osteo. Ex'rs, 708 F.2d 1466, 1468–69 (9th Cir.1983), briefly describes the interesting history of the relationship of osteopaths and allopaths in California:

> Osteopathy is a school of medicine founded by Dr. Andrew Taylor Still in the late 19th century. It is based on the principal that the body contains its own defense mechanisms against disease and that, through the process of physical manipulation of skeletal and muscular tissues, it may be brought back to health.
>
> While in its early development osteopathy was primarily a drugless, non-surgical form of medical treatment, it has since moved much closer to the allopathic school of medical practice. Oliver v. Morton, 361 F.Supp. 1262, 1264 (N.D.Ga.1973). At the present time the differences between the schools of osteopathy and allopathy are minor; often the same basic curricula and texts are used. Osteopaths are admitted to internships and

residencies approved by the American Medical Association (A.M.A.), and local medical associations are allowed to accept osteopaths as members and such osteopaths are then eligible for membership in the A.M.A. California law now provides that "holders of M.D. degrees and D.O. degrees shall be accorded equal professional status and privileges as licensed physicians and surgeons."

* * * In 1961, the California Medical Association and the California Osteopathic Association signed an agreement to unify the two organizations. The agreement provided that arrangements would be made to provide existing osteopaths in California with an M.D. degree. They would then have become subject to the jurisdiction of the Medical Board. At the same time, the Osteopathic Board was to be stripped of its power to license any new osteopaths. The parties agreed to jointly sponsor legislation to achieve these ends.

As part of the agreement, the sole school of osteopathy in California, the College of Osteopathic Physicians and Surgeons, was converted to a medical school, and [t]he state legislature then amended § 2275 of the Medical Practice Act to permit licensees of the Osteopathic Board holding an M.D. degree issued prior to September 30, 1962 to use the term M.D. Approximately 2,500 osteopaths employed this one-time opportunity to become M.D.s. Finally, the two organizations were successful in gaining the passage of an initiative by the voters entitled the Osteopathic Act of 1962. This Act placed the newly-created M.D.s under the jurisdiction of the Medical Board and barred licensing of new osteopaths in the state.

Then, in 1974, this framework of cooperation collapsed when the California Supreme Court declared the 1962 Act unconstitutional. In D'Amico v. Board of Medical Examiners, 520 P.2d 10 (Cal.1974), the state Supreme Court held that the 1962 initiative Act's prohibition of future licensing of osteopaths violated the Equal Protection Clause of both the federal and state constitutions, because the state could not demonstrate a rational relation to a legitimate governmental objective. Following the *D'Amico* decision, the Osteopathic Board resumed granting licenses to osteopaths under its original authority granted by the 1922 Act, and the two Boards, the Medical Board and the Osteopathic Board, resumed their traditional practice of separate jurisdiction and authority over their licensees.

Dr. Brandwein was a holder of a D.O. degree, who after being licensed as an osteopath in California in 1975, began representing himself as an M.D. Although charges against him for misrepresenting himself in violation of the medical practice act were dropped, he brought suit claiming, unsuccessfully, that the state regulatory scheme violated his first amendment rights by forcing him to identify himself by the title "D.O." when his personal philosophy of medicine was better reflected by the title "M.D."

Do you think osteopathy should be "merged" into medicine? (Would an antitrust analysis be helpful in resolving this issue?) Although many individual osteopaths would like to be called "M.D.," some osteopathic interests, such as educators, wish to preserve their separate identities. In the absence of a legal merger of licensing schemes (such as the one attempted unsuccessfully in California), most courts have said that the distinction maintained in state law is valid as a way of informing consumers of possibly relevant facts. E.g., Maceluch v. Wysong, 680 F.2d 1062, 1066 (5th Cir.1982) (osteopaths' distinctive training may affect "not only the aggregate of his substantive knowledge of clinical techniques, but also his judgment as to the need for, and nature of, treatment"). See also Eatough v. Albano, 673 F.2d 671, 676–77 (3d Cir.), cert. denied, 457 U.S. 1119 (1982).

4. *Homeopaths.* In North Carolina, the medical board was permitted to revoke an M.D.'s license for using of homeopathic treatments, which practice was deemed unprofessional conduct because not conforming to "the standards of acceptable and prevailing medical practice in this State." In re Guess, 393 S.E.2d 833 (N.C.1990). Dr. Guess claimed that he had used these treatments (which involve the use in small quantities of drugs chosen because in large quantities they cause symptoms similar to those being treated) only on patients for whom allopathic treatment had failed and that the evidence showed no harm and some benefit to patients. Reversing two lower courts, the state supreme court found no legislative intent to limit the licensing statute to preventing only practices that threaten specific harm and sufficient police power to justify the regulatory result reached. A dissenting opinion characterized Dr. Guess as "a dedicated physician seeking to find new ways to relieve human suffering," who used homeopathic methods "as a last resort when allopathic medicines [were] not successful." Id. at 841.

5. *Naturopaths.* In Idaho Ass'n of Naturopathic Physicians, Inc. v. FDA, 582 F.2d 849 (4th Cir.1978), the court rejected the claim that naturopathy, defined as "the art, science and philosophy of natural healing, by application of the laws of nature to the human body for its care and to prevent disease by any means that will assist the self-healing processes of the body," is constitutionally entitled to separate recognition or status. A few states, however, e.g., Washington, Idaho, and Connecticut, do recognize naturopathy as a separate healing profession. See Rubman v. Board of Natureopathic Ex'rs, 1996 WL 434265 (Conn.Super.1996) (license to practice naturopathy could be revoked for using intravenous therapy but not for practicing acupuncture).

6. *Chiropractors.* There are some 24,000 licensed chiropractors in the U.S., and more than 18 million Americans received chiropractic care in 1996. All states license chiropractors, even though the medical profession has long accused them of "cultism" and unscientific, dangerous practices. (Recall, for example, the *Wilk* case noted in chapter 4(§B).) Should it be presumed that the state legislatures have vindicated chiropractors of this charge? Interestingly, the chiropractic profession has its own internal philosophical schism. See, e.g., Sherman College of Straight Chiropractic v. United States Comm'r of Education, 493 F.Supp. 976 (D.D.C.1980) (unsuccessful challenge to federal agency's recognition of private accrediting agency that refused to accredit plaintiff because of its belief that chiropractors should be trained to diagnose only spinal conditions, not systemic

diseases); In re Sherman College of Straight Chiropractic, 397 A.2d 362 (N.J. Super. 1979) (upholding state board's acceptance of non-mainstream chiropractic school). See also Ohio College of Limited Med. Practice v. Ohio St. Med. Bd., 670 N.E.2d 490 (Ohio App. 1995) (previously recognized field of "mechanotherapy" merged with chiropractic; legislation, with grandfather clause, upheld).

7. *Midwifery*. A number of states permit lay midwifery, and midwife-assisted births increased 50-fold from 1975 to 1988. See Nazario, Midwifery is Staging Revival as Demand for Prenatal Care, Low-tech Births Rises, Wall St. J., Sept. 25, 1990, p. B1 ("Fueling demand for midwives are poor and rural women, but also many middle-class and affluent professional women who shun more impersonal, high-tech hospital care."). States that allow lay persons to practice midwifery usually do so on the theory that pregnancy is not a "disease" the treatment of which requires medical training. Nevertheless, physician hostility to midwives creates continual frictions, many of them related to the beliefs of some that childbirth has been overly "medicalized" or unduly dominated by males.

An extremely interesting case illustrating the tension between the medical establishment and lay midwifery was Leigh v. Board of Registration in Nursing, 481 N.E.2d 1347, 1352–54 (Mass.1985), in which a licensed RN had her license suspended for practicing midwifery without statutorily required certification as a nurse midwife even though there was no state regulation of any kind of midwifery by lay persons. The suspension of Leigh's license was later affirmed. 506 N.E.2d 91 (Mass.1987). How might it make sense to hold that, whereas lay persons are allowed to practice midwifery, a licensed nurse can be barred from practicing as a midwife except within the orthodox system? See Leggett v. Tennessee Bd. of Nursing, 612 S.W.2d 476 (Tenn.App.1980) (accepting midwife's argument in case similar to *Leigh*).

The constitutional and statutory basis of midwifery restrictions is often disputed. See State Bd. of Nursing v. Ruebke, 913 P.2d 142 (Kan.1996) (upholding practice of lay midwifery in face of challenge by state medical and nursing boards). But see Sammon v. New Jersey Bd. of Med. Ex'rs, 66 F.3d 639 (3d Cir. 1995) (upholding requirements that midwives have at least 1800 hours instruction from school of midwifery or maternity hospital, rather than apprenticeship, and that their applications be endorsed by registered physician); Colorado v. Rosburg, 805 P.2d 432 (Colo.1991) (upholding prohibition of lay midwifery against claim it denies equal protection). See generally Annot., Midwifery: State Regulation, 59 A.L.R.4th 929 (1987).

8. *Acupuncture*. For a case illustrating the breadth of the prohibition of unlicensed medical practice, see People v. Amber, 349 N.Y.S.2d 604 (N.Y.Sup.Ct.1973), in which the court upheld an acupuncturist's indictment, rejecting the claim that the statute contemplated only Western medicine, not Chinese acupuncture. In the court's view, determining "the existence of a disharmony brought about by the disequilibrium of Yin and Yang" constituted diagnosis within the meaning of the medical practice act.

The court considered it significant that the practice of acupuncture requires technical skill, such as "palpating the twelve pulses to read the condition of the twelve organs and thus determine which of the twelve meridians must be used * * * to restore the vital essence of 'ch'i' or vital energy." Id. at 612. See also State v. Roos, 514 N.E.2d 993 (Ill.1987) (upholding, against constitutional arguments convincing to trial court, prosecution of acupuncturist for practicing medicine without a license).

Many states now license acupuncturists. See Mitchell v. Clayton, 995 F.2d 772 (7th Cir.1993) (statutory requirement of graduation from medical, osteopathic, or chiropractic college in order to obtain license to practice acupuncture held not to violate equal protection or due process clauses even though it means that graduates of chiropractic school where acupuncture is not taught may be licensed to practice acupuncture whereas graduates of professional acupuncture school may not be). In Andrews v. Ballard, 498 F.Supp. 1038 (S.D.Tex.1980), the court invalidated a move by the Texas Medical Licensing Board to treat acupuncture as the practice of medicine and as an "experimental procedure" requiring special safeguards. Two physicians were disciplined for allowing nonphysicians to practice acupuncture under their supervision. Because no physician in Texas was trained in acupuncture, the practical effect of the board's action was to make the service unavailable. The court ruled in favor of the consumer plaintiffs, stating

> The plaintiffs have a constitutional right, encompassed by the right of privacy, to decide to obtain acupuncture treatment. The challenged articles and rules effectively deprive them of that right, and are not necessary to serve the State's interest in protecting the patient's health.

Id. at 1057.

SECTION B: PUBLIC OVERSIGHT OF PHYSICIANS

NOTES AND QUESTIONS ON THE LICENSING AND DISCIPLINE OF PHYSICIANS

1. *Constitutionality.* In Dent v. West Virginia, 129 U.S. 114 (1889), the Supreme Court upheld a West Virginia statute that required physicians, in order to commence or continue practicing in the state, to obtain a license from the state health board. Under the statute, a practitioner had to demonstrate that he had either graduated from a "reputable" medical school or been found upon examination by the board to be qualified to practice medicine. The statute also contained a grandfather clause that waived these licensure requirements for physicians who had practiced in the state for ten years prior to the statute's enactment. The appellant, who did not qualify under the grandfather clause, was indicted for practicing without a license, which he was denied because the board had determined that the American Medical Eclectic College of Cincinnati was not reputable and because he had not submitted to examination. In rejecting appellant's

claim that the statute deprived him of his liberty without due process, the Court stated, "Everyone may have occasion to consult [a physician], but comparatively few can judge of the qualifications of learning and skill which he possesses. Reliance must be placed upon the assurance given by his license * * *."

Consider the regulatory scheme in the *Dent* case. How could an individual qualify? Could Dent claim that it was arbitrary to allow *earlier* graduates of his medical school to practice medicine merely because they had been practicing in the state for the requisite number of years? What explains such grandfather clauses? Is your explanation also a legal justification? See Watson v. Maryland, 218 U.S. 173 (1910) (law requiring registration of physicians but exempting physicians in practice prior to a specific date did not deny equal protection because state could reasonably presume their competence). In Berger v. Board of Psychologist Examiners, 521 F.2d 1056 (D.C.Cir.1975), a licensing scheme that failed to provide for grandfathering was held unconstitutional. Do you agree with that holding?

The state's "police power" to adopt licensing regulations to protect the general welfare, which is the foundation of the *Dent* holding, is of course familiar and well settled. See, e.g., Sutker v. Illinois State Dental Soc'y, 808 F.2d 632 (7th Cir.1986) (rejecting denturists' attack on dental licensing law, despite persuasive policy objections). In view of the high stakes and depth of consumer ignorance, physician licensure is usually viewed as the paradigm case, the one in which the need of the consumer for protection is clearest. Consider, however, whether the state of medicine in the 1880s was such that the state could reasonably distinguish those practitioners likely to do good from those likely to cause harm. In the first half of the 19th century, a rich variety of "sectarian" and "cultist" practitioners flourished. These types stood in contrast to the so-called "regular" professions, which were generally associated with heroic practices, typically involving heavy bloodletting and use of dangerous purgatives and emetics. Whether the "regular" professionals were more or less dangerous than other practitioners is an open question. Scientific medicine began to appear only toward the end of the nineteenth century.

See generally S. Gross, Of Foxes and Hen Houses: Licensing and the Health Professions (1994); P. Starr, The Social Transformation of American Medicine (1982); R. Derbyshire, Medical Licensure and Discipline in the United States 7–12 (1969); R. Shryock, Medical Licensing in America, 1650–1965 (1967).

2. *The Nature of Physician Licensure.* Most state laws on physician licensure define the practice of medicine in some manner and prohibit any unlicensed person from engaging in it. A notable feature of statutory definitions is the breadth of the prohibition they represent or the authority they confer, as the case may be. In general, the authority granted by a license to practice medicine is unlimited except by the criminal law and the law of medical malpractice, both of which incorporate social and professional norms of conduct. The physician's unlimited license can be contrasted with the narrowly limited "scope of practice" specified in licensure laws covering all other categories of health personnel who are subject to licensure.

Another notable feature of physician licensure is its permanence. Despite the fast-changing nature of medical science, a license usually need not be renewed, or, if it is subject to renewal, no substantial new demonstration of competence is required. See Gellhorn, Periodic Physician Recredentialing, 265 J.A.M.A. 752 (1991) (reporting New York proposal to require recredentialing). See also L. Finnochio et al., Reforming Health Care Workforce Regulation: Policy Considerations for the 21st Century 25–28 (Pew Health Professions Comm'n, 1995); Jost, Oversight of the Competence of Healthcare Professionals, in Regulation of the Healthcare Professions 17, 32–34 (T. Jost, ed., 1997) (noting increasing interest in competency reevaluation and stating some principles). Many states have imposed some requirements for continuing medical education, but these have usually been formal requirements only, which are satisfied merely by attendance, irrespective of what was learned. For evidence on the effectiveness of continuing medical education in improving the quality of patient care, see Davis et al., Changing Physician Performance: A Systematic Review of the Effect Continuing Medical Education Strategies, 274 J.A.M.A. 700 (1995) (concluding that ordinary CME has minimal effects on practitioner performance and outcomes).

Obviously, the physician's license, being unlimited in scope and duration, permits the physician to perform many functions for which he or she may be ill-equipped by either training or experience. Thus, the minimum standard fixed as a quality-assurance measure is in no sense a guarantee of competence throughout the range of authorized practice. Do you therefore conclude that physician licensure provides poor protection for the public? How would you state the premises of the licensing system in order to defend it against such a charge? Is there a danger that consumers are unduly lulled by state licensure into assuming a higher level of competence and a higher degree of homogeneity among physicians than exist in fact? See W. Bogdanich, The Great White Lie: How America's Hospitals Betray Our Trust and Endanger Our Lives 29 (1991) ("The great white lie [of American medicine] is a myth holding that hospitals and doctors are equally good and deserving of our complete, unquestioning trust.").

3. *The Licensing Function.* State boards of medical examiners are charged with administering the state's medical practice act and, in most states, exercise both licensing and disciplinary powers. See generally Jost, Oversight of the Competence of Healthcare Professionals, in Regulation of the Healthcare Professions 17 (T. Jost, ed., 1997). Statutory requirements for licensure are quite uniform. Applicants are generally evaluated under four types of criteria: educational attainments, post-graduate training and experience, scores on a licensing examination, and moral and personal fitness. Applicants must graduate from an approved medical or osteopathic school, and all states rely for this purpose on the accrediting programs of the Liaison Committee on Medical Education (a joint venture of the AMA and the AAMC) and the American Osteopathic Association. (As discussed later in this chapter, special provision is made for foreign medical graduates.) Three quarters of the states require at least one year of postgraduate training (internship). Since 1979, all states have used the same licensing examination; the Federation Licensing Examination, known as FLEX, is prepared for the Federation of State Medical Boards by the National Board of Medical Examiners (NBME), a private organization with close links to organized medicine. The FLEX is not the main route to licensure, however, because nearly all states will also accept another exam prepared by the NBME or the National Board of Examiners for Osteopathic Physicians and Surgeons; the so-called National Boards are given in three parts as the student progresses through training. Despite heavy reliance on them, however, it is very far from clear that competency exams accurately measure physician competence in treating patients. See Tamblyn, Is the Public Being Protected? Prevention of Suboptimal Medical Practice Through Training Programs and Credentialing Examinations, 15 Evaluation & Health Profs. 153 (1994).

A physician holding an out-of-state license may apply for licensure in another state by endorsement, simply by proving passage of the NBME exam. Some states, however, will not endorse out-of-state licenses in the absence of a reciprocity agreement under which both states agree to endorse each other's licenses. In dentistry, such reciprocity has been found to correlate with lower professional fees and dentists' incomes. Shepard, Licensing Restrictions and the Cost of Dental Care, 21 J.L. & Econ. 187 (1978). Strikingly, one study has shown reciprocity to be no more common in licensing dentists than in licensing lawyers, despite what would seem to be differences in the transportability of knowledge. Holen, Effects of Professional Licensing Arrangements on Interstate Labor Mobility and Resource Allocation, 73 J. Pol. Econ. 492 (1965). In Benson v. Arizona St. Bd. of Dental Examiners, 673 F.2d 272 (9th Cir.1982), some dentists licensed by other states complained, unsuccessfully, of an Arizona licensure system that denied them full licenses but allowed them to provide uncompensated dental care under "restricted permits" in charitable clinics. See also Pierce v. Alabama Bd. of Optometry, 835 F.Supp. 593 (M.D.Ala.1993) (upholding Alabama law prohibiting optometrists from obtaining a state license without completing a four-year optometry program, despite plaintiff's completion of a three-year program and fifteen years experience teaching optometry at various universities, including the University of Alabama). For a proposal to provide a federal remedy for nonresident dentists subjected to discriminatory licensing requirements, see Note, The Dental Health Care Professionals Nonresidence Licensing Act: Will It Effectuate the Final Decay of Discrimination against Out-of-State Dentists?, 26 Rutgers L. Rev. 187 (1994).

4. *Discipline.* Although a licensing program may not be especially effective in preventing incompetent or unscrupulous physicians and other practitioners from entering the field, it at least provides a mechanism for removing professional bad apples from the ranks of practitioners—a function the state should probably perform on behalf of information-deprived consumers. Yet it is not easy to discipline marginal physicians for anything less

than criminal or quasi-criminal conduct. See generally Kinney, Administrative Law Issues in Professional Regulation, in Regulation of the Healthcare Professions 103 (T. Jost, ed., 1997) (describing procedural requirements in both rulemaking and adjudication and the nature and scope of judicial review of disciplinary actions).

Few licenses are revoked for disciplinary reasons. The grounds for revocation or suspension are usually egregious acts, often involving drug or sexual offenses. The AMA has proposed a model Disabled Physician Act as a way of dealing effectively but fairly with a doctor's mental or other, perhaps temporary, incapacity. See Corder v. Kansas Bd. of Healing Arts, 889 P.2d 1127 (Kan.1994) (licensing board required to initiate formal proceedings against a physician before it could require him to submit to an inpatient psychiatric examination on which to base a license revocation; although there was no specific danger to patients, physician had predicted an earthquake and a presidential assassination and had claimed to have been contacted by extraterrestrials). May a state revoke a physician's license for transgressions unrelated to patient care? Most courts have held that insurance filing is related to the practice of medicine and can be grounds for discipline. But the issue is essentially statutory. See Annot., Filing of False Insurance Claims for Medical Services as Ground for Disciplinary Action Against Dentist, Physician, or Other Medical Practitioner, 70 A.L.R. 4th 132 (1989).

There have been surprisingly few licenses revoked for incompetence or negligence. Indeed, not all statutes explicitly list such grounds for disciplinary action. Cf. Chastek v. Anderson, 416 N.E.2d 247 (Ill.1981) (license of dentist guilty of repeated acts of negligence revoked for "unprofessional conduct," one of 20 statutory grounds; statute held not unconstitutionally vague). Some licensing officials have contended that establishing professional negligence—malpractice—is so difficult that it is unrealistic to expect them to police the profession effectively. See In re Williams, 573 N.E.2d 638 (Ohio 1991) (expert testimony not required in physician disciplinary action since board includes physician members, but board action must be supported by substantial evidence); In re Schramm, 414 N.W.2d 31 (S.D.1987) (disciplinary action against dentist for incompetence requires expert testimony establishing the area standard of care, as in a malpractice action). Some courts have held that a license cannot be revoked or suspended on the basis of a mere preponderance of the evidence. E.g., Ettinger v. Board of Med. Quality Assurance, 185 Cal.Rptr. 601 (Cal.App.1982) (requiring "clear and convincing proof to a reasonable certainty"; allegation of "incompetent and grossly negligent" treatment of a single patient).

The number and proportion of physicians disciplined by state regulatory boards varies significantly from state to state. Mississippi, with 4,621 practicing physicians, carried out 45 disciplinary actions in 1996; the percentage of physicians disciplined (0.97%) was the highest in any state in that year. In the same year, California took action against 339 of 78,169 physicians (0.43%), and New York, with over 53,000 physicians, took 313 actions (0.59%). The number of actions taken nationwide has increased in recent years. For example, in 1982 Florida reported the highest percentage of physicians subject to disciplinary action (.74%), whereas in 1996 twenty-one states pursued actions against a greater percentage of physicians. This trend is attributable in part to states' enactment of stronger measures to police physicians in conjunction with reforms in the law of medical malpractice that arguably diminished the effect of tort law in correcting negligence. New powers conferred on licensing boards were not always accompanied by additional funding, however.

5. *The National Practitioner Data Bank.* At one time, a physician could migrate to a different state after encountering serious difficulties in a particular practice setting. Not only did licensing authorities have difficulty in discovering matters of record in another jurisdiction (despite a clearinghouse maintained by the Federation of State Licensing Boards and the AMA's "Masterfile"), but hospitals and prior employers were not necessarily candid about a physician's past performance, either because they wished to be rid of him or because they feared reprisal litigation. In response to this problem, Congress created the National Practitioner Data Bank in the Health Care Quality Improvement Act of 1986 (HCQIA), as amended, 42 U.S.C. §§ 11101–11152 (1994). (Other portions of the HCQIA, including the supporting congressional "findings," were noted in chapter 5(§C).) See 42 C.F.R. §§ 60.1–60.14 (1997). See generally U.S. Public Health Service, National Practitioner Data Bank Guidebook (1994) (providing discussion of the rationale behind the Data Bank and practical information on its utilization); Oshel et al., The National Practitioner Data Bank: The First Four Years, 110 Pub. Health Rep. 383 (1995).

The HCQIA provides for mandatory reporting to the bank as follows: Any entity making a payment in settlement of a malpractice claim must report the particulars of such claim to the data bank and to the appropriate state licensing board. State boards must report to the data bank the particulars of any disciplinary actions taken. A hospital or any HMO, group practice, or professional society that maintains a formal peer-review program for quality assurance must report to the appropriate state board (for retransmittal to the data bank) any professional review action adversely affecting the clinical privileges of a physician for more than thirty days, including investigations or threatened investigations that result in voluntary restrictions on the physician's practice. Shortly after the original enactment creating the data bank, 1987 legislation widened its sweep beyond physicians to include adverse actions taken against all licensed, certified, or registered health care practitioners, as well as health care entities.

The HCQIA provides that the information reported is considered confidential and may be disclosed only for use "with respect to professional review activity [or] with respect to medical malpractice actions." Since only hospitals, group medical practices, professional societies, federally designated peer review organizations (PROs), various state and federal agencies (including fraud and abuse and other enforcement officials), and the affected practitioners themselves have access to data bank information, it is not available, despite the latter clause quoted, to prospective or actual malpractice plaintiffs. State law governs disclosure by parties to whom the information had been lawfully disclosed. Hospitals are declared to have a "duty" to consult the file at least every two years. A physician may discover the contents of his or her own file, and provision is made for resolving disputes over its accuracy.

The reporting requirements raise the stakes of health care providers in many administrative actions taken in private settings, thus increasing their resistance to such actions. It may therefore be more difficult than previously to settlement of malpractice claims or to place limitations on physicians' clinical privileges in hospitals. Does the following report suggest that the data bank's reporting requirements may have curtailed, rather than merely publicized, certain kinds of private oversight of health care professionals?

> The Data Bank does not have information concerning the extent to which hospitals and other entities take disciplinary actions lasting 30 days or less or whether the existence of the Data Bank's more than 30 days requirement has skewed actions taken by hospitals and other entities. Clearly, hospitals and other entities have taken reportable actions far less frequently than State licensure boards since the opening of the Data Bank. In addition, most professional societies never or rarely report professional review actions affecting the membership of a practitioner.

Oshel et al., supra (reporting, inter alia, that from 1990 through 1994 the data bank received only 4160 reports of adverse actions on physicians' hospital privileges). Because of data bank concerns, some physicians apparently preferred—or were legally advised to prefer—arrangements with managed-care plans under which they could be terminated without cause, thus giving up job security in return for protection against possible blemishes on their public record.

Among the issues raised by the data bank are the following:

- whether there should be a floor below which payments need not be reported, enabling physicians and insurers better to deal with frivolous lawsuits. (The law states that making a payment is "not to be construed as creating a presumption that medical malpractice has occurred," 42 U.S.C. § 1137(d) (1994), but the efficacy of this disclaimer is uncertain.)
- whether malpractice insurers should be allowed access to the files. (Is this a moot point since an insurer could presumably condition coverage on the physician's making his file available?)
- whether the means for dealing with inaccurate information is adequate.
- whether consumer groups should be allowed access to the files. (The AMA and others contend that unrestricted access to data bank information, which is very abbreviated, is not in consumers' best interests, but consumer groups disagree.)

• how long certain types of information should remain in the system.

How valuable is the information provided by the data bank in identifying marginal practitioners? Reporting entities apparently vary widely in the frequency with which they report problems, suggesting that reports may be more a function of the reporting institution's zeal in pursuing quality than of any individual doctor's competence. Oshel et al., supra. On the other hand, while "at the end of 1994, the mean number of disclosable reports per practitioner was 1.3[, s]everal practitioners had more than 100 reports." Id. Hospitals and managed-care plans do query the data bank, but, even though a few (e.g., 2–3% of hospitals) report being influenced by their findings, most queries are the result of regulatory or accrediting requirements, not voluntary demonstrations of the information's value.

Payments on malpractice claims represent about 83% of the reports to the data bank. Is the absence or infrequency of paid malpractice claims in a physician's file a reliable indicator of the physician's competence? The annual rate of malpractice claims reported per 1000 physicians varied widely by state—from 7.5 (Ala.) to 45.6 (Mont.)—suggesting some unevenness in detecting actionable behavior. More ominously, as chapter 7 will reveal, the tort system has severe shortcomings as a method of bringing actual incompetence to light; indeed, only a tiny fraction of actionable, injury-causing negligence ever becomes the subject of a malpractice claim (let alone a successful one). If information concerning malpractice claims is of very limited value in revealing quality problems, of what value is the data bank itself?

6. *Policy Implications*. Do you sense that public licensing and discipline of physicians is not adequately protecting the public against marginal physicians or encouraging the promotion of quality across the full spectrum of medical care? If licensure is an unreliable source of consumer protection, what are the implications for policy? For example, should managed-care plans or provider networks undertaking to provide services on a prepaid, risk-bearing basis have more explicit responsibility for performing their own credentialing functions (as hospitals do)? How should that responsibility be created and enforced? Consider, for example, whether policy toward managed-care plans should focus on "inputs" (e.g., public prescription of physician eligibility for plan participation), "process" (e.g., legal requirements concerning the methods health plans employ in selecting physicians and monitoring their performance), or "outcomes" (e.g., vicarious legal liability for physician malpractice, etc.). Reconsider these issues in your study of chapter 8.

Rather than continuing to engage in regulation that barely scratches the surface of the quality problem, might government be more useful if it concentrated on providing verified information on which health plans and other private actors could rely in selecting physicians? See Kinney, supra, at 120 ("Indeed, in terms of regulation for purposes of consumer protection, information dissemination may actually be more effective than aggressive enforcement against individual errant practitioners."). Or does the experience of the National Practitioners Data Bank suggest that government's ability to help consumers is limited and that, once again, government's efforts, being more symbolic than practically valuable, may be counterproductive? Although the data bank is likely to survive because it seems consistent with the dominant policy of building a better health care marketplace, is it really helping to decentralize health care decision making and responsibility for the quality of care?

Participation in Medicare; PROs

Greene v. Bowen

United States District Court, Eastern District California, 1986.
639 F.Supp. 554.

■ KARLTON, CHIEF JUDGE.

On May 28, 1986, plaintiff Frank P. Greene, M.D. filed a complaint for declaratory and injunctive relief against the Acting Commissioner, Department of Health and Human Services, and California Medical Review, Inc. On the same date, plaintiff ex parte sought a temporary restraining order. The plaintiff sought to restrain the department from excluding Dr. Greene from the Medicare program and from publishing a notice of the exclusion, pending administrative review.

* * *

The facts necessary for resolution of the question of whether a preliminary injunction should issue may be stated relatively briefly. The plaintiff is a physician living and practicing medicine in Tehama County, California. He is a fellow of the American College of Surgeons, President of the Tehama County Medical Society, and one of two board-certified general surgeons currently serving the Tehama County area.

The court can take judicial notice of the fact that Tehama County is a physically large county, with a small population of approximately 38,000 people. The doctor has testified that in the fiscal year April 1985 to April 1986, he received approximately $115,000 in reimbursement from Medicare, which represented approximately 65% of his gross income for that year.

In October 1985, California Medical Review, Inc., a PRO,[6] while engaging in its routine review process, identified possible quality of care problems at Corning Memorial Hospital. As a follow-up, the PRO randomly selected various Federal Medicare admissions at the hospital for a further in-depth review. Based on that review, the PRO identified two cases in

6. A PRO (peer review organization) is either composed of licensed doctors of medicine and osteopathy practitioners in the area who are representative of the practicing physicians in the area, or alternatively, has the services of such physicians available to it. 42 U.S.C. § 1320c–1. The Secretary of the Department of Health and Human Services is authorized to establish geographic areas throughout the nation within which PRO's may be designated, and to contract with PRO's to perform a review of the professional activities of physicians and other health care practitioners within these specific geographical areas. 42 U.S.C. § 1320c–3.

which there was a suggestion of a possible "gross and flagrant violation," see 42 U.S.C. § 1320c–5(b), by the plaintiff of his duties under the Act. Accordingly, the PRO forwarded a letter to Dr. Greene on November 20, 1985, informing him of the concerns and of his right to submit to the PRO additional information or a written request for a meeting.

* * *

After [considering plaintiff's responses and] further review by a variety of doctors, the PRO notified plaintiff on February 25, 1986, that it had determined that he had in two cases grossly and flagrantly violated his obligations to provide care which meets professionally recognized standards. Accordingly, the PRO recommended to the Office of the Inspector General of the Department of Health and Human Services that the plaintiff be excluded from participation in the Medicare program for a two-year period. The letter further informed the plaintiff that he could submit additional material relating to the exclusion recommendation to the Office of the Inspector General within thirty (30) days.

The Office of the Inspector General conducted a further review [and] notified Dr. Greene in writing on May 8, 1986, that it had determined that in two cases he had grossly and flagrantly violated his obligations to provide care of a quality which meets professionally recognized standards, and that in the third case, he had substantially failed to provide care of a quality which met professionally recognized standards.[7]

By virtue of the latter determination, the doctor, although he has a right to a full administrative hearing, 42 U.S.C. § 1320c–5(b)(4) and 42 U.S.C. § 405(b), will be excluded from further treatment of Medicare patients, and that fact will be published in a local newspaper, 42 C.F.R. § 474.52(d). The doctor seeks a restraining order as to both consequences.

* * *

[On a motion for a preliminary injunction,] it is clear that the moving party must demonstrate some chance of success on the merits. The Government asserts that the plaintiff has no chance of success on the merits whatsoever, since this court lacks subject matter jurisdiction. I first consider that issue.

The Social Security Act provides, in pertinent part, that any health care provider:

> ... who is dissatisfied with a determination made by the Secretary under [42 U.S.C. § 1320c–5(b)(1)] shall be entitled to reasonable notice and

7. The PRO's recommendation was premised upon the treatment of three patients. M.J., a 72–year old patient, had been admitted with a perforated ulcer and generalized peritoneal spillage. In particular, the PRO regarded the plaintiff's failure to provide post-operative care within 48 hours after performing surgery as falling below the standard.

Concerning patient E.M., the PRO determined that once again Dr. Greene had inadequately evaluated and treated post-operatively.

Finally, the PRO considered the case of H.V., which related to an allegation of premature discharge from acute care to a lower level of care.

> opportunity for a hearing thereon by the Secretary to the same extent as is provided in [42 U.S.C.] section 405(b) ... and to judicial review of the Secretary's final decision after such hearing as is provided in [42 U.S.C.] section 405(g).

42 U.S.C. § 1320c–5(b)(4).

As the Government notes, under § 405(g), the decision sought to be reviewed must be "final," which in this context means the Appeal Council decision upon review of the administrative law judge's decision, or the Appeal Council's dismissal of a request for review. See 42 C.F.R. §§ 405.1566B.1568. Because an administrative law judge has not yet rendered a decision, it is the position of the United States that this court is without subject matter jurisdiction.

* * * [P]laintiff tenders a series of arguments to demonstrate that the issues raised in his lawsuit are collateral to the administrative hearing, and thus subject to waiver of the exhaustion [of administrative remedies] requirement. Plaintiff's position, perhaps somewhat oversimplified, may be summarized as tendering three essential propositions. First, plaintiff asserts that given the grave consequences of the doctor's exclusion, he is entitled to a hearing preceding his exclusion. Second, he contends that the PRO failed to follow the Secretary's regulations concerning, for example, the amount of time a health care provider is to be given to respond to claims of a violation of statutory duties. Finally, he asserts that the determination made by the PRO that the plaintiff had been guilty of a willful and flagrant violation of his obligations was made by the application of an inappropriate standard of care. In essence, he argues that given * * * the fact that there are only two board-certified general surgeons in Tehama County, his practice of turning post-operative care over to the referring physician (ordinarily a general practitioner) was well within the standard of care in Tehama County. He notes, however, that the PRO determination appears to have been made by the application of the standard of care in San Francisco, a compact geographic community where there are, if anything, a surfeit of physicians. He thus argues that the determination of willful and flagrant violations, upon which both the suspension and publication are predicated, was the result of the application of an inappropriate medical standard. It is upon this question that the court will focus its attention. Put succinctly, the issue is whether the contention that the PRO applied an inappropriate standard of care is sufficiently collateral to the question of entitlement, so that the plaintiff is not required to exhaust his administrative remedies before seeking relief in the district court.

The Government rejects the contention by asserting not only that the question is not collateral, but also that it is a non-issue. It asserts that the statute does not define willful and flagrant violations, but that under the regulations, the standard of care appropriate to a geographic area is irrelevant.

The applicable regulation provides that:

> "Gross and flagrant violation" means a violation of an obligation has occurred in one or more instances which presents an imminent danger to

the health, safety or well-being of a Medicare beneficiary or places the beneficiary unnecessarily in high-risk situations.

42 C.F.R. § 474.0(b).

* * *

The definition is predicated upon the violation of an "obligation." * * * [T]he Act defines an obligation, in pertinent part, as the requirement that "any health care practitioner ... assure, to the extent of his authority that services ... (2) will be of a quality which meets professionally recognized standards of health care." 42 U.S.C. § 1320c–5(a). Thus, by its terms, the statute requires examination of alleged failures under "professionally recognized standards of health care." Given that requirement, the question of what standards, and where they are applicable, is tendered by the very language of the statute. Moreover, other provisions of this reticulated statute further suggest that the standard of care in a particular community may be relevant. Thus, the statute provides that the PRO:

> [S]hall, consistent with the provisions of its contract under this part, apply professionally developed norms of care, diagnosis, and treatment based upon typical patterns of practice within the geographic area served by the organization as principal points of evaluation of review, taking into consideration national norms where appropriate.

42 U.S.C. § 1320c–3(a)(6).

Moreover, the second test contained in the regulatory definition of "gross and flagrant violation" does not require a standard independent of local standards of practice. That test defines gross and flagrant violations as those which place beneficiaries in "unnecessarily" high risk situations. The question of necessity, however, suggests the need at least to consider local medical conditions. A single example will perhaps illustrate the court's point. Assume for a moment that the question is whether a doctor in a remote area of Alaska has placed patients at an unnecessarily high risk by receiving telephone inquiries from nurses in Eskimo villages at even more remote areas and attempting to prescribe by phone. Clearly, such conduct would violate the standard of care in San Francisco, and, in San Francisco, would place his patients in an "unnecessarily" high risk situation. For the doctor in Alaska, on the other hand, this method of consultation may be the only possible one, and thus not at all unnecessary or a gross and flagrant violation.[5]

The court's view that the statute and regulations may reasonably be read to require a consideration of the standard of care relevant to the community in which the doctor practices is supported by other textual material. Thus the regulation requires that:

> For the conduct of review a PRO must—

5. The court does not mean even to suggest that the situation in Tehama justified Dr. Greene's conduct. On the contrary, the point which the court seeks to make is only that the question of necessity by its terms requires consideration of the realities and possibilities of local medical practice.

(1) Establish written criteria based upon typical patterns of practice in the PRO area, or use national criteria where appropriate; ... [varying criteria and standards].

A PRO may establish specific criteria and standards to be applied to certain locations and facilities in the PRO area if the PRO determines that—

(1) The patterns of practice in those locations and facilities are substantially different from patterns in the remainder of the PRO area; and

(2) There is a reasonable basis for the difference which makes the variation appropriate.

42 C.F.R. § 466.100(c) and (d).

I conclude from the above that plaintiff's argument that a PRO must consider the standard of care in a particular community is not without substance. That conclusion, of course, does not resolve the issue of whether the question is collateral. It appears to the court that although the definition of a collateral issue is not wholly certain, the issue tendered is collateral to the hearing before the administrative law judge.

* * * Having rejected the Government's assertion that plaintiff has no chance of prevailing on the merits because this court is without subject matter jurisdiction, I turn to the question of whether, given subject matter jurisdiction, a preliminary injunction should be granted.

* * *

The Government argues that preliminary injunctive relief is inappropriate because the plaintiff has failed to demonstrate the existence of irreparable injury. It argues that at most plaintiff tenders only two forms of injury, namely, the loss of income and the loss of reputation. It argues that neither threatened injury is irreparable within the meaning of the cases.

[The court held that "the monetary deprivation that the doctor will experience during the pendency of his suspension and prior to his reinstatement (if such should be the case) is irreparable in every ordinary meaning of the term" and that "the publication of the doctor's suspension in the local newspapers in a small county such as Tehama will have a devastating effect on his professional reputation far beyond his Medicare practice."]

I thus find that under the circumstances, the doctor has demonstrated a threat of immediate irreparable injury. I now turn to the question of the balance of hardships and the public interest.

* * * Under the circumstances, it would appear to the court that an injunction could and should be framed in such a manner as to require the doctor to personally provide post-operative care to patients upon whom he has operated, and that, so drawn, an injunction will limit any hardship to the Government and serve the public interest.

Accordingly, the court [enjoined defendants from "Suspending plaintiff as a provider of medical services under the Medicare Act, or publishing any statement to the effect that he is so suspended, provided that the plaintiff shall not perform any surgery upon any patient under circumstances in which he cannot personally provide post-operative care."]

NOTES AND QUESTIONS ON FEDERAL OVERSIGHT OF PHYSICIANS

1. *Participation in Public Programs.* Although Congress originally relied upon state licensure and regulation to maintain the quality of care, it moved in the Medicare and Medicaid Patient and Program Protection Act of 1987 to strengthen the authority of DHHS to exclude physicians and other practitioners or entities, including hospitals, from participation in virtually all federal and federally assisted health care programs on the basis of various kinds of unfitness. 42 U.S.C.A. § 1320a–7 (West Supp. 1998); 42 C.F.R. pt. 1001 (1998). A five-year mandatory exclusion accompanies conviction of any criminal offense relating to the delivery of services under any federal program or conviction of an offense involving neglect or abuse of patients; a state may request an exception for a sole community provider of a particular service. A long list of other events or offenses may also trigger exclusion, at DHHS's discretion. These include loss, suspension, or surrender (under pressure) of a license to practice even though the practitioner may be licensed in another state.

2. *The PRO Program.* PROs were examined at some length in a note in chapter 4(§B). As that discussion and the principal case show, they are private contractors working for the Medicare program and have, among other duties, a responsibility for detecting substandard medical care. Note that, under the statute, Dr. Greene could be suspended from participation in Medicare on the basis of the PRO action alone and before receiving the hearing to which he is entitled before an administrative law judge. See generally 42 C.F.R. pt. 1004 (1998). The denial of a full presuspension hearing has been upheld in several cases. E.g., Varandani v. Bowen, 824 F.2d 307 (4th Cir.1987), cert. dismissed, 484 U.S. 1052 (1988); Cassim v. Bowen, 824 F.2d 791 (9th Cir.1987) (court also denied preliminary injunction to physician found by PRO to have performed unnecessary surgery; "balance of hardships" favored government). Under 42 U.S.C.A. § 1320c–3(a)(3) (West Supp. 1998), a PRO may not notify a patient or a carrier of its adverse findings without first providing "an opportunity for discussion and review of the proposed determination." More formal review is available at a later point. Because the publicity given a PRO action may adversely affect a physician's practice, hospital privileges, or liability insurance, the opportunity for at least an informal hearing before the PRO is of crucial importance.

Was the PRO program given too broad a mandate? A 1995 report from the DHHS Office of the Inspector General (OIG) concluded that PROs are failing to identify poorly performing hospitals and physicians and rarely follow up on cases of poor care referred to them. Medicare & Medicaid Guide (CCH) ¶ 43,977 (Dec. 1995). The report advised HCFA to continue employing PROs in the larger effort to improve the overall quality of care and to encourage PROs to rely more on state medical boards to address individual cases.

3. *What Standard of Care?* The issue of local versus national standards appears in several places in these materials, but is presented in a particularly vivid fashion in the *Greene* case. (Recall the similar issue in the *Koefoot* case adverted to in chapter 4(§B).) Reflecting congressional concerns that PROs were targeting and evaluating rural doctors unfairly (one administrative law judge concluded that a physician had been "accused and convicted of being a country doctor"), a provision enacted in 1987 requires PRO norms to "take into account the special problems associated with delivering care in remote rural areas." 42 U.S.C.A. § 1320c–3(a)(6) (West Supp. 1998). Should a PRO, in deciding whether to suspend a physician, consider the effect of the suspension on patients in an underdoctored rural area? Under another provision in enacted in 1987, rural physicians cannot be summarily excluded from the program without special findings by an administrative law judge. 42 U.S.C.A. § 1320c–5(b)(5) (West Supp. 1998).

In 1992, DHHS, rejecting a request that regulations recognize variations in standards between localities, said that quality "will be assessed in light of all the surrounding circumstances, including the capabilities of the facility." 57 Fed. Reg. 3301 (1992). Should clinical practice guidelines be used as standards of care in evaluating physician performance in treating federal beneficiaries? According to a government spokesman in 1991, guidelines "will not dictate standards of practice; rather, they are designed to provide physicians and health care consumers with options available and improved decision making in the diagnosis, treatment, and management of a specific clinical condition." Clinton, Physician Input Invited on Clinical Guideline Development, 265 J.A.M.A. 1508 (1991). Given recognized problems with the quality of care, was the agency being too deferential to physician concerns about "cookbook medicine"?

The Supply of Physicians

NOTES AND QUESTIONS ON CONTROLLING THE NUMBER AND DISTRIBUTION OF PHYSICIANS

1. *Early Standardization of Medical Education Under Professional Control.* Some observers have believed that the organized medical profession long controlled the production of physicians in U.S. medical schools and the influx of foreign-trained physicians. See, e.g., Kessel, The A.M.A. and the Supply of Physicians, 35 Law & Contemp. Probs. 267 (1970). Certainly it is true that the profession gained substantial influence over the nature and availability of medical education at an early date. According to Starr, physicians and educators at the turn of the century saw the introduction of more rigorous and scientific medical education as a means to improve not only medical care but also the income and status of physicians. Licensing laws alone were not enough to achieve the profession's purposes; control of

the production of physicians was also necessary. See generally P. Starr, The Social Transformation of American Medicine 112–27 (1982).

Between 1870 and 1900, medical education developed along two tracks. The first track was comprised of proprietary medical schools; licensing laws induced proliferation of these schools, which recruited both male and female students from the working and lower-middle classes. The second and "higher" track began to appear in the 1870s, when Harvard greatly increased the length and rigor of required training. Other prestigious schools, fearing a loss of either reputation or students, followed suit. In 1890, these schools formed a national association—now the Association of American Medical Colleges (AAMC)—dedicated to raising the standards of medical education.

Other professional organizations joined the effort. In 1901, the AMA adopted a federal structure by incorporating state medical associations, making them more effective in influencing state legislatures and licensing boards. In 1904, the AMA established its Council on Medical Education and made reform of medical schools a top priority. The Council invited the Carnegie Foundation to report on the status of medical education, and in 1910 the prestigious and influential Flexner Report resulted. A. Flexner, Medical Education in the United States and Canada (1910). That report, prepared by an educator who was not a physician or otherwise schooled in medical science, advocated enormous cutbacks in the number of medical schools and much higher requirements for entrance and graduation. The Report dismissed fears that opportunities for middle and working class students would be reduced and that poor people and rural areas would not be adequately served as a result of its proposals.

Starr describes developments following the Flexner Report as follows:

> The process of consolidation in medical education moved apace in the decade after 1910. By 1915 the number of schools had fallen from 131 to 95, and the number of graduates from 5,440 to 3,536. Mergers were common among Class A and B schools; Class C schools were often disbanded for want of students. In five years, the schools requiring at least one year of college work grew from thirty-five to eighty-three, or from 27 percent of the total in 1910 to 80 percent in 1915. Licensing boards demanding college work increased from eight to eighteen. In 1912 a number of boards formed a voluntary association, the Federation of State Medical Boards, which accepted the AMA's rating of medical schools as authoritative. The AMA Council effectively became a national accrediting agency for medical schools, as an increasing number of states adopted its judgments of unacceptable institutions. In the fall of 1914, a year of college work as a prerequisite for admission became essential for a Class A rating from the AMA; two years of college were required in 1918. By 1922 thirty-eight states were requiring two years of college in preliminary work, the number of medical schools had fallen to 81, and graduates to 2,529. Even though no legislative body ever set up either the Federation of State Medical Boards or the AMA Council on Medical Education, their decisions came to have the force of law. This was an extraordinary achievement for the organized profession. Only a few decades earlier, many people had

> believed that the decentralized character of American government precluded any effective regulation of medical education. If one state raised its requirements, students would simply gravitate to schools elsewhere. Short of federal intervention, control seemed impossible. But the medical profession had carried its effort to every state, and its success was a measure of how far it had come since the mid–1800s.

Starr, supra, at 120–21.

2. *Manpower Planning and the Supply of Physicians.* Although the early reforms limited the supply of physicians by raising the cost of entry into medicine and by limiting the educational opportunities available, the medical profession eventually lost most of its ability to control the number of physicians trained. During the 1960s and the early 1970s, concerns about a physician shortage led Congress to give increasing subsidies to medical education and to condition them on the schools' willingness to increase their enrollments. The expanded "pipeline" soon began to produce physicians at a dramatically increased rate, leading in due course to concerns about a physician "glut." See, e.g., Report of the Graduate Medical Education National Advisory Committee [GMENAC] to the Secretary of Health and Human Services (1980) (prestigious national commission's report warning that nation would have surplus 70,000 physicians by 1990). For a critique of this exercise in manpower planning, see Comanor, Health Manpower and Government Planning, Regulation, May–June 1981, p. 47. A study in 1992–93 found that two mature staff-model HMOs had physician/patient ratios of 180 per 100,000, a number similar to the ratio in the nation as a whole. Hart et al., Physician Staffing Ratios in Staff–Model HMOs: A Cautionary Tale, Health Affs., Jan.-Feb. 1997, p. 55.

In 1995, a bipartisan national panel of health care experts recommended reducing the size of U.S. medical school classes by 20%–25% and cutting the number of health care professionals by the year 2005 in response to the "new health care market." Pew Health Professions Commission, Critical Challenges: Revitalizing the Health Professions for the Twenty–First Century (1995). For another warning that the supply of physicians is outstripping needs, requiring action aimed at limiting subsidies for graduate medical education (GME), see Institute of Medicine, The Nation's Physician Workforce: Options for Balancing Supply and Demand (1996). Largely in response to such recommendations, the 1997 Balanced Budget Act included provisions conditioning Medicare payments (both indirect education allowances and direct GME payments) in such a way as to reduce significantly the number of residency positions in the U.S. The legislation caps the total number of residency positions in most hospitals and provides continued GME funds, in decreasing amounts, only for institutions that reduce their number of residency positions by substantial percentages over time.

How does one decide that there is an oversupply of physicians? Does society worry in a similar way about the supply of other types of manpower? What are the dangers associated with an oversupply of physicians? What might account for an oversupply of physicians? List *all* the factors that appear to have contributed to the alleged problem. What items on this list could government appropriately address? One item on your list should be government subsidies to medical education, particularly state subsidies to state university medical schools. Who are the beneficiaries of these subsidies? Are such subsidies a sensible way to improve access of disadvantaged persons to either medical training or medical care? What could government do about other sources of the oversupply problem that you have identified?

What benefits have flowed, arguably, from the increased supply of physicians? Was the federal government's decision in the 1960s to pay medical schools to expand their enrollments an example of wise central planning? Were intensification of economic competition and the emergence of market forces as the principal source of discipline in the health care marketplace among the intended consequences? Serious doubts were expressed by some observers concerning the policy of increasing the overall physician supply in order to overcome shortages. Because many areas—mostly prosperous urban and suburban ones—were deemed to be oversupplied yet able to support even more physicians, such a policy was viewed as more likely to exacerbate existing problems than to cure undersupply in backward areas.

What, if anything, can the medical profession do collectively about the alleged oversupply of physicians? about an excessive number of specialists of a particular type? Later discussion of educational accreditation and of antitrust issues may suggest some answers to these questions.

3. *The National Health Service Corps; Primary Care Specialists*. Underserved areas have apparently benefitted from the National Health Services Corps (NHSC), a part of the Public Health Service that uses tuition support to induce medical students to sign contracts under which they will accept assignment to underserved areas following completion of their training. But see Politzer et al., Primary Care Physician Supply and the Medically Underserved: A Status Report and Recommendations, 266 J.A.M.A. 104 (1991) (expressing concern about the supply of primary care physicians due to reductions in NHSC funding and in the proportion of medical school seniors planning to work in primary care). More recent developments include an intensification for demand for primary care physicians and increased interest in the field on the part of medical students.

Are the restrictive covenants in NHSC contracts enforceable? By what sanction? See United States v. Swanson, 618 F.Supp. 1231 (E.D.Mich.1985) (three times government outlay plus interest held payable as liquidated damages, not a penalty). See also United States v. Hatcher, 922 F.2d 1402 (9th Cir.1991) (applying administrative law, not contract, principles), and Annot., 108 A.L.R. Fed. 313 (1992). According to a 1987 report, "more than 10% of the program's 13,600 participants ha[d] defaulted on their scholarship obligations, including 500 who [we]re suing the corps over what they say are abusive placement practices." James, Despite Federal Aid, Doctors Are Still in Short Supply in Rural Areas, Wall St. J., June 23, 1987, p. 33.

Selman v. Harvard Medical School

United States District Court, Southern District New York, 1980.
494 F.Supp. 603.

■ DUFFY, DISTRICT JUDGE:

Plaintiff, Burton Selman, was a medical student at Universidad Autonama of Guadalajara, Mexico [hereinafter referred to as "UAG"] whose transfer applications to numerous medical schools in the United States were rejected. The instant action was instituted in February, 1979, against several United States medical schools, individual employees of those schools, and the Association of American Medical Colleges [hereinafter referred to as "AAMC"]. Selman brought suit on behalf of himself as well as all similarly situated qualified applicants from foreign medical schools who applied for admission to defendant medical schools under the "Federal Transfer Program" and were rejected.

* * *

Plaintiff's third cause of action is based on the Foreign Medical School Transfer Program. Health Professions Educational Assistance Act Pub.L. No. 94–484, 90 Stat. 2243, 2296 (1976). It is interesting to note that this program which originally provided for a "Match List" matching qualified foreign medical school applicants with participating United States schools was repealed before it went into effect. Public Health Service Act Amendments Pub.L. No. 95–215, 91 Stat. 1503 (1977).

In its place, there is now a "capitation grant" program providing for annual grants to schools of medicine which comply with various requirements. 42 U.S.C. §§ 292 et seq. One such prerequisite to participation in the program is the assurance by participating medical schools that they will increase enrollment of full time third-year students. 42 U.S.C. § 295f–1(b) (Supp.1978). This provision would presumably encourage participating medical schools to accept transfer students from foreign schools.

It is contended that the above capitation program creates a federal statutory right to fair consideration, the violation of which may properly be redressed under 42 U.S.C. § 1983. Plaintiff maintains that the arbitrary admissions criteria used by defendant medical schools violate this statutory right as well as the due process clauses of the Fifth and Fourteenth Amendments.

* * *

In [another] cause of action, plaintiff charges defendants with unlawful combinations, contracts, and agreements in restraint of trade under the Sherman Act. As part of these supposed unlawful combinations, defendants allegedly engaged in a successful "boycott" to change the "Match List" program thereby enabling them to consider applicants on the basis of their own arbitrary criteria. It is contended that defendants' unlawful activities prevent and prohibit free competition by preventing plaintiffs and members of the class the opportunity to become doctors. Consequently, the quality of health services available to the public is allegedly severely restricted.

* * *

B. Private Right of Action Under the Public Health Service Act

* * *

Plaintiff and defendants disagree as to whether or not Congress intended the provisions concerning increased third year enrollment to be for the especial benefit of foreign medical students seeking transfer. Plaintiff points to one passage in the legislative history in support of his position: "the legislation is designed to preserve a reasonable opportunity for U.S. citizens studying abroad to complete their medical education in the United States ..." H.R.Rep. No. 95–707, 95th Cong., 1st Sess. (1977) at 4.

Defendants, on the other hand, argue, that the legislation was at least, in part, a reaction to the "relatively uncontrolled entrance into the United States medical care system by foreign medical graduates of widely varying training, background and competence [which] is severely diluting the quality of the United States health-care system." H.R.Rep. No. 94–266, 94th Cong., 1st Sess. (1975) at 54.

At the same time that Congress was trying to quell the influx of less qualified medical students from foreign schools, it was concerned that many of these students were Americans trying to come home. Certain provisions were adopted to assist these Americans. Yet, Congress stated that "[i]n authorizing grants and contracts for these purposes, the Committee in no way means to imply that it approves of the process of enrollment in foreign schools and remedial training before and during subsequent enrollment in United States medical schools." Id. at 59.

It is apparent that Congress, in passing the Public Health Service Act balanced many factors. Even assuming, for the moment, that the third year provisions were created for the benefit of qualified American students at foreign medical schools, it still must be determined whether or not Congress impliedly intended to create in them a private right of action. I think not.

The Health Professions Educational Assistance Act of 1976 originally created a "match list" which identified a pool of transfer students who were to be matched with schools of medicine receiving capitation. This provision never went into effect. Instead, the present 42 U.S.C. 295f–1(b)(3) was enacted. This compromise was in "respon[se] to the objections of some schools of medicine that existing law infringes on their academic freedom to apply their own selection criteria in the admissions process." H.R.Rep. No. 95–707, 95th Cong., 1st Sess. (1977) at 4.

In recognizing medical schools' academic freedom in the selection process, Congress certainly did not intend to give "all qualified applicants who were rejected" a private right to sue. At best, § 295f–1(b) encourages

United States medical schools to provide additional places in third-year classes.

* * *

C. 1983 Claim

* * *

Plaintiff has * * * failed to assert a "property" or "liberty" interest whose deprivation without due process would give rise to a Fourteenth Amendment claim. It is plaintiff's contention that he has a "liberty" or "property" interest in his admission to medical school.

In making his "liberty" interest argument, plaintiff relies on Board of Curators of University of Missouri v. Horowitz, 435 U.S. 78 (1978), in which a medical student at the University of Missouri–Kansas City Medical School was dismissed for academic reasons during her final year. This case might more appropriately be cited in opposition to plaintiff's contentions.

The Court in *Horowitz* did not reach the "liberty" interest question but hinted that based on Bishop v. Wood, 426 U.S. 341 (1976), a mere dismissal without the publication of harmful allegations would not deprive the respondent of an opportunity to seek admission elsewhere. Certainly, plaintiff does not contend that defendant medical schools published any damaging information which hurt his chances for admission at other schools.

Horowitz, as well as the other cases cited by plaintiff, all involved deprivations occasioned by individuals who were dismissed from school or their employment. Rejection of an application for admission is a far cry from dismissal once a person has already been admitted. In *Horowitz,* the Court expressed a desire to avoid "judicial intrusion into academic decision making." *A fortiori,* a court should be more reluctant to interfere where the "interest" involved has not even risen to that of an attending student.

Turning to the "property" interest claim, it is clear that plaintiff has not met the test established by the Supreme Court to determine the existence of such an interest for due process purposes. In Board of Regents v. Roth, 408 U.S. 564, it was clearly stated that to have a property interest, "a person must have more than an abstract need or desire. . . . He must have more than a unilateral expectation. . . . He must, instead have a legitimate claim of entitlement."

One would be hard pressed to come up with a better example of a case in which there is no such "legitimate claim of entitlement." Plaintiff cannot possibly be heard to say that every qualified student at a foreign medical school is *entitled* to transfer admission into a United States school.

In accordance with the reasoning above, plaintiff's third claim is dismissed.

* * *

E. Sherman Act

Plaintiff's fifth claim charges defendants with wrongfully engaging in "unlawful combinations, contracts and agreements in restraint of trade and commerce among the several states" in violation of 15 U.S.C. § 1. This claim must also be dismissed.

In Apex Hosiery Co. v. Leader, 310 U.S. 469 (1940), the Supreme Court discussed at length the purpose of the Sherman Act which was to prevent "restraints to free competition in business and commercial transactions which tended to restrict production, raise prices or otherwise control the market to the detriment of purchasers or consumers." The aims of the Sherman Act, according to the *Apex Hosiery* Court, must be viewed in the context of the period during which it was enacted, to wit: the era of "trusts" and "combinations" of businesses.

The pronouncements of the Supreme Court in *Apex Hosiery* have led at least one court to conclude that

> the proscriptions of the Sherman Act were 'tailored ... for the business world,' not for the non-commercial aspects of the liberal arts and the learned professions. In these contexts, an incidental restraint of trade, absent an intent or purpose to affect the commercial aspects of the profession, is not sufficient to warrant application of the antitrust laws.

Marjorie Webster Junior College, Inc. v. Middle States Association of Colleges and Secondary Schools, Inc., 432 F.2d 650, 654 (D.C.Cir.) (footnotes omitted), *cert. denied,* 400 U.S. 965 (1970).

As plaintiff correctly points out, however, there is no blanket exemption to the antitrust laws for "learned professions." Rather, the Supreme Court recognized that professions do have business aspects. Thus, in *Goldfarb v. Virginia State Bar,* the Court held that a claim based on a minimum fee schedule for title examinations published by the Fairfax, Virginia County Bar Association fell within the scope of the Sherman Act. The Court in that case, however, was quite careful to point out that "[i]t would be unrealistic to view the practice of professions as interchangeable with other business activities" and went on to say that they "intimate[d] no view on any other situation than the one with which we are confronted today."

Unlike the situation in *Goldfarb,* plaintiff does not challenge a fee schedule which would have a direct effect on the consuming public. Plaintiff here challenges a distinctly non-commercial aspect of the practice of the "learned professions;" to wit: admissions criteria.

Plaintiff alleges that by virtue of defendants' admissions policies, "the quality of care given to the public is ... severely restricted and the costs of health services are markedly elevated." Plaintiff offers no facts in support of this allegation. Moreover, the connection between defendants' admission policies and the alleged harm to the consuming public is, at best, tenuous.

Academic admissions criteria may well have a purely incidental effect on the commercial aspects of the medical profession. They are, however, non-commercial in nature. The Sherman Act was certainly not intended to provide a forum wherein disgruntled applicants to medical school could challenge their rejections. Therefore, plaintiff's sixth claim is dismissed.

Conclusion

Courts are properly reluctant to intrude into the academic decision-making process except where invidious abuses are indicated. Thus, the Supreme Court recently stated that "the freedom of a university to make its own judgments as to education includes the selection of its student body." Regents of University of California v. Bakke, 438 U.S. 265, 312 (1978).

The reluctance to intrude must be that much stronger, where, as here, the complaint is vague and overreaching. Throughout each and every claim in plaintiff's complaint, he alleges no more than the fact that he is a disappointed applicant who wishes he were able to get his medical education in the United States.

In accordance with all of the foregoing, defendants' motion to dismiss is granted and plaintiff's cross-motion to certify the class is denied.

NOTES AND QUESTIONS ON FOREIGN MEDICAL GRADUATES

1. *FMGs and USFMGs.* Over 23 percent of the physicians currently practicing in the U.S. are graduates of foreign medical schools. These foreign medical graduates (FMGs) are unevenly distributed throughout the nation, however, being found principally in some intensely urban and some relatively remote rural areas. A high percentage of the hospital positions filled by FMGs are in inner-city, rural, and mental hospitals, to which graduates of U.S. medical schools are not attracted. See Mick & Lee, The Safety–Net Role of International Medical Graduates, Health Affs., July–Aug. 1997.

For many years, the vast majority of who sought postgraduate medical training and eventually licensure in the U.S. were from such third-world countries as India, the Philippines, and Egypt. Later, increasing numbers of U.S. citizens, unable to gain admission to U.S. medical schools, sought medical training abroad, especially in Mexico and in newly created proprietary schools in the Caribbean basin. After 1983, these "USFMGs" constituted a majority of the FMGs enrolled in accredited residency programs in the U.S.

What explains the open-door immigration policy towards FMGs that prevailed for so many years? Was there an inconsistency between the high standards of and restricted access to medical education in the U.S. and the acceptance of numerous FMGs trained under very different circumstances? Was there an implication that the health care system required second-class physicians to fill certain jobs but was unwilling to acknowledge this fact by tolerating different types of medical education in U.S. schools? Can you speculate on why the medical profession, which was for so long receptive to alien FMGs, was been especially troubled by the influx of USFMGs?

2. *The ECFMG.* Ordinarily, graduates of unaccredited medical schools are ineligible to fill places in accredited residency programs or to sit for state licensing exams—a fact that explains why there are no such schools in the U.S. Some provision had to be made for foreigners, however, and this was done by creating the Educational Council for Foreign Medical Graduates (ECFMG), a joint undertaking of the AMA, several other industry groups, and the Federation of State Medical Boards. For a foreign-trained physician, certification by the ECFMG is a prerequisite to admission to an accredited residency program and thus to licensure in most states. The main route to ECFMG certification is by presentation of a degree from a school listed by the World Health Organization and satisfactory performance on an English-language examination and on a rigorous examination in the medical sciences (FMGEMS). What are the implications of allowing the ECFMG, a private organization, to preside over the influx of FMGs into the U.S.?

3. Any effort to curtail the supply of physicians by reducing the size of residency programs in U.S. hospitals raises the question of who will care for the poor in inner cities and rural communities "if the institutions serving these areas are unable to recruit foreign-trained physicians for the residencies and staff practices that are generally shunned by graduates of American medical schools." Iglehart, The Quandary Over Graduates of Foreign Medical Schools in the United States, 334 N. Eng. J. Med. 1679 (1996). Although the Balanced Budget Act of 1997 uses Medicare funds to induce cutbacks in the number of residency slots, it seems clear that FMGs will continue to provide a disproportionate share of services in underserved areas, either as residents or as permanent house staff.

4. *Questions on the Selman Case.* What was the problem to which the legislation in *Selman* was addressed? How did the medical schools respond to the legislation? Should their action have been subject to scrutiny under the Sherman Act? If not, why not? Do you agree that agreements on admissions criteria do not raise concerns of the kind that underlie the antitrust laws? Did the court look for anticompetitive effects in the right market?

Training Tomorrow's Physicians; Educational Accreditation

Clark C. Havighurst, J.D., & Gaylord Cummins, Ph.D., Letter to Ernest L. Boyer, U.S. Commissioner of Education (Designate)

March 9, 1977.

Dear Dr. Boyer:

By this letter, we respectfully submit for your consideration our views with respect to the petition of the Liaison Committee on Medical Education (LCME) for continued designation by you as the nationally recognized accrediting agency for medical schools in the United States. It is our hope that this statement will assist you in appreciating the full importance of the issues raised by the LCME's petition and the challenge thereto by the Bureau of Competition of the Federal Trade Commission (FTC).

* * * Some observers believe that the medical profession's domination of the U.S. health care system has inhibited needed change and that the LCME is now, and has long been, an important bulwark in this dominance and an obstacle to the health care system's evolution in the public interest. Fortunately, it is not necessary for the Commissioner of Education to accept any particular diagnosis of the health care system's problems and the causes thereof in order to resolve the issues in this proceeding as we suggest he should. [Under the Commissioner's own stated criteria, t]he narrower and more appropriate object of the Commissioner's inquiry is the openness and responsiveness of the educational process itself, in particular its freedom from or domination by a professional orthodoxy which may not be wholly congruent with the public's needs. Specific concern for such educational values is reflected in the [stated criteria].

The power to define how a doctor is educated is the power to define what a doctor is, and this is more than a straightforward, technical undertaking which can be safely entrusted to organized professional interests. We attempt to demonstrate in this statement the existence of a substantial danger that the LCME, by reason of its control by organized medicine and the medical education establishment, imposes on medical education a particular professional ideology, deeply rooted in a particular perception of the physician's role in society and antagonistic to educational endeavors premised on different perceptions. The U.S. Commissioner of Education, above all people, should recognize the dangers of allowing a single point of view to dominate an entire educational system. We have tried in this statement to supply enough evidence that this has occurred in medicine—and enough evidence suggesting its adverse effects on the public interest—to persuade objective observers that a different accrediting process would serve the public better. * * *

* * * The power to accredit medical schools could, of course, be used either to advance or to frustrate the achievement of state and national policy objectives. We find a number of signs that suggest that the values fostered by the nation's medical schools, operating under the accreditation process dominated by the AMA and the AAMC, are inconsistent with some current objectives of public policy. * * *

Primary Care. The public has an interest in the education of physicians to provide primary care. The problem is not new or even newly visible. * * *

The problem has been traced in part to the door of the nation's medical schools, with their commitment to acute care and scientific medicine. Alpert and Charney state that

> in addition to the external factors we have listed, there have been problems within medical education that have resulted in inadequate preparation for primary care practice. These problems have a common feature; namely, that preparation for primary care practice has not been a specific goal of

> most current medical education programs and has not been the specific responsibility of any one group.

One of the problems within medical education has been that "these programs needed to be developed in the very settings that had proved so hostile in the past; namely, the teaching hospital and the medical schools." * * *

We do not know for certain, of course, whether creating a different type of doctor would be a good or bad idea, nor do we know whether one new kind of physician would be enough. But a differently constituted accrediting body would better assure a disinterested evaluation. This example precisely illustrates the problem of entrusting to organized professional interests the power to define what a doctor is: professional ideology plays a large part—too large a part, we submit—in the educational decision.

Costs. A critically important function of the physician is to define the patient's need for services, not only those that the physician renders, but also those provided by the rest of the health care system. A combination of consumer ignorance and third-party payment for many services allows physicians to define and create demand for health services and to fuel health care cost escalation without significant restraint. Victor Fuchs, one of the most respected students of the health care economy, has explained how the cost of care is related to medical education:

> During their medical school and residency training, physicians are 'imprinted' with what they understand to be 'best medical practice,' to which they try to conform throughout their careers. This can be a mixed blessing because it is closely related to what I have called the 'technological imperative'—namely, the desire of the physician to do everything that he has been trained to do, regardless of the benefit-cost ratio.

* * *

It would be surprising if the "quality imperative" and unwillingness to consider trade-offs between costs and the quality or technological sophistication of care did not carry over into the LCME's accrediting activities. It is reasonable to expect AMA and AAMC representatives to see their professional commitment to the "quality of care," as defined under the prevailing ideology, as overriding all other considerations and to encourage anything that could conceivably result in better treatment of patients as defined by professional norms and to discourage anything that could conceivably result in worse treatment defined in the same way. * * *

To appreciate fully the implications of professional ideology for accreditation, suppose that a large, reputable health maintenance organization—say, the Kaiser Foundation Health Plan, Inc.—proposed to open a medical school to educate physicians to work in prepaid group practices, with emphasis on ambulatory care, minimal dependence on the hospital, and cost-effectiveness in the treatment of disease. Given the traditional resistance of organized medicine to the HMO concept, it is hard to anticipate that such a medical school would encounter no unusual problems or delay in achieving accreditation. It is also hard to believe that major concessions to the prevailing ideology would not be required, just as internship and residency programs in Kaiser Foundation hospitals have tended to be "rather traditional." * * *

Innovation in Medical Education

The history of medical education reveals a substantial amount of innovation in recent years. Nevertheless, three considerations suggest that this record should not obscure the specific threats to innovation posed by the LCME. First, there was very little innovation between the Flexner reforms implemented after 1910 and the end of World War II, indicating that the accreditation process put in place at the early date contributed to the stifling of change and that accreditation can indeed be the enemy of innovation in medical education. Second, the presence of some innovation is no sign that the climate is conducive to needed experimentation and variety. Third, there are signs that the trend of recent innovation has been biased in certain directions and that many desirable kinds of innovation have been repressed.

In reviewing the fruits of his work fifteen years later (in 1925), Flexner wrote:

> The desire to stamp out unfit medical schools has also operated to strengthen regimentation.... Our present fetters were forged in order to compel wretched medical schools to give unfit medical students a better training. Now that the end has been measurably accomplished, the means have become a fetish, blocking further improvement.

Apparently the fetters remained largely intact for much longer, for Reuben Kessel wrote in 1970:

> The implementation of the Flexner report has, until relatively recently, sharply reduced experimentation in the training of physicians. As a result, there was a hiatus of over 40 years in the search for better curricula and teaching methods.... It is only in recent years, in the decade of the 1960s, that the fetters imposed by the Flexner report have been loosened.

He wrote further that "to this day, there probably is less variation in medical training than in almost any other field." This history confirms that the power to accredit can be used to stymie innovation, even bring it to a standstill.

* * * [T]he close connection between the academy and the practitioner may * * * foreclose certain other types of educational innovation—namely, those which might threaten the values and interests of practitioners, including the important practitioners who constitute clinical faculties of the medical schools themselves. It is no accident that schools of public health and departments of community medicine, focusing on medicine's nontechnical aspects, are either independent of or step-children within the medical schools or that the findings emanating from these academic sources have been much more difficult to introduce into medical education and practice than the "breakthroughs" of scientific research and technological development—even when those breakthroughs have been socially questionable because of their high costs or other considerations. Again, the dominance of

orthodoxy must be cited as the cause of the educational system's less than satisfactory performance.

[The letter concluded with a discussion of options open to the Commissioner, concluding that] it would be preferable to reject the LCME petition altogether and to invite new applications. It is quite likely that one or more organizations would step forward with proposals and that one or more * * * private foundations would welcome the chance to catalyze the formation of a new body indisputably meeting the Commissioner's criteria and capable of performing in the public interest the important function of accrediting the nation's medical schools.

NOTES AND QUESTIONS ON MEDICAL EDUCATION AND THE ACCREDITING OF EDUCATIONAL PROGRAMS

1. Medical schools, together with the sophisticated and technologically advanced hospitals with which they are closely linked through a wide variety of corporate and contractual arrangements, represent one of the most powerful elements in the American health care system. Viewed as a total enterprise, the modern academic medical center is much more than an educational institution, by far the greater proportion of its effort and resources being devoted to patient care and biomedical and clinical research. Cross-subsidization is a prominent feature of these institutions, and it has been extremely difficult to isolate the costs of their myriad activities, particularly education. Medical school tuitions have increased greatly in recent years, but only a few private institutions charge anything approaching the true costs of training.

Medical educators are extremely conscious of their central role in programming future physicians, and there is a great deal of soul searching, open discussion, and internal debate concerning these matters. E.g., Commission on Medical Education, Medical Education in Transition (Robert Wood Johnson Found. 1992). It would be hard to prove that the educational establishment has not always been conscientious in discharging the responsibilities it has assumed. The issues raised in the Havighurst–Cummins letter were based on a different thesis, however. (What was that thesis?)

2. What do you gather from the foregoing was the function of the U.S. Office of Education with respect to the LCME and similar organizations? (This function is now performed by the Office of Post Secondary Education of the Department of Education.) The federal government's involvement in recognizing private accreditors began when it undertook to subsidize individuals' education under such programs as the "G.I. Bill" after World War II and wished not to support poor-quality educational programs ("diploma mills"). It has been argued that the standards employed in recognizing private accrediting programs are overly regulatory, that they are designed to foster monopoly in accrediting in particular fields, and that they are not warranted by the statute under which the program was created. See Finkin, Reforming the Federal Relationship to Educational Accreditation, 57 N.C.L.Rev. 379 (1979). See also Martin, Recent Developments Concern-

ing Accrediting Agencies in Postsecondary Education, Law & Contemp. Probs., Autumn 1994, p. 121. In your view, what additional benefits might flow from the Department's efforts in this field, besides assurance that federal funds are put to good use?

3. What was the FTC's interest in the accreditation of medical schools in 1977? The FTC challenge to the LCME appeared to reflect primarily a concern that the AMA might use it to limit the supply of physicians, as it had allegedly done in earlier eras. Would it be appropriate for the FTC, an antitrust and consumer protection agency, to embrace the concerns voiced by Havighurst and Cummins? In what way might the policies underlying the antitrust laws have been offended if the Havighurst–Cummins concerns about the LCME had merit?

4. *Multiple Accreditors?* Should the Department of Education (DOE) recognize more than one private body to accredit medical schools or any other type of educational program? There are a number of fields (e.g., legal education) where more than one accreditor co-exist. Although the DOE long tended to enfranchise a single accreditor for each type of educational program in each geographic area, in 1988 it rejected suggestions that it should discourage competition among accreditors as a way of avoiding public confusion, stating as follows: "Arbitrarily limiting the number of accrediting bodies serves no educational purpose. The Secretary wishes to foster appropriate competition among accrediting bodies and does not wish to see the recognition process used in such a way as to create a monopoly in any educational field." 53 Fed. Reg. 25,096 (1988).

5. *The Marjorie Webster Case*. Accrediting bodies like the LCME exercise substantial power to dictate the nature and content of educational programs. In Marjorie Webster Jr. College, Inc. v. Middle States Ass'n of Colleges and Secondary Schools, Inc., 432 F.2d 650 (D.C.Cir.), cert. denied, 400 U.S. 965 (1970), the court applied common-law principles in allowing an educational accreditor to refuse to accredit a proprietary school solely on the ground that it operated on a for-profit rather than a not-for-profit basis. Although one might have expected the court to sympathize with the plaintiff, a small business struggling to compete with the dominant institutions comprised in the defendant association, it chose to view the question as one of "educational philosophy." It also observed that the plaintiff was "free to join with other proprietary institutions in setting up an association for the accreditation of institutions of such character." 432 F.2d at 658. Was this suggestion realistic? Should the court have been more protective of the plaintiff? (Judicial review of accrediting standards and other actions by private organizations will be considered further below.)

6. Private accrediting and similar standard-setting organizations are common throughout the health care field and shape many features of important institutions, justifying some intensive consideration of them here. Discussion below will focus on whether private standard setting, accreditation, and certification are appropriate activities for professional organizations to engage in. Assuming that they are, consider whether the courts or the government, through programs such as that of the Department of

Education, should closely scrutinize and regulate the standards employed in private accreditation in order to ensure that private evaluation serves the public interest. Does educational accrediting differ in some substantial way from other forms of accrediting, so that a more laissez-faire attitude is arguably more justifiable?

See generally Symposium, Private Accreditation in the Regulatory State, Law & Contemp. Probs., Autumn 1994 (including articles focusing specifically on accrediting in the fields of education and health care).

7. *Problem*. Consider a current plan by the American Council on Pharmaceutical Education (ACPE) to discontinue accrediting five-year training programs for pharmacists and to accredit only six-year (Pharm.D.) programs. This proposal to extend the length of pharmacist training illustrates tellingly how a private accreditor enjoying a publicly granted virtual monopoly over standard setting in a professional field can dominate the making of crucial policy, effectively preempting both legislative and consumer choice. Although it is certainly arguable that future pharmacists should be required to have more training than the five-year minimum course required in the past, the processes currently in place for resolving this policy question lack democratic legitimacy. One source of difficulty is the DOE's recognition of the ACPE as the sole accreditor of pharmacy schools. More crucial, however, is the almost universal delegation to the ACPE by state legislatures or regulators of the authority to determine which training programs can qualify their graduates for licensure as pharmacists. This delegation makes it probable that, unless a special campaign can be mounted, the ACPE, which is dominated by educators and practicing pharmacists, will be able to effect the policy change its members desire.

Can you devise a legal remedy for the preemption of policy making encountered here? (The possibility of an antitrust challenge will be raised at a later point, but it is not obvious that such a challenge would succeed. Moreover, the ACPE has designed its change in policy to be phased in over ten years, at the end of which there are likely to be no five-year training programs remaining and no graduates of such programs that have not been absorbed into the profession and thus protected as if by a grandfather clause.) It would be be difficult for a court to declare that the ACPE's proposal to require six years' training for pharmacists reflects anything other than an honest opinion—a matter of "philosophy," such as impressed the court in *Marjorie Webster*. In any event, because it is impossible in most cases to identify dishonesty or an anticompetitive intent in the statement of an opinion (which is essentially what the new accrediting standard is), courts will rarely be in a position to ensure that accrediting programs serve public rather than predominantly private interests.

8. *Interest Groups and Educational Accrediting*. In the 1992 amendments to the Higher Education Act, 20 U.S.C. § 1099b (1994), Congress required that an accreditor recognized by the DOE be "separate and independent" from any "trade association or membership organization." It provided a definition of "separate and independent," however, that was almost a

contradiction in terms since it permitted governance by a self-perpetuating board dominated (by as much as 6 to 1) by members of an interested group. There was also a grandfather clause exempting from the independence requirement any professional body (including virtually all the medical profession's accrediting programs) that was recognized prior to 1991 and could demonstrate that "the existing relationship has not served to compromise the independence of its accreditation process." Application of the antitrust in ways suggested later in this section might cause some of the entities seemingly blessed by these well-lobbied provisions to be reconstituted so as to be truly "separate and independent" of special interests.

SECTION C: PRIVATE CREDENTIALING OF HEALTH CARE PERSONNEL

Certifying Health Workers

Clark C. Havighurst & Nancy M.P. King, Private Credentialing in the Health Care Field

Excerpt from Havighurst & King, Private Credentialing of Health Care Personnel: An Antitrust Perspective (pt. 1), 9 Am.J.L. & Med. 131, 138–50 (1983).

A. Physician Certification

The most extensive private personnel credentialing system anywhere is probably that maintained for certifying medical specialists. Twenty-three specialty boards, certifying physicians in carefully delineated areas of specialized practice, are recognized by the American Board of Medical Specialties (ABMS). A roughly equivalent number of physician-certifying entities exists outside the ABMS system, but these are of only limited importance. Many of the non-ABMS programs certify nonphysicians as well as physicians in specialized fields, but few certify physicians in areas that compete or overlap with specialties recognized by the ABMS. The ABMS system is so pervasive that health care professionals generally understand "board certification" to mean certification by an ABMS board.

Although virtually all physicians limit their practices to one or at most a few specialized areas, only about half are certified specialists. In the past twenty years, however, almost all new physicians have sought specialty certification, and the percentage of board-certified physicians among those who hold themselves out as specialists continued to grow—from 62 percent in 1970 to some 70 percent in 1980. The creation of the specialty of family practice in 1969 accounts for much of the growth in the percentage of physicians seeking certified specialty status, since general practitioners, who had previously provided the care that is now the province of family practice specialists, had not been viewed as specialists at all. It has been projected that, by 1990, ninety percent of all physicians will have some certification and that, by 2010, the figure will be close to one hundred percent.

In order to receive ABMS recognition—a form of accreditation—a specialty board must be sponsored by existing professional groups, such as one or more specialty societies and the appropriate scientific section of the American Medical Association (AMA). The four newest boards, each of which covers an area of practice that overlaps specialties established earlier, are also sponsored by the boards representing those related specialties. All but the three newest boards are "primary" boards, which determine their own policies and select board members from nominees designated by their sponsoring organizations. Membership on the remaining three "conjoint" boards must be approved by the sponsoring primary boards, under whose auspices they were established. The boards' activities are financed by examination fees charged to candidates for certification and in some cases by annual dues paid by diplomates (the boards' designation for certified specialists).

Because all twenty-three specialty boards are accredited by the ABMS according to its "Essentials for Approval of Examining Boards in Medical Specialties," their certification procedures are similar. Each board requires candidates to have received specialty training in an accredited program of graduate medical education and to pass a comprehensive examination developed and administered by the board. Some variation among the boards may be found, however, in the length of required preliminary and residency training and in the range and variety of their nonmandatory continuing education and recertification guidelines.

Each applicant for board certification must complete a residency program that has been approved by the Accreditation Council for Graduate Medical Education (ACGME). The ACGME, which is comprised of representatives of the AMA, the ABMS, and other concerned organizations, develops and applies accreditation standards, called Essentials, for residency programs in each specialty. The Essentials are developed in conjunction with the appropriate specialty board, are regularly modified to correspond with changes in specialty board requirements, and must be approved by the AMA Council on Medical Education. Thus, educational accreditation processes and specialty certification processes are highly interdependent and subject to a high degree of central control.

Although specialty board certification is generally considered indicative of superior technical competence, the boards and the associated specialty societies are usually careful in the claims they make, disclaiming an intent to draw invidious distinctions. Yet, because such disclaimers are not widely heard, questions may be raised concerning the validity of the information that certification conveys. Medical practice is a complex mixture of science and art, and it is not clear that the certifying bodies are capable of measuring all of the factors that determine professional competence. Some studies question whether the ability to pass the examinations offered by the boards correlates with high-quality medical practice. More seriously, there is a question whether the boards, which are controlled by incumbent members of each specialty, are wholeheartedly committed to disseminating accurate quality information. One sign of this problem is their failure to take some available quality-assurance measures. For example, few boards seriously attempt to evaluate an individual's qualifications at any time after initial certification. Although eleven boards provide for some type of periodic recertification, only four require it by issuing time-limited certificates; of those four, only one—family practice—has as yet administered a recertification exam. Only the four boards that require recertification require any continuing medical education, and the continuing education requirements that do exist, whether mandatory or voluntary, are not rigorous. Finally, recertification exams are not likely to be as challenging as those administered to new applicants; the passing rate on recertification exams has been upwards of ninety-five percent.

The value of the information conveyed by certification is further reduced by the presence, in every recognized specialty, of practitioners who were certified under some form of grandfather clause. One type of grandfather clause permits physicians who gained practical experience in the specialty before establishment of the board to become board-certified without fulfilling the requirements for new entrants into the specialty. Although this problem disappears in time as the original members of the specialty retire, another form of grandfathering continues to impair the quality of the information conveyed by certification. The boards periodically raise the requirements facing new candidates for certification without imposing corresponding new requirements on incumbent diplomates. Thus, the physicians certified in a specialty have not all met the same standards. The boards' failure to adopt mandatory recertification requirements takes on even greater significance in light of the continual upgrading of the requirements for initial certification.

The ABMS, in its capacity as accreditor of certifying boards, might be expected to act to rectify some of these problems in order to enhance the value of the information generated. However, because the ABMS consists almost entirely of representatives of the recognized boards, ABMS requirements have not offset the boards' protectiveness toward incumbent specialists. Indeed, ABMS policies generally reflect the interests of the existing boards. In particular, the ABMS has adopted the policy of recognizing only one board in each specialty and of minimizing overlap between specialties. In so doing, it refuses to recognize the possible informational value of competing certification schemes.

As a consequence of the division of the entire field of medicine into specialties, new boards have found it more and more difficult to achieve ABMS recognition. The three most recently approved boards—Allergy and Immunology, Nuclear Medicine, and Emergency Medicine—were made conjoint boards, thus allowing the pre-existing primary boards to retain control of their fields by requiring candidates for conjoint board certification to be certified or undergo training in one of the sponsoring primary specialties. Many of the boards also offer certification in various subspecialty areas, and several offer general certification in more than one area. Thus, the boards have been able to accommodate the growth of subspecialization without losing control of the originally recognized field. The boards' method of handling the proliferation of subspecialties closely resembles earlier efforts by the profession to prevent specialization from fragmenting the profession as a whole.

The dominance of established ABMS specialty boards in physician certification is further enhanced by some hospitals' refusal to employ or grant staff privileges to non-board-certified physicians. In this respect, hospitals are influenced by the Joint Commission on Accreditation of Hospitals (JCAH), which, while not requiring hospitals to make board certification a precondition to the granting of privileges, labels it "an excellent benchmark" of physician competence. Medical staffs may also exert pressure on hospitals to make certification a requirement. As a result of the dominance of the ABMS certification scheme, consumers seeking health care in a given field generally have as alternatives to board-certified specialists only uncertified but self-proclaimed specialists, a few specialists certified by non-ABMS boards, specialists certified in other fields, and the dwindling ranks of general practitioners.

Although there is little direct competition with the ABMS certification scheme, the hospital privilege system can serve as one alternative form of certification. Whether or not board certification is a factor in the granting of privileges, consumers may regard a physician's possession of admitting privileges at a particular hospital as good evidence of his or her competence. Where there is more than one hospital in a community, consumers can compare physicians on the basis of the relative prestige of the hospital or hospitals at which they have staff privileges. In addition, consumers may also rely upon a physician's membership in any of a variety of state and national specialty societies as an indication of professional distinction. Such membership is usually indicative not of specific attainments but of general professional achievement and of the approbation of one's peers. There are many specialty societies having greatly varying prestige and standards. The two most prominent are the American College of Surgeons (ACS), for certified surgical specialists, and the American College of Physicians (ACP), for specialists in internal medicine and related areas. Fellows, or full voting members of the Colleges, are permitted to indicate their status with the initials F.A.C.S. or F.A.C.P.

Although consumers and others have several sources to which they may turn for useful information concerning the abilities and qualifications of medical specialists, more sources of information would almost certainly serve them better. As Part Two of this Article shows, the medical profession's system for certifying specialists is not in fact intended to facilitate consumers' purchasing decisions but rather is a crucial tactic in a larger effort to standardize medical care and to limit the flow of information concerning differences among physicians and in medical practice. In general, the medical profession has prospered by maintaining—both in reality and, perhaps to an even greater degree, in appearance—an artificial homogeneity among practitioners. Specialty certification, though seeming to draw qualitative (horizontal) distinctions among physicians, is in fact a way of fostering both actual and apparent homogeneity. Now that nearly all

U.S. medical graduates are achieving certified status, it is clear that certification primarily draws not horizontal lines but vertical lines between specialties. Thus, certification serves principally as a professional trademark indicating that the holder is the product of a controlled educational and training process rather than as an indicator of relative quality. The absence of competing trademarks is an appropriate cause for public concern.

B. Nonphysician Certification

The credentialing process for the large number of categories of nonphysician health care personnel is more varied and on the whole less organized and integrated than the system for certifying physician specialists. There is more conflict and controversy, more competition among certifiers, and more overlap among categories of certified personnel. In contrast to medical specialty certification, credentialing of nonphysician health care personnel is seldom used to create distinctions within a licensed class. Instead, certification of nonphysician personnel tends either to contemplate the same scope of practice permitted by state licensure laws or to serve as a private alternative to exclusionary licensure.

Most nonphysician certification schemes, like the physician certification system, prescribe educational requirements and administer an examination. Although some credentialers require a candidate to receive training in programs accredited by a particular body as a prerequisite for examination, more accept completion of any of a wide range of educational programs. A few credentialers permit candidates to substitute apprentice-type training or other on-the-job experience for educational requirements. Others provide for certification upon successful completion of prescribed education without requiring a separate comprehensive examination. Although the system currently includes many diverse schemes, pressures toward greater standardization of requirements always exist. The paradigm of a tightly structured credentialing system, such as that maintained by the medical profession, holds great appeal for organizations certifying nonphysician health care personnel, and departures from it are usually viewed as problems to be solved by cooperative efforts.

The role of physicians in the certification of nonphysicians varies widely and is a source of much tension and conflict. Because physicians have plenary authority over all aspects of the practice of medicine, some organizations of nonphysician health care professionals have sought the collaboration of the AMA in establishing credentialing programs. Thus, some nonphysician certifying bodies are partially composed of, or even dominated by, physicians in related specialty fields. Other groups, however, including some certifying in the same personnel categories, are independent of physicians. For example, both the American Society of Clinical Pathologists, a physician specialty group, and the National Certifying Agency for Medical Laboratory Personnel, a nonphysician group, certify medical laboratory technicians, medical technologists, and nuclear medicine technologists.

Educational programs for the various categories of nonphysician health care personnel are generally accredited by bodies sponsored by the national association representing workers in the particular field. Some programs, however, are accredited through systems of state or regional vocational, secondary, or postsecondary institutional accreditation. Physician organizations also play an important role in accrediting nonphysician education programs, with the AMA Committee on Allied Health Education and Accreditation (CAHEA) being the most prominent accreditor in the field. CAHEA accredits educational programs offered in a wide variety of schools and health facilities for all twenty-six "allied" health occupations that have been recognized by the AMA's Council on Medical Education (CME), applying the "Essentials" developed by each occupation and approved by the CME.

In a few instances, more than one educational accreditor exists in a given field. For example, CAHEA accredits physical therapy education programs in association with the National Association of Physical Therapists and the United States Physical Therapy Association, but, in addition, the American Physical Therapy Association, which has no AMA affiliation, independently accredits such programs. CAHEA accreditation is nonetheless highly influential; many hospitals hire graduates of only those programs accredited by CAHEA and credentialing bodies frequently prefer graduates of such programs. Thus, the close connection between accreditation and certification that exists in the medical specialty credentialing system also exists in the credentialing of "allied" health care professionals.

A "second-tier" accreditor of certifiers of nonphysician health care personnel, corresponding to the ABMS in the field of physician certification, is the recently established National Commission for Health Certifying Agencies (NCHCA). This private body, which is funded through membership dues and federal grants, "sets standards for competency evaluation programs for health occupations in the United States." Currently, twenty-one health professional certifying associations and other interested groups are members of NCHCA. NCHCA's extensive standards cover the development, administration, and scoring of examinations, academic and training requirements, membership and independence of certification boards, and appeals from failures to certify. NCHCA is currently the only accreditor of bodies engaged in certifying nonphysician health care personnel. [In 1987, NCHCA became a subdivision of a new National Organization for Competency Assurance.—Eds.]

Finally, two higher-tier credentialing organizations exist to accredit accreditors of nonphysician health care professional education programs. One is the Office of Postsecondary Education in the U.S. Department of Education. The other is a private body, the Council on Postsecondary Accreditation (COPA). Unlike its public counterpart, however, COPA does not hesitate to accredit more than one accreditor in a given field. [COPA disbanded in 1993 and was succeeded by the Commission on Recognition of Postsecondary Accreditation (CORPA).—Eds.]

Among the various categories of nonphysician personnel, the independent professions such as dentistry, whose members market their services directly to consumers, frequently use self-certification in much the same way that the medical profession uses specialty certification—to control the flow of information useful in consumer choice and to standardize personnel. Occupations that are not practiced independently of physicians are also subjected to credentialing primarily to achieve standardization, which, in addition to serving the needs of would-be employers, may aid the certified practitioners themselves by minimizing competition across and within occupational boundaries. Certification may also be used to further the monopolistic objectives of a dominant profession that sponsors or otherwise controls the credentialing of a dependent personnel group. As discussion in Part Two of this Article explains, a dominant profession's control of credentialing of a subservient occupation may narrow the prospects for innovation in education and retard competitively inspired change in the delivery of services.

NOTES AND QUESTIONS ON PRIVATE CREDENTIALING

1. Consider how private credentialing differs from public credentialing (e.g., licensure). How would you characterize private credentialing programs for the purpose of analyzing their potential benefits and harms? You will shortly be invited to consider such programs from an antitrust perspective, and it is not too soon to begin distinguishing their procompetitive and anticompetitive effects.

2. What economic function does private personnel credentialing perform? Institutional accreditation of educational institutions, hospitals, managed-care organizations, and the like performs a similar function in those respective fields and is indistinguishable from personnel credentialing for most legal purposes. Likewise, industrial products are subject to a vast array of standard-setting and certification programs. See American Soc'y of Mechanical Engineers v. Hydrolevel Corp., 456 U.S. 556, 570 (1982); FTC Bureau of Consumer Protection, Standards and Certification (1983). Again the legal issues presented should not differ appreciably given the similar economic objectives being served.

3. How do privately conferred credentials differ from trademarks or trade names? Do the credentials issued by educational institutions more resemble trademarks or personnel certification?

4. Educational institutions perform a personnel certifying function and are in turn themselves certified by private accrediting organizations. Many of these latter organizations are themselves recognized through the earlier-noted program operated by the Department of Education and through the private Commission on Recognition of Postsecondary Accreditation (CORPA). What accounts for these multiple tiers of certifiers of certifiers?

5. What kinds of organizations might undertake to evaluate and certify the qualifications of individuals or the quality of institutions or products? What motives might inspire such efforts? Would some organizations be more vulnerable to legal attack than others? How does an organization like Consumers Union (publisher of *Consumer Reports*) differ from the private credentialers of health care personnel?

6. Are private credentialers of health care personnel engaged in "self-regulation"? What is "regulation" and who is entitled to engage in it? Is there another way to characterize private personnel credentialing?

7. Many credentialing programs attempt to disclaim an intent to draw invidious distinctions. In their official statements, the ABMS and the individual specialty boards do not claim that a diplomate is necessarily a better practitioner than an uncertified specialist in the field but claim nevertheless that board certification indicates either competence or excellence. A typical example of a board's disclaimers is the following:

> Certification * * * recognizes excellence in the discipline of internal medicine. * * * The ABIM does not intend either to interfere with or to restrict the professional activities of a licensed physician because the physician is not certified * * *.

American Board of Internal Medicine, Policies and Procedures (July 1997). The boards' reasons for limiting their claims probably include both the absence of hard evidence that specialty certification correlates well with good medical performance and a belief that underplaying their explicit claims may reduce their exposure to legal risks.

Recall the observation by Goode, in the selection reproduced at the beginning of chapter 3, of the reluctance of organized professions to publish rankings of their members. Do the credentialing programs described above confirm Goode's observation? Note also Goode's explanation of grandfather clauses.

8. A recent development is the creation by the American Medical Association of a new credentialing program—the American Medical Accreditation Program (AMAP)—for physicians. This program was questioned by the editor of the *New England Journal of Medicine*. Kassirer, The New Surrogates for Board Certification: What Should the Standards Be?, 337 New Eng. J. Med. 43 (1997). In response, an AMA official wrote that AMAP is not

> a "surrogate" for board certification. * * * AMAP accreditation is based not only on education and training but also on such personal characteristics as ethical behavior, involvement in a biennial self-assessment, willingness to be reviewed by peer reviewers, and participation in programs of clinical-data collection and feedback. Furthermore, the AMAP on-site review addresses the practice's safety, facilities, administrative systems, staffing, and medical records with a standardized set of review criteria. * * * AMA membership is not required * * *.
>
> Despite the breadth of AMAP accreditation and its different focus, * * * certification and recertification by a board recognized by the [ABMS] carry more weight than any other factor in qualifying a physician for AMAP accreditation.

Smoak, Letter to the Editor, 337 New Eng. J. Med. 857 (1997). One object of the program is to relieve physicians of having to submit to multiple assessments by managed-care plans with which they contract.

NOTES AND QUESTIONS ON JUDICIAL REVIEW OF MEMBERSHIP AND CREDENTIALING DECISIONS

1. A prestigious professional organization that expels or excludes a competing professional from membership or revokes or denies some similarly valuable credential (certification or some other seal of approval) is apt to be sued occasionally, either to reverse its action or to obtain damages for the harm done to the plaintiff's practice. Consider the following discussion from an Illinois case involving the plaintiff physician's rejection for membership in a professional association:

> We disagree with the plaintiff's contention that Illinois courts use the words "expulsion" and "exclusion" interchangeably. A review of the decisions concerning the expulsion or exclusion of a doctor from a private hospital's staff supports our position. Although Illinois courts will require a hospital to follow its by-laws in revoking a physician's staff privileges, they will not review the denial of an application for appointment to the medical staff.
>
> In determining whether we should permit judicial review of the denial of the plaintiff's membership application, we must weigh the importance of two values which are in conflict in this situation. On the one hand, we recognize the necessity of judicial restraint from interfering with or regulating the affairs and decisions of a private, voluntary association. However, we also find it unconscionable that a private association could deprive an individual of the right to pursue his or her profession because of a personality conflict, his or her race or religion, or, as the plaintiff suggests in his brief, testimony on behalf of plaintiffs in malpractice actions.
>
> Balancing these two interests, we hold that our courts can review the application procedures of a private association when membership in the organization is an economic necessity. We approve of [earlier opinions] which hold that a medical society cannot arbitrarily deny membership to an applicant when the society controls access to local hospital facilities and thus can deprive the applicant of his ability to practice medicine.
>
> We find, however, that the plaintiff has not alleged that membership in the American Academy of Orthopedic Surgeons is an economic necessity. Membership is not a requisite to hospital staff privileges as evidenced by the fact that the plaintiff is a member of the attending staff at seven Chicago hospitals. In addition, the plaintiff was board-certified and licensed by the State without academy membership.
>
> The plaintiff's complaint alleges that membership in the academy is a "practical necessity ... to realize maximum potential achievement and recognition in [his] specialty," language used by the California Supreme Court in [Pinsker v. Pacific Coast Soc'y of Orthodontists, 526 P.2d 253 (Cal.1974) (in bank)]. We refrain from following *Pinsker,* however, because such a holding would result in complaints for judicial review of every

> application rejection by a voluntary association since membership in most organizations results in some professional or economic benefits. * * *
>
> Although in this case we sympathize with the plaintiff's frustration with the academy's refusal to give him the courtesy of an explanation of the denial of his application, we believe the courts must refrain from interfering in the affairs of a private association absent a showing of economic necessity.

Treister v. American Acad. of Orthopeadic Surgeons, 396 N.E.2d 1225, 1231–32 (Ill.App.1979).

2. What is the source of judicial power to regulate the membership or accrediting practices of private organizations? Recall that the same question was asked with respect to hospital staff privileges in chapter 5(§C). Is there perhaps a clearer legal basis for scrutinizing an expulsion from membership or a revocation of privately conferred credentials than for regulating exclusions or denials? When, if ever, might procedural fairness or due process by required?

3. What facts should determine the reviewability of the membership, accrediting, or credentialing criteria of a private association or of their application in a particular case? In *Treister* and some other cases, courts have seemed to feel that the more power an organization has to affect an individual's livelihood, the more closely it should be supervised by courts. See also Potvin v. Metropolitan Life Ins. Co., 63 Cal.Rptr.2d 202 (Cal. App.), review granted, 941 P.2d 1121 (Cal. 1997) (surprising decision—note that it was on appeal at this writing—imposing California's especially demanding procedural and substantive due process requirements on a health insurer terminating physician from its provider network); *Pinsker*, quoted significantly in *Treister* excerpt, supra (dentist excluded from prestigious orthodontists' society for noncompliance with rule against sharing orthodonics patents with persons less qualified—i.e., against delegating orthodontics tasks to licensed dentists unqualified for society membership; court accepted society's rule but required society to reconsider application using fair procedures to ascertain whether plaintiff had complied or not); *Marjorie Webster Jr. College*, supra (denial of accreditation to proprietary school upheld in part because school could operate without accreditation; "the extent to which deference is due to the professional judgment of the association will vary both with the subject matter in issue and with the degree of harm resulting from the association's action"). Do you agree with using a "sliding scale" to determine the intensity of judicial review of the actions of private organizations? (Where, if anywhere, could the court find a legal warrant for imposing such a test?) Can you see any problem in adopting a test that puts successful, influential associations at more legal risk than others?

4. A number of jurisdictions appear willing to scrutinize to some extent the membership or credentialing decisions of private associations, the staff privilege decisions of private hospitals, or both. Excluding those cases dealing with hospital privileges (how do such cases differ?), membership, accrediting, or credentialing standards or procedural practices of private associations have actually been invalidated in only a few jurisdictions. See, e.g., *Pinsker*; *Potvin;* Falcone v. Middlesex County Med. Soc'y, 170 A.2d 791 (N.J.1961) (membership requirement of graduation from AMA-approved school invalidated); Higgins v. American Soc'y of Clinical Pathologists, 238 A.2d 665 (N.J.1968) (substantive standards); Hatley v. American Quarter Horse Ass'n, 552 F.2d 646 (5th Cir.1977) (procedures). On the proper scope of judicial authority over private organizations, compare Note, Exclusion from Private Associations, 74 Yale L.J. 1315 (1965) (advocating expansion of judicial involvement), with Note, Judicial Intervention in Admissions Decisions of Private Professional Associations, 49 U.Chi.L.Rev. 840 (1982) (criticizing trend toward greater public accountability for private groups).

5. If judicial review is deemed appropriate, what standard of review should courts apply in evaluating substantive standards adopted or applied by private entities? In *Treister*, for example, if the Academy's membership had been truly vital for the plaintiff's professional survival, could the Academy have rejected him for membership on the ground that his expert testimony appeared biased or otherwise unreliable? (Should the Academy have to prove his professional incompetence? Or should it be allowed to make unreviewable subjective judgments?) Must a private organization's rules be upheld if they have a rational basis—that is, are not arbitrary—or may the court consider whether they are truly in the public interest? Would you have upheld the society's rule in *Pinsker*, supra? Similar issues arise in antitrust analysis of cases such as these—as the following materials will show.

Antitrust Issues in Competitor–Sponsored Credentialing, etc.

NOTES AND QUESTIONS ON ANTITRUST ISSUES IN PRIVATE CREDENTIALING

1. In a 1983 report, the staff of the FTC's Bureau of Consumer Protection (not the agency's antitrust arm, it should be noted) outlined the antitrust principles applicable to industry standard-setting and certification programs as follows:

> Joint action is prohibited by the antitrust laws when it results "in restraint of trade or commerce." The restraint element is satisfied when an organization imposes or adopts a practice that interferes with the free play of market forces. * * * Evidence on the rulemaking record * * * points out the restraint on market forces that standards can cause due to reliance by buyers, government regulatory agencies, and others.

Bureau of Competition, FTC, Standards and Certification 247 (Final Staff Report 1983). At another point, the report stated, "The standard is the product of joint action and restrains trade by directing business from one competitor to another." Id. at 275. Do you agree that accrediting and credentialing programs "restrain trade" to the extent that they are influential? Recall the *Schachar* case in chapter 4(§B), where this issue first arose.

2. Is a denial of accreditation or certification a "boycott"? Is it a "concerted refusal to deal"? Do you agree with the FTC staff (id. at 249) that "standards activities are similar to some group boycotts in that the effect of a standard is to influence purchasers not to deal with producers whose products do not comply with the standard"?

3. Courts have generally not applied a per se rule in such cases. What inquiry should courts undertake under the Rule of Reason? Must the standard be supported by objective evidence of validity? Was there any such evidence supporting the standard in the *Marjorie Webster* case, supra (involving a policy of not accrediting for-profit schools)? Will most requirements be objectively verifiable? If an issue were raised concerning the ACPE's attempt to raise the educational requirements for licensure as a pharmacist (see Problem, supra), should a court attempt to judge the validity of the new accrediting requirement, increasing the training of all pharmacists to six years? Is verification of technical standards of private organizations a proper function for courts to perform? Does the first amendment have any bearing on these issues?

4. Does the following case provide satisfying answers to these questions? See generally Havighurst & Brody, Accrediting and the Sherman Act, Law & Contemp. Probs., Autumn 1994, p. 199.

Kreuzer v. American Academy of Periodontology

United States Court of Appeals, District of Columbia Circuit, 1984.
735 F.2d 1479.

■ MACKINNON, SENIOR CIRCUIT JUDGE:

This private antitrust action challenges the legality of one of the American Academy of Periodontology's ("AAP" and "Periodontists") requirements for active membership, specifically the "limited practice requirement". The plaintiff-appellant is Donald W. Kreuzer, D.M.D., a periodontist who practices in the District of Columbia. The defendant-appellees are the AAP and the American Dental Association ("ADA"). Dr. Kreuzer contends that the limited practice requirement is an unreasonable restraint of trade in violation of Section 1 of the Sherman Antitrust Act.

On motions of the Periodontists and the ADA, the District Court held that Dr. Kreuzer had failed to establish that a conspiracy existed between the Periodontists and the ADA to restrain trade and granted summary judgment in favor of the ADA. In addition, the District Court held that the limited practice requirement, tested under the rule of reason, was a reasonable restraint of trade because "there is no evidence of anticompetitive intent" and granted summary judgment in favor of the Periodontists.

Dr. Kreuzer has appealed * * *

I. Background

The dental profession is composed of general dentistry and eight dental specialties.[4] Periodontics is that recognized dental specialty concerned with the treatment of diseases of the tissues surrounding the teeth. To practice periodontics or any dental specialty, one need only be a graduate of an approved dental school and licensed as a dentist. A licensed dentist may perform any dental process. Thus, many general dentists become proficient in one or more dental specialties by virtue of continuing education or practical experience.

Dr. Kreuzer is a licensed dentist. In addition, he holds a certificate in periodontology from the graduate program at the University of Pennsylvania, an ADA accredited dental school. Dr. Kreuzer also obtained special training at the University of Pennsylvania in periodontal prosthesis.[6] Periodontal prosthesis involves the restoration and prosthetic treatment of advanced periodontal disease. Periodontal prosthesis developed as a subfield of periodontology concerned with saving teeth that might otherwise be extracted due to advanced periodontal disease. Periodontal prosthesis is not recognized by the ADA as a dental specialty.

The ADA is the most prominent national organization for dentists. Among the many activities of the ADA are promulgation of its Principles of Ethics, definition of dental specialists, accreditation of dental schools and graduate programs and recognition of specialty organizations such as the AAP. Because of its role in defining and recognizing dental specialties, the ADA also serves as a mediator and arbiter of the scope of dental specialties.

The AAP is a non-profit corporation organized "to advance the art and science of periodontology, and by its application, maintain and improve the health of the public." The AAP's principal functions are publication of the Journal of Periodontology and various consumer education materials, conduct of an annual scientific session, issuance of scholarships and grants, formation of standards for advancing training and formulation of procedures to facilitate reimbursement of practitioners by third-party payment plans. In addition, the Periodontist's association publishes an annual directory of its members.

The AAP has eight membership classifications. The "highest" degree of membership is active membership. To qualify for active membership, an applicant must meet several criteria including being "[e]thically qualified as a specialist in periodontics according to the requirements of the American Dental Association." To meet this criterion, a dentist must be educationally qualified in the specialty of periodontics according to the ADA, and *must "limit* [...] *his practice exclusively to the special areas approved by the American Dental Association"* ("the limited practice requirement"). ADA Principles of Ethics, § 18, R.E. 155 (emphasis added). The ADA's Council on Judicial Procedures, Constitution and Bylaws, whose responsi-

4. These specialties are endodontics, orthodontics, pedodontics, oral pathology, oral surgery, dental public health, prosthodontics and periodontics.

6. The graduate periodontics program at the University of Pennsylvania is a two year program. Students such as Dr. Kreuzer who also receive training in periodontal prothesis, however, follow a three year training program. Cohen Dep.Ex. 30, R.E. 133–152.

bility it is to interpret that body's Principles of Ethics, has ruled that the practice of periodontal prosthesis is not within the definition of periodontics. Therefore, a dentist who in part practices periodontal prothesis does not limit his practice to periodontics as required by the AAP and is ineligible for active membership in the AAP.[7]

All members of the AAP are entitled to certain benefits. Active members, however, receive additional benefits. The economic value of these additional benefits has been a contested issue in this case.

An active member is entitled to the additional benefits of the right to vote, hold office, and serve on standing committees in the AAP. These rights make possible opportunities for professional development which are likely to enhance a professional reputation and lead to a higher earning capacity. In addition, active members are listed in the AAP membership directory as specialists. AAP members are listed in the directory alphabetically and by geographic region. Alongside each name appears a numerical code and a letter or letters. The numerical code denotes the membership category. Active members are designated by the code "00", while associate members are designated by the code "10". The ADA takes no part in the publication of the directory.

The membership directory is used frequently to make referrals and generally persons who do not have a "00" code are automatically excluded from consideration. This inability of dentists who *in part* practice periodontics to become active members and to obtain referrals allegedly has a particularly adverse impact on Dr. Kreuzer. The District Court noted that because of "the unusually transient nature of the Washington metropolitan population, referral business is of particular importance to those who practice here as does plaintiff."

Dr. Kreuzer applied for active membership in the AAP in 1975. * * * Two active members who practice in the District of Columbia challenged Dr. Kreuzer's application on the grounds that he did not limit his practice to periodontics. After receipt of these complaints and further inquiry, the Membership Committee determined that Dr. Kreuzer did not limit his practice and therefore his name was not recommended to the 1975 General Assembly for active membership.

Dr. Kreuzer objected to this decision and was granted a special hearing before the Membership Committee prior to the 1976 General Assembly meeting. The Membership Committee decided after the hearing to recommend Dr. Kreuzer to the General Assembly for active membership. The 1976 General Assembly, however, voted to refer the issue of those periodontists who also practice periodontal prosthesis to a special task force. Largely because the General Assembly had made this determination to defer

7. Under the Bylaws of the AAP, such a dentist who does not exclusively practice periodontics may join the AAP as an associate member. Associate members are granted all privileges of active membership except the right to vote, to make nominations, and to hold office in the AAP. In addition, an associate member is listed in a different manner than an active member in the membership directory. As set forth infra, this is a significant difference.

further consideration of the role of those practicing periodontal prosthesis, it voted to deny Dr. Kreuzer active membership.

Dr. Kreuzer requested his application remain pending. Before the special task force could present its recommendations on periodontal prosthesis to the 1977 General Assembly this suit was initiated.[10] No further action has been taken on Dr. Kreuzer's membership application. Therefore, his application may technically still be pending.

After what the District Court referred to as "mountainous discovery", * * * the District Court granted the Periodontists' motion [for summary judgment]. Because the AAP's limited practice requirement had a "non-commercial purpose" and because the AAP is a professional organization, the District Court held that the limited practice requirement was not *per se* illegal, but rather should be tested under a rule of reason analysis. In conducting its rule of reason analysis, the District Court concluded that "there is no evidence of anticompetitive intent—only a philosophical difference of opinion...."

* * *

Appellant argues that the limited practice requirement constitutes a group boycott. Appellant draws our attention to the Supreme Court's recent decision in Arizona v. Maricopa County Medical Society, 457 U.S. 332 (1982), which, it is asserted, requires application of a *per se* rule to conduct of professionals which would be illegal *per se* for nonprofessionals, unless the conduct at issue is premised on ethical norms which would enhance the quality of the professional service. Appellant concludes that because there was no proof that the limited practice requirement was premised on ethical considerations and because group boycotts are treated as *per se* illegal for nonprofessionals the District Court erred in not finding the limited practice requirement *per se* illegal.

* * *

The Periodontists argue that the District Court did not err in refusing to rule the limited practice requirement *per se* illegal. The AAP seems to contend that the District Court's finding that the limited practice requirement was noncommercial was the equivalent of finding that it was premised on public service. Therefore, under *Maricopa,* the limited practice requirement should be tested under the rule of reason because a professional organization is involved. The United States, in an *amicus curiae* brief, also forcefully argues that *per se* treatment is not the correct approach in this case. The United States asserts that a professional organization is the group best suited to judge the competence of its members to hold themselves out to the public as specialists. It is possible then that membership rules such as the limited practice requirement could serve to inform the public and serve a procompetitive function. Thus, this procompetitive potential should be weighed against any alleged anticompetitive potential,

10. The task force recommended retention of the limited practice requirement. This was accepted by the 1978 General Assembly.

argues the United States. This weighing process is, of course, only possible under the rule of reason.

* * * To outlaw all activity which might be labelled a group boycott is dangerous in that it might discourage certain reasonable concerted activity.

In this case the attributes of *per se* illegality discernible in *Klor's* and *Fashion Originators' Guild* are not present. The AAP is a membership organization enforcing its membership rules. There is no clear showing of a purpose to exclude competitors. Numerous cases in the context of organized sports indicate that courts should be hesitant to fasten tags such as "group boycott" and "*per se*" in order to preclude inquiry into the business necessity occasioned by particular rules or practices. Because sanctioning or membership organizations do not actually compete with the individual member who is affected by a questioned practice, *per se* treatment is inadvisable. This is also true of professional organizations. When a conspiracy of this sort is alleged in the context of one of the learned professions, the nature and extent of its anticompetitive effect are often too uncertain to be amenable to *per se* treatment. See Wilk v. American Medical Association, 719 F.2d 207 (7th Cir.1983). Nor is this conclusion undercut by *Maricopa*. Under *Maricopa* an agreement to fix prices will not escape *per se* treatment simply because it is entered into by professionals and accompanied by unsupported ethical protestations. In the context of an alleged group boycott, however, if a serious argument is made that the questioned practice amounts to a public service, sufficient questions of competitive effect are raised to allow release from *per se* treatment. Therefore, we also affirm this aspect of the District Court decision.

* * *

The District Court found that the limited practice requirement passed muster under the rule of reason. The District Court decision, however, premised this solely on the fact that it found no anticompetitive *intent* in the Periodontist's adoption of a limited practice requirement. The District Court seems to have felt that where a defendant to a Section 1 claim presents a justification for a questioned practice the absence of anticompetitive intent is determinative. This is an erroneous application of the rule of reason and necessitates reversal of the District Court decision pertaining to this aspect of the case.

* * *

The significance of the District Court's exclusive reliance on the AAP's lack of anticompetitive intent is easily lost in the court's silence on the potential anticompetitive effect of the limited practice requirement. Once the potential for anticompetitive impact that the limited practice requirement poses is set forth, the error of the District Court becomes clear. A first possible effect of the rule is to prevent periodontists who wish to keep the advantages of active membership in the AAP from competing with general dentists. An active member of the AAP may not engage in general dentistry under the limited practice requirement. A second possible effect is to prevent periodontists who do decide to compete with general dentists from fully competing with other periodontists who are active members. The evidence indicates that only active AAP members are referred to prospective patients thus eliminating non-AAP periodontists from this lucrative referral business. Finally, the consumer may be disadvantaged in two ways. The consumer of periodontal services is allegedly never referred to periodontists who are not active members. This artificially limits the number of periodontists available to the consumer with a corresponding increase in the market price for periodontal services. Likewise, the consumer cannot go to a periodontist who is an active member of the AAP for his restorative dental needs. This results in additional cost and inconvenience to the patient with complicated dental needs who is deprived of the cost efficiencies which would otherwise be generated by one stop dental service.

On the other side of the balance, however, is the issue of service to the public—a dentist who devotes his *entire* working hours to practice as a periodontist, undoubtedly in the great majority of cases, will develop into a better and more skillful periodontist than a dentist who practices generally, or a dentist who has some basic skill as a periodontist but does not devote his entire practice to that specialty. In this instance, the AAP has asserted that its concerted refusal to deal with Dr. Kreuzer (in the form of the limited practice requirement) is premised not on an anticompetitive intent to exclude Dr. Kreuzer from the marketplace. Rather, the AAP asserts that this particular group boycott serves to advance a desirable social goal unrelated to the group's economic interests. Specifically, the AAP argues that the limited practice requirement allows the AAP to remain under the control of dentists who devote themselves exclusively to the practices of periodontics. This is the only way, the AAP contends, to insure that the AAP's mission to advance the art and science of periodontology and to educate the public about periodontal disease is not diluted. In short, the AAP argues that the limited practice requirement improves the quality of care of periodontal patients. Other courts have labelled such justifications for group boycotts the "patient care motive". Wilk v. American Medical Association, 719 F.2d 207, 226 (7th Cir.1983).

The leading case in this circuit demonstrating application of the rule of reason analysis to a professional association's justification of a group boycott under a patient care motive remains American Medical Association v. United States, 130 F.2d 233 (D.C.Cir.1942), aff'd, 317 U.S. 519 (1943). In that case the Medical Society of the District of Columbia barred from use of area hospitals two former members expelled from the society for participation in a group prepaid medical practice. The society argued that the exclusion was a matter of ethical concern over patient care. This court held that even if that were true, because the conduct affected doctor income more than patient care it was illegal. In that instance, however, the court viewed little rational nexus between the professional rule and public protection. Where the rational nexus between the professional rule and public protection is much closer, courts are more willing to uphold self-regulation enforced by a group boycott. See United States v. Oregon State Medical Society, 343 U.S. 326, 336 (1952). From this we can set the following standard for application of a rule of reason analysis to questioned conduct of professional associations justified under a patient care motive. When the economic self-interest of the boycotting group and its proffered justifications merge the rule of reason will seldom be satisfied. When, however, the justification for the boycott is closely related to a lawful purpose the rule of reason will generally be satisfied.

In the District Court, the Periodontists asserted that the limited practice requirement had a procompetitive effect and worked to increase the quality of patient care. The AAP now makes the same argument to this court. The District Court, however, made no such finding. Accordingly, we are constrained in making such a finding in the first instance. Moreover, even if evidence existed in the record to support the asserted justification that the limited practice requirement improved the quality of patient care, it must be shown that the means chosen to achieve that end are the least restrictive available. Silver v. New York Stock Exchange, 373 U.S. 341 (1963). Here appellant has suggested a number of plausible less restrictive alternatives to the limited practice requirement such as a minimum number of hours per week devoted to the practice of periodontics. Impractical as such suggestion might appear at first blush, because the AAP has failed to demonstrate that the limited practice requirement is the least restrictive method available to achieve the asserted goal it is, at this stage of the proceeding, an insufficient justification for a practice that in other respects has an anticompetitive potential—albeit minimal.

* * *

III. Conclusion

Finally, we wish to make clear in the strongest possible terms that the antitrust laws do not bar the formation of associations with membership limited to classes of similarly situated persons and dedicated to the joint pursuit of their common interests. It is only in that rare instance when such membership limitations have the effect of unreasonably restraining trade that the concerns of the antitrust laws are triggered. In this particular instance, one cannot help but feel that absent publication of the AAP Membership Directory as a referral guide, there would have been no concern of an antitrust violation. We hope, however, that the wrong lesson will not be drawn from this decision. This decision should not be viewed as raising any new barriers to the formation or operation of professional associations. Rather, this decision should only serve to caution such organizations to be aware that a practice intended to benefit the public may have a collateral adverse effect on competition. If it does, then such a practice must be the least restrictive means of achieving the desired goal and the public benefit rendered must outweigh the adverse effect on competition. Otherwise, this court reiterates its strong support for professional associations dedicated to furthering the public good, such as the AAP.

Affirmed in part, reversed in part and remanded for action consistent with this opinion.

FURTHER NOTES AND QUESTIONS ON ANTITRUST ISSUES

1. The foregoing is typical of many antitrust opinions that characterize the actions of a single competitor-sponsored entity as a "group boycott" or "concerted refusal to deal." It is also typical, however, in refusing to apply to such actions the per se rule ordinarily applicable to true or classic boycotts. Obviously, the actions of such entities must always be viewed in the context of the larger joint undertaking. The *Kreuzer* opinion is offered here more for its facts than as a model of legal analysis. For another interesting set of facts, see Koefoot v. American College of Surgeons, 652 F.Supp. 882 (N.D.Ill.1986) (surgeon operating in rural hospitals left patients under care of general practitioners, thereby violating College's rule against "itinerant surgery").

2. Did the AAP members in *Kreuzer* restrain trade? How? By excluding Kreuzer? (Are the antitrust laws designed to protect competitors against unfair treatment?) By agreeing to limit their practice to periodontics as they define it? If the AAP rule restrained trade at all, was it a valid restraint? Or was it arguably ancillary to the creation of the AAP as a specialty society furthering several procompetitive objectives? Did the directory and its coding system harm competition or help it? How would the court answer these questions?

3. Did the AAP make the best available defense? The limited-practice rule and the directory may be interpreted as an effort to differentiate member specialists from other dentists and to attract business away from competitors, including Kreuzer. Is there anything illegal about that purpose? Was the AAP on firmer ground in proclaiming that its purpose was to protect patients and promote quality dentistry? Can a worthy purpose save an anticompetitive practice? Is it necessary to say so in order to save the AAP and its rule? A selective directory similar to the one in *Kreuzer* was upheld in Machovec v. Council for the National Register of Health Service Providers in Psychology, Inc., 616 F.Supp. 258 (E.D.Va.1985) (directory affords "access to accurate information which may form the basis of independent decision making in the marketplace").

4. Do you agree with the *Kreuzer* court that a private organization should be required to adopt an available less restrictive standard if it can achieve essentially the same quality objective? Would a stringent requirement of this kind chill standard setting? Is the less-restrictive-alternative requirement an excuse for closely regulating standard-setting, credentialing, and accrediting programs? The FTC staff report on standards and certification, supra, appears to say that if a better standard—that is, one technically sounder or less arbitrarily exclusionary—is available, it must be adopted. Do you agree?

5. Note how the District Court characterized the dispute in *Kreuzer*—as "only a philosophical difference of opinion." In what other case did the court find a professional organization free to express its own philosophy to the detriment of an applicant for its official recognition? In Sherman College of Straight Chiropractic v. United States Comm'r of Educ., 493

F.Supp. 976 (D.D.C.1980), the court rejected the plaintiff's challenge to the Commissioner's recognition of a chiropractic accrediting body that had refused to accredit plaintiff for philosophic reasons. The court explained, "Plaintiffs themselves emphasize their distinct view of the chiropractic profession. The proper channel for their efforts is to establish their own chiropractic accrediting agency and secure federal recognition for it." Id. at 980. Do these cases suggest that these issues have a first-amendment dimension? Is the AAP's rule properly viewed as the expression of an opinion? If so, is the AAP entitled to constitutional protection against attack under the Sherman Act? Or is there any conflict between free-speech guarantees and antitrust policy? Should the Sherman Act be construed not to regulate the expression of such opinions?

6. There is, of course, little first amendment protection for false and deceptive advertising. Can the antitrust laws be used to control false and deceptive credentialing? Was the AAP rule false and deceptive? Give an example of a false and deceptive credentialing scheme. The FTC has challenged several standardless seal-of-approval programs, and standards not even arguably related to the applicant's competence would also seem subject to attack. See, e.g., Higgins v. American Soc'y of Clinical Pathologists, 51 N.J. 191, 238 A.2d 665 (1968) (physician organization not permitted, under common law, to refuse credential because applicant worked in lab not supervised by an M.D.); Bogus v. American Speech & Hearing Ass'n, 582 F.2d 277 (3d Cir.1978) (questioning requirement making issuance of credential contingent on paying substantial membership dues). Would a rational basis test be appropriate, making competitor groups free within a wide margin to express their opinions on technical subjects—that is, to set their own standards as long as they do not enforce them by illegal boycotts? Most common-law and antitrust cases do indeed give only such limited scrutiny to private credentialing and accrediting standards. Consider each of the cases in this section to see what test was employed and whether a sensible result was reached.

7. How would you answer the argument that, even though the standards of the AAP are not enforced (membership is voluntary), their effect is powerful? If the world accepts the AAP's directory and coding system and prefers those periodontists with a "00" classification, isn't that just the market speaking? Where did Judge Bazelon tell Marjorie Webster and other proprietary schools to seek a remedy for their alleged mistreatment? Should the court have told Dr. Kreuzer the same thing?

8. Do you have a lingering concern about the AAP's limited-practice rule? Can you identify the ultimate source of your concern in the facts given? Can the problem you sense—not just harm to Kreuzer, but the stifling effect of a rule that, de facto, binds nearly all periodontists—be addressed without undertaking to regulate the membership or credentialing standards set by all influential private organizations? Isn't your concern related more to the dominant influence wielded by the AAP than to the rule itself? What is the source of that influence? Is the American Dental Association implicated? What is the arrangement between the ADA, the AAP, and other dental specialties? Does the law have anything to say about these arrangements? Antitrust law (section 2 of the Sherman Act) prohibits monopolization but not monopoly itself. Is there a monopoly here—that is, a single supplier? Even if the provision of periodontists' services is not monopolized, is there another monopoly and any conduct that could be called "monopolizing"? Would consumers benefit if this monopoly and the agreements that sustain it could be broken up?

9. Consider the arrangements among the medical specialties recounted in the Havighurst–King excerpt? Do the antitrust laws have any bearing on the delineation of specialties or the relationships fostered by the ABMS among the specialty boards? Although the specialties do not overlap very much, conflict has emerged between plastic surgeons and otolaryngologists over their respective ability to perform facial plastic surgery, especially on the nose. A libel verdict for derogating the latter's surgical skills was returned against a state society of plastic surgeons in a Georgia case. Anderson v. Georgia Soc'y of Plastic Surgeons, reported in Health L.Dig. Feb. 1987, at 61 (Fulton County Super.Ct., Ga.1986). (Note that falsely impugning the abilities of a professional is usually regarded as libel per se. Should it be?) For an earlier indication that the FTC might attempt to referee the plastic surgeons/otolaryngologists dispute, see Randall, The FTC and the Plastic Surgeons, 299 New Eng.J.Med. 1464 (1978).

10. Consider the following reply by Havighurst and King, 10 Am.J.L. & Med. 459 (1985), to a response to their article from which the earlier excerpt was taken:

> The response by James W. Rankin and Bruce A. Hubbard[1] (R & H) to our article, Private Credentialing of Health Care Personnel, challenges our "hypothetical academic theories" and our suggestion that the antitrust laws should be applied to prohibit intraprofessional agreements that have the net effect of eliminating sustainable competition in the production of information and opinion concerning the quality or qualifications of various types of health care providers. They aver that the existing voluntary system for accrediting and credentialing has "worked well, stood the test of time and rendered substantial benefits to the health care profession and the public at large." (p. 200). We, of course, have no doubt that the medical profession has benefitted from this system. Our concern is that some of the benefits to the profession have been derived at the expense of the general public, resulting from artificial suppression of competition and diversity in the production of information useful to consumers in purchasing health services. Although we do not disagree with R & H that individual physicians active in the accrediting and credentialing effort sincerely believe that they are working for the public good, it is not necessary to impugn anyone's sincerity in order to believe that self-interest frequently shapes conviction and action. We would also observe that, as R & H have noted (p. 193), antitrust law turns only on effects on competition, not on good

1. Rankin & Hubbard, Private Credentialing of Health Care Personnel: A Pragmatic Response to Academic Theory, 10 Am.J.L. & Med. 189 (1984).

intentions—or even, for that matter, on proof of what is in some ultimate sense in the public's best interest.

* * *

It is clear that R & H disagree with our sense that an unencumbered market for information and opinion, policed by the antitrust laws, would serve consumers well. Although they call our preference for competition and diversity in the production of information and opinion "peculiar" (p. 190), we would have thought that the idea of letting citizens decide for themselves the correctness of several competing views could not be so characterized in a nation that has long fostered competition in the marketplace of ideas as well as in economic markets. Indeed, Americans generally disapprove of regimes in which a dominant elite works out its differences internally, promulgates a "party line," and frowns on taking matters "to the people." The first amendment tradition, which distinguishes the United States from such regimes, strongly suggests the importance of diversity in information sources. The diversity we seek is not "artificial," as R & H state, but is the natural state of a market freed of artificial restraints imposed by those who agree not to disagree publicly.

We are not persuaded that one-party rule has a place in medicine. We are impressed instead that the history of science is replete with examples of scientific establishments which defended, sometimes viciously, apparently objective theories only to have those theories subsequently found to be invalid as a result of the work of unconventional outsiders. These lessons seem relevant to the attempt by R & H to demonstrate that "unitary"—that is, monopolistic—accrediting and credentialing systems protect the public and are therefore preferable to a market in which conflicting opinions are aired for consumers' benefit. In our view, the search for the one system that is objectively "best" obscures the existence of the nonobjective factors that are hidden within *any* concept of the best. Moreover, forcing consumers to rely on a single authoritative source of guidance reduces their opportunity to choose alternatives that might espouse values not highly regarded by the dominant system or that might simply be less costly. (Although we are impressed by the threat of ideological monopoly in medical care, we did not mean to imply that professional control of information and opinion does not also have important economic consequences.)

To us, the most interesting legal issue, on which R & H shed no new light, is whether information and opinion produced by competitors in the form of accreditation or certification are articles of "trade or commerce" whose production and dissemination may be illegally restrained. R & H's assertion that this is not commercial activity is only that—an assertion. Production of information in this form is supported not by charitable gifts but by fees and dues paid by those who benefit in the marketplace from the possession of credentials. Consumers also value the information produced and would undoubtedly pay for it were it not for the market failure that makes it impossible for producers of a public good to collect from those who benefit from it. We have already observed how fundamental values embedded in the first amendment (including the [protection now accorded to] commercial speech) and elsewhere in American culture strongly support the desirability of a multiplicity of information sources. We believe that it would be highly desirable and easily within traditional antitrust notions to focus antitrust attention on intraprofessional agreements that affect the supply of commercially valuable information.

Some such agreements are clearly procompetitive, in that they permit the production of information and opinion that would otherwise not be available. Part One of our article was a vigorous defense of competitor collaboration to create accrediting and credentialing programs. Although R & H wish we had stopped there, we did not. Instead, we proceeded to ask whether the scale and sponsorship of some such intraprofessional efforts might cause them to have, on balance, an anticompetitive effect, restricting the diversity of views available to consumers. We found, for example, that the 23 specialty boards recognized by the American Board of Medical Specialties have agreed to divide the market—not the market for physician services, as R & H imply, but the market for information itself. By mutually agreeing on the precise definition and limits of each specialty, the ABMS boards have effectively agreed that each will publish only a certain type of information not produced by the others, thus ensuring that the public will hear only one authoritative opinion as to who is competent to provide each professional service. Although R & H are correct that competition between different types of specialists is not totally suppressed, market-division agreements are normally per se violations, so that there should be no need for proof of the specific adverse effects of this collaboration—not that it would be impossible to show any.

* * *

We welcome further discussion of these issues, not only because the legal stakes are high but also because it is important to understand the function of information in health care markets and the precise role of professional organizations in informing consumers.

11. *The ACPE Problem Revisited.* Does the foregoing discussion suggest a possible way of approaching the ACPE's attempt, through educational accrediting standards, to dictate new educational requirements for licensing pharmacists? What is the arguable significance of the fact that the ACPE is made up of representatives of the American Pharmaceutical Association (comprised of practicing pharmacists), the American Association of Colleges of Pharmacy, and the National Association of Boards of Pharmacy? Does antitrust law provide a possible warrant for requiring the ACPE to expand its membership to include pharmaceutical manufacturers, chain drug stores, organized health plans, pharmacy benefit managers, and consumer groups?

12. *Competing Accreditors?* If joint ventures in accrediting were broken up, would there be any accrediting at all?

Some might fear that breaking up an accrediting joint venture would undermine the ability of a successor accreditor to support a costly program, and any resulting loss in the quality of accrediting might be urged as a basis for permitting the more broadly based effort. Consumers might be better served, however, by sacrificing some economies of scale that permit more rigorous accrediting in return for greater diversity of ideas about

> what constitutes quality in the accredited field. In any event, changing the sponsorship of an accrediting program would not, in itself, affect the accreditor's ability to realize scale economies or even to operate as a natural monopoly.

Havighurst & Brody, Accrediting and the Sherman Act, Law & Contemp. Probs., Autumn 1994, p. 199, 239–40 n.138. In any event, there are a several fields (law schools and physical therapy training, for example) where multiple accreditors having different standards satisfactorily co-exist. Competing accreditors have recently been recognized by the Health Care Financing Administration in the home health field. See 58 Fed. Reg. 35007 (June 30, 1993) (recognition of Joint Commission on Accreditation of Healthcare Organizations); 57 Fed. Reg. 22773 (May 29, 1992) (recognizing Community Health Accreditation Program of the National League for Nursing). For extensive consideration of the role of accrediting in public programs, especially health care and education, see Symposium, Private Accreditation in the Regulatory State, Law & Contemp. Probs., Autumn 1994.

PROBLEM

You are an attorney in the office of the state Attorney General and have been asked to render an opinion on a proposal by the State Board of Dental Examiners (BDE). Acting under its statutory power to prevent "false, misleading, or deceptive advertising" by licensed dentists, the BDE has proposed to issue the following regulation:

> No dentist ... may claim in any announcement or advertisement in any form to "specialize," or to be a "specialist," in a particular branch of dentistry unless he is a diplomate in good standing of the certifying board in that particular specialty that is recognized by the American Dental Association (ADA), *provided* that a dentist ... may declare, if it be the fact, that his practice is limited or confined to a particular specialty field if he also states that he is not certified by an ADA-approved body as a specialist in that field.

Unlike some states (e.g., Kentucky and Missouri), the state makes no provision for licensing dental specialists separately from general practitioners. Many dentists specialize in particular fields but are not certified therein for a variety of reasons, including their election not to seek the formal training required or their entry into active practice before certification became available. A study of the yellow pages of phone books throughout the state reveals that 12% of the dentists listed under various specialty headings are not certified in the field. Cf. Reade & Ratzan, Yellow Professionalism: Advertising by Physicians in the Yellow Pages, 316 New Eng. J.Med. 1315 (1987).

In 1965, the ADA changed its ethical code so that dentists entering into specialty practice without formal certification could no longer ethically claim to limit their practice to a particular field. That provision was dropped in 1979 as a result of a consent decree entered into with the FTC.

Be prepared to discuss the proposed regulation, addressing both the legal and policy issues. See, e.g., Parker v. Commonwealth of Kentucky, 818 F.2d 504 (6th Cir.1987); Parmley v. Missouri Dental Bd., 719 S.W.2d 745 (Mo.1986).

SECTION D: PUBLIC AND PRIVATE OVERSIGHT OF INSTITUTIONAL PROVIDERS

Private Accreditation

NOTES AND QUESTIONS ON INSTITUTIONAL ACCREDITING AND THE JCAHO

1. *Standard Setting and Accrediting in Policy and Antitrust Perspective.* The materials in the previous section concerning the accreditation of educational institutions and the private credentialing of health care personnel provide a valuable introduction to the legal and policy issues raised by private accrediting of health care institutions. Like other voluntary programs for setting standards for goods or services and for certifying compliance with such standards, private accreditation involves (or should involve) nothing more than the formal expression of a private organization's authoritative opinion concerning the quality and acceptability—under objective standards fairly applied—of the services rendered by certain institutional providers. The presumptive purpose of accrediting is to provide quality information and reassurance to consumers and other users of an industry's products or services. But private accrediting is commonly sponsored by special interests in the affected field, meaning that its goals may be less consumer-oriented than its sponsors would have policymakers and the public believe. One possible objective—apparent in the managed-care field in recent years (see chapter 8(§C))—is the political one of assuaging public concerns that might lead government to regulate the field or to regulate it more aggressively; where government already has a regulatory presence, a private group may hope that the regulators will respect its standards and seal of approval instead of exercising independent prescriptive authority.

Accrediting is commonly thought of as a form of industry self-regulation. Unlike public licensure, however, it is not exclusionary, and, standing alone, it lacks the direct sanctions that only government can lawfully impose. (Recall the law on collective sanctions and boycotts from chapter 4(§B).) Indeed, whatever effects accreditation (or the lack of it) may have can be said to flow from independent choices by those who elect to rely on it, not from the collective action of the accreditors themselves. Of course, one might think it naive to draw a sharp distinction between coercive regulation and the publication of information and opinion, since the latter may have equally devastating effects on individual competitors and their ability to make independent choices about the services they provide. What do you think? This conceptual issue is important, since the distinction drawn bears not only on the public policy rationale for encouraging private accrediting but also on the applicability of antitrust law to this kind of concerted action.

Recall the *Schachar* case reproduced in chapter 4(§B) (involving a professional association's disapproval of radial keratotomy). In *Schachar*, Judge Easterbrook stated, "There can be no restraint of trade without a restraint," and went on to hold that merely expressing an opinion, however influential, did not "restrain trade." The Supreme Court has observed, however, in a case involving certification of only one kind of electrical conduit, that "agreement on a product standard is, after all, implicitly an agreement not to manufacture, distribute, or purchase certain types of products." Allied Tube & Conduit Corp. v. Indian Head, 486 U.S. 492, 500 (1988). To be sure, the Supreme Court is probably right that there is enough concerted action in these cases to warrant antitrust scrutiny. But, as you are aware from your earlier consideration of antitrust principles, competitors are permitted to collaborate for a procompetitive purpose as long as they employ means that are no more dangerous to competition than is necessary to accomplish their legitimate objectives. Thus, it would seem that, as long as collaborators in accrediting respect the "less-restrictive-alternative" requirement—by avoiding *explicit* anticompetitive agreements and by disclaiming any intention to curb independent action—, any remaining hazard to competition should probably be viewed, under the *Allied Tube* dictum, as a lawful ancillary restraint.

In any event, private accrediting is not unlawful on its face even when it disables lawful competitors in the marketplace, and it is therefore a powerful tool by which private interests can dictate standards for an entire industry. Certainly private accrediting can be put to anticompetitive uses, either in targeting and disadvantaging specific competitors or in setting standards based on industry preferences rather than overall consumer welfare. But accrediting can also be an efficient, procompetitive response to the information problems that consumers and others inevitably encounter in shopping for complex services. Information and opinion concerning commercial goods and services are, after all, classic examples of so-called "public goods" because they are not consumed when they are used; because a producer of information cannot easily prevent its use by those who have not paid for it, there is little incentive for unsubsidized entrepreneurs to produce it at all. It is for these reasons that commercial information is underproduced and that most of it, including advertising as well as private accreditation, originates from firms or industry groups that have an economic or ideological interest in influencing consumers in a certain way. Although information from such sources has social value, consumers can easily be misled, especially if they lack alternative sources of authoritative information. Questions in the preceding section addressed the role of courts in policing possible abuses of the power that accreditors inevitably possess.

2. *The Joint Commission*. Recall the brief description of the Joint Commission on Accreditation of Healthcare Organizations (JCAHO) in chapter 5(§A), particularly its domination by physician interests (although representatives of organized medicine no longer constitute a majority of voting members).

> Although the [JCAHO's] hospital accreditation program is its oldest and best known program, the JCAHO enjoys similar authority over ambulatory care, long-term care, and psychiatric facilities, as well as home care programs. It has recently established an accreditation program for health care networks. In addition, the JCAHO produces a variety of publications and offers technical assistance and consulting services to health care facilities.
>
> Hospitals accredited by the JCAHO are surveyed at least once every three years. At minimum, a survey team includes a hospital administrator, a physician, and a nurse. The survey generally lasts three days. At the conclusion of the survey, the surveyors score each of hundreds of applicable standards on a scale from one to five. These scores are then aggregated using complex algorithms to reach an accreditation decision. While approximately one-quarter of surveyed hospitals receive full accreditation, most receive accreditation with contingencies that must be resolved through further reports or inspections. Less than one percent of the hospitals surveyed are denied accreditation.
>
> The JCAHO updates its accreditation standards regularly, based on input from its staff, advisory committees, and outside experts. Traditionally, JCAHO accreditation standards focused on the structural inputs (policies, equipment, staffing) found within hospitals. [Since the late 1980s], the Commission has aggressively pursued its Agenda for Change, which shifts its focus toward an emphasis on processes and outcomes. Under the Agenda for Change, the JCAHO is revising its accreditation manuals to streamline its standards, redirect its standards from their current focus on departmental organization to a focus on institutional functions or processes, stress the interdisciplinary task of assessing and improving quality, increase the flexibility afforded providers in complying with the standards, and emphasize performance. It is also developing outcome indicators that will allow hospitals to monitor trends and patterns of care with the aim of improving patient care. Finally, it is concurrently revising its survey process to make it more timely, consistent, and useful to accredited institutions.

Jost, Medicare and the Joint Commission on Accreditation of Healthcare Organizations, Law & Contemp. Probs., Autumn 1994, p. 15, 16–17.

As noted by Jost, the JCAHO had long emphasized inputs and processes rather than outcomes in evaluating hospitals. (Recall and evaluate in this connection the JCAHO standards reproduced in chapter 5(§A).) Although the JCAHO began in the 1980s to explore the possibility of requiring outcome-oriented hospital quality review programs, it has not found it easy to measure quality accurately or in ways that hospitals would tolerate. See Schroeder, Outcome Assessment 70 Years Later: Are We Ready?, 316 New Eng.J.Med. 160 (1987) ("The success of the new [JCAHO] policy of using outcome data for hospital accreditation will ultimately depend on whether the current method of outcome assessment is sufficiently specific, sensitive, and feasible to warrant its widespread application."). Its effort, however, eventually linked up with enthusiasm for so-called "continuous quality improvement," resulting in what the JCAHO now calls its "ORYX" initiative. Under this program, a hospital's accreditation will be based on whether it has installed a number of so-called "performance measurement systems" that provide useful outcomes information on a substantial fraction of its patients. Although difficult to implement and controversial because of the burdens they impose on hospitals, these new accrediting methods appear to represent a significant new departure by the JCAHO. Query, however, whether the JCAHO is any less beholden today than previously to the interest groups that control it.

3. *The Antitrust Status of the JCAHO*. In 1977, the State of Ohio charged the Joint Commission with antitrust violations for maintaining an accrediting standard that required hospitals to limit the admitting privileges of clinical psychologists in such a way as to preclude the psychologists from practicing their profession to the full extent of their state-conferred licenses. The state further alleged that the accreditation standards in question reflected the domination of the Joint Commission by physicians interested in protecting their prerogatives within hospitals against incursions by nonphysician health care professionals. The case was eventually mooted by a change in the challenged standard. Under the antitrust principles explored in the previous section, however, how strong was the state's case? How should an antitrust court have approached the issues?

Do you see any legal basis for questioning the sponsorship of the JCAHO? Is it desirable to have the four most prominent provider organizations (the AMA, the AHA, the American College of Physicians, and the American College of Surgeons) combining to speak with one voice on questions of hospital quality? Would these organizations be likely to share the same opinion on precisely what it takes to operate a good hospital? Is it desirable that they resolve their differences so that they can express a single authoritative opinion? Can you argue that the JCAHO restrains trade? in what "market"? See Havighurst & Brody, Accrediting and the Sherman Act, Law & Contemp. Probs., Autumn 1994, p. 199, 230–41; Havighurst & King, Private Credentialing of Health Care Personnel: An Antitrust Perspective (Part Two), 9 Am. J.L. & Med. 264, 314–25 (1983).

4. *Private Accrediting and Medicare*. Hospitals and other institutional providers seeking to participate in the Medicare and Medicaid programs are required by law to meet the federal government's "conditions of participation." See, e.g., 42 C.F.R. pt. 482 (1997) (Medicare/Medicaid Conditions of Participation for Hospitals). See also 62 Fed. Reg. 66726 (Dec. 19, 1997) (HCFA's proposed new conditions of participation for hospitals, purporting to focus on patient care and outcomes—specifically on the maintenance of systems to monitor and improve quality—rather than, as previously, on inputs, process, and structural features of the institution). Technically, HCFA's requirements, although highly detailed, are not true regulatory standards but only the minimum requirements that providers must meet if

they want to do business with the government. But, obviously, a hospital is unlikely to stay in business long without Medicare or Medicaid patients. In any event, the Medicare conditions are not in fact enforced as such against most hospitals—for reasons indicated in the following excerpt:

> Since its inception, the Medicare program has accepted, or "deemed," Joint Commission accreditation as equivalent to compliance with Medicare certification standards. That is, the federal government accepts accredited hospitals as Medicare providers without additional direct review. The original 1965 Medicare statute acknowledged JCAHO authority not only by granting deemed status to JCAHO-accredited hospitals, but also by prohibiting the federal government from imposing any additional requirements on such hospitals. Furthermore, the statute made no provision for federal auditing of the Joint Commission's accreditation process. Indeed, [HEW, the predecessor of DHHS or "HHS"] did not even have access to JCAHO accreditation reports to determine the basis (or lack thereof) for accreditation decisions.
>
> In the late 1970s, several consumer groups expressed dissatisfaction with using JCAHO accreditation as conclusive evidence of acceptable quality in hospitals. This dissatisfaction led to the filing of a lawsuit challenging deemed status. Amendments to the Social Security Act in 1972 responded to these concerns. Statutory changes permitted HEW to require accredited hospitals to comply with Medicare certification standards more stringent than those of the JCAHO, required random and complaint-based inspections by state agencies to validate JCAHO judgments, permitted decertification of accredited hospitals that failed to comply with JCAHO requirements, and compelled accredited hospitals to release Joint Commission survey reports to HEW for validation survey purposes. The 1972 amendments established the basic framework for the ongoing relationship between Medicare and the Joint Commission.
>
> In the intervening two decades, there have been adjustments of that relationship with respect to information disclosure and validation procedures. In 1975, in response to a consumer organization's Freedom of Information Act request, HEW released copies of letters that the Joint Commission had sent to hospitals identifying deficiencies and that HEW had received from those hospitals under the 1972 amendments. The Joint Commission sued to maintain the confidentiality of its accreditation documents. The parties settled the suit with an agreement that HEW would not release to the public Joint Commission accreditation letters or accompanying recommendations or comments.
>
> In 1989, Congress amended the Medicare law to grant [HHS] more extensive access to accreditation documents. That legislation required all deemed status hospitals to authorize the Joint Commission to release, upon request, to HHS or to a state survey agency a copy of the most recent Joint Commission accreditation survey, whether or not the facility was undergoing a validation survey. These amendments respected the 1975 compromise, however, authorizing HHS to redisclose

> accreditation information only to the extent it related to an enforcement action taken by the Secretary of HHS.
>
> In 1990 and 1991, the General Accounting Office ("GAO") released several reports expressing concern about the federal government's validation process for deemed status hospitals, and congressional hearings were held to review these concerns. In response, HHS attempted to tighten up the validation process, in particular, committing itself to creating an annual "crosswalk" to determine the congruence between Joint Commission accreditation standards and the Medicare conditions of participation on which deemed status depends. This crosswalk, which HHS now attempts to create annually, is intended to assure that compliance with accreditation standards in fact equates with compliance with the Medicare conditions of participation.

Jost, supra, at 18–20. About two-thirds of the states likewise rely on the JCAHO, in whole or in part, in licensing hospitals.

The JCAHO continues to be a lightning rod for criticism. E.g., J. Stieber & S. Wolfe, Who's Watching Our Hospitals? (Public Citizen 1994); Schlosberg & Jackson, Assuring Quality: The Debate over Private Accreditation and Public Certification of Health Care Facilities, 30 Clearinghouse Rev. 699 (1996) (questioning reliance on private accreditors). Because the JCAHO accredits hospitals that attain a "passing score" despite identified deficiencies, access to information about those deficiencies is a natural concern of consumer groups. But see 42 U.S.C.A. § 1395bb(c) (West Supp. 1998) ("The Secretary may not disclose any accreditation survey (other than a survey with respect to a home health agency) made and released to him by [any] national accreditation body, of an entity accredited by such body, except * * * to the extent such survey and information relate to an enforcement action"). See generally Jost, Confidentiality and Disclosure in Accreditation, Law & Contemp. Probs., Autumn 1994, p. 171. See also Variety Children's Hosp. v. Mishler, 670 So.2d 184 (Fla.App.1996) (JCAHO surveys and responses protected from discovery by state peer review statute). The JCAHO's position with respect to its obligation to disclose its survey results is that it is not, and should not be treated as, a public agency or regulator. Instead, it has long contended that it is essentially a quality-control consultant to accredited institutions, paid by them and responsible to the medical care industry. Under this conception, it provides confidential reports of deficiencies to surveyed hospitals and allows the hospital to use the Joint Commission's imprimatur for whatever it is worth in dealing with purchasers, including government.

Medicare also relies upon private accreditation in qualifying institutional providers other than hospitals for program participation. For example, the Clinical Laboratories Improvement Act of 1967, as amended, 42 U.S.C.A. § 263a (West Supp. 1998), permits deemed status for accredited laboratories upon a determination by DHHS that the accreditating agency meets HHS requirements for frequency of inspections, stringency of standards, etc. Later legislation specifically instructs DHHS to grant "deemed status" to a wide variety of accredited institutions if the Secretary finds that accreditation by a national accreditor (note that local accrediting programs need not apply) demonstrates that Medicare's conditions are met. 42 U.S.C.A. § 1395bb (West Supp. 1998); 42 C.F.R. pts. 401, 488, 489 (1997). The institutions potentially eligible for deemed status include psychiatric hospitals, skilled nursing facilities, home health agencies, ambulatory surgical centers, rural health clinics, comprehensive outpatient rehabilitation facilities, hospices, and clinics, rehabilitation agencies, and public health agencies providing outpatient physical therapy, occupational therapy, or speech pathology services.

5. *The Issue of Delegation.* Although political considerations undoubtedly account for government's willingness to entrust major responsibilities to private groups, what might be the policy rationale for delegating to private organizations the public function of deciding which providers are qualified to render services under public programs? What legal issues (some of which, as Jost reports, were raised in the past by consumer groups objecting to the Joint Commission's unsupervised authority) are presented by a delegation of government policy-making responsibilities to private interests? These and other questions are addressed in the following excerpt:

> One explanation [for such delegation under Medicare] might be that government is simply privatizing the enforcement of publicly established standards in an effort to reduce the public payroll, to move enforcement costs off-budget, and to finance regulation through fees paid by firms seeking accreditation. It is unclear whether HCFA, in selecting accreditors of home health agencies (HHAs), [for example,] has simply enlisted private entities to enforce federally prescribed standards at providers' expense or has given private accreditors some discretion both in setting standards and in verifying compliance. In its 1987 proposal to recognize both the JCAHO and the Community Health Accreditation Program of the National League for Nursing (CHAP) as accreditors of HHAs, HCFA seemed willing to overlook some major differences between Medicare's written standards and a private accreditor's requirements. Although it stressed that the precise requirements and procedures adopted were less important than the general reliability of the private organization to detect deficient services, its later notice recognizing CHAP indicated that CHAP had tailored most if not all of its accreditation requirements and procedures to be "equal or superior to" HCFA's requirements and procedures. HCFA's more recent regulations require a "crosswalk" between Medicare's requirements and those of the private accreditor. But HCFA's comments stress that, although an accreditor's "standards, taken as a whole, [must be] at least as stringent as those established by HCFA," they need not be identical. It would seem significant that, HCFA, rather than hiring private entities to enforce public standards against HHAs, selected two organizations that have not only different sponsorship but significantly different philosophies of health care.
>
> Another possible reason for public reliance on private accrediting might be a desire on the part of government to delegate policymaking

responsibilities to private interests. Such delegation would raise constitutional questions. In *Cospito v. Heckler*, [742 F.2d 72 (3d Cir.1984),] a federal appeals court, perhaps seeking to avoid a constitutional issue, adopted a highly strained construction of legislation (since repealed) under which the predecessor of the JCAHO not only accredited psychiatric hospitals to participate in Medicare but was also apparently expected to set the standards to be used by HCFA in appraising such hospitals. Although the court acknowledged that "Congress may seek private assistance in 'matters of a more or less technical nature,' " it is questionable whether quality standards for psychiatric hospitals are merely technical in character. There are real policy choices to be made, after all, between the values of the medical profession and the interests of patients and taxpayers. It seems probable that, in *Cospito*, the Joint Commission, representing the interests and views of psychiatrists, was using disaccreditation, despite its adverse effect on institutionalized patients, to advance professional objectives against political resistance to paying higher costs. Indeed, professionals often use threats of disaccreditation strategically or collusively to strengthen their colleagues' claims on institutional or public resources. (This occurs most obviously perhaps in higher education, where the demands of particular programs on university administrators are often backed by their accreditors.) In any event, the general authority of the JCAHO to confer so-called "deemed status" on hospitals is not unconstitutional, because HCFA retains the authority to revoke such status if it finds that the accreditor is not providing adequate assurance of compliance with federal standards, either in general or in a specific instance. Comparable "look-behind" authority is generally provided whenever private accreditors are recognized by government.

The constitutional issue of delegation aside, there remains in each case the important policy question whether government has conferred excessive self-regulatory power on dominant private interests. Government recognition places the physician-dominated JCAHO, for example, in a good position to resolve innumerable important questions about how hospitals should be operated and evaluated; indeed, the Joint Commission for many years appeared to be more interested in organizational issues in hospitals than in the outcomes of patient care—that is, to be more concerned about how well a hospital treats its physicians than about how well it treats its patients. At both the state and federal levels, medical and other professional organizations enjoy comparable regulatory powers because of government reliance on a designated private accreditor. * * *

Perhaps the most appealing reason why government might rely on private accreditation is to foster pluralism in the regulatory state. Here again it is important whether one is witnessing merely privatized enforcement of public standards or government reliance on the judgment of reputable private organizations having their own standards and their own ideas about what constitutes quality and how it should be measured. Although it might seem that a delegation issue arises if a

> recognized accrediting body sets its own standards rather than enforcing the government's, that problem would seem to disappear if the government, in addition to periodically evaluating the accreditor's integrity under general statutory criteria, were willing to recognize alternative accreditors. In that case, the accreditor would not be performing tasks tantamount to regulation; institutions which it refuses to accredit could qualify by obtaining recognition by another accreditor meeting minimum government criteria. By encouraging competition rather than monopoly in accrediting, government could foster pluralism in the market for accredited services while still providing meaningful protection for consumers.

Havighurst, Foreword: The Place of Private Accrediting Among the Instruments of Government, Law & Contemp. Probs., Autumn 1994, p. 1, 7–10. See also Schlosberg & Jackson, supra; Michael, Federal Agency Use of Audited Self–Regulation as a Regulatory Technique, 47 Admin. L. Rev. 171 (1995) (proposal to the Administrative Conference that more regulatory tasks be delegated, under standards and supervision, to private entities).

Legislation in 1996 modified 42 U.S.C. § 1395bb(b)(1) to require a finding that a private accreditor's accreditation "demonstrates that all of the applicable conditions or requirements of this subchapter * * * are met or exceeded." Previously, accreditation had only to provide "reasonable assurance that any or all of the conditions * * * are met." Does this statutory change defeat Havighurst's apparent hope that private accreditors might introduce an element of pluralism into federal programs?

Recall the ACPE problem in the previous section of this chapter (involving an accrediting body's prescription of longer training for pharmacists), which illustrates the way in which states rely on private accreditation in defining minimum educational requirements for aspirants seeking various kinds of professional licensure. Is the delegation problem more or less serious in educational accrediting, where, partly because the first amendment precludes direct control of education, government has not sought to impose its own regulatory standards but has chosen instead to accept the judgments of reputable private accrediting programs, which employ standards of their own making? Is it open to HCFA—as it moves to implement the Medicare+Choice program, for example—to decentralize decisions on at least some quality-of-care issues, subject to ultimate accountability both to consumers exercising choice and and to government exercising oversight responsibility? Recall, from the discussion of clinical practice guidelines in chapter 2(§B), the suggestion that the federal government might allow alternative, conflicting guidelines to coexist but certify guidelines as meeting minimum criteria. What might be the advantage in having government proceed, not by certifying guidelines itself, but by accrediting private entities that perform that function?

When government adopts a private accrediting program's conclusions, does that action increase the legal accountability of the private program? State as precisely as you can one or more possible legal rationales for that result. Have you convinced yourself? How do you respond to the argument that, even when government itself adopts an accreditor's opinion as its own for regulatory purposes, it is that act of government, not the action of the private body, that has the crucial exclusionary effect? Do you yet accept the idea that effects achieved by publishing advice that others may follow are fundamentally (and legally) distinguishable, in a democracy, from effects achieved by coercive means, public or private?

6. *Competing Accreditors?* Would it be plausible, realistic, or desirable—as Havighurst seems to think—to maintain more than one accreditor of health care institutions in each discrete field? Would a multiplicity of accreditors simply confuse consumers rather than informing them better? Would the loss of scale economies cause the quality of accrediting to suffer? Would each reputable provider feel compelled to obtain every available seal of approval? Would accreditors simply compete simply by lowering the bar and laxity in applying standards? Addressing these and other issues, Havighurst, Foreword, supra, at 9–14, still argues (id. at 5) that

> a strong case can be made for actively preserving and encouraging competition in accrediting and, more generally, for maintaining a dynamic marketplace of ideas in which information flows from a plurality of sources and in which the quality of information produced by each supplier is subject to constant evaluation and criticism. In economic markets as in politics, control of information is a potent instrument of power. Government, it would seem, should avoid complicity with private groups that dominate the production of authoritative information on which underinformed consumers must rely in making market choices.

As Havighurst notes in the earlier excerpt, HCFA recognizes both the JCAHO and the National League for Nursing's [NLN's] CHAP program as an accreditor of home health agencies (HHAs). See 57 Fed. Reg. 22,773 (May 29, 1992) (final HCFA regulation recognizing CHAP); 58 Fed. Reg. 35,007 (June 30, 1993) (JCAHO). On the challenge of surveying and ensuring the quality of home health care (which takes place in hard-to-monitor locations), see GAO, Medicare: Assuring the Quality of Home Health Services (Oct. 1989); Kinney et al., Quality Improvement in Community-based Long-term Care: Theory and Reality, 20 Am. J.L. & Med. 59 (1994); Kane, Perspectives on Home Care Quality, 16 Health Care Fin. Rev. 69 (1994) (considering use of outcomes measures in evaluating home care providers); Johnson, Quality–Control Regulation of Home Health Care, 26 Hous. L. Rev. 901 (1989).

The NLN at one time complained that the Joint Commission had attempted to monopolize the accrediting of HHAs by requiring any hospital that maintained an affiliation with a HHA to have it surveyed by the JCAHO (at an additional charge to the hospital) as part of the hospital's own accreditation survey—unless the HHA already had JCAHO accreditation. Could the NLN have brought a successful antitrust suit, arguing that this policy was a kind of "tying arrangement" that, by making it cheaper for hospitals to deal with JCAHO-accredited HHAs, caused HHAs to prefer accreditation by the Joint Commission?

PROBLEM

[The following problem is partly hypothetical but also partly based on developments in the early 1980s, when the Reagan DHHS proposed deemed status for nursing homes accredited by the Joint Commission. As in the problem, this proposal met strong opposition from consumer groups, which feared a weakening of state and federal efforts to enforce quality of care standards in nursing homes; DHHS eventually abandoned its proposal.]

The administration has proposed regulations to reform federal regulation of nursing homes. The stated purpose of the proposal is to "simplify and streamline the procedures by which a long-term care facility is approved for participation in Medicare and Medicaid." According to HCFA, "the changes are necessary because many of the current procedures have proved cumbersome and expensive for the federal and state agencies to administer and either unnecessary or ineffective in ensuring the quality of health care services." In general, HCFA wants to reduce reporting requirements, lengthen the duration of "provider agreements" between nursing homes and the government, require fewer on-site surveys of homes with good compliance records, and allow more flexibility in enforcement. HCFA's most far-reaching proposal would provide that nursing homes accredited by the JCAHO are "deemed" to meet the Conditions of Participation of Medicare and Medicaid. Government surveys to validate JCAHO conclusions on nursing home quality would be made both on a regular selective-sample basis and in response to a "substantial allegation of significant deficiencies."

Congressional reaction to the HCFA proposal has been vigorous. In hearings, one senator told HCFA officials, "I would have to say that you have just about zero support for using the JCAHO for what you have proposed." A Florida senator opined that "this is just tearing out federal protection of helpless people." At another hearing, a New Jersey representative expressed apprehension about "all of this flexibility and deregulation coming at the same time that resources available for long-term care are being reduced." A bill has been introduced to impose a moratorium on finalizing the proposed regulations. Although ostensibly intended to allow Congress time to study the matter, this bill is generally understood as a test of the merits of the HCFA proposal.

As a legislative aide to a Republican congresswoman from the State of Nirvana, you are asked to educate her on the issues and to critique the HCFA proposal to substitute JCAHO review for direct federal and state supervision of nursing homes. She is interested in more than free-market rhetoric but is hesitant to endorse direct federal regulation of the private sector unless the need is clear. She has asked you for a presentation of the issues as they affect her district. Accordingly, you have inquired into the nursing home situation in Nirvana.

Your inquiries have disclosed that the nursing homes in Nirvana are about equally divided between for-profit and nonprofit facilities, the latter being operated by diverse, mostly religious groups. The proprietary homes are mostly represented by the Nirvana Health Care Association, which maintains certain membership standards as a way of improving the image of the investor-owned sector of the industry. Several multi-institutional systems, both for-profit and nonprofit, exist, and these chains are expanding both by acquisition and by constructing new facilities. A few homes are maintained as rehabilitation facilities by integrated health care systems. As in other states, well over half of the total revenues of Nirvana nursing homes are earned in caring for Medicaid patients; some homes take no Medicaid patients, however, while others cater predominantly to that population. Because of very strict limits on coverage, the federal Medicare program pays only about 10% of the total cost of nursing home care.

The Nirvana Department of Health licenses nursing homes and has issued extensive regulations governing all homes. These regulations closely correspond to the federal Medicare/Medicaid Conditions of Participation. Compliance is ensured through regular, on-site inspections by teams of nurses and other experts. The sanction available for noncompliance is license revocation or suspension. This regulatory program has not prevented two tragic nursing home fires and a number of scandals in which homes have been found to abuse patients through neglect and overuse of sedatives. A grievance system is maintained and generates a steady flow—though not a flood—of complaints from discontented patients, families, and others interested in patients' well-being.

The Department of Health also administers the state certificate-of-need (CON) program, which is currently being reconsidered by the legislature with an eye to possible repeal. One goal of the CON program has been to prevent proliferation of nursing homes. As a result of its operation, a chronic excess demand for nursing beds by Medicaid patients exists, and paying patients also have trouble finding an empty bed when it is needed. Administrators of the Medicaid program believe that the waiting list for nursing care created by CON regulation has forced desirable rationing of beds by physicians, social workers, and other decision makers and that this rationing has saved the program money. The state Medicaid administrators also believe that quality-of-care problems in nursing homes are kept under adequate control by the Department of Health, and they profess to fear the consequences of relaxing that regulation.

Your presentation to your congresswoman should include a broad evaluation of the appropriateness of the mechanisms employed to assure the quality of nursing home care in Nirvana. In this context, you should consider whether HCFA's proposal to involve the JCAHO would be a desirable move and whether your congresswoman might propose any modifications of that proposal or of the pending moratorium.

1. Why does the market fail to yield acceptable quality in nursing homes? Is it simply a problem of poor information? What strategies are available besides direct regulation?

2. Does nursing home regulation focus primarily on inputs, process, or outcomes? What alternative approaches are available? What measures of outcome would you use? Is it feasible to evaluate the process of care?

3. Is the JCAHO a good candidate for reviewing the quality of nursing home care? Given its sponsorship, would it be more or less reliable in this role than in accrediting hospitals? (Only a small fraction of nursing homes nationwide are JCAHO–accredited.)

4. Your assessment of the JCAHO's capability as an accreditor of nursing homes would benefit from reading the rest of this section, which highlights both the values implemented in public regulation of such complex institutions and the practical difficulties encountered by government in regulating using command-and-control methods. Could the JCAHO (or any other private accreditor) do any better?

Regulating Nursing Homes

Estate of Smith v. Heckler

United States Court of Appeals, Tenth Circuit, 1984.
747 F.2d 583.

■ McKAY, CIRCUIT JUDGE.

Plaintiffs, seeking relief under 42 U.S.C. § 1983 (1982), brought this class action on behalf of medicaid recipients residing in nursing homes in Colorado. They alleged that the Secretary of Health and Human Services (Secretary) has a statutory duty under Title XIX of the Social Security Act, 42 U.S.C. §§ 1396–1396n (1982), commonly known as the Medicaid Act, to develop and implement a system of nursing home review and enforcement designed to ensure that medicaid recipients residing in medicaid certified nursing homes actually receive the optimal medical and psychosocial care that they are entitled to under the Act. The plaintiffs contended that the enforcement system developed by the Secretary is "facility oriented," not "patient oriented" and thereby fails to meet the statutory mandate. The district court found that although a patient care or "patient oriented" management system is feasible, the Secretary does not have a duty to introduce and require the use of such a system.

The primary issue on appeal is whether the trial court erred in finding that the Secretary does not have a statutory duty to develop and implement a system of nursing home review and enforcement which focuses on and ensures high quality patient care. * * *

Background

The factual background of this complex lawsuit is fully discussed in the district court's opinion. In re Estate of Smith v. O'Halloran, 557 F.Supp. 289 (D.Colo.1983). Briefly, plaintiffs instituted the lawsuit in an effort to improve the deplorable conditions at many nursing homes. They presented evidence of the lack of adequate medical care and of the widespread knowledge that care is inadequate. Indeed, the district court concluded that care and life in some nursing homes is so bad that the homes "could be characterized as orphanages for the aged." Id. at 293.

* * *

The Medicaid Act

An understanding of the Medicaid Act (the Act) is essential to understand plaintiffs' contentions. The purpose of the Act is to enable the federal government to assist states in providing medical assistance to "aged, blind or disabled individuals, whose income and resources are insufficient to meet the costs of necessary medical services, and ... rehabilitation and other services to help such ... individuals to attain or retain capabilities for independence or self care." 42 U.S.C. § 1396 (1982). To receive funding, a state must submit to the Secretary and have approved by the Secretary a plan for medical assistance which meets the requirements of 42 U.S.C. § 1396a(a).

* * * A state seeking plan approval must establish or designate a single state agency to administer or supervise administration of the state plan, and must provide reports and information as the Secretary may require. Further, the state agency is responsible for establishing and maintaining health standards for institutions where the recipients of the medical assistance under the plan receive care or services. The plan must include descriptions of the standards and methods the state will use to assure that medical or remedial care services provided to the recipients "are of high quality."

The state plan must also provide "for a regular program of medical review ... of each patient's need for skilled nursing facility care ..., a written plan of care, and, where applicable, a plan of rehabilitation prior to admission to a skilled nursing facility...." Id. § 1396a(a)(26)(A). Further, the plan must provide for periodic inspections by medical review teams of:

> (i) the care being provided in such nursing facilities ... to persons receiving assistance under the State plan; (ii) with respect to each of the patients receiving such care, the adequacy of the services available in particular nursing facilities ... to meet the current health needs and promote the maximum physical well-being of patients receiving care in such facilities ...; (iii) the necessity and desirability of continued placement of such patients in such nursing facilities ...; and (iv) the feasibility of meeting their health care needs through alternative institutional or noninstitutional services.

Id. § 1396a(a)(26)(B).

The state plan must provide that any skilled nursing facility receiving payment comply with 42 U.S.C. § 1395x(j), which defines "skilled nursing facility" and sets out standards for approval under a state plan. The key requirement for purposes of this lawsuit is that a skilled nursing facility must meet "such other conditions relating to the health and safety of individuals who are furnished services in such institution or relating to the physical facilities thereof as the Secretary may find necessary...." Id. § 1395x(j)(15).

The state plan must provide for the appropriate state agency to establish a plan, consistent with regulations prescribed by the Secretary, for professional health personnel to review the appropriateness and quality of care and services furnished to Medicaid recipients. The appropriate state agency must determine on an ongoing basis whether participating institutions meet the requirements for continued participation in the Medicaid program. While the state has the initial responsibility for determining whether institutions are meeting the conditions of participation, section 1396a(a)(33)(B) gives the Secretary the authority to "look behind" the state's determination of facility compliance, and make an independent and binding determination of whether institutions meet the requirements for participation in the state Medicaid plan. Thus, the state is responsible for conducting the review of facilities to determine whether they comply with the state plan. In conducting the review, however, the states must use federal standards, forms, methods and procedures. * * *

The Secretary "shall approve" any plan which fulfills the requirements of section 1396a(a). Once the state plan is approved, the Secretary reimburses the states according to percentages set out in section 1396b. If the state fails to show that it has an effective program of "utilization control" as defined in section 1396b(g)(3), the Secretary must reduce the percentage of reimbursement to the state. If after approving a state plan the Secretary determines that the plan has been so changed that it no longer complies with section 1396a(a), or that it complies on paper but not in its actual administration, the Secretary is required to terminate payments to the state, effectively disapproving the plan.

Implementing Regulations

Congress gave the Secretary a general mandate to promulgate rules and regulations necessary to the efficient administration of the functions with which the Secretary is charged by the Act. Pursuant to this mandate the Secretary has promulgated standards for the care to be provided by skilled nursing facilities and intermediate care facilities. Among other things, the regulations provide for the frequency and general content of patients' attending physician evaluations, nursing services with policies "designed to ensure that each patient receives treatments, medications, ... diet as prescribed, ... rehabilitative nursing care as needed ..., is kept comfortable, clean, well-groomed, [is] protected from accident, injury, an infection, and [is] encouraged, assisted, and trained in self-care and group activities." 42 C.F.R. § 405.1124(c). The rehabilitative nursing care is to be directed toward each patient achieving an optimal level of self-care and independence. The regulations require a written patient care plan to be developed and maintained for each patient. * * * Finally, the regulations provide for treatment of the social and emotional needs of recipients.

The Secretary has established a procedure for determining whether state plans comply with the standards set out in the regulations. This enforcement mechanism is known as the "survey/certification" inspection system. Under this system, the states conduct reviews of nursing homes pursuant to 42 U.S.C. § 1396a(a)(33). The Secretary then determines, on the basis of the survey results, whether the nursing home surveyed is eligible for certification and, thus, eligible for Medicaid funds. The states must use federal standards, forms, methods and procedures in conducting the survey. At issue in this case is the form SSA–1569, which the Secretary requires the states to use to show that the nursing homes participating in Medicaid under an approved state plan meet the conditions of participation contained in the Act and the regulations. Plaintiffs contend that the form is "facility oriented," in that it focuses on the theoretical capability of the facility to provide high quality care, rather than "patient oriented," which would focus on the care actually provided. The district court found, with abundant support in the record, that the "facility oriented" characterization is appropriate and that the Secretary has repeatedly admitted that the form is "facility oriented."

The Plaintiffs' Claims

Plaintiffs contend that the statutory requirements regarding the content of state plans create a correlative entitlement for Medicaid recipients to quality care. They argue that the Secretary has an enforcement obligation to insure compliance with the approved state plan. More specifically, plaintiffs argue that the Secretary has a statutory duty to develop an enforcement system whereby to receive medicaid funds states would be forced to use a patient care management system. Such a system would ensure, through the review process of section 1396a(a)(33), that Medicaid recipients residing in nursing homes certified for Medicaid participation are "actually, continuously receiving their Medicaid entitlements to optimal medical and psychosocial care in a safe, sanitary, rehabilitatively supportive, accessible, personalized environment and in a context of full civil liberties as a condition of such facilities' receipt of Federal and State financial reimbursement from the Medicaid Program."

The plaintiffs do not challenge the substantive medical standards, or "conditions of participation," which have been adopted by the Secretary and which states must satisfy to have their plans approved. See 42 C.F.R. § 405.1101–.1137. Rather, plaintiffs challenge the enforcement mechanism the Secretary has established. The plaintiffs contend that the federal forms, form SSA–1569 in particular, which states are required to use, evaluate only the physical facilities and theoretical capability to render quality care. They claim that the surveys assess the care provided almost totally on the basis of the records, documentation and written policies of the facility being reviewed. Further, out of the 541 questions contained in the Secretary's form SSA–1569 which must be answered by state survey and certification inspection teams, only 30 are "even marginally related to patient care or might require any patient observation...." Appellants' brief at 10. Plaintiffs contend that the enforcement mechanism's focus on the facility, rather than on the care actually provided in the facility, results only in "paper compliance" with the substantive standards of the Act. Thus, plaintiffs contend, the Secretary has violated her statutory duty to assure that federal Medicaid monies are paid only to facilities which meet the substantive standards of the Act—facilities which actually provide high quality medical, rehabilitative and psychosocial care to resident Medicaid recipients.

The District Court's Holding

After hearing the evidence, the district court found the type of patient care management system advocated by plaintiffs clearly feasible and characterized the current enforcement system as "facility oriented." However, the court concluded that the failure to implement and require the use of a "patient oriented" system is not a violation of the Secretary's statutory duty. The essence of the district court's holding was that the State of Colorado, not the federal government, is responsible for developing and enforcing standards which would assure high quality care in nursing homes and, thus, the State of Colorado, not the federal government, should have been the defendant in this case.

The district court found that the duty lies with the state because the Medicaid Act provides that states are responsible for establishing and maintaining health standards for provider institutions, and the states determine what kind and how many professional medical and supporting personnel will be used to administer the state plan. The state plan must include standards and methods which the state will use to assure that the medical assistance provided is of high quality. Section 1396a(a)(33) provides that the responsibility for inspecting nursing homes for survey and certification purposes lies with the state.

The district court also concluded that the "look behind" provision of section 1396a(a)(33)(B), authorizing the Secretary to reject a survey/certification performed by the state agency and substitute her own independent and binding determination, is "nothing more than permitted authority to intervene for the purpose of protecting the public funds used to reimburse the state." Nor did the district court believe that section 1302, the general mandate to make rules and regulations, imposes by itself a rulemaking duty on the Secretary. * * *

The district court also found it significant that under Colorado law, the State of Colorado is responsible for licensing nursing homes, suspending a license if the public health or welfare is endangered, for regulating nursing home administration, and licensing and regulating the various professions which provide care in nursing homes. The district court found that these state statutes provided further credibility to its interpretation of the statute: that the state is primarily responsible for administering and enforcing the Medicaid Act and that the role of the federal government is essentially limited to providing financial assistance to states which meet the statutory requirements for participation.

The Secretary's Duty

After carefully reviewing the statutory scheme of the Medicaid Act, the legislative history, and the district court's opinion, we conclude that the district court improperly defined the Secretary's duty under the statute. The federal government has more than a passive role in handing out money to the states. The district court erred in finding that the burden of enforcing the substantive provisions of the Medicaid Act is on the states. The Secretary of Health and Human Services has a duty to establish a system to adequately inform herself as to whether the facilities receiving federal money are satisfying the requirements of the Act. These requirements include providing high quality patient care. This duty to be adequately informed is not only a duty to be informed at the time a facility is originally certified, but is a duty of continued supervision.

Nothing in the Medicaid Act indicates that Congress intended the physical facilities to be the end product. Rather, the purpose of the Act is to provide medical assistance and rehabilitative services. The Act repeatedly focuses on the care to be provided, with facilities being only part of that care. For example, the Act provides that health standards are to be developed and maintained, and that states must inform the Secretary what methods they will use to assure high quality care. In addition to the "adequacy of the services available," the periodic inspections must address "the care being provided" in nursing facilities. State plans must provide review of the "appropriateness and quality of care and services furnished," and do so on an ongoing basis.

While the district court correctly noted that it is the state which develops specific standards and actually conducts the inspection, there is nothing in the Act to indicate that the state function relieves the Secretary of all responsibility to ensure that the purposes of the Act are being accomplished. The Secretary, not the states, determines which facilities are eligible for federal funds. While participation in the program is voluntary, states who choose to participate must comply with federal statutory requirements. The inspections may be conducted by the states, but the Secretary approves or disapproves the state's plan for review. Further, the inspections must be made with federal forms, procedures and methods.

It would be anomalous to hold that the Secretary has a duty to determine whether a state plan meets the standards of the Act while holding that the Secretary can certify facilities without informing herself as to whether the facilities actually perform the functions required by the state plan. The Secretary has a duty to ensure more than paper compliance. The federal responsibility is particularly evident in the "look behind" provision. We do not read the Secretary's "look behind" authority as being "nothing more than permitted authority . . . ," as the district court found. Rather, we find that the purpose of that section is to assure that compliance is not merely facial, but substantive.

The legislative history makes clear that the "look behind" provision was added to the Act because the states were not properly carrying out the function of making sure that facilities were providing high quality care. The House report states:

> [T]he Committee is concerned that, without the authority to validate State agency compliance reviews and to make an independent judgment as to the extent of compliance by particular facilities, the Secretary lacks the means necessary to assure that Federal matching funds are being used to reimburse only those [skilled nursing facilities] and [intermediate care facilities] that actually comply with medicaid requirements.

H.R.Rep. No. 1167, 96th Cong., 2d Sess., reprinted in 1980 U.S.Code Cong. & Ad.News 5526, 5570. The district court's conclusion that this section merely provides the Secretary the authority to go behind a state's determination of compliance if and when the Secretary wants to, but imposes no duty on the Secretary, ignores the purpose of the section and eliminates its effectiveness.

By enacting section 1302 Congress gave the Secretary authority to promulgate regulations to achieve the functions with which she is charged. The "look-behind" provision and its legislative history clearly show that Congress intended the Secretary to be responsible for assuring that federal Medicaid money is given only to those institutions that actually comply with Medicaid requirements. The Act's requirements include providing high quality medical care and rehabilitative services. In fact, the quality of the care provided to the aged is the focus of the Act. Being charged with this function, we must conclude that a failure to promulgate regulations that allow the Secretary to remain informed, on a continuing basis, as to whether facilities receiving federal money are meeting the requirements of the Act, is an abdication of the Secretary's duty. While the Medicaid Act is admittedly very complex and the Secretary has "exceptionally broad authority to prescribe standards for applying certain sections of the Act," Schweiker v. Gray Panthers, 453 U.S. 34, 43 (1981), the Secretary's authority cannot be interpreted so as to hold that that authority is merely permissive authority. The Secretary must insure that states comply with the congressional mandate to provide high quality medical care and rehabilitative services.

The district court made a factual finding that the Secretary's current method of informing herself as to whether the facilities in question are satisfying the statutory requirements is "facility oriented," rather than "patient oriented." This characterization is fully supported by the record. Having determined that the purpose and the focus of the Act is to provide high quality medical care, we conclude that by promulgating a facility oriented enforcement system the Secretary has failed to follow that focus and such failure is arbitrary and capricious.[3]

Remedy

[The court remanded the case for further proceedings, finding that "mandamus is an appropriate remedy. The Secretary has a duty to promulgate regulations which will enable her to be informed as to whether the

3. Our conclusions are further evidenced by Congress' recent amendment to the Medicaid Act. Tax Reform Act of 1984, Pub.L. No. 98–369 (1984). Directly in response to the district court's opinion in this case, Congress amended the Act specifically imposing upon the Secretary a duty to assure that Medicaid patients in skilled nursing and intermediate care facilities receive high quality medical care. The legislative history indicates that Congress was merely reaffirming the Secretary's duty under existing law because Congress believed the district court misinterpreted the statute. We do not address the issue of whether a current legislature's comment on the intent of a previous legislature is binding. However, the amendment and its legislative history make the Secretary's duty under the Act even more clear.

nursing facilities receiving federal Medicaid funds are actually providing high quality medical care. This conclusion is fully supported by the statute and its legislative history. The statute vests broad discretion in the Secretary as to how that duty is best accomplished. The court is not a 'super agency' and cannot control the specifics of how the Secretary satisfies the duty. This is not a question of controlling the Secretary's discretion because the Secretary has failed to discharge her statutory duty altogether."]

Michigan Association of Homes and Services for the Aging, Inc. v. Shalala

United States Court of Appeals, Sixth Circuit, 1997.
127 F.3d 496.

■ MERRITT, CIRCUIT JUDGE.

An association of Michigan nursing homes brings a facial challenge to Medicare and Medicaid regulations and the defendants' policies and practices regarding nursing home examinations, certification, administration and enforcement and appeal. These regulations and policies implement the Omnibus Budget Reconciliation Act of 1987, which sought to reform the nursing home industry in response to class action litigation and studies critical of the industry.

In a comprehensive opinion, District Judge Edmunds dismissed the suit for lack of subject matter jurisdiction, concluding that the Association must exhaust its administrative remedies before pursuing an action in federal court. The Medicare Act, 42 U.S.C. §§ 1395cc(h)(1) and 1395ii, incorporates by reference the judicial review provisions for old age and disability claims under the Social Security Act. These provisions, 42 U.S.C. §§ 405(g) and (h), allow for judicial review "after any final decision of the Secretary" and disallow judicial review "except as herein provided." Section 405(h) then expressly disallows judicial review of administrative action under the general provisions supporting federal question jurisdiction found in 28 U.S.C. §§ 1331 and 1346. The courts have read Section 405(g) to require presentment of claims to the Secretary and exhaustion of administrative remedies, as in social security cases. The question before us is whether we should make an exception to the presentment and exhaustion of remedies requirements for this systemic, frontal attack on the regulatory scheme developed under the 1987 Act.

The plaintiff nursing home group argues that its case comes within the exception to the exhaustion requirement that the Supreme Court recognized in Bowen v. Michigan Academy of Family Physicians, 476 U.S. 667 (1986), and asserts that this exception includes general, systemic challenges to administrative rules, procedures, practices and customs used by the agency to evaluate nursing home care. It claims that it may bypass the restrictions on judicial review found in § 405(g) and (h) by attacking such agency policies generally.

We agree with the Court below that the plaintiff nursing homes must comply with the federal statutes requiring exhaustion of administrative remedies before coming to federal court.

I.

The Michigan Association of Homes and Services for the Aging's members provide nursing home services under both the Medicare and Medicaid programs. * * *

The regulations require regular provider surveys or inspections which are the subject of the current litigation. State teams perform certification surveys for both Medicare and Medicaid. The federal Health Care Financing Administration sets guidelines and trains the state survey teams, and can perform its own "look behind" surveys. Should these surveys reveal deficiencies, either federal or state agencies may seek and implement remedies.

The same set of federal regulations governs certification under both Medicare and Medicaid. There are twelve different outcomes available under the survey regulations. The least serious three represent a finding of "substantial compliance" and result in no sanction. The other nine represent a finding of noncompliance and may result in sanctions. The most serious six outcomes represent a finding of "substandard quality of care" and carry a more severe mix of remedies. Once regulators determine that a facility is not in substantial compliance, federal and state agencies have some discretion in imposing and choosing remedies.

In carrying out the goal of Congress to prevent backsliding nursing homes from continuing to operate within a cycle of noncompliance and then temporary compliance through short term plans of correction, the regulations authorize a broad range of remedies. Agencies may (1) disclose a finding of substandard quality of care to referring physicians and licensing boards, (2) place a ban on nurse aid training and competency evaluations, (3) direct a plan of correction, (4) initiate state monitoring through frequent inspections, (5) impose temporary agency management, (6) place a ban on payment for new admissions, (7) impose civil money penalties, and (8) terminate a provider from the Medicare and Medicaid programs. See 42 C.F.R. §§ 488.325(g),(h), 483.151, 488.406; see also 42 U.S.C. § 1395i-3(h)(2)(B).

These remedies are not available until a finding of noncompliance is made and they are appealable administratively. The imposition of state monitoring, which is not appealable administratively, is an exception. The loss of approval for a nurse aide training program would seem to be another exception, but under 42 C.F.R. § 483.151 would apparently only flow from the imposition of other remedies, which may be appealed. The regulations allow an administrative appeal of the initial determination of whether a provider is in substantial compliance; they do not allow an administrative appeal of the regulators' choice of remedy.

The Association challenges the regulatory scheme on four basic grounds. (1) It contends that the regulations are vague and hence violate the Due Process Clause. In particular, it argues that "substantial compliance" and "substandard quality of care," the terms that determine whether a facility is subject to sanctions and what sanction it will receive, are inadequately defined. According to the Association's complaint, these terms cannot be, and are not being, applied consistently. (2) The Association argues that the defendants have failed to carry out a statutory mandate to "measure and reduce inconsistency" of state surveys and enforcement. Though the government has undertaken fairly extensive training, has developed State Operations Manuals, and continues to update its recommendations to the states, the Association presents statistics that purportedly suggest that survey results vary substantially from state to state. (3) The Association attacks these same State Operations Manuals, training materials, and other communications between the Health Care Financing Administration and the state agencies as violative of the Administrative Procedure Act's notice and comment provisions. The government responds that these materials are interpretive only, and do not add to the substance of the regulations and statute. (4) The Association argues that the scheme violates procedural due process. It notes that the regulations do not allow administrative appeal of the regulators' choice of remedy. Moreover, it contends that due process requires an opportunity to correct a deficiency before sanctions are imposed.

II.

The issue before us is whether a federal district court has jurisdiction over a facial statutory and constitutional challenge to Medicare and Medicaid survey regulations and other materials despite the fact that the plaintiffs have not presented their challenge to the agency on a case-by-case basis or exhausted their administrative remedies and judicial remedies. * * *

* * *

The current plaintiffs * * *, though they concede that a claim that arises solely under the Medicare Act is subject to the statutory limitation [requiring presentment and exhaustion,] argue that federal question jurisdiction is appropriate because their claims also "arise under" the Fifth Amendment's Due Process Clause and the Administrative Procedure Act. The Supreme Court's decision in Weinberger v. Salfi, 422 U.S. 749 (1975), forecloses this approach. The *Salfi* Court held that the fact that a plaintiff's claim arises under the Constitution as well as the Social Security Act does not provide a way around the requirements of sections 405(h) and 405(g). This logic extends to the Association's Administrative Procedure Act claim as well.

The purposes of exhaustion, as articulated in *Weinberger v. Salfi*, would be undermined by allowing the Association to avoid presenting its specific claims to the Secretary. The *Salfi* Court pointed out that exhaustion is required

> as a matter of preventing premature interference with agency processes, so that the agency may function efficiently and so that it may have an opportunity to correct its own errors, to afford the parties and the courts the benefit of its experience and expertise, and to compile a record which is adequate for judicial review.

Salfi, 422 U.S. at 765. It is true that the Association's suit purports to challenge the constitutionality of the agency's regulations and other materials on their face. Its challenge relates, however, to how these materials operate procedurally, procedures that the Association itself complains are difficult to pin down. For instance, though the Association contends that the government has not taken adequate steps to reduce inconsistency, it also attacks the government's ongoing, informal attempts to produce consistency by training state surveyors and disseminating information to the states. The Association paints a picture of a system that is still struggling to implement a radical legislative change in direction, but the Association demands to be heard before the system has fully implemented the change and applied it to specific cases. Under these circumstances, requiring exhaustion will allow the parties to compile a record that will place the Association's procedural claims in a clearer light. In such circumstances, courts need an administrative record to review. They function best on a case-by-case basis, leaving broad legislative attacks to be determined by Congress.

* * *

The Association argues that even if section 405(h) would ordinarily preclude subject matter jurisdiction, the exception to section 405(h) articulated in Bowen v. Michigan Academy of Family Physicians, 476 U.S. 667 (1986), should apply in these circumstances. Courts have interpreted *Bowen* to allow federal question jurisdiction over statutory and constitutional challenges to regulations promulgated by the Secretary under the Medicare Act when there is no other avenue of judicial review.

* * *

[T]he Association contends [inter alia] that some of the lesser, alternative remedies are imposed without judicial review as a purely practical matter. Though the facilities could challenge the imposition of a remedy once it is applied, most would prefer to submit a plan to correct the deficiencies and avoid sanctions. Few of its members, asserts the Association, would choose to fight the imposition of a sanction and incur the costs and reputational damage that would result, even if the determination that led to the sanction would ultimately be overturned. Even minor sanctions, the Association claims, would force many of its members to close their doors. While we acknowledge these practical concerns, they are not dispositive. In Case v. Weinberger, 523 F.2d 602 (2d Cir.1975), the Second Circuit addressed a provider's claim to pre-termination due process. The provider argued that the denial of reimbursements would deal her business a blow from which it would never recover. The court determined, however, that

> [t]his anticipated damage to [the provider], which is certainly serious, does not compare favorably with the government's interest in the safety of her

> patients.... We must ... place [the provider's interest in participation] in proper perspective with regard to the health and safety expectations of the patients, which expectations the Secretary has a valid interest in protecting.

Id. at 607. In the instant case, the Association's practical concerns do not foreclose judicial review for the purposes of the *Bowen* exception. In particular, we note that one of the main purposes of the reforms introduced in the Omnibus Budget Reconciliation Act of 1987 was to prevent nursing homes from submitting a plan of correction to avoid sanctions over and over again in the short term, only to slide back into noncompliance—the very behavior that the Association argues its members are privileged to adopt under the *Bowen* exception. * * * If the government's surveys are as arbitrary as the Association's counsel contended during oral argument, we are confident that at least one of its members will find a test case worth pursuing through which the Association's constitutional and statutory claims may be heard.

III.

In the alternative, the Association argues that though it is true that its claims arise under the Medicare statute, its claims arise equally—and indeed principally—under the Medicaid statute, which does not incorporate section 405(h). * * * Even if we were to interpret the Association's claim as arising under the Medicaid Act, the Association would still be required to exhaust its administrative remedies. * * * The Medicaid Act's inclusion of § 405(g) is clear textual support for the proposition that Congress intended the exhaustion of administrative remedies to apply in cases such as the instant one. The similar structures of the two Acts, evasion concerns, and considerations of judicial economy and orderliness support this conclusion as well.

* * *

Conclusion

Though we hold that the Association's members must present their claims to the Secretary according to section 405(h), we emphasize that we express no opinion on the merits their statutory and constitutional claims. Agencies must, of course, operate within the limits of the Administrative Procedure Act, the enabling act that put them in business, and the procedural safeguards of the Constitution. In this context, however, it is not surprising that broad legislative reforms intended to effect a major change in nursing home certification and enforcement would require serious adjustment on behalf of both the industry and government regulators. We should hardly be surprised that regulated institutions have found standards based on patient outcomes more difficult to implement across large corporate structures than rule-like minimum requirements, or that institutions that formerly avoided sanctions over the short term with plans of correction have had difficulties making more permanent changes to the way they treat residents. Nor should we be surprised that different government surveyors have interpreted these standards in different ways as the reforms are slowly implemented. Yet Congress, faced with serious problems in the nursing home industry, mandated these reforms to protect nursing home residents. The Association may still bring its claims within the limitations of section 405(h).

The judgment of the district court is AFFIRMED.

NOTES AND QUESTIONS ON CONTROLLING THE QUALITY OF CARE RENDERED BY INSTITUTIONAL PROVIDERS

1. *In General.* The materials here focus on nursing home regulation as a way of illustrating the problems encountered in using government regulation to ensure the quality of health services rendered by institutional providers. In addition to the difficulty of defining and measuring quality in various health care settings, both state governments and federal programs face major technical problems in defining the institutions that are subject to a particular regulatory regime and in designing appropriate oversight mechanisms for each type of institution. Consider the appropriateness and feasibility of focusing on inputs, process, and outcomes in evaluating the quality of care provided by different institutional providers.

In late 1997, HCFA proposed new conditions of participation for hospitals, purporting to focus on patient care and outcomes—specifically on the maintenance of systems to monitor and improve quality. 62 Fed. Reg. 66726 (Dec. 19, 1997) (to be codified at 42 C.F.R. pts. 416, 482, 485, 489). See also 62 Fed. Reg. 11004 (Mar. 10, 1997) (proposed new conditions for home health agencies, offered in same new regulatory spirit). The new conditions for hospitals were said to be designed, consistent with the Clinton administration's "Reinventing Government" initiative, to lower the costs of compliance and to facilitate flexibility in achieving quality goals. The new focus is on the hospital's measures for assessing each patient's particular needs; advising patients of their rights with respect to privacy, advance directives, grievances, etc.; monitoring the quality of care (including patient satisfaction as well as errors in medication, etc.); and for achieving continuous quality improvement. The proposed rules emphasize the overall responsibility of the hospital governing board but would not specify the hospital's organizational structure or the organization or composition of the medical staff. Special attention is paid to encouraging donation of organs. For general discussions of HCFA efforts to rethink its approach to quality assurance, relying more on measurement of outcomes and provision of information, see Gagel, Health Care Quality Improvement Program: A New Approach, 16 Health Care Fin. Rev. 15 (1995) (HCFA spokesperson describes program implementing Clinton administration's general policy of making regulation "more flexible, effective, and user-friendly"); Edelman, Health Care Financing Administration Retreats from Regulatory Role, 30 Clearinghouse Rev. 236 (1997) (informative critical assessment).

2. *Regulatory Challenges.* The challenges in regulating the quality of care in institutions lies in part in the great variety of public and private entities providing some kind of health care services, many of which entities do not fit neatly into well-defined regulatory categories. In addition to entire acute care hospitals with their wide array of discrete service offerings, the list of facilities subject to some form of regulation both under state law and under conditions of participation (or the equivalent) in federal programs includes mental hospitals, psychiatric units in acute care hospitals, and outpatient psychiatric services such as mental health clinics and day-care centers; substance abuse treatment centers; rehabilitation hospitals and other specialized institutions; emergency rooms and freestanding urgent care centers; pharmacies; clinical laboratories; home health agencies; ambulatory surgical facilities; dialysis centers; infusion and radiation therapy centers; hospices; and numerous types of long-term care facilities, ranging from retirement homes with assisted-living and infirmary care to skilled nursing homes. A notable omission from the list of facilities subject to institutional regulation is physician offices and physician-staffed clinics, which often provide many services other than those of physicians themselves. Both within each state and from state to state, statutory and regulatory regimes are likely to differ from each other in small but practically significant respects.

Further complicating the regulatory challenge are both the inevitable changes in that occur over time in the nature and function of existing institutions and the emergence of new entities to meet new needs or to meet old needs in new, possibly more efficient ways. Changes in the nature or condition of the patients treated by a particular type of provider may be either gradual or sudden but reflect changes in physicians' practice patterns, possibly influenced by changing payment policies. For example, home health agencies increased greatly in importance in the early 1990s as a result of changes in Medicare payment policies aimed at getting patients out of acute-care hospitals into what was hoped would be lower-cost settings. See Vladeck & Miller, The Medicare Home Health Initiative, 16 Health Care Fin. Rev. 7 (1994) (Medicare spending on home health care quintupled in 5 years). The emergence of new technologies also causes shifts in referral patterns and in the quality problems that regulators must address. In many respects, command-and-control regulatory techniques are not well adapted to addressing the provision of a full spectrum of care through networks of loosely integrated freestanding providers.

3. *Regulating Nursing Homes*. The quality of care in nursing homes has long been a major public concern. See, e.g., Institute of Medicine, Improving the Quality of Care in Nursing Homes (1986); B. Vladeck, Unloving Care: The Nursing Home Tragedy (1980); M. Mendelson, Tender Loving Greed (1974). For revealing evaluations of earlier efforts to regulate nursing homes, see U.S. General Accounting Office, Medicare and Medicaid—Stronger Enforcement of Nursing Home Requirements Needed (1987), reproduced in Medicare & Medicaid Guide (CCH) ¶ 36,702 (study of compliance with federal requirements, noting serious failings in one third of the homes inspected); Butler, Assuring the Quality of Care and Life in Nursing Homes: The Dilemma of Enforcement, 57 N.C. L. Rev. 1317 (1979). On state regulation of nursing homes generally, see S. Johnson, N. Terry & M.

Wolff, Nursing Homes and the Law: State Regulation and Private Litigation (1985); Annot., Licensing and Regulation of Nursing or Rest Homes, 53 A.L.R.4th 689 (1987). For a case vividly documenting abuses, finding understaffing an unfair business practice under a state consumer protection law, and rejecting "impossibility of compliance" and "industry-wide noncompliance" defenses, see People v. Casa Blanca Convalescent Homes, Inc., 206 Cal.Rptr. 164 (Cal.App.1984). See also California Ass'n of Health Facils. v. Department of Health Servs., 940 P.2d 323 (Cal.1997) ("reasonable licensee defense" to administrative action held not to preclude licensee's vicarious responsibility for unreasonable acts of its employee but only to preclude strict liability).

The earlier problem and the principal cases illustrate the challenge of trying to make nursing homes conform to reasonable public expectations. In the 1980s, in response to proposals by the Reagan administration similar to those outlined in the problem, Congress pressured HCFA to hold off on its deregulatory effort and funded the major Institute of Medicine study cited supra. This study was completed in 1986 and called for a major strengthening of regulatory efforts along lines similar to those visualized by the court order in *Estate of Smith.* The IOM report provided the basis for extensive new legislation included in OBRA § 87, Pub. L. No. 100–203 §§ 4201–18 (codified in 42 U.S.C. §§ 1395i–3(a) to (h), 1396r(a) to (h)). The *Michigan Association* case, reproduced supra, reveals some of the complexities of the new regulatory regime as well as some issues of administrative law encountered in rulemaking and enforcement under the Medicare and Medicaid programs. On the latter, see generally Kinney, Rule and Policy Making for the Medicaid Program: A Challenge to Federalism, 51 Ohio St. L.J. 855 (1990).

A contemporary summary of the substantive and procedural innovations in the important 1987 legislation by the House Committee on Energy and Commerce follows:

> P.L. 100–203 contains provisions revising (1) the requirements which nursing homes must meet in order to participate in the Medicare and Medicaid programs, (2) the "survey and certification" process by which compliance with those requirements is monitored, and (3) the remedies available to the States and to the Federal government to deter or sanction noncompliance. The basic purpose of these provisions is to improve the quality of care for nursing home residents. This summary describes only provisions affecting Medicaid.
>
> Requirements for Nursing Facilities (Sec. 4211)
>
> * * *
>
> *Provision of Services.*—Facilities must (1) maintain or enhance the quality of life of each resident, and operate a quality assurance committee; (2) provide services in accordance with a written plan of care; (3) conduct and periodically update a standardized, reproducible assessment of each resident's functional capacity; (4) provide, or arrange for the provision of, nursing and related services, medically-related social

services, pharmaceutical services, dietary services, activities, and dental services that meet professional standards of quality; (5) use only nurse aides who have completed an approved training and competency evaluation program and are competent to provide care; (6) provide health care under the supervision of a physician and maintain clinical records; (7) in the case of a facility with more than 120 beds, have at least 1 social worker employed full-time.

With respect to nurse staffing, facilities must have at least one registered nurse on duty 8 hours per day, 7 days per week, and at least one licensed nurse on duty 24 hours per day, 7 days per week. A State may waive these requirements if (1) a facility demonstrates that it has been unable, despite diligent efforts (including offering wages at the community prevailing rate for nursing personnel) to recruit appropriate staff, (2) the waiver will not endanger the health and safety of residents, and (3) a registered nurse or physician is obligated to respond immediately to telephone calls from the facility. If the Secretary finds that a State has shown a clear pattern and practice of allowing waivers in the absence of diligent efforts by facilities to meet the staffing requirements, the Secretary must exercise the State's waiver authority.

Residents' Rights.—A nursing facility must protect and promote the specified rights of each resident relating to (1) choice of physician, (2) freedom from restraints, (3) privacy, (4) confidentiality, (5) accommodation of individual needs, (6) voicing of grievances, (7) participation in resident and family groups, (8) participation in social, religious, and community activities, (9) examination of survey results, and (10) any other rights established by the Secretary. Facilities must inform residents of these and other legal rights at the time of admission.

A facility may transfer or discharge a resident only under certain specified circumstances, and only if written notice is given to the resident (or the resident's immediate family member or legal representative) prior to the transfer or discharge. Each facility must establish a written "bed hold" policy under which Medicaid-eligible residents who are transferred for hospitalization or therapeutic leave will be readmitted.

A facility must allow immediate access to any resident by the resident's physician, immediate family members, and representatives of Federal and State agencies.

A facility must establish and maintain identical policies and practices regarding transfer, discharge, and the provision of services for all individuals regardless of source of payment.

A facility must follow admissions practices that do not (1) require individuals to waive their rights to Medicare or Medicaid benefits, (2) require a third party guarantee of payment, or (3) require Medicaid eligibles to make any payment as a precondition for admission or continued stay.

A facility must manage and account for the personal funds of each resident, and must purchase a surety bond or make other satisfactory assurance of the security of resident personal funds.

Administration and Other Matters.—A nursing facility must (1) be efficiently administered, (2) be licensed under State law, (3) meet fire and safety code requirements, (4) maintain an infection control program, (5) comply with all applicable Federal and State laws relating to professional standards, and (6) meet any health and safety and physical plant requirements established by the Secretary.

The current law requirement that States license nursing facility administrators is retained. In addition, administrators will be required to meet minimum standards established by the Secretary.

* * *

Survey and Certification Process (Sec. 4212)

Effective October 1, 1990, * * * [t]he Secretary will be responsible for determining the compliance of all State nursing facilities; States will be responsible for certifying the compliance of all other nursing facilities. The Secretary will also be responsible for assuring the adequacy of State survey activities by conducting onsite "validation" surveys of at least 5 percent of the facilities surveyed by the State each year.

In general, certification will be based upon a two-step survey process. Every nursing facility participating in Medicaid will be subject to an unannounced standard survey which occurs, on average, at least annually. The standard survey will be conducted by a multidisciplinary team and will review, for a case-mix stratified sample of residents, the quality of care (as measured by certain indicators), the written plans of care and resident assessments, and compliance with residents' rights.

Each nursing facility found, under a standard survey, to have provided substandard quality of care will be subject to an extended survey. * * * Both the standard and extended surveys will be conducted on the basis of protocols developed, tested, and validated by the Secretary. Results of all standard and extended surveys will be public information, and must be posted by each nursing facility in a place readily accessible to residents.

Medicare & Medicaid Guide (CCH) ¶ 36,784 (Jan. 5, 1988). Regulations implementing these extensive regulatory reforms were not finally adopted until November 1994, 59 Fed. Reg. 56116 (1994), and now appear mostly at 42 C.F.R. pt. 488 (1997). See Vladeck, The Past, Present, and Future of Nursing Home Quality, 275 J.A.M.A. 425 (1996) (HCFA administrator's explanation of new regulations in historical context; reporting major declines in overuse of physical restraints, certain sedatives, indwelling catheters, etc.); Edelman, Final Survey, Certification, and Enforcement Rules for

Nursing Facilities, 29 Clearinghouse Rev. 117 (1995) (helpfully summarizing complex rules). The regulations make provision for recognizing "substantial compliance" but do not include survey protocols, etc., of the sort that the court of appeals in *Estate of Smith* found indicative of actual policies. For a later ruling in the *Smith* case requiring HCFA to publish its survey process as an agency rule, see Estate of Smith v. Bowen, 675 F.Supp. 586 (D.Colo.1987).

The *Michigan Association* case, reproduced supra, provides a summary of the enforcement process established by OBRA § 87 and of the variety of graduated sanctions for noncompliance. Before 1980, the states' only remedy was to terminate a home's participation in Medicaid, a remedy that could not be invoked without imposing hardships on patients, who would find it difficult or impossible to move to another facility. Legislation adopted in that year created the alternative sanction of terminating payments for new admissions only.

4. *Private Rights of Action.* Some states allow private enforcement of state regulatory legislation. The Illinois Nursing Home Care Reform Act of 1979, as amended, 201 Ill. Comp. Stat. Ann. 45/1 to 130 (West 1993 & Supp. 1997), allows actions by nursing home residents to place the facility under the control of a receiver (if the situation presents immediate danger), to obtain injunctive relief, and to recover treble damages for injuries resulting from statutory violations. The act also sets forth a residents' "bill of rights," including a provision that residents shall not be abused or neglected. In Harris v. Manor Healthcare Corp., 489 N.E.2d 1374 (Ill.1986), the court held that the legislature could allow treble damages for ordinary negligence in order to induce private enforcement by plaintiffs (many of them elderly) whose actual damages might not be enough to warrant instituting an action. The court also recognized the possibility of punitive damages in lieu of treble damages.

Other states have similar bills of rights but vary as to the kind of private actions allowed. In North Carolina, residents may obtain injunctive relief but not damages. Makas v. Hillhaven, Inc., 589 F.Supp. 736 (M.D.N.C.1984) (stating that the statutory bill of rights was "to promote the interests and well-being of the patients" but is "so general and nebulous that a trier of fact [in an action charging negligence per se] could not determine whether the standard had been violated"). Some states allow actions for damages, including punitive damages and attorney fees. E.g., Beverly Enter.—Fla., Inc. v. Spilman, 661 So.2d 867 (Fla.App.1995) (evidence of neglect by home and its employees supported punitive damages award under bill of rights statute); Stiffelman v. Abrams, 655 S.W.2d 522 (Mo.1983) (action under Omnibus Nursing Home Act held not barred by wrongful death statute). See generally S. Johnson, N. Terry & M. Wolff, supra, §§ 1–21 to 1–28.

In states that have not enacted regulatory statutes prescribing nursing home duties, courts may apply a general rule that "the proprietors of a nursing home are under a duty to exercise reasonable care to avoid injuries to patients, and the reasonableness of such care is to be assessed in the light of the patient's physical and mental condition." Juhnke v. Evangelical Lutheran Good Samaritan Soc'y, 6 Kan.App.2d 744, 634 P.2d 1132, 1136 (1981). See also Brown v. University Nursing Home, Inc., 496 S.W.2d 503 (Tenn.App.1972). Some cases may involve intentional torts. Such cases may be more attractive to the private plaintiffs' lawyer because of the potential for punitive damages. In cases alleging negligence, there would be a question whether the standard is one of ordinary care not requiring proof of industry custom or is instead based on professional custom, requiring expert testimony. See generally S. Johnson, N. Terry & M. Wolff, supra, ch. 3.

CHAPTER 7

LIABILITY FOR MEDICAL ACCIDENTS

SECTION A: OF CRISIS AND REFORM

Policy and Historical Perspectives on Medical Injuries, Liability, and Liability Insurance

INTRODUCTORY NOTES AND QUESTIONS ON THE REPARATIONS SYSTEM FOR MEDICAL MALPRACTICE

1. As a subcategory of the law of torts, the law of medical malpractice deals with injuries arising out of medical care provided in doctors' offices, in hospitals, or elsewhere. In addition to raising many policy questions of its own, malpractice law also has implications for broader health care policy. Although it is generally presumed that the threat of liability induces providers to maintain the quality of care, that premise is open to question (as we shall see), leaving quality issues to be addressed by other mechanisms as well. Moreover, to the extent that the legal system goes beyond merely enforcing minimum standards of carefulness and skill to be exercised in each case and presumes also to prescribe specific precautions that providers must take to reduce risks of injury, health care costs are affected, perhaps substantially. Be alert throughout this chapter both to the quality-assurance aspect of the tort system and to the distinction between policing "sins of commission" and penalizing "sins of omission."

These introductory notes provide some factual, policy, and historical background for this chapter's study of the malpractice system. After providing this background, this section of the chapter will focus on issues related to legislative reforms that in recent decades have increasingly set malpractice law apart from tort law generally.

2. *Overview.* Major empirical research on the incidence of iatrogenic injuries, negligence, and malpractice suits was undertaken in New York State in the 1980s by a team of investigators from Harvard University. See Harvard Medical Practice Study, Patients, Doctors, and Lawyers: Medical Injury, Malpractice Litigation, and Patient Compensation in New York (1990). In a later report, the Harvard researchers offered the following brief description and critique of the prevailing method of dealing with adverse medical events. (See if you can anticipate where the authors are heading with their specific criticisms of the fault system.)

> Medical practice and injuries are governed by certain well-established principles of the common-law tort system that also define liability for motor vehicle and consumer product (but not workplace) injuries.

- If a patient is injured as a result of the wrongful behavior of another (a physician or other medical care provider), then the victim is entitled to recover for all losses—both financial and nonpecuniary—caused by such fault.
- In the absence of negligent behavior, a doctor is not legally responsible for injuries suffered by his or her patients; instead, such losses must be borne by the victims personally or by the broader community through its various programs of public and private loss insurance.
- Disputes over whether an instance of medical treatment was careless and over what injuries the victim suffered as a result are ultimately resolvable in a civil trial before a jury, although in practice some 90 percent of such claims are settled by the parties and their lawyers through voluntary negotiation before a trial.
- If some legal fault and liability are established through this process, compensation will almost invariably be paid to the victim not by the individual who was careless, but rather by a liability insurer for an independently practicing doctor or by the institution that employed the doctor or other provider in question (or by that institution's insurer).

This system of fault-based tort liability has traditionally been credited with securing two distinct though generally compatible objectives. First, the values of corrective justice and fairness require that losses that have already occurred as a result of careless action should be shifted (as far as is possible) from the innocent patient-victim to the culpable party. Second, the prospect of being sued and having to pay for such losses will serve as a financial and emotional incentive to doctors to provide more careful treatment to their patients in the future. The flip side of this policy rationale for the fault system is that if a patient injury was produced as a purely accidental by-product of careful medical treatment, imposing liability is not justified. To do so would unfairly single out innocent doctors (from among everyone else in the community) to bear financial responsibility for the plight of their injured patients, and could not deter substandard care because poor care was not the reason for imposing liability.

The foregoing is, we believe, a fair statement of the core assumptions of the common law of tort-fault liability. Among legal scholars, however, the corrective justice rationale is no longer in general favor. A principal reason is that with the emergence of widespread, often mandatory liability insurance, the careless doctor no longer pays the tort bill for the patient's injuries. Instead, the individual doctor's insurer pays the tort award with funds accumulated from liability insurance premiums paid by all doctors in the relevant specialty and region. * * * In turn, doctors (and hospitals) pay for their often sizable insurance premiums with money collected from patients for medical services. And the vast majority of these doctors' fees are actually paid by private or public health insurance programs funded by premiums charged to individuals and employers or by taxes collected by governments. In other words, we now have an elaborate set of insurance arrangements in which healthy citizens are required, in effect, to purchase a form of disability insurance against the risk of at least some injuries arising out of their medical treatment.

Tort litigation, then, serves as a port of entry into this socially generated disability fund by determining which injured patients are to collect and how much. From that perspective, traditional concerns about securing corrective justice as between an injured victim and an individually culpable actor have little relevance. Rather, a more pragmatic policy analysis would be appropriate, one that would address the following questions:

> How sensibly does the entire tort system distribute compensation to injured patients from the funds contributed by the broader constituency of the health care system?
>
> How economic is administration of this disability insurance program in terms of money, time, and emotional demands on the parties?
>
> How effective is such a program in preventing substandard medical treatment, so that all patients may be protected from iatrogenic injuries before they occur?

Compensation

The tort system is designed to compensate all losses of patient-victims injured through the fault of their doctors, but in fact it compensates no losses of injured patients who cannot establish physician culpability. Tort critics charge that this substantive policy accounts for two crucial deficiencies of the system as a vehicle for compensatory insurance.

The most obvious flaw concerns the plight of patients who recover nothing after suffering severe injuries, even though the injuries create real needs for financial help to pay for additional medical care and rehabilitation and to serve as a source of income during the period when the patient is unable to work. The needs of the injured patient are exactly the same irrespective of whether the carelessness of a doctor contributed to the original incident. Thus, from this perspective it seems arbitrary and unfair to deny this large category of needy victims any access at all to the disability insurance fund that has accumulated in the manner described.

More recently, tort law has been charged with a second, contrasting defect. The commitment to full compensation of victims who establish the fault prerequisite appears to some to be incompatible of these principles of loss insurance. The most apparent violation of these principles occurs when large, unconstrained monetary damages are awarded for such essentially nonpecuniary losses as pain and suffering or loss of companionship. A similar failing appears in the right to full replacement of all lost earnings or treatment costs without any application of the deductible of coinsurance formulas that are standard in both private and public insurance. Although there are historic reasons for this dichotomy in the tort regime between full compensation and no compensation, such a substantive policy simply cannot be justified as a sensible insurance program.

Administration

Irrespective of whether any substantive grounds can be advanced for the fault principle, it is clear that the fault ingredient entails a substantial administrative burden for the tort system. To make the crucial judgment about whether the doctor was careless involves reconstruction of an event that occurred years earlier, and a contest between expert witnesses trying to educate a lay jury about how to assess what are often complex and subtle questions about the appropriate standard of medical care. Even if such judgments can be made accurately and reliably, the litigation process is certainly expensive in terms of time and money. Malpractice insurers in New York now spend an average of well over $10,000 to defend every malpractice claim, meritorious or not, while successful patient-claimants pay their own lawyers a fee that is generally one-third of more of the total award. Thus, even when one leaves aside the cost of securing and investing insurance funds and focuses simply on the process of claims administration and distribution, only about 40 percent of the total amount expended in the claims process actually reaches injured patients as compensation for their injuries.

Prevention

Even defenders of the tort system would generally concede that this program is not a particularly sensible of economic mode of insurance and compensation. In their view, however, the admitted problems created by hinging the patient's compensation on proof of the doctor's negligence are a price worth paying in the effort to deter careless medical practice by all doctors. The response from critics of the tort system is that malpractice litigation is actually not an effective instrument for improving the quality of medical care.

There are two aspects to this critique. One is that any monetary sanction that is imposed upon a negligent doctor itself depends on the fortuitous occurrence and severity of the patient's injuries, rather than on the degree of the doctor's culpability. For example, a momentary inadvertent slip by a surgeon who is ordinarily attentive and meticulous, but whose mistake in this case inflicts permanent long-term brain damage on a patient, can make this doctor liable for millions of dollars in tort damages. On the other hand, another doctor whose deviation from appropriate standards of care is both deliberate and egregious, but whose patient suffers a much less serious injury (or no injury), will escape with only moderate financial liability (or none at all). Indeed, unless the potential recoverable damages are reasonably large, there will be no liability in practice, because neither the patient nor a lawyer will have sufficient incentive to make the substantial initial investment required to institute a suit against the doctor. [As will appear shortly below, a major finding of the Harvard study was that, for whatever reason, only a very small percentage of negligently caused patient injuries ever become the subject of a claim for damages, making it unlikely that the system sends a clear enough signal to work as an effective incentive to prevent bad outcomes.—Eds.]

[Deterrence can also be questioned because, rather than the negligent provider of care, a] liability insurer actually pays all these awards, whether large or small. What doctors pay is a standardized insurance premium that depends on the nature of their specialty and geographic location. * * * One might, of course, adjust the size of the doctor's insurance premium in light of individual claims experience * * *. However, there is considerable doubt whether a meaningful and actuarially credible experience rating program can be devised for liability insurance against malpractice claims, which occur so rarely for an individual doctor (by contrast, for example, with the much more extensive workers' compensation experience of a large employer).

Still, to suggest that liability insurance fully insulates doctors from the impact of the tort system is somewhat unrealistic. A far more significant factor than even a demerit adjustment in an insurance premium is the loss of practice time and earnings, as well as personal morale and professional reputation, when the quality of the doctor's medical care is attacked through tort litigation. [M]any of these costs are visited upon doctors from the mere act of being sued, not only in cases in which they are found liable. * * * A final critique of the tort system, then, is that its deterrent instrument is much too crude in operation: that it serves primarily to induce unnecessary and wasteful modes of defensive medicine designed to decrease doctors' likelihood of being sued rather than patients' likelihood of being cured.

P. Weiler et al., A Measure of Malpractice: Medical Injury, Malpractice Litigation, and Patient Compensation 14–19 (1993).

Weiler et al. hypothesize two goals for the medical malpractice system: compensation of injured patients and prevention (or deterrence) of future injuries. They also suggest, however, that, if compensation were truly a central object of public policy here, there would be no basis for conditioning payment on a demonstration that the injury resulted from someone's fault; compensation could be accomplished much more efficiently through first-party or social insurance. It is also not clear that they system fills an important social need in providing compensation since financial protection against injuries is already provided in substantial measure by various public and private insurance and income-replacement programs. Realistically, the tort system can fill very few of the gaps in this larger system. Such compensation as it provides is highly contingent, frequently duplicative, and often comes long after the necessitating event.

But, despite frequent lip service paid to it in discussions of the malpractice system, is compensation really an objective in itself? Or is the predominant justification for shifting the costs of certain injuries simply the expectation, or hope, that health care providers facing those potential costs will take appropriate actions to prevent similar injuries from occurring? In any event, is it sensible for the legal system to attempt simultaneously to pursue two coequal, possibly competing objectives? When might the two goals conflict? Would the system operate more coherently if deterrence were recognized as its principal objective?

3. *The Theory of Deterrence.* Economist Patricia Danzon has argued that

the primary economic rationale for tort liability is deterrence. In principle, the law of negligence can create an incentive structure designed to induce physicians to invest optimally in injury prevention. Since injuries are costly but prevention is also not free, optimal prevention requires balancing the costs and benefits of reducing injury risk.

Why are physicians and other professionals subject to liability for their professional acts * * *? The reason is that the efficient functioning of markets requires that consumers be informed about the risks and benefits of alternative services and be able to monitor the quality of care actually delivered. These assumptions are obviously violated to some degree in the case of medical and other professional services, where the professional is trained to have superior knowledge and expertise. Tort liability can be viewed as a device to correct the inefficiencies that could result from market signals when consumers misperceive risk.

The Optimal Prevention of Injury

Injuries are costly. Most obvious are the costs of medical treatment, rehabilitation, and wages lost as a result of temporary or permanent disability. Harder to measure but no less real are the pain and suffering and the diminution in the quality of life that result from physical impairment. These are irreplaceable losses that cannot be recompensed by monetary compensation. In addition, there are administrative and overhead costs of effecting compensation. In the case of medical malpractice, these overhead costs add up to roughly twice as much as the compensation actually received by the victim.

On the other hand, injury prevention is also costly. Averting medical injuries requires time of physicians and other personnel, perhaps additional tests and other procedures. But injury prevention, like most activities, is subject to the law of diminishing returns. The initial dollars spent on basic safety measures—sterilizing medical instruments, checking labels—have a large payoff. But as more is spent, the reduction in risk per dollar spent diminishes. Thus the marginal or incremental costs of injury prevention rise as we attempt to reduce injury rates to lower and lower levels. Since resources devoted to prevention must be diverted from other socially valuable uses, the elimination of all injuries is not feasible. Although we may say we would pay any price to avoid an injury, our behavior in innumerable contexts—driving speed, dangerous sports—reveals that we do make trade-offs between risk reduction and other valuable uses of times and money.

* * *

Several policy tools are available for achieving the prevention and compensation of injuries. The government may attempt to regulate safety directly, by setting standards[, or may mandate private, or provide public, insurance against certain losses].

In contrast to direct regulation of safety standards and insurance coverage, liability rules are an indirect method of regulation. A liability rule determines in the first instance who should pay for an injury and, if someone other than the victim is assigned liability, how much should be paid. But the assignment of liability, in addition to compensating victims retrospectively, also has prospective impact. The anticipation of liability affects the incentives of persons involved in hazardous activities to take preventive measures and to buy liability insurance. Thus liability rules are an indirect way of influencing private choices with respect to safety precautions and insurance, through incentives rather than regulatory fiat.

* * *

Injuries arising out of medical treatment—iatrogenic injuries—are currently governed by a negligence rule of liability which is a hybrid of first-party and third-party liability. Under this rule a medical provider is liable for injury to a patient if the injury was the result of failure to meet the "due" standard of care. But if the injury is judged an adverse outcome consistent with the normal risk of non-negligent care, then the medical provider is not liable and the patient bears the cost. Whether the victim or the injurer is liable depends on whether or not the injurer's level of care met or fell short of the due-care standard. Again, the initial assignment of liability does not necessarily determine who ultimately bears the loss, because of the intermediation of insurance. The person at risk typically has first-party health and disability insurance that covers injuries which are part of the normal risk of the activity—those which occur even when the due-care standard is met. Defendants typically carry liability insurance to cover costs in the event of suit.

Thus a liability rule performs two functions: first, a distributive function, to determine who should pay for the injury; and second, in the long run, an allocative function, to determine the total societal cost of injuries. This societal cost of injuries depends on the incentives of people to invest in injury prevention and to buy insurance, which in turn depend on their expectations about the assignment of liability for future injuries.

* * *

Although at first sight the rules of caveat emptor, strict liability, and negligence appear to assign injury costs very differently and hence create very different incentives for injury prevention, in fact under certain conditions the liability assignment does not matter. In his seminal article on liability rules [Coase, The Problem of Social Cost, 3 J.L. & Econ. 1 (1963)], Ronald Coase showed that if both parties are fully informed about risks and if the costs of contracting are negligible, then the allocation of resources to loss prevention will by unaffected by who is held liable. * * *

This conclusion, that the allocation of resources and the distribution of income are invariant to the liability rule, holds only under the extreme assumption that patients and physicians are equally well informed about the risks and benefits of alternative procedures, and that patients can easily monitor the quality of care actually delivered. But in general, if the consumer has imperfect information about the quality of a product or service, either because he lacks the technical expertise to evaluate its risks and benefits or because he cannot monitor whether the product actually delivered is the one he thought he had contracted for, then the rule assigning liability for injuries will affect the quality and quantity of services that are produced, the allocation of resources to injury prevention, and the frequency of injury.

To see the effect of consumer misperceptions in the medical context, consider the extreme case in which the patient is totally oblivious to the risk. With first-party liability, the fee for the test would simply be the $100 resource cost. The patient would not insure and would be willing to have the test if it yielded only $100 in expected benefits. Thus if patients tend to systematically underestimate risk, they will underinsure and will incur more risk and more injuries than they would wish to if they comprehended the risks they were incurring. Conversely, if patients systematically overestimate risk, they will overinsure and will incur higher costs of prevention and fewer injuries than they would choose to if fully informed.

Transferring liability from a poorly informed patient to a better informed physician provides a means of correcting these distortions. If the physician correctly estimates the risk of injury, when he is liable he will charge a fee of $150, composed of $100 for the resource cost and $50 for the expected liability cost. The patient confronted with a $150 fee will now only have the procedure if he values it at $150. Despite his ignorance of the risks, he is induced to make the optimal decision about risk taking and to purchase the optimal amount of insurance, which is implicit in the fee. Thus placing liability on producers provides a means of correcting the inefficiencies that would result from consumer misperception of risks. This correction of defective market signals is the economic justification for holding manufacturers liable for product-related injuries and for the professional liability of physicians, attorneys, architects, and engineers.

Obviously the example just given is a gross oversimplification of medical decision making. Nevertheless, because of their information advantage, physicians have considerable discretion in guiding the choice of quantity and quality of services. Most providers may well try to act as a perfect agent for the patient, making those choices the patient would have made if he were fully informed. Medical training, codes of ethics, and norms of decent human conduct are conducive to this end. But financial gain and preference for leisure create incentives that conflict with the patient's interests. The physician who orders unnecessary treatments, fails to refer a difficult case to a specialist, skimps on taking a history, or hurries through a procedure can increase his income, but thereby exposes the patient to more risk. If patients accurately perceived these risks, they would adjust their demand for the physician's services, thereby transferring or "internalizing" to the physician the risk consequences of his level of care. But if patients do not accurately perceive the risks, then the costs of injuries or, equivalently, the benefits of reduction in risk of injury are not internalized to the physician, and his financial incentives to engage in risk reduction are suboptimal.

P. Danzon, Medical Malpractice: Theory, Evidence, and Public Policy 9–15 (1985). Are you comfortable with the goal of allocative efficiency posited by Danzon? It implies that the tort system should aim at minimizing the *sum* of the costs of injuries and the costs of preventing injuries.

What specific reasons are there to doubt that the tort system effectively, or optimally, deters medical accidents? What is the precise nature of the incentives it creates? Consider the following four notes.

4. *Experience Rating?* The theory of deterrence may break down if liability insurance effectively insulates the negligent doctor from bearing the cost of the injuries he causes? As Weiler suggests, this would not be a problem if insurance coverage is "experience-rated"—that is, priced to reflect individual physicians' claims experience. But malpractice insurers have engaged in experience rating to only a limited degree, since it has been thought both that malpractice claims are very nearly random in their incidence and that their infrequency in any doctor's practice makes the signal too intermittent to be valid. See generally P. Weiler, Malpractice on Trial 75–82 (1991) ("Inevitably there is a random quality to an event that is as infrequent in the life of any one doctor as a malpractice suit."). But see Schwartz & Komesar, Doctors, Damages and Deterrence: An Economic View of Medical Malpractice, 298 New Eng.J.Med. 1282, 1287 (1978):

> the thesis that suits are brought randomly is not supported by a recent study of 8000 physicians in the Los Angeles area. In a four-year period, 46 physicians (0.6 per cent of the 8000) accounted for 10 per cent of all claims and 30 per cent of all payments made by the insurance plan. The average number of suits against the 46 doctors was 1 1/4 per year. Analysis indicates that doctors against whom multiple suits are brought do, indeed, represent a higher-risk population than their colleagues.

See also Bovbjerg & Petroni, The Relationship between Physicians' Malpractice Claims History and Later Claims, 272 J.A.M.A. 1421 (1994) (finding claims history had predictive value, even with unpaid claims); Rolph, Merit Rating for Physicians' Malpractice Premiums: Only a Modest Deterrent, 54 Law & Contemp. Probs, Spring 1991, p. 65 ("the 'targeting' achievable from past paid-claims history is only moderately accurate"; but "adding information on an individual physician's demographic characteristics and practice patterns increases predictive accuracy"; "physicians may find the potential stigma and economic consequences of premium surcharges substantial enough to cause them to improve * * * "); Luft, Katz & Pinney, Risk Factors for Hospital Malpractice Exposure: Implications for Managers and Insurers, in id. at 43 (finding reasons to justify experience rating of hospitals); Sloan et al., Medical Malpractice Experience of Physicians: Predictable or Haphazard?, 262 J.A.M.A. 3291 (1989) (physicians incurring malpractice liability in the 1970s were found to be especially prone to suits in the 1980s, suggesting appropriateness of experience rating).

In recent years, malpractice insurers, including some physician-owned ones, have increasingly employed experience rating, creating subcategories of higher-risk physicians based on actual claims experience. Indeed, in New York, reform legislation required the insurance superintendent to implement a system of merit rating using discounts and surcharges. The resulting regulatory formula, based on up to twenty years' claims experience, was challenged by a professional organization, and the challenge survived a motion to dismiss. New York State Soc'y of Obstetricians & Gynecologists, Inc. v. Corcoran, 525 N.Y.S.2d 457 (N.Y.Sup.Ct.1987).

What other incentives, besides financial ones, may induce physicians to improve their practice skills?

5. *Deterrence in Practice.* How reliable is the tort system likely to be in inducing appropriate medical practice? Although this question cannot be answered directly, there is some evidence that health care providers do change their behavior in response to perceived liability risks. Hospital "risk-management" and quality-assurance programs were installed following the 1970s' malpractice crisis and appear to be more than just attempts to assuage criticism or to comply minimally with statutory requirements. See, e.g., J. Orlikoff & A. Vanagunas, Malpractice Prevention and Liability Control for Hospitals (2d ed. 1988); G. Troyer & S. Salman, Handbook of Health Care Risk Management (1986); W. Robertson, Medical Malpractice: A Preventive Approach (1985) (a physician's report on risk management in Washington State). But see Morlock & Malitz, Do Hospital Risk Management Programs Make A Difference?, Law & Contemp. Probs., Spring 1991, p. 1 (finding little effect of risk management, other than certain educational activities, on malpractice claims experience in 40 hospitals).

Although physicians often maintain that the medical malpractice system only drives up costs and does not affect the quality of care, researchers connected with the Harvard malpractice study found through interviews that physicians made changes in their practices as a result of malpractice litigation pressure. See Lawthers et al., Physicians' Perceptions of the Risk of Being Sued, 17 J. Health Pol., Pol'y & L. 463 (1992) (also finding that physicians greatly exaggerate the risk of suit, leading to protective behavior). See also Bell, Legislative Intrusions into the Common Law of Medical Malpractice: Thoughts about the Deterrent Effect of Tort Liability, 35 Syracuse L.Rev. 939 (1984) (concluding that "medical malpractice liability probably is resulting in safer medical behavior").

6. *The Possibility of Overdeterrence: "Defensive Medicine."* A common allegation about the medical malpractice system is that the incentives it sets up encourage so-called "defensive medicine"—that is, the prescription of unnecessary or inappropriate tests and other precautions solely, or principally, to protect the provider against a charge of malpractice (by omission rather than commission) rather than to protect the patient's health. Although this charge has been difficult to document, its implications for efficiency and the cost of care are obvious.

It is plausible that providers, fearing not only liability but also involvement in stressful lawsuits, spend resources unnecessarily in an effort to make themselves look good on paper and in any later deposition or cross-examination. Certainly the indemnity-based financing system traditionally made resources rather freely available for extra tests, x-rays, and other services without regard to whether those costs were incurred to protect patients against bad medical outcomes or only to protect providers against perceived legal risks. Litigation fears may also cause physicians to refuse to treat individuals whom they identify as litigious and to avoid difficult cases or high-risk, but beneficial, procedures because they are more likely to result in injury and suits. It would not be surprising if physicians, not understanding the legal system but perceiving it to be irrational in its demands, sought to conform to standards that they and others would agree are unreasonable. Indeed, even if the law were quite evenhanded and fair in assessing fault, physicians might be driven by worst-case scenarios (they are known to overestimate the actual risk of being sued) to waste valuable resources.

Research on defensive medicine provides mixed evidence. An AMA-sponsored study in the 1980s estimated the costs of defensive medicine at that time at $15 billion a year. Rizzo & Gonzalez, The Cost of Medical Professional Liability, 257 J.A.M.A. 2776 (1987). An extensive study sponsored by the congressional Office of Technology Assessment, however, concluded that the cost of defensive medicine to the medical care system was probably negligible and found no evidence of adverse effects on access to medical care. Office of Technology Assessment, Defensive Medicine and Medical Malpractice (OTA H-602, 1994); see also Klingman et al., Measuring Defensive Medicine Using Clinical Scenario Surveys, 21 J. Health Pol., Pol'y & L. 185 (1996) (describing OTA study). In this study, practicing physicians in several specialties were presented with clinical scenarios and asked to rate the factors that determined their clinical choices. In most scenarios, defensive medicine did not play a significant role, leading the OTA to conclude that only a small percentage of diagnostic procedures, probably less than eight percent, are induced primarily by conscious concern about medical malpractice liability. On the other hand, the OTA was forced to conclude that it is almost impossible to quantify the effects of defensive medicine since, to the extent it occurs at all, it may have some benefit for the patient. Moreover, defensive practices that have become part of the standard of care may have acquired clinical rationales in the minds of the physicians queried. (To many physicians, defensive medicine is often what *other* doctors do.) In any event, because of these and other uncertainties, other estimates of the costs of defensive medicine have been significantly higher than the OTA's. See, e.g., Kessler & McClellan, Do Doctors Practice Defensive Medicine?, 111 Q.J. Econ. 353 (1996) (comparing expenditures and outcomes in treating elderly heart patients in states with and without recent tort reforms and estimating that greater intensity of care associated with higher malpractice risks, but not with better outcomes, raised costs 5% to 9%); Lewin-VHI Inc., Estimating the Costs of Defensive Medicine (Report prepared for MMI Companies, Inc., Fairfax, Va., Jan. 27, 1993).

7. *Is Optimal Deterrence a Realistic Objective?* Is it realistic to think, in accordance with Danzon's theory, that requiring health care providers to compensate injured patients on a wide scale would, by "internalizing" costs, achieve "optimal" deterrence of medical accidents? (Can you define these concepts?) In other words, is it reasonable to expect that making health care providers liable for injuries they cause will induce them to resolve safety/cost trade-offs efficiently—that is, to choose appropriately between incurring the costs of additional increments of safety and paying for such injuries as occur? Or does the moral hazard associated with both liability insurance and health insurance suggest that seeking optimization through cost internalization would be a vain hope?

If efficient prevention is not fostered by the present system, should we stop pursuing that objective? Danzon concludes that

> the fault-based system is worth retaining if the benefits, in terms of injuries deterred, exceed the costs of litigating over fault and other associated costs, such as defensive medicine. Unfortunately, a full cost-benefit evaluation is impossible because we cannot measure the number of injuries that are prevented as a result of the additional care exercised by medical providers in response to the threat of liability. But * * * rough calculation suggests that if the number of negligent injuries is, generously, 20 percent lower than it otherwise would be because of the incentives for care created by the malpractice system, the system is worth retaining, despite its costs.

Id. at 225–26. Although she defends the malpractice system against some of its detractors, she is no apologist, recommending numerous reforms (some of which will be mentioned later in this section).

If one lacks confidence in the ability of the tort system to achieve efficiency, should we then embrace social insurance—that is, compensation of injured persons—as the dominant goal? (The report by the Harvard researchers, Weiler et al., excerpted earlier in this section was intended in part to open this possibility for consideration.) If this seems the wisest policy after all, why stop with compensating victims of iatrogenic injuries only? Would providing compensation only to persons injured in medical treatment imply that the true purpose of the reform was to protect, not injured persons against economic losses, but medical professionals against lawsuits? (Materials in § D of this chapter will mention several so-called "no-fault" possibilities.)

If the malpractice system fails to do its job(s) well, should it simply be abolished, leaving patients to bear the costs of all injuries (or to procure their own insurance against such costs), even injuries attributable to provider negligence (which might policed through intensified disciplinary activities)? Or is the public's desire for corrective justice so strong that it would not tolerate total immunization of health care providers from liability for tortious conduct? (Danzon observes that justice in an ethical or moral sense "may be an elusive goal to pursue: the person made liable for an injury in the first instance may not end up ultimately bearing the cost, because of the operation of markets and insurance mechanism." Id. at 12. Moreover, the force of any moral messages the fault system intends to send will vary with the conscientiousness of the professionals being sanctioned, rolling off the back of the less ethical while being perhaps too devastating to those who are already committed to the welfare of their patients.) In any event, it seems clear that the right to register grievances against providers—by litigation, if necessary—is highly prized in public opinion and could not easily be abrogated. Note in the materials that follow in this section, however, how the right to sue doctors has been increasingly circumscribed by legislatures responding either to policy arguments against traditional tort remedies or to political pressure from the medical community.

Although the malpractice system is frequently and persuasively criticized on several levels (e.g., by Weiler et al.), it is not likely to go away. Should a major effort therefore be made to improve the system so that it can perform the deterrence function better than it currently appears to do?

Consider whether the coming of managed care, with its new potential for comparing costs and benefits, might make malpractice liability a more effective force for attaining efficiency goals. Would it make sense, for example, to shift liability away from individual physicians to entities further up the contractual chain linking the financing and organization of care to its delivery? Presumably such entities would pay experience-rated insurance premiums (or self-insure) and thus be motivated to prevent compensable injuries. They would also seem to be in a good position to monitor and control, or at least influence, the quality of care and to resolve trade-offs between cost and quality. Professor Grady makes the important point that much of negligence theory is concerned with inducing "durable precautions," such as the installation of better systems and methods, and not with punishing mere human errors. Grady, Why Are People Negligent? Technology, Nondurable Precautions, and the Medical Malpractice Explosion, 82 Nw. U.L. Rev. 293 (1988). Recall, in this connection, the excerpt from an article by Lucian Leape, Error in Medicine, 272 J.A.M.A. 1851 (1994), in chapter 6(§A), which observed the need for system-oriented solutions to quality problems, a need captured in the movements for "Continuous Quality Improvement" and "Total Quality Management."

Assuming that placing liability on parties more strategically placed to make systematic changes in health care delivery makes sense as a policy matter, which entities are the best candidates for such "enterprise liability"? This question, which was raised in chapter 5(§B), will be addressed more fully in chapter 8(§A) (relating to managed-care organizations). See generally Abraham & Weiler, Enterprise Medical Liability and the Evolution of the American Health Care System, 108 Harv. L. Rev. 381 (1994).

Before embracing "enterprise liability" of any kind, it might seem desirable to consider major substantive and procedural reforms in the system for identifying and appropriately assigning liability for iatrogenic injuries. Materials later in this chapter will raise possibilities for improving a system that, however dysfunctional it appears today, still seems to have great potential value as a mechanism for improving the outcomes of medical care. Is the legal system capable, however, of designing and operating a reparations system that delivers on this theoretical promise? Consider, in addition to the doctrinal and operational problems to be canvassed throughout this chapter, the particular inadequacies of the malpractice system revealed in the following note.

8. *Patient Injury and Malpractice Litigation*. The "Harvard Study" alluded to above provides an extraordinary insight into the actual workings of the malpractice system. Among its most important findings was a surprising lack of congruence between the large universe of medical injuries (the Harvard findings on the incidence of iatrogenic injuries were summarized in chapter 6(§A)) and what turned out to be, despite impressions to the contrary, a relatively small number of resulting malpractice claims based on those injuries. The Harvard researchers summarized the study's findings on this subject as follows:

[W]e set out to learn exactly what was happening within the legal system. How many malpractice claims were being brought, and in what kinds of cases? Certainly most American doctors fervently believe that present-day malpractice litigation is excessive and erratic in its operation. Acting on that belief, physician associations have persuaded most state legislatures to enact legal obstacles to the filing of such patient suits: shorter and tighter statutes of limitations, procedures for claims screening and certification, restrictions on the size of contingent fees that patients can pay lawyers to take on the chancier cases. To assess the validity of these popular and political impressions we used the files of New York State's Department of Health to document the incidence and the distribution of malpractice litigation.

Actually, scholarly opinion has not been of the persuasion that there are too many malpractice claims. On the contrary, the medical setting has provided the strongest evidence that the real tort crisis may consist in *too few* claims.

Frequently cited in support of this scholarly understanding is the work done by Patricia Danzon, who followed up on the California Medical Association's *Medical Insurance Feasibility Study*. Danzon compared the study's estimates of injuries taking place in California hospitals in 1974 with data collected by the National Association of Insurance Commissioners (NAIC) in its survey of malpractice claims closed from 1975 through 1978 in California and elsewhere across the nation. Danzon found that for every ten negligent adverse events—that is, instances of torts—actually occurring within the health care system, only one malpractice claim was lodged in the liability insurance system, even at the height of the tort crisis in that state in the mid–1970s. * * *

* * * The true risk that a negligent adverse event will produce a malpractice claim (according to Danzon, in California that risk was at most 10 percent in the mid-1970s and 5 percent in the mid–1980s) can be measured only under the tacit assumption that all the claims filed reflect negligent injuries actually suffered (even if nowhere nearly all the injuries suffered do generate filed claims). Yet on reflection that assumption is unlikely to be entirely valid. The very inability of so many patients to connect their present disability to past medical maltreatment and the persuade a lawyer that prospects of success are good enough to warrant suit also makes it likely that many patients and lawyers will mistakenly make such a connection and will file suits even if the patient was not really the victim of medical negligence.

As a second major feature of our litigation review, then, we set out to test these assumptions directly by documenting which malpractice claims were valid and which were not. We did so by matching our judgments from the medical record review about which patients had legitimate tort claims, with our litigation data about which patients actually filed claims.

The immediate objective of that investigation was to determine whether the litigation system was reasonably accurate or was quite erratic in targeting true cases of provider negligence and patient injury. If there was considerable inaccuracy in the tort selection process, such that some malpractice claims were filed even though negligent adverse events had not occurred, the aggregate injury/claims ratio derived from the earlier phase of the litigation review would in fact understate the true litigation gap. In other words, for every claim we found that was not matched to a negligent adverse event, another negligent adverse event would not have produced a malpractice claim to be incorporated in the aggregate claims total.

* * * [S]lightly more than 7 patients suffered a negligent adverse event for every patient who filed a tort claim. Although the likelihood of suit is somewhat greater than the 10–to–1 ratio estimated for California in the mid–1970s, it is significantly smaller than the less than 5–to–1 ratio we expected for New York in the mid–1980s.

* * *

One would not, of course, expect that every negligent adverse event—which we defined as including any disability lasting for at least a day—would produce a tort claim. The medical records indicated that most physical disabilities were modest and short-lived. Many of the more serious injuries or fatalities were inflicted on elderly patients, whose consequent financial losses would probably be comparatively low. Thus, nearly 80 percent (10,026 out of 12,859) of the patients who suffered a negligent injury but did not sue were either fully recovered from the injury within six months or were more than 70 years old when the injury occurred.

* * *

The foregoing aggregate ratios sharply understate the true litigation gap, because they assume that all claims made and paid were brought for true negligent injuries. Yet the key finding of our detailed matching procedure was that in only 8 of the 47 claims filed by our patients as a result of their 1984 hospitalization was there an actual negligent adverse event in the treatment. Ten claims involved hospitalization that had produced injuries, though not due to provider negligence; and another 3 cases exhibited some evidence of medical causation, but not enough to pass our probability threshold. That left 26 malpractice claims, more than half the total of 47 in our sample, which provided no evidence of medical injury, let alone medical negligence.

* * *

We noted earlier that a common physicians' complaint about malpractice litigation is that it is excessive and erratic. Our investigation of the incidence and distribution of litigation in New York demonstrates that while the legal system does in fact operate erratically, it hardly operates excessively. Indeed, precisely because so many claims brought by patients are misdirected, earlier comparisons of the totals of negligent injuries and malpractice claims actually disguised how small are the odds that a potentially legitimate tort claim will be brought.

* * * [I]t is clear that a substantial majority of malpractice claims that are filed by patients do not flow from true negligent injuries inflicted by doctors or other health care providers. Although the legal system appears to do a surprisingly accurate job of sifting out the valid from the invalid claims (in the latter cases paying the claimants nothing or just a small amount of damages), the fact is that many innocent doctors are subjected to unwarranted tort suits. Malpractice litigation appears, then, to be

sending as confusing a signal as would our traffic laws if the police regularly gave out more tickets to drivers who go through green lights than to those who go through red lights. * * *

From this perspective, one can understand the appeal of legislative efforts to inhibit the filing of "false positive" claims against innocent doctors, for example by requiring, as a prelude to suit, medical certification of the validity of a malpractice claim or preliminary evaluation of the validity of a claim by an independent review panel. But we must not lose sight of the impact that such legislative policies probably have on the litigation gap itself.

P. Weiler et al., *A Measure of Malpractice*, supra, at 61–64, 69–71, 73, 75.

Like all of tort law, medical malpractice law requires the successful plaintiff to demonstrate the following four elements: dutiful relationship, injury, negligent conduct, and a causal connection between negligence and injury. As in tort law generally, the law of medical malpractice implicitly assumes that claims usually arise when there has been negligent injury in fact, that most claims brought are valid ones, and that very few claims arise in its absence of negligent injury. As observed in the foregoing extract, however, one of the demonstrated deficiencies of the medical malpractice system is the incongruity between the universe of negligent injuries and the universe of claims actually filed. Moreover, as will appear below, claims rates have been hectic over time and appear to be dictated less by the rate of negligent injury than by other factors. What factors might explain both the relative infrequency with which valid malpractice claims are lodged (the many potential claims that never materialize) and the changes over time in the frequency (number) and severity (magnitude) of tort claims for medical injuries?

In reading the materials that follow, consider how the reforms that have been considered and adopted correlate with the policy questions raised by the Harvard study.

9. *Recurrent Crises in the Malpractice Liability System.* The malpractice system is financed, for the most part, through liability insurance purchased by individual physicians and by hospitals, which may also cover some losses through self-insurance or a combination of self-insurance and "excess" liability coverage. Although malpractice law has always been a matter of concern to medical practitioners, it was only when significant problems developed in the market for malpractice liability insurance—first, in the mid 1970s and again in the 1980s—that physicians finally were able to attract legislative attention to their supposed grievances. The resulting interventions in the malpractice system by state legislatures have increasingly distinguished the malpractice compensation system from other areas of tort liability. The following summary of the apparent crises in malpractice insurance is a prelude to the study of legislative reforms:

Most policy makers awoke to medical malpractice as a public issue during the first major insurance crisis in 1974–76. Interrelated sets of events compelled public attention: First, numerous medical malpractice insurance companies suddenly withdrew from selected state markets or announced very large price rises. Some physicians could not find coverage at virtually any price, at least in the key states of California and New York. Second, as a result, some doctors conducted "slow-downs" of medical services and even seriously discussed strikes. Medical groups lobbied heavily for remedial legislation. Both California and New York passed emergency statutes during 1975. The New York and California crises were repeated in less severe fashion across the country. The crisis or fear of incipient crisis triggered remedial or preventive legislation in most states, even those without such significant problems.

* * *

The mid–1970s' crisis had several roots. One was an unexpected surge in claims; rating bureau data show that the mild frequency growth in 1966–70 was followed by great rises in the early 1970s—12 percent a year for the whole period but 19 percent annually for 1971–73. Severity—the mean amount paid on a claim—rose more consistently throughout this period. These rises in insurance costs coincided with the post-oil-shock recession, which reduced earnings on insurers' investments. Insurers may have been too slow to react, and regulatory lag did not improve their financial posture.

By some counts, the 1970s' crisis was not the first but the third in modern medical malpractice insurance. In the 1950s, malpractice insurance was an exceedingly stable line of coverage. Agents typically sold policies to individual physicians as a sideline to coverage for automobile and premises liability. The chance of a claim's ever being made for professional negligence was very small. One American Medical Association study found that only one physician in seven had ever faced a claim in his professional lifetime. Very large recoveries were exceedingly rare, and policies were priced accordingly. Insurance rating had only two classes of insureds—physicians and surgeons—and rate-making was extremely simple.

In the late 1950s and early 1960s, however, tort doctrines became more liberal, claimants more assertive, and physicians more willing to give expert testimony. Claims frequency and costs rose, and the old order vanished. Under new cost pressure, the market became more sophisticated and specialized. * * *

The late 1960s saw further rises, with claims frequency again playing a leading role. Also rising steadily was claims severity. Malpractice concerns claimed national attention for the first time, and Congress held hearings. Overall, the malpractice premium volume (physicians and hospitals) increased fivefold in nominal dollars during the 1960s—from about $65 million in 1960 to $330 million in 1970. In 1971, President Richard Nixon directed the Secretary of Health, Education and Welfare to create a study commission, which in turn commissioned the first collection of empirical information about many facets of malpractice. The Secretary's Commission concluded that no crisis existed in the early 1970s, as insurance was readily available from numerous insurers. Of course, no sooner had the report appeared than the much more serious crisis reclaimed attention in 1974.

Industry and Legislative Response

The 1970s' crisis generally abated within two years, however, as indicated by the renewed availability of insurance. Several factors contributed to the increase: New provider-run insurers entered the market, underwriting the higher levels of coverage that were needed and committing their companies to stay for the long term. The first such physician company was founded in mid–1975; by the end of 1977, more than 15 were in operation. Ten years later 41 companies were based in 33 states, many beginning to offer coverage beyond their home states. (The hospital market is separate; there, too, provider companies have developed, but hospital self-insurance or insurance through a "captive" insurer is common.)

* * *

Stability in the insurance market also benefitted from a shift from "occurrence" to "claims-made" policies. Claims-made policies cover only claims actually filed in the policy year, rather than covering incidents occurring during the year, so long as they arose at an earlier time when a policy from the same company was also in force. * * * The new policy basis greatly simplified adjustment of rates in response to changes in frequency and expected future payouts on claims. That insurers and regulators agreed on the need to increase premiums naturally also helped stabilize the market. Total premiums passed the billion dollar mark in 1976.

* * * By the end of the 1970s and the beginning of the 1980s, * * * there was, if anything, a surplus of capacity to provide malpractice coverage. Real prices even declined in some instances, although experience varied by state. Claims frequency was down; claims severity, although up, seemed predictable; and insurers could earn high real rates of return on their investment of reserves.

Renewed Crisis in the 1980s

By the early 1980s, the situation had once again deteriorated, with rising claims and falling net revenues for insurers. Large premium hikes again appeared, this time building on a far higher base. Total malpractice insurance premiums approached $3 billion by 1983 as the next crisis gathered. * * * The American Medical Association declared a new crisis in 1984.

This time, however, the malpractice crisis was more general affecting many other insureds. Frequency of claims again rose markedly for physicians' malpractice coverage in the early 1980s. Premiums rose swiftly as costs rose and insurance capacity shrank, particularly in reinsurance (where, by some accounts, many reinsurers lost confidence that the results of the tort system were predictable over time). Investment earnings were also squeezed by a decline in interest rates. The rises in premiums and the increasingly unequal burden across specialty rating groups caused particular concern. Noteworthy in their problems were obstetricians, who were on the cutting edge of difficulties, a position relinquished since the 1970s by the anesthesiologists.

Availability was much less of an issue for physicians in the 1980s, however. The presence of physician-sponsored insurers in most states seems to have helped prevent the major upheavals in the marketplace that had occurred in some states in the 1970s. Nonetheless, there are reliable reports of limits on insurance capacity. The St. Paul, the nation's leading malpractice carrier, took the unusual step of announcing in 1986 that it would no longer underwrite new applicants for coverage. Existing insureds were covered, the company noted, but the legal-regulatory climate was too uncertain to justify committing new capital. The same company and others also withdrew altogether from several states. Anecdotally, it is said that reinsurance also contracted during this period, but data are unavailable to quantify this effect. To judge from informal reports, the situation was far more critical for many other liability insureds, public and private, including small businesses, municipal officers, and nurse midwives.

* * *

The 1980s saw a resurgence of reform efforts. * * * At the state level most enactments resemble the 1970s' versions in attempting to curb the numbers and size of awards. Three major differences are discernible between the decades, however: First, the 1980s saw far more generic tort reform, aimed at all personal injury lawsuits, rather than purely malpractice reform. Second, the federal government directly intervened for the first time—to promote insurance availability through the Risk Retention Act and to document instances of malpractice and physician discipline through the Health Care Quality Improvement Act. Third, lawmakers in the 1980s were ready to consider more sweeping reforms of today's system of tort law and liability insurance, such as the Neurologically Impaired Infants Acts of Virginia and Florida. These acts created a new compensation system for this category of severe birth injuries to replace the system of tort law and liability insurance that traditionally covers malpractice.

In the late 1980s and early 1990s, even more broadly sweeping changes in traditional tort law and insurance practice were receiving serious attention. At the same time, the crisis, measured in terms of both premium increases and claims frequency were subsiding, probably again only temporarily. * * *

Malpractice insurance is a public issue for three main reasons: First, its availability and price affect physicians' well-being. Second, these factors may indirectly affect patients' access to care and the prices that patients and other health care payers have to pay. Third, insurance developments may affect the quality of care available.

F. Sloan, R. Bovbjerg & P. Githens, Insuring Medical Malpractice 4–7, 10 (1991).

Included in the developments triggered by the crises just described was something of a revolution in the malpractice liability insurance system itself. How might the appearance of provider-owned or provider-operated liability insurers help to prevent future crises? What are the benefits of shifting from occurrence to so-called "claims-made" coverage? What is the downside of claims-made coverage from the physician's point of view?

Malpractice Reform Legislation: Constitutional and Other Issues

Carson v. Maurer

Supreme Court of New Hampshire, 1980.
120 N.H. 925, 424 A.2d 825.

■ PER CURIAM.

The plaintiffs in these consolidated appeals challenge the constitutionality of RSA ch. 507–C (Supp.1979), governing actions for medical injury.

The plaintiffs here are also plaintiffs in underlying actions for medical injury; the defendants are medical care providers. * * *

I. INTRODUCTION

The statute in question is part of an effort by the legislature to address the problems of the medical injury reparations system. In enacting RSA ch. 507–C (Supp.1979), the legislature set forth rigorous standards for qualified expert testimony, created a two-year statute of limitations applicable to most medical malpractice actions, required that notice of intent to sue be given at least sixty days before commencing the action, prohibited the statement of the total damages claimed as an ad damnum or otherwise, abolished the collateral source rule, limited the amount of damages recoverable for non-economic loss to $250,000, empowered the court to order periodic payments of any future damages in excess of $50,000, and established a contingent fee scale for attorneys in medical malpractice actions.

In enacting RSA ch. 507–C (Supp.1979), the legislature sought to contain the costs of the medical injury reparations system by revising and codifying the applicable tort law. In its statement of findings and purpose, the legislature found

> "... that substantial increases in the incidence and size of claims for medical injury pose a major threat to effective delivery of medical care in the state and that the risks and consequences of medical injury must be stabilized in order to encourage continued provision of medical care to the public at reasonable cost, the continued existence of medical care institutions and the continued readiness of individuals to enter the medical care field."

Laws 1977, ch. 417:1. Accordingly, RSA ch. RSA 507–C (Supp.1979) was intended to codify and stabilize the law governing medical malpractice actions and to improve the availability of adequate liability insurance for health care providers at reasonable cost.

The plaintiffs first argue that RSA ch. RSA 507–C (Supp.1979) violates the equal protection guarantees of the United States and New Hampshire Constitutions, in that it improperly singles out victims of medical negligence, as distinct from victims of other kinds of negligence, for harsh treatment by restricting the means by which they may sue and the damages they may recover for their injuries.

The medical malpractice statute establishes several classifications. First, it confers certain benefits on tortfeasors who are health care providers that are not afforded to other tortfeasors. Conversely, it distinguishes between those tort claimants whose injuries were caused by medical malpractice and all other tort claimants. The statute also distinguishes between medical malpractice victims whose non-economic loss exceeds $250,000 and those whose non-economic loss is $250,000 or less and between malpractice victims whose future damage awards exceed $50,000 and those who are awarded $50,000 or less for future damages. The issue is whether any of these classifications violates the equal protection mandate that "those who are similarly situated be similarly treated."

The plaintiffs contend that RSA ch. RSA 507–C (Supp.1979) impinges upon the exercise of their allegedly fundamental right to be indemnified for personal injuries, and that the statute is therefore unconstitutional unless supported by a compelling state interest. We have held, however, that the right to recover for one's injuries is not a fundamental right * * * Furthermore, none of the classifications created by RSA ch. RSA 507–C (Supp. 1979) involves the type of suspect classification, such as race, alienage or nationality, that would require strict scrutiny.

Although the right to recover for personal injuries is not a "fundamental right," * * * the rights involved herein are sufficiently important to require that the restrictions imposed on those rights be subjected to a more rigorous judicial scrutiny than allowed under the rational basis test. Consequently, the classifications created by RSA ch. RSA 507–C (Supp.1979) "must be reasonable, not arbitrary, *and* must rest upon some ground of difference having a fair and substantial relation to the object of the legislation" in order to satisfy State equal protection guarantees. (Emphasis added.) State v. Scoville, 113 N.H. 161, 163, 304 A.2d 366, 369 (1973), quoting F.S. Royster Guano Co. v. Virginia, 253 U.S. 412, 415 (1920).

We recognize that recently the United States Supreme Court has restricted its application of this substantial relationship test to cases involving classifications based upon gender and illegitimacy. In interpreting our State constitution, however, we are not confined to federal constitutional standards and are free to grant individuals more rights than the Federal Constitution requires. Indeed, we have applied the "fair and substantial relation" test not only in scrutinizing gender-based classifications, but also in examining economic and social legislation and ordinances which did not involve distinctions based upon gender or illegitimacy.

We therefore hold that, in determining whether RSA ch. RSA 507–C (Supp.1979) denies medical malpractice victims equal protection of the laws, the test is whether the challenged classifications are reasonable and have a fair and substantial relation to the object of the legislation. Accord, Arneson v. Olson, 270 N.W.2d 125, 133 (N.D.1978). Whether the malpractice statute can be justified as a reasonable measure in furtherance of the public interest depends upon whether the restriction of private rights sought to be imposed is not so serious that it outweighs the benefits sought to be conferred upon the general public.

In applying this equal protection test, however, we will not independently examine the factual basis for the legislative justification for the statute. In the absence of a "suspect classification" or a "fundamental right," courts will not second-guess the legislature as to the wisdom of or necessity for legislation. New Orleans v. Dukes, 427 U.S. 297, 303 (1976). Our sole inquiry is whether the legislature could reasonably conceive to be true the facts on which the challenged legislative classifications are based. The legislature had before it facts from which it could reasonably conclude that there had been substantial increases in the size and incidence of medical malpractice claims, which in turn posed a threat to the continued effective delivery of health care at a reasonable cost in the State. [Apparently, there were only three malpractice claims paid in New Hampshire in 1976.—Eds.] From these facts the legislature could also conclude that these problems required special legislative treatment. Whether we would have come to the same conclusion is not material * * *.

With this analytical framework in mind, we turn to our examination of those provisions of RSA ch. RSA 507–C (Supp.1979) which the plaintiffs assert deny them equal protection of the laws. The only issues we address are whether the statute has a fair and substantial relation to this legitimate legislative objective and whether it imposes unreasonable restrictions on private rights.

* * *

III. STATUTE OF LIMITATIONS.

The plaintiffs next challenge the constitutionality of the statute of limitations for medical injury actions, although they do not specify the alleged constitutional infirmity. RSA 507–C:4 (Supp.1979) requires that a medical malpractice plaintiff bring his action within two years of the alleged negligence or, if the "action is based upon the discovery of a foreign object in the body of the injured person which is not discovered and could not reasonably have been discovered within such 2 year period, the action may be commenced within 2 years of the date of discovery or of the date of discovery of facts which would reasonably lead to discovery, whichever is earlier." The statute also provides that a child less than eight years old at the time of the alleged negligence shall have until his tenth birthday to commence an action for medical injury. Prior to the enactment of RSA ch. RSA 507–C (Supp.1979), a six-year limitation period applied to malpractice actions and to most other personal actions. RSA 508:4 (Supp.1979).

* * *

RSA 507–C:4 (Supp.1979) is invalid insofar as it makes the discovery rule unavailable to all medical malpractice plaintiffs except those whose actions are based upon the discovery of a foreign object in the injured person's body. Under the discovery rule a cause of action does not accrue until the plaintiff discovers or, in the exercise of reasonable diligence, should have discovered both the fact of his injury and the cause thereof. The rule is premised on "the manifest unfairness of foreclosing an injured person's cause of action before he has had even a reasonable opportunity to discover its existence." Brown v. Mary Hitchcock Memorial Hosp., 117 N.H. 739, 741–42, 378 A.2d 1138, 1139–40 (1977). Although the discovery rule was initially employed in this State in a "foreign-object" case, we made it clear in *Brown v. Mary Hitchcock Memorial Hosp.* that the rule and the fundamental equitable considerations underlying it applied to medical malpractice cases generally. As such, the legislature may not abolish the discovery rule with respect to any one class of medical malpractice plaintiffs. We therefore hold that in *all* medical malpractice cases in which the cause of action is not discovered and could not reasonably be discovered during the applicable limitation period, that period will not begin to run until the time the plaintiff discovers both his injury and its cause. Since the issue is not before us, we do not consider whether *Brown* went too far in extending the discovery rule beyond discovery of the existence and cause of the injury to discovery of negligence on the defendant's part.

We also find that RSA 507–C:4 (Supp.1979) is unconstitutional insofar as it extinguishes rights conferred by RSA 508:8, which provides: "An infant or mentally incompetent person may bring a personal action within two years after such disability is removed." RSA 508:8 is a saving statute, the purpose of which is to protect minors and mental incompetents from the destruction of their rights by the running of the statute of limitations. The legislature may not, consistent with equal protection principles, deny only this class of medical malpractice plaintiffs the protection afforded all other persons by the saving statute. In doing so, RSA 507–C:4 (Supp.1979) does not substantially further the legislative object of containing the costs of the medical injury reparations system because the number of malpractice claims brought by or on behalf of minors or mental incompetents is comparatively small. See Jenkins, California's Medical Injury Compensation Reform Act: An Equal Protection Challenge, 52 S.Cal.L.Rev. 829, 960–61 (1979). At the same time, the statute operates to extinguish a cause of action of which the plaintiff, due to his disability, may not have learned until after the limitations period has expired. The last sentence of RSA 507–C:4 (Supp.1979) unfairly burdens and discriminates against medical malpractice plaintiffs, and we therefore hold that it denies such plaintiffs equal protection of the laws.

IV. NOTICE COMPLIANCE.

We next turn to RSA 507–C:5 (Supp.1979), which provides that no action for medical injury shall be commenced until at least sixty days after service upon the defendant, by registered or certified mail, of a written notice of claim setting forth, under oath, the nature and circumstances of the alleged injuries and the damages claimed. * * *

The legislative history indicates that the purpose of RSA 507–C:5 (Supp.1979) is to provide the malpractice defendant with some sort of warning before the commencement of expensive litigation. This would give the defendant an opportunity to evaluate the claim and consider the possibility of settlement before costly litigation is undertaken.

This notice requirement does not, however, fairly and substantially relate to any legitimate legislative objective. The malpractice defendant gets all the notice he needs when he is served with process (RSA ch. 510 (Supp.1979)), because he still has ample time to review the claim and initiate settlement negotiations before the trial begins. Any expenses incurred in doing so would likewise be incurred if the investigatory and settlement process was commenced prior to suit. Thus, the special treatment afforded medical care providers by the notice provision at issue bears no reasonable relationship to the stated purposes of RSA ch. RSA 507–C (Supp.1979).

Furthermore, by placing numerous pitfalls in the path of unsuspecting plaintiffs, the effect of this notice requirement is to unjustly hinder the prosecution of many claims. The fact that three of the plaintiffs in these consolidated appeals had their suits dismissed for failure to strictly comply with RSA 507–C:5 (Supp.1979), even though the trial court found that the defendants in fact had notice of the impending litigation, demonstrates that this section is a procedural trap for the unwary and not an effective means to encourage pretrial settlement or investigation. Of course, these plaintiffs may still institute a second suit to recover for their medical injuries, because a dismissal for failure to comply with a statutory notice requirement such as RSA 507–C:5 (Supp.1979) is not a judgment on the merits * * * Nevertheless, the notice requirement is a procedural hurdle which has the potential to prolong the time and increase the cost of medical malpractice litigation. Because of this, it unfairly postpones the time at which a malpractice victim may expect to recover for his injuries. Any conceivable public benefit conferred by RSA 507–C:5 (Supp.1979) is outweighed by the restrictions it imposes on private rights. The statute is therefore unconstitutional and void.

* * *

V. DAMAGES.

The plaintiffs also challenge the constitutionality of RSA 507–C:7 (Supp.1979), which governs the damages recoverable in an action for medical injury. RSA 507–C:7 I (Supp.1979) provides that the defendant may introduce evidence of the plaintiff's compensation from collateral sources, that the plaintiff may then offer evidence of any costs incurred in securing such compensation, and that the jury shall be instructed to reduce the award for economic loss by a sum equal to the difference between the total benefits received and the total amount paid by the plaintiff to secure such benefits. RSA 507–C:7 II (Supp.1979) limits awards for non-economic loss to $250,000. RSA 507–C:7 III (Supp.1979) requires the jury to state separately its awards for past and future damages. It also provides that the jury shall not be informed of the limit for non-economic loss and that the court shall reduce any award which exceeds the limit to conform to the limit. RSA 507–C:7 IV (Supp.1979) empowers the court, at the request of either party, to order that future damages exceeding $50,000 be paid by periodic payments on such terms as the court deems equitable. It also provides that in the event the injured person dies prior to completion of the installment payments, "upon motion of any party at interest the court shall modify the order by deducting from the remaining balance the amount thereof representing unpaid compensation for future non-economic loss and future expenses of care and by ordering the remainder to be paid to the estate of the decedent." RSA 507–C:7 IV (Supp.1979).

The plaintiffs argue that RSA 507–C:7 I (Supp.1979), by making the collateral source rule unavailable to a single class of tort claimants, unreasonably discriminates against them. Under the collateral source rule, a plaintiff is permitted to recover in full from the defendant tortfeasor even though he receives compensation from sources other than the defendant. Moulton v. Groveton Papers Co., 114 N.H. 505, 509, 323 A.2d 906, 909 (1974). By abolishing the collateral source rule and thereby eliminating the "duplicate recovery" factor that exists in some cases where the rule is applied, the legislature sought to reduce malpractice awards and contain costs in the medical injury reparations system.

We first note that,

> "[a]bolition of the [collateral source] rule ... presents the anomalous result that an injured party's insurance company may be required to compensate the victim even though the negligent tortfeasor is fully insured. Not only does this abolition patently discriminate against the victim's insurer, it may eventually result in an increased insurance burden on innocent parties."

Jenkins, 52 S.Cal.L.Rev., at 948. Thus, although RSA 507–C:7 I (Supp. 1979) may result in lower malpractice insurance rates for health care providers, it may also increase the cost of insurance for members of the general public because they are potential victims of medical negligence.

Furthermore, when the collateral benefits received by the malpractice plaintiff include workmen's compensation payments, RSA 507–C:7 I (Supp. 1979) will operate to prevent the plaintiff from recovering in full for his economic losses. This is so because RSA 281:14 I and II (Supp.1979) give the workmen's compensation carrier a lien on any damages recovered by the plaintiff, less certain costs and expenses incurred by the plaintiff, up to the amount paid in compensation benefits. The plaintiff-employee in a non-malpractice action, then, will not receive more or less than is necessary to make him whole nor will the defendant be obliged to pay more than that amount. The malpractice plaintiff, however, will have the amount of compensation benefits deducted from his award for economic loss even though his collateral payor has a lien, to the extent of the compensation, on the amount of damages he recovers. The amount of compensation payments is, in effect, being deducted twice from the plaintiff's damage award.

Finally, although the collateral source rule operates so as to place some plaintiffs in a better financial position than before the alleged wrong, its abolition will result in a windfall to the defendant tortfeasor or the tortfeasor's insurer. Moreover, this windfall will sometimes be at the expense of the plaintiff, because "in many instances the plaintiff has paid for these [collateral] benefits in the form of * * * concessions in the wages he received because of such fringe benefits." Moulton v. Groveton Papers Co., 114 N.H. at 509, 323 A.2d at 909. Thus, when the collateral payments represent employment benefits, the price for the public benefit derived from RSA 507–C:7 I (Supp.1979) will be paid solely by medical malpractice plaintiffs.

The above considerations make it apparent that RSA 507–C:7 I (Supp. 1979) arbitrarily and unreasonably discriminates in favor of the class of health care providers. Although the statute may promote the legislative objective of containing health care costs, the potential cost to the general public and the actual cost to many medical malpractice plaintiffs is simply too high. We therefore hold that RSA 507–C:7 I (Supp.1979) violates the State's equal protection clauses.

The plaintiffs next challenge the constitutionality of RSA 507–C:7 II (Supp.1979). The purpose of this section is to stabilize insurance risks and reduce malpractice insurance rates. It attempts to achieve this goal by providing that insurers will not have to pay out damages for "pain and suffering or other non-economic loss" in excess of $250,000. The plaintiffs contend that this provision denies them equal protection of the law, in that it creates an arbitrary damage limitation and thereby precludes only the most seriously injured victims of medical negligence from receiving full compensation for their injuries. We agree.

* * * We find that the necessary relationship between the legislative goal of rate reduction and the means chosen to attain that goal is weak for two reasons:

> "First, paid-out damage awards constitute only a small part of total insurance premium costs. Second, and of primary importance, few individuals suffer non-economic damages in excess of $250,000."

Jenkins, 52 S.Cal.L.Rev., at 951.

It is also clear that the cap on damage recovery distinguishes not only between malpractice victims and victims of other torts but also "between malpractice victims with non-economic losses that exceed $250,000 and those with less egregious non-economic losses." Jenkins, 52 S.Cal.L.Rev., at 951. We agree with the North Dakota Supreme Court that

> "the limitation of recovery does not provide adequate compensation to patients with meritorious claims; on the contrary, it does just the opposite for the most seriously injured claimants. It does nothing toward the elimination of nonmeritorious claims. Restrictions on recovery may encourage physicians to enter into practice and remain in practice, but do so only at the expense of claimants with meritorious claims."

Arneson v. Olson, 270 N.W.2d at 135–36. It is simply unfair and unreasonable to impose the burden of supporting the medical care industry solely upon those persons who are most severely injured and therefore most in need of compensation.

The defendants argue that the damage ceiling is saved because it applies only to non-economic loss and does not prevent the badly injured patient from recovering for all of his medical expenses and other economic loss. It is clear, however, that a tort victim "gains" nothing from the jury's award for economic loss, since that money merely replaces that which he has actually lost. It is only the award above the out-of-pocket loss that is available to compensate in some way for the pain, suffering, physical impairment or disfigurement that the victim must endure until death. In New Hampshire "pain and suffering is a very material element of damages in tort cases. . . . " Duguay v. Gelinas, 104 N.H. 182, 185, 182 A.2d 451, 453 (1962). We do not permit any formula or mathematical tool to be used in computing such damages. Id. If there is an excessive verdict, a remittitur is always available to control excessive jury awards.

The defendants also contend that Estate of Cargill v. City of Rochester, 119 N.H. 661, 406 A.2d 704 (1979) compels the conclusion that the $250,000 damage limit is constitutional. In that case, a divided court reluctantly upheld at $50,000 statutory limitation on tort recovery for bodily injury against governmental subdivisions. In doing so, however, we noted that there had been no common-law right to sue a municipality, that a governmental tortfeasor was different from other tortfeasors, and that payment was guaranteed the tort victim under RSA 507–B:8 (Supp.1979). RSA 507–C:7 II (Supp.1979) is deficient on all three grounds.

The defendants' reliance on RSA 556:13, which limits recovery in actions for wrongful death, is likewise misplaced because such actions were unknown at common law and survive "only to the extent and in the manner provided by the legislature." Hebert v. Hebert, 120 N.H. 369, 415 A.2d 679, 680 (1980). * * *

Finally, the New Hampshire Workmen's Compensation Act, RSA ch. 281, in no way supports the defendants' claim that the malpractice damage ceiling is constitutional, for the workmen's compensation law provides a *quid pro quo* for potential tort victims whose common-law rights of action are supplanted by the statute. In this regard, the Illinois Supreme Court said:

> "Defendants argue that there is a societal *quid pro quo* in that the loss of recovery potential to some malpractice victims is offset by 'lower insurance premiums and lower medical care costs for all recipients of medical care.' This *quid pro quo* does not extend to the seriously injured medical malpractice victim and does not serve to bring the limited recovery provision within the rationale of the cases upholding the constitutionality of the Workmen's Compensation Act."

Wright v. Central DuPage Hosp. Ass'n, 347 N.E.2d [736, 742 (Ill.1976)]. This same analysis was utilized by the two dissenters in Opinion of the Justices, 113 N.H. at 215, 304 A.2d at 881, in rejecting a "no-fault" insurance bill that substantially altered the traditional tort reparation system in this State:

> "In our opinion, abolition of the rights of a class of persons injured in automobile accidents to recover damages for their injuries in full would contravene the plain language of article 14, part I of the New Hampshire constitution, *in the absence of provision of a satisfactory substitute;* and certainly recovery of only a limited portion of such damages cannot be equivalent to recovery of the damages in full. Society cannot escape its responsibility to provide justice by simply eliminating the rights of its citizens."

(Emphasis added.) (Duncan and Grimes, JJ., dissenting.) We have said enough to make it apparent that RSA 507–C:7 II (Supp.1979) denies medical malpractice plaintiffs the equal protection of the law guaranteed them by the New Hampshire Constitution, and we so hold.

The plaintiffs next attack RSA 507–C:7 IV (Supp.1979) on equal protection grounds. The provision allowing the court to order periodic payments in certain circumstances is apparently designed to ensure that the claimant with substantial injuries requiring long-term treatment would have money available to pay for future medical care. The purpose of the provision relating to payments following the death of the injured person is to reduce medical reparations system costs by eliminating a "bonus element," namely, the payment of portions of the award no longer required to compensate the malpractice victim.

Regardless whether the provision substantially furthers its stated purpose, we conclude that it unreasonably discriminates in favor of health care defendants and unduly burdens seriously injured malpractice plaintiffs. RSA 507–C:7 IV (Supp.1979) makes no reference to interest payments for amounts withheld under the statute and we can only conclude that such payments are not contemplated. Thus, malpractice plaintiffs are prevented from obtaining lump sum judgments but are not able to accumulate interest on the unpaid portions of their awards. Moreover, although there may be a windfall to the claimant's family if the periodic payments are not terminated at the claimant's death, there is also a windfall benefit to the defendant's insurer under RSA 507–C:7 IV (Supp.1979) if the claimant dies. Furthermore, the money represented by the judgment becomes the plaintiff's property when he obtains a judgment. Yet he is denied the right to dispose of that property, as and when he pleases. In return he obtains only the questionable benefit of having money available to meet future expenses, which money, it may turn out, he does not even need. Finally, a statute which singles out seriously injured malpractice victims whose future damages exceed $50,000 and requires one class to shoulder the burden inherent in a periodic payments scheme from which the general public benefits offends basic notions of fairness and justice. Accordingly, we hold that RSA 507–C:7 IV (Supp.1979) is an unreasonable exercise of the legislature's police power and violates the State's equal protection guarantees.

VI. ATTORNEYS' FEES.

Lastly, the plaintiffs question the constitutionality of RSA 507–C:8 (Supp.1979), which establishes a contingent fee scale for attorneys representing parties in medical injury actions. The purpose of this provision is to assure that the malpractice victim receives the bulk of any award, thereby increasing the cost effectiveness of awards to plaintiffs and of the medical reparations system as a whole.

The relationship between this provision and the overall purpose of RSA ch. RSA 507–C (Supp.1979)—the containment of medical injury reparations system costs—is questionable. There is no "direct evidence that juries consider attorney's fees in coming to a verdict . . . "and "at least one study shows that juries do not include an assessment of the lawyer's contingency fee in their allotment of damages." Jenkins, 52 S.Cal.L.Rev., at 943.

Reapportionment of damage awards, therefore, is likely to have an insignificant effect on the size of awards, thereby doing little to reduce medical malpractice insurance rates or to control health care costs.

Moreover, RSA 507–C:8 (Supp.1979) unfairly burdens malpractice plaintiffs and, to a lesser extent, their attorneys. The regulation of attorney's fees solely in the area of medical malpractice inevitably will make such cases less attractive to the plaintiff bar. Consequently, RSA 507–C:8 (Supp.1979) "will at least somewhat deter the litigation of legitimate causes of actions, thus creating a potential impediment to injured individuals' access to courts and counsel." Jenkins, supra at 944. This statute also unjustly discriminates by interfering with the freedom of contract between a single class of plaintiffs and their attorneys. It does not regulate contingency fees generally not does it apply to defense counsel in medical malpractice cases, whose fees consume approximately the same percentage of the insurance premium dollar as do those of the plaintiff bar. Id. at 943 n. 687. We therefore hold that RSA 507–C:8 (Supp.1979) is unconstitutional.

VII. SEVERABILITY.

* * * We * * * hold that the valid provisions of RSA ch. 507–C are not separable from the remainder of the statute and declare the chapter void.

* * *

Reversed and remanded.

Fein v. Permanente Medical Group

Supreme Court of the United States, 1985.
474 U.S. 892, 106 S.Ct. 214, 88 L.Ed.2d 215.

The appeal is dismissed for want of a substantial federal question.

■ JUSTICE WHITE, dissenting.

Cal.Civ.Code Ann. § 3333.2 (West) establishes a $250,000 maximum limitation in medical malpractice actions for "noneconomic losses to compensate for pain, suffering, inconvenience, physical impairment, disfigurement, and other non-pecuniary damage." This statute is part of the Medical Injury Compensation Act of 1975 [sometimes referred to as "MICRA"—Ed.] enacted by the California legislature in response to the dramatic rise in consumer medical costs caused by the increase in both monetary awards in medical malpractice actions and medical malpractice insurance premiums.

Appellant brought a medical malpractice action against appellee, Permanente Medical Group, a partnership of physicians, for failing to diagnose and prevent a myocardial infarction. The jury awarded appellant total damages of $1,287,783, including $500,000 for noneconomic losses. The trial judge, however, pursuant to § 3333.2, reduced the amount of noneconomic damages to $250,000.

The California Supreme Court affirmed, rejecting appellant's challenge that § 3333.2 contravenes both the Due Process and Equal Protection clauses of the federal Constitution. The court found no Due Process violation based on the theory that "the Legislature retains broad control over *the measure* as well as *the timing* of damages that a defendant is obligated to pay and a plaintiff is entitled to receive, and ... the Legislature may expand or limit recoverable damages so long as its action is rationally related to a legitimate state interest." Fein v. Permanente Medical Group, 695 P.2d 665, 680 (1985) (emphasis in original). The court then reasoned that the limitation imposed by § 3333.2 was a rational response to the problem of rising medical malpractice insurance costs.

Similarly, the court found that § 3333.2 did not improperly discriminate either between medical malpractice plaintiffs and other tort plaintiffs, or within the class of medical malpractice plaintiffs by denying full recovery to those with noneconomic damages exceeding $250,000. The Legislature's decision to limit the application of § 3333.2 to medical malpractice cases, and within those cases to those with large non-economic damage awards, the court reasoned, was a rational response to escalating malpractice insurance rates.

California thus joins Indiana as the only two states to uphold the constitutionality of this type of medical malpractice damage limits. See Johnson v. St. Vincent Hospital, Inc., 273 Ind. 374, 404 N.E.2d 585, 598–601 (1980). Four other states which have addressed similar damage limitations have invalidated the challenged provisions on federal constitutional grounds. Baptist Hospital of Southeast Texas v. Baber, 672 S.W.2d 296, 298 (Tex.App.1984) ($500,000 limit on damages other than medical expenses); Carson v. Maurer, 120 N.H. 925, 941–943, 424 A.2d 825, 836–838 (1980) ($250,000 limit on "noneconomic" damages); Arneson v. Olson, 270 N.W.2d 125, 135–136 (N.D.1978) ($300,000 limit on total damages); Simon v. St. Elizabeth Medical Center, 3 Ohio Ops.3d 164, 166, 355 N.E.2d 903, 906–907 (Com.Pl.1976) ($200,000 limit on "general" damages).*

One of the reasons for the division among the state courts is a question left unresolved by this Court in Duke Power Co. v. Carolina Environmental Study Group, 438 U.S. 59 (1978). In that case, the Court upheld the provisions of the Price–Anderson Act 42 U.S.C. § 2210 (1983 ed.) which place a dollar limit on total liability that would be incurred by a defendant in the event of a nuclear accident. One of the objections raised against the liability limitation provision was that it violated Due Process by failing to provide those injured by a nuclear accident with an adequate quid pro quo for the common law right of recovery which the Act displaced. The Court noted that "it is not at all clear that the Due Process Clause in fact requires that a legislatively enacted compensation scheme either duplicate the recovery at common law or provide a reasonable substitute remedy.

* In addition, at least one other court has struck down a similar medical malpractice damage cap as violative of its state constitution. Wright v. Central DuPage Hospital Association, 63 Ill.2d 313, 329–330, 347 N.E.2d 736, 743 (1976).

However, we need not resolve this question here...." Id., at 88 (footnote omitted).

The North Dakota Supreme Court in *Arneson,* supra, followed *Duke Power Co.,* and refused to hold that the legislature may not limit a preexisting right without providing a quid pro quo. 270 N.W.2d, at 134–135. Nevertheless, the court went on to find that the imposition of a damage cap on malpractice claims did not provide a sufficient quid pro quo for the severely injured malpractice plaintiff, as his loss of recovery was offset only by lower medical costs for all recipients of medical care, and he received no specific benefit in return. Id., at 136, citing Wright v. Central DuPage Hospital Association, 63 Ill.2d 313, 328, 347 N.E.2d 736, 743 (1976). This approach has been followed by the courts in Texas and New Hampshire. See Baptist Hospital of Southeast Texas, supra, 672 S.W.2d, at 298; Carson, supra, 120 N.H., at 941–943, 424 A.2d, at 837–838. In the instant case, however, the California Supreme Court concluded that "it would be difficult to say that the preservation of a viable medical malpractice insurance industry in this state was not an adequate benefit for the detriment the legislation imposes on malpractice plaintiffs." 695 P.2d, at 681–682, n. 18.

Whether Due Process requires a legislatively enacted compensation scheme to be a quid pro quo for the common law or state law remedy it replaces, and if so, how adequate it must be, thus appears to be an issue unresolved by this Court, and one which is dividing the appellate and highest courts of several states. The issue is important, and is deserving of this Court's review. Moreover, given the continued national concern over the "malpractice crisis," it is likely that more states will enact similar types of limitations, and that the issue will recur. I find, therefore, that the federal question presented by this appeal is substantial, and dissent from the Court's conclusion to the contrary.

NOTES AND QUESTIONS ON MOVEMENTS FOR MALPRACTICE REFORM

1. Describe the so-called malpractice "crises" of the 1970s and 1980s. Were the crises real or—as alleged by the trial bar and some others (e.g., Ralph Nader)—only imagined or contrived by the insurance industry? Considering the reform movement in these terms should yield some practical and theoretical insights into the institution of liability insurance and the factors that affect its availability and cost.

2. *Frequency and Severity of Claims*. Consider specifically what caused the underlying increases in the frequency and severity of medical malpractice claims. From your prior study of tort law, what specific changes in legal doctrine may have contributed? Although it is hard to assign causality to particular changes in legal rules (many of which long preceded the burst of malpractice claims), they may have created a climate more hospitable to claims, making them more attractive to plaintiffs' lawyers and gradually fostering a rise in litigiousness. Did the trends reflect a deterioration of standards in medicine? Although there are more grievous iatrogenic injuries today, many of these are the downside of the successes of medical technology and are not necessarily indicative of a decline in quality. On the other hand, these injuries may signify a new urgency about getting increasingly complex systems to perform better, such as by implementing the strategies of Continuous Quality Improvement or Total Quality Management.

3. *Insurance "Cycles."* Although higher frequency and severity of claims were the precipitating cause of the so-called crises, the crises themselves were precipitated by the manner in which the actuaries' new fears were translated into premiums. Indeed, insurers appeared to discover the need for much higher premiums all at once and all of a sudden. Although the health care industry probably could have absorbed the higher costs fairly easily if they had accrued gradually, the suddenness and magnitude of the premium increases induced panic among providers, supplying the impetus for an effective political campaign for legislative reform.

Thus, the critical events occasioning the legal reforms in medical malpractice arguably originated in the frequently observed phenomenon of insurance "cycles," in which (*a*) good times, high investment returns, and high profits induce new entry into a particular insurance field; (*b*) competition increases, driving premiums down for a time; (*c*) industry reserves shrink below levels needed to survive even mild shocks in either investment or claims experience, and profits begin to suffer; (*d*) some insurers begin to withdraw from the market while others raise their premiums precipitously, possibly triggering a political response restoring apparent stability to the market, and (*e*) restored stability and profit margins invite new entry, starting the process all over again. See generally Priest, The Current Insurance Crisis and Modern Tort Law, 96 Yale L.J. 1521 (1987); Huber, Injury Litigation and Liability Insurance Dynamics, Science, Oct. 2, 1987, at 3; Posner, Trends in Medical Malpractice Insurance, 1970–1985, Law & Contemp.Probs., Spring 1986, at 37, 46–48. Most objective observers of the malpractice insurance crises concluded that such competitive circumstances, coupled with actuarial factors, rather than collusion among insurers, caused the premium increases and underwriting decisions that gave rise to the political pressures for reform.

4. *Policy Questions.* Were the insurance crises of such a nature that government had a good policy justification for intervening to ameliorate them? Was the fact that insurance premiums seemed very high a sufficient reason for government to act? Should government at least have acted when high insurance costs in the 1980s induced providers to discontinue vital services in certain areas (e.g., obstetrics in rural North Carolina)? Or should policy makers have taken the position that there is no objective basis for saying that malpractice insurance costs are "too high" and that, if the market (including health insurers and public programs) will not support higher prices reflecting higher liability insurance costs, then there is really little need for the service after all? Although the latter argument may seem weak, policy makers should worry when needed services are priced out of the reach of some consumers because they must buy not only the service itself (e.g., obstetrical care) but also all the costly legal rights that the tort system ties to the service. Is it possible that certain features of the tort system are not worth their marginal cost to consumers? If so, what should the legal system do?

Actual unavailability of insurance, which characterized the crisis of the 1970s more than that of the 1980s (when "affordability" was the main problem), arguably presented a more serious problem for policy makers. Legislatures of course are moved mostly by the concern that insurance unavailability will cause providers not to provide needed care. A sounder, nonpolitical reason for intervening, however, is that the refusal of private insurers to provide coverage signifies a serious malfunction in the insurance marketplace, in insurance regulation, or elsewhere. What were the precise circumstances that drove insurers from the market in the 1970s? How was the availability problem eventually solved? Were public initiatives vital? Which ones helped the most, and which ones made the most sense? Note that such legal reforms as caps on recoveries, the tapping of collateral sources, shortened statutes of limitations, changed rules of evidence, and screening panels can all be viewed as efforts to make risks more predictable and thus more readily insurable. Insurance reforms (claims-made policies, state compensation funds, provider-owned insurers, JUAs, etc.) were also aimed at making private insurance more dependably available.

Have you yet identified anything really to worry about as a matter of public policy? Aside from a few transitory and isolated problems of insurance availability, nothing has been identified besides rising frequency and severity of claims and the associated higher costs—which may indicate only that the system was working better than ever. Do you see any additional, more fundamental problems? How would you measure the *social* costs of the system? What do we get in return for the high costs incurred?

NOTES AND QUESTIONS ON CONSTITUTIONAL ISSUES IN MALPRACTICE REFORM

1. *A Rational Basis?* Constitutional scrutiny of malpractice reforms has most often been undertaken in the name of equal protection (or its state constitutional equivalent) rather than due process guarantees. Attention has thus focused on the distinctions and classifications implicit in the statutory scheme—in particular, on the distinctions drawn between malpractice victims and victims of other torts, between medical and nonmedical tortfeasors as objects of legislative protection, and between seriously injured patients and other citizens as losers and winners, respectively, under certain reforms. Under federal precedents, various discriminations warrant different degrees of judicial vigilance, thus raising the question of how demanding courts should be in assessing malpractice reforms.

Federal courts reviewing state malpractice reforms under the federal Constitution have consistently required only that the legislation have a rational basis—that is, a recognizable relationship to a legitimate legislative objective. See, e.g., Boyd v. Bulala, 877 F.2d 1191, 1196–97 (4th Cir.1989) (upholding Virginia's absolute limit on total damages in malpractice actions against equal protection and other constitutional objections); Lucas v. United States, 807 F.2d 414 (5th Cir.1986) (upholding Texas legislation limiting malpractice damages to $500,000 plus medical expenses); Hoffman v. United States, 767 F.2d 1431 (9th Cir.1985) (upholding the same California cap on noneconomic damages that was challenged in *Fein*). Many state courts have accorded similar deference to legislative judgments by adopting this undemanding standard in their own constitutional reviews of malpractice reforms. See, e.g., Etheridge v. Medical Center Hosps., 376 S.E.2d 525 (Va.1989) (upholding legislation challenged in *Boyd*, supra); Bernier v. Burris, 497 N.E.2d 763 (Ill.1986) (upholding several reforms); State ex rel. Strykowski v. Wilkie, 261 N.W.2d 434 (Wis.1978) ("classification is plainly germane to the act's purposes"). Although use of the rational-basis standard usually results in an affirmance of the legislature's choice, the Rhode Island Supreme Court overturned a 1981 law requiring submission of malpractice claims to an extrajudicial screening panel on the ground that there was no malpractice crisis in 1981. Boucher v. Sayeed, 459 A.2d 87 (R.I.1983).

In the *Fein* case, the California Supreme Court employed the traditional requirement of a rational relationship to legitimate state interests in upholding the cap on noneconomic damages as not inconsistent with federal and state due process or equal protection guarantees. Chief Justice Bird, dissenting, did not object to the standard of review adopted but argued that rejection of a higher level of equal-protection scrutiny should not imply less than meaningful review of malpractice reforms. Her conclusions were as follows:

> Millions of health care consumers stand to gain from whatever savings the limit produces. Yet, the entire burden of paying for this benefit is concentrated on a handful of badly injured victims—fewer than 15 in the year MICRA was enacted. Although the Legislature normally enjoys wide latitude in distributing the burdens of personal injuries, the singling out of such a minuscule and vulnerable group violates even the most undemanding standard of under inclusiveness.
>
> * * * [T]here is no rational basis for singling out the most severely injured victims of medical negligence to pay for special relief to health care providers and their insurers. Hence, the $250,000 limit on noneconomic damages cannot withstand any meaningful level of judicial scrutiny.

695 P.2d at 692. The majority disavowed the charge that it had conducted anything less than "a serious and genuine judicial inquiry into the correspondence between the classification and the legislative goals." Id. at 684.

A legislature's decision to limit its reforms (specifically, a damage cap) to the field of medical malpractice has been defended in the following terms:

> Given the fact that serious problems do exist; that, while not all of them are unique to the medical malpractice area, it is that area in which they appear most acute; that health care costs affect virtually all persons; that "A statutory discrimination will not be set aside if any

> state of facts reasonably may be conceived to justify it" (McGowan v. Maryland (1961), 366 U.S. 420, 426); that "reform may take one step at a time, addressing itself to the phase of the problem which seems most acute to the legislative mind"; and that "the legislature may select one phase of one field and apply a remedy there, neglecting the others" (Williamson v. Lee Optical of Oklahoma, Inc. (1955), 348 U.S. 483, 489); and that the $500,000 limitation still affords entirely adequate protection to the vast majority of victims of medical malpractice, I am not prepared to hold it an impermissible exercise of legislative discretion.

Wright v. Central DuPage Hosp. Ass'n, 347 N.E.2d 736, 746 (Ill.1976) (dissenting opinion).

2. *Other Constitutional Tests.* Several state courts, like the one in the *Carson* case, have viewed patients' tort rights with special solicitude and used an "intermediate" level of scrutiny to evaluate particular malpractice reforms under state constitutional provisions. E.g., Arneson v. Olson, 270 N.W.2d 125 (N.D.1978). In most such cases, the choice of this level of scrutiny has led to invalidation of the reforms. But see University of Miami v. Echarte, 618 So.2d 189 (Fla.1993) (finding state had shown "overpowering public necessity" for reform legislation). The test employed by these courts is often referred to as "means scrutiny," because the idea is not to limit the legislature in its choice of objects but only to ensure that the distinctions it makes have a "substantial relationship" to the objectives it declares. See generally Gunther, In Search of Evolving Doctrine on a Changing Court: A Model for a Newer Equal Protection, 86 Harv.L.Rev. 1 (1972) (advocating more than minimal scrutiny of legislation affecting economic rights).

The use of means scrutiny to review medical malpractice legislation has been questioned as constitutional doctrine. See Redish, Legislative Response to the Medical Malpractice Insurance Crisis: Constitutional Implications, 55 Tex.L.Rev. 759, 773–78 (1977). The U.S. Supreme Court, for example, seems to have confined means scrutiny to cases involving discrimination on the basis of gender or illegitimacy. On the other hand, it has been suggested that state courts applying their own constitutional norms are free to adopt a stricter standard of review:

> State court judges possess the *political* power to declare laws unconstitutional, whereas federal courts are restrained by concepts of federalism from overturning state laws on constitutional grounds. There are several reasons for the distinctive judicial review powers of state courts. Most notable among these are:
>
> (1) state courts occupy a different institutional position in the state court system than does the Supreme Court in the federal system;
>
> (2) state courts routinely engage in fashioning general common law—a power denied to federal courts since *Erie Railroad v. Tompkins*;

(3) state constitutional rights may differ qualitatively from federal constitutional rights;

(4) federal courts are obliged to pay due deference to state laws out of concerns for federalism; and

(5) unlike federal courts, state courts are not courts of limited jurisdiction and are often invested with broad general jurisdictional powers to adjudicate cases.

Smith, Battling a Receding Tort Frontier: Constitutional Attacks on Medical Malpractice Laws, 38 Okla.L.Rev. 195, 208 (1985). Each of the decisions cited by Justice White in *Fein* as applying doubtful federal constitutional principles also relied upon the state's own constitution, a fact presumably accounting for the Supreme Court's dismissal of the *Fein* appeal.

Why might a state court be suspicious of legislative reforms that single out the field of medical malpractice for special attention? Is it really because the distinctions drawn create constitutionally suspect classifications? (Indeed, viewed ex ante rather than ex post, aren't the reforms neutral, not discriminatory in the usual constitutional sense?) Or is it that state judges are activated by different concerns than federal courts bring to equal-protection review of state laws? Several courts have viewed malpractice reforms as possible instances of "special legislation"—that is, legislation of less than general application benefitting some preferred group or special interest, which is prohibited or otherwise guarded against in many state constitutions. E.g., Jones v. State Bd. of Medicine, 555 P.2d 399, 416–17 (Idaho 1976) (distinguishing the functions of the federal equal protection clause and the state constitution's prohibition of "special laws"); *Wright*, supra, 347 N.E.2d 736, 741–43 (invalidating damage cap as a "special law").

Should a court charged with detecting and preventing "special legislation" undertake closer scrutiny than federal courts provide? See *Bernier*, supra, 497 N.E.2d at 768 ("although the guarantee of equal protection and the prohibition against special legislation are not identical, they are 'generally judged by the same standard' "). Would a public-choice theorist have anything to contribute to this discussion? What is the significance in this context of the observation by sociologist Paul Starr that "a crisis can be a truly marvelous mechanism for the withdrawal or suspension of established rights, and the acquisition and legitimation of new privileges"? Quoted in *Fein,* 695 P.2d at 687 (dissenting opinion). Is it clear that common-law tort rights are worth what they cost consumers and that legislative decisions to narrow them are necessarily anticonsumer measures? Is the battle over malpractice reform a "zero-sum game" between consumers and providers? Who should be the final judge of which set of tort rights is most beneficial?

As Justice White observes in *Fein,* several courts, including the one in the *Carson* case, have taken the position—presumably by analogy to the due process requirement of compensation for a taking—that legislatures cannot cut back on common-law rights without a "quid pro quo." Thus, the Illinois Supreme Court in the *Wright* case, supra, in a passage quoted in

Carson, rejected the idea that malpractice reforms yielded a "societal quid pro quo," holding that seriously injured patients could not be forced to give up their common-law right to unlimited compensation for society's general benefit. Did this court (and others) make a mistake in viewing patients' interests ex post rather than ex ante? Should the Supreme Court have taken the opportunity presented in *Fein* to resolve the question whether the federal Constitution allows legislatures to abrogate common-law rights without supplying an adequate substitute?

Cases decided after *Fein* indicate that some state courts still look for a constitutional quid pro quo when analyzing caps on damages and other reforms. See, e.g., *Echarte*, supra, (finding that state had shown "overpowering public necessity" for cap on noneconomic damages where a party requests arbitration, that statute provides commensurate benefit to plaintiffs, and that no alternative, less onerous method of addressing crisis had been shown); Smith v. Department of Insurance, 507 So.2d 1080 (Fla. 1987); Lucas v. United States, 757 S.W.2d 687 (Tex.1988).

Other state constitutional provisions that have been used to overturn malpractice reforms include state guarantees of ready access to the courts for redress of injuries. A few courts have construed such "open courts" provisions to fix common-law definitions of redressable injuries in stone or at least to require some quid pro quo if a common-law tort right is to be extinguished or reduced. See, e.g., Smith v. Department of Ins., 507 So.2d 1080 (Fla.1987) (invalidating $450,000 cap on noneconomic damages in all tort actions); Lucas v. United States, 757 S.W.2d 687 (Tex.1988) (holding Texas malpractice damage cap invalid). But see *Jones*, supra, 555 P.2d at 404–05 (rejecting such a construction of Idaho's "open courts" clause).

State and federal guarantees of the right to jury trial have occasionally been invoked in challenges to limits on malpractice damages. Although the right to a jury trial is most directly implicated perhaps in provisions restricting access to courts (discussed below), some courts in the late 1980s and early 1990s were willing to find it violated by reforms restricting the range of damages or otherwise constraining jury discretion. E.g., Moore v. Mobile Infirmary, 592 So.2d 156 (Ala.1991) (invalidating $400,000 limit on noneconomic damages as violation of right to jury trial); Sofie v. Fibreboard Corp., 771 P.2d 711 (Wash.1989) (sliding scale caps on noneconomic damages held to violate right to jury trial). But see *Boyd*, supra, 877 F.2d. at 1196 (federal law: "If a legislature may completely abolish a cause of action without violating the right of trial by jury, we think it permissibly may limit damages recoverable for a cause of action as well."); *Etheridge*, supra, 376 S.E.2d at 528–29 (upholding same damage cap as in *Boyd* under state law against similar challenge). Certain other reforms have been challenged on the ground that they intrude in some way on functions of the judicial branch.

A few state constitutions have unusual provisions that expressly prohibit the abrogation or limitation of rights to recover damages for personal injuries. Such a provision caused the Arizona Supreme Court to employ strict scrutiny in evaluating a statutory limitation of the discovery exception to the statute of limitations applicable to malpractice actions. See Kenyon v. Hammer, 142 Ariz. 69, 688 P.2d 961 (1984) (invalidating same).

3. *Probing the Legislature's Purpose.* Should a court undertaking means scrutiny take the legislature at its word regarding its objective, or should it consider whether there is another legitimate purpose that the legislation might serve? Is it possible to be more specific than was the New Hampshire legislature in the statute invalidated in the *Carson* case concerning the benefits that the public might expect to derive from efforts to ensure the availability and affordability of malpractice insurance? How would you draft a statement of legislative purpose for such a law? See *Echarte*, supra, 618 So. 2d at 191–92 nn.12, 13 (setting forth extensive preamble and findings in Fla. reform legislation).

A 1976 Idaho case involved a challenge to legislation capping damages in most medical malpractice actions at the low level of $150,000 per claim ($300,000 per occurrence). Adopting means scrutiny as its test, the state supreme court discussed the issues as follows:

> [We] are unable to ascertain how the classification between various victims of malpractice relate[s] to the asserted purpose of assuring medical care to the people of Idaho * * *. It is asserted, however, that because of the increasing number of medical malpractice claims premium rates for medical malpractice insurance have dramatically increased and that Idaho's heretofore principal medical malpractice insurance carrier has withdrawn any coverage of 500 of the state's 900 doctors. It is argued that by limiting the amount of recovery it was intended to create a more stable basis for prediction of malpractice losses and thereby encourage the entry into Idaho of new insurance carriers at lower, more reasonable and more competitive rates. We are unable to judge the accuracy or completeness of these assertions on the record presented here.
>
> It is argued that the Act is a necessary legislative response to a "crisis in medical malpractice insurance" in Idaho, but the record does not demonstrate any such "crisis." Further, there is no evidentiary basis presented here to either support or refute the relationship between the limitations created by the Act and the abatement of the alleged crisis. As heretofore stated, the sole evidentiary record is found in the affidavit of the Director of the State Department of Insurance.
>
> Although that affidavit is conclusory in stating that the Act was a "response to the medical malpractice insurance crisis" which crisis is indicated by increased premium rates and unavailability of insurance carriers, and that the Act was designed to stabilize the medical malpractice insurance market by providing a predictable level of recovery, other matters are contained therein which cast doubt on the validity of these conclusions. Simultaneous with the passage of the Act in question here, there was enacted additional legislation authorizing creation of a temporary joint underwriting association (JUA) of liability insurance carriers in the field of medical malpractice insurance. The formation of that association was contingent upon a finding by the

Director of the Department of Insurance that medical malpractice insurance was unavailable under the standards of I.C. § 41–1405 in a voluntary market. Attached to the affidavit of the Director of the Department of Insurance are the findings of the hearing held by him to consider the necessity of forming the underwriting association. Therein it is indicated that although two insurance carriers are withdrawing from the malpractice field in Idaho, seven remain, one of whom is offering to insure physicians left uninsured by the recent withdrawals. It is further found that the rates offered by the remaining companies "are based on *competent actuarial considerations* and appear to be adequate but not excessive or unfairly discriminatory." (Emphasis supplied) And, the Director concluded that it was thus unnecessary to activate the underwriting association * * *

At the very least the findings of the Director resulting from that hearing present a differing and conflicting view of the alleged "crisis" upon which the Act is said to have been predicated.

* * * We are troubled by the clear inference * * * that the "crisis" in response to which the subject Act was adopted results in part from economic fluctuations and resultant unsuccessful investment practices.

* * *

One further problem is posed by the affidavit of the Director of Insurance in determining the relationship between the means (restriction on claims) as related to the objective of the Act. Therein it is stated that the $150,000–300,000 limitation placed upon malpractice recoveries "would have covered all claims to date." The implication arising therefrom is that no judgment or settlement in a medical malpractice action in Idaho has to the knowledge of the Director exceeded the recovery limits of the Act.

In these regards the affidavit of the Director of the Department of Insurance sheds no light and provides no assistance to this Court, but rather as indicated, poses additional unsolved problems in our application of the test to the classification created by the Act and the challenge that such classification is violative of equal protection.

While we are as aware as any other member of the public of assertions of growing problems in the medical malpractice insurance field, the record here presents no factual basis for understanding the nature and scope of the alleged medical malpractice crisis nationally or in Idaho. It is thus impossible for this Court to assess the necessity for this legislation and whether or not the limitations on medical malpractice recovery set forth in the Act bear a fair and substantial relationship to the asserted purpose of the Act.

Is there indeed a medical malpractice insurance crisis in Idaho? Are physicians and hospitals in Idaho being charged excessive, grossly unfair premiums for medical malpractice insurance (and if so, what is the position of the Director of the Department of Insurance of the

State of Idaho in relation to duties imposed upon him), or are the monumental increases in medical malpractice insurance premiums reasonably attributable to the costs of doing business in the medical malpractice insurance field? Is medical malpractice insurance unavailable at reasonable rates in the absence of legislative enactments? Is the threat of unavailability of health care to the people of Idaho a reality or not? Has there been, as suggested, an increased rash of claims and sizable recoveries or settlements in favor of persons alleged to have suffered as the result of medical malpractice in Idaho? Finally and most importantly, if there is indeed a medical malpractice insurance crisis in Idaho, what is the effect or will be the effect of the limits of recovery and the other provisions of the subject Act with respect to forestalling or abating the crisis? In the absence of any factual information bearing on these questions, if indeed there are answers, no decision can be made by this Court in the area of the equal protection challenge to the Act.

In an effort to find some answer outside the parameters of the record in this case we have examined some of the growing body of literature on medical malpractice insurance. * * *

In the case at bar the Act has been described by the appellants as a "local response to a national problem." The * * * literature casts some light on the existence of a so-called "crisis" and some of the problems inherent in that crisis. The record before us contains no attempt to relate any findings of national scope to Idaho and this Court lacks the ability to extrapolate any such relation from the national literature. * * *

It is necessary, therefore, that the case at bar be remanded to the district court for additional evidence, findings and conclusions consistent with this opinion.

Jones, supra, 555 P.2d at 411–14, 416. What is your reaction to the court's proposal that the trial court hold a hearing on whether there was truly a malpractice crisis justifying the legislature's actions? What alternatives does an appellate court have?

For some reason, the trial court in the *Jones* case did not complete its work on the remand until 1980. It found, however, that, although the legislature had a rational basis for acting as it did, the legislation it enacted was not so likely to achieve its declared purpose that it could survive closer scrutiny. Jones v. State Bd. of Medicine, Nos. 55527 and 55586 (4th Dist. Idaho, Nov. 3, 1980). The case was not further appealed, apparently because the legislation was finally repealed.

Is it not somewhat artificial to center discussion on whether or not a "crisis" exists or existed? Although this characterization helps to galvanize political constituencies and get the legislature's attention, it may obscure basic policy issues. Have courts tended to ignore the possibility that the tort system may not be well designed to serve the overall interests of consumers?

Questions about the validity of tort crises generally evaporated after the second crisis of the mid 1980s. Courts increasingly accepted that the medical malpractice insurance market would be unstable without fine-tuning through legislative tort reform.

4. *Federal Reforms?* Because many malpractice reforms have not survived constitutional challenges in state courts, it has long been suggested that reform must be achieved through federal legislation, raising interesting issues of federalism. See Smith, Battling a Receding Tort Frontier: Constitutional Attacks on Medical Malpractice Laws, 38 Okla.L.Rev. 195, 229–31 (1985). Do you agree that the federal government has a role in solving these problems? The principal legislative actions taken at the federal level include the Health Care Quality Improvement Act, described in chapters 5(§B) and 6(§A) and the Liability Risk Retention Act, which was originally passed in 1981 to benefit those exposed to products liability but which was expanded to facilitate pooling of other risks in 1986. 15 U.S.C. §§ 3901–06 (1994). These measures reflected federalism concerns in not significantly preempting, but instead supplementing, state law. The Risk Retention Act, however, aimed at overcoming obstacles to private solutions to insurance availability problems by overriding some state regulation. The act provided for so-called "risk-retention groups," under which persons facing liability risks can pool them with others similarly situated. Once licensed in a single state, a statutory group is allowed under federal law to qualify to do business as an insurer in other states without having to satisfy local regulatory requirements (other than those governing marketing). See Insurance Co. of State of Pennsylvania v. Corcoran, 850 F.2d 88 (2d Cir.1988) (nurse practitioners, whose previous carrier had quit the market, formed purchasing group to buy coverage from plaintiff; act held not to exempt group policy from New York requirement of prior approval of rates and policy forms). Provision is also made for the formation of "purchasing groups" to facilitate the purchase of group, rather than individual, liability coverage.

In the 1980s, action at the federal level was largely limited to studies of the problem. See, e.g., DHHS, Report of the Task Force on Medical Liability and Malpractice (1987); GAO, Medical Malpractice: A Framework for Action (1987) (final report of a series); DHEW, Report of the Secretary's Commission on Medical Malpractice (1973). Numerous bills were introduced in Congress, however, to demonstrate members' concerns about the difficulties their physician constituents were facing. Several of these would have altered the rights of Medicare patients and included provisions designed to induce the states to enact similar reforms. See, e.g., H.R. 3084, 99th Cong., 1st Sess. (1985) (the Moore–Gephardt bill, implementing ideas of Professor Jeffrey O'Connell).

In the early 1990s, efforts to pass federal reform became far more assertive. Illustrating Professor Eleanor Kinney's notion of "generations" of malpractice reform measures, the federal efforts built primarily on the second generation of reform efforts in the states, which emphasized the importance of creating a more rational and predictable medical malpractice system. See Kinney, Malpractice Reform in the 1990s: Past Disappointments, Future Successes, 20 J. Health Pol., Pol'y & L. 99 (1995). The second generation reforms generally included damage caps and collateral source offsets, as well as mandatory alternative dispute resolution and scheduling of damages.

In 1989, Congress established the Agency for Health Care Policy and Research with a mandate to address medical malpractice issues. Moreover the Bush administration emphasized malpractice reforms as part of its overall health care initiative. The growth of interest in malpractice reform is reflected in the fact that there were ten proposals for such reform in the 102d Congress and thirty in the 103rd Congress. Id. at 111. Although the Clinton Health Security Act proposed extensive changes in medical malpractice, those proposals died with the bill itself.

After the Republican landslide in 1994, the emphasis on federal malpractice reforms shifted slightly, with the general goal of passing a nationwide cap on noneconomic damages, eliminating joint and several liability, and restricting the award of punitive damages. See Weiler, Fixing the Tail: The Place of Malpractice in Health Care Reform, 47 Rutgers L. Rev. 1157 (1995); Note, A Review of Federal Medical Malpractice Tort Reform Alternatives, 19 Seton Hall Legis. J. 599 (1995).

As you consider the particular state-initiated reforms examined below, ask yourself whether such matters should be left in the hands of state courts and legislatures or dealt with at the federal level. Do any of the reforms being contemplated go to the heart of national health policy? How great is the financial stake of the federal government in the malpractice system? Would the federal government's possible perception that the states are too slow to adopt desirable malpractice reforms justify overriding federalism concerns? Also consider the federal government's constitutional power to preempt state law for such purposes. The approaches employed in most of federal proposals are to sponsor "demonstrations" at the state level or to condition federal payments to the state under various health programs on state compliance with the federal government's wishes. The Bush administration, for example, proposed to reduce Medicaid payments to states that fail to adopt damage caps and other reforms. (What is your opinion of making Medicaid beneficiaries hostages to overcome state resistance to such federal demands?)

NOTES AND QUESTIONS ON REFORMS RELATING TO DAMAGES

1. *Ceilings on Awards.* In addition to raising constitutional issues, legislative ceilings on tort recoveries present significant policy issues. The majority of the California Supreme Court that approved the $250,000 ceiling on noneconomic damages in the *Fein* case discussed the merits of the legislation as follows:

> It is worth noting * * * that in seeking a means of lowering malpractice costs, the Legislature *placed no limits whatsoever on a plaintiff's right to recover for all of the economic, pecuniary damages—*

such as medical expenses or lost earnings—resulting from the injury, but instead confined the statutory limitations to the recovery of *noneconomic damages,* and—even then—permitted up to a $250,000 award for such damages. Thoughtful jurists and legal scholars have for some time raised serious questions as to the wisdom of awarding damages for pain and suffering in any negligence case, noting, inter alia, the inherent difficulties in placing a monetary value on such losses, the fact that money damages are at best only imperfect compensation for such intangible injuries and that such damages are generally passed on to, and borne by, innocent consumers.[16] While the general propriety of such damages is, of course, firmly imbedded in our common law jurisprudence no California case of which we are aware has ever suggested that the right to recover for such noneconomic injuries is constitutionally immune from legislative limitation or revision.

Faced with the prospect that, in the absence of some cost reduction, medical malpractice plaintiffs might as a realistic matter have difficulty collecting judgments for *any* of their damages—pecuniary as well as nonpecuniary—the Legislature concluded that it was in the public interest to attempt to obtain some cost savings by limiting noneconomic damages. Although reasonable persons can certainly disagree as to the wisdom of this provision,[17] we cannot say that it is not rationally related to a legitimate state interest.

16. Justice Traynor, in a dissenting opinion in Seffert v. Los Angeles Transit Lines (1961) 56 Cal.2d 498, 511, 15 Cal.Rptr. 161, 364 P.2d 337, observed: "There has been forceful criticism of the rationale for awarding damages for pain and suffering in negligence cases. (Morris, Liability for Pain and Suffering, 59 Columb.L.Rev. 476; Plant, Damages for Pain and Suffering, 19 Ohio L.J. 200; Jaffe, Damages for Personal Injury: The Impact of Insurance, 18 Law and Contemporary Problems 219; Zelermyer, Damages for Pain and Suffering, 6 Syracuse L.Rev. 27.) Such damages originated under primitive law as a means of punishing wrongdoers and assuaging the feelings of those who had been wronged. They become increasingly anomalous as emphasis shifts in a mechanized society from ad hoc punishment to orderly distribution of losses through insurance and the price of goods or of transportation. Ultimately such losses are borne by a public free of fault as part of the price for the benefits of mechanization. [¶] Nonetheless, this state has long recognized pain and suffering as elements of damages in negligence cases [citations]; *any change in this regard must await reexamination of the problem by the Legislature.*" (Italics added.)

17. In its comprehensive report on the medical malpractice insurance crisis, the American Bar Association's Commission on Medical Professional Liability recommended that no dollar limit be imposed on recoveries for economic loss, but expressly "[took] no position on whether it is appropriate to place a ceiling on the recovery of non-economic loss." (Rep. of Com. on Medical Professional Liability (1977) 102 ABA Ann.Rep. 786, 849.) The commission explained its conclusions as follows: "When liability has been demonstrated, the first priority of the tort system is to compensate the injured party for the economic loss he has suffered. While it is legitimate in the Commission's view to deduct payments to or for the benefit of the plaintiff by collateral sources, it is unconscionable to preclude a plaintiff, by an arbitrary ceiling on recovery, from recovering all his economic damages, even though some lowering of medical malpractice premiums may result from the enactment of such a ceiling. [¶] The Commission has taken no position, however, on whether it is appropriate to place a statutory ceiling on the recovery of non-economic loss. The arguments in favor of limiting noneconomic loss are that a ceiling on general

Fein, supra, 695 P.2d at 680–81.

On the implementation of the California cap, a California court has said,

> Plaintiff's contention that defendant, having failed to request a jury instruction or verdict form explaining the $250,000 limit, may not now have the damage award reduced is equally unavailing. At bottom, the argument misconceives the duties of both the court and jury in a medical malpractice action tried under MICRA. While the jury possesses the ultimate responsibility for computing the measure of damages which flow from a particular act of negligence, it is for the trial court to determine the actual amount of the judgment to be entered by giving effect to rules which may increase or decrease the verdict as rendered. From our reading of Civil Code section 3333.2, we think it obvious the Legislature never intended a jury be informed of the limitations imposed by the statute or that it consider such limitations in assessing damages. First, and perhaps most importantly, the fact that an award will be reduced if it exceeds $250,000 is irrelevant to the jury's function of calculating the dollar amount of a plaintiff's injury. Second, an instruction based on the terms of the statute would only serve to increase the possibility that a jury may simply label damages that otherwise would have been denominated noneconomic as economic losses. Moreover, in those instances where a plaintiff's noneconomic loss is relatively small jurors, told of the $250,000 limit, may feel compelled to award the maximum where they otherwise would have awarded less. The Legislature's intent in limiting damages in medical malpractice litigation would be frustrated in either event. To avoid such results, the reduction of an award for noneconomic loss must be accomplished by the court as a matter of law without interference from the jury. Such a practice insures that neither party will be prejudiced by a potentially misleading instruction.

Green v. Franklin, 235 Cal.Rptr. 312, 322–23 (Cal.App.1987) (depublished opinion).

What is your view on the need to preserve a right to recover for "pain and suffering"? Is it relevant that consumers do not insure themselves against such losses in other contexts (but must pay indirectly for covering

damages would contain jury awards within realistic limits, reduce the exposure of insurers (which reductions could be reflected in lowered premiums), lead to more settlements and less litigation, and enable insurance carriers to set more accurate rates because of the greater predictability of the size of judgments. [¶] The arguments against limiting non-economic loss are that medical malpractice should not be distinguished from other areas of professional malpractice or personal injury actions which have no ceiling on general damages, that general damages are as real to the plaintiff as economic loss, that a wrongdoer should pay for all the losses he has caused, including pain and suffering, and that the general damages portion of an award provides a fund out of which the plaintiff's attorney's fees can be deducted without leaving the plaintiff economically undercompensated. In addition, it is argued that no immediate cost or premium savings will be generated by a ceiling on non-economic losses because questions regarding the constitutionality of such statutes would have to be finally resolved before the insurance companies would reflect any potential savings in their rates; and because the ceiling might prove to be the norm." (*Ibid.*)

them through the malpractice system)? Is provision for such damages defensible as a way of providing extra funds out of which an injured person may pay his attorney (and still have money to cover his out-of-pocket costs)? Should such caps be adjustable for inflation? (Not all are.)

Caps on noneconomic damages have been adopted in over twenty states, most of them following the California example of a $250,000 limit. Most such caps have been upheld. E.g., Scholz v. Metropolitan Pathologists, 851 P.2d 901 (Colo.1993); Murphy v. Edmonds, 601 A.2d 102 (Md.1992); Adams v. Childrens Mercy Hosp., 832 S.W.2d 898 (Mo.1992); Robinson v. Charleston Area Med. Center, 414 S.E.2d 877 (W.Va.1991). For successful constitutional challenges, however, see Brannigan v. Usitalo, 587 A.2d 1232 (N.H.1991) (following *Carson*, noneconomic damage cap of $875,000 held to violate state equal protection clause); Moore v. Mobile Infirmary, 592 So.2d 156 (Ala.1991); Kansas Malpractice Victims Coalition v. Bell, 757 P.2d 251 (Kan.1988). In Ohio, following a ruling that a $200,000 cap on noneconomic damages state substantive due process requirements, Morris v. Savoy, 576 N.E.2d 765 (Ohio 1991), the legislature passed new legislation with new legislative findings. Ohio Rev. Code Ann. § 2323.54 (Banks–Baldwin Supp. 1998). Other states recently passing caps on noneconomic damage caps, include North Dakota, N.D. Cent. Code § 32–42–02 (1996), and Texas, Tex. Rev. Civ. Stat. art. 4590i § 11.02 (West Supp. 1998).

Caps on total damages are obviously even more controversial. Two early statutes were upheld in Johnson v. St. Vincent Hosp., Inc., 404 N.E.2d 585 (Ind.1980) ($500,000 limit on total damages), and Prendergast v. Nelson, 256 N.W.2d 657 (Neb.1977) (upholding cap on total damages, which was subsequently liberalized, Neb. Rev. Stat. § 44–2825 (1997)). Several states have followed Indiana's pathbreaking example by establishing a patient compensation fund out of which awards above a certain level are made but with limits on total recovery. See, e.g., Williams v. Kushner, 549 So.2d 294 (La.1989) (upholding a $500,000 cap on medical malpractice damages, recoverable from state-run patient compensation fund). Only a few states have followed Nebraska in putting a flat cap in place for all tort damages, but such caps have generally survived constitutional challenge. E.g., Etheridge v. Medical Center Hosps., 376 S.E.2d 525 (Va.1989) (upholding $750,000 cap on medical malpractice claims, which legislature subsequently increased to $1 million).

See generally Annot., 26 A.L.R.5th 245 (1995). On policy issues bearing on the appropriateness of caps on damage awards, see Bovbjerg, Juries and Justice: Are Malpractice and Other Personal Injuries Created Equal?, Law & Contemp. Probs., Winter 1991, p. 5 (awards for the same injury found consistently higher in malpractice cases than in other tort cases); Metzloff, Resolving Malpractice Disputes: Imaging the Jury's Shadow, in id. at 43 (based on empirical study, "it is no wonder that insurers' files are replete with grumblings about the difficulty of predicting [the amount of] jury awards"); Sloan & van Wert, Cost and Compensation of Injuries in Medical Malpractice, in id. at 131 (study of 187 birth-related and emergency room cases of permanent injury in Florida, a noncap state, revealed that "a claimant receiving much more than economic loss in compensation more nearly appears to be the exception than the norm").

2. *Tapping Collateral Sources.* The common-law collateral source rule, which keeps juries from being aware of other compensation that the patient stands to receive for his injuries, has been amended by statute in many states to eliminate what may be seen as overcompensation. The ABA Commission on Medical Professional Liability (ABA Commission) took the following position in 1977:

> *Recommendations*
>
> Recovery of damages should be reduced by collateral source payments received by the plaintiff as the result of government, employment-related, individually-purchased and gratuitously-conferred benefits. * * * The amounts to be set off should be deducted by the judge from the jury's assessment of damages against the defendant. Subrogation should not be allowed to any collateral source for medical benefits thus set off. * * *
>
> *Supporting Reasons*
>
> Traditionally, the tort law has sanctioned a partial or total double recovery by an injured plaintiff by refusing to reduce a liability judgment by the amounts the plaintiff has received from collateral insurers. This result is grounded on the notion that it is better to allow some overlapping of payments to the innocent plaintiff than to allow the wrongdoer to benefit by the plaintiff's collateral protection.
>
> The Commission does not agree that a plaintiff should retain collateral payments and receive full compensation from the defendant in a medical malpractice action.
>
> The idea of a windfall runs counter to the basic aim of the tort law, which is to make the plaintiff whole, not to overcompensate him. The extent to which the defendant must respond in damages is better measured by the plaintiff's harm than by the degree of the defendant's fault. However, even if "fault" is an appropriate basis for refusing to permit the defendant to lessen his liability, it is a very rough and unfair basis upon which to punish defendants whose culpability in the moral sense may run from almost nil to severe. Finally, the notion of a wrongdoing defendant is increasingly anachronistic in this age of widespread malpractice insurance and growing sources of compensation for injured patients. In this context, the aim should be to assure the plaintiff fair compensation from available sources, but no more.
>
> The argument for allowing the plaintiff to retain collateral benefits and receive full tort compensation is strongest where the plaintiff has purchased an individual health insurance or disability policy. Yet, even here, the argument for overcompensation is not persuasive. One does not purchase accident insurance in the hope of a double recovery. (This is evidenced by the fact that the purchaser is almost never aware whether or not the collateral insurer has retained a subrogation right). Rather, one is paying for the security of prompt and guaranteed payments in the event of loss, regardless of whether one's injury or illness is due to anyone's fault or whether one is likely to recover damages by pursuing litigation. In receiv-

ing payment from an accident or health insurer, the injured or ill person receives exactly what he bargained for, and there is no reason a defendant should duplicate the plaintiff's recovery from this source.

Assuming that the collateral source rule is repealed, the next question is whether collateral insurers which have made payments to the plaintiff should be entitled to be made whole through subrogation. The Commission recognizes that subrogation rights vary from jurisdiction to jurisdiction, and that collateral insurers have different policies with respect to enforcing contractual or statutory indemnification and subrogation rights. However, since accident and health insurers are generally more efficient than liability insurers in making a higher percentage of premium dollars available to claimants, and since shifting losses from the former to the latter source costs money, the Commission has concluded that there is a strong argument for denying subrogation. In effect, denying subrogation would tend to make the more efficient, high-volume accident and health insurers the *primary* insurers for malpractice losses and the liability insurers the *secondary* or excess layer insurers.

Because of the possible legal and business complications in connection with such collateral sources as wage, disability and workmen's compensation payments, the Commission has not made a final decision on subrogation in these areas. It sees no reason, however, why subrogation should ever be allowed with respect to government or private health insurance payments.

The set-off of collateral source payments should be mandated as a matter of law rather than left to the jury's discretion. Moreover, legislation should require that the trial judge deduct all collateral source payments from the jury's award before entering judgment. The jury would be instructed to resolve any dispute as to the amount of a collateral source payment.

ABA Commission, Report, 102 ABA Ann. Rep. 786, 849–50 (1977). Since the mid 1980s, modification of the collateral source rule has been a highly popular approach to tort reform.

There are various ways in which the collateral source rule may be modified to lower malpractice insurance costs. One possibility, illustrated in *Carson v. Maurer,* supra, is simply to allow the introduction of evidence concerning a plaintiff's other sources of support. See also Barme v. Wood, 689 P.2d 446 (Cal.1984) (upholding such a statute); Farley v. Engelken, 740 P.2d 1058 (Kan.1987) (finding that such a statute violates equal protection guarantees under heightened scrutiny). In Tennessee, damages awarded may not include amounts reimbursed or replaced by public or private collateral sources other than private insurance purchased individually (and not by an employer). See McDaniel v. General Care Corp., 627 S.W.2d 129 (Tenn.App.1981) (plaintiff not allowed to prove such reimbursed losses). On the application of the collateral source rule, see Harlow v. Chin, 545 N.E.2d 602, 609–11 (Mass.1989) (quadriplegic's damages held not subject to reduction for more than $200,000 of federal—mostly Medicaid—benefits received; statute modifying collateral source rule had exception for benefits provided by an entity "whose right of subrogation is based in any federal law," and this language was construed to exempt Medicare and Medicaid benefits, but not Social Security disability payments, from the offset requirement; note that, under the law of subrogation, these funds are now subject to recovery by the state from the plaintiff); Bandel v. Friedrich, 584 A.2d 800 (N.J.1991) (plaintiff's misdiagnosed illness rendered him incapable of caring for himself, and his mother exclusively provided for his care and supervision; held that "defendant's obligation to pay full compensatory damages * * * is not abated by gratuitous provision of services"). See generally Annot., Validity and Construction of State Statute Abrogating Collateral Source Rule as to Medical Malpractice Actions, 74 A.L.R.4th 32 (1991).

The Illinois statute reads as follows:

> § 2–1205. Reduction in amount of recovery. An amount equal to the sum of (i) 50% of the benefits provided for lost wages or private or governmental disability income programs, which have been paid, or which have become payable to the injured person by any other person, corporation, insurance company or fund in relation to a particular injury, and (ii) 100% of the benefits provided for medical charges, hospital charges, or nursing or caretaking charges, which have been paid, or which have become payable to the injured person by any other person, corporation, insurance company or fund in relation to a particular injury, shall be deducted from any judgment in an action to recover for that injury based on an allegation of negligence or other wrongful act, not including intentional torts, on the part of a licensed hospital or physician; provided, however, that:
>
> (1) Application is made within 30 days to reduce the judgment;
>
> (2) Such reduction shall not apply to the extent that there is a right of recoupment through subrogation, trust agreement, lien, or otherwise;
>
> (3) The reduction shall not reduce the judgment by more than 50% of the total amount of the judgment entered on the verdict;
>
> (4) The damages awarded shall be increased by the amount of any insurance premiums or the direct costs paid by the plaintiff for such benefits in the 2 years prior to plaintiff's injury or death or to be paid by the plaintiff in the future for such benefits; and
>
> (5) There shall be no reduction for charges paid for medical expenses which were directly attributable to the adjudged negligent acts or omissions of the defendants found liable.

735 Ill. Comp. Stat. Ann. § 2–1205 (1992). This clause was upheld in Bernier v. Burris, 497 N.E.2d 763, 774–76 (Ill.1986). What is the purpose and effect of clause (2)?

3. *Punitive Damages.* In response to the general tort crisis of the mid-1980s, many states limited punitive damages, mostly to shield product manufacturers. See, e.g., N.C. Gen. Stat. § 1D–25 (1996) (cap of the greater of $250,000 or 3 times compensatory damages); Ind. Code Ann. § 34–4–34–4 (Michie 1997) (maximum of 3 times compensation award or $50,000); Wackenhut Applied Technologies Ctr., Inc. v. Sygnetron Protection Systems, Inc., 979 F.2d 980 (4th Cir.1992); Gordon v. State, 608 So.2d 800 (Fla.1992) (per curiam), cert. denied, 507 U.S. 1005 (1993). See generally Annot., 35 A.L.R.5th 145 (1996). More recently, the Supreme Court has ruled that punitive damages may, in some circumstances, represent a denial of constitutional due process. BMW v. Gore, 517 U.S. 559 (1996) (condemning grossly excessive awards exceeding state's legitimate interest in punishing unlawful conduct, excessiveness to be judged by reprehensibility of defendant's conduct, ratio of compensatory to punitive damages, and difference between award and other sanctions that could be imposed for such misconduct).

Specific attention to punitive damages in medical malpractice cases mostly came later, as the number and median value of such awards increased. According to one study, there were only one to two punitive awards for medical malpractice each year into the 1970s but more than 25 per year by the late 1980s. Rustad & Koenig, Reconceptualizing Punitive Damages in Medical Malpractice: Targeting Amoral Corporations not Moral Monsters, 47 Rutgers L. Rev. 975 (1995) (median size of such awards, in constant 1983 dollars, also increased, from $25,000 in 1963–73 to $397,000 in 1989–93). See also DHHS, Report of the Task Force on Medical Liability and Malpractice 130 (1987) (noting trend toward allowing punitive damages not only in cases of intentional harm but also where a jury might find " 'merely' willful or wanton misbehavior or gross negligence"). The ABA Commission, supra, at 851, argued that the medical disciplinary system and the criminal law sufficiently deter serious abuses and that a demand for punitive damages "is counterproductive in that it heightens the adversary nature of medical malpractice litigation and needlessly complicates settlement negotiations."

In Alabama, a jurisdiction that does not recognize compensatory damages in wrongful death actions (and therefore sees relatively punitive high awards), a $1,000,000 statutory cap on punitive damages in malpractice cases was struck down as an infringement of the right to jury trial and equal protection. Smith v. Schulte, 671 So.2d 1334 (Ala.1995), cert. denied, 517 U.S. 1220 (1996).

4. *EMTALA*. Recall the federal Emergency Medical Treatment and Active Labor Act. From what you learned in chapter 1(§B), are suits in federal court under EMTALA subject to damage caps provided for in state law?

5. *Periodic Payments; Structured Settlements.* Tort awards have traditionally been made in a lump sum in the expectation that, properly invested, it will replace the plaintiff's lost future income and finance future medical care needed as a result of the injury. One popular reform, again illustrated in *Carson v. Maurer,* has been to provide that damages of more than a certain amount will be paid in installments or periodic payments. Even before such awards became mandatory by statute in some states, settlements of personal injury claims often took this form. See generally Annot., 41 A.L.R.4th 275 (1985).

Periodic payments are favored in part because they provide assurance that the damage award will serve its intended purpose and will not be squandered in bad investments (e.g., a tavern or gas station) or otherwise, leaving the plaintiff destitute. (What is your opinion of this paternalistic justification for denying a plaintiff his damages?) Another perceived benefit is the reduction of liability if the injured person should have a miraculous recovery or die prematurely, thus reducing the need for income maintenance and custodial care. Finally, the costs of the malpractice system may be much reduced, because the cost to the liability insurer of purchasing an annuity covering future living expenses and exigencies is apt to be much less than some juries would award in the case; an insurer selling an annuity can pool risks and need not reserve against the worst-case scenario, as juries may feel they must do.

Statutes mandating periodic payment of awards in medical malpractice suits were overturned in *Carson* and in the *Arneson* case in North Dakota in the course of invalidating reform legislation having many other features that the courts found objectionable. Other states have generally upheld provisions for periodic payments. See, e.g., State ex rel. Strykowski v. Wilkie, 261 N.W.2d 434 (Wis.1978).

What practical problems can you foresee in the implementation of this fairly sensible idea? How should the jury be instructed? What expert witnesses are needed? How should the lawyer's contingent fee be calculated? When and out of which proceeds should it be paid? What should happen upon the death of the plaintiff or upon his return to active employment? How and under what controls should medical expenditures be reimbursed? What are the tax implications of various arrangements? (Since 1982, most periodic payments under both settlements and judgments have been exempt from federal income tax. IRC § 104(a)(2).) See generally D. Hindert et al., Structured Settlements and Periodic Payment Judgments (1986 looseleaf) (discussing various arrangements, their practical and legal complexities, and the responsibilities of legal counsel, and proposing model law); National Conference of Commissioners on Uniform State Laws, Uniform Periodic Payment of Judgment Act (1990); Henderson, Designing a Responsible Periodic–Payment System for Tort Awards: Arizona Enacts a Prototype, 32 Ariz. L. Rev. 22 (1990) (a useful general assessment as well as a description of the Arizona law).

6. *Joint and Several Liability.* A reform measure that has received some attention, although not primarily in the medical malpractice context, is the modification of the rule that joint tortfeasors are jointly and severally liable for the total amount of the plaintiff's injuries. In the malpractice context, this rule encourages suit against multiple parties, settlement with one (frequently the most culpable), and pursuit of the party with the deepest pocket (frequently the hospital), whose fault may be negligible, in hope of a big award. Reforms in this area typically provide for the apportionment of damages in proportion to fault (with various exceptions) in all tort actions.

7. *Scheduling Damages.* Danzon has argued that

> any measure which reduces the range of variability of possible court outcomes would reduce expenditure on litigation and, by making claim costs more predictable, reduce the cost of malpractice insurance. A strong

case can be made for using a schedule of awards for different types of injury in place of the current rules of compensable damages, which attempt to estimate damages incurred by each individual patient. Individual determination of damages adds to litigation costs, while adding very little to deterrence, because awards are unpredictable, often occurring many years after the event causing the injury, and because such detail is currently and is likely to remain nullified by the averaging process of rating insurance premiums. Although scheduled awards are usually associated with a no-fault liability rule, the proposal advanced here would adopt a schedule for damages but retain a fault-based liability rule.

Danzon, An Economic Analysis of the Medical Malpractice System, 1 Behav. Sci. & L. 39, 51 (1983). See also Blumstein et al., Beyond Tort Reform: Developing Better Tools for Assessing Damages for Personal Injury, 8 Yale J. on Reg. 171 (1991); Bovbjerg et al., Valuing Life and Limb in Tort: Scheduling "Pain and Suffering," 83 Nw. U.L. Rev. 908 (1989).

NOTES AND QUESTIONS ON REFORMS LIMITING ACCESS TO COURTS

1. *Statutes of Limitations.* The role of the "long tail" of malpractice claims in precipitating the insurance crisis has caused many states to shorten their statutes of limitations applicable to such cases. The ABA Commission, supra, at 847–48, recommended as follows:

> (a) An action for medical malpractice should be commenced within two years from the time the incident which gave rise to the action occurred, or within one year from the time the existence of an actionable injury is discovered or in the exercise of reasonable care should have been discovered, whichever is longer. Except for cases involving a foreign object or fraudulent concealment, no action should be brought more than eight years after the occurrence of the incident which gave rise to the injury.
>
> (b) Where a foreign object has been left in the body, a patient should have one year after the object is discovered in which to bring an action.
>
> (c) Where fraudulent concealment of material facts by a health care provider has prevented the discovery of the injury or the alleged negligence, the patient should have one year after discovering that an actionable injury exists in which to bring suit.
>
> (d) The statute of limitations should be tolled during continuous treatment by the same health care provider for the same condition or for complications arising from the original treatment.
>
> (e) The statute of limitations should apply equally to adults and minors alike, except that a minor's representative should have until the minor's eighth birthday to commence a suit, regardless of how many years earlier the cause of action accrued.
>
> *Supporting Reasons*
>
> Statutes of limitations are designed to prevent the injured person from sleeping on his claim so that witnesses, memories and evidence can be reached while still fresh, so that intervening factors will not have operated

to obscure and make the effect of the original actor's tortious conduct difficult to determine, and so that the prospective defendant's fears of being sued can be quieted after a just period of time. Because of the complex nature of medical malpractice cases, which requires that the facts of the incident be ascertained as quickly as possible, and because of the insurance crisis, a relatively short (two year) period of limitations is proposed in order to speed up the claims process. Such a shortened period will still give the patient time in which to decide to bring suit (unless the injury and its cause have not become apparent, in which case the discovery exception will prevent the statutory period from commencing), while it promotes fairness to the defendant and relieves the court of the burden of trying stale claims.

If the general statute of limitations is applied in the situation where the patient does not have a reasonable basis until after the statute has run for concluding that he may have been negligently injured, it will work an unfairness to the patient.

In applying the discovery rule, courts have had difficulty in determining when the cause of action accrues. One view holds that the discovery of an injury by the patient is enough, without more, to trigger the running of the statute. The other view is that before the statute of limitations can begin to run the patient must not only discover his injury but must also be aware of facts which suggest that his injury may have been the result of negligence. The proposed position adopts this second view by requiring the patient to discover the existence of an actionable injury. The fairness of this position is supported by numerous cases in which medical injuries have manifested themselves through vague symptoms long before their connection with negligent treatment could possibly have been discovered. In many cases of surgical malpractice, for example, a later exploratory operation in which the negligent mistakes of the first surgical procedure are discovered is performed only after years of patient complaints of pain and discomfort.

However, since the statute of limitations is also a device for giving prospective defendants respite from suits after enough time has gone by, it seems fair to include an absolute limitation, subject to certain exceptions, of eight years from the occurrence of the incident. Where fraudulent concealment has prevented the patient's discovery of the negligence, or where a foreign object, which is evidence in itself of negligence, is found, the equities are such that the defendant should not be given the benefit of an absolute cutoff of his own liability. Other cases of misdiagnosis and mistreatment, though, do not have similar compelling reasons for an open-ended discovery rule. The medical procedures used in many cases may have changed dramatically over time, making it increasingly difficult to determine the relevant standard of care against which to measure the alleged malpractice. In addition, unlike the foreign object situation where the instrumentality causing the harm retains its identity in the body and is itself probative of negligence, there will often be no clear evidence of improper treatment and no clear evidence, given the intervening years, of the proximate cause of the injury. Even though the financial impact of such an absolute limit may not be substantial (because only a very small percentage of malpractice claims remain unreported after eight years), in those cases not involving a foreign object or fraudulent concealment, principles of fairness to the defendant justify bringing his liability to an end after a reasonable period of time. Moreover, an absolute limitation on medical malpractice actions, even one of eight years duration, should have a stabilizing effect on premiums, because by eliminating much of the long tail of malpractice claims, the uncertainties of rate-setting should be reduced.

A continuous treatment tolling provision is important in that it encourages a patient to seek recourse first through remedial care rather than through the courts. It also prevents the physician from possibly escaping liability by extending treatment beyond the period of limitation, and it obviates the need to determine the point at which, during a course of treatment, the negligence occurred which resulted in injury. Routine follow-up visits and examinations undertaken at the request of the patient for the sole purpose of ascertaining his condition should not be considered to be "treatment" for this purpose.

The Commission has concluded that minors' representatives should be able to bring an action until the minor's eighth birthday, even though the injury occurred long enough before that date that the general statute of limitations would have precluded an action. In so recommending, the Commission has reached what it considers to be a reasonable compromise between the needs of injured minors and those of potential defendants and insurers. Below a certain age, the child may not realize that something is wrong or may be unable to communicate his complaint adequately. Moreover, since a young child is developing rapidly during his early years, many injuries are difficult to detect and evaluate. However, there is also legitimacy in the argument of many physicians and insurers that a rule which protects a minor until he reaches adulthood is unfair, since facts become stale, medical standards change and the risk of actions many years in the future cannot be predicted by actuaries. The argument is also made that the law relies on a minor's parents or other legal representative to protect his rights in many other contexts, and that there is no reason not to do so in the medical malpractice situation.

It seems fair, therefore, that there should be a minimum age until which a minor's representative may sue, even though the general statute of limitations would have expired.

The area of toxic torts, featuring long latency periods between exposure to a hazardous substance and development of disease, has put pressure on the entire notion of statutes of limitations. See, e.g., Green, The Paradox of Statute of Limitations in Toxic Substance Litigation, 76 Calif. L. Rev. 965 (1988) (questioning appropriateness of limitations statutes).

Courts have been quite sensitive to the unfairness of cutting off an injured person's right to sue for medical malpractice when the injury did not reveal itself before the limitations period expired. This impulse is especially manifest in holdings that the clock begins to run, not when the injury first comes to light, but when the plaintiff first realizes or should realize that it was caused by negligence. E.g., Hamilton v. Smith, 773 F.2d

461 (2d Cir.1985) (so construing Connecticut statute providing that cause of action accrues upon discovery of injury). Most courts have been clear, however, that significant symptoms start the limitations period running. E.g., Bryant v. Crider, 434 S.E.2d 161 (Ga.App.1993) (symptoms, not diagnosis of Asherman's Syndrome, trigger statute); Enfield v. Hunt, 208 Cal.Rptr. 584 (Cal.App.1984) (plaintiff's failure to investigate cause of injuries despite their severity and duration reflected lack of reasonable diligence).

A number of statutes—often called "statutes of repose"—purport to abolish or limit the discovery rule and to cut off the right to sue even for negligence that was undiscoverable. E.g., Conn. Gen. Stat. Ann. § 52–584 (West 1991) (malpractice suits must be commenced within two years after "the date when injury is first sustained or discovered" or should have been discovered but in no event more than three years after "the date of the act or omission complained of"). Note the even greater stringency of the New Hampshire statute invalidated in the *Carson* case. Note also in *Carson* the special provisions governing claims of minors, which resemble provisions in other states and which were also invalidated. See also Weiner v. Wasson, 900 S.W.2d 316 (Tex.1995) (restrictive statute of limitations invalidated as applied to minors; in case of "minors and persons of unsound mind, [the state constitution's access-to-courts guarantee] extends beyond merely ensuring their access to courts"); Lyons v. Lederle Laboratories, 440 N.W.2d 769 (S.D.1989) ("statute requiring minors to file malpractice claim during childhood violates equal protection"). But see Dowd v. Rayner, 655 A.2d 679 (R.I.1995) (holding minor's rights could be modified without offending state constitution; minimal scrutiny); Miller v. Kretz, 531 N.W.2d 93 (Wis.App.1995) (upholding statute of limitations for minor over age 10).

Changes in limitations periods and statutes of repose have usually been held constitutional in their general application. E.g., Bonin v. Vannaman, 929 P.2d 754 (Kan.1996) (8–year statute of repose for claims of persons under legal disability does not violate equal protection or due process clauses as it affects minors); Holmes v. Iwasa, 657 P.2d 476 (Idaho 1983); Horn v. Citizens Hosp., 425 So.2d 1065 (Ala.1982); Allen v. Intermountain Health Care, 635 P.2d 30 (Utah 1981). But see McCollum v. Sisters of Charity of Nazareth Health Corp., 799 S.W.2d 15 (Ky.1990) (statute barring malpractice actions more than five years after date of alleged negligent act violates open-courts provision). Many cases, however, have revealed judicial vigilance on behalf of plaintiffs threatened with loss of tort rights through no fault of their own. E.g., Makos v. Wisconsin Mason's Health Care Fund, 564 N.W.2d 662 (Wis.1997) (invalidating strict five-year statute of repose where patient did not discover misdiagnosis until four years after limitations period expired); Barrio v. San Manuel Div. Hosp. for Magma Copper Co., 692 P.2d 280 (Ariz.1984) (suit for injuries suffered in childbirth brought 20 years later; special provisions of Arizona constitution protecting common-law tort rights held violated by statute of repose); Austin v. Litvak, 682 P.2d 41 (Colo.1984) (claim for negligent misdiagnosis brought after sixteen years, during which patient thought he had brain tumor and could not lead normal life; no rational basis found for statute giving benefit of discovery rule only to plaintiffs alleging concealment by physician or nonremoval of foreign object during surgery); Hardy v. VerMeulen, 512 N.E.2d 626 (Ohio 1987) (plaintiff did not discover injury until eleven years after surgery; statute of repose unconstitutional under open courts guarantee, which allows substantive changes in common-law rights but not arbitrary limitations on opportunity to pursue same).

2. *Notice; Pleading.* Note the holding in the *Carson* case invalidating a requirement of advance notice of intent to sue. The object of such requirements has been to save expense, facilitate settlements, and avoid unnecessary publicity and animosity. ABA Commission, supra, at 836. See, e.g., DeLuna v. St. Elizabeth's Hosp., 588 N.E.2d 1139 (Ill.1992) (resolving split in appellate courts in favor of constitutionality of requiring a certificate of merit); Mahoney v. Doerhoff Surgical Services, Inc., 807 S.W.2d 503 (Mo. 1991) (upholding requirement that plaintiff file a certificate of merit based on medical expert's opinion before pursuing claim); Henke v. Dunham, 450 N.W.2d 595 (Minn.App.1990) (upholding requirement but not applying it in preclusive manner, because "the primary objective of the law [is] to dispose of cases on the merits"); Sisario v. Amsterdam Mem. Hosp., 552 N.Y.S.2d 989 (N.Y.App.Div.1990) (certificate-of-merit requirement held reasonably related to the state's interests in encouraging physicians to practice in New York and in keeping malpractice insurance premiums down by preventing frivolous lawsuits).

Another popular reform (in nearly all states) has been a prohibition of pleadings specifying a particular amount of damages suffered. For a holding that such legislation prohibiting ad damnum clauses in pleadings improperly intrudes upon the judicial branch of state government, see White v. Fisher, 689 P.2d 102 (Wyo.1984). What possible benefit could there be in such a prohibition since the plaintiff must prove his damages in either event? Does the answer have something to do with standards of journalism?

3. *Screening Panels; Arbitration.* A major goal of the malpractice reform effort has been to move cases out of the courts. One approach has been to provide for the screening of claims by special panels before litigation commences in order to discourage nonmeritorious claims and to encourage settlements. Arbitration has also been encouraged. These reforms are taken up separately in § D of this chapter.

Roa v. Lodi Medical Group, Inc.

Supreme Court of California, 1985.
37 Cal.3d 920, 211 Cal.Rptr. 77, 695 P.2d 164.

■ KAUS, JUSTICE.

* * * In this case we address a challenge to Business and Professions Code section 6146, which places limits on the amount of fees an attorney may obtain in a medical malpractice action when he represents a party on a contingency fee basis. * * * [W]hile we express no view as to the wisdom of the measure, we conclude that the legislation is constitutional.

[Plaintiffs sought and obtained court approval of a settlement (for $500,000) of a malpractice claim brought on behalf of their minor son. They also requested the court to approve a payment to their attorneys of 25% of the minor's recovery pursuant to a contingent-fee contract. This amount exceeded by $30,000 the amount payable under the statutory fee schedule, which was enacted as part of the Medical Injury Compensation Reform Act of 1975 (MICRA) and which authorized 40% of the first $50,000, 33⅓% of the next $50,000, 25% of the next $100,000, and 10% of any amount over $200,000. The plaintiffs' standing was predicated on the fee limits' allegedly adverse effects on their right to retain competent counsel and on their lawyers' incentive to pursue the remaining defendants in the case. The court expressed no opinion on the conflict of interests between plaintiffs and their attorneys, which might seem to call for their separate representation in prosecuting the appeal. The court noted that amicus curiae briefs filed in the case ensured adequate airing of the issues.

[The lower court upheld the statute against plaintiffs' constitutional challenge and approved the lower fee.]

A

Plaintiffs' due process argument rests on the claim that the statute impermissibly infringes on the right of medical malpractice victims to retain counsel in malpractice actions. Although the right to be represented by retained counsel in civil actions is not expressly enumerated in the federal or state Constitution, our cases have long recognized that the constitutional due process guarantee does embrace such a right. Section 6146, however, does not in any way abrogate the right to retain counsel, but simply limits the compensation that an attorney may obtain when he represents an injured party under a contingency fee arrangement.

Statutory limits on attorney fees are not at all uncommon, either in California or throughout the country generally. In this state, attorney fees have long been legislatively regulated both in workers' compensation proceedings and in probate matters. Some states have adopted maximum fee schedules which apply to all personal-injury contingency fee arrangements; others have enacted limits which, like section 6146, apply only in a specific area, such as medical malpractice. (See, e.g., Johnson v. St. Vincent Hospital, Inc. (1980) 273 Ind. 374, 404 N.E.2d 585, 602–603; Prendergast v. Nelson (1977) 199 Neb. 97, 256 N.W.2d 657, 669–670; DiFilippo v. Beck (D.Del.1981) 520 F.Supp. 1009, 1016.) * * *

The validity of such legislative regulation of attorney fees is well established. * * *

Plaintiffs contend, however, that even if statutory limitations on attorney fees are generally permissible, the limits established by section 6146 are invalid because the authorized fees are so low that in practice the statute will make it impossible for injured persons to retain an attorney to represent them. The adequacy of the fees permitted by the statute is in large measure an empirical matter, and plaintiffs have made no showing to support their factual claim. Furthermore, a comparison of the fees permitted by section 6146 with the fees authorized under the numerous statutory schemes noted above suggests that section 6146's limits are not usually [sic] low. Under the circumstances, we certainly cannot hold that the amount of the fees permitted renders the statute unconstitutional on its face.

Plaintiffs alternatively challenge the "sliding scale" nature of the fee schedule, asserting that the decreasing percentage permitted for larger recoveries creates a conflict of interest between attorney and client, reducing the attorney's incentive to pursue a higher award. As a number of commentators have explained, however, potential conflicts of interest are inherent in all contingent fee arrangements. (See generally MacKinnon, Contingent Fees for Legal Services (1964) pp. 196–200; Schwartz & Mitchell, An Economic Analysis of the Contingent Fee in Personal–Injury Litigation (1970) 22 Stan.L.Rev. 1125, 1136–1139.) On the one hand, whenever a contingency fee agreement provides for either a flat percentage rate regardless of the amount of recovery or a declining percentage with an increase in recovery, "it may be to the lawyer's advantage to settle [the case] quickly, spending as little time as possible on the small claim where the increment in value through rigorous bargaining or trial, while significant to the client, is not significant or perhaps compensatory to the lawyer...." (MacKinnon, supra, at p. 198.) On the other hand, "[w]here the rate is graduated according to the stage of litigation at which recovery is attained ... the increase in the rate of fee may lead the lawyer to bring suit or start trial, for example, solely to increase his rate from 25% to 33⅓%, without actually doing that much additional work and without the likelihood of a comparable increment to the client." (Ibid.) Furthermore, no matter how the particular percentage fee is calculated, "[t]he difference in the financial position of the lawyer and client may make for a complete disparity in their willingness to take a risk on a large recovery as against no recovery at all. In the same way the use of delay to increase the eventual recovery on a claim may have an entirely different impact on the injured and uncompensated claimant than it does on the lawyer, who is busy with other claims and regards this as one of a series which are ripening on the vine.... " (Id. at p. 199.) Thus, though the sliding scale arrangement embodied in section 6146 may affect the settings in which the attorney's and client's interests diverge, it does not create the basic conflict of interest problem.

Indeed, section 6146's decreasing sliding-scale approach has been recommended as the preferable form of regulation by a number of studies that have examined the question. As a report of an American Bar Association commission explained: "[I]n order to relate the attorney's fee more to the amount of legal work and expense involved in handling a case and less to the fortuity of the plaintiff's economic status and degree of injury, a decreasing maximum schedule of attorney's fees, reasonably generous in the lower recovery ranges and thus unlikely to deny potential plaintiffs access to legal representation, should be set on a state-by-state basis." (Rep. of Com. on Medical Professional Liability (1977) 102 ABA Annual Rep. 786, 851.) For just these reasons, the Legislature could rationally have determined that this aspect of the statutory scheme would promote the fairness of attorney fees. The sliding scale schedule certainly does not unconstitutionally impinge on a malpractice victim's right to counsel.

Finally, plaintiffs suggest that because the fee limits of section 6146 apply only to medical malpractice actions, the statute will operate to drive the most competent attorneys out of medical malpractice litigation into other areas of personal injury practice; they argue that this amounts to an unconstitutional infringement of a malpractice victim's right to counsel. Once again, plaintiffs have failed to make any showing to support the factual premise of their contention. In addition, a similar claim could, of course, be raised with respect to every statutory provision which creates legislative limits on attorney fees in a particular field. As we have seen, such statutes are commonplace. Suffice it to say that we know of no authority which suggests that due process requires a single, uniform attorney fee schedule for all areas of practice.

B

We turn to the equal protection claim. Here plaintiffs' principal contention—somewhat related to their final due process argument—rests on the assertion that the Legislature acted arbitrarily in selectively imposing section 6146's attorney fee limits only in medical malpractice actions.

* * *

We cannot agree that the limits on contingency fees embodied in section 6146 bear no rational relationship to the objectives of MICRA. In the first place, it is unrealistic to suggest that such limits will not reduce the costs to malpractice defendants and their insurers in the large number of malpractice cases that are resolved through settlement. A plaintiff is quite naturally concerned with what a proposed settlement will yield to him personally, and because section 6146 permits an attorney to take only a smaller bite of a settlement, a plaintiff will be more likely to agree to a lower settlement since he will obtain the same net recovery from the lower settlement. Accordingly, the Legislature could reasonably have determined that the provision would serve to reduce malpractice insurance costs.

Second, the Legislature may also have imposed limits on contingency fees in this area as a means of deterring attorneys from either instituting frivolous suits or encouraging their clients to hold out for unrealistically high settlements. Although plaintiffs contend that there is no evidence to suggest that unregulated contingency fee agreements pose special problems in the medical malpractice field, plaintiffs themselves stress—in another context—that an unusually high percentage of medical malpractice cases that go to trial result in defense verdicts. While there may be many explanations for this phenomenon, the Legislature could rationally have believed that unregulated contingency fee contracts—calling for potentially huge attorney fee awards if cases are won—play at least some part in leading so many plaintiffs to pursue malpractice claims that ultimately prove unsuccessful. Of course, even when defendants ultimately win such lawsuits, they and their insurers incur considerable expense in defending the action. Thus, by reducing plaintiffs' attorneys' incentive to encourage their clients to pursue marginal claims, section 6146 again bears a rational relation to the legislative objective of reducing insurance costs.

Finally, section 6146's limits are rationally related to the MICRA scheme in yet another respect. In order to reduce malpractice insurance costs, MICRA incorporated a number of provisions that place special limits on, or that at least may tend to reduce, a malpractice plaintiff's recovery, provisions that are not applicable to other personal injury plaintiffs. The Legislature may reasonably have concluded that a limitation on contingency fees in this field was an "appropriate means of protecting the already diminished compensation" of such plaintiffs from further reduction by high contingency fees. Accordingly, there is no merit to plaintiffs' initial equal protection claim.[9]

Plaintiffs alternatively contend that the statute violates equal protection because it places limits on the fees that *plaintiffs'* attorneys may charge but imposes no limits on *defense* counsel's fees. As we have already seen, there are a host of statutes—both in California and in other jurisdictions—that place similar limits on contingency fees without limiting attorney fees that are earned on some other basis. Here, as in those instances, the Legislature could have determined that there was a special need (1) to protect plaintiffs from having their recoveries diminished by high contingency fees, and (2) "to reduce the temptation to adopt improper methods of prosecution which contracts for large fees contingent upon success have sometimes been supposed to encourage."[10]

Finally, plaintiffs argue that the decreasing-sliding-scale component of section 6146 unconstitutionally discriminates against more seriously injured malpractice victims. They suggest that in light of the lower percentage fee which the statute authorizes for higher recoveries, the provision makes it more difficult to obtain an attorney who will be willing to undertake the additional effort required to obtain such awards. As we have already noted, however, the Legislature could reasonably have concluded that the sliding-scale approach in fact produces more equitable fees than the traditional flat contingency fee, helping to ensure that an attorney does not obtain a "windfall" simply because his client is very seriously injured

9. As already noted, a number of the medical malpractice reform statutes enacted in the mid–1970s imposed limits on attorney fees which apply only to medical malpractice litigation. Most courts that have addressed equal protection challenges to such provisions have rejected the challenges. (See, e.g., Johnson v. St. Vincent Hospital, Inc., supra, 404 N.E.2d 585, 602; DiFilippo v. Beck, supra, 520 F.Supp. 1009, 1016.) To our knowledge, only one case has sustained such an attack (Carson v. Maurer (N.H.1980) 120 N.H. 925, 424 A.2d 825, 838–839), and in Carson the court applied an "intermediate scrutiny" equal protection standard that is inconsistent with the standard applied by this court * * *

10. The dissent's suggestion that a statute which draws a distinction between plaintiffs' and defendants' attorney fees violates the First Amendment's ban on "content discrimination" not only is unsupported by any authority, but is also quite shortsighted. Numerous statutes contain provisions authorizing successful plaintiffs to recover attorney fees under circumstances in which successful defendants may not so recover. Surely, the dissent does not intend to suggest that all such statutes are unconstitutional.

and guaranteeing that the most seriously injured plaintiffs will retain the lion's share of any recovery secured on their behalf.

* * *

■ BIRD, CHIEF JUSTICE, dissenting.

* * * In effect, section 6146 prohibits severely injured victims of medical negligence from paying the general market rate for legal services, while permitting defendants to pay whatever is necessary to obtain high quality representation.

Out of practical necessity, virtually all plaintiffs use contingent fee arrangements. In fact, for clients of limited means "the contingent fee arrangement offers the only realistic hope of establishing a legal claim."

Section 6146 imposes heavy burdens on the ability of severely injured plaintiffs to obtain adequate legal representation. It sets forth a sliding scale of fee limits—the greater the recovery, the lower the allowable percentage. The effect of this approach is to impose drastically low limits on fees in precisely those cases which require a large recovery to make the plaintiff economically whole. For example, in a case involving a $1 million recovery, the allowable rate would be about 15 percent, less than half of the 33–⅓ percent rate that is generally available outside the medical malpractice field.

Other provisions of MICRA interact with section 6146 to further discourage attorneys from representing severely injured plaintiffs. The collateral source provision can substantially reduce the damage award, and thus the contingent fee, without decreasing the attorney's workload. The periodic payment provision may have the same effect and, in addition, could delay the attorney's compensation for years.[2] Further, the $250,000 limit on non-economic damages sharply reduces the recovery without relieving the attorney of the most difficult aspects of the malpractice action—proving negligence and causation.

Since section 6146 affects only medical malpractice cases, attorneys may avoid these problems by refusing to represent medical malpractice victims. Only those lawyers not sufficiently competent or well-established to attract unrestricted business have any financial incentive to represent a severely injured medical malpractice victim.

Section 6146 hampers a victim's ability to obtain high quality legal representation precisely in those cases where such representation is most essential. Defendants can be expected to concentrate their legal resources on the potential high recovery cases. The statute prohibits plaintiffs from responding in kind. Hence, the legal contest becomes a lopsided mismatch with tort victims on the losing end.

This problem is aggravated by the fact that medical malpractice plaintiffs are even more in need of high quality legal representation than

2. The precise impact of section 667.7 on attorney fees is open to question, since the statute does not explicitly preclude the possibility that the attorney fees could be paid in a lump sum at the time of judgment.

other personal injury plaintiffs. Even MICRA's principal sponsor has acknowledged that "a malpractice case is extremely difficult to prove, demands a great deal of research into causal factors and exhausts a tremendous amount of time on the part of the attorney."

Further, the risk of a zero recovery is high, and the fees collected in successful cases must also compensate the attorney for his or her work on the unsuccessful ones. (See, e.g., [references showing "50 percent of medical malpractice cases are disposed of with no recovery" and "of the malpractice claims that go to trial, 60 percent obtain zero gross recovery"].)[5]

* * *

I.

Plaintiffs urge that the fee limits imposed by section 6146 infringe on their constitutional right to petition the government for redress of grievances. They contend that their ability to obtain competent legal representation, which is essential for the effective prosecution of a medical malpractice complaint, is heavily burdened. Further, they suggest that selective imposition of restrictions on "person[s] *seeking* damages" for injuries due to medical malpractice (§ 6146, emphasis added) impermissibly discriminates among litigants according to the content of the views they wish to present to the courts. *Only plaintiffs* are prohibited from hiring attorneys at the market rate, while defendants are free to pay any amount—by contingent fee or otherwise—which may be necessary to obtain quality representation.

* * *

Since representation by counsel is essential to the effective exercise of an individual's First Amendment rights to petition and to access [to the courts for redress of private disputes], the right to obtain counsel can only be restricted where necessary to achieve a compelling state interest.

The attorney-fee limitation should be subjected to particularly vigorous scrutiny since it also runs afoul of the constitutional ban on content discrimination. In regulating the exercise of First Amendment rights, the government may not pick and choose what views may be heard.

* * *

Allowing plaintiffs to retain a greater percentage of their recovery is a legitimate interest. However, it is *not* a compelling one. * * * [S]uch a paternalistic argument is disfavored in the context of the First Amend-

5. The majority imply that the high rate of zero recovery in medical malpractice cases is due to an inordinate number of frivolous or meritless claims. The more likely explanation is that there is a "salient difference between litigation for medical malpractice and other forms of accident liability." Modern medicine is highly complex and technical, and there is often a significant lag time between the date of the wrongful act and the date an injury is perceived. These factors present special difficulties in gathering evidence and proving negligence in medical malpractice cases.

ment. It is entirely inappropriate for the state to "protect" an individual by suppressing his or her exercise of a First Amendment right.

Moreover, section 6146 is not necessary to protect a plaintiff's recovery. Section 6146 will often operate to force the early settlement of meritorious claims, resulting in a *reduction* in a plaintiff's recovery in many cases. Curiously, in cases involving serious injuries with potentially large recoveries, attorneys may be discouraged from taking meritorious cases to trial even though to do so might significantly increase the plaintiff's recovery. In cases involving smaller potential recoveries, section 6146 may actually *increase* the attorney's contingent fee since the fee schedule set out in section 6146 can be expected "to provide a floor, as well as a ceiling, on the percentage rate charged."

It is also argued that section 6146 serves MICRA's overall purpose of preserving medical malpractice insurance. * * *

Section 6146 can provide relief to defendants and their insurers only by forcing plaintiffs to settle claims for amounts far below their actual value and/or by reducing the number of claims filed. Indeed, at the time that MICRA was enacted, the Auditor General pointed out that "[u]nless the amount of medical malpractice settlements continue[s] to increase in the future there will be *little if any effect* on medical malpractice rates as a result of limitations imposed on attorney contingency fees." * * *

Section 6146 significantly infringes on plaintiff's First Amendment right to petition and does so based on the content of a plaintiff's claim. Therefore, it must be shown to be necessary to achieve a compelling state interest. Defendant has not met this burden. Accordingly, section 6146 is invalid.

II.

Next, plaintiffs contend that section 6146 violates plaintiffs' right to due process of law. * * * The limits imposed by section 6146 must be rationally related to the Legislature's purposes in enacting the statute.

The majority conclude that limiting the compensation that plaintiffs' attorney may receive does not violate due process because it "does not in any way abrogate the right to retain counsel." However, section 6146 *does* significantly interfere with the right of certain victims of medical malpractice to retain counsel. Further, it exacerbates the conflict of interest between plaintiffs and their attorneys inherent in the contingent fee arrangement.

In support of their holding, the majority cite a number of existing attorney-fee limits which have withstood legal challenge. * * *

* * * [F]ee restrictions in the workers compensation and probate contexts are not likely to discourage attorneys from working in those fields, since the legal work is relatively simple, the risks are low and compensation is available which is commensurate to the services performed.

Contrast this situation with that of the plaintiff's attorney in a malpractice action with a contingent fee arrangement. The attorney will receive no compensation unless there is a recovery in the case. One study indicates that over 400 attorney hours are spent on the average malpractice case which results in a "zero recovery" after trial. (Contingent Fees, supra, at p. 218, fn. 22.) Faced with the combined effect of the fee limitation and other MICRA provisions (e.g., the collateral source provisions, the $250,000 ceiling on noneconomic damages, and the periodic installment provision, many attorneys can be expected to cease to represent malpractice victims with valid claims). As a result, the most severely injured clients may be unable to secure representation, especially if their cases involve complex or difficult factual issues, problems of proof, or expensive expert testimony.

The majority stress that in some states (e.g., New Jersey and New York) limits on the contingent fees available to attorneys in *all* personal injury action have been upheld. However, rather than lending support to the majority's position, reference to the New Jersey and New York schemes highlights two of the most pernicious aspects of section 6146.

First, section 6146 singles out and imposes a burden on only one narrow subclass of personal injury victims. Attorneys may still find ample unrestricted work elsewhere. When the risks and cost associated with general personal injury work are not as great as for medical malpractice, and the potential compensation is much greater, common sense tells us that attorneys will abandon the medical malpractice field. By contrast, the New Jersey and New York schemes restrict broad fields of practice, leaving attorneys little room for escape.

Second, unlike the New Jersey and New York schemes, section 6146 has no provision for higher fees in exceptionally difficult cases. * * *

Simple calculations indicate that section 6146 will often operate to discourage litigation in a manner which results in a *reduction* rather than an increase in a plaintiff's recovery. An example serves to illustrate the point. This example assumes a medical malpractice case which would result in a $250,000 verdict after trial.

Studies indicate that plaintiffs who settle before trial receive approximately 75 percent of their potential verdict. (Danzon & Lillard, Settlement Out of Court: The Disposition of Medical Malpractice Claims (1983) 12 J. Legal Stud. 345, 375.) Plaintiffs and amici note that, prior to MICRA, most plaintiff attorneys employed contingent fee agreements in which the attorney received a greater percentage of the recovery if the case proceeded to trial than if it settled before trial—typically 25 percent to 33 percent if the case settled and 40 percent or more if the case went to trial.

[Chief Justice Bird developed her example to show how], after MICRA, if the case settles before trial, the attorney's compensation is not significantly less than if the case had gone to trial. However, the plaintiff's recovery is reduced by almost $55,000. * * *

* * * [Thus, a]fter MICRA, although a plaintiff might significantly increase his or her recovery by going to trial, the marginal increase in

attorney fees might not cover the expenses involved in producing expert witnesses, marshalling exhibits, and conducting the trial itself. The pressure on a plaintiff's attorney to settle a meritorious case before trial is overwhelming.

Thus, section 6146 will produce a greater number of settlements with lower recoveries. However, it will do so at a heavy price both to the injured plaintiff and his or her relationship with the attorney. Rather than helping the malpractice victim as the majority contend, section 6146 will often result in a *smaller* recovery for the plaintiff and a significant ethical dilemma for the attorney. "Limits on contingent fees decrease settlement size, increase the likelihood that a case is dropped, and decrease the likelihood of litigation to verdict.... [F]ee constraints will limit expenditure on litigation at the cost of reduced compensation to plaintiffs." (Danzon & Lillard, Settlement Out of Court: The Disposition of Medical Malpractice Claims, supra, 12 J.Legal Stud. at p. 375.) These results are exactly contrary to those forecast by the majority.

* * *

While discouraging frivolous and meritless suits is a legitimate state interest, there is no evidence that the number of frivolous claims in the medical malpractice field is high, or that such claims contribute to the cost of medical malpractice premiums. On the contrary, the difficulty in proving medical malpractice and the high risk of zero recovery make attorneys very selective about the cases they are willing to pursue. Even insurers have acknowledged that attorneys reject the vast majority of malpractice claims they see.

The absence of any evidence that prior to the enactment of MICRA there was an inordinate number of frivolous medical malpractice claims filed strongly suggests that section 6146 actually operates to discourage the filing of *meritorious* claims. The attempt to reduce malpractice premiums by reducing the number of meritorious malpractice claims filed is exactly the sort of "arbitrary and oppressive" legislative action which the due process guarantees must operate to prevent.

* * *

III.

Section 6146 also violates the equal protection clause of the California Constitution. section 6146 creates several classifications. First, it affects only those tort victims who are injured by medical malpractice. Second, it disproportionately burdens the most seriously injured medical malpractice victims. Third, it places restrictions only on medical malpractice *plaintiffs,* not defendants.

* * *

Section 6146 is grossly under inclusive with regard to the objective of reducing premiums. It is not disputed that defendant and plaintiff legal fees consume about the same proportion of the premium dollar. Furthermore, according to a systematic study of medical malpractice attorney fees, plaintiff fees are not significantly greater than defendant fees. Hence, there is no rational basis for cutting costs by restricting plaintiffs while leaving defendants free from restrictions.

Indeed, restrictions on defense fees would yield a far greater potential reduction on premiums than equivalent restrictions on plaintiff fees. Defense fees are paid directly out of insurance funds. A $1 reduction in the fee could yield a $1 reduction in premiums. By contrast, plaintiff fees are paid out of the plaintiff's recovery. * * *

If anything, MICRA's other provisions provide a rational basis for *higher* contingent rates in the medical malpractice area. As explained above, several of these provisions reduce the plaintiff's recovery without decreasing his or her attorney's work load. Hence, to obtain the same fees that are available to them elsewhere, attorneys would have to charge higher percentage rates.

* * *

■ MOSK, J., and MCCLOSKY, J. PRO. TEM., concur.

NOTES AND QUESTIONS ON REFORMS TARGETING ATTORNEYS

1. *Public Policy*. What is the public policy rationale for regulating attorneys' fees in malpractice or other personal injury cases? Usually price regulation is introduced to protect consumers against supracompetitive prices resulting from some defect in the competitive market. Is there such a market failure here? If so, does California-style regulation address it? Or was regulation adopted for another reason altogether? Is this the same kind of economic regulation that has traditionally benefitted from judicial deference to legislative judgment?

2. *Contingent Fees as Insurance*. What functions do contingent fees perform? Do you see how they are analogous to insurance? Have contingent fees contributed to the malpractice "crises"? Do they, as physicians often assert, encourage the bringing of suits of doubtful merit? Might a legislature believe that high contingent-fee rates make lawyers unduly willing to take cases in which, although liability is questionable, the patient's injuries are so grievous and the potential award so large that the case is worth the gamble because the jury may be sympathetic? What other incentive effects would you anticipate from a damage cap?

3. *Challenges to Contingency Fee Restrictions*. As a concession carefully negotiated with trial lawyers, California raised its contingent-fee rates in malpractice cases as part of package of tort reforms enacted in 1987. Cal. Bus. & Prof. Code § 6146 (a) (West 1990) (allowing diminishing percentages up to $600,000 and 15% thereafter). Several states, instead of prescribing a fee schedule, have simply given the courts the power to regulate contingent fees by rule.

Note from the *Roa* court's citations how such regulation has fared in the courts, and recall *Carson v. Maurer*. See also Annot., 12 A.L.R.4th 23 (1982). The Indiana malpractice reforms, which were more sweeping even than California's and included a flat 15% cap on the attorney's share of the award, were upheld in Johnson v. St. Vincent Hosp., Inc., 404 N.E.2d 585 (Ind. 1980). In Newton v. Cox, 878 S.W.2d 105 (Tenn.), cert. denied, 513 U.S. 869 (1994), medical malpractice plaintiffs who had signed a contract to pay an attorney 50 percent of any recovery sued successfully to recover the difference between that amount and the third of all damages permitted by Tenn. Code Ann. § 29–26–120 (1980). The court used a rational basis test in ruling the statute constitutional. Should the original contract between the plaintiff and his attorney have been abrogated?

4. *Sanctions for Frivolous Actions; Countersuits.* A number of states, following precedents like that of Rule 11 of the Federal Rules of Civil Procedure, have taken actions allowing the award of costs against attorneys who file "frivolous" malpractice actions (or the equivalent). See, e.g., N.Y. C.P.L.R. 8303–a (costs and attorney fees allowable to defendants in frivolous malpractice actions) (McKinney Supp. 1997); Weber v. Kessler, 516 N.Y.S.2d 390 (N.Y.Sup.Ct.1987) (nonresident plaintiff required to post bond to cover costs under foregoing statute). See also Annot., 84 A.L.R.3d 555 (1978). Amendments to Rule 11 in 1993 increased judicial discretion in sanctioning attorneys and created several safe harbors. See generally Armour, Practice Makes Perfect: Judicial Discretion in the 1993 Amendments to Rule 11, 24 Hofstra L. Rev. 677 (1996); Cain, Frivolous Litigation, Discretionary Sanctioning in a Safe Harbor: The 1993 Revision of Rule 11, 43 Kan. L. Rev. 207 (1994).

Florida at one time had (but subsequently repealed) a statute that required losing parties in medical malpractice suits (other than indigents) to pay the winning party's costs—that is, adopted essentially the British over the American rule on legal costs. See Florida Patient's Compensation Fund v. Rowe, 472 So.2d 1145 (Fla.1985) (upholding fee shifting statute); Englander v. St. Francis Hosp., Inc., 506 So.2d 423 (Fla.App.1987) (fees payable upon voluntary dismissal). What incentive effects would you expect the Florida statute, which applied to the parties and not their attorneys, to have? How should contingent fee arrangements be handled in such a fee-shifting scheme?

Physician resentment against attorneys has resulted in a number of so-called (but rarely successful) "countersuits," in which an attorney for an unsuccessful plaintiff in a malpractice case is accused of negligently or maliciously exposing the defendant (now plaintiff) physician to the expense and other hardships of defending what is now alleged to have been a frivolous claim. A typical case would be one in which one of several defendants sued alleges that the case against him had no colorable merit and was brought without adequate inquiry or for strategic or other purposes.

The legal theories of countersuits have included negligence, abuse of process, and malicious prosecution. Negligence actions are unlikely to succeed because they require holding, anomalously, that a plaintiff's attorney has a duty to prospective defendants. See Friedman v. Dozorc, 312 N.W.2d 585, 589–94 (Mich.1981) (an exhaustive and widely cited opinion on the validity of countersuits). Abuse of process is unlikely to be found if the attorney truly sought money damages and was not using the suit for some ulterior purpose. Id. at 594–95. Malicious prosecution suits are difficult because of the requirement of malice. See, e.g., Kaiman v. Myers, 234 Cal.Rptr. 758 (Cal.App.1987) (lack of probable cause held no basis for inferring malice); Dalton v. Breaux, 510 So.2d 1277 (La.App.1987) (failure to allege that attorney acted out of personal malice); *Friedman*, supra, at 603–08. But see Peerman v. Sidicane, 605 S.W.2d 242 (Tenn.App.1980) (attorney liable for continuing groundless claims, including allegation of fee splitting, against doctor without client knowledge). Some courts require special damages. E.g., *Friedman*, supra, at 595–603; Stopka v. Lesser, 402 N.E.2d 781 (Ill.App.1980) (enforcing, but advocating reassessment of, special damages requirement). Do you agree with the view that anxiety, loss of time, attorney fees, and the necessity for defending one's reputation should be regarded simply as unfortunate incidents of lawsuits?

Empirical Evidence on the Effects of Malpractice Reforms

Paul C. Weiler, J.D., The Impact of Malpractice Legislation

Excerpt from P. Weiler, Medical Malpractice on Trial 33, 35–37 (1991).

* * *

Medical malpractice has served as the major testing ground not only for new tort doctrines but also for empirical research about the real-world impact of new laws. Although most of the common law changes in the sixties occurred in a fairly short time, as did the legislative changes in the mid-seventies, various states acted at different times and in different ways—some not acting at all. That divergence among jurisdictions has enabled scholars to compare the impact of different laws in states with similar background conditions, and of similar laws in states with different conditions, so as to isolate the specific contribution of legal reform. * * *

Frank Sloan studied the factors influencing changes in premiums paid from 1974 through 1978 by general practitioners, ophthalmologists, and orthopedic surgeons. He looked in particular for the effect of twelve statutory changes (taken individually, not cumulatively), including caps on damages, collateral source offsets, informed consent, *res ipsa*, contingency fees, screening panels, and the statute of limitations. The only legal change that had a negative and statistically significant effect on either the level or the rate of change in premiums was the mandatory screening panel.

[Patricia] Danzon also explored the influence of statutory rules on the frequency, severity, and total cost of claims closed by insurers from 1975 through 1978. Of the various legislative changes she analyzed, the most effective were the collateral source rule, for which a mandatory offset reduced the severity of awards by 50 percent (though the discretionary use of evidence of such sources had no apparent impact), and a cap on the damage award, which reduced severity by 19 percent. The apparent effect of limits on contingent fees on claims severity and claims costs was not statistically significant. Changes in neither the statute of limitations nor such substantive doctrines as the locality rule, *res ipsa*, or informed consent had any visible impact.

The research projects described above studied the possible effect of legislation in the years just after the laws were enacted. Such a limited time frame might not give a fair picture of the longer-term impact once the parties and the courts had adjusted to the statutes. Two studies, however, have traced mid-seventies legislation over a more extended period of time.

The first was conducted by Danzon, who updated her research to look at claims closed through 1984, and who discovered some interesting revisions of her earlier findings. In the later study the reduction in the limitations period showed a statistically significant effect on claims frequency, reducing claims by 8 percent for every year by which the limitation period was reduced. While there is no longer a discernible difference between the mandatory and the discretionary versions of the collateral source offset, adopting such a rule reduces claims severity by between 11 and 19 percent and claims frequency by around 14 percent—presumably, the prospect of lower recoveries was reducing the incentive to file a claim. Although the cumulative result of caps on damage awards was to reduce the claim severity factor by 23 percent, the device had no such effect on the plaintiff's propensity to initiate claims. Danzon's verdict about the screening panel procedure was that it had no significant impact on either the frequency or the severity of awards.

Sloan and colleagues combined data from one survey of claims closed in the years 1976–1978 and from a later survey of claims closed in 1984 in order to test the longer-term effectiveness of the mid-seventies' legislative reforms. Because their analysis assumed that a claim had been filed, these investigators were able to test only the likelihood and the amount that a given claim would be paid, not the frequency of claims made relative to some independent index of injuries. Nevertheless, their research involved a closer look at the details of each statute and the timing of each malpractice claim—differentiating, for example, between caps on total damages and caps on noneconomic damages—and included a determination for each claim of whether a particular law was in effect at the time it was filed or resolved. Their findings about the impact of statutory changes, controlling for a number of other variables, can be summarized as follows. Legislative alterations in common law liability rules such as *res ipsa* or informed consent had no discernible effect; alterations in access rules such as statutes of repose or limits on attorney fees had only a modest effect on both the likelihood and the amount of recovery; but alterations to damage rules had a powerful effect. In particular a mandatory collateral source offset reduced insurer costs (both plaintiff indemnity and defendant adjustment expenses) by 21 percent on average; a cap on noneconomic damages reduced insurer costs by 23 percent; and a cap on total damages produced a reduction of fully 39 percent.

Looking back, then, at what is now a substantial body of research employing quite disparate data sets and methodologies, a general convergence about the impact of tort reform emerges from the various findings.

Standards of liability. Variations in the standards of liability make little difference in aggregate outcome, a result that should not be particularly surprising. As long as juries are still asked to apply the basic common law paradigm of physician fault, tinkering with doctrines such as informed consent or *res ipsa* is unlikely to have a pronounced effect on claims or premium levels, even though the new rules will make some difference in the disposition of particular cases.

Access rules. Variation in access rules—limitations periods, screening procedures, and attorney fees—had an overall impact of modest proportions. Such rules are more likely to affect the timing and tactics employed by the parties in tort litigation, thereby influencing the types of medical accidents that will be channeled into the tort process; but they will not generally have a large impact on the amount of litigation doctors have to face or the premiums they have to pay.

Limits on damages. More striking results ensue from legislation that limits the amount of damages to be awarded, through either offsets of collateral sources or caps on damages. Imposing a blunt, mandatory ceiling on possible tort verdicts is far more difficult for attorneys or juries to finesse; moreover, it has both a direct effect on the average payment in those claims that are made and a further dampening effect on the readiness of patients and their attorneys to file claims in the first place, given the limit on the potential return from a litigation investment. It is also unsurprising that the impact of damage caps has become more powerful over time. When they were first enacted, the ceilings tended to be set a levels that would accommodate the vast bulk of settlements then begin reached in the tort process; as a result, they constrained only a few outlying jury verdicts. However, because few of these dollar caps were made adjustable to subsequent inflation, they became significantly more binding in the eighties, and consequently more helpful to their intended beneficiaries.

NOTES AND QUESTIONS

1. *Other References.* On the effects of reforms, see also Office of Technology Assessment, Impact of Legal Reforms on Medical Malpractice Costs (OTA BP–H–119, 1993) (concluding that flat caps on total awards and nonmonetary damages, such as pain and suffering; changes in collateral source offset rules; and shortening statute of limitations all had significant impact on the number of claims brought); Symposium, Medical Malpractice: Lessons for Reform, Law & Contemp. Probs., Winter & Spring 1991 (including several reports of empirical studies, many of them carried out with support from the Robert Wood Johnson Foundation). For overviews and analyses touching on all aspects of the malpractice liability problem, see Symposium, Medical Malpractice: External Influences and Controls, Law & Contemp. Probs., Winter–Spring 1997; F. Sloan et al., Suing for

Medical Malpractice (1993); P. Weiler, Medical Malpractice on Trial, supra (thoughtful review of the issues by participant in the Harvard study of medical injuries in New York hospitals and the American Law Institute's tort reform project, leading to recommendations for a "no-fault" strategy).

2. What more would you like to know about the effects of tort law on medical practice? In general, it is surprising how little we know about tort law's contribution to the quality of care. In the last analysis, the system is probably retained primarily because it provides a channel—indeed, virtually the only channel—through which consumers can effectively voice dissatisfaction with doctors and hospitals. This feature gets providers' attention and probably causes them not only to strive to achieve good outcomes but also to cultivate a good "bedside manner" and rapport with their patients. Although both consumer choice and the law of informed consent help to make providers respect their patients as persons, the patient's right to sue in the event of a bad result may contribute more in this respect than is commonly appreciated.

3. In any event, although the fault system may have certain benefits, nothing suggests that it could not be greatly improved by measures lowering its administrative costs or enhancing its inducement of optimal accident avoidance. The concluding section of this chapter suggests some more far-reaching reform ideas, including some that might be achieved by private agreements rather than legislative reform.

SECTION B: THE LEGAL STANDARD OF CARE

NOTES AND QUESTIONS ON THE LEGAL DUTIES OF PHYSICIANS

1. To be successful in a suit for medical malpractice, a plaintiff must prove the following four propositions: (1) that there was a dutiful relationship between the doctor and the patient; (2) that some injury was sustained as a result of medical practice and not as a result of the disease process itself; (3) that there was a breach of the legal standard of care, (i.e., negligence); and (4) that there was a causal relationship between the negligence and the injury. Before taking up the precise nature of the duties that physicians owe their patients under the law of torts, these notes address different aspects of the first of these items, the doctor/patient relationship—which was also touched upon in the discussion of abandonment and related issues in chapter 1(§§ A & B).

2. *Contract or Tort?* Physician duties, it appears, arise out of an implied contract but are not truly contractual. Thus, although a doctor/patient relationship is entered into voluntarily on both sides, the incidents of that relationship, once established, are largely prescribed by law. See generally Atiyah, Medical Malpractice and the Contract/Tort Boundary, Law & Contemp.Probs., Spring 1986, p. 286 (summarizing how tort principles replaced contract notions in personal injury law). One court has stated that the parties' voluntary arrangement is most aptly seen as creating "a status or relation rather than a contract." Kennedy v. Parrott, 90 S.E.2d 754, 757 (N.C.1956). A relationship giving rise to professional duties may be established even though there is to be no charge for the service—that is, there is no consideration for the doctor's promise.

A continuing theme throughout this chapter is the potential role of private contracts in defining the legal duties of health care providers, including the standard of care to which they are held. Discussion in § E will consider whether health care providers may limit their exposure to malpractice liability by express contracts modifying the rights that the legal system confers on patients. As one might anticipate, courts and lawyers have viewed such contracts skeptically. Contracts subjecting a physician to a *higher* duty than the law itself imposes have also raised questions, as the next paragraph reveals.

3. *Contractual Guarantees of Cure.* A plaintiff's allegation that a physician made a contractual commitment to effectuate a particular medical result is likely to be closely scrutinized. In one case, an entertainer complained that a plastic surgeon breached a specific undertaking to enhance, and instead impaired, her beauty by an operation on her nose. The court addressed some of the problems raised by alleged guarantees or warranties of cure as follows:

> It is not hard to see why the courts should be unenthusiastic or skeptical about the contract theory. Considering the uncertainties of medical science and the variations in the physical and psychological conditions of individual patients, doctors can seldom in good faith promise specific results. Therefore it is unlikely that physicians of even average integrity will in fact make such promises. Statements of opinion by the physician with some optimistic coloring are a different thing, and may indeed have therapeutic value. But patients may transform such statements into firm promises in their own minds, especially when they have been disappointed in the event, and testify in that sense to sympathetic juries. If actions for breach of promise can be readily maintained, doctors, so it is said, will be frightened into practicing "defensive medicine." On the other hand, if these actions were outlawed, leaving only the possibility of suits for malpractice, there is fear that the public might be exposed to the enticements of charlatans, and confidence in the profession might ultimately be shaken. The law has taken the middle of the road position of allowing actions based on alleged contract, but insisting on clear proof. Instructions to the jury may well stress this requirement and point to tests of truth, such as the complexity or difficulty of an operation as bearing on the probability that a given result was promised.

Sullivan v. O'Connor, 296 N.E.2d 183, 186 (Mass.1973). The court's opinion also considered the appropriate measure of damages in such a case, rejecting "expectancy" and "restitution" damages and opting for an award based on the patient's reliance on the representations made. Would a physician's malpractice insurance be likely to cover damages awarded in a breach of contract action?

What advantages might a plaintiff hope to derive from basing his claim on a contract rather than a tort theory? Statutes of limitations applicable to contract actions are often more liberal, and some charitable and sovereign immunities may not extend to actions based on contract. In addition, proof of a breach of contract to achieve a specific result does not require establishing a legal standard of care and may not require an expert witness. But see Steinmetz v. Francis J. Lowry, D.D.S. & Assocs., Inc., 477 N.E.2d 671 (Ohio App. 1984) (court required plaintiff to produce expert even in case seeking to recover only cost of dentures that did not fit). You should also consider, when you reach § C, how a breach of contract action differs from an action based upon a physician's misrepresentations leading to a failure to obtain the patient's informed consent to treatment.

Some courts have been receptive to actions based on alleged contractual undertakings. E.g., Zehr v. Haugen, 855 P.2d 1127 (Or.App.1993) (failed sterilization gave rise to action for breach of contract); Murray v. University Hosp., 490 A.2d 839 (Pa.Super. 1985) (parol evidence admitted to show guarantee against future pregnancies); Guilmet v. Campbell, 188 N.W.2d 601 (Mich.1971) (upholding jury verdict based on plaintiff's recollection of extensive reassurances but not of express guarantee). Other courts have been harder to satisfy. E.g., Rogala v. Silva, 305 N.E.2d 571 (Ill.App.1973) (sterilization procedure failed; court indicated that contract claim would require proof of separate consideration and of patient's specific reliance on promise as inducement to accept service). A number of states HAVE made their statutes of frauds, requiring a written agreement, applicable to contracts warranting a specific medical result. E.g., Ind. Code Ann. § 27–12–12–1 (Burns 1993); Mich. Comp. Laws Ann. § 566.132(g) (West 1996).

4. *When Does a Doctor/Patient Relationship Exist?* A physician's eligibility to be sued for malpractice (for acting negligently or for abandonment of a patient, for example) depends upon whether a doctor/patient relationship was ever created. In general, the law respects the physician's freedom to choose those with whom to establish a professional relationship. There is thus, for physicians, no analogue to the public-utility-like duties imposed on hospitals (see chapter 1(§B)) to render at least emergency care to patients seeking it. Nevertheless, Professor King notes some judicial "willingness to seize on the slightest association or actions as evidence that the physician has undertaken to care for a patient, thereby creating a duty of care." J. King. The Law of Medical Malpractice in a Nutshell 12 (2d ed. 1986). See, e.g., Dillon v. Silver, 520 N.Y.S.2d 751 (N.Y.A.D.1987) (patient was referred by ER physician to on-call specialist, who refused to respond; because hospital required on-call physician to provide care in such cases, there was a factual issue whether relationship existed); Easter v. Lexington Mem. Hosp., Inc., 278 S.E.2d 253 (N.C.1981) (ER physician assigned another doctor, arguably unqualified, to treat burn patient; jury could find first physician had assumed responsibility to patient and could be sued for negligent referral). See also Annot., What Constitutes Physician–Patient Relationship for Malpractice Purposes, 17 A.L.R.4th 132 (1981).

5. *Duties of Physicians Retained by Third Parties.* What obligations should a physician have to an individual whom he examines, not for the patient's primary benefit, but for a nontherapeutic purpose on behalf of, say, an employer, an insurance company, or a government agency? Vital diagnostic information may be uncovered in such an examination, but physicians providing physicals for insurers are generally not held to have a duty to disclose such information. E.g., Saari v. Litman, 486 N.W.2d 813 (Minn.App.1992) (exam for insurer did not create doctor/patient relationship). Is it relevant that the insurer's action on the matter constitutes some notice that a problem was found?

At least in cases of employment-related physical exams, courts have not been so shortsighted as to make the obligation to disclose such information to the examinee turn solely on whether a physician/patient relationship was created. E.g., Daly v. United States, 946 F.2d 1467 (9th Cir.1991) (government could be sued for failure of V.A. radiologist to disclose abnormality found in pre-employment physical); Green v. Walker, 910 F.2d 291, 296 (5th Cir.1990) (finding physician conducting exam for employment purposes has duties attendant on doctor/patient relationship); Hoover v. Williamson, 203 A.2d 861 (Md.1964) (silicosis discovered in employer-required physical but not revealed; court found physician liable, observing "general rule that one who assumes to act, even though gratuitously, may thereby become subject to the duty of acting carefully"). See also Crocker v. Synpol, Inc., 732 S.W.2d 429 (Tex.App.1987) (employee consulted employer-paid physician for job-related back injury; physician held obligated to keep confidential any information—here, evidence of drug use—that might jeopardize employee's employment). Should it be a different question whether there is a duty not just to disclose, but also to exercise care to discover, any problem the examinee has? See Webb v. T.D., 951 P.2d 1008 (Mont. 1997) (physician examining patient for workers' compensation fund held obligated to use due care in detecting dangerous condition, to advise patient about such condition if discovered, and to adhere to standard of care in giving any additional advice); Ranier v. Frieman, 682 A.2d 1220 (N.J. Super. 1996) (government-retained ophthalmologist failed to diagnose disability claimant's brain tumor; court held physician could be liable for resulting personal injuries); Lotspeich v. Chance Vought Aircraft, 369 S.W.2d 705 (Tex.App.1963) (no liability for failure to diagnose disease from pre-employment chest x-ray). See generally Postol, Suing the Doctor: Lawsuits by Injured Workers Against the Occupational Physician, 31 J. Occupational Med. 891 (1989).

Should the examining physician in these situations have any enforceable obligations to the examinee with respect to the reports filed, which may affect eligibility for employment, insurance, or some other valuable privilege? Some cases turn on the nature of the relationship established. See, e.g., Ahnert v. Wildman, 376 N.E.2d 1182 (Ind.App.1978) (distinguishing between a "treating" and an "examining" physician and holding that the latter had no enforceable duty to complete and return forms to employer, which retained physician); Davis v. Tirrell, 443 N.Y.S.2d 136 (N.Y.Sup.Ct.1981) (suit dismissed against school physician whose report resulted in denial of handicapped status to student; confidentiality of information gained in a therapeutic relationship deemed to support distinction between "treating" and "examining" physician); Ferguson v. Wolkin, 499 N.Y.S.2d 356 (N.Y.Sup.Ct.1986) (dismissing action in which employee claimed doctor's report forced her to return to work prematurely and to suffer injury as a result). In California, however, "the courts have not used status alone as a means of determining liability." Keene v. Wiggins, 138 Cal.Rptr. 3, 7 (Cal.App.1977) (patient consulted doctor at request of workers' compensation insurer; court found minimal relationship and that report was for insurer only). See also Brousseau v. Jarrett, 141 Cal.Rptr. 200 (Cal.App.1977) (patient sued physician, who treated him following auto accident, because report to insurer concerning his disability was unduly conservative; over vigorous dissent, negligence action was allowed based on physician/patient relationship).

Physicians employed by third parties for nontherapeutic purposes may have obligations to those employers. In Wharton Transp. Corp. v. Bridges, 606 S.W.2d 521 (Tenn.1980), a physician who conducted a negligent physical of applicant for a position as a truck driver was held liable to the employer for damages awarded a third party as a result of driver's incompetence.

6. *Physicians' Duties to Strangers.* Physicians are also subject to suits by parties with whom they have no contractual relationship, and courts may sometimes hold them to duties variously defined. Consider the *Wharton Transport* case cited in the previous note. Should the third party injured by the driver's undetected incompetence have had a cognizable claim directly against the physician (thus avoiding the circuity of actions)? Cf. North American Co. for Life and Health Ins. v. Berger, 648 F.2d 305 (5th Cir.1981), cert. denied, 454 U.S. 1084 (1981) (psychiatric consultant to FAA certified total disability for 154 air traffic controllers; disability insurer could sue him to enforce duty to exercise reasonable care in diagnosis). Note the questions that might arise as to whether a physician's malpractice insurance policy covers liabilities of the kinds suggested here.

A physician may also owe a duty to strangers put in jeopardy by his patient's health condition. In Duvall v. Goldin, 362 N.W.2d 275 (Mich.App. 1984), failure to prescribe a drug or to warn an epileptic patient against driving led to a physician's liability to a party injured in a seizure-related accident with the patient. The foreseeability of the harm led the court to recognize "a duty to persons operating motor vehicles on the public highway." See also Joy v. Eastern Maine Med. Center, 529 A.2d 1364 (Me.1987) (negligence in failure to warn patient wearing eye patch not to drive). But see Estate of Witthoeft v. Kiskaddon, 676 A.2d 1223 (Pa. Super.1996) (although ophthalmologist failed to report patient's bad eyesight to state as required by law, court found no duty to bicyclist killed by patient driving auto); Kirk v. Michael Reese Hosp. and Med. Center, 513 N.E.2d 387 (Ill.1987) (no liability to third party absent special relationship). For other instances of duties to third parties, see DiMarco v. Lynch Homes—Chester County, 583 A.2d 422 (Pa.1990) (patient afflicted with communicable disease, hepatitis; physician owes duty to patient's sex partner, as one "within the foreseeable orbit of risk of harm," to give patient correct advice concerning risk of transmission); Annot., Liability of Doctor or Other Health Practitioner to Third Party Contracting Contagious Disease from Doctor's Patient, 3 A.L.R.5th 370 (1992). The HIV epidemic has triggered many lawsuits of this kind.

In the famous *Tarasoff* case, a psychiatrist was held liable for failing to warn his patient's former girl friend of the patient's homicidal (as it turned out) inclination. Tarasoff v. Regents of the Univ., 551 P.2d 334 (Cal.1976). See also Thompson v. County of Alameda, 614 P.2d 728 (Cal.1980) (en banc) (limiting *Tarasoff* duty to warn to persons "readily identifiable" as potential victims); California Evidence Code § 1024 (1995) (limiting psychiatrist/patient evidentiary privilege along lines of the *Tarasoff* holding); In Re Kevin F., 261 Cal.Rptr. 413 (Cal.App.1989) (construing cited statute to allow psychotherapist to testify as to patient's confession of arson in order to protect innocent persons; held that evidentiary privilege is not suspended only where specific individual is threatened). Some cases have gone beyond the *Tarasoff-Thompson* approach and found a duty to the general public. E.g., Davis v. Puryear, 673 So.2d 1298 (La.App.1996) (finding duty to protect general public by institutionalizing patient who was voluntarily admitted to institution but who institution *should have known* was dangerous); Hamman v. County of Maricopa, 775 P.2d 1122 (Ariz.1989) (psychiatrist held to have duty to protect persons within "zone of danger" against patient with general tendency to violence); McIntosh v. Milano, 403 A.2d 500 (N.J. Super. 1979) (extending liability to psychiatrist by analogy to duty to protect public from infectious diseases). Note that the *Davis* case suggests there may be liability to remote third parties for failure to diagnose, not just for failure to protect against known dangers.

7. *"Good Samaritan" Laws.* Picture a situation in which an individual needs emergency care and a physician is on the scene and could assist, but has no relationship with the patient obligating her to act. Consistent with the general rule that there is no duty to rescue, the physician is not required to get involved, and she may hesitate to do so out of fear of liability risks, perhaps because her skills in treating such cases are rusty or because she lacks the usual back-up. Physicians, troubled by the conflict in such situations between their professional duty and the perceived risk (it was in fact greatly exaggerated) of being held to an unrealistic legal standard of care, persuaded legislatures some time ago to enact so-called "Good Samaritan" statutes. These laws typically and clearly excuse a physician acting at the scene of an accident from liability for ordinary negligence. Questions sometimes arise as to whether a hospital emergency room or another location in the hospital can be the site of an emergency covered by state statute. Holdings frequently turn on whether the doctor was officially on call and thus obligated to provide care. E.g., Hirpa v. IHC Hosps., Inc., 948 P.2d 785 (Utah 1997) (doctor responding to in-hospital emergency without duty to do so held protected by Good Samaritan statute). But see Beckerman v. Gordon, 618 N.E.2d 56 (Ind.App.1993) (standard of care should not depend upon this technical distinction). See generally Annot., Construction of "Good Samaritan" Statutes Excusing from Civil Liability One Rendering Care in Emergency, 68 A.L.R.4th 294 (1993).

The California Good Samaritan statute, in addition to extending immunity for all but willful acts or omissions, provides that hospital emergency rooms will be considered "the scene of an emergency" in the event of an officially declared "medical disaster." Cal.Bus. & Prof.Code § 2395 (1990). The implication that an ER cannot otherwise be so viewed was apparently intended, as a legislative reaction to McKenna v. Cedars of Lebanon Hosp., Inc., 155 Cal.Rptr. 631 (Cal.App.1979) (chief resident not specifically "on call" in ER held immune, under earlier statute, for care rendered in ER emergency). See also Burciaga v. St. John's Hosp., 232 Cal.Rptr. 75 (Cal.App.1986) (hospital staff pediatrician held protected by Good Samaritan law when he treated another doctor's newborn patient in response to an emergency call in the hospital); Lowry v. Henry Mayo Newhall Mem. Hosp., 229 Cal.Rptr. 620 (Cal.App.1986) (special statute protecting members of hospital "Code Blue" teams applies, unlike Good Samaritan law, where doctor is not a volunteer).

Some state statutes make Good Samaritan immunity conditional on the care's being gratuitous. For cases stressing this requirement and illustrating the laws' protections, see Johnson v. Matviuw, 531 N.E.2d 970 (Ill.App.1988) (physician with staff privileges held immune in treating in-hospital emergency as a volunteer partly because hospital did not charge for his services); Tatum v. Gigliotti, 583 A.2d 1062 (Md.1991) (emergency medical technician carrying out assigned duties held protected by Good Samaritan statute; even though salaried, technician did not directly charge injured person).

8. *Confidentiality.* One of the incidents of a doctor/patient relationship is a duty of nondisclosure of personal information. See, e.g., Fairfax Hosp. v. Curtis, 492 S.E.2d 642 (Va. 1997) (recognizing cause of action in tort where hospital had disclosed confidential information concerning patient to nurse who was co-defendant in malpractice action against hospital; statute stating such information was not privileged where patient's medical condition was an issue in tort action held not automatically to authorize disclosure made); McCormick v. England, 494 S.E.2d 431 (S.C. App. 1997) (in custody proceeding, husband introduced letter from physician "to whom it may concern" concerning wife's psychiatric condition; in subsequent tort action by wife against physician, court recognized cause of action for unauthorized disclosure but left open possibility that disclosure could be justified as a protection for patient's children). See generally 1 B. Furrow et al., Health Law §§ 4–32, 4–33 (1995); Gellman, Prescribing Privacy: The Uncertain Role of the Physician in the Protection of Patient Privacy, 62 N.C.L. Rev. 255 (1984); Annot., Physician's Tort Liability for Unauthorized Disclosure of Confidential Information About Patient, 48 A.L.R.4th 668 (1986). Other health care providers, including institutions, also have duties to protect patient information. Nevertheless, because a wide variety of persons—other health professionals, third-party payers, researchers, attorneys, and law enforcement agencies—have legitimate interests in patient records, difficult issues are frequently encountered. Moreover, health care providers are also subject to numerous mandatory disclosure laws, covering such subjects as child abuse, infections and venereal disease, gunshot wounds, and other forms of violence. Although these obligations to keep confidential and disclose patient information are not examined here, the student should be aware of them. See generally W. Roach et al., Medical Records and the Law (1994).

Issues of confidentiality have recently become more salient with the computerization of medical records in hospitals and health plans, the creation of larger and larger research data banks of patients with specific diseases, and the heightened sensitivity of genetic and other health information (e.g., HIV status). To guard against inappropriate access, many state legislatures and federal authorities are considering or enacting legislation. See generally Gostin, Health Information Privacy, 80 Cornell L. Rev. 451 (1995) (describing nature, technology, and roles of information in modern health care and balancing interests in privacy against various needs for information); Gostin, Genetic Privacy, 23 J.L. Med. & Ethics 320 (1995). The area will be of increasing practical difficulty as well as social importance in the future.

9. This section of the chapter is principally concerned with the legal tests for health care provider liability. The old McCoid article, which follows, was once a classic. It summarizes some reasons for employing a professional standard in judging the performance of professionals. Note that a professional standard serves as a shield against liability as well as a benchmark for establishing it. In effect, the law allows a profession to set its own standards rather than being bound by standards set by other means, public or private. Consider in your study why, and whether, this should be so.

Holding Doctors to Standards

Allan H. McCoid, The Care Required of Medical Practitioners

12 Vand.L.Rev. 549, 558–60, 605–09 (1959).

THE STANDARD OF CONDUCT

In General

When the average layman is charged with negligence in a personal injury action, his conduct is evaluated by the jury in terms of the hypothetical conduct of a reasonable and prudent man under the same or similar circumstances, a standard which may differ considerably from what the defendant and those like him in fact do. Yet one of the circumstances to be taken into account in determining this hypothetical conduct is the special knowledge or skill of which the defendant is possessed or purports to be possessed. To this extent the standard becomes somewhat subjectively related to the specific defendant.

In medical malpractice cases a somewhat similar non-subjective standard which takes into account specialized knowledge or skill is applied. However, the standard is more precisely defined as follows:

> This legal duty requires that the physician undertaking the care of a patient possess and exercise that reasonable and ordinary degree of learning, skill and care commonly possessed and exercised by reputable physicians practicing in the same locality, or in similar localities, in the care of similar cases; it requires also that the physician, in caring for the patient, exercise his best judgment at all times.[51]
>
> Good medical practice is the standard; it comprehends what the average careful, diligent and skillful physician in the community or like communities, would do or not do in the care of similar cases.[52]
>
> The duty imposed on a physician or surgeon is to employ such reasonable skill and diligence as is ordinarily exercised in his profession in the same general neighborhood having due regard to the advanced state of the profession at the time of the treatment. . . . The physician must use such ordinary skill and diligence and apply the means and methods generally used by physicians and surgeons of ordinary skill and learning in the practice of the profession, i.e., in the same general line of practice in like cases to determine the nature of the ailment and to act upon his honest opinion and conclusions.[53]
>
> [The physician] assumes toward the patient the obligation to exercise such reasonable care and skill in that behalf as is usually exercised by physicians or surgeons of good standing, of the same system or school of practice in the community in which he resides, having due regard to the condition of medical and surgical science at that time.[54]

While by no means exhausting the various verbal formulations of the test the foregoing suggest that the common elements to be found are:

(1) a reasonable or ordinary degree of skill and learning;

(2) commonly possessed and exercised by members of the profession

(3) who are of the same school or system as the defendant

(4) and who practice in the same or similar localities;

(5) and exercise of the defendant's good judgment.

* * *

The two principal aspects of the somewhat varied standards just described are: (1) That the physician or medical practitioner is not only to be held to the standard of practice generally accepted by his branch of the profession but is to be protected by this standard since compliance with accepted practice is generally taken as conclusive evidence of due care, and;

51. Regan, Doctor and Patient and the Law 17 (3d ed. 1956).

52. Id. at 30.

53. McHugh v. Audet, 72 F.Supp. 394, 399 (M.D.Pa.1947).

54. Loudon v. Scott, 58 Mont. 645, 654, 194 Pac. 488, 491 (1920).

(2) that the patient-plaintiff in most cases is compelled to rely upon expert medical testimony to establish his case. * * *

CUSTOMARY PRACTICE AS THE STANDARD OF CARE

Evidence of custom or a relatively well defined and regular usage among a group of persons, frequently a trade or occupational group, is generally admissible in determination of the proper standard of conduct in negligence actions, although * * * evidence of compliance or non-compliance with custom is really relevant only to the determination of (a) whether an imposition of liability upon the defendant will have an unduly disrupting effect on existing business practices, (b) whether some other precautions than those taken by the defendant are feasible or practicable, and (c) whether the defendant had an opportunity to know of other precautions from the existing practices of others. With few exceptions, however, evidence of customary practice is not conclusive on the question of the care to be taken.

When we examine cases of medical negligence, however, we find that custom does become, almost exclusively, the measure of due care. As one author has put it, "Good medical practice is the standard,"[265] and it is a standard to be established by expert medical testimony as to what is accepted as good practice by reputable members of the profession practicing under similar conditions. * * *

Reliance upon professional custom as the primary test of conduct might be explained historically by the fact that before the law of negligence had developed or the "reasonable and prudent man" had seen the full light of day, the older English cases had dealt with physicians and surgeons in terms of the knowledge, skill and care which they held themselves out to the public as possessing, i.e., at least that commonly had by members of their "profession." This is not a wholly satisfactory explanation, however, since other persons engaged in "common callings" such as innkeepers, ferrymen and common carriers failed to achieve any special "immunity" on the basis of reliance on accepted practices of their trade. In fact the courts tended to impose a stricter standard of care on the persons engaging in such common callings than on the general run of mankind.

A second, and somewhat more persuasive, explanation for the reliance on custom of the profession is the lack of capacity of any layman trier of fact, be he judge or juryman, to adequately evaluate the conduct of a doctor or to determine what a reasonable and prudent man under the same circumstances (including specialized training and knowledge of the physician or surgeon) would have done or refrained from doing. This is, of course, reflected in the general requirement that expert medical testimony is essential on the issue of the standard of care and breach thereof. But again, the answer is not wholly satisfactory for in some cases the court

265. Regan, op. cit. supra note [51], at 30.

permits the jury to evaluate medical conduct without expert medical testimony.[269]

A third explanation seems even more persuasive. The "preferred position" granted by the courts to the medical profession (and to other professions) may be in recognition of the peculiar nature of the "professional" activity. The qualified practitioner of medicine has undertaken long years of study to acquire knowledge of man, his body and its illnesses and the means of combatting such ailments, coupled with an intensive training of the senses and mind of the physician to respond to stimuli in a manner best described as "the healing art." A large measure of judgment enters into the practice of this art. That judgment should be free to operate in the best interests of the patient. If the "judge" is himself to be judged by some outsider who relies on after-acquired knowledge of unsatisfactory results or unfortunate consequences in reaching a decision as to liability, the medical judgment may be hampered and the doctor may become hesitant to rely upon his developed instinct in diagnosis and treatment. If, on the other hand, the doctor knows that his conduct is to be evaluated in terms of what other highly trained medical practitioners would have done or would accept as competent medical practice, he is more likely to pursue his own judgment when he is confident of the diagnosis and line of treatment, and is more likely to provide good medical service for his patient.

I believe that the courts are fully justified in taking a position which accepts customary medical practice as the standard of care. This does not protect the activities of the quack or charlatan. It does not condone malafide practice nor slipshod methods, except as the medical profession itself approves these. There is no persuasive evidence that the profession does so approve. At most it recognizes human weakness and is somewhat less blinded to the inadequacies of its own members than is the average layman. Knowing that inherent inadequacies of judgment and skill do exist, the medical profession may be hesitant to judge too harshly the conduct of its members.

All of this, however, does not bring much comfort to the maimed, the injured and the infirm, nor to their families. In this day of increasing emphasis upon "loss distribution" and "adequate compensation" by business enterprises for the injuries caused by their activities, those who suffer injuries in the course of medical treatment may argue that it is appropriate to impose the burden of loss upon the professional practitioner who can then distribute it in the form of increased fees to all persons who benefit from his ministrations or by insurance to all who benefit from medical practice. [However,] the imposition of liability in malpractice cases involves a great deal more than mere loss distribution. The doctor who is sued for malpractice is immediately under some suspicion; the doctor against whom such a claim is successful is branded as professionally incompetent or worse. While many of the defendants against whom verdicts are rendered

269. The most notable examples are [those involving the doctrine of *res ipsa loquitur*].

may be lacking in professional competence, it seems not unlikely that many are also guilty only of a single act of deviation from competent practice. Moreover, the increasing number of malpractice claims * * * points to a substantial danger of undermining public confidence in the medical profession unless such claims are measured by a standard determined by persons fully cognizant of the perils and practicalities of medical practice.

Jones v. Porretta

Supreme Court of Michigan, 1987.
428 Mich. 132, 405 N.W.2d 863.

■ BOYLE, JUSTICE.

We granted leave in these cases to resolve the question whether it is error in a medical malpractice action for the trial court to instruct the jury that a doctor or surgeon is not a guarantor of results. In *Dziurlikowski,* we hold that the instruction given was erroneous, and we reverse the jury's verdict and remand the case for a new trial. We affirm the jury's verdict in *Jones* because we find that the guarantor instruction was balanced by the duty of care instruction and was not erroneously given in the context of the case.

* * *

I

FACTS

In *Jones,* the plaintiffs claimed that the defendant doctor had negligently failed to diagnose and treat fractures of his leg and ankle, breaching the standard of care in several regards: in failing to take the appropriate x-rays of the injured left ankle and leg, in failing to properly perform a reduction of the fractured bones before applying the cast, in failing to apply a proper cast, in failing to order no weight-bearing, in failing to conduct a proper and thorough examination when the defendant first saw Mr. Jones, and in failing to refer Mr. Jones to a specialist or to request a consultation.

The defense presented by Dr. Porretta was that, even if the second fracture had been discovered, the treatment would have been the same as that prescribed in this case. The defendant further argued that Mr. Jones' diabetes and its complications (diabetic neuropathy and Charcot's joint) were the proximate cause of the plaintiff's injuries and damage.

At the close of proofs (and after giving the standard jury instruction on professional negligence) the court, over the plaintiffs' objections, added the instruction at issue in this case:

> "No physician can be required to guarantee results, but the law demands that they [sic] bring and apply to the case at hand that degree of skill and care, knowledge and attention ordinarily possessed and exercised by other orthopedic surgeons in the same specialty under like circumstances."

The jury returned a verdict for the defendant and the plaintiffs moved for a new trial on the basis of the additional instruction. The court denied the motion and plaintiffs appealed in the Court of Appeals.

The Court of Appeals agreed with the plaintiffs that the additional instruction was a deviation from a standard jury instruction and was erroneously given in this case. It then reversed the jury's verdict [, and] we granted leave to appeal.

In *Dziurlikowski,* the plaintiffs, Ronald and Mary Ann Dziurlikowski, claimed that the defendants, Dr. Thomas Morley, M.D., South Oakland Anesthesia Associates, P.C., Elizabeth Kurcherenko, C.R.N.A., and William Beaumont Hospital had breached the standard of care by failing to follow proper procedures in the giving of anesthetic to the plaintiff husband.

Mr. Dziurlikowski was admitted to William Beaumont Hospital suffering from bleeding ulcers. While in the hospital, he underwent recommended surgery, during which the doctors also found it necessary to remove his gall bladder. This additional complication extended the anticipated length of the surgery from approximately two hours to approximately four hours.

After the surgery, Mr. Dziurlikowski experienced difficulty with movement in his right arm and underwent physical therapy. His condition was diagnosed as a brachial plexus palsy, and at the time of trial he was still unable to use his arm as before.

The plaintiffs claimed that the injury was caused by the anesthesiology team which, they alleged, had failed either to properly position his arm on the operating table or to notice that his arm had been moved during the surgery. The defendants argued that there was no negligence and that brachial plexus palsy was a relatively rare and unfortunate but occasionally unavoidable consequence of extended anesthesia.

At trial, the testimony of several experts was presented, and during the cross-examination of one of the defendants' experts, counsel for the plaintiffs attempted to impeach the testimony by the use of an article in the journal *Anesthesiology.* The witness testified that the periodical was a reliable authority, but that he did not agree with the author of the particular article being referred to by the plaintiffs' counsel. The defendants objected to the use of the article, and the court sustained the objection, [but the plaintiff failed to respond to the court's invitation to reopen the question later, thus failing to preserve the issue for appeal.]

* * * At the close of proofs, the trial court instructed the jury with the appropriate standard jury instructions and then added the disputed instruction[:

> "The difficulties and uncertainties in the practice of medicine and surgery are such that no one can be required to guarantee results and all the law demands is that the individuals involved bring and apply to the case in hand that degree of skill, care, knowledge and attention ordinarily possessed and exercised by practitioners of the medical profession under like circumstances. The mere fact that an adverse result may occur following surgery is not in itself evidence of negligence."]

The jury returned a verdict for the defendants, and the plaintiffs moved for a new trial * * *. The trial court denied the motion, and the plaintiffs appealed the issues in the Court of Appeals [, which found] that the plaintiffs were correct in their contention that the "guarantor" instruction was erroneously given * * *

III

GUARANTOR INSTRUCTION IN STANDARD MEDICAL MALPRACTICE CASE

We first turn to the guarantor instruction given in *Jones*. We are not convinced that the guarantor instruction in this case was erroneously given. Although it could be viewed as argumentative and prejudicial in a case with different facts, we agree with the defendants that, in this case, it was nothing more than an innocuous recitation of what a reasonable juror already understands. We note that a part of the plaintiffs' argument was that Dr. Porretta made a mistake in judgment and that "[h]e's a physician; he's to heal." The defendant's request for the "no guarantor" charge was apparently focused on the position that a physician is not liable for an error of judgment if the physician has acted within the appropriate standard of care. We find that the instruction, along with a statement which reiterated the correct standard of care applicable to a finding of professional negligence, was not erroneously given.

A physician is not normally held liable in a fault-based system unless it is shown that the conduct violated the standard of professional care. A "no guarantor/bad result" instruction states "well nigh universally recognized principles of medical malpractice law." While use of the term "guarantor" is a somewhat formalistic means of advising a jury as to the standard of care in a professional medical malpractice case, it is not a misleading statement when it is followed, as it was in the *Jones* case, with a reiteration of the level of care that a physician owes to a patient.

* * *

We reverse the decision of the Court of Appeals in *Jones*. No presumption of error arises as a result of a deviation from or addition to the Standard Jury Instructions, and, in the context of this case, the instruction given was not erroneous.

IV

GUARANTOR/BAD RESULT NO EVIDENCE OF NEGLIGENCE INSTRUCTION IN RES IPSA LOQUITUR MEDICAL MALPRACTICE CASE

We begin our analysis in *Dziurlikowski* by noting first that the plaintiffs and the defendants acknowledge that the case went forward at trial on a theory of res ipsa loquitur. Having held in *Jones* that the "no guarantor" instruction was not erroneous, we now consider whether the "no guarantor/bad result no evidence of negligence" instruction was error in this context.

We are well aware of the long-standing debate as to whether this state recognizes the doctrine of res ipsa loquitur. * * *

* * * [A]s late as 1981, in Wilson v. Stilwill, 411 Mich. 587, 607, n. 5, 309 N.W.2d 898 (1981), Justice Moody, writing for the Court, noted in a footnote:

> "Michigan has not formally adopted the doctrine of *res ipsa loquitur*. However, the underlying concepts of *res ipsa loquitur,* which are circumstantial evidence and negligence concepts, have been applied in Michigan."

Whether phrased as res ipsa loquitur or "circumstantial evidence of negligence," it is clear that such concepts have long been accepted in this jurisdiction. The time has come to say so. We, therefore, acknowledge the Michigan version of res ipsa loquitur which entitles a plaintiff to a permissible inference of negligence from circumstantial evidence.

recognizes RIL

The major purpose of the doctrine of res ipsa loquitur is to create at least an inference of negligence when the plaintiff is unable to prove the actual occurrence of a negligent act. According to Prosser & Keeton, Torts (5th ed.), § 39, p. 244, in order to avail themselves of the doctrine, plaintiffs in their cases in chief must meet the following conditions:

> "(1) the event must be of a kind which ordinarily does not occur in the absence of someone's negligence;
>
> "(2) it must be caused by an agency or instrumentality within the exclusive control of the defendant;
>
> "(3) it must not have been due to any voluntary action or contribution on the part of the plaintiff."

In Wilson v. Stilwill, supra, 411 Mich. at p. 607, 309 N.W.2d 898, this Court noted these conditions,[5] as well as a fourth criterion: " 'Evidence of the true explanation of the event must be more readily accessible to the defendant than to the plaintiff.' "

Application of the rule of res ipsa loquitur is limited in medical malpractice cases. "It is the general rule, in actions for malpractice, that there is no presumption of negligence from the mere failure of judgment on the part of a doctor in the diagnosis or in the treatment he has prescribed, or from the fact that he has been unsuccessful in effecting a remedy, or has failed to bring about as good a result as someone else might have accomplished, or even from the fact that aggravation follows his treatment." Shain, Res ipsa loquitur, 17 S.Cal.L.R. 187, 217 (1944). As a result, and because the jury often cannot rely on its own experience in such cases, expert evidence must usually be presented. "What this means is that

5. In *Wilson*, supra, this Court seems to have approved the continued viability of the requirement that there have been no contribution on the part of the plaintiff, even after this Court's adoption of the doctrine of comparative negligence in Placek v. Sterling Heights, 405 Mich. 638, 275 N.W.2d 511 (1979). While we do not have occasion in this case to examine this issue, we do note that Prosser & Keeton, § 39, p. 254, question its viability under such circumstances:

"[T]he advent of comparative fault should logically eliminate this element from the doctrine, unless the plaintiff's negligence would appear to be the sole proximate cause of the event, since comparative fault by its nature converts the plaintiff's contributing fault from its traditional function of barring liability into one of merely reducing damages."

ordinarily laymen are not qualified to say that a good doctor would not go wrong, and that expert testimony is indispensable before any negligence can be found." Prosser & Keeton, supra, § 39, p. 256.[7]

* * * [I]n a California case, Justice Roger Traynor expounded on these same concepts:

> "A physician's duty is to exercise that degree of care and skill ordinarily possessed and exercised by members of his profession under similar circumstances. He does not guarantee a cure. The doctrine of res ipsa loquitur cannot properly be invoked to make him an insurer of the recovery of persons he treats. The Latin words cannot obliterate the fact that much of the functioning of the human body remains a mystery to medical science and that risks inherent in a given treatment may occur unexplainably though the treatment is administered skillfully. The occurrence of an injury that is a calculated risk of an approved course of conduct, standing alone, does not permit an inference of negligence.
>
> "Such an inference must be based on more than speculation. If it is to be drawn from the happening of an accident, there must be common knowledge or expert testimony that when such an accident occurs, it is more probably than not the result of negligence." Clark v. Gibbons, 66 Cal.2d 399, 421–422, 58 Cal.Rptr. 125, 426 P.2d 525 (1967).

Thus, in a normal professional negligence case, a bad result, *of itself,* is not evidence of negligence sufficient to raise an issue for the jury. This does not mean that a bad result cannot be presented by plaintiffs as part of their evidence of negligence, but, rather, that, standing alone, it is not adequate to create an issue for the jury. Something more is required, be it the common knowledge that the injury does not ordinarily occur without negligence or expert testimony to that effect.

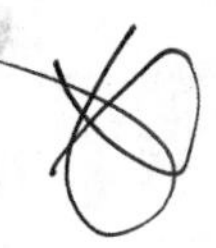

In a case where there is no expert evidence that "but for" negligence this result does not ordinarily occur, and in which the judge finds that such a determination could not be made by the jury as a matter of common understanding, a prima facie case has not been made, and a directed verdict is appropriate. However, if there is such evidence, even if it is disputed, or if such a determination could be made as a matter of common understanding, the jury is to determine whether plaintiff has proven whether it is more likely than not that defendant's negligence caused plaintiff's injury. The court may grant a motion for a directed verdict only if it is determined that reasonable minds could not differ that this result could ordinarily happen without negligence.

In cases where reasonable minds could differ as to whether this result could ordinarily happen "but for" negligence, the plaintiff is entitled to have the case submitted to the jury, which, acting in its traditional fact finding role, will decide the liability issue. In appropriate cases, the defen-

7. As Prosser & Keeton note: "There are ... some medical and surgical errors on which any layman is competent to pass judgment and conclude from common experience that such things do not happen if there has been proper skill and care." Id. They further note that these would include cases where a surgical instrument is left in the body or where an inappropriate part of the anatomy is removed.

dant is entitled to have the jury advised in some form that there are "risks inherent in ... treatment" and that an unfortunate result, standing alone, does not establish a lack of proper care, skill, or diligence. In this case, however, where the proofs have established a res ipsa case for the jury, such a statement as that given is, without additional guidance for the jury, at best, an incomplete instruction on the function of res ipsa loquitur in creating a permissible inference from circumstantial evidence.[10] A res ipsa case is a circumstantial evidence case. In a proper res ipsa loquitur medical case, a jury is permitted to infer negligence from a result which they conclude would not have been reached unless someone was negligent.

We agree with plaintiffs' observation in *Dziurlikowski* that, when coupled with the instruction that an adverse result is not evidence of negligence, the instruction had the potential to mislead the jury as to a permissible inference which the jury might draw from the plaintiffs' proofs. While it is correct to state that a bad result alone does not raise an inference of negligence, it is also an accurate statement that the bad result did permit the jury to infer negligence if it credited the testimony of plaintiffs' expert witness that such a result did not ordinarily occur in the absence of someone's negligence. The testimony of that witness was such that the trier of fact could have concluded that the defendant was negligent and the jury should have been instructed in some form to enable it to infer negligence if it found that the proofs supported the conclusion that the injury would not have occurred otherwise. Moreover, such language would be an incorrect statement of law in those classes of medical malpractice cases where common experience indicates that injury does not occur if there is proper skill and care. Where such an instruction is granted, plaintiffs also have a right to have the jury instructed on all of the aspects of a res ipsa case, not just those favorable to the defendant.[11]

Plaintiffs attempted to prove that "but for" negligence, such a complication does not ordinarily occur after surgery.[12] As the basis for this

10. A *balanced* instruction on the effect of an undesirable result in a *res ipsa* case has been found not erroneous in other jurisdictions. See, e.g., Kennedy v. Gaskell, 274 Cal. App.2d 244, 250, 78 Cal.Rptr. 753 (1969). In *Gaskell,* the plaintiff suffered a sudden loss of blood pressure after administration of anesthetic and thereafter expired. The court found that the anesthesiologist could have been found negligent under a res ipsa loquitur theory and that an instruction was not erroneous which stated:

> " 'A physician is not to be charged ... with negligence merely because the result is not what was desired. The law recognizes that, in spite of all his skill and learning, there are many factors over which he has no control.' "

The California courts, however, have also noted the necessity, in the res ipsa context, that the instruction be balanced by one which correctly instructs the jury on the inferences which may, but are not required to, be drawn from the evidence.

11. The bench and bar are respectfully advised that * * * the Court has this day notified the Committee on Standard Jury Instructions to prepare and publish for comment standard jury instructions which would be applicable in cases in which the plaintiffs have pleaded res ipsa loquitur or circumstantial evidence of negligence.

12. [12]No testimony was presented at trial which indicated that Mr. Dziurlikowski's arm had been moved or hyperextended during surgery, the basis of plaintiffs' theory of negligence. As plaintiffs point out, such evi-

contention was not in the general knowledge of the lay person, plaintiffs were required to, and did, present expert testimony by Dr. Mervin Jeffries to this effect. Although defendants disputed the testimony of plaintiffs' expert, the jury, if it had believed Dr. Jeffries, could have found that "but for" negligence this result would not ordinarily occur. However, while the jury was given the standard circumstantial evidence instruction, the jury was not instructed on any of these points, and, rather, was told that it could not find that the injury was evidence of negligence. We agree with plaintiffs that this instruction substantially "interfered with the circumstantial inference of negligence which Plaintiffs were entitled to have the jury consider," a material part of this case. Thus, we agree that plaintiffs have demonstrated that affirmance of the jury's verdict in *Dziurlikowski* would be "inconsistent with substantial justice," and we affirm the decision of the Court of Appeals granting the plaintiffs a new trial.

* * *

We affirm the decision of the Court of Appeals in *Dziurlikowski* and remand the case to the trial court for a new trial. In *Jones*, the decision of the Court of Appeals is reversed, and the jury's verdict is affirmed.

NOTES AND QUESTIONS ON BASIC ISSUES IN ASSIGNING LIABILITY FOR MEDICAL INJURIES

1. Why are courts so protective of physicians that they do not apply to them the strict-liability notions that have gained such wide acceptance in other areas of tort law? Why do they instead instruct juries, as in the *Jones* portion of *Jones v. Porretta,* that there are no warranties and, as in the case cited in footnote 10 in *Jones,* that accidents do happen? The following paragraphs may suggest some answers to these questions.

2. *Strict Liability?* Trends in tort law in the last generation, particularly in products liability, have reflected substantial emphasis on providing compensation for injured persons, especially those who cannot insure themselves. See, e.g., Helene Curtis Indus., Inc. v. Pruitt, 385 F.2d 841, 862 (5th Cir.1967) ("Until Americans have a comprehensive scheme of social insurance, courts must resolve by a balancing process the head-on collision between the need for adequate recovery and viable [business] enterprises. * * * This balancing task should be approached with a realization that the basic consideration involves a determination of the most just allocation of the risk of loss * * *.") See also Priest, The Current Insurance Crisis and Modern Tort Law, 96 Yale L.J. 1521, 1534–36 (1987) (noting the courts' widespread "acceptance of a coherent and powerful theory that justified the use of tort law to compensate injured parties, a theory its founders called 'enterprise liability' "). Should concepts from the field of products liability, such as implied warranty, strict liability in tort, and enterprise liability, apply equally in the medical realm?

dence was only within the knowledge of defendants. Neither plaintiffs nor their expert witness could know what happened while Mr. Dziurlikowski was under anesthetic.

For the most part, as illustrated by the rulings in *Jones v. Porretta,* the courts have resisted the idea of imposing on health care providers strict liability for any failure of treatment without regard to whether it resulted from proven negligence. Of course, liberality in the definition of negligence and in the rules by which it is established—particularly in the use of the principle of *res ipsa loquitur* and other pro-plaintiff rules of evidence—may sometimes yield strict liability *de facto.* Nevertheless, the nominal rule has remained conservative. Thus, in Hoven v. Kelble, 256 N.W.2d 379 (Wis. 1977), the Wisconsin Supreme Court rejected the plaintiff's broad argument that strict-liability notions from the field of products liability should be imported into the medical field and that recoveries should be allowed based on the "reasonable expectations of the consumer." (This argument drew heavily upon Greenfield, Consumer Protection in Service Transactions—Implied Warranties and Strict Liability in Tort, 1974 Utah L.Rev. 661.) The court admitted that "many of the justifications for strict liability [including consumer ignorance, plaintiffs' difficulty in proving fault, the desirability of spreading the costs of injuries, and liability's deterrent effect] have force regarding professional medical services." Nevertheless, the uncertainty of medical practice and the potential cost of strict liability appeared to deter the court from embracing the plaintiff's theory.

What is your opinion of strict liability for medical accidents? Why (or why not) should cost be a concern? Would the *Hoven* plaintiff's theory based on "reasonable expectations" greatly change the manner in which cases are tried or reduce the costs of litigation? Are physicians fit candidates for "enterprise liability"? If not, why not? Does McCoid's argument on this point amount to anything more than the observation that physicians, unlike corporations, have feelings? (Did physicians' increasing wealth in the 1960s and 1970s perhaps cause this distinction to count for less than in earlier days?) Is McCoid's argument a policy rationale or simply a demonstration that tort law rests on primitive (retributive)—or political (redistributive)—foundations? As the movement towards corporate involvement in medicine grows, would you expect strict-liability concepts to receive a more favorable hearing? The subject of strict liability will arise again at several later points.

3. *Standards of Care?* In judging the quality of medical care, does the tort system focus primarily on inputs, process, or outcome? Nearly all formulations of the law purport to leave the cost of adverse medical *outcomes* where they fall unless there is some affirmative reason associated with deterrence—that is, a culpable failure of *process*—to shift them. A large set of questions, to be canvassed in the pages ahead, has to do with the standard of care itself and the courts' ability to serve as regulatory overseers of clinical practices and processes. You will have occasion to question whether the legal system is administratively capable of defining the specific conduct that it wants to deter and of applying its definition reasonably in particular cases.

One famous legal test for negligence is described by Danzon:

The tort system of liability for negligence, in principle, corrects [for inadequate incentives to practice with care, which result from consumers' inability to evaluate the relative carefulness of individual providers,] by "internalising" to the physician the costs of injuries due to negligence. A precise definition of the legal standard of negligence was formulated by Judge Learned Hand in United States v. Carroll Towing Co.[,159 F.2d 169 (2d Cir.1947)]. By this definition, negligence occurs if there is a failure to take preventive measures that cost less than their expected benefit, i.e. the reduction in the probability of an injury times the damages suffered if it occurs. But this is precisely the economic definition of the efficient level of investment in injury prevention. Thus negligence is failure to take cost-effective precautions. If found negligent, the tort-feasor is liable for a "fine" equal to the damages suffered by the victim. Ideally, this liability rule transfers from the patient to the physician the expected costs of injuries which the patient would be willing to pay to prevent. It thereby creates incentives for the physician to provide the efficient quality of care. In the case of medical and other professional liability, courts usually defer to the customary practice of the profession to define the due standard of care, rather than apply a cost-benefit calculus to each case. The efficiency of the tort system is preserved to the extent customary practice is efficient.[2]

Danzon, An Economic Analysis of the Medical Malpractice System, 1 Behav. Sci. & L. 39, 41 (1983). How realistic is the efficiency justification for malpractice liability? Is it likely that courts and juries have the tools they need to establish a coherent, efficient standard of medical care and to enforce it consistently?

Subsequent discussion of the standard of care will invite further efficiency-oriented law-and-economics theorizing about tort liability in medical contexts. See generally G. Calabresi, The Cost of Accidents (1970) (defining the object of accident law as being the minimization of the aggregate costs of accidents and accident avoidance); W. Landes & R. Posner, The Economic Structure of Tort Law (1987) (setting forth a "positive economic theory of tort law," which asserts that common-law courts have instinctively but systematically gravitated toward efficiency); Grady, Why Are People Negligent? Technology, Nondurable Precautions, and the Medical Malpractice Explosion, 82 Nw. U.L. Rev. 293 (1988) (addressing the difference between penalizing episodic human error and inducing improvements in systems and methods); Grady, A New Positive Economic Theory of Negligence, 92 Yale L.J. 799 (1983) (focusing specifically on comparing the benefits and costs of precautions not taken).

4. *Customary Practice as a Benchmark.* Compare the standard that the tort system employs for judging the conduct of natural persons or ordinary business firms with its methods of assessing the performance of professionals? Should professionals, as McCoid seemed to think, be permitted to hide behind standards of their own making? What is the role of industry custom

2. Even if customary practice is not efficient, because of insurance and other factors, tort liability still deters deviations from the norms which patients have come to expect.

in ordinary negligence cases? Why should it be different in medical malpractice cases? Is custom a better guide to efficiency in one case than in the other?

What specific questions can be raised concerning the appropriateness of conventional practice standards as a benchmark for judging a physician's conduct? Materials later in this section concern the possibility that the professional standard might be "too low." Is there any reason to think that professional standards might sometimes be "too high"? (In what sense?) Does the notion of "defensive medicine" suggest one set of problems? Does the system by which medical care was traditionally financed present a reason for concern? What information have you (from chapter 2(§B), for example) concerning the uniformity of clinical practice and the efficacy of conventional practice methods that would be relevant to this discussion?

Now imagine that you are assigned to draft a contract fully specifying a physician's—or, more realistically, an HMO's—duty to patients in all possible exigencies. It should quickly become obvious to you that the only way to write an agreement that is both manageable in length and enforceable in court is to make reference to the practices of other professionals. Indeed, it may be a distinguishing characteristic of a profession that the duties of its practitioners cannot be defined with any precision without reference to what other ethical and competent practitioners would do in similar circumstances. Note that this explanation of why professional custom is employed as a legal benchmark—both in explicit contracts and in the implied contract for medical care on which the tort of medical malpractice is based—does not imply that customary practice is necessarily optimal or right.

5. *Contractual Deviations from Standard Practice*. Now consider how you might write a contract for *non*customary care, to be purchased through a health plan on a prepaid basis. (Recall the earlier notes on contract vs. tort and contractual guarantees.) Why might your health plan client want you to draft such a contract? Note that the contract might have any of several goals: to offer less costly health care appealing to persons of moderate income, to attract up-scale enrollees by promising higher-quality care than is customarily available, to free the plan's participating providers from slavish obedience to custom when they might be able to deliver equivalent or better outcomes by alternative means, or simply to lower the liability risks of the plan and its physicians.

On the possible desirability of varying standards by contract, see C. Havighurst, Health Care Choices: Private Contracts as Instruments of Health Reform (1995); Morreim, Medicine Meets Resource Limits: Restructuring the Standard of Care, U. Pitt. L. Rev. 1 (1997); Henderson & Siciliano, Universal Health Care and the Continued Reliance on Custom in Determining Medical Malpractice, 79 Cornell L.Rev. 1382 (1994); Siciliano, Wealth, Equity and the Unitary Medical Malpractice Standard, 77 Va. L.Rev. 439 (1991).

6. *Is Custom Still an Appropriate Source of Standards?* Some authors have begun to argue that custom is no longer a useful test for detecting medical malpractice:

> Courts traditionally have been more willing to defer to completely to professional custom in the medical care context then they have in other areas where customs may be available as guideposts for reasonable behavior. Such deference makes sense if one assumes the courts can easily identify medical custom, but becomes problematic once one considers the impediments to the formation of any stable custom, let alone reasonable custom, among health care providers.
>
> First, the medical profession is increasingly confronted with sets of problems and corresponding solutions that are vastly more complicated then those of relatively simple settings * * *. [P]atients, even those with the "same" illness or injury, may require different approaches based on a host of individual conditions, including age, gender, weight, and other health related criteria, none of which are susceptible to standardization by the forces that shape custom. * * *
>
> The variance within the patient population is matched by a diversity of therapeutic responses. Although health care providers of a generation ago may have had only a limited array of options in the diagnosis and treatment of illness and injury, the growth of technology in recent years has had greatly added to the number of possible responses. Many medical conditions can now be treated in a wide variety of ways, each with different costs, risks, and benefits. Moreover, the relentless growth of medical care technologies during the last quarter-century expands this array of caretaking approaches on an almost daily basis. * * *
>
> In light of this plethora of caretaking technologies, the first factor essential to the formation of custom—a common base of knowledge among relevant decisionmakers—may not emerge, even for simple and straightforward conditions.

Henderson & Siciliano, supra, at 1389–91.

Consider also the increasing proliferation of managed-care arrangements, which may be deemed to be charged in the marketplace, not merely with financing and delivering standardized medical treatments, but with improving the efficiency and efficacy of medical care and with offering consumers a variety of options featuring different marginal trade-offs between cost and quality. Are you struck that the law has yet to come to grips with the economic realities of medicine in the real world of decentralized health care, in which many individuals pay their own way into the expensive fee-for-service system, while others are supported by public funds and still others enroll in HMOs, etc., that, whether explicitly or implicitly, economize in the use of resources? Is there any practical way in which the tort system, with its necessarily simplistic formulations, its inability to resolve value conflicts, its poor access to reliable, pertinent information, and its responsiveness to the irrational impulses of juries and judges, can be led to accept the idea that standards may legitimately vary with circumstances?

There have been a number of scholarly efforts to come to grips with the problem of defining standards of care that are realistic about economic trade-offs. For the insights of an ethicist, see Morreim, Cost Containment and the Standard of Medical Care, 75 Cal. L. Rev. 1719 (1987), which observes that, "in allowing a defense based on the economic constraints that providers face, we are not conceding that substantial differences of care for rich and poor are morally acceptable, but only that we shall not hold the health care provider culpable for such discrepancies." Do you find it striking that this thought—that the law should not be primarily concerned with making moral statements—should come from a nonlawyer? See also Morreim, Medicine Meets Resource Limits: Restructuring the Legal Standard of Care, 59 U. Pitt. L. Rev. 1 (1997) (proposing "a basic distinction between expertise and resources," with issues concerning skill and judgment to be resolved according to traditional tort rules while issues concerning resource us are treated as matters of contract). For another approach, see Siciliano, Wealth, Equity, and the Unitary Medical Malpractice Standard, 77 Va. L. Rev. 439 (1991), which

> suggests that the malpractice standard be modified to expressly encompass patient resources as a factor bearing on the legal adequacy of the care provided. Such a step is undoubtedly painful in its symbolic connotations. It exposes an embarrassing discrepancy between the ideals we preach and the actions we are actually prepared to take. And adoption of a resource-sensitive malpractice standard runs the risk of making tort law appear to "against the poor." But surface appearances easily deceive, and, as this Article suggests, the proposed modification of the malpractice standard may far better serve the poor's interest in receiving adequate health care than tort law's current effort to mandate equity by fiat.
>
> * * * [T]hrough its adherence to the unitary ideal, tort law may end up killing the poor with an unthinking and misguided kindness.

Id. at 444–45, 487. For an AMA attorney's comments on the debate concerning whether the standard of care should be less focused on the individual patient's interests in order to accommodate society's interest in controlling health care costs, see Hirshfeld, Economic Considerations in Treatment Decisions and the Standard of Care in Medical Malpractice Litigation, 264 J.A.M.A. 2004 (1990).

Just how, as a practical matter, can the legal system introduce efficiency considerations into the definition of the standard of care? For the view that malpractice standards can evolve toward efficiency under the "respectable minority" principle, see Hall, The Malpractice Standard of Care under Health Care Cost Containment, 17 Law, Med. & Health Care 347 (1989); Schuck, Malpractice Liability and the Rationing of Care, 59 Tex. L. Rev. 1421 (1981) (decision by health care provider to ration care should expose practitioner to malpractice liability unless "at least a respectable minority would make a similar rationing decision under similar circumstances"; rationing decision must include some form of informed consent by patient). But see Havighurst, Practice Guidelines as Legal Standards Governing Physician Liability, Law & Contemp. Probs., Spring 1991, p. 87, 98:

> In theory, of course, the legal system should be able to detect shifts toward more economical practices and to excuse physicians who follow such shifts. Even in theory, however, tort law allows departures from dominant practice only after the new practices have come to be followed by a so-called "respectable minority" of physicians. Thus, in theory as well as practice, the legal system continues to expose innovators to serious liability risks. In addition, juries often remain free as a practical matter to find liability solely on the basis that more could have been done for the individual patient.

See § E of this chapter for further ideas about how the legal system might accommodate responsible economizing.

Proving Physician Negligence: Experts, Standards, and Practice Guidelines

NOTES AND QUESTIONS ON EXPERT TESTIMONY IN MALPRACTICE CASES

1. Expert testimony provides the link between medical practice and scientific knowledge, on the one hand, and the legal system on the other. Its importance not only in establishing the prevailing standard of care and whether it was breached in a given case but also in determining causation and damage issues, such as prognosis and long-term effects, makes it appropriate subject for separate treatment. These notes address its weaknesses, its strengths, and a number of rules and circumstances surrounding its use in litigation.

What rationale does McCoid's article give for relying on expert testimony as a principal source of standards for the law to employ in regulating providers' conduct? What conception of the medical profession is implicit in this rationale? Does the rationale presume greater wisdom, greater professional responsibility, greater uniformity of practice, or stronger incentives for efficiency than are found in medical care today?

2. *The Conspiracy of Silence.* Did the customary practice standard allow the medical profession to become a law unto itself? Whatever can be said in its theoretical defense, the adoption of an approach requiring a plaintiff to present the testimony of medical experts may have provided physicians with a better shield against liability than the courts intended. Would-be plaintiffs often encountered difficulty in finding a physician willing to testify against a professional colleague. (Recall the references in chapter 3(§A) noting professionals' reluctance to criticize each other in public.) Indeed, judicial recognition of the so-called "conspiracy of silence" helped to prompt the pro-plaintiff legal developments of the 1950s and 1960s, many of which were essentially relaxations of the expert witness requirement; the emergence of the doctrine of *res ipsa loquitur* in medical malpractice cases, allowing some plaintiffs to get to the jury without an expert, was a case in point. See Salgo v. Leland Stanford Jr. Univ. Bd. of Trustees, 317 P.2d 170, 175 (Cal.App.1957) (observing that a " 'conspiracy of silence' * * * forced the courts to attempt to equalize the situation"). Courts also became more receptive to textbook evidence and to the testimony of experts from a "similar" rather than the same community as the defendant. But see Ogletree v. Willis–Knighton Mem. Hosp., 530 So.2d 1175 (La.App.1988) (although defense lawyer had referred to plaintiff's witnesses as "out-of-town hired guns," plaintiff's attorney was not allowed to query out-of-state expert concerning conspiracies of silence without some evidence of actual conspiracy by local doctors).

What changes in the medical profession have caused the "conspiracy of silence," such as it was, to become less effective? (Plaintiffs' lawyers in some areas complain that reputable local physicians are still reluctant to testify for plaintiffs even in a meritorious case.)

3. *Res Ipsa Loquitur.* This doctrine, infamous to most physicians, allows a plaintiff to survive a directed verdict when, even though he has not offered expert testimony, "common knowledge" tells the court that the bad medical outcome would probably not have occurred in the absence of negligence. Most of the cases in which the doctrine operates are those, such as cases involving "foreign objects" left behind after surgery or operations on the wrong limb or organ, in which nearly all physicians would agree with the court's intuition; liability insurers quickly settle most such cases. Although some states restricted use of the doctrine in the aftermath of earlier malpractice crises, most still permit its routine use in medical malpractice cases. See, e.g., National Bank of Commerce v. Quirk, 918 S.W.2d 138 (Ark.1996).

The *Dziurlikowski* case (in *Jones v. Porretta*) indicates the utility of the *res ipsa* principle in cases where "common knowledge" does not suffice. It permits expert witnesses who cannot determine the precise nature of the negligence in a particular case to lay a foundation for an inference of negligence based on outcome. See also Connors v. University Assocs. in Obstetrics and Gynecology, Inc., 4 F.3d 123, 128 (2d Cir.1993) ("Whether the knowledge required to evaluate the likelihood of negligent conduct inferred from an accident comes from common or specialized knowledge, the key question is still whether the accident would normally occur in the ordinary course of events."). See also Morgan v. Children's Hosp., 480 N.E.2d 464 (Ohio 1985) (oxygen deprivation and brain damage during surgery; plaintiff's experts were held to have laid groundwork for *res ipsa* instruction while also offering a specific theory of how negligence occurred); Buckelew v. Grossbard, 435 A.2d 1150 (N.J.1981) (bladder cut during urological procedure; "expert testimony to the effect that the medical community recognizes that an event does not ordinarily occur in the absence of negligence may afford a sufficient basis for the application of the doctrine of *res ipsa loquitur*"). For cases barring reliance on *res ipsa* when expert testimony is employed (on the ground that expert judgment alone should suffice), see Meda v. Brown, 569 A.2d 202 (Md.1990) (anesthesia case; expert testimony, though based on inference, was held not based on *res ipsa* and therefore admissible); Anderson v. Gordon, 334 So.2d 107, 109 (Fla.App.1976).

In addition to developing as a response to a profession-wide "conspiracy of silence," the *res ipsa* doctrine has also been employed, especially in anesthesia situations, to allow juries to detect cover-ups in specific cases. The facts in the leading case of Ybarra v. Spangard, 154 P.2d 687 (Cal. 1944), resembled those in *Dziurlikowski* in that there were also multiple defendants and the plaintiff, who was anesthetized when the injury occurred (to a limb not involved in the surgery), could not prove directly who controlled the essential instruments or what caused the harm. Apparently believing that the various defendants could not be expected to testify candidly under oath, the court (even without an expert-laid foundation) applied the *res ipsa* principle, shifting to them the burden of coming forward with an explanation. See also Marrero v. Goldsmith, 486 So.2d 530 (Fla.1986) (facts similar to *Dziurlikowski;* court allowed *res ipsa* theory against multiple defendants even though exclusive control by any or all defendants was not established). But see Hoven v. Rice Mem. Hosp., 396 N.W.2d 569 (Minn.1986) (rejecting *Ybarra* theory on similar facts and requiring proof that injury would not ordinarily occur without negligence). See generally Annot., Medical Malpractice: Res Ipsa Loquitur in Negligent Anesthesia Cases, 49 A.L.R.4th 63 (1986). In another effort to aid plaintiffs having difficulty in getting essential evidence, courts have allowed a presumption of negligence where the defendants failed to maintain or preserve medical records. E.g., Public Health Trust of Dade Cty. v. Valcin, 507 So.2d 596 (Fla.1987).

Some of the anesthesia cases and perhaps a few others may seem to confirm physicians' sense that there is a campaign to make them responsible for any bad medical result rather than only for demonstrable deviations from professional standards. See also Chapman v. Pollock, 317 S.E.2d 726 (N.C.App.1984) (without invoking *res ipsa loquitur* by name, court found it "a matter of common knowledge * * * that doctors who have patients with persistent, continuing abdominal pain and other symptoms of appendicitis usually attempt to ascertain the cause of the pain and other signs and symptoms by some means and usually do not remain inactive for two or three days while the conditions are not only continuing, but getting worse"). Nevertheless, despite providers' distress at being held accountable to lay arbiters for bad results, would you argue that courts are justified in occasionally giving effect to patients' seemingly reasonable expectations and natural impressions and imposing on providers a duty to explain? After all, the *res ipsa loquitur* doctrine applies only in circumstances that seem to require some explanation and does nothing more than enable the plaintiff to meet his initial burden of proof. For cases in which courts, seemingly reluctant to allow *res ipsa* instructions to expose doctors to liability for rare bad outcomes where negligence did not affirmatively appear, refused to widen the *res ipsa* exception to the usual requirement of expert testimony to establish a breach of the standard of care, see Simmons v. Egwu, 662 N.E.2d 657 (Ind.App.1996); Orkin v. Holy Cross Hosp., 569 A.2d 207 (Md.1990); Savina v. Sterling Drug, Inc., 795 P.2d 915 (Kan.1990).

The ABA Commission on Medical Professional Liability recommended adoption of the following statute (a revision of an AMA proposal with the commission's changes indicated by brackets and italics):

> No liability for personal injury or death shall be imposed against any provider of medical care based on alleged negligence in the performance of such care unless expert medical testimony is presented as to the alleged deviation from the accepted standard of care in the specific circumstances of the case and as to the causation of the alleged personal injury or death, except that such expert medical testimony shall not be required and a [rebuttable] *permissible* inference that the personal injury or death was caused by negligence shall arise where evidence is presented that the personal injury or death occurred in any one or more of the following circumstances: (1) A foreign [substance] *object* other than medication or a prosthetic device was unintentionally left within the body of a patient following surgery, (2) an explosion or fire originating in a substance used in treatment occurred in the course of treatment, (3) an unintended burn caused by heat, radiation, or chemicals was suffered in the course of medical care, [(4) an injury was suffered during the course of treatment to a part of the body not directly involved in such treatment or proximate thereto,] or (5) a surgical procedure was performed on the wrong patient or the wrong organ, limb or part of a patient's body.

ABA Commission, *supra,* at 849. A number of states have enacted laws to this or similar effect. Should such a law be held to violate equal protection guarantees or, as was held in Arneson v. Olson, 270 N.W.2d 125, 131–38 (N.D.1978), to intrude upon the constitutional prerogatives of the judicial branch?

4. *The Battle of Partisan Experts.* Malpractice cases would appear to present in an acute form the problem of partisan experts, chosen by the parties from a large universe of experts on the basis of their willingness and ability to swear credibly to different versions of the truth. See generally I. Freckelton, The Trial of The Expert 123–50 (1987) (a general critique of the procurement and use of expert witnesses in the common-law world). Although it is customary in our adversary system to regard a jury trial as a "black box" the outcomes of which (on nonlegal questions) are granted a powerful presumption of legitimacy, realism compels recognition that juries are often poorly positioned to choose reliably between the well argued, but often highly confusing, theories of the two sides' experts. As a result, they often fall back on such irrelevancies as the witnesses' demeanor and style of presentation or sympathy for the plaintiff's plight or the defendants' reputation.

In Trower v. Jones, 520 N.E.2d 297 (Ill.1988), the court upheld the trial court's discretion to allow cross-examination of plaintiff's expert witness concerning his income from testifying in malpractice actions and the frequency of his appearance for plaintiffs. For judicial refusals, on public policy grounds, to enforce a contract under which a witness-procurement firm would receive a portion of any recovery, see First Nat'l Bank v. Malpractice Research, Inc., 688 N.E.2d 1179 (Ill. 1997); Dupree v. Malpractice Research, Inc., 445 N.W.2d 498 (Mich.App.1989) (subsequent state statute confirmed state's aversion to such contracts; damages based on quantum meruit also denied); Polo v. Gotchel, 542 A.2d 947 (N.J. Super.1987). But see Schackow v. Medical–Legal Consulting Serv., Inc., 416

A.2d 1303 (Md.1980) (contingent fee allowed where witness broker agreed only to locate experts who would review case, not reach any particular conclusion). Do you agree with the premise of the latter holding? What argument could you make for contingent fees in this context? See generally Note, Contingent Expert Witness Fees: Access and Legitimacy, 64 S. Cal. L. Rev. 363 (1991). For a case refusing to condemn a contingency arrangement with a medical-legal consulting service as long as statutory attorney fee limits are respected, see Ojeda v. Sharp Cabrillo Hosp., 10 Cal.Rptr.2d 230 (Cal.App.1992).

Consider the role of experts and the adversary system in establishing the appropriate standard of care in the ensuing materials. Can you imagine a role for impartial, court-appointed experts? See Fed. R. Evid. 706 (authorizing judicial appointment of experts with costs chargeable to parties); I. Freckleton, supra, at 203–44 (comparative perspectives). For some reason, the idea of impartial medical testimony received more active consideration in the 1950s and 1960s than it receives today, as attorneys remain reluctant to move for a court-appointed expert and trial judges remain largely reluctant to take an affirmative role in searching for the truth. Consider also the function of panels for pretrial screening of malpractice claims established by law in numerous states and examined more fully in § D of this chapter; in some states, panel findings are admissible in evidence in a subsequent trial.

6. *The Difficulty of Judging Negligence.* Although experts testifying in medical malpractice cases rely on a great deal of evidence, much their opinion must be based on what is documented in the medical record. Recent research on the complex nature of these judgments has suggested that expert physicians may not make reliable judgments about the presence of negligence. See, e.g., Localio et al., Identifying Adverse Events Caused by Medical Care: Degree of Physician Agreement in a Retrospective Chart Review, 125 Annals of Internal Med. 457 (1996) (finding that independent reviewers agreed only slightly more frequently than predicted by mere chance in judging presence of negligence from medical records). Although the reliability of their judgments might be improved by structuring their reviews, such structure is rarely applied in medical malpractice cases.

7. *A Statutory Formulation of the Malpractice Cause of Action.* Reform legislation in Florida in 1976 included the following provisions on the standards to be used in judging medical professional liability:

> **768.45. Medical negligence; standards of recovery**
>
> (1) In any [negligence action against a health care provider], the claimant shall have the burden of proving by the greater weight of evidence that the alleged actions of the health care provider represented a breach of the prevailing professional standard of care for that health care provider. The prevailing professional standard of care for a given health care provider shall be that level of care, skill, and treatment which, in light of all relevant surrounding circumstances, is recognized as acceptable and appropriate by reasonably prudent similar health care providers.

(2)(a) If the health care provider whose negligence is claimed to have created the cause of action is not certified by the appropriate American board as being a specialist, is not trained and experienced in a medical specialty, or does not hold himself or herself out as a specialist, a "similar health care provider" is one who:

1. Is licensed by the appropriate regulatory agency of this state;

2. Is trained and experienced in the same discipline or school of practice; and

3. Practices in the same or similar medical community.

(b) If the health care provider whose negligence is claimed to have created the cause of action is certified by the appropriate American board as a specialist, is trained and experienced in a medical specialty, or holds himself or herself out as a specialist, a "similar health care provider" is one who:

1. Is trained and experienced in the same specialty; and

2. Is certified by the appropriate American board in the same specialty.

However, if any health care provider described in this paragraph is providing treatment or diagnosis for a condition which is not within his or her specialty, a specialist trained in the treatment or diagnosis for that condition shall be considered a "similar health care provider."

(c) The purpose of this subsection is to establish a relative standard of care for various categories and classifications of health care providers. Any health care provider may testify as an expert in any action if he or she:

1. Is a similar health care provider pursuant to paragraph (a) or paragraph (b); or

2. Is not a similar health care provider pursuant to paragraph (a) or paragraph (b) but, to the satisfaction of the court, possesses sufficient training, experience, and knowledge as a result of practice or teaching in the specialty of the defendant or practice or teaching in a related field of medicine, so as to be able to provide such expert testimony as to the prevailing professional standard of care in a given field of medicine. Such training, experience, or knowledge must be as a result of the active involvement in the practice or teaching of medicine within the 5-year period before the incident giving rise to the claim.

(3)(a) If the injury is claimed to have resulted from the negligent affirmative medical intervention of the health care provider, the claimant must, in order to prove a breach of the prevailing professional standard of care, show that the injury was not within the necessary or reasonably foreseeable results of the surgical, medicinal, or diagnostic procedure constituting the medical intervention, if the intervention from which the injury is alleged to have resulted was carried out in accordance with the prevailing professional standard of care by a reasonably prudent similar health care provider.

(b) The provisions of this subsection shall apply only when the medical intervention was undertaken with the informed consent of the patient in compliance with the provisions of § 766.103.

(4) The existence of a medical injury shall not create any inference or presumption of negligence against a health care provider, and the claimant must maintain the burden of proving that an injury was proximately caused by a breach of the prevailing professional standard of care by the health care provider. However, the discovery of the presence of a foreign body, such as a sponge, clamp, forceps, surgical needle, or other paraphernalia commonly used in surgical, examination, or diagnostic procedures, shall be prima facie evidence of negligence on the part of the health care provider.

(5) The Legislature is cognizant of the changing trends and techniques for the delivery of health care in this state and the discretion that is inherent in the diagnosis, care, and treatment of patients by different health care providers. The failure of a health care provider to order, perform, or administer supplemental diagnostic tests shall not be actionable if the health care provider acted in good faith and with due regard for the prevailing professional standard of care.

(6) [A claim of negligence in an emergency room must be supported by an expert with recent "substantial professional experience" in providing ER services].

Fla.Stat.Ann. § 766.102 (1997 & Supp. 1998). What are the innovations here?

8. *Expert Qualifications.* Like Florida, several states have legislated on the qualifications of expert witnesses in medical malpractice cases. Tennessee, for example, requires that a witness must come from Tennessee or a contiguous state. The Tennessee statute was upheld and applied in Ralph v. Nagy, 749 F.Supp. 169 (M.D. Tenn. 1990). Although finding the statute's requirement to be procedural rather than substantive (do you agree?), the court nevertheless found it applicable in a diversity action in federal court because of Fed. R. Evid. 601, which makes the competency of witnesses in such suits turn on state law. The statute was deemed to have a rational basis even with respect to the New York experts whom plaintiff proffered to testify only on causation, because such experts might not be able to avoid opining on the standard of care. See also Sutphin v. Platt, 720 S.W.2d 455 (Tenn.1986) (upholding statute as advancing legitimate state interest in fairness in litigation). Ohio requires that an expert witness must, to be qualified, devote at least a certain fraction of his or her professional time to clinical practice (or university instruction). Ohio R. Evid. 601(D); Ohio Rev. Code Ann. § 2743.43 (1993). Such restrictions significantly limit the supply of experts available to plaintiffs in particular.

Such statutes counteract earlier efforts by courts to assist plaintiffs in obtaining expert witnesses despite the "conspiracy of silence." One approach was to allow "cross-over" testimony by professionals in a specialty different from that of the defendant. Unless barred by statute, courts regularly allow one kind of specialist to testify against another if the proffered expert has relevant knowledge. E.g., Soteropulos v. Schmidt, 556 So.2d 276 (La.App.1990) (orthopedic surgeon allowed to testify as expert against vascular surgeon as to amputations involving patients with vascular disease; knowledge of subject rather than expert's specialty is determinative). On the other hand, nonphysicians are rarely competent to testify as to the medical standard of care. See, e.g., Young v. Key Pharmaceuticals, Inc., 770 P.2d 182 (Wash.1989) (despite expertise, pharmacist could not testify about physician standard of care in prescribing medication); Courteau v. Dodd, 773 S.W.2d 436 (Ark.1989) (affidavit of respiratory therapist laid no foundation for testimony as expert concerning standard of care for radiologist's interpretation of x-ray). But see Thompson v. Carter, 518 So.2d 609 (Miss.1987) (nonphysician pharmacologist could testify on physician practices in prescribing particular drug; drug's "package insert" also held admissible as evidence of standard of care under exception to hearsay rule).

On treatises as evidence of the standard of care, see Lipton et al., Rethinking the Admissibility of Medical Treatises as Evidence, 17 Am. J.L. & Med. 209 (1991) (questioning reliability). On the relevance of practice guidelines in proving the standard of care, see *Kramer v. Milner*, reproduced infra, and accompanying notes.

9. *Admitting Scientific Evidence.* In an important 1993 decision, the Supreme Court reinterpreted the Federal Rules of Evidence and created a new test for the admissibility of expert scientific evidence in federal courts. Daubert v. Merrell Dow Pharmaceuticals, Inc., 509 U.S. 579 (1993), overruling the long-standing test of Frye v. United States, 293 Fed. 1013 (D.C.Cir.1923), which held that expert testimony was admissible if it was accepted by a scientific community. *Daubert* held that admissibility determinations should also include an inquiry into the validity of the science underlying the testimony—e.g., whether the theory has been reported and tested in peer-reviewed scientific journals. See also General Electric Co. v. Joiner, 118 S.Ct. 512 (1997) (district court's exclusion of expert evidence held reviewable only under "abuse of discretion" standard and upheld).

Similar admissibility issues are now being raised in state medical malpractice litigation. E.g., Reese v. Stroh, 907 P.2d 282 (Wash.1995) (en banc) (lower court opinion substituting *Daubert* test for general-acceptance test upheld on other grounds). Courts that endorse the *Daubert* standard are in a position to be more selective about the qualifications of expert witnesses than has been customary. Would you expect the *Daubert* approach, aimed at limiting the admissibility of so-called "junk science," to undermine the rule of custom in medical malpractice cases, replacing it with more scientifically based testimony on safety and efficacy?

Kramer v. Milner

Appellate Court of Illinois, First District, 1994.
639 N.E.2d 157.

■ JUSTICE O'CONNOR delivered the opinion of the court:

Milton Kramer's wife, Lillian Kramer, died of breast cancer on August 13, 1990, at the age of 74. The cancer was detected in October 1988, after a screening mammogram had been recommended by her then doctor, Noel Browdy, M.D. [Treatment was unsuccessful.]

Plaintiffs Milton Kramer, Lillian's husband, and Donald P. Kramer, the executor of Lillian's estate, brought this action against defendant Larry S. Milner, M.D., alleging that Dr. Milner had been negligent in * * * failing to recommend or order a screening mammogram for Lillian at any time between the date he began treating her as her general physician on November 1, 1985 and the date she left his care on September 9, 1988. A jury found Dr. Milner not negligent. The Kramers appeal. We reverse and remand for a new trial.

On appeal, the relevant evidence concerns exclusively the standard of care between November 1985 and September 1988 regarding the detection of breast cancer in women over the age of 50. * * *

Plaintiff * * * presented the expert testimony of Dr. William D. Shorey, a general surgeon. Dr. Shorey testified that between 1985 and 1988, the time period during which Dr. Milner treated Lillian, the standard of care required that an annual mammogram be ordered for all women over 50 whose mother or sister had had breast cancer. [Lillian's sister had had breast cancer and was also treated by Dr. Milner.] Dr. Shorey based his opinion regarding the standard of care on publications from the American College of Radiology, the National Cancer Institute (NCI), the American Medical Association, and the American College of Physicians. Dr. Shorey concluded that Dr. Milner violated the standard of care by not referring Lillian for mammography between 1985 and 1988.

Dr. Shorey conceded that certain recommendations as to care by the American Cancer Society (ACS) and the NCI were only guidelines, rather than requirements. Nonetheless, he testified that a doctor, such as Dr. Milner, who did not follow these guidelines, violated the standard of care. Had Lillian's cancer been detected at a much earlier stage, she would have had an 80% chance of survival.

Dr. Shorey testified that he concluded from the ACS survey that his opinion represented the standard of care because the ACS survey showed that between 1985 and 1988, 80% to 90% of doctors followed the recommendations of the ACS. * * *

Defendant presented the expert testimony of Harvey Morris Golomb, M.D., a specialist in hematology, who was familiar with the ACS guidelines for screening mammography in women over age 50. He testified that the ACS guidelines, as well as recommendations made by other medical organizations, were only "signposts" to assist an internist in practice and were "clearly not standards of practice." Specifically, he asserted that the ACS guidelines in existence on November 1, 1985, recommending screening mammography for women over 50 years old did not establish the standard of care for a specialist in internal medicine in 1985. He stated likewise for NCI recommendations. Golomb further stated that since the time screening mammography had first been recommended by the ACS in 1976, the various medical associations had not been able to establish a uniform guideline for practitioners.

Dr. Golomb testified that Dr. Milner did not violate the standard of care in treating Lillian. * * *

Dr. Golomb said that the fact that Lillian's sister had breast cancer was not relevant given Lillian's age. As women increase in age, and certainly when a woman is over 70, family history shrinks in importance and age becomes the primary indicator for treatment. Plaintiff's expert, Dr. Storey, agreed with this assessment.

Dr. Milner testified that he considered his treatment of Lillian to be within the standard of care. He generally orders screening mammography on all women over 40, and for women over 50, orders them every one to three years. However, if an asymptomatic 70 year-old woman comes to Dr. Milner with no prior history of cancer and does not register complaints about her breasts and does not request a mammogram, he would not order one. However, he said that in such cases, he increases the frequency of office visits and breast examinations to three or four per year.

A jury found Dr. Milner not negligent in his care of Lillian. Dr. Kramer appeals.

Kramer argues that the trial court improperly instructed the jury on the applicable standard of care. The trial judge gave Illinois Pattern Jury Instruction (IPI), Civil, No. 105.01 (3d Ed.1990), which states:

> "In providing professional services to (patient's name), a (insert appropriate professional person) must possess and apply the knowledge and use the skill and care ordinarily used by a reasonable well-qualified (insert appropriate professional person) practicing in the same or similar localities under the circumstances similar to those shown by the evidence. A failure to do so is professional negligence.
>
> [The only way in which you may decide whether (a) (any) defendant possessed and applied the knowledge and used the skill and care which the law required of him is from (expert testimony) (and) (or) (evidence of professional standards or conduct) presented in the trial. You must not attempt to determine this question from any knowledge you have.]"

In giving the instruction, the trial judge excluded the parenthetical "evidence of professional standards or conduct." Kramer contends that this was error. The parenthetical at issue was added to IPI 105.01 in 1990 and has not yet been the subject of appellate review.

The IPI Notes on Use state that the parenthetical "may be used in situations where the proper standard of care may be proven by other than expert testimony." Thus, although a party is entitled to have the jury instructed on his theory of the case, * * * the usage notes indicate that inclusion of this parenthetical is discretionary with the trial court, and an appellate court will not disturb a trial court's ruling on jury instructions absent a clear abuse of discretion.

In excluding the parenthetical, the trial court noted that in this case, there was no evidence of professional standards, but rather various guidelines, the impact of which the experts disagreed. The trial court was concerned about confusing the jury by instructing them about the presence of professional "standards," as such. Furthermore, the judge explained that to the extent there was evidence of professional standards, it came in through the expert testimony. Thus, the judge was concerned about being either duplicative or misleading the jury.

Kramer argues that because the experts' testimony was based in part on surveys of physician practice conducted by various medical associations, the record included evidence of professional standards and conduct, and hence, the trial court should have included the parenthetical. Dr. Milner counters that in this case, the experts did not agree on the weight that the professional community accorded the surveys at issue and that * * * the parenthetical should only be given where there is nonconflicting evidence of professional standards. We cannot agree with this view of IPI 105.01, and therefore, we find that the trial court's decision to withhold the parenthetical was an abuse of discretion requiring a new trial in this matter.

* * *

The "evidence of other professional standards" upon which Kramer bases his argument consisted of published medical association guidelines from which the experts deduced a standard of care. Although these surveys were not admitted into evidence, the expert witnesses relied extensively on them, to the point of opining whether the publications stated the applicable standard of care. Dr. Shorey, plaintiff's expert, stated that the surveys did establish the standard of care. Dr. Golomb, defendant's expert, stated they did not establish the standard of care. Thus, the jury was well-exposed to the contents of these documents.

The trend in Illinois has been to admit a range of evidence, beyond mere expert testimony, to enable a plaintiff to establish the standard of care in a medical malpractice case. * * * This trend is embodied by the amendment of IPI 105.01 to include the parenthetical at issue.

We do not agree that inclusion of the parenthetical requires, as Dr. Milner urges, that the record contain uncontested "evidence of professional standards or conduct." Indeed, medical expert testimony, by its very nature is contradictory. Two qualified experts on opposing sides of litigation, viewing the same injury, invariably reach different conclusions as to causation. Likewise, the experts in this case analyzing the same statistical data interpreted it differently. We are concerned that in a case like this one, to not include the parenthetical, might mislead the jury into believing that it was not entitled to consider the basis of the expert opinion.

In any event, the expert testimony analyzing the compliance rates of doctors with ACS and other organizations' recommendations—evidence offered by the defense—constitutes "evidence of professional . . . conduct" as contemplated in IPI 105.01. Thus, we believe the trial court abused its discretion in not including the parenthetical phrase in the jury instructions. Thus, we reverse the judgment below and remand this case for a new trial.

* * *

NOTES AND QUESTIONS ON PRACTICE GUIDELINES AS LEGAL STANDARDS

1. *Guidelines and the Malpractice System.* Recall the discussion of practice guidelines in chapter 2(§B). The source there quoted, Havighurst, Practice Guidelines as Legal Standards Governing Physician Liability, Law & Contemp. Probs., Spring 1991, p. 87, found "no reason to doubt the conventional expectation that the administration of the law of medical malpractice as a program of quality-assurance regulation will improve substantially as medical standards are increasingly codified in practice guidelines." Id. at 116. Similar conclusions have been reached by other commentators. E.g., Hall, The Defensive Effect of Medical Practice Policies in Malpractice Litigation, Law & Contemp. Probs., Spring 1991, p. 119, at 128–29; Brennan, Practice Guidelines and Malpractice Litigation: Collision or Cohesion?, 16 J. Health Pol., Pol'y & L. 67 (1991).

Do you agree with Havighurst's characterization of malpractice law as "a program of quality-assurance regulation"? In what sense is it a regulatory program? So understood, what are its shortcomings? Note that customary professional standards, while they are deemed to serve as benchmarks to guide physician practice, are not in fact declared until after the adverse event. Indeed, the standard used to judge physician negligence is never announced definitively but is instead left to be inferred from a jury verdict based on conflicting testimony. If the tort system were to be evaluated as a command-and-control regulatory program, would it be deemed to provide due process? Will the availability of clinical practice guidelines cure this deficiency?

How might the appearance of practice guidelines affect the propensity of physicians to practice "defensive medicine"?

2. *Admissibility; Effect.* Consider how practice guidelines might be admitted as evidence of the standard of care in a malpractice case. Without legislation, could a particular set of guidelines be admitted without expert testimony? What foundation must the expert lay? How would the *Daubert* approach to scientific evidence affect the admissibility of practice guidelines or expert opinions based thereon? Would it be enough for the expert to say that the guidelines are evidence of good practice? Even if a court was satisfied that a set of guidelines was probative of customary practice (how might it be?), would a physician's adherence to or departure from the guidelines be conclusive on the issue of negligence? In the *Kramer* case, did it make sense, for Dr. Shorey to testify that, while the ACS and NCI recommendations "were only guidelines, rather than requirements," Dr. Milner's failure to follow them "violated the standard of care"?

Consider the foregoing questions in light of the *Kramer* case and the following excerpt:

A plaintiff's or defendant's counterevidence to the effect that actual practice departed from some specific guideline norm would presumably also be admissible. Moreover, if the guidelines left significant room for alternative practices or allowed variation within a range—as professionally developed guidelines in particular will often do—, a plaintiff might attempt to litigate which practices, within the permissible range, were customary in fact. For example, if availability of financing induced physicians generally to practice at the top end of the specified range, the guidelines might provide no certain defense for care that met only the minimum standard. Or specialists might be held to the higher standard as a matter of course. On the other hand, a physician who met only the minimum standard but could demonstrate that it enjoyed some acceptance might be exonerated under the rule recognizing custom among a "respectable minority." The same exception—or the similar one acknowledging the legitimacy of a separate "school of thought"—might even be invoked in defense of conduct falling outside the guidelines altogether. For these reasons, it seems clear that, at least as long as courts follow the narrow logic of the customary-practice rule, guidelines will not eliminate as much uncertainty, or save as much in litigation expense, as they would if the guidelines were embodied in a statute or binding regulation. Although guidelines might often predetermine the outcome of a case by adding credibility to the testimony of one party's expert witness, they would not entirely obviate the battle of the experts.

* * *

Even though guidelines produced by a dominant professional organization and approved under the federal guidelines program would not enjoy exactly the same status in malpractice cases as a statute or binding regulation, the distinction between guidelines and regulations may prove to be more apparent than real. Some courts, perceiving guidelines as professional standards that they are charged with implementing, may implicitly or explicitly drop their adherence to the customary-practice rule and the requirement of a definite nexus between guidelines and actual medical practice. Authoritative guidelines might thus become the object of judicial notice, obviating expert testimony that physicians actually follow them. Whether or not courts go this far, they are certain to receive authoritative guidelines in evidence under some theory, and juries can be expected to accord them great weight, particularly where they are offered by a plaintiff to establish a physician's negligence. [Did this happen in *Kramer*?—Eds.] In this latter respect at least, the tort system is likely to treat advisory guidelines, to the extent applicable, as essentially binding legal requirements. [Did this?] Thus, the introduction of authoritative practice guidelines into the tort system could easily make it even more obviously a system of command-and-control regulation centralizing crucial decision making largely in professional hands.

* * *

While any injury-causing violation of [an applicable] practice guideline is very likely to be treated by a jury as negligence per se even if it is not regarded as such in law, the situation is not symmetrical: Compliance with a guideline would not be as likely to insulate a physician from liability.

Thus, a plaintiff who could not show a guideline violation would probably still be entitled to have his case submitted to a jury if he could offer credible evidence that the guideline was too general to define appropriate care in the particular case, that custom required doing more than the minimum contemplated by the guideline, or that the guideline minimum was itself a negligent standard. * * *

Such asymmetry in the practical impact of practice guidelines in litigation—giving plaintiffs more help in proving negligence than defendants receive in proving due care—might lead physician groups and others to seek legislation directing courts to treat practice guidelines not merely as evidence of the standard of care but as the standard itself. Such legislation might stop short of making violations of practice guidelines negligence per se but still declare that compliance with a guideline is a complete defense. * * * At a minimum, any legislative attempt to immunize physicians for compliance with professional standards would probably have to limit the inquiry on the due care issue to whether the guideline applied and was complied with.

Would such legislation be a good idea? Many physicians would object to it despite the marginal protection it might provide them, on the ground that it subjects the medical profession to "cookbook medicine" and devalues the element of judgment in treating particular patients. They might also argue that, because a plaintiff could almost always allege that a guideline was inapplicable to the particular case because of some circumstance not contemplated by the guideline makers, the profession would gain little protection from surrendering its members' professional freedom. Plaintiffs' lawyers would argue against making guidelines conclusive evidence of the standard of care on the grounds that they would usually be too general to resolve specific cases and might not reflect the advancing state of the art and medical custom.

Because compliance with an authoritative practice guideline would certainly impress a jury even if it did not conclusively resolve the issue in the case, it may be that no statutory immunity that was qualified enough to take account of the inevitable shortcomings of guidelines as actual rules for medical practice could significantly improve the current situation. Like the immunity provision of the PRO law [see note infra—Eds.], any such enactment would make little practical difference in the conduct of lawsuits or the practice of medicine. The problem of defensive medicine could probably be addressed as effectively by good guidelines alone as by a statutory provision declaring that practitioners are never required to go beyond the guidelines in caring for an individual patient.

An even stronger argument against a statutory provision obligating a physician only to comply with applicable practice guidelines is that such a provision requires officially singling out one set of guidelines and giving them the effect of public policy.

Havighurst, supra, at 101–03, 105–07. See also Hirshfeld, Practice Parameters and the Malpractice Liability of Physicians, 263 J.A.M.A. 1556 (1990) (AMA attorney opines that practice "parameters" or guidelines are designed only to assist physicians in clinical practice in delivering high-quality, cost-effective care and, as advisory documents, should serve merely as another source of evidence available to litigants seeking to prove the standard of care and not as an inflexible standard, deviation from which is negligence per se).

3. *State Experimentation with Guidelines.* In 1990, Maine put into effect unique legislation of the sort anticipated by Havighurst, supra, establishing an experiment with practice guidelines officially developed for use in malpractice litigation. See generally Begel, Maine Physician Practice Guidelines: The Implications for Medical Malpractice Litigation, 47 Maine L. Rev. 69 (1994). Under this legislation, adherence to a guideline would be a complete defense for the defendant physician; the legislature also purported, however, to bar the guidelines' use by plaintiffs seeking to establish the standard of care. Me. Rev. Stat. Ann. tit. 24, § 2975(1) (West 1997) ("only the physician or the physician's employer may introduce into evidence, as an affirmative defense, the existence of the practice parameters and risk management protocols developed and adopted pursuant to [the project]"). How do you explain the provision preventing the use of guidelines as a "sword" and useable only as a "shield"? Does it create a constitutional problem by denying plaintiffs the right to a jury trial? Does the common law provide a more attractive way to use practice guidelines than Maine's statutory effort? No cases have been reported under the Maine experiment.

4. *An Exculpatory Federal Law.* It may be noted, at least as a curiosity (since, as far as is known, it has never been invoked in litigation), that a federal statute dating from 1972 gives a physician substantial immunity from civil liability in federal and state courts "on account of any action taken by him in compliance with or reliance upon professionally developed norms of care and treatment" adopted and applied by PROs (which might easily adopt practice guidelines or the equivalent in evaluating medical practitioners). 42 U.S.C. § 1320c–6(c) (1994). One likely explanation for the statute's nonuse is found in language limiting the immunity granted to cases in which the provider "exercised due care in all professional conduct taken or directed by him and reasonably related to, and resulting from, the actions taken in compliance with or reliance upon such professionally accepted norms of care and treatment."

5. *Competing Guidelines.* Note that, in the *Kramer* case, there were several authoritative organizations pronouncing on appropriateness in using mammography. What if the guidelines had been inconsistent on the question in issue? Havighurst, supra, endorses pluralism in guideline development on the theory that a single standard ought not to govern all medical care. Yet the legal system would be hard pressed to know what to make of conflicting guidelines. Consider the following:

> A world featuring a multiplicity of inconsistent practice guidelines would present even more uncertainties for physicians than one in which even complete compliance with the dominant guidelines did not guarantee immunity from malpractice liability. But these uncertainties would be largely dispelled if one set of guidelines were known to govern a particular doctor/patient relationship. In theory, at least, physicians and patients are

> free to select one set of guidelines and incorporate them by reference in a contract for professional services. Although there may be some difficulties in getting courts to recognize such contracts, they have much to offer to both parties. * * * [T]hey are attractive as a way of providing physicians with clear statements of their obligations to particular patients without legislation effectively subjecting all physicians and all patients to the same possibly inappropriate standards.

Havighurst, supra, at 107.

Although pluralism in guideline development would seem compatible with new policies encouraging decentralized, cost-conscious decision making on clinical issues, the existence of conflicting guidelines is often deemed regrettable by devotees of the old paradigm of medical care. An interesting example of professional effort to eliminate differences between practice guidelines was a 1990 conference sponsored by the Council of Medical Specialty Societies (CMSS) for the express purpose of developing "a process for resolving conflicts that may arise when practice policies of specialty societies differ." Report of Proceedings, CMSS Conference on Resolving Conflict in the Design and Implementation of Practice Policies, Chicago, Ill., March 4–5, 1990, at 1. The main thrust of the focal presentation by David Eddy, M.D., Ph.D., was toward reaching principled resolution of conflicts occasioned by poor analysis of available evidence, and he reportedly counselled against pursuing objectives such as "increased income, personal gain, extend [*sic*] turf of a subspecialty, increased use of an exciting new technology, etc." During discussion, "it was pointed out * * * that if a conflict [between] two different policies is not resolved, a third party (e.g., government) could step in and choose either one or the other option for a variety of reasons (e.g., financial). [¶]At this point the audience agreed to the need to develop a strategy to resolve conflicts * * *."

Although Dr. Eddy was correct in wanting to see the scientific rationales for different conclusions tested, the reconciliation of scientific disputes is not necessarily in the public interest. Indeed, if two organizations were to unite behind a single conclusion the apparent consensus could conceivably be questioned under the antitrust laws. Thus, it has been argued that agreements between independent professional organizations not to produce inconsistent opinions on commercially important issues should be subject to antitrust scrutiny as agreements denying consumers the benefit of competition in the production of information. Havighurst, Applying Antitrust Law to Collaboration in the Production of Information: The Case of Medical Technology Assessment, Law & Contemp. Probs., Spring 1988, p 341. Should efforts like the CMSS initiative described above might be scrutinized by antitrust authorities? Certainly they might find in the attitudes revealed at the CMSS conference some reason to be concerned with the suppression of competition in the production of practice guidelines.

6. *Screening Mammograms.* The medical issue in *Kramer v. Milner*, the utilization of mammography as a screening mechanism for breast cancer, has been a subject of extensive debate, as major professional organizations have differed over both the intervals between mammograms and the ages at which routine screening is recommended. See Kaluzny et al., The National Cancer Institute to End Guideline Development: Lessons from the Breast Cancer Screening Controversy, 86 J. Nat'l Cancer Inst. 901 (1994). Although a blue-ribbon panel has addressed the issue of mammography between the ages of 40 and 50, the experts were broadly split. See Leitch et al., American Cancer Society Guidelines for the Early Detection of Breast Cancer: Update 1997, 47 CA: Cancer J. for Clinicians 1 (1997). The panel's official recommendation was for women to make their own decisions about use of mammography in their forties. See also Ernster, Mammography Screening for Women Age 40 through 49: A Guidelines Saga and a Call for Informed Decision Making, 87 Am. J. Pub. Health 1103 (1997). Although a policy of giving patients extensive information and letting them make their own decisions might seem to comport with those who advocate wider use of contracts to define physician obligations, it leaves the issue for resolution by individual patients (presumably without responsibility for paying for the examination if requested), not as health plan policy. Can you visualize how malpractice law might work if competing health plans, with different prices reflecting their greater or lesser conservatism on clinical matters, made different decisions concerning the uses of mammography?

7. *Attorney Use of Practice Guidelines.* There is evidence that some malpractice attorneys are integrating practice guideline technology into their efforts to build a case. In fact, the more expert the attorney, in terms of the proportion of his or her practice devoted to medical malpractice, the more likely he or she is to be cognizant of, and have a facility with practice guidelines. See Hyams et al., Practice Guidelines and Malpractice Litigation: A Two–Way Street, 122 Annals of Int. Med. 450 (1995). Hyams et al. also found that the guidelines were being used as frequently for inculpatory purposes as they were exculpatory purposes. The health services researchers advocating the use of guidelines have not been pleased with the information that they are being used by plaintiffs' attorneys. See, e.g., Hirshfeld, supra. Should guidelines promulgated by medical societies include an explicit disclaimer concerning their relevance in establishing a binding standard of care in medical malpractice litigation?

Legal Tests for Negligence

Hood v. Phillips

Supreme Court of Texas, 1977.
554 S.W.2d 160.

■ SAM D. JOHNSON, JUSTICE.

Seeking both actual and exemplary damages, Shelton Hood sued Dr. John R. Phillips alleging he suffered injuries from surgery which was not a medically accepted method of treatment for emphysema. * * *

At trial, Dr. Phillips described the accepted medical treatment for emphysema as follows: (1) encourage the patient to stop smoking and to move to a dry, pollution-free climate; (2) use medication to lessen the bronchial spasm; (3) use machines to aid the patient in breathing; and (4) employ oxygen therapy. Dr. Phillips related that when he first examined Mr. Hood in 1966 he had emphysema. Attempting to reduce Mr. Hood's suffering, Dr. Phillips removed one of the carotid bodies from his neck.[2] Dr. Phillips testified he had employed this surgery since 1962 and by 1966 he had performed it between 1,200 and 1,500 times. In his experience, 85 percent of his patients were helped to some extent and 15 percent were not helped at all. He acknowledged that the use of this surgery was not generally accepted and was in fact highly controversial.

In contrast to the testimony of Dr. Phillips that carotid surgery generally produced beneficial results, three physicians testifying for Hood characterized carotid surgery as an unaccepted mode of treatment for emphysema, as a treatment not supported by medical evidence, and as a surgical procedure which had been tried by a number of physicians, found ineffectual, and abandoned.

[One expert testified that he] had no knowledge of any medical support for carotid surgery as a cure for emphysema and no knowledge of any reputable physician using this method, as of 1966, to cure or relieve the symptoms of severe emphysema.

[Another expert] stated: "[T]he procedure has been proposed really without much scientific rationale, tried by a number of physicians worldwide; found ineffectual and abandoned. In my own judgment, the procedure is not only not beneficial, but potentially harmful." He described the accepted treatment for emphysema as a combination of the use of drugs, the systematic use of inhaled aerosol to help combat the disease, and the application of physical medicine techniques designed to improve breathing efficiency and to promote the physical reconditioning of the patient.

According to the testimony of Dr. Phillips on the issue of informed consent, the doctor told Mr. Hood of the risks of the surgical removal of the carotid body in accordance with medically accepted standards. * * *

Contrary to the testimony of Dr. Phillips, Mr. Hood stated upon deposition that Dr. Phillips did not tell him 15 percent of those undergoing this surgery did not receive any relief. Mr. Hood insisted Dr. Phillips guaranteed to cure his emphysema. Mr. Hood also stated that Dr. Phillips represented the incision would be small and that he would no longer need medication for emphysema after the operation. He asserted Dr. Phillips did not tell him that the operation would require the removal of nerves from his neck, did not mention his heart in any way, and did not inform him that the operation might result in high blood pressure.

2. As described by Dr. Phillips, this surgical procedure involved the removal of the carotid body and the nerves surrounding it. The carotid body is a receptor for chemical stimuli "sensitive to the concentration of carbon dioxide in the blood, and assist[s] in reflex control of respiration." Henry Gray, F.R.S., Anatomy of the Human Body, at 895 (29th Am. ed. 1973). At trial, Dr. Phillips explained the surgical removal of the carotid body as an attempt to improve the airflow to the lungs by lessening the spasms of the involuntary muscles in the bronchial tubes.

Mrs. Hood, who was present during the conversation between her husband and Dr. Phillips, [confirmed his version of the facts].

The trial court refused to submit plaintiff Hood's issue on informed consent and ordinary negligence. It did submit an issue on whether the carotid surgery was gross negligence on the part of Dr. Phillips, and the jury refused to find Dr. Phillips grossly negligent.

The court of civil appeals reversed and remanded on the grounds the plaintiff, Hood, should not have been required to meet the higher burden imposed by a gross negligence standard but rather should have been required to meet the following ordinary negligence standard:

> "[A] physician is not guilty of malpractice where the method of treatment used is supported by a *respectable minority of physicians*, as long as the physician has adhered to the acceptable procedures of administering the treatment as espoused by the minority." [Emphasis added.]

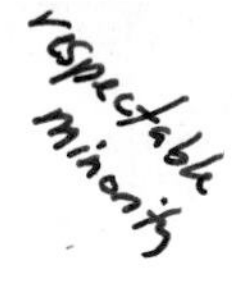

At this juncture, we note that the above standard articulated by the court of civil appeals was intended to apply to a negligence suit based on allegations that the mode or form of medical treatment was not a proper remedy for the diagnosed condition. It was not intended to apply to an action based on the negligent performance of the correct remedy for the diagnosed condition.

The court of civil appeals also held: (1) there was no evidence to support the submission of the issue of whether Dr. Phillips failed to obtain the consent to surgery of Mr. Hood; and (2) the trial court acted properly in quashing subpoenas directing Dr. Phillips to produce records in his possession * * *.

Both Dr. Phillips and Hood applied for writs of error to this court and both writs were granted.

THE NEGLIGENCE STANDARD

It should be noted at the outset that Hood does not assert that the surgical removal of the carotid body was unskillfully or negligently performed. Nor does Hood contend that Dr. Phillips' diagnosis of emphysema was incorrect. Instead, the patient-plaintiff maintains that it was negligence to utilize this particular surgical procedure as a method of treating emphysema.

Both Hood and Dr. Phillips assert the court of civil appeals erred in adopting the "respectable minority" negligence standard. There are at least four standards that may be applied to a medical malpractice suit based on the assertion that the mode or form of treatment was not a remedy for the diagnosed condition.

Respectable Minority: The "respectable minority" standard approved in the instant case by the court of civil appeals was adopted in [several cases].

In McHugh v. Audet, 72 F.Supp. 394, 400 (M.D.Pa.1947), the court adopted a slightly different standard: "Where *competent* medical authority is divided a physician or surgeon will not be held responsible if in the exercise of his judgment he followed the course of treatment advocated by a *considerable number* of his professional brethren in good standing in his community." [Emphasis added.]

Reasonable Surgeons Would Disagree: Dr. Phillips maintains it was error for the court of civil appeals to adopt the "respectable minority" standard. He proposes the following test:

> "When *reasonable surgeons would disagree* as to either the need for an operation or the procedure employed, the decision is a matter of surgical judgment, and the surgeon will not be liable even if it subsequently appears that the organ removed was healthy or the operation itself was not needed or was unsuccessful." [Emphasis added.]

Any Variance: Some courts have held any variance from the accepted mode of treatment renders the physician liable. In Jackson v. Burnham, 20 Colo. 532, 39 P. 577, 580 (1895), it was stated that "when a particular mode of treatment is upheld by a consensus of opinion among the members of the profession, it should be followed by the ordinary practitioner; and if a physician sees fit to experiment with some other mode, he should do so at his peril."

Reasonable and Prudent Doctor: The following standard has been applied in Texas in other medical malpractice suits—" . . . what a reasonable and prudent doctor would have done under the same or similar circumstances." Snow v. Bond, 438 S.W.2d 549, 550 (Tex.1969).

This review of the various standards reveals most courts have not attempted to articulate a distinction among "experimental," "outmoded," "rejected," and "accepted" surgical procedures. Instead, the majority of courts have attempted to draw a line between the reasonable and prudent physician who, as a last resort, turns to an "experimental" or a "rejected" treatment in the hope of assisting the patient and the individual practitioner who attempts to beguile his patient with false or distorted promises. These courts have recognized, as we do, that physicians should be allowed to exercise their professional judgment in selecting a mode or form of treatment. Further, physicians should be allowed to experiment in order that medical science can provide greater benefits for humankind. Consequently, we reject the "any variance" standard.

The "respectable minority" standard adopted by the court of civil appeals and "considerable number" test could convey to a jury the incorrect notion that the standard for malpractice is to be determined by a poll of the medical profession. Accordingly, these standards are rejected.

Dr. Phillips' proposed "reasonable surgeons would disagree" standard and the "what a reasonable and prudent doctor would have done" standard, which has been applied in other medical malpractice suits, appear to be simply different ways of reaching the same objective—preclude the imposition of liability on the reasonable and prudent physician and permit liability on the one who is not. We are of the opinion that the statement of the law most serviceable to this jurisdiction is as follows: A physician who undertakes a mode or form of treatment which a reasonable and prudent member of the medical profession would undertake under the same or similar circumstances shall not be subject to liability for harm caused thereby to the patient. The question which conveys to the jury the standard which should be applicable is as follows: Did the physician undertake a mode or form of treatment which a reasonable and prudent member of the medical profession would not undertake under the same or similar circumstances? Generally this standard should be applied whether the mode or form of treatment is "experimental," "outmoded," or "rejected."

The burden of proof is on the patient-plaintiff to establish that the physician-defendant has undertaken a mode or form of treatment which a reasonable and prudent member of the medical profession would not have undertaken under the same or similar circumstances. The circumstances to be considered include, but are not limited to, the expertise of and means available to the physician-defendant, the health of the patient, and the state of medical knowledge. Unless the mode or form of treatment is a matter of common knowledge or is within the experience of the layman, expert testimony will be required to meet this burden of proof. In the instant case there was expert medical testimony characterizing carotid surgery as an unaccepted mode of treatment for emphysema, as a controversial procedure, as a treatment not supported by medical evidence, and as a surgical procedure which had been tried by a number of physicians, found ineffectual, and abandoned. Although the trial court refused to submit an issue regarding ordinary negligence, this evidence would raise a question of fact for the jury on the issue of ordinary negligence and such issue should have been submitted.

GROSS NEGLIGENCE

* * * [T]he record in this case is such that not only was Hood entitled to an issue regarding ordinary negligence, but also an issue concerning gross negligence.

The issue of gross negligence has been submitted to the jury in several Texas medical malpractice cases. * * *

This court has defined gross negligence as "that entire want of care which would raise the belief that the act or omission complained of was the result of a conscious indifference to the right or welfare of the person or persons to be affected by it." With respect to the instant case, the testimony by doctors Petty, Thompson, and Longfield that carotid surgery is not an acceptable method for the treatment of emphysema and the further testimony that the method had been rejected and was not being employed by reputable physicians would raise a fact issue as to whether Dr. Phillips performed this type of surgery with conscious indifference to the welfare of Hood. The testimony in the instant case would therefore entitle Hood to a submission to the jury of an issue concerning gross negligence and, accordingly, an issue regarding exemplary damages.

INFORMED CONSENT

Hood next argues it was error for the trial court to refuse to submit the issue of informed consent to the jury. This court, in Wilson v. Scott, 412

S.W.2d 299, 301 (Tex.1967), held "[p]hysicians and surgeons have a duty to make a reasonable disclosure to a patient of risks that are incident to medical diagnosis and treatment." The court also held the patient had the burden to prove by expert medical evidence what a reasonable practitioner of the same school and same or similar community under the same or similar circumstances would have disclosed to the patient and that such medical standard of disclosure may be proven by testimony of the physician-defendant.

The evidence in this case was such that the issue of informed consent should have been submitted to the jury. * * *

[SUBPOENAS]

Hood next asserts the court of civil appeals erred in upholding the trial court's action in quashing subpoenas requiring Dr. Phillips to produce records in his possession * * *

Some of the items sought from Dr. Phillips included:

1. "All reports or correspondence with any patient in which carotid body surgery was performed reporting to Dr. Phillips as to the effect of such surgery."
2. "All records of the 189 patients in which he claims attained 85% relief in [an article he published]."
3. "All of the patient records and follow-up records of the 200 surgical cases referred to in [another article]."

Since these three items were sought for the purpose of establishing whether Dr. Phillips' claimed results were substantiated by his records, they would be material and relevant to the issues of whether Dr. Phillips did inform Hood of the actual success rate of carotid surgery, whether Dr. Phillips had reason to believe this operation could assist an individual suffering from emphysema, and whether Dr. Phillips performed the surgery with conscious indifference to the welfare of Hood.

In view of the holding that Dr. Phillips' records are not protected by [statute], the trial court should review not only the three items referred to previously, but all items sought from Dr. Phillips to ascertain whether they are discoverable. In order to protect the privacy of Dr. Phillips' patients, the trial court may order an *in camera* inspection of these records. * * *

The judgment of the court of civil appeals, which reversed the trial court judgment and remanded the cause to the trial court, is affirmed.

NOTES AND QUESTIONS ON STANDARDS FOR JUDGING PHYSICIANS' PERFORMANCE

1. *Medical Orthodoxy and Expert Hindsight in Hood v. Phillips?* Might customary practice, used as a sword as well as a shield, enforce unwarranted adherence to orthodox methods and discourage responsible experimentation? If research later shows an innovative technique to have been inefficacious or dangerous, is the innovator left out to dry? Consider the procedure at issue in *Hood*.

Unilateral carotid body resection (UCBR) was first used in Japan, and favorable results were reported in this country in the early 1960s. "Early reports of successes following UCBR for patients with asthma or emphysema made this a popular technique for the treatment of severe obstructive airway disease. These enthusiastic reports, however, were later followed by studies showing less positive results." National Center for Health Services Research and Health Care Technology Assessment, Bilateral Carotid Body Resection 2–3 (Health Technology Assessment Rep. No. 12, 1985). Specifically, these later studies suggested that the successes were due to the "placebo effect," since reported benefits were frequently short-lived and patients undergoing sham procedures experienced similar improvement. The Medicare program refused to pay for UCBR on the ground that it lacked "general acceptance of the professional medical community" and is not supported by controlled clinical studies. 45 Fed.Reg. 71431–32 (1980). The procedural validity of this ruling was contested unsuccessfully in Heckler v. Ringer, 466 U.S. 602 (1984), revealing that some physicians and patients still favored the procedure.

The literature review in the technology assessment quoted supra (which, incidentally, includes a citation to an article by Dr. Phillips) suggests that the evidence on UCBR as of 1966, when Hood was operated upon, may not have been as clear as it afterward became (although the medical rationale for using the procedure to treat emphysema was apparently never as strong as the case for using it for asthma). How would you defend Dr. Phillips against the charge that he was a "practitioner who attempts to beguile his patients with false or distorted promises"? Could you persuade a jury that he was a victim of medical orthodoxy? of 20–20 hindsight?

On the problem of determining the standard of care at a particular point in time through experts having the benefit of later scientific knowledge, see Bellardini v. Krikorian, 537 A.2d 700 (N.J.Super.1988). In that case, plaintiff alleged that it was negligent to administer the drug Tofranil to a pregnant woman in 1962. The only evidence of negligence was the testimony of an expert who had not yet entered medical school at that date. The court held that because expertise can be gained by means other than direct experience, the expert could testify.

2. *The "Reasonable and Prudent Doctor" Standard.* Recall that customary practice is employed as a standard, not because it is demonstrably correct as a matter of public policy, but in default of a better, or contractually determined, one. If one views professional custom as a dubious guide to efficiency in medical practice and as nothing more than a convenient point of departure in specifying professional duties, how strong should be the presumption against the physician who departs from prevailing standards? Does the test for negligence adopted in *Hood v. Phillips* provide a satisfactory alternative standard?

The *Hood* court states its test in more than one way. Are the different formulations interchangeable, or do they put the issue in slightly different lights? For example, is the test what a hypothetical reasonable and prudent doctor would do or whether the defendant himself acted reasonably and prudently? Does a formulation along the latter lines reduce the pressure to adhere to outmoded or inefficient standards? Does this standard assign a proper role to the jury?

3. *Respectable Minority.* The court in *Hood* rejects the "respectable minority" test adopted by the intermediate court. Other courts have allowed physicians to take refuge in the standards of a separate "school" or respectable minority of practitioners, thus avoiding the worst extremes of enforced orthodoxy. See, e.g., Chumbler v. McClure, 505 F.2d 489 (6th Cir.1974) ("The test for malpractice and for community standards is not to be determined solely by a plebiscite." Where two or more schools of thought exist among competent members of the medical profession concerning proper medical treatment for a given ailment, each of which is supported by responsible medical authority, it is not malpractice to be among the minority in a given city); Leech v. Bralliar, 275 F.Supp. 897 (D.Ariz.1967) ("prolotherapy" for whiplash injury was practiced by only 65 physicians nationally, as patient was informed; defendant was judged negligent in deviating from standards of prolotherapists).

A later Texas case relied on *Hood v. Phillips* in holding the following instruction improper:

> If you find from the credible evidence that other plastic surgeons recognized more than one method for performing augmentation mammoplasties at the time in question you are instructed that Dr. Rothenberg was at liberty to select any of such methods. A doctor is not negligent merely because he made a choice of a recognized alternative method for the procedures he followed in the treatment of a patient, if he exercised the required skill and care in administering and following the method of his choice. This would be true even though other medical witnesses may not agree with the choice he made.

Henderson v. Heyer–Schulte Corp., 600 S.W.2d 844, 847 (Tex.App.1980). The court observed that, under the instruction, "there is no requirement that the 'other' surgeons be reasonable or prudent or that they be prepared to employ that method under circumstances similar to those Dr. Rothenberg faced, the two factors most stressed in *Hood*." Despite this holding, does the *Hood* test allow sufficient leeway for the exercise of independent professional judgment?

4. *Honest Error.* Some formulations of tort duties expressly recognize that uncertainty frequently necessitates professional judgment and protect the physician against liability for errors or mistakes that do not reflect a lack of skill or care. In Perkins v. Walker, 406 N.W.2d 189 (Iowa 1987), the plaintiff contended that her prior use of steroid skin creams had lowered her adrenal function, creating a risk (which materialized) that her blood pressure could not be maintained during surgery. The defendant physician, charged with either not recognizing the problem or not protecting against the risk, obtained instructions that "a doctor cannot be found negligent merely because he makes a mistake in the diagnosis and treatment of a patient" and that "any error in diagnosis and treatment does not in and of itself constitute negligence." A defense verdict based on these instructions was upheld. (How could you argue that one instruction should have been given but not the other?) Cf. Senesac v. Associates in Obstetrics and Gynecology, 449 A.2d 900 (Vt.1982) (uterus perforated during abortion; doctor's admission that she made a mistake and was sorry could not substitute for expert testimony that standard of care had been breached). See also Rogers v. Meridian Park Hosp., 772 P.2d 929 (Or.1989) (rejecting jury instruction to the effect that physician would not be liable for error in judgment unless he failed to use reasonable care and skill in exercising judgment, on ground that, by seeming to excuse "error," it could confuse jury).

Some formulations excuse "honest" or "good faith" errors. In one case, the Minnesota Supreme Court held that a previously approved standard jury instruction vindicating the physician "for an honest error in judgment in choosing between accepted methods of treatment" was too subjective and possibly misleading; the court set forth the following new instruction:

> A doctor is not negligent simply because his or her efforts prove unsuccessful. The fact a doctor may have chosen a method of treatment that later proves to be unsuccessful is not negligence if the treatment chosen was an accepted treatment on the basis of the information available to the doctor at the time a choice had to be made; a doctor must, however, use reasonable care to obtain the information needed to exercise his or her professional judgment, and an unsuccessful method of treatment chosen because of a failure to use such reasonable care would be negligence.

Ouellette by Ouellette v. Subak, 391 N.W.2d 810, 816 (Minn.1986) (decision whether to allow a difficult pregnancy to continue or to induce labor occurred "at a time when reasonable doubt existed as to the stage of the pregnancy").

5. Consider the following comment on the utility of the foregoing defenses:

> Given the remarkable divergence of opinion on most questions of medical practice, one would expect the respectable minority and error in judgment rules to be invoked frequently in a preclusive fashion in procedural motions such as those for summary judgment or directed verdict. In fact, these doctrines are usually used only in framing instructions to the jury. Litigants have learned that the pre-emptive effect of these rules is easily avoided by eliciting from their physician witnesses not merely a difference in opinion as to the proper course of treatment, but an expression that the opposing opinion is illegitimate. Thus, it is usually a simple matter to create a factual dispute over the respectability of an alternative practice, if not its existence, leaving the jury to decide which of two opposing treatment methods is correct. This breakdown between theory and practice essentially allows the jury to impose, based on its own

> independent judgment, the governing standard of care—the very result malpractice law [with its reliance on professional norms] attempts to avoid.

Hall, The Defensive Effect of Medical Practice Policies in Malpractice Litigation, Law & Contemp. Probs., Spring 1991, p. 119, at 128–29. Might the new skepticism toward expert testimony signified by the *Daubert* case correct the problem that Hall notes?

What If the Customary Standard Is Too Low?

Gates v. Jensen

Supreme Court of Washington, 1979.
92 Wn.2d 246, 595 P.2d 919.

■ HOROWITZ, JUSTICE.

Petitioners in this suit for malpractice raise two important questions regarding a physician's duties of care and disclosure to a patient, and the rules of law which apply when a physician allegedly breaches that duty. The first question is whether the doctrine of informed consent requires a physician to inform a patient of a bodily abnormality discovered during a routine examination and of diagnostic procedures which may be taken to determine the significance of that abnormality. The second question raised is whether the rule of Helling v. Carey, 83 Wash.2d 514, 519 P.2d 981 (1974), that reasonable prudence may require a standard of care higher than that exercised by the relevant professional group, prevails even after the enactment of RCW 4.24.290. We answer both these questions affirmatively, reverse the trial court, and remand for a new trial.

In May 1972 petitioner Elisabeth Gates consulted Dr. James Hargiss, an ophthalmologist with the respondent Eye Clinic of Seattle. She complained of difficulty in focusing, blurring, and gaps in her vision. Mrs. Gates was 54 years old at the time and had a severe myopia which doubled her risk of glaucoma. Dr. Hargiss took eye pressure readings with a Schiotz tonometer and found the pressure in each eye registered 23.8 on the Goldman scale. This reading indicated Mrs. Gates was in the borderline area for glaucoma. Dr. Hargiss then examined Mrs. Gates' optic nerves with a direct ophthalmoscope to determine whether the discs, or surfaces, of the nerves showed the exacerbated "cupping" which is characteristic of glaucoma. There was evidence at trial that observation of the nerve discs in Mrs. Gates' case was particularly difficult with the direct ophthalmoscope when the pupils were not dilated. Nonetheless Dr. Hargiss did not dilate Mrs. Gates' pupils. He could see no evidence of abnormality and made no further tests for glaucoma. In response to Mrs. Gates' inquiry about the pressure test, he said he had checked for glaucoma but found everything all right. He diagnosed her problem as difficulties with the contact lenses she wore and treated her accordingly.

The significant facts in this case are that Dr. Hargiss neither told Mrs. Gates he had found high pressure in both eyes which put her in a borderline glaucoma area, nor that her risk of glaucoma was increased considerably by this high pressure and her myopia. Furthermore, Dr.

Hargiss had available to him two additional diagnostic tests for glaucoma which are simple, inexpensive, and risk free. The first was to use the standard drops for dilating the pupils to obtain a better view of the optic nerve discs. The second was to have Mrs. Gates take a visual field examination to determine whether she had suffered any loss in her field of vision. Dr. Hargiss did not tell Mrs. Gates of the existence of these simple procedures, and he did not administer the tests.

Over the next 2 years Mrs. Gates revisited the clinic 12 times complaining of blurring, fog, and gaps in her vision, as well as loss in visual acuity. Shortly after her first visit Dr. Hargiss made another pressure reading and found pressures in both eyes to be within the high range of normal. There was evidence at trial that in the early stages of glaucoma pressures can vary drastically from normal to positive glaucoma readings within a 24–hour period. Dr. Hargiss concluded, however, that the first high readings were misleading because they were caused by Mrs. Gates' tension at being subjected to the pressure testing procedure, which requires placing an instrument directly on the eye. Adhering to Dr. Hargiss' initial diagnosis of difficulty adjusting to contact lenses, the doctors at the clinic did not dilate the pupils nor administer a visual field test over the next 2 years. Mrs. Gates' symptoms gradually worsened.

In April 1974 doctors at the clinic diagnosed Mrs. Gates as having open angle glaucoma. This diagnosis was confirmed by other specialists outside the clinic. The clinic's own glaucoma expert suggested that part of Mrs. Gates' vision loss was attributable to an acute nerve disease which is untreatable and could not have been detected before it occurred. This finding was made at a time when Mrs. Gates' glaucoma had already been diagnosed and the clinic's expert had access to the records indicating that dilation and field examinations had not been previously made. The diagnosis of nerve disease was contested at trial by other expert testimony. By the time Mrs. Gates' glaucoma was discovered her vision had deteriorated from near 20/20 with glasses to 20/200 with glasses. Mrs. Gates is now functionally blind.

At trial petitioners requested instructions on the doctrine of informed consent and the reasonable prudence rule established by this court in *Helling v. Carey,* supra. The court refused both instructions. The jury reached a verdict for the respondent doctors and the court entered judgment accordingly. The Court of Appeals considered five assignments of error and affirmed the judgment for respondents. We granted the petition for review of the trial court's refusal to give the two requested instructions.

We reverse.

Informed Consent

Petitioners' proposed Supplemental Instruction No. 2[2] is based on the evidence presented at trial that the doctors at the Eye Clinic failed to

2. Petitioners' proposed supplemental instruction No. 2 reads as follows:

inform Mrs. Gates that she had high pressures in her eyes, that she was in a high risk group for glaucoma, or that there were alternative diagnostic procedures available to determine conclusively whether she had glaucoma. It is petitioners' contention that the doctors had a duty to tell her these facts so she could make an informed choice about treatments she would undergo, and that if she had been informed of these facts she would have requested the additional tests and glaucoma would have been discovered. There was evidence at trial that if glaucoma had been detected when Mrs. Gates first visited the Eye Clinic, the condition could have been stabilized and a great part of her vision saved. It is respondents' contention, however, that the doctrine of informed consent does not apply to questions of appropriate diagnostic procedures and the requested instruction was properly rejected. We do not agree.

In a thorough and comprehensive statement of the doctrine of informed consent which was adopted by this court, the Court of Appeals held that a physician has a fiduciary duty to inform a patient of abnormalities in his or her body. Miller v. Kennedy, 11 Wash.App. 272, 282, 522 P.2d 852 (1974), affirmed 85 Wash.2d 151, 530 P.2d 334 (1975). The basis of this duty is that the patient has a right to know the material facts concerning the condition of his or her body, and any risks presented by that condition, so that an informed choice may be made regarding the course which the patient's medical care will take. The patient's right to know is not confined to the choice of treatment once a disease is present and has been conclusively diagnosed. Important decisions must frequently be made in many non-treatment situations in which medical care is given, including procedures leading to a diagnosis, as in this case. These decisions must all be taken with the full knowledge and participation of the patient. The physician's duty is to tell the patient what he or she needs to know in order to make them. The existence of an abnormal condition in one's body, the presence of a high risk of disease, and the existence of alternative diagnostic procedures to conclusively determine the presence or absence of that disease are all facts which a patient must know in order to make an informed decision on the course which future medical care will take.

"You are instructed that an ophthalmologist has a duty to advise his patient of all relevant, material information concerning the condition of the patient's eyes that the patient will need to make an informed decision respecting the alternative methods of examination for eye disease, of the reasonably foreseeable risks of each alternative, and of no such examination at all. Failure to so advise the patient is negligence."

"The plaintiff-patient must prove the following elements to establish a case of negligence against the ophthalmologist for failing to impart information so the course of examination could be chosen intelligently: (1) The defendant-doctor failed to inform the plaintiff-patient of the condition of the patient's eyes, of the availability of alternative examination procedures for detecting eye disease, of the reasonably foreseeable material risks of each alternative, and of no examination at all. (2) A reasonable person in the plaintiff-patient's position would have chosen a different course of examination had the alternatives and the material risks of each been made known. (3) The plaintiff has been injured as a result of submitting to the course of examination proposed by the physician."

Contrary to respondents' contention, application of the doctrine of informed consent to circumstances other than treatment of a diagnosed disease is nothing new. *Miller v. Kennedy* itself involved evaluating the risks of a diagnostic procedure, a kidney biopsy. In Young v. Group Health Cooperative of Puget Sound, 85 Wash.2d 332, 534 P.2d 1349 (1975), the doctrine was applied to a determination whether childbirth should take a natural course, where this question again was not one of treatment of a known disease. The physician's duty of disclosure arises, therefore, whenever the doctor becomes aware of an abnormality which may indicate risk or danger. The facts which must be disclosed are all those facts the physician knows or should know which the patient needs in order to make the decision. To require less would be to deprive the patient of the capacity to choose the course his or her life will take.

In this case jury questions were raised as to whether Dr. Hargiss disclosed all the facts which he had a duty to disclose and, if not, whether Mrs. Gates was injured thereby. We conclude the trial court erred in refusing the requested Supplemental Instruction No. 2.

REASONABLE PRUDENCE IN MEDICAL PRACTICE

Petitioners' requested Supplemental Instruction No. 3[3] was based on the rule of *Helling v. Carey,* supra, that reasonable prudence may require a standard of practice which is higher than that exercised by the relevant professional community. Respondents contend the *Helling* rule does not apply in this case, and further that the rule was abrogated by RCW 4.24.290. We do not agree.

Helling v. Carey was an unusual case. The plaintiff there, like Mrs. Gates, had glaucoma. The evidence showed the disease could have been detected and successfully treated early enough to prevent her severe vision loss if routine pressure tests had been administered when she first reported troubling symptoms to her doctor. The tests were not given, however, because the doctor did not suspect glaucoma and the standard of practice among ophthalmologists at that time was not to give routine pressure tests to persons under the age of 40. The plaintiff was only 32. The pressure tests, which were then routinely given to persons over 40, are simple, inexpensive, reliable and risk-free. The court held that reasonable prudence required the use of this test on persons under the age of 40 as well, and that failure to give the test to the plaintiff was negligence. The unusual

3. Petitioners' proposed supplemental instruction No. 3 reads as follows:

"Irrespective of whether you find that any defendant met or failed to meet the applicable standard of care followed by practicing ophthalmologists in the diagnosis of glaucoma, if you find that Mrs. Gates had glaucoma and that the statistical risk of sight loss from glaucoma is serious enough in cases such as Mrs. Gates' that reasonable prudence under the circumstances required the administration of additional diagnostic tests before April 22, 1974, you are instructed that failure to perform those tests before that date would constitute negligence. In determining whether reasonable prudence would require giving the tests in question you should consider, among other facts, the cost, ease or difficulty of administration, risk to the patient and relative reliability of the tests in question."

features of the case included the nature of the disease glaucoma, which may go undetected for years until severe loss of vision is unavoidable, and the existence of a simple and harmless test which can prevent this terrible result.

The instant case presents the same unusual features. The disease is the same. The treating physicians had available to them at least two additional diagnostic procedures—dilation of the pupils for a better view of the optic nerve discs, and a vision field examination—which are simple, inexpensive, conclusive and risk free. These tests need only be used when other diagnostic procedures are inconclusive for some reason, or when a red flag of warning has been raised by some abnormality suggesting the risk of glaucoma. When a patient's condition does indicate the necessity for further examination, however, reasonable prudence requires the use of the alternative tests.

The evidence in this case showed that Mrs. Gates' physical condition—her severe myopia and her initial borderline glaucoma pressure readings—indicated a high risk of glaucoma. Other evidence tended to show Dr. Hargiss complied with the applicable professional standard of care by examining Mrs. Gates' optic nerve discs with a direct ophthalmoscope. A jury could find, however, that where the risk of glaucoma was high and the pressure tests arguably inconclusive, reasonable prudence required the physician to dilate the pupils for a better view of the optic nerve discs and administer a visual field examination. The doctrine of *Helling v. Carey,* that reasonable prudence may require a higher standard of care applies; petitioners were entitled to have their proposed instruction given to the jury.

Respondents contend, though, that the *Helling* rule was abrogated by legislative enactment. RCW 4.24.290 provides, in part:

> In any civil action for damages based on professional negligence against ... a member of the healing arts ... the plaintiff in order to prevail shall be required to prove by a preponderance of the evidence that the defendant or defendants failed to exercise that degree of skill, care and learning possessed by other persons in the same profession ...

The original house bill would have established the standard of care as that skill and care practiced by others in the same profession and specialty. HB 246, 44th Regular Sess. (1975). Respondent contends the clear intent of this bill was to abrogate the *Helling* rule. The original bill was amended though. The statute as passed requires physicians to exercise the skill, care and learning *possessed* by others in the same profession. This standard is much broader than the one embodied in the original bill, and allows ample scope for the application of the limited *Helling* rule. It is not argued that respondent and other ophthalmologists did not possess the skill, care and learning required to choose and administer the two alternative, simple and risk-free tests. We therefore find no bar to the requested instruction under RCW 4.24.290.

The judgment is reversed and the case remanded for a new trial.

■ DOLLIVER, JUSTICE (concurring in part, dissenting in part).

I do not quarrel with the analysis and result of the majority on the issue of informed consent. I do disagree, however, with its position on reasonable prudence in medical practice.

Proposed supplemental instruction No. 3 is taken directly from Helling v. Carey, 83 Wash.2d 514, 519 P.2d 981 (1974). * * *

The issue in *Helling* and in this case is the standard of care to be applied by the jury in measuring the defendants' conduct. The standard of care is a rule of law which provides the trier of fact with the controlling test for negligence. In most negligence actions, the standard of care to which the defendant must conform is that degree of care which, in the jury's view, a reasonable person of ordinary prudence would have exercised in the defendant's place in the same or similar circumstances. In medical malpractice actions, however, the standard of care traditionally had been that degree of skill, care and learning which is possessed and exercised by members of the medical profession in good standing. In short, the standard of care generally has been held to be the standard of the profession.

In *Helling,* however, we held that, regardless of the standards of the profession of ophthalmology, reasonable prudence required the "timely giving of this simple, harmless pressure test [for glaucoma] to this plaintiff and that, in failing to do so, the defendants were negligent". Citing Judge Learned Hand, we quoted with approval his observation that "*Courts must in the end say what is required; there are precautions so imperative that even their universal disregard will not excuse their omission*". The T.J. Hooper, 60 F.2d 737 (2d Cir.1932). The *Helling* decision represented a deviation from the "standard of the profession" test used in medical malpractice actions. It rested on the "reasonably prudent person" standard which is applied in ordinary tort cases.

In 1975, the legislature considered and passed Substitute House Bill No. 246—RCW 4.24.290. The purpose of the bill was stated in the bill report of the House Committee on Judiciary, 44th Legislature, 1st Ex.Sess. That report said:

> Purpose of Bill and Effect on Existing Law: This bill is occasioned by a recent holding by the Wash. State Supreme Court regarding the standard of care required of physicians. In *Helling v. Carey* the court held that in a malpractice suit it is sufficient for plaintiff to prove that the physician failed to provide reasonable and prudent care in light of all of the circumstances—even though he in fact adhered to that standard of care expected of the average practitioner in his field. *Helling* says, regardless of established practice, if the facts involved indicate that a certain duty to perform should exist then the professional is liable for breaches of that duty. The bill as introduced would re-establish the pre-*Helling* standards of negligence that have been developed through case law in Washington.
>
> Effect of SUBSTITUTE BILL: Requires medical malpractice plaintiff to show that defendant failed to exercise the degree of skill, care and learning possessed by others in the same profession and that such failure caused damages. Excludes from this requirement actions based on failure to obtain informed consent of a patient.

The question is whether this purpose was successfully accomplished.

The majority points out that the original bill referred to the "skill and care *practiced* by others in the same profession" (italics mine), while Substitute House Bill No. 246, now RCW 4.24.290, substitutes the word *possessed* for *practiced.* * * * I do not believe that the change of the word "practiced" to "possessed" frustrated the legislature's purpose in enacting RCW 4.24–290. The issue is not whether members of the profession possessed, practiced, followed or exercised a certain degree of skill. Rather, it is whether the standard of the profession should be used to measure the defendants' conduct instead of the *Helling* standard of "reasonably prudent under the circumstances".

RCW 4.24.290 says that a "plaintiff in order to prevail shall be required to prove by a preponderance of the evidence that the defendant or defendants failed to exercise that degree of skill, care and learning possessed by other persons in the same profession". Plaintiffs' proposed supplemental instruction No. 3 says that even if the defendants met "the applicable standard of care followed by practicing ophthalmologists in the diagnosis of glaucoma" the jury could still find defendants negligent. This is absolutely contrary to the mandate of the legislature. The plaintiff must prove a violation of the standard of the profession. Failure to do so bars recovery.

The trial court did not commit error in refusing to give the instruction.

NOTES AND QUESTIONS ON RAISING INADEQUATE STANDARDS TO DETER POOR PRACTICE

1. *Helling v. Carey.* In this well-known case, which is perhaps already familiar to you from your previous study of torts, the Washington court reasoned as follows:

> The issue is whether the defendants' compliance with the standard of the profession of ophthalmology, which does not require the giving of a routine pressure test to persons under 40 years of age, should insulate them from liability under the facts in this case where the plaintiff has lost a substantial amount of her vision due to the failure of the defendants to timely give the pressure test to the plaintiff.
>
> The defendants argue that the standard of the profession, which does not require the giving of a routine pressure test to persons under the age of 40, is adequate to insulate the defendants from liability for negligence because the risk of glaucoma is so rare in this age group. * * *
>
> The incidence of glaucoma in one out of 25,000 persons under the age of 40 may appear quite minimal. However, that one person, the plaintiff in this instance, is entitled to the same protection, as afforded persons over 40, essential for timely detection of the evidence of glaucoma where it can be arrested to avoid the grave and devastating result of this disease. The test is a simple pressure test, relatively inexpensive. There is no judgment factor involved, and there is no doubt that by giving the test the evidence of glaucoma can be detected. The giving of the test is harmless if the

physical condition of the eye permits. The testimony indicates that although the condition of the plaintiff's eyes might have at times prevented the defendants from administering the pressure test, there is an absence of evidence in the record that the test could not have been timely given. * * *

Under the facts of this case reasonable prudence required the timely giving of the pressure test to this plaintiff. The precaution of giving this test to detect the incidence of glaucoma to patients under 40 years of age is so imperative that irrespective of its disregard by the standards of the ophthalmology profession, it is the duty of the courts to say what is required to protect patients under 40 from the damaging results of glaucoma.

We therefore hold, as a matter of law, that the reasonable standard that should have been followed under the undisputed facts of this case was the timely giving of this simple, harmless pressure test to this plaintiff and that, in failing to do so, the defendants were negligent * * *.

519 P.2d at 982–83. The court's justification for imposing its own standard of care was Judge Learned Hand's famous pronouncement in *The T.J. Hooper* (cited in *Gates*) that, because "a whole calling may have unduly lagged in the adoption of new and available devices," custom should not necessarily be controlling.

Note in *Gates* what happened to the court's ruling in the legislature and the court's reaction to that legislation. In yet another glaucoma screening case, Harris v. Robert C. Groth, M.D., Inc., 663 P.2d 113, 118 (Wash.1983), the Washington court finally discovered a more respectable way—besides issuing medical judgments of its own—of improving upon customary practice; the test it adopted was similar to that in *Hood:* "whether a reasonably prudent [doctor], possessing the degree of skill, care, and learning possessed by other ophthalmologists in the state of Washington, and acting in the same or similar circumstances as the defendant," would have performed the particular procedure or test. Under this standard, both the *Helling* and *Gates* cases would seem to have been readily resolvable against the defendant physicians, who in each case failed to respond to clear signs that they had not properly diagnosed the problem.

2. *Cost Effectiveness; Benefit/Cost Analysis.* Now consider whether the *Helling* ruling contributed to efficiency. In order to apply Learned Hand's famous efficiency-oriented calculus for identifying negligence (from the *Carroll Towing* case), one must compare the potential harm (discounted by its probability) with the cost of preventing it, finding liability only if the latter cost is less. The following excerpt sets forth an efficiency justification for both the usual-and-customary practice rule and the *Helling* result:

Because judges and juries may find it exceedingly difficult to evaluate a medical dispute, the courts have largely accepted "customary standards of medical practice" as a measure of reasonable investment in mishap avoidance. The physician can plead that he has followed customary practice in his care of the patient, and the courts will usually substitute expert testimony about professional custom for a more specific accounting by the negligence standard.

This substitution reflects the faith of the legal system that physicians as a group, or at least those who set standards, are correctly investing in mishap avoidance and that medical custom can be used as the bench mark of adequate performance. And it conforms to the view, held both by providers of health care and by observers of the system, that most physicians tend to guard the welfare of their patients without need for external regulation. The malpractice system exists to discipline the occasional physician who does not (or cannot) protect his patients.

In the face of conflicting testimony about what constitutes customary and acceptable practice, the courts may undertake more explicit (if informal) application of the Learned Hand Rule. Even if a defendant can show that his performance has met the accepted standard of medical practice, the courts retain ultimate responsibility for determining whether that standard also constitutes "reasonable care." And they may find that it does not.

For example, custom has been rejected as the defense in a suit brought by a 32-year-old woman who became blind from glaucoma because tonometry was not performed. The appellate court weighed the cost of the test ("inexpensive" and "harmless") against the probability that glaucoma would develop in a young person ("one in 25,000") and the magnitude of the loss (blindness). The court concluded that "reasonable prudence" required the test and faulted the profession for not routinely carrying out tonometry in patients under the age of 40. Here, custom did not meet the standard of efficiently allocating resources; the court measured custom against the Hand standard and set custom aside. This decision, when expressed quantitatively, yields a result consistent with the Learned Hand Rule. If we take cost of tonometry as not exceeding \$5 and the average jury verdict for total or legal blindness at \$678,000 (for period 1973–1977), we arrive at the following formulation:

$$\$5 < 1/25{,}000 \times \$678{,}000$$
$$\$5 < \$27$$

No reasonable adjustment of the figure for the cost of avoidance would alter this conclusion. Cases like this one indicate that professional custom serves only as a provisional substitute for the negligence rule.

Schwartz & Komesar, Damages and Deterrence: An Economic View of Medical Malpractice, 298 New Eng.J.Med. 1282, 1283–84 (1978).

Despite the back-of-the-envelope calculation in the foregoing excerpt, a closer look at the diagnostic test in question reveals problems. Indeed, an extensive review of the medical literature published in 1983 cast surprising doubt upon even the customary professional practice of screening patients *over* 40 for glaucoma. See Eddy et al., The Value of Screening for Glaucoma with Tonometry, 23 Survey of Ophthalmology 194 (1983), the abstract of which read as follows:

This paper estimates the value of performing Schiotz tonometry to detect glaucoma in an asymptomatic patient. About 9% of adults over 40

> will be found on a single Schiotz tonometry test to have elevated intraocular pressure (IOP). On work-up, about 1 out of 50 of these individuals with high IOP will be found to have glaucoma. Tonometry, however, will miss about half of all patients with glaucoma because they do not have elevated IOPs at the time of the test. Pilocarpine or epinephrine are the most commonly used drugs to treat the disease, but they are not always effective in lowering a patient's IOP or in stopping the progression of field defects. From the available evidence it does not appear that earlier diagnosis makes a substantial difference in the patient's outcome. If all individuals over 40 years of age in a city of 1,000,000 were screened, the total cost of finding and treating about 484 people with chronic simple glaucoma would be on the order of $4,944,866 or about $13,000 per patient potentially benefitted.

This study especially observed the highly inconclusive character of the evidence on the efficacy of treatment. The most positive study on treatment for IOP involved only 19 eyes, and the authors found that all the studies together did not rule out "the hypothesis that treatment has no effect, or is even harmful." Treatment of glaucoma itself "has such strong historical roots (pilocarpine was introduced more than one hundred years ago) that no randomized controlled trials have been conducted, and the available information is from uncontrolled studies, clinical impressions, and inferences drawn from studies of patients with ocular hypertension." On this basis, the authors concluded, "Screening with tonometry does not appear to be warranted." See also Comment, Rational Health Policy and the Legal Standard of Care: A Call for Judicial Deference to Medical Practice Guidelines, 77 Cal. L. Rev. 1483, 1502–05 (1989).

What are you led to conclude concerning the use of customary practice as a guide to medical practice? How can courts compensate for its shortcomings in providing both inefficiently low and inefficiently high standards of care? Interestingly, it did not appear to one investigator that Washington ophthalmologists much changed their glaucoma screening practices following *Helling*. See Wiley, The Impact of Judicial Decisions on Professional Conduct: An Empirical Study, 55 S. Cal. L. Rev. 345 (1981). But see Givelber et al., *Tarasoff*, Myth and Reality: An Empirical Study of Private Law in Action 1984 Wis. L. Rev. 443, 488–90 & n.131 (questioning Wiley study methodology).

Finally, imagine that you must defend a physician for failing in the 1980s to screen a now-blind 45-year-old for glaucoma. Would you invoke the Learned Hand Test for negligence, arguing to the jury or the judge that the benefits to society do not warrant incurring the large aggregate cost of screening? Could you make essentially the same argument in terms better calculated to persuade your audience? What evidence would you offer to support your case? Under what formulations of the standard of care would you stand the best chance of prevailing? What would you do about the later research on the value of tonometry reported in the next paragraph?

More recent studies of the cost effectiveness of screening for open angle glaucoma reach new but still differing conclusions. See, e.g., Tucks & Crick, The Cost Effectiveness of Various Modes of Screening for Primary

Open Angle Glaucoma, 4 Ophthalmological Epidemiology 3 (1997); Bovin et al., Cost–Effectiveness of Screening for Primary Open Angle Glaucoma, 3 J. Med. Screening 154 (1996). The latter study found, under certain assumptions, that screening in a population 40 to 79 prevented blindness at a cost of $100,000 (Canadian) per year of disease avoided. When screening was restricted to subjects age 65 to 79, it was estimated to prevent 81% of the cases of blindness prevented by the broader use of screening, and the cost per year of blindness prevented was reduced to $42,000. Although this study concluded that screening should be applied only to those over 65, the later study by Tucks & Crick, supra, concluded that screening for the 40 to 59 age group was as cost effective as screening for an older population. Note that there has been no revision of the medical profession's view of the question in *Helling*.

3. *"Acceptable Practice."* Professor Joseph King has argued against "customary practice" and in favor of "acceptable practice" as the standard for assessing physician negligence. According to King, the focus should be on whether a practice was approved by the profession at large, not whether it was actually followed:

> This "acceptable practice" standard would not depend exclusively on the historical conduct of the profession, or on what its members customarily did, but on what a reasonably competent member of the profession practicing in the same specialty as the defendant would be expected to do in order to conform to acceptable professional practice. The reasonable expectations and collective sense of members of the profession as to what constitutes sound medicine would be the controlling inquiry.

J. King, The Law of Medical Malpractice in a Nutshell 44 (2d ed. 1986). See also King, In Search of a Standard of Care for the Medical Profession: The "Accepted Practice" Formula, 28 Vand.L.Rev. 1213 (1975).

Professor King cites Incollingo v. Ewing, 444 Pa. 263, 282 A.2d 206 (1971), as a case coming close to adopting the acceptable-practice formula. An osteopath was sued for authorizing refills of a prescription for chloromycetin without monitoring the patient during the course of therapy. The patient developed aplastic anemia, a lethal disease associated with repeated use of the antibiotic. The court held that the doctor was not exculpated by evidence that there was widespread indiscriminate use of the antibiotic in the community. Although there was expert testimony critical of the osteopath's conduct, there was no testimony that he had violated community standards. The court held, however, that a prima facie case of malpractice can be made without evidence of departure from community standards. The court emphasized that a physician must "give due regard to the advanced state of the profession and [must] exercise the care and judgment of a reasonable man in the exercise of medical skill and knowledge." According to King, *Incollingo* presents a situation where a physician's course of conduct was customary but not acceptable by professional standards.

How does Professor King's rationale for rejecting medical custom as a defense differ from that in *Helling v. Carey?* Does his formulation leave any room for introducing cost considerations into the calculus?

4. *The "Best Judgment" Rule.* Some courts have held that a physician must not only conform to the accepted community standards of practice but must also use his "best judgment." See, e.g., Burton v. Brooklyn Doctor's Hosp., 452 N.Y.S.2d 875 (N.Y.App.Div.1982); Toth v. Community Hosp., 239 N.E.2d 368 (N.Y.1968). Thus, a physician who is aware of dangers associated with customary practice has a duty to employ his best judgment to take steps to avoid those dangers. If a physician fails to employ his own best judgment, he cannot insulate himself from liability for resulting injury merely by demonstrating that he adhered to community practice.

Under this test, a physician with greater knowledge and skill will be held to a higher standard of care than other physicians in the community. For example, in the *Burton* case, supra, a physician at an academic medical center was held liable for blindness resulting from administering higher-dose oxygen therapy to premature infants. The infant was included in a clinical study of such therapy, the protocol of which called for placing one out of three premature infants in a high-oxygen environment. Although such therapy was commonly used at the time, the physician was aware of preliminary evidence from the study that suggested that high-dose oxygen increased the risk of retrolental fibroplasia and blindness. The court concluded:

> Although the conventional medical wisdom at the time believed that increased oxygen was essential to the survival of premature babies, the hospital and Dr. Engle cannot avail themselves of the shield of acceptable medical practice when a number of studies, including their own, had already indicated that increased oxygen was both unnecessary and dangerous, particularly for an otherwise healthy baby, and especially when the attending physician, who had primary responsibility for the patient's health, had recommended a decrease. "[A] physician should use his best judgment and whatever superior knowledge, skill and intelligence he has."

452 N.Y.S.2d at 879–80 (quoting *Toth,* supra).

What questions do you have about this case? Was the experiment ethical? What might make it so? Are the experimenters in such a clinical trial obligated to call it off as soon as preliminary evidence suggests that one treatment or the other is more beneficial? How could society get the benefit of clinical experimentation if courts found doctors negligent in giving any treatment the safety or efficacy of which they have some reason to doubt? The issues raised here are beyond the scope of these materials but are related to issues raised in *Hood v. Phillips,* supra, and in § C, infra.

5. *Raising Local Standards.* If standard practice in a local community of physicians is out of step with practice elsewhere, how might a plaintiff establish the negligence of physicians practicing in accordance with that standard? In Naccarato v. Grob, 180 N.W.2d 788 (Mich.1970), the plaintiff complained of failure of defendants, Detroit pediatricians, to screen a newborn for phenylketonuria (PKU), a disease that had become amenable to effective treatment (if promptly diagnosed) by the time of the alleged negligence (1960). As described by the intermediate court, the trial court had ruled that plaintiff's expert, a Los Angeles expert on PKU, could not testify as to the standard of care in Detroit:

> The basis for the decision was that Dr. Koch was required to make too many assumptions, which were contradicted by testimony of the Detroit area physicians, as to the standards in the Detroit area so that Detroit was shown not to be a "similar" community to Los Angeles despite Dr. Koch's belief that the existence of medical centers engaged in PKU research in both cities made them "similar".
>
> The standards set by Los Angeles medical centers actively engaged in PKU research could not be applied to the Detroit area medical centers, according to the trial court, where testimony showed that these centers were not known by the general practitioner in the Detroit area to have been engaged in PKU research at this time. The trial court found that the experts, although familiar with the practice and standards in a similar urban community, were not sufficiently familiar with Detroit practices in light of the contradictory testimony. The requisite degree of familiarity with Detroit procedures was thus not shown by the plaintiff's witnesses, for the communities in question were not "similar".
>
> The trial court also took judicial notice of the rarity of PKU in the time period involved and the gradual development of a test for PKU, which was not then widely known.

162 N.W.2d 305, 308 (Mich.App.1968). The intermediate court affirmed the trial court's ruling, stating, "One may not be pleased with the thoroughness of the PKU diagnostic procedures of Detroit area pediatricians during the time period in question, but it is the law of this state that a defendant physician is not to be held to a greater standard of practice than that customarily expected of his fellow physicians in the community." Id. at 309.*

What do you think of the ruling on whether Los Angeles was "similar" to Detroit? Why did courts originally permit plaintiffs to call witnesses who could testify to practice standards in similar communities? Does this case suggest that inviting testimony from similar localities might also be useful in upgrading backward standards and inducing the faster spread of new technology and learning? See Favalora v. Aetna Cas. & Surety Co., 144 So.2d 544, 551 (La.App.1962) ("To relieve a member of the medical profession from liability for injury to a patient on the ground that he

* Screening of newborns for metabolic disorders, primarily PKU, is now mandated by statute in most states. Should such regulation be relied upon to establish the standard of care in other respects? Why was regulation employed here? In Massachusetts Department of Health, Cost–Benefit Analysis of Newborn Screening for Metabolic Disorders, 291 New Eng.J.Med. 1414 (1974), the cost of screening and treatment was compared to the "averted costs" to the commonwealth of institutional care for the mentally retarded victims of undiagnosed PKU, and a "substantial net saving" was found. What do you think of the analysis? What explains the state's decision to treat screening for PKU as a public health matter? Why not rely on the law of medical malpractice to induce physicians to screen for PKU?

followed a degree or standard of care practiced by others in the same locality is, in our opinion, unthinkable when the degree or standard of care in question is shown to constitute negligence because it fails to meet the test of reasonable care and diligence required of the medical profession"); Pederson v. Dumouchel, 431 P.2d 973, 977 (Wash.1967) ("Negligence cannot be excused on the ground that others in the same locality practice the same kind of negligence").

The Michigan Supreme Court reversed the lower court in *Naccarato,* holding plaintiff's witness competent to testify under a completely different theory:

> It is * * * unnecessary to consider in this opinion whether a standard of parochial negligence can obviate the requirement of reasonable care by a local practitioner. At issue here is the standard of care owed to a patient by a community of specialists. Whatever the considerations were that allowed the area practice to set the standard for the country general practitioners—they are not relevant to a metropolitan specialist * * *.
>
> The reliance of the public upon the skills of a specialist and the wealth and sources of his knowledge are not limited to the geographic area in which he practices. Rather his knowledge is a specialty. He specializes so that he may keep abreast. Any other standard for a specialist would negate the fundamental expectations and purpose of a specialty. The standard of care for a specialist should be that of a reasonable specialist practicing medicine in the light of present day scientific knowledge. Therefore, geographical conditions or circumstances control neither the standard of a specialist's care nor the competence of an expert's testimony.

180 N.W.2d at 790–91.

The following case deals with the so-called "locality rule," its exceptions and current status. Should the locality rule be thought of primarily in the light suggested by the current context—that is, as an exception to the customary practice rule necessary so that backward standards will not be sheltered and so that plaintiffs will not be unfairly denied access to expert witnesses? Or should the trend toward national standards for all practitioners be regarded as a salutary sign that doctors are being held to higher standards and that the quality of care is being improved?

The Locality Rule

Shilkret v. Annapolis Emergency Hospital Association

Court of Appeals of Maryland, 1975.
276 Md. 187, 349 A.2d 245.

■ LEVINE, JUDGE.

In this appeal, which stems from a negligence action brought against several physicians and a hospital, we are asked to decide upon the proper standard of care to be applied in medical malpractice cases.

At the trial of the case in the Circuit Court for Anne Arundel County, the court (Wray, J.) ruled that the standard to be applied was the "strict locality" rule (the standard of care exercised by physicians in the defendant's own community or locality), and since appellants, who were plaintiffs below, had failed to meet the requirements of that rule, directed a verdict for appellees. * * * We granted certiorari for the limited purpose of deciding whether the Court of Special Appeals was correct in holding "that [in Maryland] the 'Strict Locality Rule' must be applied" in medical malpractice cases.

According to the agreed statement of facts filed in lieu of a record extract, the infant plaintiff, Mark Alan Shilkret, was born at the Anne Arundel General Hospital (Anne Arundel) on December 22, 1968, and has been continuously institutionalized since that date because of brain damage that appellants allege resulted from intracranial bleeding caused by negligence at delivery. This was allegedly complicated by subsequent treatment rendered by appellees, the various attending physicians and the hospital. The several physicians who are appellees here include two obstetricians who treated the mother throughout the prenatal stage and then delivered the infant, an anesthesiologist in attendance at birth, and a pediatrician at the hospital who allegedly examined the infant the day after his birth.

At the trial, after excerpts from the depositions of the four defendant-physicians had been admitted in evidence, argument ensued over the applicable standard of care. When the court indicated that it would apply "the strict locality rule," appellants conceded that they could not prove their case against appellees under that standard and requested leave to make a proffer of expert medical testimony which "could meet any other rule in medical negligence cases." They were afforded this opportunity and proceeded with extensive statements of what their two experts, an obstetrician-gynecologist and a neurosurgeon, would say if called as witnesses. Each expert had an impressive curriculum vitae.

The proffered testimony of the obstetrician-gynecologist established that Anne Arundel belongs to the American Hospital Association, one of several members of the accrediting body known as the Joint Commission on Accreditation of Hospitals. It was his opinion that all hospitals belonging to this group meet a national standard in caring for obstetrical patients. At the time of the infant's birth, the witness had been chief of the obstetrical-gynecological services at the U.S. Army Hospital at Aberdeen Proving Ground. He believed that in this branch of medicine, the standards at Anne Arundel were the same as those observed at Aberdeen and at all other accredited hospitals in the United States. Similarly, as a member of the American College of Gynecologists and Obstetricians, and being board certified, he believed that a national standard of care applied to those with the same qualifications. He then detailed how the failure of the four physicians and the hospital to meet the national standards of care applicable to them resulted in the injury to the plaintiff.

The other expert witness whose testimony was proffered would have stated in some detail that he was employed as a neurosurgeon at the National Institutes of Health at Bethesda, Maryland, that a national standard of care is observed in the diagnosis and treatment of neurological diseases, the knowledge of which is also possessed by general practitioners, and that each of the defendants had violated what he believed to be a national standard regarding the care of newborn infants.

Following these proffers, the trial judge granted each appellee's motion for a directed verdict. He adhered to his previously pronounced belief that the "strict locality" standard applies in Maryland, rather than the "national" (in which the standard of care is not tied to a particular geographic locality) or "similar locality" (the standard of care observed by physicians of ordinary skill and care in either the defendant-physician's locality or in a similar community) tests urged by appellants, and therefore ruled that the latter had failed to present a sufficient case for the jury. The Court of Special Appeals affirmed, holding that its own prior cases—and the decisions of this Court—compelled this result. For reasons that follow, we reverse.

The general principles which ordinarily govern in negligence cases also apply in medical malpractice claims. Therefore, as in any other case founded upon negligent conduct, the burden of proof rests upon the plaintiff in a medical malpractice case to show a lack of the requisite skill or care on the part of the defendant. Id. But, whereas the conduct of the average layman charged with negligence is evaluated in terms of the hypothetical conduct of a reasonably prudent person acting under the same or similar circumstances, the standard applied in medical malpractice cases must also take into account the specialized knowledge or skill of the defendant. W. Prosser, Torts § 32 (4th ed. 1971); McCoid, The Care Required Of Medical Practitioners, 12 Vand.L.Rev. 549, 558 (1959). The formulation of a standard of care that is consistent with these well established tort principles, but which is fair to both the patient and his physician, has troubled the courts for the past century.

Recently, in Raitt v. Johns Hopkins Hospital, 274 Md. 489, 499–500, 336 A.2d 90 (1975), where we held that an expert medical witness need not necessarily reside or practice in the defendant's community to testify as to the applicable standard of care in a medical malpractice case, we intimated that despite the plethora of reported medical malpractice decisions in Maryland, this Court actually had never been confronted with the need to adopt a standard of care from among the three we have mentioned.

* * * [W]e now explicitly decide for the first time this question of the standard of care to be applied in medical malpractice cases. It should hardly come as a surprise that appellants advocate the adoption of the national standard or, alternatively, the similar locality rule. They claim that their proof satisfied both tests. Appellees, on the other hand, contend for the strict locality rule.

In addressing this issue, we note at the outset that we are dealing with two types of defendants, physicians and hospitals.

(1)

THE STANDARD OF CARE APPLICABLE TO PHYSICIANS

The earliest traces of the strict locality rule appeared a century ago. It is an exclusive product of the United States; possibly because of the difference in the size of the two countries, the English courts have never developed such a principle. Waltz, The Rise And Gradual Fall Of The Locality Rule In Medical Malpractice Litigation, 18 DePaul L.Rev. 408 (1969). The rule was unquestionably developed to protect the rural and small town practitioner, who was presumed to be less adequately informed and equipped than his big city brother. The court reasoned with what was then unassailable logic in Tefft v. Wilcox, [6 Kan. 46, 63–64 (1870).]

> "... In the smaller towns and country, those who practice medicine and surgery, though often possessing a thorough theoretical knowledge of the highest elements of the profession do not enjoy so great opportunities of daily observation and practical operations, where the elementary studies are brought into every day use, as those have who reside in the metropolitan towns, and though just as well informed in the elements and literature of their profession, they should not be expected to exercise that high degree of skill and practical knowledge possessed by those having greater facilities for performing and witnessing operations, and who are, or may be constantly observing the various accidents and forms of disease. ..."

In short, the rationale underlying the development of the strict locality rule a century ago was grounded in the manifest inequality existing in that day between physicians practicing in large urban centers and those practicing in remote rural areas.

Ultimately, the rule came under sharp attack on two grounds. First, "[i]t effectively immunized from malpractice liability any doctor who happened to be the sole practitioner in his community. He could be treating bone fractures by the application of wet grape leaves and yet remain beyond the criticism of more enlightened practitioners from other communities." Waltz, supra at 411. Secondly, a "conspiracy of silence" in the plaintiff's locality could effectively preclude any possibility of obtaining expert medical testimony.

Whatever may have justified the strict locality rule fifty or a hundred years ago, it cannot be reconciled with the realities of medical practice today.[4] "New techniques and discoveries are available to all doctors within a short period of time through medical journals, closed circuit television presentations, special radio networks for doctors, tape recorded digests of medical literature, and current correspondence courses." Note, An Evaluation Of Changes In The Medical Standard Of Care, 23 Vand.L.Rev. 729, 732 (1970). More importantly, the quality of medical school training itself has improved dramatically in the last century. Where early medical education consisted of a course of lectures over a period of six months, which was supplemented by apprenticeships with doctors who had even less formal

4. The absurdity of coupling the standard of care with the doctor's community is aptly illustrated in Brune v. Belinkoff, 354 Mass. 102, 235 N.E.2d 793 (1968) * * * In *Brune,* which involved an act of alleged malpractice in the City of New Bedford, slightly more than 50 miles from Boston, the trial judge had instructed the jury: "' ... If, in a given case, it were determined by a jury that the ability and skill of the physician in New Bedford were fifty percent inferior to that which existed in Boston, a defendant in New Bedford would be required to measure up to the standard of skill and competence and ability that is ordinarily found by physicians in New Bedford.' "

education, there now exists a national accrediting system which has contributed to the standardization of medical schools throughout the country.

A distinct minority of states, however, cling to the strict locality rule. Nevertheless, recognizing the significant developments which have occurred in the training and practice of medicine, and the population shifts which have marked the increased urbanization of our society, a majority of American courts have now abandoned the strict locality rule as being too narrow. We, too, conclude that it can be sustained no longer given the current state of medical science.

* * *

A plurality, if not a majority, of states apply the similar locality rule.

The similar locality rule answers some of the criticism aimed at the strict locality standard by enabling the plaintiff to obtain expert witnesses from different communities, thus reducing the likelihood of their acquaintance with the defendant. It does not, however, effectively alleviate the other potential problem, a low standard of care in some of the smaller communities, because the standard in similar communities is apt to be the same. Another criticism leveled at the similar locality rule is the difficulty which arises in defining a "similar" locality.[5] For these reasons, the similar locality rule is regarded as no more than a slight improvement over the stricter standard.

These deficiencies in the locality rules and the increasing emphasis on the availability of medical facilities have led some courts to dilute the rules by extending geographical boundaries to include those centers that are readily accessible for appropriate treatment. This expanded rule, expressed in terms of "medical neighborhood" or "medical locality," has paved the way for the national standard. In any event, the trend continues away from standards which rest solely on geographic considerations.

Ever-increasing emphasis on medical specialization has accelerated the erosion of the locality rules and the concomitant emergence of the so-called national standard. Even within the framework of the locality rules, it has been generally accepted that where a physician holds himself out as a specialist, he is held to a higher standard of knowledge and skill than a general practitioner. Some courts, therefore, have abandoned the locality rules for a national standard only as to specialists. * * * This is consistent

5. One standard which has been applied is geographic proximity between communities, which retains much of the "same" locality flavor. Other courts have considered socioeconomic factors such as population, type of economy, size of city, and income of inhabitants. Most courts applying this standard, however, have adopted the view that "similar" locality should be defined in terms of medical factors such as the existence of research and laboratory facilities, medical schools, teaching hospitals and modern equipment in the localities to be compared. The commentators agree that this is the most logical application of the rule when measured against a major reason for its adoption—the availability of resources which will enable the physician to maintain the standard of his practice.

with the position of the American Law Institute which otherwise adopts the similar locality rule.[8]

Were we to adopt a standard tied to locality for specialists, we would clearly be ignoring the realities of medical life. As we have indicated, the various specialties have established uniform requirements for certification. The national boards dictate the length of residency training, subjects to be covered, and the examinations given to the candidates for certification. Since the medical profession itself recognizes national standards for specialists that are not determined by geography, the law should follow suit.

The courts in another group of cases, however, have gone further, and have adopted this same standard of care—one which is not governed by the locality of the defendant—for all physicians regardless of whether they are specialists or not.

We agree with these courts that justification for the locality rules no longer exists. The modern physician bears little resemblance to his predecessors. As we have indicated at length, the medical schools of yesterday could not possibly compare with the accredited institutions of today, many of which are associated with teaching hospitals. But the contrast merely begins at that point in the medical career: vastly superior postgraduate training, the dynamic impact of modern communications and transportation, the proliferation of medical literature, frequent seminars and conferences on a variety of professional subjects, and the growing availability of modern clinical facilities are but some of the developments in the medical profession which combine to produce contemporary standards that are not only much higher than they were just a few short years ago, but also are national in scope.

In sum, the traditional locality rules no longer fit the present-day medical malpractice case.

Moreover, while a specialist may be held to greater skill and knowledge in his particular field than would be required of a general practitioner under the same or similar circumstances, one standard can be fashioned for all physicians as the Kentucky, Washington and Wisconsin courts have carefully demonstrated. To that extent, there is no valid basis for distinguishing between general practitioners and specialists in applying standards of care. Although national board certification in the specialties has contributed significantly to standardization on a nationwide scale, all of the other reasons which justify a national standard of care apply with equal validity to general practitioners.

8. "Unless he represents that he has greater or less skill or knowledge, one who undertakes to render services in the practice of a profession or trade is required to exercise the skill and knowledge normally possessed by members of that profession or trade in good standing in similar communities." Restatement (Second) of Torts § 299 A (1965).

Comment d provides:

"An actor undertaking to render services may represent that he has superior skill or knowledge, beyond that common to his profession or trade. ...Thus a physician who holds himself out as a specialist in certain types of practice is required to have the skill and knowledge common to other specialists. . . ."

Nevertheless, in one important respect there is even a difference of opinion among those three courts and the Massachusetts court. As we noted earlier, the Massachusetts court articulated two standards, one for the "*average* qualified practitioner" and the other for the "*average* member of the profession practicing [a] specialty." Brune v. Belinkoff, [235 N.E.2d 793, 798 (Mass.1968)] (emphasis added). Similarly, the Washington court framed its standard in terms of "an *average*, competent practitioner," Pederson v. Dumouchel [431 P.2d 973, 978 (Wash.1967)] (emphasis added), and the Wisconsin court postulated its rule for the "*average* practitioner," Shier v. Freedman, [206 N.W.2d 166, 174 (Wis.1973)] (emphasis added). The Kentucky Court of Appeals, however, substituted "the term 'reasonably competent' for the term 'average' used in the Washington Court's definition." Blair v. Eblen, [461 S.W.2d 370, 373 (Ky.1970)].

In eschewing the term "average," the Kentucky court sided with the American Law Institute, which, in comment e to Restatement (Second) of Torts § 299 A (1965), states:

> "... [The standard] is not that of the most highly skilled, nor is it that of the average member of the profession ..., since those who have less than median or average skill may still be competent and qualified. Half of the physicians of America do not automatically become negligent in practicing medicine at all, merely because their skill is less than the professional average. On the other hand, the standard is not that of the charlatan, the quack, the unqualified or incompetent individual who has succeeded in entering the profession...."

Or, as one learned scholar aptly stated, " ... a true 'average' would involve an uneasy aggregation of the best and the worst, the experienced and the inexperienced, the quack and the specializing medical doctor. It has never been suggested that the law strikes the average from so diverse a grouping." Waltz, supra at 409 n. 1. Although "average" is probably expressed in the sense of "ordinary," this meaning may not be conveyed to the jury despite an explicit instruction on the point.

We align ourselves with the Kentucky court and hold that a physician is under a duty to use that degree of care and skill which is expected of a reasonably competent practitioner in the same class to which he belongs, acting in the same or similar circumstances. Under this standard, advances in the profession, availability of facilities, specialization or general practice, proximity of specialists and special facilities, together with all other relevant considerations, are to be taken into account.

(2)

THE STANDARD OF CARE APPLICABLE TO HOSPITALS

In reviewing some of our medical malpractice decisions earlier, we intimated that neither of the locality rules has been applied in Maryland where a hospital has been the defendant. Equally significant is the absence in our prior cases of any distinction between physicians and hospitals regarding the applicable standard of care. As the court stated in Pederson v. Dumouchel, supra, 431 P.2d at 978, "[m]uch that we have said [in articulating the standard of care applicable to physicians] also applies to the jury instructions given concerning hospitals. They, too, are members of national organizations and subject to accreditation." Courts elsewhere have tended to apply the same standards to hospitals that they apply to physicians.

The only case, of which we are aware, to make a distinction of any kind between physicians and hospitals is Duling v. Bluefield Sanitarium, Inc., 149 W.Va. 567, 142 S.E.2d 754, 764 (1965). There, the court, although adhering to the similar locality rule in medical malpractice cases, held that an action brought against a hospital because of a nurse's carelessness, as distinguished from that of a physician, is founded solely on negligence and want of due care. Hence, the proper standard was held to be "reasonable care."

In Dickinson v. Mailliard, 175 N.W.2d 588, 596, 36 A.L.R.3d 425 (Iowa 1970), the court, in adopting as a standard "that which obtains in hospitals generally under similar circumstances," stated:

> "... It is doubtful today if there is any substantial difference from one locality to another in the type of hospital services rendered. Hospitals must now be licensed and accredited. They are subject to statutory regulation. In order to obtain approval they must meet certain standard requirements. ...It is no longer justifiable, if indeed it ever was, to limit a hospital's liability to that degree of care which is customarily practiced in its own community. ...[M]any communities have only one hospital. Adherence to such a rule, then, means the hospital whose conduct is assailed is to be measured only by standards which it has set for itself. There is no other hospital to which it may be compared."

We think the same reasoning is apposite here. Hospitals in general, and Anne Arundel in particular, are accredited by the Joint Commission on Accreditation. This group establishes national standards to which all hospitals seeking accreditation must conform. In addition, hospitals in Maryland are subject to a rigorous regulatory scheme which promotes statewide standards. These factors, together with much of what we said earlier regarding physicians, warrant the adoption of a standard of care for hospitals which conforms to that applied in cases against physicians.

We hold, therefore, that a hospital is required to use that degree of care and skill which is expected of a reasonably competent hospital in the same or similar circumstances. As in cases brought against physicians, advances in the profession, availability of special facilities and specialists, together with all other relevant considerations, are to be taken into account.

Here, there was evidence that there is a national standard of care for accredited hospitals in the prenatal, intrapartum and perinatal periods of pregnancy. Similarly, the evidence proffered by appellants showed national standards of care for child delivery, infant care, and the treatment of neurological problems generally, and the measure of vital functions specifically, that are observed by specialists and general practitioners alike. Under our holdings here, this evidence was sufficient to take the standard of care issue to the jury as to all of the appellees. Our review, as we observed at the outset, has been limited to this question. Whether the evidence was sufficient to establish a failure to comply with the applicable standards of care, and, if so, whether said failure directly caused the injuries sustained by the infant plaintiff, are questions which we do not reach here.

NOTES AND QUESTIONS ON THE LOCALITY RULE

1. *"Medical Neighborhood."* Note the *Shilkret* court's observation that earlier cases expanded the "medical neighborhood" and its assertion that this territorial extension "paved the way for the national standard." Do you agree with this interpretation of the trend? Might the rationale of these cases have been merely that better transportation was widening the area in which the patient might be referred for treatment? Might the appropriate area for judging standards vary with the patient's condition and the benefit/cost ratio of going a greater distance for needed care? For another case abandoning the locality rule and simultaneously stressing the importance of national standards, see Morrison v. MacNamara, 407 A.2d 555 (D.C.1979).

2. *"Similar Locality."* The "strict" version of the locality rule first gave way as courts, responding to the problems of plaintiffs in getting local physicians to serve as expert witnesses, allowed experts from "similar" communities to testify. To the extent the locality rule survives at all today, it almost always takes the modified, similar-locality form. See, e.g., Mosley v. Owens, 816 P.2d 1198, 1201 (Ore. App. 1991) (expert found to possess knowledge of what constitutes proper medical treatment in a similar community); Chapel v. Allison, 785 P.2d 204 (Mont.1990) (similar locality rule for general practitioners adopted and extended to allow evidence from similar communities in other states, but not a national standard, where general practitioner treated condition most often treated by orthopedic specialists); Pederson v. Dumouchel, 431 P.2d 973 (Wash. 1967) (en banc) (early leading case overturning strict locality rule). For a case stretching the modified locality standard rather far, see Kobialko v. Lopez, 576 N.E.2d 1044 (Ill.App.1991) (Swedish plastic surgeon held competent to testify on standard of care in Chicago under similar-locality rule).

Is it possible, as was suggested in the discussion of *Naccarato v. Grob*, supra, that courts adopted the similar-locality rule in part as a way of raising standards in medically backward but otherwise similar communities?

3. *A National Standard for Specialists.* The next step in the rollback of the locality rule was the adoption of a national standard for specialists, as in *Naccarato* and *Shilkret.* This now seems to be the almost universal rule for board-certified specialists except where statutes have reintroduced a more localized standard. See, e.g., Jordan v. Bogner, 844 P.2d 664, 666 (Colo.1993) (en banc) ("a physician who holds himself or herself out as a specialist in a particular field of medicine is measured against a standard commensurate with that of a reasonable physician practicing in that specialty"; "[a] non-specialist physician must act consistently with the standards required of the medical profession in the community where he or she practices"); Grimes v. Green, 746 P.2d 978 (Idaho 1987) (under statute, outside obstetrician experts were required to show familiarity with the local standard in Twin Falls, which was said to deviate from national standard in use of amniocentesis); Robbins v. Footer, 553 F.2d 123 (D.C.Cir.1977) (obstetrician held to national standard). The cases on board-certified specialists typically emphasize the standardization of training and the national certification exam. Does the Restatement rule (see note 8 in *Shilkret*) suggest that specialists of other kinds (e.g., self-styled ones) should also be expected to meet national standards? Should a board-certified family practitioner in an under-doctored rural community be deemed a specialist subject to a national standard of care?

Certain subspecialists have been found to use more resources in treating comparable patients than general internists, who in turn used somewhat more resources than family physicians. Greenfield et al., Variations in Resource Utilization Among Medical Specialties and Systems of Care, 267 J.A.M.A. 1624 (1992). Does this suggest that consumers contract for different levels of intensity of care, as well as different levels of qualification, in choosing their physicians? Does the law conceptualize the transaction in this way? (Note that managed-care plans usually put some limits on patient choice.) Can a plaintiff avoid the lower standard of care by alleging a generalist's negligence in failing to refer to a specialist, if one was available?

To what standard should a recent medical graduate be held? In Centman v. Cobb, 581 N.E.2d 1286 (Ind.App.1991), interns and residents were deemed "practitioners of medicine bound to possess and exercise the reasonable degree of skill, care, and diligence generally possessed, exercised and accepted by members of their profession, including physicians with unlimited licenses, who practice in the same or similar localities."

4. *Current Status with Respect to General Practitioners.* As the *Shilkret* opinion notes, there is something of a trend toward the abandonment of the locality rule even for general practitioners. In Hall v. Hilbun, 466 So.2d 856 (Miss.1985), the Mississippi Supreme Court extended to the national boundaries an earlier holding widening the relevant locality to the entire state plus a reasonable distance beyond. The court's new "competence-based duty of care" was described as follows:

> Each physician may with reason and fairness be expected to possess or have reasonable access to such medical knowledge as is commonly possessed [by] or reasonably available to minimally competent physicians in the same specialty or general field of practice throughout the United States, to have a realistic understanding of the limitations on his or her knowledge or competence, and, in general, to exercise minimally adequate medical judgment. Beyond that, each physician has a duty to have a practical working knowledge of the facilities, equipment, resources (including personnel in health related fields and their general level of knowledge and competence), and options (including what specialized services or facili-

> ties may be available in larger communities, e.g., Memphis, Birmingham, Jackson, New Orleans, etc.) reasonably available to him or her as well as the practical limitations on same.
>
> In the care and treatment of each patient, each physician has a non-delegable duty to render professional services, consistent with that objectively ascertained minimally acceptable level of competence he may be expected to apply given the qualifications and level of expertise he holds himself out as possessing and given the circumstances of the particular case. The professional services contemplated within this duty concern the entire caring process, including but not limited to examination, history, testing, diagnosis, course of treatment, medication, surgery, follow-up, after-care and the like.

Id. at 871. The court added, "The content of the duty of care may be informed by local medical custom but never subsumed by it." Other cases setting aside the locality rule for general practitioners include Drs. Lane, Bryant, Eubanks & Dulaney v. Otts, 412 So.2d 254 (Ala.1982); Logan v. Greenwich Hosp. Ass'n, 465 A.2d 294 (Conn.1983).

The similar-locality rule for nonspecialists still survives in some places. See, e.g., Purtill v. Hess, 489 N.E.2d 867 (Ill.1986) (retaining locality rule but allowing outside expert to testify to minimum standards alleged to be uniform throughout the country); Gambill v. Stroud, 258 Ark. 766, 531 S.W.2d 945 (1976) (small-town surgeon); Annot., Modern Status of "Locality Rule" in Malpractice Action Against Physician Who Is Not a Specialist, 99 A.L.R.3d 1133 (1980). How would you argue for preserving the locality rule in response to the arguments for eliminating it?

The ABA Commission, in its 1977 report cited earlier in this chapter (at 852), recommended retention of the locality rule for nonspecialists, and a number of state legislatures, responding to the 1970s' "crisis," enacted statutory definitions of the standard of care that preserved the locality rule in some form. E.g., the Florida legislation reproduced supra; La. Rev. Stat. § 9:2794 (1997) ("similar locality" rule preserved for nonspecialists); N.C. Gen. Stat. § 90–21.12 (1997) (no liability unless care "was not in accordance with the standards of practice among members of the same health care profession with similar training and experience situated in the same or similar communities at the time of the alleged act giving rise to the cause of action").

5. *Who May Testify?* Note that the locality rule has an evidentiary as well as a substantive thrust, since the competence of an expert to testify turns on his familiarity with the standard in question. (Recall earlier discussion of rules and legislation on the qualifications of expert witnesses.) In *Hall v. Hilbun*, supra, at 873–75, the court, in addition to adopting a national "competence-based" standard, held that any qualified medical expert could testify in Mississippi, provided he was made familiar (perhaps through a "properly predicated and phrased hypothetical question") with the "facilities, resources, services and options available." Many other cases also involve an intertwining of the evidentiary and the substantive issues. See, e.g., First Commercial Trust Company v. Rank, 915 S.W.2d 262 (Ark.1996) (emergency medicine physician from Panama City, Fla., held qualified to testify as an expert on family practitioner's diagnosis of child abuse in Hot Springs, Ark., under statute setting standard as that for "the same type of practice or specialty in the [same or] similar locality"); Medlin v. Crosby, 583 So.2d 1290 (Ala.1991) (construing statute defining who is a specialist for purpose of determining who can testify against another specialist; board-certified internist permitted to testify on standard of care in emergency rooms, in which both expert and defendant family care specialist practiced). See also Annot., 37 A.L.R.3d 420 (1972).

6. *The Problem of Limited Facilities.* Do local circumstances matter at all anymore where the locality rule has been dispensed with? In *Hall v. Hilbun*, supra, at 872–73, the Mississippi court, in adopting its national "competence-based duty of care" for physicians, offered what it called a "resources-based caveat":

> [W]e regard that there remains a core of validity to the premises of the old locality rule.
>
> For reasons well known to all, the facilities, equipment, health care personnel, and other such resources reasonably available to Mississippi's physicians vary from community to community. * * *
>
> Because of these differences in facilities, equipment, etc., what a physician may reasonably be expected to do in the treatment of a patient in rural Humphreys County or Greene County may vary from what a physician in Jackson may be able to do. A physician practicing in Noxubee County, for example, may hardly be faulted for failure to perform a CAT scan when the necessary facilities and equipment are not reasonably available. In contradistinction, objectively reasonable expectations regarding the physician's knowledge, skill, capacity for sound medical judgment and general competence are, consistent with his field of practice and the facts and circumstances in which the patient may be found, *the same everywhere.*

One of the cases which started the present trend toward judicial abolition of the old locality rule, Pederson v. Dumouchel, 72 Wash.2d 73, 431 P.2d 973 (1967), perceived that the quality of care a physician was obligated to render should be consistent

> with the medical and professional *means* available in those centers that are readily accessible for appropriate treatment of the patient.

Another such case, Brune v. Belinkoff, 354 Mass. 102, 235 N.E.2d 793 (1968), similarly permits consideration of "the medical resources available to the physician".

Justice Hawkins spoke closer to home in his separate opinion in [King v. Murphy, 424 So.2d 547, 551 n. 1 (Miss.1982)]:

> . . . [S]mall town practitioners whose daily practice requires them to treat patients in what might be deemed less than ideal circumstances should not be penalized or obligated to . . . utilize the same equipment of a medical specialist in a metropolitan hospital.

some courts still

As a result of its resources-based component, the physician's non-delegable duty of care is this: given the circumstances of each patient, each physician has a duty to use his or her knowledge and therewith treat through maximum reasonable medical recovery, each patient, with such reasonable diligence, skill, competence, and prudence as are practiced by minimally competent physicians in the same specialty or general field of practice throughout the United States, who have available to them the same general facilities, services, equipment and options.

7. *Assessment.* Is there any doubt that the trend to national standards is both wise and inevitable? Does (or did) the locality rule serve any purpose other than to protect backward practices? What additional facts might you wish to know about a locality besides those that the courts have treated as relevant? Would efficiency analysis focus on other factors?

Should it matter whether an area is affluent or not? Perhaps you are offended by the idea that a court might countenance medical standards that vary according to patients' ability to pay. (Whatever your policy preference, should tort law be shaped by judges to fit their own or their perception of the public's tolerance for inequity?) Despite concerns one might have about ratifying second-class medical care, the reality may be that an area has fewer physicians per capita than other areas and that those few doctors are unable to give high-quality care without denying care to some patients altogether. Moreover, financial resources may be lacking to provide what would otherwise be routine precautions, and physicians may be overworked to the extent that they cannot keep current in all phases of their practice. See generally Karlson & Erwin, Medical Malpractice: Informed Consent to the Locality Rule, 12 Ind.L.Rev. 653 (1979). In these circumstances, would a locality rule of some kind make sense? Do the various new formulations of the legal standard of care leave adequate room to defend physicians based on the prevailing circumstances?

Ironically, despite the alleged unfairness of holding all physicians to the same standard, rural physicians are sued less often than their urban counterparts. Indeed, "urbanization" has been a major predictor of claims frequency and severity.

NOTES AND QUESTIONS ON THE TORT LIABILITIES OF HOSPITALS

1. *Standard of Care.* Does the *Shilkret* case mean that all accredited hospitals are subject to the same national standard? Should expert testimony be required to establish that standard? Or is the JCAHO accreditation manual the appropriate source? See Van Iperen v. Van Bramer, 392 N.W.2d 480 (Iowa 1986) (a case from the same state as *Dickinson v. Mailliard,* quoted in *Shilkret*; holding that violation of an accrediting standard was not negligence per se because standard not "self-authenticating"). What if state regulators are less demanding than the accreditors? How should unaccredited hospitals be treated? See generally Annot., Locality Rule as

Governing Hospital's Standard of Care to Patient and Expert's Competency to Testify Thereto, 36 A.L.R.3d 440 (1971).

Louisiana expressly rejects a local or community standard of care for hospitals, applying a more general reasonableness test based on the conditions and circumstances of each case. See, e.g., Keyworth v. Southern Baptist Hosps., 524 So.2d 56 (La.App.1988); Shackleford v. State Dep't of Health & Human Resources, 534 So.2d 38 (La.App.1988).

2. *Facilities and Equipment.* Suits against hospitals may focus on failures to provide adequate equipment, etc. See, e.g., Washington v. Washington Hosp. Center, 579 A.2d 177 (D.C.App.1990) (late–1987 anesthesia injury that could have been prevented if cardiac monitor had been present in OR; held that national standard requiring monitor was established by expert from Los Angeles, 1986 *J.A.M.A.* article, 1986 guidelines of professional society, and department chairman's early–1987 request to hospital for equipment, citing new standard of care); Lauro v. Travelers Ins. Co., 261 So.2d 261, 50 A.L.R.3d 1130 (La.App.1972) (no duty to have latest equipment, which would allegedly have prevented incorrect diagnosis of breast cancer). Can allowance be made for such circumstances as limited demand for particular equipment or such barriers to its acquisition as certificate-of-need regulation? See Smith v. Hospital Auth. of Terrell Cty., 288 S.E.2d 715 (Ga.App.1982) ("a hospital owes to its patients only the duty of exercising ordinary care to furnish equipment and facilities reasonably suited to the uses intended and such as are in general use under the same, or similar, circumstances in hospitals in the area"). There may be a duty to inform or transfer a patient if facilities are not adequate to treat his condition properly. E.g., Hernandez v. Smith, 552 F.2d 142 (5th Cir.1977) (14–bed hospital not equipped for cesarean delivery).

3. *Vicarious Liability.* Many suits against hospitals are based on vicarious liability, thus calling attention to the standards applicable to the hospital's employees, who may themselves be professionals subject to their own standard of care. The standards governing nonphysician health professionals will be the subject of notes concluding this section.

Confronting Trade-offs Between Cost and Quality

NOTES AND QUESTIONS ON CASES INVOLVING A FAILURE TO DIAGNOSE

1. The plaintiffs in *Kramer v. Milner*, *Helling v. Carey*, and *Gates v. Jensen* each claimed that the defendant doctor had negligently failed to make an accurate diagnosis, with dire consequences. Such failure-to-diagnose claims are increasing in frequency and have proved troublesome for courts, which are more comfortable policing errors in the performance of discrete procedures—errors of commission (not omission) having a straightforward causal connection to the patient's injury. In cases involving a failure to diagnose, the issue is apt to be whether there was a culpable error of omission or simply a mistaken judgment based on benefit/cost analysis or possibly on inconsistent professional standards relating to resource use.

Failure-to-diagnose cases typically involve ambulatory care either in a physician's office or in a hospital emergency department. In either setting, the physician sees each individual patient among many others with a variety of complaints. In the nature of things, the physician may fail to take each complaint with total seriousness or to run down every possibility suggested by the patient's symptoms. Although recent estimates suggest that only .04 percent of ambulatory visits lead to adverse events, there are as many as 100 times more ambulatory visits than hospital stays, so that even more preventable morbidity and mortality may result from ambulatory care than from care in hospitals. Most of these injuries result from failures to diagnose, which may result in turn from inattention (e.g., in reading x-rays or test results) or from errors of omission (e.g., in failing to order additional tests or more costly scans and images).

This kind of litigation promises to expand further as patients increasingly seek to attribute physician failures to diagnose their problems to the new influence of managed care. And, indeed, the new methods of paying plans and providers may discourage more than just unnecessary testing, creating real quality problems as capitated physicians reduce both the time spent with each patient and the resources expended on tests and referrals to specialists. (As a variant on the failure-to-diagnose theme, recall the failure to refer to a cardiologist in *Shea v. Esensten*, reproduced in chapter 2(§C).) On the other hand, the whole point of introducing managed care was to address marginal benefit/marginal cost issues and to get away from the old notion (detectable, for example, in the *Helling* case) that resources should be invested whenever a patient might possibly benefit. Do you now see the huge challenge facing the medical malpractice system as it tries to sort out valid from invalid claims for physicians' failures to diagnose relatively rare but serious diseases that are notoriously difficult to detect at reasonable cost in populations of many patients presenting similar symptoms? The large question that still lacks a clear answer is how the legal system can make allowances for cost considerations and particularly for the possibility that a patient's ex ante choice of a health plan implied acceptance of a certain degree of risk. Unless notions of contract law can somehow be introduced into these cases, the situation will continue to be highly unstable, and the legal environment will continue to be hostile to appropriate as well as inappropriate economizing on health services.

The two conditions that are the most common subject of claims for failure to diagnose are probably breast cancer and myocardial infarction. For a revealing graphic illustration of alternative, economics-driven diagnostic options in evaluating patients with shortness of breath for myocardial infarction, see C. Havighurst, Health Care Choices: Private Contracts as Instruments of Health Reform 259–64 (1995).

2. *What to Do about a "Lost Chance."* A recent development that adds to the potential threat of failure-to-diagnose cases is the willingness of some courts to award damages for a so-called "lost chance." Even if medical negligence is established in a particular case, there may remain a question whether it made any difference in the outcome. Negligent failure to diagnose cancer, for example, may be inconsequential because treatment is often ineffective in preventing death. Many courts, however, now routinely allow damages where a plaintiff establishes causation in the sense of a substantial "lost chance" of recovery. See Annot., Medical Malpractice: "Loss of Chance" Causality, 54 A.L.R.4th 10 (1987); King, Causation, Valuation, and Chance in Personal Injury Torts Involving Preexisting Conditions and Future Consequences, 90 Yale L.J. 1353 (1981) (seminal article leading many courts to find compensation for injuries that might have been, but were not clearly, avoidable by proper diagnosis and treatment); Delaney v. Cade, 873 P.2d 175 (Kan.1994) (extensive opinion relying on King article and recognizing cause of action for lost chance of recovery and setting forth standards of proof for such claims). Arguably, the loss of chance cases simply built on relaxed notions of causation that had infiltrated tort law well before King's seminal article. Nevertheless, although courts were already familiar with proportionate liability and had rejected all-or-nothing approaches to plaintiffs' contributory negligence, recognition of recovery for a lost chance apparently required Professor King's advocacy. At least part of the barrier to recognizing lost chances was a general judicial preference for crisp notions of active causation and discomfort with statistical notions. See, e.g., Brennan, Causal Chains and Statistical Links: The Role of Scientific Uncertainty in Hazardous Substance Litigation, 73 Cornell L. Rev. 469 (1988) (observing that judges have long avoided or misunderstood evidence relating to probabilities).

There is a split over how great the chance must be before its loss is compensable. The court in *Delaney v. Cade*, supra, at 183–85, described the various doctrines as follows (itself adopting the "middle ground" approach):

> Although a variety of approaches has emerged among jurisdictions which have examined the loss of chance theory, three general approaches are utilized by courts confronted with the theory and the standard of proof to be adopted: (1) the all or nothing approach; (2) the relaxed standard of proof approach; and (3) the any loss of chance approach.
>
> The all or nothing approach, or traditional approach, is that approach followed by jurisdictions which refuse to recognize the "lost chance" as a distinct and compensable injury. These jurisdictions, which are now probably the minority, strictly adhere to the principle that the plaintiff must prove that the defendant's negligence was the proximate cause of the injury or death suffered by the plaintiff. As such, the plaintiff must establish that there existed a better-than even chance of avoiding the physical injury or resulting death. If the plaintiff meets this burden, compensation is awarded for the particular injury or wrongful death suffered, not the lost chance of a better recovery or survival. Thus, these jurisdictions refuse to relax the traditional view of proximate cause in medical malpractice actions. * * *
>
> The relaxed standard of proof approach, commonly referred to as the "substantial chance" approach, requires plaintiff to present evidence that a

substantial or significant chance of survival or better recovery was lost. If plaintiff meets this initial threshold, the causation issue is submitted to the jury, using the traditional proximate cause standard to ascertain whether, in fact, the alleged malpractice resulted in the loss of a substantial or significant chance. Thus, the jury must find by a preponderance of the evidence that the alleged negligence was the proximate cause of the lost chance, but the lost chance itself need only be a substantial or significant chance, for a better result, absent any malpractice, rather than a greater than 50 percent chance of a better result.

An example of this approach is found in Herskovits v. Group Health, 99 Wash.2d 609, 664 P.2d 474 (1983). In *Herskovits*, representatives of decedent's estate brought a medical malpractice action against defendant for failing to properly diagnose decedent's lung cancer. Defendant's negligence led to a six-month delay in the detection of decedent's cancer. Expert testimony opined that plaintiff lost a 14 percent chance of surviving five years. [T]he Washington Supreme Court held that compensation for the loss of 14 percent was appropriate because "[t]o decide otherwise would be a blanket release from liability for doctors and hospitals any time there was less than a 50 percent chance of survival, regardless of how flagrant the negligence." * * *

At the other end of the spectrum is the third, or any loss of chance, approach. Under this approach, the courts permit the jury to determine the loss of chance of survival or better recovery no matter how small such chance may be. Thus, plaintiffs are not required to meet any threshold but merely must prove that there was some chance, even one percent, of a better recovery. If the plaintiff is able to provide evidence that the defendant's conduct resulted in any lost chance, even a de minimis amount, summary judgment would be precluded and the case submissible to the jury.

Under this approach, courts generally base their determination on an increased risk of harm approach as stated in Restatement (Second) of Torts § 323(a) (1963).

Do cases recognizing that the loss of a chance of survival or recovery is a real injury that should be compensable in order to deter negligent diagnosis carry a risk of overdeterrence—that is, of inducing overspending on marginally beneficial (in a statistical sense) tests and other measures? Is the problem reduced by allowing damages only in proportion to the chance lost? Two distinct methods of calculating damages have been described as follows in *Delaney v. Cade*, supra, at 187:

> The first approach, and the minority view among applicable jurisdictions, is the valuation approach. Under this method, the court or jury is left without instruction or guidance in ascertaining the appropriate damage figure. Instead, the trier of fact is permitted to use its experience, judgment, and common sense in determining the appropriate value for the lost chance. Although this method is the simplest because the introduction of statistical evidence is unnecessary, the goal of reaching some degree of precision in determining the loss allocation is lacking.

The second and most logical approach is the proportional damage approach recommended by Professor King. See McKellips v. Saint Francis Hosp., Inc. 741 P.2d 467 (Okla.1987). Under the proportional damage approach, the amount recoverable equals the total sum of damages ordinarily recovered for the underlying injury or death multiplied by the percent of lost chance. Because this method requires expert medical testimony in ascertaining the appropriate (percent) amount of damages recoverable, courts employing this method eliminate the risks of compensating the plaintiff for anything other than the value of the lost chance.

PROBLEM: CUSTOMARY PRACTICE AND FETAL MONITORING IN A MANAGED-CARE PLAN

The administrator of a prepaid group-practice HMO reports to you that her plan's physicians feel compelled to provide electronic fetal monitoring (EFM) for all pregnant women because that is the standard of care prevailing in the community. The physicians are persuaded that this practice is not good medicine because EFM has been shown to be of no benefit in low-risk pregnancies; in addition, EFM carries some risks to the fetus and increases the rate of cesarean deliveries. See Booth, When Medical High Tech Isn't Necessarily Better, Wash. Post, Oct. 29, 1991, p. 1 ("nine large, controlled studies done in the 1980s found that for most patients in most cases, there is little or no difference in the outcome of a pregnancy whether a fetus is monitored electronically or with a stethoscope"; yet EFM "is now the standard of care at most settings"); Huber, Medical Experts and the Ghost of Galileo, Law & Contemp. Probs., Summer 1991, p. 119, at 140–54 (arguing, with technical evidence, that liability fears distort obstetrical care); Leveno et al., A Prospective Comparison of Selective and Universal Electronic Fetal Monitoring in 34,995 Pregnancies, 315 New Eng.J.Med. 615 (1986). A few of the physicians are impressed by findings that continuous EFM is of no benefit even in high-risk patients as compared to periodic auscultation (listening to the fetal heart rate with a special stethoscope). See Luthy et al., A Randomized Trial of Electronic Fetal Monitoring in Preterm Labor, 69 Obstetrics & Gynecology 687 (1987).

Assume that the custom in the local community, with a relatively upscale population and heavily supplied with obstetricians, is to use EFM in every case. The standard is different, however, in some similar communities around the nation. On the legal standard of care, see Schifrin, Weissman & Wiley, Electronic Fetal Monitoring and Obstetrical Malpractice, 13 Law, Med. & Health Care 100 (1985) (advising general use of EFM); Gilfix, Electronic Fetal Monitoring: Physician Liability and Informed Consent, 10 Am.J.L. & Med. 31 (1984) (arguing against regarding EFM as standard).

The administrator reports that, after listening to those physicians who still regard the case against EFM's efficacy as unproven, she is persuaded that continuous EFM is not worth its cost. Accordingly, she asks you to consider how the HMO can go about altering its EFM practice without paying a malpractice claim whenever a jury, advised that a departure from customary practice has occurred, thinks that a bad outcome might have been prevented. You are aware of the difficulty of defending such failure-to-diagnose cases, where a jury may be sensitive that not everything possible was done and willing to award damages for a loss of a chance at a good outcome. What legal arguments or malpractice defenses might work? Would you argue, for example, for a kind of reverse similar-locality rule, allowing evidence of *less* demanding standards in other similar communities to be introduced? How about arguing for a reverse *Helling* rule, allowing the court to rule as a matter of law that the local standard is uneconomically and unscientifically demanding? What formulations of the physician's duty would provide the best prospects for a favorable verdict? Is this an appropriate case for the doctrine permitting a practitioner to adhere to the standards of a "respectable minority" that might exist within the profession? See Bovbjerg, The Medical Malpractice Standard of Care: HMOs and Customary Practice, 1975 Duke L.J. 1375 (arguing for a variation on this doctrine that would look to "HMO custom"). Can the HMO's limited financial resources be invoked by a defendant HMO physician as a circumstance possibly justifying his economizing move? Is the HMO itself potentially liable? (See chapter 8(§§ A & B).) Could you reasonably hope to resolve the HMO's problem by contract? Would you propose offering the patient the option of paying for EFM out of pocket in cases where the plan does not cover it?

Liability for Defective Products

Porter v. Rosenberg

District Court of Appeal of Florida, Fourth District, 1995.
650 So.2d 79.

■ PARIENTE, JUDGE.

Appellant, Kay Porter (plaintiff), a recipient of an allegedly defective breast implant, appeals the dismissal of her strict liability count against appellee, Robert Kent Rosenberg, M.D. (physician) who implanted the device, urging the court to extend the doctrine of strict liability to physicians. She claims that a physician who places a breast implant in a patient should be held strictly liable as any other distributor or seller of the product.

* * * The rationale for applying strict liability to distributors is that:

> Retailers like manufacturers are engaged in the business of distributing goods to the public. They are an integral part of the overall producing and marketing enterprise that should bear the cost of injuries resulting from defective products.

Adobe Bldg. Ctrs.[, Inc. v. Reynolds, 403 So.2d 1033,] 1037 (Hurley, J., concurring), citing Traynor, J., in Vandermark v. Ford Motor Co., 391 P.2d 168, 171 (Cal.1964).

Plaintiff argues that the rationale for imposing strict liability on distributors should apply in this case. Where a physician actually transfers the product to the patient, thereby profiting from the distribution of a product, plaintiff asserts the physician should share in the losses to a consumer when that product is found to be defective.

The fundamental purpose underlying the doctrine of strict products liability is to further public safety in the use of consumer goods, by imposing liability without fault upon entities that have the ability to adequately compensate the injured party, distribute the risk of loss, and deter further production of defective products. Courts, however, have been reluctant to extend strict liability to a health care provider who utilizes the product incidental to its primary function of providing medical services.

In explaining the rationale for treating health care providers differently, the Pennsylvania appellate court in Cafazzo v. Central Medical Health Servs., Inc., 635 A.2d 151, 154 (1993), explained:

> Physicians, like hospitals, are providers of medical services. The physician's expertise lies in the diagnosis, treatment and cure of illness, not in the research or development of prosthetics of devices used to aid medical diagnosis or treatment. A physician is not in the business of selling products, but rather is in the profession of providing medical services. Products such as the prosthetic device in this case are supplied and utilized only as needed to deliver the professional medical service. They are incidental, or integral, to a physician's service, but they are not the focus of the physician's delivery of health care.

In many cases the health care provider is in fact more akin to the consumer or user of the product, especially where the product is not transferred to the patient but utilized incidental to the provision of medical services. * * *

We recognize, however, that there are instances when a physician transfers a product to a patient via a medical procedure in which the physician may be performing a role that has some attributes similar to a retailer or other seller of a product. The manufacturer may be relying on the physician to promote its particular product within the chain of distribution to the general public. We further note that there is a qualitative difference between a physician distributing breast implants through implantation and utilizing a defective metal pin in a hip reconstruction. In the case of the breast implant, the procedure is being performed to implant the product; in the case of the metal pin, the use of the pin is incidental to the main procedure.

Nonetheless, we cannot ignore the fact that even with a product, such as a breast implant, a physician is exercising his or her professional judgment in determining what medical procedure to perform and then in selecting the appropriate product to utilize in connection with the procedure. The provision of the product is integrally related to the professional services and skill offered by the medical care provider. Compare Thomas v. St. Joseph Hosp., 618 S.W.2d 791 (Tex.Civ.App.1981) (where provision of product such as hospital gown is unrelated to the essential professional relationship, strict liability may be applied.)

When a physician is engaged in providing services involving the exercise of medical judgment, causes of action arising from personal injuries or death in connection with the rendering of medical services are governed by legislative enactment. Ch. 766, Fla.Stat. (1993). Although an implant may be considered a product for purposes of strict liability, we must determine whether the adoption of the comprehensive medical malpractice statute precludes all other common law theories against physicians, hospitals or other health care providers not filed in compliance with the statute, including a strict liability action for a defective product. The medical malpractice act sets forth the method and manner for bringing a cause of action, both procedurally and substantively. An injured person would be impermissibly circumventing the requirements and restrictions of the medical malpractice statute by selectively claiming that the physician was only acting in his role as a distributor of a product when in fact the distribution was incidental to the provision of medical services.

* * * [W]e conclude that whether or not a plaintiff may bring an action against a physician, hospital, or other health care provider for strict liability depends upon the essence of the physician-patient relationship for the particular transaction. If the medical services could not have been rendered without utilizing the product, then strict liability does not apply. If the predominant purpose of the physician-patient relationship for that transaction is the provision of medical services based upon the physician's medical judgment, skill, or expertise, the malpractice statute applies and strict liability is inapplicable.

The fact that the physician or health care provider is not solely or primarily in the business of distributing products is not the determinative factor for application of strict liability as long as distributing products is part of its business. *See* Restatement (Second) of Torts § 402A, cmt. f (1977). Therefore, if distributing products is part of the health care provider's business and the sales or distribution aspect in the particular transaction between the health care provider and the patient predominates over the services aspect an action in strict liability may lie against the health care provider.[2]

Nevertheless, we decline to extend the doctrine of strict liability under the circumstances of this case. In her complaint, plaintiff has sued multiple defendants from manufacturers to distributors of the breast implant on multiple theories including strict liability. We perceive of no overriding public policy argument which would justify an obvious circumvention of the medical malpractice statute and an extension of strict liability to physicians under the circumstances presented here.

AFFIRMED.

2. Such examples might include a nutrition doctor selling diet products or a dentist selling electric toothbrushes. Some manufacturers may rely solely or mainly on utilizing health care professionals for distribution of their products and the health care professional may rely on selling the products as part of its business as additional profit separate from provision of other medical services.

Kozup v. Georgetown University

United States District Court, District of Columbia, 1987.
663 F.Supp. 1048, aff'd in part & vacated in part, 851 F.2d 437 (D.C.Cir.1988).

■ FLANNERY, DISTRICT JUDGE.

* * * On December 26, 1982, Susan Kozup was admitted to the High Risk Obstetrical Unit of Georgetown University Hospital, when it appeared that delivery of her child would involve complications. On January 9, 1983, Mrs. Kozup went into labor. Matthew was born at 9:15 a.m. on January 10, 1983, and shortly thereafter, Georgetown began giving Matthew blood transfusions for hypovolemia, a condition associated with premature birth. Over the course of two days, January 12 and 13, Matthew received three transfusions which were contaminated with the virus now known to transmit Acquired Immune Deficiency Syndrome (AIDS).

Defendant ARC [The American Red Cross] supplied the contaminated blood to Georgetown. According to ARC records, the blood had been donated in October, 1982, by an individual who subsequently developed AIDS, and died from opportunistic infections associated with the disease. At the time of his donation, however, the donor was in good health.

* * * On July 10, 1986, Matthew died, allegedly from complications related to infection with the AIDS virus.

Plaintiffs filed the present action * * * alleging negligence, breach of implied warranty, strict liability, [and other causes of action.]

* * *

In December, 1982, the Center for Disease Control reported a case of "Possible Transfusion–Associated AIDS—California." In that case, an infant received blood platelets under circumstances similar to those surrounding Matthew Kozup's birth, and subsequently was diagnosed as suffering from AIDS. The infant did not fit into any of the previously noted high risk categories for AIDS, and thus the transfusions he received became the focus of the medical community's attention.

In January, 1983, a Workgroup to Identify Opportunities for the Prevention of AIDS was convened * * *. At the meeting, a consensus was reached for the proposition that members of high risk groups for AIDS should somehow be excluded from donating blood. However, the Report indicates that "no consensus was reached as to the best method for doing this."

* * *

On January 13, 1983, the ARC, the American Association of Blood Bankers, and the Council of Community Blood Banks issued a "Joint Statement on AIDS Related to Transfusion." The Joint Statement concluded that "evidence [was] inconclusive" as to the hypothesis that AIDS was transmissible by blood. The hypothesis was referred to as a "possibility, still unproven." * * *

On March 4, 1983, [a committee of the U.S. Public Health Service] issued its promised recommendations for donor screening, which paralleled those issued weeks later by the Bureau of Biologics ("BoB") of the Food and Drug Administration. Both recommended that, prior to donating blood, donors be given pamphlets describing high risk groups, so that they could self-screen based on the information in the pamphlets. The BoB recommended improved educational programs for blood bank personnel, so that they could better assist donors in recognizing the symptoms of AIDS. Neither recommended use of surrogate tests. These guidelines were promptly implemented by the ARC.

In April, 1984, scientists identified the virus HTLV–III as the cause of AIDS. By May, 1985, an enzyme-linked immunosorbent assay (ELISA) test was made available, which screens for the antibodies sensitive to HTLV–III. Once it was available, the Center for Disease Control issued guidelines for implementing the ELISA test. This laboratory test has proven 98.6% effective in detecting exposure to AIDS. When coupled with a second test, the Western Blot Analysis, the rate of detection for exposure to AIDS rises to 100%.

With this chronology in mind, the court can now turn to the various theories of liability presented by plaintiffs.

* * *

V. STRICT LIABILITY IN TORT AND IMPLIED WARRANTIES

Plaintiffs seek relief under the theory of strict liability in tort for an unreasonably dangerous product, under the Restatement (Second) of Torts § 402A. They also allege a cause of action for breach of the implied warranties of merchantability and fitness for a particular purpose under the Uniform Commercial Code * * *. Both these theories are rooted in the conception of blood as a product and the ARC's provision of blood to Georgetown as a sale of a product. These conceptions are threshold requirements for application of the strict liability theories which plaintiffs allege in Counts V and VI of their Amended Complaint.

The District of Columbia's Court of Appeals has held that "the current doctrines of implied warranty and strict liability in tort are but two labels for the same legal right and remedy, as the governing principles are identical." Cottom v. McGuire Funeral Service, Inc., 262 A.2d 807, 808 (D.C.App.1970), cited in Fisher v. Sibley Memorial Hospital, 403 A.2d 1130, 1133 (D.C.App.1979). Thus, plaintiffs' two separate Counts may be viewed together in determining whether summary judgment for defendants is appropriate. Largely for the reasons stated in *Fisher,* supra, summary judgment for both Georgetown and the ARC is proper.

In *Fisher,* plaintiff sought relief from a hospital for infection with hepatitis as a result of a blood transfusion supplied by the hospital. Plaintiff alleged the same two causes of action alleged by plaintiffs here. The District of Columbia Court of Appeals rejected plaintiff's claims with respect to blood, finding that "characterizing blood plasma as a product governed by strict tort liability is as unnatural as forcing a blood transfusion into the commercial sales mold." Neither theory was justified by public policy, the court found.

The court noted that, rather than being an unreasonably dangerous product, giving rise to strict tort liability, blood should instead be viewed as unavoidably unsafe because the "scientific inability to screen all carriers of viral hepatitis despite due care," combined with the "public interest in assuring the ready availability of blood," compelled such a result. Critical to the court's holding was "the difficulty of detecting hepatitis in blood given the current state of medical knowledge." In addition, the court noted that under a strict liability regime, "the hospital, no matter how careful, would be held responsible, virtually as an insurer, if the patient were harmed as a result of impure blood." For these reasons, the court concluded that strict liability theories should not be applied to a hospital's provision of blood to its patients.

* * * [T]here is no principled basis on which to limit *Fisher*'s holding to hospitals alone. The *Fisher* case represents a reasoned public policy decision which applies with equal if not greater force to the facts of this case, and to the ARC as a defendant. Moreover, in searching for an appropriate public policy regarding liability of a blood bank for provision of blood to hospitals, the court should be guided by the fact that every state except one has barred such liability, based on a concern for the adequacy of the nation's blood supply. Rather than reaching a contrary result because the District of Columbia has no "blood shield statute," the court should clarify the *Fisher* holding to be coextensive with these 47 legislative and two judicial enactments of sound public policy.

To begin with, the scientific rationale for *Fisher* is squarely applicable here. The state of medical knowledge about AIDS at the time of Matthew's transfusion was even less advanced than was medical knowledge of hepatitis at the time of the *Fisher* opinion. There was not even a consensus of the medical community as to the fact that AIDS was transmitted by a blood-borne viral agent, much less identification of that agent or of a test to screen it out of the blood supply. Thus, the *Fisher* court's emphasis on the "scientific inability to screen all carriers ... despite due care" as a reason for refusing to label blood "unreasonably dangerous" compels a similar result with respect to the ARC's provision of blood prior to the development of the ELISA test for exposure to AIDS. It is relevant that the court in *Fisher* applied Comment K to § 402A of the Restatement (Second) of Torts, which excludes from strict liability:

> those products, drugs in particular, which in the present state of human knowledge, are incapable of being made safe for their intended and ordinary use (i.e. rabies vaccine), but where existing medical experience justifies the marketing and use of the product despite the risk.

This language is in no way limited to hospitals as providers, and applies equally cogently to the ARC in the context of AIDS in blood in 1983.

The inability to detect the "defect" in blood was also one of the *Fisher* court's grounds for rejecting plaintiff's conception of the provision of blood by plaintiff hospital as a sale. The court plainly held that "the furnishing of blood is more in the nature of a service than of a sale of goods," in part because to hold otherwise would force the supplier of blood into the role of insurer, which the court declined to do. This reasoning again applies equally well to the ARC as to hospitals.

In sum, there is nothing in the language of *Fisher* to suggest that the court would have reached a different result had the defendant been a blood bank and not a hospital. The policy considerations are all relevant to the case before this court, and compel summary judgment for both Georgetown and the ARC. This result is consonant with that of nearly every jurisdiction, and avoids the aberrational result that the ARC would be strictly liable in the District of Columbia for conduct that would not be actionable in 49 of our 50 states.

* * *

NOTES AND QUESTIONS ON LIABILITY FOR POOR–QUALITY BLOOD AND OTHER HEALTH CARE PRODUCTS

1. *Defective Medical Devices, etc.* Although the court in *Porter v. Rosenberg* rejected the plaintiff's strict-liability theory on the basis of legislation governing actions for medical malpractice, its opinion can be read as leaving the door open for future strict liability claims. In general, in drug-or device-related litigation, the physician is treated as a learned intermediary between the manufacturer of the drug or device and the patient. As such, the physician is responsible for using due care in prescribing or using the drug or device and for transmitting information regarding its risks and benefits to the patient. Does adherence to a negligence standard in suits against physicians and to a strict liability standard in suits against drug or device manufacturers make sense?

The principal cases highlight the choice between liability based on negligence and strict liability for health care providers supplying products for use in patient care and blood for transfusion purposes. Like physicians, hospitals are usually not liable, without more, for latent defects in products provided or in equipment. E.g., Ayyash v. Henry Ford Health Systems, 533 N.W.2d 353 (Mich.App.1995) (physician and hospital not liable for implanting defective joint, since essence of transaction was provision of service, not sale of product); North Miami Gen. Hosp. v. Goldberg, 520 So.2d 650 (Fla.App.1988) (strict liability inapplicable to hospital or physician using defective medical implement; hospital is consumer, not producer or distributor, of product). See also Annots., 100 A.L.R.3d 1205 (1980); 54 A.L.R.3d 258 (1974); 14 A.L.R.3d 1254 (1967). Although the principles governing liability for injuries caused by defective blood products were eventually determined largely by statute, the legal doctrines employed to impose liability in some blood cases have occasionally been adopted with respect to other services and products supplied to patients by hospitals. See, e.g., Karibjanian v. Thomas Jefferson Univ. Hosp., 717 F.Supp. 1081 (E.D.Pa.

1989) (hospital sued for exposing patient to radiology contrast agent; court refused to dismiss case because plaintiff might show that defective product was sold from hospital's inventory and was regularly supplied to other patients, making hospital more than an occasional seller and thus possibly subject to liability under Restatement (Second) of Torts § 402(a)); Skelton v. Druid City Hosp. Bd., 459 So.2d 818 (Ala.1984) (hospital held liable under implied warranty for injuries caused by defective reusable suturing needle despite claim that transaction was not a sale but a service); Thomas v. St. Joseph Hosp., 618 S.W.2d 791 (Tex.Civ.App.1981) (flammable hospital gown). But see Hector v. Cedars–Sinai Med. Center, 225 Cal.Rptr. 595 (Cal.App.1986) (no strict liability for hospital supplying defective heart pacemaker when surgeon selected product and hospital's 85% markup on it was represented not as a profit but as a cross-subsidy to other hospital operations).

2. *Blood Shield Statutes: Caveat Emptor.* Plaintiffs injured by defective blood products have uniformly sought to recover under legal theories that would not require them to establish the defendant's negligence. However, in the leading case of Perlmutter v. Beth David Hosp., 123 N.E.2d 792 (N.Y.1954), the claim that the defective blood breached implied warranties of fitness and merchantability under the Uniform Commercial Code was rejected on the ground that there was no sale, only a contract for the provision of services. Many other courts followed this lead in rejecting warranty claims and claims based on strict liability in tort. E.g., Roberts v. Suburban Hosp. Ass'n, 532 A.2d 1081 (Md.App.1987) (AIDS case; blood held a service, not a product carrying a warranty). A few courts, however, held hospitals liable for post-transfusion hepatitis under implied warranties or similar theories. E.g., Cunningham v. MacNeal Mem. Hosp., 266 N.E.2d 897 (Ill.1970) (relying on sale characterization and § 402A of the Restatement (Second) of Torts); Community Blood Bank, Inc. v. Russell, 196 So.2d 115 (Fla.1967) (sale); Hoffman v. Misericordia Hosp., 267 A.2d 867 (Pa. 1970) (implied warranty applied to service).

In every state in which a court adopted a non-fault-based theory allowing recovery for blood-transmitted diseases, however, the legislature rapidly reversed the court's decision. Indeed, as the *Kozup* court observes, by the end of the 1980's nearly every state had a "blood-shield" statute blocking one or more of the no-fault theories that might be advanced by plaintiffs in these cases. See Advincula v. United Blood Services, 678 N.E.2d 1009 (Ill.1996) (reversing lower court's construction of statute that had allowed jury to judge reasonableness of blood bank's practices in early days of AIDS crisis by other than professional standards, unless experts opined that standards themselves were negligent); Coffee v. Cutter Biological, 809 F.2d 191 (2d Cir.1987) (applying Connecticut statute to protect commercial manufacturers of blood products against strict liability for AIDS). Although some statutes might have been read to leave room for a new ground of recovery, many courts probably learned that pro-plaintiff adventurism in this field would almost certainly be met by legislative rebuke, as powerful hospital and blood lobbies obtained reenactment of the rule of caveat emptor. See, e.g., Faucheaux v. Alton Ochsner Med. Found.

Hosp. & Clinic, 468 So.2d 720 (La.App.1985) (recounting quick legislative response to narrow construction of blood-shield statute).

Do you agree with the rule of caveat emptor and its application in the *Kozup* case? How do you account for it? Is it a new version of charitable immunity? Are the statutes reversing judicial decisions to impose liability constitutional? Are they vulnerable as "special legislation"? No court has found a problem with these laws. E.g., McDonald v. Sacramento Med. Found. Blood Bank, 133 Cal.Rptr. 444 (Cal.App.1976) (ensuring blood supply is legitimate legislative purpose).

3. *The Profit Motive.* Among the reasons given for exempting blood suppliers from liability was the view that the product could not be made entirely risk-free. In addition, in the health sector, it is widely believed that nonprofit organizations, run by dedicated professionals, should not be subject to liability that they cannot entirely avoid by good practice. Many believe as well that blood is a qualitatively different kind of product that should not be treated as an ordinary article of commerce. Under this view, commercial firms should not be encouraged to participate in the industry, and donated blood is to be preferred to blood that is purchased from donors. Recall, in these connections, the *Community Blood Bank* case noted in chapters 3(§C) and 4(§B).

Reflecting attitudes of the kind described, some state legislation on the subject of liability discriminates between for-profit and nonprofit suppliers of blood or treats blood differently according to whether it was obtained from paid or volunteer donors. E.g., Idaho Code § 39–3702 (1993) (allowing damage suits under strict liability theory only against for-profit blood banks); Wash. Rev. Code Ann. § 70.54.120 (West 1992) (blood shield statute "shall not apply to any transaction in which the donor receives compensation"). The Washington statute just cited was held, however, not to imply that a commercial manufacturer of blood products from purchased blood should be strictly liable for HIV-infected blood. Rogers v. Miles Laboratories, Inc., 802 P.2d 1346 (Wash.1991) (en banc) ("There is nothing in the statutory language which suggests that the Legislature intended to distinguish between for-profit and nonprofit entities"; common law and Restatement (Second) of Torts held to impose liability only for failure to warn about unavoidably unsafe product).

For a well-known (though now dated) book-length comparison of the British and American blood-collection systems, noting the higher incidence of post-transfusion hepatitis in the more commercial U.S. system, see R. Titmuss, The Gift Relationship: From Human Blood to Social Policy (1971). Titmuss's attempt to draw from his findings broad conclusions critical of all commercial enterprise (Titmuss was a Fabian socialist) was criticized for failing to recognize the possible contribution of poorly designed liability rules (caveat emptor) to the U.S. problem of poor-quality blood. See Kessel, Transfused Blood, Serum Hepatitis, and the Coase Theorem, 17 J.L. & Econ. 265 (1974); Havighurst, Legal Responses to the Problem of Poor-Quality Blood, in Blood Policy: Issues and Alternatives 21 (D. Johnson ed. 1977).

4. *Negligence in Blood Collection, Testing, and Use*. Because strict-liability theories are almost totally barred in blood cases, plaintiffs have attempted to prove negligence in the collection, testing, or use of blood products. They have regularly encountered, however, the defense that, despite the bad outcome, the defendants' practices conformed to professional or industry standards. See, e.g., Doe v. Miles Laboratories, Inc., 927 F.2d 187 (4th Cir.1991) (blood clotting product held not "unreasonably dangerous" because it was extremely useful, there was no substitute for it, there was no scientific test capable of detecting HIV at the time of the contamination, and the risk of disease transmission was relatively small; the product was therefore not subject to strict liability; court also rejected a negligence theory because the donor screening and testing procedures argued for were not part of the standard of care at the time plaintiff received the blood product); Hoemke v. New York Blood Center, 912 F.2d 550 (2d Cir. 1990) (holding neither hospital nor blood center liable for failing to screen donors or test blood or for not having an established autologous blood donor program, since the incident occurred before AIDS was definitely linked to blood; noting that decision might have been different if incident had occurred even a short time later); Spann v. Irwin Memorial Blood Centers, 40 Cal.Rptr.2d 360, 364 (Cal.App.1995) (blood bank held to a professional standard of care as defined by custom and practice); Doe v. American Red Cross Blood Services, 377 S.E.2d 323, 326 (S.C.1989) (same).

Several courts, however, have refused to limit blood banks' liability to instances where they deviate from professional custom or local usage. E.g., Brown v. United Blood Services, 858 P.2d 391, 396–97 (Nev.1993) (blood bank conformed to the industry-wide standard of care and therefore could not be held liable for failing to adopt three procedures for detecting HIV-infected blood, but court noted plaintiff could have attempted to show that the industry standards were deficient); United Blood Services v. Quintana, 827 P.2d 509, 523–24 (Colo.1992) (although blood banks should be held to a professional standard of care, the plaintiff could attempt on remand to show that the blood banking community's standard of care was deficient); Snyder v. Mekhjian 582 A.2d 307, 313 (N.J.Super. 1990) (where HIV-infected blood was transfused in August 1984, summary judgment was precluded by questions of fact regarding the reasonableness of the defendant blood bank's conduct in collecting and distributing blood without using surrogate testing, regardless of whether it followed trade association's guidelines); Hernandez v. Nueces County Med. Soc'y Community Blood Bank, 779 S.W.2d 867 (Tex.App.1989) (blood bank's compliance with federal and published industry standards did not conclusively absolve it from liability for negligence, especially where evidence suggested blood bank lagged in adopting new screening procedures for hepatitis).

5. *Responding to the AIDS Crisis*. Some of the decisions just cited appear to have been driven by judicial impressions that the blood industry did not respond well in the early days of the AIDS crisis. The matter is one of continuing controversy. See, e.g., E. DePrince, Cry Bloody Murder: A Tale of Tainted Blood (1997) (hemophiliac's story); Institute of Medicine (IOM), HIV and the Blood Supply: An Analysis of Crisis Decisionmaking (1995). In fact, the short period from late 1982 to early 1984 featured many meetings by blood bankers, blood products manufacturers, etc., often with or in anticipation of meetings with FDA representatives. Were such meetings and the discussions and agreements produced therein sheltered from antitrust scrutiny by the *Noerr-Pennington* doctrine studied in chapter 4(§C)? Although it is unlikely that an antitrust case would be brought charging industry members with coordinating their interpretations of and responses to the emerging evidence, at least one case (subsequently settled) raised the question whether possible antitrust violations could be cited to support a claim of industry-wide joint and several liability, overcoming the hemophiliac plaintiff's problem of proving which blood fractionator's product caused his injury. In any event, the close cooperation among politically nervous bureaucrats and collaborating industry interests may have prevented independent competitive responses to the problem that would have saved numerous lives.

For an example of the concerns supporting the dominant view that liability is inappropriate in these cases, see the following from an opinion by a lower court judge in the *Advincula* case in Illinois, cited supra:

> We should focus in this case upon just how little we knew of AIDS in early 1984. What the majority sees today, relying on expert testimony aided by over a decade of hindsight, as reasonable responses to the threat to the blood supply, were at the time neither so reasonable nor apparent. For instance, contrary to the implication of the majority opinion, although by February 1984 the possibility of surrogate testing of blood was discussed and suggested by some people in the medical community, it was neither recommended nor required by any professional association or regulatory agency. In any event, the majority notes that surrogate testing for Hepatitis B is between 66 percent and 88 percent accurate in identifying potentially HIV infected blood. In a worst-case scenario, that would mean 34 out of 100 donors of blood who were HIV-positive would not have been screened out by surrogate testing. Even a best-case scenario would have resulted in the donation of a significant amount of HIV-positive blood. Dr. Francis acknowledged as much. Altruistic blood donors who honestly answered self-deferment questions might result in the same or better statistics, which is precisely the type of reasoning that the blood banking community was engaged in at the time. Given this, I fail to see the exalting of surrogate testing as having (*a*) been the panacea to the blood supply crisis, and (*b*) in hindsight, set the standard of care to which the blood banking industry should be held when no professional association or regulatory agency saw fit to so deem it. As our supreme court has stated in a related context, "medicine is not an exact science. It is rather a profession which involves the exercise of individual judgment within the framework of established procedures. Differences in opinion are consistent with the exercise of due care."

Advincula v. United Blood Services, 654 N.E.2d 644, 655 (Ill.App.1995) (dissenting opinion), rev'd, 678 N.E.2d 1009 (Ill.1996). What if the full record showed that government scientists recommended the implementation of "surrogate" testing (for the Hepatitis B core antibody, which was believed to be associated with HIV infection) in January of 1983 (see IOM, supra, at 106) but that members of the blood fractionation industry agreed among themselves both to delay FDA action to require testing (by establishing a Testing Study Group and delaying its report to the FDA until July 1984, by which time surrogate testing had become almost a moot issue) and not to engage in independent testing in a competitive effort to offer a safer product to consumers? Implementation of testing, while possibly yielding marginally safer products, would have entailed financial costs to industry members (both the costs of the testing itself and the loss of plasma already drawn from persons who would test positive for the antibody).

Ironically, the AIDS crisis might have been handled better by the FDA and other public health officials but for the government's earlier experience with "swine flu." Anticipating an epidemic that never materialized, public health officials took aggressive action, including a vaccine program that itself caused several deaths. Fearful of being seen to overreact again, officials were somewhat slow to acknowledge the AIDS danger and hesitant to act on less than solid evidence that its measures would work. See IOM, supra. Industry interests naturally encouraged this hesitancy.

6. *Incentives.* What difference would a different liability rule for blood products make? Are you satisfied with the performance of the health care system in dealing with the AIDS virus in the blood supply, as described here and in the *Kozup* case? Might it have performed better if liability were not based solely on fault?

Some useful insights on the deterrence benefits of a strict liability rule may be gained by considering how, in earlier days, the risk of post-transfusion hepatitis might have been reduced even if there was no scientific test that could conclusively establish blood's safety. (Current technology allows screening blood for Hepatitis B, but it was not always so, and Hepatitis C, affecting some 4.5 million persons with potentially fatal long-term effects, still presents a significant problem. See Search On To Find Hidden HCV in U.S., Blood Weekly, Mar. 23, 1998.) There are in fact many things that might be done by suppliers and providers fearful of bad outcomes, and it is not clear that the courts, using a negligence test, could successfully compel the right combination of practices. Blood collection using paid donors (which might actually be less costly than relying on less dependable volunteers) might focus on a small number of regular donors; payments to them might vary depending upon the donor's progress in establishing the quality of his blood; to reduce donors' incentives to conceal health problems, church groups, clubs, etc., might be encouraged to use blood donation as a fund-raising technique. Blood may be tested in several ways, but the decision whether the tests are worth their cost depends in part on the reliability of the blood collection system. In transfusion practice, there are again many possibilities for increasing safety, especially in avoiding unnecessary use of blood products. (At one time, blood was frequently used post-surgery just to restore color to the patient's cheeks.) Given the complexity of the task of procuring and using blood safely and efficiently, can public regulation, private standard-setting, and professional educational efforts, all backed by tort liability for negligence, accomplish all that is needed?

Would strict liability help further to improve the quality of care? Or would it, according to the predicate of the blood-shield statutes, interfere with the nation's blood supply? In this connection, consider the following letter to an editor from a physician in charge of a hospital blood bank:

> Court decisions of medicolegal cases, in general, have resulted in a great influence on the quality of a patient's care. In the field of blood banking, an impact by a medicolegal case has been no exception to this. In the *Cunningham* case[, supra,] in October, 1970, a hospital was held strictly liable to a patient who allegedly contracted hepatitis after a blood transfusion. This has had national repercussions. The impact has been especially great on our hospital, a 675–bed general hospital, located within 20 miles of the hospital in which the case took place. In view of this, a study was made to evaluate the scope and extent of the effects of the case on blood usage in our hospital.
>
> The study included assessment of 341 charts of patients who received single-unit transfusions in the past three years. In addition, data were collected from the records of the blood bank from 1960 through 1971. There was a significant change in the trends of blood usage between the periods before and after the court decisions. The use of packed cells substantially increased in 1971 * * *. A significant increase of "necessary" single-unit transfusions was seen in 1971 * * *. "Unnecessary" transfusions, on the other hand, declined markedly in 1971 * * *.
>
> Many approaches to proper use of blood have appeared in literature. Almost all of the reports have dealt with the necessity of educational programs for medical staff, establishing a blood bank committee in a hospital, evaluating single-unit transfusions, or establishing a hepatitis follow-up system of patients who received blood. There were, however, very few reports delineating which factors played the most effective role in improving blood usage or the extent of the effects after implementing the proposed program. As a part of educational programs for the medical staff in our hospital, we have regularly issued a news bulletin in the past four years. At the end of 1969, a blood bank committee was set up in our hospital, reviewing all single-unit transfusions. At the same time, a hepatitis follow-up system has been established, sending a letter to the physician whose patient received blood transfusions three months previously. Despite these activities, this study showed no significant changes in the trends of blood usage in 1970.
>
> There has been a general feeling among those engaged in blood banking that the trend of blood usage has changed significantly after the court decision. This study appears to substantiate that feeling. The *Cunningham* case and the repercussions that followed the case have had, directly or indirectly, a great impact on the minds of physicians, and have played a decisive role in the changes of trends of blood usage.
>
> The impact by the case has been far greater than that by various educational activities hitherto taken in our hospital.

Okuno, The Cunningham Case and Blood Usage, 220 J.A.M.A. 1015 (1972). (The Illinois legislature, of course, subsequently reversed *Cunningham.*) Several commentators have argued strongly for strict liability for blood banks, in part because they are in the best position to take cost-effective precautions. E.g., Eckert, The AIDS Blood–Transfusion Cases: A Legal and Economic Analysis of Liability, 29 San Diego L. Rev. 203 (1992); Havighurst, supra; Kessel, supra. (Ross D. Eckert, the economist-author of the first article cited, was a hemophiliac who died of transfusion-transmitted AIDS in 1995.)

Should the imposition of strict liability depend on how preventable the hazard is? On prevention technology, see Bove, Transfusion–Associated Hepatitis and AIDS: What Is the Risk? 317 New Eng.J.Med., 242 (1987). On the legal issue, see the comment k exception for "unavoidably unsafe" products to § 402A of the Restatement (Second) of Torts (1965); compare Rogers v. Miles Laboratories, Inc., 802 P.2d 1346 (Wash.1991) (en banc) (common law and Restatement held to impose liability for AIDS on blood products manufacturer only if it failed to warn about unavoidably unsafe product), with *Cunningham,* supra. See also Va. Code § 32.1–297 (1997) (when blood defects are detectable by accepted methods, implied warranty is appropriate). For possible clues to future doctrine, see Note, Section 8(c) of the Proposed Restatement (Third) of Torts: Is It Really What the Doctor Ordered?, 82 Cornell L. Rev. 644 (1997) (discussing proposal to modify comment k exception).

Would strict liability spur the adoption of known preventive measures and the search for new ones? Or is the health care system sufficiently motivated without this additional inducement?

7. *Liability of Standard–Setting Organizations.* In Snyder v. American Association of Blood Banks, 676 A.2d 1036 (N.J.1996), the leading trade association of voluntary blood banks was held liable for having negligently failed to recommend surrogate testing of blood donors in the early phase of the AIDS crisis. Do you agree that such bodies should be subject to having their advisory efforts penalized by juries evaluating their performance after the fact? There is some, though conflicting, authority for liability on the part of such standard-setting organizations. E.g., King v. National Spa & Pool Inst., Inc., 570 So.2d 612 (Ala.1990) (trade association promulgating safety standards for diving board installation in swimming pools held to owe duty of care to the owner and user of a pool manufactured and installed in accordance with such standards); Wissel v. Ohio High School Athletic Ass'n, 605 N.E.2d 458 (Ohio App. 1992) (voluntary nonprofit association engaged in setting safety standards for high school athletic equipment owed a duty of care to an injured football player left quadriplegic after being tackled). But see Harmon v. National Auto Parts Ass'n, 720 F.Supp. 79 (N.D. Miss. 1989). See generally Schuck, Tort Liability for Those Injured by Negligent Accreditation Decisions, Law & Contemp. Probs., Autumn 1994, p. 185 (noting and exploring conflicting theories of liability for organizations setting and applying standards for various goods and services). Should it be relevant whether the sponsors of the standard-setting effort had a conflict of interests, such as was earlier suggested with respect to the blood fractionators in determining whether to engage in surrogate testing?

The *Snyder* case naturally raises the issue of liability for entities promulgating clinical practice guidelines in medical care. In *Snyder*, the doctrine of charitable immunity was held not to protect the association. Will the risk of such liability, or of lawsuits alleging it, chill the interest of voluntary associations in developing important guidelines? For example, the American College of Cardiology promulgates six to eight guidelines per year, many of them designed to decrease unnecessary procedures in hospitals. If an individual is arguably injured because health care providers relied on such guidelines, should they be able to bring suit against the College?

NOTES ON THE STANDARDS APPLICABLE TO NONPHYSICIAN HEALTH CARE PERSONNEL

1. *Allied Health Professionals.* In *Fein v. Permanente Medical Group,* to which extensive reference was made in § A, a significant issue (separate from the constitutional question) involved the standard of care applicable to a nurse employed by the defendant medical group, which provided medical services under contract to enrollees of an HMO. The nurse, a licensed nurse practitioner, had examined the 34–year–old patient for chest pain and given him a drug prescribed by her supervising doctor that was not suitable for the heart condition he had. The court stated:

> Defendant next contends that the trial court misinstructed the jury on the standard of care by which Nurse Welch's conduct should be judged. In addition to the general BAJI instruction on the duty of care of a graduate nurse, the court told the jury that "the standard of care required of a nurse practitioner is that of a physician and surgeon ... when the nurse practitioner is examining a patient or making a diagnosis."[4]
>
> We agree with defendant that this instruction is inconsistent with recent legislation setting forth general guidelines for the services that may properly be performed by registered nurses in this state. Section 2725 of the Business and Professions Code, as amended in 1974, explicitly declares a legislative intent "to recognize the existence of overlapping functions between physicians and registered nurses and to permit additional sharing

4. The relevant instruction read in full: "It is the duty of one who undertakes to perform the service of a trained or graduate nurse to have the knowledge and skill ordinarily possessed, and to exercise the care and skill ordinarily used in like cases, by trained and skilled members of the nursing profession practicing their profession in the same or similar locality and under similar circumstances. Failure to fulfill either of these duties is negligence. [¶] I instruct you that the standard of care required of a nurse practitioner is that of a physician and surgeon duly licensed to practice medicine in the state of California when the nurse practitioner is examining a patient or making a diagnosis."

The initial paragraph of this instruction tracks BAJI No. 6.25; the second paragraph was an added instruction given at plaintiff's request.

> of functions within organized health care systems which provide for collaboration between physicians and registered nurses." Section 2725 also includes, among the functions that properly fall within "the practice of nursing" in California, the "[o]bservation of signs and symptoms of illness, reactions to treatment, general behavior, or general physical condition, and ... determination of whether such signs, symptoms, reactions, behavior or general appearance exhibit abnormal characteristics...." In light of these provisions, the "examination" or "diagnosis" of a patient cannot in all circumstances be said—as a matter of law—to be a function reserved to physicians, rather than registered nurses or nurse practitioners. Although plaintiff was certainly entitled to have the jury determine (1) whether defendant medical center was negligent in permitting a nurse practitioner to see a patient who exhibited the symptoms of which plaintiff complained and (2) whether Nurse Welch met the standard of care of a reasonably prudent nurse practitioner in conducting the examination and prescribing treatment in conjunction with her supervising physician, the court should not have told the jury that the nurse's conduct in this case must—as a matter of law—be measured by the standard of care of a physician or surgeon.

695 P.2d at 673–74. See Note, Nurse Malpractice in North Carolina: The Standard of Care, 65 N.C.L.Rev. 579 (1987) (including general references).

It appears to be generally true that each professional, acting within his lawful scope of practice, is held only to the standards of his own profession. E.g., Wade v. John D. Archbold Mem. Hosp., 311 S.E.2d 836 (Ga.1984) ("the judgment of a physical therapist should not vary according to the location of his or her hospital"; "the standard of care * * * is that ordinarily employed by the profession generally"); Creasey v. Hogan, 292 Or. 154, 637 P.2d 114 (1981) (podiatrist; "medical practitioners are entitled to have their treatment of a patient tested by the principles of the school of medicine to which they belong"); Mohr v. Jenkins, 393 So.2d 245 (La.App. 1980) (nurse anesthetist held to standards of her profession and "recognized specialty," per statute). But see McKee v. American Home Prods. Corp., 782 P.2d 1045 (Wash.1989) (5–4 decision; pharmacist had no duty to warn patient of risks of taking addictive diet drug containing amphetamines for ten years; sole responsibility lay with prescribing physician).

2. *Who May Testify?* Whether physicians may testify as experts on the standards applicable to nonphysician practitioners is a common question. See *Creasey v. Hogan*, supra ("Where the principles, techniques, methods, practices or procedures of one branch of the healing arts concur or are generally the same as those of another branch, opinion evidence on a point concerning such matter from a practitioner in another branch is permissible"). The issue may be made quite controversial by antagonisms between the two disciplines. For conflicting views on orthopedists' eligibility to testify against podiatrists, see Melville v. Southward, 791 P.2d 383 (Colo. 1990) (orthopedic surgeon allowed to testify against podiatrist); Marshall v. Yale Podiatry Group, 496 A.2d 529 (Conn.App.1985) (same); Botehlo v. Bycura, 320 S.E.2d 59 (S.C.App.1984).

3. *Alternative Medicine*. For a collection of cases involving claims against unconventional medical healers, such as chiropractors, osteopaths, and homeopaths, see Annot., Liability of Chiropractors and Other Drugless Practitioners for Medical Malpractice, 77 A.L.R.4th 273 (1990). Legal treatment of providers of alternative medicine generally falls into two categories. For those alternative providers who are licensed by the state, courts have long applied a standard of care enunciated by experts in the field itself. See, e.g., Bowman v. Woods, 1 Greene 441, 444 (Iowa 1848) ("The people are free to select from the various classes of medical men, who are accountable to their employers for all injuries resulting from a want of ordinary diligence and skill in their respective systems of treating diseases. It is to be lamented that so many of our citizens are disposed to trust health and life to novices and empirics, to new nostrums and new methods of treatment. But these are evils which courts of justice possess no adequate power to remedy."); Boudreaux v. Panger, 481 So.2d 1382 (La. App.) (chiropractors), aff'd, 490 So.2d 1083 (La.1986); Brodersen v. Sioux Valley Memorial Hosp., 902 F.Supp. 931 (N.D.Iowa 1995) (same). Only if licensed alternative medicine providers stray outside of their school are they held accountable to the prevailing standards of allopaths. See, e.g., Epstein v. Hirschon, 33 N.Y.S.2d 83 (N.Y.Sup.1942) (chiropractic standard held no defense if chiropractor held himself out as competent to practice medicine). See generally M. Cohen, Complementary and Alternative Medicine: Legal Boundaries and Regulatory Perspectives (1998).

On the other hand, certain areas of alternative medicine do not have universal licensure. For instance, just over half the states license acupuncturists, and somewhat fewer license massage therapists. In cases where the alternative provider is not licensed, negligence allegations are judged according to conventional medical standards or lay standards. For example, a New York court has evaluated a homeopathic physician's treatment of end-stage HIV infection under the standards of conventional medical practice. Metzler v. New York State Bd. for Professional Med. Conduct, 610 N.Y.S.2d 334 (N.Y. App. Div. 1994) (homeopathy not recognized as a separate branch of medicine in N.Y.).

SECTION C: THE PHYSICIAN'S OBLIGATION TO OBTAIN THE PATIENT'S INFORMED CONSENT

Cobbs v. Grant

Supreme Court of California, 1972.
8 Cal.3d 229, 104 Cal.Rptr. 505, 502 P.2d 1.

■ MOSK, JUSTICE.

This medical malpractice case involves two issues: first, whether there was sufficient evidence of negligence in the performing of surgery to sustain a jury verdict for plaintiff; second, whether, under plaintiff's alternative theory, the instructions to the jury adequately set forth the nature of a medical doctor's duty to obtain the informed consent of a patient before undertaking treatment. * * *

Plaintiff was admitted to the hospital in August 1964 for treatment of a duodenal ulcer. [Surgery was advised and undertaken, with injury to the patient's spleen (a 5% risk in such surgery), which was removed in a second operation. The patient developed a gastric ulcer, another risk of the first surgery, and was operated on a third time—a gastrectomy to remove 50% of his stomach—with still further complications.]

Plaintiff brought this malpractice suit against his surgeon, Dr. Grant. * * * The jury * * * returned a general verdict against defendant Grant in the amount of $23,800. He appeals.

The jury could have found for plaintiff either by determining that defendant negligently performed the operation, or on the theory that defendant's failure to disclose the inherent risks of the initial surgery vitiated plaintiff's consent to operate. [Because the court could not find enough evidence of negligence to support the jury's general verdict, it reversed the judgment and remanded for a new trial.]

Since the question of informed consent is likely to arise on retrial, we address ourselves to that issue. In giving its instruction the trial court relied upon Berkey v. Anderson (1969) 1 Cal.App.3d 790, 803, 82 Cal.Rptr. 67, a case in which it was held that if the defendant failed to make a sufficient disclosure of the risks inherent in the operation, he was guilty of a "technical battery". While a battery instruction may have been warranted under the facts alleged in *Berkey,* in the case before us the instruction should have been framed in terms of negligence.

Where a doctor obtains consent of the patient to perform one type of treatment and subsequently performs a substantially different treatment for which consent was not obtained, there is a clear case of battery. * * *

However, when an undisclosed potential complication results, the occurrence of which was not an integral part of the treatment procedure but merely a known risk, the courts are divided on the issue of whether this should be deemed to be a battery or negligence. * * * California authorities have favored a negligence theory. * * *

Dean Prosser surveyed the decisions in this area and concluded, "The earliest cases treated this as a matter of vitiating the consent, so that there was liability for battery. Beginning with a decision in Kansas in 1960 [Natanson v. Kline (1960), 187 Kan. 186 [354 P.2d 670]], it began to be recognized that this was really a matter of the standard of professional conduct.... [T]he prevailing view now is that the action ... is in reality one for negligence in failing to conform to the proper standard...." (Prosser on Torts (4th ed. 1971) pp. 165–166.)

Although this is a close question, either prong of which is supportable by authority, the trend appears to be towards categorizing failure to obtain informed consent as negligence. That this result now appears with growing frequency is of more than academic interest; it reflects an appreciation of the several significant consequences of favoring negligence over a battery theory. As will be discussed infra, most jurisdictions have permitted a doctor in an informed consent action to interpose a defense that the disclosure he omitted to make was not required within his medical community. However, expert opinion as to community standard is not required in a battery count, in which the patient must merely prove failure to give informed consent and a mere touching absent consent. Moreover a doctor could be held liable for punitive damages under a battery count, and if held liable for the intentional tort of battery he might not be covered by his malpractice insurance. Additionally, in some jurisdictions the patient has a longer statute of limitations if he sues in negligence.

We agree with the majority trend. The battery theory should be reserved for those circumstances when a doctor performs an operation to which the patient has not consented. When the patient gives permission to perform one type of treatment and the doctor performs another, the requisite element of deliberate intent to deviate from the consent given is present. However, when the patient consents to certain treatment and the doctor performs that treatment but an undisclosed inherent complication with a low probability occurs, no intentional deviation from the consent given appears; rather, the doctor in obtaining consent may have failed to meet his due care duty to disclose pertinent information. In that situation the action should be pleaded in negligence.

The facts of this case constitute a classic illustration of an action that sounds in negligence. Defendant performed the identical operation to which plaintiff had consented. The spleen injury, development of the gastric ulcer, gastrectomy and internal bleeding as a result of the premature absorption of a suture, were all links in a chain of low probability events inherent in the initial operation.

III

Since this is an appropriate case for the application of a negligence theory, it remains for us to determine if the standard of care described in the jury instruction on this subject properly delineates defendant's duty to inform plaintiff of the inherent risks of the surgery. In pertinent part, the court gave the following instruction: "A physician's duty to disclose is not governed by the standard practice in the community; rather it is a duty imposed by law. A physician violates his duty to his patient and subjects himself to liability if he withholds any facts which are necessary to form the basis of an intelligent consent by the patient to the proposed treatment."

Defendant raises two objections to the foregoing instruction. First, he points out that the majority of the California cases have measured the duty to disclose not in terms of an absolute, but as a duty to reveal such information as would be disclosed by a doctor in good standing within the medical community. One commentator has imperiously declared that "good medical practice is good law." (Hagman, The Medical Patient's Right to Know (1970) 17 U.C.L.A.L.Rev. 758, 764.) Moreover, with one state and one federal exception every jurisdiction that has considered this question

has adopted the community standard as the applicable test.[1] Defendant's second contention is that this near unanimity reflects strong policy reasons for vesting in the medical community the unquestioned discretion to determine if the withholding of information by a doctor from his patient is justified at the time the patient weighs the risks of the treatment against the risks of refusing treatment.

The thesis that medical doctors are invested with discretion to withhold information from their patients has been frequently ventilated in both legal and medical literature. Despite what defendant characterizes as the prevailing rule, it has never been unequivocally adopted by an authoritative source. Therefore we probe anew into the rationale which purportedly justifies, in accordance with medical rather than legal standards, the withholding of information from a patient.

Preliminarily we employ several postulates. The first is that patients are generally persons unlearned in the medical sciences and therefore, except in rare cases, courts may safely assume the knowledge of patient and physician are not in parity. The second is that a person of adult years and in sound mind has the right, in the exercise of control over his own body, to determine whether or not to submit to lawful medical treatment. The third is that the patient's consent to treatment, to be effective, must be an informed consent. And the fourth is that the patient, being unlearned in medical sciences, has an abject dependence upon and trust in his physician for the information upon which he relies during the decisional process, thus raising an obligation in the physician that transcends arms-length transactions.

From the foregoing axiomatic ingredients emerges a necessity, and a resultant requirement, for divulgence by the physician to his patient of all information relevant to a meaningful decisional process. In many instances, to the physician, whose training and experience enable a self-satisfying evaluation, the particular treatment which should be undertaken may seem evident, but it is the prerogative of the patient, not the physician, to determine for himself the direction in which he believes his interests lie. To enable the patient to chart his course knowledgeably, reasonable familiarity with the therapeutic alternatives and their hazards becomes essential.

Therefore, we hold, as an integral part of the physician's overall obligation to the patient there is a duty of reasonable disclosure of the available choices with respect to proposed therapy and of the dangers inherently and potentially involved in each.

A concomitant issue is the yardstick to be applied in determining reasonableness of disclosure. This defendant and the majority of courts have related the duty to the custom of physicians practicing in the community. The majority rule is needlessly overbroad. Even if there can be said to be a medical community standard as to the disclosure requirement for any

1. The one state jurisdiction adopting a requirement of full disclosure is New Mexico. (Woods v. Brumlop (1962) 71 N.M. 221, 377 P.2d 520.) The federal case is Canterbury v. Spence (D.C.Cir.1972) 464 F.2d 772. * * *

prescribed treatment, it appears so nebulous that doctors become, in effect, vested with virtual absolute discretion. The court in *Canterbury v. Spence*, supra, 464 F.2d 772, 784, bluntly observed: "Nor can we ignore the fact that to bind the disclosure obligation to medical usage is to arrogate the decision on revelation to the physician alone. Respect for the patient's right of self-determination on particular therapy demands a standard set by law for physicians rather than one which physicians may or may not impose upon themselves." Unlimited discretion in the physician is irreconcilable with the basic right of the patient to make the ultimate informed decision regarding the course of treatment to which he knowledgeably consents to be subjected.

A medical doctor, being the expert, appreciates the risks inherent in the procedure he is prescribing, the risks of a decision not to undergo the treatment, and the probability of a successful outcome of the treatment. But once this information has been disclosed, that aspect of the doctor's expert function has been performed. The weighing of these risks against the individual subjective fears and hopes of the patient is not an expert skill. Such evaluation and decision is a nonmedical judgment reserved to the patient alone. A patient should be denied the opportunity to weigh the risks only where it is evident he cannot evaluate the data, as for example, where there is an emergency or the patient is a child or incompetent. For this reason the law provides that in an emergency consent is implied, and if the patient is a minor or incompetent, the authority to consent is transferred to the patient's legal guardian or closest available relative. In all cases other than the foregoing, the decision whether or not to undertake treatment is vested in the party most directly affected: the patient.

The scope of the disclosure required of physicians defies simple definition. Some courts have spoken of "full disclosure" and others refer to "full and complete" disclosure but such facile expressions obscure common practicalities. Two qualifications to a requirement of "full disclosure" need little explication. First, the patient's interest in information does not extend to a lengthy polysyllabic discourse on all possible complications. A mini-course in medical science is not required; the patient is concerned with the risk of death or bodily harm, and problems of recuperation. Second, there is no physician's duty to discuss the relatively minor risks inherent in common procedures, when it is common knowledge that such risks inherent in the procedure are of very low incidence.[2] When there is a common procedure a doctor must, of course, make such inquiries as are required to determine if for the particular patient the treatment under consideration is contraindicated—for example, to determine if the patient has had adverse reactions to antibiotics; but no warning beyond such

2. For example, the risks inherent in the simple process of taking a common blood sample are said to include hematoma, dermatitis, cellulitis, abscess, osteomyelitis, septicemia, endocarditis, thrombophlebitis, pulmonary embolism and death, to mention a few. One commentator states that California law does not require that the "patient be told too much." (Hagman, The Medical Patient's Right to Know, supra, 17 U.C.L.A.L.Rev. 758, 766.)

inquiries is required as to the remote possibility of death or serious bodily harm.

However, when there is a more complicated procedure, as the surgery in the case before us, the jury should be instructed that when a given procedure inherently involves a known risk of death or serious bodily harm, a medical doctor has a duty to disclose to his patient the potential of death or serious harm, and to explain in lay terms the complications that might possibly occur. Beyond the foregoing minimal disclosure, a doctor must also reveal to his patient such additional information as a skilled practitioner of good standing would provide under similar circumstances.

In sum, the patient's right of self-decision is the measure of the physician's duty to reveal. That right can be effectively exercised only if the patient possesses adequate information to enable an intelligent choice. The scope of the physician's communications to the patient, then, must be measured by the patient's need, and that need is whatever information is material to the decision. Thus the test for determining whether a potential peril must be divulged is its materiality to the patient's decision. (*Canterbury v. Spence*, supra, 464 F.2d 772, 786.)

We point out, for guidance on retrial, an additional problem which suggests itself. There must be a causal relationship between the physician's failure to inform and the injury to the plaintiff. Such causal connection arises only if it is established that had revelation been made consent to treatment would not have been given. Here the record discloses no testimony that had plaintiff been informed of the risks of surgery he would not have consented to the operation.

The patient-plaintiff may testify on this subject but the issue extends beyond his credibility. Since at the time of trial the uncommunicated hazard has materialized, it would be surprising if the patient-plaintiff did not claim that had he been informed of the dangers he would have declined treatment. Subjectively he may believe so, with the 20/20 vision of hindsight, but we doubt that justice will be served by placing the physician in jeopardy of the patient's bitterness and disillusionment. Thus an objective test is preferable: i.e., what would a prudent person in the patient's position have decided if adequately informed of all significant perils. (*Canterbury v. Spence*, supra, 464 F.2d 772, 787.)

The burden of going forward with evidence of nondisclosure rests on the plaintiff. Once such evidence has been produced, then the burden of going forward with evidence pertaining to justification for failure to disclose shifts to the physician.

Whenever appropriate, the court should instruct the jury on the defenses available to a doctor who has failed to make the disclosure required by law. Thus, a medical doctor need not make disclosure of risks when the patient requests that he not be so informed. Such a disclosure need not be made if the procedure is simple and the danger remote and commonly appreciated to be remote. A disclosure need not be made beyond that required within the medical community when a doctor can prove by a preponderance of the evidence he relied upon facts which would demonstrate to a reasonable man the disclosure would have so seriously upset the patient that the patient would not have been able to dispassionately weigh the risks of refusing to undergo the recommended treatment. Any defense, of course, must be consistent with what has been termed the "fiducial qualities" of the physician-patient relationship.

The judgment is reversed.

NOTES AND QUESTIONS ON THE LEGAL DUTY TO DISCLOSE THE RISKS OF TREATMENT

1. The legal and ethical requirement of informed consent to medical treatment, while important as a practical matter in day-to-day patient care, is so very widely discussed because it symbolizes so much. These materials attempt to put the subject in both a practical and policy perspective, observing but not wrestling with the moral implications of the subject. On the ethical themes, see generally T. Brennan, Just Doctoring: Medical Ethics in the Liberal State (1991). R. Faden & T. Beauchamp (with N. King), A History and Theory of Informed Consent (1986); J. Katz, The Silent World of Doctor and Patient (1984) (hereinafter The Silent World); President's Commission for the Study of Ethical Problems in Medicine and Biomedical and Behavioral Research, Making Health Care Decisions: The Ethical and Legal Implications of Informed Consent in the Patient–Practitioner Relationship (3 vols. 1982). For an enlightening new, more pragmatic view of the subject, see Schuck, Rethinking Informed Consent, 103 Yale L.J. 899 (1994). On the legal issues, see generally F. Rozovsky, Consent to Treatment (2d ed., 1990) (looseleaf).

In examining these materials, consider whether the power shifts observable in the evolution of the law of informed consent mirror in any way the modern trend to a more consumer-driven market for health services.

2. *Battery or Negligence?* How would you explain the origins of the requirement of informed consent to a physician friend? Would you begin by observing that the law originally characterized an unauthorized touching, even for a benign and therapeutic purpose, as a "battery"? See, e.g., Mohr v. Williams, 104 N.W. 12 (Minn.1905) (patient consented to operation on right ear but doctor found left ear worse and operated on it instead; good intentions held no defense to claim of battery). If so, would your friend conclude, as many other physicians have done, that lawyers—if they so label physicians' well intended ministrations—have lost touch with reality? Perhaps you could explain more fully that the common law has long protected dignitary interests. Whatever the terminology employed, you might say, the patient's autonomy and right of self-determination, which the law defends by requiring informed consent, is a widely shared moral value.

The law's essential idea in viewing early physicians as potential perpetrators of dignitary torts was expressed by Justice Benjamin Cardozo in 1914: "Every human being of adult years and sound mind has a right to determine what shall be done with his own body; and a surgeon who performs an operation without his patient's consent commits an assault." Schloendorff v. Society of New York Hosp., 105 N.E. 92, 93 (N.Y.1914). Nevertheless, as surgery became more accepted and less risky than it was in 1914, this opprobrious characterization of unauthorized surgery may have come to seem less apt. In addition, the famous 1957 case of Salgo v. Leland Stanford Jr. Univ. Bd. of Trustees, 317 P.2d 170 (Cal.App.1957), shifted attention away from whether the physician had sought consent at all and focused more on whether the consent obtained was based on full disclosure. Indeed, the *Salgo* court, although still adhering to the battery characterization, was the first to speak of the necessity for "informed" consent and of the physician's duty to make whatever disclosures were necessary to make informed consent possible. This new emphasis on the arguably technical issue of what specific medical information should have been given to the patient paved the way for a new perception of the tort as a breach of a professional obligation—that is, as a form of professional negligence.

Beginning with the Kansas Supreme Court's landmark 1960 decision in Natanson v. Kline, 350 P.2d 1093 (rehearing) (Kan. 1960), the classification of failures to obtain informed consent under the heading of negligence began to take hold. This view is now the dominant one, with the battery cause of action being largely reserved for instances in which the physician acted without any consent at all or with intent to harm or deceive. E.g., Kohoutek v. Hafner, 383 N.W.2d 295, 299 (Minn.1986) ("To argue that consent that is inadequately informed is no consent at all, and hence a battery, is to ignore the practical differences underlying the distinction between battery and negligent nondisclosure"). But see Gray v. Grunnagle, 223 A.2d 663 (Pa.1966) (showing how Pennsylvania maintained disclosure requirements without switching theories). On various kinds of liability for fraudulent or negligent misrepresentation of treatment hazards, see Annot., 42 A.L.R.4th 543 (1985).

Is something lost in characterizing a failure to obtain informed consent as negligence? What becomes of the law's original and primary focus on the dignitary interests of patients? As you study these materials, consider whether the quality of the doctor/patient relationship has been improved by employing legal sanctions in the effort to make physicians treat their patients more like autonomous human beings.

3. *The Standard of Disclosure.* Perceiving failure to obtain a patient's informed consent to treatment as a form of negligence made it natural to look to the medical community for standards by which to measure a physician's disclosure practice. As the *Natanson* court put it, "the duty of the physician to disclose * * * is limited to those disclosures which a reasonable medical practitioner would make under the same or similar circumstances." 350 P.2d at 1106. This test is probably, by a small margin, the majority rule. See generally Annot., 88 A.L.R.3d 1008 (1978) (reflecting case law, not statutes).

In the famous case of *Canterbury v. Spence*, cited and relied upon in *Cobbs v. Grant*, a federal court of appeals, applying law of the District of Columbia, stated its reservations about a profession-dictated standard of disclosure:

> To begin with, the reality of any discernible custom reflecting a professional consensus on communication of option and risk information to patients is open to serious doubt. We sense the danger that what in fact is no custom at all may be taken as an affirmative custom to maintain silence, and that physician-witnesses to the so-called custom may state merely their personal opinions as to what they or others would do under given conditions. We cannot gloss over the inconsistency between reliance on a general practice respecting divulgence and, on the other hand, realization that the myriad of variables among patients makes each case so different that its omission can rationally be justified only by the effect of its individual circumstances. Nor can we ignore the fact that to bind the disclosure obligation to medical usage is to arrogate the decision on revelation to the physician alone. Respect for the patient's right of self-determination on particular therapy demands a standard set by law for physicians rather than one which physicians may or may not impose upon themselves.

464 F.2d at 783–84.

What is the California Supreme Court's test for adequate disclosure in *Cobbs*? Its test is essentially a paraphrase of language in *Canterbury*. See 464 F.2d at 786–87. Although both courts adopted a materiality test that turned on patient need for information rather than on professional consensus concerning appropriate disclosure, they stopped short of letting the plaintiff himself set the standard. Instead, they opted for an "objective" test:

> The scope of the standard is not subjective as to either the physician or the patient; it remains objective with due regard for the patient's informational needs and with suitable leeway for the physician's situation. In broad outline, we agree that "[a] risk is thus material when a reasonable person, in what the physician knows or should know to be the patient's position, would be likely to attach significance to the risk or cluster of risks in deciding whether or not to forego the proposed therapy."

Canterbury, 464 F.2d at 787. The court's quotation is from Waltz & Scheuneman, Informed Consent to Therapy, 64 Nw.U.L.Rev. 628, 640 (1970), on which the court relied in other respects as well. Other courts adopting this "objective," "reasonable-person" standard of disclosure include Carr v. Strode, 904 P.2d 489 (Haw.1995); Wheeldon v. Madison, 374 N.W.2d 367 (S.D.1985) (amniocentesis); Cowman v. Hornaday, 329 N.W.2d 422 (Iowa 1983) (vasectomy; "the paternalistic or authoritarian rationale underlying the professional rule—that to inform the patient of the risks of the surgery or procedure would be counterproductive in the management of his or her illness or prompt the patient to forgo the therapy the physician believes the patient really needs—has no application in the circumstances before us"); Logan v. Greenwich Hosp. Ass'n, 465 A.2d 294 (Conn.1983) (even more hazardous options required to be disclosed if relevant to reasonable patient's informed decision); Wilkinson v. Vesey, 295 A.2d 676

(R.I.1972). Under this rule, professional expert testimony may be needed to establish the nature and significance of the various risks and options so that a jury can assess what should have been communicated. See, e.g., Cross v. Trapp, 294 S.E.2d 446, 455 (W.Va.1982) (identifying subjects requiring expert evidence).

The Maine Supreme Court has expressed its view of the appropriate measure of the physician's duty to disclose risks as follows:

> At trial the plaintiffs seasonably objected to the jury instruction of the presiding Justice that the defendant's obligation to apprise Linda Woolley of the risks of the proposed surgery was limited to those disclosures which would be made by a reasonable medical practitioner. In Downer v. Veilleux, 322 A.2d 82 (Me.1974), this Court recognized the doctrine of informed consent as an actionable species of medical negligence:
>
>> The doctrine is based on the general principle of law that a physician has a duty adequately to disclose to his patient the proposed diagnostic, therapeutic or surgical procedure to be undertaken, the material risks involved therein and the alternatives available, if any, so that a patient of ordinary understanding, confronted with these disclosures and faced with a choice of undergoing the proposed treatment, or selecting an alternative process, or preferring refusal of all medical relief, may, in reaching a decision, intelligently exercise his judgment by balancing the probable risks against the probable benefits.
>
> Our decision in *Downer* raised, but expressly left unresolved, the scope of the physician's duty to disclose * * *.
>
> Although it is well settled that the law imposes on a physician a general duty reasonably to disclose to his patient significant information concerning treatment, jurisdictions differ on the scope of this disclosure obligation. Many courts hold that the duty of a physician to make adequate disclosure is, as in other cases of medical malpractice, measured by the standard of the reasonable medical practitioner under the same or similar circumstances. Under this "professional" disclosure standard, therefore, whether and to what extent a physician has an obligation to disclose a particular risk must in most cases be determined by expert medical testimony establishing the prevailing standard of practice and the defendant's departure therefrom.
>
> On the other hand, an increasing number of courts hold that because a physician's obligation to disclose therapeutic risks and alternatives arises from the patient's right of physical self-determination, the disclosure duty should be measured by the patient's need for information rather than by the standards of the medical profession. These courts reason that physicians have a legal obligation adequately to disclose risk and option information that is material to the patient's decision to undergo treatment and that expert testimony as to medical standards is not required to establish this duty. Under this "material-risk" standard, although expert medical testimony may be necessary to establish the undisclosed risk as a known danger of the procedure, the jury can decide without the necessity of a medical expert whether a reasonable person in the patient's position would have considered the risk significant in making his decision.

A basic principle of medical malpractice law is that the physician is not an insurer. "A poor result, standing alone, is insufficient to establish liability." Downer v. Veilleux, supra, 322 A.2d at 87. Thus, under no view of the doctrine of informed consent can liability be found for every failure to disclose a risk that has later materialized; despite solicitude for the informational needs of patients, liability for non-disclosure must still be based on fault. Underlying the conflict in the cases is a disagreement over the fundamental question whether fault in informed consent actions should be predicated on deviation from the professional standard of care or on interference with a patient's interest in physical self-determination. Consistent with our view of informed consent as a form of professional malpractice, we believe that fault must be measured by reference to the reasonable medical practitioner in the same branch of medicine and not according to some variable lay standard of "materiality."

When a patient alleges that an unrevealed hazard has caused him injury, the jury must determine whether, under the facts of the case, the physician has deviated from the standard of care of the reasonable practitioner. Although the unreasonableness of a particular nondisclosure may be " 'sufficiently obvious as to lie within common knowledge ...,' "[6] in most cases expert medical testimony is just as necessary to establish negligence in failing adequately to disclose as it is to prove negligence in diagnosis or treatment. Whether the physician has acted unreasonably is often a question of professional judgment. In determining whether and how much he should disclose, the physician must consider the probable impact of disclosure on the patient, taking into account his peculiar knowledge of the patient's psychological, emotional and physical condition, and must evaluate the magnitude of the risk, the frequency of its occurrence and the viability of alternative therapeutic measures. "This determination involves medical judgment as to whether disclosure of possible risks may have such an adverse effect on the patient as to jeopardize success of the proposed therapy, no matter how expertly performed." Aiken v. Clary, 396 S.W.2d 668, 674 (Mo.1965).[7] Conceivably, full disclosure under some circumstances could constitute bad medical practice.

Moreover, a rule that allows a plaintiff to establish the existence and extent of the defendant-physician's disclosure obligation without regard to medical standards hardly diminishes the importance of expert medical testimony or absolves the plaintiff from producing such evidence on other issues in the case. The courts that have adopted this rule recognize the necessity, in the usual case, of medical evidence to identify the known risks of treatment, the nature of available alternatives and the cause of any injury or disability suffered by the plaintiff, and would allow the defendant

6. Additionally, there may be circumstances in which the professional standard is so clearly inadequate as to permit the conclusion that the entire profession is negligent.

7. Courts that have rejected the need for medical evidence on the disclosure obligation nevertheless acknowledge that valid medical reasons may warrant nondisclosure. These courts posit that a physician has a "privilege" to withhold information for justifiable therapeutic reasons. Just how the concept of a "privilege" fits into a negligence action is unclear, but the net effect is to place upon the physician the burden of showing the reasonableness of his conduct. Presumably, the physician would raise this privilege by way of expert medical testimony.

to show by expert testimony that his conduct comported with medical standards.[8] Furthermore, when the patient also claims negligent diagnosis or treatment, he will have secured medical experts to testify to the applicable standard of care. Bly v. Rhoads, 222 S.E.2d 783, 787 (Va.1976). It certainly adds little to the burden of the plaintiff on his informed consent claim to require him to produce medical evidence that the physician's nondisclosure departed from prevailing standards of practice.

In addition, we are not unmindful of the practical implications of dispensing with the requirement of expert medical testimony to establish the existence and extent of the disclosure duty in a given case. Inherent in such a rule is the potential danger that a jury, composed of laymen and gifted with the benefit of hindsight, will divine the breach of a disclosure obligation largely on the basis of the unfortunate result. In *Bly v. Rhoads,* supra, the Virginia court expressed a similar concern:

> The matters involved in the disclosure syndrome, more often than not, are complicated and highly technical. To leave the establishment of such matters to lay witnesses, in our opinion, would pose dangers and disadvantages which far outweigh the benefits and advantages a "modern trend" rule would bestow on patient-plaintiffs. In effect, the relaxed "modern trend" rule permits lay witnesses to express, when all is said and done, what amounts to a medical opinion.

Finally, we believe that legal principles designed to provide compensation to persons injured by bad professional practice should not unduly intrude upon the intimate physician-patient relationship. Although the "material-risk" theory may make it easier for some plaintiffs to recover, it does so by placing good medical practice in jeopardy. The physician's attention must be focused on the best interests of his patient and not on what a lay jury, unschooled in medicine, may, after the fact, conclude he should have disclosed. As a North Carolina court noted,

> [t]o adopt the ["material-risk" standard] would result in requiring every doctor to spend much unnecessary time in going over with every patient every possible effect of any proposed treatment. The doctor should not have to practice his profession with the knowledge that every consultation with every patient with respect to future treatment contains a potential lawsuit and his advice and suggestions must necessarily be phrased with the possible defense of a lawsuit in mind. This would necessarily result in the doctor's inability to give the best interest of his patient primary importance. Butler v. Berkeley, 213 S.E.2d 571, 581–82 (N.C.App.1975).

Woolley v. Henderson, 418 A.2d 1123, 1128–31 (Me.1980). Note the differing roles of expert witnesses under the two tests. Also consider how the question of "therapeutic privilege" is handled under each formulation; there are many dicta but few holdings on this subject. See Patterson, The

8. Even these courts recognize limits on a physician's disclosure obligation. * * * Nevertheless, these limitations on the disclosure duty are unlikely to afford a physician much guidance in his daily interactions with patients. Rather than relying on his professional judgment, a physician practicing in a "material-risk" jurisdiction may well feel compelled at his peril to disclose every imaginable risk and alternative to treatment.

Therapeutic Justification for Withholding Medical Information: What You Don't Know Can't Hurt You, Or Can It?, 64 Neb.L.Rev. 721 (1985).

Jay Katz, M.D., sees the tensions in the law of informed consent as reflecting "a conflict between [the law's] vision of human beings as autonomous persons and its deference to paternalism, another powerful vision of man's interaction with man"; conflicting perceptions on this point, he says, reflect "a thoroughgoing ambivalence about human beings' capacities for taking care of themselves and need for care-taking." Katz, Informed Consent: A Fairy Tale? Law's Vision, 39 U.Pitt.L.Rev. 137, 139 (1977). Is the *Canterbury/Cobbs* "reasonable-person" test consistent with the policy of protecting the patient's personal autonomy? Several commentators have argued that only a subjective test is true to the underlying ethical principle; under this approach, the question would be whether the doctor's disclosures truly aided the patient, as a specific, autonomous person, in making an informed choice satisfactory to himself. E.g., J. Katz, The Silent World, supra at 75–78; Capron, Informed Consent in Catastrophic Disease Research and Treatment, 123 U.Pa.L.Rev. 340, 364 (1974). Would such a test be fair to the physician, who may not be able to guess what each particular patient regards as material with respect to risks and benefits? Or is the whole point to get away from disclosures made only in obedience to legal requirements and to encourage instead real communication eliciting the patient's true needs? What might be the jury's role here?

One jurisdiction has attempted to blend the professional and "reasonable person" tests for appropriate disclosure:

> A physician must disclose risks of death or serious bodily harm which are of significant probability; to this there is no contention. Risks which a skilled practitioner of good standing in the community would reveal must also be disclosed and all medical experts testifying agreed the surgical complications affecting the plaintiff here were such risks. Lastly, to the extent a doctor is or can be aware that his patient attaches particular significance to risks not generally considered by the medical profession serious enough to require discussion with the patient, these too must be brought out. In determining whether risks of particular importance to the patient existed and whether his physician should have been aware of their importance, a jury must look to what a reasonable person in what the physician knows or should have known to be the plaintiff's position would consider significant when contemplating surgery.

Kinikin v. Heupel, 305 N.W.2d 589, 595 (Minn.1981). Note the emphasis on the patient's special needs or fears insofar as they are known to the physician.

In 1985, the British House of Lords ruled on a case involving a failure to obtain the patient's informed consent to a surgical procedure that resulted in partial paralysis. In Sidaway v. Bethlem Royal Hosp. and Maudsley Hosp. Health Auth., 1985 App.Cas. 871, no liability was found under the professional standard. A dissenting lord, however, argued for a test like the patient-oriented one in *Canterbury*.

4. *Causation.* Note that the *Cobbs* court, like the *Canterbury* court before it, introduced a significant additional proof burden for a patient injured by a procedure about which he was underinformed by the physician; this burden is also imposed on plaintiffs in jurisdictions applying the professional standard of disclosure. To recover, the patient must demonstrate that the failure to disclose a particular risk was a proximate cause of his injury, because he would have declined the procedure if he had been fully informed of the associated risks. (Query whether nondisclosure of a risk other than the one that materialized could logically be the basis of a claim.) Because many procedures are not truly elective in the sense that there are good alternatives, it will often be difficult to prove that more information would have caused the plaintiff to forgo the procedure. It is probably the causation requirement, more than anything else, that makes cases in which informed consent is the sole basis for the plaintiff's suit fairly rare—certainly in comparison with the amount of academic writing on the subject.

Note that the *Cobbs* court adopted another "objective" test for causation. See also *Canterbury*, supra, at 790–91. This approach is followed by the great majority of courts. E.g., Fain v. Smith, 479 So.2d 1150 (Ala.1985) (plaintiff's testimony relevant, but judge could characterize it as "self-serving" and benefitting from "hindsight" in charge to jury). Is the objective test for causation true to the professed purpose of giving individual patients a chance to choose for themselves?

For another view on how causation should be established, consider the following:

> A major issue in informed consent cases is what standard to use in determining proximate causation. A subjective standard requires the jury to determine whether, if informed, this particular patient would have foregone treatment. An objective standard requires the jury to determine whether, if informed, a reasonable, prudent person under all the surrounding circumstances would have foregone treatment.
>
> The problem with a subjective standard is that the only evidence usually available is the plaintiff's bald assertion, tempered by hindsight, as to what he would have done had he known all the facts. The apparent inequity of a jury basing its decision solely on such testimony has troubled courts, once even to the extreme of excluding the plaintiff's testimony on this issue.
>
> The detriments of the objective standard are more severe, however. In determining liability by whether a reasonable person would have submitted to treatment had he known of the risk that the defendant failed to relate, no consideration is given to the peculiar quirks and idiosyncracies of the individual. His supposedly inviolable right to decide for himself what is to be done with his body is made subject to a standard set by others. The right to base one's consent on proper information is effectively vitiated for those with fears, apprehensions, religious beliefs, or superstitions outside the mainstream of society.

> Therefore, we hold that the subjective test is the proper standard to apply in determining whether a patient would have undergone treatment had he known of the risks the physician neglected to relate to him.

McPherson v. Ellis, 287 S.E.2d 892, 896–97 (N.C.1982). The North Carolina test was subsequently changed by statute, however, to an objective standard. N.C. Gen. Stat. § 90–21.13(a)(3) (1997).

For cases adopting the subjective test, see Cheung v. Cunningham, 520 A.2d 832 (N.J.Super.1987); Arena v. Gingrich, 748 P.2d 547 (Or.1988). The jury instructions given in *Fain v. Smith,* supra, and cases such as these suggest some blurring of the distinction between the tests. Interestingly, because an operation performed without valid, informed consent is a technical battery in Pennsylvania, the patient need not show that he would have refused treatment if more information had been disclosed. Gouse v. Cassel, 615 A.2d 331 (Pa.1992); Sagala v. Tavares, 533 A.2d 165 (Pa.Super.1987).

5. *Waiver; Consent Forms.* What did the *Cobbs* court say about the possibility that a patient might waive his right to a full exposition of a treatment's risks? What are the dangers of recognizing such waivers? How might a paternalistic physician approach her disclosure task if she did not really believe that her patient was capable of forming a sound judgment? What are the dangers of not recognizing waivers? Might a patient rationally choose to forgo a recitation of the dangers he faces and to put himself instead entirely in his doctor's hands?

With the increase in patient claims based on lack of informed consent, most hospitals have employ specific consent forms, which are intended as a basis for discussions between doctors and patients and must be signed by the patient before a planned procedure may occur. Courts have tended to view consent forms as evidence to be considered by the jury but have not found them to be dispositive, except against a claim of battery. Should signing a consent form under circumstances where more information could have been obtained for the asking constitute a waiver of the patient's right to fuller disclosure? Courts have generally been unconvinced by arguments that a signed consent form amounts to such a waiver or an assumption of risk or that a plaintiff's failure to read a consent form before signing it constitutes contributory negligence. See Keomaka v. Zakaib, 811 P.2d 478 (Haw. App. 1991). Even when legislation provides that a signed consent form creates a presumption that the patient was fully informed, courts have been unwilling to grant summary judgment on the basis of the form alone. E.g., Hondroulis v. Schuhmacher, 553 So.2d 398 (La.1988) (statute creating rebuttable presumption held not to alter informed consent doctrine); Parikh v. Cunningham, 493 So.2d 999 (Fla.1986) (upholding statute giving conclusive effect to a "consent which is evidenced in writing" by construing it to require consent meeting traditional standards).

How do you, as a lawyer, react to the recurring disparagement of consent forms? One study involved questioning patients concerning procedures that they had consented to in writing one day before:

> Only 60 per cent understood the purpose and nature of the procedure, and only 55 per cent correctly listed even one major risk or complication. We found that three factors were related to inadequate recall: education, medical status, and the care with which patients thought they had read their consent forms before signing. Only 40 per cent of the patients had read the form "carefully." Most believed that consent forms were meant to "protect the physician's rights." Although most thought that consent forms were necessary and comprehensible and that they contained worthwhile information, the legalistic connotations of the forms appeared to lead to cursory reading and inadequate recall.

Cassileth et al., Informed Consent—Why Are Its Goals Imperfectly Realized? 302 New Eng.J.Med. 896 (1980).

6. *Materiality*. "Full" disclosure is not required under any standard, but appropriate disclosure may extend to a wide range of relevant factors—including the patient's diagnosis, the full range of diagnostic or therapeutic options, the prognosis under various modes of treatment, and the risks associated with each alternative. (Some additional, more controversial disclosure requirements appear in the next two cases reproduced below.)

On the duty to disclose very remote risks, see Precourt v. Frederick, 481 N.E.2d 1144 (Mass.1985) (although aseptic necrosis was listed in the *Physician's Desk Reference* as 1 of 41 potential complications known to be associated with prolonged use of Prednisone, a defense expert found no report of this side effect in a computer search of 29,000 articles on the subject; disclosure not required as a matter of law); see also Curran, Informed Consent in Malpractice Cases, 314 New Eng.J.Med. 429 (1986) (discussing evidence in *Precourt*). What is the possible relevance of the fact that the *Precourt* plaintiff's second eye operation, requiring 55 days of Prednisone medication in addition to 90 days' earlier exposure to the drug, was represented as having only a 10% chance of restoring sight?

On the duty to disclose alternative courses of action, recall *Gates v. Jensen* in § B of this chapter (failure to disclose additional diagnostic test). See also *Johnson v. Kokemoor*, reproduced below; Martin v. Richards, 531 N.W.2d 70 (Wis.1995) (jury permitted to decide that physician should have advised patient that CT scan, available only at another hospital, would rule out intracranial bleeding, which could, and did, cause brain damage); Logan v. Greenwich Hosp. Ass'n, 465 A.2d 294 (Conn.1983) (urologist would be liable if he failed to disclose "all viable alternatives" to needle biopsy of kidney, including some that were more hazardous but still relevant to informed decision); Annot., 38 A.L.R.4th 900 (1985). The potential significance of this duty in the new era of managed care will be observed more fully at the end of this section.

Although it is generally assumed that the patient-centered test is significantly more demanding than the professional standard with respect to the specific disclosures that must be made, would this necessarily be so in practice? It might not be so difficult under the professional standard to find a qualified expert who would support relatively full disclosure, leaving the issue in the jury's lap—where it might easily come out the same way as under the objective standard. There is, in any event, some empirical evidence that actual disclosure practices of clinicians do not differ according to the rule prevailing in the particular jurisdiction. See R. Faden & T. Beauchamp, supra, at 33.

A widely noted case involving the nature of the disclosures required was Arato v. Avedon, 858 P.2d 598 (Cal.1993). Its notoriety was triggered by the state appeals court's surprising ruling that the patient, who was diagnosed with fatal pancreatic cancer, should have been informed specifically of the high statistical risk of his imminent death, in part so that he could get his personal affairs in order. (His business failed after his death, and his estate suffered significant tax consequences.) The California Supreme Court reversed that result, ruling that disclosure of statistical information or of facts possibly desired for reasons unrelated to therapy should be governed by a professional, not a patient-oriented, standard. In particular, the court accepted the view expressed by experts that disclosure of the specific statistical improbability of a good outcome would mislead patients (statistics being only statistics) and might adversely affect their already dim prospects for survival. (Does freeing doctors from the need to disclose the direness of prospects, at least if the patient indicates an interest in knowing them, possibly allow them to foist chemotherapy and other high-cost, questionably beneficial treatments on them? The *Arato* plaintiffs argued that "had [Mr. Arato] known the bleak truth concerning his life expectancy, he would not have undergone the rigors of an unproven therapy, but would have chosen to live out his last days at peace with his wife and children, and arranging his business affairs." Id. at 602.)

7. *Refusals of Consent to Life-saving Treatment.* It is generally recognized that patients can refuse life-saving treatment—another acknowledgment of their right of self-determination. But what are the damages if they are treated despite their refusal of consent? In Anderson v. St. Francis–St. George Hosp., 671 N.E.2d 225 (Ohio 1996), the court refused to allow damages for "wrongful living" where a nurse had resuscitated an 82–year-old patient by defibrillation despite a "do-not-resuscitate" order entered on the patient's instruction. The patient suffered stroke two days later, was partially paralyzed, and died two years later, having himself filed the lawsuit, which his estate continued. The court observed that the stroke itself was not caused by the resuscitation and that some negligent acts may not have a legal remedy. But see Estate of Leach v. Shapiro, 469 N.E.2d 1047 (Ohio App. 1984) (allowing tort action against physicians who took heroic measures in violation of the patient's wishes). Cf. Strachan v. John F. Kennedy Mem. Hosp., 507 A.2d 718 (N.J.Super. 1986) (no liability to family for lack of procedure for expeditious turning off of respirator sustaining brain-dead suicide victim).

What if a hospital sought to collect from the family (or from Medicare) for services rendered following an unauthorized resuscitation? In First Healthcare Corp. v. Rettinger, 467 S.E.2d 243 (N.C.1996) (per curiam), reversing 456 S.E.2d 347 (N.C.App.1995), a nursing home sought to collect for the cost of care rendered after the patient's wife had asked to have treatment stopped. Although the patient had executed a living will, the state supreme court found no evidence that the conditions that might justify removing his life support had been satisfied. It therefore summarily approved a grant of summary judgment for the nursing home.

8. *Informed Consent in Radiology.* Some practical observations on informed consent are provided in the following excerpt:

> One question currently being debated among radiologists is whether the patient needs to be informed of the 1 in 40,000 risk of death associated with the intravenous injection of contrast agents for intravenous pyelography, computed tomography, or intravenous angiography. The answer to this depends on whether the procedure is being done in a "reasonable physician" or "reasonable person" type of jurisdiction. In the latter, a "reasonable person" probably would want to know about a chance of death, even though it is only 1 in 40,000. In "reasonable physician" jurisdictions, the radiologist needs to inform the patient only of the risks and complications that reasonable physicians in a similar locality would inform their patients of under similar circumstances. However, the locality rule for radiologists has generally been expanded to a national standard of practice. This obviously includes radiologists from "reasonable person" as well as "reasonable physician" jurisdictions, and the plaintiff could relatively easily get expert testimony that the risk of death is revealed. Although this problem has not yet arisen, the standard of practice in a "reasonable physician" jurisdiction should probably be given only by experts from other "reasonable physician" jurisdictions.
>
> Other problems radiologists have with informed consent derive from the episodic and impersonal relationship they have with the patient. Patients frequently feel more comfortable about discussing medical procedures with their internist or surgeon than with someone whom they have never met before. The radiologist also may be uncomfortable with the role of informing the patient about alternative procedures, many of which would be performed by nonradiologists. Finally, almost all radiologists have had the experience of going to the patient to obtain consent for a radiological procedure, only to find that the patient has never been informed of the need for the procedure in the first place. All of these problems lead radiologists to prefer that the consent be obtained by the patient's physician. However, radiologists must obtain the consent themselves. The reasons are threefold. First, confusion about who is to obtain the consent may result in the radiologist and clinician each thinking that the other has obtained the consent when, in fact, neither has. Second, the time during which the radiologist obtains consent may be the only opportunity he or she has to develop any type of patient-physician relationship prior to the procedure, and even the smallest degree of a relationship will be of great value if anything untoward occurs during the procedure. Moreover, the person who will be doing the procedure should be the one to obtain the consent, rather than having it obtained by agents, such as nurses, office personnel, or house staff. In two recent appellate decisions, the court has appropriately held that the responsibility for obtaining the consent lies with the radiologist performing the procedure, not with the referring

physician. However, the attending physician is best advised to verify this fact.

Because the issues of informed consent have become an important part of malpractice litigation, radiologists have shown great interest in detailed consent forms that specify all of the potential complications of a procedure and their relative incidence. Although the use of such forms should certainly not be encouraged for all procedures, prepared forms *may* have value in the many radiological and angiographic procedures for which complications are relatively few and their incidence is well documented.

However, detailed consent forms are a two-edged sword. Although they do an excellent job of memorializing the complications of which the patient has been informed, by implication they also reveal that the patient has not been informed of any complications that do not appear on the printed form. For this reason, many defense attorneys do not like detailed consent forms, preferring to have the physician make a notation in the chart that the patient has been informed of the risks, complications, and alternative procedures. Juries tend to believe timely notes in patients' charts, and at the time of the trial, the defendant physician can inform the jury about which complications he usually informs patients of prior to doing various procedures. If the procedure is in any way experimental or unproven, however, detailed consent forms are essential. In one such case, a very well-worded consent form was of great benefit to Dr. Cooley when his first artificial heart implant failed.

Reuter, Legal Aspects of Angiography and Interventive Radiology, 13 Legal Aspects of Med. Prac. 1, 2–3 (1985).

9. *Consent to Experimentation.* Note the reference in the preceding excerpt to the need for consent to experimentation. The case referred to, Karp v. Cooley, 493 F.2d 408 (5th Cir.1974), involved an emergency implantation in a patient of a wholly experimental mechanical heart, with quickly fatal results. The implantation was therapeutic in the sense that the purpose was to aid the patient, who was in a desperate situation anyway. The court found the detailed consent form helpful in finding no liability.

In what case that you have read did an issue of consent to an experimental procedure arise? See also Estrada v. Jaques, 321 S.E.2d 240, 253–54 (N.C.App.1984) (finding duty to disclose experimental nature of procedure; "the surgeons presented a full picture of the risks of the surgical procedure * * * without informing him of its experimental nature and their consequent lack of knowledge of the risks of whether it would fail or not"); Schneider v. Revici, 817 F.2d 987 (2d Cir.1987) (patient consented to unconventional, investigatory therapy for breast cancer and sued when it failed; verdict awarding 50% damages under comparative fault statute set aside to allow affirmative complete defense of express assumption of risk). In general, a higher standard of disclosure appears to apply whenever the procedure, even though therapeutic, is experimental. See *Estrada*, supra, for fuller discussion.

10. *Is the Law's Objective Realistic?* Is it realistic to expect patients to make intelligent choices concerning their treatment? Do the same psychological findings (some of them cited in chapter 2(§B)) that make one distrustful of consumers as decision makers in the economic marketplace (especially in weighing remote risks) cast doubt on the validity of patient sovereignty in making decisions about medical care? The way in which patients' options are framed has been shown to influence their choices. McNeil et al., On the Elicitation of Preferences for Alternative Therapies, 306 New Eng.J.Med. 1259 (1982). See also Rodwin, Physician's Conflicts of Interest, 320 New Eng. J. Med. 1405 (1989) (assessing, with sources, the efficacy of informed consent laws and standards):

> [E]vidence suggests that full disclosure still occurs relatively infrequently and not as envisioned by the law. One observer has suggested that physicians sometimes couch their disclosures in terms designed to promote more costly procedures. Psychological studies also indicate that even with accurate disclosure, patients may not understand the information provided or its implications. * * * The detailed written forms used in obtaining consent sometimes obscure understanding. Patients often treat them as meaningless paperwork and do not remember what they have signed.

It seems likely that a physician might satisfy the law's letter without really surrendering dominance in the doctor/patient relationship.

Even though it may be easy to doubt that patients are competent decision makers and that the law can successfully compel physicians to relate to their patients in ethically satisfying ways, maintaining a highly visible and much discussed expectation of interpersonal communication may have symbolic value, affecting ethical attitudes and, indirectly, some conduct. To be sure, one can argue that it is ethically useful to remind physicians that patients, despite their technical ignorance, are to be dealt with as competent, autonomous human beings. But empirical evidence supporting the existence of this or any other kind of benefit from the law's requirements is not substantial. See C. Lidz et al., Informed Consent: A Study of Decisionmaking in Psychiatry 326–27 (1984) ("It is not unduly harsh to conclude that current informed consent policy has been a dismal failure in the [psychiatric] settings we studied, at least when measured against the loftier goals of the doctrine. We simply did not witness a consistent pattern of behavior by staff members that was directed toward providing patients with adequate information on the basis of which they might make intelligent decisions; nor did we witness much enthusiasm by patients for making decisions when they were given the opportunity to do so."); Meisel & Roth, Toward an Informed Discussion of Informed Consent: A Review and Critique of the Empirical Studies, 25 Ariz.L.Rev. 265, 336 (1983) ("Despite the tomes that have been written about informed consent, * * * we know almost nothing about its operation.").

Whatever the empirical research shows, however, is the law still right to encourage physicians to be straight with patients? Medical folklore has long maintained that a good "bedside manner" is an excellent protection against malpractice suits when results disappoint patient expectations. Consider the following synthesis of legal and medical considerations:

> Informed consent need not be a mere formality with a limited medicolegal function. Rather, it can be a focal point in establishing a therapeutic alliance. Seen as a dialogue in which both the cognitive and affective implications of uncertainty are acknowledged and shared, informed consent is a powerful clinical tool. Through its use, helplessness is replaced by a degree of control as the patient becomes a coexperimenter rather than a passive object of experimentation. Hopelessness is replaced by a degree of hope as the patient comes to see that uncertainty does not imply irrationality, defeat, or abandonment. Finally, the alliance between the patient and physician, instead of being undermined by the specious denial of uncertainty, is strengthened by the mutuality of its acceptance.
>
> The legal benefits flow from the clinical ones. The usual perfunctory approach to informed consent can be characterized as a form of defensive medicine. Undertaken primarily to protect the physician from legal liability, it often fails to do even that. In contrast, the therapeutic use of informed consent to enlist the patient in an active alliance with the physician discourages overly simplistic blaming and reduces the alienation from the physician that leads the patient to seek legal remedies for dissatisfaction. This is true malpractice prevention, which offers the physician stronger legal protection by allowing both doctor and patient to deepen their understanding while building a supportive and trusting relationship—a relationship based not on unrealistic certainty but on honesty in facing the uncertainty inherent in clinical practice.

Gutheil et al., Malpractice Prevention through the Sharing of Uncertainty: Informed Consent and the Therapeutic Alliance, 311 New Eng.J.Med. 49, 51 (1984). Query, however, whether the law truly succeeds in instilling respect for patient autonomy, since physicians seem often to reduce the law's expectations to a formalistic checklist and to obey the law's letter rather than its spirit.

11. *The Trade-offs in Mandating Disclosure.* Does informed consent have costs? Obviously, time and effort that physicians spend in informing patients in detail about various aspects of their disease and treatment cannot be spent in caring for others. In an interesting reexamination of informed-consent doctrine, Professor Peter Schuck writes,

> [T]he cases evince little systematic judicial interest in the doctrine's actual consequences, especially its costs. Instead, courts tend to invoke the values of autonomy and improved decisionmaking and then analyze the implications of those values, while maintaining a silence on the issue of costs. This mode of analysis assumes that the costs of advancing these values are either de minimis or not worth analyzing.

Schuck, Rethinking Informed Consent, 103 Yale L.J. 899, 939 (1994). Schuck also observes that patients differ in their desire to know the risks and benefits of various treatment options: "Some patients seem to prefer leaving some or all medical treatment decisions to their physicians * * * [while] others—I call them (us) 'information junkies'—more closely approximate the conventional 'rational consumer' * * *." He then proposes that, where consumers are represented by an appropriate agent bargaining with providers on their behalf, "the law should permit such groups to contract with providers over the appropriate features of informed consent." Because health care is being increasingly provided in different settings—in integrated health plans as well as by individual physicians with some discretion in spending a third party's funds—, Schuck suggests that consent requirements might be permitted to vary with the context in which the patient elects to be treated. Notes at the end of this section will explore further the possibilities adumbrated here.

Johnson v. Kokemoor

Supreme Court of Wisconsin, 1996.
199 Wis.2d 615, 545 N.W.2d 495.

■ SHIRLEY S. ABRAHAMSON, J.

* * *

This case presents the issue of whether the circuit court erred in admitting evidence that the defendant, in undertaking his duty to obtain the plaintiff's informed consent before operating to clip an aneurysm, failed (1) to divulge the extent of his experience in performing this type of operation; (2) to compare the morbidity and mortality rates for this type of surgery among experienced surgeons and inexperienced surgeons like himself; and (3) to refer the plaintiff to a tertiary care center staffed by physicians more experienced in performing the same surgery. The admissibility of such physician-specific evidence in a case involving the doctrine of informed consent raises an issue of first impression in this court and is an issue with which appellate courts have had little experience.

* * *

We conclude that all three items of evidence were material to the issue of informed consent in this case. As we stated in Martin v. Richards, 192 Wis. 2d 156, 174, 531 N.W.2d 70 (1995), "a patient cannot make an informed, intelligent decision to consent to a physician's suggested treatment unless the physician discloses what is material to the patient's decision, i.e., all of the viable alternatives and risks of the treatment proposed." In this case information regarding a physician's experience in performing a particular procedure, a physician's risk statistics as compared with those of other physicians who perform the procedure, and the availability of other centers and physicians better able to perform that procedure would have facilitated the plaintiff's awareness of "all of the viable alternatives" available to her and thereby aided her exercise of informed consent. We therefore conclude that under the circumstances of this case, the circuit court did not erroneously exercise its discretion in admitting the evidence.

I

* * *

On the advice of her family physician, the plaintiff underwent a CT scan to determine the cause of her headaches. Following the scan, the family physician referred the plaintiff to the defendant, a neurosurgeon in the Chippewa Falls area. The defendant diagnosed an enlarging aneurysm at the rear of the plaintiff's brain and recommended surgery to clip the aneurysm. The defendant performed the surgery in October of 1990.

The defendant clipped the aneurysm, rendering the surgery a technical success. But as a consequence of the surgery, the plaintiff, who had no neurological impairments prior to surgery, was rendered an incomplete quadriplegic. * * *

At trial, the plaintiff introduced evidence that the defendant overstated the urgency of her need for surgery and overstated his experience with performing the particular type of aneurysm surgery which she required. According to testimony introduced during the plaintiff's case in chief, when the plaintiff questioned the defendant regarding his experience, he replied that he had performed the surgery she required "several" times; asked what he meant by "several," the defendant said "dozens" and "lots of times."

In fact, however, the defendant had relatively limited experience with aneurysm surgery. He had performed thirty aneurysm surgeries during residency, but * * * had operated on basilar bifurcation aneurysms only twice and had never operated on a large basilar bifurcation aneurysm such as the plaintiff's aneurysm.[11]

The plaintiff also presented evidence that the defendant understated the morbidity and mortality rate associated with basilar bifurcation aneurysm surgery. According to the plaintiff's witnesses, the defendant had told the plaintiff that her surgery carried a two percent risk of death or serious impairment[. I]nformation in treatises and articles which the defendant reviewed in preparation for the plaintiff's surgery set the morbidity and mortality rate at approximately fifteen percent for a basilar bifurcation aneurysm. The plaintiff also introduced expert testimony that the morbidity and mortality rate for basilar bifurcation aneurysm operations performed by one with the defendant's relatively limited experience would be between twenty and thirty percent, and "closer to the thirty percent range."

Finally, the plaintiff introduced into evidence testimony and exhibits stating that a reasonable physician in the defendant's position would have advised the plaintiff of the availability of more experienced surgeons and would have referred her to them. The plaintiff also introduced evidence stating that patients with basilar aneurysms should be referred to tertiary care centers—such as the Mayo Clinic, only 90 miles away—which contain the proper neurological intensive care unit and microsurgical facilities and

11. The defendant testified that he had failed to inform the plaintiff that he was not and never had been board certified in neurosurgery and that he was not a subspecialist in aneurysm surgery.

which are staffed by neurosurgeons with the requisite training and experience to perform basilar bifurcation aneurysm surgeries.

In his testimony at trial, the defendant denied having suggested to the plaintiff that her condition was urgent and required immediate care. He also denied having stated that her risk was comparable to that associated with an angiogram or minor surgical procedures such as tonsillectomy or appendectomy. While he acknowledged telling the plaintiff that the risk of death or serious impairment associated with clipping an aneurysm was two percent, he also claims to have told her that because of the location of her aneurysm, the risks attending her surgery would be greater, although he was unable to tell her precisely how much greater. In short, the defendant testified that his disclosure to the plaintiff adequately informed her regarding the risks she faced.

The defendant's expert witnesses testified that the defendant's recommendation of surgery was appropriate, that this type of surgery is regularly undertaken in a community hospital setting, and that the risks attending anterior and posterior circulation aneurysm surgeries was comparable. They placed the risk accompanying the plaintiff's surgery at between five and ten percent, although one of the defendant's experts also testified that such statistics can be misleading. The defendant's expert witnesses also testified that when queried by a patient regarding their experience, they would divulge the extent of that experience and its relation to the experience of other physicians performing similar operations.

* * *

IV

The defendant contends that the circuit court erred in allowing the plaintiff to introduce evidence regarding the defendant's limited experience in operating upon aneurysms comparable to the plaintiff's aneurysm. Wisconsin's law of informed consent, the defendant continues, requires a physician to reveal only those risks inherent in the treatment. Everyone agrees, argues the defendant, that he advised the plaintiff regarding those risks: the potential perils of death, a stroke or blindness associated with her surgery.

The defendant argues that the circuit court's decision to admit evidence pertaining to his surgical experience confused relevant information relating to treatment risks with irrelevant and prejudicial information that the defendant did not possess the skill and experience of the very experienced aneurysm surgeons. Therefore, according to the defendant, the jury's attention was diverted from a consideration of whether the defendant made required disclosures regarding treatment to the question of who was performing the plaintiff's operation. Thus, the defendant contends, the circuit court transformed a duty to reasonably inform into a duty to reasonably perform the surgery, even though the plaintiff was not alleging negligent treatment.

The doctrine of informed consent should not, argues the defendant, be construed as a general right to information regarding possible alternative procedures, health care facilities and physicians. Instead, urges the defendant, the doctrine of informed consent should be viewed as creating a "bright line" rule requiring physicians to disclose only significant complications intrinsic to the contemplated procedure. The defendant interprets Wis. Stat. § 448.30 as an embodiment of this more modest definition of informed consent. In sum, the defendant urges that the statutory provisions require disclosure of risks associated with particular "treatments" rather than the risks associated with particular physicians.

We reject the defendant's proposed bright line rule that it is error as a matter of law to admit evidence in an informed consent case that the physician failed to inform the patient regarding the physician's experience with the surgery or treatment at issue. The prudent patient standard adopted by Wisconsin in [Scaria v. St. Paul Fire & Marine Ins. Co., 68 Wis.2d 1, 227 N.W.2d 647 (1975) (setting forth common-law rule codified in Wis. Stat. § 448.30)] is incompatible with such a bright line rule.

* * *

In this case, the plaintiff introduced ample evidence that had a reasonable person in her position been aware of the defendant's relative lack of experience in performing basilar bifurcation aneurysm surgery, that person would not have undergone surgery with him. * * * We conclude that the circuit court did not erroneously exercise its discretion in admitting evidence regarding the defendant's lack of experience and the difficulty of the proposed procedure. A reasonable person in the plaintiff's position would have considered such information material in making an intelligent and informed decision about the surgery.

We also reject the defendant's claim that even if this information was material, it should have been excluded because its prejudicial effect outweighed its probative value. The defendant contends that the admission of such evidence allowed the jury to infer that the plaintiff's partial paralysis was a product of the defendant's lack of experience and skill rather than a consequence of his alleged failure to inform.

We disagree with the defendant's claim that evidence pertaining to the defendant's experience was unduly and unfairly prejudicial. While a jury might confuse negligent failure to disclose with negligent treatment, the likelihood of confusion is nonexistent or de minimis in this case. The plaintiff dismissed her negligent treatment claim before trial. It is thus unlikely that the jury would confuse an issue not even before it with the issue that was actually being tried. * * *

V

The defendant next argues that the circuit court erred in allowing the plaintiff to introduce evidence of morbidity and mortality rates associated with the surgery at issue. The defendant particularly objects to comparative risk statistics purporting to estimate and compare the morbidity and mortality rates when the surgery at issue is performed, respectively, by a physician of limited experience such as the defendant and by the acknowledged masters in the field. * * *

The defendant asserts that admission of these morbidity and mortality rates would lead the jury to find him liable for failing to perform at the level of the masters rather than for failing to adequately inform the plaintiff regarding the risks associated with her surgery. Furthermore, contends the defendant, statistics are notoriously inaccurate and misleading.

* * *

The defendant concedes that the duty to procure a patient's informed consent requires a physician to reveal the general risks associated with a particular surgery. The defendant does not explain why the duty to inform about this general risk data should be interpreted to categorically exclude evidence relating to provider-specific risk information, even when that provider-specific data is geared to a clearly delineated surgical procedure and identifies a particular provider as an independent risk factor. When different physicians have substantially different success rates, whether surgery is performed by one rather than another represents a choice between "alternate, viable medical modes of treatment" under § 448.30.

For example, while there may be a general risk of ten percent that a particular surgical procedure will result in paralysis or death, that risk may climb to forty percent when the particular procedure is performed by a relatively inexperienced surgeon. It defies logic to interpret this statute as requiring that the first, almost meaningless statistic be divulged to a patient while the second, far more relevant statistic should not be. Under *Scaria* and its progeny as well as the codification of *Scaria* as Wis. Stat. § 448.30, the second statistic would be material to the patient's exercise of an intelligent and informed consent regarding treatment options. A circuit court may in its discretion conclude that the second statistic is admissible.

The doctrine of informed consent requires disclosure of "all of the viable alternatives and risks of the treatment proposed" which would be material to a patient's decision. We therefore conclude that when different physicians have substantially different success rates with the same procedure and a reasonable person in the patient's position would consider such information material, the circuit court may admit this statistical evidence.[32]

We caution, as did the court of appeals, that our decision will not always require physicians to give patients comparative risk evidence in

32. See Aaron D. Twerski & Neil B. Cohen, Comparing Medical Providers: A First Look at the New Era of Medical Statistics, 58 Brook. L.Rev. 5 (1992). Professors Twerski and Cohen note that the development of sophisticated data regarding risks of various procedures and statistical models comparing the success rates of medical providers signal changes in informed consent law. Specifically, they state,

The duty to provide information may require more than a simple sharing of visceral concerns about the wisdom of undertaking a given therapeutic procedure. Physicians may have a responsibility to identify and correlate risk factors and to communicate the results to patients as a predicate to fulfilling their obligation to inform.

* * *

statistical terms to obtain informed consent. Rather, we hold that evidence of the morbidity and mortality outcomes of different physicians was admissible under the circumstances of this case.

* * *

VI

The defendant also asserts that the circuit court erred as a matter of law in allowing the plaintiff to introduce expert testimony that because of the difficulties associated with operating on the plaintiff's aneurysm, the defendant should have referred her to a tertiary care center containing a proper neurological intensive care unit, more extensive microsurgical facilities and more experienced surgeons. While evidence that a physician should have referred a patient elsewhere may support an action alleging negligent treatment, argues the defendant, it has no place in an informed consent action.

The court of appeals agreed with the defendant that this evidence should have been excluded, and it further concluded that admission of this evidence created "a serious danger [that] the jury may confuse a duty to provide average quality care with a duty to adequately inform of medical risks."

We share the concern expressed by the court of appeals and underscored by the defendant, but their concern is misplaced in this case. Here, the plaintiff was not asserting a claim for negligent performance. Just because expert testimony is relevant to one claim does not mean that it is not relevant to another.

* * *

The plaintiff's medical experts testified that given the nature and difficulty of the surgery at issue, the plaintiff could not make an intelligent decision or give an informed consent without being made aware that surgery in a tertiary facility would have decreased the risk she faced. One of the plaintiff's experts, Dr. Haring J.W. Nauta, stated that "it's not fair not to bring up the subject of referral to another center when the problem is as difficult to treat" as the plaintiff's aneurysm was. * * * Articles from the medical literature introduced by the plaintiff also stated categorically that the surgery at issue should be performed at a tertiary care center while being "excluded" from the community setting because of "the limited surgical experience" and lack of proper equipment and facilities available in such hospitals.

* * * [T]he defendant argues that if his duty to procure the plaintiff's informed consent includes an obligation to disclose that she consider seeking treatment elsewhere, then there will be no logical stopping point to what the doctrine of informed consent might encompass. We disagree with the defendant. As the plaintiff noted in her brief to this court, "it is a rare exception when the vast body of medical literature and expert opinion agree that the difference in experience of the surgeon performing the operation will impact the risk of morbidity/mortality as was the case here," thereby requiring referral. At oral argument before this court, counsel for the

plaintiff stated that under "many circumstances" and indeed "probably most circumstances," whether or not a physician referred a patient elsewhere would be "utterly irrelevant" in an informed consent case. In the vast majority of significantly less complicated cases, such a referral would be irrelevant and unnecessary.

Moreover, we have already concluded that comparative risk data distinguishing the defendant's morbidity and mortality rate from the rate of more experienced physicians was properly before the jury. A close link exists between such data and the propriety of referring a patient elsewhere. A physician who discloses that other physicians might have lower morbidity and mortality rates when performing the same procedure will presumably have access to information regarding who some of those physicians are. When the duty to share comparative risk data is material to a patient's exercise of informed consent, an ensuing referral elsewhere will often represent no more than a modest and logical next step.

Given the difficulties involved in performing the surgery at issue in this case, coupled with evidence that the defendant exaggerated his own prior experience while downplaying the risks confronting the plaintiff, the circuit court properly exercised its discretion in admitting evidence that a physician of good standing would have made the plaintiff aware of the alternative of lower risk surgery with a different, more experienced surgeon in a better-equipped facility.

For the reasons set forth, we conclude that the circuit court did not erroneously exercise its discretion in admitting the evidence at issue, and accordingly, we reverse the decision of the court of appeals and remand the cause to the circuit court for further proceedings consistent with this opinion.

NOTES AND QUESTIONS ON DUTIES WITH RESPECT TO PROVIDER–SPECIFIC RISKS

1. While provocative, the holding in the principal case is unusual. See, e.g., Ditto v. McCurdy, 947 P.2d 952 (Haw. 1997), in which the plaintiff claimed fraud in that the surgeon who performed her disfiguring breast augmentation, although certified in cosmetic surgery, failed to disclose his lack of certification in plastic surgery, which was normally a prerequisite for hospital privileges to perform the operation in Hawaii. The defendant offered evidence that a "turf war" between plastic and cosmetic surgeons explained the latter fact. The court dismissed the fraud count, holding that the law of informed consent should govern the case and, as codified in Hawaii, did not require the disclosure in question.

2. *Duty to Refer.* That a primary care physician has a duty to refer certain cases to specialists seems clear enough. But should one specialist (e.g., a neurosurgeon) have a duty to refer a patient to a more experienced one (or to a better-equipped institution) in certain situations? The logic behind such a requirement is strong in some circumstances (as in the principal case) both because experience in performing a procedure contributes to proficiency and because institutions with a high volume of particular procedures are reported to have better outcomes (providing, as noted in chapter 5(§D), a possible rationale of certificate-of-need regulation). On the other hand, should any bad result, even one not caused by provable negligence, trigger an inquiry into whether it might have been prevented by referral to a more competent practitioner? Presumably the duty will be deemed to exist only in cases, like the principal one, in which the differences between practitioners are sufficiently great to trigger a special obligation to disclose those differences.

In other markets, how often are consumers informed by one competitor that another one may offer a better product? In the current age of consumerism in health care, should the primary burden of choosing the right doctor be deemed to fall on the patient (and perhaps on his referring primary care physician), not on the first doctor chosen? The general publication of provider-specific outcomes is a popular idea with some reformers, suggesting that consumers should be expected to take some responsibility on themselves. Alternatively, one might look to managed-care organizations to steer patients to better providers. (Is this a realistic expectation? See notes at the end of this section and chapter 8.)

3. *Disclosing Other Risks*. Must physicians, or the hospitals they work for, reveal personal characteristics of the physician that might, but do not necessarily, affect performance. Several courts have considered whether knowledge of a physician's history of alcoholism or drug abuse is necessary before truly informed consent can be obtained. In Hidding v. Williams, 578 So.2d 1192 (La.App.1991), a physician who had been suspended from practice for habitual drunkenness and was again abusing alcohol was held to have a duty to disclose his condition to a surgical patient, along with other risks of surgery. However, in Kaskie v. Wright, 589 A.2d 213 (Pa.Super.1991), the court affirmed summary judgment for a physician and hospital in a case raising nondisclosure of alcoholism and of problems with the physician's license to practice. The court said, "Matters such as personal weaknesses and professional credentials of those who provide health care are the responsibility of the hospitals employing them, the professional corporations who offer their services, or the associations which are charged with oversight. Their failure to fulfill their obligations in this regard becomes a matter of negligence, and it is from them that recovery must be sought." Id. at 217. Do you agree that principles of corporate negligence offer a better way to address these problems than stretching the law of informed consent?

A special issue has been the duty of practitioners to disclose HIV infection. In Behringer v. Medical Center at Princeton, 592 A.2d 1251 (N.J. Super. 1991), the court had to balance an HIV-positive doctor's right under New Jersey law not to be discriminated against against the patient's right to know material facts before consenting to treatment. The court eventually upheld the Medical Center's decision to require the physician to disclose his HIV infection to any surgical patients. A similar result was reached in Maryland under a reasonable-patient standard, Faya v. Almaraz, 620 A.2d

327 (Md.1993), but that decision has been criticized by other courts. The subject attracted considerable scholarly attention. See, e.g., Daniels, HIV–Infected Health Care Professionals: Public Threat or Public Sacrifice?, 70 Milbank Q. 3 (1992); Glantz et al., Risky Business: Setting Public Health Policy for HIV-Infected Health Care Professionals, in id. at 43. So-called "look back" studies done on patients operated on by physicians infected with HIV have disclosed almost no associated risk. Should this mean that HIV infection is not a material issue? What should a "reasonable patient" expect? Is a professional or a reasonable-patient standard best applied in these cases? Cf. Brennan, Ensuring Adequate Health Care for the Sick: The Challenge of the Acquired Immunodeficiency Syndrome as an Occupational Disease, 1988 Duke L.J. 29, 35–47 (discussing duties of health care providers with respect to HIV-positive patients).

NOTE ON LEGISLATION CONCERNING INFORMED CONSENT

The seeming trend toward more patient-oriented doctrines concerning informed consent ran directly into the tort crises of the 1970s and 1980s. Although in this period individuals seeking health care were increasingly seen as consumers and not just as patients, the pressure to raise barriers to legal actions against physicians brought about some setbacks in the movement to vindicate patient autonomy through the law of informed consent.

Like Wisconsin in *Johnson v. Kokemoor*, somewhat more than half the states now have statutes dealing specifically with informed consent to medical treatment, some of them (as in *Johnson*) simply codifying earlier judicial holdings while others seek to reverse or head off a trend seen as encouraging unwarranted litigation. Most of these laws were enacted in their original form during the 1970s' malpractice crisis and take one of two basic approaches. Some of them proceed by listing the types of information that a health care provider must give a patient and then provide that such disclosure gives rise to a presumption of informed consent. Other states proceeded by listing the elements of a cause of action based on a failure to obtain informed consent and the defenses that may be offered to such a claim. See generally Meisel & Kabnick, Informed Consent to Medical Treatment: An Analysis of Recent Legislation, 41 U.Pitt.L.Rev. 407 (1980).

Within these frameworks, the statutes may address any of the following specific topics: (1) battery vs. negligence; (2) the standard of disclosure; (3) causation; (4) who can give informed consent on behalf of an incapacitated patient; (5) implied consent (in cases of emergency where no one capable of giving consent is available); (6) patient comprehension (and whether disclosure must be sufficient to communicate to the patient himself or only to a "reasonable person"); (7) therapeutic privilege (where disclosure is judged harmful to the patient's well-being); (8) patient waiver; (9) consent forms; and (10) evidentiary and procedural issues.

The findings of an exhaustive state-by-state examination of the early informed-consent statutes, published in 1980, were summarized as follows:

The number of jurisdictions in which, in our estimate, such changes are likely to *significantly* reduce the likelihood of recovery totals only four.[905] The most significant change involves the standard of disclosure—usually the change from a lay to a professional standard, but possibly the adoption of a professional standard against the background of an unclear on non-existent common-law standard. Thus, at most, four jurisdictions have made recovery for lack of informed consent substantially more difficult, and in a way which precludes judicial circumvention of the statutory changes. In three other jurisdictions, significant structural changes in the doctrine make it less likely that patients will recover. In Oregon, this structural change involves placing the burden on the patient to seek information above a minimal amount of statutorily mandated disclosure; in Hawaii and Texas, the content of disclosure is determined not by reference to a word-formula in the time-honored, common-law fashion, but by reference to an administratively promulgated list. However, in these three jurisdictions, the nature of the changes still allows for some judicial maneuvering.

In many jurisdictions, the statutes make changes in the common law which appear to make recovery more difficult, but should not actually do so. For instance, a statute which recognizes more exceptions to the duty to obtain informed consent than did the common law seems to provide the doctor with greater latitude for withholding disclosure or obtaining consent than did the common law. But on closer analysis, we find that the common law, while not explicitly recognizing certain exceptions, had never rejected them either. Given that the rationale for the exceptions is to be found in deeply-seated societal values and in the exigencies of medical practice, it is almost impossible that a court would fail to recognize an exception if the issue were to be presented for decision.

Although few jurisdictions have adopted statutes which are likely to make recovery substantially more difficult, none of the statutes will make recovery easier. Perhaps, then, the most significant among the effects that some of the statutes may have is that they will preclude the possibility of judicial liberalization of common-law rules in a manner that might favor patients. The trend toward the rejection of a professionally determined standard of care initiated by [*Cobbs* and *Canterbury*] may have eased; indeed substitution of a lay standard for a professional standard will be precluded in seven jurisdictions in which the common-law professional standard was codified in statute * * *. By contrast, the potential for the judicial definition and application of the exceptions to informed consent in a manner that will protect the overriding interest in patient self-determination remains unaffected, since the statutes do little more than *recognize* various exceptions, without *defining* them in a manner which is either inconsistent with this interest or which precludes judicial definition.

[We] can say with a high degree of confidence that, in the overwhelming majority of cases, the informed consent statutes are little more than window-dressing, creating the appearance of change without the substance. The legislatures have, by enacting informed consent statutes, conveyed the

905. Maine, Nebraska, New York, and Vermont.

> message to the medical profession that they are responsive to the profession's concerns. It is, however, the act of legislating, per se, that conveys this message and not the content of the legislation.

Meisel & Kabnick, supra, at 562–63.

Some more recent statutory developments include enactment of a lenient standard of general disclosure in South Dakota, where the physician need only show a good faith belief that a patient does or does not have the capacity to give informed consent to justify nondisclosure actions. S.D. Codified Laws § 34–12C–7 (Michie 1994). Georgia altered its informed consent requirement to set out specific requirements for disclosure, but provided, "A failure to comply with the requirements of this Code section shall not constitute a separate cause of action but may give rise to an action for medical malpractice." Ga. Code Ann. § 31–9–6(d) (Supp. 1990). Texas created a Medical Disclosure Panel "to determine which risks and hazards related to medical care and surgical procedures must be disclosed by health care providers or physicians to their patients or persons authorized to consent for their patients and to establish the general form and substance of such disclosure." Tex. Rev. Civ. Stat. Ann. art. 4590i § 6.03(a) (West 1998). Illinois enacted a law requiring the state Department of Public Health to publish a summary of methods for detecting and diagnosing breast cancer, as well as medically viable alternative methods for treatment, with a view to informing patients of the advantages and risks of various procedures. 20 Ill. Comp. Stat. Ann. 2310/55.49 (West Supp. 1997). Similar attempts standardize information flow have occurred in other states.

In the face of lobbying from physician groups, several state legislatures have sought to roll back the more subjective patient-based standard and to restore the professional test for appropriate disclosure. In Idaho, for example, where the state supreme court had adopted the standard enunciated in *Cobbs v. Grant*, LePelley v. Grefenson, 614 P.2d 962 (Idaho 1980), the court was forced to conclude in 1991 that "to interpret the language [in a new statute] to be a subjective patient-based standard of disclosure is contrary to the ordinary and usual meaning of the words used." Sherwood v. Carter, 805 P.2d 452 (Idaho 1991). See also Savina v. Sterling Drug, Inc., 795 P.2d 915 (Kan.1990); Roybal v. Bell, 778 P.2d 108 (Wyo.1989). Some courts have, however, remained steadfast in their support for the reasonably prudent patient standard. See Christensen v. Munsen, 867 P.2d 626 (Wash.1994).

Truman v. Thomas

Supreme Court of California, 1980.
27 Cal.3d 285, 165 Cal.Rptr. 308, 611 P.2d 902.

■ BIRD, CHIEF JUSTICE.

This court must decide whether a physician's failure to inform a patient of the material risks of not consenting to a recommended pap smear, so that the patient might make an informed choice, may have breached the physician's duty of due care to his patient, who died from cancer of the cervix.

I

Respondent, Dr. Claude R. Thomas, is a family physician engaged in a general medical practice. He was first contacted in April 1963 by appellants' mother, Rena Truman, in connection with her second pregnancy. He continued to act as the primary physician for Mrs. Truman and her two children until March 1969. During this six-year period, Mrs. Truman not only sought his medical advice, but often discussed personal matters with him.

* * *

Appellants are Rena Truman's two children. They brought this wrongful death action against Dr. Thomas for his failure to perform a pap smear test on their mother[, who died in 1970 of cervical cancer at the age of 30]. At the trial, expert testimony was presented which indicated that if Mrs. Truman had undergone a pap smear at any time between 1964 and 1969, the cervical tumor probably would have been discovered in time to save her life. There was disputed expert testimony that the standard of medical practice required a physician to explain to women patients that it is important to have a pap smear each year * * *.

Although Dr. Thomas saw Mrs. Truman frequently between 1964 and 1969, he never performed a pap smear test on her. Dr. Thomas testified that he did not "specifically" inform Mrs. Truman of the risk involved in any failure to undergo the pap smear test. Rather, "I said, 'You should have a pap smear.' We don't say by now it can be Stage Two [in the development of cervical cancer] or go through all of the different lectures about cancer. I think it is a widely known and generally accepted manner of treatment and I think the patient has a high degree of responsibility. We are not enforcers, we are advisors." * * *

[Dr. Thomas also testified, "]I am sure we discussed it with her so often that she couldn't [have] fail[ed] to realize that we wanted her to have a complete examination, breast examination, ovaries and pap smear." Dr. Thomas also testified that on at least two occasions when he performed pelvic examinations of Mrs. Truman she refused him permission to perform the test, stating she could not afford the cost. Dr. Thomas offered to defer payment, but Mrs. Truman wanted to pay cash.

Appellants * * * asked that the jury be instructed that it "is the duty of a physician to disclose to his patient all relevant information to enable the patient to make an informed decision regarding the submission to or refusal to take a diagnostic test. [¶] Failure of the physician to disclose to his patient all relevant information including the risks to the patient if the test is refused renders the physician liable for any injury legally resulting from the patient's refusal to take the test if a reasonably prudent person in the patient's position would not have refused the test if she had been adequately informed of all the significant perils." [The instructions was refused, and no instruction was given on this theory of liability.]

The jury rendered a special verdict, finding Dr. Thomas free of any negligence that proximately caused Mrs. Truman's death. This appeal followed.

II

The central issue for this court is whether Dr. Thomas breached his duty of care to Mrs. Truman when he failed to inform her of the potentially fatal consequences of allowing cervical cancer to develop undetected by a pap smear.

In *Cobbs v. Grant*, this court * * * stated that a patient must be apprised not only of the "risks inherent in the procedure [prescribed, but also] the risks of a decision not to undergo the treatment, and the probability of a successful outcome of the treatment." This rule applies whether the procedure involves treatment or a diagnostic test. On the one hand, a physician recommending a risk-free procedure may safely forego discussion beyond that necessary to conform to competent medical practice and to obtain the patient's consent. If a patient indicates that he or she is going to *decline* the risk-free test or treatment, then the doctor has the additional duty of advising of all material risks of which a reasonable person would want to be informed before deciding not to undergo the procedure. On the other hand, if the recommended test or treatment is itself risky, then the physician should always explain the potential consequences of declining to follow the recommended course of action.

Nevertheless, Dr. Thomas contends that *Cobbs* does not apply to him because the duty to disclose applies only where the patient *consents* to the recommended procedure. He argues that since a physician's advice may be presumed to be founded on an expert appraisal of the patient's medical needs, no reasonable patient would fail to undertake further inquiry before rejecting such advice. Therefore, patients who reject their physician's advice should shoulder the burden of inquiry as to the possible consequences of their decision.

This argument is inconsistent with *Cobbs*. The duty to disclose was imposed in *Cobbs* so that patients might meaningfully exercise their right to make decisions about their own bodies. The importance of this right should not be diminished by the manner in which it is exercised. Further, the need for disclosure is not lessened because patients reject a recommended procedure. Such a decision does not alter "what has been termed the 'fiducial qualities' of the physician-patient relationship," since patients who reject a procedure are as unskilled in the medical sciences as those who consent. To now hold that patients who reject their physician's advice have the burden of inquiring as to the potential consequences of their decisions would be to contradict *Cobbs*. It must be remembered that Dr. Thomas was not engaged in an arms-length transaction with Mrs. Truman. Clearly, under *Cobbs,* he was obligated to provide her with all the information material to her decision.

Dr. Thomas next contends that, as a matter of law, he had no duty to disclose to Mrs. Truman the risk of failing to undergo a pap smear test because "the danger [is] remote and commonly appreciated to be remote." (*Cobbs,* supra.) The merit of this contention depends on whether a jury could reasonably find that knowledge of this risk was material to Mrs. Truman's decision.

The record indicates that the pap smear test is an accurate detector of cervical cancer. Although the probability that Mrs. Truman had cervical cancer was low, Dr. Thomas knew that the potential harm of failing to detect the disease at an early stage was death. [T]he risk * * * was the principal reason why Dr. Thomas recommended that she undergo a pap smear.

Little evidence was introduced on whether this risk was commonly known. Dr. Thomas testified that the risk would be known to a reasonable person. Whether such evidence is sufficient to establish that there was no general duty to disclose this risk to patients is a question of fact for the jury. Moreover, even assuming such disclosure was not generally required, the circumstances in this case may establish that Dr. Thomas did have a duty to inform Mrs. Truman of the risks she was running by not undergoing a pap smear.

Dr. Thomas testified he never specifically informed her of the purpose of a pap smear test. There was no evidence introduced that Mrs. Truman was aware of the serious danger entailed in not undergoing the test. However, there was testimony that Mrs. Truman said she would not undergo the test on certain occasions because of its cost or because "she just didn't feel like it." Under these circumstances, a jury could reasonably conclude that Dr. Thomas had a duty to inform Mrs. Truman of the danger of refusing the test because it was not reasonable for Dr. Thomas to assume that Mrs. Truman appreciated the potentially fatal consequences of her conduct. Accordingly, this court cannot decide as a matter of law that Dr. Thomas owed absolutely no duty to Mrs. Truman to make this important disclosure that affected her life.

* * * [T]he rejected instruction would have correctly indicated that satisfaction of the prudent person test for causation established in *Cobbs* was necessary but not sufficient for plaintiffs to recover. If the jury were to reasonably conclude that Mrs. Truman would have unreasonably refused a pap smear in the face of adequate disclosure, there could be no finding of proximate cause. Though awkwardly phrased, the rejected instruction accurately reflected the law and a theory of liability applicable to the facts of this case.

* * *

■ CLARK, JUSTICE, dissenting.

* * *

I. DUTY

A primary consideration in determining whether a new duty should be imposed upon a defendant is the "extent of the burden to the defendant and consequences to the community" in imposing the duty.

The burden of explaining the purposes of a pap smear and the potential risks in failing to submit to one may not appear to be great, but the newly imposed duty upon physicians created by today's majority opinion goes far beyond. The instruction requires disclosure of all "relevant information to enable the patient to make an informed decision regarding the submission to or refusal to take a diagnostic test." In short, it applies not only to pap smears, but to all diagnostic procedures allegedly designed to detect illness which could lead to death or serious complication if not timely treated.

Carried to its logical end, the majority decision requires physicians to explain to patients who have not had a recent general examination the intricacies of chest examinations, blood analyses, X-ray examinations, electrocardiograms, urine analyses and innumerable other procedures. In short, today's ruling mandates doctors to provide each such patient with a summary course covering most of his or her medical education. * * *

When a patient chooses a physician, he or she obviously has confidence in the doctor and intends to accept proffered medical advice. When the doctor prescribes diagnostic tests, the patient is aware the tests are intended to discover illness. It is therefore reasonable to assume that a patient who refuses advice is aware of potential risk.

Moreover, the physician-patient relationship is based on trust, and forcing the doctor in a hard sell approach to his services can only jeopardize that relationship.

* * *

Nothing in *Cobbs v. Grant* warrants imposition of such an onerous duty—to the contrary, that case expressly rejected any such duty. In *Cobbs,* a doctor performed risky ulcer surgery on a patient which resulted in severe complications. While the surgeon explained the nature of the operation to the patient, he did not discuss the inherent risks.

We pointed out that bodily intrusion is actionable either on the basis of battery or negligence unless the patient consents. The court reasoned that because patients ordinarily are unlearned in medical science, an adult of sound mind "in the exercise of control over his own body" has a right to determine for himself whether to submit to proposed medical treatment, and that consent to intrusion must be informed to be effective. We held that the physician who ordinarily has superior knowledge had a "duty of reasonable disclosure of the available choices with respect to proposed therapy and of the dangers inherently and potentially involved in each."

In *Cobbs,* we expressly circumscribed the duty of the doctor, holding that a "mini-course in medical science is not required," that "there is no physician's duty to discuss the relatively minor risks inherent in common procedures, when it is common knowledge that such risks inherent in the procedure are of very low incidence," that as to common procedures "no warning" is "required as to the remote possibility of death or serious bodily harm," and that recovery would be permitted only if a "prudent person in the patient's position" adequately informed of the perils would have declined treatment.

Thus, *Cobbs* is not helpful to the majority because the duty of disclosure in that case was imposed to assure consent to the intrusion would be effective. When no intrusion takes place, no need for consent—effective or otherwise—arises.

Furthermore, contrary to the express limitations in *Cobbs,* today's decision requires not only an explanation of the risks of a single procedure but also a "mini-course in medical science," if not a maxi-course. Similarly, because discovery of serious illness in a general examination of an apparently healthy person is remote, the doctor, contrary to *Cobbs,* is now required to disclose remote possibilities of illness. Moreover, the *Cobbs* duty to warn in cases where an adequately informed prudent person would have declined treatment shows a concern for preventing over-selling of services by physicians. By contrast, today's duty appears designed to increase selling of medical services.

II. THE INSTRUCTION

A trial court has no duty to modify or edit an instruction offered by either side in a civil case. If the instruction is incomplete or erroneous the trial judge may, as he did here, properly refuse it.

The majority opinion and the record reveal factual issues remain to be resolved even if the new duty is imposed. The offered instruction made no mention of those issues. Thus the instruction was deficient and erroneous. * * *

Before refusing the instruction, the trial judge indicated he was sympathetic to its theory but felt it confusing. He pointed out that a duty to disclose "all relevant" information was too broad, substituted "proximate cause" for "legally resulting," and made an effort to rewrite the last portion of the instruction to avoid confusing the jury. When his attempts at simplification failed, he advised counsel he would consider a revised version of the instruction. However, counsel presented no revision. * * *

Refusal to give the requested instruction does not warrant reversal. I would affirm the judgment.

QUESTIONS ON TRUMAN v. THOMAS

1. Are you surprised by the result here? Why might you be? What other case that you have read reached a similar conclusion with respect to the duty to disclose the risks of nontreatment? What relationship do these cases bear to the early tort from which the informed consent requirement grew?

2. Is the decision in *Truman* consistent with the high regard for patient self-determination that underlies the legal requirement of informed consent? Does it reflect opposition to physician paternalism? Given the statistically small risk involved in forgoing a Pap smear, the patient's probable awareness of the purpose of the test, and the patient's professed concern about the cost, would it have been reasonable to hold that Ms. Truman waived her right to further information? What relevance would you attach to psychological research showing that human beings (even trained scientists) are poor processors of information regarding very small risks? See, e.g., Tversky & Kahneman, Judgment Under Uncertainty: Heuristics and Biases, 185 Sci. 1124 (1974). How should the jury be instructed on the causation issue when the case is retried?

3. If a patient, having been informed of all the risks of surgery, turns it down, is the physician now compelled, under the *Truman* case, to urge strongly all the reasons why that decision was mistaken? Does Justice Clark make a good point when he observes that physicians must now push their services on reluctant patients? Was not the original requirement of informed consent based in part on a concern that physicians might abuse their powerful position to oversell their services? Do physicians now have a duty, enforceable in tort law, to overcome their patients' natural sales resistance?

4. Are *Truman v. Thomas* and *Gates v. Jensen* really informed consent cases at all? In *Gates,* was it not fairly clear that the court's real concern was not the patient's right to participate in decisions concerning her eyesight but the care and competence of the practitioners who examined her? Similarly, was not the real issue in *Truman* the physician's negligence in performing his professional duty of advising his patient on health hazards? Do you sense that one reason for requiring a physician to lay out risks and benefits is to ensure that the physician knows and has thought about them?

NOTES AND QUESTIONS ON DISCLOSURE REQUIREMENTS AND CONSENT IN THE MANAGED CARE ERA

1. *Informed Consent in Policy Perspective.* The movement to enforce and expand the disclosure obligations of physicians obviously reflected increasing judicial concern about the imbalance of power between physicians and patients and about the conflict of interests that physicians often face in making clinical choices; in recognition of these same problems, ethical standards of the medical profession have also always embraced the duty of professionals to inform patients of the risks and choices they face. It is notable, however, that the powerlessness of patients did not result solely from inequality in expertise and failures of physicians to obtain informed consent. It was also to some degree an artifact of the old paradigm of medical care, under which consumers were deemed not to be good decision makers in shopping for health care, were systematically denied meaningful information about providers, were prevented from enlisting middlemen to assist them in purchasing professional services, and had only limited opportunities to make meaningful, informed choices at earlier stages in the transaction—when they were still only "consumers," not yet "patients" under a particular doctor's care. Indeed, the medical profession's recogni-

tion of an ethical duty to obtain patient consent might be seen as part of a larger effort to legitimize the considerable power and authority that individual physicians exercised under the old paradigm by virtue of their immunity from certain forms of competition. Did allowing patients finally to make informed choices at the point of treatment adequately compensate for denying them opportunities to make *consumer* choices—by such actions as limiting professional advertising and restricting their right, if they chose, to be represented by corporate intermediaries?

2. *Enter Consumer Choice and Managed Care.* How does the doctrine of informed consent relate to the recent expansion of consumers' opportunities to make meaningful choices in the competitive marketplace? Now that market developments have given consumers a somewhat stronger hand in some of their dealings with physicians (mostly by interposing middlemen capable of negotiating lower prices and lowering the overall cost of care), the role of informed consent may have to be rethought. To be sure, the basic asymmetry in the distribution of information and power remains, but its implications have changed. No longer is there the same danger that physicians will force nonessential, overly risky services on uninformed patients; indeed, health plans are now on the lookout for such inappropriate care. On the other hand, managed-care plans and the physicians they enlist are now in a position to exploit consumers' ignorance in another way—by denying them desirable, possibly even essential, services. Indeed, if a health plan can coopt physicians and induce them to keep patients ignorant of their options, the problem could be particularly severe. Do you see how the law of informed consent, though developed in response to problems in a largely fee-for-service, physician-dominated world, might provide important new protections for patients in a world dominated by managed care?

3. *Disclosing Alternatives.* Although physicians have a clear duty to disclose alternative modes of diagnosis and treatment, that duty may take on new importance in the new era of managed care, helping to ameliorate risks of undertreatment. Thus, the duty to disclose other treatment options could prove especially important in a case where a health plan has limited the options it will pay for or where a physician, paid under a capitation or other incentive scheme, has elected a less costly, but not necessarily irresponsible, course. Note how the dramatic changes in health care markets have created a new rationale for older requirements. Whereas the old paradigm empowered physicians to act in their own interests in overselling their services to patients, the greater risk today is that, under the influence of managed-care plans, they will withhold beneficial treatments.

Should a physician always be required to disclose treatment options? If the patient obviously lacks the means of paying for the service out of pocket, then disclosing the availability of an alternative may be nothing more than a distressing reminder of the economizing choice he made in enrolling in the plan? On the other hand, if the plan's denial of coverage is debatable under the contract, the patient might want the opportunity to appeal it. In these circumstances, the physician might be legally obligated not only to provide information that would make such an appeal possible but also even to assist the patient in making the appeal.

As chapter 8(§B) will describe more fully in discussing the duty to disclose alternative treatments in managed-care contexts, some health plans have allegedly sought to constrain the provision of such information to patients either through so-called "gag clauses" in their contracts with physicians or through intimidation of doctors whose loyalty to their patients is deemed inconsistent with loyalty to the plan. It will also be suggested in chapter 8 that making health plans vicariously liable for the torts of their physician agents (including nondisclosure of vital information concerning treatment alternatives) might have beneficial effects not only on the quality of care but also on plan/provider relations, reducing current tensions and inducing cooperation toward the goals of providing better quality, more personal service, and appropriate information to consumers.

4. *Waivers in Health Plan Contracts?* Although it can be argued that a health plan or an individual physician should be required to disclose an intention to omit certain services, some consumers might not wish to be confronted with such information and be willing instead to entrust their welfare to the plan and its doctors. One possibility is that a health plan would include in its contract with subscribers a provision limiting the obligation of plan physicians to make such disclosures. Do you agree that informed consent is an area where health plans might validly differentiate themselves from one another and offer consumers a range of choices instead of requiring them to accept the law's prescription of provider duties? It would certainly be regrettable if the requirement of informed consent were relaxed in ways that unnecessarily ceded patient autonomy or depersonalized health care transactions, and patients should therefore be deemed to have an explicit right to know their self-pay and appeal options. But should that right be subject to waiver by enrolling in a plan, such as a staff-or group-model HMO, that expressly limits patient choice at the time that treatment is prescribed? See generally C. Havighurst, Health Care Choices: Private Contracts as Instruments of Health Reform 208–09, 246–49, 283–84 (1995); Schuck, supra. (Materials in the next section of this chapter will address the possibility that other rights normally enjoyed by patients under the law of medical malpractice might be modified by private contract.)

Why should a court object if a health plan undertook only to care for patients according to its own standards, without making disclosure in every case where its doctors omit some arguably desirable service or even depart in some respect from customary practice? Note that ordinary malpractice claims could be brought against plan providers if they failed to provide services mandated under the applicable standard of care—professional, legal, or contractual, as the case may be. Wouldn't that be enough? In other words, would a duty to disclose options any longer serve a valuable purpose? Indeed, once providers were no longer motivated to overtreat patients and were more than willing to withhold services that patients do not want, wouldn't the law's main policy objective in requiring informed consent be achieved?

Or do you still see a value in preserving the patient's right to be informed of omissions that occur? When a physician withholds not only treatment required by the applicable standard of care but also information that a reasonable patient under managed care would want to have, would it not be just as well if the plaintiff's lawyer in a suit against the physician (or perhaps against the plan itself) could use the nondisclosure to underscore how conflicts of interests can induce physician disloyalty to a patient under the new financing arrangements (just as they did under the old)? Consider these questions again after studying chapter 8.

SECTION D: OTHER REFORMS

Alternative Mechanisms for Resolving Claims

NOTES AND QUESTIONS ON PRETRIAL SCREENING PANELS

1. *Legislation.* So-called screening panels, designed to evaluate malpractice claims prior to their resolution by a court, were provided for in legislation in some 31 states in the aftermath of the 1970s' malpractice crisis. See, e.g., Gronne v. Abrams, 793 F.2d 74 (2d Cir.1986) (describing and upholding constitutionality of N.Y. legislation creating a more or less typical program). The states' object was to facilitate the early and authoritative (but nonbinding) assessment of claims as a way of encouraging settlement of valid claims and the dropping of invalid ones. Sophisticated panels, usually including a medical professional as one member, were expected to produce more accurate and consistent applications of the law's requirements than lay juries would deliver. Antecedents of the statutory panels may be found in a number of early voluntary programs, in some of which local medical and bar associations cooperated. See generally A. Holder, Medical Malpractice Law 408–13 (2d ed. 1978). Such interprofessional cooperation was sometimes possible because physicians offered to set aside the "conspiracy of silence" and provide the lawyers with expert witnesses who would support any claims found valid. See, e.g., Marsello v. Barnett, 236 A.2d 869 (N.J.1967) (court-sponsored program; only plaintiff's attorney, not plaintiff himself, was held bound by agreement—made in return for a promise of three witnesses to support a valid claim—to drop case if panel disapproved).

How would you structure a pretrial review system? For a thorough overview see Macchiaroli, Medical Malpractice Screening Panels: Proposed Model Legislation to Cure Judicial Ills, 58 Geo. Wash. L. Rev. 181 (1990). Would your purpose be to encourage settlements, to screen out dubious claims, to facilitate discovery of each side's evidence, to assist plaintiffs in finding an expert, to limit the jury's discretion, or something else? How would you prevent the panel hearing from becoming just another costly procedural step?

A majority of states that required screening required submission of the case before a complaint was filed, apparently in the hope that settlements would be easier while the matter was still private. Several states made submission of cases voluntary (on the part of one or both parties). Most states allowed panel findings to be introduced in evidence. But see Beeler v. Downey, 442 N.E.2d 19 (Mass.1982) (panel finding held inadmissible on ground that Massachusetts panels differed from those in other states, which provide fuller discovery, cross-examination of witnesses, and rulings on merits as opposed to reasonable cause). Some states provided that only unanimous panel decisions could be given such evidentiary effect.

Two cases from Virginia are instructive: Raines v. Lutz, 341 S.E.2d 194 (Va.1986) (though admissible, panel finding favorable to a plaintiff could not take place of expert testimony concerning defendant's compliance with the legal standard of care; although plaintiff could have called professional panel members themselves as experts, "the jury has not lost to a panel of experts its prerogative to determine whether the standard was violated"; panel had not specified standard of care, thus denying jury chance to verify it); Klarfeld v. Salsbury, 355 S.E.2d 319 (Va.1987) (allowing parties to depose panel members concerning not only medical circumstances but also panel deliberations themselves). Since, as *Klarfeld* shows, the parties had an opportunity to test the validity of a panel decision, was the court wrong in *Raines* to force the plaintiff to adhere to the traditional method of proving his case? Cf. Perna v. Pirozzi, 457 A.2d 431 (N.J.1983) (allowing plaintiff to show bias of panel physician without calling him as witness; also allowing impeachment of defendant by prior inconsistent statements before panel despite absence of transcript).

Even though expert testimony might be required at trial, it was not always necessary before the screening panel, which often included an expert or could appoint a neutral one. Local practices varied, but one lawyer familiar with the Indiana system "stated his opinion that most discovery involving the parties actually occurs during the review panel stage while the 'expert phase of the trial preparation' takes place after the medical review panel has rendered its opinion." Cha v. Warnick, 476 N.E.2d 109, 111 (Ind.1985).

2. *Current Status.* Most screening panel legislation weathered challenges to its constitutionality. See, e.g., Jarrell v. American Med. Int'l, 552 So.2d 756 (La.App.1989) (statute held to further state's interest in preventing nonmeritorious lawsuits); Keyes v. Humana Hosp. Alaska, Inc., 750 P.2d 343 (Alaska1988) (prelitigation review requirement upheld; statute also provided that the panel's report was admissible in evidence and that any member of the panel could be cross-examined by any party to the action); Colton v. Riccobono, 496 N.E.2d 670 (N.Y.1986) (upholding same New York statute upheld in *Gronne*, supra); *Perna v. Pirozzi*, supra. But see Hoem v. State, 756 P.2d 780 (Wyo.1988) (requirement of prelitigation review held to deny equal protection; for subsequent legislation, see Wyo. Stat. Ann. §§ 9–2–1801 to 1812 (Michie 1997)); State ex rel. Cardinal Glennon Mem. Hosp.

v. Gaertner, 583 S.W.2d 107 (Mo.1979) (screening requirement held to create unconstitutional limit on access to courts).

Several statutes passed in the midst of the 1970s' crisis were challenged on the ground that the crisis was over and could no longer support legislation so restrictive of important rights. E.g., Borja v. Phoenix Gen. Hosp., Inc., 727 P.2d 355 (Ariz.App.1986) (statute upheld; "repeal of obsolescent statutes is properly a legislative decision"). Cf. Boucher v. Sayeed, 459 A.2d 87 (R.I.1983) (legislation passed to replace earlier, unsuccessful "mediation panel" system struck down on ground that, by time of later enactment, the crisis justifying discriminations in earlier reform no longer existed). Courts in Florida and Pennsylvania, where screening requirements were initially upheld, later changed their minds when it appeared that the states' screening panel systems were burdensome to litigants in practice and did not realize the expected benefits. Aldana v. Holub, 381 So.2d 231 (Fla.1980) ("practical operation and effect of the statute has rendered it unconstitutional"); Mattos v. Thompson, 421 A.2d 190 (Pa.1980). But see *Cha v. Warnick*, supra (holding that Indiana's legislative purpose was to cure the crisis, not to expedite claims disposition as intended in the Pennsylvania legislation invalidated in *Mattos*).

In general, screening panels are no longer important in many jurisdictions, having been invalidated or repealed in many states and having fallen into disuse in others. See Goldschmidt, Where Have All the Screening Panels Gone? A History of the Arizona Medical Liability Review Panel, 23 Ariz. St. L.J. 1013 (1992). Their effects were studied with inconclusive results. There were complaints, and some evidence, that submission to screening panels delayed the process of getting to trial (see *Aldana* and *Mattos* cases, supra) and that some parties saw the procedure as a way to probe the other party's case, not to reveal their own. Although some claims were effectively screened out for lack of merit, it was not clear whether those claims would have been pursued in the panel's absence. See generally Kemper et al., Reform Revisited: A Review of the Indiana Medical Malpractice Act Ten Years Later, 12 Ind. L. Rev. 1129, 1132–35 (1986) (noting delays and reasons therefor); Shmanske & Stevens, The Performance of Medical Malpractice Review Panels, 11 J. Health Pol., Pol'y & L. 525 (1986) (Arizona plan).

More recently, attention has focused on other alternative methods of resolving disputes, including arbitration (both binding and nonbinding) and mediation.

Thomas B. Metzloff, J.D., Arbitrating Malpractice Disputes: Insights From the Real World

Duke Law Magazine, Spring 1996, p. 7.

Those interested in alleviating problems with the current litigation system for medical malpractice cases have long suggested the use of binding arbitration. Indeed, the very first governmental report on malpractice written in 1973, just before the first malpractice crisis erupted, included a reference to arbitration as a "better way" to handle malpractice cases, even though there was no evidence that it would be an improvement. During the first malpractice "crisis" in the 1970s, a number of state legislatures supposedly provided some impetus to arbitration by enacting malpractice specific statutes designed to facilitate its use.

What does arbitration potentially offer? For its proponents, arbitration offers several benefits, including the use of more qualified decision makers. Many arbitration advocates question the ability of lay juries to decide complex malpractice disputes and have looked to alternative dispute resolution (ADR) to provide a more qualified decisionmaker. Proponents also regularly cite arbitration's potential to reduce the high costs associated with the current litigation system. Malpractice litigation is undoubtedly expensive. If administered properly, arbitration offers the potential for significantly shorter "trial" time. Arbitration hearings can be shorter than trials in part because there is no need to select, instruct, or manage a jury. In addition, conflicts over evidentiary issues are minimized because arbitration hearings are typically less formal than a jury trial. In addition, arbitration hopefully reduces the amount of discovery required. Traditional malpractice litigation takes an emotional toll on the parties, particularly the doctor accused of malpractice. Physicians perceive suits as allegations of almost criminal misconduct. Arbitration reduces the emotional drain by being more private as well as less lengthy.

It is important to remember that unlike other ADR mechanisms, arbitration is not a process designed to promote voluntary settlement. Rather, it is an alternative method of reaching a decision on the merits of the case. In addition, the parties to an arbitration have substantial power to determine for themselves the particular details of the arbitration procedure. Procedural variables relating to the conduct of an arbitration hearing include, among others: the length of the arbitration hearing, the number of arbitrators, the required qualification of arbitrators, the process for selecting arbitrators, and the amount of discovery permitted to be conducted. Significantly, arbitration does not change the basic tort theory of liability; most arbitration clauses require the arbitrators to apply the applicable substantive law. To be sure, however, arbitrators are not subject to the same level of appellate review as judges and, thus, might have greater flexibility to ignore specific substantive law requirements.

Yet, it is clear that, to date, few malpractice cases have been resolved through arbitration. In other litigation contexts, such as securities and construction disputes, arbitrations have become routine. But for malpractice, arbitration remains an exception to the norm of traditional litigation heading towards trial by jury. For example, in Michigan—a state that made a concerted effort to promote malpractice arbitration—a recent study indicated that during a thirteen year period, only 247 malpractice disputes out of a total pool of approximately 20,000 claims were arbitrated. In another study of all malpractice claims closed in 1984, the U.S. General

Accounting Office (GAO) estimated that well less than 1 percent of malpractice claims were arbitrated.

Why Hasn't Malpractice Arbitration Become Predominant?

What combination of legal, social, structural, and political factors explains this failure? The differing explanations cannot all be simultaneously true. For example, it cannot be the case that an arbitration system, on the one hand, is inherently derogatory of patient's rights, while, on the other hand, it is likely to result in an explosion of successful and lucrative awards to plaintiffs. The combination of these explanations reveals the difficult challenges that lie ahead for developing arbitration programs in the current malpractice climate.

Judicial Hostility and Legal Uncertainty: Conventional wisdom says that part of the lack of use of arbitration is a function of judicial hostility to malpractice arbitration. To be sure, there are cases from the mid–1970s and 1980s relying on such contract notions as the unconscionability doctrine to void or significantly modify malpractice arbitration agreements. One of the supposed benefits of arbitration is to avoid prolonged preliminary disputes. If plaintiffs can routinely challenge the validity of an arbitration agreement on a case-by-case basis, a major advantage of arbitration has been denied.

[Despite recent Supreme Court rulings under the FAA and numerous state cases authorizing the routine use of arbitration,] issues about the basic validity of malpractice arbitration continue to be raised. Recently, the California Supreme Court granted review of a case that challenges the underlying legality of the arbitration program operated by Kaiser Permanente, the acknowledged leader in requiring malpractice arbitrations. Other courts continue to entertain claims that malpractice arbitration clauses are unconscionable under particular facts indicating overreaching by health care professionals.

State Statutes Designed to Promote Arbitration Did Nothing of the Sort: In retrospect, many of the malpractice-specific arbitration statutes passed during the first wave of malpractice "reform" measures in the 1970s did little to promote the use of arbitration. In Michigan, for example, the malpractice arbitration statute details the specific form that arbitration hearings must follow, thus defeating one of the advantages of arbitration—party control over a flexible procedure. Georgia's provision is even more restrictive in that the malpractice arbitration agreement will be enforced only if the claimant's consent occurs after the date of the physician's alleged negligence and only if the patient has consulted with an attorney. A statute that truly promotes malpractice arbitration would simply need to announce that the public policy of a particular state was to encourage the use of arbitration * * *.

Comfort with the Current System: Malpractice insurers and defense counsel are clearly repeat players in the litigation system. As such, they are cognizant of the many potential advantages that the litigation system affords to malpractice defendants. Thus, while physicians might be highly critical of juries, insurers and defense counsel might be less so. Aware of the results that doctors fare well before juries, insurers and defense counsel are understandably reticent about trading the known quantity of the current litigation system for what is the unknown of arbitration. This comfort level is not necessarily nefarious; it is, in part, simply a recognition that the current system provides extensive opportunities for defendants to obtain the vindication that many physicians seem to desire. By the same token, malpractice insurers are in a better position than patients to use the inherent expense associated with the current litigation system to create incentives for plaintiffs to drop cases or to settle cheaply.

Need for Active Judicial Involvement: * * * Many of the procedural tools available through the court system provide physicians with strategic advantages. For example, one benefit of having cases proceed in court is the availability of the judge to resolve discovery motions or motions for summary judgment. Such motions are common in malpractice cases and are often successful in either narrowing the issues or resulting in outright victories for defendants. While arbitration forums must provide some mechanism to resolve discovery disputes, the procedures for such matters are not well understood. Additionally, in arbitration there is no clear analog for a summary judgment motion. Instead, the norm is that the matter proceeds to the arbitration hearing where non-meritorious cases will be so adjudged. Defenders may also value procedural rules designed to sanction attorneys or parties for filing non-meritorious claims; arbitrators rarely engage in such considerations.

The Lack of Empirical Information: * * * The scant evidence that does exist suggests that the arbitration process is not inherently pro-physician as some have contended. A recent study by the GAO, for example, found that plaintiffs prevailed slightly more often in arbitration than traditional litigation and that the process was less time consuming. Surprisingly, however, the GAO study found that the average cost to the litigants of resolving the cases was comparable, and not cheaper as expected.

There is at least one HMO that has extensive experience with arbitration over an extended period of time. Kaiser * * * has used arbitration as the exclusive remedy for its subscribers in California since the mid–1970s. To date, however, Kaiser has not permitted a detailed analysis of the outcome of its experience. More general accounts suggest that arbitration leads to quicker results and that plaintiffs achieve similar or even better results than in the trial system. By the same token, without more rigorous empirical scrutiny, these generalized assessments lack any predictive force.

Fundamental Flaws of the Litigation Process: Arbitration in and of itself does not radically change how a dispute is litigated apart from the identity of the decisionmaker. Discovery might be somewhat limited and the hearing itself is hopefully shorter. But beyond such tinkering, the use of an arbitration format does not usually alter many of the procedural elements that malpractice defenders find objectionable. For example, arbitration is not thought of as a means to limit plaintiff's attorneys' contingency fees, to impose more effective offer of settlement rules, or to develop more elaborate cost-shifting mechanisms.

Nor does the use of arbitration in and of itself solve the uncertainties inherent in the process of determining pain and suffering. To be sure, it changes the decisionmaker, moving from a panel of jurors to an arbitrator or panel of arbitrators. But without some additional change in the applicable substantive law to be applied, the arbitrators must make the same subjective determination about the value of non-economic damages as are made by jurors. While some would argue that arbitrators are less likely to make a runaway award of the type that juries are occasionally accused of making, a counterargument exists that because of their own higher incomes and sophistication, arbitrators may tend to award more money in certain cases because they value interference with the enjoyment of life in greater absolute dollar terms than lay jurors.

Many academics see arbitration, even if done well, as little more than a band-aid that would cover up the far more serious shortcomings. Most would prefer significant reform of the controlling liability principles * * *.

Understanding Policy Priorities: Policy leaders within the medical establishment have not made arbitration, or ADR for that matter, a priority in recent years; it is a relatively low-level concern among those interested in pursuing tort reform options. As a policy choice, arbitration must be considered in a political context in which a host of policy alternatives are being simultaneously considered. Put simply, the American Medical Association (AMA) is at this point more interested in establishing meaningful caps on damages than it is in developing ADR programs.

Perceived Failure: Defenders have been turned off from pursuing arbitration by the perceived past failures of ADR efforts in alleviating the problems of malpractice. The foremost example is the experience of states that adopted, at the urging of the medical profession, "pre-trial screening panels" for medical malpractice cases * * *. A common criticism of the panels is that they were administratively cumbersome and that they often led to long delays. Other concerns were that the process came too early in the evolution of the claim before the parties had conducted sufficient investigation. The conventional wisdom is that these panels, which looked something like arbitration panels, were ineffective in impacting the culture or reality of malpractice litigation; indeed, several states have recently abandoned their programs.

Proponents of Other ADR Forms: Even those who are not ADR evangelists do not necessarily support the use of binding arbitration. For example, one area of rapid growth in the ADR field is the development of court-sponsored ADR programs. Concerned with burgeoning dockets, numerous state and federal courts have initiated mandatory, non-binding ADR procedures. Such ADR initiatives have the advantage of not engendering active opposition from patient advocates since these programs are non-binding, meaning that the plaintiff can obtain a traditional jury trial if desired, and because they fall under the supervision of the court.

Still others who believe in the desirability of litigation alternatives would rather invest their time and energy not in arbitration, but in alternative systems seeking early identification and resolution of potential claims. Such approaches would rely on the use of mediation rather than arbitration. The mediator's role is primarily to facilitate the parties' understanding of the nature of the dispute and to explore practical solutions, even if these solutions are not necessarily required by applicable substantive law principles. For some, the use of mandatory arbitration is simply substituting one inflexible method for another. The challenge of ADR as learning how to choose intelligently among a range of procedures—to "fit the forum to the fuss." [R]ealizing the full benefits of ADR requires a careful matching of specific malpractice disputes with the particular ADR process best suited to that case.

Letting the Genie Out of the Bottle: The malpractice insurers' lack of interest also represents, in part, a concern that if a truly expedited process for asserting malpractice claims were established, the number of malpractice claims would skyrocket. It is generally thought that health care providers would be the beneficiaries of arbitration, based in large part upon the fact that those providers were the ones who initially raised the idea. This simplistic notion is no longer uncritically accepted. The interest in developing binding arbitration has no doubt been cooled by recent evidence of the large, currently untapped pool of potential malpractice claims. * * * Moreover, the available empirical evidence did not support the claim that plaintiffs routinely won their cases. This insight logically requires rethinking of the premise of arbitration as a means primarily of limiting the filing of non-meritorious suits. If an effective and efficient arbitration system were in fact developed, plaintiffs now excluded from the current system might find it easier to file claims and pursue claims.

"Splitting the Baby" Concerns: Some malpractice defenders do not have sufficient faith in the process of arbitration to seek routine submission of malpractice disputes. Anecdotal experiences have served to give them serious pause. Perhaps the most widespread concern is that arbitrators tend to make compromise decisions that do not fully vindicate their clients' interests. Especially in malpractice, where physicians are often interested in vindicating their conduct, the perception that arbitrators "split the baby" represents a serious, potential difficulty. * * * Other anecdotal accounts criticize arbitrators who step in to help unprepared plaintiffs or who feel compelled to make some award to a plaintiff regardless of the proof offered.

Anti-Arbitration Sentiment: Plaintiffs' advocate groups continue to strongly oppose the use of binding arbitration in most contexts, including medical malpractice. Why is this position held so strongly despite the clear evidence that the current system hardly operates to the benefit of patients? * * * In the simplistic nature of the tort reform debates, patient advocates are against it because doctors are for it; arbitration has become a prisoner of war. The general suspicion with which consumer groups view arbitration is also based on the fact that contractual relationships of this sort are not necessarily limited to procedural as opposed to substantive law changes. They are concerned that arbitration clauses will be used as a front to mask more direct assaults upon plaintiffs' rights. Certainly, there are those who advocate the use of private contracts as vehicles for altering legal rules in this area.

Another factor is the role played by plaintiffs' counsel who serve as spokespeople, almost by default, for the interest of patients. It is generally assumed, for example, that plaintiffs' attorneys are suspicious of arbitration and desire strongly to have a jury. As a result, plaintiffs are likely to challenge arbitration agreements vigorously, and such challenges would defeat a central benefit of arbitration, namely, expedited resolution on the merits.

After reviewing the lengthy list of reasons, it should hardly come as a surprise that malpractice arbitration has largely been a non-starter. Among those who litigate malpractice cases day to day, there is no common understanding that the current system has failed. Lacking a clear empirical basis for believing that arbitration would be better, why face the hassles of legal review to force arbitration down the throats of patients who apparently believe that arbitration is a bad idea? In reviewing the list, however, there is one important truth. Despite conventional wisdom, there is no clear understanding that arbitration is demonstrably "better" for physicians. Indeed, some of the reasons why there has not been greater use of arbitration is the suspicion that arbitration would benefit plaintiffs in a number of important ways. As a result, in looking to the future, there is no reason based upon the present record to assume that arbitration is somehow inappropriate or inherently unfair in the malpractice context. Its possible virtues should be considered unencumbered by the ill-informed claims and counterclaims made in the heat of "tort reform" battles.

The Future of Malpractice Arbitration

In looking towards the future, one is confronted by a number of questions about the possible role of arbitration. If one accepts a broad view of patient interests—one that focuses not just on those slight minority of patients who currently have a malpractice claim—is arbitration a good idea? As a policy matter, should its use in malpractice be tolerated or indeed encouraged? Is there anything unique about malpractice cases that make them inappropriate for arbitration? What arbitrator qualifications should be most sought after in forming panels? Will arbitrators be as willing as juries apparently are to award defendants outright victories when they perceive the case to be non-meritorious? Will they be as able or better than juries when it comes to valuing meritorious claims? Will malpractice arbitrations in fact prove to be more cost-efficient than traditional litigation? Will arbitration deal more effectively with the special challenges of using experts?

These questions cannot at this time be answered with any confidence. Nonetheless, my opinion is that arbitration—if well-administered—can be a particularly effective dispute-resolution method in malpractice. This conclusion is based upon my own involvement [in] coordinating malpractice arbitrations. [The author then recounts some experience and empirical studies supporting the conclusion that a well-designed and well-administered ADR program employing binding arbitration would represent an improvement over traditional litigation.]

Arbitration Legislation

Colorado Permanente Medical Group, P.C. v. Evans

Supreme Court of Colorado, 1996.
926 P.2d 1218.

■ JUSTICE KOURLIS delivered the Opinion of the Court.

Susan Evans (Evans) brought a medical malpractice and wrongful death suit arising out of the death of her husband, Michael Evans (decedent), against Kaiser Foundation Health Plan (Kaiser), Colorado Permanente Medical Group (CPMG), Dr. David Guidot, and several Kaiser employees [(the defendants other than Kaiser are referred to hereafter as the Providers)]. The threshold issue presented to us by certiorari is whether the arbitration clause in the Kaiser Permanente Group Medical and Hospital Service Agreement (Kaiser Agreement) was unenforceable under section 13–64–403, 6A C.R.S. (1996 Supp.), of the Health Care Availability Act (HCAA). We hold * * * that the HCAA does apply to the Kaiser Agreement; that the Kaiser Agreement did not comport with the requirements of section 13–64–403; and therefore that the arbitration clause was not enforceable.

* * *

At the time of his death, the decedent was 35 years old, a husband and father of three minor children, and was employed as a computer programmer. Through his employment, the decedent had health care coverage for himself and his family with Kaiser pursuant to the Kaiser Agreement which he had executed in July 1989. The Kaiser Agreement contained a clause requiring the arbitration of any claims brought by the decedent or his family against Kaiser or any "health care providers" rendering professional services under the agreement. * * *

Notwithstanding the arbitration clause, Evans filed suit in district court on her own behalf, as the guardian of her children, and as representative of the decedent's estate. In her complaint, Evans alleged that the Providers had negligently failed to diagnose and treat the decedent's condition. * * *

The Providers and Kaiser filed a motion to stay the district court proceeding and compel arbitration pursuant to the arbitration clause in the Kaiser Agreement. The trial court held that the arbitration clause was unenforceable because it did not comply with the format and language prescribed by section 13–64–403 of the HCAA.

* * *

On appeal * * * [t]he Providers asserted in part that the trial court had erred in holding the arbitration clause unenforceable. The court of appeals affirmed the unenforceability of the arbitration clause under section 13–64–403. * * *

III.

We turn then to the central issue of whether sections 13–64–403(3) and (4), 6A C.R.S. (1996 Supp.), of the HCAA render the arbitration provision in the Kaiser Agreement unenforceable as against the Providers. Section 13–64–403(3) requires language that informs the patient of the intentions and understandings of the parties and discloses various substantive rights, including the patient's right to seek counsel and to rescind the arbitration agreement within 90 days of its execution. Section 13–64–403(4) requires that every arbitration agreement include a four paragraph, 10–point, boldface warning to the patient that he or she is agreeing to arbitrate medical malpractice claims. * * *

A.

The Providers do not dispute that the Kaiser Agreement did not comply with the requirements of the HCAA. Rather, they assert that section 13–64–403 applies only to agreements entered into between patients and health care providers directly. They claim that Kaiser, as an HMO, does not fall within the statutory definition of a health care provider, and, thus, the Kaiser Agreement is not covered by the HCAA. The Providers further argue that the HCAA does not apply to HMOs because HMOs are governed exclusively by Part 4 of the Colorado Health Care Coverage Act (Coverage Act). * * *

B.

* * * [O]ur task is to evaluate whether the Kaiser Agreement propounded by the Providers in this case, is subject to the requirements of the HCAA. The Kaiser Agreement requires arbitration of all disputes arising between the decedent and Kaiser, its employees, and contracting physicians. The Providers in this case were employees and contracting physicians of Kaiser. It is the Providers who here seek to enforce the arbitration provisions. Kaiser is not a party to this case, and there are no direct claims against Kaiser that are at issue.

Hence, we must determine whether the Providers may enforce the arbitration provision of the Kaiser Agreement even though it is undisputed that the provision does not comply with section 13–64–403. On that issue we hold that the Kaiser Agreement must comply with the HCAA requirements in order to be enforceable by the Providers.

* * * Section 13–64–403(2) states that:

> Any agreement for the provision of medical services which contains a provision for binding arbitration of any dispute as to professional negligence of a health care provider that conforms to the provisions of this section shall not be deemed contrary to the public policy of this state....

In addition, the final portion of Part 4 of the HCAA provides that "[t]his part 4 shall take effect July 1, 1988, and shall apply * * * to agreements for medical services containing a binding arbitration provision on or after said date."

It is undisputed that the Kaiser Agreement is for the provision of medical services and that it provides for the binding arbitration of professional negligence claims against health care providers. If the Providers had entered into the Kaiser Agreement directly with the decedent, the HCAA would clearly apply. Nothing in the statute suggests that the identity of the contracting party requires a different result.[16] Thus, despite the fact that the decedent contracted with Kaiser and not directly with the individual health care providers who were charged with malpractice in this case, section 13–64–403, applies to the Kaiser Agreement.[17]

C.

The Providers rely upon the existence of the Coverage Act as a shield for HMOs against the HCAA. They maintain that HMOs are governed exclusively by the Coverage Act and are not required to comply with the HCAA.

Part 4 of the Coverage Act Governs the organization and activities of HMOs in Colorado. The statute does not set out any specific requirements regarding arbitration agreements between HMOs and enrollees; it does, however, mandate that each HMO establish and maintain a complaint system approved by the Commissioner of Insurance to provide reasonable procedures for the resolution of written complaints initiated by enrollees concerning health care services. The commissioner, in turn, has promulgated a regulation that concerns arbitration agreements used by HMOs. This regulation provides:

16. The basis of the Providers' argument that the HCAA only applies to agreements between a health care provider and a patient is the following language: "It is the intent of the general assembly that an arbitration agreement be a voluntary agreement between a patient and a health care provider...." § 13–64–403(1). The Providers argue that this criterion would only be satisfied if an arbitration agreement were actually signed by a health care provider. Such a narrow application would enable health care providers to avoid the requirements of the statute simply by having non-health care providers sign arbitration agreements on their behalf. * * *

17. We note that this interpretation of the HCAA is consistent with the legislative history. * * * Senator Strickland expressed his concern for "the patients in this country and in this state," and stated that one purpose of the bill was to provide these patients with an option to settle their claims in a timely fashion through arbitration. However, Senator Strickland and other legislators * * * were cognizant of the danger that patients might waive their rights to sue in court because of duress or lack of information. To protect against this danger, the Senate specifically included safeguards in § 13–64–403, such as the patient's right of rescission and the requirement of precise language informing the patient of his or her rights. Because these safeguards were intended for the protection of all patients, it is clear that the legislature was focusing on any agreement concerning arbitration of medical malpractice claims without regard to the capacities of the parties to that agreement.

> If an enrollee's complaints and grievances may be resolved through a specified arbitration agreement, the enrollee shall be advised in writing of his rights and duties under the agreement at the time the complaint is registered. Any such agreement must be accompanied by a statement setting forth in writing the terms and conditions of binding arbitration. Any health maintenance organization that makes such binding arbitration a condition of enrollment must fully disclose this requirement to its enrollees in the contract and evidence of coverage

Hence, dispute resolution procedures and arbitration agreements used by HMOs are controlled to some degree by the statutes and regulations that specifically apply to HMOs.

While the Coverage Act provides that HMOs act under the general supervision of the Commissioner of Insurance, there is nothing in the Coverage Act that would exempt HMOs from the HCAA when the HMOs enter into arbitration agreements on behalf of their employees and the other health care providers with whom they contract. * * *

Furthermore, there is no conflict between the legislative mandates of the Coverage Act and the HCAA. Under the Coverage Act, dispute resolution procedures must meet the commissioner's approval and arbitration agreements must conform to the requirements set forth * * *. Under the HCAA, an agreement requiring arbitration of claims against health care providers must contain the language required by section 13–64–403(3) and (4) and must comport with the other measures in the section designed to protect patients. The requirements of the two acts with regard to arbitration agreements are not contradictory and we conclude that HMOs must comply with both.

D.

Next, the Providers assert that section 13–64–403 is preempted by the Federal Arbitration Act (FAA), 9 U.S.C. § 2 (1994). * * *

* * * Neither the Providers nor Kaiser [which was a party to the case when the issue first arose] raised the preemption argument in the trial court, and they did not raise it on appeal to the court of appeals. There is no reason why they could not have done so. Although two important United States Supreme Court cases[22] post-date the trial court proceedings, the question of federal preemption of state laws regulating arbitration clauses was framed as early as 1984 in Southland Corp. v. Keating, 465 U.S. 1, 10–11 (1984). The issue is not newly minted.

* * *

■ JUSTICE MULLARKEY concurring in part and dissenting in part:

* * *

The issue now before the court arises because of an apparent conflict between the Coverage Act and the HCAA. * * * Under the Coverage Act,

22. See Doctor's Assocs., Inc. v. Casarotto, 517 U.S. 681, 116 S.Ct. 1652 (1996); Allied–Bruce Terminix Cos. v. Dobson, 513 U.S. 265, 115 S.Ct. 834 (1995).

Colorado HMOs operate subject to the general authority of the Commissioner of Insurance. With respect to dispute resolution, the Coverage Act requires the HMO to adopt, and submit for approval to the Commissioner of Insurance, "reasonable procedures" for resolving enrollee complaints concerning health care services. The purpose of the complaint system required * * * is to facilitate resolution of complaints "concerning health care services." This provision allows HMOs the flexibility to fairly resolve disputes while still maintaining reasonable costs to their enrollees. Furthermore, by requiring that the plan be reviewed and approved by the Insurance Commissioner, the Coverage Act provides a level of protection not offered to patients who are treated by private practitioners or practice groups.

The more general HCAA was enacted in 1988 with the express purpose of protecting "the continued availability of adequate health care services ... by containing the significantly increasing costs of malpractice insurance for medical care institutions and licensed medical care professions." Among other things, the legislature intended the act to ensure "that an arbitration agreement be a voluntary agreement between a patient and a health care provider." Under the HCAA, in order for a health care provider and a patient to agree to binding arbitration, the agreement must strictly conform to the provisions of the section

The plain language of section 13–64–403(1) limits the application of its requirements to "health care providers." The statute defines a "health care provider" as any person licensed or certified by the state of Colorado to deliver health care and any clinic, health dispensary, or health facility licensed by the state of Colorado. The term includes any professional corporation or other professional entity comprised of such health care providers as permitted by the laws of this state. As an HMO, Kaiser is a legislatively created entity with the power to provide services by contracting with or employing "health care providers." Kaiser is not certified or licensed to deliver health care, nor is Kaiser a health dispensary or facility. Therefore, while an HMO may contract with and employ "health care providers," the HMO itself is not a "health care provider" under the statute's own definition.

The majority finds the HCAA applicable to an HMO only by ignoring the fact that Kaiser is not a "health care provider" as defined by that act. * * * [T]he majority infers from subsection (2) of 13–64–403, which refers to "any agreement for the provision of medical services," that the statute applies irrespective of the capacities of the parties to the agreement. In my view, this construction reads too much into the HCAA. This passing reference in subsection (2) of 13–64–403 is too slight and insignificant to be the basis for a major policy decision by the legislature requiring HMOs to comply with the HCAA.

NOTES AND QUESTIONS ON STATE MALPRACTICE ARBITRATION ACTS

1. Nearly all states have general arbitration statutes, many of which would authorize private agreements to arbitrate future medical malpractice

claims. Like Colorado, however, a number of states have enacted arbitration statutes specifically applicable to medical liability. See, e.g., Cal. Civ. Proc. Code § 1295 (West 1982) (malpractice arbitration act similar to Colorado's, but expressly inapplicable to regulated HMOs); Cal. Health & Safety Code § 1363.1 (West 1998) (provision of Knox–Keene Health Care Service Plan Act of 1975 governing disclosure of arbitration clauses in HMO contracts). See generally U.S. General Accounting Office, Medical Malpractice: Alternatives to Litigation (GAO/HRD–92–28 1992) (noting features of state laws, including prescription of size and constitution of arbitration panels and methods for selecting same).

Although malpractice-specific arbitration statutes serve to clarify the status of agreements to arbitrate claims for medical malpractice (possibly with a view to encouraging rather than discouraging their use), they do not always reflect a policy strongly favoring the arbitration alternative. (Was the statute in the *Evans* case pro-or anti-arbitration?) The widely noted Michigan statute, for example, like several others that expressly allow agreements covering future as well as existing disputes, hedged the options by imposing extensive protections and restrictions and by providing for the revocation of agreements during a limited period following the provision of services. (Note the ambivalence revealed by the latter provision). See Morris v. Metriyakool, 344 N.W.2d 736 (Mich.1984) (upholding Michigan act against constitutional challenges, including challenge based on alleged bias of physician members of arbitration panels, both "subliminal bias" and bias resulting from opportunity to lower liability insurance premiums). The Michigan statute was also unusual in requiring that hospitals offer the arbitration option to their patients. (Even so, as noted by Metzloff, only a very few of the malpractice cases in Michigan were arbitrated.)

Even though state malpractice arbitration acts displace jury trials, there has been little question about their compatibility with state constitutions, since most of them are essentially only enabling acts allowing private waiver agreements. See *Morris*, supra.

2. *Questions on the Evans Case*. In *Evans*, did the court correctly construe the Colorado "Health Care Availability Act"? When the Providers argued that the statute did not apply to Kaiser because Kaiser, as an HMO, was not a "health care provider," were they arguing only a technicality? Or was there a policy point to be made? What specific problem was the HCAA intended to solve? Did the Kaiser Agreement present this problem in the same way as other arbitration clauses might?

Could you argue that the state HMO Act (the "Coverage Act") superseded the HCAA with respect to HMOs like Kaiser? Note that the HCAA says only that arbitration clauses meeting its conditions "shall not be deemed contrary to the public policy of this state." Did it thus leave room for the argument that it creates only a "safe harbor" and that a contract might still be enforceable even if it did not satisfy all the HCAA's specific requirements? Could you argue, a fortiori, that a contract meeting the Insurance Commissioner's requirements should be enforced?

3. *Effect of the Federal Arbitration Act.* Although the court in *Evans* did not reach the question of federal preemption under the FAA, the issue is a real one. This 1925 legislation provides, "A written provision in * * * a contract evidencing a transaction involving commerce to settle by arbitration a controversy thereafter arising out of such contract or transaction * * * shall be valid, irrevocable, and enforceable, save upon such grounds as exist at law or in equity for the revocation of any contract." 9 U.S.C. § 2 (1994). In recent years, this provision has been deemed to preclude state courts and legislatures from enforcing various limitations they might wish to impose on the use of arbitration to resolve commercial disputes. See Prima Paint Corp. v. Flood & Conklin Mfg. Co., 388 U.S. 395 (1967) (holding that, in adopting the FAA, Congress exercised its authority under the Commerce Clause, thus creating a preemptive substantive rule of law, not merely a procedural rule applicable only in federal courts); Southland Corp. v. Keating, 465 U.S. 1, 10 (1984) (holding FAA enforceable in both state and federal courts; "Congress declared a national policy favoring arbitration and withdrew the power of the states to require a judicial forum for the resolution of claims which the contracting parties agreed to resolve by arbitration"); Allied–Bruce Terminix Cos. v. Dobson, 513 U.S. 265 (1995) (interpreting phrase "involving commerce" generously, making FAA's reach coextensive with Congress's authority under Commerce Clause); Doctor's Assocs. v. Casarotto, 517 U.S. 681 (1996) (discussed infra).

Although the Supreme Court has thus firmly established that the FAA preempts any state law that conflicts with the federal policy favoring arbitration (including, most clearly, state laws prohibiting the use of arbitration in certain settings), what about a state law that merely regulates the form of contracts containing arbitration clauses? In *Casarotto*, supra, the Court held that the FAA preempted a Montana law requiring all contracts with an arbitration clause to contain a notice thereof in underlined capital letters on the first page. Consider the following argument, advanced by the respondent in the Supreme Court in *Casarotto* (which, despite the petitioner's name, did not involve medical care):

> What neither Congress nor this Court has done, but what petitioners now ask, is to extend FAA preemption to even those minimal state attempts to ensure that parties know that the contract they are signing includes an arbitration provision. Thus, petitioners seek preemption even though Montana's notice requirement does not "stand[ ] as an obstacle to the accomplishment and execution of the full purposes and objectives of Congress." * * * The Montana statute does not prohibit arbitration; instead, it sets out a minimal notice requirement that is easily satisfied. In so doing, it provides a significant benefit to both parties entering an arbitration agreement: it ensures notice to adhering parties and establishes a bright line rule for those designing standardized contracts.

Brief for Respondent at 25–26, *Casarotto*, supra. Would your assessment of the result in *Casarotto* depend on whether, as the respondent contended, Montana is a pro-arbitration state, in which arbitration clauses are generally enforced? Should it matter that the franchise agreement in *Casarotto* was eleven pages long or that it required disputes arising anywhere to to be arbitrated in Bridgeport, Conn.? See generally Carrington & Haagen, Contract and Jurisdiction, 1996 Sup. Ct. Rev. 331, 379–91 (criticizing the overriding of state protections against oppressive arbitration clauses).

Although the FAA has been given broad effect, does it clearly preempt state restrictions on the freedom of parties to agree to arbitrate future claims for medical malpractice? For example, is a tort action arising out of the provision of medical care a "controversy * * * arising out of [a contract evidencing a transaction involving commerce]"? Cf. Dukes v. U.S. Healthcare, Inc., 57 F.3d 350 (3d Cir.1995) (reproduced in chapter 8(§A)) (finding no ERISA preemption of ordinary malpractice actions against HMO providing benefits under employee benefit plans, because such claims arise under state law, not under employee benefit plan itself). Might there be a question whether interstate commerce was involved when the contract was between only a single patient and a single doctor (or hospital)? Although few cases have considered whether the FAA, with its recently broadened construction, applies to agreements to arbitrate run-of-the-mill malpractice claims, a federal district court, in another case brought against Kaiser physicians in Colorado, held that the federal statute preempts the arbitration statute applied by the state court in *Evans*. Morrison v. Colorado Permanente Med. Group, P.C., 983 F.Supp. 937 (D.Colo.1997).

Note that the FAA does not purport to interfere with the ability of state courts to invalidate arbitration clauses on "such grounds as exist at law or in equity for the revocation of any contract." The next principal case introduces some materials on the application of principles of contract law not only to arbitration clauses but also to other attempts to modify patients' malpractice rights by contract.

4. *ERISA Preemption?* Did it occur to you in reading *Evans* that ERISA might preempt Colorado's effort to dictate the form and content of arbitration clauses like the Kaiser Agreement (which was part of an employee benefits plan)? Although you will not study ERISA in malpractice contexts until chapter 8, you might have seen the point based on your study of the *Travelers* case in chapter 1(§B). You will, in any event, be reminded of the *Evans* case again in chapter 8(§A) and asked whether ERISA might indeed preempt state requirements respecting the form and content of such clauses.

NOTES AND QUESTIONS ON ALTERNATIVE DISPUTE RESOLUTION IN MALPRACTICE CASES

1. *Arbitration*. Metzloff's article partially reproduced above is a shortened version of Metzloff, The Unrealized Potential of Malpractice Arbitration, 31 Wake Forest L. Rev. 203 (1996). His report that arbitration is rarely used in malpractice cases is consistent with a study showing that arbitration clauses are not often used in health care contracts. Rolph et al., Arbitration Agreements in Health Care: Myths and Reality, Law & Contemp. Probs., Winter 1997, p. 153 (examining use and legal environment of arbitration agreements, particularly in California). The objections to arbitration as a tool for resolving malpractice cases were earlier reviewed by Terry, The Technical and Conceptual Flaws of Medical Malpractice Arbitration, 30 St. Louis U.L.J. 571 (1986).

2. *Mediation, Nonbinding Arbitration, etc.* As Metzloff reports, any of several nonbinding mechanisms for airing disputes and encouraging settlements may be easier to implement than binding arbitration. Among other things, such ADR techniques are less controversial because they do not deprive plaintiffs of the right to a jury trial. For overviews of the utility of different ADR methods in malpractice cases, see Center for Public Resources, Health Industry Dispute Resolution: Strategies and Tools for Effective Dispute Management (1993) (considering uses of ADR in all types of disputes arising in health care field); Metzloff, Alternative Dispute Resolution Strategies in Medical Malpractice, 9 Alaska L. Rev. 429 (1992) (describing and comparing mediation, binding and nonbinding arbitration, summary jury trials, early neutral evaluation, early offers of settlement, etc.).

On mediation in particular, see, e.g., Metzloff et al., Empirical Perspectives on Mediation and Malpractice, Law & Contemp. Probs., Winter 1997, p. 107 (study of court-ordered mediation program, finding little benefit in "those cases in which the parties are not inclined to settle"); Meschievitz, Mediation and Medical Malpractice: Problems with Definition and Implementation, Law & Contemp. Probs., Winter 1991, p. 196.

3. *More Radical Proposals for Employing Nonjudicial Decision Makers*. In 1988, the American Medical Association proposed a wide-ranging reform that, among other things, would have substituted a state-operated system of administrative adjudication for the existing court/jury system. See Johnson et al., A Fault–Based Administrative Alternative for Resolving Medical Malpractice Claims, 42 Vand. L. Rev. 1365 (1989). Under the proposal, a state Medical Practices Review Board would have adjudicated all malpractice claims. Costs to claimants were to be reduced by providing them with staff attorneys at state expense—a reflection of the AMA's antipathy to plaintiff's lawyers. A four-stage process was designed to weed out nonmeritorious claims and to promote settlement by mandating settlement offers at two stages, with imposition of sanctions at the second stage if a party should reject a settlement award and not procure a "more favorable" final award. In addition to procedural reforms, the AMA proposal also addressed issues of substantive law.

For a radical proposal to use federal power to force malpractice cases out of the courts and into alternative forums, see Medical Injury Compensation Fairness Act of 1991, S. 1232, 102d Cong., 1st Sess. (June 6, 1991) (introduced by Senator Pete V. Domenici). Under S. 1232, "any person accepting or providing health care to be paid for, in whole or in part, directly or indirectly, with [any federal funds would] be deemed to have agreed" to submit all malpractice claims for final resolution (subject to only limited appeal rights) to a public or private dispute resolution service certified by the Secretary of HHS. (Private health plans benefitting from favorable tax treatment would likewise have been required to incorporate an "agreement" to submit all claims for binding resolution under such auspices.) Although S. 1232 would have been aggressively prescriptive of consumer rights and preemptive of state law in the foregoing respects, it was also notable for its forebearance in not using federal power to prescribe all the details of all the reforms it would initiate. It would not, for example, specify the design and procedures of ADR mechanisms that the Secretary could certify, thus opening the field to experimentation by competing ADR services and ultimately to private discretion and choice. See Havighurst & Metzloff, S. 1232—A Late Entry in the Race for Malpractice Reform, Law & Contemp. Probs., Spring 1991, p. 179.

4. *Evaluating the Jury System.* Underlying many proposals to use ADR (and the AMA proposal described above) is a belief that civil juries are not to be trusted and, indeed, are a major cause of malpractice "crises." The evidence, however, appears not to support at least the strongest criticisms. See, e.g., N. Vidmar, Medical Malpractice and the American Jury: Confronting the Myths about Jury Incompetence, Deep Pockets, and Outrageous Damage Awards (1995) (reporting empirical studies refuting claims that juries favor claimants, are too quick to find doctors negligent, overcompensate injuries, award excessive general damages, etc.); S. Daniels, Civil Juries and the Politics of Reform (1995); Vidmar et al., Jury Awards in Medical Malpractice: A Profile of Awards, Proportions for Noneconomic Damages, and Post–Verdict Adjustments, DePaul L. Rev. (forthcoming 1998) (study of medical malpractice verdicts in New York City and surrounding counties in 1985–97; though many awards, including portions for noneconomic damages, were generous, many were reduced following the verdict, yielding on average 62% of original amount, and some were still subject to reduction).

5. *Kaiser HMOs and Arbitration.* It is noteworthy that Kaiser Foundation health plans, unlike most other HMOs (see chapter 8(§A)), accept corporate responsibility for the torts of their physicians. See Sage & Jorling, A World That Won't Stand Still: Enterprise Liability by Private Contract, 43 DePaul L. Rev. 1007, 1032 (1994) (explaining that Kaiser will defend any malpractice suit in which a Permanente Medical Group physician is named defendant). As illustrated in the *Evans* case and in the next case reproduced below, several Kaiser plans employ arbitration clauses in their contracts with employers and with subscribers, having done so in California from an early date. The majority of Kaiser plans, however (e.g., those in Georgia, Ohio, and North Carolina), do not have arbitration clauses in their subscriber contracts. Moreover, the Oregon plan dropped the arbitration clause in its contracts not long ago, citing reasons such as Metzloff offers for rejecting arbitration. As Metzloff notes, researchers have not been permitted to study the Kaiser experience.

The Kaiser arbitration system was overhauled in the late 1990s as a direct result of Engalla v. Permanente Medical Group, Inc., 938 P.2d 903 (Cal.1997), in which the California Supreme Court found serious problems in the Kaiser arbitration system. Although it refused to find the arbitration clause unconscionable per se, id. at 925 ("although the present contract has some attributes of adhesion, it does not, on its face, lack 'minimum levels of integrity' "), the court held that the plaintiff had presented evidence that might support a finding that Kaiser either fraudulently induced the plaintiff's agreement to arbitration or waived its right to enforce the agreement by operating the system in a dilatory way. The evidence showed that, despite a representation that arbitrators would be appointed within 60 days of a claim's filing, delays in appointing arbitrators averaged about 22 months. Likewise, although Kaiser represented that claims were typically resolved within a few months, a typical claim took 28 months to resolve.

After the *Engalla* decision, Kaiser appointed a task force to revamp its system, which has sometimes been accused of breeding favoritism among potential arbitrators seeking repeat business. See Neaman v. Kaiser Foundation Hosp., 11 Cal.Rptr.2d 879 (Cal.App.1992) (failure to disclose that a retired judge selected as "neutral" third arbitrator had served as Kaiser's designated arbitrator on several previous 3–person panels held to create impression of possible bias, warranting invalidation of abitral award). The new Kaiser system is likely to be administered by an independent entity, not by Kaiser itself, and to introduce protections against abuses of the kind that have been alleged to exist in the system in the past.

Can you see a reason, not enumerated by Metzloff as a rationale for arbitrating malpractice disputes, why Kaiser might have preferred arbitration in the early days and might still prefer it in its bigger plans today? What else might explain Kaiser's decision not to require arbitration in the majority of jurisdictions in which it does business and to drop it in Oregon? Might a similar reason explain its failure to operate its arbitration system in a manner that achieves the vaunted benefits of arbitration? (How would an efficient program that lowers the cost of bringing claims against Kaiser physicians be likely to affect the volume of claims?)

Reforming Tort Law by Private Contract: Arbitration Clauses

Madden v. Kaiser Foundation Hospitals

Supreme Court of California, 1976.
17 Cal.3d 699, 131 Cal.Rptr. 882, 552 P.2d 1178.

■ TOBRINER, JUSTICE.

Defendants appeal from an order denying enforcement of an arbitration provision in a medical services contract entered into between the Board of Administration of the State Employees Retirement System (hereafter board) and defendant Kaiser Foundation Health Plan.[1] Plaintiff, a

1. We shall refer collectively to all defendants who have appealed from the trial court order as "Kaiser." These defendants are Kaiser Foundation Health Plan, which contracted with the board to furnish medical services to state employees; the Kaiser Foundation Hospitals and Southern California Permanente Group, which contracted with Kaiser Foundation Health Plan to provide the hospital and medical services required by

state employee who enrolled under the Kaiser plan, contends that she is not bound by the provision for arbitration. The instant appeal presents the issue whether an agent or representative, contracting for medical services on behalf of a group of employees, has implied authority to agree to arbitration of malpractice claims of enrolled employees arising under the contract.

* * *

1. *Summary of proceedings.*

In 1945 the Legislature enacted the State Employees' Retirement Act (Gov.Code, § 20000 et seq.) and delegated the administration of the act to a board [of which] at least one-third of the board members must be persons elected to that office by the public employees enrolled under the State Employees Retirement System.

[Later legislation] authorized the board to enter into renewable one-year contracts with carriers offering basic health plans. The act provides that state employees may enroll under any medical plan embodied in a contract negotiated between the board and the carriers; the state and the employees each contribute a portion of the cost of the plan. The act requires that contracts must include a grievance procedure to protect the rights of the employees, but neither expressly grants nor withholds authority for the board to agree to arbitration of employees' malpractice claims.

Pursuant to the provisions of the act, the board negotiated an agreement with Kaiser Foundation Health Plan, a corporation, to provide medical, hospital, and related health care benefits to state employees and their families. The agreement states that it is "subject to amendment ... by mutual agreement between [Kaiser] and ... Board without the consent or concurrence of the Members. By electing medical and hospital coverage pursuant to this Agreement, or accepting benefits hereunder, all Members ... agree to all terms, conditions and provisions hereof."

When plaintiff first enrolled under the Kaiser plan in 1965, it did not contain an arbitration provision. On April 1, 1971, however, the Kaiser Foundation Health Plan, anticipating the inclusion of an arbitration provision, mailed to all subscribers a brochure which, in describing the terms and benefits of the plan, stated that claims involving professional liability and personal injury must be submitted to arbitration. Shortly thereafter, on May 28, 1971, the Kaiser Foundation Health Plan and the board amended their contract in several respects and included a provision for binding arbitration of "any claim arising from the violation of a legal duty incident to this Agreement."

On August 1, 1971, plaintiff underwent a hysterectomy at the Kaiser Hospital in Los Angeles. During the surgery, her bladder was perforated; blood transfusions were required; plaintiff thereafter contracted serum hepatitis.

the contract with the board; and Angela Young, M.D., a surgeon associated with the Southern California Permanente Health Group.

Plaintiff filed a malpractice complaint against Kaiser and the blood banks. Kaiser moved to stay the action and compel arbitration. Opposing this motion, plaintiff filed a declaration stating that because of absence from work by reason of illness she had not received the April 1971 brochure, that she was not aware of the execution of the arbitration agreement in May of 1971, and thus had no knowledge that the Kaiser plan, at the time of her operation, required arbitration of malpractice claims.

By order of April 22, 1974, the trial court denied the motion to stay the action and compel arbitration. Kaiser appeals from that order.

2. *The board, as agent for the employees, had implied authority to provide for arbitration of malpractice claims.*

Government Code sections 22774, 22790 and 22793 authorize the board to negotiate contracts for group medical plans for state employees. In negotiating such agreements and amendments the board acts as the agent or representative of the employees. The acts of an agent within the scope of his authority bind the principal (see Civ.Code, § 2330); application of this rule in the present context yields the conclusion that contract provisions, as well as amendments to the contract, negotiated by the board within the scope of its authority as an agent, bind those employees who enroll under the contract.

This preliminary doctrinal recitation sets the stage for the principal issue of this appeal: whether the board, as agent of the employees, had implied authority to agree to a contract which provided for arbitration of all disputes, including malpractice claims, arising under that contract. That issue turns on the application of Civil Code section 2319, which authorizes a general agent "To do everything necessary or proper and usual . . . for effecting the purpose of his agency." For the reasons explained below, we conclude that arbitration is a "proper and usual" means of resolving malpractice disputes, and thus that an agent empowered to negotiate a group medical contract has the implied authority to agree to the inclusion of an arbitration provision.

In Crofoot v. Blair Holdings Corp. (1953) 119 Cal.App.2d 156, 183–184, 260 P.2d 156, 170, Justice Peters summarized the evolution of legal attitudes toward arbitration. "Arbitration has had a long and troubled history. The early common law courts did not favor arbitration, and greatly limited the powers of arbitrators. But in recent times a great change in attitude and policy has taken place. Arbitrations are now usually covered by statutory law, as they are in California. Such statutes evidence a strong public policy in favor of arbitrations, which policy has frequently been approved and enforced by the courts." Subsequent decisions confirm the self-evident fact that arbitration has become an accepted and favored method of resolving disputes, praised by the courts as an expeditious and economical method of relieving overburdened civil calendars.

The transformation of legislative and judicial attitudes toward arbitration has encouraged a dramatic development in the use of this procedure. A

1952 study estimated that "aside from personal injury cases and cases in which the government is a party, more than 70 percent of the total civil litigation is decided through arbitration rather than by the courts" (Mentschikoff, The Significance of Arbitration—A Preliminary Inquiry (1952) 17 Law & Contemp.Probs. 698). In the following decades arbitration further expanded its role to encompass in certain circumstances disputes requiring evaluation of personal injury claims: California and many other states now require arbitration of uninsured motorist claims and proposals for no-fault automobile insurance frequently provide for arbitration.

Plaintiff nevertheless recites judicial authority holding that a provision for arbitration frames an extraordinary method of resolving disputes and that consequently the authority of an agent to agree to arbitration must be specially conferred. The only decisions which support that proposition, however, are cases from other states which date from an era of judicial hostility to arbitration. The agent today who consents to arbitration follows a "proper and usual" practice "for effecting the purpose" of the agency; he merely agrees that disputes arising under the contract be resolved by a common, expeditious, and judicially-favored method.

The matter becomes even clearer if we narrow our focus to arbitration of disputes arising under group contracts. In collective bargaining agreements, which, like the present contract, are negotiated by elected representatives on behalf of a group of employees, arbitration has become a customary means of resolving disputes. Negotiators have invariably accepted without question the authority of the union representative to agree to such arbitration provisions. A New York decision confirms the equivalent right of a trade association representative to agree to an arbitration clause on behalf of the employers. (Mencher v. B. & S. Abeles & Kahn (1948) 274 A.D. 585, 84 N.Y.S.2d 718, 723.) The viability of these thousands of agreements for arbitration should certainly not be sacrificed on the altar of an exotic and arid legalism that in all these years has not even occurred to the parties.

Finally, we observe the growing interest in and use of arbitration to cope with the increasing volume of medical malpractice claims. The authority of an agent to agree to the arbitration of such claims finds an illustration in our decision in Doyle v. Giuliucci (1965) 62 Cal.2d 606, 43 Cal.Rptr. 697, 401 P.2d 1. In *Doyle,* the father of an injured minor entered into a contract with the Ross–Loos Medical Group which provided for arbitration of tort and contract claims arising under the contract. In an unanimous opinion authored by Chief Justice Traynor, we held that the minor was bound by the provision of the agreement to submit her malpractice claim to arbitration. "[T]he power to enter into a contract for medical care that binds the child to arbitrate any dispute arising thereunder," we stated, "is implicit in a parent's right and duty to provide for the care of his child." Rejecting the contention that the arbitration clause unreasonably limited the minor's rights, we replied, "The arbitration provision in such contracts is a reasonable restriction, for it does no more than specify a forum for the settlement of disputes."

We do not believe *Doyle* can be distinguished from the instant case because it involves a parent contracting on behalf of a child instead of an agent contracting on behalf of its principal. Both parent and agent serve as fiduciaries with limited powers, and if, as *Doyle* holds, the implied authority of a parent includes the power to agree to arbitration of the child's malpractice claims, we perceive no reason why the implied authority of an agent should not similarly include the power to agree to arbitration of the principal's malpractice claims.

We therefore conclude that an agent or other fiduciary who contracts for medical treatment on behalf of his beneficiary retains the authority to enter into an agreement providing for arbitration of claims for medical malpractice.[11]

3. *The principles that govern contracts of adhesion do not bar enforcement of the arbitration amendment.*

Plaintiff asserts that she was unaware of the arbitration amendment and should not be bound by its terms. Although she must acknowledge the general rule that one who assents to a contract is bound by its provisions and cannot complain of unfamiliarity with the language of the instrument, she points to an exception to that rule in the instance of a contract of adhesion. As we have frequently explained, courts will not enforce provisions in adhesion contracts which limit the duties or liability of the stronger party unless such provisions are "conspicuous, plain and clear" and will not operate to defeat the reasonable expectations of the parties.

Contending that the Kaiser contract is one of adhesion, plaintiff argues that the courts should refuse to enforce its arbitration clause on the ground that the clause is inconspicuous, unexpected, and disrupts the members' reasonable expectation that a malpractice claim will be adjudicated by trial by jury. We explain our reason for concluding that the principles governing adhesion contracts do not cover the present case.

The concept that a contract of adhesion should be interpreted and enforced differently from an ordinary contract has evolved from cases which have involved contractual provisions drafted and imposed by a party enjoying superior bargaining strength—provisions which unexpectedly and

11. Amicus suggests that we should fashion a new rule to the effect that no arbitration provision in a group insurance policy will bind the beneficiary absent proof of the beneficiary's *actual* knowledge of that provision. In the present case, Kaiser provided plaintiff with a brochure describing the Kaiser plan, including the arbitration provision. Apart from plaintiff's own testimony, neither the Board nor Kaiser have any way of proving whether or not plaintiff read all or part of that brochure. The orderly administration of the plan would be impossible if it were to depend on such proof. Amicus acknowledges as much; it does not maintain that no provision of the Kaiser plan can be enforced against a beneficiary who enrolls without actual knowledge of that provision; it would, instead provide only that arbitration provisions cannot be enforced without actual knowledge. But amicus' proposal for a special rule which discriminates against enforcement of arbitration clauses would be viable only if arbitration were an extraordinary procedure, and one especially disadvantageous for the beneficiary—propositions which we have rejected in Doyle and other cases cited in this opinion.

often unconscionably limit the obligations and liability of the party drafting the contract. The present case resembles those precedents only in that the members were offered the Kaiser plan on a "take it or leave it" basis without opportunity for individual bargaining. The Kaiser contract, however, lacks those oppressive features which have characterized the contracts adjudicated in the prior decisions.

In the characteristic adhesion contract case, the stronger party drafts the contract, and the weaker has no opportunity, either personally or through an agent, to negotiate concerning its terms. The Kaiser plan, on the other hand, represents the product of negotiation between two parties, Kaiser and the board, possessing parity of bargaining strength. Although plaintiff did not engage in the personal negotiation of the contract's terms, she and other public employees benefitted from representation by a board, composed in part of persons elected by the affected employees, which exerted its bargaining strength to secure medical protection for employees on more favorable terms than any employee could individually obtain.

In many cases of adhesion contracts, the weaker party lacks not only the opportunity to bargain but also any realistic opportunity to look elsewhere for a more favorable contract; he must either adhere to the standardized agreement or forego the needed service. Plaintiff, on the other hand, enjoyed the opportunity to select from among several medical plans negotiated and offered by the board, some of which did not include arbitration provisions, or to contract individually for medical care.

Finally, in all prior contract of adhesion cases, the courts have concerned themselves with weighted contractual provisions which served to limit the obligations or liability of the stronger party. The arbitration amendment, by way of contrast, bears equally on Kaiser and the members. It does not detract from Kaiser's duty to use reasonable care in treating patients, nor limit its liability for breach of this duty, but merely substitutes one forum for another.

Although plaintiff asserts that the arbitration amendment promotes Kaiser's interest to the disadvantage of the members enrolled under the Kaiser plan, she overlooks the benefits of the arbitral forum. The speed and economy of arbitration, in contrast to the expense and delay of jury trial, could prove helpful to all parties; the simplified procedures and relaxed rules of evidence in arbitration may aid an injured plaintiff in presenting his case. Plaintiffs with less serious injuries, who cannot afford the high litigation expenses of court or jury trial, disproportionate to the amount of their claim, will benefit especially from the simplicity and economy of arbitration; that procedure could facilitate the adjudication of minor malpractice claims which cannot economically be resolved in a judicial forum. Thus plaintiff's charge that the board surrendered the members' rights to jury trial without receiving an adequate quid pro quo must fail. Moreover, to the extent that arbitration reduces Kaiser's litigation expense, it may enable Kaiser to offer medical care to members at rates lower than otherwise would be the case.

To support her contract of adhesion argument, plaintiff points to Tunkl v. Regents of University of California, supra, 60 Cal.2d 92, 32 Cal.Rptr. 33, 383 P.2d 441; that decision, however, serves instead to illuminate by contrast the nonoppressive character of the contract in the present case. In *Tunkl,* defendant hospital presented to all incoming patients a document entitled "Conditions of Admission," which provided that the patient *release* the hospital from liability for negligent or wrongful acts. We observed that the "would-be patient is in no position to reject the proffered agreement, to bargain with the hospital, or in lieu of agreement to find another hospital." Thus, the patient had no realistic choice but to assent to a standardized agreement under which he waived his right to recover for negligently inflicted injuries.

As we have explained, plaintiff, in contrast to *Tunkl,* benefitted from the board's assertion of equal power on her behalf, enjoyed the opportunity to choose from among alternative medical plans, and waived no substantive right. We conclude that *Tunkl* is not controlling in the instant setting; the principles of adhesion contracts, as elucidated and applied in *Tunkl* and the other cases we have cited, do not bar enforcement of terms of a negotiated contract which neither limit the liability of the stronger party nor bear oppressively upon the weaker. Accordingly, such principles do not bar enforcement of the arbitration amendment against plaintiff Madden.

4. *Enforcement of the arbitration provision does not violate constitutional or statutory protections of the right to trial by jury.*

* * *

Plaintiff * * * contends that the arbitration provision in the Kaiser contract fails because it does not expressly waive the parties' constitutional right to jury trial. But to predicate the legality of a consensual arbitration agreement upon the parties' express waiver of jury trial would be as artificial as it would be disastrous.

When parties agree to submit their disputes to arbitration they select a forum that is alternative to, and independent of, the judicial—a forum in which, as they well know, disputes are not resolved by juries. Hence there are literally thousands of commercial and labor contracts that provide for arbitration but do not contain express waivers of jury trial. Courts have regularly enforced such agreements * * *. Relying on this consistent pattern of judicial decision, contracting parties, such as Kaiser and the board in the case at bar, continue to draft arbitration provisions without express mention of any right to jury trial. Before today no one has so much as imagined that such agreements are consequently invalid; to destroy their viability upon an extreme hypothesis that they fail expressly to negative jury trials would be to frustrate the parties' interests and destroy the sanctity of their mutual promises.

5. *Plaintiff cannot avoid arbitration with Kaiser by joining other parties as defendants in her malpractice suit.*

Plaintiff contends that a stay of her action with respect to Kaiser will lead to piecemeal and protracted litigation because she has also named as defendants the two blood banks. We agree that plaintiff may properly join the blood banks as parties defendant, but that right does not empower her to avoid her duty to arbitrate any dispute with Kaiser. We point out that under these circumstances, the trial court is not required to stay all proceedings against the defendants who are not entitled to arbitration; the court may, in its discretion, sever the action as to the blood banks or limit any stay to those issues subject to arbitration.

6. *Conclusion.*

Under the aegis of permissive legislation and favorable judicial decisions, arbitration has become a proper and usual means of resolving civil disputes, including disputes relating to medical malpractice. We should not now turn the judicial clock backwards to an era of hostility toward arbitration. We should not fetter that institution with artificial requirements that a contracting agent must secure express authorization to enter into an arbitration provision or that the provision itself must explicitly waive rights to jury trial. We should not impose debilitating obstructions, such as those urged by plaintiffs, which could very well jeopardize the legality of the huge number of presently functioning and efficacious arbitration agreements.

We conclude that the trial court erred in denying Kaiser's motion to compel arbitration and in refusing to stay the action against Kaiser. The trial court's refusal to stay the action as to the blood bank defendants is not challenged on appeal, but the trial court may wish to reconsider its order with respect to those defendants in light of our disposition of Kaiser's appeal.

The order of April 22, 1974, denying Kaiser's motion to stay further proceedings and compel arbitration is reversed, and the cause remanded for further proceedings consistent with the views expressed herein. The appeal from the order of May 22, 1974, denying Kaiser's petition for reconsideration, is dismissed.

■ MOSK, JUSTICE (dissenting). [Opinion omitted.]

NOTES AND QUESTIONS ON THE ENFORCEABILITY OF ARBITRATION AGREEMENTS

1. *Agency*. Note the agency principles operating in the *Madden* case. See also Leong v. Kaiser Found. Hosps., 788 P.2d 164 (Haw.1990) (arbitration agreement negotiated by state as employer held not a contract of adhesion). Would the California court be equally content with a deal struck between an HMO and a *private* employer pursuant to which patients lost their right to a jury trial, the HMO got the benefits of arbitration, and the employer may have gotten a price reduction? Consider this question carefully. Do you believe courts should sit in judgment on all such transactions (on the theory that employer-dictated terms are a contract of adhesion requiring judicial approval), or do you think that the labor market and the market for

health care provide adequate checks on the opportunities of each party to exploit the others?

Why did the court think that the Kaiser plan had a duty to tell the subscribers of the deal made for them by their (employer) agent? Wouldn't principals normally look to their agent for disclosure of the contract terms negotiated on their behalf? Does the answer here lie in the concept of "multiple choice"—that is, the employees' ultimate opportunity to choose between several health plans competing for their business?

Note the special problems surrounding parents' contracts binding their minor and unborn children. In addition to *Doyle v. Giuliucci,* cited and discussed in *Madden*, see Pietrelli v. Peacock, 16 Cal.Rptr.2d 688 (Cal.App. 1993) (enforcing against child an agreement made by mother before child was conceived). Whereas the power of a parent to bind a child may be rooted in the parent's right and duty to care for the child, it may be less clear that a husband or wife can bind a nonsigning spouse to arbitration. See, e.g., Gross v. Recabaren, 253 Cal.Rptr. 820 (Cal.App.1988) (husband's signature on contract for medical services solely for himself held to require wife to arbitrate loss of consortium claim arising from husband's injuries); Hawkins v. Superior Court, 152 Cal.Rptr. 491 (Cal.App.1979) (arbitration agreement signed by husband as part of comprehensive contract with Kaiser held to bind enrolled spouse).

2. *Issues Surrounding the Enforcement of Contracts.* The *Madden* case was distinguished in Wheeler v. St. Joseph Hosp., 133 Cal.Rptr. 775 (Cal.App.1976), which involved an agreement to arbitrate included in a hospital's admission form; although the provision was not a mandatory condition of admission and was revocable for a period of time following discharge, the court viewed it as an adhesion contract, unlike the negotiated agreement in *Madden. Madden* was also narrowly interpreted in McLaughlin v. Connecticut Gen. Life Ins. Co., 565 F.Supp. 434, 447–49 (N.D.Cal.1983) (rejecting argument that *Madden* undercuts the rule that ambiguities in health insurance policies are resolved against the insurer); Fields v. Blue Shield, 209 Cal.Rptr. 781, 786–88 (Cal.App.1985) (viewing *Madden* as a threat to "long-established public policy principles in this state aimed at protection of the general public against highly refined legalistic [insurance policies] carefully designed for the benefit of the insurer"); Beynon v. Garden Grove Med. Group, 161 Cal.Rptr. 146, 149–52 (Cal.App.1980) (rejecting *Madden* as authority for an alleged agent to negotiate an especially burdensome arbitration clause). In general, however, California's legislature and its courts have been "equally supportive of arbitration." Rolph et al., supra, at 164.

Courts may enforce reasonable arbitration clauses in malpractice cases even if they have elements of adhesion contracts. E.g., Buraczynski v. Eyring, 919 S.W.2d 314 (Tenn.1996) (agreements with two different patients undergoing knee reconstructions enforced; though contracts of adhesion because presented by physician on take-it-or-leave-it basis, the agreements were found not unconscionable or oppressive), affirming 1994 WL 677487 (Tenn.App.1994) (court emphasized state version of Uniform Arbitration Act, resembling FAA, in enforcing agreements that it otherwise found distasteful). But see Valenti v. Petmecky, 669 So.2d 1 (La.App.1996) (holding enforcement could be refused where adhesion contract signed on occasion of allergy treatment was later invoked by different doctor following surgical procedure); Broemmer v. Abortion Servs. of Phoenix, Ltd., 840 P.2d 1013 (Ariz.1992) (en banc) (adhesion contract; enforcement denied on this basis, and because outside expectations of patient, without appreciable regard to reasonableness of clause as such); Obstetrics & Gynecologists v. Pepper, 693 P.2d 1259 (Nev.1985) (clinic offered arbitration agreement on take-it-or-leave-it basis, resulting in finding of adhesion contract, which was held unenforceable in absence of evidence of plaintiff's knowing assent); Sanchez v. Sirmons, 467 N.Y.S.2d 757, 760 (N.Y.Sup.Ct.1983) ("to effectively waive a fundamental constitutional right, there must be a knowing, voluntary and intelligent waiver"; arbitration clause was concealed, unintentionally, in form entitled "Consent To Abortion").

3. *Effect of the FAA.* Recall that the Federal Arbitration Act (assuming it applies to agreements to arbitrate malpractice claims) permits state courts to invalidate arbitration clauses covered by the act on, and only on, "such grounds as exist at law or in equity for the revocation of any contract." 9 U.S.C. § 2 (1994). In the *Casarotto* case, supra, the Supreme Court expressly mentions unconscionability as one of the grounds that "may be applied to invalidate arbitration clauses without contravening Section 2." 116 S. Ct. at 1656. Are there any issues in the *Madden* case that the FAA (again assuming it is applicable) might foreclose? Much like the FAA, the California general arbitration legislation provides, "A written agreement to submit to arbitration an existing controversy or a controversy thereafter arising is valid, enforceable and irrevocable, save upon such grounds as exist for the revocation of any contract." Cal. Civ. Proc. Code § 1281 (West 1981).

Reforming Tort Law by Private Contract: Substantive Reform

Emory University v. Porubiansky

Supreme Court of Georgia, 1981.
248 Ga. 391, 282 S.E.2d 903.

■ CLARKE, JUSTICE.

We granted certiorari to review the opinion in Porubiansky v. Emory University, 156 Ga.App. 602, 275 S.E.2d 163 (1980), which held a general release from liability used by the Emory University School of Dentistry Clinic to be unenforceable as against public policy. We agree that the form in question is invalid as a defense in this case and affirm.

Diane Porubiansky became a patient at the dental clinic in 1976. Prior to treatment she was required to execute an "Information–Consent" form. The clinic is part of the School of Dentistry and offers dental services to the public at fees that, on the average, are less than the average price of those of private practitioners. The form explains that patients are accepted based upon the training needs of the school and that treatment will proceed more slowly than in a private office. There is also a statement that complete dental treatment cannot be assured. The last paragraph of this form provides: "In consideration of Emory University School of Dentistry performing dental treatment, I do hereby expressly waive and relinquish any and all claims of every nature I or my minor child or ward may have against Emory University, its officers, agents, employees, or students, their successors, assignees, administrators, or executors; and further agree to hold them harmless as the result of any claims by such minor child or ward, arising out of any dental treatment rendered, regardless of its nature or extent."

In April of 1977 Mrs. Porubiansky had an impacted tooth removed by Dr. Haddad, an employee of the dental clinic. She alleges that as a result of negligent treatment her jaw was broken during the surgical procedure and filed suit against Emory University and Dr. Haddad. The defendants denied any negligent treatment and further asserted that the signing of the Information–Consent form was a complete bar to the action. The trial court granted summary judgment to the defendants based upon the exculpatory clause in the form. The Court of Appeals held the clause in question to be void as against public policy.

The appellants here, Emory University and Dr. Haddad, contend that the form is a valid covenant not to sue which would prohibit recovery for negligent dental treatment. They argue that a doctor and patient may bargain for a shifting of liability without offending any policy of this state and further contend that the Emory University School of Dentistry occupies a unique position in that it services the public need by training dental professionals and offering dental services to the general public.

We agree that through the dental clinic Emory provides a worthwhile service of lower cost professional care and in the training of dental professionals. We also agree that because the clinic is part of a teaching facility it may require that prospective patients waive the right to insist on complete treatment. However, the attempt to relieve the clinic, its employees and students from the statutory duty of care for licensed professional medical services conflicts with and frustrates the policies of the state as expressed through our General Assembly.

The practice of dentistry is a profession licensed and controlled by the state. One who charges a fee for performing certain dental services is defined as "practicing dentistry" by Code Ann. § 84–701. The Emory University School of Dentistry is authorized by law to engage in the practice of dentistry and charge fees for services performed by training students under the supervision of licensed demonstrators. Dr. Haddad and the Emory University School of Dentistry are engaged in the practice of dentistry. The legislature has established a minimum standard of care for the medical profession. "A person professing to practice surgery or the administering of medicine for compensation must bring to the exercise of his profession a reasonable degree of care and skill. Any injury resulting from a want of such care and skill shall be a tort for which a recovery may be had." Code Ann. § 84–924. This standard also governs the duties and responsibilities of a dentist.

Since this is a dental malpractice case, Mrs. Porubiansky must necessarily establish that the above standard of care was violated. The appellants argue that the exculpatory clause is a valid covenant not to sue as defined in Cash v. Street & Trail, Inc., 136 Ga.App. 462, 221 S.E.2d 640 (1975), and that the covenant protects them from a suit based upon failure to conform to this standard. The court in *Cash* stated "all people who are capable of contracting shall be extended the full freedom of doing so if they do not in some manner violate the public policy of this state." We agree that *Cash* properly follows the rule stated in Phenix Insurance Co. v. Clay, 101 Ga. 331, 332, 28 S.E. 853 (1897), that "It is well settled that contracts will not be avoided by the courts as against public policy, except 'where the case is free from doubt and an injury to the public clearly appears'." In examining this case we also follow the rule that the courts must exercise extreme caution in declaring a contract void as against public policy and should do so "only in cases free from doubt."

In *Cash,* supra, the court held that a clause releasing a retailer of motorcycles from liability for claims arising from injury during a test drive does not offend any policy of this state. However, we find the policy considerations in this case to be different. A contract between a medical practitioner and a patient must be examined in light of the strong policy of the state to protect the health of its citizens and to regulate those professionals that it licenses. It is this strong interest of the state in the health and health care of its citizens which gives the state the right to regulate the health professional. Geiger v. Jenkins, 316 F.Supp. 370 (N.D.Ga.1970) aff'd 401 U.S. 985, 91 S.Ct. 1236, 28 L.Ed.2d 525 (1971). "The right to practice medicine is a conditional right which is subordinate to the state's power and duty to safeguard the public health, and it is the universal rule that in the performance of such duty and in the exercise of such power, the state may regulate and control the practice of medicine and those who engage therein, subject only to the limitation that the measures adopted must be reasonable, necessary, and appropriate to accomplish the legislature's valid objective of protecting the health and welfare of its occupants." Geiger, supra at 374.

The duty of one engaged in the practice of dentistry and medicine to "bring to the exercise of his profession a reasonable degree of care and skill" is an affirmative statutory duty imposed upon those who engage in professional practice. The obligation to practice under this standard must be viewed as a condition to the licensure of the state to engage in the practice of medicine and dentistry.

We find that it is against the public policy of this state to allow one who procures a license to practice dentistry to relieve himself by contract of the duty to exercise reasonable care. "A purported exemption from statutory liability is void, unless the purpose of the statute is merely to give an added remedy which is not based on any strong policy." 15 Williston, Contracts, 1750A (3d Ed.1972). We agree with the reasoning of the court in

Olson v. Molzen, 558 S.W.2d 429, 430 (Tenn.1977), a case which held a release from medical negligence void, that "rules that govern tradesmen in the market place are of little relevancy in dealing with professional persons who hold themselves out as experts and whose practice is regulated by the state."

The status of doctor and patient controls the duty to exercise reasonable care. "The law imposes upon persons of professional standing performing medical ... and like skilled services, pursuant to their contracts with their clients, an obligation to exercise a reasonable degree of care, skill and ability, such as is ordinarily exercised under similar conditions and like circumstances by persons employed in the same or similar professions.... This is a duty apart from any express contractual obligation." Mauldin v. Sheffer, 113 Ga.App. 874, 880, 150 S.E.2d 150 (1966). The relationship of the parties is relevant in determining whether or not a contract is in contravention of public policy because "some relationships are such that once entered upon they involve a status requiring of one party greater responsibility than that required of the ordinary person, and therefore, a provision avoiding liability is peculiarly obnoxious." 15 Williston, Contracts 1751 (3d ed. 1972).

The status of the Emory University School of Dentistry as primarily a training institution does not allow for an exemption from the duty to exercise reasonable care. The clinic in offering services to the public is engaged in the practice of dentistry. The legislature while allowing such clinics to operate has not exempted them from the standard of care necessary for the protection of the public. The only exception involving liability of medical practitioners which has been made by the legislature is found in Code Ann. § 84–930. This applies only to good faith emergency medical care and is not applicable here.

We do not hold that licensed professionals may not enter into binding contracts with their patients and clients. Nor do we infer [*sic*] that such contracts might shift certain obligations which would otherwise arise in the relationship. However, we do conclude that the release used in the present case may not relieve the practitioner from the duty to exercise reasonable care and skill in the performance of his practice. Consequently, the attempt to plead the signing of the agreement as a complete defense to this action must fail. The Court of Appeals was correct in reversing the summary judgment and allowing Mrs. Porubiansky to proceed on her allegations that Dr. Haddad and Emory University did not exercise the requisite degree of care and skill required by law in performing the dental services in question.

Judgment affirmed.

NOTES AND QUESTIONS ON CONTRACTUAL MODIFICATION OF TORT RIGHTS

1. *Exculpatory Clauses.* The leading case striking down an exculpatory clause in a health care setting is the *Tunkl* case from California, cited and discussed in the *Madden* case, supra. In *Tunkl*, a patient signed the release

as a condition of admission to the hospital, but the court struck it down, not just as an adhesion contract, but as a violation of public policy. The court's reasoning has been described and analyzed as follows:

> The court sought to draw a line between exculpatory contracts that involved mere "private interests" and those affecting the "public interest."
>
> The court considered several general criteria for defining public interest: (1) the party seeking immunity is engaged in performing a service thought suitable for public regulation or one of great public "importance" and "practical necessity"; (2) the party seeking immunity holds himself out as willing to perform this service to any member of the public (or any member meeting "certain established standards"); (3) as a result of the "essential nature of the service" and in the "economic setting of the transaction" there is a "decisive advantage of bargaining strength" favoring the party seeking immunity; (4) the exculpatory contract is a "standardized contract of adhesion" and makes no provision whereby the other party may pay "additional reasonable fees" and obtain protection; (5) the person or property of the purchaser (patient) is under the control of the party seeking immunity and thereby subject to the risk of that party's carelessness.
>
> Of the criteria listed above, the first two seem either irrelevant or question-begging. Whether health care is a matter suitable for public regulation only begs the question of what kinds of public regulation are suitable—in particular whether judicial interference with contractual risk allocation is appropriate. The criterion of holding out to the public is simply the mindless adaptation of an ancient rule for common carriers. It begs the question of what is the proper scope of the holding out; in *Tunkl* the extent of the holding out was presumably limited by the contractual conditions of admission, which included a waiver. The third and fourth criteria fit conventional doctrine supporting judicial scrutiny of contractual bargains generally, and they warrant some attention. The fifth criterion is a bit nebulous, but it may be interpreted—rather freely, perhaps—to denote a concern over the loss of deterrence and the creation of moral hazard.

Robinson, Rethinking the Allocation of Medical Malpractice Risks Between Patients and Providers, Law & Contemp. Probs., Spring 1986, at 173, 184–85.

How does the *Emory University* case square with *Madden* and *Tunkl?* For other cases invalidating exculpatory clauses, see Ash v. New York Univ. Dental Center, 564 N.Y.S.2d 308 (N.Y.A.D.1990) (like *Emory University*, flatly invalidating exculpatory clause even though relief from liability rather clearly facilitated low-cost dental care); Tatham v. Hoke, 469 F.Supp. 914 (W.D.N.C.1979); Olson v. Molzen, 558 S.W.2d 429 (Tenn.1977); Meiman v. Rehabilitation Center, Inc., 444 S.W.2d 78 (Ky.1969). An Illinois statute provides as follows:

> Any contract or agreement signed by any person prior to, or as a condition of, such person receiving medical treatment in any form, which releases from liability any physician, hospital or other health care provider for any malfeasance, misfeasance or nonfeasance in the course of administering

> any medical treatment or service is void and against the public policy of the State of Illinois.

225 Smith–Hurd Ill. Comp. Stat. Ann. § 60/29 (West 1993).

What would you say about an exculpatory clause offered as a condition of providing prenatal and obstetrical care by a rural general practitioner who could not afford the extra cost of malpractice coverage for liabilities arising out of deliveries? Note that the patient's alternative may be no care at all. Would some less far-reaching alteration of the patient's tort rights fare better in your eyes?

2. *Limitations on Recoverable Damages.* In light of *Madden, Emory University,* and *Tunkl,* how would you advise an HMO that desired to introduce into its subscriber contract a clause that sought to limit the damages recoverable in any negligence action? Consider clauses that seek to (1) limit total damages payable in any case to $500,000; (2) foreclose or limit damages recoverable for noneconomic loss; (3) require reduction of awards to the extent that they duplicate compensation obtainable from collateral sources; (4) foreclose claims for punitive damages; (5) provide for periodic payments, suitably guaranteed; (6) provide for reduction of awards to present value; or (7) provide a first-refusal right for the HMO to provide needed medical care in kind. Would such a clause be rendered unenforceable by a statute like the Illinois one quoted or a prior judicial decision invalidating a statutory reform to the same effect? Would a court distinguish between a pure exculpatory clause, as in *Emory University* and *Tunkl,* and a modest or not-so-modest modification of tort rights? How would you argue that it should do so? See generally C. Havighurst, Health Care Choices: Private Contracts as Instruments of Health Reform 277–80, 304–14 (1995). For an effective defense even of exculpatory clauses, see Robinson, supra.

What would the *Madden* court be likely to say about contractual provisions of the kind suggested in the foregoing paragraph? Would it be easier defend such modifications of patient tort rights if the contract also contained a fair, fully disclosed, well-administered arbitration clause? Why couple substantive and procedural reforms in this way? Might the latter be fairly represented as a quid pro quo for the former?

3. *Problem: HMOs and EFM.* Recall the problem in § B of this chapter in which you were asked to advise an HMO on how it might alter its practice with respect to electronic fetal monitoring (EFM). Now consider whether the HMO's subscriber contracts should be rewritten to exclude EFM as a covered service in the absence of specified clinical indications. Would contractual fine print be enough to deter a court from holding an HMO physician liable for omitting the service if it was customary in the community? Or should the contract be backed by expert testimony showing that the standard was reasonable? Obviously, the HMO would wish to avoid having to litigate the standard's reasonableness. How can the contract be made presumptively enforceable? Would it help to ask the consumer advisory panel maintained by the plan to approve the omission of the service in appropriate cases?

Would you advise the HMO to make EFM available at an extra charge in those instances where the HMO doctors conclude that it is not cost-effective? Would the HMO and its doctors be happy with this advice? Or would they reject it because it violates the HMO's conception of itself as a fully integrated medical plan committed to providing a single style of prepaid care? (Is there an echo here of the larger system's traditional ostensible adherence to a single set of professionally designed standards?) Would the decision whether to present a choice of this kind raise questions under the law of informed consent? What kind of questions?

How might clinical practice guidelines assist you in writing the HMO's subscriber contract to address both the problem of its physicians' exposure to malpractice suits (and perhaps many similar problems in other areas of medical care) and the problem of defining and appropriately limiting the plan's coverage obligations? Would it be desirable if the plan's various contracts could coordinate its doctors' (and its own) exposure to tort-type liability with the plan's coverage obligations? See C. Havighurst, *Health Care Choices*, supra, at 166–78 (recommending "integrating the parties in a single transaction"). Would it be productive to undertake in the contract that care will conform to certain guidelines promulgated by reputable independent organizations? What problem bedeviling all health care financing and delivery—and referred to in chapter 2(§C)—would such incorporation by reference help to solve? See generally id. at ch. 6 (entitled "Practice Guidelines as Tools for Health Care Contracting").

4. *Altering the Legal Standard of Care.* Consider how an HMO's subscriber contract might be written to allow it to defend its physicians' responsible deviations from customary practice. What is your reaction to the following proposed contract term:

> *The Duty of the Plan's Physicians to You.* The Plan warrants that each of its physicians possesses at least the skill and knowledge of a reasonably competent medical practitioner in his or her specialty and undertakes to you that its physicians will exercise that skill and knowledge in a reasonable and prudent manner in your case. In so doing, a Plan physician may sometimes depart from practices customary among other physicians. Such departures shall not be deemed to breach the foregoing undertaking, however, unless they are expressly found to have been unreasonable and imprudent; evidence to support such a finding shall include the testimony of experts knowledgeable about scientific research concerning the outcomes and effectiveness of care of the type in question and about what, in the light of all the circumstances (including the cost and benefits of alternative measures), constitutes appropriate medical care. You agree that the undertaking in this paragraph fully defines the duties of the Plan's physicians to you.

Cf. Schneider v. Revici, 817 F.2d 987 (2d Cir.1987) (patient sought and expressly consented to unconventional therapy; court allowed defendant to offer assumption of risk as affirmative defense, rejecting public policy argument against waiver of right to standard treatment).

On possibilities for reformulating the general duty of health care providers in health care contracts, see C. Havighurst, *Health Care Choices*, supra, at 287–96.

5. Consider whether a fee-for-service provider—a doctor or a hospital (or provider of low-cost dental care)—should have the same degree of freedom as an HMO to contract with patients for a modification of tort rights. Why might a court be harder to persuade that such contracts ought to be enforced according to their terms? Do you agree with these arguments? Should a court consider that allowing HMOs greater freedom in this regard may place traditional practitioners at a competitive disadvantage?

6. *Recovery for Gross Negligence Only?* Assume a contract that abrogates the patient's right to recover at all unless he can prove gross negligence, suitably defined. Should such a contract be enforced? Although this term might seem extreme in depriving the injured patient of tort compensation in cases of ordinary negligence, there is anecdotal evidence that many patients currently forgo pursuit of promising tort rights either out of loyalty to the provider (perhaps because of his "bedside manner") or out of distaste for the legal system or for other reasons. Cf. Clayton et al., Doctor–Patient Relationships, in Suing for Medical Malpractice 50 (F. Sloan et al., eds, 1993) (finding communication with patients a factor in preventing lawsuits); Lloyd–Bostock, Fault and Liability for Accidents: The Accident Victim's Perspective, in Compensation and Support for Illness and Injury 139 (1984) ("contrary to what one might expect, the victim's attribution of fault for the accident does not predict whether he or she takes steps towards claiming damages under the tort system"). Do you think that consumers who are thus disposed not to sue should be allowed to obtain a price concession for expressing their disposition in advance, thus avoiding the necessity for contributing to an insurance fund on which they are unlikely to make claims? See generally C. Havighurst, *Health Care Choices*, supra, at 296–300.

7. *O'Connell's "Neo–No–Fault" Proposals.* Professor Jeffrey O'Connell has suggested making advance arrangements with an insurer to tender automatically to victims of particular injuries their net economic loss; such payments would be conditioned, however, on a release of tort rights. O'Connell predicts that such funded tenders, made without regard to fault, would induce more settlements. O'Connell, Offers That Can't be Refused: Foreclosure of Personal Injury Claims by Defendants' Prompt Tender of Claimants' Net Economic Losses, 77 Nw.U.L.Rev. 589 (1982). O'Connell has also suggested extending this idea by making prior contractual arrangements with patients under which the provider could extinguish a patient's right to sue for economic losses by voluntarily tendering net economic loss within a fixed period following an injury. Consider the enforceability of the release in the first case and the contract in the second and the practical dynamics of both approaches. O'Connell's take-it-or-leave-it approach was once embodied in a much-discussed federal legislative proposal, H.R. 3084, 99th Cong., 1st Sess. (1985), which would have provided that, even without a prior contractual arrangement, a provider's voluntary tender of net

economic loss would cut off a patient's tort claim for economic losses. See O'Connell, Neo–No–Fault Remedies for Medical Injuries: Coordinated Statutory and Contractual Alternatives, Law & Contemp. Probs., Spring 1986 at 125.

8. *Encountering Judicial (and Other) Skepticism.* Do any of the "private reforms" suggested above—or some combination thereof—strike you as reasonable enough that courts ought to be willing to enforce them if they are generally satisfied by the bargaining circumstances? See generally C. Havighurst, *Health Care Choices*, supra, 304–14; Symposium, Medical Malpractice: Can the Private Sector Find Relief?, Law & Contemp. Probs., Spring 1986, at 1, 143–320. Are you troubled by the idea that tort rules might be varied by contract? Professor Richard A. Epstein has argued as follows:

> When malpractice cases are treated as though they raise only tort [as opposed to contract] issues, there is the unmistakable tendency to treat the judicial rules as the inflexible commands of positive law. It becomes, therefore, a natural if unfortunate tendency for courts to overlook the possibility, indeed the desirability, of having the rules that they have laid down varied by the agreements between the parties. Where the situation is looked upon as contractual, the basic rules governing the relationship between physician and patient are then best understood as approximations of the rules which the parties themselves would choose to govern their own relationship. * * * The problem with medical malpractice is that the legal relationships fashioned by the courts do not begin to approximate on many points the contractual solutions that the parties would choose, or have chosen, for themselves. The problem with much of the modern approach to medical malpractice lies in the great willingness, even eagerness, of both courts and legislatures to respond to private law problems with public policy solutions. * * * And the rules that have been adopted and proposed, whether concerned with informed consent, the place of custom in setting the standard of care, the measure of damages, or any of the other issues discussed in the body of this paper, are very poor substitutes [for contractual rules] indeed. We need in the context of medical malpractice less government, and not more government; we need greater respect for private initiative and control; and we need a return to the passive virtues of both judicial and legislative statesmanship.

Epstein, Medical Malpractice: The Case for Contract, 1 Am. B. Found. Research J. 87, 94–95 (1976). But see Atiyah, Medical Malpractice and the Contract/Tort Boundary, Law & Contemp. Probs., Spring 1986, p. 287 (resisting reintroduction of contract notions but acknowledging "at the end of the day" that sound legislative reform is so difficult politically in the U.S., as compared to the United Kingdom, that the contractual alternative may have a place).

For a critique of proposals for contractual reform, anticipating that they would lead to complete exculpation of providers and a loss of deterrence rather than modification of tort rights and remedies, see P. Weiler, Medical Malpractice on Trial 93–113 (1991) ("although I favor some loosening of the legal reins on experimenting with contractual alternatives to malpractice litigation, I am highly dubious about the brave new world of no-liability, which would likely be the denouement of full-scale freedom of contract to determine who will assume the legal and financial responsibility for medical accidents: doctors, hospitals, or patients"). Do you agree that the ultimate outcome of permitting physicians, hospitals, and health plans greater contractual freedom would be a "brave new world of no-liability"? What counterforces would operate to prevent such an outcome?

Whatever you think about private reforms in theory, would you advise your hospital, physician, or health plan clients to consider contractual modifications of the liability rules to which they are subject? Most lawyers would regard the idea as impractical, believing that courts cannot be depended upon to enforce such contracts. Are these lawyers too conservative? Are they passing up an opportunity for creative lawyering both in the drafting and in the defense of such agreements? How would you defend a contractual modification of patients' tort rights, recognizing that the court will be confronted with a plaintiff who now regrets the choice that he made, knowingly or unknowingly? Would you argue only that "a contract is a contract"? What policy arguments might you make as well?

What does the skepticism of lawyers and judges toward private reform of tort-law dogma say about the legal system? That it is vigilant in defending valuable individual rights? Or that it is vigilant in defending its own monopoly in defining rights and lawyers' lucrative role in enforcing them? Are you aware of other professions that have tried to deny consumers the right to choose something different (and more economical) than the profession itself believed was good for them? See generally C. Havighurst, *Health Care Choices*, supra, at 157–66.

What might a legislature do to facilitate private reforms? Outline a bill to accomplish this purpose. See Havighurst & Metzloff, S. 1232—A Late Entry in the Race for Malpractice Reform, Law & Contemp. Probs., Spring 1991, p. 179. What form would the legislative campaign take? Outline the arguments for and against the bill.

9. *Prospects.* Even if there were no insurmountable legal obstacles to the reform of malpractice law through private contract and consumer choice, would you expect it to occur? Consider the following:

> The education of consumers in this area could be a slow process, requiring as it does instillation of an appreciation that the rights to be surrendered are of limited value and that the potential cost savings to be realized, while not large for any individual, are worth obtaining. The educational problem may be exacerbated in the context of collective choices made in the employment setting. Because of the unlikelihood that any one individual's "vote" will determine the group decision, no individual has much incentive to inform himself of the merits of the choice being made. See generally M. Olson, The Logic of Collective Action (1971). Similarly, if employers or union leaders perceive that a reform will be misinterpreted by the mass of uninformed workers as a retraction rather than a conferral of benefits, they will pass up the opportunity to effectuate it. An HMO may

likewise fear that any effort on its part to change liability rules will be misconstrued by consumers.

The alternative to collective choice is individual choice, allowing a consumer a discount if he waives particular rights. In these circumstances, the consumer's incentive to inform himself is increased (though the discount may still not be enough to induce him to master the complexities of the subject). The most promising model is perhaps an employer-negotiated option for individuals to choose care from a single provider with or without his full tort rights. Such options might be tendered together with disinterested advice on the advantages and disadvantages of each.

Whether liability insurers will pass on to providers savings proportional to their success in negotiating waivers of tort rights with their patients is another problematic question. Unless they do, of course, the cost savings and thus the incentive to change approaches would be minimal, except for self-insured providers.

Despite these reasons for doubting that private reforms will soon or ever be forthcoming in the real world, it still seems desirable for the legal system to make room for them. It is generally desirable to let individuals benefit from economizing choices. In time, consumers may learn where their true interests lie and become less enamored of a legal system that ostentatiously holds out "rights" while systematically hiding the price tag.

Havighurst, Private Reform of Tort–Law Dogma: Market Opportunities and Legal Obstacles, Law & Contemp. Probs., Spring 1986, p. 143, 171 n. 91. See generally C. Havighurst, *Health Care Choices*, supra.

No-Fault and Strict-Liability Alternatives

NOTES AND QUESTIONS ON NO–FAULT COMPENSATION

1. *Applying Social Insurance Concepts to Medical Injuries*. The high cost of litigating fault issues in the medical field has inspired proposals to create a social insurance program of some kind for persons injured in receiving medical treatment. To be sure, medical costs attributable to iatrogenic injuries are already spread to a substantial extent through public and private health insurance, and welfare programs provide some income protection for the seriously disabled. But the idea of directly and more fully compensating victims of iatrogenic injuries appeals to many who are frustrated by the high cost of the fault-based tort system and by its poor record in detecting and penalizing negligence, in compensating injured persons, and in inducing efficient levels of precaution against medical injury. Indeed, several other nations, most notably Sweden and New Zealand, have adopted compensation systems covering victims of medical accidents. See generally Danzon, The Swedish Patient Compensation System: Lessons for the United States, 15 J. Leg. Med. 199 (1994) (describing system for compensating injuries deemed "avoidable" though not necessarily the result of anyone's fault); Miller, An Analysis and Critique of the 1992 Changes to New Zealand's Accident Compensation Scheme, 52 Md. L. Rev. 1070 (1993) (describing scheme in which negligence determination was largely dropped from personal injury law in favor of overarching administrative compensation scheme providing damages for injured parties and seeking deterrence through experience-rated insurance premiums). Although these programs were the result of those nations' stronger traditions of social insurance and not of unsatisfactory experience with tort liability, they have been looked to as precedents for possible "no-fault" compensation in the United States. See, e.g., Studdert et al., Can the United States Afford a "No–Fault" System of Compensation for Medical Injury, Law & Contemp. Probs., Spring 1997, p. 1 (article from Harvard School of Public Health estimating costs of compensating injured patients in Utah and Colorado under principles developed in Swedish no-fault system).

For a proposal for a comprehensive no-fault program of compensation recommended for adoption in states where the current malpractice system was deemed most out of control (i.e., Florida and New York), see P. Weiler, Medical Malpractice on Trial 114–58 (1991). Professor Weiler, who participated in the Harvard Medical Practice Study, concludes that the data on injuries from that study "make no-fault at least a 'thinkable' idea." See also Weiler et al., Proposal for Medical Liability Reform, 267 J.A.M.A. 2355 (1992); Studdert et al., supra (costing out a similar concept).

In keeping with social insurance concepts, some of the U.S. proposals have focused principally on the problem of compensating more injured persons. (In some cases, of course, the main motive behind a proposal may have been to relieve health care providers of exposure to the unpleasantness of the fault-based tort system; in other cases, the proposal may have been driven by a sense that the health care industry's distress could be counted on to induce political support for an otherwise improbable social insurance scheme.) These proposals attach little importance, or only as an afterthought, to placing the cost of injuries on health care providers as a way of preserving or strengthening incentives to adopt appropriate precautions. Under these proposals, it is assumed that quality problems would be addressed either in the marketplace or by regulatory means. In this discussion, no-fault *compensation* schemes are distinguished from no-fault *liability* schemes, which seek to shift injury costs from injured persons to providers not because such persons should be singled out for special compensation but because providers are in a position to reduce such costs in the future.

2. *Compensating Severe Birth–Related Injuries*. In 1986, one of the three insurers writing liability coverage for obstetricians (OBs) in Virginia withdrew from the business, and the remaining insurers refused to accept new risks. The resulting insurance availability crisis led the Virginia legislature to pass the Virginia Birth–Related Neurological Injury Compensation Act. Va. Code Ann. § 38.2–5000 et seq. (Michie 1994). (A comparable program was adopted in Florida, at about the same time. Fla. Stat. ch. 766.301–.316 (1997)) The Virginia statute provides, as a substitute for tort remedies, automatic compensation to any newborn suffering "injury to the brain or spinal cord caused by the deprivation of oxygen or mechanical injury occurring in the course of labor, delivery or resuscitation in the immediate post-delivery period in a hospital which renders the infant permanently

nonambulatory, aphasic, incontinent, and in need of assistance in all phases of daily living." The narrowness of this definition, which leaves many birth-related injuries uncompensated and was estimated to cover only about 40 cases per year in the state, suggests that compensation of injured persons was not the legislature's primary object. Instead, its purpose was to remove from the tort system one class of injuries that, although rare, were so severe that they threatened to render OBs' liability risks uninsurable. Thus, although the Virginia program (and Florida's as well) takes the form of social insurance, its roots lie more in the need to fix the tort liability insurance system than in social welfare concerns.

The Virginia law provides for claims to be processed through the state workers' compensation board. The $20 million per year that is estimated to be needed to cover the program's cost is raised by assessing OBs $5000 per year, other physicians $250 per year, and hospitals $50 per delivery. Although OBs are not required by law to participate in the scheme (and thus to enjoy the resulting immunity from tort actions), liability insurers and hospitals will undoubtedly insist that they do so. The law seeks to preserve the quality of care by requiring that all compensable events be reported to state licensing authorities for investigation.

The Virginia and Florida programs have been much commented upon. E.g., Epstein, Market and Regulatory Approaches to Medical Malpractice: The Virginia Obstetrical No-Fault Statute, 74 Va. L.Rev. 1451 (1988); O'Connell, Pragmatic Constraints on Market Approaches: A Reply to Professor Epstein, id. at 1475. They have also been closely examined for lessons on the administration of no-fault benefits, on claiming behavior, and so forth. See, e.g., Sloan et al., The Road from Medical Injury to Claims Resolution: How No-Fault and Tort Differ, Law & Contemp. Probs., Spring 1997, p. 35 (noting, among other things, the small number of claims paid in each state); Bovbjerg et al., Administrative Performance of "No–Fault" Compensation for Medical Injury, id. at 71; Horwitz & Brennan, No–Fault Compensation for Medical Injury: A Case Study, Health Affs., Winter 1995, p. 164.

NOTES AND QUESTIONS ON NO–FAULT (STRICT) LIABILITY

1. *Keeping the Focus on Deterrence*. Some other proposals for rectifying problems in the malpractice liability system have focused not on compensating more injured persons as an end in itself but on the need to remove the fault issue from the liability equation in order to lower the cost of identifying compensable events and to make liability more effective in inducing efforts to avoid bad treatment outcomes. One key objective is to save the high administrative costs of determining fault on a case-by-case basis. Another goal is to bring more injuries into the system in order to strengthen rather than to minimize the signals sent to providers concerning the quality of care they are providing. Precisely because so few cases of actual negligence come to light, it is believed, liability should be broadened to cover other unfortunate outcomes—specifically those that, while perhaps not attributable to negligence as legally defined (or attributable at reasonable cost and accuracy through tort litigation), could be prevented in many instances if providers had appropriate incentives to discover and take appropriate precautions. In effect, proposals to dispense with fault determinations in assigning liability are not "no-fault" proposals in the usual sense but are more accurately characterized as "strict liability."

2. *"Medical Adversity Insurance."* For the earliest proposal of no-fault liability, see Havighurst & Tancredi, "Medical Adversity Insurance"—A No–Fault Approach to Medical Malpractice and Quality Assurance, 51 Milbank Mem. Fund Q. 125 (1973). See also Havighurst, "Medical Adversity Insurance"—Has Its Time Come?, 1975 Duke L.J. 1233 (noting that earlier proposal was originally offered as "a theoretically sound model for further study and as a conceptual benchmark for evaluating both the fault system and existing quality-assurance mechanisms"). The essentials of "Medical Adversity Insurance" (MAI) were "(1) advance specification of a limited list of automatically compensable events, carefully drawn up by medical experts * * *, and (2) design of the insurance scheme to keep providers in some measure financially accountable for the results of treatment in order to preserve and strengthen their incentives to avoid medical accidents and obtain better medical results." Id. at 1233–34. Both because this proposal is conceptually helpful and because the idea of no-fault liability continues to receive some attention in reform discussions, this original proposal may be usefully considered here.

3. *"Designated Compensable Events."* In the late 1970s, an ABA commission examined several no-fault options for medical injuries and settled upon an MAI-type scheme for further study:

> The Commission concluded that the most promising alternative of those considered is a designated compensable event (DCE) system which would predefine compensable outcomes according to established criteria. Such a DCE approach would largely but not solely predicate the payment of compensation on the conclusion of a representative group of clinicians that an injury probably would have been avoidable by adherence to accepted medical practice. Thus if a medical mishap resulting in injury is an occurrence which has been predefined, the patient would receive reparation without the necessity of bringing a tort liability claim and proving negligence. Mishaps not covered by the list of designated compensable events would remain under the tort liability system.
>
> The Commission cited the following reasons in its 1977 Report for selecting the DCE approach for study (at pages 94–95):
>
> 1. The DCE approach offers a conceptually sound "middle ground" between retaining negligence as the basis for compensation and compensating all who are medically injured. It offers an opportunity to retain a general relationship between avoidable conduct and compensation while not restricting the system to a "fault" label or to a costly case-by-case determination of negligence.
> 2. DCE is a flexible tool. It permits a modest start on the enumeration of compensable events and the periodic expansion and updating of any

such list. Such an incremental approach permits program costs to be taken into account in deciding whether to expand the number of covered events.

3. DCE offers the possibility of creating links between quality of care efforts, malpractice prevention, and compensation. The health care and tort systems now relate only in jarring, discordant ways. By predefining compensable events and by relating those events to general quality of care efforts (particularly in the hospital setting), a strong impetus can be given to prevention efforts.

4. DCE might improve the predictability of outcomes by setting forth in detail the outcomes which would give rise to compensation. To the extent that predictability of outcomes increases, the practice of defensive medicine should decrease.

5. If the decision to compensate or not follows fairly automatically when there has been an injury, based upon enumerated outcomes, then transaction costs should be considerably reduced and claims closed out much more quickly than under the present system.

* * *

It is the consensus of the Commission that the feasibility of developing lists of designated compensable events has been established by this study. The Commission recognizes that the study has not proved the feasibility of a DCE compensation system. This will only be established after a DCE–based compensation system has been constructed and tested.

ABA Commission on Medical Professional Liability, Designated Compensable Event System: A Feasibility Study 2–3, 5 (1979).

Although never subjected to a formal field test, the basic model of DCE/MAI has been fleshed out more fully in a series of studies and articles proposing liability for "accelerated-compensation events" (ACEs). See, e.g., Tancredi & Bovbjerg, Rethinking Responsibility for Patient Injury: Accelerated–Compensation Events, A Malpractice and Quality Reform Ripe for a Test, Law & Contemp. Probs., Spring 1991, p. 148 (redesignating "DCEs" as "ACEs" in recognition of the promptness and automaticity of compensation); Bovbjerg et al., Obstetrics and Malpractice: Evidence on the Performance of a Selective No-Fault System, 265 J.A.M.A. 2836 (1991) (application of list of compensable events to large data base of malpractice claims in obstetrics suggested feasibility of concept; roughly two thirds of currently paid claims, representing three quarters of dollar payouts, would be replaced by automatic compensation).

The original proposal for MAI contemplated legislative adoption, but the idea might also be adopted by private contract between an institutional provider (e.g., a hospital or HMO) and its patients. See ABA Commission, supra at 53–61; Tancredi, Designing a No-fault Alternative, Law & Contemp.Probs., Spring 1986, at 277. What would be the political prospects for legislation implementing DCE/MAI? Would obtaining enforcement of the contract be easier or harder than it was in, say, the *Madden* case?

Consider the numerous design questions that would have to be faced in implementing a DCE/MAI program. To what extent should damages be based on a schedule—as with worker's compensation (to which DCE/MAI may be usefully compared in many other respects as well)—as opposed to being individualized and determined case-by-case? How should wage loss be handled for non-wage-earners? Should an allowance be made for pain and suffering? How long must the list of compensable events be to satisfy a court's probable expectation of a "quid pro quo"?

4. *Defining Compensable Events*. It has not escaped the notice of proponents of no-fault compensation systems that it would be costly to compensate all patients suffering unfortunate consequences in the course of receiving medical care. As a result, their proposals have been characterized as "selective no-fault," with the compensation of events not deemed automatically compensable left for compensation, if at all, through the tort system (as it might be modified). Even the Swedish program mentioned above incorporates "avoidability" as a criterion in defining compensable events:

> Use of avoidability principles to simplify the compensation inquiry will not be foreign to tort scholars in this country: [DCEs and ACEs] employ this general concept as their basis. DCEs are predetermined categories of medical injuries that are identified by medical experts as preventable "in a specified share of cases receiving good care." [Bovbjerg et al., supra.] For example, inadvertent laceration of a woman's bladder during a hysterectomy procedure is the kind of event that may be automatically qualify for compensation under this formulaic approach. Proposals for systematic use of such devices have been termed "selective no-fault." Only those medical injuries selected for coverage by professional judgment are included, and the association with fault is blurred by use of statistical preventability, rather than individualized judgments, in determining compensation.

Studdert et al., supra, at 3–4. The following excerpt from Havighurst & Tancredi, supra, at 132–43, provides some further sense of the possibilities for designing a no-fault, strict-liability system that, by focusing exclusively on the outcomes of care and ignoring the processes by which those outcomes were achieved, aims at inducing improvement in the quality of medical care:

> The difficulty of defining a compensable event is self-evident to nearly everyone, but particularly to physicians. Bad results of medical treatment can be regarded as incidents of the original disease or condition or of the probabilistic character of most therapies just as easily as they can be seen as results of errors or negligence in the health care system. Others who have considered the prospects for a no-fault system in this field have very nearly despaired of reducing medical outcomes to a list of compensable events, and our study only began when it was recognized that it would not be necessary to handle all cases of possible negligence under the scheme we were proposing. Our object then became to develop a list of compensable events which, without being all-inclusive, would remove the greater number of cases from the fault-liability system, regularize compensation, and strengthen quality-promoting incentives. We began by devising an empiri-

cal study to delineate in a rough manner some possible compensable events in one area of medical care having substantial experience with malpractice claims—orthopedic surgery.

Appellate cases involving orthopedic care over the past 40 years were reviewed to sort out those which presented a strong medical presumption that the event was avoidable, in the sense that good care would have prevented the adverse outcome. After these cases were collated under various categories to develop a tentative listing of compensable events, a small meeting of orthopedic specialists, law professors, and lawyers was convened to consider it. Following a briefing on the purpose of the exercise and the principles that in our view should be applied in including an outcome on the "list," the group examined the items in the preliminary listing and proposed a number of significant additions. The resulting list, although still regarded as highly tentative, included the outcomes found to be negligently caused in the great majority of the cases previously reviewed.

The orthopedists who participated in the meeting appeared enthusiastic about the scheme as presented. As the list illustrates, they were quite free in their willingness to include items. In addition to demonstrating that some agreement could be reached by medical specialists on the overall concept and a list of appropriate compensable events, the meeting provided the opportunity for examining the complex medical, economic, and social issues which must be addressed in developing the list.

The compensable events tentatively identified fell into three broad groupings. The first grouping consisted of medical care sequelae which can affect the nonorthopedic as well as the orthopedic patient and which arise from the overall surgical treatment and postoperative course of patients. The suggested list included [postoperative infections; thrombophlebitis and embolism; catheter infections; allergic and toxic reactions to antibiotics and other drugs; blood transfusion reactions; foreign bodies; hospital accidents; adverse consequences during experimental treatment; and secondary injuries from surgery].

Many of these events are relatively frequent occurrences and will be controversial. We would emphasize, however, that their inclusion here is meant to be suggestive only, that greater specification would be needed, and that a complete examination of each item has yet to be undertaken. * * *

The second category of compensable events consisted of those which [specifically] involve diagnosis and treatment of orthopedic conditions. This list, also highly tentative, was somewhat more specific[, including growth deformity secondary to bone injury; Volkmann's contracture and other consequences of improperly administered casts; failure of healing of fractures (including malunion, nonunion, and delayed union); the consequences of bone pathology errors; and the consequences of misreading skeletal X-rays].

A third category of events was also identified. Entitled "Consequences of Conduct Appropriate for Specific Sanctions," this group included the adverse consequences of failure to obtain informed consent, abandonment of the patient, gross negligence, intentional misconduct, and illegal behavior. Because these behavioral lapses relate to special societal expectations regarding professional conduct, they seemed inappropriate for treatment in a no-fault system. * * *

* * * [A]ny list that is developed to test the [MAI] idea in practice is likely to include, for the most part, things which the courts have frequently identified as compensable events. Our analytical method may ultimately lead well beyond such events, however, resulting in the listing of adverse outcomes which have seldom been the subject of a lawsuit. It is at this point that medical adversity insurance would begin to be seen more as a new and more finely tuned instrument of quality assurance in medicine and less predominantly as a means of providing physicians relief from the stigma and trauma of malpractice claims. The open-ended character of our list is well-suited to gradual evolution in this direction as experience with the easy cases indicates the system's capacity to deal with harder ones.

Relative Avoidability (Perceived Fairness).—The first criterion for use in deciding about inclusion of an outcome on the list is relative avoidability. By this term, we invoke epidemiological probabilities and call attention to the difficulties of designing a system which meets providers' general expectations of fairness. Having removed the attribution of actual fault as either the main object or a by-product of the system, we have shifted substantially outward the boundary at which perceived unfairness sets in and have thereby improved the prospects for acceptance of compensation, even though the outcome in a significant proportion of the cases is arguably unavoidable. Nevertheless, until a good deal of education has been done, the medical community can be expected to resist treating as compensable a set of outcomes over which they consider that they have little control.[2]

So long as MAI's purpose is seen primarily as one of replacing the judicially administered system of malpractice law, the judgment of the minimum degree of avoidability required for a compensable event will be relatively straightforward. The issue would be simply whether the benefits (in increased fairness) of maintaining the opportunity for a fault-related inquiry are worth the cost. This opens up, first of all, the frequency with which the adverse outcome could be expected to have a satisfactory explanation which would exculpate the provider.[3] But this is only a small

2. Fairness is likely to be overemphasized as a concern by physicians accustomed to the fault system. Workmen's compensation, covering all industrial accidents, makes no pretense at limiting compensation to cases in which the employer could have prevented the event. In fact, a substantial percentage of the cases in which compensation is paid involve actual fault on the part of the injured employee himself. Although there are many factors which may outweigh fairness concerns, we adhere to a fairness requirement as a means of recognizing the impracticality of turning providers of medical care into guarantors of life and health for all.

3. On the question of fairness, our conception of the compensable though possibly unavoidable event may be compared with malpractice claims which fall under the legal doctrine of *res ipsa loquitur.* * * * Doctors often object to this doctrine on two fairness grounds: first, that the presumption of negligence is sometimes factually unwarranted and, second, that, although theoretically rebuttable by an affirmative showing of due care, the presumption is practically conclu-

part of the problem. One must also contend realistically with the imperfections of whatever fact-finding system may be adopted and with the problems and costs of getting proof which will adequately reveal whether the case was, in fact, one of unavoidability, negligence, or what. The risks of encouraging unproductive, litigation-inspired kinds of "defensive medicine" must also be counted. Given these imperfections in any system requiring extensive fact-and fault-finding, as well as the high costs of maintaining such a system, a substantial degree of seeming arbitrariness in a no-fault system could be justified.[4]

Once MAI has proved its capacity for effective quality assurance in areas previously policed with some frequency by malpractice suits, the process of moving it into other areas would be merely evolutionary. To the extent that a greater number of seemingly arbitrary payments were compelled, there would be desirable incentives to find ways, through research and otherwise, to avoid currently "unavoidable" occurrences. Moreover, the plan could appropriately be regarded as containing an element of social insurance, under which providers would initially bear some of the burden of the population's unavoidable illnesses. So regarded, the scheme should not seem unfair since, to the extent that unavoidable compensable events are randomly distributed, providers would have little trouble in passing the costs on to consumers through higher charges, thus spreading the burden throughout the population. There would be no windfalls to patients or large legal fees included in the payments, and no doctor would have reason to feel victimized, as physicians so often do now, by an *ad hoc* judgment against him and his professional reputation by a seemingly hostile agency of the state.

To arrive at an estimate of relative avoidability, it is necessary first to estimate the frequency with which an event is therapy-induced (iatrogenic) and the extent to which it can, in fact, be prevented, or detected and treated if it should develop. Iatrogenicity would usually be comparatively easy to determine, but it would not be conclusive on compensability because it is common in medical practice for a treatment regimen to be selected with full awareness and expectation of its side effects. In these

sive in a jury's hands. Although under our theory, likewise, occurrence of an event included on the list makes compensation automatic, the fundamental difference is that there is no imputation of fault to the physician. Indeed, avoidability is explicitly a relative matter in our formulation. We would not require compensation to be confined only to highly avoidable events, since that would be to reintroduce fault through the back door. Another important difference between MAI and *res ipsa loquitur* lies in the medical input into the process of defining compensable events. The criteria and the data used by medical experts in defining compensable events would go well beyond anything that enters a judge's mind in deciding whether to apply the doctrine of *res ipsa loquitur*.

4. The law frequently sacrifices the parties' opportunities for a full factual inquiry of the kind which might be deemed necessary for perfect justice. Strict tort liability for defective products and the use of "per se" rules in antitrust law are two examples. One senses, however, that there is a greater willingness to indulge in such conclusive presumptions where corporations, rather than individuals, are thus imposed upon. Whether a physician is a fit candidate for "enterprise liability" is no longer an open question, however, since the doctrines of *respondeat superior,* the "borrowed servant," and the "captain of the ship" all reflect judicial acceptance of nonfault liability for medical practitioners.

cases, the therapy may indeed be the best available, in which event the side effects may appropriately be regarded as unavoidable incidents of the condition which occasioned the therapy.

A decision to make an event compensable must also reflect a judgment of unexpectedness and of preventability through correct application of medical knowledge. Although perfect preventability is not a necessary condition, it may often be possible, by further classification and subcategorizing, to identify events having a higher degree of avoidability. Thus, for example, a particular adverse drug reaction, usually tolerable, might be compensated when it occurs in pregnant women but not otherwise, if pregnancy is a particular contraindication. Moreover, even if a side effect were predictable and acceptable, it might still be made compensable (perhaps with a higher deductible) if medical science was capable of initiating early and effective treatment once it develops, reducing concomitant morbidity or mortality. Other fairness problems might be dealt with by adjustments in experience-rating formulas. * * *

The important thing about relative avoidability as a criterion is that it provides no absolute guide. A lesser degree of avoidability, that is, a greater proportion of seemingly arbitrary payments, can be justified by a perceived opportunity to obtain substantially improved outcomes in the small percentage of cases where the adverse outcome is avoidable, by a need to stimulate greater attention (perhaps research) to increasing preventability, by a need to balance incentives resulting from classifying another outcome as compensable, or by other pragmatic factors. The issue to be faced is simply the effect on the system's overall credibility and workability and the value of the quality inducements achieved. At the outset, however, in order to assure acceptance by physicians and to prevent the social insurance element (and costs, if insurer subsidies are unavailable) from becoming too large, the list would probably include only events which were regarded as avoidable in a high percentage of cases.

Impact on Quality.—The second criterion for use in defining a compensable event is the impact on the quality of care. The quality-improving dimension of medical adversity insurance rests, as does much of the theory underlying the tort of malpractice, on an expectation that the consequences attached to a bad outcome will induce efforts to avoid it. The challenge is to arrange cost-bearing in such a way as to harness such efforts and direct them toward achieving net gains in quality. Incentives are difficult to order perfectly, however, and some parties are in a better position to influence certain outcomes than are others. Identifying the compensable event will often call for additional judgments, beyond specification of the event itself, which will contribute to a greater positive effect on quality.

The selection of the appropriate risk bearer is a more complex question than first appears. One obvious question illustrating this complexity is which provider's MAI policy—the physician's or the hospital's—should bear a particular loss. We visualize distinct lists of compensable events in the two policies and would expect a risk to be assigned to one policy or the other in accordance with a judgment about which provider was best able to organize to reduce or eliminate it. Thus, for example, postoperative staph infections would probably be on the hospital's list, whereas the surgeon would likely bear the primary responsibility for, say, antibiotic reactions. Although this allocation of burdens will often seem arbitrary because responsibility is shared to a large degree,[5] it may prove inconsequential from a quality point of view because the hospital and the medical staff relate in ways which enable them to work together to minimize adverse outcomes. Bargaining between them would surely be initiated whichever way the responsibility was initially assigned, and it is probable that the same preventive actions would be taken whichever party bore the initial loss ([G.] Calabresi, [The Costs of Accidents: A Legal and Economic Analysis 150–52 (1970)]; Coase, [The Problem of Social Cost, 3 J.L. & Econ. 1 (1960)]). It is an important insight that MAI would create incentives not only for direct action, but also for initiating bargaining with others who are in a position to contribute to obtaining better outcomes. Thus, continuing to hold the surgeon responsible for the sponge count would make sense if one wished to see the surgeon remain in control of the operating room and thought that the surgical staff would be effective in persuading the hospital to hire better counters.

* * *

In the last analysis, a decision not to make an event compensable is equivalent to imposing the risk on the patient himself, subject to the possibility of his recovering for malpractice. Whether the loss should be so assigned is a question which ultimately should be explicitly considered. There will be cases where the patient is indeed in the best position to control costs. One such case would be where patients' frequent failures to follow doctors' orders produce the harms and where it seems unreasonable (or costly) to rely primarily on the doctors' ability to take special steps to follow up with the patient or to maintain the regimen. Relegating the patient to his malpractice remedy would, of course, allow his contributory negligence to be put in issue * * *.

* * * [P]recisely because we have chosen to take a piecemeal approach in developing our list of compensable events, we must be concerned about introducing unwarranted biases into the choice of treatment. One would expect, of course, that a physician faced with a choice of two treatment modes would select the one which had the least likelihood of resulting in a compensable event. But, if the adverse results of one method of treatment were on the list while the results of another available method were not, the physician might be led to adopt the latter method, even if it was not the best in the circumstances. The problem in defining compensable events is to encourage proper choices, all things considered, and to avoid creating incentives which distort doctors' judgments. Thus, if tetanus infections are to be made compensable, so must adverse reactions from tetanus toxoid, since to prevent one is to invite the other, and the object is to induce the physician to consider the trade-offs.

Because of the need for a "systems" approach to the large disease categories, special rules of compensability may occasionally be necessary. Thus, although certain surgical mishaps might be generally compensable,

5. For example, staph infections may prove to be more resistant to preventive measures if hospital physicians have used antibiotics indiscreetly over time.

exceptions might be made in the case of particular disease conditions where surgery was to be encouraged and the results of not operating could, for some reason, not be made compensable. Occasionally a high degree of seeming arbitrariness would have to be tolerated in order that a "closed system" could be achieved. * * *

A final risk to be considered is whether MAI might induce physicians either to refuse to treat patients whose conditions involved a high probability of resulting in a compensable event * * *. If professional fees reflect higher risks, as they should, these problems would not be significant. Although physicians would be induced to avoid handling cases where they lacked confidence in their ability to measure up to the professional average, this is a desirable effect and should promote consultations and referrals. * * *

Administrative Simplicity.—Our third and last criterion is administrative simplicity. The necessity for defining compensable events so that they can be easily recognized in practice can hardly be overemphasized. In cases where the etiology of an outcome may be in doubt, the event must nevertheless be defined to avoid disputes. For example * * *, hepatitis contracted within six months following a blood transfusion might be paid for from the transfuser's insurance, even though the casual connection could be disputed. Thus, a relatively low degree of avoidability and an element of arbitrariness in attributing causation are accepted as the price of obtaining desirable incentives without extensive (and probably inconclusive) fact-finding efforts.

Issues of administrative simplicity are implicit in much of the foregoing discussion of criteria. Thus, relative avoidability will often have to be sacrificed for simplicity, and responsibility for particular harms may sometimes have to be arbitrarily assigned to a particular risk bearer to avoid disputes and to provide a starting point for bargaining directed to improving outcomes.

These and other difficulties illustrate the complexity of system design, but our judgment is that enlightened practicality together with high-level medical expertise could design a system which would be capable at the outset of taking most malpractice litigation out of the courts or other forums and ultimately of expanding to provide quality-inducing incentives in most areas of medical care. A high level of sophistication would be called for, but we believe dedicated medical specialists would be capable of making the system work.

5. *Costs.* Would MAI raise the cost of medical care? (Or would it merely bring into the open, as an explicit cost of care, costs that injured persons already bear privately?) Would it cost too much? How should its net costs be calculated. Studdert et al. undertook to estimate the cost of compensating all injuries compensable under Swedish no-fault principles in Utah and Colorado in 1992. Studdert et al., supra. Under certain assumptions concerning the amount and nature of compensation, they concluded that in Colorado, for example, the cost of the no-fault scheme would have been $78 million, compared to the $45–50 million current cost of the malpractice system (a difference equal to about a third of one percent of total health care costs in the state). The scheme would have compensated 973 individuals, about three times the number of successful tort claimants.

Would the method of calculating costs employed by Studdert et al. in evaluating a hypothetical no-fault *compensation* scheme be appropriate for measuring the net cost of a no-fault *liability* scheme like DCE/MAI? What factor have they omitted? In order to suggest both the costs and the benefits of MAI, Havighurst & Tancredi, supra, at 154–55, provided a rough cost estimate of making all post-transfusion hepatitis compensable. Using data from the 1960s, they determined that about 24% of the cost represented by the current incidence of hepatitis from blood transfusions was irreducible using then current technology and best practices. The remaining 76% of the aggregate cost, they suggested, should be regarded "more as an estimate of maximum potential benefits than as an estimate of potential costs." Do you see their point? (Recall the discussion in § B of this chapter of the various ways in which strict liability might induce improvements in the collection and use of blood products.)

Would DCE/MAI produce optimal deterrence of bad medical results? Or would it encourage costly defensive medical practice? At the time Havighurst and Tancredi wrote, the best that could be hoped for was that providers would cease providing "flat-of-the-curve" services but would do everything they could think of to avoid a compensable event. Would a DCE/MAI today be more likely to induce careful weighing of costs and benefits? What has changed in the meantime? The next chapter will allow you an occasion to consider whether no-fault liability might be a better idea in the age of managed care than it was when Havighurst and Tancredi first proposed it.

Would MAI be fair to providers? How important is fairness as a goal? Would physicians refer the hard cases to other providers in order to avoid the risk of having to pay for a bad outcome? Would such referrals necessarily be such a bad thing? Would the better physicians, who attract the harder cases, have the poorest results and thus be forced to pay higher premiums? Could they charge higher fees to cover their higher costs and still make money? Should we be uncomfortable in subjecting individual physicians to "enterprise liability"? Does the appearance of managed care open some new possibilities for addressing this problem?

How would a working MAI system affect the need for other quality-assurance mechanisms? How would it affect hospital/physician and physician/patient relationships? How would it affect the organization and operation of managed-care plans? What adverse consequences might flow from changing the system from a discretionary grievance mechanism into an automatic compensation system? (Recall the possible benefits of the fault system, and the discretion patients have in invoking it, in inducing physicians to cultivate patient trust and ethically satisfying doctor/patient relationships.)

6. *Variations on the Theme.* Should MAI be offered to patients on an optional basis, with or without a price difference? (Would there be an adverse selection problem?) An attractive approach might be for a provider to offer the patient a chance to purchase (perhaps at a provider-subsidized price) insurance against all the risks of, say, a particular hospitalization. (How could such coverage be priced?) Such coverage might be conditioned on a waiver of tort rights or at least on an agreement to offset the proceeds against any tort award (reducing attorneys' interest in any possible claim). Many variations of this approach, which may be likened to "flight insurance," can be imagined. In studying the materials in the next chapter, consider what new possibilities are opened up. (Should no-fault liability be mandated by statute, or might it be expected to emerge naturally in a marketplace where employers are increasingly demanding that health plans demonstrate their commitment to providing good-quality care?)

PART IV

Health Care Law in a Period of Rapid Change

CHAPTER 8

MANAGED CARE AND THE LAW

SECTION A: MCO ACCOUNTABILITY FOR THE QUALITY OF CARE

NOTE ON MODERN HEALTH CARE CONTRACTS

Consider the potential liabilities of health plans to patients under the contractual relationships described in the following excerpt:

> **Plan Contracts and Provider–Patient Relationships.** In general, the plan/subscriber contracts reviewed in this study do not purport to govern relationships between subscribers, on the one hand, and physicians, hospitals, and other providers of plan-financed services, on the other. Instead, the contracts embody the paradigmatic notion that financing entities do not provide health care but merely enable its provision by licensed providers, who have direct, independent obligations to patients. This paradigm-inspired view of health care transactions is maintained even when the plan significantly limits the subscriber's freedom to select a provider * * *.
>
> Some health plan contracts attempt to convey to the subscriber the nature of the relationship that prevails between the health plan and its participating providers * * *. Thus, one indemnity plan defines a *participating provider* as "a professional provider who has an effective participating contract with [the plan]." That definition implies a somewhat looser connection between plan and provider than the definition employed by another plan, an IPA-model HMO: "a physician who has contracted with [the plan] to provide care to persons covered under this contract." The contract of one staff-model HMO calls attention to the even closer connection implied in an employment relationship by adopting the following definition: "a physician ... who is employed by [the plan] or is under contract to provide care through [the plan's] facilities." Despite these subtle differences in defining the degree of integration of providers into the plan, however, all contracts maintain the convention that provider/patient relationships are not themselves governed by the plan/subscriber contract.
>
> Many of the contracts reviewed seek to reinforce the notion that the plan merely pays for care and is not responsible for its quality. The ease with which a plan can plausibly deny responsibility for the quality of medical care provided varies, however, with the type of plan and the amount of control it can exercise over physicians or the degree to

which it limits the consumer's choice of provider. Thus, one insurer offering both indemnity and IPA–HMO coverage includes in its indemnity contract the bald assertion that "[the plan] is not responsible for the quality of medical care" but omits this provision from its otherwise similar HMO contract. Not all closed-panel plans are similarly reluctant, however, to deny responsibility for the quality of care provided by contracting providers. For example, one IPA-model HMO contract states, "Plan Providers are solely responsible for any health services rendered to their Member patients. [The] Plan makes no express or implied warranties or representations concerning the qualifications ... of any physician, hospital, or other Plan Provider." Another HMO contract similarly demonstrates a concern about the plan's potential liability for corporate negligence in selecting participating providers by stating, "Inclusion or exclusion of a Provider or Covered Facility in any network is not an indication of the Provider's or Facility's quality or skill."

A persistent criticism of IPAs and preferred-provider arrangements as they emerged in the 1980s was their emphasis on obtaining price discounts and imposing utilization review rather than integrating financing and delivery and attempting to ensure quality. The contracts reviewed in this study indicate that, on paper at least, such plans continue to run away from legal responsibility for the quality of care. The most common approach of plans seeking to avoid such responsibility is to emphasize the independence of physicians and hospitals by calling attention to the independent relationship between provider and patient. A group-model HMO's contract, for example, states, "The relationship between a provider and any member is that of health care provider and patient. The provider is solely responsible for health care provided to any member." * * *

Thus, instead of themselves defining the obligations of providers to patients, drafters of health plan contracts put most of their energy into attempting to ensure that the plan itself will not be held liable for provider negligence under some agency principle justifying imposition of enterprise liability. In addition to seeking to avert liability, the contracts generally embody the paradigmatic notion that professional norms and standards alone protect patients against underservice and incompetent care. Only staff-model HMOs, which cannot hope to avoid vicarious liability for the torts of their physician employees, fail to stress the independent obligations that run from their physicians to plan subscribers. It is a testimonial to the strength of the professional paradigm of medical care that * * * even staff-model HMOs are rarely sued directly for physician torts. In general, health care contracts have not departed, even in the case of staff-model HMOs, from the fiction that corporations do not provide health care, providers do. * * *

Plan/Provider Contracts. [T]he separate contracts that virtually all plans maintain with their participating providers * * * have great commercial significance but deal mainly with such matters as the form and amount of the provider's compensation, utilization management and other administrative requirements, and the terms on which a provider's participation may be terminated. Although some of them state in general terms the provider's substantive obligation to care for patients, such contracts usually do no more than track similar language in the plan/subscriber agreement. In addition, provider obligations are generally not specified in unusual or innovative ways. One plan, however, obligates the physician to "provide health services to all Members in accordance with the standard of practice of the community in which Physician renders health services and in a manner so as to assure quality of care and treatment." Such a contract might be enforceable by a patient as a third-party beneficiary. If so, it also might, in conjunction with comparable language in the subscriber agreement, make the physician accountable only under a local rather than a national, regional, or similar-community standard of care. In general, however, plan/provider contracts are likely to have little substantive effect on patients' rights against either the plan or the provider.

* * *

Although plan/provider contracts have little to say about a patient's right to receive care of a certain kind, they may nevertheless impact patient care indirectly. Such contracts frequently introduce financial incentives by which the plan hopes to discourage overutilization. Such incentives could have a foreseeable detrimental effect on the care provided to individual patients. Indeed, capitation payments, which create a fixed budget with which to care for a given population, have long been valued precisely because they induce providers to economize. Physician gatekeepers are sometimes directly penalized financially if utilization exceeds certain norms, a feature that has prompted some criticism and even some congressional concern. In other plans, participating providers may be subject to periodic review of their spending proclivities under an implicit or explicit threat that utilization deemed excessive by plan administrators may result in exclusion from continued participation in the plan.

For present purposes, the striking fact about incentive arrangements in plan/provider agreements is that they are generally not disclosed or alluded to in plan/subscriber contracts. On the contrary, the latter contracts often deny any plan responsibility for the quality of care or hold out reassuringly that participating providers are governed by professional norms and standards. Such disclaimers and reassurances might be deemed to be misleading or unfair to consumers.

C. Havighurst, Health Care Choices: Private Contracts as Instruments of Health Reform 118–22 (1995). Throughout this chapter, consider the actual or potential role of the operative contracts in defining patient rights and plan and provider obligations.

Vicarious Liability for Physician Torts?

Boyd v. Albert Einstein Medical Center

Superior Court of Pennsylvania, 1988.
547 A.2d 1229.

■ OLSZEWSKI, JUDGE:

[The trial court had granted summary judgment in favor of defendant/appellee, Health Maintenance Organization of Pennsylvania ("HMO"), and the appeal raised the question whether, on the pleadings and depositions, there existed a question of material fact as to whether participating physicians were the ostensible agents of the HMO.

[Appellant's decedent was seen by Dr. Rosenthal, the primary care physician she had selected from the HMO's roster, and was referred to Dr. Cohen, a surgeon who was also a participating HMO physician. Various allegations were made.]

Appellant's theory of recovery before the trial court was primarily one of vicarious liability under the ostensible agency theory. See Capan v. Divine Providence Hospital, 287 Pa.Super. 364, 430 A.2d 647 (1980). * * *

In adopting the theory of ostensible agency [in *Capan*, supra, which allowed a jury instruction on vicarious liability for physician negligence in a hospital emergency room], we noted * * * two factors which contributed to the conclusion by other courts that, although a physician holds independent contractor status with respect to the hospital, he may nevertheless be an agent of the hospital with respect to the patient. First, there is a likelihood that patients will look to the institution rather than the individual physician for care due to the changing role of the hospital in today's society. Second, "where the hospital 'holds out' the physician as its employee[,]" a justifiable finding is that there is an ostensible agency relationship between the hospital and the physician. * * *

We must * * * decide whether there is an issue of material fact as to participating physicians being the ostensible agents of HMO. In order to make these determinations, we will discuss, initially, the arrangement between HMO and participating doctors and their relationship with HMO members. The record reflects that, through his employer, appellant became eligible for and ultimately chose to participate in a group plan provided by [HMO].[6] As part of its services, HMO provided its members with a brochure explaining, in general outline form only, the main features of the program of benefits. The brochure also provided a directory of participating

6. In a document entitled "Why offer HMO–PA?", HMO reasoned to employers that HMO "is a total care program which not only insures its subscribers, but provides medical care, guarantees the quality of the care and controls the costs of health care services." The document also claimed that "HMO–PA is more than just another health insurance plan. HMO–PA is an entire health care system. HMO–PA provides the physicians, hospitals and other health professionals needed to maintain good health. HMO–PA assures complete security, when illness or injury arises." Finally, the document provided that HMO–PA "[a]ssumes responsibility for quality and accessibility."

primary physicians and declared that the complete terms and conditions of the plan were set forth in the group master contract.

The group master contract provides that HMO "operates a comprehensive prepaid program of health care which provides health care services and benefits to Members in order to protect and promote their health, and preserve and enhance patient dignity."[7] HMO was incorporated in 1975 under the laws of Pennsylvania and converted from a non-profit to a for-profit corporation in 1981. HMO is based on the individual practice association model (hereinafter IPA), which means that HMO is comprised of participating primary physicians who are engaged in part in private practice in the HMO service area. Under the plan, IPA contracts with HMO to provide medical services to HMO members. IPA selects its primary and specialist physicians and enters into an agreement with them obligating the physician to perform health services for the subscribers of HMO.

[The court described the HMO's extensive credentialing process for physicians applying for membership in the IPA.]

The membership committee makes a recommendation to the executive committee, which makes the final decision regarding the applicant. Those accepted into the IPA are called by an IPA coordinator, who schedules an office orientation. [According to various plan documents, t]he primary physician's role is defined as the "gatekeeper into the health care delivery system." "An HMO member must consult with his primary physician before going to a specialist and/or the hospital." If the primary physician deems it necessary, he arranges a consultation with an HMO participating specialist, which constitutes a second opinion. "Basically, with the primary physicians 'screening' the members' illnesses, excessive hospitalization and improper use of specialists can be reduced."

Member-patients use a physician directory and choose a conveniently located office of a participating primary physician. HMO members will only receive reimbursement from non-participating providers when the condition requiring treatment was of an immediate nature. Determinations of immediacy are made by the HMO quality assurance committee. In any event, persons desiring emergency non-provider benefits must notify HMO or their primary physician of the emergency within forty-eight hours and must give written proof of the occurrence within ninety days after service is rendered. Reimbursement for emergency care by a non-participating provider is limited to expenses incurred prior to the time the member's condition, "in the opinion of HMOPA, reasonably permitted him or her to travel or be transported to the nearest HMOPA Participating Provider, or to receive follow-up care from a Participating Provider, upon referral by the Member's Participating Primary Physician."

Primary physicians are paid through a mechanism termed "capitation." Capitation is an actuarially determined amount prepaid by HMO to

7. The introduction to the group master contract also provides that "HMOPA operates on a direct service rather than indemnity basis. The interpretation of the Contract shall be guided by the direct service nature of HMOPA's prepaid program."

the primary physician for each patient who has chosen his office. The dollar amount is based upon a pre-determined rate per age group. The primary physicians are paid 80% of the capitation amount and the remaining 20% is pooled by IPA and goes back into a pooled risk-sharing fund as a reserve against specialty referral costs and hospital stays. Each primary care office has its own specialist fund and hospital fund established by allocating a pre-determined amount each month for each member who has chosen that primary care office. The surplus from the specialist fund is returned to the primary care office. The hospital fund, however, is governed by a hospital risk/incentive-sharing scheme which anticipates a number of inpatient days per members per year. If the actual hospital utilization is less than anticipated, the HMO and IPA each receive 50% of the savings. IPA must place the savings in the Special IPA risk-sharing account and must use the funds to offset losses resulting from unanticipated physician costs. If utilization is greater than anticipated, IPA is responsible for 50% of the loss up to the amount of uncommitted funds in the Special IPA risk sharing account.

* * *

HMO asserts that because the theory of ostensible agency has been applied in Pennsylvania only to the relationship between hospitals and independent contractor physicians, the theory is not appropriate in the instant situation. We emphasize, however, that when this Court introduced the concept of ostensible agency to this Commonwealth in *Capan*, supra, we based that decision in large part upon "the changing role of the hospital in society [which] creates a likelihood that patients will look to the institution" for care. Because the role of health care providers has changed in recent years, the *Capan* rationale for applying the theory of ostensible agency to hospitals is certainly applicable in the instant situation.

* * * [W]e find that there is an issue of material fact as to whether the participating physicians were the ostensible agents of HMO. We conclude, therefore, that the trial court erred when it granted HMO's motion for summary judgment on the ground that the participating physicians were not the ostensible agents of HMO. * * *

■ McEWEN, JUDGE, concurring. [Opinion omitted.]

NOTES AND QUESTIONS ON VICARIOUS AND OTHER LIABILITY OF MCOS

1. Do you agree with the *Boyd* court's conclusion on ostensible agency? Argue the facts both ways. Should it have been significant, as the trial judge thought, that the quoted plan documents were provided only to employers, not employees, and that the employees were not themselves parties to, or likely even to see, the "group master contract"?

In a Michigan case, an inferior state court, relying on *Grewe v. Mount Clemens General Hospital*, reproduced in chapter 5(§B), said, "Applying that holding to this case the question is:

> Whether Plaintiffs, at the time they sought treatment for John's arm, looked to the HMO for that treatment, or merely for the payment of those services? BCN contends that it is a health care insurer, not a health care provider, and that Plaintiffs in fact viewed it as such. BCN argues that by way of affidavit and deposition Plaintiffs admitted that they looked to it for health insurance. BCN contends that this, in conjunction with the Deckers' ability to independently choose their doctor, evidences their non-reliance on the HMO. BCN reasons that the Plaintiffs expected actual health care only from Dr. Saini, their primary care physician—and not their HMO, per se. On the other hand the Plaintiffs argue that they obtained Dr. Saini's name from BCN which restricted their choice of physician to a list of participating doctors. Plaintiffs submitted evidence that they believed BCN hired the best doctors as members and that they chose Dr. Saini because he belonged to BCN. Further, Plaintiffs point out that they paid BCN a membership fee and that BCN paid the doctors. Plaintiffs did not pay their doctor directly; the point being that the primary relationship for the Plaintiffs was with BCN, not the doctor. In further support of their argument Plaintiffs rely on BCN's brochure wherein it promised the "best care" available. According to Plaintiffs, the bottom line is that BCN held itself out as a health care provider, as well as a health care insurer, and they relied on that representation.
>
> It is clear from the proofs submitted by the Plaintiffs that there is evidence to support each of the three (3) elements of ostensible agency in this case. That is, there is evidence that:
>
> 1. Plaintiffs reasonably believed that Dr. Saini was BCN's agent,
> 2. That belief was generated by the representations of BCN and
> 3. Plaintiffs' reliance was not negligent.
>
> * * *
>
> As a matter of public policy, the Court notes that imposing vicarious liability on HMOs for the malpractice of their member physicians would strongly encourage them to select physicians with the best credentials. Otherwise, HMOs would have no such incentive and might be driven by economics to retain physicians with the least desirable credentials, for the lowest prices. In the interest of encouraging high standards of health care it behooves the Courts to hold HMOs liable for the conduct of their participating physicians, when the facts so merit.

Decker v. Saini, 1991 WL 277590 at *4 (Mich.Cir.Ct., 1991). See also Petrovich v. Share Health Plan, Inc., 1998 WL 122990 (Ill. App. 1998) (holding, on basis of control exercised over primary care physician and other factors, that plaintiff might have been able to show reliance despite plan's disclaimer of agency relationship); Dunn v. Praiss, 656 A.2d 413 (N.J.1995) (recognizing liability based on combination of respondeat superior, vicarious liability, and contract).

How difficult would it be for an MCO to avoid liability of the kind contemplated in *Boyd* and *Decker*?

2. *Assigning Liability for Physician Negligence.* Should the liability of an HMO or other modern health plan for the torts of participating physicians be determined by the contractual relationship between the plan and the provider, by the individual plaintiff's reasonable beliefs concerning that relationship, by the terms of the plan/subscriber contract, by the objective tenor of the various representations made by the plan, by the degree of control actually exercised over the physician, or by some other factor? Courts faced with assigning liability to an MCO will naturally consult case law concerning the corporate responsibility of hospitals for the torts of physicians. How valid and precise is the analogy, however? Is the hospital or the MCO the more logical candidate for vicarious liability? (This question will be raised again below.)

What factors should common-law courts consider in deciding which entity—physician, hospital, or plan—should bear primary responsibility for injuries caused by physician negligence? Should the outcome depend solely on the nature of the particular HMO? Presumably, the easiest case would be one in which an actual employment relationship exists, as in a staff-model HMO. In Sloan v. Metropolitan Health Council, Inc., 516 N.E.2d 1104 (Ind.App.1987), the court held the HMO liable for the negligence of an employee physician despite the defense that "the professional must exercise professional judgment that the principal [the HMO employer] may not properly control." The court observed that HMO physicians were subject to some control by the plan's medical director.

Do you agree with the rulings favorable to vicarious liability for the acts of non-employee physicians in the *Boyd* and *Decker* cases? By the same token, would you let an IPA-type HMO, or the IPA itself, off the hook if the operative contracts and sales literature conformed to conventional notions of (1) the doctor/patient relationship and (2) the appropriate role of corporate entities in providing medical care? In Raglin v. HMO Illinois, Inc., 595 N.E.2d 153, 157–58 (Ill.App.1992), the court distinguished *Boyd* and held that an IPA-type HMO was not vicariously liable for physician negligence despite the limitations it placed on patient choice. The court stated that "this is the manner in which all HMOs operate" and "[t]herefore ... should not be the dispositive factor upon which the question of apparent agency turns." The court also held that the plan's so-called Quality Assurance Compliance Program, which it maintained pursuant to state regulatory requirements and "with which medical groups and physicians contracting with HMOI must abide, is not the type of control from which agency arises."

On making "control" a factor in determining whether vicarious liability should be imposed, consider Chase v. Independent Practice Ass'n, 583 N.E.2d 251 (Mass.App.1991). Because the HMO entity itself had been dismissed as a defendant (presumably pursuant to a settlement), the court addressed the liability of the defendant "IPA." Finding no vicarious liability, the court stated:

> * * * VHP [the plan] did not employ physicians directly. Instead, it contracted with IPA to arrange for medical services to its members. IPA in turn contracted with HCGO [an incorporated ob/gyn group], who in turn employed Dr. Kaufman. IPA does not pay any physician employees and

> functions in effect as a third-party broker, arranging for services on behalf of VHP mem'ers.
>
> That IPA did not retain any right to control the professional activities of Dr. Kaufman and HCGO is clear from the IPA–HCGO agreement. While IPA did check the credentials of the agencies with whom it contracted, it did not have the right to hire and fire individual physicians, nor to set their salaries, work schedules, or term of employment. More importantly, IPA did not control the actual medical decisions made by HCGO and Dr. Kaufman. Although the agreement between IPA and HCGO does provide for certain cost-containment and utilization-review measures, it also makes clear that responsibility for the actual provision medical treatment rests with HCGO and its physician-employees.

Id. at 254. Note the attenuated relationship between the HMO, which was contractually committed to arranging care for its members, and Dr. Kaufman, who ultimately provided the service. Recalling the discussion of today's health plans in chapter 2(§C), do you regard this arrangement as unusual? Are health plans that engage principally in paying for care and that have no obvious ability, or inclination, to influence or control individual practitioners the kind of distinctive, innovative entities visualized by the original supporters of a market-oriented health care system? Should a lack of organizational integration (and the consequent inability to control physician performance) be a basis for immunizing plans from liability for bad outcomes caused by independent-contractor physicians? Or might an MCO's hands-off policy in dealing with the physicians it selects (and compensates in ways possibly antithetical to the quality of care) be seen as a reason to impose vicarious liability rather than as a reason not to?

3. *Enterprise Liability?* Would some form of "enterprise liability," under which plaintiffs would have to prove no additional facts to establish the plan's responsibility for a physician's negligence, be desirable as a way of focusing responsibility on health plans and thereby inducing closer integration of financing and delivery, greater selectivity in contracting with physicians, and appropriate attention to the quality of care? For articles embracing enterprise liability for quality failings as a logical consequence of corporate assumption of responsibility for the cost of care, see Havighurst, Making Health Plans Accountable for the Quality of Care, 31 Ga. L. Rev. 587 (1997) (developing ideas suggested in these notes); Studdert & Brennan, Deterrence in a Divided World: Emerging Problems for Malpractice law in and Era of Managed Care, 15 Behav. Sci. & L. 21 (1997) (concluding that enterprise liability, though "no panacea for achieving sharp deterrence in the malpractice sphere[, is] capable of correcting some aspects of the incompatibility between malpractice law and new organizational models"); Sage et al., Enterprise Liability for Medical Malpractice and Health Care Quality Improvement, 20 Am. J.L. & Med. 1 (1994) (joining "a chorus of voices that proposes to refocus liability for medical malpractice on the organizations that will increasingly bear practical responsibility for providing health services"); Comment, Tort Liability of Health Care Delivery Systems: Beyond Enterprise Liability, 29 Wake Forest L. Rev. 305 (1994). On the potential for improvements in the quality of MCO-financed care

(including adoption of "continuous quality improvement" or "total quality management" methods employed in manufacturing industries), see T. Brennan & D. Berwick, New Rules: Regulation, Markets, and the Quality of American Medical Care ch. 6 (1996); Sage et al., supra, at 12–15. Might exposure to liability for physician malpractice and other torts provide the wake-up call that some experts see as needed to induce correction of systemic quality failings in American medicine?

Can you explain why a legal system that has finally seen fit to empower MCOs to control the cost of health care remains fastidious about making them also responsible for its quality? If you were counseling the managed-care industry, would you advise it to resist enterprise liability? Or might you suggest to the industry that accepting liability would help legitimize it and its methods in the public eye and diminish the political backlash it is confronting?

A tentative proposal to implement MCO enterprise liability was floated prominently in May 1993 by the task force that formulated the Clinton administration's health reform initiative that failed to survive the political process in 1994. The task force suggested publicly that MCOs should be liable for the negligent acts of health care providers and that physicians affiliated with such plans should no longer be personally liable for their own negligence; only physicians maintaining traditional solo practices would retain individual liability. Proponents of the measure anticipated that, in addition to getting health plans to take more responsibility for patient well-being and outcomes, enterprise liability could eliminate costly multi-defendant litigation and encourage more or faster settlement of cases. In addition, physicians in solo practice were expected to join organized health plans to escape liability and the need to pay malpractice insurance premiums. See generally Sage et al., supra (endorsement of enterprise liability by architects of Clinton proposal).

The Clinton task force proposal was quickly taken off the table when it encountered strong opposition throughout the health care industry. See Abraham & Weiler, Enterprise Liability and the Evolution of the American Health Care System, 108 Harv. L. Rev. 381, 382–84 (suggesting reasons for industrywide criticism); Sage & Jorling, A World That Won't Stand Still: Enterprise Liability by Private Contract, 43 DePaul L. Rev. 1007, 1010–12 (1994) (describing quick and harsh condemnation of proposal by both organized medicine and managed care industry). The themes of that opposition—from organized medicine, health insurers, and the managed care industry—reveal both the implications that the locus of tort responsibility has for the control of medical practice and the degree of comfort of the major players with a state of affairs in which health plans are not legally accountable for the quality of care. Thus, the AMA's general counsel cited physician fears about the loss of professional autonomy: "[The proposal] says to doctors, 'We are going to be there, at your side, with procedure guidelines, with oversight, with second guessing.' " A lawyer for the leading trade association of HMOs stated that the proposal "assumes a lot more control over physicians by HMOs and other managed care organizations than is the case," and an executive of Aetna Health Plans stated, "It gets us involved in the practice of medicine." Are you surprised by physician resistance to a proposal to relieve them of all personal liability for professional negligence? The irony of the physicians' position was compounded by the fact that plaintiffs' lawyers also opposed the Clinton enterprise-liability proposal.

Professors Kenneth Abraham and Paul Weiler, two influential supporters of the concept of enterprise liability for physician negligence, would assign liability (at least in the absence of a contractual reallocation of risk) not to managed-care plans or risk-bearing provider networks but to hospitals. See Abraham & Weiler, supra, at 415–419 (1994). Their reasons for concluding that liability should fall, as a default rule, on delivery entities, such as hospitals, include the following: (1) The historical expansion of hospital liability has already inspired the creation of effective or potentially effective quality-assurance mechanisms at the hospital level. (2) Financing entities are "one step removed" from affecting quality directly. (3) Assigning liability to financing entities would increase litigation costs by inducing legal finger-pointing at hospitals under traditional hospital liability theories, unless the plans were, somewhat arbitrarily, made accountable "not only for treating physicians but for hospitals as well." A drawback of their plan is that it would require hospitals to be accountable for physician negligence occurring outside the hospital, necessitating arbitrary assignment of such liability to one of several hospitals a physician might use. How would you assign liability?

4. *Nondelegable Duty?* Assume that a court senses an impropriety in allowing an MCO to profit as a middleman in health care transactions while denying responsibility for the quality of care. Might it decide to hold MCOs vicariously liable for physician negligence on the theory that the duty to provide nonnegligent medical care was nondelegable to independent contractors? See, e.g., Restatement (Second) of Agency § 214 (1958) ("A * * * principal who is under a duty * * * to have care used to protect others * * * and who confides the performance of such duty to a servant or other person is subject to liability to such others for harm caused to them by the failure of such agent to perform the duty."). Would any of the cases imposing vicarious liability on hospitals for negligence by hospital-based physicians (see chapter 5(§B)) support such a holding?

To be sure, as was observed in the case of hospital liability, calling a function nondelegable by a corporate entity is difficult when public policy has traditionally viewed that function as an illegitimate one for a corporation (rather than a licensed individual) to perform. Nevertheless, might a court consider that public policy now contemplates—if not explicitly, at least in practice—that MCOs will exercise a high degree of corporate influence over the nature and content of people's medical care? Is it within the province of a common-law court to conclude that, if an MCO can restrict subscribers' freedom to select a provider, can select physicians on the basis of the low fees they can command or the low costs they incur in treating patients, and can reward physicians for economizing in patient care, it cannot delegate legal responsibility for the quality of care to physician independent contractors?

Another way to rationalize enterprise liability would be to draw from the law of products liability an implied warranty that the care provided will meet at least a minimum standard of quality. See generally Brewbaker, Medical Malpractice and Managed Care Organizations: The Implied Warranty of Quality, Law & Contemp. Probs., Spring 1997, p. 117. Do you see any practical or policy reasons for choosing between reaching enterprise liability by this route and achieving a similar result by holding plans vicariously liable under agency principles for the torts of professionals whose services they procure for their enrollees?

5. *The Effect of Legislation.* Many state HMO enabling acts empower MCOs to select physicians in a competitive market, to contract with them on the plan's own terms, and to profit by retailing their services to consumers while simultaneously declaring that MCOs are not engaged in "the practice of medicine." E.g., Colo. Rev. Stat. § 10–16–421(3) (1994) ("Any health maintenance organization authorized under * * * this article * * * shall not be deemed to be practicing medicine * * *."); N.Y. Pub. Health Law § 4410 (McKinney 1993) ("[T]he provision of comprehensive health services directly or indirectly by a health maintenance organization through its comprehensive health services plan shall not be considered the practice of * * * medicine by such organization or plan."). Several courts have interpreted such statutes as precluding HMO liability for physician negligence. E.g., Freedman v. Kaiser Found. Health Plan, Inc., 849 P.2d 811, 816 (Colo.App.1992); Dalton v. Peninsula Hosp. Ctr., 626 N.Y.S.2d 362–364 (Sup.Ct.1995). Is it correct to give such statutes such substantive effect? Or is it more likely that they were intended only to ensure that HMOs meeting the act's requirements would not run afoul of the corporate practice rule?

In a Texas case, Williams v. Good Health Plus, Inc., 743 S.W.2d 373, 379 (Tex.App.1987), the court held that a group-practice HMO could not be vicariously liable for physician negligence because Texas had a strict statutory prohibition against the corporate practice of medicine. In 1997, the Texas legislature, seeking to make MCOs more responsible for the quality of care rendered under their auspices, effectively overruled the *Williams* case by providing that no law prohibiting an MCO from practicing medicine could be asserted as a defense in any action. Tex. Civ. Prac. & Rem. Code Ann. § 88.002(h) (West 1997). The Texas law stopped short, however, of imposing vicarious liability for physician torts, preserving the requirement that there be proof of ostensible agency and stating that the mere listing of a physician as an approved physician would not constitute such proof. Id. at § 88.002(i). In 1997, Missouri dropped a disclaimer about corporate practice in the (reasonable?) expectation that expanded liability would follow. Mo. H.B. 335. See Legislation Seeks to Hold HMOs Liable for Medical Outcomes, 6 Health L. Rep. (BNA) 400 (1997) (discussing intent of Missouri proposal).

Legislatures of a few states have granted MCOs express immunity from liability for provider torts. E.g., Ala. Code § 27–21A–23(d) (1986); Mo. Ann. Stat. § 354.125 (West 1991). In Robbins v. HIP of New Jersey, 625 A.2d 45 (N.J.Super.1993), however, the court, in addition to rejecting immunity under a statute stating that an HMO "shall not be deemed to be practicing medicine," refused to read the following statute (which, incidentally, is identical to the Alabama statute) as conferring immunity for negligence of an HMO's physician employees:

> No person participating in the arrangements of a health maintenance organization other than the actual provider of health care services or supplies directly to enrollees and their families shall be liable for negligence, misfeasance, nonfeasance or malpractice in connection with the furnishings of such services and supplies.

N.J. Stat. Ann. § 26:2J–25(d) (West 1996).

6. Assuming that enterprise liability would be a good idea, how should the law be changed? by legislation? by common-law adjudication? What are the drawbacks of these two methods of adapting the law to modern conditions? Is there any other way to change the locus of legal responsibility for physician torts? Might an employer or an accrediting body, for example, make voluntary assumption of such responsibility a condition of contracting with or certifying a plan? Leaving the matter to these arbiters would presumably leave consumers with two options: Either they could choose a plan that would be primarily responsible for their care, or they could choose traditional coverage, under which they would look to an individual professional as the responsible party. Although the Clinton task force proposal contemplated that all health plans would assume legal responsibility for provider negligence, an alternative approach might have been to make that assignment of liability the "default" position that prevails in the absence of a contrary contractual provision and from which bargaining therefore proceeds. Would you place any limits on the freedom of a health plan to allocate legal responsibilities by contract—as many of them now purport to do (as revealed in the excerpt at the beginning of this section)?

7. *Nonphysician Providers.* If a legislature or court were to decide that MCOs should be automatically liable for the torts of their participating physicians, would it necessarily follow that MCOs would also be responsible for the negligence of nonphysician independent contractors employed in treating their enrollees? MCOs typically designate the hospitals, outpatient surgical facilities, diagnostic centers, clinical laboratories, pharmacies, home health agencies, and so forth to which its enrollees may be referred by participating physicians. And there is certainly some risk that they will preselect these providers on the basis of cost considerations alone or with inadequate regard for quality. Arguably, however, the decision to impose enterprise liability should reflect efficiency concerns, such as whether the plan or the independent contractor is in a better position to monitor the latter's quality problems, to make appropriate trade-offs between quality and cost, and to take (or induce others to take) indicated steps to prevent patient injuries. See, e.g., G. Calabresi, The Costs of Accidents: A Legal and

Economic Analysis 135–73 (1970) (recommending a general deterrence approach to accident liability, including assigning liability in such a way as to create incentives to ensure appropriate attention to quality and to target parties who, given transaction costs, are generally in the best position directly or indirectly to control quality and to influence outcomes).

Compare the efficiency case for MCO enterprise liability in the case of nonphysician providers and in the case of physicians. Recall that the principal economic function of MCOs is to curb moral hazard by integrating physicians' clinical decisions and health care finance. Might a court reasonably conclude that automatic vicarious (enterprise) liability for the negligence of contracting providers would be a realistic, practical, efficient, and just allocation of responsibility for the quality of care in the case of physicians but not in the case of nonphysicians?

8. *Referral Physicians*. Another question might be whether only primary care physicians, and not medical specialists, should be deemed sufficiently integrated into an MCO to warrant making the plan vicariously liable for their negligent acts. After all, the arrangements that MCOs make to obtain specialists' services often resemble their arrangements with nonphysician providers more than they resemble their contracts with primary care gatekeepers. One option might be for the court to try to ascertain in each case the degree of integration and the amount of control exercised by the plan over the referral physician. Alternatively, a court might find automatic enterprise liability to be the sounder policy, not only because it would avoid immersing courts in inconsequential facts, but also because it would obviate MCO efforts to escape liability by distancing themselves from providers, thus limiting their ability to ensure quality. Arguably, the policy goal should be to make MCOs more, not less, effective proxies for consumers in purchasing professional services, the quality of which consumers are inevitably unable to assess reliably for themselves.

In any event, two courts have already held that, even without many special facts, HMOs can be held vicariously liable for the negligence of nonmember specialists to whom patients are referred by panel doctors. Schleier v. Kaiser Found. Health Plan, 876 F.2d 174, 177 (D.C.Cir.1989) (finding HMO vicariously liable for negligence of outside medical consultant because "Kaiser had some ability to control [the consultant's] behavior in that he answered to [the] primary care-taker, a Kaiser doctor"); *Decker*, supra, at *5 ("it would be against public policy to allow HMOs, as a matter of law, to escape liability for their members' treatment by simply referring them outside the HMO plan"). Recall that, as the next note indicates, MCOs and their physicians probably have an independent responsibility to select nonphysician providers with appropriate care and to monitor the course of treatment. Cf. Dunn v. Praiss, 656 A.2d 413, 420 (N.J.1995) (finding HMO can be liable for breach of contract to provide care when participating physician commits malpractice by improper patient follow-up).

9. *Corporate Negligence*. Should MCOs be subject to liability for corporate negligence under principles similar to those employed with respect to hospitals? See chapter 5(§B). In McClellan v. HMO, 604 A.2d 1053 (Pa.Super.1992), the court considered the applicability of earlier case law governing hospitals to the same IPA-type HMO that was sued in the *Boyd* case:

> While HMO PA could be viewed as having "assumed the role of a comprehensive health center," only two of the four duties defined by the Court in [an earlier hospital case] could be imposed upon a modified IPA model HMO since such an HMO has no facilities or equipment and thus cannot "oversee ... patient care [within its walls]." It is reasonable, however, to require that an IPA model HMO "select and retain only competent physicians" and "formulate, adopt and enforce adequate rules and policies to ensure quality care for [its subscribers]."

Id. at 1059. See also Elsesser v. Hospital of Phila. College, 802 F.Supp. 1286, 1291 (E.D.Pa.1992) (recognizing duty triggered by representations of selectivity). But see Harrell v. Total Health Care, Inc., 781 S.W.2d 58, 60 (Mo.1989) (relying on state statute, court declined to allow suit against HMO for negligently retaining allegedly incompetent physician). Although it is not known how successful plaintiffs have been in finally proving MCOs' corporate negligence, it does not appear that, absent enterprise liability, the law gives MCOs much reason to worry about whether their doctors are negligence-prone. Even if representations in advertising or otherwise may expose plans to some risk, the one-free-bite principle observed in hospital liability law would presumably apply to MCOs as well. Cf. Santitoro v. Evans, 935 F.Supp. 733 (E.D.N.C.1996) (HMO's obstetrician accused of engaging in repeated sexual abuse of patients).

A later ruling in the *McClellan* case raised the issue of the discoverability of plan credentialing records under the state statute protecting the confidentiality of peer review. The supreme court held that the IPA-type HMO was not a "professional health care provider" within the meaning of the statute, operating instead as a "quasi-insurer." McClellan v. HMO, 686 A.2d 801 (Pa.1996).

10. *Incentives to Underserve.* Might an HMO be legally vulnerable because of its efforts, through financial arrangements and otherwise, to induce physicians to economize? Such a question arose in one early case in which the plaintiffs claimed that, "because the health plan represented itself to be a 'nonprofit' organization, and in fact had a system whereby the individual doctors were encouraged, by an incentive payment plan, to be conservative with reference to unnecessary tests and treatments, [the subscribers] were fraudulently led to believe that they would receive 'the best quality' of care and treatment." The court went on:

> As defendants point out, the health plan itself is nonprofit; as we understand, it, the gravamen of plaintiffs' complaint is that, although admittedly the individual doctors acted "for profit," they had believed that that profit was measured solely by a flat salary and did not include extra compensation for rendering less expensive care and treatment [than] ultra caution might suggest. We note, as defendants point out, that the use of such "incentive" plans is not only recommended by professional organiza-

> tions as a means of reducing unnecessarily high medical costs, but that they are specifically required by [the federal HMO Act of 1973]. We can see in the plan no suggestion that individual doctors act negligently or that they refrain from recommending whatever diagnostic procedures or treatments the accepted standards of their profession require.

Pulvers v. Kaiser Foundation Health Plan, Inc., 99 Cal.App.3d 560, 565, 160 Cal.Rptr. 392, 393 (1979). Do you detect here a desire to protect an "infant industry"? Would a court today be as likely to overlook undisclosed incentive arrangements? See Madsen v. Park Nicollet Med. Center, 419 N.W.2d 511, 515 (Minn.App.) (upholding discretionary exclusion in malpractice case of evidence concerning possibility that HMO's incentives might have affected physician's decision not to hospitalize patient; observing that such evidence was "only marginally relevant [on issue of malpractice], and potentially very prejudicial"), rev'd on other grounds, 431 N.W.2d 855 (Minn.1988).

In deciding whether incentive arrangements should be open to question or to discovery in malpractice cases, what weight should be given to federal and state legislation defining permissible compensation arrangements? (Recall material on physician incentive plans in chapter 3(§D).) See *McClellan*, supra, at 1056 n. 6 ("The fundamental prerogative and duty of considering and establishing social policy, including, of course, the regulation of health care providers, is vested solely in the legislature.").

Lawyers are increasingly raising the question whether an HMO might be liable simply for maintaining incentive arrangements that may induce underservice and cause harm. On the other hand, other than the *Pulvers* and *Madsen* cases, there are few reported cases addressing this issue under the common law. But see the widely cited case of Bush v. Dake, No. 86–25767–NM2, Saginaw County Circuit Ct., (Mich., April 27, 1989) (unreported), in which a gatekeeper physician whose fees were subject to a partial withhold omitted to order a pap smear that might have detected the patient's cervical cancer; while the incentive arrangement had been approved by the state legislature, the court nevertheless found enough evidence that the HMO's incentive system contributed to inferior medical treatment to preclude summary judgment. Recall *Shea v. Esensten* (8th Cir. 1997), reproduced in chapter 2(§C).

11. *Disclosure of Financial Incentives.* Should courts penalize plans that do not disclose any financial conflicts of interests they have created for professionals treating plan enrollees? Or should physicians be expected to disclose such conflicts to their patients? Which arrangements are most troublesome? capitation payments to large medical groups? gatekeeper arrangements under which a portion of fees are withheld contingent on the volume of referrals and use of ancillary services? bonuses for good performance? penalties for bad performance? As will be seen later in this chapter, several states have mandated limited disclosure by plans of incentive arrangements that might affect a physician's loyalty to a patient.

Although there are no cases clearly requiring a physician to disclose financial arrangements with a health plan that might compromise clinical decisions, several cases dealing with other kinds of conflicts of interests raise the possibility that courts, using principles akin to the requirement of informed consent, will find liability. In one case, for example, the physician was in a position to profit from selling tissue obtained from the plaintiff in surgery, and the court opined that "a physician must disclose personal interests unrelated to the patient's health, whether research or economic, that may affect the physician's professional judgment." Moore v. Regents of the Univ. of Calif., 793 P.2d 479 (Cal.1990). (Although quotable, this dictum is of questionable relevance since the case involved, not personal injury, but the doctor's appropriation of the tissue's value.) See also Hidding v. Williams, 578 So.2d 1192 (La.App.1991) ("by failing to disclose his chronic alcohol abuse Dr. Williams violated the informed consent doctrine"); Estate of Behringer v. Medical Center at Princeton, 592 A.2d 1251, 1283 (N.J.Super.1991) (finding physician had duty to disclose HIV-positive status so that patient could be "ultimate arbiter" of risk).

Professor Mark Hall has proposed adapting the doctrine of informed consent to cover situations created by managed care, including disclosure of incentive arrangements at the time of enrolling subscribers. Hall, A Theory of Economic Informed Consent, 31 Ga. L. Rev. 511, 516–26 (1997). Hall observes that expansive notions of informed consent, designed to promote patient autonomy, developed in the field of bioethics in the 1960s and 1970s, a time when physicians were deemed unduly inclined to take risky but profitable measures without regard to the preferences of patients. In his view, "[t]he fundamental incompatibility of conventional informed consent theory and modern economic reality requires that a new theory of economic informed consent be developed." Id. at 512. See also M. Hall, Making Medical Spending Decisions: The Law, Ethics, and Economics of Rationing Mechanisms ch. 6 (1997). Do you agree that the issues here should be resolved within the ethical/legal paradigm of full disclosure and informed consent? Or has the time come to jettison informed consent as the primary principle under which individuals exercise autonomy in procuring health care and to embrace instead principles of contract law and consumer choice?

Would enterprise liability for MCOs, by making a health plan or its provider network stand behind the work of its professionals, obviate the need for disclosure of the precise economic relationship between a provider and a health plan?

ERISA and Malpractice Claims Against MCOs

Dukes v. U.S. Healthcare, Inc.

United States Court of Appeals, Third Circuit, 1995.
57 F.3d 350.

■ STAPLETON, CIRCUIT JUDGE:

The plaintiffs in these two cases filed suit in state court against health maintenance organizations ("HMOs") organized by U.S. Healthcare, Inc., claiming damages, under various theories, for injuries arising from the medical malpractice of HMO-affiliated hospitals and medical personnel. The defendant HMOs removed both cases to federal court, arguing (1) that the injured person in each case had obtained medical care as a benefit from a welfare-benefit plan governed by [ERISA], (2) that removal is proper under the "complete preemption" exception to the "well-pleaded complaint rule," and (3) that the plaintiffs' claims are preempted by § 514(a) of ERISA. The district courts agreed with these contentions and dismissed the plaintiffs' claims against the HMOs. The plaintiffs appeal those rulings and ask that their claims against the HMOs be remanded to state court.

We hold that on the record before us, the plaintiffs' claims are not claims "to recover [plan] benefits due . . . under the terms of [the] plan, to enforce . . . rights under the terms of the plan, or to clarify . . . rights to future benefits under the terms of the plan" as those phrases are used in § 502(a)(1)(B) of ERISA. Accordingly, we hold that *Metropolitan Life*'s "complete preemption" exception is inapplicable and that removal of these claims from state court was improper. We will reverse the judgments of the district courts and will remand each case to district court with instructions to remand the cases to the state courts from which they were removed.

I.

[The two cases consolidated on appeal were similar. The facts of one (*Visconti*) are given here.]

Ronald and Linda Visconti are the biological parents of Serena Visconti, who was stillborn. During the third trimester of her pregnancy with Serena, Linda apparently developed symptoms typical of preeclampsia. The Viscontis claim that Linda's obstetrician, Dr. Wisniewski, negligently ignored these symptoms and that this negligence caused Serena's death.

Like Darryl Dukes, Linda received her medical treatment through a federally qualified HMO organized by U.S. Healthcare. This HMO was called the Health Maintenance Organization of Pennsylvania/New Jersey. The Viscontis received their membership in the HMO through an ERISA-covered welfare plan.

Ronald Visconti, as administrator of Serena's estate, and Ronald and Linda, in their own right (collectively, "the Viscontis"), brought suit in the Philadelphia County Court of Common Pleas. They attempted to hold the HMO liable for Dr. Wisniewski's malpractice under ostensible and actual agency theories, alleging that when Linda became pregnant, the HMO held out Dr. Wisniewski as a competent and qualified participating obstetrician/gynecologist. They also sued the HMO under a direct negligence theory, claiming, among other things, that the HMO was negligent in its selection, employment, and oversight of the medical personnel who performed the actual medical treatment.

The HMO removed the case to federal court, asserting that the Viscontis' claims were completely preempted by ERISA. It then filed a motion to dismiss, and the Viscontis filed a motion to remand, contending that removal was improper and that ERISA did not preempt their state law claims. The district court denied the Viscontis' motion but granted the HMO's motion to dismiss. * * *

II.

The HMOs removed these cases to federal court pursuant to 28 U.S.C. § 1441, alleging that the district courts had original jurisdiction over the claims, because the claims "[arose] under the Constitution, treaties or laws of the United States." § 1441(b); 28 U.S.C. § 1331. To determine whether a claim "arises under" federal law—and thus is removable—we begin with the "well-pleaded complaint rule." See Metropolitan Life Ins. Co. v. Taylor, 481 U.S. 58, 63 (1987).

Under the well-pleaded complaint rule, a cause of action "arises under" federal law, and removal is proper, only if a federal question is presented on the face of the plaintiff's properly pleaded complaint. Franchise Tax Bd. v. Construction Laborers Vacation Trust, 463 U.S. 1, 9–12 (1983). A federal defense to a plaintiff's state law cause of action ordinarily does not appear on the face of the well-pleaded complaint, and, therefore, usually is insufficient to warrant removal to federal court. Thus, it is well-established that the defense of preemption ordinarily is insufficient justification to permit removal to federal court. Caterpillar, Inc. v. Williams, 482 U.S. 386, 398 (1987) ("The fact that a defendant might ultimately prove that a plaintiff's claims are pre-empted under [a federal statute] does not establish that they are removable to federal court.").

The Supreme Court has recognized an exception to the well-pleaded complaint rule—the "complete preemption" exception—under which "Congress may so completely pre-empt a particular area that any civil complaint raising this select group of claims is necessarily federal in character." *Metropolitan Life*, 481 U.S. at 63–64. The complete preemption doctrine applies when

> the pre-emptive force of [the federal statutory provision] is so powerful as to displace entirely any state cause of action [addressed by the federal statute]. Any such suit is purely a creature of federal law, notwithstanding the fact that state law would provide a cause of action in the absence of [the federal provision].

Franchise Tax Bd., 463 U.S. at 23.

The Supreme Court has determined that Congress intended the complete-preemption doctrine to apply to state law causes of action which fit within the scope of ERISA's civil-enforcement provisions. *Metropolitan Life*, 481 U.S. at 66. It explained:

> [T]he legislative history consistently sets out [Congress's] clear intention to make § 502(a)(1)(B) suits brought by participants or beneficiaries federal questions for the purposes of federal court jurisdiction in like manner as § 301 of [the Labor Management Relations Act of 1947, 29 U.S.C. § 185.] * * *

Thus, courts have found that the *Metropolitan Life* complete-preemption doctrine permits removal of state law causes of action in a host of different ERISA-related circumstances. [Citations omitted.]

That the Supreme Court has recognized a limited exception to the well-pleaded complaint rule for state law claims which fit within the scope of § 502 by no means implies that all claims preempted by ERISA are subject to removal. Instead, as the U.S. Court of Appeals for the Sixth Circuit wrote recently, "[r]emoval and preemption are two distinct concepts." Warner v. Ford Motor Co., 46 F.3d 531, 535 (6th Cir.1995). Section 514 of ERISA defines the scope of ERISA preemption, providing that ERISA "supersede[s] any and all State laws insofar as they may now or hereafter *relate to* any employee benefit plan described in [§§ 4(a) of ERISA] and not exempt under [§ 4(b) of ERISA]." (Emphasis added.) The *Metropolitan Life* complete-preemption exception, on the other hand, is concerned with a more limited set of state laws, those which fall within the scope of ERISA's civil enforcement provision, § 502. State law claims which fall outside of the scope of § 502, even if preempted by § 514(a), are still governed by the well-pleaded complaint rule and, therefore, are not removable under the complete-preemption principles established in *Metropolitan Life*.

The difference between preemption and complete preemption is important. When the doctrine of complete preemption does not apply, but the plaintiff's state claim is arguably preempted under § 514(a), the district court, being without removal jurisdiction, cannot resolve the dispute regarding preemption. It lacks power to do anything other than remand to the state court where the preemption issue can be addressed and resolved.

III.

The district courts in these cases found that the plaintiffs' state law claims against the U.S. Healthcare HMOs fall within the scope of § 502(a)(1)(B) and that the *Metropolitan Life* complete-preemption doctrine therefore permits removal. We disagree.

To determine whether the state law claims fall within the scope of § 502(a)(1)(B), we must determine whether those claims, properly construed, are "to recover benefits due ... under the terms of [the] plan, to enforce ... rights under the terms of the plan, or to clarify ... rights to future benefits under the terms of the plan." In making that determination, it would be helpful to have a complete understanding in each case of the relationships among the HMO, the employer, and the other defendants, the nature of the plan benefits, and the rights of participants and beneficiaries under the plan. We are somewhat hampered here because these cases come to us on appeal from orders granting motions to dismiss. Because of this procedural status, the parties have had little chance to develop the records and, accordingly, we know very little about the nature of the plan benefits or about the role—if any—that U.S. Healthcare's HMOs play in the respective ERISA welfare plans.

We recognize that there are issues in dispute. The plaintiffs and the Department of Labor as amicus curie, for example, claim that the U.S.

Healthcare HMOs are separate from the ERISA plans and that the sole benefit that participants and beneficiaries receive from each plan is the plaintiffs' membership in the HMOs. In their view, the plaintiffs' claims thus have nothing at all to do with § 502(a)(1)(B) because no one contests that the plaintiffs in fact have received their plan benefits (their membership in the HMO). Instead, under their view, the plaintiffs' claims merely attack the behavior of an entity completely external to the ERISA plan. U.S. Healthcare, on the other hand, claims that the plan benefits are more than just the plan participants' or beneficiaries' memberships in the respective HMOs; it argues that the medical care received is itself the plan benefit. As a corollary to that position, it also disagrees with the plaintiffs' view that the HMOs are completely distinct from the respective ERISA plans, arguing that the HMOs in fact play a role in the delivery of plan benefits. It further maintains that ERISA is implicated because both the plaintiffs' agency claims and their direct negligence claims relate to the quality of the plan benefits and the HMOs' role as the entity that arranges for those benefits for the ERISA plans.

We need not here resolve these disputes about how to characterize the plan benefits or the HMOs' role in the respective ERISA plans. We will assume, without deciding, that the medical care provided (and not merely the plaintiffs' memberships in the respective HMOs) is the plan benefit for the purposes of ERISA. We will also assume that the HMOs, either as a part of or on behalf of the ERISA plans, arrange for the delivery of those plan benefits. We thus assume, for example, that removal jurisdiction would exist if the plaintiffs were alleging that the HMOs refused to provide the services to which membership entitled them.

Given those assumptions, we nevertheless conclude that removal was improper. We are compelled to this conclusion because the plaintiffs' claims, even when construed as U.S. Healthcare suggests, merely attack the quality of the benefits they received: The plaintiffs here simply do not claim that the plans erroneously withheld benefits due. Nor do they ask the state courts to enforce their rights under the terms of their respective plans or to clarify their rights to future benefits. As a result, the plaintiffs' claims fall outside of the scope of § 502(a)(1)(B) and these cases must be remanded to the state courts from which they were removed.

A.

Nothing in the complaints indicates that the plaintiffs are complaining about their ERISA welfare plans' failure to provide benefits due under the plan. [For example,] the Viscontis do not contend that Serena's death was due to their welfare plan's refusal to pay for or otherwise provide for medical services. Instead of claiming that the welfare plans in any way withheld some quantum of plan benefits due, the plaintiffs in both cases complain about the low quality of the medical treatment that they actually received and argue that the U.S. Healthcare HMO should be held liable under agency and negligence principles.

We are confident that a claim about the quality of a benefit received is not a claim under § 502(a)(1)(B) to "recover benefits due ... under the terms of [the] plan." To reach that conclusion, "we begin as we do in any exercise of statutory construction with the text of the provision in question, and move on, as need be, to the structure and purpose of the Act in which it occurs." New York State Conference of Blue Cross & Blue Shield Plans v. Travelers Ins. Co., 514 U.S. 645 (1995) [reproduced in chapter 1(§B)—Eds.].

The text lends no support to U.S. Healthcare's argument. On its face, a suit "to recover benefits due ... under the terms of [the] plan" is concerned exclusively with whether or not the benefits due under the plan were actually provided. The statute simply says nothing about the quality of benefits received.

Nor does anything in the legislative history, structure, or purpose of ERISA suggest that Congress viewed § 502(a)(1)(B) as creating a remedy for a participant injured by medical malpractice. When Congress enacted ERISA it was concerned in large part with the various mechanisms and institutions involved in the funding and payment of plan benefits. That is, Congress was concerned "that owing to the inadequacy of current minimum [financial and administrative] standards, the soundness and stability of plans with respect to adequate funds to pay promised benefits may be endangered." § 2, 29 U.S.C. § 1001(a). Thus, Congress sought to assure that promised benefits would be available when plan participants had need of them and § 502 was intended to provide each individual participant with a remedy in the event that promises made by the plan were not kept. We find nothing in the legislative history suggesting that § 502 was intended as a part of a federal scheme to control the quality of the benefits received by plan participants. Quality control of benefits, such as the health care benefits provided here, is a field traditionally occupied by state regulation and we interpret the silence of Congress as reflecting an intent that it remain such. See, e.g., *Travelers Ins. Co.*, at 657–61 (noting that while quality standards and work place regulations in the context of hospital services will indirectly affect the sorts of benefits an ERISA plan can afford, they have traditionally been left to the states, and there is no indication in ERISA that Congress chose to displace general health care regulation by the states).

B.

We also reject the HMOs' attempts to characterize the plaintiffs' state court complaints as attempts to enforce their "rights under the terms of the [respective welfare] plan[s]." That phrase is included, we believe, so as to provide a means of enforcing any contract rights other than the right to benefits, as for example the various plan-created rights of plan participants to benefit-claim and benefit-eligibility procedures. Just as § 502(a)(1)(B) provides the means by which a participant can insist on the promised benefits, so too does it provide the means for insisting on the plan-created rights other than plan benefits.[4]

4. ERISA ordinarily requires that welfare plans set out a description of the rights of the participants and their beneficiaries in a summary plan description ("SPD")[, which

The HMOs point to no plan-created right implicated by the plaintiffs' state law medical malpractice claims. The best they can do is assert that the plaintiffs' medical malpractice claims "attempt to define a participant's rights under the plan." (Appellee's bf. in *Visconti*, at 9.) We cannot accept that characterization. The plaintiffs are not attempting to define new "rights under the terms of the plan"; instead, they are attempting to assert their already-existing rights under the generally-applicable state law of agency and tort. Inherent in the phrases "rights under the terms of the plan" and "benefits due ... under the terms of [the] plan" is the notion that the plan participants and beneficiaries will receive something to which they would not be otherwise entitled. But patients enjoy the right to be free from medical malpractice regardless of whether or not their medical care is provided through an ERISA plan.

* * *

D.

We recognize that the distinction between the quantity of benefits due under a welfare plan and the quality of those benefits will not always be clear in situations like this where the benefit contracted for is health care services rather than money to pay for such services. There well may be cases in which the quality of a patient's medical care or the skills of the personnel provided to administer that care will be so low that the treatment received simply will not qualify as health care at all. In such a case, it well may be appropriate to conclude that the plan participant or beneficiary has been denied benefits due under the plan. This is not such a case, however. While * * * the Viscontis claim that Dr. Wisniewski was incompetent, there is no indication that he was not performing health care services at the time he allegedly committed the malpractice charged.

We also recognize the possibility that an ERISA plan may describe a benefit in terms that can accurately be described as related to the quality of the service. Thus, for example, a plan might promise that all X-rays would be analyzed by radiologists with a prescribed level of advanced training. A plan participant whose X-ray was analyzed by a physician with less than the prescribed training might well be entitled to enforce the plan's promise through a suit under § 502(a)(1)(B) to secure a denied benefit.

under regulations must "apprise the plan's participants and beneficiaries of their rights and obligations under the plan," state any "conditions pertaining to eligibility to receive benefits," identify "circumstances which may result in disqualification, ineligibility, or denial, loss, forfeiture or suspension of any benefits," and describe "[t]he procedures to be followed in presenting claims for benefits under the plan and the remedies available under the plan for the redress of claims which are denied in whole or in part"]. That requirement is relaxed in situations where the ERISA plan chooses to provide benefits through a qualified HMO. Under 29 C.F.R. § 2520.102–5(a), if health benefits are provided through an HMO, the SPD need not contain the usual description of the rights of participants or beneficiaries, provided the SPD contains a notice stating, among other things, that plan participants will receive membership "in one or more qualified health maintenance organizations," § 2520.102–5(b)(1), and that upon request each available HMO will provide [information comparable to that ordinarily provided in the SPD].

Much of the HMOs' argument in these cases is at root a contention that the employer and the HMO impliedly contracted that the health care services provided would be of acceptable quality and, accordingly, that these damage suits rest on a failure to provide services of acceptable quality. Since we do not have before us the documents reflecting the agreements between the employers and the HMOs, we are not in a position to determine whether such a commitment was implicit in their respective agreements. However, the burden of establishing removal jurisdiction rests with the defendant. Accordingly, the HMO is not in a position to press this argument.

Moreover, we hasten to add that while we have no doubt that all concerned expected the medical services arranged for by the HMOs to be of acceptable quality, this seems to us beside the point. The relevant inquiry is not whether there was an expectation of acceptably competent services, but rather whether there was an agreement to displace the quality standard found in the otherwise applicable law with a contract standard.

It may well be that an employer and an HMO could agree that a quality of health care standard articulated in their contract would replace the standards that would otherwise be supplied by the applicable state law of tort. We express no view on whether an ERISA plan sponsor may thus by contract opt out of state tort law and into a federal law of ERISA contract. We will reserve that issue until a case arises presenting it.[5] Nothing in this record suggests an agreement to displace the otherwise applicable state laws of agency and tort.

V.

For the foregoing reasons, the district courts' judgments in these cases will be reversed and remanded with instructions to remand the cases to the state courts from which they came. Our holding that the districts courts lack removal jurisdiction, of course, leaves open for resolution by the state courts the issue of whether the plaintiffs' claims are preempted under § 514(a).

NOTES AND QUESTIONS ON ERISA PREEMPTION OF STATE MALPRACTICE LAW

1. *"Complete Preemption" (ERISA § 502).* Whenever an HMO providing services under an employee benefit plan is sued in a state court for medical malpractice, it will almost certainly remove the case to federal court, arguing that, under ERISA, a federal question is presented (or would be presented on the face of a "well-pleaded complaint"). As in the *Dukes* case,

5. It would seem to Judge Roth that, if a plan were to adopt its own standard of acceptable health care to be made available to beneficiaries, the plan should provide concurrently, through insurance or otherwise, an appropriate remedy to beneficiaries for any failure of the plan care providers to meet that standard or, in the alternative, should inform plan beneficiaries that tort law remedies for medical malpractice would not be available to them under the plan.

however, when the complaint states only a claim under state malpractice law, the federal court will remand the case to the state court unless the defendant HMO can establish that the claim really arises under ERISA § 502(a), 29 U.S.C. § 1132(a) (1994). Section 502(a) provides that a beneficiary of an ERISA plan may maintain a federal civil action against a plan administrator "to recover benefits due * * * under the terms of [the] plan, to enforce rights, * * * or to clarify * * * benefits under the terms of the plan." Because § 502(a) has been construed to provide exclusive remedies, it "completely preempts" actions in state court that are simply disguised efforts to recover benefits due, or to enforce or clarify rights arising, under a benefit plan. One court of appeals has described the situation as follows:

> This jurisdictional doctrine [of "complete preemption"] provides that "to the extent that Congress has displaced a plaintiff's state law claim, that [congressional] intent informs the well-pleaded complaint rule, and a plaintiff's attempt to utilize the displaced state law is properly 'recharacterized' as a complaint arising under federal law." Rice v. Panchal, 65 F.3d 637, 640 (7th Cir.1995). Thus, federal subject matter jurisdiction exists if the complaint concerns an area of law "completely preempted" by federal law, even if the complaint does not mention a federal basis of jurisdiction.

Jass v. Prudential HealthCare Plan, Inc., 88 F.3d 1482, 1487 (7th Cir. 1996).

2. *"Conflict Preemption" (ERISA § 514).* ERISA also includes the so-called "conflict preemption" provision that was construed in the *Travelers* case in chapter 1(§B). This provision, § 514(a) of ERISA, 29 U.S.C. § 1144(a) (1994), preempts state law insofar as it "may now or hereafter relate to any employee benefit plan." In the arcane field of ERISA law, this preemption is not "complete preemption," such as is provided in § 502(a), since it does not create federal jurisdiction, and it therefore does not require or permit removal of the case to federal court. It can, however, be invoked as a defense in a state proceeding. Federal decisions involving the preemptive effects of ERISA on malpractice cases and vicarious liability claims have for the most part involved only the application of § 502(a).

3. *The Case Law.* Claims for medical malpractice brought against MCOs under theories of vicarious liability for the negligence of affiliated physicians are probably not preempted by ERISA. A number of courts, as well as the one in *Dukes*, have allowed such cases to proceed in state court and to be resolved there in accordance with state law alone. For example, in Pacificare, Inc. v. Burrage, 59 F.3d 151 (10th Cir.1995), the court quoted approvingly the following language from an earlier district court opinion: "When an HMO plan elects to directly provide medical services or leads a participant to reasonably believe that it has [so elected], rather than simply arranging and paying for treatment, a vicarious liability medical practice claim based on substandard treatment by an agent of the HMO is not preempted." Id. at 155, quoting Haas v. Group Health Plan, Inc., 875 F.Supp. 544, 548 (S.D.Ill.1994). Previously, several district courts had used the necessity to interpret plan documents as the key to preemption and, on this basis, had found vicarious liability claims to be preempted. E.g., Pomeroy v. Johns Hopkins Med. Servs., Inc., 868 F.Supp. 110, 113–14 (D.Md.1994) (relying explicitly on the district court ruling in *Dukes* to hold that ERISA preempts medical malpractice claim against HMO based on vicarious liability because determining whether plan held out the providers as its employees would require focus on the terms of the plan itself). The court in *Pacificare*, however, although recognizing that a vicarious liability claim requires reference to plan documents to determine the contractual relationship between an MCO and the physician, stated that such reference "does not implicate the concerns of ERISA preemption." *Pacificare*, 59 F.3d at 155; see also Rice v. Panchal, 65 F.3d 637, 645, 646 (7th Cir.1995) (finding no preemption because, "[w]hile the Plan will serve as evidence of [the doctor's] apparent agency, the alleged agency does not necessarily rise and fall with the Plan" and because the claim "can be resolved without interpreting an ERISA plan").

In ruling that vicarious liability claims are not preempted, the court in *Pacificare* appeared to accept the argument that "ERISA does not preempt 'laws of general application—not specifically targeting ERISA plans—that involve traditional areas of state regulation and do not affect relations among the principal ERISA entities [the employer, the plan, the plan fiduciaries, and the beneficiaries].' " *Pacificare*, 59 F.3d at 154 (quoting two of its earlier opinions). The *Dukes* decision reinforces this conclusion by citing the *Travelers* case. Presumably, the courts were not impressed by the probability that the liability risk would induce MCOs to rethink and restructure their relationships with providers. Although enterprise liability might affect the administration of an ERISA plan, it would not directly compel plans to change their practices. See also Chaghervand v. CareFirst, 909 F.Supp. 304 (D.Md.1995) (finding vicarious liability claim held not preempted by ERISA because based on common law negligence, which does not purport to regulate employee benefit plans; indirect economic effect upon plans held too tenuous to raise concerns under ERISA).

The issue of MCO vicarious liability for physician negligence is not free from doubt, however. In the *Jass* case, supra, for example, the Seventh Circuit court of appeals held that ERISA preempted at least one kind of vicarious liability claim against an HMO. In that case, however, the court interpreted the complaint as alleging not merely negligent treatment by the treating doctor, but a "negligent failure to treat"—which was in turn attributable, not to the physician's independent judgment, but to the plan's refusal to authorize continued treatment. 88 F.3d at 1493. Although this latter fact might seem to strengthen the plaintiff's claim against the plan, it has the opposite effect in the never-never land of ERISA law, where claims for improper denial of benefits are federally preempted. See, e.g., *Corcoran v. United Healthcare, Inc.*, reproduced later in this section. Indeed, in *Jass*, the court had already scotched an effort by the plaintiff, apparently recognizing that she had a preemption problem, to cast her claim for benefit denial as a claim that the nurse-employee who refused to authorize the treatment had committed professional malpractice. 88 F.3d at 1489–90. Thus, the court's holding in *Jass* may be read narrowly to permit

MCOs to avoid state malpractice suits only when the claim can be characterized as an indirect challenge to the plan's method of administering benefits.

Nevertheless, the *Jass* court also suggested in dictum that ERISA's policy of protecting employers from having to comply with diverging state requirements precluded vicarious liability suits of all kinds. Id. at 1494 ("To allow a vicarious liability claim against an ERISA Plan for the alleged negligence of a listed physician would require multi-state plans to vary their plan administration to avoid strict vicarious liability under differing state laws."). To be sure, the court recognized that some state legal requirements "may affect employee benefit plans in too tenuous, remote, or peripheral a manner to warrant a finding" of preemption. Id. (quoting *Pacificare*, 59 F.3d at 154). But it viewed state imposition of vicarious liability as intruding too far into areas of plan administration that Congress meant to protect from state action. In reaching this conclusion, the court did not consider the effect of the *Travelers* decision, in which the Supreme Court retreated from some earlier expansionist readings of ERISA and held that state laws of general application that are aimed at advancing general state goals, such as assuring the quality of care, may avoid preemption if they do not specifically target or disproportionately burden employee benefit plans. Also, the court in *Jass* did not take account of *Dukes*, where the court relied upon both *Travelers* and its view that the underlying malpractice claim concerned only "the quality of the benefits" received, not the quantity thereof, and upon its belief that ERISA was not "intended as a part of a federal scheme to control the quality of the benefits received by plan participants." See generally Jordan, Tort Liability for Managed Care: The Weakening of ERISA's Protective Shield, 25 J.L. Med. & Ethics 160 (1997).

4. *Preemption under Section 514(a)?* The manner in which the *Dukes* court relied upon the *Travelers* case suggested—as did the court in *Pacificare*—that, despite the possible impact on MCOs' administrative arrangements with their physicians, the vicarious liability claim could be resolved under state law without further regard for ERISA. Although the court observed that an ERISA preemption defense under § 514(a) could be offered in state court, its discussion suggested that state agency law, as law of general application that is focused on the quality of care and not directed at employee benefit plans as such, would not be preempted. There would therefore seem to be little room for questioning the MCO's vicarious liability under ERISA in the state proceeding. For another opinion purporting to address preemption only under § 502(a) that nevertheless applies tests developed under § 514(a) and thus implies that neither type of preemption would be found with respect to vicarious liability claims, see *Rice v. Panchal*, supra.

In short, it does not appear that ERISA would block state courts in imposing enterprise liability on MCOs if they were inclined to do so. See generally Note, New York Conference of Blue Cross & Blue Shield Plans v. Travelers Insurance Co.: Vicarious Liability Malpractice Claims Against

Managed Care Organizations Escaping ERISA's Grasp, 37 B.C. L. Rev. 813 (1996). Thus, if state courts were willing to find vicarious liability under, say, a theory of nondelegable duty, there would probably be no federal impediment to their creating a legal environment in which MCOs must truly integrate their doctors into their health plans, taking real responsibility for the services provided, and no longer acting merely as cost controllers. If this crucial step were taken, would you expect liability law to have a significantly beneficial impact on the medical care industry, correcting incongruities inherited from the past and permitting the public to enjoy in relative safety the efficiencies of corporate medical care? Or is the law of medical malpractice too poorly conceived in theory, too poorly administered in practice, or too random or arbitrary in its impact to motivate the industry to adopt methods of "continuous quality improvement" and to seek optimal trade-offs between costs and benefits? Even if you have reservations about relying on tort law as an instrument for overcoming the difficulties consumers and their agents face in purchasing care with an eye to quality as well as cost, do you see ways (based on your study of chapter 7) in which it might be made a more reliable source of incentives for health plans and providers? Does the opinion in *Dukes* suggest a way in which a health plan might tailor the obligations of its providers to ensure that liability tracks more closely the expectations of consumers and the plan?

5. *Direct Negligence in Selecting, Monitoring Providers.* What became of the claims in *Dukes* that the HMOs were negligent in selecting or retaining the physicians responsible for the plaintiffs' injuries? Should these claims be subject to resolution under state law to the same extent as claims of vicarious liability for physician negligence under an agency theory? See, e.g., Kearney v. U.S. Healthcare, Inc., 859 F.Supp. 182, 187 (E.D.Pa.1994) ("A claim that an operator or administrator of a plan failed to use due care in selecting those with whom it contracted to perform services relates to the manner in which benefits are administered or provided and [is therefore] preempted."). Under which section of ERISA do you suppose the court in *Kearney* found the claim preempted? See also Santitoro v. Evans, 935 F.Supp. 733, 737 (E.D.N.C.1996) (remanding claim for negligent selection to state court because not "completely" preempted under § 502(a) of ERISA but not addressing whether § 514(a) might preempt it in state court). See generally Jordan, supra, at 168–71.

6. *Arbitration Clauses in MCO Contracts?* Recall *Colorado Permanente Med. Group, P.C. v. Evans*, 926 P.2d 1218 reproduced in chapter 7(§D). That case involved the enforcement of state restrictions on the form and content of arbitration clauses in HMO contracts with employers but did not address the possibility of federal preemption. The clause in that case required arbitration of malpractice claims against Kaiser physicians, and the state purported to regulate the form and content of contracts containing such clauses in two ways (under a general malpractice arbitration act and under regulations of the Commissioner of Insurance applicable specifically to HMOs). An arbitration clause in a health plan contract might govern claims other than ones for malpractice, including claims against the plan itself for mistakes in the administration of benefits (see § B of this chapter).

Would ERISA preempt state requirements concerning the form and content of arbitration clauses in HMO contracts? in self-insured employee benefit plans? Under which section of ERISA would preemption be most likely? Recall that "ERISA does not preempt 'laws of general application—not specifically targeting ERISA plans—that involve traditional areas of state regulation and do not affect relations among the principal ERISA entities [the employer, the plan, the plan fiduciaries, and the beneficiaries].' " *Pacificare*, supra, 59 F.3d at 154. See also *Travelers* and *Dukes* (especially note 4).

SECTION B: LEGAL ISSUES IN THE ADMINISTRATION OF HEALTH BENEFITS

"Bad-faith" Actions; Interpretation of Health Care Contracts

Sarchett v. Blue Shield of California

Supreme Court of California, 1987.
43 Cal.3d 1, 233 Cal.Rptr. 76, 729 P.2d 267.

■ BROUSSARD, JUSTICE.

This dispute arose when defendant Blue Shield of California (Blue Shield) denied plaintiff John Sarchett's claim for hospitalization benefits in the amount of $1,203.05. Sarchett sued Blue Shield for the hospital expenses and also for a breach of the implied covenant of good faith and fair dealing. The trial court directed a verdict for Sarchett on breach of the covenant of good faith and fair dealing, and the jury awarded his hospital costs, $20,000 in compensatory damages and $80,000 in punitive damages. Blue Shield appeals from this verdict.

Facts and Procedural Background

In 1966, John Sarchett, a Los Angeles County employee, elected to be insured under a group policy provided by Blue Shield. In January 1976, Sarchett was hospitalized for three days by his family physician, Dr. Bruce Van Vranken, who is a member physician of Blue Shield. Dr. Van Vranken testified that Sarchett, usually a healthy and robust person, reported symptoms during January of fatigue, tremor, disorientation, painful swelling and distension of the stomach and back, changing bowel habits and peculiar stools. His blood test showed low hemoglobin and low white blood cell counts. Sarchett's condition appeared to be deteriorating rapidly during January, and Dr. Van Vranken feared Sarchett might be suffering from a life-threatening bleeding duodenal ulcer or leukemia.

Blue Shield paid Sarchett's medical and diagnostic testing bills, but denied his claim for the hospital stay, amounting to $1,203.05. Its denial was based on two separate provisions of Sarchett's policy: (1) an exclusion for "[s]ervices when hospitalized primarily for *diagnostic purposes* or medical observation, rest or convalescent care ..." (italics added) and (2) exclusion for services not "medically necessary." The latter exclusion reads as follows: "Medical Necessity: Benefits will be provided under this contract only for such services, whether provided on an Inpatient or Outpatient basis, as are reasonably intended, in the exercise of good medical practice, for the treatment of illness or injury." Blue Shield contended that Dr. Van Vranken's orders for Sarchett's care in the hospital were inconsistent with a belief that Sarchett was seriously ill and hospitalized for medical treatment.[3]

Plaintiff, Dr. Van Vranken, and the hospital utilization review committee protested the denial of coverage. The matter was submitted to arbitration, but the arbitrator's award in favor of plaintiff was vacated by the superior court. The matter was then set for trial de novo in the superior court.

* * *

I.

The trial court found that the Blue Shield policy was ambiguous because it did not indicate who would determine when the diagnostic services or medical necessity exclusion barred coverage. Construing that ambiguity in favor of the member, it concluded that he should be able to rely on the judgment of his treating physician as to the purpose and necessity of hospitalization, and that Blue Shield could not question that judgment. Blue Shield contends that the trial court erred in interpreting the policy, and that its right to review claims is inherent in the insurance contract. Sarchett, on the other hand, maintains that only the addition of an explicit statement asserting the insurer's right of retrospective review would cure the ambiguity and, going beyond the ruling of the trial judge, argues that regardless of policy language retrospective review should be banned as contrary to public policy.

* * *

At oral argument, * * * counsel for Blue Shield explained that the diagnostic exclusion is intended as a subset of the implied exclusion for unnecessary medical treatment, and that the insurer would cover "medically necessary" hospitalization even if done for diagnostic purposes. Consequently, coverage for plaintiff's hospitalization does not turn on whether he was hospitalized for diagnosis, but simply on whether hospitalization was "medically necessary." Furthermore, strict necessity is not required. The policy language requires only that the services be "reasonably intended ... for the treatment of illness or injury." The intent in question is apparently that of the treating physician, and "treatment," Blue Shield acknowledges,

3. For instance, Dr. Van Vranken's admitting orders allowed Sarchett to ambulate and to eat the regular house diet, and he did not order [several steps that] Blue Shield claims should have been taken if the admitting physician actually suspected a bleeding duodenal ulcer or leukemia. * * *

includes hospitalization required by the subscriber's medical condition even if further diagnosis is essential for further treatment.

Plaintiff's insurance coverage would therefore appear to depend upon three questions of fact: (1) whether Dr. Van Vranken ordered hospitalization with the intention of treating plaintiff's illness or injury, (2) whether the physician's intention was reasonable, and (3) whether that intention conforms to good medical practice. Blue Shield concedes the question of good medical practice, but disputes the other issues, claiming that Dr. Van Vranken did not reasonably believe plaintiff's medical condition called for hospital treatment.

Plaintiff, however, seeks to eliminate even these factual questions, arguing that the policy is ambiguous as to who decides whether hospitalization is medically necessary. * * *

Upon review of the entire policy, * * * we find no ambiguity in this respect. It is true that neither the diagnostic exclusion nor the medical necessity provision provides expressly how coverage disputes will be resolved, but neither does any other exclusionary clause.[6] Instead, Blue Shield has provided a separate provision, entitled "Settlement of Disputes," which applies to all disputes under the policy. That section first provides that "[a] dispute concerning the therapeutic justification for any services rendered to the member shall be resolved by the decision of the appropriate review committee of that medical society ... for the geographical area in which such services were provided...." It then states that "all other disputes, including disputes with respect to the decisions of the medical society ... shall be resolved ... in accordance with the Rules of the American Arbitration Association."

* * * [S]ince the policy itself provides unambiguously how disputes are to be resolved, including disputes concerning the "medical necessity" of hospitalization, there is no room for the argument that the policy contains an ambiguity which, construed in plaintiff's favor, would vest the final determination of medical necessity in the treating physician.

Sarchett relies on the decision of the Illinois Court of Appeal in Van Vactor v. Blue Cross Association (1977) 50 Ill.App.3d 709, 365 N.E.2d 638. *Van Vactor* was a class action by members who had been denied coverage for hospitalization for oral surgery. The policy provided for payment of hospital bills incident to removal of impacted teeth where hospitalization was "medically necessary." The court held that since "nowhere does either the master contract or the brochure provide that a judgment on medical necessity for such inpatient hospitalization is required to be made by anyone other than the duly licensed treating physician as a condition to payment of benefits, there is no justification for the denial of benefits *solely* on the ground that the insurer disagrees with the honest judgment of the

6. Besides the exclusions at issue in this case, the policy also generally excluded coverage for, e.g., mental disorders, routine eye refractions, routine physical examinations, hospitalization for tuberculosis, physical therapy, dental services, organ transplants, and treatment for alcoholism and narcoticism.

treating physician." The court then interpreted the policy to provide that the "determination of whether and to what extent hospital services are medically necessary is 'vested solely and exclusively in the judgment and discretion of the treating physician.' "

The *Van Vactor* decision, however, stands alone. It has not been followed by any other court. Numerous decisions from other jurisdictions take the position that "medical necessity" or similar policy language is an objective standard to be applied by the trier of fact, not a delegation of power to the treating physician.

We note in particular * * * Lockshin v. Blue Cross of Northeast Ohio, [70 Ohio App.2d 70, 434 N.E.2d 754 (1980)]. In that case Blue Cross denied a subscriber's claim for two days of private nursing care following a Cesarean section on the ground that care was ordered to "allay ... misapprehension" and was not "necessary" within the purview of the insurance policy. "The trial court held that the term 'necessary' was ambiguous, vis-a-vis who must ultimately decide what is 'necessary.' Consequently, the trial court strictly construed the policy against the drafter and found for the claimant (plaintiff)." The Court of Appeal, however, rejected this view, stating: "[A] function, basic to the insurer, is the right ' ... to determine whether ... [a] claim should be allowed or rejected.' The function of reviewing claims is obviously reserved by the insurer and implied by the mandatory process of submitting a proof of claim. [Citations.] Without such a right, an orderly establishment, administration and dispensation of insurance benefits would be virtually impossible." "While the decision of a physician is both relevant and probative on the issue of necessity, it is not dispositive of the question...."

In short, we find the policy unambiguous on the question of who decides "medical necessity": in the event of a dispute the decision is made by an impartial review committee, subject to further review through arbitration. * * * Thus we conclude that the trial court erred in directing a verdict that Blue Shield violated its duty of good faith and fair dealing by disagreeing with the judgment of the treating physician on retrospective review.

Plaintiff argues, however, even if the policy is not ambiguous upon close reading, it should still be construed in light of the "reasonable expectation of the insured." The subscriber under a Blue Shield policy, he contends, would reasonably expect to be covered for hospitalization recommended by the treating physician. We do not question this description of the subscriber's expectations, but we doubt that it arises from any belief that Blue Shield will cover all treatment recommended by a physician, however unreasonable the recommendation. Instead, the subscriber expects coverage because he trusts that his physician has recommended a reasonable treatment consistent with good medical practice. Consequently we believe the subscriber's expectations can be best fulfilled not by giving his physician an unreviewable power to determine coverage, but by construing the policy language liberally, so that uncertainties about the reasonableness of treatment will be resolved in favor of coverage.

Finally, plaintiff argues that, entirely apart from the policy language, the courts as a matter of public policy should bar insurers from refusing coverage for hospitalization ordered by the treating physician.[13] He points to the dilemma faced by the subscriber when his doctor tells him that hospitalization is necessary. Unless a physician himself, the subscriber lacks competence to question his doctor's recommendation. If he follows the recommendation, he takes the risk that the insurer may later deny coverage, leaving the subscriber liable for a hospital bill he cannot afford. Yet if he does not follow the recommendation, he may be foregoing needed treatment. Faced with this dilemma, most subscribers would follow their doctor's recommendation and risk the denial of insurance coverage. Subscribers purchase insurance not only for financial advantage, but to obtain the peace of mind and sense of security that follows from assured payment, and retrospective review frustrates those objectives.

There are, however, countervailing policy considerations. Sarchett had a choice between the Blue Shield plan, which offered him unlimited selection of physicians but provided for retrospective review, and alternative plans which would require him to choose from among a limited list of physicians but guaranteed payment. A holding that retrospective review is against public policy would narrow the range of choices available to the prospective subscriber, since it is unlikely that any insurer could permit the subscriber free selection of a physician if it were required to accept without question the physician's view of reasonable treatment and good medical practice. If the treating physician makes the final decision whether the treatment he prescribes is covered by the policy, inevitably a few will abuse that power by overutilization of medical procedures, imposing excessive costs on the insurer.

* * *

13. Sarchett cites two decisions to support his contention, Lopez v. Blue Cross of Louisiana (La.1981) 397 So.2d 1343, 1345, and Weissman v. Blue Cross of Western New York, Inc., 116 Misc.2d 1063, 457 N.Y.S.2d 392(1982), revd. (Erie Cty.Ct.1984) 482 N.Y.S.2d 659. In *Lopez* the Louisiana Supreme Court upheld a judgment for a Blue Cross subscriber whose hospitalization claim for depressive mental neurosis was denied under a medical necessity clause. The court found that denial of the subscriber's claim based on a mere reading of the records, without examining her, was unreasonable despite the fact that the policy expressly provided that medical necessity would be determined "in the judgment of the Carrier." The court imposed a statutory double penalty for Blue Cross' wrongful denial of the claim.

Weissman found unconscionable a contract clause providing that private nursing services would be covered "only if Blue Cross and Blue Shield, in their sole judgment determine that the medical condition of the member requires private duty nursing care." The court found that the health policy was a contract of adhesion and that "no reasonable person would accept these terms unless they had to accept the coverage due to necessity," since "the entire decision [whether the disputed care was necessary] will be based on the review by the party who may be paying for the services."

Both cases are distinguishable from the present case. Sarchett's policy did not vest the insurer with final authority to decide questions of medical necessity, but provided for decision by an impartial review committee and arbitration.

Both the federal Medicare program and the state MediCal program, which permit the patient free choice of physician, also contemplate retrospective review. We cannot declare contrary to public policy a feature found necessary whenever the public, through its representatives, itself sets out the terms of a health insurance program.

In summary, we appreciate the plight of the subscriber, forced to decide whether to follow his doctor's recommendation without assurance that his policy will cover the expense. We do not, however, believe it would be alleviated by requiring the insurer to insert redundant language into the policy to make doubly clear to the subscriber that he really is in a dilemma and cannot count on coverage. And although a judicial ruling that retrospective review violates public policy would protect against retrospective denial of coverage, subscribers would pay the price in reduced insurance alternatives and increased premiums.

The problem of retrospective denial of coverage can be reduced through the growing practice of preadmission screening of nonemergency hospital admissions. When such screening is not feasible, as in the present case, we think the best the courts can do is give the policy every reasonable interpretation in favor of coverage.[14] We trust that, with doubts respecting coverage resolved in favor of the subscriber, there will be few cases in which the physician's judgment is so plainly unreasonable, or contrary to good medical practice, that coverage will be refused.

II.

The second ground for the trial court's finding of a violation of the good faith duty was that Blue Shield repeatedly denied Sarchett's claim for hospital benefits without advising him of his contractual right to impartial review and arbitration of the disputed claim. * * *

In Davis v. Blue Cross of Northern California (1979) 25 Cal.3d 418, 158 Cal.Rptr. 828, 600 P.2d 1060, we held that "the insurer's implied duty of good faith and fair dealing include[s] a responsibility to inform its insureds of their rights under the policy's arbitration clause." In *Davis,* Blue Cross breached the covenant of good faith and fair dealing by attempting to compel arbitration after subscribers had filed suit against it for denial of claims. The basis of the breach was that Blue Cross had earlier failed "timely or adequately to apprise them of the availability of the arbitration procedure." The trial court found that "*even after learning that its insureds did not agree with its determinations as to the benefits available under the policy, Blue Cross had failed to bring the arbitration procedure to its insureds' attention. Instead it had simply reiterated in unequivocal terms its rejection of the insureds' claim.* [¶] The [trial] court found that in this context Blue Cross' failure to inform its insureds of the policy's arbitration provision amounted to *an 'implied misrepresentation ... that such subscribers have no recourse but to accept the Blue Cross determination....'*

14. The rule requiring interpretation of insurance policies in favor of coverage applies even if the policy, negotiated on a group basis, is not a contract of adhesion.

Indeed, the court additionally determined that Blue Cross had adopted its course of conduct 'for the purpose of inducing subscribers to give up their rights under the Blue Cross insurance contracts.' "([I]talics added.)

Blue Cross argued that "the inclusion of the arbitration clause in the hospitalization policy should have been sufficient to put an insured on notice of the availability of arbitration and that it was under no additional duty to call such a remedy to its insured's attention or to explain how the remedy could be invoked." We responded that "[i]n advancing this contention, Blue Cross ignores the special nature of the insurer-insured relationship and the resultant duties which an insurer owes to its insureds." Among those duties, we stated, is the duty of "each contracting party to refrain from doing anything to injure the right of the other to receive the benefits of the agreement." Thus, " '[the insurer] . . . must give at least as much consideration to the [insured's] interest as it does to its own.' * * * *In particular, in situations in which an insured's lack of knowledge may potentially result in a loss of benefits or a forfeiture of rights, an insurer has been required to bring to the insured's attention relevant information so as to enable the insured to take action to secure rights afforded by the policy.*" ([I]talics added.)

* * *

In the present case, Blue Shield failed to bring relevant information about the right to impartial review and arbitration to its insured's attention at the appropriate time. In *Davis* the policy's arbitration provision was obscurely placed in fine print, whereas here it was adequately set out with a bold-face heading. However, Blue Shield had reason to know that Sarchett was uninformed of his rights, since he repeatedly protested the denial without demanding review by an impartial panel of physicians. Blue Shield nevertheless denied Sarchett's claim several times without mentioning his right to review by anyone other than the single hired consultant who initially and repeatedly denied the claim. This course of conduct appears designed to mislead subscribers into forfeiting their contractual right to impartial review and arbitration of disputed claims, and therefore we must affirm the trial court's ruling on this issue.

III.

* * *

We conclude that the judgment must be reversed, and the case remanded. * * *

[Two justices concurred in the entire foregoing opinion, one dissented from Part II, and three dissented from Part I.]

Hughes v. Blue Cross of Northern California

California Court of Appeal, First District, Division 1, Nov. 14, 1989.
215 Cal.App.3d 832, 263 Cal.Rptr. 850, cert. denied, 495 U.S. 944 (1990).

■ NEWSOM, ASSOCIATE JUSTICE.

This appeal arises from an action brought by Sally Hughes (hereafter Mrs. Hughes) * * * against Blue Cross of California (hereafter Blue Cross) alleging several causes of action arising from the denial of insurance benefits for their son's hospitalization. Upon petition of Blue Cross, the plaintiffs' right to the disputed benefits was referred to arbitration and the arbitrator ordered payment. Mrs. Hughes then proceeded to trial to recover damages for Blue Cross's alleged breach of its implied covenant of good faith and fair dealing. The jury rendered a special verdict awarding her $150,000 in compensatory damages and $700,000 in punitive damages. * * *

[Patrick Hughes, 21, had a series of psychotic episodes and was hospitalized on several occasions over a one-year period.]

As an employee of Ralph K. Davies Medical Center, Sally Hughes and her dependents were covered by group medical insurance offered by Blue Cross of California. This action concerns the periods of hospitalization at Belmont Hills [Psychiatric Center] from October 26 to December 18, 1981, and July 13 to August 15, 1982. For these periods, Mrs. Hughes submitted claims for hospital expenses totalling $23,698.69. Blue Cross consented to pay only $6,598.69, disallowing the balance on the ground that the hospitalizations were not medically necessary. The insurance company denied coverage for the portion of the 1981 hospitalization between November 21st and December 18th, and for all of the period of hospitalization in July–August, 1982.

Blue Cross asserts that there was no substantial evidence to support the jury's verdict. The contention calls for examination of the record [to see whether there is any substantial evidence, contradicted or uncontradicted, which will support the conclusion reached by the jury].

Mrs. Hughes submitted her first claim for the October–December hospitalization in November 1981. After a preliminary clerical screening, the claim was referred to the medical review department of Blue Cross. This department allows certain claims that fall within very restrictive guidelines. The remaining claims are referred to a psychiatric consultant. The function of the medical review department is limited to procuring the necessary records, handling claim correspondence, and implementing the medical consultant's recommendation.

Shortly after receiving her claim, the medical review department sent a form to the Belmont Hills clinic that indicated, by checks in a series of boxes, a request for the following records: "History and Physical Examination (Complete)," "Physician's Orders," "Progress Notes," "Discharge Summary," "Consultation Reports," and "Nurses Notes." At trial the claim file contained only three categories of records from Belmont Hills: physician's orders, progress notes, and nurses' notes. It did not include the discharge summary, a detailed statement by the attending physician of the patient's history, treatment, and diagnosis. The medical consultant was confident he remembered reading the summary, but the clerk in the medical review department thought that it might not have been obtained. In any event, it is undisputed that the claim file did not contain the record of the patient's earlier treatment at Mary's Help Hospital or the "Nursing Referral and Care Plan" that documented discharge planning. Moreover, the file contained no record of a concurrent utilization review program at the Belmont Hills clinic. Under this program, an independent psychiatric consultant, Dr. Burton White, visited the clinic each week and reviewed the charts of all patients to determine the necessity of continued hospitalization. Dr. White had consistently approved Patrick's stay at Belmont Hills.

Upon receiving this limited medical record, the Blue Cross consultant, Dr. Ronald Hayman, requested a letter from the utilization review committee at the Belmont Hills clinic explaining the need for "acute level of care" after November 15, 1981. * * * [T]he attending physician, Dr. Lofthouse, finally wrote a one-page letter dated May 13, 1982, advising among other things that within two weeks of his discharge Patrick "became progressively more despondent and suicidal" and was again hospitalized. * * *

The case was next reviewed by a registered nurse on the Blue Cross staff who transmitted the file to Dr. Ronald Mintz, a psychiatric consultant in Southern California, with the recommendation that coverage be disapproved after December 1, 1981. On July 9, 1982, Dr. Mintz jotted the following recommendation on the medical consultant review report: "By 11/21, following 11 weeks intensive [inpatient] treatment a lower level of care is medically appropriate. Discharge planning was seriously delayed, and is the reason for the custodial period 11/21—discharge. Accept 10/26–11/20 and non-cover 11/21—discharge."

Dr. Mintz was a person of undoubted professional credentials who had 14 years of experience working for Blue Cross. But in the course of adverse examination under Evidence Code section 776 respondent raised questions about the care and standards that he employed in reviewing claims. Certain testimony, seized upon in respondent's oral argument, suggested that he devoted an average of only 12 minutes per claim. He didn't know of the program of concurrent utilization review at the Belmont Hills clinic. He considered that Dr. Lofthouse's letter contained no helpful information even though it alerted him to the patient's suicide attempt two weeks after the disputed discharge. Most damaging, Dr. Mintz disclaimed any responsibility to secure all relevant records before making a recommendation. He testified, "I felt that it was the responsibility of the treating doctor to put any information that he wanted considered in the review of these records into the records." Conceding that "the patient is the one that pays" if the records are incomplete, he still affirmed that it was not his practice to contact the utilization review committee of the treating hospital before denying a claim. If the hospital had additional information pertinent to the claim, it was the hospital's option to submit it to Blue Cross with a request for reconsideration. He would make no effort to obtain the information.

The jury could reasonably infer that Dr. Mintz employed a standard of medical necessity markedly at variance from that of the psychiatric community in California. He testified that over the years he recommended disapproval of about 30 percent of the claims he reviewed. He was unswayed by the fact that his recommendation conflicted with that of other psychiatrists, such as Dr. Lofthouse, Dr. De Lorente, and Dr. Hayman, who were familiar with the case, and evinced little interest in the opinion of Dr. White who reviewed the patient's charts to make the same determination of medical necessity each week of his hospitalization. "It is not an accounting contest," he insisted. In repeated questioning, respondent sought to elicit an admission that Dr. Mintz' definition of medical necessity differed from profession standards. While conceding that the consensus of the psychiatric community was "one of the things to be considered," the latter confirmed that he employed independent judgment and once seemed to allow that his standard of medical necessity might be more restrictive than the generally accepted professional standard. The wording of his recommendation, stating that a "lower level of care is medically appropriate," appeared to reflect independent opinion at odds with the judgment of the treating physicians.

According to its normal procedures, Blue Cross sent the treating physician, Dr. Lofthouse, a standard form letter notifying him of its intention to deny the claim for hospitalization after November 20th. The letter stated: "Based on our review of the medical records we have received to date, it is our determination that it was not medically necessary for this patient to have been hospitalized at the acute level after November 20, 1981. [¶] To allow all possible contract coverage, we are asking if you have any further medical information that can be provided regarding this patient's admission." The letter did not inform the physician of the medical grounds for the denial or identify the records Blue Cross had reviewed. Dr. Lofthouse testified that he was "very unclear" how to respond and chose not to answer. He explained, "I didn't know what to believe, because I had written an initial letter and still I was getting more letters." Receiving no response from Dr. Lofthouse, Blue Cross sent a letter dated October 5, 1982, to the patient, Patrick Hughes, denying the claim for hospitalization between November 20th and December 18th.

The processing of respondent's claim for the period of hospitalization of the Belmont Hills clinic from July 13 to August 15, 1982, followed a very similar pattern. The Blue Cross medical review department evidently conveyed to Dr. Mintz only the physician's orders, progress notes, and nursing notes for the patient's hospitalization during this period. At trial, the file evidently contained an admission summary dated July 13th but no discharge summary. Although the progress notes alluded to the patient's involuntary confinement, the file did not include the certification of need for intensive care signed by Dr. Lofthouse and Blue Cross' own consultant, Dr. Hayman. The testimony of Dr. Mintz contains no indication that he considered—or received—any records pertaining to the patient's earlier hospitalization at Belmont Hills on June 11th and July 6th, the clinic's concurrent utilization review, or the two periods of hospitalization at Mary's Help Hospital.

Dr. Mintz arrived at a recommendation based on the records he received without requesting additional documentation or making further inquiries. In a report dated September 14, 1982, he concluded, "[t]his appears to be a custodial stay for the purpose of disposition planning.... Noncover."

Before denying the claim, Blue Cross sent the attending physician, Dr. Lofthouse, the same form letter informing him of its determination that the hospitalization was not medically necessary. The letter again did not disclose the medical grounds for the determination or the records on which it had been based. Dr. Lofthouse complained, "[t]here was the sense of frustration of how to respond to the letters. I didn't know quite what did they want." Again, he failed to reply. On November 10, 1982, Blue Cross sent the patient a letter denying the claim for his hospitalization.

The covenant of good faith and fair dealing implied in all contracts requires each contracting party to refrain from doing anything to impair " 'the right of the other to receive the benefits of the agreement.' "(*Murphy v. Allstate Ins. Co.* (1976) 17 Cal.3d 937, 940.) As applied to insurance contracts, it does not merely "connote the absence ... of positive misconduct of a malicious or immoral nature...." (*Neal v. Farmers Ins. Exchange* (1978) 21 Cal.3d 910, 922, fn. 5); it demands that the insurer act reasonably. (Id. at p. 925, 148 Cal.Rptr. 389, 582 P.2d 980.) As stated in *Gruenberg v. Aetna Ins. Co.* (1973) 9 Cal.3d 566, 573, the covenant entails "a duty not to withhold unreasonably payments due under a policy." Although the record here contains much conflicting testimony as to the merits of the insured's claim, viewing the entire record in a light most favorable to the judgment, we find ample evidence to support a finding that the insurer acted unreasonably in denying benefits.

The presence of good faith implies " 'consistency with the justified expectations of the other party.' "(*Neal v. Farmers Ins. Exchange, supra*, 21 Cal.3d at p. 922, fn. 5.) As observed in *Egan v. Mutual of Omaha Ins. Co.* (1979) 24 Cal.3d 809, 819, "[t]he insured in a contract like the one before us does not seek to obtain a commercial advantage by purchasing the policy—rather, he seeks protection against calamity.... The purchase of such insurance provides peace of mind and security...." In a medical insurance policy, the insured's expectation of security is relevant to the interpretation of medical necessity. The issue is framed by *Sarchett v. Blue Shield of California* (1987) 43 Cal.3d 1, where the court considered whether the duty of good faith requires an insurer to defer to the judgment of the treating physician on the issue of medical necessity. It refused to adopt this extreme position, holding that " 'medical necessity' or similar policy language is an objective standard to be applied by the trier of fact, ..." (*Id.* at p. 9.) But the court emphasized that the " 'reasonable expectation of the insured' "requires that the policy language be construed liberally "so that uncertainties about the reasonableness of treatment will be resolved in favor of coverage." (*Id.* at p. 10.) The court emphasized "that, with doubts respecting coverage resolved in favor of the subscriber, there will be few cases in which the physician's judgment is so plainly unreasonable, or contrary to good medical practice, that coverage will be refused." (*Id.* at p. 13.)

If the insurer employs a standard of medical necessity significantly at variance with the medical standards of the community, the insured will accept the advice of his treating physician at a risk of incurring liability not likely foreseen at the time of entering the insurance contract. Such a restricted definition of medical necessity, frustrating the justified expectations of the insured, is inconsistent with the liberal construction of policy language required by the duty of good faith. It is true that the practice of retroactive review, which the *Sarchett* decision sanctions, will inevitably introduce a degree of uncertainty as to insurance coverage. But good faith demands a construction of medical necessity consistent with community medical standards that will minimize the patient's uncertainty of coverage in accepting his physician's recommended treatment. Here, the jury could reasonably infer from the testimony of Dr. Mintz that Blue Cross employed a standard of medical necessity sufficiently at variance with community standards to constitute bad faith.

Equally relevant to the present case, the Supreme Court has held "that an insurer may breach the covenant of good faith and fair dealing when it fails to properly investigate its insured's claim." (*Egan v. Mutual of Omaha Ins. Co., supra*, 24 Cal.3d 809, 817.) In reviewing the medical necessity of hospitalization, this duty of investigation surely entails an obligation to make reasonable efforts to obtain all medical records relevant to the hospitalization. The record discloses a failure of the appellant's staff to forward all significant documents to the medical consultant, Dr. Mintz, who in turn exhibited an apparent lack of concern for securing complete documentation. It might be argued that these failures can be ascribed to the fallibility inherent in all organizations, falling short of actual bad faith. But the two Blue Cross letters to the treating physician plainly bring its conduct within the sphere of bad faith. By not identifying the records on which the consultant's recommendation was based, the letters tended to assure that the staff's earlier failure to secure all relevant records would go undetected. And by omitting any explanation of the medical grounds for the intended denial of coverage, the letters placed an undue burden of inquiry on the insured's physician. The Blue Cross witnesses, in fact, defended the letters on the ground that the physician was free to write or call the medical review department to gain more information. The covenant of good faith and fair dealing, however, places the burden on the insurer to seek information relevant to the claim. This requires that the necessary letters to a treating physician be drafted in a manner calculated to elicit an informed response.

* * *

Punitive damages are appropriate only in cases of egregiously tortious conduct. * * * But the award of punitive damages finds a justification where it serves to deter socially unacceptable corporate policies. * * * Thus, in *Neal v. Farmers Ins. Exchange, supra*, 21 Cal.3d 910, 923, a judgment of punitive damages was upheld where evidence indicated that an insurer's actions "were all part of a conscious course of conduct, firmly grounded in established company policy, . . .".

In the case at bar, there was evidence that the denial of respondent's claim was not simply the unfortunate result of poor judgment but the product of the fragmentary medical records, a cursory review of the records, the consultant's disclaimer of any obligation to investigate, the use of a standard of medical necessity at variance with community standards, and the uninformative follow-up letters sent to the treating physicians. The jury could reasonably infer that these practices, particularly the reliance on a restrictive standard of medical necessity and the unhelpful letter to the treating physician, were all rooted in established company practice. The evidence hence was sufficient to support a finding that the review process operated in conscious disregard of the insured's rights.

* * *

Finally, we reject Blue Cross' claim that the trial court erred in instructing the jury that the insurer's duty to process claims fairly and in good faith was a non-delegable duty. The instruction properly states the holding of *Garner v. American Mut. Liability Ins. Co.* (1973) 107 Cal.Rptr. 604, with which we agree.

After the opening briefs had been filed in this appeal, the United States Supreme Court rendered its decision in *Pilot Life Ins. Co. v. Dedeaux* (1987) 481 U.S. 41, 107 S.Ct. 1549, 95 L.Ed.2d 39, dealing with the scope of federal preemption of state law under [ERISA]. Relying on *Pilot Life*, Blue Cross raised the issue of federal preemption for the first time in its reply brief. We held that the issue had not been timely raised, and Blue Cross petitioned the California Supreme Court for review of this portion of the decision. Our high court has remanded the case to this court "with directions to vacate [our] opinion and to reconsider * * *." We now present a more detailed analysis of the issue, giving particular attention to the precedents the Supreme Court has recommended for our consideration.

Under *Pilot Life*, ERISA clearly preempts causes of action for breach of the implied covenant of good faith in an employee welfare benefit plan as defined in [ERISA]. Subsequent California decisions have in fact extended the reach of ERISA preemption to statutory causes of action under Insurance Code section 790.03. But while the scope of federal preemption is now clear, the right of a litigant to raise the issue for the first time on appeal turns on other complex questions. [The court held, at length, that the defense of ERISA preemption is subject to waiver because it involves a choice of law and not the court's subject matter jurisdiction and that Blue Cross's failure to raise the matter as an affirmative defense constituted such a waiver.]

NOTES AND QUESTIONS ON THE DUTY OF GOOD FAITH AND FAIR DEALING

1. *"Bad–Faith" Suits*. Under either common law or state statute, insurers of all kinds (not just health insurers) are generally deemed to have a special duty of fair and careful dealing in administering their policies. As a result, they can face punitive damages for acting in "bad faith" if they deny claims

too casually or insist too strenuously upon narrow constructions of their contracts. In addition to the principal cases, see Taylor v. Prudential Ins. Co., 775 F.2d 1457 (11th Cir.1985) (jury permitted to decide whether insurer was guilty of bad faith in refusing to pay for hospitalization under "Medigap" policy largely on the basis of determination by Medicare—"a financially interested party"—that inpatient care was unnecessary); Hanson v. Prudential Ins. Co., 772 F.2d 580 (9th Cir.1985) (upholding plaintiff's claim for benefits but concluding that insurer's conduct in investigating claim, "in accord with insurance industry practice," did not constitute bad faith). See generally S. Ashley, Bad Faith Actions: Liability and Damages (1994); W. Shernoff et al., Insurance Bad Faith Litigation (1984 & Supp.); Symposium, The Law of Bad Faith in Contract and Insurance, 72 Tex. L. Rev. 1203 (1994); Sykes, "Bad Faith" Breach of Contract by First–Party Insurers 25 J. Legal Studies 405 (1996).

2. *Policy*. What do you think of the bad-faith tort as a policy matter? Is it an appropriate legal response to the insurer's temptation to stonewall a legitimate or possibly legitimate claim in the hope that the insured will go away or accept a settlement for less than the amount owed? See generally Sykes, supra, at 443 ("the remedy may be worse than the problem [because] the courts seem to find tortious conduct on the part of insurers who have bona fide disputes with their policyholders over the terms of the policy or over factual issues"). What other mechanisms does the legal system have, or might it develop, to discourage insurers from adopting a "So-sue-me!" stance?

Are bad faith-suits designed to correct a problem specifically associated with the administration of insurance contracts, or do they vindicate more general commercial and consumer interests? Note that the court in the *Hughes* case refers to "the covenant of good faith and fair dealing implied in *all* contracts." (Emphasis added.) The next note reveals the surprising significance of this point in determining how ERISA affects state law in this area.

3. *ERISA*. Although suits alleging bad faith by health plans and health insurers continue to be a concern, ERISA preempts such claims when they arise in connection with the administration of an employee benefit plan. Surprisingly (to the defendant in the *Hughes* case, among others), an ordinary health insurer administering an employer-purchased policy can invoke ERISA. Thus, in the *Pilot Life* case, referred to at the end of the *Hughes* opinion, the Supreme Court held that Mississippi's common-law tort remedy for bad-faith breaches of contract was not so specifically directed toward insurers as to be a state law that "regulates insurance," which would be preserved from preemption by the "saving clause" of ERISA. Pilot Life Ins. Co. v. Dedeaux, 481 U.S. 41 (1987). See also Metropolitan Life Ins. Co. v. Taylor, 481 U.S. 58 (1987) (holding complaints in state court purporting to plead state common-law causes of action against insurer are removable under ERISA to federal court). Might a statutory bad-faith remedy aimed at conventional health insurers survive ERISA preemption?

In any event, it seems clear that bad-faith suits under state law that are directed against administrators of employee health plans "relate to" such plans and thus are preempted by ERISA § 514(a). Moreover, enrollees must pursue their claims for benefit denials under ERISA's own enforcement provision, § 502(a), which provides for shifting attorney fees but not for punitive damages.

4. Do you agree with the findings of bad faith in *Sarchett* and *Hughes*? A dissenting justice in *Sarchett* said that Blue Shield, having provided information concerning plaintiff's appeal rights, "should not have to act as a paternalistic overseer." Do you agree with the court's requirement that insurers must bend over backwards to ensure that an insured is aware of the procedures available for contesting coverage denials? Do you agree that the insurer in *Hughes* did not do enough to verify the claim?

The holdings in both cases underscore the importance of maintaining effective procedures for administering and interpreting health care contracts. Is it the courts' role, however, to require insurers to provide such procedures? Or is that a matter for state administrative regulation (to the extent that ERISA does not preclude it)? Do insurers have reasons of their own for installing sound procedures and making sure they work well? What is the role of "claims adjusters" in the administration of health coverage? In studying the rest of this chapter, consider possible administrative procedures that plans might adopt to ensure accurate, evenhanded interpretation of health care contracts in day-to-day transactions.

5. *Physician Responsibilities*. In the *Hughes* case, did Dr. Lofthouse, the treating physician, bear any responsibility for the insurer's denial of coverage? Should the physician's failure to respond to inquiries relieve the insurer of responsibility for any mistake that was made?

If the insurers in *Sarchett* and *Hughes* had been finally absolved of responsibility for the plaintiffs' hospital bills, would the treating physicians have been liable to their patients for the cost of those bills, on the theory that they ordered unnecessary hospitalization? Presumably liability would be appropriately imposed only if the physician had breached a professionally determined standard of care. Would the standard of medical necessity governing insurance coverage be the same as the standard determining the physician's liability for exposing his patient, without consent, to a bill for services falling outside his insurance coverage? Although these points have been little litigated, they provide food for thought. See Ferguson v. New Eng. Mut. Life Ins. Co., 554 N.E.2d 1013 (Ill.App.1990) (holding complaint stated cause of action against physician for breach of express or implied contract where insured alleged detrimental reliance on physician's assurances that treatments for obesity were medically appropriate and reasonably necessary); Eisenberg & Rosoff, Physician Responsibility for the Cost of Unnecessary Medical Services, 299 New Eng.J.Med. 76 (1978). Cf. Rudolph v. Pennsylvania Blue Shield, 679 A.2d 805 (Pa.Super.1996) (holding that physicians, having contracted with Blue Shield, could not obtain de novo judicial review of plan committee's determinations of medical necessity).

The issue of physicians' role and legal responsibilities in administering health coverage will reappear later in this section.

6. *Retrospective vs. Prospective Determinations of Coverage*. The court in *Sarchett* observes the differences between retrospective denial of claims and prospective and concurrent review of treatment plans to determine eligibility for coverage. What are the respective advantages and disadvantages of each method of administering coverage? (Recall the discussion of such matters in chapter 2(§C).) In the principal cases, would a pre-admission or continued-stay certification requirement have avoided the problems encountered? Or would precertification of coverage expose a plan to a different kind of liability? This possibility will be considered below.

NOTES AND QUESTIONS ON THE INTERPRETATION AND ENFORCEMENT OF CONTRACTUAL LIMITS ON COVERAGE

1. *Enforceability*. Would you recommend that a health plan rewrite its contracts with subscribers in an attempt to ensure and expand the freedom of the plan and its providers to economize in the benefit/cost no-man's land illustrated in chapter 2(§B)? Would contracts substantially derogating from conventional entitlements be enforced by the courts? Consider the following:

> Enforceability of innovative health care contracts [promising something substantially less than, or different from, mainstream medical care] would be even [*sic*] less problematic for coverage provisions than for provisions narrowing the tort rights of patients. The contractual basis of the financing obligations of health plans has never been questioned. Although courts regularly consult professional standards in coverage disputes, they do so, not because adherence to such standards is mandated by law, but because such standards have almost universally been incorporated, implicitly or explicitly, in health plan contracts, most often in the commitment to cover all "medically necessary" care. As with tort doctrine, it is efficient to have a general standard that serves both as a default rule in the absence of an explicit contract and as the baseline from which parties can begin to bargain if bargaining is feasible. Efficiency requires, however, that the parties be free to vary the general standard by contract to accommodate whatever degree of economizing suits the preferences and circumstances of plan subscribers. Because the nominal source of patient rights against a health plan has always been the health plan contract rather than the legal system itself, most coverage limits in such contracts, if they do not violate specific statutory requirements [e.g., mandates to cover particular services in state law], will probably not be open to challenge on public policy grounds at the courthouse door.
>
> The probability that courts would enforce a new generation of health care contracts * * * would be further increased by the circumstances under which such contracts are likely to be entered into. Courts have never refused to enforce a health care contract in a case where the consumer was represented by an effective bargaining agent and where the consumer had access to both real options and accurate information on the import of the

contract. [Economizing contracts should, however,] spell out a convincing rationale for restrictions that they impose and indicate how consumers themselves benefit [ex ante] from the reforms implemented. Such explanations should help not only to demonstrate the plan's good faith but also to educate a court on the desirability of enabling consumers to trade some customary rights for lower prices or added benefits.

Most courts appear not to judge the validity of clauses in health care contracts strictly on the basis of their substantive content or effect. Instead, the key issue is usually the circumstances under which the contract was adopted and, specifically, whether the contract had any element of a contract of adhesion, undermining the presumption that it represented a voluntary consumer choice. In [the *Madden* case, reproduced in chapter 7(§D)], for example, the court approved the arbitration clause expressly because the situation was not one in which "the weaker party lacks not only the opportunity to bargain but also any realistic opportunity to look elsewhere for a more favorable contract." Because the Kaiser plan in that case was selected by the plaintiff over more conventional options, there was no basis for invoking the rule that "courts will not enforce provisions in adhesion contracts which limit the duties or liability of the stronger party unless such provisions are 'conspicuous, plain, and clear' and will not operate to defeat the reasonable expectations of the parties." If [innovative health care contracts] were similarly marketed, with full disclosure and with reasonable alternatives, lawyers could be quite confident that courts would enforce them.[12]

* * *

THE PROBLEM OF INTERPRETATION

Even if the courts are willing to enforce innovative health care contracts, they may fail to do so according either to their letter or to their spirit and may adopt instead interpretations of contractual language that defeat the contract's economizing purpose. Most judges would find it easier, after all, to be generous to sympathy-inspiring plaintiffs than to hold them strictly to the terms of a contract entered into without much thought and under different circumstances. And, indeed, judge-made state law governing the interpretation of insurance contracts provides ample authority for ignoring contractual language or interpreting it systematically in favor of insureds. Reflecting a primary concern for spreading risks and losses, the common law of insurance contracts attaches little importance to maintaining the freedom of insurers to allocate some risks to policyholders in order to avoid specific moral hazards or otherwise keep premiums affordable. A significant question for present purposes is wheth-

12. [A]n alternative legal regime embodied in an innovative contract [arguably] achieves democratic legitimacy by being chosen in competition with alternative regimes, not through individuals' actual informed consent to each and every contract term. The legal doctrine summarized in the text here captures this essential concern for democracy by focusing on the conditions under which choice is exercised. It also demonstrates how close the nation is to having in place all the institutions needed to maintain a working, democratic market in which a matter as critically important to individuals as health care—and as fraught with moral hazard and the need for collective choices at various levels—can be kept generally responsive to consumers.

> er courts, employing interpretive principles typically used in reading the fine print in insurance policies, would effectively eviscerate a new generation of health care contracts.

C. Havighurst, Health Care Choices: Private Contracts as Instruments of Health Reform 310–11, 314–15 (1995).

2. *"Reasonable Expectations."* As the *Sarchett* and *Hughes* cases illustrate, courts sometimes require insurers to honor the "reasonable expectations" of the insured—with the result that insurers may find themselves offering judge-made rather than contractually defined coverage. See generally J. Stempel, Interpretation of Insurance Contracts 203–08 (1994); R. Keeton & A. Widiss, Insurance Law § 6.3 (1988); Rahdert, Reasonable Expectations Reconsidered, 18 Conn. L. Rev. 323 (1986); Abraham, Judge–Made Law and Judge–Made Insurance: Honoring the Reasonable Expectations of the Insured, 67 Va. L. Rev. 1151 (1981). The doctrine of reasonable expectations may mean only that an insurer must not encourage, and must take steps to dispel, erroneous assumptions about coverage that unsophisticated insureds are likely to make to their detriment. See, e.g., Saltarelli v. Bob Baker Group Med. Trust, 35 F.3d 382, 385–87 (9th Cir.1994) (citing doctrine as basis for requiring conspicuous disclosure of exclusion for "pre-existing condition" in case where patient changed coverage just prior to diagnosis of cancer). Or it may be nothing more than a version of the closely related rule (also appearing in *Sarchett* and further discussed below) that ambiguities in insurance policies should be construed against the insurer. On the other hand, the reasonable expectations rule also invites judges to make coverage conform to their judicial vision of the protection that insureds should have—without regard to whether the expectations to be honored were induced by anything in the policy. Such a strong version of the rule would permit even unambiguous provisions to be read out of the contract.

Do the holdings in the principal cases portend such judicial liberality in giving effect to "reasonable expectations" that private contracts cannot be relied upon to put limits on health care spending? Or is it significant that these cases concerned only an insurer's refusal to reimburse the patient for expenses already incurred in reliance on the treating physician rather than a refusal to finance a service that the treating physician had proposed to a plan's utilization manager? In what respect might the difference between retrospective review and concurrent or prospective review affect the weight given to the "reasonable expectations" of an insured?

3. *Contracts of Adhesion?* Insurance law is highly protective of insureds. This protectiveness rests partly on a perception that consumers are generally unequal to the task of negotiating fair terms with insurers. Indeed, courts customarily view insurance contracts as contracts of adhesion that, because of their fine print and take-it-or-leave-it character, must be construed liberally in favor of the insured. See, e.g., Goodwin, Disputing Insurance Coverage Disputes, 43 Stan. L. Rev. 779, 787 (1991) (reviewing B. Ostrager & T. Newman, Handbook on Insurance Coverage Disputes (3d ed. 1990)) ("[B]ecause insureds almost never have any bargaining power vis-a-vis their insurance carrier, insurance policies are often characterized as 'contracts of adhesion,' meaning courts should give the benefit of the doubt to the insured because the insured had little or no choice about the selection of the policy language.").

Should it make a difference whether a consumer seeking a generous reading of an insurance policy had other allies in setting the contract's terms? For example, should a court feel a need to protect consumer interests where the contract language in question was acceptable to state insurance regulators, who are themselves charged with looking out for consumers? To be sure, commercial contracts for group health insurance are not usually among those that are closely regulated by state officials. Presumably, however, the states' *laissez-faire* policy toward such contracts reflects a belief that employers purchasing such coverage can be trusted to look out for themselves—and for their workers. In practice, it does not appear that courts modify their vigilance on behalf of insureds in such cases—except where the agreement was collectively bargained, e.g., Eley v. Boeing Co., 945 F.2d 276 (9th Cir.1991)—or that they recognize any irony in using their perception that health care contracts are contracts of adhesion as an excuse for imposing their own terms on the parties.

Did the *Sarchett* court view the contract in that case as adhesive? Note that the court's footnote 14 states that all insurance contracts, whether adhesive or not, are to be construed in favor of coverage. In what circumstances could such a cost-increasing interpretive policy be most persuasively justified?

4. *The Rule of Contra Proferentem*. The common judicial practice of reading insurance contracts generously is frequently justified on the

ground that the party drafting an agreement should bear the consequences of any ambiguity. One federal court has stated the policy as follows in construing a health insurance contract:

> Insurance policies are almost always drafted by specialists employed by the insurer. In light of the drafters' expertise and experience, the insurer should be expected to set forth any limitations on its liability clearly enough for a common layperson to understand; if it fails to do this, it should not be allowed to take advantage of the very ambiguities that it could have prevented with greater diligence.

Kunin v. Benefit Trust Life Ins. Co., 910 F.2d 534, 540 (9th Cir.1990). Do you gather from this statement that interpretive rules favorable to insureds are premised on an assumption that consumers actually study and agree to every clause in a contract in electing to subscribe to it? Is this realistic? Or should consumers be deemed to have accepted the total package, ambiguities included? In any event, "[t]here are literally thousands of judicial opinions resolving insurance coverage disputes in favor of claimants on the basis that a provision of the insurance policy at issue was ambiguous and therefore should be construed against the insurer." R. Keeton & A. Widiss, supra, at 629.

Although the principle that contracts should be construed *contra proferentem* (against the proffering party) is widely employed in interpreting health care contracts, its application in these cases can be questioned on policy (efficiency) grounds. See generally Rappaport, The Ambiguity Rule and Insurance Law: Why Insurance Contracts Should Not Be Construed Against the Drafter, 30 Ga. L. Rev. 171 (1995). For one thing, the ambiguity that triggers pro-plaintiff interpretation lies to a considerable extent in the eye of the judge interpreting the document ex post. And, indeed, judges have often been quick to discover ambiguity, thus enabling themselves to exercise their interpretive authority to reach pleasing, pro-consumer results rather than intended or efficient ones. E.g., Hanson v. Prudential Ins. Co., 772 F.2d 580 (9th Cir.1985) (construing "hospital [with] nursing service" to include residential facility for pre-adolescents); Meade v. Prudential Ins. Co., 477 A.2d 726 (D.C.App.1984) (crowns and inlays held covered as treatment of jaw disease despite exclusion for "mouth conditions * * * involving any of the teeth"); Duncan v. J.C. Penney Life Ins. Co., 388 So.2d 470 (La. 1980) ("necessarily confined" held too ambiguous to permit denial of claim for hospitalization for lack of medical necessity); Davidson v. Aetna Life & Cas. Ins. Co., 101 Misc.2d 1, 420 N.Y.S.2d 450 (1979) (despite exclusion of "cosmetic surgery," sex change operation held covered). See generally Cline & Rosten, The Effect of Policy Language on the Containment of Health Care Cost, 21 Tort & Ins. L.J. 120 (1985).

Judicial activism in stretching terms of insurance contracts may have gained added legitimacy as a result of recent academic theorizing addressed to the problem of interpretation. Extending insights of earlier "legal realists" and postmodern (deconstructionist) literary critics, some scholars have begun to denigrate the capacity of constitutional, statutory, or contractual language—indeed, language of any kind—to convey precise meaning. See, e.g., Fish, Fish v. Fiss, 36 Stan. L. Rev. 1325 (1984). While the limitations of language are undeniable, emphasizing them tends to diminish the legitimacy that private contracts enjoy as products of voluntary agreement and, by the same token, to enhance the authority and prescriptive power of the legal system's designated interpreters.

Even where contracts are clearly ambiguous (so to speak), the logic of the *contra proferentem* principle, or at least of its automatic invocation to ensure consumer protection in every case, can still be doubted. The rule is based, after all, on the assumption that the norm in contracts of all kinds is clarity and completeness and that ambiguity represents a failure of draftsmanship that must be deterred by judicial activism. At least in the case of health care contracts, however, some ambiguity is practically unavoidable due to technical nature of the subject matter. Moreover, the incompleteness of a particular contract may represent an appropriate (efficient) concession to the high transaction costs (and counterproductiveness) of anticipating and attempting to provide for all eventualities. For these reasons, it is at least arguable that courts, instead of invoking automatically a principle based on the paradigm of complete, fully bargained contracts, should make some allowances for the inevitable deficiencies of contracts and contract language as instruments for precisely defining rights and obligations in health care and should seek to enforce such contracts in accordance with their best reading of the drafter's intention.

Ironically, when health insurers have tried to be technically precise in writing their contracts, they have not necessarily been more successful in persuading courts to enforce contractual terms. See, e.g., Ponder v. Blue Cross, 193 Cal.Rptr. 632 (Cal.App.1983) (refusing to enforce unambiguous exclusion stated in highly technical language on a page with 2000 words). See also Hall & Anderson, Health Insurers' Assessment of Medical Necessity, 140 U. Pa. L. Rev. 1637, 1684 (1992) (observing that, although courts frequently cite a lack of contractual specificity as a ground for finding a service covered, they are apt to object to the contract's opacity when confronted with a highly technical explicit exclusion—as in the *Ponder* case just cited). An extensive review of coverage disputes found that patients won in a majority of the decided cases and that the clarity with which the insurer expressed the exclusion was not a variable influencing the outcome. Hall et al., Judicial Protection of Managed Care Consumers: An Empirical Study of Insurance Coverage Disputes, 26 Seton Hall L. Rev. 1055 (1996).

Although the *contra proferentem* principle permits courts to realize the "reasonable expectations" of the weaker party, it inevitably increases the cost of insurance:

> The *contra proferentem* rule is highly wasteful because it forces parties constantly to revise terms to override judicial rulings that are overly protective of the nonproffering parties. In addition, the rule makes it harder for parties to adopt innovative contract terms, for an innovative term will leave the parties uncertain about what "ambiguities" courts will find to resolve against the drafter.
>
> Nor can the *contra proferentem* rule redistribute between the proffering and nonproffering parties. [Citing Kennedy, Redistributive and Paternalist Motives in Contract and Tort Law, With Special Reference to Compulsory Terms and Unequal Bargaining Power, 41 Md. L. Rev. 563, 609 (asserting desirable redistributive effect of principle of *contra proferentem*).] The proffering party that recognizes that the *contra proferentem* rule will be applied in various contingencies not clearly covered by express contract language will simply "price" the probability of such contingencies * * *.

Charny, Hypothetical Bargains: The Normative Structure of Contract Interpretation, 89 Mich. L. Rev. 1815, 1854–55 (1991). See also Rappaport, supra.

5. *Medical Necessity*. The *Sarchett* and *Hughes* cases both illustrate the application of the standard of "medical necessity," which, as described in chapter 2(§C), is almost universally employed as the test for coverage in plan/subscriber contracts. Although a contract may specify a process for evaluating medical necessity, some courts have been inclined to give substantial, if not conclusive, weight to the judgment of the treating physician. Compare the *Van Vactor* case, described in *Sarchett,* with Franks v. Louisiana Health Servs. & Indem. Co., 382 So.2d 1064 (La.App.1980) (denying coverage where contract clearly stated that treating physician's judgment was not determinative). See also Schroeder v. Blue Cross and Blue Shield, 450 N.W.2d 470 (Wis.App.1989) (court said Blue Cross had no contractual or statutory right to deny a claim on the basis of an in-house determination that procedure was not medically necessary; holding determination should be left to insured's physician).

In any event, because "medical necessity" is inherently ambiguous, courts have been free to adopt expansive readings, requiring coverage of anything that did not offend the standards of the medical profession. See generally Annot., What Services, Equipment, or Supplies Are "Medically Necessary" for Purposes of Coverage under Medical Insurance, 75 A.L.R.4th 763 (1990). For cases in which courts exercised their own judgments on medical necessity, see Tudor v. Metropolitan Life Ins. Co., 539 N.Y.S.2d 690 (Dist.Ct.1989) (stating patient should not be required to "satisfy a committee, a board, or produce a plethora of testimonials from the mainstream of the medical establishment"); Aetna Life Ins. Co. v. Lavoie, 470 So.2d 1060 (Ala.1984) (rejecting insurer's argument that hospitalization was not medically necessary because services could have been performed on an outpatient basis); Lockshin v. Blue Cross of Northeast Ohio, 434 N.E.2d 754 (Ohio App.1980) (denying coverage of private nursing following uncomplicated caesarean delivery). More recent cases are mostly resolved under ERISA and are discussed at a later point.

As noted in chapter 2(§C), a second problem with the medical-necessity standard is its implicit acceptance of professional norms and standards as determinants of the proper scope of insurance coverage. Note that, in *Sarchett,* the question of medical necessity was to be submitted to a peer review committee of the local medical society. (The PSRO program under Medicare and, to a lesser extent, its successor, the PRO program, reflected government's similar commitment to pay for everything that organized physicians would not find inappropriate.) How did the *Hughes* court react to Dr. Mintz's apparent application of standard departing from professional norms? Do these cases, dealing with retrospective denials of claims, threaten to limit a health plan's ability to adopt restrictive interpretations of its contracts when engaging in prospective or concurrent review?

6. Obviously, a coverage limit that was in the consumer's interest judged ex ante may seem oppressive when judged ex post. Do the doctrines of *contra proferentem* and reasonable expectations invite judges to rewrite contracts in the interests of insureds to such an extent as to undermine efforts by health plans to contain moral hazard by writing innovative contracts? Certainly, when coupled with the threat of bad-faith suits and punitive damages, these doctrines, which are deeply embedded in the law, must deter insurers from resisting any benefit claim having a colorable basis. As later materials will show, ERISA provides some protection for plans administering employee benefits. But ERISA preemption may soon be eliminated or replaced by new federal remedies as Congress responds to the political backlash against managed care. If ERISA is in fact removed as a protection for managed-care organizations against incurring extracontractual damages in claims review, what will happen? Is it possible that the interpretation of a health care contract might vary depending upon whether the effect of the reading is a retrospective denial of payment (as in *Sarchett* and *Hughes*) or a prospective refusal to certify coverage of a particular treatment? Materials later in this section, dealing with ERISA and prospective denials of coverage, will allow a return to these issues.

Liability for Errors in Utilization Management

Wickline v. State

Court of Appeal of California, Second District, Division 5, 1986.
192 Cal.App.3d 1630, 239 Cal.Rptr. 810 (1986), review dismissed, 239 Cal.Rptr. 805, 741 P.2d 613 (1987).

■ ROWEN, ASSOCIATE JUSTICE.

This is an appeal from a judgment for plaintiff entered after a trial by jury. For the reasons discussed below, we reverse the judgment.

Principally, this matter concerns itself with the legal responsibility that a third party payor, in this case, the State of California, has for harm caused to a patient when a cost containment program is applied in a manner which is alleged to have affected the implementation of the treating physician's medical judgment.

The plaintiff, respondent herein, Lois J. Wickline (plaintiff or Wickline) sued defendant, appellant herein, State of California (State or Medi-Cal). The essence of the plaintiff's claim is found in paragraph 16 of her second amended complaint which alleges: "Between January 6, 1977, and January 21, 1977, Doe I an employee of the State of California, while acting within the scope of employment, negligently discontinued plaintiff's Medi-Cal eligibility, causing plaintiff to be discharged from Van Nuys Community Hospital prematurely and [while] in need of continuing hospital care. As a result of said negligent act, plaintiff suffered a complete occlusion of the right infra-renoaorta, necessitating an amputation of plaintiff's right leg."

I

Responding to concerns about the escalating cost of health care, public and private payors have in recent years experimented with a variety of cost containment mechanisms. We deal here with one of those programs: The prospective utilization review process.

At the outset, this court recognizes that this case appears to be the first attempt to tie a health care payor into the medical malpractice causation chain and that it, therefore, deals with issues of profound importance to the health care community and to the general public. * * *

Traditionally, quality assurance activities, including utilization review programs, were performed primarily within the hospital setting under the general control of the medical staff. The principal focus of such quality assurance review schema was to prevent overutilization due to the recognized financial incentives to both hospitals and physicians to maximize revenue by increasing the amount of service provided and to insure that patients were not unnecessarily exposed to risks as a result of unnecessary surgery and/or hospitalization.

Early cost containment programs utilized the retrospective utilization review process. In that system the third party payor reviewed the patient's chart after the fact to determine whether the treatment provided was medically necessary. If, in the judgment of the utilization reviewer, it was not, the health care provider's claim for payment was denied.

In the cost containment program in issue in this case, prospective utilization review, authority for the rendering of health care services must be obtained before medical care is rendered. Its purpose is to promote the well recognized public interest in controlling health care costs by reducing unnecessary services while still intending to assure that appropriate medical and hospital services are provided to the patient in need. However, such a cost containment strategy creates new and added pressures on the quality assurance portion of the utilization review mechanism. The stakes, the risks at issue, are much higher when a prospective cost containment review process is utilized than when a retrospective review process is used.

A mistaken conclusion about medical necessity following retrospective review will result in the wrongful withholding of payment. An erroneous decision in a prospective review process, on the other hand, in practical consequences, results in the withholding of necessary care, potentially leading to a patient's permanent disability or death.

II

[Wickline's ailment was diagnosed as Leriche's Syndrome, an arteriosclerotic condition inhibiting circulation. Because she was eligible for Medi–Cal benefits, her physicians submitted a request for authorization of treatment to Medi–Cal, which approved vascular surgery and ten days of hospitalization. After surgery, Wickline experienced a "stormy" recovery, necessitating additional surgery, which was performed. Concerned about possible infections and blood clots, the physicians concluded that she should remain in the hospital for an additional eight days for observation and treatment.]

In order to secure an extension of Wickline's hospital stay, it was necessary to complete and present to Medi–Cal a form called "Request for Extension of Stay in Hospital," commonly referred to as an "MC–180" or "180." It is the hospital's responsibility to prepare the 180 form. The hospital must secure necessary information about the patient from the responsible physician. It then submits the 180 form to Medi–Cal's representative and obtains appropriate authorization for the hospital stay extension.

The physician's responsibility in the preparation of the 180 form is to furnish (to the hospital's representative) the patient's diagnosis, significant history, clinical status and treatment plan in sufficient detail to permit a reasonable, professional evaluation by Medi–Cal's representative, either the "on-site nurse" or/and the Medi–Cal Consultant, a doctor employed by the State for just such purpose.

[The hospital's request was reviewed by a Medi–Cal nurse, who was authorized to approve it but not to reject it or to authorize fewer days than were requested. Unwilling to approve an eight-day extension, she telephoned a consultant, who, without reviewing any records or conferring with the treating physicians, authorized four additional hospital days.]

Complying with the limited extension of time authorized by Medi–Cal, Wickline was discharged from Van Nuys on January 21, 1977. Drs. Polonsky and Daniels each wrote discharge orders. At the time of her discharge, each of plaintiff's three treating physicians were aware that the Medi–Cal Consultant had approved only four of the requested eight-day hospital stay extension. While all three doctors were aware that they could attempt to obtain a further extension of Wickline's hospital stay by telephoning the Medi–Cal Consultant to request such an extension, none of them did so.

Dr. Polonsky, the senior man on the Wickline matter, and the specialist brought in specifically to treat Wickline's condition, was acknowledged by his associates as the doctor with primary responsibility in making decisions regarding her case. It would appear that both Drs. Daniels and Kovner, observing nothing that looked threatening to the patient, deferred to Dr. Polonsky and allowed Wickline to be discharged at the expiration of the period authorized by Dr. Glassman, the Medi–Cal Consultant.

At trial, Dr. Polonsky testified that in the time that had passed since the first extension request had been communicated to Medi–Cal, on January 16th or 17th, and the time of her scheduled discharge on January 21, 1977, Wickline's condition had neither deteriorated nor become critical. In Dr. Polonsky's opinion no new symptom had presented itself and no additional factors had occurred since the original request was made to have formed the basis for a change in the Medi–Cal Consultant's attitude regarding Wickline's situation. In addition, he stated that at the time of Wickline's discharge it did not appear that her leg was in any danger.

Dr. Polonsky testified that at the time in issue he felt that Medi–Cal Consultants had the State's interest more in mind than the patient's welfare and that that belief influenced his decision not to request a second extension of Wickline's hospital stay. In addition, he felt that Medi–Cal had the power to tell him, as a treating doctor, when a patient must be discharged from the hospital. Therefore, while still of the subjective, non-communicated, opinion that Wickline was seriously ill and that the danger to her was not over, Dr. Polonsky discharged her from the hospital on January 21, 1977. He testified that had Wickline's condition, in his medical judgment, been critical or in a deteriorating condition on January 21, he would have made some effort to keep her in the hospital beyond that day even if denied authority by Medi–Cal and even if he had to pay her hospital bill himself.

Dr. Daniels testified that he believed it was medically proper to discharge Wickline from the hospital on January 21, 1977. * * *

All of the medical witnesses who testified at trial agreed that Dr. Polonsky was acting within the standards of practice of the medical community in discharging Wickline on January 21, 1977.

[Wickline testified that she began to suffer severe pain in her right leg within a few days. Nine days later she was readmitted to the hospital with both clotting in the leg and an infection. After unsuccessful attempts to save the leg, it was amputated.]

Had the eight-day extension requested on Wickline's behalf been granted by Medi–Cal, she would have remained in the hospital through the morning hours of January 25, 1977. In Dr. Polonsky's medical opinion, based upon hypothetical questions derived from Wickline's recollection of her course subsequent to her discharge from the hospital, had she been at Van Nuys on January 22, 23 or 24, he would have observed her leg change color, would have formed the opinion that she had clotted and would have taken her back into surgery and reopened the graft to remove the clot again, not an uncommon procedure in this type of case. * * * In addition thereto, Dr. Polonsky testified that had Wickline developed an infection while she was in the hospital, it could have been controlled with the vigorous use of antibiotics.

In Dr. Polonsky's opinion, to a reasonable medical certainty, had Wickline remained in the hospital for the eight additional days, as originally requested by him and her other treating doctors, she would not have suffered the loss of her leg.

* * *

Dr. Polonsky testified that in his medical opinion, the Medi–Cal Consultant's rejection of the requested eight-day extension of acute care hospitalization and his authorization of a four-day extension in its place did not conform to the usual medical standards as they existed in 1977. * * *

III

From the facts thus presented, appellant takes the position that it was not negligent as a matter of law. Appellant contends that the decision to discharge was made by each of the plaintiff's three doctors, was based upon the prevailing standards of practice, and was justified by her condition at the time of her discharge. It argues that Medi–Cal had no part in the plaintiff's hospital discharge and therefore was not liable even if the decision to do so was erroneously made by her doctors.

* * *

IV

* * *

Dr. Kaufman, the chief Medi–Cal Consultant for the Los Angeles field office, was called to testify on behalf of the defendant. He testified that in January 1977, the criteria, or standard, which governed a Medi–Cal Consultant in acting on a request to consider an extension of time was founded on title 22 of the California Administrative Code. That standard was "the medical necessity" for the length and level of care requested. That, Dr. Kaufman contended, was determined by the Medi–Cal Consultant from the information provided him in the 180 form. The Medi–Cal Consultant's decision required the exercise of medical judgment and, in doing so, the Medi–Cal Consultant would utilize the skill, knowledge, training and experience he had acquired in the medical field.

Dr. Kaufman supported Dr. Glassman's decision. He testified, based upon his examination of the MC–180 form in issue in this matter, that Dr. Glassman's four-day hospital stay extension authorization was ample to meet the plaintiff's medically necessary needs at that point in time. Further, in Dr. Kaufman's opinion, there was no need for Dr. Glassman to seek information beyond that which was contained in Wickline's 180 form.

* * * Dr. Kaufman also stated that Medi–Cal Consultants did not initiate telephone calls to patient's treating doctors because of the volume of work they already had in meeting their prescribed responsibilities. Dr. Kaufman testified that any facts relating to the patient's care and treatment that was not shown on the 180 form was of no significance.

As to the principal issue before this court, i.e., who bears responsibility for allowing a patient to be discharged from the hospital, her treating physicians or the health care payor, each side's medical expert witnesses agreed that, in accordance with the standards of medical practice as it existed in January 1977, it was for the patient's treating physician to decide the course of treatment that was medically necessary to treat the ailment. It was also that physician's responsibility to determine whether or not acute care hospitalization was required and for how long. Finally, it was agreed that the patient's physician is in a better position than the Medi–Cal Consultant to determine the number of days medically necessary for any required hospital care. The decision to discharge is, therefore, the responsibility of the patient's own treating doctor.

Dr. Kaufman testified that if, on January 21, the date of the plaintiff's discharge from Van Nuys, any one of her three treating doctors had decided that in his medical judgment it was necessary to keep Wickline in the hospital for a longer period of time, they, or any of them, should have filed another request for extension of stay in the hospital, that Medi–Cal would expect those physicians to make such a request if they felt it was indicated, and upon receipt of such a request further consideration of an additional extension of hospital time would have been given.

Title 22 of the California Administrative Code section 51110, provided, in pertinent part, at the relevant time in issue here, that: "The determination of need for acute care shall be made in accordance with the usual standards of medical practice in the community."

The patient who requires treatment and who is harmed when care which should have been provided is not provided should recover for the injuries suffered from all those responsible for the deprivation of such care, including, when appropriate, health care payors. Third party payors of health care services can be held legally accountable when medically inappropriate decisions result from defects in the design or implementation of cost containment mechanisms as, for example, when appeals made on a patient's behalf for medical or hospital care are arbitrarily ignored or unreasonably disregarded or overridden. However, the physician who complies without protest with the limitations imposed by a third party payor, when his medical judgment dictates otherwise, cannot avoid his ultimate responsibility for his patient's care. He cannot point to the health care payor as the liability scapegoat when the consequences of his own determinative medical decisions go sour.

There is little doubt that Dr. Polonsky was intimidated by the Medi–Cal program but he was not paralyzed by Dr. Glassman's response nor rendered powerless to act appropriately if other action was required under the circumstances. If, in his medical judgment, it was in his patient's best interest that she remain in the acute care hospital setting for an additional four days beyond the extended time period originally authorized by Medi–Cal, Dr. Polansky should have made some effort to keep Wickline there. He himself acknowledged that responsibility to his patient. It was his medical judgment, however, that Wickline could be discharged when she was. All the plaintiff's treating physicians concurred and all the doctors who testified at trial, for either plaintiff or defendant, agreed that Dr. Polonsky's medical decision to discharge Wickline met the standard of care applicable at the time. Medi–Cal was not a party to that medical decision and therefore cannot be held to share in the harm resulting if such decision was negligently made.

In addition thereto, while Medi–Cal played a part in the scenario before us in that it was the resource for the funds to pay for the treatment sought, and its input regarding the nature and length of hospital care to be provided was of paramount importance, Medi–Cal did not override the medical judgment of Wickline's treating physicians at the time of her discharge. It was given no opportunity to do so. Therefore, there can be no viable cause of action against it for the consequences of that discharge decision.

The California Legislature's intent, in enacting the Medi–Cal Act, was to provide "mainstream" medical care to the indigent. The Legislature had expressly declared that Medi–Cal recipients should be able "whenever possible and feasible . . ., to the extent practical, . . . to secure health care in the same manner employed by the public generally, and without discrimination or segregation based purely on their economic disability." (Welf. & Inst.Code, § 14000.)

Welfare and Institutions Code section 14132 provided, in pertinent part, as follows: "The following is the schedule of benefits under this chapter: [¶] (b) In-patient hospital services, . . . are covered subject to utilization controls." Welfare and Institutions Code section 14133, provided, in pertinent part: "Utilization controls that may be applied to the services set forth in section 14132 which are subject to utilization controls shall be limited to: [¶] (a) Prior authorization, which is approval by a department [of health] consultant, of a specified service in advance of the rendering of that service based upon a determination of medical necessity."

Title 22 of the California Administrative Code set forth the pertinent regulations applicable to the State's Medi–Cal program. Section 51327 thereof, dealt with inpatient hospitalization for other than emergency services and stated, in pertinent part, as follows: "(a)(2) Nonemergency hospitalization is covered only if prior authorization is obtained from the Medi–Cal Consultant before the hospital admission is effected. The Medi–Cal Consultant's authorization shall be for a specified number of days of hospital care. Continued necessary hospitalization beyond the specified number of days shall be covered after approval by the Medi–Cal Consultant has been obtained by the hospital on or before the last day of the previously approved period of hospitalization."

In the case before us, the Medi–Cal Consultant's decision, vis-a-vis the request to extend Wickline's hospital stay, was in accord with then existing statutory law.

V

This court appreciates that what is at issue here is the effect of cost containment programs upon the professional judgment of physicians to prescribe hospital treatment for patients requiring the same. While we recognize, realistically, that cost consciousness has become a permanent feature of the health care system, it is essential that cost limitation programs not be permitted to corrupt medical judgment. We have concluded, from the facts in issue here, that in this case it did not.

For the reasons expressed herein, this court finds that appellant is not liable for respondent's injuries as a matter of law. That makes unnecessary any discussion of the other contentions of the parties.

The judgment is reversed.

NOTES AND QUESTIONS ON PAYER LIABILITY FOR DENIAL OF PRIOR AUTHORIZATION

1. Although the payer and utilization manager (the state) was not held liable in the *Wickline* case, the court suggests that liability for personal injuries might be imposed in an appropriate case of benefit denial. What legal liabilities should a private health plan or independent benefit manager face when a claims reviewer erroneously refuses to authorize payment for a recommended treatment or expenditure? See generally Blum, An Analysis of Legal Liability in Health Care Utilization Review and Case Management, 26 Houston L. Rev. 191 (1989). How does the legal theory here differ, if at all, from that underlying "bad-faith" suits? See McEvoy v. Group Health Coop., 570 N.W.2d 397 (Wis.1997) (HMO that terminated out-of-network referral of anorexic patient to allow treatment by network providers held held not entitled to summary judgment in suit for bad faith under doctrine previously applicable only to insurers; "bad faith actions

may arise where * * * financial considerations were given unreasonable weight in the decision maker's cost-benefit analysis").

2. *The Wilson Case.* Another California case sheds further light on the issue at hand. In Wilson v. Blue Cross of Southern California, 271 Cal.Rptr. 876 (Cal.App.1990), a patient with severe depression was discharged after ten days of hospitalization even though his physician believed a longer stay was required. Relying on *Wickline*, the utilization management company argued that, without an appeal by the physician, it could not be liable for the patient's subsequent suicide. The court characterized as "dicta" the language relied upon in *Wickline* and ruled (id. at 884–885) that

> the failure of Dr. Taff to follow an informal policy allowing for reconsideration by Western Medical did not warrant granting summary judgment. * * * [N]o defendant has proven that such a reconsideration request would have been granted. Also, there is a triable issue as to whether the refusal to allow the decedent to stay in the hospital was a "substantial factor" in bringing about his death and the availability of an avenue of appeal fails to prove as a matter of law that his demise was unrelated to his denial of benefits. In summary, *Wickline* is a different case from the present lawsuit. There remain triable issues of material fact as to Western Medical's * * * role in causing the wrongful death of the decedent.

3. *Clinical vs. Coverage Decisions.* Is a health plan that makes predeterminations of coverage of the kind seen in the two principal cases (or an independent contractor it hires to perform such utilization or case management functions) engaged in the practice of medicine? (Recall that some state HMO acts provide in general that HMOs shall not be deemed to be practicing medicine. E.g., Ala. Code § 27–21A–23(c)(1986).) Are its utilization reviewers—nurses or physicians, as the case may be—themselves practicing medicine? Cf. Morris v. District of Columbia Bd. of Med., 701 A.2d 364 (D.C.1997) (holding medical director of Blue Cross plan was not practicing medicine without a license); Murphy v. Board of Med. Examiners, 949 P.2d 530 (Ariz.App.1997) (board permitted to investigate prior authorization decisions by licensed but nonpracticing physician employed as medical director of health plan).

In Hand v. Tavera, 864 S.W.2d 678 (Tex. App. 1993), an ER doctor telephoned the physician designated by the patient's health plan to authorize hospital admissions, that doctor recommended outpatient treatment, and the patient subsequently suffered a stroke. The court held that "when the health-care plan's insured shows up at a participating hospital emergency room, and the plan's doctor on call is consulted about treatment or admission, there is a physician-patient relationship between the doctor and the insured." Do you agree with the *Hand* court's apparent view that a physician-reviewer (or possibly the plan itself) should be vulnerable to medical malpractice claims for failing to authorize payment for care that is subsequently deemed to be "medically necessary"? (Would the ER doctor in the *Hand* case satisfy his duty to the patient by simply going along with the plan doctor's determination?) For a particularly interesting case illustrating how the line between clinical and coverage decisions can become blurred in practice, see Long v. Great West Life & Annuity Ins. Co., 1998 WL 181968 (Wyo. 1998) (where UR physicians not only denied preauthorization of surgical procedure but also recommended alternative procedure not approved by experts in subsequent evaluations, patient was entitled to sue on ground that decision was medical; patient rather than his non-network physician had dealt directly with insurer, and insurer's policy required copayment of 20% of first $5000 for authorized surgery but would pay 60% of cost if surgery was unauthorized).

How would you argue that liability of a plan or its agents should not be on the same basis as a professional's liability but should be limited to using due care and good faith in ensuring that it is following the terms of the health care contract? Is it convincing to observe that the patient and the providers were free to proceed with treatment in the absence of prior authorization, either at the patient's or the providers' own expense or in the expectation that the payer or a court could subsequently be persuaded to see the treatment's medical merit and order payment? In other words, can one argue that the payer makes only a decision on coverage (a matter of statutory or contractual entitlement) and that the medical decision is another thing entirely? Are you willing to concede that the plan is rationing, not health care, but only health care financing? See Association of American Physicians and Surgeons v. Weinberger, 395 F.Supp. 125 (N.D.Ill.1975) (upholding early federal utilization review against the claim that restrictions on reimbursement improperly interfered with medical practice; distinguishing between a statutory limitation on government's financing obligation and an outright statutory prohibition of care of a particular type, such as abortion). See also the *Corcoran* case, reproduced below.

NOTES AND QUESTIONS ON THE ROLE OF PHYSICIANS IN THE ADMINISTRATION OF BENEFITS

1. Were the physicians in *Wickline* and *Wilson* negligent in discharging their respective patients from the hospital? When, if ever, might a provider have a duty to render or order costly services for which the patient cannot pay? Recall chapter 1(§§ A & B). Should the medical judgments of the physicians in either case be evaluated without regard to the availability of financing?

Are there other ways, besides deciding to discharge their patients, in which the physicians in *Wickline* and *Wilson* may have failed in their professional duties? Consider the following paragraphs.

2. *Duty to Appeal?* Since the advent of managed care, physicians are no longer free to spend the payer's money without appreciable restraint. But physicians might be acknowledged to have another set of professional duties in mediating between patients and the administrators of their health coverage and in helping patients cope with situations in which a payer resists paying for a service that the physician believes the patient should receive. Health plan contracts typically include some provision for appeals

from initial denials of coverage. Should a physician be deemed to have a legal duty to make such an appeal? Cf. Murphy v. Godwin, 303 A.2d 668, 673 (Del.Super.1973) (though "novel," "a duty [to complete insurance forms enabling patient to recover benefits] may be found * * * by reference to established tort theory and recognized incidents of the doctor-patient relationship").

What factors might lead physicians not to appeal rulings with which they do not agree? When would it be reasonable not to challenge a plan's determination? Does a physician have a duty to "go public" when, after all internal appeals, a plan still fails to resolve an important matter to her satisfaction or if she regards the plan as generally deficient in responding to physician prescriptions? (Such a public appeal might generate either charitable contributions or public sympathy that puts political pressure on the plan to reverse itself in a given case or to modify its conduct more generally.) Would a health plan want to retain such a whistle-blower? On the other hand, if a physician objects strongly to the plan's overall policies and practices, is it ethical for her to continue to participate in that plan—that is, to take fees from an organization that she regards as exploiting patients in order to enrich its shareholders?

Could a health plan argue that a physician's failure to appeal a denial of benefits or to bring additional facts to the plan's attention was an intervening cause relieving it of liability for a mistaken ruling? (Do you agree with the *Wilson* court's position on this question? What showing should the utilization manager make at trial?) Would a patient's failure to make such an appeal (perhaps because he was unaware of the opportunity or of the likelihood of success) constitute either an intervening cause or contributory negligence? How would you argue that a plan can reasonably treat the patient and his physician as having the burden of coming forward with evidence on the need for the treatment in the particular case? What administrative and cost-containment benefits would accompany such a plan policy? Would such a policy simply ensure that "squeaky wheels" receive more generous benefits than patients who are less assertive or less articulate or whose physicians are less willing or able to go to bat for them? How would you design a plan that could be administered to minimize such discrimination?

What light do the *Sarchett* and *Hughes* cases, reproduced earlier in this section, throw on these questions?

3. *Duty to Disclose Alternative Treatments?* If a health plan, rightly or wrongly, will not pay for a particular course of diagnosis or treatment and all internal appeals have been exhausted, should the physician be expected to inform the patient that there is an alternative path that might be taken? What might be the physician's motive in so doing? to make the plan look bad and to divert the patient's possible anger in the event the option should come to light later? to give the patient the option of appealing the decision in court? to give the patient the option of paying for the service by other means? Should a physician, in some circumstances at least, have a legal duty to make such a disclosure? Reread in this connection the concluding notes in chapter 7(§C) on informed consent. See also M. Hall, Making Medical Spending Decisions: The Law, Ethics, and Economics of Rationing Mechanisms ch. 6 (1997) (discussing legal requirements of informed consent in context of managed care).

Is the possibility of self-payment to be taken seriously? After all, it will frequently be the case that the patient cannot pay for the service for which coverage is denied. See, e.g., *Wilson*, 271 Cal. Rptr. at 883 ("The sole reason for the discharge * * * was that the decedent had no insurance or money to pay for any further in-patient benefits.") Nevertheless, in a plan designed to curb moral hazard, some services might be excluded from coverage precisely because, while desirable, they are not so obviously necessary that they should be financed by the plan in all cases. Not only would self-payment allow the patient to receive the service—which, by hypothesis, the physician conscientiously recommends and the patient reasonably desires—but it would also preserve the possibility of later seeking reimbursement from the plan under ERISA, claiming the original disallowance was improper under the terms of the plan contract. But what if the patient clearly lacks the means of paying for the service out of pocket? Should the physician withhold information about alternatives in order to spare the patient the worrisome knowledge that he is not getting the best treatment? Or might disclosure trigger either a judicial appeal or a search for some other source of payment?

Under the right circumstances, might a patient be allowed to waive the right to receive such information by contract—by enrolling in a plan that expressly disclaimed its doctors' responsibility to make such information available? See C. Havighurst, Health Care Choices, supra, at 163–64, 208–09, 246–49, 283–84 (1995) (discussing making disclosure obligations a matter of express contract between plan and consumers, some of whom might rationally prefer to leave choices to plan rather than being burdened with difficult, usually impractical, choices); M. Hall, supra (arguing that with some disclosure of rationing incentives and rules at time of enrollment in health care plan, subsequent rationing may be done without disclosure under either prior consent theory or waiver of consent theory).

4. *"Gag Clauses."* Controversy arose at one point over reports that MCOs were including so-called "gag clauses" in their contracts with physicians. These clauses were alleged to prohibit the physician from disparaging the plan or, in their most extreme form, from revealing to the patient alternative treatment options for which the plan was not prepared to pay. See generally Martin & Bjerknes, The Legal and Ethical Implications of Gag Clauses in Physician Contracts, 22 Am. J.L. & Med. 433 (1996) (surveying forms of gag clauses in physician contracts, evaluating legality of these clauses and physicians' ethical obligations, and offering responses to use of gag clauses). However, a study by the U.S. General Accounting Office, Managed Care: Explicit Gag Clauses Not Found in HMO Contracts, But Physician Concerns Remain (GAO/HEHS–97–175, Aug. 29, 1997), cast substantial doubt on the seriousness of the problem, concluding as follows:

(1) the managed care industry, physicians, and health care attorneys have different views regarding contract language that could limit a physician's ability to advise patients of all medically appropriate treatment options; (2) there is general agreement that a clause that prohibits discussion of procedures or providers not covered by the plan, and, to a lesser extent, one that requires physicians to consult with the plan before discussing treatment options with enrollees, is a gag clause; (3) however, some physicians and health care lawyers believe that other clauses could restrict the information and advice that physicians provide about a patient's medical options; (4) other physician groups, lawyers, and the HMO industry disagree that such clauses limit medical communication and contend that these are standard contract clauses designed and used only to protect HMOs' business interests; (5) of the 529 HMOs in GAO's study, none used contract clauses that specifically restricted physicians from discussing all appropriate medical options with their patients; (6) two-thirds of responding plans and 60 percent of the contracts submitted had a nondisparagement, nonsolicitation, or confidentiality clause that could be interpreted by physicians as limiting communication about all treatment options; (7) contracts with such business clauses often contained anti-gag language stating that the contract or a specific provision should not be construed as restricting physician medical advice to patients or generally encouraging open communication; (8) of those contracts with one or more of these business clauses, anti-gag language was found in 67 percent of them; (9) this combination could mitigate the potential for business clauses to be read by physicians as limiting discussion of a patient's treatment options; (10) it appears that HMO contract provisions that may be interpreted as limiting the medical information that physicians may provide patients are not likely to have a significant impact on physician practice; (11) physicians GAO interviewed maintained that they freely communicate with their patients regarding all medically appropriate care because habitual practice, professional ethics, and fear of medical liability are stronger influences on their behavior than contract requirements; and (12) physicians also pointed out that the increasing power of HMOs in the health care marketplace and their ability to terminate physician contracts can bring significant pressure to bear on physicians to modify their practice patterns or discussions with patients, without relying on the clauses discussed above.

Can an agreement between a plan and a physician alter the physician's legal duties to patients? If not, the furor surrounding gag clauses is understandable, since such clauses suggest that health plans are seeking to prevent physicians from doing what they are legally and ethically obligated to do. But the greater concern may not be that physicians who are eager to communicate with their patients about their options are having their communications squelched by health plans. Instead, the more serious problem may be that physicians are too quick to wash their hands of responsibility and to acquiesce in plan decisions—as the physicians in *Hughes*, *Wickline*, and *Wilson* may have done. Interestingly, most state statutes adopted to curb the use of gag clauses (see § C below) appear to treat disclosures to patients as if they were discretionary with the physician and to focus only on preventing interference with that discretion. If the greater problem is too-ready acceptance by physicians of plan decisions, however, a better legislative response to the problems of managed care might be to underscore by statute that physicians have the legal duties stated above, which no gag clause then could alter.

5. *Enterprise Liability?* If a treating physician should fail in performing any of the duties suggested above, should the MCO that retains his services be liable vicariously for any resulting injuries? To be sure, it may be difficult to imagine many lawsuits for breaches of such duties since there is little precedent for them other than a few rulings requiring informed consent to nontreatment. E.g., *Alexander v. Gonser*, reproduced in chapter 5(§C); *Gates v. Jensen*, reproduced in chapter 7(§B); Madsen v. Park Nicollet Med. Center, 431 N.W.2d 855, 861 (Minn.1988) ("Physician liability is imposed by [the informed consent/nondisclosure doctrine] only for failure to secure the patient's informed consent to treatment which results in harm which the patient would have avoided by declining the treatment or by choosing an alternative treatment."). See also chapter 7(§C); M. Hall, supra, at ch. 6. Nevertheless, it would seem not only that such duties have always existed in theory but also that they have become (vitally) important with the advent of managed care, with its tendencies to undermine physicians' loyalty to patients.

Imagine that the courts (or new legislation) imposed "enterprise liability" on health plans for physician failures (1) to advocate the contractual rights of patients competently and with reasonable vigor within the framework established by the plan and (2) to inform the patient of any diagnostic or treatment options that the plan refuses (rightly or wrongly) to cover but that might provide a significant medical benefit to the patient. What would be the effect on the design and operation of today's managed-care plans? (Recall the description and discussion of such plans in chapter 2(§C).) How might such a change in legal accountability affect relationships between such plans and physicians, which tend to be so adversarial today? How would professionalism, which is often thought to be in jeopardy under managed care, be affected by making health plans legally accountable when professional duties of these kinds are breached?

ERISA's Effects on Legal Actions Alleging Mistakes in Benefit Administration

Corcoran v. United HealthCare, Inc.

United States Court of Appeals, Fifth Circuit, 1992.
965 F.2d 1321.

■ KING, CIRCUIT JUDGE:

This appeal requires us to decide whether ERISA pre-empts a state-law malpractice action brought by the beneficiary of an ERISA plan against a company that provides "utilization review" services to the plan. We also address the availability under ERISA of extracontractual damages. The district court granted the defendants' motion for summary judgment, holding that ERISA both pre-empted the plaintiffs' medical malpractice claim and precluded them from recovering emotional distress damages. We affirm.

I. BACKGROUND

The basic facts are undisputed. Florence Corcoran, a long-time employee of South Central Bell Telephone Company (Bell), became pregnant in early 1989. In July, her obstetrician, Dr. Jason Collins, recommended that she have complete bed rest during the final months of her pregnancy. * * * As Mrs. Corcoran neared her delivery date, Dr. Collins ordered her hospitalized so that he could monitor the fetus around the clock.

Mrs. Corcoran was a member of Bell's Medical Assistance Plan (MAP or "the Plan"). MAP is a self-funded welfare benefit plan which provides medical benefits to eligible Bell employees. It is administered by defendant Blue Cross and Blue Shield of Alabama (Blue Cross) pursuant to an Administrative Services Agreement between Bell and Blue Cross. The parties agree that it is governed by ERISA. Under a portion of the Plan known as the "Quality Care Program" (QCP), participants must obtain advance approval for overnight hospital admissions and certain medical procedures ("pre-certification"), and must obtain approval on a continuing basis once they are admitted to a hospital ("concurrent review"), or plan benefits to which they otherwise would be entitled are reduced.

QCP is administered by defendant United HealthCare (United) pursuant to an agreement with Bell. United performs a form of cost-containment service that has commonly become known as "utilization review." * * * The Summary Plan Description (SPD) explains QCP as follows:

> The Quality Care Program (QCP), administered by United HealthCare, Inc., assists you and your covered dependents in securing quality medical care according to the provisions of the Plan while helping reduce risk and expense due to unnecessary hospitalization and surgery. They do this by providing you with information which will permit you (in consultation with your doctor) to evaluate alternatives to surgery and hospitalization when those alternatives are medically appropriate. In addition, QCP will monitor any certified hospital confinement to keep you informed as to whether or not the stay is covered by the Plan.
>
> * * *

In accordance with the QCP portion of the plan, Dr. Collins sought pre-certification from United for Mrs. Corcoran's hospital stay. Despite Dr. Collins's recommendation, United determined that hospitalization was not necessary, and instead authorized 10 hours per day of home nursing care. Mrs. Corcoran entered the hospital on October 3, 1989, but, because United had not pre-certified her stay, she returned home on October 12. On October 25, during a period of time when no nurse was on duty, the fetus went into distress and died.

Mrs. Corcoran and her husband, Wayne, filed a wrongful death action in Louisiana state court alleging that their unborn child died as a result of various acts of negligence committed by Blue Cross and United. Both sought damages for the lost love, society and affection of their unborn child. In addition, Mrs. Corcoran sought damages for the aggravation of a pre-existing depressive condition and the loss of consortium caused by such aggravation, and Mr. Corcoran sought damages for loss of consortium. The defendants removed the action to federal court on grounds that it was pre-empted by ERISA and that there was complete diversity among the parties.

Shortly thereafter, the defendants moved for summary judgment. They argued that the Corcorans' cause of action, properly characterized, sought damages for improper handling of a claim from two entities whose responsibilities were simply to administer benefits under an ERISA-governed plan. They contended that their relationship to Mrs. Corcoran came into existence solely as a result of an ERISA plan and was defined entirely by the plan. Thus, they urged the court to view the claims as "relating to" an ERISA plan, and therefore within the broad scope of state law claims pre-empted by the statute. In their opposition to the motion, the Corcorans argued that "[t]his case essentially boils down to one for malpractice against United HealthCare...." They contended that * * * their cause of action must be classified as a state law of general application which involves an exercise of traditional state authority and affects principal ERISA entities in their individual capacities. This classification, they argued, together with the fact that pre-emption would contravene the purposes of ERISA by leaving them without a remedy, leads to the conclusion that the action is permissible notwithstanding ERISA.

The district court, relying on the broad ERISA pre-emption principles developed by the Supreme Court and the Fifth Circuit, granted the motion. * * *

III. PRE-EMPTION OF THE STATE LAW CAUSE OF ACTION

A. The Nature of the Corcorans' State Law Claims

* * *

The Corcorans based their action against United on Article 2315 of the Louisiana Civil Code, which provides that "[e]very act whatever of man that causes damage to another obliges him by whose fault it happened to repair it." * * * Whether Article 2315 permits a negligence suit against a third party provider of utilization review services, however, has yet to be decided by the Louisiana courts. The potential for imposing liability on these entities is only beginning to be explored, with only one state explicitly permitting a suit based on a utilization review company's allegedly negligent decision about medical care to go forward. [*Wilson*; *Wickline*].

[A]ssuming that on these facts the Corcorans might be capable of stating a cause of action for malpractice, our task now is to determine whether such a cause of action is pre-empted by ERISA.

B. Principles of ERISA Pre-emption

* * * It is by now well-established that the "deliberately expansive" language of [section 514(a) of ERISA] is a signal that it is be construed extremely broadly. The key words "relate to" are used in such a way as to expand pre-emption beyond state laws that relate to the specific subjects covered by ERISA, such as reporting, disclosure and fiduciary obligations. Thus, state laws "relate[ ] to" employee benefit plans in a much broader sense—whenever they have "a connection with or reference to such a plan." This sweeping pre-emption of state law is consistent with Congress's decision to create a comprehensive, uniform federal scheme for the regulation of employee benefit plans.

The most obvious class of pre-empted state laws are those that are specifically designed to affect ERISA-governed employee benefit plans. But a law is not saved from pre-emption merely because it does not target employee benefit plans. Indeed, much pre-emption litigation involves laws of general application which, when applied in particular settings, can be said to have a connection with or a reference to an ERISA plan. See [Pilot Life Ins. Co. v. Dedeaux, 481 U.S. 41, 47–48 (1987)] (common law tort and contract causes of action seeking damages for improper processing of a claim for benefits under a disability plan are pre-empted). On the other hand, the Court has recognized that not every conceivable cause of action that may be brought against an ERISA-covered plan is pre-empted. * * *

C. Pre-emption of the Corcorans' Claims

Initially, we observe that the common law causes of action advanced by the Corcorans are not that species of law "specifically designed" to affect ERISA plans, for the liability rules they seek to invoke neither make explicit reference to nor are premised on the existence of an ERISA plan. Rather, applied in this case against a defendant that provides benefit-related services to an ERISA plan, the generally applicable negligence-based causes of action may have an effect on an ERISA-governed plan. In our view, the pre-emption question devolves into an assessment of the significance of these effects.

1. United's position—it makes benefit determinations, not medical decisions

United's argument in favor of pre-emption is grounded in the notion that the decision it made concerning Mrs. Corcoran was not primarily a medical decision, but instead was a decision made in its capacity as a plan fiduciary about what benefits were authorized under the Plan. All it did, it argues, was determine whether Mrs. Corcoran qualified for the benefits provided by the plan by applying previously established eligibility criteria. The argument's coup de grace is that under well-established precedent [*Pilot Life*, supra], participants may not sue in tort to redress injuries flowing from decisions about what benefits are to be paid under a plan. * * *

In support of its argument, United points to its explanatory booklet and its language stating that the company advises the patient's doctor "what the medical plan will pay for, based on a review of [the patient's] clinical information and nationally accepted medical guidelines for the treatment of [the patient's] condition." It also relies on statements to the effect that the ultimate medical decisions are up to the beneficiary's doctor. It acknowledges at various points that its decision about what benefits would be paid was based on a consideration of medical information, but the thrust of the argument is that it was simply performing commonplace administrative duties akin to claims handling.

Because it was merely performing claims handling functions when it rejected Dr. Collins's request to approve Mrs. Corcoran's hospitalization, United contends, the principles of *Pilot Life* and its progeny squarely foreclose this lawsuit. In *Pilot Life*, [t]he Court made clear that ERISA pre-empts state-law tort and contract actions in which a beneficiary seeks to recover damages for improper processing of a claim for benefits. United suggests that its actions here were analogous to those of the insurance company in *Pilot Life*, and therefore urges us to apply that decision.

2. The Corcorans' position—United makes medical decisions, not benefit determinations

The Corcorans assert that *Pilot Life* and its progeny are inapposite because they are not advancing a claim for improper processing of benefits. Rather, they say, they seek to recover solely for United's erroneous medical decision that Mrs. Corcoran did not require hospitalization during the last month of her pregnancy. This argument, of course, depends on viewing United's action in this case as a medical decision, and not merely an administrative determination about benefit entitlements. Accordingly, the Corcorans, pointing to the statements United makes in the QCP booklet concerning its medical expertise, contend that United exercised medical judgment which is outside the purview of ERISA pre-emption.

The Corcorans suggest that a medical negligence claim is permitted under the analytical framework we have developed for assessing pre-emption claims. [T]hey contend that we should not find the state law under which they proceed pre-empted because it (1) involves the exercise of traditional state authority and (2) is a law of general application which, although it affects relations between principal ERISA entities in this case, is not designed to affect the ERISA relationship.

3. Our view—United makes medical decisions incident to benefit determinations

We cannot fully agree with either United or the Corcorans. Ultimately, we conclude that United makes medical decisions—indeed, United gives medical advice—but it does so in the context of making a determination about the availability of benefits under the plan. Accordingly, we hold that the Louisiana tort action asserted by the Corcorans for the wrongful death of their child allegedly resulting from United's erroneous medical decision is pre-empted by ERISA.

Turning first to the question of the characterization of United's actions, we note that the QCP booklet and the SPD lend substantial support to the Corcorans' argument that United makes medical decisions. United's own booklet tells beneficiaries that it "assess[es] the need for surgery or hospitalization and ... determine[s] the appropriate length of stay for a hospitalization, based on nationally accepted medical guidelines." United "will discuss with your doctor the appropriateness of the treatments recommended and the availability of alternative types of treatments." Further, "United's staff includes doctors, nurses, and other medical professionals knowledgeable about the health care delivery system. Together with your doctor, they work to assure that you and your covered family members receive the most appropriate medical care." According to the SPD, United will "provid[e] you with information which will permit you (in consultation with your doctor) to evaluate alternatives to surgery and hospitalization when those alternatives are medically appropriate."

United makes much of the disclaimer that decisions about medical care are up to the beneficiary and his or her doctor. While that may be so, and while the disclaimer may support the conclusion that the relationship between United and the beneficiary is not that of doctor-patient, it does not mean that United does not make medical decisions or dispense medical advice. In response, United argues that any such medical determination or advice is made or given in the context of administering the benefits available under the Bell plan. Supporting United's position is the contract between United and Bell, which provides that "[United] shall contact the Participant's physician and based upon the medical evidence and normative data determine whether the Participant should be eligible to receive full plan benefits for the recommended hospitalization and the duration of benefits."

United argues that the decision it makes in this, the prospective context, is no different than the decision an insurer makes in the traditional retrospective context. The question in each case is "what the medical plan will pay for, based on a review of [the beneficiary's] clinical information and nationally accepted medical guidelines for the treatment of [the beneficiary's] condition." See QCP Booklet at 4. A prospective decision is, however, different in its impact on the beneficiary than a retrospective decision. In both systems, the beneficiary theoretically knows in advance what treatments the plan will pay for because coverage is spelled out in the plan documents. But in the retrospective system, a beneficiary who embarks on the course of treatment recommended by his or her physician has only a potential risk of disallowance of all or a part of the cost of that treatment, and then only after treatment has been rendered. In contrast, in a prospective system a beneficiary may be squarely presented in advance of treatment with a statement that the insurer will not pay for the proposed course of treatment recommended by his or her doctor and the beneficiary has the potential of recovering the cost of that treatment only if he or she can prevail in a challenge to the insurer's decision. A beneficiary in the latter system would likely be far less inclined to undertake the course of treatment that the insurer has at least preliminarily rejected.

By its very nature, a system of prospective decisionmaking influences the beneficiary's choice among treatment options to a far greater degree than does the theoretical risk of disallowance of a claim facing a beneficiary in a retrospective system. Indeed, the perception among insurers that prospective determinations result in lower health care costs is premised on the likelihood that a beneficiary, faced with the knowledge of specifically what the plan will and will not pay for, will choose the treatment option recommended by the plan in order to avoid risking total or partial disallowance of benefits. When United makes a decision pursuant to QCP, it is making a medical recommendation which—because of the financial ramifications—is more likely to be followed.

Although we disagree with United's position that no part of its actions involves medical decisions, we cannot agree with the Corcorans that no part of United's actions involves benefit determinations. In our view, United makes medical decisions as part and parcel of its mandate to decide what benefits are available under the Bell plan. As the QCP Booklet concisely puts it, United decides "what the medical plan will pay for." When United's actions are viewed from this perspective, it becomes apparent that the Corcorans are attempting to recover for a tort allegedly committed in the course of handling a benefit determination. The nature of the benefit determination is different than the type of decision that was at issue in *Pilot Life*, but it is a benefit determination nonetheless. The principle of *Pilot Life* that ERISA pre-empts state-law claims alleging improper handling of benefit claims is broad enough to cover the cause of action asserted here.

Moreover, allowing the Corcorans' suit to go forward would contravene Congress's goals of "ensur[ing] that plans and plan sponsors would be subject to a uniform body of benefits law" and "minimiz[ing] the administrative and financial burden of complying with conflicting directives among States or between States and the Federal Government." Ingersoll–Rand Co. [v. McClendon, 498 U.S. 133, 142 (1990)]. Thus, statutes that subject plans to inconsistent regulatory schemes in different states, thereby increasing inefficiency and potentially causing the plan to respond by reducing benefit levels, are consistently held pre-empted. [A]lthough imposing liability on United might have the salutary effect of deterring poor quality medical decisions, there is a significant risk that state liability rules would be applied differently to the conduct of utilization review companies in different states. The cost of complying with varying substantive standards would increase the cost of providing utilization review services, thereby increasing the cost to health benefit plans of including cost containment features such as the Quality Care Program (or causing them to eliminate this sort of cost containment program altogether) and ultimately decreasing the pool of plan funds available to reimburse participants.

* * * Congress may pre-empt state-law causes of action which seek to enforce various duties when it determines that such actions would interfere with a carefully constructed scheme of federal regulation. See *Pilot Life*, 481 U.S. at 48. The acknowledged absence of a remedy under ERISA's civil enforcement scheme for medical malpractice committed in connection with a plan benefit determination does not alter our conclusion. While we are not unmindful of the fact that our interpretation of the pre-emption clause leaves a gap in remedies within a statute intended to protect participants in employee benefit plans, the lack of an ERISA remedy does not affect a pre-emption analysis. Congress perhaps could not have predicted the interjection into the ERISA "system" of the medical utilization review process, but it enacted a pre-emption clause so broad and a statute so comprehensive that it would be incompatible with the language, structure and purpose of the statute to allow tort suits against entities so integrally connected with a plan.

IV. EXTRACONTRACTUAL DAMAGES

The Corcorans argue in the alternative that the damages they seek are available as "other appropriate equitable relief" under ERISA § 502(a)(3). * * *

* * * Assuming without deciding * * * that § 502(a)(3) permits the award of make-whole relief as "other appropriate equitable relief," we hold that the emotional distress and mental anguish damages sought here by the Corcorans are not recoverable.

* * *

The result ERISA compels us to reach means that the Corcorans have no remedy, state or federal, for what may have been a serious mistake. This is troubling for several reasons. First, it eliminates an important check on the thousands of medical decisions routinely made in the burgeoning utilization review system. With liability rules generally inapplicable, there is theoretically less deterrence of substandard medical decisionmaking. Moreover, if the cost of compliance with a standard of care (reflected either in the cost of prevention or the cost of paying judgments) need not be factored into utilization review companies' cost of doing business, bad medical judgments will end up being cost-free to the plans that rely on these companies to contain medical costs. ERISA plans, in turn, will have one less incentive to seek out the companies that can deliver both high quality services and reasonable prices.

Second, in any plan benefit determination, there is always some tension between the interest of the beneficiary in obtaining quality medical care and the interest of the plan in preserving the pool of funds available to compensate all beneficiaries. In a prospective review context, with its greatly increased ability to deter the beneficiary (correctly or not) from embarking on a course of treatment recommended by the beneficiary's physician, the tension between interest of the beneficiary and that of the plan is exacerbated. A system which would, at least in some circumstances, compensate the beneficiary who changes course based upon a wrong call for the costs of that call might ease the tension between the conflicting interests of the beneficiary and the plan.

Finally, cost containment features such as the one at issue in this case did not exist when Congress passed ERISA. While we are confident that the result we have reached is faithful to Congress's intent neither to allow state-law causes of action that relate to employee benefit plans nor to provide beneficiaries in the Corcorans' position with a remedy under ERISA, the world of employee benefit plans has hardly remained static since 1974. Fundamental changes such as the widespread institution of utilization review would seem to warrant a reevaluation of ERISA so that it can continue to serve its noble purpose of safeguarding the interests of employees. Our system, of course, allocates this task to Congress, not the courts, and we acknowledge our role today by interpreting ERISA in a manner consistent with the expressed intentions of its creators.

V. CONCLUSION

For all the foregoing reasons, we find that ERISA pre-empts the Corcorans' tort claim against United and that the Corcorans may not recover damages for emotional distress under § 502(a)(3) of ERISA. Accordingly, the judgment of the district court is AFFIRMED.

NOTES AND QUESTIONS ON ERISA AND UTILIZATION MANAGEMENT

1. *Remedy*. On the question of remedy for personal injuries in actions under ERISA, see Kuhl v. Lincoln National Health Plan of Kansas City, Inc., 999 F.2d 298 (8th Cir.1993) (holding ERISA preempted claims for delay in scheduling deceased's heart surgery):

> We have previously held that monetary damages are not available under section 502(a)(3)(B)(i). Novak v. Andersen Corp., 962 F.2d 757, 759 (8th Cir.1992), cert. denied, 508 U.S. 959 (1993). In *Novak*, we expressly rejected the Warren court's reasoning and held that an award of monetary damages is a legal remedy, not an equitable one. This interpretation has recently been vindicated by the Supreme Court. Mertens v. Hewitt Assocs., 508 U.S. 248 (1993). After an extensive review of the history of equitable remedies and the statutory language of section 502(a)(3), the Court concluded that damages do not constitute "other equitable relief." The district court properly held that the Kuhls' claim for monetary damages was not cognizable under section 502(a)(3)(B)(i).

See also Varity Corp. v. Howe, 516 U.S. 489 (1996) (holding that § 502 (a)(3) allows individuals, as well as plan itself, to bring actions against plan administrators for breach of fiduciary duties).

2. Is there any doubt that the *Corcoran* court construed ERISA correctly? See also Bast v. Prudential Ins. Co., 1998 WL 279217 (9th Cir. 1998) (ERISA held to preempt patients' survivors claims for denial of coverage for autologous bone marrow transplant and related treatment); Turner v.

Fallon Community Health Plan Inc., 127 F.3d 196 (1st Cir. 1997) (finding ERISA preemption of state remedies, and no federal remedy other than equitable ones under ERISA, where plan allegedly denied benefits improperly); Cannon v. Group Health Serv., Inc., 77 F.3d 1270 (10th Cir.), cert. denied, 117 S. Ct. 66 (1996) (preemption of state remedies found despite lack of adequate ERISA remedy); Tolton v. American Biodyne, Inc., 48 F.3d 937 (6th Cir.1995) (patient committed suicide after ERISA plan administrator refused to authorize inpatient mental health care; wrongful death claim found preempted, following *Corcoran*).

Consider the argument by the plaintiffs in *Dukes* to the effect that the only benefit that the employees received from their ERISA plan was their enrollment in the HMO and that, once that enrollment occurred, any problems between the HMO and the employee should be resolved under state law. How did the court in *Dukes* respond to this argument? How would you respond? Is the argument applicable in *Corcoran*? In any event, it is arguable that virtually any employer-sponsored health plan, even including most of those funded by ordinary group insurance, are entitled to the benefits of ERISA preemption. See, e.g., Kidder v. H & B Marine, Inc., 932 F.2d 347 (5th Cir.1991) (setting forth criteria for treating group coverage as an ERISA plan). The point is one of considerable confusion, however.

3. Do you agree with the *Corcoran* court's conclusion, unnecessary to its holding, "that United makes medical decisions"? Did United also, as the court states, "dispense medical advice"? Assume a similar case in which the defendant cannot assert ERISA preemption, either because it is an insurance company administering ordinary insurance coverage (and excluded from ERISA preemption by the so-called "savings clause") or because it is administering a plan for state employees. What standard should the court apply in evaluating its decisions in utilization management? Does language in *Corcoran* imply that the standard is a professional one and that the decisions should be evaluated qua "medical decisions"? How else might one frame the question in such a case?

4. For lower court cases attempting to reconcile the *Dukes*, *Pacificare*, and *Rice v. Panchal* line of cases (examined in § A of this chapter) with *Corcoran*, see Lancaster v. Kaiser Foundation Health Plan, Inc., 958 F.Supp. 1137 (E.D.Va.1997) (suit for personal injuries based on allegation that physician incentives caused undertreatment held preempted as a suit for a denial of benefits that should have been brought under ERISA); Ouellette v. Christ Hosp., 942 F.Supp. 1160 (S.D.Ohio 1996) (claim not preempted because allegation that plan provided financial incentives to hospitals for shortening length-of-stays focused on relationship of plan to hospital, not plan to member, and because allegation focused on quality, not quantity of benefits). One noteworthy case has found in the *Travelers* case, reproduced in chapter 1(§B), a basis for narrowing ERISA's preemption in cases of the foregoing kind—where allegations go to the design or operation of the plan's cost-containment measures. In Pappas v. Asbel, 675 A.2d 711 (Pa.Super.1996), review granted, 686 A.2d 1312 (Pa.1996), the injury to the patient was attributed to a delay in authorizing transfer from an emergency room to a hospital that was equipped to deal with the patient's problem and that also had a working arrangement with the patient's HMO. The state court cited the statement in *Travelers* that "a law operating as an indirect source of merely economic influence on administrative decisions * * * should not suffice to trigger preemption," 514 U.S. at 662, as a justification for allowing an action in state court challenging the plan's policies and practices. The court opined, "We do not believe that Congress can have intended, prior even to invention of the cost containment system which inheres in [the HMO's] review process, to foreclose recovery to plan beneficiaries injured by negligent medical decisions." 675 A.2d at 718. In the pending appeal, the AMA filed a brief amicus curiae urging the Pennsylvania Supreme Court to read ERISA the same way.

One commentator draws the following lesson from foregoing case and a few others like it:

> Recognizing *Travelers*'s more pragmatic and restrictive view of when preemption is appropriate should at least render it less likely that a court would find that ERISA preempts a direct negligence claim against a plan for failure to use reasonable care in formulating plan policies and procedures and in using cost-containment procedures. * * * Without ERISA's protective shield, state courts could develop tort law compelling HMOs and managed care plans to use greater care in designing policies and procedures to avoid the risk of liability.

Jordan, supra, at 173. Do you agree that ERISA, as interpreted in *Travelers*, leaves room for lawsuits of the kind contemplated?

5. Would you propose—as the court in *Corcoran* does—that Congress reevaluate ERISA? What changes would you propose? Would it be wise policy to open state courts to claimants who wish to challenge a coverage determination that turned out badly? There is strong interest in Congress in revising ERISA. Can you imagine amending ERISA without imperiling freedom of contract and weakening consumer choice as the ultimate driving force in allocating resources to health care? Is this an argument against amending it?

6. The following case returns to the problem of contract interpretation, this time in the context of ERISA. The notes following will provide additional opportunities to ponder the question of how to ensure that payers exercise due care in the administration of coverage.

Phillips v. Lincoln National Life Insurance Co.

United States Court of Appeals, Seventh Circuit, 1992.
978 F.2d 302.

■ COFFEY, CIRCUIT JUDGE.

Gordon B. Phillips ("Phillips"), as guardian for his dependent son, James G. Phillips ("James"), brought this action in the district court under

[ERISA] against Lincoln National Life Insurance Company ("Lincoln") seeking recovery of benefits under an employee welfare benefit plan ("the Plan") established by his employer, Seedboro Equipment Company ("Seedboro"), pursuant to its purchase of an insurance policy from Lincoln. Both parties agree that the Plan is an employee welfare benefit plan governed by ERISA. Phillips argued in the district court that Lincoln erroneously applied the Plan's mental illness benefit limitation to Phillips' benefits claim for expenses incurred in the treatment of James' illness. The district court entered summary judgment in favor of Phillips, and Lincoln appeals. We affirm.

I. BACKGROUND

* * * Phillips, who is Seedboro's president, and his dependent son James were eligible participants in the Plan[, which included a lifetime benefit limit of $1 million but established a separate limit of $25,000 for "mental illness(es)," an undefined term].

In December, 1981, when he was 16 years old, James was diagnosed as suffering from * * * "organic brain syndrome." * * * James' disorder manifests itself in numerous and varied behavioral episodes. * * * .

* * *

According to the record, medical science has been unable to implement a treatment program to successfully attack and contain the mental affliction from which James suffers. Therefore, doctors are forced to confine their efforts to helping James control and function with the behavioral manifestations of his illness. [Viewing the $25,000 limitation as applicable to the case, Lincoln refused to reimburse Phillips for any of the subsequent expenses arising from his son's treatment. An appeals committee affirmed the original claim determination, and Phillips filed a complaint in the district court.] Both parties filed motions for summary judgment.

In a published opinion, the district court explained that Phillips and Lincoln advanced "competing reasonable interpretations" of the Plan term "mental illness". The court noted that Phillips argued in his summary judgment motion that the term "mental illness" referred only to those illnesses with non-physical causes, "such as illnesses traceable to abuse suffered in one's childhood or to other types of traumatic experiences. According to [Phillips], behavioral problems traceable to an organic or physical cause are other than 'mental illnesses.'" Lincoln's summary judgment motion took issue with Phillips' definition of mental illness, arguing that the cause of a behavioral illness does not determine whether it is a mental illness. In Lincoln's view, an illness is a mental illness if its symptoms include extremely abnormal behavior.

The district court * * * read the ambiguity in the Plan in Phillips' favor, ruling that, as a matter of law, the Plan's mental illness limitation did not apply to James' condition. * * *

II. STANDARD OF REVIEW

Phillips brought his suit against Lincoln under [§ 502(a)(1)(B)] of ERISA which authorizes a plan participant to bring a civil action "to recover benefits due to him under the terms of his plan...." The Supreme Court has made clear that "a denial of benefits challenged under [§ 502(a)(1)(B)] is to be reviewed under a de novo standard unless the benefit plan gives the administrator or fiduciary discretionary authority to determine eligibility for benefits or to construe the terms of the plan." Firestone Tire & Rubber Company v. Bruch, 489 U.S. 101, 115 (1989). The district court action in reviewing Lincoln's denial of Phillips' benefits claim de novo was proper as neither of these exceptions apply here.

We, in turn, "review de novo a district court's grant of summary judgment." * * *

III. ANALYSIS

In Hammond v. Fidelity and Guaranty Life Insurance Company, 965 F.2d 428 (7th Cir.1992), * * * we faced [the same question that] reappears in the instant case: whether "state laws governing insurance policy interpretation [are] preserved under ERISA." We decided that they were not so preserved because "state rules of contract interpretation" did not "regulate insurance" within the meaning of ERISA and because Congress intended "uniformity of decisions under ERISA. * * * We therefore conclude[d] that ERISA preempts state decisional rules [of contract interpretation], and that any ambiguities in ERISA plans and insurance policies should be resolved by referring to the federal common law rules of contract interpretation." In *Hammond*, we summarized the relevant rules of federal common law contract interpretation as follows: "[W]e interpret the terms of the [ERISA-governed] policy 'in an ordinary and popular sense as would a [person] of average intelligence and experience.' Ambiguous terms in an insurance contract will be strictly construed in favor of the insured. However, we will 'not artificially create ambiguity where none exists.'" *Hammond*, 965 F.2d at 430 [citations of quoted cases omitted].

With these interpretive principles in mind, we turn to the questions raised in this appeal. We agree with the district court that the term "mental illness" in the disputed ERISA plan is ambiguous. Lincoln acknowledges that the Plan provides no definition of the term mental illness, but nevertheless insists that the term plainly encompasses illnesses like the one afflicting James because "the average layperson, by merely observing James' broad range of psychiatric and behavioral symptoms and the nature of his treatment, would conclude that he was suffering from and being treated for a mental illness or disorder". In Lincoln's view, the cause of an illness is irrelevant in determining whether an illness is physical or mental. This is in direct conflict with Phillips' view that because James' condition flows from an organic defect, he is suffering from a physical illness, with behavioral and emotional manifestations.

* * *

[W]e turn now to the crux of Lincoln's position: its contention that a mental illness ought to be defined as a condition whose primary observable symptoms are behavioral. This view was adopted by a panel of the Eighth Circuit in Brewer v. Lincoln National Life Insurance Company, 921 F.2d 150 (8th Cir.1990), cert. denied, 501 U.S. 1238 (1991). *Brewer* presented facts similar to the instant case: a father, as guardian for his son, sued an insurance company for its refusal to reimburse the full costs of his son's treatment for affective mood disorder, a condition which had been successfully treated with a combination of drugs and psychotherapy. The *Brewer* court, citing ERISA's directive, contained in 29 U.S.C. § 1022(a)(1), that summary plan descriptions "be written in a manner calculated to be understood by the average plan participant," stated that terms in insurance policies governed by ERISA "should be accorded their ordinary, and not specialized, meanings." The court then applied that interpretive rule to the case at hand: "[t]he cause of a disease is a judgment for experts, while laymen know and understand symptoms. * * * By focusing upon the disease's etiology, the district court considered factors that are important to experts but not to laypersons. The court thus failed to examine the term 'mental illness' as a layperson would have, which is the examination we concluded ERISA and federal common law require."

* * *

The *Brewer* court, [thus], did embrace Lincoln's preferred definition of mental illness, and the appellant's main argument is that we, like the *Brewer* court, ought to conclude that the term "mental illness" can only be understood as a description of the symptoms of a condition, and that a condition's cause is irrelevant to its classification.

* * *

[L]ike Lincoln, Phillips is able to point to a federal court of appeals decision approving its preferred definition of "mental illness." A panel of the Ninth Circuit, in Kunin v. Benefit Trust Life Insurance Company, 910 F.2d 534 (9th Cir.), cert. denied, 498 U.S. 1013 (1990), upheld a finding of the district court that autism was not a mental illness under an ERISA employee welfare benefit plan because "mental illness refers to a behavioral disturbance with no demonstrable organic or physical basis.... [I]t stems from reaction to environmental conditions as distinguished from organic causes." Since autism has an organic cause, it did not qualify as a mental illness.

Faced with these competing definitions of "mental illness" which have divided not only the litigants but also federal and state courts, we have no trouble agreeing with the district court's finding that the term "mental illness" as used in the Plan is ambiguous. * * *

Following *Hammond*, which states that federal common law rules of contract interpretation require us to construe "[a]mbiguous terms in an insurance contract ... strictly ... in favor of the insured," we hold that the district court correctly ruled that the Plan's mental illness limitation does not apply to James' condition. * * *

Lincoln argues that the application of the rule of *contra proferentem* in the ERISA context was foreclosed by the Supreme Court in *Firestone*. We disagree. In *Firestone*, the Court considered the question of the appropriate standard of review for ERISA actions brought under [ERISA § 502(a)(1)(B)], challenging denials of benefits by ERISA plan administrators. The Court concluded that de novo review was required, also making clear that principles of trust law are useful guides in the development of federal common law in ERISA cases. In its discussion of relevant trust law principles, the Court stated that as "they do with contractual provisions, courts construe terms in a trust agreement without deferring to either party's interpretation." The Court also noted that in actions challenging an employer's denial of benefits before the enactment of ERISA "[i]f the plan did not give the employer or administrator discretionary or final authority to construe uncertain terms, the court reviewed the employee's claim as it would have any other contract claim—by looking to the terms of the plan and other manifestations of the parties' intent."

Lincoln argues that this language in *Firestone* precludes application of the rule of *contra proferentem* in ERISA actions because that rule is inconsistent with the Supreme Court's instruction that the intent of the parties to an ERISA plan should be the focus of the inquiry. We [agree with the *Kunin* court] * * * "that the *Firestone* Court intended no wholesale rejection of prevailing principles of plan interpretation when it looked to trust law on the subject of the appropriate standard of judicial review."

The *Kunin* court also set out persuasive reasons for applying the rule of *contra proferentem* to cases such as the instant one: "[T]he *contra proferentem* rule is followed in all fifty states and the District of Columbia, and with good reason. * * *." As the Second Circuit reasoned in applying the rule of *contra proferentem* to an ERISA-governed employee health insurance plan, "application of this rule of interpretation to de novo review of ERISA insurance plans is an appropriate implementation of the congressional expectation that the courts will develop a 'federal common law of rights and obligations under ERISA-regulated plans.' * * * Moreover, 'ERISA abounds with the language and terminology of trust law,' ... and application of this rule to resolve ambiguities in an ERISA insurance plan on de novo review is consistent with the basic principle of trust law that trust property is to be dealt with for the benefit of the beneficiary." Masella v. Blue Cross & Blue Shield of Connecticut, Inc., 936 F.2d 98, 107 (2d Cir.1991) [quoting *Firestone*]. * * *

Lincoln mistakenly asserts that ERISA's requirement that plan descriptions be "written in a manner calculated to be understood by the average plan participant," 29 U.S.C. § 1022(a)(1), prevented it from providing any definition of mental illness. The requirement that a plan description be accessible to the average plan participant is no excuse for failing to supply any definition at all of the term "mental illness." * * * Lincoln is not being forced to provide benefits "upon every remotely colorable claim of plan ambiguity," Appellant's Brief at 44, but upon an ambiguity in a central plan limitation. Lincoln urges us to reject the application of *contra* *proferentem* and simply determine the intent of the parties as to the mental illness limitation. This is precisely what we are unable to do because the Plan term "mental illness" is ambiguous. Moreover, contrary to Lincoln's protestations, reading such ambiguities against the insurer is not in contravention of the underlying purpose of ERISA, which is "to promote the interests of employees and their beneficiaries in employee benefit plans ... and to protect contractually defined benefits." *Firestone*, 489 U.S. at 113. We serve that purpose today by holding that a plan participant cannot be denied benefits under a limitation which is ambiguous as to its application to his benefit claim.

* * *

IV.

Insurance policies are almost always drafted by insurers, and they should be certain that limitations in their coverage are clear enough for a layperson to understand. Insurers should not be permitted to exploit policy term ambiguities, which they could have avoided, to deny coverage to an unsuspecting insured. We hold that the Plan's mental illness limitation does not apply to James' condition, and therefore the district court's entry of summary judgment in favor of Phillips is AFFIRMED. We REMAND to the district court for a determination of the amount owed by Lincoln to Phillips pursuant to Lincoln's obligations under the Plan.

■ BAUER, CHIEF JUDGE, dissenting. [Opinion omitted.]

FURTHER NOTES AND QUESTIONS ON COVERAGE DISPUTES AND THE INTERPRETATION OF HEALTH CARE CONTRACTS

1. Although ERISA preserves state regulation of the business of insurance, federal law purports to centralize everything else. Thus, judicial review of both retrospective and prospective denials of coverage by employer-sponsored health benefit plans—even plans funded by conventional health insurance—occurs in federal court under ERISA itself. Compare Kidder v. H. & B Marine, Inc., 932 F.2d 347 (5th Cir.1991) (defining ERISA plans broadly to include most employer-sponsored group health insurance) with Kornman v. Blue Cross/Blue Shield , 662 So.2d 498 (La.App.1995) (rejecting Fifth Circuit's reading of ERISA). Because ERISA mandates no specific coverage, the issues addressed by the court are at least nominally contractual. The *Phillips* case addresses the interesting question whether employee benefit plans, while escaping the threat of personal-injury actions under state law (see *Pilot Life*, supra), are nevertheless subject to the same principles of contract interpretation that have allowed state courts to be generally and especially protective of consumers vis-a-vis insurers. See also Saltarelli v. Bob Baker Group Med. Trust, 35 F.3d 382 (9th Cir.1994) (holding ERISA does not prevent reliance on "reasonable expectations" doctrine in construing coverage of ERISA plan). Have the federal courts achieved Congress's purpose of establishing a nationally uniform legal environment for employee health benefit plans? For a later ruling by the court that held in the *Brewer* case (described in *Phillips*) that ERISA preempted the state rule of *contra proferentem*, see Delk v. Lincoln Nat'l Life Ins. Co., 959 F.2d 104 (8th Cir.1992) ("As a matter of federal common law, a court construing plans governed by ERISA should construe ambiguities against the drafter only if, after applying ordinary principles of construction, giving language its ordinary meaning and admitting extrinsic evidence, ambiguities remain."). Several courts have held that the *contra proferentem* rule does not apply to collectively bargained agreements. E.g., Eley v. Boeing Co., 945 F.2d 276 (9th Cir.1991).

Phillips involves only a retrospective claim for benefits, since the employer had dropped Lincoln as its carrier. (The facts, as stated, suggest a possible reason why.) How does the case differ factually from *Sarchett* and *Hughes*, reproduced earlier in this section? Did Mr. Phillips rely upon a particular reading of the contract such that a court might be justified in honoring his reasonable expectations as "an unsuspecting insured"? Some ERISA cases involve challenges to prospective denials of coverage. The most striking of these are those involving so-called "experimental" treatments, cases in which the issue is not your money but (arguably) your life. Such cases are most often resolved by the issuance or denial of a preliminary injunction ordering the plan to pay for the treatment sought and only rarely reach appellate courts. On the other hand, cases involving prospective coverage of chronic conditions (e.g., behavioral problems) or elective procedures (e.g., in vitro fertilization) do provide frequent opportunities for federal courts of appeals to address coverage questions. Should the principles of contract interpretation be the same in all cases, or do special considerations operate in cases directly affecting a patient's course of treatment rather than his pocketbook?

2. *The Arbitrary-and-Capricious Standard of Review.* In Firestone Tire & Rubber Co. v. Bruch, 489 U.S. 101, 110–15 (1989), the Supreme Court addressed the question whether a court should review a benefit plan administrator's interpretation of the plan documents de novo or under a more permissive standard:

> ERISA abounds with the language and terminology of trust law [e.g., *participant, beneficiary, fiduciary, trustee, fiduciary duties*]. ERISA's legislative history confirms that the Act's fiduciary responsibility provisions "codif[y] and mak[e] applicable to [ERISA] fiduciaries certain principles developed in the evolution of the law of trusts." H.R.Rep. No. 93–533, p. 11 (1973). Given this language and history, we have held that courts are to develop a "federal common law of rights and obligations under ERISA-regulated plans." Pilot Life Ins. Co. v. Dedeaux, [481 U.S. 41,] 56 [(1987)]. See also Franchise Tax Board v. Construction Laborers Vacation Trust, 463 U.S. 1, 24, n. 26 (1983) (" '[A] body of Federal substantive law will be developed by the courts to deal with issues involving rights and obligations under private welfare and pension plans' ") (quoting 129 Cong.Rec. 29942 (1974) (remarks of Sen. Javits)). In determining the appropriate standard of review for actions under [ERISA § 502(a)(1)(B)], we are guided by principles of trust law. Central States, Southeast and Southwest Areas Pension Fund v. Central Transport, Inc., 472 U.S. 559, 570 (1985).

Trust principles make a deferential standard of review appropriate when a trustee exercises discretionary powers. See Restatement (Second) of Trusts § 187 (1959) ("[w]here discretion is conferred upon the trustee with respect to the exercise of a power, its exercise is not subject to control by the court except to prevent an abuse by the trustee of his discretion"). See also G. Bogert & G. Bogert, Law of Trusts and Trustees § 560, pp. 193–208 (2d rev. ed. 1980). A trustee may be given power to construe disputed or doubtful terms, and in such circumstances the trustee's interpretation will not be disturbed if reasonable. Id., § 559, at 169–171. Whether "the exercise of a power is permissive or mandatory depends upon the terms of the trust." 3 W. Fratcher, Scott on Trusts § 187, p. 14 (4th ed. 1988). Hence, over a century ago we remarked that "[w]hen trustees are in existence, and capable of acting, a court of equity will not interfere to control them in the exercise of a *discretion vested in them by the instrument* under which they act." Nichols v. Eaton, 91 U.S. 716, 724–725 (1875) (emphasis added). See also *Central States, Southeast and Southwest Areas Pension Fund v. Central Transport, Inc.*, supra, 472 U.S., at 568 ("The trustees' determination that the trust documents authorize their access to records here in dispute has significant weight, for the trust agreement explicitly provides that 'any construction [of the agreement's provisions] adopted by the Trustees in good faith shall be binding upon the Union, Employees, and Employers' ").

* * * Consistent with established principles of trust law, we hold that a denial of benefits challenged under [§ 502(a)(1)(B)] is to be reviewed under a de novo standard unless the benefit plan gives the administrator or fiduciary discretionary authority to determine eligibility for benefits or to construe the terms of the plan.

For a case finding a denial of coverage for private duty nursing to be arbitrary in light of evidence of patient need, see Zuckerbrod v. Phoenix Mut. Life Ins. Co., 78 F.3d 46 (2d Cir.1996).

3. *Trust Law Principles*. Note the emphasis placed by courts on trust law as a source of principles for interpreting ERISA. Do you agree with the view, quoted in *Phillips* from the *Masella* case, that application of the *contra proferentem* principle in these cases "is consistent with the basic principle of trust law that trust property is to be dealt with for the benefit of the beneficiary"? Is the plaintiff in these cases the only "beneficiary" for whose benefit the "trust" is to be administered? Does the court truly clinch its case, as it seems to believe, by quoting *Firestone*, 489 U.S. at 113, to the effect that "the underlying purpose of ERISA * * * is 'to promote the interests of employees and their beneficiaries in employee benefit plans ... and to protect contractually defined benefits' "? See also Bedrick v. Travelers Ins. Co., 93 F.3d 149, 154 (4th Cir.1996) ("ERISA commands undivided loyalty to plan participants. Travelers did not evaluate Ethan's physical and occupational therapy claims in a manner consistent with this duty.").

Can trust law provide useful guidance on how a trustee, making decisions without definitive guidance in the trust instrument, can mediate among individual patients, other beneficiaries, and premium payers—including not only employers but also employees, whose take-home pay will inevitably suffer if their employers face higher health care costs? See generally Stein, ERISA and the Limits of Equity, Law & Contemp. Probs., Winter 1993, p. 71, 94–100 ("trust law has not been especially helpful to courts in formulating the appropriate standard for review of benefit denials under ERISA plans"); Hall & Anderson, Health Insurers' Assessment of Medical Necessity, 140 U. Pa. L. Rev. 1637, 1697–98 (1992) ("trust law does not offer much guidance on how to resolve conflicts among the beneficiaries or between one beneficiary and the group"); Fischel & Langbein, ERISA's Fundamental Contradiction: The Exclusive Benefit Rule, 55 U. Chi. L. Rev. 1105 (1988) (examining tension between duties to beneficiaries and to the common fund). But see Hall & Anderson, supra, at 1668 n.123 (observing that in ERISA cases the employer creating the plan and those administering it on the employer's behalf are more apt to be regarded as fiduciaries with a responsibility for protecting the fund for the benefit of the employees as a group).

4. *Conflict of Interests*. Because ERISA incorporates fiduciary principles from trust law, courts reviewing administrators' actions are alert to apparent conflicts of interests on the part of the decision maker. See *Firestone*, 489 U.S. at 115 ("if a benefit plan gives discretion to an administrator or fiduciary who is operating under a conflict of interest, that conflict must be weighed as a 'facto[r] in determining whether there is an abuse of discretion' "), quoting Restatement (Second) of Trusts § 187, Comment d (1959). Thus, judicial review of coverage disputes under ERISA may not be as permissive as the arbitrary-or-capricious standard would suggest. For examples of the ease with which some courts, citing conflicts of interests, have substituted their own interpretations for those of ERISA plan administrators, see *Bedrick*, supra (finding insurer's physicians' doubts that therapies would benefit patient inadequate to support denial, given insurer's financial stake in decision); Salley v. E.I. DuPont de Nemours & Co., 966 F.2d 1011 (5th Cir.1992) (abuse of discretion found in refusal to cover continued inpatient care for troubled adolescent; questioning applicability, however, of so-called "treating physician rule," under which deference is given to physician's judgment in certain types of cases); Brown v. Blue Cross & Blue Shield, 898 F.2d 1556 (11th Cir.1990), cert. denied, 498 U.S. 1040 (1991) (lengthy opinion virtually reestablishing *de novo* review where a conflict of interests is perceived). But see Sullivan v. LTV Aerospace & Defense Co., 82 F.3d 1251, 1255–56 (2d Cir. 1996) ("we decline to concur with the rule in *Brown*[, supra,] and adhere to the arbitrary and capricious standard of review in cases turning on whether the decision was based on an alleged conflict of interest, unless the conflict affected the choice of reasonable interpretation").

5. *Exclusions of "Experimental" or Nonstandard Treatments*. Recall the discussion of this topic in chapter 2(§C). Almost by definition, an experimental procedure cannot be precisely identified very far in advance for the purpose of unambiguously excluding it from coverage under the contract. Moreover, in addition to being inherently ambiguous and interpretable only with the help of partisan experts, such exclusions usually come before the court on a motion for preliminary relief. In these circumstances, instead of

finally interpreting the contract, the court "balances the equities," which often means weighing the insurer's money against the patient's (unproved) claim that his life is in the balance. It is particularly easy in such cases to forget that more than the cost of a single medical emergency is at stake. Recall from discussion of *Bradley v. Empire Blue Cross*, reproduced in chapter 2(§C), the possibility that physician experts testifying in favor of coverage in these cases are not themselves unbiased.

A series of widely publicized cases involving coverage of costly autologous bone-marrow transplants (ABMT), coupled with high-dose chemotherapy (HDC), as a treatment for cancer in its advanced stages have demonstrated that ambiguities are easy to find and to resolve in the patient's favor. E.g., Bailey v. Blue Cross & Blue Shield, 67 F.3d 53 (4th Cir.1995) (provision that ABMT "with high dose chemotherapy or radiation are not covered" concededly excluded HDC, but was ambiguous as to coverage of AMBT alone); Dahl–Eimers v. Mutual of Omaha Life Ins. Co., 986 F.2d 1379 (11th Cir.1993), cert. denied, 510 U.S. 964 (1993) (without provision for how "experimental" status of treatment would be determined, exclusion was ambiguous, justifying preliminary injunction for plaintiff); Pirozzi v. Blue Cross–Blue Shield, 741 F.Supp. 586 (E.D.Va.1990) (ERISA case; coverage found on strength of physicians' testimony that treatment was not experimental); Cole v. Blue Cross & Blue Shield, 738 F.Supp. 42 (D.Mass. 1990) (coverage found despite evidence that treatment is successful in only 9% of cases); Lubeznik v. HealthChicago, Inc., 644 N.E.2d 777 (Ill.App. 1994) (affirming issuance of preliminary injunction ordering coverage on basis of treating oncologist's opinion, ambiguity found in a contract's reference to the opinion of "appropriate medical technology boards," and plan medical director's failure to consult opinions of NIH, etc., until after ruling in first instance).

Other courts have seen the ABMT problem differently, however. See Martin v. Blue Cross & Blue Shield, Inc., 115 F.3d 1201 (4th Cir.1997) (upholding denial of ABMT coverage in case of epithelial ovarian cancer); Whitney v. Empire Blue Cross & Blue Shield, 106 F.3d 475 (2d Cir.1997) (vacating and remanding denial of ABMT coverage found arbitrary by district court under improperly reduced level of deference to determinations by administrators of ERISA plan; patient had received treatment but died anyway); Holder v. Prudential Ins. Co., 951 F.2d 89 (5th Cir.1992) (finding ABMT treatment experimental); Harris v. Mutual of Omaha Cos., 1992 WL 421489 (S.D.Ind.1992) (extensively apologizing for tragic outcome, district judge upholds federal Office of Personnel Management decision upholding denial of ABMT to federal employee); Sweeney v. Gerber Prods. Co. Med. Benefits Plan, 728 F.Supp. 594 (D.Neb.1989) (ERISA case; coverage not found). See also Henderson v. Bodine Aluminum Co., 70 F.3d 958 (8th Cir.1995) (ordering preliminary injunction requiring coverage of ABMT for breast cancer on ground that patient was likely to prove procedure's acceptance and thus to win on claim that exclusion of treatment for breast cancer while covering it for other cancers violated Americans with Disabilities Act). See generally Hall & Anderson, supra (thoughtful and extensive exposition of entire problem of defining coverage and implementing limitations, focusing on ABMT cases, which are described at pp. 1637–41).

For additional cases on the exclusion of nonstandard, arguably discredited treatments, see Jones v. Laborers Health and Welfare Trust Fund, 906 F.2d 480 (9th Cir.1990) (allowing denial of coverage for hyperthermia as treatment for breast cancer because experimental); Dallis v. Aetna Life Ins. Co., 768 F.2d 1303 (11th Cir.1985) (necessity for unproven "immuno-augmentative" cancer therapy held a question of fact); Zuckerberg v. Blue Cross & Blue Shield, 487 N.Y.S.2d 595 (App.Div.1985), affirmed on other grounds 490 N.E.2d 839 (1986) (denying coverage for nutritional therapy provided in Mexico). See generally Ferguson et al., Court-ordered Reimbursement for Unproven Medical Technology: Circumventing Technology Assessment, 269 J.A.M.A. 21116 (1993) (identifying 17 cases involving treatments of unproven efficacy, in 14 of which court ordered payment).

6. *Coverage of Infertility Treatments*. An interesting area of coverage disputes has been the treatment of infertility, particularly in vitro fertilization (IVF). See, e.g., Egert v. Connecticut Gen. Life Ins. Co., 900 F.2d 1032 (7th Cir.1990) (held arbitrary for insurer in ASO role, but with a stake in issue in its other business, not to classify in vitro fertilization as "treatment" for an "illness"); Reilly v. Blue Cross and Blue Shield United, 846 F.2d 416 (7th Cir.), cert. denied, 488 U.S. 856 (1988) (held arbitrary for Blue plan, acting as third-party administrator of ERISA plan, to find in vitro fertilization an uncovered "experimental" procedure where court sensed conflict of interests); Ralston v. Connecticut Gen. Life Ins. Co., 625 So.2d 156 (La.1993) (remanding case for determination "whether such infertility is a sickness under the policy, whether in vitro fertilization is a treatment, and whether the treatment was necessary or essential"). See generally Annot., Coverage of Artificial Insemination Procedures or Other Infertility Treatments by Health, Sickness, or Hospitalization Insurance, 80 A.L.R.4th 1059 (1990). On the larger policy and insurance issues raised by IVF, see Neumann, Should Health Insurance Cover IVF? Issues and Options, 22 J. Health Pol., Pol'y & L. 1215 (1997); Note, In Vitro Fertilization: Insurance and Consumer Protection, 109 Harv. L. Rev. 2092 (1996).

7. *"Reasonable Expectations" in Prospective Determinations of Coverage.* Although courts might reasonably require insurers to honor the "reasonable expectations" of insureds who incur expenses on the advice of a trusted physician, the expectations of patients seeking prior authorization of coverage for a particular treatment, such as an arguably "experimental" procedure, may create weaker claims for coverage. For a variety of reasons, today's consumers expect a great deal from the health care system, perhaps more than some of them are willing to pay for. Thus, a judicial policy giving presumptive weight to their expectations in interpreting their contractual entitlements could misallocate resources. Can you see a specific reason why, counterintuitively, a court should not listen very sympathetically to a consumer's claim that he selected the health plan in question because he interpreted it as promising coverage of a service for which he or his dependent had a particular need?

Although there are a number of cases construing coverage prospectively in which the notion of medical necessity has been stretched very far or a contractual exclusion from coverage has been narrowly construed, many courts continue to respect contractual limitations. One source suggests that, at least where consumers elect the more limited coverage (as in a multiple-choice situation), policy exclusions are usually enforced. Abraham, Judge–Made Law and Judge–Made Insurance: Honoring the Reasonable Expectations of the Insured, 67 Va.L.Rev. 1151, 1155 (1981) ("In cases where such coverage is available [from other sources], the courts do not find a fictional expectation in order to create coverage where in fact it does not exist."). See also Marsh v. Reserve Life Ins. Co., 516 So.2d 1311, 1313–14 (La.App.1987): "Courts must give legal effect to the insurance policy provisions according to the true intent of the parties, which intent is determined by the words of the policy when these are clear and explicit and lead to no absurd consequences. * * * It is further well-established that insurers have the same right as individuals to limit their liability and impose whatever conditions they please in the absence of conflicts with laws or public policy."

8. How should courts go about interpreting health care contracts? In the *Phillips* case, would it be helpful to consider why limitations on coverage of "mental illness" are typically included in health plans? (Note that such limits are no longer permissible under the federal Kassebaum–Kennedy legislation, which prohibits differentiating in coverage limits between physical and mental illness.) Does the answer to this question give you some ideas about whether the term should have been construed to apply to James's condition?

PROBLEM ON THE ADMINISTRATION OF COVERAGE

Your firm's client is an IPA-model HMO that seeks to achieve a degree of economizing across the board by carefully defining and administering an efficient level of coverage and by avoiding spending on unproven technologies—both new ones still in an investigational stage and old ones that lack substantial support either in clinical research or among knowledgeable, cost-conscious practitioners. Because a health care contract can never define a precise boundary between all covered and all excluded services, however, the plan has begun to look for some other way to achieve consistency in defining and delivering on its contractual commitments in individual cases and to facilitate resistance to claims that it finds unreasonable. Although it regards reasonableness, evenhandedness, and efficiency in dispensing benefits as good business in any event, it also seeks to ensure that any dispute will be handled fairly enough that a court will not undertake to define the plan's obligations itself or to construe the contract de novo under generous principles of interpretation.

The best strategy, the plan has concluded, is to create in its contract with subscribers an exclusive procedure for interpreting the plan's standards and applying them in specific cases. To be sure, the federal HMO Act has long required that federally qualified HMOs maintain "meaningful procedures for hearing and resolving grievances." 42 U.S.C. § 300e(c)(5) (1994). And state legislation regulating HMOs and other managed-care plans typically includes similar requirements. (See § C of this chapter.) But merely complying with these regulatory requirements, the plan believes, will not be enough to protect it against the risk that a court will rewrite or creatively interpret its contracts. The plan has therefore asked its lawyers to come up with something better. Although the contract might simply declare the judgments of the plan itself or of a plan-sponsored committee to be final and binding, courts are not likely to be receptive to such an agreement. See, e.g., Franks v. Louisiana Health Servs. & Indem. Co., 382 So.2d 1064 (La.App.1980) (citing policy against "potestative" contracts—i.e., those in which one party's performance is discretionary—but only to impose on insurer a duty to refer matter to its own physician experts). Presumably, therefore, the procedure adopted must be designed to give effect to a real pre-existing commitment. It must also ensure enough accuracy, consistency, and fairness in the decisions reached that courts will allow the plan's decision-making apparatus to function within fairly wide limits and will resist calls to serve as the final arbiters of the contract's meaning.

In pursuit of these objectives, the plan's lawyers and medical personnel have developed a new subscriber contract and submitted it for your firm's review. You have been asked to consider and comment upon the following provisions, identifying the specific problems they attempt to solve and noting any practical or legal problems you anticipate if they are adopted:

§ X.2 RULES GOVERNING INTERPRETATION OF THE CONTRACT AND DISPUTES

§ X.2.1 *Your Acceptance of Coverage Determinations by the Plan's Medical Consultants*. You agree that interpretations of the coverage of this Contract by the Plan's medical consultants shall finally govern in any dispute, if such interpretations are not arbitrary or capricious. (The Plan's medical consultants are licensed physicians whose compensation by the Plan is determined independently of their decisions in particular cases.) Specifically, you agree that, even when this Contract is ambiguous or incomplete in not providing a clear rule to govern a situation that arises, the Plan's medical consultants shall interpret the Contract and determine the Plan's coverage in accordance with the definition of covered services in § ___. You also agree that determinations of coverage by the Plan's medical consultants shall be final and binding unless such consultants failed to follow reasonable procedures in eliciting the relevant facts and circumstances or unless their determination was clearly unreasonable in light of the Plan's contractual commitment. Your doctor can and should assist you in making sure that the Plan and its consultants are aware of all relevant facts concerning your condition.

§ X.2.2 *Dispute Resolution; Your Acceptance of Limitations on Your Right to Challenge Coverage Determinations in Court*. You agree that, if a dispute arises concerning an interpretation of this Contract or a determination of the Plan's coverage, that dispute will be submitted first for resolution through the Plan's grievance procedure described in Appendix ___. You further agree that, if you are not satisfied with the results of that procedure and wish to obtain further review, you will submit it, not to a court of law, but to the alternative dispute resolution process administered by the Private Adjudication Center, Inc. (a nonprofit affiliate of the Duke University School of Law, which has been selected as a reliable, independent, and efficient manager of disputes). Under that dispute resolution process, the arbiter of the dispute—

(a) will be selected under and will operate according to rules adopted by the Private Adjudication Center (which make due provision for expediting proceedings in cases requiring prompt action);

(b) will be charged only with determining whether the interpretation of the Plan's coverage by its medical consultants was arbitrary or capricious or otherwise failed to meet the standards stated in § X.2.1; and

(c) will have only limited powers, as follows:

(1) In a dispute over whether the Plan should pay for care yet to be rendered, the arbiter will be empowered only to require the Plan's consultants to reconsider and redecide the question (subject to further review as provided herein), not to order the Plan to cover the care in question.

(2) In any dispute in which it is alleged that the Plan or its providers failed to provide a service required under this Contract, the arbiter will be permitted to award money damages for personal or other injuries only if it finds that you had no reasonable opportunity to challenge the determination of the Plan's coverage prior to the alleged omission. Such money damages will be awarded, however, only if the arbiter finds that the alleged omission either violated specific standards established by the Plan or reflected an interpretation of the Plan's coverage that was arbitrary or capricious or otherwise failed to meet the standards stated in § X.2.1.

(3) In any dispute over a determination of the Plan's coverage, the arbiter may award punitive damages in a discretionary amount up to (but not exceeding) $100,000 if it finds that the Plan or its consultants not only acted arbitrarily and capriciously but were also guilty of gross negligence or bad faith.

(4) In any dispute in which the arbiter finds that it was clearly reasonable for you to pursue your alleged rights under this Contract, it shall order the Plan to pay up to (but not exceeding) $10,000 to cover actual expenses reasonably incurred by you in seeking a resolution of the dispute.

You further agree that the resolution of the dispute under the dispute resolution process described here shall be final and binding on you and that you will not seek to challenge the resolution in a court of law except for fraud or other impropriety on the part of the arbiter.

§ X.2.3 *Your Waiver of Certain Protective Rules Sometimes Used by Courts in Contract Interpretation*. You agree that this Contract shall be interpreted literally or, where it is ambiguous or incomplete, in accordance with its apparent or most probable intended meaning. Accordingly, you hereby expressly waive your right to have it interpreted under any of the special interpretive rules, more favorable to individual insureds, that courts sometimes employ in reading insurance contracts. This means, for example, that, in any dispute arising under this Contract, you or your lawyer will not be allowed to invoke, and the court or other arbiter will not apply, (*a*) the principle of *contra proferentem*, a legal doctrine under which ambiguous provisions are construed against the insurer, or (*b*) the principle of "reasonable expectations," under which insureds are sometimes granted coverage beyond that contemplated in the policy because they may have expected broader protection.

§ X.2.4 *Your Reasons for Accepting Restrictions on Your Legal Rights*. You acknowledge that your agreement to the foregoing rules governing the interpretation and enforcement of your legal rights and the resolution of disputes is given in order to facilitate the Plan's efforts to protect the Plan's reserves as a common fund to which you and other Plan subscribers must contribute periodically in amounts equal to its anticipated obligations and in consideration of (*a*) the agreement by other Plan subscribers to accept the same rules and (*b*) the lower Plan premiums that such agreements make possible.

See C. Havighurst, Health Care Choices: Private Contracts as Instruments of Health Reform 200–15 (1995) (setting forth foregoing draft provision, with commentary).

On procedural issues in benefits administration, see generally Kinney, Procedural Protections for Patients in Capitated Health Plans, 22 Am. J.L. & Med. 301 (1996) (reviewing procedural issues in both public and private health plans; expressing concern that "private ADR procedures are not always designed in ways that enhance the patient's power vis-a-vis the plan"); Stayn, Securing Access to Care in Health Maintenance Organizations: Toward a Uniform Model of Grievance and Appeal Procedures, 94 Colum. L. Rev. 1674 (1994) (detailed structural and practical comparison of grievance and appeal rights of Medicare beneficiaries enrolled in HMOs with rights of other HMO enrollees, concluding that the latter are not adequately protected and calling for uniform procedure including a Federal Health Plan Review Board, to be created by amending the federal HMO Act); Hall & Anderson, supra, at 1689–1709 (helpfully discussing procedural issues at length and proposing that health plan coverage decisions be subject to judicial review analogous to the review given by courts to the actions of public administrative agencies).

SECTION C: REGULATION OF MANAGED-CARE ORGANIZATIONS

NOTES AND QUESTIONS ON THE HISTORY AND NATURE OF HMO REGULATION

1. *The Federal Health Maintenance Organization Act of 1973.* Some history of this early initiative, which is codified as amended at 42 U.S.C.A. § 300e (West 1991 & Supp. 1997), was given in chapter 2(§C). The HMO Act represented an effort by the federal government to encourage the development of HMOs through a variety of measures, including the provision of financial subsidies. In order to enjoy the act's benefits, however, an HMO had to accept a number of requirements of a regulatory nature, many of which continue in effect today. See 42 C.F.R. § 417 (1997). In many respects, the HMO Act was an important early step in kicking off the modern health care revolution. The act, its evolution, and its contribution have been described as follows:

> Under this act, still in effect today although modified periodically over the past twenty years, HMOs had to provide basic health services for a periodic payment assessed without regard to the date, frequency, extent, or kind of services required. So defined, the HMO contrasted sharply with indemnity insurance and fee-for-service medicine that were still the rule in 1975. The basic services that HMOs had to provide in order to qualify under federal law included physician care, hospital inpatient and outpatient care, crisis intervention, treatment or referral for alcohol or addiction services, home health services, and preventive services. Supplemental health services such as podiatric care were also mandated when the act was first passed, although in 1976 these became optional.
>
> HMOs were not required to be federally qualified, but [many] sought this status because of a competitive advantage that was the result of two critical provisions. First, the act prohibited [i.e., preempted] all state laws or practices that served as barriers to the formation of ["federally qualified"] HMOs, regardless of whether there was a direct conflict with federal regulation or not. This prohibition included any state regulations requiring the approval of a medical society before an HMO could be licensed, provisions that physicians make up a certain percentage of an HMO's governing body, and insurance regulations concerning capitalization or financial reserves to prevent insolvency. States were also prohibited from regulating advertising by HMOs.
>
> In addition, federal law required a mandatory dual choice policy. Any employer with more than twenty-five employees and required by law to pay the minimum wage had to offer an HMO option as part of

its health benefits and could not charge less than was charged for indemnity insurance. This requirement meant that employers could not discriminate via payroll deductions or contributions against those who chose to receive coverage through an HMO rather than through a fee-for-service plan. The indemnity plan would provide a floor for HMO premiums. Employers were originally forced to offer the HMO option if there was a federally qualified HMO in their area, but in 1976 the act was modified so that an HMO had to request that it become part of an employer's health plan.

Before 1973, many state laws had enforced a ban on the corporate practice of medicine (employment of physicians by corporate entities). This stymied HMO development in many jurisdictions. Moreover, benefits managers simply were not used to offering the managed care organization as an option. The 1973 legislation therefore opened the door for HMO development and ensured that there would be a niche for them in the marketplace.

Perhaps more significantly, the HMO Act was an example of regulation that modified the peculiar medical care market so as to allow a more socially optimal delivery system to emerge. * * *

The legislation slowly evolved. As already mentioned, amendments in 1976 made availability of supplemental services optional. To encourage existing health care plans to move to an HMO status, a forty-eight-month phase-in period for community rating (rating premiums based on the health of communities, not individuals) was offered for plans already offering prepaid health services. It is notable that the federal legislation has consistently maintained that HMOs must "community rate" patient premiums, with only certain modifications available.

In 1978, in order to maintain the integrity of HMOs by encouraging an exclusive and responsive staff, contracts with physicians were limited by law to those physicians already in an independent practice association (IPA) or medical group. To accommodate the growing variation in HMOs and promote the development of point-of-service plans (managed care plans in which enrolled patients may opt to receive care from an out-of-plan physician, usually at an additional cost), Congress allowed HMOs to impose a reasonable deductible when members obtained a basic service from a physician who was not a member of a staff IPA or a group HMO plan. However, 90 percent of services still had to be provided by an affiliated physician.

In the past decade, Congress (and Republican administrations) have acknowledged that HMOs are ready to compete in the marketplace and have removed some of the advantageous protections given to them under the 1973 legislation. In 1983, Congress decided that it was no longer necessary to provide loans to HMOs. More important, amendments required that the attractive dual choice provisions be eliminated by 1995 and relaxed the equal contribution requirement that obliged an employer to make the same financial contribution to an HMO as would be made to a traditional health plan.

> Federal preemption of state laws provided a rich culture for the growth of HMOs. The preemptive effect of the federal HMO Act of 1973 has been challenged several times, but courts have largely deferred to the federal government's grant of authority. The only exceptions are those cases in which state courts have sought to coordinate benefits with other state programs, thereby limiting the applicability of the HMO Act.

T. Brennan & D. Berwick, New Rules: Regulation, Markets, and the Quality of American Health Care 152–54 (1995).

As noted in chapter 2(§C), some commentators have questioned whether the HMO Act materially helped the growth of HMOs. Although the act conferred certain advantages, its regulatory requirements increased plan costs and eventually had to be relaxed to enable federally qualified HMOs to compete more effectively with conventional health coverage. Other requirements were also modified in later years to reflect market realities and to permit HMOs more competitive freedom. (Can you explain the probable rationale for some the particular modifications reported by Brennan and Berwick? For example, why did Congress remove the requirement that employers make equal contributions for employees choosing HMOs over other forms of coverage?) HMOs still have the option of foregoing federal qualification, and many plans, especially smaller ones, are subject to state regulation alone.

2. *State HMO Legislation*. Beginning even before Congress felt it necessary to override specific state laws restricting HMO development, states began to pass HMO enabling acts. Many of the current statutes resemble model legislation adopted by the National Association of Insurance Commissioners (NAIC). NAIC, Health Maintenance Organization Model Act (1991), reprinted in M. Hall & W. Brewbaker, eds., Managed Care 1–126 to 1–179 (Health Care Corporate Law series, 1996). All states have explicit HMO enabling legislation today except Oregon and Wisconsin, which permit HMOs to be organized under other statutes. Operation under these laws typically requires a certificate of authority from the state insurance department. Definitions of "HMO" are quite broad, and only a few states (most notably, Minnesota) make any appreciable distinction between nonprofit and for-profit plans. The following paragraphs discuss several features of state HMO laws as they evolved in the 1970s and 1980s. See generally Garvin, Health Maintenance Organizations, in Hall & Brewbaker, supra, at § 1.5.

3. *Corporate Practice*. As noted in chapter 3(§C), a key reason for enacting state HMO acts was to create an exception to the (usually) implicit prohibition of the corporate practice of medicine. Many state laws declare that an HMO shall not be deemed to be engaged in the practice of medicine, inviting the argument (adverted to in § A of this chapter) that the HMO cannot be held legally responsible for the care provided. Most statutes expressly authorize HMOs to employ physicians or to provide health services either directly or through arrangements with others.

4. *Mandated Benefits*. State HMO acts typically include a recitation of basic health services that HMOs must provide—including preventive services, which were early touted as a particular strength of HMOs. In addition, a smaller number of states also mandate coverage of such other services as mental health and substance abuse care, home health care, certain organ transplants (including ABMT), treatment of jaw disorders, infertility treatment, and post-mastectomy breast reconstruction. Many of these mandates appear in laws applicable to health insurers as well as to HMOs and reflect lobbying by provider interests as well as interested consumer groups.

Under ERISA, of course, state benefit mandates cannot be applied to self-insured employee benefit plans. In Metropolitan Life Ins. Co. v. Massachusetts, 471 U.S. 724 (1985), however, a state's mandate to insurers to cover mental health needs was held to constitute insurance regulation not preempted by ERISA (due to the so-called "saving clause"). Although this holding means that state law may prescribe the coverage offered by conventional health insurers, does it also mean that states can prescribe HMO benefit packages? In other words, can a state prevent a multi-state employer from obtaining uniform coverage for its employees through state-regulated, risk-bearing HMOs? In Washington Physicians Service Ass'n v. Gregoire, 1998 WL 318759 (9th Cir. 1998), the court upheld, under ERISA, a "mandated-provider" statute in the State of Washington requiring health insurers and HMOs to cover the services of "every category of health care provider," including naturopaths, chiropractors, etc. Noting that the statute "does not force any carrier to contract with any particular provider" (that is, does not preclude selective contracting with providers of each kind), the court held that the statute did not "relate to" ERISA plans and that, even if it did, it would be saved from preemption by ERISA's "saving clause." Summarizing the effect of its holding, the court stated as follows (id. at *3, *4):

> Thus, if ABC Corp. wishes to offer its employees health insurance by purchasing an HMO plan, it will find that all of the options available to it in the market cover alternative medicine because it is simply not legal for an HMO to offer any other kind of plan. By contrast, if ABC Corp. were itself the health self-insurer for its employees, the Act would not apply at all, and ABC Corp. could structure its benefits in any way it chose. Accordingly, the Act does not operate directly on the ERISA plan, but only indirectly by limiting the options available in the market—if the plan should choose to purchase health insurance on the market, rather than providing it itself or not providing it at all.
>
> * * * After *Travelers*, ERISA plans no longer have a Midas touch that allows them to deregulate every product they choose to buy as part of their employee benefit plan.

Is there a principled policy basis for substituting public regulation for marketplace determinations of the scope of health insurance or health plan coverage? When coverage is purchased on a group basis and not by individuals, persons desiring coverage of particular services (or the services of particular providers) may not be able to get it, suggesting that regulation may be justified to compensate for majoritarian influences in employment groups. In what direction, however, do concerns about costs, moral hazard, and adverse selection point?

The policy issues raised by benefit mandates are identified in a 1997 Washington statute, which, like a 1984 predecessor, is similar in its intent to other "mandate awareness" bills passed in at least 22 other states, mostly in 1989–90:

> The legislature finds that there is a continued interest in mandating certain health coverages or offering of health coverages by health carriers; and that improved access to these health care services to segments of the population which desire them can provide beneficial social and health consequences which may be in the public interest.
>
> The legislature finds further, however, that the cost ramifications of expanding health coverages is of continuing concern; and that the merits of a particular mandated benefit must be balanced against a variety of consequences which may go far beyond the immediate impact upon the cost of insurance coverage. The legislature hereby finds and declares that a systematic review of proposed mandated benefits, which explores all the ramifications of such proposed legislation, will assist the legislature in determining whether mandating a particular coverage or offering is in the public interest. The purpose of this chapter is to establish a procedure for the proposal, review, and determination of mandated benefit necessity.

Wash. Rev. Code Ann. § 48.47.005 (Supp. 1998). The statute goes on to require proponents of such legislation to submit a report discussing the "social" and "financial impact" of the proposal and reporting evidence, if any, of the efficacy of the service to be made the subject of a mandate. Id. §§ 48.47.010–.030. Some states have provided for waivers of mandates to facilitate the offering of low-cost coverage to small employers. See generally Jensen, Regulating the Content of Health Plans, in R. Helms, ed., American Health Policy: Critical Issues for Reform 167 (1993).

5. *Quality of Care*. The NAIC Model Act, adopted at least in part in many states, requires that HMOs establish procedures to ensure that enrollees receive care meeting "reasonable standards of quality of care consistent with prevailing professionally recognized standards of medical practice." The quality-assurance program must include peer review activities. Although the Model Act contemplates delegating oversight of quality matters to an appropriate state health official, many states entrust HMO regulation only to the insurance commissioner, whose ability to address quality-related issues would seem open to question. In general, there is little uniformity in the nature or intensity of special state efforts to verify and enhance the quality of care rendered to HMO enrollees.

6. *Consumer Protection*. Among the various consumer protections appearing in early state HMO laws were requirements that HMOs demonstrate

that their arrangements with providers were sufficient to allow them to meet their obligations—that is, that they had the capacity, either through employees or independent contractors, to meet the expected demand for services. Most state insurance departments were also required to obtain assurances concerning the methods each HMO employed in managing utilization and controlling costs. Certain requirements concerning the plan's subscriber contracts were also usually included in early HMO legislation. The typical statute also provided for limited oversight of HMO charges, requiring actuarial soundness and also generally prohibiting charges that are excessive or unfairly discriminatory.

In varying degrees, states have been concerned about information asymmetries in health care, about the accuracy and comparability of marketing information provided by HMOs to prospective enrollees, and about abuses in marketing some plans. Consequently, most states have required that HMOs provide standard information to all subscribers on available services and highlight the circumstances under which subscribers might be denied coverage or have to pay for services themselves. The vices of marketing methods have been detailed by public-interest groups, particularly in the context of plans that are marketed, not to employers in the first instance, but directly to individuals, particularly the elderly and the poor. Special disclosure and marketing requirements for Medicare + Choice and Medicaid plans are provided in the federal Social Security Act, and the states likewise deal separately with the marketing of HMOs to Medicaid recipients.

7. *Grievance Procedures*. As noted in the problem just preceding this section, the states have, from the beginning of HMO regulation, required that plans maintain a procedure for dealing with consumer complaints. Many states follow requirements proposed in NAIC, Health Carrier Grievance Procedure Act §§ 4–6 (1997). Generally, organizations are required to develop their own methods and criteria for adjudicating disputes. It is common for states to specify that accelerated adjudication must be available when the patient requires urgent treatment. E.g., N.Y. Public Health Law § 4408–a (McKinney 1986 & Supp. 1997); Wis. Stat. § 609.5 (West 1989 & Supp. 1997). As noted below, this is an area in which requirements have recently been strengthened.

8. *Solvency; Capital Requirements*. A primary concern in early state HMO acts was, of course, the solvency and financial stability of plans. Should the states regulate the financial condition of HMOs in precisely the same manner in which they regulate health insurers? State insurance commissioners sought to regulate the rates and other features of early prepaid group practices on the theory that they were engaged in the business of insurance. In the leading case of Jordan v. Group Health Ass'n, 107 F.2d 239 (D.C.Cir.1939), an HMO was held not to be an insurer under District of Columbia legislation because it provided its benefits in kind rather than in cash. Can you see how this feature might obviate regulation as an insurer? Note that a plan's financial stability and provision for insolvency are still matters of legitimate public concern. When an HMO or other managed-care entity is appropriately deemed to be an insurer is a question that arises in many different contexts (e.g., under ERISA's saving clause).

How do HMOs differ from traditional "service-benefit" prepayment plans, such as those long offered exclusively by Blue Cross and Blue Shield? These plans, which were usually set up under special state enabling acts subjecting them to special regulation by the state insurance department, also provided services through contracting hospitals or physicians. Unlike the situation in HMOs, however, patients had no contractual right to receive service, only a right to have the plan cover the cost of services received. Under the plan's arrangements with providers, the latter (rather than the corporation) bore some of the risk that premiums would prove insufficient to pay the full cost of care. See California Physicians' Service v. Garrison, 28 Cal.2d 790, 172 P.2d 4 (1946) (early service-benefit plan held not subject to insurance regulation because providers bore the risk). In which plans—HMOs or traditional Blue plans—may consumers be more at risk? See chapter 9(§A) for discussion of the application of insurance regulation to risk-bearing provider networks.

Under state HMO acts, HMOs are subject to special financial oversight by state insurance regulators, whose primary concern is to ensure the plans' solvency and financial reliability. A fairly typical HMO act enacted in Alabama in 1986, Ala. Code §§ 27–21A–1 to 32 (1986 & Supp. 1997), requires HMOs to participate in a state-sponsored guaranty fund, which is intended to protect enrollees in the event of insolvency or impairment. The statute also has provisions for working capital and capital reserves and for other protections against insolvency, including permission for the HMO to purchase stop-loss coverage or reinsurance. Provider contracts in Alabama are required to include a hold-harmless clause, protecting HMO enrollees from liability to providers for fees and charges if the plan, due to insolvency or otherwise, should fail to pay them.

Many states strengthened their solvency requirements in the late 1980s in the wake of some widely publicized HMO bankruptcies. Maryland, for instance, now demands that new HMOs have an initial surplus, exceeding its liabilities, of at least $1.5 million, Md. Code Ann. § 19–710 (Michie 1996 & Supp. 1997); moreover, once operating, a Maryland HMO must maintain a surplus equal to the lesser of 5% of annual subscription income or $3 million. Many states allow their non-federally qualified HMOs to utilize experience rating, reducing the risk that their solvency will be threatened by adverse selection.

9. *Certificate-of-Need Regulation*. The interesting experience of HMOs under state CON laws was noted at the end of chapter 5(§D). About half the states still have CON laws that apply in some respect to HMOs.

10. *ERISA*. Recall earlier discussions of ERISA—e.g., chapter 1(§B) and earlier references in this chapter—and the fact that it preempts state regulation that directly impacts employee benefit plans. To be sure, states may regulate HMOs as entire entities (e.g., prescribing structural features and measures to ensure solvency) under the "saving clause" that preserves state regulation of the business of insurance. But, as suggested above in discussing mandated benefits, state law may be preempted when it has the effect of prescribing the benefits an employer must purchase. Likewise, ERISA appears to bar states from directly impinging upon the administration of employee health benefits. (Thus, state claims for negligence in the determination of coverage are apparently blocked under the principle of the *Corcoran* case; likewise, ERISA would appear to preempt state remedies for corporate negligence in an HMO's selection or monitoring of its physicians.)

Despite ERISA, state law effectively governs, as a practical matter, most employee benefits obtained through HMOs, simply because most employers elect to purchase the HMO's regular (regulated) offering rather than attempting to negotiate a customized package of employee benefits. In your view, however, could a multi-state employer make a special arrangement with a multi-state HMO (or several local HMOs) under which all of its employees would receive identical benefits prescribed by it rather than by state law, would be treated by networks of providers selected without regard to state requirements (other than licensure), and would have fewer, or different, procedural protections than state law requires the plan to confer on its other customers?

11. *Backlash Against Managed Care*. Throughout the 1980s, HMOs enjoyed something of a honeymoon with employers and consumers, as well as with investors. Although occasional problems appeared, both the cost savings enjoyed by employers and consumers and booming HMO stock prices generally obscured the tensions inherent in the concept of managed care. Managed care began to come under increasing scrutiny in the 1990s, however, as the media began to publicize anecdotes that were both newsworthy and indicative of possible larger problems. Organized providers, invoking values anchored in the old paradigm of medical care, opportunistically took up the cry against managed care. Ultimately, the managed-care industry became the target of a full-blown public backlash, which led inevitably to increased activity on the legislative/regulatory front.

The honeymoon-is-over experience of the public and the managed-care industry was predictable. It was inevitable, after all, that health plans and the public, following their early romance, would eventually come face-to-face with the hard—and potentially divisive—realities of health care economics. Initially, of course, trimming health care costs was easy, and both consumers and investors could enjoy substantial windfalls gained either at the expense of providers or by eliminating health services of no marginal benefit. But people quickly came to take MCOs' cost-saving accomplishments for granted, asking only what managed care had done for them lately. And, as the price gap between traditional and managed-care coverage widened, more and more consumers selected, or were forced into, a managed-care plan solely on the basis of its lower price without realizing or accepting the limitations it would place on their treatment options. Although managed care managed to bring health care's share of GDP to a stable 13.6% for four straight years from 1993 to 1996, that stability was harder to maintain each passing year as costly new technologies and treatment options continued to appear and costs could be kept in line with GDP only by rationing access to some of them. Increasingly, cost battles were being fought in the benefit/cost no man's land, not on the "flat of the curve," increasing the public's fear that economizing meant denying them their entitlements. The media naturally played on this fear, focusing public attention on both real and imagined abuses in the managed-care world and on the seeming contradictions of managed care itself. Partly because ERISA bars claims for errors in benefit administration (and also because of the situation described in § A of this chapter), the public came increasingly to perceive significant gaps in the accountability of managed-care plans for the quality of the care received by their enrollees.

Beginning around 1995, state legislatures began to reflect the public's new concerns about managed care. By one count, some 400 bills to regulate various features of the industry were introduced in state legislatures in the first six months of 1996. Labeled "patient-rights" and "patient-protection" acts by their proponents (often organized medicine), these bill were called "anti-managed care" bills by others. Some of the features of the recent proposals and reforms will be examined below, and you will be asked to consider whether they intrude too far into the making of clinical and economic choices and which of them has a solid policy rationale, rather than a merely plausible one. See generally Miller, Managed Care Regulation: In the Laboratory of the States, 278 J.A.M.A. 1102 (1997); Rodwin, Consumer Protection and Managed Care: Issues, Reform Proposals, and Trade-offs, 32 Hous. L. Rev. 1319 (1996).

12. *Private Accreditation; Self-Regulation.* Partly to increase consumer confidence in managed care and partly to ward off public regulation, the managed-care industry has submitted to private accrediting. The National Committee for Quality Assurance (NCQA) was originally created in 1979 by the leading industry trade groups, the Group Health Association of America (GHAA) and the American Managed Care and Review Association (AMCRA), but became independent in 1990—with a board including employer representatives and experts on quality issues as well as industry representatives. NCQA accrediting covers all types of HMO (but not PPOs), relies heavily on the data set known as HEDIS, and focuses on six areas: preventive services; records; utilization management; enrollee rights; credentialing of providers; and quality improvement activities (including, it is claimed, the approach known as Continuous Quality Improvement). NCQA is also interested in issuing so-called "report cards," permitting comparative evaluation of health plans. See generally Brennan & Berwick, supra, at 159–62.

The JCAHO also accredits HMOs, leading some to question whether overlapping accreditation is wasteful. Should this "duplication of effort" be eliminated? Should government accept private accreditation as a substitute for public inspections? To be sure, the methodology for evaluating HMOs and other MCOs is imperfect. Is it reasonable to expect, however, that competition among accreditors will stimulate improvement and a greater flow of reliable information to purchasers of managed care?

Another initiative the managed-care industry was the adoption in 1997 by the American Association of Health Plans (AAHP)—the new trade association formed by a merger of GHAA and AMCRA—of a program labeled "Putting Patients First." See Jones, "Putting Patients First": A Philosophy in Practice, Health Affs., Nov.-Dec. 1997, p. 115. Under this program, all AAHP members are expected to conform to certain principles, so that AAHP membership can be taken by employers and consumers as a sign of consumer-friendliness. What questions might you ask about this program? Are you reassured by Jones's observations that the AAHP, as a "partnership" and "community of health plans," possesses the "leverage" needed to make the industry as a whole "accountable for constantly adhering to high standards of quality and service," to realize the industry's commitment to quality improvement "across the board," and to ensure that consumers all obtain "the right care, at the right time, and in the right setting"? (Recall that organized medicine, in justifying its earlier stewardship of American health care, always claimed that it was "putting patients first.")

13. *Federal Regulation*? Inevitably, political interest in regulating managed care spread to Washington. Federal officials and legislators not only came to recognize the degree to which ERISA frustrates state regulation of managed care, but many of them were as concerned as their counterparts in state capitals about what they saw as the potential abuses of managed care. The result was a welter of new federal proposals in the 105th Congress to regulate managed care more extensively than ever before. The executive branch's effort to provide a foundation for managed care regulation resulted in a "consumer bill of rights," reproduced below, which was promptly translated into a number of bills to implement its vision. Other proposals contemplated even more extensive regulation. Indeed, some mainstream Republicans proposed sweeping regulatory reforms aimed at the managed-care field. E.g., H.R. 1415, 105th Cong., 1st Sess. (1997) (proposed Patient Access to Responsible Care Act of 1997, sponsored by Rep. Norwood). Urgency about regulating managed care at the federal level had come to encompass more than just those plans enrolling Medicare and Medicaid patients.

Although the respective roles of federal and state regulation of managed care had yet to be determined at this writing, the likelihood of federal action seemed fairly strong:

> From the managed care industry side, a growing (if until now highly private) consensus is emerging that at the end of the day, federal regulation may not be all that bad—provided that it conveys the benefits of federal preemption of diverse state efforts to regulate the same matters. Whereas most managed care entities are inherently local in character, the companies that own them have become increasingly regional—even national—in scale and find themselves having to contend with these issues in dozens of different statehouses around the country. In many of these states, key provider groups have far more political clout than a coalition of "out-of-town gunslinger" HMO com-

panies has. Given the emerging legislative and regulatory track record in the states, an increasing number of managed care industry executives are wondering whether it would not be better to take their chances before the Republican Congress.

Moran, Federal Regulation of Managed Care: An Impulse in Search of a Theory?, Health Affs., Nov.-Dec. 1997, p. 7, 9–10. See also Brennan & Berwick, supra, ch. 5.

Protecting Consumers in the Age of Managed Care

Advisory Commission on Consumer Protection and Quality in the Health Care Industry, Consumer Bill of Rights and Responsibilities

Report to the President of the United States.
November 1997.

EXECUTIVE SUMMARY

The Advisory Commission on Consumer Protection and Quality in the Health Care Industry was appointed by President Clinton on March 26, 1997, to "advise the President on changes occurring in the health care system and recommend measures as may be necessary to promote and assure health care quality and value, and protect consumers and workers in the health care system." As part of its work, the President asked the Commission to draft a "consumer bill of rights" [which the Commission summarized as follows]:

I. Information Disclosure

Consumers have the right to receive accurate, easily understood information and some require assistance in making informed health care decisions about their health plans, professionals, and facilities.

This information should include:

- **Health plans:** Covered benefits, cost-sharing, and procedures for resolving complaints; licensure, certification, and accreditation status; comparable measures of quality and consumer satisfaction; provider network composition; the procedures that govern access to specialists and emergency services; and care management information.
- **Health professionals:** Education and board certification and recertification; years of practice; experience performing certain procedures; and comparable measures of quality and consumer satisfaction.
- **Health care facilities:** Experience in performing certain procedures and services; accreditation status; comparable measures of quality and worker and consumer satisfaction; procedures for resolving complaints; and community benefits provided.

Consumer assistance programs must be carefully structured to promote consumer confidence and to work cooperatively with health plans, providers, payers and regulators. Sponsorship that ensures accountability to the interests of consumers and stable, adequate funding are desirable characteristics of such programs.

II. Choice of Providers and Plans

Consumers have the right to a choice of health care providers that is sufficient to ensure access to appropriate high-quality health care.

To ensure such choice, health plans should provide the following:

Provider Network Adequacy: All health plan networks should provide access to sufficient numbers and types of providers to assure that all covered services will be accessible without unreasonable delay—including access to emergency services 24 hours a day and seven days a week. If a health plan has an insufficient number or type of providers to provide a covered benefit with the appropriate degree of specialization, the plan should ensure that the consumer obtains the benefit outside the network at no greater cost than if the benefit were obtained from participating providers. Plans also should establish and maintain adequate arrangements to ensure reasonable proximity of providers to the business or personal residence of their members.

Access to Qualified Specialists for Women's Health Services: Women should be able to choose a qualified provider offered by a plan—such as gynecologists, certified nurse midwives, and other qualified health care providers—for the provision of covered care necessary to provide routine and preventative women's health care services.

Access to Specialists: Consumers with complex or serious medical conditions who require frequent specialty care should have direct access to a qualified specialist of their choice within a plan's network of providers. Authorizations, when required, should be for an adequate number of direct access visits under an approved treatment plan.

Transitional Care: Consumers who are undergoing a course of treatment for a chronic or disabling condition (or who are in the second or third trimester of a pregnancy) at the time they involuntarily change health plans or at a time when a provider is terminated by a plan for other than cause should be able to continue seeing their current specialty providers for up to 90 days (or through completion of postpartum care) to allow for transition of care. Providers who continue to treat such patients must accept the plan's rates as payment in full, provide all necessary information to the plan for quality assurance purposes, and promptly transfer all medical records with patient authorization during the transition period.

Public and private group purchasers should, wherever feasible, offer consumers a choice of high-quality health insurance products. Small employers should be provided with greater assistance in offering their workers and their families a choice of health plans and products.

III. Access to Emergency Services

Consumers have the right to access emergency health care services when and where the need arises. Health plans should provide payment when a consumer presents to an emergency department with acute symptoms of sufficient severity—including severe pain—such that a "prudent layperson" could reasonably expect the absence of medical attention to result in placing that consumer's health in serious jeopardy, serious impairment to bodily functions, or serious dysfunction of any bodily organ or part.

To ensure this right:

- Health plans should educate their members about the availability, location, and appropriate use of emergency and other medical services; cost-sharing provisions for emergency services; and the availability of care outside an emergency department.
- Health plans using a defined network of providers should cover emergency department screening and stabilization services both in network and out of network without prior authorization for use consistent with the prudent layperson standard. Non-network providers and facilities should not bill patients for any charges in excess of health plans' routine payment arrangements.
- Emergency department personnel should contact a patient's primary care provider or health plan, as appropriate, as quickly as possible to discuss follow-up and post-stabilization care and promote continuity of care.

IV. Participation in Treatment Decisions

Consumers have the right and responsibility to fully participate in all decisions related to their health care. Consumers who are unable to fully participate in treatment decisions have the right to be represented by parents, guardians, family members, or other conservators.

In order to ensure consumers' right and ability to participate in treatment decisions, physicians and other health care professionals should:

- Provide patients with sufficient information and opportunity to decide among treatment options consistent with the informed consent process. Specifically,
    - Discuss all treatment options with a patient in a culturally competent manner, including the option of no treatment at all.
    - Ensure that persons with disabilities have effective communications with members of the health system in making such decisions.
    - Discuss all current treatments a consumer may be undergoing, including those alternative treatments that are self-administered.
    - Discuss all risks, benefits, and consequences to treatment or nontreatment.

- Give patients the opportunity to refuse treatment and to express preferences about future treatment decisions.
- Discuss the use of advance directives—both living wills and durable powers of attorney for health care—with patients and their designated family members.
- Abide by the decisions made by their patients and/or their designated representatives consistent with the informed consent process.

To facilitate greater communication between patients and providers, health care providers, facilities, and plans should:

- Disclose to consumers factors—such as methods of compensation, ownership of or interest in health care facilities, or matters of conscience—that they know or should have known could influence advice or treatment decisions.
- Ensure that provider contracts do not contain any so-called "gag clauses" or other contractual mechanisms that restrict health care providers' ability to communicate with and advise patients about medically necessary treatment options.
- Be prohibited from penalizing or seeking retribution against health care professionals or other health workers for advocating on behalf of their patients.

V. Respect and Nondiscrimination

Consumers have the right to considerate, respectful care from all members of the health care system at all times and under all circumstances. An environment of mutual respect is essential to maintain a quality health care system.

Consumers must not be discriminated against in the delivery of health care services consistent with the benefits covered in their policy or as required by law based on race, ethnicity, national origin, religion, sex, age, mental or physical disability, sexual orientation, genetic information, or source of payment.

Consumers who are eligible for coverage under the terms and conditions of a health plan or program or as required by law must not be discriminated against in marketing and enrollment practices based on race, ethnicity, national origin, religion, sex, age, mental or physical disability, sexual orientation, genetic information, or source of payment.

VI. Confidentiality of Health Information

Consumers have the right to communicate with health care providers in confidence and to have the confidentiality of their individually identifiable health care information protected. Consumers also have the right to review and copy their own medical records and request amendments to their records.

In order to ensure this right:

- With very few exceptions, individually identifiable health care information can be used without written consent for health purposes only, including the provision of health care, payment for services, peer review, health promotion, disease management, and quality assurance.
- In addition, disclosure of individually identifiable health care information without written consent should be permitted in very limited circumstances where there is a clear legal basis for doing so. Such reasons include: medical or health care research for which a institutional review board has determined anonymous records will not suffice, investigation of health care fraud, and public health reporting.
- To the maximum feasible extent in all situations, nonidentifiable health care information should be used unless the individual has consented to the disclosure of individually identifiable information. When disclosure is required, no greater amount of information should be disclosed than is necessary to achieve the specific purpose of the disclosure.

VII. Complaints and Appeals

All consumers have the right to a fair and efficient process for resolving differences with their health plans, health care providers, and the institutions that serve them, including a rigorous system of internal review and an independent system of external review.

Internal appeals systems should include:

- Timely written notification of a decision to deny, reduce, or terminate services or deny payment for services. Such notification should include an explanation of the reasons for the decisions and the procedures available for appealing them.
- Resolution of all appeals in a timely manner with expedited consideration for decisions involving emergency or urgent care consistent with time frames consistent with those required by Medicare (i.e., 72 hours).
- A claim review process conducted by health care professionals who are appropriately credentialed with respect to the treatment involved. Reviews should be conducted by individuals who were not involved in the initial decision.
- Written notification of the final determination by the plan of an internal appeal that includes information on the reason for the determination and how a consumer can appeal that decision to an external entity.
- Reasonable processes for resolving consumer complaints about such issues as waiting times, operating hours, the demeanor of health care personnel, and the adequacy of facilities.

External appeals systems should:

- Be available only after consumers have exhausted all internal processes (except in cases of urgently needed care).

- Apply to any decision by a health plan to deny, reduce, or terminate coverage or deny payment for services based on a determination that the treatment is either experimental or investigational in nature.
- Apply when such a decision is based on a determination that such services are not medically necessary and the amount exceeds a significant threshold or the patient's life or health is jeopardized.[1]
- Be conducted by health care professionals who are appropriately credentialed with respect to the treatment involved and subject to conflict-of-interest prohibitions. * * *
- Follow a standard of review that promotes evidence-based decisionmaking and relies on objective evidence.
- Resolve all appeals in a timely manner * * *.

VIII. Consumer Responsibilities

In a health care system that protects consumers' rights, it is reasonable to expect and encourage consumers to assume reasonable responsibilities. Greater individual involvement by consumers in their care increases the likelihood of achieving the best outcomes and helps support a quality improvement, cost-conscious environment.

Such responsibilities include:

- Take responsibility for maximizing healthy habits, such as exercising, not smoking, and eating a healthy diet.
- Become involved in specific health care decisions. Work collaboratively with health care providers in developing and carrying out agreed-upon treatment plans.
- Disclose relevant information and clearly communicate wants and needs.
- Use the health plan's internal complaint and appeal processes to address concerns that may arise.
- Avoid knowingly spreading disease.
- Recognize the reality of risks and limits of the science of medical care and the human fallibility of the health care professional.
- Be aware of a health care provider's obligation to be reasonably efficient and equitable in providing care to other patients and the community.
- Become knowledgeable about his or her health plan coverage and health plan options (when available) including all covered benefits, limitations, and exclusions, rules regarding use of network providers, coverage and referral rules, appropriate processes to secure additional information, and the process to appeal coverage decisions.
- Show respect for other patients and health workers.

1. The right to external appeals does not apply to denials, reductions, or terminations of coverage or denials of payment for services that are specifically excluded from the consumer's coverage as established by contract.

- Make a good-faith effort to meet financial obligations.
- Abide by administrative and operational procedures of health plans, health care providers, and Government health benefit programs.
- Report wrongdoing and fraud to appropriate resources or legal authorities.

NOTES AND QUESTIONS ON NEW TRENDS IN REGULATING MANAGED CARE

1. *Finding a Rationale for Managed–Care Regulation.* Consider the following discussion of the new interest in regulating MCOs:

> While the impulse toward federal regulation of the managed care industry is clear, what is far less clear is the theory of regulation under which the federal government might produce a coherent regulatory scheme. Although forceful arguments have been made to support specific regulatory interventions, no advocate of federal regulation has laid out a framework that permits us to see where federal regulation of the health benefits industry may ultimately lead.
>
> This state of affairs is unusual. Advocates of regulation in most industries bend over backward to justify regulatory interventions by appealing to a comprehensive theory of regulation. The rationale typically proceeds from a diagnosis of "market failure"—that is, that the unfettered free market, left to its own devices, would produce socially suboptimal results because of specific structural flaws in the way the market works. The regulatory regime being advanced is then typically characterized as the lowest-cost intervention in the marketplace sufficient to remedy the identified defects and produce results closer to the desired optimal outcome.
>
> In the electric utility industry, for example, the case for regulation has historically been premised on the assumption that there are "increasing returns to scale" in the generation and distribution businesses that create a natural tendency toward monopoly. * * *
>
> The theory of environmental regulation is typically built around the idea of "negative externalities." * * *
>
> In the current debate over federal regulation of the managed care industry, by contrast, we have yet to hear from regulatory advocates how the specific regulatory activities being advanced fit into any context for which a coherent rationale has been advanced. * * *
>
> Market Failure In Health Care: A Moving Target?
>
> For most of the postwar era, federal intervention in the health care industry has been routinely justified by the well-known aphorism that "markets don't work in health care." Four aspects of health care market performance [information problems; health insurance, including moral hazard; supplier-induced demand; and concerns about the

uninsured] have been most commonly cited as defects requiring active remediation.

* * *

These four factors, taken together, can be seen to inform the great majority of postwar federal regulatory efforts in health care. Policy proceeded from the presumption that there was an inherent inflationary bias in the structure of the U.S. health care system that inevitably would frustrate the normal role of market forces in balancing supply and demand, while at the same time leaving an unacceptably large number of Americans uninsured.

The rapid growth and diffusion of managed care plans, however, has called this presumption into question. Managed care benefit designs are a market-based response to many of the perceived market deficiencies just described. In the managed care business model, a new actor—the medical management structure of the health plan—is superimposed on a selected portion of the health care delivery system. In effect, the medical management structure of the health plan is a mechanism designed to overcome the historic information imbalances in health care. * * *

In medical management systems, independent judgments about the medical necessity of various clinical practices are developed to use as benchmarks against which to examine the level of provision that prevailed in the old order. Operating within a framework of voluntary private contracts, health plans are empowered to manage away many of the previously cost-increasing forces in the system. These management techniques, in actual operation, act to negate the historic effects of third-party insurance by providing a private regulatory check on health plans' willingness to pay for services that providers would otherwise want to deliver.

Whatever one thinks of these efforts, they appear to work as intended. Although patients and providers increasingly complain about the intrusion of managed care into the physician/patient relationship, service use is being restrained. The decelerating trend in health care growth over the past few years, whatever its sustainability, suggests that something fundamentally different is going on in the system.

New Concerns About Managed Care

Although many concerns about the cost-increasing tendencies of the health care system appear to have been addressed by managed care, cost containment is not costless. Even as payers' concerns about cost trends have been mitigated, they have been replaced with new concerns about the emerging operation of the marketplace.

* * * Based on our experience in most other markets, we might expect competing health plans to view consumer dissatisfaction as a business opportunity to be exploited with new products and programs aimed directly at the concerns of disgruntled buyers. Consider, for example, the "drive-through delivery" controversy. [See the problem at

the end of chapter 1(§A)—Eds.] Within days after the public firestorm hit the covers of the national newsweeklies, a substantial number of health plans had revised or clarified their policies regarding maternity length-of-stay and were actively advertising that fact. Their competitors quickly followed, so that the various legislative efforts that were promulgated to remedy this problem appeared well after the problem had disappeared from the market.

The controversy over regulating access stems from the fact that different observers draw different conclusions from the facts just described. To some, the swift realignment of industry operating practices to address consumers' concerns demonstrates the self-regulating capacity of the private marketplace. To others, the swift response of the public sector to the cries of its constituents was the driving force that dragged a reluctant industry into compliance with the wishes of the American people. A purely objective observer would probably have to say that the reactions of all parties were so swift and contemporaneous that it is impossible to sort out what would have happened in the absence of public intervention.

* * *

The Regulatory Tool Kit

There are three main sets of "tools" available to address concerns about market performance in managed care.

* * *

The third option [after information strategies and private litigation under some form of "enterprise liability"] is, of course, some form of active regulation over some or all aspects of transactions involving managed care organizations. It would be possible to create a statutory scheme that both required the development of standards for various transactions and provided for the active scrutiny of transactions to ensure compliance with standards. The scope of regulation could include "above-the-line" transactions between health plans and their customers, as well as "below-the-line" transactions between health plans and their providers and suppliers.

Most efforts in this direction now fall within the province of state regulation of HMOs and other health benefits products. Rather than constituting active day-to-day oversight, state enforcement efforts typically concentrate on issues at two points in time: at the "front end," when health plans are seeking licensure; and at the "back end," if and as problems arise that affect the ongoing viability of the licensed entity.

On the front end, states' major issues are financial viability and operating structure. Health plans seeking to do business in different forms (that is, HMO versus insurance company) face various requirements for financial solvency and reserve adequacy. States also typically scrutinize the structure of the health plan—that is, the scope and reach of the health plan's proposed provider network—to ensure that beneficiaries who enroll in those plans will have the promised access (at least geographic access) to network providers. On the back end, state regulators typically are involved in enforcing a full range of consumer-protection activities and enforcement actions that revolve around the continued financial viability of health plans that run into financial difficulty.

As we ponder the prospect of federal regulation, it is possible to visualize an expanded supervisory role in the "middle"—focusing on the day-to-day transactions among health plans, providers, and patients. However, translating that possibility into a practical regulatory program would involve finding answers to several troubling questions about what such regulation might accomplish.

* * *

The dilemma for public policy is that the sort of regulatory tools we have do not match up well against the essence of the problem that any meaningful policy needs to address. At its core, the true market failure we are experiencing in health benefits is that (1) a growing number of Americans face restricted choices in health care; (2) those Americans lack the ability to determine whether the effects of those restrictions will be harmful to their health; and (3) they do not automatically trust either health plans or providers to act in their best interest in the emerging market environment.

Short of a legislated reversion to the *status quo ante* of, say, 1975, it is unclear how government action could address these concerns. While government could, in theory, purport to address the problem through information-related regulation, it is difficult to visualize the information that would be needed to materially affect public confidence on so fundamental a question.

* * *

The problem here is that nobody knows the answer to the question that consumers really want answered: "Will I turn out not to need the services which, under managed care, I'll no longer get?" At the end of the day, the answer to this most basic of questions does not lie within the boundaries of existing clinical and scientific knowledge. Although it is tempting to think that governmental efforts could be directed toward manufacturing answers to all known clinical controversies, it is naive to believe that the American people would trust the outcome of such a process any more than they trust capitated health plans and providers.

Is there light at the end of this tunnel? While it is easy to be pessimistic about the prospects for ameliorating the American people's concerns in the short run, the long-run picture looks much better. Whatever else policymakers find themselves having to do to address immediate political concerns, government at all levels can be expected to continually strive to enhance the public information environment in health care. Meanwhile, we can expect ongoing innovation in the private sector to find health benefits products that the public will find more palatable and to increase public confidence in the positive aspects of products that now exist. As more and more Americans come to receive their health benefits though some form of managed care mechanism, we can expect those mechanisms to evolve—in response to both public and private pressure—into institutions that ultimately are responsive to the public's concerns. As long as we avoid the mistake of locking evolving clinical practice into regulatory stasis, there is reason for confidence that this will turn out all right.

Moran, Federal Regulation of Managed Care: An Impulse in Search of a Theory?, Health Affs., Nov.-Dec. 1997, p. 7, 10–16, 20–21.

Consider the theoretical arguments for regulating various features of managed care. Recall in particular from chapter 6(§A) both the possible economic justifications for setting minimum standards in licensing health (and other) occupations and the likelihood that, in practice, democratic political systems will set such standards well above the efficient (optimal) level. How do those observations (offered with respect to personnel licensure) carry over to the regulation of managed-care plans? Does the political "backlash" against managed care increase the risk that standards will be set too high? Is the principal concern only that many consumers (mostly lower-income ones) will be forced to pay marginally more for health coverage than they would choose to pay if all health plans did not have to comply with regulatory requirements? Or is there another, perhaps more serious concern? (Recall the studies of Carroll & Gaston reported in chapter 6(§A).) How might the fact that most consumer/voters are not fully aware of the true cost of their health coverage (because it is paid for by their employers in the first instance) affect the outcome of the political movement to regulate managed care?

Should the case for regulation also be examined in light of considerations other than those mentioned in the Moran excerpt—for example, agency problems, contract failure (that is, the difficulty of specifying entitlements in private contracts), and the many impediments to effective monitoring of performance and to enforcement of legal obligations? Would changes in liability rules—e.g., some form of MCO enterprise liability—be preferable to, or an adequate substitute for, command-and-control regulation? Which types of regulation described in the following paragraphs (or contemplated in the foregoing Bill of Rights) are least (most) consistent with market principles? Are disclosure strategies likely to be sufficient? If not, what additional regulatory measures would you advocate?

2. *Mandating the Standard of Care.* In the mid–1990s, in an effort to referee the power struggle between MCOs and physicians, many state legislatures began to explore new ways to reverse what they understood to be the excesses of managed care. The most striking example of legislators' scramble to lead the fight against perceived abuses was the enactment of laws against "drive-through deliveries" (as described in the problem at the end of chapter 1(§A)). See also Annas, Women and Children First, 333 New Eng. J. Med. 1647 (1995). A few states also legislated, or threatened to legislate, a mandatory hospital stay following a mastectomy, including even so-called "lumpectomies." Such measures, like other mandated benefits that legislatures have frequently enacted, appear to be based more on political pressures, intuition, and emotionalism than on clinical evidence. See, e.g., Mandl et al., Effects of Moderate Reductions in Post–Partum Length of Stay, 151 Archs. of Ped. & Adolesc. Med. 915 (1997) (reporting studies supporting safety of early discharge with appropriate follow-up care).

After the early flurry of mandated lengths of stay, legislatures came to resist their most prescriptive impulses. See, e.g., Me.Rev.Stat.Ann. tit. 24 § 2318–A (West Supp. 1996) (mandating adherence to guidelines of American College of Obstetricians and Gynecologists rather than specific length of stay). Moreover, length-of-stay requirements for other conditions, such as mastectomy and lymph node dissections, have been much slower to take hold. Nonetheless, some provider interests continue to support length-of-stay mandates. Despite having fought all past efforts to legislate the standard of care, the battle against managed care may be inducing physicians to change their position. Would it be in the long-term interest of physicians to accept government prescription of clinical standards?

3. *External Grievance Procedures*. As noted earlier, federal and state HMO acts have long required that HMOs provide grievance procedures for enrollees who believe they have been improperly denied benefits or otherwise harmed by managed-care practices. Medicare has likewise specified such procedures for its contract HMOs. In the 1990s, however, numerous states began to strengthen appellate mechanisms—as Congress also did in the Medicare+Choice program. An increasingly common approach, reflected in the "Bill of Rights" reproduced above, was to require that some form of independent external review be available for aggrieved individuals. See, e.g., N.J. Stat. Ann. § 26.2J–12 (West 1996) (requiring availability of independent utilization review organization to resolve disputes over medical necessity and other coverage issues); 1997 Conn. Acts 97–99 § 20 (Reg. Sess.) (providing that enrollee appeals from existing grievance procedures will be referred by the Department of Insurance to an impartial entity empowered to issue binding decisions).

Although consumer groups have called for much broader use of independent review organizations, some observers doubt that grievance procedures, including those with external reviewers, can effectively address the structural problem of sub rosa rationing and the likelihood that it will frequently result in de facto denials of contractual entitlements; moreover, those consumers who at greatest risk for treatment denial may be those least capable of using whatever mechanisms are in place. See, e.g., Rodwin, Consumer Protection in Managed Care: Issues, Reform Proposals, and Trade-offs, 32 Hous. L. Rev. 1319, 1347–49 (1996). Indeed, if health plans and their primary care physicians—that is, the "gatekeepers" on whom many plans rely to ensure that only appropriate care is rendered to each patient—gauge their liberality according to individual enrollees' relative awareness of their rights, articulateness, and probable propensity to litigate, systematic discrimination in the allocation of scarce resources (among patients paying identical premiums) could occur. Do you share Moran's hopefulness that competition for the business of increasingly well-informed consumers can eventually ameliorate the worst consequences of both explicit and implicit rationing? What regulatory or other remedies can you see for working out this problem, which lies at the heart not only of the consumer distrust noted by Moran but also of the managed-care strategy itself? Do you now see the aptness of the "no-man's-land" metaphor introduced in chapter 2(§C)?

4. *Access to Care*. So-called direct-access statutes require that MCOs allow their enrollees to go directly to specialists without a referral, bypassing their primary care physicians. Most enactments of this kind concern obstetrics and gynecology, reflecting both the importance of choice to consumers of these services and the lobbying skill of the American College of Obstetrics and Gynecology. See, e.g., Colo. Rev.Stat. § 10–16–107 (Michie 1997); Va. Code Ann. § 38.2–3407.11 (Michie Supp. 1997). Other medical specialties lobbying for similar legislation have been less successful. These laws clearly represent attempts to stymie the care-limiting impulse of MCOs. Significantly, however, they pit specialists against primary care physicians—not only in the political arena but also in individual health plans, where the latter may bear capitated risks that direct access makes harder to control.

A similar kind of legislative reform of managed care has concerned patients' access to emergency departments. On the assumption that MCOs were creating inappropriate obstacles for patients needing, or thinking they might need, emergency care, many state legislatures passed corrective legislation. The most common approach was to require MCOs to pay for care provided in a hospital emergency department if the patient reasonably believed (as a "prudent lay-person") that he or she needed such care. See, e.g., Ga. Code Ann. § 33–20A–3(2) (Supp. 1997). On the alleged problem to which such laws are addressed, see G. Anders, Health Against Wealth: HMOs and the Breakdown of Medical Trust 1–13, 132–34, 148–49 (1996) (journalistic account emphasizing a single tragic event, seemingly traceable only to a nurse's negligence in responding to a patient's phone inquiry, to discredit managed care in general; later disclosing, however, how a national a phone bank, used by many MCOs to respond to similar inquiries, responded correctly and instantaneously in an identical circumstance). Query whether legislation of this kind is preferable to leaving health plans free to discover triage methods that effectively identify true emergencies, reassure anxious individuals, and save costly and unnecessary emergency department visits.

5. *Regulating Risk*. Another strategy used to regulate managed care has focused on the financial risks imposed on individual providers to induce economizing behavior. The problems inherent in such financial incentives were highlighted in connection with *Shea v. Esensten*, reproduced in chapter 2(§C). HCFA's approach to so-called "physician incentive plans" used by Medicare and Medicaid contractors was examined in chapter 3(§D). State legislation generally resembles the HCFA approach of emphasizing

disclosure, imposing special requirements only when individual providers bear "substantial financial risk."

Provider Protection or Consumer Protection?

CIGNA Healthplan of Louisiana, Inc. v. Louisiana ex rel. Ieyoub

United States Court of Appeals, Fifth Circuit, 1996.
82 F.3d 642, cert. denied, 117 S.Ct. 387 (1996).

■ WIENER, CIRCUIT JUDGE:

Plaintiffs–Appellees CIGNA Healthplan of Louisiana (CIGNA) and Connecticut General Life Insurance Company (CGLIC) filed suit against Defendant–Appellant the State of Louisiana, ex rel. Richard P. Ieyoub, Attorney General (Ieyoub), seeking inter alia (1) a declaratory judgment holding that Louisiana's Any Willing Provider statute is preempted by [ERISA]; and (2) an injunction prohibiting the commencement of any action against them for alleged violations of the Any Willing Provider statute. The district court granted summary judgment declaring that ERISA preempts the Any Willing Provider statute insofar as it applies to third party administrators and health care plans that provide services to ERISA-qualified benefit plans, and issued an injunction barring enforcement of the statute against CIGNA and CGLIC. Concluding that the Any Willing Provider statute relates to employee benefit plans within the meaning of ERISA's preemption clause, and that the statute is not exempted from preemption by ERISA's insurance savings clause, we affirm.

I.

FACTS AND PROCEEDINGS

A. FACTS

1. The Any Willing Provider Statute

In 1984, in an attempt to reduce health care costs without jeopardizing the quality of care received by patients, the Louisiana legislature enacted the Health Care Cost Control Act (the Act).[8] The Act specifically authorizes the formation of preferred provider organizations (PPOs), which are defined as "contractual . . . agreements between a provider or providers and a group purchaser or purchasers to provide for alternative rates of payment. . . ." The definitional section of the Act contains a definition of "group purchaser," then follows the definition with an illustrative list of some of the types of entities that may be included in that category. According to the Act, "group purchasers" may include "[e]ntities which contract for the benefit of their insured, employees, or members"; and "[e]ntities which serve as brokers for the formation of [contracts with providers], including health care financiers, third party administrators, . . . or other intermediaries."

8. See LA.REV.STAT.ANN. §§ 40:2201 et seq. (West 1992 & Supp.1996).

The Any Willing Provider statute, which is incorporated as § 2202(5)(c) of the Act, mandates that "[n]o licensed provider ... who agrees to the terms and conditions of the preferred provider contract shall be denied the right to become a preferred provider." According to an advisory opinion issued by the Louisiana Attorney General's office in February 1993, the arbitrary exclusion from a PPO of a licensed physician who is "willing and able to accede to the terms and conditions of the preferred provider contract" constitutes both a violation of the Any Willing Provider statute and an unfair trade practice under Louisiana law.

2. The Parties

Both CIGNA and CGLIC constitute "group purchasers" under the terms of the Act. CIGNA is a licensed health maintenance organization (HMO) that provides prepaid health care coverage to enrolled subscribers—including the sponsors of ERISA-qualified employee benefit plans—by contracting with selected physicians, hospitals, and other health care suppliers (collectively, providers). The chosen providers agree to comply with CIGNA's quality control requirements and to offer health care services to CIGNA's subscribers at a discounted rate.

In Louisiana, CIGNA's provider network is marketed by CGLIC, a licensed health insurer. CGLIC also contracts with CIGNA for the right to use the provider network in conjunction with the insured and self-funded health benefit plans that CGLIC offers to, and administers for, its clients. Like CIGNA's subscribers, CGLIC's clients include the sponsors of ERISA-qualified employee welfare benefit plans.

3. Impact of the Any Willing Provider Statute

* * * CIGNA has received, and would like to reject, applications from a number of physicians seeking inclusion in its network of providers.

* * *

II.

ANALYSIS

* * *

1. Preemption Doctrine

The first question we must address is whether the Any Willing Provider statute is preempted pursuant to § 514(a) of ERISA. Section 514(a) states that ERISA "shall supersede any and all State laws insofar as they may now or hereafter relate to any employee benefit plan" that is covered by the federal statute. Courts have interpreted this preemption clause broadly, observing that its deliberatively expansive language was designed "to establish ... plan regulation as exclusively a federal concern."

The Supreme Court has given the phrase "relate to" a "broad common-sense meaning."[21] A state law relates to an ERISA plan "in the

21. Pilot Life Ins. Co. v. Dedeaux, 481 U.S. 41, 47 (1987).

normal sense of the phrase if it has connection with or reference to such a plan."[22] A state law can relate to an ERISA plan even if that law was not specifically designed to affect such plans, and even if its effect is only indirect. If a state law does not expressly concern employee benefit plans, it will still be preempted insofar as it applies to benefit plans in particular cases. Of particular significance to our analysis today is the fact that the Supreme Court has repeatedly held that ERISA preempts "state laws that mandat[e] employee benefit structures or their administration."[23]

Nevertheless, ERISA preemption is not without limits. The Supreme Court has cautioned that "[s]ome state actions may affect employee benefit plans in too tenuous, remote, or peripheral a manner to warrant a finding that the law 'relates to' the plan."[26] A unanimous Supreme Court has recently held in this regard that ERISA does not preempt state laws that have "only an indirect economic effect on the relative costs of various health insurance packages" available to ERISA-qualified plans.[27]

ERISA itself contains provisions which limit the scope of preemption. For the purposes of the instant appeal, it is relevant that under § 514(b)(2)(A) of ERISA, preemption stops short of "any law of any State which regulates insurance."

2. Application of § 514(a) to the Instant Appeal

As discussed above, § 514(a) of ERISA provides for the preemption of state laws that either refer to or have a connection with an ERISA-qualified plan. The Any Willing Provider statute qualifies for preemption on both counts. First, it refers to ERISA-qualified plans. * * *

Moreover, the statute "relates to" ERISA plans in the sense that it is connected with such plans. The Supreme Court has emphasized [in *Travelers*] that preemption is appropriate on this ground when statutes "mandat[e] employee benefit structures or their administration." In the instant case, ERISA plans that choose to offer coverage by PPOs are limited by the statute to using PPOs of a certain structure—i.e., a structure that includes every willing, licensed provider. Stated another way, the statute prohibits those ERISA plans which elect to use PPOs from selecting a PPO that does not include any willing, licensed provider. As such, the statute connects with ERISA plans.

Neither is it of any consequence that plans might not choose to offer coverage by PPOs: It is sufficient for preemption purposes that the statute eliminates the choice of one method of structuring benefits. The fact that neither CIGNA nor CGLIC is itself an ERISA plan is likewise inconsequential: By denying insurers, employers, and HMOs the right to structure their benefits in a particular manner, the statute is effectively requiring ERISA plans to purchase benefits of a particular structure when they contract

22. Shaw [v. Delta Air Lines,Inc.], 463 U.S. [85,] 96–97 [(1983)].

23. New York State Conference of Blue Cross & Blue Shield Plans v. Travelers Ins. Co., 115 S.Ct. 1671, 1678 (1995) [hereinafter *Travelers*].

26. *Shaw*, 463 U.S. at 100 n. 21.

27. *Travelers*, 115 S.Ct. at 1680.

with organizations like CIGNA and CGLIC.[39] In that regard, the statute "bears indirectly but substantially on all insured plans,"[40] and is accordingly preempted by ERISA.[41]

* * *

Unlike the New York statute at issue in *Travelers*, Louisiana's Any Willing Provider statute specifically mandates that certain benefits available to ERISA plans must be constructed in a particular manner. In other words, the Louisiana statute does not merely raise the cost of the implicated benefits; it delineates their very structure. As such, the statute falls outside the purview of the limited *Travelers* holding: The Court there repeatedly recognized that ERISA preempts "state laws that mandat[e] employee benefit structures."[48] Accordingly, we hold that the *Travelers* decision leaves undisturbed our conclusion that Louisiana's Any Willing Provider statute is preempted by ERISA.

3. The Insurance Exception

Determining that the Louisiana statute "relates to" ERISA plans and is therefore covered by ERISA's broad preemption provision does not complete our inquiry. We must next consider whether the statute is nonetheless saved from preemption by one of the exceptions embodied in ERISA's savings clause. This clause provides that "nothing in this title shall be construed to exempt or relieve any person from any law of any State which regulates insurance, banking, or securities." In [*Metropolitan Life*, cited supra note 39], the Supreme Court delineated the requirements that a statute must meet to come within the insurance facet of the savings clause. As we have noted in prior opinions, the Court took a conjunctive two-step approach:

> First, the court determined whether the statute in question fitted the common sense definition of insurance regulation. Second, it looked at three factors: (1) Whether the practice (the statute) has the effect of spreading the policyholders' risk; (2) whether the practice is an integral part of the policy relationship between the insurer and the insured; and (3) whether

39. See Metropolitan Life Ins. Co. v. Massachusetts, 471 U.S. 724 (1985) (holding that a statute "relates to" ERISA plans for the purposes of preemption if it "requires [the plans] to purchase the ... benefits specified in the statute when they purchase a certain kind of common insurance policy.").

40. See *Metropolitan Life*, 471 U.S. at 739.

41. Cf. Stuart Circle Hosp. Corp. v. Aetna Health Management, 995 F.2d 500, 502 (4th Cir.) (holding that Virginia statute prohibiting insurance companies from unreasonably discriminating in establishing PPOs is covered by ERISA's preemption provision because it "restricts the ability of an insurance company to limit the choice of providers that otherwise would confine the participants of an employee benefit plan to those preferred by the insurer") (also holding that the statute was saved from preemption by ERISA's insurance savings clause), cert. denied, 510 U.S. 1003 (1993); Blue Cross and Blue Shield of Alabama v. Nielsen, 917 F.Supp. 1532 (1996) (holding that Alabama's equivalent of the Any Willing Provider statute is preempted by ERISA).

48. [*Travelers*,] 115 S.Ct. at 1678; see also id. at 1679 (distinguishing New York law from preempted laws on ground that it "does not bind plan administrators to any particular choice").

the practice is limited to entities within the insurance industry. If the statute fitted the common sense definition of insurance regulation and the court answered "yes" to each of the questions in the three part test, then the statute fell within the savings clause exempting it from ERISA preemption.[51]

Thus, if a statute fails either to fit the common sense definition of insurance regulation or to satisfy any one element of the three-factor *Metropolitan Life* test, then the statute is not exempt from preemption by the ERISA insurance savings clause.

When we begin to apply that test to Louisiana's Any Willing Provider Statute, we may start and finish with the third factor of the *Metropolitan Life* test: On its face, Louisiana's statute obviously is not "limited to entities within the insurance industry." Even though the statute lists insurers as one group covered by its terms, it also specifies, in a non-exclusive list, that it applies to "self-funded organizations, Taft–Hartley trusts, or employers who establish or participate in self funded trusts or programs," as well as "health care financiers, third party administrators, providers, or other intermediaries." As the statute fails to meet the third factor of the *Metropolitan Life* test, we affirm the district court's holding that the statute is not saved from preemption by the insurance exception of § 514(b) of ERISA.

III.
CONCLUSION

For the foregoing reasons, we affirm the district court's grant of summary judgment declaring that ERISA preempts the Any Willing Provider Statute insofar as it relates to third party administrators and health care plans that provide services to ERISA-qualified benefit plans. We also affirm the court's grant of an injunction barring Ieyoub from enforcing the statute against CIGNA and CGLIC.

NOTES AND QUESTIONS ON PLAN/PROVIDER RELATIONS

1. *Selective Contracting*. The importance to modern health plans of the freedom to contract selectively for providers' services was noted in chapter 2(§C). This vital cost-containment tool was a natural target for a political counterattack by physician interests:

> Selective contracting, a fundamental method of managing care, has become a focal point in the larger struggle between managed care plans and independent providers. The central premise behind selective contracting is that managed care organizations (MCOs) can provide high quality care at a lower cost than traditional indemnity insurance plans by limiting the number and balancing the types of providers that plan enrollees may visit. MCOs consider the ability to select only certain

51. Tingle v. Pac. Mut. Ins. Co., 996 F.2d 105, 108 (5th Cir.1993) (citations omitted); see also NGS Am., Inc. v. Barnes, 998 F.2d 296, 299 (5th Cir.1993).

providers as essential to control utilization, lower costs, and maintain quality. Legislative restrictions on selective contracting are intended to maintain patient access to almost all providers, and provider access to all patients, insofar as state law can. The leading mechanisms require plans to contract with any willing provider (AWP) or to give their enrollees freedom of choice (FOC) of any provider at the time of service.

Marsteller et al., The Resurgence of Selective Contracting Restrictions, 22 J. Health Pol., Pol'y & L. 1133, 1134 (1997).

2. *"Any-Willing-Provider" Laws*. State laws requiring health plans to empanel "any willing provider" (AWP) may cover all types of health plans or only a subset of managed-care arrangements, such as PPOs. They may benefit providers of all kinds, only physicians, or only nonphysician providers, such as pharmacies. Many such laws allow plans to place some limitations on the number and mix of providers permitted to participate; others make no provision for such limitations. A few AWP laws simply require an open process for determining which providers may participate in a plan. See generally Marsteller et al., supra (exhaustively listing, describing, and categorizing state AWP laws). It is of interest that some AWP laws seem based on the assumption that each health plan enlists and pays all providers in a given category on the same basis and terms. Yet one can imagine a plan's paying certain providers more or less depending on supply and demand, their qualifications and skills, their location, or other factors that might make them especially attractive to consumers (and thus to a plan seeking to maintain or increase enrollment).

By the late 1990s, only a handful of states had AWP provisions of the strongest kind, including Arkansas, Alabama, Idaho, and Wyoming. Moreover, state legislative interest in enacting such laws was waning. Marsteller et al., supra, at 1155. In addition to doubts about the enforceability of such laws under ERISA, legislators became concerned about the impact of such laws on the cost of care. Indeed, an influential study in 1995 suggested that AWP laws and mandatory point-of-service laws could raise health expenditures by more than $150 billion over the next half decade. J. Sheils et al., The Costs of Legislative Restrictions on Contracting Practices: The Cost to Governments, Employers and Families (Lewin–VHI, Inc., 1995). Precisely how do AWP-type laws raise health plan costs?

3. *ERISA*. For other cases (in addition to *CIGNA*) holding that ERISA preempts an AWP law, see Texas Pharmacy Ass'n v. Prudential Ins. Co., 105 F.3d 1035 (5th Cir.1997) (Texas AWP law for pharmacies held preempted); Blue Cross & Blue Shield v. Nielsen, 917 F.Supp. 1532 (1996) (holding Alabama's AWP-type statute preempted by ERISA). Cf. Washington Physicians Service Ass'n v. Gregoire, 1998 WL 318759 (9th Cir. 1998) (ERISA held not to preempt state "mandated-provider" law, requiring that alternative providers as well as physicians be eligible to provide covered services; court noted, however, that statute did not "force any carrier to contract with any particular provider"). Even though Congress did not write ERISA with managed health care in mind, the legislative history of

ERISA indicates that Congress did intend to preclude the states from imposing AWP-type requirements on employer-sponsored prepaid legal services plans. See 120 Cong. Rec. S15757 (daily ed., Aug. 22, 1974) (statement of Sen. Javits) ("the State, directly or indirectly through the bar, is preempted from regulating the form and content of a legal service plan, for example, open or closed panels").

The preemption issue is apparently not entirely free from doubt in the courts, however. See, e.g., Stuart Circle Hosp. Corp. v. Aetna, 995 F.2d 500 (4th Cir.) (cited in *CIGNA*, note 41; finding Virginia's AWP law applicable to insurer-sponsored PPOs to be saved from preemption by ERISA's savings clause), cert. denied, 510 U.S. 1003 (1993). Moreover, as ERISA has gained an increasingly bad name as an unintended impediment to allegedly progressive state health legislation, some federal judges have become harder to persuade of its preemptive power. See, e.g., American Drug Stores, Inc. v. Harvard Pilgrim Health Care, Inc., 973 F.Supp. 60 (D.Mass.1997) (discounting earlier precedent and holding AWP law for pharmacies not preempted; law deemed not to "relate to" employee benefit plans and to qualify as insurance regulation under saving clause despite application to HMOs as well as health insurers); Napoletano v. CIGNA Healthcare, Inc., 680 A.2d 127 (Conn.1996) (upholding under ERISA a state statute requiring HMOs to adopt and adhere to written criteria for selecting physicians on ground that this requirement does not "relate to" plan administration). Despite the latter rulings, it is hard to see any intelligible reason—since selecting providers is a principal (though under-appreciated) service that ERISA plans perform in administering employee health benefits—why ERISA should not be construed to preempt state interference with the formation and maintenance of provider networks.

4. *Gag Clauses*. So-called "gag clauses," which were highlighted in a note in § B of this chapter and in a problem illustrating the antitrust treatment of professional boycotts in chapter 4(§B), are another feature of relationships between MCOs and providers that attracted legislative attention during the mid 1990s. In addition to receiving mention in the "Bill of Rights," supra, gag clauses were the subject of new laws in sixteen states in 1996. E.g., N.Y. Pub. Health Law § 4406–c (McKinney Supp. 1997). See Jaklevic, A Good Year for Patient Protection Laws, Mod. Healthcare, Oct. 28, 1996, p. 22. As noted earlier, however, contractual provisions clearly aimed at silencing physicians in communicating with their patients proved to be far less common than critics had alleged. Moreover, many MCOs quickly rewrote their contracts with providers to remove even the appearance of censoring physician communications with patients (although some retained disparagement of the plan as a ground for termination). In any event, it rapidly became clear that, as a practical matter, explicit contract language was not necessary to give plans the power to terminate a trouble-making physician, since, as the next paragraph shows, most plans retain the power to terminate a physician at will.

5. *"Deselection."* Recall from chapter 5(§C) the struggle of physicians, both collectively and individually, to check the power of hospitals to exclude or expel physicians from their medical staffs. Physicians are now engaged in an analogous struggle to achieve job security and to preserve some professional autonomy in MCOs by somehow curbing the ability of MCOs to select (and "deselect") physicians at will and without judicial review. Although many health plans maintain some procedural protections for physicians, it is uncommon to find in MCOs anything resembling the typical hospital's self-governing medical staff. See generally Blum, The Evolution of Physician Credentialing into Managed Care Selective Contracting, 22 Am. J.L. & Med. 173 (1996).

Should physicians have statutory or other legal protection against arbitrary termination by health plans, or should they have only whatever contractual protection they can obtain from plans seeking to attract the physicians they need? In other words, should MCOs be free to treat physicians as "at-will" suppliers of services, to include "termination-without-cause" clauses in plan/provider contracts, and to sever relationships arbitrarily for, say, economic reasons alone? In Harper v. Healthsource New Hampshire, Inc., 674 A.2d 962 (N.H.1996), the New Hampshire Supreme Court found public policy grounds for preventing health plans from invoking termination-without-cause clauses without an affirmative demonstration that the termination was consistent with good faith and fair dealing and did not offend (unspecified) public policy. A California appellate court has extended to managed-care plans that state's somewhat peculiar doctrine conferring extensive procedural rights and access to judicial review on any individual expelled from a private organization (such as a hospital) if he or she can show significant economic hardship. Potvin v. Metropolitan Life Ins. Co., 63 Cal.Rptr.2d 202 (Cal.App.), review granted, 941 P.2d 1189 (Cal.1997). (On the California doctrine in question, recall not only the cases noted in chapter 5(§C) but also the *Pinsker* case cited in chapter 6(§C).) For an extensive statutory enactment aimed at curbing arbitrary deselection, see N.Y. Pub. Health Law § 4406–d (McKinney Supp. 1997) (requiring written explanation and hearing prior to termination, closely regulating practice of "profiling" by which plans compare physicians' performance, and prohibiting termination for advocating patient interests).

How do the New Hampshire and California rulings and the New York statute look under ERISA? Would the *Potvin* ruling, at least (assuming it survives on appeal), be defensible under *Travelers* as a state law "with only an indirect economic effect on the relative costs of various health insurance packages in a given State"? *Travelers*, 514 U.S. at 662. It may be the case that an MCO's substantive criteria and procedural machinery for selecting physicians to treat patients who are not enrolled through ERISA plans must comply with state law even if that compliance creates burdens for ERISA plans. See, e.g., Napoletano v. CIGNA Healthcare, Inc., 680 A.2d 127 (Conn.1996) (upholding under ERISA a state statute requiring HMOs to adopt and adhere to written selection criteria on ground that this requirement does not "relate to" plan administration). But what would happen if an HMO, pursuant to express contracts with employers, maintained a separate, differently selected network for its ERISA plans? Recall that the *Dukes* case, reproduced in § A of this chapter, suggested that an explicit contract between an employer and an HMO might bring within ERISA's protection particular features of the plan/provider/patient relationship that would otherwise be governed by state law.

In any event, watch for continuing skirmishes in physicians' battle to gain greater job security and to minimize their accountability to cost-conscious corporate agents of their consumer-patients. Recall from chapter 5(§C) that state courts recognize occasional public-policy exceptions to the employment-at-will doctrine. Might this body of law provide a way to resolve cases in which a physician is terminated simply for performing his or her professional obligation to a patient? If health plans faced possible vicarious liability whenever one of their physicians fails to perform such an obligation—e.g., to advocate a patient's case in a reasonable manner or to advise the patient of treatment options—would you expect the tensions between health plans and their physicians, so obvious in the struggles over AWP laws, to diminish?

6. *Continuity of Care*. Patients also have a stake when their physicians cease to be eligible to care for them under the health plan to which they subscribe. See, e.g., Maltz v. Aetna Health Plans, Inc., 114 F.3d 9 (2d Cir.1997) (children had no ERISA right to continued treatment by physicians who resigned from health plan, where subscriber contract provided no right to continued relationship). Recent legislation in several states (e.g., Kansas, Maryland, Minnesota, New York, Texas, and Virginia) has focused on ensuring that patients who are under the care of a physician for a particular medical problem can continue to be treated by that physician for a limited period after the physician is dropped (or voluntarily withdraws) from the plan.

CHAPTER 9

MAINTAINING COMPETITION IN HEALTH CARE FINANCING AND DELIVERY

SECTION A: PHYSICIAN-SPONSORED ARRANGEMENTS

Antitrust Challenges to Physician Control

United States v. Oregon State Medical Society

Supreme Court of the United States, 1952.
343 U.S. 326, 72 S.Ct. 690, 96 L.Ed. 978.

■ MR. JUSTICE JACKSON delivered the opinion of the Court.

This is a direct appeal by the United States from dismissal by the District Court of its complaint seeking an injunction to prevent and restrain violations of §§ 1 and 2 of the Sherman Act.

Appellees are the Oregon State Medical Society, eight county medical societies, Oregon Physicians' Service (an Oregon corporation engaged in the sale of prepaid medical care), and eight doctors who are or have been at some time responsible officers in those organizations.

This controversy centers about two forms of "contract practice" of medicine. In one, private corporations organized for profit sell what amounts to a policy of insurance by which small periodic payments purchase the right to certain hospital facilities and medical attention. In the other, railroad and large industrial employers of labor contract with one or more doctors to treat their ailing or injured employees. Both forms of "contract practice," for rendering the promised medical and surgical service, depend upon doctors or panels of doctors who cooperate on a fee basis or who associate themselves with the plan on a full-or part-time employment basis.

Objections of the organized medical profession to contract practice are both monetary and ethical. Such practice diverts patients from independent practitioners to contract doctors. It tends to standardize fees. The ethical objection has been that intervention by employer or insurance company makes a tripartite matter of the doctor-patient relation. Since the contract doctor owes his employment and looks for his pay to the employer or the insurance company rather than to the patient, he serves two masters with conflicting interests. In many cases companies assumed liability for medical or surgical service only if they approved the treatment in advance. There was evidence of instances where promptly needed treatment was delayed while obtaining company approval, and where a lay insurance official disapproved treatment advised by a doctor.

In 1936, five private associations were selling prepaid medical certificates in Oregon, and doctors of that State, alarmed at the extent to which private practice was being invaded and superseded by contract practice, commenced a crusade to stamp it out. A tooth-and-claw struggle ensued between the organized medical profession, on the one hand, and the organizations employing contract doctors on the other. The campaign was bitter on both sides. State and county medical societies adopted resolutions and policy statements condemning contract practice and physicians who engaged in it. They brought pressure on individual doctors to decline or abandon it. They threatened expulsion from medical societies, and one society did expel several doctors for refusal to terminate contract practices.

However, in 1941, seven years before this action was commenced, there was an abrupt about-face on the part of the organized medical profession in Oregon. It was apparently convinced that the public demanded and was entitled to purchase protection against unexpected costs of disease and accident, which are catastrophic to persons without reserves. The organized doctors completely reversed their strategy, and, instead of trying to discourage prepaid medical service, decided to render it on a nonprofit basis themselves.

In that year, Oregon Physicians' Service, one of the defendants in this action, was formed. It is a nonprofit Oregon corporation, furnishing prepaid medical, surgical, and hospital care on a contract basis. As charged in the complaint, "It is sponsored and approved by the Oregon State Medical Society and is controlled and operated by members of that society. It sponsors, approves, and cooperates with component county societies and organizations controlled by the latter which offer prepaid medical plans." After seven years of successful operation, the Government brought this suit against the doctors, their professional organizations and their prepaid medical care company, asserting * * * that they conspired to restrain and monopolize the business of providing prepaid medical care in the State of Oregon. * * *

The District Judge, after a long trial, dismissed the complaint on the ground that the Government had proved none of its charges by a preponderance of evidence. The direct appeal procedure does not give us the benefit of review by a Court of Appeals of findings of fact.

The appeal brings to us no important questions of law or unsettled problems of statutory construction. * * * Its issues are solely ones of fact. The record is long, replete with conflicts in testimony, and includes quantities of documentary material * * *. [Although the trial judge wrote no formal opinion, his] notes indicated his disposition of the issues, but the Government predicates a suggestion of bias on irrelevant soliloquies on socialized medicine, socialized law, and the like, which they contained. Admitting that these do not add strength or persuasiveness to his opinion, they do not becloud his clear disposition of the main issues of the case, in all of which he ruled against the Government. Counsel for the doctors submitted detailed findings in accordance therewith. The Government did not submit requests to find, but by letter raised objections to various proposals of the appellees.

The trial judge found that appellees did not conspire to restrain or attempt to monopolize prepaid medical care in Oregon in the period 1936–1941, and that, even if such conspiracy during that time was proved, it was abandoned in 1941 with the formation of Oregon Physicians' Service marking the entry of appellees into the prepaid medical care business. He ruled that what restraints were proved could be justified as reasonable to maintain proper standards of medical ethics. * * *

The Government asks us to overrule each of these findings as contrary to the evidence * * *.

The trial court rejected a grouping by the Government of its evidentiary facts into four periods, 1930–1936, the year 1936, 1936–1941, and 1941 to trial. That proposal projected the inquiry over an eighteen-year period before the action was instituted. The court accepted only the period since the organization of Oregon Physicians' Service as significant and rejected the earlier years as "ancient history" of a time "when the Doctors were trying to find themselves. * * * It was a period of groping for the correct position to take to accord with changing times." Of course, present events have roots in the past, and it is quite proper to trace currently questioned conduct backwards to illuminate its connections and meanings. But we think the trial judge was quite right in rejecting pre-1941 events as establishing the cause of action the Government was trying to maintain, and adopt his division of the time involved into two periods, 1936–1941, and 1941 to trial.

It will simplify consideration of such cases as this to keep in sight the target at which relief is aimed. The sole function of an action for injunction is to forestall future violations. * * *

When defendants are shown to have settled into a continuing practice or entered into a conspiracy violative of antitrust laws, courts will not assume that it has been abandoned without clear proof. It is the duty of the courts to beware of efforts to defeat injunctive relief by protestations of repentance and reform, especially when abandonment seems timed to anticipate suit, and there is probability of resumption.

But we find not the slightest reason to doubt the genuineness, good faith or permanence of the changed attitude and strategy of these defendant-appellees which took place in 1941. It occurred seven years before this suit was commenced and, so far as we are informed, before it was predictable. It did not consist merely of pretensions or promises but was an overt and visible reversal of policy, carried out by extensive operations which have every appearance of being permanent because wise and advantageous for the doctors. The record discloses no threat or probability of resumption of the abandoned warfare against prepaid medical service and the contract practice it entails. We agree with the trial court that conduct discontinued in 1941 does not warrant the issuance of an injunction in 1949.

Appellees, in providing prepaid medical care, may engage in activities which violate the antitrust laws. They are now competitors in the field and restraints, if any are to be expected, will be in their methods of promotion and operation of their own prepaid plan. Our duty is to inquire whether any restraints have been proved of a character likely to continue if not enjoined.

Striking the events prior to 1941 out of the Government's case, except for purposes of illustration or background information, little of substance is left. The case derived its coloration and support almost entirely from the abandoned practices. It would prolong this opinion beyond useful length, to review evidentiary details peculiar to this case. We mention what appear to be some highlights.

Only the Multnomah County Medical Society resorted to expulsions of doctors because of contract-practice activities, and there have been no expulsions for such cause since 1941. There were hints in the testimony that Multnomah was reviving the expulsion threat a short time before this action was commenced, but nothing came of it, and what that Society might do within the limits of its own membership does not necessarily indicate a joint venture or conspiracy with other appellees.

* * *

The record contains a number of letters from doctors to private associations refusing to accept checks directly from them. Some base refusal on a policy of their local medical society, others are silent as to reasons. Some may be attributed to the writers' personal resistance to dealing directly with the private health associations, for it is clear that many doctors objected to filling out the company forms and supplying details required by the associations, and preferred to confine themselves to direct dealing with the patient and leaving the patient to deal with the associations. Some writers may have mistaken or misunderstood the policy of local associations. Others may have avoided disclosure of personal opposition by the handy and impersonal excuse of association "policy." The letters have some evidentiary value, but it is not compelling and, weighed against the other post–1941 evidence, does not satisfy us that the trial court's findings are "clearly erroneous."

Since no concerted refusal to deal with private health associations has been proved, we need not decide whether it would violate the antitrust laws. We might observe in passing, however, that there are ethical considerations where the historic direct relationship between patient and physician is involved which are quite different than the usual considerations prevailing in ordinary commercial matters. This Court has recognized that forms of competition usual in the business world may be demoralizing to the ethical standards of a profession. Semler v. Oregon State Board of Dental Examiners, 294 U.S. 608.

Appellees' evidence to disprove conspiracy is not conclusive, is necessarily largely negative, but is too persuasive for us to say it was clear error to accept it. In 1948, 1,210 of the 1,660 licensed physicians in Oregon were members of the Oregon State Medical Society, and between January 1, 1947, and June 30, 1948, 1,085 Oregon doctors billed and received payment directly from the Industrial Hospital Association, only one of the several private plans operating in the State. Surely there was no effective boycott, and ineffectiveness, in view of the power over its members which the Government attributes to the Society, strongly suggests the lack of an attempt to boycott these private associations. A parade of local medical society members from all parts of the State, apparently reputable, credible, and informed professional men, testified that their societies now have no policy of discrimination against private health associations, and that no attempts are made to prevent individual doctors from cooperating with them. Members of the governing councils of the State and Multnomah County Societies testified that since 1940 there have been no suggestions in their meetings of attempts to prevent individual doctors from serving private associations. The manager of Oregon Physicians' Service testified that at none of the many meetings and conferences of local societies attended by him did he hear any proposal to prevent doctors from cooperation with private plans.

If the testimony of these many responsible witnesses is given credit, no finding of conspiracy to restrain or monopolize this business could be sustained. Certainly we cannot say that the trial court's refusal to find such a conspiracy was clearly erroneous.

* * *

We conclude that the Government has not clearly proved its charges. Certainly the court's findings are not clearly erroneous. * * *

NOTES AND QUESTIONS ON THE OSMS CASE

1. Recall the discussions of this case in chapter 4(§§A & B), which focused on the alleged group boycott of the hospital associations, the sufficiency of the evidence thereof, and the Court's extraordinary dictum stating the legal test applicable to such a boycott, if proved. The case is taken up here in order to observe the specifics of the plans to which professional interests objected, to encourage speculation concerning the purpose and effects of the doctors' actions, and to consider whether there was other concerted action that the government might have challenged.

2. *The "Hospital Associations."* Some indication of the character of the "hospital associations" in the *OSMS* case can be gleaned from the following selections from record extracts appearing in appendices to the medical society's brief:

Appendix B

Extracts from letters from commercial hospital associations to doctors, prior to 1941, illustrative of interference in doctor-patient relationship, questioning honesty or good faith of doctors, imposing burdensome details upon them and related matters, all written by laymen; also extracts from fee schedule.

"However, before authorizing the G.I. study we believe it would be well to await the results of the tonsil operation as the infected tonsils may be causing his intestinal disorder."

"In checking over these statements ... we find that out of the forty-two patients who consulted you charges were made for complete examinations in twenty of these cases, and in fourteen of them an additional charge of $2.00 was made for routine office laboratory work.

"Considering the total number of patients who consulted you the number requiring special examination seems to be entirely out of proportion."

"Your bill for $71.00 indicates that the case did not respond to your treatments as you had expected and you gave many more treatments than were authorized or contemplated ...

"The question now confronts us as to whether it is right that we should assume all the added expense, or is it fair to expect the doctor to bear part of the loss when a case does not respond to his treatment and runs into a bill much higher than such cases usually do or should cost us. ...

"Financial necessity therefore compels us to question bills that run higher than authorized or higher than the usual cost of any particular case."

"You are not the only doctor we are dealing with and we believe you will agree that some doctors are not to be trusted."

"It has come to my attention that several times recently you boys have performed operations without first taking the matter up with this Association as is required.

"Exceptions are always made in emergencies if, after investigation, it is shown that the person is eligible to care at the Association's expense. Will you please mention this to the other boys and let us have your cooperation in the future."

"This service included an X-ray, but the film has not been received at this office. Please send the film in order that your account may have our attention."

[Letter to employer]: "Our experience has demonstrated to us that when we get too large a staff of doctors it is impossible to give the amount of service we are endeavoring to furnish for the fees charged."

"The fees paid by the Association in the Astoria district are as follows:

First office or hospital visit	$2.00
Subsequent visits	1.00
Residence visits	2.00
Mileage	5¢ per mile"

Appendix C

Extracts from testimony of doctors on practices of commercial hospital associations and the doctors' reasons for opposing them.

> "I did not study medicine for the purpose of having some third party broker my services without my knowledge and without my consent."
>
> "You can't measure the practice of medicine entirely in terms of dollars and cents."
>
> "They told me when I could take GI Studies; they told me when I could take x-rays; they told me when I could do surgery."
>
> "They took contracts to furnish medical aid to industrial groups in our area and then would allow the local physicians to do first aid work and that is about all."
>
> "They questioned your procedure to the point where it was insulting, when it came to almost questioning your ethics, and I just got fed up with it."
>
> "Every time I would send them a bill, say, for instance, for four calls or five calls, they would cut about one call off and then send a long cock-and-bull story about they didn't allow so many treatments for that kind of a case, until I got sick and tired of it."
>
> "I found myself working for the National Hospital Association and not for my patients which I did not like and I could not tolerate it longer. I had to get permission to do anything that I did."

Quoted in Goldberg & Greenberg, The Effect of Physician–Controlled Health Insurance: U.S. v. Oregon State Medical Society, 2 J. Health Pol., Pol'y & L. 48, 69–73 (1977).

Were the doctors' grievances legitimate or merely self-serving? Do they constitute an antitrust defense? If a comparable case were brought today, might you expect to see similar evidence emphasized in the *government's* brief? Cf. FTC v. Indiana Fed'n of Dentists, 476 U.S. 447 (1986) (reproduced in chapter 4(§B)). Compare the associations' somewhat primitive cost-containment efforts with the methods employed by health plans today.

3. *Effect on Competition?* Following the events described in this case, OPS prospered. The hospital associations remained in business, however. Although their market share declined so that by 1943 OPS alone had more of the market than they did collectively, the overall market for health insurance was growing rapidly.

By 1948, OPS's market share had declined somewhat from its earlier high level. One physician explained why he resumed "taking tickets" of the independent plans in 1948—that is, accepted assignment of patients' indemnification rights rather than requiring them to pay and seek reimbursement from their plan:

> By that time the hospital associations themselves had assumed the role of insurance companies. They no longer interfered with the relationship of the physician with the patient. They allowed the patient to choose any

> doctor in the community.... They did not attempt to dictate to the physician what he should do for the patient. Their fee schedule had been adjusted upward so that it was comparable to the schedule of OPS, which is our own organization. It ran a little less, but they usually pay 100 per cent, so it balanced out about the same.

Quoted in Goldberg & Greenberg, supra, at 61.

If the associations remained in business and eventually got physicians once again to accommodate their subscribers by "taking tickets," was any harm done? Did the Oregon physicians fail to achieve their objective? For helpful background, see Note, The American Medical Association: Power, Purpose, and Politics in Organized Medicine, 63 Yale L.J. 937, 976–96 (1954).

4. Are you convinced by the Court's explanation of why the Oregon doctors changed their policy toward contract practice in 1941? What else happened around that time (hint: consult chapter 4(§A), not world history) that might have influenced the doctors?

5. Although the evidence of a concerted refusal to "take tickets" of the hospital associations was fairly strong (see Goldberg & Greenberg, supra, at 56–62), assume that the OSMS and the county societies did nothing besides organizing OPS, an early Blue Shield plan. Did the government raise any issue concerning that concerted action, which might also have been subject to scrutiny under section 1 of the Sherman Act? Is there any issue that the government might have raised? The Court attributes a procompetitive purpose to the physicians. Is that a complete defense under the Rule-of-Reason analysis suggested in chapter 4(§B)?

Arizona v. Maricopa County Medical Society

Supreme Court of the United States, 1982.
457 U.S. 332, 102 S.Ct. 2466, 73 L.Ed.2d 48.

■ JUSTICE STEVENS delivered the opinion of the Court.

The question presented is whether § 1 of the Sherman Act has been violated by agreements among competing physicians setting, by majority vote, the maximum fees that they may claim in full payment for health services provided to policyholders of specified insurance plans. The United States Court of Appeals for the Ninth Circuit held that the question could not be answered without evaluating the actual purpose and effect of the agreements at a full trial. Because the undisputed facts disclose a violation of the statute, we * * * reverse.

* * *

II

The Maricopa Foundation for Medical Care is a nonprofit Arizona corporation composed of licensed doctors of medicine, osteopathy, and podiatry engaged in private practice. Approximately 1,750 doctors, representing about 70% of the practitioners in Maricopa County, are members.

The Maricopa Foundation was organized in 1969 for the purpose of promoting fee-for-service medicine and to provide the community with a competitive alternative to existing health insurance plans.[7] The foundation performs three primary activities. It establishes the schedule of maximum fees that participating doctors agree to accept as payment in full for services performed for patients insured under plans approved by the foundation. It reviews the medical necessity and appropriateness of treatment provided by its members to such insured persons. It is authorized to draw checks on insurance company accounts to pay doctors for services performed for covered patients. In performing these functions, the foundation is considered an "insurance administrator" by the Director of the Arizona Department of Insurance. Its participating doctors, however, have no financial interest in the operation of the foundation.

The Pima Foundation for Medical Care, which includes about 400 member doctors,[8] performs similar functions. For the purposes of this litigation, the parties seem to regard the activities of the two foundations as essentially the same. No challenge is made to their peer review or claim administration functions. Nor do the foundations allege that these two activities make it necessary for them to engage in the practice of establishing maximum-fee schedules.

At the time this lawsuit was filed, each foundation made use of "relative values" and "conversion factors" in compiling its fee schedule. The conversion factor is the dollar amount used to determine fees for a particular medical specialty. Thus, for example, the conversion factors for "medicine" and "laboratory" were $8 and $5.50, respectively, in 1972, and $10 and $6.50 in 1974. The relative value schedule provides a numerical weight for each different medical service—thus, an office consultation has a lesser value than a home visit. The relative value was multiplied by the conversion factor to determine the maximum fee. The fee schedule has been revised periodically. The foundation board of trustees would solicit advice from various medical societies about the need for change in either relative values or conversion factors in their respective specialties. The board would then formulate the new fee schedule and submit it to the vote of the entire membership.[10]

7. Most health insurance plans are of the fee-for-service type. Under the typical insurance plan, the insurer agrees with the insured to reimburse the insured for "usual, customary, and reasonable" medical charges. The third-party insurer, and the insured to the extent of any excess charges, bears the economic risk that the insured will require medical treatment. An alternative to the fee-for-service type of insurance plan is illustrated by the health maintenance organizations authorized under the [HMO Act of 1973]. * * *

8. The record contains divergent figures on the percentage of Pima County doctors that belong to the foundation. A 1975 publication of the foundation reported 80%; a 1978 affidavit by the executive director of the foundation reported 30%.

10. The parties disagree over whether the increases in the fee schedules are the cause or the result of the increases in the prevailing rate for medical services in the relevant markets. There appears to be agreement, however, that 85–95% of physicians in Maricopa County bill at or above the maximum reimbursement levels set by the Maricopa Foundation.

The fee schedules limit the amount that the member doctors may recover for services performed for patients insured under plans approved by the foundations. To obtain this approval the insurers—including self-insured employers as well as insurance companies[11]—agree to pay the doctors' charges up to the scheduled amounts, and in exchange the doctors agree to accept those amounts as payment in full for their services. The doctors are free to charge higher fees to uninsured patients, and they also may charge any patient less than the scheduled maxima. A patient who is insured by a foundation-endorsed plan is guaranteed complete coverage for the full amount of his medical bills only if he is treated by a foundation member. He is free to go to a nonmember physician and is still covered for charges that do not exceed the maximum-fee schedule, but he must pay any excess that the nonmember physician may charge.

The impact of the foundation fee schedules on medical fees and on insurance premiums is a matter of dispute. The State of Arizona contends that the periodic upward revisions of the maximum-fee schedules have the effect of stabilizing and enhancing the level of actual charges by physicians, and that the increasing level of their fees in turn increases insurance premiums. The foundations, on the other hand, argue that the schedules impose a meaningful limit on physicians' charges, and that the advance agreement by the doctors to accept the maxima enables the insurance carriers to limit and to calculate more efficiently the risks they underwrite and therefore serves as an effective cost-containment mechanism that has saved patients and insurers millions of dollars. Although the Attorneys General of 40 different States, as well as the Solicitor General of the United States and certain organizations representing consumers of medical services, have filed *amicus curiae* briefs supporting the State of Arizona's position on the merits, we must assume that the respondents' view of the genuine issues of fact is correct.

This assumption presents, but does not answer, the question whether the Sherman Act prohibits the competing doctors from adopting, revising, and agreeing to use a maximum-fee schedule in implementation of the insurance plans.

III

The respondents recognize that our decisions establish that price-fixing agreements are unlawful on their face. But they argue that the *per se* rule does not govern this case because the agreements at issue are horizontal and fix maximum prices, are among members of a profession, are in an industry with which the judiciary has little antitrust experience, and are alleged to have procompetitive justifications. Before we examine each of

11. Seven different insurance companies underwrite health insurance plans that have been approved by the Maricopa Foundation, and three companies underwrite the plans approved by the Pima Foundation. The record contains no firm data on the portion of the health care market that is covered by these plans. The State relies upon a 1974 analysis indicating that insurance plans endorsed by the Maricopa Foundation had about 63% of the prepaid health care market, but the respondents contest the accuracy of this analysis.

these arguments, we pause to consider the history and the meaning of the *per se* rule against price-fixing agreements.

[The majority here defends at length the merits of *per se* rules in the administration of the antitrust laws.]

Our decisions foreclose the argument that the agreements at issue escape *per se* condemnation because they * * * fix maximum prices. * * * The *per se* rule "is grounded on faith in price competition as a market force [and not] on a policy of low selling prices at the price of eliminating competition." Rahl, Price Competition and the Price Fixing Rule—Preface and Perspective, 57 Nw.U.L.Rev. 137, 142 (1962). In this case the rule is violated by a price restraint that tends to provide the same economic rewards to all practitioners regardless of their skill, their experience, their training, or their willingness to employ innovative and difficult procedures in individual cases. Such a restraint also may discourage entry into the market and may deter experimentation and new developments by individual entrepreneurs. It may be a masquerade for an agreement to fix uniform prices, or it may in the future take on that character.

Nor does the fact that doctors—rather than nonprofessionals—are the parties to the price-fixing agreements support the respondents' position. In Goldfarb v. Virginia State Bar, 421 U.S. 773, 788, n. 17, (1975), we stated that the "public service aspect, and other features of the professions, may require that a particular practice, which could properly be viewed as a violation of the Sherman Act in another context, be treated differently." See National Society of Professional Engineers v. United States, 435 U.S. 679, 696 (1978). The price-fixing agreements in this case, however, are not premised on public service or ethical norms. The respondents do not argue, as did the defendants in *Goldfarb* and *Professional Engineers,* that the quality of the professional service that their members provide is enhanced by the price restraint. The respondents' claim for relief from the *per se* rule is simply that the doctors' agreement not to charge certain insureds more than a fixed price facilitates the successful marketing of an attractive insurance plan. But the claim that the price restraint will make it easier for customers to pay does not distinguish the medical profession from any other provider of goods or services.

We are equally unpersuaded by the argument that we should not apply the *per se* rule in this case because the judiciary has little antitrust experience in the health care industry. The argument quite obviously is inconsistent with *Socony-Vacuum.* In unequivocal terms, we stated that, "[w]hatever may be its peculiar problems and characteristics, the Sherman Act, so far as price-fixing agreements are concerned, establishes one uniform rule applicable to all industries alike." 310 U.S. 150, 222 (1940). We also stated that "[t]he elimination of so-called competitive evils [in an industry] is no legal justification" for price-fixing agreements, id., at 220, 60 S.Ct., at 843, yet the Court of Appeals refused to apply the *per se* rule in this case in part because the health care industry was so far removed from the competitive model. * * * [T]he result of this reasoning was the adoption by the Court of Appeals of a legal standard based on the reasonableness of the fixed prices, an inquiry we have so often condemned.[22] Finally, the argument that the *per se* rule must be rejustified for every industry that has not been subject to significant antitrust litigation ignores the rationale for *per se* rules, which in part is to avoid "the necessity for an incredibly complicated and prolonged economic investigation into the entire history of the industry involved, as well as related industries, in an effort to determine at large whether a particular restraint has been unreasonable—an inquiry so often wholly fruitless when undertaken." Northern Pacific R. Co. v. United States, 356 U.S. 1, 5 (1958).

The respondents' principal argument is that the *per se* rule is inapplicable because their agreements are alleged to have procompetitive justifications. The argument indicates a misunderstanding of the *per se* concept. The anticompetitive potential inherent in all price-fixing agreements justifies their facial invalidation even if procompetitive justifications are offered for some.[23] Those claims of enhanced competition are so unlikely to prove significant in any particular case that we adhere to the rule of law that is justified in its general application. Even when the respondents are given every benefit of the doubt, the limited record in this case is not inconsistent with the presumption that the respondents' agreements will not significantly enhance competition.

The respondents contend that their fee schedules are procompetitive because they make it possible to provide consumers of health care with a uniquely desirable form of insurance coverage that could not otherwise exist. The features of the foundation-endorsed insurance plans that they stress are a choice of doctors, complete insurance coverage, and lower premiums. The first two characteristics, however, are hardly unique to these plans. Since only about 70% of the doctors in the relevant market are members of either foundation, the guarantee of complete coverage only applies when an insured chooses a physician in that 70%. If he elects to go to a nonfoundation doctor, he may be required to pay a portion of the doctor's fee. It is fair to presume, however, that at least 70% of the doctors in other markets charge no more than the "usual, customary, and reasonable" fee that typical insurers are willing to reimburse in full. Thus, in Maricopa and Pima Counties as well as in most parts of the country, if an insured asks his doctor if the insurance coverage is complete, presumably in about 70% of the cases the doctor will say "Yes" and in about 30% of the cases he will say "No."

22. In National Society of Professional Engineers v. United States, 435 U.S. 679, 689 (1978), we referred to Judge Taft's "classic rejection of the argument that competitors may lawfully agree to sell their goods at the same price as long as the agreed-upon price is reasonable." See United States v. Addyston Pipe & Steel Co., 85 F. 271 (CA6 1898), aff'd, 175 U.S. 211 (1899). * * *

23. "Whatever economic justification particular price-fixing agreements may be thought to have, the law does not permit an inquiry into their reasonableness. They are all banned because of their actual or potential threat to the central nervous system of the economy." United States v. Socony–Vacuum Oil Co., 310 U.S. 150, 226, n. 59 (1940).

It is true that a binding assurance of complete insurance coverage—as well as most of the respondents' potential for lower insurance premiums[25] —can be obtained only if the insurer and the doctor agree in advance on the maximum fee that the doctor will accept as full payment for a particular service. Even if a fee schedule is therefore desirable, it is not necessary that the doctors do the price fixing.[26] The record indicates that the Arizona Comprehensive Medical/Dental Program for Foster Children is administered by the Maricopa Foundation pursuant to a contract under which the maximum-fee schedule is prescribed by a state agency rather than by the doctors. This program and the Blue Shield plan challenged in Group Life & Health Insurance Co. v. Royal Drug Co., 440 U.S. 205 (1979), indicate that insurers are capable not only of fixing maximum reimbursable prices but also of obtaining binding agreements with providers guaranteeing the insured full reimbursement of a participating provider's fee. In light of these examples, it is not surprising that nothing in the record even arguably supports the conclusion that this type of insurance program could not function if the fee schedules were set in a different way.

The most that can be said for having doctors fix the maximum prices is that doctors may be able to do it more efficiently than insurers. The validity of that assumption is far from obvious,[28] but in any event there is

25. We do not perceive the respondents' claim of procompetitive justification for their fee schedules to rest on the premise that the fee schedules actually reduce medical fees and accordingly reduce insurance premiums, thereby enhancing competition in the health insurance industry. Such an argument would merely restate the long-rejected position that fixed prices are reasonable if they are lower than free competition would yield. It is arguable, however, that the existence of a fee schedule, whether fixed by the doctors or by the insurers, makes it easier—and to that extent less expensive—for insurers to calculate the risks that they underwrite and to arrive at the appropriate reimbursement on insured claims.

26. According to a Federal Trade Commission staff report: "Until the mid–1960's, most Blue Shield plans determined in advance how much to pay for particular procedures and prepared fee schedules reflecting their determinations. Fee schedules are still used in approximately 25 percent of Blue Shield contracts." Bureau of Competition, Federal Trade Commission, Medical Participation in Control of Blue Shield and Certain Other Open–Panel Medical Prepayment Plans 128 (1979). We do not suggest that Blue Shield plans are not actually controlled by doctors. Indeed, as the same report discusses at length, the belief that they are has given rise to considerable antitrust litigation. Nor does this case present the question whether an insurer may, consistent with the Sherman Act, fix the fee schedule and enter into bilateral contracts with individual doctors. That question was not reached in Group Life & Health Insurance Co. v. Royal Drug Co., 440 U.S. 205 (1979). In an *amicus curiae* brief, the United States expressed its opinion that such an arrangement would be legal unless the plaintiffs could establish that a conspiracy among providers was at work. Our point is simply that the record provides no factual basis for the respondents' claim that the doctors must fix the fee schedule.

28. In order to create an insurance plan under which the doctor would agree to accept as full payment a fee prescribed in a fixed schedule, someone must canvass the doctors to determine what maximum prices would be high enough to attract sufficient numbers of individual doctors to sign up but low enough to make the insurance plan competitive. In this case that canvassing function is performed by the foundation; the foundation then deals with the insurer. It would seem that an insurer could simply bypass the foundation by performing the canvassing function and dealing with the doctors itself. Under the foundation plan, each doctor must look at the maximum-fee schedule fixed by his competi-

no reason to believe that any savings that might accrue from this arrangement would be sufficiently great to affect the competitiveness of these kinds of insurance plans. It is entirely possible that the potential or actual power of the foundations to dictate the terms of such insurance plans may more than offset the theoretical efficiencies upon which the respondents' defense ultimately rests.[29]

* * *

IV

Having declined the respondents' invitation to cut back on the *per se* rule against price fixing, we are left with the respondents' argument that their fee schedules involve price fixing in only a literal sense. For this argument, the respondents rely upon Broadcast Music, Inc. v. Columbia Broadcasting System, Inc., 441 U.S. 1 (1979).

In *Broadcast Music* we were confronted with an antitrust challenge to the marketing of the right to use copyrighted compositions derived from the entire membership of the American Society of Composers, Authors and Publishers (ASCAP). The so-called "blanket license" was entirely different from the product that any one composer was able to sell by himself.[31] * * * We held that the delegation by the composers to ASCAP of the power to fix the price for the blanket license was not a species of the price-fixing agreements categorically forbidden by the Sherman Act. The record disclosed price fixing only in a "literal sense."

This case is fundamentally different. Each of the foundations is composed of individual practitioners who compete with one another for patients. Neither the foundations nor the doctors sell insurance, and they derive no profits from the sale of health insurance policies. The members of the foundations sell medical services. Their combination in the form of the foundation does not permit them to sell any different product. Their combination has merely permitted them to sell their services to certain customers at fixed prices and arguably to affect the prevailing market price of medical care.

The foundations are not analogous to partnerships or other joint arrangements in which persons who would otherwise be competitors pool their capital and share the risks of loss as well as the opportunities for profit. In such joint ventures, the partnership is regarded as a single firm

tors and vote for or against approval of the plan (and, if the plan is approved by majority vote, he must continue or revoke his foundation membership). A similar, if to some extent more protracted, process would occur if it were each insurer that offered the maximum-fee schedule to each doctor.

29. In this case it appears that the fees are set by a group with substantial power in the market for medical services, and that there is competition among insurance companies in the sale of medical insurance. Under these circumstances the insurance companies are not likely to have significantly greater bargaining power against a monopoly of doctors than would individual consumers of medical services.

31. "Thus, to the extent the blanket license is a different product, ASCAP is not really a joint sales agency offering the individual goods of many sellers, but is a separate seller offering its blanket license, of which the individual compositions are raw material." 441 U.S., at 22 (footnote omitted).

competing with other sellers in the market. The agreement under attack is an agreement among hundreds of competing doctors concerning the price at which each will offer his own services to a substantial number of consumers. It is true that some are surgeons, some anesthesiologists, and some psychiatrists, but the doctors do not sell a package of three kinds of services. If a clinic offered complete medical coverage for a flat fee, the cooperating doctors would have the type of partnership arrangement in which a price-fixing agreement among the doctors would be perfectly proper. But the fee agreements disclosed by the record in this case are among independent competing entrepreneurs. They fit squarely into the horizontal price-fixing mold.

The judgment of the Court of Appeals is reversed.

■ JUSTICE BLACKMUN and JUSTICE O'CONNOR took no part in the consideration or decision of this case.

■ JUSTICE POWELL, with whom THE CHIEF JUSTICE and JUSTICE REHNQUIST join, dissenting.

The medical care plan condemned by the Court today is a comparatively new method of providing insured medical services at predetermined maximum costs. It involves no coercion. Medical insurance companies, physicians, and patients alike are free to participate or not as they choose. On its face, the plan seems to be in the public interest.

* * * I do not think today's decision on an incomplete record is consistent with proper judicial resolution of an issue of this complexity, novelty, and importance to the public. I therefore dissent.

* * * [O]n this record we must find that insurers represent consumer interests. Normally consumers search for high quality at low prices. But once a consumer is insured[5]—*i.e.,* has chosen a medical insurance plan—he is largely indifferent to the amount that his physician charges if the coverage is full, as under the foundation-sponsored plan.

* * *

The insurer, however, is *not* indifferent. To keep insurance premiums at a competitive level and to remain profitable, insurers—including those who have contracts with the foundations—step into the consumer's shoes with his incentive to contain medical costs. Indeed, insurers may be the only parties who have the effective power to restrain medical costs, given the difficulty that patients experience in comparing price and quality for a professional service such as medical care.

On the record before us, there is no evidence of opposition to the foundation plan by insurance companies—or, for that matter, by members of the public. Rather seven insurers willingly have chosen to contract out to the foundations the task of developing maximum-fee schedules.[6] Again, on

5. At least seven insurance companies are competing in the relevant market. At this stage of the case we must infer that they are competing vigorously and successfully.

6. The State introduced no evidence on its summary judgment motion supporting its apparent view that insurers effectively can perform this function themselves, without

the record before us, we must infer that the foundation plan—open as it is to insurers, physicians, and the public—has in fact benefited consumers by "enabl[ing] the insurance carriers to limit and to calculate more efficiently the risks they underwrite." Nevertheless, even though the case is here on an incomplete summary judgment record, the Court conclusively draws contrary inferences to support its *per se* judgment.

III

It is settled law that once an arrangement has been labeled as "price fixing" it is to be condemned *per se*. But it is equally well settled that this characterization is not to be applied as a talisman to every arrangement that involves a literal fixing of prices. Many lawful contracts, mergers, and partnerships fix prices. But our cases require a more discerning approach. * * *

In sum, the fact that a foundation-sponsored health insurance plan *literally* involves the setting of ceiling prices among competing physicians does not, of itself, justify condemning the plan as *per se* illegal. Only if it is clear from the record that the agreement among physicians is "so plainly anticompetitive that no elaborate study of [its effects] is needed to establish [its] illegality" may a court properly make a *per se* judgment. National Society of Professional Engineers v. United States, supra, at 692. And, as our cases demonstrate, the *per se* label should not be assigned without carefully considering substantial benefits and pro-competitive justifications. This is especially true when the agreement under attack is novel, as in this case.

* * * [T]he plaintiff here has not yet discharged its burden of proving that respondents have entered a plainly anticompetitive combination without a substantial and procompetitive efficiency justification. In my view, the District Court therefore correctly refused to grant the State's motion for summary judgment.[13] This critical and disputed issue of fact remains unresolved.

physician participation. It is clear, however, that price and quality of professional services—unlike commercial products—are difficult to compare. Cf. Bates v. State Bar of Arizona, 433 U.S. 350, 391–395 (1977) (opinion of POWELL, J.). This is particularly true of medical service. Presumably this is a reason participating insurers wish to utilize the foundations' services.

13. Medical services differ from the typical service or commercial product at issue in an anti-trust case. The services of physicians, rendered on a patient-by-patient basis, rarely can be compared by the recipient. A person requiring medical service or advice has no ready way of comparing physicians or of "shopping" for quality medical service at a lesser price. Primarily for this reason, the foundations—operating the plan at issue—perform a function that neither physicians nor prospective patients can perform individually. On a collective—and average—basis, the physicians themselves express a willingness to render certain identifiable services for not more than specified fees, leaving patients free to choose the physician. We thus have a case in which we derive little guidance from the conventional "perfect market" analysis of anti-trust law. I would give greater weight than the Court to the uniqueness of medical services, and certainly would not invalidate on a *per se* basis a plan that may in fact perform a uniquely useful service.

V

I believe the Court's action today loses sight of the basic purposes of the Sherman Act. As we have noted, the antitrust laws are a "consumer welfare prescription." Reiter v. Sonotone Corp., 442 U.S. 330, 343 (1979). In its rush to condemn a novel plan about which it knows very little, the Court suggests that this end is achieved only by invalidating activities that *may* have some potential for harm. But the little that the record does show about the effect of the plan suggests that it is a means of providing medical services that in fact benefits rather than injures persons who need them.

* * *

NOTES AND QUESTIONS ON THE MARICOPA COUNTY MEDICAL SOCIETY CASE

1. *The Character of Per Se Rules.* As a matter of general antitrust doctrine, the majority opinion probably overstates the unbending and potentially perverse character of per se rules. Speaking for only a four-justice majority, Justice Stevens seemed to go out of his way to approve per se rules that are formulated and applied in such a way that they sometimes penalize procompetitive, efficiency-enhancing collaboration. Certainly, one must wonder why the Supreme Court would feel itself bound by rules of its own making even when a new set of facts suggested a need for an exception. In a revealing omitted passage, Justice Stevens said, "Congress may consider the exception that we are not free to read into the statute."

The Court's treatment of per se rules in *Maricopa* can be traced to its earlier application of such a rule in United States v. Topco Associates, Inc., 405 U.S. 596 (1972), which the Court cited favorably at four different points. 457 U.S. at 343, 344 n.16, 354, 355 n.30. In that case, several independent grocery chains with very modest market shares formed a joint venture to develop a private brand of products as a way of competing more effectively with national grocery chains. In aid of that effort, they undertook that they would not sell Topco products in each other's territories; they could compete in all other respects but could not free-ride on consumer loyalty to the Topco brand developed by another partner. At the government's behest, the Court found that the restrictive agreement violated the per se rule against horizontal market division, even though the agreement was clearly and reasonably ancillary to what was in all respects a procompetitive purpose.

The best explanation for the questionable outcome in the *Topco* case is that both the government and the Court saw the Topco brand as only a promotional gimmick—a new label on the same old peas—and not as a new or useful product for which (as they saw it) a time-honored antitrust rule could be bent. Instead of asking whether the joint venturers were trying to

Affirmance of the District Court's holding would not have immunized the medical service plan at issue. Nor would it have foreclosed an eventual conclusion on remand that the arrangement should be deemed *per se* invalid. And if the District Court had found that petitioner had failed to establish a *per se* violation of the Sherman Act, the question would have remained whether the plan comports with the rule of reason.

compete in ways that were compatible with dynamic competition in the market for groceries, the government and the Court seemingly made an implicit judgment that consumer welfare would not suffer much if the joint venture were prohibited from employing the territorial restriction. Query whether such regulatory value judgments should have a place in antitrust law. Note, in any event, that the *Topco* approach is fundamentally inconsistent with the Rule-of-Reason analysis suggested in chapter 4(§ A), which contemplated a law concerned solely with maintaining competitive conditions.

The Supreme Court's decision in *Topco* thus gave the antitrust agencies and courts the power to condemn as per se violations not only certain types of naked restraint (for which per se rules were originally designed) but also any ancillary restraint falling literally in one of the per se categories if the authorities deem its object unworthy as a matter of general public policy. To be sure, the *Broadcast Music* (*BMI*) case, cited in *Maricopa*, allowed for exceptions to per se rules where the challenged conduct fell in a prohibited category only in a "literal sense." 441 U.S. at 31 ("Literalness is overly simplistic and often overbroad."). But the *Maricopa* majority seemingly returned to the *Topco* approach, under which a per se rule could be used as a trump card whenever a product of a competitor-sponsored joint venture did not—like Topco's peas—seem "new" or desirable enough to warrant a waiver of the rule. The upshot therefore seemed to be that the antitrust agencies and courts, rather than letting consumers decide which products they prefer, could assume a regulatory stance, substituting their own judgments for those of the very marketplace and market forces they were supposed to foster. As later materials will show, the *Topco/Maricopa* approach created problems in the administration of joint venture law, including the analysis of new forms of collaboration among competing health professionals.

2. *Rhetoric vs. Method.* Putting aside Justice Stevens's rhetoric about per se rules and his invocation of the per se rule against price fixing, what do you think of his discussion of the foundations' practice of setting maximum fees to be charged to cooperating insurers? Did he in fact apply the per se rule automatically and without regard to whether the maximum price-fixing scheme was or was not procompetitive in fact? Is it arguable that the majority actually took a "quick look" before finding a violation—that is, considered and rejected the foundations' claim that their price fixing was not incompatible with vigorous competition and with the decentralized pricing and output decisions that competition contemplates? Did the Court in fact decide the case on the basis of a conclusive presumption that the practice, because it involved an agreement on prices, was harmful to competition?

3. *Maximum-price Fixing.* Is it reasonable to equate the fixing of maximum prices with agreements on minimum prices in order to apply to it the per se rule applicable to the latter? (The Supreme Court subsequently overruled the primary precedent supporting the per se illegality of vertical maximum price fixing. State Oil Co. v. Khan, 118 S.Ct. 275 (1997),

overruling Albrecht v. Herald Co., 390 U.S. 145 (1968).) Consider the specific dangers that Justice Stevens identifies as possible harms flowing from the foundations' maximum-price fixing:

(a) Is there a possibility that the foundations were "a masquerade for an agreement to fix uniform prices" and that a maximum fee set for a particular procedure was really the minimum fee? (What incentive would a physician have to charge less than the insurers had agreed to pay?)

(b) How might the scheme "discourage entry into the market"? (If the purpose was to discourage HMO development, was that an anticompetitive purpose? Or was the fixing of maximum prices procompetitive in the sense that the doctors were seeking to lower insurance costs in response to actual or potential HMO competition? If it is all right for a lawful monopolist to set a "limit-entry" price, does it follow that an organization of competing physicians can do the same?)

(c) The Court suggests that maximum-price fixing might "deter experimentation and new developments by individual entrepreneurs." What particular innovations might the physicians have wanted to discourage? (Does Justice Stevens suggest some possibilities?)

(d) What conclusion should be drawn from the foundations' tendency to equalize fees for participating physicians "regardless of their skill, their experience, their training, or their willingness to employ innovative and difficult procedures in individual cases"?

Should the foundations' maximum-price fixing have been held unlawful on the limited evidence presented? How would you apply the Rule-of-Reason analysis suggested in chapter 4(§A)? Consider the following note.

4. *Procompetitive or Anticompetitive?* Do you agree with the dissenting justices that the foundations' setting of maximum fees was procompetitive and beneficial to consumers? In this connection, wasn't the Court bound to accept, for summary judgment purposes, the foundations' allegation that the fee controls had "saved patients and insurers millions of dollars"? Is it possible that the practice was cost-reducing without being procompetitive? Are price effects (or effects on output) the ultimate issue? Or is it something else?

Was there another basis, besides price effects, for claiming that the restraint was procompetitive? For example, could the defendants claim that theirs was an ancillary, not a naked, restraint? How would the Court answer this argument? Must the Court's opinion be read as stating that it makes no difference? A more satisfying reading of the opinion might be that the Court found that, because a less restrictive alternative was so obviously available ("it is not necessary that the doctors do the price fixing"), the procompetitive purpose alleged was too unconvincing to be accepted as the collaborators' real purpose. On that basis, the price restriction could appropriately be condemned as a naked restraint without regard to the market power possessed by the collaborators (which the incomplete record left in doubt, at least in Pima County).

Perhaps the physicians were just being socially responsible, seeking to prevent some of their number from exploiting the insurance system and consumers by overcharging. Is it appropriate, and permissible under the antitrust laws, for a dominant professional organization to assume responsibility for controlling runaway medical costs attributable to flaws in the market for insured services? What if the doctors' purpose was to forestall public regulation or other government interference?

Could one argue that the restraint in question was defensible as a response to market failure? (Recall the discussion of such antitrust defenses in chapter 4.) What market failure in particular? Note that lowering or moderating physician fees would have the effect of lowering the price of medical insurance, thus increasing the demand and output of physician services? Are you convinced by Justice Stevens's response to the argument that the restraint was procompetitive?

The *Maricopa* decision was criticized. E.g., Gerhart, The Supreme Court and Antitrust Analysis: The (Near) Triumph of the Chicago School, 1982 Sup.Ct.Rev. 319, 344–48; see also Easterbrook, Maximum Price Fixing, 48 U.Chi.L.Rev. 886 (1981) (article preceding Court's decision but arguing against per se rule). Other articles, however, approved the result though not necessarily the Court's analysis. See, e.g., Weller, Antitrust and Health Care: Provider–Controlled Health Plans and the *Maricopa* Decision, 8 Am.J.L. & Med. 223, 233–43 (1982); Leffler, Arizona v. Maricopa County Medical Society: Maximum–Price Agreements in Markets with Insured Buyers, 2 Sup.Ct.Econ.Rev. 187 (1983).

5. *The Insurers.* The dissenting justices viewed the insurers as agents of the consumer, equally concerned about excessive physician charges. Is there any reason to doubt the insurers' dedication to keeping costs low? Is it possible that insurers would be happier knowing that the costs they face are the same as their competitors' and that they do not have to worry further about cost containment? Was there a danger, then, that the insurers would see the foundations' offer as an invitation to agree tacitly among themselves to accept the "quiet life" (which monopolists are said to prefer) rather than vigorously pursuing innovative cost-containment strategies? What particular strategies, alluded to by Justice Stevens, might they have pursued? Were the foundations interested in discouraging such "experimentation and new developments by individual entrepreneurs"? Note that an insurer must have its plan approved by the foundations in order for the doctors to accept scheduled fees as payment in full.

Was there a reasonable chance that the foundations would be successful in curbing insurer competition that would be detrimental to physicians? Or is entry into the health insurance business easy enough that consumers would be well served despite the doctors' efforts?

6. *Peer Review.* Note that the foundations in the *Maricopa* case also engaged in "review[ing] the medical necessity and appropriateness of treatment by [their] members" to persons enrolled in approved insurance plans. Recall the notes in chapter 4(§B) on the antitrust issues raised by profession-sponsored peer review activities. Should the plaintiff in *Marico-*

pa have challenged that feature of the foundations as well as their price-fixing activities?

7. *Relative Value Scales.* The majority opinion explains how relative value scales (RVSs) work and how they were used by the defendants to set maximum fees for medical and surgical procedures. Recall from chapter 2(§D) that RVSs have been employed by the Medicare program in setting physician fee schedules. Are professional groups likely to go about constructing an RVS in the same manner as a public or private third-party payer?

Should the antitrust laws be interpreted to prevent a dominant professional organization from using its technical and other resources to develop an RVS for its members' use? (The foundations in the *Maricopa* case, of course, went beyond promulgating an RVS; their members also agreed upon "conversion factors," thus converting the table of relative values into an actual price schedule.) Although an RVS is not itself a fee schedule, its adoption by a dominant medical organization might be deemed to violate the antitrust laws if it significantly enhanced physicians' ability to fix minimum prices. (Note that, with an RVS in place, competitors would have to agree only on a conversion factor, not a full range of prices, and could more readily detect and discipline price cutters.) In the only antitrust case involving RVSs to reach a decision on the merits, however, a district court refused to condemn a specialty society's RVS as a per se violation. United States v. American Soc'y of Anesthesiologists, Inc., 473 F.Supp. 147 (S.D.N.Y.1979). Even though there was evidence in that case that the RVS had been used for local price fixing, the court appeared to view effective price competition among anesthesiologists as such an unlikely prospect that the problem was de minimis. It was also impressed that the RVS was only advisory and not binding on the members. Cf. Goldfarb v. Virginia State Bar, 421 U.S. 773, 781 (1975) (if lawyers' minimum fee schedule had been "purely advisory," a "different question" would have been presented).

Now that insurers actively negotiate with providers over prices, RVSs no longer present an antitrust problem. At one time, however, professionally sponsored RVSs did appear to threaten competition not only among physicians in setting their fees but also among private third-party payers in developing independent cost-containment strategies. See Havighurst & Kissam, The Antitrust Implications of Relative Value Studies in Medicine, 4 J. Health Pol., Pol'y & L. 48 (1979).

Physician Collaboration in Today's Markets

Statement of Department of Justice and Federal Trade Commission Enforcement Policy on Physician Network Joint Ventures

Statement 8, U.S Department of Justice & FTC, Statements of Antitrust Enforcement Policy in Health Care (August 1996).

Introduction

In recent years, health plans and other purchasers of health care services have developed a variety of managed care programs that seek to reduce the costs and assure the quality of health care services. Many physicians and physician groups have organized physician network joint ventures, such as individual practice associations ("IPAs"), preferred provider organizations ("PPOs"), and other arrangements to market their services to these plans.[29] Typically, such networks contract with the plans to provide physician services to plan subscribers at predetermined prices, and the physician participants in the networks agree to controls aimed at containing costs and assuring the appropriate and efficient provision of high quality physician services. By developing and implementing mechanisms that encourage physicians to collaborate in practicing efficiently as part of the network, many physician network joint ventures promise significant procompetitive benefits for consumers of health care services.

As used in this statement, a physician network joint venture is a physician-controlled venture in which the network's physician participants collectively agree on prices or price-related terms and jointly market their services. * * *

This statement of enforcement policy describes the Agencies' antitrust analysis of physician network joint ventures, and presents several examples of its application to specific hypothetical physician network joint ventures. Before describing the general antitrust analysis, the statement sets forth antitrust safety zones that describe physician network joint ventures that are highly unlikely to raise substantial competitive concerns, and therefore will not be challenged by the Agencies under the antitrust laws, absent extraordinary circumstances.

The Agencies emphasize that merely because a physician network joint venture does not come within a safety zone in no way indicates that it is unlawful under the antitrust laws. On the contrary, such arrangements may be procompetitive and lawful, and many such arrangements have received favorable business review letters or advisory opinions from the Agencies. The safety zones use a few factors that are relatively easy to apply, to define a category of ventures for which the Agencies presume no anticompetitive harm, without examining competitive conditions in the particular case. A determination about the lawfulness of physician network joint ventures that fall outside the safety zones must be made on a case-by-case basis according to general antitrust principles and the more specific analysis described in this statement.

A. Antitrust Safety Zones

* * * The antitrust safety zones differ for "exclusive" and "non-exclusive" physician network joint ventures. In an "exclusive" venture, the network's physician participants are restricted in their ability to, or do not

29. An IPA or PPO typically provides medical services to the subscribers of health plans but does not act as their insurer. In addition, an IPA or PPO does not require complete integration of the medical practices of its physician participants. Such physicians typically continue to compete fully for patients who are enrolled in health plans not served by the IPA or PPO, or who have indemnity insurance or pay for the physician's services directly "out of pocket."

in practice, individually contract or affiliate with other network joint ventures or health plans. In a "non-exclusive" venture, on the other hand, the physician participants in fact do, or are available to, affiliate with other networks or contract individually with health plans. * * *

1. Exclusive Physician Network Joint Ventures That The Agencies Will Not Challenge, Absent Extraordinary Circumstances

The Agencies will not challenge, absent extraordinary circumstances, an exclusive physician network joint venture whose physician participants share substantial financial risk and constitute 20 percent or less of the physicians in each physician specialty with active hospital staff privileges who practice in the relevant geographic market. In relevant markets with fewer than five physicians in a particular specialty, an exclusive physician network joint venture otherwise qualifying for the antitrust safety zone may include one physician from that specialty, on a non-exclusive basis, even though the inclusion of that physician results in the venture consisting of more than 20 percent of the physicians in that specialty.

2. Non–Exclusive Physician Network Joint Ventures That The Agencies Will Not Challenge, Absent Extraordinary Circumstances

The Agencies will not challenge, absent extraordinary circumstances, a non-exclusive physician network joint venture whose physician participants share substantial financial risk and constitute 30 percent or less of the physicians in each physician specialty with active hospital staff privileges who practice in the relevant geographic market. * * *

3. Indicia Of Non–Exclusivity

* * * The Agencies will determine whether a physician network joint venture is exclusive or non-exclusive by its physician participants' activities, and not simply by the terms of the contractual relationship. In making that determination, the Agencies will examine the following indicia of non-exclusivity, among others:

(1) that viable competing networks or managed care plans with adequate physician participation currently exist in the market;

(2) that physicians in the network actually individually participate in, or contract with, other networks or managed care plans, or there is other evidence of their willingness and incentive to do so;

(3) that physicians in the network earn substantial revenue from other networks or through individual contracts with managed care plans;

(4) the absence of any indications of significant de-participation from other networks or managed care plans in the market; and

(5) the absence of any indications of coordination among the physicians in the network regarding price or other competitively significant terms of participation in other networks or managed care plans.

Networks also may limit or condition physician participants' freedom to contract outside the network in ways that fall short of a commitment of full exclusivity. If those provisions significantly restrict the ability or willingness of a network's physicians to join other networks or contract individually with managed care plans, the network will be considered exclusive for purposes of the safety zones.

4. Sharing Of Substantial Financial Risk By Physicians In A Physician Network Joint Venture

To qualify for either antitrust safety zone, the participants in a physician network joint venture must share substantial financial risk in providing all the services that are jointly priced through the network.[35] The safety zones are limited to networks involving substantial financial risk sharing not because such risk sharing is a desired end in itself, but because it normally is a clear and reliable indicator that a physician network involves sufficient integration by its physician participants to achieve significant efficiencies.[36] Risk sharing provides incentives for the physicians to cooperate in controlling costs and improving quality by managing the provision of services by network physicians.

The following are examples of some types of arrangements through which participants in a physician network joint venture can share substantial financial risk:

(1) agreement by the venture to provide services to a health plan at a "capitated" rate;[38]

(2) agreement by the venture to provide designated services or classes of services to a health plan for a predetermined percentage of premium or revenue from the plan;[39]

(3) use by the venture of significant financial incentives for its physician participants, as a group, to achieve specified cost-containment goals. Two methods by which the venture can accomplish this are:

(a) withholding from all physician participants in the network a substantial amount of the compensation due to them, with distribution of that amount to the physician participants based on group performance in meeting the cost-containment goals of the network as a whole; or

(b) establishing overall cost or utilization targets for the network as a whole, with the network's physician participants subject

35. Physician network joint ventures that involve both risk-sharing and non-risk-sharing arrangements do not fall within the safety zones. * * *

36. The existence of financial risk sharing does not depend on whether, under applicable state law, the network is considered an insurer.

38. A "capitated" rate is a fixed, predetermined payment per covered life (the "capitation") from a health plan to the joint venture in exchange for the joint venture's (not merely an individual physician's) providing and guaranteeing provision of a defined set of covered services to covered individuals for a specified period, regardless of the amount of services actually provided.

39. This is similar to a capitation arrangement, except that the amount of payment to the network can vary in response to changes in the health plan's premiums or revenues.

to subsequent substantial financial rewards or penalties based on group performance in meeting the targets; and

(4) agreement by the venture to provide a complex or extended course of treatment that requires the substantial coordination of care by physicians in different specialities offering a complementary mix of services, for a fixed, predetermined payment, where the costs of that course of treatment for any individual patient can vary greatly due to the individual patient's condition, the choice, complexity, or length of treatment, or other factors.[40]

The Agencies recognize that new types of risk-sharing arrangements may develop. The preceding examples do not foreclose consideration of other arrangements through which the participants in a physician network joint venture may share substantial financial risk in the provision of medical services through the network. Organizers of physician networks who are uncertain whether their proposed arrangements constitute substantial financial risk sharing for purposes of this policy statement are encouraged to take advantage of the Agencies' expedited business review and advisory opinion procedures.

B. The Agencies' Analysis Of Physician Network Joint Ventures That Fall Outside The Antitrust Safety Zones

Physician network joint ventures that fall outside the antitrust safety zones also may have the potential to create significant efficiencies, and do not necessarily raise substantial antitrust concerns. For example, physician network joint ventures in which the physician participants share substantial financial risk, but which involve a higher percentage of physicians in a relevant market than specified in the safety zones, may be lawful if they are not anticompetitive on balance. Likewise, physician network joint ventures that do not involve the sharing of substantial financial risk also may be lawful if the physicians' integration through the joint venture creates significant efficiencies and the venture, on balance, is not anticompetitive.

The Agencies emphasize that it is not their intent to treat such networks either more strictly or more leniently than joint ventures in other industries, or to favor any particular procompetitive organization or structure of health care delivery over other forms that consumers may desire. Rather, their goal is to ensure a competitive marketplace in which consumers will have the benefit of high quality, cost-effective health care and a wide range of choices, including new provider-controlled networks that expand consumer choice and increase competition.

1. Determining When Agreements Among Physicians In A Physician Network Joint Venture Are Analyzed Under The Rule Of Reason

40. Such arrangements are sometimes referred to as "global fees" or "all-inclusive case rates." * * *

Antitrust law treats naked agreements among competitors that fix prices or allocate markets as per se illegal. Where competitors economically integrate in a joint venture, however, such agreements, if reasonably necessary to accomplish the procompetitive benefits of the integration, are analyzed under the rule of reason. In accord with general antitrust principles, physician network joint ventures will be analyzed under the rule of reason, and will not be viewed as per se illegal, if the physicians' integration through the network is likely to produce significant efficiencies that benefit consumers, and any price agreements (or other agreements that would otherwise be per se illegal) by the network physicians are reasonably necessary to realize those efficiencies.[44]

Where the participants in a physician network joint venture have agreed to share substantial financial risk as defined in Section A.4. of this policy statement, their risk-sharing arrangement generally establishes both an overall efficiency goal for the venture and the incentives for the physicians to meet that goal. The setting of price is integral to the venture's use of such an arrangement and therefore warrants evaluation under the rule of reason.

Physician network joint ventures that do not involve the sharing of substantial financial risk may also involve sufficient integration to demonstrate that the venture is likely to produce significant efficiencies. Such integration can be evidenced by the network implementing an active and ongoing program to evaluate and modify practice patterns by the network's physician participants and create a high degree of interdependence and cooperation among the physicians to control costs and ensure quality. This program may include: (1) establishing mechanisms to monitor and control utilization of health care services that are designed to control costs and assure quality of care; (2) selectively choosing network physicians who are likely to further these efficiency objectives; and (3) the significant investment of capital, both monetary and human, in the necessary infrastructure and capability to realize the claimed efficiencies.

The foregoing are not, however, the only types of arrangements that can evidence sufficient integration to warrant rule of reason analysis, and the Agencies will consider other arrangements that also may evidence such integration. However, in all cases, the Agencies' analysis will focus on substance, rather than form, in assessing a network's likelihood of produc-

44. In some cases, the combination of the competing physicians in the network may enable them to offer what could be considered to be a new product producing substantial efficiencies, and therefore the venture will be analyzed under the rule of reason. See Broadcast Music, Inc. v. Columbia Broadcasting System, Inc., 441 U.S. 1, 21–22 (1979) (competitors' integration and creation of a blanket license for use of copyrighted compositions results in efficiencies so great as to make the blanket license a "different product" from the mere combination of individual competitors and, therefore, joint pricing of the blanket license is subject to rule of reason analysis, rather than the per se rule against price fixing). The Agencies' analysis will focus on the efficiencies likely to be produced by the venture, and the relationship of any price agreements to the achievement of those efficiencies, rather than on whether the venture creates a product that can be labeled "new" or "different."

ing significant efficiencies. To the extent that agreements on prices to be charged for the integrated provision of services are reasonably necessary to the venture's achievement of efficiencies, they will be evaluated under the rule of reason.

In contrast to integrated physician network joint ventures, such as those discussed above, there have been arrangements among physicians that have taken the form of networks, but which in purpose or effect were little more than efforts by their participants to prevent or impede competitive forces from operating in the market. These arrangements are not likely to produce significant procompetitive efficiencies. Such arrangements have been, and will continue to be, treated as unlawful conspiracies or cartels, whose price agreements are per se illegal.

Determining that an arrangement is merely a vehicle to fix prices or engage in naked anticompetitive conduct is a factual inquiry that must be done on a case-by-case basis to determine the arrangement's true nature and likely competitive effects. However, a variety of factors may tend to corroborate a network's anticompetitive nature, including: statements evidencing anticompetitive purpose; a recent history of anticompetitive behavior or collusion in the market, including efforts to obstruct or undermine the development of managed care; obvious anticompetitive structure of the network (e.g., a network comprising a very high percentage of local area physicians, whose participation in the network is exclusive, without any plausible business or efficiency justification); the absence of any mechanisms with the potential for generating significant efficiencies or otherwise increasing competition through the network; the presence of anticompetitive collateral agreements; and the absence of mechanisms to prevent the network's operation from having anticompetitive spillover effects outside the network.

2. Applying The Rule Of Reason

A rule of reason analysis determines whether the formation and operation of the joint venture may have a substantial anticompetitive effect and, if so, whether that potential effect is outweighed by any procompetitive efficiencies resulting from the joint venture. The rule of reason analysis takes into account characteristics of the particular physician network joint venture, and the competitive environment in which it operates, that bear on the venture's likely effect on competition.

A determination about the lawfulness of a network's activity under the rule of reason sometimes can be reached without an extensive inquiry under each step of the analysis. For example, a physician network joint venture that involves substantial clinical integration may include a relatively small percentage of the physicians in the relevant markets on a nonexclusive basis. In that case, the Agencies may be able to conclude expeditiously that the network is unlikely to be anticompetitive, based on the competitive environment in which it operates. In assessing the competitive environment, the Agencies would consider such market factors as the number, types, and size of managed care plans operating in the area, the extent of physician participation in those plans, and the economic importance of the managed care plans to area physicians. Alternatively, for example, if a restraint that facially appears to be of a kind that would always or almost always tend to reduce output or increase prices, but has not been considered per se unlawful, is not reasonably necessary to the creation of efficiencies, the Agencies will likely challenge the restraint without an elaborate analysis of market definition and market power.[45]

The steps ordinarily involved in a rule of reason analysis of physician network joint ventures are set forth below.

Step one: Define the relevant market. The Agencies evaluate the competitive effects of a physician network joint venture in each relevant market in which it operates or has substantial impact. In defining the relevant product and geographic markets, the Agencies look to what substitutes, as a practical matter, are reasonably available to consumers for the services in question.[46] The Agencies will first identify the relevant services that the physician network joint venture provides. Although all services provided by each physician specialty might be a separate relevant service market, there may be instances in which significant overlap of services provided by different physician specialties, or in some circumstances, certain nonphysician health care providers, justifies including services from more than one physician specialty or category of providers in the same market. For each relevant service market, the relevant geographic market will include all physicians (or other providers) who are good substitutes for the physician participants in the joint venture.

Step two: Evaluate the competitive effects of the physician joint venture. The Agencies examine the structure and activities of the physician network joint venture and the nature of competition in the relevant market to determine whether the formation or operation of the venture is likely to have an anticompetitive effect. Two key areas of competitive concern are whether a physician network joint venture could raise the prices for physician services charged to health plans above competitive levels, or could prevent or impede the formation or operation of other networks or plans.

In assessing whether a particular network arrangement could raise prices or exclude competition, the Agencies will examine whether the network physicians collectively have the ability and incentive to engage in such conduct. The Agencies will consider not only the proportion of the physicians in any relevant market who are in the network, but also the incentives faced by physicians in the network, and whether different groups of physicians in a network may have significantly different incentives that would reduce the likelihood of anticompetitive conduct. The Department of Justice has entered into final judgments that permit a network to include a relatively large proportion of physicians in a relevant market where the percentage of physicians with an ownership interest in the network is

45. See FTC v. Indiana Federation of Dentists, 476 U.S. 447, 459–60 (1986).

46. A more extensive discussion of how the Agencies define relevant markets is contained in the Agencies' 1992 Horizontal Merger Guidelines.

strictly limited, and the network subcontracts with additional physicians under terms that create a sufficient divergence of economic interest between the subcontracting physicians and the owner physicians so that the owner physicians have an incentive to control the costs to the network of the subcontracting physicians.[47] Evaluating the incentives faced by network physicians requires an examination of the facts and circumstances of each particular case. The Agencies will assess whether different groups of physicians in the network actually have significantly divergent incentives that would override any shared interest, such as the incentive to profit from higher fees for their medical services. The Agencies will also consider whether the behavior of network physicians or other market evidence indicates that the differing incentives among groups of physicians will not prevent anticompetitive conduct.

If, in the relevant market, there are many other networks or many physicians who would be available to form competing networks or to contract directly with health plans, it is unlikely that the joint venture would raise significant competitive concerns. The Agencies will analyze the availability of suitable physicians to form competing networks, including the exclusive or non-exclusive nature of the physician network joint venture.

The Agencies recognize that the competitive impact of exclusive arrangements or other limitations on the ability of a network's physician participants to contract outside the network can vary greatly. For example, in some circumstances exclusivity may help a network serve its subscribers and increase its physician participants' incentives to further the interests of the network. In other situations, however, the anticompetitive risks posed by such exclusivity may outweigh its procompetitive benefits. Accordingly, the Agencies will evaluate the actual or likely effects of particular limitations on contracting in the market situation in which they occur.

An additional area of possible anticompetitive concern involves the risk of "spillover" effects from the venture. For example, a joint venture may involve the exchange of competitively sensitive information among competing physicians and thereby become a vehicle for the network's physician participants to coordinate their activities outside the venture. Ventures that are structured to reduce the likelihood of such spillover are less likely to result in anticompetitive effects. For example, a network that uses an outside agent to collect and analyze fee data from physicians for use in developing the network's fee schedule, and avoids the sharing of such sensitive information among the network's physician participants, may reduce concerns that the information could be used by the network's physician participants to set prices for services they provide outside the network.

47. See, e.g., Competitive Impact Statements in United States v. Health Choice of Northwest Missouri, Inc., Case No. 95–6171–CV–SJ–6 (W.D. Mo.; filed Sept. 13, 1995), 60 Fed. Reg. 51808, 51815 (Oct. 3, 1995); United States and State of Connecticut v. HealthCare Partners, Inc., Case No. 395–CV–01946–RNC (D. Conn.; filed Sept. 13, 1995), 60 Fed. Reg. 52018, 52020 (Oct. 4, 1995).

Step three: Evaluate the impact of procompetitive efficiencies.[48] This step requires an examination of the joint venture's likely procompetitive efficiencies, and the balancing of these efficiencies against any likely anticompetitive effects. The greater the venture's likely anticompetitive effects, the greater must be the venture's likely efficiencies. In assessing efficiency claims, the Agencies focus on net efficiencies that will be derived from the operation of the network and that result in lower prices or higher quality to consumers. The Agencies will not accept claims of efficiencies if the parties reasonably can achieve equivalent or comparable savings through significantly less anticompetitive means. In making this assessment, however, the Agencies will not search for a theoretically least restrictive alternative that is not practical given business realities.

Experience indicates that, in general, more significant efficiencies are likely to result from a physician network joint venture's substantial financial risk sharing or substantial clinical integration. However, the Agencies will consider a broad range of possible cost savings, including improved cost controls, case management and quality assurance, economies of scale, and reduced administrative or transaction costs.

In assessing the likelihood that efficiencies will be realized, the Agencies recognize that competition is one of the strongest motivations for firms to lower prices, reduce costs, and provide higher quality. Thus, the greater the competition facing the network, the more likely it is that the network will actually realize potential efficiencies that would benefit consumers.

Step four: Evaluation of collateral agreements. This step examines whether the physician network joint venture includes collateral agreements or conditions that unreasonably restrict competition and are unlikely to contribute significantly to the legitimate purposes of the physician network joint venture. The Agencies will examine whether the collateral agreements are reasonably necessary to achieve the efficiencies sought by the joint venture. For example, if the physician participants in a physician network joint venture agree on the prices they will charge patients who are not covered by the health plans with which their network contracts, such an agreement plainly is not reasonably necessary to the success of the joint venture and is an antitrust violation.[49] Similarly, attempts by a physician network joint venture to exclude competitors or classes of competitors of the network's physician participants from the market could have anticompetitive effects, without advancing any legitimate, procompetitive goal of the network. This could happen, for example, if the network facilitated agreements among the physicians to refuse to deal with such competitors outside the network, or to pressure other market participants to refuse to deal with such competitors or deny them necessary access to key facilities.

48. If steps one and two reveal no competitive concerns with the physician network joint venture, step three is unnecessary, and the analysis continues with step four, below.

49. This analysis of collateral agreements also applies to physician network joint ventures that fall within the safety zones.

[The Agencies then set forth seven examples illustrating how the foregoing principles would be applied in specific cases.]

NOTES AND QUESTIONS ON ANTITRUST ENFORCEMENT AND PHYSICIAN NETWORKS

1. *The Statements of Enforcement Policy*. In 1993, responding to uncertainty in the legal and provider communities, the antitrust agencies began issuing formal statements of their enforcement policies with respect to certain collaborative arrangements in the health care industry. (The topics covered by the nine current statements—or guidelines, as they are sometimes called—include hospital mergers; hospital joint ventures to procure costly equipment or provide services; joint purchasing by health care providers; exchanges by providers of sensitive price and cost information; collective provision of price and other information to purchasers of health services; and the formation of physician and multiprovider networks.) The 1996 version of the statements included major revisions of both Statement 8 (reproduced above) and Statement 9 (multiprovider networks, including PHOs), as those policy statements had been been previously revised in 1994. Like the Merger Guidelines commented upon in chapter 5(§E), the health care statements are intended only as a guide to enforcement policy; they are neither legally binding on the agencies nor intended to codify the underlying law.

2. *Safety Zones*. Why did the agencies create antitrust "safety zones" for certain physician networks? What is the difference between the two zones recognized? Do you agree with the market share tests adopted? How do you suppose they were they arrived at? What would you tell your clients if their proposed venture failed to qualify for one of the safe harbors?

3. *Per Se vs. Rule-of-Reason Treatment*. Do you agree with the tests the agencies employ in deciding whether to apply a per se rule or the Rule of Reason to an arrangement whereby competing physicians combine to market themselves to managed-care plans? Assume that five solo practitioners in a very large metropolitan market appoint one of their number as an agent to negotiate the terms, including prices, on which the five would participate in particular PPOs, HMOs, or self-insured health plans. How would the agencies treat their arrangement under the policy statement? How would you defend it? Does antitrust doctrine leave room for your defense? This hypothetical should suggest a possible conceptual difficulty with the agencies' approach. Can you see it and explain how and why the agencies went wrong? Are *Maricopa* and the *Topco* case (described in a note following *Maricopa*) implicated here? Cf. Havighurst, Are the Antitrust Agencies Overregulating Physician Networks?, 8 Loyola Cons. L. Rep. 78 (1995–96) (criticizing 1994 guidelines for prescribing the specific forms that networks must take to qualify for Rule-of-Reason treatment).

For examples of provider networks that the Department of Justice has condemned on the basis that they are not sufficiently integrated and are merely vehicles for price fixing by the members, see United States v.

Woman's Hosp. Found., 1996–2 Trade Cas. (CCH) 71,561 (M.D. La. 1996) (hospital allegedly sought to monopolize maternity care by forming PHO with local OBs, allowing collective bargaining with managed-care plans and raising fee levels); United States v. Health Choice of Northwest Mo., 1996–2 Trade Cas. (CCH) 71,606 (W.D. Mo. 1995) (85% of local doctors, in collaboration with only hospital, allegedly formed exclusive network, without sharing financial risk, thereby obtaining favorable terms from managed-care plans). Although these networks were formed with rather obvious anticompetitive intent, the agencies have been criticized for being unduly arbitrary in refusing Rule-of-Reason treatment for some physician networks—as indicated in the following note.

4. *The 1996 Revision of Statement 8.* The 1994 version of Statement 8 was criticized by the American Medical Association and some other observers (e.g., Havighurst, supra) on the ground that it unduly restricted the formation of physician-sponsored networks that would be more procompetitive than anticompetitive. That criticism prompted proposals in Congress to declare that certain physician networks were entitled as a matter of law to Rule-of-Reason treatment. E.g., H.R. 2925, 104th Cong., 2d Sess. (1996) (providing that arrangements meeting statutory definition of "health care provider network" must be "judged on the basis of its reasonableness" for antitrust purposes). Partly in response to this threat of legislative action, the FTC and Department of Justice undertook to revise Statements 8 and 9.

The 1994 enforcement policy stated that physician network joint ventures having a price-fixing feature "will be reviewed under a rule of reason analysis and not viewed as per se illegal either if the physicians in the joint venture *share substantial financial risk* or if the combining of the physicians into a joint venture enables them to *offer a new product* producing substantial efficiencies." (Emphasis added.) These requirements were not laid down merely as conditions that had to be met to qualify for a "safety zone." Instead, the two conditions applied to any joint venture having a price-fixing feature. Moreover, a footnote underscored that the Rule of Reason would apply only if "the joint venture is not likely merely to restrict competition and decrease output, such as, for example, an agreement among physicians who do not share substantial financial risk that fixes the price that each physician will charge." Thus, the guidelines put the government on record as conclusively deeming any physician network joint venture of any size to be unlawful unless it was demonstrably something more than a joint selling agency wholesaling the services of the doctors in the group. Should the government have been more tolerant of physicians seeking only to improve their ability to market themselves in the world of managed care?

Criticisms of the 1994 policy included the claim that the agencies were unduly hostile to physician collaboration because of the frequency with which physicians had in the past attempted to prevent competition from taking hold. Responding to this charge, an FTC official stated,

> The central challenge of sound antitrust enforcement in health care markets is to distinguish anticompetitive resistance to market forces from innovative adaptation to those same market forces. While most instances of provider collaboration are legitimate efforts to adapt to changing markets—many providers are eager to join managed care plans or to compete against them on the merits—the danger of concerted provider opposition to market forces has not been eliminated.

Address by Mark D. Whitener, Antitrust, Medicare Reform and Health Care Competition, American Enterprise Institute for Public Policy Research, Dec. 5, 1995, Washington D.C. But see Havighurst, supra, at 81:

> Although there remain some places where the doctor's old strategies may still be capable of heading off unwanted change, the market forces that have been unleashed in most communities cannot easily be reversed by counter-revolutionary professional action. In most circumstances, antitrust enforcers should no longer presume that physician collaboration that is not certifiably innocuous is intended to restrain trade rather than to achieve efficiencies or to offer purchasers a fuller range of health care options. Suspicions that were well justified when physicians possessed the means of controlling their economic environment are not generally justified today.

To be sure, there are some (particularly rural and local) markets in which physicians' efforts to foreclose competitive innovation might be effective in preventing it. See, e.g., Physicians Group, Inc., FTC Dkt C–360 (Mar. 12, 1996) (consent order; action against physician group in Danville, Va., allegedly organized to resist managed care); Medical Staff of Broward Gen. Med. Center, 114 F.T.C. 542 (1991) (consent order; alleged concerted efforts of local physicians to prevent Cleveland Clinic from establishing a 200–bed satellite operation in South Florida); Southbank IPA, Inc., 114 F.T.C. 783 (1991) (consent order settling allegations that 23 ob-gyn specialists in Jacksonville, Fla., formed an exclusive IPA as a vehicle for boycotting an HMO and foreclosing competition in fee setting); see also footnote 47 in Statement 8, supra. The problem presented in paragraph 7 below is set in an immature market of the kind that was once typical but is increasingly rare today.

Another criticism of the 1994 guidelines was that the agencies' policy, in addition to "looking backward to the time when it was reasonable to presume that physicians collaborated only for anticompetitive purposes," also suffered,

> like many a wayward golf shot, * * * from looking ahead, away from the object at hand and toward an intended goal. Thus, the agencies appear to be anticipating where they think the health care marketplace is headed and attempting to steer physician-sponsored networks in that foreordained direction. Therefore, their prescription of the form that such networks must take reflects a prejudgment of the way physician services should, and will eventually, be bought and sold in the future health care marketplace.
>
> * * * [I]t is dangerous for regulators to dictate market outcomes on the basis of *a priori* assumptions about what is and what is not efficient or responsive to the needs and preferences of purchasers. Current antitrust

> enforcement policy with respect to physician networks is an exercise of prosecutorial discretion that, in attempting to provide guidance to the industry, has become overly regulatory and prescriptive, foreclosing options that might attract followers in a competitive market.

Havighurst, supra, at 89. What policy reasons might be offered for not unduly limiting the opportunities of physicians to organize network joint ventures that are not demonstrably anticompetitive? Are there reasons why physicians might not be capable of organizing health plans that meet the guideline requirements from the outset? Is it possible that some physician-sponsored networks not meeting the agencies' current requirements might prove attractive to consumers and major purchasers in a competitive environment?

Did the 1996 revision of policy statement 8 adequately respond the charge that the agencies were overregulating physician networks? Most observers concluded that the new guidelines did eliminate most of the problems with the earlier version. Do you agree, based on your assessment of the hypothetical in the preceding note? Should Congress enact legislation along the lines of H.R. 2925?

5. *Applying the Rule of Reason*. Do you agree with the agencies' method of analyzing physician joint ventures once they have decided to apply the Rule of Reason to a particular transaction? Are there elements that might appropriately receive somewhat more explicit weight? Recall the methodology proposed in chapter 4(§A).

6. *Using So-called "Messenger" Techniques in Negotiating Prices*. Lawyers for physicians not wishing to integrate their practices or to share financial risks but desiring to market themselves through a common agent have designed some ingenious arrangements that avoid the noncompetitive fixing of prices for the services of the individual physicians in the group. Such "messenger" arrangements, as they are called, permit the physicians to obtain some of the efficiencies of joint marketing while preserving a semblance of price competition. Statement 9 of the DOJ/FTC policy statements explains the use of these mechanisms as follows:

> Some networks that are not substantially integrated use a variety of "messenger model" arrangements to facilitate contracting between providers and payers and avoid price-fixing agreements among competing network providers. Arrangements that are designed simply to minimize the costs associated with the contracting process, and that do not result in a collective determination by the competing network providers on prices or price-related terms, are not per se illegal price fixing.
>
> Messenger models can be organized and operate in a variety of ways. For example, network providers may use an agent or third party to convey to purchasers information obtained individually from the providers about the prices or price-related terms that the providers are willing to accept. In some cases, the agent may convey to the providers all contract offers made by purchasers, and each provider then makes

an independent, unilateral decision to accept or reject the contract offers. In others, the agent may have received from individual providers some authority to accept contract offers on their behalf. The agent also may help providers understand the contracts offered, for example by providing objective or empirical information about the terms of an offer (such as a comparison of the offered terms to other contracts agreed to by network participants).

The key issue in any messenger model arrangement is whether the arrangement creates or facilitates an agreement among competitors on prices or price-related terms. Determining whether there is such an agreement is a question of fact in each case. The Agencies will examine whether the agent facilitates collective decision-making by network providers, rather than independent, unilateral, decisions. In particular, the Agencies will examine whether the agent coordinates the providers' responses to a particular proposal, disseminates to network providers the views or intentions of other network providers as to the proposal, expresses an opinion on the terms offered, collectively negotiates for the providers, or decides whether or not to convey an offer based on the agent's judgment about the attractiveness of the prices or price-related terms. If the agent engages in such activities, the arrangement may amount to a per se illegal price-fixing agreement.

At a later point, the policy statement provides the following hypothetical to illustrate how the agencies will view different methods of price setting:

The PHO contracts on a fee-for-service basis. The physicians and other health care providers who are participants in the PHO do not share substantial financial risk or otherwise integrate their services so as to provide significant efficiencies. The payers prefer to continue to use their existing third-party administrators for contract administration and utilization management, or to do it in-house.

There is no agreement among the PHO's participants to deal only through the PHO, and many of them participate in other networks and HMOs on a variety of terms. Some payers have chosen to contract with the hospital and some or all of the PHO physicians and other providers without going through the PHO, and a significant proportion of the PHO's participants contract with payers in this manner.

In an effort to avoid horizontal price agreements among competing participants in the PHO while facilitating the contracting process, the PHO considers using the following mechanisms:

A. An agent of the PHO, not otherwise affiliated with any PHO participant, will obtain from each participant a fee schedule or conversion factor that represents the minimum payment that participant will accept from a payer. The agent is authorized to contract on the participants' behalf with payers offering prices at this level or better. The agent does not negotiate pricing terms with the payer and does not share pricing information among competing participants. Price offers that do not meet the authorized fee are conveyed to the individual participant.

B. The same as option A, with the added feature that the agent is authorized, for a specified time, to bind the participant to any contract offers with prices equal, to or better than, those in a contract that the participant has already approved.

C. The same as option A, except that in order to assist payers in developing contract offers, the agent takes the fee authorizations of the various participants and develops a schedule that can be presented to a payer showing the percentages of participants in the network who have authorized contracts at various price levels.

D. The venture hires an agent to negotiate prices with payers on behalf of the PHO's participants. The agent does not disclose to the payer the prices the participants are willing to accept, as in option C, but attempts to obtain the best possible prices for all the participants. The resulting contract offer then is relayed to each participant for acceptance or rejection.

How do you suppose the agencies viewed each of the four options?

Do messenger arrangements qualify as "less restrictive alternatives"? Should every physician-sponsored joint selling agency therefore be required to use them? To be sure, they are *theoretically* less restrictive than letting the joint venturers agree on price. But because they are cumbersome to operate, they are not equally satisfactory as alternatives for getting the marketing job done. Their use therefore sacrifices some of the efficiency that joint marketing can otherwise create. In an effort to reduce this unwieldiness, some networks have employed "modified" messenger arrangements, which may take the form of a standing offer of individual physicians' services on uniform terms that a purchaser is free to accept or reject. Such arrangements have never been approved by enforcement officials, however. Although it is hard to judge the relative efficiency of all the possible messenger arrangements, the antitrust agencies might somewhat improve the situation by tolerating modified versions whenever competition in the market as a whole is healthy and not likely to be in danger.

Arguably, insistence on a second-best alternative is appropriate in antitrust enforcement and under the Rule of Reason only if a specific risk to competition outweighs the efficiencies forgone. To be sure, use of a messenger model should be required in many circumstances, often identifiable with only a "quick look." But in instances where the danger of anticompetitive harm is unclear, a more extensive evaluation should probably be required. Such an analysis would consider such factors as whether the physicians sponsoring the marketing effort are in an aggressive competitive posture rather than in a defensive, anticompetitive one; the percentage of competing physicians engaged in the effort; their freedom to participate in competing ventures; their actual participation in other marketing schemes; the sophistication, effectiveness, and preferences of the purchasers with which they deal, and the overall vigor of competition in the market being served. Even if a network was the exclusive marketer for its member doctors, there would still be no threat to competition if the market featured a variety of other plans. In such a mature market, purchasers could decide for themselves whether to patronize physician groups that have not expressly undertaken to share financial risk, to integrate their practices, or to maintain any kind of independent pricing. Indeed, the availability of meaningful purchaser options itself puts the collaborating physicians at risk of contract nonrenewal and should go far toward satisfying government officials that competition is not in danger.

7. *Problem: A Medical Society IPA.* Since the 1970s, the Oz County Medical Society has been a forum for its members' apprehensions about the deplorable things that were happening to the practice of medicine elsewhere and could, the members feared, also happen in Oz County. At a society meeting in the mid–1980s, the members heard a report that Better Health Systems, Inc., was exploring the possibility of establishing a group model HMO in Emerald City. The chairman of the society's Professional Affairs Committee told the membership that, even though they might be opposed to the idea of prepaid medical care, they should consider developing an HMO of their own, one in which they, rather than lay administrators, would call the shots. "If we don't do it ourselves," he said, "they are going to do it to us!" The ultimate result was the formation of OZIPA, a nonprofit HMO of the IPA variety.

Half of OZIPA's governing board are local laypersons drawn largely from civic organizations and the nonprofit sector, while the remainder are physicians. The board was originally named by the medical society but is now self-perpetuating. Forty-five percent of the physicians in Oz County participate in OZIPA, although membership is open to all. These physicians staff the IPA's committees and see its patients on a fee-for-service basis. The plan pays them on the basis of usual, customary, and reasonable (UCR) fees, but withholds 25% of all payments until year end to ensure that the plan can meet its obligations.

OZIPA now serves about 20% of the county residents having private health coverage. It has reduced hospitalization rates from 768 days per 1000 subscribers in the early 1980s to 326, largely by persuading those physicians detected as over-utilizers through utilization review to change their admitting practices. Financially, the plan has done well, paying its physicians 100 cents on the dollar in the last few years and building significant reserves. Only in the first three years did the physicians suffer a significant loss of income. That was the period during which Better Health was threatening to enter the market and it was necessary to quote low premiums to several employment groups tempted by Better Health's offer. By and large, OZIPA's employer customers credit it with slowing the rate of increase in the cost of their employee health benefits.

It appears that, in Oz County, only the hospitals are unhappy with OZIPA, because their occupancy has fallen and it is harder for them to meet their many obligations. One of them, Emerald City General Hospital

(ECGH), the lowest-cost facility in the community, had some expectation that Better Health would bring it more patients, and it was disappointed when Better Health changed its mind about starting an HMO in Emerald City. ECGH has lately explored the idea of starting its own hospital-based PHO with its staff physicians, but they have not been receptive. ECGH senses that OZIPA, while somewhat interested in cutting hospitalization costs, is not interested in increasing patronage of the low-cost facility by doing anything that would either disrupt staffing at the different hospitals or tempt patients to change physicians.

What legal or business advice could you give the hospital? If you were on the staff of the FTC, what would you say about the situation in Oz County? Consider the following:

(a) Is OZIPA anything more than a joint-selling agency likely to attract per se treatment? Cf. Virginia Excelsior Mills, Inc. v. FTC, 256 F.2d 538 (4th Cir.1958) (joint selling per se unlawful if competitive independence lost). Or is the element of utilization review and the imposition of fee withholds sufficient to attract Rule-of-Reason treatment? Can OZIPA argue that it is procompetitive because it offers a "different product" (see *Maricopa*, supra, at n. 31) and is sufficiently integrated that any restraints it imposes are properly deemed ancillary to a legitimate business purpose? Is it significant that the fee withholds have in recent years not reduced physicians' incomes?

(b) Is OZIPA guilty of price fixing? Should the use of UCR limits fare any better than the maximum-price fixing in *Maricopa?* Why would physicians choose to pay UCR fees? Is it because, up to the limits of the formula, it gives patients no reason to prefer one physician over another because of the fees charged?

(c) The IPA was clearly formed in response to the competitive threat posed by Better Health. Does this make it anticompetitive—or procompetitive? The doctors will claim that they simply sought to improve the quality of the insurance coverage available in Oz County in order that fee-for-service physicians could more effectively compete with Better Health or any other would-be entrant. Are there any flaws in that argument? For evidence that most modern IPAs differ from the defensive, profession-dominated plans of the past, see Welch, The New Structure of Individual Practice Associations, 12 J.Health Pol., Pol'y & L. 723 (1987). Recall the discussion of different types of health plans in chapter 2(§C).

(d) Is the problem here that the collaborators were too powerful? By what measure? When market power appears in conjunction with a legitimate procompetitive purpose in a joint venture antitrust case, what should happen?

(e) Assume that, instead of being organized by the Oz County Medical Society, the network was formed by a subset of local physicians pursuant to a request from Ozzie Industries, the county's largest employer, to organize physicians who would become "preferred providers" under the Ozzie Employees (self-insured) Health Plan. Under the plan, services obtained from preferred providers would be covered on preferential terms for Ozzie employees and their families. Does it make any difference in the antitrust analysis that Ozzie Industries, a large employer, pressed for the network to be formed?

(f) Suppose that, instead of paying the physicians on a fee-for-service basis, the network proposes a system of capitation payments. Would your analysis change?

(g) Assume that, rather than being an open network, OZIPA proposes to become exclusive so that its members may not contract with other networks. Does explicit exclusivity raise or reduce the anticompetitive risks associated with the network? On the one hand, exclusivity might lock up the market and serve to bind physicians to one network. On the other hand, however, exclusive arrangements may promote loyalty and commitment among affiliated providers and prevent free-riding by ensuring that physicians see enough subscribers to make it likely that they will engage in cost-effective practices. At what point are the competitive risks likely to outweigh the benefits? See generally Greaney, Managed Competition, Integrated Delivery Systems and Antitrust, 79 Cornell L. Rev. 1507, 1586–87 (1994) (arguing the need for guidelines to establish the threshold at which exclusivity may change "from a factor that promotes competition to one that retards it").

(h) Assume that you find many physicians grousing about OZIPA and the controls it imposes on them. Does this discontent prove that the plan is not being run in the doctors' interest and is therefore not a restraint of trade? Or would you expect to find differences of opinion over the correct price and output limitations in any cartel? There have been numerous lawsuits by providers challenging insurer practices that were developed in collaboration with provider interests. E.g., Brillhart v. Mutual Med. Ins., Inc., 768 F.2d 196 (7th Cir.1985) (unsuccessful physician challenge to traditional Blue Shield plan); Hoffman v. Delta Dental Plan, 517 F.Supp. 564 (D.Minn.1981) (nonparticipating dentists sued prepayment plan originated by dental society and controlled by 95% of dentists in state). Would you expect the plaintiffs in such cases to focus the courts' attention on the true nature and source of the possible harm to competition?

(i) It would not be implausible to argue that any plan under the control of a dominant physician organization engages in price fixing simply by choosing a method of paying physicians that limits price competition (as almost any arrangement does). Nevertheless, before applying the per se rule, an assessment of procompetitive benefits and anticompetitive harms should be undertaken. In making this assessment, what is the relevance of OZIPA's actual effect on health care costs and physician fees? If the medical society and OZIPA can show that overall costs and physician fees have been lowered, should they win? Or is the effect on competition a distinct issue?

(j) If you were an FTC commissioner trying to decide whether to issue a complaint in this case, how would you respond to the argument, such as was made by DHHS in the 1970s, that organizations like OZIPA were approved in the federal HMO Act of 1973 and are effective in controlling costs? See Egdahl et al., Fee-for-Service Health Maintenance Organizations, 241 J.A.M.A. 588 (1979). As a matter of prosecutorial discretion, should such a "bird in the hand" be sacrificed because of a theoretical faith that competition will one day bring costs under control? Should the HMO Act be construed to exempt OZIPA from the Sherman Act or the FTC Act?

(k) Can you describe specific ways in which competition was, or might have been, harmed by the formation of OZIPA? It has been argued that a controlled IPA might serve physicians as a "fighting ship" in warding off new entrants and as a vehicle for maintaining solidarity and slowing changes in the status quo. See Havighurst & Hackbarth, Enforcing the Rules of Free Enterprise in Imperfect Markets: The Case of Individual Practice Associations, in A New Approach to the Economics of Health Care 377, 381–96 (M. Olson ed. 1981). Do you see manifestations of these dangers here? Can the Oz County physicians defend themselves by arguing that a lawful monopolist does not violate the law by charging low but profitable "limit-entry" prices designed to discourage new market entrants?

(*l*) Consider Hassan v. Independent Practice Assocs., P.C., 698 F.Supp. 679 (E.D.Mich.1988). Hassan, an allergist, sued IPA for excluding him, making the usual antitrust allegations. IPA was an IPA-type HMO established in 1979 by the local medical society and controlled by physicians. The court was impressed that it faced competition on a number of fronts and seemed not to respond primarily to its physicians' preferences in setting prices. The court also stated that "[p]rice fixing agreements can be lawful if they are a necessary part of an integration of resources—a joint venture." Unlike the foundations in *Maricopa*, IPA set only the prices charged to subscribers of a single HMO, not to a larger community, and the physicians shared the risk of treatment costs through a "risk withhold." IPA was thus offering a new product, complete medical care for a prepaid premium. No anticompetitive motive was shown. The court also rejected Hassan's claim of "boycott," finding no market power and plausible business reasons for his exclusion.

Providers of Care or Insurers Against Financial Risk?

NOTES AND QUESTIONS ON INSURANCE REGULATION OF RISK–BEARING PROVIDER NETWORKS

1. Should provider-controlled organizations that assume various kinds of risk with respect to the health care needs of an enrolled population be regulated as health insurers? Recall from chapter 2(§D) that, under the Balanced Budget Act of 1997, provider-sponsored organizations (PSOs) that confine themselves to enrolling Medicare beneficiaries under the Medicare+Choice program can, for a limited time, escape state regulation and be regulated with respect to solvency, etc., only by the federal government. State regulatory policy with respect to other risk-bearing provider networks (and to Medicare-only PSOs when, and if, their waivers expire) is another matter, however.

2. *The NAIC White Paper*. In 1996, a working group of the National Association of Insurance Commissioners (NAIC) issued a draft "white paper" on the whole subject of how to regulate entities that assume "health insurance risk." NAIC, The Regulation of Health Risk–Bearing Entities (Dec. 1996 draft), reprinted in 6 Health L. Rep. (BNA) 73 (1997) [NAIC White Paper]. The white paper framed the basic issues as follows:

> Notably, some arrangements that technically involve insurance risk do not give rise to the same degree of public policy concerns as other arrangements. The courts have struggled with cases that present close public policy questions about whether an arrangement involves insurance risk and should be governed by state insurance regulation and those which involve what the courts have called service risk. * * *
>
> To provide guidance on how to grapple with the inconsistent outcomes of these lower court opinions, academic commentator Robert Keeton identified two factors that should be considered when determining whether an entity is engaged in service risk or insurance risk. These factors rest upon the nature and characteristics of the transaction:
>
>> (1) Did the specific transaction or general line of business at issue involve one or more of the concerns at which the regulatory statutes were aimed?
>>
>> (2) Were the elements of risk transference and risk distribution central to and relatively important elements of the transactions (or merely incidental to other elements that gave the transactions their distinctive character)?[17]
>
> In the health insurance context, state insurance regulators have developed an overwhelming consensus that arrangements that involve insurance risk invoke the public policy concerns that insurance regulation is designed to address. While states are still exploring issues related to the regulation of the range of risk-bearing arrangements, this consensus applies even if the entity assuming the financial risk is also providing the service. Irrespective of the type of entity assuming the risk, the potential for inaccurate actuarial projections related to cost or intensity or severity or frequency of service is always present. Further, the consequences of adverse outcomes associated with insurance risk is disruptive for the failed entity, the consumer, and other players in the health insurance market (including contracting providers and HMOs) regardless of the form of the organization assuming the insurance risk.
>
> Some lower court cases have declined to categorize as insurance risk certain service contract transactions, such as those involving

17. Keeton & Widiss, Insurance Law: A Guide to Fundamental Principles, Legal Doctrines & Commercial Practices, Section 8.3(c), 951 (1988).

warranties, which involve risk assumed by the entities responsible for manufacturing or repairing the products. However, not only are the holdings of these and similar types of cases highly inconsistent, they do not neatly apply to the health insurance market. In health care, the service at issue relates to the human body, not products. Risk-bearing entities, whether or not service providers, do not have the capacity to build the human body. Nor do risk-bearing entities control the panoply of risks to which the human body is subject. It is not possible for a risk-bearing entity to predict or control the full range of conditions arising from personal habit, heredity, accident or epidemic which may require medical care.

Further, while the ability to provide services may or may not meaningfully reduce the actuarial risks present in the health care context depending on the specifics of the arrangement, it will rarely reduce the actuarial risk to a de minimis level. The risk would probably be reduced if the risk-bearing entity is an organization owned, in whole or in part, by providers who render clinical services through the organization. However, even if some service providers are willing to work on greatly reduced or nonexistent additional income (an assertion which some question), the risk-bearing entity still may be responsible for a wide range of expenses necessary to support the provision of health care services. Examples of additional expenses may include those related to other clinical personnel, administrative services, laboratory tests, services provided by others, debt service, business expenses, and other liabilities.

In addition, the transfer and spreading of risk is an essential and important element of the transactions developing in today's marketplace. Entities operating in or seeking to operate in the managed care market are struggling to remain competitive by combining the financing and delivery of health care services. It is the nature of the risk inherent in these financing activities that gives rise to public policy concerns in the insurance context.

The issue that most concerned the NAIC was the dependability of PSOs. Although a PSO may simply contract with a licensed entity (e.g., an HMO, a Blue Cross and Blue Shield plan, or a traditional indemnity insurer) to provide services on a capitated or fee-for-service, it may also seek to contract directly with employers to care for particular employment groups. The following paragraphs discuss the regulatory issues raised in the two situations.

3. *Direct Contracting Arrangements*. As the NAIC White Paper observes,

Some * * * PSOs are structured to engage in direct contracting activities with individuals, employers, and other groups[. For example,] SecureCare of Iowa is a PHO that is licensed under the laws of Iowa as an organized delivery system (ODS). * * * The organization is affiliated with Mercy Hospital Medical Center, which is SecureCare's only hospital owner, and has 380 physicians who are stockholders. Of the 380 physician-owners, 100 are primary care physicians and 280 are specialty physicians. The physicians as a group and the hospital each own 50 percent of the organization. SecureCare of Iowa contracts with about 100 employer groups. It currently does not contract with any individuals. It is discussing with other carriers and physician-hospital organizations the possibility of "renting out" its network but has not yet entered into any contracts to do so.

* * * There is a strong difference of opinion among industry representatives about whether contracting provider groups should be able to contract directly with employers and individuals without being subject to similar requirements as HMOs. Some provider representatives assert that regulatory requirements for HMOs do not accommodate PSOs' organizational structures and advocate for a distinct regulatory framework. At the same time, they argue that, while they do not oppose state regulation, ERISA preempts state regulation of provider-sponsored direct contracting arrangements.

Employers have been a powerful, effective, and important driving force behind many innovative initiatives to enhance competition, lower costs, and improve health care quality. They view opportunities to contract directly with PSOs as a method of further reducing costs for their plans. Some employers have expressed concern that attempts by regulators to develop a framework that levels the playing field will protect, albeit inadvertently, existing licensed entities, and thus, discourage competition and hinder the success of new initiatives. Instead, these employers argue for relatively free entry and exit for risk-bearing [PSOs] into the insurance market without regulatory barriers.

On the other hand, traditional players in the managed care market, which include currently licensed provider-sponsored risk-bearing entities, dispute the contention that comprehensive regulatory standards should not apply to [PSOs]. They argue that risk-bearing PSOs do not markedly differ from HMOs and contend that developing a separate and less stringent regulatory structure will only serve to enhance the competitive advantage of PSOs at the HMO community's expense. They also assert that providers assuming similar levels and forms of risk as HMOs should face the same level of consumer protection and solvency standards as applied to HMOs.

Insurance regulators are primarily concerned with ensuring that, regardless of the nature of the entity, consumers receive adequate protection from insolvency and from incentives to deliver inadequate care. In their own states and through the NAIC, many insurance regulators have stressed the importance of creating a level playing field while at the same time fostering a regulatory environment that permits the development of new organizational forms which can also deliver quality care in a cost-effective manner.

* * *

The regulatory approaches being pursued by state insurance regulators include:

- applying current regulatory requirements to all participants in the health insurance market. These requirements may vary depending upon the level of the risk being assumed;
- creating a separate category for provider-sponsored entities that reflect similar solvency and other consumer protection standards applicable to HMOs; and
- creating a separate category for [PSOs] that imposes different solvency and consumer protection requirements on [PSOs] than are currently imposed on HMOs.

Most states have not created distinct legal requirements for PSOs. In a great number of states, provider-sponsored entities engaged in activities which meet the state's definition of the business of insurance are licensed as HMO's. * * *

In 1993, Iowa became the first state to enact a statute specifically related to provider networks. Chapter 158 of the 1993 Iowa Acts was enacted to provide flexibility for the development of integrated delivery systems, called organized delivery systems (ODS), including antitrust immunity for the entities. Of particular concern was the ability of these systems to develop in rural areas of the state. While the ODS is licensed and monitored by the state's Department of Public Health, the Department of Insurance conducts the financial reviews of ODSs.

These health delivery systems may assume risk but must comply with solvency requirements. They must maintain the greater of $1 million or three times the average monthly claims for third-party providers. * * *

While the financial and quality requirements of ODS regulations differ from HMOs, the ODS laws are still comprehensive in scope. The capital requirements are higher for the ODS than for the HMO. Since enactment, only one organization, SecureCare of Iowa, has become operational as an ODS. SecureCare complies with the state's HMO regulations. The state has seen a marked increase in HMO applications due in part to the efforts of providers to enter the Medicaid managed care market, which in Iowa requires a HMO license.

* * *

A very few states have indicated that they are unlikely to regulate certain PSO arrangements. In April 1996, the Illinois Department of Insurance issued a bulletin which stated that a contracting provider group is not subject to regulation by the Department of Insurance when it engages in an arrangement with an employer or licensed entity in which the [PSO] assumes no risk, full risk, partial risk or downstream risk and the employer or licensed entity remains on risk for health care costs should the provider group fail to perform. The bulletin states that the provider group is subject to department regulation when the provider group [as opposed to an employer] is the ultimate risk-bearer and is directly obligated to provide, arrange or pay for medical services.

In Idaho, the Department of Insurance reviews provider arrangements on a case-by-case basis. The Department notes that it would probably not require an insurance license if a provider enters into an arrangement with a licensed insurer or self-funded employer and the responsibility to members remains with the insurer or self-funded employer. Similarly, it is the South Carolina Department's position that it may be preempted by ERISA from regulating any provider network which contracts only with self-insured, single employer health plans.

Most state insurance regulators believe that just as states may regulate traditional insurers which accept insurance risk, the state's ability to regulate provider-based entities which have begun to bear insurance risk does not conflict with ERISA. Where the state regulates a [PSO] entering into a contract with an individual, employer or other group to deliver services on a risk basis in a similar manner as any other managed care organization, the state regulation does not have any more of an effect on the purchaser than the regulation governing other managed care entities which engage in the business of insurance.

4. *Downstream Risk Arrangements.* The NAIC White Paper also discussed arrangements between licensed insurers or HMOs and subcontracting provider entities (organizations or individuals) under which the latter assume some part of the licensed entity's risk:

Many provider organizations are beginning to assume risk downstream for some of the same reasons that provider organizations are beginning to assume risk directly. [HMOs], in some markets, have an increased interest in sharing their risk with providers. Providers view the acceptance of downstream risk as a way to remain competitive in the marketplace. However, many providers that accept downstream risk are not seeking to contract directly with individuals, employers, or other groups (although they would like to be able to do so legally if they chose).

The reluctance to engage in direct contracting activities can stem from an unwillingness to enter into competition with well-established health plans in the local market with whom the provider [organization] has or seeks to have good relations. It may also stem from a strategic decision to invest in the provider organization's "core competencies." Many provider organizations do not have the infrastructure, skills, and resources necessary for assuming risk directly. Alternatively, provider organizations that do have the resources available to develop the infrastructure decide to invest those resources in initiatives related more closely to patient care and quality measurement activities. Additionally, a provider organization may decide to remain only in downstream risk arrangements because the PSO does not have the geographic reach to serve adequately a direct contracting purchaser.

Both the provider community and traditional players in the managed care market seem to agree that PSOs which contract with licensed insurers to provide services on a risk basis should not be subject to licensure requirements that are as strict as those imposed on HMOs. The licensed entity, which is held to state solvency and other regulatory standards, also may be required by the state to monitor the ability of the contracting provider group to continue to provide services from both a solvency and quality perspective.

State Regulatory Response

Regulators have been exploring whether they can achieve consumer protection objectives in the downstream context without imposing duplicative regulations on an additional level of organizations. * * * The vast majority of states do not require a downstream contractor to obtain an insurance license to accept insurance risk.

State regulators are, however, concerned about the nature of the risk arrangements between licensed entities and provider networks. Some regulators continue to inquire whether having a licensed entity involved in the arrangement is enough to address consumer protection concerns. They are exploring many issues such as the question of when the risk and responsibilities of the PSO transform the contract from one between a HMO and provider group to one between a HMO and a subcontracting HMO. Additionally, some state regulators have expressed very strong concern about circumstances under which provider groups are taking on far more risk than they can handle, particularly in a global capitation context, and placing the continuity and quality of beneficiary services in jeopardy.

States are striving to design regulations that minimize the duplication of regulatory standards while still achieving regulatory objectives. A number of states are doing so by relying upon the licensed entity in the arrangement to ensure that consumer protection standards are in place. Nevertheless, states recognize that if the licensed entity does not monitor effectively the contracting provider group or the provider group takes on too much risk, the insolvency of the provider group may considerably harm the solvency of the HMO and the ability of plan enrollees to receive health care services. Consequently, several states * * * have begun to impose explicit requirements upon the licensed entity to monitor the financial solvency of its subcontractors and perhaps more minimal requirements on the subcontracting organization.

5. *Questions.* When is licensure and regulation of a PSO by a state insurance department appropriate? If an employer or licensed health plan contracts with a physician network to provide health services to a particular enrollee group, is it necessarily up to the state to ensure the provider group's ability to perform its obligations?

How would you answer Keeton's second question (as posed in the first excerpt from the NAIC White Paper) in a situation where the only reason for transferring financial risk to providers was to induce economizing in the provision of care? Is it the business of insurance commissioners to ensure that PSO providers do not overeconomize in treating patients? Or should they confine their attention to other matters? Would a state health department be appreciably better at regulating risk and its effects on provider behavior? Can regulators of any kind reasonably be expected to oversee the exquisite details of clinical decision making?

In discussing either direct contracting or "downstream risk," does the NAIC White Paper take adequate account of the fact that, in an integrated delivery system (IDS), the risk stream may divide and narrow as it flows down through lower levels of the system? In fact, an IDS may lay off risk on such entities as primary care physicians, group practices (both primary and specialty care), hospitals or PHOs, nonphysician provider networks (pharmacies, home health agencies, labs, etc.), and entities responsible for "carve-out" services (e.g., managers of behavioral health services or "PBMs"—pharmacy benefit managers). In addition, some such risk-bearing entities may in turn pass on some risk to lower-tier components. Various components can also be compensated in various ways, including subcapitation, global fees, and fees for service (which may or may not be subject to a withhold or supplemented by bonuses or penalties). Finally, all providers are inevitably at some "risk" of losing their positions in the chain (that is, of being "deselected") if their performance is deemed sub-par in some respect. Since risk bearing can take so many forms and can change dramatically at each branch in the stream, can state-based (or federal) insurance regulators really hope to assess the risks accurately and to control the manner in which they are borne? Would you conclude that, for better or for worse, we have no good alternative but to trust employers, private contracts, and the "market," supplemented by liability laws, to ensure that consumers get what they pay for?

Note that an IDS or PSO may or may not have solid, enforceable contractual guarantees that its providers will stick with it even if it encounters bad experience or is otherwise overcommitted. Indeed, one can imagine many circumstances in which providers would benefit from withdrawing from the plan and the commitments it represents. How serious do you suppose this problem to be? Does the law of abandonment offer any protection against the risk of provider disaffection? Are state insurance regulators the most appropriate place to look for consumer protection on this front?

How would you resolve the ERISA questions raised in the foregoing excerpts from the NAIC White Paper?

SECTION B: DOMINANT HEALTH PLANS

The "Blues," Then and Now

Travelers Insurance Company v. Blue Cross of Western Pennsylvania

United States Court of Appeals, Third Circuit, 1973.
481 F.2d 80, cert. denied 414 U.S. 1093 (1973).

■ VAN DUSEN, CIRCUIT JUDGE.

Travelers Insurance Company appeals from the January 6, 1972, district court order dismissing its complaint against Blue Cross of Western

Pennsylvania, which order was entered after a trial to the court. Travelers had charged Blue Cross with restraining trade, in violation of section 1 of the Sherman Act and with monopolizing and attempting to monopolize, in violation of section 2 of that Act. To prevail, Travelers had also to establish that either Blue Cross' conduct did not come within the protective umbrella provided by the language of the McCarran–Ferguson Act or was excluded from the protection of that Act by the presence of boycott, coercion, or intimidation. After a lengthy non-jury trial, the district court concluded that Blue Cross' conduct was immunized by the McCarran–Ferguson Act and that, even absent such protection, the conduct did not violate the antitrust laws. We agree with the district court on both points.

The relevant market consists of 29 counties in Western Pennsylvania. Blue Cross provides hospitalization insurance for 51% of the population of this area: and during a relevant period Blue Cross accounted for 62% of all the patient days which were covered by commercial insurance.

Travelers objects to a standard contract which Blue Cross has with 101 hospitals in this area which prescribes the amounts and terms under which Blue Cross pays for the services rendered its subscribers. Blue Cross reimburses hospitals only for audited costs subject to a ceiling [that varies for nine categories of hospitals]; and these costs do not include any portion of the general hospital expenses of capital construction, of providing free services to indigents, and of providing service to patients who default. Because of these limitations, Blue Cross pays some 14–15% less than the amounts that non–Blue Cross patients are charged.[8] Consequently, Blue Cross quotes rates for hospitalization insurance correspondingly lower than the rates of private insurance companies such as Travelers.

Whether the McCarran–Ferguson Act exempts Blue Cross' arrangement with these hospitals from antitrust scrutiny depends, first, on the scope of the statutory term "business of insurance," second, on the extent of state regulation of this arrangement, and, third, on the presence or absence of boycott, coercion or intimidation.

* * *

In the present case, the district court found that the interrelationship of hospital payments and subscribers' rates was such that Blue Cross' arrangement with hospitals should be considered part of the "business of insurance." This conclusion is a sound construction of the law and is amply supported by the evidence.[9]

8. The district court opinion makes clear that the volume of Blue Cross subscribers and its cooperative coverage of many poor risk subscribers (such subsidization amounted to $27,000,000 in the years 1960–1970) are important factors in its ability to negotiate favorable contracts with the hospitals subject to the approval of the State Insurance Department.

9. One witness, Herbert S. Denenberg, the present Insurance Commissioner, testified as follows:

"* * * [W]e think that these two items, the contract with the hospitals and the

Also, the evidence supports the district court finding that the state regulates the arrangement here in question. Section 4 of the Nonprofit Hospital Plan Act provides that:

> "The rates charged to subscribers by nonprofit corporations, ... all rates of payments to hospitals made by such corporations pursuant to the contracts provided for in this act, ... and any and all contracts entered into by any such corporation with any hospital, shall at all times, be subject to the prior approval of the Insurance Department."

* * * [T]he record here shows aggressive state regulation. In fact, as the district court found, the features of the contract which Travelers finds objectionable were mandated by Insurance Department guidelines designed to encourage high quality care at reasonable costs. Auditing hospital costs and establishing a ceiling were thought to help hold down rising hospital costs by forcing administrative efficiency. Blue Cross was not to contribute to the care of indigents because this responsibility belonged to the state, not to the subscribers of Blue Cross. Finally, Blue Cross was not to support hospital construction for two reasons: such construction was usually financed by the state, the federal government, or private philanthropy; and, historically, hospitals serving the same area have needlessly duplicated expensive specialized services.

By its terms the McCarran–Ferguson Act does not protect "boycott, coercion, or intimidation." * * * Travelers asserts that Blue Cross used "coercion" to extract concessions from the hospitals. The district court held, and we agree with its conclusion, that the economic inducements which made the Blue Cross contract acceptable to hospitals[12] did not amount to "coercion." Especially is that true where, as here, the hospitals negotiated jointly and the resulting contract was approved by the Insurance Department.

Even if the McCarran–Ferguson Act were inapplicable and Blue Cross was subject to antitrust scrutiny, we agree with the district court that Blue Cross could withstand such scrutiny. In arriving at this result, we have not reached the determination of whether Blue Cross possesses enough market power to have "monopoly power." Even assuming that such power exists, we have concluded that Blue Cross' arrangement with hospitals neither illegally restrains trade in violation of section 1 of the Sherman Act nor constitutes, in violation of section 2, "the willful acquisition or maintenance of that power as distinguished from growth or development as a consequence of a superior product, business acumen, or historic accident." United States v. Grinnell Corp., 384 U.S. 563, 570–571 (1966).

* * *

rates to the subscribers are part of the same package and we have to regulate both of them together * * *."

12. If a hospital refused to agree to the contract, Blue Cross would reimburse the hospital on a per diem basis by an amount insufficient to cover the hospital's costs. A hospital would have to make up any deficiency by charging the patient directly. We note that this procedure is typical of the indemnification plans offered by private insurance companies.

In its negotiating with hospitals, Blue Cross has done no more than conduct its business as every rational enterprise does, i.e., get the best deal possible. This pressure encourages hospitals to keep their costs down; and, for its own competitive advantage, Blue Cross passes along the saving thus realized to consumers. To be sure, Blue Cross' initiative makes life harder for commercial competitors such as Travelers. The antitrust laws, however, protect competition, not competitors; and stiff competition is encouraged, not condemned. It must be pointed out that the size of its competitors does not give Blue Cross the freedom to conduct other than fair competition for business. The dependence of the community on health facilities requires that anti-competitive practices not be tolerated.

* * * [T]he evidence does not support the proposition that Travelers or other companies could not have achieved some price reductions.[13] * * * Furthermore, there is no reason to suppose that, even if commercial insurers such as Travelers were currently unable to compete with Blue Cross, they could not immediately re-enter the hospitalization insurance business if it became profitable to do so.

In regard to the Sherman Act § 2 question, we agree with the district court's determination that Blue Cross achieved its present status in a permissible manner. It was first suggested in United States v. Aluminum Co. of America, 148 F.2d 416, 429–430 (2d Cir.1945), that a monopoly may be "thrust upon" a producer "merely by virtue of his superior skill, foresight and industry," and that such a result would not be violative of section 2. In United States v. Grinnell Corp., quoted above, the Supreme Court reaffirmed this position. The district court found, on ample evidence, that Blue Cross owes its success to the completeness of its coverage. From the time of its organization in the late 1930s, Blue Cross has reimbursed hospitals for all covered services rendered its subscribers. Private companies, on the other hand, have, until relatively recently, provided only that their policyholders would be indemnified up to a set dollar ceiling.[15] Blue Cross thus has exposed itself to considerably greater risk because of the possibility that treatment would be extensive and because of the probability that hospital costs would rise. By shouldering the risk, Blue Cross has made itself considerably more attractive to consumers. The antitrust laws were not intended to condemn such conduct.

* * *

The judgment of the District Court will be affirmed.

13. * * * Travelers calls our attention to the testimony of various of its witnesses. However, almost all of this evidence suggests not that Travelers was unable to obtain any price reduction from hospitals, but rather that Travelers assumed its inability to do so and, therefore, did not press the matter. Moreover, it is not clear that Travelers was willing to adopt a full-cost reimbursement scheme comparable to that of Blue Cross (as opposed to the typical indemnification arrangement) as a quid pro quo.

15. The commercial companies are now willing to write complete coverage for at least large-group plans. It appears that Blue Cross is still alone in offering this arrangement to small groups and to high-risk individuals.

NOTES AND QUESTIONS ON THE HISTORY OF BLUE CROSS AND BLUE SHIELD

1. Blue Cross and Blue Shield plans (the "Blues") are less distinctive today than they once were, but their history includes important lessons about competition in the health care sector. The following report, as of the mid–1980s, provides useful background:

> Set up in the depths of the Great Depression, before the advent of the commercial insurance industry, the first Blue Cross plans had the dual goal of helping strapped individuals pay for hospital care and helping strapped hospitals get more paying patients.
>
> Unlike commercial plans, which pay a fixed percentage of hospital charges in cash, Blue Cross simply covered any hospital services that patients used. Established in close collaboration with hospitals, Blue Cross based its premium charges not so much on customers' risks as on hospitals' costs. With strong ties to the hospitals and market dominance in many parts of the country, the Blue Cross plans often negotiated discounts with hospitals. In 1939, Blue Shield plans began offering similar coverage for doctors' services.
>
> The plans' broad coverage, plus the lack of deductibles and co-payments, made them popular with patients. The plans were open to all comers, regardless of health risks, and under their "community rating" system, everyone in the same place paid the same rates—thus providing a safety net for the hard-to-insure. The plans were set up under special state legislation and were tax-exempt. For many Americans, Blue Cross and Blue Shield became synonyms for health insurance.
>
> * * *
>
> Although the plans are still by far the nation's largest private insurer, their national market share dropped from about 43 per cent in 1976 to about 33 per cent in 1985. * * *
>
> Some hallmarks of the plans became liabilities. Employers who once valued the comprehensive coverage because it spared [employees] out-of-pocket costs started saying the plans didn't provide safeguards against excessive use. Some employers who had appreciated the plans' discounts started viewing with suspicion the cozy relations with doctors and hospitals. And employers increasingly shunned the Blues' community-rated contracts, which they believed saddled them with higher-cost, higher-risk subscribers outside their own pool of employees. The changed environment presented the Blues with a dilemma: How could they compete without losing their founding mission?
>
> Different plans have answered the question differently. In some states and areas, the plans have opted for a tough, businesslike approach, putting heavy emphasis on alternative health plans and diversification.

The Blues Are Displaying New Hues, Nat'l J., Apr. 18, 1987, at 938. For a review of economic evidence on the Blues' historical performance, see H. Frech, Competition and Monopoly in Medical Care 108–30 (1996).

Although the Blues were originally controlled by provider interests, such direct relationships were questioned by many, became attenuated over time, and had been severed in most cases well before the FTC made an early antitrust move against them. See FTC, Physician Agreements to Control Medical Prepayment Plans, 46 Fed. Reg. 48982 (Oct. 5, 1981) (statement of enforcement policy). An interesting question, which should be pondered in connection with the materials in this chapter, is why provider interests surrendered control of the Blues without a bigger fight.

Recent years have seen a number of Blue plans merging with others, sometimes across state lines. Several plans have converted to for-profit status, and all have in some manner joined the managed-care revolution.

2. *The "Blue" Trademarks.* The key to the Blue Cross/Blue Shield system has been the "Blue" trademarks, which belong to the national Blue Cross and Blue Shield Association (BCBSA), a creature of all the Blue plans. The marks have long been licensed to individual plans with territorial restrictions, mostly limiting plans to using them only within their respective states. In the 1980s, the BCBSA sought to enforce such geographic limits against one of several Blue plans in Ohio, where a messy situation of overlapping Blue Cross and Blue Shield plans had developed. The defendant plan countered with an antitrust suit charging unlawful "market division"—that is, a BCBSA-sponsored horizontal agreement among Blue plans not to compete in each other's territories. The lawsuit was eventually settled in a way that left all the Ohio plans free at least temporarily to compete throughout the state. Can you visualize, however, the antitrust arguments for and against the territorial restrictions in these trademark licenses? During the period in question, would the market for health care financing have been more competitive and have served consumers better if plans using the Blue trademarks had been free to compete with each other?

For more recent developments in Ohio, see Blue Cross & Blue Shield Mutual of Ohio v. BCBSA, 110 F.3d 318 (6th Cir.1997), upholding termination of a local Blue plan's trademark license in circumstances where the plan was about to be acquired by Columbia/HCA. Why might BCBSA object to transactions of this kind? In North Carolina, the possibility arose that, following a method employed in converting some California plans, the local Blue plan would be converted to a stock company, with the stock held by a charitable foundation. Could the foundation, as a practical matter, sell the company (that is, all the stock) to another for-profit insurer that sees ways to turn it into a more efficient (more valuable) operation, perhaps by combining it with other operations or by dislodging the incumbent management? Would BCBSA be likely to allow such a new company to use the cross and shield trademarks in North Carolina? If not, why not?

3. *Cost Reimbursement.* Note the basis on which the Blue Cross plan in the *Travelers* case paid the hospitals. From an early date, most Blue Cross plans similarly paid hospitals on the basis of their retrospectively determined costs. Can you see why hospitals, in organizing Blue Cross plans and establishing their payment policies, would prefer cost reimbursement to other methods of payment? In the 1960s and 1970s, some state insurance departments (including Pennsylvania's, in the manner observable in the *Travelers* opinion) used their regulatory authority over Blue Cross rates to scrutinize, and indirectly to control, hospital costs.

4. *Blue Cross Discounts.* For many years, Blue Cross plans were generally able to purchase hospital services at substantial "discounts," such as the one about which Travelers complained. Similarly, Blue Shield plans often paid physicians less than their usual fees, sometimes merely by withholding a portion of allowable fees until year end to ensure the plan's financial health. Several studies showed a correlation between the size of provider discounts and Blue plans' market share. E.g., Feldman & Greenberg, The Relation Between the Blue Cross Share and the Blue Cross "Discount" on Hospital Charges, 48 J. Risk & Ins. 235 (1981); Frech, Monopoly in Health Insurance: The Economics of *Kartell v. Blue Shield of Massachusetts*, in H. Frech, ed., Health Care in America: The Political Economy of Hospitals and Health Insurance 293, 301–06 (1988) (study of 17 large Blue Shield plans, showing discounts more or less correlating with Blue Shield market share and ranging from 28% in Massachusetts to 1% in Chattanooga). The following materials invite you to explain the origin of these discounts and to consider their significance and legality.

5. *Did Blue Cross Really "Get the Best Deal Possible"?* Are you satisfied by the court's explanation of how the Blue Cross plan in *Travelers* obtained favorable rates from hospitals? Why did Travelers assume that the same discounts that Blue Cross received would not also be available to it? (As the court observes, it did not "press the matter.") Was Travelers' problem simply that it lacked the "clout" needed to extract price concessions from local hospitals? Or was it instead that, like other commercial health insurers at the time, it respected the principle of "free choice of provider" and thus had no means of steering its insureds to lower-priced hospitals—that is, of rewarding price cutters with increased patronage? Although commercial insurers in that era contended that their small market shares in many markets (many of their accounts were large national employers with relatively few employees in individual markets) deprived them of the purchasing power needed to obtain discounts from providers, subsequent history has shown that competing hospitals are not indifferent to even small losses of patronage.

Was *Travelers* simply a case, as the court suggests, of a large buyer using its lawfully obtained buying power, which the commercial insurers could not match, to "get the best deal possible"—that is, to force its suppliers to give it low prices? Were the hospitals in fact forced to grant the discounts by competition for Blue Cross's business? What is the significance of the fact that the discounts were "negotiated jointly"? Recognizing that the discounts (uniform across all hospitals because built into the cost-reimbursement formula) were granted collectively and not competitively, what alternative hypotheses can you offer to explain them? In other words, why would a hospital cartel be prepared to give a large discount and therefore a cost advantage to one favored buyer? Did Blue Cross do anything in return?

It seems probable that Blue Cross could have gotten even larger discounts by playing the hospitals off against each other. Why did it not do so? Assuming that Blue Cross was no longer under hospital control, what did it gain by keeping the hospital cartel intact and accepting a uniform discount? Can you formulate a plausible alternative story and supporting legal theory that might have gotten Travelers some relief?

Consider whether the Blue plans in the next two principal cases got "the best deal possible."

6. *The McCarran–Ferguson Act*. This 1945 statute, which the *Travelers* court describes, exempts the "business of insurance"—but not insurance companies as such—from the reach of federal antitrust law insofar as it is regulated by the state. The issue of when the McCarran Act should be construed to protect regulated Blue plans from antitrust suits will be raised again in connection with the *Ocean State* case later in this section.

Ball Memorial Hospital, Inc. v. Mutual Hospital Insurance, Inc.

United States Court of Appeals, Seventh Circuit, 1986.
784 F.2d 1325.

■ EASTERBROOK, CIRCUIT JUDGE.

* * *

The plaintiffs in this case are 80 acute-care hospitals (the Hospitals). All 80 provide care on a fee for service basis, and all 80 receive payments from many insurance plans and administered self-insurance plans as well as from patients. Some of the 80 also offer PPO plans; others are preparing to do so. Forty of the 80 plaintiffs have appealed.

The Blues [Indiana Blue Cross and Blue Shield] have been losing market share in Indiana for some years. In 1980 the Blues insured almost two million of Indiana's 5.5 million population. By 1984 they insured only about 1.45 million people.

* * * Concerned about this [loss of business], the Blues decided to offer a PPO of their own, in addition to their traditional service benefit plans. * * * The Blues asked for bids from all acute-care hospitals in Indiana and invited each to bid a percentage discount from its regular fees. * * * The hospitals that offer PPO plans saw the Blues' decision as a threat to their success. All hospitals saw a PPO plan as a threat to revenues—those who participated in the plan might collect less per service rendered, and those outside the plan might lose volume.

Ninety-one of Indiana's 115 acute-care hospitals submitted bids, and the Blues signed up 61 of the 91. Forty-two of the 80 plaintiffs are among the 61. Eleven plaintiffs did not bid, and 27 bid but were not selected. All

80 remain eligible to participate in the regular service benefit plan offered by the Blues, which is the Blues' most popular product. All hospitals in Indiana also may provide services to patients covered by the Blues' PPO, but the Blues will reimburse only 75% of the hospitals' fees; the patients must pay the rest. The Blues will reimburse 100% of the agreed charges when insureds use hospitals within the PPO.

* * * The Hospitals began this suit on November 14, 1984, seeking injunctive relief against the Blues' proposed PPO under sections 1 and 2 of the Sherman Act, 15 U.S.C. §§ 1 and 2, and provisions of Indiana law.

* * *

We start with a proposition established by Brillhart v. Mutual Medical Insurance, Inc., 768 F.2d 196 (7th Cir.1985): the Blues are financial intermediaries, purchasing agents for the consumers of medical services. See also Kartell v. Blue Shield of Massachusetts, Inc., 749 F.2d 922 (1st Cir.1984), cert. denied, 471 U.S. 1029 (1985). The Blues, as financial intermediaries, may drive any bargains open to the consumers of services. The Rule of Reason rather than the *per se* rule supplies the standard of analysis.

The analysis of the adoption of the PPO plan must begin with an assessment of market power. Market power is a necessary ingredient in every case under the Rule of Reason. Unless the defendants possess market power, it is unnecessary to ask whether their conduct may be beneficial to consumers. Firms without power bear no burden of justification. The Hospitals say that the Blues have a large share of the market for medical insurance in Indiana, and that this establishes market power.

In many cases a firm's share of current sales does indicate power. * * *

In other cases, however, a firm's share of current sales does not reflect an ability to reduce the total output in the market, and therefore it does not convey power over price. * * *

The district court found that each of the factors suggesting that market share does not imply market power is present in the market for medical insurance. New firms may enter easily. Existing firms may expand their sales quickly; the district court pointed out that insurers need only a license and capital, and that firms such as Aetna and Prudential have both. There are no barriers to entry—other firms may duplicate the Blues' product at the same cost the Blues incur in furnishing their coverage. The Blues and other nonprofits may have an edge because of the lower tax Indiana places on premiums paid to them, but this sort of advantage is not pertinent here. Other mutual insurance carriers (including Prudential) can get the same tax break. A PPO plan does not exploit the tax advantage [any more than] any other plan the Blues could offer. The tax benefits may or may not be desirable as a matter of state policy, but this is no concern of antitrust law.

The Blues do not own any assets that block or delay entry. * * * The "productive asset" of the insurance business is money, which may be supplied on a moment's notice, plus the ability to spread risk, which many firms possess and which has no geographic boundary. The district court emphasized that every firm can expand its sales quickly if the price is right, that no firm has captive customers, and that many firms want to serve this market. The conclusion that the Blues face vigorous and effective competition is not clearly erroneous.

* * *

Although the district court did not make findings concerning the Blues' intent, the Hospitals say that the record reeks of bad intent. The Blues evidently wanted to drive down the price they paid to the providers, which entails bad intent; more, the Blues engaged in calculated planning to preserve or enlarge their market share. * * * In January 1983 the Blues circulated an internal report stating in part:

> *The Proposition:* That [the Blues] use its market position and its control over substantial sums of health care dollars to negotiate lower fees for provider services ... Blue Cross plans that enjoy major discounts in their hospital reimbursement contracts do have considerable advantage over competitors. It appears that these discount arrangements reinforce what is a common perception among both political leaders and businessmen. Which is that our control of so many health care dollars should put us in a position to negotiate lower prices for provider services....
>
> *The Recommended Response:* [The Blues are] in a unique position to serve as a broker between what might appear to be the conflicting interests of financially threatened providers and cost conscious group purchasers.... We also control an overwhelming share of the marketplace in key areas.... In short, the time seems right for an aggressive new stance in the financing of health care benefits.... The growth of competitive forces poses a grave threat, and will grow worse without counteraction.

Res ipsa loquitur, the Hospitals say. If the Blues lack market power, how come their own planning documents talk this way? The Hospitals say that the district court should have inferred power from intent, and that given this intent to prevent competition the district court also was required to enjoin the adoption of the PPO.

We assume without deciding that a court sometimes may infer market power from a sufficiently clear demonstration that a firm believes that it possesses power. Even so, an argument about evil intent in antitrust requires us to ask: "intent to do what?" The Hospitals seem to think that intent to get the best price is a bad intent. * * *

Competition is a ruthless process. A firm that reduces cost and expands sales injures rivals—sometimes fatally. The firm that slashes costs the most captures the greatest sales and inflicts the greatest injury. The deeper the injury to rivals, the greater the potential benefit. These injuries to rivals are byproducts of vigorous competition, and the antitrust laws are not balm for rivals' wounds. The antitrust laws are for the benefit of competition, not competitors. * * *

* * *

What of other "intents"? One intent reflected in the Blues' documents is to buy medical care for less. Again, though, this is just another description for hard bargaining. Even a monopolist may bargain hard. * * *

* * * [A]nother approach is to ask whether the defendant intends to (and can) raise its rivals' costs of doing business. When a firm finds a way to confront its rivals with higher costs, it may raise its own prices to consumers without drawing increased output from them. Exclusive dealing arrangements and boycotts sometimes may raise rivals' costs. But the Blues have not insisted that hospitals in the Blues' PPO refrain from joining other PPOs, so rivals have access to hospitals on the same basis as the Blues. Some hospitals participate in more than three different PPO plans.

The Hospitals urge on us a version of an argument that the Blues' PPO will raise rivals' costs. The argument, which the parties call the "cost-shifting" argument, starts from the premise that hospitals raise just enough revenue to break even each year. The hospitals offer discounts to the Blues in order to participate in their PPO. They therefore receive less revenue from patients covered by the PPO. To break even they must obtain more revenue from other patients. This means they must "shift" to their other patients their costs of operation. When the hospitals raise their prices to other insurance plans (including the hospitals' own PPO plans), these plans will be unable to compete with the Blues. The Blues' PPO will have raised its rivals' costs, in violation of § 2.

* * * The cost-shifting argument * * * assumes that the price charged to the patients in the Blues' PPO plan is below the appropriate measure of cost; the Hospitals contend that they must raise prices elsewhere to subsidize these patients. But the district court found that the PPO genuinely saves on the costs of care, and this too is not clearly erroneous. If the discounts given on patients covered by the PPO are justified by reductions in cost, there is nothing to "shift" to other patients.

We do not imply by this discussion that the Blues must demonstrate that the prices charged to the PPO patients are "cost-justified." * * * There is certainly no burden of justification in the absence of market power—no rational hospital sells below cost to a buyer without market power * * *. It is also hard to see why, if the Hospitals can raise their prices to other buyers of their services, they do not do so whether or not they join the Blues' PPO plan. * * *

* * *

[The district court rejected the Hospitals'] arguments under state law. The principal law in question, Ind.Code § 27–8–11–3, became effective on December 31, 1984. Subsection (a) allows insurers to establish PPO plans. The other pertinent provisions state:

> (b) Before entering into any agreement ... an insurer shall establish terms and conditions that must be met by providers wishing to enter into an agreement with the insurer.... These terms and conditions may not discriminate unreasonably against or among provid-

ers.... [N]either differences in prices among hospitals or other institutional providers produced by a process of individual negotiation nor price differences among other providers in different geographical areas or different specialties constitutes unreasonable discrimination.

(c) No hospital, physician, pharmacist, or other provider ... willing to meet the terms and conditions offered to it by an insurer may be denied the right to enter into an agreement....

The Hospitals' strongest argument is that the Blues have discriminated unreasonably among providers, contrary to the prohibition of subsection (b). [The court construed the anti-discrimination statute in question, a modest version of an "any-willing-provider" law, to permit the purchasing methods adopted by the plan.]

Affirmed.

NOTES AND QUESTIONS ON THE POWER OF PURCHASERS IN MARKETS FOR PROVIDERS' SERVICES

1. *Price-fixing or Boycott?* As was mentioned in connection with the "OZIPA" problem in § A of this chapter, individual physicians, dentists, and other health care providers in the 1970s and 1980s occasionally invoked the antitrust laws against financing plans controlled by their own respective professions in generally unsuccessful efforts to escape plan-imposed restrictions on their pricing and other practices. Providers had even more to lose, however, when entities they did *not* control began to create PPOs or other provider networks or otherwise to engage in selectively contracting for provider services. Such plans, as they saw it, raised antitrust issues because they "fixed" the fees practitioners could charge and limited "competition" by preventing them from competing to serve certain patients. Hospital and physician interests were particularly galled, even alarmed, to see Blue plans they had themselves created turn into monsters bent on destroying the old order they had been invented to defend. The policy memorandum quoted in the *Ball Memorial* case evidences the decision by one Blue plan to turn its guns around the other way.

It was ironic that providers attempting to fend off the new competition turned to the antitrust laws for possible relief. Among the first provider attempts to use the antitrust laws to restrain selective contracting—competition's essential ingredient—was a series of cases brought by pharmacists to challenge what they perceived as anticompetitive insurer discrimination in favor of large discount pharmacies and against smaller, service-oriented retailers. The leading case was *Royal Drug,* in which the Supreme Court initially wiped out the insurers' first line of defense—the claim that the McCarran–Ferguson Act, exempting the "business of insurance" from the antitrust laws, extended its protection to selective contracting. Group Life & Health Ins. Co. v. Royal Drug Co., 440 U.S. 205 (1979). On remand of the case, however, the pharmacies failed to convince the court of appeals that, by engaging in selective contracting, the defendant Blue Cross plan, which was wholly independent of the pharmacies themselves, was "fixing prices" (horizontally or vertically) or causing its insureds to "boycott" nonparticipating ("nonpar") pharmacies. Royal Drug Co. v. Group Life & Health Ins. Co., 737 F.2d 1433 (5th Cir.1984), cert. denied 469 U.S. 1160 (1985); see also Medical Arts Pharmacy of Stamford, Inc. v. Blue Cross & Blue Shield of Connecticut, Inc., 675 F.2d 502 (2d Cir.1982). Similar claims—although health care providers may not like the analogy—were also made (also unsuccessfully) by auto body shops against auto insurers seeking to obtain repair services at low prices. See, e.g., Quality Auto Body, Inc. v. Allstate Ins. Co., 660 F.2d 1195 (7th Cir.1981), cert. denied 455 U.S. 1020 (1982); Chick's Auto Body v. State Farm Mut. Auto. Ins. Co., 401 A.2d 722, 729 (N.J.Super.1979) ("Under the guise of a 'price-fixing' claim, plaintiffs seek not to further price competition, but to avoid it."). All these cases consistently characterized the insurers simply as purchasers seeking the best price in a competitive market.

Physicians and dentists had no better luck than pharmacists and body shops in invoking antitrust law as a protection against price competition. In Barry v. Blue Cross, 805 F.2d 866 (9th Cir.1986), the court approved summary judgment against physicians' claims that California Blue Cross's "Prudent Buyer Plan" was the product of a horizontal physician conspiracy to fix prices and to organize a boycott of nonpar physicians. Although the plan consulted with its Physicians Relations Committee in setting up the plan, the court could see no evidence that Blue Cross had not acted independently and in its own interest. Physicians' widespread adherence to the plan—"conscious parallelism"—was insufficient by itself to establish a conspiracy. The court also found the vertical agreements between plan and physicians to be nothing more than buyer/seller agreements, the adverse effects of which on other physicians are an essential consequence of competition itself. Cf. Brillhart v. Mutual Med. Ins., Inc., 768 F.2d 196 (7th Cir.1985) (dismissing physician challenge to traditional Blue Shield par/nonpar arrangement, without fully examining allegation that Blue Shield board was "controlled by physicians"); Pennsylvania Dental Ass'n v. Medical Serv. Ass'n, 745 F.2d 248 (3d Cir.1984) (Blue Shield dental plan employing UCR fee limits upheld; independent plan's "action taken to find a market price so that purchaser-insurer does not overpay does not constitute price-fixing"). See also Ambroze v. Aetna Health Plans, Inc., 1996 WL 282069 (S.D.N.Y.1996) (impatiently dismissing complaint, though "dressed up in terms of competition for better quality services," for not pleading "antitrust injury" and for targeting instead "the very concept of managed care"), remanded to permit amendment of complaint, 107 F.3d 2 (2d Cir.1997).

2. *Unlawful Monopsony?* The principal claim of the plaintiff hospitals in *Ball Memorial* was not that their prices had been unlawfully fixed or that they were victims of a boycott. Instead, they contended (under section 2 of the Sherman Act) that Blue Cross exercised unlawful market power as a dominant (monopsonistic) buyer and was therefore in a position to exploit providers by paying excessively low prices—just as a dominant seller (a monopolist) can exploit its customers by charging high prices. Many providers have felt victimized by what they perceive as the unfair concentration of buying power arrayed against them in the marketplace. Recall both from chapter 4 and from § A of this chapter the interest among physicians in unionizing or in organizing in some other way for the purpose of collective bargaining, in order to exercise what is sometimes called "countervailing power."

Do you agree that the Indiana Blue plan in *Ball Memorial*, despite its substantial market share, lacked market power (which may not amount to "monopoly" power)? The question of defining a proper market in which to test the dominance of a particular health plan for antitrust purposes will arise again later in this section.

Even if the Blues in *Ball Memorial* possessed monopoly (or monopsony) power, the result might well have been the same. Mere possession of market power is not unlawful, since the statute prohibits monopolization, not monopoly as such. As the case next reproduced below will explain, a monopoly is unlawful only if it was gotten in the first instance by unlawful (predatory) conduct or, having been gained by lawful means, was thereafter unlawfully maintained. Might there be a question, however, whether any monopoly power enjoyed by a typical Blue plan was lawfully obtained? Recall the *Oregon State Medical Society* case, and consider why there was no challenge to its market power as such. Should a dominant health plan's past affiliation and close cooperation with dominant hospital or physician interests—which in turn stonewalled the Blues' commercial competitors (as appears to have occurred in the *Travelers* case)—be viewed as an "exclusionary practice," opening the plan to a possible monopolization charge? Should providers, who created the Blues and allied themselves closely with them over many years, be entitled to question the origins of the plans' market power now that they themselves must contend with that power?

If the Indiana Blues had been found to possess monopoly (or monopsony) power but to have obtained it by lawful means, what should be the result? Is it the function of antitrust law to regulate how lawful market power is exercised? Should a firm with a dominant position that was fairly gained in the marketplace be prevented either from selling at high prices or from purchasing at low ones? Or is the aim of the law only to ensure that firms do not obtain such power by improper means? In one important case, Kartell v. Blue Shield of Massachusetts, Inc., 749 F.2d 922 (1st Cir.1984), cert. denied 471 U.S. 1029 (1985), the dominant Blue Shield plan had adopted a strategy much like the one that Justice Stevens (in the *Maricopa County Medical Society* case) had earlier anticipated that an insurer might adopt: selective contracting coupled with fee limits and a prohibition against balance-billing of its subscribers. The plan also included a lock-in feature—a refusal to cover (that is, pay anything at all for) services provided by nonpar physicians. Physicians, feeling coerced and exploited (since they felt they had no alternative but to participate in Blue Shield), sued the plan under the antitrust laws. The court of appeals assumed, without deciding, that Blue Shield possessed market power (it insured about 74% of the privately insured citizens of the commonwealth but accounted for only 13–14% of "physician practice revenue") but still found no violation. Judge (later Justice) Breyer stated the court's view that Blue Shield, an insurer legitimately aggregating the purchasing power of its many subscribers, should be regarded simply as a purchaser for the account of others. In the court's view, antitrust law does not contemplate judicial regulation of the prices charged (or paid) by firms with lawful market power.

Is monopsony likely to be a serious problem in health care (or, indeed, in any other market)? If providers were being underpaid, some of them would leave the area, and few new ones would move in to replace those who retire. Pressure to raise compensation levels to maintain access to provider services would therefore eventually become intense. Even in the short run, competing sellers of health coverage could enter the market, offering more competitive prices to the better providers and thus inducing them to leave the dominant plan and to market themselves through the new outlet. Indeed, if providers were dissatisfied, they could organize their own competing financing plan or network (assuming antitrust concerns could be overcome).

3. *Joint Purchasing.* The issue of buying power in health care markets may also arise in other contexts. See generally Havighurst, Antitrust Issues in the Joint Purchasing of Health Care, 1995 Utah L. Rev. 409. For example, in many communities employers have formed coalitions for the purpose of mutual assistance in the procurement of health care for their employees, often including some form of joint purchasing. Likewise, the 1990s saw a movement to encourage the formation of so-called "health insurance purchasing cooperatives" through which small employers and individuals could procure or bargain for health coverage. Hospitals have formed numerous alliances for the joint purchasing of hospital supplies and services. See, e.g., White & White, Inc. v. American Hosp. Supply Corp., 723 F.2d 495 (6th Cir.1983). Hospitals have encountered antitrust challenges, however, when they have combined their purchasing of nurses' services in local markets. E.g., All Care Nursing Serv., Inc. v. Bethesda Mem. Hosp., Inc., 887 F.2d 1535 (11th Cir.1989) (refusing to apply per se rule to hospital joint purchasing of temporary nursing services from nurse staffing agencies); Utah Hospitals Resolve DOJ Charge of Exchanging Nurse Salary Data, 3 Health Law Rep. (BNA) 333 (1994) (reporting consent decree to protect hospital competition in hiring nurses). See also Sullivan, Monopsony Power in the Market for Nurses, 32 J. L. & Econ. S135 (1989) (finding that hospitals enjoy significant monopsony power in purchasing nurses' services).

In general, joint purchasing is viewed favorably by antitrust enforcers, who have announced a "safety zone" for arrangements that aggregate no more than 35 percent of the purchases of a particular good or service. U.S Department of Justice & FTC, Statement of Enforcement Policy on Joint Purchasing Arrangements among Health Care Providers (Statement 7, 1996).

Exclusionary Practices?

Ocean State Physicians Health Plan, Inc. v. Blue Cross & Blue Shield of Rhode Island

United States Court of Appeals, First Circuit, 1989.
883 F.2d 1101, cert. denied, 494 U.S. 1027 (1990).

■ LEVIN H. CAMPBELL, CHIEF JUDGE.

* * *

I. FACTUAL BACKGROUND

Defendant Blue Cross, a non-profit corporation established in 1939, has long been the largest health insurer in Rhode Island. It purchases health services from physicians, hospitals, and other health care providers on behalf of its subscribers. Blue Cross underwrites the cost of these purchases by spreading the risk of health care expenses among its subscriber groups. Plaintiff Ocean State is a for-profit health maintenance organization ("HMO") that began operations in 1984. Like Blue Cross, Ocean State contracts with physicians to provide medical care to its subscribers, and then pays its contracted physicians on a fee-for-service basis. While Blue Cross will reimburse its subscribers even for certain services performed by non-participating physicians, Ocean State does not pay for services by non-participating physicians. Eighty percent of the shares of the Ocean State corporation are owned by its participating physicians. A physician may participate in more than one health insurance program. Thus, a physician may contract with Blue Cross, with Ocean State, or with both.

From its inception, Ocean State grew rapidly. Like Blue Cross, it was offered to subscribers through employers. Apparently because Ocean State provided more coverage and charged lower premiums, many subscribers switched from Blue Cross to Ocean State. By the spring of 1986, Blue Cross had lost approximately 30,000 of its 543,015 enrollees, while Ocean State's enrollment had exceeded all expectations, growing to 70,000. Because Blue Cross was experiencing financial problems, it had to raise its premiums in order to maintain adequate financial reserves. As it raised its premiums, it lost more enrollees—which, in turn, forced further rate increases. In short, Blue Cross "was faced with a serious competitive problem."

In the spring of 1986, to meet the challenge presented by Ocean State, Blue Cross instituted a three-pronged attack:

First, Blue Cross launched its own HMO "look-alike," dubbed HealthMate, which it marketed to employers who were offering the Ocean State plan to their employees. * * * In those employer groups in which employees were required to contribute to their premiums, HealthMate was offered at 5 percent below the cost of traditional Blue Cross.

Second, Blue Cross instituted an "adverse selection" policy of pricing. "Adverse selection" refers to the tendency for younger and healthier people to opt for HMOs such as Ocean State when they are made available, leaving older and sicker people (on the average) in the standard Blue Cross pool. Because of such adverse selection, Blue Cross expected the health care costs for standard Blue Cross to be higher in those employer groups that offered an HMO option than in those employer groups that did not. With the approval of the Rhode Island Department of Business Regulation ("DBR"), Blue Cross instituted a pricing plan that took account of this projected difference in health expenses. * * * Under this policy, employers were offered three different rates for traditional Blue Cross coverage. The rate was lowest for an employer who offered only traditional Blue Cross, intermediate for an employer who also offered a competing HMO (usually Ocean State) and HealthMate, and highest for an employer who also offered a competing HMO but declined to offer HealthMate.

Third, Blue Cross initiated a policy, which it called "Prudent Buyer," of not paying a physician more for any service or procedure than that physician was accepting from any other health care cost provider (such as Ocean State). Blue Cross established this policy after it became apparent that Ocean State's contracting physicians were accepting about 20 percent less for their services from Ocean State than they were receiving from Blue Cross. Ocean State had withheld 20 percent of its physicians' fees in 1985, with the expectation that if the corporation made a profit the withhold would be returned. Ocean State did not turn a profit, however, and the withhold was not returned. In 1986 Ocean State again withheld 20 percent of its physicians fees, which it again failed to return after the end of the year. In order to ensure that it was getting the physicians' best prices, Blue Cross required each of its participating physicians to certify that he or she was not accepting any lower fees from other providers than he or she was receiving from Blue Cross for the same service. If the provider failed to provide such certification, Blue Cross reduced that physician's fees by 20 percent. As a result of the Prudent Buyer policy, Blue Cross achieved significant cost savings. After the implementation of Prudent Buyer, about 350 of Ocean State's 1200 physicians resigned, in many cases apparently in order to avoid a reduction in their Blue Cross fees.

II. PROCEDURAL BACKGROUND

Ocean State, together with a certified class of its participating physicians, brought this suit against Blue Cross. Ocean State * * * alleged that Blue Cross's conduct violated, inter alia, section 2 of the Sherman Act, which makes it unlawful to "monopolize ... any part of the trade or commerce among the several States." * * * Ocean State charged that Blue Cross launched HealthMate not because it was a viable long-term product, but in order to put Ocean State out of business. Through the adverse selection policy, Ocean State claimed, Blue Cross was able to raise its rates for standard Blue Cross for employer groups offering HealthMate—which, in turn, influenced employers not to make HealthMate available. Finally, Ocean State claimed that Blue Cross instituted the Prudent Buyer policy not in order to save money, but rather to induce physicians to resign from Ocean State. * * *

After a lengthy trial, the jury found Blue Cross "guilty" on the section 2 claim, but it awarded no damages on this claim. * * *

In its opinion, the district court granted Blue Cross's motion for judgment notwithstanding the verdict * * *. [T]he court held that, quite aside from the "no damages" verdict, Ocean State plaintiffs had failed to show that Blue Cross's actions were anything other than legitimate acts of competition. * * *

* * *

IV. THE ANTITRUST CLAIM

In addressing Ocean State's antitrust claim, we first consider the effects on that claim of the jury's "guilty/no damages" verdict. We decline to utilize the jury's failure to award damages as a basis for upholding the lower court's entry of judgment notwithstanding the verdict for Blue Cross. We then consider the applicability of the McCarran–Ferguson Act, which under certain circumstances exempts the "business of insurance" from the antitrust laws. We conclude that by reason of McCarran–Ferguson both HealthMate and the adverse selection policy are exempt from antitrust scrutiny. Finally, we consider whether the Prudent Buyer policy can as a matter of law be found to be an instance of prohibited monopolization, rather than legitimate competitive activity, and we conclude that it cannot.

* * *

B. The Effect of the McCarran–Ferguson Act

The McCarran–Ferguson Act ("the Act"), 15 U.S.C. §§ 1012(b), 1013(b), exempts from the antitrust laws all conduct that is (1) part of the "business of insurance"; (2) "regulated by State law"; and (3) not in the form of "boycott, coercion, or intimidation." * * *

1. *The "business of insurance."* The central issue with respect to the applicability of the McCarran–Ferguson Act is whether HealthMate and adverse selection are part of the "business of insurance." The Supreme Court has identified "three criteria relevant in determining whether a particular practice is part of the 'business of insurance' exempted from the antitrust laws": first, whether a particular practice has the effect of transferring or spreading a policyholder's risk; second, whether the practice is an integral part of the policy relationship between the insurer and the insured; and third, whether the practice is limited to entities within the insurance industry. Union Labor Life Insurance Co. v. Pireno, 458 U.S. 119, 129 (1982). * * *

Both HealthMate and the adverse selection policy qualify as the "business of insurance" under these criteria. HealthMate is an insurance policy which operates by spreading policyholders' risk; adverse selection is a pricing policy that inherently involves risk-spreading. Both HealthMate and adverse selection directly involve the relationship between the insurer (Blue Cross) and the insured (its policyholders). Such policies are, more or less by definition, limited to entities in the "insurance industry" as broadly construed. * * *

* * *

2. *Regulation by state law.* Turning to the second requirement for exemption under the Act, it is clear that both HealthMate and the adverse selection policy were "regulated by state law." The Rhode Island Department of Business Regulation approved the marketing of HealthMate, as well as the adverse selection rating formula. Ocean State protests that DBR did not approve the specific elements of HealthMate and adverse selection that Ocean State is challenging—for example, the decisions as to where and at what price to offer HealthMate, and the specific projections (which were plugged into the adverse selection formula) of the number of employees who would switch from standard Blue Cross to HMOs. In demanding this level of specificity, however, Ocean State misinterprets the provision of the Act that limits the exemption to conduct that is "regulated by State law." The Supreme Court has suggested that this requirement is satisfied by general standards set by the state. * * *

3. *"Boycott, coercion, or intimidation."* The McCarran–Ferguson Act specifically excepts from the exemption any "act of boycott, coercion, or intimidation." * * * Ocean State does not point to any evidence that any employer was coerced to offer HealthMate or not to offer Ocean State. Even the one personnel manager who testified that the adverse selection policy served to dissuade his company from offering Ocean State did not suggest that the policy left him no choice in the matter. * * *

We conclude that the challenged actions of Blue Cross with respect to HealthMate and adverse selection are exempt from antitrust scrutiny under the McCarran–Ferguson Act.

C. The Prudent Buyer Policy

The Prudent Buyer policy involves Blue Cross's relationships not with its subscribers but with its provider physicians. Blue Cross makes no claim that this policy is protected by the McCarran–Ferguson exemption. * * * We agree with the district court, however, that the Prudent Buyer policy—through which Blue Cross ensured that it would not pay a provider physician any more for any particular service than she was accepting from Ocean State or any other private health care purchaser—is, as a matter of law, not violative of section 2 of the Sherman Act.

Section 2 of the Sherman Act Makes It Unlawful to "Monopolize ... Any Part of the Trade or Commerce Among the Several States." the Offense of Monopolization Has Two Elements:

> (1) the possession of monopoly power in the relevant market and (2) the willful acquisition or maintenance of that power as distinguished from growth or development as a consequence of a superior product, business acumen, or historic accident.

United States v. Grinnell Corp., 384 U.S. 563, 570–71 (1966). On this appeal, Blue Cross does not dispute its monopoly power in the market for health care insurance in Rhode Island. Ocean State, for its part, concedes that Blue Cross acquired its historical advantages legitimately. The issue in dispute is whether Blue Cross maintained its monopoly position through improper means.

Section 2 Does Not Prohibit Vigorous Competition on the Part of a Monopoly. to the Contrary, the Primary Purpose of the Antitrust Laws Is to Encourage Competition. * * * What Section 2 Does Prohibit Is "Exclusionary" Conduct by a Monopoly, Often Defined as "Behavior That Not Only (1) Tends to Impair the Opportunities of Rivals, but Also (2) Either Does Not Further Competition on the Merits or Does So in an Unnecessarily Restrictive Way." 3 P. Areeda & D. Turner, Antitrust Law ¶ 626B at 78 (1978). * * * to Decide Whether the Prudent Buyer Policy Can Reasonably Be Found to Be Exclusionary, We Must Ask Whether Blue Cross's Conduct "Went Beyond the Needs of Ordinary Business Dealings, Beyond the Ambit of Ordinary Business Skill, and 'Unnecessarily Excluded Competition' "From the Health Care Insurance Market. * * *

In the case at hand, the record amply supports Blue Cross's view that Prudent Buyer was a bona fide policy to ensure that Blue Cross would not pay more than any competitor paid for the same services. According to the policy, when physicians provided data on the lowest prices they accepted for particular services, and these prices were lower than those allowed by Blue Cross, Blue Cross lowered its price to match the lowest price accepted. When Ocean State physicians did not provide this price information, Blue Cross reduced its fee to the physicians by 20%, to correspond to Ocean State's 20% withhold. Blue Cross estimated that it saved $1,900,000 through this policy.

We agree with the district court that such a policy of insisting on a supplier's lowest price—assuming that the price is not "predatory" or below the supplier's incremental cost—tends to further competition on the merits and, as a matter of law, is not exclusionary. It is hard to disagree with the district court's view: "As a naked proposition, it would seem silly to argue that a policy to pay the same amount for the same service is anticompetitive, even on the part of one who has market power. This, it would seem, is what competition should be all about."

This conclusion is also compelled by this court's holding in Kartell v. Blue Shield of Massachusetts, 749 F.2d 922 (1st Cir.1984), cert. denied, 471 U.S. 1029 (1985) that a health insurer's unilateral decisions about the prices it will pay providers do not violate the Sherman Act—unless the prices are "predatory" or below incremental cost—even if the insurer is assumed to have monopoly power in the relevant market.

Kartell concerned Blue Shield of Massachusetts's ban on balance billing, a price policy according to which Blue Shield paid participating physicians only if they agreed not to make any additional charges to the subscriber. We held that, for antitrust purposes, a health insurer like Blue Shield must be viewed "as itself the purchaser of the doctors' services." As such, the insurer—like any buyer of goods or services—is lawfully entitled to bargain with its providers for the best price it can get. "[E]ven if the buyer has monopoly power, an antitrust court ... will not interfere with a buyer's (nonpredatory) determination of price." In the present case, Ocean State does not contend that the prices paid under the Prudent Buyer policy were "predatory" or below anyone's incremental cost. As Blue Cross argues, the legality of the Prudent Buyer policy rests *a fortiori* upon the holding in *Kartell*. In that case, Blue Shield sought to limit the fees to be charged by the physician to the subscriber; here, Blue Cross is limiting the price that it pays to the physician for services it is purchasing.

* * * The physicians [in *Kartell*] argued that Blue Shield's pricing policy enabled it to attract more subscribers, thus "increasing its dominance in the health insurance business." We rejected this argument, noting that it "comes down to saying that Blue Shield can attract more subscribers because it can charge them less." Such an outcome—more business at lower prices—would not ordinarily run afoul of the antitrust laws. Citing [*Travelers*,] a case that centered on an allegation of injury by a horizontal competitor, we concluded that "Blue Shield seems simply to be acting 'as every rational enterprise does, i.e., [to] get the best deal possible.' "

* * * Ocean State contends that although the Prudent Buyer policy was neutral on its face, Blue Cross in fact applied it only to Ocean State physicians. But even if we assume for argument's sake that Blue Cross selectively applied Prudent Buyer in this way, its conduct remains legitimate. It was primarily Ocean State physicians who were selling their services at a lower price to another provider (Ocean State) than to Blue Cross. Indeed, it was Ocean State's lower pricing policy—in particular, its 1986 decision not to return its participating physicians' withholds for 1985—that gave rise to Prudent Buyer. Therefore, it seems only logical—and not illegitimate—for Blue Cross to have focused its efforts in applying Prudent Buyer on Ocean State physicians.

* * *

Finally, Ocean State points to evidence in the record that Blue Cross officials hoped that Prudent Buyer—together with HealthMate and adverse selection—would have the effect of destroying or weakening Ocean State. For example, there was testimony that Blue Cross's president had expressed—in none-too-polite terms—a desire to emasculate Ocean State. Another Blue Cross executive wrote in a handwritten note that "not one guy in the state isn't going to know the implication of signing with Ocean State." The jury may reasonably have concluded, on the basis of this and other evidence, that Blue Cross's leadership desired to put Ocean State out of business. But the desire to crush a competitor, standing alone, is insufficient to make out a violation of the antitrust laws. As this court has noted, " 'intent to harm' without more offers too vague a standard in a world where executives may think no further than 'Let's get more business,' and long-term effects on consumers depend in large measure on competitors' responses." Barry Wright [Corp. v. ITT Grinnell Corp., 724 F.2d 227,] 232 [(1st Cir.1983)]. As long as Blue Cross's course of conduct was itself legitimate, the fact that some of its executives hoped to see Ocean State disappear is irrelevant. Under these circumstances Blue Cross is no more guilty of an antitrust violation than a boxer who delivers a perfectly legal punch—hoping that it will kill his opponent—is guilty of attempted murder.

* * *

Affirmed.

Brief of American Managed Care and Review Association as Amicus Curiae Supporting Petitioners

Ocean State Physicians Health Plan, Inc. v. Blue Cross & Blue Shield of Rhode Island, Supreme Court of the United States, 1990.
494 U.S. 1027, 110 S.Ct. 1473, 108 L.Ed.2d 610 (1990) (cert. denied).

* * *

III. The Court of Appeals Egregiously Misconstrued Blue Cross' Prudent Buyer Plan in Viewing It, as a Matter of Law, as a Cost–Reducing Measure That "Tends to Further Competition on the Merits"

In characterizing the Prudent Buyer plan as nothing more than "insisting on a supplier's lowest price," the court of appeals chose to see Blue Cross' effort only as a cost-reduction strategy. The court of appeals was wrong on three counts—first, in believing that Blue Cross was truly and primarily interested in reducing its costs; second, in believing that Blue Cross' method was calculated to "get the lowest possible price" or "the best deal possible"; and third, in believing that allowing the practice would "bring low price benefits to the consumer." Far from justifying the court's view of the case, the evidence in the record easily supports the jury's apparent conclusion that the program was part of a scheme to pay physicians, not less, but more—as long as they did not sell their services at a discount to Ocean State. This strategy was specifically intended to perpetuate Blue Cross' position as the physicians' exclusive marketing agent, to raise Ocean State's costs, and to enhance Blue Cross' power over price. The record shows that consumers paid higher prices, not lower, as a consequence of Ocean State's reduced ability to check Blue Cross' premium increases.

That Blue Cross was not interested in getting "the best deal possible" from physicians is easily demonstrated by comparing what it did with the actions of comparable insurers in the *Kartell* and *Ball Memorial* cases. In those cases, the courts (in opinions by Judges Breyer and Easterbrook, respectively) upheld health insurers' aggressive cost reduction efforts against antitrust challenges lodged by the affected providers. Those insurers, in demanding that providers accept the plan's allowances as payment in full (*Kartell*) or that they offer their best price in competitive bidding (*Ball Memorial*), were plainly engaged in efforts to "get the best deal possible" for their subscribers. Despite the view of the court of appeals that the result in *Ocean State* was "compelled" by its earlier holding in *Kartell*, the Rhode Island plan followed a policy fundamentally different from the aggressive cost containment seen in both *Kartell* and *Ball Memorial*.

Thus, Blue Cross allowed "balance billing" by nonparticipating physicians and sought lower fees only from those physicians that persisted in dealing with Ocean State—hardly the way to "get the best deal possible" from physicians. Thus, instead of concluding that Blue Cross was seeking only to pay lower prices, the court should have said that Blue Cross was offering to pay *more* to each physician who eschewed marketing at a discount through other outlets.[19] Despite its euphemistic name, the Prudent Buyer program was not calculated to obtain low physician fees in general, but only to penalize Ocean State doctors. Indeed, the record shows rather strikingly that Blue Cross' mind was more on raising Ocean State's costs than on lowering its own.

A possible interpretation of Blue Cross' action, seemingly adopted by the court of appeals, is that it was simply targeting those doctors who had already signified their willingness to accept lower fees—in other words, that it was merely defending itself against price discrimination being practiced against it by its suppliers. But the notion that a buyer with an 80% market share was a *victim* of price discrimination is patently absurd. Far from demonstrating that Blue Cross was seeking to "get the best deal possible," this circumstance reveals that Blue Cross had assiduously *refrained* from exercising its buying power against physicians and that it was Ocean State that finally brought competition to the market for physician services in Rhode Island. Of course, if Blue Cross had used its buying power to the fullest in the consumer's interest instead of using it selectively to obtain an unnatural market advantage, there would have been no basis for Ocean State to complain. But it is Blue Cross that is price-discriminating—in what it pays physicians—obviously hoping by such discrimination to discourage doctors from embarking on the competitive path of discounting their services and selling through alternative outlets.

IV. Monopolistic Practices by Insurers of the Particular Kind Involved in This Case Threaten Competition Not Only in the Market for Private Health Care Financing But, Even More Importantly, in the Market for Physicians' Services

Nonprofit health insurance offered under the Blue Cross and Blue Shield trademarks has a long and venerated history in the United States. As the market for health insurance has evolved in different places, however, two essential types of "Blue" plans have emerged—one selling services on behalf of providers and the other purchasing services on behalf of its subscribers. Although nearly all Blue plans began life as monopolistic joint selling agencies controlled by the providers whose services they sold, provider control gradually eroded. Some plans evolved into ordinary insur-

19. Ironically, the first case to approve efforts by a Blue Cross or Blue Shield plan to "get the best deal possible"—indeed, the case from which the *Kartell* and *Ocean State* courts quoted that phrase—also misconstrued the plan's actions and excused what was in fact a monopolistic rather than simply a cost-containment strategy. [*Travelers.*] * * *

ers, purchasing services as consumers' agents. But others, particularly those with very large market shares, found that their corporate interests were still served best by remaining the ally of providers rather than by becoming aggressive purchasers of their services. The respondent in this action is a prime example of a plan whose monopoly made this a feasible strategy—as was the Blue Cross plan in the 1973 *Travelers* case. The plans in *Kartell* and *Ball Memorial* are examples of plans with a different orientation.

In expressly characterizing the Rhode Island plan as one that "purchases health services ... on behalf of its subscribers," the *Ocean State* court signified its failure to focus on the crucial distinction between that plan and the plans in *Ball Memorial* and *Kartell*. In that distinction lies one of the keys to this case. The Blue Cross monopolist, hoping to enjoy the benefits of its dominant market position, undertook to induce exclusive dealing by strategic pricing, charging more to employers who offered the Ocean State option and paying less to physicians who marketed through an alternative plan. These strategies were aimed at stamping out alternative health plans and raising the costs of any that survived. Under the Blue Cross monopoly, there would be virtually no opportunity for a physician to engage in price competition—that is, to increase patient volume by lowering price. Thus, Blue Cross suppressed the competition from which consumers had the most to gain (and Blue Cross had the most to lose).

The ultimate reason why the court of appeals could see little potential harm to consumers in what Blue Cross did to Ocean State is that it overlooked entirely the possibility that a dominant nonprofit health insurer might have monopolistic reasons of its own for *not* seeking to "get the best deal possible"[23] and for instead allying itself explicitly or implicitly with providers and suppressing competition among them.[24] In fact, however, a

23. The practice of paying physicians supracompetitive fees in order to raise rivals' costs could easily qualify for condemnation as a predatory practice under the rationale routinely used in condemning predatory pricing. Significant current outlays aimed, not at increased efficiency, but only at gaining or keeping a monopoly are appropriate targets for policing under Section 2. R. Bork, [*The Antitrust Paradox*] 137–48 [(1978)].

24. The theory that Blue Cross sought to monopolize by specifically refraining from efforts to "get the best deal possible"—from everyone, that is, except Ocean State physicians—must be examined to see whether it makes "economic sense." *Matsushita* [*Electric Industrial Co. v. Zenith Radio Corp.*], 475 U.S. [574,] 598 [(1986)] (approving grant of summary judgment against plaintiffs on the ground that complaint, which contemplated a decades-long, improbable conspiracy to practice predatory pricing, "simply [made] no economic sense"). After all, it might be argued, a rational Blue Cross monopolist would not choose to incur unnecessarily high costs in the short run if it could not realistically hope to recover them in the long run—either because the firm is subject to price regulation or because its nonprofit character precludes anyone's direct enjoyment of future monopoly profits. But a business strategy of serving provider rather than consumer interests would appeal to a nonprofit, regulated insurer precisely because it is regulated and has no significant interest in profits as such. Such a firm can enjoy the nonpecuniary benefits that flow from monopolizing the marketing of physician services—e.g., large size and cash flow, with the attendant prestige, perquisites, and job security for corporate managers—while regulation, which regards the costs in-nonprofit, regulated health insurer has little reason not to overpay providers if it can thereby prevent the emergence of alternative outlets through which they can sell their services. Only if this Court corrects the errors made by the court of appeals in this case can Section 2 be used to prevent similar abuses in other health care markets.

V. The Practices Immunized by the Court of Appeals in Applying the McCarran-Ferguson Act Are Potentially Destructive of Important Competition in Provider Markets as Well as in "the Business of Insurance." A Different Reading of the Act Would Provide Needed Protection Against Such Abuses

Although this Court reasonably might elect in this case to review only those issues related to Blue Cross' Prudent Buyer program, the issues raised under the McCarran–Ferguson Act are of equal practical significance. Indeed, actions of the kind treated by the court of appeals as immune from antitrust attack under the McCarran Act also have the potential for destroying the market opportunities of HMOs and other innovative health plans and for foreclosing competition among providers. If dominant health insurers are able to practice differential pricing, ostensibly to offset the effects of adverse selection, without meaningful regulatory oversight, emerging HMOs and other competitive medical plans will be easy targets for predatory pricing. Moreover, regulated nonprofit insurers like Blue Cross have less of a disincentive to engage in predatory pricing than other would-be monopolists because they have reserves that can be used to defray current losses and that can be replaced through higher rates once the threat is past. In addition, they operate over geographic areas larger than most HMOs, yet can target their price cuts and sail their "fighting ship" HMOs wherever competition threatens to get a foothold. They may also be able to reduce their payments to providers (an apparently procompetitive move) as a way of financing a predatory campaign, a practice that many providers may approve as a way of staving off competition that they too wish to avoid. Even if regulators are alert, they may be hard-pressed to prevent pricing strategies that are exclusionary in fact. If the regulators fail, as in this case, even to consider the specific practices that carry the risk of abuse, antitrust immunity is an invitation to suppress the most promising forms of price competition in the in health care industry.

Certainly the insurance regulatory scheme in this case left Blue Cross the opportunity to engage in predation with impunity. As petitioners argue, this Court should consider the significance of the fact that the state's oversight in this case was clearly insufficient to constitute active "state supervision" under the two-part test for "state-action" immunity laid down in *California Retail Liquor Dealers Association v. Midcal Aluminum, Inc.,* 445 U.S. 97 (1980). *See also Patrick v. Burget,* 486 U.S. 94 (1988).

There is some authority for the view that the McCarran exemption, being explicit, is broader than the comity-inspired implied exemption for state action. However, the McCarran Act was passed well before the courts,

curred for physician services simply as an expense to be passed on to consumers, allows the physicians to enjoy the monetary rewards.

construing the Sherman Act not to preempt the states as economic policy makers, finally defined what a state must do before federal antitrust policy will give way. This Court should take this occasion to consider the argument that the McCarran Act, in requiring state regulation as a condition of exemption, was simply a precursor of the state-action doctrine and did not provide any more sweeping immunity than that which this Court subsequently inferred from the Sherman Act itself. It seems unlikely, for example, that Congress, in the same statute that expressly barred state insurance regulators from authorizing predatory "boycott[s], coerçion or intimidation," intended to free private insurers to set possibly predatory prices without actual state supervision. * * *

NOTES AND QUESTIONS

1. *Ocean State*. Are you persuaded by the AMCRA brief that the courts failed to detect a serious section 2 violation? What significance do you attach to the fact that Ocean State survived the loss of 29 percent of its physicians and was still able, perhaps "leaner and meaner," to compete with Blue Cross—that is, that Blue Cross did not succeed in gaining a monopoly, if that was its intent? If Blue Cross had required its physicians to dedicate themselves exclusively to serving its insureds (plus Medicare and Medicaid beneficiaries), would the effect on competition have been greater or less than under the Prudent Buyer program?

What do you make of Blue Cross's claim that adverse selection requires it to charge higher rates to employers offering HMO or other options, a policy which encourages exclusive dealing? Would predatory pricing or practices in insurance markets be easy to detect and punish? Explain the characterization of Blue Cross's HMO as a "fighting ship."

2. *"Most-Favored-Nation" Clauses*. The "Prudent Buyer" policy in the *Ocean State* case took the form of a so-called "most-favored-nation" (MFN) clause in Blue Cross's contract with participating physicians. A MFN clause is simply a proviso added to the price term of a long-term contract that gives the purchaser the benefit of any lower price that the seller may charge someone else. Ostensibly, its purposes are to save the transaction cost of renegotiating the price term every time price levels change and to prevent price discrimination against the buyer. Although there can be no objection to such a clause in isolated transactions, adverse effects on consumer welfare can occur if the MFN clause blankets an entire industry. Competition may be adversely affected in either the seller's market or the buyer's market.

The potential of a MFN clause for dampening price competition among sellers (e.g., physicians or hospitals) is not difficult to see. Whenever a MFN clause is in effect, a price cut to get the business of a particular buyer (e.g., Ocean State) is more expensive to the seller, who must give the same discount to the buyer with the MFN clause (e.g., Blue Cross). The price cut would therefore seem less likely to be granted. To be sure, there is no reason to fear for competition if other sellers are not similarly bound. (The more hesitant other sellers are to discount their services, the more lucrative it would be for any one seller to cut price and attract greater volume.) Nevertheless, price cuts may be inhibited if all or nearly all sellers are bound by enforceable MFN clauses with one or more large buyers. Indeed, oligopolistic or colluding sellers might find the universal use of such clauses extremely valuable in suppressing price competition. In an ordinary cartel or tight oligopoly, each member must fear that the other members will "cheat" by shading their prices to certain buyers, thus taking business from those who adhere to the tacitly or explicitly agreed-upon price. To the extent MFN clauses are enforceable, they amount to firm commitments by the sellers to have their pricing monitored and to pay a penalty for engaging in price competition. They could thus serve the purpose of strengthening horizontal collusion.

MFN clauses may also suppress beneficial competition among buyers (e.g., health plans)—as they were alleged to do in *Ocean State*. A dominant purchaser (e.g., Blue Shield or Blue Cross) that observes some of its suppliers (e.g., physicians or hospitals) granting discounts to smaller competitors (e.g., an HMO such as Ocean State) might introduce a MFN clause to ensure that those competitors do not get any price advantage from their aggressive purchasing efforts. By raising the input cost of a competitor, an already dominant firm arguably could entrench its position even against more efficient competitors and a would-be monopolist might be able to achieve market power. See Krattenmaker & Salop, Anticompetitive Exclusion: Raising Rivals' Costs to Achieve Power Over Price, 96 Yale L.J. 209 (1986). What market conditions must prevail before this threat is a significant concern?

In the *Marshfield Clinic* case, reproduced below, Judge Posner characterizes the use of MFN clauses as a method by which payers "try to bargain for low prices" and also as "the sort of conduct that the antitrust laws seek to encourage." In response to several briefs amicus curiae questioning the generality of that statement, the court amended its original opinion by adding a final qualifying sentence to the paragraph in question. See infra.

Despite the holding in *Ocean State*, the Justice Department challenged a number of MFN clauses, obtaining consent decrees prohibiting their use. E.g., United States v. Delta Dental of Rhode Island, 943 F.Supp. 172 (D.R.I.1996) (plan sought, unsuccessfully, to rely on *Ocean State* as a precedent for vindicating its MFN clause), 1997 WL 527669 (D.R.I.1997) (consent decree); United States v. Oregon Dental Serv., 1995–2 Trade Cas. (CCH) ¶ 71,062 (N.D. Cal. 1995); United States v. Delta Dental Plan of Arizona, Inc., 1995–1 Trade Cas. (CCH) ¶ 71,048 (D. Ariz. 1995); United States v. Vision Serv. Plan, 1996–1 Trade Cas. (CCH) ¶ 71,404 (D.D.C. 1996), 60 Fed. Reg. 5210 (1995) (proposed final judgment and competitive impact statement regarding *Vision Service* consent decree); see also FTC, RxCare of Tennessee, Inc.; Consent Agreement With Analysis To Aid Public Comment, 61 Fed. Reg. 2833 (Jan. 29, 1996) (pharmacy benefit plan). In each of these cases, however, the defendant or respondent was arguably under the control of, or involved in a conspiracy with, the providers of services. In what way did *Ocean State* present a different issue?

3. In Reazin v. Blue Cross & Blue Shield of Kansas, Inc., 635 F.Supp. 1287 (D.Kan.1986), the Kansas Blues plan terminated Wesley Hospital as a participating provider. Wesley, the largest hospital in Wichita, had recently been acquired by Hospital Corporation of America, which also owned the largest HMO in Wichita and had recently acquired a health insurance subsidiary. HCA sued the Blues, alleging that the Blues' move against Wesley (and the implied threat to other hospitals) was an attempt to exclude HCA as a competitor in health care financing. In denying summary judgment, the district court entertained a conspiracy theory, based on support of the Blues by the other Wichita hospitals, and a monopolization theory, based on the Blues' unilateral termination of Wesley, an action that betrayed predatory intent because it actually made the Blues' insurance less valuable to subscribers. The court found the evidence of the Blues' market power sufficient to warrant a trial—which resulted in a verdict for HCA on both counts and another lengthy opinion by the court upholding same. 663 F.Supp. 1360 (D.Kan.1987).

Successful Group Practice or Vicious Medical Monopoly?

Blue Cross & Blue Shield United of Wisconsin v. Marshfield Clinic

United States Court of Appeals, Seventh Circuit, 1995.
65 F.3d 1406, cert. denied, 516 U.S. 1184 (1996).

■ POSNER, CHIEF JUDGE

Blue Cross & Blue Shield United of Wisconsin ("Blue Cross" for short), and its subsidiary, Compcare Health Services Insurance Corporation, a health maintenance organization (HMO), brought suit last year under sections 1 and 2 of the Sherman Act against the Marshfield Clinic and its HMO subsidiary, Security Health Plan of Wisconsin, Inc. * * *

The two plaintiffs have distinct though overlapping claims. Compcare, Blue Cross's HMO, claims that the Marshfield Clinic—a nonprofit corporation owned by the 400 physicians whom it employs—has a monopoly which it acquired and has maintained by improper practices that have excluded Compcare from the HMO "market" in the counties of north central Wisconsin in which the Marshfield Clinic and its HMO subsidiary (Security) operate. This is a section 2 monopolization charge. Blue Cross claims that Marshfield, partly through its own monopoly power and partly by collusion with other providers of medical services, charged supracompetitive prices to patients insured by Blue Cross. This is a section 2 monopolization charge combined with a section 1 price-fixing and division-of-markets charge.

Although Marshfield is a town of only 20,000 people in a largely rural region, the Marshfield Clinic is the fifth largest physician-owned clinic in North America, with annual revenues in excess of $200 million. The Clinic has its main office in Marshfield but it has 21 branch offices scattered throughout the 14 counties of north central Wisconsin. Oddly, we cannot find in the record, nor were counsel able to inform us at argument, what percentage the 400 physicians employed by the Clinic comprise of all the physicians in the 14 counties. We do know that the Clinic employs all the physicians in Marshfield itself and in several other towns—but one of these towns has only one physician—and all the physicians in one entire county—but a county that has only 12 physicians. Security, the Marshfield Clinic's HMO subsidiary, serves its subscribers through the physicians employed by the Clinic plus almost 900 other physicians with whom Security has contracts. These contracts are not exclusive—the physicians are free to work for other HMOs as well as to practice fee-for-service medicine—and in fact work for Security generates only 6 percent of these physicians' total income. * * * In nine of the 14 counties in the north central region, Security has more than 90 percent of all subscribers to HMOs.

Compcare persuaded the jury that HMOs constitute a separate market, much as banks are a separate market from currency exchanges; and if there is a reasonable basis for this finding in the evidence, we are bound to accept it regardless of what we might think as an original matter. But we have searched the record in vain for evidence that under contemporary principles of antitrust law would justify such a finding. An HMO is not a distinctive organizational form or assemblage of skills, as is plain from the fact that the physicians retained by Security, whether they are employees of the Marshfield Clinic or completely independent, to serve its subscribers serve other patients on a fee-for-service basis. An HMO is basically a method of pricing medical services [that] gives the HMO an incentive to minimize the procedures that it performs, since the marginal revenue it derives from each procedure is zero. Hence HMOs are thought to reduce "waste" and to encourage preventive care, although those hostile to the HMO concept believe that the principal effect is merely to reduce the amount of medical care that patients receive. * * * Compcare complains that Security's contracts with physicians require them to refer their patients to the Clinic rather than to "independent" physicians. But that is of the essence of an HMO: the subscriber must take the service offered by the physicians whom the HMO has enlisted.

Compcare's principal argument is that Security has enlisted such a large fraction of the physicians in the 14–county north central region that Compcare cannot find enough "independent" physicians to be able to offer HMO services competitive with Security's—hence Security's huge market shares in 9 of the 14 counties. Supposing this is true—as seems unlikely since Security's almost 900 independent physicians are available to join other HMOs, along with an unknown number of physicians neither employed by the Marshfield Clinic nor retained by Security—it has monopolistic significance only if HMOs constitute a market separate from other contractual forms in which many of the same physicians sell their services. Of this we cannot find any evidence.

In defining a market, one must consider substitution both by buyers and by sellers[. L]et us start with buyers. The record shows, what is anyway well known, that individuals, and their employers, and medical insurers (the real "buyers" of medical services, according to the plaintiffs) regard HMOs as competitive not only with each other but also with the various types of fee-for-service provider, including "preferred provider" plans * * *. HMOs, though they have made great strides in recent years because of the widespread concern with skyrocketing medical costs, remain relative upstarts in the market for physician services. Many people don't like them because of the restriction on the patient's choice of doctors or because they fear that HMOs skimp on service * * *. HMOs compensate for these perceived drawbacks by charging a lower price than fee-for-service plans.

We do not wish to associate ourselves with the critics of HMOs. All that is important to our consideration of this appeal is that many people believe—whether rightly or wrongly is of no moment—that HMOs are not an unalloyed blessing; and this means that the price that an HMO can charge is constrained not only by competition from other HMOs but also by competition from forms of medical-services contracting that are free from the perceived perverse incentive effects of the HMO form. * * *

We do not understand Compcare to be contending that insurance companies cannot find enough physicians in the north central region willing to sign contracts with them to staff preferred-provider plans. This has a dual significance. Such plans are particularly close substitutes for HMOs, since they use the insurer's clout with physicians to drive down price. And if, as the record shows, they are feasible even in areas supposedly dominated by the Marshfield Clinic, and even without including any physicians employed by the Clinic, it is impossible to understand what barrier there could be to the formation of HMOs. All that is needed is an array of physicians who among them provide a broad range of medical services, and the same thing is needed for a preferred-provider plan. Ability to create a preferred-provider plan therefore implies ability to create an HMO, and so implies in turn that if Security raised its prices above competitive levels, and if people had a strong preference for HMOs over preferred-provider plans despite the similarities between the two systems for providing medical care, the operators of those plans would convert them to HMOs. If so, those plans are part of the same market with HMOs. So Blue Cross and Blue Shield of Indiana argued in Ball Memorial Hospital, Inc. v. Mutual Hospital Ins., Inc., 784 F.2d 1325 (7th Cir.1986), and we accepted its argument.

As we said earlier, the definition of a market depends on substitutability on the supply side as well as on the demand side. Even if two products are completely different from the consumer's standpoint, if they are made by the same producers an increase in the price of one that is not cost-justified will induce producers to shift production from the other product to this one in order to increase their profits by selling at a supracompetitive price. The services offered by HMOs and by various fee-for-service plans are both provided by the same physicians, who can easily shift from one type of service to another if a change in relative prices makes one type more lucrative than others.

We thus do not believe that a reasonable jury, confronting the record compiled in the district court, could find that HMOs constitute a separate market. * * * Nor, if we examine a more plausible market such as all physician services in north central Wisconsin and thus shift our focus from Security, the HMO, to the Marshfield Clinic itself, is there any basis in the record for treating the Clinic not as the alliance of 400 physicians that is the Marshfield Clinic but instead as the almost 1300 physicians who are either employed by the Clinic or have contracts with Security. The 900 independent contractors derive only a small fraction of their income from those contracts, as we have seen, and the contracts do not forbid them to join other HMOs or otherwise compete with Security or with the Marshfield Clinic.

It is true that because of the sparsity of the physician population in north central Wisconsin the physicians employed by the Clinic have a large share of the market for physician services, since, for primary care anyway (an important qualification—people will go a long way for a liver transplant), that market is a local one. Remember, there is one entire county in which all the physicians are employed by the Clinic. We do not understand Compcare to be arguing that this is the market that the Clinic monopolized; the damages to Compcare from being excluded (if it was excluded—we do not know) from that tiny market would be tiny. Compcare paints with a broader brush, drawing a dizzying series of concentric circles around the Clinic's offices and counting the physicians who can serve people living in the circles. It would have been much simpler and we suppose just as good—having in mind the desirability of avoiding a hunt for the snark of delusive exactness—to have treated the counties as the markets. But whatever the precise method chosen, Compcare is unable to show that in what it chooses to regard as the relevant geographic market or series of linked geographic markets for physician services the Marshfield Clinic employed 50 percent or more of the physicians serving the market. Fifty percent is below any accepted benchmark for inferring monopoly power from market share, and the Clinic has given us no reason for lowering the mark. * * * If the Clinic overprices a particular procedure, other physicians capable of performing that procedure will have an added incentive to do so, knocking down the excessive price.

Compcare also asked the jury to infer monopoly power directly from the Clinic's high prices, and high rate of return, relative to the prices and rates of return of its competitors. But when dealing with a heterogeneous product or service, such as the full range of medical care, a reasonable finder of fact cannot infer monopoly power just from higher prices—the difference may reflect a higher quality more costly to provide—and it is always treacherous to try to infer monopoly power from a high rate of return. Taking the second point first, not only do measured rates of return reflect accounting conventions more than they do real profits (or losses), as an economist would understand these terms, but there is not even a good economic theory that associates monopoly power with a high rate of return. Firms compete to become and to remain monopolists, and the process of competition erodes their profits. Conversely, competitive firms may be highly profitable merely by virtue of having low costs as a result of superior efficiency, yet not sufficiently lower costs than all other competitors to enable the firm to take over its market and become a monopolist. As for high prices, one of the complaints against HMOs, remember, is that they skimp on service. One HMO may charge higher prices than other HMOs (and Security does charge higher prices) not because it has a monopoly but because it is offering better service than the other HMOs in its market. Compcare itself stresses the quality of the Marshfield Clinic's doctors, as part of its argument that it cannot succeed unless the Clinic is forced to join it. Generally you must pay more for higher quality.

So Security is not a monopolist of HMO services, because, subject to our earlier qualification, HMOs are not a market. The Marshfield Clinic, its parent, is not a monopolist either. It does not control its independent contractors; and once they are excluded, the Clinic (which is to say the physicians who own and are employed by it—who are the firm, functionally speaking) does not have a monopoly of physician services in the north central region or in any parts of the region other than parts too small to support more than a handful of physicians. If the Marshfield Clinic is a monopolist in any of these areas it is what is called a "natural monopolist," which is to say a firm that has no competitors simply because the market is too small to support more than a single firm. If an entire county has only 12 physicians, one can hardly expect or want them to set up in competition with each other. We live in the age of technology and specialization in medical services. Physicians practice in groups, in alliances, in networks, utilizing expensive equipment and support. Twelve physicians competing in a county would be competing to provide horse-and-buggy medicine. Only as part of a large and sophisticated medical enterprise such as the Marshfield Clinic can they practice modern medicine in rural Wisconsin.

* * *

[Blue Cross argued that the Clinic was a so-called "essential facility" and, as such, should be required to accept referrals from Compcare. In this connection, it claimed that] the Clinic's reputation is so superb that no one will sign up with an HMO or preferred-provider plan that does not have the Clinic on its roster. The suggestion that the price of being "best" is to be brought under the regulatory aegis of antitrust law and stripped of your power to decide whom to do business with does not identify an interest that the antitrust laws protect. "The successful competitor, having been urged to compete, must not be turned upon when he wins." United States v. Aluminum Co. of America, [148 F.2d 416, 430 (2d Cir.1945) (L. Hand, J.)].

Since monopoly power was not proved, we need not evaluate the practices by which the Clinic acquired or maintained it. But we will not conceal our skepticism that they are exclusionary in an invidious sense. Compcare argues that the Clinic refused to allow its employees to "cross-cover" with "independent" physicians, in the sense of physicians not employed by or affiliated by contract with the Clinic (that is, agree to care for another physician's patients when that physician is on vacation or otherwise unavailable in exchange for a reciprocal agreement by the other physician), discouraged hospitals that its staff controlled from joining HMOs that compete with Security, and restricted staff privileges at those hospitals of "independent" physicians at those hospitals. All these practices are ambiguous from the standpoint of competition and efficiency. Hospitals are not public utilities, required to grant staff privileges to anyone with a medical license. The Marshfield Clinic's reputation for high quality implies selectivity in the granting of staff privileges at hospitals affiliated with the Clinic. Physicians employed by the Clinic, which has its own HMO, are hardly to be expected to steer their patients to another HMO, as they would be doing if they used their control of hospital staffs to induce the hospital to join another HMO. And given the extensive network constituted by the physicians either employed by or contracting with the Clinic, they would have little occasion to "cross-cover" with other physicians and would be reluctant to do so if, as is completely consistent with Compcare's version of the "essential facilities" doctrine, the Clinic maintains a reputation for high quality by being selective about the physicians to whom it entrusts its customers. But the important point is that, even if these practices are as we doubt tortious interferences with Compcare's business, they do not constitute monopolizing in violation of section 2 of the Sherman Act in the absence of acceptable proof, here lacking, of monopoly power.

We turn to Blue Cross's case. Blue Cross claims that it was overcharged by the Clinic. Many of the individuals whom Blue Cross insures in north central Wisconsin are customers of the Marshfield Clinic, paying for the services they receive from the Clinic on a fee-for-service basis. (The Clinic's doctors devote only a small part of their time to Security's HMO clientele.) Blue Cross pays the Clinic directly the portion of the fee that Blue Cross has agreed with its insureds to cover. The Clinic seeks to head off Blue Cross's claim at the pass, arguing that since the Clinic's fee-for-service contracts are with the patients themselves—it has no contract with Blue Cross—only the patients have "standing" * * * to complain about the alleged overcharging.

* * *

We note a tension between Blue Cross's claim and Compcare's. Blue Cross claims that the Clinic overcharged. The higher its prices, the greater the opening for competitors, such as Compcare. Even if Compcare could not get a foothold in the HMO "market," it could, of course, provide medical services through other means, such as a preferred-provider plan; and the higher the prices charged by the Marshfield Clinic, the more attractive such a plan offered by Compcare would be to employers and other purchasers of medical plans. To put the point differently, Blue Cross has a dual role in this case, as a buyer of medical services from Marshfield Clinic and, through its Compcare subsidiary, as a competitor of the Clinic. As a competitor its interest is in the Clinic's charging high prices, but as a buyer its interest is in the Clinic's charging low prices. Damages to Compcare are windfalls to Blue Cross, and vice versa. The damages awarded by the jury to the two plaintiffs (since they are economically one entity) should have been netted against each other rather than aggregated.

But that is a detail, since Compcare, for the reasons discussed earlier, was not entitled to recover any damages at all. Forget Compcare, then, and think of Blue Cross solely as a purchaser of medical services. Insofar as it paid high prices because the Marshfield Clinic was a monopolist, its claim must fail because the Clinic was not shown to be an illegal monopolist; a lawful monopolist can charge what it wants. But Blue Cross also claims that the Clinic colluded with competitors to raise prices above competitive levels. That claim is independent of the Clinic's being a monopolist.

Two forms of collusion are charged, with various furbelows and arabesques that can be ignored. The first is collusion between the Clinic and its affiliated (as distinct from employed) physicians. [T]he only evidence of collusion is that the Clinic, when buying services from the affiliated physicians either directly or through Security, would not pay them more than what these physicians charge their other patients. This is said to put a floor underneath these physicians' prices, since if they cut prices to their other patients their reimbursement from the Clinic will decline automatically. This is an ingenious but perverse argument. "Most favored nations" clauses are standard devices by which buyers try to bargain for low prices, by getting the seller to agree to treat them as favorably as any of their other customers. The Clinic did this to minimize the cost of these physicians to it, and that is the sort of conduct that the antitrust laws seek to encourage. It is not price-fixing. Perhaps, as the Department of Justice believes, these clauses are misused to anticompetitive ends in some cases; but there is no evidence of that in this case.

The other form of collusion alleged is more troublesome. The Clinic is said to have agreed with some of its competitors, in particular the North Central Health Protection Plan, an HMO that had 37,000 subscribers, to divide markets, a practice that violates section 1 of the Sherman Act. The analogy between price-fixing and division of markets is compelling. It would be a strange interpretation of antitrust law that forbade competitors to agree on what price to charge, thus eliminating price competition among them, but allowed them to divide markets, thus eliminating all competition among them.

The charge of a division of markets in this case is backed up by some pretty strong documents. In one of them an executive of the Marshfield Clinic, after noting that "at the time in which management of Marshfield Clinic and North Central Health Protection Plan established the Free Flow arrangements, the parties involved purposely chose not to place in writing clear descriptions of their respective Plan service areas so as to minimize any risk in terms of violation of antitrust laws," remarks that some years ago physicians affiliated with the NCHPP "wished to establish a practice in Marshfield and we took the position that the Free Flow agreement did not support that activity"—and they backed off. The implications of this only slightly Aesopian wording are backed up by statistics showing that Security had fewer than 30 percent of the HMO subscribers in the two counties in which NCHPP was active, while in the counties surrounding those two counties on three sides it had more than 90 percent of the HMO subscribers.

We think the evidence of a division of markets, though a little scanty, was sufficient to sustain the jury's verdict on this (and only this) aspect of the case * * *.

We conclude that the jury verdict on liability must stand insofar as the charge of a division of markets is concerned, and therefore the provisions of the injunction * * * that forbid the Clinic to divide markets with competing plans or groups. The rest of the injunction falls with the charges that we have held to be without legal or factual basis. No part of the award of damages or of costs and attorneys' fees can stand, because these items were not segregated by offense. There must be a new trial limited to damages for dividing markets. The burden will be on Blue Cross to show how much less it would have paid the Clinic had the Clinic refrained from that illegal practice. * * *

NOTES AND QUESTIONS ON THE MARSHFIELD CLINIC CASE

1. Consider Judge Posner's application of economic theory to the situation in north central Wisconsin. Although the so-called "Chicago-school" antitrust theorists (of whom Judge Posner was an early leader) have made important contributions to antitrust analysis, the presumptions they derive from economic theory may create excessively heavy burdens of proof for plaintiffs alleging monopolistic conduct. Moreover, because health care markets (like the Almighty) sometimes work in mysterious ways, trial lawyers and expert witnesses face a daunting challenge in trying to explicate for juries—as well as for judges, both trial and appellate—the causes and effects of business practices that have a potential for both procompetitive good and anticompetitive evil. The *Marshfield Clinic* case is itself a valuable clinic in which to diagnose a particular market, to evaluate conduct, and to understand relationships between players in the new economic game in which health insurers (including the Blues), managed-care plans, and health care providers are engaged.

For an insightful critique of Judge Posner's assessment of the situation in *Marshfield*, see Sage, Judge Posner's RFP: Antitrust Law and Managed Care, Health Affs., Nov.-Dec. 1997, p. 44 (concluding with a call for "empirical research * * * to generate a clear vocabulary [for health care antitrust litigation], to formulate a standard analytical approach, to frame the key issues, and to support or refute common assertions about managed care markets"). As Professor Sage notes, there is a certain irony in Judge Posner's special commendation of the parties for "the [unusual] speed with which this complex case was brought to trial" and his hypercritical evaluation of the plaintiffs' evidence. (His own opinion was issued just six weeks after oral argument.)

2. *Are HMOs a Distinct Product Market*? Like Judge Easterbrook in *Ball Memorial*, Judge Posner found insufficient evidence of a distinct HMO market. He emphasized, however, that this finding was based on "the record compiled in the district court." What evidence might persuade a court that HMOs constitute a narrower market than "health care financing"?

Is an HMO merely "a method of pricing medical services," like PPOs and ordinary health insurance? Does its lower price merely compensate for perceived quality differences so that, as Judge Posner suggests, an HMO could never exercise monopoly power even in the absence of other HMOs?

In its famous but now widely questioned *"Cellophane"* decision, the Supreme Court, rejecting the notion that functional differences alone define markets, treated cellophane (in which duPont had a 75% market share) as part of a much larger market for "flexible packaging materials." United States v. E.I. du Pont de Nemours & Co., 351 U.S. 377 (1956). Because it detected "cross-elasticity of demand" (that is, substitution of one product for another when the price of either changed), the Court thought duPont's control of cellophane could not constitute a monopoly. In reaching this conclusion, however, the Court ignored duPont's large profit margin on cellophane (as compared to, say, rayon), the discretion duPont enjoyed in setting its price and output, the inability of its competitors to respond in any way to the large and damaging reductions of cellophane's price over time (reflecting duPont's falling production costs), and the fact that any monopolist will naturally set its price at a level where some substitution occurs (that is, where demand is more elastic rather than less). In deciding that HMOs probably do not constitute a distinct market capable of being "monopolized," did Judge Posner make a *Cellophane*-type error?

Or was the true issue in the *Marshfield* case not the power exercised by the Clinic's HMO alone but the power of the Clinic itself, in combination with other providers, in the market for physician services? (See paragraph 4 below.) How was the Security HMO helpful in maintaining the Clinic's market power? Was it employed in the same manner as HealthMate, Blue Cross's HMO in *Ocean State*? Was Security's low market share a function of consumer distrust (as Judge Posner hypothesized)? Or did it reflect instead its relatively high price and its control by the Clinic, which was principally committed to fee-for-service practice? See Sage, supra, at 55 ("Marshfield's core business is delivering specialized medical care, making Security's HMO the tail of a very large fee-for-service dog.").

3. *Ease of Entry*. Entry conditions are relevant both in defining the market and in assessing the power exercised by a firm dominant in the market, once defined. In *Ball Memorial*, the issue was the purchasing power of a dominant health insurer, which operated a PPO. The court doubted that health care financing was a market capable of being monopolized as such, largely because entry into the health insurance business is relatively easy. Would it be appreciably more difficult, however, to develop and sell a competitive product effectively integrating financing and delivery, either in a single organization (as in staff-and group-model HMOs) or by contract (as in other HMOs and PPOs). Although provider networks have proved easy enough to organize and provide some competition for more closely integrated plans, an argument can still be made that plans of the latter type constitute a separate market in which market power might be exercised even in the presence of alternative financing arrangements. See Reazin v. Blue Cross & Blue Shield of Kansas, Inc., 663 F.Supp. 1360 (D.Kan.1987) (rejecting analysis of *Ball Memorial* and finding market power on different facts). Does the *Marshfield* court recognize that forming an effective HMO, with all the administrative and service capabilities needed, is more complicated than selling indemnity insurance?

4. *Power in the Market for Medical Services.* Now consider the claim that the Marshfield Clinic effectively monopolized the delivery of medical care in the relevant area. Its market share was never calculated but is signified by its 400 doctors, a minority in the area as a whole (though undoubtedly more in particular specialties). As the court observes, "50 percent is below any accepted benchmark for inferring monopoly power from market share." Recall that the antitrust agencies set 30% as the upper limit of their "safety zone" for evaluating nonexclusive physician network joint ventures. Is there an inconsistency here, or are there good reasons to assess market power differently when a single firm's dominance is under challenge and when competitor collaboration is being evaluated?

Although the Clinic's market share alone may not have reflected monopoly power in markets for physician services, the Clinic had arrangements with 900 other doctors. What were those arrangements and how might they increase the power that the Clinic could exercise? What evidence is there that the Clinic did in fact exercise market power in the market for physician services? Are you persuaded by Judge Posner's discounting of the Clinic's high prices and profits? Was it crucial to the maintenance of the Clinic's market position that independent HMOs not get a foothold in the region? Or was the ability of Compcare to launch a PPO alone enough (as Judge Posner seemed to think) to counteract whatever market power the Clinic might hope to possess?

5. *Exclusionary Practices?* If the court had found a monopoly in any market (HMOs or physician services), the inquiry would then have focused on the conduct by which it was gained or maintained. The court focuses on alleged collusion with competitors, which, if proved to constitute a section 1 violation, would also constitute an exclusionary practice under section 2. The court finds that the Marshfield Clinic's use of most-favored-nation clauses in its contracts with 900 independent physicians participating in its HMO (Security) was permissible for the same reason as in *Ocean State* (which the court did not cite). How did these contracts affect Compcare's ability to sign up a significant number of physicians for its HMO? Are you satisfied that the potential reduction of their fees on the work they did for Security (6% of their patients in the aggregate) adequately explains why the independents refused to deal with Compcare, a new HMO that might have sent them a greater volume of patients? Is it helpful to consider the refusal by nearly 900 physicians to deal with Compcare as an instance of "conscious parallelism" (considered in a problem in chapter 4(§B)) that, while not decisive on the question of conspiracy, invites a look for so-called "plus" factors? Did the independents act in their individual, or their collective, self-interest in refusing to deal with Compcare?

What other factors besides the possibility of income loss must have entered into the thinking of independent practitioners in deciding whether to cooperate with Compcare? How free were they, as a practical matter, to take action that the Marshfield Clinic would regard as unfriendly? Note that the MFN clause gave Security (controlled by the Clinic) the right to inquire about a doctor's prices to other purchasers. Note also that the Clinic's doctors were influential in or controlled the hospitals in the region, and recall in this connection *Patrick v. Burget*, noted in chapter 5(§C). What is significant about the fact that the Clinic was also the area's principal referral center, with an excellent reputation for quality.

From what you have gathered here, was the Marshfield Clinic a highly successful multi-specialty group practice or a vicious monopoly? On the basis of the insights you have gained in studying health care law and policy, do you think that you could prepare and try a similar case well enough to win a jury verdict for the plaintiff and to sustain it through a motion for judgment NOV and on appeal? See Sage, supra, at 58 ("evidence presented at trial must be both emotionally resonant to the jury and logically satisfying to the judge").

6. *Market Division*. The plaintiffs in *Marshfield* later suffered summary judgment on the one claim remaining after the appeal, because they could not demonstrate damages resulting from the market-allocation scheme. Another set of plaintiffs, however, brought suit on a similar theory and survived a motion for summary judgment. Rozema v. Marshfield Clinic, 977 F.Supp. 1362 (W.D.Wis.1997). In that case, the Clinic et al. argued—cleverly, but unsuccessfully—that antitrust injuries can arise only from increased prices and decreased output, whereas some of the damages claimed by plaintiffs were from overutilization of services.

INDEX

References are to Pages

1-56662-617-x
9 781566 626170
90000